Professional and Occupational Licensing Directory

Highlights

Professional and Occupational Licensing Directory (POLD) brings together for the first time detailed information on licensing requirements from more than 1,000 state and federal agencies and boards. More than 500 occupational categories comprising over 1,000 job titles are represented in this convenient, comprehensive source.

POLD covers virtually every professional license that:

- Is *required* in order for a person to work at an occupation or use a given professional title
- Is held by an *individual*, as opposed to those issued to businesses
- Is issued to a person for the purpose of working at a *specific profession or occupation*

Optional, voluntary professional licenses are not included, nor are any county or municipal certifications.

Detailed entries serve many users

Students preparing for their first professional jobs; career changers and other job seekers; professionals trained outside the United States; vocational counselors, outplacement consultants, personnel managers, and other business users; consumers with concerns about licensed practitioners; and governmental licensing officials all will find *POLD* a helpful resource.

POLD goes beyond *Occupational Outlook Handbook (OOH)* to identify what states require licenses and whether federal credentials are necessary for each occupational category. For each license, *POLD* details:

- Specific job title used for licensing
- Full contact information on the licensing board or agency, including fax numbers, if available
- Educational, experience, and other requirements
- Examination to be taken, whether written, oral, practical, or performance
- Activities authorized by the license
- Exemptions and reciprocity
- Fees

Designed for ease of use

POLD has separate chapters for each occupational category, using standard *OOH* terms as chapter titles. A Master List of Professions and Occupations guides users from variant job titles to these terms. Each chapter starts with a checklist to tell at a glance which states require licenses. Within the chapter, licenses are arranged by state. The Geographic Index gives an overall picture of occupational licensing in each state and on the federal level. Two appendixes cover Occupations Rarely Licensed and State Licensing Information Sources.

ISSN 1070-3322

Professional and Occupational Licensing Directory

A Descriptive Guide to State and Federal Licensing, Registration, and Certification Requirements

First Edition

David P. Bianco, Editor

 **Gale Research Inc.** • DETROIT • WASHINGTON, D.C. • LONDON

David P. Bianco, *Editor*
Susan M. Hill, Allison A. Jones, and Michael P. Smith, *Editorial Assistants*

Karen Hill, *Project Coordinator*
Joseph M. Palmisano, *Contributing Editor*
Ned Burels, Joyce Jakubiak, and Diane Sawinski, *Contributing Associate Editors*
Paula M. Labbe and Wendy H. Mason, *Contributing Assistant Editors*
Linda S. Hubbard, *Senior Editor*

Theresa A. Rocklin, *Supervisor of Systems and Programming*
Joseph D. Krutulis, *Programmer*

Mary Beth Trimper, *Production Director*
Mary Kelley, *Production Assistant*

Arthur Chartow, *Technical Design Director*
Cynthia Baldwin, *Art Director*

Benita L. Spight, *Data Entry Supervisor*
Gwendolyn S. Tucker, *Data Entry Group Leader*
Marjorita Onyekuru and Nancy K. Sheridan, *Data Entry Associates*

While every effort has been made to ensure the reliability of the information presented in this publication, Gale Research, Inc. does not guarantee the accuracy of the data contained herein. Gale accepts no payment for listing; and inclusion in the publication of any organization, agency, institution, publication, service, or individual does not imply endorsement of the editors or publisher.

Errors brought to the attention of the publisher and verified to the satisfaction of the publisher will be corrected in future editions.

The paper used in this publication meets the minimum requirements of American National Standard for Information Sciences--Permanence Paper for Printed Library Materials, ANSI Z39.48-1984. ∞™

This book is printed on recycled paper that meets Environmental Protection Agency standards.

This publication is a creative work fully protected by all applicable copyright laws, as well as by misappropriation, trade secret, unfair competition, and other applicable laws. The authors and editors of this work have added one or more of the following: unique and original selection, coordination, expression, arrangement, and classification of the information.

All rights to this publication will be vigorously defended.

Copyright © 1993
Gale Research Inc.
835 Penobscot Bldg.
Detroit, MI 48226-4094

ISBN 0-8103-8894-4
ISSN 1070-3322

Printed in the United States of America

Published simultaneously in the United Kingdom
by Gale Research International Limited.
(An affiliated company of Gale Research)

The trademark **ITP** is used under license.

10 9 8 7 6 5 4 3 2

Contents

Highlights	ii
Contents	v
Dedication	vii
Introduction	ix
User's Guide	xi
Master List of Job Titles	xv
Professional and Occupational Licenses	1

Accountants and Auditors	1	Dental Assistants	304
Acupuncturists	16	Dental Hygienists	306
Adjusters, Investigators, and Collectors	21	Dental Laboratory Technicians	314
Administrative Services Managers	30	Dentists	316
Adult and Vocational Education Teachers	33	Designers, Including Interior Designers and Florists	324
Agricultural Scientists	53	Detectives, Except Public	326
Air Traffic Controllers	56	Dietitians and Nutritionists	332
Aircraft Mechanics, Engine Specialists, and Parachute Riggers	60	Dispensing Opticians	338
Aircraft Pilots	64	Education Administrators	342
Animal Caretakers and Trainers, Except Farm	71	Electricians	366
Architects	102	Elevator Installation and Repair Occupations	384
Athletes, Coaches, Umpires, and Referees	109	Emergency Medical Technicians	387
Auctioneers	147	Engineering, Science, and Data Processing Managers	402
Automotive Body Repairers and Mechanics	151	Farm Operators and Managers	404
Bail Bond Occupations	153	Financial Managers	405
Barbers and Cosmetologists	155	Firefighting Occupations	408
Blue-Collar Worker Supervisors	191	Fishers, Hunters, and Trappers, Including Guides	410
Boilermakers and Boiler Operators and Tenders	198	Food and Beverage Service Occupations	416
Busdrivers	201	Foresters and Conservation Scientists and Workers	419
Cashiers	205	Funeral Directors and Morticians	423
Chiropractors	207	Gambling Occupations Other Than Racetrack	436
Clinical Laboratory Technologists and Technicians	215	Gardeners, Horticulture Workers, and Groundskeepers	449
Communications Equipment Repairers, Including T.V. and Radio	219	General Managers and Top Executives	452
Communications, Transportation, and Utilities Operations Managers	222	Geologists and Geophysicists	465
Construction and Building Inspectors	228	Guards	468
Construction Contractors and Managers	244	Handlers, Equipment Cleaners, Helpers, and Laborers	476
Counselors	281		

Health Services Managers	479
Hearing Aid Dealers and Fitters	488
Heating, Air-Conditioning, and Refrigeration Mechanics	497
Human Services Workers	505
Inspectors and Compliance Officers, Except Construction	508
Inspectors, Testers, and Graders	524
Instructors and Coaches, Sports and Physical Training	530
Insulation/Asbestos Workers	535
Insurance Agents and Brokers	543
Janitors and Cleaners	562
Kindergarten and Elementary School Teachers	566
Landscape Architects	600
Lawyers	608
Librarians	615
Licensed Practical Nurses	625
Lobbyists	632
Manufacturers' and Wholesale Sales Representatives	644
Marketing, Advertising, and Public Relations Managers and Promoters	645
Material Moving Equipment Operators	650
Medical Assistants	652
Mining, Quarrying, and Tunneling Occupations	654
Notary Publics	667
Nuclear Medicine Technologists	673
Nursery Workers	675
Nursing Aides and Psychiatric Aides	677
Occupational Therapists	680
Occupational Therapy Assistants and Aides	689
Optometrists	697
Personnel, Training, and Labor Relations Specialists and Managers	705
Pest Controllers and Assistants	708
Pharmacists	735
Photographers and Camera Operators	746
Physical and Corrective Therapy Assistants and Aides	749
Physical Therapists	755
Physician Assistants	765
Physicians	772
Plumbers and Pipefitters	794

Podiatrists	813
Police, Detectives, and Special Agents	819
Polygraph Examiners and Assistants	822
Power Plant Systems Operators and Managers	828
Precision Instrument Repairers	832
Preschool Workers	834
Professional Engineers	841
Property and Real Estate Managers	854
Psychologists	855
Racetrack Occupations	868
Radio, T.V., and Other Announcers and Newscasters	975
Radiologic Technologists	978
Real Estate Agents, Brokers, and Appraisers	986
Registered Nurses	1021
Respiratory Therapists	1036
Retail Sales Workers	1042
Science Technicians	1054
Secondary School Teachers	1056
Secretaries	1089
Securities and Financial Services Sales Representatives	1091
Services Sales Representatives	1115
Social Workers	1120
Speech-Language Pathologists and Audiologists	1133
Stenographers and Court Reporters	1147
Surveyors	1153
Tax Examiners, Collectors, and Revenue Agents	1164
Taxi Drivers and Chauffeurs	1167
Taxidermists	1170
Telephone, Telegraph, and Teletype Operators	1172
Truckdrivers	1175
Ushers, Lobby Attendants, and Ticket Takers	1182
Veterinarians	1184
Visual Artists	1196
Water Transportation Occupations	1197
Water and Wastewater Treatment Plant Operators	1206
Wholesale and Retail Buyers and Merchandise Managers	1223

Appendix 1: Occupations Rarely Licensed ... 1225
Appendix 2: State Licensing Information Sources ... 1253
Geographic Index ... 1259

Dedication

To the memory of Robert C. Thomas (1925-1993): mentor, friend, colleague.

Introduction

Professional and Occupational Licensing Directory (POLD) is the only publication to offer detailed information on national and state licensing in all career areas for the entire United States. This work covers more than 500 different occupations (and hundreds of additional specific job titles) that require state or federal licensure, certification, or registration. Previously this information was available only in scattered sources covering a particular state or profession, if at all. Now a wide range of interested users will benefit from a convenient source of detailed information obtained from more than 1,000 individual state and federal licensing agencies and boards.

Serves a variety of users

The detailed information on professional requirements offered by *POLD* meets the needs of many types of people, from students still planning their career education to job-seekers looking to relocate or to change careers and wondering how their present credentials or experience might apply. Professionals trained outside the U.S. will also find it useful. Vocational counselors and outplacement consultants will find help in referring clients over a wide area. Personnel departments and other business users may refer to *POLD* to ensure compliance with licensing requirements for new positions. Consumers of any licensed service can use it to check the requirements in their field of interest or to address complaints. Government officials concerned with licensing will be able to compare requirements across fields or across geographic areas conveniently through *POLD*.

Types of licenses covered

POLD is a comprehensive resource on the licenses that meet these criteria:

- The license must be *required* in order for an individual to practice or work at a profession or occupation or to use a particular professional or occupational title.
- An *individual* must be able to apply for the license. In some cases a partnership or a corporation may also be eligible to apply for the same license. As explained below, licenses that apply to businesses as such are not included.
- The license must be issued to the individual for the purpose of allowing the person to work at a *specific profession or occupation*.

Professional certification that is voluntary, not required by law, is not included in *POLD*, nor are county and municipal licenses of any kind.

State and federal boards also license and regulate a wide range of businesses and activities that are outside the scope of *POLD*, which does *not* cover:

- Licenses granted exclusively to corporations or businesses, not to individuals
- Facility licenses that allow someone to engage in an occupation only at a specific facility, such as a day care site
- Owner licenses, which restrict ownership, not the operation of a business
- Privilege licenses, such as a restaurant liquor license.

Finally, since *POLD* is intended as a guide to current licensing practice, discontinued licenses are omitted.

Hundreds of occupations represented

POLD provides comprehensive national and state licensing information on the hundreds of job categories used in the U.S. Department of Labor's *Occupational Outlook Handbook (OOH)*, 1992-93 edition, probably the most widely held career resource available. *POLD* also includes licensed occupations not covered in *OOH*, which were either assigned to existing *OOH* categories or, as necessary, to newly created categories.

Among the new categories that appear as chapter headings are: Acupuncturists, Auctioneers, Bail Bond Occupations, Hearing Aid Dealers and Fitters, Lobbyists, Notary Publics, Polygraph Examiners, and Racetrack Occupations.

Full details included on each license

While the *OOH* gives brief, general licensing information in its career profiles, *POLD* fills in the details for each state and federal professional license, including:

- Specific job title used on the license, which can vary from state-to-state
- Full contact information on the licensing board or agency
- Summary of requirements, examination, scope, exemptions and reciprocity, and fees. The governing statute that applies to the license may also be noted.

Consult the User's Guide that follows this Introduction for a complete explanation of the elements in a *POLD* listing.

Appendixes and index enhance use

In addition to the chapters devoted to specific career areas, *POLD* also includes two appendixes. The first identifies over 200 licenses for job titles that are required in fewer than six states; they may be in emerging fields, regional activities, or simply unusual occupations. Licensing officials may find this appendix especially useful, as well as the second appendix, which presents contact information for the State Occupational Information Coordinating Committees (SOICCs) and other general professional licensing boards and offices. The Geographic Index shows all the occupations licensed in each state and on a national level.

Compilation methods

More than 1,000 individual federal and state licensing agencies and boards provided information for the first edition of *Professional and Occupational Licensing Directory*. In addition to mail and telephone contacts with these organizations, the editor researched their publications and those issued by national trade and professional associations and by state occupational information coordinating committees. Compilations of state laws were also consulted.

Acknowledgments

This book originated in an observation by Shirley Gershen, adult services librarian at the West Islip P.L., Long Island, New York, of the need for a convenient, comprehensive source of licensing information. The editor also thanks Pamela L. Brinegar, executive director of the Council on Licensure, Enforcement and Regulation (CLEAR), for sharing her expertise, and the many licensing officials who provided information for this edition.

The editor would also like to acknowledge the contributions of the dedicated individuals who helped make this book possible, including Barbara Beach, Karen Hill, Linda Hubbard, and other members of the Gale editorial team. For their skilled assistance, the editor gratefully thanks Susan Hill, Allison Jones, and Michael P. Smith.

Comments and suggestions are welcome

Users can make an important contribution to future editions of *POLD* by passing along comments and suggestions regarding the format, coverage, and usefulness of this publication. Please address remarks to:

Professional and Occupational Licensing Directory
Gale Research Inc.
835 Penobscot Bldg.
Detroit, MI 48226-4094
Phone: (313) 961-2242
(800) 877-GALE
Fax: (313) 961-6083

User's Guide

Professional and Occupational Licensing Directory (POLD) is designed for easy consultation. It has these section types:

- Master List of Job Titles
- Chapters devoted to the license requirements of a particular occupational category, from abstractor to wrestler
- Appendix 1: Occupations Rarely Licensed
- Appendix 2: State Licensing Information Sources
- Geographic Index

How to find a specific requirement

Turn to the appropriate occupational chapter. Because states do not use uniform terminology for the job titles on licenses, consult the **Master List of Job Titles** for cross references from the many alternative terms to the standard occupation names that act as chapter titles in *POLD*. The chapters are arranged alphabetically by these standard occupation names.

Scan the checklist that appears at the chapter opening. This identifies whether or not federal licensing applies and provides an at-a-glance list of all states that had their own requirements when *POLD* went to press.

Find the listings for the state(s) of interest. Federal requirements, of course, apply throughout the country and appear first in the chapter, if applicable. States follow in alphabetical order.

Scan the numbered job titles under that state for the appropriate choice. The standard occupation name that defines the chapter may encompass a number of similar or related job types. For example, the Aircraft Pilot chapter includes licenses that apply for helicopters, balloons, gliders, as well as for airplanes. Such job titles are arranged alphabetically within the state's listings.

If multiple credential types apply to a specific job title--as with a progression of licenses from apprentice level through full certification--they are arranged with the most widely held license first and the trainee and/or advanced credentials following in logical order. The rubric "Credential Type" flags each level within a given job title.

What's in an entry

Entries provide full contact information and details on the requirements for licensing, the applicability of the credential, exemptions and reciprocity, and more. The ficticious sample entry on the following page indicates the full range of possible elements; an explanation of each follows.

Sample Entry

---

① **352**

② Ship Pilot

③ Law Enforcement Div.
Dept. of Natural Resources
PO Box 30028
Lansing, MI 48909
(313) 555-1212

④ **Credential Type:** License. ⑤ **Duration:** Two years. ⑥ **Authorization:** All persons who pilot passenger, cargo excursion, or charter boats on the inland waters of the State must be licensed by the Department of Natural Resources. ⑦ **Requirements:** At least 18 years of age. At least one year of experience on the type of vessel for which a license is being applied. Be in good physical condition and have good vision. Have not been convicted of a marine law violation in the past five years. Have not been convicted of violations of narcotics laws. ⑧ **Examination:** Written exam. ⑨ **Exemptions:** A person who holds a valid United States Coast Guard Pilot's license is not required to be licensed by the Department. ⑩ **Reciprocity:** Yes, provided home state maintains equal standards and extends similar privileges of reciprocity to Michigan. ⑪ **Fees:** $5 initial exam and license fee. $5 renewal fee. ⑫ **Governing Statute:** Vessels Carrying Passengers for Hire Act, Act 228 of 1965.

---

① **Sequential Entry Number.** This number marks the start of a listing of the credentials for a specific occupation name. References in the Geographic Index use these entry numbers, not page numbers.

② **Occupation Name.** The job title that appears here is the one used for licensing purposes by the individual state and so it may not match the chapter name; for example, some states may use "sheriff" for licenses in the Police, Detectives, and Special Agents chapter.

③ **Licensing Agency.** Full name, address, telephone number, and, if available, fax number for the board that issues the credential. Federal licensing agencies may be represented by both a headquarters address and by regional contact points for more convenient consultation by users seeking application forms or information packets.

④ **Credential Type.** Distinguishes between "license," a legal document necessary in order to practice a particular vocation; "certification," which indicates an individual meets competency requirements; and "registration," which implies that an individual furnishes name, address, and qualifications to a central registry. When the latter two types are mandatory, as they would be in any *POLD* listing, they achieve the same restrictiveness as licensing.

⑤ **Duration.** Length of time before renewal is necessary.

⑥ **Authorization.** Defines the activities authorized by the license, if such are not obvious.

⑦ **Requirements.** Identifies the education, experience, and training needed to qualify for the license. May also include minimum age, character, citizenship, residency, and professional references required, if any.

User's Guide

Applicants can contact the board directly to determine what documentation is necessary as verification.

(8) Examination. Indicates mandatory tests that may be part of the licensing process. Whenever possible, the type of examination (written, oral, practical, performance) is given, as is the name of the examination in the case of those nationally recognized. Users can contact the licensing board to obtain a current testing schedule.

(9) Exemptions. Notes when professionals with other licenses are exempt from one or more requirements. Some licensing boards waive requirements on a case-by-case basis for a wide variety of special situations; users are advised to contact the local board if they feel they may qualify for individual exemptions.

(10) Reciprocity. Licensing boards may be authorized to give special consideration to those who already hold a license from another state and seek licensure from the board. They may:

- recognize another state's license as equivalent (known as "reciprocity");
- issue a license based on the individual having met similar requirements out-of-state ("endorsement" or "license by credentials");
- credit equivalent out-of-state training, education, and examinations ("comity"). This item alerts those who are relocating to opportunities to expedite the credentialing process.

(11) Fees. Provides information about the following types of fees, when available: application fee, license fee, examination fee, renewal fee. Other types of fees may also be included, though fees for late renewals, re-examinations, and duplicate documents are not stated. Fees are those in effect as *POLD* went to press, but they are subject to change.

(12) Governing Statute. Cites the appropriate state or federal law that governs the licensing activity, when available. Federal citations are to the Code of Federal Regulations. State citations are given to state law or code. Boards may issue rules and regulations that clarify and implement various aspects of licensing and have the effect of law.

Appendixes and index provide additional information

Appendix 1: Occupations Rarely Licensed.
Emerging fields just beginning to be licensed, regional occupations, and other unusual jobs that are licensed by less than six states are highlighted here. While some of these entries are also included in the main chapters if they logically fit, many of them are so unique that they appear only in this appendix. Licensing professionals may find this chapter useful for charting trends.

Appendix 2: State Licensing Information Sources.
A network of State Occupational Information Coordinating Committees (SOICCs) and a National OICC was mandated by Congress in 1976 to improve coordination and communication among developers and users of occupational information. Contact information for these valuable resources and for other state boards involved in licensing in general is included here for users with interests in a specific state.

Geographic Index.
Consult the Geographic Index for a complete list of the occupations licensed in a particular state or by the U.S. government. Federal listings appear first, followed by those for all fifty states and the District of Columbia. Citations to licenses are by entry number, speeding access to the details.

Master List of Job Titles

Cross-references over 1300 job titles, occupation names, and key terms contained within job titles found in POLD's 126 chapters.

Abstractor *See* Appendix 1: Occupations Rarely Licensed 1225
Accident reconstruction specialist *See* Appendix 1: Occupations Rarely Licensed 1225
Accountant, Certified Public *See* Accountants and auditors 1
Accounting practitioner *See* Accountants and auditors 1
Accountants and auditors 1
Acupuncturists 16
Addiction counselor *See* Human services workers 281
Adjuster, insurance *See* Adjusters, investigators, and collectors 21
Adjuster, public *See* Adjusters, investigators, and collectors 21
Adjusters, investigators, and collectors 21
Administrative services managers 30
Adoption investigator *See* Appendix 1: Occupations Rarely Licensed 1225
Adult and vocational education teachers ... 33
Adult home care manager *See* Health services managers 479
Aerospace engineer *See* Professional engineers 841
Aesthetician *See* Barbers and cosmetologists .. 155
Agricultural broker *See* Wholesale and retail buyers and merchandise managers 1223
Agricultural consultant *See* Pest controllers and assistants 708
Agricultural scientists 53
Air conditioning contractor *See* Construction contractors and managers 244
Air conditioning technician *See* Heating, air-conditioning, and refrigeration mechanics 497
Air monitoring technician *See* Insulation/asbestos workers 535
Air school instructor *See* Adult and vocational education teachers 33
Air traffic control en route specialist *See* Air traffic controllers 56
Air traffic control flight service specialist *See* Air traffic controllers 56
Air traffic control operator *See* Air traffic controllers 56
Air traffic control terminal specialist *See* Air traffic controllers 56
Air traffic controllers 56
Air transport pilot *See* Aircraft pilots 64
Aircraft dispatcher *See* Air traffic controllers . 56
Aircraft mechanics, engine specialists, and parachute riggers 60
Aircraft pilots 64
Aircraft repair person *See* Aircraft mechanics, engine specialists, and parachute riggers ... 60
Airplane repairers *See* Aircraft mechanics, engine specialists, and parachute riggers 60
Airport manager *See* Appendix 1: Occupations Rarely Licensed 1225
Alarm system contractor *See* Construction contractors and managers 244
Alarm system installer and repairer *See* Electricians 366
Alarm system operator and manager *See* Communications, transportation, and utilities operations managers 222
Alarm system salesperson *See* Services sales representatives 1115
Alcohol abuse counselor *See* Human services workers 505
Alcoholic beverage worker *See* Food and beverage service occupations 416
Ambulance attendant *See* Emergency medical technicians 387
Amusement ride inspector *See* Appendix 1: Occupations Rarely Licensed 1225
Animal breeder *See* Agricultural scientists ... 53
Animal caretakers and trainers, except farm 71
Animal control officer *See* Inspectors and compliance officers, except construction ... 508
Animal dealer *See* Animal caretakers and trainers, except farm 71
Animal health technologist *See* Animal caretakers and trainers, except farm 71
Animal technician *See* Animal caretakers and trainers, except farm 71
Announcer *See* Radio, T.V., and other announcers and newscasters 975

xv

Antenna service dealer *See* Services sales representatives 1115
Antenna technician *See* Communications equipment repairers, including T.V. and radio 219
Appliance plumbing contractor *See* Construction contractors and managers 244
Appliance plumbing installer *See* Plumbers and pipefitters 794
Aquaculturist *See* Farm operators and managers 404
Arborist *See* Foresters and conservation scientists and workers 419
Architects 102
Armed courier *See* Guards 468
Armored car guard *See* Guards 468
Art therapist (school) *See* Visual artists 1196
Artificial inseminator *See* Appendix 1: Occupations Rarely Licensed 71
Artist (school) *See* Visual artists 1196
Asbestos abatement contractor/supervisor *See* Construction contractors and managers 244
Asbestos abatement worker *See* Insulation/asbestos workers 535
Asbestos air sampling professional *See* Construction and building inspectors 228
Asbestos consultant *See* Insulation/asbestos workers 535
Asbestos employee *See* Insulation/asbestos workers 535
Asbestos employer *See* Construction contractors and managers 244
Asbestos handler *See* Insulation/asbestos workers 535
Asbestos inspector *See* Construction and building inspectors 228
Asbestos investor *See* Insulation/asbestos workers 535
Asbestos management planner *See* Construction contractors and managers 244
Asbestos project designer *See* Construction contractors and managers 244
Asbestos project supervisor *See*
  Construction contractors and managers 244
  Blue-collar worker supervisors 191
Asbestos training provider *See* Adult and vocational education teachers 33
Asbestos transporter *See* Truckdrivers 1175
Asbestos waste disposal manager *See* Insulation/asbestos workers 535
Assayer *See* Appendix 1: Occupations Rarely Licensed 1225
Assessor *See* Real estate agents, brokers, and appraisers 986
Athlete agent *See* Athletes, coaches, umpires, and referees 109
Athletes, coaches, umpires, and referees ... 109
Athletic manager *See* Athletes, coaches, umpires, and referees 109
Athletic promoter/matchmaker *See* Marketing, advertising, and public relations managers and promoters 645
Athletic trainer *See* Instructors and coaches, sports and physical training 530
Attorney *See* Lawyers 608
Auctioneers 147
Audiologist *See* Speech-language pathologists and audiologists 1133
Automatic sprinkler system designer *See* Electricians 366
Automobile appraiser *See* Adjusters, investigators, and collectors 21
Automobile dealer *See* Retail sales workers . 1042
Automobile mechanic *See* Automotive body repairers and mechanics 151
Automobile repossessor *See* Adjusters, investigators, and collectors 21
Automobile salesperson *See* Retail sales workers 1042
Automotive body repairers and mechanics . 151
Automotive parts recycler *See* Retail sales workers 1042
Bail bond agent *See* Bail bond occupations ... 153
Bail bond occupations 153
Bail bond runner *See* Bail bond occupations .. 153
Bail bondsman *See* Bail bond occupations ... 153
Barber *See* Barbers and cosmetologists 155
Barber instructor *See* Adult and vocational education teachers 33
Barber technician *See* Barbers and cosmetologists 155
Barbers and cosmetologists 155
Barge supervisor *See* Water transportation occupations 1197
Bartender *See* Food and beverage service occupations 416
Beauty operator *See* Barbers and cosmetologists 155
Bedding and upholstered furniture repairer *See* Appendix 1: Occupations Rarely Licensed . 1225
Bedding and upholstered furniture sterilizer *See* Appendix 1: Occupations Rarely Licensed . 1225
Bingo game manager *See* Gambling occupations other than racetrack 436
Bio-analytical laboratory director *See* Engineering, science, and data processing managers 402
Blacksmith (racetrack) *See* Racetrack occupations 868

Master List of Job Titles

Blaster (Mining) *See* Mining, quarrying, and tunneling occupations 654
Blaster (Non-Mining) *See* Handlers, equipment cleaners, helpers, and laborers 476
Blue-collar worker supervisors 191
Boat operator *See* Water transportation occupations 1197
Boiler inspector *See*
  Construction and building inspectors 228
  Inspectors and compliance officers, except construction 508
Boiler installer *See* Boilermakers and boiler operators and tenders 198
Boiler repairer *See* Boilermakers and boiler operators and tenders 198
Boilermakers and boiler operator and tenders 198
Bondsman *See* Bail bond occupations 153
Box office employee *See* Ushers, lobby attendants, and ticket takers 1182
Boxer *See* Athletes, coaches, umpires, and referees 109
Boxing/wrestling manager *See* Athletes, coaches, umpires, and referees 109
Boxing/wrestling promoter *See* Marketing, advertising, and public relations managers and promoters 645
Boxing/wrestling referee *See* Athletes, coaches, umpires, and referees 109
Breath analyzer operator *See* Inspectors and compliance officers, except construction ... 508
Breeder, game fish *See* Farm operators and managers 404
Breeder, wild animals and birds *See* Agricultural scientists 53
Bricklayer *See* Appendix 1: Occupations Rarely Licensed 1225
Broker-dealer agent *See* Securities and financial services sales representatives ... 1091
Broker-dealer, principal *See* Securities and financial services sales representatives ... 1091
Building construction official *See* Construction and building inspectors 228
Building inspector *See* Construction and building inspectors 228
Building service mechanic *See* Heating, air-conditioning, and refrigeration mechanics 497
Burglar alarm contractor *See* Construction contractors and managers 244
Burglar alarm installer *See* Electricians 366
Burglar alarm operator/servicer *See* Communications, transportation, and utilities operations managers 222

Burglar alarm service and installation company manager *See* General managers and top executives 452
Burglar alarm service and installation company technician *See* Electricians 366
Burglar alarm service and installation company salesman *See* Services sales representatives 1115
Busdrivers 201
Butter grader *See* Inspectors, testers, and graders 524
Cameraman (racetrack) *See* Photographers and camera operators 746
Cardiac technician *See* Appendix 1: Occupations Rarely Licensed 1225
Carpenter *See* Appendix 1: Occupations Rarely Licensed 1225
Carpet installer *See* Appendix 1: Occupations Rarely Licensed 1225
Cashiers 205
Casino floor employee *See* Gambling occupations other than racetrack 436
Casino manager *See* Gambling occupations other than racetrack 436
Casino reservations manager *See* Gambling occupations other than racetrack 436
Casualty adjuster *See* Adjusters, investigators, and collectors 21
Cement mason *See* Appendix 1: Occupations Rarely Licensed 1225
Cemetery broker *See* Real estate agents, brokers, and appraisers 986
Cemetery salesperson *See* Real estate agents, brokers, and appraisers 986
Ceramic engineer *See* Professional engineers . 841
Certified mobile laser operator *See* Appendix 1: Occupations Rarely Licensed 1225
Certified Public Accountant *See* Accountants and auditors 1
Chaplain (racetrack) *See* Appendix 1: Occupations Rarely Licensed 1225
Charitable solicitor *See* Services sales representatives 1115
Charter boat operator *See* Water transportation occupations 1197
Chauffeur *See* Taxi drivers and chauffeurs .. 1167
Cheese grader *See* Appendix 1: Occupations Rarely Licensed 1225
Check casher *See* Cashiers 205
Check seller *See* Cashiers 205
Chef (gaming or gambling) *See* Gambling occupations other than racetrack 436
Chemical dependency specialist/counselor *See* Human services workers 505

Chemical engineer *See* Professional engineers . 841
Chemists (racetrack) *See* Racetrack occupations 868
Chest x-ray technologist *See* Radiologic
 technologists 978
Chief engineer *See* Water transportation
 occupations 1197
Chief operating officer *See* General managers
 and top executives 452
Child care administrator *See* Health services
 managers 479
Child care aide/provider *See* Preschool workers 834
Child health associate *See* Preschool workers . 834
Chiropractors 207
Civil engineer *See* Professional engineers 841
Claims adjuster *See* Adjusters, investigators,
 and collectors 21
Clerk of scales *See* Inspectors and compliance
 officers, except construction 508
Clinical laboratory director *See* Engineering,
 science, and data processing managers 215
**Clinical laboratory technologists and
 technicians** 215
Clinical mental health counselor *See* Counselors 281
Clocker (racing) *See* Racetrack occupations . . 868
Coal mine worker *See* Mining, quarrying, and
 tunneling occupations 654
Coast Guard *See* Water transportation
 occupations 1197
Cocktail waitress (gaming) *See* Gambling
 occupations other than racetrack 436
Collection agency worker *See* Adjusters,
 investigators, and collectors 21
Commercial applicator *See* Pest controllers and
 assistants 708
Commercial driver *See*
 Taxi drivers and chauffeurs 1167
 Truckdrivers 1175
Commercial fisher *See* Fishers, hunters, and
 trappers, including guides 410
Commercial pilot (aircraft) *See* Aircraft pilots . 64
Commercial marine license *See* Water
 transportation occupations 1197
Commission chemist (racetrack) *See* Appendix 1:
 Occupations Rarely Licensed 1225
Commodity broker-dealer *See* Securities and
 financial services sales representatives . . . 1091
**Communications equipment repairers, including
 T.V. and radio** 219
**Communications, transportation, and utilities
 operations managers** 222
Community college teacher *See* Appendix 1:
 Occupations Rarely Licensed 1225
Community planner *See* Appendix 1: Occupations
 Rarely Licensed 1225
Computer programmer *See* Appendix 1:
 Occupations Rarely Licensed 1225
Concert promoter *See* Appendix 1: Occupations
 Rarely Licensed 1225
Concrete technician *See* Appendix 1: Occupations
 Rarely Licensed 1225
Condominium hotel operator *See* Appendix 1:
 Occupations Rarely Licensed 1225
Condominium managing agent *See* Property and
 real estate managers 854
Construction and building inspectors 228
Construction code official *See* Construction and
 building inspectors 228
Construction contractors and managers . . . 244
Contractor *See* Construction contractors and
 managers 244
Cook (gaming) *See* Appendix 1: Occupations
 Rarely Licensed 1225
Coroner *See* Appendix 1: Occupations Rarely
 Licensed 1225
Correction officer *See* Appendix 1: Occupations
 Rarely Licensed 1225
Cosmetologist *See* Barbers and cosmetologists . 155
Cosmetology instructor *See* Adult and vocational
 education teachers 33
Counselor, associate *See* Counselors 281
Counselor, professional *See* Counselors 281
Counselors 281
Counterintelligence licensee *See* Appendix 1:
 Occupations Rarely Licensed 326
Court reporter *See* Stenographers and court
 reporters 1147
Crane operator *See* Material moving equipment
 operators 650
Cross-connection control device inspector *See*
 Appendix 1: Occupations Rarely Licensed 1225
Custom applicator *See* Pest controllers and
 assistants 708
Customs broker *See* Inspectors and compliance
 officers, except construction 508
Cytotechnologist *See* Clinical laboratory
 technologists and technicians 215
Dairy technician *See* Appendix 1: Occupations
 Rarely Licensed 1225
Dance therapist (school) *See* Appendix 1:
 Occupations Rarely Licensed 1225
Day care administrator *See* Administrative services
 managers 30
Day care center teacher/caregiver *See* Preschool
 workers 834
Day care home teacher/caregiver *See* Preschool
 workers 834

Master List of Job Titles

Dealer/repairer of weighing and measuring devices *See* Precision instrument repairers 832
Debt adjuster *See* Securities and financial services sales representatives 1091
Debt collector *See* Adjusters, investigators, and collectors 21
Debt consolidation agent *See* Appendix 1: Occupations Rarely Licensed 1225
Dental assistants 304
Dental hygienists 306
Dental laboratory technicians 314
Dental specialist *See* Dentists 316
Dental technician *See* Dental laboratory technicians 314
Dental x-ray technologist *See* Dental laboratory technicians 314
Dentists 316
Denturist *See* Dental laboratory technicians .. 314
Designated duty engineer *See* Water transportation occupations 1197
Designers, including interior designers and florist 324
Detection of deception examiner *See* Polygraph examiners and assistants 822
Detective, private *See* Detectives, except public 326
Detectives, except public 326
Diagnostic x-ray technologist *See* Radiologic technologists 978
Dietitians and nutritionists 332
Direct disposer *See* Appendix 1: Occupations Rarely Licensed 1225
Dishwasher/kitchen utility helper (gaming) *See* Appendix 1: Occupations Rarely Licensed 1225
Dispatchers ....
Dispensing opticians 338
Dispensing optician assistant *See* Medical assistants 652
Diver *See* Fishers, hunters, and trappers, including guides 410
Drinking water treatment and distribution system operator *See* Water and wastewater treatment plant operators 1206
Driver education instructor *See* Adult and vocational education teachers 33
Driving instructor *See* Adult and vocational education teachers 33
Drug abuse counselor *See* Human services workers 505
Drug auctioneer *See* Appendix 1: Occupations Rarely Licensed 1225
Drug researcher *See* Biological scientists ......
Education administrators 342
Education program specialist *See*

Adult and vocational education teachers 33
Education administrators 342
Egg grader *See* Inspectors, testers, and graders 524
Electric power generating plant workers *See* Power plant systems operators and managers 828
Electric sign contractor *See* Construction contractors and managers 244
Electric sign installer *See* Electricians 366
Electrical administrator *See* Construction and building inspectors 228
Electrical contractor *See* Construction contractors and managers 244
Electrical and electronics engineer *See* Professional engineers 841
Electrical hoisting engineer (coal mine) *See* Mining, Quarrying, and Tunneling Occupations 654
Electrical inspector *See* Construction and building inspectors 228
Electricians 366
Electrician (mine) *See* Mining, quarrying, and tunneling occupations 654
Electrologist *See* Barbers and cosmetologists .. 155
Electrology instructor *See* Adult and vocational education teachers 33
Electronic criminal surveillance officer *See* Appendix 1: Occupations Rarely Licensed 1225
Electronic technician *See* Communications equipment repairers, including T.V. and radio 219
Elementary principal *See* Education administrators 342
Elementary school teacher *See* Kindergarten and elementary school teachers 566
Elevator and lifting device Inspector *See* Construction and building inspectors 228
Elevator apprentice *See* Elevator installation and repair occupations 384
Elevator construction electrician *See* Electricians 366
Elevator contractor *See* Construction contractors and managers 244
Elevator craftsman *See* Elevator installation and repair occupations 384
Elevator helper *See* Elevator installation and repair occupations 384
Elevator inspector *See* Construction and building inspectors 228
Elevator installation and repair occupations 384
Elevator journeyman *See* Elevator installation and repair occupations 384
Elevator mechanic *See* Elevator installation and repair occupations 384
Elevator operator *See* Material moving equipment operators 650

xix

Embalmer *See* Funeral directors and morticians 423
Embalmer apprentice *See* Funeral directors and morticians 423
Emergency medical services - instructor *See* Adult and vocational education teachers 33
Emergency medical technicians 387
Emergency rescue technician (ERT) *See* Emergency medical technicians 387
Employment agency counselor *See* Counselors 281
Employment agency manager *See* Personnel, training, and labor relations specialists and managers 705
Employment agency operator *See* Personnel, training, and labor relations specialists and managers 705
Employment agent *See* Personnel, training, and labor relations specialists and managers 705
Endodontist *See* Dentists 316
Engine department, qualified member *See* Water transportation occupations 1197
Engineer *See*
　Material moving equipment operators 650
　Mining, Quarrying, and Tunneling Occupations 654
　Professional engineers 841
　Water transportation occupations 1197
Engineer, assistant *See* Water transportation occupations 1197
Engineer, chief *See* Water transportation occupations 1197
Engineer, designated duty *See* Water transportation occupations 1197
Engineer in training *See* Professional engineers 841
Engineer (ship or riverboat) *See* Water transportation occupations 1197
Engineering, science, and data processing managers 402
Entertainer (riverboat gambling) *See* Appendix 1: Occupations Rarely Licensed 1225
Environmental health specialist *See* Inspectors and compliance officers, except construction . . . 508
Environmental sanitarian *See* Inspectors and compliance officers, except construction . . . 508
Equine dentist *See* Dentists 316
Equipment inspector *See* Inspectors and compliance officers, except construction 508
Escrow agent *See* Real estate agents, brokers, and appraisers 986
Exercise rider (racetrack) *See* Racetrack occupations 868
Explosives dealer *See* Retail sales workers . . 1042
Explosives handler (mining) *See* Mining, quarrying, and tunneling occupations 654

Explosives handler (non-mining) *See* Handlers, equipment cleaners, helpers, and laborers . . 476
Exterminator *See* Pest controllers and assistants 708
Facialist *See* Barbers and cosmetologists 155
Family day care provider *See* Preschool workers 834
Farm bulk milk hauler *See* Truckdrivers . . . 1175
Farm labor contractor *See* Appendix 1: Occupations Rarely Licensed 1225
Farm operators and managers 404
Farrier (racetrack) *See* Racetrack occupations . 868
Film patrol/video tape operator and projectionist (racetrack) *See* Photographers and camera operators 746
Financial managers 405
Financial officer *See* Financial managers 405
Financial services sales representative *See* Securities and financial services sales representatives 1091
Fire alarm service and installation company installer/technician *See* Electricians 366
Fire alarm service and installation company manager *See* Communications, transportation, and utilities operations managers 222
Fire alarm service and installation company salesman *See* Services sales representatives 1115
Fire alarm sprinkler company technician *See* Electricians 366
Fire boss (underground) *See* Mining, quarrying, and tunneling occupations 654
Fire detection systems and lightning rods installer *See* Electricians 366
Fire detection and lightning rods seller *See* Services sales representatives 1115
Fire equipment distributor *See* Services sales representatives 1115
Fire equipment employee *See* Firefighting occupations 408
Fire fighter *See* Firefighting occupations 408
Fire fighter training instructor *See* Adult and vocational education teachers 33
Fire protection inspector *See* Construction and building inspectors 228
Fire protection sprinkler apprentice *See* Plumbers and pipefitters 794
Fire protection sprinkler contractor *See* Construction contractors and managers 244
Fire protection sprinkler journeyman *See* Plumbers and pipefitters 794
Firearms trainer *See* Instructors and coaches, sports and physical training 530
Firefighting occupations 408
Fireman engineer *See* Firefighting occupations 408

Master List of Job Titles

Fireworks shooter *See* Handlers, equipment cleaners, helpers, and laborers 476
First responder *See* Emergency medical technicians 387
Fish dealer *See* Retail sales workers 1042
Fish farmer *See* Farm operators and managers 404
Fisher, commercial *See* Fishers, hunters, and trappers, including guides 410
Fishers, hunters, and trappers, including guides 410
Fishing area operator *See* Fishers, hunters, and trappers, including guides 410
Fishing guide *See* Fishers, hunters, and trappers, including guides 410
Flight engineer *See* Aircraft pilots 64
Flight instructor *See* Adult and vocational education teachers 33
Flight navigator *See* Aircraft pilots 64
Floor and carpet layer *See* Appendix 1: Occupations Rarely Licensed 1225
Florists *See* Designers, including interior designers and florists 324
Food and beverage service occupations 416
Food inspector *See* Inspectors and compliance officers, except construction 508
Food processor/packer *See* Food and beverage service occupations 416
Food service sanitation manager *See* Food and beverage service occupations 416
Forest products operator *See* Farm operators and managers 404
Foresters and conservation scientists and workers 419
Franchise broker/dealer *See* Services sales representatives 1115
Fundraiser *See* Services sales representatives 1115
Fundraising counsel *See* Services sales representatives 1115
Funeral directors and morticians 423
Funeral director apprentice *See* Funeral directors and morticians 423
Funeral service licensee *See* Funeral directors and morticians 423
Fur buyer *See* Appendix 1: Occupations Rarely Licensed 1225
Fur dealer *See* Appendix 1: Occupations Rarely Licensed 1225
Fur processor *See* Appendix 1: Occupations Rarely Licensed 1225
Fur tanner and dyer *See* Appendix 1: Occupations Rarely Licensed 1225
Gambling occupations other than racetrack . 436
Gardeners, horticulture workers, and groundskeepers 449
Gas and petroleum plant and systems occupations *See* Power plant systems operators and managers 828
Gas fitter *See* Plumbers and pipefitters 794
Gas fitter supervisor *See* Plumbers and pipefitters 794
Gas fitter trainee *See* Plumbers and pipefitters . 794
General contractor *See* Construction contractors and managers 244
General managers and top executives 452
Geoduck diver *See* Appendix 1: Occupations Rarely Licensed 1225
Geologists and geophysicists 465
Geophysicist *See* Geologists and geophysicists . 465
Gift shop manager (casino) *See* Gambling occupations other than racetrack 436
Gift shop salesperson (casino) *See* Gambling occupations other than racetrack 436
Glaziers *See* Appendix 1: Occupations Rarely Licensed 1225
Grain warehouseman *See* Communications, transportation, and utilities operations managers 222
Greyhound clerk of scales *See* Racetrack occupations 868
Greyhound commission judge *See* Racetrack occupations 868
Greyhound commission veterinarian *See* Veterinarians 1184
Greyhound kennel manager *See* Racetrack occupations 868
Greyhound lead-out *See* Racetrack occupations 868
Greyhound mutuels director *See* Racetrack occupations 868
Greyhound paddock judge *See* Racetrack occupations 868
Greyhound presiding judge *See* Racetrack occupations 868
Greyhound racing director *See* Racetrack occupations 868
Greyhound racing secretary *See* Racetrack occupations 868
Greyhound starter *See* Racetrack occupations . 868
Greyhound trainer *See* Racetrack occupations . 868
Greyhound trainer assistant *See* Racetrack occupations 868
Groom (racetrack) *See* Racetrack occupations . 868
Groundskeeper *See* Gardeners, horticulture workers, and groundskeepers 449
Guard dog service employee *See* Guards 468
Guard, security or private *See* Guards 468
Guards 468

Guide, Fishing or Hunting *See* Fishers, hunters, and trappers, including guides 410
Guide, tourist *See* Appendix 1: Occupations Rarely Licensed 1225
Guide dog instructor *See* Appendix 1: Occupations Rarely Licensed 1225
Habilitation aide *See* Occupational therapy assistants and aides 689
Handicapper *See* Racetrack occupations 868
Handlers, equipment cleaners, helpers, and laborers 476
Harbor pilot *See* Water transportation occupations 1197
Harness race driver *See* Racetrack occupations 868
Hauler *See* Truckdrivers 1175
Hazardous waste disposal facility inspector *See* Inspectors and compliance officers, except construction 508
Hazardous waste disposal facility operator *See* Communications, transportation, and utilities operations managers 222
Hazardous waste hauler *See* Truckdrivers .. 1175
Health facility administrator *See* Health services managers 479
Health officer *See* Inspectors and compliance officers, except construction 508
Health planner *See* Health services managers . 479
Health service provider in psychology *See* Psychologists 855
Health services managers 479
Hearing aid dealers and fitters 488
Hearing aid dispenser *See* Hearing aid dealers and fitters 488
Heating, air-conditioning, and refrigeration mechanics 497
Heating-cooling apprentice *See* Heating, air-conditioning, and refrigeration mechanics .. 497
Heating-cooling contractor *See* Construction contractors and managers 244
Heating-cooling journeyman *See* Heating, air-conditioning, and refrigeration mechanics .. 497
Heavy equipment operator *See* Material moving equipment operators 650
Highway superintendent *See* General managers and top executives 452
Histologic technician *See* Clinical laboratory technologists and technicians 215
Hoisting engineer (underground) *See* Material moving equipment operators 650
Home health aide *See* Appendix 1: Occupations Rarely Licensed 1225
Home improvement/repair Contractor *See* Construction contractors and managers 244

Home improvement/repair salesperson *See* Services sales representatives 1115
Homeopathic physician *See* Physicians 772
Horse exerciser *See* Racetrack occupations ... 868
Horse race starter *See* Racetrack occupations . 868
Horse riding stable operator *See* Animal caretakers and trainers, except farm 71
Horse trainer *See* Racetrack occupations 868
Horse trainer assistant *See* Racetrack occupations 868
Horseshoer (racetrack) *See* Racetrack occupations 868
Horticulturist *See* Agricultural Scientists 53
Hospital maintenance plumber *See* Plumbers and pipefitters 794
Hospital maintenance plumber trainee *See* Plumbers and pipefitters 794
Hospital maintenance plumbing supervisor *See* Plumbers and pipefitters 794
Human services workers 505
Hunting area operator *See* Fishers, hunters, and trappers, including guides 410
Hunting guide *See* Fishers, hunters, and trappers, including guides 410
Hypertrichologist *See* Clinical laboratory technologists and technicians 215
Hypnotherapist *See* Appendix 1: Occupations Rarely Licensed 1225
Industrial engineer *See* Professional engineers . 841
Industrial hygienist *See* Health services managers 479
Industrial maintenance electrician *See* Electricians 366
Industrial radiographer *See* Radiologic technologists 97
In-plant inspector *See* Inspectors and compliance officers, except construction 508
Inspector, Vehicle Emission Testing *See* Inspectors and compliance officers, except construction 508
Inspectors and compliance officers, except construction 508
Inspectors, testers, and graders 524
Instructor, community college *See* Appendix 1: Occupations Rarely Licensed 1225
Instructor, vocational-technical *See* Adult and vocational education teachers 33
Instructors and coaches, sports and physical training 530
Insulation installer *See* Insulation/asbestos workers 535
Insulation/asbestos workers 535
Insurance adjuster *See* Adjusters, investigators, and collectors 21

Master List of Job Titles

Insurance administrator (third party) *See* Administrative services managers 30
Insurance agents and brokers 543
Insurance appraiser *See* Adjusters, investigators, and collectors 21
Insurance broker *See* Insurance agents and brokers 543
Insurance company/independent firm adjuster *See* Adjusters, investigators, and collectors 21
Insurance consultant *See* Insurance agents and brokers 543
Insurance inspector (boiler) *See* Inspectors and compliance officers, except construction ... 508
Insurance producer *See* Insurance agents and brokers 543
Insurance representative (limited) *See* Insurance agents and brokers 543
Insurance sales agent *See* Insurance agents and brokers 543
Insurance solicitor *See* Insurance agents and brokers 543
Interior designer *See* Designers, including interior designers and florists 324
Interpreter for the Deaf *See* Appendix 1: Occupations Rarely Licensed 1225
Invention developer *See* Appendix 1: Occupations Rarely Licensed 1225
Investigator, private *See* Detectives, except public 326
Investment advisor *See* Securities and financial services sales representatives 1091
Irrigation contractor *See* Construction contractors and managers 244
Issuer agent *See* Securities and financial services sales representatives 1091
Itinerant vendor *See* Retail sales workers ... 1042
Jailer *See* Appendix 1: Occupations Rarely Licensed 1225
Janitors and cleaners 562
Jockey *See* Racetrack occupations 868
Jockey *See* Athletes, coaches, umpires, and referees 109
Jockey agent *See* Racetrack occupations 868
Jockey apprentice *See* Racetrack occupations . 868
Jockey room custodian *See* Racetrack occupations 868
Journeyman electrician *See* Electricians 366
Journeyman pipeline welder *See* Appendix 1: Occupations Rarely Licensed 1225
Journeyman plumber *See* Plumbers and pipefitters 794
Journeyman sheet metal worker *See* Appendix 1: Occupations Rarely Licensed 1225

Kindergarten and elementary school teachers 566
Kitchen employee (riverboat gambling) *See* Appendix 1: Occupations Rarely Licensed 1225
Laboratory analysis technician *See* Clinical laboratory technologists and technicians 215
Laboratory director *See* Engineering, science, and data processing managers 402
Land development representative *See* Real estate agents, brokers, and appraisers 986
Land surveyor *See* Surveyors 1153
Land surveyor in training *See* Surveyors ... 1153
Landfarming operator *See* Farm operators and managers 404
Landfill operator *See* Communications, transportation, and utilities operations managers 222
Landscape architects 600
Landscape contractor *See* Construction contractors and managers 244
Landscape designer *See* Landscape architects . 600
Landscape gardener *See* Gardeners, horticulture workers and groundskeepers 449
Landscape horticulturist *See* Landscape architects 600
Landscape planter *See* Gardeners, horticulture workers and groundskeepers 449
Law enforcement officer *See* Police, detectives, and special agents 819
Lawyers 608
Lay midwife *See* Nursing aides and psychiatric aides 677
Lead hazard abatement contractor *See* Construction contractors and managers 244
Lead hazard abatement worker *See* Handlers, equipment cleaners, helpers, and laborers .. 476
Lead pony rider *See* Racetrack occupations .. 868
Librarians 615
Librarian, school *See* Librarians 615
Licensed practical nurses 625
Licensed vocational nurse *See* Licensed practical nurses 625
Lie detector operator *See* Polygraph examiners and assistants 822
Lifeboatman *See* Water transportation occupations 1197
Lifeguard *See* Appendix 1: Occupations Rarely Licensed 1225
Lightning rods and fire detection systems installer *See* Electricians 366
Lightning rods and fire detection systems seller *See* Services sales representatives 1115
Lineman *See* Electricians 366

xxiii

Liquefied petroleum gas appliance servicer *See* Appendix 1: Occupations Rarely Licensed . 1225
Liquefied petroleum gas installer *See* Plumbers and pipefitters 794
Liquefied petroleum gas safety supervisor *See* Communications, transportation, and utilities operations managers 222
Liquefied petroleum gas truck driver *See* Truckdrivers 1175
Liquid industrial waste remover *See* Truckdrivers 1175
Live bait seller *See* Appendix 1: Occupations Rarely Licensed 1225
Loan originator *See* Securities and financial services sales representatives 1091
Loan solicitor *See* Securities and financial services sales representatives 1091
Lobbyists 632
Lobster seller *See* Appendix 1: Occupations Rarely Licensed 1225
Locksmith *See* Appendix 1: Occupations Rarely Licensed 1225
Long boom crane operator *See* Material moving equipment operators 650
Manager (boxing/wrestling) *See* Athletes, coaches, umpires, and referees 109
Manicurist *See* Barbers and cosmetologists . . . 155
Manufactured and mobile home plumbing contractor or installer *See* Plumbers and pipefitters 794
Manufactured home dealer/broker *See* Real estate agents, brokers, and appraisers 986
Manufactured home installer or mechanic *See* Construction contractors and managers 244
Manufactured home salesperson *See* Real estate agents, brokers, and appraisers 986
Manufacturers' and wholesale sales representatives 644
Marine radio operator *See* Telephone, telegraph, and teletype operators 1172
Marital mediator *See* Counselors 281
Marketing, advertising, and public relations managers and promoters 645
Marriage and family therapist *See* Counselors . 281
Marriage counselor *See* Counselors 281
Massage therapist *See* Physical therapists 755
Massage therapist apprentice *See* Physical therapists 755
Massage therapy instructor *See* Appendix 1: Occupations Rarely Licensed 1225
Masseur/masseuse *See* Physical therapists . . . 755
Master *See* Water transportation occupations 1197
Mate *See* Water transportation occupations . . 1197
Material moving equipment operators 650

Materials engineer *See* Professional engineers . 841
Mechanic, automobile *See* Automotive body repairers and mechanics 151
Mechanical contractor *See* Construction contractors and managers 244
Mechanical engineer *See* Professional engineers 841
Mechanical inspector *See* Construction and building inspectors 228
Mechanical journeyperson *See* Heating, air conditioning, and refrigeration mechanics . . 497
Medical assistants 652
Medical laboratory technician *See* Clinical laboratory technologists and technicians 215
Medical technician *See* Clinical laboratory technologists and technicians 215
Medical training student *See* Appendix 1: Occupations Rarely Licensed 1225
Medication aide *See* Nursing aides and psychiatric aides 677
Mental health counselor *See* Counselors 281
Merchant mariner *See* Water transportation occupations 1197
Metallurgical engineer *See* Professional engineers 841
Middle school teacher *See* Secondary school teachers 1056
Midwife *See*
  Nursing aides and psychiatric aides 677
  Registered nurses 1021
Midwife, lay *See* Nursing aides and psychiatric aides 677
Midwife, nurse *See* Registered nurses 1021
Milk dealer *See* Food and beverage service occupations 416
Milk distributor *See* Truckdrivers 1175
Milk Hauler *See* Truckdrivers 1175
Milk sampler/weigher *See* Inspectors, testers, and graders 524
Milk tester *See* Inspectors, testers, and graders 524
Mine Electrician *See* Mining, quarrying, and tunneling occupations 654
Mine examiner *See* Inspectors and compliance officers, except construction 508
Mine fireboss *See* Mining, quarrying, and tunneling occupations 654
Mine foreman *See* Mining, quarrying, and tunneling occupations 654
Mine inspector *See* Inspectors and compliance officers, except construction 508
Mine shot firer (underground) *See* Mining, quarrying, and tunneling occupations 654
Mine surveyor *See* Surveyors 1153

Master List of Job Titles

Miner *See* Mining, quarrying, and tunneling occupations 654
Mining engineers *See* Mining, quarrying, and tunneling occupations 654
Mining, quarrying, and tunneling occupations 654
M.I.S. manager/technical supports systems operator (gaming) *See* Appendix 1: Occupations Rarely Licensed 1225
Mobile home dealer/broker *See* Real estate agents, brokers, and appraisers 986
Mobile home installer/mechanic *See* Construction contractors and managers 244
Mobile home plumbing contractor *See* Plumbers and pipefitters 794
Mobile home plumbing installer *See* Plumbers and pipefitters 794
Mobile home salesperson *See* Real estate agents, brokers, and appraisers 986
Mobile intensive care technician *See* Emergency medical technicians 387
Mobile laser operator, certified *See* Appendix 1: Occupations Rarely Licensed 1225
Monitoring well contractor *See* Mining, quarrying, and tunneling occupations 654
Mortgage banker/broker *See* Securities and financial services sales representatives 1091
Mortician *See* Funeral directors and morticians 423
Motor vehicle damage appraiser *See* Adjusters, investigators, and collectors 21
Motor vehicle dismantler *See* Appendix 1: Occupations Rarely Licensed 1225
Motor vehicle inspector *See* Inspectors and compliance officers, except construction 508
Motor vehicle operator *See* Taxi drivers and chauffeurs 1167
Motor vehicle salesperson *See* Retail sales workers 1042
Motor vehicle transporter *See* Truckdrivers 1175
Motor vehicle wrecker *See* Automotive body repairers and mechanics 151
Movers and warehousemen *See* Communications, transportation, and utilities operations managers 222
Municipal accountant or auditor *See* Accountants and auditors 1
Music therapist (school) *See* Appendix 1: Occupations Rarely Licensed 1225
Nail technician *See* Barbers and cosmetologists 155
Naturopath *See* Physicians 772
Notary publics 667
Nuclear engineer *See* Power plant systems operators and managers 828

Professional engineers 841
Nuclear facility operator *See* Power plant systems operators and managers 828
Nuclear medicine technologists 673
Nuclear pharmacist *See* Pharmacists 735
Nuisance wildlife control operator *See* Appendix 1: Occupations Rarely Licensed 1225
Nurse aide *See* Nursing aides and psychiatric aides 677
Nurse aide/practical nurse instructor *See* Adult and vocational education teachers 33
Nurse anesthetist *See* Registered nurses 1021
Nurse, licensed practical *See* Licensed practical nurses 625
Nurse, licensed vocational *See* Licensed practical nurses 625
Nurse midwife *See* Registered nurses 1021
Nurse practitioner *See* Registered nurses 1021
Nurse, psychiatric mental health *See* Registered nurses 1021
Nurse, registered *See* Registered nurses 1021
Nurse, school *See* Registered nurses 1021
Nursery dealer *See* Nursery workers 675
Nursery workers 675
Nurseryman *See* Nursery workers 675
Nursing aides and psychiatric aides 677
Nursing assistant *See* Nursing aides and psychiatric aides 677
Nursing home activity director *See* Appendix 1: Occupations Rarely Licensed 1225
Nursing home administrator *See* Health services managers 479
Nutritionist *See* Dietitians and nutritionists 332
Occupational therapists 680
Occupational therapy assistants and aides 689
Ocean freight forwarder *See* Communications, transportation, and utilities operations 222
Ocularist *See* Optometrists 697
Oil and gas broker *See* Securities and financial services sales representatives 1091
Oil and gas wellhead welder *See* Appendix 1: Occupations Rarely Licensed 1225
Oil burner technician *See* Plumbers and pipefitters 794
Oil tank installer *See* Construction contractors and managers 244
Operating engineer *See* Material moving equipment operators 650
Operator of uninspected towing vessel *See* Water transportation occupations 1197
Operator of uninspected passenger vessel *See* Water transportation occupations 1197
Ophthalmic dispenser *See* Dispensing opticians 338

Ophthalmic laboratory technicians *See* Appendix 1: Occupations Rarely Licensed 1225
Optician assistant, dispensing *See* Medical assistants 652
Optician, dispensing *See* Dispensing opticians . 338
Optician technician *See* Appendix 1: Occupations Rarely Licensed 1225
Optometrists 697
Oral surgeon *See* Dentists 316
Orthopedic x-ray technologist *See* Radiologic technologists 978
Orthopist *See* Appendix 1: Occupations Rarely Licensed 1225
Osteopathic physician and surgeon *See* Physicians 772
Outfitter *See* Fishers, hunters, and trappers, including guides 410
Outrider (racetrack) *See* Racetrack occupations 868
Paddock judge *See* Racetrack occupations ... 868
Painter *See* Appendix 1: Occupations Rarely Licensed 1225
Parachute rigger *See* Aircraft mechanics, engine specialists, and parachute riggers 60
Paramedic *See* Emergency medical technicians 387
Pari-mutuel employee *See* Racetrack occupations 868
Parking Lot Attendant *See* Handlers, equipment cleaners, helpers, and laborers 476
Parole/Probation Officer *See* Appendix 1: Occupations Rarely Licensed 1225
Passenger vessel operator *See* Water transportation occupations 1197
Pasteurizer operator *See* Appendix 1: Occupations Rarely Licensed 1225
Pastoral counselor *See* Appendix 1: Occupations Rarely Licensed 1225
Patrol judge *See* Racetrack occupations 868
Pawnbroker *See* Retail sales workers 1042
Peace officer *See* Police, detectives, and special agents 819
Peddler *See* Retail sales workers 1042
Percolation test technician *See* Inspectors, testers, and graders 524
Pedodontist *See* Dentists 316
Periodontist *See* Dentists 316
Personal property examiner *See* Tax examiners, collectors, and revenue agents 1164
Personnel consultant *See* Counselors 281
Personnel service manager *See* Personnel, training, and labor relations specialists and managers . 705
Personnel, training, and labor relations specialists and managers 705
Pest control applicator *See* Pest controllers and assistants 708
Pest control operator *See* Pest controllers and assistants 708
Pest controllers and assistants 708
Pest exterminator *See* Pest controllers and assistants 708
Pesticide applicator *See* Pest controllers and assistants 708
Pesticide consultant *See* Pest controllers and assistants 708
Pesticide dealer *See* Pest controllers and assistants 708
Pesticide operator *See* Pest controllers and assistants 708
Petroleum device technician *See* Appendix 1: Occupations Rarely Licensed 1225
Petroleum engineer *See* Professional engineers 841
Pharmacists 735
Pharmacist intern *See* Pharmacists 735
Pharmacy assistants and technicians *See* Appendix 1: Occupations Rarely Licensed 1225
Pharmacy preceptor *See* Appendix 1: Occupations Rarely Licensed 1225
Photo manager (racetrack) *See* Photographers and camera operators 746
Photofinish operator (racetrack) *See* Photographers and camera operators 746
Photographer, itinerant *See* Photographers and camera operators 746
Photographer (racetrack) *See* Photographers and camera operators 746
Photographers and camera operators 746
Physical and corrective therapy assistants and aides 749
Physical therapists 755
Physical therapist assistant *See* Physical and corrective therapy assistants and aides 749
Physician assistants 765
Physician/surgeon *See* Physicians 772
Physicians 772
Pilot, commercial and airline transportation *See* Aircraft pilots 64
Pilot, private (aircraft) *See* Aircraft pilots ... 64
Pilot, ship's *See* Water transportation occupations 1197
Pipefitter *See* Plumbers and pipefitters 794
Piping systems inspector *See* Construction and building inspectors 228
Placing judge *See* Racetrack occupations 868
Plans examiner *See* Appendix 1: Occupations Rarely Licensed 1225
Plant breeder *See* Agricultural scientists 53

Master List of Job Titles

Plant dealer *See* Nursery workers 675
Plant grower *See* Agricultural scientists 53
Plasterers *See* Appendix 1: Occupations Rarely Licensed 1225
Plater (racetrack) *See* Racetrack occupations .. 868
Plumbers and pipefitters 794
Plumber apprentice *See* Plumbers and pipefitters
Plumbing and gas inspector *See* Construction and building inspectors 228
Plumbing, heating, and air conditioning contractor *See* Construction contractors and managers . 244
Plumbing Inspector *See* Construction and building inspectors 228
Plumbing-piping apprentice *See* Plumbers and pipefitters 794
Plumbing-piping contractor *See* Construction contractors and managers 244
Plumbing-piping journeyman *See* Plumbers and pipefitters 794
Podiatrists 813
Police, detectives, and special agents 819
Police officer *See* Police, detectives, and special agents 819
Polygraph examiners and assistants 822
Polygraph intern *See* Polygraph examiners and assistants 822
Pony rider (racetrack) *See* Racetrack occupations 868
Post-mortem examiner *See* Appendix 1: Occupations Rarely Licensed 1225
Powder-actuated tool operator *See* Appendix 1: Occupations Rarely Licensed 1225
Power plant systems operators and managers 828
Practical nurse/nurse aide instructor *See* Adult and vocational education teachers 33
Precision instrument repairers 832
Precision tank tester *See* Precision instrument repairers 832
Pre-need contract agent *See* Appendix 1: Occupations Rarely Licensed 1225
Preschool workers 834
Preserve area operator *See* Animal caretakers and trainers, except farm 71
Principal, school *See* Education administrators 342
Private investigator *See* Detectives, except public 326
Private patrol operator *See* Guards 468
Private security contractor *See* Guards 468
Private security guard agency owner/operator *See* Guards 468
Professional engineers 841
Promoter (boxing/wrestling) *See* Marketing, advertising, and public relations managers and promoters 645
Property and real estate managers 854
Property manager *See* Property and real estate managers 854
Property valuation administrator *See* Tax examiners, collectors, and revenue agents . 1164
Prosthetist *See* Appendix 1: Occupations Rarely Licensed 1225
Prosthodontist *See* Dentists 316
Protective agent *See* Guards 468
Psychiatric aide *See* Nursing aides and psychiatric aides 677
Psychiatric mental health nurse *See* Registered nurses 1021
Psychiatric technician *See* Nursing aides and psychiatric aides 677
Psychological associate *See* Psychologists ... 855
Psychological examiner *See* Psychologists ... 855
Psychological stress evaluator (PSE) *See* Psychologists 855
Psychologists 855
Psychologist assistant *See* Nursing aides and psychiatric aides 677
Public accountant *See* Accountants and auditors . 1
Public adjuster *See* Adjusters, investigators, and collectors 21
Public health officer *See* Inspectors and compliance officers, except construction 508
Pump and pitless unit contractor *See* Construction contractors and managers 244
Pump Installer *See* Construction contractors and managers 244
Purchasing manager/agent (gaming) *See* Appendix 1: Occupations Rarely Licensed 1225
Purser *See* Water transportation occupations . 1197
Pyrotechnic operator *See* Appendix 1: Occupations Rarely Licensed 1225
Qualified member of the engine department *See* Water transportation occupations 1197
Racehorse owner *See* Racetrack occupations .. 868
Racehorse trainer *See* Racetrack occupations .. 868
Racehorse trainer, assistant *See* Racetrack occupations 868
Racehorse veterinarian *See* Veterinarians ... 1184
Racetrack occupations 868
Racetrack steward *See* Racetrack occupations . 868
Racetrack vendor *See* Racetrack occupations .. 868
Racing agent *See* Racetrack occupations 868
Racing secretary *See* Racetrack occupations .. 868
Racing worker *See* Racetrack occupations ... 868
Radar observer *See* Water transportation occupations 1197

Radiation technician *See* Radiologic
  technologists 978
Radiation therapy technologist *See* Radiologic
  technologists 978
**Radio, T.V., and other announcers and
  newscasters** 975
Radio and television technician *See*
  Communications equipment repairers, including
  T.V. and radio 219
Radio electronics service dealer *See*
  Communications equipment repairers, including
  T.V. and radio 219
Radio electronics service dealer *See* Services
  sales representatives 1115
Radio electronics service technician *See*
  Communications equipment repairers, including
  T.V. and radio 219
Radio officer *See* Water transportation
  occupations 1197
Radio service technician *See* Communications
  repairers, including T.V. and radio 219
Radiographer *See* Radiologic technologists ... 978
Radiologic technologists **978**
Radiotelephone/telegraph operator *See* Telephone,
  telegraph, and teletype operators 1172
Radon measurement specialist *See* Inspectors and
  compliance officers, except construction ... 508
Radon mitigation specialist *See* Inspectors and
  compliance officers, except construction ... 508
Railroad police officer *See* Police, detectives,
  and special agents 819
Real estate agents, brokers, and appraisers . 986
Real estate appraiser *See* Real estate agents,
  brokers, and appraisers 986
Real estate auctioneer *See* Appendix 1: Occupations
  Rarely Licensed 1225
Real estate broker *See* Real estate agents, brokers,
  and appraisers 986
Real estate inspector *See* Real estate agents,
  brokers, and appraisers 986
Real estate instructor *See* Adult and vocational
  education teachers 33
Real estate property manager *See* Property and real
  estate managers 854
Real estate sales agent *See* Real estate agents,
  brokers, and appraisers 986
Real estate timeshare salesperson *See* Real estate
  agents, brokers, and appraisers 986
Rebuilder of salvage vehicles *See* Appendix 1:
  Occupations Rarely Licensed 1225
Receiving barn custodian *See* Racetrack
  occupations 868
Recreation administrator *See* Appendix 1:
  Occupations Rarely Licensed 1225
Recreation supervisor *See* Appendix 1: Occupations
  Rarely Licensed 1225
Recreational therapists *See* Appendix 1:
  Occupations Rarely Licensed 1225
Referee (boxing/wrestling) *See* Athletes, coaches,
  umpires, and referees 109
Refrigeration contractor *See* Construction
  contractors and managers 244
Refrigeration engineer *See* Power plant systems
  operators and managers 828
Refrigeration mechanic *See* Heating, air
  conditioning, and refrigeration mechanics .. 497
Refrigeration technician *See* Heating, air
  conditioning, and refrigeration mechanics .. 497
Registered nurses 1021
Registered nurse practitioner *See* Registered
  nurses 1021
Rehabilitation counselor *See* Human services
  workers 505
Remittance agent *See* Cashiers 205
Repossessor *See* Appendix 1: Occupations Rarely
  Licensed 1225
Reptile/amphibian caretaker, commercial *See*
  Animal caretakers and trainers, except farm . 71
Reptile amphibian catcher, commercial *See*
  Appendix 1: Occupations Rarely Licensed 1225
Research animal dealer *See* Appendix 1:
  Occupations Rarely Licensed 1225
Residential builder *See* Construction contractors and
  managers 244
Residential care facility administrator *See* Health
  services managers 479
Residential maintenance and alteration contractor
  See Construction contractors and managers . 244
Residential builder salesperson *See* Manufacturers'
  and wholesale sales representatives 644
Respiratory care practitioner *See* Respiratory
  therapists 1036
Respiratory therapists 1036
Retail sales workers 1042
Riding instructor *See* Adult and vocational
  education teachers 33
Ring announcer *See* Radio, T.V., and other
  announcers and newscasters 975
River pilot *See* Water transportation
  occupations 1197
Riverboat gambling Worker *See* Gambling
  occupations other than racetrack 436
Roofer *See* Appendix 1: Occupations Rarely
  Licensed 1225
Roofing contractor *See* Construction contractors
  and managers 244

Master List of Job Titles

Rotary driller *See* Mining, quarrying, and tunneling occupations 654
Safety inspection mechanic (Automobiles) *See* Automotive body repairers and mechanics ... 151
Salvage vehicle buyer *See* Wholesale and retail buyers and merchandise managers 1223
Salvage yard dealer or pool operator *See* Appendix 1: Occupations Rarely Licensed   1225
Sanitarian *See* Inspectors and compliance officers, except construction 508
Sanitarian-in-Training *See* Inspectors and compliance officers, except construction ... 508
Sanitary inspector *See* Inspectors and compliance officers, except construction 508
Sanitary pumper *See* Water and wastewater treatment plant operators 1206
Scale technician *See* Precision instrument repairers 832
School administrator *See* Education administrators 342
School Business Official *See* General managers and top executives 452
School counselor *See* Counselors 281
School librarian *See* Librarians 615
School nurse *See* Registered nurses 1021
School principal *See* Education administrators . 342
School psychologist *See* Psychologists 855
School superintendent *See* Education administrators 342
Science technicians 1054
Scientific collector *See* Appendix 1: Occupations Rarely Licensed 1225
Scrap processor *See* Appendix 1: Occupations Rarely Licensed 1225
Seaman *See* Water transportation occupations 1197
Secondary school teachers 1056
Secretaries 1089
Securities agent *See* Securities and financial services sales representatives 1091
Securities and financial services sales representatives 1091
Securities broker-dealer *See* Securities and financial services sales representatives 1091
Securities dealer *See* Securities and financial services sales representatives 1091
Securities issuer *See* Securities and financial services sales representatives 1091
Security alarm agent *See* Services sales representatives 1115
Security alarm dealer *See* Services sales representatives 1115
Security director (Gaming) *See* Gambling occupations other than racetrack 436

Security director (Racetrack) *See* Racetrack occupations 868
Security guard *See* Guards 468
Security guard agency owner/operator *See* Guards 468
Security guard, armed *See* Guards 468
Security guard provider *See* Guards 468
Seed treatment commercial applicator *See* Pest controllers and assistants 708
Septic tank cleaner *See* Janitors and cleaners .. 562
Services sales representatives 1115
Sewage system contractor *See* Construction contractors and managers 244
Sewage treatment plant superintendent *See* Water and wastewater treatment plant operators .. 1206
Sewer and water plumbing contractor *See* Construction contractors and managers 244
Sewer and water plumbing contractor ....
Sheep dealer *See* Appendix 1: Occupations Rarely Licensed 1225
Sheet-metal workers ....
Shellfish diver *See* Appendix 1: Occupations Rarely Licensed 1225
Sheriff *See* Police, detectives, and special agents 819
Ship's doctor *See* Water transportation occupations 1197
Ship's nurse *See* Water transportation occupations 1197
Ship's pilot *See* Water transportation occupations 1197
Shooting area operator *See* Fishers, hunters, and trappers, including guides 410
Shot firer *See* Mining, quarrying, and tunneling occupations 654
Slot mechanic *See* Gambling occupations other than racetrack 436
Slot technician *See* Gambling occupations other than racetrack 436
Social service worker *See* Human services workers 505
Social work technician *See* Social workers .. 1120
Social workers 1120
Soil classifier *See* Agricultural scientists 53
Soil scientist *See* Agricultural scientists 53
Solar apprentice *See* Heating, air-conditioning, and refrigeration mechanics 497
Solar contractor *See* Construction contractors and managers 244
Solar contractor *See* Heating, air-conditioning, and refrigeration mechanics 497
Solar journeyman *See* Heating, air-conditioning, and refrigeration mechanics 497

Solicitor (Debt collector) *See* Adjusters, investigators, and collectors 21
Solicitor (Fundraiser) *See* Services sales representatives 1115
Solid fuel burner technician *See* Plumbers and pipefitters 794
Solid waste collector *See* Communications, transportation, and utilities operations managers 222
Solid waste facility operator *See* Communications, transportation, and utilities operations managers 222
Solid waste site operator *See* Communications, transportation, and utilities operations managers 222
Special gas fitter *See* Plumbers and pipefitters . 794
Speech-language pathologists and audiologists 1133
Speech pathologist *See* Speech-language pathologists and audiologists 1133
Sports *See* Athletes, coaches, umpires, and referees 109
Sportswriter (racetrack) *See* Appendix 1: Occupations Rarely Licensed 1225
Sprinkler systems *See* Plumbers and pipefitters 794
Stable attendant (racetrack) *See* Racetrack occupations 868
Stable employee (racetrack) *See* Racetrack occupations 868
Stable foreman (racetrack) *See* Racetrack occupations 868
State trooper *See* Police, detectives, and special agents 819
Stationary engineers *See*
   Power plant systems operators and managers 828
   Professional engineers 841
Statistician (racetrack) *See* Appendix 1: Occupations Rarely Licensed 1225
Steam engineer *See*
   Power plant systems operators and managers 828
   Professional engineers 841
Steamfitter/Pipefitter *See* Plumbers and pipefitters 794
Stenographers and court reporters 1147
Stockbroker *See* Securities and financial services sales representatives 1091
Structural engineer *See* Professional engineers . 841
Structural pest control applicator or operator *See* Pest controllers and assistants 708
Substance abuse counselor *See* Human services workers 505
Superintendent, school *See* Education administrators 342
Superintendent (underground) *See* Mining, quarrying, and tunneling occupations 654
Surface blaster *See* Mining, quarrying, and tunneling occupations 654
Surface supervisor *See* Mining, quarrying, and tunneling occupations 654
Surgeon *See* Physicians 772
Surplus lines broker *See* Insurance agents and brokers 543
Surveyors 1153
Swimming pool operator *See* Appendix 1: Occupations Rarely Licensed 1225
Tankerman *See* Water transportation occupations 1197
Tattoo artist *See* Appendix 1: Occupations Rarely Licensed 1225
Tax consultant *See* Tax examiners, collectors, and revenue agents 1164
Tax examiners, collectors, and revenue agents 1164
Tax interviewer *See* Tax examiners, collectors, and revenue agents 1164
Tax preparer *See* Tax examiners, collectors, and revenue agents 1164
Tax professional *See* Tax examiners, collectors, and revenue agents 1164
Taxi drivers and chauffeurs 1167
Taxidermists 1170
Teacher aides ....
Teacher, agriculture education *See* Adult and vocational education teachers 33
Teacher, business education *See* Adult and vocation education teachers 33
Teacher, career orientation *See* Adult and vocational education teachers 33
Teacher, early childhood special education *See*
   Preschool workers 834
   Kindergarten and elementary school teachers 566
Teacher, elementary school *See* Kindergarten and elementary school teachers 566
Teacher, general cooperative education *See* Adult and vocational education teachers 33
Teacher, health occupations education *See* Adult and vocational education teachers 33
Teacher, home economics education *See* Adult and vocational education teachers 33
Teacher, kindergarten through 12th grade *See*
   Kindergarten and elementary school teachers 566
   Secondary school teachers 1056
Teacher, secondary school *See* Secondary school teachers 1056
Teacher/Specialist, public school *See*
   Kindergarten and elementary school teachers 566

Master List of Job Titles

Secondary school teachers 1056
Teacher, vocational-trade and industrial (Secondary) *See* Adult and vocational education teachers 33
Telephone, telegraph, and teletype operators 1172
Television electronics service dealer *See* Communications equipment repairers, including T.V. and radio 219
Television electronics service dealer *See* Services sales representatives 1115
Television electronics technician *See* Communications equipment repairers, including T.V. and radio 219
Therapeutic recreation specialist *See* Appendix 1: Occupations Rarely Licensed 1225
Therapy technician (Masseur/Masseuse) *See* Physical therapists 755
Ticket seller or taker *See* Ushers, lobby attendants, and ticket takers 1182
Timber buyer *See* Appendix 1: Occupations Rarely Licensed 1225
Timekeeper *See* Racetrack occupations 868
Timeshare salesperson *See* Real estate agents, brokers, and appraisers 986
Tow truck operator *See* Truckdrivers 1175
Towing vessel operator *See* Water transportation occupations 1197
Track superintendent *See* Racetrack occupations 868
Track veterinarian *See* Veterinarians 1184
Tractor-trailer truck driver *See* Truckdrivers . 1175
Trade and education instructor *See* Adult and vocational education teachers 33
Trainer, athletic *See* Instructors and coaches, sports and physical training 530
Trainer, greyhound *See* Racetrack occupations 868
Trainer, racehorse *See* Racetrack occupations . 868
Transient merchant *See* Retail sales workers 1042
Transportation operations managers *See* Communications, transportation, and utilities operations managers 222
Trapper *See* Fishers, hunters, and trappers, including guides 410
Travel agent *See* Appendix 1: Occupations Rarely Licensed 1225
Tree expert *See* Foresters and conservation scientists and workers 419
Tree injector (Forest Worker) *See* Foresters and conservation scientists and workers 419
Tree surgeon *See* Foresters and conservation scientists and workers 419
Truckdrivers 1175
Underground miner *See* Mining, quarrying, and tunneling occupations 654

Underground storage tank installer *See* Construction contractors and managers 244
Urban Planner *See* Appendix 1: Occupations Rarely Licensed 1225
Urologic x-ray technologist *See* Radiologic technologists 978
Ushers, lobby attendants, and ticket takers 1182
Utilities operations managers *See* Communications, transportation, and utilities operations managers 222
Valet *See* Racetrack occupations 868
Vehicle emission testing inspector *See* Inspectors and compliance officers, except construction . 508
Vehicle repairer *See* Automotive body repairers and mechanics 151
Vendor *See* Retail sales workers 1042
Vendor, itinerant *See* Retail sales workers .. 1042
Veterinarians 1184
Veterinarian assistant *See* Animal caretakers and trainers, except farm 71
Video operator (racetrack) *See* Photographers and camera operators 746
Vision screening technician *See* Appendix 1: Occupations Rarely Licensed 1225
Visual artists 1196
Vocational administrator *See* Educational administrators 342
Voice stress analyst *See* Polygraph examiners and assistants 822
Waitress, cocktail (gaming) *See* Gambling occupations other than racetrack 436
Waste disposal facility inspector *See* Inspectors and compliance officers, except construction ... 508
Waste disposal facility operator *See* Communications, transportation, and utilities operations managers 222
Wastewater disposal facility inspector *See* Inspectors and compliance officers, except construction 508
Wastewater system operator *See* Water and wastewater treatment plant operators 1206
Wastewater treatment plant operator *See* Water and wastewater treatment plant operators 1206
Water and wastewater treatment plant operators 1206
Water conditioner plumbing contractor *See* Construction contractors and managers 244
Water conditioner plumbing installer *See* Plumbers and pipefitters 794
Water hauler *See* Truckdrivers 1175
Water laboratory analyst *See* Science technicians 1054
Water rights examiner *See* Inspectors and

compliance officers, except construction . . . 508
Water supply operator *See* Water and wastewater treatment plant operators 1206
Water transportation occupations 1197
Water treatment facility operator *See* Water and wastewater treatment plant operators 1206
Water well driller *See* Mining, quarrying, and tunneling occupations 654
Water well pump installation contractor *See* Mining, quarrying, and tunneling occupations 654
Water works operator *See* Water and wastewater treatment plant operators 1206
Weather modifier *See* Appendix 1: Occupations Rarely Licensed 1225
Weighing and measuring device dealer/repairer *See* Precision instrument repairers 832
Weighmaster *See* Inspectors and compliance officers, except construction 508
Welders *See* Appendix 1: Occupations Rarely Licensed 1225
Well Driller *See* Mining, quarrying, and tunneling occupations 654
Whitewater rafting guide *See* Appendix 1: Occupations Rarely Licensed 1225
Wholesale and retail buyers and merchandise managers 1223
Wild game and bird breeder *See* Appendix 1: Occupations Rarely Licensed 1225
Wildlife control operator *See* Animal caretakers and trainers, except farm 71
Wildlife exhibitor *See* Appendix 1: Occupations Rarely Licensed 1225
Wildlife propagator *See* Appendix 1: Occupations Rarely Licensed 1225
Wireman *See* Electricians 366
Wrestler *See* Athletes, coaches, umpires, and referees 109

Professional and Occupational Licensing Directory

Accountants and Auditors

The following states grant licenses in this occupational category as of the date of publication:

Alabama	District of	Iowa	Minnesota	New Mexico	Rhode Island	Washington
Alaska	Columbia	Kansas	Mississippi	New York	South Carolina	West Virginia
Arizona	Florida	Kentucky	Missouri	North Carolina	South Dakota	Wisconsin
Arkansas	Georgia	Louisiana	Montana	North Dakota	Tennessee	Wyoming
California	Hawaii	Maine	Nebraska	Ohio	Texas	
Colorado	Idaho	Maryland	Nevada	Oklahoma	Utah	
Connecticut	Illinois	Massachusetts	New Hampshire	Oregon	Vermont	
Delaware	Indiana	Michigan	New Jersey	Pennsylvania	Virginia	

Alabama

Certified Public Accountant
Alabama State Board of Public
  Accountancy
12 Commerce Row
529 S. Perry St.
Montgomery, AL 36104-3503
Phone: (205)242-5700

Credential Type: CPA Certificate and permit to practice. **Duration of License:** One year. **Requirements:** Citizen of the United States or declaration of intent to become a citizen. 19 years of age. Good moral character. Meet specified educational requirements. Pass the Uniform CPA Examination. Pass the American Institute of Certified Public Accountants' course "Professional Ethics for CPAs."

Must hold a baccalaureate from an accredited college or university. A candidate may sit for the exam without being in public accounting if he/she possesses a degree with a major in accounting or its equivalent. After January 1, 1995, any person who has not previously sat for the uniform written CPA examination must have completed a total of 150 semester hours or 225 quarter hours of postsecondary education, including a baccalaureate at a college or university accredited by a regional accreditation board. The total education program must include an accounting concentration as defined by the Board of Accountancy and such other course work as the board may require by regulation.

Two years experience in public accounting required for permit to practice. Continuing professional education requirement is 40 hours each fiscal year by September 30. **Examination:** Uniform CPA Examination. **Reciprocity:** An applicant for a reciprocal CPA certificate based on a certificate issued by another state must be a citizen of the United States or have declared an intent to become a citizen. Must also be 19 years of age and good moral character. Must have satisfactorily passed an ethics examination acceptable to the board.

Foreign accountants holding a certificate, license, or degree in a foreign country may be issued a permit to practice at the discretion of the board. **Fees:** $50 application. $125 examination. $25 reexamination registration, plus fees for the following exam parts: $50 for accounting practice; $25 for auditing; $25 for business law; and $25 for accounting theory. $150 reexamination (all parts). $50 reciprocal certificate. $35 annual permit. $25 inactive certificate registration.

Credential Type: Temporary permit. **Authorization:** Granted to an out-of-state CPA to fulfill specific engagements contracted for outside Alabama. **Fees:** $35.

Alaska

Certified Public Accountant
Alaska State Board of Public
  Accountancy
Dept. of Commerce
Div. of Occupational Licensing
PO Box D
Juneau, AK 99811-0800
Phone: (907)465-2580

Credential Type: CPA Certificate and permit to practice. **Duration of License:** Two years. **Requirements:** 19 years of age. Good moral character. Meet specified educational and experience requirements. Pass the Uniform CPA Examination. Pass an examination in professional ethics.

Minimum of two years of study at a recognized college or university, or show graduation from a recognized university with either an accounting or non-accounting baccalaureate. Such study, if two years in length, must include at least 12 semester hours of accounting.

Four years of professional accounting experience are required if applicant has completed two years of study; three years if applicant holds a baccalaureate with a non-accounting major; or two years if applicant holds a baccalaureate with a major in accounting. **Examination:** Uniform CPA Examination. **Reciprocity:** No. **Fees:** $30 application. $70 examination. $70 reexamination (all parts). $180 active permit (biennial). $95 inactive registration (biennial). $30 nonresident permit application. $100 partnership or corporation biennial permit/license. $30 application for general permit to practice (annual). $90 general permit to practice (annual).

Credential Type: Temporary permit. **Duration of License:** Six months. **Authorization:** Granted to out-of-state CPAs. **Requirements:** Must meet all CPA requirements except residency, having a place of business, or be regularly employed in Alaska. **Fees:** No fee.

Arizona

Certified Public Accountant
Arizona State Board of Accountancy
3110 N. 19th Ave., Ste. 140
Phoenix, AZ 85015-6038
Phone: (602)255-2648

Credential Type: CPA Certificate and permit to practice. **Duration of License:** Two years. **Requirements:** Resident of Arizona. 18 years of age. Good moral character.

Arkansas 4

Certified Public Accountant, continued

Meet specified education and experience requirements. Pass the Uniform CPA Examination. Pass course in professional ethics.

Must hold a bachelor's degree from one of the universities or state colleges of this state or from a recognized college or university with 24 semester hours in accounting and 18 in related subjects. May sit for examination if educational requirements are met within 90 days of written examination.

Two years of experience in public accounting or experience in industry or government as approved by Board are required. Those holding a master's degree in accounting or business administration require one year of experience. **Examination:** Uniform CPA Examination. **Reciprocity:** A reciprocal CPA certificate may be issued to a CPA of another state who is a resident of Arizona. Must have two years experience that is acceptable to the Board of Accountancy. Must meet educational and examination requirements of the Arizona Accountancy Law. American Institute of Certified Public Accountants' professional ethics exam may be required if not previously passed. Original certificate must be in good standing with the state of issue. **Fees:** $60 preexamination. $175 examination. $50 reexamination (per part). $175 reexamination (all parts). $175 proctoring (out-of-state). $50 reciprocal certificate. $100 registration (biennial). $100 firm registration.

Arkansas
4

Accountant
Arkansas State Board of Public Accountancy
1515 W. 7th St., Ste. 320
Little Rock, AR 72202
Phone: (501)682-1520

Credential Type: License. **Requirements:** Bachelor's degree in accounting or equivalent. Resident of Arkansas or regular employee in the state. Two years of acceptable work experience (a Master's degree may waive one year of experience). **Examination:** Yes. **Fees:** $150 ($30 per part) for written examination.

California
5

Certified Public Accountant
California State Board of Accountancy
2135 Butano Dr., Ste 112
Sacramento, CA 985825-045
Phone: (916)920-7121

Credential Type: CPA Certificate and permit to practice. **Duration of License:** Two years. **Requirements:** Meet specified educational and experience requirements. Pass the Uniform CPA Examination and a course in professional ethics.

Must hold a baccalaureate with a concentration in accounting from an accredited college or university or have completed a two-year course of study at college level with studies in accounting and related courses for a period of four years. May be able to sit for examination if candidate expects to meet the educational requirements within 120 days following written exam. Education requirement may also be satisfied by the successful completion of a special examination approved by the board.

Three years of public accounting experience are required for applicant who holds a baccalaureate with concentration in accounting; four years experience are required of applicants not holding baccalaureates. Private or government experience, not to exceed four years, may be accepted. **Examination:** Uniform CPA Examination. **Reciprocity:** A CPA certificate may be issued to a CPA of another state who has a residence or office in California and is actively engaged in the practice of public accounting. Must meet experience and educational requirements in effect in California at the time the original certificate was issued. Professional ethics exam may be required. Must have completed 40 hours of continuing education in the 12 months prior to filing an application. Following licensure, 20 hours of continuing professional education must be completed for each six months between the date of licensure and the next renewal date. **Fees:** $185 examination. $25 reexamination (per part). $185 reexamination (all parts). $200 reciprocal certificate. $200 biennial permit renewal.

Credential Type: Temporary Permit. **Authorization:** Permitted on business incident to regular home business. Applicant who has filed an application for a certificate may practice temporarily until the Board approves or rejects his application. **Fees:** No fee.

Colorado
6

Certified Public Accountant
Colorado State Board of Accountancy
1525 Sherman St., Rm. 617
Denver, CO 80203-1719
Phone: (303)866-2869

Credential Type: CPA Certificate and permit to practice. **Duration of License:** Two years. **Requirements:** Meet the specified educational and experience requirements. Successfully complete the Uniform CPA Examination and the American Institute of Certified Public Accountants' (AICPA) course and examination.

Must hold baccalaureate with a concentration in accounting or its equivalent, or a non-accounting concentration supplemented by what the Board determines to be the equivalent. A concentration in accounting requires 27 semester hours in accounting subjects, at least three hours must be in auditing, and no more than three hours may be in accounting-related computer and information systems. Must have 21 semester hours in business-related subjects. No more than six hours may be in any one area. Applicant may be eligible to sit for examination if he expects to successfully complete the educational requirements within 60 days of the written exam.

One year public accounting experience or equivalent required for permit to practice. In lieu of experience, the Board will accept a master's degree or 30 semester hours of graduate credit. In addition, to qualify in lieu of experience, an applicant must have 45 hours in accounting subjects, of which at least six hours must be in auditing and not more than six in accounting-related computer and information systems. Also, the applicant must have 36 hours of business-related courses with not more than nine in any one area. **Examination:** Uniform CPA Examination; AICPA Ethics Examination. **Reciprocity:** A reciprocal CPA certificate may be issued to a CPA of another state who meets educational and experience requirements in effect in Colorado at the time that the original certificate was issued. A course and examination in professional ethics is required as a condition to receiving a certificate by reciprocity. **Fees:** $130 examination. $50 reexamination (one part). $70 reexamination (two parts). $90 reexamination (three parts). $120 reexamination (all parts). $35 proctoring exam. $110 reciprocal certificate. $96 biennial permit (individual). $125 biennial permit (firm). $69 original registration of firm.

Credential Type: Temporary Permit. **Authorization:** Temporary practice by an

Accountants and Auditors

District of Columbia

out-of-state accountant is permitted on professional business incident to regular out-of-state practice. **Fees:** No fee.

Connecticut

7

Certified Public Accountant
Connecticut State Board of
    Accountancy
30 Trinity St.
Hartford, CT 06106
Phone: (203)566-7835

Credential Type: CPA Certificate and permit to practice. **Duration of License:** One year. **Requirements:** Must be a resident of, or have a place for the regular transaction of business in, Connecticut. Must be 18 years of age. Meet specified educational and experience requirements. Pass the Uniform CPA Examination.

To sit for the Uniform CPA Examination, an applicant must hold a baccalaureate from an accredited four-year institution. Must have at least 46 semester hours in the study of accounting and related subjects of which 24 hours must be in accounting; three hours in economics; three hours in finance; three hours in business law; and 13 hours in business-related subjects.

Individuals employed in public accounting prior to April 27, 1983, are required to verify two years of experience. Those who began employment after this date have the option of verifying three years of experience or verifying two years of experience with 42 semester hours of accounting and 36 semester hours of business-related subjects. **Examination:** Uniform CPA Examination. **Reciprocity:** A reciprocal CPA certificate and license may be issued to a CPA of another state who resides in, or has a place for the regular transaction of business in, Connecticut. Applicant must practice public accounting as his/her principal occupation. Must have three years of public accounting experience. Must meet educational requirements in effect in Connecticut at the time that the original certificate was issued. The state of the applicant's original issuance must also grant a similar privilege to Connecticut CPAs. **Fees:** $220 examination. $220 reexamination (all parts). $150 reciprocal certificate application. $25 initial license. $150 license renewal (annual) $25 initial firm permit. $25 renewal firm permit.

Credential Type: Temporary permit. **Authorization:** Granted to an out-of-state accountant on professional business incident to his/her regular practice out of state. A limited permit may be issued to render public accounting services only to clients specified in the application for such permit. All permits expire on December 31 of the year in which they were issued. **Fees:** $25.

8

Internal Auditor (Racetrack)
Connecticut Div. of Special Revenue
Russell Rd.
PO Box 11424
Newington, CT 06111-0424
Phone: (203)566-2756

Credential Type: License Registration. **Requirements:** Submit application and fingerprint card. Pay fee. **Fees:** $5 registration fee.

Delaware

9

Certified Public Accountant
Delaware State Board of
    Accountancy
PO Box 1401
Dover, DE 19903
Phone: (302)736-4522

Credential Type: CPA Certificate and permit to practice. **Duration of License:** Two years. **Requirements:** Must be at least 18 years of age. Good moral character. Meet specified educational requirements. Pass Uniform CPA Examination. Pass an examination in professional ethics.

Applicant must hold a two-year degree with a concentration in accounting, or complete 21 semester hours of accounting or equivalent courses, from a recognized two-year college or university. Applicants may be able to sit for examination if they expect to meet the educational requirement within 120 days of the written examination.

Four full years of public accounting experience or eight years of full-time experience either as an owner, principal, or employee of a recognized firm engaged in the practice of public accountancy or in government, industry, or a related field are required for a permit to practice. In the alternative, an applicant holding a baccalaureate with a concentration in accounting is required to meet two years of acceptable experience under the guidance of a certified public accountant or four years under the supervision of a public accountant. An applicant with a master's degree with a concentration in accounting, or its equivalent, must have one year of experience under a certified public accountant or two years of experience under a public accountant. **Examination:** Uniform CPA Examination. **Reciprocity:** A reciprocal CPA certificate may be issued to a CPA of another state who is engaged full-time in public accountancy in Delaware. Must have two years public accounting experience; four years experience required with a two-year degree. Must meet the educational requirements in effect in Delaware at the time of filing the application. **Fees:** $150 examination. $100 reexamination (one, two, or three parts). $125 reexamination (all parts). $150 reciprocal certificate. $100 biennial permit (individual). $50 to $100 biennial permit (firm); fee dependant on the number of principals.

Credential Type: Temporary permit. **Duration of License:** One year. **Authorization:** May be issued to an out-of-state CPA practicing full time in the state of Delaware for a period of one year. **Fees:** $150.

District of Columbia

10

Certified Public Accountant
District of Columbia Board of
    Accountancy
Dept. of Consumer and Regulatory
    Affairs
614 H St., NW, Rm. 923
Washington, DC 20515-6019
Phone: (202)727-7468

Credential Type: CPA Certificate and permit to practice. **Duration of License:** One or two years. **Requirements:** 18 years of age. Resident of the District of Columbia or has been employed in the District for six months prior to the final date for accepting applications for the written examinations. If an employee of a District CPA firm, must have been a bona fide resident of a foreign country for at least 18 months and is not qualified to be examined in the state of last residence solely because of such foreign residence. Good moral character. Meet the specified educational requirements. Pass the Uniform CPA Examination.

Baccalaureate with a concentration in accounting, or what the board determines to be the equivalent, is required.

Certificate holders must have two years experience acceptable to the board in auditing or reviewing financial statements before being issued a permit to practice (including acceptable auditing and accounting experience in a governmental agency.) **Examination:** Uniform CPA Examination. **Reciprocity:** A CPA permit to practice by endorsement may be granted to a licensed CPA from another state who meets all qualifications and requirements (except residency and employment in the District) for an original CPA license. Must intend to practice public accounting in the District on a full-time basis. **Fees:** $120 application for examination. $120 reexamination fee (all parts). $20 CPA certificate. $80 endorse-

Certified Public Accountant, continued

ment application fee (reciprocity). $25 permit to practice (initial). $20 permit to practice (endorsement—one year). $40 permit to practice (endorsement—two years). $40 biennial permit (individual). $60 biennial permit (partnership or professional corporation).

Credential Type: Temporary permit. **Authorization:** Out-of-state accountants may temporarily or periodically perform specific accounting engagements in the District of Columbia on professional business, provided such practice is incident to their regular practice outside of the District and is conducted in conformity with the rules of professional conduct. **Fees:** No fee.

Florida

11

Certified Public Accountant
Florida Board of Accountancy
4001 NW 43rd St., Ste.16
Gainesville, FL 32606-4598
Phone: (904)336-2165

Credential Type: CPA Certificate and permit to practice. **Duration of License:** Two years. **Requirements:** May sit for the Uniform CPA Examination in Florida if of good moral character and meets the specified educational requirements. A CPA certificate will be granted upon passing the Uniform CPA Examination and an examination on the accountancy laws and rules.

To sit for the CPA Examination, an applicant must have a baccalaureate with a major in accounting, or its equivalent, from an accredited college or university and an additional 45 quarter hours which include a concentration in accounting and business courses as specified by the board. This includes 54 quarter hours in accounting education, above the elementary level. Must include no less than 18 quarter hours in financial accounting, eight quarter hours in auditing, eight quarter hours in taxation, and not more than four quarter hours in internship programs. Also 58 quarter hours in general business, including eight quarter hours in business law, are required.

No formal experience requirements for those applying after August 2, 1983. **Examination:** Uniform CPA Examination. **Reciprocity:** A certificate may be issued to a CPA of another state. Must meet the requirements in effect in Florida when their original license was issued and hold an active license to practice or meet certification requirements in effect in Florida at time of application. "Fifth year" requirement may be waived for those with five years experience in public accounting after licensure. Any person who received his/her original certificate after 1955 must be a graduate of a four-year accredited college with a major in accounting. Applicants must present evidence of completion of continuing professional education equal to that required of a Florida license in the two years immediately preceding application. After receiving reciprocal certificate, applicants must complete the required continuing education. **Fees:** $175 examination (non-refundable). $30 reexamination (per part). $150 reexamination (all parts). $150 reciprocal certificate (endorsement; nonrefundable). $100 biennial registration (individual) $150 biennial registration (partnership or professional service corporation).

Credential Type: Temporary permit. **Duration of License:** 90 days. **Authorization:** May be issued to out-of-state practitioners to fulfill specific engagements. Not valid for more than 90 days. Will not be granted to practitioners who are residents or maintain full-time staff in Florida. **Fees:** $200.

Georgia

12

Certified Public Accountant
Georgia State Board of Accountancy
166 Pryor St. SW
Atlanta, GA 30303
Phone: (404)656-3941

Credential Type: CPA Certificate and permit to practice. **Duration of License:** Two years. **Requirements:** 18 years of age. Good moral character. Meet specified educational and experience requirements. Pass Uniform CPA Examination.

Must hold a baccalaureate with a major in accounting, or a non-accounting major with supplementary classes that are the equivalent, from a recognized college or university. Applicant may be eligible to sit for examination if he/she expects to meet the educational requirements within 120 days of the written examination.

Two years experience in public accounting preceding the date of application for certificate are required. Or may fulfill requirement with five years of continuous employment in the accounting field in industry, government, or college teaching. **Examination:** Uniform CPA Examination. **Reciprocity:** Reciprocal permit will be issued to a CPA who holds a current permit to practice in another jurisdiction if he/she passes an examination equivalent to that required by the Georgia board. Must meet equivalent educational and experience requirements in Georgia. Ten years of public accounting experience may be accepted in lieu of the examination requirement. State where permit was originally issued must grant similar privilege to Georgia CPAs. **Fees:** $150 examination. $45 reexamination (one part). $65 reexamination (two parts). $90 reexamination (three parts). $140 reexamination (all parts). $20 application fee for certificate of registration. $120 reciprocal certificate. $50 biennial permit. $50 firm/office registration.

Credential Type: Temporary permit. **Duration of License:** 90 days. **Authorization:** Granted to individuals or firms not residing in Georgia but holding valid permits from another jurisdiction. Allows the performance of specific professional engagements involving the practice of public accounting. Valid for 90 days and limited to a single, specific, professional engagement. **Fees:** $120.

13

Foreign Accountant
State Board of Accountancy
Professional Examining Boards
166 Pryor St., SW
Atlanta, GA 30303
Phone: (404)656-3933

Credential Type: License. **Requirements:** Contact licensing body for application information.

14

Registered Public Accountant
State Board of Accountancy
Professional Examining Boards
166 Pryor St., SW
Atlanta, GA 30303
Phone: (404)656-3933

Credential Type: License. **Requirements:** Contact licensing body for application information.

Hawaii

15

Certified Public Accountant
Hawaii Board of Public Accountancy
Dept. of Commerce and Consumer Affairs
PO Box 3469
Honolulu, HI 96801
Phone: (808)548-7471

Credential Type: License. **Requirements:** 18 years of age. Bachelor's degree in accounting plus 30 semester hours of graduate-level business-related subjects or 30 months of public accounting practice; or a bachelor's degree in another field plus 18 semester hours of graduate level accounting/auditing, plus 30 semester hours of graduate-level business-related courses or 30 months of experience with a public accounting firm; or 1,500 chargable hours in auditing involving generally accepted accounting principles; or two years of professional work experience in public accounting practice. Three "Certificates of Competence." **Examination:** American Institute of Certified Public Accountants (AICPA) Uniform CPA Exam. Open-book laws and ethics exam. **Fees:** $225 CPA exam fee. $95 to $135 certification fee. $55 to $125 permit to practice fee.

Idaho

16

Certified Public Accountant
Idaho State Board of Accountancy
500 S. 10th St., Ste.104
Statehouse Mail
Boise, ID 83720
Phone: (208)334-2490

Credential Type: CPA Certificate and permit to practice. **Duration of License:** One year. **Requirements:** 18 years of age. Good moral character. Meet the specified educational and experience requirements. Pass the Uniform CPA Examination. Pass course in professional ethics. Presently is, has been, or plans to be a resident of Idaho.

Must hold a baccalaureate with 30 semester hours in business administration subjects, of which at least 20 semester hours are in accounting, from a recognized college or university. Applicants may be eligible to sit for examination if they expect to complete the educational requirements within 90 days of the written examination.

One year of public accounting experience is required or two years of accounting experience which the board recognizes as being equivalent. **Examination:** Uniform CPA Examination. **Reciprocity:** Reciprocal permits may be granted to out-of-state CPAs who meet general qualifications and the educational and experience requirements of the board. An examination in professional ethics is required. **Fees:** $100 examination. $30 reexamination (one part). $30 reexamination (each additional part). $100 reexamination (all parts). $50 reciprocal certificate. $75 annual license. $40 annual license (over 65).

Credential Type: Temporary permit. **Duration of License:** 30 days. **Authorization:** Temporary practice by an out-of-state accountant is permitted on business incident to his/her regular practice and is not to exceed 30 days in any calendar year. **Fees:** No fee.

Illinois

17

Certified Public Accountant
Illinois Dept. of Professional
 Regulation
Licensing and Enforcement
Public Accountancy Section
320 W. Washington St., 3rd Fl.
Springfield, IL 62786-0001
Phone: (217)785-0800

Credential Type: CPA Certificate and permit to practice. **Duration of License:** Two years. **Requirements:** 18 years of age. Meet specified education requirements. Pass the Uniform CPA Examination.

Before sitting for the Uniform CPA Examination, candidates must complete 120 semester hours of college/university level credits of which at least 27 hours must be in accounting, auditing, and business law (limiting business law to no more than six semester hours).

Experience is not required for the issuance of a certificate. However, before a CPA desiring to practice may register, he/she must have at least one year of experience on the professional staff of a practicing public accountant, in a responsible audit position in a governmental agency, or experience of an equivalent nature. **Examination:** Uniform CPA Examination. **Reciprocity:** An individual may be issued a reciprocal certificate if he/she holds a valid, unrevoked certificate issued under the laws of any jurisdiction and granted on the basis of the written examination and educational requirements in effect in Illinois at the time. A reciprocal license may be issued to any public accountant licensed under the laws of another jurisdiction with requirements equivalent to Illinois at the time of issue. **Fees:** $180 CPA certificate examination. $90 reexamination (one part). CPA Certificate: $105 reexamination (two parts); $120 reexamination (three parts); $145 reexamination (all parts); $170 reciprocal certificate (endorsement); $170 transfer of grades. License: $75 application (individual); $40 biennial renewal (individual); $75 initial fee (partnership); $80 renewal fee (partnership); $100 reciprocal certificate (endorsement).

Credential Type: Temporary permit. **Authorization:** Granted to out-of-state CPAs for professional business incident to regular practice in another jurisdiction. **Fees:** No fee.

18

General Accountant (Gaming)
Illinois Gaming Board
PO Box 19474
Springfield, IL 62794-9474
Phone: (217)524-0228

Credential Type: General Accountant License. **Duration of License:** One year. **Requirements:** At least 18 years of age. U.S. citizen. No felony convictions. High school graduate or equivalent. Six months experience in an accounting office. Good computer skills. **Reciprocity:** No. **Fees:** $75 application/initial license fee. $50 renewal fee. **Governing Statute:** Illinois Revised Statutes, Chapter 120.

Indiana

19

Accounting Practitioner
Indiana State Board of Public
 Accountancy
Professional Licensing Agency
1021 State Office Bldg.
Indianapolis, IN 46204
Phone: (317)232-3898

Credential Type: License. **Requirements:** Contact licensing body for application information.

20

Certified Public Accountant
Indiana State Board of Public
 Accountancy
Professional Licensing Agency
1021 State Office Bldg.
Indianapolis, IN 46204
Phone: (317)232-3898

Credential Type: CPA Certificate and permit to practice. **Duration of License:** Two years. **Requirements:** 18 years of age. Good moral character. Meet specified educational and experience requirements. Pass Uniform CPA Examination. Pass special examination in professional ethics. Must live in Indiana at least 60 days immediately preceding submission of application or must have maintained a permanent residence in Indiana for the preceding six months.

Must hold a baccalaureate with 40 or more semester hours (60 quarter hours) at the undergraduate level in accounting, business administration and economics. Twenty semester hours (30 quarter hours) must be in accounting and/or business law (limiting business law to six hours.) Applicants receiving credit for 30 or more semester

Indiana 21

Certified Public Accountant, continued

hours (45 quarter hours) at the graduate level in accounting, business administration, and economics must have at least 16 semester hours (24 quarter hours) in accounting and/or business law with no more than four hours in business law. Applicants may be eligible to sit for exam if they expect to meet the educational requirements within 60 days of taking the written exam.

To qualify for a certificate, applicants must have three years of experience in public accounting or three to six years of experience in industry, government, or college teaching which, in the opinion of the board, is equivalent. A recognized master's degree in accounting or business administration may be substituted for one year of public accounting experience. **Examination:** Uniform CPA Examination. **Reciprocity:** A reciprocal certificate may be issued to an out-of-state CPA who is a resident of Indiana or maintains an office and practices public accounting in Indiana. Must have three years of public accounting experience or its equivalent. Must meet educational requirements as determined by the board. Original state of issue must provide reciprocity to Indiana's CPAs. **Fees:** $135 examination. $90 reexamination (one to three parts). $135 reexamination (all parts). $75 reciprocal certificate. $30 permit to practice. $50 biennial registration. $60 proctoring (out-of-state candidates).

Credential Type: Temporary permit. **Authorization:** Granted to an out-of-state CPA on business incident to his/her regular practice, provided that such practice is conducted in conformity with the board's rules. **Fees:** $30.

21

Public Accountant
Indiana State Board of Public Accountancy
Professional Licensing Agency
1021 State Office Bldg.
Indianapolis, IN 46204
Phone: (317)232-3898

Credential Type: License. **Requirements:** Contact licensing body for application information.

Iowa

22

Accountant (Riverboat Gambling)
Iowa Racing and Gaming Commission
Lucas State Office Bldg.
Des Moines, IA 50319
Phone: (515)281-7352

Credential Type: License Registration. **Requirements:** Submit application and pay fees. **Fees:** $50 license fee.

23

Accounting Practitioner
Iowa Accountancy Examining Board
1918 SE Hulsizer
Ankeny, IA 50021
Phone: (515)281-7363

Credential Type: License. **Duration of License:** Two years. **Requirements:** Two years of continuous experience as an accounting practitioner in the employ of a CPA or AP; or a graduate of a four-year, accredited college with a major in accounting; or a graduate in accounting from an accredited business or correspondence school. **Examination:** Two parts of the Uniform CPA Examination. **Fees:** $150 exam fee. $20 license fee. $20 renewal fee.

24

Auditor (Riverboat Gambling)
Iowa Racing and Gaming Commission
Lucas State Office Bldg.
Des Moines, IA 50319
Phone: (515)281-7352

Credential Type: License Registration. **Requirements:** Submit application and pay fees. **Fees:** $50 license fee.

25

Certified Public Accountant
Iowa Accounting Examining Board
1918 SE Hulsizer
Ankeny, IA 50021
Phone: (515)281-7363

Credential Type: Certificate. **Duration of License:** Two years. **Requirements:** The applicant must be a final semester senior with a concentration in accounting, a college graduate with a concentration in accounting, or have three years of qualifying public accounting experience. **Examination:** Uniform CPA Examination. **Reciprocity:** Yes. **Fees:** $150 exam fee. $20 renewal fee.

Kansas

26

Certified Public Accountant
Kansas Board of Accountancy
Landon State Office Bldg.
900 SW Jackson St., Ste. 556
Topeka, KS 66612-1220
Phone: (913)296-2162

Credential Type: CPA Certificate and permit to practice. **Duration of License:** One or two years. **Requirements:** Must be a resident of, have a place of business for public accounting in, or be permanently employed in public accounting in Kansas. Meet specified educational and experience requirements. Pass the Uniform CPA Examination. Pass the American Institute of Certified Public Accountants' (AICPA) course in professional ethics.

To sit for the examination, an applicant must hold a baccalaureate or higher degree with a concentration in accounting, as defined by board regulations, from a recognized college or university or a baccalaureate or higher degree and complete two years of acceptable public accounting experience. Candidates who expect to complete their educational requirements within 90 days of taking the written examination may be eligible to sit for the Uniform CPA Examination.

An applicant who meets the general, educational, and examination requirements will be approved for a Kansas CPA certificate upon application. A permit (license) to hold out and practice as a CPA will only be issued to a Kansas CPA who meets one of the following experience requirements: (a) two years of practical public accounting experience under a practicing, licensed CPA, including at least six months of auditing, or (b) master's or higher degree with a concentration in accounting, as defined by the board, and six months of practical public accounting auditing experience under a licensed, practicing CPA. Kansas CPAs not performing any type of services for the public which are normally done by public accountants may use the designation CPA without a permit. **Examination:** Uniform CPA Examination. **Reciprocity:** A reciprocal certificate may be issued to an out-of-state CPA who becomes a resident of, has a place of business as a public accountant in, or is permanently employed in public accounting in Kansas. Must meet the same educational and experience requirements for a permit as required of Kansas CPAs. Must agree to meet continuing education requirements as defined by Board.

Fees: $125 CPA certificate (includes initial examination fee). $50 reexamination (one part). $60 reexamination (two parts). $75 reexamination (three parts). $100 reexamination (all parts). $125 reciprocal certificate or transfer of grades from another state. $90 biennial permit to practice. $45 permit to practice (one year or less). $135 late permit renewal or reinstatement (biennial); $67.50 (annual).

Credential Type: Temporary permit. **Authorization:** Temporary permits are required for out-of-state CPAs wishing to practice in Kansas on business not incidental to their practice in another state. Temporary practice is permitted without a permit for professional business incidental to regular practice in another state. The board determines what is considered to be incidental practice. **Fees:** $50.

Kentucky

27

Certified Public Accountant
Kentucky State Board of Accountancy
332 W. Broadway, Ste. 310
Louisville, KY 40202-2115
Phone: (502)588-3037

Credential Type: CPA Certificate and permit to practice. **Duration of License:** One year. **Requirements:** Must be a resident, have an office in, or are regularly employed in Kentucky at the time of admission to the Uniform CPA Examination. 18 years of age. Good moral character. Pass the Uniform CPA examination. Pass an examination in professional ethics.

Must have a baccalaureate with a major or concentration (39 semester hours of business related courses of which 27 hours must be accounting courses) from a recognized college or university.

Must have affidavits from his/her employer attesting that the applicant has attained two years of public accounting experience to be granted a permit to practice; one year must be full-time and the other may be satisfied with part-time experience, which will be accorded half credit. Those holding a master's degree in public accounting or business administration must have one year of public accounting experience. All candidates must have a portfolio of qualifying experience which includes 500 hours in audit and review work and documentation of participation in 10 of 17 analytical procedures and techniques specified in the regulations. **Examination:** Uniform CPA Examination. **Reciprocity:** Issued to CPA of another state who is a resident of or has an office in Kentucky. Must meet experience and educational requirements in Kentucky at the time the original certificate was issued or have four years of public accounting experience within the 10 years immediately preceding application. An open-book examination on the law, regulations, and rules of professional conduct is required. **Fees:** $125 examination. $25 reexamination (per part). $125 reexamination (all parts). $25 certificate. $25 reciprocal certificate. $50 annual permit.

Credential Type: Temporary permit. **Duration of License:** Six months. **Authorization:** May be issued to out-of-state CPA to fulfill specific engagements in Kentucky. Permit is valid for six months after issuance then must be renewed to continue practice. Firms renewing after six months must comply with the stipulations of the board's Quality Enhancement Program. **Fees:** $50.

Louisiana

28

Accountant/Certified Public Accountant
State Board of Certified Public Accountants of Louisiana
1515 World Trade Center
2 Canal St.
New Orleans, LA 70130
Phone: (504)566-1244

Credential Type: License. **Duration of License:** One year. **Requirements:** Two years of public accounting experience or its equivalent. A master's degree shall be considered the equivalent to one year of public accounting experience. At least 120 hours of continuing education every three years. **Examination:** Yes. **Reciprocity:** Yes. **Fees:** $100 exam fee. $50 certification fee. $50 license fee.

Maine

29

Certified Public Accountant
Maine State Board of Accountancy
Dept. of Professional and Financial Regulation
Div. of Licensing and Enforcement
State House Station 35
Augusta, ME 04333
Phone: (207)582-8723

Credential Type: License. **Duration of License:** One year. **Requirements:** Must be a resident of Maine and have a place of business in or be regularly employed in Maine. 18 years of age. Good moral character. Meet specified educational and experience requirements. Pass the Uniform CPA Examination.

Must hold a baccalaureate from a recognized college or university. Applicant who expects to meet the educational requirement within 120 days of the written examination may be eligible to sit for examination.

Must present evidence of two years experience in public accounting to be granted certificate. One year of experience is required with a master's degree. **Examination:** Uniform CPA Examination. **Reciprocity:** Granted to CPA from another state who is a resident of Maine. Must have one or two years of public accounting experience (determined by years of schooling) and meet the educational requirement in effect at the time that the original certificate was issued. **Fees:** $120 examination. $30 reexamination (one part). $120 reexamination (all parts). $35 annual registration permit.

Credential Type: Temporary permit. **Authorization:** Temporary practice by an out-of-state accountant is permitted on professional business incident to his/her regular practice outside the state. **Fees:** No fee.

Maryland

30

Certified Public Accountant
Maryland State Board of Public Accountancy
501 St. Paul Pl., 9th Fl.
Baltimore, MD 21202-2222
Phone: (301)333-6322

Credential Type: CPA Certificate and permit to practice. **Duration of License:** Two years. **Requirements:** 18 years of age. Good moral character. Meet specified educational requirements. Pass Uniform CPA Examination. Pass course in professional ethics.

Must hold a baccalaureate with a major in accounting, or a substantial equivalent, and a minimum of 45 semester hours in accounting and related subjects. At least 30 hours must consist of one or more courses each in auditing, financial accounting, cost accounting, federal income tax, and business law; 15 must consist of one course each in statistics, computer science (information systems or data processing), economics, corporation or business finance and management. **Examination:** Uniform CPA Examination. **Reciprocity:** A CPA of another state may be issued a permit if he/she meets the educational requirements in effect in Maryland at the time the original license was issued. Examination in professional ethics is required. **Fees:** $120 exami-

Massachusetts 31

Certified Public Accountant, continued

nation. $60 reexamination (less than all parts). $80 reexamination (all parts). $50 reciprocal certificate. $80 biennial registration (active); $40 (inactive).

Credential Type: Temporary permit. **Duration of License:** One year. **Authorization:** Individuals may secure a limited license, and corporations or partnerships a limited permit. Issued for one year and is for practice on a specified job. **Requirements:** File application and pay fee. Meet requirements of board. **Fees:** As determined by board.

Massachusetts 31

Certified Public Accountant
Massachusetts Board of Public
  Accountancy
Saltonstall Bldg., Rm. 1514
100 Cambridge St.
Boston, MA 02202-0001
Phone: (617)727-1753

Credential Type: CPA Certificate and permit to practice. **Duration of License:** Two years. **Requirements:** 18 years of age. Good moral character. Meet specified education and experience requirements. Pass Uniform CPA Examination.

Must hold a baccalaureate (or be in final semester) from a recognized college or university with 24 hours in accounting or related subjects to sit for examination.

Must have three years of experience in public accounting. An applicant with a master's degree and 24 semester hours of accounting is required to have two years of experience. Board may grant one year of experience for every two or three full years of equivalent experience with the U.S. Government, the Commonwealth of Massachusetts, or a subdivision thereof. **Examination:** Uniform CPA Examination. **Reciprocity:** May be issued to a CPA of another state who meets all current requirements in Massachusetts at the time the application is made or the requirements in effect at the time the original certificate was issued. A CPA who passes all requirements except that he/she passed the Uniform CPA Examination under conditional credit provisions different from those in Massachusetts, must have been engaged in full time practice as a CPA licensed in another state for five of the last 10 years. **Fees:** $200 examination. $120 reexamination (one part). $135 reexamination (two parts). $160 reexamination (three parts). $200 reexamination (all parts). $20 biennial continuing professional education (maximum) $260 reciprocal certificate. $135 biennial permit.

Michigan 32

Certified Public Accountant
Michigan Board of Accountancy
Dept. of Licensing and Regulation
PO Box 30018
Lansing, MI 48909-7518
Phone: (517)373-0682

Credential Type: CPA Certificate and permit to practice. **Duration of License:** Two years. **Requirements:** 18 years of age. Good moral character. Meet specified education and experience requirements. Pass Uniform CPA Examination.

Must hold a baccalaureate with a concentration in accounting from an educational institution recognized by the board. Must be a resident of, have a place of business in, or be regularly employed in Michigan before candidate is eligible to sit for examination.

Must have two years experience in a responsible audit position in public accounting, or the equivalent experience in government, within six years of application. Candidates holding advanced degrees in accounting, or their equivalent, may have the equivalent of one year of experience. Candidates holding graduate degrees in accounting, or their equivalent, and have two years experience in teaching (above the elementary level), within a period of six years prior to application, are considered to have one year of experience. **Examination:** Uniform CPA Examination. **Reciprocity:** May be issued to a CPA of another state or territory of the United States if an equivalent exam has been passed or he/she has maintained an office for the practice of public accounting for not less than 10 years. Must meet the equivalent continuing professional education requirements when application is made for a license to practice. **Fees:** $120 examination. $40 reexamination (one part). $55 reexamination (two parts). $70 reexamination (three parts). $85 reexamination (all parts). $100 reexamination (all parts). $35 application processing fee. $50 biennial license. $20 biennial registration form.

Credential Type: Temporary permit. **Duration of License:** One year. **Authorization:** May obtain a temporary permit if certified properly outside the state for a one-year period to work directly under a licensed individual supervisor. **Fees:** $15.

Minnesota 33

Certified Public Accountant
Minnesota State Board of
  Accountancy
133 E. 7th St., 3rd Fl.
St. Paul, MN 55101
Phone: (612)296-7937

Credential Type: CPA Certificate and permit to practice. **Duration of License:** One year. **Requirements:** 18 years of age. Good moral character. Meet specified education and experience requirements. Pass Uniform CPA Examination. Pass written examination on professional ethics.

Must hold a diploma as a graduate of an accredited high school, or have equivalent education, and meet specified experience requirement to sit for examination. Those who meet additional education requirement, as specified by Board, may waive the experience requirement.

An applicant who has graduated from an accredited high school must have five years of experience to sit for examination and six years to be granted a license, or if applicant has completed two years of study in an accredited college or university, he/she must have three years experience to sit for examination and five years for a license. If candidate has a baccalaureate with an accounting major from an accredited college or university, he/she may sit for examination with no experience but must have two years of experience before being granted a license or one year if the applicant holds a master's degree. Experience may include public accounting experience and experience as an auditor or examiner with an agency of government, as approved by the board. **Examination:** Uniform CPA Examination. **Reciprocity:** May be granted to a CPA of another state who meets the required educational and experience standards and demonstrates, to the satisfaction of the Board, a need for a Minnesota license. Ethics examination required if not previously passed. **Fees:** $115 examination. $30 reexamination (per part). $115 reexamination (all parts). $100 reciprocal license. $100 initial registration for corporation. $30 annual license (individual) $35 annual license (partnership or corporation).

Mississippi

34

Certified Public Accountant
Mississippi State Board of Public
    Accountancy
961 Highway 80 E., Ste. A
Clinton, MS 39056-5246
Phone: (601)924-8457

Credential Type: CPA Certificate and permit to practice. **Duration of License:** One year. **Requirements:** Certificate requirements: Resident of Mississippi. Good moral character. Meet specified education and experience requirements. Pass Uniform CPA Examination. License requirements: Hold certificate in good standing. Meet the experience requirements.

Must have a degree from a recognized four-year college.

A license to practice may be issued to a certificate holder who has passed the Uniform CPA Examination, has a four-year college degree with a major in accounting and one year of public accounting experience on the staff of a licensed, practicing CPA, including a minimum of 500 hours in auditing work. Three years experience in industry, business, government, or college teaching, approved by the board, may be accepted in lieu of one year of public accounting experience. Candidates with a four-year college degree, with a major other than accounting, will be required to complete one additional year of public accounting or four years of acceptable equivalent experience. **Examination:** Uniform CPA Examination. **Reciprocity:** May be issued to a CPA of another state who has been in public practice as a CPA for three of the past 10 years, or who otherwise meets the educational and experience requirements for obtaining an original Mississippi certificate and license. Will only issue certificates and licenses to individuals from states that grant similar privileges to Mississippi CPAs. **Fees:** $107 examination. $27 reexamination (one part). $42 reexamination (two parts). $57 reexamination (three parts). $87 reexamination (all parts). $100 reciprocal certificate and license. Annual registration fees: $15 original certificate. $25 reciprocal certificate. $25 license to practice.

Credential Type: Temporary permit. **Duration of License:** 30 days in a calendar year. **Authorization:** Granted to a CPA from another state to practice on a temporary basis if such practice is incident to the practitioner's regular practice out-of-state. Temporary is defined as less than 30 days during a year and does not include engagements with a Mississippi domiciled entity. **Fees:** No fee.

Missouri

35

Certified Public Accountant
Missouri State Board of Accountancy
PO Box 613
Jefferson City, MO 65102-0613
Phone: (314)751-0012

Credential Type: CPA Certificate and permit to practice. **Duration of License:** One year. **Requirements:** A certificate shall be granted to a person who is a resident of, has a place of business in, or is regularly employed in Missouri. Must be 21 years of age. Good moral character. Meet specified educational requirements. Pass the Uniform CPA Examination. Pass a course in professional ethics.

Must hold a baccalaureate conferred by an accredited college or university with a concentration in accounting or what the board determines to be equivalent.

Experience is required before a permit to practice is issued to certificate holders. Must have two years experience in public accounting under the supervision of a licensed CPA. Only one year of experience is required of an internal revenue agent who has at least four years experience with the Internal Revenue Service. Also acceptable are two to four years experience in the practice of governmental accounting, budgeting, and auditing as an employee of the state, a political subdivision of this state, or the U.S. government under the supervision of a licensed CPA. **Examination:** Uniform CPA Examination. **Reciprocity:** May be issued to a CPA of another state who meets the general qualifications required of Missouri candidate. **Fees:** $150 examination. $30 reexamination (per part). $150 reexamination (all parts). $150 reciprocal certificate. $25 issuance of certificate. $150 professional corporate permit. $150 partnership permit. $114 annual permit.

Credential Type: Temporary permit. **Authorization:** Out-of-state CPAs who have Missouri clients may practice temporarily on professional business incident to regular practice. **Requirements:** Must conform with Missouri law and Board rules. Must be licensed. **Fees:** No fee.

Montana

36

Accountant
Montana Board of Public
    Accountants
111 N. Jackson
Helena, MT 59620
Phone: (406)444-3739

Credential Type: Certificate. **Duration of License:** One year. **Requirements:** Bachelor's degree in accounting or equivalent. 120 hours of continuing education every three years. **Examination:** Written. **Fees:** $100 exam fee. $60 certificate fee. $60 renewal fee. **Governing Statute:** Montana Code Annotated 37-50-301 through 37-50-342.

37

Auditor (Racetrack)
State of Montana Board of Horse
    Racing
Dept. of Commerce
1424 9th Ave.
Helena, MT 59620
Phone: (406)444-4287

Credential Type: License Registration. **Requirements:** Submit application and fingerprint card. Pay fee. **Fees:** $20 registration fee.

Nebraska

38

Accountant (CPA)
Nebraska Board of Public
    Accountancy
Gold's Galleria, Ste. 548
PO Box 94725
Lincoln, NE 68509
Phone: (402)471-3595

Credential Type: License. **Duration of License:** One year. **Requirements:** Must have a four-year degree from a recognized college. Must have two years of experience. **Examination:** Yes. **Fees:** $160 CPA examination fee. $45 ethics examination fee. $85 renewal fee. $30 inactive renewal fee.

Nevada

Accountant/Auditor
Nevada State Board of Accountancy
1 E. Liberty, Ste. 311
Reno, NV 89501
Phone: (702)786-0231

Credential Type: Certification. **Duration of License:** One year. **Requirements:** Bachelor's degree with a major in accounting. Two years of accounting experience. One-thousand hours in the attest function, which includes a minimum of 700 audit hours. **Examination:** Uniform CPA Examination. **Reciprocity:** Yes. **Fees:** $125 exam fee. $120 license fee. $120 renewal fee.

New Hampshire

Certified Public Accountant
New Hampshire Board of Accountancy
57 Regional Dr.
Concord, NH 03301
Phone: (603)271-3286

Credential Type: CPA Certificate and permit to practice. **Duration of License:** Two years. **Requirements:** 21 years of age. Good professional character. Pass the Uniform CPA Examination. Satisfy the specified educational and experience requirements.

Must complete a four-year college degree program or equivalent, to be eligible to sit for examination.

Two years experience required in public and/or governmental accounting, acceptable to the Board, to be issued a certificate. One year of experience is required of a candidate with a master's degree in business administration or accounting. **Examination:** Uniform CPA Examination. **Reciprocity:** May be issued to a CPA of another state who meets the general qualifications and experience and educational requirements for a New Hampshire certificate. Will be issued only to applicants from states that issue such certificates to New Hampshire CPAs. **Fees:** $200 examination. $50 reexamination (per part). $170 reexamination (all parts). $200 reciprocal certificate. $50 biennial permit. $25 review of continuing professional education. permit. $30 initial reciprocal certificate (plus $20 for wall certificate). $40 course in professional ethics.

Credential Type: Temporary permit. **Authorization:** A CPA of another state may practice in New Hampshire after acquiring a foreign account practice permit. This is required of all engagements however incidental. **Requirements:** Must acquire a foreign account practice permit. **Fees:** No fee.

New Jersey

Accountant
New Jersey State Board of Accountancy
1100 Raymond Blvd., Rm. 507A
Newark, NJ 07102
Phone: (201)648-3240

Credential Type: Certified Public Accountant. **Duration of License:** Two years. **Requirements:** A baccalaureate degree, or its equivalent, based upon an approved curriculum. Two years of experience in public accounting and auditing; or four years of experience as an Internal Revenue Agent; or four years of experience in the office of a public accountant; or four years of experience in the employment of a state or political subdivision of the U.S. 18 years of age. 48 hours of continuing education before renewal. **Examination:** Written. **Reciprocity:** Yes. **Fees:** $100 exam fee. $40 registration fee. $6 certificate fee. **Governing Statute:** NJSA 45:2B. NJAC 13:29.

Municipal Accountant
New Jersey State Board of Accountancy
1100 Raymond Blvd., Rm. 507A
Newark, NJ 07102
Phone: (201)648-3240

Credential Type: Registered Municipal Accountant. **Duration of License:** Two years. **Requirements:** Completion of 48 hours of continuing education each two-year registration period. **Examination:** Written. **Fees:** $100 exam fee. $40 biennial registration fee. **Governing Statute:** NJSA 45:2B. NJAC 13:29.

Public School Accountant
New Jersey State Board of Accountancy
1100 Raymond Blvd., Rm. 507A
Newark, NJ 07102
Phone: (201)648-3240

Credential Type: License. **Requirements:** Applicants must show they are fully acquainted with New Jersey laws governing the fiscal affairs of school districts and that they are competent and experienced auditors. **Fees:** $5 registration fee. **Governing Statute:** NJSA 45:2B. NJAC 13:29.

New Mexico

Certified Public Accountant
New Mexico State Board of Public Accountancy
4125 Carlisle NE
Albuquerque, NM 87107
Phone: (505)841-6524

Credential Type: CPA Certificate and permit to practice. **Duration of License:** One year. **Requirements:** 18 years of age. Good moral character. Meet specified education and experience requirements. Pass Uniform CPA Examination. Pass written examination on professional ethics. Must be resident of or maintain an office in New Mexico for the practice of public accounting.

To sit for examination, a candidate must have a baccalaureate from a college or university recognized by the Board with a major, or the equivalent, in accounting.

One year of public accounting experience required to obtain a CPA certificate. **Examination:** Uniform CPA Examination. **Reciprocity:** May be granted to an out-of-state CPA provided that the standards established in the state of origin are equivalent to the standards in New Mexico and that such other state grants similar privileges to New Mexico CPAs. An applicant who has held a valid permit or license to practice and has practiced public accounting for a period of not less than five years shall be deemed to have met the requirements. Must take, or have previously taken, an ethics examination. **Fees:** $125 examination. $125 reexamination. $30 initial certificate (plus $20 for wall certificate). $40 permit. $30 initial reciprocal certificate (plus $20 for wall certificate). $40 course in professional ethics.

Credential Type: Temporary permit. **Authorization:** Out-of-state accountants may temporarily practice in New Mexico on professional business by filing an application for reciprocity with the board. **Requirements:** Reciprocal certificate. **Fees:** $30.

Accountants and Auditors

45

State Auditor (Racetrack)
New Mexico State Racing
 Commission
PO Box 8576, Highland Station
Albuquerque, NM 87198
Phone: (505)841-4644

Credential Type: License Registration. **Requirements:** Submit application and fingerprint card. Pay fees. **Fees:** $21 registration fee. $1 notary fee. $23 fingerprint card processing fee.

New York

46

Certified Public Accountant
State Education Dept.
Div. of Professional Licensing
 Services
Cultural Education Center
Empire State Plaza
Albany, NY 12230
Phone: (518)474-5170

Credential Type: License. **Duration of License:** Three years. **Requirements:** Bachelor's degree with a major in accountancy or equivalent. Two years of accounting and auditing experience under the supervision of a CPA. 21 years of age. **Examination:** Written. **Fees:** $370 license fee. $210 renewal fee. **Governing Statute:** Title VIII Articles 130, 149 of the Education Law.

North Carolina

47

Certified Public Accountant
North Carolina State Board of
 Certified Public Accountants
PO Box 12827
Raleigh, NC 27605
Phone: (919)733-4222

Credential Type: License. **Duration of License:** One year. **Requirements:** Bachelor's degree from an accredited school including 24 semester hours of accounting; or 60 semester hours from an accredited school, including 24 specified semester hours of accounting and two years of work experience; or completion of a special Board-approved examination. In addition to the educational requirements, applicants must have two years of experience in the field under the supervision of a CPA or five years in the field of accountancy or teaching. **Examination:** National exam. **Fees:** $140 exam fee. $50 certification fee. $35 renewal fee.

North Dakota

48

Auditor (Racetrack)
North Dakota Racing Commission
State Capitol Bldg.
Bismarck, ND 58505
Phone: (701)224-2210

Credential Type: License Registration. **Requirements:** Submit application and fingerprint card. Pay fee. **Fees:** $10 license fee. $10 duplicate license fee.

49

Certified Public Accountant
North Dakota State Board of
 Accountancy
University Station
PO Box 8104
Grand Forks, ND 58202
Phone: (701)777-3869

Credential Type: CPA Certificate and permit to practice. **Duration of License:** One year. **Requirements:** Resident of North Dakota. 18 years of age. Good moral character. Meet specified education and experience requirements. Pass Uniform CPA Examination. Pass course and written examination in professional ethics.

A degree from an accredited four-year college or university with emphasis in accounting is required unless candidate satisfies the experience requirement.

Four years of practice in public accounting or four years in an accounting or auditing position with a federal or state government agency are required unless candidate meets the educational requirement. **Examination:** Uniform CPA Examination. **Reciprocity:** Issued to a CPA who is not a resident of North Dakota. Must meet the general qualifications (except residency) and the educational and experience requirements imposed on North Dakota candidates. Must be licensed in a state that extends reciprocity to North Dakota CPAs. **Fees:** $125 examination. $60 reexamination (accounting practice). reexamination $30 (all other parts; per part). $125 reexamination (all parts). $100 reciprocal certificate. $50 annual permit (in-state). $40 annual permit (out-of-state).

Credential Type: Temporary permit. **Authorization:** Out-of-state accountant may temporarily practice in North Dakota on business incidental to a regular practice provided it is conducted in conformity with Board rules. **Fees:** No fee.

Ohio

50

Certified Public Accountant
Accountancy Board of Ohio
77 S. High St., 18th Fl.
Columbus, OH 43266-0301
Phone: (614)466-4135

Credential Type: CPA Certificate and permit to practice. **Duration of License:** Three years. **Requirements:** Resident of, has place of business in, or is regularly employed in Ohio. 18 years of age. Good moral character. Meet specified education and experience requirements. Pass Uniform CPA Examination. Pass special written examination in professional ethics.

A baccalaureate from a recognized college or university with a concentration in accounting, or the successfull completion of an equivalency examination.

Two years of acceptable public accounting experience or experience in private or governmental accounting, which the Board deems equivalent, is required for certificate. A candidate holding a master's degree in accounting or business administration and who has completed an approved number of semester hours in accounting, business administration, economics and other related subjects, is required to have one year of experience. **Examination:** Uniform CPA Examination. **Reciprocity:** May be issued to a CPA of another state who meets all of the general qualifications, education, and experience requirements that were in effect in Ohio at the time of application or at the time that the original certificate was issued. **Fees:** $140 examination. $70 reexamination (one part). $80 reexamination (two parts). $90 reexamination (three parts). $105 reexamination (four parts). $120 reexamination (all parts). $100 reciprocal certificate. $90 triennial permit. $15 nonpracticing triennial registration. $15 firm registration (per licensed individual).

Credential Type: Temporary permit. **Authorization:** Granted to out-of-state accountant for temporary practice in Ohio on professional business incident to the accountant's regular practice in another state, provided such practice in conducted in conformity with Board rules. **Fees:** No fee.

Oklahoma

51

Accountant, Certified Public (CPA)
Oklahoma State Board of Public
 Accountancy
4545 North Lincoln Blvd., Ste. 165
Oklahoma City, OK 73105-3413
Phone: (405)521-2397

Credential Type: Certificate. **Duration of License:** One year. **Requirements:** Bachelor's degree in a related field or qualification by experience through individual Board review. Twenty-four hours of continuing education required each year. 21 years of age. Good moral character. State resident for one year. High school graduate. Conviction of a felony or any crime involving dishonesty or fraud is subject to individual Board review. **Examination:** Uniform Certified Public Accountant Exmaination. **Fees:** $100 exam fee. $100 application fee. $25 annual registration fee. $25 renewal fee.

52

Accountant, Public (PA)
Oklahoma State Board of Public
 Accountancy
4545 North Lincoln Blvd., Ste. 165
Oklahoma City, OK 73105-3413
Phone: (405)521-2397

Credential Type: License. **Duration of License:** One year. **Requirements:** Bachelor's degree in a related field or qualification by experience through individual Board review. Twenty-four hours of continuing education required each year. 21 years of age. Good moral character. State resident for one year. High school graduate. Conviction of a felony or any crime involving dishonesty or fraud is subject to individual Board review. **Examination:** Uniform Public Accountant Examination. **Fees:** $60 exam fee. $60 application fee. $25 registration fee. $25 renewal fee.

Oregon

53

Certified Public Accountant
Oregon State Board of Accountancy
158 12th St. NE
Salem, OR 97310
Phone: (503)378-4181

Credential Type: License. **Requirements:** Must be a graduate of a college with coursework in accounting, business law, economics and finance; or present satisfactory evidence of graduation from high school or have an equivalent education and have at least two years of public accounting experience or the equivalent. **Examination:** Yes. **Fees:** $150 exam fee. $100 license fee. $100 renewal fee. **Governing Statute:** ORS 673.010 to 673.455.

54

Municipal Auditor
Oregon State Board of Accountancy
158 12th St. NE
Salem, OR 97310
Phone: (503)378-4181

Credential Type: License. **Requirements:** Must be a Certified Public Accountant or Public Accountant in good standing. Document specific continuing professional education. **Fees:** $80 license fee. $30 renewal fee. **Governing Statute:** ORS 673.040 to 673.455.

55

Public Accountant
Oregon State Board of Accountancy
158 12th St. NE
Salem, OR 97310
Phone: (503)378-4270

Credential Type: License. **Duration of License:** Two years. **Requirements:** Graduation from a recognized college or university, and have 30 more semester hours or the equivalent in accounting, business law, economics and finance; or graduation from high school or equivalent, and have at least two years of public accounting experience or the equivalent. **Examination:** Yes. **Fees:** Exam fees set per subject. $100 license fee. $100 renewal fee. **Governing Statute:** ORS 673.010 to 673.455.

Pennsylvania

56

Certified Public Accountant
Pennsylvania State Board of
 Accountancy
613 Transportation and Safety Bldg.
PO Box 2649
Harrisburg, PA 17105-2649
Phone: (717)783-1404

Credential Type: CPA Certificate and permit to practice. **Duration of License:** Two years. **Requirements:** Resident of, is enrolled in a college or university in, or is engaged in public accounting in Pennsylvania at the time he/she sits for examination. 18 years of age. Good moral character. Meet specified education and experience requirements. Pass Uniform CPA Examination.

Must have a baccalaureate, or its equivalent, and the completion of 12 semester hours in accounting subjects acceptable to the Board to sit for examination. Candidates expecting to meet the required education requirements within 90 days of the written examination may also be eligible to sit for examination.

Must have at least two years of experience in public or government accounting approved by Board to sit for examination and be granted a certificate. Candidates with a master's degree in accounting or business administration may be required to have one year of experience. Candidates with a baccalaureate, master's, or doctor's degree and who have completed at least 24 semester hours in accounting subjects acceptable to the Board may sit for examination without meeting any experience requirement. However, candidates must meet the required public accounting experience required before a CPA certificate will be granted. **Examination:** Uniform CPA Examination. **Reciprocity:** Issued to a CPA of another state who meets the general qualifications, complies with the requirements of continuing professional education, has passed the Uniform CPA Examination, and has at least two years of public accounting experience. **Fees:** $103.75 examination. $43.75 reexamination (one part). $58.75 reexamination (two parts). $73.75 reexamination (three parts). $88.75 reexamination (four parts). $103.75 reexamination (all parts). $50 reciprocal application. $50 corporate, partnership, or professional association application. $45 biennial license.

Credential Type: Temporary permit. **Authorization:** An out-of-state accountant engaged in public practice may temporarily practice in Pennsylvania on professional business incident to his/her regular practice provided such practice is conducted in conformity with Board rules. **Fees:** No fee.

Rhode Island

57

Certified Public Accountant
Rhode Island Board of Accountancy
Dept. of Business Regulation
233 Richmond St., Ste. 236
Providence, RI 02903-4236
Phone: (401)277-3185

Credential Type: CPA Certificate and permit to practice. **Duration of License:** One year. **Requirements:** Principal residence or primary place of employment is in Rhode Island. Good moral character. Meet education and experience requirements. Pass the

Accountants and Auditors | **Texas**

Uniform CPA Examination. Pass an open-book professional ethics examination.

Baccalaureate from a recognized college or university with a concentration in accounting (30 semester hours in accounting and related courses).

Two years of public accounting experience are required of candidates holding baccalaureates. One year of experience is required of candidates holding master's or doctor's degrees in accounting or business administration as approved by the Board. Candidates may sit for examination without completing the experience requirement, but this requirement must be met before being issued a certificate. **Examination:** Uniform CPA Examination. **Reciprocity:** Granted to applicants who meet all current requirements in Rhode Island at time of application or meet all requirements in the state of Rhode Island at the time the original certificate was issued or have five years of experience in the practice of public accounting within the last 10 years prior to application. All applicants must pay fee. **Fees:** $140 examination. $80 reexamination (one part). $100 reexamination (two parts). $140 reexamination (three to all parts). $20 certificate. $50 reciprocal certificate. $80 annual license permit.

Credential Type: Temporary permit. **Authorization:** Temporary practice is permitted by a licensed accountant of another state on business incident to regular practice provided that the applicant registers with the Board and complies with its regulations. **Fees:** No fee.

South Carolina

58

Accountant
South Carolina Board of Accountancy
800 Dutch Square Blvd., Ste. 260
Columbia, SC 29210
Phone: (803)737-9266

Credential Type: Certified Public Accountant License. **Requirements:** State resident. 18 years of age. No history of dishonest or felonious acts. Bachelor's degree with 24 hours in accounting subjects. Two years of qualifying experience. **Examination:** Yes. **Fees:** $80 license fee.

Credential Type: Accounting Practitioner License. **Requirements:** State resident. 18 years of age. No history of dishonest or felonious acts. Either a bachelor's degree with a major in accounting or passing the Practice and Theory sections of the CPA examination. **Fees:** $80 license fee.

South Dakota

59

Certified Public Accountant
South Dakota Board of Accountancy
301 E. 14th St., Ste. 200
Sioux Falls, SD 57104
Phone: (605)339-6746

Credential Type: License. **Duration of License:** One year. **Requirements:** Good character. Meet education requirements. Pass Uniform CPA Examination. Pass professional ethics examination.

Associate's or bachelor's degree from an accredited college, university, or business college with a major in accounting, or Board-approved equivalent, is required to sit for examination. A candidate may sit for examination if he/she is within 100 days of completion of the educational requirement.

Before beginning practice as a CPA, candidates must present proof of two years in public accounting, or one year and 30 semester hours in accounting or business administration, and an examination in professional ethics. **Examination:** Uniform CPA Examination. **Reciprocity:** Must apply for permit to practice in South Dakota and have a certificate in good standing from another state. Must fulfill the two-year experience and ethics examination requirements. **Fees:** $175 examination and certificate. $25 reexamination (per part). $125 reexamination (all parts). $65 individual permit (initial and annual renewal). Firm permit fees vary with number of individuals and location.

Tennessee

60

Accountant
Tennessee Board of Accountancy
500 James Robertson Pky.
Nashville, TN 37245-1141
Phone: (615)741-2250

Credential Type: License. **Duration of License:** Two years. **Requirements:** Pass Exam. Two years experience in public accounting. Degree in accounting, or other degree with 24 semester hours in accounting. Must take 80 hours of continuing education every two years. **Examination:** Certified Public Accountants (CPA) examination every two years. **Reciprocity:** Yes. **Fees:** $150 Application. $100 Renewal.

61

Certified Public Accountant
Tennessee State Board of Accountancy
500 James Robertson Pky., 2nd Fl.
Nashville, TN 37219
Phone: (615)741-2550

Credential Type: CPA Certificate and permit to practice. **Duration of License:** Two years. **Requirements:** Resident of Tennessee, has a place of business therein, or is regularly employed therein. Meet the specified educational and experience requirements. Pass the Uniform CPA Examination. Pass examination in professional ethics.

Must have a baccalaureate with a major in accounting (24 semester hours). In 1993 the Board will require the completion of 150 college credit hours prior to a candidate's consideration for a certificate.

A candidate holding a baccalaureate must have two years of public accounting experience, two years in state audit, three years in private industry/auditing, or approved equivalent to be issued a permit. One year of experience is required of a candidate with a master's degree in accounting or business administration. **Examination:** Uniform CPA Examination. **Reciprocity:** Issued to CPA from another state who resides in Tennessee or maintains an office within the state having one or more general partners residing in the state. State of origin must have similar licensing requirements to that of Tennessee and be licensed in a state that extends reciprocity to Tennessee CPAs. **Fees:** $150 examination. $100 reexamination (all parts). $35 reciprocal permit and processing (per year). $100 biennial registration. $50 annual firm (practice unit) registration.

Texas

62

Certified Public Accountant
Texas State Board of Public Accountancy
1033 LaPosada, Ste. 340
Austin, TX 78752-3892
Phone: (512)451-0241

Credential Type: CPA Certificate and permit to practice. **Duration of License:** One year. **Requirements:** Citizen of the United States or has lived in Texas for 90 days preceding application or has maintained permanent legal residence in Texas for six months prior to filing application. 18 years of age. Good moral character. Meet speci-

Certified Public Accountant, continued

fied requirements of education and experience. Pass the Uniform CPA Examination.

Requires a baccalaureate or graduate degree with not less than 30 semester hours in accounting, of which at least 20 semester hours are in core accounting subjects. Also required are at least two years of accounting experience under the supervision of a licensed CPA or equivalent, as determined by the board. Should the candidate hold a baccalaureate with 20 semester hours in accounting the experience requirement would be four years. A candidate who meets the educational requirements will be eligible to sit for examination, however, he/she will not be licensed to practice until the experience requirements are met. **Examination:** Uniform CPA Examination. **Reciprocity:** Reciprocal certificate may be issued to a CPA from another state who meets specified educational and experience requirements in Texas or if applicant has four years of experience in public accounting in the 10 years immediately preceding application and has passed the Uniform CPA Examination. Applicant must meet the continuing education requirements that apply to Texas during the three license years preceding the date of application. **Fees:** $100 examination fee. $100 reexamination (all parts). $100 reciprocity certificate. $26 annual license permit. $10 retired or permanently disabled license fee. $25 certificate fee.

Credential Type: Temporary permit. **Duration of License:** 180 days. **Authorization:** Licensed accountant of another state may practice temporarily on professional business incident to his/her regular practice. A permit is valid for 180 days and Board will not issue more than one permit to a person in any three-year period. **Fees:** $100.

Utah

63

Certified Public Accountant
Utah Board of Accountancy
160 East 300 South
PO Box 45802
Salt Lake City, UT 84145-0802
Phone: (801)530-6628

Credential Type: CPA Certificate and permit to practice. **Duration of License:** Two years. **Requirements:** Good moral character. Meet specified educational and experience requirements. Pass Uniform CPA examination. Pass examination in professional ethics.

Before July 1, 1994: Baccalaureate degree with a concentration in accounting, auditing, and business as approved by the Board and a required one year of associate experience which includes applying accounting and auditing skills under the licensed supervision of a CPA to sit for examination. Plus an additional three years of associate experience before being granted a license to practice. After July 1, 1994: A total of 150 semester hours (225 quarter hours) with a concentration in accounting, auditing, and business, including a baccalaureate or its equivalent, and an associated experience requirement for licensure of one year is required. **Examination:** Uniform CPA Examination. **Reciprocity:** Must hold a license or a certificate as a CPA issued by another state, district, or territory of the United States. Must have passed a qualifying examination and meet all current requirements in this state for issuance of a license at the time the application for license is made. **Fees:** $70 application. $165 examination/reexamination (all parts), or fees for the following exam parts: $25 for business law; $25 for accounting theory; $40 for accounting practice; and $25 for auditing. $25 reexamination administration. $70 reciprocity (endorsement). $40 biennial renewal.

Credential Type: Temporary permit. **Authorization:** Granted to out-of-state accountant if the practice is incidental to his/her regular out-of-state business. **Requirements:** Must conform to Utah's laws and rules. **Fees:** No fee.

Vermont

64

Accountant, Certified Public
Board of Public Accounting
Secretary of State
Licensing and Registration
Pavilion Office Bldg.
Montpelier, VT 05602
Phone: (802)828-2372

Credential Type: License. **Duration of License:** Two years. **Requirements:** Good moral character. High school education plus 60 college credits including 30 credit hours in accounting and related subjects. Two years experience in public accounting in the employ of a licensed public accountant. Renewal requires 80 hours of continuing education in accounting. **Examination:** CPA Exam, RPA Exam. **Reciprocity:** Yes. **Fees:** $40 application (CPA/RPA). $130 CPA examination fee. $105 RPA examination fee. $10 registration temporary license. $20 late renewal. $10 biennial renewal. **Governing Statute:** Title 26, VSA Sect. 31-82.

65

Accountant, Registered Public
Board of Public Accounting
Secretary of State
Licensing and Registration
Pavilion Office Bldg.
Montpelier, VT 05602
Phone: (802)828-2372

Credential Type: License. **Duration of License:** Two years. **Requirements:** Good moral character. High school education plus 60 college credits, including 30 credit hours in accounting and related subjects. Two years experience in public accounting in the employ of a licensed public accountant. Renewal requires 80 hours of continuing education in accounting. **Examination:** RPA exam (five parts) **Reciprocity:** Yes, with 12 other states. **Fees:** $105 full RPA exam. $25/part for five-part exam. $50/part for retake. $40 license by reciprocity. $10 biennial renewal. **Governing Statute:** Title 26, VSA Sect. 31-82.

Virginia

66

Accountant (CPA)
Virginia State Board of Accountancy
Dept. of Commerce
3600 W. Broad St.
Richmond, VA 23230
Phone: (804)367-8590

Credential Type: License. **Duration of License:** Two years. **Requirements:** Bachelor's degree from an accredited college, with specified accounting and business courses, and two to four years of work experience. Good character and references. **Examination:** AICPA Examination. **Fees:** $100 application fee. $50 license fee.

Washington

67

Certified Public Accountant
Washington State Board of
  Accountancy
210 E. Union, Ste. H
PO Box 9131
Olympia, WA 98504-2321
Phone: (206)753-2585

Credential Type: License. **Duration of License:** Two years. **Requirements:** Good moral character. Meet specified education and experience requirements. Pass the Uniform CPA Examination. Pass examination in professional ethics.

Accountants and Auditors

70 Wyoming

Baccalaureate with a concentration in accounting from a college or university recognized by the Board or equivalent education as approved by the Board.

Applicant for initial license must have one year (or equivalent) in public practice including 500 hours attest experience. **Examination:** Uniform CPA Examination. **Reciprocity:** Granted to a CPA of another state who meets the same requirements as candidates for original Washington CPA certificates. **Fees:** $125 examination. $75 reexamination (one part). $75 reexamination (two parts). $100 reexamination (three parts). $125 reexamination (all parts). $40 reciprocity certificate. $40 transfer of credits. $80 biennial public accounting license. $50 firm license for sole proprietor with employees ($0 without employees). $100 partnership/corporation. $10 biennial renewal of CPA Certificate.

Credential Type: Temporary permit. **Authorization:** Granted to out-of-state accountant practicing on business incident to his/her regular practice. **Requirements:** Must inform the board in writing, giving the name of the client and assurance that he/she is temporarily practicing on business incident to his/her practice. **Fees:** $10.

West Virginia

68

Accountant (CPA)
State Board of Accountancy
201 L&S Bldg.
812 Quarrier St.
Charlestown, WV 25301
Phone: (304)348-3557

Credential Type: License. **Duration of License:** One year. **Requirements:** U.S. citizen. State resident. 18 years old. Four-year college degree in accounting. Good moral character. Never convicted of a felony. **Examination:** Yes. **Fees:** $40 Application. $100 Examination. $10 License. $10 Renewal.

Wisconsin

69

Accountant/Certified Public
Regulations and Licensing Dept.
Accounting Board
PO Box 8935
Madison, WI 53708-8935
Phone: (608)266-8609

Credential Type: License. **Requirements:** Bachelor's degree or higher with a major in accounting from an accredited school.

Three years of accounting experience with at least 18 months at the senior level. 18 years of age. **Examination:** Written. **Reciprocity:** Yes.

Wyoming

70

Accountant, Certified Public
Board of CPA's
Barrett Bldg., 3rd Fl.
2301 Central Ave.
Cheyenne, WY 82002
Phone: (307)777-7551

Credential Type: License. **Duration of License:** One year. **Requirements:** Must have a Bachelors degree with 24 hours of accounting course work. Two years experience in public accounting which includes tax work and the preparation of financial statements. Pay an annual permit fee. 19 years of age. Pass a professional ethics examination. Pass the Uniform Certified Public Accountant Examination, or qualify by reciprocity with another state or nation. **Examination:** Yes. **Reciprocity:** Yes. **Fees:** $175 Original Examination. $40 Repeat examination. $100 Annual active participating certificate. $50 Annual inactive practicing certificate.

Acupuncturists

The following states grant licenses in this occupational category as of the date of publication:

Alaska	District of Columbia	Hawaii	Massachusetts	New Mexico	Pennsylvania	Virginia
Arkansas		Louisiana	Montana	New York	Rhode Island	Washington
California	Florida	Maine	Nevada	North Carolina	Utah	Wisconsin
Colorado	Georgia	Maryland	New Jersey	Oregon	Vermont	

Alaska

71

Licensed Acupuncturist (L.Ac.)
Dept. of Commerce and Economic Development
Div. of Occupational Licensing, Acupuncture
PO Box D-Lic
Juneau, AK 99811-0800
Phone: (907)465-2541

Credential Type: Acupuncturist License. **Duration of License:** Two years. **Requirements:** 21 years of age. Good moral character. National Commission for the Certification of Acupuncture (NCCA) certification. Complete a course of study consistent with the core curriculum and guidelines of the National Council of Acupuncture Schools and Colleges at an approved school. **Examination:** NCCA written examination. **Exemptions:** Medical doctors and dentists are exempt from this statute but the dental board may set requirements of experience or education for dentists. **Reciprocity:** Reciprocity exists for applicants who are licensed to practice acupuncture in another jurisdiction that has licensing requirements equivalent to those of Alaska. **Fees:** $30 application. $400 initial license fee. $400 renewal fee. **Governing Statute:** Alaska Statutes 08.01-03; AS 08.06; Regulations 12 AAC 02.

Arkansas

72

Acupuncturist
Arkansas State Medical Board
PO Box 102
Harrisburg, AR 72432
Phone: (501)578-2448

Credential Type: License. **Requirements:** Bachelor's degree and completion of a two year program of study in acupuncture. Completion of an accredited tutorial program in acupuncture. Hold an Arkansas license to practice medicine and surgery. Affidavits from two licensed and reputable doctors of chiropractic medicine. **Examination:** Written and Oral examination. **Fees:** $75 application fee. $85 Renewal.

California

73

Certified Acupuncturist (C.A.)
Dept. of Consumer Affairs
Medical Board, Acupuncture Committee
1420 Howe Ave., Ste. 14
Sacramento, CA 95825-3233
Phone: (916)924-2642

Credential Type: Acupuncturist Certificate. **Duration of License:** One year. **Requirements:** 18 years of age. Graduate from an approved school and complete four academic years of education with a minimum of 1548 hours of theory including biology, organic chemistry, biochemistry, psychology, anatomy and physiology, pathology, nutrition and vitamins (400 hours), history of medicine, medical terminology (30 hours), CPR, Tai Chi (660 hours), ethics (30 hours), herbology (300 hours including botany), and 800 hours of clinical training.

An apprenticeship under a tutorial supervisor who has 10 years of experience and takes no more than two trainees at a time must include 2850 hours of training. The tutorial must include 200 hours of Western science, anatomy, physiology, and pathology and must include a written agreement and on-site supervision.

Licensee must have 30 approved hours of continuing education every two years as a condition of renewal. **Examination:** California examination. **Exemptions:** Licensed medical doctors, dentists, and podiatrists may practice without an acupuncture license provided they have had adequate training in acupuncture. **Reciprocity:** No **Fees:** $75 application. $200 exam and license. $325 initial license or annual license.

Colorado

74

Acupuncturist
Dept. of Regulatory Agencies
Office of Acupuncturists Registration
1560 Broadway, Ste. 1300
Denver, CO 80202
Phone: (303)894-7690

Credential Type: Acupuncturist Registration. **Duration of License:** Two years. **Requirements:** National Commission for the Certification of Acupuncture (NCCA) certification which includes 1000 hours of entry-level acupuncture education (700 academic hours and 250 clinical hours).

Apprenticeship must consist of 4000 contact hours under direct supervision completed in no less than three years and no more than six years.

To meet experience requirements, an applicant must be able to document four years of practice with a minimum of 500 patient visits on no less than 100 different patients of which 70 percent must be in general health care. **Examination:** NCCA written examination. **Reciprocity:** No. **Fees:** $628 application or initial fee. $300 biennial renewal.

District of Columbia

75

Acupuncturist
Advisory Committee on Acupuncture
D.C. Board of Medicine
605 G St. NW, Rm. LL 202
Washington, DC 20001
Phone: (202)727-5365

Credential Type: Acupuncturist License. **Duration of License:** Two years. **Requirements:** Complete three academic years of instruction in a school for acupuncture, including 500 hours of clinic, or two academic years of instruction plus 1500 hours of apprenticeship.

An apprenticeship must be a tutorial of at least three years with a minimum of 4500 contact hours.

The Board may approve the education and training of an applicant who documents three years of experience prior to October 1989 with a minimum of 100 patients and 500 patient visits each year in general health care. **Examination:** National Commission for the Certification of Acupuncture (NCCA) written exam. **Exemptions:** Physicians with 250 hours of acupuncture instruction may practice acupuncture. **Reciprocity:** Must pass the NCCA exam before practicing. **Fees:** $41 application. $28 license or renewal.

Florida

76

Acupuncturist
Board of Acupuncture
Div. of Medical Quality Assurance
Dept. of Professional Regulation
1940 N. Monroe St.
Tallahassee, FL 32399-0761
Phone: (904)488-6039

Credential Type: Certificate to practice. **Duration of License:** Two years. **Requirements:** Be at least 18 years of age. Be either a citizen of the United States, a permanent resident of the United States, or be a legal alien who has resided in the United States for the past six months. Meet one of the following sets of requirements: (1) Complete a two-year course of study that meets standards established by the board. (2) Complete a two-year tutorial program that meets standards established by the board. (3) Have at least five years of experience as an acupuncturist. **Examination:** 3-part examination consisting of (1) a state written examination, (2) the written examination developed by the National Commission for the Certification of Acupuncturists (NCCA), and (3) the written and hands-on clean needle technique examination developed by the NCCA. **Exemptions:** Applicants who have previously taken parts two or three in another state may be exempts from retaking them. A license may be granted to an applicant who has completed a board-approved national certification process upon completion of state written examination.

Medical doctors or osteopaths may practice acupuncture. Chiropractors may practice acupuncture with 100 hours of training, but may not advertise themselves as acupuncturists. **Reciprocity:** An applicant who is actively licensed in a state that has substantially equivalent examination requirements may be granted a license without examination. **Fees:** $300 application fee. $350 NCCA written portion exam fee. $350 people's portion exam fee. $250 clean needle technique exam fee. $200 examination fee (endorsement). $500 initial certification fee. $700 renewal fee. **Governing Statute:** Florida Statutes, Chapter 457. Florida Administrative Code, Rules 21-AA.

Georgia

77

Acupuncturist
Composite State Board of Medical Examiners
Professional Examining Boards
166 Pryor St., SW
Atlanta, GA 30303
Phone: (404)656-3913

Credential Type: Acupuncturist License. **Requirements:** Only medical doctors can apply to be acupuncturists in Georgia. Additional training is required and must be approved by the board. **Fees:** No fees.

Hawaii

78

Acupuncturist
Hawaii Board of Acupuncture
Dept. of Commerce and Consumer Affairs
1010 Richards St.
PO Box 3469
Honolulu, HI 96801
Phone: (808)548-7697

Credential Type: License. **Duration of License:** Two years. **Requirements:** Completion of a formal acupuncture program with a diploma from a Board-approved institute. At least two years of academic training and a one year internship supervised by a licensed acupuncturist. **Examination:** National Commission for the Certification of Acupuncturists and State Jurisprudence exams. **Exemptions:** Licensed physicians and dentists do not need a license to practice acupuncture. **Fees:** $50 application fee. $240 exam fee. $175 license fee. $30 Compliance Resolution Fund fee. $150 renewal fee.

Louisiana

79

Acupuncture Assistant
State Board of Medical Examiners
830 Union St., Ste. 100
New Orleans, LA 70112
Phone: (504)524-6763

Credential Type: Certificate to Practice. **Duration of License:** One year. **Authorization:** Must work under the supervision of a licensed physician. **Requirements:** Complete 36 months of training in a school or clinic of traditional Chinese acupuncture. **Fees:** $100 processing fee. $25 renewal fee. **Governing Statute:** R.S. 37:1356-1360.

Maine

80

Licensed Acupuncturist (L.Ac.)
Dept. of Professional and Financial Regulation
Div. of Licensing and Enforcement
State House Station No. 35
Augusta, ME 04333
Phone: (207)582-8723

Credential Type: Acupuncturist License. **Duration of License:** Two years. **Requirements:** 21 years of age. National Commission for the Certification of Acupuncture (NCCA) certified. Must show a minimum

Licensed Acupuncturist (L.Ac.), continued

of 1000 hours of classroom instruction in acupuncture and 300 hours of clinic. Must have a B.S., B.A., R.N. or P.A. degree. Tutorials may be accepted at the discretion of the Board.

Licensee must have 30 hours of continuing education every two years in order to renew a license. Courses must be certified by the American Association for Acupuncture and Oriental Medicine (AAAOM) or offered by member schools of the National Council of Acupuncture Schools and Colleges (NCASC) or be equivalent. **Examination:** NCCA written examination in English. **Exemptions:** Exemption language is provided for individuals practicing acupuncture within the scope of their license. **Reciprocity:** Reciprocity is possible with a current, valid license to practice acupuncture from another state which has requirements at least equal to Maine's requirements. **Fees:** $25 application. $250 original license. $250 renewal.

Maryland
81

Registered Acupuncturist
Physician Quality Assurance
4201 Patterson Ave.
Baltimore, MD 21215
Phone: (301)764-4770

Credential Type: Acupuncturist Registration. **Duration of License:** Two years. **Requirements:** 21 years of age. Demonstrate the ability to communicate in English. Must submit three letters of recommendation in English or by certified translation into English. Minimum of 1200 hours of instruction, of which at least 300 hours must be clinical, over not more than a three year period. An applicant need not take the examination if the educational requirement is met.

A license may be granted through experience if the applicant has three years of acupuncture practice, with a minimum of 500 patientss per year preceding the date of application outside the state. Examination would be waived under these conditions. All registrants must have 40 hours of continuing education every two years to renew a registration. **Examination:** National Commissiion for the Certification of Acupuncture (NCCA) examination (required for those not meeting educational, experience, or reciprocity requirements). **Exemptions:** Dentists may perform acupuncture with regard to dentistry without meeting the requirements. **Reciprocity:** Reciprocity is possible if an applicant shows a license, certificate, or authorization from another jurisdiction demonstrating equivalent training or experience. **Fees:** $150 application fee. $50 renewal fee.

Massachusetts
82

Licensed Acupuncturist
Board of Registration in Medicine
Acupuncture Unit
10 West St., 3rd Fl.
Boston, MA 02111
Phone: (617)727-3086

Credential Type: Acupuncturist License. **Duration of License:** Two years. **Requirements:** 18 years of age. Good moral character. Demonstrate sufficient knowledge of the English language to be understood or have a translator available to communicate with patients. Must graduate from a committee approved acupuncture school with a minimum of 1350 clinical/didactic hours combined. Applicant must document 100 hours of clinic with sole responsibility for diagnosis and treatment of patients within the required 1350 hours of acupuncture education. Or applicant may attend an accredited university/college for two academic years. Must include three semester hours each of human anatomy, physiology, and general biology. After receiving a license, applicants must have 30 hours of approved continuing education every two years. Fifteen of these hours must be directly related to acupuncture. Western medical or professional activity courses are allowed for the remaining 15. **Examination:** National Commission for the Certification of Acupuncture (NCCA) written examination. NCCA PEPLS and the National Council of Acupuncture Schools and Colleges (NCASC) CNT practical examinations. **Exemptions:** Exemption language is provided for physical therapists for transcutaneous nerve stimulation and for licensed physicians. **Reciprocity:** No. **Fees:** $150 application. $100 renewal.

Credential Type: Temporary Permit. **Duration of License:** One year. **Authorization:** Temporary licenses are available for clinical instructors in an approved educational seminar or program that demonstrates clinical techniques to patients. **Fees:** $75 temporary license (per year).

Montana
83

Acupuncturist
Montana Board of Medical
  Examiners
111 N. Jackson
Helena, MT 59620
Phone: (406)444-4284

Credential Type: License. **Duration of License:** One year. **Requirements:** 18 years of age. Graduation from an approved school of acupuncture or equivalent. **Examination:** National board exam. **Fees:** $350 investigation fee. $20 license fee. $20 renewal fee. **Governing Statute:** Montana Code Annotated 37-13-301 through 37-13-316.

Nevada
84

Acupuncturist
Nevada State Board of Oriental
  Medicine
434 10th St.
Sparks, NV 89431
Phone: (702)359-7025

Credential Type: Acupuncturist License. **Requirements:** The state of Nevada recognizes four levels of acupuncture practice. To be licensed to practice as a Doctor of Traditional Oriental Medicine, an applicant must have successfully completed four years in traditional Oriental medicine totaling 1800 hours, show a minimum of six years of practice and demonstrate the ability to speak English. To be licensed as a Doctor of Acupuncture, an applicant must complete a three year course in acupuncture totaling 1400 hours, show a minimum of six years of practice, and demonstrate the ability to speak English. To be licensed as a Doctor of Herbology, an applicant must complete a three year course of study in herbal medicine, show a minimum of six years of practice, and demonstrate the ability to speak English. To be licensed as an Acupuncture Assistant, an applicant must complete a three year course of study in acupuncture (no experience or English requirement). **Examination:** Nevada examination. **Reciprocity:** No. **Fees:** $100 application fee. $300 exam fee. $300 investigation fee.

New Jersey

85

Acupuncturist
Acupuncture Examining Board
28 W. State St.
Trenton, NJ 08608
Phone: (609)292-4843

Credential Type: Certified Acupuncturist. **Duration of License:** Two years. **Requirements:** A bachelor's degree and completion of a two-year program of study in acupuncture; or successful completion of a board-approved tutorial program in acupuncture; or a state license to practice medicine and surgery; or three years of board-approved experience in the practice of acupuncture completed between January 18, 1983 and January 17, 1986. **Examination:** Written and oral exams. **Fees:** $325 exam fee. $25 processing fee. $120 registration fee.

New Mexico

86

Licensed Acupuncturist (L.Ac.)
Acupuncture Board
PO Box 25101
Santa Fe, NM 87504
Phone: (505)827-7160

Credential Type: Acupuncturist License. **Duration of License:** Two years. **Requirements:** Good moral character. Must have completed a course in acupuncture and received a certificate or diploma from an institute approved by the Board. The course in acupuncture must be at least three academic years and 1800 hours in length. It should include 750 hours of supervised clinical practice of which 250 hours must be spent performing complete treatments as the primary practitioner. Or applicant may complete an apprenticeship of at least 1800 hours, over not less than three years, including 750 clinical hours with a minimum of 250 hours spent performing complete treatments as the primary student practitioner. The preceptor must have a minimum of 10 years of experience and the student-teacher ratio shall not exceed four to one at any time. **Examination:** National Commission for the Certification of Acupuncture (NCCA) written examination. New Mexico practical examination. **Exemptions:** Other health care practitioners may practice acupuncture within the scope of practice, but may not advertise themselves to be "acupuncturists" unless they are licensed. **Reciprocity:** Reciprocity is possible if the applicant is licensed in a state with substantially the same requirements, has passed a written and practical examination, and if that state permits a New Mexico practitioner to practice without examination. **Fees:** $100 application. $350 exam cost. $200 biennial renewal.

New York

87

Acupuncturist
State Education Dept.
Div. of Professional Licensing
  Services
Cultural Education Center
Empire State Plaza
Albany, NY 12231
Phone: (518)474-3279

Credential Type: License. **Duration of License:** Three years. **Requirements:** Acceptable license as a Doctor of Acupuncture, Herb Physician or Doctor of Traditional Chinese Medicine. 10 years of accupuncture experience. Proficiency in English language. **Examination:** Examination requirement not yet established. **Fees:** $285 license fee. $155 renewal fee. **Governing Statute:** Title VIII Articles 130, 130 of the Education Law.

North Carolina

88

Acupuncturist
North Carolina State Board of
  Medical Examiners
PO Box 26808
Raleigh, NC 27611
Phone: (919)876-3885

Credential Type: License. **Requirements:** 18 years of age. Three letters of recommendation. Completion of four years of medical school. Serve as a resident-in-training for one year. **Examination:** Federation Licensing Examination. **Fees:** $50 registration fee. $615 exam fee. $25 resident-in-training fee.

Oregon

89

Licensed Acupuncturist (L.Ac.)
Board of Medical Examiners
620 Crown Plaza
1500 SW First Ave.
Portland, OR 97201-5770
Phone: (503)229-5770

Credential Type: Acupuncturist License. **Duration of License:** Two years. **Requirements:** Good moral character. Have the ability to communicate in English. Must graduate from a program with a minimum of 750 hours of acupuncture and 484 hours of Western medicine, including 45 anatomy, 45 physiology, 90 pathology, 90 survey of Western diagnosis and clinical medicine and 30 pharmacology. Program must include 12 months of clinical training with 250 hours of clinical observation, 500 hours of treatment and diagnosis in not less than nine months, a minimum of 350 supervised treatments and 50 hours of case presentation. Clinic instructors must have a minimum of five years of experience. **Examination:** National Commission for the Certification of Acupuncture (NCCA) written exam (CDR is accepted in lieu of NCCA written exam). NCCA PEPLS exam. Oregon practical exam. **Exemptions:** Medical doctors and osteopaths may practice acupuncture without training. **Reciprocity:** No. **Fees:** $245 application fee. $250 renewal fee.

Pennsylvania

90

Acupuncturist
The State Board of Medicine
PO Box 2649
Harrisburg, PA 17105
Phone: (717)783-1400

Credential Type: Acupuncturist License. **Duration of License:** Two years. **Requirements:** Graduates of U.S. programs must show two academic years of acupuncture training plus one academic year of a college level educational program. Graduates of foreign programs must graduate from a college with a program of study including Oriental medicine and document 300 class hours of study in acupuncture training. **Examination:** National Commission for the Certification of Acupuncture (NCCA) written examination. (Other state exams taken prior to January 1, 1987 are accepted.) **Exemptions:** Medical doctors with 200 hours of Category I continuing medical education credits in acupuncture may practice acupuncture after registering with the board. **Reciprocity:** No **Fees:** $15 application fee. $25 renewal.

Rhode Island

Doctor of Acupuncture
State of Rhode Island and Providence Plantations
Dept. of Health
Cannon Bldg.
Three Capitol Hill
Providence, RI 02908
Phone: (401)277-2827

Credential Type: Acupuncturist License. **Duration of License:** One year. **Requirements:** Good moral character. Applicant must successfully complete an accredited course of study at a foreign or domestic college satisfactory to the department. Must be certified by the National Commission for the Certification of Acupuncture (NCCA) and pass the examination. **Examination:** NCCA written examination. **Exemptions:** Exemption language exists for physicians. **Reciprocity:** No. **Fees:** $100 application. $250 annual renewal.

Utah

Acupuncturist
Dept. of Professional Regulation
Div. of Occupational and Professional Licensing
Heber M. Wells Bldg.
PO Box 45802
Salt Lake City, UT 84145
Phone: (801)530-6628

Credential Type: Acupuncturist License. **Duration of License:** Two years. **Requirements:** 21 years of age. Resident of Utah. High school graduate. Pass the National Commission for the Certification of Acupuncture (NCCA) exam. Foreign trained applicants must have their credentials evaluated and bear the expense.

Applicants trained in the U.S. must have two years of undergraduate work with an emphasis in biology, human anatomy, and physiology and a course in acupuncture in a school accredited by the National Council of Acupuncture Schools and Colleges (NCASC) or the equivalent of at least two years plus 500 hours of post graduate training under a licensed acupuncture practitioner. Applicants holding licenses or certificates from another state or country may qualify after at least two years of equivalent training. **Examination:** NCCA written examination. Utah Law and Rules examination. NCCA, CNT, and Utah practical examinations. **Exemptions:** Medical doctors may practice acupuncture, but may not represent themselves as "acupuncture practitioners." **Reciprocity:** No. **Fees:** $100 application. $75 renewal.

Vermont

Acupuncturist
Acupuncturist Licensing
Secretary of State
Licensing and Registration
Pavilion Office Bldg.
Montpelier, VT 05602
Phone: (802)828-2373

Credential Type: License. **Requirements:** Fill out application. **Examination:** No. **Fees:** $50 with application.

Virginia

Licensed Acupuncturist (L.Ac. or Lic. Ac.)
Virginia Board of Medicine
1601 Rolling Hills Dr.
Richmond, VA 23229-5055
Phone: (804)662-9908

Credential Type: Acupuncturist License. **Duration of License:** Not yet determined. **Requirements:** Not yet determined. Contact licensing body for application information. **Examination:** Not yet determined. **Exemptions:** Not yet determined. **Reciprocity:** Not yet determined. **Fees:** Not yet determined.

Washington

Certified Acupuncturist
Dept. of Health Professional Licensing Services
1300 SE Quince St. EY-21
Olympia, WA 98504
Phone: (206)753-3095

Credential Type: Acupuncturist Certification. **Duration of License:** One year. **Requirements:** Applicant must show two years of academic coursework including anatomy, physiology, bacteriology or microbiology, biochemistry, pathology, hygiene and a survey of Western clinical sciences. Clinical work must be completed over a minimum of one academic year, include 29 quarter credits of supervised practice with 1000 hours of observation and document at least 400 patient visits with 100 different patients. The rules specify 45 academic credits of Western science (450 hours) plus CPR and 75 credits of acupuncture sciences (750 hours). **Examination:** National Commission for the Certification of Acupuncture (NCCA) written examination in English. NCCA practical examination. CNT in English. **Exemptions:** Exemption language is provided for medical doctors and osteopaths, but they may not hold themselves out to be "certified acupuncturists". **Reciprocity:** Endorsement is possible if the other state's requirements are equivalent or greater than Washington's. **Fees:** $200 application. $600 annual renewal.

Wisconsin

Acupuncturist
Regulations and Licensing Dept.
Acupuncture Board
PO Box 8935
Madison, WI 53708-8935
Phone: (608)266-8609

Credential Type: License. **Requirements:** Successful completion of clean needle technique. Graduation from an accredited school and completion of a residency program. **Examination:** NCCA exam. **Reciprocity:** Yes.

Adjusters, Investigators, and Collectors

The following states grant licenses in this occupational category as of the date of publication:

Alaska	Delaware	Illinois	Massachusetts	New Hampshire	Oklahoma	Utah
Arizona	District of	Indiana	Michigan	New Mexico	Oregon	Vermont
Arkansas	Columbia	Iowa	Minnesota	New York	Pennsylvania	Washington
California	Florida	Kentucky	Montana	North Carolina	Rhode Island	Wisconsin
Colorado	Georgia	Maine	Nebraska	North Dakota	Tennessee	Wyoming
Connecticut	Idaho	Maryland	Nevada	Ohio	Texas	

Alaska

97

Collection Agency Operator
Dept. of Commerce and Economic Development
Div. of Occupational Licensing
Collection Agencies and Operators
PO Box D-LIC
Juneau, AK 99811-0800
Phone: (907)465-2541
Fax: (907)465-2974

Credential Type: Collection Agency Operator License. **Duration of License:** Two years. **Authorization:** All collection agencies and branch offices must be under the management and control of a licensed operator. **Requirements:** At least 19 years of age. High school graduate or equivalent. Good moral character. No violation of state licensing laws or convictions of a felony or crime of larceny or embezzlement or a crime involving moral turpitude. Not be a disbarred attorney or have filed bankruptcy. **Fees:** $30 resident application fee. $60 non-resident application fee. $100 resident license fee. $200 non-resident license fee. **Governing Statute:** Alaska Statutes 08.24.

98

Independent Insurance Adjuster
Div. of Insurance
Dept. of Commerce and Economic Development
State Office Bldg., 9th Fl.
33 Willoughby Ave.
PO Box 110805
Juneau, AK 99811-0805
Phone: (907)465-2579
Phone: (907)465-2575
Phone: (907)465-2578

Credential Type: Independent Adjuster License. **Duration of License:** Two years. **Requirements:** Contact licensing body for application information. **Fees:** $50 resident fee. $100 non-resident fee. **Governing Statute:** Alaska Statutes, Title 21.

Credential Type: Trainee License. **Duration of License:** Two years. **Requirements:** Contact licensing body for application information. **Fees:** $50 resident fee. **Governing Statute:** Alaska Statutes, Title 21.

Arizona

99

Insurance Adjuster
Dept. of Insurance
Licensing Section
Abacus Towers 1100
3030 N. 3rd St.
Phoenix, AZ 85012
Phone: (602)255-5605

Credential Type: Insurance Adjuster License. **Duration of License:** Two years. **Requirements:** Prove sufficient experience and training. **Fees:** $35.65 license fee.

Arkansas

100

Claims Adjuster
Arkansas Insurance Dept.
400 University Tower Bldg.
12th & University St.
Little Rock, AR 72204
Phone: (501)371-1421

Credential Type: License. **Duration of License:** Two years. **Requirements:** 18 years of age. Resident of Arkansas or other state which has reciprocity with Arkansas to act as adjusters. Experience or special training in the handling of loss claims. **Examination:** Yes. **Reciprocity:** Yes. **Fees:** $25 General examination. $25 License. $25 Renewal.

101

Collection Agency Collector
State Board of Collection Agencies
1120 John Hardin Dr.
PO Box 585
Jacksonville, AR 72076
Phone: (501)982-2778

Credential Type: License. **Duration of License:** One year. **Requirements:** Must possess patience, persistence and tact, and be skilled in telephone and written communications. **Examination:** No. **Fees:** $15 License. $15 Renewal.

Arkansas 102

102

Collection Agency Manager
State Board of Collection Agencies
1120 John Hardin Dr.
PO Box 585
Jacksonville, AR 72076
Phone: (501)982-2778

Credential Type: License. **Duration of License:** One year. **Requirements:** Must have either one year experience in a collection agency or pass a manager's examination. **Examination:** Yes. **Fees:** $125 License. $125 Renewal.

California

103

Insurance Adjuster
Dept. of Insurance
700 L St.
Sacramento, CA 95814
Phone: (916)322-3555
Phone: (415)557-1126

Credential Type: Insurance Adjuster License. **Duration of License:** Two years. **Requirements:** Contact licensing body for application information. Must be a California resident. **Fees:** $47 application fee. $190 license fee. $190 renewal fee.

104

Public Insurance Adjuster
Dept. of Insurance
700 L St.
Sacramento, CA 95814
Phone: (916)322-3555
Phone: (415)557-1126

Credential Type: Public Insurance Adjuster License. **Duration of License:** Two years. **Requirements:** Contact licensing body for application information. Must be a California resident. **Fees:** $41 application fee. $160 license fee. $160 renewal fee.

105

Repossession Company Operator
Bureau of Collection and
  Investigative Services
400 R St., Ste. 2001
Sacramento, CA 95814-6234
Phone: (916)445-7366

Credential Type: Repossession Company Operator License. **Requirements:** At least one year or 2000 hours of compensated experience as an employee of a licensed repossession agency in California during the past five years, or in recovering personal property sold under a security agreement in California. **Examination:** Written examination. **Fees:** $750 license application fee. $27 fingerprint processing fee.

Credential Type: Qualified Manager Certificate. **Authorization:** Required of the person who is in active charge of the business. **Requirements:** Be at least 18 years of age. At least one year or 2000 hours of compensated experience as an employee of a licensed repossession agency in California during the past five years, or in recovering personal property sold under a security agreement in California. **Examination:** Written examination. **Fees:** $250 application and qualification certificate fee. $27 fingerprint processing fee.

Colorado

106

Collections Manager
Dept. of Law
Office of the Attorney General
State Services Bldg.
1525 Sherman St., 5th Fl.
Denver, CO 80203
Phone: (303)866-4500
Phone: (303)866-3611
Fax: (303)866-5691

Credential Type: Collection manager license. **Duration of License:** Three years. **Requirements:** Submit application and pay fees. Pass written examination to test competency. Must be registered as a debt collector. **Examination:** Written competency examination. **Governing Statute:** Colorado Revised Statutes, Title 12, Chapter 14, Colorado Fair Debt Collection Practices Act. Collection Agency Board Rules.

107

Debt Collector
Dept. of Law
Office of the Attorney General
State Services Bldg.
1525 Sherman St., 5th Fl.
Denver, CO 80203
Phone: (303)866-4500
Phone: (303)866-3611
Fax: (303)866-5691

Credential Type: Debt collector certificate of registration. **Duration of License:** Three years. **Requirements:** Submit application and pay fees. **Governing Statute:** Colorado Revised Statutes, Title 12, Chapter 14, Colorado Fair Debt Collection Practices Act. Collection Agency Board Rules.

108

Insurance Adjuster
Dept. of Regulatory Agencies
Div. of Insurance
303 W. Colfax, Ste. 500
Denver, CO 80204
Phone: (303)866-6248

Credential Type: Professional license. **Duration of License:** Two years. **Requirements:** Complete a 65-hour training course or pass an Adjuster-All Lines examination. **Examination:** Adjuster-All Lines examination. **Reciprocity:** Yes, but restricted as to states involved. **Fees:** $67 exam fee. $29 license fee.

Connecticut

109

Automobile Physical Damage Appraiser
Licensing and Investigations Div.
Insurance Dept.
PO Box 816
Hartford, CT 06142-0816
Phone: (203)297-3841

Credential Type: Resident Automobile Physical Damage Appraiser License. **Duration of License:** Two years. **Requirements:** Submit application and fees. Pass examination. **Examination:** Yes. **Fees:** $25 application filing fee. $40 examination fee. $40 license fee.

Credential Type: Non-Resident Automobile Physical Damage Appraiser License. **Duration of License:** Two years. **Requirements:** May be issued without examination provided the applicant holds the same or similar license from the state in which applicant resides. **Fees:** $25 application filing fee. $40 license fee.

110

Casualty Adjuster
Licensing and Investigations Div.
Insurance Dept.
PO Box 816
Hartford, CT 06142-0816
Phone: (203)297-3841

Credential Type: Resident Casualty Adjuster License. **Duration of License:** Two years. **Requirements:** Submit application and pay fees. Pass examination. **Examination:** Connecticut Casualty Adjuster Examination. **Fees:** $25 application filing fee. $10 examination fee. $40 license fee.

Credential Type: Non-Resident Casualty Adjuster License. **Duration of License:**

Two years. **Requirements:** May be issued without examination provided the applicant holds the same or similar license from the state in which applicant resides. **Fees:** $25 application filing fee. $40 license fee.

111

Insurance Investigator (Racetrack)
Connecticut Div. of Special Revenue
Russell Rd.
PO Box 11424
Newington, CT 06111-0424
Phone: (203)566-2756

Credential Type: License Registration. **Requirements:** Submit application and fingerprint card. Pay fee. **Fees:** $5 registration fee.

112

Public Insurance Adjuster
Licensing and Investigations Div.
Insurance Dept.
PO Box 816
Hartford, CT 06142-0816
Phone: (203)297-3841

Credential Type: Resident Public Insurance Adjuster License. **Duration of License:** Two years. **Requirements:** Submit application and pay fees. Pass examination. **Examination:** Connecticut Public Adjuster's Examination. **Fees:** $25 application filing fee. $7 examination fee. $125 license fee.

Credential Type: Non-Resident Public Insurance Adjuster License. **Duration of License:** Two years. **Requirements:** May be issued without examination provided the applicant holds the same or similar license from the state in which applicant resides. **Fees:** $25 application filing fee. $125 license fee.

Delaware

113

Insurance Adjuster
Dept. of Insurance
841 Silver Lake Blvd.
Rodney Bldg.
Dover, DE 19901
Phone: (302)739-4251

Credential Type: Insurance Adjuster License and Certificate of Authority. **Duration of License:** Permanent. **Requirements:** Must be at least 18 years of age. Be competent, trustworthy, financially responsible, and of good reputation. Demonstrate competency by completing qualification examination. Submit examination report from ASI. In addition, non-residents must provide Letter of Certification from home state or Delaware examination report from ASI. **Examination:** Yes. **Exemptions:** Exam may be waived for applicants who have completed all phases of the Insurance Institute of America qualification requirements. **Fees:** $30 application fee.

Credential Type: Apprentice Adjuster's License. **Duration of License:** One year. **Requirements:** Must be a full-time employee of a licensed Insurance Adjuster. Must be at least 18 years of age. Be competent, trustworthy, financially responsible, and of good reputation. **Fees:** $10 application fee.

114

Motor Vehicle Appraiser
Dept. of Insurance
841 Silver Lake Blvd.
Rodney Bldg.
Dover, DE 19901
Phone: (302)739-4251

Credential Type: Motor Vehicle Appraiser License and Certificate of Authority. **Duration of License:** Permanent. **Requirements:** Must be at least 18 years of age. Be competent, trustworthy, financially responsible, and of good reputation. Demonstrate competency by completing qualification examination. Submit examination report from ASI. In addition, non-residents must provide Letter of Certification from home state or Delaware examination report from ASI. **Examination:** Yes. **Fees:** $30 application fee.

Credential Type: Apprentice Appraiser's License. **Duration of License:** One year. **Requirements:** Must be a full-time employee of a licensed Motor Vehicle Appraiser. Must be at least 18 years of age. Be competent, trustworthy, financially responsible, and of good reputation. **Fees:** $10 application fee.

District of Columbia

115

Auto Repossessor
License and Certification Div.
Occupational and Professional Licensure Administration
Consumer and Regulatory Affairs Dept.
PO Box 37200
Washington, DC 20013-7200
Phone: (202)727-7823
Phone: (202)727-7480

Alternate Information: 614 H St., NW, Washington, DC 20001 **Requirements:** Contact licensing body for application information.

116

Solicitor
License and Certification Div.
Occupational and Professional Licensure Administration
Consumer and Regulatory Affairs Dept.
PO Box 37200
Washington, DC 20013-7200
Phone: (202)727-7823
Phone: (202)727-7480

Alternate Information: 614 H St., NW, Washington, DC 20001 **Requirements:** Contact licensing body for application information.

Florida

117

Insurance Adjuster
Dept. of Insurance
Bureau of Agent and Agency Licensing
The Capitol
Tallahassee, FL 32399-0300
Phone: (904)922-3137

Credential Type: Resident Adjuster License. **Duration of License:** Two years. **Authorization:** Licenses are issued for the following lines of insurance: All Lines, Property and Casualty, Motor Vehicle Physical Damage, Workers' Compensation, and Health. **Requirements:** Contact licensing body for application information.

Credential Type: Nonresident Adjuster License. **Duration of License:** Two years. **Authorization:** Licenses are issued for the following lines of insurance: All Lines, Property and Casualty, Motor Vehicle Physical Damage, Workers' Compensa-

Insurance Adjuster, continued

tion, and Health. **Requirements:** Contact licensing body for application information. **Fees:** $50 application fee. $58 fingerprint processing fee. $5 license fee.

Georgia

118

Insurance Adjuster
State Insurance Dept.
Agents Licensing Div.
Box 101208
Atlanta, GA 30392-1208
Phone: (404)656-2056
Fax: (404)656-7628

Credential Type: Independent Adjuster License. **Requirements:** Complete a 40-hour classroom pre-licensing course. **Examination:** ASI Examination. **Fees:** $15 application fee. $50 license fee. $90 exam fee.

Credential Type: Company Adjuster License. **Requirements:** Complete a 40-hour classroom pre-licensing course. **Examination:** ASI Examination. **Fees:** $15 application fee. $50 license fee. $90 exam fee.

119

Public Adjuster
State Insurance Dept.
Agents Licensing Div.
Box 101208
Atlanta, GA 30392-1208
Phone: (404)656-2056
Fax: (404)656-7628

Credential Type: Adjuster License. **Requirements:** Complete a 40-hour classroom pre-licensing course. Post appropriate bond. **Examination:** ASI Examination. **Fees:** $15 application fee. $50 license fee. $90 exam fee.

Idaho

120

Solicitor/collector
Dept. of Finance
Statehouse Mail
Boise, ID 83720-2700
Phone: (208)334-2945

Credential Type: Solicitor/collector license. **Duration of License:** One year. **Authorization:** A license is required for all solicitors and collectors as well as for all principal officers, owners, or partners of a licensed collection agency. **Requirements:** Submit application and pay fee. **Fees:** $20 license fee. $20 renewal fee. **Governing Statute:** Idaho Code, Chap. 22, Title 26.

Illinois

121

Collection Agent
Illinois Dept. of Professional
  Regulations
320 W. Washington St.
Springfield, IL 62786
Phone: (217)782-8556

Credential Type: Collection Agent License. **Duration of License:** Two years. **Requirements:** At least 18 years of age. U.S. citizen or legal alien. Good moral character. One year experience in credit or related fields. Have an acceptable credit rating. Post a $25,000 surety bond. **Reciprocity:** No. **Fees:** $75 initial license fee. $60 renewal fee. **Governing Statute:** The Collection Agency Act, Illinois Revised Statutes 1991, Chapter 111.

122

Public Insurance Adjuster
Illinois Dept. of Insurance
320 W. Washington
Springfield, IL 62767
Phone: (217)782-6366

Credential Type: Public Insurance Adjuster License. **Duration of License:** One year. **Requirements:** At least 18 years of age. Background in property insurance. Submit application and pay fee. **Examination:** Public Insurance Adjuster Examination. **Reciprocity:** Yes, if applicant holds a valid license from another state. **Fees:** $55 examination fee. $10 application fee. $30 initial license fee. $30 renewal fee. **Governing Statute:** Illinois Insurance Code, Chapter 73.

Indiana

123

Insurance Adjuster
Insurance Dept.
311 W. Washington St., Ste. 300
Indianapolis, IN 46204-2787
Phone: (317)232-2385
Fax: (317)232-5251

Credential Type: License. **Requirements:** Contact licensing body for application information.

Iowa

124

Adoption Investigator
Dept. of Inspections and Appeals
Lucas State Office Bldg.
Des Moines, IA 50319
Phone: (515)281-6377

Credential Type: License. **Duration of License:** Three years. **Requirements:** Graduation from a four-year accredited college plus three years of full-time adoption experience; or graduation from four-year accredited college with a bachelor's degree in social work, plus two years of full-time adoption experience; or a master's degree in social work plus one year of full-time adoption experience.

Kentucky

125

Insurance Adjuster
Kentucky Dept. of Insurance
PO Box 517
Frankfort, KY 40602
Phone: (502)564-3630

Credential Type: License. **Duration of License:** Two years. **Requirements:** 21 years of age. Must be a law school graduate, a full time employee of a licensed insurance adjusting firm, a salaried employee of an admitted property and casualty insurer or have other special claims experience indicating competence. Must file a $1,000 surety bond. **Examination:** Yes. **Fees:** $50 exam fee. $50 renewal fee.

Maine

126

Debt Collector
Dept. of Professional and Financial
  Regulation
Bureau of Consumer Protection
State House Station 35
Augusta, ME 04333-0035
Phone: (207)582-8718
Fax: (207)582-5415

Credential Type: Debt Collector License. **Duration of License:** Two years. **Requirements:** Submit application and pay fee. Must have minimum net worth of $10,000. Post bond based on debt collection activities to be conducted: $20,000 if applicant will undertake direct collections; $15,000 if applicants will undertake repossessions only; $5,000 if applicant will be letter writing only (no direct collections). **Fees:** $400 license fee. $400 renewal fee. **Governing Statute:** 32 M.R.S.A., Chap. 111, Section 11031. Bureau of Consumer Credit Protection Rule 300.

127

Insurance Adjuster
Bureau of Insurance
Dept. of Professional and Financial Regulation
State House Station 34
Augusta, ME 04333
Phone: (207)582-8707
Fax: (207)582-8716

Credential Type: Insurance Adjuster License. **Requirements:** Contact licensing body for application information.

Maryland

128

Debt Collector
Commissioner of Consumer Credit
Dept. of Licensing and Regulation
501 St. Paul Pl.
Baltimore, MD 21202-2272
Phone: (410)333-6330

Credential Type: Collection Agency License. **Duration of License:** One year. **Requirements:** Submit application and pay fee. Post $5,000 surety bond. **Fees:** $150 license fee.

129

Public Adjuster
Insurance Div.
Dept. of Licensing and Regulation
501 St. Paul Pl.
Baltimore, MD 21202-2272
Phone: (410)333-4057

Credential Type: Public Adjuster License. **Duration of License:** Two years. **Requirements:** Resident of Maryland for at least one year. At least five years experience in property and casualty or claims adjusting. **Examination:** Public Adjuster Examination. **Fees:** $33 exam fee.

Massachusetts

130

Motor Vehicle Damage Appraiser
Motor Vehicle Damage Appraisers Board
Div. of Insurance
280 Friend St.
Boston, MA 02114
Phone: (617)727-7189

Credential Type: License. **Requirements:** Contact licensing body for application information.

Michigan

131

Adjuster for the Insured
Licensing Section
Michigan Insurance Bureau
Michigan Department of Commerce
PO Box 30220
Lansing, MI 48909
Phone: (517)373-0220

Credential Type: License. **Duration of License:** One year. **Requirements:** Not be employed by, own stock in, be an officer or director of, or in any other manner be connected with a fire repair contractor. Abide by the rules and regulations of the Michigan Insurance Bureau. **Examination:** Written exam. **Fees:** $10 application fee. $5 initial license fee. $5 renewal fee. **Governing Statute:** Insurance Code, Act 218 of 1956, as amended.

132

Collection Agency Manager
Collection Practices Board
Bureau of Occupational & Professional Regulation
Dept. of Commerce
PO Box 30018
Lansing, MI 48909
Phone: (517)373-9153

Credential Type: License. **Duration of License:** One year. **Requirements:** At least 18 years of age. High school diploma or equivalent. Six months of full-time experience in the collection of accounts. Provide the Board with a credit bureau report and information for a criminal record check. Abide by the rules and regulations of the Board. Be of good moral character. **Examination:** Written exam. **Fees:** $25 application processing fee. $50 initial exam fee. $50 initial license fee. $50 renewal fee. **Governing Statute:** The Occupational Code, Act 299 of 1980, as amended.

133

Insurance Adjuster
Licensing Section
Insurance Bureau
Dept. of Commerce
PO Box 30220
Lansing, MI 48909
Phone: (517)373-9153

Credential Type: License. **Duration of License:** One year. **Requirements:** Must not be employed by, own stock in, be an officer or director of, or in any other manner be connected with a fire repair contractor. Abide by the rules and regulations of the Michigan Insurance Bureau. **Examination:** Written exam. **Reciprocity:** There is complete reciprocity with all other states extending similar courtesies to Michigan residents. **Fees:** $10 application fee. $5 initial license fee. $5 renewal fee. **Governing Statute:** Insurance Code, Act 218 of 1956, as amended.

Minnesota

134

Debt Collector
Dept. of Commerce
Licensing Unit
133 E. 7th St.
St. Paul, MN 55101
Phone: (612)296-6319

Credential Type: Debt Collector License. **Duration of License:** Two years. **Requirements:** Submit application and pay fee. **Fees:** $10 license fee.

135

Independent Insurance Adjustor
Dept. of Commerce
Licensing Unit
133 E. 7th St.
St. Paul, MN 55101
Phone: (612)296-6319

Credential Type: Independent Adjustor License. **Duration of License:** One year. **Authorization:** Available for Fire, Casualty, or Multiple Lines. **Requirements:** Must have at least one year of experience. **Examination:** ASI Examination, parts 1 and 2. **Fees:** $20 license fee. $41 exam fee.

Minnesota

136

Public Insurance Adjustor
Dept. of Commerce
Licensing Unit
133 E. 7th St.
St. Paul, MN 55101
Phone: (612)296-6319

Credential Type: Public Adjustor License. **Duration of License:** One year. **Authorization:** Available for Fire, Casualty, or Multiple Lines. **Requirements:** Must have at least one year of experience. Post $10,000 bond. **Examination:** ASI Examination, parts 1 and 2. **Fees:** $20 license fee. $41 exam fee.

Montana

137

Adjuster
Montana Insurance Dept.
PO Box 4009
Helena, MT 59604
Phone: (406)444-2040

Credential Type: License. **Duration of License:** One year. **Requirements:** 18 years of age. Current full-time employment in an adjusting firm, or equivalent experience. An office in Montana. **Fees:** $15 license fee. $15 renewal fee. **Governing Statute:** Montana Code Annotated 13-17-301 through 13-17-301.

Nebraska

138

Solicitor
Nebraska Collection Agency
  Advisory Board
Secretary of State
State Capitol Bldg., Ste. 2300
Lincoln, NE 68509
Phone: (402)471-2008

Credential Type: Solicitor's Certificate. **Duration of License:** One year. **Requirements:** Must be employed by a licensed collection agency. **Governing Statute:** Nebraska Revised Statutes, Chap. 45, Article 6.

Nevada

139

Claims Adjuster/Examiner
Nevada State Dept. of Commerce
Insurance Div.
Bradley Bldg.
2501 E. Sahara Ave., Rm. 302
Las Vegas, NV 89104
Phone: (702)486-4009

Credential Type: License. **Requirements:** State resident for 90 days. Two years of experience handling claims. Fingerprint card. 21 years of age. **Examination:** Yes. **Fees:** $78 application fee. $82 exam fee. $15 Recovery Fund fee.

140

Collection Agent/Manager
Nevada State Dept. of Commerce
Financial Institutions Div.
406 E. Second St.
Carson City, NV 89710
Phone: (702)687-4259

Credential Type: License. **Duration of License:** One year. **Requirements:** Two years of applicable experience. **Examination:** Yes. **Fees:** $75 investigation fee. $20 license fee. $20 renewal fee.

141

Motor Vehicle Damage Appraiser
Nevada State Dept. of Commerce
Insurance Div.
Bradley Bldg.
2501 E. Sahara Ave., Rm. 302
Las Vegas, NV 89158
Phone: (702)486-4009

Credential Type: License. **Requirements:** 21 years of age. $2,500 bond. Fingerprint card. **Fees:** $78 license fee.

142

Repossessor
Office of the Attorney General
Private Investigator's Licensing
  Board
198 S. Carson St.
Carson City, NV 89710
Phone: (702)687-5534

Credential Type: License. **Duration of License:** One year. **Requirements:** Five years of applicable experience. $200,000 of liability insurance. **Examination:** Yes. **Fees:** $16.50 application fee. $100 exam fee. $50 abeyance fee. $360 license fee. $360 renewal fee. $750 investigation deposit.

New Hampshire

143

Insurance Adjuster
New Hampshire Insurance Dept.
169 Manchester St.
Concord, NH 03301
Phone: (603)271-2261

Credential Type: Insurance Adjuster License. **Duration of License:** Two years. **Requirements:** Good moral character. Submit application which must include the following information: age; sex; domicile; line or lines of insurance applicant will be working in; and place of business. **Examination:** Examination administered by the Insurance Testing Corporation (ITC). **Reciprocity:** Yes, providing applicant has been engaged in business for at least six months. **Fees:** $15 (per line) application fee. $25 resident license fee. $25 biennial renewal fee. $5 express registration fee. $63 New Hampshire Laws and Regulations Exam. $77 Life, Accident, & Health Exam fee. $77 Property & Casualty Exam fee. $63 Worker's Compensation Exam fee.

144

Public Insurance Adjuster
New Hampshire Insurance Dept.
169 Manchester St.
Concord, NH 03301
Phone: (603)271-2261

Credential Type: Public Adjuster License. **Duration of License:** Two years. **Requirements:** Submit application. Good personal and business reputations. Be trustworthy and financially responsible. Post bond of $10,000. Be a resident of New Hampshire or of a state granting similar licenses. Have at least five years of experience in the insurance business, involved in sales, underwriting, or claims. **Examination:** Examination as required by Board. **Reciprocity:** No. **Fees:** $15 application fee. $100 resident license fee. $100 biennial renewal fee. $63 examination fee. $5 express registration fee.

New Mexico

145

Collection Agency Manager
Regulation and Licensing Dept.
Financial Institutions Div.
PO Box 25101
725 St. Michael's Dr.
Santa Fe, NM 97504
Phone: (505)827-7100
Fax: (505)827-7107

Credential Type: Collection Agency Manager's License. **Duration of License:** One year. **Requirements:** Must be a citizen of the United States. Have reached age of majority. Not have been convicted of a felony or crime involving moral turpitude. Have been a resident of New Mexico for at least six months prior to filing application. High school graduate or equivalent. Must have been actively and continuously engaged or employed in the collection of accounts receivable for at least two of the five years preceding application. Must have a good credit record. **Examination:** Written examination. **Fees:** $50 exam fee. $35 renewal fee. **Governing Statute:** Section 61-18A-1 et seq. NMSA 1978.

146

Solicitor
Regulation and Licensing Dept.
Financial Institutions Div.
PO Box 25101
725 St. Michael's Dr.
Santa Fe, NM 97504
Phone: (505)827-7100
Fax: (505)827-7107

Credential Type: Solicitor's Certificate. **Duration of License:** One year. **Requirements:** Be at least 18 years of age. Not have been convicted of a felony or crime involving moral turpitude. Must have a good credit record. **Fees:** $75 certification fee. **Governing Statute:** Section 61-18A-1 et seq. NMSA 1978.

New York

147

Adjuster (Insurance)
New York State Insurance Dept.
Licensing Unit
Agency Bldg. One
Empire State Plaza
Albany, NY 12257
Phone: (518)474-4570

Credential Type: License. **Duration of License:** One year. **Requirements:** Must be observant of physical details during inspections of loss or damage. Verbal ability to settle claims. No felony convictions. Character references. Fingerprint record card. **Examination:** Written. **Fees:** $25 license fee. $20 exam fee. $25 renewal fee. **Governing Statute:** Section 2108 of the Insurance Law.

North Carolina

148

Insurance Company/Independent Firm Adjuster
Dept. of Insurance
Agent Services Div.
PO Box 26267
Raleigh, NC 27611
Phone: (919)733-7487

Credential Type: License. **Duration of License:** One year. **Requirements:** 18 years of age. Must be sponsored by an insurance company or adjusting firm. **Examination:** Written. **Fees:** $10 registration fee. $16 exam fee. $50 license fee (billed to the employer). $50 renewal fee (billed to the employer).

149

Motor Vehicle Damage Appraiser
Dept. of Insurance
Agent Services Div.
PO Box 26267
Raleigh, NC 27611
Phone: (919)733-7487

Credential Type: License. **Duration of License:** One year. **Requirements:** 18 years of age. **Fees:** $50 license fee. $10 registration fee. $50 renewal fee.

150

Self-Employed Insurance Adjuster
Dept. of Insurance
Agent Services Div.
PO Box 26267
Raleigh, NC 27611
Phone: (919)733-7487

Credential Type: License. **Duration of License:** One year. **Requirements:** 18 years of age. **Examination:** Written. **Fees:** $16 exam fee. $50 license fee. $10 registration fee. $50 renewal fee.

North Dakota

151

Debt Collector
Dept. of Banking and Financial Institutions
State Capitol
600 E. Blvd. Ave., 13th Fl.
Bismarck, ND 58505-0080
Phone: (701)224-2253
Fax: (701)224-3000

Credential Type: Debt Collector's Certificate. **Duration of License:** One year. **Requirements:** Must be employed by a licensed collection agency. Employing agency must submit names and addresses of all appointed debt collectors to receive certificates. **Governing Statute:** North Dakota Century Code, Chap. 13-05. North Dakota Administrative Rules, Chap. 13-04-02.

Ohio

152

Public Adjuster
Licensing Div.
Dept. of Insurance
2100 Stella Ct.
Columbus, OH 43266-0566
Phone: (614)644-2665

Credential Type: Public Adjuster License. **Duration of License:** One year. **Requirements:** Pre-licensing education consisting of 40 hours of training is required. **Examination:** Insurance Testing Corporation (ITC) examination. **Reciprocity:** Yes, provided proof of certification is submitted. **Fees:** $10 application fee. $100 license fee. $50 renewal fee. **Governing Statute:** Ohio Revised Code 3901.01. Ohio Insurance and Administrative Code.

Oklahoma

153

Insurance Adjuster
Oklahoma State Insurance Commission
1901 N. Walnut
PO Box 53408
Oklahoma City, OK 73152
Phone: (405)521-3916

Credential Type: License. **Duration of License:** One year. **Requirements:** A working knowledge of the occupation is necessary. **Examination:** Insurance Adjuster Exam. **Fees:** $20 exam fee. $15 application fee. $15 renewal fee.

Oregon

154

Independent Adjusters
Insurance Div.
Labor & Industries Bldg., Rm. 440
Salem, OR 97310
Phone: (503)378-4511

Credential Type: License. **Duration of License:** Two years. **Requirements:** 18 years of age. Oregon resident. Experience or education handling loss claims under insurance policies. **Examination:** Yes. **Fees:** $81 exam fee. $60 license fee. $60 renewal fee. **Governing Statute:** ORS 744.505 to 744.575.

Pennsylvania

155

Public Adjuster
State Insurance Dept.
Div. of Agents and Brokers
1300 Strawberry Sq.
Harrisburg, PA 17120
Phone: (717)787-3840

Credential Type: Public Adjuster License. **Requirements:** Post $40,000 surety bond. **Examination:** Public Adjuster Examination. **Fees:** $10 application fee. $100 license fee.

Credential Type: Mediclaim Adjuster License. **Requirements:** Post $40,000 surety bond. **Examination:** Accident and Health Examination. **Fees:** $10 application fee. $100 license fee.

156

Public Adjuster Solicitor
State Insurance Dept.
Div. of Agents and Brokers
1300 Strawberry Sq.
Harrisburg, PA 17120
Phone: (717)787-3840

Credential Type: Public Adjuster Solicitor License. **Requirements:** Post $8,000 surety bond. Must be employed by a licensed public adjuster. **Examination:** Public Adjuster Solicitor Examination. **Fees:** $10 application fee. $50 license fee.

Rhode Island

157

Insurance Appraiser
Office of the Insurance
 Commissioner
Insurance Div.
Rhode Island Dept. of Business
 Regulation
233 Richmond St.
Providence, RI 02903
Phone: (401)277-2223

Credential Type: Insurance Appraiser License. **Duration of License:** Three years. **Requirements:** At least 18 years of age. Pass a screening by the State Police Bureau of Criminal Identification. Knowledge of real and personal property value. **Examination:** Written examination. **Reciprocity:** Yes. **Fees:** $10 application fee. $50 license fee. $150 renewal fee.

158

Insurance Claim Adjuster/Public Adjuster
Office of the Insurance
 Commissioner
Insurance Div.
Rhode Island Dept. of Business
 Regulation
233 Richmond St.
Providence, RI 02903
Phone: (401)277-2223

Credential Type: Claim Adjuster License. **Duration of License:** One year. **Requirements:** At least 18 years of age. Good moral character. Approved training. Must pass examinations if not affiliated with an insurance company under an approved program. **Examination:** Written and oral examination. **Exemptions:** The following persons are exempt from licensing requirements: Attorneys; Insurance Agents; Insurance Brokers; Insurance Solicitors; or employees or agents of companies acting in settling claims of $2,500 or less. **Reciprocity:** No. **Fees:** $20 filing fee. $10 examination fee. $50 license fee.

159

Motor Vehicle Damage Appraiser
Office of the Insurance
 Commissioner
Insurance Div.
Rhode Island Dept. of Business
 Regulation
233 Richmond St.
Providence, RI 02903
Phone: (401)277-2223

Credential Type: Motor Vehicle Damage Appraiser License. **Duration of License:** Three years. **Requirements:** Have knowledge of the pricing of motor vehicle parts. Submit application and pay fee. **Examination:** Written examination. **Reciprocity:** No. **Fees:** $10 examination fee. $50 initial license fee. $150 renewal fee.

Tennessee

160

Collection Service Location Manager
Dept. of Commerce and Insurance
Collection Service Board
500 James Robertson Pky.
Nashville, TN 37219
Phone: (615)741-1741

Credential Type: Collection Service Location Manager License. **Duration of License:** One year. **Authorization:** Every collection service must have, for each location at which it conducts business, a licensed location manager. **Requirements:** High school graduate or equivalent. Meet one of the following sets of requirements: (1) Must have been employed by a licensed collection service in a position directly related to the collection of debts and/or the solicitation of accounts receivable for at least one year within the past three years. (2) Must demonstrate adequate experience within the past three years in a business governed by laws similar to those governing collection services. **Examination:** Location manager examination. **Fees:** $100 application fee. **Governing Statute:** Tennessee Code Annotated, Title 62, Chap. 20.

Texas

161

Insurance Adjuster
Texas Dept. of Insurance
Agents License Div.
1110 San Jacinto
Austin, TX 78701
Phone: (512)322-4191

Credential Type: License. **Duration of License:** One year. **Requirements:** Texas residency. 18 years of age. Experience, education, or training sufficient to allow applicant to fulfill the responsibilities of an adjuster. **Examination:** Written state examination or examination upon completion of course study. **Fees:** $50 application fee. $27 exam fee. $48 renewal fee. **Governing Statute:** Insurance Code 21.07-4, Section 7:1-6.

Utah

162

Insurance Adjuster
Utah State Insurance Dept.
3110 State Office Bldg.
Salt Lake City, UT 84114
Phone: (801)538-3855

Credential Type: Insurance agent license. **Requirements:** Must be 18 years of age. Must complete an approved state pre-license study program. Pass license examination. **Examination:** Yes. **Fees:** $61 examination-combined license fee. $55 examination-single line fee. $40 license fee.

Vermont

163

Insurance Adjuster
Dept. of Banking and Insurance
120 State St.
Montpelier, VT 05602
Phone: (802)828-3301

Credential Type: License. **Duration of License:** One year. **Requirements:** 18 years of age. Good personal and business reputation. Two years minimum experience or special training in loss claims. In lieu of above—employed for three years directly under licensed adjuster immediately prior to application. **Examination:** Yes. **Reciprocity:** Yes. **Fees:** $20 Application fee. $20 License fee. $20 Renewal. **Governing Statute:** Title 8, VSA Sections 4791-4793 and 4803.

164

Insurance Appraiser
Dept. of Banking and Insurance
120 State St.
Montpelier, VT 05602
Phone: (802)828-3301

Credential Type: License. **Duration of License:** One year. **Requirements:** 18 years of age. Good personal and business reputation. Two years of experience or special training in appraising; or employed under direct supervision of a licensed appraiser who has worked in Vermont for three years immediately prior to application. **Examination:** Yes. **Reciprocity:** Yes. **Fees:** $20 Application fee. $20 License fee. $20 Renewal. **Governing Statute:** Title 8, VSA Sections 4791-4793 and 4803.

165

Public Adjuster
Dept. of Banking and Insurance
120 State St.
Montpelier, VT 05602
Phone: (802)828-3301

Credential Type: License. **Duration of License:** One year. **Requirements:** 18 years of age. Good personal and business reputation. At least two years experience or special training with respect to handling loss claims of sufficient duration and scope to prove competency; or, employed under the direct supervision of a Public Adjuster who has been in business in Vermont for three years immediately prior to applying. **Examination:** No. **Reciprocity:** Yes. **Fees:** $20 Application. $100 License. $100 Renewal. **Governing Statute:** Title 8, VSA Sections 4791-4793 and 4803.

Washington

166

Independent Insurance Adjuster
Insurance Commissioner
Insurance Bldg., AQ-21
Olympia, WA 98504-0321
Phone: (206)753-7307

Credential Type: Independent Insurance Adjuster License. **Duration of License:** One year. **Requirements:** At least 18 years of age. Submit to background investigation. Complete specified education and experience requirements. Submit fingerprint cards and Certificate of Affiliation. Non-resident requirements retaliatory with applicant's home state. **Examination:** ASI examination. **Fees:** $25 resident license fee. $5 filing fee. $45 examination fee. $10 fee for each Certificate of Affiliation.

167

Insurance Claims Adjuster
Insurance Commission
Insurance Bldg., AQ-21
Olympia, WA 98504-0321
Phone: (206)753-7307

Credential Type: Insurance Claims Adjuster License. **Duration of License:** One year. **Requirements:** At least 18 years of age. Submit to background investigation. Submit fingerprint card. Complete education and experience requirements related to specialty. Submit Certificate of Affiliation. Non-resident requirements retaliatory with applicant's home state. **Examination:** Written examination. **Fees:** $25 resident license fee. $45 examination fee. $5 filing fee. $10 fee for each Certificate of Affiliation.

Wisconsin

168

Debt Collector
Office of Commissioner of Banking
Consumer Credit Div.
131 W. Wilson St., 8th Fl.
PO Box 7876
Madison, WI 53707-7876
Phone: (608)266-1621

Credential Type: Solicitor/Collector License. **Duration of License:** One year. **Requirements:** Must be employed by a license collection agency. **Fees:** $2 license fee. $2 renewal fee. **Governing Statute:** Wisconsin Statutes, Sect. 218.04.

Wyoming

169

Claims Adjuster
Wyoming Insurance Dept.
Herschler Building, 3rd Fl.
122 W. 25th St.
Cheyenne, WY 82002
Phone: (307)777-7319

Credential Type: License. **Duration of License:** One year. **Requirements:** Must be an adult. Must be a Wyoming resident. Must be trustworthy and of good reputation. Must be a full time salaried employee of a licensed adjuster, or graduate from an accredited law school or have experience dealing with loss claims. Pass the examination. **Examination:** Yes. **Reciprocity:** No. **Fees:** $58 Pre-registered examination ($28 in Rock Springs). $75 Walk-in examination ($45 in Rock Springs). $25 Annual license.

Administrative Services Managers

The following states grant licenses in this occupational category as of the date of publication: California, Connecticut, Florida, Georgia, Iowa, Kansas, Kentucky, Michigan, North Carolina.

California

170

Assistant Manager (Racetrack)
California Horse Racing Board
1010 Hurley Way, Ste. 190
Sacramento, CA 95825
Phone: (916)920-7178

Credential Type: License Registration. **Requirements:** Submit application and fingerprint card. Pay fee. **Fees:** $75 registration fee.

Connecticut

171

Administrator (Racetrack)
Connecticut Div. of Special Revenue
Russell Rd.
PO Box 11424
Newington, CT 06111-0424
Phone: (203)566-2756

Credential Type: License Registration. **Requirements:** Submit application and fingerprint card. Pay fee. **Fees:** $5 registration fee.

172

Assistant Manager (Racetrack)
Connecticut Div. of Special Revenue
Russell Rd.
PO Box 11424
Newington, CT 06111-0424
Phone: (203)566-2756

Credential Type: License Registration. **Requirements:** Submit application and fingerprint card. Pay fee. **Fees:** $5-$20 registration fee.

173

Assistant Operations Manager (Racetrack)
Connecticut Div. of Special Revenue
Russell Rd.
PO Box 11424
Newington, CT 06111-0424
Phone: (203)566-2756

Credential Type: License Registration. **Requirements:** Submit application and fingerprint card. Pay fee. **Fees:** $5 registration fee.

174

Assistant Plant Superintendent (Racetrack)
Connecticut Div. of Special Revenue
Russell Rd.
PO Box 11424
Newington, CT 06111-0424
Phone: (203)566-2756

Credential Type: License Registration. **Requirements:** Submit application and fingerprint card. Pay fee. **Fees:** $5 registration fee.

175

Facility Supervisor (Racetrack)
Connecticut Div. of Special Revenue
Russell Rd.
PO Box 11424
Newington, CT 06111-0424
Phone: (203)566-2756

Credential Type: License Registration. **Requirements:** Submit application and fingerprint card. Pay fee. **Fees:** $20 registration fee.

Florida

176

Association Manager/Supervisor (Racetrack)
Florida Dept. of Business
Div. of Pari-Mutuel Wagering
Licensing Section
725 S. Bronough St.
Tallahassee, FL 32399-1037
Phone: (904)488-9161

Credential Type: License Registration Code 1005. **Authorization:** Authorizes work in the following positions: admissions manager, chief of security, concession manager or owner, general manager, mutuels manager, parking director, public relations director, plant superintendent, and track superintendent. **Requirements:** Submit application and fingerprint card. Pay fee. **Fees:** $40 registration fee.

Georgia

177

Recreation Administrator
State Board of Recreation Examiners
Allied Health Fields Section
Professional Examining Boards
166 Pryor St., SW
Atlanta, GA 30303
Phone: (404)656-3921

Credential Type: Recreation Administrator License. **Duration of License:** Two years. **Authorization:** A recreation administrator is the executive head or management level position administering a permanent full-time recreation or park program. **Requirements:** Meet one of the following criteria: (1) Have a baccalaureate degree in recreation from an accredited college or university. Have 12 months full-time recreation experience. (2) Have a baccalaureate degree in a related field from an accredited college or university. Have 24 months full-time recreation experience. (3) Have a baccalaureate degree from an accredited college or university. Have 36 months full-time recreation experience. (4) Have 10 or more years full-time recreation or park specialty experience in an administrative or management capacity normally requiring the possession of a baccalaureate degree. **Examination:** Recreation Administrator License Examination. **Reciprocity:** No. **Fees:** $20 application fee. $40 exam fee. $100 renewal fee. **Governing Statute:** Official Code of Georgia Annotated 43-41.

Iowa

178

Administrator (Racetrack)
Iowa State Racing Commission
Lucas State Office Bldg.
Des Moines, IA 50319
Phone: (515)281-7352

Credential Type: License Registration. **Requirements:** Submit application and fingerprint card. Pay fee. **Fees:** $5 registration fee.

179

Assistant Manager (Racetrack)
Iowa State Racing Commission
Lucas State Office Bldg.
Des Moines, IA 50319
Phone: (515)281-7352

Credential Type: License Registration. **Requirements:** Submit application and fingerprint card. Pay fee. **Fees:** $20 registration fee.

180

Assistant Manager (Racetrack)
Iowa State Racing Commission
Lucas State Office Bldg.
Des Moines, IA 50319
Phone: (515)281-7352

Credential Type: License Registration. **Requirements:** Submit application and fingerprint card. Pay fee. **Fees:** $20 registration fee.

181

Manager (Racetrack)
Iowa State Racing Commission
Lucas State Office Bldg.
Des Moines, IA 50319
Phone: (515)281-7352

Credential Type: License Registration. **Requirements:** Submit application and fingerprint card. Pay fee. **Fees:** $20 registration fee.

Kansas

182

Administrator (Racetrack)
Kansas Racing Commission
3400 VanBuren
Topeka, KS 66611-2228
Phone: (913)296-5800

Credential Type: License Registration. **Requirements:** Submit application and fingerprint card. Pay fee. **Fees:** $20 registration fee.

183

Assistant Manager (Racetrack)
Kansas Racing Commission
3400 VanBuren
Topeka, KS 66611-2228
Phone: (913)296-5800

Credential Type: License Registration. **Requirements:** Submit application and fingerprint card. Pay fee. **Fees:** $20 registration fee.

Kentucky

184

Admission Department Manager/ Employee(Racetrack)
Kentucky State Racing Commission
PO Box 1080
Lexington, KY 40588
Phone: (606)254-7021

Credential Type: Association Employee and Occupational License. **Requirements:** Submit application and fingerprint card. Pay fee. **Fees:** $10 license fee.

Michigan

185

Insurance Administrative Services Manager (Third Party)
Licensing Section
Insurance Bureau
Dept. of Commerce
PO Box 30220
Lansing, MI 48909
Phone: (517)373-9153

Credential Type: License. **Duration of License:** Permanent. **Requirements:** Submit to the Michigan Insurance Bureau a written authority or statement from an authorized Insurance Administrator (Third Party) to act on its behalf. Be honest, trustworthy, and of good moral character. Abide by the rules and regulations of the Michigan Insurance Bureau. **Examination:** Written exam. **Fees:** $10 initial license fee. **Governing Statute:** Third Party Administrator Act, Act 218 of 1984.

186

Insurance Administrator (Third Party)
Licensing Section
Insurance Bureau
Dept. of Commerce
PO Box 30220
Lansing, MI 48909
Phone: (517)373-9153

Credential Type: Certificate of Authority. **Duration of License:** Permanent. **Requirements:** Apply on forms prescribed by the Insurance Commissioner, as well as, submit a copy of such organizational documents as the articles of incorporation, by-laws, articles of association, and trade name certificate. Be domiciled in Michigan, or have a blanket consent to service if not domiciled in Michigan. To obtain a blanket consent to service, insurance administrators must execute a power of attorney appointing the Insurance Commissioner as their attorney, upon whom legal action or proceedings may be served. Submit a copy of their most recent financial statement. Employ at least one licensed insurance administrative services manager (third party) who would be responsible for the daily operations. Have adequate facilities, personnel, and managers. Abide by the rules and regulations of the Michigan Insurance Bureau. **Fees:** $200 initial application fee. $25 initial certificate of authority fee. $25 filing fee for annual statement. **Governing Statute:** Third Party Administrator Act, Act 218 of 1984.

North Carolina

Day Care Administrator
Dept. of Human Resources
Child Day Care Section
701 Barbour Dr.
Raleigh, NC 27603
Phone: (919)733-4801

Credential Type: Registration. **Duration of License:** Two years. **Requirements:** High school diploma or GED, two years of full-time day care or early childhood experience, and verification of successful completion, or current enrollment in, three credit hours of training in the area of child care program administration. 21 years of age. Valid driver's license. Continuing education required.

Adult and Vocational Education Teachers

One or more occupations in this chapter require a federal license. Additionally, the following states grant licenses as of the date of publication:

Alabama	Delaware	Kansas	Minnesota	New York	South Carolina	Washington
Alaska	Florida	Kentucky	Missouri	North Carolina	South Dakota	West Virginia
Arizona	Georgia	Louisiana	Montana	North Dakota	Tennessee	
Arkansas	Idaho	Maine	Nebraska	Ohio	Texas	
California	Illinois	Maryland	New Hampshire	Oklahoma	Utah	
Colorado	Indiana	Massachusetts	New Jersey	Pennsylvania	Vermont	
Connecticut	Iowa	Michigan	New Mexico	Rhode Island	Virginia	

Federal Licenses

188

Flight Instructor
Federal Aviation Administration
800 Independence Ave., SW
Washington, DC 20591
Phone: (202)267-3484

Credential Type: Flight Instructor Certificate. **Authorization:** Authorized to give flight instruction, ground instruction, or a home study course for a pilot certificate or rating. Authorized to give ground and flight instruction for a flight instructor certificate and rating. **Requirements:** 18 years old. Read, speak, and understand English.

Hold a commercial or airline transport pilot certificate with appropriate aircraft rating. Complete a course of instruction in subjects relating to aeronautical instruction. Have logged ground instruction in all of the subjects in which ground instruction is required for a private and commercial pilot certificate.

For an instrument or airplane instructor rating, must hold an instrument rating. Have logged ground instruction for an instrument rating.

For additional rating, must hold an effective pilot certificate with appropriate ratings. Have at least 15 hours as pilot in command in the category and class of aircraft. Pass the written and practical test prescribed for the rating sought. Additional ratings include airplane-single engine, airplane-multiengine, rotorcraft-helicopter, rotorcraft-gyroplane, instrument-airplane, and instrument-helicopter. **Examination:** Written test on subjects in which ground instruction is required. Practical oral and flight test covering items selected by the inspector or examiner. **Governing Statute:** Federal Aviation Regulations, 14 CFR Ch. 1, part 61, subpart G.

Alabama

189

Cosmetology Instructor
Alabama Board of Cosmetology
Altus Bank Bldg., Ste. 801
100 Commerce St.
Montgomery, AL 36130
Phone: (205)242-5613
Phone: (205)242-5614

Credential Type: License. **Duration of License:** Two years. **Requirements:** Must hold a license in cosmetology. Must complete a teacher's training course. Must have educational equivalent to the completion of 12 grades in school. **Examination:** Written and practical examinations. **Fees:** $40 examination fee. $30 license fee. $15 renewal fee.

Alaska

190

Barber Instructor
Dept. of Commerce and Economic Development
Div. of Occupational Licensing
Board of Barbers and Hairdressers
PO Box D-LIC
Juneau, AK 99811-0800
Phone: (907)465-2541
Fax: (907)465-2974

Credential Type: Barber Instructor License by Examination. **Duration of License:** Two years. **Requirements:** Hold a current barber practitioner license. Have at least three years of practice as a licensed barber in Alaska or in another licensing jurisdiction; or one year of practice as a licensed barber in Alaska or in another licensing jurisdiction followed by 600 hours of student instructor training in a school approved by the board or approved by another licensing jurisdiction. **Examination:** State-administered practical examination. Applicant must furnish tools and supplies for examination and secure his or her own model. **Fees:** $30 application fee. $100 license fee. $25 examination fee. **Governing Statute:** Alaska Statutes 08.13. Professional Regulations 12 AAC 09.

Credential Type: Barber License by Credentials. **Duration of License:** Two years. **Requirements:** Hold a current barber instructor license issued by another licensing jurisdiction. Training and work experience equivalent to at least three years of practice as a licensed barber in Alaska or in another licensing jurisdiction; or one year of practice as a licensed barber in Alaska or in another licensing jurisdiction followed by 600 hours of student instructor training in a school approved by the board or approved by another licensing jurisdiction. **Fees:** $30 application fee. $100 license fee. **Governing Statute:** Alaska Statutes 08.13. Professional Regulations 12 AAC 09.

Credential Type: Temporary Permit. **Duration of License:** Six months. **Requirements:** Hold a current valid barber instructor license from a board of barbering in another state. Apply for a permanent license. **Fees:** $30 application fee. $20 temporary permit fee. **Governing Statute:** Alaska Statutes 08.13. Professional Regulations 12 AAC 09.

191

Cosmetologist Instructor
Dept. of Commerce and Economic Development
Div. of Occupational Licensing
Board of Barbers and Hairdressers
PO Box D-LIC
Juneau, AK 99811-0800
Phone: (907)465-2541
Fax: (907)465-2974

Credential Type: Cosmetologist Instructor License by Examination. **Duration of License:** Two years. **Requirements:** Hold a current cosmetologist practitioner license. Have at least three years of practice as a licensed cosmetologist in Alaska or in another licensing jurisdiction; or one year of practice as a licensed cosmetologist in Alaska or in another licensing jurisdiction followed by 600 hours of student instructor training in a school approved by the board or approved by another licensing jurisdiction. **Examination:** State-administered practical examination. Applicant must furnish tools and supplies for examination and secure his or her own model. **Fees:** $30 application fee. $100 license fee. $25 examination fee. **Governing Statute:** Alaska Statutes 08.13. Professional Regulations 12 AAC 09.

Credential Type: Cosmetologist Instructor License by Credentials. **Duration of License:** Two years. **Requirements:** Hold a current cosmetologist instructor license issued by another state. Equivalent of at least three years of practice as a licensed cosmetologist in Alaska or in another licensing jurisdiction; or one year of practice as a licensed cosmetologist in Alaska or in another licensing jurisdiction followed by 600 hours of student instructor training in a school approved by the board or approved by another licensing jurisdiction. **Fees:** $30 application fee. $100 license fee. **Governing Statute:** Alaska Statutes 08.13. Professional Regulations 12 AAC 09.

Credential Type: Temporary Permit. **Duration of License:** Six months. **Requirements:** Hold a current valid cosmetologist instructor license from a board of cosmetology in another state. Apply for a permanent license. **Fees:** $30 application fee. $20 temporary permit fee. **Governing Statute:** Alaska Statutes 08.13. Professional Regulations 12 AAC 09.

192

Hairdresser Instructor
Dept. of Commerce and Economic Development
Div. of Occupational Licensing
Board of Barbers and Hairdressers
PO Box D-LIC
Juneau, AK 99811-0800
Phone: (907)465-2541
Fax: (907)465-2974

Credential Type: Hairdresser Instructor License by Examination. **Duration of License:** Two years. **Requirements:** Hold a current hairdresser practitioner license. Have at least three years of practice as a licensed hairdresser in Alaska or in another licensing jurisdiction; or one year of practice as a licensed hairdresser in Alaska or in another licensing jurisdiction followed by 600 hours of student instructor training in a school approved by the board or approved by another licensing jurisdiction. **Examination:** State-administered practical examination. Applicant must furnish tools and supplies for examination and secure his or her own model. **Fees:** $30 application fee. $100 license fee. $25 examination fee. **Governing Statute:** Alaska Statutes 08.13. Professional Regulations 12 AAC 09.

Credential Type: Hairdresser Instructor License by Credentials. **Duration of License:** Two years. **Requirements:** Hold a current hairdresser instructor license issued by another licensing jurisdiction. Training and work experience equivalent to at least three years of practice as a licensed hairdresser in Alaska or in another licensing jurisdiction; or one year of practice as a licensed hairdresser in Alaska or in another licensing jurisdiction followed by 600 hours of student instructor training in a school approved by the board or approved by another licensing jurisdiction. **Fees:** $30 application fee. $100 license fee. **Governing Statute:** Alaska Statutes 08.13. Professional Regulations 12 AAC 09.

Credential Type: Temporary Permit. **Duration of License:** Six months. **Requirements:** Hold a current valid hairdresser instructor license from a board of hairdressing in another state. Apply for a permanent license. **Fees:** $30 application fee. $20 temporary permit fee. **Governing Statute:** Alaska Statutes 08.13. Professional Regulations 12 AAC 09.

193

Real Estate Instructor
Dept. of Commerce and Economic Development
Div. of Occupational Licensing
Real Estate Commission
PO Box D
Juneau, AK 99811-0800
Phone: (907)465-2534
Fax: (907)465-2974

Credential Type: Approved Real Estate Instructor. **Duration of License:** Two years. **Requirements:** A bachelor's degree, two years experience as a real estate broker, and 30 contact hours of experience teaching adults; or a bachelor's degree, three years experience as an associate real estate broker, and 30 contact hours of experience teaching adults; or five years experience as a real estate licensee and 60 contact hours of experience teaching adults; or a juris doctorate or equivalent degree from an accredited law school and three years experience in the areas of proposesd instruction; or three years experience in a specialized area related to real estate that is the proposed area of instruction, and 30 contact hours of experience teaching adults; or another combination of experience and education that the commision finds sufficient.

Successful completion of an instructor workshop sponsored by the National Association of Real Estate License Law Officials or the National Association of Realtors may be substituted for 30 contact hours of teaching experience. **Fees:** $100 instructor approval fee. **Governing Statute:** Alaska Statutes 08.88. Professional Regulations 12 AAC 64.

Credential Type: Temporary Real Estate Instructor Approval. **Duration of License:** Five days. **Requirements:** Currently certified by a nationally recognized organization that requires similar instructor standards or have sufficient experience in the specific area of real estate to be covered by that course. **Fees:** $50 temporary instructor approval **Governing Statute:** Alaska Statutes 08.88. Professional Regulations 12 AAC 64.

194

Vocational Education Teacher
Dept. of Education, Certification Analyst
Box F
Juneau, AK 99811-0500
Phone: (907)465-2810
Phone: (907)465-2831

Credential Type: Vocational Trades Certificate—Type D. **Duration of License:**

Two years. **Requirements:** Completion of at least four years of full-time work experience in a trade or vocational pursuit, of which not more than two years of formal training (trade school or technical institute) are acceptable. Letters of reference from former employers must be submitted. Must have proof of employment in the trade or vocational area by a school district in Alaska.

Renewal requirements include three semester hours of professional courses related to applicant's field of employment, or additional training and/or work experience acceptable to the Commissioner, all of which must have been completed within the two years immediately preceding the expiration date of the current certificate. Must have proof of employment in the trade or vocational area by a school district in Alaska . **Fees:** $43 fingerprint card processing fee. $125 application fee. $10 endorsement fee.

Arizona

195

Aesthetic Instructor
Arizona State Board of Cosmetology
1645 W. Jefferson, Rm. 125
Phoenix, AZ 85007
Phone: (602)542-5301

Credential Type: Instructor license. **Requirements:** High school graduate. GED Certificate with passing score. Graduate from a cosmetology school with at least 500 hours of instructor training. Be a licensed aesthetician. Have at least one year of work experience. Pass Instructor Practical Examination. **Examination:** Instructor Practical Examination. **Fees:** $35 exam fee.

196

Barber Instructor
Board of Barbers
1645 W. Jefferson
Phoenix, AZ 85007
Phone: (602)542-4498

Credential Type: Instructor license. **Duration of License:** Two years. **Requirements:** At least 19 years of age. High school graduate. Must have practiced barbering for two years and have at least 500 hours of training. Must have at least one year work experience if being licensed by reciprocity. Pass written and practical examination. **Examination:** Instructor License Examination. **Reciprocity:** Yes, with 24 states. **Fees:** $40 license fee. $100 examination fee. $150 license by reciprocity fee.

197

Nail Technology Instructor
Arizona State Board of Cosmetology
1645 W. Jefferson, Rm. 125
Phoenix, AZ 85007
Phone: (602)542-5301

Credential Type: Instructor license. **Requirements:** High school graduate. GED Certificate with passing score. Graduate from a cosmetology school with at least 350 hours of instructor training. Be a licensed nail technician. Have at least one year of work experience. Pass Instructor Practical Examination. **Examination:** Instructor Practical Examination. **Fees:** $35 exam fee.

198

Traffic Survival School Instructor
Dept. of Transportation
Motor Vehicle Div.
Traffic Safety Office
1801 W. Jefferson
Phoenix, AZ 85007
Phone: (602)255-7173

Credential Type: Traffic Survival School Instructor Certificate. **Duration of License:** Indefinite, provided instructor remains active with an approved school. **Requirements:** Be at least 21 years of age and a high school graduate. Pass Professional Driver Training School Examination. Complete approved curriculum workshop. Have an acceptable personal driving record. Be accepted for employment by an approved school. Be of good moral character. **Examination:** Professional Driver Training School Examination. **Exemptions:** Individuals certified to teach driver education by the State Dept. of Education are exempt from the examination. **Fees:** No examination or certificate fee.

Arkansas

199

Agriculture Education Teacher
Office of Teacher Education and
 Licensure
State Education Bldg., Rm. 107B
4 Capitol Mall
Little Rock, AR 72201-1071
Phone: (501)682-4344

Credential Type: License. **Requirements:** Graduate in four year curriculum in agriculture education designed for certification. Minimum of 24 semester hours in science. Minimum of 35 semester hours in technical agriculture. 15 hours in mechanical technology. **Examination:** Yes. **Fees:** $30 Professional Knowledge Core Battery Test. $45 Specialty area test. $45 Renewal in specialty area test.

200

Barber Instructor
State Board of Barber Examiners
Donaghey Bldg., Rm. 212
Little Rock, AR 72201
Phone: (501)682-4035

Credential Type: License. **Duration of License:** One year. **Requirements:** 12th grade education. Meet all requirements for a barber. Complete a postgraduate course in barber-teacher technology theory in accredited school. **Examination:** Yes. **Fees:** $40 for written, oral and practical examination. $20 License. $20 Renewal. $25 Restoration after Sept. 1.

201

Business Education Teacher
Arkansas Dept. of Education
Office of Teacher Education and
 Licensure
State Educational Bldg., Rm. 107B
4 Capitol Mall
Little Rock, AR 72201-1071
Phone: (501)682-4344

Credential Type: License. **Requirements:** Bachelor's degree and teaching certificate in Business Education. Highly recommended that a Master's be obtained. Education must include nine semester hours of vocational education; six hours per year after initial employment begins. **Examination:** Yes. **Fees:** $30 Professional Knowledge Core Battery Test. $45 National Teacher Examination (NTE) Specialty Area Test. $45 NTE specialty Area Test Renewal.

202

Career Orientation Teacher
Arkansas Dept. of Education
Office of Teacher Education and
 Licensure
State Educational Bldg., Rm. 107B
4 Capitol Mall
Little Rock, AR 72201-1071
Phone: (501)682-4344

Credential Type: License. **Requirements:** Must be certified to teach in one of the Vocational Education fields. Three semester hours in each class of; Methods of organizing and teaching Career Orientation Courses to middle and Junior high students, Providing Vocational Guidance, Providing

Arkansas 203

Career Orientation Teacher, continued

Hands-on Activities and Observation Experiences for Career Orientation Courses. Teacher deficient in course work shall obtain a minimum of six semester hours toward the elimination of the deficiencies each fiscal year until they are eliminated. **Examination:** Yes. **Fees:** $30 Professional Knowledge Core Battery Test. $45 National Teacher Examination (NTE) Specialty Area Test. $45 NTE specialty Area Test Renewal.

203

Coordinated Career Education Teacher
Arkansas Dept. of Education
Office of Teacher Education and Licensure
State Education Bldg., Rm. 107B
Capitol Mall 4
Little Rock, AR 72201-1071
Phone: (501)682-4344

Credential Type: License. **Requirements:** Must have or acquire 12 semester hours of Special Education and/or Special Needs Vocational Education and additional training that would indicate ability and interest in working with Special Needs Students at the secondary level. Certified Special Education Teachers must have or acquire 12 hours of vocational education courses. Teachers deficient in course work shall obtain a minimum of six semester hours toward the elimination of the deficiencies each fiscal year until they are eliminated. **Examination:** Yes. **Fees:** $30 Professional Knowledge Core Battery Test. $45 National Teacher Examination (NTE) Specialty Area Test. $45 NTE Specialty renewal.

204

Cosmetology Instructor
Arkansas State Board of Cosmetology
1515 Bldg., Ste. 400
1515 W. Seventh St.
Little Rock, AR 72202
Phone: (501)682-2168

Credential Type: License. **Requirements:** 16 years of age. 12th grade education or equivalent. Licensed as a cosmetologist. Graduate of an advanced 600 hour course in cosmetology. **Examination:** Yes. **Fees:** $30 Written and practical examinations.

205

Driving Instructor (Commercial School)
Office of Driver Services
Driver's License Issuance Section
7th and Wolfe St.
Little Rock, AR 72203
Phone: (501)682-7058

Credential Type: License. **Requirements:** 21 years of age. High School graduate. Physically able to operate a motor vehicle. Good moral character. Completed an approved training course as a driving instructor (from an approved school). **Examination:** Yes. **Fees:** $14.25 Class D operator.

206

Electrology Instructor
Arkansas State Board of Cosmetology
1515 Bldg., Ste. 400
1515 W. Seventh St.
Little Rock, AR 72202
Phone: (501)371-2168

Credential Type: License. **Requirements:** Three years experience as an electrologist. Pass the written and practical test. **Examination:** Yes. **Fees:** $30 Written and practical tests.

207

General Cooperative Education Teacher
Arkansas Dept. of Education
Office of Teacher Education
State Education Bldg., Rm. 107B
Capitol Mall 4
Little Rock, AR 72201-1071
Phone: (501)682-4344

Credential Type: License. **Requirements:** Bachelors degree and be a certified secondary teacher. Have or obtain within two years nine semester hours in vocational education courses approved by Supervisor. Six semester hours must be earned each year until requirements are satisfied. 40 hours of inservice training may be substituted for three semester hours. Teaching coordinator shall have had 2000 hours of work experience other than teaching in two or more occupational areas. **Examination:** Yes. **Fees:** $45 National Teacher Examination (NTE) Specialty Area Test. $30 Professional Knowledge Core Battery Test. $45 Renewal of Specialty Area Test.

208

Health Occupations Education Teacher
Arkansas Dept. of Education
Office of Teacher Education and Licensure
State Education Bldg., Rm. 107B
Capitol Mall 4
Little Rock, AR 72201-1071
Phone: (501)682-4344

Credential Type: License. **Requirements:** Bachelors degree with a major related to the health care occupations and two years experience working in the health care system. Work experience must be immediately prior to application (may be waived under certain circumstances). Life Science majors can meet the experience requirements by completing an internship in a hospital accredited by the Arkansas Department of Health, plus partial time of not less than 180 hours in a 12 week period in a clinic. Within one calendar year of employment, the teacher must complete six hours of vocational education courses. By the end of the second year, the teacher must have completed at least nine hours. **Examination:** Yes. **Fees:** $30 National Teacher Examination (NTE) Professional Knowledge Core Battery Test. $45 NTE Specialty Area Test. $45 NTE Specialty Area renewal.

209

Home Economics Education Teacher
Arkansas Dept. of Education
Office of Teacher Education and Licensure
State Education Bldg., Rm. 107B
Capitol Mall 4
Little Rock, AR 72201-1071
Phone: (501)682-4344

Credential Type: License. **Requirements:** Bachelors degree in Home Economics. Meet general education requirements for a secondary teaching certificate. Have a minimum of six semester hours in related art and 32 semester hours in Technical Home Economics. Completed the following classes ; Child Development with Nursery School Observation and Participation, Methods of Teaching Home Economics, Directed Teaching in Home Economics. **Examination:** Yes. **Fees:** $30 National Teacher Examination (NTE) Professional Knowledge Core Battery Test. $45 NTE Specialty Area Test. $45 NTE Specialty Area Test renewal.

Adult and Vocational Education Teachers

210

Marketing and Distributive Education Teacher
Arkansas Dept. of Education
Office of Teacher Education and Licensure
State Education Bldg., Rm. 107B
4 Capitol Mall
Little Rock, AR 72201-1071
Phone: (501)682-4344

Credential Type: License. **Requirements:** Bachelors degree which includes nine semester hours in Vocational Education, nine semester hours in technical marketing courses and either one full year of employment in sales and marketing or 3000 hours of part-time employment. Deficiencies must be worked off within three years. Must maintain expertise in the field through employment or classes. **Examination:** Yes. **Fees:** $30 Professional Knowledge Core Battery Test. $45 Specialty Area Test. $45 Renewal of Specialty Area.

211

Trade and Industrial Education Instructor
Arkansas Dept, of Education
Office of Teacher Education and Licensure
State Education Bldg., Rm. 107B
Capitol Mall 4
Little Rock, AR 72201-1071
Phone: (501)682-4344

Credential Type: License. **Requirements:** The coordinator of Industrial Cooperative Training must have a bachelors degree. Within two years after employment, the Coordinator must complete nine semester hours in vocational educational courses. Teachers of exploratory industrial education classes must meet certification requirements of industrial education coordinator or trade teacher. Trade and industrial teachers must have high school or equivalent education and five years of recent experience, or two years recent experience and pass the National Competency Test for the trade to be sought. Within three years of employment, the shop instructor should complete 90 clock hours or nine semester hours of teacher education in vocational educational courses. **Examination:** Yes. **Fees:** $30 Professional Knowledge Core Battery Test. $45 NTE Specialty area Test. $15 National Competency Test in Trade. $45 NTE Specialty area test renewal.

California

212

Barber Instructor
Board of Barbering and Cosmetology
PO Box 944226
Sacramento, CA 94244-2260
Phone: (916)445-7061
Phone: (916)445-7008

Credential Type: Barber License. **Requirements:** Contact licensing body for application information.

213

Cosmetology Instructor
Board of Barbering and Cosmetology
PO Box 944226
Sacramento, CA 94244-2260
Phone: (916)445-7061
Phone: (916)445-7008

Credential Type: Cosmetology Instructor License and Registration. **Duration of License:** Two years. **Requirements:** High school graduate or equivalent. Hold a valid California license as a cosmetologist. Meet one of the following sets of requirements: (1) Complete at least 600 hours of teacher training. (2) Have one year of practical experience within the previous three years in all branches of cosmetology, except electrology, in a licensed cosmetology establishment.

Renewal requires 30 clock hours of continuing education. **Examination:** Written and practical examination. **Reciprocity:** No. **Governing Statute:** The Cosmetology Act, Business and Professions Code, Div. 3, Chap. 10, Sect. 7300 et seq.

Colorado

214

Vocational Education Teacher
Teacher Certification
State Dept. of Education
201 E. Colifax
Denver, CO 80203
Phone: (303)866-6628

Credential Type: Vocational Teacher Certificate—Type C. **Duration of License:** Five years. **Requirements:** Initial teacher certification which requires the following: Bachelor's degree. Completion of an approved program of teacher preparation from a four year, regionally accredited, degree granting institution which must include student teaching. Six semester hours of credit applicable to the certificate being sought, and/or general education, and/or child abuse, taken within the past five years from date of application. Course work in the exceptional child, covering the full range of exceptionalities, gifted through handicapped, and course work in the theory, methods, and related practice of the teaching of reading. Passage of the spelling, language, and mathematics sections of Level 19 of the California Achievement Test and oral English competence which is met by having a B—or better in a public speaking course taken from a regionally accredited college or passing an oral English panel assessment. Completed and signed appropriate application. Institutional recommendation from the school(s) where the teacher preparation work was completed. Official original transcripts from all applicable institutions.

In addition applicants must demonstrate Vocational Basic Skills in the field in which the endorsement is being sought, by passing a state or nationally validated occupational competency examination as approved by CDE, or the appropriate State Licensing Examination. Additional qualifying requirements are five years of successful experience, which may include a maximum of two years of specialized schooling. The remaining work experience must be beyond the learner level in the applicant's instructional occupation and must be verified through previous employers. **Examination:** California Achievement Test Level 19 (spelling, language, and mathematics sections). Occupational competency examination. **Fees:** $45 initial certification application fee. $40 fingerprint card processing fee.

Connecticut

215

Instructor (Racetrack)
Connecticut Div. of Special Revenue
Russell Rd.
PO Box 11424
Newington, CT 06111-0424
Phone: (203)566-2756

Credential Type: License Registration. **Requirements:** Submit application and fingerprint card. Pay fee. **Fees:** $5 registration fee.

Delaware

216

Cosmetology Instructor
Board of Cosmetology and Barbering
Dept. of Administrative Services
Div. of Professional Regulation
PO Box 1401
Dover, DE 19903
Phone: (302)739-4522

Credential Type: Instructor's License. **Duration of License:** Two years. **Requirements:** Have at least an 8th-grade education. Must be a licensed cosmetologist. Have at least six months teacher's training course in cosmetology in a registered school of cosmetology; or have at least two years experience as an active practicing cosmetologist, supplemented by not less than three months of teacher's training in cosmetology in a registered school of cosmetology. **Examination:** Written and oral test. Practical demonstrations. **Reciprocity:** Yes, with other states, territories, the District of Columbia, or foreign country, state, or province. Applicant must have five years continuous experience and pay appropriate fees. **Fees:** $75 license fee. $75 renewal fee. **Governing Statute:** Delaware Code, Title 24, Chapter 6.

217

Electrologist Instructor
Board of Cosmetology and Barbering
Dept. of Administrative Services
Div. of Professional Regulation
PO Box 1401
Dover, DE 19903
Phone: (302)739-4522

Credential Type: Electrologist Instructor Certificate. **Duration of License:** Two years. **Requirements:** Have at least an 8th-grade education. Complete an advanced course in electrolysis of at least 100 hours of training. Have been engaged in the active and full-time practice of electrology for 12 months preceding application. **Examination:** Written and oral test. Practical demonstrations. **Reciprocity:** Yes, with other states, territories, the District of Columbia, or foreign country, state, or province. Applicant must have five years continuous experience and pay appropriate fees. **Fees:** $50 license fee. $50 renewal fee. **Governing Statute:** Delaware Code, Title 24, Chapter 6.

218

Student Instructor in Cosmetology
Board of Cosmetology and Barbering
Dept. of Administrative Services
Div. of Professional Regulation
PO Box 1401
Dover, DE 19903
Phone: (302)739-4522

Credential Type: Student instructor's registration. **Requirements:** Have at least an 8th-grade education. Must be a licensed cosmetologist. Must be enrolled in a school of cosmetology as a student instructor. **Fees:** $10 registration fee. **Governing Statute:** Delaware Code, Title 24, Chapter 6.

Florida

219

Real Estate Instructor
Florida Real Estate Commission
Hurston North Tower
400 W. Robinson St., Rm. 309
Orlando, FL 32801-1772
Phone: (407)423-6053

Credential Type: Real Estate Instructor License. **Duration of License:** Two years. **Requirements:** Contact licensing body for application information. **Reciprocity:** No. **Fees:** $50 license fee. $50 renewal fee. **Governing Statute:** Florida Statutes, Chapter 475, Part I. Florida Administrative Code, Rules 21-V.

Georgia

220

Barber Teacher
State Board of Barbers
Barber and Cosmetology Boards
  Section
Professional Examining Boards
166 Pryor St., SW
Atlanta, GA 30303
Phone: (404)656-3909

Credential Type: Barber Teacher License. **Duration of License:** Two years. **Requirements:** High school education or equivalent. Complete 750 hours of teacher training at a board-approved school. **Examination:** Barber Teacher Examination, written and practical. **Reciprocity:** Yes, with states that have an equal training requirement of 750 hours. **Fees:** $50 exam and license fee. $60 renewal fee.

221

Cosmetology Teacher
State Board of Cosmetology
Barber and Cosmetology Boards
  Section
Professional Examining Boards
166 Pryor St., SW
Atlanta, GA 30303
Phone: (404)656-3909

Credential Type: Cosmetology Teacher License. **Duration of License:** Two years. **Requirements:** High school education or equivalent. Hold a current Master Cosmetologist License. Complete 1500 hours of instructor training in a board-approved school. Renewal requires 10 hours of continuing education per two-year period. **Examination:** Cosmetology Teacher Examination, written and practical. **Fees:** $50 exam fee. $65 renewal fee.

Idaho

222

Barber Instructor
Board of Examiners of Barbers
Bureau of Occupational Licenses
1109 Main St., Ste. 220
Boise, ID 83702-5642
Phone: (208)334-3233

Credential Type: Barber Instructor License. **Duration of License:** One year. **Requirements:** Must have been a registered master barber in Idaho for at least three years. Must complete 20 hours of continuing education within the 12 months preceding application, of which 12 hours are in educational training and eight hours in seminars, trade shows, etc. **Examination:** Barber Teacher Certification Examination. **Fees:** $100 exam fee. $30 original license fee. $30 renewal fee. **Governing Statute:** Idaho Code, Title 54, Chap. 5. Rules of the Idaho Board of Examiners of Barbers.

223

Cosmetology Instructor
Board of Cosmetology
Bureau of Occupational Licenses
1109 Main St., Ste. 220
Boise, ID 83702-5642
Phone: (208)334-3233

Credential Type: Cosmetology Instructor License. **Duration of License:** One year. **Requirements:** Complete 12 semester college credit hours or equivalent, or pass examination. Meet one of the following sets of requirements: (1) Have one year experience as a licensed cosmetologist in a registered cosmetological establishment or school. Complete six months of teacher's training in a school of cosmetology. (2) Have two years experience as a licensed cosmetologist in a registered cosmetological establishment or school. Complete three months of teacher's training in a school of cosmetology. (3) Have five years experience as a licensed cosmetologist immediately preceding application. **Examination:** Written and practical examination. **Reciprocity:** License by endorsement may be granted, provided applicant has three years practical experience within the past five years or holds a license from a state with requirements equal to Idaho's. Applicant must meet basic educational requirements. **Fees:** $25 license fee. $25 renewal fee. $35 exam fee. **Governing Statute:** Idaho Code, Title 54, Chap. 8. Idaho Board of Cosmetology Rules.

Illinois

224

Barber Teacher
Illinois Dept. of Professional Regulation
320 W. Washington St.
Springfield, IL 62786
Phone: (217)782-8556

Credential Type: Barber Teacher License. **Duration of License:** Two years. **Requirements:** At least 18 years of age. Good moral character. High school graduate or equivalent. Hold an Illinois Barber License. Three years of barbering experience. Must have 500 hours of teacher training in an accredited barber school in a period of not less than three months and not more than two years or 1,000 hours of teachers training in an approved barbershop over a period of not less than six months and not more than two years. **Examination:** Barber Licensing Exam. **Reciprocity:** Yes, with an Illinois Barber License and a barber teacher license from another state, providing the licensing state has requirements substantially equivalent to those of Illinois. **Fees:** $58.30 examination fee. $25 initial license fee. $35 license by endorsement fee. $40 renewal fee. **Governing Statute:** The Barber, Cosmetology, Esthetics, and Nail Technology Act Illinois Revised Statutes 1991, Chapter 111.

225

Cosmetology Teacher
Illinois Dept. of Professional Regulation
320 W. Washingtion St.
Springfield, IL 62786
Phone: (217)782-8556

Credential Type: Cosmetology Teacher. **Duration of License:** Two years. **Requirements:** At least 18 years of age. High school graduate or equivalent. Illinois Cosmetologist License in good standing. Two years experience under an Illinois Cosmetologist License and 1,000 hours of teacher training in an approved Cosmetology School. Renewal requires 10 hours of continuing education biennially. **Examination:** Cosmetology Teacher Examination. **Reciprocity:** Yes, if qualifications in the state of licensure are substantially equivalent to those of the state of Illinois. **Fees:** $58.30 examination fee. $25 initial license fee. $35 license by endorsement fee. $40 renewal fee. **Governing Statute:** The Barber, Cosmetology, Esthetics, and Nail Technology Act of 1985, Illinois Revised Statutes 1991, Chapter 111.

226

Driver Training Instructor
Illinois Secretary of State
Commercial Driver Training
650 Roppolo Drive
Elk Grove Village, IL 60007
Phone: (708)437-3953

Credential Type: Driver Training Instructor License. **Duration of License:** One year. **Requirements:** At least 21 years of age. Resident of Illinois. High school graduate or equivalent. Pass examinations. Teen instructor requires additional training. **Examination:** Driver Training Instructor Examination. CDL Accreditation Examination. **Reciprocity:** No. **Fees:** $35 application/initial license fee. $35 renewal fee. $10 reinstatement fee. **Governing Statute:** Illinois Vehicle Code, Chapter 95 1/2.

227

Driver Training Instructor (Third Party Certification)
Secretary of State
Commercial Driver Training
605 Roppolo Drive
Elk Grove, IL 60007
Phone: (708)437-3953

Credential Type: Third Party Certification License. **Duration of License:** Three years. **Authorization:** Authorizes holder to provide behind the wheel testing for driver license applicants. **Requirements:** At least 21 years of age. Must be an Illinois resident or a resident of a state adjacent to Illinois. Must conduct certification program pursuant to Chapter 95 1/2, section 60508 of the Illinois Vehicle Code. **Reciprocity:** No. **Fees:** No fee. **Governing Statute:** Illinois Vehicle Code 95 1/2.

228

Education Provider (Insurance)
Illinois Dept. of Insurance
320 W. Washington
Springfield, IL 62767
Phone: (217)782-6366

Credential Type: Registration. **Duration of License:** One year. **Requirements:** Must have a bachelor's degree or three years experience in the course subject matter. Submit application and pay fee. **Reciprocity:** No. **Fees:** $50 initial provider license registration. $25 each course license registration. $50 renewal provider. $10 renewal each course. **Governing Statute:** Section 494.1 of the Illinois Insurance Code, Chapter 73.

229

Esthetician Teacher
Illinois Dept. of Professional Regulation
320 W. Washington St.
Springfield, IL 62786
Phone: (217)782-8556

Credential Type: Esthetician Teacher License. **Duration of License:** Two years. **Requirements:** At least 18 years of age. High school graduate or its equivalent. Hold an active license as an Esthetician or Cosmetologist. Complete 500 hours of teachers training. Complete two years of practice as an esthetician or cosmetologist within five years of examination or 1,000 hours of approved teacher's training from an esthetics or cosmetology school. **Examination:** Written examination. **Reciprocity:** Yes, considered on an individual basis. **Fees:** $60.30 examination fee. $25 initial license fee. $35 license by endorsement fee. $40 renewal fee. **Governing Statute:** The Barber, Cosmetology, Esthetics, and Nail Technology Act, Illinois Revised Statutes 1991, Chapter 111.

230

Food Service Sanitation Manager Certification Instructor
Illinois Dept. of Health
Div. of Foods, Drugs, and Dairies
525 W. Jefferson
Springfield, IL 62761
Phone: (217)785-2439

Credential Type: Food Service Sanitation Manager Certification Instructor Certificate. **Duration of License:** Five years. **Requirements:** High school graduate or equivalent. Must complete a Department approved Food Service Sanitation Certification course. Pass examination with a score of at least 75 percent. Renewal requires attendance of at least one five-hour training seminar on food safety every two years. **Examination:** Food Services Sanitation Certification Exam. **Reciprocity:** No. **Governing Statute:** Illinois Revised Statutes 1991, Chapter 56 1/2.

Indiana

231

Barber Instructor
State Board of Barber Examiners
1021 State Office Bldg.
100 N. Senate Ave.
Indianapolis, IN 46204
Phone: (317)232-2531

Credential Type: License. **Requirements:** Contact licensing body for application information.

232

Cosmetology Instructor
Board of Cosmetology
Licensing Division
Professional Licensing Agency
1021 State Office Bldg.
100 N. Senate Ave.
Indianapolis, IN 46204
Phone: (317)232-2980

Credential Type: License. **Requirements:** Contact licensing body for application information.

Iowa

233

Emergency Medical Services - Instructor
Iowa Dept. of Public Health
Emergency Medical Services
Lucas State Office Bldg.
Des Moines, IA 50319
Phone: (515)281-3239

Credential Type: License. **Duration of License:** Two years. **Requirements:** An applicant must have a current EMS certification or its equivalent, experience in an EMS-related field, a recommendation by an approved training program, and a minimum of 40 classroom hours. **Examination:** Written and practical.

234

Instructor, Community College or Vocational-Technical School
Bureau of Practitioner Preparation and Licensure
Dept. of Education
Grimes State Office Bldg.
Des Moines, IA 50319
Phone: (515)281-3611

Credential Type: License. **Duration of License:** Five years. **Requirements:** Instructors teaching arts and sciences subjects that are transferable to a four-year institution must hold a master's degree from an accredited institution. Graduate specialization is required in a field or instruction offered in the arts and sciences division of an area community college. Also required are at least six semester hours of professional preparation appropriate for college teaching or completion of an approved program. Occupational instructors qualify for their teaching positions on the basis of their occupational background, knowledge of subject area, and a competency test. **Fees:** $15 license fee. $15 renewal fee.

235

Teacher of English As A Second Language
Board of Educational Examiners
Grimes State Office Bldg.
Des Moines, IA 50319-0147
Phone: (515)281-3245

Credential Type: Provisional Certificate. **Duration of License:** Two years. **Requirements:** Baccalaureate degree. Complete approved teacher program. Complete approved human relations component. Complete course work or evidence of competency in: structure of American education; philosophies of education; professional ethics and legal responsibilities; psychology of teaching; audiovisual/media/computer technology; evaluation techniques; human development; exceptional learner; classroom management; instructional planning; curriculum; methods of teaching; pre-student field-based experiences; and student teaching in desired subject area and grade level. Complete 24 semester hours of course work in ESOL. Certificate is renewable for a second two-year term.

Credential Type: Education Certificate. **Duration of License:** Five years. **Requirements:** Provisional Certificate. Two years of successful teaching experience based on a local evaluation process. Renewable.

Credential Type: Professional Teacher's Certificate. **Duration of License:** Five years. **Requirements:** Holder of or eligible for an Education Certificate. Five years of teaching experience. Master's degree in the area of a teaching endorsement. Renewable.

Kansas

236

Cosmetology Instructor
Cosmetology Board
717 Kansas Ave.
Topeka, KS 66603
Phone: (913)296-3155

Credential Type: Instructor's permit. **Duration of License:** Two years. **Requirements:** Must be a licensed cosmetologist. Must have completed high school. Renewal requires completion of at least 100 clock hours of training approved by the board, including at least 60 clock hours of teacher training and 40 clock hours of training in advanced hair styling. **Fees:** Contact board for fee. **Governing Statute:** Kansas Statutes Annotated 65-1901 through 65-1912, Rules and Regulations 69-1 ff.

Credential Type: Instructor's license. **Duration of License:** Three years. **Requirements:** Must be a licensed cosmetologist. Must have completed high school. Renewal requires completion of at least 100 clock hours of training approved by the board, including at least 60 clock hours of teacher training and 40 clock hours of training in advanced hair styling. **Fees:** Contact board for fee. **Governing Statute:** Kansas Statutes Annotated 65-1901 through 65-1912, Rules and Regulations 69-1 ff.

Adult and Vocational Education Teachers

237

Emergency Medical Instructor-Coordinator
Board of Emergency Medical Services
109 SW 6th St.
Topeka, KS 66603-3805
Phone: (913)296-7299

Credential Type: Instructor-Coordinator Certificate. **Duration of License:** One year. **Requirements:** Must be at least 18 years of age. Have at least one year of experience as an ambulance attendant. Be certified for at least one year as an Emergency Medical Technician or higher. Complete board-approved course of training in instructing and coordinating attendant training programs.

Renewal requires at least 30 hours of continuing education. **Examination:** Yes. **Governing Statute:** Kansas Statutes Annotated 65-6101 ff. Kansas Administrative Regulations 109-1 through 109-12.

Kentucky

238

Driver Training Instructor
Kentucky State Police Driver Testing Section
919 Versailles Rd.
Frankfort, KY 40601
Phone: (502)695-6338

Credential Type: License. **Duration of License:** One year. **Requirements:** High school diploma or equivalent. 21 years of age. Must hold a current Kentucky operator's license and have a good driving record. Must be employed by a driver training school licensed by the State Police. **Examination:** Yes. **Reciprocity:** No. **Fees:** $20 license fee. $20 renewal fee.

239

Law Enforcement Training Instructor
Dept. of Criminal Justice Training
Eastern Kentucky University
Stratton Bldg., Rm. 112
Richmond, KY 40475
Phone: (606)622-6165

Credential Type: License. **Requirements:** Three years experience as a police officer, judiciary or related criminal justice experience or expertise. Bachelor's degree from an accredited college or university. No criminal record. Excellent physical and mental condition. **Examination:** Yes.

240

Mining Safety Instructor
Dept. of Mines and Minerals
PO Box 14080
Lexington, KY 40512
Phone: (606)254-0367

Credential Type: License. **Duration of License:** One year. **Requirements:** Must be a Kentucky resident. Must have 10 years of work experience in coal mines after the age of 18, of which two years must be in a Kentucky mine. A bachelor's degree in mining engineering from a recognized institution will substitute for two years of work experience. An associate degree in mining technology will count for one year of work experience. Must possess an underground mine foreman certificate and a mine safety underground mine instructor's certificate issued by the Department. 16 hours of retraining are required annually. **Examination:** Yes. **Fees:** $50 exam fee.

241

Teacher of Vocational Education - Industrial Education
Dept. of Education
Teacher Education and Certification
Capital Plaza Tower, 18th Fl.
Frankfort, KY 40601
Phone: (502)564-4606

Credential Type: License. **Duration of License:** One year. **Requirements:** High school diploma or equivalent. Must have four years of successful and appropriate occupational experience in the area to be taught, two of which must have been completed within the last five years. Successful completion of an internship is required. Continuing education required. **Examination:** Yes. **Fees:** $50 exam fee.

Louisiana

242

Flight Instructor (Ultralight Aircraft)
Dept. of Transportation and Development
PO Box 94245
Baton Rouge, LA 70804-7437
Phone: (504)342-7437

Credential Type: Instructor License. **Duration of License:** Two years. **Requirements:** Contact board for requirements. **Examination:** Written examination. **Fees:** $15 license fee.

243

Practical Nurse and Nurse Aide Instructor
Louisiana State Dept. of Education
Teacher Certification
PO Box 94064
Baton Rouge, LA 70804
Phone: (504)342-3490

Credential Type: Certificate. **Duration of License:** One year. **Requirements:** Graduation from a licensed nursing school. Two years of experience in staff nursing or nursing education within the past four years. Continuing education requirements must be met before renewal.

244

Teacher Vocational-Trade & Industrial (Secondary)
Louisiana State Dept. of Education
PO Box 94064
Baton Rouge, LA 70804
Phone: (504)342-3530

Credential Type: License. **Duration of License:** One year until continuing education requirements are met, at which time the license becomes permanent. **Requirements:** High school diploma or equivalent. At least four years of full-time experience in the trade or technical field in which the applicant is to teach. Educational credit can be substituted for up to two years of the required work experience.

Maine

245

Barber Instructor
State Board of Barbering and Cosmetology
Dept. of Professional and Financial Regulation
State House Station 62
Augusta, ME 04333
Phone: (207)582-8745
Fax: (207)582-5415

Credential Type: Barber Instructor License. **Duration of License:** One year. **Requirements:** Must hold high school diploma or equivalent. Valid Maine barber license. Complete a course of study for the preparation of instructors in a licensed school of barbering within the past three years; or complete at least 500 hours of training in a course for the preparation of instructors in a licensed school of barbering, and have at least three years shop experience as a barber within the past five years. **Examination:** Barber instructor

Maine

Barber Instructor, continued

exam, practical and written. **Fees:** $45 exam fee. $25 license fee.

246

Commercial Driver Education Instructor
Board of Commercial Driver Instruction
Dept. of Professional and Financial Regulation
State House Station 35
Augusta, ME 04333
Phone: (207)582-8723

Credential Type: Class A Commercial Driver Education Instructor License. **Duration of License:** One year. **Authorization:** May teach both the classroom and behind-the-wheel or road phases of driver education. **Requirements:** Must be at least 21 years of age. Must be employed by or associated with a licensed commercial driver education school. Must possess a valid operator's license or endorsement for the class or type of vehicle in which instruction is to be given. Must have four years of driving experience as a licensed operator and a conviction-free motor vehicle record for one year prior to application. Must maintain a good driving record.

Applicant for a Class A license must complete an educational program in the teaching of driver education, including at least college level courses or equivalent in the teaching of driver education and in psychology or teaching methods. **Examination:** Knowledge, vision, and road tests. **Fees:** $125 license fee. $125 renewal fee. **Governing Statute:** 32 M.S.R.A., Chap. 95.

Credential Type: Class B Commercial Driver Education Instructor License. **Duration of License:** One year. **Authorization:** May teach only the behind-the-wheel or road phases of driver education. **Requirements:** Must be at least 21 years of age. Must be employed by or associated with a licensed commercial driver education school. Must possess a valid operator's license or endorsement for the class or type of vehicle in which instruction is to be given. Must have four years of driving experience as a licensed operator and a conviction-free motor vehicle record for one year prior to application. Must maintain a good driving record. **Examination:** Knowledge, vision, and road tests. **Fees:** $125 license fee. $125 renewal fee. **Governing Statute:** 32 M.S.R.A., Chap. 95.

Credential Type: Truck Training Supplemental Instructor License. **Duration of License:** One year. **Authorization:** May teach both the classroom and behind-the-wheel or road phases of driver education for trucks. **Requirements:** Must be at least 21 years of age. Must be employed by or associated with a licensed commercial driver education school. Must possess a valid operator's license or endorsement for the class or type of vehicle in which instruction is to be given. Must have four years of driving experience as a licensed operator and a conviction-free motor vehicle record for one year prior to application. Must maintain a good driving record. **Examination:** Knowledge, vision, and road tests. **Fees:** $125 license fee. $125 renewal fee. **Governing Statute:** 32 M.S.R.A., Chap. 95.

247

Cosmetology Instructor
State Board of Barbering and Cosmetology
Dept. of Professional and Financial Regulation
State House Station 62
Augusta, ME 04333
Phone: (207)582-8745
Fax: (207)582-5415

Credential Type: Cosmetology Instructor License and Certificate. **Duration of License:** Two years. **Requirements:** Meet one of the following sets of requirements: (1) High school diploma or equivalent. Valid Maine cosmetology license. Complete a course of instruction for the preparation of cosmetology instructors of at least 1000 hours in a licensed school of cosmetology; or complete 1000 hours in a cosmetology instructor course in an approved school within the past three years. (2) High school diploma or equivalent. Valid Maine cosmetology license. Have three years of beauty shop experience within the past five years. Have 12 credits from a postsecondary school, college, or university in courses related to teaching. **Examination:** Cosmetology instructor exam, practical and written. **Fees:** $50 exam and initial license fee. $16 renewal fee.

Maryland

248

Air School Instructor
State Aviation Administration
Dept. of Transportation
PO Box 8766
BWI Airport
Baltimore, MD 21240
Phone: (410)859-7100

Credential Type: License. **Requirements:** Contact licensing body for application information.

249

Barber Instructor
Board of Barber Examiners
Dept. of Licensing and Regulation
501 St. Paul Pl.
Baltimore, MD 21202-2272
Phone: (410)333-6320

Credential Type: Barber Instructor License. **Requirements:** Contact licensing body for application information.

250

Cosmetology Instructor
Board of Cosmetologists
Dept. of Licensing and Regulation
501 St. Paul Pl.
Baltimore, MD 21202-2272
Phone: (410)333-6320

Credential Type: License. **Requirements:** Contact licensing body for application information.

251

Driver Training Instructor
Motor Vehicle Administration
Dept. of Transportation
6601 Ritchie Hwy.
Glen Burnie, MD 21062
Phone: (301)768-7254
Phone: (301)768-7275

Credential Type: License. **Requirements:** Contact licensing body for application information.

252

Electrology Instructor
Board of Electrologists
Dept. of Health and Mental Hygiene
4201 Patterson Ave.
Baltimore, MD 21215-2299
Phone: (410)764-4727

Credential Type: License. **Duration of License:** Two years. **Requirements:** Be a licensed electrologist. Have practiced electrology actively for at least five years immediately prior to application. **Examination:** Oral and written examinations. **Fees:** Contact board for fees. **Governing Statute:** Annotated Code of Maryland, Title 6. Code of Maryland Regulations, Title 10, Subtitle 53.

253

Vocational Education Teacher
Dept. of Certification 18100
State Dept. of Education
200 W. Baltimore St.
Baltimore, MD 21201
Phone: (301)333-2142

Credential Type: Provisional Non-Degree Certificate. **Requirements:** Degree is not a requirement, however applicant must complete a pre-service teacher preparation program as approved by the Maryland State Dept. of Education.

Credential Type: Advanced Professional Certificate. **Authorization:** Issued in vocational education areas to a teacher who is not required to hold a bachelor's degree. **Requirements:** Three years of successful teaching experience. Completes vocational education program of 34 semester hours May have a maximum of six inservice credits.

Massachusetts

254

Approved Asbestos Training Provider
Dept. of Labor and Industries
Bureau of Technical Services
100 Cambridge St., Rm. 1101
Boston, MA 02202-0003
Phone: (617)727-1932
Phone: (617)727-1933

Credential Type: Certification. **Requirements:** Submit application and pay fee. Submit a list of training courses to be provided, outlines of all courses, manuals to be used, description of teaching methods, and other information concerning training program to be offered. **Fees:** $850 certification fee. **Governing Statute:** M.G.L. c149, ss 6-6F. 453 CMR 6.01 ff.

255

Barber Instructor
Board of Registration of Barbers
Div. of Registration
100 Cambridge St., 15th fl.
Boston, MA 02202
Phone: (617)727-7367

Credential Type: Barber Instructor Registration. **Duration of License:** One year. **Requirements:** Have at least five years working experience as a registered Master Barber. **Examination:** Practical and written examinations. **Fees:** $150 license and examination fee.

256

Cosmetologist Instructor
Board of Registration of Hairdressers
Div. of Registration
100 Cambridge St.
Boston, MA 02202
Phone: (617)727-9940
Phone: (617)727-3067

Credential Type: Instructor's License. **Duration of License:** Two years. **Requirements:** Complete a 1000-hour program. Two years work experience. Be a fully licensed cosmetologist. **Examination:** Practical and written instructor's examination. **Exemptions:** Anyone holding a Junior Assistant Instructor License may take the exam after two years. **Reciprocity:** Yes. **Fees:** $25 exam fee. $100 license fee.

Credential Type: Junior Assistant Instructor License. **Duration of License:** Two years. **Requirements:** Contact licensing body for application information. **Reciprocity:** Yes.

257

Riding Instructor
Div. of Animal Health
Dept. of Food and Agriculture
100 Cambridge St., 21st Fl.
Boston, MA 02202
Phone: (617)727-3018

Credential Type: License. **Duration of License:** One year. **Requirements:** Demonstrate appropriate experience. **Examination:** Written examination. **Fees:** $10 application fee. $15 license fee.

258

Teacher of English as a Second Language
Massachusetts Dept. of Education
1385 Hancock St.
Quincy, MA 02169
Phone: (617)770-7500

Credential Type: Teaching Certificate with an English as a Second Language Endorsement. **Requirements:** Proficiency in reading, writing, and speaking American English as established by state administered test procedures. ESL content course. Satisfy the five Standards established by the Massachusetts Dept. of Education. Standard I includes 36 semester hours of course work in the following areas: stages and characteristics of normal child development; sensory, motor, social, emotional and cognitive development; learning theory in general; and basic studies of early childhood education which include reading, communication, the arts, mathematics, science, social studies, health, and physical education. Plus 21 semester hours of prepracticum experience and, in addition, complete a successful ESL practicum of 300 clock hours.

Michigan

259

Barber Instructor
Board of Barber Examiners
Bureau of Occupational & Professional Regulation
Dept. of Commerce
PO Box 30018
Lansing, MI 48909
Phone: (517)373-9153

Credential Type: License. **Duration of License:** Two years. **Requirements:** Completed the 12th grade or its equivalent. Worked at least two years as a barber. Completed one year of schooling as a student instructor (learning the theory and practice of an instructor), or have completed 60 semester or 90 term hours in an approved course of instruction at a college and have six months of schooling as a student instructor. Be of good moral character. Abide by the rules of the Board of Barber Examiners. **Examination:** Written and practical exam. **Reciprocity:** None. However, a person who has been licensed by his/her state, jurisdiction, or country to instruct others in barbering may substitute one year of experience in barber instruction for the required training. The two-year barber experience and the examination requirements shall not be waived on the basis of prior experience as an instructor. **Fees:** $15 application pro-

Barber Instructor, continued

cessing fee. $75 complete exam fee. $35 written exam fee. $45 practical exam fee. $20 exam review fee. $25 initial barber instructor license fee. $15 initial student instructor license fee. $25 barber instuctor renewal fee. $15 student instructor renewal fee. **Governing Statute:** The Occupational Code, Act 299 of l980, as amended.

260

Cosmetology Instructor
Board of Cosmetology
Bureau of Occupational &
  Professional Regulation
Dept. of Commerce
PO Box 30018
Lansing, MI 48909
Phone: (517)373-9153

Credential Type: License. **Duration of License:** Two years. **Requirements:** Completed the 12th grade. Possess a valid Michigan cosmetology license. 500 hours of instructor training. Abide by the rules and regulations of the Board. Three years of experience as a cosmetologist, or two years of teaching experience and one year experience as a cosmetologist. **Examination:** Written, practical, and oral exam. **Fees:** $10 application processing fee. $25 complete initial exam fee ($15 written exam, $15 practical exam). $20 exam review fee. $12 initial license fee, per year. $12 renewal fee, per year. **Governing Statute:** The Occupational Code, Act 299 of 1980, as amended.

Credential Type: Limited License. **Duration of License:** Two years. **Requirements:** Completed the 12th grade. Possess a valid Michigan cosmetology license. 500 hours of instructor training. Abide by the rules and regulations of the Board. **Examination:** Written, practical, and oral exam. **Fees:** $10 application processing fee. $25 complete initial exam fee ($15 written exam, $15 practical exam). $20 exam review fee. $12 initial license fee, per year. $12 renewal fee, per year. **Governing Statute:** The Occupational Code, Act 299 of 1980, as amended.

261

Driver Training Instructor (Commercial)
Driver Training School Div.
Bureau of Driver Improvement
Dept. of State
7064 Crowner Dr.
Lansing, MI 48918
Phone: (517)322-1460

Credential Type: License. **Duration of License:** One year. **Requirements:** Physically qualified to operate a motor vehicle, as evidenced by a medical examination report which has been completed by a Michigan licensed physician. Valid driver's license which has been in continuous effect for the three years prior to application. Have not received a six-point conviction or three or more points in conjunction with a fatal accident. Have not accumulated 12 or more points within a 24-month period or received convictions of six moving violations within a 36-month period. Have not been involved in three or more accidents within the preceding 24-month period which resulted in personal injury or property damage and for which he/she received a conviction in conjunction with each accident.

Commercial driver training instructors of youth under 18 years of age must also meet these requirements: Be at least 21 years of age. Have a personal driving record with no more than six points for moving traffic violation convictions during the two years prior to application. Have earned at least eight semester hours of specific university credit in the field of Traffic Safety Education. **Fees:** $2 initial license fee. $2 renewal fee. **Governing Statute:** Driver Training Schools, Act 369 of 1974. Michigan Vehicle Code, Act 300 of 1949, as amended.

262

Driver Training Instructor (School)
Driver Training School Div.
Bureau of Driver Improvement
Dept. of State
7064 Crowner Dr.
Lansing, MI 48918
Phone: (517)322-1460

Credential Type: License. **Duration of License:** One year. **Authorization:** Required for approval as public or private school instructors of youth under 18 years of age. **Requirements:** Possess a valid Michigan teaching certificate. Possess a valid driver's license. Be at least 21 years of age. Have a personal driving record with no more than six points for moving traffic violation convictions during the two years prior to application. Have earned at least eight semester hours of specific university credit in the field of Traffic Safety Education. **Fees:** No fees. **Governing Statute:** Driver Training Schools, Act 369 of 1974. Michigan Vehicle Code, Act 300 of 1949, as amended.

263

Emergency Medical Technician Instructor-Coordinator
Div. of Emergency Medical Services
Dept. of Public Health
3423 N. Logan
PO Box 30195
Lansing, MI 48909
Phone: (517)335-8000

Credential Type: Certificate. **Duration of License:** Three years. **Requirements:** Be a licensed emergency medical technician. Must have at least two years of practical experience in the field of emergency health care and possess demonstrated teaching ability. Completed an emergency medical technician instructor-coordinator training program. Abide by the rules of the Department of Public Health. Renewal requires completion of an ongoing education program each year. **Examination:** Written and practical exam. **Governing Statute:** Public Health Code, Act 368 of 1978, as amended.

264

Fire Fighter Training Instructor
Fire Fighters Training Council
Fire Marshall Div.
Dept. of State Police
7150 Harris Dr.
Lansing, MI 48913
Phone: (517)332-2521

Credential Type: Fire Fighter Training Instructor Certification. **Duration of License:** Lifelong. **Authorization:** All persons employed as a fire fighter training instructor must be certified by the Fire Fighters Training Council of the Michigan Department of State Police. **Requirements:** Minimum of five years experience in fire suppression service. Certification as a Fire Fighter I. Have received one positive evaluation and recommendation by a Fire Fighters Training Council representative, while a provisional instructor. Completed the Fire Fighters Training Council Basic Instructional Methodological (16 hour) Course, or its equivalent. **Fees:** No fees. **Governing Statute:** Fire Fighters Training Council Act of 1966, Act 291 of 1966, as amended.

Credential Type: Associate Instructor Certification. **Duration of License:** Lifelong. **Authorization:** All persons employed as a fire fighter training instructor

Adult and Vocational Education Teachers

must be certified by the Fire Fighters Training Council of the Michigan Department of State Police. **Requirements:** Have a minimum of three years experience in the specialized area or subject to be taught. Have received the recommendation and approval of a certified fire service instructor or recognized authority in the area to be taught. Abide by the rules of the Fire Fighters Training Council. **Fees:** No fees. **Governing Statute:** Fire Fighters Training Council Act of 1966, Act 291 of 1966, as amended.

Credential Type: Provisional Instructor Certification. **Duration of License:** Lifelong. **Authorization:** All persons employed as a fire fighter training instructor must be certified by the Fire Fighters Training Council of the Michigan Department of State Police. **Requirements:** Have a minimum of three years experience in fire suppression service. Have successfully completed the Fire Fighters Training Council Fire Fighter I curriculum. Have received the recommendation and approval of their fire chief or governing municipality official. Abide by the rules of the Fire Fighters Training Council. **Fees:** No fees. **Governing Statute:** Fire Fighters Training Council Act of 1966, Act 291 of 1966, as amended.

Credential Type: Fire Instructor Advisor Certification. **Duration of License:** Lifelong. **Authorization:** All persons employed as a fire fighter training instructor must be certified by the Fire Fighters Training Council of the Michigan Department of State Police. **Requirements:** Have certification as a Fire Fighter II and Fire Fighter Training Instructor. Have instructed in a minimum of five (5) Fire Fighters Training Council recognized programs. Have received three positive evaluations and recommendations by Fire Fighters Training Council representatives, while a Fire Fighter Training Instructor. Have completed the Fire Fighters Training Council Advanced Instructional Methodological Course, or its equivalent. **Fees:** No fees. **Governing Statute:** Fire Fighters Training Council Act of 1966, Act 291 of 1966, as amended.

Credential Type: Fire Training Administrator Certification. **Duration of License:** Lifelong. **Authorization:** All persons employed as a fire fighter training instructor must be certified by the Fire Fighters Training Council of the Michigan Department of State Police. **Requirements:** Have certification as a Fire Fighter II and a Fire Instructor Advisor. Have managed, supervised, or instructed in a minimum of 10 Fire Fighters Training Council recognized programs. **Fees:** No fees. **Governing Statute:** Fire Fighters Training Council Act of 1966, Act 291 of 1966, as amended.

265

Teacher, Vocational
Teacher
Administrator Preparation and Certification Services
Dept. of Education
PO Box 30008
Lansing, MI 48909
Phone: (517)373-3324

Credential Type: Secondary provisional certificate with vocational endorsement. **Duration of License:** Varies, with three-year renewal periods. **Authorization:** For individuals completing approved teacher training programs with a major or minor in a vocational area. **Requirements:** Completed an approved teacher education program. Completed a major or minor in an occupational area in an approved program. Two years of recent and relevant work experience in the occupational area or have completed a supervised work experience program at a teacher training institution. **Examination:** Basic skills exam and subject area exam. **Fees:** $50 endorsement fee. **Governing Statute:** The School Code Act, Act 269 of 1955, as amended. Act 287 of 1964, as amended. The School Code of 1976, Act 451 of 1976, as amended.

Credential Type: Temporary vocational authorization certificate. **Duration of License:** Up to six years, with three-year renewal periods. **Authorization:** For individuals who have not completed a professional teacher training program. **Requirements:** Have a bachelor's degree. Have completed a major or minor in the occupational area or equivalent graduate credit. Have two years of recent and relevant work experience in the occupational area or have completed a college-planned program of directed and supervised work experience in vocational education. **Examination:** Basic skills exam and subject area exam. **Fees:** $125 authorization fee. **Governing Statute:** The School Code Act, Act 269 of 1955, as amended. Act 287 of 1964, as amended. The School Code of 1976, Act 451 of 1976, as amended.

Credential Type: Occupational Education Certificate. **Duration of License:** Five years. **Authorization:** Issued to new teachers as of July 1, 1992. **Requirements:** Have three years of successful teaching experience in the field of vocational education. Have completed a minimum of 10 semester hours of college vocational credit approved by a sponsoring Michigan teacher training institution. **Examination:** Basic skills exam and subject area exam. **Fees:** $125 certification fee. **Governing Statute:** The School Code Act, Act 269 of 1955, as amended. Act 287 of 1964, as amended. The School Code of 1976, Act 451 of 1976, as amended.

Credential Type: Professional Education Certificate. **Duration of License:** Five years. **Authorization:** Issued to new teachers as of July 1, 1992. **Requirements:** Have three years of successful teaching experience in the appropriate subject area. Have completed 18 semester hours of credit in a course of study "planned" by an approved teacher training institution and include a minimum of 10 semester hours of relevant vocational education credit. A person with an earned master's or higher degree from an approved teacher education institution is not required to complete the 18 semester hour planned program. **Examination:** Basic skills exam and subject area exam. **Fees:** $125 certification fee. **Governing Statute:** The School Code Act, Act 269 of 1955, as amended. Act 287 of 1964, as amended. The School Code of 1976, Act 451 of 1976, as amended.

Minnesota

266

Barber Instructor
Board of Barber Examiners
Iris Park Place Bldg.
1885 University Ave. W., Ste. 335
St. Paul, MN 55104-3403
Phone: (612)642-0489

Credential Type: Barber Instructor License. **Duration of License:** One year. **Requirements:** Submit application and pay fees. Pass examination. Renewal requires continuing education. **Examination:** Yes. **Fees:** $35 license fee. $150 exam fee. **Governing Statute:** Minnesota Statutes, Chap. 154. Minnesota Rules 2100.

267

Cosmetologist Instructor
Dept. of Commerce
Licensing Unit
133 E. 7th St.
St. Paul, MN 55101
Phone: (612)296-6319

Credential Type: Cosmetologist Instructor's License. **Requirements:** Be a licensed cosmetologist. Complete 38 hours of teacher training. Complete 1400 hours of work experience within the past three years. **Examination:** Written and practical exams. **Fees:** $60 license fee. **Governing Statute:** Minnesota Statutes, Chap. 155A. Cosmetology Rules, Chap. 2640.

Missouri

268

Cosmetology Instructor
Board of Cosmetology
3605 Missouri Blvd.
PO Box 1062
Jefferson City, MO 65102-1062
Phone: (314)751-1052
Phone: (314)751-2334

Credential Type: Instructor Trainee License. **Duration of License:** A definite period needed to complete training requirements. **Requirements:** Good moral character. Good physical and mental health. High school graduate or equivalent. Hold a Missouri license to practice as a cosmetologist or manicurist. **Fees:** $10 trainee enrollment fee. **Governing Statute:** Laws of Missouri, Chap. 329. Rules and Regulations, four CSR 90.

Credential Type: Instructor License. **Duration of License:** Two years. **Requirements:** Good moral character. Good physical and mental health. High school graduate or equivalent. Hold a Missouri license to practice as a cosmetologist or manicurist. Complete 1200 hours of instructor training in a licensed cosmetology school. Renewal requires attendance at one or more teacher training seminars or workshops every two years. **Examination:** Instructor examination. **Reciprocity:** Yes, provided other state has equivalent requirements. **Fees:** $30 exam fee. $24 license fee. $24 renewal fee. $54 reciprocity fee. **Governing Statute:** Laws of Missouri, Chap. 329. Rules and Regulations, four CSR 90.

Montana

269

Barber Instructor
Montana Board of Barbers
111 N. Jackson
Helena, MT 59620
Phone: (406)444-3738

Credential Type: License. **Duration of License:** One year. **Requirements:** Contact licensing body for application information. **Fees:** $50 license fee. $25 renewal fee. **Governing Statute:** Montana Code Annotated 37-30-301 through 37-30-311.

270

Vocational Education Teacher
Teacher Certification
Office of Public Instruction
State Capitol
Helena, MT 59620
Phone: (406)444-3150

Credential Type: Class 4 Vocational Certificate. **Duration of License:** Five years. **Requirements:** Must present training and experience as required by the United States Office of Education or by the special needs required in the vocational area. Requirements vary with the situation. Renewable upon verification of one year of successful teaching experience and six quarter credits during the valid term of the certificate.

Nebraska

271

Driving Instructor
Nebraska Dept. of Motor Vehicles
301 Centennial Mall S.
PO Box 94789
Lincoln, NE 68509
Phone: (402)471-2281

Credential Type: License. **Duration of License:** One year. **Requirements:** 21 years of age. Must be a high school graduate. Must have held a Nebraska drivers license and had no more than two moving violations for at least two years preceding the application. **Examination:** Yes. **Fees:** $10 licensed instructor fee. $50 licensed school fee. $10 instructor renewal fee. $50 school renewal fee.

New Hampshire

272

Cosmetology Instructor
Board of Barbering, Cosmetology, and Esthetics
Health and Welfare Bldg.
Hazen Dr.
Concord, NH 03301
Phone: (603)271-3608

Credential Type: Cosmetology Instructor's License. **Duration of License:** Two years. **Requirements:** Must be a licensed cosmetologist, barber, manicurist, or esthetician. Complete at least one year of practice in a licensed shop. Complete 1000 hours of training or 700 hours as a student instructor. Renewal requires 28 hours of continuing education every two years. **Examination:** Written or oral examination of the National Interstate Council of State Boards of Cosmetology. Practical examination. **Reciprocity:** Yes, provided other state's licensing requirements are substantially equivalent. **Fees:** $25 license fee. $30 renewal fee. $60 reciprocity fee. **Governing Statute:** RSA 313-A. Code of Administrative Rules.

Credential Type: Temporary Permit. **Duration of License:** Until next examination. **Requirements:** Must have applied for a license and be eligible to take the examination. **Governing Statute:** RSA 313-A. Code of Administrative Rules.

273

Driver Education Instructor
NH Dept. of Safety
James Hayes Safety Bldg.
10 Hazen Drive
Concord, NH 03301
Phone: (603)271-2485

Credential Type: Commercial Motor Vehicle School Provisional Certificate. **Duration of License:** One year. **Requirements:** At least 21 years of age. Good moral character. U.S. citizen. No criminal record or any major motor vehicle convictions within the last three years. Valid driver's license for five or more years. Current medical physical. High school graduate or equivalent. Complete two 3-credit courses which meet the certification competencies of the state of New Hampshire. **Examination:** State examination. **Reciprocity:** Yes, with state approval. **Fees:** $25 provisional certificate fee.

Credential Type: Commercial Motor Vehicle School Standard Certificate. **Duration of License:** Three years. **Requirements:** Meet requirements for provisional certificate. Have supervised teaching experience in New Hampshire within the last two years. Must include a minimum of 60 hours of classroom instruction and 140 hours of actual driving instruction. Complete two 3-credit courses which meet the certification competencies of the state of New Hampshire. Renewal requires 50 clock hours of professional growth work and 20 hours of courses which pertain directly to driver's education every three years. **Examination:** State examination. **Fees:** $40 standard certification fee.

Adult and Vocational Education Teachers

274

Vocational Education Teacher
Bureau of Teacher Education and Professional Standards
State Dept. of Education
101 Pleasant St.
Concord, NH 03301
Phone: (603)271-2407

Credential Type: Beginning Educator Certificate. **Duration of License:** Three years. **Requirements:** Be recommended under the Critical Staffing Claus of New Hampshire. Demonstrate vocational competence. Four years of recent, successful, full-time work experience in the appropriate area or completion of a two year vocational technical program plus two years of full time work experience. Demonstrate competence in the basic skills of reading, writing, and mathematics.

Credential Type: Experienced Educator Certificate. **Duration of License:** Three years. **Requirements:** Must have recommendation of the Superintendent of Schools during the life of the Beginning Educator Certificate. Must have met all requirements for previous level of certification or successfully completed an approved graduate program that extends clinical experience to a full year under supervision.

New Jersey

275

Cosmetology Instructor
Board of Cosmetology and Hairstyling
1100 Raymond Blvd., Rm. 311
Newark, NJ 07102
Phone: (201)648-2450

Credential Type: Cosmetology and Hairstyling Teacher. **Duration of License:** Two years. **Requirements:** High school diploma or equivalent. Completion of a teacher training course of 500 hours at a licensed school. Completion of a 30-hour teaching methods course conducted by an approved college. Hold a cosmetologist-hairstylist license or an operator license from the state board. 18 years of age. **Examination:** Written, oral and practical exam. **Fees:** $30 exam fee. $30 biennial license fee. **Governing Statute:** NJSA 45:5B. NJAC 13:2B.

276

Real Estate Instructor
New Jersey Real Estate Commission
20 W. State St., 10th Fl.
Trenton, NJ 08625-0325
Phone: (609)292-7055

Credential Type: License. **Requirements:** 18 years of age. A member of the faculty of an accredited college or university and have previously taught at least one course in real estate or a related subject; or have actively practiced as a licensed attorney at law in New Jersey for at least three years and have substantial experience in real estate; or hold a recent bachelor's degree in real estate; or hold a bachelor's degree and possess at least 15 credits in real estate or a related subject, and hold a teaching certificate; or be a New Jersey licensed real estate broker with five years of experience as a New Jersey licensee; or otherwise possess the competency to effectively teach real estate subjects. Good moral character.

New Mexico

277

Barber Instructor
Board of Barber Examiners
Dept. of Regulation and Licensing
PO Box 25101
725 St. Michael's Dr.
Santa Fe, NM 87504
Phone: (505)827-7176

Credential Type: Certificate of Registration. **Duration of License:** One year. **Requirements:** Be at least 18 years of age. Good moral character and temperate habits. Complete a course of barbering of at least 1200 hours. Pass instructor's exam. **Examination:** Practical demonstration. Written and oral examination. **Reciprocity:** Yes. **Fees:** $50 exam fee. $25 certificate fee. $25 renewal fee. **Governing Statute:** New Mexico Board of Barber Examiners Statutes 61-17-1 et seq. New Mexico Board of Barber Examiners Rules.

278

Cosmetology Teacher
Cosmetology Board
Dept. of Regulation and Licensing
PO Box 25101
725 St. Michael's Dr.
Santa Fe, NM 87504
Phone: (505)827-7176

Credential Type: Cosmetology Teacher's License. **Duration of License:** One year. **Requirements:** High school graduate or equivalent. Must be a licensed cosmetologist with three years experience or 1000 hours of instructor training. **Examination:** State examination. **Reciprocity:** Yes, provided applicant meets state requirements for training, age, and education. **Fees:** $25 exam fee. $25 license fee. $25 renewal fee. $100 reciprocity fee.

279

Massage Therapy Instructor
Massage Therapy Board
Dept. of Regulation and Licensing
PO Box 25101
Santa Fe, NM 87504
Phone: (505)827-7113

Credential Type: Massage Therapy Instructor Registration. **Requirements:** Must be a licensed massage therapist in New Mexico. Complete at least two years experience in massage therapy. **Fees:** $10 registration fee. **Governing Statute:** 61-12C-1 et seq. NMSA 1978. New Mexico Board of Massage Therapy Rules, Rule 92-1 et seq.

New York

280

Driving Instructor
New York State Dept. of Motor Vehicles
Office of Communications
Empire State Plaza
Albany, NY 12228
Phone: (518)474-0877

Credential Type: Certificate. **Duration of License:** One or two years. **Requirements:** High school diploma or equivalency plus 30-hour instructors' course. Minimum of two years of driving experience. Must be endorsed by a licensed driving school wishing to employ the applicant. **Examination:** Vision, written and road tests. **Fees:** $10 certificate fee. $10 renewal fee. **Governing Statute:** Section 394 of the Vehicle and Traffic Law. Part 76 of the Regulations of the Commissioner of Motor Vehicles.

North Carolina

281

Barber Instructor
North Carolina State Board of Barber Examiners
3901 Barrett Dr., Ste. 300
Raleigh, NC 27609
Phone: (919)733-3650

Credential Type: Registration. **Duration of License:** One year. **Requirements:**

Barber Instructor, continued

Must be a registered and practicing barber in North Carolina. **Examination:** Written, oral and practical. **Fees:** $35 registration fee. $85 exam fee. $35 renewal fee.

282

Cosmetologist Instructor
North Carolina State Board of Cosmetic Arts
4101 North Blvd., Ste. H
Raleigh, NC 27604
Phone: (919)790-8460

Credential Type: License. **Duration of License:** Two years. **Requirements:** Must be a licensed cosmetologist for five consecutive years, or a licensed cosmetologist for six months and completed 400 clock hours of teaching courses. **Examination:** Theoretical and practical questions. **Fees:** $50 exam fee. $10 license fee. $15 registration fee. $10 renewal fee.

283

Driver Education Specialist
Dept. of Transportation
School Bus and Traffic Safety Section
1100 New Bern Ave.
Raleigh, NC 27697
Phone: (919)733-3046

Credential Type: License. **Duration of License:** One year. **Requirements:** High school education or GED. Presently employed by a licensed commercial driver's training school. Completion of a two-semester-hour college course in traffic safety or the equivalent. Four years of experience as a licensed driver. 20 years of age. Good driving record and moral character. **Examination:** Written and road test. **Fees:** $8 license fee. $8 renewal fee.

284

Vocational Education Teacher
Certification Section
State Dept. of Public Instruction
Raleigh, NC 27603
Phone: (919)733-4125

Credential Type: Vocational Education Certificate. **Duration of License:** Five years. **Requirements:** Complete at least four or more years of full-time appropriate work experience in a trade or vocational pursuit, of which not less than two years of formal training (trade school or technical institute) are acceptable. Letters of reference from former employees must be submitted, or proof of two years of full-time work experience. Demonstrate vocational competence. Proof of employment in the trade or vocational area by an L.E.A. If requirements have not all been completed, it may be possible to hold position as a vocational education teacher subject to yearly evaluations, until all requirements are satisfied. A minimum of six semester hours of course work or the equivalent work experience would be required during the life time of each 12 month extension. **Fees:** $30 application fee. $30 renewal fee.

North Dakota

285

Cosmetology Instructor
State Board of Cosmetology
Box 2177
Bismarck, ND 58502-2177
Phone: (701)224-9800

Credential Type: Instructor License. **Duration of License:** One year. **Requirements:** Be at least 18 years of age. High school graduate or equivalent. Meet one of the following sets of requirements: (1) Complete instructor's training course in cosmetology of 960 hours. (2) Have at least one year experience as an active practicing cosmetologist, supplemented by at least 480 hours of instructor's training in cosmetology. (3) Possess a current North Dakota license as a cosmetologist. Have been engaged as an active practicing cosmetologist for at least three years prior to application, supplemented by at least 160 hours of instructor's training in cosmetology.

Renewal requires attendance at an approved seminar. **Examination:** Practical Examination. National Teacher Examination. North Dakota Law and Sanitation Examination. **Reciprocity:** No reciprocity for instructors. **Fees:** $10 application fee. $50 exam fee. $30 license fee. **Governing Statute:** North Dakota Century Code 43-11-01 et seq.

Credential Type: Student Instructor Registration. **Requirements:** Must register upon enrollment in a school of cosmetology. Must have completed a four-year high school education or equivalent. Must hold a license as a cosmetologist. **Governing Statute:** North Dakota Century Code 43-11-01 et seq.

Ohio

286

Cosmetology Instructor
Ohio Board of Cosmetology
8 E. Long, Ste. 1000
Columbus, OH 43215
Phone: (614)466-3834

Credential Type: Cosmetology Instructor License. **Duration of License:** Two years. **Requirements:** Good moral character. Have the equivalent of a 12th-grade education. Hold a current managing cosmetologist license. Complete one year of practice as a cosmetologist in a licensed beauty salon, or complete 1000 hours of cosmetology instructor training in a licensed school of cosmetology as an apprentice instructor. **Examination:** Yes. **Reciprocity:** Yes. **Fees:** $21 application fee. $25 license fee. $25 renewal fee. $50 reciprocity fee. **Governing Statute:** Ohio Revised Code, Chap. 4713. Administrative Code, 4713-1 et seq.

287

Esthetics Instructor
Ohio Board of Cosmetology
8 E. Long, Ste. 1000
Columbus, OH 43215
Phone: (614)466-3834

Credential Type: Esthetics Instructor License. **Duration of License:** Two years. **Requirements:** Be at least 18 years of age. Good moral character. Have the equivalent of a 12th-grade education. Hold a current managing cosmetologist or managing esthetician license. Complete one year of practice as a managing cosmetologist or managing esthetician in a licensed beauty salon, or complete 500 hours of training in a licensed school of cosmetology as an assistant esthetics instructor. **Examination:** Yes. **Reciprocity:** Yes. **Fees:** $21 application fee. $25 license fee. $25 renewal fee. $50 reciprocity fee. **Governing Statute:** Ohio Revised Code, Chap. 4713. Administrative Code, 4713-1 et seq.

288

Manicurist Instructor
Ohio Board of Cosmetology
8 E. Long, Ste. 1000
Columbus, OH 43215
Phone: (614)466-3834

Credential Type: Manicurist Instructor License. **Duration of License:** Two years. **Requirements:** Be at least 18 years of age. Hold a current managing cosmetologist or managing manicurist license. Complete an additional 1000 hours of training in manicuring in a licensed school of cosmetology. **Examination:** Yes. **Reciprocity:** Yes. **Fees:** $21 application fee. $25 license fee. $25 renewal fee. $50 reciprocity fee. **Governing Statute:** Ohio Revised Code, Chap. 4713. Administrative Code, 4713-1 et seq.

289

Vocational Education Teacher
Teacher Education and Certification
State Dept. of Education
65 S. Front St., Rm. 1012
Columbus, OH 43266-0308
Phone: (614)466-3593

Credential Type: Provisional Vocational Education Certificate. **Requirements:** Baccalaureate degree. Good moral character. Complete an approved program of teacher preparation including an examination. Recommendation of preparing institution. 30 semester hours of general education courses distributed over the humanities, mathematics, natural sciences, and social sciences. 20 semester hours of professional education courses, both clinical and fieldbased, designed for teaching vocational education. 45 semester hours of curriculum content courses in technical work. Two years recent related work experience in the teaching area or a directed occupational experience under the supervision of a vocational educator. Teaching fields in which an applicant may be certified are: agriculture education; business education; marketing education; home economics/consumer homemaking education; home economics/job training; health occupations; and trade and industrial education.

Oklahoma

290

Cosmetology Instructor
Oklahoma State Board of
  Cosmetology
2200 Classen Blvd., Ste. 1530
Oklahoma City, OK 73106
Phone: (405)521-2441

Credential Type: License. **Duration of License:** One year. **Requirements:** High School degree. 1,000 hours of instructor courses at a licensed school of cosmetology plus 1,500 hours of training in basic cosmetology courses. 16 years of age. Must hold a current cosmetologist license at time of application. **Examination:** National Cosmetology Teachers Test. **Fees:** $10 exam fee. $15 license fee. $15 renewal fee.

291

Driver Training Instructor (Commercial Driving School)
Oklahoma Dept. of Public Safety -
  Troop N
3600 N. Martin Luther King Ave.
PO Box 11415
Oklahoma City, OK 73136
Phone: (405)521-6223

Credential Type: License. **Duration of License:** One year. **Requirements:** Six semester hours in Driver Education I and Driver Education II. A minimum of three semester hours of General Safety Education. 20 hours of training each year. Valid Oklahoma driver's license. 21 years of age. Approved driving record. No felony convictions. **Examination:** Driver's Examination (Class A). Vision test. Standard road test. **Fees:** $5 exam fee. $5 license fee. $5 renewal fee.

292

Vocational Education Teacher 9-12
Teacher Education and Certification
State Dept. of Education
2500 N. Lincoln Blvd., Rm. 211
Oklahoma City, OK 73105
Phone: (405)521-3337

Credential Type: Provisional Level II Vocational-Technical Certificate. **Duration of License:** Five years. **Requirements:** High school diploma or G.E.D. Pass an occupational competency examination approved by the State Dept. of Vocational-Technical Education. Provide evidence of three years of appropriate experience in the field to be taught that has occurred within the five years preceding initial certification. Complete 48 semester hours of approved credit of which a maximum of 24 semester hours may be earned by passing an occupational competency examination approved by the State Dept. of Vocational-Technical Education. Recommendation from the appropriate State Vocational-Technical Supervisor. Present a statement from the preparing institution that states that the applicant has an approved plan of study which will lead to a Standard Certificate. **Examination:** State approved competency examination.

Credential Type: Provisional Level I Vocational-Technical Certificate. **Duration of License:** One year. **Requirements:** High school diploma or G.E.D. Provide evidence of three years of appropriate experience in the field to be taught that has occurred within the five years preceding initial certification. Complete the Vocational-Technical Orientation Training Program during the first 60 days of the school year for which the original certificate is used. Recommendation for the Provisional Level I Certificate from the appropriate State Vocational-Technical Supervisor and from the employing Superintendent. Present a statement that proves the applicant has an approved plan of study for the Provisional II Vocational-Technical Certificate and the Standard Certificate. Pass an occupational competency examination approved by the State Dept. of Vocational-Technical Education for yearly renewal of this certificate.

Credential Type: Standard Vocational-Technical Certificate—Undergraduate. **Duration of License:** Five years. **Requirements:** Complete an approved certificate program at an accredited college or university which includes a minimum of the following: a baccalaureate degree; 50 semester hours in general education; 30 semester hours in professional education; and 40 semester hours in course work pertaining to vocational education. Pass the state certified test(s) in vocational education competencies. Successfully complete the Entry-Year Assistance Program as a licensed teacher. Complete a course of two or more semester hours in the education of the exceptional child. **Examination:** State certification tests pertaining to vocational education.

Pennsylvania

293

Barber Teacher
State Board of Barber Examiners
Bureau of Professional and
  Occupational Affairs
Dept. of State
Transportation and Safety Bldg., 6th
  Fl.
Harrisburg, PA 17120
Phone: (717)787-8503

Credential Type: Barber Teacher License. **Duration of License:** Two years. **Requirements:** At least 23 years of age. High school graduate. Five year's experience as a licensed barber or be a manager-barber who has trained for 1,250 hours under a licensed teacher in a licensed barber school as a teacher trainee. **Examination:** State barber teacher examination. **Fees:** $40 complete examination fee. $30 examination fee (practical only). $30 examination fee (theory only). $20 initial license. $67 biennial renewal.

294

Cosmetology Teacher
State Board of Cosmetology
Bureau of Professional and Occupational Affairs
Dept. of State
Transportation and Safety Bldg., 6th Fl.
Harrisburg, PA 17120
Phone: (717)787-8503

Credential Type: Cosmetology Teacher. **Duration of License:** Two years. **Authorization:** Qualifies holder to perform the functions of a cosmetology teacher, manager, cosmetologist, cosmetician or manicurist. **Requirements:** At least 18 years of age. Complete the 12th grade or its equivalent. Hold a current cosmetologist license. Complete 500 hours of instruction for cosmetology teachers in a licensed school of cosmetology. **Examination:** State cosmetology teacher examination. **Reciprocity:** Holders of out-of-state licenses may be granted reciprocity with board approval. **Fees:** $52.50 complete examination fee. $24 examination fee (practical only). $28.50 examination fee (theory only). $25 reciprocal license fee. $10 initial license fee. $36 biennial renewal.

Credential Type: Cosmetology Manager License. **Duration of License:** Two years. **Authorization:** Qualifies the holder to perform the functions of manager, cosmetologist, cosmetician, or manicurist. **Requirements:** At least 18 years of age. Complete the 10th grade or its equivalent. Hold a current cosmetology license. Complete one of the following requirements: (1) Complete 300 hours of courses for cosmetology managers in a licensed school of cosmetology. (2) Have a minimum of 18 month's experience in a licensed cosmetology shop working as a full-time cosmetologist. **Examination:** State cosmetology manager examination. **Reciprocity:** Holders of out-of-state licenses may be granted reciprocity with board approval. **Fees:** $28.50 examination fee. $25 reciprocal license fee. $10 initial license fee. $25 biennial renewal fee.

295

Supervisor of Vocational Education
Bureau of Certification
Dept. of Education
333 Market St.
Harrisburg, PA 17126-0333
Phone: (717)787-2967

Credential Type: Supervisor of Comprehensive Vocational Education I Certificate—Provisional. **Requirements:** Three years of satisfactory service in a vocational field. Complete an approved preparation/certification program for supervision in all fields of vocational education. Recommendation of the preparing institution.

All new applicants must produce a background clearance as required in Act 34. A Pennsylvania State Police background check is required for Pennsylvania residents and an F.B.I. background check is required for out-of-state residents. Applicants may not work in Pennsylvania public schools without this clearance.

Credential Type: Supervisor of Comprehensive Vocational Education II Certificate—Permanent. **Duration of License:** Permanent. **Requirements:** Three years of satisfactory service on a Supervisor of Vocational Education I Certificate.

296

Vocational Education Teacher
Bureau of Certification
Dept. of Education
333 Market St.
Harrisburg, PA 17126-0333
Phone: (717)787-2967

Credential Type: Vocational Instructional Intern Certificate. **Duration of License:** Three years. **Requirements:** High school graduate or equivalent. Complete one of the five following forms of qualification: 1-Pass occupational competency examination of the Dept.; 2—Acceptance of credentials and adequate work experience by the Dept. for those competency areas where examinations do not exist; 3—State licensure; 4—Occupational accreditation by a Board of Examiners; 5—Certification from another state with criteria similar to those of Pennsylvania. Must have acceptance for enrollment in an approved vocational teacher preparation program and complete 18 semester hours of course work in this program during the life of the certificate. Recommendation of preparing institution.

All new applicants must produce a background clearance as required in Act 34. A Pennsylvania State Police background check is required for Pennsylvania residents and an F.B.I. background check is required for out-of-state residents. Applicants may not work in Pennsylvania public schools without this clearance.

Credential Type: Vocational Instructional I Certificate—Provisional. **Duration of License:** Seven years. **Duration of License:** Permanent. **Authorization:** Valid only in areas for which occupational competency credential is held. **Requirements:** Two years of wage-earning experience. Successful completion of NTE Basic Skills test and Occupational Competency test. Complete 18 credit hours of an approved program of vocational teacher education. Recommendation of preparing institution. Nonrenewable. Candidate must complete requirements for Vocational Instructional II Certificate during the life of this certificate.

All new applicants must produce a background clearance as required in Act 34. A Pennsylvania State Police background check is required for Pennsylvania residents and an F.B.I. background check is required for out-of-state residents. Applicants may not work in Pennsylvania public schools without this clearance. **Requirements:** Three years of satisfactory service on the Vocational Instructional I Certificate. Complete 60 semester hours in an approved program in the appropriate vocational field. Satisfactory completion of the NTE General Knowledge and Professional Knowledge tests. Complete a department approved induction program. **Examination:** NTE Basic Skills and Occupational Competency tests. Vocational Instructional II Certificate—Permanent. **Examination:** NTE General Knowledge and Professional Knowledge tests.

Rhode Island

297

Barber Instructor
Board of Examiners in Barbering
Div. of Professional Regulation
Rhode Island Dept. of Health
3 Capitol Hill
Providence, RI 02908
Phone: (401)277-2827

Credential Type: Instructor License. **Duration of License:** One year. **Requirements:** Complete all requirements for Barber License. Submit application and pay fees. **Examination:** Written and practical examinations. **Reciprocity:** No. **Fees:** $100 application fee. $50 annual renewal fee.

298

Driving Instructor
Div. of Motor Vehicles
Research Section
Rhode Island Dept. of Transportation
345 Harris Ave.
Providence, RI 02909
Phone: (401)277-2991

Credential Type: Driving Instructor License. **Duration of License:** One year. **Requirements:** At least 21 years of age. Valid Rhode Island driver's license for type of vehicle used for instruction. **Reciprocity:** No. **Fees:** $15 application fee. $15 annual renewal fee.

South Carolina

299

Cosmetologist Instructor
South Carolina State Board of Cosmetology
1209 Blanding St.
Columbia, SC 29201
Phone: (803)253-6222

Credential Type: Cosmetology Instructor License. **Requirements:** Must be initially licensed as a cosmetologist. Completion of 45 clock hours in teaching methods. High school diploma or equivalent. **Examination:** Yes. **Fees:** $50 license fee. $30 renewal fee.

South Dakota

300

Cosmetology Instructor
Cosmetology Commission
Dept. of Commerce and Regulation
PO Box 127
Pierre, SD 57501
Phone: (605)224-5072

Credential Type: Senior Instructor's License. **Duration of License:** One year. **Requirements:** Be at least 18 years of age. High school graduate or equivalent. Have at least two years experience as a licensed operator cosmetologist or one year experience as a junior instructor. Must hold a current valid manager-operator's license. Must have attended at least 10 hours of board-approved seminars conducted for cosmetology instructors during the 12 months prior to application. **Fees:** $15 license fee. $15 renewal fee. **Governing Statute:** South Dakota Codified Laws, Chap. 36-15.

Credential Type: Junior Instructor's License. **Duration of License:** One year. **Authorization:** Must work in a licensed beauty school under the direct supervision of a licensed senior instructor. **Requirements:** Be at least 18 years of age. High school graduate or equivalent. Must hold a current valid operator's license. Must have attended at least 10 hours of board-approved seminars conducted for cosmetology instructors during the 12 months prior to application. License may be granted conditionally provided applicant takes 10 hours of seminars within six months. **Fees:** $15 license fee. $15 renewal fee. **Governing Statute:** South Dakota Codified Laws, Chap. 36-15.

Tennessee

301

Vocational Education Teacher
Office of Teaching Licensing
Dept. of Education
Cordell Hull Bldg.
Nashville, TN 37219-5335
Phone: (615)741-1644

Credential Type: Trade Shop License. **Duration of License:** 10 years. **Requirements:** High school diploma or GED. Minimum of two years of appropriate employment experience and successful completion of the appropriate probationary and apprentice teacher period. Renewable.

Texas

302

Asbestos Training Provider
Texas Dept. of Health
Occupational Health Div.
Asbestos Licensing Section
1100 W. 49th St.
Austin, TX 78756
Phone: (512)834-6600

Credential Type: Asbestos Training Provider License. **Duration of License:** One year. **Authorization:** License required to offer and conduct asbestos training for fulfillment of specific training requirements prerequisite to licensing or registration by the Texas Department of Health. **Requirements:** Instructors must meet one of the following requirements: (1) At least two years of actual hands-on experience in asbestos-related activities with training accreditation from the Environmental Protection Agency (EPA). A high school diploma. Completion of one or more teacher education courses in vocational or industrial teaching; or

(2) A college degree in natural or physical sciences or a related field. One year of actual hands-on experience in asbestos-related activities. Current accreditation in at least one EPA asbestos course; or

(3) At least three years teaching experience in Hazmat or HazWoper or EPA approved asbestos courses. Completion of one or more teacher education courses in vocational or industrial teaching from an accredited junior college or university; or

(4) Qualification on an individual basis of professional persons for the purpose of teaching their specialty; or

(5) A vocational teacher with certification from the Texas Education Agency. One year of actual hands-on experience in asbestos-related activities. Current accreditation in at least one EPA asbestos course. **Fees:** $500 license fee. **Governing Statute:** Texas Civil Statutes, Article 4477-3a. Texas Asbestos Health Protection Rules, Section 295.

Utah

303

Driver's Education Teacher
Teacher Certification
250 E. 500 S.
Salt Lake City, UT 84111
Phone: (801)538-7740

Credential Type: License. **Requirements:** Must hold a valid teaching certificate for secondary schools. Must hold a valid Utah operators license and satisfactory record. Must have 24 quarter-hours in drivers education. **Fees:** $10 renewal fee.

Vermont

304

Driver Education Instructor (Public Schools)
Licensing Office
State Dept. of Education
120 State St.
Montpelier, VT 05602
Phone: (802)828-2445
Phone: (802)828-3126

Credential Type: License. **Requirements:** Valid License (level I or II). Valid Vermont Motor Vehicle Operator's License. Evidence of safe driving record. 18 total semester hours including basic drivers education, advanced drivers education and behavioral science plus nine semester hours devoted to related topics. **Examination:** No. **Reciprocity:** No. **Fees:** No. **Governing Statute:** Title 23, VSA Sections 701-711.

305

Driver Instructor, Commercial
Vermont State Dept. of Motor Vehicles
120 State St.
Montpelier, VT 05603
Phone: (802)828-2000

Credential Type: License. **Duration of License:** One year. **Requirements:** 21 years of age. Physically able. Five years as a licensed operator. Responsible driving record. Pass the examination. **Examination:** Yes. **Reciprocity:** No. **Fees:** $25 Original School License. $15 Renewal. $10

Vermont 306

Driver Instructor, Commercial, continued

Original Instructor license. $5 Renewal. **Governing Statute:** Title 23, VSA Sections 701-711.

306

Vocational Education Teacher
Teacher Licensure
State Dept. of Education
Montpelier, VT 05602-2703
Phone: (802)828-2445

Credential Type: Initial License. **Requirements:** High School diploma or equivalent. Complete an approved program in industrial education and two years of trade experience or two years of recent trade experience beyond the recognized training/apprenticeship period or a total of six or more years of trade experience. Expertise in one of the 26 identified vocational skill areas and the specific competencies as required by the Standards Board.

Virginia

307

Vocational Education Teacher
Administrative Director
Office of Professional Development
  and Teacher Education
Dept. of Education
PO Box 6-Q
Richmond, VA 23216-2060
Phone: (804)225-2094

Credential Type: Vocational Education Certificate. **Authorization:** Endorsements may be granted to allow teaching in the following areas: Agriculture; Business; Marketing; Health Occupations; Home Economics; Technology; and Trade and Industrial. **Requirements:** Pass the National Teacher Examination (NTE). Complete an approved course of study for the Vocational Education Instructor and meet experience and preparation requirements for the area of specialization.

Washington

308

Driver Training Instructor (Commercial Driving School)
Dept. of Licensing
Driver Services
Highways-Licenses Bldg., PB-01
Olympia, WA 98504-8001
Phone: (206)754-2487

Credential Type: Driver Training Instructor License. **Duration of License:** One year. **Requirements:** At least 21 years of age. High school graduate. Must have 60 hours of driver training instruction which includes 12 hours of instruction in behind-the-wheel teaching methods. Must have six hours of supervised behind-the-wheel teaching experience. Requalification examination must be taken every five years. **Examination:** Qualification examination. **Fees:** $25 initial license fee. $5 renewal fee.

309

Pharmacy Preceptor
Dept. of Health
Board of Pharmacy
1300 SE Quince, EY-20
Olympia, WA 98504
Phone: (206)753-6834

Credential Type: Certification. **Duration of License:** Five years. **Authorization:** Required to ensure that preceptors are qualified to instruct pharmacy interns. **Requirements:** Be at least 19 years of age. Must be a United States citizen or registered alien. Have a B.S. in pharmacy and one year of practice. Must be employed in a Class A pharmacy. Recertification requires 15 hours of continuing education per year. **Fees:** No fees.

West Virginia

310

Instructor, Barber and Beautician
State Board of Barbers and
  Beauticians
Guthrie Cntr.
4860 Brenda Ln.
Charleston, WV 25312
Phone: (304)348-3450
Phone: (304)348-2924

Credential Type: License. **Duration of License:** One year. **Requirements:** 18 years of age for student instructor. 21 years of age for regular instructor. High school graduate. 250 hours of instructor training in beauty/barber school. 2000 hours of beauty training or 1800 hours barber training. One year experience for student instructor., or three years experience for regular instructor. While training, must complete 15 hours of college credits. **Examination:** Yes. **Fees:** $25 Examination. $50 License. $50 Renewal.

Agricultural Scientists

The following states grant licenses in this occupational category as of the date of publication: Alabama, Arkansas, California, Illinois, Louisiana, Maine, Michigan, Mississippi, New Hampshire, North Dakota, South Carolina, Virginia.

Alabama

311

Landscape Horticulturist
Dept. Agricultural and Industries
Div. of Agricultural Chemistry and Plant Industry
Beard Bldg.
PO Box 3336
Montgomery, AL 36193
Phone: (205)242-2656

Credential Type: License. **Duration of License:** One year. **Requirements:** Must submit a written statement outlining training and experience in this field. **Examination:** Written examination. **Fees:** $10 examination fee. $25 renewal fee.

Arkansas

312

Agricultural Consultant
Arkansas State Plant Board
1 Natural Resources Dr.
PO Box 1069
Little Rock, AR 72203
Phone: (501)225-1598

Credential Type: License. **Requirements:** Masters or Phd from an accredited college or university in an appropriate discipline. Pass a written examination given by the board. Three years experience waives the test; or, a Bachelor's degree from an accredited school and one year experience and pass the exam given by the board; or, completed two years of training with an accredited school, three years of experience and passes the written examination given by the board. **Examination:** Written examination. **Fees:** $50 License fee.

313

Plant Breeders
Arkansas State Plant Board
No. 1 Natural Resources Dr.
PO Box 1069
Little Rock, AR 72203
Phone: (501)225-1598

Credential Type: License. **Requirements:** Any person having a Doctorate degree in Plant Breeding and three years experience is not required to take the examination. **Examination:** Yes.

314

Soil Classifier
Arkansas State Board of Registration for Professional Soil Classifiers
2801 Briarcliff Ave.
Fort Smith, AR 72903
Phone: (501)646-6255

Credential Type: License. **Duration of License:** One year. **Requirements:** Must have at least four years of college with a Bachelor of Science degree in Agriculture, with at least 15 hours in soil science; or, four years of college with a Bachelors degree in Agriculture or Biological Science and 30 hours in biological, physical and earth science with a minimum of nine hours in soil science. Must have one or two years of field experience depending on education. **Examination:** Yes. **Fees:** $20 Written examination. $60 License. $20 Renewal.

California

315

Agricultural Pest Control Adviser
California Environmental Protection Agency
Dept. of Pesticide Regulation
1220 N St.
PO Box 942871
Sacramento, CA 94271-0001
Phone: (916)654-0606
Fax: (916)654-1427

Credential Type: Agricultural Pest Control Adviser (APCA) License. **Duration of License:** One year. **Authorization:** License is required for any individual who offers a recommendation on any agricultural use. **Requirements:** Meet one of the following sets of requirements: (1) Have a bachelors degree in agricultural sciences, biological science, or pest management. (2) Have completed at least 60 semester hours (90 quarter hours) of college level curriculum in agricultural sciences, biological science, or pest management. Complete 24 months of technical experience as an assistant to an APCA or equivalent.

At least 40 hours of continuing education are required every two years for renewal. **Examination:** Laws and Regulations Examination. At least one category examination. **Fees:** $50 application fee. $30 annual renewal fee.

Illinois

316

Animal Breeder (Fur Bearing)
Illinois Dept. of Conservation
524 S. Second St.
Springfield, IL 62701-1787
Phone: (217)785-3423

Credential Type: Animal Breeder License. **Duration of License:** One year. **Requirements:** Must be Illinois resident for at least 30 days. Submit application and pay fee. **Reciprocity:** No. **Fees:** $25 initial license fee. $25 renewal fee. **Governing Statute:** Illinois Revised Statutes, Chapter 61. Illinois Conservation Law-Wildlife.

317

Wild Game and Bird Breeder
Illinois Dept. of Conservation
524 South 2nd St.
Springfield, IL 62701-1787
Phone: (217)785-3423

Credential Type: Class A (Non-Commercial) License. **Duration of License:** One year. **Requirements:** Must be an Illinois resident for at least 30 days. Submit application and pay fee. **Reciprocity:** No. **Fees:** $10 initial license fee. $10 renewal fee. **Governing Statute:** Illinois Revised Statutes, Chapter 61.

Credential Type: Class B (Commercial) License. **Duration of License:** One year. **Requirements:** Must be an Illinois resident for at least 30 days. Submit application and pay fee. **Reciprocity:** No. **Fees:** $20 initial license fee. $20 renewal fee. **Governing Statute:** Illinois Revised Statutes, Chapter 61.

Louisiana

318

Agricultural Consultant
Dept. of Agriculture
Agricultural and Environmental Programs
PO Box 44153, Capitol Sta.
Baton Rouge, LA 70804
Phone: (504)342-7011

Credential Type: Certification. **Duration of License:** One year followed by three-year renewal periods. **Requirements:** Have at least a bachelor's degree from an accredited university. Have worked for a minimum of four crop seasons. **Examination:** Certification examination. **Fees:** $5 certification fee. $5 exam fee. **Governing Statute:** R.S. 3:3246.

Credential Type: License. **Duration of License:** One year. **Authorization:** All agricultural consultants operating as a business and charging a fee must be licensed. **Requirements:** Must be or must employ a certified agricultural consultant. All field checkers must be registered with the Department. **Fees:** $25 license fee. $25 annual renewal fee. $5 per field scout.]GOV R.S. 3:3246.

319

Horticulturist
Horticulture Commission
PO Box 3118
Baton Rouge, LA 70821
Phone: (504)925-7772

Credential Type: License. **Duration of License:** One year. **Examination:** Written. **Fees:** $35 exam fee. $35 license fee.

320

Plant Breeder
Dept. of Agriculture
Seed Commission
Director of Seed Program
PO Box 18190-B
Baton Rouge, LA 70893
Phone: (504)342-5809

Credential Type: Certification. **Duration of License:** Indefinite. **Requirements:** Meet one of the following sets of requirements: (1) An advanced degree with plant breeding as a major; (2) An advanced degree in agronomy or horticulture with one year of experience assisting as a plant breeder; (3) Bachelor's degree in agronomy or horticulture with at least one course in plant breeding, and two years of experience; (4) Bachelor's degree in general agriculture and two years of experience. **Fees:** None.

Maine

321

Soil Scientist
Board of Certification for Geologists and Soil Scientists
Dept. of Professional and Financial Regulation
State House Station 35
Augusta, ME 04333
Phone: (207)582-8723

Credential Type: Soil Scientist Certification. **Duration of License:** Two years. **Requirements:** Graduate from an approved four-year college curriculum leading to a Baccalaureate Degree, in which applicant has completed a minimum of 15 credit hours of soil or soil-related courses of a pedological nature. Have three years or more experience in soil science. Summer employment and teaching pedological courses in a college or university may be counted toward the experience requirement. Each degree beyond the Bachelor's Degree is counted as one year of experience. **Examination:** Yes. **Fees:** $20 exam fee. $45 certification fee. $45 renewal fee. **Governing Statute:** 32 M.S.R.A., Chap. 73.

Michigan

322

Breeder, Wild Animals and Birds
Wildlife Div.
Dept. of Natural Resources
Stevens T. Mason Bldg.
PO Box 30028
Lansing, MI 48909
Phone: (517)373-1220

Credential Type: License. **Duration of License:** Three years. **Requirements:** Have obtained wildlife in a lawful manner, as evidenced by a receipted invoice or other document. Provide humane and sanitary conditions for wildlife. Provide pens, cages, or enclosures of sufficient size to prevent the crowding of wildlife. Provide wildlife with food and water. Submit pens and wildlife to an inspection by a conservation officer. Comply with the Game Breeder's Law and the rules of the Department of Natural Resources. **Fees:** $45 minimum—$150 maximum initial license fee (which is based either on the size of the area or on the number of animals enclosed). Same renewal fee as initial fee. **Governing Statute:** The Game Breeders Law, Act 191 of 1929, as amended.

323

Plant Grower
Pesticide and Plant Pest Management Div.
Dept. of Agriculture
Ottawa Bldg., N.
PO Box 30017
Lansing, MI 48909
Phone: (517)373-1104

Credential Type: License. **Duration of License:** One year. **Requirements:** Receive a valid certificate of inspection each growing season. Abide by the rules of the Department of Agriculture. **Fees:** $20 initial license fee. $20 renewal fee. Nonresident plant growers are required to pay a $20 license fee. **Governing Statute:** Insect

Pests and Plant Diseases Act, Act 189 of 1931, as amended.

Mississippi

324

Landscape Horticulturist
Dept. of Agriculture and Commerce
Div. of Plant Industry
PO Box 5207
Mississippi State, MS 39762
Phone: (601)325-3390

Credential Type: Horticulturist License. **Duration of License:** Indefinite. **Requirements:** Meet one of the following sets of requirements: (1) Graduate from a college or university with at least 15 semester hours or the equivalent in the field for which a license is requested. (2) Have at least two years of college or university training, with special training in the field for which a license is requested. (3) Be a high school graduate or equivalent and have at least one year of experience with a licensed horticulturist within the past two years. (4) If applicant is not a high school graduate, must have completed at least two years of experience with a licensed horticulturist within the past three years.

Renewal requires attending an approved training course every three years. **Examination:** Written examination in landscape gardening. **Reciprocity:** Exam may be waived if applicant is licensed in a state with standards equal to those of Mississippi and that state will honor the Mississippi Examination.

New Hampshire

325

Soil Scientist
Joint Board of Architects, Engineers, Land Surveyors, and Natural Scientists
57 Regional Drive
Concord, NH 03301
Phone: (603)271-2219

Credential Type: Soil Scientist Certificate. **Duration of License:** Two years. **Requirements:** Graduate of a four-year college curriculum with one of the following: (1) 30 semester hours of physical, biological, and earth science which includes 15 semester hours in soil science and three or more years of experience in the practice of soil science; (2) 15 semester hours in soil science and four or more years of experience in the practice of soil science; (3) six or more years of experience in the practice of soil science. Experience may include teaching, summer employment, apprentice programs, or advanced degree. Renewal requires 10 continuing education hours every two years. **Examination:** Examination as required by Board. **Reciprocity:** Yes. **Fees:** $70 resident certificate without exam. $170 non-resident certificate without exam. $70 certificate by reciprocity. $220 resident certificate upon exam. $320 non-resident certificate upon exam. $100 biennial renewal. $35 apprentice certificate. $5 replacement certificate.

North Dakota

326

Soil Classifier
State Board of Registration for Professional Soil Classifiers
1141 W. 12th Ave.
Dickinson, ND 58601
Phone: (701)225-5113

Credential Type: Professional Soil Classifier-in-Training Certification. **Duration of License:** Four years. **Requirements:** Graduate of an approved soils curriculum; or if a graduate from an unapproved curriculum, have at least four years experience in soil classification. **Examination:** Fundamentals of Soil Classification. **Fees:** $25 exam fee.

Credential Type: Professional Soil Classifier Registration. **Duration of License:** One year. **Requirements:** Be certified as a Professional Soil Classifier-in-Training. Pass a field examination. Submit five letters of reference, three of which must be from Registered Professional Soil Classifiers. In addition, meet one of the following requirements: (1) Have four years work experience if a graduate of an approved soils curriculum. (2) Have eight years work experience if a graduate of a non-approved soils curriculum. (3) Have four years of teaching and/or research in the classification field and two years of additional experience. **Examination:** Field examination. **Fees:** $100 exam fee. $10 annual license fee (non-practicing). $90 aannual license fee (practicing).

South Carolina

327

Professional Soil Classifier
Board of Registration for Professional Soil Classifiers
2221 Devine St., Ste. 222
Columbia, SC 29205
Phone: (803)734-9100

Credential Type: Soil Classifier Registration. **Requirements:** Contact licensing body for application information. **Examination:** Yes. **Fees:** $5 application fee. $15 license fee.

Credential Type: Soil Classifier-in-training Registration. **Requirements:** Contact licensing body for application information. **Examination:** Yes. **Fees:** $5 application fee. $15 license fee.

Virginia

328

Soil Scientist
Board of Profesional Soil Scientists
Dept. of Commerce
3600 W. Broad St.
Richmond, VA 23230
Phone: (804)367-2194

Credential Type: License. **Requirements:** A bachelor's degree in the natural sciences. Must have four to five years of experience in soil evaluation. A total of eight years of experience may be substituted for the bachelor's degree. **Examination:** Yes. **Fees:** $75 examination fee.

Air Traffic Controllers

Occupations in this chapter require federal licenses.

Federal Contacts

Federal Aviation Administration
800 Independence Ave., SW
Washington, DC 20591
Phone: (202)267-3484

Alabama

FAA FSDO-9
Municipal Airport, FSS-WB Bldg.
6500 43rd Ave., N.
N. Birmingham, AL 35206

Alaska

FAA Flight Standards AAL-200
222 W. 7th St.
Anchorage, AK 99513

FAA FSDO-03
4510 W. International Airport Rd., Ste. 302
Anchorage, AK 99502

FAA FSDO-01
6348 Old Airport Way
Fairbanks, AK 99709

FAA-FSDO-05
1910 Alex Holden Way, Ste. A
Juneau, AK 99801

Arizona

FAA AWP FSDO-19
Sky Harbor International Airport
4122 E. Airlane Dr.
Phoenix, AZ 85034

FAA FSDO-7
15041 N. Airport Dr.
Scottsdale, AZ 85260

Arkansas

FAA FSDO-11
1701 Bond St.
Little Rock, AR 72202-5733

California

FSDO
Bldg. B, Rm. 105
831 Mitten Rd.
Burlingame, CA 94010-1303

FAA FSDO-4
Fresno Air Terminal
4955 E. Anderson, Ste. 110
Fresno, CA 93727

FAA FSDO-5
2815 E. Spring St.
Long Beach, CA 90806-2485

FAA AWP-200/Western Pacific Region
PO Box 92007
Worldway Postal Center
Los Angeles, CA 90009-2007

FSDO-10
5885 W. Imperial Way
Los Angeles, CA 90045

FAA OAK FSDO-14
PO Box 2397
Airport Station
Oakland, CA 94614

FAA FSDO-8
6961 Flight Rd.
Riverside Municipal Airport
Riverside, CA 92504

FAA FSDO-12
6650 Belleau Wood Ln.
Sacramento Executive Airport
Sacramento, CA 95822

FAA FSDO-9
8525 Gibbs Dr., Ste. 120
San Diego, CA 92123

FAA FSDO-2
1250 Aviation Ave., Ste. 295
San Jose, CA 95110-1119

FAA FSDO-1
Skylane Bldg., Ste. 330
16501 Sherman Way
Van Nuys, CA 91406

Colorado

FAA Denver FSDO-3
5440 Roslyn St., Ste. 201, Rm. 202
Denver, CO 80216

Connecticut

FAA FSDO-3
Bldg. 85-214, 1st Fl.
Bradley International Airport
Windsor Locks, CT 06096

District of Columbia

FAA
PO Box 17325
Washington Dulles Airport
Washington, DC 20041-0325

Florida

ASO FSDO-15
Terminal Bldg. W. Wing
St. Petersburg-Clearwater Airport
Clearwater, FL 34622

FAA FSDO-17
286 SW 34th St.
Ft. Lauderdale-Hollywood International Airport
Ft. Lauderdale, FL 33315

FSDO
FAA Bldg., Craig Field
855 St. John's Bluff Rd.
Jacksonville, FL 32211

ASO FSDO-19
PO Box 592015
Miami, FL 33159

FAA FSDO-15
9677 Tradeport Dr., Ste. 100
International Airport
Orlando, FL 32827-5397

Georgia

FAA Southern Region, ASO-200
PO Box 20636
Atlanta, GA 30320

FAA Mid-South FSDO-11
1680 Phoenix Pky., 2nd Fl.
College Park, GA 30349

Air Traffic Controllers — Federal Contacts

Hawaii
FAA
90 Nakola Pl., Rm. 215
Honolulu, HI 96819

Idaho
FAA Boise FSDO-8
Boise Airport
3975 Rickenbacker St.
Boise, ID 83705

Illinois
FAA AGL-200
Great Lakes Region
2300 E. Devon Ave.
Des Plaines, IL 60018

AGL FSDO-31
O'Hare Aerospace Center
9950 W. Lawrence Ave., Ste. 400
Shiller Park, IL 60176

FSDO-19
No. 3 N. Airport Dr.
Capital Airport
Springfield, IL 62708

FAA FSDO-3
31W775 N. Ave.
DuPage County Airport
W. Chicago, IL 60185-1056

Indiana
FAA FSDO-11
6801 Pierson Dr.
International Airport
Indianapolis, IN 46241

FSDO-17
Michiana Regional Airport
1843 Commerce Dr.
South Bend, IN 46628

Iowa
FAA FSDO-1
3021 Army Post Rd.
Des Moines, IA 50321

Kansas
FAA FSDO-7
FAA Bldg., Rm. 103
1801 Airport Rd.
Mid-Continent Airport
Wichita, KS 67209

Kentucky
FAA FSDO-1
Bowman Field
Kaden Bldg., 5th Fl.
6100 Dutchman's Ln.
Louisville, KY 40205

Louisiana
FAA FSDO-03
FAA Bldg.
9191 Plank Rd.
Ryan Airport
Baton Rouge, LA 70811

Maine
FAA FSDO-5
2 Al McKay Ave.
Portland International Airport
Portland, ME 04102

Maryland
Baltimore FSDO-7
PO Box 8747
Baltimore-Washington International
Baltimore, MD 21240-8747

Massachusetts
FAA FSDO-1
L.G. Hanscom Field
Civil Air Terminal, 2nd Fl.
Bedford, MA 01730

FAA ANE FSDO-02
Logan International Airport
1 Massachusetts Tech Center
Boston, MA 02128

FAA ANE-200
New England Region
12 New England Executive Park
Burlington, MA 01803-5299

Michigan
FAA FSDO-23
Willow Run Airport
8800 Beck Rd. - East Side
Belleville, MI 48111

FAA FSDO-9
PO Box 888879
Grand Rapids, MI 49588-8879

Minnesota
FAA AGL CMO-01
6020 28th Ave., Rm. 202
Minneapolis, MN 55450

FSDO-15
6020 28th Ave., S., Rm. 201
Minneapolis-St. Paul International Airport
Minneapolis, MN 55450

Mississippi
FAA FSDO-7
FAA Bldg, Ste. C
120 N. Hangar Dr.
Jackson Municipal Airport
Jackson, MS 39208

Missouri
FAA ACE-200
Federal Bldg., Rm. 1664
601 E. 12th St.
Kansas City, MO 64106

FAA FSDO-5
525 Mexico City Ave.
Kansas City International Airport
Kansas City, MO 64153

FAA Building, FSDO-3
10801 Pear Tree Ln., Ste. 200
St. Ann, MO 63074

Montana
FAA Helena FSDO-5
FAA Bldg., Rm. 3
Helena Airport
Helena, MT 59601

Nebraska
FAA FSDO-9
General Aviation Bldg.
Municipal Airport
Lincoln, NE 68524

Nevada
FAA FSDO-19
6020 S. Spencer Ave., Ste. A7
Las Vegas, NV 89119

FAA FSDO-11
601 S. Rock Blvd., Ste. 102
Reno, NV 89502

New Jersey
FAA Teterboro FSDO-25
150 Fred Wehran Dr., Rm. 5
Teterboro Airport
Teterboro, NJ 07608

New Mexico
FAA FSDO-01
1601 Randolph Rd., SE, Ste. 200 N.
ABQ International Airport
Albuquerque, NM 87106

New York
FAA Albany FSDO-1
CFR & M Bldg.
Albany County Airport
Albany, NY 12211

FAA Farmingdale FSDO-11
Admin. Bldg., Ste. 235
Republic Airport
Route 110
Farmingdale, NY 11735

FAA Eastern Region, AEA-200
Fitzgerald Federal Bldg., Rm. 229
JFK International Airport
Jamaica, NY 11430

Rochester FSDO-23
1 Airport Way, Ste. 110
Greater International Airport
Rochester, NY 14624

AEA FSDO-15
181 S. Franklin Ave., 4th Fl.
Valley Stream, NY 11581

North Carolina
ASO FSDO-8
FAA Bldg.
5318 Morris Field Dr.
Municipal Airport
Charlotte, NC 28208

FAA FSDO-6
2000 Aerial Center Pky., Ste. 120
Morrisville, NC 27623-0428

Federal Aviation Administration, continued

FSDO-5
8025 N. Point Blvd., Rm. 250
Smith Reynold Airport
Winston-Salem, NC 27106

North Dakota

FAA FSDO-21
PO Box 5496
Fargo, ND 58105

Ohio

FAA FSDO-05
Executive Bldg., Ground Fl.
4242 Airport Rd.
Lunken Airport
Cincinatti, OH 45226

FAA FSDO-25
Federal Facilities Bldg.
Cleveland Hopkins International Airport
Cleveland, OH 44135

FAA FSDO-07
4393 International Gateway, 2nd Fl.
Port Columbus International Airport
Columbus, OH 43219-1798

Oklahoma

FAA FSDO-15
1300 S. Meridan, Ste. 601
Oklahoma City, OK 73108

Oregon

FAA Portland FSDO-9
3355 NE Cornell Rd.
Portland-Hillsboro Airport
Hillsboro, OR 97124

Pennsylvania

Allentown FSDO-5
RAS Aviation Center Bldg.
Allentown-Bethlehem Easton Airport
Allentown, PA 18103

AEA FSDO-19
One Thorn Run Center, Ste. 200
1187 Thorn Run Extension
Corapolis, PA 15108

FAA Harrisburg FSDO-13
Admin. Bldg., Rm. 201
Capitol City Airport
New Cumberland, PA 17070

FAA Philadelphia FSDO-17
Scott Plaza 2, 2nd Fl.
Philadelphia, PA 19113

Pittsburgh FSDO-3
Terminal Bldg., Rm. 213
Allegheny County Airport
West Mifflin, PA 15122

Puerto Rico

FAA/FSDO-21
Luis Munoz Marin International Airport,
 Rm. 203-A
San Juan, PR 00913

South Carolina

FAA FSDO-13
2819 Aviation Way
Columbia Metro Airport
West Columbia, SC 29169

South Dakota

FAA FSDO-27
Rural Rt. 2, Box 4750
Rapid City, SD 57701

Tennessee

FAA FSDO-03
2285 Airways Blvd., Ste. 115
Memphis, TN 38116

FAA FSDO-3
No. 2 International Plaza Dr., Ste. 700
Nashville, TN 37217

Texas

FAA FSDO-05
7701 N. Stemmons Fwy., Ste. 300
Lockbox 5
Dallas, TX 75247

FSDO
PO Box 619020
Dallas, TX 75261

FAA ASW FSDO-19
2260 Alliance Blvd.
Fort Worth Allian Airport
Fort Worth, TX 76177

FAA Southwest Region, ASW-200
Flight Standards Division
Fort Worth, TX 76193

FAA FSDO-09
8800 Paul B. Koonce Dr., Rm. 152
Hobby Airport
Houston, TX 77061

FAA FSDO-13
S. End Old Terminal Bldg.
Lubbock International Airport
Rte. 3, Box 51
Lubbock, TX 79401

FAA FSDO-17
10100 Reunion Pl., Ste. 200
International Airport
San Antonio, TX 78216

Utah

FAA Salt Lake City FSDO-7
116 N. 2400 W.
Salt Lake City, UT 84116

Virginia

FAA-AEA-FSDO-21
Terminal Bldg., 2nd Fl.
Richmond International Airport
Sandston, VA 23150-2594

Washington

FAA ANM-200
Northwest Mountain Region
1601 Lind Ave., SW
Renton, WA 98055-4056

FAA Seattle FSDO-1
1601 Lind Ave., SW
Renton, WA 98055-4056

West Virginia

Charleston FSDO-9
301 Eagle Mountain, Rm. 144
Yeager Airport
Charleston, WV 25311

Wisconsin

FAA FSDO-13
4915 S. Howell Ave., 4th Fl.
Milwaukee, WI 53207

Wyoming

FAA Casper FSDO-60A
Terminal Bldg., 2nd Fl.
Natrona County International Airport
Casper, WY 82604

Federal Licenses

329

Air-Traffic Control-Tower Operator

Credential Type: Air-Traffic Control-Tower Operator Certificate. **Authorization:** Facility rating required for an air-traffic control-tower operator at an air-traffic control tower in connection with civil aircraft. Senior rating may perform similar duties only under the supervision of a holder of a facility rating. Individual with a junior rating must be under the supervision of a holder of either a facility rating or a senior rating. **Requirements:** 18 years old. Good moral character. Read, speak, and understand English. Pass medical examination. For a facility rating, must have served at least six months at that facility with no facility rating, or at another facility for at least six months with a facility rating. Pass written and practical tests.

For a senior rating, must pass written and practical tests. For a junior rating, must pass a written test. **Examination:** Written and practical tests. **Governing Statute:** Federal Aviation Regulations, 14 CFR Ch. 1, part 65.

330

Aircraft Dispatcher

Credential Type: Aircraft Dispatcher Certificate. **Requirements:** 23 years old. Read, speak, and understand English. For two of the previous three years, must have experience in scheduled aircraft operations, air traffic control, or equivalent; or for one of the two previous years have experience as an assistant in dispatching scheduled aircraft performing the duties of an aircraft dispatcher under the direct supervision of a certified dispatcher; or a combination of the above experience totalling at least two years; or within 90 days prior to application complete an FAA-approved course of instruction. **Examination:** Written and practical tests. **Governing Statute:** Federal Aviation Regulations, 14 CFR Ch. 1, part 65.

Aircraft Mechanics, Engine Specialists, and Parachute Riggers

Occupations in this chapter require federal licenses.

Federal Contacts

Federal Aviation Administration
800 Independence Ave., SW
Washington, DC 20591
Phone: (202)267-3484

Alabama

FAA FSDO-9
Municipal Airport, FSS-WB Bldg.
6500 43rd Ave., N.
N. Birmingham, AL 35206

Alaska

FAA Flight Standards AAL-200
222 W. 7th St.
Anchorage, AK 99513

FAA FSDO-03
4510 W. International Airport Rd., Ste. 302
Anchorage, AK 99502

FAA FSDO-01
6348 Old Airport Way
Fairbanks, AK 99709

FAA-FSDO-05
1910 Alex Holden Way, Ste. A
Juneau, AK 99801

Arizona

FAA AWP FSDO-19
Sky Harbor International Airport
4122 E. Airlane Dr.
Phoenix, AZ 85034

FAA FSDO-7
15041 N. Airport Dr.
Scottsdale, AZ 85260

Arkansas

FAA FSDO-11
1701 Bond St.
Little Rock, AR 72202-5733

California

FSDO
Bldg. B, Rm. 105
831 Mitten Rd.
Burlingame, CA 94010-1303

FAA FSDO-4
Fresno Air Terminal
4955 E. Anderson, Ste. 110
Fresno, CA 93727

FAA FSDO-5
2815 E. Spring St.
Long Beach, CA 90806-2485

FAA AWP-200/Western Pacific Region
PO Box 92007
Worldway Postal Center
Los Angeles, CA 90009-2007

FSDO-10
5885 W. Imperial Way
Los Angeles, CA 90045

FAA OAK FSDO-14
PO Box 2397
Airport Station
Oakland, CA 94614

FAA FSDO-8
6961 Flight Rd.
Riverside Municipal Airport
Riverside, CA 92504

FAA FSDO-12
6650 Belleau Wood Ln.
Sacramento Executive Airport
Sacramento, CA 95822

FAA FSDO-9
8525 Gibbs Dr., Ste. 120
San Diego, CA 92123

FAA FSDO-2
1250 Aviation Ave., Ste. 295
San Jose, CA 95110-1119

FAA FSDO-1
Skylane Bldg., Ste. 330
16501 Sherman Way
Van Nuys, CA 91406

Colorado

FAA Denver FSDO-3
5440 Roslyn St., Ste. 201, Rm. 202
Denver, CO 80216

Connecticut

FAA FSDO-3
Bldg. 85-214, 1st Fl.
Bradley International Airport
Windsor Locks, CT 06096

District of Columbia

FAA
PO Box 17325
Washington Dulles Airport
Washington, DC 20041-0325

Florida

ASO FSDO-15
Terminal Bldg. W. Wing
St. Petersburg-Clearwater Airport
Clearwater, FL 34622

FAA FSDO-17
286 SW 34th St.
Ft. Lauderdale-Hollywood International Airport
Ft. Lauderdale, FL 33315

FSDO
FAA Bldg., Craig Field
855 St. John's Bluff Rd.
Jacksonville, FL 32211

ASO FSDO-19
PO Box 592015
Miami, FL 33159

FAA FSDO-15
9677 Tradeport Dr., Ste. 100
International Airport
Orlando, FL 32827-5397

Georgia

FAA Southern Region, ASO-200
PO Box 20636
Atlanta, GA 30320

FAA Mid-South FSDO-11
1680 Phoenix Pky., 2nd Fl.
College Park, GA 30349

Hawaii

FAA
90 Nakola Pl., Rm. 215
Honolulu, HI 96819

Idaho

FAA Boise FSDO-8
Boise Airport
3975 Rickenbacker St.
Boise, ID 83705

Illinois

FAA AGL-200
Great Lakes Region
2300 E. Devon Ave.
Des Plaines, IL 60018

AGL FSDO-31
O'Hare Aerospace Center
9950 W. Lawrence Ave., Ste. 400
Shiller Park, IL 60176

FSDO-19
No. 3 N. Airport Dr.
Capital Airport
Springfield, IL 62708

FAA FSDO-3
31W775 N. Ave.
DuPage County Airport
W. Chicago, IL 60185-1056

Indiana

FAA FSDO-11
6801 Pierson Dr.
International Airport
Indianapolis, IN 46241

FSDO-17
Michiana Regional Airport
1843 Commerce Dr.
South Bend, IN 46628

Iowa

FAA FSDO-1
3021 Army Post Rd.
Des Moines, IA 50321

Kansas

FAA FSDO-7
FAA Bldg., Rm. 103
1801 Airport Rd.
Mid-Continent Airport
Wichita, KS 67209

Kentucky

FAA FSDO-1
Bowman Field
Kaden Bldg., 5th Fl.
6100 Dutchman's Ln.
Louisville, KY 40205

Louisiana

FAA FSDO-03
FAA Bldg.
9191 Plank Rd.
Ryan Airport
Baton Rouge, LA 70811

Maine

FAA FSDO-5
2 Al McKay Ave.
Portland International Airport
Portland, ME 04102

Maryland

Baltimore FSDO-7
PO Box 8747
Baltimore-Washington International
Baltimore, MD 21240-8747

Massachusetts

FAA FSDO-1
L.G. Hanscom Field
Civil Air Terminal, 2nd Fl.
Bedford, MA 01730

FAA ANE FSDO-02
Logan International Airport
1 Massachusetts Tech Center
Boston, MA 02128

FAA ANE-200
New England Region
12 New England Executive Park
Burlington, MA 01803-5299

Michigan

FAA FSDO-23
Willow Run Airport
8800 Beck Rd. - East Side
Belleville, MI 48111

FAA FSDO-9
PO Box 888879
Grand Rapids, MI 49588-8879

Minnesota

FAA AGL CMO-01
6020 28th Ave., Rm. 202
Minneapolis, MN 55450

FSDO-15
6020 28th Ave., S., Rm. 201
Minneapolis-St. Paul International Airport
Minneapolis, MN 55450

Mississippi

FAA FSDO-7
FAA Bldg, Ste. C
120 N. Hangar Dr.
Jackson Municipal Airport
Jackson, MS 39208

Missouri

FAA ACE-200
Federal Bldg., Rm. 1664
601 E. 12th St.
Kansas City, MO 64106

FAA FSDO-5
525 Mexico City Ave.
Kansas City International Airport
Kansas City, MO 64153

FAA Building, FSDO-3
10801 Pear Tree Ln., Ste. 200
St. Ann, MO 63074

Montana

FAA Helena FSDO-5
FAA Bldg., Rm. 3
Helena Airport
Helena, MT 59601

Nebraska

FAA FSDO-9
General Aviation Bldg.
Municipal Airport
Lincoln, NE 68524

Nevada

FAA FSDO-19
6020 S. Spencer Ave., Ste. A7
Las Vegas, NV 89119

FAA FSDO-11
601 S. Rock Blvd., Ste. 102
Reno, NV 89502

New Jersey

FAA Teterboro FSDO-25
150 Fred Wehran Dr., Rm. 5
Teterboro Airport
Teterboro, NJ 07608

New Mexico

FAA FSDO-01
1601 Randolph Rd., SE, Ste. 200 N.
ABQ International Airport
Albuquerque, NM 87106

New York

FAA Albany FSDO-1
CFR & M Bldg.
Albany County Airport
Albany, NY 12211

FAA Farmingdale FSDO-11
Admin. Bldg., Ste. 235
Republic Airport
Route 110
Farmingdale, NY 11735

FAA Eastern Region, AEA-200
Fitzgerald Federal Bldg., Rm. 229
JFK International Airport
Jamaica, NY 11430

Rochester FSDO-23
1 Airport Way, Ste. 110
Greater International Airport
Rochester, NY 14624

AEA FSDO-15
181 S. Franklin Ave., 4th Fl.
Valley Stream, NY 11581

North Carolina

ASO FSDO-8
FAA Bldg.
5318 Morris Field Dr.
Municipal Airport
Charlotte, NC 28208

FAA FSDO-6
2000 Aerial Center Pky., Ste. 120
Morrisville, NC 27623-0428

Federal Aviation Administration, continued

FSDO-5
8025 N. Point Blvd., Rm. 250
Smith Reynold Airport
Winston-Salem, NC 27106

North Dakota

FAA FSDO-21
PO Box 5496
Fargo, ND 58105

Ohio

FAA FSDO-05
Executive Bldg., Ground Fl.
4242 Airport Rd.
Lunken Airport
Cincinatti, OH 45226

FAA FSDO-25
Federal Facilities Bldg.
Cleveland Hopkins International Airport
Cleveland, OH 44135

FAA FSDO-07
4393 International Gateway, 2nd Fl.
Port Columbus International Airport
Columbus, OH 43219-1798

Oklahoma

FAA FSDO-15
1300 S. Meridan, Ste. 601
Oklahoma City, OK 73108

Oregon

FAA Portland FSDO-9
3355 NE Cornell Rd.
Portland-Hillsboro Airport
Hillsboro, OR 97124

Pennsylvania

Allentown FSDO-5
RAS Aviation Center Bldg.
Allentown-Bethlehem Easton Airport
Allentown, PA 18103

AEA FSDO-19
One Thorn Run Center, Ste. 200
1187 Thorn Run Extension
Corapolis, PA 15108

FAA Harrisburg FSDO-13
Admin. Bldg., Rm. 201
Capitol City Airport
New Cumberland, PA 17070

FAA Philadelphia FSDO-17
Scott Plaza 2, 2nd Fl.
Philadelphia, PA 19113

Pittsburgh FSDO-3
Terminal Bldg., Rm. 213
Allegheny County Airport
West Mifflin, PA 15122

Puerto Rico

FAA/FSDO-21
Luis Munoz Marin International Airport,
Rm. 203-A
San Juan, PR 00913

South Carolina

FAA FSDO-13
2819 Aviation Way
Columbia Metro Airport
West Columbia, SC 29169

South Dakota

FAA FSDO-27
Rural Rt. 2, Box 4750
Rapid City, SD 57701

Tennessee

FAA FSDO-03
2285 Airways Blvd., Ste. 115
Memphis, TN 38116

FAA FSDO-3
No. 2 International Plaza Dr., Ste. 700
Nashville, TN 37217

Texas

FAA FSDO-05
7701 N. Stemmons Fwy., Ste. 300
Lockbox 5
Dallas, TX 75247

FSDO
PO Box 619020
Dallas, TX 75261

FAA ASW FSDO-19
2260 Alliance Blvd.
Fort Worth Allian Airport
Fort Worth, TX 76177

FAA Southwest Region, ASW-200
Flight Standards Division
Fort Worth, TX 76193

FAA FSDO-09
8800 Paul B. Koonce Dr., Rm. 152
Hobby Airport
Houston, TX 77061

FAA FSDO-13
S. End Old Terminal Bldg.
Lubbock International Airport
Rte. 3, Box 51
Lubbock, TX 79401

FAA FSDO-17
10100 Reunion Pl., Ste. 200
International Airport
San Antonio, TX 78216

Utah

FAA Salt Lake City FSDO-7
116 N. 2400 W.
Salt Lake City, UT 84116

Virginia

FAA-AEA-FSDO-21
Terminal Bldg., 2nd Fl.
Richmond International Airport
Sandston, VA 23150-2594

Washington

FAA ANM-200
Northwest Mountain Region
1601 Lind Ave., SW
Renton, WA 98055-4056

FAA Seattle FSDO-1
1601 Lind Ave., SW
Renton, WA 98055-4056

West Virginia

Charleston FSDO-9
301 Eagle Mountain, Rm. 144
Yeager Airport
Charleston, WV 25311

Wisconsin

FAA FSDO-13
4915 S. Howell Ave., 4th Fl.
Milwaukee, WI 53207

Wyoming

FAA Casper FSDO-60A
Terminal Bldg., 2nd Fl.
Natrona County International Airport
Casper, WY 82604

Federal Licenses

331

Aircraft Mechanic

Credential Type: Aircraft Mechanic Certificate. **Requirements:** 18 years old. Read, speak, and understand English. Pass appropriate tests within 24 months of application for certificate. Two ratings are available: Airframe and Powerplant. Applicant must pass written and practical-oral tests appropriate to the rating(s) sought.

Must complete a course from a certified aviation maintenance technician school; or have at least 18 months practical experience appropriate to the rating(s) sought; or have at least 30 months practical experience concurrently performing duties of both Airframe and Powerplant ratings. **Examination:** Written and practical-oral tests. **Governing Statute:** Federal Aviation Regulations, 14 CFR Ch. 1, part 65, subpart D.

Credential Type: Inspection Authorization. **Duration of License:** One year. **Requirements:** Must hold a current aircraft mechanic certificate with both Airframe and Powerplant ratings. Must have been actively engaged for two years in maintaining aircraft. Must have a fixed base of operations and have equipment, facilities, and inspection data available to perform inspection of airframes, powerplants, propellors, or related parts or appliances.

Renewal of inspection authorization requires passing a refresher course of at least eight hours. Pass an oral test. Perform at least one annual inspection for each 90 days, or an inspection of at least two major repairs for each 90 days, or one progressive inspection. **Examination:** Written test on ability to inspect. **Governing Statute:** Fed-

332

Aircraft Repairer

Credential Type: Aircraft Repairman Certificate. **Authorization:** May perform or supervise maintenance or alteration of aircraft and aircraft components only in connection with duties related to employment. **Requirements:** 18 years old. Read, speak, and understand English. Be specially qualified to perform maintenance on an aircraft. Be employed for a specific job requiring these special qualifications by a certificated repair station or commercial operator. Be recommended for certification by employer.

Have 18 months of practical experience in aircraft maintenance duties, or complete appropriate and approved formal training. **Governing Statute:** Federal Aviation Regulations, 14 CFR Ch. 1, part 65, subpart E.

Credential Type: Aircraft Repairman Certificate, Experimental Aircraft Builder. **Requirements:** 18 years old. Be the primary builder of the aircraft to which the privileges of the certificate are applicable. Have the requisite skill to determine whether the aircraft is in a condition for safe operations. Be a citizen of the United States, or a foreign citizen who has lawfully been admitted for permanent residence in the United States. **Governing Statute:** Federal Aviation Regulations, 14 CFR Ch. 1, part 65, subpart E.

333

Parachute Rigger

Credential Type: Senior Parachute Rigger Certificate. **Authorization:** Certificate required to pack, maintain, or alter any personnel-carrying parachute intended for emergency use in connection with civil aircraft of the United States. Also required to pack, maintain, or alter any main parachute of a dual parachute pack to be used for intentional jumping in connection with civil aircraft of the United States. **Requirements:** 18 years old. Read, speak, and understand English, unless employed in Puerto Rico or outside the United States by a U.S. air carrier. Have packed at least 20 parachutes of each type for which a rating is sought. Separate ratings are given for seat, back, chest, and lap parachutes. **Examination:** Written test. Practical-oral test. **Exemptions:** Active military riggers or those discharged within the past 12 months do not need to take the practical-oral test, if they have the requisite experience. **Governing Statute:** Federal Aviation Regulations, 14 CFR Ch. 1, part 65, subpart F.

Credential Type: Master Parachute Rigger Certificate. **Authorization:** Certificate required to pack, maintain, or alter any personnel-carrying parachute intended for emergency use in connection with civil aircraft of the United States. Also required to pack, maintain, or alter any main parachute of a dual parachute pack to be used for intentional jumping in connection with civil aircraft of the United States. **Requirements:** 18 years old. Read, speak, and understand English, unless employed in Puerto Rico or outside the United States by a U.S. air carrier. Have at least three years experience as a parachute rigger and have packed at least 100 parachutes of each of two types in common use while a certificated senior parachute rigger or while under the supervision of a certificated senior parachute rigger. Separate ratings are given for seat, back, chest, and lap parachutes. **Examination:** Written test. Practical-oral test. **Exemptions:** Holders of a senior parachute rigger certificate need not take the written test. **Governing Statute:** Federal Aviation Regulations, 14 CFR Ch. 1, part 65, subpart F.

Aircraft Pilots

One or more occupations in this chapter require a federal license. Additionally, the following states grant licenses as of the date of publication: Arizona, Louisiana, Maryland, Washington.

Federal Contacts

Federal Aviation Administration
800 Independence Ave., SW
Washington, DC 20591
Phone: (202)267-3484

Alabama

FAA FSDO-9
Municipal Airport, FSS-WB Bldg.
6500 43rd Ave., N.
N. Birmingham, AL 35206

Alaska

FAA Flight Standards AAL-200
222 W. 7th St.
Anchorage, AK 99513

FAA FSDO-03
4510 W. International Airport Rd., Ste. 302
Anchorage, AK 99502

FAA FSDO-01
6348 Old Airport Way
Fairbanks, AK 99709

FAA-FSDO-05
1910 Alex Holden Way, Ste. A
Juneau, AK 99801

Arizona

FAA AWP FSDO-19
Sky Harbor International Airport
4122 E. Airlane Dr.
Phoenix, AZ 85034

FAA FSDO-7
15041 N. Airport Dr.
Scottsdale, AZ 85260

Arkansas

FAA FSDO-11
1701 Bond St.
Little Rock, AR 72202-5733

California

FSDO
Bldg. B, Rm. 105
831 Mitten Rd.
Burlingame, CA 94010-1303

FAA FSDO-4
Fresno Air Terminal
4955 E. Anderson, Ste. 110
Fresno, CA 93727

FAA FSDO-5
2815 E. Spring St.
Long Beach, CA 90806-2485

FAA AWP-200/Western Pacific Region
PO Box 92007
Worldway Postal Center
Los Angeles, CA 90009-2007

FSDO-10
5885 W. Imperial Way
Los Angeles, CA 90045

FAA OAK FSDO-14
PO Box 2397
Airport Station
Oakland, CA 94614

FAA FSDO-8
6961 Flight Rd.
Riverside Municipal Airport
Riverside, CA 92504

FAA FSDO-12
6650 Belleau Wood Ln.
Sacramento Executive Airport
Sacramento, CA 95822

FAA FSDO-9
8525 Gibbs Dr., Ste. 120
San Diego, CA 92123

FAA FSDO-2
1250 Aviation Ave., Ste. 295
San Jose, CA 95110-1119

FAA FSDO-1
Skylane Bldg., Ste. 330
16501 Sherman Way
Van Nuys, CA 91406

Colorado

FAA Denver FSDO-3
5440 Roslyn St., Ste. 201, Rm. 202
Denver, CO 80216

Connecticut

FAA FSDO-3
Bldg. 85-214, 1st Fl.
Bradley International Airport
Windsor Locks, CT 06096

District of Columbia

FAA
PO Box 17325
Washington Dulles Airport
Washington, DC 20041-0325

Florida

ASO FSDO-15
Terminal Bldg. W. Wing
St. Petersburg-Clearwater Airport
Clearwater, FL 34622

FAA FSDO-17
286 SW 34th St.
Ft. Lauderdale-Hollywood International Airport
Ft. Lauderdale, FL 33315

FSDO
FAA Bldg., Craig Field
855 St. John's Bluff Rd.
Jacksonville, FL 32211

ASO FSDO-19
PO Box 592015
Miami, FL 33159

FAA FSDO-15
9677 Tradeport Dr., Ste. 100
International Airport
Orlando, FL 32827-5397

Georgia

FAA Southern Region, ASO-200
PO Box 20636
Atlanta, GA 30320

FAA Mid-South FSDO-11
1680 Phoenix Pky., 2nd Fl.
College Park, GA 30349

Aircraft Pilots — Federal Contacts

Hawaii

FAA
90 Nakola Pl., Rm. 215
Honolulu, HI 96819

Idaho

FAA Boise FSDO-8
Boise Airport
3975 Rickenbacker St.
Boise, ID 83705

Illinois

FAA AGL-200
Great Lakes Region
2300 E. Devon Ave.
Des Plaines, IL 60018

AGL FSDO-31
O'Hare Aerospace Center
9950 W. Lawrence Ave., Ste. 400
Shiller Park, IL 60176

FSDO-19
No. 3 N. Airport Dr.
Capital Airport
Springfield, IL 62708

FAA FSDO-3
31W775 N. Ave.
DuPage County Airport
W. Chicago, IL 60185-1056

Indiana

FAA FSDO-11
6801 Pierson Dr.
International Airport
Indianapolis, IN 46241

FSDO-17
Michiana Regional Airport
1843 Commerce Dr.
South Bend, IN 46628

Iowa

FAA FSDO-1
3021 Army Post Rd.
Des Moines, IA 50321

Kansas

FAA FSDO-7
FAA Bldg., Rm. 103
1801 Airport Rd.
Mid-Continent Airport
Wichita, KS 67209

Kentucky

FAA FSDO-1
Bowman Field
Kaden Bldg., 5th Fl.
6100 Dutchman's Ln.
Louisville, KY 40205

Louisiana

FAA FSDO-03
FAA Bldg.
9191 Plank Rd.
Ryan Airport
Baton Rouge, LA 70811

Maine

FAA FSDO-5
2 Al McKay Ave.
Portland International Airport
Portland, ME 04102

Maryland

Baltimore FSDO-7
PO Box 8747
Baltimore-Washington International
Baltimore, MD 21240-8747

Massachusetts

FAA FSDO-1
L.G. Hanscom Field
Civil Air Terminal, 2nd Fl.
Bedford, MA 01730

FAA ANE FSDO-02
Logan International Airport
1 Massachusetts Tech Center
Boston, MA 02128

FAA ANE-200
New England Region
12 New England Executive Park
Burlington, MA 01803-5299

Michigan

FAA FSDO-23
Willow Run Airport
8800 Beck Rd. - East Side
Belleville, MI 48111

FAA FSDO-9
PO Box 888879
Grand Rapids, MI 49588-8879

Minnesota

FAA AGL CMO-01
6020 28th Ave., Rm. 202
Minneapolis, MN 55450

FSDO-15
6020 28th Ave., S., Rm. 201
Minneapolis-St. Paul International Airport
Minneapolis, MN 55450

Mississippi

FAA FSDO-7
FAA Bldg, Ste. C
120 N. Hangar Dr.
Jackson Municipal Airport
Jackson, MS 39208

Missouri

FAA ACE-200
Federal Bldg., Rm. 1664
601 E. 12th St.
Kansas City, MO 64106

FAA FSDO-5
525 Mexico City Ave.
Kansas City International Airport
Kansas City, MO 64153

FAA Building, FSDO-3
10801 Pear Tree Ln., Ste. 200
St. Ann, MO 63074

Montana

FAA Helena FSDO-5
FAA Bldg., Rm. 3
Helena Airport
Helena, MT 59601

Nebraska

FAA FSDO-9
General Aviation Bldg.
Municipal Airport
Lincoln, NE 68524

Nevada

FAA FSDO-19
6020 S. Spencer Ave., Ste. A7
Las Vegas, NV 89119

FAA FSDO-11
601 S. Rock Blvd., Ste. 102
Reno, NV 89502

New Jersey

FAA Teterboro FSDO-25
150 Fred Wehran Dr., Rm. 5
Teterboro Airport
Teterboro, NJ 07608

New Mexico

FAA FSDO-01
1601 Randolph Rd., SE, Ste. 200 N.
ABQ International Airport
Albuquerque, NM 87106

New York

FAA Albany FSDO-1
CFR & M Bldg.
Albany County Airport
Albany, NY 12211

FAA Farmingdale FSDO-11
Admin. Bldg., Ste. 235
Republic Airport
Route 110
Farmingdale, NY 11735

FAA Eastern Region, AEA-200
Fitzgerald Federal Bldg., Rm. 229
JFK International Airport
Jamaica, NY 11430

Rochester FSDO-23
1 Airport Way, Ste. 110
Greater International Airport
Rochester, NY 14624

AEA FSDO-15
181 S. Franklin Ave., 4th Fl.
Valley Stream, NY 11581

North Carolina

ASO FSDO-8
FAA Bldg.
5318 Morris Field Dr.
Municipal Airport
Charlotte, NC 28208

FAA FSDO-6
2000 Aerial Center Pky., Ste. 120
Morrisville, NC 27623-0428

Federal Aviation Administration, continued

FSDO-5
8025 N. Point Blvd., Rm. 250
Smith Reynold Airport
Winston-Salem, NC 27106

North Dakota

FAA FSDO-21
PO Box 5496
Fargo, ND 58105

Ohio

FAA FSDO-05
Executive Bldg., Ground Fl.
4242 Airport Rd.
Lunken Airport
Cincinatti, OH 45226

FAA FSDO-25
Federal Facilities Bldg.
Cleveland Hopkins International Airport
Cleveland, OH 44135

FAA FSDO-07
4393 International Gateway, 2nd Fl.
Port Columbus International Airport
Columbus, OH 43219-1798

Oklahoma

FAA FSDO-15
1300 S. Meridan, Ste. 601
Oklahoma City, OK 73108

Oregon

FAA Portland FSDO-9
3355 NE Cornell Rd.
Portland-Hillsboro Airport
Hillsboro, OR 97124

Pennsylvania

Allentown FSDO-5
RAS Aviation Center Bldg.
Allentown-Bethlehem Easton Airport
Allentown, PA 18103

AEA FSDO-19
One Thorn Run Center, Ste. 200
1187 Thorn Run Extension
Corapolis, PA 15108

FAA Harrisburg FSDO-13
Admin. Bldg., Rm. 201
Capitol City Airport
New Cumberland, PA 17070

FAA Philadelphia FSDO-17
Scott Plaza 2, 2nd Fl.
Philadelphia, PA 19113

Pittsburgh FSDO-3
Terminal Bldg., Rm. 213
Allegheny County Airport
West Mifflin, PA 15122

Puerto Rico

FAA/FSDO-21
Luis Munoz Marin International Airport,
Rm. 203-A
San Juan, PR 00913

South Carolina

FAA FSDO-13
2819 Aviation Way
Columbia Metro Airport
West Columbia, SC 29169

South Dakota

FAA FSDO-27
Rural Rt. 2, Box 4750
Rapid City, SD 57701

Tennessee

FAA FSDO-03
2285 Airways Blvd., Ste. 115
Memphis, TN 38116

FAA FSDO-3
No. 2 International Plaza Dr., Ste. 700
Nashville, TN 37217

Texas

FAA FSDO-05
7701 N. Stemmons Fwy., Ste. 300
Lockbox 5
Dallas, TX 75247

FSDO
PO Box 619020
Dallas, TX 75261

FAA ASW FSDO-19
2260 Alliance Blvd.
Fort Worth Allian Airport
Fort Worth, TX 76177

FAA Southwest Region, ASW-200
Flight Standards Division
Fort Worth, TX 76193

FAA FSDO-09
8800 Paul B. Koonce Dr., Rm. 152
Hobby Airport
Houston, TX 77061

FAA FSDO-13
S. End Old Terminal Bldg.
Lubbock International Airport
Rte. 3, Box 51
Lubbock, TX 79401

FAA FSDO-17
10100 Reunion Pl., Ste. 200
International Airport
San Antonio, TX 78216

Utah

FAA Salt Lake City FSDO-7
116 N. 2400 W.
Salt Lake City, UT 84116

Virginia

FAA-AEA-FSDO-21
Terminal Bldg., 2nd Fl.
Richmond International Airport
Sandston, VA 23150-2594

Washington

FAA ANM-200
Northwest Mountain Region
1601 Lind Ave., SW
Renton, WA 98055-4056

FAA Seattle FSDO-1
1601 Lind Ave., SW
Renton, WA 98055-4056

West Virginia

Charleston FSDO-9
301 Eagle Mountain, Rm. 144
Yeager Airport
Charleston, WV 25311

Wisconsin

FAA FSDO-13
4915 S. Howell Ave., 4th Fl.
Milwaukee, WI 53207

Wyoming

FAA Casper FSDO-60A
Terminal Bldg., 2nd Fl.
Natrona County International Airport
Casper, WY 82604

Federal Licenses

334

Airline Transport Pilot (Airplanes)

Credential Type: Airline Transport Pilot Certificate with an Airplane Rating. **Authorization:** Pilot in command of an aircraft carrying persons or property for compensation or hire. Give flight instructions subject to limitation. **Requirements:** 23 years old. Read, speak, and understand English. Have a first-class medical certificate. Be a high school graduate or equivalent.

Hold a commercial pilot certificate or a foreign airline transport pilot or commercial pilot license without limitations, issued by a member state of ICAO, or be a pilot in an Armed Forces branch of the United States whose military experience qualifies applicant for a commercial pilot certificate. Have at least 250 hours of flight time as pilot in command of an airplane, or as a copilot performing the duties of a pilot under supervision of a pilot in command, at least 100 hours of which were crosscountry time and 25 hours of which were night flight time. At least 1500 hours of flight time as a pilot, including at least 500 hours of cross-country flight time, 100 hours of night flight time, and 75 hours of actual or simulated instrument time, of which at least 50 hours were in actual flight.

Have at least 100 hours, including at least 15 hours at night, of airplane flight time as pilot in command or as second in command performing the duties of pilot under supervision of a pilot in command; or complete a training program conducted by a certificated air carrier or other approved agency requiring at least 75 hours of airplane flight time. **Examination:** Written exam. Practical oral and flight test covering items selected by the inspector or examiner. **Gov-**

erning Statute: Federal Aviation Regulations, 14 CFR Ch. 1, part 61, subpart F.

335

Airline Transport Pilot (Rotorcrfaft and Helicopters)

Credential Type: Airline Transport Pilot Certificate with a Rotorcraft-Helicopter Rating. **Authorization:** Pilot in command of an aircraft carrying persons or property for compensation or hire. Give flight instructions subject to limitation. **Requirements:** 23 years old. Read, speak, and understand English. Have a first-class medical certificate. Be a high school graduate or equivalent.

Hold a commercial pilot certificate or a foreign airline transport pilot or commercial pilot license without limitations, issued by a member state of ICAO, or be a pilot in an Armed Forces branch of the United States whose military experience qualifies applicant for a commercial pilot certificate. At least 1200 hours of flight time as a pilot, including at least 500 hours of cross-country flight time, 100 hours of night flight time, and 75 hours of actual or simulated instrument time, of which at least 50 hours were in actual flight with at least 25 hours in helicopters as pilot in command or as second in command performing the duties of pilot under supervision of a pilot in command.

Have at least 100 hours, including at least 15 hours at night, of rotorcraft flight time as pilot in command or as second in command performing the duties of pilot under supervision of a pilot in command; or complete a training program conducted by a certificated air carrier or other approved agency requiring at least 75 hours of rotorcraft flight time. **Examination:** Written exam. Practical oral and flight test covering items selected by the inspector or examiner. **Governing Statute:** Federal Aviation Regulations, 14 CFR Ch. 1, part 61, subpart F.

336

Commercial Pilot, Airplanes

Credential Type: Commercial Pilot Certificate with an Airplane Rating. **Authorization:** Pilot in command of an aircraft carrying persons or property for compensation or hire. **Requirements:** 18 years old. Read, speak, and understand English. Hold at least a second-class medical certificate. Logged ground instruction from an authorized instructor or completed course of instruction or home study in appropriate areas of aeronautical knowledge. Logged instruction from an authorized flight instructor in appropriate pilot operations. Receive endorsement by an authorized flight instructor. Hold a private pilot certificate with an airplane rating; or meet flight experience requirements for a private pilot certificate and airplane rating and pass applicable written and practical tests. Hold an instrument rating (airplane), or certificate will be endorsed with a limitation. Have at least 250 hours of flight time as a pilot, which may not include more than 50 hours of instruction and must include at least 100 hours in powered aircraft and 100 hours of pilot-in-command time. **Examination:** Written exam appropriate to aircraft rating sought. Oral and flight test appropriate to aircraft rating and covering items selected by the inspector or examiner. **Governing Statute:** Federal Aviation Regulations, 14 CFR Ch. 1, part 61, subpart E.

337

Commercial Pilot, Airships

Credential Type: Commercial Pilot Certificate with an Airship Rating. **Authorization:** Pilot in command of an aircraft carrying persons or property for compensation or hire. Give flight instructions in airships. **Requirements:** 18 years old. Read, speak, and understand English. Hold at least a second-class medical certificate. Logged ground instruction from an authorized instructor or completed course of instruction or home study in appropriate areas of aeronautical knowledge. Logged instruction from an authorized flight instructor in appropriate pilot operations. Receive endorsement by an authorized flight instructor. Have at least 200 hours of flight time as pilot, including 50 hours of flight time as pilot in airships, 30 hours of flight time performing the duties of pilot in command in airships, and 40 hours of instrument time, of which at least 20 hours must be in flight with 10 hours of that flight time in airships. **Examination:** Written exam appropriate to aircraft rating sought. Oral and flight test appropriate to aircraft rating and covering items selected by the inspector or examiner. **Governing Statute:** Federal Aviation Regulations, 14 CFR Ch. 1, part 61, subpart E.

338

Commercial Pilot, Free Balloons

Credential Type: Commercial Pilot Certificate with a Free Balloon Rating. **Authorization:** Pilot in command of an aircraft carrying persons or property for compensation or hire. Give flight instructions in free balloons. **Requirements:** 18 years old. Read, speak, and understand English. No known medical deficiency that would prevent individual from piloting a free balloon. Logged ground instruction from an authorized instructor or completed course of instruction or home study in appropriate areas of aeronautical knowledge. Logged instruction from an authorized flight instructor in appropriate pilot operations. Receive endorsement by an authorized flight instructor. For gas balloon or hot air balloon with an airborne heater, at least 35 hours of flight time, including 20 hours in free balloons and 10 flights in free balloons. For a hot air balloon without an airborne heater, 10 flights in free balloons including at least two solo flights and six flights under the supervision of a commercial free balloon pilot. **Examination:** Written exam appropriate to aircraft rating sought. Oral and flight test appropriate to aircraft rating and covering items selected by the inspector or examiner. **Governing Statute:** Federal Aviation Regulations, 14 CFR Ch. 1, part 61, subpart E.

339

Commercial Pilot, Gliders

Credential Type: Commercial Pilot Certificate with a Glider Rating. **Authorization:** Pilot in command of an aircraft carrying persons or property for compensation or hire. **Requirements:** 18 years old. Read, speak, and understand English. No known medical deficiency that would prevent individual from piloting a glider. Logged ground instruction from an authorized instructor or completed course of instruction or home study in appropriate areas of aeronautical knowledge. Logged instruction from an authorized flight instructor in appropriate pilot operations. Receive endorsement by an authorized flight instructor. Have at least 25 hours of pilot time in aircraft, including 20 hours in gliders, and a total of 100 glider flights as pilot in command, including 25 flights during which 360-degree turns were made; or a total of 200 hours of pilot time in heavier-than-air aircraft, including 20 glider flights as pilot in command during which 360-degree turns were made. **Examination:** Written exam appropriate to aircraft rating sought. Oral and flight test appropriate to aircraft rating and covering items selected by the inspector or examiner. **Governing Statute:** Federal Aviation Regulations, 14 CFR Ch. 1, part 61, subpart E.

340

Commercial Pilot, Rotorcraft (Helicopters and Gyrocraft)

Credential Type: Commercial Pilot Certificate with a Rotorcraft Rating. **Authorization:** Pilot in command of an aircraft

Commercial Pilot, Rotorcraft (Helicopters and Gyrocraft), continued

carrying persons or property for compensation or hire. **Requirements:** 18 years old. Read, speak, and understand English. Hold at least a second-class medical certificate. Logged ground instruction from an authorized instructor or completed course of instruction or home study in appropriate areas of aeronautical knowledge. Logged instruction from an authorized flight instructor in appropriate pilot operations. Receive endorsement by an authorized flight instructor. For helicopters, have 150 hours of flight time, including at least 100 hours in powered aircraft, 50 hours of which must be in a helicopter, including 40 hours of flight instruction from an authorized flight instructor, and 100 hours of pilot-in-command flight time, 35 hours of which must be in a helicopter. For gyroplanes, have 150 hours of flight time, including at least 100 hours in powered aircraft, of which 25 hours must be in a gyroplane, including 40 hours of flight instruction from an authorized flight instructor, 10 hours of which must be in a gyroplane, and 100 hours of pilot-in-command flight time, 15 hours of which must be in a gyroplane. **Examination:** Written exam appropriate to aircraft rating sought. Oral and flight test appropriate to aircraft rating and covering items selected by the inspector or examiner. **Governing Statute:** Federal Aviation Regulations, 14 CFR Ch. 1, part 61, subpart E.

341

Flight Engineer

Credential Type: Flight Engineer Certificate. **Requirements:** 21 years old. Read, speak, and understand English, or have an appropriate limitation placed on the certificate. Hold at least a second-class medical certificate. Ratings are given for reciprocating engine powered aircraft, turbopropellor powered, and turbojet powered. Knowledge and experience must be appropriate to the rating sought.

Pass flight test, or complete an approved flight engineer training program.

Provide evidence of one of the following: (1) Have at least three years of diversified practical experience in aircraft and aircraft engine maintenance, of which one year was in maintaining multi-engine aircraft with engines rated at least 800 horsepower each, or the equivalent in turbine engine powered aircraft, and at least five hours of flight training in the duties of a flight engineer; or

(2) Graduate from at least a two-year specialized aeronautical training course in maintaining aircraft and aircraft engines, of which six months were in maintaining multi-engine aircraft with engines rated at least 800 horsepower each, or the equivalent in turbine engine powered aircraft, and at least five hours of flight training in the duties of a flight engineer; or

(3) Degree in aeronautical, electrical, or mechanical engineering, and at least six months practical experience in maintaining multi-engine aircraft with engines rated at least 800 horsepower each, or the equivalent in turbine engine powered aircraft, and at least five hours of flight training in the duties of a flight engineer; or

(4) At least a commercial pilot certificate with an instrument rating and at least five hours of flight training in the duties of a flight engineer; or

(5) At least 200 hours of flight time in a transport category airplane as pilot in command or second in command performing the functions of a pilot in command under the supervision of a pilot in command; or

(6) At least 100 hours of flight time as a flight engineer; or

(7) Within 90 days prior to application complete an approved flight engineer ground and flight course of instruction. **Examination:** Written test. Practical-oral test. **Exemptions:** The holder of a foreign flight engineer license issued by a contracting state to the Convention on International Civil Aviation, and who meets the above requirements, may be issued a flight engineer certificate. **Governing Statute:** Federal Aviation Regulations, 14 CFR Ch. 1, part 65, subpart B.

342

Flight Instructor

Credential Type: Flight Instructor Certificate. **Authorization:** Authorized to give flight instruction, ground instruction, or a home study course for a pilot certificate or rating. Authorized to give ground and flight instruction for a flight instructor certificate and rating. **Requirements:** 18 years old. Read, speak, and understand English.

Hold a commercial or airline transport pilot certificate with appropriate aircraft rating. Complete a course of instruction in subjects relating to aeronautical instruction. Have logged ground instruction in all of the subjects in which ground instruction is required for a private and commercial pilot certificate.

For an instrument or airplane instructor rating, must hold an instrument rating.

Have logged ground instruction for an instrument rating.

For additional rating, must hold an effective pilot certificate with appropriate ratings. Have at least 15 hours as pilot in command in the category and class of aircraft. Pass the written and practical test prescribed for the rating sought. Additional ratings include airplane-single engine, airplane-multiengine, rotorcraft-helicopter, rotorcraft-gyroplane, instrument-airplane, and instrument-helicopter. **Examination:** Written test on subjects in which ground instruction is required. Practical oral and flight test covering items selected by the inspector or examiner. **Governing Statute:** Federal Aviation Regulations, 14 CFR Ch. 1, part 61, subpart G.

343

Flight Navigator

Credential Type: Flight Navigator Certificate. **Requirements:** 21 years old. Read, speak, and understand English. Hold at least a second-class medical certificate. Must be a graduate of an approved flight navigator course. If not a graduate of such a course, must have satisfactorily determined his position in flight at least 25 times by night by celestial observation and at least 25 times by day by celestial observation in conjunction with other aids; and have at least 200 hours of satisfactory flight navigation, including celestial and radio navigation and dead reckoning. **Examination:** Written test. Practical-oral test. **Governing Statute:** Federal Aviation Regulations, 14 CFR Ch. 1, part 65, subpart C.

344

Private Pilot, Airplanes

Credential Type: Private Pilot Certificate with Airplane Rating. **Authorization:** Solo airplane flight subject to limitations. **Requirements:** 17 years old. Read, speak, and understand English. Hold at least a third-class medical certificate. Logged ground instruction from an authorized instructor or completed course of instruction or home study in appropriate areas of aeronautical knowledge. Logged instruction from an authorized flight instructor in appropriate pilot operations. Receive endorsement by an authorized flight instructor. Have at least a total of 40 hours of flight instruction and solo flight time, including at least 20 hours of flight instruction from an authorized flight instructor and 20 hours of solo flight time. **Examination:** Written test on subject areas on which instruction or home study is required. Oral and flight test on procedures and maneuvers selected by an FAA inspector or examiner. **Governing Statute:** Federal Aviation Regulations, 14 CFR Ch. 1, part 61, subpart D.

345

Private Pilot, Airships

Credential Type: Private Pilot Certificate with Lighter-than-Air Rating for Airships. **Authorization:** Solo flight subject to limitations. **Requirements:** 17 years old. Read, speak, and understand English. Hold at least a third-class medical certificate. Logged ground instruction from an authorized instructor or completed course of instruction or home study in appropriate areas of aeronautical knowledge. Logged instruction from an authorized flight instructor in appropriate pilot operations. Receive endorsement by an authorized flight instructor. At least 50 hours of flight time as pilot with at least 25 hours in airships, including at least five hours of solo flight time in airships or performing the functions of a pilot in an airship for which more than one pilot is required. **Examination:** Written test on subject areas on which instruction or home study is required. Oral and flight test on procedures and maneuvers selected by an FAA inspector or examiner. **Governing Statute:** Federal Aviation Regulations, 14 CFR Ch. 1, part 61, subpart D.

346

Private Pilot, Balloons

Credential Type: Private Pilot Certificate with Lighter-than-Air Rating for Balloons. **Authorization:** Solo flight subject to limitations. **Requirements:** 16 years old. Read, speak, and understand English. No known medical deficiency that would make individual unable to pilot a balloon. Logged ground instruction from an authorized instructor or completed course of instruction or home study in appropriate areas of aeronautical knowledge. Logged instruction from an authorized flight instructor in appropriate pilot operations. Receive endorsement by an authorized flight instructor. For gas balloons or hot air balloons with an airborne heater, a total of 10 hours in free balloons with at least six flights under the supervision of a person holding a commercial pilot certificate with a free balloon rating. For hot air balloons without an airborne heater, six flights under the supervision of a commercial balloon pilot with at least one solo flight. **Examination:** Written test on subject areas on which instruction or home study is required. Oral and flight test on procedures and maneuvers selected by an FAA inspector or examiner. **Governing Statute:** Federal Aviation Regulations, 14 CFR Ch. 1, part 61, subpart D.

347

Private Pilot, Gliders

Credential Type: Private Pilot Certificate with Glider Rating. **Authorization:** Solo flight subject to limitations. **Requirements:** 16 years old. Read, speak, and understand English. No known medical deficiency that would make individual unable to pilot a glider. Logged ground instruction from an authorized instructor or completed course of instruction or home study in appropriate areas of aeronautical knowledge. Logged instruction from an authorized flight instructor in appropriate pilot operations. Receive endorsement by an authorized flight instructor. Have logged at least 70 solo glider flights, including 20 during which 360-degree turns were made; or logged at least seven hours of solo flights in gliders; or have 40 hours of flight time in gliders and single-engine airplanes, including 10 solo glider flights during which 360-degree turns were made. **Examination:** Written test on subject areas on which instruction or home study is required. Oral and flight test on procedures and maneuvers selected by an FAA inspector or examiner. **Governing Statute:** Federal Aviation Regulations, 14 CFR Ch. 1, part 61, subpart D.

348

Private Pilot, Rotorcraft (Helicopters and Gyrocraft)

Credential Type: Private Pilot Certificate with Rotorcraft Rating. **Authorization:** Solo flight subject to limitations. **Requirements:** 17 years old. Read, speak, and understand English. Hold at least a third-class medical certificate. Logged ground instruction from an authorized instructor or completed course of instruction or home study in appropriate areas of aeronautical knowledge. Logged instruction from an authorized flight instructor in appropriate pilot operations. Receive endorsement by an authorized flight instructor. Have at least a total of 40 hours of flight instruction and solo flight time, including at least 20 hours of flight instruction from an authorized flight instructor and 20 hours of solo flight time, of which 15 must be in a helicopter for a helicopter rating or 10 in a gyroplane for a gyroplane rating. **Examination:** Written test on subject areas on which instruction or home study is required. Oral and flight test on procedures and maneuvers selected by an FAA inspector or examiner. **Governing Statute:** Federal Aviation Regulations, 14 CFR Ch. 1, part 61, subpart D.

349

Student and Recreational Pilot, Airplanes

Credential Type: Student Pilot Certificate. **Duration of License:** 90 days. **Authorization:** Solo airplane flight subject to general limitations. **Requirements:** 16 years old. Read, speak, and understand English. Hold at least a third-class medical certificate. Receive appropriate presolo flight instruction and training. Receive endorsement by authorized flight instructor. **Examination:** Written exam administered and graded by instructor who endorses the student's pilot certificate for solo flight. **Governing Statute:** Federal Aviation Regulations, 14 CFR Ch. 1, part 61, subpart C.

Credential Type: Recreational Pilot Certificate. **Authorization:** Solo airplane flight subject to general limitations. **Requirements:** 17 years old. Read, speak, and understand English. Hold at least a third-class medical certificate. Receive ground instruction from an authorized instructor or demonstrate completion of a course of instruction or home study. Logged instruction from an authorized flight instructor for appropriate flight operations. Have at least a total of 30 hours of flight instruction and solo flight time, including at least 15 hours of flight instruction from an authorized flight instructor and 15 hours of solo flight time in airplanes. **Examination:** Written exam on aeronautical knowledge. Oral and flight test on maneuvers and procedures selected by an FAA inspector or designated pilot examiner. **Governing Statute:** Federal Aviation Regulations, 14 CFR Ch. 1, part 61, subpart C.

350

Student and Recreational Pilot, Gliders and Balloons

Credential Type: Student Pilot Certificate. **Duration of License:** 90 days. **Authorization:** Solo flight subject to general limitations. **Requirements:** 14 years old. Read, speak, and understand English. No known medical deficiency that makes individual unable to pilot a glider or free balloon. Receive appropriate pre-solo flight instruction and training. Receive endorsement by authorized flight instructor. **Examination:** Written exam administered and graded by instructor who endorses the student's pilot certificate for solo flight. **Governing Statute:** Federal Aviation Regulations, 14 CFR Ch. 1, part 61, subpart C.

351

Student and Recreational Pilot, Rotorcraft (Helicopters and Gyroplanes)

Credential Type: Recreational Pilot Certificate. **Authorization:** Solo airplane flight subject to general limitations. **Requirements:** 17 years old. Read, speak, and understand English. Hold at least a third-class medical certificate. Receive ground instruction from an authorized instructor or demonstrate completion of a course of instruction or home study. Logged instruction from an authorized flight instructor for appropriate flight operations. For a helicopter rating, have at least a total of 30 hours of flight instruction and solo flight time, including at least 15 hours of flight instruction from an authorized flight instructor and 15 hours of solo flight time in helicopters. For a gyroplane rating, have at least a total of 30 hours of flight instruction and solo flight time, including at least 15 hours of flight instruction from an authorized flight instructor and 10 hours of solo flight time in gyroplanes. **Governing Statute:** Federal Aviation Regulations, 14 CFR Ch. 1, part 61, subpart C.

Arizona

352

Agricultural Aircraft Pilot
Environmental Services Div.
Dept. of Agriculture
PO Box 1586
Mesa, AZ 85211
Phone: (602)833-5442

Credential Type: License. **Requirements:** FAA Commercial Pilot's Certificate. **Examination:** Written. **Fees:** $50 license fee.

Louisiana

353

Flight Instructor (Ultralight Aircraft)
Dept. of Transportation and Development
PO Box 94245
Baton Rouge, LA 70804-7437
Phone: (504)342-7437

Credential Type: Instructor License. **Duration of License:** Two years. **Requirements:** Contact board for requirements. **Examination:** Written examination. **Fees:** $15 license fee.

354

Pilot (Ultralight Aircraft)
Dept. of Transportation and Development
PO Box 94245
Baton Rouge, LA 70804-7437
Phone: (504)342-7437

Credential Type: Ultralight Pilot License. **Duration of License:** Two years. **Requirements:** Complete written exam and flight check from designated examiner. **Fees:** $10 license fee.

Maryland

355

Air School Instructor
State Aviation Administration
Dept. of Transportation
PO Box 8766
BWI Airport
Baltimore, MD 21240
Phone: (410)859-7100

Credential Type: License. **Requirements:** Contact licensing body for application information.

Washington

356

Pilot
Dept. of Transportation
Transportation Bldg., KF-01
Olympia, WA 98504-5201
Phone: (206)764-4131

Credential Type: Pilot License. **Duration of License:** One year. **Authorization:** State license required for pilots who fly in Washington state. **Requirements:** At least 16 years of age. Federal Pilot Certification through an F.A.A. program. **Fees:** $10 maximum license fee (fee varies).

Animal Caretakers and Trainers, Except Farm

The following states grant licenses in this occupational category as of the date of publication:

Alabama	Florida	Kentucky	Mississippi	New York	Rhode Island	Washington
Arizona	Georgia	Louisiana	Missouri	North Carolina	South Carolina	West Virginia
Arkansas	Idaho	Maine	Montana	North Dakota	South Dakota	Wisconsin
California	Illinois	Maryland	Nebraska	Ohio	Tennessee	Wyoming
Colorado	Indiana	Massachusetts	Nevada	Oklahoma	Texas	
Connecticut	Iowa	Michigan	New Jersey	Oregon	Vermont	
Delaware	Kansas	Minnesota	New Mexico	Pennsylvania	Virginia	

Alabama

357

Veterinarian Technician
Veterinary Board
PO Box 1767
Decatur, AL 35602
Phone: (205)353-3544

Credential Type: Veterinary Technician Certificate. **Duration of License:** One year. **Requirements:** Must hold diploma from an American Veterinary Medical Association (AVMA) accredited program. **Examination:** National Examination. **Reciprocity:** None. **Fees:** $25 application fee. $60 examination fee. $15 renewal fee. **Governing Statute:** Title 46, Code of Alabama.

Arizona

358

Cool-out (Racetrack)
Arizona Dept. of Racing
Investigations and Licensing Div.
800 W. Washington, Rm. 515
Phoenix, AZ 85007
Phone: (602)542-5151

Credential Type: Cool-out license. **Duration of License:** One or three years. **Requirements:** At least 16 years of age. Not have been convicted of a felony or any crime involving moral turpitude within the last five years. **Fees:** $15 license fee (3 years). $7 license fee (1 year).

359

Exercise Rider (Racetrack)
Arizona Dept. of Racing
Investigations and Licensing Div.
800 W. Washington, Rm. 515
Phoenix, AZ 85007
Phone: (602)542-5151

Credential Type: Exercise rider license. **Duration of License:** Three years. **Requirements:** At least 16 years of age. Not have been convicted of a felony or any crime involving moral turpitude within the last five years. If applicant has not been previously licensed in this category in Arizona or in another recognized racing association state with pari-mutuel wagering, then applicant must be screened and approved by the Board of Stewards. **Fees:** $15 license fee.

360

Groom (Racetrack)
Arizona Dept. of Racing
Investigations and Licensing Div.
800 W. Washington, Rm. 515
Phoenix, AZ 85007
Phone: (602)542-5151

Credential Type: Groom license. **Duration of License:** Three years. **Requirements:** At least 16 years of age. Not have been convicted of a felony or any crime involving moral turpitude within the last five years. **Fees:** $15 license fee.

361

Lead-out (Racetrack)
Arizona Dept. of Racing
Investigations and Licensing Div.
800 W. Washington, Rm. 515
Phoenix, AZ 85007
Phone: (602)542-5151

Credential Type: Lead-out license. **Duration of License:** One or three years. **Requirements:** At least 16 years of age. Not have been convicted of a felony or any crime involving moral turpitude within the last five years. **Fees:** $15 license fee (3 years). $7 license fee (1 year).

362

Outrider (Racetrack)
Arizona Dept. of Racing
Investigations and Licensing Div.
800 W. Washington, Rm. 515
Phoenix, AZ 85007
Phone: (602)542-5151

Credential Type: Outrider license. **Duration of License:** Three years. **Requirements:** At least 16 years of age. Not have been convicted of a felony or any crime involving moral turpitude within the last five years. If applicant has not been previously licensed in this category in Arizona or in another recognized racing association state with pari-mutuel wagering, then applicant must be screened and approved by the Board of Stewards. **Fees:** $15 license fee.

363

Pony Rider (Racetrack)
Arizona Dept. of Racing
Investigations and Licensing Div.
800 W. Washington, Rm. 515
Phoenix, AZ 85007
Phone: (602)542-5151

Credential Type: Pony rider license. **Duration of License:** Three years. **Requirements:** At least 16 years of age. Not have been convicted of a felony or any crime involving moral turpitude within the last five years. If applicant has not been previously licensed in this category in Arizona or in another recognized racing association state with pari-mutuel wagering, then applicant must be screened and approved by the Board of Stewards. **Fees:** $15 license fee.

364

Trainer (Racetrack)
Arizona Dept. of Racing
Investigations and Licensing Div.
800 W. Washington, Rm. 515
Phoenix, AZ 85007
Phone: (602)542-5151

Credential Type: Trainer license. **Duration of License:** Three years. **Requirements:** At least 18 years of age. Not have been convicted of a felony or any crime involving moral turpitude within the last five years. If applicant has not been previously licensed as a trainer in Arizona or in another recognized racing association state with pari-mutuel wagering, then applicant must pass a written and practical examination administered by the Board of Stewards. Animal registration papers must be on file in the Racing Secretary's office of the track before being licensed. **Examination:** Written and practical examination administered by the Board of Stewards (new trainer license applications only). **Fees:** $36 license fee.

Credential Type: Assistant trainer license. **Duration of License:** Three years. **Requirements:** At least 18 years of age. Not have been convicted of a felony or any crime involving moral turpitude within the last five years. If applicant has not been previously licensed as a trainer in Arizona or in another recognized racing association state with pari-mutuel wagering, then applicant must pass a written examination administered by the Board of Stewards. **Examination:** Written examination administered by the Board of Stewards (new license applications only). **Fees:** $36 license fee. $5 administrative fee if applicant is already licensed as a trainer.

365

Veterinary Technician
Veterinary Board
1645 W. Jefferson, Rm. 410
Phoenix, AZ 85007
Phone: (602)542-3093
Phone: (602)542-3095

Credential Type: Veterinary Technician Certificate. **Duration of License:** Two years. **Requirements:** Must hold diploma from a two-year American Veterinary Medical Association (AVMA) accredited program in veterinary technology; or have been employed for at least two years as a veterinary assistant under the supervision of an Arizona licensed veterinarian, and be recommended by the employing veterinarian. **Examination:** National examination. **Fees:** $120 application/examination fee. $30 maximum certificate fee. $30 biennial renewal fee. **Governing Statute:** Practice law.

Arkansas

366

Animal Technician
Veterinary Medical Examination Board
1 Natural Resources Dr.
PO Box 5497
Little Rock, AR 72215
Phone: (501)224-2836

Credential Type: License. **Requirements:** Citizen of the United States. Good moral character. Possess a diploma or equivalent from a two year college level program accredited by the AVMA. Satisfactory completion of the National Boards. Letter of recommendation from a licensed veterinarian. **Examination:** Yes. **Fees:** $40 for written examination. $35 Temporary permit. $85 National Board Exam.

367

Farrier (Horse Racing)
Arkansas State Racing Commission
Ledbetter Bldg., Rm. G08
7th & Wolfe St.
PO Box 3076
Little Rock, AR 72203
Phone: (501)682-1467

Credential Type: License. **Duration of License:** One year. **Requirements:** Application must be approved by the Stewards. **Examination:** Yes. **Fees:** $3 License. $3 Renewal.

368

Greyhound Kennel Manager (Racing)
Arkansas State Racing Commission
Ledbetter Bldg., Rm. G08
7th & Wolfe St.
PO Box 3076
Little Rock, AR 72203
Phone: (501)682-1467

Credential Type: License. **Duration of License:** One year. **Requirements:** Must not be associated with any bookmaking practices which are illegal or would be detrimental to the public or the sport of racing. Never convicted of a crime. Qualified as to ability and integrity of license sought and have endorsement of employer. Not be habitually intoxicated or addicted to drugs. Declare ownership or interest in any greyhound. Application must contain no falsehoods. 16 years of age. Application approved by Director of Racing. **Examination:** No **Fees:** $3 License. $3 Renewal.

369

Greyhound Lead-Out (Racing)
Arkansas State Racing Commission
Ledbetter Bldg., Rm. G08
7th & Wolfe St.
PO Box 3076
Little Rock, AR 72203
Phone: (501)682-1467

Credential Type: License. **Duration of License:** One year. **Requirements:** Must not be associated with any bookmaking practices which are illegal or would be detrimental to the public or the sport of racing. Never convicted of a crime. Qualified as to ability and integrity of license sought and have endorsement of employer. Not be habitually intoxicated or addicted to drugs. Declare ownership or interest in any greyhound. Application must contain no falsehoods. 16 years of age. Application approved by Director of Racing. **Examination:** No **Fees:** $3 License. $3 Renewal.

370

Greyhound Trainer Assistant (Racing)
Arkansas State Racing Commission
Ledbetter Bldg., Rm. G08
7th & Wolfe St.
PO Box 3076
Little Rock, AR 72203
Phone: (501)682-1467

Credential Type: License. **Duration of License:** One year. **Requirements:** Must not be associated with any bookmaking

Animal Caretakers and Trainers, Except Farm

practices which are illegal or would be detrimental to the public or the sport of racing. Never convicted of a crime. Qualified as to ability and integrity of license sought and have endorsement of employer. Not be habitually intoxicated or addicted to drugs. Declare ownership or interest in any greyhound. Application must contain no falsehoods. 16 years of age. Application approved by Director of Racing. **Examination:** No **Fees:** $15 License. $15 Renewal.

371

Greyhound Trainer (Racing)
Arkansas State Racing Commission
Ledbetter Bldg., Rm. G08
7th & Wolfe St.
PO Box 3076
Little Rock, AR 72203
Phone: (501)682-1467

Credential Type: License. **Duration of License:** One year. **Requirements:** Must not be associated with any bookmaking practices which are illegal or would be detrimental to the public or the sport of racing. Never convicted of a crime. Qualified as to ability and integrity of license sought and have endorsement of employer. Not be habitually intoxicated or addicted to drugs. Declare ownership or interest in any greyhound. Application must contain no falsehoods. 16 years of age. Application approved by Director of Racing. **Examination:** No **Fees:** $15 License. $15 Renewal.

372

Horse Exerciser (Racing)
Arkansas State Racing Commission
Ledbetter Bldg., Rm. G08
7th & Wolfe St.
PO Box 3076
Little Rock, AR 72203
Phone: (501)682-1467

Credential Type: License. **Duration of License:** One year. **Requirements:** Application must be approved by the Stewards. Must be qualified as to ability and integrity of license sought and have the endorsement of the employer. Must be 16 years of age. Never convicted of a crime. Must not be habitually intoxicated or addicted to drugs. Must not be engaged in any activity or practice which is illegal, undesirable, or detrimental to the best interest of the public and the sport of racing. **Examination:** Yes. **Fees:** $3 License. $3 Renewal.

373

Horse Trainer Assistant (Racing)
Arkansas State Racing Commission
Ledbetter Bldg., Rm. G08
7th & Wolfe St.
PO Box 3076
Little Rock, AR 72203
Phone: (501)682-1467

Credential Type: License. **Duration of License:** One year. **Requirements:** Application must be approved by the Stewards. **Examination:** Yes. **Fees:** $15 License. $15 Renewal.

374

Horse Trainer (Racing)
Arkansas State Racing Commission
Ledbetter Bldg., Rm. G08
7th & Wolfe St.
PO Box 3076
Little Rock, AR 72203
Phone: (501)682-1467

Credential Type: License. **Requirements:** Application must be approved by the Stewards. **Examination:** Yes, unless valid license is currently held from another racing jurisdiction and is in good standing with all jurisdictions. **Fees:** $15 License. $15 Renewal.

375

Lead Pony Rider (Racing)
Arkansas State Racing Commission
Ledbetter Bldg., Rm. G08
7th & Wolfe St.
PO Box 3076
Little Rock, AR 72203
Phone: (501)682-1467

Credential Type: License. **Duration of License:** One year. **Requirements:** Application approved by the Stewards. Qualified as to ability and integrity of license sought and have the endorsement of employer. 16 years of age. Never convicted of a crime. Not be habitually addicted to drugs. Not be engaged in any activity or practice which is illegal, undesirable, or detrimental to the best interest of the public or the sport of racing. **Examination:** No **Fees:** $3 License. $3 Renewal.

376

Receiving Barn Custodian (Racing)
Arkansas State Racing Commission
Ledbetter Bldg., Rm. G08
7th & Wolfe St.
PO Box 3076
Little Rock, AR 72203
Phone: (501)862-1467

Credential Type: License. **Duration of License:** One year. **Requirements:** Application must be approved by the Stewards. Must be qualified as to ability and integrity of license sought and have the endorsement of employer. 16 years of age. Never convicted of a crime. Not be habitually addicted to drugs or intoxicated. Must not be engaged in any activity which is illegal, undesirable or detrimental to the best interest of the public and the sport of racing. **Examination:** No **Fees:** $3 License. $3 Renewal.

377

Stable Attendant (Racing)
Arkansas State Racing Commission
Ledbetter Bldg., Rm. G08
7th & Wolfe St.
PO Box 3076
Little Rock, AR 72203
Phone: (501)682-1467

Credential Type: License. **Duration of License:** One year. **Requirements:** Application must be approved by the Stewards. Must be qualified as to ability and integrity of license sought and have the endorsement of employer. 16 years of age. Never convicted of a crime. Not be habitually addicted to drugs or intoxicated. Must not be engaged in any activity which is illegal, undesirable or detrimental to the best interest of the public and the sport of racing. **Examination:** No **Fees:** $3 License. $3 Renewal.

California

378

Animal Health Technician
Animal Health Technician Examining Committee
1420 Howe Ave., Ste. 6
Sacramento, CA 95825
Phone: (916)920-7688

Credential Type: Animal Health Technician License and Certification. **Duration of License:** Two years. **Requirements:** Meet one of the following sets of requirements: (1) Must have a B.S. degree in a field related to animal science. Complete 12 months (1560 hours) practical experience under the direct supervision of a licensed

California

Animal Health Technician, continued

veterinarian. (2) Graduate from an approved animal health technician program. No practical experience required. (3) Graduate from a non-approved animal health technician, two-year community college curriculum. Complete 18 months (2234 hours) practical experience under the direct supervision of a licensed veterinarian. (4) Graduate from a private approved animal health technician program. (5) Complete at least 50 semester or 75 quarter hours of postsecondary education in appropriate courses. Complete 36 months (4680 hours) practical experience under the direct supervision of a licensed veterinarian. (6) Be registered as an animal health technician in another state with an equivalent licensing examination. Complete 36 months (4680 hours) practical experience under the direct supervision of a licensed veterinarian. **Examination:** California Animal Health Techician Examination. **Fees:** $50 application and exam fee.

379

Assistant Trainer (Racetrack)
California Horse Racing Board
1010 Hurley Way, Ste. 190
Sacramento, CA 95825
Phone: (916)920-7178

Credential Type: License Registration. **Requirements:** Submit application and fingerprint card. Pay fee. **Fees:** $150 registration fee.

380

Assistant to the Veterinarian (Racetrack)
California Horse Racing Board
1010 Hurley Way, Ste. 190
Sacramento, CA 95825
Phone: (916)920-7178

Credential Type: License Registration. **Requirements:** Submit application and fingerprint card. Pay fee. **Fees:** $75 registration fee.

381

Exercise Rider (Racetrack)
California Horse Racing Board
1010 Hurley Way, Ste. 190
Sacramento, CA 95825
Phone: (916)920-7178

Credential Type: License Registration. **Requirements:** Submit application and fingerprint card. Pay fee. **Fees:** $75 registration fee.

382

Groom or Stable Employee (Racetrack)
California Horse Racing Board
1010 Hurley Way, Ste. 190
Sacramento, CA 95825
Phone: (916)920-7178

Credential Type: License Registration. **Requirements:** Submit application and fingerprint card. Pay fee. **Fees:** $35 registration fee. $20 annual renewal fee.

383

Guide Dog Instructor
Board of Guide Dogs for the Blind
830 K St., Rm. 222
Sacramento, CA 95814
Phone: (916)445-9041

Credential Type: License. **Requirements:** Must complete a three-year apprenticeship. **Fees:** $75 license fee.

384

Horseshoer (Racetrack)
California Horse Racing Board
1010 Hurley Way, Ste. 190
Sacramento, CA 95825
Phone: (916)920-7178

Credential Type: License Registration. **Requirements:** Submit application and fingerprint card. Pay fee. **Fees:** $75 registration fee.

385

Outrider (Racetrack)
California Horse Racing Board
1010 Hurley Way, Ste. 190
Sacramento, CA 95825
Phone: (916)920-7178

Credential Type: License Registration. **Requirements:** Submit application and fingerprint card. Pay fee. **Fees:** $75 registration fee.

386

Paddock Attendant (Racetrack)
California Horse Racing Board
1010 Hurley Way, Ste. 190
Sacramento, CA 95825
Phone: (916)920-7178

Credential Type: License Registration. **Requirements:** Submit application and fingerprint card. Pay fee. **Fees:** $75 registration fee.

387

Pony Rider (Racetrack)
California Horse Racing Board
1010 Hurley Way, Ste. 190
Sacramento, CA 95825
Phone: (916)920-7178

Credential Type: License Registration. **Requirements:** Submit application and fingerprint card. Pay fee. **Fees:** $75 registration fee.

388

Trainer (Racetrack)
California Horse Racing Board
1010 Hurley Way, Ste. 190
Sacramento, CA 95825
Phone: (916)920-7178

Credential Type: License Registration. **Requirements:** Submit application and fingerprint card. Pay fee. **Fees:** $150 registration fee.

Colorado

389

Animal Technician
CVMA Board
1780 S. Bellaire, Ste. 701
Denver, CO 80222
Phone: (303)759-1251

Credential Type: Animal Technician Certificate. **Duration of License:** One year. **Requirements:** Complete Animal Technician program. **Examination:** State examination. **Fees:** $25 examination fee. $10 renewal fee. **Governing Statute:** Practice act.

Animal Caretakers and Trainers, Except Farm

390

Artificial Inseminator
Board of Veterinary Medicine
Dept. of Regulatory Agencies
Div. of Registrations
1560 Broadway, Ste. 1340
Denver, CO 80202
Phone: (303)894-7755

Credential Type: License. **Requirements:** Contact licensing body for application information.

391

Assistant Trainer (Greyhound Racing)
Colorado Racing Commission
Dept. of Regulatory Agencies
1560 Broadway, Ste. 1540
Denver, CO 80202
Phone: (303)894-2990
Fax: (303)894-7580

Credential Type: Assistant Trainer License. **Duration of License:** Three years. **Requirements:** Submit application, pay fees, and pass examination. **Examination:** Assistant Trainer's Test. **Fees:** $33 application/exam/license fee.

392

Assistant Trainer (Horse Racing)
Colorado Racing Commission
Dept. of Regulatory Agencies
1560 Broadway, Ste. 1540
Denver, CO 80202
Phone: (303)894-2990
Fax: (303)894-7580

Credential Type: Assistant Trainer License. **Duration of License:** Three years. **Requirements:** Submit application, pay fees, and pass examination. **Examination:** Assistant Trainer's Test. **Fees:** $59 application/exam/license fee.

393

Exercise Person (Horse Racing)
Colorado Racing Commission
Dept. of Regulatory Agencies
1560 Broadway, Ste. 1540
Denver, CO 80202
Phone: (303)894-2990
Fax: (303)894-7580

Credential Type: Exercise Person License. **Requirements:** Submit application and pay fee. **Fees:** $24 license fee.

394

Groom (Greyhound Racing)
Colorado Racing Commission
Dept. of Regulatory Agencies
1560 Broadway, Ste. 1540
Denver, CO 80202
Phone: (303)894-2990
Fax: (303)894-7580

Credential Type: Groom License. **Requirements:** Submit application and pay fee. **Fees:** $24 license fee.

395

Groom (Horse Racing)
Colorado Racing Commission
Dept. of Regulatory Agencies
1560 Broadway, Ste. 1540
Denver, CO 80202
Phone: (303)894-2990
Fax: (303)894-7580

Credential Type: Groom License. **Requirements:** Submit application and pay fee. **Fees:** $24 license fee.

396

Kennel Helper (Greyhound Racing)
Colorado Racing Commission
Dept. of Regulatory Agencies
1560 Broadway, Ste. 1540
Denver, CO 80202
Phone: (303)894-2990
Fax: (303)894-7580

Credential Type: Kennel Helper License. **Duration of License:** Three years. **Requirements:** Submit application and pay fee. **Fees:** $24 license fee.

397

Plater (Horse Racing)
Colorado Racing Commission
Dept. of Regulatory Agencies
1560 Broadway, Ste. 1540
Denver, CO 80202
Phone: (303)894-2990
Fax: (303)894-7580

Credential Type: Plater License. **Duration of License:** Three years. **Requirements:** Submit application and pay fee. **Fees:** $59 license fee.

398

Pony Person (Racing)
Colorado Racing Commission
Dept. of Regulatory Agencies
1560 Broadway, Ste. 1540
Denver, CO 80202
Phone: (303)894-2990
Fax: (303)894-7580

Credential Type: Pony Person License. **Duration of License:** Three years. **Requirements:** Submit application and pay fee. **Fees:** $24 license fee.

399

Trainer (Greyhound Racing)
Colorado Racing Commission
Dept. of Regulatory Agencies
1560 Broadway, Ste. 1540
Denver, CO 80202
Phone: (303)894-2990
Fax: (303)894-7580

Credential Type: Trainer License. **Duration of License:** Three years. **Requirements:** Submit application, pay fees, and pass examination. **Examination:** Trainer's Test. **Reciprocity:** Yes. **Fees:** $59 application/exam/license fee.

400

Trainer (Horse Racing)
Colorado Racing Commission
Dept. of Regulatory Agencies
1560 Broadway, Ste. 1540
Denver, CO 80202
Phone: (303)894-2990
Fax: (303)894-7580

Credential Type: Trainer License. **Duration of License:** Three years. **Requirements:** Submit application, pay fees, and pass examination. **Examination:** Trainer's Test. **Fees:** $59 application/exam/license fee.

Connecticut

401

Assistant Trainer (Racetrack)
Connecticut Div. of Special Revenue
Russell Rd.
PO Box 11424
Newington, CT 06111-0424
Phone: (203)566-2756

Credential Type: License Registration. **Requirements:** Submit application and fingerprint card. Pay fee. **Fees:** $20 registration fee.

Connecticut

402

Kennel Helper (Racetrack)
Connecticut Div. of Special Revenue
Russell Rd.
PO Box 11424
Newington, CT 06111-0424
Phone: (203)566-2756

Credential Type: License Registration.
Requirements: Submit application and fingerprint card. Pay fee. **Fees:** $5 registration fee.

403

Trainer (Racetrack)
Connecticut Div. of Special Revenue
Russell Rd.
PO Box 11424
Newington, CT 06111-0424
Phone: (203)566-2756

Credential Type: License Registration.
Requirements: Submit application and fingerprint card. Pay fee. **Fees:** $20 registration fee.

Delaware

404

Groom (Racetrack)
Delaware Harness Racing
 Commission
2320 S. DuPont Hwy.
Dover, DE 19901
Phone: (302)739-4811

Credential Type: License Registration.
Requirements: Submit application and fingerprint card. Pay fee. **Fees:** $5 registration fee.

405

Horse Trainer (Racetrack)
Delaware Harness Racing
 Commission
2320 S. DuPont Hwy.
Dover, DE 19901
Phone: (302)739-4811

Credential Type: License Registration.
Requirements: Submit application and fingerprint card. Pay fee. **Fees:** $10 registration fee.

406

Thoroughbred Trainer (Racetrack)
Delaware Thoroughbred Racing
 Commission
820 French St., 3rd Level
Wilmington, DE 19801
Phone: (302)577-3288

Credential Type: License Registration.
Requirements: Contact licensing body for application information.

407

Veterinarian Assistant (Racetrack)
Delaware Harness Racing
 Commission
2320 S. DuPont Hwy.
Dover, DE 19901
Phone: (302)739-4811

Credential Type: License Registration.
Requirements: Submit application and fingerprint card. Pay fee. **Fees:** $5 registration fee.

Florida

408

Blacksmith/Plater (Racetrack)
Florida Dept. of Business
Div. of Pari-Mutuel Wagering
Licensing Section
725 S. Bronough St.
Tallahassee, FL 32399-1037
Phone: (904)488-9161

Credential Type: License Registration Code 1055. **Requirements:** Submit application and fingerprint card. Pay fee. **Fees:** $10 registration fee.

409

Exercise Person (Racetrack)
Florida Dept. of Business
Div. of Pari-Mutuel Wagering
Licensing Section
725 S. Bronough St.
Tallahassee, FL 32399-1037
Phone: (904)488-9161

Credential Type: License Registration Code 1053. **Requirements:** Submit application and fingerprint card. Pay fee. **Fees:** $10 registration fee.

410

Greyhound Trainer/Assistant (Racetrack)
Florida Dept. of Business
Div. of Pari-Mutuel Wagering
Licensing Section
725 S. Bronough St.
Tallahassee, FL 32399-1037
Phone: (904)488-9161

Credential Type: License Registration Code 6050. **Requirements:** Submit application and fingerprint card. Pay fee. **Fees:** $40 registration fee.

411

Harness Trainer/Assistant (Racetrack)
Florida Dept. of Business
Div. of Pari-Mutuel Wagering
Licensing Section
725 S. Bronough St.
Tallahassee, FL 32399-1037
Phone: (904)488-9161

Credential Type: License Registration Code 4050. **Requirements:** Submit application and fingerprint card. Pay fee. **Fees:** $40 registration fee.

412

Quarter Horse Trainer/Assistant (Racetrack)
Florida Dept. of Business
Div. of Pari-Mutuel Wagering
Licensing Section
725 S. Bronough St.
Tallahassee, FL 32399-1037
Phone: (904)488-9161

Credential Type: License Registration Code 5050. **Requirements:** Submit application and fingerprint card. Pay fee. **Fees:** $40 registration fee.

413

Stable/Kennel Helper (Racetrack)
Florida Dept. of Business
Div. of Pari-Mutuel Wagering
Licensing Section
725 S. Bronough St.
Tallahassee, FL 32399-1037
Phone: (904)488-9161

Credential Type: License Registration Code 1056. **Authorization:** Authorizes work in the following positions: groom, horse clipper, hot walker, pony rider, outrider, kennel help, and similar positions. **Requirements:** Submit application and fin-

gerprint card. Pay fee. **Fees:** $10 registration fee.

414

Thoroughbred Trainer/Assistant (Racetrack)
Florida Dept. of Business
Div. of Pari-Mutuel Wagering
Licensing Section
725 S. Bronough St.
Tallahassee, FL 32399-1037
Phone: (904)488-9161

Credential Type: License Registration Code 3050. **Requirements:** Submit application and fingerprint card. Pay fee. **Fees:** $40 registration fee.

415

Veterinarian Assistant (Racetrack)
Florida Dept. of Business
Div. of Pari-Mutuel Wagering
Licensing Section
725 S. Bronough St.
Tallahassee, FL 32399-1037
Phone: (904)488-9161

Credential Type: License Registration Code 1061. **Requirements:** Submit application and fingerprint card. Pay fee. **Fees:** $10 registration fee.

Georgia

416

Veterinary Technician
State Examining Boards/Health Care Practitioners Section
166 Pryor St. SW
Atlanta, GA 30303
Phone: (404)656-3912

Credential Type: Veterinary Technician Certificate. **Requirements:** Graduate from an accredited school of animal technician training. **Examination:** State examination. **Governing Statute:** Chapter 43-50, Veterinary Practice Act.

Idaho

417

Assistant Trainer (Racetrack)
Idaho State Horse Racing Commission
6133 Corporal Lane
Boise, ID 83704
Phone: (208)327-7105

Credential Type: License Registration. **Requirements:** Submit application and fingerprint card. Pay fee. **Fees:** $20 registration fee.

418

Exercise Boy/Girl (Racetrack)
Idaho State Horse Racing Commission
6133 Corporal Lane
Boise, ID 83704
Phone: (208)327-7105

Credential Type: License Registration. **Requirements:** Submit application and fingerprint card. Pay fee. **Fees:** $10 registration fee.

419

Groom (Racetrack)
Idaho State Horse Racing Commission
6133 Corporal Lane
Boise, ID 83704
Phone: (208)327-7105

Credential Type: License Registration. **Requirements:** Submit application and fingerprint card. Pay fee. **Fees:** $10 registration fee.

420

Kennel Employee (Racetrack)
Idaho State Horse Racing Commission
6133 Corporal Lane
Boise, ID 83704
Phone: (208)327-7105

Credential Type: License Registration. **Requirements:** Submit application and fingerprint card. Pay fee. **Fees:** $20 registration fee.

421

Plater (Racetrack)
Idaho State Horse Racing Commission
6133 Corporal Lane
Boise, ID 83704
Phone: (208)327-7105

Credential Type: License Registration. **Requirements:** Submit application and fingerprint card. Pay fee. **Fees:** $25 registration fee.

422

Pony Boy/Girl (Racetrack)
Idaho State Horse Racing Commission
6133 Corporal Lane
Boise, ID 83704
Phone: (208)327-7105

Credential Type: License Registration. **Requirements:** Submit application and fingerprint card. Pay fee. **Fees:** $10 registration fee.

423

Stable Employee (Racetrack)
Idaho State Horse Racing Commission
6133 Corporal Lane
Boise, ID 83704
Phone: (208)327-7105

Credential Type: License Registration. **Requirements:** Submit application and fingerprint card. Pay fee. **Fees:** $20 registration fee.

424

Trainer (Racetrack)
Idaho State Horse Racing Commission
6133 Corporal Lane
Boise, ID 83704
Phone: (208)327-7105

Credential Type: License Registration. **Requirements:** Submit application and fingerprint card. Pay fee. **Fees:** $25 registration fee.

Illinois

425

Animal Breeder (Fur Bearing)
Illinois Dept. of Conservation
524 S. Second St.
Springfield, IL 62701-1787
Phone: (217)785-3423

Credential Type: Animal Breeder License. **Duration of License:** One year. **Requirements:** Must be Illinois resident for at least 30 days. Submit application and pay fee. **Reciprocity:** No. **Fees:** $25 initial license fee. $25 renewal fee. **Governing Statute:** Illinois Revised Statutes, Chapter 61. Illinois Conservation Law-Wildlife.

426

Animal Health Technician (Racetrack)
Illinois Racing Board
100 W. Randolph St., Ste. 11-100
Chicago, IL 60601
Phone: (312)814-2600

Credential Type: License Registration. **Requirements:** Submit application and fingerprint card. Pay fee. **Fees:** $15 registration fee. $2 photo fee. $10 fingerprint card fee.

427

Apprentice Blacksmith (Racetrack)
Illinois Racing Board
100 W. Randolph St., Ste. 11-100
Chicago, IL 60601
Phone: (312)814-2600

Credential Type: License Registration. **Requirements:** Submit application and fingerprint card. Pay fee. **Fees:** $25 registration fee. $2 photo fee. $10 fingerprint card fee.

428

Assistant Trainer (Racetrack)
Illinois Racing Board
100 W. Randolph St., Ste. 11-100
Chicago, IL 60601
Phone: (312)814-2600

Credential Type: License Registration. **Requirements:** Submit application and fingerprint card. Pay fee. **Fees:** $15 registration fee. $2 photo fee. $10 fingerprint card fee.

429

Blacksmith (Racetrack)
Illinois Racing Board
100 W. Randolph St., Ste. 11-100
Chicago, IL 60601
Phone: (312)814-2600

Credential Type: License Registration. **Requirements:** Submit application and fingerprint card. Pay fee. **Fees:** $25 registration fee. $2 photo fee. $10 fingerprint card fee.

430

Exercise Person (Racetrack)
Illinois Racing Board
100 W. Randolph St., Ste. 11-100
Chicago, IL 60601
Phone: (312)814-2600

Credential Type: License Registration. **Requirements:** Submit application and fingerprint card. Pay fee. **Fees:** $10 registration fee. $2 photo fee. $10 fingerprint card fee.

431

Groom (Racetrack)
Illinois Racing Board
100 W. Randolph St., Ste. 11-100
Chicago, IL 60601
Phone: (312)814-2600

Credential Type: License Registration. **Requirements:** Submit application and fingerprint card. Pay fee. **Fees:** $5 registration fee. $2 photo fee. $10 fingerprint card fee.

432

Hotwalker (Racetrack)
Illinois Racing Board
100 W. Randolph St., Ste. 11-100
Chicago, IL 60601
Phone: (312)814-2600

Credential Type: License Registration. **Requirements:** Submit application and fingerprint card. Pay fee. **Fees:** $5 registration fee. $2 photo fee. $10 fingerprint card fee.

433

Nuisance Wildlife Control Operator
Illinois Dept. of Conservation
524 South 2nd St.
Springfield, IL 62706
Phone: (217)785-6834

Credential Type: License Permit. **Duration of License:** One year. **Requirements:** At least 18 years of age. Submit application. **Examination:** Written examination. **Reciprocity:** No. **Fees:** No fee. **Governing Statute:** Illinois Revised Statutes, Chapter 61, Illinois Administrative Code, Part 525.

434

Owner-Assistant Trainer (Racetrack)
Illinois Racing Board
100 W. Randolph St., Ste. 11-100
Chicago, IL 60601
Phone: (312)814-2600

Credential Type: License Registration. **Requirements:** Submit application and fingerprint card. Pay fee. **Fees:** $25 registration fee. $2 photo fee. $10 fingerprint card fee.

435

Owner-Trainer (Racetrack)
Illinois Racing Board
100 W. Randolph St., Ste. 11-100
Chicago, IL 60601
Phone: (312)814-2600

Credential Type: License Registration. **Requirements:** Submit application and fingerprint card. Pay fee. **Fees:** $25 registration fee. $2 photo fee. $10 fingerprint card fee.

436

Pony Person (Racetrack)
Illinois Racing Board
100 W. Randolph St., Ste. 11-100
Chicago, IL 60601
Phone: (312)814-2600

Credential Type: License Registration. **Requirements:** Submit application and fingerprint card. Pay fee. **Fees:** $10 registration fee. $2 photo fee. $10 fingerprint card fee.

437

Preserve Area Operator
Illinois Dept. of Conservation
524 South 2nd St.
Springfield, IL 62701-1787
Phone: (217)785-3423

Credential Type: Preserve Area Operator License. **Duration of License:** One year. **Authorization:** Allows applicant to operate a preserve for breeding and hunting of game birds. **Requirements:** Must be an Illinois resident for at least 30 days. Submit application and pay fee. **Reciprocity:** No. **Fees:** $100 initial license fee. $100 renewal fee. **Governing Statute:** Illinois Revised Statutes, Chapter 61, Illinois Conservation Law—Wildlife.

438

Trainer (Racetrack)
Illinois Racing Board
100 W. Randolph St., Ste. 11-100
Chicago, IL 60601
Phone: (312)814-2600

Credential Type: License Registration. **Requirements:** Submit application and fingerprint card. Pay fee. **Fees:** $25 registration fee. $2 photo fee. $10 fingerprint card fee.

439

Veterinarian Assistant (Racetrack)
Illinois Racing Board
100 W. Randolph St., Ste. 11-100
Chicago, IL 60601
Phone: (312)814-2600

Credential Type: License Registration. **Requirements:** Submit application and fingerprint card. Pay fee. **Fees:** $15 registration fee. $2 photo fee. $10 fingerprint card fee.

440

Wild Game and Bird Breeder
Illinois Dept. of Conservation
524 South 2nd St.
Springfield, IL 62701-1787
Phone: (217)785-3423

Credential Type: Class A (Non-Commercial) License. **Duration of License:** One year. **Requirements:** Must be an Illinois resident for at least 30 days. Submit application and pay fee. **Reciprocity:** No. **Fees:** $10 initial license fee. $10 renewal fee. **Governing Statute:** Illinois Revised Statutes, Chapter 61.

Credential Type: Class B (Commercial) License. **Duration of License:** One year. **Requirements:** Must be an Illinois resident for at least 30 days. Submit application and pay fee. **Reciprocity:** No. **Fees:** $20 initial license fee. $20 renewal fee. **Governing Statute:** Illinois Revised Statutes, Chapter 61.

Indiana

441

Veterinary Technician
Health Professions Bureau
402 W. Washington St., Rm. 041
Indianapolis, IN 46204
Phone: (317)233-4407
Fax: (317)233-4236

Credential Type: Veterinary Technician Certificate. **Duration of License:** Two years. **Requirements:** 18 years of age. High school graduate or equivalent. No felony convictions that would impair his/her ability to practice competency. Complete an approved program of veterinary technology. **Examination:** Indiana written and oral-practical examinations. **Fees:** $85 written examination fee. $50 oral-practical examination fee. $10 registration fee. $20 biennial renewal fee. **Governing Statute:** New Veterinary Practice Act.

Iowa

442

Assistant Trainer (Racetrack)
Iowa State Racing Commission
Lucas State Office Bldg.
Des Moines, IA 50319
Phone: (515)281-7352

Credential Type: License Registration. **Requirements:** Submit application and fingerprint card. Pay fee. **Fees:** $10 registration fee.

443

Exercise Rider (Racetrack)
Iowa State Racing Commission
Lucas State Office Bldg.
Des Moines, IA 50319
Phone: (515)281-7352

Credential Type: License Registration. **Requirements:** Submit application and fingerprint card. Pay fee. **Fees:** $5 registration fee.

444

Groom (Racetrack)
Iowa State Racing Commission
Lucas State Office Bldg.
Des Moines, IA 50319
Phone: (515)281-7352

Credential Type: License Registration. **Requirements:** Submit application and fingerprint card. Pay fee. **Fees:** $5 registration fee.

445

Kennel Helper (Racetrack)
Iowa State Racing Commission
Lucas State Office Bldg.
Des Moines, IA 50319
Phone: (515)281-7352

Credential Type: License Registration. **Requirements:** Submit application and fingerprint card. Pay fee. **Fees:** $5 registration fee.

446

Lead Out (Racetrack)
Iowa State Racing Commission
Lucas State Office Bldg.
Des Moines, IA 50319
Phone: (515)281-7352

Credential Type: License Registration. **Requirements:** Submit application and fingerprint card. Pay fee. **Fees:** $5 registration fee.

447

Outrider (Racetrack)
Iowa State Racing Commission
Lucas State Office Bldg.
Des Moines, IA 50319
Phone: (515)281-7352

Credential Type: License Registration. **Requirements:** Submit application and fingerprint card. Pay fee. **Fees:** $10 registration fee.

448

Owner-Trainer (Racetrack)
Iowa State Racing Commission
Lucas State Office Bldg.
Des Moines, IA 50319
Phone: (515)281-7352

Credential Type: License Registration. **Requirements:** Submit application and fingerprint card. Pay fee. **Fees:** $20 registration fee.

Iowa

449

Trainer (Racetrack)
Iowa State Racing Commission
Lucas State Office Bldg.
Des Moines, IA 50319
Phone: (515)281-7352

Credential Type: License Registration. **Requirements:** Submit application and fingerprint card. Pay fee. **Fees:** $10 registration fee.

450

Veterinarian Assistant/Animal Technician
Iowa Board of Veterinary Medicine
Public Health Dept.
Wallace State Office Bldg., 2nd Fl.
Des Moines, IA 50319
Phone: (515)281-6762

Credential Type: Certificate. **Requirements:** Two years of animal technology in an approved college. **Examination:** Written. **Fees:** $95 exam fee.

Kansas

451

Assistant Trainer (Racetrack)
Kansas Racing Commission
3400 VanBuren
Topeka, KS 66611-2228
Phone: (913)296-5800

Credential Type: License Registration. **Requirements:** Submit application and fingerprint card. Pay fee. **Fees:** $10 registration fee.

452

Blacksmith (Racetrack)
Kansas Racing Commission
3400 VanBuren
Topeka, KS 66611-2228
Phone: (913)296-5800

Credential Type: License Registration. **Requirements:** Submit application and fingerprint card. Pay fee. **Fees:** $10 registration fee.

453

Exercise Person (Racetrack)
Kansas Racing Commission
3400 VanBuren
Topeka, KS 66611-2228
Phone: (913)296-5800

Credential Type: License Registration. **Requirements:** Submit application and fingerprint card. Pay fee. **Fees:** $5 registration fee.

454

Farrier (Racetrack)
Kansas Racing Commission
3400 VanBuren
Topeka, KS 66611-2228
Phone: (913)296-5800

Credential Type: License Registration. **Requirements:** Submit application and fingerprint card. Pay fee. **Fees:** $10 registration fee.

455

Groom/Hot Walker (Racetrack)
Kansas Racing Commission
3400 VanBuren
Topeka, KS 66611-2228
Phone: (913)296-5800

Credential Type: License Registration. **Requirements:** Submit application and fingerprint card. Pay fee. **Fees:** $5 registration fee.

456

Kennel Helper (Racetrack)
Kansas Racing Commission
3400 VanBuren
Topeka, KS 66611-2228
Phone: (913)296-5800

Credential Type: License Registration. **Requirements:** Submit application and fingerprint card. Pay fee. **Fees:** $5 registration fee.

457

Kennel Master (Racetrack)
Kansas Racing Commission
3400 VanBuren
Topeka, KS 66611-2228
Phone: (913)296-5800

Credential Type: License Registration. **Requirements:** Submit application and fingerprint card. Pay fee. **Fees:** $20 registration fee.

458

Lead Out (Racetrack)
Kansas Racing Commission
3400 VanBuren
Topeka, KS 66611-2228
Phone: (913)296-5800

Credential Type: License Registration. **Requirements:** Submit application and fingerprint card. Pay fee. **Fees:** $5 registration fee.

459

Outrider (Racetrack)
Kansas Racing Commission
3400 VanBuren
Topeka, KS 66611-2228
Phone: (913)296-5800

Credential Type: License Registration. **Requirements:** Submit application and fingerprint card. Pay fee. **Fees:** $10 registration fee.

460

Paddock Attendant (Racetrack)
Kansas Racing Commission
3400 VanBuren
Topeka, KS 66611-2228
Phone: (913)296-5800

Credential Type: License Registration. **Requirements:** Submit application and fingerprint card. Pay fee. **Fees:** $5 registration fee.

461

Plater (Racetrack)
Kansas Racing Commission
3400 VanBuren
Topeka, KS 66611-2228
Phone: (913)296-5800

Credential Type: License Registration. **Requirements:** Submit application and fingerprint card. Pay fee. **Fees:** $10 registration fee.

462

Pony Person (Racetrack)
Kansas Racing Commission
3400 VanBuren
Topeka, KS 66611-2228
Phone: (913)296-5800

Credential Type: License Registration. **Requirements:** Submit application and fingerprint card. Pay fee. **Fees:** $5 registration fee.

Animal Caretakers and Trainers, Except Farm

463

Stable Trainer/Agent (Racetrack)
Kansas Racing Commission
3400 VanBuren
Topeka, KS 66611-2228
Phone: (913)296-5800

Credential Type: License Registration. **Requirements:** Submit application and fingerprint card. Pay fee. **Fees:** $10 registration fee.

464

Trainer (Racetrack)
Kansas Racing Commission
3400 VanBuren
Topeka, KS 66611-2228
Phone: (913)296-5800

Credential Type: License Registration. **Requirements:** Submit application and fingerprint card. Pay fee. **Fees:** $10 registration fee.

Kentucky

465

Animal Technician
Kentucky Board of Veterinary Examiners
PO Box 456
Frankfort, KY 40602
Phone: (502)564-3296
Fax: (502)564-4818

Credential Type: Animal Technician Certificate. **Duration of License:** One year. **Requirements:** High school graduate. Complete an approved course in the care and treatment of animals. **Examination:** National Boards for Animal Technicians. **Reciprocity:** $25 examination fee. $15 renewal fee. **Governing Statute:** Chapter 321 of Kentucky Revised Statutes.

466

Assistant Trainer (Racetrack)
Kentucky State Racing Commission
PO Box 1080
Lexington, KY 40588
Phone: (606)254-7021

Credential Type: License Registration. **Requirements:** Submit application and fingerprint card. Pay fee. **Fees:** $35 registration fee.

467

Blacksmith (Racetrack)
Kentucky State Racing Commission
PO Box 1080
Lexington, KY 40588
Phone: (606)254-7021

Credential Type: License Registration. **Requirements:** Submit application and fingerprint card. Pay fee. **Fees:** $35 registration fee.

468

Dental Technician (Racetrack)
Kentucky State Racing Commission
PO Box 1080
Lexington, KY 40588
Phone: (606)254-7021

Credential Type: License Registration. **Requirements:** Submit application and fingerprint card. Pay fee. **Fees:** $35 registration fee.

469

Farrier/Apprentice Farrier (Racetrack)
Kentucky State Racing Commission
PO Box 1080
Lexington, KY 40588
Phone: (606)254-7021

Credential Type: Farrier/Apprentice Farrier License. **Requirements:** Submit application and fingerprint card. Pay fee. **Fees:** $35 license fee.

470

Outrider (Racetrack)
Kentucky State Racing Commission
PO Box 1080
Lexington, KY 40588
Phone: (606)254-7021

Credential Type: Association Employee and Occupational License. **Requirements:** Submit application and fingerprint card. Pay fee. **Fees:** $10 license fee.

471

Stable Employee (Racetrack)
Kentucky State Racing Commission
PO Box 1080
Lexington, KY 40588
Phone: (606)254-7021

Credential Type: Stable Employee License. **Authorization:** Authorizes work in the following positions: foreman, exercise boy, groom, hotwalker, watchman, or pony boy. **Requirements:** Submit application and fingerprint card. Pay fee. **Fees:** $5 license fee.

472

Trainer (Racetrack)
Kentucky State Racing Commission
PO Box 1080
Lexington, KY 40588
Phone: (606)254-7021

Credential Type: License Registration. **Requirements:** Submit application and fingerprint card. Pay fee. **Fees:** $35 registration fee.

473

Veterinarian Assistant (Racetrack)
Kentucky State Racing Commission
PO Box 1080
Lexington, KY 40588
Phone: (606)254-7021

Credential Type: License Registration. **Requirements:** Submit application and fingerprint card. Pay fee. **Fees:** $25 registration fee.

Louisiana

474

Exercise Rider (Racetrack)
Louisiana State Racing Commission
320 N. Carrollton Ave., Ste. 2-B
New Orleans, LA 70119-5111
Phone: (504)483-4000

Credential Type: License Registration. **Duration of License:** One year initial license. **Requirements:** At least 18 years of age or 16 years of age with permit. Abide by state rules and regulations. Submit application and pay fees. **Fees:** $25 registration fee. $75 three year renewal fee.

475

Groom (Racetrack)
Louisiana State Racing Commission
320 N. Carrollton Ave., Ste. 2-B
New Orleans, LA 70119-5111
Phone: (504)483-4000

Credential Type: License Registration. **Duration of License:** One year. **Requirements:** At least 18 years of age. Abide by state rules and regulations. Submit application and pay fees. **Fees:** $12.50 registration fee.

Louisiana

476

Hot Walker (Racetrack)
Louisiana State Racing Commission
320 N. Carrollton Ave., Ste. 2-B
New Orleans, LA 70119-5111
Phone: (504)483-4000

Credential Type: License Registration. **Duration of License:** One year. **Requirements:** At least 18 years of age. Abide by state rules and regulations. Submit application and pay fees. **Fees:** $12.50 registration fee.

477

Outrider (Racetrack)
Louisiana State Racing Commission
320 N. Carrollton Ave., Ste. 2-B
New Orleans, LA 70119-5111
Phone: (504)483-4000

Credential Type: License Registration. **Duration of License:** One year. **Requirements:** At least 18 years of age. Abide by state rules and regulations. Submit application and pay fees. **Fees:** $25 registration fee.

478

Pony Boy/Pony Girl (Racetrack)
Louisiana State Racing Commission
320 N. Carrollton Ave., Ste. 2-B
New Orleans, LA 70119-5111
Phone: (504)483-4000

Credential Type: License Registration. **Duration of License:** One year. **Requirements:** At least 18 years of age. Abide by state rules and regulations. Submit application and pay fees. **Fees:** $25 registration fee.

479

Racehorse Trainer
Louisiana State Racing Commission
320 N. Carrollton Ave., Ste. 2-B
New Orleans, LA 70119
Phone: (504)483-4000

Credential Type: y. **Duration of License:** One or three years. **Requirements:** 18 years of age. Two years of racing experience. Two recommendations. **Examination:** Yes. **Fees:** $25 one-year license fee. $75 three-year license fee.

Maine

480

Animal Technician
Dept. of Professional and Financial Regulation
Div. of Licensing and Enforcement
State House Station 35
Augusta, ME 04333
Phone: (207)582-8723
Fax: (207)582-5415

Credential Type: Animal Technician Certificate. **Duration of License:** One year. **Requirements:** Graduate of a two year college animal technician program. **Examination:** State examination. **Fees:** $50 examination fee. $10 annual registration fee. **Governing Statute:** Maine Statutes.

Maryland

481

Assistant Trainer (Thoroughbred Racing)
Maryland Racing Commission
Stanbalt Bldg., 14th Fl.
501 St. Paul Place
Baltimore, MD 21202
Phone: (301)333-6267

Credential Type: License Registration. **Requirements:** Submit application, fingerprint card, and three passport size photos. Pay fee. **Fees:** $25 registration fee.

482

Farrier (Harness Racing)
Maryland Racing Commission
Stanbalt Bldg., 14th Fl.
501 St. Paul Place
Baltimore, MD 21202
Phone: (301)333-6267

Credential Type: License Registration. **Requirements:** Submit application, fingerprint card, and three passport size photos. Pay fee. **Fees:** $10 registration fee.

483

Farrier (Thoroughbred Racing)
Maryland Racing Commission
Stanbalt Bldg., 14th Fl.
501 St. Paul Place
Baltimore, MD 21202
Phone: (301)333-6267

Credential Type: License Registration. **Requirements:** Submit application, fingerprint card, and three passport size photos. Pay fee. **Fees:** $10 registration fee.

484

Stable Employee (Harness Racing)
Maryland Racing Commission
Stanbalt Bldg., 14th Fl.
501 St. Paul Place
Baltimore, MD 21202
Phone: (301)333-6267

Credential Type: License Registration. **Requirements:** Submit application, fingerprint card, and three passport size photos. Pay fee. **Fees:** $5 registration fee.

485

Stable Employee (Thoroughbred Racing)
Maryland Racing Commission
Stanbalt Bldg., 14th Fl.
501 St. Paul Place
Baltimore, MD 21202
Phone: (301)333-6267

Credential Type: License Registration. **Requirements:** Submit application, fingerprint card, and three passport size photos. Pay fee. **Fees:** $5 registration fee.

486

Trainer (Harness Racing)
Maryland Racing Commission
Stanbalt Bldg., 14th Fl.
501 St. Paul Place
Baltimore, MD 21202
Phone: (301)333-6267

Credential Type: License Registration. **Requirements:** Submit application, fingerprint card, and three passport size photos. Pay fee. **Fees:** $25 registration fee.

487

Trainer (Thoroughbred Racing)
Maryland Racing Commission
Stanbalt Bldg., 14th Fl.
501 St. Paul Place
Baltimore, MD 21202
Phone: (301)333-6267

Credential Type: License Registration. **Requirements:** Submit application, fingerprint card, and three passport size photos. Pay fee. **Fees:** $50 original registration fee. $25 renewal fee.

488

Wildlife Exhibitor
Wildlife Div.
Dept. of Natural Resources
Tawes State Office Bldg.
Annapolis, MD 21401
Phone: (410)296-2230

Credential Type: Exhibitor License. **Duration of License:** Varies. **Requirements:** Submit application with copies of appropriate federal permits. **Fees:** No fee.

Massachusetts

489

Blacksmith (Racetrack)
Massachusetts State Racing Commission
1 Ashburton Place, Rm. 1313
Boston, MA 02108
Phone: (617)727-2581

Credential Type: License Registration. **Requirements:** Submit application and fingerprint card. Pay fee. **Fees:** $20 registration fee.

490

Greyhound Assistant Trainer (Racetrack)
Massachusetts State Racing Commission
1 Ashburton Place, Rm. 1313
Boston, MA 02108
Phone: (617)727-2581

Credential Type: License Registration. **Requirements:** Submit application and fingerprint card. Pay fee. **Fees:** $20 registration fee.

491

Greyhound Trainer (Racetrack)
Massachusetts State Racing Commission
1 Ashburton Place, Rm. 1313
Boston, MA 02108
Phone: (617)727-2581

Credential Type: License Registration. **Requirements:** Submit application and fingerprint card. Pay fee. **Fees:** $25 registration fee.

492

Outrider (Racetrack)
Massachusetts State Racing Commission
1 Ashburton Place, Rm. 1313
Boston, MA 02108
Phone: (617)727-2581

Credential Type: License Registration. **Requirements:** Submit application and fingerprint card. Pay fee. **Fees:** $10 registration fee.

493

Stable Employee (Racetrack)
Massachusetts State Racing Commission
1 Ashburton Place, Rm. 1313
Boston, MA 02108
Phone: (617)727-2581

Credential Type: License Registration. **Requirements:** Submit application and fingerprint card. Pay fee. **Fees:** $5 registration fee.

494

Thoroughbred Trainer (Racetrack)
Massachusetts State Racing Commission
1 Ashburton Place, Rm. 1313
Boston, MA 02108
Phone: (617)727-2581

Credential Type: License Registration. **Requirements:** Submit application and fingerprint card. Pay fee. **Fees:** $25 registration fee.

Michigan

495

Assistant Trainer (Racetrack)
Michigan Office of Racing Commissioner
37650 Professional Center Dr.
Livonia, MI 48154-1114
Phone: (313)462-2400

Credential Type: License Registration. **Requirements:** Submit application and fingerprint card. Pay fee. **Fees:** $20 registration fee. $5 duplicate license fee.

496

Blacksmith (Racetrack)
Michigan Office of Racing Commissioner
37650 Professional Center Dr.
Livonia, MI 48154-1114
Phone: (313)462-2400

Credential Type: License Registration. **Requirements:** Submit application and fingerprint card. Pay fee. **Fees:** $20 registration fee. $5 duplicate license fee.

497

Breeder, Wild Animals and Birds
Wildlife Div.
Dept. of Natural Resources
Stevens T. Mason Bldg.
PO Box 30028
Lansing, MI 48909
Phone: (517)373-1220

Credential Type: License. **Duration of License:** Three years. **Requirements:** Have obtained wildlife in a lawful manner, as evidenced by a receipted invoice or other document. Provide humane and sanitary conditions for wildlife. Provide pens, cages, or enclosures of sufficient size to prevent the crowding of wildlife. Provide wildlife with food and water. Submit pens and wildlife to an inspection by a conservation officer. Comply with the Game Breeder's Law and the rules of the Department of Natural Resources. **Fees:** $45 minimum—$150 maximum initial license fee (which is based either on the size of the area or on the number of animals enclosed). Same renewal fee as initial fee. **Governing Statute:** The Game Breeders Law, Act 191 of 1929, as amended.

498

Farrier (Racetrack)
Michigan Office of Racing Commissioner
37650 Professional Center Dr.
Livonia, MI 48154-1114
Phone: (313)462-2400

Credential Type: License Registration. **Requirements:** Submit application and fingerprint card. Pay fee. **Fees:** $20 registration fee. $5 duplicate license fee.

499

Groom (Racetrack)
Michigan Office of Racing
  Commissioner
37650 Professional Center Dr.
Livonia, MI 48154-1114
Phone: (313)462-2400

Credential Type: License Registration. **Requirements:** Submit application and fingerprint card. Pay fee. **Fees:** $10 registration fee. $5 duplicate license fee.

500

Horse Riding Stable Operator
Animal Industry Div.
Dept. of Agriculture
Ottawa Bldg., N.
PO Box 30017
Lansing, MI 48909
Phone: (517)373-1104

Credential Type: License. **Duration of License:** One year. **Requirements:** Follow all rules and regulations of the Department of Agriculture. **Fees:** $25 initial license fee. $25 renewal fee. **Governing Statute:** Horse Riding Stables and Sales Barns Act, Act 93 of 1974, as amended.

501

Plater (Racetrack)
Michigan Office of Racing
  Commissioner
37650 Professional Center Dr.
Livonia, MI 48154-1114
Phone: (313)462-2400

Credential Type: License Registration. **Requirements:** Submit application and fingerprint card. Pay fee. **Fees:** $20 registration fee. $5 duplicate license fee.

502

Reptile/Amphibian Catcher, Commercial
Fisheries Div.
Dept. of Natural Resources
Stevens T. Mason Bldg.
PO Box 30028
Lansing, MI 48909
Phone: (517)373-1220

Credential Type: License. **Duration of License:** One year. **Requirements:** Must provide a record of their catch by species on a monthly basis to the Department. **Fees:** $150 initial license fee. $150 renewal fee. **Governing Statute:** Michigan Sports Fishing Law, Act 165 of 1929, as amended.

503

Research Animal Dealer
Animal Industry Div.
Dept. of Agriculture
Ottawa Bldg., N.
PO Box 30017
Lansing, MI 48909
Phone: (517)373-1104

Credential Type: License. **Duration of License:** Lifelong. **Requirements:** Be of good moral character. Never have been convicted of cruelty to animals or a violation of this Act. Pass an inspection of premises. Conduct business in a permanent structure or building. Abide by the rules put into effect by the Department of Agriculture. **Fees:** $25 initial license fee. **Governing Statute:** Animals for Research Act, Act 224 of 1969.

504

Stable Helper (Racetrack)
Michigan Office of Racing
  Commissioner
37650 Professional Center Dr.
Livonia, MI 48154-1114
Phone: (313)462-2400

Credential Type: License Registration. **Requirements:** Submit application and fingerprint card. Pay fee. **Fees:** $10 registration fee. $5 duplicate license fee.

505

Trainer (Racetrack)
Michigan Office of Racing
  Commissioner
37650 Professional Center Dr.
Livonia, MI 48154-1114
Phone: (313)462-2400

Credential Type: License Registration. **Requirements:** Submit application and fingerprint card. Pay fee. **Fees:** $20 registration fee. $5 duplicate license fee.

506

Veterinary Technician
State Board of Veterinary Medicine
Dept. of Commerce
611 W. Ottawa
PO Box 30018
Lansing, MI 48909
Phone: (517)373-3596
Fax: (517)373-2179

Credential Type: License to practice. **Duration of License:** Two years. **Requirements:** Graduation from an approved program in veterinary technical training. **Examination:** State veterinary technician examination. **Fees:** $150 examination fee. $20 license fee. $20 biennial renewal fee. **Governing Statute:** Public Health Code, Act 368, Articles 1, 7, and 15.

507

Wildlife Exhibitor (Animals and Birds)
Wildlife Div.
Dept. of Natural Resources
Stevens T. Mason Bldg.
PO Box 30028
Lansing, MI 48909
Phone: (517)373-1220

Credential Type: License. **Duration of License:** One year. **Requirements:** Have obtained animals and birds in a lawful manner, as evidenced by a receipted invoice or other document. Confine animals and birds in pens or fenced areas which meet the department's minimum specifications. Provide humane and sanitary conditions. Provide water and food. Submit to an inspection of pens and surrounding premises by a Department officer. Comply with the rules of the Department of Natural Resources. **Fees:** $15 initial permit fee. $15 renewal fee. **Governing Statute:** Game Law, Act 286 of 1929, as amended.

Minnesota

508

Exercise Rider (Racetrack)
Minnesota Racing Commission
11000 W. 78th St., Ste. 201
Eden Prairie, MN 55344
Phone: (612)341-7555

Credential Type: License Registration. **Requirements:** Submit application and fingerprint card. Pay fee. **Fees:** $15 registration fee.

509

Farrier (Racetrack)
Minnesota Racing Commission
11000 W. 78th St., Ste. 201
Eden Prairie, MN 55344
Phone: (612)341-7555

Credential Type: License Registration. **Requirements:** Submit application and fingerprint card. Pay fee. **Fees:** $25 registration fee.

Animal Caretakers and Trainers, Except Farm — Missouri

510

Farrier's Assistant (Racetrack)
Minnesota Racing Commission
11000 W. 78th St., Ste. 201
Eden Prairie, MN 55344
Phone: (612)341-7555

Credential Type: License Registration. **Requirements:** Submit application and fingerprint card. Pay fee. **Fees:** $10 registration fee.

511

Groom/Hotwalker (Racetrack)
Minnesota Racing Commission
11000 W. 78th St., Ste. 201
Eden Prairie, MN 55344
Phone: (612)341-7555

Credential Type: License Registration. **Requirements:** Submit application and fingerprint card. Pay fee. **Fees:** $5 registration fee.

512

Pony Rider (Racetrack)
Minnesota Racing Commission
11000 W. 78th St., Ste. 201
Eden Prairie, MN 55344
Phone: (612)341-7555

Credential Type: License Registration. **Requirements:** Submit application and fingerprint card. Pay fee. **Fees:** $10 registration fee.

513

Stable Foreman (Racetrack)
Minnesota Racing Commission
11000 W. 78th St., Ste. 201
Eden Prairie, MN 55344
Phone: (612)341-7555

Credential Type: License Registration. **Requirements:** Submit application and fingerprint card. Pay fee. **Fees:** $5 registration fee.

514

Trainer Assistant (Racetrack)
Minnesota Racing Commission
11000 W. 78th St., Ste. 201
Eden Prairie, MN 55344
Phone: (612)341-7555

Credential Type: License Registration. **Requirements:** Submit application and fingerprint card. Pay fee. **Fees:** $15 registration fee.

515

Trainer (Racetrack)
Minnesota Racing Commission
11000 W. 78th St., Ste. 201
Eden Prairie, MN 55344
Phone: (612)341-7555

Credential Type: License Registration. **Requirements:** Submit application and fingerprint card. Pay fee. **Fees:** $25 registration fee.

516

Veterinary Assistant (Racetrack)
Minnesota Racing Commission
11000 W. 78th St., Ste. 201
Eden Prairie, MN 55344
Phone: (612)341-7555

Credential Type: License Registration. **Requirements:** Submit application and fingerprint card. Pay fee. **Fees:** $25 registration fee.

Mississippi

517

Animal Technician
Board of Veterinary Medicine
209 S. Lafayette St.
Starkville, MS 39759
Phone: (601)324-0235

Credential Type: Animal Technician Certificate. **Duration of License:** One year. **Requirements:** Pass examination. Renewal requires applicant to be actively working for a licensed veterinarian. **Examination:** State examination **Fees:** $25 examination fee. $5 annual renewal fee. **Governing Statute:** The Veterinary Practice Law (Sections 73-39-1 to 73-39-7).

Missouri

518

Assistant Trainer (Racetrack)
Missouri Horse Racing Commission
PO Box 754
Jefferson City, MO 65102
Phone: (314)751-3565

Credential Type: License Registration. **Requirements:** Submit application and fingerprint card. Pay fee. **Fees:** $20 registration fee. $4 duplicate registration fee.

519

Exercise Rider (Racetrack)
Missouri Horse Racing Commission
PO Box 754
Jefferson City, MO 65102
Phone: (314)751-3565

Credential Type: License Registration. **Requirements:** Submit application and fingerprint card. Pay fee. **Fees:** $15 registration fee. $4 duplicate registration fee.

520

Farrier Assistant (Racetrack)
Missouri Horse Racing Commission
PO Box 754
Jefferson City, MO 65102
Phone: (314)751-3565

Credential Type: License Registration. **Requirements:** Submit application and fingerprint card. Pay fee. **Fees:** $10 registration fee. $4 duplicate registration fee.

521

Farrier (Racetrack)
Missouri Horse Racing Commission
PO Box 754
Jefferson City, MO 65102
Phone: (314)751-3565

Credential Type: License Registration. **Requirements:** Submit application and fingerprint card. Pay fee. **Fees:** $50 registration fee. $4 duplicate registration fee.

522

Owner-Trainer (Racetrack)
Missouri Horse Racing Commission
PO Box 754
Jefferson City, MO 65102
Phone: (314)751-3565

Credential Type: License Registration. **Requirements:** Submit application and fingerprint card. Pay fee. **Fees:** $25 registration fee. $4 duplicate registration fee.

523

Stable Employee (Racetrack)
Missouri Horse Racing Commission
PO Box 754
Jefferson City, MO 65102
Phone: (314)751-3565

Credential Type: License Registration. **Requirements:** Submit application and fingerprint card. Pay fee. **Fees:** $5 registration fee. $4 duplicate registration fee.

524

Veterinarian Assistant (Racetrack)
Missouri Horse Racing Commission
PO Box 754
Jefferson City, MO 65102
Phone: (314)751-3565

Credential Type: License Registration.
Requirements: Submit application and fingerprint card. Pay fee. **Fees:** $10 registration fee. $4 duplicate registration fee.

525

Veterinary Technician
Veterinary Medical Board
PO Box 633
Jefferson City, MO 65102
Phone: (314)751-0031

Credential Type: Veterinary Technician Certificate. **Duration of License:** One year. **Requirements:** Pass examination. Renewal requires applicant to be actively working for a licensed veterinarian. **Examination:** Professional Examination Service examination. **Fees:** $85 examination fee. $15 renewal fee. **Governing Statute:** Original practice act.

Montana

526

Assistant Trainer (Racetrack)
State of Montana Board of Horse Racing
Dept. of Commerce
1424 9th Ave.
Helena, MT 59620
Phone: (406)444-4287

Credential Type: License Registration.
Requirements: Submit application and fingerprint card. Pay fee. **Fees:** $30 registration fee.

527

Exercise Person (Racetrack)
State of Montana Board of Horse Racing
Dept. of Commerce
1424 9th Ave.
Helena, MT 59620
Phone: (406)444-4287

Credential Type: License Registration.
Requirements: Submit application and fingerprint card. Pay fee. **Fees:** $20 registration fee.

528

Groom (Racetrack)
State of Montana Board of Horse Racing
Dept. of Commerce
1424 9th Ave.
Helena, MT 59620
Phone: (406)444-4287

Credential Type: License Registration.
Requirements: Submit application and fingerprint card. Pay fee. **Fees:** $20 registration fee.

529

Hot Walker (Racetrack)
State of Montana Board of Horse Racing
Dept. of Commerce
1424 9th Ave.
Helena, MT 59620
Phone: (406)444-4287

Credential Type: License Registration.
Requirements: Submit application and fingerprint card. Pay fee. **Fees:** $20 registration fee.

530

Outrider (Racetrack)
State of Montana Board of Horse Racing
Dept. of Commerce
1424 9th Ave.
Helena, MT 59620
Phone: (406)444-4287

Credential Type: License Registration.
Requirements: Submit application and fingerprint card. Pay fee. **Fees:** $20 registration fee.

531

Plater (Racetrack)
State of Montana Board of Horse Racing
Dept. of Commerce
1424 9th Ave.
Helena, MT 59620
Phone: (406)444-4287

Credential Type: License Registration.
Requirements: Submit application and fingerprint card. Pay fee. **Fees:** $30 registration fee.

532

Pony Person (Racetrack)
State of Montana Board of Horse Racing
Dept. of Commerce
1424 9th Ave.
Helena, MT 59620
Phone: (406)444-4287

Credential Type: License Registration.
Requirements: Submit application and fingerprint card. Pay fee. **Fees:** $20 registration fee.

533

Stable Foreman (Racetrack)
State of Montana Board of Horse Racing
Dept. of Commerce
1424 9th Ave.
Helena, MT 59620
Phone: (406)444-4287

Credential Type: License Registration.
Requirements: Submit application and fingerprint card. Pay fee. **Fees:** $20 registration fee.

534

Trainer (Racetrack)
State of Montana Board of Horse Racing
Dept. of Commerce
1424 9th Ave.
Helena, MT 59620
Phone: (406)444-4287

Credential Type: License Registration.
Requirements: Submit application and fingerprint card. Pay fee. **Fees:** $30 registration fee.

535

Veterinarian Assistant (Racetrack)
State of Montana Board of Horse Racing
Dept. of Commerce
1424 9th Ave.
Helena, MT 59620
Phone: (406)444-4287

Credential Type: License Registration.
Requirements: Submit application and fingerprint card. Pay fee. **Fees:** $20 registration fee.

Nebraska

536

Animal Technician
Nebraska Board of Examiners in Veterinary Medicine & Surgery
PO Box 95007
301 Centennial Mall S.
Lincoln, NE 68509
Phone: (402)471-2115

Credential Type: License. **Duration of License:** One year. **Requirements:** Must be a graduate of an approved animal technician program and work under the supervision of a licensed veterinarian or group of veterinarians approved by the board. **Fees:** $5 application fee. $5 renewal fee.

537

Assistant Trainer (Racetrack)
Nebraska Racing Commission
PO Box 95014
301 Centennial Mall S.
Lincoln, NE 68509
Phone: (402)471-4155

Credential Type: License Registration. **Duration of License:** One year. **Requirements:** At least 16 years of age. No felony convictions. Secure employment and submit application completed and signed by management. Pay fees. **Examination:** Tested by Board of Stewards. **Fees:** $20 license fee. $20 renewal fee.

538

Exercise Rider (Racetrack)
Nebraska Racing Commission
PO Box 95014
301 Centennial Mall S.
Lincoln, NE 68509
Phone: (402)471-4155

Credential Type: License Registration. **Duration of License:** One year. **Requirements:** At least 16 years of age. No felony convictions. Secure employment and submit application completed and signed by management. Pay fees. **Examination:** Tested by Board of Stewards. **Fees:** $20 license fee. $20 renewal fee.

539

Groom
Nebraska Racing Commision
PO Box 95014
Lincoln, NE 68509
Phone: (402)471-2577

Credential Type: License. **Duration of License:** One year. **Requirements:** 16 years of age. **Fees:** $10 license fee. $10 renewal fee.

540

Horseshoer (Racetrack)
Nebraska Racing Commission
PO Box 95014
301 Centennial Mall S.
Lincoln, NE 68509
Phone: (402)471-4155

Credential Type: License Registration. **Duration of License:** One year. **Requirements:** At least 16 years of age. No felony convictions. Secure employment and submit application completed and signed by management. Pay fees. **Examination:** Tested by Board of Stewards. **Fees:** $20 license fee. $20 renewal fee.

541

Pony Person (Racetrack)
Nebraska Racing Commission
PO Box 95014
301 Centennial Mall S.
Lincoln, NE 68509
Phone: (402)471-4155

Credential Type: License Registration. **Duration of License:** One year. **Requirements:** At least 16 years of age. No felony convictions. Secure employment and submit application completed and signed by management. Pay fees. **Examination:** Tested by Board of Stewards. **Fees:** $20 license fee. $20 renewal fee.

542

Trainer (Race Horse)
Nebraska Racing Commission
PO Box 95014
Lincoln, NE 68509
Phone: (402)471-2477

Credential Type: License. **Duration of License:** One year. **Requirements:** 16 years of age. Must be approved by the Board of Stewards. A felony conviction may be grounds for denial of license. **Examination:** Yes. **Fees:** $25 license fee. $25 renewal fee.

543

Veterinarian's Assistant (Racetrack)
Nebraska Racing Commission
PO Box 95014
301 Centennial Mall S.
Lincoln, NE 68509
Phone: (402)471-4155

Credential Type: License Registration. **Duration of License:** One year. **Requirements:** At least 16 years of age. No felony convictions. Secure employment and submit application completed and signed by management. Pay fees. **Fees:** $10 license fee. $10 renewal fee.

Nevada

544

Animal Caretaker
Nevada State Board of Veterinary Medical Examiners
1005 Terminal Way, Ste. 246
Reno, NV 89502
Phone: (702)322-9422

Credential Type: License. **Duration of License:** One year. **Requirements:** Pass a college-level course in animal technology conforming to the standards of the American Veterinary Medical Association. **Examination:** Yes. **Fees:** $100 exam/licensing fee. $50 renewal fee.

545

Animal Technician
Board of Veterinary Medical Examiners
Executive Plaza
1005 Terminal Way, Ste. 246
Reno, NV 89502
Phone: (702)322-9422
Fax: (702)322-1926

Credential Type: Animal Technician Certificate. **Requirements:** Pass examination. **Examination:** State examination. **Fees:** $100 license fee. **Governing Statute:** Practice law.

546

Assistant Trainer (Racetrack)
Nevada Racing Commission
4820 Alpine Ct., Ste. 203
Las Vegas, NV 89107
Phone: (702)486-7619

Credential Type: License Registration. **Requirements:** Submit application and fin-

Assistant Trainer (Racetrack), continued

gerprint card. Pay fee. **Fees:** $20 registration fee.

547

Euthanasia Technician
Board of Veterinary Medical Examiners
Executive Plaza
1005 Terminal Way, Ste. 246
Reno, NV 89502
Phone: (702)322-9422
Fax: (702)322-1926

Credential Type: Euthanasia Technician Certificate. **Requirements:** Pass examination. **Examination:** State examination. **Fees:** $200 application/examination fee. **Governing Statute:** Practice law.

548

Kennel Helper (Racetrack)
Nevada Racing Commission
4820 Alpine Ct., Ste. 203
Las Vegas, NV 89107
Phone: (702)486-7619

Credential Type: License Registration. **Requirements:** Submit application and fingerprint card. Pay fee. **Fees:** $10 registration fee.

549

Lead Out (Racetrack)
Nevada Racing Commission
4820 Alpine Ct., Ste. 203
Las Vegas, NV 89107
Phone: (702)486-7619

Credential Type: License Registration. **Requirements:** Submit application and fingerprint card. Pay fee. **Fees:** $15 registration fee.

550

Owner-Trainer (Racetrack)
Nevada Racing Commission
4820 Alpine Ct., Ste. 203
Las Vegas, NV 89107
Phone: (702)486-7619

Credential Type: License Registration. **Requirements:** Submit application and fingerprint card. Pay fee. **Fees:** $45 registration fee.

551

Trainer (Racetrack)
Nevada Racing Commission
4820 Alpine Ct., Ste. 203
Las Vegas, NV 89107
Phone: (702)486-7619

Credential Type: License Registration. **Requirements:** Submit application and fingerprint card. Pay fee. **Fees:** $35 registration fee.

New Jersey

552

Groom
New Jersey Racing Commission
CN088
Trenton, NJ 08625-0088
Phone: (609)292-0613

Credential Type: License. **Requirements:** 16 years of age. U.S. citizen or valid immigration card. **Fees:** $5 license fee. **Governing Statute:** NJSA 5:5. NJAC 13:70-4.

553

Plater (Racetrack)
New Jersey Racing Commission
200 Woolverton St.
Trenton, NJ 08625-0088
Phone: (609)292-0613

Credential Type: License Registration. **Requirements:** At least 18 years of age or 16 years of age with working papers. U.S. citizen or valid immigration card. No drug convictions. No convictions of crimes involving moral turpitude. Submit application and fingerprint card. Pay fees. **Fees:** $29 registration fee. $15 registration fee.

New Mexico

554

Exercise Boy (Racetrack)
New Mexico State Racing Commission
PO Box 8576, Highland Station
Albuquerque, NM 87198
Phone: (505)841-4644

Credential Type: License Registration. **Requirements:** Submit application and fingerprint card. Pay fees. **Fees:** $16 registration fee. $1 notary fee. $23 fingerprint card processing fee.

555

Groom (Racetrack)
New Mexico State Racing Commission
PO Box 8576, Highland Station
Albuquerque, NM 87198
Phone: (505)841-4644

Credential Type: License Registration. **Requirements:** Submit application and fingerprint card. Pay fees. **Fees:** $12 registration fee. $1 notary fee. $23 fingerprint card processing fee.

556

Outrider (Racetrack)
New Mexico State Racing Commission
PO Box 8576, Highland Station
Albuquerque, NM 87198
Phone: (505)841-4644

Credential Type: License Registration. **Requirements:** Submit application and fingerprint card. Pay fees. **Fees:** $16 registration fee. $1 notary fee. $23 fingerprint card processing fee.

557

Plater (Racetrack)
New Mexico State Racing Commission
PO Box 8576, Highland Station
Albuquerque, NM 87198
Phone: (505)841-4644

Credential Type: License Registration. **Requirements:** Submit application and fingerprint card. Pay fees. **Fees:** $21 registration fee. $1 notary fee. $23 fingerprint card processing fee.

558

Pony Boy (Racetrack)
New Mexico State Racing Commission
PO Box 8576, Highland Station
Albuquerque, NM 87198
Phone: (505)841-4644

Credential Type: License Registration. **Requirements:** Submit application and fingerprint card. Pay fees. **Fees:** $16 registration fee. $1 notary fee. $23 fingerprint card processing fee.

559

Stable Area Gateman (Racetrack)
New Mexico State Racing
    Commission
PO Box 8576, Highland Station
Albuquerque, NM 87198
Phone: (505)841-4644

Credential Type: License Registration.
Requirements: Submit application and fingerprint card. Pay fees. **Fees:** $13 registration fee. $1 notary fee. $23 fingerprint card processing fee.

560

Stable Foreman (Racetrack)
New Mexico State Racing
    Commission
PO Box 8576, Highland Station
Albuquerque, NM 87198
Phone: (505)841-4644

Credential Type: License Registration.
Requirements: Submit application and fingerprint card. Pay fees. **Fees:** $16 registration fee. $1 notary fee. $23 fingerprint card processing fee.

561

Trainer Assistant (Racetrack)
New Mexico State Racing
    Commission
PO Box 8576, Highland Station
Albuquerque, NM 87198
Phone: (505)841-4644

Credential Type: License Registration.
Requirements: Submit application and fingerprint card. Pay fees. **Fees:** $21 registration fee. $1 notary fee. $23 fingerprint card processing fee.

562

Trainer (Racetrack)
New Mexico State Racing
    Commission
PO Box 8576, Highland Station
Albuquerque, NM 87198
Phone: (505)841-4644

Credential Type: License Registration.
Duration of License: Three years. **Requirements:** Submit application and fingerprint card. Pay fees. **Fees:** $105.50 registration fee. $1 notary fee. $23 fingerprint card processing fee.

563

Veterinarian Assistant (Racetrack)
New Mexico State Racing
    Commission
PO Box 8576, Highland Station
Albuquerque, NM 87198
Phone: (505)841-4644

Credential Type: License Registration.
Requirements: Submit application and fingerprint card. Pay fees. **Fees:** $14 registration fee. $1 notary fee. $23 fingerprint card processing fee.

564

Veterinary Technician
Board of Veterinary Examiners
1650 University Blvd. NE
Albuquerque, NM 87102
Phone: (505)841-9112

Credential Type: Veterinary Technician Certificate. **Duration of License:** One year. **Requirements:** Good moral character. Industrious. Responsible. Must have at least two years of training in an approved veterinary technician program. Renewal requires eight hours of continuing education annually. **Examination:** State examination. **Reciprocity:** None. **Fees:** $50 application fee. $20 annual registration fee. **Governing Statute:** New Mexico 1978 annotated Chapter 61:Professional and Occupational Licenses—Pamphlet 97:Medical Services Providers 612-1 through 61-1-19—Article 14 Veterinary Medicine 61-14-1 through 61-14-19.

New York

565

Animal Health Technologist (Veterinary Technologist)
State Education Dept.
Div. of Professional Licensing
    Services
Cultural Education Center
Empire State Plaza
Albany, NY 12231
Phone: (518)474-3279

Credential Type: License. **Duration of License:** Three years. **Requirements:** Associate's Degree in veterinary science technology. **Examination:** Three part written, and State Board developed practical. **Fees:** $165 license fee. $80 renewal fee. **Governing Statute:** Title VIII Articles 130, 135 of the Education Law.

566

Assistant Trainer (Thoroughbred Racing)
New York State Racing and
    Wagering Board
400 Broome St.
New York, NY 10013
Phone: (212)219-4230

Credential Type: License Registration.
Duration of License: One year. **Requirements:** Submit application, F.B.I fingerprint card, New York state fingerprint card, and three photos. Pay fees. **Fees:** $30 registration fee. $44 New York state fingerprint card processing fee (valid for five years).

567

Farrier (Harness or Quarter Horse Racing)
New York State Racing and
    Wagering Board
400 Broome St.
New York, NY 10013
Phone: (212)219-4230

Credential Type: License Registration.
Duration of License: One year. **Requirements:** Submit application, F.B.I fingerprint card, New York state fingerprint card, and three photos. Pay fees. **Fees:** $20 registration fee. $44 New York state fingerprint card processing fee (valid for five years).

568

Farrier (Thoroughbred Racing)
New York State Racing and
    Wagering Board
400 Broome St.
New York, NY 10013
Phone: (212)219-4230

Credential Type: License Registration.
Duration of License: One year. **Requirements:** Submit application, F.B.I fingerprint card, New York state fingerprint card, and three photos. Pay fees. **Fees:** $20 registration fee. $44 New York state fingerprint card processing fee (valid for five years).

569

Groom (Harness or Quarter Horse Racing)
New York State Racing and
    Wagering Board
400 Broome St.
New York, NY 10013
Phone: (212)219-4230

Credential Type: License Registration.
Duration of License: One year. **Require-

New York

Groom (Harness or Quarter Horse Racing), continued

ments: Submit application, F.B.I fingerprint card, New York state fingerprint card, and three photos. Pay fees. **Fees:** $5 registration fee. $44 New York state fingerprint card processing fee (valid for five years).

570

Stable Worker (Thoroughbred Racing)
New York State Racing and Wagering Board
400 Broome St.
New York, NY 10013
Phone: (212)219-4230

Credential Type: License Registration. **Duration of License:** One year. **Requirements:** Submit application, F.B.I fingerprint card, New York state fingerprint card, and three photos. Pay fees. **Fees:** $5 registration fee. $44 New York state fingerprint card processing fee (valid for five years).

571

Trainer/Assistant Trainer (Harness or Quarter Horse Racing)
New York State Racing and Wagering Board
400 Broome St.
New York, NY 10013
Phone: (212)219-4230

Credential Type: License Registration. **Duration of License:** One year. **Requirements:** Submit application, F.B.I fingerprint card, New York state fingerprint card, and three photos. Pay fees. **Fees:** $20 registration fee. $44 New York state fingerprint card processing fee (valid for five years).

572

Trainer (Thoroughbred Racing)
New York State Racing and Wagering Board
400 Broome St.
New York, NY 10013
Phone: (212)219-4230

Credential Type: License Registration. **Duration of License:** One year. **Requirements:** Submit application, F.B.I fingerprint card, New York state fingerprint card, and three photos. Pay fees. **Fees:** $30 registration fee. $44 New York state fingerprint card processing fee (valid for five years).

North Carolina

573

Veterinary Technician
Veterinary Medical Board
PO Box 12587
Raleigh, NC 27605
Phone: (919)733-7689

Credential Type: Certification. **Duration of License:** Two years. **Requirements:** High school diploma or equivalent. Completion of a two-year accredited veterinary technician program from an approved school. 18 years of age. Two recommendations. **Examination:** National and state exams. **Fees:** $90 exam fee. $10 renewal fee.

North Dakota

574

Assistant Veterinarian (Racetrack)
North Dakota Racing Commission
State Capitol Bldg.
Bismarck, ND 58505
Phone: (701)224-2210

Credential Type: License Registration. **Requirements:** Submit application and fingerprint card. Pay fee. **Fees:** $25 license fee. $10 duplicate license fee.

575

Exercise Person (Racetrack)
North Dakota Racing Commission
State Capitol Bldg.
Bismarck, ND 58505
Phone: (701)224-2210

Credential Type: License Registration. **Requirements:** Submit application and fingerprint card. Pay fee. **Fees:** $10 license fee. $10 duplicate license fee.

576

Groom (Racetrack)
North Dakota Racing Commission
State Capitol Bldg.
Bismarck, ND 58505
Phone: (701)224-2210

Credential Type: License Registration. **Requirements:** Submit application and fingerprint card. Pay fee. **Fees:** $10 license fee. $10 duplicate license fee.

577

Hot Walker (Racetrack)
North Dakota Racing Commission
State Capitol Bldg.
Bismarck, ND 58505
Phone: (701)224-2210

Credential Type: License Registration. **Requirements:** Submit application and fingerprint card. Pay fee. **Fees:** $10 license fee. $10 duplicate license fee.

578

Owner-Trainer (Racetrack)
North Dakota Racing Commission
State Capitol Bldg.
Bismarck, ND 58505
Phone: (701)224-2210

Credential Type: License Registration. **Requirements:** Submit application and fingerprint card. Pay fee. **Fees:** $50 license fee. $5 additional fee for each horse owned over three horses in number. $10 duplicate license fee.

579

Pony Person (Racetrack)
North Dakota Racing Commission
State Capitol Bldg.
Bismarck, ND 58505
Phone: (701)224-2210

Credential Type: License Registration. **Requirements:** Submit application and fingerprint card. Pay fee. **Fees:** $10 license fee. $10 duplicate license fee.

580

Stable Foreman (Racetrack)
North Dakota Racing Commission
State Capitol Bldg.
Bismarck, ND 58505
Phone: (701)224-2210

Credential Type: License Registration. **Requirements:** Submit application and fingerprint card. Pay fee. **Fees:** $10 license fee. $10 duplicate license fee.

581

Trainer (Racetrack)
North Dakota Racing Commission
State Capitol Bldg.
Bismarck, ND 58505
Phone: (701)224-2210

Credential Type: License Registration. **Requirements:** Submit application and fin-

gerprint card. Pay fee. **Fees:** $25 license fee. $10 duplicate license fee.

Ohio

582

Animal Technician
Veterinary Medical Board
77th S. High St., 16th Fl.
Columbus, OH 43266-0116
Phone: (614)644-5281

Credential Type: Animal Technician Certificate. **Duration of License:** Two years. **Requirements:** Graduate of an approved American Veterinary Medical Association (AVMA) program for animal technicians. Renewal requires four hours of continuing education annually. **Fees:** $25 registration fee. $25 biennial renewal fee. **Governing Statute:** Ohio Revised Code Chapter 4741 and Ohio Administrative Code Chapter 474-1.

583

Assistant Trainer (Thoroughbred, Standardbred, and Quarter Horse Racing)
Ohio State Racing Commission
State Office Tower
77 S. High St., 18th Fl.
Columbus, OH 43266-0416
Phone: (614)466-2757

Credential Type: License Registration. **Requirements:** Submit application and fingerprint card. Pay fee. **Fees:** $25 registration fee.

584

Exercise Boy/Girl (Thoroughbred and Quarter Horse Racing)
Ohio State Racing Commission
State Office Tower
77 S. High St., 18th Fl.
Columbus, OH 43266-0416
Phone: (614)466-2757

Credential Type: License Registration. **Requirements:** Submit application and fingerprint card. Pay fee. **Fees:** $10 registration fee.

585

Groom (Thoroughbred, Standardbred, and Quarter Horse Racing)
Ohio State Racing Commission
State Office Tower
77 S. High St., 18th Fl.
Columbus, OH 43266-0416
Phone: (614)466-2757

Credential Type: License Registration. **Requirements:** Submit application and fingerprint card. Pay fee. **Fees:** $10 registration fee.

586

Horseshoer (Thoroughbred, Standardbred, and Quarter Horse Racing)
Ohio State Racing Commission
State Office Tower
77 S. High St., 18th Fl.
Columbus, OH 43266-0416
Phone: (614)466-2757

Credential Type: License Registration. **Requirements:** Submit application and fingerprint card. Pay fee. **Fees:** $25 registration fee.

587

Outrider (Thoroughbred, Standardbred, and Quarter Horse Racing)
Ohio State Racing Commission
State Office Tower
77 S. High St., 18th Fl.
Columbus, OH 43266-0416
Phone: (614)466-2757

Credential Type: License Registration. **Requirements:** Submit application and fingerprint card. Pay fee. **Fees:** $10 registration fee.

588

Trainer (Thoroughbred, Standardbred, and Quarter Horse Racing)
Ohio State Racing Commission
State Office Tower
77 S. High St., 18th Fl.
Columbus, OH 43266-0416
Phone: (614)466-2757

Credential Type: License Registration. **Requirements:** Submit application and fingerprint card. Pay fee. **Fees:** $25 registration fee.

589

Veterinarian's Assistant (Thoroughbred, Standardbred, and Quarter Horse Racing)
Ohio State Racing Commission
State Office Tower
77 S. High St., 18th Fl.
Columbus, OH 43266-0416
Phone: (614)466-2757

Credential Type: License Registration. **Requirements:** Submit application and fingerprint card. Pay fee. **Fees:** $10 registration fee.

Oklahoma

590

Animal Technician
Oklahoma Board of Veterinary Medicine Examiners
PO Box 18256
Oklahoma City, OK 73154
Phone: (405)848-6841

Credential Type: License. **Duration of License:** One year. **Requirements:** Associate degree in applied science. 8-week preceptor at a veterinary clinic under a licensed veterinarian. Six hours continuing education each year. No felony convictions. **Examination:** National Professional Examination Service Veterinary Technician Exam and Oklahoma State Examination. **Fees:** $160 exam fee (included in application). $160 application fee (includes exam fee). $25 renewal fee.

591

Assistant Trainer (Racetrack)
Oklahoma Horse Racing Commission
6501 N. Broadway, Ste. 180
Oklahoma City, OK 73116
Phone: (405)848-0404

Credential Type: License Registration. **Duration of License:** One year. **Requirements:** Submit application and fingerprint card. Pay fee. **Fees:** $50 registration fee. $50 annual renewal.

592

Blacksmith (Racetrack)
Oklahoma Horse Racing Commission
6501 N. Broadway, Ste. 180
Oklahoma City, OK 73116
Phone: (405)848-0404

Credential Type: License Registration. **Duration of License:** One year. **Requirements:** Submit application and fingerprint

Oklahoma

Blacksmith (Racetrack), continued

card. Pay fee. **Fees:** $50 registration fee. $50 annual renewal. $120 triennial renewal.

593

Exercise Person (Racetrack)
Oklahoma Horse Racing Commission
6501 N. Broadway, Ste. 180
Oklahoma City, OK 73116
Phone: (405)848-0404

Credential Type: License Registration. **Duration of License:** One year. **Requirements:** Submit application and fingerprint card. Pay fee. **Fees:** $25 registration fee. $25 annual renewal.

594

Groom (Racetrack)
Oklahoma Horse Racing Commission
6501 N. Broadway, Ste. 180
Oklahoma City, OK 73116
Phone: (405)848-0404

Credential Type: License Registration. **Duration of License:** One year. **Requirements:** Submit application and fingerprint card. Pay fee. **Fees:** $25 registration fee. $25 annual renewal.

595

Outrider (Racetrack)
Oklahoma Horse Racing Commission
6501 N. Broadway, Ste. 180
Oklahoma City, OK 73116
Phone: (405)848-0404

Credential Type: License Registration. **Duration of License:** One year. **Requirements:** Submit application and fingerprint card. Pay fee. **Fees:** $25 registration fee. $25 annual renewal.

596

Owner/Assistant Trainer (Racetrack)
Oklahoma Horse Racing Commission
6501 N. Broadway, Ste. 180
Oklahoma City, OK 73116
Phone: (405)848-0404

Credential Type: License Registration. **Duration of License:** One year. **Requirements:** Submit application and fingerprint card. Pay fee. **Fees:** $50 registration fee. $50 annual renewal.

597

Owner/Trainer (Racetrack)
Oklahoma Horse Racing Commission
6501 N. Broadway, Ste. 180
Oklahoma City, OK 73116
Phone: (405)848-0404

Credential Type: License Registration. **Duration of License:** One year. **Requirements:** Submit application and fingerprint card. Pay fee. **Fees:** $50 registration fee. $50 annual renewal. $120 triennial renewal.

598

Pony Rider (Racetrack)
Oklahoma Horse Racing Commission
6501 N. Broadway, Ste. 180
Oklahoma City, OK 73116
Phone: (405)848-0404

Credential Type: License Registration. **Duration of License:** One year. **Requirements:** Submit application and fingerprint card. Pay fee. **Fees:** $25 registration fee. $25 annual renewal.

599

Racehorse Trainer
Oklahoma Horse Racing Commission
6501 N. Broadway, Ste. 180
Oklahoma City, OK 73116
Phone: (405)848-0404

Credential Type: License. **Duration of License:** One and three years. **Requirements:** 18 years of age. **Examination:** Oklahoma Horse Racing Commission Trainers Examination. **Fees:** $50 exam fee. $50 application fee. $50 renewal fee.

600

Racehorse Trainer, Assistant
Oklahoma Horse Racing Commission
6501 N. Broadway, Ste. 180
Oklahoma City, OK 73116
Phone: (405)848-0404

Credential Type: License. **Duration of License:** One year. **Requirements:** 18 years of age. **Examination:** Oklahoma Horse Racing Commission Trainers Exam. **Fees:** $50 exam fee. $50 application fee. $50 renewal fee.

601

Trainer (Racetrack)
Oklahoma Horse Racing Commission
6501 N. Broadway, Ste. 180
Oklahoma City, OK 73116
Phone: (405)848-0404

Credential Type: License Registration. **Duration of License:** One year. **Requirements:** Submit application and fingerprint card. Pay fee. **Fees:** $50 registration fee. $50 annual renewal. $120 triennial renewal.

602

Veterinarian Assistant (Racetrack)
Oklahoma Horse Racing Commission
6501 N. Broadway, Ste. 180
Oklahoma City, OK 73116
Phone: (405)848-0404

Credential Type: License Registration. **Duration of License:** One year. **Requirements:** Submit application and fingerprint card. Pay fee. **Fees:** $25 registration fee. $25 annual renewal.

Oregon

603

Animal Health Technician
Veterinary Medical Examining Board
PO Box 231
Portland, OR 97207
Phone: (503)229-5286

Credential Type: Animal Health Technician Certificate. **Duration of License:** One year. **Requirements:** Graduate of American Veterinary Medical Association (AVMA) veterinary college program or four years of training and experience in the veterinary field. **Examination:** State Board examination. **Fees:** $40 application/examination fee. $15 annual renewal fee. **Governing Statute:** Chapter 686, Veterinary Practice Act.

604

Assistant Trainer (Racetrack)
Oregon Racing Commission
113 State Office Bldg.
1400 SW Fifth
Portland, OR 97201
Phone: (503)229-5820

Credential Type: License Registration. **Requirements:** Submit application and fingerprint card. Pay fee. **Fees:** $30 registration fee. $6 duplicate fee.

Animal Caretakers and Trainers, Except Farm

605

Exercise Person (Racetrack)
Oregon Racing Commission
113 State Office Bldg.
1400 SW Fifth
Portland, OR 97201
Phone: (503)229-5820

Credential Type: License Registration.
Requirements: Submit application and fingerprint card. Pay fee. **Fees:** $30 registration fee. $6 duplicate fee.

606

Groom/Hot Walker (Racetrack)
Oregon Racing Commission
113 State Office Bldg.
1400 SW Fifth
Portland, OR 97201
Phone: (503)229-5820

Credential Type: License Registration.
Requirements: Submit application and fingerprint card. Pay fee. **Fees:** $30 registration fee. $6 duplicate fee.

607

Horseshoer/Plater (Racetrack)
Oregon Racing Commission
113 State Office Bldg.
1400 SW Fifth
Portland, OR 97201
Phone: (503)229-5820

Credential Type: License Registration.
Requirements: Submit application and fingerprint card. Pay fee. **Fees:** $30 registration fee. $6 duplicate fee.

608

Kennel Employee (Racetrack)
Oregon Racing Commission
113 State Office Bldg.
1400 SW Fifth
Portland, OR 97201
Phone: (503)229-5820

Credential Type: License Registration.
Requirements: Submit application and fingerprint card. Pay fee. **Fees:** $30 registration fee. $6 duplicate fee.

609

Lead Out (Racetrack)
Oregon Racing Commission
113 State Office Bldg.
1400 SW Fifth
Portland, OR 97201
Phone: (503)229-5820

Credential Type: License Registration.
Requirements: Submit application and fingerprint card. Pay fee. **Fees:** $30 registration fee. $6 duplicate fee.

610

Pony Person (Racetrack)
Oregon Racing Commission
113 State Office Bldg.
1400 SW Fifth
Portland, OR 97201
Phone: (503)229-5820

Credential Type: License Registration.
Requirements: Submit application and fingerprint card. Pay fee. **Fees:** $30 registration fee. $6 duplicate fee.

611

Trainer (Racetrack)
Oregon Racing Commission
113 State Office Bldg.
1400 SW Fifth
Portland, OR 97201
Phone: (503)229-5820

Credential Type: License Registration.
Requirements: Submit application and fingerprint card. Pay fee. **Fees:** $30 registration fee. $6 duplicate fee.

612

Veterinary Technician
Oregon State Veterinary Medical Examining Board
800 NE Oregon
PO Box 14450
Portland, OR 97214
Phone: (503)731-4051

Credential Type: License. **Duration of License:** One year. **Requirements:** Graduation from a two-year accredited program in Veterinary Technology, or have four years on-the-job training as a veterinary assistant. **Examination:** Yes. **Fees:** $40 exam fee. $15 renewal fee. **Governing Statute:** ORS 686.

Pennsylvania

613

Assistant Trainer (Horse Racing)
Pennsylvania State Horse Racing Commission
2301 N. Cameron St., Rm. 306, 4th Fl.
Harrisburg, PA 17110-9408
Phone: (717)787-1942

Credential Type: License Registration.
Duration of License: Three years. **Requirements:** Submit application, two photos, and fingerprint card. Pay fee. **Fees:** $30 registration fee. $2 duplicate license.

614

Blacksmith (Harness Racing)
Pennsylvania State Harness Racing Commission
2301 N. Cameron St.
Harrisburg, PA 17110-9408
Phone: (717)787-5196

Credential Type: License Registration.
Duration of License: Three years. **Requirements:** Submit application, three photos, and fingerprint card. Pay fee. **Fees:** $30 registration fee. $5 duplicate license. $33 fingerprint processing fee.

615

Driver/Groom (Harness Racing)
Pennsylvania State Harness Racing Commission
2301 N. Cameron St.
Harrisburg, PA 17110-9408
Phone: (717)787-5196

Credential Type: License Registration.
Duration of License: Three years. **Requirements:** Submit application, three photos, and fingerprint card. Pay fee. **Fees:** $45 registration fee. $5 duplicate license. $33 fingerprint processing fee.

616

Driver/Trainer/Groom (Harness Racing)
Pennsylvania State Harness Racing Commission
2301 N. Cameron St.
Harrisburg, PA 17110-9408
Phone: (717)787-5196

Credential Type: License Registration.
Duration of License: Three years. **Requirements:** Submit application, three photos, and fingerprint card. Pay fee. **Fees:** $75

Pennsylvania 617

Driver/Trainer/Groom (Harness Racing), continued

registration fee. $5 duplicate license. $33 fingerprint processing fee.

617

Farrier (Horse Racing)
Pennsylvania State Horse Racing Commission
2301 N. Cameron St., Rm. 306, 4th Fl.
Harrisburg, PA 17110-9408
Phone: (717)787-1942

Credential Type: License Registration. **Duration of License:** Three years. **Requirements:** Submit application, two photos, and fingerprint card. Pay fee. **Fees:** $45 registration fee. $2 duplicate license.

618

Groom (Harness Racing)
Pennsylvania State Harness Racing Commission
2301 N. Cameron St.
Harrisburg, PA 17110-9408
Phone: (717)787-5196

Credential Type: License Registration. **Duration of License:** Three years. **Requirements:** Submit application, three photos, and fingerprint card. Pay fee. **Fees:** $15 registration fee. $5 duplicate license. $33 fingerprint processing fee.

619

Owner/Driver/Groom (Harness Racing)
Pennsylvania State Harness Racing Commission
2301 N. Cameron St.
Harrisburg, PA 17110-9408
Phone: (717)787-5196

Credential Type: License Registration. **Duration of License:** Three years. **Requirements:** Submit application, three photos, and fingerprint card. Pay fee. **Fees:** $75 registration fee. $5 duplicate license. $33 fingerprint processing fee.

620

Owner/Groom (Harness Racing)
Pennsylvania State Harness Racing Commission
2301 N. Cameron St.
Harrisburg, PA 17110-9408
Phone: (717)787-5196

Credential Type: License Registration. **Duration of License:** Three years. **Requirements:** Submit application, three photos, and fingerprint card. Pay fee. **Fees:** $60 registration fee. $5 duplicate license. $33 fingerprint processing fee.

621

Owner/Trainer/Driver/Groom (Harness Racing)
Pennsylvania State Harness Racing Commission
2301 N. Cameron St.
Harrisburg, PA 17110-9408
Phone: (717)787-5196

Credential Type: License Registration. **Duration of License:** Three years. **Requirements:** Submit application, three photos, and fingerprint card. Pay fee. **Fees:** $75 registration fee. $5 duplicate license. $33 fingerprint processing fee.

622

Owner/Trainer/Groom (Harness Racing)
Pennsylvania State Harness Racing Commission
2301 N. Cameron St.
Harrisburg, PA 17110-9408
Phone: (717)787-5196

Credential Type: License Registration. **Duration of License:** Three years. **Requirements:** Submit application, three photos, and fingerprint card. Pay fee. **Fees:** $75 registration fee. $5 duplicate license. $33 fingerprint processing fee.

623

Owner/Trainer (Harness Racing)
Pennsylvania State Harness Racing Commission
2301 N. Cameron St.
Harrisburg, PA 17110-9408
Phone: (717)787-5196

Credential Type: License Registration. **Duration of License:** Three years. **Requirements:** Submit application, three photos, and fingerprint card. Pay fee. **Fees:** $60 registration fee. $5 duplicate license. $33 fingerprint processing fee.

624

Stable Employee (Horse Racing)
Pennsylvania State Horse Racing Commission
2301 N. Cameron St., Rm. 306, 4th Fl.
Harrisburg, PA 17110-9408
Phone: (717)787-1942

Credential Type: License Registration. **Duration of License:** Three years. **Requirements:** Submit application, two photos, and fingerprint card. Pay fee. **Fees:** $15 registration fee. $2 duplicate license.

625

Trainer/Groom (Harness Racing)
Pennsylvania State Harness Racing Commission
2301 N. Cameron St.
Harrisburg, PA 17110-9408
Phone: (717)787-5196

Credential Type: License Registration. **Duration of License:** Three years. **Requirements:** Submit application, three photos, and fingerprint card. Pay fee. **Fees:** $45 registration fee. $5 duplicate license. $33 fingerprint processing fee.

626

Trainer (Harness Racing)
Pennsylvania State Harness Racing Commission
2301 N. Cameron St.
Harrisburg, PA 17110-9408
Phone: (717)787-5196

Credential Type: License Registration. **Duration of License:** Three years. **Requirements:** Submit application, three photos, and fingerprint card. Pay fee. **Fees:** $30 registration fee. $5 duplicate license. $33 fingerprint processing fee.

627

Trainer (Horse Racing)
Pennsylvania State Horse Racing Commission
2301 N. Cameron St., Rm. 306, 4th Fl.
Harrisburg, PA 17110-9408
Phone: (717)787-1942

Credential Type: License Registration. **Duration of License:** Three years. **Requirements:** Submit application, two photos, and fingerprint card. Pay fee. **Fees:** $45 registration fee. $2 duplicate license.

Animal Caretakers and Trainers, Except Farm

Rhode Island

628

Kennel Employee (Racetrack)
Rhode Island Dept. of Business
  Regulations
Div. of Racing & Athletics
233 Richmond St., Ste. 234
Providence, RI 02903-4234
Phone: (401)277-6541

Credential Type: License Registration. **Duration of License:** Three years. **Requirements:** Submit application and fingerprint card. Pay fee. **Fees:** $5 registration fee.

629

Lead Out (Racetrack)
Rhode Island Dept. of Business
  Regulations
Div. of Racing & Athletics
233 Richmond St., Ste. 234
Providence, RI 02903-4234
Phone: (401)277-6541

Credential Type: License Registration. **Duration of License:** Three years. **Requirements:** Submit application and fingerprint card. Pay fee. **Fees:** $5 registration fee.

630

Trainer (Racetrack)
Rhode Island Dept. of Business
  Regulations
Div. of Racing & Athletics
233 Richmond St., Ste. 234
Providence, RI 02903-4234
Phone: (401)277-6541

Credential Type: License Registration. **Duration of License:** Three years. **Requirements:** Submit application and fingerprint card. Pay fee. **Fees:** $20 registration fee.

631

Wildlife Propagator
Office of Boat Registration and
  Licensing
Rhode Island Dept. of Environmental
  Management
22 Hayes St.
Providence, RI 02908
Phone: (401)277-3576

Credential Type: Wildlife Propagator License. **Duration of License:** One year. **Requirements:** Premises must be inspected for suitability of facility for work with species permitted. Submit application and pay fee. **Reciprocity:** No. **Fees:** $5 non-commercial license. $25 commercial license.

South Carolina

632

Animal Technician
South Carolina State Board of
  Veterinary Medical Examiners
PO Box 210786
Columbia, SC 29221
Phone: (803)772-8411

Credential Type: Animal Health Technician License. **Requirements:** 18 years of age. Graduation from an accredited school of animal technology. Good physical and mental health. **Examination:** Yes. **Fees:** $25 exam fee. $20 renewal fee.

South Dakota

633

**Assistant Trainer (Greyhound
  Racing)**
South Dakota Racing Commission
c/o 500 East Capitol
Pierre, SD 57501
Phone: (605)773-6050

Credential Type: License Registration. **Requirements:** Submit application and fingerprint card. Pay fee. **Fees:** $15 registration fee.

634

Exercise Rider (Horse Racing)
South Dakota Racing Commission
c/o 500 East Capitol
Pierre, SD 57501
Phone: (605)773-6050

Credential Type: License Registration. **Requirements:** Submit application and fingerprint card. Pay fee. **Fees:** $10 registration fee.

635

Groom (Horse Racing)
South Dakota Racing Commission
c/o 500 East Capitol
Pierre, SD 57501
Phone: (605)773-6050

Credential Type: License Registration. **Requirements:** Submit application and fingerprint card. Pay fee. **Fees:** $10 registration fee.

636

Kennel Helper (Greyhound Racing)
South Dakota Racing Commission
c/o 500 East Capitol
Pierre, SD 57501
Phone: (605)773-6050

Credential Type: License Registration. **Requirements:** Submit application and fingerprint card. Pay fee. **Fees:** $7.50 registration fee.

637

**Kennel Master (Greyhound
  Racing)**
South Dakota Racing Commission
c/o 500 East Capitol
Pierre, SD 57501
Phone: (605)773-6050

Credential Type: License Registration. **Requirements:** Submit application and fingerprint card. Pay fee. **Fees:** $15 registration fee.

638

**Kennel Operator (Greyhound
  Racing)**
South Dakota Racing Commission
c/o 500 East Capitol
Pierre, SD 57501
Phone: (605)773-6050

Credential Type: License Registration. **Requirements:** Submit application and fingerprint card. Pay fee. **Fees:** $15 registration fee.

639

Kennel Owner (Greyhound Racing)
South Dakota Racing Commission
c/o 500 East Capitol
Pierre, SD 57501
Phone: (605)773-6050

Credential Type: License Registration. **Requirements:** Submit application and fingerprint card. Pay fee. **Fees:** $15 registration fee.

640

Lead Out (Greyhound Racing)
South Dakota Racing Commission
c/o 500 East Capitol
Pierre, SD 57501
Phone: (605)773-6050

Credential Type: License Registration. **Requirements:** Submit application and fin-

South Dakota

Lead Out (Greyhound Racing), continued

gerprint card. Pay fee. **Fees:** $7.50 registration fee.

641

Outrider (Horse Racing)
South Dakota Racing Commission
c/o 500 East Capitol
Pierre, SD 57501
Phone: (605)773-6050

Credential Type: License Registration. **Requirements:** Submit application and fingerprint card. Pay fee. **Fees:** $10 registration fee.

642

Owner/Trainer (Greyhound Racing)
South Dakota Racing Commission
c/o 500 East Capitol
Pierre, SD 57501
Phone: (605)773-6050

Credential Type: License Registration. **Requirements:** Submit application and fingerprint card. Pay fee. **Fees:** $25 registration fee.

643

Owner/Trainer (Horse Racing)
South Dakota Racing Commission
c/o 500 East Capitol
Pierre, SD 57501
Phone: (605)773-6050

Credential Type: License Registration. **Requirements:** Submit application and fingerprint card. Pay fee. **Fees:** $40 registration fee.

644

Plater (Horse Racing)
South Dakota Racing Commission
c/o 500 East Capitol
Pierre, SD 57501
Phone: (605)773-6050

Credential Type: License Registration. **Requirements:** Submit application and fingerprint card. Pay fee. **Fees:** $10 registration fee.

645

Pony Rider (Horse Racing)
South Dakota Racing Commission
c/o 500 East Capitol
Pierre, SD 57501
Phone: (605)773-6050

Credential Type: License Registration. **Requirements:** Submit application and fingerprint card. Pay fee. **Fees:** $10 registration fee.

646

Trainer (Greyhound Racing)
South Dakota Racing Commission
c/o 500 East Capitol
Pierre, SD 57501
Phone: (605)773-6050

Credential Type: License Registration. **Requirements:** Submit application and fingerprint card. Pay fee. **Fees:** $15 registration fee.

647

Trainer (Horse Racing)
South Dakota Racing Commission
c/o 500 East Capitol
Pierre, SD 57501
Phone: (605)773-6050

Credential Type: License Registration. **Requirements:** Submit application and fingerprint card. Pay fee. **Fees:** $25 registration fee.

648

Veterinarian Assistant (Horse Racing)
South Dakota Racing Commission
c/o 500 East Capitol
Pierre, SD 57501
Phone: (605)773-6050

Credential Type: License Registration. **Requirements:** Submit application and fingerprint card. Pay fee. **Fees:** $10 registration fee.

Tennessee

649

Animal Dealer, Livestock
Tennessee Dept. of Agriculture
Animal Industries
PO Box 40627
Nashville, TN 37204
Phone: (615)360-0120

Credential Type: License. **Duration of License:** One year. **Fees:** $25 License. $25 Renewal.

650

Animal Technician
Board of Veterinary Medical Examiners
Bureau of Manpower and Facilities
283 Plus Park Blvd.
Nashville, TN 37217
Phone: (615)367-6225
Fax: (615)367-6397

Credential Type: Animal Technician Certificate. **Requirements:** Complete a two year American Veterinarian Medical Association (AVMA) accredited course for animal technicians. **Examination:** National Board Examination. **Fees:** $85 application/examination fee. $25 renewal fee. **Governing Statute:** Practice act.

651

Assistant Trainer (Racetrack)
Tennessee State Racing Commission
500 James Robertson Pky., 2nd Fl.
Nashville, TN 37243
Phone: (615)741-1952

Credential Type: License Registration. **Requirements:** Submit application and fingerprint card. Pay fee. **Fees:** $20 registration fee.

652

Exercise Rider (Racetrack)
Tennessee State Racing Commission
500 James Robertson Pky., 2nd Fl.
Nashville, TN 37243
Phone: (615)741-1952

Credential Type: License Registration. **Requirements:** Submit application and fingerprint card. Pay fee. **Fees:** $15 registration fee.

Animal Caretakers and Trainers, Except Farm

653

Farrier Assistant (Racetrack)
Tennessee State Racing Commission
500 James Robertson Pky., 2nd Fl.
Nashville, TN 37243
Phone: (615)741-1952

Credential Type: License Registration.
Requirements: Submit application and fingerprint card. Pay fee. **Fees:** $10 registration fee.

654

Farrier (Racetrack)
Tennessee State Racing Commission
500 James Robertson Pky., 2nd Fl.
Nashville, TN 37243
Phone: (615)741-1952

Credential Type: License Registration.
Requirements: Submit application and fingerprint card. Pay fee. **Fees:** $50 registration fee.

655

Stable Employee (Racetrack)
Tennessee State Racing Commission
500 James Robertson Pky., 2nd Fl.
Nashville, TN 37243
Phone: (615)741-1952

Credential Type: License Registration.
Requirements: Submit application and fingerprint card. Pay fee. **Fees:** $10 registration fee.

656

Trainer (Racetrack)
Tennessee State Racing Commission
500 James Robertson Pky., 2nd Fl.
Nashville, TN 37243
Phone: (615)741-1952

Credential Type: License Registration.
Requirements: Submit application and fingerprint card. Pay fee. **Fees:** $25 registration fee.

657

Veterinarian Assistant (Racetrack)
Tennessee State Racing Commission
500 James Robertson Pky., 2nd Fl.
Nashville, TN 37243
Phone: (615)741-1952

Credential Type: License Registration.
Requirements: Submit application and fingerprint card. Pay fee. **Fees:** $10 registration fee.

Texas

658

Assistant Trainer/Owner (Racetrack)
Texas Racing Commission
PO Box 12080
Austin, TX 78711
Phone: (512)794-8461

Credential Type: License Registration.
Requirements: Submit application and fingerprint card. Pay fee. **Fees:** $75 registration fee.

659

Assistant Trainer (Racetrack)
Texas Racing Commission
PO Box 12080
Austin, TX 78711
Phone: (512)794-8461

Credential Type: License Registration.
Requirements: Submit application and fingerprint card. Pay fee. **Fees:** $75 registration fee.

660

Cool Out (Racetrack)
Texas Racing Commission
PO Box 12080
Austin, TX 78711
Phone: (512)794-8461

Credential Type: License Registration.
Requirements: Submit application and fingerprint card. Pay fee. **Fees:** $20 registration fee.

661

Exercise Rider (Racetrack)
Texas Racing Commission
PO Box 12080
Austin, TX 78711
Phone: (512)794-8461

Credential Type: License Registration.
Requirements: Submit application and fingerprint card. Pay fee. **Fees:** $20 registration fee.

662

Farrier/Plater/Blacksmith (Racetrack)
Texas Racing Commission
PO Box 12080
Austin, TX 78711
Phone: (512)794-8461

Credential Type: License Registration.
Requirements: Submit application and fingerprint card. Pay fee. **Fees:** $65 registration fee.

663

Groom (Racetrack)
Texas Racing Commission
PO Box 12080
Austin, TX 78711
Phone: (512)794-8461

Credential Type: License Registration.
Requirements: Submit application and fingerprint card. Pay fee. **Fees:** $20 registration fee.

664

Kennel Helper (Racetrack)
Texas Racing Commission
PO Box 12080
Austin, TX 78711
Phone: (512)794-8461

Credential Type: License Registration.
Requirements: Submit application and fingerprint card. Pay fee. **Fees:** $20 registration fee.

665

Kennel Owner/Trainer (Racetrack)
Texas Racing Commission
PO Box 12080
Austin, TX 78711
Phone: (512)794-8461

Credential Type: License Registration.
Requirements: Submit application and fingerprint card. Pay fee. **Fees:** $75 registration fee.

666

Lead Out (Racetrack)
Texas Racing Commission
PO Box 12080
Austin, TX 78711
Phone: (512)794-8461

Credential Type: License Registration.
Requirements: Submit application and fin-

Lead Out (Racetrack), continued

gerprint card. Pay fee. **Fees:** $20 registration fee.

667

Outrider (Racetrack)
Texas Racing Commission
PO Box 12080
Austin, TX 78711
Phone: (512)794-8461

Credential Type: License Registration. **Requirements:** Submit application and fingerprint card. Pay fee. **Fees:** $20 registration fee.

668

Pony Person (Racetrack)
Texas Racing Commission
PO Box 12080
Austin, TX 78711
Phone: (512)794-8461

Credential Type: License Registration. **Requirements:** Submit application and fingerprint card. Pay fee. **Fees:** $20 registration fee.

669

Stable Foreman (Racetrack)
Texas Racing Commission
PO Box 12080
Austin, TX 78711
Phone: (512)794-8461

Credential Type: License Registration. **Requirements:** Submit application and fingerprint card. Pay fee. **Fees:** $50 registration fee.

670

Trainer (Racetrack)
Texas Racing Commission
PO Box 12080
Austin, TX 78711
Phone: (512)794-8461

Credential Type: License Registration. **Requirements:** Submit application and fingerprint card. Pay fee. **Fees:** $75 registration fee.

671

Veterinarian Assistant (Racetrack)
Texas Racing Commission
PO Box 12080
Austin, TX 78711
Phone: (512)794-8461

Credential Type: License Registration. **Requirements:** Submit application and fingerprint card. Pay fee. **Fees:** $20 registration fee.

Vermont

672

Assistant Trainer (Greyhound Racing)
Vermont Racing Commission
State Office Bldg.
Montpelier, VT 05602
Phone: (802)828-3429

Credential Type: License Registration. **Requirements:** Submit application and fingerprint card. Pay fee. **Fees:** $20 registration fee. $5 duplicate license.

673

Blacksmith (Racetrack)
Vermont Racing Commission
State Office Bldg.
Montpelier, VT 05602
Phone: (802)828-3429

Credential Type: License Registration. **Requirements:** Submit application and fingerprint card. Pay fee. **Fees:** $2 registration fee. $2 duplicate license.

674

Exercise Boy (Racetrack)
Vermont Racing Commission
State Office Bldg.
Montpelier, VT 05602
Phone: (802)828-3429

Credential Type: License Registration. **Requirements:** Submit application and fingerprint card. Pay fee. **Fees:** $2 registration fee. $2 duplicate license.

675

Groom (Racetrack)
Vermont Racing Commission
State Office Bldg.
Montpelier, VT 05602
Phone: (802)828-3429

Credential Type: License Registration. **Requirements:** Submit application and fingerprint card. Pay fee. **Fees:** $2 registration fee. $2 duplicate license.

676

Guard Dog Handler
State Board of Private Investigative and Security Service Licensing
Pavilion Office Bldg.
Montpelier, VT 05602
Phone: (802)828-2363

Credential Type: License. **Duration of License:** Two years. **Requirements:** 18 years of age. File a surety bond of $25,000. Favorable background investigation. Prior approval is required before carrying a firearm or using a guard dog. **Examination:** Yes. **Reciprocity:** No. **Fees:** $60 Application for license. $100 Renewal. $25 Late renewal penalty. **Governing Statute:** Title 26, VSA Sections 3151-3179.

677

Hot Walker (Racetrack)
Vermont Racing Commission
State Office Bldg.
Montpelier, VT 05602
Phone: (802)828-3429

Credential Type: License Registration. **Requirements:** Submit application and fingerprint card. Pay fee. **Fees:** $2 registration fee. $2 duplicate license.

678

Kennel Helper (Greyhound Racing)
Vermont Racing Commission
State Office Bldg.
Montpelier, VT 05602
Phone: (802)828-3429

Credential Type: License Registration. **Requirements:** Submit application and fingerprint card. Pay fee. **Fees:** $5 registration fee. $5 duplicate license.

Animal Caretakers and Trainers, Except Farm

679

Kennel Master (Greyhound Racing)
Vermont Racing Commission
State Office Bldg.
Montpelier, VT 05602
Phone: (802)828-3429

Credential Type: License Registration. **Requirements:** Submit application and fingerprint card. Pay fee. **Fees:** $20 registration fee. $5 duplicate license.

680

Outrider (Racetrack)
Vermont Racing Commission
State Office Bldg.
Montpelier, VT 05602
Phone: (802)828-3429

Credential Type: License Registration. **Requirements:** Submit application and fingerprint card. Pay fee. **Fees:** $20 registration fee. $2 duplicate license.

681

Pony Boy (Racetrack)
Vermont Racing Commission
State Office Bldg.
Montpelier, VT 05602
Phone: (802)828-3429

Credential Type: License Registration. **Requirements:** Submit application and fingerprint card. Pay fee. **Fees:** $2 registration fee. $2 duplicate license.

682

Trainer (Greyhound Racing)
Vermont Racing Commission
State Office Bldg.
Montpelier, VT 05602
Phone: (802)828-3429

Credential Type: License Registration. **Requirements:** Submit application and fingerprint card. Pay fee. **Fees:** $20 registration fee. $5 duplicate license.

683

Trainer (Thoroughbred Racing)
Vermont Racing Commission
State Office Bldg.
Montpelier, VT 05602
Phone: (802)828-3429

Credential Type: License Registration. **Requirements:** Submit application and fingerprint card. Pay fee. **Fees:** $5 registration fee. $2 duplicate license.

Virginia

684

Assistant Trainer (Racetrack)
Virginia Racing Commission
PO Box 1123
Richmond, VA 23208
Phone: (804)371-7363

Credential Type: License Registration. **Requirements:** Submit application and fingerprint card. Pay fee. **Fees:** $10 registration fee.

685

Exercise Rider (Racetrack)
Virginia Racing Commission
PO Box 1123
Richmond, VA 23208
Phone: (804)371-7363

Credential Type: License Registration. **Requirements:** Submit application and fingerprint card. Pay fee. **Fees:** $10 registration fee.

686

Farrier (Racetrack)
Virginia Racing Commission
PO Box 1123
Richmond, VA 23208
Phone: (804)371-7363

Credential Type: License Registration. **Requirements:** Submit application and fingerprint card. Pay fee. **Fees:** $10 registration fee.

687

Groom/Hotwalker (Racetrack)
Virginia Racing Commission
PO Box 1123
Richmond, VA 23208
Phone: (804)371-7363

Credential Type: License Registration. **Requirements:** Submit application and fingerprint card. Pay fee. **Fees:** $5 registration fee.

688

Outrider (Racetrack)
Virginia Racing Commission
PO Box 1123
Richmond, VA 23208
Phone: (804)371-7363

Credential Type: License Registration. **Requirements:** Submit application and fingerprint card. Pay fee. **Fees:** $10 registration fee.

689

Pony Rider (Racetrack)
Virginia Racing Commission
PO Box 1123
Richmond, VA 23208
Phone: (804)371-7363

Credential Type: License Registration. **Requirements:** Submit application and fingerprint card. Pay fee. **Fees:** $10 registration fee.

690

Stall Superintendent (Racetrack)
Virginia Racing Commission
PO Box 1123
Richmond, VA 23208
Phone: (804)371-7363

Credential Type: License Registration. **Requirements:** Submit application and fingerprint card. Pay fee. **Fees:** $10 registration fee.

691

Trainer (Racetrack)
Virginia Racing Commission
PO Box 1123
Richmond, VA 23208
Phone: (804)371-7363

Credential Type: License Registration. **Requirements:** Submit application and fingerprint card. Pay fee. **Fees:** $10 registration fee.

692

Veterinarian Technician
Board of Veterinary Medicine
1601 Rolling Hills Dr.
Richmond, VA 23229
Phone: (804)662-9915
Fax: (804)662-9943

Credential Type: License to practice. **Duration of License:** One year. **Requirements:** Degree in veterinary technology.

Virginia

Veterinarian Technician, continued

Pass examination including state exam on jurisprudence. **Examination:** National Board Examination. State board examination. **Fees:** $75 National Board Examination. $25 State board examination. $25 annual license renewal. **Governing Statute:** Code of Virginia, Sections 54.1-3800 through 54.1-3810.

693

Veterinary Assistant
Board of Veterinary Medicine
1601 Rolling Hills Dr.
Richmond, VA 23229
Phone: (804)662-9920

Credential Type: Certificate. **Duration of License:** One year. **Requirements:** 18 years of age. A degree in Veterinary Technology approved by the American Veterinary Medical Association. **Examination:** Yes. **Fees:** $75 application fee. $25 renewal fee.

Washington

694

Animal Technician
Veterinary Board of Governors
1300 SE Quince
Olympia, WA 98504
Phone: (206)586-6355
Phone: (206)586-6350

Credential Type: Animal Technician Certificate. **Requirements:** Pass examination. **Examination:** National Board Examination. State Board examination. **Reciprocity:** Granted to the holder of any out-of-state license that is deemed substantially equivalent and which extends reciprocity to Washington licensees. **Fees:** $100 State examination fee. $95 National Board Examination fee. $60 renewal fee. **Governing Statute:** Chapter 18.92 Revised Code of Washington and Chapter 246-933 Washington Administrative Code.

695

Owner/Trainer (Racetrack)
Washington Horse Racing
   Commission
3700 Martin Way, Ste. 101
Olympia, WA 98506
Phone: (206)459-6462

Credential Type: License Registration. **Duration of License:** One year. **Requirements:** Submit application and fingerprint card. Pay fee. **Fees:** $30 registration fee. $5 duplicate license fee.

696

Plater (Racetrack)
Washington Horse Racing
   Commission
3700 Martin Way, Ste. 101
Olympia, WA 98506
Phone: (206)459-6462

Credential Type: License Registration. **Duration of License:** One year. **Requirements:** Submit application and fingerprint card. Pay fee. **Fees:** $10 registration fee. $5 duplicate license.

697

Trainer (Racetrack)
Washington Horse Racing
   Commission
3700 Martin Way, Ste. 101
Olympia, WA 98506
Phone: (206)459-6462

Credential Type: License Registration. **Duration of License:** One year. **Requirements:** Submit application and fingerprint card. Pay fee. **Fees:** $15 registration fee. $5 duplicate license fee.

West Virginia

698

Animal Technician
Board of Veterinary Medicine
712 MacCorkle Ave.
S. Charleston, WV 25303
Phone: (304)744-4721

Credential Type: License. **Duration of License:** One year. **Requirements:** U.S. citizen. 18 years old. Graduate of a two year approved course in an accredited school. Never convicted of a felony. **Examination:** Yes. **Fees:** $25 Application. $10 Renewal.

Wisconsin

699

Animal Technician
Regulations and Licensing Dept.
Veterinary Board
PO Box 8935
Madison, WI 53708-8935
Phone: (608)266-8609

Credential Type: License. **Requirements:** Completion of a two-year, approved animal technician course. Two years of experience under a state licensed veterinarian. 18 years of age. **Examination:** Written and practical.

700

Assistant Trainer (Dog Racing)
Wisconsin Racing Board
PO Box 7975
Madison, WI 53707-7975
Phone: (608)267-3291

Credential Type: License Registration. **Requirements:** Submit application and two sets of fingerprint cards. Pay fee. **Fees:** $20 registration fee. $20 duplicate license.

701

Kennel Helper (Dog Racing)
Wisconsin Racing Board
PO Box 7975
Madison, WI 53707-7975
Phone: (608)267-3291

Credential Type: License Registration. **Requirements:** Submit application and two sets of fingerprint cards. Pay fee. **Fees:** $20 registration fee. $20 duplicate license.

702

Kennel Master (Racetrack)
Wisconsin Racing Board
PO Box 7975
Madison, WI 53707-7975
Phone: (608)267-3291

Credential Type: License Registration. **Requirements:** Submit application and two sets of fingerprint cards. Pay fee. **Fees:** $20 registration fee. $20 duplicate license.

703

Kennel Operator (Racetrack)
Wisconsin Racing Board
PO Box 7975
Madison, WI 53707-7975
Phone: (608)267-3291

Credential Type: License Registration. **Requirements:** Submit application and two sets of fingerprint cards. Pay fee. **Fees:** $80 registration fee. $20 duplicate license.

Animal Caretakers and Trainers, Except Farm

704

Lead Out (Racetrack)
Wisconsin Racing Board
PO Box 7975
Madison, WI 53707-7975
Phone: (608)267-3291

Credential Type: License Registration. **Requirements:** Submit application and two sets of fingerprint cards. Pay fee. **Fees:** $20 registration fee. $20 duplicate license.

705

Owner/Trainer (Dog Racing)
Wisconsin Racing Board
PO Box 7975
Madison, WI 53707-7975
Phone: (608)267-3291

Credential Type: License Registration. **Requirements:** Submit application and two sets of fingerprint cards. Pay fee. **Fees:** $50 registration fee. $20 duplicate license.

706

Trainer (Dog Racing)
Wisconsin Racing Board
PO Box 7975
Madison, WI 53707-7975
Phone: (608)267-3291

Credential Type: License Registration. **Requirements:** Submit application and two sets of fingerprint cards. Pay fee. **Fees:** $50 registration fee. $20 duplicate license.

Wyoming

707

Artificial Inseminator of Animals
Board of Veterinary Medicine
Herschler Bldg., 3rd Fl.
122 W. 25th St.
Cheyenne, WY 82002
Phone: (307)777-7515

Credential Type: License. **Duration of License:** One year. **Requirements:** Good moral character. Graduate from an approved course in artificial insemination of animals. **Examination:** Yes. **Fees:** $10 Application. $5 Renewal. $7.50 Renewal (non-resident).

708

Exerciser (Racetrack)
Wyoming State Pari-Mutuel
  Commission
Barrett Bldg., 3rd Fl.
Cheyenne, WY 82002
Phone: (307)777-5887

Credential Type: License Registration. **Requirements:** Submit application and fingerprint card. Pay fee. **Fees:** $20 registration fee. $10 duplicate license.

709

Groom (Racetrack)
Wyoming State Pari-Mutuel
  Commission
Barrett Bldg., 3rd Fl.
Cheyenne, WY 82002
Phone: (307)777-5887

Credential Type: License Registration. **Requirements:** Submit application and fingerprint card. Pay fee. **Fees:** $10 registration fee. $10 duplicate license.

710

Outrider (Racetrack)
Wyoming State Pari-Mutuel
  Commission
Barrett Bldg., 3rd Fl.
Cheyenne, WY 82002
Phone: (307)777-5887

Credential Type: License Registration. **Requirements:** Submit application and fingerprint card. Pay fee. **Fees:** $20 registration fee. $10 duplicate license.

711

Plater (Racetrack)
Wyoming State Pari-Mutuel
  Commission
Barrett Bldg., 3rd Fl.
Cheyenne, WY 82002
Phone: (307)777-5887

Credential Type: License Registration. **Requirements:** Submit application and fingerprint card. Pay fee. **Fees:** $20 registration fee. $10 duplicate license.

712

Pony Rider (Racetrack)
Wyoming State Pari-Mutuel
  Commission
Barrett Bldg., 3rd Fl.
Cheyenne, WY 82002
Phone: (307)777-5887

Credential Type: License Registration. **Requirements:** Submit application and fingerprint card. Pay fee. **Fees:** $20 registration fee. $10 duplicate license.

713

Roper (Racetrack)
Wyoming State Pari-Mutuel
  Commission
Barrett Bldg., 3rd Fl.
Cheyenne, WY 82002
Phone: (307)777-5887

Credential Type: License Registration. **Requirements:** Submit application and fingerprint card. Pay fee. **Fees:** $20 registration fee. $10 duplicate license.

714

Trainer/Assistant Trainer (Racetrack)
Wyoming State Pari-Mutuel
  Commission
Barrett Bldg., 3rd Fl.
Cheyenne, WY 82002
Phone: (307)777-5887

Credential Type: License Registration. **Requirements:** Submit application and fingerprint card. Pay fee. **Fees:** $20 registration fee. $10 duplicate license.

715

Veterinarian Assistant (Racetrack)
Wyoming State Pari-Mutuel
  Commission
Barrett Bldg., 3rd Fl.
Cheyenne, WY 82002
Phone: (307)777-5887

Credential Type: License Registration. **Requirements:** Submit application and fingerprint card. Pay fee. **Fees:** $20 registration fee. $10 duplicate license.

Architects

The following states grant licenses in this occupational category as of the date of publication:

Alabama	District of	Iowa	Minnesota	New Mexico	Rhode Island	Washington
Alaska	Columbia	Kansas	Mississippi	New York	South Carolina	West Virginia
Arizona	Florida	Kentucky	Missouri	North Carolina	South Dakota	Wisconsin
Arkansas	Georgia	Louisiana	Montana	North Dakota	Tennessee	Wyoming
California	Hawaii	Maine	Nebraska	Ohio	Texas	
Colorado	Idaho	Maryland	Nevada	Oklahoma	Utah	
Connecticut	Illinois	Massachusetts	New Hampshire	Oregon	Vermont	
Delaware	Indiana	Michigan	New Jersey	Pennsylvania	Virginia	

Alabama

716

Architect
Board of Registration of Architects
1115 S. Court St.
Montgomery, AL 36104
Phone: (205)242-4179

Credential Type: License. **Duration of License:** One year. **Requirements:** Must hold five-year degree and have three years training experience under the direct supervision of an architect. **Examination:** Yes. **Fees:** $310 examination fee. $75-$100 registration fee.

Alaska

717

Architect
Alaska Board of Architects,
 Engineers and Land Surveyors
Dept. of Commerce and Economic
 Development
Div. of Occupational Licensing
PO Box D-LIC
Juneau, AK 99811
Phone: (907)465-2540

Credential Type: Architect license. **Duration of License:** Two years. **Requirements:** Three years acceptable architectural experience, or equivalent, required with National Architectural Accrediting Board accredited degree. Graduation from an approved school of architecture. Pass an arctic and sub-arctic engineering course approved by the board. **Examination:** National Council of Architectural Registration Boards (NCARB) Architect Registration Examination. **Reciprocity:** Yes. **Fees:** $30 exam application fee. $130 application fee. $100 registration fee. $100 renewal fee. $50 for having exam proctored out of state. **Governing Statute:** Alaska Statutes 08.48. Professional Regulations 12 AAC 36.

Arizona

718

Architect
Arizona State Board of Technical
 Registrations for Architects
1951 W. Camelback Rd., Ste. 250
Phoenix, AZ 85015
Phone: (602)255-4053

Credential Type: Architect license. **Requirements:** Three years acceptable architectural experience, or equivalent, required with National Architectural Accrediting Board accredited degree; five years required with a four year pre-professional degree in architecture; or eight years experience with a high school education. **Examination:** National Council of Architectural Registration Boards (NCARB) Architect Registration Examination.

Arkansas

719

Architect
Arkansas State Board of Architects
1515 Bldg., Rm. 512
1515 W. Seventh St.
Little Rock, AR 72202
Phone: (501)375-1310

Credential Type: License. **Duration of License:** One year. **Requirements:** Must hold a Bachelor's or Master's of Architecture. Completed three years internship in acceptable work. **Examination:** Yes. **Fees:** Fee for written exam is actual cost of examination materials plus administrative charge. $40 Registration. $25 License. $25 Renewal (annual).

California

720

Architect
California Board of Architectural
 Examiners
1021 "O" St., Rm. A-102
Sacramento, CA 94244-2580
Phone: (916)445-3394
Fax: (916)443-1601

Credential Type: Architect license. **Requirements:** 18 years of age. Three years acceptable architectural experience, or equivalent, required with National Architectural Accrediting Board accredited degree; four and one-half years required with a four year pre-professional degree in architecture; or eight years experience with a high school education. **Examination:** National Council of Architectural Registration Boards (NCARB) Architect Registration Examination.

Colorado

721

Architect
Colorado Board of Examiners of
 Architects
617 State Services Bldg.
1525 Sherman St.
Denver, CO 80203
Phone: (303)866-2271
Fax: (303)866-2018

Credential Type: Architect license. **Requirements:** 700 value units of acceptable architectural experience, or equivalent, required with National Architectural Accrediting Board accredited degree; 2,350 value units required with a four year pre-professional degree in architecture or with a high school education. **Examination:** National Council of Architectural Registration Boards (NCARB) Architect Registration Examination.

Connecticut

722

Architect
Connecticut Architectural Licensing Board
State Office Bldg., Rm. G-1
165 Capitol Ave.
Hartford, CT 06106
Phone: (203)566-2093

Credential Type: Architect license. **Requirements:** 18 years of age. Three years acceptable architectural experience, or equivalent, required with National Architectural Accrediting Board accredited degree. **Examination:** National Council of Architectural Registration Boards (NCARB) Architect Registration Examination.

Delaware

723

Architect
Delaware Board of Architects
Margaret O'Neil Bldg.
PO Box 1401
Dover, DE 19903
Phone: (302)736-4522

Credential Type: Architect license. **Requirements:** Three years acceptable architectural experience, or equivalent, required with National Architectural Accrediting Board accredited degree. **Examination:** National Council of Architectural Registration Boards (NCARB) Architect Registration Examination.

District of Columbia

724

Architect
D.C. Dept. of Consumer and Regulatory Affairs
Occupational and Professional Licensing Administration
PO Box 37200, Rm. 923
Washington, DC 20013-7200
Phone: (202)727-7468

Credential Type: Architect license. **Requirements:** 18 years of age. Three years of acceptable architectural experience, or equivalent, required with National Architectural Accrediting Board accredited degree. **Examination:** National Council of Architectural Registration Boards (NCARB) Architect Registration Examination.

Florida

725

Architect
Florida Board of Architecture and Interior Design
The Norwood Center
1940 N. Monroe, Ste. 60
Tallahassee, FL 32399-0750
Phone: (904)488-6685

Credential Type: Architect license. **Requirements:** An applicant holding a National Architectural Accrediting Board accredited bachelor's degree, with a major in architecture, is required to have three years of acceptable architectural experience. An applicant holding a master's degree, with a major in architecture, is required to obtain two years experience. **Examination:** National Council of Architectural Registration Boards (NCARB) Architect Registration Examination.

Georgia

726

Architect
Georgia State Board of Architects
Examining Boards Div.
166 Pryor St., SW
Atlanta, GA 30303
Phone: (404)656-2281
Fax: (404)651-9532

Credential Type: Certificate of registration. **Duration of License:** Two years. **Requirements:** 21 years of age. Three years acceptable architectural experience, or equivalent, required with National Architectural Accrediting Board accredited degree; six years required with a four year pre-professional degree in architecture; or 10 years experience with a high school education. **Examination:** National Council of Architectural Registration Boards (NCARB) Architect Registration Examination. **Fees:** $20 application fee. $45 renewal fee.

Hawaii

727

Architect
Hawaii Board of Engineers, Architects, Surveyors and Landscape Artists
Dept. of Commerce and Consumer Affairs
1010 Richards St.
PO Box 3469
Honolulu, HI 96801
Phone: (808)548-8542

Credential Type: License. **Duration of License:** Six months. **Requirements:** Master's Degree in architecture from an approved institution, graduated from a five-year architectural curriculum of an approved school, and two years of architectural experience, or graduation from a five-year architectural curriculum and three years of architectural experience, or graduation from a four-year architectural, pre-architectural, or arts and science curriculum and five years of architectural experience, or graduation from a two-year architectural technology curriculum and eight years of experience, or 11 years of architectural experience. Statements from three architect's certifying experience and reputation. **Examination:** Given in June. **Exemptions:** Exam may be waived if applicant has passed an equivalent exam in another state and has a valid registration from that state. **Fees:** $50 application fee. $360 exam fee. $30 license fee. $15 $30 Compliance Resolution Fund fee. $30 renewal fee.

Idaho

728

Architect
Bureau of Occupational Licenses
2417 Bank Dr., Rm. 312
Boise, ID 83705
Phone: (208)334-3233

Credential Type: Architect license. **Requirements:** Resident of Idaho. Three years of acceptable architectural experience, or equivalent, required with National Architectural Accrediting Board accredited

Architect, continued

degree. **Examination:** National Council of Architectural Registration Boards (NCARB) Architect Registration Examination.

Illinois

729

Architect
Dept. of Professional Regulation
320 W. Washington St., 3rd Fl.
Springfield, IL 62786
Phone: (217)782-0458
Fax: (217)782-7645

Credential Type: Architect license. **Requirements:** An applicant holding a National Architectural Accrediting Board accredited bachelor's degree, with a major in architecture, is required to have three years of acceptable architectural experience. An applicant holding a master's degree, with a major in architecture, is required to obtain two years experience. An applicant with a four year pre-professional degree in architecture is required to have five years experience. **Examination:** National Council of Architectural Registration Boards (NCARB) Architect Registration Examination.

Indiana

730

Architect
Indiana Professional Licensing Agency
State Office Bldg., Rm. 1021
Indianapolis, IN 47204-2246
Phone: (317)232-2980

Credential Type: Architect license. **Requirements:** 18 years of age. National Architectural Accrediting Board accredited degree only and three years of acceptable architectural experience. **Examination:** National Council of Architectural Registration Boards (NCARB) Architect Registration Examination.

Iowa

731

Architect
Iowa Architectural Examining Board
1918 SE Hulsizer
Ankeny, IA 50021
Phone: (515)281-5910

Credential Type: License. **Duration of License:** Two years. **Requirements:** A five-year degree from an accredited school or architecture plus three years of training under a registered architect. **Examination:** Architect Registration Examination. **Fees:** $435 exam fee. $140 registration fee. $140 renewal fee.

Kansas

732

Architect
Kansas State Board of Technical Professions
900 Jackson St., Ste. 507
Topeka, KS 66612-1214
Phone: (913)296-3053

Credential Type: Architect license. **Requirements:** Resident of Kansas. Three years acceptable architectural experience, or equivalent, required with National Architectural Accrediting Board accredited degree; six years required with a four year pre-professional degree in architecture; or 10 years experience with a high school education. **Examination:** National Council of Architectural Registration Boards (NCARB) Architect Registration Examination.

Kentucky

733

Architect
State Board of Examiners and Registration of Architects
Box 22097-40522
Lexington, KY 40522
Phone: (606)277-3312

Credential Type: Architect license. **Requirements:** Resident of Kentucky. National Architectural Accrediting Board accredited degree only and three years of accepted architectural experience. **Examination:** National Council of Architectural Registration Boards (NCARB) Architect Registration Examination.

Louisiana

734

Architect
Architectural Licensing Board
1987 Dallas Dr.
Baton Rouge, LA 70806
Phone: (504)925-4802

Credential Type: License. **Duration of License:** One year. **Requirements:** 21 years of age. Must have a professional degree. Completion and verification of the intern-architect development program. **Examination:** Written. **Fees:** $300 exam fee. $50 license fee.

Maine

735

Architect
Maine State Board of Registrations of Architects and Landscape Architects
142 High St., Rm. 614
Portland, ME 04101
Phone: (207)774-0039

Credential Type: Architect license. **Requirements:** Approved degree with a major in architecture. **Examination:** National Council of Architectural Registration Boards (NCARB) Architect Registration Examination.

Maryland

736

Architect
Maryland Architectural Registration Board
Div. of Occupational and Professional Licensing
501 St. Paul Pl., Rm. 902
Baltimore, MD 21202
Phone: (301)333-6322
Fax: (301)333-1229

Credential Type: Architect license. **Requirements:** Three years acceptable architectural experience, or equivalent, required with National Architectural Accrediting Board accredited degree; seven years required with a four year pre-professional degree in architecture; or 13 years experience with a high school education. **Examination:** National Council of Architectural Registration Boards (NCARB) Architect Registration Examination.

Massachusetts

737

Architect
Board of Registration of Architects
Leverett Saltonstall Bldg.
100 Cambridge St., Rm. 1513
Boston, MA 02202
Phone: (617)727-3072

Credential Type: Architect license. **Requirements:** 21 years of age. Approved degree with major in architecture. **Examination:** National Council of Architectural Registration Boards (NCARB) Architect Registration Examination.

Michigan

738

Architect
Board of Architects
Dept. of Licensing and Regulation
Box 30018
611 W. Ottawa
Lansing, MI 48909
Phone: (517)335-1669

Credential Type: Architect license. **Requirements:** National Architectural Accrediting Board accredited degree, or equivalent degree, and three years acceptable architectural experience required. **Examination:** National Council of Architectural Registration Boards (NCARB) Architect Registration Examination.

Minnesota

739

Architect
Board of Architecture, Engineering, Land Surveying and Landscape Architecture
402 Metro Square Bldg.
121 E. 7th Pl.
St. Paul, MN 55101
Phone: (612)296-2388
Fax: (612)297-5310

Credential Type: Architect license. **Requirements:** 25 years of age. National Architectural Accrediting Board accredited degree, or equivalent degree, and three years of acceptable architectural experience. **Examination:** National Council of Architectural Registration Boards (NCARB) Architect Registration Examination.

Mississippi

740

Architect
Mississippi State Board of Architecture
239 N. Lamar St., Ste. 502
Jackson, MS 39201-1311
Phone: (601)359-6029
Fax: (601)957-1790

Credential Type: Architect license. **Requirements:** National Architectural Accrediting Board accredited degree only and three years of acceptable architectural experience. **Examination:** National Council of Architectural Registration Boards (NCARB) Architect Registration Examination.

Missouri

741

Architect
Missouri Board for Architects, Professional Engineers, and Land Surveyors
PO Box 184
3523 N. Ten Mile Dr., Rm 218
Jefferson City, MO 65102
Phone: (314)751-2334
Fax: (314)751-4176

Credential Type: Architect license. **Requirements:** 21 years of age. Three years acceptable architectural experience, or equivalent, required with National Architectural Accrediting Board accredited degree; eight years required with a four year pre-professional degree in architecture; or 12 years experience with a high school education. **Examination:** National Council of Architectural Registration Boards (NCARB) Architect Registration Examination.

Montana

742

Architect
Montana Board of Architects
111 N. Jackson
Helena, MT 59620
Phone: (406)444-3745

Credential Type: License. **Duration of License:** One year. **Requirements:** Bachelor's degree in architecture or equivalent. Three years of training with at least one year under a registered architect. **Examination:** National board exam. **Reciprocity:** Yes. **Fees:** $329 exam fee. $20 license fee. $100 reciprocity fee. $40 renewal fee. **Governing Statute:** Montana Code Annotated 37-65-301 through 37-65-323.

Nebraska

743

Architect
Nebraska Board of Examiners for Professional Engineers and Architects
PO Box 94751
Lincoln, NE 68509
Phone: (402)471-2021

Credential Type: License. **Duration of License:** One year. **Requirements:** 24 years of age. Must have a professional degree from an approved school of architecture. Must have three years experience. **Examination:** Yes. **Fees:** $65 examination fee. $390 initial examination fee. $30 renewal fee.

Nevada

744

Architect
Nevada State Board of Architecture
2080 E. Flamingo Rd., Ste. 319
Las Vegas, NV 89119
Phone: (702)486-7300

Credential Type: License. **Duration of License:** Two years. **Requirements:** Degree from an accredited architect program. Completion of an Intern-architect Development Program. **Examination:** Yes. **Reciprocity:** Yes. **Fees:** $25 application fee. $125 certificate fee. $500 exam fee. $200 renewal fee.

New Hampshire

745

Architect
Joint Board of Engineers, Architects, Land Surveyors, Natural Scientists, and Foresters
57 Regional Dr.
Concord, NH 03301
Phone: (603)271-2219

Credential Type: Architect license. **Requirements:** Resident of New Hampshire. Three years acceptable architectural experience, or equivalent, required with National Architectural Accrediting Board accredited degree; seven years required with a four year pre-professional degree in architecture; or 13 years experience with a high

Architect, continued

school education. **Examination:** National Council of Architectural Registration Boards (NCARB) Architect Registration Examination.

New Jersey

746

Architect
Board of Architects and Certified Landscape Architects
1100 Raymond Blvd., Rm. 511
Newark, NJ 07102
Phone: (201)648-2378

Credential Type: License. **Duration of License:** Two years. **Requirements:** A professional degree in architecture from an accredited school, plus three years of experience under the direct supervision of a registered architect. 21 years of age. **Examination:** Yes. **Reciprocity:** Yes. **Fees:** $25 application fee. $350 exam fee. $100 registration fee. **Governing Statute:** NJSA 45:3-3. NJAC 13:27-6.1.

New Mexico

747

Architect
New Mexico State Board of Examiners for Architects
Box 509
112 W. Marcy St., Ste. 400
Santa Fe, NM 87504
Phone: (505)827-6375
Fax: (505)827-6373

Credential Type: Architect license. **Requirements:** National Architectural Accrediting Board accredited degree only and three years acceptable architectural experience. **Examination:** National Council of Architectural Registration Boards (NCARB) Architect Registration Examination.

New York

748

Architect
State Education Dept.
Div. of Professional Licensing Services
Cultural Education Center
Empire State Plaza
Albany, NY 12230
Phone: (518)474-3326

Credential Type: License. **Duration of License:** Three years. **Requirements:** Bachelor's Degree in architecture. Eight years of experience. 21 years of age. **Examination:** Written nine-part exam. **Fees:** $555 exam fee. $210 renewal fee. **Governing Statute:** Title VIII Articles 130, 147 of the Education Law.

North Carolina

749

Architect
North Carolina State Board of Architecture
501 N. Blount St.
Raleigh, NC 27604
Phone: (919)733-9544

Credential Type: License. **Duration of License:** One year. **Requirements:** Five years of professional education with a degree in architecture or the equivalent, from an accredited college, plus three years of practical training in the office of a registered architect. 18 years of age. **Examination:** Architectural Registration Examination. **Fees:** $25 application fee. $300 exam fee. $40 renewal fee.

North Dakota

750

Architect
North Dakota State Board of Architecture
2705 4th Ave., NW
Minot, ND 58701
Phone: (701)852-4178
Fax: (701)852-4179

Credential Type: Architect license. **Requirements:** 21 years of age. National Architectural Accrediting Board accredited degree, or equivalent degree, and three years acceptable architectural experience. **Examination:** National Council of Architectural Registration Boards (NCARB) Architect Registration Examination.

Ohio

751

Architect
Ohio State Board of Examiners of Architects
77 S. High St., 16th Fl.
Columbus, OH 43266-0303
Phone: (614)466-2316
Fax: (614)644-9048

Credential Type: Architect license. **Requirements:** 18 years of age. Three years acceptable architectural experience, or equivalent, required with National Architectural Accrediting Board accredited degree; five years required with a four year pre-professional degree in architecture; or 13 years experience with a high school education. **Examination:** National Council of Architectural Registration Boards (NCARB) Architect Registration Examination.

Oklahoma

752

Architect
Board of Governors of the Licensed Architects and Landscape Architects of Oklahoma
6801 N. Broadway, Ste. 201
Oklahoma City, OK 73116
Phone: (405)848-6596

Credential Type: License. **Duration of License:** Two years (expires June 30). **Requirements:** Bachelor's degree in architecture from an accredited program or the substitution of obtained educational credits and additional training. Three years of approved training under an architect or completion of Intern Development Program. Good moral character. 21 years of age. Legal resident of Oklahoma if applying for initial registration. No felony convictions. **Examination:** Architect Registration Examination. **Fees:** $390 exam fee plus $75 administrative fee. $100 application fee for reciprocal license. $150 license fee in odd years, $75 in even years. $150 renewal fee.

Oregon

753

Architect
Board of Architect Examiners
750 Front St. NE, Ste. 260
Salem, OR 97310
Phone: (503)378-4270

Credential Type: License. **Duration of License:** One year. **Requirements:** Must have a first professional degree in architecture from a program of architecture accredited by the National Architectural Accrediting Board (NAAB) and 700 Value Units of training requirements evaluated as per the NBRB table on Training Requirements for the Intern-Architect Developement Program; or have completed five education credits, evaluated per Appendix A of the 1983 Circular of Information No. One and 700 Value Units of training requirements evaluated as per the National Council of Architectural Registration Boards (NCARB) table on Training Requirements for the Intern-Architect Development. **Examination:** Yes. **Fees:** $250 (resident) or $300 (non-resedent) examination fee. $65 license fee. $70 renewal fee. **Governing Statute:** ORS 671.010 to 671.220 and Administrative Rules Chapter 806.

Pennsylvania

754

Architect
Pennsylvania State Architects Licensure Board
Dept. of State
PO Box 2649
Harrisburg, PA 17105-2649
Phone: (717)783-1261

Credential Type: Architect license. **Requirements:** 20 years of age. Resident of Pennsylvania. National Architectural Accrediting Board accredited degree, or equivalent degree, and three years acceptable architectural experience. **Examination:** National Council of Architectural Registration Boards (NCARB) Architect Registration Examination.

Rhode Island

755

Architect
Board of Examinations and Registration of Architects
50 Holden St.
Providence, RI 02908
Phone: (401)272-1730
Fax: (401)273-7156

Credential Type: Architect license. **Requirements:** 21 years of age. Resident of Rhode Island. National Architectural Accrediting Board accredited degree, or equivalent degree, and three years acceptable architectural experience. **Examination:** National Council of Architectural Registration Boards (NCARB) Architect Registration Examination.

South Carolina

756

Architect
South Carolina State Board of Architectural Examiners
3710 Landmark Dr., Ste. 206
Columbia, SC 29204
Phone: (803)734-1080

Credential Type: License. **Duration of License:** One year. **Requirements:** High school education or equivalent. Eight years of experience under a registered practicing architect, or graduation from an accredited architecture school and three years of experience. **Examination:** Yes. **Reciprocity:** Yes. **Fees:** $85 application fee. $50 initial annual fee by examination. $90 initial annual fee by reciprocity. $55 in-state renewal fee. $85 out-of-state renewal fee.

South Dakota

757

Architect
Engineering and Architectural Examiners
2040 W. Main St., Ste. 304
Rapid City, SD 57702-2497
Phone: (605)394-2510

Credential Type: Architect license. **Requirements:** Resident of South Dakota. Three years acceptable architectural experience, or equivalent, required with National Architectural Accrediting Board accredited degree; five years required with a four year pre-professional degree in architecture; or 12 years experience with a high school education. As of 1993, only a National Architectural Accrediting Board accredited degree in architecture and three years of architectural experience will be accepted. **Examination:** National Council of Architectural Registration Boards (NCARB) Architect Registration Examination.

Tennessee

758

Architect
Tennessee Board of Architectural and Engineering Examiners
3rd Fl., Volunteer Plaza Bldg.
500 James Robertson Pky.
Nashville, TN 37243-1142
Phone: (615)741-3221

Credential Type: License. **Duration of License:** One year. **Requirements:** Must have experience (at least three years) based upon education. Degree in Architecture. Pass the exam. Good moral character. Must speak and write English. **Examination:** National Council of Architectural Registration Boards (NCARB) and Architect Registration Examination (ARE). **Reciprocity:** Yes. **Fees:** $75 Application. $100 Application (without exam). Examination fees extra.

Texas

759

Architect
Texas Board of Architectural Examiners
8213 Shoal Creek Blvd., Ste. 107
Austin, TX 78758
Phone: (512)458-1363

Credential Type: License. **Duration of License:** One year. **Requirements:** National Architectural Accrediting Board-accredited professional degree in architecture, plus three years experience in the offices of registered architects; or other combinations of eight years experience and education. **Examination:** Architect Registration Examination. **Fees:** $210 application fee. $430 exam fee. $250 renewal fee. **Governing Statute:** VACS 249a, 22 TAC 1.

Utah

760

Architect
Dept. of Commerce
Div. of Occupational and
  Professional Licensing
160 E. 300 S.
PO Box 45802
Salt Lake City, UT 84145
Phone: (801)530-6628

Credential Type: License. **Duration of License:** Two years. **Requirements:** Must hold a bachelor of architecture degree or a master of architecture degree, or educational/experience equivalent. Must complete a program of diversified practical experience in accordance with a schedule adopted by the Board. **Examination:** Yes. **Fees:** $100 license fee. $35 renewal fee.

Vermont

761

Architect
Vermont Board of Architects
Secretary of State
Licensing and Registration
Pavilion Office Bldg.
Montpelier, VT 05602
Phone: (802)828-2373

Credential Type: Certificate. **Duration of License:** Two years. **Requirements:** Attain age of majority. Graduate from an approved architectural school and have three years practical experience under supervision of a practicing architect(s) who has been licensed for more than three years, or has had nine years of diversified practical experience. Credits from an accredited post-secondary educational institution may be substituted for up to four years of the experience requirements. Training equivalent to the above. **Examination:** Yes. **Reciprocity:** Yes. **Fees:** $35 application. $430 examination. $10 certificate. $30 biennial renewal. $5 late renewal penalty. $10 replacement. **Governing Statute:** Title 26, VSA Sect. 201-210.

Virginia

762

Architect
Virginia Board of Architects,
  Professional Engineers, Land
  Surveyors, and Certified Landscape
  Architects
Seaboard Bldg., 5th Fl.
3600 W. Broad St.
Richmond, VA 23230
Phone: (804)367-8514

Credential Type: Architect license. **Requirements:** 18 years of age. Three years acceptable architectural experience, or equivalent, required with National Architectural Accrediting Board accredited degree; seven years required with a four year pre-professional degree in architecture; or 13 years experience with a high school education. As of 1993, only a National Architectural Accrediting Board accredited degree in architecture and three years of architectural experience will be accepted. **Examination:** National Council of Architectural Registration Boards (NCARB) Architect Registration Examination.

Washington

763

Architect
Dept. of Licensing
Professional Licensing Services
2424 Bristol Ct., SW
Olympia, WA 98504
Phone: (206)753-1153

Credential Type: Architect License. **Duration of License:** Three years. **Requirements:** At least 18 years of age. Complete eight years of training and experience or be a graduate in architecture and have three years of experience. **Examination:** Written, graphic, and oral examinations. **Reciprocity:** Yes. **Fees:** $100 application fee (by examination). $350 application fee (by reciprocity). $345 full exam fee. $135 initial license fee. $135 renewal fee.

West Virginia

764

Architect
Board of Architects
910 4th St., Ste. 412
Huntington, WV 25701-1434
Phone: (304)528-5825

Credential Type: License. **Duration of License:** One year. **Requirements:** U.S. citizen. 21 years old. Accredited degree. Three years experience. Never convicted of a felony. **Examination:** Yes. **Fees:** $150 Application. $350 Examination, first time, $200 retake. $40 License. $25 Renewal.

Wisconsin

765

Architect
Regulations and Licensing Dept.
Architects & Engineers Board
PO Box 8935
Madison, WI 53708-8935
Phone: (608)266-8609

Credential Type: License. **Requirements:** National Architectural Accrediting Board (NAAB) degree and two years of experience; or seven years of experience with credit allowed for education. **Examination:** Written. **Reciprocity:** Yes.

Wyoming

766

Architect
State Board of Architecture
Barrett Bldg., 3rd Fl.
Cheyenne, WY 82002
Phone: (307)777-6313

Credential Type: License. **Duration of License:** Two years. **Requirements:** Must be an adult. Good moral character and reputation. Hold a professional degree in architecture from an accredited school, or have equivalent education and experience as determined by the Board. Pass the examination. **Examination:** Yes. **Fees:** $50 Application. $50 Renewal.

Athletes, Coaches, Umpires, and Referees

The following states grant licenses in this occupational category as of the date of publication:

Alabama	Delaware	Iowa	Michigan	New Mexico	Rhode Island	Virginia
Alaska	Florida	Kansas	Minnesota	New York	South Carolina	Washington
Arizona	Georgia	Kentucky	Missouri	North Dakota	South Dakota	Wisconsin
Arkansas	Hawaii	Louisiana	Montana	Ohio	Tennessee	Wyoming
California	Idaho	Maine	Nebraska	Oklahoma	Texas	
Colorado	Illinois	Maryland	Nevada	Oregon	Utah	
Connecticut	Indiana	Massachusetts	New Jersey	Pennsylvania	Vermont	

Alabama

767

Professional Wrestler
State Athletic Commission
50 N. Ripley St., Rm. 4121
Montgomery, AL 36132
Phone: (205)242-1380

Credential Type: License. **Duration of License:** One year. **Requirements:** Succesfully pass physical exam. **Fees:** $20 registration fee. $20 renewal fee.

768

Wrestling Judge
State Athletic Commission
50 N. Ripley St., Rm. 4121
Montgomery, AL 36132
Phone: (205)242-1380

Credential Type: License. **Duration of License:** One year. **Fees:** $5 license fee.

769

Wrestling Manager
State Athletic Commission
50 N. Ripley St., Rm. 4121
Montgomery, AL 36132
Phone: (205)242-1380

Credential Type: License. **Duration of License:** One year. **Fees:** $20 license fee.

770

Wrestling Referee
State Athletic Commission
50 N. Ripley St., Rm. 4121
Montgomery, AL 36132
Phone: (205)242-1380

Credential Type: License. **Duration of License:** One year. **Fees:** $5 license fee.

771

Wrestling Second (Substitute)
State Athletic Commission
50 N. Ripley St., Rm. 4121
Montgomery, AL 36132
Phone: (205)242-1380

Credential Type: License. **Duration of License:** One year. **Fees:** $5 license fee.

772

Wrestling Time Keeper
State Athletic Commission
50 N. Ripley St., Rm. 4121
Montgomery, AL 36132
Phone: (205)242-1380

Credential Type: License. **Duration of License:** One year. **Fees:** $5 license fee.

Alaska

773

Boxer
Dept. of Commerce and Economic Development
Div. of Occupational Licensing
Athletic Commission
PO Box D-LIC
Juneau, AK 99811-0800
Phone: (907)465-2534
Fax: (907)465-2974

Credential Type: License. **Duration of License:** One year. **Requirements:** At least 18 years of age. Pass a blood test. Written statement from a licensed examining physician. **Fees:** $10 license fee. **Governing Statute:** Alaska Statutes 05.05 and 08.10. Professional Regulations 12 AAC 06.

774

Boxing Manager
Dept. of Commerce and Economic Development
Div. of Occupational Licensing
Athletic Commission
PO Box D-LIC
Juneau, AK 99811-0800
Phone: (907)465-2534
Fax: (907)465-2974

Credential Type: License. **Duration of License:** One year. **Fees:** $50 license fee. **Governing Statute:** Alaska Statutes 05.05 and 08.10. Professional Regulations 12 AAC 06.

Alaska

775

Boxing Referee
Dept. of Commerce and Economic Development
Div. of Occupational Licensing
Athletic Commission
PO Box D-LIC
Juneau, AK 99811-0800
Phone: (907)465-2534
Fax: (907)465-2974

Credential Type: License. **Duration of License:** One year. **Requirements:** At least 21 years of age. One year experience in either amateur or professional boxing as a referee or judge. Submit verifications from three persons of proficiency as a referee or judge. Pass physical examination within 30 days of initial application or renewal date. **Fees:** $10 license fee. **Governing Statute:** Alaska Statutes 05.05 and 08.10. Professional Regulations 12 AAC 06.

776

Boxing Second
Dept. of Commerce and Economic Development
Div. of Occupational Licensing
Athletic Commission
PO Box D-LIC
Juneau, AK 99811-0800
Phone: (907)465-2534
Fax: (907)465-2974

Credential Type: License. **Duration of License:** One year. **Exemptions:** A licensed manager may act as a second without a second's license. **Fees:** $10 license fee. **Governing Statute:** Alaska Statutes 05.05 and 08.10. Professional Regulations 12 AAC 06.

777

Professional Wrestler
Dept. of Commerce and Economic Development
Div. of Occupational Licensing
Athletic Commission
PO Box D-LIC
Juneau, AK 99811-0800
Phone: (907)465-2534
Fax: (907)465-2974

Credential Type: License. **Duration of License:** One year. **Requirements:** At least 18 years of age. Pass physical examination by licensed examining physician. **Fees:** $10 license fee. **Governing Statute:** Alaska Statutes 05.05 and 08.10. Professional Regulations 12 AAC 06.

Arizona

778

Apprentice Jockey
Arizona Dept. of Racing
Investigations and Licensing Div.
800 W. Washington, Rm. 515
Phoenix, AZ 85007
Phone: (602)542-5151

Credential Type: Jockey apprentice certificate. **Duration of License:** Three years. **Requirements:** At least 16 years of age. Not have been convicted of a felony or any crime involving moral turpitude within the last five years. If applicant has not been previously licensed as a jockey apprentice in Arizona or in another recognized racing association state with pari-mutuel wagering, then application will be reviewed by the Board of Stewards. **Fees:** $75 license fee.

779

Authorized Agent
Arizona Dept. of Racing
Investigations and Licensing Div.
800 W. Washington, Rm. 515
Phoenix, AZ 85007
Phone: (602)542-5151

Credential Type: Authorized agent license. **Duration of License:** Three years. **Requirements:** At least 16 years of age. Not have been convicted of a felony or any crime involving moral turpitude within the last five years. Application must be signed by the principal(s) and clearly set forth the powers of the agent. **Fees:** $36 license fee if not licensed in another category. $5 license fee if licensed in another category.

780

Boxer
Boxing Commission
1645 W. Jefferson, Rm. 212
Phoenix, AZ 85007
Phone: (602)542-1417

Credential Type: License. **Requirements:** Contact the commission for an application.

781

Boxing Judge
Boxing Commission
1645 W. Jefferson, Rm. 212
Phoenix, AZ 85007
Phone: (602)542-1417

Credential Type: License. **Requirements:** Contact the commission for an application.

782

Jockey
Arizona Dept. of Racing
Investigations and Licensing Div.
800 W. Washington, Rm. 515
Phoenix, AZ 85007
Phone: (602)542-5151

Credential Type: Jockey license. **Duration of License:** Three years. **Requirements:** At least 16 years of age. Not have been convicted of a felony or any crime involving moral turpitude within the last five years. If applicant has not been previously licensed as a jockey in Arizona or in another recognized racing association state with pari-mutuel wagering, then application will be reviewed by the Board of Stewards. **Fees:** $75 license fee.

783

Jockey Agent
Arizona Dept. of Racing
Investigations and Licensing Div.
800 W. Washington, Rm. 515
Phoenix, AZ 85007
Phone: (602)542-5151

Credential Type: Jockey agent license. **Duration of License:** Three years. **Requirements:** At least 16 years of age. Not have been convicted of a felony or any crime involving moral turpitude within the last five years. Must be accompanied by the jockey(s) the applicant represents. No jockey agent may represent more than two jockeys and one apprentice jockey at any one time. A jockey agent cannot be licensed in more than one category at any track. **Fees:** $75 license fee.

784

Referee
Boxing Commission
1645 W. Jefferson, Rm. 212
Phoenix, AZ 85007
Phone: (602)542-1417

Credential Type: License. **Requirements:** Contact the commission for an application.

785

Second Manager
Boxing Commission
1645 W. Jefferson, Rm. 212
Phoenix, AZ 85007
Phone: (602)542-1417

Credential Type: License. **Requirements:** Contact the commission for an application.

Athletes, Coaches, Umpires, and Referees

786

Timekeeper
Boxing Commission
1645 W. Jefferson, Rm. 212
Phoenix, AZ 85007
Phone: (602)542-1417

Credential Type: License. **Requirements:** Contact the commission for an application.

787

Track Official
Arizona Dept. of Racing
Investigations and Licensing Div.
800 W. Washington, Rm. 515
Phoenix, AZ 85007
Phone: (602)542-5151

Credential Type: Track official license. **Duration of License:** Three years. **Authorization:** A track official license allows the license holder to serve in any of the following positions without additional licensing: director of racing, mutuel manager, clerk of the scales, track veterinarian, jockey room custodian, mechanical lure operator, track superintendent, handicapper, kennel master, patrol judge, starter, timer, announcer, chief of security, chart writer, racing secretary, paddock judge, horsemen's bookkeeper. One person may serve in more than one official position with the consent and approval of the department. **Requirements:** At least 16 years of age. Not have been convicted of a felony or any crime involving moral turpitude within the last five years. **Fees:** $36 license fee.

Arkansas

788

Athletic Manager
Arkansas Athletic Commission
Quawpaw Towers, Rm. 2A
Little Rock, AR 72201
Phone: (501)371-2110

Credential Type: License. **Duration of License:** One year. **Requirements:** License based on experience listed on application. License must be granted and signed by the Post Commander of a local unit of a statewide patriotic organization, chartered by a special Act of Congress. (VFW or American Legion). **Examination:** No. **Fees:** $25 License fee. $25 Renewal.

789

Boxing/Wrestling Referee
Arkansas Athletic Commission
Quawpaw Towers, Rm. 2A
Little Rock, AR 72201
Phone: (501)371-2110

Credential Type: License. **Duration of License:** One year. **Requirements:** License based on experience listed on application. License must be granted by the Post Commander of a local unit of a statewide patriotic organization, chartered by a special Act of Congress (VFW or American Legion). **Examination:** No **Fees:** $25 License. $25 Renewal.

790

Commission Clocker
Arkansas State Racing Commission
Ledbetter Bldg., Rm. G08
7th & Wolfe St.
PO Box 3076
Little Rock, AR 72203
Phone: (501)682-1467

Credential Type: License. **Duration of License:** One year. **Requirements:** Application must be approved by the Stewards. Must be qualified as to ability and integrity, and have endorsement by employer. Must be 16 years of age. Never convicted of a crime, excluding minor traffic offenses. Not be habitually intoxicated or addicted to drugs. Must not be engaged in any activity or practice which is illegal, undesirable, or detrimental to the best interest of the public and the sport of racing. **Examination:** No. **Fees:** $3 License. $3 Renewal.

791

Greyhound Commission Judge
Arkansas State Racing Commission
Ledbetter Bldg., Rm. G08
7th & Wolfe St.
PO Box 3076
Little Rock, AR 72203
Phone: (501)682-1467

Credential Type: License. **Duration of License:** One year. **Requirements:** Must not be associated with any bookmaking practices which are illegal or would be detrimental to the public or the sport of racing. Never convicted of a crime. Qualified as to ability and integrity of license sought and have endorsement of employer. Not be habitually intoxicated or addicted to drugs. Declare ownership or interest in any greyhound. Application must contain no falsehoods. 16 years of age. Application approved by Director of Racing. **Examination:** No **Fees:** $3 License. $3 Renewal.

792

Greyhound Paddock Judge
Arkansas State Racing Commission
Ledbetter Bldg., Rm. G08
7th & Wolfe St.
PO Box 3076
Little Rock, AR 72203
Phone: (501)682-1467

Credential Type: License. **Duration of License:** One year. **Requirements:** Must not be associated with any bookmaking practices which are illegal or would be detrimental to the public or the sport of racing. Never convicted of a crime. Qualified as to ability and integrity of license sought and have endorsement of employer. Not be habitually intoxicated or addicted to drugs. Declare ownership or interest in any greyhound. Application must contain no falsehoods. 16 years of age. Application approved by Director of Racing. **Examination:** No **Fees:** $3 License. $3 Renewal.

793

Greyhound Presiding Judge
Arkansas State Racing Commission
Ledbetter Bldg., Rm. G08
7th & Wolfe St.
PO Box 3076
Little Rock, AR 72203
Phone: (501)682-1467

Credential Type: License. **Duration of License:** One year. **Requirements:** Must not be associated with any bookmaking practices which are illegal or would be detrimental to the public or the sport of racing. Never convicted of a crime. Qualified as to ability and integrity of license sought and have endorsement of employer. Not be habitually intoxicated or addicted to drugs. Declare ownership or interest in any greyhound. Application must contain no falsehoods. 16 years of age. Application approved by Director of Racing. **Examination:** No **Fees:** $3 License. $3 Renewal.

794

Greyhound Racing Secretary
Arkansas State Racing Commission
Ledbetter Bldg., Rm. G08
7th & Wolfe St.
PO Box 3076
Little Rock, AR 72203
Phone: (501)682-1467

Credential Type: License. **Duration of License:** One year. **Requirements:** Must not be associated with any bookmaking practices which are illegal or would be detrimental to the public or the sport of racing.

Arkansas 795

Greyhound Racing Secretary, continued

Never convicted of a crime. Qualified as to ability and integrity of license sought and have endorsement of employer. Not be habitually intoxicated or addicted to drugs. Declare ownership or interest in any greyhound. Application must contain no falsehoods. 16 years of age. Application approved by Director of Racing. **Examination:** No **Fees:** $3 License. $3 Renewal.

795

Greyhound Starter
Arkansas State Racing Commission
Ledbetter Bldg., Rm. G08
7th & Wolfe St.
PO Box 3076
Little Rock, AR 72203
Phone: (501)682-1467

Credential Type: License. **Duration of License:** One year. **Requirements:** Must not be associated with any bookmaking practices which are illegal or would be detrimental to the public or the sport of racing. Never convicted of a crime. Qualified as to ability and integrity of license sought and have endorsement of employer. Not be habitually intoxicated or addicted to drugs. Declare ownership or interest in any greyhound. Application must contain no falsehoods. 16 years of age. Application approved by Director of Racing. **Examination:** No **Fees:** $3 License. $3 Renewal.

796

Horse Race Starter
Arkansas State Racing Commission
Ledbetter Bldg., Rm. G08
7th & Wolfe St.
PO Box 3076
Little Rock, AR 72203
Phone: (501)682-1467

Credential Type: License. **Duration of License:** One year. **Requirements:** Application must be approved by the Stewards. Must be qualified as to ability and integrity of license sought and have the endorsement of the employer. Must be 16 years of age. Never convicted of a crime. Must not be habitually intoxicated or addicted to drugs. Must not be engaged in any activity or practice which is illegal, undesirable, or detrimental to the best interest of the public and the sport of racing. **Examination:** No **Fees:** $3 License. $3 Renewal.

797

Jockey
Arkansas State Racing Commission
Ledbetter Bldg., Rm. G08
7th & Wolfe St.
PO Box 3076
Little Rock, AR 72203
Phone: (501)682-1467

Credential Type: License. **Duration of License:** One year. **Requirements:** 18 years of age. Must not be an owner of any horse racing in Arkansas. Application must be approved by the Stewards. **Examination:** No **Fees:** $15 License. $15 Renewal.

798

Jockey Agent
Arkansas State Racing Commission
Ledbetter Bldg., Rm. G08
7th & Wolfe St.
PO Box 3076
Little Rock, AR 72203
Phone: (501)682-1467

Credential Type: License. **Duration of License:** One year. **Requirements:** Application must be approved by the Stewards. **Examination:** No **Fees:** $15 License. $15 Renewal.

799

Jockey Apprentice
Arkansas Sate Racing Commission
Ledbetter Bldg., Rm. G08
7th & Wolfe St.
PO Box 3076
Little Rock, AR 72203
Phone: (501)682-1467

Credential Type: License. **Duration of License:** One year. **Requirements:** Between ages of 18 and 25. Provide evidence of date of birth. Not have been licensed as a jockey in any country. Be bound to an owner or trainer for no less than three years, but no longer than five years. Proof of at least two years service with a racing stable. Application approved by the Stewards. **Examination:** No **Fees:** $15 License. $15 Renewal.

800

Paddock Judge
Arkansas State Racing Commission
Ledbetter Bldg., Rm. G08
7th & Wolfe St.
PO Box 3076
Little Rock, AR 72203
Phone: (501)268-4351

Credential Type: License. **Duration of License:** One year. **Requirements:** Applications must be approved by the Stewards. Must be qualified as to ability and integrity of license sought. Must be 16 years of age. Must have endorsement of employer. Never convicted of a crime. Must not be habitually intoxicated or addicted to drugs. Must not be engaged in any activity or practice which is illegal or undesirable, or detrimental to the best interest of the public or the sport of racing. **Examination:** No **Fees:** $3 License. $3 Renewal.

801

Patrol Judge
Arkansas State Racing Commission
Ledbetter Bldg., Rm. G08
7th & Wolfe St.
PO Box 3076
Little Rock, AR 72203
Phone: (501)682-1467

Credential Type: License. **Duration of License:** One year. **Requirements:** Applications must be approved by the Stewards. Must be qualified as to ability and integrity of license sought. Must be 16 years of age. Must have endorsement of employer. Never convicted of a crime. Must not be habitually intoxicated or addicted to drugs. Must not be engaged in any activity or practice which is illegal or undesirable, or detrimental to the best interest of the public or the sport of racing. **Examination:** No **Fees:** $3 License. $3 Renewal.

802

Placing Judge
Arkansas State Racing Commission
Ledbetter Bldg., Rm. G08
7th & Wolfe St.
PO Box 3076
Little Rock, AR 72203
Phone: (501)682-1467

Credential Type: License. **Duration of License:** One year. **Requirements:** Application must be approved by the Stewards. Must be qualified as to ability and integrity of license sought and have the endorsement of employer. 16 years of age. Never convicted of a crime. Not be habitually ad-

Athletes, Coaches, Umpires, and Referees

dicted to drugs or intoxicated. Must not be engaged in any activity which is illegal, undesirable or detrimental to the best interest of the public and the sport of racing. **Examination:** No **Fees:** $3 License. $3 Renewal.

803

Professional Boxer
Arkansas Athletic Commission
Quawpaw Towers, Rm. 2A
Little Rock, AR 72201
Phone: (501)371-2110

Credential Type: License. **Duration of License:** One year. **Requirements:** Pass a physical examination. License must be granted by the Post Commander of a local unit of a statewide patriotic organization (American Legion or VFW). **Examination:** Yes. **Fees:** $10 License. $10 Renewal.

804

Professional Wrestler
Arkansas Athletic Commission
Quawpaw Towers, Rm. 2A
Little Rock, AR 72201
Phone: (501)371-2110

Credential Type: License. **Duration of License:** One year. **Requirements:** Pass the physical examination. License must be granted by a local chapter of either the VFW or the American Legion. **Examination:** Yes. **Fees:** $20 License. $20 Renewal.

805

Racetrack Steward
Arkansas State Racing Commission
Ledbetter Bldg., Rm. G08
7th & Wolfe St.
PO Box 3076
Little Rock, AR 72203
Phone: (501)682-1467

Credential Type: License. **Requirements:** Must have held a position related to race meeting prior to application; duration must be at least 60 days during the last three years. **Examination:** No **Fees:** None

806

Racing Agent
Arkansas State Racing Commission
Ledbetter Bldg., Rm. G08
7th & Wolfe St.
PO Box 3076
Little Rock, AR 72203
Phone: (501)682-1467

Credential Type: License. **Duration of License:** One year. **Requirements:** Meet all requirements listed in the Arkansas State Racing Commission Rules and Regulations. Must be approved by the Stewards. **Examination:** No **Fees:** $5 License (per owner or trainer represented per year).

807

Racing Secretary
Arkansas State Racing Commission
Ledbetter Bldg., Rm. G08
7th & Wolfe St.
PO Box 3076
Little Rock, AR 72203
Phone: (501)682-1467

Credential Type: License. **Duration of License:** One year. **Requirements:** Application must be approved by the Stewards. Must be qualified as to ability and integrity of license sought and have the endorsement of employer. 16 years of age. Never convicted of a crime. Not be habitually addicted to drugs or intoxicated. Must not be engaged in any activity which is illegal, undesirable or detrimental to the best interest of the public and the sport of racing. **Examination:** No **Fees:** $3 License. $3 Renewal.

808

Timekeeper
Arkansas Athletic Commission
Quawpaw Towers, Rm. 2A
Little Rock, AR 72201
Phone: (501)371-2110

Credential Type: License. **Duration of License:** One year. **Requirements:** License must be granted a local unit of either the VFW or the American Legion. **Examination:** No **Fees:** $10 License. $10 Renewal.

California

809

Apprentice Jockey (Racetrack)
California Horse Racing Board
1010 Hurley Way, Ste. 190
Sacramento, CA 95825
Phone: (916)920-7178

Credential Type: License Registration. **Requirements:** Submit application and fingerprint card. Pay fee. **Fees:** $150 registration fee.

810

Assistant Starter (Racetrack)
California Horse Racing Board
1010 Hurley Way, Ste. 190
Sacramento, CA 95825
Phone: (916)920-7178

Credential Type: License Registration. **Requirements:** Submit application and fingerprint card. Pay fee. **Fees:** $75 registration fee.

811

Driver (Racetrack)
California Horse Racing Board
1010 Hurley Way, Ste. 190
Sacramento, CA 95825
Phone: (916)920-7178

Credential Type: License Registration. **Requirements:** Submit application and fingerprint card. Pay fee. **Fees:** $150 registration fee.

812

Jockey Agent (Racetrack)
California Horse Racing Board
1010 Hurley Way, Ste. 190
Sacramento, CA 95825
Phone: (916)920-7178

Credential Type: License Registration. **Requirements:** Submit application and fingerprint card. Pay fee. **Fees:** $150 registration fee.

813

Jockey (Racetrack)
California Horse Racing Board
1010 Hurley Way, Ste. 190
Sacramento, CA 95825
Phone: (916)920-7178

Credential Type: License Registration. **Requirements:** Submit application and fin-

Jockey (Racetrack), continued

gerprint card. Pay fee. **Fees:** $150 registration fee.

814

Judge (Amateur Boxing, Kickboxing, or Martial Arts)
Athletic Commission
1424 Howe Ave., Ste. 33
Sacramento, CA 95814-6200
Phone: (916)920-7300

Credential Type: License. **Duration of License:** One year. **Requirements:** Submit application and pay fee. **Fees:** $25 license fee. $25 renewal fee.

815

Judge (Professional Boxing, Kickboxing, or Martial Arts)
Athletic Commission
1424 Howe Ave., Ste. 33
Sacramento, CA 95814-6200
Phone: (916)920-7300

Credential Type: License. **Duration of License:** One year. **Requirements:** Submit application and pay fee. **Fees:** $60 license fee. $60 renewal fee.

816

Marshal (Racetrack)
California Horse Racing Board
1010 Hurley Way, Ste. 190
Sacramento, CA 95825
Phone: (916)920-7178

Credential Type: License Registration. **Requirements:** Submit application and fingerprint card. Pay fee. **Fees:** $75 registration fee.

817

Professional Boxer
Athletic Commission
1424 Howe Ave., Ste. 33
Sacramento, CA 95814-6200
Phone: (916)920-7300

Credential Type: License. **Duration of License:** One year. **Requirements:** Submit application and pay fee. **Fees:** $25 license fee. $25 renewal fee.

818

Professional Kickboxer
Athletic Commission
1424 Howe Ave., Ste. 33
Sacramento, CA 95814-6200
Phone: (916)920-7300

Credential Type: License. **Duration of License:** One year. **Requirements:** Submit application and pay fee. **Fees:** $25 license fee. $25 renewal fee.

819

Professional Martial Arts Fighter
Athletic Commission
1424 Howe Ave., Ste. 33
Sacramento, CA 95814-6200
Phone: (916)920-7300

Credential Type: License. **Duration of License:** One year. **Requirements:** Submit application and pay fee. **Fees:** $25 license fee. $25 renewal fee.

820

Racing Official (Racetrack)
California Horse Racing Board
1010 Hurley Way, Ste. 190
Sacramento, CA 95825
Phone: (916)920-7178

Credential Type: License Registration. **Requirements:** Submit application and fingerprint card. Pay fee. **Fees:** $150 registration fee.

821

Referee (Amateur Boxing, Kickboxing, or Martial Arts)
Athletic Commission
1424 Howe Ave., Ste. 33
Sacramento, CA 95814-6200
Phone: (916)920-7300

Credential Type: License. **Duration of License:** One year. **Requirements:** Submit application and pay fee. **Fees:** $25 license fee. $25 renewal fee.

822

Referee (Professional Boxing, Kickboxing, or Martial Arts)
Athletic Commission
1424 Howe Ave., Ste. 33
Sacramento, CA 95814-6200
Phone: (916)920-7300

Credential Type: License. **Duration of License:** One year. **Requirements:** Submit application and pay fee. **Fees:** $60 license fee. $60 renewal fee.

823

Second (Boxing, Kickboxing, or Martial Arts)
Athletic Commission
1424 Howe Ave., Ste. 33
Sacramento, CA 95814-6200
Phone: (916)920-7300

Credential Type: License. **Duration of License:** One year. **Requirements:** Submit application and pay fee. **Fees:** $25 license fee. $25 renewal fee.

824

Steward (Racetrack)
California Horse Racing Board
1010 Hurley Way, Ste. 190
Sacramento, CA 95825
Phone: (916)920-7178

Credential Type: License Registration. **Requirements:** Submit application and fingerprint card. Pay fee. **Fees:** $150 registration fee.

825

Timekeeper (Boxing, Kickboxing, or Martial Arts)
Athletic Commission
1424 Howe Ave., Ste. 33
Sacramento, CA 95814-6200
Phone: (916)920-7300

Credential Type: License. **Duration of License:** One year. **Requirements:** Submit application and pay fee. **Fees:** $25 license fee. $25 renewal fee.

Colorado

826

Apprentice Jockey (Horse)
Colorado Racing Commission
Dept. of Regulatory Agencies
1560 Broadway, Ste. 1540
Denver, CO 80202
Phone: (303)894-2990
Fax: (303)894-7580

Credential Type: Apprentice Jockey License. **Requirements:** Submit application and pay fee. **Fees:** $44 license fee.

Athletes, Coaches, Umpires, and Referees

827

Assistant Starter (Horse)
Colorado Racing Commission
Dept. of Regulatory Agencies
1560 Broadway, Ste. 1540
Denver, CO 80202
Phone: (303)894-2990
Fax: (303)894-7580

Credential Type: Assistant Starter License. **Requirements:** Submit application and pay fee. **Fees:** $24 license fee.

828

Jockey (Horse)
Colorado Racing Commission
Dept. of Regulatory Agencies
1560 Broadway, Ste. 1540
Denver, CO 80202
Phone: (303)894-2990
Fax: (303)894-7580

Credential Type: Jockey License. **Requirements:** Submit application and pay fee. **Fees:** $44 license fee.

829

Racing Official (Greyhound)
Colorado Racing Commission
Dept. of Regulatory Agencies
1560 Broadway, Ste. 1540
Denver, CO 80202
Phone: (303)894-2990
Fax: (303)894-7580

Credential Type: Steward/Judge, Racing Official License. **Duration of License:** Three years. **Requirements:** Submit application, pay fees, and pass examination. **Examination:** Steward/Judge Exam. **Fees:** $44 application/exam/license fee.

830

Racing Official (Horse)
Colorado Racing Commission
Dept. of Regulatory Agencies
1560 Broadway, Ste. 1540
Denver, CO 80202
Phone: (303)894-2990
Fax: (303)894-7580

Credential Type: Steward/Judge, Racing Official License. **Duration of License:** Three years. **Requirements:** Submit application, pay fees, and pass examination. **Examination:** Steward/Judge Exam. **Fees:** $44 application/exam/license fee.

Connecticut

831

Assistant Racing Secretary (Racetrack)
Connecticut Div. of Special Revenue
Russell Rd.
PO Box 11424
Newington, CT 06111-0424
Phone: (203)566-2756

Credential Type: License Registration. **Requirements:** Submit application and fingerprint card. Pay fee. **Fees:** $20 registration fee.

832

Assistant Starter (Racetrack)
Connecticut Div. of Special Revenue
Russell Rd.
PO Box 11424
Newington, CT 06111-0424
Phone: (203)566-2756

Credential Type: License Registration. **Requirements:** Submit application and fingerprint card. Pay fee. **Fees:** $20 registration fee.

833

Authorized Agent (Greyhound Track)
Connecticut Div. of Special Revenue
Russell Rd.
PO Box 11424
Newington, CT 06111-0424
Phone: (203)566-2756

Credential Type: License Registration. **Requirements:** Submit application and fingerprint card. Pay fee. **Fees:** $5 registration fee.

834

Boxer
Athletic Div.
Consumer Protection Dept.
165 Capitol Ave.
Hartford, CT 06106
Phone: (203)566-3843

Credential Type: License. **Requirements:** Contact licensing body for application information.

835

Deputy Judge (Racetrack)
Connecticut Div. of Special Revenue
Russell Rd.
PO Box 11424
Newington, CT 06111-0424
Phone: (203)566-2756

Credential Type: License Registration. **Requirements:** Submit application and fingerprint card. Pay fee. **Fees:** $20 registration fee.

836

Harness Driver (Racetrack)
Connecticut Div. of Special Revenue
Russell Rd.
PO Box 11424
Newington, CT 06111-0424
Phone: (203)566-2756

Credential Type: License Registration. **Requirements:** Submit application and fingerprint card. Pay fee. **Fees:** $5 registration fee.

837

Jockey (Racetrack)
Connecticut Div. of Special Revenue
Russell Rd.
PO Box 11424
Newington, CT 06111-0424
Phone: (203)566-2756

Credential Type: License Registration. **Requirements:** Submit application and fingerprint card. Pay fee. **Fees:** $5 registration fee.

838

Judge (Boxing and Wrestling)
Athletic Div.
Consumer Protection Dept.
165 Capitol Ave.
Hartford, CT 06106
Phone: (203)566-3843

Credential Type: License. **Requirements:** Contact licensing body for application information.

839

Judge (Racetrack)
Connecticut Div. of Special Revenue
Russell Rd.
PO Box 11424
Newington, CT 06111-0424
Phone: (203)566-2756

Credential Type: License Registration. **Requirements:** Submit application and fingerprint card. Pay fee. **Fees:** $20 registration fee.

840

Manager (Boxing and Wrestling)
Athletic Div.
Consumer Protection Dept.
165 Capitol Ave.
Hartford, CT 06106
Phone: (203)566-3843

Credential Type: License. **Requirements:** Contact licensing body for application information.

841

Official (Racetrack)
Connecticut Div. of Special Revenue
Russell Rd.
PO Box 11424
Newington, CT 06111-0424
Phone: (203)566-2756

Credential Type: License Registration. **Requirements:** Submit application and fingerprint card. Pay fee. **Fees:** $20 registration fee.

842

Paddock Judge (Racetrack)
Connecticut Div. of Special Revenue
Russell Rd.
PO Box 11424
Newington, CT 06111-0424
Phone: (203)566-2756

Credential Type: License Registration. **Requirements:** Submit application and fingerprint card. Pay fee. **Fees:** $20 registration fee.

843

Patrol Judge (Racetrack)
Connecticut Div. of Special Revenue
Russell Rd.
PO Box 11424
Newington, CT 06111-0424
Phone: (203)566-2756

Credential Type: License Registration. **Requirements:** Submit application and fingerprint card. Pay fee. **Fees:** $20 registration fee.

844

Player Judge (Racetrack)
Connecticut Div. of Special Revenue
Russell Rd.
PO Box 11424
Newington, CT 06111-0424
Phone: (203)566-2756

Credential Type: License Registration. **Requirements:** Submit application and fingerprint card. Pay fee. **Fees:** $20 registration fee.

845

Racing Secretary (Racetrack)
Connecticut Div. of Special Revenue
Russell Rd.
PO Box 11424
Newington, CT 06111-0424
Phone: (203)566-2756

Credential Type: License Registration. **Requirements:** Submit application and fingerprint card. Pay fee. **Fees:** $20 registration fee.

846

Referee (Boxing and Wrestling)
Athletic Div.
Consumer Protection Dept.
165 Capitol Ave.
Hartford, CT 06106
Phone: (203)566-3843

Credential Type: License. **Requirements:** Contact licensing body for application information.

847

Second (Boxing and Wrestling)
Athletic Div.
Consumer Protection Dept.
165 Capitol Ave.
Hartford, CT 06106
Phone: (203)566-3843

Credential Type: License. **Requirements:** Contact licensing body for application information.

848

Starter (Racetrack)
Connecticut Div. of Special Revenue
Russell Rd.
PO Box 11424
Newington, CT 06111-0424
Phone: (203)566-2756

Credential Type: License Registration. **Requirements:** Submit application and fingerprint card. Pay fee. **Fees:** $20 registration fee.

849

Timekeeper (Boxing and Wrestling)
Athletic Div.
Consumer Protection Dept.
165 Capitol Ave.
Hartford, CT 06106
Phone: (203)566-3843

Credential Type: License. **Requirements:** Contact licensing body for application information.

850

Wrestler
Athletic Div.
Consumer Protection Dept.
165 Capitol Ave.
Hartford, CT 06106
Phone: (203)566-3843

Credential Type: License. **Requirements:** Contact licensing body for application information.

Delaware

851

Assistant Racing Secretary (Racetrack)
Delaware Harness Racing
  Commission
2320 S. DuPont Hwy.
Dover, DE 19901
Phone: (302)739-4811

Credential Type: License Registration.
Requirements: Submit application and fingerprint card. Pay fee. **Fees:** $10 registration fee.

852

Associate Judge (Racetrack)
Delaware Harness Racing
  Commission
2320 S. DuPont Hwy.
Dover, DE 19901
Phone: (302)739-4811

Credential Type: License Registration.
Requirements: Submit application and fingerprint card. Pay fee. **Fees:** $15 registration fee.

853

Horse Driver (Racetrack)
Delaware Harness Racing
  Commission
2320 S. DuPont Hwy.
Dover, DE 19901
Phone: (302)739-4811

Credential Type: License Registration.
Requirements: Submit application and fingerprint card. Pay fee. **Fees:** $10 registration fee.

854

Paddock Judge (Racetrack)
Delaware Harness Racing
  Commission
2320 S. DuPont Hwy.
Dover, DE 19901
Phone: (302)739-4811

Credential Type: License Registration.
Requirements: Submit application and fingerprint card. Pay fee. **Fees:** $10 registration fee.

855

Patrol Judge (Racetrack)
Delaware Harness Racing
  Commission
2320 S. DuPont Hwy.
Dover, DE 19901
Phone: (302)739-4811

Credential Type: License Registration.
Requirements: Submit application and fingerprint card. Pay fee. **Fees:** $10 registration fee.

856

Presiding Judge (Racetrack)
Delaware Harness Racing
  Commission
2320 S. DuPont Hwy.
Dover, DE 19901
Phone: (302)739-4811

Credential Type: License Registration.
Requirements: Submit application and fingerprint card. Pay fee. **Fees:** $20 registration fee.

857

Racing Secretary (Racetrack)
Delaware Harness Racing
  Commission
2320 S. DuPont Hwy.
Dover, DE 19901
Phone: (302)739-4811

Credential Type: License Registration.
Requirements: Submit application and fingerprint card. Pay fee. **Fees:** $20 registration fee.

858

Starter (Racetrack)
Delaware Harness Racing
  Commission
2320 S. DuPont Hwy.
Dover, DE 19901
Phone: (302)739-4811

Credential Type: License Registration.
Requirements: Submit application and fingerprint card. Pay fee. **Fees:** $15 registration fee.

859

State Steward (Racetrack)
Delaware Harness Racing
  Commission
2320 S. DuPont Hwy.
Dover, DE 19901
Phone: (302)739-4811

Credential Type: License Registration.
Requirements: Submit application and fingerprint card. Pay fee. **Fees:** $15 registration fee.

860

Thoroughbred Jockey (Racetrack)
Delaware Thoroughbred Racing
  Commission
820 French St., 3rd Level
Wilmington, DE 19801
Phone: (302)577-3288

Credential Type: License Registration.
Requirements: Contact licensing body for application information.

861

Thoroughbred Racing Official (Racetrack)
Delaware Thoroughbred Racing
  Commission
820 French St., 3rd Level
Wilmington, DE 19801
Phone: (302)577-3288

Credential Type: License Registration.
Requirements: Contact licensing body for application information.

862

Timer (Racetrack)
Delaware Harness Racing
  Commission
2320 S. DuPont Hwy.
Dover, DE 19901
Phone: (302)739-4811

Credential Type: License Registration.
Requirements: Submit application and fingerprint card. Pay fee. **Fees:** $5 registration fee.

Florida

863

Agent, Jockey (Racetrack)
Florida Dept. of Business
Div. of Pari-Mutuel Wagering
Licensing Section
725 S. Bronough St.
Tallahassee, FL 32399-1037
Phone: (904)488-9161

Credential Type: License Registration Code 1054. **Requirements:** Submit application and fingerprint card. Pay fee. **Fees:** $40 registration fee.

864

Alternate Racing/Game Official (Racetrack)
Florida Dept. of Business
Div. of Pari-Mutuel Wagering
Licensing Section
725 S. Bronough St.
Tallahassee, FL 32399-1037
Phone: (904)488-9161

Credential Type: License Registration Code 1067. **Requirements:** Submit application and fingerprint card. Pay fee. **Fees:** $10 registration fee.

865

Athlete Agent
Dept. of Professional Regulation
1940 N. Monroe St.
Tallahassee, FL 32399-0777
Phone: (904)488-7487

Credential Type: Athlete Agent License. **Duration of License:** Two years. **Requirements:** Complete application and pay fee. **Reciprocity:** No. **Fees:** $500 license fee. $440 renewal fee. **Governing Statute:** Florida Statutes, Chapter 468, Part IX.

866

Authorized Agent (Racetrack)
Florida Dept. of Business
Div. of Pari-Mutuel Wagering
Licensing Section
725 S. Bronough St.
Tallahassee, FL 32399-1037
Phone: (904)488-9161

Credential Type: License Registration Code 1047. **Requirements:** Submit application and fingerprint card. Pay fee. **Fees:** $40 registration fee.

867

Greyhound Judge (Racetrack)
Florida Dept. of Business
Div. of Pari-Mutuel Wagering
Licensing Section
725 S. Bronough St.
Tallahassee, FL 32399-1037
Phone: (904)488-9161

Credential Type: License Registration Code 6035. **Requirements:** Submit application and fingerprint card. Pay fee. **Fees:** $40 registration fee.

868

Harness Driver (Racetrack)
Florida Dept. of Business
Div. of Pari-Mutuel Wagering
Licensing Section
725 S. Bronough St.
Tallahassee, FL 32399-1037
Phone: (904)488-9161

Credential Type: License Registration Code 4027. **Requirements:** Submit application and fingerprint card. Pay fee. **Fees:** $40 registration fee.

869

Jai-Alai Judge
Florida Dept. of Business
Div. of Pari-Mutuel Wagering
Licensing Section
725 S. Bronough St.
Tallahassee, FL 32399-1037
Phone: (904)488-9161

Credential Type: License Registration Code 2035. **Requirements:** Submit application and fingerprint card. Pay fee. **Fees:** $40 registration fee.

870

Jai-Alai Player
Florida Dept. of Business
Div. of Pari-Mutuel Wagering
Licensing Section
725 S. Bronough St.
Tallahassee, FL 32399-1037
Phone: (904)488-9161

Credential Type: License Registration Code 2037. **Requirements:** Submit application and fingerprint card. Pay fee. **Fees:** $40 registration fee.

871

Jockey/Apprentice Jockey (Racetrack)
Florida Dept. of Business
Div. of Pari-Mutuel Wagering
Licensing Section
725 S. Bronough St.
Tallahassee, FL 32399-1037
Phone: (904)488-9161

Credential Type: License Registration Code 1028. **Requirements:** Submit application and fingerprint card. Pay fee. **Fees:** $40 registration fee.

872

Paddock/Patrol/Placing Judge (Racetrack)
Florida Dept. of Business
Div. of Pari-Mutuel Wagering
Licensing Section
725 S. Bronough St.
Tallahassee, FL 32399-1037
Phone: (904)488-9161

Credential Type: License Registration Code 1035. **Requirements:** Submit application and fingerprint card. Pay fee. **Fees:** $40 registration fee.

873

Players' Manager/Assistant/Matchmaker (Jai-Alai)
Florida Dept. of Business
Div. of Pari-Mutuel Wagering
Licensing Section
725 S. Bronough St.
Tallahassee, FL 32399-1037
Phone: (904)488-9161

Credential Type: License Registration Code 1042. **Requirements:** Submit application and fingerprint card. Pay fee. **Fees:** $40 registration fee.

874

Racing Secretary (Racetrack)
Florida Dept. of Business
Div. of Pari-Mutuel Wagering
Licensing Section
725 S. Bronough St.
Tallahassee, FL 32399-1037
Phone: (904)488-9161

Credential Type: License Registration Code 1042. **Requirements:** Submit application and fingerprint card. Pay fee. **Fees:** $40 registration fee.

875

Starter (Racetrack)
Florida Dept. of Business
Div. of Pari-Mutuel Wagering
Licensing Section
725 S. Bronough St.
Tallahassee, FL 32399-1037
Phone: (904)488-9161

Credential Type: License Registration Code 1044. **Requirements:** Submit application and fingerprint card. Pay fee. **Fees:** $40 registration fee.

876

Steward (Racetrack)
Florida Dept. of Business
Div. of Pari-Mutuel Wagering
Licensing Section
725 S. Bronough St.
Tallahassee, FL 32399-1037
Phone: (904)488-9161

Credential Type: License Registration Code 1045. **Requirements:** Submit application and fingerprint card. Pay fee. **Fees:** $40 registration fee.

Georgia

877

Athlete Agent
Georgia Athlete Agent Commission
Health and Consumer Services Section
Professional Examining Boards
166 Pryor St., SW
Atlanta, GA 30303
Phone: (404)656-3933

Credential Type: Athlete Agent Registration. **Duration of License:** Two years. **Requirements:** Provide street address of principal place of business. Submit evidence of formal training or practical experience in at least one of the following areas: contracts, contract negotiation, complaint resolution, arbitration, or civil resolution of contract disputes. Deposit a surety bond of $10,000. **Fees:** $100 application fee. $100 renewal fee. **Governing Statute:** Rules of the Georgia Athlete Agent Commission, Chap. 54.

Credential Type: Temporary Registration. **Requirements:** Submit application. Post surety bond of $10,000. Pay fee. **Fees:** $100 application fee. **Governing Statute:** Rules of the Georgia Athlete Agent Commission, Chap. 54.

Hawaii

878

Boxer
Hawaii State Boxing Commission
Dept. of Commerce and Consumer Affairs
PO Box 3469
Honolulu, HI 96801
Phone: (808)548-7461

Credential Type: License. **Requirements:** At least 18 and not more than 38 years of age. Satisfactory physical and mental health. **Fees:** $15 application fee. $15 Compliance Resolution Fund fee.

Idaho

879

Apprentice Jockey (Racetrack)
Idaho State Horse Racing Commission
6133 Corporal Lane
Boise, ID 83704
Phone: (208)327-7105

Credential Type: License Registration. **Requirements:** Submit application and fingerprint card. Pay fee. **Fees:** $20 registration fee.

880

Boxer
State Athletic Dept.
1224 Vista Ave.
Boise, ID 83705
Phone: (208)334-3888

Credential Type: Boxing License. **Duration of License:** One year. **Requirements:** Submit application and pay fee. **Fees:** $10 license fee.

881

Jockey Agent (Racetrack)
Idaho State Horse Racing Commission
6133 Corporal Lane
Boise, ID 83704
Phone: (208)327-7105

Credential Type: License Registration. **Requirements:** Submit application and fingerprint card. Pay fee. **Fees:** $25 registration fee.

882

Jockey (Racetrack)
Idaho State Horse Racing Commission
6133 Corporal Lane
Boise, ID 83704
Phone: (208)327-7105

Credential Type: License Registration. **Requirements:** Submit application and fingerprint card. Pay fee. **Fees:** $20 registration fee.

883

Official (Racetrack)
Idaho State Horse Racing Commission
6133 Corporal Lane
Boise, ID 83704
Phone: (208)327-7105

Credential Type: License Registration. **Requirements:** Submit application and fingerprint card. Pay fee. **Fees:** $25 registration fee.

884

Wrestler
State Athletic Dept.
1224 Vista Ave.
Boise, ID 83705
Phone: (208)334-3888

Credential Type: Wrestling License. **Duration of License:** One year. **Requirements:** Submit application and pay fee. **Fees:** $10 license fee.

Illinois

885

Apprentice Jockey (Racetrack)
Illinois Racing Board
100 W. Randolph St., Ste. 11-100
Chicago, IL 60601
Phone: (312)814-2600

Credential Type: License Registration. **Requirements:** Submit application and fingerprint card. Pay fee. **Fees:** $25 registration fee. $2 photo fee. $10 fingerprint card fee.

Illinois 886

886

Assistant Starter (Racetrack)
Illinois Racing Board
100 W. Randolph St., Ste. 11-100
Chicago, IL 60601
Phone: (312)814-2600

Credential Type: License Registration. **Requirements:** Submit application and fingerprint card. Pay fee. **Fees:** $5 registration fee. $2 photo fee. $10 fingerprint card fee.

887

Authorized Agent (Racetrack)
Illinois Racing Board
100 W. Randolph St., Ste. 11-100
Chicago, IL 60601
Phone: (312)814-2600

Credential Type: License Registration. **Requirements:** Submit application and fingerprint card. Pay fee. **Fees:** $25 registration fee. $2 photo fee. $10 fingerprint card fee.

888

Driver-Trainer (Racetrack)
Illinois Racing Board
100 W. Randolph St., Ste. 11-100
Chicago, IL 60601
Phone: (312)814-2600

Credential Type: License Registration. **Requirements:** Submit application and fingerprint card. Pay fee. **Fees:** $25 registration fee. $2 photo fee. $10 fingerprint card fee.

889

Gloveman (Boxing/Wrestling)
Illinois Dept. of Professional
  Regulations
State of Illinois Ctr.
100 W. Randolph, Ste. 9-300
Chicago, IL 60601
Phone: (312)814-2719

Credential Type: Registration. **Duration of License:** Lifetime. **Requirements:** Submit registration to board. Must re-register if original information changes. **Reciprocity:** No. **Governing Statute:** The Illinois Professional Boxing and Wrestling Act. Illinois Revised Statutes 1991, Chapter 111.

890

Jockey Agent (Racetrack)
Illinois Racing Board
100 W. Randolph St., Ste. 11-100
Chicago, IL 60601
Phone: (312)814-2600

Credential Type: License Registration. **Requirements:** Submit application and fingerprint card. Pay fee. **Fees:** $25 registration fee. $2 photo fee. $10 fingerprint card fee.

891

Jockey (Racetrack)
Illinois Racing Board
100 W. Randolph St., Ste. 11-100
Chicago, IL 60601
Phone: (312)814-2600

Credential Type: License Registration. **Requirements:** Submit application and fingerprint card. Pay fee. **Fees:** $25 registration fee. $2 photo fee. $10 fingerprint card fee.

892

Owner-Driver (Racetrack)
Illinois Racing Board
100 W. Randolph St., Ste. 11-100
Chicago, IL 60601
Phone: (312)814-2600

Credential Type: License Registration. **Requirements:** Submit application and fingerprint card. Pay fee. **Fees:** $25 registration fee. $2 photo fee. $10 fingerprint card fee.

893

Owner-Driver-Trainer (Racetrack)
Illinois Racing Board
100 W. Randolph St., Ste. 11-100
Chicago, IL 60601
Phone: (312)814-2600

Credential Type: License Registration. **Requirements:** Submit application and fingerprint card. Pay fee. **Fees:** $25 registration fee. $2 photo fee. $10 fingerprint card fee.

894

Professional Boxer
Illinois Dept. of Professional
  Regulation
State of Illinois Ctr.
100 W. Randolph, Ste. 9-300
Chicago, IL 60601
Phone: (312)814-2719

Credential Type: Professional Boxer License. **Duration of License:** Two years. **Requirements:** At least 18 years of age. Complete physical examination and statement by a licensed physician attesting that applicant is fit and qualified to participate in boxing matches. Submit application which includes amateur record, total number of bouts, break down of wins and losses, names of opponents, result of each fight and two recent photos. Training Quarters Evaluation by the Professional Boxing and Wrestling Board of Illinois Staff is required. **Reciprocity:** No. **Fees:** $20 initial license fee. $20 renewal fee. **Governing Statute:** The Professional Box and Wrestling Act, Illinois Revised Statutes 1991.

895

Professional Boxing Judge
Illinois Dept. of Professional
  Regulation
State of Illinois Ctr.
100 W. Randolph, Ste. 9-300
Chicago, IL 60601
Phone: (312)814-2719

Credential Type: Professional Boxing Judge License. **Duration of License:** Two years. **Requirements:** Good moral character. Not in violation of any laws governing boxing. Satisfactory experience in boxing and judging at the amateur level. Must have attended Department of Professional Regulation medical seminars pertaining to boxing. Submit application with two recent pictures. **Examination:** Score card evaluation. **Reciprocity:** No. **Fees:** $10 initial license fee. $10 renewal fee. **Governing Statute:** The Professional Boxing and Wrestling Act, Illinois Revised Statutes 1991.

896

Professional Boxing Manager
Illinois Dept. of Professional
  Regulation
State of Illinois Ctr.
100 W. Randolph, Ste. 9-300
Chicago, IL 60601
Phone: (312)814-2719

Credential Type: Professional Boxing Manager License. **Duration of License:**

Athletes, Coaches, Umpires, and Referees

Two years. **Requirements:** Good moral character. Not in violation of any laws governing boxing. Satisfactory experience in managing boxers. Must have participated in medical seminars on boxing contests. Knowledge of boxing safety requirements. **Examination:** Boxing Manager Test (Given in English or Spanish). **Reciprocity:** No. **Fees:** $50 initial license fee. $50 renewal fee. **Governing Statute:** The Professional Boxing and Wrestling Act, Public Act 85-1209, Illinois Revised Statutes 1991.

897

Professional Boxing Referee
Illinois Dept. of Professional
    Regulation
State of Illinois Ctr.
100 W. Randolph, Ste. 9-300
Chicago, IL 60601
Phone: (312)814-2719

Credential Type: Professional Boxing Referee License. **Duration of License:** Two years. **Requirements:** Good moral character. Minimum of three years experience at the amateur level officiating fights. Very knowledgeable in boxing techniques. Submit application and letter from physician attesting to the applicant's good health. **Examination:** Performance examination in four round bouts. **Reciprocity:** No. **Fees:** $100 initial license fee. $100 renewal fee. **Governing Statute:** The Professional Boxing and Wrestling Act, Illinois Revised Statutes 1991.

898

Racing Official (Racetrack)
Illinois Racing Board
100 W. Randolph St., Ste. 11-100
Chicago, IL 60601
Phone: (312)814-2600

Credential Type: License Registration. **Requirements:** Submit application and fingerprint card. Pay fee. **Fees:** $25 registration fee. $2 photo fee. $10 fingerprint card fee.

899

Starter (Racetrack)
Illinois Racing Board
100 W. Randolph St., Ste. 11-100
Chicago, IL 60601
Phone: (312)814-2600

Credential Type: License Registration. **Requirements:** Submit application and fingerprint card. Pay fee. **Fees:** $25 registration fee. $2 photo fee. $10 fingerprint card fee.

900

Steward (Racetrack)
Illinois Racing Board
100 W. Randolph St., Ste. 11-100
Chicago, IL 60601
Phone: (312)814-2600

Credential Type: License Registration. **Requirements:** Submit application and fingerprint card. Pay fee. **Fees:** $25 registration fee. $2 photo fee. $10 fingerprint card fee.

901

Timekeeper (Boxing and Wrestling)
Illinois Dept. of Professional
    Regulations
State of Illinois Ctr.
100 W. Randolph, Ste. 9-300
Chicago, IL 60601
Phone: (312)814-2719

Credential Type: Timekeeper License. **Duration of License:** Indefinite. **Requirements:** Must have experience in amateur booking events. Submit two recent photos with application. Must have own equipment (stop watches, whistle, back-up gong, etc.). Must be evaluated by Athletic Board Staff. **Reciprocity:** No. **Fees:** $50 license fee. **Governing Statute:** The Illinois Professional Boxing and Wrestling Act, Illinois Revised Statutes 1987, Chapter 111.

902

Wrestler
Illinois Dept. of Professional
    Regulations
State of Illinois Ctr.
100 W. Randolph, Ste. 9-300
Chicago, IL 60601
Phone: (312)814-2719

Credential Type: Wrestler Mandatory Registration. **Duration of License:** Indefinite. **Requirements:** Submit application which must include ring name, social security number, address, and phone. **Reciprocity:** No. **Fees:** No fee. **Governing Statute:** The Illinois Professional Boxing and Wrestling Act, Illinois Revised Statutes 1991, Chapter 111.

Indiana

903

Boxer
Boxing Commission
Examination Administrative Div.
Professional Licensing Agency
1021 State Office Bldg.
Indianapolis, IN 46204
Phone: (317)232-3897

Credential Type: License. **Requirements:** Contact licensing body for application information.

904

Judge (Boxing)
Boxing Commission
Examination Administrative Div.
Professional Licensing Agency
1021 State Office Bldg.
Indianapolis, IN 46204
Phone: (317)232-3897

Credential Type: License. **Requirements:** Contact licensing body for application information.

905

Manager (Boxing)
Boxing Commission
Examination Administrative Div.
Professional Licensing Agency
1021 State Office Bldg.
Indianapolis, IN 46204
Phone: (317)232-3897

Credential Type: License. **Requirements:** Contact licensing body for application information.

906

Referee (Boxing)
Boxing Commission
Examination Administrative Div.
Professional Licensing Agency
1021 State Office Bldg.
Indianapolis, IN 46204
Phone: (317)232-3897

Credential Type: License. **Requirements:** Contact licensing body for application information.

Indiana

907

Time Keeper (Boxing)
Boxing Commission
Examination Administrative Div.
Professional Licensing Agency
1021 State Office Bldg.
Indianapolis, IN 46204
Phone: (317)232-3897

Credential Type: License. **Requirements:** Contact licensing body for application information.

Iowa

908

Apprentice Jockey (Racetrack)
Iowa State Racing Commission
Lucas State Office Bldg.
Des Moines, IA 50319
Phone: (515)281-7352

Credential Type: License Registration. **Requirements:** Submit application and fingerprint card. Pay fee. **Fees:** $10 registration fee.

909

Assistant Racing Secretary (Racetrack)
Iowa State Racing Commission
Lucas State Office Bldg.
Des Moines, IA 50319
Phone: (515)281-7352

Credential Type: License Registration. **Requirements:** Submit application and fingerprint card. Pay fee. **Fees:** $10 registration fee.

910

Authorized Agent (Racetrack)
Iowa State Racing Commission
Lucas State Office Bldg.
Des Moines, IA 50319
Phone: (515)281-7352

Credential Type: License Registration. **Requirements:** Submit application and fingerprint card. Pay fee. **Fees:** $10 registration fee.

911

Driver/Jockey (Racetrack)
Iowa State Racing Commission
Lucas State Office Bldg.
Des Moines, IA 50319
Phone: (515)281-7352

Credential Type: License Registration. **Requirements:** Submit application and fingerprint card. Pay fee. **Fees:** $10 registration fee.

912

Jockey Agent (Racetrack)
Iowa State Racing Commission
Lucas State Office Bldg.
Des Moines, IA 50319
Phone: (515)281-7352

Credential Type: License Registration. **Requirements:** Submit application and fingerprint card. Pay fee. **Fees:** $10 registration fee.

913

Official (Racetrack)
Iowa State Racing Commission
Lucas State Office Bldg.
Des Moines, IA 50319
Phone: (515)281-7352

Credential Type: License Registration. **Requirements:** Submit application and fingerprint card. Pay fee. **Fees:** $10 registration fee.

914

Owner-Trainer-Driver(Racetrack)
Iowa State Racing Commission
Lucas State Office Bldg.
Des Moines, IA 50319
Phone: (515)281-7352

Credential Type: License Registration. **Requirements:** Submit application and fingerprint card. Pay fee. **Fees:** $20 registration fee.

915

Racing Secretary (Racetrack)
Iowa State Racing Commission
Lucas State Office Bldg.
Des Moines, IA 50319
Phone: (515)281-7352

Credential Type: License Registration. **Requirements:** Submit application and fingerprint card. Pay fee. **Fees:** $20 registration fee.

Kansas

916

Apprentice Jockey (Racetrack)
Kansas Racing Commission
3400 VanBuren
Topeka, KS 66611-2228
Phone: (913)296-5800

Credential Type: License Registration. **Requirements:** Submit application and fingerprint card. Pay fee. **Fees:** $10 registration fee.

917

Assistant Racing Secretary (Racetrack)
Kansas Racing Commission
3400 VanBuren
Topeka, KS 66611-2228
Phone: (913)296-5800

Credential Type: License Registration. **Requirements:** Submit application and fingerprint card. Pay fee. **Fees:** $10 registration fee.

918

Assistant Starter (Racetrack)
Kansas Racing Commission
3400 VanBuren
Topeka, KS 66611-2228
Phone: (913)296-5800

Credential Type: License Registration. **Requirements:** Submit application and fingerprint card. Pay fee. **Fees:** $5 registration fee.

919

Authorized Agent (Racetrack)
Kansas Racing Commission
3400 VanBuren
Topeka, KS 66611-2228
Phone: (913)296-5800

Credential Type: License Registration. **Requirements:** Submit application and fingerprint card. Pay fee. **Fees:** $10 registration fee.

Athletes, Coaches, Umpires, and Referees

920

Driver (Racetrack)
Kansas Racing Commission
3400 VanBuren
Topeka, KS 66611-2228
Phone: (913)296-5800

Credential Type: License Registration.
Requirements: Submit application and fingerprint card. Pay fee. **Fees:** $10 registration fee.

921

Jockey Agent (Racetrack)
Kansas Racing Commission
3400 VanBuren
Topeka, KS 66611-2228
Phone: (913)296-5800

Credential Type: License Registration.
Requirements: Submit application and fingerprint card. Pay fee. **Fees:** $10 registration fee.

922

Jockey (Racetrack)
Kansas Racing Commission
3400 VanBuren
Topeka, KS 66611-2228
Phone: (913)296-5800

Credential Type: License Registration.
Requirements: Submit application and fingerprint card. Pay fee. **Fees:** $10 registration fee.

923

Official (Racetrack)
Kansas Racing Commission
3400 VanBuren
Topeka, KS 66611-2228
Phone: (913)296-5800

Credential Type: License Registration.
Requirements: Submit application and fingerprint card. Pay fee. **Fees:** $10 registration fee.

924

Paddock Judge (Racetrack)
Kansas Racing Commission
3400 VanBuren
Topeka, KS 66611-2228
Phone: (913)296-5800

Credential Type: License Registration.
Requirements: Submit application and fingerprint card. Pay fee. **Fees:** $10 registration fee.

925

Patrol Judge (Racetrack)
Kansas Racing Commission
3400 VanBuren
Topeka, KS 66611-2228
Phone: (913)296-5800

Credential Type: License Registration.
Requirements: Submit application and fingerprint card. Pay fee. **Fees:** $10 registration fee.

926

Racing Secretary (Racetrack)
Kansas Racing Commission
3400 VanBuren
Topeka, KS 66611-2228
Phone: (913)296-5800

Credential Type: License Registration.
Requirements: Submit application and fingerprint card. Pay fee. **Fees:** $20 registration fee.

927

Starter (Racetrack)
Kansas Racing Commission
3400 VanBuren
Topeka, KS 66611-2228
Phone: (913)296-5800

Credential Type: License Registration.
Requirements: Submit application and fingerprint card. Pay fee. **Fees:** $10 registration fee.

928

Timer (Racetrack)
Kansas Racing Commission
3400 VanBuren
Topeka, KS 66611-2228
Phone: (913)296-5800

Credential Type: License Registration.
Requirements: Submit application and fingerprint card. Pay fee. **Fees:** $10 registration fee.

Kentucky

929

Jockey Agent (Racetrack)
Kentucky State Racing Commission
PO Box 1080
Lexington, KY 40588
Phone: (606)254-7021

Credential Type: License Registration.
Requirements: Submit application and fingerprint card. Pay fee. **Fees:** $45 license fee.

930

Jockey Apprentice (Racetrack)
Kentucky State Racing Commission
PO Box 1080
Lexington, KY 40588
Phone: (606)254-7021

Credential Type: License Registration.
Requirements: Submit application and fingerprint card. Pay fee. **Fees:** $25 registration fee.

931

Jockey (Racetrack)
Kentucky State Racing Commission
PO Box 1080
Lexington, KY 40588
Phone: (606)254-7021

Credential Type: License Registration.
Requirements: Submit application and fingerprint card. Pay fee. **Fees:** $35 registration fee.

932

Paddock Judge (Racetrack)
Kentucky State Racing Commission
PO Box 1080
Lexington, KY 40588
Phone: (606)254-7021

Credential Type: License Registration.
Requirements: Submit application and fingerprint card. Pay fee. **Fees:** $35 registration fee.

933

Patrol Judge (Racetrack)
Kentucky State Racing Commission
PO Box 1080
Lexington, KY 40588
Phone: (606)254-7021

Credential Type: License Registration.
Requirements: Submit application and fingerprint card. Pay fee. **Fees:** $35 registration fee.

Kentucky

934

Placing Judge (Racetrack)
Kentucky State Racing Commission
PO Box 1080
Lexington, KY 40588
Phone: (606)254-7021

Credential Type: License Registration. **Requirements:** Submit application and fingerprint card. Pay fee. **Fees:** $35 registration fee.

935

Racing Official (Racetrack)
Kentucky State Racing Commission
PO Box 1080
Lexington, KY 40588
Phone: (606)254-7021

Credential Type: License Registration. **Requirements:** Submit application and fingerprint card. Pay fee. **Fees:** $35 registration fee.

936

Racing Secretary/Assistant Racing Secretary (Racetrack)
Kentucky State Racing Commission
PO Box 1080
Lexington, KY 40588
Phone: (606)254-7021

Credential Type: License Registration. **Requirements:** Submit application and fingerprint card. Pay fee. **Fees:** $35 registration fee.

937

Starter/Assistant Starter (Racetrack)
Kentucky State Racing Commission
PO Box 1080
Lexington, KY 40588
Phone: (606)254-7021

Credential Type: License Registration. **Requirements:** Submit application and fingerprint card. Pay fee. **Fees:** $35 registration fee.

938

Steward (Racetrack)
Kentucky State Racing Commission
PO Box 1080
Lexington, KY 40588
Phone: (606)254-7021

Credential Type: License Registration. **Requirements:** Submit application and fingerprint card. Pay fee. **Fees:** $35 registration fee.

939

Timer (Racetrack)
Kentucky State Racing Commission
PO Box 1080
Lexington, KY 40588
Phone: (606)254-7021

Credential Type: License Registration. **Requirements:** Submit application and fingerprint card. Pay fee. **Fees:** $35 registration fee.

Louisiana

940

Assistant Starter (Racetrack)
Louisiana State Racing Commission
320 N. Carrollton Ave., Ste. 2-B
New Orleans, LA 70119-5111
Phone: (504)483-4000

Credential Type: License Registration. **Duration of License:** One year. **Requirements:** At least 18 years of age. Abide by state rules and regulations. Submit application and pay fees. **Fees:** $25 registration fee.

941

Boxer/Wrestler
Louisiana State Boxing and
  Wrestling Commission
201 S. Broad St.
New Orleans, LA 70119
Phone: (504)821-7761

Credential Type: License. **Duration of License:** One year. **Requirements:** 16 years of age to box four to six rounds. 18 years of age to box six rounds or more. **Examination:** Medical exams are required before each contest. **Fees:** $5 fee for preliminary. $10 fee for main entrant.

942

Jockey
Louisiana State Racing Commission
320 N. Carrollton Ave., Ste. 2-B
New Orleans, LA 70119
Phone: (504)483-4000

Credential Type: Apprentice Jockey Certificate. **Duration of License:** One year. **Requirements:** 18 years of age, or 16 years of age with a permit. Approval by the stewards. **Fees:** $25 certificate fee.

Credential Type: Jockey License. **Duration of License:** One or three years. **Requirements:** 18 years of age, or 16 years of age with a permit. Approval by the stewards. **Fees:** $25 license fee for one year license. $75 license fee for three year license.

943

Jockey Agent
Louisiana State Racing Commission
320 N. Carrollton Ave., Ste 2-B
New Orleans, LA 70119
Phone: (504)483-4000

Credential Type: License. **Duration of License:** One or three years. **Requirements:** 18 years of age. **Examination:** Yes. **Fees:** $25 license fee for one year. $75 license fee for three years.

944

Steward (Racetrack)
Louisiana State Racing Commission
320 N. Carrollton Ave., Ste. 2-B
New Orleans, LA 70119-5111
Phone: (504)483-4000

Credential Type: License Registration. **Duration of License:** One year. **Requirements:** At least 18 years of age. Abide by state rules and regulations. Submit application and pay fees. **Examination:** Written examination. **Fees:** Contact Commission for fees.

Maine

945

Boxer
Athletic Commission
Dept. of Professional and Financial
  Regulation
Div. of Licensing and Enforcement
State House Station 35
Augusta, ME 04333
Phone: (207)582-8723

Credential Type: License. **Duration of License:** One year. **Requirements:** Knowledge of laws and rules. Submit application and pay fee. **Fees:** $15 license fee. **Governing Statute:** 32 M.S.R.A. Chap. 115.

946

Boxing Judge
Athletic Commission
Dept. of Professional and Financial
  Regulation
Div. of Licensing and Enforcement
State House Station 35
Augusta, ME 04333
Phone: (207)582-8723

Credential Type: License. **Duration of License:** One year. **Requirements:** Knowledge of laws and rules. Submit application and pay fee. **Fees:** $10 license fee. **Governing Statute:** 32 M.S.R.A. Chap. 115.

947

Boxing Knock-Down Timekeeper
Athletic Commission
Dept. of Professional and Financial
  Regulation
Div. of Licensing and Enforcement
State House Station 35
Augusta, ME 04333
Phone: (207)582-8723

Credential Type: License. **Duration of License:** One year. **Requirements:** Knowledge of laws and rules. Submit application and pay fee. **Fees:** $10 license fee. **Governing Statute:** 32 M.S.R.A. Chap. 115.

948

Boxing Manager
Athletic Commission
Dept. of Professional and Financial
  Regulation
Div. of Licensing and Enforcement
State House Station 35
Augusta, ME 04333
Phone: (207)582-8723

Credential Type: License. **Duration of License:** One year. **Requirements:** Knowledge of laws and rules. Submit application and pay fee. **Fees:** $15 license fee. **Governing Statute:** 32 M.S.R.A. Chap. 115.

949

Boxing Referee
Athletic Commission
Dept. of Professional and Financial
  Regulation
Div. of Licensing and Enforcement
State House Station 35
Augusta, ME 04333
Phone: (207)582-8723

Credential Type: License. **Duration of License:** One year. **Requirements:** Knowledge of laws and rules. Submit application and pay fee. **Fees:** $15 license fee. **Governing Statute:** 32 M.S.R.A. Chap. 115.

950

Boxing Second
Athletic Commission
Dept. of Professional and Financial
  Regulation
Div. of Licensing and Enforcement
State House Station 35
Augusta, ME 04333
Phone: (207)582-8723

Credential Type: License. **Duration of License:** One year. **Requirements:** Knowledge of laws and rules. Submit application and pay fee. **Fees:** $15 license fee. **Governing Statute:** 32 M.S.R.A. Chap. 115.

951

Boxing Timekeeper
Athletic Commission
Dept. of Professional and Financial
  Regulation
Div. of Licensing and Enforcement
State House Station 35
Augusta, ME 04333
Phone: (207)582-8723

Credential Type: License. **Duration of License:** One year. **Requirements:** Knowledge of laws and rules. Submit application and pay fee. **Fees:** $10 license fee. **Governing Statute:** 32 M.S.R.A. Chap. 115.

952

Kickboxer
Athletic Commission
Dept. of Professional and Financial
  Regulation
Div. of Licensing and Enforcement
State House Station 35
Augusta, ME 04333
Phone: (207)582-8723

Credential Type: License. **Duration of License:** One year. **Requirements:** Knowledge of laws and rules. Submit application and pay fee. **Fees:** $15 license fee. **Governing Statute:** 32 M.S.R.A. Chap. 115.

953

Kickboxing Assistant Scorekeeper
Athletic Commission
Dept. of Professional and Financial
  Regulation
Div. of Licensing and Enforcement
State House Station 35
Augusta, ME 04333
Phone: (207)582-8723

Credential Type: License. **Duration of License:** One year. **Requirements:** Knowledge of laws and rules. Submit application and pay fee. **Fees:** $10 license fee. **Governing Statute:** 32 M.S.R.A. Chap. 115.

954

Kickboxing Judge
Athletic Commission
Dept. of Professional and Financial
  Regulation
Div. of Licensing and Enforcement
State House Station 35
Augusta, ME 04333
Phone: (207)582-8723

Credential Type: License. **Duration of License:** One year. **Requirements:** Knowledge of laws and rules. Submit application and pay fee. **Fees:** $10 license fee. **Governing Statute:** 32 M.S.R.A. Chap. 115.

955

Kickboxing Kick Judge
Athletic Commission
Dept. of Professional and Financial
  Regulation
Div. of Licensing and Enforcement
State House Station 35
Augusta, ME 04333
Phone: (207)582-8723

Credential Type: License. **Duration of License:** One year. **Requirements:** Knowledge of laws and rules. Submit application and pay fee. **Fees:** $10 license fee. **Governing Statute:** 32 M.S.R.A. Chap. 115.

Maine

956

Kickboxing Knock-down Timekeeper
Athletic Commission
Dept. of Professional and Financial Regulation
Div. of Licensing and Enforcement
State House Station 35
Augusta, ME 04333
Phone: (207)582-8723

Credential Type: License. **Duration of License:** One year. **Requirements:** Knowledge of laws and rules. Submit application and pay fee. **Fees:** $10 license fee. **Governing Statute:** 32 M.S.R.A. Chap. 115.

957

Kickboxing Manager
Athletic Commission
Dept. of Professional and Financial Regulation
Div. of Licensing and Enforcement
State House Station 35
Augusta, ME 04333
Phone: (207)582-8723

Credential Type: License. **Duration of License:** One year. **Requirements:** Knowledge of laws and rules. Submit application and pay fee. **Fees:** $10 license fee. **Governing Statute:** 32 M.S.R.A. Chap. 115.

958

Kickboxing Referee
Athletic Commission
Dept. of Professional and Financial Regulation
Div. of Licensing and Enforcement
State House Station 35
Augusta, ME 04333
Phone: (207)582-8723

Credential Type: License. **Duration of License:** One year. **Requirements:** Knowledge of laws and rules. Submit application and pay fee. **Fees:** $15 license fee. **Governing Statute:** 32 M.S.R.A. Chap. 115.

959

Kickboxing Scorekeeper
Athletic Commission
Dept. of Professional and Financial Regulation
Div. of Licensing and Enforcement
State House Station 35
Augusta, ME 04333
Phone: (207)582-8723

Credential Type: License. **Duration of License:** One year. **Requirements:** Knowledge of laws and rules. Submit application and pay fee. **Fees:** $10 license fee. **Governing Statute:** 32 M.S.R.A. Chap. 115.

960

Kickboxing Second
Athletic Commission
Dept. of Professional and Financial Regulation
Div. of Licensing and Enforcement
State House Station 35
Augusta, ME 04333
Phone: (207)582-8723

Credential Type: License. **Duration of License:** One year. **Requirements:** Knowledge of laws and rules. Submit application and pay fee. **Fees:** $15 license fee. **Governing Statute:** 32 M.S.R.A. Chap. 115.

961

Kickboxing Timekeeper
Athletic Commission
Dept. of Professional and Financial Regulation
Div. of Licensing and Enforcement
State House Station 35
Augusta, ME 04333
Phone: (207)582-8723

Credential Type: License. **Duration of License:** One year. **Requirements:** Knowledge of laws and rules. Submit application and pay fee. **Fees:** $10 license fee. **Governing Statute:** 32 M.S.R.A. Chap. 115.

962

Wrestling Manager
Athletic Commission
Dept. of Professional and Financial Regulation
Div. of Licensing and Enforcement
State House Station 35
Augusta, ME 04333
Phone: (207)582-8723

Credential Type: License. **Duration of License:** One year. **Requirements:** Knowledge of laws and rules. Submit application and pay fee. **Fees:** $10 license fee. **Governing Statute:** 32 M.S.R.A. Chap. 115.

963

Wrestling Referee
Athletic Commission
Dept. of Professional and Financial Regulation
Div. of Licensing and Enforcement
State House Station 35
Augusta, ME 04333
Phone: (207)582-8723

Credential Type: License. **Duration of License:** One year. **Requirements:** Knowledge of laws and rules. Submit application and pay fee. **Fees:** $15 license fee. **Governing Statute:** 32 M.S.R.A. Chap. 115.

964

Wrestling Timekeeper
Athletic Commission
Dept. of Professional and Financial Regulation
Div. of Licensing and Enforcement
State House Station 35
Augusta, ME 04333
Phone: (207)582-8723

Credential Type: License. **Duration of License:** One year. **Requirements:** Knowledge of laws and rules. Submit application and pay fee. **Fees:** $10 license fee. **Governing Statute:** 32 M.S.R.A. Chap. 115.

Maryland

965

Boxer
State Athletic Commission
Dept. of Licensing and Regulation
501 St. Paul Pl.
Baltimore, MD 21202-2272
Phone: (410)333-6313

Credential Type: License. **Requirements:** Submit application and pay fee. Amateur boxing experience required. **Examination:** Neurological, opthalmalogical, and routine medical examinations. **Fees:** $20 license fee.

Athletes, Coaches, Umpires, and Referees

966

Boxing Referee
State Athletic Commission
Dept. of Licensing and Regulation
501 St. Paul Pl.
Baltimore, MD 21202-2272
Phone: (410)333-6313

Credential Type: License. **Requirements:** Contact licensing body for application information.

967

Driver (Harness Racing)
Maryland Racing Commission
Stanbalt Bldg., 14th Fl.
501 St. Paul Place
Baltimore, MD 21202
Phone: (301)333-6267

Credential Type: License Registration. **Requirements:** Submit application, fingerprint card, and three passport size photos. Pay fee. **Fees:** $25 registration fee.

968

Jockey Agent (Thoroughbred Racing)
Maryland Racing Commission
Stanbalt Bldg., 14th Fl.
501 St. Paul Place
Baltimore, MD 21202
Phone: (301)333-6267

Credential Type: License Registration. **Requirements:** Submit application, fingerprint card, and three passport size photos. Pay fee. **Fees:** $25 registration fee.

969

Jockey/Apprentice Jockey (Thoroughbred Racing)
Maryland Racing Commission
Stanbalt Bldg., 14th Fl.
501 St. Paul Place
Baltimore, MD 21202
Phone: (301)333-6267

Credential Type: License Registration. **Requirements:** Submit application, fingerprint card, and three passport size photos. Pay fee. **Fees:** $25 registration fee.

Massachusetts

970

Greyhound Authorized Agent (Racetrack)
Massachusetts State Racing Commission
1 Ashburton Place, Rm. 1313
Boston, MA 02108
Phone: (617)727-2581

Credential Type: License Registration. **Requirements:** Submit application and fingerprint card. Pay fee. **Fees:** $20 registration fee.

971

Jockey Agent (Racetrack)
Massachusetts State Racing Commission
1 Ashburton Place, Rm. 1313
Boston, MA 02108
Phone: (617)727-2581

Credential Type: License Registration. **Requirements:** Submit application and fingerprint card. Pay fee. **Fees:** $50 registration fee.

972

Jockey Apprentice (Racetrack)
Massachusetts State Racing Commission
1 Ashburton Place, Rm. 1313
Boston, MA 02108
Phone: (617)727-2581

Credential Type: License Registration. **Requirements:** Submit application and fingerprint card. Pay fee. **Fees:** $50 registration fee.

973

Jockey (Racetrack)
Massachusetts State Racing Commission
1 Ashburton Place, Rm. 1313
Boston, MA 02108
Phone: (617)727-2581

Credential Type: License Registration. **Requirements:** Submit application and fingerprint card. Pay fee. **Fees:** $50 registration fee.

974

Judge (Boxing)
State Boxing Commission
Dept. of Public Safety
One Ashburton Pl., Rm. 1310
Boston, MA 02108
Phone: (617)727-3296

Credential Type: License. **Requirements:** Submit application and pay fee. **Fees:** Contact commission for fee. **Governing Statute:** Annotated Laws of Massachusetts, Chap. 147.

975

Manager (Boxing)
State Boxing Commission
Dept. of Public Safety
One Ashburton Pl., Rm. 1310
Boston, MA 02108
Phone: (617)727-3296

Credential Type: License. **Requirements:** Submit application and pay fee. **Fees:** Contact commission for fee. **Governing Statute:** Annotated Laws of Massachusetts, Chap. 147.

976

Professional Boxer
State Boxing Commission
Dept. of Public Safety
One Ashburton Pl., Rm. 1310
Boston, MA 02108
Phone: (617)727-3296

Credential Type: License. **Requirements:** Submit application and pay fee. **Fees:** Contact commission for fee. **Governing Statute:** Annotated Laws of Massachusetts, Chap. 147.

977

Racing Official (Racetrack)
Massachusetts State Racing Commission
1 Ashburton Place, Rm. 1313
Boston, MA 02108
Phone: (617)727-2581

Credential Type: License Registration. **Requirements:** Submit application and fingerprint card. Pay fee. **Fees:** $20 registration fee.

Massachusetts

978

Referee (Boxing)
State Boxing Commission
Dept. of Public Safety
One Ashburton Pl., Rm. 1310
Boston, MA 02108
Phone: (617)727-3296

Credential Type: License. **Requirements:** Submit application and pay fee. **Fees:** Contact commission for fee. **Governing Statute:** Annotated Laws of Massachusetts, Chap. 147.

979

Second (Boxing)
State Boxing Commission
Dept. of Public Safety
One Ashburton Pl., Rm. 1310
Boston, MA 02108
Phone: (617)727-3296

Credential Type: License. **Requirements:** Submit application and pay fee. **Fees:** Contact commission for fee. **Governing Statute:** Annotated Laws of Massachusetts, Chap. 147.

980

Timekeeper (Boxing)
State Boxing Commission
Dept. of Public Safety
One Ashburton Pl., Rm. 1310
Boston, MA 02108
Phone: (617)727-3296

Credential Type: License. **Requirements:** Submit application and pay fee. **Fees:** Contact commission for fee. **Governing Statute:** Annotated Laws of Massachusetts, Chap. 147.

Michigan

981

Authorized Agent (Racetrack)
Michigan Office of Racing
  Commissioner
37650 Professional Center Dr.
Livonia, MI 48154-1114
Phone: (313)462-2400

Credential Type: License Registration. **Requirements:** Submit application and fingerprint card. Pay fee. **Fees:** $10 registration fee. $5 duplicate license fee.

982

Driver (Racetrack)
Michigan Office of Racing
  Commissioner
37650 Professional Center Dr.
Livonia, MI 48154-1114
Phone: (313)462-2400

Credential Type: License Registration. **Requirements:** Submit application and fingerprint card. Pay fee. **Fees:** $20 registration fee. $5 duplicate license fee.

983

Driver-Trainer (Racetrack)
Michigan Office of Racing
  Commissioner
37650 Professional Center Dr.
Livonia, MI 48154-1114
Phone: (313)462-2400

Credential Type: License Registration. **Requirements:** Submit application and fingerprint card. Pay fee. **Fees:** $40 registration fee.

984

Jockey Agent (Racetrack)
Michigan Office of Racing
  Commissioner
37650 Professional Center Dr.
Livonia, MI 48154-1114
Phone: (313)462-2400

Credential Type: License Registration. **Requirements:** Submit application and fingerprint card. Pay fee. **Fees:** $20 registration fee. $5 duplicate license fee.

985

Jockey/Apprentice Jockey (Racetrack)
Michigan Office of Racing
  Commissioner
37650 Professional Center Dr.
Livonia, MI 48154-1114
Phone: (313)462-2400

Credential Type: License Registration. **Requirements:** Submit application and fingerprint card. Pay fee. **Fees:** $20 registration fee. $5 duplicate license fee.

986

Racing Official (Racetrack)
Michigan Office of Racing
  Commissioner
37650 Professional Center Dr.
Livonia, MI 48154-1114
Phone: (313)462-2400

Credential Type: License Registration. **Requirements:** Submit application and fingerprint card. Pay fee. **Fees:** $20 registration fee. $5 duplicate license fee.

Minnesota

987

Boxer
Board of Boxing
133 E. 7th and Robert Sts.
St. Paul, MN 55101
Phone: (612)296-2501

Credential Type: License. **Duration of License:** One year. **Requirements:** Submit application and pay fee. **Fees:** $5 license fee (professional). No license fee (amateur). **Governing Statute:** Minnesota Statutes, Chap. 341. Minnesota Rules 2200-2299.

988

Driver (Racetrack)
Minnesota Racing Commission
11000 W. 78th St., Ste. 201
Eden Prairie, MN 55344
Phone: (612)341-7555

Credential Type: License Registration. **Requirements:** Submit application and fingerprint card. Pay fee. **Fees:** $25 registration fee.

989

Jockey Agent (Racetrack)
Minnesota Racing Commission
11000 W. 78th St., Ste. 201
Eden Prairie, MN 55344
Phone: (612)341-7555

Credential Type: License Registration. **Requirements:** Submit application and fingerprint card. Pay fee. **Fees:** $25 registration fee.

990

Jockey Apprentice (Racetrack)
Minnesota Racing Commission
11000 W. 78th St., Ste. 201
Eden Prairie, MN 55344
Phone: (612)341-7555

Credential Type: License Registration. **Requirements:** Submit application and fingerprint card. Pay fee. **Fees:** $25 registration fee.

991

Jockey (Racetrack)
Minnesota Racing Commission
11000 W. 78th St., Ste. 201
Eden Prairie, MN 55344
Phone: (612)341-7555

Credential Type: License Registration. **Requirements:** Submit application and fingerprint card. Pay fee. **Fees:** $25 registration fee.

992

Kick Boxer
Board of Boxing
133 E. 7th and Robert Sts.
St. Paul, MN 55101
Phone: (612)296-2501

Credential Type: License. **Duration of License:** One year. **Requirements:** Submit application and pay fee. **Fees:** $5 license fee (professional). No license fee (amateur). **Governing Statute:** Minnesota Statutes, Chap. 341. Minnesota Rules 2200-2299.

993

Manager (Boxing and Kick Boxing)
Board of Boxing
133 E. 7th and Robert Sts.
St. Paul, MN 55101
Phone: (612)296-2501

Credential Type: License. **Duration of License:** One year. **Requirements:** Submit application and pay fee. **Fees:** $10 license fee (professional). No license fee (amateur). **Governing Statute:** Minnesota Statutes, Chap. 341. Minnesota Rules 2200-2299.

994

Racing Official (Racetrack)
Minnesota Racing Commission
11000 W. 78th St., Ste. 201
Eden Prairie, MN 55344
Phone: (612)341-7555

Credential Type: License Registration. **Requirements:** Submit application and fingerprint card. Pay fee. **Fees:** $25 registration fee.

995

Referee (Boxing and Kick Boxing)
Board of Boxing
133 E. 7th and Robert Sts.
St. Paul, MN 55101
Phone: (612)296-2501

Credential Type: License. **Duration of License:** One year. **Requirements:** Submit application and pay fee. **Fees:** $25 license fee (professional). $10 license fee (amateur). **Governing Statute:** Minnesota Statutes, Chap. 341. Minnesota Rules 2200-2299.

996

Second (Boxing and Kick Boxing)
Board of Boxing
133 E. 7th and Robert Sts.
St. Paul, MN 55101
Phone: (612)296-2501

Credential Type: License. **Duration of License:** One year. **Requirements:** Submit application and pay fee. **Fees:** $5 license fee (professional). $2 license fee (amateur). **Governing Statute:** Minnesota Statutes, Chap. 341. Minnesota Rules 2200-2299.

Missouri

997

Contestant (Boxing, Wrestling, or Karate)
Office of Athletics
Dept. of Economic Development
3605 Missouri Blvd.
PO Box 1335
Jefferson City, MO 65102
Phone: (314)751-0243

Credential Type: License. **Duration of License:** One year. **Requirements:** Application for license must be submitted no later than 10 business days prior to a professional exhibition and seven days prior to an amateur exhibition. **Fees:** $20 professional license fee. No amateur license fee. **Governing Statute:** four CSR 40.

998

Driver (Racetrack)
Missouri Horse Racing Commission
PO Box 754
Jefferson City, MO 65102
Phone: (314)751-3565

Credential Type: License Registration. **Requirements:** Submit application and fingerprint card. Pay fee. **Fees:** $50 registration fee. $4 duplicate registration fee.

999

Jockey Agent (Racetrack)
Missouri Horse Racing Commission
PO Box 754
Jefferson City, MO 65102
Phone: (314)751-3565

Credential Type: License Registration. **Requirements:** Submit application and fingerprint card. Pay fee. **Fees:** $25 registration fee. $4 duplicate registration fee.

1000

Jockey (Racetrack)
Missouri Horse Racing Commission
PO Box 754
Jefferson City, MO 65102
Phone: (314)751-3565

Credential Type: License Registration. **Requirements:** Submit application and fingerprint card. Pay fee. **Fees:** $25 registration fee. $4 duplicate registration fee.

1001

Judge (Boxing, Wrestling, or Karate)
Office of Athletics
Dept. of Economic Development
3605 Missouri Blvd.
PO Box 1335
Jefferson City, MO 65102
Phone: (314)751-0243

Credential Type: License. **Duration of License:** One year. **Requirements:** Application for license must be submitted no later than 10 business days prior to a professional exhibition and seven days prior to an amateur exhibition. **Fees:** $10 professional license fee. No amateur license fee. **Governing Statute:** four CSR 40.

1002

Manager (Boxing, Wrestling, or Karate)
Office of Athletics
Dept. of Economic Development
3605 Missouri Blvd.
PO Box 1335
Jefferson City, MO 65102
Phone: (314)751-0243

Credential Type: License. **Duration of License:** One year. **Requirements:** Application for license must be submitted no later than 10 business days prior to a professional exhibition and seven days prior to an amateur exhibition. **Fees:** $10 license fee. **Governing Statute:** four CSR 40.

1003

Official (Racetrack)
Missouri Horse Racing Commission
PO Box 754
Jefferson City, MO 65102
Phone: (314)751-3565

Credential Type: License Registration. **Requirements:** Submit application and fingerprint card. Pay fee. **Fees:** $10 registration fee. $4 duplicate registration fee.

1004

Referee (Boxing, Wrestling, or Karate)
Office of Athletics
Dept. of Economic Development
3605 Missouri Blvd.
PO Box 1335
Jefferson City, MO 65102
Phone: (314)751-0243

Credential Type: License. **Duration of License:** One year. **Requirements:** Application for license must be submitted no later than 10 business days prior to a professional exhibition and seven days prior to an amateur exhibition. **Fees:** $10 license fee. **Governing Statute:** four CSR 40.

1005

Second (Boxing, Wrestling, or Karate)
Office of Athletics
Dept. of Economic Development
3605 Missouri Blvd.
PO Box 1335
Jefferson City, MO 65102
Phone: (314)751-0243

Credential Type: License. **Duration of License:** One year. **Requirements:** Application for license must be submitted no later than 10 business days prior to a professional exhibition and seven days prior to an amateur exhibition. **Fees:** $10 license fee. **Governing Statute:** four CSR 40.

1006

Timekeeper (Boxing, Wrestling, or Karate)
Office of Athletics
Dept. of Economic Development
3605 Missouri Blvd.
PO Box 1335
Jefferson City, MO 65102
Phone: (314)751-0243

Credential Type: License. **Duration of License:** One year. **Requirements:** Application for license must be submitted no later than 10 business days prior to a professional exhibition and seven days prior to an amateur exhibition. **Fees:** $10 license fee. **Governing Statute:** four CSR 40.

Montana

1007

Authorized Agent (Racetrack)
State of Montana Board of Horse Racing
Dept. of Commerce
1424 9th Ave.
Helena, MT 59620
Phone: (406)444-4287

Credential Type: License Registration. **Requirements:** Submit application and fingerprint card. Pay fee. **Fees:** $20 registration fee.

1008

Jockey Agent (Racetrack)
State of Montana Board of Horse Racing
Dept. of Commerce
1424 9th Ave.
Helena, MT 59620
Phone: (406)444-4287

Credential Type: License Registration. **Requirements:** Submit application and fingerprint card. Pay fee. **Fees:** $30 registration fee.

1009

Jockey Apprentice (Racetrack)
State of Montana Board of Horse Racing
Dept. of Commerce
1424 9th Ave.
Helena, MT 59620
Phone: (406)444-4287

Credential Type: License Registration. **Requirements:** Submit application and fingerprint card. Pay fee. **Fees:** $30 registration fee.

1010

Jockey (Racetrack)
State of Montana Board of Horse Racing
Dept. of Commerce
1424 9th Ave.
Helena, MT 59620
Phone: (406)444-4287

Credential Type: License Registration. **Requirements:** Submit application and fingerprint card. Pay fee. **Fees:** $20 registration fee.

1011

Paddock Judge (Racetrack)
State of Montana Board of Horse Racing
Dept. of Commerce
1424 9th Ave.
Helena, MT 59620
Phone: (406)444-4287

Credential Type: License Registration. **Requirements:** Submit application and fingerprint card. Pay fee. **Fees:** $20 registration fee.

1012

Patrol Judge (Racetrack)
State of Montana Board of Horse Racing
Dept. of Commerce
1424 9th Ave.
Helena, MT 59620
Phone: (406)444-4287

Credential Type: License Registration. **Requirements:** Submit application and fingerprint card. Pay fee. **Fees:** $20 registration fee.

Athletes, Coaches, Umpires, and Referees

1013

Placing Judge (Racetrack)
State of Montana Board of Horse Racing
Dept. of Commerce
1424 9th Ave.
Helena, MT 59620
Phone: (406)444-4287

Credential Type: License Registration. **Requirements:** Submit application and fingerprint card. Pay fee. **Fees:** $20 registration fee.

1014

Racing Secretary Assistant (Racetrack)
State of Montana Board of Horse Racing
Dept. of Commerce
1424 9th Ave.
Helena, MT 59620
Phone: (406)444-4287

Credential Type: License Registration. **Requirements:** Submit application and fingerprint card. Pay fee. **Fees:** $20 registration fee.

1015

Racing Secretary (Racetrack)
State of Montana Board of Horse Racing
Dept. of Commerce
1424 9th Ave.
Helena, MT 59620
Phone: (406)444-4287

Credential Type: License Registration. **Requirements:** Submit application and fingerprint card. Pay fee. **Fees:** $30 registration fee.

1016

Starter (Racetrack)
State of Montana Board of Horse Racing
Dept. of Commerce
1424 9th Ave.
Helena, MT 59620
Phone: (406)444-4287

Credential Type: License Registration. **Requirements:** Submit application and fingerprint card. Pay fee. **Fees:** $20 registration fee.

1017

Steward (Racetrack)
State of Montana Board of Horse Racing
Dept. of Commerce
1424 9th Ave.
Helena, MT 59620
Phone: (406)444-4287

Credential Type: License Registration. **Requirements:** Submit application and fingerprint card. Pay fee. **Fees:** $20 registration fee.

1018

Timer (Racetrack)
State of Montana Board of Horse Racing
Dept. of Commerce
1424 9th Ave.
Helena, MT 59620
Phone: (406)444-4287

Credential Type: License Registration. **Requirements:** Submit application and fingerprint card. Pay fee. **Fees:** $20 registration fee.

Nebraska

1019

Apprentice Jockey (Racetrack)
Nebraska Racing Commission
PO Box 95014
301 Centennial Mall S.
Lincoln, NE 68509
Phone: (402)471-4155

Credential Type: License Registration. **Duration of License:** One year. **Requirements:** At least 16 years of age. No felony convictions. Secure employment and submit application completed and signed by management. Pay fees. **Examination:** Tested by Board of Stewards. **Fees:** $25 license fee. $25 renewal fee.

1020

Assistant Starter (Racetrack)
Nebraska Racing Commission
PO Box 95014
301 Centennial Mall S.
Lincoln, NE 68509
Phone: (402)471-4155

Credential Type: License Registration. **Duration of License:** One year. **Requirements:** At least 16 years of age. No felony convictions. Secure employment and submit application completed and signed by management. Pay fees. **Examination:** Tested by Board of Stewards. **Fees:** $10 license fee. $10 renewal fee.

1021

Boxer
Nebraska Athletic Commission
301 Centennial Mall S.
PO Box 94743
Lincoln, NE 68509
Phone: (402)471-2009

Credential Type: License. **Duration of License:** One year. **Requirements:** Must have a physical examination before being allowed to compete in a sporting event. Must be in training at least seven days before the event. **Fees:** $5 license fee. $5 renewal fee.

1022

Jockey
Nebraska Racing Commission
301 Centennial Mall S.
PO Box 95014
Lincoln, NE 68509
Phone: (402)471-2577

Credential Type: License. **Duration of License:** One year. **Requirements:** 16 years of age. **Examination:** Yes. **Fees:** $25 license fee. $25 renewal fee.

1023

Official (Racetrack)
Nebraska Racing Commission
PO Box 95014
301 Centennial Mall S.
Lincoln, NE 68509
Phone: (402)471-4155

Credential Type: License Registration. **Duration of License:** One year. **Requirements:** At least 16 years of age. No felony convictions. Secure employment and submit application completed and signed by management. Pay fees. **Fees:** $20 license fee. $20 renewal fee.

Nevada

1024

Association Racing Official (Racetrack)
Nevada Racing Commission
4820 Alpine Ct., Ste. 203
Las Vegas, NV 89107
Phone: (702)486-7619

Credential Type: License Registration. **Requirements:** Submit application and fingerprint card. Pay fee. **Fees:** $25 registration fee.

1025

Authorized Agent (Racetrack)
Nevada Racing Commission
4820 Alpine Ct., Ste. 203
Las Vegas, NV 89107
Phone: (702)486-7619

Credential Type: License Registration. **Requirements:** Submit application and fingerprint card. Pay fee. **Fees:** $25 registration fee.

New Jersey

1026

Boxer
State Athletic Control Board
CN180
Trenton, NJ 08625-0180
Phone: (609)292-0317

Credential Type: License. **Requirements:** 18 years of age. **Examination:** Physical exam. **Fees:** $5 license fee. **Governing Statute:** NJSA 5:2A. NJAC 13:46.

1027

Boxing Manager
State Athletic Control Board
CN180
Trenton, NJ 08625-0180
Phone: (609)292-0317

Credential Type: License. **Fees:** $15 license fee. **Governing Statute:** NJSA 5:2A. NJAC 13:46.

1028

Clocker (Racetrack)
New Jersey Racing Commission
200 Woolverton St.
Trenton, NJ 08625-0088
Phone: (609)292-0613

Credential Type: License Registration. **Requirements:** At least 18 years of age or 16 years of age with working papers. U.S. citizen or valid immigration card. No drug convictions. No convictions of crimes involving moral turpitude. Submit application and fingerprint card. Pay fees. **Fees:** $14 application fee. $5 registration fee.

1029

Harness Race Driver
New Jersey Racing Commission
200 Woolverton St., CN088
Trenton, NJ 08625-0613
Phone: (609)292-0613

Credential Type: License. **Requirements:** Requirements are based on the class of license requested. U.S citizen or valid immigration card. 16 years of age. **Examination:** Written. **Fees:** $50 license fee. **Governing Statute:** NJSA 5:5. NJAC 13:71-7.

1030

Jockey
New Jersey Racing Commission
200 Woolverton St., CN088
Trenton, NJ 08625-0088
Phone: (609)292-0613

Credential Type: License. **Requirements:** 16 years of age with working papers. Good moral character. U.S. citizen or valid immigration card. **Fees:** $25 license fee. **Governing Statute:** NJSA 5:5. NJAC 13:70-9.

1031

Starter (Racetrack)
New Jersey Racing Commission
200 Woolverton St.
Trenton, NJ 08625-0088
Phone: (609)292-0613

Credential Type: License Registration. **Requirements:** At least 18 years of age or 16 years of age with working papers. U.S. citizen or valid immigration card. No drug convictions. No convictions of crimes involving moral turpitude. Submit application and fingerprint card. Pay fees. **Fees:** $14 application fee. $5 registration fee.

1032

Timer (Racetrack)
New Jersey Racing Commission
200 Woolverton St.
Trenton, NJ 08625-0088
Phone: (609)292-0613

Credential Type: License Registration. **Requirements:** At least 18 years of age or 16 years of age with working papers. U.S. citizen or valid immigration card. No drug convictions. No convictions of crimes involving moral turpitude. Submit application and fingerprint card. Pay fees. **Fees:** $14 application fee. $5 registration fee.

New Mexico

1033

Assistant Racing Secretary (Racetrack)
New Mexico State Racing Commission
PO Box 8576, Highland Station
Albuquerque, NM 87198
Phone: (505)841-4644

Credential Type: License Registration. **Requirements:** Submit application and fingerprint card. Pay fees. **Fees:** $16 registration fee. $1 notary fee. $23 fingerprint card processing fee.

1034

Authorized Agent (Racetrack)
New Mexico State Racing Commission
PO Box 8576, Highland Station
Albuquerque, NM 87198
Phone: (505)841-4644

Credential Type: License Registration. **Requirements:** Submit application and fingerprint card. Pay fees. **Fees:** $21 registration fee. $1 notary fee. $23 fingerprint card processing fee.

1035

Clocker (Racetrack)
New Mexico State Racing Commission
PO Box 8576, Highland Station
Albuquerque, NM 87198
Phone: (505)841-4644

Credential Type: License Registration. **Requirements:** Submit application and fingerprint card. Pay fees. **Fees:** $16 registration fee. $1 notary fee. $23 fingerprint card processing fee.

1036

Jockey Agent (Racetrack)
New Mexico State Racing
 Commission
PO Box 8576, Highland Station
Albuquerque, NM 87198
Phone: (505)841-4644

Credential Type: License Registration.
Requirements: Submit application and fingerprint card. Pay fees. **Fees:** $21 registration fee. $1 notary fee. $23 fingerprint card processing fee.

1037

Jockey Apprentice (Racetrack)
New Mexico State Racing
 Commission
PO Box 8576, Highland Station
Albuquerque, NM 87198
Phone: (505)841-4644

Credential Type: License Registration.
Requirements: Submit application and fingerprint card. Pay fees. **Fees:** $16 registration fee. $1 notary fee. $23 fingerprint card processing fee.

1038

Jockey (Racetrack)
New Mexico State Racing
 Commission
PO Box 8576, Highland Station
Albuquerque, NM 87198
Phone: (505)841-4644

Credential Type: License Registration.
Duration of License: Three years. **Requirements:** Submit application and fingerprint card. Pay fees. **Fees:** $105.50 registration fee. $1 notary fee. $23 fingerprint card processing fee.

1039

Judge (Boxing, Wrestling, Martial Arts, and Kick Boxing)
Athletic Commission
Dept. of Regulation and Licensing
PO Box 25101
725 St. Michael's Dr.
Santa Fe, NM 87504
Phone: (505)827-7172

Credential Type: License. **Duration of License:** One year. **Requirements:** Must have appropriate experience. **Examination:** Local written examination. **Fees:** $10 license fee.

1040

Paddock Judge (Racetrack)
New Mexico State Racing
 Commission
PO Box 8576, Highland Station
Albuquerque, NM 87198
Phone: (505)841-4644

Credential Type: License Registration.
Requirements: Submit application and fingerprint card. Pay fees. **Fees:** $16 registration fee. $1 notary fee. $23 fingerprint card processing fee.

1041

Placing Judge (Racetrack)
New Mexico State Racing
 Commission
PO Box 8576, Highland Station
Albuquerque, NM 87198
Phone: (505)841-4644

Credential Type: License Registration.
Requirements: Submit application and fingerprint card. Pay fees. **Fees:** $16 registration fee. $1 notary fee. $23 fingerprint card processing fee.

1042

Professional Boxer
Athletic Commission
Dept. of Regulation and Licensing
PO Box 25101
725 St. Michael's Dr.
Santa Fe, NM 87504
Phone: (505)827-7172

Credential Type: License. **Duration of License:** One year. **Requirements:** Must have appropriate experience. **Fees:** $10 license fee.

1043

Professional Kick Boxer
Athletic Commission
Dept. of Regulation and Licensing
PO Box 25101
725 St. Michael's Dr.
Santa Fe, NM 87504
Phone: (505)827-7172

Credential Type: License. **Duration of License:** One year. **Requirements:** Must have appropriate experience. **Fees:** $10 license fee.

1044

Professional Martial Arts Fighter
Athletic Commission
Dept. of Regulation and Licensing
PO Box 25101
725 St. Michael's Dr.
Santa Fe, NM 87504
Phone: (505)827-7172

Credential Type: License. **Duration of License:** One year. **Requirements:** Must have appropriate experience. **Fees:** $10 license fee.

1045

Professional Wrestler
Athletic Commission
Dept. of Regulation and Licensing
PO Box 25101
725 St. Michael's Dr.
Santa Fe, NM 87504
Phone: (505)827-7172

Credential Type: License. **Duration of License:** One year. **Requirements:** Must have appropriate experience. **Fees:** $25 license fee.

1046

Racing Secretary (Racetrack)
New Mexico State Racing
 Commission
PO Box 8576, Highland Station
Albuquerque, NM 87198
Phone: (505)841-4644

Credential Type: License Registration.
Requirements: Submit application and fingerprint card. Pay fees. **Fees:** $21 registration fee. $1 notary fee. $23 fingerprint card processing fee.

1047

Referee (Boxing, Wrestling, Martial Arts, and Kick Boxing)
Athletic Commission
Dept. of Regulation and Licensing
PO Box 25101
725 St. Michael's Dr.
Santa Fe, NM 87504
Phone: (505)827-7172

Credential Type: License. **Duration of License:** One year. **Requirements:** Must have appropriate experience. **Examination:** Local written examination. **Fees:** $15 license fee.

New Mexico

1048

Starter (Racetrack)
New Mexico State Racing
 Commission
PO Box 8576, Highland Station
Albuquerque, NM 87198
Phone: (505)841-4644

Credential Type: License Registration.
Requirements: Submit application and fingerprint card. Pay fees. **Fees:** $21 registration fee. $1 notary fee. $23 fingerprint card processing fee.

1049

Timekeeper (Boxing, Wrestling, Martial Arts, and Kick Boxing)
Athletic Commission
Dept. of Regulation and Licensing
PO Box 25101
725 St. Michael's Dr.
Santa Fe, NM 87504
Phone: (505)827-7172

Credential Type: License. **Duration of License:** One year. **Requirements:** Must have appropriate experience. **Fees:** $5 license fee.

1050

Timer (Racetrack)
New Mexico State Racing
 Commission
PO Box 8576, Highland Station
Albuquerque, NM 87198
Phone: (505)841-4644

Credential Type: License Registration.
Requirements: Submit application and fingerprint card. Pay fees. **Fees:** $16 registration fee. $1 notary fee. $23 fingerprint card processing fee.

1051

Track Steward (Racetrack)
New Mexico State Racing
 Commission
PO Box 8576, Highland Station
Albuquerque, NM 87198
Phone: (505)841-4644

Credential Type: License Registration.
Requirements: Submit application and fingerprint card. Pay fees. **Fees:** $21 registration fee. $1 notary fee. $23 fingerprint card processing fee.

New York

1052

Authorized Agent (Thoroughbred Racing)
New York State Racing and
 Wagering Board
400 Broome St.
New York, NY 10013
Phone: (212)219-4230

Credential Type: License Registration. **Duration of License:** One year. **Requirements:** Submit application, F.B.I fingerprint card, New York state fingerprint card, and three photos. Pay fees. **Fees:** $5 registration fee. $44 New York state fingerprint card processing fee (valid for five years).

1053

Driver (Harness or Quarter Horse Racing)
New York State Racing and
 Wagering Board
400 Broome St.
New York, NY 10013
Phone: (212)219-4230

Credential Type: License Registration. **Duration of License:** One year. **Requirements:** Submit application, F.B.I fingerprint card, New York state fingerprint card, and three photos. Pay fees. **Fees:** $20 registration fee. $44 New York state fingerprint card processing fee (valid for five years).

1054

Jockey Agent (Thoroughbred Racing)
New York State Racing and
 Wagering Board
400 Broome St.
New York, NY 10013
Phone: (212)219-4230

Credential Type: License Registration. **Duration of License:** One year. **Requirements:** Submit application, F.B.I fingerprint card, New York state fingerprint card, and three photos. Pay fees. **Fees:** $20 registration fee. $44 New York state fingerprint card processing fee (valid for five years).

1055

Jockey/Apprentice Jockey (Thoroughbred Racing)
New York State Racing and
 Wagering Board
400 Broome St.
New York, NY 10013
Phone: (212)219-4230

Credential Type: License Registration. **Duration of License:** One year. **Requirements:** Submit application, F.B.I fingerprint card, New York state fingerprint card, and three photos. Pay fees. **Fees:** $50 registration fee. $44 New York state fingerprint card processing fee (valid for five years).

1056

Racing Official (Thoroughbred Racing)
New York State Racing and
 Wagering Board
400 Broome St.
New York, NY 10013
Phone: (212)219-4230

Credential Type: License Registration. **Duration of License:** One year. **Requirements:** Submit application, F.B.I fingerprint card, New York state fingerprint card, and three photos. Pay fees. **Fees:** $10 registration fee. $44 New York state fingerprint card processing fee (valid for five years).

North Dakota

1057

Authorized Agent (Racetrack)
North Dakota Racing Commission
State Capitol Bldg.
Bismarck, ND 58505
Phone: (701)224-2210

Credential Type: License Registration. **Requirements:** Submit application and fingerprint card. Pay fee. **Fees:** $25 license fee. $10 duplicate license fee.

1058

Boxer
North Dakota Secretary of State
600 E. Blvd. Ave.
Capitol Bldg., 1st Fl.
Bismarck, ND 58505
Phone: (701)224-4284

Credential Type: License. **Duration of License:** One year. **Requirements:** Submit application and pay fee. **Fees:** $10 license fee. (The license fee for individuals holding

1059

Boxing Cornerperson
North Dakota Secretary of State
600 E. Blvd. Ave.
Capitol Bldg., 1st Fl.
Bismarck, ND 58505
Phone: (701)224-4284

Credential Type: License. **Duration of License:** One year. **Requirements:** Submit application and pay fee. **Fees:** $10 license fee. (The license fee for individuals holding more than one license is the highest of the applicable license fees.)

1060

Boxing Judge
North Dakota Secretary of State
600 E. Blvd. Ave.
Capitol Bldg., 1st Fl.
Bismarck, ND 58505
Phone: (701)224-4284

Credential Type: License. **Duration of License:** One year. **Requirements:** Submit application and pay fee. **Fees:** $25 license fee. (The license fee for individuals holding more than one license is the highest of the applicable license fees.)

1061

Boxing Manager
North Dakota Secretary of State
600 E. Blvd. Ave.
Capitol Bldg., 1st Fl.
Bismarck, ND 58505
Phone: (701)224-4284

Credential Type: License. **Duration of License:** One year. **Requirements:** Submit application and pay fee. **Fees:** $25 license fee. (The license fee for individuals holding more than one license is the highest of the applicable license fees.)

1062

Boxing Referee
North Dakota Secretary of State
600 E. Blvd. Ave.
Capitol Bldg., 1st Fl.
Bismarck, ND 58505
Phone: (701)224-4284

Credential Type: License. **Duration of License:** One year. **Requirements:** Submit application and pay fee. **Fees:** $25 license fee. (The license fee for individuals holding more than one license is the highest of the applicable license fees.)

1063

Boxing Timekeeper
North Dakota Secretary of State
600 E. Blvd. Ave.
Capitol Bldg., 1st Fl.
Bismarck, ND 58505
Phone: (701)224-4284

Credential Type: License. **Duration of License:** One year. **Requirements:** Submit application and pay fee. **Fees:** $10 license fee. (The license fee for individuals holding more than one license is the highest of the applicable license fees.)

1064

Jockey Agent (Racetrack)
North Dakota Racing Commission
State Capitol Bldg.
Bismarck, ND 58505
Phone: (701)224-2210

Credential Type: License Registration. **Requirements:** Submit application and fingerprint card. Pay fee. **Fees:** $25 license fee. $10 duplicate license fee.

1065

Jockey Apprentice (Racetrack)
North Dakota Racing Commission
State Capitol Bldg.
Bismarck, ND 58505
Phone: (701)224-2210

Credential Type: License Registration. **Requirements:** Submit application and fingerprint card. Pay fee. **Fees:** $25 license fee. $10 duplicate license fee.

1066

Jockey-Driver (Racetrack)
North Dakota Racing Commission
State Capitol Bldg.
Bismarck, ND 58505
Phone: (701)224-2210

Credential Type: License Registration. **Requirements:** Submit application and fingerprint card. Pay fee. **Fees:** $100 license fee. $10 duplicate license fee.

1067

Kickboxer
North Dakota Secretary of State
600 E. Blvd. Ave.
Capitol Bldg., 1st Fl.
Bismarck, ND 58505
Phone: (701)224-4284

Credential Type: License. **Duration of License:** One year. **Requirements:** Submit application and pay fee. **Fees:** $10 license fee. (The license fee for individuals holding more than one license is the highest of the applicable license fees.)

1068

Paddock Judge (Racetrack)
North Dakota Racing Commission
State Capitol Bldg.
Bismarck, ND 58505
Phone: (701)224-2210

Credential Type: License Registration. **Requirements:** Submit application and fingerprint card. Pay fee. **Fees:** $10 license fee. $10 duplicate license fee.

1069

Patrol Judge (Racetrack)
North Dakota Racing Commission
State Capitol Bldg.
Bismarck, ND 58505
Phone: (701)224-2210

Credential Type: License Registration. **Requirements:** Submit application and fingerprint card. Pay fee. **Fees:** $10 license fee. $10 duplicate license fee.

1070

Placing Judge (Racetrack)
North Dakota Racing Commission
State Capitol Bldg.
Bismarck, ND 58505
Phone: (701)224-2210

Credential Type: License Registration. **Requirements:** Submit application and fingerprint card. Pay fee. **Fees:** $10 license fee. $10 duplicate license fee.

North Dakota

1071

Racing Secretary Assistant (Racetrack)
North Dakota Racing Commission
State Capitol Bldg.
Bismarck, ND 58505
Phone: (701)224-2210

Credential Type: License Registration.
Requirements: Submit application and fingerprint card. Pay fee. **Fees:** $10 license fee. $10 duplicate license fee.

1072

Racing Secretary (Racetrack)
North Dakota Racing Commission
State Capitol Bldg.
Bismarck, ND 58505
Phone: (701)224-2210

Credential Type: License Registration.
Requirements: Submit application and fingerprint card. Pay fee. **Fees:** $25 license fee. $10 duplicate license fee.

1073

Starter (Racetrack)
North Dakota Racing Commission
State Capitol Bldg.
Bismarck, ND 58505
Phone: (701)224-2210

Credential Type: License Registration.
Requirements: Submit application and fingerprint card. Pay fee. **Fees:** $10 license fee. $10 duplicate license fee.

1074

Steward (Racetrack)
North Dakota Racing Commission
State Capitol Bldg.
Bismarck, ND 58505
Phone: (701)224-2210

Credential Type: License Registration.
Requirements: Submit application and fingerprint card. Pay fee. **Fees:** $25 license fee. $10 duplicate license fee.

1075

Timer (Racetrack)
North Dakota Racing Commission
State Capitol Bldg.
Bismarck, ND 58505
Phone: (701)224-2210

Credential Type: License Registration.
Requirements: Submit application and fingerprint card. Pay fee. **Fees:** $10 license fee. $10 duplicate license fee.

Ohio

1076

Apprentice Jockey (Thoroughbred and Quarter Horse Racing)
Ohio State Racing Commission
State Office Tower
77 S. High St., 18th Fl.
Columbus, OH 43266-0416
Phone: (614)466-2757

Credential Type: License Registration.
Requirements: Submit application and fingerprint card. Pay fee. **Fees:** $25 registration fee.

1077

Assistant Racing Secretary (Thoroughbred, Standardbred, and Quarter Horse Racing)
Ohio State Racing Commission
State Office Tower
77 S. High St., 18th Fl.
Columbus, OH 43266-0416
Phone: (614)466-2757

Credential Type: License Registration.
Requirements: Submit application and fingerprint card. Pay fee. **Fees:** $25 registration fee.

1078

Assistant Starter (Thoroughbred, Standardbred, and Quarter Horse Racing)
Ohio State Racing Commission
State Office Tower
77 S. High St., 18th Fl.
Columbus, OH 43266-0416
Phone: (614)466-2757

Credential Type: License Registration.
Requirements: Submit application and fingerprint card. Pay fee. **Fees:** $25 registration fee.

1079

Authorized Agent (Thoroughbred, Standardbred, and Quarter Horse Racing)
Ohio State Racing Commission
State Office Tower
77 S. High St., 18th Fl.
Columbus, OH 43266-0416
Phone: (614)466-2757

Credential Type: License Registration.
Requirements: Submit application and fingerprint card. Pay fee. **Fees:** $25 registration fee.

1080

Driver/Trainer (Standardbred Racing)
Ohio State Racing Commission
State Office Tower
77 S. High St., 18th Fl.
Columbus, OH 43266-0416
Phone: (614)466-2757

Credential Type: License Registration.
Requirements: Submit application and fingerprint card. Pay fee. **Fees:** $25 registration fee.

1081

Jockey Agent (Thoroughbred and Quarter Horse Racing)
Ohio State Racing Commission
State Office Tower
77 S. High St., 18th Fl.
Columbus, OH 43266-0416
Phone: (614)466-2757

Credential Type: License Registration.
Requirements: Submit application and fingerprint card. Pay fee. **Fees:** $25 registration fee.

1082

Jockey (Thoroughbred and Quarter Horse Racing)
Ohio State Racing Commission
State Office Tower
77 S. High St., 18th Fl.
Columbus, OH 43266-0416
Phone: (614)466-2757

Credential Type: License Registration.
Requirements: Submit application and fingerprint card. Pay fee. **Fees:** $25 registration fee.

1083

Judge (Standardbred Racing)
Ohio State Racing Commission
State Office Tower
77 S. High St., 18th Fl.
Columbus, OH 43266-0416
Phone: (614)466-2757

Credential Type: License Registration.
Requirements: Submit application and fingerprint card. Pay fee. **Fees:** $25 registration fee.

1084

Paddock Judge (Thoroughbred, Standardbred, and Quarter Horse Racing)
Ohio State Racing Commission
State Office Tower
77 S. High St., 18th Fl.
Columbus, OH 43266-0416
Phone: (614)466-2757

Credential Type: License Registration.
Requirements: Submit application and fingerprint card. Pay fee. **Fees:** $25 registration fee.

1085

Patrol Judge (Thoroughbred and Quarter Horse Racing)
Ohio State Racing Commission
State Office Tower
77 S. High St., 18th Fl.
Columbus, OH 43266-0416
Phone: (614)466-2757

Credential Type: License Registration.
Requirements: Submit application and fingerprint card. Pay fee. **Fees:** $25 registration fee.

1086

Placing Judge (Thoroughbred and Quarter Horse Racing)
Ohio State Racing Commission
State Office Tower
77 S. High St., 18th Fl.
Columbus, OH 43266-0416
Phone: (614)466-2757

Credential Type: License Registration.
Requirements: Submit application and fingerprint card. Pay fee. **Fees:** $25 registration fee.

1087

Racing Secretary (Thoroughbred, Standardbred, and Quarter Horse Racing)
Ohio State Racing Commission
State Office Tower
77 S. High St., 18th Fl.
Columbus, OH 43266-0416
Phone: (614)466-2757

Credential Type: License Registration.
Requirements: Submit application and fingerprint card. Pay fee. **Fees:** $25 registration fee.

1088

Starter (Thoroughbred, Standardbred, and Quarter Horse Racing)
Ohio State Racing Commission
State Office Tower
77 S. High St., 18th Fl.
Columbus, OH 43266-0416
Phone: (614)466-2757

Credential Type: License Registration.
Requirements: Submit application and fingerprint card. Pay fee. **Fees:** $25 registration fee.

1089

Steward (Thoroughbred and Quarter Horse Racing)
Ohio State Racing Commission
State Office Tower
77 S. High St., 18th Fl.
Columbus, OH 43266-0416
Phone: (614)466-2757

Credential Type: License Registration.
Requirements: Submit application and fingerprint card. Pay fee. **Fees:** $25 registration fee.

1090

Timer (Thoroughbred, Standardbred, and Quarter Horse Racing)
Ohio State Racing Commission
State Office Tower
77 S. High St., 18th Fl.
Columbus, OH 43266-0416
Phone: (614)466-2757

Credential Type: License Registration.
Requirements: Submit application and fingerprint card. Pay fee. **Fees:** $10 registration fee.

Oklahoma

1091

Apprentice Jockey (Racetrack)
Oklahoma Horse Racing Commission
6501 N. Broadway, Ste. 180
Oklahoma City, OK 73116
Phone: (405)848-0404

Credential Type: License Registration.
Duration of License: One year. **Requirements:** Submit application and fingerprint card. Pay fee. **Fees:** $50 registration fee. $50 annual renewal. $120 triennial renewal.

1092

Authorized Agent (Racetrack)
Oklahoma Horse Racing Commission
6501 N. Broadway, Ste. 180
Oklahoma City, OK 73116
Phone: (405)848-0404

Credential Type: License Registration.
Duration of License: One year. **Requirements:** Submit application and fingerprint card. Pay fee. **Fees:** $50 registration fee. $50 annual renewal.

1093

Jockey Agent (Racetrack)
Oklahoma Horse Racing Commission
6501 N. Broadway, Ste. 180
Oklahoma City, OK 73116
Phone: (405)848-0404

Credential Type: License Registration.
Duration of License: One year. **Requirements:** Submit application and fingerprint card. Pay fee. **Fees:** $50 registration fee. $50 annual renewal.

1094

Jockey (Racetrack)
Oklahoma Horse Racing Commission
6501 N. Broadway, Ste. 180
Oklahoma City, OK 73116
Phone: (405)848-0404

Credential Type: License Registration.
Duration of License: One year. **Requirements:** Submit application and fingerprint card. Pay fee. **Fees:** $50 registration fee. $50 annual renewal. $120 triennial renewal.

1095

Racing Official (Racetrack)
Oklahoma Horse Racing Commission
6501 N. Broadway, Ste. 180
Oklahoma City, OK 73116
Phone: (405)848-0404

Credential Type: License Registration. **Duration of License:** One year. **Requirements:** Submit application and fingerprint card. Pay fee. **Fees:** $50 registration fee. $50 annual renewal.

1096

Sports Official, High School
Oklahoma Secondary Schools
   Activities Assn.
222 N.E. 27th
Oklahoma City, OK 73152
Phone: (405)528-3385

Credential Type: License. **Duration of License:** One year. **Requirements:** High school diploma. Must attend five rules meetings each year. **Examination:** Examinations given according to sport. **Fees:** $25 license fee for first sport. $10 license fee for each additional sport. $25 renewal fee for first sport. $10 renewal fee for each additional sport.

Oregon

1097

Apprentice Jockey (Racetrack)
Oregon Racing Commission
113 State Office Bldg.
1400 SW Fifth
Portland, OR 97201
Phone: (503)229-5820

Credential Type: License Registration. **Requirements:** Submit application and fingerprint card. Pay fee . **Fees:** $30 registration fee. $6 duplicate fee.

1098

Jockey Agent (Racetrack)
Oregon Racing Commission
113 State Office Bldg.
1400 SW Fifth
Portland, OR 97201
Phone: (503)229-5820

Credential Type: License Registration. **Requirements:** Submit application and fingerprint card. Pay fee. **Fees:** $30 registration fee. $6 duplicate fee.

1099

Jockey (Racetrack)
Oregon Racing Commission
113 State Office Bldg.
1400 SW Fifth
Portland, OR 97201
Phone: (503)229-5820

Credential Type: License Registration. **Requirements:** Submit application and fingerprint card. Pay fee. **Fees:** $30 registration fee. $6 duplicate fee.

1100

Official (Racetrack)
Oregon Racing Commission
113 State Office Bldg.
1400 SW Fifth
Portland, OR 97201
Phone: (503)229-5820

Credential Type: License Registration. **Requirements:** Submit application and fingerprint card. Pay fee. **Fees:** $30 registration fee. $6 duplicate fee.

1101

Starter/Assistant Starter (Racetrack)
Oregon Racing Commission
113 State Office Bldg.
1400 SW Fifth
Portland, OR 97201
Phone: (503)229-5820

Credential Type: License Registration. **Requirements:** Submit application and fingerprint card. Pay fee. **Fees:** $30 registration fee. $6 duplicate fee.

1102

Timer (Racetrack)
Oregon Racing Commission
113 State Office Bldg.
1400 SW Fifth
Portland, OR 97201
Phone: (503)229-5820

Credential Type: License Registration. **Requirements:** Submit application and fingerprint card. Pay fee. **Fees:** $30 registration fee. $6 duplicate fee.

Pennsylvania

1103

Apprentice Jockey (Horse Racing)
Pennsylvania State Horse Racing
   Commission
2301 N. Cameron St., Rm. 306, 4th
   Fl.
Harrisburg, PA 17110-9408
Phone: (717)787-1942

Credential Type: License Registration. **Duration of License:** Three years. **Requirements:** Submit application, two photos, and fingerprint card. Pay fee. **Fees:** $30 registration fee. $2 duplicate license.

1104

Authorized Agent (Horse Racing)
Pennsylvania State Horse Racing
   Commission
2301 N. Cameron St., Rm. 306, 4th
   Fl.
Harrisburg, PA 17110-9408
Phone: (717)787-1942

Credential Type: License Registration. **Duration of License:** Three years. **Requirements:** Submit application, two photos, and fingerprint card. Pay fee. **Fees:** $30 registration fee. $2 duplicate license.

1105

Driver/Groom (Harness Racing)
Pennsylvania State Harness Racing
   Commission
2301 N. Cameron St.
Harrisburg, PA 17110-9408
Phone: (717)787-5196

Credential Type: License Registration. **Duration of License:** Three years. **Requirements:** Submit application, three photos, and fingerprint card. Pay fee. **Fees:** $45 registration fee. $5 duplicate license. $33 fingerprint processing fee.

1106

Driver (Harness Racing)
Pennsylvania State Harness Racing
   Commission
2301 N. Cameron St.
Harrisburg, PA 17110-9408
Phone: (717)787-5196

Credential Type: License Registration. **Duration of License:** Three years. **Requirements:** Submit application, three photos, and fingerprint card. Pay fee. **Fees:** $30 registration fee. $5 duplicate license. $33 fingerprint processing fee.

1107

Driver/Trainer/Groom (Harness Racing)
Pennsylvania State Harness Racing Commission
2301 N. Cameron St.
Harrisburg, PA 17110-9408
Phone: (717)787-5196

Credential Type: License Registration. **Duration of License:** Three years. **Requirements:** Submit application, three photos, and fingerprint card. Pay fee. **Fees:** $75 registration fee. $5 duplicate license. $33 fingerprint processing fee.

1108

Driver/Trainer (Harness Racing)
Pennsylvania State Harness Racing Commission
2301 N. Cameron St.
Harrisburg, PA 17110-9408
Phone: (717)787-5196

Credential Type: License Registration. **Duration of License:** Three years. **Requirements:** Submit application, three photos, and fingerprint card. Pay fee. **Fees:** $60 registration fee. $5 duplicate license. $33 fingerprint processing fee.

1109

Jockey Agent (Horse Racing)
Pennsylvania State Horse Racing Commission
2301 N. Cameron St., Rm. 306, 4th Fl.
Harrisburg, PA 17110-9408
Phone: (717)787-1942

Credential Type: License Registration. **Duration of License:** Three years. **Requirements:** Submit application, two photos, and fingerprint card. Pay fee. **Fees:** $30 registration fee. $2 duplicate license.

1110

Jockey (Horse Racing)
Pennsylvania State Horse Racing Commission
2301 N. Cameron St., Rm. 306, 4th Fl.
Harrisburg, PA 17110-9408
Phone: (717)787-1942

Credential Type: License Registration. **Duration of License:** Three years. **Requirements:** Submit application, two photos, and fingerprint card. Pay fee. **Fees:** $30 registration fee. $2 duplicate license.

1111

Official (Horse Racing)
Pennsylvania State Horse Racing Commission
2301 N. Cameron St., Rm. 306, 4th Fl.
Harrisburg, PA 17110-9408
Phone: (717)787-1942

Credential Type: License Registration. **Duration of License:** Three years. **Requirements:** Submit application, two photos, and fingerprint card. Pay fee. **Fees:** $30 registration fee. $2 duplicate license.

1112

Officials (Harness Racing)
Pennsylvania State Harness Racing Commission
2301 N. Cameron St.
Harrisburg, PA 17110-9408
Phone: (717)787-5196

Credential Type: License Registration. **Duration of License:** Three years. **Requirements:** Submit application, three photos, and fingerprint card. Pay fee. **Fees:** $60 registration fee. $5 duplicate license. $33 fingerprint processing fee.

1113

Owner/Driver/Groom (Harness Racing)
Pennsylvania State Harness Racing Commission
2301 N. Cameron St.
Harrisburg, PA 17110-9408
Phone: (717)787-5196

Credential Type: License Registration. **Duration of License:** Three years. **Requirements:** Submit application, three photos, and fingerprint card. Pay fee. **Fees:** $75 registration fee. $5 duplicate license. $33 fingerprint processing fee.

1114

Owner/Driver (Harness Racing)
Pennsylvania State Harness Racing Commission
2301 N. Cameron St.
Harrisburg, PA 17110-9408
Phone: (717)787-5196

Credential Type: License Registration. **Duration of License:** Three years. **Requirements:** Submit application, three photos, and fingerprint card. Pay fee. **Fees:** $60 registration fee. $5 duplicate license. $33 fingerprint processing fee.

1115

Owner/Trainer/Driver/Groom (Harness Racing)
Pennsylvania State Harness Racing Commission
2301 N. Cameron St.
Harrisburg, PA 17110-9408
Phone: (717)787-5196

Credential Type: License Registration. **Duration of License:** Three years. **Requirements:** Submit application, three photos, and fingerprint card. Pay fee. **Fees:** $75 registration fee. $5 duplicate license. $33 fingerprint processing fee.

1116

Owner/Trainer/Driver (Harness Racing)
Pennsylvania State Harness Racing Commission
2301 N. Cameron St.
Harrisburg, PA 17110-9408
Phone: (717)787-5196

Credential Type: License Registration. **Duration of License:** Three years. **Requirements:** Submit application, three photos, and fingerprint card. Pay fee. **Fees:** $60 registration fee. $5 duplicate license. $33 fingerprint processing fee.

Rhode Island

1117

Professional Boxer
Div. of Racing and Athletics
Rhode Island Dept. of Business Regulation
233 Richmond St.
Providence, RI 02903
Phone: (401)277-6541

Credential Type: Professional Boxer License. **Duration of License:** One year. **Requirements:** Between 18 and 35 years of age (unless waived by licensing agency). Foreign born must show proof of legal entry into the U.S. Physical examination required before each bout and drug test required after each bout. **Reciprocity:** Yes. **Fees:** $5 license fee.

Rhode Island

1118

Professional Wrestler
Div. of Racing and Athletics
Rhode Island Dept. of Business Regulation
233 Richmond St.
Providence, RI 02903
Phone: (401)277-6541

Credential Type: Professional Wrestler License. **Duration of License:** One year. **Requirements:** At least 18 years of age. Foreign born must show proof of legal entry into U.S. Physical exam before each bout. Blood test after each bout. **Reciprocity:** Yes. **Fees:** $5 license fee.

South Carolina

1119

Boxer
State Athletic Commission
PO Box 2461
Columbia, SC 29202
Phone: (803)254-3661

Credential Type: License. **Requirements:** Submit application and pay fee. **Fees:** $10 license fee.

1120

Boxing-Wrestling Judge
State Athletic Commission
PO Box 2461
Columbia, SC 29202
Phone: (803)254-3661

Credential Type: License. **Requirements:** Submit application and pay fee. **Fees:** $10 license fee.

1121

Boxing-Wrestling Referee
State Athletic Commission
PO Box 2461
Columbia, SC 29202
Phone: (803)254-3661

Credential Type: License. **Requirements:** Submit application and pay fee. **Fees:** $10 license fee.

1122

Boxing-Wrestling Timekeeper
State Athletic Commission
PO Box 2461
Columbia, SC 29202
Phone: (803)254-3661

Credential Type: License. **Requirements:** Submit application and pay fee. **Fees:** $10 license fee.

1123

Kickboxer
State Athletic Commission
PO Box 2461
Columbia, SC 29202
Phone: (803)254-3661

Credential Type: License. **Requirements:** Submit application and pay fee. **Fees:** $10 license fee.

1124

Manager (Boxing)
State Athletic Commission
PO Box 2461
Columbia, SC 29202
Phone: (803)254-3661

Credential Type: License. **Requirements:** Submit application and pay fee. **Fees:** $20 license fee.

1125

Professional Wrestler
State Athletic Commission
PO Box 2461
Columbia, SC 29202
Phone: (803)254-3661

Credential Type: License. **Requirements:** Submit application and pay fee. **Fees:** $10 license fee.

1126

Second (Boxing)
State Athletic Commission
PO Box 2461
Columbia, SC 29202
Phone: (803)254-3661

Credential Type: License. **Requirements:** Submit application and pay fee. **Fees:** $10 license fee.

South Dakota

1127

Apprentice Jockey (Horse Racing)
South Dakota Racing Commission
c/o 500 East Capitol
Pierre, SD 57501
Phone: (605)773-6050

Credential Type: License Registration. **Requirements:** Submit application and fingerprint card. Pay fee. **Fees:** $25 registration fee.

1128

Assistant Starter (Horse Racing)
South Dakota Racing Commission
c/o 500 East Capitol
Pierre, SD 57501
Phone: (605)773-6050

Credential Type: License Registration. **Requirements:** Submit application and fingerprint card. Pay fee. **Fees:** $10 registration fee.

1129

Associate Judge (Greyhound Racing)
South Dakota Racing Commission
c/o 500 East Capitol
Pierre, SD 57501
Phone: (605)773-6050

Credential Type: License Registration. **Requirements:** Submit application and fingerprint card. Pay fee. **Fees:** $15 registration fee.

1130

Authorized Agent (Greyhound Racing)
South Dakota Racing Commission
c/o 500 East Capitol
Pierre, SD 57501
Phone: (605)773-6050

Credential Type: License Registration. **Requirements:** Submit application and fingerprint card. Pay fee. **Fees:** $15 registration fee.

1131

Authorized Agent (Horse Racing)
South Dakota Racing Commission
c/o 500 East Capitol
Pierre, SD 57501
Phone: (605)773-6050

Credential Type: License Registration.
Requirements: Submit application and fingerprint card. Pay fee. **Fees:** $15 registration fee.

1132

Jockey Agent (Horse Racing)
South Dakota Racing Commission
c/o 500 East Capitol
Pierre, SD 57501
Phone: (605)773-6050

Credential Type: License Registration.
Requirements: Submit application and fingerprint card. Pay fee. **Fees:** $20 registration fee.

1133

Jockey (Horse Racing)
South Dakota Racing Commission
c/o 500 East Capitol
Pierre, SD 57501
Phone: (605)773-6050

Credential Type: License Registration.
Requirements: Submit application and fingerprint card. Pay fee. **Fees:** $25 registration fee.

1134

Official (Horse Racing)
South Dakota Racing Commission
c/o 500 East Capitol
Pierre, SD 57501
Phone: (605)773-6050

Credential Type: License Registration.
Requirements: Submit application and fingerprint card. Pay fee. **Fees:** $15 registration fee.

1135

Paddock Judge (Greyhound Racing)
South Dakota Racing Commission
c/o 500 East Capitol
Pierre, SD 57501
Phone: (605)773-6050

Credential Type: License Registration.
Requirements: Submit application and fingerprint card. Pay fee. **Fees:** $15 registration fee.

1136

Presiding Judge (Greyhound Racing)
South Dakota Racing Commission
c/o 500 East Capitol
Pierre, SD 57501
Phone: (605)773-6050

Credential Type: License Registration.
Requirements: Submit application and fingerprint card. Pay fee. **Fees:** $15 registration fee.

1137

Racing Secretary (Greyhound Racing)
South Dakota Racing Commission
c/o 500 East Capitol
Pierre, SD 57501
Phone: (605)773-6050

Credential Type: License Registration.
Requirements: Submit application and fingerprint card. Pay fee. **Fees:** $15 registration fee.

1138

Starter (Greyhound Racing)
South Dakota Racing Commission
c/o 500 East Capitol
Pierre, SD 57501
Phone: (605)773-6050

Credential Type: License Registration.
Requirements: Submit application and fingerprint card. Pay fee. **Fees:** $15 registration fee.

1139

Starter (Horse Racing)
South Dakota Racing Commission
c/o 500 East Capitol
Pierre, SD 57501
Phone: (605)773-6050

Credential Type: License Registration.
Requirements: Submit application and fingerprint card. Pay fee. **Fees:** $15 registration fee.

1140

Timer (Greyhound Racing)
South Dakota Racing Commission
c/o 500 East Capitol
Pierre, SD 57501
Phone: (605)773-6050

Credential Type: License Registration.
Requirements: Submit application and fingerprint card. Pay fee. **Fees:** $15 registration fee.

Tennessee

1141

Driver/Jockey (Racetrack)
Tennessee State Racing Commission
500 James Robertson Pky., 2nd Fl.
Nashville, TN 37243
Phone: (615)741-1952

Credential Type: License Registration.
Requirements: Submit application and fingerprint card. Pay fee. **Fees:** $25 registration fee.

1142

Jockey Agent (Racetrack)
Tennessee State Racing Commission
500 James Robertson Pky., 2nd Fl.
Nashville, TN 37243
Phone: (615)741-1952

Credential Type: License Registration.
Requirements: Submit application and fingerprint card. Pay fee. **Fees:** $25 registration fee.

1143

Official (Racetrack)
Tennessee State Racing Commission
500 James Robertson Pky., 2nd Fl.
Nashville, TN 37243
Phone: (615)741-1952

Credential Type: License Registration.
Requirements: Submit application and fingerprint card. Pay fee. **Fees:** $10 registration fee.

1144

Trainer/Driver (Racetrack)
Tennessee State Racing Commission
500 James Robertson Pky., 2nd Fl.
Nashville, TN 37243
Phone: (615)741-1952

Credential Type: License Registration.
Requirements: Submit application and fin-

Texas

Trainer/Driver (Racetrack), continued

gerprint card. Pay fee. **Fees:** $25 registration fee.

Texas

1145

Apprentice Jockey (Racetrack)
Texas Racing Commission
PO Box 12080
Austin, TX 78711
Phone: (512)794-8461

Credential Type: License Registration. **Requirements:** Submit application and fingerprint card. Pay fee. **Fees:** $65 registration fee.

1146

Assistant Starter (Racetrack)
Texas Racing Commission
PO Box 12080
Austin, TX 78711
Phone: (512)794-8461

Credential Type: License Registration. **Requirements:** Submit application and fingerprint card. Pay fee. **Fees:** $20 registration fee.

1147

Association Judge (Racetrack)
Texas Racing Commission
PO Box 12080
Austin, TX 78711
Phone: (512)794-8461

Credential Type: License Registration. **Requirements:** Submit application and fingerprint card. Pay fee. **Fees:** $65 registration fee.

1148

Athlete Agent
Secretary of State, Athlete Agent Registration
PO Box 12887
Austin, TX 78711
Phone: (512)463-5558

Credential Type: License. **Duration of License:** One year. **Requirements:** $100,000 surety bond, if agent offers financial services to athlete. Information concerning business or occupation for five years preceding application. Five professional references, if requested. Complete list of present and previous athlete clients for three years immediately preceding application. All formal training, practical experience and educational background relating to applicant's professional activities as an athlete agent must be submitted. **Examination:** No. **Fees:** $1,000 registration fee. $1,000 renewal fee. **Governing Statute:** VACS 8871, one TAC 781.

1149

Authorized Agent (Racetrack)
Texas Racing Commission
PO Box 12080
Austin, TX 78711
Phone: (512)794-8461

Credential Type: License Registration. **Requirements:** Submit application and fingerprint card. Pay fee. **Fees:** $10 registration fee.

1150

Boxer
Texas Dept. of Licensing & Regulation
PO Box 12157
Austin, TX 78711
Phone: (512)463-5522

Credential Type: License. **Requirements:** Submit application and pay fee. **Fees:** $15 license fee. **Governing Statute:** VACS 8501-1, 16 TAC 61.1.

1151

Boxing Manager
Texas Dept. of Licensing & Regulation
PO Box 12157
Austin, TX 78711
Phone: (512)463-5522

Credential Type: License. **Requirements:** Submit application and pay fee. **Fees:** $75 license fee. **Governing Statute:** VACS 8501-1, 16 TAC 61.1.

1152

Boxing Referee
Texas Dept. of Licensing & Regulation
PO Box 12157
Austin, TX 78711
Phone: (512)463-5522

Credential Type: License. **Requirements:** Submit application and pay fee. **Fees:** $25 license fee. **Governing Statute:** VACS 8501-1, 16 TAC 61.1.

1153

Boxing Second
Texas Dept. of Licensing & Regulation
PO Box 12157
Austin, TX 78711
Phone: (512)463-5522

Credential Type: License. **Requirements:** Submit application and pay fee. **Fees:** $10 license fee. **Governing Statute:** VACS 8501-1, 16 TAC 61.1.

1154

Jockey Agent (Racetrack)
Texas Racing Commission
PO Box 12080
Austin, TX 78711
Phone: (512)794-8461

Credential Type: License Registration. **Requirements:** Submit application and fingerprint card. Pay fee. **Fees:** $75 registration fee.

1155

Jockey (Racetrack)
Texas Racing Commission
PO Box 12080
Austin, TX 78711
Phone: (512)794-8461

Credential Type: License Registration. **Requirements:** Submit application and fingerprint card. Pay fee. **Fees:** $75 registration fee.

1156

Official (Racetrack)
Texas Racing Commission
PO Box 12080
Austin, TX 78711
Phone: (512)794-8461

Credential Type: License Registration. **Requirements:** Submit application and fingerprint card. Pay fee. **Fees:** $75 registration fee.

Utah

1157

Boxer
Dept. of Commerce
Div. of Occupational and
  Professional Licensing
160 E. 300 S.
PO Box 45802
Salt Lake City, UT 84145
Phone: (801)530-6628

Credential Type: Registration. **Requirements:** Contact licensing body for application information.

Vermont

1158

Association Official (Greyhound Racing)
Vermont Racing Commission
State Office Bldg.
Montpelier, VT 05602
Phone: (802)828-3429

Credential Type: License Registration. **Requirements:** Submit application and fingerprint card. Pay fee. **Fees:** $20 registration fee. $5 duplicate license.

1159

Authorized Agent (Greyhound Racing)
Vermont Racing Commission
State Office Bldg.
Montpelier, VT 05602
Phone: (802)828-3429

Credential Type: License Registration. **Requirements:** Submit application and fingerprint card. Pay fee. **Fees:** $20 registration fee. $5 duplicate license.

1160

Authorized Agent (Racetrack)
Vermont Racing Commission
State Office Bldg.
Montpelier, VT 05602
Phone: (802)828-3429

Credential Type: License Registration. **Requirements:** Submit application and fingerprint card. Pay fee. **Fees:** $5 registration fee. $2 duplicate license.

1161

Boxing, Professional
Boxing Control Board
Pavilion Office Bldg.
Montpelier, VT 05602
Phone: (802)828-2363

Credential Type: License. **Requirements:** License required to conduct a boxing contest. License required to participate as : Participant, manager, promoter and referee. **Examination:** No. **Reciprocity:** No. **Fees:** $5 (not to exceed) Annual, contestants and seconds. $15 (not to exceed) Manager, contestant. $25 (not to exceed) Promoters. $10 (not to exceed) Referees. **Governing Statute:** Title 31 VSA, Sections 105-107.

1162

Jockey Agent (Racetrack)
Vermont Racing Commission
State Office Bldg.
Montpelier, VT 05602
Phone: (802)828-3429

Credential Type: License Registration. **Requirements:** Submit application and fingerprint card. Pay fee. **Fees:** $5 registration fee. $2 duplicate license.

1163

Jockey Apprentice (Racetrack)
Vermont Racing Commission
State Office Bldg.
Montpelier, VT 05602
Phone: (802)828-3429

Credential Type: License Registration. **Requirements:** Submit application and fingerprint card. Pay fee. **Fees:** $5 registration fee. $2 duplicate license.

1164

Jockey (Racetrack)
Vermont Racing Commission
State Office Bldg.
Montpelier, VT 05602
Phone: (802)828-3429

Credential Type: License Registration. **Requirements:** Submit application and fingerprint card. Pay fee. **Fees:** $5 registration fee. $2 duplicate license.

1165

Judge (Greyhound Racing)
Vermont Racing Commission
State Office Bldg.
Montpelier, VT 05602
Phone: (802)828-3429

Credential Type: License Registration. **Requirements:** Submit application and fingerprint card. Pay fee. **Fees:** $20 registration fee. $5 duplicate license.

1166

Official (Racetrack)
Vermont Racing Commission
State Office Bldg.
Montpelier, VT 05602
Phone: (802)828-3429

Credential Type: License Registration. **Requirements:** Submit application and fingerprint card. Pay fee. **Fees:** $5 registration fee. $2 duplicate license.

1167

Paddock Judge (Greyhound Racing)
Vermont Racing Commission
State Office Bldg.
Montpelier, VT 05602
Phone: (802)828-3429

Credential Type: License Registration. **Requirements:** Submit application and fingerprint card. Pay fee. **Fees:** $20 registration fee. $5 duplicate license.

1168

Patrol Judge (Greyhound Racing)
Vermont Racing Commission
State Office Bldg.
Montpelier, VT 05602
Phone: (802)828-3429

Credential Type: License Registration. **Requirements:** Submit application and fingerprint card. Pay fee. **Fees:** $20 registration fee. $5 duplicate license.

1169

Racing Secretary (Greyhound Racing)
Vermont Racing Commission
State Office Bldg.
Montpelier, VT 05602
Phone: (802)828-3429

Credential Type: License Registration. **Requirements:** Submit application and fin-

Vermont

Racing Secretary (Greyhound Racing), continued

gerprint card. Pay fee. **Fees:** $20 registration fee. $5 duplicate license.

1170

Starter (Greyhound Racing)
Vermont Racing Commission
State Office Bldg.
Montpelier, VT 05602
Phone: (802)828-3429

Credential Type: License Registration. **Requirements:** Submit application and fingerprint card. Pay fee. **Fees:** $20 registration fee. $5 duplicate license.

1171

Timer (Greyhound Racing)
Vermont Racing Commission
State Office Bldg.
Montpelier, VT 05602
Phone: (802)828-3429

Credential Type: License Registration. **Requirements:** Submit application and fingerprint card. Pay fee. **Fees:** $20 registration fee. $5 duplicate license.

1172

Trainer/Driver (Harness Racing)
Vermont Racing Commission
State Office Bldg.
Montpelier, VT 05602
Phone: (802)828-3429

Credential Type: License Registration. **Requirements:** Submit application and fingerprint card. Pay fee. **Fees:** $5 registration fee. $2 duplicate license.

Virginia

1173

Apprentice Jockey (Racetrack)
Virginia Racing Commission
PO Box 1123
Richmond, VA 23208
Phone: (804)371-7363

Credential Type: License Registration. **Requirements:** Submit application and fingerprint card. Pay fee. **Fees:** $10 registration fee.

1174

Assistant Racing Secretary (Racetrack)
Virginia Racing Commission
PO Box 1123
Richmond, VA 23208
Phone: (804)371-7363

Credential Type: License Registration. **Requirements:** Submit application and fingerprint card. Pay fee. **Fees:** $10 registration fee.

1175

Assistant Starter (Racetrack)
Virginia Racing Commission
PO Box 1123
Richmond, VA 23208
Phone: (804)371-7363

Credential Type: License Registration. **Requirements:** Submit application and fingerprint card. Pay fee. **Fees:** $5 registration fee.

1176

Authorized Agent (Racetrack)
Virginia Racing Commission
PO Box 1123
Richmond, VA 23208
Phone: (804)371-7363

Credential Type: License Registration. **Requirements:** Submit application and fingerprint card. Pay fee. **Fees:** $10 registration fee.

1177

Clocker (Racetrack)
Virginia Racing Commission
PO Box 1123
Richmond, VA 23208
Phone: (804)371-7363

Credential Type: License Registration. **Requirements:** Submit application and fingerprint card. Pay fee. **Fees:** $10 registration fee.

1178

Driver (Racetrack)
Virginia Racing Commission
PO Box 1123
Richmond, VA 23208
Phone: (804)371-7363

Credential Type: License Registration. **Requirements:** Submit application and fingerprint card. Pay fee. **Fees:** $10 registration fee.

1179

Jockey Agent (Racetrack)
Virginia Racing Commission
PO Box 1123
Richmond, VA 23208
Phone: (804)371-7363

Credential Type: License Registration. **Requirements:** Submit application and fingerprint card. Pay fee. **Fees:** $10 registration fee.

1180

Jockey (Racetrack)
Virginia Racing Commission
PO Box 1123
Richmond, VA 23208
Phone: (804)371-7363

Credential Type: License Registration. **Requirements:** Submit application and fingerprint card. Pay fee. **Fees:** $10 registration fee.

1181

Paddock Judge (Racetrack)
Virginia Racing Commission
PO Box 1123
Richmond, VA 23208
Phone: (804)371-7363

Credential Type: License Registration. **Requirements:** Submit application and fingerprint card. Pay fee. **Fees:** $10 registration fee.

1182

Patrol Judge (Racetrack)
Virginia Racing Commission
PO Box 1123
Richmond, VA 23208
Phone: (804)371-7363

Credential Type: License Registration. **Requirements:** Submit application and fingerprint card. Pay fee. **Fees:** $10 registration fee.

Athletes, Coaches, Umpires, and Referees

1183

Placing Judge (Racetrack)
Virginia Racing Commission
PO Box 1123
Richmond, VA 23208
Phone: (804)371-7363

Credential Type: License Registration. **Requirements:** Submit application and fingerprint card. Pay fee. **Fees:** $10 registration fee.

1184

Racing Secretary (Racetrack)
Virginia Racing Commission
PO Box 1123
Richmond, VA 23208
Phone: (804)371-7363

Credential Type: License Registration. **Requirements:** Submit application and fingerprint card. Pay fee. **Fees:** $10 registration fee.

1185

Starter (Racetrack)
Virginia Racing Commission
PO Box 1123
Richmond, VA 23208
Phone: (804)371-7363

Credential Type: License Registration. **Requirements:** Submit application and fingerprint card. Pay fee. **Fees:** $10 registration fee.

1186

Timer (Racetrack)
Virginia Racing Commission
PO Box 1123
Richmond, VA 23208
Phone: (804)371-7363

Credential Type: License Registration. **Requirements:** Submit application and fingerprint card. Pay fee. **Fees:** $10 registration fee.

Washington

1187

Announcer/Timekeeper (Professional Boxing & Wrestling)
Boxing Commission
414 12th Ave., PH-21
Olympia, WA 98504-8321
Phone: (206)753-3713

Credential Type: Announcer/Timekeeper License. **Duration of License:** One year. **Requirements:** Submit application with current photo. **Fees:** No fee.

1188

Authorized Agent (Racetrack)
Washington Horse Racing Commission
3700 Martin Way, Ste. 101
Olympia, WA 98506
Phone: (206)459-6462

Credential Type: License Registration. **Duration of License:** One year. **Requirements:** Submit application and fingerprint card. Pay fee. **Fees:** $5 registration fee. $5 duplicate license fee.

1189

Inspector (Professional Boxing/Wrestling)
Professional Athletic Commission
2626 12th Court, GT-17
Olympia, WA 98504-8321
Phone: (206)753-3713

Credential Type: Inspector License. **Duration of License:** One year. **Requirements:** Submit application with current photo. **Fees:** No fee.

1190

Jockey Agent (Racetrack)
Washington Horse Racing Commission
3700 Martin Way, Ste. 101
Olympia, WA 98506
Phone: (206)459-6462

Credential Type: License Registration. **Duration of License:** One year. **Requirements:** Submit application and fingerprint card. Pay fee. **Fees:** $5 registration fee. $5 duplicate license fee.

1191

Jockey (Racetrack)
Washington Horse Racing Commission
3700 Martin Way, Ste. 101
Olympia, WA 98506
Phone: (206)459-6462

Credential Type: License Registration. **Duration of License:** One year. **Requirements:** Submit application and fingerprint card. Pay fee. **Fees:** $15 registration fee. $5 duplicate license fee.

1192

Judge (Professional Boxing/Wrestling)
Professional Athletic Commission
2626 12th Court, GT-17
Olympia, WA 98504-8321
Phone: (206)753-3713

Credential Type: Judge License. **Duration of License:** One year. **Requirements:** Submit application with current photo. **Fees:** No fee.

1193

Manager (Professional Boxing/Wrestling)
Professional Athletic Commission
2626 12th Court, GT-17
Olympia, WA 98504-8321
Phone: (206)753-3713

Credential Type: Manager License. **Duration of License:** One year. **Requirements:** Submit application with current photo. **Fees:** $40 license fee.

1194

Professional Boxer
Boxing Commission
2626 12th Court SW, GT-17
Olympia, WA 98504-8321
Phone: (206)753-3713

Credential Type: Professional Boxer License. **Duration of License:** One year. **Requirements:** Submit application with fee and current photos. Must have a complete physical. **Fees:** $15 license fee.

Washington

1195

Professional Boxing Referee
Professional Athletic Commission
2626 12th Court SW, GT-17
Olympia, WA 98504-8321
Phone: (206)753-3713

Credential Type: Professional Boxing Referee License. **Duration of License:** One year. **Requirements:** Submit application, current photos, and fee. Requires a physical examination. **Fees:** $15 license fee.

1196

Professional Wrestler
Boxing Commission
2626 12th Court SW, GT-17
Olympia, WA 98504-8321
Phone: (206)753-3713

Credential Type: Professional Wrestler License. **Duration of License:** One year. **Requirements:** Submit application with fee and current photos. Must have a complete physical. **Fees:** $15 license fee.

1197

Second (Professional Boxing/ Wrestling)
Professional Athletic Commission
2626 12th Court SW, GT-17
Olympia, WA 98504-8321
Phone: (206)753-3713

Credential Type: Second License. **Duration of License:** One year. **Requirements:** Submit application, current photos, and fee. **Fees:** $15 license fee.

Wisconsin

1198

Assistant Racing Secretary (Racetrack)
Wisconsin Racing Board
PO Box 7975
Madison, WI 53707-7975
Phone: (608)267-3291

Credential Type: License Registration. **Requirements:** Submit application and two sets of fingerprint cards. Pay fee. **Fees:** $20 registration fee. $20 duplicate license.

1199

Association Steward (Racetrack)
Wisconsin Racing Board
PO Box 7975
Madison, WI 53707-7975
Phone: (608)267-3291

Credential Type: License Registration. **Requirements:** Submit application and two sets of fingerprint cards. Pay fee. **Fees:** $50 registration fee. $20 duplicate license.

1200

Authorized Agent (Dog Racing)
Wisconsin Racing Board
PO Box 7975
Madison, WI 53707-7975
Phone: (608)267-3291

Credential Type: License Registration. **Requirements:** Submit application and two sets of fingerprint cards. Pay fee. **Fees:** $25 registration fee. $20 duplicate license.

1201

Paddock Judge (Racetrack)
Wisconsin Racing Board
PO Box 7975
Madison, WI 53707-7975
Phone: (608)267-3291

Credential Type: License Registration. **Requirements:** Submit application and two sets of fingerprint cards. Pay fee. **Fees:** $50 registration fee. $20 duplicate license.

1202

Racing Secretary (Racetrack)
Wisconsin Racing Board
PO Box 7975
Madison, WI 53707-7975
Phone: (608)267-3291

Credential Type: License Registration. **Requirements:** Submit application and two sets of fingerprint cards. Pay fee. **Fees:** $50 registration fee. $20 duplicate license.

1203

Timer (Racetrack)
Wisconsin Racing Board
PO Box 7975
Madison, WI 53707-7975
Phone: (608)267-3291

Credential Type: License Registration. **Requirements:** Submit application and two sets of fingerprint cards. Pay fee. **Fees:** $20 registration fee. $20 duplicate license.

Wyoming

1204

Agent (Racetrack)
Wyoming State Pari-Mutuel Commission
Barrett Bldg., 3rd Fl.
Cheyenne, WY 82002
Phone: (307)777-5887

Credential Type: License Registration. **Requirements:** Submit application and fingerprint card. Pay fee. **Fees:** $20 registration fee. $10 duplicate license.

1205

Assistant Starter (Racetrack)
Wyoming State Pari-Mutuel Commission
Barrett Bldg., 3rd Fl.
Cheyenne, WY 82002
Phone: (307)777-5887

Credential Type: License Registration. **Requirements:** Submit application and fingerprint card. Pay fee. **Fees:** $10 registration fee. $10 duplicate license.

1206

Jockey/Apprentice Jockey (Racetrack)
Wyoming State Pari-Mutuel Commission
Barrett Bldg., 3rd Fl.
Cheyenne, WY 82002
Phone: (307)777-5887

Credential Type: License Registration. **Requirements:** Submit application and fingerprint card. Pay fee. **Fees:** $20 registration fee. $10 duplicate license.

1207

Racing Secretary (Racetrack)
Wyoming State Pari-Mutuel Commission
Barrett Bldg., 3rd Fl.
Cheyenne, WY 82002
Phone: (307)777-5887

Credential Type: License Registration. **Requirements:** Submit application and fingerprint card. Pay fee. **Fees:** $20 registration fee. $10 duplicate license.

Auctioneers

The following states grant licenses in this occupational category as of the date of publication:

Alabama	Florida	Kentucky	Nebraska	Ohio	South Dakota	Washington
Arkansas	Georgia	Louisiana	New Hampshire	Pennsylvania	Tennessee	
District of Columbia	Illinois	Maine	North Carolina	Rhode Island	Texas	
	Indiana	Massachusetts	North Dakota	South Carolina	Vermont	

Alabama

1208

Auctioneer
Alabama State Board of Auctioneers
Downtown Plaza, Ste. 109
Cullman, AL 35055
Phone: (205)739-0548

Credential Type: Yes. **Requirements:** 18 years of age. Must be a graduate of an approved auctioneering school and must complete a one-year apprenticeship. **Examination:** Yes. **Reciprocity:** Yes. **Fees:** $70 renewal fee. $60 auctioneer fee. $50 exam fee.

Arkansas

1209

Auctioneer
Arkansas Auctioneer Licensing Board
221 West Second, Ste. 228
Little Rock, AR 72201
Phone: (501)375-3858

Credential Type: License. **Duration of License:** One year. **Requirements:** 18 years of age. Citizen of the US. Never been convicted of a crime of moral turpitude or a felony. **Examination:** Yes. **Fees:** $50 Examination. $50 License. $50 Renewal. $2,000 Cash or Surety Bond.

District of Columbia

1210

Auctioneer
License and Certification Div.
Occupational and Professional Licensure Administration
Consumer and Regulatory Affairs Dept.
PO Box 37200
Washington, DC 20013-7200
Phone: (202)727-7823
Phone: (202)727-7480

Alternate Information: 614 H St., NW, Washington, DC 20001.

Credential Type: License. **Requirements:** Contact licensing body for application information.

Florida

1211

Auctioneer
Auctioneers Board
Dept. of Professional Regulation
1940 N. Monroe St.
Tallahassee, FL 32399-0750
Phone: (904)488-5189

Credential Type: Auctioneer License. **Duration of License:** Two years. **Requirements:** Submit application and pay fees. Pass examination. **Examination:** 150-question Auctioneer Examination. **Reciprocity:** Yes. **Fees:** $300 exam fee. $300 license fee. $375 license by reciprocity fee.

1212

Auctioneer Apprentice
Auctioneers Board
Dept. of Professional Regulation
1940 N. Monroe St.
Tallahassee, FL 32399-0750
Phone: (904)488-5189

Credential Type: Auctioneer License. **Duration of License:** Two years. **Requirements:** Submit application and pay fees. **Fees:** $300 apprentice license fee.

Georgia

1213

Apprentice Auctioneer
Georgia Auctioneers Commission
Businesses and Occupations Section
Professional Examining Boards
166 Pryor St., SW
Atlanta, GA 30303
Phone: (404)656-2282

Credential Type: Auctioneer Apprentice License. **Duration of License:** Two years. **Requirements:** After passing apprentice examination, submit name of sponsor and license fee. **Examination:** Apprentice Examination, written. **Reciprocity:** Yes. **Fees:** $50 application/exam fee. $75 license fee. $150 Auctioneers Recovery Fund fee.

Credential Type: Non-resident Apprentice License. **Requirements:** Submit application, letter of certification of licensure in home state, and notarized letter from sponsoring auctioneer. Sponsoring auctioneer must be licensed in Georgia. **Examination:** Apprentice Examination, written. **Fees:** $50 application/exam fee. $75 license fee. $150 Auctioneers Recovery Fund fee.

147

Georgia 1214

1214

Auctioneer
Georgia Auctioneers Commission
Businesses and Occupations Section
Professional Examining Boards
166 Pryor St., SW
Atlanta, GA 30303
Phone: (404)656-2282

Credential Type: Auctioneer License. **Duration of License:** Two years. **Requirements:** Serve an apprenticeship of at least 12 months under the supervision of a sponsoring auctioneer in at least 10 auctions exclusive of charity auctions; or graduate from an approved auctioneer school and serve an apprenticeship of at least six months under the supervision of a sponsoring auctioneer. **Examination:** Auctioneer Examination, written. **Reciprocity:** Yes. **Fees:** $50 application/exam fee. $150 license fee. $150 Auctioneers Recovery Fund fee.

Credential Type: Non-resident Auctioneer License. **Duration of License:** Two years. **Requirements:** Submit application, letter of certification of licensure in home state, escrow account information, and designation of agent for the service of process. **Fees:** $50 application/exam fee. $150 license fee. $150 Auctioneers Recovery Fund fee.

Illinois

1215

Vehicle Auctioneer
Secretary of State
Centennial Bldg., Rm. 008
Springfield, IL 62756
Phone: (217)782-7817

Credential Type: Vehicle Auctioneer License. **Duration of License:** One year. **Requirements:** Submit application and pay fee. Requires ID cards. **Reciprocity:** No. **Fees:** $50 initial license fee. $50 renewal fee. **Governing Statute:** Illinois Vehicle Code 95 1/2 5-701.

Indiana

1216

Auctioneer
Licensing Division
Professional Licensing Agency
1021 State Office Bldg.
100 N. Senate Ave.
Indianapolis, IN 46204
Phone: (317)232-5955

Credential Type: License. **Requirements:** Contact licensing body for application information.

Kentucky

1217

Auctioneer
Kentucky Board of Auctioneers
400 Sherburn Ln., Ste. 343
Louisville, KY 40207
Phone: (502)588-4453

Credential Type: Apprentice License. **Duration of License:** One year. **Requirements:** 18 years of age. **Examination:** Yes. **Fees:** $75 exam fee. $50 license fee. $30 Auctioneer's Education Research and Recovery Fund fee. $50 renewal fee.

Credential Type: Auctioneer License. **Duration of License:** One year. **Requirements:** 18 years of age. High school diploma or equivalent. Completion of two-year internship. Must have been the bid-caller in at least ten sales during apprenticeship. **Examination:** Yes. **Fees:** $100 exam fee. $80 license fee. $75 renewal fee.

Credential Type: Auction House Operator License. **Duration of License:** One year. **Requirements:** 18 years of age. Must be the owner/operator of an auction house at a fixed site. **Examination:** Yes. **Fees:** $100 exam fee. $75 renewal fee.

Louisiana

1218

Auctioneer
Louisiana Auctioneers Licensing Board
8017 Jefferson Hwy., Ste. B-3
Baton Rouge, LA 70809
Phone: (504)925-3921

Credential Type: License. **Duration of License:** One year. **Requirements:** Completion of an auctioneers school or apprenticeship. **Examination:** Written and oral. **Reciprocity:** Out-of-state auctioneers may be licensed in Louisiana if their home state will extend the same right to Louisiana auctioneers. **Fees:** $75 exam fee. $75 application fee. $150 license fee. $150 renewal fee. $10,000 bond.

Maine

1219

Auctioneer
Board of Licensing of Auctioneers
Dept. of Professional and Financial Regulation
Div. of Licensing and Enforcement
State House Station 35
Augusta, ME 04333
Phone: (207)582-8723

Credential Type: License. **Duration of License:** Two years. **Requirements:** Submit application and pay fee. **Fees:** $50 resident license fee. $100 non-resident license fee. **Governing Statute:** 32 M.S.R.A. Chap. 5-A.

Massachusetts

1220

Auctioneer
Div. of Standards
One Ashburton Pl.
Boston, MA 02108
Phone: (617)727-3480

Credential Type: Auctioneer License. **Duration of License:** One year. **Requirements:** Submit application and pay fee. **Reciprocity:** Yes. **Fees:** $100 license fee.

Nebraska

1221

Auctioneer
Lincoln City Clerk's Office
555 S. 10th St.
Lincoln, NE 68508
Phone: (402)471-7437

Credential Type: License. **Duration of License:** Three or 12 months. **Fees:** $50 12 month license fee. $15 three month license fee. $50 12 month renewal fee. $15 three month renewal fee.

New Hampshire

1222

Auctioneer
New Hampshire Board of Auctioneers
Secretary of State's Office
State House, Rm. 204
Concord, NH 03301
Phone: (603)271-3242

Credential Type: Auctioneer License. **Requirements:** U.S. citizen. Must submit affidavit of competency. $10,000 bond required. **Examination:** Written examination. **Reciprocity:** No. **Fees:** $100 resident license fee. $150 non-resident license fee.

North Carolina

1223

Auctioneer
North Carolina Auctioneer Licensing Board
3509 Haworth Dr.
Raleigh, NC 27609
Phone: (919)733-2182

Credential Type: License. **Duration of License:** One year. **Requirements:** 18 years of age. Graduation from an approved school of auctioneering or completion of a two-year apprenticeship and 100 hours of practical auctioneering experience. **Examination:** Written. **Fees:** $75 license fee. $25 application and exam fee. $50 recovery fund fee. $75 renewal fee.

North Dakota

1224

Auctioneer
Public Service Commission
State Capitol, 12th Fl.
Bismarck, ND 58505

Credential Type: Auctioneer's License. **Duration of License:** One year. **Requirements:** Be at least 18 years of age. Complete an approved course of study related to auctioneering. Post $3000 surety bond. **Fees:** $35 license fee. $35 renewal fee. **Governing Statute:** North Dakota Century Code, Chap. 51-05.

Credential Type: Clerk's License. **Duration of License:** One year. **Requirements:** Be at least 18 years of age. Complete an approved course of study related to auctioneering. Post $10,000 surety bond. **Fees:** $35 license fee. $35 renewal fee. **Governing Statute:** North Dakota Century Code, Chap. 51-05.

Ohio

1225

Auctioneer
Licensing Div.
Commerce Dept.
77 S. High St., 23rd Fl.
Columbus, OH 43266-0544
Phone: (614)466-4130

Credential Type: Auctioneer License. **Requirements:** Complete an apprenticeship of one year. Attend an approved school of auctioneering. Have bid calling experience at 12 or more sales under the direct supervision of a sponsoring auctioneer. **Examination:** Yes. **Fees:** $25 application and exam fee. $100 license fee. $100 renewal fee.

Credential Type: Apprentice Auctioneer License. **Authorization:** May call auctions only under the supervision of the licensed sponsor. **Requirements:** Must be sponsored by a currently licensed auctioneer. Must post surety bond of $10,000. **Fees:** $15 application and exam fee. $100 license fee. $100 renewal fee.

Pennsylvania

1226

Auctioneer
State Board of Auctioneer Examiners
Bureau of Professional and Occupational Affairs
Dept. of State
Transportation and Safety Bldg., 6th Fl.
Harrisburg, PA 17120
Phone: (717)787-8503

Credential Type: Auctioneer License. **Duration of License:** Two years. **Requirements:** Good reputation for honesty, truthfulness, integrity and competence to transact business in a manner to safeguard the interest of the public. Must complete twenty credit hours of instruction (a credit hour of instruction is defined as 15 standard hours of instruction) at a board-approved school that covers the following areas of study: audience communication; procurement of merchandise for auction; appraisal; auction law; preparation for auction; and conducting an auction. Or, in lieu of the education requirement, an applicant may serve an apprenticeship as a licensed apprentice auctioneer for a period of at least two years in the employ of a qualified auctioneer and participate, for compensation, in at least 30 auctions. **Examination:** State examination. **Reciprocity:** Reciprocity may be granted to license holders from other states with board approval.

Credential Type: Apprentice Auctioneer License. **Duration of License:** Two years. **Requirements:** Must be sponsored and employed for compensation by a licensed auctioneer who employees no more than one other apprentice. **Reciprocity:** Reciprocity may be granted to license holders from other states with board approval.

1227

Real Estate Auctioneer
Real Estate Commission
Transportation and Safety Bldg., Rm. 611
PO Box 2649
Harrisburg, PA 17105-2649
Phone: (717)783-3658

Credential Type: Real Estate Auctioneer License. **Requirements:** Contact licensing body for application information.

Rhode Island

1228

Auctioneer
Div. of Licensing and Consumer Protection
Rhode Island Dept. of Business Regulation
233 Richmond St.
Providence, RI 02903
Phone: (401)277-3857

Credential Type: Apprentice Auctioneer License. **Duration of License:** Three years. **Requirements:** At least 16 years of age. Foreign born must show proof of legal entry into the U.S. Post $2,000 bond. Submit application and pay fees. **Reciprocity:** Yes. **Fees:** $10 application fee. $60 apprentice license fee.

Credential Type: Auctioneer License. **Duration of License:** Three years. **Requirements:** At least 18 years of age. Foreign born must show proof of legal entry into the U.S. Post $2,000 bond. Must have at least six months experience under supervision of a licensed auctioneer or three months experience after graduating from an approved school of auctioneering. Pass examination. **Examination:** Written examination. **Reciprocity:** Yes. **Fees:** $10 application fee. $105 resident license fee. $225 nonresident license fee. $15 examination fee.

Rhode Island

1229

Drug Auctioneer
State Board of Pharmacy
Div. of Drug Control
Rhode Island Dept. of Health
3 Capitol Hill
Providence, RI 02908
Phone: (401)277-2837

Credential Type: Drug Auctioneer License. **Duration of License:** New license must be obtained for each auction. **Requirements:** Good moral character. Foreign born must show proof of legal entry into the U.S. Must be familiar with pharmaceutics. No addiction to alcohol or controlled substances. No felony convictions or violations of any drug statutes. **Reciprocity:** No. **Fees:** $75 license fee.

South Carolina

1230

Auctioneer
South Carolina State Auctioneers Commission
PO Box 807
Columbia, SC 29202
Phone: (803)734-3193

Credential Type: Auctioneer License. **Requirements:** 18 years of age. State resident. Two years as an apprentice auctioneer, or completion of 80 hours of instruction in auctioneering at an approved institution. **Examination:** Yes. **Fees:** $150 license fee.

Credential Type: Apprentice Auctioneer License. **Fees:** $150 license fee.

South Dakota

1231

Real Estate Auctioneer
South Dakota Real Estate Commission
PO Box 490
Pierre, SD 57501-0490
Phone: (605)773-3600
Phone: (605)773-3150

Credential Type: Real Estate Auctioneer License. **Duration of License:** Two years. **Requirements:** Submit application and pay fees. **Examination:** State-administered auctioneer's examination. **Exemptions:** Real estate brokers do not need an auctioneer's license. **Fees:** $100 application and license fee. $80 renewal fee.

Tennessee

1232

Auctioneer
Auctioneer Commission
500 James Robertson Pky.
Nashville, TN 37243-1141
Phone: (615)292-6619

Credential Type: License. **Duration of License:** Two years. **Requirements:** Two year apprenticeship. 80 hours education, prior to apprentice exam. 30 hours prior to auctioneers exam. **Examination:** Yes. **Reciprocity:** Yes. **Fees:** $25 Examination. $100 Application (apprentice), $150 Application (auctioneer). $100 Renewal.

Texas

1233

Auctioneer
Texas Dept. of Licensing and Regulation
PO Box 12157
Austin, TX 78711
Phone: (512)463-5522

Credential Type: License. **Duration of License:** One year. **Requirements:** U.S. citizen or legal alien. 18 years of age. Sales tax number or exemption. Knowledge of the auction business and laws pertaining to it; or apprenticeship with a licensed auctioneer for one year and participation in at least five auctions. **Examination:** Written or oral. **Fees:** $25 exam fee. $100 auctioneer license. $100 renewal fee. **Governing Statute:** VACS 8700, 16 TAC 67.1.

Vermont

1234

Auctioneer
Secretary of State
Pavilion Office Bldg.
Montpelier, VT 05602
Phone: (802)828-2363

Credential Type: License. **Duration of License:** Two years. **Requirements:** Filing a surety bond. **Examination:** No. **Reciprocity:** No. **Fees:** $25 (resident); $50 (non-resident) License. $25 (resident); $50 (non-resident) Renewal. **Governing Statute:** Title 32, VSA Sections 7601-7606.

Washington

1235

Auctioneer
Dept. of Licensing
Professional Licensing Services
2424 Bristol Court SW
Olympia, WA 98504
Phone: (206)753-2803

Credential Type: Auctioneer License. **Duration of License:** One year. **Requirements:** At least 18 years of age. Post a $25,000 security bond or other security based on value of sales. (Company bond may cover auctioneers who are sole proprietors or partners.) Must have a Washington State Revenue Tax Number. Submit financial certification affidavit. **Fees:** $110 initial license fee. $110 renewal fee.

Automotive Body Repairers and Mechanics

The following states grant licenses in this occupational category as of the date of publication: District of Columbia, Georgia, Hawaii, Illinois, Michigan, North Carolina, Washington.

District of Columbia

1236

Master Mechanic
License and Certification Div.
Occupational and Professional Licensure Administration
Consumer and Regulatory Affairs Dept.
PO Box 37200
Washington, DC 20013-7200
Phone: (202)727-7823
Phone: (202)727-7480

Alternate Information: 614 H St., NW, Washington, DC 20001

Credential Type: Master Mechanic License. **Requirements:** Contact licensing body for application information.

Georgia

1237

Motor Vehicle Dismantler
State Board of Registration for Used Motor Vehicle Dismantlers, Rebuilders, and Salvage Dealers
Businesses and Occupations Section
Professional Examining Boards
166 Pryor St., SW
Atlanta, GA 30303
Phone: (404)656-3900

Credential Type: Motor Vehicle Dismantler License. **Requirements:** Submit application and pay fees. Post a $10,000 surety bond and have liability insurance in the amount of $50/100/25 or single limits of $125,000. Must have a state sales tax number and fixed place of business. **Fees:** $175 application fee.

1238

Rebuilder
State Board of Registration for Used Motor Vehicle Dismantlers, Rebuilders, and Salvage Dealers
Businesses and Occupations Section
Professional Examining Boards
166 Pryor St., SW
Atlanta, GA 30303
Phone: (404)656-2282

Credential Type: License. **Requirements:** Contact licensing body for application information.

Hawaii

1239

Automobile Mechanic
Hawaii Motor Vehicle Repair Industry Board
1010 Richards St.
PO Box 3469 (ZIP 96801)
Honolulu, HI 96813
Phone: (808)548-7452

Credential Type: License. **Duration of License:** Two years. **Requirements:** Two or more years of full-time, "hands-on" working experience as an automotive technician. One year of experience may be substituted with formal training. Completion of a three- or four-year apprenticeship program may satisfy the two-year working requirement. **Examination:** ASE exam. **Fees:** $10 application fee. $40 license fee. $15 exam fee per category. $20 recertification exam fee. $20 registration fee. $40 biennial license fee. $20—$40 Compliance Resolution Fund fee.

Illinois

1240

Rebuilder of Salvage Vehicles
Secretary of State
Centennial Bldg., Rm. 008
Springfield, IL 62756
Phone: (217)782-7817

Credential Type: Rebuilder License. **Duration of License:** One year. **Authorization:** Allows holder to restore vehicles for which a salvage certificate has been issued. **Requirements:** Submit application and pay fees. Requires ID card. **Reciprocity:** No. **Fees:** $50 initial license fee. $50 renewal fee. $2 ID card fee. **Governing Statute:** Illinois Vehicle Code 95 1/2 5-301.

1241

Vehicle Repairer
Secretary of State
Centennial Bldg., Rm. 008
Springfield, IL 62756
Phone: (217)782-7817

Credential Type: Repairer License. **Duration of License:** One year. **Authorization:** Allows holder to restore and repair vehicles other than those for which a salvage certificate have been issued. **Requirements:** Submit application and pay fee. Requires ID card. **Reciprocity:** No. **Fees:** $50 initial license fee. $50 renewal fee. $2 ID card fee. **Governing Statute:** Illinois Vehicle Code 95 1/2 5-301.

Michigan

1242

Automotive Mechanic
Bureau of Automotive Regulation
Repair Facility Div.
Dept. of State
208 N. Capitol Ave.
Lansing, MI 48918
Phone: (517)322-1460

Credential Type: Master Mechanic Certification. **Duration of License:** One year. **Requirements:** Must pass all 17 motor vehicle repair category tests. **Examination:** 17 separate written motor vehicle repair category tests. **Fees:** $6 per test initial exam fee. $25 initial certificate fee. $20 renewal fee. $25 trainee permit fee. **Governing Statute:** Motor Vehicle Service and Repair Act, Act 300 of 1974, as amended.

Credential Type: Specialty Mechanic Certification. **Duration of License:** One year. **Authorization:** Specialty certification is issued for each category of test passed. **Requirements:** Pass at least one of the 17 motor vehicle repair category tests. **Examination:** Choose from 17 separate written motor vehicle repair category tests. **Fees:** $6 per test initial exam fee. $25 initial certificate fee. $20 renewal fee. $25 trainee permit fee. **Governing Statute:** Motor Vehicle Service and Repair Act, Act 300 of 1974, as amended.

North Carolina

1243

Safety Inspection Mechanic
Dept. of Transportation
Div. of Motor Vehicles
1100 New Bern Ave.
Raleigh, NC 27697
Phone: (919)733-0133

Credential Type: License. **Duration of License:** Permanent. **Requirements:** 16 years of age. Valid driver's license. Completion of one four-hour course from an accredited school. **Examination:** Written and practical.

Washington

1244

Motor Vehicle Wrecker
Dept. of Licensing
Vehicle Services - Dealers
Highways-Licenses Bldg., PB-01
Olympia, WA 98504-8001
Phone: (206)753-6954

Credential Type: Motor Vehicle Wrecker License. **Duration of License:** One year. **Requirements:** Submit to background investigation and inspection of facility. Post a $1,000 bond. Submit Environmental Impact Statement and Legal History. Additional locations must be licensed separately. **Fees:** $25 initial license fee. $10 renewal fee. $6 original plates fee. $3 additional plates fee. $2 renewable tabs fee. $5 fee to renew first plate. $2.50 fee to renew additional plates.

Bail Bond Occupations

The following states grant licenses in this occupational category as of the date of publication: Alaska, Arizona, Arkansas, California, Colorado, Maryland, Minnesota, New Hampshire, New York, North Carolina, Oklahoma, Rhode Island.

Alaska

1245

Bail Bond Person
Div. of Insurance
Dept. of Commerce and Economic Development
State Office Bldg., 9th Fl.
33 Willoughby Ave.
PO Box 110805
Juneau, AK 99811-0805
Phone: (907)465-2579
Phone: (907)465-2575
Phone: (907)465-2578

Credential Type: Bail Bond Limited License. **Duration of License:** Two years. **Requirements:** Contact licensing body for application information. **Fees:** $50 resident fee. **Governing Statute:** Alaska Statutes, Title 21.

Arizona

1246

Bail Bond Agent
Dept. of Insurance
Licensing Section
Abacus Towers 1100
3030 N. 3rd St.
Phoenix, AZ 85012
Phone: (602)255-5605

Credential Type: Bail Bond Agent License. **Duration of License:** Two years. **Requirements:** Pass security clearance with the Arizona Department of Public Safety and the Federal Bureau of Investigation. Pass appropriate exam. Post $10,000 surety bond. **Examination:** Bail Bond Agent Exam, Series 13-35. **Fees:** $53 exam fee. $35.65 license fee.

Arkansas

1247

Bail Bondsman
Arkansas Insurance Department
University Tower Bldg., Ste. 400
12th and University
Little Rock, AR 72204
Phone: (501)371-1325

Credential Type: License. **Duration of License:** One year. **Requirements:** Three character references. Must be fingerprinted. Never convicted of a felony or any offense involving moral turpitude. **Examination:** Yes. **Fees:** $25 for written examination. $5,000 Bond fee. $500 License. $500 Renewal.

California

1248

Bail Bond Agent
Dept. of Insurance
700 L St.
Sacramento, CA 95814
Phone: (916)322-3555
Phone: (415)557-1126

Credential Type: Bail Bond Agent License. **Duration of License:** One year. **Requirements:** Contact licensing body for application information. Must be a California resident. **Fees:** $190 license fee. $56 renewal fee.

1249

Bail Bond Solicitor
Dept. of Insurance
700 L St.
Sacramento, CA 95814
Phone: (916)322-3555
Phone: (415)557-1126

Credential Type: Bail Bond Solicitor License. **Duration of License:** One year. **Requirements:** Contact licensing body for application information. Must be a California resident. **Fees:** $190 license fee. $56 renewal fee.

Colorado

1250

Bailbondsman
Dept. of Regulatory Agencies
Div. of Insurance
303 W. Colfax, Ste. 500
Denver, CO 80204
Phone: (303)866-6248

Credential Type: Professional license. **Duration of License:** Two years. **Requirements:** Pass bail bond test with ASI. **Examination:** Bail bond test. **Fees:** $67 test fee. $19 license fee. $19 appointment fee.

Maryland

1251

Bail Bondsman
Insurance Div.
Dept. of Licensing and Regulation
501 St. Paul Pl.
Baltimore, MD 21202-2272
Phone: (410)333-4057

Credential Type: License. **Requirements:** Contact licensing body for application information.

Minnesota

1252

Bail Bond Agent
Dept. of Commerce
Licensing Unit
133 E. 7th St.
St. Paul, MN 55101
Phone: (612)296-6319

Credential Type: Bail Bond License. **Duration of License:** One year. **Requirements:** Submit application and pay fee. Renewal requires 20 hours of continuing education per year. **Fees:** $25 license fee. $25 renewal fee.

New Hampshire

1253

Professional Bail Bondsman
Bureau of Securities Regulation
Dept. of State
State House, Rm. 204
Concord, NH 03301
Phone: (603)271-1463
Fax: (603)224-1427

Credential Type: Professional Bail Bondsman License. **Duration of License:** One year. **Requirements:** Must hold a license as a Property and Casualty Insurance Agent. **Examination:** Written examination. **Reciprocity:** No. **Fees:** $400 application and examination fee. $100 annual filing fee (per county).

New York

1254

Bail Bond Agent
New York State Insurance Dept.
Licensing Unit
Agency Bldg. One
Empire State Plaza
Albany, NY 12257
Phone: (518)474-7159

Credential Type: License. **Duration of License:** One year. **Requirements:** Good perceptual skill in evaluating people. **Examination:** Essay. **Fees:** $20 exam fee. $25 license fee. $25 renewal fee. **Governing Statute:** Article 68, Section 6801-6802 of the Insurance Law.

North Carolina

1255

Bail Bond Agent
Dept. of Insurance
Div. of Special Services
430 N. Salisbury St.
Raleigh, NC 27611
Phone: (919)733-2200

Credential Type: License. **Duration of License:** One year. **Requirements:** Applicants must be familiar with North Carolina General Statute 85C in order to successfully pass the examination. 18 years of age. No felony convictions. $5,000 minimum bail bond security. **Examination:** Written. **Fees:** $60 license fee. $15 exam fee. $30 renewal fee.

1256

Bail Bond Runner
Dept. of Insurance
Div. of Special Services
430 N. Salisbury St.
Raleigh, NC 27611
Phone: (919)733-2200

Credential Type: License. **Duration of License:** One year. **Requirements:** 18 years of age. No felony convictions. **Examination:** Written. **Fees:** $20 license fee. $10 exam fee. $10 renewal fee.

Oklahoma

1257

Bail Bondsman
State of Oklahoma Insurance Commission
Bailbond Forfeitures and Licensing
1901 N. Walnut
Oklahoma City, OK 73105
Phone: (405)521-2828

Credential Type: License. **Duration of License:** One year. **Requirements:** 20 hours of pre-license education sponsored by the Oklahoma Bondsman Association 10 hours of continuing education each year. U.S. citizenship. 21 years of age. State resident for one year. **Examination:** Bail Bond License Examination. **Fees:** $450 application fee. $100 exam fee. $100 renewal fee.

Rhode Island

1258

Professional Bondsman
Office of Presiding Justice of Superior Court
Rhode Island Superior Court
250 Benefit St.
Providence, RI 02903
Phone: (401)277-3212

Credential Type: Professional Bondsman License. **Duration of License:** One year. **Requirements:** Show evidence of ability to pledge real estate in exchange for bail or surety. Submit application. **Reciprocity:** No. **Fees:** No fee.

Barbers and Cosmetologists

The following states grant licenses in this occupational category as of the date of publication:

Alabama	District of	Iowa	Minnesota	New Mexico	Rhode Island	Washington
Alaska	Columbia	Kansas	Mississippi	New York	South Carolina	West Virginia
Arizona	Florida	Kentucky	Missouri	North Carolina	South Dakota	Wisconsin
Arkansas	Georgia	Louisiana	Montana	North Dakota	Tennessee	Wyoming
California	Hawaii	Maine	Nebraska	Ohio	Texas	
Colorado	Idaho	Maryland	Nevada	Oklahoma	Utah	
Connecticut	Illinois	Massachusetts	New Hampshire	Oregon	Vermont	
Delaware	Indiana	Michigan	New Jersey	Pennsylvania	Virginia	

Alabama

1259

Cosmetologist

Alabama Board of Cosmetology
Altus Bank Bldg., Ste. 801
100 Commerce St.
Montgomery, AL 36130
Phone: (205)242-5613
Phone: (205)242-5614

Credential Type: License. **Duration of License:** Two years. **Requirements:** 16 years of age. Must submit certification of health. Must have equivalent to the completion of 10 grades in school. Must complete course of cosmetology of not less than 1200 credit hours in a school of cosmetology, or serve an apprenticeship in a beauty shop of not less than 3000 hours over at least one year. **Examination:** Written and practical examinations. **Fees:** Contact board for fees.

1260

Cosmetology Instructor

Alabama Board of Cosmetology
Altus Bank Bldg., Ste. 801
100 Commerce St.
Montgomery, AL 36130
Phone: (205)242-5613
Phone: (205)242-5614

Credential Type: License. **Duration of License:** Two years. **Requirements:** Must hold a license in cosmetology. Must complete a teacher's training course. Must have educational equivalent to the completion of 12 grades in school. **Examination:** Written and practical examinations. **Fees:** $40 examination fee. $30 license fee. $15 renewal fee.

Alaska

1261

Barber

Dept. of Commerce and Economic Development
Div. of Occupational Licensing
Board of Barbers and Hairdressers
PO Box D-LIC
Juneau, AK 99811-0800
Phone: (907)465-2541
Fax: (907)465-2974

Credential Type: Barber License by Examination. **Duration of License:** Two years. **Requirements:** 1,650 hours of course work in a school approved by the board; or 2,000 hours of training in an apprenticeship program; or a board-approved combination of course work and apprenticeship. **Examination:** State-administered practical examination. Applicant must furnish tools and supplies for examination and secure his or her own model. **Fees:** $30 application fee. $100 license fee. $25 examination fee. **Governing Statute:** Alaska Statutes 08.13. Professional Regulations 12 AAC 09.

Credential Type: Barber License by Credentials. **Duration of License:** Two years. **Requirements:** Hold a current license to practice barbering issued by another state. Training and work experience equivalent to 1,650 hours of course work in a school approved by the board; or 2,000 hours of training in an apprenticeship program; or at least one year full-time work experience as a licensed barber averaging no less than 32 hours per week, and a minimum of 1,000 hours of training in an approved school or an apprenticeship program approved by the board or by another licensing jurisdiction. **Fees:** $30 application fee. $100 license fee. **Governing Statute:** Alaska Statutes 08.13. Professional Regulations 12 AAC 09.

Credential Type: Temporary Permit. **Duration of License:** Six months. **Requirements:** Hold a current valid license from a board of barbering in another state. Apply for a permanent license. **Fees:** $30 application fee. $20 temporary permit fee. **Governing Statute:** Alaska Statutes 08.13. Professional Regulations 12 AAC 09.

1262

Barber Instructor

Dept. of Commerce and Economic Development
Div. of Occupational Licensing
Board of Barbers and Hairdressers
PO Box D-LIC
Juneau, AK 99811-0800
Phone: (907)465-2541
Fax: (907)465-2974

Credential Type: Barber Instructor License by Examination. **Duration of License:** Two years. **Requirements:** Hold a current barber practitioner license. Have at least three years of practice as a licensed barber in Alaska or in another licensing jurisdiction; or one year of practice as a licensed barber in Alaska or in another licensing jurisdiction followed by 600 hours of student instructor training in a school approved by the board or approved by another licensing jurisdiction. **Examination:** State-administered practical examination. Applicant must furnish tools and supplies for examination and secure his or her own model. **Fees:** $30 application fee. $100 license fee. $25 examination fee. **Governing Statute:** Alaska Statutes 08.13. Professional Regulations 12 AAC 09.

Credential Type: Barber License by Credentials. **Duration of License:** Two years. **Requirements:** Hold a current barber instructor license issued by another licensing jurisdiction. Training and work experience

Alaska 1263

Barber Instructor, continued

equivalent to at least three years of practice as a licensed barber in Alaska or in another licensing jurisdiction; or one year of practice as a licensed barber in Alaska or in another licensing jurisdiction followed by 600 hours of student instructor training in a school approved by the board or approved by another licensing jurisdiction. **Fees:** $30 application fee. $100 license fee. **Governing Statute:** Alaska Statutes 08.13. Professional Regulations 12 AAC 09.

Credential Type: Temporary Permit. **Duration of License:** Six months. **Requirements:** Hold a current valid barber instructor license from a board of barbering in another state. Apply for a permanent license. **Fees:** $30 application fee. $20 temporary permit fee. **Governing Statute:** Alaska Statutes 08.13. Professional Regulations 12 AAC 09.

1263

Cosmetologist
Dept. of Commerce and Economic Development
Div. of Occupational Licensing
Board of Barbers and Hairdressers
PO Box D-LIC
Juneau, AK 99811-0800
Phone: (907)465-2541
Fax: (907)465-2974

Credential Type: Cosmetologist License by Examination. **Duration of License:** Two years. **Requirements:** 350 hours of cosmetology training in an approved school, apprenticeship program, or a board-approved combination of training and apprenticeship. **Examination:** State-administered practical examination. Applicant must furnish tools and supplies for examination and secure his or her own model. **Fees:** $30 application fee. $100 license fee. $25 examination fee. **Governing Statute:** Alaska Statutes 08.13. Professional Regulations 12 AAC 09.

Credential Type: Cosmetologist License by Credentials. **Duration of License:** Two years. **Requirements:** Hold a current license to practice cosmetology issued by another state. Equivalent of 350 hours of cosmetology training in an approved school, apprenticeship program, or a board-approved combination of training and apprenticeship. **Fees:** $30 application fee. $100 license fee. **Governing Statute:** Alaska Statutes 08.13. Professional Regulations 12 AAC 09.

Credential Type: Temporary Permit. **Duration of License:** Six months. **Requirements:** Hold a current valid license from a board of cosmetology in another state. Apply for a permanent license. **Fees:** $30 application fee. $20 temporary permit fee. **Governing Statute:** Alaska Statutes 08.13. Professional Regulations 12 AAC 09.

1264

Cosmetologist Instructor
Dept. of Commerce and Economic Development
Div. of Occupational Licensing
Board of Barbers and Hairdressers
PO Box D-LIC
Juneau, AK 99811-0800
Phone: (907)465-2541
Fax: (907)465-2974

Credential Type: Cosmetologist Instructor License by Examination. **Duration of License:** Two years. **Requirements:** Hold a current cosmetologist practitioner license. Have at least three years of practice as a licensed cosmetologist in Alaska or in another licensing jurisdiction; or one year of practice as a licensed cosmetologist in Alaska or in another licensing jurisdiction followed by 600 hours of student instructor training in a school approved by the board or approved by another licensing jurisdiction. **Examination:** State-administered practical examination. Applicant must furnish tools and supplies for examination and secure his or her own model. **Fees:** $30 application fee. $100 license fee. $25 examination fee. **Governing Statute:** Alaska Statutes 08.13. Professional Regulations 12 AAC 09.

Credential Type: Cosmetologist Instructor License by Credentials. **Duration of License:** Two years. **Requirements:** Hold a current cosmetologist instructor license issued by another state. Equivalent of at least three years of practice as a licensed cosmetologist in Alaska or in another licensing jurisdiction; or one year of practice as a licensed cosmetologist in Alaska or in another licensing jurisdiction followed by 600 hours of student instructor training in a school approved by the board or approved by another licensing jurisdiction. **Fees:** $30 application fee. $100 license fee. **Governing Statute:** Alaska Statutes 08.13. Professional Regulations 12 AAC 09.

Credential Type: Temporary Permit. **Duration of License:** Six months. **Requirements:** Hold a current valid cosmetologist instructor license from a board of cosmetology in another state. Apply for a permanent license. **Fees:** $30 application fee. $20 temporary permit fee. **Governing Statute:** Alaska Statutes 08.13. Professional Regulations 12 AAC 09.

1265

Hairdresser
Dept. of Commerce and Economic Development
Div. of Occupational Licensing
Board of Barbers and Hairdressers
PO Box D-LIC
Juneau, AK 99811-0800
Phone: (907)465-2541
Fax: (907)465-2974

Credential Type: Hairdresser License by Examination. **Duration of License:** Two years. **Requirements:** 1,650 hours of course work in a school approved by the board; or 2,000 hours of training in an apprenticeship program; or a board-approved combination of course work and apprenticeship. **Examination:** State-administered practical examination. Applicant must furnish tools and supplies for examination and secure his or her own model. **Fees:** $30 application fee. $100 license fee. $25 examination fee. **Governing Statute:** Alaska Statutes 08.13. Professional Regulations 12 AAC 09.

Credential Type: Hairdresser License by Credentials. **Duration of License:** Two years. **Requirements:** Hold a current license to practice hairdressing issued by another state. Training and work experience equivalent to 1,650 hours of course work in a school approved by the board; or 2,000 hours of training in an apprenticeship program; or at least one year full-time work experience as a licensed hairdresser averaging no less than 32 hours per week, and a minimum of 1,000 hours of training in an approved school or an apprenticeship program approved by the board or by another licensing jurisdiction. **Fees:** $30 application fee. $100 license fee. **Governing Statute:** Alaska Statutes 08.13. Professional Regulations 12 AAC 09.

Credential Type: Temporary Permit. **Duration of License:** Six months. **Requirements:** Hold a current valid license from a board of hairdressing in another state. Apply for a permanent license. **Fees:** $30 application fee. $20 temporary permit fee. **Governing Statute:** Alaska Statutes 08.13. Professional Regulations 12 AAC 09.

1266

Hairdresser Instructor
Dept. of Commerce and Economic Development
Div. of Occupational Licensing
Board of Barbers and Hairdressers
PO Box D-LIC
Juneau, AK 99811-0800
Phone: (907)465-2541
Fax: (907)465-2974

Credential Type: Hairdresser Instructor License by Examination. **Duration of License:** Two years. **Requirements:** Hold a current hairdresser practitioner license. Have at least three years of practice as a licensed hairdresser in Alaska or in another licensing jurisdiction; or one year of practice as a licensed hairdresser in Alaska or in another licensing jurisdiction followed by 600 hours of student instructor training in a school approved by the board or approved by another licensing jurisdiction. **Examination:** State-administered practical examination. Applicant must furnish tools and supplies for examination and secure his or her own model. **Fees:** $30 application fee. $100 license fee. $25 examination fee. **Governing Statute:** Alaska Statutes 08.13. Professional Regulations 12 AAC 09.

Credential Type: Hairdresser Instructor License by Credentials. **Duration of License:** Two years. **Requirements:** Hold a current hairdresser instructor license issued by another licensing jurisdiction. Training and work experience equivalent to at least three years of practice as a licensed hairdresser in Alaska or in another licensing jurisdiction; or one year of practice as a licensed hairdresser in Alaska or in another licensing jurisdiction followed by 600 hours of student instructor training in a school approved by the board or approved by another licensing jurisdiction. **Fees:** $30 application fee. $100 license fee. **Governing Statute:** Alaska Statutes 08.13. Professional Regulations 12 AAC 09.

Credential Type: Temporary Permit. **Duration of License:** Six months. **Requirements:** Hold a current valid hairdresser instructor license from a board of hairdressing in another state. Apply for a permanent license. **Fees:** $30 application fee. $20 temporary permit fee. **Governing Statute:** Alaska Statutes 08.13. Professional Regulations 12 AAC 09.

Arizona

1267

Aesthetic Instructor
Arizona State Board of Cosmetology
1645 W. Jefferson, Rm. 125
Phoenix, AZ 85007
Phone: (602)542-5301

Credential Type: Instructor license. **Requirements:** High school graduate. GED Certificate with passing score. Graduate from a cosmetology school with at least 500 hours of instructor training. Be a licensed aesthetician. Have at least one year of work experience. Pass Instructor Practical Examination. **Examination:** Instructor Practical Examination. **Fees:** $35 exam fee.

1268

Aesthetician
Arizona State Board of Cosmetology
1645 W. Jefferson, Rm. 125
Phoenix, AZ 85007
Phone: (602)542-5301

Credential Type: Aesthetics license. **Requirements:** High school graduate. GED Certificate with passing scores in English. Graduate from a cosmetology school with at least 600 hours of training. Pass Aesthetician Practical Examination. **Examination:** Aesthetician Practical Examination. **Fees:** $22 exam fee.

1269

Barber
Board of Barbers
1645 W. Jefferson
Phoenix, AZ 85007
Phone: (602)542-4498

Credential Type: Barber license. **Duration of License:** Two years. **Requirements:** At least 16 years of age. Have at least a 10th grade education. Must have at least one year work experience if being licensed by reciprocity. Pass written and practical examination. **Examination:** Barber License Examination. **Reciprocity:** Yes, with 24 states. **Fees:** $30 license fee. $75 examination fee. $150 license by reciprocity fee.

1270

Barber Instructor
Board of Barbers
1645 W. Jefferson
Phoenix, AZ 85007
Phone: (602)542-4498

Credential Type: Instructor license. **Duration of License:** Two years. **Requirements:** At least 19 years of age. High school graduate. Must have practiced barbering for two years and have at least 500 hours of training. Must have at least one year work experience if being licensed by reciprocity. Pass written and practical examination. **Examination:** Instructor License Examination. **Reciprocity:** Yes, with 24 states. **Fees:** $40 license fee. $100 examination fee. $150 license by reciprocity fee.

1271

Cosmetologist
Arizona State Board of Cosmetology
1645 W. Jefferson, Rm. 125
Phoenix, AZ 85007
Phone: (602)542-5301

Credential Type: Cosmetology license. **Requirements:** High school graduate. GED Certificate with passing scores in English. Graduate from a cosmetology school with at least 1600 hours of training. Pass Cosmetologist Practical Examination. **Examination:** Cosmetologist Practical Examination. **Fees:** $25 exam fee.

1272

Cosmetology Instructor
Arizona State Board of Cosmetology
1645 W. Jefferson, Rm. 125
Phoenix, AZ 85007
Phone: (602)542-5301

Credential Type: Instructor license. **Requirements:** High school graduate. GED Certificate with passing score. Graduate from a cosmetology school with at least 650 hours of instructor training. Be a licensed cosmetologist. Have at least one year of work experience. Pass Instructor Practical Examination. **Examination:** Instructor Practical Examination. **Fees:** $35 exam fee.

Arizona

1273

Nail Technician
Arizona State Board of Cosmetology
1645 W. Jefferson, Rm. 125
Phoenix, AZ 85007
Phone: (602)542-5301

Credential Type: Nail technology license. **Requirements:** High school graduate. GED Certificate with passing scores in English. Graduate from a cosmetology school with at least 300 hours of training. Pass Nail Technician Practical Examination. **Examination:** Nail Technician Practical Examination. **Fees:** $20 exam fee.

1274

Nail Technology Instructor
Arizona State Board of Cosmetology
1645 W. Jefferson, Rm. 125
Phoenix, AZ 85007
Phone: (602)542-5301

Credential Type: Instructor license. **Requirements:** High school graduate. GED Certificate with passing score. Graduate from a cosmetology school with at least 350 hours of instructor training. Be a licensed nail technician. Have at least one year of work experience. Pass Instructor Practical Examination. **Examination:** Instructor Practical Examination. **Fees:** $35 exam fee.

Arkansas

1275

Aesthetician
Arkansas State Board of
  Cosmetology
1515 West Seventh, Rm. 400
Little Rock, AR 72201
Phone: (501)682-2168

Credential Type: License. **Requirements:** 16 years of age. Good moral character and temperate habits. Completed two years of high school or the equivalent. Completed 600 hours of practical and theoretical training. **Examination:** Written and practical exams. **Fees:** $30 exam fee. $12 Renewal.

1276

Barber Instructor
State Board of Barber Examiners
Donaghey Bldg., Rm. 212
Little Rock, AR 72201
Phone: (501)682-4035

Credential Type: License. **Duration of License:** One year. **Requirements:** 12th grade education. Meet all requirements for a barber. Complete a postgraduate course in barber-teacher technology theory in accredited school. **Examination:** Yes. **Fees:** $40 for written, oral and practical examination. $20 License. $20 Renewal. $25 Restoration after Sept. 1.

1277

Barber Technician
State Board of Barber Examiners
Donaghey Bldg., Rm. 212
Little Rock, AR 72201
Phone: (501)372-4035

Credential Type: License. **Duration of License:** One year. **Requirements:** 12th grade education. 20 days study at an accredited school of barbering or 60 days apprenticeship program in a licensed barber shop under direction of a registered barber. **Examination:** Yes. **Fees:** $17 for written, oral and practical examination. $17 License. $17 Renewal. $25 Restoration after Sept. 1.

1278

Cosmetologist
Arkansas State Board of
  Cosmetology
1515 Bldg., Ste. 400
1515 W. Seventh St.
Little Rock, AR 72201
Phone: (501)682-2168

Credential Type: License. **Requirements:** 16 years of age. 10th grade education or equivalent. Graduate of an accredited school of cosmetology consisting of 1500 hours. **Examination:** Yes. **Fees:** $30 Examination. $10 Registration.

1279

Cosmetology Instructor
Arkansas State Board of
  Cosmetology
1515 Bldg., Ste. 400
1515 W. Seventh St.
Little Rock, AR 72202
Phone: (501)682-2168

Credential Type: License. **Requirements:** 16 years of age. 12th grade education or equivalent. Licensed as a cosmetologist. Graduate of an advanced 600 hour course in cosmetology. **Examination:** Yes. **Fees:** $30 Written and practical examinations.

1280

Electrologist
Arkansas State Board of
  Cosmetology
1515 Bldg., Ste. 400
1515 West Seventh St.
Little Rock, AR 72202
Phone: (501)371-2168

Credential Type: License. **Requirements:** 18 years of age. 12th grade education or equivalent. 100 hour course for licensed cosmetologist. 200 hour course for person not licensed as a cosmetologist. **Examination:** Yes. **Fees:** $30 Written and practical examinations. $5 Registration.

1281

Electrology Instructor
Arkansas State Board of
  Cosmetology
1515 Bldg., Ste. 400
1515 W. Seventh St.
Little Rock, AR 72202
Phone: (501)371-2168

Credential Type: License. **Requirements:** Three years experience as an electrologist. Pass the written and practical test. **Examination:** Yes. **Fees:** $30 Written and practical tests.

1282

Manicurist
Arkansas State Board of
  Cosmetology
1515 Bldg., Ste. 400
1515 W. 7th St.
Little Rock, AR 72202
Phone: (501)371-2168

Credential Type: License. **Requirements:** 16 years of age. 10th grade education or equivalent. Graduate of a 350 hour course of instruction at an approved school of cosmetology. **Examination:** Yes. **Fees:** $20 Written and practical examination. $5 Registration.

1283

Registered Barber
State Board of Barber Examiners
Donaghey Bldg., Rm. 212
Little Rock, AR 72201
Phone: (501)682-4035

Credential Type: License. **Duration of License:** One year. **Requirements:** Proof of graduation from the 8th grade or equivalent. 18 years of age. Good moral character and temperate habits. Must have at least

1500 hours of instruction, to be completed in not less than nine months from an approved school of barbering. Pass the examination given by the Board. **Examination:** Yes. **Fees:** $25 Written, oral and practical examinations. $20 License. $17 Renewal. $25 Restoration after September 1.

California

1284

Barber
Board of Barbering and Cosmetology
PO Box 944226
Sacramento, CA 94244-2260
Phone: (916)445-7061
Phone: (916)445-7008

Credential Type: Barber License. **Requirements:** Contact licensing body for application information.

Credential Type: Apprentice Barber License. **Requirements:** Contact licensing body for application information.

1285

Barber Instructor
Board of Barbering and Cosmetology
PO Box 944226
Sacramento, CA 94244-2260
Phone: (916)445-7061
Phone: (916)445-7008

Credential Type: Barber License. **Requirements:** Contact licensing body for application information.

1286

Cosmetician/Esthetician
Board of Barbering and Cosmetology
PO Box 944226
Sacramento, CA 94244-2260
Phone: (916)445-7061
Phone: (916)445-7008

Credential Type: Esthetician License and Registration. **Duration of License:** Two years. **Requirements:** Be at least 17 years of age. Complete at least the 10th grade. Meet one of the following sets of requirements: (1) Complete at least 600 hours of training, at least 150 of which were received within five years preceding application. The training requirement may be met with a combination of training and work experience. 100 hours of credit is granted for each three months of full-time training and/or work experience. (2) Have practiced as a cosmetician for at least 18 months outside of this state within five years preceding application. Each three months of practice shall count toward 100 hours of the training requirement. **Examination:** Written and practical examination. **Reciprocity:** No. **Governing Statute:** The Cosmetology Act, Business and Professions Code, Div. 3, Chap. 10, Sect. 7300 et seq.

1287

Cosmetologist
Board of Barbering and Cosmetology
PO Box 944226
Sacramento, CA 94244-2260
Phone: (916)445-7061
Phone: (916)445-7008

Credential Type: Cosmetologist License and Registration. **Duration of License:** Two years. **Requirements:** Be at least 17 years of age. Complete at least the 10th grade or have 10 years of public education. Meet one of the following sets of requirements: (1) Complete at least 1600 hours of training. The training requirement may be met with a combination of training and work experience. 100 hours of credit is granted for each three months of full-time training and/or work experience. (2) Complete a course in cosmetology from a board-approved school. (3) Be a licensed barber and complete the cosmetology crossover course in a board-approved school. (4) Complete a barbering course in a board-approved school and complete a cosmetology crossover course in a board-approved school. **Examination:** Written and practical examination. **Reciprocity:** No. **Governing Statute:** The Cosmetology Act, Business and Professions Code, Div. 3, Chap. 10, Sect. 7300 et seq.

Credential Type: Junior Operator License. **Duration of License:** Three years. **Authorization:** Includes individuals who are learning the occupation of cosmetologist under the direct supervision of a licensed cosmetologist in a licensed cosmetology establishment. May practice cosmetology upon a patron only after receiving 350 hours of instruction. **Requirements:** Be at least 16 years of age. Complete at least the 10th grade. Training must be conducted under the direct supervision of a licensed cosmetologist in a licensed cosmetology establishment.

1288

Cosmetology Instructor
Board of Barbering and Cosmetology
PO Box 944226
Sacramento, CA 94244-2260
Phone: (916)445-7061
Phone: (916)445-7008

Credential Type: Cosmetology Instructor License and Registration. **Duration of License:** Two years. **Requirements:** High school graduate or equivalent. Hold a valid California license as a cosmetologist. Meet one of the following sets of requirements: (1) Complete at least 600 hours of teacher training. (2) Have one year of practical experience within the previous three years in all branches of cosmetology, except electrology, in a licensed cosmetology establishment.

Renewal requires 30 clock hours of continuing education. **Examination:** Written and practical examination. **Reciprocity:** No. **Governing Statute:** The Cosmetology Act, Business and Professions Code, Div. 3, Chap. 10, Sect. 7300 et seq.

1289

Electrologist
Board of Barbering and Cosmetology
PO Box 944226
Sacramento, CA 94244-2260
Phone: (916)445-7061
Phone: (916)445-7008

Credential Type: Electrologist License and Registration. **Duration of License:** Two years. **Requirements:** Be at least 17 years of age. Complete at least the 12th grade or have 12 years of public education. Meet one of the following sets of requirements: (1) Complete at least 500 hours of training. The training requirement may be met with a combination of training and work experience. 100 hours of credit is granted for each three months of full-time training and/or work experience. (2) Complete a course in electrolysis from a board-approved school. (3) Have practiced electrolysis for at least 18 months outside of this state within a period of time equivalent to a complete training course in electrolysis. **Examination:** Written and practical examination. **Reciprocity:** No. **Governing Statute:** The Cosmetology Act, Business and Professions Code, Div. 3, Chap. 10, Sect. 7300 et seq.

Credential Type: Junior Electrologist License. **Duration of License:** Three years. **Authorization:** Includes individuals who are learning the occupation of electrolysis under the direct supervision of a licensed electrologist in a licensed cosmetology es-

Electrologist, continued

tablishment. May practice electrolysis upon a patron only after receiving 150 hours of instruction. **Requirements:** Be at least 17.5 years of age. Complete at least the 12th grade. Training must be conducted under the direct supervision of a licensed electrologist in a licensed cosmetology establishment. **Governing Statute:** The Cosmetology Act, Business and Professions Code, Div. 3, Chap. 10, Sect. 7300 et seq.

1290

Manicurist

Board of Barbering and Cosmetology
PO Box 944226
Sacramento, CA 94244-2260
Phone: (916)445-7061
Phone: (916)445-7008

Credential Type: Manicurist License and Registration. **Duration of License:** Two years. **Requirements:** Be at least 17 years of age. Complete at least the 10th grade. Meet one of the following sets of requirements: (1) Complete at least 350 hours of training. The training requirement may be met with a combination of training and work experience. 100 hours of credit is granted for each three months of full-time training and/or work experience. (2) Have practiced as a manicurist for at least 10.5 months outside of this state within five years preceding application. Each three months of practice shall count toward 100 hours of the training requirement. **Examination:** Written and practical examination. **Reciprocity:** No. **Governing Statute:** The Cosmetology Act, Business and Professions Code, Div. 3, Chap. 10, Sect. 7300 et seq.

Colorado

1291

Barber

Board of Barbers and Cosmetologists
Dept. of Regulatory Agencies
Div. of Registrations
1560 Broadway, Ste. 1340
Denver, CO 80202
Phone: (303)894-7772

Credential Type: Barber license. **Duration of License:** Two years. **Requirements:** Be at least 16 years of age. Graduate from an approved barber school. Complete at least 1000 hours of training. **Examination:** Board administered written and practical examination. **Reciprocity:** A license by reciprocity will be issued to anyone who is licensed to practice in another state and possesses credentials and qualifications which are substantially equivalent to requirements in Colorado. **Fees:** $39 exam fee. $24 initial license fee. $49 license renewal fee. **Governing Statute:** Colorado Statutes, Title 12, Article 8.

1292

Cosmetician

Board of Barbers and Cosmetologists
Dept. of Regulatory Agencies
Div. of Registrations
1560 Broadway, Ste. 1340
Denver, CO 80202
Phone: (303)894-7772

Credential Type: Cosmetician license. **Duration of License:** Two years. **Requirements:** Be at least 16 years of age. Graduate from an approved beauty school. Complete at least 550 hours of training. **Examination:** Board administered written and practical examination. **Reciprocity:** A license by reciprocity will be issued to anyone who is licensed to practice in another state and possesses credentials and qualifications which are substantially equivalent to requirements in Colorado. **Fees:** $27 exam fee. $24 initial license fee. $49 license renewal fee. **Governing Statute:** Colorado Statutes, Title 12, Article 8.

1293

Cosmetologist

Board of Barbers and Cosmetologists
Dept. of Regulatory Agencies
Div. of Registrations
1560 Broadway, Ste. 1340
Denver, CO 80202
Phone: (303)894-7772

Credential Type: Cosmetologist license. **Duration of License:** Two years. **Requirements:** Be at least 16 years of age. Graduate from an approved beauty school. Complete at least 1000 hours of training. **Examination:** Board administered written and practical examination. **Reciprocity:** A license by reciprocity will be issued to anyone who is licensed to practice in another state and possesses credentials and qualifications which are substantially equivalent to requirements in Colorado. **Fees:** $39 exam fee. $24 initial license fee. $49 license renewal fee. **Governing Statute:** Colorado Statutes, Title 12, Article 8.

1294

Manicurist

Board of Barbers and Cosmetologists
Dept. of Regulatory Agencies
Div. of Registrations
1560 Broadway, Ste. 1340
Denver, CO 80202
Phone: (303)894-7772

Credential Type: Manicurist license. **Duration of License:** Two years. **Requirements:** Be at least 16 years of age. Graduate from an approved beauty school. Complete at least 350 hours of training. **Examination:** Board administered written and practical examination. **Reciprocity:** A license by reciprocity will be issued to anyone who is licensed to practice in another state and possesses credentials and qualifications which are substantially equivalent to requirements in Colorado. **Fees:** $27 exam fee. $24 initial license fee. $49 license renewal fee. **Governing Statute:** Colorado Statutes, Title 12, Article 8.

Connecticut

1295

Barber

Dept. of Health Services
Div. of Medical Quality Assurance
150 Washington St.
Hartford, CT 06106
Phone: (203)566-1042

Credential Type: Master Barber License. **Duration of License:** One year. **Requirements:** Have at least an 8th grade education. Complete at least 1500 hours of professional education in a barber school. **Examination:** Barber examination. **Reciprocity:** A license without examination may be issued to any person licensed as a barber in a state with equivalent or higher requirements, provided that state grants similar privileges to applicants from Connecticut. **Fees:** $50 application fee. $50 exam fee. $25 renewal fee.

1296

Cosmetician

Dept. of Health Services
Div. of Medical Quality Assurance
150 Washington St.
Hartford, CT 06106
Phone: (203)566-1042

Credential Type: Cosmetician License and Registration. **Duration of License:** One year. **Requirements:** Have at least a 9th grade education. Complete at least 1500 hours of professional education in an approved school. **Examination:** Written examination. **Reciprocity:** A license without examination may be issued to any person licensed as a cosmetologist in a state with equivalent or higher requirements, provided that state grants similar privileges to applicants from Connecticut. **Fees:** $50 application fee. $50 exam fee. $25 renewal fee.

1297

Electrologist
Dept. of Health Services
State Board of Cosmetology
150 Washington St.
Hartford, CT 06106
Phone: (203)566-1042

Credential Type: License to practice. **Requirements:** 18 years of age. High school graduate or equivalent. Complete 600 hours of study. Pass the American Electrology Association (AEA)/ETS examination. **Examination:** AEA/ETS Examination.

1298

Hairdresser
Dept. of Health Services
Div. of Medical Quality Assurance
150 Washington St.
Hartford, CT 06106
Phone: (203)566-1042

Credential Type: Hairdresser License and Registration. **Duration of License:** One year. **Requirements:** Have at least a 9th grade education. Complete at least 1500 hours of professional education in an approved school. **Examination:** Written examination. **Reciprocity:** A license without examination may be issued to any person licensed as a hairdresser in a state with equivalent or higher requirements, provided that state grants similar privileges to applicants from Connecticut. **Fees:** $50 application fee. $50 exam fee. $25 renewal fee.

Delaware

1299

Barber
Board of Cosmetology and Barbering
Dept. of Administrative Services
Div. of Professional Regulation
PO Box 1401
Dover, DE 19903
Phone: (302)739-4522

Credential Type: Master Barber License and certificate of registration. **Duration of License:** One year. **Requirements:** Have at least an 8th-grade education. Must be at least 19 years of age. Good moral character. Free from contagious disease. Must have studied for at least three years as an apprentice under a qualified and practicing barber, or practiced as a barber in another state for at least two years.

A licensed physician or surgeon may obtain a certificate of registration as a barber upon passing examination. **Examination:** Written and oral examination. **Reciprocity:** Yes, with other states, territories, the District of Columbia, or foreign country, state, or province. Applicant must have trained as a registered student in a registered barber school for at least 20 consecutive weeks. **Fees:** $50 examination and license fee. $10 annual renewal fee. **Governing Statute:** Delaware Code, Title 24, Chapter 4.

1300

Barber Apprentice
Board of Cosmetology and Barbering
Dept. of Administrative Services
Div. of Professional Regulation
PO Box 1401
Dover, DE 19903
Phone: (302)739-4522

Credential Type: Apprentice Barber License and certificate of registration. **Duration of License:** One year. **Requirements:** Have at least an 8th-grade education. Must be at least 16 years of age. Must be employed by a licensed barber. **Fees:** $10 registration fee. $10 annual renewal fee. **Governing Statute:** Delaware Code, Title 24, Chapter 4.

1301

Cosmetologist
Board of Cosmetology and Barbering
Dept. of Administrative Services
Div. of Professional Regulation
PO Box 1401
Dover, DE 19903
Phone: (302)739-4522

Credential Type: Cosmetologist License. **Duration of License:** Two years. **Requirements:** Have at least an 8th-grade education. Complete a course in cosmetology of at least 1500 hours of continuous training in a registered school of cosmetology, or 3000 hours of formal training in a registered beauty salon as an apprentice. **Examination:** Written and oral test. Practical demonstrations. **Reciprocity:** Yes, with other states, territories, the District of Columbia, or foreign country, state, or province. Applicant must have five years continuous experience and pay appropriate fees. **Fees:** $50 license fee. $50 renewal fee. **Governing Statute:** Delaware Code, Title 24, Chapter 6.

1302

Cosmetologist Apprentice
Board of Cosmetology and Barbering
Dept. of Administrative Services
Div. of Professional Regulation
PO Box 1401
Dover, DE 19903
Phone: (302)739-4522

Credential Type: Cosmetologist Apprentice Registration. **Duration of License:** Two years. **Requirements:** Be at least 16 years of age. Have at least an 8th-grade education. Must take cosmetologist examination after completing 3000 hours of training. **Fees:** $10 registration fee. $10 renewal fee. **Governing Statute:** Delaware Code, Title 24, Chapter 6.

1303

Cosmetology Demonstrator
Board of Cosmetology and Barbering
Dept. of Administrative Services
Div. of Professional Regulation
PO Box 1401
Dover, DE 19903
Phone: (302)739-4522

Credential Type: Demonstrator License. **Duration of License:** Two years. **Requirements:** Have at least an 8th-grade education. Must be a licensed cosmetologist or have continuously practiced as a cosmetologist for at least three years. **Examination:** Written and oral test. Practical demonstrations. **Reciprocity:** Yes, with other states, territories, the District of Columbia, or foreign country, state, or province. Applicant must have five years continuous experience and pay appropriate fees. **Fees:** $20 license fee. $20 renewal fee. **Governing Statute:** Delaware Code, Title 24, Chapter 6.

1304

Cosmetology Instructor
Board of Cosmetology and Barbering
Dept. of Administrative Services
Div. of Professional Regulation
PO Box 1401
Dover, DE 19903
Phone: (302)739-4522

Credential Type: Instructor's License. **Duration of License:** Two years. **Requirements:** Have at least an 8th-grade education. Must be a licensed cosmetologist. Have at least six months teacher's training course in cosmetology in a registered

Cosmetology Instructor, continued

school of cosmetology; or have at least two years experience as an active practicing cosmetologist, supplemented by not less than three months of teacher's training in cosmetology in a registered school of cosmetology. **Examination:** Written and oral test. Practical demonstrations. **Reciprocity:** Yes, with other states, territories, the District of Columbia, or foreign country, state, or province. Applicant must have five years continuous experience and pay appropriate fees. **Fees:** $75 license fee. $75 renewal fee. **Governing Statute:** Delaware Code, Title 24, Chapter 6.

1305

Cosmetology Student
Board of Cosmetology and Barbering
Dept. of Administrative Services
Div. of Professional Regulation
PO Box 1401
Dover, DE 19903
Phone: (302)739-4522

Credential Type: Student registration. **Requirements:** Have at least an 8th-grade education. Must be at least 16 years of age. Must be enrolled in a registered school of cosmetology. **Fees:** $10 registrration fee. **Governing Statute:** Delaware Code, Title 24, Chapter 6.

1306

Electrologist
Board of Cosmetology and Barbering
Dept. of Administrative Services
Div. of Professional Regulation
PO Box 1401
Dover, DE 19903
Phone: (302)739-4522

Credential Type: Electrologist License. **Duration of License:** Two years. **Requirements:** Have at least an 8th-grade education. Complete a course in electrolysis of at least 300 hours of continuous training, not to exceed eight hours in any one day; or have 600 hours of experience as an apprentice in a place of business for training over a minimum period of six months, not to exceed eight hours in any one day. **Examination:** Written and oral test. Practical demonstrations. **Reciprocity:** Yes, with other states, territories, the District of Columbia, or foreign country, state, or province. Applicant must have five years continuous experience and pay appropriate fees. **Fees:** $30 license fee. $30 renewal fee. **Governing Statute:** Delaware Code, Title 24, Chapter 6.

1307

Electrologist Instructor
Board of Cosmetology and Barbering
Dept. of Administrative Services
Div. of Professional Regulation
PO Box 1401
Dover, DE 19903
Phone: (302)739-4522

Credential Type: Electrologist Instructor Certificate. **Duration of License:** Two years. **Requirements:** Have at least an 8th-grade education. Complete an advanced course in electrolysis of at least 100 hours of training. Have been engaged in the active and full-time practice of electrology for 12 months preceding application. **Examination:** Written and oral test. Practical demonstrations. **Reciprocity:** Yes, with other states, territories, the District of Columbia, or foreign country, state, or province. Applicant must have five years continuous experience and pay appropriate fees. **Fees:** $50 license fee. $50 renewal fee. **Governing Statute:** Delaware Code, Title 24, Chapter 6.

1308

Managing Cosmetologist
Board of Cosmetology and Barbering
Dept. of Administrative Services
Div. of Professional Regulation
PO Box 1401
Dover, DE 19903
Phone: (302)739-4522

Credential Type: Managing Cosmetologist License. **Duration of License:** Two years. **Authorization:** License required to manage or conduct a beauty salon or school of cosmetology. **Requirements:** Have at least an 8th-grade education. Have at least one year of experience as a licensed cosmetologist. **Examination:** Written and oral test. Practical demonstrations. **Exemptions:** A holder of a valid cosmetology instructor's license does not need additional licensing to own or manage a beauty salon. **Reciprocity:** Yes, with other states, territories, the District of Columbia, or foreign country, state, or province. Applicant must have five years continuous experience and pay appropriate fees. **Fees:** $75 license fee. $75 renewal fee. **Governing Statute:** Delaware Code, Title 24, Chapter 6.

1309

Manicurist
Board of Cosmetology and Barbering
Dept. of Administrative Services
Div. of Professional Regulation
PO Box 1401
Dover, DE 19903
Phone: (302)739-4522

Credential Type: Manicurist License. **Duration of License:** Two years. **Requirements:** Have at least an 8th-grade education. Complete a course of training of not less than 125 hours in a school of cosmetology or 250 hours as an apprentice in a beauty salon. **Examination:** Written and oral test. Practical demonstrations. **Reciprocity:** Yes, with other states, territories, the District of Columbia, or foreign country, state, or province. Applicant must have five years continuous experience and pay appropriate fees. **Fees:** $25 license fee. $25 renewal fee. **Governing Statute:** Delaware Code, Title 24, Chapter 6.

1310

Shampooist
Board of Cosmetology and Barbering
Dept. of Administrative Services
Div. of Professional Regulation
PO Box 1401
Dover, DE 19903
Phone: (302)739-4522

Credential Type: Shampooist License. **Duration of License:** Two years. **Requirements:** Have at least an 8th-grade education. Have 100 hours of formal training in a registered school of cosmetology, or 200 hours of formal training in a registered beauty salon as an apprentice. **Reciprocity:** Yes, with other states, territories, the District of Columbia, or foreign country, state, or province. Applicant must have five years continuous experience and pay appropriate fees. **Fees:** $25 license fee. $25 renewal fee. **Governing Statute:** Delaware Code, Title 24, Chapter 6.

1311

Student Barber
Board of Cosmetology and Barbering
Dept. of Administrative Services
Div. of Professional Regulation
PO Box 1401
Dover, DE 19903
Phone: (302)739-4522

Credential Type: Student Barber License and certificate of registration. **Duration of License:** One year. **Requirements:** Have at least an 8th-grade education. Must be a graduate of a bona fide barber school, completing a course of instruction of at least 1500 hours. A student barber must serve 12 months with a licensed barber before applying for examination to be duly licensed as a barber. **Examination:** Written and oral examination. **Fees:** $50 examination and license fee. $10 annual renewal fee. **Governing Statute:** Delaware Code, Title 24, Chapter 4.

1312

Student Instructor in Cosmetology
Board of Cosmetology and Barbering
Dept. of Administrative Services
Div. of Professional Regulation
PO Box 1401
Dover, DE 19903
Phone: (302)739-4522

Credential Type: Student instructor's registration. **Requirements:** Have at least an 8th-grade education. Must be a licensed cosmetologist. Must be enrolled in a school of cosmetology as a student instructor. **Fees:** $10 registration fee. **Governing Statute:** Delaware Code, Title 24, Chapter 6.

District of Columbia

1313

Barber
Board of Barber Examiners
614 H St., NW, Rm. 9213
Washington, DC 20001
Phone: (202)727-7468

Credential Type: License. **Requirements:** Contact licensing body for application information.

Florida

1314

Barber
Barber's Board
Dept. of Professional Regulation
1940 N. Monroe St.
Tallahassee, FL 32399-0796
Phone: (904)488-5702

Credential Type: Barber's License. **Duration of License:** Two years. **Requirements:** Contact licensing body for application information. **Examination:** Licensing Examination to Practice Barbering, written and practical sections. **Reciprocity:** License may be granted by endorsement. **Fees:** $100 application fee. $50 initial license fee. $50 renewal fee. **Governing Statute:** Florida Statutes, Chapter 476.

1315

Cosmetologist
Board of Cosmetology
Dept. of Professional Regulation
1940 N. Monroe St.
Tallahassee, FL 32399-0790
Phone: (904)488-5702

Credential Type: Cosmetologist license. **Duration of License:** Two years. **Requirements:** Contact licensing body for application information. **Examination:** Cosmetology Examination, including written theory, written laws and rules, and written clinical. **Reciprocity:** License may be granted by endorsement. **Fees:** $50 exam fee. $50 license by endorsement fee. $20 initial license fee. $20 renewal fee. **Governing Statute:** Florida Statutes, Chapter 477.

Credential Type: Specialist license. **Duration of License:** Two years. **Requirements:** Contact licensing body for application information. **Reciprocity:** License may be granted by endorsement. **Fees:** $30 license by endorsement fee. $20 initial license fee. $20 renewal fee. **Governing Statute:** Florida Statutes, Chapter 477.

1316

Electrologist
Florida Board of Cosmetology
1940 N. Monroe St.
Tallahassee, FL 32399-0750
Phone: (904)488-5702

Credential Type: License to practice. **Requirements:** 18 years of age. High school graduate or equivalent. Complete 120 hours of study. Pass examination. **Examination:** Yes.

Georgia

1317

Barber
State Board of Barbers
Barber and Cosmetology Boards Section
Professional Examining Boards
166 Pryor St., SW
Atlanta, GA 30303
Phone: (404)656-3909

Credential Type: Master Barber License. **Duration of License:** Two years. **Requirements:** Ninth-grade education. Must have nine months and 1500 school hours training. Must complete 18 months and 3000 hours apprenticeship. **Examination:** Barber Examination, written and practical. **Reciprocity:** Yes, with all states. **Fees:** $45 exam fee. $30 renewal fee.

Credential Type: Barber Student License. **Requirements:** Ninth-grade education. Be a registered barber student in a board-approved school. **Fees:** $15 student license fee.

Credential Type: Barber Apprentice License. **Requirements:** Ninth-grade education. Must have nine months and 1500 school hours training. **Fees:** $30 apprentice license fee.

1318

Barber Teacher
State Board of Barbers
Barber and Cosmetology Boards Section
Professional Examining Boards
166 Pryor St., SW
Atlanta, GA 30303
Phone: (404)656-3909

Credential Type: Barber Teacher License. **Duration of License:** Two years. **Requirements:** High school education or equivalent. Complete 750 hours of teacher training at a board-approved school. **Examination:** Barber Teacher Examination, written and practical. **Reciprocity:** Yes, with states that have an equal training requirement of 750 hours. **Fees:** $50 exam and license fee. $60 renewal fee.

1319

Cosmetology Teacher
State Board of Cosmetology
Barber and Cosmetology Boards Section
Professional Examining Boards
166 Pryor St., SW
Atlanta, GA 30303
Phone: (404)656-3909

Credential Type: Cosmetology Teacher License. **Duration of License:** Two years. **Requirements:** High school education or equivalent. Hold a current Master Cosmetologist License. Complete 1500 hours of instructor training in a board-approved school.

Renewal requires 10 hours of continuing education per two-year period. **Examination:** Cosmetology Teacher Examination, written and practical. **Fees:** $50 exam fee. $65 renewal fee.

Georgia 1320

1320

Esthetician
State Board of Cosmetology
Barber and Cosmetology Boards Section
Professional Examining Boards
166 Pryor St., SW
Atlanta, GA 30303
Phone: (404)656-3909

Credential Type: Esthetician License. **Duration of License:** Two years. **Requirements:** Ninth-grade education. Complette 750 hours of school training and 1500 hours of apprenticeship. **Examination:** Esthetician Examination, written and practical. **Fees:** $45 exam fee. $35 renewal fee.

1321

Manicurist
State Board of Cosmetology
Barber and Cosmetology Boards Section
Professional Examining Boards
166 Pryor St., SW
Atlanta, GA 30303
Phone: (404)656-3909

Credential Type: Manicurist License. **Duration of License:** Two years. **Requirements:** Ninth-grade education. Complete 320 hours of school training and 640 hours of apprenticeship in a shop. **Examination:** Manicurist Examination, written and practical. **Fees:** $45 exam fee. $35 renewal fee.

1322

Master Cosmetologist
State Board of Cosmetology
Barber and Cosmetology Boards Section
Professional Examining Boards
166 Pryor St., SW
Atlanta, GA 30303
Phone: (404)656-3909

Credential Type: Master Cosmetologist License. **Duration of License:** Two years. **Requirements:** Be at least 17 years of age. Ninth-grade education. Complete nine months and 1500 hours of school training. Complete 18 months and 3000 hours of apprenticeship. **Examination:** Master Cosmetology Examination, written and practical. **Reciprocity:** All states except Florida (unless licensed prior to 8-1-86), California, Rhode Island, Virgin Islands, and Hawaii. **Fees:** $45 exam fee. $35 renewal fee.

Hawaii

1323

Barber
Hawaii Board of Barbers
Dept. of Commerce and Consumer Affairs
PO Box 3469
Honolulu, HI 96801
Phone: (808)548-3952

Credential Type: License. **Duration of License:** Six months. **Requirements:** 17 years of age. Six months as a registered apprentice. **Examination:** Given four times per year. **Fees:** $10 application fee. $10 license fee. $15 Compliance Resolution Fund fee. $15 renewal fee.

1324

Beauty Operator
Hawaii Board of Cosmetology
Dept. of Commerce and Consumer Affairs
PO Box 3469
Honolulu, HI 96801
Phone: (808)548-3952

Credential Type: License. **Duration of License:** Six months. **Examination:** Given three times per year. **Fees:** $10 application fee. $15 license fee. $15—$30 Compliance Resolution Fund fee. $15 renewal fee. $10 temporary permit.

1325

Electrologist
Board of Cosmetology
Professional & Vocational Licensing
Dept. of Consumer Affairs
PO Box 3649
Honolulu, HI 96801
Phone: (808)548-4100

Credential Type: License to practice. **Requirements:** 18 years of age. High school graduate or equivalent. Complete 600 hours of study or an 800 hr. apprenticeship. Pass the American Electrology Association (AEA)/ETS examination. **Examination:** AEA/ETS Examination.

Idaho

1326

Barber
Board of Examiners of Barbers
Bureau of Occupational Licenses
1109 Main St., Ste. 220
Boise, ID 83702-5642
Phone: (208)334-3233

Credential Type: Certificate of Registration. **Duration of License:** One year. **Requirements:** Be at least 16.5 years of age. Good moral character. Complete two years of high school (tenth grade) or equivalent. Complete and graduate from a course consisting of at least 1700 hours within a period of 10.5 months in a school of barbering approved by the board.

Applicant who fails to pass examination must take an additional course of three months of not less than 500 hours in a school of barbering approved by the board. **Examination:** Barber's Examination (practical, written, and oral). **Reciprocity:** Yes, provided applicant is at least 18 years of age. Must hold a valid license from a state or country with substantially the same requirements, or have practiced for at least three years as a licensed barber. An examination may be required at the discretion of the board. **Fees:** $25 application fee. $75 exam fee. $30 original certificate fee. $30 renewal fee. $80 endorsement fee. **Governing Statute:** Idaho Code, Title 54, Chap. 5. Rules of the Idaho Board of Examiners of Barbers.

Credential Type: Temporary Permit. **Duration of License:** Until results of examination are available. **Requirements:** Temporary permit may be issued to an applicant who has not previously been issued a temporary permit and whose application and fees are accepted as being completed. **Fees:** $15 temporary permit fee. **Governing Statute:** Idaho Code, Title 54, Chap. 5. Rules of the Idaho Board of Examiners of Barbers.

1327

Barber Apprentice
Board of Examiners of Barbers
Bureau of Occupational Licenses
1109 Main St., Ste. 220
Boise, ID 83702-5642
Phone: (208)334-3233

Credential Type: Apprentice Barber License. **Duration of License:** One year. **Requirements:** Be at least 16.5 years of age. Good moral character. Complete two years of high school (tenth grade) or equivalent. **Fees:** $25 application fee. $30 original certificate fee. $30 renewal fee. **Governing

Statute: Idaho Code, Title 54, Chap. 5. Rules of the Idaho Board of Examiners of Barbers.

Credential Type: Temporary Permit. **Requirements:** Temporary permit may be issued to an applicant who has not previously been issued a temporary permit and whose application and fees are accepted as being completed. **Fees:** $15 temporary permit fee. **Governing Statute:** Idaho Code, Title 54, Chap. 5. Rules of the Idaho Board of Examiners of Barbers.

1328

Barber Instructor
Board of Examiners of Barbers
Bureau of Occupational Licenses
1109 Main St., Ste. 220
Boise, ID 83702-5642
Phone: (208)334-3233

Credential Type: Barber Instructor License. **Duration of License:** One year. **Requirements:** Must have been a registered master barber in Idaho for at least three years. Must complete 20 hours of continuing education within the 12 months preceding application, of which 12 hours are in educational training and eight hours in seminars, trade shows, etc. **Examination:** Barber Teacher Certification Examination. **Fees:** $100 exam fee. $30 original license fee. $30 renewal fee. **Governing Statute:** Idaho Code, Title 54, Chap. 5. Rules of the Idaho Board of Examiners of Barbers.

1329

Cosmetologist
Board of Cosmetology
Bureau of Occupational Licenses
1109 Main St., Ste. 220
Boise, ID 83702-5642
Phone: (208)334-3233

Credential Type: Cosmetologist Registration and License. **Duration of License:** One year. **Authorization:** Must practice in a licensed establishment. **Requirements:** Complete two years of high school or equivalent. Graduate from and complete 2,000 hours training in a school of cosmetology, or 4,000 hours training as an apprentice. **Examination:** National Interstate Council of State Boards of Cosmetology written examination. Practical examination. **Reciprocity:** License by endorsement may be granted, provided applicant has three years practical experience within the past five years or holds a license from a state with requirements equal to Idaho's. Applicant must meet basic educational requirements. **Fees:** $20 registration/license fee. $20 renewal fee. $35 exam fee. **Governing Statute:** Idaho Code, Title 54, Chap. 8. Idaho Board of Cosmetology Rules.

1330

Cosmetology Apprentice
Board of Cosmetology
Bureau of Occupational Licenses
1109 Main St., Ste. 220
Boise, ID 83702-5642
Phone: (208)334-3233

Credential Type: Cosmetology Apprentice License. **Duration of License:** No renewal required. **Requirements:** Must be at least 16.5 years of age. Must have completed at least two years of high school or equivalent. **Fees:** $20 license fee. **Governing Statute:** Idaho Code, Title 54, Chap. 8. Idaho Board of Cosmetology Rules.

1331

Cosmetology Instructor
Board of Cosmetology
Bureau of Occupational Licenses
1109 Main St., Ste. 220
Boise, ID 83702-5642
Phone: (208)334-3233

Credential Type: Cosmetology Instructor License. **Duration of License:** One year. **Requirements:** Complete 12 semester college credit hours or equivalent, or pass examination. Meet one of the following sets of requirements: (1) Have one year experience as a licensed cosmetologist in a registered cosmetological establishment or school. Complete six months of teacher's training in a school of cosmetology. (2) Have two years experience as a licensed cosmetologist in a registered cosmetological establishment or school. Complete three months of teacher's training in a school of cosmetology. (3) Have five years experience as a licensed cosmetologist immediately preceding application. **Examination:** Written and practical examination. **Reciprocity:** License by endorsement may be granted, provided applicant has three years practical experience within the past five years or holds a license from a state with requirements equal to Idaho's. Applicant must meet basic educational requirements. **Fees:** $25 license fee. $25 renewal fee. $35 exam fee. **Governing Statute:** Idaho Code, Title 54, Chap. 8. Idaho Board of Cosmetology Rules.

1332

Cosmetology Student
Board of Cosmetology
Bureau of Occupational Licenses
1109 Main St., Ste. 220
Boise, ID 83702-5642
Phone: (208)334-3233

Credential Type: Cosmetology Student Certificate. **Duration of License:** No renewal required. **Requirements:** Must be at least 16.5 years of age. Must have completed at least two years of high school or equivalent. **Fees:** $20 certificate fee. **Governing Statute:** Idaho Code, Title 54, Chap. 8. Idaho Board of Cosmetology Rules.

1333

Electrologist/Esthetician
Board of Cosmetology
Bureau of Occupational Licenses
1109 Main St., Ste. 220
Boise, ID 83702-5642
Phone: (208)334-3233

Credential Type: Electrologist License. **Duration of License:** One year. **Requirements:** Must be at least 16.5 years of age. Must have completed at least two years of high school or equivalent. Must have completed and graduated from at least 800 hours of training in a board-approved school, or 1600 hours as an apprentice under the direct personal supervision of a licensed electrologist/electrician. **Examination:** Written and practical examination. **Reciprocity:** License by endorsement may be granted, provided applicant has three years practical experience within the past five years or holds a license from a state with requirements equal to Idaho's. Applicant must meet basic educational requirements. **Fees:** $22 license fee. $22 renewal fee. $35 exam fee. **Governing Statute:** Idaho Code, Title 54, Chap. 8. Idaho Board of Cosmetology Rules.

1334

Esthetician
Board of Cosmetology
Bureau of Occupational Licenses
1109 Main St., Ste. 220
Boise, ID 83702-5642
Phone: (208)334-3233

Credential Type: Esthetician License. **Duration of License:** One year. **Requirements:** Must be at least 16.5 years of age. Must have completed at least two years of high school or equivalent. Must have completed and graduated from at least 500 hours of training in a board approved

Esthetician, continued

school. **Examination:** Written and practical examination. **Reciprocity:** License by endorsement may be granted, provided applicant has three years practical experience within the past five years or holds a license from a state with requirements equal to Idaho's. Applicant must meet basic educational requirements. **Fees:** $22 license fee. $22 renewal fee. $35 exam fee. **Governing Statute:** Idaho Code, Title 54, Chap. 8. Idaho Board of Cosmetology Rules.

1335

Manicurist/Nail Technician
Board of Cosmetology
Bureau of Occupational Licenses
1109 Main St., Ste. 220
Boise, ID 83702-5642
Phone: (208)334-3233

Credential Type: Manicurist Registration. **Duration of License:** One year. **Requirements:** Must be at least 16.5 years of age. Must have completed at least two years of high school or equivalent. Must have completed and graduated from at least 300 hours of training in a boardapproved school. **Examination:** Written and practical examination. **Reciprocity:** Registration by endorsement may be granted, provided applicant has three years practical experience within the past five years or holds a license from a state with requirements equal to Idaho's. Applicant must meet basic educational requirements. **Fees:** $20 license fee. $20 renewal fee. $35 exam fee. **Governing Statute:** Idaho Code, Title 54, Chap. 8. Idaho Board of Cosmetology Rules.

Illinois

1336

Barber
Illinois Dept. of Professional Regulation
320 W. Washington St.
Springfield, IL 62786
Phone: (217)782-8556

Credential Type: Barber License. **Duration of License:** Two years. **Requirements:** At least 16 years of age. Good moral character. High school graduate or its equivalent or over the age of mandatory school attendance. Graduate from an approved barbering school in a period of not less than nine months and not more than three years. **Examination:** Barber Licensing Exam. **Reciprocity:** Yes, with an active barber's license in another state that has requirements substantially equivalent to those of Illinois. **Fees:** $53.15 examination fee. $25 initial license fee. $35 license by endorsement fee. $40 renewal fee. **Governing Statute:** The Barber, Cosmetology, Esthetics, and Nail Technology Act Illinois Revised Statutes 1991, Chapter 111.

1337

Barber Teacher
Illinois Dept. of Professional Regulation
320 W. Washington St.
Springfield, IL 62786
Phone: (217)782-8556

Credential Type: Barber Teacher License. **Duration of License:** Two years. **Requirements:** At least 18 years of age. Good moral character. High school graduate or equivalent. Hold an Illinois Barber License. Three years of barbering experience. Must have 500 hours of teacher training in an accredited barber school in a period of not less than three months and not more than two years or 1,000 hours of teachers training in an approved barbershop over a period of not less than six months and not more than two years. **Examination:** Barber Licensing Exam. **Reciprocity:** Yes, with an Illinois Barber License and a barber teacher license from another state, providing the licensing state has requirements substantially equivalent to those of Illinois. **Fees:** $58.30 examination fee. $25 initial license fee. $35 license by endorsement fee. $40 renewal fee. **Governing Statute:** The Barber, Cosmetology, Esthetics, and Nail Technology Act Illinois Revised Statutes 1991, Chapter 111.

1338

Cosmetologist
Illinois Dept. of Professional Regulation
320 W. Washington St.
Springfield, IL 62786
Phone: (217)782-8556

Credential Type: Cosmetologist License. **Duration of License:** Two years. **Requirements:** At least 16 years of age. Good moral character. Eighth grade graduate or equivalent. Complete a program of not less than 1,500 hours in an approved Cosmetology school over a period of not less than nine months, nor more than three years. A maximum of 500 hours of study in an approved barbering school may be credited towards the 1,500 hours needed for the cosmetology license. Renewal requires 20 hours of continuing education biennially. **Examination:** Registered Cometologist Examination. **Reciprocity:** Yes, if qualifications in the state of licensure are substantially equivalent to those of the state of Illinois or if applicant has verification of three years of lawful practice. **Fees:** $62.42 examination fee. $25 initial license fee. $35 license by endorsement fee. $40 renewal fee. **Governing Statute:** The Barber, Cosmetology, Esthetics, and Nail Technology Act of 1985, Illinois Revised Statutes 1991, Chapter 111.

1339

Cosmetology Teacher
Illinois Dept. of Professional Regulation
320 W. Washingtion St.
Springfield, IL 62786
Phone: (217)782-8556

Credential Type: Cosmetology Teacher. **Duration of License:** Two years. **Requirements:** At least 18 years of age. High school graduate or equivalent. Illinois Cosmetologist License in good standing. Two years experience under an Illinois Cosmetologist License and 1,000 hours of teacher training in an approved Cosmetology School. Renewal requires 10 hours of continuing education biennially. **Examination:** Cosmetology Teacher Examination. **Reciprocity:** Yes, if qualifications in the state of licensure are substantially equivalent to those of the state of Illinois. **Fees:** $58.30 examination fee. $25 initial license fee. $35 license by endorsement fee. $40 renewal fee. **Governing Statute:** The Barber, Cosmetology, Esthetics, and Nail Technology Act of 1985, Illinois Revised Statutes 1991, Chapter 111.

1340

Esthetician
Illinois Dept. of Professional Regulation
320 W. Washington St.
Springfield, IL 62786
Phone: (217)782-8556

Credential Type: Esthetician License. **Duration of License:** Two years. **Requirements:** At least 16 years of age. High school graduate, its equivalent, or beyond the age of mandatory school attendance. Graduate from an approved school licensed to teach esthetics. Program must include 750 hours in the study of esthetics in a period of not less than five months nor more than two years. **Examination:** Written examination. **Reciprocity:** Yes, considered on an individual basis. **Fees:** $64.42 examination fee. $25 initial license fee. $35 license by endorsement fee. $40 renewal fee. **Governing Statute:** The Barber, Cosmetology, Esthetics, and Nail Technology Act, Illinois Revised Statutes 1991, Chapter 111.

1341

Esthetician Teacher
Illinois Dept. of Professional Regulation
320 W. Washington St.
Springfield, IL 62786
Phone: (217)782-8556

Credential Type: Esthetician Teacher License. **Duration of License:** Two years. **Requirements:** At least 18 years of age. High school graduate or its equivalent. Hold an active license as an Esthetician or Cosmetologist. Complete 500 hours of teachers training. Complete two years of practice as an esthetician or cosmetologist within five years of examination or 1,000 hours of approved teacher's training from an esthetics or cosmetology school. **Examination:** Written examination. **Reciprocity:** Yes, considered on an individual basis. **Fees:** $60.30 examination fee. $25 initial license fee. $35 license by endorsement fee. $40 renewal fee. **Governing Statute:** The Barber, Cosmetology, Esthetics, and Nail Technology Act, Illinois Revised Statutes 1991, Chapter 111.

Indiana

1342

Barber
State Board of Barber Examiners
1021 State Office Bldg.
100 N. Senate Ave.
Indianapolis, IN 46204
Phone: (317)232-2531

Credential Type: License. **Requirements:** Contact licensing body for application information.

1343

Barber Instructor
State Board of Barber Examiners
1021 State Office Bldg.
100 N. Senate Ave.
Indianapolis, IN 46204
Phone: (317)232-2531

Credential Type: License. **Requirements:** Contact licensing body for application information.

1344

Cosmetology Hairdresser
Board of Cosmetology
Licensing Division
Professional Licensing Agency
1021 State Office Bldg.
100 N. Senate Ave.
Indianapolis, IN 46204
Phone: (317)232-2980

Credential Type: License. **Requirements:** Contact licensing body for application information.

1345

Cosmetology Instructor
Board of Cosmetology
Licensing Division
Professional Licensing Agency
1021 State Office Bldg.
100 N. Senate Ave.
Indianapolis, IN 46204
Phone: (317)232-2980

Credential Type: License. **Requirements:** Contact licensing body for application information.

1346

Electrologist
State Board of Beauty Culturists
Board of Examiners
100 N. Senate Ave.
Indianapolis, IN 46204
Phone: (317)232-2980

Credential Type: License to practice. **Requirements:** 18 years of age. Minimum 10th grade education or equivalent. Must hold a beauty culture license which requires completion of a 1000-hr. beauty culture course. Must also complete 200 hours in the study of electrology and pass the American Electrology Association (AEA)/ETS examination. **Examination:** AEA/ETS Examination.

1347

Esthetician
Board of Cosmetology
Licensing Division
Professional Licensing Agency
1021 State Office Bldg.
100 N. Senate Ave.
Indianapolis, IN 46204
Phone: (317)232-2980

Credential Type: License. **Requirements:** Contact licensing body for application information.

1348

Manicurist
Board of Cosmetology
Licensing Division
Professional Licensing Agency
1021 State Office Bldg.
100 N. Senate Ave.
Indianapolis, IN 46204
Phone: (317)232-2980

Credential Type: License. **Requirements:** Contact licensing body for application information.

1349

Shampoo Operator
Board of Cosmetology
Licensing Division
Professional Licensing Agency
1021 State Office Bldg.
100 N. Senate Ave.
Indianapolis, IN 46204
Phone: (317)232-2980

Credential Type: License. **Requirements:** Contact licensing body for application information.

Iowa

1350

Barber
Board of Barber Examiners
Lucas State Office Bldg.
Des Moines, IA 50319
Phone: (515)281-5596

Credential Type: License. **Duration of License:** Two years. **Requirements:** 16 years of age. 10th grade education. Graduation from a licensed barber school. Completion of 2,100 hours of training within a 10-month period. **Examination:** Written and practical. **Reciprocity:** Reciprocity with some states. $100 fee. **Fees:** $75 license and exam fee. $60 renewal fee.

Credential Type: License. **Duration of License:** Two years. **Requirements:** 16 years of age. 10th grade education. 160 hours of practical instruction, demonstration, and lecture or 1,000 hours of barber or cosmetology training. **Fees:** $25 license fee. $5 renewal fee.

Iowa

1351

Cosmetologist
Board of Cosmetology Examiners
Dept. of Public Health
Lucas State Office Bldg.
Des Moines, IA 50319
Phone: (515)281-6762

Credential Type: License. **Duration of License:** Two years. **Authorization:** Written and practical exam **Requirements:** A high school diploma or equivalent, plus 2,100 hours of training that lasts at least ten months. **Examination:** Written and practical. **Reciprocity:** Yes. **Fees:** $25 exam and license fee. $20 renewal fee.

Credential Type: License. **Duration of License:** Two years. **Requirements:** 19 years of age. Must be a licensed cosmetologist and take a course prescribed by the board. High school graduate or equivalent, and have 1,000 hours of teacher training or two years of experience in cosmetology. **Fees:** $20 license fee. $20 renewal fee.

1352

Electrologist
Board of Cosmetology
Dept. of Public Health
Lucas State Office Bldg.
321 E. 12th St.
Des Moines, IA 50319-0075
Phone: (515)281-4422

Credential Type: License to practice. **Requirements:** Complete 125 hours of study in electrology that includes a minimum of 25 hours of instruction in hair removal using electronic tweezers. Must also hold a cosmetologist's license that requires completion of a 2100-hr. cosmetology course. Pass examination. **Examination:** Yes.

Kansas

1353

Barber
Board of Barbering
717 S. Kansas Ave.
Topeka, KS 66603-3811
Phone: (913)296-2211

Credential Type: License. **Requirements:** Contact licensing body for application information.

1354

Cosmetologist
Cosmetology Board
717 Kansas Ave.
Topeka, KS 66603
Phone: (913)296-3155

Credential Type: Cosmetologist license. **Duration of License:** Two years. **Requirements:** Be at least 17 years of age. High school graduate or equivalent; if not, must be at least 25 years of age. Be free from contagious and infectious diseases. Complete 1500 hours of apprenticeship training in a licensed school, or 3000 hours in a licensed salon. **Examination:** Written and practical examinations. **Reciprocity:** Yes. **Fees:** $20 license fee. $15 exam fee. $35 out-of-state application fee. **Governing Statute:** Kansas Statutes Annotated 65-1901 through 65-1912, Rules and Regulations 69-1 ff.

1355

Cosmetology Apprentice
Cosmetology Board
717 Kansas Ave.
Topeka, KS 66603
Phone: (913)296-3155

Credential Type: Apprentice license. **Authorization:** Allows licensee to practice in a licensed school. **Requirements:** Submit application within 15 days of enrollment in a licensed cosemtology school. **Fees:** $10 license fee. **Governing Statute:** Kansas Statutes Annotated 65-1901 through 65-1912, Rules and Regulations 69-1 ff.

1356

Cosmetology Instructor
Cosmetology Board
717 Kansas Ave.
Topeka, KS 66603
Phone: (913)296-3155

Credential Type: Instructor's permit. **Duration of License:** Two years. **Requirements:** Must be a licensed cosmetologist. Must have completed high school. Renewal requires completion of at least 100 clock hours of training approved by the board, including at least 60 clock hours of teacher training and 40 clock hours of training in advanced hair styling. **Fees:** Contact board for fee. **Governing Statute:** Kansas Statutes Annotated 65-1901 through 65-1912, Rules and Regulations 69-1 ff.

Credential Type: Instructor's license. **Duration of License:** Three years. **Requirements:** Must be a licensed cosmetologist. Must have completed high school. Renewal requires completion of at least 100 clock hours of training approved by the board, including at least 60 clock hours of teacher training and 40 clock hours of training in advanced hair styling. **Fees:** Contact board for fee. **Governing Statute:** Kansas Statutes Annotated 65-1901 through 65-1912, Rules and Regulations 69-1 ff.

1357

Cosmetology Technician
Cosmetology Board
717 Kansas Ave.
Topeka, KS 66603
Phone: (913)296-3155

Credential Type: Cosmetology Technician license. **Duration of License:** Two years. **Requirements:** Be at least 17 years of age. High school graduate or equivalent; if not, must be at least 25 years of age. Be free from contagious and infectious diseases. Complete 1000 hours of apprenticeship training in a licensed school. **Examination:** Written and practical examinations. **Reciprocity:** Yes. **Fees:** $14 license fee. $15 exam fee. $35 out-of-state application fee. **Governing Statute:** Kansas Statutes Annotated 65-1901 through 65-1912, Rules and Regulations 69-1 ff.

1358

Electrologist
Cosmetology Board
717 Kansas Ave.
Topeka, KS 66603
Phone: (913)296-3155

Credential Type: Electrologist license. **Duration of License:** Two years. **Requirements:** Be at least 17 years of age. High school graduate or equivalent; if not, must be at least 25 years of age. Be free from contagious and infectious diseases. Complete 500 hours of apprenticeship training in a licensed school, or 1000 hours in a licensed salon. **Examination:** Written and practical examinations. **Reciprocity:** Yes. **Fees:** $20 license fee. $15 exam fee. $35 out-of-state application fee. **Governing Statute:** Kansas Statutes Annotated 65-1901 through 65-1912, Rules and Regulations 69-1 ff.

1359

Manicurist
Cosmetology Board
717 Kansas Ave.
Topeka, KS 66603
Phone: (913)296-3155

Credential Type: Manicurist license. **Duration of License:** Two years. **Requirements:** Be at least 17 years of age. High school graduate or equivalent; if not, must be at least 25 years of age. Be free from contagious and infectious diseases. Complete 350 hours of apprenticeship training in a licensed school, or 700 hours in a licensed salon. **Examination:** Written and practical examinations. **Reciprocity:** Yes. **Fees:** $16 license fee. $15 exam fee. $35 out-of-state application fee. **Governing Statute:** Kansas Statutes Annotated 65-1901 through 65-1912, Rules and Regulations 69-1 ff.

Kentucky

1360

Barber
Kentucky Board of Barbering
400 Sherburn, Ste. 405
Louisville, KY 40207
Phone: (502)895-4117

Credential Type: Barber License. **Duration of License:** One year. **Requirements:** High school diploma or equivalent. 1,500 hours in an accredited or licensed school of barbering. 18 years of age. Good health. 18 months of on-the-job training. **Examination:** Yes. **Fees:** $100 exam fee. $30 renewal fee.

Credential Type: Apprentice License. **Duration of License:** One year. **Requirements:** High school diploma or equivalent. 1,500 hours in an accredited or licensed school of barbering. 16 1/2 years of age. Good health. **Examination:** Yes. **Fees:** $100 exam fee. $50 license fee. $30 renewal fee.

Credential Type: Barber Instructor License. **Duration of License:** One year. **Requirements:** High school diploma or equivalent. 1,500 hours in an accredited or licensed school of barbering. **Examination:** Yes. **Fees:** $100 exam fee. $50 license fee. $30 renewal fee.

1361

Cosmetologist
Kentucky State Board of Hairdressers and Cosmetologists
314 W. Second St.
Frankfort, KY 40601
Phone: (502)564-4262

Credential Type: Apprentice License. **Duration of License:** One year. **Requirements:** 10th grade education. 1,800 hours in an approved school of cosmetology. 16 years of age. **Examination:** Yes. **Fees:** $25 exam fee. $12 license fee. $10 renewal fee.

Credential Type: Hairdresser License. **Duration of License:** One year. **Requirements:** 10th grade education. 1,800 hours in an approved school of cosmetology. 16 years of age. Six months of work experience as an apprentice in a licensed beauty salon. **Examination:** Yes. **Fees:** $35 exam fee.

Credential Type: Cosmetologist Instructor. **Duration of License:** One year. **Requirements:** High school diploma or equivalent. 1,000 hours in an approved school of cosmetology as an apprentice instructor. 16 years of age. One year of work experience in a licensed beauty salon. **Examination:** Yes. **Fees:** $50 exam fee. $35 license fee. $25 renewal fee.

Louisiana

1362

Barber
State Board of Barber Examiners
1000 Scenic Hwy.
Baton Rouge, LA 70801
Phone: (504)342-3099

Credential Type: License. **Duration of License:** One year. **Requirements:** High school diploma. 18 years of age. Completion of an accredited barber school. **Examination:** Written and practical exams. **Reciprocity:** Yes. **Fees:** $40 license fee. $32 exam fee.

1363

Cosmetologist/Beautician/Beauty Operator
Louisiana State Board of Cosmetology
11622 Sunbelt Court Industriplex, Rm. 412
Baton Rouge, LA 70816
Phone: (504)568-5267

Credential Type: License. **Duration of License:** One year. **Requirements:** 16 years of age. 10th grade education or equivalent. Graduation from an accredited cosmetology school. **Examination:** Written and practical exams. **Fees:** $15 initial fee. $19—$38 license fee.

1364

Electrologist
Louisiana State Board of Electrolysis Examiners
PO Box 1468
Baton Rouge, LA 70821
Phone: (504)336-1409

Credential Type: License. **Duration of License:** One year. **Requirements:** 18 years of age. Free of infectious disease. State resident. High school graduate. Completion of a course in practical training in electrolysis in an approved school of electrology, or completion of a like number of hours in an approved apprenticeship program. **Examination:** Yes. **Fees:** $150 application fee. $75 renewal fee.

Maine

1365

Aesthetician
State Board of Barbering and Cosmetology
Dept. of Professional and Financial Regulation
State House Station 62
Augusta, ME 04333
Phone: (207)582-8745
Fax: (207)582-5415

Credential Type: Aesthetician License. **Duration of License:** Two years. **Requirements:** Must be at least 17 years of age. Complete at least 10th grade of a secondary school education or equivalent. Within the past three years, complete a course of instruction in aesthetics of at least 750 hours in not less than five months in a licensed beauty school, or complete 1250 hours of apprentice training in not less than seven months. **Examination:** National Written Examination, practical examination, and State Law Quiz. **Reciprocity:** Yes, with states that grant similar reciprocity and have similar requirements. **Fees:** $15 exam fee. $15 license fee. $35 renewal fee. **Governing Statute:** 32 M.S.R.A., Chap. 126.

1366

Aesthetician Apprentice
State Board of Barbering and
   Cosmetology
Dept. of Professional and Financial
   Regulation
State House Station 62
Augusta, ME 04333
Phone: (207)582-8745
Fax: (207)582-5415

Credential Type: Apprentice Registration. **Duration of License:** One year. **Authorization:** Must work under the direct supervision of a licensed individual in a licensed shop. **Requirements:** Must be at least 17 years of age. Complete at least 10th grade of a secondary school education or equivalent. Must have place of employment. **Fees:** $25 registration fee. **Governing Statute:** 32 M.S.R.A., Chap. 126.

1367

Barber
State Board of Barbering and
   Cosmetology
Dept. of Professional and Financial
   Regulation
State House Station 62
Augusta, ME 04333
Phone: (207)582-8745
Fax: (207)582-5415

Credential Type: Barber License. **Duration of License:** One year. **Requirements:** Must be at least 17 years of age. Complete at least 10th grade of a secondary school education or equivalent. Within the past three years, complete a course of instruction in barbering of at least 1500 hours in not less than nine months in a licensed barber school, or complete 2500 hours of apprentice training in not less than 18 months. **Examination:** Written and practical examination. **Reciprocity:** Yes, with states that grant similar reciprocity and have similar requirements. **Fees:** $25 exam fee. $40 license fee. $40 renewal fee. **Governing Statute:** 32 M.S.R.A., Chap. 126.

1368

Barber Apprentice
State Board of Barbering and
   Cosmetology
Dept. of Professional and Financial
   Regulation
State House Station 62
Augusta, ME 04333
Phone: (207)582-8745
Fax: (207)582-5415

Credential Type: Apprentice Registration. **Duration of License:** 18 months. **Authorization:** Must work under the direct supervision of a licensed individual in a licensed shop. **Requirements:** Must be at least 17 years of age. Complete at least 10th grade of a secondary school education or equivalent. Must have place of employment. **Fees:** $25 registration fee. **Governing Statute:** 32 M.S.R.A., Chap. 126.

1369

Barber Instructor
State Board of Barbering and
   Cosmetology
Dept. of Professional and Financial
   Regulation
State House Station 62
Augusta, ME 04333
Phone: (207)582-8745
Fax: (207)582-5415

Credential Type: Barber Instructor License. **Duration of License:** One year. **Requirements:** Must hold high school diploma or equivalent. Valid Maine barber license. Complete a course of study for the preparation of instructors in a licensed school of barbering within the past three years; or complete at least 500 hours of training in a course for the preparation of instructors in a licensed school of barbering, and have at least three years shop experience as a barber within the past five years. **Examination:** Barber instructor exam, practical and written. **Fees:** $45 exam fee. $25 license fee.

1370

Barber Student
State Board of Barbering and
   Cosmetology
Dept. of Professional and Financial
   Regulation
State House Station 62
Augusta, ME 04333
Phone: (207)582-8745
Fax: (207)582-5415

Credential Type: Student Permit. **Duration of License:** 12 months. **Authorization:** Any training or services rendered to the general public must be under the direct supervision of a licensed instructor in a licensed school. **Requirements:** Must be at least 16 years of age. Complete at least 10th grade of a secondary school education or equivalent. Must be enrolled in a licensed school. **Fees:** $25 permit fee. **Governing Statute:** 32 M.S.R.A., Chap. 126.

1371

Cosmetologist
State Board of Barbering and
   Cosmetology
Dept. of Professional and Financial
   Regulation
State House Station 62
Augusta, ME 04333
Phone: (207)582-8745
Fax: (207)582-5415

Credential Type: Cosmetologist License. **Duration of License:** Two years. **Requirements:** Must be at least 17 years of age. Complete at least 10th grade of a secondary school education or equivalent. Within the past three years, complete a course of instruction in cosmetology of at least 1500 hours in not less than nine months in a licensed beauty school, or complete 2500 hours of apprentice training in not less than 18 months.

Requirement for a licensed barber is a course of instruction in cosmetology of at least 500 hours in a licensed beauty school, or 900 hours of apprentice training. **Examination:** National Practical Examination, National Written Examination, and State Law Quiz. **Reciprocity:** Yes, with states that grant similar reciprocity and have similar requirements. **Fees:** $15 exam fee. $15 license fee. $35 renewal fee. **Governing Statute:** 32 M.S.R.A., Chap. 126.

1372

Cosmetology Apprentice
State Board of Barbering and
   Cosmetology
Dept. of Professional and Financial
   Regulation
State House Station 62
Augusta, ME 04333
Phone: (207)582-8745
Fax: (207)582-5415

Credential Type: Apprentice Registration. **Duration of License:** 18 months. **Authorization:** Must work under the direct supervision of a licensed individual in a licensed shop. **Requirements:** Must be at least 17 years of age. Complete at least 10th grade of a secondary school education or equivalent. Must have place of employment. **Fees:**

$25 registration fee. **Governing Statute:** 32 M.S.R.A., Chap. 126.

1373

Cosmetology Instructor
State Board of Barbering and Cosmetology
Dept. of Professional and Financial Regulation
State House Station 62
Augusta, ME 04333
Phone: (207)582-8745
Fax: (207)582-5415

Credential Type: Cosmetology Instructor License and Certificate. **Duration of License:** Two years. **Requirements:** Meet one of the following sets of requirements: (1) High school diploma or equivalent. Valid Maine cosmetology license. Complete a course of instruction for the preparation of cosmetology instructors of at least 1000 hours in a licensed school of cosmetology; or complete 1000 hours in a cosmetology instructor course in an approved school within the past three years. (2) High school diploma or equivalent. Valid Maine cosmetology license. Have three years of beauty shop experience within the past five years. Have 12 credits from a postsecondary school, college, or university in courses related to teaching. **Examination:** Cosmetology instructor exam, practical and written. **Fees:** $50 exam and initial license fee. $16 renewal fee.

1374

Cosmetology Student
State Board of Barbering and Cosmetology
Dept. of Professional and Financial Regulation
State House Station 62
Augusta, ME 04333
Phone: (207)582-8745
Fax: (207)582-5415

Credential Type: Student Permit. **Duration of License:** 12 months. **Authorization:** Any training or services rendered to the general public must be under the direct supervision of a licensed instructor in a licensed school. **Requirements:** Must be at least 16 years of age. Complete at least 10th grade of a secondary school education or equivalent. Must be enrolled in a licensed school. **Fees:** $25 permit fee. **Governing Statute:** 32 M.S.R.A., Chap. 126.

1375

Manicurist
State Board of Barbering and Cosmetology
Dept. of Professional and Financial Regulation
State House Station 62
Augusta, ME 04333
Phone: (207)582-8745
Fax: (207)582-5415

Credential Type: Manicurist License. **Duration of License:** Two years. **Requirements:** Must be at least 17 years of age. Complete at least 10th grade of a secondary school education or equivalent. Within the past three years, complete a course of instruction in manicuring of at least 200 hours in not less than five weeks in a licensed beauty school, or complete 400 hours of apprentice training in not less than 10 weeks. **Examination:** National Written Examination, practical examination, and State Law Quiz. **Reciprocity:** Yes, with states that grant similar reciprocity and have similar requirements. **Fees:** $15 exam fee. $15 license fee. $35 renewal fee. **Governing Statute:** 32 M.S.R.A., Chap. 126.

1376

Manicurist Apprentice
State Board of Barbering and Cosmetology
Dept. of Professional and Financial Regulation
State House Station 62
Augusta, ME 04333
Phone: (207)582-8745
Fax: (207)582-5415

Credential Type: Apprentice Registration. **Duration of License:** Six months. **Authorization:** Must work under the direct supervision of a licensed individual in a licensed shop. **Requirements:** Must be at least 17 years of age. Complete at least 10th grade of a secondary school education or equivalent. Must have place of employment. **Fees:** $25 registration fee. **Governing Statute:** 32 M.S.R.A., Chap. 126.

Maryland

1377

Apprentice Cosmetologist
Board of Cosmetologists
Dept. of Licensing and Regulation
501 St. Paul Pl.
Baltimore, MD 21202-2272
Phone: (410)333-6320

Credential Type: Apprentice Cosmetologist License. **Requirements:** Completion of at least the ninth grade. **Fees:** $10 license fee.

1378

Barber
Board of Barber Examiners
Dept. of Licensing and Regulation
501 St. Paul Pl.
Baltimore, MD 21202-2272
Phone: (410)333-6320

Credential Type: Journey Barber License. **Requirements:** Complete 1200 hours of study in a barber school or 2250 hours of experience as an Apprentice Master Barber. **Examination:** Theory and practical examination. **Fees:** $50 license fee. $41 exam fee.

Credential Type: Master Barber License. **Requirements:** Complete 15 months of working experience as a Journey Barber. **Examination:** Theory examination. **Fees:** $50 license fee. $46 exam fee.

1379

Barber Apprentice
Board of Barber Examiners
Dept. of Licensing and Regulation
501 St. Paul Pl.
Baltimore, MD 21202-2272
Phone: (410)333-6320

Credential Type: Apprentice License. **Requirements:** Submit application and pay fee. **Fees:** $10 license fee.

1380

Barber Instructor
Board of Barber Examiners
Dept. of Licensing and Regulation
501 St. Paul Pl.
Baltimore, MD 21202-2272
Phone: (410)333-6320

Credential Type: Barber Instructor License. **Requirements:** Contact licensing body for application information.

Maryland

1381

Beauty Shop Manager
Board of Cosmetologists
Dept. of Licensing and Regulation
501 St. Paul Pl.
Baltimore, MD 21202-2272
Phone: (410)333-6320

Credential Type: License. **Requirements:** Completion of at least the ninth grade. Complete two years of working experience as a Licensed Cosmetologist. **Examination:** Senior Cosmetologist examination, theory. **Fees:** $50 license fee. $46 exam fee.

1382

Cosmetologist
Board of Cosmetologists
Dept. of Licensing and Regulation
501 St. Paul Pl.
Baltimore, MD 21202-2272
Phone: (410)333-6320

Credential Type: Cosmetologist License. **Requirements:** Completion of at least the ninth grade. Complete 1500 hours of training in a cosmetology school or 24 months of working experience as an apprentice. **Examination:** Theory and practical examination. **Fees:** $50 license fee. $41 exam fee.

1383

Cosmetology Instructor
Board of Cosmetologists
Dept. of Licensing and Regulation
501 St. Paul Pl.
Baltimore, MD 21202-2272
Phone: (410)333-6320

Credential Type: License. **Requirements:** Contact licensing body for application information.

1384

Demonstrator Hairdresser
Board of Cosmetologists
Dept. of Licensing and Regulation
501 St. Paul Pl.
Baltimore, MD 21202-2272
Phone: (410)333-6320

Credential Type: License. **Requirements:** Complete a board-approved program for make-up artist licensing. **Fees:** $50 license fee.

1385

Electrologist
Board of Electrologists
Dept. of Health and Mental Hygiene
4201 Patterson Ave.
Baltimore, MD 21215-2299
Phone: (410)764-4727

Credential Type: License. **Requirements:** Be at least 18 years of age. High school graduate or equivalent. Complete 300 hours of training in an approved electrology school, including at least 118 hours of theory and 182 hours of clinical practice.

Renewal requires 10 clock hours or one CEU of continuing education for each year. **Examination:** Practical, theory, and laws and regulations examinations. **Reciprocity:** Yes, but applicants must take all three licensing examinations. **Fees:** Contact board for fees. **Governing Statute:** Annotated Code of Maryland, Title 6. Code of Maryland Regulations, Title 10, Subtitle 53.

1386

Electrology Instructor
Board of Electrologists
Dept. of Health and Mental Hygiene
4201 Patterson Ave.
Baltimore, MD 21215-2299
Phone: (410)764-4727

Credential Type: License. **Duration of License:** Two years. **Requirements:** Be a licensed electrologist. Have practiced electrology actively for at least five years immediately prior to application. **Examination:** Oral and written examinations. **Fees:** Contact board for fees. **Governing Statute:** Annotated Code of Maryland, Title 6. Code of Maryland Regulations, Title 10, Subtitle 53.

1387

Manicurist
Board of Cosmetologists
Dept. of Licensing and Regulation
501 St. Paul Pl.
Baltimore, MD 21202-2272
Phone: (410)333-6320

Credential Type: Manicurist License. **Requirements:** Completion of at least the ninth grade. Complete 100 hours of training in a cosmetology school or three months of working experience as an apprentice. **Examination:** Theory and practical examination. **Fees:** $50 license fee. $41 exam fee.

Massachusetts

1388

Aesthetician
Board of Registration of Hairdressers
Div. of Registration
100 Cambridge St.
Boston, MA 02202
Phone: (617)727-9940
Phone: (617)727-3067

Credential Type: Aesthetician 7 License. **Duration of License:** Two years. **Requirements:** License issued upon completion of a 300-hour aesthetic program. **Examination:** Practical and written examination. **Reciprocity:** Yes. **Fees:** $60 exam fee. $50 license fee.

Credential Type: Aesthetician 6 License. **Duration of License:** Two years. **Requirements:** Complete two years of experience after being issued an Aesthetician 7 License. **Reciprocity:** Yes.

1389

Barber
Board of Registration of Barbers
Div. of Registration
100 Cambridge St., 15th fl.
Boston, MA 02202
Phone: (617)727-7367

Credential Type: Master Barber Registration. **Duration of License:** Two years. **Requirements:** Complete apprentice schooling of six months (1000 hours) in a licensed school. Complete 18 months as an apprentice working under a registered Master Barber. **Examination:** Practical and written examinations. **Reciprocity:** Yes. **Fees:** $100 exam fee. $60 license fee.

Credential Type: Apprentice Barber Registration. **Duration of License:** Two years. **Requirements:** Be at least 16 years of age. Complete six months (1000 hours) in a licensed school. **Examination:** Practical and written examinations. **Reciprocity:** Yes. **Fees:** $65 license and exam fee. $100 endorsement fee.

1390

Barber Instructor
Board of Registration of Barbers
Div. of Registration
100 Cambridge St., 15th fl.
Boston, MA 02202
Phone: (617)727-7367

Credential Type: Barber Instructor Registration. **Duration of License:** One year. **Requirements:** Have at least five years working experience as a registered Master Barber. **Examination:** Practical and written examinations. **Fees:** $150 license and examination fee.

1391

Cosmetologist
Board of Registration of Hairdressers
Div. of Registration
100 Cambridge St.
Boston, MA 02202
Phone: (617)727-9940
Phone: (617)727-3067

Credential Type: Operator's License. **Duration of License:** Two years. **Requirements:** License issued upon completion of a 1000-hour training program in a cosmetology school. **Examination:** Practical and written examination. **Reciprocity:** Yes. **Fees:** $60 exam fee. $50 license fee.

Credential Type: Cosmetologist License. **Duration of License:** Two years. **Requirements:** Complete two years of experience after being issued an Operator's License. **Reciprocity:** Yes.

1392

Cosmetologist Instructor
Board of Registration of Hairdressers
Div. of Registration
100 Cambridge St.
Boston, MA 02202
Phone: (617)727-9940
Phone: (617)727-3067

Credential Type: Instructor's License. **Duration of License:** Two years. **Requirements:** Complete a 1000-hour program. Two years work experience. Be a fully licensed cosmetologist. **Examination:** Practical and written instructor's examination. **Exemptions:** Anyone holding a Junior Assistant Instructor License may take the exam after two years. **Reciprocity:** Yes. **Fees:** $25 exam fee. $100 license fee.

Credential Type: Junior Assistant Instructor License. **Duration of License:** Two years. **Requirements:** Contact licensing body for application information. **Reciprocity:** Yes.

1393

Electrologist
Board of Cosmetology
Leverett Saltonstall Bldg., Rm. 1512
100 Cambridge St.
Boston, MA 02202
Phone: (617)727-9942

Credential Type: License to practice. **Requirements:** 18 years of age. High school graduate or equivalent. Complete an 1100-hr. course of study. Pass examination. **Examination:** Yes.

1394

Manicurist
Board of Registration of Hairdressers
Div. of Registration
100 Cambridge St.
Boston, MA 02202
Phone: (617)727-9940
Phone: (617)727-3067

Credential Type: License. **Duration of License:** Two years. **Requirements:** Complete a 100-hour manicuring program. **Examination:** Practical and written examination. **Reciprocity:** Yes. **Fees:** $60 exam fee. $50 license fee.

Michigan

1395

Barber
Board of Barber Examiners
Bureau of Occupational &
 Professional Regulation
Dept. of Commerce
PO Box 30018
Lansing, MI 48909
Phone: (517)373-9153

Credential Type: License. **Duration of License:** Two years. **Requirements:** At least 17 years of age. Completed the 10th grade or its equivalent. Completed 2,000 hours of training at an approved barber school. Be of good moral character. Abide by the rules of the Board of Barber Examiners. **Examination:** Written and practical exam. **Reciprocity:** Reciprocity may be granted to a person who has held a license in another state, jurisdiction, or country for one out of the three years prior to the date of application, if the requirements of the home state are substantially equivalent to those of Michigan. **Fees:** $15 application processing fee. $75 complete exam fee. $35 written exam fee. $45 practical exam fee. $20 exam review fee. $15 initial license fee. $15 renewal fee. $45 reciprocity fee. **Governing Statute:** The Occupational Code, Act 299 of 1980, as amended.

1396

Barber Instructor
Board of Barber Examiners
Bureau of Occupational &
 Professional Regulation
Dept. of Commerce
PO Box 30018
Lansing, MI 48909
Phone: (517)373-9153

Credential Type: License. **Duration of License:** Two years. **Requirements:** Completed the 12th grade or its equivalent. Worked at least two years as a barber. Completed one year of schooling as a student instructor (learning the theory and practice of an instructor), or have completed 60 semester or 90 term hours in an approved course of instruction at a college and have six months of schooling as a student instructor. Be of good moral character. Abide by the rules of the Board of Barber Examiners. **Examination:** Written and practical exam. **Reciprocity:** None. However, a person who has been licensed by his/her state, jurisdiction, or country to instruct others in barbering may substitute one year of experience in barber instruction for the required training. The two-year barber experience and the examination requirements shall not be waived on the basis of prior experience as an instructor. **Fees:** $15 application processing fee. $75 complete exam fee. $35 written exam fee. $45 practical exam fee. $20 exam review fee. $25 initial barber instructor license fee. $15 initial student instructor license fee. $25 barber instuctor renewal fee. $15 student instructor renewal fee. **Governing Statute:** The Occupational Code, Act 299 of 1980, as amended.

1397

Cosmetologist
Board of Cosmetology
Bureau of Occupational &
 Professional Regulation
Dept. of Commerce
PO Box 30018
Lansing, MI 48909
Phone: (517)373-9153

Credential Type: License. **Duration of License:** Two years. **Requirements:** At least 17 years of age. Completed the 9th grade or equivalent. Completed a 1500 hour approved course in cosmetology or a two-year apprenticeship and present a diploma. Submit the names of three personal references to the Board. Abide by the rules and regulations of the Board. Be of good moral

Cosmetologist, continued

character. **Examination:** Written and practical exam. **Reciprocity:** Licensed cosmetologists from other states whose backgrounds meet Michigan standards may be licensed without examination. **Fees:** $10 application processing fee. $25 complete initial exam fee ($15 written exam, $15 practical exam). $20 exam review fee. $12 initial license fee, per year. $12 renewal fee, per year. $20 reciprocity fee. **Governing Statute:** The Occupational Code, Act 299 of 1980, as amended.

1398

Cosmetology Instructor
Board of Cosmetology
Bureau of Occupational &
   Professional Regulation
Dept. of Commerce
PO Box 30018
Lansing, MI 48909
Phone: (517)373-9153

Credential Type: License. **Duration of License:** Two years. **Requirements:** Completed the 12th grade. Possess a valid Michigan cosmetology license. 500 hours of instructor training. Abide by the rules and regulations of the Board. Three years of experience as a cosmetologist, or two years of teaching experience and one year experience as a cosmetologist. **Examination:** Written, practical, and oral exam. **Fees:** $10 application processing fee. $25 complete initial exam fee ($15 written exam, $15 practical exam). $20 exam review fee. $12 initial license fee, per year. $12 renewal fee, per year. **Governing Statute:** The Occupational Code, Act 299 of 1980, as amended.

Credential Type: Limited License. **Duration of License:** Two years. **Requirements:** Completed the 12th grade. Possess a valid Michigan cosmetology license. 500 hours of instructor training. Abide by the rules and regulations of the Board. **Examination:** Written, practical, and oral exam. **Fees:** $10 application processing fee. $25 complete initial exam fee ($15 written exam, $15 practical exam). $20 exam review fee. $12 initial license fee, per year. $12 renewal fee, per year. **Governing Statute:** The Occupational Code, Act 299 of 1980, as amended.

1399

Electrologist
Board of Cosmetology
Dept. of Licensing and Regulation
611 W. Ottawa
PO Box 30244
Lansing, MI 48909
Phone: (517)373-0580

Credential Type: License to practice. **Requirements:** 18 years of age. Minimum 9th grade education or equivalent. Complete 300 hours of study or a 12-month apprenticeship. Pass examination. **Examination:** Yes.

1400

Manicurist
Board of Cosmetology
Bureau of Occupational &
   Professional Regulation
Dept. of Commerce
PO Box 30018
Lansing, MI 48909
Phone: (517)373-9153

Credential Type: License. **Duration of License:** Two years. **Requirements:** At least 17 years of age. Completed 300 hours of training in a cosmetology school or a six month approved apprenticeship. Abide by the rules and regulations of the Board. Be of good moral character. **Examination:** Written and practical exam. **Reciprocity:** Applicants from other states whose backgrounds meet the requirements of Michigan may be licensed without examination. All others must meet the same requirements as new applicants. **Fees:** $10 application processing fee. $25 initial exam fee ($15 written exam, $15 practical exam). $20 exam review fee. $12 initial license fee, per year. $12 renewal fee, per year. $12 reciprocity fee. **Governing Statute:** The Occupational Code, Act 299 of 1980, as amended.

Minnesota

1401

Barber
Board of Barber Examiners
Iris Park Place Bldg.
1885 University Ave. W., Ste. 335
St. Paul, MN 55104-3403
Phone: (612)642-0489

Credential Type: Registered Barber License. **Duration of License:** One year. **Requirements:** Submit application and pay fees. Pass examination. **Examination:** Yes. **Fees:** $55 exam and certificate fee. **Governing Statute:** Minnesota Statutes, Chap. 154. Minnesota Rules 2100.

Credential Type: Registered Apprentice License. **Duration of License:** One year. **Requirements:** Submit application and pay fees. Pass examination. **Examination:** Yes. **Fees:** $50 exam and certificate fee. **Governing Statute:** Minnesota Statutes, Chap. 154. Minnesota Rules 2100.

Credential Type: Temporary Apprentice Permit. **Requirements:** Submit application and pay fees. **Fees:** $25 temporary permit fee. **Governing Statute:** Minnesota Statutes, Chap. 154. Minnesota Rules 2100.

Credential Type: Student Permit. **Requirements:** Submit application and pay fees. **Fees:** $10 student permit fee. **Governing Statute:** Minnesota Statutes, Chap. 154. Minnesota Rules 2100.

1402

Barber Instructor
Board of Barber Examiners
Iris Park Place Bldg.
1885 University Ave. W., Ste. 335
St. Paul, MN 55104-3403
Phone: (612)642-0489

Credential Type: Barber Instructor License. **Duration of License:** One year. **Requirements:** Submit application and pay fees. Pass examination. Renewal requires continuing education. **Examination:** Yes. **Fees:** $35 license fee. $150 exam fee. **Governing Statute:** Minnesota Statutes, Chap. 154. Minnesota Rules 2100.

1403

Cosmetologist
Dept. of Commerce
Licensing Unit
133 E. 7th St.
St. Paul, MN 55101
Phone: (612)296-6319

Credential Type: Cosmetologist License. **Authorization:** Authorizes cosmetic care of hair, skin, and nails. **Requirements:** Complete 1550 hours of training. **Examination:** Practical exam from cosmetology school attended. Educational Testing Service—Cosmetology Multistate Licensing Program (ETSCMLP) cosmetologist test. Minnesota state test for cosmetologist, manicurist, and esthetician candidates. **Fees:** $45 license fee (includes $15 student registration fee). $32 exam fee (preregistered). $17 additional exam fee for walk-ins. (Exam fee covers both ETSCMLP and state exams.) **Governing Statute:** Minnesota Statutes, Chap. 155A. Cosmetology Rules, Chap. 2640.

Barbers and Cosmetologists — Minnesota

Credential Type: License by Reciprocity. **Requirements:** If initial license was issued within three years of application, must pass state laws portion of Minnesota cosmetology exam and submit licensing history. If initial license was issued over three year prior to application, must pass state laws portion of Minnesota cosmetology exam and submit licensing history; in addition, applicant must meet one of the following sets of requirements: (1) Complete 1800 hours of work experience within the past three years. (2) Complete a Minnesota-approved 40-hour refresher course. (3) Complete a Minnesota-approved reactivation course and both portions of the written exam (Uniform and state laws). **Examination:** Minnesota state laws. **Fees:** $45 license fee. **Governing Statute:** Minnesota Statutes, Chap. 155A. Cosmetology Rules, Chap. 2640.

1404

Cosmetologist Instructor
Dept. of Commerce
Licensing Unit
133 E. 7th St.
St. Paul, MN 55101
Phone: (612)296-6319

Credential Type: Cosmetologist Instructor's License. **Requirements:** Be a licensed cosmetologist. Complete 38 hours of teacher training. Complete 1400 hours of work experience within the past three years. **Examination:** Written and practical exams. **Fees:** $60 license fee. **Governing Statute:** Minnesota Statutes, Chap. 155A. Cosmetology Rules, Chap. 2640.

1405

Cosmetologist Manager
Dept. of Commerce
Licensing Unit
133 E. 7th St.
St. Paul, MN 55101
Phone: (612)296-6319

Credential Type: Cosmetologist Manager's License. **Authorization:** Authorizes cosmetic care of hair, skin, and nails. **Requirements:** Be a licensed cosmetologist. Complete 2700 hours of work experience within the past three years. **Examination:** Minnesota state test for managers. **Fees:** $60 license fee. $32 exam fee (preregistered). $17 additional exam fee for walk-ins. **Governing Statute:** Minnesota Statutes, Chap. 155A. Cosmetology Rules, Chap. 2640.

1406

Esthetician
Dept. of Commerce
Licensing Unit
133 E. 7th St.
St. Paul, MN 55101
Phone: (612)296-6319

Credential Type: Esthetician License. **Authorization:** Authorizes cosmetic care of skin only. **Requirements:** Complete 600 hours of training. **Examination:** Practical exam from cosmetology school attended. Educational Testing Service—Cosmetology Multistate Licensing Program (ETSCMLP) esthetician test. Minnesota state test for cosmetologist, manicurist, and esthetician candidates. **Fees:** $45 license fee (includes $15 student registration fee). $32 exam fee (preregistered). $17 additional exam fee for walk-ins. (Exam fee covers both ETS-CMLP and state exams.) **Governing Statute:** Minnesota Statutes, Chap. 155A. Cosmetology Rules, Chap. 2640.

Credential Type: License by Reciprocity. **Requirements:** If initial license was issued within three years of application, must pass state laws portion of Minnesota cosmetology exam and submit licensing history. If initial license was issued over three year prior to application, must pass state laws portion of Minnesota cosmetology exam and submit licensing history; in addition, applicant must meet one of the following sets of requirements: (1) Complete 1800 hours of work experience within the past three years. (2) Complete a Minnesota-approved 40-hour refresher course. (3) Complete a Minnesota-approved reactivation course and both portions of the written exam (Uniform and state laws). **Examination:** Minnesota state laws. **Fees:** $45 license fee. **Governing Statute:** Minnesota Statutes, Chap. 155A. Cosmetology Rules, Chap. 2640.

1407

Esthetician Manager
Dept. of Commerce
Licensing Unit
133 E. 7th St.
St. Paul, MN 55101
Phone: (612)296-6319

Credential Type: Esathetician Manager's License. **Authorization:** Authorizes cosmetic care of skin only. **Requirements:** Be a licensed esthetician. Complete 2700 hours of work experience within the past three years. **Examination:** Minnesota state test for managers. **Fees:** $60 license fee. $32 exam fee (preregistered). $17 additional exam fee for walk-ins. **Governing Statute:** Minnesota Statutes, Chap. 155A. Cosmetology Rules, Chap. 2640.

1408

Manicurist
Dept. of Commerce
Licensing Unit
133 E. 7th St.
St. Paul, MN 55101
Phone: (612)296-6319

Credential Type: Manicurist License. **Authorization:** Authorizes cosmetic care of nails only. **Requirements:** Complete 350 hours of training. **Examination:** Practical exam from cosmetology school attended. Educational Testing Service—Cosmetology Multistate Licensing Program (ETSCMLP) manicurist test. Minnesota state test for cosmetologist, manicurist, and esthetician candidates. **Fees:** $45 license fee (includes $15 student registration fee). $32 exam fee (preregistered). $17 additional exam fee for walk-ins. (Exam fee covers both ETS-CMLP and state exams.) **Governing Statute:** Minnesota Statutes, Chap. 155A. Cosmetology Rules, Chap. 2640.

Credential Type: License by Reciprocity. **Requirements:** If initial license was issued within three years of application, must pass state laws portion of Minnesota cosmetology exam and submit licensing history. If initial license was issued over three year prior to application, must pass state laws portion of Minnesota cosmetology exam and submit licensing history; in addition, applicant must meet one of the following sets of requirements: (1) Complete 1800 hours of work experience within the past three years. (2) Complete a Minnesota-approved 40-hour refresher course. (3) Complete a Minnesota-approved reactivation course and both portions of the written exam (Uniform and state laws). **Examination:** Minnesota state laws. **Fees:** $45 license fee. **Governing Statute:** Minnesota Statutes, Chap. 155A. Cosmetology Rules, Chap. 2640.

1409

Manicurist Manager
Dept. of Commerce
Licensing Unit
133 E. 7th St.
St. Paul, MN 55101
Phone: (612)296-6319

Credential Type: Manicurist Manager's License. **Authorization:** Authorizes cosmetic care of nails only. **Requirements:** Be a licensed manicurist. Complete 2700 hours of work experience within the past three

Manicurist Manager, continued

years. **Examination:** Minnesota state test for managers. **Fees:** $60 license fee. $32 exam fee (preregistered). $17 additional exam fee for walk-ins. **Governing Statute:** Minnesota Statutes, Chap. 155A. Cosmetology Rules, Chap. 2640.

Mississippi

1410

Barber
State Board of Barber Examiners
510 George St., Rm. 234
PO Box 603
Jackson, MS 39205
Phone: (601)359-1015

Credential Type: License. **Requirements:** Contact licensing body for application information.

Missouri

1411

Barber
State Board of Barber Examiners
3605 Missouri Blvd.
PO Box 1335
Jefferson City, MO 65102
Phone: (314)751-0805

Credential Type: License. **Requirements:** Contact licensing body for application information.

1412

Cosmetologist
Board of Cosmetology
3605 Missouri Blvd.
PO Box 1062
Jefferson City, MO 65102-1062
Phone: (314)751-1052
Phone: (314)751-2334

Credential Type: Registration and License. **Duration of License:** Two years. **Requirements:** Be at least 17 years of age. Complete at least the 10th grade or equivalent. Meet one of the following sets of requirements: (1) If an apprentice, must complete at least 3000 hours under the supervision of a licensed cosmetologist. (2) If a student, must complete at least 1500 hours of training in a licensed school. **Examination:** State examination. **Reciprocity:** Yes, provided other state has equivalent requirements. **Fees:** $20 exam fee. $40 renewal fee. $40 reciprocity fee. **Governing Statute:** Laws of Missouri, Chap. 329. Rules and Regulations, four CSR 90.

1413

Cosmetology Instructor
Board of Cosmetology
3605 Missouri Blvd.
PO Box 1062
Jefferson City, MO 65102-1062
Phone: (314)751-1052
Phone: (314)751-2334

Credential Type: Instructor Trainee License. **Duration of License:** A definite period needed to complete training requirements. **Requirements:** Good moral character. Good physical and mental health. High school graduate or equivalent. Hold a Missouri license to practice as a cosmetologist or manicurist. **Fees:** $10 trainee enrollment fee. **Governing Statute:** Laws of Missouri, Chap. 329. Rules and Regulations, four CSR 90.

Credential Type: Instructor License. **Duration of License:** Two years. **Requirements:** Good moral character. Good physical and mental health. High school graduate or equivalent. Hold a Missouri license to practice as a cosmetologist or manicurist. Complete 1200 hours of instructor training in a licensed cosmetology school. Renewal requires attendance at one or more teacher training seminars or workshops every two years. **Examination:** Instructor examination. **Reciprocity:** Yes, provided other state has equivalent requirements. **Fees:** $30 exam fee. $24 license fee. $24 renewal fee. $54 reciprocity fee. **Governing Statute:** Laws of Missouri, Chap. 329. Rules and Regulations, four CSR 90.

1414

Cosmetology Student/Apprentice
Board of Cosmetology
3605 Missouri Blvd.
PO Box 1062
Jefferson City, MO 65102-1062
Phone: (314)751-1052
Phone: (314)751-2334

Credential Type: Registration. **Requirements:** Be enrolled in a licensed school or employed in a licensed shop. Be at least 17 years of age. Complete at least the 10th grade or equivalent. **Fees:** $10 student enrollment fee. $25 apprentice enrollment fee. **Governing Statute:** Laws of Missouri, Chap. 329. Rules and Regulations, four CSR 90.

1415

Manicurist
Board of Cosmetology
3605 Missouri Blvd.
PO Box 1062
Jefferson City, MO 65102-1062
Phone: (314)751-1052
Phone: (314)751-2334

Credential Type: Registration and License. **Duration of License:** Two years. **Requirements:** Be at least 17 years of age. Complete at least the 10th grade or equivalent. Meet one of the following sets of requirements: (1) If an apprentice, must complete at least 700 hours under the supervision of a licensed cosmetologist. (2) If a student, must complete at least 350 hours of training in a licensed school. **Examination:** State examination. **Reciprocity:** Yes, provided other state has equivalent requirements. **Fees:** $20 exam fee. $40 renewal fee. $40 reciprocity fee. **Governing Statute:** Laws of Missouri, Chap. 329. Rules and Regulations, four CSR 90.

Montana

1416

Barber
Montana Board of Barbers
111 N. Jackson
Helena, MT 59620
Phone: (406)444-3738

Credential Type: License. **Duration of License:** One year. **Requirements:** 18 years of age. Eighth grade education. Graduation from a licensed barber school, including completion of 2000 hours of barbering instruction, or equivalent. Health certificate. **Examination:** National Board Examinations. Practical examination. Law and rules examination. **Fees:** $20 exam fee. $15 license fee. $15 renewal fee. **Governing Statute:** Montana Code Annotated 37-30-301 through 37-30-311.

1417

Barber Instructor
Montana Board of Barbers
111 N. Jackson
Helena, MT 59620
Phone: (406)444-3738

Credential Type: License. **Duration of License:** One year. **Requirements:** Contact licensing body for application information. **Fees:** $50 license fee. $25 renewal fee. **Governing Statute:** Montana Code Annotated 37-30-301 through 37-30-311.

1418

Cosmetologist
Montana Board of Cosmetologists
111 N. Jackson
Helena, MT 59620
Phone: (406)444-4288

Credential Type: License. **Duration of License:** One year. **Requirements:** 18 years of age. Eighth grade education. Graduation from a registered school of cosmetology or equivalent. **Examination:** Written and practical. **Fees:** $20 exam fee. $25 license fee. $10 renewal fee. **Governing Statute:** Montana Code Annotated 37-31-301 through 37-31-334.

1419

Electrologist
Montana Board of Cosmetologists
111 N. Jackson
Helena, MT 59620
Phone: (406)444-4288

Credential Type: License. **Duration of License:** One year. **Requirements:** 18 years of age. High school graduation or equivalent. Completion of an approved electrology program. **Examination:** State board exam. **Fees:** $50 exam fee. $25 license fee. $10 renewal fee. **Governing Statute:** Montana Code Annotated 37-32-301 through 37-32-311.

1420

Manicurist
Montana Board of Cosmetologists
111 N. Jackson
Helena, MT 59620
Phone: (406)444-4288

Credential Type: License. **Duration of License:** One year. **Requirements:** 18 years of age. High school diploma or equivalent. Graduation from a registered school of manicuring or equivalent. **Examination:** Written and practical. **Fees:** $40 exam fee. $25 license fee. $10 renewal fee. **Governing Statute:** Montana Code Annotated 37-31-301 through 37-31-334.

Nebraska

1421

Barber
Nebraska Board of Barber Examiners
301 Centennial Mall S.
PO Box 94723
Lincoln, NE 68509
Phone: (402)471-2051

Credential Type: License. **Duration of License:** One year. **Requirements:** 17 years of age. Must have a high school diploma. Must have completed 2,100 hours at an accredited barber school. **Examination:** Yes. **Fees:** $50 examination fee. $10 license fee. $30 renewal fee.

1422

Cosmetologist
Nebraska Board of Examiners in Cosmetology
301 Centennial Mall S.
PO Box 95007
Lincoln, NE 68509
Phone: (402)471-2115

Credential Type: License. **Duration of License:** Two years. **Requirements:** 17 years of age. Must have no infectius or contagious diseases. Must hold a high school diploma. Must have completed a first aid course. Must have graduated from an accredited school of cosmetology. **Examination:** Yes. **Fees:** Cosmetologist, $40 license and $25 renewal fees. Instructor, $25 license and $25 renewal fees. School of Cosmetology, $3000 license and $400 renewal fees.

1423

Electrologist
Arizona Institute of Electrolysis
4002 E. Main, Ste. 2
Mesa, AZ 85205
Phone: (602)832-8999

Credential Type: Certificate. **Requirements:** Must complete the required course hours at an accredited school.

Nevada

1424

Barber
Nevada State Board of Barber Examiners
606 E. Sahara Ave.
Las Vegas, NV 89104
Phone: (702)731-1966

Credential Type: License. **Requirements:** Completion of a 1,500 hour barber school course. **Examination:** Yes. **Fees:** $10 application fee. $75 exam and license fee. $40 renewal fee.

1425

Cosmetologist
State Board of Cosmetology
1785 E. Sahara Ave., Ste. 255
Las Vegas, NV 89104
Phone: (702)486-6542

Credential Type: Cosmetologist License. **Duration of License:** Two years. **Requirements:** Completion of 1,800 hours in a licensed school of cosmetology. Completion of 10th grade or equivalent. 18 years of age. **Examination:** Student written and practical examinations. **Fees:** $15 application fee. $55 exam and license fee. $30 renewal fee.

Credential Type: License by Reciprocity. **Duration of License:** Two years. **Requirements:** Be at least 18 years of age. Must hold a current license from at least one state. Must have passed a national written examination. Must have at least one year of full-time experience within the past three years. If applicant has insufficient experience, then applicant must take student written and practical examinations. **Examination:** National written examination (if not already passed). Written Nevada Law test. Student written and practical examinations (if insufficient experience). **Fees:** $100 reciprocity fee. $40 national written exam fee. $55 student exam fee.

1426

Electrologist
Board of Cosmetology
1785 E. Sahara, Ste. 180
Las Vegas, NV 89104
Phone: (702)486-6542

Credential Type: License to practice. **Requirements:** 18 years of age. High school graduate or equivalent. Complete a 500-hr. course of study or a 1000-hr. apprenticeship. Pass examination. **Examination:** Yes.

Nevada

1427

Hair Stylist
Nevada State Board of Cosmetology
1785 E. Sahara Ave., Ste. 180
Las Vegas, NV 89104
Phone: (702)486-6542

Credential Type: License. **Duration of License:** Two years. **Requirements:** Completion of 1,800 hours in a licensed school of cosmetology. Completion of 10th grade or equivalent. 18 years of age. **Fees:** $15 application fee. $55 exam and license fee. $30 renewal fee.

New Hampshire

1428

Barber
Board of Barbering, Cosmetology, and Esthetics
Health and Welfare Bldg.
Hazen Dr.
Concord, NH 03301
Phone: (603)271-3608

Credential Type: Barber's License. **Duration of License:** Two years. **Requirements:** High school graduate or equivalent. Meet one of the following sets of requirements: (1) Complete 1500 hours of training over a period of at least one year in an approved school of barbering. (2) Complete at least 3000 hours of training over a period of at least two years under a licensed barber who has engaged in the practice of barbering within the state for at least two years. **Examination:** Written or oral examination of the National Interstate Council of State Boards of Cosmetology. Practical examination. **Reciprocity:** Yes, provided other state's licensing requirements are substantially equivalent. **Fees:** $25 license fee. $30 renewal fee. $60 reciprocity fee. **Governing Statute:** RSA 313-A. Code of Administrative Rules.

Credential Type: Temporary Permit. **Duration of License:** Until next examination. **Authorization:** Authorizes holder to work temporarily under the guidance of a licensed practitioner in a registered salon or barbershop. **Requirements:** Must have applied for a license and be eligible to take the examination. **Governing Statute:** RSA 313-A. Code of Administrative Rules.

Credential Type: Apprentice Registration. **Requirements:** Be at least 16 years of age. **Fees:** $20 registration fee. $20 renewal fee. **Governing Statute:** RSA 313-A. Code of Administrative Rules.

1429

Cosmetologist
Board of Barbering, Cosmetology, and Esthetics
Health and Welfare Bldg.
Hazen Dr.
Concord, NH 03301
Phone: (603)271-3608

Credential Type: Cosmetologist's License. **Duration of License:** Two years. **Requirements:** High school graduate or equivalent. Meet one of the following sets of requirements: (1) Complete 1500 hours of training over a period of at least one year in an approved school of cosmetology. (2) Complete at least 3000 hours of training over a period of at least two years under a licensed cosmetologist who has engaged in the practice of cosmetology within the state for at least two years. **Examination:** Written or oral examination of the National Interstate Council of State Boards of Cosmetology. Practical examination. **Reciprocity:** Yes, provided other state's licensing requirements are substantially equivalent. **Fees:** $25 license fee. $30 renewal fee. $60 reciprocity fee. **Governing Statute:** RSA 313-A. Code of Administrative Rules.

Credential Type: Temporary Permit. **Duration of License:** Until next examination. **Authorization:** Authorizes holder to work temporarily under the guidance of a licensed practitioner in a registered salon or barbershop. **Requirements:** Must have applied for a license and be eligible to take the examination. **Governing Statute:** RSA 313-A. Code of Administrative Rules.

Credential Type: Apprentice Registration. **Requirements:** Be at least 16 years of age. **Fees:** $20 registration fee. $20 renewal fee. **Governing Statute:** RSA 313-A. Code of Administrative Rules.

1430

Cosmetology Instructor
Board of Barbering, Cosmetology, and Esthetics
Health and Welfare Bldg.
Hazen Dr.
Concord, NH 03301
Phone: (603)271-3608

Credential Type: Cosmetology Instructor's License. **Duration of License:** Two years. **Requirements:** Must be a licensed cosmetologist, barber, manicurist, or esthetician. Complete at least one year of practice in a licensed shop. Complete 1000 hours of training or 700 hours as a student instructor. Renewal requires 28 hours of continuing education every two years. **Examination:** Written or oral examination of the National Interstate Council of State Boards of Cosmetology. Practical examination. **Reciprocity:** Yes, provided other state's licensing requirements are substantially equivalent. **Fees:** $25 license fee. $30 renewal fee. $60 reciprocity fee. **Governing Statute:** RSA 313-A. Code of Administrative Rules.

Credential Type: Temporary Permit. **Duration of License:** Until next examination. **Requirements:** Must have applied for a license and be eligible to take the examination. **Governing Statute:** RSA 313-A. Code of Administrative Rules.

1431

Electrologist
Board of Cosmetology
Health and Welfare Bldg.
6 Hazen Dr.
Concord, NH 03301
Phone: (603)271-3608

Credential Type: License to practice. **Requirements:** 18 years of age. High school graduate or equivalent. Complete an 1100-hr. course of study. Pass the American Electrology Association (AEA)/ETS examination. **Examination:** AEA/ETS Examination.

1432

Esthetician
Board of Barbering, Cosmetology, and Esthetics
Health and Welfare Bldg.
Hazen Dr.
Concord, NH 03301
Phone: (603)271-3608

Credential Type: Esthetician's License. **Duration of License:** Two years. **Requirements:** High school graduate or equivalent. Meet one of the following sets of requirements: (1) Complete 450 hours of training in an approved school of cosmetology. (2) Receive equivalent training as an apprentice in a beauty salon. **Examination:** Written or oral examination of the National Interstate Council of State Boards of Cosmetology. Practical examination. **Reciprocity:** Yes, provided other state's licensing requirements are substantially equivalent. **Fees:** $25 license fee. $30 renewal fee. $60 reciprocity fee. **Governing Statute:** RSA 313-A. Code of Administrative Rules.

Credential Type: Temporary Permit. **Duration of License:** Until next examination. **Authorization:** Authorizes holder to work temporarily under the guidance of a licensed practitioner in a registered salon or barbershop. **Requirements:** Must have applied for a license and be eligible to take the examination. **Governing Statute:** RSA 313-A. Code of Administrative Rules.

Credential Type: Apprentice Registration. **Requirements:** Be at least 16 years of age. **Fees:** $20 registration fee. $20 renewal fee. **Governing Statute:** RSA 313-A. Code of Administrative Rules.

1433

Manicurist
Board of Barbering, Cosmetology, and Esthetics
Health and Welfare Bldg.
Hazen Dr.
Concord, NH 03301
Phone: (603)271-3608

Credential Type: Manicurist's License. **Duration of License:** Two years. **Requirements:** High school graduate or equivalent. Meet one of the following sets of requirements: (1) Complete a course of at least six weeks, including at least 150 hours of professional training in manicuring in an approved school. (2) Receive equivalent training as an apprentice in a beauty salon. **Examination:** Written or oral examination of the National Interstate Council of State Boards of Cosmetology. Practical examination. **Reciprocity:** Yes, provided other state's licensing requirements are substantially equivalent. **Fees:** $25 license fee. $30 renewal fee. $60 reciprocity fee. **Governing Statute:** RSA 313-A. Code of Administrative Rules.

Credential Type: Temporary Permit. **Duration of License:** Until next examination. **Authorization:** Authorizes holder to work temporarily under the guidance of a licensed practitioner in a registered salon or barbershop. **Requirements:** Must have applied for a license and be eligible to take the examination. **Governing Statute:** RSA 313-A. Code of Administrative Rules.

Credential Type: Apprentice Registration. **Requirements:** Be at least 16 years of age. **Fees:** $20 registration fee. $20 renewal fee. **Governing Statute:** RSA 313-A. Code of Administrative Rules.

New Jersey

1434

Cosmetologist/Hairstylist
Board of Cosmetology and Hairstyling
1100 Raymond Blvd., Rm. 311
Newark, NJ 07102
Phone: (201)648-2450

Credential Type: License. **Duration of License:** Two years. **Requirements:** High school diploma or equivalent. Completion of a 1,200-hour course in cosmetology and hair styling at an approved school. 17 years of age. **Examination:** Written, oral and practical exam. **Fees:** $30 exam fee. $30 license fee. $30 renewal fee. **Governing Statute:** NJSA 45:5B. NJAC 13:28.

1435

Cosmetology Instructor
Board of Cosmetology and Hairstyling
1100 Raymond Blvd., Rm. 311
Newark, NJ 07102
Phone: (201)648-2450

Credential Type: Cosmetology and Hairstyling Teacher. **Duration of License:** Two years. **Requirements:** High school diploma or equivalent. Completion of a teacher training course of 500 hours at a licensed school. Completion of a 30-hour teaching methods course conducted by an approved college. Hold a cosmetologist-hairstylist license or an operator license from the state board. 18 years of age. **Examination:** Written, oral and practical exam. **Fees:** $30 exam fee. $30 biennial license fee. **Governing Statute:** NJSA 45:5B. NJAC 13:2B.

1436

Manicurist
Board of Cosmetology and Hairstyling
1100 Raymond Blvd., Rm. 311
Newark, NJ 07102
Phone: (201)648-2450

Credential Type: License. **Duration of License:** Two years. **Requirements:** High school diploma or equivalent. Completion of an approved course in manicuring. 17 years of age. **Examination:** Written, oral and practical exam. **Fees:** $30 exam fee. $30 biennial license fee. **Governing Statute:** NJSA 45:5B. NJAC 13:28.

New Mexico

1437

Barber
Board of Barber Examiners
Dept. of Regulation and Licensing
PO Box 25101
725 St. Michael's Dr.
Santa Fe, NM 87504
Phone: (505)827-7176

Credential Type: Certificate of Registration. **Duration of License:** One year. **Requirements:** Be at least 18 years of age. Good moral character and temperate habits. Complete a course of barbering of at least 1200 hours. **Examination:** Practical demonstration. Written and oral examination. **Reciprocity:** Yes. **Fees:** $50 exam fee. $45 certificate fee. $45 renewal fee. **Governing Statute:** New Mexico Board of Barber Examiners Statutes 61-17-1 et seq. New Mexico Board of Barber Examiners Rules.

1438

Barber Instructor
Board of Barber Examiners
Dept. of Regulation and Licensing
PO Box 25101
725 St. Michael's Dr.
Santa Fe, NM 87504
Phone: (505)827-7176

Credential Type: Certificate of Registration. **Duration of License:** One year. **Requirements:** Be at least 18 years of age. Good moral character and temperate habits. Complete a course of barbering of at least 1200 hours. Pass instructor's exam. **Examination:** Practical demonstration. Written and oral examination. **Reciprocity:** Yes. **Fees:** $50 exam fee. $25 certificate fee. $25 renewal fee. **Governing Statute:** New Mexico Board of Barber Examiners Statutes 61-17-1 et seq. New Mexico Board of Barber Examiners Rules.

1439

Cosmetologist
State Board of Cosmetologists
Regulation and Licensing Dept.
PO Box 25101
725 St. Michael's Dr.
Santa Fe, NM 87504
Phone: (505)827-7176

Credential Type: Cosmetologist License. **Duration of License:** One year. **Requirements:** Complete at least two years of high school or equivalent. Be at least 16 years of age. Complete 1600 hours of training in a cosmetology school. **Examination:** Yes.

Cosmetologist, continued

Reciprocity: Yes, provided applicant meets state requirements for training, age, and education. **Fees:** $20 license fee. $25 exam fee. $12.50 renewal fee. $100 reciprocity fee.

1440

Cosmetology Teacher
Cosmetology Board
Dept. of Regulation and Licensing
PO Box 25101
725 St. Michael's Dr.
Santa Fe, NM 87504
Phone: (505)827-7176

Credential Type: Cosmetology Teacher's License. **Duration of License:** One year. **Requirements:** High school graduate or equivalent. Must be a licensed cosmetologist with three years experience or 1000 hours of instructor training. **Examination:** State examination. **Reciprocity:** Yes, provided applicant meets state requirements for training, age, and education. **Fees:** $25 exam fee. $25 license fee. $25 renewal fee. $100 reciprocity fee.

1441

Electrologist
Cosmetology Board
Dept. of Regulation and Licensing
PO Box 25101
725 St. Michael's Dr.
Santa Fe, NM 87504
Phone: (505)827-7176

Credential Type: Electrologist License. **Duration of License:** One year. **Requirements:** High school graduate or equivalent. Be at least 17 years of age. Complete 500 hours of training in a cosmetology school. **Examination:** Yes. **Reciprocity:** Yes, provided applicant meets state requirements for training, age, and education. **Fees:** $20 license fee. $35 exam fee. $12.50 renewal fee. $100 reciprocity fee.

1442

Manicurist
Cosmetology Board
Dept. of Regulation and Licensing
PO Box 25101
725 St. Michael's Dr.
Santa Fe, NM 87504
Phone: (505)827-7176

Credential Type: Manicurist License. **Duration of License:** One year. **Requirements:** Complete at least two years of high school or equivalent. Be at least 16 years of age. Complete 500 hours of training in a cosmetology school. **Examination:** Yes. **Reciprocity:** Yes, provided applicant meets state requirements for training, age, and education. **Fees:** $12.50 license fee. $25 exam fee. $7.50 renewal fee. $100 reciprocity fee.

1443

Skin Care Specialist (Esthetician)
Cosmetology Board
Dept. of Regulation and Licensing
PO Box 25101
725 St. Michael's Dr.
Santa Fe, NM 87504
Phone: (505)827-7176

Credential Type: Skin Care License. **Duration of License:** One year. **Requirements:** Complete at least two years of high school or equivalent. Be at least 16 years of age. Complete 900 hours of training in a cosmetology school. **Examination:** Yes. **Reciprocity:** Yes, provided applicant meets state requirements for training, age, and education. **Fees:** $20 license fee. $25 exam fee. $12.50 renewal fee. $100 reciprocity fee.

New York

1444

Barber
New York State Dept. of State
Div. of Licensing Services
162 Washington Ave.
Albany, NY 12231
Phone: (518)474-2650

Credential Type: License. **Duration of License:** Two years. **Requirements:** Completion of course of study in barber school. 18 months of experince as an apprentice with schooling, or 24 months of experience without schooling. 17 years of age. Certificate of health. **Examination:** Practical. **Fees:** $15 exam fee. $20—$30 license fee. $20—$30 renewal fee. **Governing Statute:** Article 28 of the General Business Law.

1445

Cosmetologist (Hairdresser/Stylist, Manicurist, Beautician)
New York State Dept. of State
Div. of Licensing Services
162 Washington Ave.
Albany, NY 12231
Phone: (518)474-2650

Credential Type: License. **Duration of License:** Two years. **Requirements:** Beauty school plus proof of eighth-grade education. 17 years of age. Health certificate. Two recent photographs. **Examination:** Written and practical. **Fees:** $15 exam fee. $20 application fee. $10 license fee. $20 renewal fee. **Governing Statute:** Article 27, General Business Law.

North Carolina

1446

Barber
North Carolina State Board of Barber Examiners
3901 Barrett Dr., Ste. 300
Raleigh, NC 27609
Phone: (919)733-3650

Credential Type: License. **Duration of License:** One year. **Requirements:** Eighth-grade education. Completion of 1,528 clock hours of study from an approved barber's school. Pass an apprentice exam and serve one year as a full-time apprentice under a registered barber. **Examination:** Practical and multiple choice. **Fees:** $20 registration fee. $80 exam fee. $20 renewal fee.

1447

Barber Instructor
North Carolina State Board of Barber Examiners
3901 Barrett Dr., Ste. 300
Raleigh, NC 27609
Phone: (919)733-3650

Credential Type: Registration. **Duration of License:** One year. **Requirements:** Must be a registered and practicing barber in North Carolina. **Examination:** Written, oral and practical. **Fees:** $35 registration fee. $85 exam fee. $35 renewal fee.

1448

Cosmetologist
North Carolina State Board of Cosmetic Arts
4101 North Blvd., Ste. H
Raleigh, NC 27604
Phone: (919)790-8460

Credential Type: License. **Duration of License:** Three years. **Requirements:** 17 years of age. High school diploma or equivalent. 1,500 clock hours at an approved beauty college or serve as an apprentice. An apprentice must complete 1,200 clock hours at an approved beauty school and receive six months of experience under the direct supervision of a licensed cosmetologist. **Examination:** Practical and theoretical. **Fees:** $33 license fee. $10 exam fee. $15 registration fee. $33 renewal fee.

1449

Cosmetologist Instructor
North Carolina State Board of Cosmetic Arts
4101 North Blvd., Ste. H
Raleigh, NC 27604
Phone: (919)790-8460

Credential Type: License. **Duration of License:** Two years. **Requirements:** Must be a licensed cosmetologist for five consecutive years, or a licensed cosmetologist for six months and completed 400 clock hours of teaching courses. **Examination:** Theoretical and practical questions. **Fees:** $50 exam fee. $10 license fee. $15 registration fee. $10 renewal fee.

1450

Electrologist
State Board of Cosmetic Arts
4101 N. Blvd., Ste. H
Raleigh, NC 27604
Phone: (919)790-8460

Credential Type: License to practice. **Requirements:** 18 years of age. High school graduate or equivalent. Complete a 100-hr. course of study. Pass examination. **Examination:** Yes.

1451

Manicurist
North Carolina State Board of Cosmetic Arts
4101 North Blvd., Ste. H
Raleigh, NC 27604
Phone: (919)790-8460

Credential Type: License. **Duration of License:** One year. **Requirements:** High School diploma or equivalent. 17 years of age. Completion of 150 clock hours of training at a board approved beauty school. **Examination:** Written and practical. **Fees:** $5 exam fee. $5 license fee. $5 renewal fee.

North Dakota

1452

Barber
State Board of Barber Examiners
Box 885
Bowman, ND 58623
Phone: (701)523-3327
Phone: (701)574-3172

Credential Type: License. **Requirements:** Contact licensing body for application information.

1453

Beauty Shop Manager/Operator
State Board of Cosmetology
Box 2177
Bismarck, ND 58502-2177
Phone: (701)224-9800

Credential Type: Manager Operator License. **Duration of License:** One year. **Requirements:** High school graduate or equivalent. Must hold a current North Dakota cosmetology operator license. Must have practiced as a license cosmetology operator for at least 125 days. **Examination:** National Cosmetology Manager Written Examination. North Dakota Law and Sanitation Examination. **Reciprocity:** No reciprocity for manager operators. **Fees:** $20 exam fee. $20 license fee. **Governing Statute:** North Dakota Century Code 43-11-01 et seq.

1454

Cosmetologist
State Board of Cosmetology
Box 2177
Bismarck, ND 58502-2177
Phone: (701)224-9800

Credential Type: Cosmetologist (Operator) License. **Duration of License:** One year. **Requirements:** High school graduate or equivalent. Complete 1800 hours of school training in cosmetology. **Examination:** National Practical Examination. National Cosmetology Theory Examination. North Dakota Law and Sanitation Examination. **Reciprocity:** Granted to applicants from states whose requirements are equal and who grant the same privileges to North Dakota licensees. **Fees:** $20 exam fee. $10 license fee. **Governing Statute:** North Dakota Century Code 43-11-01 et seq.

1455

Cosmetology Instructor
State Board of Cosmetology
Box 2177
Bismarck, ND 58502-2177
Phone: (701)224-9800

Credential Type: Instructor License. **Duration of License:** One year. **Requirements:** Be at least 18 years of age. High school graduate or equivalent. Meet one of the following sets of requirements: (1) Complete instructor's training course in cosmetology of 960 hours. (2) Have at least one year experience as an active practicing cosmetologist, supplemented by at least 480 hours of instructor's training in cosmetology. (3) Possess a current North Dakota license as a cosmetologist. Have been engaged as an active practicing cosmetologist for at least three years prior to application, supplemented by at least 160 hours of instructor's training in cosmetology.

Renewal requires attendance at an approved seminar. **Examination:** Practical Examination. National Teacher Examination. North Dakota Law and Sanitation Examination. **Reciprocity:** No reciprocity for instructors. **Fees:** $10 application fee. $50 exam fee. $30 license fee. **Governing Statute:** North Dakota Century Code 43-11-01 et seq.

Credential Type: Student Instructor Registration. **Requirements:** Must register upon enrollment in a school of cosmetology. Must have completed a four-year high school education or equivalent. Must hold a license as a cosmetologist. **Governing Statute:** North Dakota Century Code 43-11-01 et seq.

North Dakota

1456

Electrologist
Board of Cosmetology
PO Box 2177
Bismark, ND 58502-2177
Phone: (701)224-9800

Credential Type: License to practice. **Requirements:** 18 years of age. High school graduate or equivalent. Complete a 600-hr. course of study or pass the American Electrology Association (AEA)/ETS examination.

1457

Esthetician
State Board of Cosmetology
Box 2177
Bismarck, ND 58502-2177
Phone: (701)224-9800

Credential Type: Esthetician License. **Duration of License:** One year. **Requirements:** High school graduate or equivalent. Complete esthetician course of 900 hours. **Examination:** Practical Examination. National Esthetician Examination. North Dakota Law and Sanitation Examination. **Reciprocity:** Granted to applicants from states whose requirements are equal and who grant the same privileges to North Dakota licensees. **Fees:** Contact board for fees. **Governing Statute:** North Dakota Century Code 43-11-01 et seq.

1458

Manicurist
State Board of Cosmetology
Box 2177
Bismarck, ND 58502-2177
Phone: (701)224-9800

Credential Type: Manicurist License. **Duration of License:** One year. **Requirements:** High school graduate or equivalent. Complete manicurist course of 350 hours. **Examination:** Practical Examination. National Manicurist Examination. North Dakota Law and Sanitation Examination. **Reciprocity:** Granted to applicants from states whose requirements are equal and who grant the same privileges to North Dakota licensees. **Fees:** Contact board for fees. **Governing Statute:** North Dakota Century Code 43-11-01 et seq.

Ohio

1459

Barber
State Barber Board
77 S. High St., 16th Fl.
Columbus, OH 43266-0304
Phone: (614)466-5003

Credential Type: License. **Requirements:** Contact licensing body for application information.

1460

Cosmetologist
Ohio Board of Cosmetology
8 E. Long, Ste. 1000
Columbus, OH 43215
Phone: (614)466-3834

Credential Type: Cosmetologist License. **Duration of License:** Two years. **Requirements:** Be at least 16 years of age. Good moral character. Have the equivalent of an eighth-grade education. Complete at least 1500 hours of instruction in a licensed school of cosmetology. **Examination:** Yes. **Reciprocity:** Yes. **Fees:** $21 application fee. $20 license fee. $20 renewal fee. $50 reciprocity fee. **Governing Statute:** Ohio Revised Code, Chap. 4713. Administrative Code, 4713-1 et seq.

1461

Cosmetology Instructor
Ohio Board of Cosmetology
8 E. Long, Ste. 1000
Columbus, OH 43215
Phone: (614)466-3834

Credential Type: Cosmetology Instructor License. **Duration of License:** Two years. **Requirements:** Good moral character. Have the equivalent of a 12th-grade education. Hold a current managing cosmetologist license. Complete one year of practice as a cosmetologist in a licensed beauty salon, or complete 1000 hours of cosmetology instructor training in a licensed school of cosmetology as an apprentice instructor. **Examination:** Yes. **Reciprocity:** Yes. **Fees:** $21 application fee. $25 license fee. $25 renewal fee. $50 reciprocity fee. **Governing Statute:** Ohio Revised Code, Chap. 4713. Administrative Code, 4713-1 et seq.

1462

Electrologist
Board of Cosmetology
8 E. Long, Ste. 100
Columbus, OH 43215
Phone: (614)466-3834

Credential Type: License to practice. **Duration of License:** Two years. **Requirements:** 18 years of age. High school graduate or equivalent. Complete a 600-hr. course of study. Pass examination. Renewal requires 2.5 Continuing Education Units. **Examination:** Yes.

1463

Esthetician
Ohio Board of Cosmetology
8 E. Long, Ste. 1000
Columbus, OH 43215
Phone: (614)466-3834

Credential Type: Esthetician License. **Duration of License:** Two years. **Requirements:** Be at least 16 years of age. Good moral character. Have the equivalent of an eighth-grade education. Complete at least 600 hours of instruction in a licensed school of cosmetology. **Examination:** Yes. **Reciprocity:** Yes. **Fees:** $21 application fee. $20 license fee. $20 renewal fee. $50 reciprocity fee. **Governing Statute:** Ohio Revised Code, Chap. 4713. Administrative Code, 4713-1 et seq.

1464

Esthetics Instructor
Ohio Board of Cosmetology
8 E. Long, Ste. 1000
Columbus, OH 43215
Phone: (614)466-3834

Credential Type: Esthetics Instructor License. **Duration of License:** Two years. **Requirements:** Be at least 18 years of age. Good moral character. Have the equivalent of a 12th-grade education. Hold a current managing cosmetologist or managing esthetician license. Complete one year of practice as a managing cosmetologist or managing esthetician in a licensed beauty salon, or complete 500 hours of training in a licensed school of cosmetology as an assistant esthetics instructor. **Examination:** Yes. **Reciprocity:** Yes. **Fees:** $21 application fee. $25 license fee. $25 renewal fee. $50 reciprocity fee. **Governing Statute:** Ohio Revised Code, Chap. 4713. Administrative Code, 4713-1 et seq.

Barbers and Cosmetologists | **Oklahoma**

1465

Managing Cosmetologist
Ohio Board of Cosmetology
8 E. Long, Ste. 1000
Columbus, OH 43215
Phone: (614)466-3834

Credential Type: Managing Cosmetologist License. **Duration of License:** Two years. **Requirements:** Good moral character. Have the equivalent of an eighth-grade education. Meet one of the following sets of requirements: (1) Complete at least 300 hours of board-approved instruction related to advanced cosmetology, business management, and supervision, in a licensed school of cosmetology. (2) Complete one year of practice as a cosmetologist in a licensed beauty salon. **Examination:** Yes. **Reciprocity:** Yes. **Fees:** $21 application fee. $20 license fee. $20 renewal fee. $50 reciprocity fee. **Governing Statute:** Ohio Revised Code, Chap. 4713. Administrative Code, 4713-1 et seq.

1466

Managing Esthetician
Ohio Board of Cosmetology
8 E. Long, Ste. 1000
Columbus, OH 43215
Phone: (614)466-3834

Credential Type: Managing Esthetician License. **Duration of License:** Two years. **Requirements:** Good moral character. Have the equivalent of an eighth-grade education. Meet one of the following sets of requirements: (1) Complete an additional 150 hours of board-approved instruction in management training in a licensed school of cosmetology. (2) Complete one year of practice in esthetics as a cosmetologist or esthetician in a licensed beauty salon. **Examination:** Yes. **Reciprocity:** Yes. **Fees:** $21 application fee. $20 license fee. $20 renewal fee. $50 reciprocity fee. **Governing Statute:** Ohio Revised Code, Chap. 4713. Administrative Code, 4713-1 et seq.

1467

Managing Manicurist
Ohio Board of Cosmetology
8 E. Long, Ste. 1000
Columbus, OH 43215
Phone: (614)466-3834

Credential Type: Managing Manicurist License. **Duration of License:** Two years. **Requirements:** Good moral character. Have the equivalent of an eighth-grade education. Meet one of the following sets of requirements: (1) Complete an additional 100 hours of board-approved instruction in advanced subjects. (2) Complete one year of practice as a manicurist in a licensed beauty salon. **Examination:** Yes. **Reciprocity:** Yes. **Fees:** $21 application fee. $20 license fee. $20 renewal fee. $50 reciprocity fee. **Governing Statute:** Ohio Revised Code, Chap. 4713. Administrative Code, 4713-1 et seq.

1468

Manicurist
Ohio Board of Cosmetology
8 E. Long, Ste. 1000
Columbus, OH 43215
Phone: (614)466-3834

Credential Type: Manicurist License. **Duration of License:** Two years. **Requirements:** Be at least 16 years of age. Good moral character. Have the equivalent of an eighth-grade education. Complete at least 200 hours of instruction in a licensed school of cosmetology. **Examination:** Yes. **Reciprocity:** Yes. **Fees:** $21 application fee. $20 license fee. $20 renewal fee. $50 reciprocity fee. **Governing Statute:** Ohio Revised Code, Chap. 4713. Administrative Code, 4713-1 et seq.

1469

Manicurist Instructor
Ohio Board of Cosmetology
8 E. Long, Ste. 1000
Columbus, OH 43215
Phone: (614)466-3834

Credential Type: Manicurist Instructor License. **Duration of License:** Two years. **Requirements:** Be at least 18 years of age. Hold a current managing cosmetologist or managing manicurist license. Complete an additional 1000 hours of training in manicuring in a licensed school of cosmetology. **Examination:** Yes. **Reciprocity:** Yes. **Fees:** $21 application fee. $25 license fee. $25 renewal fee. $50 reciprocity fee. **Governing Statute:** Ohio Revised Code, Chap. 4713. Administrative Code, 4713-1 et seq.

Oklahoma

1470

Barber
Oklahoma State Dept. of Health
1000 N.E. Tenth St.
Oklahoma City, OK 73152
Phone: (405)271-5217

Credential Type: License. **Duration of License:** One year. **Requirements:** Graduate of nine-month barber college of completion of 18 months as a barber apprentice. 16 years of age. Reading ability. **Examination:** Barber's License Examination. **Fees:** $35 exam fee. $25 license fee. $25 renewal fee.

1471

Cosmetologist
Oklahoma State Board of Cosmetology
2200 Classen Blvd., Ste. 1530
Oklahoma City, OK 73106
Phone: (405)521-2441

Credential Type: License. **Duration of License:** One year. **Requirements:** Eighth-grade education or equivalent. 1,500 hours of training in an approved beauty school or an apprenticeship of 3,000 hours. 17 years of age. **Examination:** National Cosmetology Test. **Fees:** $10 license fee. $10 exam fee. $10 renewal fee.

1472

Cosmetology Instructor
Oklahoma State Board of Cosmetology
2200 Classen Blvd., Ste. 1530
Oklahoma City, OK 73106
Phone: (405)521-2441

Credential Type: License. **Duration of License:** One year. **Requirements:** High School degree. 1,000 hours of instructor courses at a licensed school of cosmetology plus 1,500 hours of training in basic cosmetology courses. 16 years of age. Must hold a current cosmetologist license at time of application. **Examination:** National Cosmetology Teachers Test. **Fees:** $10 exam fee. $15 license fee. $15 renewal fee.

1473

Electrologist
Board of Cosmetology
2200 N. Classen Blvd., Ste. 1530
Oklahoma City, OK 73106
Phone: (405)521-2441

Credential Type: License to practice. **Requirements:** 21 years of age. Bachelor's degree with an approved major. Internship or a program of planned professional experience. Pass examination. **Examination:** Yes.

Oklahoma

1474

Facialist
Oklahoma State Board of
 Cosmetology
2200 Classen Blvd., Ste. 1530
Oklahoma City, OK 73106
Phone: (405)521-2441

Credential Type: License. **Duration of License:** One year. **Requirements:** Eighth-grade education. 17 years of age. **Examination:** The Oklahoma State Board Facialist Examination. **Fees:** $10 exam fee. $10 license fee. $10 renewal fee.

1475

Manicurist
Oklahoma State Board of
 Cosmetology
2200 Classen Blvd., Ste. 1530
Oklahoma City, OK 73106
Phone: (405)521-2441

Credential Type: License. **Duration of License:** One year. **Requirements:** Eighth-grade education or equivalent. 300 clock hours at an approved beauty school or 600 clock hours of beauty school curriculum. 17 years of age. **Examination:** National Manicuring and Sculptured Nail Test. **Fees:** $10 exam fee. $10 license fee. $10 renewal fee.

Oregon

1476

Barber and Hairdresser
Oregon State Board of Barbers and
 Hairdressers
750 Front St. NE, Ste. 200
Salem, OR 97310
Phone: (503)378-8667

Credential Type: License. **Duration of License:** Two years. **Requirements:** Must complete all courses of a school of hair design or barber school; or have a license from another state. **Examination:** Yes. **Reciprocity:** Yes. **Fees:** $15 exam fee. $20 license fee. $40 renewal fee. **Governing Statute:** ORS 345.010 to 345.470.

1477

Electrologist
Electrologist Licensing
750 Front St., NE, Ste. 200
Salem, OR 97310
Phone: (503)378-8667

Credential Type: License. **Duration of License:** One year. **Requirements:** Graduation from a school of electrolysis or an equivalent education and experience from another state. **Examination:** Yes. **Fees:** $100 exam fee. $150 license fee. $150 renewal fee. **Governing Statute:** ORS 690.350 to 690.998.

1478

Facial Technician
Oregon State Board of Barbers &
 Hairdressers
750 Front St. NE, Ste. 200
Salem, OR 97310
Phone: (503)378-8667

Credential Type: License. **Duration of License:** Two years. **Requirements:** Successful completion of all courses in a school permitted to teach facial technology. **Examination:** Yes. **Reciprocity:** Yes. **Fees:** $15 exam fee. $20 license fee. $40 renewal fee. **Governing Statute:** ORS 690.005 to 690.235.

1479

Manicurist
Oregon State Board of Barbers &
 Hairdressers
750 Front St. NE, Ste. 200
Salem, OR 97310
Phone: (503)378-8667

Credential Type: License. **Duration of License:** Two years. **Requirements:** Must have successfully completed all courses a school permitted to teach manicure is required to teach to be licensed. **Examination:** Yes. **Reciprocity:** Yes. **Fees:** $15 exam fee. $20 license fee. $40 renewal fee. **Governing Statute:** ORS 690.005 to 690.235

Pennsylvania

1480

Barber
State Board of Barber Examiners
Bureau of Professional and
 Occupational Affairs
Dept. of State
Transportation and Safety Bldg., 6th
 Fl.
Harrisburg, PA 17120
Phone: (717)787-8503

Credential Type: Barber License. **Duration of License:** Two years. **Requirements:** At least 16 years of age. Eighth grade education or equivalent. Physical examination and blood test proving no evidence of contagious or infectious disease. Complete a barbering study and training period of at least 1,250 hours (in not less than nine months) at a licensed barber shop or school under the instruction of a licensed teacher. **Examination:** State barber examination. **Reciprocity:** Barbers currently licensed in other states may be eligible for licensure in Pennsylvania if the state in which they were licensed has substantially the same licensing requirements as Pennsylvania. **Fees:** $40 complete examination fee. $30 examination fee (practical only). $30 examination fee (theory only). $20 initial license. $15 reciprocal license fee. $42 biennial renewal fee.

Credential Type: Manager-Barber License. **Duration of License:** Two years. **Requirements:** Hold a current barber license. Actively engage in the practice of barbering for one year. **Examination:** State manager-barber examination. **Fees:** $30 examination fee. $20 initial license fee. $62 biennial renewal.

1481

Barber Teacher
State Board of Barber Examiners
Bureau of Professional and
 Occupational Affairs
Dept. of State
Transportation and Safety Bldg., 6th
 Fl.
Harrisburg, PA 17120
Phone: (717)787-8503

Credential Type: Barber Teacher License. **Duration of License:** Two years. **Requirements:** At least 23 years of age. High school graduate. Five year's experience as a licensed barber or be a manager-barber who has trained for 1,250 hours under a licensed teacher in a licensed barber school as a teacher trainee. **Examination:** State barber teacher examination. **Fees:** $40 complete examination fee. $30 examination fee (practical only). $30 examination fee (theory only). $20 initial license. $67 biennial renewal.

1482

Cosmetician
State Board of Cosmetology
Bureau of Professional and
 Occupational Affairs
Dept. of State
Transportation and Safety Bldg., 6th
 Fl.
Harrisburg, PA 17120
Phone: (717)787-8503

Credential Type: Cosmetician License. **Duration of License:** Two years. **Requirements:** Must have completed 300 hours of skin care instruction in a licensed school of cosmetology. **Examination:** State cosmetician examination. **Reciprocity:** Holders of out-of-state licenses may be granted reciprocity with board approval. **Fees:** $52.50 complete examination fee. $24 examination fee (practical only). $28.50 examination fee (theory only). $25 reciprocal license fee. $5 initial license fee. $21 biennial renewal fee.

1483

Cosmetologist
State Board of Cosmetology
Bureau of Professional and Occupational Affairs
Dept. of State
Transportation and Safety Bldg., 6th Fl.
Harrisburg, PA 17120
Phone: (717)787-8503

Credential Type: Cosmetologist License. **Duration of License:** Two years. **Authorization:** Qualifies holder to perform the functions of a cosmetologist, cosmetician, or manicurist. **Requirements:** At least 16 years of age. Must have one of the following qualifications: (1) Have a 10th grade education or its equivalent; (2) Receive training from the Bureau of Rehabilitation in the Department of Labor and Industry; (3) Be a veteran; (4) Be 35 years of age or older. Must have completed one of the following education requirements: (1) Complete 1250 hours of day-time cosmetology instruction, in not less than eight consecutive months, as a student in a licensed cosmetology school; (2) Complete 1250 hours of night-time cosmetology instruction, in not less than 15 consecutive months, as a student in a licensed cosmetology school; (3) Complete 2000 hours of training as an apprentice in a Board approved cosmetology program. **Examination:** State cosmetologist examination. **Reciprocity:** Holders of out-of-state licenses may be granted reciprocity with board approval. **Fees:** $47.50 complete examination fee. $24 examination fee (practical only). $23.50 examination fee (theory only). $35 apprentice registration fee. $5 initial license fee. $25 reciprocal license fee. $23 biennial renewal fee.

Credential Type: Temporary License. **Duration of License:** Nine months or until the next available examination. **Authorization:** Allows temporary cosmetology practice, under the supervision of a licensed cosmetologist, until applicant can achieve a passing grade on the state cosmetologist examination. **Requirements:** Must meet all qualifications for a cosmetologist license, with the exception of completing examination.

1484

Cosmetology Teacher
State Board of Cosmetology
Bureau of Professional and Occupational Affairs
Dept. of State
Transportation and Safety Bldg., 6th Fl.
Harrisburg, PA 17120
Phone: (717)787-8503

Credential Type: Cosmetology Teacher. **Duration of License:** Two years. **Authorization:** Qualifies holder to perform the functions of a cosmetology teacher, manager, cosmetologist, cosmetician or manicurist. **Requirements:** At least 18 years of age. Complete the 12th grade or its equivalent. Hold a current cosmetologist license. Complete 500 hours of instruction for cosmetology teachers in a licensed school of cosmetology. **Examination:** State cosmetology teacher examination. **Reciprocity:** Holders of out-of-state licenses may be granted reciprocity with board approval. **Fees:** $52.50 complete examination fee. $24 examination fee (practical only). $28.50 examination fee (theory only). $25 reciprocal license fee. $10 initial license fee. $36 biennial renewal.

Credential Type: Cosmetology Manager License. **Duration of License:** Two years. **Authorization:** Qualifies the holder to perform the functions of manager, cosmetologist, cosmetician, or manicurist. **Requirements:** At least 18 years of age. Complete the 10th grade or its equivalent. Hold a current cosmetology license. Complete one of the following requirements: (1) Complete 300 hours of courses for cosmetology managers in a licensed school of cosmetology. (2) Have a minimum of 18 month's experience in a licensed cosmetology shop working as a full-time cosmetologist. **Examination:** State cosmetology manager examination. **Reciprocity:** Holders of out-of-state licenses may be granted reciprocity with board approval. **Fees:** $28.50 examination fee. $25 reciprocal license fee. $10 initial license fee. $25 biennial renewal fee.

1485

Manicurist
State Board of Cosmetology
Bureau of Professional and Occupational Affairs
Dept. of State
Transportation and Safety Bldg., 6th Fl.
Harrisburg, PA 17120
Phone: (717)787-8503

Credential Type: Manicurist License. **Duration of License:** Two years. **Requirements:** Complete 200 hours of manicurist instruction in a licensed school of cosmetology. **Examination:** State manicurist examination. **Reciprocity:** Holders of out-of-state licenses may be granted reciprocity with board approval. **Fees:** $47.50 complete examination fee. $24 examination fee (practical only). $23.50 examination fee (theory only). $25 reciprocal license fee. $5 initial license fee. $21 biennial renewal fee.

Credential Type: Temporary License. **Duration of License:** Nine months or until the next available examination. **Authorization:** Allows temporary practice as a manicurist, under the supervision of a licensed cosmetologist, until applicant can achieve a passing grade on the state manicurist examination. **Requirements:** Must meet all qualifications for a manicurist license, with the exception of completing examination.

Rhode Island

1486

Barber
Board of Examiners in Barbering
Div. of Professional Regulation
Rhode Island Dept. of Health
3 Capitol Hill
Providence, RI 02908
Phone: (401)277-2827

Credential Type: Apprentice Barber License. **Duration of License:** One year. **Requirements:** At least 16 years of age. Foreign born must show proof of legal entry into the U.S. Free of infections or contagious disease. Complete 10 years of school or equivalent. Submit application and pay fees. **Reciprocity:** No. **Fees:** $5 apprentice application fee. $5 apprentice annual renewal fee.

Credential Type: Barber License. **Duration of License:** One year. **Requirements:** At least 18 years of age. Foreign born must show proof of legal entry into the U.S. Free of infections or contagious disease. Complete 10 years of school or equivalent. Submit application and pay fees. Complete a two year course of study in an approved

Rhode Island

Barber, continued

barber school or complete a two-year apprenticeship under the supervision of a licensed barber. **Examination:** Written and practical examinations. **Reciprocity:** No. **Fees:** $25 application fee. $10 annual renewal fee.

1487

Barber Instructor
Board of Examiners in Barbering
Div. of Professional Regulation
Rhode Island Dept. of Health
3 Capitol Hill
Providence, RI 02908
Phone: (401)277-2827

Credential Type: Instructor License. **Duration of License:** One year. **Requirements:** Complete all requirements for Barber License. Submit application and pay fees. **Examination:** Written and practical examinations. **Reciprocity:** No. **Fees:** $100 application fee. $50 annual renewal fee.

1488

Cosmetologist
State Board of Hairdressing
Div. of Professional Regulation
Rhode Island Dept. of Health
3 Capitol Hill
Providence, RI 02908
Phone: (401)277-2511

Credential Type: Cosmetologist License. **Duration of License:** Two years. **Requirements:** At least 18 years of age. Foreign born must show proof of legal entry into U.S. High school graduate or equivalent. Complete an approved 1500 hour course in cosmetology. Be free from contagious and infectious diseases. **Examination:** Written and practical examination. **Reciprocity:** Yes. **Fees:** $15 application fee. $30 cosmetologist license fee. $30 biennial renewal fee.

1489

Electrologist
Board of Cosmetology
3 Capitol Bldg., Rm. 209
Providence, RI 02908
Phone: (401)277-2511

Credential Type: License to practice. **Requirements:** 18 years of age. High school graduate or equivalent. Complete a 650-hr. apprenticeship. Pass the American Electrology Association (AEA)/ETS examination. **Examination:** AEA/ETS examination.

1490

Esthetician
State Board of Hairdressing
Div. of Professional Regulation
Rhode Island Dept. of Health
3 Capitol Hill
Providence, RI 02908
Phone: (401)277-2511

Credential Type: Esthetician License. **Duration of License:** Two years. **Requirements:** At least 18 years of age. Foreign born must show proof of legal entry into U.S. High school graduate or equivalent. Complete an approved 600-hour esthetician course within a four-month period. Be free from contagious and infectious diseases. **Examination:** Written and practical examination. **Reciprocity:** Yes. **Fees:** $15 application fee. $30 esthetician license fee. $30 biennial renewal fee.

1491

Hairdresser
State Board of Hairdressing
Div. of Professional Regulation
Rhode Island Dept. of Health
3 Capitol Hill
Providence, RI 02908
Phone: (401)277-2511

Credential Type: Hairdresser License. **Duration of License:** Two years. **Requirements:** At least 18 years of age. Foreign born must show proof of legal entry into U.S. High school graduate or equivalent. Complete an approved 1500 hour course in hairdressing. Be free from contagious and infectious diseases. **Examination:** Written and practical examination. **Reciprocity:** Yes. **Fees:** $15 application fee. $30 hairdresser license.

Credential Type: Hairdressing Instructor License. **Duration of License:** Two years. **Requirements:** At least 18 years of age. Foreign born must show proof of legal entry into U.S. High school graduate or equivalent. Hold a hairdressing license. Complete an approved 300 hour hairdressing instructor course. Be free from contagious and infectious diseases. **Examination:** Written and practical examinations. **Reciprocity:** Yes. **Fees:** $15 application fee. $30 Hairdressing instructor license fee. $30 biennial renewal fee.

1492

Manicurist
State Board of Hairdressing
Div. of Professional Regulation
Rhode Island Dept. of Health
3 Capitol Hill
Providence, RI 02908
Phone: (401)277-2511

Credential Type: Manicurist License. **Duration of License:** Two years. **Requirements:** At least 18 years of age. Foreign born must show proof of legal entry into U.S. High school graduate or equivalent. Complete an approved 300-hour manicurist course. Be free from contagious and infectious diseases. **Examination:** Written and practical examination. **Reciprocity:** Yes. **Fees:** $15 application fee. $30 manicurist license fee. $30 biennial renewal fee.

South Carolina

1493

Barber
South Carolina Board of Barber Examiners
900 Garland St.
Columbia, SC 29201
Phone: (803)732-1733

Credential Type: Barber License. **Requirements:** 18 years of age. 12 months as an apprentice under the supervision of a registered barber. **Examination:** Yes. **Fees:** $35 license fee.

Credential Type: Apprentice Barber License. **Requirements:** 16 years of age. Ninth-grade education or equivalent. Nine months in an approved barber school, or 12 months of training under the supervision of a qualified, registered barber. **Examination:** Yes. **Fees:** $25 license fee.

1494

Cosmetologist
South Carolina State Board of Cosmetology
1209 Blanding St.
Columbia, SC 29201
Phone: (803)253-6222

Credential Type: Cosmetologist License. **Requirements:** 16 years of age. 10th-grade education or equivalent. Completion of 1,500 hours in cosmetology classes at an approved school. **Examination:** Yes. **Fees:** $45 license fee. $15 renewal fee.

1495

Cosmetologist Instructor
South Carolina State Board of Cosmetology
1209 Blanding St.
Columbia, SC 29201
Phone: (803)253-6222

Credential Type: Cosmetology Instructor License. **Requirements:** Must be initially licensed as a cosmetologist. Completion of 45 clock hours in teaching methods. High school diploma or equivalent. **Examination:** Yes. **Fees:** $50 license fee. $30 renewal fee.

1496

Esthetician
South Carolina Board of Cosmetology
1209 Blanding St.
Columbia, SC 29201
Phone: (803)253-6222

Credential Type: License. **Requirements:** 16 years of age. 10th-grade education or equivalent. 450 hours in skin care classes in an approved school or comparable approved training. **Examination:** Yes. **Fees:** $45 initial fee. $15 renewal fee.

1497

Manicurist
South Carolina State Board of Cosmetology
1209 Blanding St.
Columbia, SC 29201
Phone: (803)253-6222

Credential Type: License. **Requirements:** 16 years of age. 10th-grade education or equivalent. 300 hours in manicuring classes in an approved school or comparable approved training. **Examination:** Yes. **Fees:** $45 initial fee. $15 renewal fee.

South Dakota

1498

Barber
State Board of Barber Examiners
PO Box 613
Pierre, SD 57501
Phone: (605)224-6281

Credential Type: License. **Requirements:** Contact licensing body for application information.

1499

Cosmetologist
Cosmetology Commission
Dept. of Commerce and Regulation
PO Box 127
Pierre, SD 57501
Phone: (605)224-5072

Credential Type: Operator's License. **Duration of License:** One year. **Requirements:** Be at least 18 years of age. High school graduate or equivalent. Complete 2100 hours of training in an approved and licensed beauty school or as an apprentice in a licensed beauty shop for 18 months. **Examination:** Operator's examination. **Reciprocity:** Yes, but must take examination on South Dakota cosmetology laws. **Fees:** $20 exam fee. $15 renewal fee. $6 temporary license fee. $50 reciprocity fee. **Governing Statute:** South Dakota Codified Laws, Chap. 36-15.

Credential Type: Student's License. **Requirements:** Be at least 16.5 years of age. Any person entering or enrolling in a licensed beauty school for training must apply for a student's license within 10 days after enrolling. **Fees:** $6 student license fee. **Governing Statute:** South Dakota Codified Laws, Chap. 36-15.

Credential Type: Apprentice's License. **Duration of License:** 18 months. **Requirements:** Be at least 17 years of age. Must serve apprenticeship in a licensed beauty shop. Apprenticeship period is 18 months. **Fees:** $25 apprentice license fee. **Governing Statute:** South Dakota Codified Laws, Chap. 36-15.

1500

Cosmetologist Manager
Cosmetology Commission
Dept. of Commerce and Regulation
PO Box 127
Pierre, SD 57501
Phone: (605)224-5072

Credential Type: Manager-Operator's License. **Duration of License:** One year. **Requirements:** Be at least 18 years of age. High school graduate or equivalent. Meet one of the following sets of requirements: (1) Have at least 50 weeks with an average of 40 hours per week of experience as a licensed operator cosmetologist. (2) Have taught in a licensed and approved beauty school for at least 12 months. (3) Have a combination of work and teaching experience of at least 12 months. **Fees:** $15 license fee. $15 renewal fee. **Governing Statute:** South Dakota Codified Laws, Chap. 36-15.

1501

Cosmetology Instructor
Cosmetology Commission
Dept. of Commerce and Regulation
PO Box 127
Pierre, SD 57501
Phone: (605)224-5072

Credential Type: Senior Instructor's License. **Duration of License:** One year. **Requirements:** Be at least 18 years of age. High school graduate or equivalent. Have at least two years experience as a licensed operator cosmetologist or one year experience as a junior instructor. Must hold a current valid manager-operator's license. Must have attended at least 10 hours of board-approved seminars conducted for cosmetology instructors during the 12 months prior to application. **Fees:** $15 license fee. $15 renewal fee. **Governing Statute:** South Dakota Codified Laws, Chap. 36-15.

Credential Type: Junior Instructor's License. **Duration of License:** One year. **Authorization:** Must work in a licensed beauty school under the direct supervision of a licensed senior instructor. **Requirements:** Be at least 18 years of age. High school graduate or equivalent. Must hold a current valid operator's license. Must have attended at least 10 hours of board-approved seminars conducted for cosmetology instructors during the 12 months prior to application. License may be granted conditionally provided applicant takes 10 hours of seminars within six months. **Fees:** $15 license fee. $15 renewal fee. **Governing Statute:** South Dakota Codified Laws, Chap. 36-15.

Tennessee

1502

Barber
Barbers Examining Board
500 James Robertson Pky.
Nashville, TN 37243
Phone: (615)741-2294

Credential Type: License. **Duration of License:** One year. **Requirements:** 16 years old. 1500 hours in barber school. **Examination:** Yes. **Reciprocity:** Yes, with experience and study. **Fees:** $100 Application. $40 Renewal.

Tennessee

1503

Cosmetologist
Board of Cosmetology
500 James Robertson Pky., 1st Fl.
Nashville, TN 37245-1147
Phone: (615)741-2515

Credential Type: License. **Duration of License:** Two years. **Requirements:** 16 years old. Complete 1500 hours of cosmetology school. 300 hours for manicurist only. Pass exam. Must complete 24 hours of continuing education every two years for renewal. **Examination:** Yes. **Reciprocity:** Yes, with equivalent requirements. **Fees:** $24 Initial. $15 Manicurist only. $20 Cosmetologist.

1504

Electrologist
Board of Electrolysis Examiners
283 Plus Park Blvd.
Nashville, TN 37217
Phone: (615)367-6225

Credential Type: License. **Duration of License:** one year **Requirements:** 18 years old. 600 hours electrology (23 semester hours). 10 hours continuing education per year. Good moral character, graduate of high school or equivalent. **Examination:** Yes. **Fees:** $185 Registration. $100 Examination. $100 Application. $185 Renewal.

Texas

1505

Barber
State Board of Barber Examiners
9101 Burnet Rd., Ste. 103
Austin, TX 78758
Phone: (512)835-2040

Credential Type: License. **Duration of License:** Two years. **Requirements:** 16 years of age. Good health. 1,500 hours in not less than nine months at a barbering school or practical experience from a barber during training. **Examination:** Written and practical. **Fees:** $10 exam fee. $100 license fee. $100 renewal fee. **Governing Statute:** VACS 8407a, 22 TAC 51.51.

1506

Cosmetologist
Texas Cosmetology Commission
PO Box 26700
Austin, TX 78755
Phone: (512)454-4674

Credential Type: License. **Duration of License:** Two years. **Requirements:** 16 years of age. Health certificate. Completion of 7th grade or equivalent. 1,500 hours of instruction in a licensed beauty culture school, or 1,000 hours of instruction in beauty culture courses and 500 hours of related high school vocational courses. **Examination:** Physical demonstration and theory tests. **Fees:** $25 exam fee. $35 license fee. $35 renewal fee. **Governing Statute:** VACS 8451a, 22 TAC 89.

Utah

1507

Barber
Dept. of Commerce
Div. of Occupational and
  Professional Licensing
160 E. 300 S.
PO Box 45802
Salt Lake City, UT 84145
Phone: (801)530-6628

Credential Type: Barber license. **Duration of License:** Two years. **Requirements:** Must complete an approved barber course of not less than 2,000 hours over a period of 12 months. **Examination:** Yes. **Fees:** $40 license fee. $25 renewal fee.

1508

Cosmetologist
Dept. of Commerce
Div. of Occupational and
  Professional Licensing
160 E. 300 S.
PO Box 45802
Salt Lake City, UT 84145
Phone: (801)530-6628

Credential Type: Cosmetologist license. **Duration of License:** Two years. **Requirements:** Must complete an approved cosmetologist course of not less than 2,000 hours over a period of 12 months. **Examination:** Yes. **Fees:** $40 license fee. $25 renewal fee.

1509

Electrologist
Dept. of Commerce
Div. of Occupational and
  Professional Licensing
160 E. 300 S.
PO Box 45802
Salt Lake City, UT 84145
Phone: (801)530-6628

Credential Type: License. **Duration of License:** Two years. **Requirements:** Must complete a course in electrology of at least 500 hours of training in a school approved by the division. **Examination:** Yes. **Fees:** $40 license fee. $25 renewal fee.

Vermont

1510

Barber
State Board of Barber Licensing
Pavilion Office Bldg.
Montpelier, VT 05602
Phone: (802)828-2390

Credential Type: License. **Duration of License:** Two years. **Requirements:** 18 years of age. Completion of approved barber school. Apprenticeship of 12 months (24 month apprenticeship omits need for barber school). **Examination:** Yes. **Reciprocity:** No. **Fees:** $10 Apprentice registration. $60 Barber exam fee. $10 License fee. $15 Renewal. **Governing Statute:** Title 26 VSA, Sections 261-270.

1511

Cosmetologist
State Board of Cosmetology
Pavilion Office Bldg.
Montpelier, VT 05602
Phone: (802)828-2373

Credential Type: License. **Duration of License:** Two years. **Requirements:** 17 years of age. High school graduate or equivalent. Good moral character. Complete course of 1500 hours in beauty culture. **Examination:** Yes. **Reciprocity:** Yes. **Fees:** $35 Examination fee. $5 Temporary license. $10 Original operator's license. $14 Renewal. $15 Manager operator license. $10 Manicure license. $10 Esthetician license. **Governing Statute:** Title 26, VSA Sections 651-661.

Virginia

1512

Barber
Virginia Board of Barber Examiners
Dept. of Commerce
3600 W. Broad St., 5th Fl.
Richmond, VA 23230
Phone: (804)367-8590

Credential Type: License. **Duration of License:** Two years. **Requirements:** Graduation from an approved school of barbering; or completion of a course in a public school with a curriculum in barbering approved by the State Department of Education; or have completed training as a barber in the Armed Forces; or have completed training as a barber in any state institution; or have completed an apprenticeship program approved by the Board. **Examination:** Yes. **Fees:** $50 exam fee. $30 renewal fee.

1513

Cosmetologist
Virginia Board of Cosmetology
Dept. of Commerce
3600 W. Broad St.
Richmond, VA 23230
Phone: (804)367-2175

Credential Type: License. **Duration of License:** Two years. **Requirements:** Graduated from a licensed cosmetology school or a Virginia public school in cosmetology; or completed an approved apprenticeship program with standards established by the Division of Apprenticeship Training of the Virginia Department of Labor and Industry for Apprenticeship. **Examination:** Yes. **Fees:** $35 application fee. $25 renewal fee.

Washington

1514

Barber
Dept. of Licensing
Professional Licensing Services
2424 Bristol Court SW
Olympia, WA 98504
Phone: (206)753-3834

Credential Type: Barber License. **Duration of License:** Two years. **Requirements:** At least 17 years of age. Must have a minimum of 1,000 hours of instruction in an approved barber school. **Examination:** Written examination. **Reciprocity:** Yes. **Fees:** $25 examination fee. $25 reciprocal license fee. $20 renewal fee.

1515

Cosmetologist
Dept. of Licensing
Professional Licensing Services
2424 Bristol Court SW
Olympia, WA 98504
Phone: (206)753-3834

Credential Type: Cosmetologist License. **Duration of License:** Two years. **Requirements:** At least 17 years of age. Complete an approved Cosmetology course that consists of no less than 1,600 hours of training. **Examination:** Written examination. **Fees:** $25 examination fee. $20 renewal fee. $15 duplicate license fee. $25 certification fee.

Credential Type: Cosmetology Instructor License. **Duration of License:** Two years. **Requirements:** Hold a valid cosmetologist license. Complete a 500 hour course for Cosmetology instructors. **Examination:** Written examination. **Fees:** $30 examination fee. $20 renewal fee. $15 duplicate license fee. $25 certificate fee.

1516

Manicurist
Dept. of Licensing
Professional Licensing Services
2424 Bristol Court SW
Olympia, WA 98504
Phone: (206)753-3834

Credential Type: Manicurist License. **Duration of License:** One year. **Requirements:** At least 17 years of age. Complete a 500 hour manicurist course. **Examination:** Manicurist examination. **Fees:** $25 examination fee. $20 renewal fee.

West Virginia

1517

Barber
State Board of Barbers and
  Beauticians
Guthourie Ctr.
4860 Brenda Ln.
Charleston, WV 25312
Phone: (304)348-3450
Phone: (304)348-2924

Credential Type: License. **Duration of License:** One year. **Requirements:** U.S. citizen. 8th grade education. 1800 hours of barber school training in approved school. Never convicted of a felony. **Examination:** Yes. **Fees:** $5 Application. $25 Examination. $25 License. $25 Renewal.

1518

Cosmetologist, Beautician, Beauty Operator
State Board of Barbers and
  Beauticians
Guthourie Ctr.
4860 Brenda Ln.
Charleston, WV 25312
Phone: (304)348-3450
Phone: (304)348-2924

Credential Type: License. **Duration of License:** One year. **Requirements:** 18 years of age. Completion of 8th grade. 2000 hours of beauty culture training in approved beauty school. Never convicted of a felony. **Examination:** Yes. **Fees:** $5 Application. $25 Examination. $25 License. $25 Renewal.

1519

Instructor, Barber and Beautician
State Board of Barbers and
  Beauticians
Guthrie Cntr.
4860 Brenda Ln.
Charleston, WV 25312
Phone: (304)348-3450
Phone: (304)348-2924

Credential Type: License. **Duration of License:** One year. **Requirements:** 18 years of age for student instructor. 21 years of age for regular instructor. High school graduate. 250 hours of instructor training in beauty/barber school. 2000 hours of beauty training or 1800 hours barber training. One year experience for student instructor., or three years experience for regular instructor. While training, must complete 15 hours of college credits. **Examination:** Yes. **Fees:** $25 Examination. $50 License. $50 Renewal.

1520

Manicurist
Board of Barbers and Beauticians
Guthrie Ctr.
4860 Brenda Ln.
Charleston, WV 25312
Phone: (304)348-3450
Phone: (304)348-2924

Credential Type: License. **Duration of License:** One year. **Requirements:** 18 years old. Completed 8th grade. 400 hours of training at approved beauty school. Never convicted of a felony. **Examination:** Yes. **Fees:** $5 Application. $25 Examination. $25 License. $25 Renewal.

Wisconsin

1521

Aesthetician
Regulations and Licensing Dept.
Barbering & Cosmetology Board
PO Box 8935
Madison, WI 53708-8935
Phone: (608)266-8609

Credential Type: License. **Requirements:** 450 hours in a school. **Examination:** Written and practical.

1522

Barber
Regulations and Licensing Dept.
Barbering & Cosmetology Board
PO Box 8935
Madison, WI 53708-8935
Phone: (608)266-8609

Credential Type: License. **Requirements:** 1,800 hours in a school, or 4,000 hours as an apprentice. **Examination:** Written and practical.

1523

Electrologist
Regulations and Licensing Dept.
Barbering & Cosmetology Board
PO Box 8935
Madison, WI 53708-8935
Phone: (608)266-8609

Credential Type: License. **Requirements:** 450 hours in a school. **Examination:** Written and practical.

1524

Manicurist
Regulations and Licensing Dept.
Barbering & Cosmetology Board
PO Box 8935
Madison, WI 53708-8935
Phone: (608)266-8609

Credential Type: License. **Requirements:** 300 hours in a school. **Examination:** Written and practical.

Wyoming

1525

Barber
State Barber Examiner Board
PO Box 2031
Cheyenne, WY 82003
Phone: (307)632-9700

Credential Type: License. **Duration of License:** One year. **Requirements:** Graduate from an accredited barber school. Possess a high school diploma or equivalent. Pass the written and practical examinations. **Examination:** Yes. **Fees:** $50 License. $25 Renewal. $25 Permit.

1526

Cosmetologist
Board of Cosmetology
PO Box 4480
Casper, WY 82604
Phone: (307)265-2917

Credential Type: License. **Duration of License:** One year. **Requirements:** 16 years old. Must have completed 10th grade. Must graduate from an approved cosmetology school, completing 2000 hours in course work. Pass the written and practical examinations. **Examination:** Yes. **Fees:** $20 Examination. $12 License. $12 Renewal.

Blue-Collar Worker Supervisors

The following states grant licenses in this occupational category as of the date of publication:

Alabama	Hawaii	Kentucky	Michigan	New Mexico	Rhode Island	West Virginia
Arkansas	Idaho	Louisiana	Minnesota	North Dakota	Texas	Wyoming
California	Illinois	Maine	Mississippi	Ohio	Utah	
Colorado	Indiana	Maryland	Montana	Oklahoma	Vermont	
Connecticut	Iowa	Massachusetts	Nebraska	Oregon	Virginia	

Alabama

1527

Coal Mine Foreman (surface)
Board of Mine Examiners
Div. of Safety and Inspection
1816 8th Ave. N.
PO Box 10444
Birmingham, AL 35202
Phone: (205)254-1275

Credential Type: License. **Duration of License:** One year. **Requirements:** 18 years of age. Must have worked under the supervision of a licensed surface coal mine foreman for at least one year. **Examination:** Written examination.

1528

Coal Mine Foreman (underground)
Board of Mine Examiners
Div. of Safety and Inspection
1816 8th Ave., N.
PO Box 10444
Birmingham, AL 35202
Phone: (205)254-1275

Credential Type: License. **Requirements:** 23 years of age and a U.S. citizen. Four years practical mining experience; or three years experience and a university degree; or an associate degree in mine technology. **Examination:** Written, oral, and practical examinations. **Fees:** $20 registration and exam fee.

Arkansas

1529

Gas Fitter Supervisor
Arkansas Dept. of Health
Div. of Plumbing and Natural Gas
4815 W. Markham
Little Rock, AR 72201
Phone: (501)661-2642

Credential Type: License. **Duration of License:** One year. **Requirements:** Minimum of six years of gas fitting experience. One full year as a licensed gas fitter. **Examination:** Yes. **Fees:** $125 Written and practical examination. $200 License. $200 Renewal.

1530

Hospital Maintenance Plumbing Supervisor
Arkansas Dept. of Health
Div. of Plumbing and Natural Gas
4815 W. Markham
Little Rock, AR 72201
Phone: (501)661-2642

Credential Type: License. **Duration of License:** One year. **Requirements:** Must have a minimum of six years hospital maintenance plumbing experience or its equivalent. One year of the six must have been as a licensed hospital maintenance plumber. **Examination:** Yes. **Fees:** $125 Written and practical examinations. $100 License. $100 Renewal.

1531

Liquefied Petroleum Gas Safety Supervisor
The Liquefied Petroleum Gas Board
1421 W. Sixth St.
Little Rock, AR 72201
Phone: (501)371-1008

Credential Type: License. **Duration of License:** One year. **Requirements:** Employed by a class one permit holder. Have thorough knowledge of liquefied petroleum gases and the National Fire Protection Association Pamphlet 58 and the State Liquefied Petroleum Gas Code. **Examination:** Yes. **Fees:** $5 License. $5 Renewal.

California

1532

Stable Foreman (Racetrack)
California Horse Racing Board
1010 Hurley Way, Ste. 190
Sacramento, CA 95825
Phone: (916)920-7178

Credential Type: License Registration. **Requirements:** Submit application and fingerprint card. Pay fee. **Fees:** $75 registration fee.

Colorado

1533

Pesticide Supervisor
Dept. of Agriculture
Div. of Plant Industry
Pesticide Applicator Section
700 Kipling St., Ste. 4000
Lakewood, CO 80215-5894
Phone: (303)239-4139
Phone: (303)239-4140

Credential Type: Qualified Supervisor License. **Duration of License:** Three years. **Authorization:** Required of any individual in the employ of a commercial, limited commercial, or public applicator; who, without supervision, evaluates pest problems or recommends pest controls, or who mixes, loads, or applies any pesticides, or sells any application services, or operates devices, or supervises others in these functions. **Requirements:** Demonstrate competency by passing appropriate examinations. Experience requirements vary with category. **Examination:** General exam plus appropriate category examinations. **Fees:** $75 license fee.

Connecticut

1534

Field Service Manager (Racetrack)
Connecticut Div. of Special Revenue
Russell Rd.
PO Box 11424
Newington, CT 06111-0424
Phone: (203)566-2756

Credential Type: License Registration. **Requirements:** Submit application and fingerprint card. Pay fee. **Fees:** $5 registration fee.

Hawaii

1535

Supervising Electrician
Hawaii Board of Electricians and Plumbers
Dept. of Commerce and Consumer Affairs
PO Box 3469
Honolulu, HI 96801
Phone: (808)548-3952

Credential Type: License. **Duration of License:** Six months. **Requirements:** Two years of experience as a licensed Journeyman Industrial Electrician or equivalent. **Examination:** Yes. **Fees:** $15 application fee. $40 exam fee. $10 license fee. $10 renewal fee. $15-$30 Compliance Resolution Fund fee.

1536

Supervising Industrial Electrician
Hawaii Board of Electricians and Plumbers
Dept. of Commerce and Consumer Affairs
PO Box 3469
Honolulu, HI 96801
Phone: (808)548-3952

Credential Type: License. **Duration of License:** Six months. **Requirements:** Two years of experience as a licensed Journeyman Industrial Electrician or equivalent. **Examination:** Yes. **Fees:** $15 application fee. $40 exam fee. $10 license fee. $10 renewal fee. $15—$30 Compliance Resolution Fund fee.

1537

Supervising Specialty Electrician
Hawaii Board of Electricians and Plumbers
Dept. of Commerce and Consumer Affairs
PO Box 3469
Honolulu, HI 96801
Phone: (808)548-3952

Credential Type: License. **Duration of License:** Six months. **Requirements:** Two years of experience as a licensed Journeyman Specialty Electrician. **Examination:** Yes. **Fees:** $15 application fee. $40 exam fee. $10 license fee. $10 renewal fee. $15—$30 Compliance Resolution Fund fee.

Idaho

1538

Water Well Drilling Supervisor
Dept. of Water Resources
1301 N. Orchard
Statehouse Mail
Boise, ID 83706
Phone: (208)327-7900
Phone: (208)327-7956

Credential Type: Well Drilling License. **Duration of License:** One year. **Requirements:** Must have been employed on a full-time basis for at least 30 months, under the supervision of a person holding a valid Idaho well driller's license. Up to 12 months of classroom study may be credited toward the experience requirement. Post bond of $5,000 to $20,000. **Examination:** Written and/or oral examination administered by the director. **Fees:** $25 license fee. $10 renewal fee. **Governing Statute:** Rules and Regulations, Water Well Driller's Licenses, Idaho Dept. of Water Resources.

Illinois

1539

Asbestos Project Supervisor
Illinois Dept. of Public Health
Div. of Environmental Health
525 W. Jefferson St.
Springfield, IL 62761
Phone: (217)782-3517

Credential Type: Asbestos Project Supervisor License. **Duration of License:** One year. **Requirements:** Complete an Illinois accredited asbestos Contractor/Supervisor training course or hold a current Illinois asbestos worker license. Renewal requires a one-half day refresher course for asbestos Contractors/Supervisors annually. **Examination:** Written examination. **Reciprocity:** Yes, if license was received in a state with requirements equal to or greater than those of Illinois. Must pay Illinois license fee. **Fees:** $50 initial license fee. $50 license renewal fee. $15 license reinstatement fee. **Governing Statute:** Illinois Asbestos Abatements act, Illinois Revised Statutes, Chapter 122.

1540

Housekeeping Supervisor (Gaming)
Illinois Gaming Board
PO Box 19474
Springfield, IL 62794-9474
Phone: (217)524-0228

Credential Type: Housekeeping Supervisor License. **Duration of License:** One year. **Requirements:** At least 18 years of age. U.S. citizen or legal alien as specified by the federal employment eligibility requirement. Housekeeping experience in the position of manager or supervisor. Submit application and pay fee. **Reciprocity:** No. **Fees:** $75 application fee. $50 initial license fee. $50 renewal fee. **Governing Statute:** Illinois Revised Statutes, Chapter 120.

1541

Maintenance Manager (Gaming)
Illinois Gaming Board
PO Box 19474
Springfield, IL 62794-9474
Phone: (217)524-0228

Credential Type: Maintenance Manager License. **Authorization:** Authorizes applicant to oversee the maintenance and housekeeping departments in a gaming establishment. **Requirements:** At least 18 years of age. Supervisory experience. Previous experience in maintenance preferred. U.S. citizen or legal alien as specified by the federal employment eligibility requirement. **Reciprocity:** No. **Fees:** $75 application fee. $50 initial license fee. $50 renewal fee. **Governing Statute:** Illinois Revised Statutes, Chapter 120.

1542

Maintenance Supervisor (Gaming)
Illinois Gaming Board
PO Box 19474
Springfield, IL 62794-9474
Phone: (217)524-0228

Credential Type: Maintenance Supervisor License. **Authorization:** Authorizes applicant to oversee the maintenance and cleaning of a gaming facility and its grounds. **Requirements:** At least 18 years of age. Supervisory experience. Previous experience in maintenance preferred. U.S. citizen or legal alien as specified by the federal employment eligibility requirement. **Reciprocity:** No. **Fees:** $75 application fee. $50 initial license fee. $50 renewal fee. **Governing Statute:** Illinois Revised Statutes, Chapter 120.

1543

Metal Mine Foreman
Illinois Dept. of Mines & Minerals
300 W. Jefferson St., Ste. 300
PO Box 10137
Springfield, IL 62791-0137
Phone: (217)782-6791

Credential Type: Metal Mine Foreman Certificate. **Duration of License:** Permanent. **Requirements:** At least 24 years of age. U.S. citizen. Four-year degree from an accredited engineering school and two years experience or four years experience without a degree. **Examination:** Written and oral examinations. **Reciprocity:** No. **Fees:** No fee. **Governing Statute:** 1989 Illinois Revised Statutes, Chapter 96 1/2.

1544

Security Supervisor (Gaming)
Illinois Gaming Board
PO Box 19474
Springfield, IL 62794-9474
Phone: (217)524-0228

Credential Type: Security Supervisor License. **Duration of License:** One year. **Requirements:** At least 21 years of age. U.S. citizen or legal alien as specified by Federal employability requirement. High school graduate or equivalent. Must have previous training and/or experience in the field of law enforcement. **Reciprocity:** No. **Fees:** $75 application fee. $50 initial license fee. $50 renewal fee. **Governing Statute:** Illinois Revised Statutes, Chapter 120.

1545

Shaft and Slope Supervisor (Construction and Mining)
Illinois Dept. of Mines and Minerals
300 W. Jefferson St., Ste. 300
PO Box 10137
Springfield, IL 62791-0137
Phone: (217)782-6791

Credential Type: Shaft and Slope Supervisor Certificate. **Duration of License:** Permanent. **Requirements:** At least 18 years of age. U.S. citizen. Three years of shaft and slope underground construction experience or 18 months of experience with a degree in Mining Engineering or Civil Engineering. Must complete a course in instruction of first aid. **Examination:** Written and oral examination. **Reciprocity:** No. **Fees:** No fee. **Governing Statute:** 62 Illinois Administrative Code 220.190(y).

1546

Surface Mine Supervisor
Illinois Dept. of Mines and Minerals
300 W. Jefferson St., Ste. 300
PO Box 10137
Springfield, IL 62791-0137
Phone: (217)782-6791

Credential Type: Surface Mine Supervisor Certificate. **Duration of License:** Permanent. **Requirements:** At least 18 years of age. U.S. citizen. Two years of field experience. Must pass four category examination. **Exemptions:** Written and oral examination in the following categories: (1) Overburden Stripping; (2) Drilling and Shooting; (3) Pit Coal Loading; (4) Reclamation. **Reciprocity:** No. **Fees:** No fee. **Governing Statute:** 1989 Illinois Revised Statutes, Chapter 96 1/2.

Indiana

1547

Asbestos Project Supervisor
Dept. of Environmental Management
Office of Air Management
Asbestos Section
PO Box 7060
Indianapolis, IN 46202-7060
Phone: (317)232-8232

Credential Type: Accreditation. **Duration of License:** One year. **Requirements:** Have at least six months experience as an asbestos project supervisor or as an asbestos worker. Attend an approved training course.

Renewal requires attending a refresher course. **Examination:** Training course examination. **Fees:** $100 annual accreditation fee. **Governing Statute:** 326 IAC 18-1 et seq.

Iowa

1548

Asbestos Abatement Contractor/ Supervisor
Iowa Dept. of Employment Services
Labor Services Div.
1000 E. Grand Ave.
Des Moines, IA 50319-0209
Phone: (515)281-3606

Credential Type: License. **Duration of License:** One year. **Requirements:** 18 years of age. Physically capable of performing the work safely. Successful completion of the approved training course. Passing of an Asbestos physical exam. **Reciprocity:** Licenses from other states will be reviewed. **Fees:** $50 license fee. $50 renewal fee.

1549

Maintenance Supervisor (Riverboat Gambling)
Iowa Racing and Gaming Commission
Lucas State Office Bldg.
Des Moines, IA 50319
Phone: (515)281-7352

Credential Type: License Registration. **Requirements:** Submit application and pay fees. **Fees:** $50 license fee.

Iowa

1550

Security Supervisor (Riverboat Gambling)
Iowa Racing and Gaming Commission
Lucas State Office Bldg.
Des Moines, IA 50319
Phone: (515)281-7352

Credential Type: License Registration. **Requirements:** Submit application and pay fees. **Fees:** $50 license fee.

Kentucky

1551

Mining Foreman
Dept. of Mines and Minerals
PO Box 14080
Lexington, KY 40512
Phone: (606)254-0367

Credential Type: License. **Duration of License:** One year. **Requirements:** Must have five years actual underground mining experience after reaching the 18th birthday, of which one year experience must have been at the face of the coal. An associate degree in mining technology or a four-year degree in mining engineering will count for two years of experience. Must be a resident of Kentucky or employed by a mine in Kentucky. 16 hours of retraining required annually. **Examination:** Yes. **Fees:** $50 exam fee.

Louisiana

1552

Stable Foreman (Racetrack)
Louisiana State Racing Commission
320 N. Carrollton Ave., Ste. 2-B
New Orleans, LA 70119-5111
Phone: (504)483-4000

Credential Type: License Registration. **Duration of License:** One year. **Requirements:** At least 18 years of age. Abide by state rules and regulations. Submit application and pay fees. **Fees:** $25 registration fee.

Maine

1553

Government Pesticide Supervisor
Dept. of Agriculture
Food and Rural Resources
Board of Pesticides Control
State House Station 28
Augusta, ME 04333
Phone: (207)287-2731

Credential Type: Government Pesticide Supervisor Certification. **Duration of License:** Five years. **Authorization:** There are 11 categories of certification. **Requirements:** Demonstrate competency by passing appropriate examinations. Recertification requires retesting or attending recertification training. **Examination:** General examination and appropriate category examinations. **Fees:** No fees.

Credential Type: Government Pesticide Supervisor License. **Duration of License:** One year. **Requirements:** License will be issued upon receiving certification. **Reciprocity:** Yes. **Fees:** No fees.

Maryland

1554

Mining Foreman
Bureau of Mines
Dept. of Natural Resources
PO Drawer C
Westernport, MD 21562
Phone: (301)689-4136

Credential Type: License. **Requirements:** Contact licensing body for application information.

Massachusetts

1555

Construction Supervisor
Board of Building Regulations and Standards
One Ashburton Pl., Rm. 1301
Boston, MA 02108
Phone: (617)727-3200

Credential Type: Construction Supervisor License, Restricted (1A). **Duration of License:** Three years followed by two-year renewal periods. **Authorization:** Permits supervision only of masonry-related work on one- and two-family dwellings and buildings of less than 35,000 cubic feet. **Requirements:** Be at least 18 years of age. Have three years experience in building construction or design in appropriate field. May also need to register as a Home Improvement Contractor. **Examination:** Construction Supervisor Examination, Restricted (1A). **Fees:** $150 license fee. $25 exam fee. $100 renewal fee.

Credential Type: Construction Supervisor License, Restricted (1G). **Duration of License:** Three years followed by two-year renewal periods. **Authorization:** Permits supervision of construction, reconstruction, altgeration, etc., involving the structural elements of one- and two-family dwellings only. **Requirements:** Be at least 18 years of age. Have three years experience in building construction or design in appropriate field. May also need to register as a Home Improvement Contractor. **Examination:** Construction Supervisor Examination, Restricted (1G). **Fees:** $150 license fee. $75 exam fee. $100 renewal fee.

Credential Type: Construction Supervisor License, Unrestricted. **Duration of License:** Three years followed by two-year renewal periods. **Authorization:** Permits supervision of construction, reconstruction, altgeration, etc., involving the structural elements of buildings containing less than 35,000 cubic feet, one- and two-family dwellings or accessory buildings thereto, buildings used for farm purposes, and retaining walls less than 10 feet in height. **Requirements:** Be at least 18 years of age. Have three years experience in building construction or design in appropriate field. May also need to register as a Home Improvement Contractor. **Examination:** Construction Supervisor Examination, Unrestricted. **Fees:** $150 license fee. $75 exam fee. $100 renewal fee.

Michigan

1556

Asbestos Abatement Supervisor
Asbestos Licensing
Div. of Occupational Health
Dept. of Public Health
3423 N. Logan
PO Box 30195
Lansing, MI 48909
Phone: (517)335-8000

Credential Type: Accreditation. **Duration of License:** One year. **Requirements:** Pass an Environmental Protection Agency (EPA) or state accredited four-day Asbestos Contractor/Supervisor Course. Abide by the rules and regulations of the Department. Renewal requires completion of a one-day refresher training course. **Examination:** Written exam. **Reciprocity:** Reciprocity may be granted if the requirements of the other state are equal to or exceed those of Michigan and the individual submits a certificate of successful completion of training from the other state. **Fees:** $25 initial accreditation fee. $25 renewal fee. $25 reciprocity fee. **Governing Statute:** Asbestos Workers Accreditation Act, Act 440 of 1988. Michigan Occupational and Safety Health Act, Act 154 of 1974, as amended. OSHA Construction Standard, 29 Code of Federal Regulations, 1926.58 Paragraph.

Minnesota

1557

Stable Foreman (Racetrack)
Minnesota Racing Commission
11000 W. 78th St., Ste. 201
Eden Prairie, MN 55344
Phone: (612)341-7555

Credential Type: License Registration. **Requirements:** Submit application and fingerprint card. Pay fee. **Fees:** $5 registration fee.

1558

Underground Storage Tank Supervisor
Pollution Control Agency
Tanks and Spills Section
520 N. Lafayette Rd.
St. Paul, MN 55155
Phone: (612)297-8679

Credential Type: Supervisor Certification. **Duration of License:** Four years. **Requirements:** Complete a 40-hour training program. Have at least two years of service experience. Have participated in at least five projects within the past two years. **Examination:** Yes. **Fees:** $50 application fee. $260 training fee.

Mississippi

1559

Asbestos Supervisor
Dept. of Environmental Quality
Office of Pollution Control
PO Box 10385
Jackson, MS 39289-0385
Phone: (601)961-5100

Credential Type: Certification. **Duration of License:** One year. **Requirements:** Must have a high school or GED diploma. Must attend an EPA-approved four-day contractor/supervisor course. Training must be continuous for recertification. **Examination:** EPA-approved examination for supervisor certification. **Exemptions:** Certification not required for federally owned buildings or small-scale, short duration activities. **Reciprocity:** No reciprocity. **Fees:** $200 license fee. $200 renewal fee.

Montana

1560

Asbestos Abatement Contractor/ Supervisor
Dept. of Health and Environmental Sciences
Health Services Div.
Occupational Health Bureau
1400 Broadway
Cogswell Bldg.
Helena, MT 59620
Phone: (406)444-3671

Credential Type: License and Accreditation. **Duration of License:** One year. **Requirements:** Contact licensing body for application information. Renewal requires completing a refresher course. **Fees:** $100 annual license fee. **Governing Statute:** Montana Code Annotated 75-2.

1561

Stable Foreman (Racetrack)
State of Montana Board of Horse Racing
Dept. of Commerce
1424 9th Ave.
Helena, MT 59620
Phone: (406)444-4287

Credential Type: License Registration. **Requirements:** Submit application and fingerprint card. Pay fee. **Fees:** $20 registration fee.

1562

Stable Superintendent (Racetrack)
State of Montana Board of Horse Racing
Dept. of Commerce
1424 9th Ave.
Helena, MT 59620
Phone: (406)444-4287

Credential Type: License Registration. **Requirements:** Submit application and fingerprint card. Pay fee. **Fees:** $20 registration fee.

Nebraska

1563

Stable Foreman (Racetrack)
Nebraska Racing Commission
PO Box 95014
301 Centennial Mall S.
Lincoln, NE 68509
Phone: (402)471-4155

Credential Type: License Registration. **Duration of License:** One year. **Requirements:** At least 16 years of age. No felony convictions. Secure employment and submit application completed and signed by management. Pay fees. **Fees:** $20 license fee. $20 renewal fee.

New Mexico

1564

Stable Foreman (Racetrack)
New Mexico State Racing Commission
PO Box 8576, Highland Station
Albuquerque, NM 87198
Phone: (505)841-4644

Credential Type: License Registration. **Requirements:** Submit application and fingerprint card. Pay fees. **Fees:** $16 registration fee. $1 notary fee. $23 fingerprint card processing fee.

1565

Stable Superintendent (Racetrack)
New Mexico State Racing Commission
PO Box 8576, Highland Station
Albuquerque, NM 87198
Phone: (505)841-4644

Credential Type: License Registration. **Requirements:** Submit application and fingerprint card. Pay fees. **Fees:** $16 registration fee. $1 notary fee. $23 fingerprint card processing fee.

North Dakota

1566

Asbestos Abatement Supervisor
State Dept. of Health and
  Consolidated Laboratories
Box 5520
1200 Missouri Ave.
Bismarck, ND 58502-5520
Phone: (701)224-5188

Credential Type: Asbestos Abatement Supervisor License. **Duration of License:** One year. **Requirements:** Complete an EPA-approved Asbestos Abatement Supervisor Course. Renewal requires attendance at annual refresher course. **Examination:** Written examination given as part of course. **Exemptions:** In-house non-public employees. Public employees and contractor employees disturbing less than three square feet or three line feet of asbestos-containing material. **Reciprocity:** All EPA-approved courses are recognized as acceptable. **Fees:** $25 license fee per discipline.

1567

Stable Foreman (Racetrack)
North Dakota Racing Commission
State Capitol Bldg.
Bismarck, ND 58505
Phone: (701)224-2210

Credential Type: License Registration. **Requirements:** Submit application and fingerprint card. Pay fee. **Fees:** $10 license fee. $10 duplicate license fee.

Ohio

1568

Mine Foreman
Mine Examining Board
Dept. of Industrial Relations
2323 W. Fifth Ave.
PO Box 825
Columbus, OH 43216
Phone: (614)644-2234

Credential Type: License. **Duration of License:** Permanent. **Authorization:** There are separate license categories for a foreman of a gaseous mine, a non-gaseous mine, and a clay mine or stripping pit. **Requirements:** Be able to read and write English. Have at least three years of practical experience. **Examination:** Mine foreman examination. **Fees:** $10 exam fee.

Oklahoma

1569

Mine Foreman (Underground)
State Mining Commission
4040 N. Lincoln, Ste. 107
Oklahoma City, OK 73105
Phone: (405)521-3859

Credential Type: Certificate. **Duration of License:** Lifetime. **Requirements:** State resident. First-aid certificate. Three years of practical underground experience. Completion of a two-year of four-year accredited mining program shall be credited one year of experience. **Examination:** Mine Foreman Certificate of Competency. **Fees:** $15 exam fee. $15 certification fee.

1570

Superintendent (Underground)
State Mining Commission
4040 N. Lincoln, Ste. 107
Oklahoma City, OK 73105
Phone: (405)521-3859

Credential Type: Certificate. **Duration of License:** Lifetime. **Requirements:** State resident. First-aid certificate. Five years of practical underground experience. **Examination:** Superintendent Examination. **Fees:** $20 exam fee. $20 certification fee.

1571

Surface Supervisor
State Mining Commission
4040 N. Lincoln, Ste. 107
Oklahoma City, OK 73105
Phone: (405)521-3859

Credential Type: Certificate. **Duration of License:** One year for coal certificate. Two years for non-coal. **Requirements:** First-aid certificate. One year of mining industry experience. **Examination:** Surface Supervisor Certification Examination. **Fees:** $5 exam fee. $5 certification fee.

Oregon

1572

Electrician, General Supervisor
Building Codes Agency
1535 Edgewater NW
Salem, OR 97310
Phone: (503)373-1268

Credential Type: License. **Duration of License:** Three years. **Requirements:** Must be regularly employed by either an electrical contractor or an industrial plant. Must submit proof of at least four years of employment as a General Journeyman Electrician. **Examination:** Yes. **Fees:** $10 exam fee. $100 license fee. $100 renewal fee. **Governing Statute:** ORS 479.630(2).

Rhode Island

1573

Asbestos Abatement Site Supervisor
Div. of Occupational and
  Radiological Health
Rhode Island Dept. of Health
3 Capitol Hill
Providence, RI 02908
Phone: (401)277-3601

Credential Type: Asbestos Abatement Site Supervisor License. **Duration of License:** Two years. **Requirements:** At least 18 years of age. Complete 40 hours of approved asbestos abatement training. **Examination:** Written examination. **Reciprocity:** No. **Fees:** $40 biennial renewal fee.

1574

Lead Hazard Abatement Site Supervisor
Office of Environmental Health Risk
  Assessment
Rhode Island Dept. of Health
3 Capitol Hill
Providence, RI 02908
Phone: (401)277-1417

Credential Type: Lead Hazard Abatement Site Supervisor. **Requirements:** Submit application. Contact licensing agency for additional requirements. **Examination:** Written and practical examinations.

Texas

1575

Asbestos Operations and Maintenance Supervisor
Texas Dept. of Health
Occupational Health Div.
Asbestos Licensing Section
1100 W. 49th St.
Austin, TX 78756
Phone: (512)834-6600

Credential Type: Asbestos Operations and Maintenance Supervisor License (Restricted). **Duration of License:** One year. **Authorization:** Operations and maintenance activities are restricted to small-scale, short-duration work practices and engineering controls that result in the disturbance, dislodgement, or removal of asbestos in the course of performing repairs, maintenance, renovation, installation, replacement, or cleanup operations. **Requirements:** Completion within the past 12 months of an approved training course for asbestos abatement contractors and project supervisors. Renewal requires completing the annual refresher training course. Must pass physical examination. **Fees:** $90 license fee. **Governing Statute:** Texas Civil Statutes, Article 4477-3a. Texas Asbestos Health Protection Rules, Section 295.

1576

Asbestos Project Supervisor
Texas Dept. of Health
Occupational Health Div.
Asbestos Licensing Section
1100 W. 49th St.
Austin, TX 78756
Phone: (512)834-6600

Credential Type: Asbestos Project Supervisor License (Restricted). **Duration of License:** One year. **Authorization:** License required to engage in supervision of an asbestos abatement project conducted in a public building. **Requirements:** Completion within the past 12 months of an approved training course for asbestos abatement contractors and project supervisors. Renewal requires completing the annual refresher training course. Must pass physical examination. Must have appropriate work experience of at least 90 days over a period of not less than 12 months and not more than 24 months. **Fees:** $300 license fee. **Governing Statute:** Texas Civil Statutes, Article 4477-3a. Texas Asbestos Health Protection Rules, Section 295.

1577

Stable Foreman (Racetrack)
Texas Racing Commission
PO Box 12080
Austin, TX 78711
Phone: (512)794-8461

Credential Type: License Registration. **Requirements:** Submit application and fingerprint card. Pay fee. **Fees:** $50 registration fee.

Utah

1578

Mine Foreman
The Industrial Commission of Utah
160 E. 300 S.
Salt Lake City, UT 84151-0910
Phone: (801)530-6869

Credential Type: Mine Foreman License. **Requirements:** Must have four years of varied underground coal mining experience. Must be trained in mine rescue and hold a U.S. Bureau of Mines First Aid Certificate or equivalent training. Two years experience may be credited to a mining engineering graduate of an approved four-year college; or one year's experience may be credited to a graduate of a two-year course in mining technology. **Examination:** Yes. **Fees:** $50 license fee.

1579

Surface Foreman
The Industrial Commission of Utah
160 E. 300 S.
Salt Lake City, UT 84151-0910
Phone: (801)530-6869

Credential Type: Surface Foreman License. **Requirements:** Must have three years of varied suface experience. Must have a U.S. Bureau of Mines First Aid Certificate or the equivalent training; or must hold an underground mine foreman certificate with three years of varied surface mining experience in any other industry that has substantially equivalent surface facilities, if the applicant has performed or is presently performing the duties normally required of a surface foreman. **Examination:** Yes. **Fees:** $50 license fee.

Vermont

1580

Foreman (Racetrack)
Vermont Racing Commission
State Office Bldg.
Montpelier, VT 05602
Phone: (802)828-3429

Credential Type: License Registration. **Requirements:** Submit application and fingerprint card. Pay fee. **Fees:** $2 registration fee. $2 duplicate license.

Virginia

1581

Foreman (Racetrack)
Virginia Racing Commission
PO Box 1123
Richmond, VA 23208
Phone: (804)371-7363

Credential Type: License Registration. **Requirements:** Submit application and fingerprint card. Pay fee. **Fees:** $10 registration fee.

1582

Stall Superintendent (Racetrack)
Virginia Racing Commission
PO Box 1123
Richmond, VA 23208
Phone: (804)371-7363

Credential Type: License Registration. **Requirements:** Submit application and fingerprint card. Pay fee. **Fees:** $10 registration fee.

West Virginia

1583

Mine Foreman
Dept. of Energy
State Capitol Bldg.
Charleston, WV 25305
Phone: (304)348-3500

Credential Type: License. **Requirements:** State resident. 18 years old. Foreman—five years experience with a degree in mining. Assistant—three years experience or degree in mining. **Examination:** Yes. **Fees:** $25 License.

Wyoming

1584

Mine Foreman
Mining Board of Wyoming
PO Box 1094
Rock Springs, WY 82901
Phone: (307)362-5222

Credential Type: License. **Requirements:** 23 years of age. Must have at least three years experience in the type of mine desired; or, two years of training as a mining engineer from an accredited college and one year of experience in the type of mine desired. Pass the examination. **Examination:** Yes. **Fees:** $25 License.

Boilermakers and Boiler Operators and Tenders

The following states grant licenses in this occupational category as of the date of publication: Alaska, Arkansas, Idaho, Kentucky, Michigan, New Jersey, New Mexico, Ohio, Oregon, Tennessee.

Alaska

1585

Boiler Operator
Alaska Dept. of Labor
Mechanical Inspection
PO Box 107020
Anchorage, AK 99510-7020
Phone: (907)264-2447

Credential Type: Boiler Operator's License. **Requirements:** License not required by the state but may be required by an employer. Six months experience for a third class operator's license. One year experience for a second class operator's license. Two years for a first class operator's license. **Examination:** Progressively more difficult examination, administered by the Alaska Dept. of Labor, is required for each class of license.

Arkansas

1586

Boiler Installer
Arkansas Dept. of Labor
Boiler Inspection Div.
10421 W. Markham
Little Rock, AR 72205
Phone: (501)682-4513

Credential Type: License. **Requirements:** Furnish suitable evidence of qualification to perform the duties involved with the job. **Examination:** No **Fees:** $75 License.

1587

Boiler Operator
Arkansas Dept. of Labor
Boiler Inspection Div.
10421 W. Markham
Little Rock, AR 72205
Phone: (501)628-4513

Credential Type: License. **Duration of License:** One year. **Requirements:** No less than six months on-the-job training prior to examination, proof of which must be presented by employer. **Examination:** Yes. **Fees:** $16 Written and oral examinations and Initial license fee. $12 Renewal.

1588

Boiler Repairer
Arkansas Dept. of Labor
Boiler Inspection Div.
10421 W. Markham
Little Rock, AR 72205
Phone: (501)682-4513

Credential Type: License. **Requirements:** Furnish evidence of qualification to perform this work, such as American Society of Mechanical Engineers (ASME) Section IX, Welding Code Specifications, Procedures and Qualifications. **Examination:** No **Fees:** $75 License.

Idaho

1589

Boilermaker
Dept. of Labor
State House Mail
Boise, ID 83720
Phone: (208)334-2327

Credential Type: Boilermaker Certification. **Requirements:** Contact licensing body for application information.

Kentucky

1590

Boiler Installer
Dept. of Housing, Building and Construction
1047 U.S. 127 South
Frankfort, KY 40601
Phone: (502)564-3626

Credential Type: License. **Duration of License:** One year. **Requirements:** Three years work experience. **Examination:** Yes. **Fees:** $100 exam fee. $70 renewal fee.

Michigan

1591

Boiler Installer
Boiler Div.
Bureau of Construction Codes
Dept. of Labor
7150 Harris Dr.
PO Box 30015
Lansing, MI 48909
Phone: (517)322-1287

Credential Type: License. **Duration of License:** One year. **Authorization:** There are 19 classes of boiler installer licenses. **Requirements:** At least five years of experience in the installation of boilers. A credit for two years of the required experience will be given for two years of experience in the design, construction, manufacture, maintenance, or inspection of boilers. Prior to licensure, the Boiler Division may require inspection and approval of installations previously made by the applicant. **Examination:** Written exam. **Fees:** $50 initial exam and license fee. $50 renewal fee. **Governing Statute:** Boiler Act, Act 290 of 1965.

1592

Boiler Repairer
Boiler Div.
Bureau of Construction Codes
Dept. of Labor
7150 Harris Dr.
PO Box 30015
Lansing, MI 48909
Phone: (517)322-1287

Credential Type: License. **Duration of License:** One year. **Requirements:** At least five years of experience in all phases of boiler repair allowed by the license class for which they are applying. A credit of three years toward the five years will be given for three years of experience in the design, construction, manufacture, or inspection of boilers. Prior to licensure, the Boiler Division will inspect all repairs reported on an applicant's application to establish their repair experience. **Examination:** Written exam. **Fees:** $50 initial exam and license fee. $50 renewal fee. **Governing Statute:** Boiler Act, Act 290 of 1965.

New Jersey

1593

Boiler Operator - Black Seal
New Jersey Dept. of Labor
Office of Boiler and Pressure Vessel Compliance
Trenton, NJ 08625-0392
Phone: (609)292-2921

Credential Type: Low Pressure License. **Duration of License:** Three years. **Requirements:** Three months of experience as a helper, apprentice or assistant to a licensed operator on boilers of over 100 HP. 18 years of age. **Examination:** Yes. **Fees:** $15 exam fee. $10 additional classification fee. $10 renewal fee. **Governing Statute:** NJSA 34:7. NJAC 12:90.

Credential Type: High Pressure In-Charge License. **Duration of License:** Three years. **Requirements:** Three months of experience as a helper, apprentice or assistant to a licensed operator on high pressure boilers of over 100 HP. 18 years of age. **Examination:** Yes. **Fees:** $15 exam fee. $10 additional classification fee. $10 renewal fee. **Governing Statute:** NJSA 34:7. NJAC 12:90.

Credential Type: Low Pressure In-Charge License. **Duration of License:** Three years. **Requirements:** FMN LP boiler operator license and three months of experience. 18 years of age. **Examination:** Yes. **Fees:** $15 exam fee. $10 additional classification fee. $10 renewal fee. **Governing Statute:** NJSA 34:7. NJAC 12:90.

New Mexico

1594

Journeyman Boiler Operator
Construction Industries Div.
Dept. of Regulation and Licensing
PO Box 25101
725 St. Michael's Dr.
Santa Fe, NM 87504
Phone: (505)827-7030
Fax: (505)827-7045

Credential Type: Journeyman Boiler Operator Certificate of Competence. **Duration of License:** One year. **Authorization:** Must be employed by a properly licensed contractor. **Requirements:** Be at least 18 years of age. Complete at least two years of approved experience or a course in the trade approved by the vocational educational division of the state department of public education. **Examination:** Boiler Operator Examination. **Fees:** $25 exam fee. $25 renewal fee. **Governing Statute:** Construction Industries Division Rules and Regulations. New Mexico Construction Industries Licensing Act, Chapter 60.

Ohio

1595

Boiler Operator
Div. of Examiners of Steam Engineers
Dept. of Industrial Relations
2323 W. 5th Ave.
PO Box 825
Columbus, OH 43266-0567
Phone: (614)644-2248

Credential Type: Low Pressure Boiler Operator License. **Duration of License:** One year. **Authorization:** License required of any person who operates or has charge of a stationary steam boiler of more than 30 horsepower, carrying a pressure of no more than 15 pounds per square inch. **Requirements:** Submit application and pass examination for competency. **Examination:** Low Pressure Boiler Operator Examination. **Exemptions:** Licensed Steam Engineers and Licensed High Pressure Boiler Operators. **Fees:** $50 license and exam fee. $25 renewal fee. **Governing Statute:** Ohio Revised Code 4739.13.

Credential Type: High Pressure Boiler Operator License. **Duration of License:** One year. **Authorization:** License required of any person who operates or has charge of a stationary steam boiler of more than 30 horsepower, except boilers that are in charge of a licensed engineer. **Requirements:** Submit application and pass examination for competency. **Examination:** High Pressure Boiler Operator Examination. **Fees:** $50 license and exam fee. $25 renewal fee. **Governing Statute:** Ohio Revised Code 4739.12.

Oregon

1596

Boilermaker
Building Codes Agency
1535 Edgewater
Salem, OR 97310
Phone: (503)373-1268

Credential Type: License. **Requirements:** Must have four years of experience. **Examination:** Yes. **Fees:** $25 exam fee. **Governing Statute:** ORS 480.510 to 480.990.

Tennessee

1597

Boiler Operator
Mechanical Licensing Board
160 N. Mid America Mall, Ste. 750
Memphis, TN 38103
Phone: (901)576-5280

Credential Type: License. **Duration of License:** One year. **Requirements:** 19 years old for 3rd class, 21 years old for 1st class. One year experience for 3rd class, two years for 1st class. **Examination:** Yes. **Fees:** $50 Examination. $30 Renewal.

Busdrivers

The following states grant licenses in this occupational category as of the date of publication:

Alabama	Illinois	Michigan	New York	South Dakota	Wyoming
Arizona	Iowa	Montana	North Carolina	Utah	
Hawaii	Kentucky	Nevada	Rhode Island	West Virginia	

Alabama

1598

School Bus Driver
Alabama State Board of Education,
 Transportation Section
5144 Gordon Persons Bldg.
50 N. Ripley St.
Montgomery, AL 36130-3901
Phone: (205)242-9730

Credential Type: License. **Duration of License:** One year. **Requirements:** 18 years of age. Must hold a valid drivers license. Must have attended State Dept. of Education twelve-hour driver's school. **Examination:** Yes. **Fees:** No fees.

Arizona

1599

School Bus Driver
Dept. of Transportation
Motor Vehicle Div.
1801 W. Jefferson
Phoenix, AZ 85007
Phone: (602)255-8152

Credential Type: School Bus Driver Certificate. **Duration of License:** One year. **Examination:** Final Test (School Bus Driver). **Fees:** $23 fingerprint processing fee.

Hawaii

1600

Motor Vehicle Operator, Bus Driver
City and County Motor Vehicle
 Licensing Div., Motor Vehicle
 Branch
1455 S. Beretania St.
Honolulu, HI 96814
Phone: (808)973-2730

Credential Type: License. **Requirements:** 20 or 21 years of age. Type 3 driver's license. Type 4 driver's license if bus is over 10,000 lbs. Hawaii driver's license. Certificate of health. **Examination:** Road test. **Fees:** $3 permit fee. $3 upgrade fee.

1601

Motor Vehicle Operator, School Bus Driver
City and County Motor Vehicle
 Licensing Div., Motor Vehicle
 Branch
1455 S. Beretania St.
Honolulu, HI 96814
Phone: (808)973-2730

Credential Type: License. **Requirements:** 21 years of age. Hawaii driver's license of appropriate class. Medical certificate. TB clearance. Submit a traffic violation abstract. One year of practical driving experience. No felony convictions within the past five years. No misdemeanor convictions during the last three years. **Fees:** No fees.

Illinois

1602

Commercial Driver (Truck or Bus)
Secretary of State
2701 S. Dirksen Parkway
Springfield, IL 62723
Phone: (217)782-0560

Credential Type: Commercial Driver License. **Duration of License:** Four years. **Authorization:** Allows applicant to operate a truck or bus that is over 26,000 pounds. **Requirements:** Must be at least 18 years of age to drive for-hire or within the state of Illinois. Must be at least 21 years of age to transport passengers or for interstate driving. **Examination:** Written and performance tests. **Reciprocity:** Yes, with a valid commercial license from another jurisdiction. **Fees:** $40 examination fee. $40 initial license fee. $40 renewal fee. **Governing Statute:** Chapter 95 1/2, Section 6-500, Illinois Vehicle Code.

Iowa

1603

Bus Driver
Office of Driver Services
Motor Vehicles Div.
Park Fair Mall
100 Euclid
Des Moines, IA 50306
Phone: (515)237-3153

Alternate Information: 5268 2nd Ave., NW, Des Moines, IA 50313

Credential Type: License. **Duration of License:** Two or four years. **Requirements:** 18 years of age. **Examination:** Written, driving and vision exams. **Fees:** $16 or $32 license fees. $20 exam fee.

Kentucky

1604

School Bus Driver
Dept. of Education, Pupil Transportation
Capital Plaza Tower
Frankfort, KY 40601
Phone: (502)564-4718

Credential Type: License. **Requirements:** High school diploma or GED. Completion of an 18-hour structured program developed by the Kentucky Dept. of Education. **Examination:** Yes.

Michigan

1605

Bus Driver
Bureau of Driver and Vehicles Records
Dept. of State
7064 Crowner Dr.
Lansing, MI 48918
Phone: (517)322-1460

Credential Type: Chauffeur's License. **Duration of License:** Two or four years. **Authorization:** A "Group C" designation is required for smaller passenger vehicles designed for 16 or more occupants, including the driver, that qualify as buses. **Requirements:** At least 18 years of age. Not have a physical or mental condition which may interfere with the reasonable operation of a motor vehicle. Must not be a habitual drunkard or addicted to a controlled substance. Drivers employed to operate a motor vehicle as a public or common carrier of property must also be certified by the Public Service Commission of the Department of Commerce. **Examination:** Written, vision, and practical exam. **Fees:** $5 (one year), $20 (four years) initial exam and license fee. $25 behind-the-wheel road test fee. $10 (two years), $20 (four years) renewal exam and license fee. $20 vehicle group designation initial examination and license fee (one to four years). $60 behind-the-wheel road test. **Governing Statute:** Michigan Vehicle Code, Act 300 of 1949, as amended.

1606

Motor Carrier of Passengers for Hire
Intercity Div.
Bureau of Urban and Public Transportation
Dept. of Transportation
PO Box 30050
Lansing, MI 48909
Phone: (517)373-2090

Credential Type: Certificate of authority. **Duration of License:** One year. **Requirements:** Demonstrate financial responsibility. Have a good safety record and submit a list of equipment (vehicle roster) to be used. Have motor bus(es) inspected by the Department. Submit a paid, one-year certificate of insurance with specific personal injury protection coverage and property damage coverage with a combined single limit of at least $5 million as well as $1 million Michigan basic no-fault coverage. Abide by the rules of the Department. **Examination:** Written exam. **Reciprocity:** Informal reciprocity for safety inspections of vehicles for certain states and provinces is accepted. Check with the Michigan Department of Transportation for the current list. **Fees:** $300 initial application and certificate of authority fee. $25 (times the number of motor buses used) renewal certificate of authority fee. **Governing Statute:** Motor Bus Transportation Act, Act 432 of 1982, as amended.

1607

School Bus Driver
Bureau of Driver and Vehicles Records
Dept. of State
7064 Crowner Dr.
Lansing, MI 48918
Phone: (517)322-1460

Credential Type: Chauffeur's License. **Duration of License:** Two or four years. **Authorization:** A "Group C" designation is required for smaller passenger vehicles designed for 16 or more occupants, including the driver, that qualify as buses. **Requirements:** At least 18 years of age. Must not have a physical or mental condition which may interfere with the reasonable operation of a motor vehicle. Must not be a habitual drunkard or addicted to a controlled substance. Drivers employed to operate a motor vehicle as a public or common carrier of property must also be certified by the Public Service Commission of the Department of Commerce. School bus drivers must also complete a school bus safety education course and pass a physical exam each year. **Examination:** Written, vision, and practical exam. **Fees:** $5 (one year), $20 (four years) initial exam and license fee. $25 behind-the-wheel road test fee. $10 (two years), $20 (four years) renewal exam and license fee. $20 vehicle group designation initial examination and license fee (one to four years). $60 behind-the-wheel road test. **Governing Statute:** Michigan Vehicle Code, Act 300 of 1949, as amended.

Montana

1608

Bus Driver
Montana Driver Services Bureau
303 Roberts
Helena, MT 59620
Phone: (406)444-3292

Credential Type: Driver's License—Type 1. **Duration of License:** Four years. **Authorization:** May operate anywhere in the United States. **Requirements:** A medical certificate. 21 years of age. **Examination:** Written and practical exam. **Fees:** $12 license fee. $24 renewal fee. **Governing Statute:** Montana Code Annotated 61-5-101 through 61-5-213.

Credential Type: Driver's License—Type 2. **Duration of License:** Four years. **Authorization:** May operate only in Montana. **Requirements:** A medical certificate. 18 years of age. One year of driving experience. **Examination:** Written and practical exam **Fees:**. $12 license fee. $18 renewal fee. **Governing Statute:** Montana Code Annotated 61-5-101 through 61-5-213.

Nevada

1609

Bus Driver
Dept. of Motor Vehicles
Driver's License Div.
305 Galletti Way
Reno, NV 89512
Phone: (702)688-2404

Credential Type: Class B Commercial Driver's License. **Examination:** Written, vision and driving exams. **Fees:** $85 exam fee. $85 license fee. $1 photo fee.

New York

1610

Bus Driver
New York State Dept. of Motor Vehicles
Office of Communications
Empire State Plaza
Albany, NY 12228
Phone: (518)474-0877

Credential Type: License. **Duration of License:** Four years. **Requirements:** Prelicensing classroom instruction. 18 years of age. Excellent vision. Driver's license. **Examination:** Written, vision and road tests. **Fees:** $19 exam fee. $42.50—$50.50 license fee. $33.50 renewal fee. **Governing Statute:** Articles 19 and 19-A of the Vehicle and Traffic Law.

North Carolina

1611

Bus Driver
Dept. of Transportation
Driver's License Section
1100 New Bern Ave.
Raleigh, NC 27697
Phone: (919)733-4241

Credential Type: License. **Duration of License:** Four years. **Requirements:** 18 years of age. **Examination:** Written, vision and road tests. **Fees:** $15 license fee. $15 renewal fee.

Rhode Island

1612

Commercial Driver
Div. of Motor Vehicles
Rhode Island Dept. of Transportation
2 Capitol Hill
Providence, RI 02903
Phone: (401)277-3427

Credential Type: Commercial Driver's License (CDL)—Class A. **Duration of License:** Five years. **Authorization:** Authorizes applicant to drive a commercial vehicle of 13 tons, or more, carrying over five tons. **Requirements:** At least 18 years of age. Resident of Rhode Island. A minimum of one year of driving experience. Submit application and pay fees. **Examination:** Written, road, and eye examinations (each eye must test at least 20/40). **Reciprocity:** Yes. **Fees:** $10 CDL examination fee (per exam). $100 CDL application fee. $25 CDL road test fee. $10 CDL license fee.

Credential Type: Commercial Driver's License (CDL)—Class B. **Duration of License:** Five years. **Authorization:** Authorizes applicant to drive a commercial vehicle of 13 tons, or more, but not carrying more than five tons. **Requirements:** At least 18 years of age. Resident of Rhode Island. A minimum of one year of driving experience. Submit application and pay fees. **Examination:** Written, road, and eye examinations (each eye must test at least 20/40). **Reciprocity:** Yes. **Fees:** $10 CDL examination fee (per exam). $100 CDL application fee. $25 CDL road test fee. $10 CDL license fee.

Credential Type: Commercial Driver's License (CDL)—Class C. **Duration of License:** Five years. **Authorization:** Authorizes applicant to drive a commercial vehicle not meeting Class A or B standards or carrying hazardous material or over 15 passengers, except school buses. **Requirements:** At least 18 years of age. Resident of Rhode Island. A minimum of one year of driving experience. Proper endorsements required for particular type of vehicle ("H" for hazardous material, "P" for passengers, "N" for tank vehicle, and "T" for double or triple trailers). Submit proper applications and pay fees. **Examination:** Written, road, and eye examinations (each eye must test at least 20/40). **Reciprocity:** Yes. **Fees:** $10 CDL examination fee (per exam). $100 CDL application fee. $25 CDL road test fee. $10 CDL license fee.

1613

School Bus Driver
Div. of Motor Vehicles
Rhode Island Dept. of Transportation
Two Capitol Hill
Providence, RI 02903
Phone: (401)277-2679

Credential Type: School Bus Driver License. **Duration of License:** Two years. **Requirements:** At least 21 years of age and not over 65 years of age. Rhode Island resident. Hold a motor vehicle operator license for at least one year. Complete a School Bus Driver training course of a minimum of 10 hours. Course instructor must be certified by the Rhode Island Div. of Motor Vehicles. Instruction must include classroom and behind-the-wheel training. Eye test and physical examination are required. Annual randomly administered drug test. **Reciprocity:** No. **Fees:** $10 CDL application fee. $10 fee each CDL endorsement. $2 transfer (to chauffeur) fee. $8 renewal fee.

South Dakota

1614

Bus Driver
Dept. of Commerce and Regulation
Driver Licensing Program
State Capitol
Pierre, SD 57501
Phone: (605)773-3105

Credential Type: Commercial Drivers License. **Duration of License:** Four years. **Authorization:** Required to drive a vehicle designed to transport 16 or more persons including the driver. **Requirements:** Be at least 18 years of age. Resident of South Dakota. The following endorsements are available with additional testing: passengers, school bus. **Examination:** Knowledge and skills test. **Fees:** $25 license fee (knowledge and skills test). $15 license fee (knowledge test only). $5 endorsement fee (per endorsement).

Utah

1615

Driving Occupations
Dept. of Public Safety
Drivers License Div.
4501 S. 2700 W.
PO Box 30560
Salt Lake City, UT 84130-0560
Phone: (801)965-4406

Credential Type: Commercial Driver's License. **Authorization:** CDL required for the following Commercial Motor Vehicles: single vehicle of more than 26,000 pounds; trailer of more than 10,000 pounds if gross combination weight rating is more than 26,000 pounds; vehicle designed to transport more than 15 persons (including driver); any size vehicle requiring hazardous materials placards; any size vehicle used as a school bus. **Requirements:** Submit application, pay fees, and pass tests. **Examination:** Knowledge, skills, and driving tests. **Fees:** Contact department or any local motor vehicle testing station for fees.

West Virginia

1616

Driver—School Bus
Dept. of Education
Office of Educational Personnel
 Development
1900 Washington St. E
Charleston, WV 25305
Phone: (800)982-2378

Credential Type: License. **Duration of License:** Four years. **Requirements:** West Virginia resident. May operate bus between ages 19 and 70. Thirty hours of West Virginia School Bus Operator Program. Behind the wheel instruction. Never convicted of a felony. **Examination:** Yes. **Fees:** $15 License (every four years).

Wyoming

1617

Bus Driver, School
Wyoming Dept. of Education
Administrative Services Div.
Hathaway Bldg.
2300 Capitol Ave.
Cheyenne, WY 82002
Phone: (307)777-6265

Credential Type: License. **Duration of License:** Four years. **Requirements:** Good driving record. Must be at least 18 years old. Pass physical examination. **Examination:** Yes. **Fees:** $40 Initial license. $40 Renewal.

Cashiers

The following states grant licenses in this occupational category as of the date of publication: District of Columbia, Illinois, Iowa, New Jersey, North Dakota, Rhode Island.

District of Columbia

1618

Check Seller
License and Certification Div.
Occupational and Professional Licensure Administration
Consumer and Regulatory Affairs Dept.
PO Box 37200
Washington, DC 20013-7200
Phone: (202)727-7823
Phone: (202)727-7480

Alternate Information: 614 H St., NW, Washington, DC 20001.

Credential Type: License. **Requirements:** Contact licensing body for application information.

Illinois

1619

Casino Cage Cashier (Gaming)
Illinois Gaming Board
PO Box 19474
Springfield, IL 62794-9474
Phone: (217)524-0228

Credential Type: Casino Cage Cashier License. **Duration of License:** One year. **Requirements:** At least 21 years of age. No felony convictions. U.S. citizen and resident of Illinois. High school graduate or equivalent. Previous experience in cashier transactions. Have knowledge of computers and 10 key calculators. **Reciprocity:** No. **Fees:** $75 application and initial license fee. $50 renewal fee. **Governing Statute:** Illinois Revised Statutes, Chapter 120.

1620

Change Attendant (Gaming)
Illinois Gaming Board
PO Box 19474
Springfield, IL 62794-9474
Phone: (217)524-0228

Credential Type: Change Attendant License. **Duration of License:** One year. **Requirements:** At least 21 years of age. High school graduate or equivalent. U.S. citizen and Illinois resident. No felony convictions. Excellent customer service skills. Physically capable of performing required duties. **Reciprocity:** No. **Fees:** $75 application and license fee. $50 renewal fee. **Governing Statute:** Illinois Revised Statutes, Chapter 120.

1621

Remittance Agent
Secretary of State
Centennial Bldg., Rm. 008
Springfield, IL 62756
Phone: (217)782-7817

Credential Type: Remittance Agent License. **Duration of License:** One year. **Authorization:** License required of any individual who is publicly engaged in accepting money for remittance to the State of Illinois or any of its instrumentalities or political subdivisions for the payment of vehicle taxes or license or registration fees. **Requirements:** Submit application and pay fee. **Reciprocity:** No. **Fees:** $50 license fee. **Governing Statute:** Illinois Vehicle Code 93 1/2 3-900.

1622

Restaurant Cashier (Gaming)
Illinois Gaming Board
PO Box 19474
Springfield, IL 62794-9474
Phone: (217)524-0228

Credential Type: Restaurant Cashier License. **Duration of License:** One year. **Requirements:** At least 18 years of age. Must be a U.S. citizen or legal alien as specified by the Federal employment eligibility requirement. Submit application and pay fee. **Reciprocity:** No. **Fees:** $75 application and initial license fee. $50 renewal fee. **Governing Statute:** Illinois Revised Statutes, Chapter 120.

Iowa

1623

Casino Teller (Riverboat Gambling)
Iowa Racing and Gaming Commission
Lucas State Office Bldg.
Des Moines, IA 50319
Phone: (515)281-7352

Credential Type: License Registration. **Requirements:** Submit application and pay fees. **Fees:** $20 license fee.

Iowa

1624

Non-Gaming Cashier (Riverboat Gambling)
Iowa Racing and Gaming Commission
Lucas State Office Bldg.
Des Moines, IA 50319
Phone: (515)281-7352

Credential Type: License Registration. **Requirements:** Submit application and pay fees. **Fees:** $10 license fee.

1625

Non-Gaming Change Person (Riverboat Gambling)
Iowa Racing and Gaming Commission
Lucas State Office Bldg.
Des Moines, IA 50319
Phone: (515)281-7352

Credential Type: License Registration. **Requirements:** Submit application and pay fees. **Fees:** $10 license fee.

1626

Slot Change Person (Riverboat Gambling)
Iowa Racing and Gaming Commission
Lucas State Office Bldg.
Des Moines, IA 50319
Phone: (515)281-7352

Credential Type: License Registration. **Requirements:** Submit application and pay fees. **Fees:** $20 license fee.

New Jersey

1627

Check Casher
New Jersey Dept. of Banking
Consumer Credit Bureau
CN040
Trenton, NJ 08625
Phone: (609)292-5466

Credential Type: License. **Duration of License:** Two years. **Requirements:** Applicants must have $50,000 in liquid assets available at all times for the operation of the business. **Fees:** $100 application fee. $800 registration fee. **Governing Statute:** NJSA 17:15A. NJAC 3:24.

1628

Check Seller
New Jersey Dept. of Banking
Consumer Credit Bureau
CN040
Trenton, NJ 08625-0040
Phone: (609)292-5466

Credential Type: License. **Duration of License:** Two years. **Requirements:** Applicants must file a corporate surety bond of $100,000 with the department. **Fees:** $200 investigation fee. $1,200 license fee. $1,200 renewal fee. **Governing Statute:** NJSA 17:15. NJAC 3:24-5.

North Dakota

1629

Check Seller
Commissioner of Banking and Financial Institutions
600 E. Blvd. Ave.
Bismarck, ND 58505
Phone: (701)224-2253

Credential Type: License. **Duration of License:** One year. **Requirements:** Must have a net worth of at least $50,000. Have appropriate financial responsibility and business experience. Post a $25,000 bond plus a $5000 bond for each location. **Fees:** $300 investigation fee. $200 license fee. $200 renewal fee. **Governing Statute:** North Dakota Century Code, Chap. 51-17.

Rhode Island

1630

Check Cashier
Div. of Banking
Rhode Island Dept. of Business Regulation
233 Richmond St.
Providence, RI 02903
Phone: (401)277-2405

Credential Type: Check Cashier License. **Duration of License:** One year. **Authorization:** Allows licensee to cash checks, prepare money orders, receive payment for utility bills, and transfer funds through electronic and wire transfer systems. **Requirements:** Must be financially reliable. File policy of insurance. Post surety bond of $50,00, plus $5,000 for each business location. Must submit application with the following information: (1) Financial statement which includes 1st year projected expenses and income; (2) Financial statement showing sources of all investment; (3) Business plan; (4) Location of business. **Reciprocity:** No. **Fees:** $200 application/initial license fee. $200 annual renewal fee.

Chiropractors

The following states grant licenses in this occupational category as of the date of publication:

Alabama	District of	Iowa	Minnesota	New Mexico	Rhode Island	Washington
Alaska	Columbia	Kansas	Mississippi	New York	South Carolina	West Virginia
Arizona	Florida	Kentucky	Missouri	North Carolina	South Dakota	Wisconsin
Arkansas	Georgia	Louisiana	Montana	North Dakota	Tennessee	Wyoming
California	Hawaii	Maine	Nebraska	Ohio	Texas	
Colorado	Idaho	Maryland	Nevada	Oklahoma	Utah	
Connecticut	Illinois	Massachusetts	New Hampshire	Oregon	Vermont	
Delaware	Indiana	Michigan	New Jersey	Pennsylvania	Virginia	

Alabama

1631

Chiropractor (Doctor of Chiropractic)
State Board of Chiropractic Examiners
PO Box 925
Robertsdale, AL 36567
Phone: (205)947-5838

Credential Type: License. **Duration of License:** One year. **Requirements:** High school diploma. Two years of pre-chiropractic college. Graduation from an approved college of Chiropractic. License renewal requires 15 hours of continuing education. **Examination:** National Boards, parts one and 2. **Fees:** $100 application fee. $15 license fee. $100 renewal fee.

Alaska

1632

Chiropractor
Alaska State Board of Chiropractic Examiners
333 Willoughby Ave., SOB
PO Box 110806
Juneau, AK 99811-0806
Phone: (907)465-2580
Fax: (907)465-2974

Credential Type: Chiropractic license. **Duration of License:** Two years. **Requirements:** Two years liberal arts of pre-professional education. Graduate of an approved chiropractic college. Renewal requires 12 hours of Continuing Education per complete calendar year of license. **Examination:** State written jurisprudence and x-ray. State developed and administered Practical exam. National Board Examination, Parts I, II, III, and Physiotherapy. **Reciprocity:** Credentials as per AS 08.20.140. **Fees:** $50 exam fee. $30 application fee. $100 initial license fee. $100 license renewal fee.

Arizona

1633

Chiropractor
Arizona State Board of Chiropractic Examiners
5060 N. 19th Ave., Ste. 416
Phoenix, AZ 85015
Phone: (602)255-1444
Fax: (602)255-4289

Credential Type: Chiropractic license. **Duration of License:** One year. **Requirements:** Graduate of an approved chiropractic college. **Examination:** State administered: adjusting technique, x-ray film reading, and Arizona Law. National Board Examination, Parts I, II, and III. **Reciprocity:** Reciprocity based license obtained after exam requiring Parts I, II and III of the National Boards, and state level exam on adjusting, x-ray film reading and local jurisprudence; and three years full time practice in good standing. **Fees:** $100 exam fee. $100 initial license fee. $100 license renewal fee.

Credential Type: Physiotherapy certification. **Duration of License:** One year. **Requirements:** 120 hours of additional education. **Examination:** Passing score on NBCE Physiotherapy exam waives state exam. **Fees:** $100 exam fee. $100 certification fee.

Credential Type: Acupuncture certification. **Duration of License:** One year. **Requirements:** 50 credit hours additional education. **Examination:** State level written exam. **Fees:** $100 exam fee. $100 certification fee.

Arkansas

1634

Chiropractor
Arkansas State Board of Chiropractic Examiners
2020 W. 3rd, Ste. 1C
Little Rock, AR 72205
Phone: (501)324-9870

Credential Type: License. **Duration of License:** One year. **Requirements:** 21 years of age. Good moral character. Two years (60 semester hours) of college in the field of Science. Possess a valid Doctor of Chiropractic Degree from an approved chiropractic institution. Pass the National Board Examination. **Examination:** Yes. **Fees:** $50 Orientation. $15 Written, Oral and Practical examinations. $125 License. $125 Renewal.

California

1635

Chiropractor
California State Board of Chiropractic Examiners
3401 Folsom Blvd., Ste. B
Sacramento, CA 95816
Phone: (916)739-3445

Credential Type: Chiropractic license. **Duration of License:** One year. **Requirements:** 60 college credits of pre-professional education. Graduate of an approved chiropractic college. Renewal requires 12 hours of Continuing Education per year. **Examination:** State administered optional written exam for applicants not having National Board exams; clinical competency, physiotherapy, adjustive technique, x-ray. National Board Examination, Parts I, II, and Physiotherapy. **Reciprocity:** Meet

Chiropractor, continued

same educational requirements in same areas at time of original licensure. Same reciprocation by state. No disciplinary action against the license. License must be current and valid. **Fees:** $100 application fee (includes initial license fee). $75 written examination reimbursement costs including physiotherapy. $65 written physiotherapy only. $27 fingerprint processing cost. $150 license renewal fee.

Credential Type: Physiotherapy certification. **Duration of License:** One year. **Requirements:** 120 hours of additional education. **Examination:** State physiotherapy exam. **Fees:** No additional fee.

Colorado

1636

Chiropractor
Colorado Board of Chiropractic Examiners
1560 Broadway, Ste. 1310
Denver, CO 80202
Phone: (303)894-7762
Fax: (303)894-7764

Credential Type: Chiropractic license. **Duration of License:** Two years. **Requirements:** High school diploma. Graduate of an approved chiropractic college. Renewal requires 15 hours of Continuing Education per year. **Examination:** State administered practical and jurisprudence exams. National Board Examination, Parts I, II, and III. **Reciprocity:** Practical exam in clinical subjects. Three years of full-time practice out of last five years. $282 reciprocity fee. **Fees:** $282 exam fee (includes initial license fee). $208 license renewal fee.

Credential Type: Electrotherapy certification. **Duration of License:** Two years. **Requirements:** 120 classroom hours of additional education in electrotherapy. **Examination:** No additional exam. **Fees:** No additional fee.

Connecticut

1637

Chiropractor
Connecticut State Board of Chiropractic Examiners
150 Washington St.
Hartford, CT 06106
Phone: (203)566-1031

Credential Type: Chiropractic license. **Duration of License:** One year. **Requirements:** Two years or 60 semester hours of pre-professional education. Graduate of an approved chiropractic college. **Examination:** State administered practical exam. National Board Examination, Parts I, II, III, and Physiotherapy. **Reciprocity:** No direct reciprocity. Endorsement (waiver of National Boards) available to qualifying applicants. **Fees:** $450 exam fee (includes initial license fee). $225 license renewal fee.

Delaware

1638

Chiropractor
Delaware Board of Chiropractic Examiners
PO Box 1401
Dover, DE 19903
Phone: (302)739-4522
Fax: (302)739-6148

Credential Type: Chiropractic license. **Duration of License:** Two years. **Requirements:** Graduate of an approved chiropractic college. Renewal requires 24 hours of Continuing Education per two years. **Examination:** State administered exams: diagnosis, x-ray evaluation, principles of adjusting, and physical therapy. National Board Examination, Parts I, II, and III. **Reciprocity:** Must meet full Delaware requirements. **Fees:** $200 exam fee (includes initial license fee). $150 license renewal fee.

District of Columbia

1639

Chiropractor
Government of the District of Columbia Board of Medicine
614 H. St., NW, Rm. 904
Washington, DC 20001
Phone: (202)727-5365

Credential Type: Chiropractic license. **Duration of License:** Two years. **Requirements:** Two years of pre-professional education. Graduate of an approved chiropractic college. Renewal requires 24 hours of Continuing Education per two years of active license. **Examination:** State administered exam, six parts: neurological and orthopedics, x-ray interpretation, physical examination and instrumentation, technique and clinical competency, physical diagnosis, and District of Columbia laws and regulations. National Board Examination, Parts I, II, and III. **Reciprocity:** Must take full District of Columbia examination. **Fees:** $180 exam fee. $20 initial license fee. $120 license renewal fee.

Credential Type: Ancillary procedures certification. **Duration of License:** Two years. **Examination:** NBCE Physiotherapy exam. District of Columbia Ancillary Procedures exam. **Fees:** $50 application fee.

Florida

1640

Chiropractor
Florida State Board of Chiropractic
1940 N. Monroe St.
Tallahassee, FL 32399-0752
Phone: (904)487-2395

Credential Type: Chiropractic license. **Duration of License:** Two years. **Requirements:** Bachelors degree for applicants who matriculate effective as of July 1, 1991. Graduate of an approved chiropractic college. Renewal requires 40 hours of Continuing Education every two years, five hours of which must be in risk management and four hours in AIDS. **Examination:** State administered exams: practical (including x-ray interpretation, technique, and physical diagnosis) and laws and rules. National Board Examination, Parts I, II, and III. **Reciprocity:** Qualified doctors licensed for five or more years in another state with no disciplinary actions. **Fees:** $100 application fee. $250 exam fee. $250 (2 year license), $125 (1 year license) initial license fee. $250 license renewal fee.

Credential Type: Physiotherapy certification. **Duration of License:** Two years. **Requirements:** 120 hours of additional education (PHT) at accredited institution. **Examination:** NBCE Physiotherapy exam within last 10 years of application for exam. **Fees:** $175 combined application/exam fee.

Georgia

1641

Chiropractor
Georgia State Board of Chiropractic Examiners
166 Pryor St., SW
Atlanta, GA 30303
Phone: (404)656-3912
Fax: (404)651-9532

Credential Type: Chiropractic license. **Duration of License:** Two years. **Requirements:** High school diploma. Two years of general college (60 semester hours or 90 quarter hours). Graduate of an approved chiropractic college. Renewal requires 12 hours of Continuing Education per year. **Examination:** State administered practical exam: x-ray, clinical evaluation/technique, ethics and jurisprudence. Failure in any one area requires retaking the complete exam. National Board Examination, Parts I, II, and III. **Reciprocity:** three years practice in a reciprocal state. Practical exam. **Fees:** $50 application fee. $150 exam fee (includes initial license fee). $100 license renewal fee.

Credential Type: Physiological Therapeutics certification. **Duration of License:** Two years. **Requirements:** 120 classroom hours of additional education in electrical therapeutic modalities. **Examination:** No additional exam. **Fees:** No additional fee.

Hawaii

1642

Chiropractor
Hawaii Board of Chiropractic
  Examiners
Dept. of Commerce and Consumer
  Affairs
PO Box 3469
Honolulu, HI 96801
Phone: (808)548-8590

Credential Type: License. **Duration of License:** Six months. **Requirements:** 60 semester hours in liberal arts and/or sciences. Graduation from an approved chiropractic college. **Examination:** National Board exam. Hawaii practical exam. **Reciprocity:** None. **Fees:** $25 application fee. $100 exam fee. $75 license fee. $25 $50 Compliance Resolution Fund fee. $75 renewal fee.

Idaho

1643

Chiropractor
Idaho Board of Chiropractic
  Physicians
2417 Bank Dr., Rm. 312
Boise, ID 83705-2598
Phone: (208)334-3233

Credential Type: Chiropractic license. **Duration of License:** One year. **Requirements:** Two years of college or university. Graduate of an approved chiropractic college. Renewal requires 12 hours of Continuing Education per year. **Examination:** State administered written exams: x-ray interpretation practical, adjustive technique (written and practical), jurisprudence, and nutrition. National Board Examination, Parts I, II, and III. **Reciprocity:** five consecutive years of practice. Current license in good standing. Meet requirements for Idaho licensure. Complete limited exam and NBCE Parts I and II. **Fees:** $100 application fee. $150 exam fee (includes initial license fee). $100 license renewal fee.

Credential Type: Physiotherapy certification. **Duration of License:** One year. **Requirements:** 120 hours of additional education. **Examination:** No additional exam. **Fees:** No additional fee.

Illinois

1644

Chiropractor
Illinois Medical Licensing Board
320 W. Washington, 3rd Fl.
Springfield, IL 62786
Phone: (217)782-8556
Fax: (217)782-7645

Credential Type: Chiropractic license. **Duration of License:** Three years. **Requirements:** Graduate of an approved chiropractic college. Renewal requires Continuing Education. **Examination:** National Board Examination, Parts I, II, and III. **Reciprocity:** Graduate of an approved chiropractic school or college. Requirements for the applicant's license must be equivalent to the requirements for a license to practice in the state at the date of the applicant's license. Currently licensed in another state, territory, country, or province. **Fees:** $300 initial license fee. $300 resident, $600 non-resident license renewal fee.

Indiana

1645

Chiropractor
Indiana Board of Chiropractic
  Examiners
402 W. Washington St., Rm. 041
Indianapolis, IN 46204
Phone: (317)232-1107
Fax: (317)233-4236

Credential Type: Chiropractic license. **Duration of License:** Two years. **Requirements:** Two years (60 semester hours) from an accredited college or university. Graduate of an approved chiropractic college. Renewal requires eight hours of Continuing Education per year. **Examination:** State administered exams: written, oral and practical, including chiropractic jurisprudence, orthopedic testing, neurological testing, and chiropractic technique. National Board Examination, Parts I, II, III, and Physiotherapy. **Reciprocity:** Equivalent license in good standing in another state. NBCE parts I, II, III, and Physiotherapy. **Fees:** $100 exam fee. $10 initial license fee. $50 license renewal fee ($25 inactive).

Iowa

1646

Chiropractor
Board of Chiropractic Examiners
Dept. of Public Health
Lucas State Office Bldg.
Des Moines, IA 50319
Phone: (515)281-6762

Credential Type: License. **Duration of License:** Two years. **Requirements:** An applicant must be a high school graduate, have two years of pre-chiropractic education, and have graduated from an Iowa-approved chiropractic college. **Examination:** Practical, clinical and technical exam. **Fees:** $100 exam fee. $100 renewal fee.

Kansas

1647

Chiropractor
Kansas State Board of Healing Arts
235 S. Topeka Blvd.
Topeka, KS 66603
Phone: (913)296-7413
Fax: (913)296-0852

Credential Type: Chiropractic license. **Duration of License:** One year. **Requirements:** 60 semester hours of pre-professional education. Graduate of an approved chiropractic college. Renewal requires 50 hours of Continuing Education per year. **Examination:** State administered exams: oral interview, demonstration of clinical chiropractic procedure. National Board Examination, Parts I, II, III, and Physiotherapy. **Reciprocity:** Complete Kansas exam. $150 reciprocity fee. **Fees:** $150 exam fee (includes initial license fee). $30 temporary permit fee. $150 license renewal fee.

Kentucky

1648

Chiropractor
Kentucky State Board of Chiropractic
  Examiners
211 S. Green St.
PO Box 183
Glasgow, KY 42142-0183
Phone: (502)651-2522

Credential Type: Chiropractic license. **Duration of License:** One year. **Requirements:** 60 semester hours of pre-professional education. Graduate of an approved chiropractic college. Renewal requires 12 hours of Continuing Education per year. **Examination:** State administered oral/

Louisiana 1649

Chiropractor, continued

practical clinical competency exam, including x-ray interpretation. National Board Examination, Parts I, II, and III. **Reciprocity:** Must meet licensure requirements equal to or more stringent than Kentucky. Must reciprocate with Kentucky. **Fees:** $150 exam fee (includes initial license fee). $60 license renewal fee.

Louisiana

1649

Chiropractor
State Board of Chiropractic
  Examiners
5800 One Perkins Place, Ste. 5-C
Baton Rouge, LA 70808
Phone: (504)765-2322
Fax: (504)765-2640

Credential Type: Chiropractic License. **Duration of License:** One year. **Requirements:** High school diploma and 60 hours of course work at a college or university of liberal arts or science. Graduate of an approved chiropractic college. Renewal requires 12 hours of continuing education per year and six hours of risk management every two years. **Examination:** State administered state statutes, practical x-ray, and practical techniques exams. National Board Examination, Parts I, II, III (WCEE), and Physiotherapy. **Reciprocity:** Eight years active practice in another state. License in good standing. Reciprocity fee. **Fees:** $150 application fee. $150 initial license fee. $150 license renewal fee. $200 reciprocity fee.

Maine

1650

Chiropractor
Maine Board of Chiropractic
  Examination and Registration
State House Station 35
Augusta, ME 04333
Phone: (207)582-8723
Fax: (207)582-5415

Credential Type: Chiropractic license. **Duration of License:** One year. **Requirements:** Two years of pre-professional education, including English and biology. Graduate of an approved chiropractic college. Renewal requires 12 hours of Continuing Education per year. **Examination:** State administered practical exams: x-ray interpretation, chiropractic technique, clinical diagnosis, physiological therapeutics, and jurisprudence. National Board Examination, Parts I, II, III, and Physiotherapy. **Reciprocity:** Must reciprocate with Maine. Must have requirements similar or greater than Maine. 120 hours physiological therapeutics, practical exam, required parts of NBCE exams. Clinical experience as defined by Ch. 1, Sec. 10. Active license in good standing. Proof of ten years practice and 24 hours Continuing Education per year waives all but practical exam. $225 reciprocity fee (2 year license). **Fees:** $100 exam fee. $100 initial license fee. $100 license renewal fee.

Maryland

1651

Chiropractor
Maryland State Board of Chiropractic
  Examiners
4201 Patterson Ave., 3rd Fl, Rm.
  312
Baltimore, MD 21215-2299
Phone: (301)764-4727
Fax: (301)764-5987

Credential Type: Chiropractic license. **Duration of License:** Two years. **Requirements:** Two academic years of pre-professional education, including two of the following subjects: biology, physics, chemistry (totalling 16 credit hours combined). Accredited B.S. degree. Graduate of an approved chiropractic college. Renewal requires 48 hours of Continuing Education every two years. **Examination:** State administered exams: clinical sciences, including chiropractic principles and technique, public health and hygiene, orthopedic, neurology, roentgenology, physical diagnosis, and symptomatology; optional exam in physical therapy. National Board Examination, Parts I and Physiotherapy (required to determine eligibility to take optional Maryland physical therapy exam). **Reciprocity:** Full Maryland examination. Two academic years of college are not required of applicants licensed before June 1, 1967. **Fees:** $25 application fee. $50 exam fee. $25 initial license fee. $50 license renewal fee.

Credential Type: physical therapy certification. **Duration of License:** Two years. **Requirements:** 120 hours physical therapy from accredited CCE college. **Examination:** NBCE Physiotherapy exam and Maryland Physical Therapy exam. **Fees:** No additional fee.

Massachusetts

1652

Chiropractor
Massachusetts Board of Registration
  of Chiropractors
Leverett Saltonstall Bldg., Rm. 1513
100 Cambridge St.
Boston, MA 02202
Phone: (617)727-3093

Credential Type: Chiropractic license. **Duration of License:** One year. **Requirements:** High school diploma. After December 1, 1969, proof of completion of two years in a curriculum leading to a Bachelor's Degree in Liberal Arts or Sciences. Graduate of an approved chiropractic college. Renewal requires 12 hours of Continuing Education per year. **Examination:** State administered x-ray exam, practical exams in conjunction with an outside examination service. National Board Examination, Parts I, II, and III. **Reciprocity:** Equal standards. Must reciprocate with Massachusetts. Three years practice. Massachusetts Clinical Exam. $140 reciprocity fee. **Fees:** $30 application fee. $140 exam fee. $60 initial license fee. $60 license renewal fee.

Michigan

1653

Chiropractor
Board of Chiropractic
Bureau of Occupational &
  Professional Regulation
Dept. of Commerce
PO Box 30018
Lansing, MI 48909
Phone: (517)373-7902

Credential Type: License. **Duration of License:** Two years. **Requirements:** At least 18 years of age. High school graduate or its equivalent. Graduated from a recognized four-year chiropractic college program, which included a semester of internship. Pass the Michigan examination or the National Examination, as well as the Michigan Scope of Practice exam. Be of good moral character. Working knowledge of the English language. Abide by the State law, and the rules and regulations of the Board. Renewal requires completion of at least 24 hours of continuing education. **Examination:** Written exam and the Michigan Scope of Practice exam. **Reciprocity:** A licensed chiropractor from another state may be licensed in Michigan if the requirements for licensure in that state are substantially equivalent to those of Michigan or if the applicant has passed both parts of the

National Examination. However, the applicant is still required to pass the Michigan Scope of Practice exam. **Fees:** $20 application processing fee. $100 initial exam fee. $20 exam review fee. $50 initial license fee, per year. $50 renewal fee, per year. $220 reciprocity fee. **Governing Statute:** Public Health Code, Act 368 of 1978, as amended.

Credential Type: Limited License. **Duration of License:** Six months. **Requirements:** Two years of education in a college of arts and sciences and four semesters (or six quarters) in an approved chiropractic college. **Fees:** $25 limited license fee. **Governing Statute:** Public Health Code, Act 368 of 1978, as amended.

Minnesota

1654

Chiropractor
Minnesota Board of Chiropractic Examiners
2700 W. University Ave., Ste. 20
St. Paul, MN 55114-1089
Phone: (612)642-0591

Credential Type: Chiropractic license. **Duration of License:** One year. **Requirements:** Two years of pre-professional education. Graduate of an approved chiropractic college. Renewal requires 10 hours of Continuing Education first year, 15 hours second year, 20 hours per year thereafter, eight hours professional boundary/abuse recognition every four years, and three x-ray hours per year. **Examination:** State administered written exams: jurisprudence, clinical nutrition, case management, and x-ray safety; practical exams: adjustive technique, x-ray interpretation, and case management (including orthopedics, neurology, and physical diagnosis). National Board Examination, Parts I, II, III, and Physiotherapy. **Reciprocity:** Not available. **Fees:** $150 exam fee (includes initial license fee). $150 license renewal fee.

Mississippi

1655

Chiropractor
Mississippi State Board of Chiropractic Examiners
PO Box 775
Louisville, MS 39339
Phone: (601)773-4478

Credential Type: Chiropractic license. **Duration of License:** Two years. **Requirements:** Two years of pre-professional education. Graduate of an approved chiropractic college. Renewal requires 24 hours of Continuing Education every two years. **Examination:** State administered practical exam. National Board Examination, Part I, II, III, and Physiotherapy. **Reciprocity:** No reciprocity. **Fees:** $25 application fee. $125 resident, $150 non-resident exam fee. No initial license fee. $140 licensed renewal fee (prorated when licensed during term).

Missouri

1656

Chiropractor
Missouri Board of Chiropractic Examiners
PO Box 672
Jefferson City, MO 65102-0672
Phone: (314)751-2104
Fax: (314)751-0735

Credential Type: Chiropractic license. **Duration of License:** One year. **Requirements:** 60 credit hours of pre-professional education leading to a baccalaureate degree. Graduate of an approved chiropractic college. **Examination:** State administered practical jurisprudence and x-ray exams, oral interview covering technique, orthopedics, neurology, diagnosis, physical therapy, nutrition, and x-ray. National Board Examination, Parts I, II, III, and Physiotherapy. **Reciprocity:** State laws and exams must be equivalent to Missouri. Must reciprocate with Missouri. $250 reciprocity fee. **Fees:** $250 exam fee (includes initial license fee). $100 license renewal fee.

Montana

1657

Chiropractor
Montana Board of Chiropractors
111 N. Jackson
Helena, MT 59620
Phone: (406)444-5433

Credential Type: License. **Duration of License:** One year. **Requirements:** Completion of two years of preprofessional study at an approved college or university. Graduation from an approved chiropractic college. **Examination:** Written and practical exam. **Fees:** $125 application and exam fee. $100 renewal fee. **Governing Statute:** Montana Code Annotated 37-12-301 through 37-12-324.

Nebraska

1658

Chiropractor
Nebraska Board of Examiners in Chiropractic
301 Centennial Mall S.
PO Box 95007
Lincoln, NE 68509
Phone: (402)471-2115

Credential Type: License. **Duration of License:** Two years. **Requirements:** Must be a graduate of an accredited college of chiropractic medicine. **Examination:** Yes. **Fees:** $300 application fee. $5 license fee. $250 renewal fee.

Nevada

1659

Chiropractor
Nevada State Board of Chiropractic Examiners
4600 Kietzke Ln., Ste. F-154
Reno, NV 89502
Phone: (702)826-8574

Credential Type: License. **Duration of License:** One year. **Requirements:** At least two years of pre-chiropractic college course work. Graduation from an accredited chiropractic college. **Examination:** Yes. **Fees:** $100 application fee. $100 license fee. $200 renewal fee.

Credential Type: Chiropractic Assistant License. **Duration of License:** One year. **Requirements:** 12 months, or 480 hours, of classroom training; or six months of on-the-job training. **Examination:** Yes. **Fees:** $100 application. $15 renewal fee.

New Hampshire

1660

Chiropractor
New Hampshire Board of Chiropractic Examiners
Health & Welfare Bldg.
6 Hazen Dr.
Concord, NH 03301-6527
Phone: (603)271-4560
Fax: (603)271-3745

Credential Type: Chiropractic license. **Duration of License:** Two years. **Requirements:** Graduate of an approved chiropractic college. Renewal requires 10 hours of Continuing Education per fiscal year. **Examination:** State administered exams: oral clinical proficiency exam, in-

Chiropractor, continued

cluding physical exam, neurological diagnosis, orthopedic diagnosis, differential diagnosis, and adjusting skills; written exam on New Hampshire law and Code of Administrative Rules. National Board Examination, Parts I, II, III, and Physiotherapy (for optional certification). **Reciprocity:** three years active practice. Licensing standards substantially similar to New Hampshire. May give oral clinical proficiency exam. **Fees:** $100 exam fee (includes initial license fee). $150 license renewal fee.

New Jersey

1661

Chiropractor
Board of Medical Examiners
28 W. State St., Rm. 914
Trenton, NJ 08608
Phone: (609)292-4843

Credential Type: License. **Duration of License:** Two years. **Requirements:** 21 years of age. High school diploma or equivalent. Two years of study in a school or college of arts and sciences. Doctor of Chiropractic degree from a board approved school. **Examination:** Written and clinical. **Fees:** $30 certificate fee. $150 exam fee. $120 registration fee. **Governing Statute:** NJSA 45:9. NJAC 13:35.

New Mexico

1662

Chiropractor
New Mexico Board of Chiropractic Examiners
725 St. Michael's Dr.
PO Box 25101
Santa Fe, NM 87504
Phone: (505)827-7171

Credential Type: Chiropractic license. **Duration of License:** One year. **Requirements:** Two years of pre-professional education. Graduate of an approved chiropractic college. Renewal requires 10 hours of Continuing Education per year. **Examination:** State administered four part exam consisting of three written portions and an oral/practical. Written: x-ray, chiropractic principles, chiropractic practice. Oral: day to day procedures that take place in a chiropractic office. National Board Examination, Parts I, II, and III (if graduated after June 30, 1991). **Reciprocity:** Oral/practical exam. NBCE Part III waives written exams. **Fees:** $100 exam fee. $100 initial license fee. $100 license renewal fee.

New York

1663

Chiropractor
State Education Dept.
Div. of Professional Licensing Services
Cultural Education Center
Empire State Plaza
Albany, NY 12230
Phone: (518)474-3326

Credential Type: License. **Duration of License:** Three years. **Requirements:** Graduation from professional school after at least two years of college study with emphasis in the sciences. 21 years of age. U.S. citizen or alien lawfully admitted for permanent residency. **Examination:** Written and practical. **Fees:** $50 exam fee. $330 license fee. $155 renewal fee. **Governing Statute:** Title VIII Articles 130, 132 of the Education Law.

North Carolina

1664

Chiropractor
North Carolina State Board of Chiropractic Examiners
720 W. Hargett St.
Raleigh, NC 27603
Phone: (919)828-0600

Credential Type: License. **Duration of License:** One year. **Requirements:** Two years of preprofessional chiropractic training with a minimum of 60 hours of course study before entrance into an accredited chiropractic school. Graduation from a four-year chiropractic program, plus an 18-month internship. 18 years of age. Three references. **Examination:** Written and oral. **Fees:** $100 exam and license fee. $100 renewal fee.

North Dakota

1665

Chiropractor
North Dakota Board of Chiropractic Examiners
Highway 17 West
PO Box 185
Grafton, ND 58237
Phone: (701)352-1690

Credential Type: Chiropractic license. **Duration of License:** One year. **Requirements:** Two years of pre-professional education. Graduate of an approved chiropractic college. Renewal requires 12 hours of Continuing Education per year. **Examination:** State administered exams: jurisprudence, five practical areas: x-ray, extremity adjusting, first-aid, case management, and spinal bio-mechanics. National Board Examination, Parts I, II, and III (for graduates after 1988). **Reciprocity:** Same examination procedures as new applicants. **Fees:** $150 exam fee (includes initial license fee). $100 license renewal fee.

Ohio

1666

Chiropractor
Ohio Board of Chiropractic Examiners
77 S. High St., 16th Fl.
Columbus, OH 43266-0542
Phone: (614)644-7032
Fax: (614)644-8112

Credential Type: Chiropractic license. **Duration of License:** One year. **Requirements:** 60 semester hours or 90 quarter hours of pre-professional education. Graduate of an approved chiropractic college. Renewal requires 12 hours of Continuing Education per year. **Examination:** State administered exams: clinical competency, consisting of jurisprudence, x-ray technique and interpretation, manipulative adjustive technique, principles and practice of chiropractic, rehabilitative procedures, physical, orthopedic, and neurological examination procedures; written exam for applicants who do not have NBCE exams. National Board Examination, Parts I, II, III, and Physiotherapy. **Reciprocity:** Licensing requirements equal to Ohio. Three years full-time practice within the last five years. NBCE exams depending on graduation date. Must not have previously failed Ohio Licensure exam. $250 reciprocity fee. **Fees:** $250 exam fee (includes initial license fee).

Oklahoma

1667

Chiropractor
Oklahoma State Board of Chiropractic Examiners
5700 S. Pennsylvania
Oklahoma City, OK 73119-7017
Phone: (405)682-1275

Credential Type: License. **Duration of License:** One year. **Requirements:** 60 pre-Chiropractic college hours. Doctor of Chiropractic. 12 hours of continuing education. No felony convictions. **Examination:** Oklahoma State Board Chiropractic Examination. **Fees:** $150 application fee. $150 exam fee. $150 renewal fee.

Oregon

1668

Chiropractic (Doctor of)
Board of Chiropractic Examiners
796 Winter St NE
Salem, OR 97310
Phone: (503)378-5816

Credential Type: License. **Requirements:** Must provide transcripts of grades from all colleges attended showing successful completion of at least two years of liberal arts and sciences study in an approved college. Must provide diploma and transcript from an approved chiropractic college which requires for graduation a period of actual attendance of four years of at least nine months, or equivalent, each with a schedule of minimum educational requirements enumerated in ORS 684.050 (4). Must provide an official certificate of proficiency issued by the National Board of Chiropractic Examiners. **Examination:** Yes. **Fees:** $150 exam fee. $100 license fee. $250 (active) or $150 (inactive) renewal fee. **Governing Statute:** ORS 684.

Pennsylvania

1669

Chiropractor
Pennsylvania State Board of Chiropractic Examiners
PO Box 2649
Harrisburg, PA 17105
Phone: (717)783-7156
Fax: (717)787-7769

Credential Type: Chiropractic license. **Duration of License:** Two years. **Requirements:** Two years of pre-professional education. Graduate of an approved chiropractic college. Renewal requires 24 hours of Continuing Education every two years. **Examination:** State administered chiropractic technique and jurisprudence exams. National Board Examination, Parts I, II, and III (Physiotherapy optional). **Reciprocity:** Must reciprocate with Pennsylvania. $65 reciprocity fee. **Fees:** $70 exam fee (includes initial license fee). $130 license renewal fee.

Credential Type: adjunctive procedures certification. **Duration of License:** Two years. **Requirements:** Either NBCE PHY exam or 100 or more hours in adjunctive procedures. **Examination:** Either NBCE PHY exam or 100 or more hours in adjunctive procedures. **Fees:** $25 fee.

Rhode Island

1670

Chiropractor
Rhode Island Board of Examiners in Chiropractic
104 Cannon Bldg.
Three Capital Hill
Providence, RI 02908-5097
Phone: (401)277-2827
Fax: (401)277-1272

Credential Type: Chiropractic license. **Duration of License:** One year. **Requirements:** Two years of pre-professional education. Graduate of an approved chiropractic college. Renewal requires 12 hours of Continuing Education per year. **Examination:** State administered practical exam. National Board Examination, Parts I, II, and III (Physiotherapy not required if persons are not applying for licensure also in Physiotherapy). **Reciprocity:** NBCE Parts I, II, and III, and Rhode Island board practical exam. Equal qualifications. Reciprocate with Rhode Island. **Fees:** $50 exam fee (includes initial license fee). $25 license renewal fee.

South Carolina

1671

Chiropractor
South Carolina State Board of Chiropractic Examiners
810 Dutch Square Blvd., Ste. 395
Columbia, SC 29210
Phone: (803)772-0093

Credential Type: License. **Requirements:** High school graduate. Two years of college. Graduation from an accredited chiropractic college. **Examination:** Yes. **Fees:** $115 in-state license. $57.50 out-of-state license.

South Dakota

1672

Chiropractor
South Dakota Board of Chiropractic Examiners
109 E. Second Ave.
Flandreau, SD 57028
Phone: (605)997-3733

Credential Type: Chiropractic license. **Duration of License:** One year. **Requirements:** Two years of pre-professional education. Graduate of an approved chiropractic college. Renewal requires 36 hours of Continuing Education every three years. **Examination:** State administered exams: practical for all applicants, written exam for those who have not passed NBCE part III. Exams include orthopedics, neurology, x-ray interpretation, laboratory, and physiotherapy. National Board Examination, Parts I, II, III (for those graduating after January 1989), and Physiotherapy. **Reciprocity:** Active practice for at least one year prior to exam date. Practical exam and written exam if graduated before January 1989 and have not taken Part III of the National Board. Written scores waived if 75 percent score on the practical. Letter of good standing from State Board of Examiners. **Fees:** $100 exam fee. $100 active, $25 inactive initial license fee. $100 license renewal fee.

Credential Type: acupuncture certification. **Duration of License:** One year. **Requirements:** 100 hours of Continuing Education to sit exam, then 100 hours within two years following. **Fees:** $50 fee.

Tennessee

1673

Chiropractor
Tennessee Board of Chiropractic Examiners
283 Plus Park Blvd.
Nashville, TN 37219-5407
Phone: (615)367-6393
Fax: (615)367-6397

Credential Type: Chiropractic license. **Duration of License:** One year. **Requirements:** Four years of pre-professional education. Graduate of an approved chiropractic college. Renewal requires 12 hours of Continuing Education per year. **Examination:** State administered exams: nutrition, physiotherapy, x-ray, neurological and orthopedics, clinical diagnosis, jurisprudence, and chiropractic practical. National Board Examination, Parts I, II, and Physiotherapy. **Reciprocity:** Tennessee Clinical Competency Exam. Granted only on an individual basis. Waive National Board requirement if licensed before 1975. **Fees:** $100 application fee. $200 exam fee. $80 initial license fee. $70 license renewal fee.

Texas

1674

Chiropractor
Texas Board of Chiropractic
 Examiners
8716 Mopac North, Ste. 301
Austin, TX 78759
Phone: (512)343-1895

Credential Type: License. **Duration of License:** One year. **Requirements:** 18 years of age. Sixty semester hours of acceptable health science college courses at the undergraduate level other than those in chiropractic school. Graduation from a bona fide, reputable chiropractic school. Classroom and practical studies required as part of training. At least two days of continuing education per year. **Examination:** Board-administered written and practical examination. National Board of Chiropractic Examiners Examination (all parts), including a written clinical competency examination. **Fees:** $125 application fee. $322 exam fee. $322 renewal fee. **Governing Statute:** VACS 4512b, 22 TAC 71.

Utah

1675

Chiropractor
Dept. of Commerce
Div. of Occupational and
 Professional Licensing
160 E. 300 S.
PO Box 45802
Salt Lake City, UT 84145
Phone: (801)530-6628

Credential Type: License. **Duration of License:** Two years. **Requirements:** Must be a graduate of an approved Chiropractic College. **Examination:** Yes. **Fees:** $100 license fee. $75 renewal fee.

Vermont

1676

Chiropractic Physician
Board of Chiropractic Examination
 and Registration
Pavilion Office Bldg.
Montpelier, VT 05602
Phone: (802)828-2363
Phone: (802)828-2390

Credential Type: License. **Duration of License:** Two years. **Requirements:** 18 years of age. Good moral character. High school education. Two year course of study in approved school of arts and sciences. Graduate of approved chiropractic school; minimum of four years and 4400 hours as resident student. **Examination:** Yes. **Reciprocity:** Yes. **Fees:** $50 Application with Exam fee. $5 Recording fee. $20 renewal. $75 License. **Governing Statute:** Title 26, VSA Sections 501-510.

Virginia

1677

Chiropractor
Dept. of Health Professions
 Regulatory Board
1601 Rolling Hill Dr.
Richmond, VA 23229-5005
Phone: (804)662-9920

Credential Type: License. **Duration of License:** Two years. **Requirements:** 18 years of age. Good moral character. Graduation from a recognized chiropractic college. **Examination:** Yes. **Fees:** $200 examination fee.

Washington

1678

Chiropractor
Washington Board of Chiropractic
 Examiners
PO Box 1099 - EY-21
Olympia, WA 98507
Phone: (206)753-0776
Fax: (206)586-7774

Credential Type: Chiropractic license. **Duration of License:** One year. **Requirements:** Two years of pre-professional education. Graduate of an approved chiropractic college. Renewal requires 25 hours of Continuing Education per year. **Examination:** State administered written, practical x-ray, and practical technique exams. National Board Examination, Parts I and II. **Reciprocity:** Requirements equivalent to Washington. Three years full-time practice or teaching within past five years. License in good standing. Jurisprudence and Adjustive Technique exams. Reciprocity fee. **Fees:** $300 exam fee. $200 initial license fee. $300 license renewal fee.

West Virginia

1679

Chiropractor
State Board of Chiropractic
 Examiners
142 MacCorkle Ave, SW
St. Albans, WV 25177
Phone: (304)522-2838

Alternate Information: 2703 Third Ave., Huntington, WV 25702

Credential Type: License. **Duration of License:** One year. **Requirements:** U.S. citizen. 21 years old. 60 semester hours at an academic college plus a four year degree from a Chiropractic College. Never convicted of a felony. **Examination:** Yes. **Fees:** $100 Application and license. $25 Renewal.

Wisconsin

1680

Chiropractor
Regulations and Licensing Dept.
Chiropractic Board
PO Box 8935
Madison, WI 53708-8935
Phone: (608)266-8609

Credential Type: License. **Requirements:** Two years of pre-professional education, graduation from a reputable school of chiropractic, and completion of a residence course of not less than 36 months. **Examination:** Yes.

Wyoming

1681

Chiropractor
State Board of Chiropractic
 Examiners
611 E. Main St.
Riverton, WY 82501
Phone: (307)856-4400

Credential Type: License. **Duration of License:** One year. **Requirements:** Two years of pre-professional chiropractic study including inorganic chemistry, organic chemistry, microbiology and physics. Graduate from a recognized four year school of chiropractic medicine. Pass the National Examination. **Examination:** Yes. **Reciprocity:** Yes. **Fees:** $200 Application. $75 Application by Reciprocity. $28 Renewal.

Clinical Laboratory Technologists and Technicians

The following states grant licenses in this occupational category as of the date of publication: California, Connecticut, Florida, Hawaii, Illinois, Nevada, North Carolina, North Dakota, Rhode Island, Tennessee.

California

1682

Clinical Lab Technician
Health Services Dept.
Licensing and Certification Div.
714 P St.
Sacramento, CA 95814
Phone: (916)657-1425

Credential Type: License. **Requirements:** Contact licensing body for application information.

Connecticut

1683

Hypertrichologist
Div. of Medical Quality Assurance
Health Systems Regulation Bureau
Health Services Dept.
150 Washington St.
Hartford, CT 06106
Phone: (203)566-3207

Credential Type: License. **Requirements:** Contact licensing body for application information.

Florida

1684

Clinical Lab Technician
Professional Regulation Dept.
Medical Quality Assurance Div.
1940 N. Monroe St.
Tallahassee, FL 32399-0750
Phone: (904)487-2252

Credential Type: License. **Requirements:** Contact licensing body for application information.

Hawaii

1685

Clinical Laboratory Cytotechnologist
Hawaii State Dept. of Health
Laboratories Div.
1250 Punchbowl St.
PO Box 3378
Honolulu, HI 96813
Phone: (808)548-7400

Credential Type: License. **Requirements:** Completion of two academic years in an accredited college with at least 12 semester hours of courses pertinent to the medical sciences plus one year of training in an approved cytotechnology school or six months of training in an approved cytotechnology school and six months of full-time cytotechnology experience in an acceptable laboratory; or a high school diploma and six months of cytotechnology training in a pathologist-directed laboratory and two years of full-time experience. **Examination:** National qualifying exam. **Exemptions:** Exam may be waived if applicant has Dept. of Health-acceptable certification by a national accrediting board. **Fees:** $10 initial fee. $3 renewal fee.

1686

Clinical Laboratory Technician
Hawaii State Board of Health
Laboratories Div.
1250 Punchbowl St.
PO Box 3378
Honolulu, HI 96813
Phone: (808)548-7400

Credential Type: License. **Requirements:** Associate Degree from an accredited clinical laboratory technician program; or Completion of two academic years in an accredited program with at least 12 semester hours in chemistry, bacteriology, or parasitology and three in college-level mathematics plus six months of full-time experience in an acceptable laboratory; or a high school diploma with one year of military laboratory training or one year of approved medical technician training; or high school diploma and completion of a clinical laboratory assistant training course plus three years of full-time clinical laboratory assistant experience. **Examination:** Yes. **Exemptions:** Exam may be waived for Dept. of Health-acceptable certification by a national accrediting board. **Fees:** $10 initial fee. $3 renewal fee.

Hawaii

1687

Clinical Laboratory Technologist/ Specialist
Hawaii State Dept. of Health
Laboratories Div.
1250 Punchbowl St.
PO Box 3378
Honolulu, HI 96813
Phone: (808)548-7400

Credential Type: License. **Requirements:** Bachelor's Degree from an accredited college in medical technology plus one year of training in an approved program; or completion of three academic years in an accredited college in medical technology plus a training course in an appproved medical technology school; or a Bachelor's Degree from an accredited college in chemical, physical or biological science plus one year of experience in an acceptable laboratory; or completion of three academic years in an accredited college in chemical, physical or biological science plus one year of experience in an acceptable laboratory. **Examination:** National qualifying exam. **Exemptions:** Exam may be waived if applicant has Dept. of Health-acceptable certification by a national accrediting board. **Fees:** $10 initial fee. $3 renewal fee.

Illinois

1688

Laboratory Analysis Technician
Illinois Dept. of Health
525 W. Jefferson
Springfield, IL 62761
Phone: (217)782-1571

Credential Type: Laboratory Analysis Technician Certificate. **Duration of License:** One year. **Requirements:** Five or more years experience in analytical chemistry. Submit application. **Reciprocity:** No. **Fees:** No fee. **Governing Statute:** Illinois Vehicle Code Section 11-501.2, Illinois Revised Statutes Chapter 95 1/2.

Nevada

1689

Clinical Laboratory Technologist
Bureau of Regulatory Health
 Services
505 E. King St., Rm. 202
Carson City, NV 89710
Phone: (702)687-4475

Credential Type: License. **Requirements:** Bachelor's degree in medical technology from an accredited institution, or an equivalent combination of education and experience. **Examination:** Yes. **Fees:** $25 license fee. $18 renewal fee.

1690

Cytotechnologist
Bureau of Regulatory Health
 Services
505 E. King St., Rm. 202
Carson City, NV 89710
Phone: (702)687-4475

Credential Type: License. **Requirements:** Completion of two years of coursework in an accredited institution with at least 12 semester hours in science, and completion of 12 months of training in an accredited school of cytotechnology; or an equivalent combination of education and experience. **Examination:** Yes. **Fees:** $25 license fee. $18 renewal fee.

1691

Histologic Technician
Bureau of Regulatory Health
 Services
505 E. King St., Rm. 202
Carson City, NV 89710
Phone: (702)687-4475

Credential Type: License. **Requirements:** Completion of a certified program in histotechnology, or an equivalent combination of education and experience. **Fees:** $25 license fee. $18 renewal fee.

1692

Histotechnologist
Bureau of Regulatory Health
 Services
505 E. King St., Rm. 202
Carson City, NV 89710
Phone: (702)687-4475

Credential Type: License. **Requirements:** Bachelor's degree from an accredited institution, with 32 semester hours in science, and one year of experience in a histopathology laboratory under the supervision of a certified pathologist; or an equivalent combination of education and experience. **Examination:** Yes. **Fees:** $25 license fee. $18 renewal fee.

1693

Medical Laboratory Assistant
Bureau of Regulatory Health
 Services
505 E. King St., Rm. 202
Carson City, NV 89710
Phone: (702)687-4475

Credential Type: License. **Requirements:** High school diploma. Six months of training in laboratory procedures. **Fees:** $25 license fee. $18 renewal fee.

1694

Medical Technician
Bureau of Regulatory Health
 Services
505 E. King St., Rm. 202
Carson City, NV 89710
Phone: (702)687-4475

Credential Type: License. **Requirements:** Associate degree as a medical technician; or completion of a program based on a course of study including chemistry, biology and laboratory techniques from an accredited institution; or an equivalent combination of education and experience. **Examination:** Yes. **Fees:** $25 license fee. $18 renewal fee.

North Carolina

1695

Cytotechnologist
Board of Registry
PO Box 12270
Chicago, IL 60612
Phone: (312)738-1336

Credential Type: License. **Duration of License:** One year. **Requirements:** Bachelor's degree from an accredited college, with 20 semester hours of biological science, eight semester hours of chemistry and three semester hours of mathematics. **Examination:** Written. **Fees:** $75 exam fee. $20 renewal fee.

1696

Histologic Technician
Board of Registry
PO Box 12270
Chicago, IL 60612
Phone: (312)738-1336

Credential Type: Certification. **Duration of License:** One year. **Requirements:** High school diploma or equivalent, plus a one-year, accredited histologic technician program, or two years of experience and an associate degree, or the equivalent and one year of experience. **Examination:** Multiple choice. **Fees:** $60 initial fee. $20 renewal fee.

1697

Medical Laboratory Technician
Board of Registry
PO Box 12270
Chicago, IL 60612
Phone: (312)738-1336

Credential Type: License. **Duration of License:** One year. **Requirements:** Associate degree from an approved medical laboratory technician program. **Examination:** National exam. **Fees:** $60 exam fee. $20 renewal fee.

North Dakota

1698

Clinical Laboratory Scientist
State Board of Clinical Laboratory Practice
Dept. of Health and Consolidated Laboratories
Consolidated Laboratory Branch Registration Div.
2635 E. Main
Bismarck, ND 58502-0937
Phone: (701)221-6140

Credential Type: License. **Duration of License:** Two years. **Requirements:** Bachelor's degree in a science-related discipline. **Examination:** National certifying examination. **Governing Statute:** North Dakota Century Code, Chap. 43-48.

1699

Clinical Laboratory Technician
State Board of Clinical Laboratory Practice
Dept. of Health and Consolidated Laboratories
Consolidated Laboratory Branch Registration Div.
2635 E. Main
Bismarck, ND 58502-0937
Phone: (701)221-6140

Credential Type: License. **Duration of License:** Two years. **Requirements:** Complete the academic requirements of an approved educational program. **Examination:** National certifying examination. **Governing Statute:** North Dakota Century Code, Chap. 43-48.

Rhode Island

1700

Clinical Histologic Technician
Clinical Laboratory Advisory Board
Div. of Professional Regulation
Rhode Island Dept. of Health
3 Capitol Hill
Providence, RI 02908
Phone: (401)277-2827

Credential Type: Clinical Histologic Technician License. **Duration of License:** Two years. **Authorization:** Authorizes licensee to prepare specimens of human and animal tissue for microscopic examination and to perform other routine procedures in the pathology laboratory. **Requirements:** Foreign born must show proof of legal entry into the U.S. Associate degree or complete 60 semester hours that includes: mathematics; 12 or more hours in biology and chemistry; and accredited programs in histologic technique. Alternative requirements are available through the board. **Examination:** American Society of Clinical Pathologists (ASCP) examination. **Reciprocity:** Yes, providing standards of licensing state meets those of New Hampshire. **Fees:** To be established by July, 1993.

1701

Clinical Laboratory Science Practitioner
Clinical Laboratory Advisory Board
Div. of Professional Regulation
Rhode Island Dept. of Health
3 Capitol Hill
Providence, RI 02908
Phone: (401)277-2827

Credential Type: Clinical Laboratory Science Practitioner License. **Duration of License:** Two years. **Authorization:** Authorizes licensee to hold the following positions: Teaching Supervisor Medical Technologist; Chief Medical Technologist; or Medical Technologist. **Requirements:** Foreign born must show proof of legal entry into the U.S. Hold a bachelor's degree in medical technology, biological science, chemical science, or physical science. Alternative requirements are available through the board. **Examination:** Examination as required by board. **Reciprocity:** Yes, providing standards of licensing state meets those of New Hampshire. **Fees:** To be established.

1702

Clinical Medical Laboratory Technician
Clinical Laboratory Advisory Board
Div. of Professional Regulation
Rhode Island Dept. of Health
3 Capitol Hill
Providence, RI 02908
Phone: (401)277-2827

Credential Type: Clinical/Medical Laboratory Technician License. **Duration of License:** Two years. **Requirements:** Foreign born must show proof of legal entry into the U.S. Hold an associate degree or complete 60 semester hours in an MLT (or equivalent) clinical laboratory technical program. Alternative requirements are available through the board. **Examination:** Examination as required by board. **Reciprocity:** Yes, providing standards of licensing state meets those of New Hampshire. **Fees:** To be established.

1703

Cytotechnologist
Clinical Laboratory Advisory Board
Div. of Professional Regulation
Rhode Island Dept. of Health
3 Capitol Hill
Providence, RI 02908
Phone: (401)277-2827

Credential Type: Cytotechnologist License. **Duration of License:** Two years. **Authorization:** Authorizes licensee to stain, mount, and study human cells to detect pathological conditions, such as evidence of cancer and hormonal abnormalities. **Requirements:** Foreign born must show proof of legal entry into the U.S. Bachelor's degree with 20 semester hours of biological science. Alternative licensing requirements are available by contacting the board. **Examination:** American Society of Clinical Pathology (ASCP) Examination. **Reciprocity:** Yes, providing the standards of the licensing state are equivalent to those of Rhode Island. **Fees:** To be established.

Tennessee

1704

Clinical Lab Technician
Board of Medical Examiners
283 Plus Park Blvd.
Nashville, TN 37247
Phone: (615)367-6231

Credential Type: License. **Requirements:** Contact licensing body for application information.

Communications Equipment Repairers, Including T.V. and Radio

The following states grant licenses in this occupational category as of the date of publication: Arkansas, Connecticut, Louisiana, Massachusetts, Minnesota, North Carolina, Oregon.

Arkansas

1705

Burglar Alarm Servicer, Operator
Arkansas State Police
3 Natural Resources Dr.
PO Box 5901
Little Rock, AR 72215
Phone: (501)224-3101

Credential Type: License. **Duration of License:** One year. **Requirements:** 18 years of age. High school graduate or equivalent. Never convicted of any felony or Class A misdemeanor, or crime. Never declared incompetent by reason of mental defect or disease. Not be suffering from habitual drunkenness or narcotic addiction or dependence. Not discharged from the armed services under any condition other than honorable. **Examination:** Yes. **Fees:** $50 Written and Oral examinations application. $13 License fee. $13 Renewal.

Connecticut

1706

Antenna Service Dealer
Board of Television and Radio
  Service Examiners
Occupational Licensing Div.
Consumer Protection Dept.
165 Capitol Ave.
Hartford, CT 06106
Phone: (203)566-3275

Credential Type: Certified Master Antenna Service Dealer License. **Authorization:** Restricted to contracting to install, repair, and maintain all types of television antenna systems for the public and other dealers in the trade. **Requirements:** Must pass examination and employ licensed certified antenna technicians. **Examination:** Board examination. **Governing Statute:** Connecticut Statutes, Chap. 394. State Board of Television and Radio Service Examiners Administrative Regulations.

Credential Type: Certified Service Dealer License. **Authorization:** Restricted to contracting to install, repair, and maintain individual systems, primarily used in the home, for the public and other dealers in the trade. **Requirements:** Must pass examination. **Examination:** Board examination. **Governing Statute:** Connecticut Statutes, Chap. 394. State Board of Television and Radio Service Examiners Administrative Regulations.

1707

Antenna Technician
Board of Television and Radio
  Service Examiners
Occupational Licensing Div.
Consumer Protection Dept.
165 Capitol Ave.
Hartford, CT 06106
Phone: (203)566-3275

Credential Type: Certified Antenna Technician License. **Authorization:** Restricted to television antenna installation and repair. **Requirements:** Must pass examination and be in the employ of another who is in the business of the installation, repair, and maintenance of television antenna systems. **Examination:** Board examination. **Governing Statute:** Connecticut Statutes, Chap. 394. State Board of Television and Radio Service Examiners Administrative Regulations.

1708

Apprentice Television Electronics Technician
Board of Television and Radio
  Service Examiners
Occupational Licensing Div.
Consumer Protection Dept.
165 Capitol Ave.
Hartford, CT 06106
Phone: (203)566-3275

Credential Type: Apprentice Electronics Technician License. **Duration of License:** Three years. **Requirements:** Must enroll in the state board apprentice program. Apprentice program consists of three years of on-the-job training, the first two years of which are under the supervision of a licensed certified electronics technician. **Governing Statute:** Connecticut Statutes, Chap. 394. State Board of Television and Radio Service Examiners Administrative Regulations.

1709

Radio Electronics Service Dealer
Board of Television and Radio
  Service Examiners
Occupational Licensing Div.
Consumer Protection Dept.
165 Capitol Ave.
Hartford, CT 06106
Phone: (203)566-3275

Credential Type: Certified Radio Electronics Service Dealer License. **Requirements:** Must pass examinations and have an established place of business. **Examination:** Board examinations. **Governing Statute:** Connecticut Statutes, Chap. 394. State Board of Television and Radio Service Examiners Administrative Regulations.

Connecticut

1710

Radio Electronics Service Technician
Board of Television and Radio
  Service Examiners
Occupational Licensing Div.
Consumer Protection Dept.
165 Capitol Ave.
Hartford, CT 06106
Phone: (203)566-3275

Credential Type: Certified Radio Electronics Service Technician License. **Authorization:** Restricted to repair of radio receiving equipment, phonographs, and tape recorders. **Requirements:** Must pass examination and be in the employ of another who is in the business of repairing, maintaining, and servicing radio receiving equipment, phonographs, and tape recorders. **Examination:** Board examination. **Governing Statute:** Connecticut Statutes, Chap. 394. State Board of Television and Radio Service Examiners Administrative Regulations.

1711

Television Electronics Service Dealer
Board of Television and Radio
  Service Examiners
Occupational Licensing Div.
Consumer Protection Dept.
165 Capitol Ave.
Hartford, CT 06106
Phone: (203)566-3275

Credential Type: Service Dealer Certified Electronics Technician Owner Unrestricted License. **Requirements:** Must pass examinations and have an established place of business. **Examination:** Black and white TV, color TV, practical, and oral examinations. **Governing Statute:** Connecticut Statutes, Chap. 394. State Board of Television and Radio Service Examiners Administrative Regulations.

1712

Television Electronics Technician
Board of Television and Radio
  Service Examiners
Occupational Licensing Div.
Consumer Protection Dept.
165 Capitol Ave.
Hartford, CT 06106
Phone: (203)566-3275

Credential Type: Certified Electronics Technician Unrestricted License. **Requirements:** Must pass examinations and be in the employ of another in the business of repairing, maintaining, and servicing television receiving equipment. **Examination:** Black and white TV, color TV, practical, and oral examinations. **Governing Statute:** Connecticut Statutes, Chap. 394. State Board of Television and Radio Service Examiners Administrative Regulations.

Louisiana

1713

Radio Technician
Board of Radio and Television
  Technology
Dept. of Economic Development
333 St. Charles Ave.
New Orleans, LA 70130
Phone: (504)522-9824

Credential Type: Radio Technician License. **Duration of License:** One year. **Requirements:** Submit application and pay fee. **Fees:** $25 license fee. **Governing Statute:** Revised Statutes of 1950, Title 37, Chap. 27. Act 428 of 1958.

1714

Radio and Television Technician
Board of Radio and Television
  Technology
Dept. of Economic Development
333 St. Charles Ave., Rm. 1400
New Orleans, LA 70130
Phone: (504)522-9824

Credential Type: Radio and Television Technician License. **Duration of License:** One year. **Requirements:** Submit application and pay fee. **Fees:** $45 license fee. **Governing Statute:** Revised Statutes of 1950, Title 37, Chap. 27 Act 428 of 1958.

Massachusetts

1715

Radio and Television Technician
Board of Registration of Radio and
  Television Technicians
Div. of Registration
100 Cambridge St., 15th Fl.
Boston, MA 02202
Phone: (617)727-3070

Credential Type: License. **Requirements:** Contact licensing body for application information.

Minnesota

1716

Alarm and Communication System Contractor
Board of Electricity
S-173 Griggs Midway Bldg.
1821 University Ave.
St. Paul, MN 55104
Phone: (612)642-0800

Credential Type: License. **Duration of License:** Two years. **Requirements:** Post $5000 performance bond. Have required general liability and property damage insurance. Individual or an employee must pass examination. **Examination:** Alarm and Communication Examination. **Fees:** $200 license fee. **Governing Statute:** Minnesota Statutes, Sections 326.241-326.248. Minnesota Rules 3800-3899.

1717

Alarm and Communication System Installer
Board of Electricity
S-173 Griggs Midway Bldg.
1821 University Ave.
St. Paul, MN 55104
Phone: (612)642-0800

Credential Type: Alarm and Communication License. **Duration of License:** Two years. **Requirements:** Contact licensing body for application information. **Examination:** Yes. **Fees:** $35 exam fee. No additional license fee. **Governing Statute:** Minnesota Statutes, Sections 326.241-326.248. Minnesota Rules 3800-3899.

North Carolina

1718

Alarm System Business Licensee
Alarm Systems Licensing Board
PO Box 29500
Raleigh, NC 27626
Phone: (919)779-1611

Credential Type: License. **Duration of License:** One year. **Authorization:** License allows individual to install, service, monitor, or respond to alarm signal devices, burglar alarms, or other burglary detection devices. **Requirements:** High school diploma and two years of experience within the past five years in an alarm systems business. 18 years of age. **Examination:** Written. **Fees:** $75 application fee. $150 license fee. $50 recovery fund fee. $150 renewal fee.

Oregon

1719

Consumer Electronic Entertainment Equipment Service Technician (Pick-up Point)
Bureau of Labor and Industries
Licensing Unit
State Office Bldg., Ste. 1160
Portland, OR 97232
Phone: (503)741-4074

Credential Type: License. **Duration of License:** One year. **Requirements:** Must complete application and pay fee. **Fees:** $30 license fee. $30 renewal fee. **Governing Statute:** ORS 702.010 to 702.175.

1720

Consumer Electronic Entertainment Equipment Service Technician (Service Dealers)
Bureau of Labor and Industries
State Office Bldg.
800 NE Oregon St., 32
Portland, OR 97232
Phone: (503)741-4074

Credential Type: License. **Duration of License:** One year. **Requirements:** Must prove one is a technician or employs a technician full time and is responsible for the quality of the service performed. Must be servicing consumer electronic entertainment equipment at a fixed place of business. **Fees:** $85 license fee. $85 renewal fee. **Governing Statute:** ORS 702.010 to 702.175.

1721

Consumer Electronic Entertainment Equipment Service Technician (Technician)
Bureau of Labor and Industries
State Office Bldg.
800 NE Oregon St., 32
Portland, OR 97232
Phone: (503)741-4074, ext. 237

Credential Type: License. **Duration of License:** One year. **Requirements:** Must have serviced consumer electronic entertainment equipment for at least three years or have serviced consumer electronic entertainment equipment for at least two years and have satisfactorily completed a program in the servicing of consumer electronic entertainment equipment; or have other equivalent experience or qualifications. **Examination:** Yes. **Fees:** $10—$25 exam fee. $45 license fee. $45 renewal fee. **Governing Statute:** ORS 702.010 to 702.175.

1722

Consumer Electronic Entertainment Equipment Service Technician (Technician Trainee)
Bureau of Labor and Industries
State Office Bldg.
800 NE Oregon St., 32
Portland, OR 97232
Phone: (503)741-4074

Credential Type: License. **Duration of License:** One year. **Requirements:** Must provide evidence that applicant works servicing consumer electronic entertainment equipment under the supervision of technician. Must have completed a program in electronics and the servicing of consumer electronic entertainment equipmemt. Must prove enrollment in or completion of a consumer electronics program. **Fees:** $35 license fee. $35 renewal fee. **Governing Statute:** ORS 702.010 to 702.175.

Communications, Transportation, and Utilities Operations Managers

One or more occupations in this chapter require a federal license. Additionally, the following states grant licenses as of the date of publication:

Arkansas	District of	Illinois	Minnesota	New Jersey	Ohio
California	Columbia	Kentucky	Missouri	New Mexico	Oklahoma
Connecticut	Florida	Louisiana	Montana	North Carolina	South Carolina
	Georgia	Michigan	Nebraska	North Dakota	Virginia

Federal Licenses

1723

Ocean Freight Forwarder
Bureau of Tariffs
Federal Maritime Commission
Washington, DC 20573
Phone: (202)523-5843

Credential Type: Ocean Freight Forwarder's License. **Authorization:** License allows individual to dispatch shipments from the United States via common carrier and book or otherwise arrange space for those shipments on behalf of shippers. Licensed individual may also process the documentation and perform related activities incident to those shipments. **Requirements:** Have at least three years experience in ocean freight forwarding duties in the United States. File a surety bond with the Commission in the amount of $30,000, plus $10,000 for each of the applicant's unincorporated branch offices. **Fees:** $350 application and license fee. **Governing Statute:** 46 CFR, Part 510.

Arkansas

1724

Grain Warehouseman
Arkansas State Plant Board
PO Box 1069
Little Rock, AR 72203
Phone: (501)225-1598

Credential Type: License. **Requirements:** Meet certain financial requirements. Post bond of letter of credit. Maintain records in accordance with the law and regulations. **Examination:** No **Fees:** $150 New applicant. $50 Less than 250,000 bushel capacity. $100 More than 250,000 bushel capacity.

1725

Liquefied Petroleum Gas Safety Supervisor
The Liquefied Petroleum Gas Board
1421 W. Sixth St.
Little Rock, AR 72201
Phone: (501)371-1008

Credential Type: License. **Duration of License:** One year. **Requirements:** Employed by a class one permit holder. Have thorough knowledge of liquefied petroleum gases and the National Fire Protection Association Pamphlet 58 and the State Liquefied Petroleum Gas Code. **Examination:** Yes. **Fees:** $5 License. $5 Renewal.

1726

Solid Waste Facility Operator
Dept. of Pollution Control and Ecology
Solid Waste Div.
PO Box 9583
Little Rock, AR 72219
Phone: (501)562-7444

Credential Type: License. **Duration of License:** One year. **Requirements:** Proposed rules would establish three classes of licensure, each with different experience and training requirements. Required experience ranges from no experience required to two years. Required training ranges from 20 hours to 40 hours.

Renewal requires completing six hours of approved training each year. **Examination:** Examination in appropriate class. **Governing Statute:** Arkansas Code, Title 8, Chap. 6, Subchap. 9.

California

1727

Alarm Company Operator
Bureau of Collection and Investigative Services
400 R St., Ste. 2001
Sacramento, CA 95814-6234
Phone: (916)445-7366

Credential Type: Alarm Company Operator License. **Requirements:** At least two years or 4000 hours of compensated experience in alarm company work, or equivalent. **Examination:** Written examination. **Fees:** $25 license application fee. $200 license fee. $27 fingerprint processing fee. **Governing Statute:** Alarm Company Act.

Credential Type: Qualified Manager Certificate. **Authorization:** Required of the person who is in active charge of the business. **Requirements:** Be at least 18 years of age. At least two years or 4000 hours of compensated experience in alarm company work, or equivalent. **Examination:** Written examination. **Fees:** $75 application and qualification certificate fee. $27 fingerprint processing fee.

1728

Satellite Facility Supervisor (Racetrack)
California Horse Racing Board
1010 Hurley Way, Ste. 190
Sacramento, CA 95825
Phone: (916)920-7178

Credential Type: License Registration. **Requirements:** Submit application and fingerprint card. Pay fee. **Fees:** $150 registration fee.

Connecticut

1729

Solid Waste Facility Operator
Dept. of Environmental Protection
165 Capitol Ave.
Hartford, CT 06106
Phone: (203)566-8844

Credential Type: Solid Waste Facility Operator Certificate. **Duration of License:** Five years. **Authorization:** A certified operator must be present at the solid waste facility at all times during operating hours. **Requirements:** Applicant for certification must demonstrate sufficient training in solid waste facility operational procedures to be able to oversee the operation of the solid waste facility in accordance with applicable state and federal statutes and regulations. Training may consist of on-the-job or classroom instruction. Applicant must pass a written or oral examination, or be interviewed and present documentation of training and experience.

Renewal requires completing a training course offered by the Department of Environmental Protection or, as required, passing an examination or qualification review. **Examination:** Written or oral examination. **Exemptions:** An interview may be held in lieu of an examination.

District of Columbia

1730

Solid Waste Collector
License and Certification Div.
Occupational and Professional Licensure Administration
Consumer and Regulatory Affairs Dept.
PO Box 37200
Washington, DC 20013-7200
Phone: (202)727-7823
Phone: (202)727-7480

Alternate Information: 614 H St., NW, Washington, DC 20001 **Requirements:** Contact licensing body for application information.

Florida

1731

Solid Waste Facility Operator
Dept. of Environmental Regulation
Div. of Waste Management
Bureau of Solid and Hazardous Waste
Solid Waste Section
2600 Blair Stone Rd.
Tallahassee, FL 32399-2400
Phone: (904)922-6104
Fax: (904)922-4939

Credential Type: Operator Certification. **Authorization:** Proposed rules would require that persons employed to perform the duties of an operator must be a trained operator or an interim operator. **Requirements:** Complete an approved training program. **Examination:** Training program examination. **Governing Statute:** Florida Statutes, Section 403.

Georgia

1732

Certified Landfill Operator
Dept. of Natural Resources
Environmental Protection Div.
205 Butler St., Ste. 1154
Atlanta, GA 30334
Phone: (404)656-4713

Credential Type: Landfill Operator Certification. **Duration of License:** Five years. **Authorization:** Effective July 1, 1992, certification is required for all operators of a municipal solid waste disposal facility. **Requirements:** High school graduate or equivalent. Have at least six months experience as a landfill operator. Prior to July 1, 1994, five years experience may be substituted for high school education. Complete Landfill Certification Training Course and examination. **Examination:** Landfill Operator Certification Examination. **Reciprocity:** Yes, provided that requirements for certification do not conflict and are not of a lower standard, and that state, territory, or possession of the United States has a reciprocal agreement with Georgia. **Governing Statute:** Rules of the Georgia Department of Natural Resources, Environmental Protection Division, Chapter 391-3-4.

Illinois

1733

Grain Warehouse Operator
Illinois Dept. of Agriculture
Div. of Agricultural Industry Regulation
State Fairgrounds
PO Box 19281
Springfield, IL 62794
Phone: (217)782-3817

Credential Type: Grain Warehouse Operator. **Duration of License:** Permanent. **Requirements:** At least 18 years of age. Good business reputation. Must have sufficient work experience and educational background to run a grain warehouse. Submit application and financial statement. **Reciprocity:** No. **Fees:** $100 application/initial license fee. $25 filing fee. **Governing Statute:** Illinois Revised Statutes, Chapter 114.

1734

Landfill Chief Operator
Illinois Environmental Protection Agency
2200 Churchill Rd.
Springfield, IL 62706
Phone: (217)782-0462

Credential Type: Landfill Chief Operator Certificate. **Duration of License:** One year. **Requirements:** Submit application. **Reciprocity:** No. **Fees:** No fee. **Governing Statute:** Illinois Administrative Code 35, Subtitle G.

1735

Solid Waste Site Operator
Illinois Environmental Protection Agency
2200 Churchill Rd.
Springfield, IL 62706
Phone: (217)782-1654

Credential Type: Solid Waste Operator Class A License. **Duration of License:** Three years. **Requirements:** At least 18 years of age. Must have a combination of study, training, and landfill experience. High school graduate, or equivalent education, must have a minimum of two years landfill experience. Grammar school graduate must have a minimum of 15 years landfill experience. Renewal requires reexamination. **Examination:** Landfill Operator Certification Examination. **Reciprocity:** No. **Fees:** $100 application fee. $400 examination/license fee. $400 renewal/reexamination fee. **Governing Statute:** Illinois Administrative Code 870.

Kentucky 1736

Solid Waste Site Operator, continued

Credential Type: Solid Waste Operator Class B License. **Duration of License:** Three years. **Requirements:** At least 18 years of age. Must have a combination of study, training, and landfill experience. High school graduate, or equivalent education, must have a minimum of six months landfill experience. Grammar school graduate must have a minimum of five years landfill experience. Renewal requires reexamination. **Examination:** Landfill Operator Certification Examination. **Reciprocity:** No. **Fees:** $100 application fee. $200 examination/license fee. $200 renewal/reexamination fee. **Governing Statute:** Illinois Administrative Code 870.

Credential Type: Special Waste Endorsement License. **Duration of License:** Three years. **Requirements:** At least 18 years of age. Must have a combination of study, training, and landfill experience. Renewal requires reexamination. **Examination:** Landfill Operator Certification Examination. **Reciprocity:** No. **Fees:** $100 application fee. $100 examination/license fee. $100 renewal/reexamination fee. **Governing Statute:** Illinois Administrative Code 870.

Kentucky

1736

Landfill Operator
Div. of Waste Management
18 Reilly Rd.
Frankfort, KY 40601
Phone: (502)564-6716

Credential Type: Operator Certification. **Duration of License:** Five years. **Authorization:** Each construction/demolition debris landfill and contained landfill must have at least one certified landfill operator and one certified landfill manager, or one individual certified for both categories. **Requirements:** High school graduate or equivalent. Have at least one year of experience. Additional experience may be acceptable if applicant has not graduated from high school. Complete an approved training program. **Examination:** Operator certification examination. **Reciprocity:** Yes, if training requirements are comparable.

Credential Type: Manager Certification. **Duration of License:** Five years. **Authorization:** Each construction/demolition debris landfill and contained landfill must have at least one certified landfill operator and one certified landfill manager, or one individual certified for both categories. **Requirements:** High school graduate or equivalent. Additional experience may be acceptable if applicant has not graduated from high school. Complete an approved training program. Meet one of the following sets of requirements: (1) Have at least two years of administrative experience in a related field. (2) Have two years of postsecondary education. (3) Have a combination of two years of experience and postsecondary education. **Examination:** Operator certification examination. **Reciprocity:** Yes, if training requirements are comparable.

1737

Sanitary Landfill Operator
Natural Resources & Environmental Protection Cabinet
Div. of Waste Management
14 Reilly Rd.
Frankfort, KY 40601
Phone: (502)564-6716

Credential Type: License. **Duration of License:** Five years. **Requirements:** High school diploma or equivalent required for any type landfill operation, however, experience may be substituted on a year-for-year basis. Must attend training session provided by regulatory agency. **Examination:** Yes. **Fees:** $125 exam fee.

Louisiana

1738

Solid Waste Facility Operator
Dept. of Environmental Quality
Office of Solid and Hazardous Waste
Solid Waste Div.
PO Box 82178
Baton Rouge, LA 70884-2178
Phone: (504)765-0249
Fax: (504)765-0299

Credential Type: Operator Certification—Level A. **Duration of License:** Four years. **Authorization:** Operators must be certified for all disposal facilities that receive residential or commercial solid waste. There are four categories of facilities: sanitary landfill, surface impoundment, landfarm, and open dumps. **Requirements:** High school graduate or equivalent. Meet one of the following sets of requirements: (1) Have three years responsible experience in solid waste management. (2) Have one year of responsible experience in solid waste management and three years experience as a supervisor in the construction field relating to the use of heavy equipment, good drainage practice, and other skills. (3) Have one year of responsible experience in solid waste management and either an engineering degree or a degree from a four-year program related to soils management or equipment operation. (4) Have one year of responsible experience in solid waste management and have held a Level B operator certificate for at least one year.

Recertification requires attending an approved training session. **Examination:** Operator examination. **Fees:** $100 certification fee. $100 exam fee. $100 recertification fee. **Governing Statute:** LA. R.S. 37:3154.

Credential Type: Operator Certification—Level B. **Duration of License:** Four years. **Authorization:** Operators must be certified for all disposal facilities that receive residential or commercial solid waste. There are four categories of facilities: sanitary landfill, surface impoundment, landfarm, and open dumps. **Requirements:** Meet one of the following sets of requirements: (1) Have two years responsible experience in solid waste management. (2) Have one year of responsible experience in solid waste management and two years experience as a supervisor in the construction field relating to the use of heavy equipment, good drainage practice, and other skills. (3) Have one year of responsible experience in solid waste management and either an engineering degree or a degree from a 4year program related to soils management or equipment operation. (4) Have one year of responsible experience in solid waste management and have held a Level C operator certificate for at least one year.

Recertification requires attending an approved training session. **Examination:** Operator examination. **Fees:** $100 certification fee. $100 exam fee. $100 recertification fee. **Governing Statute:** LA. R.S. 37:3154.

Credential Type: Operator Certification—Level C. **Duration of License:** Four years. **Authorization:** Operators must be certified for all disposal facilities that receive residential or commercial solid waste. There are four categories of facilities: sanitary landfill, surface impoundment, landfarm, and open dumps. **Requirements:** Meet one of the following sets of requirements: (1) Have one year of responsible experience in solid waste management. (2) Have one year of experience in the construction field relating to the use of heavy equipment, good drainage practice, and other skills. (3) Have either an engineering degree or a degree from a four-year program related to soils management or equipment operation.

Recertification requires attending an approved training session. **Examination:** Operator examination. **Fees:** $100 certification fee. $100 exam fee. $100 recertification fee. **Governing Statute:** LA. R.S. 37:3154.

Michigan

1739

Airport Manager
Safety and Services Div.
Bureau of Aeronautics
Dept. of Transportation
Capitol City Airport
Lansing, MI 48906
Phone: (517)373-2090

Credential Type: License. **Duration of License:** One year. **Requirements:** Abide by the rules and regulations of the Commission. **Examination:** Written exam. **Fees:** No fees. **Governing Statute:** Aeronautics Code, Act 327 of 1945, as amended.

Minnesota

1740

Hazardous Waste Disposal Facility Operator
Pollution Control Agency
520 N. Lafayette Rd.
St. Paul, MN 55155
Phone: (612)296-7283

Credential Type: Type I Operator Certification. **Duration of License:** Three years. **Authorization:** If three or fewer operators are employed at a facility, at least one must be certified. If 4-7 operators, then at least two must be certified. If more than eight operators, then at least three must be certified. **Requirements:** Must have a B.S. in biological, chemical, or physical sciences. Complete at least 15 hours of training within the three years immediately prior to application. Have at least six months of acceptable experience.

Renewal requires 18 contact hours of additional job-related training. **Examination:** Yes. **Fees:** $15 exam fee. $15 certification fee. $15 renewal fee. **Governing Statute:** Minnesota Statutes 116.41. Pollution Control Agency Rules 6 MCAR 4.6088 et seq.

1741

Non-Hazardous Waste Disposal Facility Operator
Pollution Control Agency
520 N. Lafayette Rd.
St. Paul, MN 55155
Phone: (612)296-7283

Credential Type: Type II Operator Certification. **Duration of License:** Three years. **Authorization:** Type II Certification covers sanitary, modified sanitary, and sludge landfills. If three or fewer operators are employed at a facility, at least one must be certified. If 4-7 operators, then at least two must be certified. If more than eight operators, then at least three must be certified. **Requirements:** High school graduate or equivalent. Complete at least 15 hours of training within the three years immediately prior to application. Have at least six months of acceptable experience.

Renewal requires 18 contact hours of additional job-related training. **Examination:** Yes. **Fees:** $15 exam fee. $15 certification fee. $15 renewal fee. **Governing Statute:** Minnesota Statutes 116.41. Pollution Control Agency Rules 6 MCAR 4.6088 et seq.

Credential Type: Type III Operator Certification. **Duration of License:** Three years. **Authorization:** Type III Certification covers demolition waste and nonhazardous source-specific industrial waste disposal facilities. If three or fewer operators are employed at a facility, at least one must be certified. If 4-7 operators, then at least two must be certified. If more than eight operators, then at least three must be certified. **Requirements:** Complete at least four hours of training within the three years immediately prior to application. Renewal requires six contact hours of additional job-related training. **Examination:** Yes. **Fees:** $15 exam fee. $15 certification fee. $15 renewal fee. **Governing Statute:** Minnesota Statutes 116.41. Pollution Control Agency Rules 6 MCAR 4.6088 et seq.

Credential Type: Type IV Operator Certification. **Duration of License:** Three years. **Authorization:** Type IV Certification covers land application sites and facilities for sewage sludge or industrial-commercial sludges. If three or fewer operators are employed at a facility, at least one must be certified. If 4-7 operators, then at least two must be certified. If more than eight operators, then at least three must be certified. **Requirements:** High school graduate or equivalent. Complete at least nine hours of training within the three years immediately prior to application. Have at least six months of acceptable experience.

Renewal requires nine contact hours of additional job-related training. **Examination:** Yes. **Fees:** $15 exam fee. $15 certification fee. $15 renewal fee. **Governing Statute:** Minnesota Statutes 116.41. Pollution Control Agency Rules 6 MCAR 4.6088 et seq.

Missouri

1742

Landfill Operator
State Dept. of Natural Resources
Div. of Environmental Quality
Solid Waste Management Program
205 Jefferson St.
PO Box 176
Jefferson City, MO 65102-0176
Phone: (314)751-5410
Phone: (314)751-3176

Credential Type: Operator Certification. **Duration of License:** Three years. **Authorization:** Every landfill must be operated by a certified individual. **Requirements:** Must take a three-day class approved by the Solid Waste Association of North America (SWANA). Must be a landfill owner, operator, or regulator in the state to take the class and examination. **Examination:** Written certification examination. **Fees:** No fees.

Montana

1743

Director at Simulcast Facility (Racetrack)
State of Montana Board of Horse Racing
Dept. of Commerce
1424 9th Ave.
Helena, MT 59620
Phone: (406)444-4287

Credential Type: License Registration. **Requirements:** Submit application and fingerprint card. Pay fee. **Fees:** $35 registration fee.

Nebraska

1744

County Highway Superintendent/ City Street Superintendent
Nebraska Board of Examiners for County Highway and City Street Superintendents
1101 Arapahoe St., Ste. 103
PO Box 94759
Lincoln, NE 68509
Phone: (402)479-4569

Credential Type: License. **Duration of License:** One year. **Requirements:** Must have four years of work experience or education following high school graduation. **Examination:** Yes. **Fees:** $25 examination and license fees. $10 renewal fee.

New Jersey

1745

Movers and Warehousemen
Board of Public Movers and Warehousemen
1100 Raymond Blvd., Rm. 511
Newark, NJ 07102
Phone: (201)648-3882

Credential Type: License. **Fees:** $225 application fee. $25 license fee. **Governing Statute:** NJSA 45:14D.

New Mexico

1746

Solid Waste Facility Operator
State Environment Dept.
Solid Waste Bureau
Regulation Section
1190 St. Francis Dr.
PO Box 26110
Santa Fe, NM 87502
Phone: (505)827-0559

Credential Type: Operator Certification. **Duration of License:** Three years. **Authorization:** Operators of the following solid waste facilities must be certified by January 1, 1994: landfills, transfer stations, recycling facilities, processing facilities, transformation facilities, and composting facilities. **Requirements:** Have at least three years of experience. High school graduation may be substituted for one year of experience. Complete an approved training course. Recertification requires taking another training course. **Examination:** Training course examination. **Fees:** No certification fees.

North Carolina

1747

Alarm System Business Licensee
Alarm Systems Licensing Board
PO Box 29500
Raleigh, NC 27626
Phone: (919)779-1611

Credential Type: License. **Duration of License:** One year. **Authorization:** License allows individual to install, service, monitor, or respond to alarm signal devices, burglar alarms, or other burglary detection devices. **Requirements:** High school diploma and two years of experience within the past five years in an alarm systems business. 18 years of age. **Examination:** Written. **Fees:** $75 application fee. $150 license fee. $50 recovery fund fee. $150 renewal fee.

1748

Solid Waste Facility Operator
Dept. of Environment, Health, and Natural Resources
Div. of Solid Waste Management
S. Central Regional Office
225 Green St., Ste. 601
Fayetteville, NC 28301
Phone: (919)486-1191

Credential Type: Operator Certification. **Requirements:** Statute requires that operators complete a certified training program no later than January 1, 1996. However, no formal state certification program is yet in place. May accept certification by the Solid Waste Association of North America (SWANA).

North Dakota

1749

Municipal Waste Incinerator Operator
State Dept. of Health and Consolidated Laboratories
Environmental Health Section
Solid Waste Program
1200 Missouri Ave.
PO Box 5520
Bismarck, ND 58502-5520
Phone: (701)221-5166
Fax: (701)221-5200

Credential Type: Incinerator Operator Certification. **Duration of License:** One year. **Authorization:** A certified operator must be on-site at all times during operation. **Requirements:** Have at least one year of operating experience. Attend an approved training session. Renewal requires attending at least one approved training course every three years. **Examination:** Written certification examination. **Fees:** $25 certification fee. $15 renewal fee.

1750

Municipal Waste Landfill Operator
State Dept. of Health and Consolidated Laboratories
Environmental Health Section
Solid Waste Program
1200 Missouri Ave.
PO Box 5520
Bismarck, ND 58502-5520
Phone: (701)221-5166
Fax: (701)221-5200

Credential Type: Landfill Operator Certification. **Duration of License:** One year. **Authorization:** A certified operator must be on-site at all times during operation. **Requirements:** Have at least one year of operating experience. Attend an approved training session. Renewal requires attending at least one approved training course every three years. **Examination:** Written certification examination. **Fees:** $25 certification fee. $15 renewal fee.

Ohio

1751

Solid Waste Facility Operator
State Environmental Protection Agency
Div. of Solid and Infectious Waste Management
PO Box 1049
1800 WaterMark Dr.
Columbus, OH 43266-0149
Phone: (614)644-3020
Phone: (614)644-2917
Fax: (614)644-2329

Credential Type: Operator Certification. **Duration of License:** Three years. **Authorization:** Proposed rules would require that all facilities have a certified operator on-site at all times during operating hours by January 1, 1996. **Requirements:** Complete an approved training course. **Examination:** Operator Examination.

Oklahoma

1752

Burglar Alarm Service and Installation Company Manager
Oklahoma State Dept. of Health
Occupational Licensing Service
1000 N.E. Tenth
PO Box 53551
Oklahoma City, OK 73152
Phone: (405)271-5217

Credential Type: License. **Duration of License:** One year. **Requirements:** 21 years of age. Two years of experience in the alarm industry. No felony convictions. Security verification clearance. **Examination:** Burglar Alarm Manager Examination. **Fees:** $50 exam fee. $50 application fee. $50 renewal fee.

1753

Fire Alarm Service and Installation Company Manager
Oklahoma State Dept. of Health
Occupational Licensing Service
1000 N.E. Tenth
PO Box 53551
Oklahoma City, OK 73152
Phone: (405)271-5217

Credential Type: License. **Duration of License:** One year. **Requirements:** 21 years of age. Security verification clearance. No felony convictions. **Examination:** Fire Alarm Manager Examination. **Fees:** $50 exam fee. $50 application fee. $50 renewal fee.

South Carolina

1754

Municipal Solid Waste Landfill Operator
Dept. of Health and Environmental Control
Div. of Solid Waste Management
2600 Bull St.
Columbia, SC 29201
Phone: (803)734-5210
Fax: (803)734-4901

Credential Type: Operator Certification. **Duration of License:** Three years. **Requirements:** Tentative requirements are as follows (regulations are in the process of being drafted). Complete an approved certification program. Solid Waste Association of North America (SWANA) or GRCDA certification may be accepted in lieu of completing the required training course. Renewal requires 15 hours of continuing education units every three years.

Virginia

1755

Solid Waste Facility Operator
Waste Management Facility Operators Board
Dept. of Commerce
3600 W. Broad St.
Richmond, VA 23230
Phone: (804)367-8534

Credential Type: Operator Certification. **Authorization:** All operators, after January 1, 1993, must obtain interim certification, which is valid until January 1, 1994. **Requirements:** Standards for full certification are being developed. For interim certification, must meet one of the following sets of requirements: (1) three years of full-time supervisory or operational experience managing a waste management facility since January of 1989. (2) two years of full-time supervisory or operational experience managing a waste management facility since January of 1989 and a high school diploma. (3) one year of full-time supervisory or operational experience managing a waste management facility since January of 1989 and an Associate's Degree or at least 60 semester hours, or the equivalent, from an accredited institution of higher learning. (4) six months of full-time supervisory or operational experience managing a waste management facility since January of 1989 and a Bachelor's Degree. **Fees:** $85 application fee. **Governing Statute:** Code of Virginia, Chap. 22.1, Title 54.1 and Chapters 1-3, Title 54.1.

Construction and Building Inspectors

The following states grant licenses in this occupational category as of the date of publication:

Alaska	Iowa	Michigan	New Jersey	Ohio	South Dakota
Arkansas	Kentucky	Mississippi	New York	Oklahoma	Texas
Illinois	Louisiana	Montana	North Carolina	Oregon	Virginia
Indiana	Massachusetts	Nebraska	North Dakota	Rhode Island	Washington

Alaska

1756

Electrical Administrator
Dept. of Commerce and Economic Development
Div. of Occupational Licensing
Board of Electrical Examiners
PO Box D
Juneau, AK 99811-0800
Phone: (907)465-2551
Fax: (907)465-2974

Credential Type: Inside Wiring Category. **Duration of License:** Two years. **Requirements:** One of the following education or experience requirements: (1) practical experience as a journeyman electrician in inside construction wiring for at least four of the six years immediately preceding date of application; or

(2) construction management experience in inside wiring as a field superintendent, field engineer, or similar position for at least four of the six years immediately preceding date of application; or

(3) a degree in electrical engineering from an accredited college or university plus practical experience as a journeyman electrician in inside construction wiring for at least one of the three years immediately preceding the date of application; or

(4) an Alaska registration as a professional electrical engineer plus management experience in the electrical construction industry as a field engineer, office engineer, or in a similar position for at least four of the six years immediately preceding date of application; or

(5) experience as a journeyman electrician in inside construction for three of the six years immediately preceding date of application and one year experience during those six years as a certified electrical inspector for a state or municipality or as a full-time electrical instructor at a school approved by the board.

Submit notarized Certificates of Support of experience and qualifications from three persons licensed in the electrical industry in any state.

Applicants licensed in another state and having taken a similar examination in another state may be granted a license by credentials without taking the Alaska examination.

License renewal requires at least one 8-hour continuing education workshop approved by the board which covers the National Electrical Code. **Examination:** Inside Wiring Examination. Applicant may not be examined for more than two electrical administrator's categories at any one scheduled examination. Passing the Inside Wiring Examination automatically qualifies the applicant to be licensed in the Residential Wiring category. **Fees:** $30 application fee. $50 examination fee. $250 license fee. **Governing Statute:** Alaska Statutes 08.40. Professional Regulations 12 AAC 32.

Credential Type: Inside Communications Category. **Duration of License:** Two years. **Requirements:** Practical experience as a journeyman in inside construction communications for at least two of the four years immediately preceding the date of application. Graduated from an accredited college or trade school in inside communication.

Submit notarized Certificates of Support of experience and qualifications from three persons employed, but not necessarily licensed, in the electrical industry in any state.

Applicants licensed in another state and having taken a similar examination in another state may be granted a license by credentials without taking the Alaska examination.

License renewal requires at least one 8-hour continuing education workshop approved by the board which covers the National Electrical Code. **Examination:** Inside Communications Examination. Applicant may not be examined for more than two electrical administrator's categories at any one scheduled examination. **Fees:** $30 application fee. $50 examination fee. $250 license fee. **Governing Statute:** Alaska Statutes 08.40. Professional Regulations 12 AAC 32.

Credential Type: Residential Wiring Category. **Duration of License:** Two years. **Requirements:** Practical experience as a journeyman residential wireman for at least two of the four years immediately preceding the date of application.

License renewal requires at least one 8-hour continuing education workshop approved by the board which covers the National Electrical Code. **Examination:** Residential Wiring Examination. Applicant may not be examined for more than two electrical administrator's categories at any one scheduled examination. Passing the Inside Wiring Examination automatically qualified the applicant to be licensed in the Residential Wiring category. **Fees:** $30 application fee. $50 examination fee. $250 license fee. **Governing Statute:** Alaska Statutes 08.40. Professional Regulations 12 AAC 32.

Credential Type: Outside Linework Category. **Duration of License:** Two years. **Requirements:** One of the following education or experience requirements: (1) practical experience as a journeyman electrician in outside construction linework for at least four of the six years immediately preceding date of application; or

(2) construction management experience in outside linework as a field superintendent,

field engineer, or similar position for at least four of the six years immediately preceding date of application; or

(3) a degree in electrical engineering from an accredited college or university plus practical experience as a journeyman lineman in outside construction linework for at least one of the three years immediately preceding the date of application; or

(4) an Alaska registration as a professional electrical engineer plus management experience in the electrical construction industry as a field engineer, office engineer, or in a similar engineering position for at least four of the six years immediately preceding date of application; or

(5) experience as a journeyman lineman in outside construction for three of the six years immediately preceding date of application and one year experience during those six years as a certified electrical inspector for a state or municipality or as a full-time electrical instructor at a school approved by the board.

Submit notarized Certificates of Support of experience and qualifications from three persons licensed in the electrical industry in any state.

Applicants licensed in another state and having taken a similar examination in another state may be granted a license by credentials without taking the Alaska examination.

License renewal requires at least one 8-hour continuing education workshop approved by the board which covers the National Electrical Safety Code. **Examination:** Outside Linework Examination. Applicant may not be examined for more than two electrical administrator's categories at any one scheduled examination. **Fees:** $30 application fee. $50 examination fee. $250 license fee. **Governing Statute:** Alaska Statutes 08.40. Professional Regulations 12 AAC 32.

Credential Type: Outside Communications Category. **Duration of License:** Two years. **Requirements:** Practical experience as a journeyman in outside construction communications for at least two of the four years immediately preceding the date of application. Graduated from an accredited college or trade school in inside communication.

Submit notarized Certificates of Support of experience and qualifications from three persons employed, but not necessarily licensed, in the electrical industry in any state.

Applicants licensed in another state and having taken a similar examination in another state may be granted a license by credentials without taking the Alaska examination.

License renewal requires at least one 8-hour continuing education workshop approved by the board which covers the National Electrical Safety Code. **Examination:** Outside Communications Examination. Applicant may not be examined for more than two electrical administrator's categories at any one scheduled examination. **Fees:** $30 application fee. $50 examination fee. $250 license fee. **Governing Statute:** Alaska Statutes 08.40. Professional Regulations 12 AAC 32.

Credential Type: Controls and Control Wiring Category. **Duration of License:** Two years. **Requirements:** Hold a current Alaska license as a mechanical administrator. Practical experience as a journeyman installing low voltage controls for at least two of the four years preceding date of application. Construction management experience in low voltage control wiring as a field superintendent, field engineer, or similar position for at least four of the six years immediately preceding date of application; or an Alaska registration as an electrical or mechanical engineer plus management experience in the electrical or mechanical low voltage control wiring industry as a field engineer or office engineer for at least two of the four years immediately preceding date of application.

Submit notarized Certificates of Support of experience and qualifications from three persons licensed in the electrical industry in any state.

Applicants licensed in another state and having taken a similar examination in another state may be granted a license by credentials without taking the Alaska examination.

License renewal requires at least one 8-hour continuing education workshop approved by the board. **Examination:** Controls and Control Wiring Examination. Applicant may not be examined for more than two electrical administrator's categories at any one scheduled examination. **Fees:** $30 application fee. $50 examination fee. $250 license fee. **Governing Statute:** Alaska Statutes 08.40. Professional Regulations 12 AAC 32.

1757

Mechanical Administrator - Dry Chemical Fire Protection Category
Dept. of Commerce and Economic Development
Div. of Occupational Licensing
Board of Mechanical Examiners
PO Box D
Juneau, AK 99811-0800
Phone: (907)465-2546
Fax: (907)465-2974

Credential Type: Mechanical administrator license—Dry Chemical Fire Protection Category. License by Credentials. **Duration of License:** Two years. **Requirements:** Verification of current or past licensure in another state. Pass an examination for mechanical administrator work that is equivalent to the examination required by Alaska. Take the Alaska specific portion of the state-administered examination. References from three persons employed in the mechanical field in any state. Submit documentation of appropriate education and experience.

One of the following:

(1) Practical experience as a journeyman in fire protection work using dry chemical systems for at least two of the four years immediately preceding date of application.

(2) Graduate of an accredited college or trade school in fire protection using dry chemical systems.

(3) Holds a valid level III certificate in Fire Protection Engineering Technology, Special Hazards Systems Layout, issued by the National Institute for Certification in Engineering Technologies (NICET). **Fees:** $30 application fee. $250 license fee. **Governing Statute:** Alaska Statutes 08.40. Professional Regulations 12 AAC 39.

Credential Type: Mechanical administrator license—Dry Chemical Fire Protection Category. License by Examination. **Duration of License:** Two years. **Requirements:** Pass the state-administered examination. References from three persons employed in the mechanical field in any state. Submit documentation of appropriate education and experience.

One of the following:

(1) Practical experience as a journeyman in fire protection work using dry chemical systems for at least two of the four years immediately preceding date of application.

(2) Graduate of an accredited college or trade school in fire protection using dry chemical systems.

(3) Holds a valid level III certificate in Fire Protection Engineering Technology, Spe-

Mechanical Administrator - Dry Chemical Fire Protection Category, continued

cial Hazards Systems Layout, issued by the National Institute for Certification in Engineering Technologies (NICET). **Examination:** State-administered examination (maximum of two categories). **Fees:** $30 application fee. $250 license fee. $50 exam fee. **Governing Statute:** Alaska Statutes 08.40. Professional Regulations 12 AAC 39.

1758

Mechanical Administrator - Heating, Cooling, and Process Piping Category
Dept. of Commerce and Economic Development
Div. of Occupational Licensing
Board of Mechanical Examiners
PO Box D
Juneau, AK 99811-0800
Phone: (907)465-2546
Fax: (907)465-2974

Credential Type: Mechanical administrator license—Heating, Cooling, and Process Piping Category. License by Credentials. **Duration of License:** Two years. **Requirements:** Verification of current or past licensure in another state. Pass an examination for mechanical administrator work that is equivalent to the examination required by Alaska. Take the Alaska specific portion of the state-administered examination. References from three persons employed in the mechanical field in any state. Submit documentation of appropriate education and experience.

One of the following:

(1) Practical experience as a journeyman in heating, cooling, and process piping work for at least four of the six years immediately preceding date of application.

(2) Construction management experience in heating, cooling, and process piping work as a field superintendent, field engineer, or similar position for at least four of the six years immediately preceding date of application.

(3) Degree in mechanical engineering from a regionally accredited college or university, plus practical experience as a journeyman pipefitter in heating, cooling, and process piping for at least one of the three years immediately preceding date of application.

(4) Alaska registration as a professional mechanical engineer, plus management experience in the mechanical contracting field as a field engineer, office engineer, or similar engineering position for at least four of the six years immediately preceding date of application. **Fees:** $30 application fee. $250 license fee. **Governing Statute:** Alaska Statutes 08.40. Professional Regulations 12 AAC 39.

Credential Type: Mechanical administrator license—Heating, Cooling, and Process Piping Category. License by Examination. **Duration of License:** Two years. **Requirements:** Pass the state-administered examination. References from three persons employed in the mechanical field in any state. Submit documentation of appropriate education and experience.

One of the following:

(1) Practical experience as a journeyman in heating, cooling, and process piping work for at least four of the six years immediately preceding date of application.

(2) Construction management experience in heating, cooling, and process piping work as a field superintendent, field engineer, or similar position for at least four of the six years immediately preceding date of application.

(3) Degree in mechanical engineering from a regionally accredited college or university, plus practical experience as a journeyman pipefitter in heating, cooling, and process piping for at least one of the three years immediately preceding date of application.

(4) Alaska registration as a professional mechanical engineer, plus management experience in the mechanical contracting field as a field engineer, office engineer, or similar engineering position for at least four of the six years immediately preceding date of application. **Examination:** State-administered examination (maximum of two categories). **Fees:** $30 application fee. $250 license fee. $50 exam fee. **Governing Statute:** Alaska Statutes 08.40. Professional Regulations 12 AAC 39

1759

Mechanical Administrator - HVAC/Sheet Metal Category
Dept. of Commerce and Economic Development
Div. of Occupational Licensing
Board of Mechanical Examiners
PO Box D
Juneau, AK 99811-0800
Phone: (907)465-2546
Fax: (907)465-2974

Credential Type: Mechanical administrator license—HVAC/Sheet Metal Category. License by Credentials. **Duration of License:** Two years. **Requirements:** Verification of current or past licensure in another state. Pass an examination for mechanical administrator work that is equivalent to the examination required by Alaska. Take the Alaska specific portion of the state-administered examination. References from three persons employed in the mechanical field in any state. Submit documentation of appropriate education and experience.

One of the following:

(1) Practical experience as a journeyman in HVAC and sheet metal work for at least four of the six years immediately preceding date of application.

(2) Management experience in HVAC and sheet metal work as a field superintendent, office engineer, or similar position for at least four of the six years immediately preceding date of application.

(3) Degree in mechanical engineering from an accredited college or university, plus practical experience as a journeyman in HVAC and sheet metal work for at least one of the three years immediately preceding date of application.

(4) Alaska registration as a professional mechanical engineer, plus management experience in the mechanical contracting field as a field engineer, office engineer, or similar engineering position for at least four of the six years immediately preceding date of application. **Fees:** $30 application fee. $250 license fee. **Governing Statute:** Alaska Statutes 08.40. Professional Regulations 12 AAC 39.

Credential Type: Mechanical administrator license—HVAC/Sheet Metal Category. License by Examination. **Duration of License:** Two years. **Requirements:** Pass the state-administered examination. References from three persons employed in the mechanical field in any state. Submit documentation of appropriate education and experience.

One of the following:

(1) Practical experience as a journeyman in HVAC and sheet metal work for at least four of the six years immediately preceding date of application.

(2) Management experience in HVAC and sheet metal work as a field superintendent, office engineer, or similar position for at least four of the six years immediately preceding date of application.

(3) Degree in mechanical engineering from an accredited college or university, plus practical experience as a journeyman in HVAC and sheet metal work for at least one of the three years immediately preceding date of application.

(4) Alaska registration as a professional mechanical engineer, plus management experience in the mechanical contracting field as a field engineer, office engineer, or simi-

lar engineering position for at least four of the six years immediately preceding date of application. **Examination:** State-administered examination (maximum of two categories). **Fees:** $30 application fee. $250 license fee. $50 exam fee. **Governing Statute:** Alaska Statutes 08.40. Professional Regulations 12 AAC 39.

1760

Mechanical Administrator - Mechanical Systems Temperature Control Category
Dept. of Commerce and Economic Development
Div. of Occupational Licensing
Board of Mechanical Examiners
PO Box D
Juneau, AK 99811-0800
Phone: (907)465-2546
Fax: (907)465-2974

Credential Type: Mechanical administrator license—Mechanical Systems Temperature Control Category. License by Credentials. **Duration of License:** Two years. **Requirements:** Verification of current or past licensure in another state. Pass an examination for mechanical administrator work that is equivalent to the examination required by Alaska. Take the Alaska specific portion of the state-administered examination. References from three persons employed in the mechanical field in any state. Submit documentation of appropriate education and experience.

One of the following:

(1) Practical experience as a journeyman in mechanical systems temperature control work for at least two of the four years immediately preceding date of application.

(2) Management experience in mechanical systems temperature control work as a field superintendent, office engineer, or similar position for at least four of the six years immediately preceding date of application.

(3) Degree in mechanical engineering from an accredited college or university, or be a graduate of an accredited college or trade school in mechanical systems temperature control. **Fees:** $30 application fee. $250 license fee. **Governing Statute:** Alaska Statutes 08.40. Professional Regulations 12 AAC 39.

Credential Type: Mechanical administrator license—Mechanical Systems Temperature Control Category. License by Examination. **Duration of License:** Two years. **Requirements:** Pass the state-administered examination. References from three persons employed in the mechanical field in any state. Submit documentation of appropriate education and experience.

One of the following:

(1) Practical experience as a journeyman in mechanical systems temperature control work for at least two of the four years immediately preceding date of application.

(2) Management experience in mechanical systems temperature control work as a field superintendent, office engineer, or similar position for at least four of the six years immediately preceding date of application.

(3) Degree in mechanical engineering from an accredited college or university, or be a graduate of an accredited college or trade school in mechanical systems temperature control. **Examination:** State-administered examination (maximum of two categories). **Fees:** $30 application fee. $250 license fee. $50 exam fee. **Governing Statute:** Alaska Statutes 08.40. Professional Regulations 12 AAC 39.

1761

Mechanical Administrator - Plumbing Category
Dept. of Commerce and Economic Development
Div. of Occupational Licensing
Board of Mechanical Examiners
PO Box D
Juneau, AK 99811-0800
Phone: (907)465-2546
Fax: (907)465-2974

Credential Type: Mechanical administrator license—Plumbing Category. License by Credentials. **Duration of License:** Two years. **Requirements:** Verification of current or past licensure in another state. Pass an examination for mechanical administrator work that is equivalent to the examination required by Alaska. Take the Alaska specific portion of the state-administered examination. References from three persons employed in the mechanical field in any state. Submit documentation of appropriate education and experience.

One of the following:

(1) Practical experience as a journeyman plumber for at least four of the six years immediately preceding date of application.

(2) Management experience in plumbing work as a field superintendent, office engineer, or similar position for at least four of the six years immediately preceding date of application.

(3) Degree in mechanical engineering from a regionally accredited college or university, plus practical experience as a journeyman plumber for at least one of the three years immediately preceding date of application.

(4) Alaska registration as a professional mechanical engineer, plus management experience in the mechanical contracting field as a field engineer, office engineer, or similar engineering position for at least four of the six years immediately preceding date of application. **Fees:** $30 application fee. $250 license fee. **Governing Statute:** Alaska Statutes 08.40. Professional Regulations 12 AAC 39.

Credential Type: Mechanical administrator license—Plumbing Category. License by Examination. **Duration of License:** Two years. **Requirements:** Pass the state-administered examination. References from three persons employed in the mechanical field in any state. Submit documentation of appropriate education and experience.

One of the following:

(1) Practical experience as a journeyman plumber for at least four of the six years immediately preceding date of application.

(2) Management experience in plumbing work as a field superintendent, office engineer, or similar position for at least four of the six years immediately preceding date of application.

(3) Degree in mechanical engineering from a regionally accredited college or university, plus practical experience as a journeyman plumber for at least one of the three years immediately preceding date of application.

(4) Alaska registration as a professional mechanical engineer, plus management experience in the mechanical contracting field as a field engineer, office engineer, or similar engineering position for at least four of the six years immediately preceding date of application. **Examination:** State-administered examination (maximum of two categories). **Fees:** $30 application fee. $250 license fee. $50 exam fee. **Governing Statute:** Alaska Statutes 08.40. Professional Regulations 12 AAC 39.

1762

Mechanical Administrator - Refrigeration Category
Dept. of Commerce and Economic Development
Div. of Occupational Licensing
Board of Mechanical Examiners
PO Box D
Juneau, AK 99811-0800
Phone: (907)465-2546
Fax: (907)465-2974

Credential Type: Mechanical administrator license—Refrigeration Category. License by Credentials. **Duration of License:** Two years. **Requirements:** Verification of current or past licensure in another state.

Mechanical Administrator - Refrigeration Category, continued

Pass an examination for mechanical administrator work that is equivalent to the examination required by Alaska. Take the Alaska specific portion of the state-administered examination. References from three persons employed in the mechanical field in any state. Submit documentation of appropriate education and experience.

One of the following:

(1) Practical experience as a journeyman in refrigeration for at least two of the four years immediately preceding date of application.

(2) Graduate of an accredited college or trade school in refrigeration. **Fees:** $30 application fee. $250 license fee. **Governing Statute:** Alaska Statutes 08.40. Professional Regulations 12 AAC 39.

Credential Type: Mechanical administrator license—Refrigeration Category. License by Examination. **Duration of License:** Two years. **Requirements:** Pass the state-administered examination. References from three persons employed in the mechanical field in any state. Submit documentation of appropriate education and experience.

One of the following:

(1) Practical experience as a journeyman in refrigeration for at least two of the four years immediately preceding date of application.

(2) Graduate of an accredited college or trade school in refrigeration. **Examination:** State-administered examination (maximum of two categories). **Fees:** $30 application fee. $250 license fee. $50 exam fee. **Governing Statute:** Alaska Statutes 08.40. Professional Regulations 12 AAC 39.

1763

Mechanical Administrator - Residential HVAC Category

Dept. of Commerce and Economic Development
Div. of Occupational Licensing
Board of Mechanical Examiners
PO Box D
Juneau, AK 99811-0800
Phone: (907)465-2546
Fax: (907)465-2974

Credential Type: Mechanical administrator license—Residential HVAC Category. License by Credentials. **Duration of License:** Two years. **Requirements:** Verification of current or past licensure in another state. Pass an examination for mechanical administrator work that is equivalent to the examination required by Alaska. Take the Alaska specific portion of the state-administered examination. References from three persons employed in the mechanical field in any state. Submit documentation of appropriate education and experience.

Practical experience as a journeyman in residential HVAC work for at least two of the four years immediately preceding date of application. **Fees:** $30 application fee. $250 license fee. **Governing Statute:** Alaska Statutes 08.40. Professional Regulations 12 AAC 39.

Credential Type: Mechanical administrator license—Residential HVAC Category. License by Examination. **Duration of License:** Two years. **Requirements:** Pass the state-administered examination. References from three persons employed in the mechanical field in any state. Submit documentation of appropriate education and experience.

Practical experience as a journeyman in residential HVAC work for at least two of the four years immediately preceding date of application. **Examination:** State-administered examination (maximum of two categories). **Fees:** $30 application fee. $250 license fee. $50 exam fee. **Governing Statute:** Alaska Statutes 08.40. Professional Regulations 12 AAC 39.

1764

Mechanical Administrator - Residential Plumbing and Hydronic Heating Category

Dept. of Commerce and Economic Development
Div. of Occupational Licensing
Board of Mechanical Examiners
PO Box D
Juneau, AK 99811-0800
Phone: (907)465-2546
Fax: (907)465-2974

Credential Type: Mechanical administrator license—Residential Plumbing and Hydronic Heating Category. License by Credentials. **Duration of License:** Two years. **Requirements:** Verification of current or past licensure in another state. Pass an examination for mechanical administrator work that is equivalent to the examination required by Alaska. Take the Alaska specific portion of the state-administered examination. References from three persons employed in the mechanical field in any state. Submit documentation of appropriate education and experience.

Practical experience as a journeyman in residential plumbing and hydronic heating work for at least two of the four years immediately preceding date of application. **Fees:** $30 application fee. $250 license fee. **Governing Statute:** Alaska Statutes 08.40. Professional Regulations 12 AAC 39.

Credential Type: Mechanical administrator license—Residential Plumbing and Hydronic Heating Category. License by Examination. **Duration of License:** Two years. **Requirements:** Pass the state-administered examination. References from three persons employed in the mechanical field in any state. Submit documentation of appropriate education and experience.

Practical experience as a journeyman in residential plumbing and hydronic heating work for at least two of the four years immediately preceding date of application. **Examination:** State-administered examination (maximum of two categories). **Fees:** $30 application fee. $250 license fee. $50 exam fee. **Governing Statute:** Alaska Statutes 08.40. Professional Regulations 12 AAC 39.

1765

Mechanical Administrator - Sprinkler System Fire Protection Category

Dept. of Commerce and Economic Development
Div. of Occupational Licensing
Board of Mechanical Examiners
PO Box D
Juneau, AK 99811-0800
Phone: (907)465-2546
Fax: (907)465-2974

Credential Type: Mechanical administrator license—Sprinkler System Fire Protection Category. License by Credentials. **Duration of License:** Two years. **Requirements:** Verification of current or past licensure in another state. Pass an examination for mechanical administrator work that is equivalent to the examination required by Alaska. Take the Alaska specific portion of the state-administered examination. References from three persons employed in the mechanical field in any state. Submit documentation of appropriate education and experience.

One of the following:

(1) Practical experience as a journeyman in fire protection work using wet agent sprinkler systems for at least two of the four years immediately preceding date of application.

(2) Graduate of an accredited college or trade school in fire protection using wet agent sprinkler systems.

(3) Holds a valid level III certificate in Fire Protection Engineering Technology, Automatic Sprinkler System Layout, issued by

Construction and Building Inspectors

the National Institute for Certification in Engineering Technologies (NICET). **Fees:** $30 application fee. $250 license fee. **Governing Statute:** Alaska Statutes 08.40. Professional Regulations 12 AAC 39.

Credential Type: Mechanical administrator license—Sprinkler System Fire Protection Category. License by Examination. **Duration of License:** Two years. **Requirements:** Pass the state-administered examination. References from three persons employed in the mechanical field in any state. Submit documentation of appropriate education and experience.

One of the following:

(1) Practical experience as a journeyman in fire protection work using wet agent sprinkler systems for at least two of the four years immediately preceding date of application.

(2) Graduate of an accredited college or trade school in fire protection using wet agent sprinkler systems.

(3) Holds a valid level III certificate in Fire Protection Engineering Technology, Automatic Sprinkler System Layout, issued by the National Institute for Certification in Engineering Technologies (NICET). **Examination:** State-administered examination (maximum of two categories). **Fees:** $30 application fee. $250 license fee. $50 exam fee. **Governing Statute:** Alaska Statutes 08.40. Professional Regulations 12 AAC 39.

Arkansas

1766

Boiler Inspector, State
Arkansas Dept. of Labor
Boiler Inspection Div.
10421 W. Markham
Little Rock, AR 72205
Phone: (501)682-4513

Credential Type: License. **Requirements:** Five years experience in construction, maintenance, installation and repair of high-pressure boilers and unfired pressure vessels. Furnish a bond in the sum of $2,000. **Examination:** Yes. **Fees:** No fees

1767

Elevator and Lifting Device Inspector
Arkansas Dept. of Labor
Elevator Safety Board
10421 W. Markham
Little Rock, AR 72205
Phone: (501)682-4530

Credential Type: License. **Requirements:** Pass the written examination. Submit a written application. **Examination:** Yes. **Fees:** $5 Written Examination. $25 License. $25 Renewal.

1768

Insurance Inspector (Boiler)
Arkansas Dept. of Labor
Boiler Inspector Div.
10421 W. Markham
Little Rock, AR 72202
Phone: (501)682-4513

Credential Type: License. **Requirements:** Must be employed by a company authorized to insure boilers against explosion. Meet all requirements and be approved by State Insurance Commission to insure boilers and machinery. Pass written examination and be issued a certificate of competency as a boiler inspector. **Examination:** Yes. **Fees:** $25 Written examination and initial license. $15 Renewal.

1769

Plumbing and Gas Inspector
Arkansas Dept. of Health
Div. of Plumbing and Natural Gas
4815 W. Markham St.
Little Rock, AR 72201
Phone: (501)661-2642

Credential Type: License. **Duration of License:** One year. **Requirements:** Must be licensed as a plumber or gas fitter. May also have sanitarian or water operators license. **Examination:** Yes. **Fees:** $5 Written examination. $25 License. $5 Renewal.

Illinois

1770

Asbestos Air Sampling Professional
Illinois Dept. of Public Health
Div. of Environmental Health
525 W. Jefferson St.
Springfield, IL 62761
Phone: (217)782-3517

Credential Type: Asbestos Air Sampling Professional License. **Duration of License:** One year. **Requirements:** Complete Illinois Registered National Institute of Occupational Safety & Health (NIOSH) 582 Course. Bachelor's degree in live, environmental, or physical science or engineering, or 12 months of experience in on-site air sampling for asbestos abatement projects. Plus have three months of experience in general indoor air pollution sampling. **Examination:** National Institute of Occupational Safety & Health (NIOSH) Examination. **Reciprocity:** Yes, if license was received in a state with requirements equal to or greater than those of Illinois. Must pay Illinois license fee. **Fees:** $50 initial license fee. $50 license renewal fee. $15 license reinstatement fee. $15 duplicate license fee. **Governing Statute:** Illinois Asbestos Abatements act, Illinois Revised Statutes, Chapter 122.

1771

Asbestos Inspector
Illinois Dept. of Public Health
Div. of Environmental Health
525 W. Jefferson St.
Springfield, IL 62761
Phone: (217)782-3517

Credential Type: Asbestos Inspector License. **Duration of License:** One year. **Requirements:** High school graduate. Complete an Illinois accredited inspector training course. At least six months experience inspecting buildings for asbestos containing materials or a minimum of 18 months experience in direct planning of construction projects and/or construction project inspection. Renewal requires a half-day refresher course for inspectors annually. **Examination:** Written examination. **Reciprocity:** Yes, if license was received in a state with requirements equal to or greater than those of Illinois. Must pay Illinois license fee. **Fees:** $50 initial license fee. $50 license renewal fee. $15 license reinstatement fee. **Governing Statute:** Illinois Asbestos Abatements act, Illinois Revised Statutes, Chapter 122.

1772

Deputy Boiler Inspector
Illinois State Fire Marshal
Div. of Boiler & Pressure Vessel Safety
1035 Stevenson Drive
Springfield, IL 62703
Phone: (217)785-1010

Credential Type: Deputy Boiler Inspector Certificate. **Duration of License:** One year. **Requirements:** Must have at least five years experience in the construction, maintenance, repair or operation of high pres-

Illinois 1773

Deputy Boiler Inspector, continued

sure boilers and unfired pressure vessels. Experience may be gained in the position of mechanical engineer, steam engineer, boiler maker, or boiler inspector. **Examination:** National Board Exam for Boiler and Pressure Vessel Inspectors. **Reciprocity:** Yes, with states that require passage of the National Board of Boiler and Pressure Vessel Inspectors Exam. **Fees:** $15 examination fee. $15 application fee. $10 initial license fee. $5 renewal fee. $10 reinstatement fee. **Governing Statute:** Boiler and Pressure Vessel Safety Act—Chapter 111.

1773

Special Boiler Inspector (Insurance Co.)
Illinois State Fire Marshal
Div. of Boiler & Pressure Vessel Safety
1035 Stevenson Drive
Springfield, IL 62703
Phone: (217)785-1010

Credential Type: Special Boiler Inspector Certificate. **Duration of License:** One year. **Authorization:** Allows inspection of boilers and pressure vessels for authorized insurance companies. **Requirements:** Must have at least three years experience in the construction, maintenance, repair or operation of high pressure boilers and pressure vessels. **Examination:** National Board Exam for Boiler and Pressure Vessel Inspectors. **Reciprocity:** Yes, with states that require passage of the National Board of Boiler and Pressure Vessel Inspectors Exam. **Fees:** $15 examination fee. $15 application fee. $10 initial license fee. $5 renewal fee. $10 reinstatement fee. **Governing Statute:** Boiler and Pressure Vessel Safety Act—Chapter 111.

Indiana

1774

Asbestos Inspector
Dept. of Environmental Management
Office of Air Management
Asbestos Section
PO Box 7060
Indianapolis, IN 46202-7060
Phone: (317)232-8232

Credential Type: Accreditation. **Duration of License:** One year. **Requirements:** High school degree or equivalent, or have two years of experience in either asbestos inspection, building construction, building maintenance, or general building inspection. Attend an approved training course. Renewal requires attending a refresher course. **Examination:** Training course examination. **Fees:** $100 annual accreditation fee. **Governing Statute:** 326 IAC 18-1 et seq.

Iowa

1775

Asbestos Inspector
Iowa Dept. of Employment Services
Labor Services Div.
1000 E. Grand Ave.
Des Moines, IA 50319
Phone: (515)281-3606

Credential Type: License. **Duration of License:** One year. **Requirements:** 18 years of age. Physically capable of performing the work safely. Successful completion of the approved training course. **Reciprocity:** Licenses from other states will be reviewed. **Fees:** $20 license fee. $20 renewal fee.

1776

Boiler Inspector
Iowa Dept. of Employment Services
Chief Boiler Inspector
1000 E. Grand Ave.
Des Moines, IA 50319
Phone: (515)281-3606

Credential Type: Commission. **Duration of License:** One year. **Requirements:** A degree in engineering plus two years of experience with high pressure boilers and pressure boilers; or an associate degree in mechanical technology plus two years of experience; or a high school diploma or equivalent plus three years of experience. **Examination:** Yes. **Reciprocity:** Yes. **Fees:** $25 National Board Commission card fee. $20 renewal fee.

1777

Special Elevator Inspector
Elevator Safety Section
Iowa Dept. of Employment Services
1000 E. Grand Ave.
Des Moines, IA 50319
Phone: (515)281-3606

Credential Type: Special Elevator Inspector Certificate. **Duration of License:** Permanent. **Authorization:** Limited to safety tests on elevators, escalators, and lifts. **Requirements:** The applicant must study the "Safety Code for Elevators and Escalators" and the "Inspector's Manual." **Examination:** Written and practical. **Fees:** None.

Credential Type: Special Elevator Inspector License. **Duration of License:** One year. **Requirements:** High school diploma or equivalent. Three years of full-time experience with elevators. Completion of a one-week course put on by the National Assn. of Elevator Authorities. **Examination:** Written and practical. **Fees:** $400—$600 course and exam fee.

Kentucky

1778

Boiler Inspector
Dept. of Housing, Building and Construction
1047 U.S. 127 South
Frankfort, KY 40601
Phone: (502)564-3626

Credential Type: License. **Requirements:** High school diploma or equivalent. Five years of experience in boiler and/or pressure vessel construction, repair, operation or maintenance inspection. **Examination:** Yes. **Fees:** $20 exam fee. $50 license fee. $25 renewal fee.

1779

Building Inspector
Dept. of Housing, Building and Construction
1047 U.S. 127 South
Frankfort, KY 40601
Phone: (502)564-8048

Credential Type: Level I License. **Duration of License:** One year. **Requirements:** High school education, plus three years experience in a construction position or three years experience in an architect's or engineer's office performing building design or drafting duties; or associate's degree in a construction related subject; or bachelor's degree in architecture, fire science, engineering, or building technology; or successful passage of at least one examination module. **Examination:** Yes. **Fees:** $45 registration fee. $30 exam fee. $25 renewal fee.

Credential Type: Level II License. **Duration of License:** One year. **Requirements:** High school education, plus three years experience in a construction position or three years experience in an architect's or engineer's office performing building design or drafting duties; or associate's degree in a construction related subject; or bachelor's degree in architecture, fire science, engineering, or building technology; or successful passage of at least one examination module. **Examination:** Yes. **Fees:** $45 registration fee. $30 exam fee. $25 renewal fee.

1780

Electrical Inspector
Dept. of Housing, Building and
 Construction
1047 U.S. 127 South
Frankfort, KY 40601
Phone: (502)564-3626

Credential Type: License. **Requirements:** Ability to speak, read and write in English language and possess a general education level to perform duties. Five years work experience in the installation and/or design of all types of residential and commercial wiring systems installed in accordance with NEC standards. **Examination:** Yes. **Fees:** $25 application fee. $25 renewal fee.

1781

Elevator Inspector
Dept. of Housing, Building and
 Construction
1047 U.S. 127 South
Frankfort, KY 40601
Phone: (502)564-3626

Credential Type: License. **Requirements:** High school diploma or Certificate of Competency. 18 years of age. **Examination:** Yes. **Reciprocity:** No. **Fees:** $10 exam fee.

1782

Fire Alarm System Inspector
Dept. of Housing, Building and
 Construction
1047 U.S. 127
Frankfort, KY 40601
Phone: (502)564-3626

Credential Type: License. **Requirements:** Within the five years preceding application, individual should have a minimum of 18 months experience in the installation, repair or testing of fire alarm systems. Educational courses and special training courses may be substituted for experience. **Examination:** Yes. **Fees:** $25 exam fee.

1783

Plans & Specifications Inspector
Dept. of Housing, Building &
 Construction
1047 U.S. 127 South
Frankfort, KY 40601
Phone: (502)564-8048

Credential Type: License. **Duration of License:** One year. **Requirements:** High school diploma or GED, plus three years experience in a responsible, directly related construction position requiring the ability to effectively read and interpret building plans and specifications or three years experience in an architect's or engineer's office performing building design or drafting duties; or an associate degree in a construction related subject; or bachelor's degree architecture, engineering, fire science or building technology; or successful passage of at least one examination module listed: 1A, 1B, 3B, 4B, 1C and 3C. **Examination:** Yes. **Fees:** $30 exam fee. $45 registration fee. $25 renewal fee.

1784

Suppression System Inspector
Dept. of Housing, Building &
 Construction
U.S. 127 South
Frankfort, KY 40601
Phone: (502)564-3626

Credential Type: License. **Requirements:** 18 months experience in the installation, repair or testing of fire suppression systems. Educational courses and special training courses may be substituted for experience. "The Kentucky Fire Prevention Code—Standards of Safety" is the document the exam is based upon. **Examination:** Yes. **Fees:** $25 exam fee.

Louisiana

1785

Boiler Inspector/Director of Boiler Inspections
State Board of Boiler Examiners
Office of State Fire Marshall
Boiler Inspection Section
1033 N. Lobdell Blvd.
Baton Rouge, LA 70806
Phone: (504)925-4911

Credential Type: License. **Duration of License:** One year. **Requirements:** High school diploma or equivalent. Must maintain a valid National Board Commission. **Fees:** $40 license fee. $20 renewal fee.

Massachusetts

1786

Asbestos Inspector
Dept. of Labor and Industries
Bureau of Technical Services
100 Cambridge St., Rm. 1101
Boston, MA 02202-0003
Phone: (617)727-1932
Phone: (617)727-1933

Credential Type: Certification. **Requirements:** Complete required training. Have at least six months work experience in a comparable occupation or two months field experience under the supervision of a certified asbestos inspector or management planner. **Fees:** $300 certification fee. (If one person is applying for certification as both an Asbestos Inspector and an Asbestos Management Planner, only one $300 certification fee is required.) **Governing Statute:** M.G.L. c149, ss 6-6F. 453 CMR 6.01 ff.

Michigan

1787

Asbestos Abatement Inspector
Asbestos Licensing
Div. of Occupational Health
Dept. of Public Health
3423 N. Logan
PO Box 30195
Lansing, MI 48909
Phone: (517)335-8000

Credential Type: Accreditation. **Duration of License:** One year. **Requirements:** At least one year of experience in asbestos-related work or not less than five years of supervising experience in school building operations and maintenance. Pass an Environmental Protection Agency (EPA) or state accredited three-day Asbestos Inspector Course. Renewal requires completion of a half-day refresher training course. **Examination:** Written exam. **Reciprocity:** Reciprocity may be granted if the requirements of the other state are equal to or exceed those of Michigan and the individual submits a certificate of successful completion of training from the other state. **Fees:** $150 initial accreditation fee. $75 renewal fee. $150 reciprocity fee. **Governing Statute:** Asbestos Workers Accreditation Act, Act 440 of 1988.

1788

Boiler Inspector
Boiler Div.
Bureau of Construction Codes
Dept. of Labor
7150 Harris Dr.
PO Box 30015
Lansing, MI 48909
Phone: (517)322-1287

Credential Type: License. **Duration of License:** One year. **Authorization:** Must be both licensed and certified competent. **Requirements:** Must be certified competent according to the National Board of Boiler and Pressure Vessel Inspectors Inspection Code. Must be employed by a company authorized to insure against loss from explosion of boilers or by a city having an authorized boiler inspection department. **Examination:** No separate licensing examination. **Exemptions:** Boiler inspectors employed by the City of Detroit are licensed by the city. **Reciprocity:** Yes. **Fees:** $30 fee covers exam, license, and certificate of competency. $15 license renewal fee. $30 reciprocity fee. **Governing Statute:** Boiler Act, Act 290 of 1965.

Credential Type: Certification. **Duration of License:** Permanent. **Authorization:** Must be both licensed and certified competent. **Requirements:** Requirements for certification include three years of practical experience in the design, construction, or operation of high pressure boilers as a mechanical engineer, steam engineer, or boilermaker, or at least three years of inspection experience as an inspector of high pressure boilers. A credit of two years of the required experience will be given to applicants holding an engineering degree from an accredited college of engineering. **Examination:** Written certification examination of the National Board of Boiler and Pressure Vessel Inspectors. **Fees:** $30 fee covers exam, license, and certificate of competency. **Governing Statute:** Boiler Act, Act 290 of 1965.

1789

Building (Construction) Official
Building Officials Advisory Board
Bureau of Construction Codes
Dept. of Labor
7150 Harris Dr.
PO Box 30015
Lansing, MI 48909
Phone: (517)322-1287

Credential Type: Registration. **Duration of License:** Three years. **Requirements:** Submit documentation confirming governmental employment with the duties of building official. Proposed requirement of at least two years work experience as a registered inspector (building, electrical, mechanical, or plumbing) or construction plan reviewer. **Fees:** $10 initial registration fee. $10 renewal fee, per year. **Governing Statute:** Building Officials and Inspectors Registration Act, Act 54 of 1986.

1790

Construction Plan Reviewer
Plan Review Div.
Bureau of Construction Codes
Dept. of Labor
7150 Harris Dr.
PO Box 30015
Lansing, MI 48909
Phone: (517)322-1287

Credential Type: Registration. **Duration of License:** Three years. **Requirements:** Three years of experience in the interpretation of construction plans; or be a Michigan licensed Architect or Engineer; or have a bachelor's degree in architecture or engineering and two years working experience; or have an appropriate trade license (such as Electrical Contractor, Mechanical Contractor, Master Plumber, Residential Builder, or Residential Maintenance and Alteration Contractor). **Fees:** $10 initial registration fee, per year. $10 renewal fee, per year. **Governing Statute:** Building Officials and Inspectors Registration Act, Act 54 of 1986.

1791

Elevator Inspector
Elevator Safety Board
Elevator Div.
Bureau of Construction Codes
Dept. of Labor
PO Box 30015
7150 Harris Dr.
Lansing, MI 48909
Phone: (517)322-1287

Credential Type: General Elevator Inspector Certification and Commission. **Duration of License:** One year (commission). **Authorization:** General Elevator Inspectors are employed by the state. **Requirements:** Must be certified competent by the Elevator Safety Board of the Department of Labor. Have three years of experience in elevator construction. Provide two letters of reference. After receiving certificate of competency, applicant is eligible for an annual commission. **Examination:** Written and oral certification exam. **Fees:** $27 certification exam and certificate of competency fee. No commission fee. **Governing Statute:** Michigan Elevator Act, Act 227 of 1967, as amended.

Credential Type: Special Elevator Inspector Certification and Commission. **Duration of License:** One year (commission). **Authorization:** Special Elevator Inspectors are employed by insurance companies or municipalities. **Requirements:** Must be certified competent by the Elevator Safety Board of the Department of Labor. Three years of experience in designing, installing, maintaining, or inspecting elevators. Provide two letters of reference. After receiving certificate of competency, applicant is eligible for an annual commission. **Examination:** Written and oral certification exam. **Fees:** $27 certification exam and certificate of competency fee. $16 initial commission fee. $11 renewal fee. **Governing Statute:** Michigan Elevator Act, Act 227 of 1967, as amended.

1792

Inspector (Building, Electrical, Mechanical, and Plumbing)
Bureau of Construction Codes
Dept. of Labor
7150 Harris Dr.
PO Box 30015
Lansing, MI 48909
Phone: (517)322-1287

Credential Type: Registration. **Duration of License:** Three years. **Requirements:** Submit documentation confirming governmental employment with the duties of inspector. Proposed requirements: (A) Have at least four years work experience in the construction trades, if applying for building inspector registration. (B) Be licensed as an electrician (journey level) for at least two years or be licensed as a master electrician, if applying for electrical inspector registration. (C) Be licensed (not by the State of Michigan) at the journey level in the trade as a journey worker, if applying for mechanical inspection registration. (D) Be licensed as a plumber (journey level) for at least two years or be licensed as a master plumber, if applying for plumbing inspection registration. **Fees:** $10 initial registration fee, per year. $10 renewal fee, per year. **Governing Statute:** Building Officials and Inspectors Registration Act, Act 54 of 1986.

Mississippi

1793

Asbestos Inspector
Dept. of Environmental Quality
Office of Pollution Control
PO Box 10385
Jackson, MS 39289-0385
Phone: (601)961-5100

Credential Type: Certification. **Duration of License:** One year. **Requirements:** Must have a high school or GED diploma. Must attend an EPA approved three-day inspector's course. Training must be continuous for recertification. **Examination:** EPA-approved examination for inspector certification. **Exemptions:** Certification not required for federally owned buildings or small-scale, short duration activities. **Reciprocity:** No reciprocity. **Fees:** $100 license fee. $100 renewal fee.

Montana

1794

Asbestos Inspector
Dept. of Health and Environmental Sciences
Health Services Div.
Occupational Health Bureau
1400 Broadway
Cogswell Bldg.
Helena, MT 59620
Phone: (406)444-3671

Credential Type: License and Accreditation. **Duration of License:** One year. **Requirements:** Contact licensing body for application information. Renewal requires completing a refresher course. **Fees:** $100 annual license fee. **Governing Statute:** Montana Code Annotated 75-2.

Nebraska

1795

Boiler/Boilerhouse Inspector
Div. of Safety, Boiler Section
301 Centennial Mall S.
PO Box 95024
Lincoln, NE 68509
Phone: (402)471-4721

Credential Type: License. **Duration of License:** Two years. **Requirements:** Must have at least 10 years experience in construction, installation, repair, and inspection of boilers. **Examination:** Yes. **Fees:** $30 examination fee. $20 initial renewal fee. $10 renewal fee.

1796

Elevator Inspections Manager
Nebraska Dept. of Labor
PO Box 95024
301 Centennial Mall S.
Lincoln, NE 68509
Phone: (402)471-2239

Credential Type: License. **Duration of License:** One year. **Requirements:** Must have at least five years experience at the journeyman level in elevator installation, maintenance, and inspection. **Examination:** Yes. **Fees:** $100 certification fee. $750 examination fee. $75 membership renewal fee. $35 regisration renewal fee.

New Jersey

1797

Building Inspector
New Jersey Dept. of Community Affairs
Bureau of Technical Services
CN816
Trenton, NJ 08625-0816
Phone: (609)530-8803

Credential Type: Residential and Small Commercial (RCS) License. **Requirements:** Three years of experience in construction design or supervision as a journeyman in a skilled trade; or three years of experience as a construction contractor; or three years of experience as a building inspector, housing inspector, or building inspector trainee; or an associate's degree in code enforcement and one year of experience; or a bachelor's degree in architecture, architectural technology, engineering, or engineering technology; or a current state license to practice as an architect or engineer. Applicant's without a degree must complete an approved RCS course. **Examination:** Yes. **Fees:** $30 license fee. **Governing Statute:** NJSA 52:27D. NJAC 5:23-1.

Credential Type: Industrial and Commercial (ICS) License. **Requirements:** Five years of experience; or an associate's degree and two years of experience; or a bachelor's degree and one year of experience; or a state license to practice architecture or engineering. Applicants without a degree must complete an approved ICS course. **Examination:** Yes. **Fees:** $30 license fee. **Governing Statute:** NJSA 52:27D. NJAC 5:23-1.

Credential Type: High-Rise Hazardous Structures (HHS) License. **Requirements:** Seven years of experience; or an associate's degree and three years of experience; or a bachelor's degree and two years of experience; or a state license in architecture or engineering. Applicants without a degree must complete an approved HHS course. **Examination:** Yes. **Fees:** $30 license fee. **Governing Statute:** NJSA 52:27D. NJAC 5:23-1.

1798

Construction Code Official
New Jersey Dept. of Community Affairs
Bureau of Technical Services
CN816
Trenton, NJ 08625-0816
Phone: (609)530-8803

Credential Type: Subcode Official License.

1799

Electrical Inspector
New Jersey Dept. of Community Affairs
Bureau of Technical Services
CN816
Trenton, NJ 08625-0816
Phone: (609)530-8803

Credential Type: Industrial and Commercial Structures (ICS) License. **Requirements:** Five years of appropriate experience; or an associate's degree in code enforcement and two years of experience; or a bachelor's degree in architecture, architectural technology, engineering or engineering technology and one year of experience. Applicants without a degree must complete the appropriate inspector course. **Examination:** Yes. **Fees:** $30 license fee. **Governing Statute:** NJSA 52:27D. NJAC 5:23-1.

Credential Type: High-Rise and Hazardous Structures (HHS) License. **Requirements:** Seven years of appropriate experience; or an associate's degree and three years of experience; or a bachelor's degree and two years of experience; or a New Jersey license to practice architecture or engineering. Applicants without a degree must complete the appropriate inspector course. **Examination:** Yes. **Fees:** $30 license fee. **Governing Statute:** NJSA 52:27D. NJAC 5:23-1.

1800

Fire Protection Inspector
New Jersey Dept. of Community Affairs
Bureau of Technical Services
CN816
Trenton, NJ 08625-0816
Phone: (609)530-8803

Credential Type: Residential and Small Commercial (RCS) License. **Requirements:** Three years of experience in the fire service or as a registered Fire Protection Inspector Trainee and successful completion of the approved training course. **Examination:** Written. **Fees:** $30 license fee. **Governing Statute:** NJSA 52:27D. NJAC 5:23-1.

Credential Type: Industrial and Commercial (ICS) License. **Requirements:** Five years of fire service experience as an officer, inspector or firefighter, or three years of experience as a contractor or journeyman in a regulated skilled trade and two years in the fire service, plus the completion of the approved training course. **Examination:** Written. **Fees:** $30 license fee. **Governing Statute:** NJSA 52:27D. NJAC 5:23-1.

Credential Type: High-Rise and Hazardous Site (HHS) License. **Requirements:** Seven years of fire service experience as an officer, inspector or firefighter, or five years of experience as a contractor or journeyman in a regulated skilled trade and two years in the fire service, plus completion of the approved training course. **Examination:** Written. **Fees:** $30 license fee. **Governing Statute:** NJSA 52:27D. NJAC 5:23-1.

1801

Plumbing Inspector
New Jersey Dept. of Community Affairs
Div. of Housing Development
CN816
Trenton, NJ 08625-0816
Phone: (609)530-8803

Credential Type: Industrial and Commercial Structure (ICS) Plumbing Inspector License. **Requirements:** Five years of experience; or two years experience and an associate's degree in code enforcement; or one year of experience and a bachelor's degree in architecture, architectural technology, engineering or engineering technology; or a New Jersey license as an architect or engineer plus completion of an approved training program. One technical CEU of continuing education is required for license renewal. **Examination:** Yes. **Fees:** $30 license fee. **Governing Statute:** NJSA 52:27D. NJAC 5:23-1.

Credential Type: High-Rise and Hazardous Structure (HHS) Plumbing Inspector License. **Requirements:** Seven years of experience; or three years experience and an associate's degree; or a New Jersey license as an architect or engineer plus completion of an approved training course. **Examination:** Yes. **Fees:** $30 license fee. **Governing Statute:** NJSA 52:27D. NJAC 5:23-1.

New York

1802

Boiler Inspector (Boiler and Pressure Vessel Inspector)
New York State Dept. of Labor
Boiler Safety Bureau
State Office Campus, Bldg. 12, Rm. 134
Albany, NY 12240-0102
Phone: (518)457-2722

Credential Type: Certificate. **Duration of License:** One year. **Requirements:** Bachelor's Degree in Mechanical Engineering plus one year of experience. Or Associate's Degree in Mechanical Technology plus two years of experience. Or High School Diploma plus three years of experience in operating boiler/pressure vessels. Must be employed by a state licensed insurance ageny to work as a boiler inspector in the private sector. **Examination:** Two day exam. Math and practical questions. **Fees:** $50 exam fee. $20 license fee. **Governing Statute:** Section 204 of the New York State Labor Law.

North Carolina

1803

Boiler Inspector
Dept. of Labor
Boiler and Pressure Vessel Div.
4 W. Edenton St.
Raleigh, NC 27601
Phone: (919)733-3034

Credential Type: License. **Duration of License:** One year. **Requirements:** High school diploma or equivalent. 18 years of age. Three years of experience with boilers and pressure vessels; or an equivalent combination of education and experience. **Examination:** National exam. **Fees:** $5 certification fee. $20 exam fee. $25 renewal fee.

1804

Building Inspector
Dept. of Insurance
Div. of Engineering and Building Codes
PO Box 26387
Raleigh, NC 27611
Phone: (919)733-3901

Credential Type: License. **Duration of License:** One year. **Requirements:** High school diploma or equivalent. Presently employed by a state or local governmental agency. At least one year of technical or trade school training, or an apprenticeship program in building construction, or six months of work under the direct supervision of a certified building inspector. There are also various alternatives to these requirements. **Examination:** 200 multiple choice questions. **Fees:** $20 application fee. $10 renewal fee.

1805

Mechanical Inspector
Dept. of Insurance
Div. of Engineering and Building Codes
PO Box 26387
Raleigh, NC 27611
Phone: (919)733-3901

Credential Type: Certification. **Duration of License:** One year. **Requirements:** High school diploma or equivalent. Currently employed by a state or local government department or agency. Completion of one year of technical or trade school, or six months under the direct supervision of a certified mechanical inspector. **Examination:** Written. **Fees:** $20 initial fee. $10 renewal fee.

1806

Plumbing Inspector
Dept. of Insurance
Div. of Engineering and Building Codes
PO Box 26387
Raleigh, NC 27611
Phone: (919)733-3901

Credential Type: License. **Duration of License:** One year. **Requirements:** High school diploma or equivalent. Must be presently employed by a state or local government department or agency. Completion of one year of trade or technical school training; or an apprenticeship program in plumbing; or six months of work experience under the direct supervision of a standard certified plumbing inspector. There are alternatives to these requirements. **Examination:** 200 multiple choice questions. **Fees:** $20 application fee. $10 renewal fee.

North Dakota

1807

Asbestos Abatement Inspector
State Dept. of Health and
  Consolidated Laboratories
Box 5520
1200 Missouri Ave.
Bismarck, ND 58502-5520
Phone: (701)224-5188

Credential Type: Asbestos Abatement Inspector License. **Duration of License:** One year. **Requirements:** Complete an EPA-approved Asbestos Abatement Inspector Course. Renewal requires attendance at annual refresher course. **Examination:** Written examination given as part of course. **Exemptions:** In-house non-public employees. Public employees and contractor employees disturbing less than three square feet or three line feet of asbestos-containing material. **Reciprocity:** All EPA-approved courses are recognized as acceptable. **Fees:** $25 license fee per discipline.

Ohio

1808

**Automatic Sprinkler System
  Inspector**
Board of Building Standards
Dept. of Industrial Relations
2323 W. 5th Ave.
PO Box 825
Columbus, OH 43266-0567
Phone: (614)644-2613

Credential Type: Class IV Automatic Sprinkler System Inspector Certification. **Duration of License:** Three years. **Requirements:** Have three years of automatic sprinkler system installation experience or at least three years of inspection experience with a certified building department. A maximum of two years as a certified automatic sprinkler system designer may be substituted for two of the required three years of experience. **Examination:** Board-administered examination. **Fees:** $30 certification fee.

1809

Boiler Inspector
Div. of Boiler Inspection
Dept. of Industrial Relations
2323 W. 5th Ave.
PO Box 825
Columbus, OH 43266-0567
Phone: (614)644-2236

Credential Type: Boiler Inspector Certification. **Duration of License:** Three years. **Requirements:** Submit application and pass examination for competency. **Examination:** Examination for Boiler and Pressure Piping Vessel Inspector. **Fees:** $50 exam fee. **Governing Statute:** Ohio Revised Code 4104.07.

1810

Building Inspector
Board of Building Standards
Dept. of Industrial Relations
2323 W. 5th Ave.
PO Box 825
Columbus, OH 43266-0567
Phone: (614)644-2613

Credential Type: Class III Building Inspector Certification. **Duration of License:** Three years. **Requirements:** Have three years of related trades, general construction, or prior building inspection experience with a certified building department. (Experience related to 1, 2, or 3-family structures does not count.) A maximum of two academic years of related vocational or technical education may be substituted for two of the required three years of experience. **Examination:** BOCA International examination, modules 1-A, 1-B, and 3-B. **Fees:** $30 certification fee.

Credential Type: Class III Trainee Certification. **Duration of License:** Three years. **Authorization:** Must work under the direct supervision of a Class III certified individual. **Requirements:** Have three years of related trades, general construction, or prior building inspection experience with a certified building department. (Experience related to 1, 2, or 3-family structures does not count.) A maximum of two academic years of related vocational or technical education may be substituted for two of the required three years of experience. **Examination:** Examination requirement to be completed within alloted time of the trainee program. **Fees:** $30 certification fee.

1811

Building Official
Board of Building Standards
Dept. of Industrial Relations
2323 W. 5th Ave.
PO Box 825
Columbus, OH 43266-0567
Phone: (614)644-2613

Credential Type: Class I Building Official Certification. **Duration of License:** Three years. **Requirements:** Meet one of the following sets of requirements: (1) Hold an Ohio Registration as an architect or engineer. Have five years of experience in building design and construction or building inspection with a certified building department. (Experience related to 1, 2, or 3-family structures does not count.) (2) Have 10 years experience as a contractor or superintendent of building construction or building inspection with a certified building department. (Experience related to 1, 2, or 3-family structures does not count.) **Examination:** Council of American Building Officials (CABO) examination covering management, legal, and technical modules. **Fees:** $30 certification fee.

1812

Electrical Safety Inspector
Board of Building Standards
Dept. of Industrial Relations
2323 W. 5th Ave.
PO Box 825
Columbus, OH 43266-0567
Phone: (614)644-2613

Credential Type: Electrical Safety Inspector Certification. **Duration of License:** Three years. **Requirements:** Submit application and pass examination for competency. **Examination:** Electrical Safety Inspector Examination. **Fees:** $300 exam fee.

1813

Elevator Inspector
Div. of Elevator Inspection
Dept. of Industrial Relations
2323 W. 5th Ave.
PO Box 825
Columbus, OH 43266-0567
Phone: (614)644-2244

Credential Type: Elevator Inspector Certification. **Duration of License:** Three years. **Requirements:** Submit application and pass examination for competency. **Examination:** General Inspector Examination. **Fees:** $50 exam fee. **Governing Statute:** Ohio Revised Code 4105.02.

1814

HVAC Inspector (Mechanical)
Board of Building Standards
Dept. of Industrial Relations
2323 W. 5th Ave.
PO Box 825
Columbus, OH 43266-0567
Phone: (614)644-2613

Credential Type: HVAC Inspector Certification. **Duration of License:** Three years. **Requirements:** Have three years of HVAC trade experience or HVAC systems review and inspection with a certified building department. (Experience related to 1, 2, or 3-family structures does not count.) A maximum of two academic years of related vocational or technical education may be substituted for two of the required three years of experience. **Examination:** BOCA International examination, modules 4-A and 4-B. **Fees:** $30 certification fee.

Credential Type: HVAC Inspector Trainee Certification. **Duration of License:** Three years. **Authorization:** Must work under the direct supervision of a HVAC certified inspector. **Requirements:** Have three years of HVAC trade experience or HVAC systems review and inspection with a certified building department. (Experience related to 1, 2, or 3-family structures does not count.) A maximum of two academic years of related vocational or technical education may be substituted for two of the required three years of experience. **Examination:** Examination requirement to be completed within alloted time of the trainee program. **Fees:** $30 certification fee.

1815

Piping System Inspector
Div. of Pressure Piping Inspection
Dept. of Industrial Relations
2323 W. 5th Ave.
PO Box 825
Columbus, OH 43266-0567
Phone: (614)644-2250

Credential Type: Piping System Inspector Certification. **Duration of License:** Three years. **Requirements:** Submit application and pass examination for competency. **Examination:** Piping System Inspector Examination. **Fees:** $25 exam fee. **Governing Statute:** Pressure Piping Systems Code, Chap. 4101:8-11.

1816

Plans Examiner
Board of Building Standards
Dept. of Industrial Relations
2323 W. 5th Ave.
PO Box 825
Columbus, OH 43266-0567
Phone: (614)644-2613

Credential Type: Class II Plans Examiner Certification. **Duration of License:** Three years. **Requirements:** Hold an Ohio Registration as an architect or engineer. Have five years of experience in building design and construction or building inspection with a certified building department. (Experience related to 1, 2, or 3-family structures does not count.) **Fees:** $30 certification fee.

Credential Type: Class II Trainee Certification. **Duration of License:** Three years. **Authorization:** Must work under the direct supervision of a Class II certified individual. **Requirements:** Be a graduate architect or engineer from an accredited university. **Fees:** $30 certification fee.

Oklahoma

1817

Building Inspector
State Dept. of Health
Occupational Licensing Div.
1000 N.E. 10th St.
PO Box 53551
Oklahoma City, OK 73152
Phone: (405)271-4953

Credential Type: License. **Duration of License:** One year. **Requirements:** Four hours of continuing education each year. **Examination:** There is no state exam. The applicant must submit certification by a National Code organization such as the Building Officials and Code Administration (BOCA), which requires the Building Officials and Code Administration Examination. **Exemptions:** Building inspectors working in cities with populations less than 10,000 do not need a license. **Fees:** $25 license fee. $25 renewal fee.

1818

Electrical Inspector
State Dept. of Health
Occupational Licensing Div.
1000 N.E. Tenth
PO Box 53551
Oklahoma City, OK 73152
Phone: (405)271-4953

Credential Type: License. **Duration of License:** One year. **Requirements:** Four hours of continuing education per year. Five years of experience practical experience in cities with a population greater than 4,000. **Examination:** There is no state exam. The applicant must submit certification by a National Code organization such as the Building Officials and Code Administration (BOCA), which requires the Building Officials and Code Administration Examination. **Exemptions:** Electrical inspectors working in cities with populations less than 10,000 do not need a license. **Fees:** $25 license fee. $25 renewal fee.

1819

Mechanical Inspector
State Dept. of Health
Occupational Licensing Div.
1000 N.E. Tenth
PO Box 53551
Oklahoma City, OK 73152
Phone: (405)271-4953

Credential Type: License. **Duration of License:** One year. **Requirements:** Four hours of state-approved courses in the mechanical trade per year. **Examination:** There is no state exam. The applicant must submit certification by a National Code organization such as the Building Officials Code Administration (BOCA) which requires the Building Officials and Code Examination. **Exemptions:** Mechanical inspectors working in cities with populations less than 10,000 do not need a license. **Fees:** $25 license fee. $25 renewal fee.

1820

Plumbing Inspector
State Dept. of Health
Occupational Licensing Div.
1000 N.E. 10th
PO Box 53551
Oklahoma City, OK 73152
Phone: (405)271-4953

Credential Type: License. **Duration of License:** One year. **Requirements:** Four hours of continuing education per year. Five years of practical experience in cities with a population larger than 4,000. **Examination:** There is no state exam. The applicant must submit certification by a National Code organization such as Building Officials and Code Administration (BOCA) which requires the Building Officials and Code Administration Examination. **Exemptions:** Inspectors working in cities with populations less than 10,000 must obtain a state license. **Fees:** $25 license fee. $25 renewal fee.

Oregon

1821

Amusement Ride Inspector
Building Codes Agency
1535 Edgewater NW
Salem, OR 97310
Phone: (503)373-1268

Credential Type: Certificate. **Requirements:** Must have two years of experience with an insurance company as an amusement ride inspector; or have two years experience inspecting amusement rides and enforcing amusement ride codes while employed by a governmental body regulating rides; or have not less than five years documented field operating maintenance experience with amusement rides and devices; or have not less than ten years documented practical experience in design, construction, matintenance, repair, field inspection and operation of amusement rides and devices as an authorized representative of a recognized manufacturer; or have a combination of training and experience deemed equivalent by the Director of the Building Codes Agency. **Fees:** $100 certification fee. **Governing Statute:** ORS 460.400.

1822

Building Official
Building Codes Agency
1535 Edgewater
Salem, OR 97310
Phone: (503)373-1268

Credential Type: License. **Requirements:** Complete application, and list work experience. **Examination:** Yes. **Fees:** $22 exam fee. **Governing Statute:** ORS 455.730 and Oregon Administrative Rule 814-03-025.

1823

Family Dwelling Electrical Inspector
Building Codes Agency
1535 Edgewater NW
Salem, OR 97310
Phone: (503)373-1268

Credential Type: Certificate. **Requirements:** Must have an Oregon Journeyman Electrician's license, or have equivalent experience and training required by a General Journeyman Electrician, or a minimum of one year inspection experience as a certified plumbing, mechanical or structural inspector. **Examination:** Yes. **Fees:** $22 exam fee. **Governing Statute:** ORS 479 and Administrative Rule 918-260-010.

1824

Limited Building Sewer Inspector
Building Codes Agency
1535 Edgewater NW
Salem, OR 97310
Phone: (503)373-1268

Credential Type: Certificate. **Requirements:** Must have a journeyman plumber license; or two years of experience in sewer design, installation or inspection; or experience and training equivalent and approved by the board. **Examination:** Yes. **Fees:** $22 exam fee. **Governing Statute:** ORS 455.730 and Oregon Administrative Rule 814-21-109(5).

1825

Manufactured Home Installation Inspector
Building Code Agency
1535 Edgewater NW
Salem, OR 97310
Phone: (503)373-1268

Credential Type: Certificate. **Requirements:** Must have two years experience as a supervisor in building construction industry; or have completed two years design work related to a building construction-related field of study; or have worked for two years as a certified building construction inspector; or have a one year certificate of completion in building inspection from a community college; or have completed two years of college education in a construction-related field; or complete an approved two and one-half month training program with a certified manufacturing home installation inspector; or have a combination of experience and education in the building construction industry equalling at least two years; and successfully complete an agency approved training program on manufacturing home installation standards. **Examination:** Yes. **Fees:** $22 exam fee. **Governing Statute:** ORS 446.230 to 446.240.

1826

Mechanical Inspector
Building Codes Agency
1535 Edgewater NW
Salem, OR 97310
Phone: (503)373-1268

Credential Type: Certificate. **Requirements:** Combination of training and experience on heating, ventilating and/or air conditioning (HVAC) equipment. **Examination:** Yes. **Fees:** $22 exam fee. **Governing Statute:** ORS 455.730 and Oregon Administrative Rule 814-03-025(A).

1827

Plans Examiner
Building Codes Agency
1535 Edgewater NW
Salem, OR 97310
Phone: (503)373-1268

Credential Type: License. **Requirements:** Combination of training and experience in building design and plans examination for building code compliance. At least one year of the required experience or education must have been within the last five years, or the applicant must have had relevant alternative experience or training during the past five years. **Examination:** Yes. **Fees:** $22 exam fee. **Governing Statute:** ORS 455.730 and Oregon Administrative Rule 814-03-025(A).

1828

Plumbing Inspector
Building Codes Agency
1535 Edgewater NW
Salem, OR 97310
Phone: (503)373-1268

Credential Type: Certificate. **Requirements:** Three years of experience as a journeyman plumber; or a degree in Mechanical Engineering or professional registration with two years work experience in plumbing design, installation or inspection; or five years experience inspecting plumbing installations or equivalent experience and training approved by the Plumbing Board. **Examination:** Yes. **Fees:** $22 exam fee. **Governing Statute:** ORS 455.730 and Oregon Administrative Rule 814-21-109(5).

1829

Structural Inspector
Building Codes Agency
1535 Edgewater NW
Salem, OR 97310
Phone: (503)373-1268

Credential Type: Certificate. **Examination:** Yes. **Fees:** $22 exam fee. **Governing Statute:** ORS 455.730 and Oregon Administrative Rule 814-03-025.

Rhode Island

1830

Elevator Inspector
Div. of Occupational Safety
Elevator Unit
220 Elmwood Ave.
Providence, RI 02907
Phone: (401)457-1860

Credential Type: Elevator Inspector License. **Duration of License:** Two years. **Requirements:** Must have a minimum of five years of mechanical and/or electrical experience and one year as an employee of a state enforcement authority. Hold a Qualified Elevator Inspector (QEI) certificate from the American Society of Mechanical Engineers or take written examination. **Reciprocity:** No. **Fees:** $10 examination/application fee. $10 application only fee. $5 biennial renewal fee.

South Dakota

1831

Electrical Inspector
South Dakota Electrical Commission
Dept. of Commerce and Regulation
125 West Capitol
Pierre, SD 57501
Phone: (605)773-3573
Phone: (605)224-8674
Phone: (800)233-7765

Credential Type: Electrical Inspector Registration and Permit. **Duration of License:** Two years. **Requirements:** Meet one of the following sets of requirements: (1) Must be a graduate of a recognized electrical and have four years experience in electrical work. (2) Have at least six years practical experience in electrical work.

Renewal requires 12 continuing education credits every two years. After July 1, 1994, the continuing education requirement will increase to 16 credits. **Examination:** Written exam for wiring permit. **Fees:** $40 permit fee. $40 exam fee. $40 renewal fee. **Governing Statute:** South Dakota Codified Laws, Chap. 36-16. Administrative Rules of South Dakota, Article 20:44.

Texas

1832

Air Monitoring Technician
Texas Dept. of Health
Occupational Health Div.
Asbestos Licensing Section
1100 W. 49th St.
Austin, TX 78756
Phone: (512)834-6600

Credential Type: Air Monitoring Technician License. **Duration of License:** One year. **Authorization:** License required to perform air monitoring services for an asbestos abatement project or related activity in a public building. **Requirements:** Completion of an approved training course for air monitoring technicians. Renewal requires completion of annual refresher training. Pass physical examination.

An upgraded license to perform analysis of airborne fibers in the field requires completion of the National Institute of Occupational Safety & Health No. 582 training course, or equivalent, titled "Analysis of Asbestos Dust" and current accreditation by the Asbestos Analyst Registry. **Fees:** $50 license fee. **Governing Statute:** Texas Civil Statutes, Article 4477-3a. Texas Asbestos Health Protection Rules, Section 295.

1833

Asbestos Inspector
Texas Dept. of Health
Occupational Health Div.
Asbestos Licensing Section
1100 W. 49th St.
Austin, TX 78756
Phone: (512)834-6600

Credential Type: Asbestos Inspector License. **Duration of License:** One year. **Authorization:** License required to conduct asbestos surveys in public buildings. If performing asbestos building surveys for hire, must be employed by a licensed asbestos consultant agency or licensed asbestos management planner. **Requirements:** High school graduate or a GED certificate. Completion of approved three-day training course for asbestos inspectors or annual refresher training. Renewal requires completing the annual refresher training course. Must pass physical examination. Must have professional liability insurance of at least $100,000 when doing work for hire, or be covered under employer's policy. Must have work experience of at least five asbestos surveys or current employment with and doing work under the supervision of a licensed management planner or asbestos consultant. **Fees:** $60 license fee. **Governing Statute:** Texas Civil Statutes, Article 4477-3a. Texas Asbestos Health Protection Rules, Section 295.

Virginia

1834

Asbestos Inspector
Dept. of Commerce
Asbestos Licensing Program
3600 W. Broad St.
Richmond, VA 23230
Phone: (804)367-2194

Credential Type: License. **Duration of License:** One year. **Requirements:** 18 years of age. Successful completion of asbestos workers training course. **Examination:** Yes. **Fees:** $35 license fee.

Washington

1835

Amusement Ride Inspector
Dept. of Labor & Industries
Building & Construction Safety
Inspection Services
General Administration Bldg., HC-101
Olympia, WA 98504
Phone: (206)753-6194

Credential Type: Amusement Ride Inspector Certificate. **Duration of License:** One year. **Requirements:** Meet one of the following requirements: (1) Have two years experience as an insurance company ride inspector; (2) Have two years experience as a ride inspector for a governmental body; (3) Have five years of documented field experience; (4) Have 10 years experience in design/construction of amusement ride equipment. **Fees:** $20 certificate fee.

1836

Boiler Inspector
Dept. of Labor & Industries
Building & Construction Safety
Inspection Services
General Administration Bldg., HC-101
Olympia, WA 98504
Phone: (206)586-0217

Credential Type: Boiler Inspector License. **Duration of License:** permanent. **Requirements:** High school graduate. Engineering degree or approved equivalent experience. Certificate of Competency. **Examination:** Written examination. **Reciprocity:** Yes. **Fees:** $40 Certificate of Competency fee. $10 annual Commission renewal fee. $25 reciprocal commission renewal fee.

1837

Electrical Administrator
Dept. of Labor and Industries
Building and Construction Safety
  Inspection Services
General Administration Bldg., HC-101
Olympia, WA 98504
Phone: (206)753-6807
Phone: (206)753-6307

Credential Type: Certification. **Duration of License:** Two years. **Requirements:** Complete approved training in electrical work, the National Electrical Code, electrical theory, and safety and administrative procedures. Continuing education required for renewal. **Examination:** Written examination. **Fees:** $25 application fee. $40 certification fee. $60 exam fee. $52 renewal fee.

Construction Contractors and Managers

The following states grant licenses in this occupational category as of the date of publication:

Alabama	Delaware	Illinois	Maryland	Nevada	Rhode Island	Washington
Alaska	District of	Indiana	Massachusetts	New Jersey	South Carolina	West Virginia
Arizona	Columbia	Iowa	Michigan	New Mexico	South Dakota	
Arkansas	Florida	Kansas	Minnesota	North Carolina	Tennessee	
California	Georgia	Kentucky	Mississippi	North Dakota	Texas	
Colorado	Hawaii	Louisiana	Montana	Oklahoma	Utah	
Connecticut	Idaho	Maine	Nebraska	Oregon	Virginia	

Alabama

1838

General Contractor
Licensing Board for General
  Contractors
125 S. Ripley St.
Montgomery, AL 36130
Phone: (205)242-2839

Credential Type: License. **Duration of License:** One year. **Requirements:** Must provide evidence of work experience, and must submit a certified financial statememt and names of professional associates for recommendations for licensing. **Fees:** $200 license fee. $100 renewal fee.

1839

Heating and Air Conditioning Contractor
Alabama State Board of Heating and
  Air Conditioning Contractors
421 S. McDonough St.
Montgomery, AL 36104
Phone: (205)242-5550

Credential Type: License. **Duration of License:** One year. **Requirements:** Must have knowledge of the trade. **Examination:** Written examination. **Fees:** $50 examination fee. $50 renewal fee.

Alaska

1840

Asbestos Abatement Contractor
Labor Dept.
Labor Standards and Safety Div.
Contractor Licensing Section
PO Box 107021
Anchorage AK, AK 99510-7021
Phone: (907)264-2435
Fax: (907)465-2974

Credential Type: License. **Requirements:** Must fulfill requirements of Specialty Construction Contractor and Asbestos Removal Worker.

1841

Construction Contractor, General
Dept. of Commerce and Economic
  Development
Div. of Occupational Licensing
Construction Contractor Section
PO Box D
Juneau, AK 99811-0800
Phone: (907)465-2546
Fax: (907)465-2974

Credential Type: Certificate of registration. **Duration of License:** Two years. **Requirements:** Submit evidence of public liability and property damage insurance. Submit evidence of workers' compensation insurance or explanation stating why workers' compensation insurance is not required. Surety bond in the amount of $10,000. **Fees:** $30 application fee. $180 license fee. **Governing Statute:** Alaska Statutes 08.18. Professional Regulations 12 AAC 21.

Credential Type: Residential Contractor Endorsement. **Duration of License:** Two years. **Requirements:** Hold certificate of registration as a general contractor. Pass a residential contractor examination offered by the department within six months preceding application. Within the two years preceding the date of application, complete either the Alaska craftsman home program sponsored by the Department of Community and Regional Affairs or its equivalent, or a postsecondary course in arctic engineering or its equivalent. Must not have been under sentence for an offense related to forgery, theft, extortion, conspiracy to defraud creditors, or a felony involving dishonesty within seven years preceding date of application.

An active general contractor in Alaska for three of the five years immediately preceding date of application may receive endorsement without examination.

Endorsement renewal requires proof of continued competency. **Examination:** Residential Contractor Examination. **Fees:** $30 application fee. $120 endorsement fee. $25 examination fee. **Governing Statute:** Alaska Statutes 08.18. Professional Regulations 12 AAC 21.

1842

Construction Contractor, Mechanical
Dept. of Commerce and Economic
  Development
Div. of Occupational Licensing
Construction Contractor Section
PO Box D
Juneau, AK 99811-0800
Phone: (907)465-2546
Fax: (907)465-2974

Credential Type: Certificate of registration. **Duration of License:** Two years. **Requirements:** Submit evidence of public liability and property damage insurance. Submit evidence of workers' compensation

Construction Contractors and Managers

insurance or explanation stating why workers' compensation insurance is not required. Surety bond in the amount of $5,000. Applicant must identify the contractor's mechanical administrator. **Fees:** $30 application fee. $180 license fee. **Governing Statute:** Alaska Statutes 08.18. Professional Regulations 12 AAC 21.

1843

Construction Contractor, Specialty
Dept. of Commerce and Economic Development
Div. of Occupational Licensing
Construction Contractor Section
PO Box D
Juneau, AK 99811-0800
Phone: (907)465-2546
Fax: (907)465-2974

Credential Type: Certificate of registration. **Duration of License:** Two years. **Requirements:** Submit evidence of public liability and property damage insurance. Submit evidence of workers' compensation insurance or explanation stating why workers' compensation insurance is not required. Surety bond in the amount of $5,000. If applicant is intending to bid on or perform electrical work, applicant must identify the contractor's electrical administrator. **Fees:** $30 application fee. $180 license fee. **Governing Statute:** Alaska Statutes 08.18. Professional Regulations 12 AAC 21.

1844

Electrical Administrator
Dept. of Commerce and Economic Development
Div. of Occupational Licensing
Board of Electrical Examiners
PO Box D
Juneau, AK 99811-0800
Phone: (907)465-2551
Fax: (907)465-2974

Credential Type: Inside Wiring Category. **Duration of License:** Two years. **Requirements:** One of the following education or experience requirements: (1) practical experience as a journeyman electrician in inside construction wiring for at least four of the six years immediately preceding date of application; or

(2) construction management experience in inside wiring as a field superintendent, field engineer, or similar position for at least four of the six years immediately preceding date of application; or

(3) a degree in electrical engineering from an accredited college or university plus practical experience as a journeyman electrician in inside construction wiring for at least one of the three years immediately preceding the date of application; or

(4) an Alaska registration as a professional electrical engineer plus management experience in the electrical construction industry as a field engineer, office engineer, or in a similar position for at least four of the six years immediately preceding date of application; or

(5) experience as a journeyman electrician in inside construction for three of the six years immediately preceding date of application and one year experience during those six years as a certified electrical inspector for a state or municipality or as a full-time electrical instructor at a school approved by the board.

Submit notarized Certificates of Support of experience and qualifications from three persons licensed in the electrical industry in any state.

Applicants licensed in another state and having taken a similar examination in another state may be granted a license by credentials without taking the Alaska examination.

License renewal requires at least one 8-hour continuing education workshop approved by the board which covers the National Electrical Code. **Examination:** Inside Wiring Examination. Applicant may not be examined for more than two electrical administrator's categories at any one scheduled examination. Passing the Inside Wiring Examination automatically qualifies the applicant to be licensed in the Residential Wiring category. **Fees:** $30 application fee. $50 examination fee. $250 license fee. **Governing Statute:** Alaska Statutes 08.40. Professional Regulations 12 AAC 32.

Credential Type: Inside Communications Category. **Duration of License:** Two years. **Requirements:** Practical experience as a journeyman in inside construction communications for at least two of the four years immediately preceding the date of application. Graduated from an accredited college or trade school in inside communication.

Submit notarized Certificates of Support of experience and qualifications from three persons employed, but not necessarily licensed, in the electrical industry in any state.

Applicants licensed in another state and having taken a similar examination in another state may be granted a license by credentials without taking the Alaska examination.

License renewal requires at least one 8-hour continuing education workshop approved by the board which covers the National Electrical Code. **Examination:** Inside Communications Examination. Applicant may not be examined for more than two electrical administrator's categories at any one scheduled examination. **Fees:** $30 application fee. $50 examination fee. $250 license fee. **Governing Statute:** Alaska Statutes 08.40. Professional Regulations 12 AAC 32.

Credential Type: Residential Wiring Category. **Duration of License:** Two years. **Requirements:** Practical experience as a journeyman residential wireman for at least two of the four years immediately preceding the date of application.

License renewal requires at least one 8-hour continuing education workshop approved by the board which covers the National Electrical Code. **Examination:** Residential Wiring Examination. Applicant may not be examined for more than two electrical administrator's categories at any one scheduled examination. Passing the Inside Wiring Examination automatically qualified the applicant to be licensed in the Residential Wiring category. **Fees:** $30 application fee. $50 examination fee. $250 license fee. **Governing Statute:** Alaska Statutes 08.40. Professional Regulations 12 AAC 32.

Credential Type: Outside Linework Category. **Duration of License:** Two years. **Requirements:** One of the following education or experience requirements: (1) practical experience as a journeyman electrician in outside construction linework for at least four of the six years immediately preceding date of application; or

(2) construction management experience in outside linework as a field superintendent, field engineer, or similar position for at least four of the six years immediately preceding date of application; or

(3) a degree in electrical engineering from an accredited college or university plus practical experience as a journeyman lineman in outside construction linework for at least one of the three years immediately preceding the date of application; or

(4) an Alaska registration as a professional electrical engineer plus management experience in the electrical construction industry as a field engineer, office engineer, or in a similar engineering position for at least four of the six years immediately preceding date of application; or

(5) experience as a journeyman lineman in outside construction for three of the six years immediately preceding date of application and one year experience during those six years as a certified electrical inspector for a state or municipality or as a full-time electrical instructor at a school approved by the board.

Electrical Administrator, continued

Submit notarized Certificates of Support of experience and qualifications from three persons licensed in the electrical industry in any state.

Applicants licensed in another state and having taken a similar examination in another state may be granted a license by credentials without taking the Alaska examination.

License renewal requires at least one 8-hour continuing education workshop approved by the board which covers the National Electrical Safety Code. **Examination:** Outside Linework Examination. Applicant may not be examined for more than two electrical administrator's categories at any one scheduled examination. **Fees:** $30 application fee. $50 examination fee. $250 license fee. **Governing Statute:** Alaska Statutes 08.40. Professional Regulations 12 AAC 32.

Credential Type: Outside Communications Category. **Duration of License:** Two years. **Requirements:** Practical experience as a journeyman in outside construction communications for at least two of the four years immediately preceding the date of application. Graduated from an accredited college or trade school in inside communication.

Submit notarized Certificates of Support of experience and qualifications from three persons employed, but not necessarily licensed, in the electrical industry in any state.

Applicants licensed in another state and having taken a similar examination in another state may be granted a license by credentials without taking the Alaska examination.

License renewal requires at least one 8-hour continuing education workshop approved by the board which covers the National Electrical Safety Code. **Examination:** Outside Communications Examination. Applicant may not be examined for more than two electrical administrator's categories at any one scheduled examination. **Fees:** $30 application fee. $50 examination fee. $250 license fee. **Governing Statute:** Alaska Statutes 08.40. Professional Regulations 12 AAC 32.

Credential Type: Controls and Control Wiring Category. **Duration of License:** Two years. **Requirements:** Hold a current Alaska license as a mechanical administrator. Practical experience as a journeyman installing low voltage controls for at least two of the four years preceding date of application. Construction management experience in low voltage control wiring as a field superintendent, field engineer, or similar position for at least four of the six years immediately preceding date of application; or an Alaska registration as an electrical or mechanical engineer plus management experience in the electrical or mechanical low voltage control wiring industry as a field engineer or office engineer for at least two of the four years immediately preceding date of application.

Submit notarized Certificates of Support of experience and qualifications from three persons licensed in the electrical industry in any state.

Applicants licensed in another state and having taken a similar examination in another state may be granted a license by credentials without taking the Alaska examination.

License renewal requires at least one 8-hour continuing education workshop approved by the board. **Examination:** Controls and Control Wiring Examination. Applicant may not be examined for more than two electrical administrator's categories at any one scheduled examination. **Fees:** $30 application fee. $50 examination fee. $250 license fee. **Governing Statute:** Alaska Statutes 08.40. Professional Regulations 12 AAC 32.

Arizona

1845

General Contractor
Registrar of Contractors
800 W. Washington, 6th Fl.
Phoenix, AZ 85007
Phone: (602)542-1502

Credential Type: General contractor license. **Authorization:** Covers residential, commercial, industrial and public works construction. Includes subcontractors, specialty contractors, floor covering contractors, landscape maintenance contractors, landscape contractors and consultants representing themselves. **Requirements:** Minimum of four years practical or management trade experience (2 of which must be within the last 10 years), a detailed financial statement, must not have had a license refused or revoked within a year prior to application. Bonding requirement: 1) contractors without a history of reporting transaction privilege tax in Arizona required to post a bond before a Transaction Privilege (Sales) Tax License is issued; 2) prime contractors based out-of-state entering into construction contracts of $50,000 or more must post a bond in an amount sufficient to cover the contractor's anticipated transaction privilege (sales) tax liability for the contract; 3) persons who are delinquent in payment of Arizona taxes or have had a history of delinquency for a previous business license. **Examination:** Written exam covering general knowledge of the building, safety, health and lien laws of the state and demonstration of understanding of the construction work and/or other related construction. **Reciprocity:** Arizona and California honor each other's licensing qualifications as long as applicants pass Arizona's Business Management Exam and California's Business and Law Exam. **Fees:** $600 General Commercial Contractor (includes General Engineering Contractor) license application and exam fee. $320 General commercial Contractor (includes General Engineering Contractor) license renewal fee. $400 Specialty Commercial Contractor license application and exam fee. $270 Specialty Commercial Contractor license renewal fee. $55 exam fee. **Governing Statute:** Arizona Statutes and Rules, November 1990, Chapter 10, Title 32.

1846

Manufactured Home Installer
Dept. of Building and Fire Safety
1540 W. Van Buren
Phoenix, AZ 85007
Phone: (602)255-4072

Credential Type: License. **Requirements:** Contact licensing body for application information. **Fees:** $40 application fee. $23 background investigation fee.

Arkansas

1847

Contractor
Contractors Licensing Board
621 East Capitol Ave.
Little Rock, AR 72202
Phone: (501)372-4661

Credential Type: License. **Requirements:** Five years of experience in type of work to be performed in Arkansas. Proof of financial responsibility. Furnish a list of equipment available for their use in performing their type of work. **Examination:** No **Fees:** $100 New application fee. $50 Renewal.

Construction Contractors and Managers

1848

Electrical Contractor
Arkansas Department of Labor
Board of Electrical Examiners
10421 W. Markham
Little Rock, AR 72205
Phone: (501)682-4547

Credential Type: License. **Duration of License:** One year. **Requirements:** Must meet the requirements of a master electrician or employ a master technician as a superintendent or manager. **Examination:** No **Fees:** $100 License. $100 Renewal.

California

1849

General Building Contractor
California State License Board
9835 Goethe Rd.
PO Box 26000
Sacramento, CA 95826
Phone: (916)366-5153
Phone: (916)327-9707
Phone: (800)321-CSLB

Credential Type: Contractor's license. **Duration of License:** Two years. **Requirements:** Must have at least four years experience within the past 10 years as a journeyman, foreman, supervising employee, or contractor in the class applied for. More than $2,500 worth of operating capital, proof of workers' compensation insurance coverage, file a Contractors Bond or cash deposit in the amount of $5,000 (except for Swimming Pool classification which requires $10,000) for the Responsible Managing Employee or the Responsible Managing Officer. **Examination:** Law and Business examination and second test covering the specific trade or certification area that the contractor is applying for. **Reciprocity:** California and Arizona honor each other's licensing qualifications as long as applicants pass Arizona's Business Management Exam and California's Business and Law Exam. Also reciprocity with Nevada and Utah. **Fees:** $150 application processing fee (plus $50 fee for each additional classification). $150 initial license fee. $200 renewal fee. **Governing Statute:** Business and Professions Code, Sections 7065-7068 and the Board Rule 816 (California Administrative Code).

1850

General Engineering Contractor
California State License Board
9835 Goethe Rd.
PO Box 26000
Sacramento, CA 95826
Phone: (916)366-5153
Phone: (916)327-9707
Phone: (800)321-CSLB

Credential Type: Contractor's license. **Duration of License:** Two years. **Authorization:** Covers contractors whose principal contracting business is in connection with fixed works requiring specialized engineering knowledge and skill. **Requirements:** Must have at least four years experience within the past 10 years as a journeyman, foreman, supervising employee, or contractor in the class applied for. More than $2,500 worth of operating capital, proof of workers' compensation insurance coverage, file a Contractors Bond or cash deposit in the amount of $5,000 (except for Swimming Pool classification which requires $10,000) for the Responsible Managing Employee or the Responsible Managing Officer. **Examination:** Law and Business examination and second test covering the specific trade or certification area that the contractor is applying for. **Reciprocity:** California and Arizona honor each other's licensing qualifications as long as applicants pass Arizona's Business Management Exam and California's Business and Law Exam. Also reciprocity with Nevada and Utah. **Fees:** $150 application processing fee (plus $50 fee for each additional classification). $150 initial license fee. $200 renewal fee. **Governing Statute:** Business and Professions Code, Sections 7065-7068 and the Board Rule 816 (California Administrative Code).

1851

Specialty Contractor
California State License Board
9835 Goethe Rd.
PO Box 26000
Sacramento, CA 95826
Phone: (916)366-5153
Phone: (916)327-9707
Phone: (800)321-CSLB

Credential Type: Contractor's license. **Duration of License:** Two years. **Authorization:** Issued in 37 license categories. Licenses are also issued in 60 limited specialty categories. **Requirements:** Must have at least four years experience within the past 10 years as a journeyman, foreman, supervising employee, or contractor in the class applied for. More than $2,500 worth of operating capital, proof of workers' compensation insurance coverage, file a Contractors Bond or cash deposit in the amount of $5,000 (except for Swimming Pool classification which requires $10,000) for the Responsible Managing Employee or the Responsible Managing Officer. **Examination:** Law and Business examination and second test covering the specific trade or certification area that the contractor is applying for. **Reciprocity:** California and Arizona honor each other's licensing qualifications as long as applicants pass Arizona's Business Management Exam and California's Business and Law Exam. Also reciprocity with Nevada and Utah. **Fees:** $150 application processing fee (plus $50 fee for each additional classification). $150 initial license fee. $200 renewal fee. **Governing Statute:** Business and Professions Code, Sections 7065-7068 and the Board Rule 816 (California Administrative Code).

Colorado

1852

Electrical Contractor
State Electrical Board
Dept. of Regulatory Agencies
Div. of Registrations
1390 Logan St., Ste. 400
Denver, CO 80203-2390
Phone: (303)894-2300

Credential Type: Electrical contractor registration. **Duration of License:** One year. **Requirements:** Register with the board, pay fee, and present evidence of compliance with state's worker's compensation and unemployment compensation laws. Either the owner or part owner of the contracting company must be a licensed master electrician, or a licensed master electrician must be employed by the contracting company. **Fees:** $100 annual license fee. **Governing Statute:** Colorado Revised Statutes Title 12, Article 23.

Connecticut

1853

Electrical Contractor
Electrical Work Examining Board
Occupational Licensing Div.
Consumer Protection Dept.
165 Capitol Ave.
Hartford, CT 06106
Phone: (203)566-3275

Credential Type: Unlimited electrical contractor's license. **Duration of License:** Two years. **Requirements:** Be of good moral character. Have an 8th grade education or equivalent. Must have served as an

Electrical Contractor, continued

electrical journeyman for not less than two years. If service was outside of state, must submit evidence that service was comparable to service in state or that applicant has education and experience and has passed an examination demonstrating competency to be an unlimited contractor. **Examination:** State licensure exam. **Reciprocity:** Yes, with selected states. **Fees:** $75 application fee. $150 license fee. **Governing Statute:** General Statutes of Connecticut, Chap. 393.

Credential Type: Limited electrical contractor's license (L-3). **Duration of License:** Two years. **Authorization:** May perform only work limited to cable splicing and its allied work. **Requirements:** Be of good moral character. Have an 8th grade education or equivalent. Must have served as an electrical journeyman for not less than two years. If service was outside of state, must submit evidence that service was comparable to service in state. **Examination:** State licensure exam. **Reciprocity:** Yes, with selected states. **Fees:** $75 application fee. $150 license fee. **Governing Statute:** General Statutes of Connecticut, Chap. 393.

Credential Type: Limited electrical contractor's license (L-5). **Duration of License:** Two years. **Authorization:** May perform only work limited to ADT, similar, or low voltage signal work, audio, and sound systems. Voltage of the system may not exceed 25 volts or five amperes, from a source of power supplied by others, and does not include wiring in new construction of buildings. **Requirements:** Be of good moral character. Have an 8th grade education or equivalent. Must have served as an electrical journeyman for not less than two years. If service was outside of state, must submit evidence that service was comparable to service in state. **Examination:** State licensure exam. **Reciprocity:** Yes, with selected states. **Fees:** $75 application fee. $150 license fee. **Governing Statute:** General Statutes of Connecticut, Chap. 393.

Credential Type: Limited electrical contractor's license (C-5). **Duration of License:** Two years. **Authorization:** May perform only work limited to ADT, similar, or low voltage signal work; audio and sound systems; or telephone-interconnect. Voltage of the system may not exceed 48 volts or five amperes, from a source of power supplied by others. **Requirements:** Be of good moral character. Have an 8th grade education or equivalent. Must have served two years as a registered apprentice, plus four years as a licensed journeyman. **Examination:** State licensure exam. **Reciprocity:** Yes, with selected states. **Fees:** $75 application fee. $150 license fee. **Governing Statute:** General Statutes of Connecticut, Chap. 393.

Credential Type: Limited electrical contractor's license (T-1). **Duration of License:** Two years. **Authorization:** May perform only work limited to telephone-interconnect systems and be from a source of power supplied by others. **Requirements:** Be of good moral character. Have an 8th grade education or equivalent. Must have served two years as a registered apprentice, plus four years as a licensed journeyman. **Examination:** State licensure exam. **Reciprocity:** Yes, with selected states. **Fees:** $75 application fee. $150 license fee. **Governing Statute:** General Statutes of Connecticut, Chap. 393.

1854

Elevator Contractor
Elevator Installation, Repair, and Maintenance Board
Occupational Licensing Div.
Consumer Protection Dept.
165 Capitol Ave.
Hartford, CT 06106
Phone: (203)566-3275

Credential Type: Unlimited contractor elevator craftsman's license (R-1). **Duration of License:** Two years. **Authorization:** Covers elevator installation, repair, and maintenance. **Requirements:** Be of good moral character. Have an 8th grade education or equivalent. Must have served as an journeyman elevator craftsman for not less than two years. If service was outside of state, must submit evidence that service was comparable to service in state or that applicant has education and experience and has passed an examination demonstrating competency to be an unlimited contractor. **Examination:** State licensure exam. **Reciprocity:** Yes, with selected states. **Fees:** $75 application fee. $150 license fee. **Governing Statute:** General Statutes of Connecticut, Chap. 393.

1855

Fire Protection Sprinkler Contractor
Fire Protection Sprinkler Systems Work Board
Occupational Licensing Div.
Consumer Protection Dept.
165 Capitol Ave.
Hartford, CT 06106
Phone: (203)566-3275

Credential Type: Unlimited fire protection sprinkler contractor license (F-1). **Duration of License:** Two years. **Requirements:** Be of good moral character. Have an 8th grade education or equivalent. Must have served at least two years as a F-2 journeyman or have equivalent experience. **Examination:** State licensure exam. **Reciprocity:** Yes, with selected states. **Fees:** $75 application fee. $150 license fee. **Governing Statute:** General Statutes of Connecticut, Chap. 393.

Credential Type: Limited fire protection sprinkler contractor license (F-3). **Duration of License:** Two years. **Authorization:** Limited to work involving foam extinguishing systems, special hazard systems, halon, and other liquid or gas fire suppression systems. **Requirements:** Be of good moral character. Have an 8th grade education or equivalent. Must have served at least two years as a F-4 journeyman or have equivalent experience. **Examination:** State licensure exam. **Reciprocity:** Yes, with selected states. **Fees:** $75 application fee. $150 license fee. **Governing Statute:** General Statutes of Connecticut, Chap. 393.

1856

Heating-Cooling Contractor
Heating, Piping, and Cooling Work Examining Board
Occupational Licensing Div.
Consumer Protection Dept.
165 Capitol Ave.
Hartford, CT 06106
Phone: (203)566-3275

Credential Type: Unlimited heating-cooling contractor's license (S-1). **Duration of License:** Two years. **Requirements:** Be of good moral character. Have an 8th grade education or equivalent. Must have served as an heating-cooling journeyman for not less than two years. If service was outside of state, must submit evidence that service was comparable to service in state or that applicant has education and experience and has passed an examination demonstrating competency to be an unlimited contractor. **Examination:** State licensure exam. **Reciprocity:** Yes, with selected states. **Fees:** $75 application fee. $150 license fee. **Governing Statute:** General Statutes of Connecticut, Chap. 393.

Credential Type: Limited heating-cooling contractor's license (S-3). **Duration of License:** Two years. **Authorization:** Limited to installation, repair, replacement, alteration, or maintenance of any apparatus of piping, appliances, devices, or accessories for heating systems and boilers, excluding sheet metal work, air conditioning, and refrigeration systems. May install hot, chilled, and condensed water, as well as steam piping in air conditioning systems. **Requirements:** Be of good moral character.

Construction Contractors and Managers

Connecticut

Have an 8th grade education or equivalent. Must have served one year as a heating-cooling apprentice, plus one year as a licensed journeyman. **Examination:** State licensure exam. **Reciprocity:** Yes, with selected states. **Fees:** $75 application fee. $150 license fee. **Governing Statute:** General Statutes of Connecticut, Chap. 393.

Credential Type: Limited heating-cooling contractor's license (S-5). **Duration of License:** Two years. **Authorization:** May perform only work limited to hot water or steam heating systems for buildings not over three stories high. Does not cover the installation or servicing of oil burners of any size. **Requirements:** Be of good moral character. Have an 8th grade education or equivalent. Must have served as a heating-cooling journeyman for not less than two years. If service was outside of state, must submit evidence that service was comparable to service in state. **Examination:** State licensure exam. **Reciprocity:** Yes, with selected states. **Fees:** $75 application fee. $150 license fee. **Governing Statute:** General Statutes of Connecticut, Chap. 393.

Credential Type: Limited heating-cooling contractor's license (S-7). **Duration of License:** Two years. **Authorization:** May perform only work limited to hot water or steam heating systems for buildings not over three stories high. May install or service oil burners handling up to five gallons per hour as well as gas piping for the work covered by this license. **Requirements:** Be of good moral character. Have an 8th grade education or equivalent. Must have served as a heating-cooling journeyman for not less than two years. If service was outside of state, must submit evidence that service was comparable to service in state. **Examination:** State licensure exam. **Reciprocity:** Yes, with selected states. **Fees:** $75 application fee. $150 license fee. **Governing Statute:** General Statutes of Connecticut, Chap. 393.

Credential Type: Limited heating-cooling contractor's license (B-1). **Duration of License:** Two years. **Authorization:** Permits the installation, service, and repair of gas or oil burners for domestic and light commercial installations consuming less than five gallons per hour. **Requirements:** Be of good moral character. Have an 8th grade education or equivalent. Must have served as a heating-cooling journeyman for not less than two years. If service was outside of state, must submit evidence that service was comparable to service in state. **Examination:** State licensure exam. **Reciprocity:** Yes, with selected states. **Fees:** $75 application fee. $150 license fee. **Governing Statute:** General Statutes of Connecticut, Chap. 393.

Credential Type: Limited heating-cooling contractor's license (B-3). **Duration of License:** Two years. **Authorization:** Permits the installation, service, and repair of any gas or oil fired burners. **Requirements:** Be of good moral character. Have an 8th grade education or equivalent. Must have served as a heating-cooling journeyman for not less than two years. If service was outside of state, must submit evidence that service was comparable to service in state. **Examination:** State licensure exam. **Reciprocity:** Yes, with selected states. **Fees:** $75 application fee. $150 license fee. **Governing Statute:** General Statutes of Connecticut, Chap. 393.

Credential Type: Limited heating-cooling contractor's license (D-1). **Duration of License:** Two years. **Authorization:** Permits the installation, service, repair, replacement, maintenance, or alteration of any warm air, air conditioning, and refrigeration system, including necessary piping and associated pumping equipment. Does not cover the installation or servicing of oil burners of any size. **Requirements:** Be of good moral character. Have an 8th grade education or equivalent. Must have served as a heating-cooling journeyman for not less than two years. If service was outside of state, must submit evidence that service was comparable to service in state. **Examination:** State licensure exam. **Reciprocity:** Yes, with selected states. **Fees:** $75 application fee. $150 license fee. **Governing Statute:** General Statutes of Connecticut, Chap. 393.

Credential Type: Limited heating-cooling contractor's license (D-3). **Duration of License:** Two years. **Authorization:** May perform only work limited to the installation, service, repair, replacement, maintenance, or alteration of all refrigeration systems included in food storage, air conditioning, and special process systems. **Requirements:** Be of good moral character. Have an 8th grade education or equivalent. Must have served as a heating-cooling journeyman for not less than two years. If service was outside of state, must submit evidence that service was comparable to service in state. **Examination:** State licensure exam. **Reciprocity:** Yes, with selected states. **Fees:** $75 application fee. $150 license fee. **Governing Statute:** General Statutes of Connecticut, Chap. 393.

Credential Type: Limited heating, piping and cooling contractor's license (G-1). **Duration of License:** Two years. **Authorization:** May perform only work limited to the installation, service, repair, replacement, maintenance, or alteration of gas piping systems and approved gas appliances, gas utilization equipment and accessories for use with LP gas. **Requirements:** Be of good moral character. Have an 8th grade education or equivalent. Must have served as a heating-cooling journeyman for not less than two years. If service was outside of state, must submit evidence that service was comparable to service in state. **Examination:** State licensure exam. **Reciprocity:** Yes, with selected states. **Fees:** $75 application fee. $150 license fee. **Governing Statute:** General Statutes of Connecticut, Chap. 393.

1857

Home Improvement Contractor
Occupational Licensing Div.
Consumer Protection Dept.
165 Capitol Ave.
Hartford, CT 06106
Phone: (203)566-3275

Credential Type: Certificate of registration. **Duration of License:** One year. **Requirements:** Submit application and pay fee. Post $10,000 surety bond. **Fees:** $60 application fee. $60 renewal fee. $100 guaranty fund fee. **Governing Statute:** Connecticut Statutes, Chap. 400.

1858

Irrigation Contractor
Plumbing and Piping Work
   Examining Board
Occupational Licensing Div.
Consumer Protection Dept.
165 Capitol Ave.
Hartford, CT 06106
Phone: (203)566-3275

Credential Type: Irrigation contractor's license. **Duration of License:** Two years. **Requirements:** Be of good moral character. Have an 8th grade education or equivalent. Have requisite skill and pass appropriate state licensure examination. **Examination:** State licensure exam. **Reciprocity:** Yes, with selected states. **Fees:** $75 application fee. $150 license fee. **Governing Statute:** General Statutes of Connecticut, Chap. 393.

1859

Plumbing-Piping Contractor
Plumbing and Piping Work
   Examining Board
Occupational Licensing Div.
Consumer Protection Dept.
165 Capitol Ave.
Hartford, CT 06106
Phone: (203)566-3275

Credential Type: Unlimited plumbing-piping contractor's license (P-1). **Duration of License:** Two years. **Requirements:** Be

Plumbing-Piping Contractor, continued

of good moral character. Have an 8th grade education or equivalent. Must have served as an plumbing-piping journeyman for not less than two years. If service was outside of state, must submit evidence that service was comparable to service in state or that applicant has education and experience and has passed an examination demonstrating competency to be an unlimited contractor. **Examination:** State licensure exam. **Reciprocity:** Yes, with selected states. **Fees:** $75 application fee. $150 license fee. **Governing Statute:** General Statutes of Connecticut, Chap. 393.

Credential Type: Contractor license—limited to gasoline station tanks and pumping equipment (P-9). **Duration of License:** Two years. **Authorization:** Limited to installation, repair, replacement, alteration, or maintenance of piping for gasoline tanks and related pumping equipment. **Requirements:** Be of good moral character. Have an 8th grade education or equivalent. Must have served one year as a plumbing-piping apprentice, plus one year as a licensed journeyman. **Examination:** State licensure exam. **Reciprocity:** Yes, with selected states. **Fees:** $75 application fee. $150 license fee. **Governing Statute:** General Statutes of Connecticut, Chap. 393.

Credential Type: Limited plumbing-piping contractor's license (J-1). **Duration of License:** Two years. **Authorization:** May perform only work limited to domestic water pumps and water conditioning. **Requirements:** Be of good moral character. Have an 8th grade education or equivalent. Must have served as a plumbing-piping journeyman for not less than two years. If service was outside of state, must submit evidence that service was comparable to service in state. **Examination:** State licensure exam. **Reciprocity:** Yes, with selected states. **Fees:** $75 application fee. $150 license fee. **Governing Statute:** General Statutes of Connecticut, Chap. 393.

Credential Type: Limited plumbing-piping contractor's license (W-9). **Duration of License:** Two years. **Authorization:** May perform only work limited to sewer and storm lines, from a point outside of a structure to the point of utility responsibility. **Requirements:** Be of good moral character. Have an 8th grade education or equivalent. Must have served as a plumbing-piping journeyman for not less than six months. **Examination:** State licensure exam. **Reciprocity:** Yes, with selected states. **Fees:** $75 application fee. $150 license fee. **Governing Statute:** General Statutes of Connecticut, Chap. 393.

Credential Type: Contractor license—limited to water, sewer, and storm lines (P-7). **Duration of License:** Two years. **Authorization:** Permits the installation, repair, replacement, alteration, or maintenance of piping limited to water, sewer, and storm lines from the point of utility reponsibility to a point immediately inside a structure. **Requirements:** Be of good moral character. Have an 8th grade education or equivalent. Must have served as a plumbing-piping apprentice for not less than one year, plus one year as a licensed journeyman. **Examination:** State licensure exam. **Reciprocity:** Yes, with selected states. **Fees:** $75 application fee. $150 license fee. **Governing Statute:** General Statutes of Connecticut, Chap. 393.

Credential Type: Contractor license—limited to lawn sprinkler lines (J-3). **Duration of License:** Two years. **Authorization:** Permits the installation, repair, replacement, alteration, or maintenance of lawn sprinkler systems. **Requirements:** Be of good moral character. Have an 8th grade education or equivalent. Must have served as a plumbing-piping apprentice for not less than one year, plus one year as a licensed journeyman.

1860

Solar Contractor
Heating, Piping, and Cooling Work Examining Board
Occupational Licensing Div.
Consumer Protection Dept.
165 Capitol Ave.
Hartford, CT 06106
Phone: (203)566-3275

Credential Type: Solar contractor's license. **Duration of License:** Two years. **Authorization:** Covers the installation, repair, replacement, alteration, or maintenance of an active, passive, or hybrid solar hot water heating system. **Requirements:** Be of good moral character. Have an 8th grade education or equivalent. Must have served as a solar journeyman for not less than two years. If service was outside of state, must submit evidence that service was comparable to service in state or that applicant has education and experience and has passed an examination demonstrating competency to be a solar contractor.

Heating-cooling contractors and plumbing-piping contractors who were licensed before July 1, 1984, or who have installed at least six fully operational solar hot water heating systems may be granted a solar contractor's license upon completion of state licensure examination. **Examination:** State licensure exam. **Reciprocity:** Yes, with selected states. **Fees:** $75 application fee. $150 license fee. **Governing Statute:** General Statutes of Connecticut, Chap. 393.

Delaware

1861

General Contractor
Division of Revenue
Carvel State Bldg.
820 N. French St.
Wilmington, DE 19801
Phone: (302)577-3369

Credential Type: General contractor license. **Duration of License:** One year. **Requirements:** Compliance with bonding requirements; compliance with unemployment and workers' compensation laws as enforced by the Department of Labor and Industrial Accident Board; register to obtain a Delaware Contractor's Business License and register as a Withholding Agent; mandatory compliance with both gross receipts and licensing provisions—Form 1280, Subcontractor Payments must be completed and attached to the gross receipts tax form for verification. Non-resident contractors (those who do not regularly maintain either a principal place of business or main office in Delaware) must also provide a Statement of Contracts awarded by general contractors, subcontractors, and construction managers; bond equal to six percent of the contract where a single contract/subcontract totals $20,000 or more—cash bonds are accepted for contracts totalling $20,000 but less than $100,000. **Fees:** $50 license fee. **Governing Statute:** Title 30, Delaware Code, chapter 25 and Chapter three (nonresident).

District of Columbia

1862

Electrical Contractor
License and Certification Div.
Occupational and Professional Licensure Administration
Consumer and Regulatory Affairs Dept.
PO Box 37200
Washington, DC 20013-7200
Phone: (202)727-7823
Phone: (202)727-7480

Alternate Information: 614 H St., NW, Washington, DC 20001

Credential Type: Electrical Contractor License. **Duration of License:** One year. **Requirements:** Must be licensed as a master electrician or have a master electrician as an employee, officer, or substantial stockholder. Post bond of $4,000. **Fees:** $50 application fee. $20 license fee. $60 annual renewal fee. **Governing Statute:** Municipal Regulations, Title 17, Chap. 2.

Credential Type: Specialty Electrical Contractor License. **Duration of License:** One year. **Requirements:** Must be licensed as a master electrician or master electrician specialist, have a master electrician or master electrician specialist as an employee, officer, or substantial stockholder. Post bond of $2,000. **Fees:** $50 application fee. $20 license fee. $60 annual renewal fee. **Governing Statute:** Municipal Regulations, Title 17, Chap. 2.

1863

Plumbing Contractor
License and Certification Div.
Occupational and Professional Licensure Administration
Consumer and Regulatory Affairs Dept.
PO Box 37200
Washington, DC 20013-7200
Phone: (202)727-7823
Phone: (202)727-7480

Alternate Information: 614 H St., NW, Washington, DC 20001 **Requirements:** Contact licensing body for application information.

1864

Refrigeration and Air Conditioning Contractor
License and Certification Div.
Occupational and Professional Licensure Administration
Consumer and Regulatory Affairs Dept.
PO Box 37200
Washington, DC 20013-7200
Phone: (202)727-7823
Phone: (202)727-7480

Alternate Information: 614 H St., NW, Washington, DC 20001.

Credential Type: Refrigeration and Air Conditioning Contractor License. **Duration of License:** One year. **Requirements:** Business must be conducted by or employ a person holding a Master Refrigeration and Air Conditioning Mechanic Limited License. Business must be conducted from a specific location. **Fees:** $50 application fee. $20 license fee. $70 annual renewal fee. **Governing Statute:** Municipal Regulations, Title 17, Chap. 3.

Florida

1865

Air Conditioning Contractor
Dept. of Professional Regulation
Construction Industry Licensing Board
PO Box 2
Jacksonville, FL 32201
Phone: (904)359-6310

Credential Type: Class A State Certified License. **Duration of License:** Two or three years. **Authorization:** Authorized to work throughout the State of Florida without taking additional examinations in this construction category. Class A air conditioning contractor services are unlimited with regard to size of unit. **Requirements:** Be at least 18 years of age. Good moral character. Meet one of the following criteria: (1) Baccalaureate degree from an accredited four-year college in the appropriate field. Have one year of proven experience or a minimum of 2000 man-hours. (2) Have at least four years of active experience, either as a workman who has learned the trade by serving an apprenticeship as a skilled workman who is able to comand the rate of a mechanic in applicant's field, or as a foreman. (3) Have a combination of not less than one year of experience as a foreman and not less than three years of credits for any accredited college-level courses; or a combination of not less than one year of experience as a foreman, one year as a skilled workman, and not less than two years of credits for any accredited college-level courses; or a combination of not less than one year of experience as a foreman, two years as a skilled workman, and not less than one year of credits for any accredited college-level courses.

Pass State Certification Examination. Must have appropriate workers' compensation coverage.

An active certified Class C (no longer issued) air conditioning contractor with four years of proven experience is eligible to take the Class A air conditioning contractors' examination. An active certified Class B air conditioning contractor with one year of proven experience is eligible to take the Class A air conditioning contractors' examination. **Examination:** State Certification Examination. **Reciprocity:** Yes. Applicant must have passed a similar national, regional, state, or U.S. territorial licensing examination. **Fees:** $254 examination fee. **Governing Statute:** Florida Statutes, Chapter 489, Part I.

Credential Type: Class A State Registered License. **Duration of License:** Two or three years. **Authorization:** Allows applicant to work only in those local areas in which applicant has complied with local requirements. Class A air conditioning contractor services are unlimited with regard to size of unit. **Requirements:** Applicant must first contact county or municipality in which applicant wishes to work for occupational and competency requirements. After meeting local requirements, applicant may apply for state registration. **Governing Statute:** Florida Statutes, Chapter 489, Part I.

Credential Type: Class B State Certified License. **Duration of License:** Two or three years. **Authorization:** Authorized to work throughout the State of Florida without taking additional examinations in this construction category. Class B air conditioning contractor services are limited to 25 tons of cooling and 500,000 BTU of heating in any one system. **Requirements:** Be at least 18 years of age. Good moral character. Meet one of the following criteria: (1) Baccalaureate degree from an accredited four-year college in the appropriate field. Have one year of proven experience or a minimum of 2000 man-hours. (2) Have at least four years of active experience, either as a workman who has learned the trade by serving an apprenticeship as a skilled workman who is able to comand the rate of a mechanic in applicant's field, or as a foreman. (3) Have a combination of not less than one year of experience as a foreman and not less than three years of credits for any accredited college-level courses; or a combination of not less than one year of experience as a foreman, one year as a skilled workman, and not less than two years of credits for any accredited college-level courses; or a combination of not less than one year of experience as a foreman, two years as a skilled workman, and not less than one year of credits for any accredited college-level courses.

Pass State Certification Examination. Must have appropriate workers' compensation coverage.

An active certified Class C (no longer issued) air conditioning contractor with three years of proven experience is eligible to take the Class B air conditioning contractors' examination. **Examination:** State Certification Examination. **Reciprocity:** Yes. Applicant must have passed a similar national, regional, state, or U.S. territorial licensing examination. **Fees:** $254 examination fee. **Governing Statute:** Florida Statutes, Chapter 489, Part I.

Credential Type: Class B State Registered License. **Duration of License:** Two or three years. **Authorization:** Allows applicant to work only in those local areas in which applicant has complied with local requirements. Class B air conditioning con-

Air Conditioning Contractor, continued

tractor services are limited to 25 tons of cooling and 500,000 BTU of heating in any one system. **Requirements:** Applicant must first contact county or municipality in which applicant wishes to work for occupational and competency requirements. After meeting local requirements, applicant may apply for state registration. **Governing Statute:** Florida Statutes, Chapter 489, Part I.

1866

Alarm System Contractor
Electrical Contractors Board
Professional Regulation Dept.
1940 N. Monroe St.
Tallahassee, FL 32399-0750
Phone: (904)488-6685

Credential Type: Alarm system contactor certificate I. **Duration of License:** Two years. **Authorization:** Business includes all types of alarm systems for all purposes. **Requirements:** Must be at least 18 years of age. Good moral character. Must possess and demonstrate the requisite skill, knowledge, and experience in the trade as an alarm system contractor. Must have public liability and property damage insurance.

Must meet one of the following requirements: (1) Have at least three years proven management experience as an alarm system contractor or educational equivalent, but not more than half of which is met by educational equivalent; or (2) Have at least six years of comprehensive, specialized training, education, or experience associated with an alarm system contracting business; or (3) Have been licensed for three years as an engineer.

Renewal of an inactive certified license requires 12 classroom hours of continuing education. **Examination:** Yes. **Reciprocity:** A holder of a valid license to practice alarm system contracting issued by another state or territory of the United States may apply for licensure by endorsement, if the criteria for issuance of such a license was substantially equivalent to Florida's. **Fees:** $50 application fee for certification examination. $150 examination fee. $200 application fee for licensure by endorsement. $200 renewal fee. **Governing Statute:** Florida Statutes, Chapter 489, Part II.

Credential Type: Alarm system contactor certificate II. **Duration of License:** Two years. **Authorization:** Business includes all types of alarm systems, other than fire, for all purposes. **Requirements:** Must be at least 18 years of age. Good moral character. Must possess and demonstrate the requisite skill, knowledge, and experience in the trade as an alarm system contractor. Must have public liability and property damage insurance.

Must meet one of the following requirements: (1) Have at least three years proven management experience as an alarm system contractor or educational equivalent, but not more than half of which is met by educational equivalent; or (2) Have at least six years of comprehensive, specialized training, education, or experience associated with an alarm system contracting business; or (3) Have been licensed for three years as an engineer.

Renewal of an inactive certified license requires 12 classroom hours of continuing education. **Examination:** Yes. **Reciprocity:** A holder of a valid license to practice alarm system contracting issued by another state or territory of the United States may apply for licensure by endorsement, if the criteria for issuance of such a license was substantially equivalent to Florida's. **Fees:** $50 application fee for certification examination. $150 examination fee. $200 application fee for licensure by endorsement. $200 renewal fee. **Governing Statute:** Florida Statutes, Chapter 489, Part II.

Credential Type: Alarm System Contractor Registration. **Duration of License:** Two years. **Authorization:** Limited to contracting only in the area and for the type of work covered by the registration, unless local licenses are issued for other areas and types of work, or unless certification is obtained. **Requirements:** Must hold a current occupational license or a current license issued by any municipality or county of the state of Florida for the type of work for which registration is requested. **Fees:** $65 initial registration fee. $50 registration renewal fee. **Governing Statute:** Florida Statutes, Chapter 489, Part II.

1867

Asbestos Abatement Contractor
Dept. of Professional Regulation
Construction Industry Licensing
 Board
PO Box 2
Jacksonville, FL 32201
Phone: (904)359-6310

Credential Type: State Certified License. **Duration of License:** Two or three years. **Authorization:** Authorized to work throughout the State of Florida without taking additional examinations in this construction category. **Requirements:** Be at least 18 years of age. Good moral character. Meet one of the following criteria: (1) Baccalaureate degree from an accredited four-year college in the appropriate field. Have one year of proven experience or a minimum of 2000 man-hours. (2) Have at least four years of active experience, either as a workman who has learned the trade by serving an apprenticeship as a skilled workman who is able to comand the rate of a mechanic in applicant's field, or as a foreman. (3) Have a combination of not less than one year of experience as a foreman and not less than three years of credits for any accredited college-level courses; or a combination of not less than one year of experience as a foreman, one year as a skilled workman, and not less than two years of credits for any accredited college-level courses; or a combination of not less than one year of experience as a foreman, two years as a skilled workman, and not less than one year of credits for any accredited college-level courses.

Pass State Certification Examination. Must have appropriate workers' compensation coverage. **Examination:** State Certification Examination. **Reciprocity:** Yes. Applicant must have passed a similar national, regional, state, or U.S. territorial licensing examination. **Fees:** $254 examination fee. **Governing Statute:** Florida Statutes, Chapter 489, Part I.

1868

Building Contractor
Dept. of Professional Regulation
Construction Industry Licensing
 Board
PO Box 2
Jacksonville, FL 32201
Phone: (904)359-6310

Credential Type: State Certified License. **Duration of License:** Two or three years. **Authorization:** Authorized to work throughout the State of Florida without taking additional examinations in this construction category. **Requirements:** Be at least 18 years of age. Good moral character. Meet one of the following criteria: (1) Baccalaureate degree from an accredited four-year college in the appropriate field. Have one year of proven experience or a minimum of 2000 man-hours. (2) Have at least four years of active experience, either as a workman who has learned the trade by serving an apprenticeship as a skilled workman who is able to comand the rate of a mechanic in applicant's field, or as a foreman. (3) Have a combination of not less than one year of experience as a foreman and not less than three years of credits for any accredited college-level courses; or a combination of not less than one year of experience as a foreman, one year as a skilled workman, and not less than two years of credits for any accredited college-level courses; or a combination of not less

Construction Contractors and Managers — Florida

than one year of experience as a foreman, two years as a skilled workman, and not less than one year of credits for any accredited college-level courses.

Pass State Certification Examination. Must have appropriate workers' compensation coverage.

An active certified residential contractor with three years of proven experience is eligible to take the building contractor's examination. **Examination:** State Certification Examination. **Reciprocity:** Yes. Applicant must have passed a similar national, regional, state, or U.S. territorial licensing examination. **Fees:** $254 examination fee. **Governing Statute:** Florida Statutes, Chapter 489, Part I.

Credential Type: State Registered License. **Duration of License:** Two or three years. **Authorization:** Allows applicant to work only in those local areas in which applicant has complied with local requirements. **Requirements:** Applicant must first contact county or municipality in which applicant wishes to work for occupational and competency requirements. After meeting local requirements, applicant may apply for state registration. **Governing Statute:** Florida Statutes, Chapter 489, Part I.

1869

Commercial Pool/Spa Contractor
Dept. of Professional Regulation
Construction Industry Licensing
 Board
PO Box 2
Jacksonville, FL 32201
Phone: (904)359-6310

Credential Type: State Certified License. **Duration of License:** Two or three years. **Authorization:** Authorized to work throughout the State of Florida without taking additional examinations in this construction category. **Requirements:** Be at least 18 years of age. Good moral character. Meet one of the following criteria: (1) Baccalaureate degree from an accredited four-year college in the appropriate field. Have one year of proven experience or a minimum of 2000 man-hours. (2) Have at least four years of active experience, either as a workman who has learned the trade by serving an apprenticeship as a skilled workman who is able to comand the rate of a mechanic in applicant's field, or as a foreman. (3) Have a combination of not less than one year of experience as a foreman and not less than three years of credits for any accredited college-level courses; or a combination of not less than one year of experience as a foreman, one year as a skilled workman, and not less than two years of credits for any accredited college-level courses; or a combination of not less than one year of experience as a foreman, two years as a skilled workman, and not less than one year of credits for any accredited college-level courses.

Pass State Certification Examination. Must have appropriate workers' compensation coverage.

An active certified swimming pool servicing contractor with four years of proven experience is eligible to take the commercial swimming pool contractors' examination. An active certified residential swimming pool contractor with one year of proven experience is eligible to take the commercial swimming pool contractors' examination. **Examination:** State Certification Examination. **Reciprocity:** Yes. Applicant must have passed a similar national, regional, state, or U.S. territorial licensing examination. **Fees:** $254 examination fee. **Governing Statute:** Florida Statutes, Chapter 489, Part I.

Credential Type: State Registered License. **Duration of License:** Two or three years. **Authorization:** Allows applicant to work only in those local areas in which applicant has complied with local requirements. **Requirements:** Applicant must first contact county or municipality in which applicant wishes to work for occupational and competency requirements. After meeting local requirements, applicant may apply for state registration. **Governing Statute:** Florida Statutes, Chapter 489, Part I.

1870

Electrical Contractor
Electrical Contractors Board
Professional Regulation Dept.
1940 N. Monroe St.
Tallahassee, FL 32399-0750
Phone: (904)488-6685

Credential Type: Unlimited electrical contractor certificate of competency. **Duration of License:** Two years. **Requirements:** Must be at least 18 years of age. Good moral character. Must possess and demonstrate the requisite skill, knowledge, and experience in the trade as an electrical contractor. Must have public liability and property damage insurance.

Must meet one of the following requirements: (1) Have at least three years proven management experience as an electrical contractor or educational equivalent, but not more than half of which is met by educational equivalent; or (2) Have at least six years of comprehensive, specialized training, education, or experience associated with an electrical or alarm system contracting business; or (3) Have been licensed for three years as an engineer.

Renewal of an inactive certified license requires 12 classroom hours of continuing education. **Examination:** Yes. **Reciprocity:** A holder of a valid license to practice electrical contracting issued by another state or territory of the United States may apply for licensure by endorsement, if the criteria for issuance of such a license was substantially equivalent to Florida's. **Fees:** $50 application fee for certification examination. $150 examination fee. $200 application fee for licensure by endorsement. $200 renewal fee. **Governing Statute:** Florida Statutes, Chapter 489, Part II.

Credential Type: Lighting Maintenance Specialty Electrical Contractor Certificate. **Duration of License:** Two years. **Requirements:** Must have three years experience in this specialty. Pass appropriate examination. **Examination:** Yes. **Fees:** $50 application fee for certification examination. $150 examination fee. $200 application fee for licensure by endorsement. $200 renewal fee. **Governing Statute:** Florida Statutes, Chapter 489, Part II.

Credential Type: Elevator Specialty Electrical Contractor Certificate. **Duration of License:** Two years. **Requirements:** Must have three years experience in this specialty. Pass appropriate examination. **Examination:** Yes. **Fees:** $50 application fee for certification examination. $150 examination fee. $200 application fee for licensure by endorsement. $200 renewal fee. **Governing Statute:** Florida Statutes, Chapter 489, Part II.

Credential Type: Electrical Outdoor Sign Specialty Electrical Contractor Certificate. **Duration of License:** Two years. **Requirements:** Must have three years experience in this specialty. Pass appropriate examination. **Examination:** Yes. **Fees:** $50 application fee for certification examination. $150 examination fee. $200 application fee for licensure by endorsement. $200 renewal fee. **Governing Statute:** Florida Statutes, Chapter 489, Part II.

Credential Type: Residential Electrical Contractor Certificate. **Duration of License:** Two years. **Requirements:** Must have three years experience in this specialty. Pass appropriate examination. **Examination:** Yes. **Fees:** $50 application fee for certification examination. $150 examination fee. $200 application fee for licensure by endorsement. $200 renewal fee. **Governing Statute:** Florida Statutes, Chapter 489, Part II.

Credential Type: Electrical Contractor Registration. **Duration of License:** Two years. **Authorization:** Limited to contracting only in the area and for the type of work covered by the registration, unless local licenses are issued for other areas and

Florida 1871

Electrical Contractor, continued

types of work, or unless certification is obtained. **Requirements:** Must hold a current occupational license or a current license issued by any municipality or county of the state of Florida for the type of work for which registration is requested. **Fees:** $65 initial registration fee. $50 registration renewal fee. **Governing Statute:** Florida Statutes, Chapter 489, Part II.

1871

General Contractor
Dept. of Professional Regulation
Construction Industry Licensing
  Board
PO Box 2
Jacksonville, FL 32201
Phone: (904)359-6310

Credential Type: State Certified License. **Duration of License:** Two or three years. **Authorization:** Authorized to work throughout the State of Florida without taking additional examinations in this construction category. **Requirements:** Be at least 18 years of age. Good moral character. Meet one of the following criteria: (1) Baccalaureate degree from an accredited four-year college in the appropriate field. Have one year of proven experience or a minimum of 2000 man-hours. (2) Have at least four years of active experience, either as a workman who has learned the trade by serving an apprenticeship as a skilled workman who is able to comand the rate of a mechanic in applicant's field, or as a foreman. (3) Have a combination of not less than one year of experience as a foreman and not less than three years of credits for any accredited college-level courses; or a combination of not less than one year of experience as a foreman, one year as a skilled workman, and not less than two years of credits for any accredited college-level courses; or a combination of not less than one year of experience as a foreman, two years as a skilled workman, and not less than one year of credits for any accredited college-level courses.

Pass State Certification Examination. Must have appropriate workers' compensation coverage.

An active certified residential contractor with four years of proven experience is eligible to take the general contractor's examination. An active certified building contractor with four years of proven experience is eligible to take the general contractor's examination. **Examination:** State Certification Examination. **Reciprocity:** Yes. Applicant must have passed a similar national, regional, state, or U.S. territorial licensing examination. **Fees:** $254 examination fee. **Governing Statute:** Florida Statutes, Chapter 489, Part I.

Credential Type: State Registered License. **Duration of License:** Two or three years. **Authorization:** Allows applicant to work only in those local areas in which applicant has complied with local requirements. **Requirements:** Applicant must first contact county or municipality in which applicant wishes to work for occupational and competency requirements. After meeting local requirements, applicant may apply for state registration. **Governing Statute:** Florida Statutes, Chapter 489, Part I.

1872

Gypsum Drywall Specialty Contractor
Dept. of Professional Regulation
Construction Industry Licensing
  Board
PO Box 2
Jacksonville, FL 32201
Phone: (904)359-6310

Credential Type: State Certified License. **Duration of License:** Two or three years. **Authorization:** Authorized to work throughout the State of Florida without taking additional examinations in this construction category. **Requirements:** Be at least 18 years of age. Good moral character. Meet one of the following criteria: (1) Baccalaureate degree from an accredited four-year college in the appropriate field. Have one year of proven experience or a minimum of 2000 man-hours. (2) Have at least four years of active experience, either as a workman who has learned the trade by serving an apprenticeship as a skilled workman who is able to comand the rate of a mechanic in applicant's field, or as a foreman. (3) Have a combination of not less than one year of experience as a foreman and not less than three years of credits for any accredited college-level courses; or a combination of not less than one year of experience as a foreman, one year as a skilled workman, and not less than two years of credits for any accredited college-level courses; or a combination of not less than one year of experience as a foreman, two years as a skilled workman, and not less than one year of credits for any accredited college-level courses.

Pass State Certification Examination. Must have appropriate workers' compensation coverage. **Examination:** State Certification Examination. **Reciprocity:** Yes. Applicant must have passed a similar national, regional, state, or U.S. territorial licensing examination. **Fees:** $254 examination fee. **Governing Statute:** Florida Statutes, Chapter 489, Part I.

Credential Type: State Registered License. **Duration of License:** Two or three years. **Authorization:** Allows applicant to work only in those local areas in which applicant has complied with local requirements. **Requirements:** Applicant must first contact county or municipality in which applicant wishes to work for occupational and competency requirements. After meeting local requirements, applicant may apply for state registration. **Governing Statute:** Florida Statutes, Chapter 489, Part I.

1873

Mechanical Contractor
Dept. of Professional Regulation
Construction Industry Licensing
  Board
PO Box 2
Jacksonville, FL 32201
Phone: (904)359-6310

Credential Type: State Certified License. **Duration of License:** Two or three years. **Authorization:** Authorized to work throughout the State of Florida without taking additional examinations in this construction category. **Requirements:** Be at least 18 years of age. Good moral character. Meet one of the following criteria: (1) Baccalaureate degree from an accredited four-year college in the appropriate field. Have one year of proven experience or a minimum of 2000 man-hours. (2) Have at least four years of active experience, either as a workman who has learned the trade by serving an apprenticeship as a skilled workman who is able to comand the rate of a mechanic in applicant's field, or as a foreman. (3) Have a combination of not less than one year of experience as a foreman and not less than three years of credits for any accredited college-level courses; or a combination of not less than one year of experience as a foreman, one year as a skilled workman, and not less than two years of credits for any accredited college-level courses; or a combination of not less than one year of experience as a foreman, two years as a skilled workman, and not less than one year of credits for any accredited college-level courses.

Pass State Certification Examination. Must have appropriate workers' compensation coverage. **Examination:** State Certification Examination. **Reciprocity:** Yes. Applicant must have passed a similar national, regional, state, or U.S. territorial licensing examination. **Fees:** $254 examination fee. **Governing Statute:** Florida Statutes, Chapter 489, Part I.

Credential Type: State Registered License. Duration of License: Two or three years. Authorization: Allows applicant to work only in those local areas in which applicant has complied with local requirements. Requirements: Applicant must first contact county or municipality in which applicant wishes to work for occupational and competency requirements. After meeting local requirements, applicant may apply for state registration. Governing Statute: Florida Statutes, Chapter 489, Part I.

1874

Plumbing Contractor
Dept. of Professional Regulation
Construction Industry Licensing
 Board
PO Box 2
Jacksonville, FL 32201
Phone: (904)359-6310

Credential Type: State Certified License. Duration of License: Two or three years. Authorization: Authorized to work throughout the State of Florida without taking additional examinations in this construction category. Requirements: Be at least 18 years of age. Good moral character. Meet one of the following criteria: (1) Baccalaureate degree from an accredited four-year college in the appropriate field. Have one year of proven experience or a minimum of 2000 man-hours. (2) Have at least four years of active experience, either as a workman who has learned the trade by serving an apprenticeship as a skilled workman who is able to comand the rate of a mechanic in applicant's field, or as a foreman. (3) Have a combination of not less than one year of experience as a foreman and not less than three years of credits for any accredited college-level courses; or a combination of not less than one year of experience as a foreman, one year as a skilled workman, and not less than two years of credits for any accredited college-level courses; or a combination of not less than one year of experience as a foreman, two years as a skilled workman, and not less than one year of credits for any accredited college-level courses.

Pass State Certification Examination. Must have appropriate workers' compensation coverage. Examination: State Certification Examination. Reciprocity: Yes. Applicant must have passed a similar national, regional, state, or U.S. territorial licensing examination. Fees: $254 examination fee. Governing Statute: Florida Statutes, Chapter 489, Part I.

Credential Type: State Registered License. Duration of License: Two or three years. Authorization: Allows applicant to work only in those local areas in which applicant has complied with local requirements. Requirements: Applicant must first contact county or municipality in which applicant wishes to work for occupational and competency requirements. After meeting local requirements, applicant may apply for state registration. Governing Statute: Florida Statutes, Chapter 489, Part I.

1875

Pollutant Storage System Specialty Contractor
Dept. of Professional Regulation
Construction Industry Licensing
 Board
PO Box 2
Jacksonville, FL 32201
Phone: (904)359-6310

Credential Type: State Certified License. Duration of License: Two or three years. Authorization: Authorized to work throughout the State of Florida without taking additional examinations in this construction category. Requirements: Be at least 18 years of age. Good moral character. Meet one of the following criteria: (1) Baccalaureate degree from an accredited four-year college in the appropriate field. Have one year of proven experience or a minimum of 2000 man-hours. (2) Have at least four years of active experience, either as a workman who has learned the trade by serving an apprenticeship as a skilled workman who is able to comand the rate of a mechanic in applicant's field, or as a foreman. (3) Have a combination of not less than one year of experience as a foreman and not less than three years of credits for any accredited college-level courses; or a combination of not less than one year of experience as a foreman, one year as a skilled workman, and not less than two years of credits for any accredited college-level courses; or a combination of not less than one year of experience as a foreman, two years as a skilled workman, and not less than one year of credits for any accredited college-level courses.

Pass State Certification Examination. Must have appropriate workers' compensation coverage. Examination: State Certification Examination. Reciprocity: Yes. Applicant must have passed a similar national, regional, state, or U.S. territorial licensing examination. Fees: $254 examination fee. Governing Statute: Florida Statutes, Chapter 489, Part I.

1876

Pool/Spa Servicing Contractor
Dept. of Professional Regulation
Construction Industry Licensing
 Board
PO Box 2
Jacksonville, FL 32201
Phone: (904)359-6310

Credential Type: State Certified License. Duration of License: Two or three years. Authorization: Authorized to work throughout the State of Florida without taking additional examinations in this construction category. Requirements: Be at least 18 years of age. Good moral character. Meet one of the following criteria: (1) Baccalaureate degree from an accredited four-year college in the appropriate field. Have one year of proven experience or a minimum of 2000 man-hours. (2) Have at least four years of active experience, either as a workman who has learned the trade by serving an apprenticeship as a skilled workman who is able to comand the rate of a mechanic in applicant's field, or as a foreman. (3) Have a combination of not less than one year of experience as a foreman and not less than three years of credits for any accredited college-level courses; or a combination of not less than one year of experience as a foreman, one year as a skilled workman, and not less than two years of credits for any accredited college-level courses; or a combination of not less than one year of experience as a foreman, two years as a skilled workman, and not less than one year of credits for any accredited college-level courses.

Pass State Certification Examination. Must have appropriate workers' compensation coverage. Examination: State Certification Examination. Reciprocity: Yes. Applicant must have passed a similar national, regional, state, or U.S. territorial licensing examination. Fees: $254 examination fee. Governing Statute: Florida Statutes, Chapter 489, Part I.

Credential Type: State Registered License. Duration of License: Two or three years. Authorization: Allows applicant to work only in those local areas in which applicant has complied with local requirements. Requirements: Applicant must first contact county or municipality in which applicant wishes to work for occupational and competency requirements. After meeting local requirements, applicant may apply for state registration. Governing Statute: Florida Statutes, Chapter 489, Part I.

1877

Residential Contractor
Dept. of Professional Regulation
Construction Industry Licensing Board
PO Box 2
Jacksonville, FL 32201
Phone: (904)359-6310

Credential Type: State Certified License. **Duration of License:** Two or three years. **Authorization:** Authorized to work throughout the State of Florida without taking additional examinations in this construction category. **Requirements:** Be at least 18 years of age. Good moral character. Meet one of the following criteria: (1) Baccalaureate degree from an accredited four-year college in the appropriate field. Have one year of proven experience or a minimum of 2000 man-hours. (2) Have at least four years of active experience, either as a workman who has learned the trade by serving an apprenticeship as a skilled workman who is able to comand the rate of a mechanic in applicant's field, or as a foreman. (3) Have a combination of not less than one year of experience as a foreman and not less than three years of credits for any accredited college-level courses; or a combination of not less than one year of experience as a foreman, one year as a skilled workman, and not less than two years of credits for any accredited college-level courses; or a combination of not less than one year of experience as a foreman, two years as a skilled workman, and not less than one year of credits for any accredited college-level courses.

Pass State Certification Examination. Must have appropriate workers' compensation coverage. **Examination:** State Certification Examination. **Reciprocity:** Yes. Applicant must have passed a similar national, regional, state, or U.S. territorial licensing examination. **Fees:** $254 examination fee. **Governing Statute:** Florida Statutes, Chapter 489, Part I.

Credential Type: State Registered License. **Duration of License:** Two or three years. **Authorization:** Allows applicant to work only in those local areas in which applicant has complied with local requirements. **Requirements:** Applicant must first contact county or municipality in which applicant wishes to work for occupational and competency requirements. After meeting local requirements, applicant may apply for state registration. **Governing Statute:** Florida Statutes, Chapter 489, Part I.

1878

Residential Pool/Spa Contractor
Dept. of Professional Regulation
Construction Industry Licensing Board
PO Box 2
Jacksonville, FL 32201
Phone: (904)359-6310

Credential Type: State Certified License. **Duration of License:** Two or three years. **Authorization:** Authorized to work throughout the State of Florida without taking additional examinations in this construction category. **Requirements:** Be at least 18 years of age. Good moral character. Meet one of the following criteria: (1) Baccalaureate degree from an accredited four-year college in the appropriate field. Have one year of proven experience or a minimum of 2000 man-hours. (2) Have at least four years of active experience, either as a workman who has learned the trade by serving an apprenticeship as a skilled workman who is able to comand the rate of a mechanic in applicant's field, or as a foreman. (3) Have a combination of not less than one year of experience as a foreman and not less than three years of credits for any accredited college-level courses; or a combination of not less than one year of experience as a foreman, one year as a skilled workman, and not less than two years of credits for any accredited college-level courses; or a combination of not less than one year of experience as a foreman, two years as a skilled workman, and not less than one year of credits for any accredited college-level courses.

Pass State Certification Examination. Must have appropriate workers' compensation coverage.

An active certified swimming pool servicing contractor with three years of proven experience is eligible to take the residential swimming pool contractors' examination. **Examination:** State Certification Examination. **Reciprocity:** Yes. Applicant must have passed a similar national, regional, state, or U.S. territorial licensing examination. **Fees:** $254 examination fee. **Governing Statute:** Florida Statutes, Chapter 489, Part I.

Credential Type: State Registered License. **Duration of License:** Two or three years. **Authorization:** Allows applicant to work only in those local areas in which applicant has complied with local requirements. **Requirements:** Applicant must first contact county or municipality in which applicant wishes to work for occupational and competency requirements. After meeting local requirements, applicant may apply for state registration. **Governing Statute:** Florida Statutes, Chapter 489, Part I.

1879

Residential Solar Water Heating Specialty Contractor
Dept. of Professional Regulation
Construction Industry Licensing Board
PO Box 2
Jacksonville, FL 32201
Phone: (904)359-6310

Credential Type: State Certified License. **Duration of License:** Two or three years. **Authorization:** Authorized to work throughout the State of Florida without taking additional examinations in this construction category. **Requirements:** Be at least 18 years of age. Good moral character. Meet one of the following criteria: (1) Baccalaureate degree from an accredited four-year college in the appropriate field. Have one year of proven experience or a minimum of 2000 man-hours. (2) Have at least four years of active experience, either as a workman who has learned the trade by serving an apprenticeship as a skilled workman who is able to comand the rate of a mechanic in applicant's field, or as a foreman. (3) Have a combination of not less than one year of experience as a foreman and not less than three years of credits for any accredited college-level courses; or a combination of not less than one year of experience as a foreman, one year as a skilled workman, and not less than two years of credits for any accredited college-level courses; or a combination of not less than one year of experience as a foreman, two years as a skilled workman, and not less than one year of credits for any accredited college-level courses.

Pass State Certification Examination. Must have appropriate workers' compensation coverage. **Examination:** State Certification Examination. **Reciprocity:** Yes. Applicant must have passed a similar national, regional, state, or U.S. territorial licensing examination. **Fees:** $254 examination fee. **Governing Statute:** Florida Statutes, Chapter 489, Part I.

Credential Type: State Registered License. **Duration of License:** Two or three years. **Authorization:** Allows applicant to work only in those local areas in which applicant has complied with local requirements. **Requirements:** Applicant must first contact county or municipality in which applicant wishes to work for occupational and competency requirements. After meeting local requirements, applicant may apply for state registration. **Governing Statute:** Florida Statutes, Chapter 489, Part I.

1880

Roofing Contractor
Dept. of Professional Regulation
Construction Industry Licensing Board
PO Box 2
Jacksonville, FL 32201
Phone: (904)359-6310

Credential Type: State Certified License. **Duration of License:** Two or three years. **Authorization:** Authorized to work throughout the State of Florida without taking additional examinations in this construction category. **Requirements:** Be at least 18 years of age. Good moral character. Meet one of the following criteria: (1) Baccalaureate degree from an accredited four-year college in the appropriate field. Have one year of proven experience or a minimum of 2000 man-hours. (2) Have at least four years of active experience, either as a workman who has learned the trade by serving an apprenticeship as a skilled workman who is able to comand the rate of a mechanic in applicant's field, or as a foreman. (3) Have a combination of not less than one year of experience as a foreman and not less than three years of credits for any accredited college-level courses; or a combination of not less than one year of experience as a foreman, one year as a skilled workman, and not less than two years of credits for any accredited college-level courses; or a combination of not less than one year of experience as a foreman, two years as a skilled workman, and not less than one year of credits for any accredited college-level courses.

Pass State Certification Examination. Must have appropriate workers' compensation coverage. **Examination:** State Certification Examination. **Reciprocity:** Yes. Applicant must have passed a similar national, regional, state, or U.S. territorial licensing examination. **Fees:** $254 examination fee. **Governing Statute:** Florida Statutes, Chapter 489, Part I.

Credential Type: State Registered License. **Duration of License:** Two or three years. **Authorization:** Allows applicant to work only in those local areas in which applicant has complied with local requirements. **Requirements:** Applicant must first contact county or municipality in which applicant wishes to work for occupational and competency requirements. After meeting local requirements, applicant may apply for state registration. **Governing Statute:** Florida Statutes, Chapter 489, Part I.

1881

Sheet Metal Contractor
Dept. of Professional Regulation
Construction Industry Licensing Board
PO Box 2
Jacksonville, FL 32201
Phone: (904)359-6310

Credential Type: State Certified License. **Duration of License:** Two or three years. **Authorization:** Authorized to work throughout the State of Florida without taking additional examinations in this construction category. **Requirements:** Be at least 18 years of age. Good moral character. Meet one of the following criteria: (1) Baccalaureate degree from an accredited four-year college in the appropriate field. Have one year of proven experience or a minimum of 2000 man-hours. (2) Have at least four years of active experience, either as a workman who has learned the trade by serving an apprenticeship as a skilled workman who is able to comand the rate of a mechanic in applicant's field, or as a foreman. (3) Have a combination of not less than one year of experience as a foreman and not less than three years of credits for any accredited college-level courses; or a combination of not less than one year of experience as a foreman, one year as a skilled workman, and not less than two years of credits for any accredited college-level courses; or a combination of not less than one year of experience as a foreman, two years as a skilled workman, and not less than one year of credits for any accredited college-level courses.

Pass State Certification Examination. Must have appropriate workers' compensation coverage. **Examination:** State Certification Examination. **Reciprocity:** Yes. Applicant must have passed a similar national, regional, state, or U.S. territorial licensing examination. **Fees:** $254 examination fee. **Governing Statute:** Florida Statutes, Chapter 489, Part I.

Credential Type: State Registered License. **Duration of License:** Two or three years. **Authorization:** Allows applicant to work only in those local areas in which applicant has complied with local requirements. **Requirements:** Applicant must first contact county or municipality in which applicant wishes to work for occupational and competency requirements. After meeting local requirements, applicant may apply for state registration. **Governing Statute:** Florida Statutes, Chapter 489, Part I.

1882

Specialty Structure Contractor
Dept. of Professional Regulation
Construction Industry Licensing Board
PO Box 2
Jacksonville, FL 32201
Phone: (904)359-6310

Credential Type: State Certified License. **Duration of License:** Two or three years. **Authorization:** Authorized to work throughout the State of Florida without taking additional examinations in this construction category. **Requirements:** Be at least 18 years of age. Good moral character. Meet one of the following criteria: (1) Baccalaureate degree from an accredited four-year college in the appropriate field. Have one year of proven experience or a minimum of 2000 man-hours. (2) Have at least four years of active experience, either as a workman who has learned the trade by serving an apprenticeship as a skilled workman who is able to comand the rate of a mechanic in applicant's field, or as a foreman. (3) Have a combination of not less than one year of experience as a foreman and not less than three years of credits for any accredited college-level courses; or a combination of not less than one year of experience as a foreman, one year as a skilled workman, and not less than two years of credits for any accredited college-level courses; or a combination of not less than one year of experience as a foreman, two years as a skilled workman, and not less than one year of credits for any accredited college-level courses.

Pass State Certification Examination. Must have appropriate workers' compensation coverage. **Examination:** State Certification Examination. **Reciprocity:** Yes. Applicant must have passed a similar national, regional, state, or U.S. territorial licensing examination. **Fees:** $254 examination fee. **Governing Statute:** Florida Statutes, Chapter 489, Part I.

Credential Type: State Registered License. **Duration of License:** Two or three years. **Authorization:** Allows applicant to work only in those local areas in which applicant has complied with local requirements. **Requirements:** Applicant must first contact county or municipality in which applicant wishes to work for occupational and competency requirements. After meeting local requirements, applicant may apply for state registration. **Governing Statute:** Florida Statutes, Chapter 489, Part I.

Florida

1883

Underground Utility Contractor
Dept. of Professional Regulation
Construction Industry Licensing Board
PO Box 2
Jacksonville, FL 32201
Phone: (904)359-6310

Credential Type: State Certified License. **Duration of License:** Two or three years. **Authorization:** Authorized to work throughout the State of Florida without taking additional examinations in this construction category. **Requirements:** Be at least 18 years of age. Good moral character. Meet one of the following criteria: (1) Baccalaureate degree from an accredited four-year college in the appropriate field. Have one year of proven experience or a minimum of 2000 man-hours. (2) Have at least four years of active experience, either as a workman who has learned the trade by serving an apprenticeship as a skilled workman who is able to comand the rate of a mechanic in applicant's field, or as a foreman. (3) Have a combination of not less than one year of experience as a foreman and not less than three years of credits for any accredited college-level courses; or a combination of not less than one year of experience as a foreman, one year as a skilled workman, and not less than two years of credits for any accredited college-level courses; or a combination of not less than one year of experience as a foreman, two years as a skilled workman, and not less than one year of credits for any accredited college-level courses.

Pass State Certification Examination. Must have appropriate workers' compensation coverage. **Examination:** State Certification Examination. **Reciprocity:** Yes. Applicant must have passed a similar national, regional, state, or U.S. territorial licensing examination. **Fees:** $254 examination fee. **Governing Statute:** Florida Statutes, Chapter 489, Part I.

Credential Type: State Registered License. **Duration of License:** Two or three years. **Authorization:** Allows applicant to work only in those local areas in which applicant has complied with local requirements. **Requirements:** Applicant must first contact county or municipality in which applicant wishes to work for occupational and competency requirements. After meeting local requirements, applicant may apply for state registration. **Governing Statute:** Florida Statutes, Chapter 489, Part I.

Georgia

1884

Conditioned Air Contractor
State Construction Industry Licensing Board
Div. of Conditioned Air Contractors
Professional Examining Boards
166 Pryor St., SW
Atlanta, GA 30303
Phone: (404)656-3939

Credential Type: Class I Conditioned Air Contractor License. **Authorization:** Restricted to 175,000 BTU of heating and five tons (60,000 BTU) of cooling. **Requirements:** Minimum of three years of primary experience gained through the direct installation of and responsibility for conditioned air systems. A maximum of one year of secondary experience or education may be substituted for the experience requirement, where secondary experience means work or training related to the installation of conditioned air systems. Submit three professional references. **Examination:** Construction Industry Licensing Board Examination for Class I Conditioned Air Contractors. **Reciprocity:** Applicant who holds a current out of state license based on passing an examination may be granted a license by endorsement, provided that applicant meets Georgia's experience requirements. **Fees:** $29 application fee. $56 exam fee. **Governing Statute:** Official Code of Georgia Annotated 43-14. Rules of the State Construction Industry Licensing Board, Chap. 121.

Credential Type: Class II Conditioned Air Contractor License. **Authorization:** Unstrcited as to the capacity of the system. **Requirements:** Minimum of three years of primary experience gained through the direct installation of and responsibility for conditioned air systems. A maximum of one year of secondary experience or education may be substituted for the experience requirement, where secondary experience means work or training related to the installation of conditioned air systems. Submit three professional references. **Examination:** Construction Industry Licensing Board Examination for Class II Conditioned Air Contractors. **Reciprocity:** Applicant who holds a current out of state license based on passing an examination may be granted a license by endorsement, provided that applicant meets Georgia's experience requirements. **Fees:** $29 application fee. $56 exam fee. **Governing Statute:** Official Code of Georgia Annotated 43-14. Rules of the State Construction Industry Licensing Board, Chap. 121.

1885

Electrical Contractor
State Construction Industry Licensing Board
Div. of Electrical Contractors
Professional Examining Boards
166 Pryor St., SW
Atlanta, GA 30303
Phone: (404)656-3939

Credential Type: Class I Statewide Electrical Contractor License. **Authorization:** Restricted to electrical contracting which involves work on single phase electrical systems not exceeding 200 amperes. Work on certain systems of 50 volts or less requires a state low voltage contractor license. **Requirements:** Be at least 21 years of age. Minimum of four years of primary experience gained through the direct installation of and responsibility for electrical systems. Secondary experience, including work, training, and education, may be credited toward the experience requirement at a rate of 50 percent, to a maximum of one year of credit (2 years secondary experience equals one year of experience credit). **Examination:** Construction Industry Licensing Board Examination for Class I Electrical Contractors. **Reciprocity:** Applicant who holds a current out of state license based on passing an examination may be granted a license by endorsement, provided that applicant meets Georgia's experience requirements. **Fees:** $29 application fee. $56 exam fee. **Governing Statute:** Official Code of Georgia Annotated 43-14. Rules of the State Construction Industry Licensing Board, Chap. 121.

Credential Type: Class II Statewide Electrical Contractor License. **Authorization:** Unrestricted as to the capacity of the system. Work on certain systems of 50 volts or less requires a state low voltage contractor license. **Requirements:** Be at least 21 years of age. Minimum of four years of primary experience gained through the direct installation of and responsibility for electrical systems. Secondary experience, including work, training, and education, may be credited toward the experience requirement at a rate of 50 percent, to a maximum of one year of credit (2 years secondary experience equals one year of experience credit). Experience must be with installations in excess of single phase, 200 amperes systems. **Examination:** Construction Industry Licensing Board Examination for Class II Electrical Contractors. **Reciprocity:** Applicant who holds a current out of state license based on passing an examination may be granted a license by endorsement, provided that applicant meets Georgia's experience requirements. **Fees:** $29 application fee. $56 exam fee. **Governing Statute:** Official

Construction Contractors and Managers

Code of Georgia Annotated 43-14. Rules of the State Construction Industry Licensing Board, Chap. 121.

1886

General Contractor
Georgia Construction Industry Licensing Board
166 Prior St., SW
Atlanta, GA 30303
Phone: (404)656-2448

Credential Type: General contractor license. **Authorization:** Covers non-resident contractors. **Requirements:** Bond established must be in the amount of 10 percent of the contract amount; the General or Prime Contractor must file Sales and Use Tax returns to the Department of Revenue on a monthly basis and is to withhold three percent of the subcontractors wage for sales and tax use. **Fees:** $10 non-resident fee (per contract). **Governing Statute:** Section 48-8-63 of the Official Code of Georgia Annotated and Regulation 560-12-2-.26.

1887

Low Voltage Contractor
State Construction Industry Licensing Board
Div. of LowVoltage Contractors
Professional Examining Boards
166 Pryor St., SW
Atlanta, GA 30303
Phone: (404)656-3939

Credential Type: Class LV-A Contractor License. **Authorization:** Restricted to alarm and general system low-voltage contracting. **Requirements:** Minimum of one year of experience in low-voltage wiring in this category. A maximum of six months of courses in electronics may be credited toward the experience requirement. **Examination:** Construction Industry Licensing Board Examination for LowVoltage Alarm System Contractors. **Reciprocity:** Applicant who holds a current out of state license based on passing an examination may be granted a license by endorsement, provided that applicant meets Georgia's experience requirements. **Fees:** $29 application fee. $33 exam fee. **Governing Statute:** Official Code of Georgia Annotated 43-14. Rules of the State Construction Industry Licensing Board, Chap. 121.

Credential Type: Class LV-T Contractor License. **Authorization:** Restricted to telecommunications and general system lowvoltage contracting. **Requirements:** Minimum of one year of experience in low-voltage wiring in this category. A maximum of six months of courses in electronics may be credited toward the experience requirement. **Examination:** Construction Industry Licensing Board Examination for LowVoltage Telecommunications Contractors. **Reciprocity:** Applicant who holds a current out of state license based on passing an examination may be granted a license by endorsement, provided that applicant meets Georgia's experience requirements. **Fees:** $29 application fee. $33 exam fee. **Governing Statute:** Official Code of Georgia Annotated 43-14. Rules of the State Construction Industry Licensing Board, Chap. 121.

Credential Type: Class LV-G Contractor License. **Authorization:** Restricted to general system low-voltage contracting. **Requirements:** Minimum of one year of experience in low-voltage wiring in this category. A maximum of six months of courses in electronics may be credited toward the experience requirement. **Examination:** Construction Industry Licensing Board Examination for LowVoltage General System Contractors. **Reciprocity:** Applicant who holds a current out of state license based on passing an examination may be granted a license by endorsement, provided that applicant meets Georgia's experience requirements. **Fees:** $29 application fee. $33 exam fee. **Governing Statute:** Official Code of Georgia Annotated 43-14. Rules of the State Construction Industry Licensing Board, Chap. 121.

Credential Type: Class LV-U Contractor License. **Authorization:** Unrestricted as to low-voltage contracting. **Requirements:** Minimum of one year of experience in low-voltage wiring in this category. A maximum of six months of courses in electronics may be credited toward the experience requirement. **Examination:** Construction Industry Licensing Board Examination for Unrestricted Low-Voltage Contractors. **Reciprocity:** Applicant who holds a current out of state license based on passing an examination may be granted a license by endorsement, provided that applicant meets Georgia's experience requirements. **Fees:** $29 application fee. $33 exam fee. **Governing Statute:** Official Code of Georgia Annotated 43-14. Rules of the State Construction Industry Licensing Board, Chap. 121.

Hawaii

1888

Contractor
Hawaii Contractors License Board
Dept. of Commerce and Consumer Affairs
PO Box 3469
Honolulu, HI 96801
Phone: (808)548-7637

Credential Type: License. **Duration of License:** Two years. **Requirements:** Three certifications of supervisory experience, at least four years of full-time experience within 10 years prior to application, under the supervision of a contractor licensed in the classification for which applying. Technical or business administration training may be accepted, but shall not count for more than one year of experience. Submission of current financial statement and other financial and insurance records. Definite place of business in an area meeting Hawaii's zoning codes for such business operations. **Examination:** Written. **Fees:** $50 application fee. $275 license fee. $150 Compliance Resolution Fund fee. $50 Biennial Compliance Resolution Fund fee.

Idaho

1889

Electrical Contractor
Idaho State Electrical Board
277 N. 6th St.
Boise, ID 83720-6000
Phone: (208)334-2183

Credential Type: Electrical Contractor License. **Duration of License:** One year. **Requirements:** An Electrical Contractor License will be issued to a Licensed Journeyman Electrician who has been licensed for at least two years upon submission of application and fee. **Fees:** $125 application fee. $100 renewal fee. **Governing Statute:** Idaho Code, Title 54, Chap. 10.

1890

General Contractor
Public Works Contractors State License Board
Statehouse Mail
500 S. 10th St., Ste. 105
Boise, ID 83720-7000
Phone: (208)334-2966

Credential Type: Public Works contractor license. **Authorization:** Covers any construction, repair, or reconstruction for the State of Idaho, any county, city, town, or

Idaho

1891

General Contractor, continued

school district. Also includes irrigation, drainage, sewer, and fire districts or any other taxing subdivision or district of any public or quasi-public corporation of the state, commission, department, or agency. **Requirements:** A current financial statement prepared by a Certified Public Accountant. **Examination:** Exam sent to the applicant in the application packet. **Fees:** $25 Class D—bid or contract limit of $50,000; $50 Class C limit of $100,000; $75 Class B—limit of $250,000; $90 Class A limit of $600,000; $100 Class AA—limit of $1,000,000; $125 Class AAA—limit of 1,000,000. **Governing Statute:** Public Works Contractors License Act, Title 54, Chapter 19.

1891

Manufactured Home Manufacturer
Manufactured Home Advisory Board
Dept. of Labor and Industrial
  Services
277 N. 6th
Statehouse Mail
Boise, ID 83720
Phone: (208)334-3950
Fax: (208)334-2683

Credential Type: Manufactured Home Manufacturer License. **Duration of License:** One year. **Requirements:** Submit application and pay fee. Post $20,000 bond with department. **Fees:** $250 license fee. **Governing Statute:** Idaho Code, Title 44, Chapt. 21.

1892

Plumbing Contractor
Plumbing Administration
Dept. of Labor and Industrial
  Services
277 N. 6th
State House Mail
Boise, ID 83720
Phone: (208)334-3442
Phone: (208)334-3950
Fax: (208)334-2683

Credential Type: Plumbing Contractor's License (Certificate of Competency). **Duration of License:** One year. **Requirements:** Complete 2.5 years experience as a licensed journeyman plumber. **Examination:** Written and practical examination. **Reciprocity:** No. **Fees:** $22.50 application fee. $35 exam fee. $75 license fee. $37.50 renewal fee. **Governing Statute:** Idaho Code, Title 54, Chap. 26.

1893

Specialty Electrical Contractor
Idaho State Electrical Board
277 N. 6th St.
Boise, ID 83720-6000
Phone: (208)334-2183

Credential Type: Specialty Electrical Contractor License. **Duration of License:** One year. **Requirements:** A Specialty Electrical Contractor License will be issued to a Licensed Specialty Electrician who has been licensed for at least two years upon submission of application and fee. **Fees:** $125 application fee. $100 renewal fee. **Governing Statute:** Idaho Code, Title 54, Chap. 10.

Illinois

1894

Asbestos Contractor
Illinois Dept. of Public Health
Div. of Environmental Health
525 W. Jefferson St.
Springfield, IL 62761
Phone: (217)782-3517

Credential Type: Asbestos Contractor License. **Duration of License:** One year. **Requirements:** Submit evidence of completing a four-day USEPA or state approved training course for contractors or supervisors. Submit the names of three former employees as character references. Submit a list of prior contracts for asbestos abatement projects and evidence of monitoring data taken before and after these projects. Include a description of any project(s) prematurely terminated and the reason for termination. Must have proof of insurance or post a bond of at least $500,000. Renewal requires a one-day refresher course for contractor/supervisor annually. **Examination:** Written examination. **Reciprocity:** Yes, if license was received in a state with requirements equal to or greater than those of Illinois. Must pay Illinois license fee. **Fees:** $250 application fee. $500 initial license fee. $500 renewal fee. $100 license reinstatement fee. **Governing Statute:** Illinois Asbestos Abatements act, Illinois Revised Statutes, Chapter 122.

1895

Asbestos Management Planner
Illinois Dept. of Public Health
Div. of Environmental Health
525 W. Jefferson St.
Springfield, IL 62761
Phone: (217)782-3517

Credential Type: Asbestos Manager Planner License. **Duration of License:** One year. **Requirements:** Complete an Illinois accredited Inspector course and a Management Planner training course. Meet one of the following requirements: (1) Be an Illinois Registered Architect; (2) Be an Illinois-licensed Structural Engineer; (3) Be an Illinois professional Engineer; (4) Be a Certified Industrial Hygienist; (5) Have a bachelor's degree or higher in architecture, engineering, mathematics, or science and a minimum of six months experience inspecting buildings for asbestos-containing materials. (6) Have a bachelor's degree or higher in architecture, engineering, mathematics, or science and two years of experience in asbestos inspections, instructions, project management, project design, or other asbestos management and control activities. Renewal requires one-half day refresher course for Management Planners and one-half day refresher course for Inspectors annually. **Examination:** Written examination. **Reciprocity:** Yes, if license was received in a state with requirements equal to or greater than those of Illinois. Must pay Illinois license fee. **Fees:** $50 initial license fee. $50 license renewal fee. $15 license reinstatement fee. **Governing Statute:** Illinois Asbestos Abatements act, Illinois Revised Statutes, Chapter 122.

1896

Asbestos Project Designer
Illinois Dept. of Public Health
Div. of Environmental Health
525 W. Jefferson St.
Springfield, IL 62761
Phone: (217)782-3517

Credential Type: Asbestos Project Designer License. **Duration of License:** One year. **Requirements:** Complete an Illinois accredited Inspector, Management Planner, and Contractor/Supervisor course. Must be one of the following: (1) an Illinois Registered Architect; (2) an Illinois Licensed Professional Engineer; (3) an Illinois Licensed Structural Engineer; (4) a Certified Industrial Hygienist. Renewal requires one-half day refresher course for Inspectors, one-half day refresher course for Management Planners, and a full day refresher course for Contractors/Supervisors. **Examination:** Written examination. **Reciproc-

Construction Contractors and Managers — Illinois

ity: Yes, if license was received in a state with requirements equal to or greater than those of Illinois. Must pay Illinois license fee. **Fees:** $50 initial license fee. $50 license renewal fee. $15 license reinstatement fee. **Governing Statute:** Illinois Asbestos Abatements act, Illinois Revised Statutes, Chapter 122.

1897

Asbestos Project Manager
Illinois Dept. of Public Health
Div. of Environmental Health
525 W. Jefferson St.
Springfield, IL 62761
Phone: (217)782-3517

Credential Type: Asbestos Project Manager License. **Duration of License:** One year. **Requirements:** Complete an Illinois accredited Contractor/Supervisor course. Must have one year, on-site working experience in building construction projects or three months on-site working experience assisting the licensed project manager on asbestos abatement projects. Renewal requires a one-half day refresher course for Contractors/Supervisors annually. **Examination:** Written examination. **Reciprocity:** Yes, if license was received in a state with requirements equal to or greater than those of Illinois. Must pay Illinois license fee. **Fees:** $50 initial license fee. $50 license renewal fee. $15 license reinstatement fee. **Governing Statute:** Illinois Asbestos Abatements act, Illinois Revised Statutes, Chapter 122.

1898

Asbestos Project Supervisor
Illinois Dept. of Public Health
Div. of Environmental Health
525 W. Jefferson St.
Springfield, IL 62761
Phone: (217)782-3517

Credential Type: Asbestos Project Supervisor License. **Duration of License:** One year. **Requirements:** Complete an Illinois accredited asbestos Contractor/Supervisor training course or hold a current Illinois asbestos worker license. Renewal requires a one-half day refresher course for asbestos Contractors/Supervisors annually. **Examination:** Written examination. **Reciprocity:** Yes, if license was received in a state with requirements equal to or greater than those of Illinois. Must pay Illinois license fee. **Fees:** $50 initial license fee. $50 license renewal fee. $15 license reinstatement fee. **Governing Statute:** Illinois Asbestos Abatements act, Illinois Revised Statutes, Chapter 122.

1899

Private Alarm Contractor
Illinois Dept. of Professional Regulations
320 W. Washington St.
Springfield, IL 62786
Phone: (217)782-8556

Credential Type: Private Alarm Contractor License. **Duration of License:** Three years. **Requirements:** At least 21 years of age. U.S. citizen or legal alien. Good moral character. No felony convictions in the last 10 years. No alcohol or drug dependency or addiction. No dishonorable discharges from the U.S. Armed Services. Never been found incompetent by any court for reason of mental or physical defect or disease. Must show proof of liability insurance appropriate for business circumstances. Must have three years experience, during the five years preceding application, as a full-time supervisor, manager or administrator for licensed private alarm contractor or meet Department of Professional Regulations standards. **Examination:** Private Alarm Contractor Examination. **Reciprocity:** Yes, if licensing state has a reciprocal agreement with Illinois and its standards for licensure are substantially equivalent to those of Illinois. **Fees:** $216.80 examination fee. $500 initial license fee. $500 license by endorsement fee. $450 renewal fee. **Governing Statute:** The Private Detective, Private Alarm And Private Security Act of 1983, Illinois Revised Statutes 1991, Chapter 111.

1900

Private Contractor (Sewage Disposal—System Pumping)
Illinois Dept. of Public Health
525 W. Jefferson
Springfield, IL 62761
Phone: (217)782-5830

Credential Type: Private Contractor License. **Duration of License:** One year. **Requirements:** Must have knowledge of the private sewage disposal code. Submit application and pay fee. **Examination:** Private Sewage Disposal Pumping Contractor Examination. **Exemptions:** Licensed Illinois plumbers are exempt from licensing fees. **Reciprocity:** No. **Fees:** $25 application fee. $50 initial license fee. $50 renewal fee. **Governing Statute:** Illinois Revised Statutes 1991, Chapter 111 1/2.

1901

Private Contractor (Sewage System Installation)
Illinois Dept. of Public Health
525 W. Jefferson
Springfield, IL 62761
Phone: (217)782-5830

Credential Type: Private Contractor License. **Duration of License:** One year. **Requirements:** Must have knowledge of the private sewage disposal code. Submit application and pay fee. **Examination:** Private Sewage Disposal Installation Contractor Examination. **Exemptions:** Licensed Illinois plumbers are exempt from licensing fees. **Reciprocity:** No. **Fees:** $25 application fee. $50 initial license fee. $50 renewal fee. **Governing Statute:** Illinois Revised Statutes 1991, Chapter 111 1/2.

1902

Roofing Contractor
Illinois Dept. of Professional Regulations
320 W. Washington St.
Springfield, IL 62786
Phone: (217)782-8556

Credential Type: Roofing Contractor Certificate. **Duration of License:** Two years. **Requirements:** Must carry acceptable amounts of liability insurance. Must also carry Worker's Compensation Insurance for employees. Submit application and pay fee. **Reciprocity:** No. **Fees:** $100 application fee. $50 initial certificate fee. $50 renewal fee. **Governing Statute:** The Illinois Roofing Industry Licensing Act, Illinois Revised Statutes 1991.

1903

Underground Storage Tank (UST) Worker
Illinois State Fire Marshal
1035 Stevenson Drive
Springfield, IL 62703
Phone: (217)785-1020

Credential Type: Underground Storage Tank (UST) Certificate. **Duration of License:** One year. **Authorization:** Allows licensee to remove, install, reline, and test underground storage tanks. **Requirements:** Submit application and pay fee. **Reciprocity:** No. **Fees:** $100 initial registration fee. $100 renewal fee. **Governing Statute:** 41 Illinois Administrative Code.

Illinois

1904

Water Well and Pump Installation Contractor
Illinois Dept. of Health
525 W. Jefferson
Springfield, IL 62761
Phone: (217)782-5830

Credential Type: Water Well and Pump Installation Contractor License. **Duration of License:** One year. **Requirements:** At least 18 years of age. U.S. citizen or declared intention to become a citizen. Must have two years experience under the supervision of a licensed water well and pump contractor. **Examination:** Water Well and Pump Installation Contractor Licensing Examination. **Reciprocity:** No. **Fees:** $80 examination fee. $80 application/initial license fee. $35 renewal fee. **Governing Statute:** Illinois Revised Statutes 1991, Chapter 111.

1905

Water Well Pump Installation Contractor
Illinois Dept. of Health
525 W. Jefferson
Springfield, IL 62761
Phone: (217)782-5830

Credential Type: Water Well Pump Installation Contractor License. **Duration of License:** One year. **Requirements:** At least 18 years of age. U.S. citizen or declared intention to become a citizen. Must have two years experience under the supervision of a licensed water well contractor. **Examination:** Water Well Pump Installation Contractor Licensing Examination. **Reciprocity:** No. **Fees:** $50 examination fee. $50 application/initial license fee. $25 renewal fee. **Governing Statute:** Illinois Revised Statutes 1991, Chapter 111.

Indiana

1906

Asbestos Contractor
Dept. of Environmental Management
Office of Air Management
Asbestos Section
PO Box 7060
Indianapolis, IN 46202-7060
Phone: (317)232-8232

Credential Type: Accreditation. **Duration of License:** One year. **Requirements:** Submit proof of financial responsibility. Attend an approved training course. A contractor may designate an employee to take the training course. Demonstrate competence. Renewal requires attending a refresher course. **Examination:** Training course examination. **Fees:** $150 annual accreditation fee. **Governing Statute:** 326 IAC 18-1 et seq.

1907

Asbestos Project Designer
Dept. of Environmental Management
Office of Air Management
Asbestos Section
PO Box 7060
Indianapolis, IN 46202-7060
Phone: (317)232-8232

Credential Type: Accreditation. **Duration of License:** One year. **Requirements:** Have an associate's degree or higher in architecture, industrial hygiene, engineering, building system design, or a related field of study; or be a high school graduate and have one year of experience in either planning, supervision, or cost estimation of building construction or asbestos projects, or in asbestos inspection or general building inspection. Attend an approved training course.

Renewal requires attending a refresher course. **Examination:** Training course examination. **Fees:** $100 annual accreditation fee. **Governing Statute:** 326 IAC 18-1 et seq.

1908

Asbestos Project Supervisor
Dept. of Environmental Management
Office of Air Management
Asbestos Section
PO Box 7060
Indianapolis, IN 46202-7060
Phone: (317)232-8232

Credential Type: Accreditation. **Duration of License:** One year. **Requirements:** Have at least six months experience as an asbestos project supervisor or as an asbestos worker. Attend an approved training course.

Renewal requires attending a refresher course. **Examination:** Training course examination. **Fees:** $100 annual accreditation fee. **Governing Statute:** 326 IAC 18-1 et seq.

1909

Plumber Contractor
Licensing Division
Professional Licensing Agency
1021 State Office Bldg.
100 N. Senate Ave.
Indianapolis, IN 46204
Phone: (317)232-5955

Credential Type: License. **Requirements:** Contact licensing body for application information.

Iowa

1910

Asbestos Abatement Contractor/ Supervisor
Iowa Dept. of Employment Services
Labor Services Div.
1000 E. Grand Ave.
Des Moines, IA 50319-0209
Phone: (515)281-3606

Credential Type: License. **Duration of License:** One year. **Requirements:** 18 years of age. Physically capable of performing the work safely. Successful completion of the approved training course. Passing of an Asbestos physical exam. **Reciprocity:** Licenses from other states will be reviewed. **Fees:** $50 license fee. $50 renewal fee.

1911

Asbestos Management Planner
Iowa Dept. of Employment Services
Labor Services Div.
1000 E. Grand Ave.
Des Moines, IA 50319
Phone: (515)281-3606

Credential Type: License. **Duration of License:** One year. **Requirements:** 18 years of age. Physically capable of performing the work safely. Successful completion of two approved training courses. **Reciprocity:** Licenses from other states will be reviewed. **Fees:** $20 license fee. $20 renewal fee.

1912

Asbestos Project Designer
Iowa Dept. of Employment Services
Labor Services Div.
1000 E. Grand Ave.
Des Moines, IA 50319
Phone: (515)281-3606

Credential Type: License. **Duration of License:** One year. **Requirements:** 18 years of age. Physically capable of performing the work safely. Completion of one of two available courses. **Reciprocity:** Licenses from other states will be reviewed. **Fees:** $50 license fee. $50 renewal fee.

1913

General Contractor
Department of Employment Services
Division of Labor
1000 E. Grand Ave.
Des Moines, IA 50319-0209
Phone: (515)281-3606

Credential Type: General contractor registration. **Authorization:** Any construction contractor performing work in Iowa must be registered with the Iowa Division of Labor. **Requirements:** Obtain an Iowa Employer Account number from Job Service of Iowa; complete registration form; Certificate of Insurance listing the Division of Labor as the certificate holder for workers compensation coverage and the completed application sent to the Division of Labor. **Fees:** $25 registration fee. **Governing Statute:** Iowa Code Chapter 91C (1989).

Credential Type: Out-of-State contractor registration. **Authorization:** Covers Out-of-State contractors. **Requirements:** Out-of-State contractors must file a surety bond with the Division of Labor if contract is in excess of $5,000—the bond must be five percent of the contract price or $1,000, whichever is greater. Out-of-State contractor may file a blanket bond with the Division of Labor in an amount no less than $50,000 in lieu of filing individual bonds for multiple contracts—if the amount of the contracts exceeds $1 million, contractor must submit a bond providing additional coverage. A Certificate of Insurance listing the Division of Labor as the certificate holder for workers compensation coverage and the completed application must be sent to the Division of Labor. **Fees:** $25 registration fee. **Governing Statute:** Iowa Code Chapter 91C (1989).

Kansas

1914

General Contractor
Department of Revenue
Division of Taxation
Robert B. Docking State Office Bldg.
Topeka, KS 66625-0001
Phone: (913)296-3160

Credential Type: Non-resident general contractor license. **Authorization:** Covers non-resident contractors and subcontractors. **Requirements:** Must register with the Director of Revenue for each contract where the total contract price or compensation to be received amounts to over $1,000; file a surety bond with the Director of Revenue before entering into a contract—the amount of the bond must be an amount equal to eight percent of the total amount of the contract or $1,000, whichever is greater (in instances where there is a sales tax exempt project, the amount of this bond need only be equal to four percent of the total contract price or $1,000, whichever is greater); register with the Director of Taxation. **Governing Statute:** Non-Residence Contractors Act, K.S.A. 79-1008 through 79-1015.

Kentucky

1915

Electrical Contractor
Dept. of Housing, Buildings and Construction
1047 U.S. 127 South
Frankfort, KY 40601
Phone: (502)564-3626

Credential Type: License. **Duration of License:** One year. **Requirements:** Ability to read, comprehend and write. Proof of $250,000 liability insurance for electrical construction work, and an affidavit to insure compliance with Kentucky Worker's Compensation and Unemployment Insurance Laws. **Examination:** Yes. **Fees:** $40 exam fee. $100 application fee. $25 renewal fee.

Louisiana

1916

Contractor
State Licensing Board for Contractors
7434 Perkins Rd.
Baton Rouge, LA 70808
Phone: (504)765-2301

Credential Type: License. **Duration of License:** One year. **Requirements:** Legal age to conduct business in the state. A minimum of $10,000 net worth. **Examination:** Yes. **Fees:** $25 exam fee. $100—$300 license fee.

1917

Fire Protection Sprinkler Contractor
Office of the State Fire Marshal
1033 N. Lobdell Blvd.
Baton Rouge, LA 70806
Phone: (504)925-4911

Credential Type: Permit. **Duration of License:** One year. **Requirements:** Complete competency test and document past year's work. **Examination:** Competency test. **Fees:** $100 permit fee. **Governing Statute:** R.S. 40:1625 et seq.

1918

Landscape Contractor
Horticulture Commission
PO Box 3118
Baton Rouge, LA 70821
Phone: (504)925-7772

Credential Type: License. **Duration of License:** One year. **Examination:** Written. **Fees:** $35 exam fee. $35 license fee. $35 renewal fee.

Maine

1919

Manufactured Home Mechanic
Dept. of Professional and Financial Regulation
Div. of Licensing and Enforcement
Manufactured Housing Board
State House Station 35
Augusta, ME 04333
Phone: (207)582-8723

Credential Type: License. **Duration of License:** Two years. **Requirements:** Submit application and pay fee. **Fees:** $140 license fee.

1920

Oil Tank Installer
Board of Underground Storage Tank
 Installers
Dept. of Environmental Protection
State House Station 17
Augusta, ME 04333
Phone: (207)289-2651

Credential Type: Class 1 Oil Storage Tank Installer Certificate. **Duration of License:** Two years. **Authorization:** Permits individuals to install and remove all types of underground oil storage tanks and facilities, excluding field-constructed tanks and impressed-current cathodically protected tanks and facilities. **Requirements:** Complete apprenticeship of 12 installations, six of which are on heavy oil tanks or facilities, and six of which are on tanks or facilities used for motor fuel or the marketing and distribution of oil. **Examination:** Written or oral initial exam. Final exam following apprenticeship. **Fees:** $200 application/exam/apprenticeship registration fee. $150 annual apprenticeship renewal fee. $250 final exam/initial certification fee. $150 biennial recertification fee.

Credential Type: Class 2 Oil Storage Tank Installer Certificate. **Duration of License:** Two years. **Authorization:** Similar to Class 1 certification, except that installer may not install heavy oil tanks and facilities. **Requirements:** Complete apprenticeship of six installations, all of which are on tanks or facilities used for motor fuel or the marketing and distribution of oil. **Examination:** Written or oral initial exam. Final exam following apprenticeship. **Fees:** $200 application/exam/apprenticeship registration fee. $150 annual apprenticeship renewal fee. $250 final exam/initial certification fee. $150 biennial recertification fee.

Credential Type: Class 3 Oil Storage Tank Installer Certificate. **Duration of License:** Two years. **Authorization:** Permits installer only to install tanks and facilities for the storage of No. Two fuel oil for consumption on the premises of the facility. **Requirements:** Complete apprenticeship of six installations, all of which are on tanks or facilities used for storage of No. Two fuel oil for consumption on the premises where stored. **Examination:** Written or oral initial exam. Final exam following apprenticeship. **Fees:** $200 application/exam/apprenticeship registration fee. $150 annual apprenticeship renewal fee. $250 final exam/initial certification fee. $150 biennial recertification fee.

1921

Underground Gasoline Tank Remover
Board of Underground Storage Tank
 Installers
Dept. of Environmental Protection
State House Station 17
Augusta, ME 04333
Phone: (207)289-2651

Credential Type: Underground Gasoline Tank Remover Certificate. **Duration of License:** Two years. **Authorization:** Allows the certified person to remove underground gasoline tanks, provided that all the tanks at a single location are removed at the same time, and no new tanks are installed at the same location for at least six months following removal. **Requirements:** Must pass on-site examination by removing a petroleum tank under the supervision of a designated employee of the Department of Environmental Protection. On-site examination must be completed within six months of passing the written or oral initial exam. **Examination:** Written or oral initial exam. **Fees:** $25 application/initial exam fee. $350 deposit for on-site exam. $350 daily fee for on-site exam. $150 certification fee. $150 recertification fee.

1922

Underground Hazardous Substance Tank Installer
Board of Underground Storage Tank
 Installers
Dept. of Environmental Protection
State House Station 17
Augusta, ME 04333
Phone: (207)289-2651

Credential Type: Underground Hazardous Substance Tank Installer Certificate. **Duration of License:** Two years. **Authorization:** Allows the certified person to install and remove underground storage tanks and facilities for the storage of legally designated hazardous substances (other than oil). **Requirements:** Must pass on-site examination by installing a hazardous substance storage tank under the supervision of a designated employee of the Department of Environmental Protection. On-site examination must be completed within six months of passing the written or oral initial exam. **Examination:** Written or oral initial exam. **Fees:** $50 application/initial exam fee. $350 deposit for on-site exam. $350 daily fee for on-site exam. $150 certification fee. $150 recertification fee.

Maryland

1923

General Contractor
State License Bureau
301 W. Preston St.
Baltimore, MD 21201-2383
Phone: (410)225-1550

Credential Type: General contractor license. **Requirements:** State construction license available for purchase in any of the counties. Corporations must first register with the Department of Assessment and Taxation. **Reciprocity:** Reciprocal with any counties in the state. **Fees:** $40 license fee in Baltimore City. $15 license fee in the county. **Governing Statute:** Article 56, Section 180 of Annotated Code of Maryland.

1924

Home Improvement Contractor
Home Improvement Commission
Dept. of Licensing and Regulation
501 St. Paul Pl.
Baltimore, MD 21202-2272
Phone: (410)333-6309

Credential Type: License. **Duration of License:** Two years. **Requirements:** Submit application, pay fees, and pass examination. **Examination:** Contractor Examination of the National Assessment Institute, written. **Fees:** $20 exam fee. $325 license fee. **Governing Statute:** Annotated Code of Maryland, Article 56. Code of Maryland Regulations, Title 09, Subtitle 08.

1925

Home Improvement Subcontractor
Home Improvement Commission
Dept. of Licensing and Regulation
501 St. Paul Pl.
Baltimore, MD 21202-2272
Phone: (410)333-6309

Credential Type: License. **Duration of License:** Two years. **Requirements:** Submit application, pay fees, and pass examination. **Examination:** Subcontractor Examination of the National Assessment Institute, written. **Fees:** $10 exam fee. $125 license fee. **Governing Statute:** Annotated Code of Maryland, Article 56. Code of Maryland Regulations, Title 09, Subtitle 08.

Massachusetts

1926

Asbestos Abatement Project Designer
Dept. of Labor and Industries
Bureau of Technical Services
100 Cambridge St., Rm. 1101
Boston, MA 02202-0003
Phone: (617)727-1932
Phone: (617)727-1933

Credential Type: Certification. **Requirements:** Have at least a bachelor's degree in industrial hygiene, occupational health, environmental science, biological science, or physical science, or be registered as an architect or engineer. Complete required training. Have at least 12 months work experience in asbestos abatement field. **Fees:** $300 certification fee. **Governing Statute:** M.G.L. c149, ss 6-6F. 453 CMR 6.01 ff.

1927

Asbestos Abatement Project Monitor
Dept. of Labor and Industries
Bureau of Technical Services
100 Cambridge St., Rm. 1101
Boston, MA 02202-0003
Phone: (617)727-1932
Phone: (617)727-1933

Credential Type: Certification. **Requirements:** Have at least an associate's or technical degree, or equivalent, or two years of college credit. Complete required training. Have at least six months work experience in a comparable occupation or two months field experience under the supervision of a certified asbestos abatement project monitor. **Fees:** $300 certification fee. **Governing Statute:** M.G.L. c149, ss 6-6F. 453 CMR 6.01 ff.

1928

Asbestos Contractor
Dept. of Labor and Industries
Bureau of Technical Services
100 Cambridge St., Rm. 1101
Boston, MA 02202-0003
Phone: (617)727-1932
Phone: (617)727-1933

Credential Type: Certification. **Requirements:** Submit application and pay fee. Designate responsibile persons and management persons having primary responsibility for asbestos work. Provide evidence of their training. Submit worker protection information, including written respirator program, medical monitoring program, and procedures for complying with personal monitoring requirements. **Fees:** $2000 certification fee. **Governing Statute:** M.G.L. c149, ss 6-6F. 453 CMR 6.01 ff.

1929

Asbestos Management Planner
Dept. of Labor and Industries
Bureau of Technical Services
100 Cambridge St., Rm. 1101
Boston, MA 02202-0003
Phone: (617)727-1932
Phone: (617)727-1933

Credential Type: Certification. **Requirements:** Have at least an associate's degree or certificate in project planning, management, environmental sciences, engineering, construction, architecture, industrial hygiene, occupational health, or a related scientific field. Complete required training. Have at least six months work experience in asbestos abatement field, including experience in asbestos management. **Fees:** $300 certification fee. (If one person is applying for certification as both an Asbestos Inspector and an Asbestos Management Planner, only one $300 certification fee is required.) **Governing Statute:** M.G.L. c149, ss 6-6F. 453 CMR 6.01 ff.

1930

Construction Supervisor
Board of Building Regulations and Standards
One Ashburton Pl., Rm. 1301
Boston, MA 02108
Phone: (617)727-3200

Credential Type: Construction Supervisor License, Restricted (1A). **Duration of License:** Three years followed by two-year renewal periods. **Authorization:** Permits supervision only of masonry-related work on one- and two-family dwellings and buildings of less than 35,000 cubic feet. **Requirements:** Be at least 18 years of age. Have three years experience in building construction or design in appropriate field. May also need to register as a Home Improvement Contractor. **Examination:** Construction Supervisor Examination, Restricted (1A). **Fees:** $150 license fee. $25 exam fee. $100 renewal fee.

Credential Type: Construction Supervisor License, Restricted (1G). **Duration of License:** Three years followed by two-year renewal periods. **Authorization:** Permits supervision of construction, reconstruction, altgeration, etc., involving the structural elements of one- and two-family dwellings only. **Requirements:** Be at least 18 years of age. Have three years experience in building construction or design in appropriate field. May also need to register as a Home Improvement Contractor. **Examination:** Construction Supervisor Examination, Restricted (1G). **Fees:** $150 license fee. $75 exam fee. $100 renewal fee.

Credential Type: Construction Supervisor License, Unrestricted. **Duration of License:** Three years followed by two-year renewal periods. **Authorization:** Permits supervision of construction, reconstruction, altgeration, etc., involving the structural elements of buildings containing less than 35,000 cubic feet, one- and two-family dwellings or accessory buildings thereto, buildings used for farm purposes, and retaining walls less than 10 feet in height. **Requirements:** Be at least 18 years of age. Have three years experience in building construction or design in appropriate field. May also need to register as a Home Improvement Contractor. **Examination:** Construction Supervisor Examination, Unrestricted. **Fees:** $150 license fee. $75 exam fee. $100 renewal fee.

1931

Elevator Constructor
Dept. of Public Safety
Div. of Inspection
Elevator Inspection Section
One Ashburton Pl.
Boston, MA 02108
Phone: (617)727-3200

Credential Type: Elevator Constructor License. **Duration of License:** One year. **Requirements:** Have at least two years of related work experience. **Examination:** Written examination. **Governing Statute:** Massachusetts General Laws, Chap. 143.

1932

General Contractor
State Board of Building Regulations and Standards
1 Ashburton Pl., Rm. 1301
Boston, MA 02108
Phone: (617)727-3200

Credential Type: Construction supervisor's license. **Duration of License:** Two or three years. **Authorization:** Includes individuals who directly supervise persons engaged in construction, reconstruction, alteration, repair, removal, or demolition involving the structural elements of: (1) buildings containing less than 25,000 cubic feet of enclosed space; (2) one and two-family dwellings or any accessory building thereto; (3) buildings used for farm purposes; and (4) retaining walls less than 10 feet in height at all points along the wall as

Massachusetts 1933

General Contractor, continued

measured from the base of the footing to the top of the wall. **Requirements:** Sign a tax statement acknowledging that contractor has filed all state tax returns and paid all state taxes required under law; work experience must be documented as a minimum of 36 months of full-time work with any employer listed on the registration form. **Examination:** three hour, 50 question, open book exam dealing with the Massachusetts State Building Code. **Fees:** $150 licensing fee (3 year period). $100 renewal fee (2 year period). $65 exam fee. **Governing Statute:** Massachusetts Building Code.

Credential Type: Restricted construction supervisor's license. **Authorization:** Covers home builders. **Requirements:** Sign a tax statement acknowledging that contractor has filed all state tax returns and paid all state taxes required under law; work experience must be documented as a minimum of 36 months of full-time work with any employer listed on the registration form. **Examination:** three hour, 50 question, open book exam dealing with the Massachusetts State Building Code. **Fees:** $150 licensing fee (3 year period). $100 renewal fee (2 year period). $65 exam fee. **Governing Statute:** Massachusetts Building Code.

1933

Home Improvement Contractor
Board of Building Regulations and Standards
One Ashburton Pl., Rm. 1301
Boston, MA 02108
Phone: (617)727-3200

Credential Type: Registration. **Authorization:** Applies to owner-occupied residential buildings with one to four units. **Requirements:** Submit application and pay fees. **Fees:** $100 registration fee. $100-500 Guaranty Fund fee, prorated based on number of employees.

1934

Refrigeration Contractor
Dept. of Public Safety
Div. of Inspection
Engineering Section
One Ashburton Pl.
Boston, MA 02108
Phone: (617)727-3200

Credential Type: Contractor License. **Authorization:** Required for installing, repairing, replacing, or maintaining any refrigeration/air conditioning system 10 tons or over. **Requirements:** Must own a refrigeration contracting business and have at least four years of experience. **Examination:** Yes. **Fees:** $150 license and exam fee. **Governing Statute:** Massachusetts General Laws, Chap. 146.

Michigan

1935

Alarm System Contractor
Private Security and Investigator Sect.
Dept. of State Police
General Office Bldg.
7150 Harris Dr.
Lansing, MI 48913
Phone: (517)322-1911

Credential Type: License. **Duration of License:** Two years. **Requirements:** At least 25 years of age. At least a high school education or equivalent. A resident of Michigan for at least one year. Must not have been convicted of a felony within the five years prior to application. Must not have been dishonorably discharged from military service. Post a bond or a liability insurance policy with the Department of State Police. Must not have been judged insane or if so judged must have been restored to full mental competency (documented by a court order). Five personal references, other than relatives. Fingerprint check and background information check. Have lawfully been engaged in the alarm system contracting business on his/her own for not less than three years; or have been an employee of a licensed alarm system contractor for not less than three years, and have had at least four years of full-time work experience as a supervisor, or pass a written exam given by the Department of State Police. Abide by the Private Security Guard law. **Examination:** Written exam. **Fees:** $500 initial license fee. $250 renewal fee. $100 fee for each additional branch office. **Governing Statute:** Private Security Guard Licensing Act, Act 330 of 1968, as amended.

1936

Asbestos Abatement Contractor
Asbestos Licensing
Div. of Occupational Health
Dept. of Public Health
3423 N. Logan
PO Box 30195
Lansing, MI 48909
Phone: (517)335-8000

Credential Type: License. **Duration of License:** One year. **Requirements:** Pass an Environmental Protection Agency (EPA) or state accredited four-day Asbestos Contractor/Supervisor Course or submit proof that an employee or agent who is responsible for, or actually involved in, the asbestos abatement project has received the required training. Proof of worker's compensation insurance. Abide by the rules and regulations of the Department. **Examination:** Written exam. **Reciprocity:** Reciprocity may be granted if the requirements of the other state are equal to or exceed those of Michigan and the individual or firm submits a certificate of successful completion of training from the other state. **Fees:** $200 initial license fee if four or fewer employees are engaged in asbestos abatement projects. $400 initial license fee if five or more employees are engaged in asbestos abatement projects. $100 renewal fee if four or fewer employees are engaged in asbestos abatement projects. $300 renewal fee if five or more employees are engaged in asbestos abatement project. $100 penalty for late renewal. Reciprocity fee same as initial fee. **Governing Statute:** Asbestos Workers Accreditation Act, Acts 439 and 440 of 1988. Asbestos Licensing Act, Act 135 of 1986. Asbestos Training Act, Act 147 of 1986. Michigan Occupational and Safety Health Act, Act 154 of 1974, as amended.

1937

Asbestos Abatement Project Designer
Asbestos Licensing
Div. of Occupational Health
Dept. of Public Health
3423 N. Logan
PO Box 30195
Lansing, MI 48909
Phone: (517)335-8000

Credential Type: Accreditation. **Duration of License:** One year. **Requirements:** At least two years experience in asbestos related work or not less than five years of supervisory experience in school building operations and maintenance. Pass an Environmental Protection Agency (EPA) or state accredited Asbestos Abatement Project Designer Course or 32-hour Asbestos Abatement Contractor/Supervisor Course. Renewal requires completion of one-day refresher training course. **Examination:** Written exam. **Reciprocity:** Reciprocity may be granted if the requirements of the other state are equal to or exceed those of Michigan, and the individual submits a certificate of successful completion of training from the other state. **Fees:** $150 initial accreditation fee. $75 renewal fee. $150 reciprocity fee. **Governing Statute:** Asbestos Workers Accreditation Act, Act 440 of 1988.

1938

Asbestos Abatement Supervisor
Asbestos Licensing
Div. of Occupational Health
Dept. of Public Health
3423 N. Logan
PO Box 30195
Lansing, MI 48909
Phone: (517)335-8000

Credential Type: Accreditation. **Duration of License:** One year. **Requirements:** Pass an Environmental Protection Agency (EPA) or state accredited four-day Asbestos Contractor/Supervisor Course. Abide by the rules and regulations of the Department. Renewal requires completion of a one-day refresher training course. **Examination:** Written exam. **Reciprocity:** Reciprocity may be granted if the requirements of the other state are equal to or exceed those of Michigan and the individual submits a certificate of successful completion of training from the other state. **Fees:** $25 initial accreditation fee. $25 renewal fee. $25 reciprocity fee. **Governing Statute:** Asbestos Workers Accreditation Act, Act 440 of 1988. Michigan Occupational and Safety Health Act, Act 154 of 1974, as amended. OSHA Construction Standard, 29 Code of Federal Regulations, 1926.58 Paragraph.

1939

Asbestos Management Planner
Asbestos Licensing
Div. of Occupational Health
Dept. of Public Health
3423 N. Logan
PO Box 30195
Lansing, MI 48909
Phone: (517)335-8000

Credential Type: Accreditation. **Duration of License:** One year. **Requirements:** At least two years experience in asbestos related work or not less than five years of supervisory experience in school building operations and maintenance. Pass an Environmental Protection Agency (EPA) or state accredited three-day Asbestos Inspector Course and two-day Asbestos Management Planner Course. Renewal requires completion of one-day refresher training course. **Examination:** Written exam. **Reciprocity:** Reciprocity may be granted if the requirements of the other state are equal to or exceed those of Michigan and the individual submits a certificate of successful completion of training from the other state. **Fees:** $150 initial accreditation fee. $75 renewal fee. $150 reciprocity fee. **Governing Statute:** Asbestos Workers Accreditation Act, Act 440 of 1988.

1940

Electrical Contractor (Class 1 Electrician)
State Electrical Administrative Board
Electrical Div.
Bureau of Construction Codes
Dept. of Labor
7150 Harris Dr.
PO Box 30015
Lansing, MI 48909
Phone: (517)322-1287

Credential Type: License. **Duration of License:** One year. **Requirements:** Over 21 years of age. Have a master electrician's license or regularly employ a person who has a master electrician's license who will be in charge of work for the applicant. Abide by the rules of the State Electrical Administrative Board. **Fees:** $75 initial license fee. $75 renewal fee. $50 homeowner construction lien fund assessment fee. **Governing Statute:** Electrical Administrative Act, Act 217 of 1956, as amended.

1941

Elevator Contractor
Elevator Safety Board
Elevator Div.
Bureau of Construction Codes
Dept. of Labor
PO Box 30015
7150 Harris Dr.
Lansing, MI 48909
Phone: (517)322-1287

Credential Type: License. **Duration of License:** One year. **Requirements:** At least five years of experience as an elevator constructor or journeyperson in the type of elevator work for which they desire the license. Provide two letters of reference. Comply with the rules and regulations of the Elevator Safety Board. **Examination:** Written exam. **Fees:** $32 initial exam fee. $53 initial license fee. $53 renewal fee. **Governing Statute:** Michigan Elevator Act, Act 227 of 1967, as amended.

1942

Mechanical (Heating/Cooling/Ventilating/Refrigerating) Contractor
Mechanical Div.
Bureau of Construction Codes
Dept. of Labor
7150 Harris Dr.
PO Box 30015
Lansing, MI 48909
Phone: (517)322-1287

Credential Type: License. **Duration of License:** One year. **Requirements:** At least three years of work experience which is acceptable to the Department. Be of good moral character. **Examination:** Two written exams. **Fees:** $25 initial examination fee. (An applicant who seeks licensure in more than one work classification on a single application is required to pay only one examination fee.) $75 initial license fee. $75 renewal fee. $50 homeowner construction lien fund assessment fee. **Governing Statute:** Forbes Mechanical Contractors Act, Act 192 of 1984, as amended.

1943

Mobile Home Installer and Repairer
Mobile Home and Land Resources Div.
Dept. of Commerce
PO Box 30222
Lansing, MI 48909
Phone: (517)373-9153

Credential Type: License. **Duration of License:** One year. **Requirements:** At least 18 years of age. Comply with all rules and regulations of the Mobile Home and Land Resources Division pertaining to licensing, and the installation and repair of mobile homes. **Fees:** $50 initial license fee. $50 renewal fee. **Governing Statute:** Mobile Home Commission Act, Act 96 of 1987, as amended.

1944

Residential Builder
Residential Builders Board
Bureau of Occupational & Professional Regulation
Dept. of Commerce
PO Box 30245
Lansing, MI 48909
Phone: (517)373-9153

Credential Type: License. **Duration of License:** One year. **Requirements:** Present articles of incorporation and a certificate of good standing, if applicable, or a copy of

Michigan

Residential Builder, continued

the assumed name certificate (if using an assumed name). Maintain a permanent business office in Michigan from which business is conducted. Have a credit report submitted directly to the Department on behalf of an individual applicant, all partners and officers, and the corporation if it is over one year old. Be of good moral character. Comply with all of the rules and regulations of the Residential Builders Board. **Examination:** Written exam. **Fees:** $15 application processing fee. $50 initial exam fee ($30 law and rules, $30 practice or trade) $30 initial license fee. $30 renewal fee. $50 homeowner construction lien fund assessment fee. **Governing Statute:** The Occupational Code, Act 299 of 1980, Article 24, as amended.

1945

Residential Maintenance and Alteration Contractor

Residential Builders Board
Bureau of Occupational & Professional Regulation
Dept. of Commerce
PO Box 30245
Lansing, MI 48909
Phone: (517)373-9153

Credential Type: License. **Duration of License:** One year. **Requirements:** Maintain a permanent business office in the state from which they conduct their business and where they maintain their records. Have a credit report submitted directly to the department on behalf of an individual applicant, all partners and officers, and the corporation if it is over one year old. Present articles of incorporation and a certificate of good standing, if applicable, or a copy of the assumed name certificate (if using an assumed name). Be of good moral character. Comply with all rules and regulations of the Residential Builders Board. **Examination:** Written exam. **Exemptions:** Some individuals such as authorized representatives of the government and officers of a court are exempt from the state law. **Fees:** $15 application processing fee. $50 initial exam fee ($30 law and rules, $30 practice or trade). $30 initial license fee. $30 renewal fee. $50 homeowner construction lien fund assessment fee. **Governing Statute:** The Occupational Code, Act 299 of 1980, Article 24, as amended.

Minnesota

1946

Asbestos Abatement Contractor

Dept. of Health
Environmental Health Div.
Asbestos Abatement Unit
717 Delaware St., SE
Box 9441
Minneapolis, MN 55440
Phone: (612)627-5089
Fax: (612)623-5043

Credential Type: Contractor License. **Requirements:** Contact licensing body for application information. **Fees:** $100 license fee.

1947

Electrical Contractor

Board of Electricity
S-173 Griggs Midway Bldg.
1821 University Ave.
St. Paul, MN 55104
Phone: (612)642-0800

Credential Type: License. **Duration of License:** Two years. **Requirements:** Individual or employee must be a licensed master electrician. Post $5000 performance bond. Have required general liability and property damage insurance. **Fees:** $200 license fee. **Governing Statute:** Minnesota Statutes, Sections 326.241-326.248. Minnesota Rules 3800-3899.

1948

Manufactured Housing Installer

Dept. of Administration
Manufactured Housing Section
50 Sherbourne Ave.
200 Administration Bldg.
St. Paul, MN 55155
Phone: (612)296-4628

Credential Type: Registration. **Duration of License:** One year. **Requirements:** Submit application and pay fee. **Fees:** $20 registration fee.

1949

Residential Contractor

Dept. of Commerce
Licensing Unit
133 E. 7th St.
St. Paul, MN 55101
Phone: (612)296-6319

Credential Type: Residential Contractor License. **Duration of License:** Two years. **Authorization:** Required for construction of residential real estate or improving residential real estate. **Requirements:** Submit application and pass examination. Additional requirements will become effective in 1993 and 1994. **Examination:** Yes. **Fees:** $135 license fee. $150 biennial renewal fee.

1950

Residential Remodeler

Dept. of Commerce
Licensing Unit
133 E. 7th St.
St. Paul, MN 55101
Phone: (612)296-6319

Credential Type: Remodeler License. **Duration of License:** Two years. **Authorization:** Authorizes improvement of existing real estate only. Remodeler's license required when contracting to perform more than one specialty. **Requirements:** Must have at least two special skills. Additional requirements will become effective in 1993 and 1994. **Examination:** Yes. **Fees:** $135 license fee. $150 biennial renewal fee.

1951

Underground Storage Tank Contractor

Pollution Control Agency
Tanks and Spills Section
520 N. Lafayette Rd.
St. Paul, MN 55155
Phone: (612)297-8679

Credential Type: Contractor Certification. **Duration of License:** Two years. **Requirements:** Contractors must provide evidence of financial responsibility and employ a certified supervisor. **Fees:** $50 application fee.

1952

Underground Storage Tank Supervisor

Pollution Control Agency
Tanks and Spills Section
520 N. Lafayette Rd.
St. Paul, MN 55155
Phone: (612)297-8679

Credential Type: Supervisor Certification. **Duration of License:** Four years. **Requirements:** Complete a 40-hour training program. Have at least two years of service experience. Have participated in at least five projects within the past two years. **Examination:** Yes. **Fees:** $50 application fee. $260 training fee.

Construction Contractors and Managers

1953

Water Conditioning Contractor
Dept. of Health
Environmental Health Div.
Water Supply and General
 Engineering Section
Plumbing Program
717 Delaware St., SE
Box 9441
Minneapolis, MN 55440
Phone: (612)627-5117
Phone: (612)627-5133
Fax: (612)623-5043

Credential Type: Contractor License. **Duration of License:** One year. **Authorization:** License required if working in community with a population of 5000 or more. **Requirements:** Submit application and pass examination. **Examination:** Written examination. **Fees:** $50 license fee. $30 exam fee. $40 bond filing fee.

1954

Water Conditioning Installer
Dept. of Health
Environmental Health Div.
Water Supply and General
 Engineering Section
Plumbing Program
717 Delaware St., SE
Box 9441
Minneapolis, MN 55440
Phone: (612)627-5117
Phone: (612)627-5133
Fax: (612)623-5043

Credential Type: Installer License. **Duration of License:** One year. **Authorization:** License required if working in community with a population of 5000 or more. **Requirements:** Submit application and pass examination. **Examination:** Written examination. **Fees:** $30 license fee. $30 exam fee.

Mississippi

1955

Asbestos Contractor
Dept. of Environmental Quality
Office of Pollution Control
PO Box 10385
Jackson, MS 39289-0385
Phone: (601)961-5100

Credential Type: Certification. **Duration of License:** One year. **Requirements:** Must have a high school or GED diploma. Must attend an EPA approved four-day contractor/supervisor course. Training must be continuous for recertification. **Examination:** EPA-approved examination for contractor certification. **Exemptions:** Certification not required for federally owned buildings or small-scale, short duration activities. **Reciprocity:** No reciprocity. **Fees:** $300 license fee. $300 renewal fee.

1956

Asbestos Management Planner
Dept. of Environmental Quality
Office of Pollution Control
PO Box 10385
Jackson, MS 39289-0385
Phone: (601)961-5100

Credential Type: Certification. **Duration of License:** One year. **Requirements:** Must be a registered professional engineer or licensed architect in the state. Must attend a 3-day inspector's course and a 2-day management planner course. Additional training must be taken annually for recertification. **Examination:** EPA-approved examination for management planner certification. **Exemptions:** Certification not required for federally owned buildings or small-scale, short duration activities. **Reciprocity:** No reciprocity. **Fees:** $100 license fee. $100 renewal fee.

1957

Asbestos Project Designer
Dept. of Environmental Quality
Office of Pollution Control
PO Box 10385
Jackson, MS 39289-0385
Phone: (601)961-5100

Credential Type: Certification. **Duration of License:** One year. **Requirements:** Must be a registered professional engineer or licensed architect in the state. Must attend an EPA-approved 3-day project designer course or an EPA-approved 4-day contractor/supervisor course. Refresher course must be taken after initial training. Additional training must be taken annually for recertification. **Examination:** EPA-approved examination for project designer certification or for contractor/supervisor certification. **Exemptions:** Certification not required for federally owned buildings or small-scale, short duration activities. **Reciprocity:** No reciprocity. **Fees:** $100 license fee. $100 renewal fee.

1958

Asbestos Supervisor
Dept. of Environmental Quality
Office of Pollution Control
PO Box 10385
Jackson, MS 39289-0385
Phone: (601)961-5100

Credential Type: Certification. **Duration of License:** One year. **Requirements:** Must have a high school or GED diploma. Must attend an EPA-approved four-day contractor/supervisor course. Training must be continuous for recertification. **Examination:** EPA-approved examination for supervisor certification. **Exemptions:** Certification not required for federally owned buildings or small-scale, short duration activities. **Reciprocity:** No reciprocity. **Fees:** $200 license fee. $200 renewal fee.

1959

General Contractor
Mississippi State Board of
 Contractors
2001 Airport Rd., Ste. 101
Jackson, MS 39208
Phone: (601)354-6161

Credential Type: General contractor Certificate of Responsibility. **Authorization:** For public contract over $50,000 and private projects over $100,000; new commercial construction under 7,500 square feet and one to two stories in height. **Requirements:** Financial statement prepared and attested to by a certified public accountant—assets must include a net worth of at least $10,000; an out-of-state, or foreign corporation must qualify to do business in Mississippi with the Secretary of State, and provide the Board with a Certificate of Proof; obtain a Mississippi state tax commission sales tax number and Mississippi income tax identification numbers. **Examination:** 50-150 question exam covering the general knowledge of the construction industry including rules and regulations, business management, trade skills, safety, contracts, and bidding. **Reciprocity:** No reciprocity. **Fees:** $100 application fee. $50 additional classification fee. $50 exam fee. **Governing Statute:** Mississippi Code of 1972 (Sec. 31-3-1 through 31-3-23) and General Laws of Mississippi, Chapter 527, 1988.

Mississippi

1960

Underground Storage Tank Installer
Dept. of Environmental Quality
Office of Pollution Control
PO Box 10385
Jackson, MS 39289-0385
Phone: (601)961-5100

Credential Type: Certification. **Requirements:** High school graduate. Proof of financial responsibility. **Examination:** Certification examinations. **Fees:** No fees.

Credential Type: Restricted Certification. **Authorization:** Authorizes individual to only work on tanks owned by individual or individual's company. **Fees:** No fees.

Montana

1961

Asbestos Abatement Contractor/ Supervisor
Dept. of Health and Environmental Sciences
Health Services Div.
Occupational Health Bureau
1400 Broadway
Cogswell Bldg.
Helena, MT 59620
Phone: (406)444-3671

Credential Type: License and Accreditation. **Duration of License:** One year. **Requirements:** Contact licensing body for application information. Renewal requires completing a refresher course. **Fees:** $100 annual license fee. **Governing Statute:** Montana Code Annotated 75-2.

1962

Asbestos Abatement Project Designer
Dept. of Health and Environmental Sciences
Health Services Div.
Occupational Health Bureau
1400 Broadway
Cogswell Bldg.
Helena, MT 59620
Phone: (406)444-3671

Credential Type: License and Accreditation. **Duration of License:** One year. **Requirements:** Contact licensing body for application information. Renewal requires completing a refresher course. **Fees:** $200 annual license fee. **Governing Statute:** Montana Code Annotated 75-2.

1963

Asbestos Management Planner
Dept. of Health and Environmental Sciences
Health Services Div.
Occupational Health Bureau
1400 Broadway
Cogswell Bldg.
Helena, MT 59620
Phone: (406)444-3671

Credential Type: License and Accreditation. **Duration of License:** One year. **Requirements:** Contact licensing body for application information. Renewal requires completing a refresher course. **Fees:** $100 annual license fee. **Governing Statute:** Montana Code Annotated 75-2.

1964

General Contractor
Department of Commerce
Building Codes Bureau
Attn: Public Contractors
1218 E. 6th Ave.
Helena, MT 59620
Phone: (406)444-3933

Credential Type: Public Contractors license. **Duration of License:** All Public Contractors licenses expire December 31, regardless of the date issued. **Authorization:** Covers public construction contracts exceeding $5,000. **Fees:** $250 Class A—value of any single contract project unlimited; $150 Class B—value not to exceed $100,000; $100 Class C—value not to exceed $25,000. **Governing Statute:** Title 37, Chapters 69 (plumbers), Chapter 68 (electricians) and Chapter 71 of the Montana Code Annotated.

1965

Underground Storage Tank Installer and Remover
Dept. of Health and Environmental Sciences
Environmental Sciences Div.
Solid and Hazardous Wastes Bureau
836 Front St.
Helena, MT 59620
Phone: (406)444-1430

Credential Type: Underground Storage Tank Installer and Remover License. **Duration of License:** Three years (annual renewal). **Requirements:** Contact licensing body for application information. During three-year license term, 16 hours of continuing education are required for renewal. **Examination:** Yes. **Fees:** $50 exam and license fee. $25 annual renewal fee. **Governing Statute:** Montana Code Annotated 75-11.

Nebraska

1966

Air Conditioning/Heating Contractor
Dept. of Building and Safety
City County Bldg.
555 S. 10th St.
Lincoln, NE 68508
Phone: (402)471-7525

Credential Type: License. **Duration of License:** One year. **Requirements:** Must have three years of experience in the field. **Examination:** Yes. **Fees:** $30 application and examination fee. $20 registration fee. $20 renewal fee.

1967

General Contractor
Nebraska Department of Revenue
PO Box 94818
Lincoln, NE 68509-4871
Phone: (402)471-5729

Credential Type: General contractor registration. **Authorization:** Covers non-residents' construction projects with a total value of more than $2,500. **Requirements:** Bonding: A bond or alternative security must be filed for each contract; the amount is based on a percentage of the total contract price of each project; the total contract price of each project may be reduced by work performed by (1) subcontractors not subject to the bond requirements, or (2) subcontractors in compliance with the bond requirements; the required bond amount is 10 percent of the contract price up to the first $100,000 plus five percent of the contract price in excess of $100,000, rounded to the nearest multiple of $1,000; contracts of $2,500 to $10,000 require a bond of $1,000; a bond is not required for contracts less than $2,500. File unemployment insurance with Nebraska Division of Employment. File taxes. **Fees:** $25 application fee for non-resident contractor registration. $25 Nebraska Tax Application fee for non-resident contractor project permit. **Governing Statute:** Nebraska Revised Statute 77-3101 through 77-3112.

Construction Contractors and Managers

Nevada

1968

General Contractor
State Contractor Board
70 Linden St.
Reno, NV 89502
Phone: (702)688-1141

Credential Type: General contractor license. **Requirements:** Establishment of minimum of four years experience as a skilled craftsman; four completed, signed, and notarized reference sheets verifying the type of work applicant is applying for; bank confirmation; financial statements (applicants seeking a monetary limit to $250,000 must present a compiled financial statement prepared by a Certified Public Accountant or Licensed Public Accountant; applicants seeking a monetary limit from $250,000 to $750,000 must provide a financial statement with full disclosures no older than six months; applicants seeking a monetary limit between $750,000 and unlimited need to provide a reviewed financial statement no older than six months or an audited financial statement no older than one year prepared by a CPA); Surety Bond not less than $1,000 or more than $50,000—fixed by the board with reference to the contractor's financial and professional responsibility; proof of registration with Nevada's State Industrial Insurance System. **Examination:** Management exam—open book; General Building Contractor exam—80 questions, closed book; Residential and Small Commercial General Building Contractor—80 questions, closed book. **Reciprocity:** Honored from the states of Arizona, California, and Utah—management exam; four references; proof of license; proof of successfully passing the exam of the state; and proof of license in good standing in the state for five of the last seven years. **Fees:** $270 application fee. $40 management exam fee. If classification requires a technical exam, both exams, $75. **Governing Statute:** Chapter 624 of Nevada Revised Statutes and Chapter 624 of Nevada Administrative Code.

New Jersey

1969

Asbestos Employer
New Jersey Dept. of Labor
Office of Asbestos Control and Licensing
CN054
Trenton, NJ 08625-0054
Phone: (609)633-3760

Credential Type: License. **Duration of License:** Two years. **Requirements:** Must employ an asbestos employee or supervisor who holds a valid permit. 18 years of age. **Fees:** $200 biennial license fee. **Governing Statute:** NJSA 34:5A-32. NJAC 12:120.

1970

Electrical Contractor
Board of Examiners of Electrical Contractors
1100 Raymond Blvd., Rm. 503
Newark, NJ 07102
Phone: (201)648-2058

Credential Type: License. **Requirements:** Five years of related experience; or a bachelor's degree in electrical engineering plus two years of experience; or a high school diploma, graduation from an accredited electrical technical school and three and one-half years of experience. 21 years of age. **Examination:** Yes. **Fees:** $40 exam fee. $75 license fee. $12.50 permit fee. $20 seal press fee. $25 application fee. **Governing Statute:** NJSA 45:5A. NJAC 13:31.

1971

Home Repair Contractor
New Jersey Dept. of Banking
Div. of Consumer Complaints
Legal and Economic Research
CN040
Trenton, NJ 08625-0040
Phone: (609)292-5340

Credential Type: License. **Duration of License:** Two years. **Requirements:** Must maintain a place of business in the state for the transaction of business. Must carry workmen's compensation and public liability insurance. **Fees:** $150 biennial license fee. **Governing Statute:** NJSA 17:16C-62. NJAC 3:19-1.1.

New Mexico

1972

Electrical Contractor
Construction Industries Div.
Dept. of Regulation and Licensing
PO Box 25101
725 St. Michael's Dr.
Santa Fe, NM 87504
Phone: (505)827-7030
Fax: (505)827-7045

Credential Type: Electrical Contractor License. **Duration of License:** Two years. **Requirements:** Be at least 18 years of age. Complete at least four years of approved experience within the past 10 years. **Examination:** Yes. **Fees:** $30 application fee. $30 exam fee. $200 license fee. $200 renewal fee. **Governing Statute:** Construction Industries Division Rules and Regulations. New Mexico Construction Industries Licensing Act, Chapter 60.

1973

General Contractor
Regulation and Licensing Department
Construction Industries Division
725 St. Michaels' Dr.
PO Box 25101
Santa Fe, NM 87504
Phone: (505)827-7054

Credential Type: General contractor license. **Duration of License:** Two years. **Requirements:** Qualifying party: any person or entity engaged in contracting within New Mexico must have a qualifying party certified by the Division; the qualifying party must have experience in the field in which he is applying and pass the exam; during any time that a business is without a qualifying party, the license will be suspended and no new bids may be made nor new work undertaken. Bonding requirement: $25,000 or less (amount of single project), $500 bond; more than $25,000/less than $200,000, $1,000 bond; more than $200,000/less than $1 million, $2,500 bond; more than $1 million, $5,000 bond. A current audited financial statement is filed initially with the license application and filed annually thereafter. **Examination:** Two part exam, one part technical and the other part business knowledge. **Fees:** $30 application fee. $30 exam fee (each exam). $8.42 fee for contractor licensing requirement packet. **Governing Statute:** Construction Industries Division Rules and Regulations and New Mexico Construction Industries Licensing Act, Chapter 60.

1974

Manufactured Housing Installer and Repairperson
Manufactured Housing Div.
Dept. of Regulation and Licensing
PO Box 25101
725 St. Michael's Dr.
Santa Fe, NM 87504
Phone: (505)827-7070

Credential Type: Installer and Repairperson License. **Requirements:** Submit application and pay fee. Demonstrate knowledge and experience of manufactured homes. **Fees:** $100 license fee.

1975

Mechanical Contractor
Construction Industries Div.
Dept. of Regulation and Licensing
PO Box 25101
725 St. Michael's Dr.
Santa Fe, NM 87504
Phone: (505)827-7030
Fax: (505)827-7045

Credential Type: Mechanical Contractor License. **Duration of License:** Two years. **Requirements:** Be at least 18 years of age. Complete at least four years of approved experience within the past 10 years. **Examination:** Yes. **Fees:** $30 application fee. $30 exam fee. $200 license fee. $200 renewal fee. **Governing Statute:** Construction Industries Division Rules and Regulations. New Mexico Construction Industries Licensing Act, Chapter 60.

North Carolina

1976

Alarm System Business License
Alarm Systems Licensing Board
PO Box 29500
Raleigh, NC 27626
Phone: (919)779-1611

Credential Type: License. **Duration of License:** One year. **Authorization:** License allows individual to install, service, monitor, or respond to alarm signal devices, burglar alarms, or other burglary detection devices. **Requirements:** High school diploma and two years of experience within the past five years in an alarm systems business. 18 years of age. **Examination:** Written. **Fees:** $75 application fee. $150 license fee. $50 recovery fund fee. $150 renewal fee.

1977

Electrical Contractor
North Carolina State Board of
  Electrical Contractors
PO Box 18727
Raleigh, NC 27619
Phone: (919)733-9042

Credential Type: License. **Duration of License:** One year. **Requirements:** 18 years of age. High school diploma or equivalent. Two years of experience while engaged actively and directly in the installation of electrical wiring and equipment. **Examination:** Multiple choice. **Fees:** $50—$200 application and license fee. $25—$100 renewal fee.

1978

General Contractor
Licensing Board for General
  Contractors
PO Box 17187
Raleigh, NC 27619
Phone: (919)781-8771

Credential Type: General contractor license. **Duration of License:** One year. **Authorization:** Covers construction projects worth $45,000 or more. **Requirements:** Financial statement: the requirement for a given limitation is established by working capital. **Examination:** Written exam. **Reciprocity:** Written exam waived if the qualifications of the applicant are equal to those of holders of similar licenses in North Carolina. **Fees:** $100 unlimited license fee; $75 intermediate license fee; $50 limited license fee. $25 exam fee. $75 unlimited renewal fee; $50 intermediate renewal fee; $25 limited renewal fee. **Governing Statute:** General Statutes of North Carolina, Chapter 87, Section one et seq.

1979

Plumbing, Heating, and Air Conditioning Contractor
North Carolina State Board of
  Examiners for Plumbing, Heating
  and Air Conditioning Contractors
PO Box 110
Raleigh, NC 27602
Phone: (919)733-9350

Credential Type: License. **Duration of License:** One year. **Requirements:** 18 years of age. **Examination:** Yes. **Fees:** $10 exam fee. $25—$50 license fee. $25—$50 renewal fee.

1980

Refrigeration Contractor
North Carolina State Board of
  Refrigeration Examiners
PO Box 10553
Raleigh, NC 27605
Phone: (919)834-5484

Credential Type: License. **Duration of License:** One year. **Requirements:** Minimum of 2,000 hours of supervised field experience. 18 years of age. **Examination:** Written. **Fees:** $40 initial fee. $40 renewal fee.

North Dakota

1981

Asbestos Abatement Contractor
State Dept. of Health and
  Consolidated Laboratories
Box 5520
1200 Missouri Ave.
Bismarck, ND 58502-5520
Phone: (701)224-5188

Credential Type: Asbestos Abatement Contractor License. **Duration of License:** One year. **Requirements:** One employee must be certified as either an Asbestos Abatement Supervisor, Designer, Inspector, Management Planner, or Project Monitor. **Examination:** Certified employee must pass examination. **Exemptions:** Contractors distrubing less than three square feet or three line feet of asbestos-containing material. **Fees:** $100 license fee. $100 renewal fee.

1982

Asbestos Abatement Management Planner
State Dept. of Health and
  Consolidated Laboratories
Box 5520
1200 Missouri Ave.
Bismarck, ND 58502-5520
Phone: (701)224-5188

Credential Type: Asbestos Abatement Management Planner License. **Duration of License:** One year. **Requirements:** Complete an EPA-approved Asbestos Abatement Management Planner Course. Renewal requires attendance at annual refresher course. **Examination:** Written examination given as part of course. **Exemptions:** In-house non-public employees. Public employees and contractor employees disturbing less than three square feet or three line feet of asbestos-containing material. **Reciprocity:** All EPA-approved courses are recognized as acceptable. **Fees:** $25 license fee per discipline.

1983

Asbestos Abatement Project Designer
State Dept. of Health and
 Consolidated Laboratories
Box 5520
1200 Missouri Ave.
Bismarck, ND 58502-5520
Phone: (701)224-5188

Credential Type: Asbestos Abatement Project Designer License. **Duration of License:** One year. **Requirements:** Complete an EPA-approved Asbestos Abatement Project Designer Course. Renewal requires attendance at annual refresher course. **Examination:** Written examination given as part of course. **Exemptions:** In-house non-public employees. Public employees and contractor employees disturbing less than three square feet or three line feet of asbestos-containing material. **Reciprocity:** All EPA-approved courses are recognized as acceptable. **Fees:** $25 license fee per discipline.

1984

Asbestos Abatement Project Monitor
State Dept. of Health and
 Consolidated Laboratories
Box 5520
1200 Missouri Ave.
Bismarck, ND 58502-5520
Phone: (701)224-5188

Credential Type: Asbestos Abatement Project Monitor License. **Duration of License:** One year. **Requirements:** Complete an EPA-approved Asbestos Abatement Course for supervisors or project desginers. Must attend a NIOSH 582 or equivalent air sampling course. Renewal requires attendance at annual refresher course. **Examination:** Written examination given as part of course. **Exemptions:** Asbestos abatement contractors performing their own air monitoring. In-house non-public employees. **Reciprocity:** All EPA-approved courses for project designer or supervisor are recognized as acceptable. **Fees:** $25 license fee per discipline.

1985

Asbestos Abatement Supervisor
State Dept. of Health and
 Consolidated Laboratories
Box 5520
1200 Missouri Ave.
Bismarck, ND 58502-5520
Phone: (701)224-5188

Credential Type: Asbestos Abatement Supervisor License. **Duration of License:** One year. **Requirements:** Complete an EPA-approved Asbestos Abatement Supervisor Course. Renewal requires attendance at annual refresher course. **Examination:** Written examination given as part of course. **Exemptions:** In-house non-public employees. Public employees and contractor employees disturbing less than three square feet or three line feet of asbestos-containing material. **Reciprocity:** All EPA-approved courses are recognized as acceptable. **Fees:** $25 license fee per discipline.

1986

General Contractor
Secretary of State
Licensing Division
Capitol Bldg., 600 E. Boulevard Ave.
Bismarck, ND 58505-0500
Phone: (701)224-3665

Credential Type: General contractor license. **Authorization:** Covers construction worth at least $500. **Requirements:** Bonding requirement: applicant must file a valid bond with the application, issued by a surety company in the state; Class D contractors only may provide a personal bond with two sureties who are acceptable to the Secretary of State. Proof of workers' compensation coverage. **Fees:** $250 Class A license fee; $150 Class B license fee; $100 Class C license fee; $50 Class D license fee. **Governing Statute:** North Dakota Century Code, Chapter 43-07.

1987

Heating and Air Conditioning Contractor
Secretary of State
Contractor's Div.
Capitol Bldg.
Bismarck, ND 58505
Phone: (701)224-2900

Credential Type: License. **Requirements:** Contact licensing body for application information.

1988

Pump and Pitless Unit Contractor
State Board of Water Well
 Contractors
900 E. Blvd.
Bismarck, ND 58505
Phone: (701)224-2754

Credential Type: Pump and Pitless Unit Contractor Certification. **Duration of License:** One year. **Requirements:** Have at least one year of experience under a qualified contractor. Post $2000 surety bond. **Examination:** Written certification examination. **Fees:** $25 certification fee. $10 exam fee. $25 renewal fee. **Governing Statute:** North Dakota Century Code 43-35.

1989

Sewer and Water Contractor
State Plumbing Board
204 W. Thayer Ave.
Bismarck, ND 58501
Phone: (701)224-4651

Credential Type: Sewer and Water Contractor License. **Duration of License:** One year. **Requirements:** Complete at least one year (1700 hours) of experience as an installer in this state. **Examination:** Written examination. **Reciprocity:** Yes, but must take examination. **Fees:** $100 license and exam fee. $100 renewal fee. **Governing Statute:** North Dakota Century Code 43-18.2-01 et seq.

1990

Sewer and Water Installer
State Plumbing Board
204 W. Thayer Ave.
Bismarck, ND 58501
Phone: (701)224-4651

Credential Type: Sewer and Water Installer License. **Duration of License:** One year. **Requirements:** Complete at least two years (3400 hours) of experience as an apprentice building sewer and water installer in this state. **Examination:** Written examination. **Reciprocity:** Yes, but must take examination. **Fees:** $25 license and exam fee. $25 renewal fee. **Governing Statute:** North Dakota Century Code 43-18.2-01 et seq.

Credential Type: Apprentice Sewer and Water Installer License. **Duration of License:** Two years with annual renewal. **Authorization:** Must work under the supervision of a licensed building sewer and water installer. **Requirements:** Submit application. Apprenticeship lasts two years (3400

North Dakota

Sewer and Water Installer, continued

hours). **Fees:** No fee. **Governing Statute:** North Dakota Century Code 43-18.2-01 et seq.

1991

Water Conditioning Contractor
State Plumbing Board
204 W. Thayer Ave.
Bismarck, ND 58501
Phone: (701)224-4651

Credential Type: Water Conditioning Contractor License and Registration. **Duration of License:** One year. **Requirements:** Be at least 21 years of age. Complete at least one year (1900 hours) of experience as a licensed water conditioning installer. **Examination:** Written examination. **Reciprocity:** Yes, but must take examination. **Fees:** $40 license and exam fee. $40 renewal fee. **Governing Statute:** North Dakota Century Code 43-18.1-01 et seq.

1992

Water Conditioning Installer
State Plumbing Board
204 W. Thayer Ave.
Bismarck, ND 58501
Phone: (701)224-4651

Credential Type: Water Conditioning Installer License and Registration. **Duration of License:** One year. **Requirements:** Meet one of the following sets of requirements: (1) Complete at least one year (1700 hours) of experience as an apprentice water conditioning installer under a licensed water conditioning contractor. (2) Graduate from the plumbing course of an accredited trade school with at least a 9-month (1020 hour) course in plumbing. **Examination:** Written examination. **Reciprocity:** Yes, but must take examination. **Fees:** $20 license and exam fee. $20 renewal fee. **Governing Statute:** North Dakota Century Code 43-18.1-01 et seq.

Credential Type: Apprentice Water Conditioning Installer License. **Authorization:** Must work under the direct supervision of a licensed water conditioning contractor or installer. **Requirements:** Submit application. Apprenticeship lasts one year (1700 hours). **Fees:** No fee. **Governing Statute:** North Dakota Century Code 43-18.1-01 et seq.

Oklahoma

1993

Asbestos Abatement Contractor
Dept. of Labor, Asbestos Div.
4001 N. Lincoln Blvd.
Oklahoma City, OK 73105-5212
Phone: (405)528-1500

Credential Type: License. **Duration of License:** One year. **Requirements:** Two 40-hour courses in asbestos abatement accredited by EPA. Continuing education. Evidence of respiratory training and equipment operation. **Examination:** Asbestos Abatement Contractor Examination. **Fees:** $300 license fee. $300 renewal fee. Included in course fee.

1994

Electrical Contractor (Residential)
Oklahoma State Health Dept.
1000 N.E. Tenth, Rm. 806
Oklahoma City, OK 73152
Phone: (405)271-5217

Credential Type: License. **Duration of License:** One year. **Requirements:** 19 years of age. Three years of work experience. **Examination:** Residential Electrical Contractor Examination. **Fees:** $50 exam fee. $50 license fee. $50 renewal fee.

1995

Electrical Contractor (Unlimited)
Oklahoma State Dept. of Health
1000 N.E. Tenth, Rm. 806
Oklahoma City, OK 73152
Phone: (405)271-5217

Credential Type: License. **Duration of License:** One year. **Requirements:** 21 years of age. Five years of experience in electrical construction; two years must be experience in commercial/industrial construction. **Examination:** Electrical Contractor Examination. **Fees:** $50 exam fee. $50 license fee. $50 renewal fee.

1996

Mechanical Contractor
Oklahoma State Health Dept., Mechanical Div.
1000 N.E. Tenth
Oklahoma City, OK 73152
Phone: (405)271-5217

Credential Type: License. **Duration of License:** One year. **Requirements:** 20 years of age. Four years of experience in the field. Two years of experience may be substituted for classroom for classroom training. **Examination:** Mechanical Contractor Examination. **Fees:** $50 exam fee. $50 license fee. $50 renewal fee.

1997

Plumbing Contractor
Oklahoma State Health Dept.
1000 N.E. Tenth, Rm. 806
Oklahoma City, OK 73152
Phone: (405)271-5217

Credential Type: License. **Duration of License:** One year. **Requirements:** 20 years of age. Four years of experience in the plumbing trade. **Examination:** Plumbing Contractor Examination. **Fees:** $50 exam fee. $50 license fee. $50 renewal fee.

1998

Underground Storage Tank Installer
Oklahoma Corp. Commission
U.S.T. Fuel Div.
2101 Lincoln
Oklahoma City, OK 73105
Phone: (405)521-6720

Credential Type: License. **Duration of License:** Two years. **Requirements:** Two years of related work experience. Experience in three U.S.T. activities. **Examination:** Underground Storage Tank Licensing Exam 0470. **Fees:** $50 application fee (includes exam). $50 license fee. $50 renewal fee.

Oregon

1999

Construction Contractor
Construction Contractor's Board
Veterans' Bldg., Ste. 300
Salem, OR 97309-5052
Phone: (503)378-4621

Credential Type: Registration. **Duration of License:** One year. **Requirements:** Must have a surety bond. Must have liability insurance. Must complete up to four hours of classes. **Fees:** $80—$100 registration fee. $65—$80 renewal fee. **Governing Statute:** ORS 701.

Construction Contractors and Managers

2000

Contractor, Registered
Construction Contractors Board
Veterans Bldg., Ste. 300
Salem, OR 97309-5052
Phone: (503)378-4621

Credential Type: Registration. **Duration of License:** One year. **Requirements:** Must have a surety bond. Must have liability insurance. Must have completed up to four hours of classes. **Fees:** $80—$100 original fee. $65—$80 renewal fee. **Governing Statute:** ORS 701.

2001

Electrical Contractor
Construction Contractors Board
700 Summer St. NE, Ste. 300
Salem, OR 97309-5052
Phone: (503)373-4621

Credential Type: Registration. **Requirements:** Must complete application and pay fees. **Fees:** $125 registration fee. $125 renewal fee. **Governing Statute:** ORS 479.630.

2002

Electrical Limited Maintenance Specialty Contractor
Building Codes Agency
1535 Edgewater
Salem, OR 97310
Phone: (503)373-1268

Credential Type: License. **Requirements:** Must have 12 months of related exprience. **Fees:** $25 license fee. $25 renewal fee. **Governing Statute:** ORS 479.630.

2003

Landscape Contractor
Landscape Contractors Board
Veterans Bldg., Ste. 300
Salem, OR 97309-5052
Phone: (503)378-4621, ext. 4032

Credential Type: License. **Requirements:** Must have two years of landscape experience or one year of experience and one year of education in landscape contracting. **Examination:** Yes. **Fees:** $25 exam fee. $30 license fee. $30 renewal fee. **Governing Statute:** ORS 671.510 to 671.990.

2004

Limited Energy Electrical Contractor
Building Codes Agency
1535 Edgewater NW
Salem, OR 97310
Phone: (503)373-1268

Credential Type: License. **Fees:** $125 license fee. $125 renewal fee. **Governing Statute:** ORS 479.630.

2005

Limited Pump Installation Contractor
Building Codes Agency
1535 Edgewater NW
Salem, OR 97310
Phone: (503)373-1268

Credential Type: License. **Requirements:** Must have at least 12 months experience in the repairing, replacing, installing new or existing pump or irrigation equipment on residential property. **Examination:** No. **Fees:** $25 application fee. $25 renewal fee. **Governing Statute:** ORS 479.630(12).

2006

Limited Sign Contractors
Building Codes Agency
1535 Edgewater NW
Salem, OR 97310
Phone: (503)373-1268

Credential Type: License. **Examination:** No. **Fees:** $125 license fee. $125 renewal fee. **Governing Statute:** ORS 479.630.

2007

Plumbing Contractor
Building Codes Agency
1535 Edgewater NW
Salem, OR 97310
Phone: (503)373-1268

Credential Type: License. **Examination:** Yes. **Fees:** $150 license fee. $150 renewal fee. **Governing Statute:** ORS 693.135.

Rhode Island

2008

Asbestos Abatement Contractor
Div. of Occupational and Radiological Health
Rhode Island Dept. of Health
3 Capitol Hill
Providence, RI 02908
Phone: (401)277-3601

Credential Type: Asbestos Abatement Contractor License. **Duration of License:** Two years. **Requirements:** At least 18 years of age. Complete 40 hours of approved asbestos abatement training. **Examination:** Written examination. **Reciprocity:** No. **Fees:** $150 biennial renewal fee.

2009

Asbestos Abatement Site Supervisor
Div. of Occupational and Radiological Health
Rhode Island Dept. of Health
3 Capitol Hill
Providence, RI 02908
Phone: (401)277-3601

Credential Type: Asbestos Abatement Site Supervisor License. **Duration of License:** Two years. **Requirements:** At least 18 years of age. Complete 40 hours of approved asbestos abatement training. **Examination:** Written examination. **Reciprocity:** No. **Fees:** $40 biennial renewal fee.

2010

Electric Sign Installer
Board of Examiners of Electricians
Div. of Professional Regulation
Rhode Island Dept. of Labor
220 Elmwood Ave.
Providence, RI 02907
Phone: (401)457-1860

Credential Type: Journeyperson License (Cert CF). **Duration of License:** One year. **Requirements:** At least 18 years of age. Complete a 6,000 hour registered apprenticeship under the supervision of a licensed electrician. **Examination:** Written examination. **Reciprocity:** No. **Fees:** $30 application fee. $10 apprentice registration fee. $30 Journeyperson (Cert CF) license fee.

Credential Type: Master Contractor License (Cert SCF). **Duration of License:** One year. **Requirements:** Hold journeyperson's license for at least one year or complete 10,000 hours of equivalent expe-

Rhode Island

2011

Electric Sign Installer, continued

rience. Alternative requirements are available by contacting the board. **Examination:** Written examination. **Reciprocity:** No. **Fees:** $30 application fee. $100 master contractor (Cert SCF) license fee.

2011

Electrical Contractor
Board of Examiners of Electricians
Div. of Professional Regulation
Rhode Island Dept. of Labor
220 Elmwood Ave.
Providence, RI 02907
Phone: (401)457-1860

Credential Type: Master Contractor License (Cert A). **Duration of License:** One year. **Requirements:** Hold journeyperson's license for at least one year or complete 10,000 hours of equivalent experience. Alternative requirements are available by contacting the board. **Examination:** Written examination. **Reciprocity:** No. **Fees:** $30 application fee. $100 master contractor (Cert A) license fee.

2012

Lead Hazard Abatement Contractor
Office of Environmental Health Risk Assessment
Rhode Island Dept. of Health
3 Capitol Hill
Providence, RI 02908
Phone: (401)277-1417

Credential Type: Lead Hazard Abatement Contractor. **Requirements:** Submit application. Contact licensing agency for additional requirements. **Examination:** Written and practical examinations.

2013

Lead Hazard Abatement Site Supervisor
Office of Environmental Health Risk Assessment
Rhode Island Dept. of Health
3 Capitol Hill
Providence, RI 02908
Phone: (401)277-1417

Credential Type: Lead Hazard Abatement Site Supervisor. **Requirements:** Submit application. Contact licensing agency for additional requirements. **Examination:** Written and practical examinations.

2014

Residential Building Contractor/ Sub-Contractor
Building Contractor's Registration Board
Rhode Island Dept. of Administration
One Capitol Hill
Providence, RI 02908
Phone: (401)277-1270

Credential Type: Residential Building Contractor/Sub-Contractor License. **Duration of License:** One year. **Requirements:** Knowledge of building codes and proper trade practices. Must carry adequate insurance to cover damage to property or injury to persons. **Examination:** Written examination. **Reciprocity:** No. **Fees:** $60 initial license/application fee. $60 renewal fee.

2015

Sewage Disposal System Installer
Div. of Air and Hazardous Materials, ISDS Section
Rhode Island Dept. of Environmental Management
291 Promenade St.
Providence, RI 02908
Phone: (401)277-2306

Credential Type: Sewage Disposal System Installer. **Duration of License:** One year. **Requirements:** Ability to use transit and to install and repair sewage disposal system. **Examination:** Written examination. **Reciprocity:** No. **Fees:** $55 application fee. $30 renewal fee.

South Carolina

2016

Burglar Alarm Contractor
South Carolina State Licensing Board for Contractors
PO Box 5737
Columbia, SC 29250
Phone: (803)734-8954

Credential Type: Burglar Alarm Contractor License. **Requirements:** Approved financial statement showing net worth. **Examination:** Yes. **Fees:** $250 license fee.

2017

Contractor
South Carolina State Licensing Board for Contractors
PO Box 5737
Columbia, SC 29250
Phone: (803)734-8954

Credential Type: General Contractor License. **Requirements:** Approved financial statement showing net worth. **Examination:** Yes. **Fees:** $110 license fee.

Credential Type: Mechanical Contractor License. **Requirements:** Approved financial statement showing net worth. **Examination:** Yes. **Fees:** $110 license fee.

2018

Fire Protection Contractor
South Carolina State Licensing Board for Contractors
PO Box 5737
Columbia, SC 29250
Phone: (803)734-8954

Credential Type: Fire Protection Contractor License. **Requirements:** Approved financial statement showing net worth. **Examination:** Yes. **Fees:** $250 license fee.

2019

Residential Home Builder
Residential Home Builders Commission
2221 Devine St., Ste. 530
Columbia, SC 29205
Phone: (803)734-9174

Credential Type: License. **Requirements:** Contact licensing body for application information. **Examination:** Yes. **Fees:** $100 license fee. $100 renewal fee. $100 exam fee.

South Dakota

2020

Appliance Installation Plumbing Contractor
State Plumbing Commission
222 E. Capitol
PO Box 807
Pierre, SD 57501
Phone: (605)773-3429
Phone: (605)224-4374

Credential Type: Appliance Installation Plumbing Contractor License. **Duration of License:** One year. **Requirements:** Have at least one year experience as an appliance plumbing installer in South Dakota. **Examination:** Written examination. **Reciprocity:** Yes, provided state has same qualifications as South Dakota. **Fees:** $110 license and exam fee. $60 renewal fee. $50 temporary license fee. **Governing Statute:** South Dakota Codified Laws, Chap. 36-25. Administrative Rules of South Dakota, Article 20:53.

2021

Electrical Contractor
South Dakota Electrical Commission
Dept. of Commerce and Regulation
125 West Capitol
Pierre, SD 57501
Phone: (605)773-3573
Phone: (605)224-8674
Phone: (800)233-7765

Credential Type: Electrical Contractor Registration and Permit. **Duration of License:** Two years. **Requirements:** Must have the necessary qualifications, training, experience, and technical knowledge to plan, lay out, and supervise the installation and repair of electrical wiring, apparatus, and equipment for electric light, heating, and power. Must have at least two years experience as a journeyman electrician or at least four years experience as a Class B electrician. Post bond of $10,000.

Renewal requires 12 continuing education credits every two years. After July 1, 1994, the continuing education requirement will increase to 16 credits. **Examination:** Written exam for wiring permit. **Reciprocity:** Yes. **Fees:** $100 permit fee. $40 exam fee. $100 renewal fee. $100 reciprocity fee. **Governing Statute:** South Dakota Codified Laws, Chap. 36-16. Administrative Rules of South Dakota, Article 20:44.

2022

Manufactured and Mobile Home Installation Plumbing Contractor
State Plumbing Commission
222 E. Capitol
PO Box 807
Pierre, SD 57501
Phone: (605)773-3429
Phone: (605)224-4374

Credential Type: Manufactured and Mobile Home Installation Plumbing Contractor License. **Duration of License:** One year. **Requirements:** Have at least one year experience as a manufactured and mobile home plumbing installer in South Dakota. **Examination:** Written examination. **Exemptions:** Manufactured and mobile home licenses not required of licensed plumbing contractors, plumbers, or plumber apprentices. **Reciprocity:** Yes, provided state has same qualifications as South Dakota. **Fees:** $110 license and exam fee. $60 renewal fee. **Governing Statute:** South Dakota Codified Laws, Chap. 36-25. Administrative Rules of South Dakota, Article 20:53.

2023

Plumbing Contractor
State Plumbing Commission
222 E. Capitol
PO Box 807
Pierre, SD 57501
Phone: (605)773-3429
Phone: (605)224-4374

Credential Type: Plumbing Contractor License. **Duration of License:** One year. **Requirements:** Complete at least six years of experience (1900 hour per year) as a plumbing contractor, plumber, or apprentice plumber, with at least two of those years as a plumbing contractor or plumber. **Examination:** Plumbing contractor examination. **Reciprocity:** Yes, provided state has same qualifications as South Dakota. **Fees:** $200 license and exam fee. $150 renewal fee. **Governing Statute:** South Dakota Codified Laws, Chap. 36-25. Administrative Rules of South Dakota, Article 20:53.

2024

Sewage and Water Installation Plumbing Contractor
State Plumbing Commission
222 E. Capitol
PO Box 807
Pierre, SD 57501
Phone: (605)773-3429
Phone: (605)224-4374

Credential Type: Sewage and Water Installation Plumbing Contractor License. **Duration of License:** One year. **Requirements:** Have at least one year experience as a sewage and water plumbing installer in South Dakota. **Examination:** Written examination. **Reciprocity:** Yes, provided state has same qualifications as South Dakota. **Fees:** $170 license and exam fee. $120 renewal fee. **Governing Statute:** South Dakota Codified Laws, Chap. 36-25. Administrative Rules of South Dakota, Article 20:53.

2025

Water Conditioning and Treatment Plumbing Contractor
State Plumbing Commission
222 E. Capitol
PO Box 807
Pierre, SD 57501
Phone: (605)773-3429
Phone: (605)224-4374

Credential Type: Water Conditioning and Treatment Plumbing Contractor License. **Duration of License:** One year. **Requirements:** Submit application and pay fees. Demonstrate qualifications. **Examination:** Written examination. **Exemptions:** Water conditioning licenses not required of licensed plumbing contractors, plumbers, or plumber apprentices. **Reciprocity:** Yes, provided state has same qualifications as South Dakota. **Fees:** $110 license and exam fee. $60 renewal fee. $50 temporary license fee. **Governing Statute:** South Dakota Codified Laws, Chap. 36-25. Administrative Rules of South Dakota, Article 20:53.

Tennessee

2026

Fire Protection Sprinkler System Contractor
Dept. of Commerce and Insurance
Div. of Fire Prevention and Engineering
500 James Robertson Pky., 3rd Fl.
Nashville, TN 37243
Phone: (615)741-7190

Credential Type: License. **Requirements:** 18 years old. Must have Responsible Managing Employee on staff. Must have $10,000 surety bond. Complete application. **Fees:** $500 Registration. $100 Application. $100 Renewal (if not filed in time).

2027

Fire Protection Sprinkler System Contractor/Responsible Managing Employee (RME)
Dept. of Commerce and Insurance
Div. of Fire Prevention and Engineering
500 James Robertson Pky., 3rd Fl.
Nashville, TN 37243
Phone: (615)741-7190

Credential Type: License. **Requirements:** 18 years old. Licensed architect or engineer in Tennessee, or complete NICET 'Level III'. Complete application. **Examination:** Yes. **Fees:** $200 Registration. $25 Applica-

Fire Protection Sprinkler System Contractor/ Responsible Managing Employee (RME), continued

tion. Renewal fees apply. Examination fees will be levied when taking the NICET.

2028

General Contractor
Board of Licensing Contractors
500 James Robertson Pky., 1st Fl.
Nashville, TN 37219
Phone: (615)741-2122

Credential Type: License. **Duration of License:** One year. **Requirements:** Must have references, and list of finances, equipment and experience. **Examination:** Yes. **Reciprocity:** Yes, with application fee. **Fees:** $35 Examination. $150 Application. $75 Reciprocity application.

2029

Home Improvement Contractor
Home Improvment Commission
500 James Robertson Pky., Rm. 110
Nashville, TN 37219
Phone: (615)741-5630

Credential Type: License. **Duration of License:** One year. **Requirements:** Pass the examinations. Must file for renewal every year. Good moral character. Financially stable. Experienced. **Examination:** Yes. **Fees:** $25 Examination. $150 Application. $50 Guaranty Fund.

Texas

2030

Air Conditioning & Refrigeration Contractor
Texas Dept. of Labor and Standards, Licensing Section
PO Box 12157
Austin, TX 78711
Phone: (512)463-2904

Credential Type: Class A License. **Duration of License:** Three years. **Authorization:** Allows holder to install, repair, and alter the type of equipment for which the license is endorsed (environmental, commercial, or both) of any size or capacity. **Requirements:** 18 years of age. Certificate of required insurance of $300,000. Three years of practical experience within the last five years; or a degree in air conditioning engineering or mechanical engineering, and one year of experience; or a combination of at least one year experience with technical education, at the rate of one month experience for each two months of education, equal to three years. **Examination:** Written or oral. **Fees:** $100 exam fee. $300 license fee. $150 renewal fee. **Governing Statute:** VACS 8861, 16 TAC 75.1.

Credential Type: Class B License. **Duration of License:** Three years. **Authorization:** Allows holder to install, repair, and alter the type of equipment for which the license is endorsed (environmental, commercial, or both) of not more than 25 tons cooling capacity and not more than 1.5 million BTU per hours output heating capacity. **Requirements:** 18 years of age. Certificate of required insurance of $100,000. Three years of practical experience within the last five years; or a degree in air conditioning engineering or mechanical engineering, and one year of experience; or a combination of at least one year experience with technical education, at the rate of one month experience for each two months of education, equal to three years. **Examination:** Written or oral. **Fees:** $100 exam fee. $150 license fee. $75 renewal fee. **Governing Statute:** VACS 8861, 16 TAC 75.1.

2031

Asbestos Abatement Contractor
Texas Dept. of Health
Occupational Health Div.
Asbestos Licensing Section
1100 W. 49th St.
Austin, TX 78756
Phone: (512)834-6600

Credential Type: Asbestos Abatement Contractor License. **Duration of License:** One year. **Authorization:** Licensee is authorized to employ currently licensed asbestos abatement supervisors and workers to carry out asbestos abatement procedures. Licensee may also employ operations and maintenance supervisors for building operations and maintenance activities. **Requirements:** Completion within the past 12 months of an approved training course for asbestos abatement contractors and project supervisors. Renewal requires completing the annual refresher training course. Must have certificate of good standing from the State Comptroller's Office that all franchise taxes have been paid. Must have State of Texas sales tax account number. Must have workers compensation insurance. Must have asbestos abatement liability insurance in the amount of $1 million when doing work for hire. Must provide a written respiratory protection plan and descriptions of various procedures and methods to be used. **Fees:** $500 license fee. **Governing Statute:** Texas Civil Statutes, Article 4477-3a. Texas Asbestos Health Protection Rules, Section 295.

2032

Asbestos Management Planner
Texas Dept. of Health
Occupational Health Div.
Asbestos Licensing Section
1100 W. 49th St.
Austin, TX 78756
Phone: (512)834-6600

Credential Type: Individual Asbestos Management Planner License. **Duration of License:** One year. **Authorization:** License required to develop an asbestos management plan. **Requirements:** Completion of Environmental Protection Agency (EPA) or state-approved inspector training courses together with the additional management planner courses of instruction within the past 12 months. Renewal requires completion of annual refresher training for management planners and inspectors. Must have an associate's degree or 60 credit hours from a college or university, or must currently be performing management plans and pass a state-administered competency test. **Examination:** Competency test. **Exemptions:** Competency test not required if applicant has an associate's degree or 60 credit hours from a college or university. **Fees:** $120 license fee. **Governing Statute:** Texas Civil Statutes, Article 4477-3a. Texas Asbestos Health Protection Rules, Section 295.

2033

Asbestos Operations and Maintenance Contractor
Texas Dept. of Health
Occupational Health Div.
Asbestos Licensing Section
1100 W. 49th St.
Austin, TX 78756
Phone: (512)834-6600

Credential Type: Asbestos Operations and Maintenance Contractor License (Restricted). **Duration of License:** One year. **Authorization:** Operations and maintenance activities are restricted to small-scale, short-duration work practices and engineering controls that result in the disturbance, dislodgement, or removal of asbestos in the course of performing repairs, maintenance, renovation, installation, replacement, or cleanup operations. **Requirements:** Completion within the past 12 months of an approved training course for asbestos abatement contractors and project supervisors. Renewal requires completing the annual refresher training course. Must have certificate of good standing from the

Construction Contractors and Managers

State Comptroller's Office that all franchise taxes have been paid. Must have State of Texas sales tax account number. Must have workers compensation insurance. Must provide a written respiratory protection plan and descriptions of various procedures and methods to be used. **Fees:** $120 license fee. **Governing Statute:** Texas Civil Statutes, Article 4477-3a. Texas Asbestos Health Protection Rules, Section 295.

2034

Asbestos Operations and Maintenance Supervisor

Texas Dept. of Health
Occupational Health Div.
Asbestos Licensing Section
1100 W. 49th St.
Austin, TX 78756
Phone: (512)834-6600

Credential Type: Asbestos Operations and Maintenance Supervisor License (Restricted). **Duration of License:** One year. **Authorization:** Operations and maintenance activities are restricted to small-scale, short-duration work practices and engineering controls that result in the disturbance, dislodgement, or removal of asbestos in the course of performing repairs, maintenance, renovation, installation, replacement, or cleanup operations. **Requirements:** Completion within the past 12 months of an approved training course for asbestos abatement contractors and project supervisors. Renewal requires completing the annual refresher training course. Must pass physical examination. **Fees:** $90 license fee. **Governing Statute:** Texas Civil Statutes, Article 4477-3a. Texas Asbestos Health Protection Rules, Section 295.

2035

Asbestos Project Manager

Texas Dept. of Health
Occupational Health Div.
Asbestos Licensing Section
1100 W. 49th St.
Austin, TX 78756
Phone: (512)834-6600

Credential Type: Asbestos Project Manager License. **Duration of License:** One year. **Authorization:** Must be licensed and employed by a licensed asbestos consultant agency to evaluate the quality of work being done on an asbestos abatement project. **Requirements:** High school graduate or a GED certificate. Completion within the past 12 months of an approved training course for asbestos abatement contractors and project supervisors. Renewal requires completing the annual refresher training course. Must pass physical examination. **Fees:** $150 license fee. **Governing Statute:** Texas Civil Statutes, Article 4477-3a. Texas Asbestos Health Protection Rules, Section 295.

2036

Asbestos Project Supervisor

Texas Dept. of Health
Occupational Health Div.
Asbestos Licensing Section
1100 W. 49th St.
Austin, TX 78756
Phone: (512)834-6600

Credential Type: Asbestos Project Supervisor License (Restricted). **Duration of License:** One year. **Authorization:** License required to engage in supervision of an asbestos abatement project conducted in a public building. **Requirements:** Completion within the past 12 months of an approved training course for asbestos abatement contractors and project supervisors. Renewal requires completing the annual refresher training course. Must pass physical examination. Must have appropriate work experience of at least 90 days over a period of not less than 12 months and not more than 24 months. **Fees:** $300 license fee. **Governing Statute:** Texas Civil Statutes, Article 4477-3a. Texas Asbestos Health Protection Rules, Section 295.

2037

Irrigator

Texas Board of Irrigators
PO Box 12337
Austin, TX 78711
Phone: (512)463-7990

Credential Type: License. **Duration of License:** One year. **Examination:** Yes. **Fees:** $75 exam fee. $85 renewal fee. **Governing Statute:** VACS 9751, 31 TAC 421.1.

2038

Underground Storage Tank Installer

Texas Water Commission
Underground Storage Tank Div.
Technical Services Section
PO Box 13087
Austin, TX 78711
Phone: (512)371-6219

Credential Type: License. **Duration of License:** One year. **Requirements:** 18 years of age. 24 months of applicable construction experience. May require up to two years experience in underground storage tank installation, underground utilities installation, or other engineering construction in Texas. Eight hours of continuing education per year per license held for license renewal. **Examination:** Examination on standards and practices. **Fees:** $50 exam fee. $200 initial license fee. $175 renewal fee. **Governing Statute:** House Bill 183, 71st Legislature, Regular Session.

Utah

2039

Contractor

Dept. of Commerce
Div. of Occupational and Processional Licensing
160 E. 300 S.
PO Box 45802
Salt Lake City, UT 84145
Phone: (801)530-6628

Credential Type: License. **Requirements:** Must provide evidence of financial responsibility. Must produce satisfactory evidence of knowledge and experience in the construction industry and knowledge of the principles of business as a contractor. **Examination:** Yes. **Fees:** $200 primary application fee. $100 primary license renewal fee. Primary supplemental: $200 application fee. $100 license renewal fee. $40 changer qualifier fee. Specialized supplemental: $100 application fee. $75 license renewal fee.

Virginia

2040

General Contractor

Commonwealth of Virginia
Department of Commerce
3600 W. Broad St.
Richmond, VA 23230-4917
Phone: (804)367-2532

Credential Type: General contractor license. **Authorization:** Class A license covers single construction contracts or projects worth at least $40,000 or construction work performed in any 12 month period worth at least $300,000. Class B license covers single construction contracts or projects worth less than $40,000 and more than $1,500, or when the work is for the purpose of constructing a water well to reach ground water as defined in the Code of Virginia. **Requirements:** Experience: Class A applicants must prove five years experience in the license classification or specialty services for which they are applying; Class B applicants must prove three years experience. Proof of good financial credit: Class A applicants must provide the Board with

279

Washington 2041

General Contractor, continued

information showing there are no outstanding past-due debts, outstanding state or federal tax obligations and defaults on bonds; Class B applicants must provide the Board with the past three years information. **Financial statement:** Class A applicants must show assets or net equity less than $45,000; Class B applicants must show assets or net equity less than $15,000 (excluding any jointly owned residence). Both must hold workers' compensation and unemployment insurance. **Examination:** Each firm seeking a contractors license must have in its fulltime employ a Designated Employee who has successfully completed the licensure exam. **Reciprocity:** Reciprocity with North Carolina: Class A applicants must meet basic requirements of Class A and have passed an exam equivalent to the Virginia exam; Class B applicants must meet the basic requirements of Class B, be a designated employee for the firm seeking reciprocal licensing, have passed an exam equivalent to the Virginia exam, and take the Virginia section of the Virginia exam; both A and B Class applicants must show proof of experience in the licensing classification of specialty service where the license is held. **Fees:** $135 Class A application fee; $115 Class B application fee. $60 exam fee. $20 reciprocity exam fee for individuals required to take the Virginia section; $40 reciprocity exam fee for individuals required to take both the Virginia and Advanced section of the Class A exam package. **Governing Statute:** Code of Virginia Statutes, Chapters 11, 1, 2, three (Title 54.1 in each) and Rules and Regulations of the Board for Contractors (VR 220-01-2).

Washington

2041

Electrical Administrator
Dept. of Labor and Industries
Building and Construction Safety
  Inspection Services
General Administration Bldg., HC-101
Olympia, WA 98504
Phone: (206)753-6807
Phone: (206)753-6307

Credential Type: Certification. **Duration of License:** Two years. **Requirements:** Complete approved training in electrical work, the National Electrical Code, electrical theory, and safety and administrative procedures. Continuing education required for renewal. **Examination:** Written examination. **Fees:** $25 application fee. $40 certification fee. $60 exam fee. $52 renewal fee.

2042

Electrical Contractor
Dept. of Labor and Industries
Building and Construction Safety
  Inspection Services
General Administration Bldg., HC-101
Olympia, WA 98504
Phone: (206)753-6807
Phone: (206)753-6307

Credential Type: License. **Duration of License:** Two years. **Authorization:** General and specialty licenses are issued. **Requirements:** Must be a certified electrical administrator or be employed by one. Post $4000 surety bond. **Fees:** $80 annual license fee.

2043

General Contractor
Department of Labor and Industries
805 Plum St.
PO Box 9689, HC-650
Olympia, WA 98507-9689
Phone: (206)586-6085

Credential Type: General contractor license. **Requirements:** Surety bond: general contractors must post $6,000 bond. Liability insurance: upon registration and re-registration, applicant needs to furnish insurance or financial responsibility of $20,000 for injury or damages to the property, and $50,000 for injury or damage including death to any one person, and $100,000 for injury or damage including death to more than one person. Supply identification number as proof of workers' compensation and unemployment compensation. **Fees:** $40 registration fee. **Governing Statute:** An Act Relating To general Contractors and Specialty Contractors (RCW 18.27, WAC 296-200).

West Virginia

2044

General Contractor
West Virginia Contractor Licensing
  Board
Bldg. 3, Rm. 319
State Capitol Complex
Charleston, WV 25305
Phone: (304)348-7890

Credential Type: General contractor license. **Authorization:** Covers all contracting work. **Requirements:** Current number of employees working in West Virginia; date applicant began business in West Virginia; Business Franchise Tax Number, which is obtained from the West Virginia Department of Tax and Revenue; Federal Taxpayers identification number; proof of registration and in compliance with the workers' compensation fund, the unemployment compensation fund and the wage bonding law, if applicable; wage bond is required for contractors who have not been actively and actually engaged in construction work for at least five consecutive years preceding the completion date of the application form—the bond is equal to the total gross payroll for four weeks at full capacity or production, plus 15 percent for benefits (wage bond is not required for contractors who only perform residential contract work). **Examination:** Each company is required to designate a qualifying individual to take the exam(s) for the firm. **Fees:** $100 application fee. $40 Business and Law exam fee; $40 (each) trade exam fee. $100 renewal fee. **Governing Statute:** West Virginia Contractor Licensing Act, Chapter 21, Article 11, Code of West Virginia.

Counselors

The following states grant licenses in this occupational category as of the date of publication:

Alabama	District of	Iowa	Minnesota	New Mexico	South Carolina	West Virginia
Arizona	Columbia	Kansas	Mississippi	New York	South Dakota	Wisconsin
Arkansas	Florida	Kentucky	Missouri	North Carolina	Tennessee	Wyoming
California	Georgia	Louisiana	Montana	North Dakota	Texas	
Colorado	Hawaii	Maine	Nebraska	Ohio	Utah	
Connecticut	Idaho	Maryland	Nevada	Oklahoma	Vermont	
Delaware	Illinois	Massachusetts	New Hampshire	Oregon	Virginia	
	Indiana	Michigan	New Jersey	Rhode Island	Washington	

Alabama

2045

Counselor
ALabama Board of Examiners in Counseling
PO Box 550397
Birmingham, AL 35255
Phone: (205)934-0498

Credential Type: License. **Duration of License:** Two years. **Requirements:** 19 years of age. U.S. citizenship. Must hold a master's degree which is primarily professional counseling in content from a regionally accredited university. Must have three years of supervised full-time experience in professional counseling. **Examination:** Board-administered examination. **Fees:** $75 registration fee. $40 examination fee. $100 license fee. $100 renewal fee.

2046

Guidance Counselor
State Dept. of Education,
Certification Officer
Montgomery, AL 36130
Phone: (205)242-9977

Credential Type: Class A Counseling and Guidance Professional Certificate. **Requirements:** Eligibility for a Class B Professional Certificate. Two years of appropriate professional experience, one of which must be in teaching. Master's degree in guidance and counseling approved by the Alabama State Board of Education or the National Council for Accreditation of Teacher Education or the National Association of State Directors of Teacher Education and Certification or ICP. A practicum of not less than 30 contact hours. A fulltime supervised internship of at least 10 weeks duration (minimum of 300 clock hours).

Credential Type: Class AA Counseling and Guidance Professional Certificate. **Requirements:** Eligibility for Class A Counseling and Guidance Certificate. Completion of a sixth year program in counseling and guidance approved by the Alabama State Board of Education.

2047

School Counselor
Alabama State Dept. of Education
Gordon Persons Bldg., Rm. 5201
Mongomery, AL 36130-3901
Phone: (205)242-9977

Credential Type: Certifcate. **Duration of License:** 10 years. **Requirements:** Must hold an Alabama teacher's certificate. Must have completed two years of profesional experience, including one full year of classroom teaching. Must have a master's degree from a regionally accredited institution including required coursework. **Fees:** $20 certification fee. $20 renewal fee.

Arizona

2048

Guidance Counselor
Teacher Certification Unit
PO Box 25609
1535 W. Jefferson
Phoenix, AZ 85002
Phone: (602)542-4368

Credential Type: Guidance Counselor Endorsement. **Requirements:** Arizona teaching certificate. Three years of successful classroom teaching in a position requiring a teaching certificate. Master's degree. Completion of an approved graduate program in school guidance and counseling to include a supervised school counseling practicum.

2049

Marriage and Family Therapist
Board of Behavioral Health
Examiners
1645 W. Jefferson
Phoenix, AZ 85007
Phone: (602)542-1882

Credential Type: Marriage and Family Therapist Certificate. **Duration of License:** Two years. **Authorization:** Voluntary certification by state board is not required by law to practice. **Requirements:** Master's degree or higher in a behavioral science, with courses in Marriage and Family Studies, Marriage and Family Therapy, Human Development, and Professional Studies and Research. At least two years of professional experience that includes 200 hours of supervision. Pass approved examination. Renewal requires 40 clock hours of continuing education. **Examination:** Examination in Marital and Family Therapy, as developed by the Association of Marital and Family Regulatory Boards. **Fees:** $160 exam fee. $200 certification fee. $200 renewal fee.

Credential Type: Associate Marriage and Family Therapist Certificate. **Duration of License:** Two years. **Authorization:** May only practice under the supervision of a certified or licensed behavioral health professional. **Requirements:** Master's degree or higher in a behavioral science, with courses in Marriage and Family Studies, Marriage and Family Therapy, Human Development, and Professional Studies and Research. Pass approved examination. Renewal requires 40 clock hours of continuing education. **Examination:** Examination in Marital and Family Therapy, as developed by the Association of Marital and Family

281

Marriage and Family Therapist, continued

Regulatory Boards. **Fees:** $160 exam fee. $200 certification fee. $200 renewal fee.

2050

Professional Counselor
Board of Behavioral Health
  Examiners
1645 W. Jefferson
Phoenix, AZ 85007
Phone: (602)542-1882

Credential Type: Professional Counselor Certificate. **Authorization:** Voluntary certification by state board is not required by law to practice. **Requirements:** Master's degree or higher with a major emphasis in couseling and of at least 48 semester hours. At least two years of professional experience, one year of which is under professional supervision. Pass approved examination. Renewal requires 40 clock hours of continuing education. **Examination:** Approved examinations include National Counselor Examination (NBCC), Certified Rehabilitation Counselor Examination (CRCC), and Clinical Mental Health Counseslors Examination (NACCMHC). **Fees:** $100 exam fee. $200 certification fee. $200 renewal fee.

Credential Type: Associate Counselor Certificate. **Authorization:** May only practice under the supervision of a certified or licensed behavioral health professional. **Requirements:** Master's degree or higher with a major emphasis in couseling and of at least 48 semester hours. Pass approved examination. Renewal requires 40 clock hours of continuing education. **Examination:** Approved examinations include National Counselor Examination (NBCC), Certified Rehabilitation Counselor Examination (CRCC), and Clinical Mental Health Counseslors Examination (NACCMHC). **Fees:** $100 exam fee. $200 certification fee. $200 renewal fee.

Arkansas

2051

Advanced School Guidance Counselor
Teacher Education and Licensure
State Dept. of Education
4 State Capitol Mall
Little Rock, AR 72201-1071
Phone: (501)682-4342

Credential Type: Advanced Guidance Counseling Certificate. **Requirements:** Hold or be eligible to hold a master's level school guidance/counseling certificate. Have three years of school experience, at least half-time work each year, as a certificated school counselor (guidance worker). Complete post-master's program of 30 or more semester hours that has professional accreditation by an accrediting agency recognized by the State Board of Education. 18 semester hours of Guidance and Counseling. Nine semester hours of electives taken from education, guidance and counseling, psychology, social work, sociology, and/or vocational education. Three semester hours of electives related to the professional practice of a school counselor.

2052

Advanced School Guidance Supervisor
Teacher Education and Licensure
State Dept. of Education
4 State Capitol Mall
Little Rock, AR 72201-1071
Phone: (501)682-4342

Credential Type: Advance Guidance Supervision Certificate. **Requirements:** Hold or be eligible to hold a master's level school guidance/counseling certificate. Have three years of school experience, at least half-time work each year, as a certificated school counselor (guidance worker). Complete post-master's program of 30 or more semester hours that has professional accreditation by an accrediting agency recognized by the State Board of Education. 12 semester hours in Administration and Supervision, including at least two semester hours of each of the following: Educational administration; Supervision; Curriculum; Vocational education. 12 semester hours in Guidance and Counseling. Six semester hours of electives in areas related to work of a supervisor of guidance programs.

2053

Associate Counselor
Arkansas Board of Examiners in
  Counseling
Southern Arkansas University
PO Box 1369
Magnolia, AR 71753
Phone: (501)235-4151

Credential Type: License. **Duration of License:** One year. **Examination:** Yes. **Fees:** Fees for examinations are set annually based on cost of processing the exams. $40 Application. $100 License. $100 Renewal.

2054

Elementary School Guidance Counselor (K-6)
Teacher Education and Licensure
State Dept. of Education
4 State Capitol Mall
Little Rock, AR 72201-1071
Phone: (501)682-4342

Credential Type: Elementary School Guidance Counselor Certificate K-6. **Requirements:** General Requirements require candidates hold or be eligible to hold a six year teaching certificate. Have one school year of full-time teaching experience (continuous or accumulated). One calendar year of non-teaching paid employment (continuous or accumulated). A program of study consisting of 36 or more graduate-level semester hours including or accompanied by a master's or higher degree; program of study must have professional accreditation by an accrediting agency recognized by the State Board of Education. Educational and guidance foundations totalling 24 semester hours, with at least two hours in each of the following: Introduction to guidance and counseling services; Student development, kindergarten through adult; Statistics, or statistics and research; Group testing; Counseling and consultation; Group guidance and counseling; Guidance information systems, kindergarten through adult; Vocational education.

Specialized requirements require nine semester hours of laboratory and supervised experience with at least two semester hours in each of the following: Case management with simulated and/or actual experiences with Elementary students including development and use of cumulative records, development and use of individualized educational plans, report writing, case conferences, placement, referral and follow-up; Practicum of supervised experience with individual and groups of elementary students, parents, teachers, and administrators; Additional practicum or Internship consisting of supervised experience in the delivery of guidance and counseling service in an elementary school setting(s). **Reciprocity:** Applicants holding a valid certificate from another state based on a master's or higher degree from an accredited program and have worked under contract one school year as a full-time counselor, or two years as a half time counselor, may receive a certificate.

2055

Professional Counselor
Arkansas Board of Examiners in Counseling
Box 1396
Southern Arkansas University
Magnolia, AR 71753
Phone: (501)234-1842
Phone: (501)235-4151

Credential Type: License. **Duration of License:** One year. **Requirements:** 18 years of age. Arkansas resident. Three years of supervised full-time work experience in professional counseling. One year of experience may be granted for each 30 graduate semester hours beyond a Masters degree, provided that such hours are clearly related to the field of counseling. Hours earned may be substituted for no more than two years of experience. **Examination:** Yes. **Fees:** Written, oral and practical examination fees are set annually. $40 Application fee. $100 License. $100 Renewal.

2056

School Counselor (Elementary and Secondary)
Arkansas Dept. of Education
Office of Teacher Education and Licensure
State Education Bldg., Rm. 107B
Capitol Mall 4
Little Rock, AR 72201-1071
Phone: (501)682-4344

Credential Type: License. **Requirements:** Eligible to hold a six year teaching certificate. One year experience as certified classroom teacher. Must have one calendar year of non-teaching paid experience. Must complete a graduate program of study in school guidance at an approved school (program must be at least 36 semester hours, including or accompanied by a Masters degree). Must complete general requirements in educational and guidance foundations. Must complete specialized requirements for Elementary Guidance K-6 and Secondary Guidance 7-12 as appropriate. Must be recommended by certifying officer of higher education institution. **Examination:** Yes. **Fees:** $45 National Teacher Examination (NTE) Specialty area test (counselor). $45 NTE Specialty area test renewal.

2057

Secondary School Guidance Counselor (7-12)
Teacher Education and Licensure
State Dept. of Education
4 State Capitol Mall
Little Rock, AR 72201-1071
Phone: (501)682-4342

Credential Type: Secondary School Guidance Counselor Certificate 7-12. **Requirements:** General Requirements require candidates hold or be eligible to hold a six year teaching certificate. Have one school year of full-time teaching experience (continuous or accumulated). One calendar year of non-teaching paid employment (continuous or accumulated). A program of study consisting of 36 or more graduatelevel semester hours including or accompanied by a master's or higher degree; program of study must have professional accreditation by an accrediting agency recognized by the State Board of Education. Educational and guidance foundations totalling 24 semester hours, with at least two hours in each of the following: Introduction to guidance and counseling services; Student development, kindergarten through adult; Statistics, or statistics and research; Group testing; Counseling and consultation; Group guidance and counseling; Guidance information systems, kindergarten through adult; Vocational education.

Specialized requirements require nine semester hours of laboratory and supervised experience with at least two semester hours in each of the following: Case management with simulated and/or actual experiences with Secondary students including development and use of cumulative records, development and use of individualized educational plans, report writing, case conferences, placement, referral and follow-up; Practicum of supervised experience with individual and groups of secondary students, parents, teachers, and administrators; Additional practicum or Internship consisting of supervised experience in the delivery of guidance and counseling service in a secondary school setting(s). **Reciprocity:** Applicants holding a valid certificate from another state based on a master's or higher degree from an accredited program and have worked under contract one school year as a full-time counselor, or two years as a half time counselor, may receive a certificate.

California

2058

Marriage, Family, and Child Counselor
Board of Behavioral Science Examiners
400 R St., Ste. 3150
Sacramento, CA 95814
Phone: (916)445-4933

Credential Type: License. **Requirements:** Master's or doctoral degree in marriage and family therapy or its equivalent from an approved school. Complete two years (3000 hours) of experience in the practice of marriage and family therapy under the supervision of a qualified marriage and family therapist, of which at least 1500 hours are postgraduate experience. **Examination:** Board administered written and oral examinations. **Fees:** $100 application fee. $100 written exam fee. $100 oral exam fee. $27 fingerprint fee.

Credential Type: Intern Registration. **Authorization:** All interns must be registered for postgraduate experience to be credited. **Requirements:** Master's or doctoral degree in marriage and family therapy or its equivalent from an approved school. Must be employed by a licensed supervisor. **Fees:** $60 application fee. $27 fingerprint fee.

2059

School Counselor
Commission on Teacher Credentialing
PO Box 944270
Sacramento, CA 94244-7000
Phone: (916)445-7254

Credential Type: Pupil Personnel Services Credential. **Authorization:** Authorizes the holder to perform school counseling at all grade levels. **Requirements:** Fifth year of study beyond the bachelor's degree. Professional preparation program in school counseling, including a practicum involving direct classroom contact (minimum grade of B on a five point scale). Passage of CBEST. Recommendation of a California institution with an approved program.

Out-of-state applicants who meet requirements may still be certified. They must verify completion of master's or higher degree of 60 semester hours beyond the bachelor's degree, including the practicum. They must also verify eligibility for the equivalent credential authorization in the state where the program was completed. **Examination:** California Basic Education Skills Test **Fees:** $60 application fee. $30

School Counselor, continued

test score recording and evaluation fee, except for CBEST.

Colorado

2060

Licensed Professional Counselor
State Board of Licensed Professional Counselor Examiners
Dept. of Regulatory Agencies
Div. of Registrations
1560 Broadway, Ste. 1340
Denver, CO 80202
Phone: (303)894-7766

Credential Type: Professional counselor's license. **Requirements:** Master's or doctoral education and training in professional counseling. Certification by the National Board for Certified Counselors or the National Academy of Certified Clinical Mental Health Counselors fulfills education requirement.

Complete one year of postdoctoral practice in applied psychotherapy under supervision, consisting of at least 1000 hours reasonably distributed over 12 months. The teaching of applied psychotherapy may count up to 300 hours of postdoctoral practice under supervision and up to 15 hours of supervision, provided teaching was supervised by an approved supervisor.

Or complete two years of post-master's practice in applied psychotherapy under supervision, consisting of at least 2000 hours reasonably distributed over 24 months. The teaching of applied psychotherapy may count up to 600 hours of postdoctoral practice under supervision and up to 30 hours of supervision, provided teaching was supervised by an approved supervisor.

Certification by the National Academy of Certified Clinical Mental Health Counselors fulfills the postdoctoral or post-master's practice under supervision requirement. **Examination:** National Board of Certified Counselors (NBCC) exam. **Fees:** $270 application fee.

Credential Type: License by endorsement. **Requirements:** Be at least 21 years of age. Hold a current license to practice professional counseling from another state. Applicant may not be subject to any injunction, malpractice judgment or claim, complaint, investigation, or disciplinary proceeding. Meet similar requirements regarding education and supervised practice as are required for a Colorado license. **Fees:** $270 application fee.

2061

Marriage and Family Therapist
Board of Marriage and Family Therapist Examiners
Dept. of Regulatory Agencies
Div. of Registrations
1560 Broadway, Ste. 1340
Denver, CO 80202
Phone: (303)894-7766

Credential Type: Marriage and family therapist license. **Duration of License:** One year. **Requirements:** Master's or doctoral degree with major in marriage or family therapy or equivalent major. If applicant has doctoral degree, must complete at least one year of approved, supervised post-degree practice in individual and marriage and family therapy. Practice must include at least 1000 hours of face-to-face contact with couples and families for the purpose of assessment and intervention. If applicant has master's degree, must complete at least two years of approved, supervised post-degree practice in individual and marriage and family therapy. Practice must include at least 1500 hours of face-to-face contact with couples and families for the purpose of assessment and intervention.

For each 1000 hours of postdoctoral practice, applicant must have 50 hours of supervision, including at least 25 hours of face-to-face individual supervision. For each 750 hours of post-master's practice, applicant must have 50 hours of supervision, including at least 25 hours of face-to-face individual supervision. **Examination:** National examination for marriage and family therapist licensure, administered under contract with the Association of Marital and Family Therapy Regulatory Boards. **Reciprocity:** Applicants holding a current license from another state and having credentials and qualifications substantially equivalent to those of Colorado will be considered for license by endorsement. **Fees:** $671 license fee. **Governing Statute:** Colorado Revised Statutes Title 12, Article 43.

Connecticut

2062

Marriage and Family Therapist
Div. of Medical Quality Assurance
Health Systems Regulation Bureau
Health Services Dept.
150 Washington St.
Hartford, CT 06106
Phone: (203)566-3207

Credential Type: License. **Requirements:** Contact licensing body for application information.

2063

School Counselor
State Dept. of Education
Teacher Certification, Chief
165 Capitol Ave.
PO Box 2219
Hartford, CT 06145
Phone: (203)566-4561

Credential Type: School Counseling Initial Certificate. **Requirements:** Holds a professional educator certificate or is eligible for an initial teaching certificate with three years of successful teaching experience or in addition to a practicum, has completed a one-year full-time internship. Master's degree. Equivalent of one year of graduate study in an approved institution, to include 30 semester hours in a planned program in school counseling. Recommendation by preparing institution of knowledge, skills, and understanding in the following areas: principles and philosophy of pupil services; psychological and sociological theory as related to children and youth; career development theory and practice; individual and group counseling procedures; organizational patterns and relationship of pupil services to total school and community program; pupil appraisal and evaluation techniques and evidence of progression of supervised experience in counseling and guidance through laboratory practicum.

Credential Type: School Counseling Provisional Certificate. **Requirements:** School Counseling Initial Certificate. Completion of beginning educator support and assessment program, as may be available from the Connecticut Board, and one school year of successful service under the interim or initial certificates or three years of successful service in the area for which the certificate is being sought, in an approved school, within 10 years prior to application.

Credential Type: School Counseling Professional Certificate. **Requirements:** Three years of successful service under the School Counseling Provisional Certificate. Completion of 45 graduate semester hours in the area of school counseling services.

Delaware

2064

Elementary School Guidance Counselor
Teacher Certification
Dept. of Public Instruction
Box 1402
Dover, DE 19903
Phone: (302)739-4688

Credential Type: Elementary School Guidance Counselor Endorsement. **Requirements:** Master's degree. Complete graduate degree program in elementary school counseling or complete graduate degree in any field plus complete 30 semester hours of graduate course work in the following studies: principles and practices of the guidance program; tools and techniques in counseling; counseling theory and interviewing; organization and administration of the guidance program; career information; testing and analysis; and a supervised practicum or internship at the elementary level. Three years' experience in and elementary school or three years of related, approved experience or a one year supervised internship in a elementary school. Must successfully complete the Educational Testing Service Pre-Professional Skills Tests with the following minimum scores: Reading 175; Writing 172; Mathematics 175. **Examination:** Educational Testing Service Pre-Professional Skills Tests.

2065

Mental Health Counselor
Board of Professional Counselors
Dept. of Administrative Services
Div. of Professional Regulation
PO Box 1401
Dover, DE 19903
Phone: (302)739-4522

Credential Type: Professional Counselor of Mental Health License. **Requirements:** Master's degree. Must have three years of full-time clinical experience concurrent with 100 hours of clinical supervision, with no less than 1400 clinical hours per year for a total of 4200 hours. **Examination:** NAC-CMHC or NBCC examination. **Reciprocity:** Yes. **Fees:** Contact board for fees.

2066

Secondary School Guidance Counselor
Teacher Certification
Dept. of Public Instruction
Box 1402
Dover, DE 19903
Phone: (302)739-4688

Credential Type: Secondary School Guidance Counselor Endorsement. **Requirements:** Master's degree. Complete graduate degree program in secondary school counseling or complete graduate degree in any field plus complete 30 semester hours of graduate course work in the following studies: principles and practices of the guidance program; tools and techniques in counseling; counseling theory and interviewing; organization and administration of the guidance program; career information; testing and analysis; and a supervised practicum or internship at the secondary level. Three years' experience in a secondary school or three years of related, approved experience or a one year supervised internship in a secondary school. Must successfully complete the Educational Testing Service Pre-Professional Skills Tests with the following minimum scores: Reading 175; Writing 172; Mathematics 175. **Examination:** Educational Testing Service Pre-Professional Skills Tests.

District of Columbia

2067

Employment Counselor
License and Certification Div.
Occupational and Professional Licensure Administration
Consumer and Regulatory Affairs Dept.
PO Box 37200
Washington, DC 20013-7200
Phone: (202)727-7823
Phone: (202)727-7480

Alternate Information: 614 H St., NW, Washington, DC 20001 **Requirements:** Contact licensing body for application information.

Florida

2068

Guidance Counselor (K-12)
Bureau of Teacher Certification
Florida Education Center
325 W. Gaines, Rm. 201
Tallahassee, FL 32399
Phone: (904)488-2317

Credential Type: Guidance Counselor Certificate. **Requirements:** Master's degree with a graduate major in guidance and counseling or counselor education which includes three semester hours in a supervised counseling practicum in an elementary or secondary school. Or master's degree with 30 semester hours of graduate credit in guidance and counseling including: three hours principles and administration guidance; three hours student appraisal; three hours education and career development; three hours learning theory and techniques; three hours counseling theories and techniques; three hours group counseling; three hours consultation skills; three hours legal and ethics issues; three hours counseling techniques for special populations; and three hours supervised practicum.

2069

Marriage and Family Therapist
Board of Clinical Social Work, Marriage and Family Therapy, and Mental Health Counseling
Dept. of Professional Regulation
1940 N. Monroe St.
Tallahassee, FL 32399-0750
Phone: (904)487-2520

Credential Type: Marriage and Family Therapist License. **Duration of License:** Two years. **Requirements:** Have at least a master's degree with major emphasis in marriage and family therapy, or a closely related field. Complete at least three years of clinical experience, during which 50 percent of the applicant's clients were receiving marriage and family therapy, two years of which were completed after receiving a master's degree, under the supervision of a licensed marriage and family therapist with at least five years experience, or equivalent. Renewal requires 30 hours of approved continuing education credit. **Examination:** Laws and rules examination. Objective multiple choice examination developed by the Examination Advisory Regulatory Board (AMFTRB) and the Professional Examination Service. **Reciprocity:** License may be granted by endorsement if applicant holds a valid license to practice from another state and has actively practiced for

Marriage and Family Therapist, continued

three of the past five years. Must meet basic educational and experience requirements. Must pass Florida laws and rules examination. **Fees:** $250 application and examination fee. $150 license by endorsement fee. $50 renewal fee. **Governing Statute:** Florida Statutes, Chapter 491. Florida Administrative Code, Rules 21-CC.

2070

Mental Health Counselor
Board of Clinical Social Work, Marriage and Family Therapy, and Mental Health Counseling
Dept. of Professional Regulation
1940 N. Monroe St.
Tallahassee, FL 32399-0750
Phone: (904)487-2520

Credential Type: Mental Health Counselor License. **Duration of License:** Two years. **Requirements:** Have at least a master's degree with major related to the practice of mental health counseling. Complete at least three years of clinical experience in mental health counseling, two years of which were completed after receiving a master's degree, under the supervision of a licensed mental health counselor or equivalent.

Renewal requires 30 hours of approved continuing education credit. **Examination:** Laws and rules examination. Objective multiple choice examination developed by the National Board for Certified Counselors. **Reciprocity:** License may be granted by endorsement if applicant holds a valid license to practice from another state and has actively practiced for three of the past five years. Must meet basic educational and experience requirements. Must pass Florida laws and rules examination. **Fees:** $250 application and examination fee. $150 license by endorsement fee. $50 renewal fee. **Governing Statute:** Florida Statutes, Chapter 491. Florida Administrative Code, Rules 21-CC.

Georgia

2071

Marriage and Family Therapist
Composite Board of Professional Counselors, Social Workers, and Marriage and Family Therapists
Health and Consumer Services Section
Professional Examining Boards
166 Pryor St., SW
Atlanta, GA 30303
Phone: (404)656-3933

Credential Type: Marriage and Family Therapist License. **Duration of License:** Two years. **Requirements:** Master's degree or a doctorate degree from an accredited institution in one of the following subjects: professional counseling, social work, marriage and family therapy, medicine, psychiatric nursing, applied psychology, pastoral counseling, applied child and family development, applied sociology, or any program accredited by the Commission on Accreditation for Marriage and Family Therapy Education. Applicant must complete a minimum of four graduate-level courses in the principles and practice of marriage and family therapy.

Applicant with a master's degree must complete four years of full-time post-master's experience under direction in the practice of professional counseling, clinical social work, or marriage and family therapy, with a minimum of two years in the practice of marriage and family therapy and a maximum of one year in an internship program.

Applicant with a doctorate degree must complete two years of full-time post-master's experience under direction in the practice of marriage and family therapy, with a maximum of one year in an internship.

An applicant with a master's degree must complete 200 hours of supervision in the practice of professional counseling, clinical social work, or marriage and family therapy, with a minimum of 100 hours of supervision in the practice of marriage and family therapy.

Applicant with a doctorate degree must complete 100 hours of supervision in the practice of marriage and family therapy, with a maximum of 50 hours as a student or intern. **Examination:** Marriage and Family Therapy Examination. **Reciprocity:** Yes, a license by examination waiver (endorsement) may be granted to a holder of a current license as a Marriage and Family Therapist from a state with substantially equal license requirements. **Fees:** $100 application fee. $50 exam fee. $100 renewal fee. **Governing Statute:** Rules of the Composite Board of Professional Counselors, Social Workers, and Marriage and Family Therapists, Chap. 135-5.

2072

Professional Counselor
Composite Board of Professional Counselors, Social Workers, and Marriage and Family Therapists
Health and Consumer Services Section
Professional Examining Boards
166 Pryor St., SW
Atlanta, GA 30303
Phone: (404)656-3933

Credential Type: Professional Counselor License. **Duration of License:** Two years. **Requirements:** Meet one of the following criteria: (1) Master's degree with program content primarily in counseling. Complete four years of postmaster's directed experience, at least one year of which must be directed experience under supervision in a work setting approved by the board. One year of a counseling practicum or internship that was part of the master's program may count toward the experience requirement. (2) Doctorate degree with program content primarily in counseling. Complete one year of practicum or internship. **Examination:** National Board of Certified Counselors Examination. **Reciprocity:** Yes, a license by examination waiver (endorsement) may be granted to a holder of a current license as a Professional Counselor from a state with substantially equal license requirements. **Fees:** $100 application fee. $50 exam fee. $100 renewal fee.

2073

School Service Associate
Div. of Teacher Education
State Dept. of Education
1452 Twin Towers East
Atlanta, GA 30334-5070
Phone: (404)656-2406

Credential Type: School Service Certificate. **Authorization:** Authorizes the holder to administer school services in one of the following occupations: Audiologist, Media Specialist, School Counselor, School Nutrition Director, School Psychometrist, School Psychologist, School Social Worker/Visiting Teacher, or Speech and Language Pathologist. **Requirements:** Bachelor's degree is required for Nutrition Director, Speech/ Language Pathologist and Media Specialist. Master's degree and sixth year program is required for Psychologist. All other occupations require a master's degree or fifth year program. Media

Specialist requires Initial Teaching Certificate. A staff development program in the Identification and Education of Children with Special Needs and a certification test is required at the master's degree level in the field of School Counseling. Three years of acceptable school experience are required of in the fields of nutrition and counseling.

Hawaii

2074

School Counselor
Dept. of Education
Office of Personnel Services
PO Box 2360
Honolulu, HI 96804
Phone: (808)548-5803

Credential Type: Initial Specialist Basic Certificate. **Requirements:** Complete a state approved teacher education program at the baccalaureate level with a major in guidance counseling. Pass the National Teachers Examination (NTE) Core Battery and Specialty Area Test. **Examination:** NTE Core Battery and Specialty Area Test.

Credential Type: Specialist Basic Certificate. **Requirements:** Initial Specialist Basic Certificate. Complete two years of successful performance in the public schools of Hawaii.

Credential Type: Initial Specialist Professional Certificate. **Requirements:** Complete a state approved teacher education program majoring in guidance counseling with a master's degree or equivalent five year university program. Pass the NTE Core Battery and Specialty Area Tests. **Examination:** NTE Core Battery and Specialty Area Test.

Credential Type: Specialist Professional Certificate. **Requirements:** Initial Specialist Professional Certificate. Two years of successful performance in the public schools of Hawaii.

Idaho

2075

Professional Counselor
Counselor Licensing Board
Bureau of Occupational Licenses
1109 Main St., Ste. 220
Boise, ID 83702-5642
Phone: (208)334-3233

Credential Type: Professional Counselor License. **Duration of License:** One year. **Requirements:** Complete a planned graduate program of 60 semester hours that is primarily counseling in nature, including six semester hours in an advanced counseling practicum and a graduate degree in a counseling field. Complete 1,000 hours of supervised experience in counseling. **Examination:** Written examination. **Reciprocity:** Yes, provided applicant meets licensing requirements. **Fees:** $75 application fee. $50 exam fee. $75 original license fee. $60 renewal fee. **Governing Statute:** Idaho Code, Title 54, Chap. 34. Rules of the Idaho Counselor Licensing Board.

2076

School Counselor
Certification Analyst
State Dept. of Education
L. B. Jordan Office Bldg.
Boise, ID 83720
Phone: (208)334-3475

Credential Type: Standard Counselor Endorsement. **Duration of License:** Five years. **Requirements:** Master's degree plus verification of completion of approved program of graduate study in guidance and counseling approved by State Board of Education. Must include a practicum in counseling K-12, plus two years of successful teaching experience or 24 cumulative months of gainful employment plus one year of supervised school counseling experience in K-12 setting or two years of successful counseling experience in a K-12 professional setting verified by the employing agency. Valid for five years and may be renewed upon completion of at least six semester credits of college courses within the period of validity.

Credential Type: Advanced Counselor Endorsement. **Duration of License:** Five years. **Requirements:** Valid Standard Counselor Endorsement. Approved Educational Specialist or doctoral degree in guidance and counseling including a practicum. Three years of satisfactory counseling experience in a N12 school setting. Valid for five years and may be renewed upon completion of at least six semester credits of college courses within the period of validity.

Illinois

2077

Private Employment Agency Counselor
Illinois Dept. of Labor
310 S. Michigan Ave., 10th Fl.
Chicago, IL 60604
Phone: (312)793-2810

Credential Type: Private Employment Agency Counselor License. **Duration of License:** One year. **Requirements:** Submit application on appropriate forms. Be employed by a licensed employment agency. Pass examination within 90 days of application. Pay fee. **Examination:** Written examination. **Reciprocity:** No. **Fees:** $50 examination/90 day permit fee. $50 application fee. $25 renewal fee. **Governing Statute:** Illinois Revised Statutes, Chapter 111.

2078

School Guidance Counselor
Certification and Placement Section
100 N. First St.
Springfield, IL 62777
Phone: (217)782-4321

Credential Type: Guidance Counselor Endorsement. **Requirements:** Good character. Good health. At least 19 years of age. Citizen of the U.S. Complete an approved program in guidance counseling. Standard teaching certificate. Master's degree. Complete a supervised practicum in guidance counseling. Complete 32 semester hours of course work that include the following areas of study: Principles and techniques of guidance; appraisal techniques; human growth and development; principles and practices in counseling; occupational, educational, personal, and social information; mental hygiene and/or personality dynamics; organization of guidance services; and research. Pass required sections of the Illinois Certification Test. **Examination:** Illinois Certification Test. **Reciprocity:** Reciprocity exists for applicants holding out-of-state certificates providing their preparation was comparable to that required by the state of Illinois. **Fees:** $44 per section of the Illinois Certification Test.

Indiana

2079

Marriage and Family Therapist
Health Professions Bureau
402 W. Washington St., Rm. 041
Indianapolis, IN 46204
Phone: (317)232-2960

Credential Type: License. **Requirements:** Contact licensing body for application information.

2080

School Counselor
Teacher Certification
Center for Professional Development
State House, Rm. 229
Indianapolis, IN 46204-2798
Phone: (317)232-9010

Credential Type: School Services Standard License. **Duration of License:** Five years. **Authorization:** Holder is eligible to serve as a counselor at all levels. **Requirements:** Complete two years of creditable teaching experience or have a valid out-of-state school counseling license and one year experience as a counselor. Master's degree in counseling or a related field from a regionally accredited institution and the completion 30 semester hours in counseling and guidance at the graduate level. Knowledge or competencies in the following areas: counseling theory; human growth and development; social and cultural foundations; the helping relationship; group dynamics; lifestyle and career development; appraisal of the individual; research and evaluation; and professional orientation.

May be renewed for one five-year period upon completion of six semester hours of graduate work in counselor education directed toward professionalization of this license and with recommendation of the institution where renewal credit was earned.

Credential Type: Professional Endorsement. **Duration of License:** 10 years. **Requirements:** School Services Standard License. Five years of experience in accredited schools as a school counselor subsequent to the issuance of the Standard License, with at least half-time in counseling. Complete 18 or more graduate hours in counselor education beyond the hours required for the Standard License, including four additional areas from the following: evaluation and accountability; consultation; advanced practicum; statistics; supervision of counseling programs; human potential; program management; and family counseling. Recommendation for the Professional License by the institution where the approved professionalization program was completed.

Iowa

2081

Elementary Counselor (K-6)
Board of Educational Examiners
Grimes State Office Bldg.
Des Moines, IA 50319-0147
Phone: (515)281-3245

Credential Type: Elementary Counselor Endorsement. **Requirements:** Master's degree. Holder of or eligible for one other teaching endorsement. One year of successful teaching experience. complete 27 semester hours focusing on guidance and counseling on the elementary level, including a practicum in elementary school counseling.

2082

Marital and Family Therapist
Board of Behavioral Science
  Examiners
Dept. of Public Health
Licas State Office Bldg.
Des Moines, IA 50319-0075
Phone: (515)281-5787
Fax: (515)281-4958

Credential Type: License. **Requirements:** Graduate degree in marital and family therapy with at least 45 semester hours or 60 quarter hours. Complete two years of postgraduate full-time supervised experience in marital and family therapy, including at least 1000 hours of marital and family therapy conducted in face-to-face contact with couples and families, of which 200 hours are in supervision. **Examination:** Examination in Marital and Family Therapy. **Reciprocity:** Yes. **Fees:** $100 application fee. $160 exam fee. **Governing Statute:** Iowa Administrative Code 645, Chap. 30.

2083

Mental Health Counselor
Board of Behavioral Science
  Examiners
Dept. of Public Health
Licas State Office Bldg.
Des Moines, IA 50319-0075
Phone: (515)281-5787
Fax: (515)281-4958

Credential Type: License. **Requirements:** Graduate degree in counseling with at least 45 semester hours or 60 quarter hours. Complete two years of postgraduate full-time supervised experience in counseling. **Examination:** National Counselor Examination (NCE), or Clinical Counselor Examination of the National Academy of Certified Clinical Mental Health Counselors. **Reciprocity:** Yes. **Fees:** $100 application fee. $100 exam fee. **Governing Statute:** Iowa Administrative Code 645, Chap. 30.

2084

Secondary Counselor (7-12)
Board of Educational Examiners
Grimes State Office Bldg.
Des Moines, IA 50319-0147
Phone: (515)281-3245

Credential Type: Secondary Counselor Endorsement. **Requirements:** Master's degree. Holder of or eligible for one other teaching endorsement. One year of successful teaching experience. complete 27 semester hours focusing on guidance and counseling on the secondary level, including a practicum in elementary school counseling.

Kansas

2085

Marriage and Family Therapist
Behavioral Sciences Regulatory
  Board
900 Jackson, Rm. 651-S
Topeka, KS 66612-1220
Phone: (913)296-3240

Credential Type: Registration. **Requirements:** Rules are being formulated for the registration process.

2086

Professional Counselor
Behavioral Sciences Regulatory
  Board
900 Jackson, Rm. 651-S
Topeka, KS 66612-1220
Phone: (913)296-3240

Credential Type: Registration. **Duration of License:** Two years. **Requirements:** Be at least 18 years of age. Complete 60 graduate semester hours including a graduate degree in counseling from a board-approved college or university, with 45 graduate semester hours in courses specified by the board. Complete three years of supervised full-time experience in professional counseling. One year of experience may be subtracted from the requirement for every 30 graduate semester hours obtained beyond the 60 hours required for registration, as long as applicant has at least one year of actual supervised experience.

Renewal requires 50 contact hours of continuing education every two years. **Examination:** Board administered written or oral examination. **Fees:** $100 application and registration fee. $100 exam fee. $100 renewal fee. **Governing Statute:** K.S.A. 65-5801 et seq. K.A.R. 102-3-1 et seq.

2087

School Counselor
Certification Specialist
Kansas State Dept. of Education
Kansas State Education Bldg.
120 E. 10th St.
Topeka, KS 66612-1103
Phone: (913)296-2288

Credential Type: School Counselor Endorsement. **Authorization:** Endorsement will allow work at the elementary or secondary level. **Requirements:** Complete a state approved graduate degree program that includes course work and a supervised practicum at the level at which endorsement is sought. Document two years of teaching experience or one year of teaching experience and one year supervised field experience. Be recommended by a teacher institution.

Kentucky

2088

Rehabilitation Counselor
Dept. of Vocational Rehabilitation
Capital Plaza Tower
Frankfort, KY 40601
Phone: (502)564-4440

Credential Type: License. **Requirements:** Bachelor's degree in rehabilitation, guidance and/or counseling, sociology, psychology, social work, special education, or education with emphasis in vocational counseling or a related field. **Examination:** Yes.

2089

School Guidance Counselor
Kentucky Dept. of Education
Div. of Teacher Education and Certification
Capitol Plaza Tower, 18th Fl.
500 Mero St.
Frankfort, KY 40601
Phone: (502)564-4606

Credential Type: Provisional Certificate. **Duration of License:** Five years. **Requirements:** Hold a Kentucky teaching certificate. Guidance counseling in grades K-8 requires an elementary certificate and grades 5-12 require a certificate valid for grades 5-8, 7-12, or 9-12. One year of successful, full-time classroom teaching. Master's degree with studies that include: history, philosophy, and principles of guidance; organization and administration of guidance and personnel services; appraisal, assessment, and understanding the individual; developmental processes, personality, and behavior change; theories and methods of individual counseling; career development and vocational planning; group processes and procedures; legal and ethical issues; social and personal issues; supervised practicum in guidance and counseling; research and evaluation procedures; and electives from general and/or professional education. Certificate is renewable upon completion of nine semester hours of graduate credit every five years, leading to a Standard Guidance Certificate.

Credential Type: Standard Certificate. **Duration of License:** Five years. **Requirements:** One year experience as a full-time guidance counselor. Graduate program of 60 semester hours which includes a master's degree, advanced instruction in guidance and counseling, and additional course work designed to increase skills and knowledge associated with counseling. Renewable for five year periods upon completion of 60 clock hours of appropriate training.

Louisiana

2090

Elementary School Counselor
Louisiana Dept. of Education
Box 94064
Baton Rouge, LA 70804-9064
Phone: (504)342-3490

Credential Type: Provisional Certificate. **Duration of License:** Three years. **Requirements:** Valid Louisiana Elementary Teaching Certificate. Three years successful experience at the elementary level. Master's degree in Guidance and Counseling from an accredited institution or a master's degree with equivalent hours and courses required for a Master's degree in Guidance and Counseling. 21 semester hours of professional courses to include one course in each of the following basic areas: principles and administration of elementary school guidance; analysis of the elementary school pupil; counseling theory and practice; orientation to the world of work; group processes in the elementary school; elementary guidance practicum; child growth and development. Must have recommendation from the institution where requirements were completed. Permanent endorsement may be added upon completion of nine semester hours of additional work from this list: human growth and development; social and cultural foundations; the helping relationship; groups (group theory, types, methods and practices); supervised experiences; specialized studies.

2091

Secondary School Counselor
Louisiana Dept. of Education
Box 94064
Baton Rouge, LA 70804-9064
Phone: (504)342-3490

Credential Type: Provisional Certificate. **Duration of License:** Three years. **Requirements:** Valid Louisiana Secondary Teaching Certificate. Three years of successful experience at secondary level, or two years at secondary level and one year of accumulated occupational experience. Master's degree in Guidance and Counseling from an accredited institution or a master's degree with equivalent hours and courses required for a Master's degree in Guidance and Counseling. 21 semester hours of professional courses to include one course in each of the following basic areas: principles and administration of guidance; occupational and educational information; individual analysis; vocational guidance; counseling theory and practice; guidance practicum; and group processes. Must have recommendation from the institution where requirements were completed. Permanent endorsement may be added upon completion of nine semester hours of additional work from this list: human growth and development; social and cultural foundations; the helping relationship; groups (group theory, types, methods and practices); supervised experiences; specialized studies.

Maine

2092

Clinical Professional Counselor
Board of Counseling Professionals Licensure
Dept. of Professional and Financial Regulation
Div. of Licensing and Enforcement
State House Station 35
Augusta, ME 04333
Phone: (207)582-8723

Credential Type: Licensed Clinical Professional Counselor. **Duration of License:** Two years. **Requirements:** Master's degree in counseling or an allied mental health field. Complete two years of experience after receiving master's degree, with a minimum of 3000 hours of supervised experience with a minimum of 100 hours of

Clinical Professional Counselor, continued

personal supervision. **Examination:** One of the following: Certified Clinical Mental Health Counselor Examination, or National Counselors Examination (NCE). **Fees:** $40 application fee. $200 license fee. $200 renewal fee. **Governing Statute:** 32 M.S.R.A. Chap. 119.

Credential Type: Conditional License. **Duration of License:** Two years. **Requirements:** Meet all requirements for licensure, except for supervised experience. **Governing Statute:** 32 M.S.R.A. Chap. 119.

Credential Type: Registered Clinical Professional Counselor. **Duration of License:** Two years. **Authorization:** Registration is required of individuals who are not licensed and who practice counseling. **Requirements:** Be at least 18 years of age. Good moral character. Adhere to Code of Ethics. Complete registration form and pay fee. **Fees:** $50 registration fee. $50 renewal fee. **Governing Statute:** 32 M.S.R.A. Chap. 119.

2093

Marriage and Family Therapist
Board of Counseling Professionals Licensure
Dept. of Professional and Financial Regulation
Div. of Licensing and Enforcement
State House Station 35
Augusta, ME 04333
Phone: (207)582-8723

Credential Type: Licensed Marriage and Family Therapist. **Duration of License:** Two years. **Requirements:** Master's degree in marriage and family therapy or equivalent, including a one-year clinical practicum. Complete two years of experience after receiving master's degree, with a minimum of 1000 hours of direct clinical contact and 200 hours of supervision, at least 100 of which shall be individual supervision. **Examination:** Association of Marital and Family Therapy Regulatory Board's Examination in Marital and Family Therapy. **Fees:** $40 application fee. $200 license fee. $200 renewal fee. **Governing Statute:** 32 M.S.R.A. Chap. 119.

Credential Type: Conditional License. **Duration of License:** Two years. **Requirements:** Meet all requirements for licensure, except for supervised experience. **Governing Statute:** 32 M.S.R.A. Chap. 119.

Credential Type: Registered Marriage and Family Therapist. **Duration of License:** Two years. **Authorization:** Registration is required of individuals who are not licensed and who practice counseling. **Requirements:** Be at least 18 years of age. Good moral character. Adhere to Code of Ethics. Complete registration form and pay fee. **Fees:** $50 registration fee. $50 renewal fee. **Governing Statute:** 32 M.S.R.A. Chap. 119.

2094

Pastoral Counselor
Board of Counseling Professionals Licensure
Dept. of Professional and Financial Regulation
Div. of Licensing and Enforcement
State House Station 35
Augusta, ME 04333
Phone: (207)582-8723

Credential Type: Licensed Pastoral Counselor. **Duration of License:** Two years. **Requirements:** Educational requirements include a Master of Divinity degree or its equivalent, with a core curriculum in the field of counseling and human relations, and clinical pastoral education consisting of a 400-contact-hour internship in a supervised ministry. In addition, two years of experience after receiving a degree are required, consisting of at least 1000 hours of direct clinical contact. Applicant must also complete 200 hours of supervision. **Examination:** One of the following: a board-approved examination, the National Counselors Examination (NCE), the Certified Clinical Mental Health Counselors Examination, the Examination in Marriage and Family Therapy, or the National Psychological Examination. **Fees:** $40 application fee. $200 license fee. $200 renewal fee. **Governing Statute:** 32 M.S.R.A. Chap. 119.

Credential Type: Conditional License. **Duration of License:** Two years. **Requirements:** Meet all requirements for licensure, except for supervised experience. **Governing Statute:** 32 M.S.R.A. Chap. 119.

Credential Type: Registered Pastoral Counselor. **Duration of License:** Two years. **Authorization:** Registration is required of individuals who are not licensed and who practice counseling. **Requirements:** Be at least 18 years of age. Good moral character. Adhere to Code of Ethics. Complete registration form and pay fee. **Fees:** $50 registration fee. $50 renewal fee. **Governing Statute:** 32 M.S.R.A. Chap. 119.

2095

Professional Counselor
Board of Counseling Professionals Licensure
Dept. of Professional and Financial Regulation
Div. of Licensing and Enforcement
State House Station 35
Augusta, ME 04333
Phone: (207)582-8723

Credential Type: Licensed Professional Counselor. **Duration of License:** Two years. **Requirements:** Master's degree in counseling or an allied mental health field. Complete two years of experience after receiving master's degree, with a minimum of 2000 hours of supervised experience. **Examination:** National Counselors Examination (NCE). **Fees:** $40 application fee. $200 license fee. $200 renewal fee. **Governing Statute:** 32 M.S.R.A. Chap. 119.

Credential Type: Conditional License. **Duration of License:** Two years. **Requirements:** Meet all requirements for licensure, except for supervised experience. **Governing Statute:** 32 M.S.R.A. Chap. 119.

Credential Type: Registered Professional Counselor. **Duration of License:** Two years. **Authorization:** Registration is required of individuals who are not licensed and who practice counseling. **Requirements:** Be at least 18 years of age. Good moral character. Adhere to Code of Ethics. Complete registration form and pay fee. **Fees:** $50 registration fee. $50 renewal fee. **Governing Statute:** 32 M.S.R.A. Chap. 119.

2096

School Guidance Counselor (K-12)
Teacher Certification
Dept. of Education
State House Station 23
Augusta, ME 04333
Phone: (207)289-5944

Credential Type: Counseling Certificate. **Duration of License:** Five years. **Requirements:** Master's degree or a doctorate from an accredited institution and an approved program to prepare school guidance counselors. Formal recommendation from the preparing institution. 33 graduate semester credit hours which include: profession of school guidance; educational philosophy and school operations; consultation skills; individual and group counseling skills; human development and behavior; career development; assessment and testing; research skills related to guidance; and a K-12 internship under the supervision of a certified guidance counselor or equivalent.

Complete approved graduate level K-12 internship or one academic year which relates to the duties of a school guidance counselor in a school setting. Two full years of work experience. Renewal requires six semester hours of approved study, preferably academic study in the certificate area.

Maryland

2097

Employment Counselor
Commissioner of Labor and Industry
Dept. of Licensing and Regulation
501 St. Paul Pl.
Baltimore, MD 21202-2272
Phone: (410)333-4211

Credential Type: License. **Duration of License:** Duration of agency employment. **Requirements:** Pass background investigation into character and integrity. **Fees:** $5 license fee.

2098

School Guidance Counselor
Dept. of Certification 18100
State Dept. of Education
200 W. Baltimore St.
Baltimore, MD 21201
Phone: (301)333-2142

Credential Type: Guidance Counselor Endorsement. **Requirements:** There are four routes of eligibility to receive the Guidance Counselor Endorsement in Maryland. Option 1—Master's degree in school guidance and counseling. National Board of Counselors certificate. Two years experience as a counselor or teacher in a school setting. Option 2—Master's degree from a program in school guidance and counseling approved on-site using NASDTEC Standards for State Approval of Teacher Education or using standards deemed comparable by the Dept. of Education. Two years experience as a teacher or counselor or a 500 clock hr. practicum in school guidance and counseling. Option 3—Master' degree in school guidance and counseling from a program approved by the Council for Accreditation of Counseling and Related Educational Programs. Option 4—Master's degree in school guidance and counseling from and approved program under the Interstate Contract agreement for support services. Two years of satisfactory performance as a teacher or counselor.

Massachusetts

2099

Guidance Counselor
Massachusetts Dept. of Education
1385 Hancock St.
Quincy, MA 02169
Phone: (617)770-7500

Credential Type: Guidance Counselor Endorsement. **Requirements:** 30 semester hr. prepracticum. In addition, complete a 300 clock hr. practicum. A candidate with a Massachusetts teaching certificate and one year of employment in a role covered by that certificate may be certified as a school guidance counselor by completing a 30 semester hr. prepracticum and 150 clock hr. practicum. Demonstrate the competencies contained in the five Standards established by the Massachusetts Dept. of Education for guidance counselors. Standard I-Knowledge of the following: developmental psychology in general; personality theory; theories of learning and their application; individual and group counseling; relationship of above areas to other fields of knowledge; recent developments in guidance and counseling; federal and state laws affecting counseling; referral agencies; methods of research and inquiry in psychology and guidance. Standard II-Communicate clearly and appropriately. Standard III-Ability to design programs and provide services. Standard IV-Ability to evaluate and assess effectiveness of guidance procedures and services. Standard V-Be equitable, sensitive, and responsive.

2100

Marriage and Family Therapist
Board of Registration of Allied
  Mental Health and Human
  Services Professions
100 Cambridge St., 15th Fl.
Boston, MA 02202
Phone: (617)727-1716

Credential Type: Marriage and Family Therapist License. **Requirements:** Master's degree in marriage and family therapy. Complete 3360 hours of post-master's degree experience, including 1000 hours of clinical experience and 200 hours of supervised clinical experience. **Examination:** Marriage and Family Therapy Regulatory Board examination. **Fees:** $90 application fee. $120 license fee. **Governing Statute:** 262 Code of Massachusetts Regulations (CMR).

2101

Mental Health Counselor
Board of Registration of Allied
  Mental Health and Human
  Services Professions
100 Cambridge St., 15th Fl.
Boston, MA 02202
Phone: (617)727-1716

Credential Type: Mental Health Counselor License. **Requirements:** Master's degree in counseling or related field. Complete 3360 hours of post-master's degree experience, including 960 hours of clinical experience and 100 hours of supervised clinical experience. **Examination:** Mental Health Counselor Examination. **Fees:** $90 application fee. $120 license fee. **Governing Statute:** 262 Code of Massachusetts Regulations (CMR).

Michigan

2102

Marriage Counselor
Board of Marriage Counselors
Bureau of Occupational &
  Professional Regulation
Dept. of Commerce
PO Box 30018
Lansing, MI 48909
Phone: (517)373-9153

Credential Type: Registration. **Duration of License:** Two years. **Requirements:** Be a resident of Michigan. Doctorate in psychology, sociology, psychiatry, marriage or pastoral counseling, or an equivalent doctorate, plus five years of professional experience including one year of specialization in marriage counseling under the direct supervision of a registered marriage counselor; or have a master's degree in social work, or marriage or pastoral counseling, from an institution approved by the Department, plus five years of professional experience. **Fees:** $25 application processing fee. $50 initial registration fee, per year. $50 renewal fee, per year. **Governing Statute:** The Occupational Code, Act 299 of 1980, as amended.

Michigan

2103

Professional Counselor
Bureau of Occupational & Professional Regulation
Dept. of Commerce
PO Box 30018
Lansing, MI 48909
Phone: (517)373-1870

Credential Type: License and Certification. **Requirements:** Contact licensing body for application information.

2104

School Guidance Counselor
Teacher Preparation and Certification
Michigan Dept. of Education
Box 30008
Lansing, MI 48909
Phone: (517)373-3310

Credential Type: Guidance Counselor Endorsement. **Requirements:** Valid Michigan teaching certificate. Minimum or 18 semester hours of appropriate guidance credit, including practicum. This credit must be in addition to requirements for the requisite basic teaching certificate.

Minnesota

2105

Elementary School Guidance Counselor
Teacher Licensing and Placement
State Dept. of Education
616 Capitol Square Bldg.
St. Paul, MN 55101
Phone: (612)296-2046

Credential Type: Elementary Guidance Counselor Endorsement. **Requirements:** Valid teacher's license based on a bachelor's degree. One year of successful elementary teaching experience. Master's degree which includes 54 quarter hours at the graduate level. Competencies must be developed in areas of coordination, counseling, consultation, developmental guidance, diagnosis, and human relations.

2106

Employment Counselor
Dept. of Labor and Industry
Labor Standards Div.
443 Lafayette Rd.
St. Paul, MN 55155
Phone: (612)296-2342

Credential Type: Counselor License. **Requirements:** Be employed by an employment agency. Pass one-hour exam. **Examination:** Yes. **Fees:** Contact board for license and exam fees. **Governing Statute:** Minnesota Statutes, Chap. 175-178, 181-184, and 326. Minnesota Rules 5200-5499.

2107

Marriage and Family Therapist
Board of Marriage and Family Therapy
2700 University Ave. W., Ste. 67
St. Paul, MN 55114
Phone: (612)643-3667

Credential Type: Marriage and Family Therapist License. **Duration of License:** One year. **Requirements:** Master's or doctoral degree in marriage and family therapy from a regionally accredited institution, or a degree in a related subject containing the required coursework. Complete at least two years of supervised post-graduate full-time employment, or equivalent in part-time employment.

Renewal requires 30 hours of continuing education every two years. **Examination:** Written examination approved by the Association for Marriage and Family Therapy Regulatory Boards. Oral examination covering rules and ethics. **Exemptions:** Written exam may be waived for applicants who have passed the national exam at or above Minnesota's cut score in another state and who have met the educational requirements. **Fees:** $200 exam application fee. $100 license application fee. $100 (maximum) license fee. $300 reciprocity fee. $115 renewal fee. **Governing Statute:** Minnesota Statutes, Section 148B. Minnesota Rules 5300.0100-5300.0360.

2108

Secondary School Guidance Counselor
Teacher Licensing and Placement
State Dept. of Education
616 Capitol Square Bldg.
St. Paul, MN 55101
Phone: (612)296-2046

Credential Type: Secondary Guidance Counselor Endorsement. **Requirements:** Valid teacher's license based on a bachelor's degree. One year of successful secondary teaching experience and one year of cumulated work experience. Master's degree which includes 54 quarter hours at the graduate level which includes one course from each of the following seven areas: principles and practice in guidance; personality structure and mental hygiene; measurement and research methods; appraisal techniques, occupational and training information and material, counseling procedure, practice in guidance and counseling. Plus one course must be chosen from the following: group guidance, organization and administration of guidance services, and psychology of learning. Not more than six credits may be in undergraduate courses.

Mississippi

2109

Licensed Professional Counselor
State Board of Examiners for Licensed Professional Counselors
PO Drawer 6239
Mississippi State, MS 39762
Phone: (601)325-8182

Credential Type: Professional Counselor License. **Duration of License:** One year. **Requirements:** Be at least 21 years of age. Be a resident of or pay income tax in Mississippi. Complete 60 semester hours or 90 quarter hours of graduate study that are primarily counseling in nature, with a graduate degree in counselor education or a related counseling program. Complete two years (3500 hours) of supervised experience, at least one-third of which includes direct counseling service to clients. One of the two years of experience may be concurrent with the pursuit of a master's degree. **Examination:** National Counselor Examination (NCE). **Fees:** $100 application fee. $50 renewal fee. **Governing Statute:** Mississippi Statutes 73-30-1 et seq. Rules and Regulations.

Missouri

2110

Elementary School Counselor (K-8)
Teacher Certification
Dept. of Elementary and Secondary Education
Box 480
Jefferson City, MO 65102
Phone: (314)751-3486

Credential Type: Initial Elementary Counselor Certificate. **Duration of License:** Five years. **Requirements:** Valid

Missouri teaching certificate. Two years of teaching experience. Master's degree with emphasis on guidance and counseling. One year of accumulated paid employment other than teaching or counseling. Completion of a course in psychology and education of the exceptional child. Recommendation for certification from the designated official of an approved college or university where preparation was completed. A planned program of at least 24 semester hours, 12 of which focused on the elementary level, that included a three semester hr. course in each of the following: personal and professional development in counseling; foundations of elementary and secondary school guidance; theories and techniques of elementary and secondary school counseling; elementary school child and school learning problems; theories and techniques of group counseling; and a practicum in counseling. Supervised practice in an elementary school guidance program for three semester hours

Renewal of certificate is possible with six semester hours of appropriate graduate credit or a planned professional development program approved by the Commissioner of Education and equivalent to six semester hours of college credit. Must also have three professional workshops/seminars totaling 15 clock hours

2111

Professional Counselor
Missouri Committee for Professional Counselors
Div. of Professional Registration
3605 Missouri Blvd.
PO Box 162
Jefferson City, MO 65102
Phone: (314)751-0018

Credential Type: License. **Requirements:** Meet one of the following sets of requirements: (1) Doctoral degree with a major in counseling, or equivalent, from an acceptable educational institution. Complete at least one year of supervised counseling experience subsequent to receipt of degree. (2) Specialist's degree with a major in counseling, or its equivalent, from an acceptable educational institution. Complete at least one year of supervised counseling experience subsequent to receipt of degree. (3) Master's degree with a major in counseling, or its equivalent, from an acceptable educational institution. Complete at least two years of supervised counseling experience subsequent to receipt of degree. **Examination:** Written examination. **Reciprocity:** Yes, provided requirements in the applicant's state, territory, country, or province were, at the date of licensure, substantially equal to the requirements then in force in this state. **Fees:** $100 application fee. $150 exam fee. $100 reciprocity fee. $125 renewal fee. **Governing Statute:** 4 CSR 95. Revised Professional Counselor Practice Act, Chap. 337.

2112

Secondary School Counselor (7-12)
Teacher Certification
Dept. of Elementary and Secondary Education
Box 480
Jefferson City, MO 65102
Phone: (314)751-3486

Credential Type: Initial Secondary School Counselor Certificate. **Duration of License:** Five years. **Requirements:** Valid Missouri teaching certificate. Two years of teaching experience. Master's degree with emphasis on guidance and counseling. One year of accumulated paid employment other than teaching or counseling. Completion of a course in psychology and education of the exceptional child. Recommendation for certification from the designated official of an approved college or university where preparation was completed. A planned program of at least 24 semester hours, 12 of which focused on the secondary level, that included a three semester hr. course in each of the following: personal and professional development in counseling; foundations of elementary and secondary school guidance; theories and techniques of elementary and secondary school counseling; secondary school child and school learning problems; theories and techniques of group counseling; and a practicum in counseling. Supervised practice in an secondary school guidance program for three semester hours

Renewal of certificate is possible with six semester hours of appropriate graduate credit or a planned professional development program approved by the Commissioner of Education and equivalent to six semester hours of college credit. Must also have three professional workshops/seminars totaling 15 clock hours

2113

Substance Abuse Counselor
Missouri Substance Abuse Counselors Certification Board
Div. of Professional Registration
3605 Missouri Blvd.
Jefferson City, MO 65102
Phone: (314)751-0018

Credential Type: Certification. **Requirements:** Contact licensing body for application information.

Montana

2114

Chemical Dependency Counselor
Montana Dept. of Institutions
Chemical Dependency Bureau
1539 11th Ave.
Helena, MT 59620
Phone: (406)444-2827

Credential Type: License. **Duration of License:** Four years. **Requirements:** 200 points based on a combination of academic preparation and work experience. Four years of approved college coursework or five years of work experience amounts to approximately 65 points. The remaining points are made up through exams. A 25-45 minute tape of a counseling session conducted by the applicant. 12 quarter hours of continuing education or equivalent every four years. **Examination:** Yes. **Fees:** $50 application and exam fee. **Governing Statute:** Montana Code Annotated 53-24-204.

2115

Licensed Professional Counselor
Montana Board of Social Work Examiners and Professional Counselors
111 N. Jackson
Helena, MT 59620
Phone: (406)444-4285

Credential Type: License. **Duration of License:** One year. **Requirements:** Master's degree in counseling from an accredited college. 2,000 hours of supervised counseling practice, half of which is post-degree. **Examination:** National board exam. **Fees:** $75 application fee. $75 exam fee. $120 license fee. $120 renewal fee. **Governing Statute:** Montana Code Annotated 37-23-201 through 37-23-212.

2116

School Guidance Counselor
Teacher Certification
Office of Public Instruction
State Capitol
Helena, MT 59620
Phone: (406)444-3150

Credential Type: Guidance and Counseling Endorsement. **Requirements:** Endorsement will be added to a valid Montana teaching certificate after applicant has completed an approved K-12 guidance and counseling program and has completed three years of successful teaching experience or the equivalent. The majority of the experience must be obtained in a school

School Guidance Counselor, continued

organization consistent with Montana's K-12 pattern.

Nebraska

2117

Counselor
Nebraska Board of Examiners in Professional Counseling
301 Centennial Mall S.
PO Box 95007
Lincoln, NE 68509
Phone: (402)471-2115

Credential Type: License. **Duration of License:** Two years. **Requirements:** Must be 21 years of age with a master's degree from an approved educational program. Must have three years of full-time experience in professional counseling. Thirty additional graduate hours may be substituted for one year experience if related. **Fees:** $200 certificate fee. $175 renewal fee.

Nevada

2118

Marriage/Family Counselor
State of Nevada Board of Examiners for Marriage and Family Therapists
2585 E. Flamingo Rd., Ste. 8
Las Vegas, NV 89121
Phone: (702)486-7388

Credential Type: License. **Duration of License:** One year. **Requirements:** Completion of residency training in psychiatry, or have a graduate degree in marriage and family therapy, psychology, or social work from an accredited institution. Completion of at least one year of postgraduate internship in marriage and family therapy. 21 years of age. Good moral character. **Fees:** $75 application fee. $200 exam fee. $150 license fee. $150 renewal fee. $50 processing fee.

2119

School Counselor
Nevada State Dept. of Education
Licensing Office
Capitol Complex, 400 W. King St.
Carson City, NV 89701
Phone: (702)687-3115

Credential Type: License. **Requirements:** Teaching license. Master's degree from an accredited college or university in counseling or a related field. Two years of teaching or school counseling. Certification by the National Board of Certified Counselors. Completion of a 36-credit graduate program with required courses. **Fees:** $84 license fee. $50 renewal fee.

New Hampshire

2120

Certified Alcohol Counselor (CAC)
Office of Alcohol & Drug Abuse Prevention
105 Pleasant St.
Concord, NH 03301
Phone: (603)271-6112
Fax: (603)271-6116

Credential Type: Alcohol Counselor Certificate. **Duration of License:** Two years. **Requirements:** At least 180 hours of training in substance abuse and/or counseling (6 hours must be in ethics). 24 hours must have been acquired within one year of application. Must have two years or 4,000 hours of supervised experience with alcohol clients. A minimum of 1,000 hours must be in the form of direct counseling. Must also complete a 220 hour practicum. Applicant must sign Code of Ethics and submit evaluation from a supervisor of six months, or longer, and two professional references. Oral interview will consist of case presentation prepared by applicant. Renewal requires 48 hours of continuing education. **Examination:** National Certification Examination. **Reciprocity:** Yes, with application to the National Certification Reciprocity Consortium. **Fees:** $10 application packet fee. $55 written examination fee. $90 certification processing fee. $50 biennial recertification fee. $100 reciprocity fee.

2121

Certified Alcohol and Drug Abuse Counselor (CADAC)
Office of Alcohol & Drug Abuse Prevention
105 Pleasant St.
Concord, NH 03301
Phone: (603)271-6112
Fax: (603)271-6116

Credential Type: Alcohol and Drug Abuse Counselor Certificate. **Duration of License:** Two years. **Requirements:** At least 270 hours of training in substance abuse and/or counseling (6 hours must be in ethics). 24 hours of training must have been acquired within one year of application. Must have three years or 6,000 hours of supervised counseling experience in alcohol and/or drug abuse. At least 2,000 hours must be spent working with alcohol clients and 2,000 hours working with drug clients. A minimum of 1,500 hours must be spent in direct counseling. A practicum of 300 hours is also required. Applicant must sign Code of Ethics and submit evaluation from a supervisor of six months, or longer, and two professional references. Oral interview will consist of case presentation prepared by applicant. Renewal requires 48 hours of continuing education. **Examination:** National Certification Examination. **Reciprocity:** Yes, with application to the National Certification Reciprocity Consortium. **Fees:** $10 application packet fee. $55 written exam fee. $90 certification processing fee. $50 biennial recertification fee. $100 reciprocity fee.

2122

Certified Drug Counselor (CDC)
Office of Alcohol & Drug Abuse Prevention
105 Pleasant St.
Concord, NH 03301
Phone: (603)271-6112
Fax: (603)271-6116

Credential Type: Drug Counselor Certificate. **Duration of License:** Two years. **Requirements:** At least 180 hours of training in substance abuse and/or counseling (6 hours must be in ethics). 24 hours must have been acquired within one year of application. Must have two years or 4,000 hours of supervised experience with drug clients. A minimum of 1,000 hours must be in the form of direct counseling. Must also complete a 220 hour practicum. Applicant must sign Code of Ethics and submit evaluation from a supervisor of six months, or longer, and two professional references. Oral interview will consist of case presentation prepared by applicant. Renewal requires 48 hours of continuing education. **Examination:** National Certification Examination. **Reciprocity:** Yes, with application to the National Certification Reciprocity Consortium. **Fees:** $10 application packet fee. $55 written examination fee. $90 certification processing fee. $50 biennial recertification fee. $100 reciprocity fee.

2123

Certified Marital Mediator
New Hampshire Mediation Program
33 Stickney Ave.
Concord, NH 03301
Phone: (603)224-8043

Credential Type: Certified Marital Mediator Certificate. **Requirements:** Complete an approved program, of at least 48 hours of study, which includes eight hours in domestic violence and components in family dynamics and relevant law. Complete a 20 hour internship. Submit application and three personal recommendations from persons familiar with applicant's marital mediation work. Eight hours of continuing education are required each year. **Reciprocity:** No.

2124

Pastoral Counselor
Board of Examiners of Psychologists
PO Box 457, 105 Pleasant St.
Concord, NH 03301
Phone: (603)226-2599

Credential Type: Pastoral Counselor Certificate. **Duration of License:** One year. **Requirements:** Complete college undergraduate degree. Hold a graduate degree from an accredited theological school. Hold a Doctoral degree in pastoral counseling. Complete at least 12 weeks of full-time clinical pastoral education in an accredited clinical center. Must have 125 hours of counseling experience that has been supervised by at least two different supervisors. Oral interview required with the certifying committee to evaluate clinical competence. Renewal requires 20 hours of continuing education annually. **Reciprocity:** Yes, provided the applicant's state has standards equal to or higher than those of New Hampshire. **Fees:** $100 initial license/application fee. $60 annual renewal fee.

New Jersey

2125

Alcohol Counselor
Alcohol and Other Drugs of Abuse Counselor Certification Board
90 Monmouth St.
Red Bank, NJ 07701
Phone: (201)741-3835

Credential Type: Certified Alcoholism Counselor. **Duration of License:** One year. **Requirements:** Completion of 240 hours of approved classroom training within five years immediately prior to application and 220 hours of supervised practical training hours. Completion of 4,000 hours of direct alcoholism counseling in an approved alcoholism facility within four years prior to application. No history or evidence of alcohol or drug abuse. 60 hours of continuing education every two years. **Examination:** Written and oral exams. **Fees:** $50 application fee. $100 case review fee. $100 certification fee. $60 renewal fee.

2126

Drug Abuse Counselor
Alcohol and Other Drugs of Abuse Counselor Certification Board
90 Manmouth St., Ste. 1
Red Bank, NJ 07701
Phone: (201)741-3835

Credential Type: Certified Drug Counselor. **Requirements:** At least 240 clock hours of approved substance abuse training experience and 220 supervised practical training hours. At least 4,000 hours of documented supervised drug counseling experience. **Fees:** $10 orientation fee. $65 application fee.

2127

Marriage Counselor
Board of Marriage Counselor Examiners
1100 Raymond Blvd., Rm. 512
Newark, NJ 07102
Phone: (201)648-2534

Credential Type: License. **Duration of License:** One year. **Requirements:** A master's degree in social work; or a post-master's degree in Marriage and Family Counseling; or a doctorate degree in a closely allied field of study. Five years experience. 21 years of age. Good moral character. **Examination:** Yes. **Reciprocity:** Yes. **Fees:** $50 examination of credentials fee. $100 exam fee. $65 annual license fee. **Governing Statute:** NJSA 45:8B. NJAC 13:34.

2128

School Counselor
Office of Teacher Certification and Academic Credentials
CN 503
Trenton, NJ 08625-0503
Phone: (609)292-2079

Credential Type: Student Personnel Services Endorsement. **Authorization:** Authorizes candidates to perform the following student personnel services: study and assessment of individual pupils; counseling with teachers, students, and parents; developing cooperative relationships with community agencies in assisting children and families. **Requirements:** Bachelor's or higher degree. Regular New Jersey instructional certificate or equivalent. One year of successful teaching experience. Passing score in specified areas of the NTE written examination or 30 post-baccalaureate semester hours to include courses in the following: six hours in guidance and counseling which includes theory and procedures in individual and group guidance, counseling and interviewing techniques, and vocational guidance; three hours in testing and evaluation; six hours in psychology which includes child and adolescent development, psychology of exceptional children, psychology of learning, and child and youth study; six hours in sociological foundations which includes community agencies, organizations, and resources, educational sociology, social problems, juvenile delinquency; and nine hours of electives in the field. **Examination:** National Teachers Examination (if applicant has not met the college study requirements).

New Mexico

2129

School Guidance Counselor K-12
Director, Professional Licensing Unit
Education Bldg.
300 Don Gaspar
Santa Fe, NM 87503
Phone: (505)827-6587

Credential Type: Initial License—Level 3—A. **Requirements:** Bachelor's degree from an accredited institution. Master's degree from a New Mexico institution which must incorporate the State Board's prescribed competencies in the area of guidance/counseling or a master's degree from an out-of-state institution in a guidance/counseling program approved by the State Board. Hold a valid Level two or higher New Mexico teaching license or three years of verified, satisfactory experience in one or more of the following areas: teaching, educational administration, school guidance/counseling, clinical practice, and/or mental health work. Verification by local superintendent or private school official that applicant has met the State Board's prescribed Level 3-A competencies.

New York

2130

School Counselor K-12
Administrator of Teacher Certification Policy
Univ. of the State of New York
State Education Dept.
Cultural Center, Rm. 5-A-11
Albany, NY 12230
Phone: (518)474-6440

Credential Type: Provisional School Counselor Certificate. **Duration of License:** Five years. **Requirements:** Complete a program that has been registered and approved by the State Education Dept. in

School Counselor K-12, continued

school counseling or hold a bachelor's degree from a regionally credited institution and complete 30 semester hours of approved graduate study in the field of school counseling, including supervised practice in guidance. Note: The city of Buffalo, New York has certification standards that are exclusive of New York State.

Credential Type: Permanent School Counselor Certificate. **Duration of License:** Permanent. **Requirements:** Hold a Provisional School Counselor Certificate. An additional 30 semester hours of graduate study in the field of school counseling. Master's degree. Two years of pupil personnel service in the elementary and/or secondary schools. Note: The city of Buffalo, New York has certification standards that are exclusive of New York State.

North Carolina

2131

Counselor
North Carolina Board of Registered Practicing Counselors
PO Box 12023
Raleigh, NC 27605
Phone: (919)515-2244

Credential Type: Registered Practicing Counselor. **Duration of License:** Two years. **Requirements:** Master's degree in counseling or related field. Complete two years of experience. Complete a supervised practicum. **Examination:** Board administered written examination. **Fees:** $75 application fee. $75 exam fee. $50 renewal fee.

2132

Marital and Family Therapist
Marital and Family Therapy Certification Board
1001 S. Marshall St., Ste. 5
Winston-Salem, NC 27101-5893
Phone: (919)724-1288

Credential Type: Certification. **Duration of License:** One year. **Requirements:** Master's degree in marital and family therapy from a recognized educational institution, with at least 45 semester hours including 27 semester hours in board specified courses. Complete at least 1500 hours of clinical experience in the practice of marital and family therapy, at least 1000 hours of which are postgraduate. **Examination:** Certification Examination. **Reciprocity:** Considered on a case-by-case basis. **Fees:** $75 application fee. $50 exam fee

2133

School Guidance Counselor K-12
Certification Section
State Dept. of Public Instruction
Raleigh, NC 27603
Phone: (919)733-4125

Credential Type: Guidance Counselor Certificate. **Duration of License:** Five years. **Requirements:** Master's or higher degree from a college or university with an approved program in guidance and/or counseling. Supervised practicum in a school setting. Pass NTE. Institutional recommendation. Complete 10 semester hours of course work within the five year period immediately preceding the date of application. **Examination:** National Teacher Examination. **Fees:** $30 application fee. $30 renewal fee.

North Dakota

2134

Addiction Counselor
State Board of Addiction Counseling Examiners
1406 Second St. NW
Mandan, ND 58554
Phone: (701)663-2321

Credential Type: Addiction Counselor License. **Duration of License:** One year. **Requirements:** Bachelor's degree plus 12 required courses. Complete at least a 9-month clinical training program, followed by one year of work experience or internship. **Examination:** Written Examination. Oral Case Presentation Examination. **Fees:** $150 license fee. $60 written exam fee. $75 oral exam fee. $75 renewal fee. **Governing Statute:** North Dakota Century Code 43-45.

2135

Associate Counselor
Board of Counselor Examiners
PO Box 8262, University Sta.
Grand Forks, ND 58202
Phone: (701)777-2729

Alternate Information: PO Box 2735, Bismarck, ND 58502

Credential Type: Associate Counselor License. **Duration of License:** Two years. **Requirements:** Master's degree in counseling or another human services field from an accredited institution. Three professional recommendations. Submit written plan covering client contact hours and supervision received. **Examination:** National Counselor Examination (NCE). **Reciprocity:** Yes, provided license was granted on the basis of national testing. **Fees:** $140 filing, processing, and administrative fee. $75 exam fee. **Governing Statute:** North Dakota Century Code 43-47-01 et seq. Administrative Rules, Title 97.

2136

Professional Counselor
Board of Counselor Examiners
PO Box 8262, University Sta.
Grand Forks, ND 58202
Phone: (701)777-2729

Alternate Information: PO Box 2735, Bismarck, ND 58502

Credential Type: Professional Counselor License. **Duration of License:** Two years. **Requirements:** Master's degree in counseling or another human services field from an accredited institution. Three professional recommendations. Complete two years of supervised experience under a licensed professional counselor. Renewal requires 30 hours of continuing education every two years. **Examination:** National Counselor Examination (NCE). **Reciprocity:** Yes, provided license was granted on the basis of national testing. **Fees:** $140 filing, processing, and administrative fee. $75 exam fee. **Governing Statute:** North Dakota Century Code 43-47-01 et seq. Administrative Rules, Title 97.

2137

School Counselor
Director of Certification
State Dept. of Public Instruction
Bismarck, ND 58505
Phone: (701)224-2264

Credential Type: Professional Credential. **Duration of License:** Five years. **Authorization:** May be endorsed to allow school guidance counseling at the elementary, secondary, or K-12 levels. **Requirements:** Master's degree with specified core guidance courses and practicum. Two years of teaching experience or related human services experience. One year of probational work. Valid North Dakota Educator's Professional Certificate.

Ohio

2138

Licensed Professional Clinical Counselor
Counselor and Social Worker Board
77 S. High St., 16th Fl.
Columbus, OH 43266
Phone: (614)466-6463
Phone: (614)466-0912

Credential Type: LPCC License. **Requirements:** Meet one of the following sets of requirements: (1) Master's degree in counseling, with a total of 90 quarter hours or 60 semester hours that include at least 30 quarter hours or 20 semester hours of advanced courses as specified by the board. Must provide evidence of meeting minimum requirements for admission to a doctoral program, including a score of 50 on the Miller Analogies Test or a combined score of 1000 on the Graduate Record Examination, and a 3.25 grade point average. Complete three years (4500 clock hours) of supervised counseling experience in a clinical setting, one year of which may be obtained prior to receiving the degree. Two of the three years must be paid experience.

(2) Doctoral degree in counseling, including at least 90 quarter hours or 60 semester hours of counseling training in a program accredited by the Council for Accreditation of Counseling and Related Educational Programs (CACREP), the Council on Rehabilitation Education (CORE), or the Ohio Counselor and Social Worker Board. At least 30 quarter hours or 20 semester hours must be in areas specified by the board. Complete two years (3000 clock hours) of supervised counseling experience, one year of which may be obtained prior to receiving the degree. One of the two years must be paid experience. **Examination:** Board administered examination.

2139

Licensed Professional Counselor
Counselor and Social Worker Board
77 S. High St., 16th Fl.
Columbus, OH 43266
Phone: (614)466-6463
Phone: (614)466-0912

Credential Type: LPC License. **Requirements:** Meet one of the following sets of requirements: (1) Master's degree in counseling, including 60 quarter hours or 40 semester hours of counseling training in a program accredited by the Council for Accreditation of Counseling and Related Educational Programs (CACREP), the Council on Rehabilitation Education (CORE), or the Ohio Counselor and Social Worker Board. Complete three years (4500 clock hours) of supervised counseling experience, one year of which may be obtained prior to receiving the degree. Two of the three years must be paid experience.

(2) Doctoral degree in counseling, including 90 quarter hours or 60 semester hours of counseling training in a program accredited by the Council for Accreditation of Counseling and Related Educational Programs (CACREP), the Council on Rehabilitation Education (CORE), or the Ohio Counselor and Social Worker Board. Complete two years (3000 clock hours) of supervised counseling experience, one year of which may be obtained prior to receiving the degree. One of the two years must be paid experience. **Examination:** Board administered examination.

2140

School Counselor
Teacher Education and Certification
State Dept. of Education
65 S. Front St., Rm. 1012
Columbus, OH 43266-0308
Phone: (614)466-3593

Credential Type: Provisional Pupil Personnel Certificate—Counseling. **Requirements:** Recommendation of university official. Complete examination prescribed by the State Board of Education. Proof of education and experience in area of specialization. Master's degree. Course work and field-based experience well distributed over the areas of counseling and guidance with practical application to programs and practices in schools. Three years of satisfactory teaching experience. **Examination:** Examination prescribed by the State Board of Education.

Oklahoma

2141

Counselor, Licensed Professional
Licensed Professional Counselors
1000 N.E. Tenth
Oklahoma City, OK 73152
Phone: (405)271-6030

Credential Type: License. **Duration of License:** Two years for first license. One year renewals. **Requirements:** Master's degree in counseling-related field. 300-hour internship in a counseling setting. 20 hours of continuing education each year. 21 years of age. Three years or 3,000 hours of work experience under a licensed professional counselor. **Examination:** National Counselor Examination. **Fees:** $90 exam fee. $145 application fee. $90 license fee. $80 renewal fee.

2142

Marital and Family Therapist
State Dept. of Health
LMFT Administrator
1000 NE 10th St.
Oklahoma City, OK 73117-1299
Phone: (405)271-7265

Credential Type: Marital and Family Therapist License. **Duration of License:** One year following initial two year period. **Requirements:** Master's degree in marital and family therapy from an accredited college or university, or a master's degree in a mental health, behavioral science, or counseling related field that includes 33 semester hours of board specified courses and a practicum or internship consisting of at least 300 clock hours. Complete two years of supervised experience. Submit three professional recommendations.

Renewal requires 20 clock hours of continuing education per year. **Examination:** Examination in Marital and Family Therapy. **Fees:** $200 application fee. $100 exam fee. $100 initial license fee (covers two years). $100 annual renewal fee.

2143

School Service Personnel K-12
Teacher Education and Certification
State Dept. of Education
2500 N. Lincoln Blvd., Rm. 211
Oklahoma City, OK 73105
Phone: (405)521-3337

Credential Type: Standard Certificate in a School Personnel Field—Graduate. **Duration of License:** Five years. **Authorization:** Endorsement will be given to persons seeking positions in the following fields: Counselor; Library Media Specialist; Elementary School Principal; Secondary School Principal; School Superintendent; School Psychometrist; School Psychologist; SpeechLanguage Pathologist; or Reading Specialist. **Requirements:** Complete an approved certificate program at an accredited college or university which includes a minimum of the following: a baccalaureate degree; 50 semester hours in general education; 30 semester hours in professional education; and 40 semester hours in course work pertaining to the area of specialization. Pass the state certified test(s) in specialization competencies. Complete State Board graduate level course requirements.

Oregon

2144

Counselor, Professional
Board of Licensed Profesional Counselors and Therapists
796 Winter NE
Salem, OR 97310
Phone: (503)378-5499

Credential Type: License. **Duration of License:** One year. **Requirements:** Must have a Master's degree in counseling. Must have three years of supervised experience. **Examination:** Yes. **Fees:** $75 exam fee. $65 license fee. $65 renewal fee. **Governing Statute:** ORS 657.705 to 675.835.

2145

Marriage and Family Therapist
Board of Licensed Professional Counselors and Therapists
796 Winter NE
Salem, OR 97310
Phone: (503)378-5499

Credential Type: License. **Duration of License:** One year. **Requirements:** Masster's degree in marriage and family therapy. Three years of supervised experience. **Examination:** Yes. **Fees:** $175 exam fee. $65 license fee. $65 renewal fee. **Governing Statute:** ORS 657.705 to 675.835.

2146

School Counselor
Teacher Standards and Practices Commission
630 Center St. NE, Ste. 200
Salem, OR 97310-0320
Phone: (503)378-3586

Credential Type: Basic Personnel Service Certificate—Counselor Endorsement. **Duration of License:** Three years. **Requirements:** Recommendation for certification by an approved teacher education institution. Evidence of recent public school personnel service experience. Passing scores on the CBEST. Out-of-state prepared applicants may submit their passing scores on the Core Battery of the National Teacher Examination, in lieu of the CBEST. Completion of an approved personnel service preparation program. Holder of, or eligible for, an Oregon teaching certificate or equivalent from other state. Two years of successful experience in the public schools or one year of successful teaching experience plus one year of a public school intern counseling experience. 24 quarter hours of graduate credit in an approved program in guidance and counseling, including a practicum. **Examination:** California Basic Education Skills Test.

Credential Type: Standard Personnel Service Certificate—Counselor Endorsement. **Duration of License:** Five years. **Requirements:** Two years of successful counseling experience in Oregon schools while holding a basic counselor endorsement. Complete 24 quarter hours of graduate credit in guidance and counseling beyond the basic counselor endorsement. A master's degree program in guidance and counseling held by an out-of-state applicant may be accepted in lieu of the above requirements.

Rhode Island

2147

Chemical Dependency Professional
Rhode Island Board for Certification of Chemical Dependency Professionals.
84 Broad St.
Pawtucket, RI 02860
Phone: (401)233-2215

Credential Type: Chemical Dependency Professional Certificate—Level I. **Duration of License:** Four years. **Requirements:** Must complete 140 hours of educational courses, of which 70 hours must be directly related to substance abuse. Complete 150 hours of clinical supervision. Complete 2,000 hours of work in a licensed substance abuse facility. **Examination:** Written examination. **Reciprocity:** No. **Fees:** $150 initial certification. $125 recertification.

Credential Type: Advanced Chemical Dependency Professional Certificate—Level II. **Duration of License:** Four years. **Requirements:** Complete a board approved program of additional work experience, education and supervision. **Examination:** Written and oral examination. **Reciprocity:** Yes. **Fees:** $150 initial certification. $125 recertification.

Credential Type: Chemical Dependency Supervisor—Level III. **Duration of License:** Four years. **Requirements:** Level II certification and complete a board approved program of additional work related education. **Reciprocity:** Yes. **Fees:** $150 initial certification. $125 recertification.

2148

Counselor in Mental Health
State Board of Mental Health Counselors and Marriage and Family Therapists
Div. of Professional Regulation
Rhode Island Dept. of Health
3 Capitol Hill
Providence, RI 02908
Phone: (401)277-2827

Credential Type: Mental Health Counselor License. **Duration of License:** Two years. **Requirements:** Good moral character. Foreign born must show proof of legal entry into the U.S. Graduate degree in counseling or therapy from an approved school plus 60 semester hours within a counseling/therapy program. Complete a supervised practicum of at least 12 hours and a post-graduate experience of at least two years that includes 100 hours of supervised case work. **Examination:** National Academy for Certified Clinical Mental Health Counselors Examination. **Reciprocity:** Yes. **Fees:** $350 initial license/application fee. $200 biennial renewal fee.

2149

Marriage and Family Therapist
State Board of Mental Health Counselors and Marriage and Family Therapists
Div. of Professional Regulation
Rhode Island Dept. of Health
3 Capitol Hill
Providence, RI 02908
Phone: (401)277-2827

Credential Type: Marriage and Family Therapist License. **Duration of License:** Two years. **Requirements:** Good moral character. Foreign born must show proof of legal entry into U.S. Hold a graduate degree in counseling or therapy from an accredited school that includes 60 semester hours of marital and family courses. Complete a 12 semester hour supervised practicum and a one-year supervised internship. Must complete a two-year program of post-graduate experience that includes 200 hours of direct client contact and at least 100 hours of supervised case work. **Examination:** American Association for Marriage and Family Therapy Certification Examination. **Reciprocity:** Yes. **Fees:** $350 license/application fee. $200 renewal fee.

Counselors

2150

School Guidance Counselor
Office of Teacher Certification
State Dept. of Education
22 Hayes St.
Providence, RI 02908
Phone: (401)277-2675

Credential Type: Provisional Guidance Counselor's Certificate. **Duration of License:** Six years. **Requirements:** Bachelor's degree. Complete an approved program for school counselors, to include 24 semester hours in guidance, counseling, and related disciplines. Hold or be eligible for a Rhode Island teaching certificate. Two years of successful teaching experience. Nonrenewable.

Credential Type: Professional Guidance Counselor's Certificate. **Duration of License:** Permanent. **Requirements:** Master's degree or 36 semester hours of approved study beyond the bachelor's degree. Complete an approved program for school counselors, to include 24 semester hours in guidance, counseling, and related disciplines. Hold or be eligible for a Rhode Island teaching certificate. Three years of successful teaching experience.

2151

School Guidance Supervisor
Office of Teacher Certification
State Dept. of Education
22 Hayes St.
Providence, RI 02908
Phone: (401)277-2675

Credential Type: Provisional Guidance Supervisor's Certificate. **Duration of License:** Six years. **Requirements:** Hold or be eligible for a Rhode Island Guidance Counselor's Certificate. Master's degree or 36 semester hours of approved study beyond the bachelor's degree. Three years of successful experience as a school counselor. 15 semester hours of graduate courses beyond the work done for the Guidance Counselor's Certificate which includes work in guidance, counseling, and related disciplines and a course in administration and organization of guidance programs.

Credential Type: Professional Guidance Supervisor's Certificate. **Duration of License:** Permanent. **Requirements:** Hold or be eligible for a Rhode Island Guidance Counselor's Certificate. Master's degree or 36 semester hours of approved study beyond the bachelor's degree. Three years of successful experience as a school counselor. 15 semester hours of graduate courses beyond the work done for the Guidance Counselor's Certificate which includes work in guidance, counseling, and related disciplines and a course in administration and organization of guidance programs. Three years of successful experience as a supervisor of guidance in Rhode Island.

South Carolina

2152

Counselor, Licensed Professional
Board of Examiners for Licensed
   Professional Counselors
PO Box 7965
Columbia, SC 29202
Phone: (803)734-2726

Credential Type: License. **Duration of License:** Two years. **Requirements:** Master's degree in counseling. Two years of experience under supervision. State resident. **Examination:** Yes. **Fees:** $100 license fee.

2153

Elementary School Guidance Counselor
Teacher Education and Certification
State Dept. of Education
Rutledge Bldg., Rm. 1015
Columbia, SC 29201
Phone: (803)734-8464

Credential Type: Elementary School Guidance Counselor Certificate. **Requirements:** Master's degree. A minimum score of 550 on the NTE in Guidance Counseling. Complete a State Board of Education approved program in counseling and guidance. **Examination:** National Teacher Examination in Guidance Counseling.

2154

Marital and Family Therapist
Board of Examiners for Licensed
   Professional Counselors, Associate
   Counselors, and Marital and
   Family Therapists
PO Box 7965
Columbia, SC 29202
Phone: (803)734-1765

Credential Type: License. **Duration of License:** Two years. **Requirements:** Master's degree in marital and family therapy or in a related behavioral science or mental health field including board-specified graduate courses. Complete two years of postgraduate full-time supervised experience in marital and family therapy, including at least 1000 hours of direct clinical contact with couples and families, of which 200 hours are in supervision. **Examination:** Written examination. **Fees:** $75 application fee. $160 exam fee. $150 license fee. **Governing Statute:** Title 40, Chap. 75, Code of Laws of South Carolina, 1976.

2155

Secondary School Guidance Counselor
Teacher Education and Certification
State Dept. of Education
Rutledge Bldg., Rm. 1015
Columbia, SC 29201
Phone: (803)734-8464

Credential Type: Secondary School Associate Guidance Counselor Certificate. **Requirements:** Bachelor's degree. Valid professional teaching certificate. A minimum score of 550 on the NTE in Guidance Counseling. 21 semester hours in professional school counseling and education. Three semester hours in each of the following: principles and philosophy of education; basic guidance course; vocational and occupational information; appraisal of the individual; and introduction to counseling. A six semester hr. supervised practicum and internship. Nine semester hours of psychology which includes the following areas: development; personality; socialization; learning; and abnormal. Six semester hours which include studies on societal forces and cultural change. **Examination:** National Teacher Examination in Guidance Counseling.

Credential Type: Secondary School Counselor Certificate—Advanced. **Requirements:** Master's degree. Qualified to hold Secondary School Associate Guidance Counselor Certificate. Nine semester hours of graduate credit beyond the guidance counselor certificate which includes work in : school counseling and guidance; education; psychology; and societal forces and cultural changes.

South Dakota

2156

School Counselor
Teacher Education and Certification
State Dept. of Education
700 Governor's Drive
Pierre, SD 57501
Phone: (605)773-3553

Credential Type: School Counselor Certificate Endorsement. **Requirements:** Complete a master's degree program in guidance and counseling at a college or university. Hold a valid teaching certificate

Tennessee 2157

School Counselor, continued

or complete 500 clock hours of internship in either elementary or secondary school or a combination of both under the supervision of a certified counselor and a counselor educator.

Tennessee

2157

Elementary School Counselor
Office of Teaching Licensing
Dept. of Education
Cordell Hull Bldg.
Nashville, TN 37219-5335
Phone: (615)741-1644

Credential Type: Professional School Service Personnel License. **Duration of License:** 10 years. **Requirements:** Valid teacher's certificate endorsed for elementary grades. Two years of teaching experience or one year of teaching and 600 contact hours 27 quarter hours of college level study to include: guidance services (principles, philosophy, organization, and administration); personality organization; growth and development; education measurement; informational services; techniques of counseling; consulting and coordinating; group methods and processes; research and analysis; learning theories and their application in schools; supervised practice in elementary school counseling and other guidance services. Renewable.

2158

Marital and Family Therapist
Board of Certification for
  Professional Counselors and
  Marital and Family Therapy
283 Plus Park Blvd.
Nashville, TN 37247
Phone: (615)367-6207

Credential Type: License. **Requirements:** 18 years old. Two years professional experience. Masters degree, major in Marital and Family Therapy or equivalent. Good moral character. **Examination:** Yes. **Fees:** $45 Registration. $70 Application.

2159

Personnel Consultant
Personnel Recruiting Services Board
500 James Robertson Pky., 2nd Fl.
Nashville, TN 37243
Phone: (615)741-4700

Credential Type: License. **Duration of License:** Two years. **Requirements:** 18 years old. Narrative of qualifications. Agency license requires a financial statement. **Examination:** Yes. **Fees:** $10 Registration. $40 Examination. $35 Application. $35 Renewal.

2160

Professional Counselor
Board of Certification for
  Professional Counselors and
  Marital and Family Therapy
283 Plus Park Blvd.
Nashville, TN 37247
Phone: (615)367-6207

Credential Type: License. **Requirements:** 18 years old. Two years professional experience. 60 graduate semester hours of study. Good moral character. **Examination:** Yes. **Fees:** $45 Registration. $70 Application.

Texas

2161

Counselor, Professional
Texas State Board of Examiners of
  Professional Counselors
1100 W. 49th St.
Austin, TX 78756
Phone: (512)458-7511

Credential Type: License. **Duration of License:** One year. **Requirements:** A graduate degree from an accredited university. Completion of planned graduate program of 45 semester hours in counseling, including 300 clock hours of supervised practicum approved by the board. 24 months or 2,000 hours of supervised experience. 75 clock hours of continuing education during each three-year period required for license renewal. **Examination:** Written examination. **Fees:** $30 application fee. $50 exam fee. $36 license fee. $40 renewal fee. **Governing Statute:** VACS 4512g, 22 TAC 681.

2162

Marriage and Family Therapist
Texas State Board of Examiners of
  Marriage and Family Therapists
Texas Dept. of Health
1100 W. 49th St.
Austin, TX 78756
Phone: (512)834-6657

Credential Type: License without Examination (until September 1, 1993). **Duration of License:** One year. **Requirements:** At least three years of supervised clinical experience in the practice of marriage and family therapy. Master's or doctorate degree from a regionally accredited institution of higher education in marriage and family therapy or a related mental health discipline. Must be licensed or certified by this state in a mental health discipline. Must be certified by an appropriate professional organization having appropriate certification and standards. **Examination:** Written. **Fees:** $30 application fee. $36 license fee. $30 renewal fee. **Governing Statute:** VACS 4512c-1, 25 TAC 128.

Utah

2163

Marriage and Family Therapist
Dept. of Commerce
Div. of Occupational and
  Professional Licensing
160 E. 300 S.
PO Box 45802
Salt Lake City, UT 84145
Phone: (801)530-6628

Credential Type: License. **Duration of License:** Two years. **Requirements:** Must have a doctorate in marriage and family counseling or the equivalent, and three years of professional experience including one year of satisfactory marriage and family counseling experience; or a masters degree in marriage and family counseling, or a related field of study with three years of approved counseling experience; or have a graduate degree in a field of religious study which includes instruction and supervision in marriage and family counseling from an approved institution, along with three years of acceptable counseling experience. **Examination:** Yes. **Fees:** $75 license fee. $55 renewal fee.

2164

School Counselor
Certification and Personnel
  Development Section
State Board of Education
250 East 500 South St.
Salt Lake City, UT 84111
Phone: (801)538-7740

Credential Type: Basic Certificate. **Duration of License:** Four years. **Requirements:** Master's degree in an approved counselor education program or 55 quarter hours of approved graduate credit for school counselors. Hold or be eligible for a Utah teaching certificate or complete a prior-approved internship under supervision of a professional counselor, in addition to the supervised counseling practicum required by the counselor education program.

Recommendation of the preparing institution.

Credential Type: Standard Certificate. **Duration of License:** Valid indefinitely with consistent employment in counseling. **Requirements:** Complete two years of successful experience as a counselor under a Basic Certificate or its equivalent. Recommendation of the employing school district. Valid indefinitely providing holder verifies appropriate employment in education of at least three years during each succeeding five year interval. May also be renewed with nine quarter hours of approved credit earned within the five year period prior to date of application if more than five years have elapsed since applicant received bachelor's or higher degree.

Vermont

2165

Clinical Mental Health Counselor
Secretary of State
Pavilion Office Bldg.
Montpelier, VT 05602
Phone: (802)828-2373

Credential Type: License. **Duration of License:** Two years. **Requirements:** Not in violation of Title 6, Chapter 65 Section 3261 et al. Master's degree in counseling from approved institution in approved courses of study. Documented proof of 3,000 hours of supervised work in mental health counseling; and 100 hours of face to face supervision after masters supervised experience. **Examination:** Yes. **Reciprocity:** Yes. **Fees:** $60 Application. $75 Renewal.

2166

School Guidance Counselor
Teacher Licensure
State Dept. of Education
Montpelier, VT 05602-2703
Phone: (802)828-2445

Credential Type: Initial License. **Requirements:** Master's degree with a concentration in school guidance or its equivalent. Complete 180 clock hours of field experience which provides for an awareness of the application of guidance services at elementary (60 hours), middle/junior high (60 hours), and senior high (60 hours) school levels. Plus complete an additional 300 clock hr. internship in school guidance. Meet competencies specified by the Standards Board.

Virginia

2167

Counselor (Licensed Professional)
Virginia Board of Professional
   Counselors
1601 Rolling Hills Dr.
Richmond, VA 23229
Phone: (804)662-9920

Credential Type: License. **Duration of License:** One year. **Requirements:** Submit five letters of recommendation. Must complete 60 semester hours of graduate study from a credited university with two years of post graduate full-time experience under supervision acceptable to the Board of Professional Counselors. **Examination:** Yes. **Fees:** $100 application fee. $150 examination fee. $75 renewal fee.

2168

School Guidance Counselor
Administrative Director
Office of Professional Development
   and Teacher Education
Dept. of Education
PO Box 6-Q
Richmond, VA 23216-2060
Phone: (804)225-2094

Credential Type: Guidance Counselor Endorsement. **Requirements:** Master's degree in guidance and counseling plus two years of full-time teaching experience. Complete graduate level work which includes the following: philosophy and principles of guidance and other pupil personnel services; theory and practice of counseling; educational and psychological measurements; career development theory; understanding the individual; group guidance and counseling; research and evaluation; guidance in area of certification; and a supervised practicum of 180 clock hours

2169

Substance Abuse Counselor
Virginia Board of Professional
   Counselors
1601 Rolling Hills Dr.
Richmond, VA 23229
Phone: (804)662-9920

Credential Type: License. **Requirements:** High school diploma. Must complete 400 hours in a substance abuse education program accredited by a college or university, or an integrated program approved by the Board. Must also complete 2,000 hours of supervised experience as specified by the Board. **Examination:** Yes.

Washington

2170

Certified Mental Health Counselor
Dept. of Health
1112 SE Quince
Olympia, WA 98504
Phone: (206)753-6936

Credential Type: Mental Health Counselor Certificate. **Duration of License:** Two years. **Requirements:** Must have a master's or doctorate degree in mental health counseling, or a related field, from an approved school or complete a minimum of 30 graduate semester hours (45 quarter hours) in mental health counseling. Must have two years of supervised postgraduate experience. Must complete a four hour course in AIDS education. **Examination:** Written examination. **Fees:** $145 examination fee. $131 application and issuance certificate fee. $120 fee to retake examination. $73 renewal fee. $50 certification verification fee. $62 duplicate certificate fee.

2171

Marriage and Family Therapist
Dept. of Health
Professional Licensing Services
Counseling Section
Eastside Plaza
1300 SE Quince St.
Olympia, WA 98504
Phone: (206)753-6936

Credential Type: Certification. **Duration of License:** Two years. **Authorization:** Certification is not required by statute. **Requirements:** Master's or doctoral degree in marriage and family therapy or its equivalent from an approved school. Complete two years of postgraduate practice of marriage and family therapy under the supervision of a qualified marriage and family therapist. **Examination:** Board administered written and oral examinations. **Reciprocity:** Yes. **Fees:** $131 application fee. $140 written exam fee. $140 oral exam fee. **Governing Statute:** RCW 18.19.130. WAC 246-810.

Washington

2172

School Guidance Counselor
Superintendent of Public Instruction
Professional Education and
 Certification
Old Capitol Bldg. FG-11
Seattle, WA 98504-3211
Phone: (206)753-6773

Credential Type: Initial Educational Staff Associate Certificate. **Duration of License:** Seven years. **Authorization:** Authorizes service in primary role of assistant to the learner, the teacher, the administrator, and/or the educational program. **Requirements:** Complete all course work (except special projects or thesis) for a master's degree with a major in guidance and counseling.

Credential Type: Continuing Educational Staff Associate Certificate. **Duration of License:** Five years. **Requirements:** Master's degree in guidance and counseling. Verification of 180 days of experience in the role. Complete a college level course which includes peer review while employed in the role. Out-of-state applicants must complete a comprehensive written examination (unless already taken as part of the master's degree). Renewable upon 150 clock hours of work in this position during the life of the certificate.

West Virginia

2173

Professional Counselor
Board of Examiners in Counseling
PO Box 6492
Charleston, WV 25362
Phone: (304)345-3852

Credential Type: License. **Requirements:** Contact licensing body for application information.

2174

School Counselor
Dept. of Education
Office of Educational Personnel
 Development
1900 Washington St. E
Charleston, WV 25305
Phone: (800)982-2378

Credential Type: Certification. **Requirements:** U.S. citizen. 18 years old. Masters and completion of state approved educational preparatory program. Never convicted of a felony. **Examination:** Yes. **Reciprocity:** Yes. **Fees:** $5 Application. $5 Renewal.

Wisconsin

2175

Marriage and Family Therapist
Bureau of Health Service Professions
Dept. of Regulation and Licensing
PO Box 8935
Madison, WI 53708
Phone: (608)266-8609

Credential Type: Certification. **Authorization:** Certification required for use of title. **Requirements:** New certification rules to be established by May 1, 1993. If applying before May 31, 1995, requirements for certification without examination are a graduate degree in marriage and family therapy or in a related field with substantial marriage and family therapy course work. Complete two years of full-time supervised clinical marriage and family therapy practice after receiving degree. **Exemptions:** A certified independent clinical social worker may use the title of "marriage and family therapist." **Fees:** $39 certification fee. **Governing Statute:** 1991 Wisconsin Act 160.

2176

Professional Counselor
Bureau of Health Service Professions
Dept. of Regulation and Licensing
PO Box 8935
Madison, WI 53708
Phone: (608)266-8609

Credential Type: Certification. **Authorization:** Certification required for use of title. **Requirements:** New certification rules to be established by May 1, 1993. If applying before May 31, 1995, requirements for certification without examination are a graduate degree in professional counseling or its equivalent from an approved program. Within the past five years, meet one of the following sets of requirements: (1) With a master's degree, have at least two years of full-time supervised clinical professional counseling experience. (2) With a doctoral degree, have at least one year of full-time supervised clinical professional counseling experience. **Fees:** $39 certification fee. **Governing Statute:** 1991 Wisconsin Act 160.

2177

Rehabilitation Counselor
Bureau of Health Service Professions
Dept. of Regulation and Licensing
PO Box 8935
Madison, WI 53708
Phone: (608)266-8609

Credential Type: Certification. **Authorization:** Certification required for use of title. **Requirements:** New certification rules to be established by May 1, 1993. If applying before May 31, 1995, requirements for certification without examination are a graduate degree in professional counseling or its equivalent from an approved program. Within the past five years, meet one of the following sets of requirements: (1) With a master's degree, have at least two years of full-time supervised clinical professional counseling experience. (2) With a doctoral degree, have at least one year of full-time supervised clinical professional counseling experience. **Fees:** $39 certification fee. **Governing Statute:** 1991 Wisconsin Act 160.

2178

School Counselor
Teacher Education, Licensing, and
 Placement
Box 7841
Madison, WI 53707-7841
Phone: (608)266-1027

Credential Type: School Counselor License. **Requirements:** Master's degree with a major in school counseling and guidance or a master's degree with 30 semester hours in an approved school counseling and guidance program with institutional endorsement. Eligibility for a Wisconsin teaching license, or completion of a program for elementary or secondary teachers and two years of successful teaching experience, or an approved one year, full-time school counseling internship, or a minimum or two years as a licensed school counselor in an assigned position of one-half time or more. Demonstrated proficiency in the many areas necessary for the improvement of school practices related to counseling and guidance.

Wyoming

2179

Chemical Dependency Specialist Counselor
Wyoming Mental Health Professions Licensing Board
PO Box 591
Cheyenne, WY 82003
Phone: (307)635-2816

Credential Type: License. **Duration of License:** Two years. **Requirements:** Age of majority. Hold a Masters, Educational Specialist, or Doctorate degree in the appropriate field from an accredited school. Have accumulated 3000 hours of supervised experience. Pass a nationally recommended examination accepted by the Board. **Examination:** Yes. **Fees:** $60 Application. $50 License. $50 Renewal. Additional cost for examination.

2180

Licensed Professional Counselor
Professional Counselors, Marriage and Family Therapists, Social Workers, and Chemical Dependency Specialists Licensing Board
Barrett Bldg., 3rd Fl.
2301 Central Ave.
Cheyenne, WY 82002
Phone: (307)777-6313
Phone: (307)777-6529
Phone: (307)777-7788
Fax: (307)777-6005

Credential Type: LPC License. **Requirements:** Master's degree in counseling from a CACREP/CORE approved program or from a regionally accredited college or university. Program must include at least 45 semester hours of graduate study distributed over 10 core course work areas required by NBCC and CACREP. Complete 3000 hours of supervised experience in counseling, including 100 hours of face to face supervision, during or after master's degree training. Submit three professional references. **Examination:** National Counselor Examination (NCE). **Fees:** $100 application fee. $100 exam fee. $75 license fee. $100 renewal fee.

2181

Marriage and Family Therapist
Professional Counselors, Marriage and Family Therapists, Social Workers, and Chemical Dependency Specialists Licensing Board
Barrett Bldg., 3rd Fl.
2301 Central Ave.
Cheyenne, WY 82002
Phone: (307)777-6313
Phone: (307)777-6529
Phone: (307)777-7788
Fax: (307)777-6005

Credential Type: Marriage and Family Therapist License. **Requirements:** Master's degree in marriage and family therapy from a regionally accredited college or university. Complete 3000 hours of supervised experience in marriage and family therapy, including 100 hours of face to face supervision, during or after master's degree training. Submit three professional references. **Examination:** Examination in Marriage and Family Therapy. **Fees:** $100 application fee. $100 exam fee. $75 license fee. $100 renewal fee.

2182

School Counselor
State Dept. of Education
Certification and Accreditation Services Unit, Hathaway Bldg.
Cheyenne, WY 82002
Phone: (307)777-7291

Credential Type: Counselor Endorsement. **Requirements:** Teacher certification and the Education Specialist certification. 24 semester hours of graduate work, including a master's degree in counseling and the following courses of study: coordination and administration of guidance services; counseling theories and techniques; practicum in counseling; career guidance or occupational and educational information; education or psychological tests and measurements; counseling in the elementary schools or consulting with parents; and behavioral sciences. One calendar year of work experience outside the field of education. Two years of classroom teaching, or supervisory, or administrative experience in a K-12 setting.

Dental Assistants

The following states grant licenses in this occupational category as of the date of publication:
Arizona, Arkansas, California, Michigan, Minnesota, Tennessee, Vermont.

Arizona

2183

Dental Assistant
Board of Dental Examiners
5060 N. 19th Ave., Ste. 406
Phoenix, AZ 85015
Phone: (602)255-3696

Credential Type: License. **Requirements:** Contact licensing body for application information.

Arkansas

2184

Dental Assistant
Arkansas State Board of Dental Examiners
Tower Bldg., Ste. 1200
4th & Center St.
Little Rock, AR 72202
Phone: (501)682-2085

Credential Type: License. **Requirements:** Graduate of a school approved by the American Dental Association (ADA); or, two years chairside experience and completion of a self-study course. **Examination:** Yes. **Fees:** $30 Application fee.

California

2185

Dental Assistant
Committee on Dental Auxiliaries
1428 Howe Ave., Ste. 58
Sacramento, CA 95825-3235
Phone: (916)920-7637

Credential Type: Registration. **Requirements:** Contact licensing body for application information.

Michigan

2186

Dental Assistant, Registered
Board of Dentistry
Bureau of Occupational & Professional Regulation
Dept. of Commerce
PO Box 30018
Lansing, MI 48909
Phone: (517)373-7902

Credential Type: Registered Dental Assistant License. **Duration of License:** Three years. **Requirements:** Complete a dental assisting program which has been accredited by the American Dental Association and approved by the Board for the teaching of expanded functions. Working knowledge of the English language. **Examination:** Written and clinical exam. **Reciprocity:** Individuals who are licensed in other states as an expanded function dental assistant are licensed by the Michigan Board on an individual basis. **Fees:** $10 application processing fee. $50 exam fee ($25 per exam part). $10 exam review fee. $5 initial license fee, per year. $5 renewal fee, per year. $15 reciprocity fee. **Governing Statute:** Public Health Code, Act 368 of 1978, as amended.

Minnesota

2187

Dental Assistant
Board of Dentistry
2700 University Ave. W., Ste. 70
St. Paul, MN 55114-1055
Phone: (612)642-0579

Credential Type: Registration. **Duration of License:** One year. **Requirements:** Submit application and fees. Pass required examinations. **Examination:** Minnesota Registration Examination. State jurisprudence examination. **Fees:** $30 registration fee. $26 renewal fee. **Governing Statute:** Minnesota Statutes, Chap. 150A and 319A. Minnesota Rules 3100-3199.

Tennessee

2188

Dental Assistant
Board of Dentistry
283 Plus Park Blvd.
Nashville, TN 37247-1010
Phone: (615)367-6228

Credential Type: License. **Duration of License:** Two years. **Requirements:** Formal training program or certified by National Board. Good moral character and reputation. **Examination:** Yes. **Fees:** $50 Registration. $15 Examination. $15 Application.

Vermont

2189

Dental Assistant, Certified
Board of Dental Examiners
Pavilion Office Bldg.
Montpelier, VT 05602
Phone: (802)828-2363
Phone: (802)828-2390

Credential Type: License. **Duration of License:** Two years. **Requirements:** Completion of dental assisting course approved by the American Dental Association. Successful completion of radiology course at approved institution. Six months continuous experience as Dental Assistant in Vermont under supervision of licensed dentist. **Examination:** Yes. **Reciprocity:** No. **Fees:** $5 Registration. $7.50 Renewal. **Governing Statute:** Title 26, VSA Secions 861-865.

2190

Dental Assistant, Traditional
Board of Dental Examiners
Pavilion Office Bldg.
Montpelier, VT 05602
Phone: (802)828-2991

Credential Type: License. **Duration of License:** Two years. **Requirements:** Six months experience as a Dental Assistant trainee within past two years; or graduate of a secondary school dental assistant program. **Examination:** No. **Reciprocity:** No. **Fees:** $5 Registration. $10 Renewal **Governing Statute:** Title 26, VSA Sections 861-865.

Dental Hygienists

The following states grant licenses in this occupational category as of the date of publication:

Alabama	District of	Iowa	Minnesota	New Mexico	Rhode Island	Washington
Alaska	Columbia	Kansas	Mississippi	New York	South Carolina	West Virginia
Arizona	Florida	Kentucky	Missouri	North Carolina	South Dakota	Wisconsin
Arkansas	Georgia	Louisiana	Montana	North Dakota	Tennessee	Wyoming
California	Hawaii	Maine	Nebraska	Ohio	Texas	
Colorado	Idaho	Maryland	Nevada	Oklahoma	Utah	
Connecticut	Illinois	Massachusetts	New Hampshire	Oregon	Vermont	
Delaware	Indiana	Michigan	New Jersey	Pennsylvania	Virginia	

Alabama

2191

Dental Hygienist
Board of Dental Examiners of Alabama
2308-B Starmount Circle
Huntsville, AL 35801
Phone: (205)533-4638

Credential Type: License. **Duration of License:** One year. **Requirements:** 19 years of age. Must be a graduate of a school of dental hygiene, or must be a graduate of the Alabama Dental Hygiene Program conducted by the ADHP. **Examination:** Yes. **Fees:** $80 application fee. $20 certificate fee. $25 renewal fee.

Alaska

2192

Dental Hygienist
Dept. of Commerce and Economic Development
Div. of Occupational Licensing
Board of Dental Examiners
PO Box D
Juneau, AK 99811-0800
Phone: (907)465-2534
Fax: (907)465-2974

Credential Type: License by examination and certificate of registration. **Duration of License:** Two years. **Requirements:** At least 18 years of age. Graduate of an accredited high school. Graduate of a dental hygiene school that requires at least a two-year course and is accredited by the Commission on Accreditation of Dental and Dental Auxilliary Education Programs of the American Dental Association. Complete the written theory examination of the American Dental Association Joint Commission on National Dental Examinations or an equivalent written examination given by the board. License renewal requirement of seven hours of continuing education credit for each complete calendar year the applicant was licensed during the concluding licensing period. **Examination:** State board conducted examination or examination given by the Western Regional Examining Board. **Exemptions:** Person enrolled as a full-time student in an accredited school of dental hygiene may perform dental hygiene procedures without a license as part of a course of study. The procedures must be performed under the direct supervision of a licensed member of the faculty and the clinical program must be board approved. **Fees:** $30 application fee. $150 board conducted examination fee. $100 license fee. $100 renewal fee. **Governing Statute:** Alaska Statutes 08.32. Professional Regulations 12 AAC 28.

Credential Type: License by credentials and certificate of registration. **Duration of License:** Two years. **Requirements:** At least 18 years of age. Graduate of an accredited high school. Graduate of a dental hygiene school that requires at least a two-year course and is accredited by the Commission on Accreditation of Dental and Dental Auxilliary Education Programs of the American Dental Association. Complete the written theory examination of the American Dental Association Joint Commission on National Dental Examinations or an equivalent written examination given by the board.

Pass a state or regional dental hygiene clinical examination that is equivalent to the Alaska clinical examination. Been in active clinical dental hygiene practice averaging no less than 14 hours per week for each of the two years immediately preceding application for state licensure.

Applicant has not failed state's clinical dental hygiene examination. Has not previously had a license to practice dental hygiene revoked. Is personally interviewed by a board member. Is not the subject of an unresolved complaint, review procedure, or disciplinary proceeding.

License renewal requirement of seven hours of continuing education credit for each complete calendar year the applicant was licensed during the concluding licensing period. **Examination:** Equivalent of state administered examination. **Fees:** $30 application fee. $50 credential review fee. $100 license fee. $100 renewal fee. **Governing Statute:** Alaska Statutes 08.32. Professional Regulations 12 AAC 28.

Credential Type: Temporary license. **Duration of License:** Expires at the time notice is given of the results of the next scheduled examination and may not be reissued. **Requirements:** At least 18 years of age. Graduate of an accredited high school. Graduate of a dental hygiene school that requires at least a two-year course and is accredited by the Commission on Accreditation of Dental and Dental Auxilliary Education Programs of the American Dental Association. Complete the written theory examination of the American Dental Association Joint Commission on National Dental Examinations or an equivalent written examination given by the board.

Pass a state or regional dental hygiene clinical examination that is equivalent to the Alaska clinical examination. Mayy have been in active clinical dental hygiene practice less than two years immediately preceding application for state licensure.

Applicant has not failed state's clinical dental hygiene examination. Has not previously had a license to practice dental hygiene revoked. Is personally interviewed by a board member. Is not the subject of an unresolved complaint, review procedure, or disciplinary proceeding.

Licensed to practice dental hygiene in another state. **Examination:** No examination required. **Fees:** $30 application fee. $20 temporary license fee.

Arizona

2193

Dental Hygienist
Arizona State Board of Dental Examiners
5060 N. 19th Ave., Ste. 406
Phoenix, AZ 85015
Phone: (602)255-3696

Credential Type: License to practice. **Duration of License:** Three years. **Requirements:** At least 18 years of age. Good moral character. Complete a course or curriculum in dental hygiene from a recognized dental hygiene school. Pass a dental hygienist examination. **Examination:** Dental hygienist examination. **Fees:** Application fee. Examination fee. License fee. Renewal fee.

Arkansas

2194

Dental Hygienist
Arkansas State Board of Dental Examiners
Tower Bldg., Ste. 1200
4th & Center St.
Little Rock, AR 72202
Phone: (501)682-2085

Credential Type: License. **Requirements:** Graduate of a dental hygiene school approved by the American Dental Association (ADA). Satisfactory completion of National Boards. Successful completion of examination given by Southern Regional Testing Agency. **Examination:** Yes. **Fees:** $100 Application. Written and practical examinations.

California

2195

Dental Hygienist
Committee on Dental Auxiliaries
1428 Howe Ave., Ste. 58
Sacramento, CA 95825-3235
Phone: (916)920-7637

Credential Type: Registration. **Requirements:** Contact licensing body for application information.

2196

School Health Services Associate
Commission on Teacher Credentialing
PO Box 944270
Sacramento, CA 94244-7000
Phone: (916)445-7254

Credential Type: Health Services Credential. **Authorization:** Authorizes the holder to perform, in preschool, grades 1-12, and adult classes, the health service designated on the credential, (Services such as audiometrist, occupational therapist, or physical therapist are not deemed health services.) Authorized services are school nurse, physician, dentist, dental hygienist, and optometrist. **Requirements:** Valid license, certificate, or registration appropriate to the health service to be designated, issued by the California agency and authorized by law to license, certify, or register persons to practice that health service in California. Additional requirements as may be prescribed by the Commission. For school nurses, a bachelor's degree, an approved program of preparation in school nursing, and two years of successful experience as a school nurse is also required. A preliminary School Nurse Services Credential (valid for five years) requires only a bachelor's degree and a valid California registered nurse license. **Fees:** $60 application fee. $30 test score recording and evaluation fee, except for CBEST.

Colorado

2197

Dental Hygienist
Board of Dental Examiners
1560 Broadway, Ste. 1310
Denver, CO 80202
Phone: (303)894-7758

Credential Type: License to practice. **Requirements:** Eligible for licensing by endorsement or pass CRDTS regional examination. **Examination:** Regional CRDTS examination.

Connecticut

2198

Dental Hygienist
Connecticut Dental Commission
Dept. of Health Services
150 Washington St.
Hartford, CT 06106
Phone: (203)566-4619

Credential Type: License. **Duration of License:** One year. **Requirements:** Complete and graduate from a two-year program from an ADA-accredited school. **Examination:** Regional board examination. **Fees:** $75 application and license fee. $50 renewal fee.

Delaware

2199

Dental Hygienist
State Board of Dental Examiners
Dept. of Administrative Services
Div. of Professional Regulation
Margaret O'Neill Bldg.
PO Box 1401
Dover, DE 19903
Phone: (302)739-4522
Fax: (302)739-6148

Credential Type: Dental hygienist certificate of registration. **Duration of License:** One or two years. **Requirements:** Be at least 18 years of age. Good moral character. Graduate from high school. Graduate from an approved dental hygiene academic program of at least two academic years in duration. Pass examination. **Examination:** Written examination and practical clinical demonstrations. **Reciprocity:** Yes, provided the state or territory has an equal standard of laws regulating the practice of dental hygiene. Applicant must have practiced dental hygiene for at least two years and pay fee of $25. Registration may be granted if applicant was registered in a state not maintaining an equal standard, provided applicant furnishes evidence of good moral character, education, and professional qualifications. **Fees:** $46 examination and initial license fee. $36 biennial renewal fee.

District of Columbia

2200

Dental Hygienist
License and Certification Div.
Occupational and Professional Licensure Administration
Consumer and Regulatory Affairs Dept.
PO Box 37200
Washington, DC 20013-7200
Phone: (202)727-7823
Phone: (202)727-7480

Alternate Information: 614 H St., NW, Washington, DC 20001.

Credential Type: License. **Requirements:** Contact licensing body for application information.

Florida

2201

Dental Hygienist
Board of Dentistry
Dept. of Professional Regulation
1940 N. Monroe St.
Tallahassee, FL 32399-0765
Phone: (904)488-6015

Credential Type: Dental Hygienist License. **Duration of License:** Two years. **Requirements:** Be 18 years of age. Graduate of a dental hygiene college or school approved by the board or accredited by the Commission on Accreditation of the American Dental Association. Complete the National Board of Dental Hygiene examination within the past 10 years.

Renewal requires 24 hours of continuing education. **Examination:** National Board of Dental Hygiene examination. Stateadministered written examination. Practical or clinical examination. **Fees:** $50 application fee. $225 exam fee. $75 licensure fee. $75 renewal fee. **Governing Statute:** Florida Statutes, Chapter 455 and 466. Florida Administrative Code, Rule 21-G.

Georgia

2202

Dental Hygienist
Georgia Board of Dentistry
166 Pryor St., SW
Atlanta, GA 30303
Phone: (404)656-3925

Credential Type: License. **Duration of License:** Two years. **Requirements:** Complete and graduate from a two-year program from an ADA-accredited school. Renewal requires continuing education. **Examination:** National Board exams. Southern regional examination. **Fees:** $50 processing fee. $125 renewal fee.

Credential Type: Temporary permit. **Requirements:** Must be licensed in another state, have applied for Georgia licensing, and be waiting for the next examination. **Fees:** $150 temporary permit fee.

Hawaii

2203

Dental Hygienist
Hawaii Board of Dental Examiners
Dept. of Commerce and Consumer Affairs
PO Box 3469
Honolulu, HI 96801
Phone: (808)548-7461

Credential Type: License. **Duration of License:** Six months. **Requirements:** High school diploma or equivalent. Graduation from an accredited, two-year American school for dental hygienists. Certification in the administration of intra-oral infiltration local anesthesia. **Examination:** National Board of Dental Hygiene exam. State exam. **Fees:** $20 application fee. $110 exam fee. $25 license fee. $15 $30 Compliance Resolution Fund fee. $12.50 renewal fee.

Idaho

2204

Dental Hygienist
Idaho State Board of Dentistry
Statehouse Mail
Boise, ID 83720
Phone: (208)334-2369

Credential Type: License to practice. **Requirements:** Pass required examinations. **Examination:** Jurisprudence examination. WREB regional examination.

Illinois

2205

Dental Hygienist
State Board of Dentistry
Licensure Maint. Unit
Dept. of Regulations and Education
320 W. Washington, 3rd Fl.
Springfield, IL 62786
Phone: (217)785-0800

Credential Type: Licenst to practice. **Duration of License:** Two years. **Requirements:** High school graduate or equivalent. Complete two years of study in an approved college of dental hygiene. Have current CPR certification. Pass required examinations. **Examination:** NERB, CRDTS, or SRTA regional examination. National Detnal Examination. **Reciprocity:** Yes, provided applicant meets Illinois education and training requirements and has practiced for three of the past five years. **Fees:** $25 license fee. $50 endorsement fee. $30 renewal fee.

Indiana

2206

Dental Hygienist
State Board of Dental Examiners
Health Professions Bureau
402 W. Washington St., Rm. 041
Indianapolis, IN 46204
Phone: (317)232-2960

Credential Type: License to practice. **Duration of License:** Two years. **Requirements:** Graduation from a board-approved school. Pass examination. **Examination:** Board-administered clinical exam. Exam on statutes and rules. **Reciprocity:** License by endorsement may be granted to applicants with a license from a state with similar requirements and who have been in active practice for five of the past seven years. **Fees:** $25 application fee. $35 exam fee. $25 license fee. $20 renewal fee. **Governing Statute:** Indiana Code 25-13. 828 Indiana Administrative Code.

Iowa

2207

Dental Hygienist
Iowa Board of Dental Examiners
Executive Hills West
1209 East Court
Des Moines, IA 50319
Phone: (515)281-5157

Credential Type: License. **Duration of License:** Two years. **Requirements:** Graduation from an accredited school of dental hygiene. **Examination:** Joint Commission on National Dental Examinations. Central Regional Dental Testing Service examination. Jurisprudence exam. **Fees:** $50 application fee. $70 renewal fee.

Kansas

2208

Dental Hygienist
Board of Dental Examiners
3601 SW 29th St., S-134
Topeka, KS 66614-2062
Phone: (913)273-0780

Credential Type: License to practice. **Duration of License:** One year. **Requirements:** Must be at least 18 years of age. Good moral character. Graduate of a board-approved school for dental hygienists.
Renewal requires at least 15 hours of continuing dental education. **Examination:** CRDTS examination. **Reciprocity:** Yes, provided applicant has practiced for three consecutive years and holds a valid license. **Fees:** $100 application fee. $5 certificate issuance fee. **Governing Statute:** Kansas Statutes Annotated, Chap. 65, Article 12. Rules and Regulations of the Kansas Dental Board.

Kentucky

2209

Dental Hygienist
Kentucky Board of Dentistry
2106 Bardstown Rd.
Louisville, KY 40205
Phone: (502)451-6832

Credential Type: License. **Duration of License:** One year. **Requirements:** High school diploma. Completion of an accredited training program in a school of dental hygiene. 18 years of age. Must have HIV course annually and CPR course biennially. Must complete continuing education courses. **Examination:** Yes.

Louisiana

2210

Dental Hygienist
Louisiana State Board of Dentistry
1515 Poydras St., Ste. 2240
New Orleans, LA 70112
Phone: (504)568-8574

Credential Type: License. **Duration of License:** One year. **Requirements:** 18 years of age. Graduation from an approved training school of dental hygienists. U.S. citizen or permanent resident. **Examination:** Yes. **Fees:** $50 exam fee. $50 renewal fee.

Maine

2211

Dental Hygienist
Board of Dental Examiners
Dept. of Professional and Financial Regulation
State House Station 143
Augusta, ME 04333
Phone: (207)289-3333

Credential Type: License. **Requirements:** Contact licensing body for application information.

Maryland

2212

Dental Hygienist
Board of Dental Examiners
Metro-Executive Center
4201 Patterson Ave.
Baltimore, MD 21215
Phone: (301)764-4730

Credential Type: License. **Duration of License:** Two years. **Requirements:** Complete and graduate from a two-year program from an ADA-accredited school. **Examination:** Northeast Regional Board Exams. Jurisprudence examination. **Fees:** $150 application and license fee. $90 renewal fee.

Massachusetts

2213

Dental Hygienist
Board of Registration in Dentistry
100 Cambridge St., Rm. 1514
Boston, MA 02202
Phone: (617)727-9928
Fax: (617)727-7378

Credential Type: License. **Duration of License:** Two years. **Requirements:** Complete and graduate from a two-year program from an ADA-accredited school. **Examination:** National Board Exams. Northeast Regional Board Exams. **Fees:** $45 application fee. $40 license fee. $40 renewal fee.

Michigan

2214

Dental Hygienist
Board of Dentistry
Dept. of Licensing and Regulation
Bureau of Health Services
PO Box 30018
Lansing, MI 48909
Phone: (517)373-6650

Credential Type: License to practice. **Requirements:** Pass required examinations. **Examination:** NERB regional examination.

Minnesota

2215

Dental Hygienist
Board of Dentistry
2700 University Ave. W., Ste. 70
St. Paul, MN 55114-1055
Phone: (612)642-0579

Credential Type: License to practice. **Duration of License:** One year. **Requirements:** Pass required examinations. **Examination:** National Board Examination. CRDTS regional examination. State jurisprudence examination. **Reciprocity:** Dental hygienists licensed in another state or Canada may apply for licensure by credentials. Must have actively practiced for one of the preceding two years. **Fees:** $55 license fee. $150 license by credentials fee. $40 renewal fee. **Governing Statute:** Minnesota Statutes, Chap. 150A and 319A. Minnesota Reules 3100-3199.

Mississippi

2216

Dental Hygienist
Board of Dental Examiners
PO Box 1960
Clinton, MS 39060
Phone: (601)924-9622

Credential Type: License. **Duration of License:** One year. **Requirements:** 18 years of age. Complete and graduate from a two-year program from an ADA-accredited school. Current CPR certificate. **Examination:** State Board Examination. **Fees:** $135 exam fee ($100 to board; $35 to dental school). $50 renewal fee.

Missouri

2217

Dental Hygienist
Missouri Dental Board
Div. of Professional Registration
3605 Missouri Blvd.
PO Box 1367
Jefferson City, MO 65102
Phone: (314)751-0040

Credential Type: Registration and license to practice. **Duration of License:** One year. **Requirements:** Good moral character. Complete a course in dental hygiene in an accredited dental hygiene school. **Examination:** CRDTS written and clinical examination. Missouri dental law and rules examination. **Fees:** $100 application and examination fee. $45 license renewal fee. **Governing Statute:** Chap. 332 RSMo (Supp 1981). 4 CSR 110.

Credential Type: Licensure by credentials. **Duration of License:** One year. **Authorization:** Issued to qualified dental hygienists coming from another jurisdiction. **Requirements:** Have passed the National Board Exam. Be a graduate of and hold a degree from an accredited school of dental hygiene. Have passed a clinical exam in another jurisdiction equivalent in its requirements to the CRDTS. Have held a current and valid license in the practice of dental hygiene for at least two years immediately preceding application. Hold current certification in CPR. Have engaged in the active practice of dental hygiene for at least two years immediately preceding application. **Examination:** Written exam on Missouri dental law and rules. **Fees:** $100 application and exam fee. $45 license renewal fee. **Governing Statute:** Chap. 332 RSMo (Supp 1981). 4 CSR 110.

Montana

2218

Dental Hygienist
Montana Board of Dentistry
111 N. Jackson
Helena, MT 59620
Phone: (406)444-3745

Credential Type: License. **Duration of License:** One year. **Requirements:** Graduation from an approved dental hygiene program. **Examination:** Western Regional Clinical Examination. Montana Jurisprudence Examination. **Reciprocity:** Yes, by credentials. **Fees:** $75 exam fee. $35 license fee. $50 renewal fee. $75 credentials application fee. **Governing Statute:** Montana Code Annotated 37-4-401 through 37-4-408.

Nebraska

2219

Dental Hygienist
Nebraska Board of Examiners in Dentistry
301 Centennial Mall S.
PO Box 95007
Lincoln, NE 68509
Phone: (402)471-2115

Credential Type: License. **Duration of License:** Two years. **Requirements:** 19 years of age. Must be a high school graduate. Must be a graduate of an approved training program. **Examination:** Yes. **Fees:** $50 initial fee. $40 renewal fee.

Nevada

2220

Dental Hygienist
Nevada State Board of Dental Examiners
PO Box 80360
Las Vegas, NV 89180
Phone: (702)258-4230

Credential Type: License. **Duration of License:** One year. **Requirements:** Graduation from an accredited school of dental hygiene. **Examination:** National Board of Dental Examiners exam. Clinical exam. **Fees:** $150 exam fee. $112.50 license fee. $112.50 renewal fee.

New Hampshire

2221

Dental Hygienist
Board of Dental Examiners
6 Hazen Dr.
Concord, NH 03301-6527
Phone: (603)271-4561

Credential Type: License to practice. **Requirements:** Pass required examinations. **Examination:** NERB regional examination.

New Jersey

2222

Dental Hygienist
State Board of Dentistry
1100 Raymond Blvd.
Newark, NJ 07102
Phone: (201)648-7087

Credential Type: License. **Requirements:** High school diploma or equivalent. Graduation from an approved school of dental hygiene. 20 hours of continuing education every four years. **Examination:** Northeast Regional Board Examination. **Fees:** $50 application fee. $30 qualifying certificate. $50 examination fee. $30 license fee. **Governing Statute:** NJSA 45:6. NJAC 13:30-2.

New Mexico

2223

Dental Hygienist
Board of Dentistry
PO Drawer 8397
Santa Fe, NM 87504-8397
Phone: (505)827-7165

Credential Type: License. Contact licensing body for application information.

New York

2224

Dental Hygienist
State Education Dept.
Div. of Professional Licensing Services
Cultural Education Center
Empire State Plaza
Albany, NY 12230
Phone: (518)474-3696

Credential Type: License. **Duration of License:** Three years. **Requirements:** Academic and clinical education at a college level. 17 years of age. U.S. citizen or alien lawfully admitted for permanent residency. **Examination:** Written and practical. **Fees:** $285 exam fee. $120 license fee. $50 renewal fee. **Governing Statute:** Title VIII Articles 130, 133 of the Education Law.

North Carolina

2225

Dental Hygienist
North Carolina State Board of Dental Examiners
PO Box 32270
Raleigh, NC 27622
Phone: (919)781-4901

Credential Type: Certification. **Duration of License:** One year. **Requirements:** High school diploma or GED. 18 years of age. Basic college preparatory course prior to entrance in a dental hygiene program. Graduation from an approved, two-year dental hygiene program. **Examination:** Written. **Fees:** $125 license, exam and application fee. $45 renewal fee.

North Dakota

2226

Dental Hygienist
Board of Dental Examiners
PO Box 179
Valley City, ND 58072
Phone: (701)845-3708

Credential Type: License and Registration. **Duration of License:** One year. **Requirements:** Good moral character. High school graduate or equivalent. Graduate of a school of dental hygiene approved by the Council on Education of the American Dental Association. Must meet continuing education requirement for renewal. **Examination:** National Board Examination or board administered examination. **Reciprocity:** Yes. **Fees:** $35 application fee. **Governing Statute:** North Dakota Century Code, Chap. 43-20

Ohio

2227

Dental Hygienist
Ohio State Dental Board
77 S. High St., 18th Fl.
Columbus, OH 43266-0306
Phone: (614)466-2580

Credential Type: License. **Duration of License:** Two years. **Requirements:** Complete and graduate from a two-year program from an ADA-accredited school. Renewal requires continuing education. **Examination:** National Board Exam. Regional board examinations. **Fees:** $37.50 application fee. $52 renewal fee.

Oklahoma

2228

Dental Hygienist
Board of Governors of Registered Dentists
2726 N. Oklahoma Ave.
Oklahoma City, OK 73105
Phone: (405)521-2350

Credential Type: Certificate. **Duration of License:** One year. **Requirements:** A certificate of dental hygiene from an accredited school. 30 hours of continuing education over a three-year period. Must pass a theoretical exam such as the National Boards. **Examination:** Oklahoma Dental Hygiene Examination. **Fees:** $100 exam fee. $100 application fee. $45 renewal fee.

Oregon

2229

Dental Hygienist
Oregon Board of Dentistry
1515 SW Fifth, Ste. 400
Portland, OR 97201
Phone: (503)229-5520

Credential Type: License. **Duration of License:** Two years. **Requirements:** Must be a graduate from an accredited dental hygiene school. **Examination:** Yes. **Fees:** $200 exam fee. $85 renewal fee. **Governing Statute:** ORS 680.010 to 680.170.

Pennsylvania

2230

Dental Hygienist
State Board of Dentistry
PO Box 2649
Harrisburg, PA 17120
Phone: (717)783-7162

Credential Type: Dental Hygienist License. **Duration of License:** Two years. **Requirements:** Must graduate from an approved two-year school of dental hygiene. Curriculum must include at least thirty-two, 30 hour weeks of instruction. **Examination:** The Pennsylvania State Dental Council and Examining Board Clinical Dental Hygiene Examination. National Board written examination. **Reciprocity:** License holders from out-of-state may be granted reciprocity upon submission of credentials and approval of the board. **Fees:** $15 license application fee. $35 criteria approval application fee. $10 verification of licensure fee. $10 certificate of license fee. $10 duplicate license fee. $25 biennial renewal fee.

Rhode Island

2231

Dental Hygienist
Board of Examiners in Dentistry
Dept. of Health
3 Capitol Hill, No. 404
Providence, RI 02908
Phone: (401)277-2151

Credential Type: License. **Duration of License:** One year. **Requirements:** Complete and graduate from a two-year program from an ADA-accredited school. Renewal requires continuing education. **Examination:** National Board Exam. State or regional board examination. **Fees:** $75 application fee. $75 renewal fee. $100 state exam fee.

South Carolina

2232

Dental Hygienist
South Carolina State Board of Dentistry
1315 Blanding St.
Columbia, SC 29201
Phone: (803)734-8904

Credential Type: License. **Requirements:** Good moral character. Graduation from an accredited school of dental hygiene. **Examination:** National Board exam. State Board exam. **Fees:** $150 license fee. $65 re-registration fee.

South Dakota

2233

Dental Hygienist
State Board of Dentistry
PO Box 8047
Rapid City, SD 57709-8047
Phone: (605)342-3026

Credential Type: License to practice. **Duration of License:** One year. **Requirements:** Graduate from an accredited dental hygiene school. Renewal requires 75 hours of continuing education every five years. **Examination:** Central Regional Dental Testing Service examination. National

Dental Hygienist, continued

board examination. Written examination on rules and regulations. **Reciprocity:** Yes. **Fees:** $50 exam fee. $20 certificate of registration fee. $100 reciprocity fee. $30 annual renewal fee. $15 annual continuing education fee.

Tennessee

`2234`

Dental Hygienist
Board of Dentistry
283 Plus Park Blvd.
Nashville, TN 37247-1010
Phone: (615)367-6228

Credential Type: License. **Duration of License:** One year. **Requirements:** 18 years old. Graduate of dental hygiene school. Good moral character and reputation. **Examination:** Yes. **Reciprocity:** No. **Fees:** $35 Registration. $25 Application.

Texas

`2235`

Dental Hygienist
Texas State Board of Dental Examiners
327 Congress Ave., Ste. 500
Austin, TX 78701
Phone: (512)477-2985

Credential Type: License. **Duration of License:** One year. **Requirements:** 18 years of age. High school diploma or equivalent. Graduation from an accredited school or college of dentistry or dental hygiene with not less than two terms of instruction, each lasting eight months. Proof of training in CPR, or proof that person is not physically able to complete CPR training. **Examination:** Written, oral, and/or practical examination. Exam in Texas law relating to dental hygiene. **Fees:** $75 exam fee. $50 annual renewal. **Governing Statute:** VACS 4551e, 22 TAC 103.

Utah

`2236`

Dental Hygienist
Dept. of Commerce
Div. of Occupational and Professional Licensing
160 E. 300 S.
PO Box 45802
Salt Lake City, UT 84145
Phone: (801)530-6628

Credential Type: License. **Duration of License:** Two years. **Requirements:** Must be a graduate of a recognized hygiene school. **Examination:** Yes. **Fees:** $40 license fee. $30 renewal fee.

Vermont

`2237`

Dental Hygienist
Board of Dental Examiners
Pavilion Office Bldg.
Montpelier, VT 05602
Phone: (802)828-2363
Phone: (802)828-2390

Credential Type: License. **Duration of License:** Two years. **Requirements:** 18 years of age. Graduate of approved school of Dental Hygiene. CPR required. Passed either Northeast or Central Region Board exam within past five years, or have been practicing for five consecutive years. Present a letter stating fulfillment of the above. **Examination:** Yes. **Reciprocity:** No. **Fees:** $25 Initial fee. $15 Renewal. **Governing Statute:** Title 26, VSA Sections 851-856.

Virginia

`2238`

Dental Hygienist
Virginia Board of Dentistry
1601 Rolling Hills Dr.
Richmond, VA 23229
Phone: (804)662-9920

Credential Type: License. **Duration of License:** Two years. **Requirements:** A graduate of an approved school of dental hygiene recognized by the Council on Dental Education of the American Dental Association and the Virginia Board of Dentistry. File a completed application accompanied by a certified transcript of grades. **Examination:** Yes. **Fees:** $120 application fee. $50 renewal fee.

Washington

`2239`

Dental Hygienist
Dept. of Health
1112 SE Quince
Olympia, WA 98504
Phone: (206)586-1867

Credential Type: License. **Duration of License:** One year. **Requirements:** Graduate from an accredited dental hygienist school. **Examination:** Written and practical examination. **Fees:** $200 application and exam fee. $95 renewal fee.

West Virginia

`2240`

Dental Hygienist
Board of Dental Examiners
PO Drawer 1459
Beckley, WV 25802-1459
Phone: (304)252-8266

Credential Type: License. **Duration of License:** One year. **Requirements:** U.S. citizen. 18 years old. Graduate of an approved dental school. Possession of an acceptable dental diploma. Never convicted of a felony. **Examination:** Yes. **Fees:** $20 Application. $5 License. $10 Renewal.

Wisconsin

`2241`

Dental Hygienist
Regulations and Licensing Dept.
Dentistry Board
PO Box 8935
Madison, WI 53708-8935
Phone: (608)266-8609

Credential Type: License. **Requirements:** High school diploma. Completion of a two-year dental hygiene course. **Examination:** Written and practical. **Reciprocity:** Yes.

Wyoming

`2242`

Dental Hygienist
Board of Dental Examiners
PO Box 1024
Powell, WY 82435
Phone: (307)754-3476

Credential Type: License. **Duration of License:** One year. **Requirements:** Complete an American Dental Association-ac-

Dental Hygienists

credited dental hygiene program. Pass the written and clinical examinations within the last five years. Pass the ADA National Board Examination. Pass the state examinations. Complete an Expanded Duties course of study previously endorsed by the Board. Services must be performed under the supervision of a licensed dentist. **Examination:** Yes. **Fees:** $120 Examination. $45 Renewal.

Dental Laboratory Technicians

The following states grant licenses in this occupational category as of the date of publication: Arizona, Florida, Idaho, Kentucky, Montana, New Jersey, Oregon, South Carolina.

Arizona

2243

Denturist
Arizona State Board of Dental Examiners
5060 N. 19th Ave., Ste. 406
Phoenix, AZ 85015
Phone: (602)255-3696

Credential Type: Certificate to practice denture technology. **Authorization:** All work by a denturist must be performed under the general supervision of a licensed dentist. **Requirements:** Good moral character. High school graduate or equivalent. Hold a diploma in denture technology granted by a school accredited by the board. Pass board-administered examination. **Examination:** Examination in denture technology. **Fees:** Application fee. Examination fee. License fee. Renewal fee.

Florida

2244

Dental Radiographer
Board of Dentistry
Dept. of Professional Regulation
1940 N. Monroe St.
Tallahassee, FL 32399-0765
Phone: (904)488-6015

Credential Type: Dental Radiographer Certificate. **Duration of License:** Two years. **Authorization:** Certificate required for dental assistants to position and expose dental radiographic films, unless they have graduated from a board-approved dental assisting program or school. **Requirements:** Dental assistant may be certified as a dental readiographer by completing at least three months of continuous on-the-job training through assisting in the positioning and exposing of dental radiographic film under the direct supervision of a Florida licensed dentist. Complete a board-approved course in dental radiography within 12 months after completing on-the-job training. **Fees:** $20 certification fee. **Governing Statute:** Florida Statutes, Chapter 455 and 466. Florida Administrative Code, Rule 21-G.

Idaho

2245

Denturist
State Board of Denturity
Bureau of Occupational Licenses
1109 Main St., Ste. 220
Boise, ID 83702-5642
Phone: (208)334-3233

Credential Type: License to practice. **Duration of License:** One year. **Requirements:** Complete formal training of at least two years duration at an accredited educational institution. Complete at least two years internship under the supervision of a licensed denturist or have equivalent experience. **Examination:** License examination. Competency examination. **Fees:** $300 license application/examination fee. $300 competency application/examination fee. $300 initial license fee. $500 annual renewal fee. **Governing Statute:** Idaho Code, Title 54, Chap. 33. Rules of the Idaho State Board of Denturity.

2246

Denturist Intern
State Board of Denturity
Bureau of Occupational Licenses
1109 Main St., Ste. 220
Boise, ID 83702-5642
Phone: (208)334-3233

Credential Type: Intern permit. **Duration of License:** One year. **Requirements:** Complete formal training of at least two years duration at an accredited educational institution, or have three years of denturitry experience within the past five years immediately preceding application. **Fees:** $300 intern application and permit fee. **Governing Statute:** Idaho Code, Title 54, Chap. 33. Rules of the Idaho State Board of Denturity.

Kentucky

2247

Dental Laboratory Technician
Kentucky Board of Dentistry
2106 Bardstown Rd.
Louisville, KY 40205
Phone: (502)451-6832

Credential Type: License. **Duration of License:** One year. **Requirements:** Graduation from an approved or accredited institution program, or at least two years training in a dental office, or two years experience in a registered dental laboratory. Each registered dental laboratory must have at least one certified dental technician. **Fees:** $10 certification fee. $10 renewal fee.

Dental Laboratory Technicians

Montana

2248

Denturist
Montana Board of Dentistry
111 N. Jackson
Helena, MT 59620
Phone: (406)444-3745

Credential Type: License. **Duration of License:** One year. **Requirements:** Completion of two years of formal training in dental technology. Completion of a two-year internship. **Examination:** Written, oral and practical exam. **Fees:** $200 application fee. $200 exam fee. $200 license fee. $50 renewal fee. **Governing Statute:** Montana Code Annotated 37-29-301 through 37-29-321.

New Jersey

2249

Dental X-Ray Technologist
New Jersey Dept. of Environmental Protection
Bureau of Revenue
CN402
Trenton, NJ 08625-0402
Phone: (609)530-5760

Credential Type: License. **Duration of License:** Two years. **Requirements:** High school diploma. Completion of a curriculum for dental radiology or its equivalent. 18 years of age. **Examination:** Yes. **Fees:** $30 exam fee. $20 biennial registration fee. $30 application fee. **Governing Statute:** NJSA 26-2D. NJAC 7:28-19.

Oregon

2250

Denturist
State Board of Denture Technology
750 Front St. NE, Ste. 200
Salem, OR 97310
Phone: (503)378-8667

Credential Type: License. **Duration of License:** One year. **Requirements:** Must complete two years of post-secondary education in denture technology or equivalant, and 1,000 hours of supervised experience during or after training. **Examination:** Yes. **Fees:** $225 exam fee. $250 license fee. $250 renewal fee. **Governing Statute:** ORS 680.500 to 680.990.

South Carolina

2251

Dental Technician
South Carolina State Board of Dentistry
1315 Blanding St.
Columbia, SC 29201
Phone: (803)734-8904

Credential Type: License. **Requirements:** 21 years of age. Good moral character. High school diploma or equivalent. Two years in an approved school for dental technological work or three years of dental technological work under licensed supervision. **Examination:** State Board exam. **Fees:** $100 license fee. $80 re-registration fee.

Dentists

The following states grant licenses in this occupational category as of the date of publication:

Alabama	District of	Iowa	Minnesota	New Mexico	Rhode Island	Washington
Alaska	Columbia	Kansas	Mississippi	New York	South Carolina	West Virginia
Arizona	Florida	Kentucky	Missouri	North Carolina	South Dakota	Wisconsin
Arkansas	Georgia	Louisiana	Montana	North Dakota	Tennessee	Wyoming
California	Hawaii	Maine	Nebraska	Ohio	Texas	
Colorado	Idaho	Maryland	Nevada	Oklahoma	Utah	
Connecticut	Illinois	Massachusetts	New Hampshire	Oregon	Vermont	
Delaware	Indiana	Michigan	New Jersey	Pennsylvania	Virginia	

Alabama

2252

Dentist
Board of Dental Examiners of
 Alabama
2308-B Starmount Circle
Huntsville, AL 35801
Phone: (205)533-4638

Credential Type: License. **Duration of License:** One year. **Requirements:** Must have completed a minimum of three years of pre-dental academic study with required coursework. Must be a graduate of a school of Dentistry. **Examination:** Yes. **Fees:** $200 examination and certificate fee. $50 renewal fee.

Alaska

2253

Dentist
Board of Dental Examiners
Dept. of Commerce and Economic
 Development
PO Box 11086
Juneau, AK 99811-0806
Phone: (907)465-2542

Credential Type: License to practice. **Duration of License:** Two years. **Requirements:** DDS or DMD or a SPEC from an American Dental Association (ADA)-accredited school. Renewal requires continuing education. **Examination:** National Board Exams. Jurisprudence examination. State or regional clinical and didactic examination. **Reciprocity:** Issues license by credentials. **Fees:** $50 application fee. $200 license fee (by exam). $200 license fee (by credentials). $250 credentials fee. $200 renewal fee.

Arizona

2254

Dentist
Board of Dental Examiners
5060 N. 19th Ave., No. 406
Phoenix, AZ 85015
Phone: (602)255-3696

Credential Type: License to practice. **Duration of License:** One year initially, then three-year renewal periods. **Requirements:** DDS or DMD from an American Dental Association (ADA)-accredited school. Graduates of nonaccredited schools may qualify with clinical examination. **Examination:** Regional WREB examination, Jurisprudence examination. **Fees:** $50 jurisprudence exam fee. $120 initial license fee (pro-rated). $360 renewal fee.

Arkansas

2255

Dentist
Arkansas State Board of Dental
 Examiners
Tower Bldg., Ste. 1200
4th & Center St.
Little Rock, AR 72202
Phone: (501)682-2085

Credential Type: License. **Requirements:** Graduate of a school approved by the American Dental Association (ADA). Satisfactory completion of National Boards. Successful completion of examination given by Southern Regional Testing Agency. **Examination:** Yes. **Fees:** $150 Application. Written and practical examinations.

California

2256

Dentist
Board of Dental Examiners
1432 Howe Ave., No. 85B
Sacramento, CA 95825
Phone: (916)263-2300

Credential Type: License to practice. **Duration of License:** Two years. **Requirements:** 21 years of age. DDS or DMD from an American Dental Association (ADA)-accredited school. Renewal requires continuing education. **Examination:** National Board Exams. State or regional clinical and didactic examination. **Fees:** $600 application and clinical exam fee. $240 renewal fee.

2257

School Health Services Associate
Commission on Teacher
 Credentialing
PO Box 944270
Sacramento, CA 94244-7000
Phone: (916)445-7254

Credential Type: Health Services Credential. **Authorization:** Authorizes the holder to perform, in preschool, grades 1-12, and adult classes, the health service designated on the credential, (Services such as audiometrist, occupational therapist, or physical therapist are not deemed health services.) Authorized services are school nurse, physician, dentist, dental hygienist, and optometrist. **Requirements:** Valid license, certificate, or registration appropriate to the health service to be designated, issued by the California agency and authorized by law to license, certify, or register persons to practice that health service in California. Additional requirements as may be prescribed by the Commission. For school nurses, a bachelor's degree, an approved program of preparation in school nursing, and two years of successful experience as a school nurse is also required. A preliminary School Nurse Services Credential (valid for five years) requires only a bachelor's degree and a valid California registered nurse license. **Fees:** $60 application fee. $30 test score recording and evaluation fee, except for CBEST.

Colorado

2258

Dentist
Board of Dental Examiners
1560 Broadway, Ste. 1310
Denver, CO 80202
Phone: (303)894-7758

Credential Type: License to practice. **Requirements:** 21 years of age. DDS or DMD from an American Dental Association (ADA)-accredited school. **Examination:** National Board Exams. Jurisprudence examination. State or regional clinical and didactic examination.

Connecticut

2259

Dentist
Connecticut Dental Commission
Dept. of Health Services
150 Washington St.
Hartford, CT 06106
Phone: (203)566-4619

Credential Type: License to practice. **Duration of License:** One year. **Authorization:** General practice only. No specialty licenses granted. **Requirements:** Good moral character. References required. DDS or DMD from an American Dental Association (ADA)-accredited school. **Examination:** National Board Exams. Jurisprudence examination. State or regional clinical and didactic examination. **Fees:** $450 application and initial license fee. $450 annual renewal fee.

Delaware

2260

Dentist
Board of Dental Examiners
O'Neil Bldg.
PO Box 1401
Dover, DE 19903
Phone: (302)739-4522
Fax: (302)739-6148

Credential Type: License to practice. **Duration of License:** Two years. **Requirements:** DDS or DMD from an American Dental Association (ADA)-accredited school. Renewal requires continuing education. **Examination:** Jurisprudence examination. State or regional clinical and didactic examination. **Fees:** $154 application, exam, and initial license fee. $144 biennial renewal fee.

District of Columbia

2261

Dentist
Dept. of Consumer and Regulatory Affairs
614 H St. NW, No. 904
Washington, DC 20001
Phone: (202)727-7454

Credential Type: License to practice. **Requirements:** DDS or DMD from an American Dental Association (ADA)-accredited school. Renewal requires continuing education. **Examination:** National Board Exams. Jurisprudence examination. State or regional clinical and didactic examination. **Reciprocity:** Yes.

Florida

2262

Dentist
Florida Board of Dentistry
1940 N. Monroe St.
Tallahassee, FL 32399
Phone: (904)488-6015

Credential Type: License to practice. **Duration of License:** Two years. **Requirements:** 18 years of age. DDS or DMD from an American Dental Association (ADA)-accredited school. Renewal requires continuing education. **Examination:** National Board Exams. State or regional clinical and didactic examination. **Fees:** $100 application fee. $425 dental examination fee. $250 manual skills examination fee. $165 license fee. $165 renewal fee. **Governing Statute:** Florida Statutes, Chapter 455 and 466. Florida Administrative Code, Rule 21-G.

Georgia

2263

Dentist
Georgia Board of Dentistry
166 Pryor St. SW
Atlanta, GA 30303
Phone: (404)656-3925

Credential Type: License to practice. **Duration of License:** Two years. **Requirements:** 18 years of age. Good moral character. References required. DDS or DMD from an American Dental Association (ADA)-accredited school. Renewal requires continuing education. **Examination:** National Board Exams. Jurisprudence examination. State or regional clinical and didactic examination. **Fees:** $100 processing fee. $250 biennial renewal fee.

Hawaii

2264

Dentist
Hawaii Board of Dental Examiners
Dept. of Commerce and Consumer Affairs
PO Box 3469
Honolulu, HI 96801
Phone: (808)548-7461

Credential Type: License. **Duration of License:** Six months. **Requirements:** 18 years of age. Graduate of an accredited dental college. Additional requirements for foreign graduates. **Examination:** National Board Written Theory exam. State exam. **Fees:** $45 application fee. $700 exam fee. $45 license fee. $20 $40 Compliance Resolution Fund fee. $37 renewal fee.

Idaho

2265

Dentist
Idaho State Board of Dentistry
Statehouse Mail
Boise, ID 83720
Phone: (208)334-2369

Credential Type: License to practice. **Duration of License:** One year. **Requirements:** Good moral character. References required. DDS or DMD or SPEC from an American Dental Association (ADA)-accredited school. Endorsement applicants must have active practice experience for five of the nine years preceding application.

Dentist, continued

Renewal requires continuing education. **Examination:** National Board Exams. Jurisprudence examination. Local Anesthesia examination. State or regional clinical and didactic examination. **Reciprocity:** Issues license by credentials. **Fees:** $100 application fee (general dentist). $100 application fee (specialist). $250 application fee (by credentials). $125 annual renewal fee.

Illinois

2266

Dentist
State Board of Dentistry
Licensure Maintenance Unit
Dept. of Regulations & Education
320 W. Washington, 3rd Fl.
Springfield, IL 62786
Phone: (217)785-0800

Credential Type: License to practice. **Duration of License:** Two years. **Requirements:** 21 years of age. Good moral character. References required. DDS or DMD from an American Dental Association (ADA)-accredited school. **Examination:** National Board Exams. State or regional clinical and didactic examination. **Fees:** $25 license fee. $100 renewal fee.

Indiana

2267

Dentist
Board of Dental Examiners
Health Professional Bureau
402 W. Washington, Rm. 041
Indianapolis, IN 46204
Phone: (317)233-4413

Credential Type: License to practice. **Duration of License:** Two years. **Requirements:** Good moral character. References required for endorsement applicants. DDS or DMD from an American Dental Association (ADA)-accredited school. Renewal will require continuing education as of 1994. **Examination:** National Board Exams. Jurisprudence examination. State or regional clinical and didactic examination. **Reciprocity:** Individuals licensed and in good standing in another state who have engaged in the active practice of dentistry for at least five of the previous nine years may be exempted from the examination requirement. **Fees:** $50 application fee. $27 supplies fee (for exam). $45 use of facility fee (for exam). $50 license fee. $60 renewal fee. **Governing Statute:** Indiana Code 25-14. 828 Indiana Administrative Code.

Iowa

2268

Dentist
Iowa Board of Dental Examiners
Executive Hills West
1209 East Court
Des Moines, IA 50319
Phone: (515)281-5157

Credential Type: License. **Duration of License:** Two years. **Requirements:** Graduation with a degree of Doctor of Dental Surgery or Doctor of Dental Medicine conferred by an accredited dental college. **Examination:** Joint Commission on National Dental Examinations. Central Regional Dental Testing Service exam. Jurisprudence exam. **Fees:** $100 application fee. $120 renewal fee.

Kansas

2269

Dentist
Kansas Dental Board
4301 Huntoon, Ste. 4
Topeka, KS 66604
Phone: (913)273-0780

Credential Type: License to practice. **Duration of License:** One year. **Requirements:** Pass required examinations. Renewal requires continuing education. **Examination:** National Board Exams. Jurisprudence examination. State or regional clinical and didactic examination. **Reciprocity:** Issues license by credentials. **Fees:** $105 application fee (by credentials). $55 application fee (by exam). $60 annual renewal fee.

Kentucky

2270

Dentist
Kentucky Board of Dentistry
2106 Bardstown Rd.
Louisville, KY 40205
Phone: (502)451-6832

Credential Type: License. **Duration of License:** One year. **Requirements:** Graduation from accredited pre-dental and dental programs. Specialists are required to secure additional educational training. 18 years of age. Must complete continuing education courses. Must have HIV course annually and CRP biennially. **Examination:** Yes. **Fees:** Exam fees are determined by the testing agencies.

Louisiana

2271

Dentist
Louisiana State Board of Dentistry
1515 Poydras St., Ste. 2240
New Orleans, LA 70112
Phone: (504)568-8574

Credential Type: License. **Duration of License:** One year. **Requirements:** Graduation from an accredited school of dentistry. U.S. citizen or permanent resident. **Examination:** Written and clinical exam. **Fees:** $100 exam fee.

Maine

2272

Dentist
Board of Dental Examiners
2 Bangor St.
State House Station 143
Augusta, ME 04333
Phone: (207)289-3333

Credential Type: License to practice. **Requirements:** 21 years of age. Good moral character. References required. DDS or DMD from an American Dental Association (ADA)-accredited school. Renewal requires continuing education. **Examination:** National Board Exams. Jurisprudence examination. State or regional clinical and didactic examination. **Reciprocity:** Yes.

Maryland

2273

Dentist
Board of Dental Examiners
Metro-Executive Center
4201 Patterson Ave.
Baltimore, MD 21215
Phone: (410)764-4730

Credential Type: License to practice. **Duration of License:** Two years. **Requirements:** 18 years of age. Good moral character. References required. DDS or DMD from an American Dental Association (ADA)-accredited school. Renewal requires continuing education. **Examination:** National Board Exams. Jurisprudence examination. State or regional clinical and didactic examination. **Exemptions:** Clinical exam may be waived if applicant has actively practiced for the past five years. **Fees:** $200 license fee (by exam). $750 license fee (by waiver of clinical exam). $130 renewal fee.

Massachusetts

2274

Dentist
Board of Registration in Dentistry
100 Cambridge St., Rm. 1514
Boston, MA 02202
Phone: (617)727-9928
Fax: (617)727-7378

Credential Type: License to practice. **Duration of License:** Two years. **Authorization:** General practice only. No specialty licenses granted. **Requirements:** 21 years of age. Good moral character. References required. DDS or DMD from an American Dental Association (ADA)-accredited school. Renewal requires continuing education. **Examination:** National Board Exams. Jurisprudence examination. State or regional clinical and didactic examination. **Fees:** $100 application fee. $100 exam fee. $120 renewal fee.

Michigan

2275

Dentist
Board of Dentistry
Dept. of Licensing and Regulation
Bureau of Health Services
PO Box 30018
Lansing, MI 48909
Phone: (517)373-6650

Credential Type: License to practice. **Requirements:** 21 years of age. DDS or DMD or SPEC from an American Dental Association (ADA)-accredited school. Beginning August 1994 renewal will require continuing education. State Specialty examination may be waived if the applicant holds an American Board Certificate. **Examination:** National Board Exams. State or regional clinical and didactic examination. Specialty examination (when applicable).

Minnesota

2276

Dentist
Board of Dentistry
2700 University Ave. W., Ste. 70
St. Paul, MN 55114-1055
Phone: (612)642-0579

Credential Type: License to practice. **Duration of License:** One year. **Authorization:** General practice only. No specialty licenses granted. **Requirements:** Good moral character. References required. DDS or DMD from an ADA accredited school. Renewal requires continuing education. **Examination:** National Board Exams. Jurisprudence examination. State or regional clinical and didactic examination. **Reciprocity:** Dentists licensed in another state or Canada may apply for licensure by credentials. Must have actively practiced for three of the preceding four years. **Fees:** $125 license fee. $700 licensure by credentials fee. $110 renewal fee. **Governing Statute:** Minnesota Statutes, Chap. 150A and 319A. Minnesota Rules 3100-3199.

Mississippi

2277

Dentist
Board of Dental Examiners
PO Box 1960
Clinton, MS 39060
Phone: (601)924-9622

Credential Type: License to practice. **Duration of License:** One year. **Requirements:** 21 years of age. Good moral character. References required. DDS or DMD or SPEC from an American Dental Association (ADA)-accredited school. Current CPR certificate. **Examination:** National Board Exams. Jurisprudence examination. State or regional clinical and didactic examination. **Reciprocity:** Began issuing license by credentials on July 1, 1993. **Fees:** $400 exam fee ($200 to board and $200 to dental school). $100 annual renewal fee.

Missouri

2278

Dental Specialist
Missouri Dental Board
Div. of Professional Registration
3605 Missouri Blvd.
PO Box 1367
Jefferson City, MO 65102
Phone: (314)751-0040

Credential Type: Certification for Licensure. **Duration of License:** One year. **Authorization:** The following specialties require examination and licensure: endodontics, oral pathology, oral surgery, orthodontics, pedodontics, periodontics, prosthodontics, and public health. **Requirements:** Be a graduate of and hold a certificate from a graduate training program in the specialty from an accredited dental school. **Examination:** Missouri specialty examination, or the examination administered by the American board in the specialty. **Fees:** $300 application and exam fee. $90 renewal fee. **Governing Statute:** Chap. 332 RSMo (Supp 1981). 4 CSR 110.

2279

Dentist
Missouri Dental Board
3605 Missouri Blvd.
Jefferson City, MO 65109
Phone: (314)751-0041
Fax: (314)751-4176

Credential Type: License to practice. **Requirements:** 21 years of age. Good moral character. References required. DDS or DMD or SPEC from an American Dental Association (ADA)-accredited school. Current CPR Certificate. **Examination:** National Board Exams. Jurisprudence examination. State or regional clinical and didactic examination. Specialty examination (when applicable).

Montana

2280

Dentist
Montana Board of Dentistry
111 N. Jackson
Helena, MT 59620
Phone: (406)444-3745

Credential Type: License. **Duration of License:** One year. **Requirements:** Graduation from an approved dental school. **Examination:** National and Regional Board Examinations. Written and oral examinations. **Fees:** $75 exam fee. $35 license fee. $70 renewal fee. **Governing Statute:** Montana Code Annotated 37-4-301 through 37-4-328.

Nebraska

2281

Dentist
Nebraska Board of Examiners in
  Dentistry
301 Centennial Mall S.
PO Box 95007
Lincoln, NE 68509
Phone: (402)471-2115

Credential Type: License. **Duration of License:** Two years. **Requirements:** Must be a graduate of an accredited college of dentistry. **Examination:** Yes. **Fees:** $50 initial fee. $70 renewal fee.

Nevada

2282

Dentist
Nevada State Board of Dental Examiners
PO Box 80360
Las Vegas, NV 89180
Phone: (702)258-4230

Credential Type: License. **Duration of License:** One year. **Requirements:** Graduation from an accredited dental school. **Examination:** National Board of Dental Examiners exam. Clinical exam. **Fees:** $300 exam fee. $300 license fee. $300 renewal fee.

New Hampshire

2283

Dentist
Board of Dental Examiners
6 Hazen Dr.
Concord, NH 03301-6527
Phone: (603)271-4561

Credential Type: License to practice. **Duration of License:** Two years. **Requirements:** 21 years of age. Good moral character. References required. DDS or DMD from an American Dental Association (ADA)-accredited school. Renewal requires continuing education. **Examination:** National Board Exams. Jurisprudence examination. State or regional clinical and didactic examination. **Fees:** $100 application fee. $150 registration fee. $150 renewal fee.

New Jersey

2284

Dentist
State Board of Dentistry
1100 Raymond Blvd.
Newark, NJ 07102
Phone: (201)648-7087

Credential Type: License. **Requirements:** High school diploma or equivalent. Two years of study at a registered college. Graduation from an approved dental school. 21 years of age. **Examination:** Written, oral and practical. **Reciprocity:** Yes. **Fees:** $75 application fee. $25 exam fee. $100 registration fee. **Governing Statute:** NJSA 45:6. NJAC 13:30.

New Mexico

2285

Dentist
Board of Dentistry
PO Drawer 8397
Santa Fe, NM 87504-8397
Phone: (505)827-7165

Credential Type: License to practice. **Requirements:** 18 years of age. Good moral character. References required. DDS or DMD from an American Dental Association (ADA)-accredited school. Current CPR certificate. Renewal requires continuing education. **Examination:** National Board Exams. Jurisprudence examination. State or regional clinical and didactic examination.

New York

2286

Dentist
State Education Dept.
Div. of Professional Licensing Services
Cultural Education Center
Empire State Plaza
Albany, NY 12230
Phone: (518)474-3696

Credential Type: License. **Duration of License:** Three years. **Requirements:** At least two years of college level pre-dentistry plus graduation from a four-year dentistry program. 21 years of age. U.S. citizen or an alien lawfully admitted for permanent residency. **Examination:** Written and practical. **Fees:** $495 exam fee. $345—$430 license fee. $210 renewal fee. **Governing Statute:** Title VIII Articles 130, 133 of the Education Law.

North Carolina

2287

Dentist
North Carolina State Board of Dental Examiners
PO Box 32270
Raleigh, NC 27622
Phone: (919)781-4901

Credential Type: License. **Duration of License:** One year. **Requirements:** Two years at an approved liberal arts college. Graduation from an accredited school of dentistry. 18 years of age. Two letters of recommendation. **Examination:** Written and clinical. **Fees:** $200 license, exam and application fee. $60 renewal fee.

North Dakota

2288

Dentist
Board of Dental Examiners
PO Box 179
Valley City, ND 58072
Phone: (701)845-3708

Credential Type: License to practice. **Duration of License:** One year. **Requirements:** Good moral character. References required. DDS or DMD from an American Dental Association (ADA)-accredited school. Renewal requires continuing education. **Examination:** National Board Exams. Jurisprudence examination. State or regional clinical and didactic examination. **Reciprocity:** Issues license by credentials. **Fees:** $200 license fee (by exam). $450 license fee (by credentials). $90 annual renewal fee.

Ohio

2289

Dentist
Ohio State Dental Board
77 S. High St., 18th Fl.
Columbus, OH 43266-0306
Phone: (614)466-2580

Credential Type: License. **Duration of License:** Two years. **Requirements:** 18 years of age. DDS or DMD from an American Dental Association (ADA)-accredited school. Renewal requires continuing education. **Examination:** National Board Exams. Jurisprudence examination. State or regional clinical and didactic examination. **Reciprocity:** Issues license by credentials. **Fees:** $75 application fee. $130 renewal fee.

Oklahoma

2290

Dentist
Board of Governors of Registered Dentists
2726 N. Oklahoma Ave.
Oklahoma City, OK 73105
Phone: (405)521-2350

Credential Type: License. **Duration of License:** One year. **Requirements:** D.D.S. or D.M.D. degree from an accredited school. 60 hours of continuing education over a three-year period. **Examination:** Oklahoma Dental Examination. **Fees:** $200 exam fee. $200 application fee. $90 renewal fee.

Oregon

2291

Dental Specialist
Oregon Board of Dentistry
1515 SW Fifth, Ste. 400
Portland, OR 97201
Phone: (503)229-5520

Credential Type: License. **Duration of License:** Two years. **Requirements:** Must be a graduate of an accredited dental school. Must have completed an accredited specialty program; or be licensed as a general dentist in another state. **Examination:** Yes. **Reciprocity:** Yes. **Fees:** $500 exam fee. $170 renewal fee. **Governing Statute:** ORS 679.010 to 679.991 and OAR 818-21-010.

2292

Dentist, General
Oregon Board of Dentistry
1515 SW Fifth, Ste. 400
Portland, OR 97201
Phone: (503)229-5520

Credential Type: License. **Duration of License:** Two years. **Requirements:** Must be a graduate of an accredited school of dentistry. **Examination:** Yes. **Fees:** $350 exam fee. $170 renewal fee. **Governing Statute:** ORS 679.010 to 679.991.

Pennsylvania

2293

Dentist
Board of Dentistry
PO Box 2649
Harrisburg, PA 17105
Phone: (717)783-7162

Credential Type: License to practice. **Requirements:** 21 years of age. DDS or DMD from an American Dental Association (ADA)-accredited school. **Examination:** National Board Exams. Jurisprudence examination. State or regional clinical and didactic examination.

Rhode Island

2294

Dentist
Board of Examiners in Dentistry
Dept. of Health
Three Capitol Hill, No. 404
Providence, RI 02908
Phone: (401)277-2151

Credential Type: License to practice. **Duration of License:** One year. **Requirements:** 21 years of age. Good moral character. References required. DDS or DMD from an American Dental Association (ADA)-accredited school. Renewal requires continuing education. **Examination:** National Board Exams. State or regional clinical and didactic examination. **Fees:** $350 application fee. $200 annual renewal fee. $100 state exam fee (if required).

South Carolina

2295

Dental Specialist
South Carolina State Board of Dentistry
1315 Blanding St.
Columbia, SC 29201
Phone: (803)734-8904

Credential Type: License. **Requirements:** Good moral character. South Carolina general dentistry license issued by South Carolina State Board of Dentistry. Approved post-graduate training in a specialty. **Examination:** State Board exam. **Fees:** $300 license fee. $115 re-registration fee.

2296

Dentist
South Carolina State Board of Dentistry
1315 Blanding St.
Columbia, SC 29201
Phone: (803)734-8904

Credential Type: License. **Requirements:** 21 years of age. Good moral character. Graduation from an accredited dental college. **Examination:** Parts I and II of the National Board exam. State Board exam. **Fees:** $300 license fee. $105 re-registration fee.

South Dakota

2297

Dentist
State Board of Dentistry
PO Box 8047
Rapid City, SD 57709-8047
Phone: (605)342-3026

Credential Type: License to practice. **Duration of License:** One year. **Requirements:** 18 years of age. Good moral character. References required. DDS or DMD or SPEC from an ADA accredited school. Renewal requires 100 hours of continuing education every five years. **Examination:** National Board Exams. Jurisprudence examination. Central Regional Dental Testing Service examination. **Reciprocity:** Yes. **Fees:** $100 exam fee. $425 reciprocity fee. $50 certificate of registration fee. $75 annual renewal fee. $15 annual continuing education fee.

Tennessee

2298

Dentist
Board of Dentistry
Regulatory Boards Admin.
283 Plus Park Blvd.
Nashville, TN 37247-1010
Phone: (615)367-6228

Credential Type: License to practice. **Duration of License:** One year. **Requirements:** 18 years of age. Good moral character. References required. DDS or DMD from an American Dental Association (ADA)-accredited school. Renewal requires 15 semester hours of continuing education and current CPR certificate. **Examination:** National Board Exams. Jurisprudence examination. State or regional clinical and didactic examination. **Reciprocity:** No. **Fees:** $35 registration. $50 application. $35 renewal.

2299

Endodontist
Board of Dentistry
283 Plus Park Blvd.
Nashville, TN 37247
Phone: (615)367-6228

Credential Type: License. **Requirements:** Dental license and two years graduate study. Pass exam. **Examination:** Yes. **Fees:** $100 Examination.

2300

Oral and Maxillofacial Surgeon
Board of Dentistry
283 Plus Park Blvd.
Nashville, TN 37247
Phone: (615)367-6228

Credential Type: License. **Requirements:** Tennessee dental license, three years advanced study in a graduate school or hospital. Good moral character and reputation. **Examination:** Yes. **Reciprocity:** No. **Fees:** $100 Examination.

2301

Oral Pathologist
Board of Dentistry
283 Plus Park Blvd.
Nashville, TN 37247
Phone: (615)367-6228

Credential Type: License. **Requirements:** Two years post graduate training at university level. Tennessee dental license. Good moral character and reputation. **Examination:** Yes. **Fees:** $100 Exam.

2302

Pedodontist
Board of Dentistry
283 Plus Park Blvd.
Nashville, TN 37247
Phone: (615)367-6228

Credential Type: License. **Requirements:** No less than two years in a graduate program. Tennessee dental license. Good moral character and reputation. **Examination:** Yes. **Fees:** $100 Examination.

2303

Periodontist
Board of Dentistry
283 Plus Park Blvd.
Nashville, TN 37247
Phone: (615)367-6228

Credential Type: License. **Requirements:** Minimum of two years post graduate training at university level. Tennessee dental license. Good moral character and reputation. **Examination:** Yes. **Fees:** $100 Examination.

2304

Prosthodontist
Board of Dentistry
283 Plus Park Blvd.
Nashville, TN 37247
Phone: (615)367-6228

Credential Type: License. **Requirements:** Two years post-doctoral education in Prosthodontics. Tennessee dental license. Good moral character and reputation. **Examination:** Yes. **Fees:** $100 Examination.

Texas

2305

Dentist
Texas State Board of Dental Examiners
327 Congress, Ste. 500
Austin, TX 78701
Phone: (512)477-2985

Credential Type: License. **Duration of License:** One year. **Requirements:** 21 years of age. Four terms of eight months each at an accredited dental college. Training in CPR. **Examination:** Written, oral, and/or practical examination. National Board of Dental Examiners Examination. **Fees:** $150 exam fee. $100 renewal fee. **Governing Statute:** VACS 4545, 22 TAC 101.

Utah

2306

Dentist
Dept. of Commerce
Div. of Occupational and Professional Licensing
160 E. 300 S.
PO Box 45802
Salt Lake City, UT 84145
Phone: (801)530-6628

Credential Type: License. **Duration of License:** Two years. **Requirements:** Must ba a graduate of an approved dental college. **Examination:** Yes. **Fees:** $100 license fee. $60 renewal fee. $90 controlled substance original fee. $50 controlled substance renewal fee.

Vermont

2307

Dentist
State Board of Dental Examiners
Pavilion Office Bldg.
Montpelier, VT 05602
Phone: (802)828-2390

Credential Type: License. **Duration of License:** Two years. **Requirements:** 18 years of age. US citizen. Good moral character. Graduate of approved dental school. Successful completion of NERB within past five years. Certificate of the National Board of Dental Examiners. **Examination:** Yes. **Reciprocity:** No. **Fees:** $50 Initial application license. $50 Renewal. **Governing Statute:** Title 26, VSA Sections 801-812.

Virginia

2308

Dentist
Virginia Board of Dentistry
1601 Rolling Hills Dr.
Richmond, VA 23229
Phone: (804)662-9920

Credential Type: License. **Duration of License:** Two years. **Requirements:** Be a graduate of an approved dental school as recognized by Commission on Dental Accreditation of the American Dental Association. File an application accompanied by a certified transcript. **Examination:** National Board of Dental Examiners exam. **Fees:** $140 application fee. $80 renewal fee.

Washington

2309

Dentist
Board of Dental Examiners
1300 SE Quince St.
Olympia, WA 98504
Phone: (206)586-6898

Credential Type: License to practice. **Duration of License:** One year. **Requirements:** DDS or DMD from an American Dental Association (ADA)-accredited school. AIDS Training. Foreign graduates must have two additional years of supervised experience. **Examination:** National Board Exams. Jurisprudence examination. State or regional clinical and didactic examination. **Fees:** $650 exam fee. $215 renewal fee.

West Virginia

2310

Dentist
Board of Dental Examiners
PO Drawer 1459
Beckley, WV 25802-1459
Phone: (304)252-8266

Credential Type: License. **Duration of License:** One year. **Requirements:** U.S. citizen. Graduate of approved dental school. Never convicted of a felony. **Examination:** Yes. **Fees:** $35 Application. $5 License. $20 Renewal.

Wisconsin

2311

Dentist
Regulations and Licensing Dept.
Dentistry Board
PO Box 8935
Madison, WI 53708-8935
Phone: (608)266-2811

Credential Type: License. **Requirements:** High school diploma. Two years of college and graduation from a dental school. **Examination:** Yes. **Reciprocity:** Yes.

Wyoming

2312

Dentist
Board of Dental Examiners
PO Box 1024
Powell, WY 82435
Phone: (307)754-3476

Credential Type: License. **Duration of License:** One year. **Requirements:** Graduate from an accredited school of dentistry. Pass the American Dental Association (ADA) National Board examination. Must have passed the Central Regional Dental Testing Services examinations within the last five years. Pass the Sate Board Examinations. **Examination:** Yes. **Fees:** $175 Application. $65 Renewal.

Designers, Including Interior Designers and Florists

The following states grant licenses in this occupational category as of the date of publication: Alabama, Connecticut, District of Columbia, Florida, Idaho, Illinois, Louisiana, New Mexico.

Alabama

2313

Interior Designer
Alabama State Board of Registation for Interior Designers
Jefferson State Junior College
2601 Carson Rd.
Birmingham, AL 35215
Phone: (205)853-1200, ext. 1265

Credential Type: Certificate. **Duration of License:** One year. **Requirements:** Must have completed 48 college semester hours of education related to the field of interior design. **Examination:** National Council for Interior Design Qualification (NCIDQ) written examination. **Fees:** $50 registration fee. $25 application fee. $150 examination fee. $50 renewal fee.

Connecticut

2314

Interior Designer
Professional Licensing Div.
Consumer Protection Dept.
165 Capitol Ave.
Hartford, CT 06106
Phone: (203)566-1549

Credential Type: Certificate of registration. **Duration of License:** One year. **Requirements:** Submit application and pay fee. Pass examination. **Examination:** National Council for Interior Design Qualifications Examination, or equivalent. **Exemptions:** Licensed architects do not need certificate of registration to use title of interior designer. **Reciprocity:** Yes, provided state has registration or licensing stanbards equal to or greater than those of Connecticut. **Fees:** Contact board for fees. **Governing Statute:** Connecticut Statutes, Chap. 396a.

District of Columbia

2315

Interior Designer
License and Certification Div.
Occupational and Professional Licensure Administration
Consumer and Regulatory Affairs Dept.
PO Box 37200
Washington, DC 20013-7200
Phone: (202)727-7823
Phone: (202)727-7480

Alternate Information: 614 H St., NW, Washington, DC 20001.

Credential Type: License to practice. **Duration of License:** One year. **Requirements:** Complete an educational program in interior design of at least two academic years at a college, university, or other accredited institution. Subsequent to the first renewal of a license by examination, five contact hours of continuing education are required for renewal. **Examination:** National Council for Interior Design Qualification (NCIDQ) examination. **Reciprocity:** Yes. **Fees:** $50 application fee. $35 license fee. $35 renewal fee. **Governing Statute:** Municipal Regulations, Title 17, Chap. 32.

Florida

2316

Interior Designer
Board of Architecture and Interior Design
Dept. of Professional Regulation
1940 N. Monroe St.
Tallahassee, FL 32399-0751
Phone: (904)488-6685

Credential Type: License by Examination. **Duration of License:** Two years. **Authorization:** To perform design services which do not necessarily require performance by an architect. **Requirements:** Meet one of the following sets of requirements: (1) Graduate from an interior design program of five years or more. Complete one year of diversified interior design experience. (2) Graduate from an interior design program of four years or more. Complete two years of diversified interior design experience. (3) Complete at least three years in an interior design curriculum. Complete three years of diversified interior design experience. (4) Graduate from an interior design program of two years or more. Complete four years of diversified interior design experience. **Examination:** National Council for Interior Design Qualifications (NCIDQ). **Fees:** $50 application fee. $525 examination fee. $200 license fee. $200 renewal fee. **Governing Statute:** Florida Statutes, Chapter 481, Part I. Florida Administrative Code, Rule 21-B.

Credential Type: License by Endorsement. **Duration of License:** Two years. **Requirements:** Meet basic educational and experience requirements, and pass a substantially equivalent examination in another jurisdiction; or hold a valid license to use the title "interior designer" issued by another jurisdiction of the United States with substantially equivalent licensure criteria. **Fees:** $50 application fee. $200 license fee. $200 renewal fee. **Governing Statute:** Florida Statutes, Chapter 481, Part I. Florida Administrative Code, Rule 21-B.

Idaho

2317

Florist
Plant Industries Div.
Agriculture Dept.
PO Box 790
Boise, ID 83701
Phone: (208)334-2986

Credential Type: Class A License. **Duration of License:** One year. **Authorization:** Required if gross business is over $1,000 per year. **Requirements:** Submit application and pay fee. **Fees:** $50 license fee per outlet. **Governing Statute:** Idaho Code, Title 22, Chap. 23.

Credential Type: Class B License. **Duration of License:** One year. **Authorization:** Required if gross business is $1,000 or less per year. **Requirements:** Submit application and pay fee. **Fees:** $15 license fee. **Governing Statute:** Idaho Code, Title 22, Chap. 23.

Illinois

2318

Interior Designer
Illinois Dept. of Professional Regulations
320 W. Washington St.
Springfield, IL 62786
Phone: (217)782-8556

Credential Type: Registration. **Duration of License:** Two years. **Requirements:** Must meet one of the following sets of requirements: (1) Graduate of a four or five-year approved interior design program with a minimum of two years of design experience; (2) Graduate of a three-year approved interior design program with at least three years of design experience; (3) Graduate of a two-year approved interior design program with at least four years of design experience; (4) Graduate from a non-approved interior design curriculum and has met board's requirements. **Examination:** National Council for Interior Design Qualifications (NCIDQ) Examination. **Reciprocity:** Yes, considered on an individual basis. **Fees:** $450 total examination fee (6 parts). $150 identification and application examination fee. $75 problem solving examination fee. $75 building and barrier free codes examination fee. $50 programming examination fee. $50 3-dimensional exercise examination fee. $50 project scenario examination fee. $100 initial registration fee. $100 registration by endorsement fee. $160 renewal fee. **Governing Statute:** The Interior Design Profession Title Act, Illinois Revised Statutes 1991, Chapter 1111.

Louisiana

2319

Interior Designer
State Board of Examiners of Interior Designers
Dept. of Economic Development
PO Box 94185
Baton Rouge, LA 70804-9185
Phone: (504)342-9171

Credential Type: License. **Duration of License:** One year. **Requirements:** Meet requirements established in the Board's rules. **Governing Statute:** R.S. 36:109(E)12. R.S. 37:3171-3183.

2320

Retail Florist
Horticulture Commission
PO Box 3118
Baton Rouge, LA 70821
Phone: (504)925-7772

Credential Type: License. **Duration of License:** One year. **Examination:** Written and practical. **Fees:** $100 exam fee. $35 license fee. $35 renewal fee.

2321

Wholesale Florist
Horticulture Commission
PO Box 3118
Baton Rouge, LA 70821
Phone: (504)925-7772

Credential Type: License. **Duration of License:** One year. **Examination:** Written. **Fees:** $35 exam fee. $35 license fee. $35 renewal fee.

New Mexico

2322

Interior Designer
Interior Design Board
Dept. of Regulation and Licensing
PO Box 25101
725 St. Michael's Dr.
Santa Fe, NM 87504
Phone: (505)827-7160

Credential Type: License. **Duration of License:** One year. **Requirements:** Submit application and pass national examination. Granting of license without examination was discontinued June 16, 1990. **Examination:** NCIDQ Examination for Interior Designers. **Reciprocity:** Yes, provided qualifications are equal to or exceed those required by New Mexico. **Fees:** $10 application packet fee. $45 application fee. $200 license fee. $200 renewal fee. **Governing Statute:** 61-24C-1 et seq. NMSA 1978. Rules of the New Mexico Board of Interior Design, Rule 89-1 et seq.

Detectives, Except Public

The following states grant licenses in this occupational category as of the date of publication:

Arizona	Florida	Kansas	Montana	New York	South Carolina
Arkansas	Georgia	Maine	Nebraska	North Carolina	Texas
California	Hawaii	Maryland	Nevada	North Dakota	Vermont
Connecticut	Illinois	Massachusetts	New Hampshire	Ohio	Virginia
District of	Indiana	Michigan	New Jersey	Oklahoma	West Virginia
Columbia	Iowa	Minnesota	New Mexico	Pennsylvania	Wisconsin

Arizona

2323

Private Investigator
Dept. of Public Safety
PO Box 6328
Phoenix, AZ 85005
Phone: (602)223-2361

Credential Type: Private investigator license. **Duration of License:** Three years. **Requirements:** Be a citizen or legal resident of the United States. Be of good moral character. No convictions of a felony or any crime involving illegal use or possession of a deadly weapon. Not have defaulted on payment of money collected or received for another. Not have had a registration certificate or license revoked in Arizona.

Have a minimum of three years full-time investigative experience. Submit a $2500 surety bond with application. **Fees:** $150 application fee, plus cost of fingerprint processing. $300 license fee. $150 renewal fee. **Governing Statute:** Arizona Revised Statutes, Title 32, Chapter 24.

Credential Type: Provisional license. **Duration of License:** 90 days. **Requirements:** Meet requirements for an Arizona private investigator's license and have a valid private investigator's license from another state or jurisdiction. **Fees:** $100 provisional license fee, plus cost of fingerprint processing. **Governing Statute:** Arizona Revised Statutes, Title 32, Chapter 24.

Arkansas

2324

Private Investigator
Arkansas State Police
3 Natural Resources Dr.
PO Box 5901
Little Rock, AR 72215
Phone: (501)224-3101

Credential Type: License. **Requirements:** 18 years of age. High school graduate or equivalent. Must not have been convicted of any felony, class A misdemeanor or crime. Must not have been declared incompetent by reason of mental defect or disease. Must not be suffering from habitual drunkenness or narcotic addiction or dependence. Must not have been discharged from the armed services under other than honorable conditions. **Fees:** $150 License. $50 Renewal.

California

2325

Private Investigator
Bureau of Collection and
  Investigative Services
400 R St., Ste. 2001
Sacramento, CA 95814-6234
Phone: (916)445-7366

Credential Type: Private Investigator License. **Requirements:** Meet one of the following sets of requirements: (1) At least three years or 6000 hours of compensated experience in investigation work. (2) Hold a law degree or complete a four-year course in police science, criminal justice, criminal law, or equivalent. Have at least two years or 4000 hours of compensated experience in investigation work.

All private investigators providing armed bodyguard services must maintain appropriate liability insurance. **Examination:** Written examination. **Fees:** $25 application fee. $100 license fee. $27 fingerprint processing fee. **Governing Statute:** Private Investigator Act, Business and Professions Code, Sect. 7541.

2326

Security Investigator (Racetrack)
California Horse Racing Board
1010 Hurley Way, Ste. 190
Sacramento, CA 95825
Phone: (916)920-7178

Credential Type: License Registration. **Requirements:** Submit application and fingerprint card. Pay fee. **Fees:** $75 registration fee.

Connecticut

2327

Private Investigator
State of Connecticut
Div. of State Police
294 Colony St.
Meriden, CT 06450-2098
Phone: (203)238-6631

Credential Type: Private Investigator License. **Requirements:** Must have acceptable experience. Fee may be required.

District of Columbia

2328

Private Detective
License and Certification Div.
Occupational and Professional Licensure Administration
Consumer and Regulatory Affairs Dept.
PO Box 37200
Washington, DC 20013-7200
Phone: (202)727-7823
Phone: (202)727-7480

Alternate Information: 614 H St., NW, Washington, DC 20001.

Credential Type: License. **Duration of License:** One year. **Requirements:** Good moral character. Post $5,000 bond. **Governing Statute:** Municipal Regulations, Title 17, Chap. 20.

Florida

2329

Private Investigator
Florida Law Enforcement Dept.
2331 Phillips Rd.
PO Box 1489
Tallahassee, FL 32308
Phone: (904)488-8771

Credential Type: Private Investigator License. **Requirements:** Must have acceptable experience. Fee may be required.

Georgia

2330

Private Detective
Board of Private Detective and Security Agencies
Businesses and Occupations Section
Professional Examining Boards
166 Pryor St., SW
Atlanta, GA 30303
Phone: (404)656-2282

Credential Type: Private Detective License. **Requirements:** Have two years of experience with a licensed private detective agency or two years of experience in law enforcement. **Examination:** Private Detective Examination, written. **Exemptions:** Law enforcement and government agents, attorneys, credit and employment agencies, and insurance claims adjusters. **Reciprocity:** No. **Fees:** $75 exam fee. $320 private detective company fee. $45 employee registration fee. $23 fingerprint processing fee.

Hawaii

2331

Detective and Guard, Private
Hawaii Board of Private Detectives and Guards
Dept. of Commerce and Consumer Affairs
PO Box 3469
Honolulu, HI 96801
Phone: (808)548-3086

Credential Type: License. **Duration of License:** Six months. **Requirements:** High school diploma or equivalent. Four years of full-time investigational work or guard service. Criminal abstract covering the past 10 years. Fingerprints for FBI clearance. $5,000 bond. **Examination:** Written and verbal. **Reciprocity:** If self-employed and licensed in another state, submission of license status verification is required. **Fees:** $50 application fee. $50 exam fee. $25 license fee. $20 $40 Compliance Resolution Fund fee. $75 renewal fee.

Illinois

2332

Private Detective
Illinois Dept. of Professional Regulation
320 W. Washington, 3rd Fl.
Springfield, IL 62786
Phone: (217)782-8556

Credential Type: Private Detective License. **Duration of License:** Three years. **Requirements:** Be at least 21 years of age. Meet one of the following sets of requirements: (1) At least three years out of the preceding five years experience as a full-time investigator for a licensed private detective agency or meet Department standards. (2) Have a Baccalaureate Degree in police science, business, or related field and one year of investigative experience. (3) Have an Associate Degree in police science or related field and two years of investigative experience. **Examination:** Private Detective Examination, written. **Reciprocity:** Yes, providing other jurisdiction grants similar privelege to applicants from Illinois. **Fees:** $216.80 exam fee. $500 license fee. $450 renewal fee. **Governing Statute:** Illinois Revised Statutes 1991, Chap. 111. 68 Ill. Adm. Code 1240.

Indiana

2333

Private Investigator
Indiana State Police
P100 N. Senate Ave.
Indianapolis, IN 46204
Phone: (317)232-8269

Credential Type: Private Investigator License. **Requirements:** Must have acceptable experience. Fee may be required.

Iowa

2334

Private Investigator
Div. of Administrative Services
Dept. of Public Safety
Wallace State Office Bldg.
Des Moines, IA 50319
Phone: (515)281-8422

Credential Type: License. **Duration of License:** Two years. **Requirements:** 18 years of age. U.S. Citizenship. No convictions for an aggravated misdemeanor or a felony. An applicant should submit pictures and fingerprints along with a completed application. Applicant must be approved for a $5,000 surety bond. **Examination:** Written. **Fees:** $100 licensing fee. $100 renewal fee.

Kansas

2335

Private Investigator
Kansas Bureau of Investigators
Attorney General's Office
1620 Tyler
Topeka, KS 66612
Phone: (913)232-6000

Credential Type: Private Investigator License. **Requirements:** Experience evaluated on an individual basis. Insurance and surety bond are required. **Examination:** Yes.

Maine

2336

Private Investigator
Public Safety Dept.
State Police Bureau
Statehouse Station 42
36 Hospital St.
Augusta, ME 04333
Phone: (207)621-1268

Credential Type: Private Investigator License. **Requirements:** Must have one year of acceptable experience. Fee may be required.

Maryland

2337

Private Detective
Licensing Div.
Maryland State Police
Pikesville, MD 21208-3899
Phone: (301)653-4435
Phone: (301)486-3101

Credential Type: Private Detective Agency License. **Duration of License:** One year. **Authorization:** An individual or corporation must be so licensed before providing private detective services in the state. **Requirements:** Be at least 25 years of age. Good character and reputation. Meet one of the following sets of requirements: (1) Have at least five years experience as a certified or licensed private detective. (2) Have at least five years experience as a full-time police officer and complete the police officer training course of the Police Training Commission. (3) Have at least three years experience in an investigative capacity as a detective while serving as a police officer with an organized police agency. (4) Have at least three years experience in an investigative capacity in any unit of the United States, or of the state, or a county or municipality of the state, for the purpose of law enforcement, and complete the police officer training required by the Police Training Commission. (5) Have at least five years experience as a full-time fire investigator for a fire department or law enforcement agency of the state or a city or county in the state.

Applicant must submit five letters of recommendation. Post $3000 bond. Must maintain an office in the state. **Fees:** $400 application fee (individual). $200 renewal fee (individual). **Governing Statute:** Annotated Code of Maryland, Title 13.

Credential Type: Private Detective Certification. **Authorization:** Authorizes individual to provide private detective services only on behalf of the agency through which certification was obtained and only while that agency is licensed in the state. **Requirements:** Meet standards set by the Superintendent of the Maryland State Police. **Fees:** $50 application fee. **Governing Statute:** Annotated Code of Maryland, Title 13.

Massachusetts

2338

Private Detective
Dept. of State Police
Special Licensing Unit
20 Somerset St., 9th Fl., Rm. 1
Boston, MA 02108
Phone: (617)566-4500

Credential Type: Private Detective Agency License. **Duration of License:** One year. **Authorization:** License required to engage in the private detective business. Employees need not be separately licensed, except for the resident manager or superintendent when the licensee is a corporation. **Requirements:** Submit three character references. Good moral character. Have at least three years of experience as a detective doing investigative work, as a former member of an investigative service of the United States, or as a former police officer of a rank or grade higher than a patrolman. Post $5000 surety bond. **Fees:** $1100 license fee. $600 renewal fee.

2339

Private Investigator
Dept. of Public Safety
License Div.
McCormack State Office Bldg., 13th Fl.
One Ashburton Pl.
Boston, MA 02108
Phone: (617)727-7775

Credential Type: Private Investigator License. **Duration of License:** One year. **Requirements:** Be at least 25 years of age. Have at least three years experience as a detective, or as a member of an investigative service of the United States, or as a police officer of a rank or grade higher than that of a patrolman. Post $5000 bond. **Fees:** Contact board for fees. **Governing Statute:** Annotated Laws of Massachusetts, Chap. 147.

Michigan

2340

Private Detective or Private Investigator
Private Security and Investigator Section
Dept. of State Police
General Office Bldg.
7150 Harris Dr.
Lansing, MI 48913
Phone: (517)332-2521

Credential Type: License. **Duration of License:** Two years. **Requirements:** Be a citizen of the United States and a resident of Michigan. At least 25 years of age. High school education or the equivalent. Have not been convicted of a felony or misdemeanor involving dishonesty or fraud, unauthorized divulgence or selling of information, impersonation of a law enforcement officer or employee of a governmental agency, or of illegally using, carrying, or possessing a dangerous weapon. Have not been dishonorably discharged from military service. Post a bond in the amount of $5,000 if the license holder is a person or $10,000 if the license holder is a partnership, firm, company, or corporation. Have been lawfully engaged in the private detective business on his/her own for not less than three years; or have been an investigative employee of a licensed private detective business for not less than three years; or have been employed as an investigator, detective, special agent, or police officer of a government agency; or have a degree in the field of police administration from an accredited university or college. Submit five reference statements. Pass a fingerprint check and background investigation. Receive the approval of the prosecuting attorney and the sheriff of the county within which the holder's office is to be located. Abide by the Private Detective License law. Be of good moral character. **Fees:** $100 (for a person), $200 (for a firm, partnership, or corporation) initial license fee. $50 (for a person), $200 (for a firm, partnership, or corporation) renewal fee. $25 fee for each additional branch office. **Governing Statute:** Private Security Guard Licensing Act, Act 330 of 1968, as amended.

Minnesota

2341

Private Investigator
Minnesota Private Detective and Protective Agent Services Board
1246 University Ave.
St. Paul, MN 55104
Phone: (612)642-0775

Credential Type: Private Investigator License. **Duration of License:** Two years. **Requirements:** Must meet board requirements. Post $10,000 surety bond. Show proof of financial responsibility. **Fees:** $500 license fee. $400 renewal fee. **Governing Statute:** Minnesota Statutes, Sections 326.32—326.339. Minnesota Rules 7506.0100-.0180.

Montana

2342

Private Investigator
Montana Board of Private Security Patrolmen and Investigators
111 N. Jackson
Helena, MT 59620
Phone: (406)444-4286

Credential Type: License. **Duration of License:** One year. **Requirements:** 21 years of age. U.S. citizenship. High school graduation or equivalent. Three years of private investigative experience or equivalent. Completion of a certified private investigator training program. Private investigators who wear or carry firearms must also complete an approved firearms training program. **Examination:** Written. **Fees:** $25 (unarmed) or $75 (armed) application fee. $25 exam fee. $20 (unarmed) or $50 (armed) renewal fee. **Governing Statute:** Montana Code Annotated 37-60-301 through 37-60-322.

Nebraska

2343

Private Investigator
Nebraska Secretary of State
PO Box 94608
State Capitol Bldg., Ste. 2300
Lincoln, NE 68509
Phone: (402)471-2554

Credential Type: License. **Duration of License:** One year. **Requirements:** 21 years of age. Must be a United States citizen. **Fees:** $100 agency license fee. $50 private investigator's license fee. $25 plain clothes investigator fee. $50 renewal fee.

Nevada

2344

Private Investigator
Nevada Attorney General's Office
Private Investigator's Licensing Board
Heroes Memorial Bldg.
198 S. Carson St.
Carson City, NV 89710-1032
Phone: (702)687-4170

Credential Type: Private Investigator License. **Requirements:** Must have acceptable experience and pass examination. Fee may be required. **Examination:** Yes.

New Hampshire

2345

Private Investigator
New Hampshire Dept. of Safety
10 Hazen Dr.
Concord, NH 03301
Phone: (603)271-2791

Credential Type: Private Investigator License. **Requirements:** Must have acceptable experience. Fee may be required.

New Jersey

2346

Private Detective
New Jersey Div. of State Police
Private Detective Unit
PO Box 7068
West Trenton, NJ 08625
Phone: (609)882-2000

Credential Type: License. **Requirements:** 25 years of age. U.S. citizen. Five years experience as an investigator or a police officer with a government agency. No criminal convictions. Must post a $3,000 surety bond. **Fees:** $250 license fee. **Governing Statute:** NJSA 45:19-8, et seq. NJAC 13:55.

New Mexico

2347

Private Investigator
Private Investigator Bureau
Dept. of Regulation and Licensing
PO Box 25101
Santa Fe, NM 87504
Phone: (505)827-7172
Fax: (505)827-7095

Credential Type: Private Investigator License. **Duration of License:** Two years. **Authorization:** Only a licensed private investigator may act as a body guard. **Requirements:** Complete three years of investigative experience within the past five years. **Examination:** Written examination on rules, regulations, and statutes. **Reciprocity:** No. **Fees:** $200 license fee.

New York

2348

Private Investigator
New York State Dept. of State
Div. of Licensing Services
162 Washington Ave.
Albany, NY 12231
Phone: (518)474-2650

Credential Type: License. **Duration of License:** Two years. **Requirements:** At least three years of regular employment as a private investigator employed by a licensed private investigator. 25 years of age. $10,000 surety bond. Two recent photographs. Fingerprint cards. **Examination:** Written. **Fees:** $15 exam fee. $400—$500 application fee. $400—$500 renewal fee.

North Carolina

2349

Counterintelligence Licensee
Private Protective Services Board
PO Box 29500
Raleigh, NC 27626
Phone: (919)779-1611

Credential Type: License. **Duration of License:** One year. **Requirements:** High school diploma. Three years of experience within the past five years in counterintelligence or completion of a board approved school in counterintelligence. 18 years of age. **Fees:** $150 application fee. $150 license fee. $50 recovery fund fee. $150 renewal fee.

North Carolina

2350

Private Investigator
Private Protective Services Board
PO Box 29500
Raleigh, NC 27626
Phone: (919)779-1611

Credential Type: License. **Duration of License:** One year. **Requirements:** High school diploma. Three years of investigative experience within the past five years. Educational credit may be given in lieu of experience. 18 years of age. **Fees:** $150 application fee. $150 license fee. $50 recovery fund fee. $150 renewal fee.

North Dakota

2351

Private Detective
Attorney General's Office
State Capitol Offices
600 E. Blvd. Ave.
Bismarck, ND 58505
Phone: (701)224-2210

Credential Type: Private Detective License. **Duration of License:** One year. **Requirements:** Be at least 18 years of age. Must be a United States citizen. Good moral character. Post $5000 surety bond. **Examination:** Yes. **Fees:** $20 exam fee. $50 license fee. $25 renewal fee. **Governing Statute:** North Dakota Century Code, Chap. 43-30.

Ohio

2352

Private Investigator
Licensing Div.
Commerce Dept.
77 S. High St., 23rd Fl.
Columbus, OH 43266-0544
Phone: (614)466-4130

Credential Type: Private Investigator License. **Requirements:** Good reputation. No conviction of a felony within the past 20 years, and no conviction of any offense involving moral turpitude. For two years prior to application must have been engaged in investigatory services work for a law enforcement or other public agency or for a private investigator, or in the practice of law, or have equivalent experience. Submit proof of insurability. **Examination:** Yes. **Fees:** $25 application and exam fee. $250 license fee. **Governing Statute:** Ohio Revised Code 4749.01 et seq.

Oklahoma

2353

Private Investigator
Council on Law Enforcement
   Education and Training
Cimarron Sta.
PO Box 11476
Oklahoma City, OK 73136
Phone: (405)425-2775

Credential Type: License. **Duration of License:** Two years. **Requirements:** Ability to read and write. 18 years of age for unarmed private investigators. 21 years of age for armed private investigators. One year of experience working for a licensed investigators. No convictions of crimes of moral turpitude. Covicted felons cannot carry firearms. **Examination:** Oklahoma State Licensing Examination for Private Investigators. **Fees:** $60—$110 license fee. $25—$75 renewal fee.

Pennsylvania

2354

Private Investigator
Pennsylvania Private Detective
   Licensing
c/o Clerk of Courts
Dauphin County Courthouse
Front and Market Sts.
Harrisburg, PA 17101

Credential Type: Private Investigator License. **Requirements:** Must have acceptable experience. Fee may be required.

South Carolina

2355

Private Detective
State Law Enforcement Div.,
   Regulatory Services
PO Box 21398
Columbia, SC 29221
Phone: (803)737-9073

Credential Type: License. **Requirements:** 18 years of age. U.S. citizen. No felony convictions or other crime involving moral turpitude. Two years of experience as a private detective with a licensed agency, supervisor in industrial security, or with a licensed private agency, member of FBI, member of state, county, or municipal police department. $10,000 surety bond. **Fees:** $200 license fee.

Texas

2356

Private Investigator
Texas Board of Private Investigators
   and Private Security Agencies
PO Box 13509, Capitol Station
Austin, TX 78711
Phone: (512)463-5545

Credential Type: License. **Requirements:** 18 years of age. Certificate of insurance. Three years of consecutive experience in investigative field for private investigation firm license. Completion of approved training course consisting of at least 30 hours. **Examination:** Exam may be required. **Fees:** $225—$340 license and renewal fee. **Governing Statute:** VACS 4413(29bb), 22 TAC 429.

Vermont

2357

Private Investigator (detective)
State Board of Private Investigative
   and Security License Services
Pavilion Office Bldg.
Montpelier, VT 05602
Phone: (802)828-2363

Credential Type: License. **Duration of License:** Two years. **Requirements:** 18 years of age. Surety bond of $25,000. Two years of investigative experience. Favorable background. **Examination:** Yes. **Reciprocity:** No. **Fees:** $6 Application for license. $100 Renewal. $25 Late Renewal Penalty. **Governing Statute:** Title 26, VSA Sections 3151-3179.

Virginia

2358

Private Investigator
Virginia Dept. of Commerce
3600 W. Broad St.
Richmond, VA 23230-4917
Phone: (804)257-8500

Credential Type: Private Investigator License. **Requirements:** Must have acceptable experience and pass examination. Fee may be required. **Examination:** Yes.

2359

Private Security Agent
Private Security Services
Dept. of Commerce
3600 W. Broad St.
Richmond, VA 23230
Phone: (804)367-8534

Credential Type: Registration. **Requirements:** Individual employees of a private securities service business who perform armored car personnel, courier, guard, guard dog handler, or private detective services must be registered with the Department of Commerce.

Firm must present evidence of a surety bond and employ a compliance agent who has passed a written examination. Compliance agent must also pass a criminal history background investigation and be registered in at least one category in which the firm offers services. **Examination:** Written examination may be required.

West Virginia

2360

Private Detective
Secretary of State
State Capitol Bldg., Rm. 157
Charleston, WV 25305
Phone: (304)345-4000

Credential Type: License. **Requirements:** 18 years old. Three years experience with police, sheriff, or government investigative service. One year training at accredited college or private investigative agency. **Examination:** No. **Fees:** $500 Non resident corporation or individual. $50 Resident individual. $100 Resident corporation.

Wisconsin

2361

Private Detective
Regulations and Licensing Dept.
Private Detective Board
PO Box 8935
Madison, WI 53708-8935
Phone: (608)266-8609

Credential Type: License. **Requirements:** 18 years of age. **Examination:** Written.

Dietitians and Nutritionists

The following states grant licenses in this occupational category as of the date of publication:

Alabama	District of	Iowa	Maine	Nebraska	Oklahoma	Texas
Arkansas	Columbia	Kansas	Maryland	New Mexico	Oregon	Utah
California	Florida	Kentucky	Mississippi	North Dakota	Rhode Island	Washington
	Georgia	Louisiana	Montana	Ohio	Tennessee	

Alabama

2362

Dietitian
Alabama Board of Examiners for Dietetic-Nutrition Practice
622 Adams Ave.
Montgomery, AL 36103
Phone: (205)242-4505

Credential Type: License to practice. **Duration of License:** Two years. **Requirements:** Baccalaureate degree. Pass examination. Academic degree validation for foreign applicants. Must have completed a course of study covering human nutrition, foods and nutrition, and dietetics. Must have 900 hours of experience in dietetic practice that is supervised by a licensed dietitian or nutritionist. Applicants will be considered fully qualified for licensure if they are currently registered with the Commission on Dietetic Registration as a dietitian. Renewal requires 30 continuing education hours. **Reciprocity:** Yes. **Fees:** $50 application fee. $50 renewal fee.

Credential Type: Temporary Dietitian's License. **Requirements:** Baccalaureate degree. Academic degree validation for foreign applicants. Must have completed a course of study covering human nutrition, foods and nutrition, and dietetics.

2363

Nutritionist
Alabama Board of Examiners for Dietetic-Nutrition Practice
622 Adams Ave.
Montgomery, AL 36103
Phone: (205)242-4505

Credential Type: License to practice. **Duration of License:** Two years. **Requirements:** Master's or doctoral degree. Pass examination. Academic degree validation for foreign applicants. Must have completed a course of study covering human nutrition, foods and nutrition, and dietetics. Must have 900 hours of experience in dietetic practice that is supervised by a licensed dietitian or nutritionist. Applicants will be considered fully qualified for licensure if they are currently registered with the Commission on Dietetic Registration as a dietitian. Renewal requires 30 continuing education hours. **Reciprocity:** Yes. **Fees:** $50 application fee. $50 renewal fee.

Credential Type: Temporary Nutritionist's License. **Requirements:** Baccalaureate degree. Academic degree validation for foreign applicants. Must have completed a course of study covering human nutrition, foods and nutrition, and dietetics.

Arkansas

2364

Dietitian
Arkansas Dietetics Licensing Board
PO Box 1016
Little Rock, AR 72115
Phone: (501)374-8212

Credential Type: License. **Requirements:** Baccalaureate or post-baccalaureate degree from a regionally accredited U.S. college in a program of human nutrition, food and nutrition, dietetics, or food systems management. Pass examination given by Commission on Dietetic Registration. **Examination:** Yes. **Fees:** $110 License. $50 Renewal. Written examination.

California

2365

Dietitian
Dept. of Health Services
Licensing and Certification Div.
714-744 P St.
Sacramento, CA 95814
Phone: (916)485-2070

Credential Type: License to practice. **Requirements:** Baccalaureate degree. Complete an approved course of study for the preparation of dietitians. Must complete six months of supervised clinical experience in the field. Applicants will be considered fully qualified for licensure if they are currently registered with the Commission on Dietetic Registration as a dietitian.

District of Columbia

2366

Dietitian
Board of Dietetics and Nutrition
Applications Div.
Occupational and Professional Licensing Admin.
Dept. of Consumer and Regulatory Affairs
PO Box 37290
614 H St., NW, Rm. 923
Washington, DC 20013
Phone: (202)727-7468

Credential Type: License to practice. **Duration of License:** Two years. **Requirements:** Baccalaureate degree. Pass examination. Academic degree validation for foreign applicants. Must have completed a course of study covering human nutrition, foods and nutrition, and dietetics. Must have 900 hours of experience in dietetic practice that is supervised by a licensed dietitian or nutritionist. Applicants will be considered fully qualified for licensure if they are currently registered with the Commission on Dietetic Registration as a dietitian. Renewal requires 30 continuing education hours. **Reciprocity:** Yes. **Fees:** $28 renewal fee. $41 reinstatement fee for inactive status application.

2367

Nutritionist
Board of Dietetics and Nutrition
Applications Div.
Occupational and Professional
    Licensing Admin.
Dept. of Consumer and Regulatory
    Affairs
PO Box 37290
614 H St., NW, Rm. 923
Washington, DC 20013
Phone: (202)727-7468

Credential Type: License to practice. **Duration of License:** Two years. **Requirements:** Baccalaureate degree. Pass examination. Academic degree validation for foreign applicants. Must have completed a course of study covering human nutrition, foods and nutrition, and dietetics. Must have 900 hours of experience in dietetic practice that is supervised by a licensed dietitian or nutritionist. Renewal requires 30 continuing education hours. **Reciprocity:** Yes. **Fees:** $28 renewal fee. $41 reinstatement fee for inactive status application.

Florida

2368

Dietitian-Nutritionist
Dietetics and Nutrition Council
Dept. of Professional Regulation
130 N. Monroe St.
Tallahassee, FL 32399
Phone: (904)487-3372

Credential Type: License to practice. **Duration of License:** Two years. **Requirements:** Baccalaureate degree. Pass examination. Academic degree validation for foreign applicants. Must have completed a course of study covering human nutrition, foods and nutrition, and dietetics. Must have 900 hours of experience in dietetic practice that is supervised by a licensed dietitian or nutritionist or equivalent education. Applicants will be considered fully qualified for licensure if they are currently registered with the Commission on Dietetic Registration as a dietitian. **Reciprocity:** Yes. **Fees:** $50 application fee. $200 renewal fee. **Governing Statute:** Florida Statutes, Chapter 468, Part X. Florida Administrative Code, Rule 21-M.

Credential Type: Temporary Dietitian-Nutritionist's License. **Requirements:** Baccalaureate degree. Academic degree validation for foreign applicants. Must have completed a course of study covering human nutrition, foods and nutrition, and dietetics. **Governing Statute:** Florida Statutes, Chapter 468, Part X. Florida Administrative Code, Rule 21-M.

Georgia

2369

Dietitian
Board of Examiners of Licensed
    Dietitians
166 Pryor St. SW
Atlanta, GA 30303
Phone: (404)656-3921

Credential Type: License to practice. **Duration of License:** Two years. **Requirements:** Baccalaureate degree. Pass examination. Academic degree validation for foreign applicants. Must have completed a course of study covering human nutrition, foods and nutrition, and dietetics. Must have 900 hours of experience in dietetic practice that is supervised by a licensed dietitian or nutritionist or equivalent education. Applicants will be considered fully qualified for licensure if they are currently registered with the Commission on Dietetic Registration as a dietitian. Renewal requires 30 continuing education hours. **Examination:** CDR Certification Exam. **Reciprocity:** Yes, by endorsement with states having similar requirements and reciprocity with Georgia. **Fees:** $90 application/examination fee. $75 application by endorsement fee. $50 renewal fee.

2370

School Service Associate
Div. of Teacher Education
State Dept. of Education
1452 Twin Towers East
Atlanta, GA 30334-5070
Phone: (404)656-2406

Credential Type: School Service Certificate. **Authorization:** Authorizes the holder to administer school services in one of the following occupations: Audiologist, Media Specialist, School Counselor, School Nutrition Director, School Psychometrist, School Psychologist, School Social Worker/Visiting Teacher, or Speech and Language Pathologist. **Requirements:** Bachelor's degree is required for Nutrition Director, Speech/ Language Pathologist and Media Specialist. Master's degree and sixth year program is required for Psychologist. All other occupations require a master's degree or fifth year program. Media Specialist requires Initial Teaching Certificate. A staff development program in the Identification and Education of Children with Special Needs and a certification test is required at the master's degree level in the field of School Counseling. Three years of acceptable school experience are required of in the fields of nutrition and counseling.

Iowa

2371

Dietitian
Board of Dietetic Examiners
Dept. of Public Health
Lucas State Office Bldg.
Des Moines, IA 50319
Phone: (515)281-6762

Credential Type: License. **Duration of License:** Two years. **Requirements:** Baccalaureate degree with major course work in nutrition, dietetics, or food management. Completion of a planned preprofessional experience component of not less than 900 hours. **Examination:** National Registration Exam. **Fees:** $100 application fee. $100 renewal fee. $25 national registraation fee.

Kansas

2372

Dietitian
Bureau of Adult & Child Care
Dept. of Health & Environment
Landon State Office Bldg.
900 SW Jackson
Topeka, KS 66612
Phone: (913)296-0056

Credential Type: License to practice. **Duration of License:** Two years. **Requirements:** Baccalaureate degree. Pass examination. Must have completed a course of study covering human nutrition, foods and nutrition, and dietetics. Must have 900 hours of experience in dietetic practice that is supervised by a licensed dietitian or nutritionist or equivalent education. Renewal requires 15 continuing education hours. **Reciprocity:** Yes.

Credential Type: Temporary Dietitian's License. **Requirements:** Baccalaureate degree. Must have completed a course of study covering human nutrition, foods and nutrition, and dietetics.

Kentucky

2373

Dietitian
Div. of Occupations & Professions
Dept. of Administration
Finance & Administration Cabinet
Frankfort, KY 40601
Phone: (502)564-3296

Credential Type: License to practice. **Requirements:** Baccalaureate degree. Complete a course of study that meets the minimum academic requirements as established by the Commission on Dietetic Registration (CDR). Must be accredited by the American Dietetic Association (ADA) or have approved experience. Applicants will be considered fully qualified for licensure if they are currently registered with the CDR as a dietitian. **Fees:** $50 (maximum) application fee.

2374

Nutritionist
Div. of Occupations & Professions
Dept. of Administration
Finance & Administration Cabinet
Frankfort, KY 40601
Phone: (502)564-3296

Credential Type: License to practice. **Requirements:** Master's degree. Complete a course of study that includes course work in human nutrition, foods and nutrition, and dietetics. Complete 12 graduate semester hours in nutrition. Applicants will be considered fully qualified for licensure if they are currently registered with the Commission on Dietetic Registration as a dietitian. **Fees:** $50 (maximum) application fee.

Louisiana

2375

Dietitian-Nutritionist
State Board of Examiners in
 Dietetics and Nutrition
PO Box 41042
Baton Rouge, LA 70838
Phone: (504)673-8043

Credential Type: License to practice. **Duration of License:** Two years. **Requirements:** Baccalaureate degree. Pass examination. Academic degree validation for foreign applicants. Must have completed a course of study covering human nutrition, foods and nutrition, and dietetics. Must have 900 hours of experience in dietetic practice that is supervised by a licensed dietitian or nutritionist or equivalent education. Applicants will be considered fully qualified for licensure if they are currently registered with the Commission on Dietetic Registration as a dietitian. Renewal requires 30 continuing education hours. **Reciprocity:** Yes. **Fees:** $45 application fee. $45 initial license fee. $60 renewal fee.

Credential Type: Temporary Dietitian-Nutritionist's License. **Requirements:** Baccalaureate degree. Academic degree validation for foreign applicants. Must have completed a course of study covering human nutrition, foods and nutrition, and dietetics.

Maine

2376

Dietetic Technician
Board of Dietetic Registration
Div. of Licensure & Enforcement
Dept. of Professional & Financial
 Regulation
State House Station 35
Augusta, ME 04333
Phone: (207)582-8723

Credential Type: License to practice. **Duration of License:** One year. **Requirements:** Associate degree from an American Dietetic Association (ADA)-approved dietetic technician program or a BS in foods and nutrition. Academic degree validation for foreign applicants. Must complete a program of study for dietetic technicians with course work in dietetic technology, nutrition care, foodservice systems management, human nutrition, foods and nutrition, and dietetics. Must complete 450 hours of experience in dietetic practice under the supervision of a licensed dietitian-nutritionist or a registered dietitian. Pass examination. Registration as a dietetic technician with the Commission on Dietetic Registration will fully qualify an applicant for licensure. Renewal requires 10 continuing education hours. **Reciprocity:** Yes. **Fees:** $25 application fee. $40 renewal fee.

Credential Type: Temporary Dietetic Technician's License. **Requirements:** Associate degree from an ADA-approved dietetic technician program or a BS in foods and nutrition. Academic degree validation for foreign applicants. Must complete a program of study for dietetic technicians with course work in dietetic technology, nutrition care, foodservice systems management, human nutrition, foods and nutrition, and dietetics.

2377

Dietitian
Board of Dietetic Registration
Div. of Licensure & Enforcement
Dept. of Professional & Financial
 Regulation
State House Station 35
Augusta, ME 04333
Phone: (207)582-8723

Credential Type: License to practice. **Duration of License:** One year. **Requirements:** Baccalaureate degree. Pass examination. Academic degree validation for foreign applicants. Must have completed a course of study covering human nutrition, foods and nutrition, and dietetics. Must have 900 hours of experience in dietetic practice that is supervised by a licensed dietitian or nutritionist or equivalent education. Must meet American Dietetic Association (ADA) academic and experience requirements or have approved equivalent. Applicants will be considered fully qualified for licensure if they are currently registered with the Commission on Dietetic Registration as a dietitian. Renewal requires 15 continuing education hours. **Reciprocity:** Yes. **Fees:** $25 application fee. $40 renewal fee.

Credential Type: Temporary Dietitian's License. **Requirements:** Baccalaureate degree. Academic degree validation for foreign applicants. Must have completed a course of study covering human nutrition, foods and nutrition, and dietetics. Must have 900 hours of experience in dietetic practice that is supervised by a licensed dietitian or nutritionist or equivalent education. Must meet ADA academic and experience requirements or have approved equivalent.

Maryland

2378

Dietitian
Board of Dietetic Practice
Div. of Health & Mental Hygiene
4701 Patterson Ave.
Baltimore, MD 21215
Phone: (301)764-4733

Credential Type: License to practice. **Duration of License:** Two years. **Requirements:** Baccalaureate degree. Pass examination. Academic degree validation for foreign applicants. Must have completed a course of study covering human nutrition, foods and nutrition, and dietetics. Must have 900 hours of experience in dietetic practice that is supervised by a licensed dietitian or nutritionist or equivalent education. Applicants will be considered fully qualified for licensure if they are currently registered with the Commission on Dietetic Registration as a dietitian. Renewal requires 30 continuing education hours. **Reciprocity:** Yes. **Fees:** $30 application fee. $50 renewal fee.

2379

Nutritionist
Board of Dietetic Practice
Div. of Health & Mental Hygiene
4701 Patterson Ave.
Baltimore, MD 21215
Phone: (301)764-4733

Credential Type: License to practice. **Duration of License:** Two years. **Requirements:** Baccalaureate, master's, or doctoral degree. Pass examination. Academic degree validation for foreign applicants. Must have completed a course of study covering human nutrition, foods and nutrition, and dietetics. Must have 900 hours of experience in dietetic practice that is supervised by a licensed dietitian or nutritionist or equivalent education. Applicants will be considered fully qualified for licensure if they are currently registered with the Commission on Dietetic Registration as a dietitian. Renewal requires 30 continuing education hours. **Reciprocity:** Yes. **Fees:** $30 application fee. $50 renewal fee.

Mississippi

2380

Dietitian
State Dept. of Health
Child Care & Special Licensure
PO Box 1700
Jackson, MS 39215
Phone: (601)960-7504

Credential Type: License to practice. **Duration of License:** One year. **Requirements:** Baccalaureate degree. Pass examination. Academic degree validation for foreign applicants. Must have completed a course of study covering human nutrition, foods and nutrition, and dietetics. Must have 900 hours of experience in dietetic practice that is supervised by a licensed dietitian or nutritionist or equivalent education. Applicants will be considered fully qualified for licensure if they are currently registered with the Commission on Dietetic Registration as a dietitian. Renewal requires 15 continuing education hours. **Reciprocity:** Yes. **Fees:** $25 application fee. $50 renewal fee.

Credential Type: Temporary Dietitian's License. **Requirements:** Must have senior status in a baccalaureate program of nutrition.

Montana

2381

Nutritionist
Montana Board of Medical
 Examiners
111 N. Jackson
Helena, MT 59620
Phone: (406)444-4284

Credential Type: Nutritionist License. **Duration of License:** One year. **Requirements:** A master's degree in dietetics, food and nutrition, or public health nutrition. Registration with the Commission of Dietetic Registration. **Fees:** $45 application and original license fee. $20 renewal fee. **Governing Statute:** Montana Code Annotated 37-25-301 through 37-25-308.

2382

Registered Dietitian
Montana Board of Medical
 Examiners
111 N. Jackson
Helena, MT 59620
Phone: (406)444-4284

Credential Type: Registration. **Duration of License:** One year. **Requirements:** A master's degree in dietetics, food and nutrition, or public health nutrition. Registration with the Commission of Dietetic Registration. **Fees:** $45 application and original license fee. $20 renewal fee. **Governing Statute:** Montana Code Annotated 37-25-301 through 37-25-308.

Nebraska

2383

Dietitian
Nebraska Dept. of Health
301 Centennial Mall S.
PO Box 95007
Lincoln, NE 68509
Phone: (402)471-2115

Credential Type: License. **Duration of License:** Two years. **Requirements:** Must hold a baccalaureate degree from an accredited college with a major course of study in human nutrition, food systems management, or the equivalent. Must have 900 hours of planned continuous experience. **Examination:** Yes. **Fees:** $175 initial certification fee. $100 renewal fee.

New Mexico

2384

Dietitian
Nutrition and Dietetics Practice
 Board
Regulation and Licensing Dept.
PO Box 25101
725 St. Michael's Dr.
Santa Fe, NM 87504
Phone: (505)827-7160

Credential Type: License to practice. **Duration of License:** One year. **Requirements:** Must meet qualifications of the Commission on Dietetic Registration and be currently registered as a Registered Dietitian. Renewal requires 15 continuing education hours. **Reciprocity:** Yes. **Fees:** $50 application fee. $150 license fee. $75 renewal fee. **Governing Statute:** 61-7A-1 et seq. NMSA 1978. Nutrition and Dietetics Practice Board Rules, Rule 92-9 et seq.

Credential Type: Provisional Permit. **Duration of License:** 30 days. **Requirements:** Must have submitted application for licensure and be registered with the board. Baccalaureate degree. Complete a program of study that includes course work in human nutrition, foods and nutrition, and dietetics.

2385

Nutrition Associate
Nutrition and Dietetics Practice
 Board
Regulation and Licensing Dept.
PO Box 25101
725 St. Michael's Dr.
Santa Fe, NM 87504
Phone: (505)827-7160

Credential Type: License to practice. **Duration of License:** One year. **Authorization:** Must work under the supervision of a licensed dietitian or nutritionist. **Requirements:** Baccalaureate degree or higher from a course of study that includes studies in human nutrition, foods and nutrition, and dietetics. Renewal requires 15 continuing education hours. **Reciprocity:** Yes. **Fees:** $50 application fee. $150 license fee. $75 renewal fee. **Governing Statute:** 61-7A-1 et seq. NMSA 1978. Nutrition and Dietetics Practice Board Rules, Rule 92-9 et seq.

New Mexico

2386

Nutritionist
Nutrition and Dietetics Practice Board
Regulation and Licensing Dept.
PO Box 25101
725 St. Michael's Dr.
Santa Fe, NM 87504
Phone: (505)827-7160

Credential Type: License to practice. **Duration of License:** One year. **Requirements:** Master's or doctoral degree, or membership in the American Institute of Nutrition or American Society for Clinical Nutrition or American Board of Nutrition. Complete a course of study that includes studies in human nutrition, foods and nutrition, and dietetics. Renewal requires 15 continuing education hours. **Reciprocity:** Yes. **Fees:** $50 application fee. $150 license fee. $75 renewal fee. **Governing Statute:** 61-7A-1 et seq. NMSA 1978. Nutrition and Dietetics Practice Board Rules, Rule 92-9 et seq.

Credential Type: Provisional Permit. **Duration of License:** 30 days. **Requirements:** Must have submitted application for licensure and be registered with the board. Baccalaureate degree. Complete a program of study that includes course work in human nutrition, foods and nutrition, and dietetics.

North Dakota

2387

Dietitian
Board of Dietetic Practice
2015 8th Ave. N
Grand Forks, ND 58201
Phone: (701)777-3752

Credential Type: License to practice. **Duration of License:** One year. **Requirements:** Must meet qualifications of the Commission on Dietetic Registration and be currently registered as a Registered Dietitian. Renewal requires 12 continuing education hours or 75 continuing education hours in a five-year period. **Reciprocity:** Yes. **Fees:** $60 application fee. $45 renewal fee.

Credential Type: Temporary Dietitian's License. **Requirements:** Baccalaureate degree. Must have completed a course of study covering human nutrition, foods and nutrition, and dietetics. Must have 900 hours of experience in dietetic practice that is supervised by a licensed dietitian or nutritionist or equivalent education.

2388

Nutritionist
Board of Dietetic Practice
2015 8th Ave. N
Grand Forks, ND 58201
Phone: (701)777-3752

Credential Type: License to practice. **Duration of License:** One year. **Requirements:** Baccalaureate, master's or doctoral degree. Complete a program of study that includes course work in human nutrition, foods and nutrition, and dietetics. Renewal requires 12 continuing education hours or 75 continuing education hours in a five-year period. **Reciprocity:** Yes. **Fees:** $60 application fee. $45 renewal fee.

Ohio

2389

Dietitian-Nutritionist
Board of Dietetics
77 S High St., 18th Fl.
Columbus, OH 43266
Phone: (614)466-3291

Credential Type: License to practice. **Duration of License:** One year. **Requirements:** Baccalaureate degree. Pass examination. Academic degree validation for foreign applicants. Must have completed a course of study that is consistent with American Dietetic Association (ADA) academic standards and covers human nutrition, foods and nutrition, and dietetics. Must have 900 hours of experience in dietetic practice that is supervised by a licensed dietitian or nutritionist or equivalent education. Experience should be ADA-approved or Commission on Dietetic Registration (CDR) equivalent. Applicants will be considered fully qualified for licensure if they are currently registered with the CDR as a dietitian. Renewal requires 15 continuing education hours. **Reciprocity:** Yes. **Fees:** $60 application fee. $45 renewal fee.

Credential Type: Temporary Dietitian-Nutritionist's License. **Requirements:** Baccalaureate degree. Academic degree validation for foreign applicants. Must have completed a course of study that is consistent with ADA academic standards and covers human nutrition, foods and nutrition, and dietetics. Must have 900 hours of experience in dietetic practice that is supervised by a licensed dietitian or nutritionist or equivalent education. Experience should be ADA-approved or CDR equivalent.

Oklahoma

2390

Licensed Dietician
State Board of Medical Licensure and Supervision
PO Box 18256
Oklahoma City, OK 73154
Phone: (405)848-6841

Credential Type: License. **Duration of License:** One year. **Requirements:** Baccalaureate degree. A minimum of 24 semester hours in human nutrition or an equivalent. Internship. 75 hours of continuing education within five years. Three recommendations. **Examination:** Registered Examination for Dietitian. **Fees:** $75 exam fee. $100 application fee. $40 renewal fee.

Oregon

2391

Dietitian
State Health Div.
1400 SW Fifth
Portland, OR 97201
Phone: (503)229-5806

Credential Type: License to practice. **Duration of License:** Two years. **Requirements:** Baccalaureate degree. Pass examination. Must have completed a course of study covering human nutrition, foods and nutrition, and dietetics. Must have 900 hours of experience in dietetic practice that is supervised by a licensed dietitian or nutritionist or equivalent education. Applicants will be considered fully qualified for licensure if they are currently registered with the Commission on Dietetic Registration as a dietitian. Must be able to demonstrate knowledge of the code of ethics of the dietetic profession. Renewal requires 30 continuing education hours. **Reciprocity:** Yes.

Rhode Island

2392

Dietitian
Dept. of Professional Regulation
Dept. of Health
75 Davis St.
Providence, RI 02908
Phone: (401)277-2827

Credential Type: License to practice. **Duration of License:** Two years. **Requirements:** Baccalaureate degree. Complete a program in nutrition and/or dietetics. Pass examination. Must have 900 hours of experience in dietetic practice that is supervised by a licensed dietitian or nutritionist or equivalent education. Applicants will be considered fully qualified for licensure if they are currently registered with the Commission on Dietetic Registration as a dietitian. **Fees:** $100 renewal fee.

Credential Type: Temporary Dietitian's License. **Requirements:** Baccalaureate degree. Academic degree validation for foreign students. Complete a program in nutrition and/or dietetics.

Tennessee

2393

Dietitian-Nutritionist
Board of Dietitian-Nutritionist
  Examiners
St. Thomas Hospital
PO Box 380
4220 Harding Rd.
Nashville, TN 37202
Phone: (615)386-6558

Credential Type: License to practice. **Duration of License:** Two years. **Requirements:** Baccalaureate degree. Pass examination. Academic degree validation for foreign applicants. Must have completed a course of study covering human nutrition, foods and nutrition, and dietetics. Must have 900 hours of experience in dietetic practice that is supervised by a licensed dietitian or nutritionist or equivalent education. Applicants will be considered fully qualified for licensure if they are currently registered with the Commission on Dietetic Registration as a dietitian. **Reciprocity:** Yes. **Fees:** $75 application fee. $100 renewal fee.

Credential Type: Temporary Dietitian-Nutritionist's License. **Requirements:** Baccalaureate degree. Must have applied to take the examination for licensure. Academic degree validation for foreign applicants. Must have completed a course of study covering human nutrition, foods and nutrition, and dietetics. Must have 900 hours of experience in dietetic practice that is supervised by a licensed dietitian or nutritionist or equivalent education.

Texas

2394

Dietitian
Board of Examiners of Dietitians
1100 W 49th St., Rm. T-502
Austin, TX 78756
Phone: (512)458-7501

Credential Type: License to practice. **Duration of License:** One year. **Requirements:** Baccalaureate degree. Pass examination. Academic degree validation for foreign applicants. Must have completed a course of study covering human nutrition, foods and nutrition, and dietetics. Board approved internship or preplanned experience program. Applicants will be considered fully qualified for licensure if they are currently registered with the Commission on Dietetic Registration as a dietitian. **Reciprocity:** Yes. **Fees:** $30 application fee. $24 renewal fee.

Credential Type: Temporary Dietitian's License. **Requirements:** Baccalaureate degree. Academic degree validation for foreign applicants. Must have completed a course of study covering human nutrition, foods and nutrition, and dietetics.

Utah

2395

Dietitian
Dept. of Commerce
Div. of Occupational and
  Professional Licensing
160 E. 300 S.
PO Box 45802
Salt Lake City, UT 84145
Phone: (801)530-6628

Credential Type: License. **Duration of License:** Two years. **Requirements:** Must hold a bachelor's or graduate degree with a major course of study in the sciences of food, dietetics, food systems management, or the equivalent. Must complete an internship in a dietetic program under a certified dietitian. **Examination:** Yes. **Fees:** $50 license fee. $30 renewal fee.

Washington

2396

Dietitian
Professional Programs Management
PO Box 9012
Olympia, WA 98504
Phone: (206)586-4565

Credential Type: License to practice. **Duration of License:** One year. **Requirements:** Baccalaureate degree. Pass examination. Academic degree validation for foreign applicants. Must have completed a course of study covering human nutrition, foods and nutrition, and dietetics. Must have 900 hours of experience in dietetic practice that is supervised by a licensed dietitian or nutritionist or equivalent education. Applicants will be considered fully qualified for licensure if they are currently registered with the Commission on Dietetic Registration as a dietitian. All applicants must have completed AIDS education and training. **Reciprocity:** Yes. for certified dietitians only. **Fees:** $75 application fee.

2397

Nutritionist
Professional Programs Management
PO Box 9012
Olympia, WA 98504
Phone: (206)586-4565

Credential Type: License to practice. **Duration of License:** One year. **Requirements:** Master's or doctoral degree. Academic degree validation for foreign applicants. Must have completed a course of study covering human nutrition, foods and nutrition, and dietetics. Applicants will be considered fully qualified for licensure if they are currently registered with the Commission on Dietetic Registration as a dietitian. All applicants must have completed AIDS education and training. **Fees:** $75 application fee.

Dispensing Opticians

The following states grant licenses in this occupational category as of the date of publication:

Alaska	Connecticut	Iowa	New Hampshire	Ohio	Vermont
Arizona	Florida	Kentucky	New Jersey	Rhode Island	Virginia
Arkansas	Georgia	Massachusetts	New York	South Carolina	Washington
California	Hawaii	Nevada	North Carolina	Tennessee	

Alaska

2398

Optician
Board of Dispensing Opticians
Dept. of Commerce and Economic Development
Div. of Occupational Licensing
PO Box D-LIC
Juneau, AK 99811
Phone: (907)465-2547

Credential Type: Optician License. **Duration of License:** Two years. **Requirements:** High school graduate. 6000 hours of apprenticeship, or 6000 hours as a practicing optician. An associate degree from a recognized program may be used for 4000 hours. 15 hours of continuing education required every four years.

Contact lens dispensing requires additional license. **Examination:** National Opticianry Competency Examination (NOCE) and two-hour practical examination. **Reciprocity:** Yes, under condition of equal qualification and mutual reciprocity. **Fees:** $30 application fee. $100 renewal fee. $50 exam fee. $20 endorsement fee.

Arizona

2399

Optician
Board of Dispensing Opticians
1645 W. Jefferson, Rm. 410
Phoenix, AZ 85007
Phone: (602)542-3095

Credential Type: Optician License. **Duration of License:** One year. **Requirements:** High school graduate. Three years of apprenticeship or one year of apprenticeship with two years of formal schooling. 1,000 hours of optical lab work may count as a portion of apprenticeship. National Opticianry Competency Examination (NOCE) and/or National Contact Lens Registry Examination (NCLE) may be accepted in place of state examinations.

Must be NCLE certified to dispense contact lenses. **Examination:** State written and practical examinations. **Reciprocity:** Yes, under condition of equal qualification. **Fees:** $50 application fee. $50 license fee. $25 initial year balance fee. $70 annual renewal fee.

Arkansas

2400

Dispensing Optician
Arkansas Board of Dispensing Opticians
107 Central Ave.
Searcy, AR 72143
Phone: (501)268-1673

Credential Type: License. **Duration of License:** One year. **Requirements:** 21 years of age. Resident of Arkansas. Good moral character. High school graduate or equivalent. Graduate of an approved school of opticianry where curriculum is approved; or, have engaged in ophthalmic dispensing for five years prior to application, of which no more than three years may consist of either working in a qualified, full service optical laboratory or providing ophthalmic dispensing services under the direct supervision of an Arkansas licensed dispensing optician. **Examination:** Yes. **Fees:** $50 Written and Practical examination. $50 License. $50 Renewal.

California

2401

Optician
Medical Board of California
Div. of Allied Health Professional
1430 Howe Ave.
Sacramento, CA 95825
Phone: (916)924-2612

Credential Type: Optician License. **Duration of License:** Two years. **Requirements:** Must pass National Opticianry Competency Examination (NOCE). Contact lens dispensing requires an additional license. **Examination:** National Opticianry Competency Examination (NOCE). **Fees:** $100 initial license fee. $150 biennial renewal fee.

Credential Type: Contact Lens Dispenser's License. **Duration of License:** Two years. **Requirements:** Must pass NCLE examination. **Examination:** National Contact Lens Registry Examination (NCLE). **Fees:** $100 application fee. $100 biennial renewal fee.

Connecticut

2402

Optician
Board of Medical Quality Assurance
Optical Dept.
150 Washington St.
Hartford, CT 06106
Phone: (203)566-1035

Credential Type: Optician License. **Duration of License:** One year. **Requirements:** Must have four years of apprenticeship or an associated degree from a COA approved program. Must pass NOCE and NCLE prior to taking state examination. **Examination:**

National Opticianry Competency Examination (NOCE). National Contact Lens Registry Examination (NCLE). State practical examination. **Reciprocity:** Yes, under condition of equal qualification. **Fees:** $75 application fee. $45 annual renewal fee. $250 optical selling permit. $25 apprentice registration and renewal.

Florida

2403

Optician
Dept. of Professional Regulation
Div. of Professions
Board of Opticianry
Northwood Center, Ste. 60
1940 N. Monroe St.
Tallahassee, FL 32399-0750
Phone: (904)487-2397

Credential Type: Optician License. **Duration of License:** Two years. **Requirements:** At least 18 years of age. High school graduate. Three years of apprenticeship or associated degree from a program approved by the COA. 20 hours of continuing education is required every two years. **Examination:** National Opticianry Competency Examination (NOCE). National Contact Lens Registry Examination (NCLE). State practical examination. State written examination. **Fees:** $100 application fee. $180 biennial license renewal fee. $325 examination fee. $50 application fee (Board Certified Optician). $10 apprentice processing fee.

Georgia

2404

Optician
Board of Dispensing Opticians
Examining Boards Division
166 Pryor St. SW
Atlanta, GA 30303
Phone: (404)656-=3912

Credential Type: Optician License. **Duration of License:** Two years. **Requirements:** At least 18 years of age. High school graduate. Two years of apprenticeship or one year of formal schooling. 10 hours of continuing education required every two years. **Examination:** National Opticianry Competency Examination (NOCE). National Contact Lens Registry Examination (NCLE). State practical examination. **Reciprocity:** Yes, under condition of equal qualification and mutual reciprocity. **Fees:** $60 biennial license renewal.

Hawaii

2405

Dispensing Optician
Hawaii Board of Dispensing
  Opticians
Dept. of Commerce and Consumer
  Affairs
PO Box 3469
Honolulu, HI 96801
Phone: (808)548-8590

Credential Type: License. **Duration of License:** Two years. **Requirements:** Graduation from an accredited opticianry course; or proof of a previous license in another jurisdiction; or a minimum of three years as a full-time practical and mechanical optical experience as an opticianry apprentice. **Examination:** National Opticianry Competence Examination. National Contact Lens Registry Examination. **Fees:** $20 application fee. $55 exam fee. $70 registration fee. $40 Compliance Resolution Fund fee.

Iowa

2406

Ophthalmic Dispenser/Optician
Ophthalmic Dispenser Certification
Dept. of Public Health
Lucas State Office Bldg.
Des Moines, IA 50319
Phone: (515)281-6762

Credential Type: Certificate. **Duration of License:** One year. **Requirements:** Completion of a course of study from an approved school of optics or school of ophthalmic dispensing; or three years or more as a registered apprentice under the direct supervision of a physician and surgeon, osteopathic physician, osteopathic physician and surgeon, or licensed optomotrist; or six years of experience as an ophthalmic dispenser and a reference from a physician, osteopathic physician, or Iowa licensed optomotrist. **Fees:** $25 certification fee. $10 renewal fee.

Kentucky

2407

Ophthalmic Dispenser - Optician
Kentucky Board of Ophthalmic
  Dispensers
640 Fourth Ave.
PO Box 1063
Louisville, KY 40201
Phone: (502)588-3149

Credential Type: License. **Duration of License:** One year. **Requirements:** Graduation from an approved school of ophthalmic dispensing, or two years training and experience as an apprentice. 18 years of age. **Examination:** Yes. **Reciprocity:** No. **Fees:** $250 exam fee. $10 renewal fee.

Massachusetts

2408

Optician
Board of Registration and Dispensing
  Opticians
Leverett Saltonstall Bldg.
100 Cambridge St.
Boston, MA 02202
Phone: (617)727-0346

Credential Type: Optician License. **Duration of License:** Two years. **Requirements:** High school graduate. Three years of apprenticeship or two years of schooling in an approved program.

Contact lens dispensing requires passage of the National Contact Lens Registry Examination (NCLE). **Examination:** National Opticianry Competency Examination (NOCE). **Reciprocity:** Yes, under condition of equal qualification. **Fees:** $25 application fee.

Nevada

2409

Optician
Nevada State Board of Dispensing
  Opticians
PO Box 50291
Henderson, NV 89014
Phone: (702)451-2122

Credential Type: License. **Duration of License:** One year. **Requirements:** Completion of a two-year accredited college program and one year of practical experience under a licensed dispensing optician or optometrist. **Examination:** Yes. **Fees:** $200 exam and license fee. $200 renewal fee.

New Hampshire

Optician, continued

Credential Type: Optician Apprentice License. **Duration of License:** One year. **Requirements:** Must be employed at least 1,900 hours per year and dispense on the retail floor in the last year of apprenticeship. Must submit proof of 12 hours of continuing education for license renewal. **Fees:** $40 license fee. $25 renewal fee.

New Hampshire

2410

Optician
Ophthalmic Dispenser Advisory Committee
Health & Welfare Bldg.
6 Hazen Dr.
Concord, NH 03301
Phone: (603)271-1203

Credential Type: Optician License. **Duration of License:** Two years. **Requirements:** Registration with the Division of Public Health Services. Contact lens dispensing requires a statement of delegation from an ophthalmologist and/or optometrist. **Fees:** $100 registration fee. $100 biennial renewal fee.

New Jersey

2411

Optician, Dispensing
Board of Examiners of Ophthalmic Dispensers and Ophthalmic Technicians
1100 Raymond Blvd., Rm. 501
Newark, NJ 07102
Phone: (201)648-2840

Credential Type: License. **Duration of License:** Two years. **Requirements:** 17 years of age. High school diploma or equivalent. An associate degree in ophthalmic science or equivalent from an accredited institution and work as a full-time apprentice for four to 12 months; or served as an apprentice for 36 months during which time the applicant has completed the required number of school hours or board approved courses in ophthalmic science; or has served as an apprentice for at least 36 months during which time the applicant has satisfactorily completed a minimum of 30 hours of board approved courses in ophthalmic science at an accredited school or college. **Examination:** Yes. **Reciprocity:** Yes. **Fees:** $100 exam fee. $75 license fee. $170 renewal fee. $75 apprentice permit. **Governing Statute:** NJSA 52:17B-41. NJAC 13:33.

New York

2412

Ophthalmic Dispenser (Optician)
State Education Dept.
Div. of Professional Licensing Services
Cultural Education Center
Empire State Plaza
Albany, NY 12230
Phone: (518)474-3827

Credential Type: License. **Duration of License:** Three years. **Requirements:** High school diploma and vocational training in ophthalmic dispensing. 18 years of age. **Examination:** Written and practical. **Fees:** $165 application fee. $50 renewal fee. **Governing Statute:** Title VIII Articles 130, 144 of the Education Law.

North Carolina

2413

Optician
North Carolina State Board of Opticians
412 N. Wilmington St.
Raleigh, NC 27601
Phone: (919)733-9321

Credential Type: License. **Duration of License:** One year. **Requirements:** High school diploma or equivalent. Associate degree in Applied Science from an accredited school of optometry; or completion of a three and a half year apprenticeship, plus a six month internship under a licensed Optician, Ophthalmologist or Optometrist. **Examination:** Written and practical exam. **Fees:** $100 exam fee. $10 license fee. $60 renewal fee.

Ohio

2414

Optician
Optical Dispenser Board
77 S. High St., 16th Fl.
Columbus, OH 43266-0328
Phone: (614)466-9707

Credential Type: Optician License. **Duration of License:** One year. **Requirements:** At least 18 years of age. Two years of apprenticeship or two years of schooling in an approved program. Four hours of spectacle and eight hours of contact lens continuing education is required annually.

Contact lens dispensing requires passage of the National Contact Lens Registry Examination (NCLE) and additional license. **Examination:** National Opticianry Competency Examination (NOCE).

Rhode Island

2415

Optician
Opticians Advisory Committee
State Dept. of Health
Div. of Professional Regulation
104 Health Dept. Bldg.
Providence, RI 02908
Phone: (401)277-2828

Credential Type: Optician License. **Duration of License:** Two years. **Authorization:** Does not allow dispensing of contact lenses. **Requirements:** At least 18 years of age. High school graduate. Three years of apprenticeship or two years of schooling in an approved program and one year apprenticeship. Six hours of continuing education required every two years. **Examination:** National Opticianry Competency Examination (NOCE). **Fees:** $30 application fee. $50 biennial renewal fee.

South Carolina

2416

Optician
South Carolina State Board of Examiners of Opticianry
PO Box 541
Fountain Inn, SC 29644
Phone: (803)271-8241

Credential Type: License. **Requirements:** High school graduate or equivalent. Certification from an accredited school of opticianry or three years of experience as an apprentice. **Examination:** Yes. **Fees:** $15 license fee. $50 renewal fee.

Tennessee

2417

Optician
Board of Dispensing Opticians
Dept. of Health
283 Plus Park Blvd.
Nashville, TN 37247-1010
Phone: (615)367-6249

Credential Type: Optician License. **Duration of License:** One year. **Requirements:** At least 18 years of age. Three years of registered apprenticeship or two years of formal schooling. Eight hours of continuing education (4 hours spectacle & four hours contact lens) are required every year. **Ex-

amination: National Opticianry Competency Examination (NOCE). National Contact Lens Registry Examination (NCLE). State practical examination. **Fees:** $100 application fee. $100 renewal fee.

Vermont

2418

Optician
State Board of Opticians
Pavilion Office Bldg.
Montpelier, VT 05602
Phone: (802)828-2390

Credential Type: License. **Duration of License:** One year. **Requirements:** High school education or equivalent. Completion of a two year program in school of ophthalmic dispensing approved by board; or, completed three years of training and experience approved by board. Note: Any person entering into training must notify board within 60 days. **Examination:** Yes. **Reciprocity:** Yes. **Fees:** $50 Exam fee. $50 Biennial renewal fee. $5 Wall Certificate. $5 Trainee Registration. $5 Annual renewal. **Governing Statute:** Title 26, VSA Sections 2671-2678 Age of Majority.

Virginia

2419

Optician
Virginia Board of Opticians
Dept. of Commerce
3600 Broad St.
Richmond, VA 23230
Phone: (804)367-8590

Credential Type: License. **Duration of License:** Two years. **Requirements:** 18 years of age. High school diploma. Must have completed a two year course from an approved school of optometry, or must have completed a three year apprenticeship in accordance with standards established by the Division of Apprenticeship Training of the State Department of Labor and Industry and approved by the Virginia State Board of Opticians. **Fees:** $100 license fee. $65 renewal fee.

Washington

2420

Optician
Dispensing Opticians Examining Committee
Dept. of Health
PO Box 1099
Olympia, WA 98507-1099
Phone: (206)753-3576

Credential Type: Optician License. **Duration of License:** One year. **Requirements:** At least 18 years of age. Must have three years of apprenticeship or two years of formal education. 30 hours of continuing education are required every three years. **Examination:** State written and practical examinations. **Fees:** Application and annual renewal fees.

Education Administrators

The following states grant licenses in this occupational category as of the date of publication:

Alabama	Delaware	Iowa	Michigan	New Hampshire	Oklahoma	Utah
Alaska	Florida	Kansas	Minnesota	New Jersey	Oregon	Vermont
Arizona	Georgia	Kentucky	Mississippi	New Mexico	Pennsylvania	Virginia
Arkansas	Hawaii	Louisiana	Missouri	New York	Rhode Island	Washington
California	Idaho	Maine	Montana	North Carolina	South Carolina	West Virginia
Colorado	Illinois	Maryland	Nebraska	North Dakota	South Dakota	Wisconsin
Connecticut	Indiana	Massachusetts	Nevada	Ohio	Tennessee	Wyoming

Alabama

2421

Administrator of Vocational Education
State Dept. of Education,
   Certification Officer
Montgomery, AL 36130
Phone: (205)242-9977

Credential Type: Class A Administrator of Vocational Education Professional Certificate. **Requirements:** Eligibility for Class B Professional Certificate in a vocational teaching field. Completion of a program for vocational administrators approved by the Alabama State Board of Education or the National Council for Accreditation of Teacher Education or the National Association of State Directors of Teacher Education and Certification or ICP. Three years of acceptable teaching experience.

Credential Type: Class AA Administrator of Vocational Education Professional Certificate. **Requirements:** Eligibility for a Class A Administrator of Vocational Education Certificate. Completion of a sixth year program approved by the Alabama State Board of Education.

2422

School Principal
State Dept. of Education,
   Certification Officer
Montgomery, AL 36130
Phone: (205)242-9977

Credential Type: Class A Principal Professional Certificate. **Requirements:** Eligibility for Class B Professional Certificate. Completion of a program for principals approved by the Alabama State Board of Education or the National Council for Accreditation of Teacher Education or the National Association of State Directors of Teacher Education and Certification or ICP. Three years of acceptable teaching experience.

Credential Type: Class AA Principal Professional Certificate. **Requirements:** Eligibility for a Class A Principal Certificate. Completion of a sixth year program approved by the Alabama State Board of Education.

2423

School Superintendent
State Dept. of Education,
   Certification Officer
Montgomery, AL 36130
Phone: (205)242-9977

Credential Type: Class A Superintendent-Professional Certificate. **Requirements:** Eligibility for a Class B Professional Certificate. Completion of a program for Superintendents approved by the Alabama State Board of Education or the National Council for Accreditation of Teacher Education or the National Association of State Directors of Teacher Education and Certification or ICP. Three years of acceptable teaching experience.

Credential Type: Class AA Superintendent-Professional Certificate. **Requirements:** Eligibility for a Class A Superintendent-Professional Certificate. Completion of a sixth-year program for superintendents approved by the Alabama State Board of Education.

2424

School Supervisor
State Dept. of Education
Montgomery, AL 36130
Phone: (205)242-9977

Credential Type: Class A Supervisor Professional Certificate. **Requirements:** Issued with endorsement for supervisor of instruction, or supervisor of attendance, vocational education, reading, school food and nutrition. Eligibility for Class B Professional Certificate. Completion of a program for supervisors approved by the Alabama State Board of Education or the National Council for Accreditation of Teacher Education or the National Association of State Directors of Teacher Education and Certification or ICP. Three years of acceptable teaching experience.

Credential Type: Class AA Supervisor Professional Certificate. **Requirements:** Eligibility for a Class A Supervisor Certificate. Completion of a sixth year program approved by the Alabama State Board of Education.

Alaska

2425

School Administrator
Dept. of Education, Certification
   Analyst
Box F
Juneau, AK 99811-0500
Phone: (907)465-2810
Phone: (907)465-2831

Credential Type: Administrative Certificate—Type B. **Duration of License:** Five years. **Requirements:** Three years of satisfactory teaching experience. Master's degree from an accredited institution, and completion of approved program in administrative specialty plus institutional recommendation or recommendation from certifying State Department. Six semester hours must have been earned in the five year period immediately preceding the date of application.

Certificate may be renewed six months before expiration date upon application and completion of six semester hours of credit during the life of the certificate. Three of the six semester hours may be in correspondence, or by completing workshops or institutes or by travel for which non-academic credit has been approved by the Commission of Education prior to the holding of the workshop, travel, or institute. First time renewals must complete three semester hours in Alaska studies and three semester hours in multicultural education.

Endorsements will be granted as recommended by the preparing institution. **Fees:** $43 fingerprint card processing fee. $125 application fee. $10 endorsement fee.

Credential Type: Temporary Certificate—Type T (For Type B). **Duration of License:** One year. **Requirements:** Meet all application requirements except the six semester hours of recency. Proof of satisfactory teaching service for at least three years. Never possessed an Alaska teacher certificate. Nonrenewable. **Fees:** $20 temporary certificate application fee.

Arizona

2426

School Principal
Teacher Certification Unit
PO Box 25609
1535 W. Jefferson
Phoenix, AZ 85002
Phone: (602)542-4368

Credential Type: Principal Certificate (K-12). **Duration of License:** Six years. **Requirements:** Master's or more advanced degree from a regionally accredited institution. Three years of verifiable teaching experience (K-12). Minimum of 54 graduate semester hours including completion of an approved program in educational administration for the principalship from a regionally accredited institution or 30 graduate semester hours of educational administrative course work which teach the following administrative skills: organizational planning; program development; staff development and evaluation; monitoring and evaluating programs. Internship for principal or two years of verifiable educational administrative experience as a principal, assistant principal, associate principal, or vice principal (K-12). Pass Arizona Teacher Proficiency Exam (ATPE) exam. Satisfy Arizona Constitution and U.S. Constitution requirements during initial year of certification. **Examination:** Arizona Teacher Proficiency Exam.

2427

School Superintendent
Teacher Certification Unit
PO Box 25609
1535 W. Jefferson
Phoenix, AZ 85002
Phone: (602)542-4368

Credential Type: Superintendent Certificate (K-12). **Duration of License:** Six years. **Requirements:** Master's or more advanced degree from a regionally accredited institution. Three years of verifiable teaching experience (K-12). Minimum of 60 graduate semester hours including completion of an approved program in educational administration for the superintendent from a regionally accredited institution or 36 graduate semester hours of educational administrative course work which teach the following administrative skills: organizational planning; program development; staff development and evaluation; evaluating productivity. Internship for educational administration for the superintendency or two years of verifiable educational administrative experience as a superintendent, assistant or associate superintendent (K-12). Pass Arizona Teacher Proficiency Exam (ATPE) exam. Satisfy Arizona Constitution and U.S. Constitution requirements during initial year of certification. **Examination:** Arizona Teacher Proficiency Examination

2428

School Supervisor
Teacher Certification Unit
PO Box 25609
1535 W. Jefferson
Phoenix, AZ 85002
Phone: (602)542-4368

Credential Type: Supervisor Certificate (K-12). **Duration of License:** Six years. **Requirements:** An Arizona Elementary, Secondary, or Special Education Certificate. Master's or more advanced degree from a regionally accredited institution. Three years successful teaching experience within grades K-12 for which a valid teaching certificate was required. Minimum of 45 graduate semester hours to include completion of approved program in educational administration or 18 graduate semester hours of educational administrative course work which teach the following administrative skills: organizational planning; program development; staff development and evaluation; monitoring and evaluating programs. Internship in educational supervision or two years of verifiable teaching experience (K-12).

Arkansas

2429

Advanced School Guidance Supervisor
Teacher Education and Licensure
State Dept. of Education
4 State Capitol Mall
Little Rock, AR 72201-1071
Phone: (501)682-4342

Credential Type: Advance Guidance Supervision Certificate. **Requirements:** Hold or be eligible to hold a master's level school guidance/counseling certificate. Have three years of school experience, at least half-time work each year, as a certificated school counselor (guidance worker). Complete post-master's program of 30 or more semester hours that has professional accreditation by an accrediting agency recognized by the State Board of Education. 12 semester hours in Administration and Supervision, including at least two semester hours of each of the following: Educational administration; Supervision; Curriculum; Vocational education. 12 semester hours in Guidance and Counseling. Six semester hours of electives in areas related to work of a supervisor of guidance programs.

2430

Elementary School Principal
Teacher Education and Licensure
State Dept. of Education
4 State Capitol Mall
Little Rock, AR 72201-1071
Phone: (501)682-4342

Credential Type: Elementary School Principal's Certificate. **Duration of License:** 10 years. **Requirements:** Hold, or be qualified to hold, at time of application, the six year elementary (K-6 or K-12) certificate. If not certified in K-6 elementary, must have six hours elementary reading and three hours elementary math. Minimum of four years teaching experience as a teacher or administrator, three of which must be in an elementary school classroom. Must have 45 semester hours graduate work in elementary related field. Must include a master's degree in elementary administration or equivalent.

Arkansas

2431

School Administrator
Teacher Education and Licensure
State Dept. of Education
4 State Capitol Mall
Little Rock, AR 72201-1071
Phone: (501)682-4342

Credential Type: Administrator's Certificate. **Duration of License:** 10 years. **Requirements:** Hold or be qualified to hold, at the time of application, the six year high school or elementary teaching certificate. Completion of 60 semester hours of graduate training with emphasis in school administration from an accredited institution authorized by the State Department of Education or accredited by the National Council for Accreditation of Teacher Education (NCATE) to grant the Diploma of Advanced Study or Specialist's Degree in school administration. Must include the master's degree in school administration (or equivalent) with a minimum of 30 hours in graduate education courses including an appropriate distribution of courses in administration, supervision and related fields. Master's degree graduates from schools not authorized to grant the Diploma of Advanced Study or Specialist's Degree in School Administration must submit a "deficiency and removal" plan to the Office of Teacher Education and Licensure. Minimum of four years experience as a teacher or administrator, three of which must be in the classroom.

2432

School Library Media Administrator
Teacher Education and Licensure
State Dept. of Education
4 State Capitol Mall
Little Rock, AR 72201-1071
Phone: (501)682-4342

Credential Type: Library Media Administrator Certificate. **Duration of License:** 10 years. **Requirements:** Master's degree plus 30 semester hours. Certified as a Library Media Specialist K-12. Minimum of four years successful experience as a classroom teacher in an accredited elementary school, secondary school and/or as a library media center Specialist in a unified school library media center (a minimum of two of the four years must have been as a Media Center Specialist).

Specialized Requirements include an additional 30 semester hours in graduate education courses including an appropriate distribution in administration, supervision and related fields.

2433

School Superintendent
Arkansas Dept. of Education
ffice of Teacher Education and Licensure
Sate Education Bldg., Rm. 107B
Capitol Mall 4
Little Rock, AR 72201-1071
Phone: (501)682-4344

Credential Type: License. **Requirements:** Must be eligible to hold a teaching certificate (elementary or secondary). Minimum of four years experience as teacher or administrator. Must complete program of study of 60 semester hours of graduate education with emphasis in school administration and Masters degree in School Administration at an approved institution. **Examination:** Yes. **Fees:** $45 National Teacher Examination (NTE) Specialty Area Test. $45 NTE Specialty Area Test renewal.

2434

Secondary School Principal
Teacher Education and Licensure
State Dept. of Education
4 State Capitol Mall
Little Rock, AR 72201-1071
Phone: (501)682-4342

Credential Type: Secondary School Principal's Certificate. **Duration of License:** 10 years. **Requirements:** Hold, or be qualified to hold, at the time of application a six year high school certificate or a K-12 certificate. Complete a minimum of 45 semester hours of graduate credit inclusive of the master's degree in school administration (or the equivalent), from an institution authorized by the State Department of Education or accredited by the National Council for Accreditation of Teacher Education (NCATE) to grant the Diploma of Advance Study or Specialist's Degree in school administration. Mater's degree graduates from institutions not authorized to grant the Diploma of Advanced Study or Specialist's Degree in school administration must submit a "deficiency and removal" plan to the Office of Teacher Education and Licensure. Minimum of four years experience as a teacher or administrator, three of which must be in the secondary school classroom.

California

2435

School Administrator
Commission on Teacher Credentialing
PO Box 944270
Sacramento, CA 94244-7000
Phone: (916)445-7254

Credential Type: Five Year Preliminary Administrative Services Credential (nonrenewable). **Duration of License:** Five years. **Requirements:** Possession of a valid California credential, which may be in: teaching; designated subjects vocational teaching; pupil personnel services; librarianship; health services/school nurse; or clinical rehabilitative services. Three years successful, full-time service on the prerequisite credential. Approved program of specialized and professional preparation in administrative services or approved one year administrative internship program from a California institution. Special education (mainstreaming). CBEST examination. Recommendation of a California college or university with an approved administrative services program. Out-of-state applicants who meet requirements may still be certified. Their approved program in school administrative services must have at least one year of postgraduate preparation and must include field work in a school situation completed with a grade of B on a five point scale. **Examination:** California Basic Education Skills Test **Fees:** $60 application fee. $30 test score recording and evaluation fee, except for CBEST.

Credential Type: Five Year Professional Administrative Credential. **Duration of License:** Five years. **Authorization:** Authorizes the holder to serve as a superintendent, associate superintendent, deputy superintendent, principal, assistant principal, supervisor, consultant, coordinator, or in an equivalent intermediate level administrative position. **Requirements:** Five Year Preliminary Administrative Credential. Two years of successful full-time experience in a position requiring the preliminary credential. Approved program of advanced study and field experience and the recommendation of the institution. **Fees:** $60 application fee. $30 test score recording and evaluation fee, except for CBEST.

Colorado

2436

School Administrator
Teacher Certification
State Dept. of Education
201 E. Colifax
Denver, CO 80203
Phone: (303)866-6628

Credential Type: Administrative Certificate—Type D. **Duration of License:** Five years. **Requirements:** Initial teacher certification and Type A General Teacher Certificate which requires the following: Bachelor's degree. Completion of an approved program of teacher preparation from a four year, regionally accredited, degree granting institution which must include student teaching. Six semester hours of credit applicable to the certificate being sought, and/or general education, and/or child abuse, taken within the past five years from date of application. Course work in the exceptional child, covering the full range of exceptionalities, gifted through handicapped, and course work in the theory, methods, and related practice of the teaching of reading. Passage of the spelling, language, and mathematics sections of Level 19 of the California Achievement Test and oral English competence which is met by having a B—or better in a public speaking course taken from a regionally accredited college or passing an oral English panel assessment. Completed and signed appropriate application. Institutional recommendation from the school(s) where the teacher preparation work was completed. Official, original transcripts from all applicable institutions.

In addition the General Teacher Certificate requires Institutional recommendation to verify satisfactory completion of teacher preparation including: student teaching; completion of grade levels, subject areas, or service specialization; passing competency examination, meeting the Recent Credit Requirement (having earned six semester or nine quarter hours within the five years prior to the date of application for the certificate) or Renewal Credit Requirement.

Administrative certification requires a master's or higher degree and an institutional recommendation verifying the satisfactory completion of an approved graduate program for School Administrators. **Examination:** California Achievement Test Level 19 (spelling, language, and mathematics sections) **Fees:** $45 initial certification application fee. $40 fingerprint card processing fee.

Connecticut

2437

Intermediate School Administrator or Supervisor
State Dept. of Education
Teacher Certification, Chief
165 Capitol Ave.
PO Box 2219
Hartford, CT 06145
Phone: (203)566-4561

Credential Type: Intermediate Administrator or Supervisor Initial Certificate. **Requirements:** Connecticut teaching certificate or eligibility for one. Master's degree from an approved institution. Five years of successful teaching experience. Recommendation of an accredited college or university approved in Connecticut for preparation of administrative and supervisory personnel, based on a program of 18 semester hours in addition to the master's degree. Graduate study in the following areas: Foundations of education; Psychological foundations of learning; Curriculum development; Educational administration and supervision.

Credential Type: Intermediate Administrator or Supervisor Provisional Certificate. **Requirements:** Intermediate Administrator or Supervisor Initial Certificate. Completion of beginning educator support and assessment program as may be available from the Connecticut Board and one school year of successful service under the interim or initial certificates or three years of successful service as a superintendent of schools, in an approved school, within 10 years prior to application.

Credential Type: Intermediate Administrator or Supervisor Professional Certificate. **Requirements:** At least three years of successful service under the Provisional Certificate. 30 hours of study beyond the master's degree. 100 hours of general education (liberal arts).

2438

Superintendent of Schools
State Dept. of Education
Teacher Certification, Chief
165 Capitol Ave.
PO Box 2219
Hartford, CT 06145
Phone: (203)566-4561

Credential Type: Superintendent of Schools Initial Certificate. **Requirements:** Connecticut teaching certificate or eligibility for one. Master's degree from an approved institution. Eight years of successful teaching or administrative experience. Three years of full-time administrative or supervisory experience in U.S. schools. Recommendation of an accredited college or university approved by the State Department of Education for preparation of superintendent of schools, based on a program of 30 semester hours in addition to the master's degree. Graduate study in the following areas: Foundations of education; Psychological foundations of learning; Curriculum development; Educational administration and supervision; and a core of related study to ensure breadth of education and scholarly background consistent with the competence expected of a superintendent of schools.

Credential Type: Superintendent of Schools Provisional Certificate. **Requirements:** Superintendent of Schools Initial Certificate. Completion of beginning educator support and assessment program as may be available from the Connecticut Board and one school year of successful service under the interim or initial certificates or three years of successful service as a superintendent of schools, in an approved school, within 10 years prior to application. Superintendent of Schools Professional Certificate. **Requirements:** Three years of successful service under the Provisional Certificate.

Delaware

2439

Elementary School Principal
Teacher Certification
Dept. of Public Instruction
PO Box 1402
Dover, DE 19903
Phone: (302)739-4688

Credential Type: Elementary Principal Endorsement. **Authorization:** Authorizes employment as an elementary school principal or assistant principal. **Requirements:** Master's degree from an accredited college. Three years of successful experience as an elementary school teacher or two years' teaching experience and one year of internship. Master's degree in an approved administration program or complete an approved graduate program in elementary school administration or a master's degree with course work in the following: general school administration; elementary school administration; supervision; curriculum development; and school business management.

Delaware

2440

School Administrative Supervisor
Teacher Certification
Dept. of Public Instruction
Box 1402
Dover, DE 19903
Phone: (302)739-4688

Credential Type: Administrative Supervisor Endorsement. **Requirements:** Master's degree from an accredited college with a major in educational supervision and curriculum or a master's degree with at least 30 semester hours of course work in advanced areas of supervision and curriculum development. Must have three years' teaching experience in area to be supervised.

2441

School Superintendent
Teacher Certification
Dept. of Public Instruction
Box 1402
Dover, DE 19903
Phone: (302)739-4688

Credential Type: Superintendent Endorsement. **Requirements:** Master's degree plus at least 30 graduate credits or a doctor's degree. Must have a major in administration that covers course work in curriculum, supervision, business administration and personnel administration. Three years' teaching experience or two years of teaching and a 60 semester hr. program for school administrators that includes a one year internship.

2442

Secondary School Principal
Teacher Certification
Dept. of Public Instruction
PO Box 1402
Dover, DE 19903
Phone: (302)739-4688

Credential Type: Secondary Principal Endorsement. **Authorization:** Authorizes employment as a secondary school principal or assistant principal. **Requirements:** Master's degree from an accredited college. Three years of successful experience as a secondary school teacher or two years' teaching experience and one year of internship. Master's degree in an approved administration program or complete an approved graduate program in secondary school administration or a master's degree with course work in the following: secondary school administration; supervision; curriculum development; and school business management; administration and supervision of tests.

Florida

2443

School Administrator or Supervisor
Bureau of Teacher Certification
Florida Education Center
325 W. Gaines, Rm. 201
Tallahassee, FL 32399
Phone: (904)488-2317

Credential Type: Professional Certificate. **Duration of License:** Five years. **Requirements:** Bachelor's degree. Six semester hours of both sociological and psychological foundations. Six semester hours of general methods of teaching, administration, supervision, and curriculum at the level where certification is sought. Two hours of special methods for teaching at the level where certification is sought. Six semester hours of a college internship program or two years of full-time teaching experience.

Credential Type: Educational Leadership Level One Certificate. **Requirements:** Three years of successful teaching experience in an elementary or secondary school. Hold a master's degree. Successfully complete the Florida Educational Leadership Core Curriculum by specified options. Six graduate credit hours in area of emphasis. Passing scores on the Florida Educational Leadership Examination. **Examination:** Florida Educational Leadership Examination.

2444

School Principal
Bureau of Teacher Certification
Florida Education Center
325 W. Gaines, Rm. 201
Tallahassee, FL 32399
Phone: (904)488-2317

Credential Type: Educational Leadership Level Two Certificate. **Requirements:** Hold a valid professional certificate covering administration/supervision. Document successful performance of the duties of school principalship. Demonstrate successful performance of the competences of the school principalship which has been documented by the Florida district school superintendent.

Credential Type: Professional School Principal Certification. **Requirements:** Hold a valid professional school principal (Level Two) certificate. Three years of successful experience as a principal in the same Florida public school district. Documented superior performance by district school superintendent.

Georgia

2445

School Administrator or Supervisor
Div. of Teacher Education
State Dept. of Education
1452 Twin Towers East
Atlanta, GA 30334-5070
Phone: (404)656-2406

Credential Type: Leadership Fifth Year Certificate. **Requirements:** Initial Teaching Certificate. Master's degree or fifth year program. Three years of acceptable school experience. Staff development program in the Identification and Education of Children with special needs that is equal to five quarter hours A certification test at the master's degree level in Administration and Supervision.

Hawaii

2446

Educational Administrator
Dept. of Education
Office of Personnel Services
PO Box 2360
Honolulu, HI 96804
Phone: (808)548-5803

Credential Type: Professional Educational Administrator Certificate. **Authorization:** Issued to district and state educational officers in positions of administration. **Requirements:** Competence as evaluated by the Department of Education. Master's degree or five years of equivalent college or university education. Minimum qualification requirements as established by the vacancy. Appointment to the position by the state Board of Education.

2447

School Administrator
Dept. of Education
Office of Personnel Services
PO Box 2360
Honolulu, HI 96804
Phone: (808)548-5803

Credential Type: Professional School Administrator Certificate. **Requirements:** Competence as evaluated by the Department of Education. Possession of a Hawaii teacher certificate. Tenure in the Department of Education. Five years of satisfactory teaching experience in grades K-12. Successful completion of the Hawaii Department of Education school administrator education program. Twenty-one semester hours of course work in educational administration as prescribed by the Hawaii Department of Education.

Idaho

2448

Director of Special Education
Certification Analyst
State Dept. of Education
L. B. Jordan Office Bldg.
Boise, ID 83720
Phone: (208)334-3475

Credential Type: Administrative Exceptional Child Certificate. **Duration of License:** Five years. **Requirements:** Three years of successful teaching experience in area of certification. Advanced Exceptional Child Certificate, or Pupil Personnel Services Certificate, endorsed for School Psychologist, Communication Disorders Specialist, or School Social Worker and demonstrated competencies or Administration Certificate plus demonstrated competencies. Valid for five years and may be renewed upon completion of at least six semester credits of college courses within the period of validity.

2449

Exceptional Child School Program Supervisor
Certification Analyst
State Dept. of Education
L. B. Jordan Office Bldg.
Boise, ID 83720
Phone: (208)334-3475

Credential Type: Administrative Exceptional Child Certificate with Supervisor Endorsement. **Duration of License:** Five years. **Requirements:** Master's degree. Advanced Exceptional Child Certificate, or Pupil Personnel Services Certificate, endorsed for School Psychologist, Communication Disorders Specialist, or School Social Worker. Three years of experience in special education. Demonstrated competencies. Valid for five years and may be renewed upon completion of at least six semester credits of college courses within the period of validity.

2450

School Principal
Certification Analyst
State Dept. of Education
L. B. Jordan Office Bldg.
Boise, ID 83720
Phone: (208)334-3475

Credential Type: Administrative Certificate with Elementary Principal Endorsement K-8. **Duration of License:** Five years. **Requirements:** Qualify for an Idaho Standard or Advanced Elementary Certificate. Master's degree from an accredited institution. Four years full-time regular and/or special education classroom teaching experience in grades K-8 while properly certified. Administrative internship or one year of experience as an administrator. Completion of an approved program of at least 30 semester credit hours of graduate study in school administration for the preparation of elementary school principals at an accredited institution to include competencies in supervision of instruction; curriculum development; school finance; administration; school law; student behavior management; and education of special populations. Valid for five years and may be renewed upon completion of at least six semester credits of college courses within the period of validity.

Credential Type: Administrative Certificate with Secondary Principal Endorsement 6-12. **Duration of License:** Five years. **Requirements:** Qualify for an Idaho Standard or Advanced Secondary Certificate. Master's degree from an accredited institution. Four years full-time regular and/or special education classroom teaching experience in grades 6-12 while properly certified. Administrative internship or one year of experience as an administrator. Completion of an approved program of at least 30 semester credit hours of graduate study in school administration for the preparation of secondary school principals at an accredited institution to include competencies in supervision of instruction; curriculum development; school finance; administration; school law; student behavior management; and education of special populations. Valid for five years and may be renewed upon completion of at least six semester credits of college courses within the period of validity.

2451

School Superintendent
Certification Analyst
State Dept. of Education
L. B. Jordan Office Bldg.
Boise, ID 83720
Phone: (208)334-3475

Credential Type: Administrative Certificate with Superintendent Endorsement. **Duration of License:** Five years. **Requirements:** Qualify for an Idaho Standard or Advanced Elementary or Secondary Certificate. Educational specialist or doctorate degree or a comparable postmaster's sixth year program at an accredited institution. Four years full-time regular and/or special education classroom teaching experience in grades K-12 while properly certified. Administrative internship or one year of experience as an administrator in grades K-12. Completion of an approved program of at least 30 semester credit hours of graduate study in school administration for the preparation of school superintendents at an accredited institution to include competencies in supervision of instruction; curriculum development; school finance; administration; school law; student behavior management; education of special populations; advanced money management and accounting principles; district-wide support services; employment practices and negotiations; school board and community relations; special services; and federal programs. Valid for five years and may be renewed upon completion of at least six semester credits of college courses within the period of validity.

Illinois

2452

Chief School Business Official
Certification and Placement Section
100 N. First St.
Springfield, IL 62777
Phone: (217)782-4321

Credential Type: Chief School Business Official Endorsement. **Duration of License:** Five years. **Requirements:** Good character. Good health. At least 19 years of age. Citizen of the U.S. Master's degree in administration from a recognized institution. Must have the following graduate level semester hr. credits: School Business Management 12; School Organization and Administration 3; School Finance and Fiscal Planning 6; and Clinical Experience (appropriate to the endorsement) while holding a certificate of comparable validity. Two years of business management experience. Pass required sections of the Illinois

Chief School Business Official, continued

Certification Test. **Examination:** Illinois Certification Test. **Reciprocity:** Reciprocity exists for applicants holding out-of-state administrative certificates providing their preparation was comparable to that required by the state of Illinois. **Fees:** $44 per section of the Illinois Certification Test.

2453

School Principal
Certification and Placement Section
100 N. First St.
Springfield, IL 62777
Phone: (217)782-4321

Credential Type: General Administrative Endorsement. **Duration of License:** Five years. **Authorization:** Authorizes employment in Illinois Public Schools as a principal, assist. principal, or assist. or associate superintendent. **Requirements:** Good character. Good health. At least 19 years of age. Citizen of the U.S. Master's degree in administration from a recognized institution. Must have the following graduate level semester hr. credits: Instructional Leadership 12; Management of Public Schools 9; Schools and Public Policy 4-6; and Clinical Experience (appropriate to the endorsement). Two years of full-time teaching experience or school service personnel experience. Pass required sections of the Illinois Certification Test. **Examination:** Illinois Certification Test. **Reciprocity:** Reciprocity exists for applicants holding out-of-state administrative certificates providing their preparation was comparable to that required by the state of Illinois. **Fees:** $44 per section of the Illinois Certification Test.

2454

School Superintendent
Certification and Placement Section
100 N. First St.
Springfield, IL 62777
Phone: (217)782-4321

Credential Type: Superintendent Endorsement. **Duration of License:** Five years. **Requirements:** Good character. Good health. At least 19 years of age. Citizen of the U.S. Master's degree in administration from a recognized institution. Must have the following graduate level semester hr. credits: Governance of Public Schools 6; Management of Public Schools 6; Educational Planning 6; Graduate Level Electives 12; and Clinical Experience (appropriate to the endorsement). Two years of school supervisory or administrative experience and possession of the general supervisory or general administrative certificate. Pass required sections of the Illinois Certification Test. **Examination:** Illinois Certification Test. **Reciprocity:** Reciprocity exists for applicants holding out-of-state administrative certificates providing their preparation was comparable to that required by the state of Illinois. **Fees:** $44 per section of the Illinois Certification Test.

2455

School Supervisor
Certification and Placement Section
100 N. First St.
Springfield, IL 62777
Phone: (217)782-4321

Credential Type: General Supervisory Endorsement. **Duration of License:** Five years. **Authorization:** Authorizes employment in Illinois Public Schools as a supervisor, curriculum director and other similar or related positions. **Requirements:** Good character. Good health. At least 19 years of age. Citizen of the U.S. Master's degree in administrative supervision from a recognized institution. Must have the following graduate level semester hr. credits: Curriculum 3; Educational Research 3; Combined work in Curriculum and Educational Research 8; Supervision and Staff Development 8; Schools and Public Policy 8-9; and Clinical Experience (appropriate to the endorsement). Two years of full-time teaching experience or school service personnel experience. Pass required sections of the Illinois Certification Test. **Examination:** Illinois Certification Test. **Reciprocity:** Reciprocity exists for applicants holding out-of-state administrative certificates providing their preparation was comparable to that required by the state of Illinois. **Fees:** $44 per section of the Illinois Certification Test.

Indiana

2456

Elementary School Administrator
Teacher Certification
Center for Professional Development
State House, Rm. 229
Indianapolis, IN 46204-2798
Phone: (317)232-9010

Credential Type: Elementary Administration and Supervision License. **Duration of License:** Five years. **Authorization:** Allows holding of administrative positions at the Elementary or Middle Junior High/Middle School levels. **Requirements:** Hold Professional License in Early Childhood, KindergartenPrimary, Elementary or Junior High/Middle School education. 45 semester hours of graduate credit to include: elementary administration; elementary supervision; elementary curriculum; elementary guidance; philosophy of education; psychology and evaluation; school-community relations; cultural awareness of minority groups; human relation; and school law. Recommendation of institution where approved qualifying program was completed. License may be renewed for the following five year period if continuing education requirements are completed. These may include additional graduate semester hours and certification renewal units (CRUs) granted for approved professional experiences.

Credential Type: Professional Endorsement. **Duration of License:** 10 years. **Requirements:** Five years' experience as an administrator and/or supervisor in an accredited elementary, junior high, or middle school subsequent to issuance of Standard License. 60 semester hours in graduate credit in school administration or cognate area from a regionally accredited institution. Recommendation for Professional License by institution where professionalization program was completed.

2457

Secondary School Administrator
Teacher Certification
Center for Professional Development
State House, Rm. 229
Indianapolis, IN 46204-2798
Phone: (317)232-9010

Credential Type: Secondary Administration and Supervision License. **Duration of License:** Five years. **Authorization:** Allows the holding of administrative positions at the Junior High/Middle School or Secondary School levels. **Requirements:** Holds Professional License in Junior High/Middle School or Secondary School education. 45 semester hours of graduate credit to include: secondary administration; secondary supervision; secondary curriculum; secondary guidance; philosophy of education; psychology and evaluation; school-community relations; cultural awareness of minority groups; human relation; and school law. Recommendation of institution where approved qualifying program was completed. License may be renewed for the following five year period if continuing education requirements are completed. These may include additional graduate semester hours and certification renewal units (CRUs) granted for approved professional experiences.

Credential Type: Professional Endorsement. **Duration of License:** 10 years. **Requirements:** Five years' experience as an administrator and/or supervisor in an accredited junior high, middle, or secondary school subsequent to issuance of Standard License. 60 semester hours in graduate credit in school administration or cognate area from a regionally accredited institution. Recommendation for Professional License by institution where professionalization program was completed.

Iowa

2458

Elementary School Principal (PK-6)
Board of Educational Examiners
Grimes State Office Bldg.
Des Moines, IA 50319-0147
Phone: (515)281-3245

Credential Type: Professional Administrator's Certificate. **Duration of License:** Five years. **Requirements:** Holder of or eligible for an Education Certificate. Fiveyears of teaching experience, at least three years of which were on the PK-6 level. Master's degree. Complete 27 semester hours of course work in elementary administration, supervision, and curriculum. Certificate is renewable.

2459

Secondary School Principal (7-12)
Board of Educational Examiners
Grimes State Office Bldg.
Des Moines, IA 50319-0147
Phone: (515)281-3245

Credential Type: Professional Administrator's Certificate. **Duration of License:** Five years. **Requirements:** Holder of or eligible for an Education Certificate. Fiveyears of teaching experience, at least three years of which were on the 7-12 grade level. Master's degree. Complete 27 semester hours of course work in secondary administration, supervision, and curriculum. Certificate is renewable.

2460

Superintendent of Schools (K-12)
Board of Educational Examiners
Grimes State Office Bldg.
Des Moines, IA 50319-0147
Phone: (515)281-3245

Credential Type: Professional Administrator's Certificate. **Duration of License:** Five years. **Requirements:** Holder of or eligible for an Education Certificate. Fiveyears of teaching experience. Master's degree, plus a least 30 semester hours of planned graduate study in administration beyond the master's degree. Overall, at least 45 semester hours of course work must be in school administration and related subjects. Three years' experience as a building principal or other PK-12 districtwide experience or have education agency administration experience. Certificate is renewable.

Kansas

2461

District School Administrator
Certification Specialist
Kansas State Dept. of Education
Kansas State Education Bldg.
120 E. 10th St.
Topeka, KS 66612-1103
Phone: (913)296-2288

Credential Type: District Administrator Endorsement. **Requirements:** Earn a graduate degree. Complete state approved district school administrator program. Complete state approved building administrator program. Three years of experience as a certified, educational professional. Recommended by a teacher education institution.

2462

School Building Administrator K-12
Certification Specialist
Kansas State Dept. of Education
Kansas State Education Bldg.
120 E. 10th St.
Topeka, KS 66612-1103
Phone: (913)296-2288

Credential Type: Building Administration Endorsement. **Requirements:** Earn a graduate degree. Complete state approved administrator program. Three years of experience as a certified, educational professional. Recommended by a teacher education institution.

Kentucky

2463

School Principal
Kentucky Dept. of Education
Div. of Teacher Education and Certification
Capitol Plaza Tower, 18th Fl.
500 Mero St.
Frankfort, KY 40601
Phone: (502)564-4606

Credential Type: Professional Certificate for School Principals. **Duration of License:** Five years. **Requirements:** Hold a standard teaching certificate valid for teaching at appropriate level, although standard certificates issued or endorsed for art, music, physical education, or speech and communication disorders will not satisfy this prerequisite. Complete three years of fulltime teaching experience. Hold a master's degree. Complete Level I program of preparation which includes a one year internship and 18 semester hours in a graduate program for school administration and instructional leadership as outlined by the Kentucky State Board of Education. Level I preparation should include studies in the following areas: modern administrative theories, processes, and techniques; research available on education for the appropriate level; school curriculum; techniques of instructional supervision including the acquisition of those skills needed to effectively monitor, evaluate, and coach instructional personnel, and to provide leadership in staff development, inservice, and program evaluation; educational and psychological testing; modern technological tools (ie, computers) in instructional and administrative processes; and the role of the school principal. Complete the Level II program of preparation which includes an additional 12 hours of graduate credit and requires studies in the following areas: business management and accounting procedures in the public school, legal aspects of education, personnel administration, and community relations. Meet guidelines for competencies for principals as established by the Board. Certificate may be renewed for five year periods providing the applicant completes 12 semester hours of graduate work in the Level II Program for his/her first renewal and, thereafter, completes two years of experience as a principal or three semester hours of additional graduate credit which relates to his/her position or 42 hours of approved training selected from programs approved for the Kentucky Effective Leadership Training Program for each subsequent renewal.

Credential Type: Early Elementary School Principal Endorsement. **Duration of License:** Five years. **Authorization:** Valid for the position of school principal for grades K-4 and also for any other sequential combination of the grades K-8 that includes any grade K-4. **Requirements:** Professional Certificate for Instructional Leadership with studies concentrated at the Early Elementary Level.

Credential Type: Middle Grade School Principal Endorsement. **Duration of License:** Five years. **Authorization:** Valid for the position of school principal for grades 5-8 and also for any other sequential combination of the grades K-12 that includes any grade 5-8. **Requirements:** Pro-

School Principal, continued

fessional Certificate for Instructional Leadership with studies concentrated at the Middle School Level.

Credential Type: Secondary School Principal Endorsement. **Duration of License:** Five years. **Authorization:** Valid for the position of school principal for grades 9-12 and also for any other sequential combination of the grades 5-12 that includes any grade 9-12. **Requirements:** Professional Certificate for Instructional Leadership with studies concentrated at the Middle School Level.

Louisiana

2464

Elementary School Principal
Louisiana Dept. of Education
Box 94064
Baton Rouge, LA 70804-9064
Phone: (504)342-3490

Credential Type: Standard Certificate. **Requirements:** Valid Type A Louisiana Teaching certificate for elementary school. Master's degree from an accredited institution. Five or more years of elementary classroom teaching experience. 33 graduate credit semester hours to include: nine hours educational administration; 18 hours which includes educational research, history, or philosophy of education, elementary school curriculum, school law, school finance, school personnel administration; and three semester hours of electives. Plus three semester hours internship or clinical supervision at the elementary school level.

2465

Parish or City School Superintendent
Louisiana Dept. of Education
Box 94064
Baton Rouge, LA 70804-9064
Phone: (504)342-3490

Credential Type: Standard Certificate. **Requirements:** Valid Type A Louisiana Teaching Certificate. Master's degree from an accredited institution. Five years of successful experience as superintendent, assist. superintendent, supervisor of instruction, or principal in a state-approved system. 48 graduate credit semester hours to include: 30 hours educational administration and supervision; 12 hours of professional educations; and six hours of electives from cognate fields. Asst. Superintendents are required to meet the same requirements.

2466

Parish or City School Supervisor of Instruction
Louisiana Dept. of Education
Box 94064
Baton Rouge, LA 70804-9064
Phone: (504)342-3490

Credential Type: Standard Certificate. **Requirements:** Valid Type A Louisiana Teaching Certificate. Master's degree from an accredited institution. 33 semester hours of graduate courses which include: 15 hours of educational administration and supervision; 15 hours professional education; and three hours of practicum in instructional supervision or internship in instructional supervision.

2467

Secondary School Principal
Louisiana Dept. of Education
Box 94064
Baton Rouge, LA 70804-9064
Phone: (504)342-3490

Credential Type: Standard Certificate. **Requirements:** Valid Type A Louisiana Teaching certificate for secondary school. Master's degree from an accredited institution. Five or more years of secondary classroom teaching experience. 33 graduate credit semester hours to include: nine hours educational administration; 18 hours which includes educational research, history, or philosophy of education, secondary school curriculum, school law, school finance, school personnel administration; and three semester hours of electives. Plus three semester hours internship or clinical supervision at the secondary school level.

Maine

2468

Assistant School Principal
Teacher Certification
Dept. of Education
State House Station 23
Augusta, ME 04333
Phone: (207)289-5944

Credential Type: Assistant Principal Certificate. **Duration of License:** Five years. **Requirements:** Bachelor's degree from an accredited institution. Three years of satisfactory public school teaching experience or three years of equivalent teaching experience. Complete course work in the following areas: community relations; school finance; supervision and evaluation of personnel; civil rights and education laws; organizational theory and planning; educational leadership; educational philosophy and theory; effective instruction; curriculum development; staff development; the exceptional student; and knowledge of the learner and the learning process. Graduate level, state approved, principal internship or practicum program of a least 15 weeks or one full year of employment as an assistant principal or mentorship program lasting one academic year in which the mentor is a school principal. Renewable.

2469

Assistant School Superintendent
Teacher Certification
Dept. of Education
State House Station 23
Augusta, ME 04333
Phone: (207)289-5944

Credential Type: Assistant Superintendent Certificate. **Duration of License:** Five years. **Requirements:** Bachelor's degree. Master's degree, preferred in educational administration. Three years teaching experience or three years equivalent teaching experience in an instructional setting. Complete course work in the following areas: community relations; school finance; supervision and evaluation of personnel; civil rights and education laws; organizational theory and planning; educational leadership; educational philosophy and theory; effective instruction; curriculum development; staff development; the exceptional student; and knowledge of the learner and the learning process. One year of previous administrative experience in schools (or equivalent experience as an administrator in an institutional setting) or one year administrator internship. Renewable.

2470

School Principal
Teacher Certification
Dept. of Education
State House Station 23
Augusta, ME 04333
Phone: (207)289-5944

Credential Type: Principal Certificate. **Requirements:** Bachelor's degree. Master's degree, preferred in educational administration. Three years teaching experience or three years equivalent teaching experience in an instructional setting. Three years of previous administrator experience in schools or equivalent experience as an administrator in an institutional setting. Complete course work in the following areas: community relations; school finance; supervision and evaluation of personnel; civil rights and education laws; organizational theory and planning; educational leadership; educational philosophy and theory; effective instruction; curriculum development; staff development; the exceptional student; and knowledge of the learner and the learning process. Graduate level, state approved, principal internship or practicum program of a least 15 weeks or one full year of employment as an assistant principal or mentorship program lasting one academic year in which the mentor is a school principal. Renewable.

2471

School Superintendent
Teacher Certification
Dept. of Education
State House Station 23
Augusta, ME 04333
Phone: (207)289-5944

Credential Type: Superintendent Certificate. **Duration of License:** Five years. **Requirements:** Bachelor's degree. Master's degree, preferred in educational administration. Three years teaching experience or three years equivalent teaching experience in an instructional setting. Three years of previous administrative experience in schools or equivalent experience as an administrator in an institutional setting. Complete course work in the following areas: community relations; school finance; supervision and evaluation of personnel; civil rights and education laws; organizational theory and planning; educational leadership; educational philosophy and theory; effective instruction; curriculum development; staff development; the exceptional student; and knowledge of the learner and the learning process. Graduate level, state approved, administrator internship or practicum program of a least 15 weeks or one full year of employment as an assistant supervisor/superintendent or mentorship program lasting one academic year in which the mentor is a school superintendent. Renewable.

Maryland

2472

School Principal
Dept. of Certification 18100
State Dept. of Education
200 W. Baltimore St.
Baltimore, MD 21201
Phone: (301)333-2142

Credential Type: Principal Endorsement. **Requirements:** Professional teaching certificate at appropriate level of assignment. Master's degree plus 15 additional hours of graduate credit. Three years of successful teaching experience. Complete a balance program of graduate courses of which 15 hours may be in State Dept. of Education approved workshops. At least 18 semester hours of supervision courses which should include work in these areas: administration; supervision; psychology of learning; guidance and counseling; group dynamics; human growth and development; oral and written communication; multi-media; and sociology of the community. Plus 12 semester hours of curriculum courses to include: curriculum design and paradigms; strategy and influences in curriculum development; curriculum appraisal; programmed instruction; and data systems. In addition, must have 15 additional semester hours in content area courses appropriate to the level of assignment.

2473

School Superintendent
Dept. of Certification 18100
State Dept. of Education
200 W. Baltimore St.
Baltimore, MD 21201
Phone: (301)333-2142

Credential Type: Superintendent Endorsement. **Requirements:** Eligible for a professional teaching certificate. Master's degree from an accredited institution. Three years of successful teaching experience and two years of administrative and/or supervisory experience. Successful completion of a two year program with graduate courses in administration and supervision. Must have a minimum of 60 semester hours of graduate work.

2474

School Supervisor
Dept. of Certification 18100
State Dept. of Education
200 W. Baltimore St.
Baltimore, MD 21201
Phone: (301)333-2142

Credential Type: Supervisor Endorsement. **Requirements:** Professional teaching certificate. Master's degree plus 15 additional hours of graduate credit. Three years of successful teaching experience. Complete a balance program of graduate courses of which 15 hours may be in State Dept. of Education approved workshops. At least 18 semester hours of supervision courses which should include work in these areas: administration; supervision; psychology of learning; guidance and counseling; group dynamics; human growth and development; oral and written communication; multi-media; and sociology of the community. Plus 12 semester hours of curriculum courses to include: curriculum design and paradigms; strategy and influences in curriculum development; curriculum appraisal; programmed instruction; and data systems. In addition, must have 15 additional semester hours in content area courses appropriate to the level of assignment.

Massachusetts

2475

School Business Administrator
Massachusetts Dept. of Education
1385 Hancock St.
Quincy, MA 02169
Phone: (617)770-7500

Credential Type: Business Administrator Endorsement. **Requirements:** Massachusetts teacher's certificate. One year of employment in role covered by certificate or three years of successful employment in a managerial role. 24 semester hr. pre-practicum. In addition, complete a 150 clock hr. practicum within one year or an 300 clock hr. internship within two years. Demonstrate the competencies contained in the four Standards established by the Massachusetts Dept. of Education for business administrators. Standard I-Knowledge of business administration in general and of recent developments in school management and education. Standard II—Communicate clearly and appropriately. Standard III—Ability to manage fiscal and other non-academic affairs. Standard IV-Ability to use evaluative procedures to assess effectiveness of systems of management and personnel.

2476

School Principal
Massachusetts Dept. of Education
1385 Hancock St.
Quincy, MA 02169
Phone: (617)770-7500

Credential Type: Principal Endorsement. **Requirements:** Massachusetts teacher's certificate. Three years of teaching experience. 24 semester hr. pre-practicum. In addition, complete a 150 clock hr. practicum within one year or an 300 clock hr. internship within two years. Must include responsibility for supervision or direction within the same area of education as candidate's teaching certificate. Demonstrate the competencies contained in the five Standards established by the Massachusetts Dept. of Education for administrators. Standard I—Know theories of curriculum design; techniques of supervision and evaluation of personnel; school law, budgeting, and plant management; human relations

Massachusetts

School Principal, continued

and community education; sociology and philosophy of education; organizational characteristics of schools. Standard IIPresent instructional goals and policies; the needs and concerns of students, parents, and the community. Standard III-Set goals and establish priorities. Standard IV—Use evaluative procedures to assess the effectiveness of program and personnel. Standard V—Deal in equitable, sensitive, and responsive manner with students, parents, and community.

2477

School Superintendent/Assistant Superintendent
Massachusetts Dept. of Education
1385 Hancock St.
Quincy, MA 02169
Phone: (617)770-7500

Credential Type: Superintendent Endorsement. **Requirements:** Massachusetts teacher's certificate. Three years of teaching experience. 24 semester hr. pre-practicum. In addition, complete a 150 clock hr. practicum within one year or an 300 clock hr. internship within two years. Must include responsibility for supervision or direction within the same area of education as candidate's teaching certificate. Demonstrate the competencies contained in the five Standards established by the Massachusetts Dept. of Education for administrators. Standard I—Know theories of curriculum design; techniques of supervision and evaluation of personnel; organizational characteristics of schools; sociology and philosophy of education; research in methods of teaching and learning. Standard II—Present instructional goals and policies; the needs and concerns of students, parents, and the community. Standard III-Set goals and establish priorities. Standard IV—Use evaluative procedures to assess the effectiveness of program and personnel. Standard V—Deal in equitable, sensitive, and responsive manner with students, parents, and community.

2478

School Supervisor/Director
Massachusetts Dept. of Education
1385 Hancock St.
Quincy, MA 02169
Phone: (617)770-7500

Credential Type: Supervisor/Director Endorsement. **Requirements:** Massachusetts teacher's certificate. Three years of teaching experience. 24 semester hr. pre-practicum. In addition, complete a 150 clock hr. practicum within one year or an 300 clock hr. internship within two years. Must include responsibility for supervision or direction within the same area of education as candidate's teaching certificate. Demonstrate the competencies contained in the five Standards established by the Massachusetts Dept. of Education for administrators. Standard I—Know theories of curriculum design; techniques of supervision and evaluation of personnel; organizational characteristics of schools; sociology and philosophy of education; research in methods of teaching and learning. Standard II—Present instructional goals and policies; the needs and concerns of students, parents, and the community. Standard III-Set goals and establish priorities. Standard IV—Use evaluative procedures to assess the effectiveness of program and personnel. Standard V—Deal in equitable, sensitive, and responsive manner with students, parents, and community.

Michigan

2479

School Administrator
Teacher Preparation and Certification
Michigan Dept. of Education
Box 30008
Lansing, MI 48909
Phone: (517)373-3310

Credential Type: Administrator Certification. **Duration of License:** Five years. **Authorization:** Valid for the positions of superintendent, principal, assistant principal, chief school business official, and those positions whose primary responsibility is supervising instructional programs and staff. **Requirements:** Michigan teaching certificate (Except chief school business official position). Approved administration program. Renewable.

Minnesota

2480

School Administrator
Teacher Licensing and Placement
State Dept. of Education
616 Capitol Square Bldg.
St. Paul, MN 55101
Phone: (612)296-2046

Credential Type: Administration Entrance License. **Authorization:** License may be granted for the following positions: superintendent of schools, elementary school principal, or secondary school principal. **Requirements:** Teaching certificate. Satisfactory completion of a program approved by the State Board in school administration for the administrative post being sought and a specialist or higher degree, or a program which results in completion of 45 quarter hours credit or equivalent, beyond a master's degree. Three years of successful teaching. Renewable with one year of appropriate administrative experience.

Credential Type: Continuing Administrative License. **Requirements:** 125 clock hours of approved administrative continuing education. Renewable.

Mississippi

2481

School Administrator
Teacher Certification
State Dept. of Education
Box 771
Jackson, MS 39205-0771
Phone: (601)359-3483

Credential Type: Provisional Certificate. **Duration of License:** One year. **Requirements:** Hold valid Mississippi teaching certificate or equivalent and passage of the Core Battery of the NTE and specialty tests. Complete an approved program in administration. Renewable for not more than two additional one year periods.

Credential Type: Standard Certificate. **Duration of License:** One year. **Requirements:** Successful completion of the provisional certification period, which includes an evaluation of on-the-job performance. Demonstrate the mastery of the administrative competencies at the prescribed level. One of four classes of the standard certificate may be issued dependent on the candidate's education and experience. The classes are A, AA, AAA, and AAAA. Certificate will be extended based on the administrator's successful completion of staff development requirements.

Missouri

2482

School Principal
Teacher Certification
Dept. of Elementary and Secondary Education
Box 480
Jefferson City, MO 65102
Phone: (314)751-3486

Credential Type: Initial Certificate. **Duration of License:** Five years. **Authorization:** Authorizes holding the position at the elementary or secondary level. **Requirements:** Valid Missouri teaching certificate at the appropriate level. Two years of teaching experience. Completion of a course in psychology and education of the exceptional child. Master's degree. Recommendation of college or university where degree was completed. Graduate credit must include two semester hours in each of the following: foundations of educational administration; elementary administration; elementary curriculum; and school supervision. Directed field experiences in administration at appropriate level of at least two semester hours Knowledge and/or competency in each of the following areas: instructional management systems; teaching learning processes; instruction in communication skills; educational measurements; evaluation of teachers; administration and coordination of special programs and services; school law; school business administration and coordination of school activities programs; philosophy of vocational education (secondary only). Certificate may be renewed one time by earning 15 semester hours toward a two year graduate program for principals approved by the Missouri Dept. of Elementary and Secondary Education.

Credential Type: Advanced Elementary and Secondary Principal Certificate. **Duration of License:** 10 years. **Requirements:** Hold or be eligible for Initial Certificate for principals at the elementary or secondary level. Complete a two year graduate program for principals approved by the Missouri Dept. of Elementary and Secondary Education. Reccommendation from the college or university where the graduate work was completed.

May be renewed by persons who have five years experience in school administration during the previous 10 years and complete a Professional Development Agreement. This agreement requires a least three of the following: annual membership in the state and national school administrator's professional organizations; participation in at least five annual state or national meetings of professional education organizations; at least 60 clock hours of participation in workshops and/or seminars on educational administration, instructional leadership, or curriculum development; participation in at least two accreditation-evaluations of schools by NCA, NCATE, or Dept. of Elementary and Secondary Education evaluation teams; completion of six semester hours of appropriate college course work.

Credential Type: Middle School Principal Endorsement. **Requirements:** Meet the requirements for and elementary or secondary principal's initial or advanced certificate. Complete a six semester hr. graduate program in courses focusing on middle school philosophy, organization, and curriculum plus the intellectual, physiological, emotional, and social development of the transcendent child (10-14 yr. old).

2483

School Superintendent
Teacher Certification
Dept. of Elementary and Secondary Education
Box 480
Jefferson City, MO 65102
Phone: (314)751-3486

Credential Type: Initial Certificate. **Duration of License:** 10 years. **Requirements:** Valid Missouri teaching certificate. Four years of teaching, supervisory, or administrative experience, or any combination thereof. Completion of a course in psychology and education of the exceptional child. Approved two year graduate program for preparation of the superintendent which must include knowledge and/or competency in each of the following areas: foundation of educational administration; city school administration; school supervision; curriculum construction; research and evaluation; school finance; school law; school staff personnel administration; school/community relations; school plant design and operation. Recommendation for certification from the designated official of the college or university.

To renew the certificate applicant must have five years of experience during the previous 10 years and complete a Professional Development Agreement which would include at least one of the following: a minimum of six semester hours of graduate credit appropriate for the superintendency; three AASA-NASE Leadership Training Seminars which are in depth sessions and are usually four or five days in length; four semester hours of graduate credit and one AASA-NASE Leadership Training Institute course; or a planned professional development program equivalent to six semester hours of approved graduate credit.

Montana

2484

Principal
Teacher Certification
Office of Public Instruction
State Capitol
Helena, MT 59620
Phone: (406)444-3150

Credential Type: Class 3 Administrative Certificate—Principal Endorsement. **Duration of License:** Five years. **Requirements:** Master's degree in school administration or the equivalent. Eligible for Class 1 or two teaching certificate. Verification of a minimum of three years of successful experience as an appropriately certified and assigned teacher at the proper level. 14 graduate semester hours credit in education or the equivalent to include: general school administration; specific area administration (elementary or secondary); administration of guidance services; supervision of instruction/evaluation at the appropriate level; school curriculum at the appropriate level; school finance (budgeting); and school law. Renewable upon verification of one year of successful experience in the area of endorsement during the valid term of the certificate. Beginning with those certificates expiring in 1992, six quarter credits will also be required for renewal.

Credential Type: Class 5 Provisional Administrative Certificate—Principal Endorsement. **Duration of License:** Three years. **Requirements:** Must have a plan of professional intent leading to Class 3 Administrative certification. May be issued to applicants who may not meet course requirements for other general areas but who, within the last five years, have been fully eligible for administrative certification endorsed in one of the following areas: elementary principal, secondary principal, superintendent, or general superintendent. May also be issued to an applicant from another state with valid certification, as long as the certification was based on not less than a master's degree program in school administration. Must be eligible for Class 1, 2, or five teaching certificate at the appropriate level. Within the term of the Class 5 certificate the applicant must complete an approved master's degree in school administration to include the following state specified courses: general school administration; specific area administration (elementary or secondary); administration of guidance services; supervision of instruction/evaluation at the appropriate level; school curriculum at the appropriate level; school finance (budgeting); and school law. Nonrenewable.

2485

School Superintendent
Teacher Certification
Office of Public Instruction
State Capitol
Helena, MT 59620
Phone: (406)444-3150

Credential Type: Class 3 Administrative Certificate. **Duration of License:** Five years. **Requirements:** Master's degree in school administration or the equivalent. Eligible for Class 1 or two teaching certificate. Full eligibility for a principal endorse-

School Superintendent, continued

ment in Montana. Eight graduate credits beyond the master's degree to include school management/facilities, school negotiation, school finance (economics of education), and public relations. Eight graduate credits in elementary education to include elementary administration and elementary curriculum if endorsed at the secondary level or secondary administration and secondary curriculum if endorsed at the elementary level. Three years of teaching experience from the date fully qualified as a principal or one year of administrative experience as an appropriately certified school administrator or one year of a supervised internship as a superintendent. Renewable upon verification of one year of successful experience in the area of endorsement during the valid term of the certificate. Beginning with those certificates expiring in 1992, six quarter credits will also be required for renewal.

Credential Type: Class 5 Administrative Certificate. **Duration of License:** Three years. **Requirements:** Must have a plan of professional intent leading to Class 3 Administrative certification. May be issued to applicants who may not meet course requirements for other general areas but who, within the last five years, have been fully eligible for administrative certification endorsed in one of the following areas: elementary principal, secondary principal, superintendent, or general superintendent. Must be eligible for Class 1, 2, or five teaching certificate. Three years of teaching experience from the date fully qualified as a principal or one year of administrative experience as an appropriately certified school administrator or one year of a supervised administrative internship. Master's degree in school administration or the equivalent to include completed school administration program for the principal. Eight graduate credits in elementary education to include elementary administration and elementary curriculum if endorsed at the secondary level or secondary administration and secondary curriculum if endorsed at the elementary level. Plan of intent must include eight graduate credits beyond the master's degree to include school management/facilities, school negotiation, school finance (economics of education), and public relations. Nonrenewable.

Nebraska

2486

School Administrator or Supervisor
Teacher Certification
State Dept. of Education
301 Centennial Mall South
Box 94987
Lincoln, NE 68509-4987
Phone: (402)471-2496

Credential Type: Standard Administrative and Supervisory Certificate. **Requirements:** Standard Teaching Certificate or equivalent. Proof of completion of an approved graduate program of preparation for school administrators and/or supervisors from preparing college or university. Master's degree in administration and/or supervision or 36 hours of graduate credit which is part of a six year program in administration and/or supervision. Course work must have an area of specialization that the applicant is prepared to administer (not valid for Superintendent of Schools). Six semester hours of course work must have been completed in the past three years prior to application.

Credential Type: Professional Administrative and Supervisory Certificate. **Requirements:** Standard Teaching Certificate or Equivalent. Proof of completion of an approved six-year program for preparation in administration and supervision. Must possess a six-year diploma or certificate.

Nevada

2487

School Administrator
Nevada Dept. of Education
State Mail Room
1850 E. Sahara, Ste. 200
Las Vegas, NV 89158
Phone: (702)386-5401

Credential Type: Limited School Administrator Endorsement. **Duration of License:** Five years. **Authorization:** Authorizes work in the following positions: superintendent, associate superintendent, assist. superintendent, principal, vice principal, supervisor, administrative assist., and program administrator. **Requirements:** Master's degree. Valid elementary, or secondary license. Three years of teaching experience at the K-12 level. Completion of 18 semester hours of graduate courses in school administration to include: administration and organization of schools; supervision of instruction; evaluation and development of personnel; school finance; and school law. Not renewable. Holder must complete requirements for Professional School Administrator during term of certificate.

Credential Type: Professional School Administrator Endorsement. **Requirements:** Hold or be eligible for Limited School Administrator Endorsement. Complete an additional nine semester hours of graduate courses in school administration.

2488

School Program Administrator
Nevada Dept. of Education
State Mail Room
1850 E. Sahara, Ste. 200
Las Vegas, NV 89158
Phone: (702)386-5401

Credential Type: Limited Program Administrator Endorsement. **Duration of License:** Five years. **Authorization:** Authorizes work in one or more of the following areas, dependent on specialized training: nursing; school psychology; speech therapy; physical therapy; and occupational therapy. **Requirements:** Master's degree. Valid special license in the program for which an endorsement is sought. Three years of experience as a licensed employee at the K-12 level. Completion of 18 semester hours of graduate courses in school administration to include: administration and organization of schools; supervision of instruction; evaluation and development of personnel; school finance; and school law. Not renewable. Holder must complete requirements for Professional Program Administrator during term of certificate.

Credential Type: Professional Program Administrator Endorsement. **Requirements:** Hold or be eligible for Limited Program Administrator Endorsement. Complete an additional nine semester hours of graduate courses considered to be part of an educational administrative degree program.

New Hampshire

2489

School Administrator
Bureau of Teacher Education and Professional Standards
State Dept. of Education
101 Pleasant St.
Concord, NH 03301
Phone: (603)271-2407

Credential Type: Administrator Endorsement. **Duration of License:** Three years. **Requirements:** Hold or be eligible for a Beginning Educator Certificate. (Business administrators are not required to hold educator's certificate.) Complete an approved program at a recognized college or university in administration. Business Administrator candidates, who have not completed an approved program may qualify with recommendation under the Critical Staffing Clause and demonstrated equivalent competence through experience in comparable business management positions.

Credential Type: Experienced Administrator Endorsement. **Duration of License:** Three years. **Requirements:** Must have recommendation of the Superintendent of Schools during the life of the Beginning Administrator Endorsement. Must have met all requirements for previous level of certification or successfully completed an approved graduate program that extends clinical experience to a full year under supervision.

New Jersey

2490

Director of Student Personnel Services
Office of Teacher Certification and Academic Credentials
CN 503
Trenton, NJ 08625-0503
Phone: (609)292-2079

Credential Type: Director of Student Personnel Services Endorsement. **Authorization:** Authorizes candidate to hold the following positions: director, administrator, or supervisor of guidance and personnel services of a school system, including the supervision of the various special services in a given school district. **Requirements:** Bachelor's degree from an accredited institution. Regular New Jersey student personnel services (counseling) endorsement or its equivalent. Three years of successful experience in school student personnel work. Passing score in specified areas of the NTE written examination or 40 post-baccalaureate semester hours to include courses in the following: 18 hours in guidance including principles of guidance, individual analysis, organization and administration of guidance programs, job analysis, research, seminar in guidance, counseling, group methods in guidance, student personnel work, occupational and educational information, placement, vocational education and a practicum; 10 hours of psychology (exclusive of introductory courses) including psychology of physical and mental growth, child and adolescent psychology, tests and measurements, psychology of parent and child relationships, mental hygiene, statistics, mental abnormalities and defects; 12 hours consisting of one course in each sociology, administration and curriculum, and supervision of instruction. **Examination:** National Teachers Examination (if applicant has not met the college study requirements).

2491

School Administrator
Office of Teacher Certification and Academic Credentials
CN 503
Trenton, NJ 08625-0503
Phone: (609)292-2079

Credential Type: Administration Endorsement. **Requirements:** Regular New Jersey instructional certificate or equivalent. Three years of successful teaching experience. Master's degree. Complete an approved program in administration or complete 30 graduate semester hours of credit of study in the following: school administration; educational supervision; curriculum development; the learner and the learning process (optional); academic disciplines related to school administration (optional).The college study requirement may be waived for an out-of-state candidate who has completed a NCATE program, a candidate holding a doctor's degree in educational administration, or a candidate who has completed a two year graduate program for the preparation of school administrators leading to the specialist in education certificate or similar diploma or degree.

Must have three years of educational administrative or supervisory experience, under a New Jersey administrative or supervisory endorsement or its equivalent, when spending at least half-time in administrative or supervisory duties. One year of an approved internship may be submitted to fulfill this requirement. One year of the experience requirement may be waived to holders of a doctor's degree in educational administration.

2492

School Principal
Office of Teacher Certification and Academic Credentials
CN 503
Trenton, NJ 08625-0503
Phone: (609)292-2079

Credential Type: Principal Endorsement. **Requirements:** Master's degree in administration, leadership, or management. Written examination. Evaluation at an assessment center. One or two years of employment under a provisional certificate in a program of continued training and supervision. **Examination:** New Jersey written examination.

2493

School Supervisor
Office of Teacher Certification and Academic Credentials
CN 503
Trenton, NJ 08625-0503
Phone: (609)292-2079

Credential Type: Supervision Endorsement. **Requirements:** Regular New Jersey instructional certificate or equivalent. Three years of successful teaching experience. Master's degree. Complete an approved program in supervision or complete 12 graduate semester hours of credit which include the following: one course in general principles of educational supervision for K-12; one course in general principles of curriculum development K-12; and additional study in supervision and/or curriculum development in particular grade levels or in special subject fields. Candidates completing their preparation in out-of-state universities will qualify if their program was approved by the NCATE.

New Mexico

2494

School Administrator K-12
Director, Professional Licensing Unit
Education Bldg.
300 Don Gaspar
Santa Fe, NM 87503
Phone: (505)827-6587

Credential Type: Initial License—Level 3-B. **Requirements:** Valid Level two or higher New Mexico teaching license. Bachelor's degree and master's degree from an accredited institution. For students first entering a college or university in Fall 1986 and thereafter, an apprenticeship is required. The apprenticeship may be a 180 clock hr. program completed through an institution with an approved educational administration program or may be completed under the supervision of a local school superintendent or a private school official. Must also have 18 semester hours of graduate credit in an approved educational administration program which incorporates the State Board's approved functional areas and related competencies in educational administration.

New York

2495

School Administrator
State Education Dept.
Office of Teaching
Cultural Education Center, Rm. 5A11
Albany, NY 12230
Phone: (518)474-6440

Credential Type: Certificate. **Requirements:** Master's Degree including course study in public school administration. U.S. citizenship. **Examination:** Written. **Fees:** $50 application fee. **Governing Statute:** Sections 3001, 3003, 3004, and 3006 of the New York State Education Law.

2496

School Administrator and/or Supervisor K-12
Administrator of Teacher Certification Policy
Univ. of the State of New York
State Education Dept.
Cultural Center, Rm. 5-A-11
Albany, NY 12230
Phone: (518)474-6440

Credential Type: Provisional School Administration and/or Supervision Certificate. **Duration of License:** Five years. **Requirements:** Master's degree. 30 semester hours of graduate study which includes 18 semester hours in the field of administration and supervision. Approved administrative-supervisory internship, or one year of full-time experience in a school administrative or supervisory position. Note: The city of Buffalo, New York has certification standards that are exclusive of New York State.

Credential Type: Permanent School Administration and/or Supervision Certificate. **Duration of License:** Permanent. **Requirements:** Hold a Provisional Certificate in administration and supervision. Two years in an administrative/supervisory position. Note: The city of Buffalo, New York has certification standards that are exclusive of New York State.

2497

School District Administrator
Administrator of Teacher Certification Policy
Univ. of the State of New York
State Education Dept.
Cultural Center, Rm. 5-A-11
Albany, NY 12230
Phone: (518)474-6440

Credential Type: Permanent School District Administration Certificate. **Duration of License:** Permanent. **Requirements:** Master's degree. Complete a graduate program registered or approved by the State Education Dept. for the preparation of school district administrator or school administrator and supervisor or complete a 60 semester hr. graduate study program which includes 24 semester hours in the field of administration and supervision. Complete approved administrative-supervisory internship or one year of full-time experience in a school administrative or supervisory position. Three years of teaching and/or administrative and/or supervisory and/or pupil personnel experience in elementary or secondary schools. Note: The city of Buffalo, New York has certification standards that are exclusive of New York State.

North Carolina

2498

School Principal K-12
Certification Section
State Dept. of Public Instruction
Raleigh, NC 27603
Phone: (919)733-4125

Credential Type: Administrator I Certificate. **Duration of License:** Five years. **Requirements:** Three years of satisfactory teaching experience or equivalent. Master's degree. Complete an approved program in administration. Pass NTE examination. Institutional recommendation. Must have 10 semester hours of college credit completed in the five-year period immediately preceding the date of application or an active certificate from a reciprocating state. **Examination:** National Teacher Examination. **Fees:** $30 application fee. $30 renewal fee.

Credential Type: Administrator II Certificate. **Duration of License:** Five years. **Requirements:** Three years of satisfactory teaching experience or equivalent. Sixth-year certificate (degree) from an accredited institution including the completion of an approved program in administration. Pass NTE examination. Institutional recommendation. Must have 10 semester hours of college credit completed in the five-year period immediately preceding the date of application. **Examination:** National Teacher Examination. **Fees:** $30 application fee. $30 renewal fee.

Credential Type: Administrator III Certificate. **Duration of License:** Five years. **Requirements:** Three years of satisfactory teaching experience or equivalent. Doctorate degree in an approved program of study. Pass NTE examination. Institutional recommendation. Must have 10 semester hours of college credit completed in the five-year period immediately preceding the date of application. **Examination:** National Teacher Examination. **Fees:** $30 application fee. $30 renewal fee.

2499

School Superintendent
Certification Section
State Dept. of Public Instruction
Raleigh, NC 27603
Phone: (919)733-4125

Credential Type: Administrator II Certificate. **Duration of License:** Five years. **Requirements:** Three years of satisfactory teaching experience or equivalent. Sixth-year certificate (degree) from an accredited institution including the completion of an approved program in administration. Pass NTE examination. Institutional recommendation. Must have 10 semester hours of college credit completed in the five-year period immediately preceding the date of application. **Examination:** National Teacher Examination. **Fees:** $30 application fee. $30 renewal fee.

Credential Type: Administrator III Certificate. **Duration of License:** Five years. **Requirements:** Three years of satisfactory teaching experience or equivalent. Doctorate degree in an approved program of study. Pass NTE examination. Institutional recommendation. Must have 10 semester hours of college credit completed in the five-year period immediately preceding the date of application. **Examination:** National Teacher Examination. **Fees:** $30 application fee. $30 renewal fee.

2500

School Supervisor and/or Program Coordinator K-12
Certification Section
State Dept. of Public Instruction
Raleigh, NC 27603
Phone: (919)733-4125

Credential Type: Supervisor and/or Program Coordinator Certificate. **Duration of License:** Five years. **Requirements:** Hold a Class "A" Teacher's certificate. Three years of satisfactory teaching experience.

Master's or more advanced degree, including competencies in administration, supervision, curriculum methods and educational research with major preparation in an area of administrative specialization. Pass NTE examination. Institutional recommendation. **Examination:** National Teacher Examination. **Fees:** $30 application fee. $30 renewal fee.

North Dakota

2501

Elementary School Principal
Director of Certification
State Dept. of Public Instruction
Bismarck, ND 58505
Phone: (701)224-2264

Credential Type: EP01 Principal Certificate. **Duration of License:** Five years. **Authorization:** Authorizes work as a principal in elementary schools with enrollment of 301 students or more. **Requirements:** Valid North Dakota Educator's Professional Certificate in elementary education. Master's degree with at least 20 semester hours of graduate work in elementary education that includes courses in elementary education, elementary supervision, elementary curriculum, as well as work in content fields. Three years of successful elementary teaching and/or elementary administrative experience, or a combination of both. Renewal is possible with four semester hours of teacher training in administration, supervision, or subject matter fields and satisfactory performance.

Credential Type: EPO2 Principal Certificate. **Duration of License:** Five years. **Authorization:** Authorizes work as a principal in elementary schools with enrollment of 151-300 students. **Requirements:** Valid North Dakota Educator's Professional Certificate in elementary education. Master's degree with at least 16 semester hours of graduate work in elementary education that includes courses in elementary education, elementary supervision, elementary curriculum, as well as work in content fields. Three years of successful elementary teaching and/or elementary administrative experience, or a combination of both. Renewal is possible with four semester hours of teacher training in administration, supervision, or subject matter fields and satisfactory performance.

Credential Type: EPO3 Principal Certificate. **Duration of License:** Five years. **Authorization:** Authorizes work as a principal in elementary schools with enrollment of 25-150 students. **Requirements:** Valid North Dakota Educator's Professional Certificate in elementary education. Master's degree with at least eight semester hours of graduate work in elementary education that includes courses in elementary education, elementary supervision, elementary curriculum, as well as work in content fields. Three years of successful elementary teaching and/or elementary administrative experience, or a combination of both. Renewal is possible with four semester hours of teacher training in administration, supervision, or subject matter fields and satisfactory performance.

2502

School Superintendent
Director of Certification
State Dept. of Public Instruction
Bismarck, ND 58505
Phone: (701)224-2264

Credential Type: Superintendent Certificate. **Duration of License:** Entrance one year, renewable for five years. **Requirements:** Master's degree in school administration. North Dakota Educator's Professional Certificate. 20 semester hours of credit in both elementary and secondary school administration. Four years experience, of which two years must be in an administrative position in an accredited system. Renewable after four semester hours of additional work or two semester hours of additional work plus attendance at state, regional, or national conferences, and successful recommendation by supervisor.

2503

Secondary School Principal
Director of Certification
State Dept. of Public Instruction
Bismarck, ND 58505
Phone: (701)224-2264

Credential Type: SPO1 Principal Certificate. **Duration of License:** Entrance two years, renewable for five years. **Authorization:** Authorizes work as a principal in secondary schools with enrollment of 351 or more students. **Requirements:** Valid North Dakota Educator's Professional Certificate in secondary education. Master's degree with a major or equivalent in secondary school administration. 20 semester hr. major to include general administration, school law, supervision, and curriculum at secondary school level. Four years of successful teaching and/or administrative experience at the secondary school level. Renewable by attending six workshops and/or conferences plus two semester hours of course work in administration or four semester hours of administrative course work.

Credential Type: SPO2 Principal Certificate. **Duration of License:** Entrance two years, renewable for five years. **Requirements:** Authorizes work as a principal in secondary schools with enrollment of 81-350 students. **Reciprocity:** Valid North Dakota Educator's Professional Certificate in secondary education. 16 semester hours of graduate courses in secondary school administration to include general administration, school law, supervision, and curriculum at secondary school level. Three years of successful teaching and/or administrative experience at the secondary school level. Renewable by attending six workshops and/or conferences plus two semester hours of course work in administration or four semester hours of administrative course work.

Credential Type: SPO3 Principal Certificate. **Duration of License:** Entrance two years, renewable for five years. **Requirements:** Authorizes work as a principal in secondary schools with enrollments of up to 80 students. **Reciprocity:** Valid North Dakota Educator's Professional Certificate in secondary education. Eight semester hours of graduate courses in secondary school administration to include general administration, school law, supervision, and curriculum at secondary school level. Two years of successful teaching and/or administrative experience at the secondary school level. Renewable by attending six workshops and/or conferences plus two semester hours of course work in administration or four semester hours of administrative course work.

Ohio

2504

School Administrator
Teacher Education and Certification
State Dept. of Education
65 S. Front St., Rm. 1012
Columbus, OH 43266-0308
Phone: (614)466-3593

Credential Type: Provisional Superintendent Certificate. **Requirements:** Master's degree. Good moral character. Successful completion of an approved 60 semester hr. program in administration with course work in the following: administration; curriculum, instructional leadership, and foundations. Pass an examination prescribed by the State Board of Education. Institutional recommendation. Three years of satisfactory experience in an administrative or supervisory position under a standard certificate. **Examination:** Examination prescribed by the State Board of Education.

School Administrator, continued

Credential Type: Provisional Assistant Superintendent Certificate. **Requirements:** Master's degree. Good moral character. Successful completion of an approved 45 semester hr. program in administration with course work in the following: administration; curriculum, instructional leadership, and foundations. Pass an examination prescribed by the State Board of Education. Institutional recommendation. Three years of satisfactory experience in an administrative or supervisory position under a standard certificate. **Examination:** Examination prescribed by the State Board of Education.

Credential Type: Educational Administrative Specialist Certificate. **Requirements:** Master's degree. Good moral character. Successful completion of an approved 45 semester hr. program in administration with course work in the following: administration; curriculum, instructional leadership, and foundations. Pass an examination prescribed by the State Board of Education. Institutional recommendation. Three years of satisfactory experience in an administrative or supervisory position under a standard certificate. Specialist certificates may be issued in any of the following areas with 15 semester hours of additional coursework in each area: business management; education of exceptional pupils; educational research; educational staff personnel administration; instructional services; pupil personnel administration; schoolcommunity relations; and/or vocational directorship.

2505

School Principal
Teacher Education and Certification
State Dept. of Education
65 S. Front St., Rm. 1012
Columbus, OH 43266-0308
Phone: (614)466-3593

Credential Type: Provisional Principal Certificate. **Authorization:** Certificate will be endorsed and allow service at the elementary, middle grade, or high school level dependent on level at which teaching experience was completed. **Requirements:** Master's degree. Good moral character. Complete an approved program, of at least 45 semester hours, that includes courses in administration, curriculum and instructional leadership, and foundations. Pass an examination prescribed by the State Board of Education. Institutional recommendation. Three years of satisfactory teaching experience in which at least two years shall have been in the appropriate grades under a standard teaching certificate. **Examination:** Examination prescribed by the State Board of Education.

Oklahoma

2506

School Service Personnel K-12
Teacher Education and Certification
State Dept. of Education
2500 N. Lincoln Blvd., Rm. 211
Oklahoma City, OK 73105
Phone: (405)521-3337

Credential Type: Standard Certificate in a School Personnel Field—Graduate. **Duration of License:** Five years. **Authorization:** Endorsement will be given to persons seeking positions in the following fields: Counselor; Library Media Specialist; Elementary School Principal; Secondary School Principal; School Superintendent; School Psychometrist; School Psychologist; SpeechLanguage Pathologist; or Reading Specialist. **Requirements:** Complete an approved certificate program at an accredited college or university which includes a minimum of the following: a baccalaureate degree; 50 semester hours in general education; 30 semester hours in professional education; and 40 semester hours in course work pertaining to the area of specialization. Pass the state certified test(s) in specialization competencies. Complete State Board graduate level course requirements.

Oregon

2507

School Administrator
Teacher Standards and Practices
  Commission
630 Center St. NE, Ste. 200
Salem, OR 97310-0320
Phone: (503)378-3586

Credential Type: Basic Administrative Certificate. **Duration of License:** Two years. **Requirements:** Master's degree. Recommendation from an approved teacher education institution or current out-of-state administrative certificate. Passing scores on CBEST. Out-of-state prepared applicants may submit their passing scores on the Core Battery of the National Teacher Examination, in lieu of the CBEST. 12 quarter hours of graduate credit in school administration, including a supervised practicum or internship of five quarter hours completed subsequent to master's degree. One year of successful administrative experience within the three-year period immediately preceding application or nine quarter hours of preparation in educational administration within the past three years. **Examination:** California Basic Educational Skills Test.

Credential Type: Standard Administrative Certificate. **Duration of License:** Five years. **Requirements:** Three years of successful administration experience in Oregon schools on a Basic Administrative Certificate. Recommendation of approved college or university where applicant completed graduate program for standard school administrator. 18 quarter hours of graduate credit in school administration, in addition to those required for the basic endorsement, completed subsequent to master's degree.

2508

School Superintendent
Teacher Standards and Practices
  Commission
630 Center St. NE, Ste. 200
Salem, OR 97310-0320
Phone: (503)378-3586

Credential Type: Basic Superintendent Endorsement. **Duration of License:** Two years. **Requirements:** Master's degree. Recommendation from an approved teacher education institution or current out-of-state administrative certificate. Passing scores on CBEST. Out-of-state prepared applicants may submit their passing scores on the Core Battery of the National Teacher Examination, in lieu of the CBEST. 18 quarter hours of graduate credit in school administration, including a supervised practicum or internship of six quarter hours and completed subsequent to master's degree. One year of successful administrative experience within the three-year period immediately preceding application or nine quarter hours of preparation in educational administration within the past three years. **Examination:** California Basic Educational Skills Test.

Credential Type: Standard Superintendent Endorsement. **Duration of License:** Five years. **Requirements:** Three years of successful administration experience in Oregon schools on a Basic Administrative Certificate. Recommendation of approved college or university where applicant completed graduate program for standard school administrator. 24 quarter hours of graduate credit in school administration, in addition to those required for the basic endorsement, completed subsequent to master's degree.

Education Administrators

2509

School Supervisor
Teacher Standards and Practices Commission
630 Center St. NE, Ste. 200
Salem, OR 97310-0320
Phone: (503)378-3586

Credential Type: Basic Personnel Service Certificate—Supervisor Endorsement. **Duration of License:** Three years. **Requirements:** Recommendation for certification by an approved teacher education institution. Evidence of recent public school personnel service experience. Passing scores on the CBEST. Out-of-state prepared applicants may submit their passing scores on the Core Battery of the National Teacher Examination, in lieu of the CBEST. Completion of an approved personnel service preparation program. Holder of, or eligible for, an Oregon standard subject matter, special education, or personnel service endorsement. Three years of successful teaching experience in the public schools. 12 quarter hours of graduate credit in an approved program in school supervision, including a practicum or supervised internship of five quarter hours **Examination:** California Basic Education Skills Test.

Credential Type: Standard Personnel Service Certificate—Supervisor Endorsement. **Duration of License:** Five years. **Requirements:** Two years of successful supervisory experience in Oregon schools while holding a basic supervisor endorsement. Complete 18 quarter hours of graduate credit in school supervision beyond the basic supervisor endorsement. A master's degree program in guidance and counseling held by an out-of-state applicant may be accepted in lieu of the above requirements.

Pennsylvania

2510

School Administrator
Bureau of Certification
Dept. of Education
333 Market St.
Harrisburg, PA 17126-0333
Phone: (717)787-2967

Credential Type: Administrative I—Provisional. **Duration of License:** Three years. **Authorization:** Authorizes employment in the positions of Principal or Vocational School Director. **Requirements:** Five years of professional school experience, with three years at the level for which the administrative certificate is sought. Completion of continuing professional development plan, determined by employing school entity and reviewed every five years. Recommendation of preparing institution.

All new applicants must produce a background clearance as required in Act 34. A Pennsylvania State Police background check is required for Pennsylvania residents and an F.B.I. background check is required for out-of-state residents. Applicants may not work in Pennsylvania public schools without this clearance.

Credential Type: Administrative II—Permanent. **Duration of License:** Permanent. **Authorization:** Authorizes employment in the positions of Principal or Vocational School Director. **Requirements:** Three years of satisfactory service on the Pennsylvania Administrative I Certificate. Completion of continuing professional development plan, determined by employing school entity and reviewed every five years.

2511

School Intermediate Unit Executive Director
Bureau of Certification
Dept. of Education
333 Market St.
Harrisburg, PA 17126-0333
Phone: (717)787-2967

Credential Type: Administrative Letters of Eligibility—I.U. Executive Director Endorsement. **Requirements:** Complete Pennsylvania approved graduate level program of educational administrative study equal to two full academic years of study or have been prepared in an approved out-of-state program. Six years of professional experience which includes three years of supervisory experience. Complete six credit hours of course work, every five years of service, as determined by the Bureau of Basic Education.

2512

School Superintendent/Assistant Superintendent
Bureau of Certification
Dept. of Education
333 Market St.
Harrisburg, PA 17126-0333
Phone: (717)787-2967

Credential Type: Administrative Letters of Eligibility—Superintendent Endorsement. **Requirements:** Complete Pennsylvania approved graduate level program of educational administrative study equal to two full academic years of study or have been prepared in an approved out-of-state program. Six years of professional, certificated school service which includes three years of supervisory or administrative experience. Recommendation of preparing institution. Complete six credit hours of course work, every five years of service, as determined by the Bureau of Basic Education.

2513

School Supervisor
Bureau of Certification
Dept. of Education
333 Market St.
Harrisburg, PA 17126-0333
Phone: (717)787-2967

Credential Type: Supervisory I—Provisional. **Duration of License:** Six years. **Authorization:** Authorizes employment in Curriculum and Instruction or Pupil Personnel Services. **Requirements:** Five years of satisfactory professional experience in the area in which certification is sought. Completion of graduate program in the endorsement area. Recommendation of preparing institution.

All new applicants must produce a background clearance as required in Act 34. A Pennsylvania State Police background check is required for Pennsylvania residents and an F.B.I. background check is required for out-of-state residents. Applicants may not work in Pennsylvania public schools without this clearance.

Credential Type: Supervisory II—Permanent. **Duration of License:** Permanent. **Authorization:** Authorizes employment in Curriculum and Instruction or Pupil Personnel Services. **Requirements:** Three years of satisfactory service on the Pennsylvania Supervisory I Certificate.

2514

Supervisor of Vocational Education
Bureau of Certification
Dept. of Education
333 Market St.
Harrisburg, PA 17126-0333
Phone: (717)787-2967

Credential Type: Supervisor of Comprehensive Vocational Education I Certificate—Provisional. **Requirements:** Three years of satisfactory service in a vocational field. Complete an approved preparation/certification program for supervision in all fields of vocational education. Recommendation of the preparing institution.

All new applicants must produce a background clearance as required in Act 34. A Pennsylvania State Police background check is required for Pennsylvania residents and an F.B.I. background check is required for out-of-state residents. Appli-

Supervisor of Vocational Education, continued

cants may not work in Pennsylvania public schools without this clearance.

Credential Type: Supervisor of Comprehensive Vocational Education II Certificate—Permanent. **Duration of License:** Permanent. **Requirements:** Three years of satisfactory service on a Supervisor of Vocational Education I Certificate.

Rhode Island

2515

Elementary School Principal
Office of Teacher Certification
State Dept. of Education
22 Hayes St.
Providence, RI 02908
Phone: (401)277-2675

Credential Type: Provisional Elementary School Principal Certificate. **Duration of License:** Three years. **Requirements:** Master's degree from an approved institution. Hold or be eligible for a Rhode Island elementary school teacher's certificate. Three years of teaching experience at the elementary school level. Complete an approved program for the preparation of elementary school principals or 24 semester hours of graduate level course work which includes work in the following areas: school/community relations; elementary curriculum development; organization/administration of the elementary school; supervision of instruction; supervision and evaluation of professional staff; educational research; program evaluation; fiscal planning; and school law. Nonrenewable.

Credential Type: Professional Elementary School Principal Certificate. **Duration of License:** Five years. **Requirements:** Complete six graduate credits in educational administration, curriculum, or supervision while under the Provisional Elementary School Principal Certificate. Three years of documented service as an elementary school principal in Rhode Island. May be renewed upon completion of nine credits and verification of continued service as an elementary school principal. Six of the required nine credits must be on the graduate level and three of the graduate credits must be in educational administration and related areas. Of the nine required credits, three may be in approved,in-service work and the rest must be done at the college level.

Credential Type: Life Professional Elementary School Principal Certificate. **Duration of License:** Permanent. **Requirements:** Doctorate degree or certificate of advanced study from an approved institution in educational administration, supervision, and curriculum or 30 semester hours of graduate credit beyond a master's degree which includes 21 semester hours in educational administration, supervision, and curriculum. Must have six years of experience as an elementary principal, of which three must be in Rhode Island.

2516

School Superintendent
Office of Teacher Certification
State Dept. of Education
22 Hayes St.
Providence, RI 02908
Phone: (401)277-2675

Credential Type: Provisional School Superintendent Certificate. **Duration of License:** Three years. **Requirements:** Doctorate, certificate of advanced graduate study, or master's degree. Complete 36 semester hours of graduate credit including work in the following areas: school/community relations; curriculum construction; school administration; supervision of instruction; supervision and evaluation of professional staff; educational research; program evaluation; school plant planning; and school finance. Hold or be eligible for a Rhode Island teaching certificate. Eight years of educational experience that includes both teaching and administration. Nonrenewable.

Credential Type: Professional Superintendent Certificate. **Duration of License:** Five years. **Requirements:** Complete six graduate credits in educational administration while on the provisional certificate. Three years of service as a superintendent of schools in Rhode Island.

Credential Type: Life Professional Superintendent Certificate. **Duration of License:** Permanent. **Requirements:** Doctorate degree or certificate of advanced study from an approved institution in educational administration, supervision, and curriculum or 30 semester hours of graduate credit beyond a master's degree which includes 21 semester hours in educational administration, supervision, and curriculum. Must have six years of experience as a superintendent of schools, of which three must be in Rhode Island.

2517

Secondary School Principal
Office of Teacher Certification
State Dept. of Education
22 Hayes St.
Providence, RI 02908
Phone: (401)277-2675

Credential Type: Provisional Secondary School Principal Certificate. **Duration of License:** Three years. **Requirements:** Master's degree from an approved institution. Hold or be eligible for a Rhode Island secondary school teacher's certificate. Three years of teaching experience at the secondary school level. Complete an approved program for the preparation of secondary school principals or 24 semester hours of graduate level course work which includes work in the following areas: school/community relations; secondary curriculum development; organization/administration of the secondary school; supervision of instruction; supervision and evaluation of professional staff; educational research; program evaluation; fiscal planning; and school law. Nonrenewable.

Credential Type: Professional Secondary School Principal Certificate. **Duration of License:** Five years. **Requirements:** Complete six graduate credits in educational administration, curriculum, or supervision while under the Provisional Secondary School Principal Certificate. Three years of documented service as a secondary school principal in Rhode Island. May be renewed upon completion of nine credits and verification of continued service as a secondary school principal. Six of the required nine credits must be on the graduate level and three of the graduate credits must be in educational administration and related areas. Of the nine required credits, three may be in approved,in-service work and the rest must be done at the college level.

Credential Type: Life Professional Secondary School Principal Certificate. **Duration of License:** Permanent. **Requirements:** Doctorate degree or certificate of advanced study from an approved institution in educational administration, supervision, and curriculum or 30 semester hours of graduate credit beyond a master's degree which includes 21 semester hours in educational administration, supervision, and curriculum. Must have six years of experience as a secondary principal, of which three must be in Rhode Island.

Education Administrators

South Carolina

2518

Elementary School Principal and Supervisor
Teacher Education and Certification
State Dept. of Education
Rutledge Bldg., Rm. 1015
Columbia, SC 29201
Phone: (803)734-8464

Credential Type: Elementary School Principal and Supervisor Certificate. **Requirements:** Valid professional teaching certificate at the elementary level. A minimum score of 590 on the NTE in Administration and Supervision. Three years of teaching experience, which includes at least one year at the elementary level. Complete an advanced program approved for the training of elementary principals. **Examination:** National Teacher Examination in Administration and Supervision.

2519

School Superintendent
Teacher Education and Certification
State Dept. of Education
Rutledge Bldg., Rm. 1015
Columbia, SC 29201
Phone: (803)734-8464

Credential Type: School Superintendent Certificate. **Requirements:** Valid Principal's or Teacher's Professional Certificate. A minimum score of 590 on the NTE in Administration and Supervision. Seven years of educational experience in teaching and administrating with a minimum of two years as a school administrator. Complete an advanced program approved for the training of school superintendents. **Examination:** National Teacher Examination in Administration and Supervision.

2520

Secondary School Principal and Supervisor
Teacher Education and Certification
State Dept. of Education
Rutledge Bldg., Rm. 1015
Columbia, SC 29201
Phone: (803)734-8464

Credential Type: Secondary School Principal and Supervisor Certificate. **Requirements:** Valid professional teaching certificate at the secondary level. A minimum score of 590 on the NTE in Administration and Supervision. Three years of teaching experience, which includes at least one year at the secondary level. Complete an advanced program approved for the training of secondary principals. **Examination:** National Teacher Examination in Administration and Supervision.

South Dakota

2521

Elementary School Principal
Teacher Education and Certification
State Dept. of Education
700 Governor's Drive
Pierre, SD 57501
Phone: (605)773-3553

Credential Type: Elementary Principal Certificate Endorsement. **Requirements:** Master's degree. Hold an elementary teaching certificate. Two years teaching experience in the elementary school. Complete a college level program for elementary school principals. One year of successful supervised associate instructor experience as a school principal or assistant school principal.

2522

School Superintendent
Teacher Education and Certification
State Dept. of Education
700 Governor's Drive
Pierre, SD 57501
Phone: (605)773-3553

Credential Type: Superintendent Certificate Endorsement. **Requirements:** Master's degree. Hold a valid teaching certificate. Three years of experience in the public schools, two years of which must be classroom teaching. Complete an approved program for superintendents at a college or university. One year of successful supervised associate instructor experience as a school principal or assistant school principal.

Credential Type: Advanced Superintendent Certificate Endorsement. **Requirements:** Hold a Superintendent Certificate Endorsement. Complete an approved six-year specialist degree or doctoral degree program for superintendents at a college or university.

2523

Secondary School Principal
Teacher Education and Certification
State Dept. of Education
700 Governor's Drive
Pierre, SD 57501
Phone: (605)773-3553

Credential Type: Secondary Principal Certificate Endorsement. **Requirements:** Master's degree. Hold an secondary teaching certificate. Two years teaching experience in the secondary school. Complete a college level program for secondary school principals. One year of successful supervised associate instructor experience as a school principal or assistant school principal.

Tennessee

2524

School Administrator or Supervisor
Office of Teaching Licensing
Dept. of Education
Cordell Hull Bldg.
Nashville, TN 37219-5335
Phone: (615)741-1644

Credential Type: Career Level I Certificate. **Duration of License:** 10 years. **Requirements:** Hold a Tennessee Professional Teacher's License endorsed for the grades to be principally supervised. Three years of acceptable classroom teaching in an approved or accredited school at the appropriate grade level. Minimum master's degree with 30 quarter hours of graduate study in Educational Administration and Supervision. Course work must include: organization and administration of public schools; educational supervision; curriculum development; school and community relations; school finance or school business management; school facilities; school law; educational foundations; and research in education or statistics.

Credential Type: Career Level II and III Administrator Certificates. **Duration of License:** 10 years. **Requirements:** Issued upon successful evaluation for these levels on the "Administrator Career Ladder." Renewable.

Utah

School Administrator or Supervisor
Certification and Personnel
   Development Section
State Board of Education
250 East 500 South St.
Salt Lake City, UT 84111
Phone: (801)538-7740

Credential Type: Basic Certificate. **Duration of License:** Four years. **Authorization:** Holder may administer or supervise at elementary, middle, or secondary level. **Requirements:** Hold a Basic or Standard Teaching Certificate. Complete a fifth year of training in a teacher education program including a master's degree or 55 quarter hours of appropriate credit beyond the bachelor's degree. Complete sufficient study/training to acquire the following competencies: administrative/supervisory processes such as discovering, diagnosing, goal setting, planning, decisionmaking, organizing, delegating, communicating, and evaluating; Administration/supervision of education programs, administration of funds and facilities, personnel administration, and continuing self-development; Understanding the crucial and dynamic role of the school; Human relations skills to select and develop school personnel; Knowledge and skills in relation to the following: the learner and the learning process, curriculum development; school organization and operation, supervision of professional and nonprofessional personnel, school board relationships, school law, professional personnel responsibilities, negotiations, school finance, public relations, relevant concepts from social and behavioral sciences, performance and interpretation of research and development, and school-community needs. Complete course work or experience to assure administrative/supervisory competence at level on which the applicant was not previously certified. Complete two years of acceptable professional experience. Recommendation of preparing institute. Note—A principal of a school with less than six teachers may perform the duties of a principal while holding only a Basic or Standard Teaching Certificate.

Credential Type: Standard Certificate. **Duration of License:** Five years. **Requirements:** Complete an approved sixth-year program for the preparation of administrators/supervisors which provides for the acquisition of the professional competencies as follows: administrative/supervisory processes such as discovering, diagnosing, goal setting, planning, decision-making, organizing, delegating, communicating, and evaluating; Administration/supervision of education programs, administration of funds and facilities, personnel administration, and continuing self-development; Understanding the crucial and dynamic role of the school; Human relations skills to select and develop school personnel; Knowledge and skills in relation to the following: the learner and the learning process, curriculum development; school organization and operation, supervision of professional and nonprofessional personnel, school board relationships, school law, professional personnel responsibilities, negotiations, school finance, public relations, relevant concepts from social and behavioral sciences, performance and interpretation of research and development, and school-community needs. Complete course work or experience to assure administrative/supervisory competence at level on which the applicant was not previously certified. Complete three years of acceptable professional experience. Recommendation of preparing institute.

Vermont

School Principal K-12
Teacher Licensure
State Dept. of Education
Montpelier, VT 05602-2703
Phone: (802)828-2445

Credential Type: Level One: Initial License. **Duration of License:** Two years. **Requirements:** Master's degree or equivalent with a concentration in educational administration. At least five years of educational experience consisting of: a minimum of three years teaching experience; a minimum of two years of successful school management experience. Meet competencies as determined by the Standards Board.

Credential Type: Level Two: Professional Administrator's License. **Duration of License:** Seven years. **Requirements:** Two years of experience under a Level One License. Demonstrate the following characteristics: ability to plan instruction; ability to maintain a positive learning environment; ability to conduct learning experiences for individuals as well as groups; knowledge of content area; and interest and motivation in continuing professional development. Renewal requires nine credit hours, or the equivalent of educational development activity, per license endorsement area.

School Superintendent
Teacher Licensure
State Dept. of Education
Montpelier, VT 05602-2703
Phone: (802)828-2445

Credential Type: Level One: Initial License. **Duration of License:** Two years. **Requirements:** Master's degree or equivalent with a concentration in educational administration. At least five years of educational experience consisting of: a minimum of three years teaching experience; a minimum of two years of successful school management experience. Meet competencies as determined by the Standards Board.

Credential Type: Level Two: Professional Administrator's License. **Duration of License:** Seven years. **Requirements:** Two years of experience under a Level One License. Demonstrate the following characteristics: ability to plan instruction; ability to maintain a positive learning environment; ability to conduct learning experiences for individuals as well as groups; knowledge of content area; and interest and motivation in continuing professional development. Renewal requires nine credit hours, or the equivalent of educational development activity, per license endorsement area.

Virginia

School Division Superintendent
Administrative Director
Office of Professional Development
   and Teacher Education
Dept. of Education
PO Box 6-Q
Richmond, VA 23216-2060
Phone: (804)225-2094

Credential Type: Division Superintendent Endorsement. **Requirements:** Master's degree or preparing a doctoral program. 60 semester hours of graduate work to include courses in: history of philosophy of education; supervision and curriculum development; administration; finance; law; personnel administration; schoolcommunity relations; school plant planning; research or statistical methods.

2529

School Principal
Administrative Director
Office of Professional Development
  and Teacher Education
Dept. of Education
PO Box 6-Q
Richmond, VA 23216-2060
Phone: (804)225-2094

Credential Type: Principal Endorsement. **Authorization:** Authorizes employment as a principal at the elementary, middle, or secondary grade level. **Requirements:** Postgraduate Professional Teaching Certificate. Leadership qualities and personal characteristics. Graduate level work in each of the following areas: school administration; supervision and evaluation of instruction and instructional programs; school curriculum; school law; school-community relations; personnel administration; and finance.

2530

School Supervisor
Administrative Director
Office of Professional Development
  and Teacher Education
Dept. of Education
PO Box 6-Q
Richmond, VA 23216-2060
Phone: (804)225-2094

Credential Type: Instructional and Supervisory Personnel Endorsement. **Requirements:** Postgraduate Professional Teaching Certificate. Leadership qualities and personal characteristics. Applicants must have endorsement in the specialized area they are employed to supervise. Three years of recent successful experience as a teacher, administrator, or supervisor. Applicants for district supervisor must have five years of recent experience and formal graduate work in two levels of curriculum. Must have graduate level work in the following areas: supervision and evaluation of instructional programs; school psychology of organizations; curriculum development; school administration; learning theory; education of exceptional individuals; and educational technology.

Washington

2531

School Principal K-12
Superintendent of Public Instruction
Professional Education and
  Certification
Old Capitol Bldg. FG-11
Seattle, WA 98504-3211
Phone: (206)753-6773

Credential Type: Initial Principal Certificate. **Duration of License:** Seven years. **Requirements:** Valid regular teaching certificate (from any state). Complete 30 quarter hours in approved graduate level program for preparation of principals. Meet experience requirement as determined by the Superintendent of Public Instruction.

Credential Type: Continuing Principal Certificate. **Duration of License:** Five years. **Requirements:** Valid regular teaching certificate (from any state). Master's degree. Renewable upon completion of 150 clock hours of full-time administration during the life of the certificate.

2532

School Program Administrator
Superintendent of Public Instruction
Professional Education and
  Certification
Old Capitol Bldg. FG-11
Seattle, WA 98504-3211
Phone: (206)753-6773

Credential Type: Initial Program Administrator Certificate. **Duration of License:** Seven years. **Requirements:** Valid teaching or Educational Staff Associate certificate (from any state). Master's degree. Complete an approved program of preparation for the program administrator.

Credential Type: Continuing Program Administrator Certificate. **Duration of License:** Five years. **Requirements:** Initial Program Administrator Certificate. Complete 15 quarter hours of graduate work subsequent to the master's degree and relevant to field of specialization. Renewable upon completion of 150 clock hours of full-time administration during the life of the certificate.

2533

School Superintendent
Superintendent of Public Instruction
Professional Education and
  Certification
Old Capitol Bldg. FG-11
Seattle, WA 98504-3211
Phone: (206)753-6773

Credential Type: Initial Superintendent Certificate. **Duration of License:** Seven years. **Requirements:** Hold or be eligible for a regular teaching or Educational Staff Associate Certificate. Master's degree. Complete an approved preparation program for the superintendency. Complete 15 quarter hours of graduate study beyond the master's degree in course work related to education.

Credential Type: Continuing Superintendent Certificate. **Duration of License:** Five years. **Requirements:** Initial Superintendent Certificate. Complete a total of 30 quarter hours of graduate study beyond the master's degree in course work related to education. Renewable upon completion of 150 clock hours of full-time administration during the life of the certificate.

West Virginia

2534

School Business Official
Dept. of Education
Office of Educational Personnel
  Development
1900 Washington St. E
Charleston, WV 25305
Phone: (800)982-2378

Credential Type: Certification. **Requirements:** U.S. citizen. 18 years old. Bachelors degree from regionally accredited college. Never convicted of a felony. **Examination:** No. **Fees:** None.

2535

School Principal
Dept. of Education
Office of Educational Personnel
  Development
1900 Washington St. E
Charleston, WV 25305
Phone: (800)982-2378

Credential Type: Certification. **Requirements:** U.S. citizen. 18 years old. Masters and completion of state approved educational program. Principals certification is requested. Never convicted of a felony. **Examination:** Yes. **Fees:** $5 Application. $5

West Virginia

School Principal, continued

Renewal (for conversion and permanent certificate).

School Superintendent
Dept. of Education
Office of Educational Personnel
  Development
1900 Washington St. E
Charleston, WV 25305
Phone: (800)982-2378

Credential Type: Certification. **Requirements:** U.S. citizen. 18 years old. Masters degree and completion of approved program. Five years educational experience in public shcools, including three years of classroom experience. Never convicted of a felony. **Examination:** Yes. **Fees:** $5 Application. $5 Renewal.

Supervisor of Instruction
Dept. of Education
Office of Educational Personnel
  Development
1900 Washington St. E
Charleston, WV 25305
Phone: (800)982-2378

Credential Type: Certification. **Requirements:** U.S. citizen. 18 years old. Masters degree and completion of approved program. Three years of classroom experience. Never convicted of a felony. **Examination:** Yes. **Fees:** $5 Application. $5 Renewal.

Vocational Administrator
Dept. of Education
Office of Educational Personnel
  Development
1900 Washington St. E
Charleston, WV 25305
Phone: (800)982-2378

Credential Type: Certification. **Requirements:** U.S. citizen. 18 years old. Masters degree and completion of approved educational preparatory program. Three years teaching experience at secondary level. Never convicted of a felony. **Examination:** Yes. **Fees:** $5 Application. $5 Renewal.

Wisconsin

Elementary or Middle School Principal
Teacher Education, Licensing, and
  Placement
Box 7841
Madison, WI 53707-7841
Phone: (608)266-1027

Credential Type: Elementary/Middle Level Principal License. **Duration of License:** Five years. **Requirements:** Master's degree or equivalent in school administration. Complete an approved program for preparation of principals. Must include 12 graduate semester hours in the following areas: principalship; coordination of special school programs; curriculum development at elementary/middle level; practicum or internship at elementary/middle level. Graduate or undergraduate course work in child psychology; early adolescent psychology; and adolescent psychology. 21 graduate semester hours in the following areas: human relations; oral and written communications; educational leadership; organization and operation of public schools; governance of education; supervision of instruction; evaluation of personnel; school law; school business administration and budgeting; and politics of education. Complete 18 semester hours of professional education course work which is not part of the approved principal program. Hold or be eligible to hold a teaching license at the elementary, middle, or secondary levels or as a school counselor, school psychologist, or social worker. Three years of successful teaching, counseling, or work as a social worker or school psychologist, with at least 540 clock hours of classroom teaching. Renewable, with six semester hours of professional credits or an approved equivalent, during the life of the license.

Middle or Secondary School Principal
Teacher Education, Licensing, and
  Placement
Box 7841
Madison, WI 53707-7841
Phone: (608)266-1027

Credential Type: Middle/Secondary Level Principal License. **Duration of License:** Five years. **Requirements:** Master's degree or equivalent in school administration. Complete an approved program for preparation of principals. Must include 12 graduate semester hours in the following areas: principalship; coordination of special school programs; curriculum development at middle/secondary level; practicum or internship at middle/secondary level. Graduate or undergraduate course work in child psychology; early adolescent psychology; and adolescent psychology. 21 graduate semester hours in the following areas: human relations; oral and written communications; educational leadership; organization and operation of public schools; governance of education; supervision of instruction; evaluation of personnel; school law; school business administration and budgeting; and politics of education. Complete 18 semester hours of professional education course work which is not part of the approved principal program. Hold or be eligible to hold a teaching license at the elementary, middle, or secondary levels or as a school counselor, school psychologist, or social worker. Three years of successful teaching, counseling, or work as a social worker or school psychologist, with at least 540 clock hours of classroom teaching. Renewable, with six semester hours of professional credits or an approved equivalent, during the life of the license.

School District Superintendent
Teacher Education, Licensing, and
  Placement
Box 7841
Madison, WI 53707-7841
Phone: (608)266-1027

Credential Type: District Superintendent License. **Duration of License:** Five years. **Requirements:** Hold or be eligible to hold a principal license. Complete an approved specialist degree program for the superintendent. Complete 12 graduate semester hours in the following studies: superintendency; advanced program planning and evaluation; economics of education; advanced politics of education; personnel administration; collective bargaining and contract administration; and a practicum or internship.

Wyoming

Educational Diagnostician
State Dept. of Education
Certification and Accreditation
Services Unit, Hathaway Bldg.
Cheyenne, WY 82002
Phone: (307)777-7291

Credential Type: Educational Diagnostician Endorsement. **Requirements:** Teacher certification and the Education Specialist certification. 45 semester hours of graduate work, including a master's degree, which includes the following areas and semester hours as specified: mental retardation 2; learning disabilities 2; emotional disturbances 2; psycho-assessment of the exceptional child or psychological assessment or assessment of reading and mathematical problems 6; prescriptive teaching and programming or classroom management or curriculum methods and materials 6; behavior modification and instructional behavior intervention 2; counseling parents of exceptional children or counseling techniques 2. Four classes from the required 45 hours must also have practicum related work. Requires two years of classroom teaching, counseling, supervisory or administrative experience in a recognized K-12 setting.

2543

School Principal
State Dept. of Education
Certification and Accreditation
Services Unit, Hathaway Bldg.
Cheyenne, WY 82002
Phone: (307)777-7291

Credential Type: Principal Endorsement. **Requirements:** Teacher certification and Education Specialist certification. 15 semester hours of graduate work, including a master's degree and the following courses of study: school administration and supervision; curriculum and instruction; staff and program evaluation; school law; introductory finance; and special phases of school administration (ie; guidance and community relations). Three years of classroom teaching experience in a K-12 setting.

2544

School Superintendent
State Dept. of Education
Certification and Accreditation
Services Unit, Hathaway Bldg.
Cheyenne, WY 82002
Phone: (307)777-7291

Credential Type: Superintendent Endorsement. **Requirements:** Teacher certification and Education Specialist certification. Sixty semester hours of graduate work, which includes a master's degree and 30 semester hours in the following courses of study: school administration and supervision; curriculum and instruction; staff and program evaluation; school law; introductory finance; and special phases of school administration (such as guidance and community relations). Three years of classroom teaching experience in a K-12 setting.

2545

School Supervisor
State Dept. of Education
Certification and Accreditation
Services Unit, Hathaway Bldg.
Cheyenne, WY 82002
Phone: (307)777-7291

Credential Type: Supervisor Endorsement. **Authorization:** Authorizes employment in the positions of Supervisor, Director, or Coordinator in the Wyoming Public Schools. **Requirements:** Education Specialist certification. Master's degree which includes work in school administration; staff and program evaluation; curriculum and instruction; and areas relevant to instructional program supervised. Three years of classroom teaching experience in a K-12 setting.

Electricians

The following states grant licenses in this occupational category as of the date of publication:

Alabama	District of	Illinois	Minnesota	New Mexico	Rhode Island	West Virginia
Alaska	Columbia	Kentucky	Montana	North Carolina	South Carolina	Wyoming
Arkansas	Florida	Maine	Nebraska	North Dakota	South Dakota	
Colorado	Georgia	Maryland	Nevada	Ohio	Utah	
Connecticut	Hawaii	Massachusetts	New Hampshire	Oklahoma	Vermont	
Delaware	Idaho	Michigan	New Jersey	Oregon	Washington	

Alabama

2546

Mine Electrician
Board of Mine Examiners
Div. of Safety and Inspection
1816 8th Ave. N.
PO Box 10444
Birmingham, AL 35202
Phone: (205)254-1300

Credential Type: Certificate. **Duration of License:** One year. **Requirements:** One year of work experience. Must have completed 90 clock hours of course work. Renewal requires 16 hours of continuing education. **Examination:** Written examination.

Alaska

2547

Electrical Administrator
Dept. of Commerce and Economic Development
Div. of Occupational Licensing
Board of Electrical Examiners
PO Box D
Juneau, AK 99811-0800
Phone: (907)465-2551
Fax: (907)465-2974

Credential Type: Inside Wiring Category. **Duration of License:** Two years. **Requirements:** One of the following education or experience requirements: (1) practical experience as a journeyman electrician in inside construction wiring for at least four of the six years immediately preceding date of application; or

(2) construction management experience in inside wiring as a field superintendent, field engineer, or similar position for at least four of the six years immediately preceding date of application; or

(3) a degree in electrical engineering from an accredited college or university plus practical experience as a journeyman electrician in inside construction wiring for at least one of the three years immediately preceding the date of application; or

(4) an Alaska registration as a professional electrical engineer plus management experience in the electrical construction industry as a field engineer, office engineer, or in a similar position for at least four of the six years immediately preceding date of application; or

(5) experience as a journeyman electrician in inside construction for three of the six years immediately preceding date of application and one year experience during those six years as a certified electrical inspector for a state or municipality or as a full-time electrical instructor at a school approved by the board.

Submit notarized Certificates of Support of experience and qualifications from three persons licensed in the electrical industry in any state.

Applicants licensed in another state and having taken a similar examination in another state may be granted a license by credentials without taking the Alaska examination.

License renewal requires at least one 8-hour continuing education workshop approved by the board which covers the National Electrical Code. **Examination:** Inside Wiring Examination. Applicant may not be examined for more than two electrical administrator's categories at any one scheduled examination. Passing the Inside Wiring Examination automatically qualifies the applicant to be licensed in the Residential Wiring category. **Fees:** $30 application fee. $50 examination fee. $250 license fee. **Governing Statute:** Alaska Statutes 08.40. Professional Regulations 12 AAC 32.

Credential Type: Inside Communications Category. **Duration of License:** Two years. **Requirements:** Practical experience as a journeyman in inside construction communications for at least two of the four years immediately preceding the date of application. Graduated from an accredited college or trade school in inside communication.

Submit notarized Certificates of Support of experience and qualifications from three persons employed, but not necessarily licensed, in the electrical industry in any state.

Applicants licensed in another state and having taken a similar examination in another state may be granted a license by credentials without taking the Alaska examination.

License renewal requires at least one 8-hour continuing education workshop approved by the board which covers the National Electrical Code. **Examination:** Inside Communications Examination. Applicant may not be examined for more than two electrical administrator's categories at any one scheduled examination. **Fees:** $30 application fee. $50 examination fee. $250 license fee. **Governing Statute:** Alaska Statutes 08.40. Professional Regulations 12 AAC 32.

Credential Type: Residential Wiring Category. **Duration of License:** Two years. **Requirements:** Practical experience as a journeyman residential wireman for at least two of the four years immediately preceding the date of application.

License renewal requires at least one 8-hour continuing education workshop approved by the board which covers the National Electrical Code. **Examination:** Residential Wiring Examination. Applicant may not be examined for more than two electrical administrator's categories at any one scheduled examination. Passing the Inside Wiring Examination automatically qualified the applicant to be licensed in the Residential Wiring category. **Fees:** $30 application fee. $50 examination fee. $250 license fee. **Governing Statute:** Alaska Statutes 08.40. Professional Regulations 12 AAC 32.

Credential Type: Outside Linework Category. **Duration of License:** Two years. **Requirements:** One of the following education or experience requirements: (1) practical experience as a journeyman electrician in outside construction linework for at least four of the six years immediately preceding date of application; or

(2) construction management experience in outside linework as a field superintendent, field engineer, or similar position for at least four of the six years immediately preceding date of application; or

(3) a degree in electrical engineering from an accredited college or university plus practical experience as a journeyman lineman in outside construction linework for at least one of the three years immediately preceding the date of application; or

(4) an Alaska registration as a professional electrical engineer plus management experience in the electrical construction industry as a field engineer, office engineer, or in a similar engineering position for at least four of the six years immediately preceding date of application; or

(5) experience as a journeyman lineman in outside construction for three of the six years immediately preceding date of application and one year experience during those six years as a certified electrical inspector for a state or municipality or as a full-time electrical instructor at a school approved by the board.

Submit notarized Certificates of Support of experience and qualifications from three persons licensed in the electrical industry in any state.

Applicants licensed in another state and having taken a similar examination in another state may be granted a license by credentials without taking the Alaska examination.

License renewal requires at least one 8-hour continuing education workshop approved by the board which covers the National Electrical Safety Code. **Examination:** Outside Linework Examination. Applicant may not be examined for more than two electrical administrator's categories at any one scheduled examination. **Fees:** $30 application fee. $50 examination fee. $250 license fee. **Governing Statute:** Alaska Statutes 08.40. Professional Regulations 12 AAC 32.

Credential Type: Outside Communications Category. **Duration of License:** Two years. **Requirements:** Practical experience as a journeyman in outside construction communications for at least two of the four years immediately preceding the date of application. Graduated from an accredited college or trade school in inside communication.

Submit notarized Certificates of Support of experience and qualifications from three persons employed, but not necessarily licensed, in the electrical industry in any state.

Applicants licensed in another state and having taken a similar examination in another state may be granted a license by credentials without taking the Alaska examination.

License renewal requires at least one 8-hour continuing education workshop approved by the board which covers the National Electrical Safety Code. **Examination:** Outside Communications Examination. Applicant may not be examined for more than two electrical administrator's categories at any one scheduled examination. **Fees:** $30 application fee. $50 examination fee. $250 license fee. **Governing Statute:** Alaska Statutes 08.40. Professional Regulations 12 AAC 32.

Credential Type: Controls and Control Wiring Category. **Duration of License:** Two years. **Requirements:** Hold a current Alaska license as a mechanical administrator. Practical experience as a journeyman installing low voltage controls for at least two of the four years preceding date of application. Construction management experience in low voltage control wiring as a field superintendent, field engineer, or similar position for at least four of the six years immediately preceding date of application; or an Alaska registration as an electrical or mechanical engineer plus management experience in the electrical or mechanical low voltage control wiring industry as a field engineer or office engineer for at least two of the four years immediately preceding date of application.

Submit notarized Certificates of Support of experience and qualifications from three persons licensed in the electrical industry in any state.

Applicants licensed in another state and having taken a similar examination in another state may be granted a license by credentials without taking the Alaska examination.

License renewal requires at least one 8-hour continuing education workshop approved by the board. **Examination:** Controls and Control Wiring Examination. Applicant may not be examined for more than two electrical administrator's categories at any one scheduled examination. **Fees:** $30 application fee. $50 examination fee. $250 license fee. **Governing Statute:** Alaska Statutes 08.40. Professional Regulations 12 AAC 32.

2548

Electrician Journeyman

Alaska Dept. of Labor
Div. of Labor Standards and Safety
Mechanical Inspection
PO Box 107020
Anchorage, AK 99510
Phone: (907)264-2447

Credential Type: Electrician Journeyman Certificate. **Duration of License:** One or three years. **Requirements:** Four years or 8,000 hours of experience. Accredited apprenticeship or classroom training may be substituted for some of the work experience required. Submit letter of experience from prior employer or union. For construction electricians, certificate of fitness or an apprentice/learner certificate. **Examination:** Yes. **Fees:** $40 annual license fee, or $75 three-year license fee.

2549

Electrician Lineman

Alaska Dept. of Labor
Div. of Labor Standards and Safety
Mechanical Inspection
PO Box 107020
Anchorage, AK 99510
Phone: (907)264-2447

Credential Type: Electrician Lineman Certificate. **Duration of License:** One or three years. **Requirements:** Four years or 8,000 hours of experience. Accredited apprenticeship or classroom training may be substituted for some of the work experience required. Submit letter of experience from prior employer or union. For construction electricians, certificate of fitness or an apprentice/learner certificate. **Examination:** Yes. **Fees:** $40 annual license fee, or $75 three-year license fee.

2550

Electrician Maintenance

Alaska Dept. of Labor
Div. of Labor Standards and Safety
Mechanical Inspection
PO Box 107020
Anchorage, AK 99510
Phone: (907)264-2447

Credential Type: Electrician Maintenance Certificate. **Duration of License:** One or

Alaska 2551

Electrician Maintenance, continued

three years. **Requirements:** Three years or 6,000 hours of experience. Accredited apprenticeship or classroom training may be substituted for some of the work experience required. Submit letter of experience from prior employer or union. For construction electricians, certificate of fitness or an apprentice/learner certificate. **Examination:** Yes. **Fees:** $40 annual license fee, or $75 three-year license fee.

2551

Electrician Residential
Alaska Dept. of Labor
Div. of Labor Standards and Safety
Mechanical Inspection
PO Box 107020
Anchorage, AK 99510
Phone: (907)264-2447

Credential Type: Electrician Residential Certificate. **Duration of License:** One or three years. **Requirements:** Two years or 4,000 hours of experience. Accredited apprenticeship or classroom training may be substituted for some of the work experience required. Submit letter of experience from prior employer or union. For construction electricians, certificate of fitness or an apprentice/learner certificate. **Examination:** Yes. **Fees:** $40 annual license fee, or $75 three-year license fee.

2552

Electrician Trainee
Alaska Dept. of Labor
Div. of Labor Standards and Safety
Mechanical Inspection
PO Box 107020
Anchorage, AK 99510
Phone: (907)264-2447

Credential Type: Electrician Trainee Certificate. **Duration of License:** One or three years. **Requirements:** Submit letter attesting applicant will work under a certified electrician. **Examination:** No **Fees:** $40 annual license fee, or $75 three-year license fee.

Arkansas

2553

Burglar Alarm Installer
Arkansas State Police
3 Natural Resources Dr.
PO Box 5901
Little Rock, AR 72215
Phone: (501)224-3101

Credential Type: License. **Duration of License:** One year. **Requirements:** 18 years of age. High school graduate or equivalent. Never convicted of any felony or Class A misdemeanor, or crime. Never declared incompetent by reason of mental defect or disease. Not be suffering from habitual drunkenness or narcotic addiction or dependence. Not discharged from the armed services under any condition other than honorable. **Examination:** Yes. **Fees:** $50 Written and oral examinations Application. $13 License. $13 Renewal.

2554

Electrical Contractor
Arkansas Department of Labor
Board of Electrical Examiners
10421 W. Markham
Little Rock, AR 72205
Phone: (501)682-4547

Credential Type: License. **Duration of License:** One year. **Requirements:** Must meet the requirements of a master electrician or employ a master technician as a superintendent or manager. **Examination:** No **Fees:** $100 License. $100 Renewal.

2555

Industrial Maintenance Electrician
Arkansas Dept. of Labor
Board of Electrical Examiners
10421 W. Markham
Little Rock, AR 72205
Phone: (501)682-4547

Credential Type: License. **Duration of License:** One year. **Requirements:** Four years experience under the supervision of an engineer or equivalent in the maintenance of electrical conductors and equipment; or, any combination of training and experience as the Board may require, such as outlined in Arkansas Act 870 of 1979. **Examination:** Yes. **Fees:** $25 Written examination. $15 License. $15 Renewal.

2556

Journeyman Electrician
Arkansas Dept. of Labor
Board of Electrical Examiners
10421 W. Markham
Little Rock, AR 72205
Phone: (501)682-4547

Credential Type: License. **Duration of License:** One year. **Requirements:** Four years experience; or, any combination of training and experience as specified in Arkansas Act 870 of 1979. **Examination:** Yes. **Fees:** $25 Written Examination. $15 License. $15 Renewal.

2557

Master Electrician
Arkansas Dept. of Labor
Board of Electrical Examiners
10421 W. Markham
Little Rock, AR 72205
Phone: (501)682-4547

Credential Type: License. **Duration of License:** One year. **Requirements:** Must hold a degree in Electrical Engineering plus one year of experience; or, six years of experience, including two years experience as a journeyman electrician; or, any combination of training and experience may be considered for approval by the Board, refer to Arkansas Act 870 of 1979. **Examination:** Yes. **Fees:** $50 Written Examination. $30 License. $30 Renewal.

Colorado

2558

Electrical Contractor
State Electrical Board
Dept. of Regulatory Agencies
Div. of Registrations
1390 Logan St., Ste. 400
Denver, CO 80203-2390
Phone: (303)894-2300

Credential Type: Electrical contractor registration. **Duration of License:** One year. **Requirements:** Register with the board, pay fee, and present evidence of compliance with state's worker's compensation and unemployment compensation laws. Either the owner or part owner of the contracting company must be a licensed master electrician, or a licensed master electrician must be employed by the contracting company. **Fees:** $100 annual license fee. **Governing Statute:** Colorado Revised Statutes Title 12, Article 23.

Electricians

2559

Journeyman Electrician
State Electrical Board
Dept. of Regulatory Agencies
Div. of Registrations
1390 Logan St., Ste. 400
Denver, CO 80203-2390
Phone: (303)894-2300

Credential Type: Journeyman electrician license. **Duration of License:** Two years. **Requirements:** Must have four years experience in wiring for light, heat, and power, including at least two years experience in commercial and/or industrial work; or at least four years apprenticeship in the electrical trade. **Examination:** Board administered written examination. **Reciprocity:** Licensees from another state may be eligible for licensure by endorsement if they have comparable credentials and qualifications. **Fees:** $44 exam and license fee. $32 temporary journeyman permit fee (1 year). $55 biennial renewal fee. **Governing Statute:** Colorado Revised Statutes Title 12, Article 23.

2560

Master Electrician
State Electrical Board
Dept. of Regulatory Agencies
Div. of Registrations
1390 Logan St., Ste. 400
Denver, CO 80203-2390
Phone: (303)894-2300

Credential Type: Master electrician's license. **Duration of License:** Two years. **Requirements:** Must have five years experience in wiring for light, heat, and power of residential and commercial buildings, including one year of planning and layout experience; or an electrical engineering degree and one year of actual construction wiring experience; or be a graduate of an electrical trade school or community college and have at least four years of practical experience in electrical work. **Examination:** Board administered written examination. **Reciprocity:** Licensees from another state may be eligible for licensure by endorsement if they have comparable credentials and qualifications. **Fees:** $44 exam and license fee. $69 temporary master permit fee (1 year). $129 biennial renewal fee. **Governing Statute:** Colorado Revised Statutes Title 12, Article 23.

2561

Residential Wireman
State Electrical Board
Dept. of Regulatory Agencies
Div. of Registrations
1390 Logan St., Ste. 400
Denver, CO 80203-2390
Phone: (303)894-2300

Credential Type: Residential wireman license. **Duration of License:** Two years. **Requirements:** Must have at least two years accredited training or practical experience in wiring one-, two-, three-, and four-unit family dwellings. **Examination:** Board administered written examination. **Reciprocity:** Licensees from another state may be eligible for licensure by endorsement if they have comparable credentials and qualifications. **Fees:** $44 exam and license fee. $28 temporary residential wireman permit fee (1 year). $47 biennial renewal fee. **Governing Statute:** Colorado Revised Statutes Title 12, Article 23.

Connecticut

2562

Electrical Apprentice
Electrical Work Examining Board
Occupational Licensing Div.
Consumer Protection Dept.
165 Capitol Ave.
Hartford, CT 06106
Phone: (203)566-3275

Credential Type: Apprentice permit. **Duration of License:** Until next licensure examination. **Authorization:** Work may be performed only under the supervision of a licensed contractor or journeyman. **Requirements:** Be of good moral character. Have an 8th grade education or equivalent. **Governing Statute:** General Statutes of Connecticut, Chap. 393.

2563

Electrical Contractor
Electrical Work Examining Board
Occupational Licensing Div.
Consumer Protection Dept.
165 Capitol Ave.
Hartford, CT 06106
Phone: (203)566-3275

Credential Type: Unlimited electrical contractor's license. **Duration of License:** Two years. **Requirements:** Be of good moral character. Have an 8th grade education or equivalent. Must have served as an electrical journeyman for not less than two years. If service was outside of state, must submit evidence that service was comparable to service in state or that applicant has education and experience and has passed an examination demonstrating competency to be an unlimited contractor. **Examination:** State licensure exam. **Reciprocity:** Yes, with selected states. **Fees:** $75 application fee. $150 license fee. **Governing Statute:** General Statutes of Connecticut, Chap. 393.

Credential Type: Limited electrical contractor's license (L-3). **Duration of License:** Two years. **Authorization:** May perform only work limited to cable splicing and its allied work. **Requirements:** Be of good moral character. Have an 8th grade education or equivalent. Must have served as an electrical journeyman for not less than two years. If service was outside of state, must submit evidence that service was comparable to service in state. **Examination:** State licensure exam. **Reciprocity:** Yes, with selected states. **Fees:** $75 application fee. $150 license fee. **Governing Statute:** General Statutes of Connecticut, Chap. 393.

Credential Type: Limited electrical contractor's license (L-5). **Duration of License:** Two years. **Authorization:** May perform only work limited to ADT, similar, or low voltage signal work, audio, and sound systems. Voltage of the system may not exceed 25 volts or five amperes, from a source of power supplied by others, and does not include wiring in new construction of buildings. **Requirements:** Be of good moral character. Have an 8th grade education or equivalent. Must have served as an electrical journeyman for not less than two years. If service was outside of state, must submit evidence that service was comparable to service in state. **Examination:** State licensure exam. **Reciprocity:** Yes, with selected states. **Fees:** $75 application fee. $150 license fee. **Governing Statute:** General Statutes of Connecticut, Chap. 393.

Credential Type: Limited electrical contractor's license (C-5). **Duration of License:** Two years. **Authorization:** May perform only work limited to ADT, similar, or low voltage signal work; audio and sound systems; or telephone-interconnect. Voltage of the system may not exceed 48 volts or five amperes, from a source of power supplied by others. **Requirements:** Be of good moral character. Have an 8th grade education or equivalent. Must have served two years as a registered apprentice, plus four years as a licensed journeyman. **Examination:** State licensure exam. **Reciprocity:** Yes, with selected states. **Fees:** $75 application fee. $150 license fee. **Governing Statute:** General Statutes of Connecticut, Chap. 393.

Electrical Contractor, continued

Credential Type: Limited electrical contractor's license (T-1). **Duration of License:** Two years. **Authorization:** May perform only work limited to telephone-interconnect systems and be from a source of power supplied by others. **Requirements:** Be of good moral character. Have an 8th grade education or equivalent. Must have served two years as a registered apprentice, plus four years as a licensed journeyman. **Examination:** State licensure exam. **Reciprocity:** Yes, with selected states. **Fees:** $75 application fee. $150 license fee. **Governing Statute:** General Statutes of Connecticut, Chap. 393.

2564

Electrical Journeyman
Electrical Work Examining Board
Occupational Licensing Div.
Consumer Protection Dept.
165 Capitol Ave.
Hartford, CT 06106
Phone: (203)566-3275

Credential Type: Unlimited electrical journeyman's license (E-2). **Duration of License:** Two years. **Authorization:** Must be in the employ of a licensed contractor. **Requirements:** Be of good moral character. Have an 8th grade education or equivalent. Complete a bona fide apprenticeship program, including not less than four years experience. Demonstrate competency by completing applicable state licensure examination. **Examination:** State licensure examination. **Reciprocity:** Yes, with selected states. **Fees:** $45 application fee. $120 license fee. **Governing Statute:** General Statutes of Connecticut, Chap. 393.

Credential Type: Limited electrical journeyman's license (L-4). **Duration of License:** Two years. **Authorization:** May perform only work limited to cable splicing and its allied work. Must be in the employ of a contractor licensed for such work. **Requirements:** Be of good moral character. Have an 8th grade education or equivalent. Complete a bona fide apprenticeship program, including experience in this specific area. Demonstrate competency by completing applicable state licensure examination. **Examination:** State licensure examination. **Reciprocity:** Yes, with selected states. **Fees:** $45 application fee. $120 license fee. **Governing Statute:** General Statutes of Connecticut, Chap. 393.

Credential Type: Limited electrical journeyman's license (L-6). **Duration of License:** Two years. **Authorization:** May perform only work limited to ADT, similar, or low voltage signal work, audio, and sound systems. Voltage of the system may not exceed 25 volts or five amperes, from a source of power supplied by others, and does not include wiring in new construction of buildings. Must be in the employ of a contractor licensed for such work. **Requirements:** Be of good moral character. Have an 8th grade education or equivalent. Complete a bona fide apprenticeship program, including experience in this specific area. Demonstrate competency by completing applicable state licensure examination. **Examination:** State licensure examination. **Reciprocity:** Yes, with selected states. **Fees:** $45 application fee. $120 license fee. **Governing Statute:** General Statutes of Connecticut, Chap. 393.

Credential Type: Limited electrical journeyman's license (C-6). **Duration of License:** Two years. **Authorization:** May perform only work limited to ADT, similar, or low voltage signal work; audio and sound systems; or telephone-interconnect. Voltage of the system may not exceed 48 volts or five amperes, from a source of power supplied by others. Must be in the employ of a contractor licensed for such work. **Requirements:** Be of good moral character. Have an 8th grade education or equivalent. Complete two years as a registered apprentice. Demonstrate competency by completing applicable state licensure examination. **Examination:** State licensure examination. **Reciprocity:** Yes, with selected states. **Fees:** $45 application fee. $120 license fee. **Governing Statute:** General Statutes of Connecticut, Chap. 393.

Credential Type: Limited electrical journeyman's license (T-2). **Duration of License:** Two years. **Authorization:** May perform only work limited to telephone-interconnect systems and be from a source of power supplied by others. Must be in the employ of a contractor licensed for such work. **Requirements:** Be of good moral character. Have an 8th grade education or equivalent. Complete two years as a registered apprentice. Demonstrate competency by completing applicable state licensure examination. **Examination:** State licensure examination. **Reciprocity:** Yes, with selected states. **Fees:** $45 application fee. $120 license fee. **Governing Statute:** General Statutes of Connecticut, Chap. 393.

2565

Electrician (Racetrack)
Connecticut Div. of Special Revenue
Russell Rd.
PO Box 11424
Newington, CT 06111-0424
Phone: (203)566-2756

Credential Type: License Registration. **Requirements:** Submit application and fingerprint card. Pay fee. **Fees:** $5 registration fee.

Delaware

2566

Electrician
Board of Electrical Examiners
Dept. of Administrative Services
Div. of Professional Regulation
PO Box 1401
Dover, DE 19903
Phone: (302)739-4522

Credential Type: Master General Electrician License. **Duration of License:** Two years. **Requirements:** At least six years of experience, of which two years may be educational. **Examination:** Yes, administered through the National Assessment Institute of Maryland. **Fees:** $10 application fee. $50 examination fee. $65 license fee.

Credential Type: Limited Electrician License. **Duration of License:** Two years. **Requirements:** At least three years of experience, of which two years may be educational. **Examination:** Yes, administered through the National Assessment Institute of Maryland. **Fees:** $10 application fee. $50 examination fee. $35 license fee.

District of Columbia

2567

Electrical Contractor
License and Certification Div.
Occupational and Professional
 Licensure Administration
Consumer and Regulatory Affairs
 Dept.
PO Box 37200
Washington, DC 20013-7200
Phone: (202)727-7823
Phone: (202)727-7480

Alternate Information: 614 H St., NW, Washington, DC 20001

Credential Type: Electrical Contractor License. **Duration of License:** One year. **Requirements:** Must be licensed as a master electrician or have a master electrician as an employee, officer, or substantial stockholder. Post bond of $4,000. **Fees:** $50 application fee. $20 license fee. $60 annual renewal fee. **Governing Statute:** Municipal Regulations, Title 17, Chap. 2.

Credential Type: Specialty Electrical Contractor License. **Duration of License:** One year. **Requirements:** Must be licensed as a master electrician or master electrician specialist, have a master electrician or master electrician specialist as an employee, officer, or substantial stockholder. Post bond of $2,000. **Fees:** $50 application fee. $20 license fee. $60 annual renewal fee. **Governing Statute:** Municipal Regulations, Title 17, Chap. 2.

2568

Electrician
License and Certification Div.
Occupational and Professional Licensure Administration
Consumer and Regulatory Affairs Dept.
PO Box 37200
Washington, DC 20013-7200
Phone: (202)727-7823
Phone: (202)727-7480

Alternate Information: 614 H St., NW, Washington, DC 20001

Credential Type: Master Electrician License. **Duration of License:** Two years. **Requirements:** Be at least 16 years of age. Meet one of the following sets of requirements: (1) Have worked as an electrician for at least four years. (2) Have at least two years of practical experience and complete a four-year course in electrical engineering. (3) Have equivalent experience in the U.S. armed forces or merchant marine, with at least two years of practical experience. **Examination:** Written. **Fees:** $10 application fee. $10 license fee. $40 exam fee. $30 annual renewal fee. **Governing Statute:** Municipal Regulations, Title 17, Chap. 2.

Credential Type: Master Electrician Specialist License. **Duration of License:** Two years. **Requirements:** Meet one of the following sets of requirements: (1) Complete four years (4000 hours) as an apprentice electrician. (2) Have equivalent experience of four years (4000 hours), which may include experience in the U.S. armed forces or merchant marine. (3) Complete a four-year course in electrical engineerng and at least one year of practical experience. (4) Complete an appropriate combination of experience and study to establish eligibility to take the examination. **Examination:** Written. **Fees:** $10 application fee. $10 license fee. $40 exam fee. $30 annual renewal fee. **Governing Statute:** Municipal Regulations, Title 17, Chap. 2.

Credential Type: Electrician's License. **Duration of License:** Two years. **Requirements:** Meet one of the following sets of requirements: (1) Complete four years (4000 hours) as an apprentice electrician. (2) Have equivalent experience of four years (4000 hours), which may include experience in the U.S. armed forces or merchant marine. (3) Complete a four-year course in electrical engineering and at least one year of practical experience. (4) Complete an appropriate combination of experience and study to establish eligibility to take the examination. **Examination:** Written. **Fees:** $10 application fee. $10 license fee. $20 exam fee. $20 annual renewal fee. **Governing Statute:** Municpal Regulations, Title 17, Chap. 2.

Credential Type: Maintenance and Repair Electrician's License. **Duration of License:** Two years. **Requirements:** Meet one of the following sets of requirements: (1) Be licensed in the District of Columbia for four years as a steam and operating engineer. (2) Complete four years (4000 hours) as an apprentice electrician. **Examination:** Written examination. **Governing Statute:** Municipal Regulations, Title 17, Chap. 2.

Credential Type: Apprentice Electrician License. **Duration of License:** Two years. **Authorization:** Must work under the direct personal supervision of a licensed master electrician, licensed master electrician specialist, licensed electrician or a licensed maintenance and repair electrician. **Requirements:** Submit application and pay fee. **Fees:** $8 license fee. $10 annual renewal fee. **Governing Statute:** Municipal Regulations, Title 17, Chap. 2.

Florida

2569

Electrical Contractor
Electrical Contractors Board
Professional Regulation Dept.
1940 N. Monroe St.
Tallahassee, FL 32399-0750
Phone: (904)488-6685

Credential Type: Unlimited electrical contractor certificate of competency. **Duration of License:** Two years. **Requirements:** Must be at least 18 years of age. Good moral character. Must possess and demonstrate the requisite skill, knowledge, and experience in the trade as an electrical contractor. Must have public liability and property damage insurance. Must meet one of the following requirements: (1) Have at least three years proven management experience as an electrical contractor or educational equivalent, but not more than half of which is met by educational equivalent; or (2) Have at least six years of comprehensive, specialized training, education, or experience associated with an electrical or alarm system contracting business; or (3) Have been licensed for three years as an engineer.

Renewal of an inactive certified license requires 12 classroom hours of continuing education. **Examination:** Yes. **Reciprocity:** A holder of a valid license to practice electrical contracting issued by another state or territory of the United States may apply for licensure by endorsement, if the criteria for issuance of such a license was substantially equivalent to Florida's. **Fees:** $50 application fee for certification examination. $150 examination fee. $200 application fee for licensure by endorsement. $200 renewal fee. **Governing Statute:** Florida Statutes, Chapter 489, Part II.

Credential Type: Lighting Maintenance Specialty Electrical Contractor Certificate. **Duration of License:** Two years. **Requirements:** Must have three years experience in this specialty. Pass appropriate examination. **Examination:** Yes. **Fees:** $50 application fee for certification examination. $150 examination fee. $200 application fee for licensure by endorsement. $200 renewal fee. **Governing Statute:** Florida Statutes, Chapter 489, Part II.

Credential Type: Elevator Specialty Electrical Contractor Certificate. **Duration of License:** Two years. **Requirements:** Must have three years experience in this specialty. Pass appropriate examination. **Examination:** Yes. **Fees:** $50 application fee for certification examination. $150 examination fee. $200 application fee for licensure by endorsement. $200 renewal fee. **Governing Statute:** Florida Statutes, Chapter 489, Part II.

Credential Type: Electrical Outdoor Sign Specialty Electrical Contractor Certificate. **Duration of License:** Two years. **Requirements:** Must have three years experience in this specialty. Pass appropriate examination. **Examination:** Yes. **Fees:** $50 application fee for certification examination. $150 examination fee. $200 application fee for licensure by endorsement. $200 renewal fee. **Governing Statute:** Florida Statutes, Chapter 489, Part II.

Credential Type: Residential Electrical Contractor Certificate. **Duration of License:** Two years. **Requirements:** Must have three years experience in this specialty. Pass appropriate examination. **Examination:** Yes. **Fees:** $50 application fee for certification examination. $150 exami-

Georgia

Electrical Contractor, continued

nation fee. $200 application fee for licensure by endorsement. $200 renewal fee. **Governing Statute:** Florida Statutes, Chapter 489, Part II.

Credential Type: Electrical Contractor Registration. **Duration of License:** Two years. **Authorization:** Limited to contracting only in the area and for the type of work covered by the registration, unless local licenses are issued for other areas and types of work, or unless certification is obtained. **Requirements:** Must hold a current occupational license or a current license issued by any municipality or county of the state of Florida for the type of work for which registration is requested. **Fees:** $65 initial registration fee. $50 registration renewal fee. **Governing Statute:** Florida Statutes, Chapter 489, Part II.

Georgia

2570

Electrical Contractor
State Construction Industry Licensing Board
Div. of Electrical Contractors
Professional Examining Boards
166 Pryor St., SW
Atlanta, GA 30303
Phone: (404)656-3939

Credential Type: Class I Statewide Electrical Contractor License. **Authorization:** Restricted to electrical contracting which involves work on single phase electrical systems not exceeding 200 amperes. Work on certain systems of 50 volts or less requires a state low voltage contractor license. **Requirements:** Be at least 21 years of age. Minimum of four years of primary experience gained through the direct installation of and responsibility for electrical systems. Secondary experience, including work, training, and education, may be credited toward the experience requirement at a rate of 50 percent, to a maximum of one year of credit (2 years secondary experience equals one year of experience credit). **Examination:** Construction Industry Licensing Board Examination for Class I Electrical Contractors. **Reciprocity:** Applicant who holds a current out of state license based on passing an examination may be granted a license by endorsement, provided that applicant meets Georgia's experience requirements. **Fees:** $29 application fee. $56 exam fee. **Governing Statute:** Official Code of Georgia Annotated 43-14. Rules of the State Construction Industry Licensing Board, Chap. 121.

Credential Type: Class II Statewide Electrical Contractor License. **Authorization:** Unrestricted as to the capacity of the system. Work on certain systems of 50 volts or less requires a state low voltage contractor license. **Requirements:** Be at least 21 years of age. Minimum of four years of primary experience gained through the direct installation of and responsibility for electrical systems. Secondary experience, including work, training, and education, may be credited toward the experience requirement at a rate of 50 percent, to a maximum of one year of credit (2 years secondary experience equals one year of experience credit). Experience must be with installations in excess of single phase, 200 amperes systems. **Examination:** Construction Industry Licensing Board Examination for Class II Electrical Contractors. **Reciprocity:** Applicant who holds a current out of state license based on passing an examination may be granted a license by endorsement, provided that applicant meets Georgia's experience requirements. **Fees:** $29 application fee. $56 exam fee. **Governing Statute:** Official Code of Georgia Annotated 43-14. Rules of the State Construction Industry Licensing Board, Chap. 121.

2571

Low Voltage Contractor
State Construction Industry Licensing Board
Div. of LowVoltage Contractors
Professional Examining Boards
166 Pryor St., SW
Atlanta, GA 30303
Phone: (404)656-3939

Credential Type: Class LV-A Contractor License. **Authorization:** Restricted to alarm and general system low-voltage contracting. **Requirements:** Minimum of one year of experience in low-voltage wiring in this category. A maximum of six months of courses in electronics may be credited toward the experience requirement. **Examination:** Construction Industry Licensing Board Examination for LowVoltage Alarm System Contractors. **Reciprocity:** Applicant who holds a current out of state license based on passing an examination may be granted a license by endorsement, provided that applicant meets Georgia's experience requirements. **Fees:** $29 application fee. $33 exam fee. **Governing Statute:** Official Code of Georgia Annotated 43-14. Rules of the State Construction Industry Licensing Board, Chap. 121.

Credential Type: Class LV-T Contractor License. **Authorization:** Restricted to telecommunications and general system lowvoltage contracting. **Requirements:** Minimum of one year of experience in low-voltage wiring in this category. A maximum of six months of courses in electronics may be credited toward the experience requirement. **Examination:** Construction Industry Licensing Board Examination for LowVoltage Telecommunications Contractors. **Reciprocity:** Applicant who holds a current out of state license based on passing an examination may be granted a license by endorsement, provided that applicant meets Georgia's experience requirements. **Fees:** $29 application fee. $33 exam fee. **Governing Statute:** Official Code of Georgia Annotated 43-14. Rules of the State Construction Industry Licensing Board, Chap. 121.

Credential Type: Class LV-G Contractor License. **Authorization:** Restricted to general system low-voltage contracting. **Requirements:** Minimum of one year of experience in low-voltage wiring in this category. A maximum of six months of courses in electronics may be credited toward the experience requirement. **Examination:** Construction Industry Licensing Board Examination for LowVoltage General System Contractors. **Reciprocity:** Applicant who holds a current out of state license based on passing an examination may be granted a license by endorsement, provided that applicant meets Georgia's experience requirements. **Fees:** $29 application fee. $33 exam fee. **Governing Statute:** Official Code of Georgia Annotated 43-14. Rules of the State Construction Industry Licensing Board, Chap. 121.

Credential Type: Class LV-U Contractor License. **Authorization:** Unrestricted as to low-voltage contracting. **Requirements:** Minimum of one year of experience in low-voltage wiring in this category. A maximum of six months of courses in electronics may be credited toward the experience requirement. **Examination:** Construction Industry Licensing Board Examination for Unrestricted Low-Voltage Contractors. **Reciprocity:** Applicant who holds a current out of state license based on passing an examination may be granted a license by endorsement, provided that applicant meets Georgia's experience requirements. **Fees:** $29 application fee. $33 exam fee. **Governing Statute:** Official Code of Georgia Annotated 43-14. Rules of the State Construction Industry Licensing Board, Chap. 121.

Hawaii

2572

Journeyman Electrician
Hawaii Board of Electricians and
  Plumbers
Dept. of Commerce and Consumer
  Affairs
PO Box 3469
Honolulu, HI 96801
Phone: (808)548-3952

Credential Type: License. **Duration of License:** Six months. **Requirements:** Four years of experience in residential and/or commercial structural wiring and installation, alteration and repair of electrical equipment, wires, and apparatus. **Fees:** $15 application fee. $40 exam fee. $10 license fee. $10 renewal fee. $15—$30 Compliance Resolution Fund fee.

2573

Journeyman Industrial Electrician
Hawaii Board of Electricians and
  Plumbers
Dept. of Commerce and Consumer
  Affairs
PO Box 3469
Honolulu, HI 96801
Phone: (808)548-3952

Credential Type: License. **Duration of License:** Six months. **Requirements:** Four years of experience in industrial electrical work, including electrical work for an employer that may not need to comply with the National Electric Code. **Fees:** $15 application fee. $40 exam fee. $10 license fee. $10 renewal fee. $15—$30 Compliance Resolution Fund fee.

2574

Journeyman Specialty Electrician
Hawaii Board of Electricians and
  Plumbers
Dept. of Commerce and Consumer
  Affairs
PO Box 3469
Honolulu, HI 96801
Phone: (808)548-3952

Credential Type: License. **Duration of License:** Six months. **Requirements:** Four years of experience in a specialized electrical field. **Examination:** Yes. **Fees:** $15 application fee. $40 exam fee. $10 license fee. $10 renewal fee. $15—$30 Compliance Resolution Fund fee.

2575

Maintenance Electrician
Hawaii Board of Electricians and
  Plumbers
Dept. of Commerce and Consumer
  Affairs
PO Box 3469
Honolulu, HI 96801
Phone: (808)548-3952

Credential Type: License. **Duration of License:** Six months. **Requirements:** One year of maintenance electrical work experience or two years of electrical trade schooling. **Examination:** Yes. **Fees:** $15 application fee. $40 exam fee. $10 license fee. $10 renewal fee. $15—$30 Compliance Resolution Fund fee.

2576

Supervising Electrician
Hawaii Board of Electricians and
  Plumbers
Dept. of Commerce and Consumer
  Affairs
PO Box 3469
Honolulu, HI 96801
Phone: (808)548-3952

Credential Type: License. **Duration of License:** Six months. **Requirements:** Two years of experience as a licensed Journeyman Industrial Electrician or equivalent. **Examination:** Yes. **Fees:** $15 application fee. $40 exam fee. $10 license fee. $10 renewal fee. $15-$30 Compliance Resolution Fund fee.

2577

Supervising Industrial Electrician
Hawaii Board of Electricians and
  Plumbers
Dept. of Commerce and Consumer
  Affairs
PO Box 3469
Honolulu, HI 96801
Phone: (808)548-3952

Credential Type: License. **Duration of License:** Six months. **Requirements:** Two years of experience as a licensed Journeyman Industrial Electrician or equivalent. **Examination:** Yes. **Fees:** $15 application fee. $40 exam fee. $10 license fee. $10 renewal fee. $15—$30 Compliance Resolution Fund fee.

2578

Supervising Specialty Electrician
Hawaii Board of Electricians and
  Plumbers
Dept. of Commerce and Consumer
  Affairs
PO Box 3469
Honolulu, HI 96801
Phone: (808)548-3952

Credential Type: License. **Duration of License:** Six months. **Requirements:** Two years of experience as a licensed Journeyman Specialty Electrician. **Examination:** Yes. **Fees:** $15 application fee. $40 exam fee. $10 license fee. $10 renewal fee. $15—$30 Compliance Resolution Fund fee.

Idaho

2579

Apprentice Electrician
Idaho State Electrical Board
277 N. 6th St.
Boise, ID 83720-6000
Phone: (208)334-2183

Credential Type: Apprentice Registration. **Duration of License:** One year. **Requirements:** During a four-year apprenticeship must complete 144 hours of education each year and 2000 hours of experience under a licensed journeyman electrician. Must be at least 16 years of age. **Fees:** $10 annual registration fee. **Governing Statute:** Idaho Code, Title 54, Chap. 10.

2580

Electrical Contractor
Idaho State Electrical Board
277 N. 6th St.
Boise, ID 83720-6000
Phone: (208)334-2183

Credential Type: Electrical Contractor License. **Duration of License:** One year. **Requirements:** An Electrical Contractor License will be issued to a Licensed Journeyman Electrician who has been licensed for at least two years upon submission of application and fee. **Fees:** $125 application fee. $100 renewal fee. **Governing Statute:** Idaho Code, Title 54, Chap. 10.

2581

Journeyman Electrician
Idaho State Electrical Board
277 N. 6th St.
Boise, ID 83720-6000
Phone: (208)334-2183

Credential Type: Journeyman Electrician License. **Duration of License:** One year. **Authorization:** May make installations of electrical wiring and equipment only as an employee of a licensed electrical contractor. Need not obtain additional specialty electrician licenses to make any specialty installations. **Requirements:** Must have at least four years experience working in the trade as a registered apprentice making electrical installations under the supervision of a qualified journeyman electrician. Must have 576 hours of vocational schooling. **Examination:** Journeyman Examination, covering National Electric Code, theory, and calculations. **Reciprocity:** With Oregon, Washington, Montana, and North Dakota only. **Fees:** $15 application fee. $25 license fee. $15 annual renewal fee. **Governing Statute:** Idaho Code, Title 54, Chap. 10.

2582

Specialty Electrical Contractor
Idaho State Electrical Board
277 N. 6th St.
Boise, ID 83720-6000
Phone: (208)334-2183

Credential Type: Specialty Electrical Contractor License. **Duration of License:** One year. **Requirements:** A Specialty Electrical Contractor License will be issued to a Licensed Specialty Electrician who has been licensed for at least two years upon submission of application and fee. **Fees:** $125 application fee. $100 renewal fee. **Governing Statute:** Idaho Code, Title 54, Chap. 10.

2583

Specialty Electrician
Idaho State Electrical Board
277 N. 6th St.
Boise, ID 83720-6000
Phone: (208)334-2183

Credential Type: Elevator, Dumbwaiter, Escalator, or Moving Walk Electrical License. **Duration of License:** One year. **Requirements:** Complete two years of experience in this specialty. **Examination:** Elevator Electrician Examination. **Exemptions:** A Licensed Journeyman Electrician may perform installations of this type without additional specialty licensing. **Reci**procity: No. **Fees:** $15 administrative fee. $25 license fee. $35 exam fee. $10 renewal fee. **Governing Statute:** Idaho Code, Title 54, Chap. 10.

Credential Type: Sign Electrical License. **Duration of License:** One year. **Requirements:** Complete two years of experience in this specialty. **Examination:** Sign Electrician Examination. **Exemptions:** A Licensed Journeyman Electrician may perform installations of this type without additional specialty licensing. **Reciprocity:** No. **Fees:** $15 administrative fee. $25 license fee. $35 exam fee. $10 renewal fee. **Governing Statute:** Idaho Code, Title 54, Chap. 10.

Credential Type: Manufacturing or Assembling Equipment Electrical License. **Duration of License:** One year. **Requirements:** Complete two years of experience in this specialty. **Examination:** Manufacturing or Assembling Equipment Electrician Examination. **Exemptions:** A Licensed Journeyman Electrician may perform installations of this type without additional specialty licensing. **Reciprocity:** No. **Fees:** $15 administrative fee. $25 license fee. $35 exam fee. $10 renewal fee. **Governing Statute:** Idaho Code, Title 54, Chap. 10.

Credential Type: Mobile Home Dealer Electrical License. **Duration of License:** One year. **Authorization:** Limited to mobile home and recreational vehicles owned by or in the possession of the dealer by whom employed. **Requirements:** Complete two years of experience in this specialty. **Examination:** Mobile Home Dealer Electrician Examination. **Exemptions:** A Licensed Journeyman Electrician may perform installations of this type without additional specialty licensing. **Reciprocity:** No. **Fees:** $15 administrative fee. $25 license fee. $35 exam fee. $10 renewal fee. **Governing Statute:** Idaho Code, Title 54, Chap. 10.

Credential Type: Limited Energy Electrical License. **Duration of License:** One year. **Authorization:** Must be employed by a licensed limited energy electrical contractor. **Requirements:** Complete two years of experience in this specialty. **Examination:** Limited Energy Electrician Examination. **Exemptions:** A Licensed Journeyman Electrician may perform installations of this type without additional specialty licensing. **Reciprocity:** No. **Fees:** $15 administrative fee. $25 license fee. $35 exam fee. $10 renewal fee. **Governing Statute:** Idaho Code, Title 54, Chap. 10.

Credential Type: Irrigation Sprinkler Electrical License. **Duration of License:** One year. **Authorization:** Must be employed by a licensed electrical contractor who is required to have a licensed employee in this specialty. **Requirements:** Complete two years of experience in this specialty. **Examination:** Irrigation Sprinkler Electrician Examination. **Exemptions:** A Licensed Journeyman Electrician may perform installations of this type without additional specialty licensing. **Reciprocity:** No. **Fees:** $15 administrative fee. $25 license fee. $35 exam fee. $10 renewal fee. **Governing Statute:** Idaho Code, Title 54, Chap. 10.

Credential Type: Well Driller and Water Pump Installer License. **Duration of License:** One year. **Authorization:** Must be employed by a licensed well driller and water pump installer electrical contractor. **Requirements:** Complete two years of experience in this specialty. **Examination:** Well Driller and Water Pump Installer Examination. **Exemptions:** A Licensed Journeyman Electrician may perform installations of this type without additional specialty licensing. **Reciprocity:** No. **Fees:** $15 administrative fee. $25 license fee. $35 exam fee. $10 renewal fee. **Governing Statute:** Idaho Code, Title 54, Chap. 10.

Credential Type: Refrigeration, Heating, and Air Conditioning Electrical Installer License. **Duration of License:** One year. **Authorization:** Must be employed by a licensed electrical contractor whose license covers this category. **Requirements:** Complete two years of experience in this specialty. **Examination:** Refrigeration, Heating, and Air Conditioning Electrical Installer Examination. **Exemptions:** A Licensed Journeyman Electrician may perform installations of this type without additional specialty licensing. **Reciprocity:** No. **Fees:** $15 administrative fee. $25 license fee. $35 exam fee. $10 renewal fee. **Governing Statute:** Idaho Code, Title 54, Chap. 10.

Illinois

2584

Fire Equipment Employee
Illinois State Fire Marshal
1035 Stevenson Drive
Springfield, IL 62703
Phone: (217)785-1010

Credential Type: Class 1 License. **Duration of License:** One year. **Requirements:** Must have knowledge of servicing engineered fire extinguishing systems. Submit application, current photographs, and fee. **Examination:** Fire Equipment Employee Examination—Class 1. **Reciprocity:** Yes, considered on an individual basis. **Fees:** $25 initial license fee. $25 renewal fee.

Governing Statute: Public Act 85-1434, Illinois Administrative Code.

Credential Type: Class 2 License. **Duration of License:** One year. **Requirements:** Must have knowledge of servicing pre-engineered fire extinguishing systems. Submit application, current photographs, and fee. **Examination:** Fire Equipment Employee Examination—Class 2. **Reciprocity:** Yes, considered on an individual basis. **Fees:** $25 initial license fee. $25 renewal fee. **Governing Statute:** Public Act 85-1434, Illinois Administrative Code.

Credential Type: Class 3 License. **Duration of License:** One year. **Requirements:** Must have knowledge of servicing engineered fire extinguishing systems. Submit application, current photographs, and fee. **Examination:** Fire Equipment Employee Examination—Class 3. **Reciprocity:** Yes, considered on an individual basis. **Fees:** $25 initial license fee. $25 renewal fee. **Governing Statute:** Public Act 85-1434, Illinois Administrative Code.

Kentucky

2585

Electrical Contractor
Dept. of Housing, Buildings and Construction
1047 U.S. 127 South
Frankfort, KY 40601
Phone: (502)564-3626

Credential Type: License. **Duration of License:** One year. **Requirements:** Ability to read, comprehend and write. Proof of $250,000 liability insurance for electrical construction work, and an affidavit to insure compliance with Kentucky Worker's Compensation and Unemployment Insurance Laws. **Examination:** Yes. **Fees:** $40 exam fee. $100 application fee. $25 renewal fee.

2586

Mining Electrical Worker
Dept. of Mines and Minerals
PO Box 14080
Lexington, KY 40512
Phone: (606)254-0367

Credential Type: License. **Duration of License:** One year. **Requirements:** One year experience of electrical work on surface mines, in underground mines, mine equipment manufacturing industry or in any other industry using or manufacturing similar equipment. Retraining is required. **Examination:** Yes.

Maine

2587

Apprentice Electrician
Electricians Examining Board
Dept. of Professional and Financial Regulations
State House Station 35
Augusta, ME 04333
Phone: (207)582-8723

Credential Type: Apprentice Electrician License. **Duration of License:** Two years. **Requirements:** Must be at least 16 years of age. Must be enrolled in the Maine Apprenticeship Program. **Fees:** $20 application fee. $20 license fee. $20 renewal fee. **Governing Statute:** 32 M.S.R.A., Chap. 17.

2588

Helper Electrician
Electricians Examining Board
Dept. of Professional and Financial Regulations
State House Station 35
Augusta, ME 04333
Phone: (207)582-8723

Credential Type: Helper Electrician License. **Duration of License:** Two years. **Authorization:** Covers persons engaged in making electrical installations under the direct supervision of a master, journeyman, or limited electrician, but does not include apprentices. **Requirements:** Must be at least 16 years of age. **Fees:** $20 application fee. $20 license fee. $20 renewal fee. **Governing Statute:** 32 M.S.R.A., Chap. 17.

2589

Journeyman Electrician
Electricians Examining Board
Dept. of Professional and Financial Regulations
State House Station 35
Augusta, ME 04333
Phone: (207)582-8723

Credential Type: Journeyman Electrician License. **Duration of License:** Two years. **Authorization:** Covers persons engaged in making electrical installations in the employment of a master electrician. **Requirements:** Meet one of the following sets of requirements: (1) Complete at least 8,000 hours of service as an apprentice or helper electrician, or have at least 8,000 hours of experience in electrical installations. Complete a program of study of 576 hours, of which 225 hours are in electrical study and 351 hours of electives are either in trade-related courses or 225 hours are trade-related and 135 are degree-related. (2) Be a graduate of an accredited regional vocational high school two-year electrical program. Have 8,000 experience working under the supervision of a master electrician or equivalent. Complete a course of at least 45 hours in the current National Electrical Code. (3) Be a graduate of an accredited Maine vocational-technical institute or Department of Corrections vocational-electrical program. Have 4,000 hours experience working under the supervision of a master electrician or equivalent. Complete a course of at least 45 hours in the current National Electrical Code. (4) Be a registered electrical apprentice and have completed 576 hours of related instruction, the 8,000-hour approved program, and a course of at least 45 hours in the current National Electrical Code. **Examination:** Yes. **Fees:** $20 application fee. $60 license fee. $60 renewal fee. $80 exam fee. **Governing Statute:** 32 M.S.R.A., Chap. 17.

2590

Journeyman-in-Training Electrician
Electricians Examining Board
Dept. of Professional and Financial Regulations
State House Station 35
Augusta, ME 04333
Phone: (207)582-8723

Credential Type: Journeyman-in-Training Electrician License. **Duration of License:** Two years. **Authorization:** Covers persons engaged in making electrical installations under the direct supervision of a master or journeyman electrician. **Requirements:** Must be at least 16 years of age. **Examination:** Yes. **Fees:** $20 application fee. $25 license fee. $25 renewal fee. $80 exam fee. **Governing Statute:** 32 M.S.R.A., Chap. 17.

2591

Limited Electrician
Electricians Examining Board
Dept. of Professional and Financial Regulations
State House Station 35
Augusta, ME 04333
Phone: (207)582-8723

Credential Type: Limited Electrician License. **Duration of License:** Two years. **Authorization:** License are limited to one or more of the following: water pumps, outdoor signs, gasoline dispensing, traffic signals, house wiring, refrigeration, and low energy including fire alarms. **Requirements:** Hours of electrical education and experience vary with each specialty. **Examination:** Yes. **Fees:** $20 application fee.

Limited Electrician, continued

$80 license fee. $80 renewal fee. $100 exam fee. **Governing Statute:** 32 M.S.R.A., Chap. 17.

2592

Master Electrician
Electricians Examining Board
Dept. of Professional and Financial Regulations
State House Station 35
Augusta, ME 04333
Phone: (207)582-8723

Credential Type: Master Electrician License. **Duration of License:** Two years. **Requirements:** Complete at least 4,000 hours of service as a journeyman electrician, or at least 12,000 hours of experience in electrical installations. Complete a program of study of 576 hours, of which 450 hours are in electrical study and 126 hours are in degree-related courses. **Examination:** Yes. **Fees:** $20 application fee. $150 license fee. $150 renewal fee. $150 exam fee. **Governing Statute:** 32 M.S.R.A., Chap. 17.

Maryland

2593

Electrician
State Board of Master Electricians
Dept. of Licensing and Regulation
501 St. Paul Pl.
Baltimore, MD 21202-2272
Phone: (410)333-6322

Credential Type: Master Electrician License. **Duration of License:** Two years. **Requirements:** Have at least seven years of experience in providing electrical services for all types of electrical equipment under the direction and supervision of a licensed master electrician or similarly qualified employee of a governmental unit. Up to three years of credit toward the experience requirement may be granted for completion of a formal course of study or professional training in electrical installation. **Examination:** Board-administered written examination. **Exemptions:** Exam may be waived for local license holders. **Reciprocity:** Yes, provided applicant's state waives the examination of licensees of Maryland to a similar extent, and that applicant has met the experience requirement. **Fees:** $35 application fee. $75 license fee. **Governing Statute:** Annotated Code of Maryland, Title 6.

Massachusetts

2594

Electrician
Board of Registration of Electricians
Div. of Registration
100 Cambridge St., 15th fl.
Boston, MA 02202
Phone: (617)727-9931

Credential Type: Master Electrician License. **Requirements:** Complete 100 hours of training and five years working experience. **Examination:** Master Electrician Examination. **Fees:** $140 license fee.

Credential Type: Journeyman Electrician License. **Requirements:** Complete 300 hours of training and four years working experience. **Examination:** Journeyman Electrician Examination. **Fees:** $85 license fee.

Michigan

2595

Electrical Contractor (Class 1 Electrician)
State Electrical Administrative Board
Electrical Div.
Bureau of Construction Codes
Dept. of Labor
7150 Harris Dr.
PO Box 30015
Lansing, MI 48909
Phone: (517)322-1287

Credential Type: License. **Duration of License:** One year. **Requirements:** Over 21 years of age. Have a master electrician's license or regularly employ a person who has a master electrician's license who will be in charge of work for the applicant. Abide by the rules of the State Electrical Administrative Board. **Fees:** $75 initial license fee. $75 renewal fee. $50 homeowner construction lien fund assessment fee. **Governing Statute:** Electrical Administrative Act, Act 217 of 1956, as amended.

2596

Electrician, Journeyperson (Class 3 Electrician)
State Electrical Administrative Board
Electrical Div.
Bureau of Construction Codes
Dept. of Labor
7150 Harris Dr.
PO Box 30015
Lansing, MI 48909
Phone: (517)322-1287

Credential Type: License. **Duration of License:** One year. **Requirements:** At least 18 years of age. Worked at least four years in the type of electrical construction or maintenance work for which a license is required, or have a combination of work experience and training at a recognized trade or technical school provided this includes at least one year of practical experience. Submit written evidence from employers and trade or technical schools showing the type of work performed and the length of time employed. Abide by the rules of the State Electrical Administrative Board. **Examination:** Written exam. **Fees:** $45 initial exam and license fee. $20 renewal fee. **Governing Statute:** Electrical Administrative Act, Act 217 of 1956, as amended.

2597

Electrician, Master (Class 2 Electrician)
State Electrical Administrative Board
Electrical Div.
Bureau of Construction Codes
Dept. of Labor
7150 Harris Dr.
PO Box 30015
Lansing, MI 48909
Phone: (517)322-1287

Credential Type: License. **Duration of License:** One year. **Requirements:** At least 21 years of age. Have been a licensed Journeyperson (Class 3) electrician for at least two years. Abide by the rules of the State Electrical Administrative Board. **Examination:** Written exam. **Fees:** $50 initial exam and license fee. $25 renewal fee. **Governing Statute:** Electrical Administrative Act, Act 217 of 1956, as amended.

Minnesota

2598

Alarm and Communication System Contractor
Board of Electricity
S-173 Griggs Midway Bldg.
1821 University Ave.
St. Paul, MN 55104
Phone: (612)642-0800

Credential Type: License. **Duration of License:** Two years. **Requirements:** Post $5000 performance bond. Have required general liability and property damage insurance. Individual or an employee must pass examination. **Examination:** Alarm and Communication Examination. **Fees:** $200 license fee. **Governing Statute:** Minnesota Statutes, Sections 326.241-326.248. Minnesota Rules 3800-3899.

2599

Electrical Contractor
Board of Electricity
S-173 Griggs Midway Bldg.
1821 University Ave.
St. Paul, MN 55104
Phone: (612)642-0800

Credential Type: License. **Duration of License:** Two years. **Requirements:** Individual or employee must be a licensed master electrician. Post $5000 performance bond. Have required general liability and property damage insurance. **Fees:** $200 license fee. **Governing Statute:** Minnesota Statutes, Sections 326.241-326.248. Minnesota Rules 3800-3899.

2600

Electrical Lineman
Board of Electricity
S-173 Griggs Midway Bldg.
1821 University Ave.
St. Paul, MN 55104
Phone: (612)642-0800

Credential Type: Electrical Lineman License. **Duration of License:** Two years. **Requirements:** Contact licensing body for application information. **Examination:** Yes. **Fees:** $30 license fee. $35 exam fee. $30 renewal fee. **Governing Statute:** Minnesota Statutes, Sections 326.241-326.248. Minnesota Rules 3800-3899.

2601

Electrician
Board of Electricity
S-173 Griggs Midway Bldg.
1821 University Ave.
St. Paul, MN 55104
Phone: (612)642-0800

Credential Type: Class A Master Electrician License. **Duration of License:** Two years. **Requirements:** Contact licensing body for application information. **Examination:** Yes. **Fees:** $80 license fee. $35 exam fee. $80 renewal fee. **Governing Statute:** Minnesota Statutes, Sections 326.241-326.248. Minnesota Rules 3800-3899.

Credential Type: Class A Journeyman Electrician License. **Duration of License:** Two years. **Requirements:** Contact licensing body for application information. **Examination:** Yes. **Fees:** $80 license fee. $35 exam fee. $80 renewal fee. **Governing Statute:** Minnesota Statutes, Sections 326.241-326.248. Minnesota Rules 3800-3899.

Credential Type: Maintenance Electrician License. **Duration of License:** Two years. **Requirements:** Contact licensing body for application information. **Examination:** Yes. **Fees:** $30 license fee. $35 exam fee. $30 renewal fee. **Governing Statute:** Minnesota Statutes, Sections 326.241-326.248. Minnesota Rules 3800-3899.

Credential Type: Class A Installer License. **Duration of License:** Two years. **Requirements:** Contact licensing body for application information. **Examination:** Yes. **Fees:** $30 license fee. $35 exam fee. $30 renewal fee. **Governing Statute:** Minnesota Statutes, Sections 326.241-326.248. Minnesota Rules 3800-3899.

Credential Type: Class B Installer License. **Duration of License:** Two years. **Requirements:** Contact licensing body for application information. **Examination:** Yes. **Fees:** $30 license fee. $35 exam fee. $30 renewal fee. **Governing Statute:** Minnesota Statutes, Sections 326.241-326.248. Minnesota Rules 3800-3899.

2602

Elevator Constructor Electrician
Board of Electricity
S-173 Griggs Midway Bldg.
1821 University Ave.
St. Paul, MN 55104
Phone: (612)642-0800

Credential Type: Master Elevator Constructor License. **Duration of License:** Two years. **Requirements:** Contact licensing body for application information. **Examination:** Yes. **Fees:** $80 license fee. $35 exam fee. $80 renewal fee. **Governing Statute:** Minnesota Statutes, Sections 326.241-326.248. Minnesota Rules 3800-3899.

Credential Type: Elevator Constructor License. **Duration of License:** Two years. **Requirements:** Contact licensing body for application information. **Examination:** Yes. **Fees:** $30 license fee. $35 exam fee. $30 renewal fee. **Governing Statute:** Minnesota Statutes, Sections 326.241-326.248. Minnesota Rules 3800-3899.

Montana

2603

Electrician
Montana State Electrical Board
111 N. Jackson
Helena, MT 59620
Phone: (406)444-4390

Credential Type: Residential Electrician License. **Duration of License:** One year. **Requirements:** Two years of apprenticeship in the electrical trade, or two years of practical electrical experience in residential structures consisting of fewer than five living units per structure. **Examination:** Written **Fees:** $10 application fee. $40 exam fee. $10 license fee. $7.50 renewal fee. **Governing Statute:** Montana Code Annotated 37-68-301 through 37-68-322.

Credential Type: Journeyworker Electrician License. **Duration of License:** One year. **Requirements:** Four years of apprenticeship in the electrical trade, or four years of practical electrical experience. **Examination:** Written. **Fees:** $10 application fee. $40 exam fee. $10 license fee. $7.50 renewal fee. **Governing Statute:** Montana Code Annotated 37-68-301 through 37-68-322.

Credential Type: Master Electrician License. **Duration of License:** One year. **Requirements:** Graduation from an electrical engineering program at an accredited college plus one year of practical electrical experience; or graduation from an electrical trade school plus four years of practical experience in electrical work or equivalent. **Examination:** Written. **Fees:** $10 application fee. $40 exam fee. $25 license fee. $20 renewal fee. **Governing Statute:** Montana Code Annotated 37-68-301 through 37-68-322.

Nebraska

2604

Electrician
Nebraska Electric Board
PO Box 95066
800 S. 13th St., Ste. 109
Lincoln, NE 68509
Phone: (402)471-3550

Credential Type: License. **Requirements:** Class A Contractor must be a graduate of an accredited four year college plus have one year experience as a licensed journeyman, or five years experience in layout, supervision, and installation. Class B Contractor must have at least three years of acceptable experience. **Examination:** Yes. **Fees:** Class A Contractor, $62 examination fee. Class A Contractor, $150 license fee. Class B Contractor, $45 examination fee. Class B Contractor, $150 license fee.

Credential Type: Master License. **Requirements:** Class A Master must be a graduate of an accredited four year college plus one year experience as a licensed journeyman, or five years experience in layout, supervision, and installation. Class B Master must have at least three years of acceptable experience. **Examination:** Yes. **Fees:** Class A Master, $62 examination fee. Class A Master, $150 license fee. Class B Master, $32 examination fee. Class B Master, $150 license fee.

Credential Type: Journeyman License. **Requirements:** Class A Journeyman must have at least four years experience acceptable to the board or three years experience and successful completion of a two year post-high school course in electrical wiring. **Examination:** Yes. **Fees:** Class A Journeyman, $12 examination fee. Class A Journeyman, $20 license fee.

Nevada

2605

Electrician
Nevada State Contractors Board
70 Linden St.
Reno, NV 89502
Phone: (702)688-1141

Credential Type: License. **Requirements:** Four years of skilled experience in the licensed field. Financial responsibility and good character. **Examination:** Yes. **Fees:** $270 application fee. $120 license fee. $120 renewal fee. $40 exam fee.

New Hampshire

2606

Electrician
Electricians Licensing Board
James Hayes Safety Bldg.
10 Hazen Drive
Concord, NH 03302
Phone: (603)271-3748

Credential Type: Journeyman Electrician License. **Duration of License:** One year. **Requirements:** At least 18 years of age. High school graduate or equivalent. Four years (8,000 hours) of experience as an apprentice electrician under the supervision of a licensed electrician. Complete a four year course (144 hours each year) of study in electricity. Renewal requires a 15 hour code course on each new edition of the National Electric Code. **Examination:** Journeyman's examination. **Reciprocity:** Yes, with the states of Massachusetts and Vermont. **Fees:** $25 examination fee. $20 license fee. $20 annual renewal fee.

Credential Type: Master Electrician License. **Duration of License:** One year. **Requirements:** Hold a Journeyman Electrician License. Complete at least one year (2,000 hours) of practical experience as a journeyman. Renewal requires a 15 hour code course on each new edition of the National Electric Code. **Examination:** Master electrician examination. **Reciprocity:** Yes, with the states of Massachusetts and Vermont. **Fees:** $25 examination fee. $60 license fee. $60 annual renewal fee.

New Jersey

2607

Electrical Contractor
Board of Examiners of Electrical Contractors
1100 Raymond Blvd., Rm. 503
Newark, NJ 07102
Phone: (201)648-2058

Credential Type: License. **Requirements:** Five years of related experience; or a bachelor's degree in electrical engineering plus two years of experience; or a high school diploma, graduation from an accredited electrical technical school and three and one-half years of experience. 21 years of age. **Examination:** Yes. **Fees:** $40 exam fee. $75 license fee. $12.50 permit fee. $20 seal press fee. $25 application fee. **Governing Statute:** NJSA 45:5A. NJAC 13:31.

New Mexico

2608

Electrical Contractor
Construction Industries Div.
Dept. of Regulation and Licensing
PO Box 25101
725 St. Michael's Dr.
Santa Fe, NM 87504
Phone: (505)827-7030
Fax: (505)827-7045

Credential Type: Electrical Contractor License. **Duration of License:** Two years. **Requirements:** Be at least 18 years of age. Complete at least four years of approved experience within the past 10 years. **Examination:** Yes. **Fees:** $30 application fee. $30 exam fee. $200 license fee. $200 renewal fee. **Governing Statute:** Construction Industries Division Rules and Regulations. New Mexico Construction Industries Licensing Act, Chapter 60.

2609

Electrician (Racetrack)
New Mexico State Racing Commission
PO Box 8576, Highland Station
Albuquerque, NM 87198
Phone: (505)841-4644

Credential Type: License Registration. **Requirements:** Submit application and fingerprint card. Pay fees. **Fees:** $14 registration fee. $1 notary fee. $23 fingerprint card processing fee.

2610

Journeyman Electrician
Construction Industries Div.
Dept. of Regulation and Licensing
PO Box 25101
725 St. Michael's Dr.
Santa Fe, NM 87504
Phone: (505)827-7030
Fax: (505)827-7045

Credential Type: Journeyman Electrician Certificate of Competence. **Duration of License:** One year. **Authorization:** Must be employed by a properly licensed contractor. **Requirements:** Be at least 18 years of age. Complete at least two years of approved experience or a course in the trade approved by the vocational educational division of the state department of public education. **Examination:** Electrical Journeyman Examination. **Fees:** $25 exam fee. $25 renewal fee. **Governing Statute:** Construction Industries Division Rules and

North Carolina

2611

Alarm Installer
Alarm Systems Licensing Board
PO Box 29500
Raliegh, NC 27626
Phone: (919)779-1611

Credential Type: Registration. **Duration of License:** One year. **Requirements:** 18 years of age. U.S. citizen or resident alien. Must be employed by a licensed alarm system company. **Fees:** $15 application fee. $10 registration fee. $15 renewal fee.

2612

Electrical Contractor
North Carolina State Board of Electrical Contractors
PO Box 18727
Raleigh, NC 27619
Phone: (919)733-9042

Credential Type: License. **Duration of License:** One year. **Requirements:** 18 years of age. High school diploma or equivalent. Two years of experience while engaged actively and directly in the installation of electrical wiring and equipment. **Examination:** Multiple choice. **Fees:** $50—$200 application and license fee. $25—$100 renewal fee.

North Dakota

2613

Electrician
State Electrical Board
Box 857
Bismarck, ND 58502-0857
Phone: (701)224-2822

Credential Type: Master Electrician License. **Duration of License:** One year. **Requirements:** Complete at least one year of work experience as a licensed journeyman electrician. **Examination:** Master Electrician Examination. **Reciprocity:** With Minnesota and South Dakota only. **Fees:** $50 license fee. $50 exam fee.

Credential Type: Journeyman Electrician License. **Duration of License:** One year. **Requirements:** Complete four years of work experience as an apprentice. **Examination:** Journeyman Electrician Examination. **Fees:** $25 license fee. $25 exam fee.

Ohio

2614

Automatic Sprinkler System Designer
Board of Building Standards
Dept. of Industrial Relations
2323 W. 5th Ave.
PO Box 825
Columbus, OH 43266-0567
Phone: (614)644-2613

Credential Type: Automatic Sprinkler System Designer Certification. **Duration of License:** Three years. **Requirements:** Submit application and pass examination for competency. **Examination:** Automatic Sprinkler System Designer Examination. **Fees:** $200 exam fee.

2615

Mine Electrician
Mine Examining Board
Dept. of Industrial Relations
2323 W. Fifth Ave.
PO Box 825
Columbus, OH 43216
Phone: (614)644-2234

Credential Type: License. **Duration of License:** Permanent. **Authorization:** Must remain employed to keep license. **Requirements:** Be able to read and write English. Have at least one year of practical experience. **Examination:** Mine electrician examination. **Fees:** $10 exam fee.

Oklahoma

2616

Burglar Alarm Service and Installation Company Technician
Oklahoma State Dept. of Health
Occupational Licensing Div.
1000 N.E. Tenth
PO Box 53551
Oklahoma City, OK 73152
Phone: (405)271-5217

Credential Type: License. **Duration of License:** One year. **Requirements:** Verified experience in burglar alarm industry. Security verification clearance. No felony convictions. **Examination:** Burglar Alarm Service and Installation Company Technician Examination. **Fees:** $25 application fee. $25 renewal fee.

2617

Electrical Contractor (Residential)
Oklahoma State Health Dept.
1000 N.E. Tenth, Rm. 806
Oklahoma City, OK 73152
Phone: (405)271-5217

Credential Type: License. **Duration of License:** One year. **Requirements:** 19 years of age. Three years of work experience. **Examination:** Residential Electrical Contractor Examination. **Fees:** $50 exam fee. $50 license fee. $50 renewal fee.

2618

Electrical Contractor (Unlimited)
Oklahoma State Dept. of Health
1000 N.E. Tenth, Rm. 806
Oklahoma City, OK 73152
Phone: (405)271-5217

Credential Type: License. **Duration of License:** One year. **Requirements:** 21 years of age. Five years of experience in electrical construction; two years must be experience in commercial/industrial construction. **Examination:** Electrical Contractor Examination. **Fees:** $50 exam fee. $50 license fee. $50 renewal fee.

2619

Electrical Journeyman (Residential)
Oklahoma State Dept. of Health
1000 N.E. Tenth, Rm. 806
Oklahoma City, OK 73152
Phone: (405)271-5217

Credential Type: License. **Duration of License:** One year. **Requirements:** 18 years of age. Two years of work experience. **Examination:** Residential Journeyman Electrician Examination. **Fees:** $25 exam fee. $15 license fee. $15 renewal fee.

2620

Electrical Journeyman (Unlimited)
Oklahoma Dept. of Health
1000 N.E. Tenth, Rm. 806
Oklahoma City, OK 73152
Phone: (405)271-5217

Credential Type: License. **Duration of License:** One year. **Requirements:** 20 years of age. Four years of experience in commercial/industrial construction. **Examination:** Journeyman Electrician Examination. **Fees:** $25 exam fee. $15 license fee. $15 renewal fee.

Regulations. New Mexico Construction Industries Licensing Act, Chapter 60.

2621

Fire Alarm Service and Installation Company Technician
Oklahoma State Dept. of Health
Occupational Licensing Service
1000 N.E. Tenth
PO Box 53551
Oklahoma City, OK 73152
Phone: (405)271-5217

Credential Type: License. **Duration of License:** One year. **Requirements:** Verified experience in the fire alarm industry. Security verification clearance. No felony convictions. **Examination:** Fire Alarm Technician Examination. **Fees:** $25 exam fee. $25 application fee. $25 renewal fee.

2622

Fire Alarm Sprinkler Company Technician
Oklahoma State Dept. of Health
Occupational Licensing Service
1000 N.E. Tenth
PO Box 53551
Oklahoma City, OK 73152
Phone: (405)271-5217

Credential Type: License. **Duration of License:** One year. **Requirements:** Verified experience working in the fire sprinkler industry. **Examination:** Fire Sprinkler Technician Examination. **Fees:** $25 exam fee. $25 application fee. $25 renewal fee.

Oregon

2623

Electrical Contractor
Construction Contractors Board
700 Summer St. NE, Ste. 300
Salem, OR 97309-5052
Phone: (503)373-4621

Credential Type: Registration. **Requirements:** Must complete application and pay fees. **Fees:** $125 registration fee. $125 renewal fee. **Governing Statute:** ORS 479.630.

2624

Electrical Limited Maintenance Specialty Contractor
Building Codes Agency
1535 Edgewater
Salem, OR 97310
Phone: (503)373-1268

Credential Type: License. **Requirements:** Must have 12 months of related exprience. **Fees:** $25 license fee. $25 renewal fee. **Governing Statute:** ORS 479.630.

2625

Electrician
Building Codes Agency
1535 Edgewater NW
Salem, OR 97310
Phone: (503)373-1268

Credential Type: License. **Duration of License:** Three years. **Requirements:** Employer verification of experience and qualifications. Four-year apprenticeship or equivalent experience. **Examination:** Yes. **Fees:** $10 exam fee. $100 license fee. $100 renewal fee. **Governing Statute:** ORS 479.630(5).

2626

Electrician, General Supervisor
Building Codes Agency
1535 Edgewater NW
Salem, OR 97310
Phone: (503)373-1268

Credential Type: License. **Duration of License:** Three years. **Requirements:** Must be regularly employed by either an electrical contractor or an industrial plant. Must submit proof of at least four years of employment as a General Journeyman Electrician. **Examination:** Yes. **Fees:** $10 exam fee. $100 license fee. $100 renewal fee. **Governing Statute:** ORS 479.630(2).

2627

Electrician, Limited Journeyman, Elevator
Building Codes Agency
1535 Edgewater NW
Salem, OR 97310
Phone: (503)373-1268

Credential Type: License. **Requirements:** Must complete Elevator Apprenticeship or equivalent experience. **Examination:** Yes. **Fees:** $10 exam fee. $15 license fee. $15 renewal fee. **Governing Statute:** ORS 479.630(6).

2628

Electrician, Limited Journeyman (Limited Energy, Sign, and Stage)
Building Codes Agency
1535 Edgewater NW
Salem, OR 97310
Phone: (503)373-1268

Credential Type: License. **Duration of License:** Three years. **Requirements:** Must have employer verification of qualifications. Must have four-year apprenticeship or equivalent experience. **Examination:** Yes. **Fees:** $10 exam fee. $100 license fee. $100 renewal fee. **Governing Statute:** ORS 479.630(5).

2629

Electrician, Limited Journeyman Manufacturing Plant
Building Codes Agency
1535 Edgewater NW
Salem, OR 97310
Phone: (503)373-1268

Credential Type: License. **Duration of License:** Three years. **Requirements:** Must have served a four year apprenticeship, or have equivalent experience as required by Oregon law. **Examination:** Yes. **Fees:** $10 exam fee. $100 license fee. $100 renewal fee. **Governing Statute:** ORS 479.630.

2630

Electrician, Limited Residential
Building Codes Agency
1535 Edgewater NW
Salem, OR 97310
Phone: (503)373-1268

Credential Type: License. **Duration of License:** Three years. **Requirements:** Must have two years apprenticeship or equivalent experience. **Examination:** Yes. **Fees:** $10 exam fee. $100 license fee. $100 renewal fee. **Governing Statute:** ORS 479.630.

2631

Electrician, Oil Module
Building Codes Agency
1535 Edgewater NW
Salem, OR 97310
Phone: (503)373-1268

Credential Type: License. **Requirements:** At least 2,000 hours of experience gained during the past five years in installing, maintaining, replacing or repairing electrical wiring or electrical products; or demonstrate continual employment in installing, maintaining, replacing or repairing electrical wiring products by an oil module manufacturer during the previous 12 months; or hold a valid general journey electrician's license or higher. **Examination:** Yes. **Reciprocity:** Yes. **Fees:** $10 exam fee. **Governing Statute:** ORS 479.630.

2632

Limited Energy Electrical Contractor
Building Codes Agency
1535 Edgewater NW
Salem, OR 97310
Phone: (503)373-1268

Credential Type: License. **Fees:** $125 license fee. $125 renewal fee. **Governing Statute:** ORS 479.630.

Rhode Island

2633

Electric Sign Installer
Board of Examiners of Electricians
Div. of Professional Regulation
Rhode Island Dept. of Labor
220 Elmwood Ave.
Providence, RI 02907
Phone: (401)457-1860

Credential Type: Journeyperson License (Cert CF). **Duration of License:** One year. **Requirements:** At least 18 years of age. Complete a 6,000 hour registered apprenticeship under the supervision of a licensed electrician. **Examination:** Written examination. **Reciprocity:** No. **Fees:** $30 application fee. $10 apprentice registration fee. $30 Journeyperson (Cert CF) license fee.

Credential Type: Master Contractor License (Cert SCF). **Duration of License:** One year. **Requirements:** Hold journeyperson's license for at least one year or complete 10,000 hours of equivalent experience. Alternative requirements are available by contacting the board. **Examination:** Written examination. **Reciprocity:** No. **Fees:** $30 application fee. $100 master contractor (Cert SCF) license fee.

2634

Electrical Contractor
Board of Examiners of Electricians
Div. of Professional Regulation
Rhode Island Dept. of Labor
220 Elmwood Ave.
Providence, RI 02907
Phone: (401)457-1860

Credential Type: Master Contractor License (Cert A). **Duration of License:** One year. **Requirements:** Hold journeyperson's license for at least one year or complete 10,000 hours of equivalent experience. Alternative requirements are available by contacting the board. **Examination:** Written examination. **Reciprocity:** No. **Fees:** $30 application fee. $100 master contractor (Cert A) license fee.

2635

Electrician
Board of Examiners of Electricians
Div. of Professional Regulation
Rhode Island Dept. of Labor
220 Elmwood Ave.
Providence, RI 02907
Phone: (401)457-1860

Credential Type: Journeyperson License (Cert B). **Duration of License:** One year. **Requirements:** At least 18 years of age. Complete a 6,000 hour registered apprenticeship under the supervision of a licensed electrician. **Examination:** Written examination. **Reciprocity:** No. **Fees:** $30 application fee. $10 apprentice registration fee. $30 Journeyperson (Cert B) license fee.

2636

Fire Alarm Installer
Board of Examiners of Electricians
Div. of Professional Regulation
Rhode Island Dept. of Labor
220 Elmwood Ave.
Providence, RI 02907
Phone: (401)457-1860

Credential Type: Fire Alarm Installer Journeyperson License (Cert BF). **Duration of License:** One year. **Requirements:** At least 18 years of age. Complete 6,000 hours of practical experience as an apprentice to a licensed fire alarm installer. Must register with licensing agency before starting training. **Examination:** Written. **Reciprocity:** No. **Fees:** $10 apprentice registration fee. $30 application fee. $30 Journeyperson's license (Cert BF) fee.

Credential Type: Fire Alarm Installer Master (Contractor) License (Cert AF). **Duration of License:** One year. **Requirements:** Hold a journeyperson's license for at least one year. Complete 10,000 hours of work on fire alarm systems. Alternative licensing requirements are available through the board. **Examination:** Written. **Reciprocity:** No. **Fees:** $30 application fee. $100 Master (Contractor) license fee.

South Carolina

2637

Electrician
Municipal Assn. of South Carolina
1529 Washington St.
Columbia, SC 29201
Phone: (803)799-9574

Credential Type: Master Electrician. **Requirements:** Four years of experience in a trade.

Credential Type: Journeyman Electrician. **Requirements:** Two years of experience in a trade. **Examination:** Yes.

South Dakota

2638

Electrical Contractor
South Dakota Electrical Commission
Dept. of Commerce and Regulation
125 West Capitol
Pierre, SD 57501
Phone: (605)773-3573
Phone: (605)224-8674
Phone: (800)233-7765

Credential Type: Electrical Contractor Registration and Permit. **Duration of License:** Two years. **Requirements:** Must have the necessary qualifications, training, experience, and technical knowledge to plan, lay out, and supervise the installation and repair of electrical wiring, apparatus, and equipment for electric light, heating, and power. Must have at least two years experience as a journeyman electrician or at least four years experience as a Class B electrician. Post bond of $10,000.

Renewal requires 12 continuing education credits every two years. After July 1, 1994, the continuing education requirement will increase to 16 credits. **Examination:** Written exam for wiring permit. **Reciprocity:** Yes. **Fees:** $100 permit fee. $40 exam fee. $100 renewal fee. $100 reciprocity fee. **Governing Statute:** South Dakota Codified Laws, Chap. 36-16. Administrative Rules of South Dakota, Article 20:44.

2639

Electrician
South Dakota Electrical Commission
Dept. of Commerce and Regulation
125 West Capitol
Pierre, SD 57501
Phone: (605)773-3573
Phone: (605)224-8674
Phone: (800)233-7765

Credential Type: Class B Electrician Registration and Permit. **Duration of License:** Two years. **Requirements:** Must have at least three years experience in the wiring, installing, and reparing of electrical apparatus and equipment under the supervision of an electrical contractor or Class B electrician. Post bond of $10,000.

Renewal requires 12 continuing education credits every two years. After July 1, 1994, the continuing education requirement will increase to 16 credits. **Examination:** Written exam for wiring permit. **Fees:** $40 permit fee. $40 exam fee. $40 renewal fee. **Governing Statute:** South Dakota Codified Laws, Chap. 36-16. Administrative Rules of South Dakota, Article 20:44.

Credential Type: Journeyman Electrician Registration and Permit. **Duration of License:** Two years. **Requirements:** Must have at least four years experience in the wiring, installing, and reparing of electrical apparatus and equipment under the supervision of an electrical contractor or Class B electrician.

Renewal requires 12 continuing education credits every two years. After July 1, 1994, the continuing education requirement will increase to 16 credits. **Examination:** Written exam for wiring permit. **Reciprocity:** Yes. **Fees:** $40 permit fee. $40 exam fee. $40 renewal fee. $40 reciprocity fee. **Governing Statute:** South Dakota Codified Laws, Chap. 36-16. Administrative Rules of South Dakota, Article 20:44.

Utah

2640

Electrician
Dept. of Commerce
Div. of Occupational and
   Professional Licensing
160 E. 300 S.
PO Box 45802
Salt Lake City, UT 84145
Phone: (801)530-6628

Credential Type: Master Electrician License. **Requirements:** A master electritcan must have graduated from an approved college or university with one year of practical experience; or graduated from an approved trade school with two years practical experience; or at least eight years of practical experience under a licensed journeyman or master electrician. **Examination:** Yes. **Fees:** $100 license fee. $75 renewal fee.

Credential Type: Journeyman Electrican License. **Requirements:** A journeyman must complete four years of full-time training and instruction as a licensed apprentice under supervision; or completion of six years of practical experience in wiring, installing, and repairing electrical apparatus under supervision. In addition a journerman must also complete two years of training in an approved program; or complete four years of experience under a licensed master, journeyman, or residential journeyman electrician. **Fees:** $100 license fee. $75 renewal fee.

2641

Mine Electrician
The Industrial Commission of Utah
160 E. 300 S.
Salt Lake City, UT 84151-0910
Phone: (801)530-6869

Credential Type: Mine Electrician License. **Requirements:** Must have at least one year of experience in performing electrical work underground in a coal mine, in the surface coal mine, in a non-coal mine, in the mine equipment manufacturing industry, or in any other industry using or manufacturing similar equipment. Must hold a U.S. Bureau of Mines First Aid Certificate or the equivalent training. **Examination:** Yes. **Fees:** $50 license fee.

Vermont

2642

Electrician, Journeyman
Electrician's Licensing Board
Dept. of Labor and Industry
120 State St.
Montpelier, VT 05602
Phone: (802)828-2107

Credential Type: License. **Duration of License:** One year. **Requirements:** Successful completion of apprenticeship in electrical wiring; or equivalent experience or training. **Examination:** Yes. **Reciprocity:** Yes. **Fees:** $60 Annual fee. **Governing Statute:** Title 26, VSA Section 903.

2643

Electrician Journeyman Type S
Electrician's Licensing Board
Dept. of Labor and Industry
120 State St.
Montpelier, VT 05602
Phone: (802)828-2107

Credential Type: License. **Duration of License:** One year. **Authorization:** Restricted to areas of specialized competence. **Requirements:** Successful completion of Type S Journeyman program in at least one field. Experience in or out of Vermont. **Examination:** Yes. **Reciprocity:** No. **Fees:** $40 per field, per year. **Governing Statute:** Title 26, VSA Section 904.

2644

Electrician, Master
Electrician's Licensing Board
Dept. of Labor and Industry
120 State St.
Montpelier, VT 05602
Phone: (802)828-2107

Credential Type: License. **Duration of License:** One year. **Requirements:** Journeyman's license held for two years or comparable experience. **Examination:** Yes. **Reciprocity:** Yes. **Fees:** $100 Annual fee. **Governing Statute:** Title 26, VSA Section 902.

2645

Installer/Seller Lightning Rods and Fire Detection Systems
Electrician's Licensing Board
Dept. of Labor and Industry
120 State St.
Montpelier, VT 05602
Phone: (802)828-2107

Credential Type: License. **Requirements:** To Install: Equipment must be approved. To Sell: Deemed qualified by State Fire Marshal. **Examination:** Installers: Yes. Sellers: No. **Reciprocity:** No. **Fees:** $10 Installers (annually). $5 Sellers (annually). **Governing Statute:** Title 9, VSA Sections 3201-3205.

Washington

2646

Electrical Administrator
Dept. of Labor and Industries
Building and Construction Safety
 Inspection Services
General Administration Bldg., HC-101
Olympia, WA 98504
Phone: (206)753-6807
Phone: (206)753-6307

Credential Type: Certification. **Duration of License:** Two years. **Requirements:** Complete approved training in electrical work, the National Electrical Code, electrical theory, and safety and administrative procedures. Continuing education required for renewal. **Examination:** Written examination. **Fees:** $25 application fee. $40 certification fee. $60 exam fee. $52 renewal fee.

2647

Electrical Contractor
Dept. of Labor and Industries
Building and Construction Safety
 Inspection Services
General Administration Bldg., HC-101
Olympia, WA 98504
Phone: (206)753-6807
Phone: (206)753-6307

Credential Type: License. **Duration of License:** Two years. **Authorization:** General and specialty licenses are issued. **Requirements:** Must be a certified electrical administrator or be employed by one. Post $4000 surety bond. **Fees:** $80 annual license fee.

2648

Electrician
Dept. of Labor & Industries
Building & Construction Safety
 Inspection Services
General Administration Bldg., HC-101
Olympia, WA 98504
Phone: (206)753-5194

Credential Type: Apprentice Electrician Certificate. **Duration of License:** One year. **Requirements:** Submit application. Must be supervised by a journeyman or specialty electrician who is employed by an electrical contractor. Must verify hours of work experience at time of certificate renewal. **Fees:** $15 initial certificate fee. $20 renewal fee.

Credential Type: Journeyman Electrician Certificate. **Duration of License:** Two years. **Requirements:** Must have four years of commercial/industrial electrical experience or two years of specialty electrical experience and two years of commercial/industrial experience. **Fees:** $20 initial certificate fee. $25 application fee. $25 examination fee. $26 renewal fee.

Credential Type: Specialty Electrician Certificate. **Duration of License:** Two years. **Requirements:** Must have four years experience in appropriate electrical specialty. **Fees:** $20 initial certificate fee. $25 application fee. $25 examination fee. $26 renewal fee.

West Virginia

2649

Electrician
West Virginia State Fire Marshal
2000 Quarrier St.
Charleston, WV 25305
Phone: (304)348-2191

Credential Type: License. **Duration of License:** One year. **Authorization:** Licenses issued for electrician helper, journeyman electrician, and master electrician. **Requirements:** 18 years old. **Examination:** Yes. **Fees:** $10 Examination. $4 License. $4 Renewal.

2650

Electrician (Mine)
Dept. of Energy
State Capitol Bldg.
Charleston, WV 25305
Phone: (304)348-3500

Credential Type: License. **Requirements:** 19 years old. One year of experience in electrical work. Eight hours of hazard training. Must obtain license legally. **Examination:** Yes. **Fees:** $15 License.

Wyoming

2651

Electrician
Wyoming State Electrical Board
Barrett Bldg.
Cheyenne, WY 82002
Phone: (307)777-7991

Credential Type: License. **Duration of License:** Journeyman—3 years. Master and limited—1 year. **Requirements:** Journeyman—4 years experience, pass written and practical examinations. Master—8 years experience, pass written examination. Limited—Pass written examination. **Examination:** Yes. **Fees:** $50 Examination administration. $25 Examination application ($50 Master and Limited). $50 License (Journeyman), $100 License (Master), $25 (Master). $25 Renewal (Journeyman and Limited), $50 Master. Other fees may apply, please contact the board.

Elevator Installation and Repair Occupations

The following states grant licenses in this occupational category as of the date of publication: Arkansas, Connecticut, Hawaii, Iowa, Kentucky, Massachusetts, Michigan, Minnesota, Nebraska, Ohio, Rhode Island.

Arkansas

2652

Elevator and Lifting Device Inspector
Arkansas Dept. of Labor
Elevator Safety Board
10421 W. Markham
Little Rock, AR 72205
Phone: (501)682-4530

Credential Type: License. **Requirements:** Pass the written examination. Submit a written application. **Examination:** Yes. **Fees:** $5 Written Examination. $25 License. $25 Renewal.

Connecticut

2653

Elevator Apprentice
Elevator Installation, Repair, and Maintenance Board
Occupational Licensing Div.
Consumer Protection Dept.
165 Capitol Ave.
Hartford, CT 06106
Phone: (203)566-3275

Credential Type: Apprentice permit. **Duration of License:** Until next licensure examination. **Authorization:** Work may be performed only under the supervision of a licensed contractor, journeyman, or elevator craftsman. **Requirements:** Be of good moral character. Have an 8th grade education or equivalent. **Governing Statute:** General Statutes of Connecticut, Chap. 393.

2654

Elevator Contractor
Elevator Installation, Repair, and Maintenance Board
Occupational Licensing Div.
Consumer Protection Dept.
165 Capitol Ave.
Hartford, CT 06106
Phone: (203)566-3275

Credential Type: Unlimited contractor elevator craftsman's license (R-1). **Duration of License:** Two years. **Authorization:** Covers elevator installation, repair, and maintenance. **Requirements:** Be of good moral character. Have an 8th grade education or equivalent. Must have served as an journeyman elevator craftsman for not less than two years. If service was outside of state, must submit evidence that service was comparable to service in state or that applicant has education and experience and has passed an examination demonstrating competency to be an unlimited contractor. **Examination:** State licensure exam. **Reciprocity:** Yes, with selected states. **Fees:** $75 application fee. $150 license fee. **Governing Statute:** General Statutes of Connecticut, Chap. 393.

2655

Elevator Craftsman
Elevator Installation, Repair, and Maintenance Board
Occupational Licensing Div.
Consumer Protection Dept.
165 Capitol Ave.
Hartford, CT 06106
Phone: (203)566-3275

Credential Type: Elevator craftsman's license. **Duration of License:** Two years. **Requirements:** Be of good moral character. Have an 8th grade education or equivalent. Complete a bona fide apprencticeship program. Have at least two years experience. Demonstrate competency by completing applicable state licensure examination. **Examination:** State licensure examination. **Reciprocity:** Yes, with selected states. **Fees:** $45 application fee. $120 license fee. **Governing Statute:** General Statutes of Connecticut, Chap. 393.

2656

Elevator Helper
Elevator Installation, Repair, and Maintenance Board
Occupational Licensing Div.
Consumer Protection Dept.
165 Capitol Ave.
Hartford, CT 06106
Phone: (203)566-3275

Credential Type: Elevator helper's license. **Duration of License:** Two years. **Authorization:** May perform only elevator maintenance under the supervision of an elevator craftsman. **Requirements:** Be of good moral character. Have an 8th grade education or equivalent. **Fees:** $45 application fee. $120 license fee. **Governing Statute:** General Statutes of Connecticut, Chap. 393.

2657

Elevator Journeyman
Elevator Installation, Repair, and Maintenance Board
Occupational Licensing Div.
Consumer Protection Dept.
165 Capitol Ave.
Hartford, CT 06106
Phone: (203)566-3275

Credential Type: Unlimited journeyman elevator craftsman's license (R-2). **Duration of License: Two years. **Authorization:** Must be in the employ of a licensed contractor. **Requirements:** Be of good moral character. Have an 8th grade education or equivalent. Complete a bona fide apprencticeship program, including not less than four years experience. Demonstrate competency by completing applicable state licensure examination. **Examination:** State licensure examination. **Reciprocity:** Yes, with selected states. **Fees:** $45 application fee. $120 license fee. **Governing Statute:** General Statutes of Connecticut, Chap. 393.

Hawaii

2658

Elevator Mechanic
Hawaii Elevator Mechanics Licensing Board
Dept. of Commerce and Consumer Affairs
PO Box 3469
Honolulu, HI 96801
Phone: (808)548-7471

Credential Type: License. **Duration of License:** Six months. **Requirements:** Two years of training as a registered apprentice elevator mechanic under the supervision of a licensed elevator mechanic. **Examination:** Written. **Fees:** $20 application fee. $35 exam fee. $20 license fee. $15 $30 Biennial Compliance Resolution Fund fee. $20 renewal fee.

Iowa

2659

Special Elevator Inspector
Elevator Safety Section
Iowa Dept. of Employment Services
1000 E. Grand Ave.
Des Moines, IA 50319
Phone: (515)281-3606

Credential Type: Special Elevator Inspector Certificate. **Duration of License:** Permanent. **Authorization:** Limited to safety tests on elevators, escalators, and lifts. **Requirements:** The applicant must study the "Safety Code for Elevators and Escalators" and the "Inspector's Manual." **Examination:** Written and practical. **Fees:** None.

Credential Type: Special Elevator Inspector License. **Duration of License:** One year. **Requirements:** High school diploma or equivalent. Three years of full-time experience with elevators. Completion of a one-week course put on by the National Assn. of Elevator Authorities. **Examination:** Written and practical. **Fees:** $400—$600 course and exam fee.

Kentucky

2660

Elevator Inspector
Dept. of Housing, Building and Construction
1047 U.S. 127 South
Frankfort, KY 40601
Phone: (502)564-3626

Credential Type: License. **Requirements:** High school diploma or Certificate of Competency. 18 years of age. **Examination:** Yes. **Reciprocity:** No. **Fees:** $10 exam fee.

Massachusetts

2661

Elevator Constructor
Dept. of Public Safety
Div. of Inspection
Elevator Inspection Section
One Ashburton Pl.
Boston, MA 02108
Phone: (617)727-3200

Credential Type: Elevator Constructor License. **Duration of License:** One year. **Requirements:** Have at least two years of related work experience. **Examination:** Written examination. **Governing Statute:** Massachusetts General Laws, Chap. 143.

2662

Elevator Maintenance Person
Dept. of Public Safety
Div. of Inspection
Elevator Inspection Section
One Ashburton Pl.
Boston, MA 02108
Phone: (617)727-3200

Credential Type: Elevator Maintenance Person License. **Duration of License:** One year. **Requirements:** Have at least two years of related work experience. **Examination:** Written examination. **Governing Statute:** Massachusetts General Laws, Chap. 143.

2663

Elevator Repairperson
Dept. of Public Safety
Div. of Inspection
Elevator Inspection Section
One Ashburton Pl.
Boston, MA 02108
Phone: (617)727-3200

Credential Type: Elevator Repairperson License. **Duration of License:** One year. **Requirements:** Have at least two years of related work experience. **Examination:** Written examination. **Governing Statute:** Massachusetts General Laws, Chap. 143.

Michigan

2664

Elevator Contractor
Elevator Safety Board
Elevator Div.
Bureau of Construction Codes
Dept. of Labor
PO Box 30015
7150 Harris Dr.
Lansing, MI 48909
Phone: (517)322-1287

Credential Type: License. **Duration of License:** One year. **Requirements:** At least five years of experience as an elevator constructor or journeyperson in the type of elevator work for which they desire the license. Provide two letters of reference. Comply with the rules and regulations of the Elevator Safety Board. **Examination:** Written exam. **Fees:** $32 initial exam fee. $53 initial license fee. $53 renewal fee. **Governing Statute:** Michigan Elevator Act, Act 227 of 1967, as amended.

2665

Elevator Inspector
Elevator Safety Board
Elevator Div.
Bureau of Construction Codes
Dept. of Labor
PO Box 30015
7150 Harris Dr.
Lansing, MI 48909
Phone: (517)322-1287

Credential Type: General Elevator Inspector Certification and Commission. **Duration of License:** One year (commission). **Authorization:** General Elevator Inspectors are employed by the state. **Requirements:** Must be certified competent by the Elevator Safety Board of the Department of Labor. Have three years of experience in elevator construction. Provide two letters of

Elevator Inspector, continued

reference. After receiving certificate of competency, applicant is eligible for an annual commission. **Examination:** Written and oral certification exam. **Fees:** $27 certification exam and certificate of competency fee. No commission fee. **Governing Statute:** Michigan Elevator Act, Act 227 of 1967, as amended.

Credential Type: Special Elevator Inspector Certification and Commission. **Duration of License:** One year (commission). **Authorization:** Special Elevator Inspectors are employed by insurance companies or municipalities. **Requirements:** Must be certified competent by the Elevator Safety Board of the Department of Labor. Three years of experience in designing, installing, maintaining, or inspecting elevators. Provide two letters of reference. After receiving certificate of competency, applicant is eligible for an annual commission. **Examination:** Written and oral certification exam. **Fees:** $27 certification exam and certificate of competency fee. $16 initial commission fee. $11 renewal fee. **Governing Statute:** Michigan Elevator Act, Act 227 of 1967, as amended.

2666

Elevator Journeyperson
Elevator Safety Board
Elevator Div.
Bureau of Construction Codes
Dept. of Labor
PO Box 30015
7150 Harris Dr.
Lansing, MI 48909
Phone: (517)322-1287

Credential Type: License. **Duration of License:** One year. **Requirements:** Three years of continuous experience in the type(s) of elevator work in which they desire to be licensed. A degree in electrical or mechanical engineering may be substituted for one year of experience. Provide two written references. Comply with the rules and regulations of the Elevator Safety Board. **Examination:** Written exam. **Fees:** $16 initial exam fee. $11 initial license fee. $11 renewal fee. **Governing Statute:** Elevator Journeyman's Act, Act 333 of 1976, as amended.

Minnesota

2667

Elevator Constructor Electrician
Board of Electricity
S-173 Griggs Midway Bldg.
1821 University Ave.
St. Paul, MN 55104
Phone: (612)642-0800

Credential Type: Master Elevator Constructor License. **Duration of License:** Two years. **Requirements:** Contact licensing body for application information. **Examination:** Yes. **Fees:** $80 license fee. $35 exam fee. $80 renewal fee. **Governing Statute:** Minnesota Statutes, Sections 326.241-326.248. Minnesota Rules 3800-3899.

Credential Type: Elevator Constructor License. **Duration of License:** Two years. **Requirements:** Contact licensing body for application information. **Examination:** Yes. **Fees:** $30 license fee. $35 exam fee. $30 renewal fee. **Governing Statute:** Minnesota Statutes, Sections 326.241-326.248. Minnesota Rules 3800-3899.

Nebraska

2668

Elevator Inspections Manager
Nebraska Dept. of Labor
PO Box 95024
301 Centennial Mall S.
Lincoln, NE 68509
Phone: (402)471-2239

Credential Type: License. **Duration of License:** One year. **Requirements:** Must have at least five years experience at the journeyman level in elevator installation, maintenance, and inspection. **Examination:** Yes. **Fees:** $100 certification fee. $750 examination fee. $75 membership renewal fee. $35 regisration renewal fee.

Ohio

2669

Elevator Inspector
Div. of Elevator Inspection
Dept. of Industrial Relations
2323 W. 5th Ave.
PO Box 825
Columbus, OH 43266-0567
Phone: (614)644-2244

Credential Type: Elevator Inspector Certification. **Duration of License:** Three years. **Requirements:** Submit application and pass examination for competency. **Examination:** General Inspector Examination. **Fees:** $50 exam fee. **Governing Statute:** Ohio Revised Code 4105.02.

Rhode Island

2670

Elevator Inspector
Div. of Occupational Safety
Elevator Unit
220 Elmwood Ave.
Providence, RI 02907
Phone: (401)457-1860

Credential Type: Elevator Inspector License. **Duration of License:** Two years. **Requirements:** Must have a minimum of five years of mechanical and/or electrical experience and one year as an employee of a state enforcement authority. Hold a Qualified Elevator Inspector (QEI) certificate from the American Society of Mechanical Engineers or take written examination. **Reciprocity:** No. **Fees:** $10 examination/application fee. $10 application only fee. $5 biennial renewal fee.

Emergency Medical Technicians

The following states grant licenses in this occupational category as of the date of publication:

Alabama	District of	Iowa	Minnesota	New Mexico	Rhode Island	Washington
Alaska	Columbia	Kansas	Mississippi	New York	South Carolina	West Virginia
Arizona	Florida	Kentucky	Missouri	North Carolina	South Dakota	Wisconsin
Arkansas	Georgia	Louisiana	Montana	North Dakota	Tennessee	Wyoming
California	Hawaii	Maine	Nebraska	Ohio	Texas	
Colorado	Idaho	Maryland	Nevada	Oklahoma	Utah	
Connecticut	Illinois	Massachusetts	New Hampshire	Oregon	Vermont	
Delaware	Indiana	Michigan	New Jersey	Pennsylvania	Virginia	

Alabama

2671

Emergency Medical Technician
State Dept. of Public Health
Emergency Medical Services Div.
669 S. Lawrence St.
Montgomery, AL 36104
Phone: (800)962-9234

Credential Type: License. **Duration of License:** Three years. **Requirements:** 18 years of age. Successful completion of an EMT Training program for Basic, Intermediate, or Paramedic levels. **Examination:** Written and practical portions of the National Registry of EMT's Board certification examination. **Fees:** $15 license fee.

Alaska

2672

Emergency Medical Technician
Alaska Dept. of Health and Social Services
Div. of Public Health
Emergency Medical Services Section
PO Box H
Juneau, AK 99811-0616
Phone: (907)465-3027

Credential Type: Emergency Trauma Technician Certificate. **Requirements:** At least 40 hours of education and training. **Examination:** Written and practical examination administered by state. **Reciprocity:** Holders of valid licenses or certificates issued by other states may be granted an Alaska certificate. **Fees:** $15 test fee for initial certification and recertification.

Credential Type: Emergency Medical Technician Certificate Level I (EMT-I). **Requirements:** At least 110 hours of education and training. **Examination:** Written and practical examination administered by state. **Reciprocity:** Holders of valid licenses or certificates issued by other states may be granted an Alaska certificate. **Fees:** $15 test fee for initial certification and recertification.

Credential Type: Emergency Medical Technician Certificate Level II (EMT-II). **Requirements:** At least 160 hours of education and training. Have six months experience as a state certified EMT-I. **Examination:** Written and practical examination administered by state. **Reciprocity:** Holders of valid licenses or certificates issued by other states may be granted an Alaska certificate. **Fees:** $15 test fee for initial certification and recertification.

Credential Type: Emergency Medical Technician Certificate Level III (EMT-III). **Requirements:** At least 210 hours of education and training. State certification as an EMT-II, plus six months experience as an EMT-II. **Examination:** Written and practical examination administered by state. **Reciprocity:** Holders of valid licenses or certificates issued by other states may be granted an Alaska certificate. **Fees:** $15 test fee for initial certification and recertification.

2673

Mobile Intensive Care Paramedic
Dept. of Commerce and Economic Development
Div. of Occupational Licensing
State Medical Board
PO Box D-LIC
Juneau, AK 99811-0800
Phone: (907)465-2541
Fax: (907)465-2974

Credential Type: Mobile Intensive Care Paramedic License. **Duration of License:** Two years. **Requirements:** At least 19 years of age. High school graduate. Complete paramedic course which meets or exceeds the U.S. Dept. of Transportation National Training Course for the Emergency Medical Technician Paramedic. Following completion of classroom and clinical portions of the board approved curriculum, complete a 480hour internship. Current certification as an Emergency Medical Technician by the National Registry of Emergency Medical Technicians or the Alaska Dept. of Health and Social Services. Pass the written and practical examination for the Emergency Medical Technician-Paramedic administered by the National Registry of Emergency Medical Technicians.

Applicants holding a current license in another state must fulfill the above requirements with the exception of the 480-hour internship and not be currently under suspension or revocation nor be the subject of an unresolved investigation, complaint review procedure, or disciplinary proceeding. **Examination:** Examination for Emergency Medical Technician-Paramedic administered by the National Registry of Emergency Medical Technicians. **Fees:** $50 application fee. $50 license fee. **Governing Statute:** Alaska Statutes 08.64. Professional Regulations 12 AAC 40.

Credential Type: Temporary Permit. **Duration of License:** Eight months. **Requirements:** Meet requirements for licensure and have applied for a permanent license. **Fees:** $50 application fee. $50 license fee. $50 temporary permit fee. **Governing Statute:** Alaska Statutes 08.64. Professional Regulations 12 AAC 40.

Arizona

2674

Emergency Medical Technician
Dept. of Health Services
Office of Emergency Medical Services
100 W. Clarendon
Phoenix, AZ 85013
Phone: (602)255-1170

Credential Type: Basic EMT certificate. **Requirements:** Pass a one-semester course on emergency medical procedures given by an Arizona community college. Pass state-administered written test. **Examination:** State-administered written test.

Credential Type: Intermediate EMT certificate. **Requirements:** Have at least one year experience as a basic EMT. Apply for advance training. Pass a written and practical examination through the National Registry. **Examination:** National Registry intermediate EMT examination. **Fees:** $35 National Registry exam fee.

2675

Paramedic
Dept. of Health Services
Office of Emergency Medical Services
100 W. Clarendon
Phoenix, AZ 85013
Phone: (602)255-1170

Credential Type: Paramedic certificate. **Requirements:** Complete a paramedic training program of at least 650 hours. Pass National Registry examination. **Examination:** National Registry paramedic examination. **Fees:** $35 National Registry exam fee.

Arkansas

2676

Emergency Medical Technician
Arkansas Dept. of Health
Div. of Emergency Medical Services
4815 W. Markham St.
Little Rock, AR 72201
Phone: (501)661-2262

Credential Type: License. **Duration of License:** One year. **Requirements:** 18 years of age. Complete the National Standard Curriculum Emergency Medical Technician course. Affiliated with or sponsored by a licensed emergency ambulance service provider. **Examination:** Yes. **Fees:** $10 Certification. $10 Renewal.

2677

Emergency Medical Technician Intermediate
Arkansas Dept. of Health
Div. of Emergency Medical Services
4815 W. Markham St.
Little Rock, AR 72201
Phone: (501)661-2262

Credential Type: License. **Duration of License:** One year. **Requirements:** 18 years of age. Complete the National Standard Curriculum Emergency Medical Technician course. Currently certified as an EMT. Affiliated with or sponsored by a licensed emergency ambulance service provider. **Examination:** Yes. **Fees:** $10 Certification. $5 Renewal.

2678

Emergency Medical Technician - Paramedic
Arkansas Dept. of Health
Div. of Emergency Medical Services
4815 W. Markham St.
Little Rock, AR 72201
Phone: (501)661-2262

Credential Type: License. **Duration of License:** One year. **Requirements:** Must be certified as an EMT. Complete an approved Paramedic training program consisting of at least 480 hours of didactic and clinical work. **Examination:** Yes. **Fees:** $10 Certification. $10 Renewal.

California

2679

Emergency Medical Technician
California EMS Authority
1930 Ninth St., Ste. 100
Sacramento, CA 95814
Phone: (916)322-4336

Credential Type: EMT-I Certification (Basic). **Duration of License:** Two years. **Authorization:** Certification is implemented by local EMS agencies according to standards determined by the state EMS Authority. **Requirements:** Be at least 18 years of age. Complete 104 hours of EMT-I training. Recertification requires completing a 24-hour refresher course every two years. **Examination:** Written and skills certifying examination.

Credential Type: EMT-II Certification (Limited Advanced Life Support). **Authorization:** Certification is implemented by local EMS agencies according to standards determined by the state EMS Authority. **Requirements:** Be at least 18 years of age. High school graduate or equivalent. Must have EMT-I certification and one year of experience as an EMT-I. Complete 306 total hours of training. Recertification requires 48 hours of continuing education every two years.

Credential Type: EMT-Paramedic Certification. **Authorization:** Certification is implemented by local EMS agencies according to standards determined by the state EMS Authority. **Requirements:** Be at least 18 years of age. High school graduate or equivalent. Must have EMT-I certification. Complete 1032 total hours of training. Recertification requires 48 hours of continuing education every two years and written retesting every four years. **Examination:** Written examination.

Colorado

2680

Emergency Medical Technician
Dept. of Health
Emergency Medical Services Div.
4210 E. 11th Ave.
Denver, CO 80220
Phone: (303)331-8630

Credential Type: Basic Certification (EMT-B). **Duration of License:** Three years. **Authorization:** Authorized to provide basic emergency medical care. **Requirements:** Must be at least 18 years of age. Must pass an EMS-Division approved training program of at least 110 hours, of which at least 100 hours are didactic and 10 hours are clinical. Training program must meet the current National Department of Transportation's standard 110-hour course and include PASG.

Recertification requires 36 hours of pre-approved continuing education, or a 36-hour refresher courrse that meet's DOT standards. Must pass EMT-Basic Practical Examination and State EMT-Basic Written Certification Examination for recertification. **Examination:** EMT-Basic Practical Examination and State EMT-Basic Written Certification Examination. **Reciprocity:** All eligible applicants for legal recognition of an out-of-state certification must take the practical and written certification examinations.

Credential Type: Intermediate Certification (EMT-I). **Duration of License:** Three years. **Authorization:** Authorized to provide advanced emergency medical care. **Requirements:** Must be at least 18 years of age. Must have been certified as an EMT-B. Must complete an additional EMS-Division approved training program of at least 176 hours, of which at least 128 hours are didactic and 48 hours are clinical.

Recertification requires 36 hours of pre-approved continuing education. Must pass EMT-Intermediate Practical Examination and State EMT-Intermediate Written Certification Examination for recertification. **Examination:** EMT-Intermediate Practical Examination and State EMT-Intermediate Written Certification Examination. **Reciprocity:** All eligible applicants for legal recognition of an out-of-state certification must take the practical and written certification examinations.

Credential Type: Paramedic Certification (EMT-P). **Duration of License:** Three years. **Authorization:** Authorized to provide advanced emergency medical care. **Requirements:** Must be at least 18 years of age. Must have been certified as an EMT-B or EMT-I. Must complete an additional EMS-Division approved training program of at least 900 hours, of which at least 300 hours are didactic, 100 hours are clinical, and 500 hours are field internship. Training program must meet the current National Department of Transportation's standard.

Recertification requires 45 hours of pre-approved continuing education, or a 36-hour refresher course that meet's DOT standards. Must document skills testing and pass State EMT-Paramedic Written Certification Examination for recertification. **Examination:** EMT-Paramedic Practical Examination and State EMT-Paramedic Written Certification Examination. **Reciprocity:** All eligible applicants for legal recognition of an out-of-state certification must take the practical and written certification examinations.

Connecticut

2681

Emergency Medical Technician
State Dept. of Health Services
Office of Emergency Medical Services
150 Washington St.
Hartford, CT 06106
Phone: (203)566-7336

Credential Type: EMT Basic Certification. **Requirements:** Complete an approved training program. Applicants certified in another state or by the National Registry may take exam without additional training. **Examination:** State administered practical examination. **Exemptions:** The following individuals may take the examination without EMT training: registered or practical nurses, medical doctors, doctors of osteopathy, certified physician's assistants, medical corpsmen with 24 months duty in the U.S. armed forces, and certified Senior National Ski Patrollers.

Delaware

2682

Emergency Medical Technician
Health and Social Services Dept.
Div. of Public Health
Emergency Medical Services
Jesse Cooper Memorial Bldg.
Wm. Penn and Federal Sts.
Dover, DE 19901
Phone: (302)739-4710

Credential Type: License. **Requirements:** Contact licensing body for application information.

District of Columbia

2683

Emergency Medical Technician
Human Services Dept.
Emergency Medical Services Office
801 N. Capitol St., NW, Ste. 900
Washington, DC 20002
Phone: (202)673-6663
Phone: (202)673-6744

Credential Type: License. **Requirements:** Contact licensing body for application information.

Florida

2684

Emergency Medical Technician
Office of Emergency Medical Services
Dept. of Health and Rehabilitative Services
1317 Winewood Blvd.
Tallahassee, FL 32399-0700
Phone: (904)487-1911

Credential Type: EMT Certification. **Duration of License:** Two years. **Requirements:** Complete training at an approved Florida training center, consisting of 110-300 hours, that meets U.S. Dept. of Transportation Emergency Medical Technician curriculum requirements. Training must include knowledge of HIV/AIDS transmission, control, treatment, and prevention. Applicants currently certified in another state or by the National Registry of EMTs are also eligible to take the certification exam. Certification exam must be taken within 12 months of training.

Recertification requires taking two hours of AIDS training and being currently certified as a Red Cross Professional Rescuer or American Heart Association Level C Provider BLS-CPR. In addition, meet one of the following requirements for recertification: (1) Complete 30 hour EMT refresher course. (2) Complete U.S. DOT Emergency Medical Technician curriculum within the previous two years. (3) Pass in one attempt the EMT certification examination. **Examination:** Written certification examination. **Fees:** $35 certification fee. $40 exam fee. $20 recertification fee.

2685

Paramedic
Office of Emergency Medical Services
Dept. of Health and Rehabilitative Services
1317 Winewood Blvd.
Tallahassee, FL 32399-0700
Phone: (904)487-1911

Credential Type: Paramedic Certification. **Duration of License:** Two years. **Authorization:** In addition to performing EMT procedures, a certified paramedic may perform advanced life support (ALS) procedures, but only under the direction of a medical doctor. **Requirements:** Complete paramedic training at an approved Florida training center, consisting of approximately 1000 hours, that meets U.S. Dept. of Transportation Paramedic curriculum requirements. Training must include knowledge of HIV/AIDS transmission, control, treatment, and prevention. Applicants currently certified as paramedics in another state or by the National Registry of EMTs are also eligible to take the certification exam. Certification exam must be taken within 12 months of training. Complete 2-person CPR certification course C or higher of the American Red Cross or the American Heart Association, or be currently certified in Advanced Cardiac Life Support by the American Heart Association.

Recertification requires taking two hours of AIDS training and being currently certified as a Red Cross Professional Rescuer or American Heart Association Level C Provider BLS-CPR or be currently certified in ACLS by the American Heart Association. In addition, meet one of the following requirements for recertification: (1) Complete 30 hours of paramedic continuing education units, including a 16-hour advanced cardiac life support course. Current ACLS certification is accepted for 16 of the required 30 hours. (2) Complete 30 hour EMT refresher course and be currently certifies in AHA ACLS. (3) Pass in one attempt the paramedic certification examination. **Examination:** Written certification examination. **Fees:** $45 certification fee. $40 exam fee. $45 recertification fee.

Florida 2686

2686

Paramedic/EMT (Racetrack)
Florida Dept. of Business
Div. of Pari-Mutuel Wagering
Licensing Section
725 S. Bronough St.
Tallahassee, FL 32399-1037
Phone: (904)488-9161

Credential Type: License Registration Code 1016. **Requirements:** Must have a Health and Rehabilitative Services (HRS) license or a Department of Professional Regulation (DPR) license. Submit application and fingerprint card. Pay fee. **Fees:** $40 registration fee.

Georgia

2687

Paramedic
Composite State Board of Medical
 Examiners
Professional Examining Boards
166 Pryor St., SW
Atlanta, GA 30303
Phone: (404)656-3913

Credential Type: Paramedic Certificate. **Duration of License:** Two years. **Requirements:** Complete 750 hours of classroom training. ACLS certification. **Examination:** Paramedic Examination. **Fees:** $50 application/exam fee. $50 renewal fee.

Hawaii

2688

Emergency Medical Technician - Ambulance
Hawaii Board of Medical Examiners
Dept. of Commerce and Consumer
 Affairs
PO Box 3469
Honolulu, HI 96801
Phone: (808)548-4392

Credential Type: Certificate. **Duration of License:** Six months. **Requirements:** Graduation from a state-approved program. **Examination:** EMT Basic National Registry exam. **Fees:** $20 application fee. $30 exam fee. $25 license fee. $15 $30 Compliance Resolution Fund fee. $15 renewal fee.

2689

Mobile Intensive Care Technician (Paramedic)
Hawaii Board of Medical Examiners
Dept. of Commerce and Consumer
 Affairs
PO Box 3469
Honolulu, HI 96801
Phone: (808)548-4392

Credential Type: Certificate. **Duration of License:** Six months. **Requirements:** Graduation from a state-approved program. **Examination:** EMT Paramedic National Registry exam. **Fees:** $20 application fee. $100 exam fee. $25 license fee. $15 $30 Compliance Resolution Fund fee. $15 renewal fee.

Idaho

2690

Advanced Emergency Medical Technician - Ambulance
Idaho State Board of Medicine
280 N. 8th St., Ste. 202
Boise, ID 83720
Phone: (208)334-2822

Credential Type: Board certification. **Duration of License:** Two years. **Requirements:** Complete basic EMT-A training and at least 50 hours of advanced training. Have received additional training by a licensed physician to administer drugs and perform other acts under written or oral authorization of a licensed physician.

Renewal requires continuing education, completion of skills maintenance standards, passage of examinations, and recommendation for recertification by the physician program director. **Examination:** Written, oral, and practical examination. **Reciprocity:** No. **Fees:** $35 certification fee. $25 renewal fee. **Governing Statute:** Idaho Code, Title 54, Chap. 37. IDAPA 22.F.

2691

Emergency Medical Technician - Paramedic
Idaho State Board of Medicine
280 N. 8th St., Ste. 202
Boise, ID 83720
Phone: (208)334-2822

Credential Type: Board certification. **Duration of License:** Two years. **Requirements:** Complete all or specified parts of the EMT-Paramedic Curriculum approved by the U.S. Dept. of Transportation and the U.S. Dept. of Health and Human Services. Must be affiliated with an approved program.

Applicants who have not participated in an approved program must provide evidence of endorsement by an approved Idaho local community adv/EMT-P committee; recommendation for eligibility by the Statewide Physician Committee on Advanced Life Support; and compliance with minimum education and experience requirements.

Renewal requires continuing education, completion of skills maintenance standards, passage of examinations, and recommendation for recertification by the physician program director. **Examination:** Written, oral, and practical examination. **Reciprocity:** No. **Fees:** $35 certification fee. $25 renewal fee. **Governing Statute:** Idaho Code, Title 54, Chap. 37. IDAPA 22.F.

Illinois

2692

Emergency Medical Technician (EMT)—Coal Mine or Ambulance
Illinois Dept. of Public Health
525 W. Jefferson
Springfield, IL 62761
Phone: (217)785-2080

Credential Type: EMT License—Coal Mine or Ambulance. **Duration of License:** Two years. **Requirements:** At least 18 years of age. High school graduate or equivalent. Complete EMT-A Course. Pass examinations. Renewal requires 40 hours of continuing education, current CPR card, and approved trauma-life support refresher course. **Examination:** Emergency Medical Technician-A State Licensure Examination. Emergency Medical Technician Practical Examination. **Fees:** $10 examination fee. **Governing Statute:** Public Act 81-1518, Illinois Administration Code 77, Chapter I 535.

2693

Emergency Medical Technician (EMT)—Intermediate
Illinois Dept. of Public Health
525 W. Jefferson
Springfield, IL 62761
Phone: (217)785-2080

Credential Type: EMT License—Intermediate. **Duration of License:** Two years. **Requirements:** At least 18 years of age. Must be a licensed EMT-A (basic). Complete approved training program. Must be recommended by the Project Medical Director to sit for examination. Renewal requires 48 hours of continuing education,

Emergency Medical Technicians

current CPR card, and approved refresher course. **Examination:** Emergency Medical Technician—Intermediate Examination. **Reciprocity:** Yes, based on individual applicant. **Fees:** $10 examination fee. **Governing Statute:** Public Act 81-1518, Illinois Administration Code 77, Chapter I 535.

2694

Emergency Medical Technician (EMT)—Paramedic
Illinois Dept. of Public Health
525 W. Jefferson
Springfield, IL 62761
Phone: (217)785-2080

Credential Type: EMT/Paramedic License. **Duration of License:** Two years. **Requirements:** At least 18 years of age. Complete EMT-A Course (basic). Complete approved training program. Must be recommended by the Project Medical Director to sit for examination. Renewal requires 40 hours of continuing education, current CPR card, and approved refresher course. **Examination:** Emergency Medical Technician—Intermediate Examination. **Reciprocity:** Yes, based on individual applicant. **Fees:** $25 examination fee. **Governing Statute:** Public Act 81-1518, Illinois Administration Code 77, Chapter I 535.

2695

Mine Rescue Station Supervisor
Illinois Dept. of Mines & Minerals
300 W. Jefferson St., Ste. 300
PO Box 10137
Springfield, IL 62791-0137
Phone: (217)782-6791

Credential Type: Mine Rescue Station Supervisor Certificate. **Duration of License:** Two years (unless currently employed in field which would allow a permanent certificate). **Requirements:** At least 18 years of age. U.S. citizen. Complete the equivalent of four years high school. Hold an Advanced First Aid and Mine Rescue Certificate of Competency issued by the Department of Mines and Minerals. Must have four years experience in underground gassy mines. Knowledge of department rules, mine rescue operation rules, and equipment and supplies. **Examination:** Written and oral examinations. **Reciprocity:** No. **Fees:** No fee. **Governing Statute:** 1989 Illinois Revised Statutes, Chapter 96 1/2.

2696

Paramedic (Boxing/Wrestling)
Illinois Dept. of Professional Regulations
State of Illinois Ctr.
100 W. Randolph, Ste. 9-300
Chicago, IL 60601
Phone: (312)814-2719

Credential Type: Registration. **Duration of License:** Lifetime. **Requirements:** Submit registration to board. Must re-register if original information changes. **Reciprocity:** No. **Governing Statute:** The Illinois Professional Boxing and Wrestling Act. Illinois Revised Statutes 1991, Chapter 111.

2697

Security/Emergency Medical Technician Officer (Gaming)
Illinois Gaming Board
PO Box 19474
Springfield, IL 62794-9474
Phone: (217)524-0228

Credential Type: Security/EMT Officer License. **Duration of License:** One year. **Requirements:** At least 21 years of age. Current Emergency Medical Technician (EMT) Certificate. CPR card. Experience preferred. Renewal requires a current EMT certificate. **Examination:** DOT 20 (Refresher Course) Examination. **Reciprocity:** No. **Fees:** $75 application fee. $50 initial license fee. $50 renewal fee. **Governing Statute:** Illinois Revised Statutes, Chapter 120.

Indiana

2698

Emergency Medical Technician
Emergency Medical Services Commission
State Office Bldg., Rm. 315
100 N. Senate Ave.
Indianapolis, IN 46204
Phone: (317)232-3980

Credential Type: License. **Requirements:** Contact licensing body for application information.

Iowa

2699

Emergency Medical Services - Instructor
Iowa Dept. of Public Health
Emergency Medical Services
Lucas State Office Bldg.
Des Moines, IA 50319
Phone: (515)281-3239

Credential Type: License. **Duration of License:** Two years. **Requirements:** An applicant must have a current EMS certification or its equivalent, experience in an EMS-related field, a recommendation by an approved training program, and a minimum of 40 classroom hours. **Examination:** Written and practical.

2700

Emergency Medical Technician - Ambulance
Iowa Dept. of Public Health
Emergency Medical Services
Lucas State Office Bldg.
Des Moines, IA 50319
Phone: (515)281-3239

Credential Type: License. **Duration of License:** Two years. **Requirements:** High school diploma or equivalent, plus a minimum or 102 classroom hours and 18 clinical hours of study. Ambulance and rescue field experience hours may be required by the training program. 24 hours of continuing education every two years. **Examination:** Written and practical.

2701

Emergency Medical Technician - Defibrillation
Iowa Dept. of Public Health
Emergency Medical Services
Lucas State Office Bldg.
Des Moines, IA 50319
Phone: (515)281-3239

Credential Type: License. **Duration of License:** Two years. **Requirements:** High school diploma or equivalent, plus completion of a minimum of four hours of classroom training. Current certification as an EMT-A. 24 hours of continuing education every two years. **Examination:** Written and practical. **Fees:** $10 certification fee. $10 renewal fee.

2702

Emergency Medical Technician - Intermediate
Iowa Dept. of Public Health
Emergency Medical Services
Lucas State Office Bldg.
Des Moines, IA 50319
Phone: (515)281-3239

Credential Type: License. **Duration of License:** Two years. **Requirements:** High school diploma or equivalent, plus current certification as an EMT-A or EMT-D, completion of a minimum of 60 classroom hours, 50 clinical hours, and 50 hours of ambulance field experience. 48 hours of continuing education experience. CPR certification. **Examination:** Written and practical. **Fees:** $10 certification fee. $10 renewal fee.

2703

Emergency Medical Technician - Paramedic
Iowa Dept. of Public Health
Emergency Medical Services
Lucas State Office Bldg.
Des Moines, IA 50319
Phone: (515)281-3239

Credential Type: License. **Duration of License:** Two years. **Requirements:** High school diploma or equivalent. Current certification as an EMT-A, EMT-D, or EMT-I, completion of a minimum of 300 classroom hours, 150 clinical hours, and 150 hours of ambulence field experience. 60 hours of continuing education every two years. Current certification in CPR and Advanced Cardiac Life Support. **Examination:** Written and practical. **Fees:** $10 certification fee. $10 renewal fee.

2704

Emergency Rescue Technician (ERT)
Iowa Dept. of Public Health
Emergency Medical Services
Lucas State Office Bldg.
Des Moines, IA 50319
Phone: (515)281-3239

Credential Type: License. **Requirements:** Certification as a First Responder, EMT-A, EMT-D, EMT-I or a Paramedic. Completion of 40 classroom hours, complete ambulance/rescue field experience hours as may be required by the training program. Completion of four specific one-hour rescue topics for recertification. **Examination:** Written and practical exam.

2705

First Responder
Iowa Dept. of Public Health
Emergency Medical Services
Lucas State Office Bldg.
Des Moines, IA 50319
Phone: (515)281-3239

Credential Type: License. **Duration of License:** Two years. **Requirements:** High school diploma or equivalent, plus a minimum of 40 classroom hours, and completion of clinical hours as required by the training program. **Examination:** Written and practical.

2706

First Responder - Defibrillation
Iowa Dept. of Public Health
Emergency Medical Services
Lucas State Office Bldg.
Des Moines, IA 50319
Phone: (515)281-3239

Credential Type: License. **Duration of License:** Two years. **Requirements:** High school diploma or equivalent, plus completion of a minimum of four hours of classroom training. Current certification as a First Responder. 14 hours of continuing education every two years. CPR certification. **Examination:** Written and practical. **Fees:** $10 certification fee. $10 renewal fee.

Kansas

2707

Ambulance Attendant
Board of Emergency Medical Services
109 SW 6th St.
Topeka, KS 66603-3805
Phone: (913)296-7299

Credential Type: Certificate. **Duration of License:** One year. **Requirements:** Must be at least 18 years of age. Complete appropriate course of instruction. **Examination:** Yes.

2708

Emergency Medical Instructor-Coordinator
Board of Emergency Medical Services
109 SW 6th St.
Topeka, KS 66603-3805
Phone: (913)296-7299

Credential Type: Instructor-Coordinator Certificate. **Duration of License:** One year. **Requirements:** Must be at least 18 years of age. Have at least one year of experience as an ambulance attendant. Be certified for at least one year as an Emergency Medical Technician or higher. Complete board-approved course of training in instructing and coordinating attendant training programs.

Renewal requires at least 30 hours of continuing education. **Examination:** Yes. **Governing Statute:** Kansas Statutes Annotated 65-6101 ff. Kansas Administrative Regulations 109-1 through 109-12.

2709

Emergency Medical Technician
Board of Emergency Medical Services
109 SW 6th St.
Topeka, KS 66603-3805
Phone: (913)296-7299

Credential Type: Emergency Medical Technician Certificate. **Duration of License:** One year. **Requirements:** Must be at least 18 years of age. Complete board-approved course of training in preliminary medical care.

Renewal requires at least 14 hours of continuing education. **Examination:** Yes. **Fees:** $35 exam fee. $15 certification fee. $15 renewal fee. **Governing Statute:** Kansas Statutes Annotated 65-6101 ff. Kansas Administrative Regulations 109-1 through 109-12.

Credential Type: Emergency Medical Technician-Intermediate Certificate. **Duration of License:** One year. **Requirements:** Must be at least 18 years of age. Be certified as an Emergency Medical Technician. Complete board-approved course of training.

Renewal requires at least 18 hours of continuing education. **Examination:** Yes. **Fees:** $35 exam fee. $15 certification fee. $15 renewal fee. **Governing Statute:** Kansas Statutes Annotated 65-6101 ff. Kansas Administrative Regulations 109-1 through 109-12.

Credential Type: Emergency Medical Technician-Defibrillator Certificate. **Duration of License:** One year. **Requirements:** Must be at least 18 years of age. Be certified as an Emergency Medical Technician. Complete board-approved course of training.

Renewal requires at least 18 hours of continuing education. **Examination:** Yes. **Fees:** $35 exam fee. $15 certification fee. $15 renewal fee. **Governing Statute:** Kansas Statutes Annotated 65-6101 ff. Kansas Administrative Regulations 109-1 through 109-12.

Credential Type: Mobile Intensive Care Technician Certificate. **Duration of License:** One year. **Requirements:** Must be at least 18 years of age. Complete board-approved course of training.

Renewal requires at least 30 hours of continuing education. **Examination:** Yes. **Fees:** $50 exam fee. $15 certification fee. $15 renewal fee. **Governing Statute:** Kansas Statutes Annotated 65-6101 ff. Kansas Administrative Regulations 109-1 through 109-12.

Credential Type: First Responder Certificate. **Duration of License:** One year. **Requirements:** Must be at least 18 years of age. Complete board-approved course of training.

Renewal requires at least eight hours of continuing education. **Examination:** Yes. **Fees:** $10 exam fee. $5 certification fee. $10 reenewal fee. **Governing Statute:** Kansas Statutes Annotated 65-6101 ff. Kansas Administrative Regulations 109-1 through 109-12.

Credential Type: Crash Injury Management Technician Certificate. **Duration of License:** One year. **Requirements:** Must be at least 18 years of age. Complete board-approved course of training.

Renewal requires at least 10 hours of continuing education. **Examination:** Yes. **Fees:** $25 exam fee. $15 certification fee. $15 renewal fee. **Governing Statute:** Kansas Statutes Annotated 65-6101 ff. Kansas Administrative Regulations 109-1 through 109-12.

2710

Emergency Medical Technician (Racetrack)
Kansas Racing Commission
3400 VanBuren
Topeka, KS 66611-2228
Phone: (913)296-5800

Credential Type: License Registration. **Requirements:** Submit application and fingerprint card. Pay fee. **Fees:** $5 registration fee.

Kentucky

2711

Emergency Medical Technician
Cabinet for Human Resources
Emergency Medical Services Branch
275 E. Main St., 1 R Center
Frankfort, KY 40601
Phone: (502)564-8950

Credential Type: License. **Duration of License:** Two years. **Requirements:** Must be able to read, speak, write and understand the English language. Must complete a prescribed training course approved by the regulatory agency. 18 years of age. Some continuing education required. **Examination:** Yes. **Fees:** $19 exam fee.

2712

Mining Emergency Medical Technician
Dept. of Mines and Minerals
PO Box 14080
Lexington, KY 40512
Phone: (606)254-0367

Credential Type: License. **Requirements:** Must have 103 hours of classroom training as required by the Cabinet for Human Resources and the Department of Mines and Minerals. Retraining required. **Examination:** Yes. **Fees:** $16 exam fee.

2713

Paramedic
Kentucky Board of Medical Licensure
310 Whittington Pky., Ste. 1 B
Louisville, KY 40222
Phone: (502)429-8046

Credential Type: License. **Requirements:** High school diploma or equivalency. Successful completion of an approved paramedic training course. 18 years of age. Good health. Must be currently certified as an EMT, EMT-Ambulance, EMT-Instructor or EMT-Instructor/Trainer. Continuing education required. **Examination:** Yes. **Fees:** $45 exam fee. $10 application fee.

Louisiana

2714

Emergency Medical Technician (EMT)
Dept. of Health and Human Resources, Bureau of EMS
200 Lafayette, 7th Fl.
Baton Rouge, LA 70801
Phone: (504)342-2600

Credential Type: Certified EMT—Basic. **Duration of License:** Two years. **Requirements:** Completion of a basic emergency medical technician course. **Examination:** Written and practical exam. **Fees:** $15 exam fee.

Credential Type: Certified EMT—Intermediate. **Duration of License:** Two years. **Requirements:** Completion of an intermediate emergency medical technician course. **Examination:** Written and practical exam. **Fees:** $35 exam fee. $25 license fee.

Credential Type: Certified EMT—Paramedic. **Duration of License:** Two years. **Requirements:** Completion of an emergency medical technician paramedic training course. **Examination:** Written and practical exam. **Fees:** $35 exam fee. $25 license fee.

Maine

2715

Emergency Medical Technician
Dept. of Human Services
Medical Services Bureau
Licensing and Certification Div.
State House Station 11
Augusta, ME 04333
Phone: (207)289-2606
Phone: (207)289-3953

Credential Type: License. **Requirements:** Contact licensing body for application information.

Maryland

2716

Emergency Medical Technician
Maryland Institute for Emergency Medical Services Systems
PO Box 22587
Baltimore, MD 21203
Phone: (410)706-3666

Credential Type: First Responder Certification. **Authorization:** Authorizes holder to provide basic life support. **Require-**

Massachusetts 2717

Emergency Medical Technician, continued

ments: Be at least 16 years of age. Complete 40 hours of approved training. **Examination:** State certification examination. **Reciprocity:** Considered on a case-by-case basis. **Fees:** $25 reciprocity fee.

Credential Type: Emergency Medical Technician-Ambulance Certification. **Authorization:** Authorizes holder to provide basic life support. **Requirements:** Be at least 16 years of age. Complete 110 hours of approved training. Must be or become affiliated with a Maryland ambulance company, rescue squad, fire company, or similar organization. Hold a current CPR card. **Examination:** State certification examination, written and practical. **Reciprocity:** Considered on a case-by-case basis. **Fees:** $25 reciprocity fee.

Credential Type: Cardiac Rescue Technician Certification. **Authorization:** Authorizes holder to provide advanced life support. **Requirements:** Be at least 18 years of age. Complete 160 hours of approved paramedic training. Must be or become affiliated with an approved Advanced Life Support Company. Must take a 20-hour CRT refresher course. **Examination:** State CRT examination. **Reciprocity:** Considered on a case-by-case basis. **Fees:** $25 reciprocity fee. $15 exam fee.

Credential Type: Emergency Medical Technician-Paramedic Certification. **Authorization:** Authorizes holder to provide advanced life support. **Requirements:** Be at least 18 years of age. Complete 300 hours of approved paramedic training. Must be or become affiliated with an approved Advanced Life Support Company. Must be currently certified as an EMT-P with the National Registry. Must complete an approved Maryland Protocol Review session. **Examination:** Maryland Protocol Examination. **Reciprocity:** Considered on a case-by-case basis. **Fees:** $25 reciprocity fee.

Massachusetts

2717

Emergency Medical Technician
Dept. of Public Health
Office of Emergency Medical Services
150 Tremont St., 2nd Fl.
Boston, MA 02111
Phone: (617)727-8338

Credential Type: Basic EMT Certification. **Duration of License:** Two years. **Requirements:** Be at least 18 years of age. Complete a department approved training course. Be certified as a Red Cross Professional Rescuer or American Heart Association Level C Provider BLS-CPR. The following applicants are also eligible to take the certification examination: (1) EMTs who are currently certified in another state or are current with the National Registry. (2) Individuals who are currently an EMT or equivalent in military service or recently discharged. (3) Physicians, registered nurses, or physician's assistants who are currently licensed in Massachusetts.

Renewal requires taking an EMT refresher course of at least 20 hours and completing an additional 28 hours of continuing education. **Examination:** EMT Certification Examination (written and practical skills). **Fees:** $75 exam fee. **Governing Statute:** 105 CMR 170.00—172.00.

Michigan

2718

Ambulance Attendant
Div. of Emergency Medical Services
Dept. of Public Health
3423 N. Logan
PO Box 30195
Lansing, MI 48909
Phone: (517)335-8000

Credential Type: License. **Duration of License:** Three years. **Requirements:** Currently certified by the American Red Cross in advanced First Aid and Emergency Care and Cardiopulmonary Resuscitation or equivalent courses approved by the Department. Physically qualified as evidenced by the submission of a medical examination report which has been completed by a Michigan licensed physician. Abide by the rules of the Department of Public Health. Renewal requires continuing education. **Examination:** Written and practical exam. **Reciprocity:** A licensed ambulance attendant from another state may be licensed in Michigan if the applicant has completed the American Red Cross's Advanced First Aid and Emergency Care Course and Cardiopulmonary Resuscitation Course and examination. In addition, there must be no disciplinary proceedings pending or sanctions imposed against the applicant in the home state. **Fees:** $5 initial license fee. $5 renewal fee. **Governing Statute:** Public Health Code, Act 368 of 1978, as amended.

2719

Emergency Medical Technician (EMT)
Div. of Emergency Medical Services
Dept. of Public Health
3423 N. Logan
PO Box 30195
Lansing, MI 48909
Phone: (517)335-8000

Credential Type: License. **Duration of License:** Three years. **Requirements:** Successfully complete an emergency medical technician-ambulance training program. Physically qualified as evidenced by the submittal of a medical examination report which has been completed by a Michigan licensed physician. Renewal requires a minimum of 30 credit hours of continuing education in areas specified by the Division. **Examination:** Written and practical exam. **Reciprocity:** A currently licensed emergency medical technician from another state may be licensed in Michigan if the applicant has completed an emergency medical technician-ambulance training course equivalent to that required by Michigan. In addition, there must be no disciplinary proceedings pending or sanctions imposed against the applicant in the home state. **Fees:** $5 initial license fee. $5 renewal fee. No reciprocity fee. **Governing Statute:** Public Health Code, Act 368 of 1978, as amended.

2720

Emergency Medical Technician (EMT), Advanced
Div. of Emergency Medical Services
Dept. of Public Health
3423 N. Logan
PO Box 30195
Lansing, MI 48909
Phone: (517)335-8000

Credential Type: License. **Duration of License:** Three years. **Requirements:** Be a Michigan licensed emergency medical technician, or have passed the Basic EMT written and practical exams. Successful completion of an advanced emergency medical technician training program. Physically qualified as evidenced by the submittal of a medical examination report which has been completed by a Michigan licensed physician. Renewal requires completion of 40 hours of Department-approved, ongoing education during the three-year licensure period. **Examination:** Written and practical exam. **Reciprocity:** A currently licensed advanced emergency medical technician from another state may be licensed in Michigan if the applicant has completed an advanced emergency medical technician training course equivalent to that required by Michigan. In addition, there must be no disciplinary proceedings pending or sanctions imposed against the applicant in the home state. **Fees:** $5 initial license fee. $5 renewal fee. No reciprocity fee. **Governing Statute:** Public Health Code, Act 368 of 1978, as amended.

2721

Emergency Medical Technician (EMT) Specialist
Div. of Emergency Medical Services
Dept. of Public Health
3423 N. Logan
PO Box 30195
Lansing, MI 48909
Phone: (517)335-8000

Credential Type: License. **Duration of License:** Three years. **Requirements:** Be a Michigan licensed emergency medical technician, or have passed Michigan basic EMT written and practical examinations. Completed an EMT specialist training program. Be physically qualified as evidenced by the submittal of a medical examination report which has been completed by a Michigan licensed physician. Be employed by a Department-approved limited advanced mobile emergency care service. Renewal requires a minimum of 30 credit hours of continuing education during the course of licensure. **Examination:** Written and practical exam. **Reciprocity:** A currently licensed EMT specialist from another state may be licensed in Michigan if the applicant has completed an EMT specialist training course equivalent to that required by Michigan. In addition, there must be no disciplinary proceedings pending or sanctions imposed against the applicant in the home state. **Fees:** $5 initial license fee. $5 renewal fee. No reciprocity fee. **Governing Statute:** Public Health Code, Act 368 of 1978, as amended.

2722

Emergency Medical Technician Instructor-Coordinator
Div. of Emergency Medical Services
Dept. of Public Health
3423 N. Logan
PO Box 30195
Lansing, MI 48909
Phone: (517)335-8000

Credential Type: Certificate. **Duration of License:** Three years. **Requirements:** Be a licensed emergency medical technician. Must have at least two years of practical experience in the field of emergency health care and possess demonstrated teaching ability. Completed an emergency medical technician instructor-coordinator training program. Abide by the rules of the Department of Public Health. Renewal requires completion of an ongoing education program each year. **Examination:** Written and practical exam. **Governing Statute:** Public Health Code, Act 368 of 1978, as amended.

Minnesota

2723

Emergency Medical Technician
Dept. of Health
Bureau of Health Delivery Systems
Emergency Medical Services Section
717 Delaware St. SE
Box 9441
Minneapolis, MN 55440
Phone: (612)623-5482

Credential Type: EMT Basic Certification. **Requirements:** Complete an approved EMT Basic training course. **Examination:** National Registry examination. **Fees:** $15 exam fee. **Governing Statute:** Minnesota Laws of 1990, Chap. 568, Article 1, Section 16.

Credential Type: EMT Intermediate Certification. **Requirements:** Complete an approved EMT Intermediate training course. **Examination:** National Registry examination. **Fees:** $35 exam fee. **Governing Statute:** Minnesota Laws of 1990, Chap. 568, Article 1, Section 16.

Credential Type: EMT Paramedic Certification. **Requirements:** Complete an approved EMT Paramedic training course. **Examination:** National Registry examination. **Fees:** $35 exam fee. **Governing Statute:** Minnesota Laws of 1990, Chap. 568, Article 1, Section 16.

Mississippi

2724

Emergency Medical Technician
State Dept. of Health
Div. of Emergency Medical Services
Training, Testing, and Certification
PO Box 1700
2423 N. State St.
Jackson, MS 39215-1700
Phone: (601)987-3880
Phone: (601)960-7400
Fax: (601)960-7948

Credential Type: EMT Certification. **Duration of License:** Two years. **Authorization:** Certification is offered at the Basic, Intermediate, and Paramedic levels. **Requirements:** Mississippi is a National Registry of Emergency Medical Technicians state. Must be registered with the National Registry of Emergency Medical Technicians. Recertification requires reregistration with the National Registry. **Fees:** $15 state certification fee.

Missouri

2725

Emergency Medical Technician
Dept. of Health
Bureau of Emergency Medical Services
PO Box 570
Jefferson City, MO 65102
Phone: (314)751-6369
Phone: (314)751-6400
Fax: (314)751-6010

Credential Type: EMT-Basic License. **Duration of License:** Three years. **Requirements:** Complete training program within the past three years. State training requirements exceed U.S. Department of Transportation guidelines and require training in the use of the esophageal obturator airway (EOA), pneumatic counter pressure device (PCPD), and the automatic external defibrillator.

Renewal requires 60 continuing education units, or completing a refresher course and retaking the written examination. **Examination:** State written and practical examinations. **Fees:** $3 license fee. $40 practical test fee.

Credential Type: EMT-Paramedic License. **Duration of License:** Three years. **Requirements:** Complete training program meeting U.S. Department of Transportation guidelines within the past three years. Renewal requires 90 continuing education units or completing a refresher course. All paramedics must retake the written examination to renew their licenses. **Examination:** State written and practical examinations. **Fees:** $3 license fee. $40 practical test fee.

Montana

2726

Emergency Medical Technician
Montana Emergency Services Bureau
Cogswell Bldg.
Helena, MT 59620
Phone: (406)444-3895

Credential Type: EMT—Basic Certificate. **Duration of License:** Two years. **Requirements:** 18 years of age. Graduation from high school or equivalent. Completion

Nebraska

Emergency Medical Technician, continued

of an EMT program. Ten hours of in-hospital clinical experience. Six months experience as an emergency care provider. **Examination:** Written and practical. **Fees:** $35 exam and certificate fee. $15 renewal fee. **Governing Statute:** Montana Code Annotated 50-6-201 through 50-6-207.

Credential Type: EMT—Advanced Certificate. **Duration of License:** Two years. **Requirements:** 19 years of age. Certification as an EMT—Basic. Current employment as an emergency care provider with at least one year of pre-hospital patient care experience. Completion of an approved intermediate or paramedic EMT program. Six months experience as an EMT—Intermediate or EMT—Paramedic. **Examination:** Written and practical. **Fees:** $60—$85 exam and certificate fee. $20—$30 renewal fee. **Governing Statute:** Montana Code Annotated 50-6-201 through 50-6-207.

Credential Type: EMT—Defibrillation Certificate. **Duration of License:** Two years. **Requirements:** Certification as an EMT—Basic. Completion of an approved EMT—Defibrillation program. Six months experience as an EMT Defibrillation. **Examination:** Written and practical. **Fees:** $35 exam and certificate fee. $15 renewal fee. **Governing Statute:** Montana Code Annotated 50-6-201 through 50-6-207.

Nebraska

2727

Emergency Medical Technician
Nebraska Bureau of Examining Boards in Advanced Emergency Medical Care
301 Centennial Mall S.
PO Box 95007
Lincoln, NE 68509
Phone: (402)471-2115

Credential Type: License. **Duration of License:** Two years. **Requirements:** 21 years of age. Must be a high school graduate. Must complete an approved training program. **Examination:** Yes.

Nevada

2728

Emergency Medical Technician
Nevada State Health Div.
Bureau of Regulatory Health Services
505 E. King St., Rm. 204
Carson City, NV 89710
Phone: (702)687-3065

Credential Type: EMT Basic License. **Requirements:** Completion of a 110-hour course. **Examination:** Written and practical exam. **Fees:** $15 license fee.

Credential Type: EMT Intermediate License. **Requirements:** Must have additional specialized training in IV therapy, esophagal airway and endotracheal treatment. **Examination:** Yes.

Credential Type: EMT Paramedic License. **Requirements:** 40 hours of continuing medical education annually. **Examination:** Written, oral and practical. **Fees:** $25 license fee.

New Hampshire

2729

Ambulance & Rescue Attendant
NH Division of Public Health Services
Bureau of Emergency Medical Services
6 Hazen Drive
Concord, NH 03301
Phone: (603)271-4568

Credential Type: Ambulance & Rescue Attendant License. **Duration of License:** One year. **Requirements:** At least 18 years of age. A recognized training program (such as the Emergency Medical Technician program). Training must include a cardiopulmonary resuscitator course and a American Red Cross Advanced First Aid and Emergency Care Course. **Examination:** Appropriate written and practical examinations. **Reciprocity:** Yes, with Emergency Medical Technician certification. **Fees:** $5.00 license fee (volunteer attendants pay no fee). $5.00 renewal fee.

2730

Emergency Medical Technician
Health and Human Services Dept.
Div. of Public Health
Emergency Medical Services Bureau
Health and Welfare Bldg.
Hazen Dr.
Concord, NH 03301
Phone: (603)271-4566
Phone: (603)271-4568

Credential Type: License. **Requirements:** Contact licensing body for application information.

New Jersey

2731

Emergency Medical Technician
Dept. of Health
Div. of Community Health Services
CN364
Trenton, NJ 08625-0364
Phone: (609)292-0782

Credential Type: EMT Certification. **Requirements:** Have current CPR certification. Complete an approved 120-hour EMT basic training course. **Examination:** Certification test.

New Mexico

2732

Emergency Medical Technician
Dept. of Health
Primary Care and EMS Bureau
1190 St. Francis Dr., Rm. N1100
PO Box 26110
Santa Fe, NM 87502-6110
Phone: (505)827-2509

Credential Type: EMT-Basic License. **Duration of License:** Two years. **Requirements:** Complete training at EMS Academy. Hold a current CPR card. Applicants holding current certification by the National Registry may be granted an initial license.

Renewal require completing an EMT-Basic Refresher Course, having current CPR certification, and completing 24 hours of approved continuing education. **Examination:** State or National Registry examination. **Fees:** $25 license and state exam fee. $15 state exam only fee. $10 license only fee. $10 renewal fee. $15 license and National Registry exam fee (optional). $15 National Registry exam fee only (optional). $10 National Registry license fee only (optional).

Credential Type: EMT-Intermediate License. Duration of License: Two years. Requirements: Complete training at EMS Academy. Hold a current CPR card. Applicants holding current certification by the National Registry may be granted an initial license. Candidates with an out-of-state license or approved training may be able to take the examination.

Renewal require completing an EMT-Basic and Intermediate Refresher Course, having current CPR certification, and completing 30 hours of approved continuing education. Examination: State or National Registry examination. Fees: $30 license and state exam fee. $20 state exam only fee. $15 license only fee. $15 renewal fee. $35 license and National Registry exam fee (optional). $35 National Registry exam fee only (optional). $15 National Registry license fee only (optional).

Credential Type: EMT-Paramedic License. Duration of License: Two years. Requirements: Complete training at EMS Academy. Hold a current CPR card. Applicants holding current certification by the National Registry may be granted an initial license. Candidates with an out-of-state license or approved training may be able to take the examination.

Renewal require completing an EMT-Paramedic Refresher Course, having current ACLS certification, and completing 48 hours of approved continuing education. Examination: State and National Registry examination. Fees: $35 license and state exam fee. $25 state exam only fee. $20 license only fee. $20 renewal fee. $35 license and National Registry exam fee (required). $35 National Registry exam fee only (required). $15 National Registry license fee only (optional).

New York

2733

Emergency Medical Technician and Paramedic
New York State Dept. of Health
Emergency Medical Services
 Program
74 State St., 4th Fl.
Empire State Plaza
Albany, NY 12207
Phone: (518)474-2219

Credential Type: Certification available at five levels. Requirements: Requirements vary for the five progressive levels of certification, beginning with Certified First Responder and continuing through EMT-Basic, EMT-Intermediate, EMT-Critical Care, and EMT-Paramedic. Fees: Contact board for fees. Governing Statute: Article 30 Public Health Law. Chap. 6, Title 10 (Health) official compilation of rules and regulations, Part 800.

North Carolina

2734

Ambulance Attendant
Dept. of Human Resources
Office of Medical Services
701 Barbour Dr.
Raleigh, NC 27603
Phone: (919)733-2285

Credential Type: Certification. Duration of License: Two years. Requirements: 18 years of age. Good physical health. Completion of an approved emergency medical technician course or a minimum of 110 hours or an approved 40 hour ambulance attendant program. A 21-hour refresher course is required upon renewal. Examination: Written and practical.

2735

Emergency Medical Technician
Dept. of Human Resources
Office of Emergency Medical
 Services
701 Barbour Dr.
Raleigh, NC 27603
Phone: (919)733-2285

Credential Type: EMT Certification. Duration of License: Two years. Requirements: 18 years of age. Completion of an approved EMT course. 27 hour refresher course every two years. Examination: Written, practical and physical.

Credential Type: EMT, Advanced Intermediate Certification. Duration of License: Two years. Requirements: EMT certification. 216 hours of training. 18 years of age. Two recommendations. Examination: Written, practical and physical.

Credential Type: EMT, Defibrillation Certification. Duration of License: Two years. Requirements: EMT certification. Completion of a 13-hour EMT-D training program. 18 years of age. Two recommendations. 72 hours of continuing education every two years. Examination: Written, practical and physical.

Credential Type: EMT, Intermediate Certification. Duration of License: Two years. Requirements: EMT certification. 98 hours of training. 18 years of age. Two recommendations. Examination: Written, practical and physical.

Credential Type: EMT, Paramedic Certification. Duration of License: Two years. Requirements: EMT certification. Completion of a 556-hour training program. 18 years of age. Two recommendations. Examination: Written, practical and physical.

North Dakota

2736

Emergency Medical Technician
Dept. of Health
Div. of Emergency Health Services
State Capitol Bldg.
600 E. Blvd.
Bismarck, ND 58504
Phone: (701)224-2388

Credential Type: Certification and License. Duration of License: One year. Authorization: May perform emergency medical services only under the direction and responsibility of a licensed physician. Requirements: Contact licensing body for application information. Fees: $10 license fee. $10 renewal fee. Governing Statute: North Dakota Century Code 50-03-03.

Ohio

2737

Emergency Medical Technician
Dept. of Highway Safety
Div. of Emergency Medical Services
240 Parsons Ave.
PO Box 7167
Columbus, OH 43266-0563
Phone: (614)466-9447
Phone: (614)466-2550

Credential Type: EMT-Basic Certification. Duration of License: Three years. Requirements: Complete training program meeting U.S. Department of Transportation guidelines. Examination: National Registry of Emergency Medical Technicians written and practical examinations. Fees: No state fees.

Credential Type: EMT-Intermediate Certification. Duration of License: Three years. Requirements: Complete training program meeting U.S. Department of Transportation guidelines. Examination: National Registry of Emergency Medical Technicians written and practical examinations. Fees: No state fees.

Credential Type: EMT-Paramedic Certification. Duration of License: Three years. Requirements: Complete training program meeting U.S. Department of Transportation guidelines. Examination: National Registry of Emergency Medical Technicians written and practical examinations. Fees: No state fees.

Oklahoma

2738

Emergency Medical Technician, Basic
Oklahoma State Dept. of Health
Emergency Medical Services Div.
1000 N.E. Tenth
Oklahoma City, OK 73152
Phone: (405)271-4027

Credential Type: License. **Duration of License:** Two years. **Requirements:** Approved Dept. of Transportation curriculum from an approved training institution. EMT Basic training. 48 hours of continuing education every two years. 18 years of age. Must maintain CPR certification. **Examination:** National Registry of Emergency Medical Technicians—EMT Basic. **Fees:** $50 application and license fee (includes exam). $10 renewal fee.

2739

Emergency Medical Technician, Intermediate
Oklahoma State Dept. of Health
Emergency Medical Services Div.
1000 N.E. Tenth
Oklahoma City, OK 73152
Phone: (405)271-4027

Credential Type: License. **Duration of License:** Two years. **Requirements:** Approved Dept. of Transportation curriculum from an approved training institution. EMT Intermediate training. 36 hours of continuing education and a 36-hour refresher course every two years. 18 years of age. EMT Basic license. CPR certification. **Examination:** National Registry of Emergency Medical Technicians—EMT Intermediate. **Fees:** $75 application and license fee (includes exam). $20 renewal fee.

2740

Emergency Medical Technician, Paramedic
Oklahoma State Dept. of Health
Emergency Medical Services Div.
1000 N.E. Tenth
Oklahoma City, OK 73152
Phone: (405)271-4027

Credential Type: License. **Duration of License:** Two years. **Requirements:** Approved Dept. of Transportation curriculum. EMT Paramedic training. 24 hours of continuing education and 48-hour refresher course every two years. 18 years of age. EMT Basic level license. CPR certification. **Examination:** National Registry of Emergency Medical Technicians—EMT Paramedic. **Fees:** $85 application and license fee (exam included). $20 renewal fee.

Oregon

2741

Emergency Medical Technician
Oregon Health Div., Emergency Medical Services Section
800 NE Oregon
Portland, OR 97232
Phone: (503)731-4011

Credential Type: EMT Certificate. **Duration of License:** Varies. **Requirements:** 18 years of age. Successful completion of an approved EMT course. Must be certified as a EMT one before applying for EMT two four certification. Must be physically and mentally qualified to act as an EMT. No substance abuse. **Examination:** Yes. **Fees:** $55—$165 certification fee. $15—$75 recertification fee. **Governing Statute:** ORS 823.010 to 823.990.

Pennsylvania

2742

Emergency Medical Technician
Dept. of Health
Div. of Emergency Medical Services
PO Box 90
Harrisburg, PA 06106
Phone: (203)566-7336

Credential Type: EMT Certification. **Requirements:** Complete a U.S. Department of Transportation approved training program. **Examination:** State administered EMT skills and knowledge examination.

Credential Type: EMT-Paramedic Certification. **Requirements:** Must be a Pennsylvania certified EMT and have completed a U.S. Department of Transportation approved training program. **Examination:** Written examination.

Rhode Island

2743

Emergency Medical Technician
Divison of Emergency Medical Services
RI Dept. of Health
3 Capitol Hill
Providence, RI 02908
Phone: (401)277-2401

Credential Type: Emergency Medical Technician—Ambulance License (EMT-A). **Duration of License:** Three years. **Requirements:** At least 18 years of age. Complete the Emergency Medical Technician-Ambulance Training Course or National Standard EMTBasic. Must be currently certified in cardiopulmonary resuscitation. **Examination:** Written and practical. **Reciprocity:** Yes. **Fees:** No fee.

Credential Type: Emergency Medical Technician—Cardiac License (EMT-C). **Duration of License:** Three years. **Requirements:** At least 18 years of age. Complete the Emergency Medical Technician-Cardiac Training Course. Must be currently certified in cardiopulmonary resuscitation. **Examination:** Written and practical. **Reciprocity:** Yes. **Fees:** No fee.

Credential Type: Emergency Medical Technician—Paramedic License (EMT-P). **Duration of License:** Two years. **Requirements:** At least 18 years of age. Complete the Emergency Medical Technician-Paramedic Training Course or National Standard EMTParamedic Training Program. Must be currently certified in cardiopulmonary resuscitation. **Examination:** Written and practical. **Reciprocity:** Yes. **Fees:** No fee.

South Carolina

2744

Emergency Medical Technician
Dept. of Health and Environmental Control
Div. of Emergency Medical Services
2600 Bull St.
Columbia, SC 29201
Phone: (803)758-8616

Credential Type: EMT Basic Certification. **Duration of License:** Three years. **Requirements:** Complete an approved 127-hour EMT basic training course. Renewal requires completing either a 36-hour EMT refresher course or a provider-based in-service training program, and taking the state board written and practical examinations. **Examination:** State board written and practical examinations. **Exemptions:** Persons who are nationally registry certified need not take state exam if they are state residents and employed by a South Carolina EMS provider.

Credential Type: EMT Advanced Certification. **Duration of License:** Three years. **Requirements:** Complete an approved 424-hour EMT advanced training course. Must be currently certified in South Carolina and have six months experience as a Basic EMT. Must be a member of a South Carolina licensed ambulance service. **Examination:** Screening test. State board written and practical examinations. **Exemptions: Persons who are nationally registry certified need not take state exam if they are state residents and employed by a South Carolina EMS provider. **Reciprocity:** Applicants currently certified in another state may take the state written and practical examination, provided they have established residency and are employed by a licensed ambulance provider.

South Dakota

2745

Emergency Medical Technician
Dept. of Health
Emergency Medical Services Div.
523 E. Capitol
Pierre, SD 57501
Phone: (605)773-3737
Phone: (605)773-4928

Credential Type: EMT Basic Certification. **Duration of License:** Two years. **Requirements:** Complete an approved EMT Basic training course that meets U.S. Department of Transportation standards. Renewal requires 30 hours of continuing education every two years. **Examination:** State written and practical examination. **Fees:** No fee.

Credential Type: EMT Intermediate License and Certification. **Duration of License:** Two years (certification) and one year (license). **Requirements:** Complete an approved EMT Intermediate training course, consisting of 36-54 hours of didactic training, 24 hours of mobile intensive care training in the field, and hospital training. Must maintain BCLC-CPR certification through continuing education. Must be working to be licensed and certified. Annual licenses are issued through the Board of Medical Examiners.

Renewal requires 40 hours of continuing education every two years. **Examination:** National Registry examination. **Reciprocity:** Yes. **Fees:** $50 license fee. $75 reciprocity fee. $15 annual renewal fee.

Credential Type: EMT Special Skills License and Certification. **Duration of License:** Two years (certification) and one year (license). **Requirements:** Complete an approved EMT training course that is a subset of the paramedic training course, consisting of cardiac and trauma technician training. Must maintain ACLS and NCLC-CPR certification through continuing education. Must be working to be licensed and certified. Annual licenses are issued through the Board of Medical Examiners.

Renewal requires 60 hours of continuing education every two years. **Examination:** State written and practical examination. **Reciprocity:** Yes. **Fees:** $50 license fee. $75 reciprocity fee. $25 annual renewal fee.

Credential Type: EMT Paramedic License and Certification. **Duration of License:** Two years (certification) and one year (license). **Requirements:** Complete an approved EMT Paramedic training course that meets U.S. Department of Transportation standards. Must maintain ACLS and BCLC-CPR certification through continuing education. Must be working to be licensed and certified. Annual licenses are issued through the Board of Medical Examiners.

Renewal requires 60 hours of continuing education every two years. **Examination:** National Registry examination. **Fees:** $50 license fee. $75 reciprocity fee. $25 annual renewal fee.

Tennessee

2746

Emergency Medical Technician
Dept. of Health and Environment
Manpower and Facilities Bureau
Div. of Emergency Medical Services
287 Plus Park Blvd.
Nashville, TN 37247-0701
Phone: (615)367-6278

Credential Type: EMT License and Certification. **Duration of License:** Two years. **Requirements:** High school graduate or equivalent. Current CPR certification. Must be a state resident. Complete an approved EMT training program, including training in epinephrine for anaphylaxis and in the pharyngeotracheal lumen airway (PTL). Have knowledge of desination guidelines.

Renewal requires two continuing education units in EMS related subjects, or passing of renewal examination. **Examination:** Tennessee certification examination. **Reciprocity:** Yes, based on training completed and examinations passed. **Fees:** $10 license fee. $10 exam fee. $10 renewal fee.

Credential Type: EMT-IV License and Certification. **Duration of License:** Two years. **Requirements:** High school graduate or equivalent. Current CPR certification. Must be a state resident. Complete an approved EMT training program, including training in epinephrine for anaphylaxis and in the pharyngeotracheal lumen airway (PTL). Have knowledge of desination guidelines. Successful completion of five venipunctures.

Renewal requires two continuing education units in EMS related subjects, or passing of renewal examination. **Examination:** Tennessee certification examination. IV Therapy Examination. **Reciprocity:** Yes, based on training completed and examinations passed. **Fees:** $10 license fee. $10 EMT exam fee. $10 I.V. Therapy exam fee. $10 renewal fee.

Credential Type: Paramedic License and Certification. **Duration of License:** Two years. **Requirements:** High school graduate or equivalent. Current CPR certification. Must be a state resident. Complete an approved paramedic training program.

Renewal requires three continuing education units in EMS related subjects, or passing of renewal examination. **Examination:** Tennessee certification examination. **Reciprocity:** Yes, based on training completed and examinations passed. **Fees:** $20 license fee. $30 exam fee. $10 renewal fee.

Texas

2747

Emergency Medical Technician
Bureau of Emergency Management
1100 W. 49th St.
Austin, TX 78756
Phone: (512)458-7550

Credential Type: Emergency Care Attendant Certificate. **Requirements:** 18 years of age. Valid driver's license. 40 hours of classroom training. **Examination:** Written and physical. **Fees:** $50 certification fee. $50 renewal fee. **Governing Statute:** Health & Safety Code, Ch. 773, 25 TAC 157.

Credential Type: Emergency Medical Technician Certificate. **Requirements:** 18 years of age. Valid driver's license. 100 hours of classroom training. 20 hours of clinical training. Completion of a field internship. **Examination:** Written and physical. **Fees:** $50 certification fee. $50 renewal fee. **Governing Statute:** Health & Safety Code, Ch. 773, 25 TAC 157.

Credential Type: Emergency Medical Technician—Intermediate Certificate. **Requirements:** 18 years of age. Valid driver's license. 60 hours of classroom training. 50 hours of clinical training. Completion of a field internship. **Examination:** Written and physical. **Fees:** $75 certification fee. $75 renewal fee. **Governing Statute:** Health & Safety Code, Ch. 773, 25 TAC 157.

Credential Type: Emergency Medical Technician—Paramedic Certificate. **Requirements:** 18 years of age. Valid driver's license. 160 hours of classroom training. 140 hours of clinical training. Completion of a field internship. **Examination:** Written and physical. **Fees:** $75 certification fee. $75 renewal fee. **Governing Statute:** Health & Safety Code, Ch. 773, 25 TAC 157.

Utah

2748

Emergency Medical Technician
Bureau of Emergency Medical
   Services
288 N. 1460 W.
PO Box 16660
Salt Lake City, UT 84116-0660
Phone: (801)538-6435

Credential Type: License. **Duration of License:** Two years. **Requirements:** Must complete an approved Emergency Medical Technician course. **Examination:** Yes. **Fees:** $37 testing fee. $31 examination fee. $7.50 certificate fee. $7.50 renewal fee.

Vermont

2749

Emergency Medical Technician
Emergency Medical Services
Vermont Dept. of Health
131 Main St. Box 70
Burlington, VT 05402
Phone: (802)863-7310

Credential Type: License. **Duration of License:** One year. **Requirements:** Sponsored by ambulance service or equivalent. Meet admission requirements of EMS district. 18 years of age upon completion of requirements. Successfully complete EMT course or curriculum. Pass clinical observation requirements. Hold a valid CPR card issued by American Heart Association or the American Red Cross. **Examination:** Yes. **Reciprocity:** Yes. **Fees:** $15 National Registry (optional).

Virginia

2750

Emergency Medical Technician
Virginia State Dept. of Health
1538 E. Parham Rd.
Richmond, VA 23228
Phone: (804)367-2102

Credential Type: Certificate. **Requirements:** 18 years of age. Must have a current and valid certifcate evidencing EMT-A Certification. Must have served one year with an emergency medical services agency. Be an active member of an emergency medical services agency. High school diploma. Complete the specified course. **Examination:** Yes.

Washington

2751

Emergency Medical Technician (EMT)
Dept. of Health
Emergency Medical Services
   Training and Licensing Section
1112 SE Quince
Olympia, WA 98504
Phone: (206)753-2095

Credential Type: Emergency Medical Technician (EMT) Certificate. **Duration of License:** Three years. **Requirements:** At least 18 years of age. Recommendation by an approved physician. Complete an approved EMT course. Renewal requires continuing education credits. **Examination:** Certification examination. **Fees:** No fee.

Credential Type: Physicians Trained Mobile Intravenous Therapy Technician Certificate. **Duration of License:** Two years. **Requirements:** Must have valid EMT Certificate. Recommendation by an approved physician. Complete an approved specialty training course in Mobile Intravenous Therapy. Renewal requires continuing education. **Examination:** Certification examination. **Fees:** No fee.

Credential Type: Physicians Trained Mobile Airway Management Technician Certificate. **Duration of License:** Two years. **Requirements:** Must have valid EMT Certificate. Recommendation by an approved physician. Complete an approved specialty training course in Mobile Airway Management. Renewal requires continuing education. **Examination:** Certification examination. **Fees:** No fee.

Credential Type: Physicians Trained Mobile Intensive Care Paramedic Certificate. **Duration of License:** Two years. **Requirements:** Must have valid EMT Certificate. Recommendation by an approved physician. Complete an approved specialty training course in Mobile Intensive Care. Renewal requires continuing education. **Examination:** Certification examination. **Fees:** No fee.

2752

First Responder
Dept. of Health
1300 SE Quince
Olympia, WA 98504
Phone: (206)753-2095

Credential Type: First Responder License. **Duration of License:** Three years. **Requirements:** At least 16 years of age to begin training. Complete a minimum of 44 hours of approved instruction. Continuing education required for renewal. **Examination:** Written and practical examination. **Fees:** No fee.

West Virginia

2753

Emergency Medical Technician
Dept. of Health
Office of Emergency Medical
   Services
Bldg. 3, Rm. 426
1800 Washington St. E.
Charleston, WV 25305
Phone: (304)348-3956

Credential Type: Emergency Medical Service Attendant Certification. **Requirements:** Must be able to read, write, and speak English. Be at least 18 years of age. Have earned a certificate in advanced first aid or equivalent and CPR.

Renewal requires completion of an approved refresher course or continuing education program. Pass recertification exam. **Governing Statute:** West Virginia Code 16-4C-1 et deq. Administrative Rules, Title 64, Series 48.

Credential Type: Emergency Medical Technician Certification. **Requirements:** Must be able to read, write, and speak English. Be at least 18 years of age. Complete an approved course on emergency care.

Renewal requires completion of an approved refresher course or continuing education program. Pass recertification exam. **Governing Statute:** West Virginia Code 16-4C-1 et deq. Administrative Rules, Title 64, Series 48.

Credential Type: Emergency Medical Technician-Ambulance Certification. **Requirements:** Must be able to read, write, and speak English. Be at least 18 years of age. Complete an approved course for certification as an EMT-A.

Renewal requires completion of an approved refresher course or continuing education program. Pass recertification exam. **Governing Statute:** West Virginia Code 16-4C-1 et deq. Administrative Rules, Title 64, Series 48.

Credential Type: Emergency Medical Technician-Intermediate Certification. **Requirements:** Must be able to read, write, and speak English. Be at least 18 years of age. Complete an approved course for certification.

Renewal requires completion of an approved continuing education program. Pass recertification exam. **Governing Statute:**

West Virginia Code 16-4C-1 et deq. Administrative Rules, Title 64, Series 48.

Credential Type: Emergency Medical Technician-Critical Care Certification. **Requirements:** Must be able to read, write, and speak English. Be at least 18 years of age. High school graduate or equivalent. Complete an approved course for certification. Be currently certified and have at least six months experience as an EMT or EMT-A.

Renewal requires completion of an approved continuing education program. Pass recertification exam. **Examination:** Competency test may be required. **Governing Statute:** West Virginia Code 16-4C-1 et deq. Administrative Rules, Title 64, Series 48.

Credential Type: Emergency Medical Technician-Paramedic Certification. **Requirements:** Must be able to read, write, and speak English. Be at least 18 years of age. High school graduate or equivalent. Complete an approved course for certification. Be currently certified and have at least six months experience as an EMT or EMT-A.

Renewal requires completion of an approved continuing education program. Pass recertification exam. **Examination:** Competency test may be required. **Governing Statute:** West Virginia Code 16-4C-1 et deq. Administrative Rules, Title 64, Series 48.

Wisconsin

2754

Emergency Medical Technician
Dept. of Health and Social Services
Div. of Health
Emergency Medical Services Section
PO Box 309
Madison, WI 53701-0309
Phone: (608)266-1568
Phone: (608)266-9781
Fax: (608)267-4853

Credential Type: EMT License. **Duration of License:** Two years. **Requirements:** Be at least 18 years of age. Complete a 120-hour training program equivalent to the U.S. Department of Transportation National Standard within the past two years. Possess current Professional Rescuer CPR certification. Must be affiliated with a Wisconsin licensed ambulance service provider.

Renewal requires completing a 30-hour refresher course every two years and annual CPR recertification. **Examination:** National Registry written and practical examination. **Exemptions:** Licensed physicians, registered nurses, and physician's assistants may function as an EMT without an EMT-Basic license or permit. **Governing Statute:** Wisconsin Statutes Sect. 146.50. Wisconsin Administrative Code, CHap. HSS 110.

Credential Type: EMT Training Permit. **Duration of License:** Two years (nonrenewable). **Authorization:** Must work with a person holding an EMT license. **Requirements:** Be at least 18 years of age. Possess current Professional Rescuer CPR certification. Must be affiliated with a Wisconsin licensed ambulance service provider. Complete one of the following: (1) 10 weeks of a Basic EMT course. (2) An approved first aid course. (3) Complete an approved First Responder course.

Credential Type: EMT-I License (Intermediate). **Duration of License:** Two years. **Authorization:** May perform limited advanced life support procedures when authorized by a physician and while working for a licensed ambulance service. **Requirements:** Be at least 18 years of age. Be currently licensed as an EMTBasic and have at least one year of experience as an EMT-Basic. Must be employed by a Wisconsin licensed ambulance service provider identified in an EMT-I plan. Complete an EMT-I course consisting of 40 classroom hours and 60 hours of supervised field experience.

Renewal requires completion of an approved EMT-I refresher course and annual CPR certification. **Examination:** National Registry EMT-I written and practical examination.

Credential Type: EMT-Paramedic License. **Duration of License:** Two years. **Requirements:** Be at least 18 years of age. Must have EMT license and one year of experience as an EMT. Complete 750 hours of additional training.

Renewal requires 48 hours of continuing education every two years, annual CPR recertification, and Advanced Cardiac Life Support recertification every two years. **Examination:** State written and practical examination.

Credential Type: EMT-Defibrillator Certification. **Duration of License:** Two years. **Authorization:** Defibrillation may be provided only under the supervision of a physician. **Requirements:** Must be employed by a Wisconsin license ambulance provider identified in an EMT-D plan. Have current license and six months experience as an EMT or EMT-I. Hold current CPR certification. Complete five hours (automatic) or 20 hours (manual) additional training in cardiac monitoring and defibrillation. **Examination:** State written and practical examination.

Wyoming

2755

Emergency Medical Technician
Office of Emergency Medical
  Services
Hathaway Bldg.
2300 Capitol Ave.
Cheyenne, WY 82002
Phone: (307)777-7955

Credential Type: License. **Requirements:** Complete 120 hours of course work. Pass the examinations. **Examination:** Yes. **Fees:** $40—60 Class.

Engineering, Science, and Data Processing Managers

The following states grant licenses in this occupational category as of the date of publication: Connecticut, Delaware, Illinois, Michigan, New Jersey, North Dakota.

Connecticut

2756

Operators Manager (Racetrack)
Connecticut Div. of Special Revenue
Russell Rd.
PO Box 11424
Newington, CT 06111-0424
Phone: (203)566-2756

Credential Type: License Registration. **Requirements:** Submit application and fingerprint card. Pay fee. **Fees:** $5 registration fee.

Delaware

2757

Laboratory Official (Racetrack)
Delaware Harness Racing Commission
2320 S. DuPont Hwy.
Dover, DE 19901
Phone: (302)739-4811

Credential Type: License Registration. **Requirements:** Submit application and fingerprint card. Pay fee. **Fees:** $5 registration fee.

Illinois

2758

M.I.S. Manager/Technical Supports Systems Operator (Gaming)
Illinois Gaming Board
PO Box 19474
Springfield, IL 62794-9474
Phone: (217)524-0228

Credential Type: M.I.S. Manager License. **Duration of License:** One year. **Requirements:** At least 18 years of age. No felony convictions. High school graduate or equivalent. Computer experience. **Reciprocity:** No. **Fees:** $75 application/initial license fee. $50 renewal fee. **Governing Statute:** Illinois Revised Statutes, Chapter 120.

Michigan

2759

Clinical Laboratory Director
Laboratory Improvement Div.
Dept. of Public Health
PO Box 30035
3500 N. Logan St.
Lansing, MI 48909
Phone: (517)335-8000

Credential Type: Certification. **Duration of License:** Lifetime. **Requirements:** Submit a completed application for a certificate of qualification. Submit supporting documents or give information which shows that they meet the minimum education and experience requirements prescribed by the Department for each field for which certification is requested. Demonstrate that they possess the character, training, and ability to properly administer the technical and scientific operation of a clinical laboratory. **Governing Statute:** Clinical Laboratories Act, Act 235 of 1968, as amended. Public Health Code, Act 368 of 1978, as amended.

New Jersey

2760

Bio-Analytical Laboratory Director
State Board of Medical Examiners
28 W. State St.
Trenton, NJ 08608
Phone: (609)292-4843

Credential Type: License. **Requirements:** A doctorate degree plus one year of experience; or a master's degree plus two years of experience; or a bachelor's degree and three years of experience. 21 years of age. Good moral character. Must be a state resident for one year. **Examination:** Written. **Fees:** $150 exam fee. $120 registration fee. **Governing Statute:** NJSA 45:9. NJAC 13:35.

2761

Laboratory Director
Board of Medical Examiners
28 W. State St.
Trenton, NJ 08608
Phone: (609)292-4843

Credential Type: Laboratory Director Specialty License. **Duration of License:** Two years. **Requirements:** A doctorate degree from an accredited university in Biochemical Genetics, Clinical Chemistry, Cytogenetics, Microbiology or Toxicology Chemistry. At least one year of experience. National certification by at least one acceptable certifying agency. **Examination:** Written. **Fees:** $150 license fee. $120 biennial registration fee. **Governing Statute:** NJSA 45:42. NJAC 8:45.

North Dakota

2762

Clinical Laboratory Scientist
State Board of Clinical Laboratory
 Practice
Dept. of Health and Consolidated
 Laboratories
Consolidated Laboratory Branch
Registration Div.
2635 E. Main
Bismarck, ND 58502-0937
Phone: (701)221-6140

Credential Type: License. **Duration of License:** Two years. **Requirements:** Bachelor's degree in a science-related discipline. **Examination:** National certifying examination. **Governing Statute:** North Dakota Century Code, Chap. 43-48.

Farm Operators and Managers

The following states grant licenses in this occupational category as of the date of publication: Illinois, Iowa, Kentucky, Maryland, Michigan, Texas.

Illinois

2763

Aquaculturist
Illinois Dept. of Conservation
524 S. Second St.
Springfield, IL 62701-1787
Phone: (217)785-3423

Credential Type: Aquaculturist License. **Duration of License:** One year. **Authorization:** Allows licensee to engage in breeding, hatching, propagating, or raising aquatic life. **Requirements:** Must be a resident of the state of Illinois for at least 30 days. Work site will be inspected by Agency Culturist. Submit application and pay fee. **Reciprocity:** No. **Fees:** $50 initial license fee. $50 renewal fee. **Governing Statute:** Illinois Revised Statutes, Chapter 56. Illinois Conservation Law—Fish.

Iowa

2764

Sheep Dealer
Dept. of Agriculture and Land
 Stewardship
Sheep Bureau
Wallace State Office Bldg.
Des Moines, IA 50319
Phone: (515)281-5736

Credential Type: License. **Duration of License:** One year. **Requirements:** An applicant must file an application with the Dept. of Agriculture. **Fees:** $5 license fee. $5 renewal fee.

Kentucky

2765

Farm Manager/Agent (Racetrack)
Kentucky State Racing Commission
PO Box 1080
Lexington, KY 40588
Phone: (606)254-7021

Credential Type: License Registration. **Requirements:** Submit application and fingerprint card. Pay fee. **Fees:** $35 registration fee.

2766

Landfarming Operator
Natural Resources and Environmental
 Protection Cabinet
Div. of Waste Management
14 Reilly Rd.
Frankfort, KY 40601
Phone: (502)564-6716

Credential Type: License. **Duration of License:** Five years. **Requirements:** High school diploma or equivalent. One year experience at a landfarming facility. Must attend a state landfarming school. **Examination:** Yes. **Fees:** $125 exam fee.

Maryland

2767

Forest Products Operator
Forestry Div.
Dept. of Natural Resources
Tawes State Office Bldg.
Annapolis, MD 21401
Phone: (410)974-3776

Credential Type: License. **Duration of License:** One year. **Requirements:** Submit application and pay fee. Submit annual harvest disclosure. **Fees:** $10 license fee.

Michigan

2768

Breeder, Game Fish
Administrative Services Div.
Dept. of Natural Resources
Stevens T. Mason Bldg.
PO Box 30028
Lansing, MI 48909
Phone: (517)373-1220

Credential Type: License. **Duration of License:** One year. **Requirements:** Must comply with laws regarding game fish breeders and rules put into effect by the Department of Natural Resources. **Fees:** $5 initial license fee. $5 renewal fee. **Governing Statute:** Fish Breeders Act, Act 196 of 1958.

Texas

2769

Fish Farmer
Texas Dept. of Agriculture
Fish Farmer Program
1700 N. Congress
Austin, TX 78711
Phone: (512)463-7624

Credential Type: Aquaculture License. **Duration of License:** Two years. **Requirements:** Submit application and pay fee. **Fees:** $100 license fee. **Governing Statute:** Agricultural Code Ch. 134, 31 TAC 361.

Financial Managers

The following states grant licenses in this occupational category as of the date of publication:

Connecticut	Iowa	Minnesota	North Dakota	Virginia
Florida	Kansas	Montana	Ohio	Wisconsin
Illinois	Kentucky	New Mexico	South Dakota	Wyoming

Connecticut

2770

Assistant Controller (Racetrack)
Connecticut Div. of Special Revenue
Russell Rd.
PO Box 11424
Newington, CT 06111-0424
Phone: (203)566-2756

Credential Type: License Registration. **Requirements:** Submit application and fingerprint card. Pay fee. **Fees:** $5 registration fee.

2771

Budget Analyst (Racetrack)
Connecticut Div. of Special Revenue
Russel Rd.
PO Box 11424
Newington, CT 06111-0424
Phone: (203)566-2756

Credential Type: License Registration. **Requirements:** Submit application and fingerprint card. Pay fee. **Fees:** $5 registration fee.

2772

Mutuel Manager and Assistant Mutuel Manager (Racetrack)
Connecticut Div. of Special Revenue
Russell Rd.
PO Box 11424
Newington, CT 06111-0424
Phone: (203)566-2756

Credential Type: License Registration. **Requirements:** Submit application and fingerprint card. Pay fee. **Fees:** $20 registration fee.

2773

Treasurer (Racetrack)
Connecticut Div. of Special Revenue
Russell Rd.
PO Box 11424
Newington, CT 06111-0424
Phone: (203)566-2756

Credential Type: License Registration. **Requirements:** Submit application and fingerprint card. Pay fee. **Fees:** $5 registration fee.

Florida

2774

Comptroller (Racetrack)
Florida Dept. of Business
Div. of Pari-Mutuel Wagering
Licensing Section
725 S. Bronough St.
Tallahassee, FL 32399-1037
Phone: (904)488-9161

Credential Type: License Registration Code 1008. **Requirements:** Submit application and fingerprint card. Pay fee. **Fees:** $40 registration fee.

2775

Horsemen's Bookkeeper (Racetrack)
Florida Dept. of Business
Div. of Pari-Mutuel Wagering
Licensing Section
725 S. Bronough St.
Tallahassee, FL 32399-1037
Phone: (904)488-9161

Credential Type: License Registration Code 1018. **Requirements:** Submit application and fingerprint card. Pay fee. **Fees:** $40 registration fee.

Illinois

2776

Cage Credit Manager (Gaming)
Illinois Gaming Board
PO Box 19474
Springfield, IL 62794-9474
Phone: (217)524-0228

Credential Type: Cage Credit Manager License. **Duration of License:** One year. **Requirements:** At least 21 years old. No felony convictions. High school graduate or equivalent. Minimum of six months as a casino cage manager. Must have knowledge of computers and 10 key calculators. Able to handle large amounts of currency. **Reciprocity:** No. **Fees:** $200 application and initial license fee. $50 renewal fee. **Governing Statute:** Illinois Revised Statutes, Chapter 120.

2777

Chief Financial Officer/Controller (Gaming)
Illinois Gaming Board
PO Box 19474
Springfield, IL 62794-9474
Phone: (217)524-0228

Credential Type: Chief Financial Officer/Controller License. **Duration of License:** One year. **Requirements:** At least 18 years of age. U.S. citizen and resident of Illinois. No felony convictions. High school graduate or equivalent. Bachelor's degree in Major Accounting. Certified Public Accountant (CPA) preferred. Must have two years experience in related field. **Reciprocity:** No. **Fees:** $1,000 application and li-

Illinois

Chief Financial Officer/ Controller (Gaming), continued

cense fee. $50 renewal fee. **Governing Statute:** Illinois Revised Statutes, Chapter 120.

2778

Chief School Business Official
Certification and Placement Section
100 N. First St.
Springfield, IL 62777
Phone: (217)782-4321

Credential Type: Chief School Business Official Endorsement. **Duration of License:** Five years. **Requirements:** Good character. Good health. At least 19 years of age. Citizen of the U.S. Master's degree in administration from a recognized institution. Must have the following graduate level semester hr. credits: School Business Management 12; School Organization and Administration 3; School Finance and Fiscal Planning 6; and Clinical Experience (appropriate to the endorsement) while holding a certificate of comparable validity. Two years of business management experience. Pass required sections of the Illinois Certification Test. **Examination:** Illinois Certification Test. **Reciprocity:** Reciprocity exists for applicants holding out-of-state administrative certificates providing their preparation was comparable to that required by the state of Illinois. **Fees:** $44 per section of the Illinois Certification Test.

2779

Internal Audit Manager (Gaming)
Illinois Gaming Board
PO Box 19474
Springfield, IL 62794-9474
Phone: (217)524-0228

Credential Type: Internal Audit Manager License. **Duration of License:** One year. **Requirements:** At least 18 years of age. U.S. citizen or legal alien as specified by the federal employment eligibility requirement. College graduate of an accounting program or equivalent training. Auditing experience. Gaming auditing experience preferred. **Reciprocity:** No. **Fees:** $1,000 application fee. $50 initial license fee. $50 renewal fee. **Governing Statute:** Illinois Revised Statutes, Chapter 120.

Iowa

2780

Mutuels Manager (Racetrack)
Iowa State Racing Commission
Lucas State Office Bldg.
Des Moines, IA 50319
Phone: (515)281-7352

Credential Type: License Registration. **Requirements:** Submit application and fingerprint card. Pay fee. **Fees:** $20 registration fee.

Kansas

2781

Horsemen's Bookkeeper (Racetrack)
Kansas Racing Commission
3400 VanBuren
Topeka, KS 66611-2228
Phone: (913)296-5800

Credential Type: License Registration. **Requirements:** Submit application and fingerprint card. Pay fee. **Fees:** $10 registration fee.

2782

Supervisor of Mutuels (Racetrack)
Kansas Racing Commission
3400 VanBuren
Topeka, KS 66611-2228
Phone: (913)296-5800

Credential Type: License Registration. **Requirements:** Submit application and fingerprint card. Pay fee. **Fees:** $20 registration fee.

Kentucky

2783

Commission Supervisor of Pari-Mutuel Betting (Racetrack)
Kentucky State Racing Commission
PO Box 1080
Lexington, KY 40588
Phone: (606)254-7021

Credential Type: License Registration. **Requirements:** Submit application and fingerprint card. Pay fee. **Fees:** $35 registration fee.

Minnesota

2784

Horsemen's Bookkeeper (Racetrack)
Minnesota Racing Commission
11000 W. 78th St., Ste. 201
Eden Prairie, MN 55344
Phone: (612)341-7555

Credential Type: License Registration. **Requirements:** Submit application and fingerprint card. Pay fee. **Fees:** $25 registration fee.

Montana

2785

Horsemen's Bookkeeper (Racetrack)
State of Montana Board of Horse Racing
Dept. of Commerce
1424 9th Ave.
Helena, MT 59620
Phone: (406)444-4287

Credential Type: License Registration. **Requirements:** Submit application and fingerprint card. Pay fee. **Fees:** $20 registration fee.

2786

Parimutuel Manager (Racetrack)
State of Montana Board of Horse Racing
Dept. of Commerce
1424 9th Ave.
Helena, MT 59620
Phone: (406)444-4287

Credential Type: License Registration. **Requirements:** Submit application and fingerprint card. Pay fee. **Fees:** $30 registration fee.

New Mexico

2787

Horsemen's Bookkeeper (Racetrack)
New Mexico State Racing Commission
PO Box 8576, Highland Station
Albuquerque, NM 87198
Phone: (505)841-4644

Credential Type: License Registration. **Requirements:** Submit application and fingerprint card. Pay fees. **Fees:** $16 registration fee. $1 notary fee. $23 fingerprint card processing fee.

2788

Pari-Mutuel Manager (Racetrack)
New Mexico State Racing Commission
PO Box 8576, Highland Station
Albuquerque, NM 87198
Phone: (505)841-4644

Credential Type: License Registration.
Requirements: Submit application and fingerprint card. Pay fees. **Fees:** $21 registration fee. $1 notary fee. $23 fingerprint card processing fee.

North Dakota

2789

Pari-Mutuel Manager (Racetrack)
North Dakota Racing Commission
State Capitol Bldg.
Bismarck, ND 58505
Phone: (701)224-2210

Credential Type: License Registration.
Requirements: Submit application and fingerprint card. Pay fee. **Fees:** $10 license fee. $10 duplicate license fee.

Ohio

2790

Horsemen's Bookkeeper (Thoroughbred, Standardbred, and Quarter Horse Racing)
Ohio State Racing Commission
State Office Tower
77 S. High St., 18th Fl.
Columbus, OH 43266-0416
Phone: (614)466-2757

Credential Type: License Registration.
Requirements: Submit application and fingerprint card. Pay fee. **Fees:** $25 registration fee.

2791

Mutuel Manager (Thoroughbred, Standardbred, and Quarter Horse Racing)
Ohio State Racing Commission
State Office Tower
77 S. High St., 18th Fl.
Columbus, OH 43266-0416
Phone: (614)466-2757

Credential Type: License Registration.
Requirements: Submit application and fingerprint card. Pay fee. **Fees:** $25 registration fee.

South Dakota

2792

Bookkeeper (Horse Racing)
South Dakota Racing Commission
c/o 500 East Capitol
Pierre, SD 57501
Phone: (605)773-6050

Credential Type: License Registration.
Requirements: Submit application and fingerprint card. Pay fee. **Fees:** $15 registration fee.

Virginia

2793

Horsemen's Bookkeeper (Racetrack)
Virginia Racing Commission
PO Box 1123
Richmond, VA 23208
Phone: (804)371-7363

Credential Type: License Registration.
Requirements: Submit application and fingerprint card. Pay fee. **Fees:** $10 registration fee.

2794

Mutuel Manager (Racetrack)
Virginia Racing Commission
PO Box 1123
Richmond, VA 23208
Phone: (804)371-7363

Credential Type: License Registration.
Requirements: Submit application and fingerprint card. Pay fee. **Fees:** $10 registration fee.

Wisconsin

2795

Mutuel Manager (Racetrack)
Wisconsin Racing Board
PO Box 7975
Madison, WI 53707-7975
Phone: (608)267-3291

Credential Type: License Registration.
Requirements: Submit application and two sets of fingerprint cards. Pay fee. **Fees:** $50 registration fee. $20 duplicate license.

Wyoming

2796

Horsemen's Bookkeeper (Racetrack)
Wyoming State Pari-Mutuel Commission
Barrett Bldg., 3rd Fl.
Cheyenne, WY 82002
Phone: (307)777-5887

Credential Type: License Registration.
Requirements: Submit application and fingerprint card. Pay fee. **Fees:** $20 registration fee. $10 duplicate license.

2797

Mutuel Official (Racetrack)
Wyoming State Pari-Mutuel Commission
Barrett Bldg., 3rd Fl.
Cheyenne, WY 82002
Phone: (307)777-5887

Credential Type: License Registration.
Requirements: Submit application and fingerprint card. Pay fee. **Fees:** $20 registration fee. $10 duplicate license.

Firefighting Occupations

The following states grant licenses in this occupational category as of the date of publication: Alabama, Illinois, Massachusetts, Michigan, New Hampshire, Texas.

Alabama

2798

Fire Fighter
Alabama Fire College and Personnel Standards Commission
2015 McFarland Blvd. E.
Tuscaloosa, AL 35405
Phone: (205)759-1508

Credential Type: License. **Requirements:** Must provide evidence of knowledge and ability to do described work. Must meet educational requirements as set forth by the hiring authority. **Examination:** Written and practical examinations. **Fees:** No fees.

Illinois

2799

Fire Equipment Employee
Illinois State Fire Marshal
1035 Stevenson Drive
Springfield, IL 62703
Phone: (217)785-1010

Credential Type: Class 1 License. **Duration of License:** One year. **Requirements:** Must have knowledge of servicing engineered fire extinguishing systems. Submit application, current photographs, and fee. **Examination:** Fire Equipment Employee Examination—Class 1. **Reciprocity:** Yes, considered on an individual basis. **Fees:** $25 initial license fee. $25 renewal fee. **Governing Statute:** Public Act 85-1434, Illinois Administrative Code.

Credential Type: Class 2 License. **Duration of License:** One year. **Requirements:** Must have knowledge of servicing pre-engineered fire extinguishing systems. Submit application, current photographs, and fee. **Examination:** Fire Equipment Employee Examination—Class 2. **Reciprocity:** Yes, considered on an individual basis. **Fees:** $25 initial license fee. $25 renewal fee. **Governing Statute:** Public Act 85-1434, Illinois Administrative Code.

Credential Type: Class 3 License. **Duration of License:** One year. **Requirements:** Must have knowledge of servicing engineered fire extinguishing systems. Submit application, current photographs, and fee. **Examination:** Fire Equipment Employee Examination—Class 3. **Reciprocity:** Yes, considered on an individual basis. **Fees:** $25 initial license fee. $25 renewal fee. **Governing Statute:** Public Act 85-1434, Illinois Administrative Code.

2800

Firefighter
Illinois State Fire Marshal
1035 Stevenson Drive
Springfield, IL 62703
Phone: (217)785-1010

Credential Type: Firefighter Certificate. **Duration of License:** Permanent. **Requirements:** Complete an approved course of study in fire science. Secure employment as a firefighter in Illinois. Submit application. **Examination:** Firefighter Certification Examination. **Reciprocity:** No. **Fees:** No fee. **Governing Statute:** Illinois Revised Statutes, Chapter 127 1/2 and 85.

Massachusetts

2801

Fireman Engineer
Dept. of Public Safety
Div. of Inspection
Engineering Section
One Ashburton Pl.
Boston, MA 02108
Phone: (617)727-3200

Credential Type: First Class Fireman License. **Duration of License:** Two years. **Requirements:** Complete at least one year of related work experience, or six months experience as a Second Class Fireman. **Examination:** Written and oral examination. **Fees:** $50 license and exam fee. **Governing Statute:** Massachusetts General Laws, Chap. 146.

Credential Type: Second Class Fireman License. **Duration of License:** Two years. **Requirements:** Be at least 18 years of age. Submit evidence of previous training. **Examination:** Written and oral examinations. **Fees:** $50 license and exam fee. **Governing Statute:** Massachusetts General Laws, Chap. 146.

Michigan

2802

Fire Fighter Training Instructor
Fire Fighters Training Council
Fire Marshall Div.
Dept. of State Police
7150 Harris Dr.
Lansing, MI 48913
Phone: (517)332-2521

Credential Type: Fire Fighter Training Instructor Certification. **Duration of License:** Lifelong. **Authorization:** All persons employed as a fire fighter training instructor must be certified by the Fire Fighters Training Council of the Michigan Department of State Police. **Requirements:** Minimum of five years experience in fire suppression service. Certification as a Fire Fighter I. Have received one positive evaluation and recommendation by a Fire Fighters Training Council representative, while a provisional instructor. Completed the Fire Fighters Training Council Basic Instructional Methodological (16 hour) Course, or its equivalent. **Fees:** No fees. **Governing Statute:** Fire Fighters Training Council Act of 1966, Act 291 of 1966, as amended.

Credential Type: Associate Instructor Certification. **Duration of License:** Lifelong. **Authorization:** All persons employed as a fire fighter training instructor must be certified by the Fire Fighters Training Council of the Michigan Department of State Police. **Requirements:** Have a minimum of three years experience in the specialized area or subject to be taught. Have received the recommendation and approval of a certified fire service instructor or recognized authority in the area to be taught. Abide by the rules of the Fire Fighters Training Council. **Fees:** No fees. **Governing Statute:** Fire Fighters Training Council Act of 1966, Act 291 of 1966, as amended.

Credential Type: Provisional Instructor Certification. **Duration of License:** Lifelong. **Authorization:** All persons employed as a fire fighter training instructor must be certified by the Fire Fighters Training Council of the Michigan Department of State Police. **Requirements:** Have a minimum of three years experience in fire suppression service. Have successfully completed the Fire Fighters Training Council Fire Fighter I curriculum. Have received the recommendation and approval of their fire chief or governing municipality official. Abide by the rules of the Fire Fighters Training Council. **Fees:** No fees. **Governing Statute:** Fire Fighters Training Council Act of 1966, Act 291 of 1966, as amended.

Credential Type: Fire Instructor Advisor Certification. **Duration of License:** Lifelong. **Authorization:** All persons employed as a fire fighter training instructor must be certified by the Fire Fighters Training Council of the Michigan Department of State Police. **Requirements:** Have certification as a Fire Fighter II and Fire Fighter Training Instructor. Have instructed in a minimum of five (5) Fire Fighters Training Council recognized programs. Have received three positive evaluations and recommendations by Fire Fighters Training Council representatives, while a Fire Fighter Training Instructor. Have completed the Fire Fighters Training Council Advanced Instructional Methodological Course, or its equivalent. **Fees:** No fees. **Governing Statute:** Fire Fighters Training Council Act of 1966, Act 291 of 1966, as amended.

Credential Type: Fire Training Administrator Certification. **Duration of License:** Lifelong. **Authorization:** All persons employed as a fire fighter training instructor must be certified by the Fire Fighters Training Council of the Michigan Department of State Police. **Requirements:** Have certification as a Fire Fighter II and a Fire Instructor Advisor. Have managed, supervised, or instructed in a minimum of 10 Fire Fighters Training Council recognized programs. **Fees:** No fees. **Governing Statute:** Fire Fighters Training Council Act of 1966, Act 291 of 1966, as amended.

New Hampshire

2803

Firefighter
Fire Standards & Training Commission
Dept. of Safety
91 Airport Rd.
Concord, NH 03301
Phone: (603)271-2661
Fax: (603)271-1091

Credential Type: Firefighter Certificate. **Requirements:** At least 18 years of age. Good moral character. High school graduate or equivalent. Pass medical and physical requirements. Complete a fire training program within one year of employment as a career firefighter. **Examination:** Physical Agility Test. **Reciprocity:** Yes, if training meets New Hampshire standards. **Fees:** $650 Level I Certification (in-state). $1,300 Level I Certification (out-of-state). $25 administrative fee for certificate.

Texas

2804

Firefighter
Texas Commission on Fire Protection
PO Box 2286
Austin, TX 78768
Phone: (512)322-3550

Credential Type: License. **Duration of License:** One year. **Requirements:** 18 years of age. Satisfactory completion of basic program of training in fire protection at a school approved or operated by the Commission. **Examination:** Written and physical. **Fees:** $20 license fee. $20 renewal fee. **Governing Statute:** VACS 4413(35), Gov't Code 419.021 Municipal, 419.071 Volunteer.

Fishers, Hunters, and Trappers, Including Guides

The following states grant licenses in this occupational category as of the date of publication:

Alaska	Colorado	Maine	Nevada	Ohio	Utah	Wyoming
Arizona	Idaho	Maryland	New Hampshire	Oregon	Washington	
Arkansas	Illinois	Michigan	New York	Rhode Island	West Virginia	
California	Kentucky	Montana	North Dakota	Texas	Wisconsin	

Alaska

2805

Assistant Guide Outfitter (hunting)
Alaska Dept. of Commerce and
  Economic Development
Div. of Occupational Licensing
State Office Bldg.
PO Box D
Juneau, AK 99811-0800
Phone: (907)465-2543

Credential Type: Assistant Guide Outfitter License. **Duration of License:** Two years. **Requirements:** At least 18 years of age. Must have hunted for at least two years in Alaska. **Examination:** Written and oral exam conducted by the Big Game Commercial Services Board, an agency of the Alaska Dept. of Commerce and Economic Development. **Fees:** $30 application fee. $25 exam fee. $200 assistant guide outfitter license fee.

Credential Type: Class A Assistant Guide Outfitter License. **Duration of License:** Two years. **Requirements:** At least 18 years of age. Be employed for at least one season as a licensed assistant guide outfitter. Have 10 years experience in the guide district. **Examination:** Written and oral exam conducted by the Big Game Commercial Services Board, an agency of the Alaska Dept. of Commerce and Economic Development. **Fees:** $30 application fee. $25 exam fee. $200 Class A assistant guide outfitter license fee.

2806

Guide Outfitter (hunting)
Alaska Dept. of Commerce and
  Economic Development
Div. of Occupational Licensing
State Office Bldg.
PO Box D
Juneau, AK 99811-0800
Phone: (907)465-2543

Credential Type: Guide Outfitter License. **Duration of License:** Two years. **Requirements:** At least 21 years of age. Must have hunted for at least five years, been licensed and employed as an assistant guide outfitter for three years. Provide proof of field experience. **Examination:** Oral exam conducted by the Big Game Commercial Services Board, an agency of the Alaska Dept. of Commerce and Economic Development. **Fees:** $30 application fee. $25 exam fee. $200 guide outfitter license fee. $150 transporter license fee. $100 commercial use permit fee.

Arizona

2807

Fishing Guide
Fisheries Branch
2221 W. Greenway Rd.
Phoenix, AZ 85023
Phone: (602)942-3000

Credential Type: Permit. **Duration of License:** One year. **Requirements:** Submit application and pay fee. **Fees:** $100 permit fee.

2808

Guide (Hunting/Fishing)
Arizona Game and Fish Dept.
2221 W. Greenway Rd.
Phoenix, AZ 85023-4312
Phone: (602)942-3000
Fax: (602)789-3920

Credential Type: Hunting guide license. **Authorization:** To act as a guide to taking wildlife, other than aquatic wildlife. **Requirements:** Be at least 18 years of age and a resident of Arizona. Have a current Arizona hunting license. Correctly answer at least 80 percent of the questions in a written examination. Within the past five years not have a felony conviction for violation of the following federal laws: Lacey Act, Endangered Species Act, Bald Eagle Protection Act, Airborne Hunting Act, and Migratory Bird Treaty Act. Applicant's privilege to take wildlife must not be currently under suspension or revocation by any state or the federal government. **Examination:** Written examination supervised and administered by the department. **Fees:** $100 license fee. **Governing Statute:** Arizona Revised Statutes, Title 17, Chapter 2.

Credential Type: Fishing guide license. **Authorization:** To act as a guide for taking aquatic wildlife only. **Requirements:** Be at least 18 years of age and a resident of Arizona. Have a current Arizona fishing license. Correctly answer at least 80 percent of the questions in a written examination. Within the past five years not have a felony conviction for violation of the following federal laws: Lacey Act, Endangered Species Act, Bald Eagle Protection Act, Airborne Hunting Act, and Migratory Bird Treaty Act. Applicant's privilege to take wildlife must not be currently under suspension or revocation by any state or the federal government. **Examination:** Written examination supervised and administered by the department. **Fees:** $100 license fee. **Governing Statute:** Arizona Revised Statutes, Title 17, Chapter 2.

Credential Type: Hunting and fishing guide license. **Authorization:** To act as a guide for taking all wildlife. **Requirements:** Be at least 18 years of age and a resident of Arizona. Have a current Arizona hunting and fishing license. Correctly answer at least 80 percent of the questions in a written examination. Within the past five years not have a felony conviction for violation of the following federal laws: Lacey Act, Endangered Species Act, Bald Eagle Protection Act, Airborne Hunting Act, and Migratory Bird Treaty Act. Applicant's privilege to take wildlife must not be currently under suspension or revocation by any state or the federal government. **Examination:** Written examination supervised and administered by the department. **Fees:** $100 license fee. **Governing Statute:** Arizona Revised Statutes, Title 17, Chapter 2.

Arkansas

2809

Fishing Guide
Arkansas Game and Fish
 Commission
2 Natural Resources Dr.
Little Rock, AR 72205
Phone: (501)223-6320

Credential Type: Guide License. **Duration of License:** One year. **Requirements:** Submit application and pay fee. **Fees:** $20 license fee.

California

2810

Professional Guide (Hunting and Fishing)
Dept. of Fish and Game
3211 S St.
Sacramento, CA 95816
Phone: (916)739-3555

Credential Type: Guide License. **Duration of License:** One year. **Authorization:** Covers sport fishing and hunting. **Requirements:** Submit application stating experience, areas of operation, and equipment, vehicles, and property to be used. Must be bonded. **Fees:** $57.75 resident license fee. $161 nonresident license fee.

Colorado

2811

Outfitter
Outfitters Registration, Dept. of
 Regulatory Agencies, Div. of
 Registrations
1560 Broadway, Ste. 1340
Denver, CO 80202
Phone: (303)894-7778

Credential Type: Outfitter registration. **Duration of License:** One year. **Authorization:** To solicit to provide or to provide for compensation facilities, guide services, or transportation for the purpose of hunting or fishing on land the outfitter does not own. **Requirements:** Be at least 21 years of age. Hold a valid instructor's card in first aid or equivalent. Have minimum liability insurance of at least $50,000 for bodily injury to one person and $100,000 for bodily injury to all persons. Submit surety bond of at least $10,000. **Fees:** $40 initial registration fee. **Governing Statute:** Colorado Statutes Title 12, Article 55.

2812

Professional Guide (Hunting and Fishing)
Natural Resources Dept.
Wildlife Div.
Fisheries Program
6060 Broadway
Denver, CO 80216
Phone: (303)291-7362

Credential Type: Guide Permit. **Duration of License:** One year. **Authorization:** Covers fishing and hunting. **Requirements:** Be at least 18 years of age. Resident of Colorado for at least six months. Hold a valid Red Cross First Aid card. **Examination:** Yes. **Fees:** $121 permit fee. $110 exam fee. $13 renewal fee.

Idaho

2813

Guide
Outfitters and Guides Licensing
 Board
1365 N. Orchard, Rm. 372
Boise, ID 83706
Phone: (208)327-7380
Fax: (208)327-7382

Credential Type: Guide License. **Duration of License:** One year. **Authorization:** Must be employed by a licensed outfitter. Guide is licensed for specific activities, and may only guide in operating areas for which employing outfitter is licensed. **Requirements:** Submit application and pay fees. Employing outfitter must verify competency to perform type of guiding activities for which licensing is sought and knowledge of operating areas. Guide applicant must also meet specific experience requirements for different specialties (e.g., hunting, boating, skiing). **Fees:** $85 license fee. **Governing Statute:** Idaho Code, Title 36, Chap. 21. Rules and Regulations of the Outfitters and Guides Licensing Board.

2814

Outfitter
Outfitters and Guides Licensing
 Board
1365 N. Orchard, Rm. 372
Boise, ID 83706
Phone: (208)327-7380
Fax: (208)327-7382

Credential Type: Outfitter License. **Duration of License:** One year. **Authorization:** License specifies activities for which applicant is licensed, designates specific operating areas for each activity, and is based on outfitter's operating plan. **Requirements:** Submit application and pay fees. Post $5,000 bond. Have interview with board. **Fees:** $250 license fee. **Governing Statute:** Idaho Code, Title 36, Chap. 21. Rules and Regulations of the Outfitters and Guides Licensing Board.

2815

Trapper
License Office
Administration Bureau
Fish and Game Dept.
PO Box 25
600 S. Walnut
Boise, ID 83707
Phone: (208)334-3717

Credential Type: License. **Requirements:** APP

Illinois

2816

Commercial Fisherman
Illinois Dept. of Conservation
524 S. Second
Springfield, IL 62701-1787
Phone: (217)782-3397

Credential Type: Commercial Fisherman License. **Duration of License:** One year (April 1—March 31 only). **Requirements:** Must reside in Illinois for at least one year to qualify for Resident License fee. Submit

Illinois

2817

Commercial Fisherman, continued

application and pay fee. **Reciprocity:** No. **Fees:** $25 resident initial license fee. $100 non-resident initial license fee. $25 resident renewal fee. $100 non-resident renewal fee. **Governing Statute:** Illinois Revised Statutes, Chapter 56, Illinois Conservation Law—Commercial Fishing.

2817

Commercial Musselor
Illinois Dept. of Conservation
524 S. Second
Springfield, IL 62701-1787
Phone: (217)785-3423

Credential Type: Commercial Musselor License. **Duration of License:** One year (April 15—August 31 only or when musseling season is scheduled). **Requirements:** Must reside in Illinois for at least one year. Submit application and pay fee. **Reciprocity:** No. **Fees:** $25 initial license fee. $25 renewal fee. **Governing Statute:** Illinois Revised Statutes, Chapter 56, Illinois Conservation Law—Commercial Fishing.

2818

Fee Fishing Area Operator
Illinois Dept. of Conservation
524 S. 2nd St.
Springfield, IL 62701-1787
Phone: (217)785-3423

Credential Type: Fee Fishing Area Operator License. **Duration of License:** One year. **Requirements:** Must be an Illinois resident for at least 30 days. Submit application and pay fee. **Reciprocity:** No. **Fees:** $50 initial license fee. $50 renewal fee.

2819

Hunting Area Operator (Exotic Game)
Illinois Dept. of Conservation
524 South 2nd St.
Springfield, IL 62701-1787
Phone: (217)785-3423

Credential Type: Exotic Game Hunting Area Operator License. **Duration of License:** One season. **Requirements:** Be an Illinois resident for at least 30 days. Submit application and pay fee. **Reciprocity:** No. **Fees:** $1,000 initial license fee. $1,000 renewal fee. **Governing Statute:** Illinois Revised Statutes, Chapter 61.

2820

Hunting Area Operator (Migratory Waterfowl)
Illinois Dept. of Conservation
524 South 2nd St.
Springfield, IL 62701-1787
Phone: (217)785-3423

Credential Type: Migratory Waterfowl Hunting Area Operator License. **Duration of License:** Limited to one duck and goose season. **Requirements:** Must be an Illinois resident for at least 30 days. Submit application and pay fee. **Reciprocity:** No. **Fees:** $15 license fee per blind. $15 renewal fee per blind. **Governing Statute:** Illinois Revised Statutes, Chapter 61.

Kentucky

2821

Professional Guide (Hunting and Fishing)
Dept. of Fish and Wildlife
1 Game Farm Rd.
Frankfort, KY 40342
Phone: (502)564-4224

Credential Type: Guide License. **Duration of License:** One year. **Authorization:** Covers fishing and hunting. **Requirements:** Be at least 18 years of age. **Fees:** $14.50 resident license fee. $42.50 nonresident license fee.

Maine

2822

Professional Guide (Hunting and Fishing)
Dept. of Inland Fisheries and Wildlife
Licensing Div.
State House Station 41
Augusta, ME 04333
Phone: (207)622-9116

Credential Type: Guide License and Registration. **Duration of License:** Three years. **Authorization:** Covers fishing and hunting. **Requirements:** Submit application and pay fee. **Fees:** $40 resident license fee. $142 nonresident license fee.

Maryland

2823

Commercial Fishing Guide
Dept. of Natural Resources
Tidewater Administration
Fisheries Dept.
Tawes State Office Bldg.
580 Taylor Ave.
Annapolis, MD 21401
Phone: (301)974-3765

Credential Type: Commercial Fishing Guide License. **Duration of License:** One year. **Requirements:** Submit application and pay fee. **Fees:** $35 resident license fee. $100 nonresident license fee.

2824

Master Hunting Guide
Wildlife Div.
Dept. of Natural Resources
Tawes State Office Bldg.
Annapolis, MD 21401
Phone: (410)974-3195

Credential Type: Master Hunting Guide License. **Duration of License:** One year. **Requirements:** Must file monthly reports. **Fees:** $100 license fee.

2825

Regulated Shooting Area Operator
Wildlife Div.
Dept. of Natural Resources
Tawes State Office Bldg.
Annapolis, MD 21401
Phone: (410)974-3195

Credential Type: Commercial License. **Duration of License:** One year. **Requirements:** Must include aerial photo and tax map with application. Area must include a minimum of 200 acres for upland game birds and 50 acres for "flighted" mallard ducks. **Fees:** $100 license fee.

Credential Type: Non-commercial License. **Duration of License:** One year. **Requirements:** Must include aerial photo and tax map with application. Area must include a minimum of 200 acres for upland game birds and 50 acres for "flighted" mallard ducks. **Fees:** $100 license fee.

2826

Trapper
Wildlife Div.
Dept. of Natural Resources
Tawes State Office Bldg.
Annapolis, MD 21401
Phone: (410)974-3776

Credential Type: Non-resident Trapping License. **Duration of License:** One year. **Requirements:** Submit fee and proof of purchase of a non-resident hunting license. **Fees:** $25.50 license fee.

Michigan

2827

Shooting Preserve Operator, Private
Wildlife Div.
Dept. of Natural Resources
Stevens T. Mason Bldg.
PO Box 30028
Lansing, MI 48909
Phone: (517)373-1220

Credential Type: License. **Duration of License:** One year. **Requirements:** Have the area to be licensed inspected by a Department officer to ensure that it meets the requirements of the Shooting Preserve Law. Show proof that they control full shooting rights for the shooting preserve. Have an area that contains at least 80 acres and not more than 640 acres. Shooting preserves on which only mallard ducks are flown and shot may contain as little as, but not less than, 50 acres. A shooting preserve usually must be contained in a single connected tract of land. Obtain all birds that are released and shot on the preserve lawfully. They must have been either reared by the shooting preserve operator or purchased from a licensed animal and bird breeder. Maintain good public relations with neighbors bordering the preserve. Comply with the Shooting Preserve Law and the rules of the Department of Natural Resources. All licensed shooting preserve operators must maintain up-to-date records of daily operations and submit an annual summary report to the Department with proof (invoice vouchers or other similar documents) that a minimum number of game birds were purchased and released. **Fees:** $60 (for a shooting preserve in excess of 320 acres), $35 (for a shooting preserve of 320 acres or less) initial license fee. Renewal fee is same as initial fee. **Governing Statute:** Shooting Preserve Law, Act 134 of 1957, as amended.

Montana

2828

Outfitter
Montana Board of Outfitters and Guides
Dept. of Commerce
111 N. Jackson
Helena, MT 59620
Phone: (406)444-3738

Credential Type: Outfitter's License. **Duration of License:** One year. **Requirements:** 18 years of age. An operations plan outlining the functions and operations of the outfitter's business. Three seasons of experience as a licensed outfitter or licensed professional guide in Montana. Verification of liability insurance for services provided. A valid wildlife conservation license. An inspection of the applicant's equipment, livestock and facilities. **Examination:** Written. **Fees:** $50 application fee. $50 exam fee. $175 investigation fee. $75 operations plan processing fee. $200 equipment inspection fee. $100 license fee. $100 renewal fee. **Governing Statute:** Montana Code Annotated 37-8-401 through 37-8-444.

2829

Professional Guide
Montana Board of Outfitters and Guides
Dept. of Commerce
111 N. Jackson
Helena, MT 59620
Phone: (406)444-3738

Credential Type: Professional Guide License. **Duration of License:** One year. **Requirements:** 18 years of age. An endorsement and recommendation from a licensed outfitter. One season of hunting or fishing experience, or completion of an approved professional guide program. A valid wildlife conservation license. **Fees:** $25 processing fee. $25 renewal fee. **Governing Statute:** Montana Code Annotated 87-4-101 through 87-4-163.

Nevada

2830

Fishing Guide
Dept. of Wildlife
Fisheries Div.
PO Box 10678
1100 Valley Rd.
Reno, NV 89520
Phone: (702)688-1530

Credential Type: Master Guide License. **Duration of License:** One year. **Requirements:** Contact licensing body for application information. **Fees:** $125 resident license fee. $250 nonresident license fee.

Credential Type: Subguide License. **Duration of License:** One year. **Requirements:** Contact licensing body for application information. **Fees:** $60 resident license fee.

New Hampshire

2831

Hunting & Fishing Guide
Fish and Game Dept.
2 Hazen Drive
Concord, NH 03301
Phone: (603)271-3421

Credential Type: Hunting & Fishing Guide License. **Duration of License:** One year. **Requirements:** At least 18 years of age. Practice safety and competence in all situations. Have the skill to use, manage, and handle boats and canoes. **Examination:** Examination administered through law enforcement agency. **Reciprocity:** No. **Fees:** $60 resident license. $201 non-resident license.

New York

2832

Guide
New York State Dept. of Environmental Conservation
Div. of Lands and Forests
50 Wolf Rd.
Albany, NY 12233
Phone: (518)457-5740

Credential Type: License. **Duration of License:** Five years. **Requirements:** American Red Cross standard first aid, CPR and water safety certification. 18 years of age. **Examination:** Written. **Fees:** $25 application fee. $75 license fee. $20 additional license fee for each additional activity. $75 renewal fee. $20 additional renewal

Guide, continued

fee for each additional activity. **Governing Statute:** Environmental Conservation Law Section 11-0533.

North Dakota

2833

Fishing Guide
Game and Fish Dept.
100 N. Bismarck Expwy.
Bismarck, ND 58501
Phone: (701)221-6300

Credential Type: Fishing Guide License. **Duration of License:** One year. **Requirements:** Must be a state resident. **Fees:** $100 license fee.

Ohio

2834

Fishing Guide
Dept. of Natural Resources
Div. of Wildlife
1840 Belcher Dr.
Columbus, OH 43224
Phone: (614)265-7040

Credential Type: Lake Erie Fishing Guide License. **Authorization:** Required for those who receive a fee to guide ice fishermen and those who provide watercraft services for a fee to fishermen on Lake Erie. **Requirements:** Submit application and pay fee. **Fees:** $50 license fee.

Oregon

2835

Outfitter/Guide
Oregon State Marine Board
435 Commercial St. NE
Salem, OR 97310
Phone: (503)373-1405

Credential Type: Registration. **Duration of License:** One year. **Requirements:** A current valid first-aid card or equivalent. Must have $300,000 of general liability insurance. **Examination:** No. **Fees:** $50 registration fee. $50 renewal fee. **Governing Statute:** ORS 704.010 to 704.990.

Rhode Island

2836

Commercial Fisher
Office of Boat Registration and Licensing
Rhode Island Dept. of Environmental Management
22 Hayes St.
Providence, RI 02908
Phone: (401)277-3576

Credential Type: Commercial Fisher Multi-purpose License. **Duration of License:** One year. **Requirements:** Rhode Island resident. First time applicants must submit an application notarized by the city or town clerk of residence. **Examination:** None. **Reciprocity:** No. **Fees:** $300 multi-purpose license fee.

Credential Type: Commercial Fisher Shellfish License. **Duration of License:** One year. **Requirements:** Rhode Island resident. First time applicants must submit an application notarized by the city or town clerk of residence. **Reciprocity:** No. **Fees:** $200 shellfish license (over age 65 license is free). $50 student shellfish license (under 24 and a student).

Credential Type: Commercial Fisher Scallops License. **Duration of License:** One year. **Requirements:** Rhode Island resident. First time applicants must submit an application notarized by the city or town clerk of residence. **Reciprocity:** No. **Fees:** $200 scallops license.

Credential Type: Commercial Fisher Lobster License. **Duration of License:** One year. **Requirements:** Rhode Island resident. First time applicants must submit an application notarized by the city or town clerk of residence. **Reciprocity:** No. **Fees:** $200 lobster license.

Credential Type: Commercial Fisher Rod & Reel License. **Duration of License:** One year. **Requirements:** Rhode Island resident. First time applicants must submit an application notarized by the city or town clerk of residence. **Reciprocity:** No. **Fees:** $200 rod & reel license.

2837

Commercial Trapper
Office of Boat Registration and Licensing
Rhode Island Dept. of Environmental Management
22 Hayes St.
Providence, RI 02908
Phone: (401)277-3576

Credential Type: Commercial Trapper License. **Duration of License:** One year. **Requirements:** Submit application and pay fee. **Reciprocity:** Yes. **Fees:** $10 resident license fee. $30 non-resident license fee.

Texas

2838

Fishing Guide
State Parks and Wildlife Dept.
4200 Smith School Rd.
Austin, TX 78744
Phone: (512)389-4818

Credential Type: Fishing Guide License. **Requirements:** Submit application and pay fee. **Fees:** $50 license fee.

Utah

2839

Hunting Guide
Natural Resources Dept.
Div. of Wildlife Resources
1596 W. North Temple
Salt Lake City, UT 84116
Phone: (801)533-9333

Credential Type: Registration. **Requirements:** Contact licensing body for application information.

Washington

2840

Commercial Fisher
Dept. of Fisheries
115 General Administration Bldg., AX-11
Olympia, WA 98504-0611
Phone: (206)753-6590

Credential Type: Commercial Fisher License. **Duration of License:** One year. **Requirements:** At least 16 years of age. U.S. resident. Must apply for endorsements for special types of fishing. Must meet moratorium requirements on special types of fishing. **Fees:** $50-$510 license fees for residents (depending on the specific type of fishing license(s) required). $100-$920 license fees for non-residents.

2841

Deckhand
Dept. of Fisheries
115 General Administration Bldg., AX-11
Olympia, WA 98504-0611
Phone: (206)753-6590

Credential Type: Deckhand License. **Duration of License:** One year. **Authorization:** Allows a crew member, fishing from a licensed charter boat, to sell salmon roe taken from fish caught for personal use. **Requirements:** Must be a bona fide U.S. resident. Submit application and pay fee. **Fees:** $20 license fee.

2842

Fishing Guide
Dept. of Wildlife
600 N. Capitol Way, GJ-11
Olympia, WA 98504-0091
Phone: (206)753-5700

Credential Type: Fishing Guide License. **Duration of License:** One year. **Requirements:** Resident of Washington state for a minimum of 90 days. Submit application and pay fee. **Fees:** $180 resident license fee. $600 non-resident license fee.

2843

Geoduck Diver
Dept. of Fisheries
115 General Administration Bldg., AX-11
Olympia, WA 98504-0611
Phone: (206)753-6590

Credential Type: Geoduck Diver License. **Duration of License:** One year. **Requirements:** At least 16 years of age. Submit application and pay fee. **Fees:** $100 resident license fee. $200 non-resident license fee.

2844

Shellfish Diver
Dept. of Fisheries
115 General Administration Bldg., ACC
Olympia, WA 98504-0611
Phone: (206)753-6590

Credential Type: Shellfish Diver License. **Duration of License:** One year. **Authorization:** Allows harvesting of shellfish other than clams. **Requirements:** At least 16 years of age. Submit application and pay fee. **Fees:** $50 resident license fee. $100 non-resident license fee.

2845

Trapper
Dept. of Wildlife
600 N. Capitol Way, GJ-11
Olympia, WA 98504-0091
Phone: (206)753-5700

Credential Type: Trapper License. **Duration of License:** One year. **Requirements:** At least 17 years of age. (Under 17 may apply for a Trapper Training Card.) Must be a resident of Washington state for at least 90 days to qualify for resident fee. Submit application and pay fee. **Fees:** $36 resident fee. $180 non-resident fee.

West Virginia

2846

Fishing Guide
Div. of Natural Resources
Wildlife Resources Div.
1900 Kanawha Blvd.
East Bldg. 3, Rm. 809
Charleston, WV 25305
Phone: (304)348-2771

Credential Type: Fishing Guide License. **Duration of License:** One year. **Requirements:** Contact licensing body for application information. **Fees:** $10 license fee.

Wisconsin

2847

Fishing Guide
Dept. of Natural Resources
Licensing Section
101 S. Webster
PO Box 7921
Madison, WI 53707
Phone: (608)266-2105

Credential Type: Fishing Guide License (Inland). **Requirements:** Be at least 18 years of age. Must be a state resident. **Fees:** $5 license fee.

Credential Type: Fishing Guide License (Outlying Waters). **Authorization:** Covers outlying waters (Lake Michigan, Green Bay, and Lake Superior). **Requirements:** Submit application and pay fee. **Fees:** $100 resident license fee. $400 nonresident license fee.

Wyoming

2848

Guide, Professional
State Board of Outfitters and Professional Guides
1750 Westland Rd.
Cheyenne, WY 82002
Phone: (307)777-5323

Credential Type: License. **Duration of License:** One year. **Requirements:** 18 years of age. Employed by a licensed outfitter. **Examination:** Yes. **Fees:** $5 New applicant. $75 License. $25 License (14 days).

2849

Outfitter
State Board of Outfitters and Guides
1750 Westland Rd.
Cheyenne, WY 82002
Phone: (307)777-5323

Credential Type: License. **Duration of License:** One year. **Requirements:** 19 years of age. Experience as a licensed Professional Guide for at least one year. Possess the necessary and applicable equipment and facilities. **Examination:** Yes. **Fees:** $100 New Applicant. $300 License. $300 Renewal.

Food and Beverage Service Occupations

The following states grant licenses in this occupational category as of the date of publication: California, Illinois, Iowa, Maryland, Michigan, New Jersey, New York, Texas, Washington.

California

2850

Food Service Person (Racetrack)
California Horse Racing Board
1010 Hurley Way, Ste. 190
Sacramento, CA 95825
Phone: (916)920-7178

Credential Type: License Registration. **Requirements:** Submit application and fingerprint card. Pay fee. **Fees:** $75 registration fee.

Illinois

2851

Bartender (Gaming Industry)
Illinois Gaming Board
PO Box 19747
Springfield, IL 62794-9474
Phone: (217)524-0228

Credential Type: Bartender License. **Duration of License:** One year. **Requirements:** At least 18 years of age. Complete a bartender training program. Must have knowledge of state liquor laws. **Reciprocity:** No. **Fees:** $75 application and license fee. $50 annual renewal fee. **Governing Statute:** Illinois Revised Statutes, Chapter 120.

2852

Cocktail Waitress (Gaming)
Illinois Gaming Board
PO Box 19474
Springfield, IL 62794-9474
Phone: (217)524-0228

Credential Type: Cocktail Waitress License. **Duration of License:** One year. **Requirements:** At least 18 years of age. U.S. citizen or legal alien as specified by the Federal employment eligibility requirement. Submit application and pay fee. **Reciprocity:** No. **Fees:** $75 initial license and application fee. $50 renewal fee. **Governing Statute:** Illinois Revised Statutes, Chapter 120.

2853

Food and Beverage Manager (Gaming)
Illinois Gaming Board
PO Box 19474
Springfield, IL 62794-9474
Phone: (217)524-0228

Credential Type: Food and Beverage Manager License. **Duration of License:** One year. **Requirements:** At least 18 years of age. U.S. citizen or legal alien as specified by the federal employment eligibility requirement. Must have at least five years experience as a Food and Beverage Manager in a full service restaurant. **Reciprocity:** No. **Fees:** $75 application/initial license fee. $50 renewal fee. **Governing Statute:** Illinois Revised Statutes, Chapter 120.

2854

Food Service Sanitation Manager
Illinois Dept.of Health
Div. of Foods, Drugs, and Dairies
525 W. Jefferson
Springfield, IL 62761
Phone: (217)785-2439

Credential Type: Food Service Sanitation Manager Certificate. **Duration of License:** Five years. **Requirements:** Must complete a course approved by the Department of Public Health. Submit application and pay fee. **Examination:** Food Services Sanitation Manager Certification Examination. **Reciprocity:** Yes, if certificate was granted on completion of similar requirements or if applicant's state has a reciprocal agreement with Illinois. **Fees:** $35 initial certificate fee. $35 renewal fee. **Governing Statute:** Illinois Revised Statutes 1991, Chapter 56 1/2.

2855

Restaurant Bus Helper (Gaming)
Illinois Gaming Board
PO Box 19474
Springfield, IL 62794-9474
Phone: (217)524-0228

Credential Type: Bus Helper License. **Duration of License:** One year. **Requirements:** At least 18 years of age. U.S. citizen or legal alien as specified by Federal employability requirement. **Reciprocity:** No. **Fees:** $75 application/initial license fee. $50 renewal fee. **Governing Statute:** Illinois Revised Statutes, Chapter 120.

2856

Restaurant Hostess/Host (Gaming)
Illinois Gaming Board
PO Box 19474
Springfield, IL 62794-9474
Phone: (217)524-0228

Credential Type: Hostess/Host License. **Duration of License:** One year. **Requirements:** At least 18 years of age. U.S. citizen or legal alien as specified by Federal employability requirement. **Reciprocity:** No. **Fees:** $75 application/initial license fee. $50 renewal fee. **Governing Statute:** Illinois Revised Statutes, Chapter 120.

2857

Restaurant Manager (Gaming)
Illinois Gaming Board
PO Box 19474
Springfield, IL 62794-9474
Phone: (217)524-0228

Credential Type: Restaurant Manger License. **Duration of License:** One year. **Requirements:** At least 18 years of age. U.S. citizen or legal alien as specified by Federal employability requirement. Must have three or more years experience as a manager in a full service restaurant. **Reciprocity:** No. **Fees:** $75 application/initial license fee. $50 renewal fee. **Governing Statute:** Illinois Revised Statutes, Chapter 120.

2858

Restaurant Server (Gaming)
Illinois Gaming Board
PO Box 19474
Springfield, IL 62794-9474
Phone: (217)524-0228

Credential Type: Restaurant Server License. **Duration of License:** One year. **Requirements:** At least 18 years of age. U.S. citizen or legal alien as specified by Federal employability requirement. Submit application and pay fee. **Reciprocity:** No. **Fees:** $75 application/initial license fee. $50 renewal fee. **Governing Statute:** Illinois Revised Statutes, Chapter 120.

2859

Sous Chef (Gaming)
Illinois Gaming Board
PO Box 19474
Springfield, IL 62794-9474
Phone: (217)524-0228

Credential Type: Sous Chef License. **Duration of License:** One year. **Requirements:** At least 18 years of age. U.S. citizen and Illinois resident. No felony convictions. Three or more years experience as a Sous Chef in a gourmet restaurant. **Reciprocity:** No. **Fees:** $75 application and license fee. $50 renewal fee. **Governing Statute:** Illinois Revised Statutes, Chapter 120.

Iowa

2860

Alcohol Server (Riverboat Gambling)
Iowa Racing and Gaming Commission
Lucas State Office Bldg.
Des Moines, IA 50319
Phone: (515)281-7352

Credential Type: License Registration. **Requirements:** Submit application and pay fees. **Fees:** $10 license fee.

2861

Food & Beverage Director (Riverboat Gambling)
Iowa Racing and Gaming Commission
Lucas State Office Bldg.
Des Moines, IA 50319
Phone: (515)281-7352

Credential Type: License Registration. **Requirements:** Submit application and pay fees. **Fees:** $50 license fee.

2862

Food Service Worker (Riverboat Gambling)
Iowa Racing and Gaming Commission
Lucas State Office Bldg.
Des Moines, IA 50319
Phone: (515)281-7352

Credential Type: License Registration. **Requirements:** Submit application and pay fees. **Fees:** $10 license fee.

2863

Host/Hostess (Riverboat Gambling)
Iowa Racing and Gaming Commission
Lucas State Office Bldg.
Des Moines, IA 50319
Phone: (515)281-7352

Credential Type: License Registration. **Requirements:** Submit application and pay fees. **Fees:** $10 license fee.

Maryland

2864

Caterer (Harness Racing)
Maryland Racing Commission
Stanbalt Bldg., 14th Fl.
501 St. Paul Place
Baltimore, MD 21202
Phone: (301)333-6267

Credential Type: License Registration. **Requirements:** Submit application, fingerprint card, and three passport size photos. Pay fee. **Fees:** $5 registration fee.

2865

Caterer (Thoroughbred Racing)
Maryland Racing Commission
Stanbalt Bldg., 14th Fl.
501 St. Paul Place
Baltimore, MD 21202
Phone: (301)333-6267

Credential Type: License Registration. **Requirements:** Submit application, fingerprint card, and three passport size photos. Pay fee. **Fees:** $5 registration fee.

Michigan

2866

Alcoholic Beverage Worker
Liquor Control Commission
Dept. of Commerce
7150 Harris Dr.
PO Box 30005
Lansing, MI 48909
Phone: (517)373-9153

Credential Type: License. **Duration of License:** Three years. **Requirements:** At least 18 years old. Comply with all rules and regulations of the Liquor Control Commission. **Examination:** No exam. **Fees:** $35 initial license fee. $35 renewal fee. **Governing Statute:** Michigan Liquor Control Act, Act eight of 1933 (extra session), as amended.

New Jersey

2867

Milk Dealer
New Jersey Dept. of Agriculture
Div. of Dairy Industry
CN332
Trenton, NJ 08625-0332
Phone: (609)292-5646

Credential Type: License. **Fees:** License fees vary depending upon the amount of milk sold and processed. **Governing Statute:** NJSA 4-12A. NJAC 2:52.

New York

2868

Food Services Employee (Harness or Quarter Horse Racing)
New York State Racing and
   Wagering Board
400 Broome St.
New York, NY 10013
Phone: (212)219-4230

Credential Type: License Registration. **Duration of License:** One year. **Requirements:** Submit application, F.B.I fingerprint card, New York state fingerprint card, and three photos. Pay fees. **Fees:** $5 registration fee. $44 New York state fingerprint card processing fee (valid for five years).

2869

Food Services Employee (Thoroughbred Racing)
New York State Racing and
   Wagering Board
400 Broome St.
New York, NY 10013
Phone: (212)219-4230

Credential Type: License Registration. **Duration of License:** One year. **Requirements:** Submit application, F.B.I fingerprint card, New York state fingerprint card, and three photos. Pay fees. **Fees:** $5 registration fee. $44 New York state fingerprint card processing fee (valid for five years).

Texas

2870

Food Service Employee (Racetrack)
Texas Racing Commission
PO Box 12080
Austin, TX 78711
Phone: (512)794-8461

Credential Type: License Registration. **Requirements:** Submit application and fingerprint card. Pay fee. **Fees:** $20 registration fee.

Washington

2871

Food Processor/Packer
Dept. of Agriculture
Food Safety and Animal Health
   Division
406 General Administration Bldg.,
   AX-41
Olympia, WA 98504-0641
Phone: (206)753-5043

Credential Type: Food Processor/Packer License. **Duration of License:** One year. **Requirements:** Submit application and pay fee. **Fees:** $25 license fee.

2872

Food Service Worker
Dept. of Health
2223 SE Quince
Olympia, WA 98504
Phone: (206)753-5871

Credential Type: Food Worker License. **Duration of License:** Two years initial; five years renewal. **Requirements:** Submit application and pay fee. Pass examination. **Examination:** Written examination. **Fees:** $5 initial license fee. $5 renewal fee.

Foresters and Conservation Scientists and Workers

The following states grant licenses in this occupational category as of the date of publication:

Alabama	Connecticut	Louisiana	Maryland	Mississippi	New Jersey	South Carolina	
Arkansas	Georgia	Maine	Michigan	New Hampshire	Rhode Island	West Virginia	

Alabama

2873

Forester
State Board of Registration for Foresters
513 Madison Ave.
Montgomery, AL 36130
Phone: (205)240-9368

Credential Type: License. **Duration of License:** One year. **Requirements:** Must hold a B.S. degree in Forestry and have two years of experience after graduation. **Examination:** Written and/or oral examinations. **Fees:** $30 registration fee. $20 renewal fee.

2874

Tree Surgeon
Dept. of Agriculture
Div. of Agricultural Chemistry and Plant Industry
Beard Bldg.
PO Box 3336
Montgomery, AL 36193
Phone: (205)242-2656

Credential Type: License. **Duration of License:** One year. **Requirements:** Must have sufficient knowledge and competency to do the work. Must submit a written statement outlining training and experience in this field. **Examination:** Written examination. **Fees:** $10 examination fee. $25 renewal fee.

Arkansas

2875

Forester
State Board of Registration for Foresters
75 Robinwood Dr.
PO Box 7424
Little Rock, AR 72207
Phone: (501)225-8619

Credential Type: License. **Requirements:** Graduate of an approved four year forestry college and if applicant has three years of experience the written test may be waived; or, six years of experience in forestry work approved by the Board and passing a written examination. **Examination:** Yes. **Fees:** $7.50 Application. $7.50 Registration.

2876

Tree Injector (Forest Worker)
Arkansas State Plant Board
1 Natural Resources Dr.
PO Box 1069
Little Rock, AR 72205
Phone: (501)225-1598

Credential Type: License. **Requirements:** Demonstrate a proficiency in tree-growth knowledge, disease control and use of herbicides. **Examination:** Yes. **Fees:** $25 License. $25 Operator in charge.

Connecticut

2877

Arborist
Tree Protection Examining Board
Consumer Protection Dept.
165 Capitol Ave.
Hartford, CT 06106
Phone: (203)566-3290

Credential Type: Arboriculture license. **Duration of License:** Five years. **Requirements:** Submit application and pay fee. Pass examination. **Examination:** Board-administered examination. **Fees:** $20 license fee. $20 renewal fee. $10 exam fee. **Governing Statute:** General Statutes of Connecticut, Chap. 451.

Georgia

2878

Forester
State Board of Registration for Foresters
Sciences and Professions Section
Professional Examining Boards
166 Pryor St., SW
Atlanta, GA 30303
Phone: (404)656-2281

Credential Type: Forester Registration. **Duration of License:** Two years. **Requirements:** Provide three professional references from foresters currently registered in Georgia. Meet one of the following sets of requirements: (1) Graduate from a school, college, or department of forestry approved by the board. Pass a board-approved examination after graduation. Complete two years experience in forestry work. (2) Graduate from a shcool of forestry not approved by the board or complete a curriculum ap-

Forester, continued

proved by the board of at least 40 quarter hours in forestry subjects. Pass a board-approved examination after graduation. Complete two years experience in forestry work. (3) Have a masters degree in addition to a bachelor's degree in forestry. Pass a board-approved examination after graduation. Complete one year of experience in forestry work. **Examination:** Yes. **Reciprocity:** Yes, with states that have equivalent requirements and reciprocity with Georgia. **Fees:** $20 application fee. $60 exam fee. $50 initial registration fee. $50 reciprocal registration fee. $50 renewal fee. **Governing Statute:** Official Code of Georgia Annotated 12-6. Rules of the State Board of Registration for Foresters, Chap. 220.

Louisiana

2879

Arborist
Horticulture Commission
PO Box 3118
Baton Rouge, LA 70821
Phone: (504)925-7772

Credential Type: License. **Duration of License:** One year. **Requirements:** Must have a certificate of insurance. **Examination:** Written. **Fees:** $35 exam fee. $35 license fee. $35 renewal fee.

Maine

2880

Apprentice Landscape Arborist
Arborist Examining Board
Dept. of Professional and Financial Regulations
State House Station 35
Augusta, ME 04333
Phone: (207)582-8723

Credential Type: Apprentice Permit. **Duration of License:** One year. **Authorization:** Must work under the on-site supervision of a First Class or Master Landscape Arborist. **Requirements:** Must be at least 18 years of age. Applicants with no prior experience must train under the direction of a First Class or Master Landscape Arborist for at least one year as an apprentice. **Fees:** $15 application fee. **Governing Statute:** 32 M.S.R.A., Chap. 29.

2881

Apprentice Utility Arborist
Arborist Examining Board
Dept. of Professional and Financial Regulations
State House Station 35
Augusta, ME 04333
Phone: (207)582-8723

Credential Type: Apprentice Permit. **Duration of License:** One year. **Authorization:** Must work under the on-site supervision of a First Class or Master Utility Arborist. A Utility Arborist may perform agricultural procedures closer than 120 feet from an energized conductor. **Requirements:** Must be at least 18 years of age. Applicants with no prior experience must train under the direction of a First Class or Master Utility Arborist for at least one year as an apprentice. **Fees:** $15 application fee. **Governing Statute:** 32 M.S.R.A., Chap. 29.

2882

Arborist (Unrestricted)
Arborist Examining Board
Dept. of Professional and Financial Regulations
State House Station 35
Augusta, ME 04333
Phone: (207)582-8723

Credential Type: Unrestricted Arborist Licence. **Duration of License:** One year. **Requirements:** Must be at least 18 years of age. Must have a minimum of five years experience as both a landscape and utility arborist. Hold a valid Maine Pesticide Applicators License in categories 3A-Outdoor Ornamentals and 6B-Utility Vegetation. **Examination:** Master Landscape Arborist Examination, written and practical. Master Utility Arborist Examination, written and practical. **Fees:** $15 application fee. $50 exam fee. $30 license fee. $30 renewal fee. **Governing Statute:** 32 M.S.R.A., Chap. 29.

2883

Landscape Arborist
Arborist Examining Board
Dept. of Professional and Financial Regulations
State House Station 35
Augusta, ME 04333
Phone: (207)582-8723

Credential Type: First Class Landscape Arborist Licence. **Duration of License:** One year. **Requirements:** Must be at least 18 years of age. Must have at least one year of prior experience or have completed one year apprenticeship. **Examination:** First Class Landscape Arborist Examination, written and practical. **Fees:** $15 application fee. $50 exam fee. $30 license fee. $30 renewal fee. **Governing Statute:** 32 M.S.R.A., Chap. 29.

Credential Type: Master Landscape Arborist Licence. **Duration of License:** One year. **Requirements:** Must be at least 18 years of age. Must have at least five years of prior experience or training. Must hold a valid Maine Pesticide Applicator license in category 3A-Outdoor Ornamentals. **Examination:** Master Landscape Arborist Examination, written and practical. **Fees:** $15 application fee. $75 exam fee. $30 license fee. $30 renewal fee. **Governing Statute:** 32 M.S.R.A., Chap. 29.

2884

Professional Forester
Board of Registration for Professional Foresters
Dept. of Professional and Financial Regulation
Div. of Licensing and Enforcement
State House Station 35
Augusta, ME 04333
Phone: (207)582-8723

Credential Type: License. **Duration of License:** Two years. **Requirements:** Graduation from a curriculum in forestry of four years or more in an approved college or school; or graduation from a postgraduate curriculum in forestry leading to a degree higher than a bachelor's degree. Applicants who have not graduated from such a curriculum may substitute two years of experience in forestry work, including internship, for each year of the undergraduate requirement.

Complete a two-year internship under the guidance of a licensed forester following completion of at least three years of an approved curriculum. The internship is not required of graduates of an approved four-year curriculum who have also completed at least two years of experience. **Examination:** Written examination. **Exemptions:** Individuals licensed on or before January 1, 1991, are not required to complete an examination as a condition for continuing licensure. **Fees:** $30 application fee. $25 license fee. $25 renewal fee. **Governing Statute:** 32 M.S.R.A. Chap. 75.

2885

Utility Arborist
Arborist Examining Board
Dept. of Professional and Financial Regulations
State House Station 35
Augusta, ME 04333
Phone: (207)582-8723

Credential Type: First Class Utility Arborist Licence. **Duration of License:** One year. **Authorization:** A Utility Arborist may perform agricultural procedures closer than 120 feet from an energized conductor. **Requirements:** Must be at least 18 years of age. Must have at least one year of prior experience or have completed one year apprenticeship. **Examination:** First Class Utility Arborist Examination, written and practical. **Fees:** $15 application fee. $50 exam fee. $30 license fee. $30 renewal fee. **Governing Statute:** 32 M.S.R.A., Chap. 29.

Credential Type: Master Utility Arborist Licence. **Duration of License:** One year. **Requirements:** Must be at least 18 years of age. Must have at least five years of prior experience or training. Must hold a valid Maine Pesticide Applicator license in category 6B-Utility Vegetation. **Examination:** Master Utility Arborist Examination, written and practical. **Fees:** $15 application fee. $75 exam fee. $30 license fee. $30 renewal fee. **Governing Statute:** 32 M.S.R.A., Chap. 29.

Maryland

2886

Forester
State Board of Registration of Foresters
Dept. of Licensing and Regulation
501 St. Paul Pl.
Baltimore, MD 21202-2272
Phone: (410)333-6322

Credential Type: Registration and license. **Duration of License:** Two years. **Requirements:** Graduation from a curriculum in forestry of four years or more in a board-approved or Society of American Foresters-accredited school or college. Two or more years experience in forestry work. **Fees:** $55 license fee. $100 renewal fee. **Governing Statute:** Annotated Code of Maryland, Title 9, Article 56. Code of Maryland Regulations 09.29.01, 09.01.02, 09.01.03.

2887

Tree Expert
Forestry Div.
Dept. of Natural Resources
Tawes State Office Bldg.
Annapolis, MD 21401
Phone: (410)974-3776

Credential Type: License. **Duration of License:** One year. **Requirements:** Meet one of the following sets of requirements: (1) two-year degree in biology, forestry, or related field. One year experience under a licensed tree expert. (2) No degree with five years experience under a licensed tree expert.

Proof of insurance is also required. **Examination:** Tree expert examination. **Reciprocity:** Yes. **Fees:** $10 license fee. $30 exam fee.

Michigan

2888

Forester, Registered
Board of Registration for Foresters
Bureau of Occupational & Professional Regulation
Dept. of Commerce
PO Box 30018
Lansing, MI 48909
Phone: (517)373-9153

Credential Type: Registration. **Duration of License:** Two years. **Requirements:** Have a minimum of a bachelor's degree in a forestry curriculum, including course work totaling not less than 30 semester hours or 45 quarter hours in the following subjects: forest biology, forest resources inventory, forestry in the social context, forest resources administration, and forest ecosystem management. A minimum of 12 semester or 18 quarter hours must be in forest ecosystem management. At least two years of experience in forestry work, in addition to college graduation. Be of good moral character. Submit the names of three references. They must be foresters who have personal or professional knowledge of the applicant's forestry experience. Comply with all rules and regulations of the Board. **Reciprocity:** A registered forester from another state may be registered in Michigan if: (1) The applicant submits proof of registration and completes application forms. (2) The requirements for registration in that state are substantially equivalent to those of Michigan. **Fees:** $50 application processing fee. $25 initial registration fee, per year. $25 renewal fee, per year. $50 reciprocity fee. **Governing Statute:** The Occupational Code, Act 299 of 1980, as amended.

Mississippi

2889

Tree Surgeon
Dept. of Agriculture and Commerce
Div. of Plant Industry
PO Box 5207
Mississippi State, MS 39762
Phone: (601)325-3390

Credential Type: Tree Surgeon License. **Duration of License:** Indefinite. **Requirements:** Meet one of the following sets of requirements: (1) Graduate from a college or university with at least 15 semester hours or the equivalent in the field for which a license is requested. (2) Have at least two years of college or university training, with special training in the field for which a license is requested. (3) Be a high school graduate or equivalent and have at least one year of experience with a licensed tree surgeon within the past two years. (4) If applicant is not a high school graduate, must have completed at least two years of experience with a licensed tree surgeon within the past three years.

Renewal requires attending an approved training course every three years. **Examination:** Written examination in tree surgery. **Reciprocity:** Exam may be waived if applicant is licensed in a state with standards equal to those of Mississippi and that state will honor the Mississippi Examination.

New Hampshire

2890

Professional Forester
Joint Board of Engineers, Architects, Land Surveyors, and Natural Scientists
57 Regional Drive
Concord, NH 03301
Phone: (603)371-2219

Credential Type: Professional Forester License. **Duration of License:** Two years. **Requirements:** Good professional character. Must meet one of the following sets of requirements: (1) four-year forestry degree and two years of experience; (2) two-year forestry degree and four years of experience; (3) four-year related degree and four years of experience; (4) two-year related degree and six years of experience. Renewal requires 20 hours of continuing education every two years. **Examination:** Written or oral examination. **Reciprocity:** Yes, with approval. **Fees:** $100 resident license fee (no exam). $40 resident exam fee. $100 state-to-state reciprocity fee. $140 non-resident license (no exam). $50

Professional Forester, continued

non-resident exam fee. $40 re-exam fee. $100 biennial renewal fee. $5 replacement certificate fee.

New Jersey

2891

Tree Expert
New Jersey Dept. of Environmental Protection
Board of Tree Experts
CN404
Trenton, NJ 08625-0404
Phone: (609)292-2520

Credential Type: Certified Tree Inspector. **Duration of License:** One year. **Requirements:** 21 years of age. Graduation from a four-year college with a degree in forestry, arborculture, ornamental horticulture, landscape architecture, or the equivalent; or five years of continuous experience as a tree expert. **Examination:** Written. **Reciprocity:** Yes. **Fees:** $10 exam fee. $5 renewal fee. **Governing Statute:** NJSA 45:15.

Rhode Island

2892

Arborist
Div. of Forest Environment
Rhode Island Dept. of Environmental Management
1037 Hartford Pike
North Scituate, RI 02857
Phone: (401)647-3367

Credential Type: Arborist License. **Duration of License:** One year. **Authorization:** Authorizes tree surgery and the pruning, planting, and spraying of trees. Use of pesticides requires a Pesticide Applicator license. **Requirements:** Knowledge of planting and pruning trees and shrubs. Submit application. Pass examination. **Examination:** Written and practical for pruning, planting, and tree surgery. Written for spraying. **Reciprocity:** Yes, for spraying only. **Fees:** $25 application fee. $25 renewal fee.

South Carolina

2893

Forester
South Carolina State Board of Registration
PO Box 21707
Columbia, SC 29221
Phone: (803)734-8800

Credential Type: License. **Requirements:** Six years of experience under a registered forester or a degree from a four-year school of forestry plus two years of experience under a registered forester. **Examination:** Yes. **Fees:** $50 registration fee. $30 renewal fee.

West Virginia

2894

Forester
State Board of Registration for Foresters
8 Kepner St.
Buckhannon, WV 26201
Phone: (304)924-6266

Credential Type: Registration. **Requirements:** Contact licensing body for application information.

Funeral Directors and Morticians

The following states grant licenses in this occupational category as of the date of publication:

Alabama	District of	Iowa	Minnesota	New Mexico	Rhode Island	Washington
Alaska	Columbia	Kansas	Mississippi	New York	South Carolina	West Virginia
Arizona	Florida	Kentucky	Missouri	North Carolina	South Dakota	Wisconsin
Arkansas	Georgia	Louisiana	Montana	North Dakota	Tennessee	Wyoming
California	Hawaii	Maine	Nebraska	Ohio	Texas	
Connecticut	Idaho	Maryland	Nevada	Oklahoma	Utah	
Delaware	Illinois	Massachusetts	New Hampshire	Oregon	Vermont	
	Indiana	Michigan	New Jersey	Pennsylvania	Virginia	

Alabama

2895

Embalmer
Alabama Board of Funeral Services
Montgomery, AL 36130
Phone: (205)242-4049

Credential Type: License. **Duration of License:** One year. **Requirements:** 18 years of age. U.S. citizenship. High school diploma or equivalent. Must complete a degree or certificate program at a school of college of mortuary science. Must have served two years as an apprentice. **Examination:** Written examination. **Fees:** $15 apprentice fee. $50 application/examination fee. $25 renewal fee.

2896

Funeral Director
Alabama Board of Funeral Services
Montgomery, AL 36130
Phone: (205)242-4049

Credential Type: License. **Duration of License:** One year. **Requirements:** 18 years of age. U.S. citizenship. Must be a high school graduate or equivalent. Must have served as an apprentice for two years. **Examination:** Written examination. **Fees:** $15 apprentice fee. $50 application/examination fee. $25 renewal fee.

Alaska

2897

Embalmer
Dept. of Commerce and Economic
  Development
Div. of Occupational Licensing
Mortuary Science Section
PO Box 110806
Juneau, AK 99811-0806
Phone: (907)465-2534
Fax: (907)465-2974

Credential Type: License to practice embalming. **Duration of License:** Two years. **Requirements:** At least 18 years of age. Graduated from an accredited school or college of mortuary science. Taken and passed examination for a license to practice embalming conducted by the department. Completed at least one year of apprnticeship as a trainee under a licensed embalmer. **Examination:** Exam conducted by the state department of licensing. **Reciprocity:** Yes. **Fees:** $20 application fee. $50 examination fee. $60 license fee. **Governing Statute:** Alaska Statutes 08.42.

Credential Type: Embalmer trainee permit. **Duration of License:** One year. **Requirements:** At least 18 years of age. Furnish evidence that a licensed embalmer will supervise the training and that training will take place in a funeral establishment that meets state requirements. **Fees:** $20 application fee. $20 permit fee. $20 renewal fee. **Governing Statute:** Alaska Statutes 08.42

2898

Funeral Director
Dept. of Commerce and Economic
  Development
Div. of Occupational Licensing
Mortuary Science Section
PO Box 110806
Juneau, AK 99811-0806
Phone: (907)465-2534
Fax: (907)465-2974

Credential Type: License to practice funeral directing. **Duration of License:** Two years. **Requirements:** At least 18 years of age. Completed at least one year at an accredited college or university. Taken and passed the examination for a license to practice funeral directing conducted by the department. Completed at least one year of apprenticeship as a trainee under a person licensed to practice funeral directing in the state. **Examination:** Exam conducted by the state department of licensing. **Reciprocity:** Yes. **Fees:** $20 application fee. $45 examination fee. $60 license fee. **Governing Statute:** Alaska Statutes 08.42.

Credential Type: Funeral director trainee permit. **Duration of License:** One year. **Requirements:** At least 18 years of age. Furnish evidence that a licensed funeral director will supervise the training and that training will take place in a funeral establishment that meets state requirements. **Fees:** $20 application fee. $20 permit fee. $20 renewal fee. **Governing Statute:** Alaska Statutes 08.42

Arizona

2899

Embalmer
Board of Funeral Directors and Embalmers
1645 W. Jefferson, Rm. 410
Phoenix, AZ 85007
Phone: (602)542-3095

Credential Type: License. **Requirements:** Contact licensing body for application information.

2900

Funeral Director
Board of Funeral Directors and Embalmers
1645 W. Jefferson, Rm. 410
Phoenix, AZ 85007
Phone: (602)542-3095

Credential Type: License. **Requirements:** Contact licensing body for application information.

Arkansas

2901

Embalmer
Arkansas State Board of Embalmers and Funeral Directors
PO Box 2673
Batesville, AR 72503-2673
Phone: (501)698-2072

Credential Type: License. **Duration of License:** One year. **Requirements:** Serve as an apprentice embalmer for one year. Assist in the embalming of at least 50 bodies. Apprenticeship must be completed within five years of date of registration. Graduate of an institution accredited by the American Board of Funeral Service Education (ABFSE) as a school of mortuary science. **Examination:** Yes. **Fees:** $100 Written and oral examinations. $50 Application. $15 License. $15 Renewal.

2902

Embalmer Apprentice
Arkansas State Board of Embalmers and Funeral Directors
PO Box 2673
Batesville, AR 72503-2673
Phone: (501)698-2072

Credential Type: License. **Duration of License:** One year. **Requirements:** 18 years of age. Completed 12th grade or equivalent. Good moral character and reputation. **Examination:** Yes. **Fees:** $100 Written and oral examinations. $50 Application. $15 License. $15 Renewal.

2903

Funeral Director
Arkansas State Board of Embalmers and Funeral Directors
PO Box 2673
Batesville, AR 72503-2673
Phone: (501)698-2072

Credential Type: License. **Duration of License:** One year. **Requirements:** Serve as a student or apprentice funeral director for two years, Provide evidence for at least 50 funerals during apprenticeship; or, graduate of an accredited embalming or funeral directors school, pass a written and oral examination, serve one year as an apprentice. **Examination:** Yes. **Fees:** $100 Written and Oral examinations. $50 Application. $15 License. $15 Renewal.

2904

Funeral Director Apprentice
Arkansas State Board of Embalmers and Funeral Directors
PO Box 2673
Batesville, AR 72503-2673
Phone: (501)698-2072

Credential Type: License. **Requirements:** Completed 12th grade or equivalent. Good moral character. Provide two sworn certificates from responsible persons. 18 years of age. **Examination:** Yes. **Fees:** $50 Application. $15 License. $15 Renewal.

California

2905

Embalmer
Board of Funeral Directors and Embalmers
400 R St., Ste. 2060
Sacramento, CA 95814-6200
Phone: (916)445-2413

Credential Type: Embalmer's License. **Duration of License:** One year. **Requirements:** Be at least 18 years of age. High school graduate or equivalent, or have been licensed and practiced as an embalmer in another state for at least three years within the past seven years. Complete at least a 9-month course in a school of mortuary science. Complete a two-year apprenticeship in California, or have been licensed and practiced as an embalmer in another state for at least three years within the past seven years. **Examination:** California Board Examination for Embalmers. (National Board Exam is not recognized in California.) **Reciprocity:** No. **Fees:** $150 application and exam fee. $100 renewal fee.

Credential Type: Apprentice Registration. **Requirements:** Be at least 18 years of age. High school graduate or equivalent, or have been licensed and practiced as an embalmer in another state for at least three years within the past seven years. Be employed in an approved funeral establishment in California. **Reciprocity:** No. **Fees:** $60 apprentice registration.

Connecticut

2906

Embalmer
Div. of Medical Quality Assurance
Health Systems Regulation Bureau
Health Services Dept.
150 Washington St.
Hartford, CT 06106
Phone: (203)566-3207

Credential Type: License. **Requirements:** Contact licensing body for application information.

2907

Funeral Director
Div. of Medical Quality Assurance
Health Systems Regulation Bureau
Health Services Dept.
150 Washington St.
Hartford, CT 06106
Phone: (203)566-3207

Credential Type: License. **Requirements:** Contact licensing body for application information.

Delaware

2908

Funeral Director
Board of Funeral Services
Dept. of Administrative Services
Div. of Professional Regulation
PO Box 1401
Dover, DE 19903
Phone: (302)739-4522

Credential Type: Funeral Service License. **Duration of License:** Two years. **Requirements:** Must be a high school graduate or equivalent. Complete two years of college and one year of mortuary science school. Complete a one-year apprentice program, submitting at least 25 embalming reports and four quarterly work reports. **Examination:** National Board Examination. State examination covering statutes. **Reciprocity:** Yes. **Fees:** $10 apprentice application fee. $75 application fee.

2909

Funeral Director Apprentice
Board of Funeral Services
Dept. of Administrative Services
Div. of Professional Regulation
PO Box 1401
Dover, DE 19903
Phone: (302)739-4522

Credential Type: Funeral Service Apprentice. **Requirements:** Must be a high school graduate or equivalent. Complete two years of college and one year of mortuary science school. **Examination:** National Board Examination. **Fees:** $10 apprentice application fee.

District of Columbia

2910

Funeral Director
Board of Funeral Directors
Occupational and Professional Licensing Administration
Dept. of Consumer and Regulatory Affairs
PO Box 37200
Washington, DC 20013-7200
Phone: (202)727-7468

Credential Type: Funeral Director License. **Duration of License:** Two years. **Requirements:** Contact licensing body for application information.

Florida

2911

Direct Disposer
Board of Funeral Directors and Embalmers
Dept. of Professional Regulation
1940 N. Monroe St.
Tallahassee, FL 32399-0754
Phone: (904)488-8690

Credential Type: Direct Disposers License. **Duration of License:** Two years. **Requirements:** Be at least 18 years of age. Possess a high school diploma or equivalent. **Examination:** Objective examination. State laws and rules examination. **Reciprocity:** License may be granted by endorsement. **Fees:** $200 objective examination fee. $110 laws and rules examination fee. $200 renewal fee. $160 license by endorsement fee. **Governing Statute:** Florida Statutes, Chapter 470.

2912

Embalmer
Board of Funeral Directors and Embalmers
Dept. of Professional Regulation
1940 N. Monroe St.
Tallahassee, FL 32399-0754
Phone: (904)488-8690

Credential Type: Embalmer License. **Duration of License:** Two years. **Requirements:** Be at least 18 years of age. Possess a high school diploma or equivalent. Complete an approved program in mortuary science. Complete one year of internship under a licensed embalmer. **Examination:** Objective examination. State laws and rules examination. **Exemptions:** Objective examination not required if applicant has passed the examination of the Conference of Funeral Service Examining Boards. **Reciprocity:** License may be granted by endorsement. **Fees:** $200 objective examination fee. $110 laws and rules examination fee. $55 renewal fee. $160 license by endorsement fee. **Governing Statute:** Florida Statutes, Chapter 470.

2913

Funeral Director
Board of Funeral Directors and Embalmers
Dept. of Professional Regulation
1940 N. Monroe St.
Tallahassee, FL 32399-0754
Phone: (904)488-8690

Credential Type: Funeral Director License. **Duration of License:** Two years. **Requirements:** Be at least 18 years of age. Possess a high school diploma or equivalent. Possess an associate of arts degree in mortuary science. Complete one year of internship under a licensed funeral director. **Examination:** Objective examination. State laws and rules examination. **Exemptions:** Objective examination not required if applicant has passed the examination of the Conference of Funeral Service Examining Boards. **Reciprocity:** License may be granted by endorsement. **Fees:** $200 objective examination fee. $110 laws and rules examination fee. $75 renewal fee. $160 license by endorsement fee. **Governing Statute:** Florida Statutes, Chapter 470.

Georgia

2914

Embalmer
State Board of Funeral Service
Health and Consumer Services Section
Professional Examining Boards
166 Pryor St., SW
Atlanta, GA 30303
Phone: (404)656-3933

Credential Type: Embalmer License. **Duration of License:** Two years. **Requirements:** Be at least 18 years of age. Good moral character. High school diploma or GED certificate. Graduate of a college of funeral service accredited by the American Board of Funeral Service Education or specifically approved by the board. Complete 3920 hours of service as an apprentice, which includes assisting in embalming at least 50 bodies. **Examination:** Funeral Service Science Examination of the National Conference of Funeral Service Examination Boards. Applicants for licensure by endorsement must pass Jurisprudence Examination. **Reciprocity:** A license by endorsement may be granted without examination to an applicant holding a valid embalmer's license in a jurisdiction whose requirements for licensure are substantially equal to those of Georgia. Applicant must pass a Jurisprudence Examination on the appropriate laws and rules of Georgia. **Fees:** $50 application fee. $70 renewal fee. $125 license by endorsement fee. $35 Jurisprudence Exam fee. **Governing Statute:** Rules of the Georgia State Board of Funeral Service, Chapter 250-5.

2915

Embalmer Apprentice
State Board of Funeral Service
Health and Consumer Services Section
Professional Examining Boards
166 Pryor St., SW
Atlanta, GA 30303
Phone: (404)656-3933

Credential Type: Apprenticeship Registration. **Duration of License:** Two years. **Requirements:** Be at least 18 years of age. Must serve apprenticeship at a board-approved funeral establishment. **Fees:** $40 application fee. **Governing Statute:** Rules of the Georgia State Board of Funeral Service, Chapter 250-5.

Georgia

2916

Funeral Director
State Board of Funeral Service
Health and Consumer Services Section
Professional Examining Boards
166 Pryor St., SW
Atlanta, GA 30303
Phone: (404)656-3933

Credential Type: Funeral Director License. **Duration of License:** Two years. **Requirements:** Be at least 18 years of age. Good moral character. High school diploma or GED certificate. Be a licensed embalmer in the state of Georgia, or complete an apprenticeship program that includes assisting with at least 50 funerals. **Examination:** Both of the Funeral Service Arts Examinations of the National Conference of Funeral Service Examining Boards. Jurisprudence Examination. **Reciprocity:** A license by endorsement may be granted without examination to an applicant holding a valid funeral director's license in a jurisdiction whose requirements for licensure are substantially equal to those of Georgia. Applicant must pass a Jurisprudence Examination on the appropriate laws and rules of Georgia. **Fees:** $50 application fee. $70 renewal fee. $125 license by endorsement fee. $35 Jurisprudence Exam fee. **Governing Statute:** Rules of the Georgia State Board of Funeral Service, Chapter 250-5.

2917

Funeral Director Apprentice
State Board of Funeral Service
Health and Consumer Services Section
Professional Examining Boards
166 Pryor St., SW
Atlanta, GA 30303
Phone: (404)656-3933

Credential Type: Apprenticeship Registration. **Duration of License:** Two years. **Requirements:** Be at least 18 years of age. Must serve apprenticeship at a board-approved funeral establishment. **Fees:** $40 application fee. **Governing Statute:** Rules of the Georgia State Board of Funeral Service, Chapter 250-5.

Hawaii

2918

Embalmer
Hawaii State Board of Health, Sanitation Branch
591 Ala Moana Blvd.
Honolulu, HI 96813
Phone: (808)548-5397

Credential Type: License. **Duration of License:** One year. **Requirements:** 18 years of age. Affidavits from three residents certifying moral character. Five years of experience under a registered embalmer; or two years of practical experience under a registered embalmer plus a high school diploma; or one year of practical experience plus a degree from an approved embalming school; or a curren embalming license. **Examination:** Written and practical. **Fees:** $25 exam fee. $10 renewal fee.

Idaho

2919

Funeral Director
State Board of Morticians
Bureau of Occupational Licenses
1109 Main St., Ste. 220
Boise, ID 83702-5642
Phone: (208)334-3233

Credential Type: Funeral Director License. **Duration of License:** One year. **Requirements:** No new funeral director's licenses issued after June 30, 1970. Existing licenses may be renewed. For new applicants, a mortician license is issued. **Fees:** $25 renewal fee. **Governing Statute:** Idaho Code, Title 54, Chap. 11. Rules of the Idaho State Board of Morticians.

2920

Mortician
State Board of Morticians
Bureau of Occupational Licenses
1109 Main St., Ste. 220
Boise, ID 83702-5642
Phone: (208)334-3233

Credential Type: Resident Mortician's License. **Duration of License:** One year. **Requirements:** Be at least 21 years of age. Good moral character. Complete at least 60 semester hours or 90 quarter hours of college credit in liberal arts, business, or science. Complete 12 months of accredited embalming school. Complete a training period under a licensed practicing mortician in Idaho of at least one year and not to exceed two years. **Examination:** Mortician Examination. **Reciprocity:** Yes, with states having substantially similar requirements. **Fees:** $25 application and license fee. **Governing Statute:** Idaho Code, Title 54, Chap. 11. Rules of the Idaho State Board of Morticians.

2921

Mortician Resident Trainee
State Board of Morticians
Bureau of Occupational Licenses
1109 Main St., Ste. 220
Boise, ID 83702-5642
Phone: (208)334-3233

Credential Type: Mortician Resident Trainee Registration. **Duration of License:** One year. **Authorization:** A maximum training period of two years is allowed. Training must be served under the direction of a qualified resident mortician licensed in Idaho. **Requirements:** Be at least 18 years of age. Good moral character. Graduate of an accredited high school or equivalent. **Fees:** $15 application and license fee. **Governing Statute:** Idaho Code, Title 54, Chap. 11. Rules of the Idaho State Board of Morticians.

Illinois

2922

Funeral Director and Embalmer
Illinois Dept. of Professional Regulation
320 W. Washington St.
Springfield, IL 62786
Phone: (217)785-0800

Credential Type: Funeral Director and Embalmer License. **Duration of License:** Two years. **Requirements:** At least 18 years of age. U.S. citizen or legal alien. Must be properly immunized against diphtheria, hepatitis B and tetanus. Must complete one year of training under the direct supervision of a licensed funeral director and embalmer and one of the following requirements: (1) Complete 30 semester hours (45 quarter hours) of college level study and graduate from a 12-month approved mortuary science program; (2) Complete an associate's degree, or its equivalent, in mortuary science; (3) Complete a bachelor's degree in mortuary science. Renewal requires 24 hours of continuing education. **Examination:** National Conference Examination. **Reciprocity:** Yes, if a reciprocal agreement exists between applicant's state and Illinois and if requirements for licensure are substantially equivalent to those of Illinois. **Fees:** $160 examination fee. $100 initial license fee. $200 license by endorsement fee. $100 renewal fee. **Governing Statute:** Illinois Revised Statutes 1989, Chapter 111.

Credential Type: Funeral Director and Embalmer Trainee License. **Duration of License:** Two years. **Authorization:** Authorizes work in funeral directing and embalming under the direct supervision of a licensed funeral director and embalmer. **Requirements:** At least 18 years of age. U.S. citizen or legal alien. Must be properly immunized against diphtheria, hepatitis B and tetanus. Must complete one of the following requirements: (1) Complete 30 semester hours (45 quarter hours) of college level study and graduate from a 12-month approved mortuary science program; (2) Complete an associate's degree, or its equivalent, in mortuary science; (3) Complete a bachelor's degree in mortuary science. **Reciprocity:** No. **Fees:** $50 initial license fee. $100 renewal fee. **Governing Statute:** Illinois Revised Statutes 1989, Chapter 111.

Indiana

2923

Funeral Director
Indiana Funeral Services Board
Professional Licensing Agency
1021 State Office Bldg.
100 N. Senate Ave.
Indianapolis, IN 46204
Phone: (317)232-7208

Credential Type: License. **Requirements:** Contact licensing body for application information.

Iowa

2924

Funeral Director
Board of Mortuary Science
 Examiners
Dept. of Public Health
Lucas State Office Bldg.
Des Moines, IA 50319
Phone: (515)281-6762

Credential Type: License. **Requirements:** An applicant must complete two academic years in a regionally accredited college or university and meet specific college credit requirements. An applicant receiving a bachelor's degree with a major in mortuary science from an accredited university is deemed to have completed the education requirements. An applicant must serve a one-year internship with an Iowa licensed funeral director. **Examination:** National Board examination, plus a written and practical exam. **Fees:** $50 exam fee.

Kansas

2925

Assistant Funeral Director
State Board of Mortuary Arts
700 SW Jackson St., Ste. 904
Topeka, KS 66603-3758
Phone: (913)296-3980

Credential Type: Assistant Funeral Director License and Registration. **Duration of License:** Two years. **Requirements:** Be a full-time employee with funeral director under which apprenticeship is to be served. Be at least 17 years of age. **Fees:** $75 application fee. $120 license fee. $120 renewal fee.

2926

Embalmer
State Board of Mortuary Arts
700 SW Jackson St., Ste. 904
Topeka, KS 66603-3758
Phone: (913)296-3980

Credential Type: Embalmer License and Registration. **Duration of License:** Two years. **Requirements:** Pre-register with the board prior to serving practicum in mortuary school. Earn an Associate Arts degree in mortuary science with at least 30 semester hours in mortuary science. Serve one-year apprenticeship under the supervision of a licensed embalmer. **Examination:** National Board examination and/or state board comprehensive examination. **Reciprocity:** Yes. **Fees:** $96 license fee. $150 exam fee. $96 renewal fee. $50 apprentice registration fee. $250 reciprocity application fee.

2927

Funeral Director
State Board of Mortuary Arts
700 SW Jackson St., Ste. 904
Topeka, KS 66603-3758
Phone: (913)296-3980

Credential Type: Funeral Director License and Registration. **Duration of License:** Two years. **Requirements:** Complete at least two years of general college education. Serve one-year apprenticeship on a full-time basis as an assistant funeral director under the supervision of a licensed funeral director. Must work with at least 25 families during apprenticeship. **Examination:** National Board examination and/or state board comprehensive examination. **Reciprocity:** Yes. **Fees:** $168 license fee. $150 exam fee. $168 renewal fee. $250 reciprocity application fee.

Kentucky

2928

Funeral Director/Embalmer
State Board of Embalmers
PO Box 335
Beaver Dam, KY 42320
Phone: (502)274-4515

Credential Type: License. **Duration of License:** One year. **Requirements:** High school diploma or equivalent. Graduation from an accredited school of mortuary science. 18 years of age. Must complete a three year apprenticeship for funeral directors, two years for embalmers. A minimum of four hours of continuing education is required for renewal. **Examination:** Yes. **Fees:** $50 exam fee. $30 renewal fee.

Louisiana

2929

Embalmer
Louisiana State Board of Embalmers
 and Funeral Directors
3500 N. Causeway Blvd., No. 1232
Metairie, LA 70002
Phone: (504)838-5019

Credential Type: License. **Duration of License:** One year. **Requirements:** 18 years of age. High school graduation. 12 months in a Mortuary Science program. One year internship. **Examination:** Written. **Fees:** $80 exam fee. $150 license fee.

2930

Funeral Director
Louisiana State Board of Embalmers
 and Funeral Directors
3500 N. Causeway Blvd., No. 1232
Metairie, LA 70002
Phone: (504)838-5109

Credential Type: License. **Duration of License:** One year. **Requirements:** 18 years of age. High school diploma plus 30 semester college credit hours. One year internship. **Examination:** Written. **Fees:** $80 exam fee. $150 license fee.

Maine

2931

Embalmer
Board of Funeral Service
Dept. of Professional and Financial Regulation
State House Station 35
Augusta, ME 04333
Phone: (207)582-8723

Credential Type: Embalmer License. **Duration of License:** One year. **Requirements:** Must be at least 18 years of age. Have 1,000 hours experience practicing embalming, including embalming of at least 25 bodies, under the direction and supervision of a licensed funeral practitioner. Graduation from a board-approved course of study in embalming.

Renewal requires 12 hours of continuing education. **Examination:** National Conference or State Conference Examination. State Law and Rule Examination. Practical examination. **Reciprocity:** Licensee from another state with similar requirements and with three years of active practice may sit for the State Law Examination. **Fees:** $40 license fee. $40 renewal fee. $60 state law and rule exam and practical exam fee (combined). $40 state law and rule exam fee only. $175 state conference exam fee. **Governing Statute:** 32 M.S.R.A., Chap. 21.

2932

Funeral Director
Board of Funeral Service
Dept. of Professional and Financial Regulation
State House Station 35
Augusta, ME 04333
Phone: (207)582-8723

Credential Type: Funeral Director License. **Duration of License:** One year. **Requirements:** Must be at least 18 years of age. Have completed two years of college-level courses. Have 2,000 hours experience practicing funeral directing under the direction and supervision of a licensed funeral practitioner. Graduation from a 12-month course of study in a school or college of mortuary science.

Renewal requires 12 hours of continuing education. **Examination:** National Conference or State Conference Examination. State Law and Rule Examination. Practical examination. **Reciprocity:** Licensee from another state with similar requirements and with three years of active practice may sit for the State Law Examination. **Fees:** $40 license fee. $40 renewal fee. $60 state law and rule exam and practical exam fee (combined). $40 state law and rule exam fee only. $175 state conference exam fee. **Governing Statute:** 32 M.S.R.A., Chap. 21.

2933

Funeral Service Practitioner
Board of Funeral Service
Dept. of Professional and Financial Regulation
State House Station 35
Augusta, ME 04333
Phone: (207)582-8723

Credential Type: Practitioner of Funeral Service License. **Duration of License:** One year. **Authorization:** May practice embalming as well as funeral directing. **Requirements:** Complete 50 credit hours of study of at least three semesters duration, at a college of mortuary science approved by the board. Complete one year of college-level courses, which requirement may be waived by the board if applicant has an Associate Degree from a college of mortuary science.

Renewal requires 12 hours of continuing education. **Examination:** National Conference or State Conference Examination. State Law and Rule Examination. Practical examination. **Reciprocity:** Licensee from another state with similar requirements and with three years of active practice may sit for the State Law Examination. **Fees:** $80 license fee. $80 renewal fee. $60 state law and rule exam and practical exam fee (combined). $40 state law and rule exam fee only. $175 state conference exam fee. **Governing Statute:** 32 M.S.R.A., Chap. 21.

2934

Funeral Service Practitioner Trainee
Board of Funeral Service
Dept. of Professional and Financial Regulation
State House Station 35
Augusta, ME 04333
Phone: (207)582-8723

Credential Type: Practitioner of Funeral Service Trainee Registration. **Duration of License:** One year. **Requirements:** Submit application and pay fee. Have interview with the board. To receive credit for time served as a practitioner trainee, applicant must serve 2,000 hours of employment with an approved funeral establishment, under the instruction and supervision of a licensed individual. **Fees:** $20 registration fee. $20 renewal fee. **Governing Statute:** 32 M.S.R.A., Chap. 21.

Maryland

2935

Embalmer
Board of Morticians
Dept. of Health and Mental Hygiene
4201 Patterson Ave.
Baltimore, MD 21215
Phone: (410)764-4792

Credential Type: License. **Requirements:** Contact licensing body for application information.

2936

Funeral Director
Board of Morticians
Dept. of Health and Mental Hygiene
4201 Patterson Ave.
Baltimore, MD 21215
Phone: (410)764-4792

Credential Type: License. **Requirements:** Contact licensing body for application information.

2937

Mortician
Board of Morticians
Dept. of Health and Mental Hygiene
4201 Patterson Ave.
Baltimore, MD 21215
Phone: (410)764-4792

Credential Type: License. **Requirements:** Contact licensing body for application information.

Massachusetts

2938

Embalmer
Board of Registration in Embalming and Funeral Directing
Div. of Registration
100 Cambridge St., 15th fl.
Boston, MA 02202
Phone: (617)727-1718

Credential Type: Registration. **Authorization:** May not arrange or conduct funeral services, but may assist licensed funeral director in the conduct of funerals. **Requirements:** Complete high school and one year of mortuary school. Complete a two-year apprenticeship. **Examination:** National and State Board Examinations. **Fees:** $50 practical exam fee.

2939

Funeral Director
Board of Registration in Embalming and Funeral Directing
Div. of Registration
100 Cambridge St., 15th fl.
Boston, MA 02202
Phone: (617)727-1718

Credential Type: License and Registration. **Authorization:** Includes embalmer and funeral director registrations. Allows registrants to arrange at-need and pre-need funeral services. Also qualified to process pre-need contracts and receive, control, or manage pre-need funds. **Requirements:** Must own at least 10 percent of the issued stock in a funeral service corporation, or an interest in a partnership. If there is only one licensee in a corporation, applicant must own controlling interest. Complete high school and one year of mortuary school. Complete a two-year apprenticeship. Must also qualify as a registered embalmer. **Examination:** National and State Board Examinations. Rules and Regulations Examination. **Fees:** $50 exam fee.

Credential Type: Registration (unlicensed). **Authorization:** May assist licensed funeral directors in funeral service procedures and are qualified to perform embalming procedures. **Requirements:** This initial form of registration indicates applicant has qualified through internship, education, and examination to be registered. Must also qualify as a registered embalmer. **Examination:** National and State Board Examinations. Rules and Regulations Examination.

Credential Type: Certified Funeral Director. **Requirements:** A licensed funeral director may certify a full-time, registered employee to allow the employee to act in the full capacity of a licensed funeral director and in the limited absence of the licensee.

Michigan

2940

Mortician
Board of Examiners in Mortuary Science
Bureau of Occupational & Professional Regulation
Dept. of Commerce
PO Box 30018
Lansing, MI 48909
Phone: (517)373-9153

Credential Type: License. **Duration of License:** Two years. **Requirements:** Be of good moral character. Graduated from a three-year program in mortuary science from an accredited school. Have served one year as a resident trainee under the direction of a licensed mortician. A portion of this requirement may be waived if the applicant has received a bachelor's degree from an accredited school. Abide by the rules and regulations of the Board and Department. **Examination:** Michigan written exam and National written exam. **Reciprocity:** Licensed morticians from other states may be licensed in Michigan if they meet or exceed the required education and training established by the Michigan Board of Examiners, show proof of passing the national examination, and pass the Michigan written exam. **Fees:** $20 application processing fee. $50 initial Michigan exam fee. $150 initial National exam fee. $25 exam review fee. $30 initial license fee, per year. $30 renewal fee, per year. $50 reciprocity fee plus exam fee. **Governing Statute:** The Occupational Code, Act 299 of 1980, as amended.

2941

Mortuary Science Resident Trainee
Board of Examiners in Mortuary Science
Bureau of Occupational & Professional Regulation
Dept. of Commerce
PO Box 30018
Lansing, MI 48909
Phone: (517)373-9153

Credential Type: License. **Duration of License:** One year. **Requirements:** Completed high school or its equivalent. Be sponsored by a Michigan licensed mortician. Abide by the rules and regulations of the Board. **Fees:** $15 application processing fee. $15 initial license fee, per year. $15 renewal fee, per year. **Governing Statute:** The Occupational Code, Act 299 of 1980, as amended.

Minnesota

2942

Mortician
State Dept. of Health
Mortician Licensing
717 Delaware St. SE
PO Box 9441
Minneapolis, MN 55440-9441
Phone: (612)623-5491
Phone: (612)623-5000

Credential Type: Mortuary Science License. **Requirements:** Complete at least two years of general college education. Complete one year of mortuary college, including graduation. Register and serve for one year as a mortuary science trainee under the supervision of a licensed mortician. **Examination:** National Board examination. Examination on Minnesota Laws and Rules. **Reciprocity:** Yes, by endorsement, provided state has comparable licensing requirements. **Fees:** $50 exam fee. $25 trainee registration fee. $50 renewal fee. $200 endorsement exam fee. **Governing Statute:** Minnesota Statutes, Chap. 282149.

Mississippi

2943

Funeral Director
State Board of Funeral Services
802 N. State St., Ste. 401
Jackson, MS 39202
Phone: (601)354-6903

Credential Type: Funeral Director License. **Duration of License:** Two years. **Requirements:** Be at least 18 years of age. High school graduate or equivalent. Serve for two years as a resident trainee under the supervision of a licensed funeral director or person licensed to practice funeral service. **Examination:** National Board examination. **Reciprocity:** Yes, provided state has comparable requirements. **Fees:** $25 application fee. $50 license fee. $10 renewal application fee. $50 renewal fee. $100 reciprocal application fee. **Governing Statute:** Mississippi Code, Section 73-11. Rules and Regulations.

2944

Funeral Service Practitioner
State Board of Funeral Services
802 N. State St., Ste. 401
Jackson, MS 39202
Phone: (601)354-6903

Credential Type: Funeral Service License. **Duration of License:** Two years. **Requirements:** Be at least 18 years of age. High school graduate or equivalent. Complete at least 12 months of academic and professional instruction from an institution accredited by the American Board of Funeral Service Education or successor organization. Serve for one year as a resident trainee under the supervision of a person licensed to practice funeral service. **Examination:** National Board examination. **Reciprocity:** Yes, provided state has comparable requirements. **Fees:** $50 application fee. $60 license fee. $30 renewal application fee. $50 renewal fee. $100 reciprocal application fee. **Governing Statute:** Mississippi Code, Section 73-11. Rules and Regulations.

Missouri

2945

Embalmer
State Board of Embalmers and
 Funeral Directors
PO Box 423
3605 Missouri Blvd.
Jefferson City, MO 65102
Phone: (314)751-0813

Credential Type: Embalmer License. **Duration of License:** One year. **Requirements:** Be at least 18 years of age. High school graduate or equivalent. Graduate from an institute of mortuary science education accredited by the American Board of Funeral Service Education. Complete an internship of at least one year under a licensed embalmer. Internship must include at least 25 supervised embalmings. **Examination:** Board administered examination or National Board Examination. Oral examination. **Reciprocity:** Yes. Must pass written reciprocity exam. **Fees:** $130 exam fee. $125 oral exam fee. $200 reciprocity fee. $40 renewal fee. $25 apprenticeship registration fee. **Governing Statute:** Chap. 333, 436, 193, 194, RSMo. Rules and Regulations.

Credential Type: Student Registration. **Authorization:** Allows student to work under direct supervision during practicum. **Requirements:** Upon entering an accredited institution of mortuary science, must register with the board. **Fees:** $25 student registration fee. **Governing Statute:** Chap. 333, 436, 193, 194, RSMo. Rules and Regulations.

2946

Funeral Director
State Board of Embalmers and
 Funeral Directors
PO Box 423
3605 Missouri Blvd.
Jefferson City, MO 65102
Phone: (314)751-0813

Credential Type: Funeral Director License. **Duration of License:** One year. **Requirements:** Be at least 18 years of age. High school graduate or equivalent. Demonstrate knowledge of state laws and rules through examination. **Examination:** Board administered examination or National Board Examination. State rules and regulations examination. **Reciprocity:** Yes. Must pass written reciprocity exam. **Fees:** $150 exam fee. $200 reciprocity fee. $40 renewal fee. **Governing Statute:** Chap. 333, 436, 193, 194, RSMo. Rules and Regulations.

Montana

2947

Mortician
Montana Board of Morticians
111 N. Jackson
Helena, MT 59620
Phone: (406)444-5433

Credential Type: Intern Mortician. **Duration of License:** One year. **Requirements:** 18 years of age. Graduation from an accredited college or mortuary science. **Examination:** National board and written exam. **Fees:** $75 application and exam fee. $30 license fee. $60 renewal fee. **Governing Statute:** Montana Code Annotated 37-19-301 through 37-19-316.

Credential Type: Mortician. **Duration of License:** One year. **Requirements:** Completion of a one-year internship. **Examination:** Yes. **Fees:** $75 application and exam fee. $60 license fee. $60 renewal fee. **Governing Statute:** Montana Code Annotated 37-19-301 through 37-19-316.

Nebraska

2948

Embalmer
Nebraska Bureau of Examining
 Boards in Embalming and Funeral
 Directing
PO Box 95007
301 Centennial Mall S.
Lincoln, NE 68509
Phone: (402)471-4115

Credential Type: License. **Duration of License:** Two years. **Requirements:** Must prove completion of 60 semester hours of college credit in addition to a full course of instruction in mortuary science college. Applicants must have completed one year of service as a student embalmer. Must have embalmed 25 bodies under the direction of a licensed embalmer. **Examination:** Yes. **Fees:** $50 initial fee. $20 renewal fee.

2949

Funeral Director
Nebraska Board of Examiners in
 Embalming and Funeral Directing
301 Centennial Mall S.
PO Box 95007
Lincoln, NE 68509
Phone: (402)471-2115

Credential Type: License. **Duration of License:** Two years. **Requirements:** Must have completed a two year course at an accredited college. Must also have completed a full course of instruction in an accredited college of mortuary science. Must have conducted no less than 25 funerals under supervision. **Examination:** Yes. **Fees:** $50 initial fee. $30 funeral establishment initial fee. $20 renewal fee. $10 funeral establishment renewal fee.

Nevada

2950

Funeral Director/Embalmer
Nevada State Board of Funeral
 Directors and Embalmers
PO Box 2462
Reno, NV 89503
Phone: (702)323-3312

Credential Type: Funeral Director's License. **Requirements:** Good moral character. Must be a licensed embalmer or employ a licensed embalmer. **Examination:** Yes. **Fees:** $35 application fee. $100 exam fee. $35 renewal fee.

Credential Type: Embalmer's License. **Requirements:** Completion of 60 semester hours or 90 quarter hours at an accredited university, and 12 hours at an embalmer's school. Completion of one year of practical experience under a licensed supervisor. **Fees:** $25 application fee. $100 examination fee. $35 renewal fee.

New Hampshire

2951

Embalmer
Board of Registation of Funeral
 Directors & Embalmers
6 Hazen Drive
Concord, NH 03301
Phone: (603)271-4651
Fax: (603)271-3745

Credential Type: Embalmer License. **Duration of License:** One year. **Requirements:** At least 18 years of age. Good professional character. Must be U.S. citizen and resident of New Hampshire. Must have completed one year (30 credit hours) of postsecondary education at an accredited institution; or be a graduate of a course in embalming prior to 1975, kept a current license since graduation, and have a letter of good standing from licensing state. Must have completed a one year apprenticeship under the supervision of a licensed embalmer within the state of New Hampshire. Successfully complete a course of instruction in an embalming school. **Examination:** Written and practical examinations. **Reciprocity:** No. **Fees:** $25 application fee.

$75 license fee. $50 practical examination fee. $100 written examination fee. $50 annual renewal fee.

2952

Funeral Director
Board of Registration of Funeral Directors & Embalmers
6 Hazen Drive
Concord, NH 03301
Phone: (603)271-4651
Fax: (603)271-3745

Credential Type: Funeral Director License. **Duration of License:** One year. **Requirements:** U.S. citizen. Resident of New Hampshire. Must hold embalmer's license. Pass examination. Renewal requires applicant to attend one educational meeting annually. **Examination:** State examination. **Reciprocity:** No. **Fees:** $100 license fee. $100 examination fee. $75 annual renewal.

New Jersey

2953

Mortician
Board of Mortuary Science
1100 Raymond Blvd., Rm. 513
Newark, NJ 07102
Phone: (201)648-2532

Credential Type: Practitioner of Mortuary Science. **Requirements:** High school diploma or equivalent. Two years of academic study at an approved college or university. One year of instruction in an approved school of mortuary science. One or two years as a registered intern. **Examination:** Written and practical exam. **Fees:** $50 intern registration fee. $150 exam fee. $100 license fee. **Governing Statute:** NJSA 45:7. NJAC 13:36.

New Mexico

2954

Funeral Service Practitioner
Board of Thanatopractice
Dept. of Regulation and Licensing
PO Box 25101
725 St. Michael's Dr.
Santa Fe, NM 87504
Phone: (505)827-7177

Credential Type: License. **Duration of License:** One year. **Requirements:** Hold a mortuary science diploma with 60 semester hours of academic study. Complete one year of resident training. **Examination:** Jurisprudence examination. **Reciprocity:** Yes. **Fees:** $125 license fee. $125 renewal fee.

New York

2955

Funeral Director
New York State Dept. of Health
Bureau of Funeral Directing
Corning Tower
Empire State Plaza
Albany, NY 12237
Phone: (518)453-1989

Credential Type: License. **Duration of License:** Two years. **Requirements:** Completion of 60 semester credits of approved college-level study in Mortuary Arts, Funeral Services and Elective Subjects. One year of training as a registered resident at an approved funeral establishment in New York State. U.S. citizenship or alien lawfully admitted for permanent residency. **Examination:** National Board Examination from the Conference of Funeral Services Examining Boards of the United States. **Fees:** $40 registration fee. **Governing Statute:** Article 34 Public Health Law and Sections 77.1 and 77.2 of the Health Commissioner's rules and regulations.

North Carolina

2956

Embalmer
North Carolina State Board of Mortuary Science
412 N. Wilmington St.
Raleigh, NC 27601
Phone: (919)733-9380

Credential Type: License. **Duration of License:** One year. **Requirements:** 18 years of age. Three references. Graduation from an approved mortuary science college, plus the completion of a 12 month training period. **Examination:** National and state exam. **Fees:** $25 license fee. $100 exam fee. $25 renewal fee.

2957

Funeral Director
North Carolina State Board of Mortuary Science
412 N. Wilmington St.
Raleigh, NC 27601
Phone: (919)733-9380

Credential Type: License. **Duration of License:** One year. **Requirements:** 32 semester hours of special instruction or graduation from a mortuary science school, plus completion of a 12-month residency as a funeral director. Five hours of continuing education are required prior to renewal. **Examination:** Written. **Fees:** $100 exam fee. $25 license fee. $25 renewal fee.

2958

Funeral Service Licensee
North Carolina State Board of Mortuary Science
412 N. Wilmington St.
Raleigh, NC 27601
Phone: (919)733-9380

Credential Type: License. **Duration of License:** One year. **Requirements:** Graduation from an approved mortuary science college and completion of a 12-month, full-time resident traineeship as a funeral service licensee. 18 years of age. Three personal references. Five hours of continuing education prior to renewal. **Examination:** Written. **Fees:** $100 exam fee. $50 license fee. $50 renewal fee.

North Dakota

2959

Embalmer/Funeral Director
State Board of Funeral Service
RR 5, Box 58A
Devils Lake, ND 58072
Phone: (701)662-2511

Credential Type: Embalmer/Funeral Director License. **Duration of License:** One year. **Requirements:** High school graduate or equivalent. Complete 60 semester hours of college, following the established course of study established by the state board. Complete a course of instruction from an accredited school of embalming. Complete a 12-month internship that includes at least 25 embalmings and 10 reports on funeral arrangements. **Examination:** Conference of Funeral Service Examining Boards national examination. North Dakota Laws and Rules Examination. **Reciprocity:** Yes, provided applicant has held a license for at least one year and state has same licensing requirements. **Fees:** $15 intern fee. $50 license fee. $50 renewal fee. $100 reciprocity fee.

Ohio

2960

Embalmer
Board of Embalmers and Funeral Directors of Ohio
77 S. High St., 16th Fl.
Columbus, OH 43266-0313
Phone: (614)466-4252

Credential Type: Embalmer and Funeral Director License and Registration. **Requirements:** Be at least 18 years of age. Be a United States citizen. Complete high school and at least two years of postsecondary general education. Complete 12 months of mortuary science college. Serve one-year embalmer and funeral director apprenticeships concurrently. **Examination:** National Board examination and/or state board comprehensive examination. Embalmer Ohio laws exam. Funeral director Ohio laws exam. **Fees:** $50 application fee. **Governing Statute:** Ohio Revised Code 4717.06(A). Administrative Rule 4717-1-10.

Credential Type: Embalmer License and Registration. **Requirements:** Be at least 18 years of age. Be a United States citizen. Complete high school and at least two years of postsecondary general education. Complete 12 months of mortuary science college. Serve one-year embalmer apprenticeship, assisting in at least 25 embalmings. **Examination:** National Board examination and/or state board comprehensive examination. Embalmer Ohio laws exam. **Fees:** $25 application fee. **Governing Statute:** Ohio Revised Code 4717.06(A). Administrative Rule 4717-1-10.

2961

Funeral Director
Board of Embalmers and Funeral Directors of Ohio
77 S. High St., 16th Fl.
Columbus, OH 43266-0313
Phone: (614)466-4252

Credential Type: Embalmer and Funeral Director License and Registration. **Requirements:** Be at least 18 years of age. Be a United States citizen. Complete high school and at least two years of postsecondary general education. Complete 12 months of mortuary science college. Serve one-year embalmer and funeral director apprenticeships concurrently. **Examination:** National Board examination and/or state board comprehensive examination. Embalmer Ohio laws exam. Funeral director Ohio laws exam. **Fees:** $50 application fee. **Governing Statute:** Ohio Revised Code 4717.06(A). Administrative Rule 4717-1-10.

Credential Type: Funeral Director License and Registration. **Requirements:** Be at least 18 years of age. Be a United States citizen. Complete high school and have a bachelor's degree. After registering with the board, assist in directing at least 25 funerals. In addition, meet one of the following sets of requirements: (1) Complete 12 months of mortuary science college. Serve a one-year apprenticeship under a licensed funeral director. (2) Complete a two-year apprenticeship under a licensed funeral director. **Examination:** National Board examination and/or state board comprehensive examination. Funeral director Ohio laws exam. **Fees:** $25 application fee. **Governing Statute:** Ohio Revised Code 4717.06(B). Administrative Rule 4717-1-12.

Oklahoma

2962

Embalmer
Oklahoma State Board of Embalmers and Funeral Directors
4545 Lincoln Blvd., Ste. 175
Oklahoma City, OK 73105
Phone: (405)525-0158

Credential Type: License. **Duration of License:** One year. **Requirements:** 60 accredited hours of study from a school of mortuary science. A one-year internship under the supervision of a licensed funeral director. Six hours of continuing education each year. 20 years of age. Legal resident of Oklahoma. U.S. citizen. No felony convictions. **Examination:** Embalmers Examination. **Fees:** $40 exam fee. $50 application fee. $50 license fee. $50 renewal fee.

2963

Funeral Director
Oklahoma State Board of Embalmers and Funeral Directors
4545 Lincoln Blvd., Ste. 175
Oklahoma City, OK 73105
Phone: (405)525-0158

Credential Type: License. **Duration of License:** One year. **Requirements:** 60 accredited hours of study from an accredited college, university or equivalent. 12-month apprenticeship under the direction of a licensed funeral director. Six hours of continuing education related to mortuary science each year. 20 years of age. U.S. citizenship. No felony convictions. **Examination:** Funeral Directors Examination. **Fees:** $40 exam fee. $50 application fee. $50 license fee. $50 renewal fee.

Oregon

2964

Embalmer
Oregon State Mortuary and Cemetary Board
800 NE Oregon St., Ste. 430
Portland, OR 97232
Phone: (503)731-4040

Credential Type: License. **Duration of License:** One year. **Requirements:** 18 years of age. High school diploma or GED. Completion of one year apprenticeship. Graduation from a course in mortuary science from an accredited school. **Examination:** Yes. **Fees:** $130 exam fee. $35 license fee. $35 renewal fee. **Governing Statute:** ORS 692.010 to 692.990.

2965

Funeral Service Practitioner
Oregon State Mortuary and Cemetary Board
800 NE Oregon St., Ste. 430
Portland, OR 97232
Phone: (503)731-4040

Credential Type: License. **Duration of License:** One year. **Requirements:** 18 years of age. High school diploma or GED. Completion of a two year apprenticeship program. **Examination:** Yes. **Fees:** $50 exam fee. $35 license fee. $35 renewal fee. **Governing Statute:** ORS 692.010 to 692.990.

Pennsylvania

2966

Funeral Director
State Board of Funeral Directors
Bureau of Professional and Occupational Affairs
Dept. of State
Transportation and Safety Bldg., 6th Fl.
Harrisburg, PA 17120
Phone: (717)787-8503

Credential Type: Funeral Director License. **Duration of License:** Two years. **Requirements:** At least 21 years of age. Good moral character. U.S. citizen. High school graduate or equivalent. Complete two years (60 semester hours) of academic work at a college or university accredited by the Dept. of Education. Complete a one year course at a mortuary college or university accredited by the American Board of Funeral Service Education, Inc. and one year as a student trainee. Complete a course of actual work in didactic and laboratory studies in a school of embalming for a period approved by the board (ranging from 900 to 2400 hours) and two years as a resident intern. **Examination:** State oral, written, and practical examinations. **Reciprocity:** Reciprocity is available to applicants from other states if their state licensure standards and qualifications are equivalent to, or higher than, those of the Commonwealth of Pennsylvania. **Fees:** $40 written examination fee. $60 oral examination fee. $60 practical examination fee. $20 initial license fee. $130 reciprocal license and examination fee. $82 biennial renewal fee. $15 student trainee registration fee.

Rhode Island

2967

Embalmer
Board of Examiners in Embalming
Div. of Professional Regulation
Rhode Island Dept. of Health
3 Capitol Hill
Providence, RI 02908
Phone: (401)277-2827

Credential Type: Embalmer License. **Duration of License:** One year. **Requirements:** At least 18 years of age. Good moral character. Foreign born must show proof of legal entry into the U.S. High school graduate or equivalent. Graduate from an accredited embalming school. Complete a two-year supervised apprenticeship under a Rhode Island licensed embalmer. Must assist in embalming at least 50 bodies before licensing. **Examination:** Written and practical examinations. **Reciprocity:** No. **Fees:** $50 application fee. $20 apprentice application fee. $10 annual renewal fee.

2968

Funeral Director
Board of Funeral Directors
Div. of Professional Regulation
Rhode Island Dept. of Health
3 Capitol Hill
Providence, RI 02908
Phone: (401)277-2827

Credential Type: Funeral Director License. **Duration of License:** One year. **Requirements:** At least 21 years of age. Rhode Island resident. Foreign born must show proof of legal entry into U.S. Must have an embalmer's license and a fixed place of business. **Reciprocity:** No. **Fees:** $50 application fee. $20 annual renewal fee.

South Carolina

2969

Embalmer
South Carolina Board of Funeral Services
PO Box 305
Johnston, SC 29832
Phone: (803)275-2509

Credential Type: Embalmer License. **Requirements:** 18 years of age. Good moral character. High school diploma or equivalent. One year in an accredited embalming college. 24 months as an apprentice under licensed supervision. **Examination:** Yes. **Fees:** $125 license fee. $50 initial license fee for National Board Certificate holders. $40 renewal fee. $50 special permit fee.

Credential Type: Embalmer Apprentice License. **Requirements:** High school education or equivalent. **Fees:** $25 registration fee.

2970

Funeral Director
South Carolina Board of Funeral Services
PO Box 305
Johnston, SC 29832
Phone: (803)275-2509

Credential Type: License. **Requirements:** 18 years of age. Good moral character. High school education or equivalent. Two years at an accredited college or one year at an accredited mortuary college. 24 months as an apprentice funeral director under the supervison of an active licensed funeral director. **Examination:** Yes. **Fees:** $125 license fee. $40 renewal fee.

South Dakota

2971

Funeral Director
Dept. of Commerce and Regulation
Board of Funeral Service
115 E. Sioux
PO Box 1115
Pierre, SD 57501
Phone: (605)224-6281

Credential Type: Funeral Director License. **Duration of License:** One year. **Requirements:** Be at least 18 years of age. High school graduate or equivalent. Complete at least two years of general college education. Complete a prescribed course of study at a mortuary college. Register and serve for one year as a full-time trainee under the supervision of a licensed funeral director. Traineeship must include at least 25 embalming case reports, assistance in at least 25 funerals, and five sets of arrangements. **Examination:** National Board examination. Examination on South Dakota Laws and Rules. **Reciprocity:** Yes. **Fees:** $25 application fee. $25 renewal fee. **Governing Statute:** South Dakota Compiled Laws, CHap. 36-19. Rules and Regulations, Article 20:45.

Credential Type: Funeral Director Trainee Registration. **Requirements:** Be at least 18 years of age. High school graduate or equivalent. Register and serve for one year as a full-time trainee under the supervision of a licensed funeral director to qualify for licensure. **Fees:** $10 trainee registration fee. **Governing Statute:** South Dakota Compiled Laws, CHap. 36-19. Rules and Regulations, Article 20:45.

Credential Type: License by Reciprocity. **Duration of License:** One year. **Requirements:** Must hold a valid license from a state with comparable requirements that has a reciprocity agreement with South Dakota. Must have practiced for at least two consecutive years immediately prior to filing application. Must be licensed as an embalmer. **Examination:** Examination on South Dakota Laws and Rules. **Fees:** $25 application fee. $25 renewal fee. **Governing Statute:** South Dakota Compiled Laws, Chap. 36-19. Rules and Regulations, Article 20:45.

Tennessee

2972

Embalmer
Board of Funeral Directors and Embalmers
500 James Robertson Pky.
Nashville, TN 37243
Phone: (615)741-2378

Credential Type: License. **Duration of License:** Two years. **Requirements:** 18 years old. One year of apprenticeship under licensed supervisor. Completion of 12 months of mortuary science training. Must furnish character references. **Examination:** Yes. **Reciprocity:** Yes, approval by Board **Fees:** $100 Renewal. $200 Late charges.

Tennessee

2973

Funeral Director
Board of Funeral Directors and Embalmers
500 James Robertson Pky.
Nashville, TN 37243
Phone: (615)741-2378

Credential Type: License. **Duration of License:** Two years. **Requirements:** 18 years old. Two years apprenticeship under licensed supervisor. Completion of mortuary school. High school diploma or equivalent. Must furnish character references. **Examination:** Yes. **Reciprocity:** Yes, with approval by Board **Fees:** $100 Renewal. $200 Late charges.

Texas

2974

Embalmer
Texas Funeral Service Commission
8100 Cameron Rd., Bldg. B 550
Austin, TX 78753
Phone: (512)834-9992

Credential Type: License. **Duration of License:** Two years. **Requirements:** Texas resident. 18 years of age. High school diploma or equivalent. Graduation from an accredited school or college of mortuary science. Apprenticeship of 12 consecutive months to a licensed embalmer. **Examination:** Written. **Fees:** $30 apprenticeship registration fee. $60 license fee. $60 renewal fee. **Governing Statute:** VACS 4582b, 22 TAC 203.

2975

Funeral Director
Texas Funeral Service Commission
8100 Cameron Rd., Bldg. B 550
Austin, TX 78753
Phone: (512)834-9992

Credential Type: License. **Duration of License:** Two years. **Requirements:** Texas resident. 18 years of age. High school diploma or equivalent. Graduation from an accredited school or college of mortuary science. Apprenticeship of 12 consecutive months to a licensed funeral director. **Examination:** Written. **Fees:** $30 apprenticeship registration fee. $60 license fee. $60 renewal fee. **Governing Statute:** VACS 4582b, 22 TAC 203.

Utah

2976

Funeral Service Director
Dept. of Commerce
Div. of Occupational and Professional Licensing
160 E. 300 S.
PO Box 45802
Salt Lake City, UT 84145
Phone: (801)530-6628

Credential Type: License. **Duration of License:** Three years. **Requirements:** Must be a high school graduate. Must have attended at least two years of college. Must have completed 12 months of academic instruction in a prescribed course at a school of funeral services. Must have served as a resident trainee for not less than 12 months under the personal supervision of a person licensed in Utah. **Examination:** Yes. **Fees:** $150 license fee. $60 renewal fee.

2977

Pre-Need Contract Agent
Dept. of Commerce
Div. of Occupational and Professional Licensing
160 E. 300 S.
PO Box 45802
Salt Lake City, UT 84145
Phone: (801)530-6628

Credential Type: License. **Duration of License:** One year. **Authorization:** To accept funds for pre-arranged funeral plans. **Requirements:** Submit application and pay fee. **Fees:** $40 license fee. $25 renewal fee.

Vermont

2978

Embalmer
Board of Funeral Service
Pavilion Office Bldg.
Montpelier, VT 05602
Phone: (802)828-2363

Credential Type: License. **Duration of License:** Two years. **Requirements:** Good moral character. Graduate of an accredited school of Funeral Service in a course of either two years, or; 12 months plus an additional 30 hours of study in approved study. A trainee-ship of 12 months full-time employment or equivalent (proof required). **Examination:** Yes. **Reciprocity:** Yes. **Fees:** $40 Application fee. $20 Resident Trainee. $20 Renewal. $90 Embalmer by exam. $55 Embalmer by endorsement. **Governing Statute:** Title 26, VSA Sections 991-996.

2979

Funeral Director
Board of Funeral Services
Pavilion Office Bldg.
Montpelier, VT 05602
Phone: (802)828-2390

Credential Type: License. **Duration of License:** Two years. **Requirements:** 18 years of age. U.S. citizen. Resident of Vermont. Good moral character. **Examination:** Yes. **Reciprocity:** Yes. **Fees:** $130 Exam fee. $5 License fee. $10 Renewal. **Governing Statute:** Title 26, VSA Sections 1251-1257.

Virginia

2980

Embalmer/Funeral Director
Virginia Board of Funeral Directors and Embalmers
1601 Rolling Hills Dr.
Richmond, VA 23229
Phone: (804)662-9920

Credential Type: License. **Duration of License:** One year. **Requirements:** High school diploma. Must have completed two years as a funeral service trainee in a program approved by the Board. **Examination:** Yes. **Fees:** $100 examination fee. $100 licensure fee. $70 renewal fee.

Washington

2981

Embalmer
Dept. of Licensing
Professional Licensing Services
2424 Bristol Court SW
Olympia, WA 98504
Phone: (206)586-4905

Credential Type: Embalmer Certificate. **Duration of License:** One year. **Requirements:** At least 18 years of age. Must have two years of college and complete an approved course at an embalming school. Must carry a 2.0 grade average and complete specified course work. Must complete a two-year (3600 hour) apprenticeship under the supervision of a licensed embalmer. **Examination:** State examination. **Fees:** $150 examination fee. $100 renewal fee. $25 certification fee. $15 duplicate certificate fee.

Credential Type: Embalmer Apprentice Certificate. **Duration of License:** One year. **Requirements:** Must register as an apprentice under the supervision of a licensed embalmer. **Fees:** $75 application fee. $45 renewal fee. $25 certificate fee. $15 duplicate certificate fee.

2982

Funeral Director
Dept. of Licensing
Professional Licensing
2424 Bristol Court SW
Olympia, WA 98504
Phone: (206)583-4905

Credential Type: Funeral Director License. **Duration of License:** One year. **Requirements:** At least 18 years of age. Complete two years of college that includes specified courses. Carry at least a 2.0 grade average. Complete a one year apprenticeship under the supervision of a licensed funeral director. **Examination:** State examination. **Fees:** $200 examination or reexamination fee. $125 license renewal fee. $25 certification fee.

Credential Type: Funeral Director Apprentice License. **Duration of License:** One year. **Requirements:** Must register under the supervision of a licensed funeral director. **Fees:** $75 application fee. $45 renewal fee. $25 certificate fee.

West Virginia

2983

Funeral Director/Mortician/ Embalmer
Board of Embalmers and Funeral Directors
305 Peoples Bldg.
Charleston, WV 26501
Phone: (304)348-0302

Credential Type: License. **Duration of License:** One year. **Requirements:** U.S. citizen. State resident. 18 years old. High school diploma. 60 hours towards Baccalaureate degree. One year apprenticeship. One year mortuary college. **Examination:** Yes. **Fees:** $100 Examination. $15 License. $15 Renewal.

Wisconsin

2984

Funeral Director
Regulations and Licensing Dept.
Funeral Directors Board
PO Box 8935
Madison, WI 53708-8935
Phone: (608)266-8609

Credential Type: License. **Requirements:** Two years of college and one year of mortuary science. 18 years of age. **Examination:** Written. **Reciprocity:** Yes.

Wyoming

2985

Embalmer
State Board of Embalming
PO Box 349
Worland, WY 82401
Phone: (307)347-4028

Credential Type: License. **Duration of License:** One year. **Requirements:** High school diploma. 21 years old. One year (26 hours) of college. One year at an accredited college of mortuary science. One year apprenticeship in Wyoming with an embalmer. Pass the State Board examination. **Examination:** Yes. **Fees:** $50 License. $30 Renewal.

2986

Funeral Director
State Board of Embalming
PO Box 349
Worland, WY 82401
Phone: (307)347-4028

Credential Type: License. **Duration of License:** One year. **Requirements:** Over 21 years of age. Good moral character. Pass the state examination. **Examination:** Yes. **Fees:** $100 License. $50 Renewal.

Gambling Occupations Other Than Racetrack

The following states grant licenses in this occupational category as of the date of publication: Illinois, Iowa, Minnesota, Nevada, New Jersey, Washington.

Illinois

2987

Accounting/Payroll Clerk (Gaming)
Illinois Gaming Board
PO Box 19474
Springfield, IL 62794-9474
Phone: (217)524-0228

Credential Type: Accounting/Payroll Clerk License. **Duration of License:** One year. **Requirements:** At least 18 years of age. U.S. citizen and Illinois resident. No felony convictions. Complete six months of experience in payroll and/or accounting office. Good computer skills. **Reciprocity:** No. **Fees:** $75 application and license fee. $50 renewal fee. **Governing Statute:** Illinois Revised Statutes, Chapter 120.

2988

Associate Director of Sales/Sales Manager (Gaming Industry)
Illinois Gaming Board
PO Box 19474
Springfield, IL 62794-9474
Phone: (217)524-0228

Credential Type: Sales Director/Manager License. **Duration of License:** One year. **Requirements:** At least 18 years of age. U.S. citizen or legal alien. College degree in marketing. Minimum of five years of marketing and/or sales experience with a service industry. **Reciprocity:** No. **Fees:** $75 application fee. $50 annual renewal fee. **Governing Statute:** Illinois Revised Statutes, Chapter 120.

2989

Bartender (Gaming Industry)
Illinois Gaming Board
PO Box 19747
Springfield, IL 62794-9474
Phone: (217)524-0228

Credential Type: Bartender License. **Duration of License:** One year. **Requirements:** At least 18 years of age. Complete a bartender training program. Must have knowledge of state liquor laws. **Reciprocity:** No. **Fees:** $75 application and license fee. $50 annual renewal fee. **Governing Statute:** Illinois Revised Statutes, Chapter 120.

2990

Boxperson (Gaming)
Illinois Gaming Board
PO Box 19474
Springfield, IL 62794-9474
Phone: (217)524-0228

Credential Type: Boxperson License. **Duration of License:** One year. **Requirements:** At least 21 years of age. High school graduate or equivalent. No felony convictions. Minimum six months experience as a casino boxperson. Knowledge of game protection. Extensive knowledge of the dice game. Excellent customer and employee relations. **Reciprocity:** No. **Fees:** $200 application fee. $50 renewal fee. **Governing Statute:** Illinois Revised Statutes, Chapter 120.

2991

Cage Credit Manager (Gaming)
Illinois Gaming Board
PO Box 19474
Springfield, IL 62794-9474
Phone: (217)524-0228

Credential Type: Cage Credit Manager License. **Duration of License:** One year. **Requirements:** At least 21 years old. No felony convictions. High school graduate or equivalent. Minimum of six months as a casino cage manager. Must have knowledge of computers and 10 key calculators. Able to handle large amounts of currency. **Reciprocity:** No. **Fees:** $200 application and initial license fee. $50 renewal fee. **Governing Statute:** Illinois Revised Statutes, Chapter 120.

2992

Casino Cage Cashier (Gaming)
Illinois Gaming Board
PO Box 19474
Springfield, IL 62794-9474
Phone: (217)524-0228

Credential Type: Casino Cage Cashier License. **Duration of License:** One year. **Requirements:** At least 21 years of age. No felony convictions. U.S. citizen and resident of Illinois. High school graduate or equivalent. Previous experience in cashier transactions. Have knowledge of computers and 10 key calculators. **Reciprocity:** No. **Fees:** $75 application and initial license fee. $50 renewal fee. **Governing Statute:** Illinois Revised Statutes, Chapter 120.

2993

Casino Floor Game Supervisor (Gaming)
Illinois Gaming Board
PO Box 19474
Springfield, IL 62794-9474
Phone: (217)524-0228

Credential Type: Casino Floor Game Supervisor License. **Duration of License:** One year. **Requirements:** At least 21 years of age. U.S. citizen and Illinois resident. No felony convictions. High school graduate or equivalent. Minimum of one year experience in all table games. Knowledge of game protection and employee relations. Physically able to stand for course of working shift. **Reciprocity:** No. **Fees:** $200 application and license fee. $50 renewal fee. **Governing Statute:** Illinois Revised Statutes, Chapter 120.

2994

Casino Manager (Gaming)
Illinois Gaming Board
PO Box 19474
Springfield, IL 62794-9474
Phone: (217)524-0228

Credential Type: Casino Manager License. **Duration of License:** One year. **Requirements:** At least 21 years of age. U.S. citizen and Illinois resident. No felony convictions. High school graduate or equivalent. Must have a minimum of 10 years experience in all facets of casino management. Knowledge of game protection and employee relations. **Reciprocity:** No. **Fees:** $1,000 application and license fee. $50 renewal fee. **Governing Statute:** Illinois Revised Statutes, Chapter 120.

2995

Casino Reservations and Ticketing Manager (Gaming)
Illinois Gaming Board
PO Box 19474
Springfield, IL 62794-9474
Phone: (217)524-0228

Credential Type: Casino Reservations and Ticketing Manager License. **Duration of License:** One year. **Requirements:** At least 18 years of age. U.S. citizen and Illinois resident. No felony convictions. On-the-job training in reservations, sales, ticketing, and/or greeter positions. **Reciprocity:** No. **Fees:** $75 application and license fee. $50 renewal fee. **Governing Statute:** Illinois Revised Statutes, Chapter 120.

2996

Casino Shift Manager (Gaming)
Illinois Gaming Board
PO Box 19474
Springfield, IL 62794-9474
Phone: (217)524-0228

Credential Type: Casino Shift Manager License. **Duration of License:** One year. **Requirements:** At least 21 years of age. High school graduate or equivalent. U.S. citizen and Illinois resident. No felony convictions. Five years experience in Casino management. Knowledge of all Casino transactions. Strong managerial skills. Knowledge of State Gaming Regulations. Knowledge of game protection and employee relations. **Reciprocity:** No. **Fees:** $200 application and license fee. $50 renewal fee. **Governing Statute:** Illinois Revised Statutes, Chapter 120.

2997

Change Attendant (Gaming)
Illinois Gaming Board
PO Box 19474
Springfield, IL 62794-9474
Phone: (217)524-0228

Credential Type: Change Attendant License. **Duration of License:** One year. **Requirements:** At least 21 years of age. High school graduate or equivalent. U.S. citizen and Illinois resident. No felony convictions. Excellent customer service skills. Physically capable of performing required duties. **Reciprocity:** No. **Fees:** $75 application and license fee. $50 renewal fee. **Governing Statute:** Illinois Revised Statutes, Chapter 120.

2998

Chef/Executive Kitchen Manager (Gaming)
Illinois Gaming Board
PO Box 19474
Springfield, IL 62794-9474
Phone: (217)524-0228

Credential Type: Chef/Executive Kitchen Manager License. **Duration of License:** One year. **Requirements:** At least 18 years of age. U.S. citizen and Illinois resident. No felony convictions. Four to five years experience as a Sous Chef. **Reciprocity:** No. **Fees:** $75 application and license fee. $50 renewal fee. **Governing Statute:** Illinois Revised Statutes, Chapter 120.

2999

Chief Financial Officer/Controller (Gaming)
Illinois Gaming Board
PO Box 19474
Springfield, IL 62794-9474
Phone: (217)524-0228

Credential Type: Chief Financial Officer/Controller License. **Duration of License:** One year. **Requirements:** At least 18 years of age. U.S. citizen and resident of Illinois. No felony convictions. High school graduate or equivalent. Bachelor's degree in Major Accounting. Certified Public Accountant (CPA) preferred. Must have two years experience in related field. **Reciprocity:** No. **Fees:** $1,000 application and license fee. $50 renewal fee. **Governing Statute:** Illinois Revised Statutes, Chapter 120.

3000

Chief Operating Officer/General Manager (Gaming)
Illinois Gaming Board
PO Box 19474
Springfield, IL 62794-9474
Phone: (217)524-0228

Credential Type: Chief Operating Officer/General Manager License. **Duration of License:** One year. **Requirements:** At least 18 years of age. U.S. citizen or legal alien as specified by the Federal employment eligibility requirement. High school graduate or equivalent. Must have extensive experience in the Gaming industry and a record of successful growth through added responsibilities. **Reciprocity:** No. **Fees:** $1,000 application fee. $50 initial license fee. $50 renewal fee. **Governing Statute:** Illinois Revised Statutes, Chapter 120.

3001

Cocktail Waitress (Gaming)
Illinois Gaming Board
PO Box 19474
Springfield, IL 62794-9474
Phone: (217)524-0228

Credential Type: Cocktail Waitress License. **Duration of License:** One year. **Requirements:** At least 18 years of age. U.S. citizen or legal alien as specified by the Federal employment eligibility requirement. Submit application and pay fee. **Reciprocity:** No. **Fees:** $75 initial license and application fee. $50 renewal fee. **Governing Statute:** Illinois Revised Statutes, Chapter 120.

3002

Computer Programmer (Gaming)
Illinois Gaming Board
PO Box 19474
Springfield, IL 62794-9474
Phone: (217)524-0228

Credential Type: Computer Programmer License. **Duration of License:** One year. **Requirements:** At least 18 years of age. U.S. citizen and resident of Illinois. No felony convictions. High school graduate or equivalent. Good computer skills. **Reciprocity:** No. **Fees:** $75 application and initial license fee. $50 renewal fee.

3003

Cook (Gaming)
Illinois Gaming Board
PO Box 19474
Springfield, IL 62749-9474
Phone: (217)524-0228

Credential Type: Cook License. **Duration of License:** One year. **Requirements:** At least 18 years of age. U.S. citizen or legal alien as specified by the federal employment eligibility requirement. One to two years of general restaurant experience. Submit application and pay fee. **Reciprocity:** No. **Fees:** $75 application and initial license fee. $50 renewal fee. **Governing Statute:** Illinois Revised Statutes, Chapter 120.

3004

Dealer (Gaming)
Illinois Gaming Board
PO Box 19474
Springfield, IL 62794-9474
Phone: (217)524-0228

Credential Type: Dealer License. **Duration of License:** One year. **Requirements:** At least 18 years of age. U.S. citizen or legal alien as specified by the federal employment eligibility requirement. Submit application and pay fee. **Reciprocity:** No. **Fees:** $75 application fee. $50 initial license fee. $50 renewal fee. **Governing Statute:** Illinois Revised Statutes, Chapter 120.

3005

Deckhand (Gaming)
Illinois Gaming Board
PO Box 19474
Springfield, IL 62794-9474
Phone: (217)524-0228

Credential Type: Deckhand License. **Duration of License:** One year. **Requirements:** At least 18 years of age. U.S. citizen or legal alien as specified by the federal employment eligibility requirement. Submit application and pay fee. **Reciprocity:** No. **Fees:** $75 application fee. $50 initial license fee. $50 renewal fee. **Governing Statute:** Illinois Revised Statutes, Chapter 120.

3006

Director of Marketing and Public Relations (Gaming)
Illinois Gaming Board
PO Box 19474
Springfield, IL 62794-9474
Phone: (217)524-0228

Credential Type: Director of Marketing License. **Duration of License:** One year. **Requirements:** At least 18 years of age. College degree in marketing. Must have five or more years experience in a service related business as a marketing manager. U.S. citizen or legal alien as specified by the federal employment eligibility requirement. **Reciprocity:** No. **Fees:** $75 application/initial license fee. $50 renewal fee. **Governing Statute:** Illinois Revised Statutes, Chapter 120.

3007

Director of Security (Gaming)
Illinois Gaming Board
PO Box 19474
Springfield, IL 62794-9474
Phone: (217)524-0228

Credential Type: Director of Security License. **Duration of License:** One year. **Requirements:** At least 21 years of age. High school graduate. College degree preferred. Must have training and experience in law enforcement. U.S. citizen or legal alien as specified by the federal employment eligibility requirement. **Reciprocity:** No. **Fees:** $1,000 application fee. $50 initial license fee. $50 renewal fee. **Governing Statute:** Illinois Revised Statutes, Chapter 120.

3008

Dishwasher/Kitchen Utility Helper (Gaming)
Illinois Gaming Board
PO Box 19474
Springfield, IL 62794-9474
Phone: (217)524-0228

Credential Type: Dishwasher/Utility License. **Duration of License:** One year. **Requirements:** At least 18 years of age. U.S. citizen or legal alien as specified by Federal employability requirement. Submit application and pay fee. **Reciprocity:** No. **Fees:** $75 application/initial license fee. $50 renewal fee. **Governing Statute:** Illinois Revised Statutes, Chapter 120.

3009

First Mate (Gaming)
Illinois Gaming Board
PO Box 19474
Springfield, IL 62794-9474
Phone: (217)534-0228

Credential Type: First Mate License. **Duration of License:** One year. **Requirements:** At least 18 years of age. Knowledge and experience in Maritime field. Must have U.S. Coast Guard license. Renewal requires reexamination every five years. **Examination:** Mate (tonnage rating) examination. **Reciprocity:** No. **Fees:** $385 examination fee. $75 application fee. $50 initial license fee. $50 renewal fee. **Governing Statute:** Illinois Revised Statutes, Chapter 120.

3010

Food and Beverage Manager (Gaming)
Illinois Gaming Board
PO Box 19474
Springfield, IL 62794-9474
Phone: (217)524-0228

Credential Type: Food and Beverage Manager License. **Duration of License:** One year. **Requirements:** At least 18 years of age. U.S. citizen or legal alien as specified by the federal employment eligibility requirement. Must have at least five years experience as a Food and Beverage Manager in a full service restaurant. **Reciprocity:** No. **Fees:** $75 application/initial license fee. $50 renewal fee. **Governing Statute:** Illinois Revised Statutes, Chapter 120.

Gambling Occupations Other Than Racetrack

3011

General Accountant (Gaming)
Illinois Gaming Board
PO Box 19474
Springfield, IL 62794-9474
Phone: (217)524-0228

Credential Type: General Accountant License. **Duration of License:** One year. **Requirements:** At least 18 years of age. U.S. citizen. No felony convictions. High school graduate or equivalent. Six months experience in an accounting office. Good computer skills. **Reciprocity:** No. **Fees:** $75 application/initial license fee. $50 renewal fee. **Governing Statute:** Illinois Revised Statutes, Chapter 120.

3012

Gift Shop Manager (Gaming)
Illinois Gaming Board
PO Box 19474
Springfield, IL 62794-9474
Phone: (217)524-0228

Credential Type: Gift Shop Manager License. **Duration of License:** One year. **Requirements:** At least 18 years of age. U.S. citizen. No felony convictions. High school graduate or equivalent. **Reciprocity:** No. **Fees:** $75 application/initial license fee. $50 renewal fee. **Governing Statute:** Illinois Revised Statutes, Chapter 120.

3013

Gift Shop Salesperson (Gaming)
Illinois Gaming Board
PO Box 19474
Springfield, IL 62794-9474
Phone: (217)524-0228

Credential Type: Gift Shop Salesperson License. **Duration of License:** One year. **Requirements:** At least 18 years of age. U.S. citizen. No felony convictions. High school graduate or equivalent. Retail experience preferred. **Reciprocity:** No. **Fees:** $75 application/initial license fee. $50 renewal fee. **Governing Statute:** Illinois Revised Statutes, Chapter 120.

3014

Hard Count Clerk (Gaming)
Illinois Gaming Board
PO Box 19474
Springfield, IL 62794-9474
Phone: (217)524-0228

Credential Type: Hard Count Clerk License. **Duration of License:** One year. **Authorization:** Authorizes applicant to remove, count, and restock tokens from electronic gaming devices. **Requirements:** At least 21 years of age. No felony convictions. High school graduate or equivalent. Physically able to perform required duties. **Reciprocity:** No. **Fees:** $75 application/initial license fee. $50 renewal fee. **Governing Statute:** Illinois Revised Statutes, Chapter 120.

3015

Hard Count/Soft Count Supervisor (Gaming)
Illinois Gaming Board
PO Box 19474
Springfield, IL 62794-9474
Phone: (217)524-0228

Credential Type: Hard Count/Soft Count Supervisor License. **Duration of License:** One year. **Requirements:** At least 21 years of age. No felony convictions. High school graduate or equivalent. Experience in handling and counting large amounts of currency. Good computer skills. Physically able to perform required duties. **Reciprocity:** No. **Fees:** $75 application/initial license fee. $50 renewal fee. **Governing Statute:** Illinois Revised Statutes, Chapter 120.

3016

Housekeeper (Gaming)
Illinois Gaming Board
PO Box 19474
Springfield, IL 62794-9474
Phone: (217)524-0228

Credential Type: Housekeeper License. **Duration of License:** One year. **Requirements:** At least 18 years of age. U.S. citizen or legal alien as specified by the federal employment eligibility requirement. Submit application and pay fee. **Reciprocity:** No. **Fees:** $75 application fee. $50 initial license fee. $50 renewal fee. **Governing Statute:** Illinois Revised Statutes, Chapter 120.

3017

Housekeeping Supervisor (Gaming)
Illinois Gaming Board
PO Box 19474
Springfield, IL 62794-9474
Phone: (217)524-0228

Credential Type: Housekeeping Supervisor License. **Duration of License:** One year. **Requirements:** At least 18 years of age. U.S. citizen or legal alien as specified by the federal employment eligibility requirement. Housekeeping experience in the position of manager or supervisor. Submit application and pay fee. **Reciprocity:** No. **Fees:** $75 application fee. $50 initial license fee. $50 renewal fee. **Governing Statute:** Illinois Revised Statutes, Chapter 120.

3018

Human Resource Manager (Gaming)
Illinois Gaming Board
PO Box 19474
Springfield, IL 62794-9474
Phone: (217)524-0228

Credential Type: Human Resource Manager License. **Duration of License:** One year. **Requirements:** At least 18 years of age. U.S. citizen or legal alien as specified by the federal employment eligibility requirement. Four-year college degree in Human Resources. Between five and seven years experience as a generalist in a medium-size company. **Reciprocity:** No. **Fees:** $75 application/initial license fee. $50 renewal fee. **Governing Statute:** Illinois Revised Statutes, Chapter 120.

3019

Internal Audit Manager (Gaming)
Illinois Gaming Board
PO Box 19474
Springfield, IL 62794-9474
Phone: (217)524-0228

Credential Type: Internal Audit Manager License. **Duration of License:** One year. **Requirements:** At least 18 years of age. U.S. citizen or legal alien as specified by the federal employment eligibility requirement. College graduate of an accounting program or equivalent training. Auditing experience. Gaming auditing experience preferred. **Reciprocity:** No. **Fees:** $1,000 application fee. $50 initial license fee. $50 renewal fee. **Governing Statute:** Illinois Revised Statutes, Chapter 120.

3020

Maintenance Manager (Gaming)
Illinois Gaming Board
PO Box 19474
Springfield, IL 62794-9474
Phone: (217)524-0228

Credential Type: Maintenance Manager License. **Authorization:** Authorizes applicant to oversee the maintenance and housekeeping departments in a gaming establishment. **Requirements:** At least 18 years of age. Supervisory experience. Previous experience in maintenance preferred. U.S. cit-

Maintenance Manager (Gaming), continued

izen or legal alien as specified by the federal employment eligibility requirement. **Reciprocity:** No. **Fees:** $75 application fee. $50 initial license fee. $50 renewal fee. **Governing Statute:** Illinois Revised Statutes, Chapter 120.

3021

Maintenance Supervisor (Gaming)
Illinois Gaming Board
PO Box 19474
Springfield, IL 62794-9474
Phone: (217)524-0228

Credential Type: Maintenance Supervisor License. **Authorization:** Authorizes applicant to oversee the maintenance and cleaning of a gaming facility and its grounds. **Requirements:** At least 18 years of age. Supervisory experience. Previous experience in maintenance preferred. U.S. citizen or legal alien as specified by the federal employment eligibility requirement. **Reciprocity:** No. **Fees:** $75 application fee. $50 initial license fee. $50 renewal fee. **Governing Statute:** Illinois Revised Statutes, Chapter 120.

3022

Maintenance Worker (Gaming)
Illinois Gaming Board
PO Box 19474
Springfield, IL 62794-9474
Phone: (217)524-0228

Credential Type: Maintenance Worker License. **Authorization:** Authorizes applicant to oversee operation of the maintenance and housekeeping departments in a gaming establishment. **Requirements:** At least 18 years of age. U.S. citizen or legal alien as specified by the federal employment eligibility requirement. Strong mechanical aptitude. Previous experience preferred. **Reciprocity:** No. **Fees:** $75 application fee. $50 initial license fee. $50 renewal fee. **Governing Statute:** Illinois Revised Statutes, Chapter 120.

3023

Marketing Assistant/Secretary (Gaming)
Illinois Gaming Board
PO Box 19474
Springfield, IL 62794-9474
Phone: (217)524-0228

Credential Type: Marketing Assistant License. **Requirements:** At least 18 years of age. No felony convictions. U.S. citizen or legal alien as specified by the federal employment eligibility requirement. High school graduate or equivalent. Good moral character. Good typing skills and computer experience. **Reciprocity:** No. **Fees:** $75 application/initial license fee. $50 renewal fee. **Governing Statute:** Illinois Revised Statutes, Chapter 120.

3024

M.I.S. Manager/Technical Supports Systems Operator (Gaming)
Illinois Gaming Board
PO Box 19474
Springfield, IL 62794-9474
Phone: (217)524-0228

Credential Type: M.I.S. Manager License. **Duration of License:** One year. **Requirements:** At least 18 years of age. No felony convictions. High school graduate or equivalent. Computer experience. **Reciprocity:** No. **Fees:** $75 application/initial license fee. $50 renewal fee. **Governing Statute:** Illinois Revised Statutes, Chapter 120.

3025

Oiler (Gaming)
Illinois Gaming Board
PO Box 19474
Springfield, IL 62794-9474
Phone: (217)524-0228

Credential Type: Oiler License. **Duration of License:** One year. **Authorization:** Authorizes applicant to maintain engines and other equipment on a casino boat. **Requirements:** At least 18 years of age. Mechanical background. Technical training. Naval experience preferred. U.S. citizen or legal alien as specified by the federal employment eligibility requirement. **Reciprocity:** No. **Fees:** $75 application fee. $50 initial license fee. $50 renewal fee. **Governing Statute:** Illinois Revised Statutes, Chapter 120.

3026

Pit Boss (Gaming)
Illinois Gaming Board
PO Box 19474
Springfield, IL 62794-9474
Phone: (217)524-0228

Credential Type: Pit Boss License. **Duration of License:** One year. **Requirements:** At least 21 years of age. U.S. citizen. Resident of Illinois. No felony convictions. High school graduate or its equivalent. Knowledge of game protection. Must have a minimum of six months experience as a Casino Floorperson. Must exhibit excellent customer/employee relations. **Reciprocity:** No. **Fees:** $200 application/initial license fee. $50 renewal fee. **Governing Statute:** Illinois Revised Statutes, Chapter 120.

3027

Purchasing Manager/Agent (Gaming)
Illinois Gaming Board
PO Box 19474
Springfield, IL 62794-9474
Phone: (217)524-0228

Credential Type: Purchasing Manager/Agent License. **Duration of License:** One year. **Requirements:** At least 21 years of age. High school graduate or equivalent. No felony convictions. One year experience in purchasing. **Reciprocity:** No. **Fees:** $75 application/initial license fee. $50 renewal fee. **Governing Statute:** Illinois Revised Statutes, Chapter 120.

3028

Regional Sales Manager (Gaming)
Illinois Gaming Board
PO Box 19474
Springfield, IL 62794-9474
Phone: (217)524-0228

Credential Type: Regional Sales Manager License. **Duration of License:** One year. **Requirements:** At least 18 years of age. U.S. citizen or legal alien as specified by Federal employability requirement. No felony convictions. Marketing degree. Must have three to five years of marketing experience in a service based industry. **Reciprocity:** No. **Fees:** $75 application/initial license fee. $50 renewal fee. **Governing Statute:** Illinois Revised Statutes, Chapter 120.

3029

Restaurant Bus Helper (Gaming)
Illinois Gaming Board
PO Box 19474
Springfield, IL 62794-9474
Phone: (217)524-0228

Credential Type: Bus Helper License. **Duration of License:** One year. **Requirements:** At least 18 years of age. U.S. citizen or legal alien as specified by Federal employability requirement. **Reciprocity:** No. **Fees:** $75 application/initial license fee. $50 renewal fee. **Governing Statute:** Illinois Revised Statutes, Chapter 120.

Gambling Occupations Other Than Racetrack — Illinois

3030

Restaurant Cashier (Gaming)
Illinois Gaming Board
PO Box 19474
Springfield, IL 62794-9474
Phone: (217)524-0228

Credential Type: Restaurant Cashier License. **Duration of License:** One year. **Requirements:** At least 18 years of age. Must be a U.S. citizen or legal alien as specified by the Federal employment eligibility requirement. Submit application and pay fee. **Reciprocity:** No. **Fees:** $75 application and initial license fee. $50 renewal fee. **Governing Statute:** Illinois Revised Statutes, Chapter 120.

3031

Restaurant Hostess/Host (Gaming)
Illinois Gaming Board
PO Box 19474
Springfield, IL 62794-9474
Phone: (217)524-0228

Credential Type: Hostess/Host License. **Duration of License:** One year. **Requirements:** At least 18 years of age. U.S. citizen or legal alien as specified by Federal employability requirement. **Reciprocity:** No. **Fees:** $75 application/initial license fee. $50 renewal fee. **Governing Statute:** Illinois Revised Statutes, Chapter 120.

3032

Restaurant Manager (Gaming)
Illinois Gaming Board
PO Box 19474
Springfield, IL 62794-9474
Phone: (217)524-0228

Credential Type: Restaurant Manger License. **Duration of License:** One year. **Requirements:** At least 18 years of age. U.S. citizen or legal alien as specified by Federal employability requirement. Must have three or more years experience as a manager in a full service restaurant. **Reciprocity:** No. **Fees:** $75 application/initial license fee. $50 renewal fee. **Governing Statute:** Illinois Revised Statutes, Chapter 120.

3033

Restaurant Server (Gaming)
Illinois Gaming Board
PO Box 19474
Springfield, IL 62794-9474
Phone: (217)524-0228

Credential Type: Restaurant Server License. **Duration of License:** One year. **Requirements:** At least 18 years of age. U.S. citizen or legal alien as specified by Federal employability requirement. Submit application and pay fee. **Reciprocity:** No. **Fees:** $75 application/initial license fee. $50 renewal fee. **Governing Statute:** Illinois Revised Statutes, Chapter 120.

3034

Riverboat Senior Master/Captain (Gaming)
Illinois Gaming Board
PO Box 19474
Springfield, IL 62794-9474
Phone: (217)524-0228

Credential Type: Senior Master/Captain License. **Duration of License:** One year. **Requirements:** At least 18 years of age. Must have the appropriate U.S. Coast Guard's Pilots License. Must have experience as a Pilot in maritime areas. **Examination:** Master Examination (exam varies dependent on tonnage). **Reciprocity:** No. **Fees:** $385 examination fee. $75 application fee. $50 initial license fee. $50 renewal fee. **Governing Statute:** Illinois Revised Statutes, Chapter 120.

3035

Sales/Ticketing/Reservations Employee (Gaming)
Illinois Gaming Board
PO Box 19474
Springfield, IL 62794-9474
Phone: (217)524-0228

Credential Type: Sales License. **Duration of License:** One year. **Requirements:** At least 18 years of age. U.S. citizen or legal alien as specified by Federal employability requirement. Good computer or typing skills. Good public relations and phone skills. **Reciprocity:** No. **Fees:** $75 application/initial license fee. $50 renewal fee. **Governing Statute:** Illinois Revised Statutes, Chapter 120.

3036

Security/Emergency Medical Technician Officer (Gaming)
Illinois Gaming Board
PO Box 19474
Springfield, IL 62794-9474
Phone: (217)524-0228

Credential Type: Security/EMT Officer License. **Duration of License:** One year. **Requirements:** At least 21 years of age. Current Emergency Medical Technician (EMT) Certificate. CPR card. Experience preferred. Renewal requires a current EMT certificate. **Examination:** DOT 20 (Refresher Course) Examination. **Reciprocity:** No. **Fees:** $75 application fee. $50 initial license fee. $50 renewal fee. **Governing Statute:** Illinois Revised Statutes, Chapter 120.

3037

Security Officer (Gaming)
Illinois Gaming Board
PO Box 19474
Springfield, IL 62794-9474
Phone: (217)524-0228

Credential Type: Security Officer License. **Duration of License:** One year. **Requirements:** At least 21 years of age. U.S. citizen or legal alien as specified by Federal employability requirement. Experience or police training preferred. **Reciprocity:** No. **Fees:** $75 application fee. $50 initial license fee. $50 renewal fee. **Governing Statute:** Illinois Revised Statutes, Chapter 120.

3038

Security Supervisor (Gaming)
Illinois Gaming Board
PO Box 19474
Springfield, IL 62794-9474
Phone: (217)524-0228

Credential Type: Security Supervisor License. **Duration of License:** One year. **Requirements:** At least 21 years of age. U.S. citizen or legal alien as specified by Federal employability requirement. High school graduate or equivalent. Must have previous training and/or experience in the field of law enforcement. **Reciprocity:** No. **Fees:** $75 application fee. $50 initial license fee. $50 renewal fee. **Governing Statute:** Illinois Revised Statutes, Chapter 120.

3039

Slot Manager (Gaming)
Illinois Gaming Board
PO Box 19474
Springfield, IL 62794-9474
Phone: (217)524-0228

Credential Type: Slot Manager License. **Duration of License:** One year. **Requirements:** At least 21 years of age. U.S. citizen or legal alien as specified by Federal employability requirement. No felony convictions. High school graduate or equivalent. Knowledge of slot information system. At least one year experience in casino slot department operations and management. **Reciprocity:** No. **Fees:** $1,000 application/initial license fee. $50 renewal fee. **Governing Statute:** Illinois Revised Statutes, Chapter 120.

3040

Slot Mechanic (Gaming)
Illinois Gaming Board
PO Box 19474
Springfield, IL 62794-9474
Phone: (217)524-0228

Credential Type: Slot Mechanic License. **Duration of License:** One year. **Requirements:** At least 21 years of age. U.S. citizen or legal alien as specified by Federal employability requirement. No felony convictions. High school graduate or equivalent. Knowledge of electronics and computer functions. At least six months experience in casino slot operations or one year in microprocessing video machines. **Reciprocity:** No. **Fees:** $75 application/initial license fee. $50 renewal fee. **Governing Statute:** Illinois Revised Statutes, Chapter 120.

3041

Slot Supervisor (Gaming)
Illinois Gaming Board
PO Box 19474
Springfield, IL 62794-9474
Phone: (217)524-0228

Credential Type: Slot Supervisor License. **Duration of License:** One year. **Requirements:** At least 21 years of age. U.S. citizen or legal alien as specified by Federal employability requirement. No felony convictions. High school graduate or equivalent. Knowledge of machine operations and basic repair. Knowledge of slot information system. At least six months experience in casino slot department operations. **Reciprocity:** No. **Fees:** $200 application/initial license fee. $50 renewal fee. **Governing Statute:** Illinois Revised Statutes, Chapter 120.

3042

Slot Technician (Gaming)
Illinois Gaming Board
PO Box 19474
Springfield, IL 62794-9474
Phone: (217)524-0228

Credential Type: Slot Technician License. **Duration of License:** One year. **Requirements:** At least 21 years of age. U.S. citizen or legal alien as specified by Federal employability requirement. No felony convictions. High school graduate or equivalent. Knowledge of electronics and computer functions. At least six months experience in casino slot department operations or one year microprocessing video machines. **Reciprocity:** No. **Fees:** $75 application/initial license fee. $50 renewal fee. **Governing Statute:** Illinois Revised Statutes, Chapter 120.

3043

Soft Count Clerk (Gaming)
Illinois Gaming Board
PO Box 19474
Springfield, IL 62794-9474
Phone: (217)524-0228

Credential Type: Soft Count Clerk License. **Duration of License:** One year. **Requirements:** At least 21 years of age. U.S. citizen or legal alien as specified by Federal employability requirement. No felony convictions. High school graduate or equivalent. Currency handling experience. Ability to count large sums of money. Good computer skills. **Reciprocity:** No. **Fees:** $75 application/initial license fee. $50 renewal fee. **Governing Statute:** Illinois Revised Statutes, Chapter 120.

3044

Sous Chef (Gaming)
Illinois Gaming Board
PO Box 19474
Springfield, IL 62794-9474
Phone: (217)524-0228

Credential Type: Sous Chef License. **Duration of License:** One year. **Requirements:** At least 18 years of age. U.S. citizen and Illinois resident. No felony convictions. Three or more years experience as a Sous Chef in a gourmet restaurant. **Reciprocity:** No. **Fees:** $75 application and license fee. $50 renewal fee. **Governing Statute:** Illinois Revised Statutes, Chapter 120.

3045

Surveillance Manager (Gaming)
Illinois Gaming Board
PO Box 19474
Springfield, IL 62794-9474
Phone: (217)524-0228

Credential Type: Surveillance Manager License. **Duration of License:** One year. **Requirements:** At least 21 years of age. U.S. citizen or legal alien as specified by Federal employability requirement. Knowledge of camera equipment and surveillance. Extensive experience in Casino operations. **Reciprocity:** No. **Fees:** $1,000 application fee. $50 initial license fee. $50 renewal fee. **Governing Statute:** Illinois Revised Statutes, Chapter 120.

3046

Surveillance Operator (Gaming)
Illinois Gaming Board
PO Box 19474
Springfield, IL 62794-9474
Phone: (217)524-0228

Credential Type: Surveillance Operator License. **Duration of License:** One year. **Requirements:** At least 21 years of age. U.S. citizen or legal alien as specified by Federal employability requirement. Knowledge of camera equipment and its operation. Casino gaming knowledge and training. **Reciprocity:** No. **Fees:** $75 application fee. $50 initial license fee. $50 renewal fee. **Governing Statute:** Illinois Revised Statutes, Chapter 120.

3047

Warehouse/Receiving Clerk (Gaming)
Illinois Gaming Board
PO Box 19474
Springfield, IL 62794-9474
Phone: (217)524-0228

Credential Type: Warehouse/Receiving Clerk License. **Duration of License:** One year. **Requirements:** At least 18 years of age. U.S. citizen. Resident of Illinois. No felony convictions. High school graduate or equivalent. Physically capable of performing required duties. **Reciprocity:** No. **Fees:** $75 application/license fee. $50 renewal fee. **Governing Statute:** Illinois Revised Statutes, Chapter 120.

Iowa

3048

Accountant (Riverboat Gambling)
Iowa Racing and Gaming
 Commission
Lucas State Office Bldg.
Des Moines, IA 50319
Phone: (515)281-7352

Credential Type: License Registration.
Requirements: Submit application and pay fees. **Fees:** $50 license fee.

3049

Accounting Employee (Riverboat Gambling)
Iowa Racing and Gaming
 Commission
Lucas State Office Bldg.
Des Moines, IA 50319
Phone: (515)281-7352

Credential Type: License Registration.
Requirements: Submit application and pay fees. **Fees:** $20 license fee.

3050

Administrative Employee (Riverboat Gambling)
Iowa Racing and Gaming
 Commission
Lucas State Office Bldg.
Des Moines, IA 50319
Phone: (515)281-7352

Credential Type: License Registration.
Requirements: Submit application and pay fees. **Fees:** $10 license fee.

3051

Alcohol Server (Riverboat Gambling)
Iowa Racing and Gaming
 Commission
Lucas State Office Bldg.
Des Moines, IA 50319
Phone: (515)281-7352

Credential Type: License Registration.
Requirements: Submit application and pay fees. **Fees:** $10 license fee.

3052

Association Member (Riverboat Gambling)
Iowa Racing and Gaming
 Commission
Lucas State Office Bldg.
Des Moines, IA 50319
Phone: (515)281-7352

Credential Type: License Registration.
Requirements: Submit application and pay fees. **Fees:** $20 license fee.

3053

Attendant (Riverboat Gambling)
Iowa Racing and Gaming
 Commission
Lucas State Office Bldg.
Des Moines, IA 50319
Phone: (515)281-7352

Credential Type: License Registration.
Requirements: Submit application and pay fees. **Fees:** $10 license fee.

3054

Auditing Employee (Riverboat Gambling)
Iowa Racing and Gaming
 Commission
Lucas State Office Bldg.
Des Moines, IA 50319
Phone: (515)281-7352

Credential Type: License Registration.
Requirements: Submit application and pay fees. **Fees:** $20 license fee.

3055

Auditor (Riverboat Gambling)
Iowa Racing and Gaming
 Commission
Lucas State Office Bldg.
Des Moines, IA 50319
Phone: (515)281-7352

Credential Type: License Registration.
Requirements: Submit application and pay fees. **Fees:** $50 license fee.

3056

Boat Engineer (Riverboat Gambling)
Iowa Racing and Gaming
 Commission
Lucas State Office Bldg.
Des Moines, IA 50319
Phone: (515)281-7352

Credential Type: License Registration.
Requirements: Submit application and pay fees. **Fees:** $10 license fee.

3057

Boat Pilot (Riverboat Gambling)
Iowa Racing and Gaming
 Commission
Lucas State Office Bldg.
Des Moines, IA 50319
Phone: (515)281-7352

Credential Type: License Registration.
Requirements: Submit application and pay fees. **Fees:** $50 license fee.

3058

Box Person (Riverboat Gambling)
Iowa Racing and Gaming
 Commission
Lucas State Office Bldg.
Des Moines, IA 50319
Phone: (515)281-7352

Credential Type: License Registration.
Requirements: Submit application and pay fees. **Fees:** $20 license fee.

3059

Captain (Riverboat Gambling)
Iowa Racing and Gaming
 Commission
Lucas State Office Bldg.
Des Moines, IA 50319
Phone: (515)281-7352

Credential Type: License Registration.
Requirements: Submit application and pay fees. **Fees:** $50 license fee.

3060

Casino Clerk (Riverboat Gambling)
Iowa Racing and Gaming Commission
Lucas State Office Bldg.
Des Moines, IA 50319
Phone: (515)281-7352

Credential Type: License Registration.
Requirements: Submit application and pay fees. **Fees:** $20 license fee.

3061

Casino Manager (Riverboat Gambling)
Iowa Racing and Gaming Commission
Lucas State Office Bldg.
Des Moines, IA 50319
Phone: (515)281-7352

Credential Type: License Registration.
Requirements: Submit application and pay fees. **Fees:** $50 license fee.

3062

Casino Teller (Riverboat Gambling)
Iowa Racing and Gaming Commission
Lucas State Office Bldg.
Des Moines, IA 50319
Phone: (515)281-7352

Credential Type: License Registration.
Requirements: Submit application and pay fees. **Fees:** $20 license fee.

3063

Count Room Employee (Riverboat Gambling)
Iowa Racing and Gaming Commission
Lucas State Office Bldg.
Des Moines, IA 50319
Phone: (515)281-7352

Credential Type: License Registration.
Requirements: Submit application and pay fees. **Fees:** $20 license fee.

3064

Count Room Supervisor (Riverboat Gambling)
Iowa Racing and Gaming Commission
Lucas State Office Bldg.
Des Moines, IA 50319
Phone: (515)281-7352

Credential Type: License Registration.
Requirements: Submit application and pay fees. **Fees:** $50 license fee.

3065

Dealer Person (Riverboat Gambling)
Iowa Racing and Gaming Commission
Lucas State Office Bldg.
Des Moines, IA 50319
Phone: (515)281-7352

Credential Type: License Registration.
Requirements: Submit application and pay fees. **Fees:** $20 license fee.

3066

Deck Hand (Riverboat Gambling)
Iowa Racing and Gaming Commission
Lucas State Office Bldg.
Des Moines, IA 50319
Phone: (515)281-7352

Credential Type: License Registration.
Requirements: Submit application and pay fees. **Fees:** $10 license fee.

3067

Director (Riverboat Gambling)
Iowa Racing and Gaming Commission
Lucas State Office Bldg.
Des Moines, IA 50319
Phone: (515)281-7352

Credential Type: License Registration.
Requirements: Submit application and pay fees. **Fees:** $50 license fee.

3068

Director of Surveillance (Riverboat Gambling)
Iowa Racing and Gaming Commission
Lucas State Office Bldg.
Des Moines, IA 50319
Phone: (515)281-7352

Credential Type: License Registration.
Requirements: Submit application and pay fees. **Fees:** $50 license fee.

3069

EDP Employee (Riverboat Gambling)
Iowa Racing and Gaming Commission
Lucas State Office Bldg.
Des Moines, IA 50319
Phone: (515)281-7352

Credential Type: License Registration.
Requirements: Submit application and pay fees. **Fees:** $20 license fee.

3070

Entertainer (Riverboat Gambling)
Iowa Racing and Gaming Commission
Lucas State Office Bldg.
Des Moines, IA 50319
Phone: (515)281-7352

Credential Type: License Registration.
Requirements: Submit application and pay fees. **Fees:** $10 license fee.

3071

Entertainment Director (Riverboat Gambling)
Iowa Racing and Gaming Commission
Lucas State Office Bldg.
Des Moines, IA 50319
Phone: (515)281-7352

Credential Type: License Registration.
Requirements: Submit application and pay fees. **Fees:** $50 license fee.

Gambling Occupations Other Than Racetrack

3072

Floor Person (Riverboat Gambling)
Iowa Racing and Gaming
    Commission
Lucas State Office Bldg.
Des Moines, IA 50319
Phone: (515)281-7352

Credential Type: License Registration.
Requirements: Submit application and pay fees. **Fees:** $50 license fee.

3073

Food & Beverage Director (Riverboat Gambling)
Iowa Racing and Gaming
    Commission
Lucas State Office Bldg.
Des Moines, IA 50319
Phone: (515)281-7352

Credential Type: License Registration.
Requirements: Submit application and pay fees. **Fees:** $50 license fee.

3074

Food Service Worker (Riverboat Gambling)
Iowa Racing and Gaming
    Commission
Lucas State Office Bldg.
Des Moines, IA 50319
Phone: (515)281-7352

Credential Type: License Registration.
Requirements: Submit application and pay fees. **Fees:** $10 license fee.

3075

Games Manager (Riverboat Gambling)
Iowa Racing and Gaming
    Commission
Lucas State Office Bldg.
Des Moines, IA 50319
Phone: (515)281-7352

Credential Type: License Registration.
Requirements: Submit application and pay fees. **Fees:** $50 license fee.

3076

Games Supervisor (Riverboat Gambling)
Iowa Racing and Gaming
    Commission
Lucas State Office Bldg.
Des Moines, IA 50319
Phone: (515)281-7352

Credential Type: License Registration.
Requirements: Submit application and pay fees. **Fees:** $50 license fee.

3077

Head Casino Cashier Supervisor (Riverboat Gambling)
Iowa Racing and Gaming
    Commission
Lucas State Office Bldg.
Des Moines, IA 50319
Phone: (515)281-7352

Credential Type: License Registration.
Requirements: Submit application and pay fees. **Fees:** $50 license fee.

3078

Host/Hostess (Riverboat Gambling)
Iowa Racing and Gaming
    Commission
Lucas State Office Bldg.
Des Moines, IA 50319
Phone: (515)281-7352

Credential Type: License Registration.
Requirements: Submit application and pay fees. **Fees:** $10 license fee.

3079

Janitorial Employee (Riverboat Gambling)
Iowa Racing and Gaming
    Commission
Lucas State Office Bldg.
Des Moines, IA 50319
Phone: (515)281-7352

Credential Type: License Registration.
Requirements: Submit application and pay fees. **Fees:** $10 license fee.

3080

Kitchen Employee (Riverboat Gambling)
Iowa Racing and Gaming
    Commission
Lucas State Office Bldg.
Des Moines, IA 50319
Phone: (515)281-7352

Credential Type: License Registration.
Requirements: Submit application and pay fees. **Fees:** $10 license fee.

3081

Maintenance Supervisor (Riverboat Gambling)
Iowa Racing and Gaming
    Commission
Lucas State Office Bldg.
Des Moines, IA 50319
Phone: (515)281-7352

Credential Type: License Registration.
Requirements: Submit application and pay fees. **Fees:** $50 license fee.

3082

Non-Gaming Cashier (Riverboat Gambling)
Iowa Racing and Gaming
    Commission
Lucas State Office Bldg.
Des Moines, IA 50319
Phone: (515)281-7352

Credential Type: License Registration.
Requirements: Submit application and pay fees. **Fees:** $10 license fee.

3083

Non-Gaming Change Person (Riverboat Gambling)
Iowa Racing and Gaming
    Commission
Lucas State Office Bldg.
Des Moines, IA 50319
Phone: (515)281-7352

Credential Type: License Registration.
Requirements: Submit application and pay fees. **Fees:** $10 license fee.

3084

Officer (Riverboat Gambling)
Iowa Racing and Gaming
  Commission
Lucas State Office Bldg.
Des Moines, IA 50319
Phone: (515)281-7352

Credential Type: License Registration.
Requirements: Submit application and pay fees. **Fees:** $50 license fee.

3085

Outside Sales Representative (Riverboat Gambling)
Iowa Racing and Gaming
  Commission
Lucas State Office Bldg.
Des Moines, IA 50319
Phone: (515)281-7352

Credential Type: License Registration.
Requirements: Submit application and pay fees. **Fees:** $10 license fee.

3086

Owner/Operator (Riverboat Gambling)
Iowa Racing and Gaming
  Commission
Lucas State Office Bldg.
Des Moines, IA 50319
Phone: (515)281-7352

Credential Type: License Registration.
Requirements: Submit application and pay fees. **Fees:** $50 license fee.

3087

Porter (Riverboat Gambling)
Iowa Racing and Gaming
  Commission
Lucas State Office Bldg.
Des Moines, IA 50319
Phone: (515)281-7352

Credential Type: License Registration.
Requirements: Submit application and pay fees. **Fees:** $10 license fee.

3088

Retail Salesperson (Riverboat Gambling)
Iowa Racing and Gaming
  Commission
Lucas State Office Bldg.
Des Moines, IA 50319
Phone: (515)281-7352

Credential Type: License Registration.
Requirements: Submit application and pay fees. **Fees:** $10 license fee.

3089

Security Director (Riverboat Gambling)
Iowa Racing and Gaming
  Commission
Lucas State Office Bldg.
Des Moines, IA 50319
Phone: (515)281-7352

Credential Type: License Registration.
Requirements: Submit application and pay fees. **Fees:** $50 license fee.

3090

Security Employee (Riverboat Gambling)
Iowa Racing and Gaming
  Commission
Lucas State Office Bldg.
Des Moines, IA 50319
Phone: (515)281-7352

Credential Type: License Registration.
Requirements: Submit application and pay fees. **Fees:** $20 license fee.

3091

Security Supervisor (Riverboat Gambling)
Iowa Racing and Gaming
  Commission
Lucas State Office Bldg.
Des Moines, IA 50319
Phone: (515)281-7352

Credential Type: License Registration.
Requirements: Submit application and pay fees. **Fees:** $50 license fee.

3092

Service Representative (Riverboat Gambling)
Iowa Racing and Gaming
  Commission
Lucas State Office Bldg.
Des Moines, IA 50319
Phone: (515)281-7352

Credential Type: License Registration.
Requirements: Submit application and pay fees. **Fees:** $10 license fee.

3093

Shift Supervisor (Riverboat Gambling)
Iowa Racing and Gaming
  Commission
Lucas State Office Bldg.
Des Moines, IA 50319
Phone: (515)281-7352

Credential Type: License Registration.
Requirements: Submit application and pay fees. **Fees:** $50 license fee.

3094

Slot Attendant (Riverboat Gambling)
Iowa Racing and Gaming
  Commission
Lucas State Office Bldg.
Des Moines, IA 50319
Phone: (515)281-7352

Credential Type: License Registration.
Requirements: Submit application and pay fees. **Fees:** $20 license fee.

3095

Slot Change Person (Riverboat Gambling)
Iowa Racing and Gaming
  Commission
Lucas State Office Bldg.
Des Moines, IA 50319
Phone: (515)281-7352

Credential Type: License Registration.
Requirements: Submit application and pay fees. **Fees:** $20 license fee.

Gambling Occupations Other Than Racetrack

3096

Slot Manager (Riverboat Gambling)
Iowa Racing and Gaming Commission
Lucas State Office Bldg.
Des Moines, IA 50319
Phone: (515)281-7352

Credential Type: License Registration. **Requirements:** Submit application and pay fees. **Fees:** $50 license fee.

3097

Slot Supervisor (Riverboat Gambling)
Iowa Racing and Gaming Commission
Lucas State Office Bldg.
Des Moines, IA 50319
Phone: (515)281-7352

Credential Type: License Registration. **Requirements:** Submit application and pay fees. **Fees:** $50 license fee.

3098

Slot Technician (Riverboat Gambling)
Iowa Racing and Gaming Commission
Lucas State Office Bldg.
Des Moines, IA 50319
Phone: (515)281-7352

Credential Type: License Registration. **Requirements:** Submit application and pay fees. **Fees:** $20 license fee.

3099

Stock Person (Riverboat Gambling)
Iowa Racing and Gaming Commission
Lucas State Office Bldg.
Des Moines, IA 50319
Phone: (515)281-7352

Credential Type: License Registration. **Requirements:** Submit application and pay fees. **Fees:** $20 license fee.

3100

Surveillance Employee (Riverboat Gambling)
Iowa Racing and Gaming Commission
Lucas State Office Bldg.
Des Moines, IA 50319
Phone: (515)281-7352

Credential Type: License Registration. **Requirements:** Submit application and pay fees. **Fees:** $20 license fee.

Minnesota

3101

Gambling Employee
Gambling Control Board
1711 W. County Rd. B, Ste. 300-S
Roseville, MN 55113
Phone: (612)639-4000

Credential Type: Gambling Employee Registration. **Duration of License:** Continuous. **Authorization:** Required of employees of nonprofit organizations that conduct charitable gambling. Only employees that are compensated and that work directly with the public must be registered. **Requirements:** Submit application. Employee receives identification badge that must be worn when working for the organization. **Fees:** No fees.

3102

Gambling Manager
Gambling Control Board
1711 W. County Rd. B, Ste. 300-S
Roseville, MN 55113
Phone: (612)639-4000

Credential Type: Gambling Manager License. **Duration of License:** One year. **Authorization:** Required of managers of nonprofit organizations that conduct charitable gambling. **Requirements:** Must have been a member of the nonprofit organization for at least the two most recent years. Pass background check. Post $10,000 fidelity bond. Complete a 2-day gambling manager seminar conducted by the board. **Fees:** $100 license fee.

Nevada

3103

Casino Management Employee
Gaming Control Board
Applicant Services Dept.
1150 E. William St.
Carson City, NV 89710
Phone: (702)687-6540

Credential Type: License. **Authorization:** Key employess are required to be licensed. Other casino employees must obtain work permits. **Requirements:** Contact licensing body for application information.

New Jersey

3104

Casino Floor Employee
New Jersey Casino Control Commission
Licensing Div.
1325 Boardwalk
Atlantic City, NJ 08401
Phone: (609)441-3030

Credential Type: License. **Duration of License:** Three years. **Requirements:** Certain occupations may have specific education or experience requirements. 18 years of age. State resident at the time the license is issued. **Fees:** $195—$275 initial fee. $180—$225 renewal fee. **Governing Statute:** NJSA 5:12-90. NJAC 19:41-1.3.

3105

Casino Hotel Employee
New Jersey Casino Contol Commission
Licensing Div.
1325 Boardwalk
Atlantic City, NJ 08401
Phone: (609)441-3030

Credential Type: Registration. **Duration of License:** Indefinite. **Authorization:** Required of employees of a licensed hotel casino in Atlantic City. **Requirements:** State residency not required. Submit application and personal history disclosure form. Employing casino must petition for registration. **Fees:** $30 registration fee. **Governing Statute:** NJSA 5:12-91. NJAC 19:41-1.3.

Washington

3106

Bingo Game Manager
Washington State Gambling
 Commission
4511 Woodview Dr. SE, QB-11
Olympia, WA 98504-8121
Phone: (206)438-7654

Credential Type: Bingo Game Manager License. **Duration of License:** One year. **Requirements:** Submit to personal and criminal background investigation. Submit application and pay fee. **Fees:** $150 initial license fee. $75 renewal fee.

3107

Distributor's Representative (Gambling)
Washington State Gambling
 Commission
Jefferson Bldg.
1110 S. Jefferson, PC-21
Olympia, WA 98504-8121
Phone: (206)438-7654

Credential Type: Distributor's Representative License. **Duration of License:** One year. **Authorization:** Allows licensee to distribute punchboard, pull tab, and pull tab dispensing devices. **Requirements:** Submit application and pay fee. **Fees:** $200 initial license fee. $125 license renewal fee.

3108

Public Card Room Employee (Gambling)
Washington State Gambling
 Commission
4511 Woodview Dr. SE, QB-11
Olympia, WA 98504-8121
Phone: (206)438-7654

Credential Type: Public Card Room Employee License. **Duration of License:** One year. **Requirements:** Submit application and pay fee. Personal/criminal background investigation. **Fees:** $150 initial license fee. $75 renewal fee.

Gardeners, Horticulture Workers, and Groundskeepers

The following states grant licenses in this occupational category as of the date of publication: Alabama, Arkansas, Connecticut, Idaho, Kentucky, Louisiana, Maine, Michigan, Montana, Nevada, Rhode Island.

Alabama

3109

Landscape Planter
Dept. of Agricultural and Industries
Div. of Agricultural Chemistry and Plant Industry
Beard Bldg.
PO Box 3336
Montgomery, AL 36193
Phone: (205)242-2656

Credential Type: Licensed. **Duration of License:** One year. **Requirements:** Must submit a written statement outlining their training and experience in this field. **Examination:** Written examination. **Fees:** $10 examination fee. $25 renewal fee.

Arkansas

3110

Nurseryman
Arkansas State Plant Board
No. 1 Natural Resources Dr.
PO Box 1069
Little Rock, AR 72205
Phone: (501)225-1598

Credential Type: License. **Requirements:** Be of sound moral and financial character. **Examination:** No. **Fees:** $10 License. $45 Inspection.

Connecticut

3111

Arborist
Tree Protection Examining Board
Consumer Protection Dept.
165 Capitol Ave.
Hartford, CT 06106
Phone: (203)566-3290

Credential Type: Arboriculture license. **Duration of License:** Five years. **Requirements:** Submit application and pay fee. Pass examination. **Examination:** Board-administered examination. **Fees:** $20 license fee. $20 renewal fee. $10 exam fee. **Governing Statute:** General Statutes of Connecticut, Chap. 451.

Idaho

3112

Nursery Agent
Plant Industries Div.
Agriculture Dept.
PO Box 790
Boise, ID 83701
Phone: (208)334-2986

Credential Type: Agent's License. **Duration of License:** One year. **Requirements:** Submit application and pay fee. **Exemptions:** Agents soliciting sales only from persons licensed as florists, nurserymen, or landsacpe designers are exempt from license fees. **Fees:** $25 fee per principal respresented. **Governing Statute:** Idaho Code, Title 22, Chap. 23.

3113

Nurseryman
Plant Industries Div.
Agriculture Dept.
PO Box 790
Boise, ID 83701
Phone: (208)334-2986

Credential Type: Class A License. **Duration of License:** One year. **Authorization:** Required if gross business is over $1,000 per year. **Requirements:** Submit application and pay fee. **Fees:** $50 license fee per outlet. **Governing Statute:** Idaho Code, Title 22, Chap. 23.

Credential Type: Class B License. **Duration of License:** One year. **Authorization:** Required if gross business is $1,000 or less per year. **Requirements:** Submit application and pay fee. **Fees:** $15 license fee. **Governing Statute:** Idaho Code, Title 22, Chap. 23.

Kentucky

3114

Groundsman (Racetrack)
Kentucky State Racing Commission
PO Box 1080
Lexington, KY 40588
Phone: (606)254-7021

Credential Type: Association Employee and Occupational License. **Requirements:** Submit application and fingerprint card. Pay fee. **Fees:** $10 license fee.

Louisiana

3115

Cut Flower Dealer
Horticulture Commission
Plant Quarantine and Horticulture Programs
PO Box 44517
Baton Rouge, LA 70804
Phone: (504)925-7772

Credential Type: Permit. **Duration of License:** One year. **Requirements:** Submit application and pay fee. **Fees:** $35 permit fee. $35 renewal fee. **Governing Statute:** R.S. 37:1961-1974.

3116

Nursery Stock Dealer
Horticulture Commission
Plant Quarantine and Horticulture Programs
PO Box 44517, Capitol Sta.
Baton Rouge, LA 70804
Phone: (504)925-7772

Credential Type: Permit. **Duration of License:** One year. **Requirements:** Submit application and pay fee. **Fees:** $65 permit fee. $35 renewal fee. **Governing Statute:** R.S. 37:1961-1974.

Maine

3117

Apprentice Utility Arborist
Arborist Examining Board
Dept. of Professional and Financial Regulations
State House Station 35
Augusta, ME 04333
Phone: (207)582-8723

Credential Type: Apprentice Permit. **Duration of License:** One year. **Authorization:** Must work under the on-site supervision of a First Class or Master Utility Arborist. A Utility Arborist may perform agricultural procedures closer than 120 feet from an energized conductor. **Requirements:** Must be at least 18 years of age. Applicants with no prior experience must train under the direction of a First Class or Master Utility Arborist for at least one year as an apprentice. **Fees:** $15 application fee. **Governing Statute:** 32 M.S.R.A., Chap. 29.

3118

Arborist (Unrestricted)
Arborist Examining Board
Dept. of Professional and Financial Regulations
State House Station 35
Augusta, ME 04333
Phone: (207)582-8723

Credential Type: Unrestricted Arborist Licence. **Duration of License:** One year. **Requirements:** Must be at least 18 years of age. Must have a minimum of five years experience as both a landscape and utility arborist. Hold a valid Maine Pesticide Applicators License in categories 3A-Outdoor Ornamentals and 6B-Utility Vegetation. **Examination:** Master Landscape Arborist Examination, written and practical. Master Utility Arborist Examination, written and practical. **Fees:** $15 application fee. $50 exam fee. $30 license fee. $30 renewal fee. **Governing Statute:** 32 M.S.R.A., Chap. 29.

3119

Landscape Arborist
Arborist Examining Board
Dept. of Professional and Financial Regulations
State House Station 35
Augusta, ME 04333
Phone: (207)582-8723

Credential Type: First Class Landscape Arborist Licence. **Duration of License:** One year. **Requirements:** Must be at least 18 years of age. Must have at least one year of prior experience or have completed one year apprenticeship. **Examination:** First Class Landscape Arborist Examination, written and practical. **Fees:** $15 application fee. $50 exam fee. $30 license fee. $30 renewal fee. **Governing Statute:** 32 M.S.R.A., Chap. 29.

Credential Type: Master Landscape Arborist Licence. **Duration of License:** One year. **Requirements:** Must be at least 18 years of age. Must have at least five years of prior experience or training. Must hold a valid Maine Pesticide Applicator license in category 3A-Outdoor Ornamentals. **Examination:** Master Landscape Arborist Examination, written and practical. **Fees:** $15 application fee. $75 exam fee. $30 license fee. $30 renewal fee. **Governing Statute:** 32 M.S.R.A., Chap. 29.

3120

Utility Arborist
Arborist Examining Board
Dept. of Professional and Financial Regulations
State House Station 35
Augusta, ME 04333
Phone: (207)582-8723

Credential Type: First Class Utility Arborist Licence. **Duration of License:** One year. **Authorization:** A Utility Arborist may perform agricultural procedures closer than 120 feet from an energized conductor. **Requirements:** Must be at least 18 years of age. Must have at least one year of prior experience or have completed one year apprenticeship. **Examination:** First Class Utility Arborist Examination, written and practical. **Fees:** $15 application fee. $50 exam fee. $30 license fee. $30 renewal fee. **Governing Statute:** 32 M.S.R.A., Chap. 29.

Credential Type: Master Utility Arborist Licence. **Duration of License:** One year. **Requirements:** Must be at least 18 years of age. Must have at least five years of prior experience or training. Must hold a valid Maine Pesticide Applicator license in category 6B-Utility Vegetation. **Examination:** Master Utility Arborist Examination, written and practical. **Fees:** $15 application fee. $75 exam fee. $30 license fee. $30 renewal fee. **Governing Statute:** 32 M.S.R.A., Chap. 29.

Michigan

3121

Nursery Dealer
Pesticide and Plant Pest Management Div.
Dept. of Agriculture
Ottawa Bldg. N.
PO Box 30017
Lansing, MI 48909
Phone: (517)373-1104

Credential Type: License. **Duration of License:** One year. **Requirements:** Submit application and pay fee. Must sell nursery stock that is free of dangerous plant pests and that is purchased from a certified source. Abide by the rules of the Department of Agriculture. **Fees:** $50 initial license fee. $50 renewal fee. Nonresident nursery dealers are required to pay the $50 license fee. **Governing Statute:** Insect Pests and Plant Diseases Act, Act 189 of 1931, as amended.

Gardeners, Horticulture Workers, and Groundskeepers

3122

Nurseryperson (Nurseryman)
Pesticide and Plant Pest Management Div.
Dept. of Agriculture
Ottawa Bldg. N.
PO Box 30017
Lansing, MI 48909
Phone: (517)373-1104

Credential Type: License. **Duration of License:** One year. **Requirements:** Submit application and pay fee. Must have nursery stock inspected for dangerous insect pests and plant diseases and certified to be apparently free of such pests and diseases by the Department or a Department-approved inspector. **Fees:** $50 initial license fee. $50 renewal fee. Nonresident nurserypersons are required to pay the $50 license fee. **Governing Statute:** Insect Pests and Plant Diseases Act, Act 189 of 1931, as amended.

3123

Plant Dealer
Pesticide and Plant Pest Management Div.
Dept. of Agriculture
Ottawa Bldg., N.
PO Box 30017
Lansing, MI 48909
Phone: (517)373-1104

Credential Type: License. **Duration of License:** One year. **Requirements:** Must sell plants that have been obtained from a Department of Agriculture certified source. Abide by the rules of the Department of Agriculture. **Fees:** $20 initial license fee. $20 renewal fee. **Governing Statute:** Insect Pests and Plant Diseases Act, Act 189 of 1931, as amended.

Montana

3124

Nurseryman
Dept. of Agriculture
Plant Industry Div.
Agriculture and Livestock Bldg.
6th and Roberts
Helena, MT 59620
Phone: (406)444-3730

Credential Type: Class A License. **Authorization:** General nursery license. **Requirements:** Submit application and pay fee. **Fees:** $50 license fee. **Governing Statute:** ARM, Title 80, Chap. 7.

Credential Type: Class B License. **Authorization:** Limited to small fruits, shrubs, and bushes. **Requirements:** Submit application and pay fee. **Fees:** $35 license fee. **Governing Statute:** ARM, Title 80, Chap. 7.

Credential Type: Class C License. **Authorization:** Limited to bulbs, perennials, and greenhouse plants. **Requirements:** Submit application and pay fee. **Fees:** $20 license fee. **Governing Statute:** Montana Code Annotated, Title 80, Chap. 7.

Nevada

3125

Groundskeeper/Gardener
Nevada State Dept. of Agriculture
Pest Control Licensing Section
PO Box 11100
Reno, NV 89510
Phone: (702)789-0180

Credential Type: License. **Duration of License:** One year. **Requirements:** Individuals applying as company principals must have two years of documented pest control experience, or a combination of 16 credits of college courses in pest control or related subjects and six months of experience. Applicators must pass the examinations, but do not need to have previous pest control experience. **Examination:** Yes. **Fees:** $15—$35 exam fee. $15 license fee. $15 renewal fee.

Rhode Island

3126

Arborist
Div. of Forest Environment
Rhode Island Dept. of Environmental Management
1037 Hartford Pike
North Scituate, RI 02857
Phone: (401)647-3367

Credential Type: Arborist License. **Duration of License:** One year. **Authorization:** Authorizes tree surgery and the pruning, planting, and spraying of trees. Use of pesticides requires a Pesticide Applicator license. **Requirements:** Knowledge of planting and pruning trees and shrubs. Submit application. Pass examination. **Examination:** Written and practical for pruning, planting, and tree surgery. Written for spraying. **Reciprocity:** Yes, for spraying only. **Fees:** $25 application fee. $25 renewal fee.

3127

Nurseryman
Div. of Agriculture
Rhode Island Dept. of Environmental Management
22 Hayes St., Rm. 120
Providence, RI 02908
Phone: (401)277-2781

Credential Type: Nurseryman License. **Duration of License:** One year. **Requirements:** Submit application and pay fee. **Fees:** $50 license fee. $50 renewal fee.

General Managers and Top Executives

The following states grant licenses in this occupational category as of the date of publication:

Alabama	Florida	Louisiana	Montana	Ohio	South Dakota	Wisconsin
Arizona	Idaho	Maine	New Jersey	Oklahoma	Texas	Wyoming
Arkansas	Illinois	Maryland	New Mexico	Oregon	Vermont	
California	Iowa	Massachusetts	New York	Pennsylvania	Virginia	
Connecticut	Kansas	Michigan	North Carolina	Rhode Island	Washington	
Delaware	Kentucky	Missouri	North Dakota	South Carolina	West Virginia	

Alabama

3128

School Superintendent
State Dept. of Education,
 Certification Officer
Montgomery, AL 36130
Phone: (205)242-9977

Credential Type: Class A Superintendent-Professional Certificate. **Requirements:** Eligibility for a Class B Professional Certificate. Completion of a program for Superintendents approved by the Alabama State Board of Education or the National Council for Accreditation of Teacher Education or the National Association of State Directors of Teacher Education and Certification or ICP. Three years of acceptable teaching experience.

Credential Type: Class AA Superintendent-Professional Certificate. **Requirements:** Eligibility for a Class A Superintendent-Professional Certificate. Completion of a sixth-year program for superintendents approved by the Alabama State Board of Education.

3129

Wrestling Director
State Athletic Commission
50 N. Ripley St., Rm. 4121
Montgomery, AL 36132
Phone: (205)242-1380

Credential Type: License. **Duration of License:** One year. **Fees:** $5 license fee.

Arizona

3130

School Superintendent
Teacher Certification Unit
PO Box 25609
1535 W. Jefferson
Phoenix, AZ 85002
Phone: (602)542-4368

Credential Type: Superintendent Certificate (K-12). **Duration of License:** Six years. **Requirements:** Master's or more advanced degree from a regionally accredited institution. Three years of verifiable teaching experience (K-12). Minimum of 60 graduate semester hours including completion of an approved program in educational administration for the superintendent from a regionally accredited institution or 36 graduate semester hours of educational administrative course work which teach the following administrative skills: organizational planning; program development; staff development and evaluation; evaluating productivity. Internship for educational administration for the superintendency or two years of verifiable educational administrative experience as a superintendent, assistant or associate superintendent (K-12). Pass Arizona Teacher Proficiency Exam (ATPE) exam. Satisfy Arizona Constitution and U.S. Constitution requirements during initial year of certification. **Examination:** Arizona Teacher Proficiency Examination

Arkansas

3131

Greyhound Mutuels Director
Arkansas State Racing Commission
Ledbetter Bldg., Rm. G08
7th & Wolfe St.
PO Box 3076
Little Rock, AR 72203
Phone: (501)682-1467

Credential Type: License. **Duration of License:** One year. **Requirements:** Must not be associated with any bookmaking practices which are illegal or would be detrimental to the public or the sport of racing. Never convicted of a crime. Qualified as to ability and integrity of license sought and have endorsement of employer. Not be habitually intoxicated or addicted to drugs. Declare ownership or interest in any greyhound. Application must contain no falsehoods. 16 years of age. Application approved by Director of Racing. **Examination:** No **Fees:** $3 License. $3 Renewal.

3132

Greyhound Racing Director
Arkansas State Racing Commission
Ledbetter Bldg., Rm. G08
7th & Wolfe St.
PO Box 3076
Little Rock, AR 72203
Phone: (501)682-1467

Credential Type: License. **Duration of License:** One year. **Requirements:** Must not be associated with any bookmaking practices which are illegal or would be detrimental to the public or the sport of racing. Never convicted of a crime. Qualified as to ability and integrity of license sought and have endorsement of employer. Not be habitually intoxicated or addicted to drugs.

Declare ownership or interest in any greyhound. Application must contain no falsehoods. 16 years of age. Application approved by Director of Racing. **Examination:** No **Fees:** $3 License. $3 Renewal.

3133

School Superintendent
Arkansas Dept. of Education
ffice of Teacher Education and
 Licensure
Sate Education Bldg., Rm. 107B
Capitol Mall 4
Little Rock, AR 72201-1071
Phone: (501)682-4344

Credential Type: License. **Requirements:** Must be eligible to hold a teaching certificate (elementary or secondary). Minimum of four years experience as teacher or administrator. Must complete program of study of 60 semester hours of graduate education with emphasis in school administration and Masters degree in School Administration at an approved institution. **Examination:** Yes. **Fees:** $45 National Teacher Examination (NTE) Specialty Area Test. $45 NTE Specialty Area Test renewal.

3134

Track Superintendent
Arkansas State Racing Commission
Ledbetter Bldg., Rm. G08
7th & Wolfe St.
PO Box 3076
Little Rock, AR 72203
Phone: (501)682-1467

Credential Type: License. **Duration of License:** One year. **Requirements:** Application must be approved by the Stewards. Must be qualified as to ability and integrity of license sought and have the endorsement of employer. 16 years of age. Never convicted of a crime. Not be habitually addicted to drugs or intoxicated. Must not be engaged in any activity which is illegal, undesirable or detrimental to the best interest of the public and the sport of racing. **Examination:** No **Fees:** $3 License. $3 Renewal.

California

3135

Officer, Director, or Partner of a Racing Association (Racetrack)
California Horse Racing Board
1010 Hurley Way, Ste. 190
Sacramento, CA 95825
Phone: (916)920-7178

Credential Type: License Registration. **Requirements:** Submit application and fingerprint card. Pay fee. **Fees:** $200 registration fee.

3136

Official and Manager of a Racing Association (Racetrack)
California Horse Racing Board
1010 Hurley Way, Ste. 190
Sacramento, CA 95825
Phone: (916)920-7178

Credential Type: License Registration. **Requirements:** Submit application and fingerprint card. Pay fee. **Fees:** $150 registration fee.

3137

Superintendent (Racetrack)
California Horse Racing Board
1010 Hurley Way, Ste. 190
Sacramento, CA 95825
Phone: (916)920-7178

Credential Type: License Registration. **Requirements:** Submit application and fingerprint card. Pay fee. **Fees:** $75 registration fee.

Connecticut

3138

Assistant Director of Security (Racetrack)
Connecticut Div. of Special Revenue
Russell Rd.
PO Box 11424
Newington, CT 06111-0424
Phone: (203)566-2756

Credential Type: License Registration. **Requirements:** Submit application and fingerprint card. Pay fee. **Fees:** $20 registration fee.

3139

Corporation Director II (Racetrack)
Connecticut Div. of Special Revenue
Russell Rd.
PO Box 11424
Newington, CT 06111-0424
Phone: (203)566-2756

Credential Type: License Registration. **Requirements:** Submit application and fingerprint card. Pay fee. **Fees:** $20 registration fee.

3140

Corporation Officer II (Racetrack)
Connecticut Div. of Special Revenue
Russell Rd.
PO Box 11424
Newington, CT 06111-0424
Phone: (203)566-2756

Credential Type: License Registration. **Requirements:** Submit application and fingerprint card. Pay fee. **Fees:** $20 registration fee.

3141

Director of Security (Racetrack)
Connecticut Div. of Special Revenue
Russell Rd.
PO Box 11424
Newington, CT 06111-0424
Phone: (203)566-2756

Credential Type: License Registration. **Requirements:** Submit application and fingerprint card. Pay fee. **Fees:** $20 registration fee.

3142

Superintendent (Racetrack)
Connecticut Div. of Special Revenue
Russell Rd.
PO Box 11424
Newington, CT 06111-0424
Phone: (203)566-2756

Credential Type: License Registration. **Requirements:** Submit application and fingerprint card. Pay fee. **Fees:** $5 registration fee.

Connecticut

3143

Superintendent of Schools
State Dept. of Education
Teacher Certification, Chief
165 Capitol Ave.
PO Box 2219
Hartford, CT 06145
Phone: (203)566-4561

Credential Type: Superintendent of Schools Initial Certificate. **Requirements:** Connecticut teaching certificate or eligibility for one. Master's degree from an approved institution. Eight years of successful teaching or administrative experience. Three years of full-time administrative or supervisory experience in U.S. schools. Recommendation of an accredited college or university approved by the State Department of Education for preparation of superintendent of schools, based on a program of 30 semester hours in addition to the master's degree. Graduate study in the following areas: Foundations of education; Psychological foundations of learning; Curriculum development; Educational administration and supervision; and a core of related study to ensure breadth of education and scholarly background consistent with the competence expected of a superintendent of schools.

Credential Type: Superintendent of Schools Provisional Certificate. **Requirements:** Superintendent of Schools Initial Certificate. Completion of beginning educator support and assessment program as may be available from the Connecticut Board and one school year of successful service under the interim or initial certificates or three years of successful service as a superintendent of schools, in an approved school, within 10 years prior to application. Superintendent of Schools Professional Certificate. **Requirements:** Three years of successful service under the Provisional Certificate.

Delaware

3144

Program Director (Racetrack)
Delaware Harness Racing Commission
2320 S. DuPont Hwy.
Dover, DE 19901
Phone: (302)739-4811

Credential Type: License Registration. **Requirements:** Submit application and fingerprint card. Pay fee. **Fees:** $5 registration fee.

3145

School Superintendent
Teacher Certification
Dept. of Public Instruction
Box 1402
Dover, DE 19903
Phone: (302)739-4688

Credential Type: Superintendent Endorsement. **Requirements:** Master's degree plus at least 30 graduate credits or a doctor's degree. Must have a major in administration that covers course work in curriculum, supervision, business administration and personnel administration. Three years' teaching experience or two years of teaching and a 60 semester hr. program for school administrators that includes a one year internship.

Florida

3146

Association Manager/Supervisor (Racetrack)
Florida Dept. of Business
Div. of Pari-Mutuel Wagering
Licensing Section
725 S. Bronough St.
Tallahassee, FL 32399-1037
Phone: (904)488-9161

Credential Type: License Registration Code 1005. **Authorization:** Authorizes work in the following positions: admissions manager, chief of security, concession manager or owner, general manager, mutuels manager, parking director, public relations director, plant superintendent, and track superintendent. **Requirements:** Submit application and fingerprint card. Pay fee. **Fees:** $40 registration fee.

3147

Association Officer/Director/Manager (Racetrack)
Florida Dept. of Business
Div. of Pari-Mutuel Wagering
Licensing Section
725 S. Bronough St.
Tallahassee, FL 32399-1037
Phone: (904)488-9161

Credential Type: License Registration Code 1066. **Requirements:** Submit application and fingerprint card. Pay fee. **Fees:** $40 registration fee.

Idaho

3148

School Superintendent
Certification Analyst
State Dept. of Education
L. B. Jordan Office Bldg.
Boise, ID 83720
Phone: (208)334-3475

Credential Type: Administrative Certificate with Superintendent Endorsement. **Duration of License:** Five years. **Requirements:** Qualify for an Idaho Standard or Advanced Elementary or Secondary Certificate. Educational specialist or doctorate degree or a comparable postmaster's sixth year program at an accredited institution. Four years full-time regular and/or special education classroom teaching experience in grades K-12 while properly certified. Administrative internship or one year of experience as an administrator in grades K-12. Completion of an approved program of at least 30 semester credit hours of graduate study in school administration for the preparation of school superintendents at an accredited institution to include competencies in supervision of instruction; curriculum development; school finance; administration; school law; student behavior management; education of special populations; advanced money management and accounting principles; district-wide support services; employment practices and negotiations; school board and community relations; special services; and federal programs. Valid for five years and may be renewed upon completion of at least six semester credits of college courses within the period of validity.

Illinois

3149

Casino Manager (Gaming)
Illinois Gaming Board
PO Box 19474
Springfield, IL 62794-9474
Phone: (217)524-0228

Credential Type: Casino Manager License. **Duration of License:** One year. **Requirements:** At least 21 years of age. U.S. citizen and Illinois resident. No felony convictions. High school graduate or equivalent. Must have a minimum of 10 years experience in all facets of casino management. Knowledge of game protection and employee relations. **Reciprocity:** No. **Fees:** $1,000 application and license fee. $50 renewal fee. **Governing Statute:** Illinois Revised Statutes, Chapter 120.

3150

Chief Operating Officer/General Manager (Gaming)
Illinois Gaming Board
PO Box 19474
Springfield, IL 62794-9474
Phone: (217)524-0228

Credential Type: Chief Operating Officer/General Manager License. **Duration of License:** One year. **Requirements:** At least 18 years of age. U.S. citizen or legal alien as specified by the Federal employment eligibility requirement. High school graduate or equivalent. Must have extensive experience in the Gaming industry and a record of successful growth through added responsibilities. **Reciprocity:** No. **Fees:** $1,000 application fee. $50 initial license fee. $50 renewal fee. **Governing Statute:** Illinois Revised Statutes, Chapter 120.

3151

Director of Security (Gaming)
Illinois Gaming Board
PO Box 19474
Springfield, IL 62794-9474
Phone: (217)524-0228

Credential Type: Director of Security License. **Duration of License:** One year. **Requirements:** At least 21 years of age. High school graduate. College degree preferred. Must have training and experience in law enforcement. U.S. citizen or legal alien as specified by the federal employment eligibility requirement. **Reciprocity:** No. **Fees:** $1,000 application fee. $50 initial license fee. $50 renewal fee. **Governing Statute:** Illinois Revised Statutes, Chapter 120.

3152

Gym Owner (Boxing/Wrestling)
Illinois Dept. of Professional Regulations
State of Illinois Ctr.
100 W. Randolph, Ste. 9-300
Chicago, IL 60601
Phone: (312)814-2719

Credential Type: Registration. **Duration of License:** Lifetime. **Requirements:** Submit registration to board. Must re-register if original information changes. **Reciprocity:** No. **Governing Statute:** The Illinois Professional Boxing and Wrestling Act. Illinois Revised Statutes 1991, Chapter 111.

3153

M.I.S. Manager/Technical Supports Systems Operator (Gaming)
Illinois Gaming Board
PO Box 19474
Springfield, IL 62794-9474
Phone: (217)524-0228

Credential Type: M.I.S. Manager License. **Duration of License:** One year. **Requirements:** At least 18 years of age. No felony convictions. High school graduate or equivalent. Computer experience. **Reciprocity:** No. **Fees:** $75 application/initial license fee. $50 renewal fee. **Governing Statute:** Illinois Revised Statutes, Chapter 120.

3154

School Superintendent
Certification and Placement Section
100 N. First St.
Springfield, IL 62777
Phone: (217)782-4321

Credential Type: Superintendent Endorsement. **Duration of License:** Five years. **Requirements:** Good character. Good health. At least 19 years of age. Citizen of the U.S. Master's degree in administration from a recognized institution. Must have the following graduate level semester hr. credits: Governance of Public Schools 6; Management of Public Schools 6; Educational Planning 6; Graduate Level Electives 12; and Clinical Experience (appropriate to the endorsement). Two years of school supervisory or administrative experience and possession of the general supervisory or general administrative certificate. Pass required sections of the Illinois Certification Test. **Examination:** Illinois Certification Test. **Reciprocity:** Reciprocity exists for applicants holding out-of-state administrative certificates providing their preparation was comparable to that required by the state of Illinois. **Fees:** $44 per section of the Illinois Certification Test.

Iowa

3155

Casino Manager (Riverboat Gambling)
Iowa Racing and Gaming Commission
Lucas State Office Bldg.
Des Moines, IA 50319
Phone: (515)281-7352

Credential Type: License Registration. **Requirements:** Submit application and pay fees. **Fees:** $50 license fee.

3156

Corporate Director/Officer (Racetrack)
Iowa State Racing Commission
Lucas State Office Bldg.
Des Moines, IA 50319
Phone: (515)281-7352

Credential Type: License Registration. **Requirements:** Submit application and fingerprint card. Pay fee. **Fees:** $10 registration fee.

3157

Director (Riverboat Gambling)
Iowa Racing and Gaming Commission
Lucas State Office Bldg.
Des Moines, IA 50319
Phone: (515)281-7352

Credential Type: License Registration. **Requirements:** Submit application and pay fees. **Fees:** $50 license fee.

3158

Director of Surveillance (Riverboat Gambling)
Iowa Racing and Gaming Commission
Lucas State Office Bldg.
Des Moines, IA 50319
Phone: (515)281-7352

Credential Type: License Registration. **Requirements:** Submit application and pay fees. **Fees:** $50 license fee.

3159

Games Manager (Riverboat Gambling)
Iowa Racing and Gaming Commission
Lucas State Office Bldg.
Des Moines, IA 50319
Phone: (515)281-7352

Credential Type: License Registration. **Requirements:** Submit application and pay fees. **Fees:** $50 license fee.

Iowa

3160

Security Director (Riverboat Gambling)
Iowa Racing and Gaming Commission
Lucas State Office Bldg.
Des Moines, IA 50319
Phone: (515)281-7352

Credential Type: License Registration. **Requirements:** Submit application and pay fees. **Fees:** $50 license fee.

3161

Superintendent of Schools (K-12)
Board of Educational Examiners
Grimes State Office Bldg.
Des Moines, IA 50319-0147
Phone: (515)281-3245

Credential Type: Professional Administrator's Certificate. **Duration of License:** Five years. **Requirements:** Holder of or eligible for an Education Certificate. Fiveyears of teaching experience. Master's degree, plus a least 30 semester hours of planned graduate study in administration beyond the master's degree. Overall, at least 45 semester hours of course work must be in school administration and related subjects. Three years' experience as a building principal or other PK-12 district-wide experience or have education agency administration experience. Certificate is renewable.

3162

Track Superintendent (Racetrack)
Iowa State Racing Commission
Lucas State Office Bldg.
Des Moines, IA 50319
Phone: (515)281-7352

Credential Type: License Registration. **Requirements:** Submit application and fingerprint card. Pay fee. **Fees:** $10 registration fee.

Kansas

3163

Director of Racing (Racetrack)
Kansas Racing Commission
3400 VanBuren
Topeka, KS 66611-2228
Phone: (913)296-5800

Credential Type: License Registration. **Requirements:** Submit application and fingerprint card. Pay fee. **Fees:** $20 registration fee.

3164

Director of Security (Racetrack)
Kansas Racing Commission
3400 VanBuren
Topeka, KS 66611-2228
Phone: (913)296-5800

Credential Type: License Registration. **Requirements:** Submit application and fingerprint card. Pay fee. **Fees:** $20 registration fee.

3165

Program Manager (Racetrack)
Kansas Racing Commission
3400 VanBuren
Topeka, KS 66611-2228
Phone: (913)296-5800

Credential Type: License Registration. **Requirements:** Submit application and fingerprint card. Pay fee. **Fees:** $20 registration fee.

3166

Track Superintendent (Racetrack)
Kansas Racing Commission
3400 VanBuren
Topeka, KS 66611-2228
Phone: (913)296-5800

Credential Type: License Registration. **Requirements:** Submit application and fingerprint card. Pay fee. **Fees:** $10 registration fee.

Kentucky

3167

Commission Director of Security (Racetrack)
Kentucky State Racing Commission
PO Box 1080
Lexington, KY 40588
Phone: (606)254-7021

Credential Type: License Registration. **Requirements:** Submit application and fingerprint card. Pay fee. **Fees:** $35 registration fee.

3168

Director of Racing (Racetrack)
Kentucky State Racing Commission
PO Box 1080
Lexington, KY 40588
Phone: (606)254-7021

Credential Type: License Registration. **Requirements:** Submit application and fingerprint card. Pay fee. **Fees:** $35 registration fee.

3169

Track Superintendent (Racetrack)
Kentucky State Racing Commission
PO Box 1080
Lexington, KY 40588
Phone: (606)254-7021

Credential Type: Association Employee and Occupational License. **Requirements:** Submit application and fingerprint card. Pay fee. **Fees:** $10 license fee.

Louisiana

3170

Parish or City School Superintendent
Louisiana Dept. of Education
Box 94064
Baton Rouge, LA 70804-9064
Phone: (504)342-3490

Credential Type: Standard Certificate. **Requirements:** Valid Type A Louisiana Teaching Certificate. Master's degree from an accredited institution. Fiveyears of successful experience as superintendent, assist. superintendent, supervisor of instruction, or principal in a state-approved system. 48 graduate credit semester hours to include: 30 hours educational administration and supervision; 12 hours of professional educations; and six hours of electives from cognate fields. Asst. Superintendents are required to meet the same requirements.

Maine

3171

Assistant School Superintendent
Teacher Certification
Dept. of Education
State House Station 23
Augusta, ME 04333
Phone: (207)289-5944

Credential Type: Assistant Superintendent Certificate. **Duration of License:** Five years. **Requirements:** Bachelor's degree.

Master's degree, preferred in educational administration. Three years teaching experience or three years equivalent teaching experience in an instructional setting. Complete course work in the following areas: community relations; school finance; supervision and evaluation of personnel; civil rights and education laws; organizational theory and planning; educational leadership; educational philosophy and theory; effective instruction; curriculum development; staff development; the exceptional student; and knowledge of the learner and the learning process. One year of previous administrative experience in schools (or equivalent experience as an administrator in an institutional setting) or one year administrator internship. Renewable.

3172

School Superintendent
Teacher Certification
Dept. of Education
State House Station 23
Augusta, ME 04333
Phone: (207)289-5944

Credential Type: Superintendent Certificate. **Duration of License:** Five years. **Requirements:** Bachelor's degree. Master's degree, preferred in educational administration. Three years teaching experience or three years equivalent teaching experience in an instructional setting. Three years of previous administrative experience in schools or equivalent experience as an administrator in an institutional setting. Complete course work in the following areas: community relations; school finance; supervision and evaluation of personnel; civil rights and education laws; organizational theory and planning; educational leadership; educational philosophy and theory; effective instruction; curriculum development; staff development; the exceptional student; and knowledge of the learner and the learning process. Graduate level, state approved, administrator internship or practicum program of a least 15 weeks or one full year of employment as an assistant supervisor/superintendent or mentorship program lasting one academic year in which the mentor is a school superintendent. Renewable.

Maryland

3173

School Superintendent
Dept. of Certification 18100
State Dept. of Education
200 W. Baltimore St.
Baltimore, MD 21201
Phone: (301)333-2142

Credential Type: Superintendent Endorsement. **Requirements:** Eligible for a professional teaching certificate. Master's degree from an accredited institution. Three years of successful teaching experience and two years of administrative and/or supervisory experience. Successful completion of a two year program with graduate courses in administration and supervision. Must have a minimum of 60 semester hours of graduate work.

Massachusetts

3174

School Superintendent/Assistant Superintendent
Massachusetts Dept. of Education
1385 Hancock St.
Quincy, MA 02169
Phone: (617)770-7500

Credential Type: Superintendent Endorsement. **Requirements:** Massachusetts teacher's certificate. Three years of teaching experience. 24 semester hr. pre-practicum. In addition, complete a 150 clock hr. practicum within one year or an 300 clock hr. internship within two years. Must include responsibility for supervision or direction within the same area of education as candidate's teaching certificate. Demonstrate the competencies contained in the five Standards established by the Massachusetts Dept. of Education for administrators. Standard I—Know theories of curriculum design; techniques of supervision and evaluation of personnel; organizational characteristics of schools; sociology and philosophy of education; research in methods of teaching and learning. Standard II—Present instructional goals and policies; the needs and concerns of students, parents, and the community. Standard III-Set goals and establish priorities. Standard IV—Use evaluative procedures to assess the effectiveness of program and personnel. Standard V—Deal in equitable, sensitive, and responsive manner with students, parents, and community.

Michigan

3175

Clinical Laboratory Director
Laboratory Improvement Div.
Dept. of Public Health
PO Box 30035
3500 N. Logan St.
Lansing, MI 48909
Phone: (517)335-8000

Credential Type: Certification. **Duration of License:** Lifetime. **Requirements:** Submit a completed application for a certificate of qualification. Submit supporting documents or give information which shows that they meet the minimum education and experience requirements prescribed by the Department for each field for which certification is requested. Demonstrate that they possess the character, training, and ability to properly administer the technical and scientific operation of a clinical laboratory. **Governing Statute:** Clinical Laboratories Act, Act 235 of 1968, as amended. Public Health Code, Act 368 of 1978, as amended.

Missouri

3176

School Superintendent
Teacher Certification
Dept. of Elementary and Secondary Education
Box 480
Jefferson City, MO 65102
Phone: (314)751-3486

Credential Type: Initial Certificate. **Duration of License:** 10 years. **Requirements:** Valid Missouri teaching certificate. Four years of teaching, supervisory, or administrative experience, or any combination thereof. Completion of a course in psychology and education of the exceptional child. Approved two year graduate program for preparation of the superintendent which must include knowledge and/or competency in each of the following areas: foundation of educational administration; city school administration; school supervision; curriculum construction; research and evaluation; school finance; school law; school staff personnel administration; school/community relations; school plant design and operation. Recommendation for certification from the designated official of the college or university.

To renew the certificate applicant must have five years of experience during the previous 10 years and complete a Professional Development Agreement which would include at least one of the following:

School Superintendent, continued

a minimum of six semester hours of graduate credit appropriate for the superintendency; three AASA-NASE Leadership Training Seminars which are in depth sessions and are usually four or five days in length; four semester hours of graduate credit and one AASA-NASE Leadership Training Institute course; or a planned professional development program equivalent to six semester hours of approved graduate credit.

Montana

3177

Chief of Security (Racetrack)
State of Montana Board of Horse Racing
Dept. of Commerce
1424 9th Ave.
Helena, MT 59620
Phone: (406)444-4287

Credential Type: License Registration. **Requirements:** Submit application and fingerprint card. Pay fee. **Fees:** $20 registration fee.

3178

Director of Racing (Racetrack)
State of Montana Board of Horse Racing
Dept. of Commerce
1424 9th Ave.
Helena, MT 59620
Phone: (406)444-4287

Credential Type: License Registration. **Requirements:** Submit application and fingerprint card. Pay fee. **Fees:** $20 registration fee.

3179

Director at Simulcast Facility (Racetrack)
State of Montana Board of Horse Racing
Dept. of Commerce
1424 9th Ave.
Helena, MT 59620
Phone: (406)444-4287

Credential Type: License Registration. **Requirements:** Submit application and fingerprint card. Pay fee. **Fees:** $35 registration fee.

3180

Director of Simulcast Network (Racetrack)
State of Montana Board of Horse Racing
Dept. of Commerce
1424 9th Ave.
Helena, MT 59620
Phone: (406)444-4287

Credential Type: License Registration. **Requirements:** Submit application and fingerprint card. Pay fee. **Fees:** $35 registration fee.

3181

Parimutuel Manager at Simulcast Network (Racetrack)
State of Montana Board of Horse Racing
Dept. of Commerce
1424 9th Ave.
Helena, MT 59620
Phone: (406)444-4287

Credential Type: License Registration. **Requirements:** Submit application and fingerprint card. Pay fee. **Fees:** $30 registration fee.

3182

Program Manager (Racetrack)
State of Montana Board of Horse Racing
Dept. of Commerce
1424 9th Ave.
Helena, MT 59620
Phone: (406)444-4287

Credential Type: License Registration. **Requirements:** Submit application and fingerprint card. Pay fee. **Fees:** $30 registration fee.

3183

School Superintendent
Teacher Certification
Office of Public Instruction
State Capitol
Helena, MT 59620
Phone: (406)444-3150

Credential Type: Class 3 Administrative Certificate. **Duration of License:** Five years. **Requirements:** Master's degree in school administration or the equivalent. Eligible for Class 1 or two teaching certificate. Full eligibility for a principal endorsement in Montana. Eight graduate credits beyond the master's degree to include school management/facilities, school negotiation, school finance (economics of education), and public relations. Eight graduate credits in elementary education to include elementary administration and elementary curriculum if endorsed at the secondary level or secondary administration and secondary curriculum if endorsed at the elementary level. Three years of teaching experience from the date fully qualified as a principal or one year of administrative experience as an appropriately certified school administrator or one year of a supervised internship as a superintendent. Renewable upon verification of one year of successful experience in the area of endorsement during the valid term of the certificate. Beginning with those certificates expiring in 1992, six quarter credits will also be required for renewal.

Credential Type: Class 5 Administrative Certificate. **Duration of License:** Three years. **Requirements:** Must have a plan of professional intent leading to Class 3 Administrative certification. May be issued to applicants who may not meet course requirements for other general areas but who, within the last five years, have been fully eligible for administrative certification endorsed in one of the following areas: elementary principal, secondary principal, superintendent, or general superintendent. Must be eligible for Class 1, 2, or five teaching certificate. Three years of teaching experience from the date fully qualified as a principal or one year of administrative experience as an appropriately certified school administrator or one year of a supervised administrative internship. Master's degree in school administration or the equivalent to include completed school administration program for the principal. Eight graduate credits in elementary education to include elementary administration and elementary curriculum if endorsed at the secondary level or secondary administration and secondary curriculum if endorsed at the elementary level. Plan of intent must include eight graduate credits beyond the master's degree to include school management/facilities, school negotiation, school finance (economics of education), and public relations. Nonrenewable.

3184

Stable Superintendent (Racetrack)
State of Montana Board of Horse Racing
Dept. of Commerce
1424 9th Ave.
Helena, MT 59620
Phone: (406)444-4287

Credential Type: License Registration. **Requirements:** Submit application and fingerprint card. Pay fee. **Fees:** $20 registration fee.

3185

Track Superintendent (Racetrack)
State of Montana Board of Horse Racing
Dept. of Commerce
1424 9th Ave.
Helena, MT 59620
Phone: (406)444-4287

Credential Type: License Registration. **Requirements:** Submit application and fingerprint card. Pay fee. **Fees:** $20 registration fee.

New Jersey

3186

Bio-Analytical Laboratory Director
State Board of Medical Examiners
28 W. State St.
Trenton, NJ 08608
Phone: (609)292-4843

Credential Type: License. **Requirements:** A doctorate degree plus one year of experience; or a master's degree plus two years of experience; or a bachelor's degree and three years of experience. 21 years of age. Good moral character. Must be a state resident for one year. **Examination:** Written. **Fees:** $150 exam fee. $120 registration fee. **Governing Statute:** NJSA 45:9. NJAC 13:35.

3187

Laboratory Director
Board of Medical Examiners
28 W. State St.
Trenton, NJ 08608
Phone: (609)292-4843

Credential Type: Laboratory Director Specialty License. **Duration of License:** Two years. **Requirements:** A doctorate degree from an accredited university in Biochemical Genetics, Clinical Chemistry, Cytogenetics, Microbiology or Toxicology Chemistry. At least one year of experience. National certification by at least one acceptable certifying agency. **Examination:** Written. **Fees:** $150 license fee. $120 biennial registration fee. **Governing Statute:** NJSA 45:42. NJAC 8:45.

New Mexico

3188

Director of Racing (Racetrack)
New Mexico State Racing Commission
PO Box 8576, Highland Station
Albuquerque, NM 87198
Phone: (505)841-4644

Credential Type: License Registration. **Requirements:** Submit application and fingerprint card. Pay fees. **Fees:** $21 registration fee. $1 notary fee. $23 fingerprint card processing fee.

3189

General Manager (Racetrack)
New Mexico State Racing Commission
PO Box 8576, Highland Station
Albuquerque, NM 87198
Phone: (505)841-4644

Credential Type: License Registration. **Requirements:** Submit application and fingerprint card. Pay fees. **Fees:** $21 registration fee. $1 notary fee. $23 fingerprint card processing fee.

3190

Security Chief (Racetrack)
New Mexico State Racing Commission
PO Box 8576, Highland Station
Albuquerque, NM 87198
Phone: (505)841-4644

Credential Type: License Registration. **Requirements:** Submit application and fingerprint card. Pay fees. **Fees:** $16 registration fee. $1 notary fee. $23 fingerprint card processing fee.

3191

Stable Superintendent (Racetrack)
New Mexico State Racing Commission
PO Box 8576, Highland Station
Albuquerque, NM 87198
Phone: (505)841-4644

Credential Type: License Registration. **Requirements:** Submit application and fingerprint card. Pay fees. **Fees:** $16 registration fee. $1 notary fee. $23 fingerprint card processing fee.

3192

Track Superintendent (Racetrack)
New Mexico State Racing Commission
PO Box 8576, Highland Station
Albuquerque, NM 87198
Phone: (505)841-4644

Credential Type: License Registration. **Requirements:** Submit application and fingerprint card. Pay fees. **Fees:** $16 registration fee. $1 notary fee. $23 fingerprint card processing fee.

New York

3193

Manager, Milk Gathering Plant
Dept. of Agriculture and Markets
Div. of Milk Control
One Winners Circle
Albany, NY 12235
Phone: (518)457-1772

Credential Type: License. **Duration of License:** Five years. **Examination:** Written and practical. **Fees:** $5 application fee. $2 renewal fee. **Governing Statute:** Article four Section 56b, 57, and 57a of Agriculture and Markets Law, and Title 1, New York Consolidated Rules and Regulations, Part 6.

3194

Track Manager (Harness or Quarter Horse Racing)
New York State Racing and Wagering Board
400 Broome St.
New York, NY 10013
Phone: (212)219-4230

Credential Type: License Registration. **Duration of License:** One year. **Requirements:** Submit application, F.B.I fingerprint card, New York state fingerprint card, and three photos. Pay fees. **Fees:** $20 regis-

New York

Track Manager (Harness or Quarter Horse Racing), continued

tration fee. $44 New York state fingerprint card processing fee (valid for five years).

3195

Track Manager (Thoroughbred Racing)
New York State Racing and Wagering Board
400 Broome St.
New York, NY 10013
Phone: (212)219-4230

Credential Type: License Registration. **Duration of License:** One year. **Requirements:** Submit application, F.B.I fingerprint card, New York state fingerprint card, and three photos. Pay fees. **Fees:** $20 registration fee. $44 New York state fingerprint card processing fee (valid for five years).

North Carolina

3196

School Superintendent
Certification Section
State Dept. of Public Instruction
Raleigh, NC 27603
Phone: (919)733-4125

Credential Type: Administrator II Certificate. **Duration of License:** Five years. **Requirements:** Three years of satisfactory teaching experience or equivalent. Sixth-year certificate (degree) from an accredited institution including the completion of an approved program in administration. Pass NTE examination. Institutional recommendation. Must have 10 semester hours of college credit completed in the five-year period immediately preceding the date of application. **Examination:** National Teacher Examination. **Fees:** $30 application fee. $30 renewal fee.

Credential Type: Administrator III Certificate. **Duration of License:** Five years. **Requirements:** Three years of satisfactory teaching experience or equivalent. Doctorate degree in an approved program of study. Pass NTE examination. Institutional recommendation. Must have 10 semester hours of college credit completed in the five-year period immediately preceding the date of application. **Examination:** National Teacher Examination. **Fees:** $30 application fee. $30 renewal fee.

North Dakota

3197

Chief of Security (Racetrack)
North Dakota Racing Commission
State Capitol Bldg.
Bismarck, ND 58505
Phone: (701)224-2210

Credential Type: License Registration. **Requirements:** Submit application and fingerprint card. Pay fee. **Fees:** $10 license fee. $10 duplicate license fee.

3198

Director of Racing (Racetrack)
North Dakota Racing Commission
State Capitol Bldg.
Bismarck, ND 58505
Phone: (701)224-2210

Credential Type: License Registration. **Requirements:** Submit application and fingerprint card. Pay fee. **Fees:** $10 license fee. $10 duplicate license fee.

3199

School Superintendent
Director of Certification
State Dept. of Public Instruction
Bismarck, ND 58505
Phone: (701)224-2264

Credential Type: Superintendent Certificate. **Duration of License:** Entrance one year, renewable for five years. **Requirements:** Master's degree in school administration. North Dakota Educator's Professional Certificate. 20 semester hours of credit in both elementary and secondary school administration. Four years experience, of which two years must be in an administrative position in an accredited system. Renewable after four semester hours of additional work or two semester hours of additional work plus attendance at state, regional, or national conferences, and successful recommendation by supervisor.

3200

Track Superintendent (Racetrack)
North Dakota Racing Commission
State Capitol Bldg.
Bismarck, ND 58505
Phone: (701)224-2210

Credential Type: License Registration. **Requirements:** Submit application and fingerprint card. Pay fee. **Fees:** $10 license fee. $10 duplicate license fee.

Ohio

3201

Chief of Security (Thoroughbred, Standardbred, and Quarter Horse Racing)
Ohio State Racing Commission
State Office Tower
77 S. High St., 18th Fl.
Columbus, OH 43266-0416
Phone: (614)466-2757

Credential Type: License Registration. **Requirements:** Submit application and fingerprint card. Pay fee. **Fees:** $25 registration fee.

3202

General Manager (Thoroughbred, Standardbred, and Quarter Horse Racing)
Ohio State Racing Commission
State Office Tower
77 S. High St., 18th Fl.
Columbus, OH 43266-0416
Phone: (614)466-2757

Credential Type: License Registration. **Requirements:** Submit application and fingerprint card. Pay fee. **Fees:** $25 registration fee.

3203

Mutuel Manager (Thoroughbred, Standardbred, and Quarter Horse Racing)
Ohio State Racing Commission
State Office Tower
77 S. High St., 18th Fl.
Columbus, OH 43266-0416
Phone: (614)466-2757

Credential Type: License Registration. **Requirements:** Submit application and fingerprint card. Pay fee. **Fees:** $25 registration fee.

Oklahoma

3204

Burglar Alarm Service and Installation Company Manager
Oklahoma State Dept. of Health
Occupational Licensing Service
1000 N.E. Tenth
PO Box 53551
Oklahoma City, OK 73152
Phone: (405)271-5217

Credential Type: License. **Duration of License:** One year. **Requirements:** 21 years of age. Two years of experience in the alarm industry. No felony convictions. Security verification clearance. **Examination:** Burglar Alarm Manager Examination. **Fees:** $50 exam fee. $50 application fee. $50 renewal fee.

3205

Fire Alarm Service and Installation Company Manager
Oklahoma State Dept. of Health
Occupational Licensing Service
1000 N.E. Tenth
PO Box 53551
Oklahoma City, OK 73152
Phone: (405)271-5217

Credential Type: License. **Duration of License:** One year. **Requirements:** 21 years of age. Security verification clearance. No felony convictions. **Examination:** Fire Alarm Manager Examination. **Fees:** $50 exam fee. $50 application fee. $50 renewal fee.

3206

Track Manager (Racetrack)
Oklahoma Horse Racing Commission
6501 N. Broadway, Ste. 180
Oklahoma City, OK 73116
Phone: (405)848-0404

Credential Type: License Registration. **Duration of License:** One year. **Requirements:** Submit application and fingerprint card. Pay fee. **Fees:** $50 registration fee. $50 annual renewal.

Oregon

3207

School Superintendent
Teacher Standards and Practices Commission
630 Center St. NE, Ste. 200
Salem, OR 97310-0320
Phone: (503)378-3586

Credential Type: Basic Superintendent Endorsement. **Duration of License:** Two years. **Requirements:** Master's degree. Recommendation from an approved teacher education institution or current out-of-state administrative certificate. Passing scores on CBEST. Out-of-state prepared applicants may submit their passing scores on the Core Battery of the National Teacher Examination, in lieu of the CBEST. 18 quarter hours of graduate credit in school administration, including a supervised practicum or internship of six quarter hours and completed subsequent to master's degree. One year of successful administrative experience within the three-year period immediately preceding application or nine quarter hours of preparation in educational administration within the past three years. **Examination:** California Basic Educational Skills Test.

Credential Type: Standard Superintendent Endorsement. **Duration of License:** Five years. **Requirements:** Three years of successful administration experience in Oregon schools on a Basic Administrative Certificate. Recommendation of approved college or university where applicant completed graduate program for standard school administrator. 24 quarter hours of graduate credit in school administration, in addition to those required for the basic endorsement, completed subsequent to master's degree.

Pennsylvania

3208

School Superintendent/Assistant Superintendent
Bureau of Certification
Dept. of Education
333 Market St.
Harrisburg, PA 17126-0333
Phone: (717)787-2967

Credential Type: Administrative Letters of Eligibility—Superintendent Endorsement. **Requirements:** Complete Pennsylvania approved graduate level program of educational administrative study equal to two full academic years of study or have been prepared in an approved out-of-state program. Six years of professional, certificated school service which includes three years of supervisory or administrative experience. Recommendation of preparing institution. Complete six credit hours of course work, every five years of service, as determined by the Bureau of Basic Education.

3209

Track Manager (Harness Racing)
Pennsylvania State Harness Racing Commission
2301 N. Cameron St.
Harrisburg, PA 17110-9408
Phone: (717)787-5196

Credential Type: License Registration. **Duration of License:** Three years. **Requirements:** Submit application, three photos, and fingerprint card. Pay fee. **Fees:** $30 registration fee. $5 duplicate license. $33 fingerprint processing fee.

Rhode Island

3210

School Superintendent
Office of Teacher Certification
State Dept. of Education
22 Hayes St.
Providence, RI 02908
Phone: (401)277-2675

Credential Type: Provisional School Superintendent Certificate. **Duration of License:** Three years. **Requirements:** Doctorate, certificate of advanced graduate study, or master's degree. Complete 36 semester hours of graduate credit including work in the following areas: school/community relations; curriculum construction; school administration; supervision of instruction; supervision and evaluation of professional staff; educational research; program evaluation; school plant planning; and school finance. Hold or be eligible for a Rhode Island teaching certificate. Eight years of educational experience that includes both teaching and administration. Nonrenewable.

Credential Type: Professional Superintendent Certificate. **Duration of License:** Five years. **Requirements:** Complete six graduate credits in educational administration while on the provisional certificate. Three years of service as a superintendent of schools in Rhode Island.

Credential Type: Life Professional Superintendent Certificate. **Duration of License:** Permanent. **Requirements:** Doctorate degree or certificate of advanced study from

School Superintendent, continued

an approved institution in educational administration, supervision, and curriculum or 30 semester hours of graduate credit beyond a master's degree which includes 21 semester hours in educational administration, supervision, and curriculum. Must have six years of experience as a superintendent of schools, of which three must be in Rhode Island.

South Carolina

3211

School Superintendent
Teacher Education and Certification
State Dept. of Education
Rutledge Bldg., Rm. 1015
Columbia, SC 29201
Phone: (803)734-8464

Credential Type: School Superintendent Certificate. **Requirements:** Valid Principal's or Teacher's Professional Certificate. A minimum score of 590 on the NTE in Administration and Supervision. Seven years of educational experience in teaching and administrating with a minimum of two years as a school administrator. Complete an advanced program approved for the training of school superintendents. **Examination:** National Teacher Examination in Administration and Supervision.

South Dakota

3212

School Superintendent
Teacher Education and Certification
State Dept. of Education
700 Governor's Drive
Pierre, SD 57501
Phone: (605)773-3553

Credential Type: Superintendent Certificate Endorsement. **Requirements:** Master's degree. Hold a valid teaching certificate. Three years of experience in the public schools, two years of which must be classroom teaching. Complete an approved program for superintendents at a college or university. One year of successful supervised associate instructor experience as a school principal or assistant school principal.

Credential Type: Advanced Superintendent Certificate Endorsement. **Requirements:** Hold a Superintendent Certificate Endorsement. Complete an approved six-year specialist degree or doctoral degree program for superintendents at a college or university.

Texas

3213

Association Officer/Director (Racetrack)
Texas Racing Commission
PO Box 12080
Austin, TX 78711
Phone: (512)794-8461

Credential Type: License Registration. **Requirements:** Submit application and fingerprint card. Pay fee. **Fees:** $75 registration fee.

Vermont

3214

Director of Racing (Greyhound Racing)
Vermont Racing Commission
State Office Bldg.
Montpelier, VT 05602
Phone: (802)828-3429

Credential Type: License Registration. **Requirements:** Submit application and fingerprint card. Pay fee. **Fees:** $20 registration fee. $5 duplicate license.

3215

School Superintendent
Teacher Licensure
State Dept. of Education
Montpelier, VT 05602-2703
Phone: (802)828-2445

Credential Type: Level One: Initial License. **Duration of License:** Two years. **Requirements:** Master's degree or equivalent with a concentration in educational administration. At least five years of educational experience consisting of: a minimum of three years teaching experience; a minimum of two years of successful school management experience. Meet competencies as determined by the Standards Board.

Credential Type: Level Two: Professional Administrator's License. **Duration of License:** Seven years. **Requirements:** Two years of experience under a Level One License. Demonstrate the following characteristics: ability to plan instruction; ability to maintain a positive learning environment; ability to conduct learning experiences for individuals as well as groups; knowledge of content area; and interest and motivation in continuing professional development. Renewal requires nine credit hours, or the equivalent of educational development activity, per license endorsement area.

Virginia

3216

Assistant General Manager (Racetrack)
Virginia Racing Commission
PO Box 1123
Richmond, VA 23208
Phone: (804)371-7363

Credential Type: License Registration. **Requirements:** Submit application and fingerprint card. Pay fee. **Fees:** $10 registration fee.

3217

Director of Security (Racetrack)
Virginia Racing Commission
PO Box 1123
Richmond, VA 23208
Phone: (804)371-7363

Credential Type: License Registration. **Requirements:** Submit application and fingerprint card. Pay fee. **Fees:** $10 registration fee.

3218

General Manager (Racetrack)
Virginia Racing Commission
PO Box 1123
Richmond, VA 23208
Phone: (804)371-7363

Credential Type: License Registration. **Requirements:** Submit application and fingerprint card. Pay fee. **Fees:** $10 registration fee.

3219

Mutuel Manager (Racetrack)
Virginia Racing Commission
PO Box 1123
Richmond, VA 23208
Phone: (804)371-7363

Credential Type: License Registration. **Requirements:** Submit application and fingerprint card. Pay fee. **Fees:** $10 registration fee.

3220

Program Director (Racetrack)
Virginia Racing Commission
PO Box 1123
Richmond, VA 23208
Phone: (804)371-7363

Credential Type: License Registration. **Requirements:** Submit application and fingerprint card. Pay fee. **Fees:** $10 registration fee.

3221

School Division Superintendent
Administrative Director
Office of Professional Development
 and Teacher Education
Dept. of Education
PO Box 6-Q
Richmond, VA 23216-2060
Phone: (804)225-2094

Credential Type: Division Superintendent Endorsement. **Requirements:** Master's degree or preparing a doctoral program. 60 semester hours of graduate work to include courses in: history of philosophy of education; supervision and curriculum development; administration; finance; law; personnel administration; schoolcommunity relations; school plant planning; research or statistical methods.

3222

Track Superintendent (Racetrack)
Virginia Racing Commission
PO Box 1123
Richmond, VA 23208
Phone: (804)371-7363

Credential Type: License Registration. **Requirements:** Submit application and fingerprint card. Pay fee. **Fees:** $10 registration fee.

Washington

3223

School Superintendent
Superintendent of Public Instruction
Professional Education and
 Certification
Old Capitol Bldg. FG-11
Seattle, WA 98504-3211
Phone: (206)753-6773

Credential Type: Initial Superintendent Certificate. **Duration of License:** Seven years. **Requirements:** Hold or be eligible for a regular teaching or Educational Staff Associate Certificate. Master's degree. Complete an approved preparation program for the superintendency. Complete 15 quarter hours of graduate study beyond the master's degree in course work related to education.

Credential Type: Continuing Superintendent Certificate. **Duration of License:** Five years. **Requirements:** Initial Superintendent Certificate. Complete a total of 30 quarter hours of graduate study beyond the master's degree in course work related to education. Renewable upon completion of 150 clock hours of full-time administration during the life of the certificate.

West Virginia

3224

School Superintendent
Dept. of Education
Office of Educational Personnel
 Development
1900 Washington St. E
Charleston, WV 25305
Phone: (800)982-2378

Credential Type: Certification. **Requirements:** U.S. citizen. 18 years old. Masters degree and completion of approved program. Five years educational experience in public shcools, including three years of classroom experience. Never convicted of a felony. **Examination:** Yes. **Fees:** $5 Application. $5 Renewal.

Wisconsin

3225

Director of Racing (Racetrack)
Wisconsin Racing Board
PO Box 7975
Madison, WI 53707-7975
Phone: (608)267-3291

Credential Type: License Registration. **Requirements:** Submit application and two sets of fingerprint cards. Pay fee. **Fees:** $50 registration fee. $20 duplicate license.

3226

**General Manager/Assistant General
 Manager (Racetrack)**
Wisconsin Racing Board
PO Box 7975
Madison, WI 53707-7975
Phone: (608)267-3291

Credential Type: License Registration. **Requirements:** Submit application and two sets of fingerprint cards. Pay fee. **Fees:** $100 registration fee. $20 duplicate license.

3227

Mutuel Manager (Racetrack)
Wisconsin Racing Board
PO Box 7975
Madison, WI 53707-7975
Phone: (608)267-3291

Credential Type: License Registration. **Requirements:** Submit application and two sets of fingerprint cards. Pay fee. **Fees:** $50 registration fee. $20 duplicate license.

3228

School District Superintendent
Teacher Education, Licensing, and
 Placement
Box 7841
Madison, WI 53707-7841
Phone: (608)266-1027

Credential Type: District Superintendent License. **Duration of License:** Five years. **Requirements:** Hold or be eligible to hold a principal license. Complete an approved specialist degree program for the superintendent. Complete 12 graduate semester hours in the following studies: superintendency; advanced program planning and evaluation; economics of education; advanced politics of education; personnel administration; collective bargaining and contract administration; and a practicum or internship.

3229

Track Superintendent (Racetrack)
Wisconsin Racing Board
PO Box 7975
Madison, WI 53707-7975
Phone: (608)267-3291

Credential Type: License Registration. **Requirements:** Submit application and two sets of fingerprint cards. Pay fee. **Fees:** $50 registration fee. $20 duplicate license.

Wyoming

3230

Mutuel Official (Racetrack)
Wyoming State Pari-Mutuel
  Commission
Barrett Bldg., 3rd Fl.
Cheyenne, WY 82002
Phone: (307)777-5887

Credential Type: License Registration. **Requirements:** Submit application and fingerprint card. Pay fee. **Fees:** $20 registration fee. $10 duplicate license.

3231

School Superintendent
State Dept. of Education
Certification and Accreditation
Services Unit, Hathaway Bldg.
Cheyenne, WY 82002
Phone: (307)777-7291

Credential Type: Superintendent Endorsement. **Requirements:** Teacher certification and Education Specialist certification. Sixty semester hours of graduate work, which includes a master's degree and 30 semester hours in the following courses of study: school administration and supervision; curriculum and instruction; staff and program evaluation; school law; introductory finance; and special phases of school administration (such as guidance and community relations). Three years of classroom teaching experience in a K-12 setting.

Geologists and Geophysicists

The following states grant licenses in this occupational category as of the date of publication:

Alabama	Arkansas	Florida	Maine	South Carolina	Wyoming
Alaska	California	Georgia	North Carolina	Tennessee	
Arizona	Delaware	Idaho	Oregon	Virginia	

Alabama

3232

Geologist
Geological Survey of Alabama
PO Box O
420 Hackberry Lane
Tuscaloosa, AL 35486-9780
Phone: (205)349-2852

Credential Type: Registration. **Requirements:** A committee has been formed to draft regulations for the professional registration of geologists.

Alaska

3233

Professional Geologist
Dept. of Commerce and Economic Development
Div. of Occupational Licensing
PO Box D
Juneau, AK 99811-0800
Phone: (907)465-2534
Fax: (907)465-2974

Alternate Information: American Institute of Professional Geologists, 7828 Vance Dr., Ste. 103, Arvada, CO 80003. Phone: (303)431-0831.

Credential Type: Professional Geologist Certification. **Duration of License:** No expiration date. **Requirements:** Licensing is based solely on the registration requirements of the American Institute of Professional Geologists. **Fees:** $30 certification fee. **Governing Statute:** Alaska Statutes 08.02. Professional Regulations 12 AAC 02.220.

Arizona

3234

Geologist
Board of Technical Registration
1951 W. Camelback, Ste. 250
Phoenix, AZ 85015
Phone: (602)255-4053

Credential Type: Registration to Practice. **Duration of License:** Three years. **Requirements:** Be of good moral character. Have at least eight years education or experience, or combination of both with at least four years of experience. Pass in-training and professional examination administered by the board. **Examination:** In-training and professional (principles and practices) examinations. **Exemptions:** The in-training exam may be waived for candidates who have a degree in geology. **Fees:** $90 application fee. $120 exam fee. $126 renewal fee.

Credential Type: Registration without examination. **Requirements:** Hold a valid registration in another state, jurisdiction, territory, or country. Meet experience and education requirements similar to those of Arizona, or have been actively engaged in the profession for at least 10 years. **Fees:** $90 application fee. $126 renewal fee.

3235

Geologist-in-Training
Board of Technical Registration
1951 W. Camelback, Ste. 250
Phoenix, AZ 85015
Phone: (602)255-4053

Credential Type: In-training registration. **Requirements:** Be of good moral character. To qualify for the in-training examination on the basis of education, must be a graduate of a four-year degree program of an accredited college or university, with a major in geology.

To qualify for the in-training examination on the basis of experience, must have at least four years of education or experience or both directly related to the practice of geology. **Examination:** In-training examination (fundamentals). **Fees:** $30 application fee. $120 exam fee.

Arkansas

3236

Geologist
Arkansas Board of Registration for Professional Geologists
3815 W. Roosevelt Rd.
Little Rock, AR 72204
Phone: (501)371-1488

Credential Type: License. **Requirements:** Good moral character; references required. Graduate of an accredited college with a major in geology, engineering geology, or geological engineering. **Examination:** Yes. **Fees:** $20 Written examination. $20 Application.

California

3237

Engineering Geologist
Board of Registration for Geologists and Geophysicists
400 R St., Ste. 4060
Sacramento, CA 95814-6200
Phone: (916)445-1920

Credential Type: License and Certification. **Duration of License:** Two years. **Requirements:** Must be a registered geologist. Have at least three years of experience

Engineering Geologist, continued

as an engineering geologist. **Examination:** Certified Engineering Geologist examination. **Reciprocity:** No. **Fees:** $100 application and registration fee.

3238

Geologist

Board of Registration for Geologists and Geophysicists
400 R St., Ste. 4060
Sacramento, CA 95814-6200
Phone: (916)445-1920

Credential Type: License and Registration. **Duration of License:** Two years. **Requirements:** Have a B.A. or B.S. in Geology. Have at least five years of experience. **Examination:** Geologist examination. **Reciprocity:** With Arizona and Idaho. **Fees:** $100 application and registration fee.

3239

Geophysicist

Board of Registration for Geologists and Geophysicists
400 R St., Ste. 4060
Sacramento, CA 95814-6200
Phone: (916)445-1920

Credential Type: License and Registration. **Duration of License:** Two years. **Requirements:** Have a B.A. or B.S. in Geophysics. Have at least five years of experience. **Examination:** Geophysicist examination. **Reciprocity:** No. **Fees:** $100 application and registration fee.

Delaware

3240

Professional Geologist

Board of Registration Geologists
Dept. of Administrative Services
Div. of Professional Regulation
PO Box 1401
Dover, DE 19903
Phone: (302)739-4522

Credential Type: Professional geologist certificate of registration. **Duration of License:** Two years. **Requirements:** Graduate of an accredited college or university with a mahor in geology; or completion of 30 credit hours of geology or its subdivisions, of which 24 credits are third or fourth year courses or graduate courses. Have five years experience in geologic work, with a minimum of three years in a position of responsible charge. Have experience, competency, and integrity satisfactory to the board. **Fees:** $25 application fee. $122 initial license fee. $122 renewal fee. **Governing Statute:** Delaware Code, Title 24, Chapter 36.

Florida

3241

Professional Geologist

Board of Professional Geologists
Dept. of Professional Regulation
1940 N. Monroe St.
Tallahassee, FL 32399-0764
Phone: (904)488-1105

Credential Type: Professional Geologist License. **Duration of License:** Two years. **Requirements:** Contact licensing body for application information. **Examination:** State examination.

Georgia

3242

Geologist

State Board of Registration for Professional Geologists
Sciences and Professions Section
Professional Examining Boards
166 Pryor St., SW
Atlanta, GA 30303
Phone: (404)656-2281

Credential Type: Geologist Certificate of Registration. **Duration of License:** Two years. **Requirements:** Be of good ethical character. Graduate from a board-approved accredited college or university, with a major in geology, engineering geology, or geological engineering, or with 45 quarter hours in geological science courses leading to a major in geology. Have at least seven years of professional geological work experience, with a minimum of three years under the supervision of a registered geologist, registered civil engineer, or other supervision acceptable to the board. Education may be substituted for the experience requirement up to a maximum of two years, with one year of undergraduate education counting as one-half year of experience and one year of graduate education counting as one year of experience. **Examination:** Written examination. **Reciprocity:** Yes, on the basis of comparable licensing requirements. **Fees:** $20 application fee. $90 initial registration fee. $90 reciprocal registration fee. $90 renewal fee. **Governing Statute:** Official Code of Georgia Annotated 43-19. Registration of Geologists Act of 1975.

Idaho

3243

Geologist

Board of Registration for Professional Geologists
Len B. Jordan Bldg.
650 W. State St., Rm. B-83
Boise, ID 83720
Phone: (208)334-2268

Credential Type: Registration. **Requirements:** Complete 30 semester units in courses in geological sciences leading to a degree in the geological sciences, with at least 24 units at the junior, senior, or graduate level. Have at least seven years of professional geological work, with a minimum of three years of professional geological work under the supervision of a registered geologist, or five years of professive experience in responsible charge of geological work. Each year of undergraduate study in the geological sciences may count as one-half year of experience up to a maximum of two years credit. Each year of graduate study in the geological sciences may count as one year of experience. Teaching in the geological sciences at the college level may also be credited year for year toward the experience requirement. In no case shall more than four years of credit toward the experience requirement be given for study or teaching. Submit three professional references. **Examination:** Board administered examination. **Reciprocity:** Only with California and Oregon. **Fees:** $100 registration fee (includes $80 application fee).

Maine

3244

Geologist

Board of Certification for Geologists and Soil Scientists
Dept. of Professional and Financial Regulation
State House Station 35
Augusta, ME 04333
Phone: (207)582-8723

Credential Type: Geologist Certification. **Duration of License:** Two years. **Requirements:** Meet one of the following sets of requirements: (1) Be a graduate of an accredited college or university with a major in geological sciences. (2) Complete 30 credits in geological sciences at an accredited college or university. (3) Have at least seven years of professional geological work, including either a minimum of three years of professional geological work under the supervision of a qualified geologist or a minimum of five years of responsible charge of geological work.

In addition, must have acquired seven years of experience in responsible charge of geological work. An undergraduate degree with 30 credit hours or more in geological science courses may count as two years of experience, and each year of graduate study in the geological sciences may count as one-half year of experience, up to a maximum of two years of credit. **Examination:** Yes. **Fees:** $20 exam fee. $45 certification fee. $45 renewal fee. **Governing Statute:** 32 M.S.R.A., Chap. 73.

North Carolina

3245

Geologist
North Carolina State Board for Licensing of Geologists
PO Box 27402
Raleigh, NC 27611
Phone: (919)781-7240

Credential Type: License. **Duration of License:** Two years. **Requirements:** Degree from an accredited college or university in geology, engineering geology or a related geological science; or the completion of 30 semester hours or the equivalent in geological science courses leading to a major in geology. **Examination:** Written. **Fees:** $55 application fee. $25 exam fee. $30—$70 renewal fee.

Oregon

3246

Engineering Geologist
Oregon State Board of Geologist Examiners
750 Front St. NE, Ste. 240
Salem, OR 97310
Phone: (503)378-4180

Credential Type: License. **Duration of License:** One year. **Requirements:** Must be a registered Professional Geologist plus have additional experience. **Examination:** Yes. **Fees:** $40 exam fee. $15 license fee. $15 renewal fee. **Governing Statute:** ORS 672.505 to 672.705.

3247

Geologist, Professional
Oregon State Board of Geologist Examiners
750 Front St. NE, Ste. 240
Salem, OR 97310
Phone: (503)378-4180

Credential Type: License. **Duration of License:** One year. **Requirements:** Seven years experience and a degree in Geology or a related earth science. **Examination:** Yes. **Fees:** $80 exam fee. $3 certificate fee. $30 renewal fee. **Governing Statute:** ORS 672.505 to 672.705.

South Carolina

3248

Geologist
State Board of Registration for Geologists
PO Box 11904
Columbia, SC 29211-1904
Phone: (803)253-4127
Fax: (803)252-3432

Credential Type: Professional Geologist Registration. **Duration of License:** One year. **Requirements:** Complete application and pass advanced GRE in Geology. Become registered as a geologist-in-training. Pass Part II of the state exam. **Examination:** Advanced GRE in Geology. Part II of state examination. **Fees:** $10 application fee. $100 registration fee. $75 renewal fee.

Credential Type: Geologist-in-Training Registration. **Requirements:** Complete application and pass advanced GRE in Geology. **Examination:** Advanced GRE in Geology. **Fees:** $10 application fee. $50 registration fee. $40 renewal fee.

Tennessee

3249

Geologist, Professional
Dept. of Commerce and Insurance
Div. of Regulatory Boards
Volunteer Plaza Bldg., 2nd Fl.
500 James Robertson Pky.
Nashville, TN 37219
Phone: (615)741-3449

Credential Type: License. **Duration of License:** Five years. **Requirements:** Geologist must have college degree in geology or geological engineering; Professional Geologist must have an additional five years experience (including graduate study). Must adhere to exemplary conduct and ethical behavior. **Reciprocity:** No. **Fees:** $25 Application.

Virginia

3250

Geologist
Virginia Board of Geology
Dept. of Commerce
3600 W. Broad St.
Richmond, VA 23230
Phone: (804)367-8595

Credential Type: License. **Requirements:** Must have a bachelor's degree from an accredited university with a major in geology or completed 30 semester hours equivalent in geological science courses leading to a major in geology. Must have seven years of work experience as specified by the Board. **Examination:** Yes.

Wyoming

3251

Geologist
State Board of Professional Geologists
Box 3008, Univ. Sta.
Laramie, WY 82071
Phone: (307)766-2490
Fax: (307)766-2605

Credential Type: Professional Geologist Registration. **Duration of License:** One year. **Requirements:** Have at least a bachelors degree in geology or associated science. Be recognized as a certified geologist-in-training. Have at least four years of active professional practice in geologic work. **Examination:** Professional geologist examination. **Fees:** $94 registration fee. $75 exam fee. $30 renewal fee. **Governing Statute:** Wyoming Statutes 33-41.

Credential Type: Geologist-in-Training Certification. **Duration of License:** One year. **Requirements:** Have at least a bachelors degree in geology or associated science. **Examination:** Fundamentals of Geology Examination. **Fees:** $47 certification fee. $75 exam fee. $10 renewal fee. **Governing Statute:** Wyoming Statutes 33-41.

Guards

The following states grant licenses in this occupational category as of the date of publication:

Alaska	Delaware	Illinois	Michigan	New Hampshire	Ohio	Utah
Arizona	District of	Iowa	Minnesota	New Mexico	Oklahoma	Vermont
Arkansas	Columbia	Kansas	Montana	New York	South Dakota	Virginia
California	Georgia	Kentucky	Nebraska	North Carolina	Tennessee	Wisconsin
Connecticut	Hawaii	Maryland	Nevada	North Dakota	Texas	Wyoming

Alaska

3252

Security Guard
Alaska State Troopers
Security Guard Licensing
5700 E. Tudor Rd.
Anchorage, AK 99507
Phone: (907)269-5594

Credential Type: Temporary Guard Permit. **Duration of License:** 180 days. **Requirements:** Complete at least eight hours of general pre-assignment training. **Fees:** $25 license fee. $43 fingerprint fee.

Credential Type: Guard License. **Duration of License:** Two years. **Authorization:** Required of those who work for an agency which contracts guard services to other businesses. **Requirements:** Complete 40 hours of in-service training within 180 days after employment. **Fees:** $25 license fee. $50 renewal fee. $43 fingerprint fee.

Credential Type: Armed Guard License. **Duration of License:** Two years. **Authorization:** Must have a firearms training certificate. Complete 40 hours of in-service training within 180 days after employment. **Fees:** $25 license fee. $50 renewal fee. $43 fingerprint fee.

Arizona

3253

Security Guard
Dept. of Public Safety
PO Box 6328
Phoenix, AZ 85005
Phone: (602)223-2361

Credential Type: Security guard registration certificate. **Duration of License:** Three years. **Requirements:** Be a citizen or legal resident of the United States. Be at least 18 years of age. No convictions of a felony or any crime involving fraud, physical violence, illegal sexual conduct, or illegal use or possession of a deadly weapon. Not have had a registration certificate or license revoked in Arizona. Not be on probation or parole for any crime nor have any outstanding arrest warrants. **Exemptions:** Regularly commissioned peace officer **Fees:** $20 certificate fee. $20 renewal fee. **Governing Statute:** Arizona Revised Statutes, Title 32, Chapter 26.

Credential Type: Provisional certificate. **Duration of License:** 180 days. **Requirements:** Comply with application requirements and appear to meet requirements for a security guard registration certificate. **Fees:** $10 application fee, plus cost of fingerprint processing. **Governing Statute:** Arizona Revised Statutes, Title 32, Chapter 26.

Arkansas

3254

Armored Car Guard
Arkansas State Police
3 Natural Resources Dr.
PO Box 5901
Little Rock, AR 72215
Phone: (501)244-3101

Credential Type: License. **Duration of License:** One year. **Requirements:** 21 years of age. High school graduate or equivalent. Complete required training course (Board rule 8.5). Never been convicted of a felony, class A misdemeanor, crime. Never declared incompetent by reason of mental defect or disease. Not suffering from habitual drunkenness or from narcotics addiction or dependence. Not been discharged from the armed services under any conditions other than honorable. **Examination:** Yes. **Fees:** No fee for the written examination. $13 License. $13 Renewal (annual).

3255

Security Guard
Arkansas State Police
3 Natural Resources Dr.
PO Box 5901
Little Rock, AR 72215
Phone: (501)224-3101

Credential Type: License. **Duration of License:** One year. **Requirements:** Must have completed training course as outlined in Board Rule 8.8. 21 years of age (18 if no weapon is carried). High school graduate or equivalent. Never convicted of a felony, class A misdemeanor or crime. Must not have been declared incompetent by reason of mental defect or disease. Must not be suffering from habitual drunkenness or from narcotics addiction or dependence. Must not have been discharged from the armed services under other than honorable conditions. **Examination:** Yes. **Fees:** $13 License. $13 Renewal.

California

3256

Private Patrol Operator
Bureau of Collection and
  Investigative Services
400 R St., Ste. 2001
Sacramento, CA 95814-6234
Phone: (916)445-7366

Credential Type: Private Patrol Operator License. **Requirements:** At least one year or 2000 hours of compensated experience as a patrolman, guard, or watchman, or equivalent.

All private patrol operators who employ armed security guards must maintain appropriate liability insurance. **Examination:** Written examination. **Fees:** $100 application fee. $350 license fee. $27 fingerprint processing fee. **Governing Statute:** Private Investigator Act, Business and Professions Code, Sect. 7541.

3257

Protection Dog Operator
Bureau of Collection and
 Investigative Services
400 R St., Ste. 2001
Sacramento, CA 95814-6234
Phone: (916)445-7366

Credential Type: Protection Dog Operator License. **Requirements:** Previous experience in training a protection dog for others. **Examination:** Written examination. **Exemptions:** Bureau license not required if individual operates exclusively in a city and/or county that has adopted a licensing and regulation ordinance that is equivalent to or greater than the requirements of the state bureau. **Fees:** $25 application fee. $250 license fee. $27 fingerprint processing fee. **Governing Statute:** Private Investigator Act, Business and Professions Code, Sect. 7541.

3258

Security Guard (Racetrack)
California Horse Racing Board
1010 Hurley Way, Ste. 190
Sacramento, CA 95825
Phone: (916)920-7178

Credential Type: License Registration. **Requirements:** Submit application and fingerprint card. Pay fee. **Fees:** $75 registration fee.

3259

Security Officer (Racetrack)
California Horse Racing Board
1010 Hurley Way, Ste. 190
Sacramento, CA 95825
Phone: (916)920-7178

Credential Type: License Registration. **Requirements:** Submit application and fingerprint card. Pay fee. **Fees:** $75 registration fee.

Connecticut

3260

Security Employee (Racetrack)
Connecticut Div. of Special Revenue
Russell Rd.
PO Box 11424
Newington, CT 06111-0424
Phone: (203)566-2756

Credential Type: License Registration. **Requirements:** Submit application and fingerprint card. Pay fee. **Fees:** $5 registration fee.

Delaware

3261

Security Employee (Racetrack)
Delaware Harness Racing
 Commission
2320 S. DuPont Hwy.
Dover, DE 19901
Phone: (302)739-4811

Credential Type: License Registration. **Requirements:** Submit application and fingerprint card. Pay fee. **Fees:** $5 registration fee.

District of Columbia

3262

Security Guard
License and Certification Div.
Occupational and Professional
 Licensure Administration
Consumer and Regulatory Affairs
 Dept.
PO Box 37200
Washington, DC 20013-7200
Phone: (202)727-7823
Phone: (202)727-7480

Alternate Information: 614 H St., NW, Washington, DC 20001

Credential Type: Certification. **Duration of License:** One year. **Requirements:** Good moral character. Pass physical examination. **Examination:** Yes. **Governing Statute:** Municipal Regulations, Title 17, Chap. 21.

Georgia

3263

Private Security Guard
Board of Private Detective and
 Security Agencies
Businesses and Occupations Section
Professional Examining Boards
166 Pryor St., SW
Atlanta, GA 30303
Phone: (404)656-2282

Credential Type: Private Security Guard License. **Requirements:** Have two years of experience with a licensed contract agency or two years of experience in law enforcement. **Exemptions:** Government and law enforcement agents. **Reciprocity:** No. **Fees:** $320 security agency fee (12 or fewer employees). $520 security agency fee (more than 12 employees). $45 employee registration fee. $23 fingerprint processing fee.

Hawaii

3264

Detective and Guard, Private
Hawaii Board of Private Detectives
 and Guards
Dept. of Commerce and Consumer
 Affairs
PO Box 3469
Honolulu, HI 96801
Phone: (808)548-3086

Credential Type: License. **Duration of License:** Six months. **Requirements:** High school diploma or equivalent. Four years of full-time investigational work or guard service. Criminal abstract covering the past 10 years. Fingerprints for FBI clearance. $5,000 bond. **Examination:** Written and verbal. **Reciprocity:** If self-employed and licensed in another state, submission of license status verification is required. **Fees:** $50 application fee. $50 exam fee. $25 license fee. $20 $40 Compliance Resolution Fund fee. $75 renewal fee.

Illinois

3265

Private Security Contractor
Illinois Dept. of Professional
 Regulations
320 W. Washington St.
Springfield, IL 62786
Phone: (217)782-8556

Credential Type: Private Security Contractor License. **Duration of License:**

Illinois

Private Security Contractor, continued

Three years. **Requirements:** At least 21 years of age. No felony convictions in the last 10 years. No alcohol or drug dependency or addiction. No dishonorable discharges from the U.S. Armed Services. Never been found incompetent by any court for reason of mental or physical defect or disease. Must show proof of liability insurance of at least $100,000 per person, $300,000 per occurrence for bodily injury, and $50,000 for property damage. Submit and be cleared of state and federal fingerprint security clearance. Meet one of the following requirements: (1) Have three years experience, during the five years preceding application, as a full-time supervisor, manager or administrator for a licensed security contractor agency; (2) Have three years experience, during the five years preceding application, as a manager or administrator of a privately owned security force that employs 30 or more personnel; (3) Have three years experience, during the five years preceding application, as a full-time supervisor in a law enforcement agency; (4) Hold a bachelor's degree in police science, or a related field, with one year experience; (5) Hold an associate's degree in police science, or a related field, with two years experience. **Examination:** Private Security Contractor Examination. **Reciprocity:** Yes, if licensing state has a reciprocal agreement with Illinois and its standards for licensure are substantially equivalent to those of Illinois. **Fees:** $216.80 examination fee. $500 initial license fee. $500 license by endorsement fee. $450 renewal fee. **Governing Statute:** The Private Detective, Private Alarm And Private Security Act of 1983, Illinois Revised Statutes 1991, Chapter 111.

3266

Security Officer (Gaming)
Illinois Gaming Board
PO Box 19474
Springfield, IL 62794-9474
Phone: (217)524-0228

Credential Type: Security Officer License. **Duration of License:** One year. **Requirements:** At least 21 years of age. U.S. citizen or legal alien as specified by Federal employability requirement. Experience or police training preferred. **Reciprocity:** No. **Fees:** $75 application fee. $50 initial license fee. $50 renewal fee. **Governing Statute:** Illinois Revised Statutes, Chapter 120.

3267

Security Supervisor (Gaming)
Illinois Gaming Board
PO Box 19474
Springfield, IL 62794-9474
Phone: (217)524-0228

Credential Type: Security Supervisor License. **Duration of License:** One year. **Requirements:** At least 21 years of age. U.S. citizen or legal alien as specified by Federal employability requirement. High school graduate or equivalent. Must have previous training and/or experience in the field of law enforcement. **Reciprocity:** No. **Fees:** $75 application fee. $50 initial license fee. $50 renewal fee. **Governing Statute:** Illinois Revised Statutes, Chapter 120.

3268

Third Party Safety Officer
Secretary of State
Commercial Driver Training
650 Roppolo Drive
Elk Grove, IL 60007
Phone: (708)437-3953

Credential Type: Third Party Safety Officer License. **Duration of License:** Three years. **Authorization:** Authorizes holder to conduct skills tests required by the Illinois Secretary of State. **Requirements:** At least 21 years of age. Must have Commercial Drivers License (CDL). Complete Safety Officer Training Session. **Reciprocity:** No. **Fees:** No fee. **Governing Statute:** Illinois Administrative Code, Chapter II.

Iowa

3269

Security Employee (Racetrack)
Iowa State Racing Commission
Lucas State Office Bldg.
Des Moines, IA 50319
Phone: (515)281-7352

Credential Type: License Registration. **Requirements:** Submit application and fingerprint card. Pay fee. **Fees:** $5 registration fee.

3270

Security Employee (Riverboat Gambling)
Iowa Racing and Gaming Commission
Lucas State Office Bldg.
Des Moines, IA 50319
Phone: (515)281-7352

Credential Type: License Registration. **Requirements:** Submit application and pay fees. **Fees:** $20 license fee.

3271

Security Guard
Div. of Administrative Serivces
Dept. of Public Safety
Wallace State Office Bldg.
Des Moines, IA 50319
Phone: (515)281-8422

Credential Type: License. **Duration of License:** Two years. **Requirements:** 18 years of age. U.S. citizenship. No convictions for an aggravated misdemeanor or a felony. An applicant should submit pictures and fingerprints along with a completed application. An applicant must be approved for a $5,000 surety bond. **Examination:** Written. **Fees:** $100 license fee. $100 renwal fee.

3272

Security Supervisor (Riverboat Gambling)
Iowa Racing and Gaming Commission
Lucas State Office Bldg.
Des Moines, IA 50319
Phone: (515)281-7352

Credential Type: License Registration. **Requirements:** Submit application and pay fees. **Fees:** $50 license fee.

3273

Surveillance Employee (Riverboat Gambling)
Iowa Racing and Gaming Commission
Lucas State Office Bldg.
Des Moines, IA 50319
Phone: (515)281-7352

Credential Type: License Registration. **Requirements:** Submit application and pay fees. **Fees:** $20 license fee.

Kansas

3274

Security Employee (Racetrack)
Kansas Racing Commission
3400 VanBuren
Topeka, KS 66611-2228
Phone: (913)296-5800

Credential Type: License Registration. **Requirements:** Submit application and fingerprint card. Pay fee. **Fees:** $5 registration fee.

Kentucky

3275

Security Department Employee (Racetrack)
Kentucky State Racing Commission
PO Box 1080
Lexington, KY 40588
Phone: (606)254-7021

Credential Type: Association Employee and Occupational License. **Authorization:** Authorizes work in the following positions: police chief, detective, policeman, watchman, fireman, and ambulance driver/attendant. **Requirements:** Submit application and fingerprint card. Pay fee. **Fees:** $10 license fee.

Maryland

3276

Security Guard
Licensing Div.
Maryland State Police
Pikesville, MD 21208-3899
Phone: (301)653-4435
Phone: (301)486-3101

Credential Type: Security Guard Certification. **Requirements:** Meet standards set by the Superintendent of the Maryland State Police. Must be an employee or applicant for employment with a licensed private detective agency.

Michigan

3277

Private Security Guard
Private Security and Investigator Section
Dept. of State Police
General Office Bldg.
7150 Harris Dr.
Lansing, MI 48913
Phone: (517)332-2521

Credential Type: Approval. **Duration of License:** Valid until the guard seeks employment with another private security guard agency or until revoked by the Department of State Police. **Requirements:** At least 18 years of age. Have not been convicted of a felony within the five years prior to application. Have not been dishonorably discharged from military service. Have not been judged insane or if so judged, must have been restored to full mental competency (documented by a court order). At least an 8th grade education or equivalent. Pass a fingerprint check prior to employment with the private security guard agency. **Fees:** $10 fingerprint processing fee. **Governing Statute:** Private Security Guard Licensing Act, Act 330 of 1968, as amended.

3278

Private Security Guard Agency Owner/Operator
Private Security and Investigator Section
Dept. of State Police
General Office Bldg.
7150 Harris Dr.
Lansing, MI 48913
Phone: (517)332-2521

Credential Type: License. **Duration of License:** Two years. **Requirements:** At least 25 years of age. High school education or the equivalent. Be a resident of Michigan for at least one year prior to application for the license. Have not been convicted of a felony within the five years prior to application. Have not been dishonorably discharged from military service. Post a bond or a liability insurance policy with the Department of State Police. Have not been judged insane or if so judged have been restored to full mental competency (documented by a court order). Submit the names of five personal references, other than relatives. Submit a fingerprint check and a background information check. Have lawfully been engaged in the private security guard business on his/her own for not less than three years; or have been an employee of a licensed private security guard business for not less than three years and have had at least four years of full-time guard work experience in a supervisory capacity with rank above that of a patrol officer; or have been in law enforcement employment on a full-time basis for at least four years with a government agency; or have been in the private security guard business as an employee or in a private business as a security administrator for at least two years on a full-time basis, and be a graduate (or the equivalent) in the field of police administration or industrial security of an accredited college or university. Abide by the Private Security Guard law. **Fees:** $200 (for a person), $300 (for a firm, partnership, company, or corporation) initial license fee. $100 (for a person), $150 (for a firm, partnership, company, or corporation) renewal fee. $50 fee for each additional branch office. **Governing Statute:** Private Security Guard Licensing Act, Act 330 of 1968, as amended.

Minnesota

3279

Protective Agent
Minnesota Private Detective and Protective Agent Services Board
1246 University Ave.
St. Paul, MN 55104
Phone: (612)642-0775

Credential Type: Protective Agent License. **Duration of License:** Two years. **Requirements:** Must meet board requirements. Post $10,000 surety bond. Show proof of financial responsibility. **Fees:** $400 license fee. $350 renewal fee. **Governing Statute:** Minnesota Statutes, Sections 326.32—326.339. Minnesota Rules 7506.0100-.0180.

3280

Security Officer (Racetrack)
Minnesota Racing Commission
11000 W. 78th St., Ste. 201
Eden Prairie, MN 55344
Phone: (612)341-7555

Credential Type: License Registration. **Requirements:** Submit application and fingerprint card. Pay fee. **Fees:** $25 registration fee.

Montana

3281

Chief of Security (Racetrack)
State of Montana Board of Horse Racing
Dept. of Commerce
1424 9th Ave.
Helena, MT 59620
Phone: (406)444-4287

Credential Type: License Registration. **Requirements:** Submit application and fingerprint card. Pay fee. **Fees:** $20 registration fee.

3282

Private Security Guard
Montana Board of Private Security Patrolmen and Investigators
111 N. Jackson
Helena, MT 59620
Phone: (406)444-4286

Credential Type: License. **Duration of License:** One year. **Requirements:** 18 years of age. U.S. citizenship. Completion of a certified private security guard training program. A certificate of liability insurance. **Examination:** Written. **Fees:** $25—$75 application fee. $25 exam fee. $20—$50 renewal fee. **Governing Statute:** Montana Code Annotated 37-60-301 through 37-60-322.

3283

Security Staff Person (Racetrack)
State of Montana Board of Horse Racing
Dept. of Commerce
1424 9th Ave.
Helena, MT 59620
Phone: (406)444-4287

Credential Type: License Registration. **Requirements:** Submit application and fingerprint card. Pay fee. **Fees:** $20 registration fee.

3284

Watchman (Racetrack)
State of Montana Board of Horse Racing
Dept. of Commerce
1424 9th Ave.
Helena, MT 59620
Phone: (406)444-4287

Credential Type: License Registration. **Requirements:** Submit application and fingerprint card. Pay fee. **Fees:** $20 registration fee.

Nebraska

3285

Security Guard (Racetrack)
Nebraska Racing Commission
PO Box 95014
301 Centennial Mall S.
Lincoln, NE 68509
Phone: (402)471-4155

Credential Type: License Registration. **Duration of License:** One year. **Requirements:** At least 16 years of age. No felony convictions. Secure employment and submit application completed and signed by management. Pay fees. **Fees:** $10 license fee. $10 renewal fee.

Nevada

3286

Security Employee (Racetrack)
Nevada Racing Commission
4820 Alpine Ct., Ste. 203
Las Vegas, NV 89107
Phone: (702)486-7619

Credential Type: License Registration. **Requirements:** Submit application and fingerprint card. Pay fee. **Fees:** $20 registration fee.

New Hampshire

3287

Security Guard
New Hampshire State Police
License and Permits Division
James Hayes Safety Bldg.
10 Hazen Drive
Concord, NH 03305
Phone: (603)271-3575

Credential Type: Security Guard License. **Duration of License:** One year. **Requirements:** At least 18 years of age. Post a surety bond of $10,000. Submit all forms in accordance with the Administrative Procedures Act. Two sets of fingerprints and firearms qualification required for armed security guards. **Reciprocity:** No. **Fees:** $100 individual license fee. $30 fee for armed guard record check.

New Mexico

3288

Private Patrol Operator
Private Investigator Bureau
Dept. of Regulation and Licensing
PO Box 25101
Santa Fe, NM 87504
Phone: (505)827-7172
Fax: (505)827-7095

Credential Type: Private Patrol Operator License. **Duration of License:** Two years. **Authorization:** License entitles individual to operate an armored car company, alarm company, and security dog company. **Requirements:** Complete three years of security or patrol experience. **Examination:** Written examination on rules, regulations, and statutes as well as CPR and first aid. **Reciprocity:** No. **Fees:** $200 license and exam fee. $75 manager's license fee. $15 security guard fee.

3289

Security Chief (Racetrack)
New Mexico State Racing Commission
PO Box 8576, Highland Station
Albuquerque, NM 87198
Phone: (505)841-4644

Credential Type: License Registration. **Requirements:** Submit application and fingerprint card. Pay fees. **Fees:** $16 registration fee. $1 notary fee. $23 fingerprint card processing fee.

3290

Security Staff Employee (Racetrack)
New Mexico State Racing Commission
PO Box 8576, Highland Station
Albuquerque, NM 87198
Phone: (505)841-4644

Credential Type: License Registration. **Requirements:** Submit application and fingerprint card. Pay fees. **Fees:** $14 registration fee. $1 notary fee. $23 fingerprint card processing fee.

3291

Watchman (Racetrack)
New Mexico State Racing Commission
PO Box 8576, Highland Station
Albuquerque, NM 87198
Phone: (505)841-4644

Credential Type: License Registration. **Requirements:** Submit application and fingerprint card. Pay fees. **Fees:** $13 registration fee. $1 notary fee. $23 fingerprint card processing fee.

New York

3292

Security Employee (Harness or Quarter Horse Racing)
New York State Racing and Wagering Board
400 Broome St.
New York, NY 10013
Phone: (212)219-4230

Credential Type: License Registration. **Duration of License:** One year. **Requirements:** Submit application, F.B.I fingerprint card, New York state fingerprint card, and three photos. Pay fees. **Fees:** $10 registration fee. $44 New York state fingerprint card processing fee (valid for five years).

3293

Security Employee (Thoroughbred Racing)
New York State Racing and Wagering Board
400 Broome St.
New York, NY 10013
Phone: (212)219-4230

Credential Type: License Registration. **Duration of License:** One year. **Requirements:** Submit application, F.B.I fingerprint card, New York state fingerprint card, and three photos. Pay fees. **Fees:** $10 registration fee. $44 New York state fingerprint card processing fee (valid for five years).

North Carolina

3294

Armed Security Guard
Private Protective Services Board
PO Box 29500
Raleigh, NC 27626
Phone: (919)779-1611

Credential Type: Registration. **Duration of License:** One year. **Requirements:** High school diploma. Completion of a basic training course in firearms for armed security guards. 18 years of age. U.S. citizen or resident alien. Good moral character. **Fees:** $17.50 registration fee. $17.50 renewal fee.

3295

Guard Dog Service Employee
Private Protective Services Board
PO Box 29500
Raleigh, NC 27626
Phone: (919)779-1611

Credential Type: License. **Duration of License:** One year. **Requirements:** High school diploma. Two years of experience performing guard dog functions within the past five years as a supervisor with a contract security company, proprietary security organization, law enforcement agency. 18 years of age. **Fees:** $150 application fee. $150 license fee. $50 recovery fund fee. $150 renewal fee.

3296

Security Guard and Patrol Licensee
Private Protective Services Board
PO Box 29500
Raleigh, NC 27626
Phone: (919)779-1611

Credential Type: License. **Duration of License:** One year. **Requirements:** High school diploma. Three years of experience performing guard and patrol functions within the past five years as a supervisor with a contract security company, a proprietary security organization, or a law enforcement agency. 18 years of age. The experience and requirements can be met in other ways, such as college education. **Fees:** $150 application fee. $150 license fee. $50 recovery fund fee. $150 renewal fee.

North Dakota

3297

Chief of Security (Racetrack)
North Dakota Racing Commission
State Capitol Bldg.
Bismarck, ND 58505
Phone: (701)224-2210

Credential Type: License Registration. **Requirements:** Submit application and fingerprint card. Pay fee. **Fees:** $10 license fee. $10 duplicate license fee.

3298

Security Employee (Racetrack)
North Dakota Racing Commission
State Capitol Bldg.
Bismarck, ND 58505
Phone: (701)224-2210

Credential Type: License Registration. **Requirements:** Submit application and fingerprint card. Pay fee. **Fees:** $10 license fee. $10 duplicate license fee.

Ohio

3299

Chief of Security (Thoroughbred, Standardbred, and Quarter Horse Racing)
Ohio State Racing Commission
State Office Tower
77 S. High St., 18th Fl.
Columbus, OH 43266-0416
Phone: (614)466-2757

Credential Type: License Registration. **Requirements:** Submit application and fingerprint card. Pay fee. **Fees:** $25 registration fee.

3300

Security Employee (Thoroughbred, Standardbred, and Quarter Horse Racing)
Ohio State Racing Commission
State Office Tower
77 S. High St., 18th Fl.
Columbus, OH 43266-0416
Phone: (614)466-2757

Credential Type: License Registration. **Requirements:** Submit application and fingerprint card. Pay fee. **Fees:** $10 registration fee.

Ohio 3301

3301

Security Guard Provider
Licensing Div.
Commerce Dept.
77 S. High St., 23rd Fl.
Columbus, OH 43266-0544
Phone: (614)466-4130

Credential Type: Security Guard Provider License. **Requirements:** Good reputation. No conviction of a felony within the past 20 years, and no conviction of any offense involving moral turpitude. For two years prior to application must have been engaged in security services work for a law enforcement or other public agency or for a security guard provider, or in the practice of law, or have equivalent experience. Submit proof of insurability. **Examination:** Yes. **Fees:** $25 application and exam fee. $250 license fee. **Governing Statute:** Ohio Revised Code 4749.01 et seq.

Oklahoma

3302

Security Employee (Racetrack)
Oklahoma Horse Racing Commission
6501 N. Broadway, Ste. 180
Oklahoma City, OK 73116
Phone: (405)848-0404

Credential Type: License Registration. **Duration of License:** One year. **Requirements:** Submit application and fingerprint card. Pay fee. **Fees:** $25 registration fee. $25 annual renewal.

3303

Security Guard/Armed Security Guard
Council on Law Enforcement Education and Training
PO Box 11476, Cimarron Station
Oklahoma City, OK 73136
Phone: (405)425-2775

Credential Type: License. **Duration of License:** Two years. **Requirements:** 18 years of age for unarmed guard. 21 years of age for armed guard. No felony convictions for armed guards. State resident. **Examination:** State Licensing Examination. **Fees:** $60—$85 license fee. $25—$50 renewal fee.

South Dakota

3304

Security Employee (Horse Racing)
South Dakota Racing Commission
c/o 500 East Capitol
Pierre, SD 57501
Phone: (605)773-6050

Credential Type: License Registration. **Requirements:** Submit application and fingerprint card. Pay fee. **Fees:** $10 registration fee.

Tennessee

3305

Security Officer
Private Security Guards
500 James Robertson Pky.
Nashville, TN 37243
Phone: (615)741-6382

Credential Type: License. **Duration of License:** Two years. **Requirements:** 18 years or 21 years, unarmed, armed. Four-hour education course for unarmed guard, an additional eight hours in classroom and four hours on firing range for armed guard. Pass a four-hour exam and spend four hours on firing range for renewal. **Examination:** Yes. **Fees:** $25 Registration. $15 Application.

Texas

3306

Security Guard
Texas Board of Private Investigators and Private Security Agencies
PO Box 13509, Capitol Station
Austin, TX 78711
Phone: (512)463-5545

Credential Type: License. **Requirements:** 18 years of age. Certificate of insurance. Three years of consecutive experience in security services field for security services firm license. Completion of approved training course consisting of at least 30 hours. **Examination:** Exam may be required. **Fees:** $225—$340 license and renewal fee. **Governing Statute:** VACS 4413(29bb), 22 TAC 429.

3307

Security Officer (Racetrack)
Texas Racing Commission
PO Box 12080
Austin, TX 78711
Phone: (512)794-8461

Credential Type: License Registration. **Requirements:** Submit application and fingerprint card. Pay fee. **Fees:** $20 registration fee.

Utah

3308

Security Guard
Office of Regulatory Licensing
4501 S. 2700 W.
Salt Lake City, UT 84119
Phone: (801)965-4484

Credential Type: Unarmed Security Guard License. **Requirements:** 18 years of age. Must not have been convicted of a felony for which a full pardon has been issued. Must not suffer from a dependence or addiction to any drugs or alcohol. Must complete four hours of approved pre-security training. An additional basic training must be completed within 90 days of employment. **Examination:** Yes. **Fees:** Unarmed: $5 security guard fee. $2 renewal fee. Armed: $15 registration fee. $10 renewal fee.

Credential Type: Armed License. **Requirements:** 18 years of age. Must not have been convicted of a felony for which a full pardon has not been granted. Must not have been declared by any court incompetent by reasons of mental defect or disease. Must not be dependent on any drug or alcohol. Must not have been discharged from any armed services of the United States under other than honorable conditions. Must have received at least eight hours of approved pre-service training. Must have received approved fire arms training as established by the Department of Public Safety. **Examination:** Yes. **Fees:** $15 registration fee. $10 renewal fee.

Vermont

3309

Armed Courier
State Board of Private Investigative
  and Security Service Licensing
Pavilion Office Bldg.
Montpelier, VT 05602
Phone: (802)828-2363

Credential Type: License. **Duration of License:** Two years. **Requirements:** 18 years of age. File a surety bond of $25,000. Favorable background investigation. Prior approval is required before carrying a firearm or using a guard dog. **Examination:** Yes. **Reciprocity:** No. **Fees:** $60 Application for license. $100 Renewal. $25 Late renewal penalty. **Governing Statute:** Title 26, VSA Sections 3151-3179.

3310

Guard Dog Handler
State Board of Private Investigative
  and Security Service Licensing
Pavilion Office Bldg.
Montpelier, VT 05602
Phone: (802)828-2363

Credential Type: License. **Duration of License:** Two years. **Requirements:** 18 years of age. File a surety bond of $25,000. Favorable background investigation. Prior approval is required before carrying a firearm or using a guard dog. **Examination:** Yes. **Reciprocity:** No. **Fees:** $60 Application for license. $100 Renewal. $25 Late renewal penalty. **Governing Statute:** Title 26, VSA Sections 3151-3179.

3311

Security Guard
State Board of Private Investigative
  and Security Service Licensing
Pavilion Office Bldg.
Montpelier, VT 05602
Phone: (802)828-2363

Credential Type: License. **Duration of License:** Two years. **Requirements:** 18 years of age. File a surety bond of $25,000. Favorable background investigation. Prior approval is required before carrying a firearm or using a guard dog. **Examination:** Yes. **Reciprocity:** No. **Fees:** $60 Application for license. $100 Renewal. $25 Late renewal penalty. **Governing Statute:** Title 26, VSA Sections 3151-3179.

Virginia

3312

Director of Security (Racetrack)
Virginia Racing Commission
PO Box 1123
Richmond, VA 23208
Phone: (804)371-7363

Credential Type: License Registration. **Requirements:** Submit application and fingerprint card. Pay fee. **Fees:** $10 registration fee.

3313

Nightwatchman (Racetrack)
Virginia Racing Commission
PO Box 1123
Richmond, VA 23208
Phone: (804)371-7363

Credential Type: License Registration. **Requirements:** Submit application and fingerprint card. Pay fee. **Fees:** $10 registration fee.

3314

Private Security Agent
Private Security Services
Dept. of Commerce
3600 W. Broad St.
Richmond, VA 23230
Phone: (804)367-8534

Credential Type: Registration. **Requirements:** Individual employees of a private securities service business who perform armored car personnel, courier, guard, guard dog handler, or private detective services must be registered with the Department of Commerce.

Firm must present evidence of a surety bond and employ a compliance agent who has passed a written examination. Compliance agent must also pass a criminal history background investigation and be registered in at least one category in which the firm offers services. **Examination:** Written examination may be required.

3315

Security Officer (Racetrack)
Virginia Racing Commission
PO Box 1123
Richmond, VA 23208
Phone: (804)371-7363

Credential Type: License Registration. **Requirements:** Submit application and fingerprint card. Pay fee. **Fees:** $10 registration fee.

Wisconsin

3316

Security Employee (Racetrack)
Wisconsin Racing Board
PO Box 7975
Madison, WI 53707-7975
Phone: (608)267-3291

Credential Type: License Registration. **Requirements:** Submit application and two sets of fingerprint cards. Pay fee. **Fees:** $20 registration fee. $20 duplicate license.

Wyoming

3317

Security Employee (Racetrack)
Wyoming State Pari-Mutuel
  Commission
Barrett Bldg., 3rd Fl.
Cheyenne, WY 82002
Phone: (307)777-5887

Credential Type: License Registration. **Requirements:** Submit application and fingerprint card. Pay fee. **Fees:** $10 registration fee. $10 duplicate license.

Handlers, Equipment Cleaners, Helpers, and Laborers

The following states grant licenses in this occupational category as of the date of publication:

Alaska	Delaware	Kansas	Michigan	Ohio	Texas
California	District of	Kentucky	New Mexico	Rhode Island	Virginia
Connecticut	Columbia	Louisiana	North Dakota	South Dakota	

Alaska

3318

Explosives Handler
Alaska Dept. of Labor
Labor Standards and Safety Div.
Occupational Health and Safety
PO Box 7-022
Anchorage, AK 99501
Phone: (907)283-3778

Credential Type: Certificate. **Duration of License:** Three years. **Requirements:** At least six months experience under the direction of another certified explosive handler, or as a chuck tender or driller. **Examination:** Written exam. **Exemptions:** Persons employed in mines do not need this certificate. **Fees:** $75 license fee.

California

3319

Jockey Room/Driver's Room Attendant (Racetrack)
California Horse Racing Board
1010 Hurley Way, Ste. 190
Sacramento, CA 95825
Phone: (916)920-7178

Credential Type: License Registration. **Requirements:** Submit application and fingerprint card. Pay fee. **Fees:** $75 registration fee.

Connecticut

3320

Parking Attendant (Racetrack)
Connecticut Div. of Special Revenue
Russell Rd.
PO Box 11424
Newington, CT 06111-0424
Phone: (203)566-2756

Credential Type: License Registration. **Requirements:** Submit application and fingerprint card. Pay fee. **Fees:** $5 registration fee.

Delaware

3321

Parking Lot Attendant (Racetrack)
Delaware Harness Racing Commission
2320 S. DuPont Hwy.
Dover, DE 19901
Phone: (302)739-4811

Credential Type: License Registration. **Requirements:** Submit application and fingerprint card. Pay fee. **Fees:** $5 registration fee.

District of Columbia

3322

Parking Lot Attendant
License and Certification Div.
Occupational and Professional Licensure Administration
Consumer and Regulatory Affairs Dept.
PO Box 37200
Washington, DC 20013-7200
Phone: (202)727-7823
Phone: (202)727-7480

Alternate Information: 614 H St., NW, Washington, DC 20001 **Requirements:** Contact licensing body for application information.

Kansas

3323

Jockey Room Attendant (Racetrack)
Kansas Racing Commission
3400 VanBuren
Topeka, KS 66611-2228
Phone: (913)296-5800

Credential Type: License Registration. **Requirements:** Submit application and fingerprint card. Pay fee. **Fees:** $5 registration fee.

3324

Parking Attendant (Racetrack)
Kansas Racing Commission
3400 VanBuren
Topeka, KS 66611-2228
Phone: (913)296-5800

Credential Type: License Registration. **Requirements:** Submit application and fingerprint card. Pay fee. **Fees:** $5 registration fee.

Kentucky

3325

Parking Manager/Employee (Racetrack)
Kentucky State Racing Commission
PO Box 1080
Lexington, KY 40588
Phone: (606)254-7021

Credential Type: Association Employee and Occupational License. **Requirements:** Submit application and fingerprint card. Pay fee. **Fees:** $10 license fee.

Louisiana

3326

Explosives Handler
Office of State Police
Explosives Control Unit
PO Box 66614
Baton Rouge, LA 70809
Phone: (504)925-6178

Credential Type: License. **Duration of License:** One year. **Authorization:** License is required of a person employed by a user who detonates or otherwise effects the explosion of an explosive or who is in immediate personal charge and supervision of one or more other persons engaged in such activity. **Requirements:** Submit application and pay fee. **Fees:** $10 license fee. **Governing Statute:** R.S. 40:1471.

Michigan

3327

Explosive Handler
Fire Marshal Div.
Dept. of State Police
7150 Harris Dr.
Lansing, MI 48913
Phone: (517)332-2521

Credential Type: License. **Duration of License:** Five years. **Requirements:** Have first obtained a temporary permit and then applied in writing for a regular license. Abide by the rules of the Department of State Police. **Fees:** $1 regular (permanent) license fee. $1 renewal fee. **Governing Statute:** Explosives Act, Act 202 of 1970.

Credential Type: Temporary License. **Duration of License:** One year. **Requirements:** At least 18 years of age. Have no felony convictions in the last five years. Must not have been judged insane or must have been restored to full mental competency (documented by a court order). **Fees:** $1 temporary license fee. $1 renewal fee. **Governing Statute:** Explosives Act, Act 202 of 1970.

New Mexico

3328

Laborer (Racetrack)
New Mexico State Racing Commission
PO Box 8576, Highland Station
Albuquerque, NM 87198
Phone: (505)841-4644

Credential Type: License Registration. **Requirements:** Submit application and fingerprint card. Pay fees. **Fees:** $13 registration fee. $1 notary fee. $23 fingerprint card processing fee.

North Dakota

3329

Attendant (Racetrack)
North Dakota Racing Commission
State Capitol Bldg.
Bismarck, ND 58505
Phone: (701)224-2210

Credential Type: License Registration. **Requirements:** Submit application and fingerprint card. Pay fee. **Fees:** $10 license fee. $10 duplicate license fee.

Ohio

3330

Parking Lot Employee (Thoroughbred and Quarter Horse Racing)
Ohio State Racing Commission
State Office Tower
77 S. High St., 18th Fl.
Columbus, OH 43266-0416
Phone: (614)466-2757

Credential Type: License Registration. **Requirements:** Submit application and fingerprint card. Pay fee. **Fees:** $10 registration fee.

Rhode Island

3331

Lead Hazard Abatement Worker
Office of Environmental Health Risk Assessment
Rhode Island Dept. of Health
3 Capitol Hill
Providence, RI 02908
Phone: (401)277-1417

Credential Type: Lead Hazard Abatement Worker. **Requirements:** Submit application. Contact licensing agency for additional requirements. **Examination:** Written and practical examinations.

South Dakota

3332

Parking Lot Employee (Horse Racing)
South Dakota Racing Commission
c/o 500 East Capitol
Pierre, SD 57501
Phone: (605)773-6050

Credential Type: License Registration. **Requirements:** Submit application and fingerprint card. Pay fee. **Fees:** $10 registration fee.

Texas

3333

Parking Attendant (Racetrack)
Texas Racing Commission
PO Box 12080
Austin, TX 78711
Phone: (512)794-8461

Credential Type: License Registration. **Requirements:** Submit application and fin-

Parking Attendant (Racetrack), continued

gerprint card. Pay fee. **Fees:** $20 registration fee.

Virginia

3334

Valet (Racetrack)
Virginia Racing Commission
PO Box 1123
Richmond, VA 23208
Phone: (804)371-7363

Credential Type: License Registration. **Requirements:** Submit application and fingerprint card. Pay fee. **Fees:** $5 registration fee.

Health Services Managers

The following states grant licenses in this occupational category as of the date of publication:

Alabama	District of	Iowa	Minnesota	New Mexico	Rhode Island	Washington
Alaska	Columbia	Kansas	Mississippi	New York	South Carolina	West Virginia
Arizona	Florida	Kentucky	Missouri	North Carolina	South Dakota	Wisconsin
Arkansas	Georgia	Louisiana	Montana	North Dakota	Tennessee	Wyoming
California	Hawaii	Maine	Nebraska	Ohio	Texas	
Colorado	Idaho	Maryland	Nevada	Oklahoma	Utah	
Connecticut	Illinois	Massachusetts	New Hampshire	Oregon	Vermont	
Delaware	Indiana	Michigan	New Jersey	Pennsylvania	Virginia	

Alabama

3335

Nursing Home Administrator
Board of Examiners of Nursing
  Home Administrators
4156 Carmichael Rd.
Montgomery, AL 36106
Phone: (205)271-6214

Credential Type: License. **Duration of License:** One year. **Requirements:** 19 years of age and a U.S. citizen. Must be a high school graduate and have obtained one year of progressively comprehensive practical experience in the nursing home administration area. Renewal requires 24 clock hours of continuing education. **Examination:** Written and oral examinations. **Fees:** $100 application fee. $150 examination fee. $100 license fee. $50 renewal fee.

Alaska

3336

Child Care Administrator (Center)
Dept. of Health and Social Services
Div. of Family and Youth Services
PO Box H-05
Juneau, AK 99811-0630
Phone: (907)465-2145

Credential Type: Child Care Center Administrator License. **Duration of License:** Two years. **Authorization:** Required of persons working in a child care center as administrators. **Requirements:** Be at least 21 years of age. Have a minimum of nine hours of college level credits in Early Childhood Development, Child Psychology, or Childhood Development or the equivalent. Submit three character references, one of which must be from a former supervisor. Applicants must submit verification they do not have tuberculosis and must be free of serious physical and mental problems. **Fees:** No fee

3337

Nursing Home Administrator
Dept. of Commerce and Economic
  Development
Board of Nursing Home
  Administrators
PO Box D-LIC
Juneau, AK 99811-0800
Phone: (907)465-2541
Fax: (907)465-2974

Credential Type: License by Examination. **Duration of License:** Two years. **Requirements:** At least 19 years of age. High school graduate or equivalent. Good moral character. Bachelor's degree from an accredited four-year college or university. One year of administrative experience in a health care institution. Good physical and mental health. **Examination:** PES examination. **Fees:** $30 application fee. $30 examination fee. $60 license fee. **Governing Statute:** Alaska Statutes, Title 8, Chapter 70. Professional Regulations, 12 AAC, Chapter 46.

Credential Type: License by Endorsement. **Duration of License:** Two years. **Requirements:** Hold a current license as a nursing home administrator from another jurisdiction. Must have passed either the NAB or the PES examination for nursing home administrators. Meet other basic requirements. **Fees:** $30 application fee. $60 license fee. **Governing Statute:** Alaska Statutes, Title 8, Chapter 70. Professional Regulations, 12 AAC, Chapter 46.

Arizona

3338

Adult Care Home Manager
Board of Examiners
Nursing Care Institution
  Administrators and Adult Care
  Home Managers
1645 W. Jefferson, Rm. 410
Phoenix, AZ 85007
Phone: (602)542-3095
Fax: (602)542-3093

Credential Type: Adult care home manager license. **Duration of License:** Two years. **Requirements:** Complete a board-approved training course. Pass state examination. **Examination:** State examination. **Exemptions:** A currently licensed registered nurse or licensed practical nurse is exempt from the training course. **Reciprocity:** No. **Fees:** $40 examination fee. $100 license fee. $25 temporary certificate fee. **Governing Statute:** Arizona Revised Statutes, Title 36, Chapter 4, Article 6.

3339

**Nursing Care Institution
  Administrator**
Board of Examiners
Nursing Care Institution
  Administrators and Adult Care
  Home Managers
1645 W. Jefferson, Rm. 410
Phoenix, AZ 85007
Phone: (602)542-3095
Fax: (602)542-3093

Credential Type: Nursing care institution administrator license. **Duration of License:** Two years. **Requirements:** Be of good moral character. Complete a board-approved course of instruction and training,

Arkansas 3340

Nursing Care Institution Administrator, continued

or provide evidence of sufficient education and training. Pass state and national examinations. **Examination:** State and national examinations. **Reciprocity:** Yes. **Fees:** $100 application fee. $250 license fee. $250 temporary license fee. **Governing Statute:** Arizona Revised Statutes, Title 36, Chapter 4, Article 6.

Arkansas

3340

Nursing Home Administrator
Arkansas Dept. of Human Services
Div. of Social Service
Office of Long Term Care
Donaghey Bldg.
7th and Main St.
PO Box 1437
Little Rock, AR 72203
Phone: (501)682-1001

Credential Type: License. **Requirements:** 21 years of age. Good moral character. Sound physical and mental health. One year of internship or direct experience in Nursing Home Administration; or an associates degree or minimum of 60 hours of Nursing Home Administration study; or two years administration or supervisory experience and the successful completion of an approved correspondence course. **Examination:** Yes. **Fees:** $100 Written examination. $100 License. $100 Renewal.

California

3341

Nursing Home Administrator
Board of Examiners of Nursing
  Home Administrators
1420 Howe Ave., Ste. 2
Sacramento, CA 95825
Phone: (916)920-6481

Credential Type: Nursing Home Administrator. **Duration of License:** Two years. **Requirements:** An associate's degree and 1000 hours of administrator-in-training program. Renewal requires 40 hours of continuing education every two years. **Examination:** National and state examinations.

Colorado

3342

Nursing Home Administrator
Board of Nursing Home
  Administrators
1560 Broadway, Ste. 1310
Denver, CO 80202
Phone: (303)894-7760
Fax: (303)894-7764

Credential Type: Nursing Home Administrator. **Duration of License:** One year. **Requirements:** Bachelor's degree or associate's degree plus two years of college level education. Must have six to 12 months of administrator-in-training program. **Examination:** National and state examinations. **Reciprocity:** Yes. **Fees:** $233 license fee (by exam). $209 license fee (by reciprocity). $194 Renewal fee.

Connecticut

3343

Nursing Home Administrator
Dept. of Health Services
Nursing Home Administrator
  Licensure
150 Washington St.
Hartford, CT 06106
Phone: (203)566-4068

Credential Type: Nursing Home Administrator. **Duration of License:** One year. **Requirements:** Bachelor's or master's degree and specified courses. Must have 500 to 900 hours of administrator-in-training program. **Examination:** National and state examinations.

Delaware

3344

Nursing Home Administrator
Board of Examiners of Nursing
  Home Administrators
O'Neil Bldg.
PO Box 1401
Wilmington, DE 19903
Phone: (302)739-4522
Fax: (302)739-6148

Credential Type: Nursing Home Administrator. **Duration of License:** Two years. **Requirements:** An associate's degree and Nursing Home Administration (NHA) courses. Must have 3-12 months of administrator-in-training program. Renewal requires 48 hours of continuing education every two years. **Examination:** National examination.

District of Columbia

3345

Nursing Home Administrator
Board of Nursing Home
  Administration
614 H St. NW, Rm. 931
Washington, DC 20009
Phone: (202)727-7480
Fax: (202)272-5384

Credential Type: Nursing Home Administrator. **Duration of License:** Two years. **Requirements:** Bachelor's degree and specified courses. Must have one year of administrator-in-training program. Renewal requires 20 hours of continuing education every year. **Examination:** National and state examinations.

Florida

3346

Nursing Home Administrator
Board of Nursing Home
  Administrators
Dept. of Professional Regulation
1940 N. Monroe St.
Tallahassee, FL 32399-0777
Phone: (904)488-7487

Credential Type: Nursing Home Administrator License. **Duration of License:** Two years. **Requirements:** Be at least 18 years of age. Starting October of 1992, must have a four-year degree. Complete a one-year Administrator-in-Training (AIT) program, or complete a college internship in health administration, or have two years of practical experience in nursing home administration.

Renewal requires 40 hours of continuing education. **Examination:** Written examination on Florida laws and rules. Written National Boards (NAB). **Reciprocity:** License may be granted by endorsement. **Fees:** $250 exam fee. $230 renewal fee. **Governing Statute:** Florida Statutes, Chapter 468, Part II.

Georgia

3347

Nursing Home Administrator
Board of Examiners for Nursing Home Administrators
166 Pryor St. SW
Atlanta, GA 30303
Phone: (404)656-3989
Fax: (404)651-9532

Credential Type: Nursing Home Administrator. **Duration of License:** Two years. **Requirements:** Bachelor's degree and two year's experience. Must have six months of administrator-in-training program. Renewal requires 40 hours of continuing education every two years. **Examination:** National and state examinations.

Hawaii

3348

Nursing Home Administrator
Hawaii Board of Examiners of Nursing Home Administrators
1010 Richards St.
PO Box 3469
Honolulu, HI 96801
Phone: (808)548-7461

Credential Type: License. **Duration of License:** Six months. **Requirements:** 21 years of age. A degree from an accredited four-year institution; or one year of satisfactory performance as an administrator of a health care institution; or a master's degree in public health, business administration or hospital administration with a health services administration specialization; or employer certification of at least one year of administrative experience in a health-related area. Completion of a satisfactory NHA correspondence course (may be exempted). **Examination:** Given in March and September. **Fees:** $100 application fee. $100 exam fee. $100 license fee. $15—$30 Compliance Resolution Fund fee. $50 renewal fee.

Idaho

3349

Nursing Home Administrator
Board of Examiners for Nursing Home Administrators
1109 Main St., Ste. 220
Boise, ID 83702-5642
Phone: (208)334-3233

Credential Type: Nursing Home Administrator. **Duration of License:** One year. **Requirements:** Bachelor's degree with specified courses and experience. Must have one year of administrator-in-training program. Renewal requires 20 hours of continuing education each year. **Examination:** National and state examinations. **Fees:** $65 temporary permit fee (administrator-in-training). $150 exam fee. $65 initial license fee. $65 renewal fee.

3350

Residential Care Facility Administrator
Board of Examiners of Residential Care Facility Administrators
Bureau of Occupational Licenses
1109 Main St., Ste. 220
Boise, ID 83702-5642
Phone: (208)334-3233

Credential Type: License and certificate of registration. **Duration of License:** One year. **Requirements:** Must be at least 21 years of age. High school diploma or equivalent. Good moral character. Complete an approved course of training and instruction, such as the Certification Program for Residential Care Facility Administrators administered by the National Residential Care Association, or equivalent courses.

Renewal requires 12 hours of continuing education per year. **Examination:** Two-part written examination. **Fees:** $25 application fee. $40 temporary license fee. $75 exam fee. $75 renewal fee. **Governing Statute:** Idaho Code, Title 54, Chap. 42. Rules of the Board of Examiners of Residential Care Facility Administrators.

Illinois

3351

Mine Rescue Station Supervisor
Illinois Dept. of Mines & Minerals
300 W. Jefferson St., Ste. 300
PO Box 10137
Springfield, IL 62791-0137
Phone: (217)782-6791

Credential Type: Mine Rescue Station Supervisor Certificate. **Duration of License:** Two years (unless currently employed in field which would allow a permanent certificate). **Requirements:** At least 18 years of age. U.S. citizen. Complete the equivalent of four years high school. Hold an Advanced First Aid and Mine Rescue Certificate of Competency issued by the Department of Mines and Minerals. Must have four years experience in underground gassy mines. Knowledge of department rules, mine rescue operation rules, and equipment and supplies. **Examination:** Written and oral examinations. **Reciprocity:** No. **Fees:** No fee. **Governing Statute:** 1989 Illinois Revised Statutes, Chapter 96 1/2.

3352

Nursing Home Administrator
Dept. of Registration and Education
320 W. Washington St., 3rd Fl.
Springfield, IL 62786
Phone: (217)785-0872
Phone: (217)782-8556
Fax: (217)782-7645

Credential Type: Nursing Home Administrator. **Duration of License:** Two years. **Requirements:** An associate's degree with specified courses and experience. Renewal requires 36 hours of continuing education every two years. **Examination:** National and state examinations. **Reciprocity:** Yes. Must pass state exam. **Fees:** $100 license fee (by exam). $150 license fee (by endorsement). $170 national exam fee. $103 state exam fee.

Indiana

3353

Health Facility Administrator
Health Facility Board
Health Professions Bureau
402 W. Washington St., Rm. 041
Indianapolis, IN 46204
Phone: (317)232-2960

Credential Type: License to practice. **Duration of License:** Two years. **Requirements:** Must have appropriate training and education. **Examination:** State examination. NAB examination. **Fees:** $40 application fee. $25 state exam fee. $125 NAB exam fee. $75 license issuance fee. $75 renewal fee. $10 temporary license fee. $50 provisional license fee. **Governing Statute:** Indiana Code 25-19. 840 Indiana Administrative Code.

3354

Nursing Home Administrator
Board of Health
Facility Administrators
1 American Sq., Ste. 1020
PO Box 82067
Indianapolis, IN 46282
Phone: (317)232-2960
Fax: (317)233-4236

Credential Type: Nursing Home Administrator. **Duration of License:** Two years. **Requirements:** An associate's degree and Long-Term Care (LTC) courses. Must have 6-9 months of administrator-in-training

Nursing Home Administrator, continued

program. Renewal requires 40 hours of continuing education every two years. **Examination:** National and state examinations.

Iowa

3355

Nursing Home Activity Director
Div. of Health Facilities
Dept. of Inspection and Appeals
Lucas State Office Bldg., 3rd Fl.
Des Moines, IA 50319
Phone: (515)281-4233

Credential Type: Certificate. **Requirements:** 16 years of age and completion of a 42-hour workshop. **Examination:** Written. **Fees:** $100 workshop fee.

3356

Nursing Home Administrator
Board of Examiners for Nursing Home Administrator
Dept. of Public Health
Lucas State Office Bldg.
Des Moines, IA 50319
Phone: (515)281-6762

Credential Type: License. **Duration of License:** Two years. **Requirements:** High school diploma or equivalent with an Associate of Arts degree in long-term health care administration; or a high school diploma or equivalent with education and training in nursing home administration. **Examination:** National and state exams. **Reciprocity:** None. **Fees:** $175 exam fee. $50 application fee. $90 renewal fee.

Kansas

3357

Nursing Home Administrator
Board of Adult Care Home Administrators
Bureau of Adult and Child Care
Landon State Office Bldg.
900 SW Jackson, Ste.901
Topeka, KS 66612-1290
Phone: (913)296-0061
Fax: (913)296-1266

Credential Type: Nursing Home Administrator. **Duration of License:** Two years. **Requirements:** Bachelor's degree and 480 hours of practical experience. Renewal requires 60 hours of continuing education every two years. **Examination:** National and state examinations. **Fees:** $100 application fee. $125 exam fee. $100 renewal fee.

Kentucky

3358

Nursing Home Administrator
Occupations and Professions Board
PO Box 456
Frankfort, KY 40602
Phone: (502)564-3296

Credential Type: License. **Duration of License:** Two years. **Requirements:** Bachelor's degree from an accredited college or university and six months of continuous management experience at a health care facility. 21 years of age. Continuing education required. **Examination:** Yes. **Fees:** $115 exam fee. $100 renewal fee.

Louisiana

3359

Nursing Home Administrator
Board of Examiners for Nursing Home Administrators
4550 North Blvd., Ste 205
Baton Rouge, LA 70806
Phone: (504)952-4591

Credential Type: License. **Duration of License:** Two years. **Requirements:** 21 years of age. Two years of college credit in a specific care curriculum with a "C" grade average. Completion of a six-month internship. **Examination:** Written. **Reciprocity:** Yes. **Fees:** $200 exam fee.

Maine

3360

Nursing Home Administrator
Nursing Home Administrators Licensing Board
Dept. of Professional & Financial Regulation
State House Station 35
Augusta, ME 04333
Phone: (207)289-3671
Fax: (207)582-5415

Credential Type: Nursing Home Administrator. **Duration of License:** One year. **Requirements:** Bachelor's degree. Must have six months of administrator-in-training program. Renewal requires 24 hours of continuing education each year. **Examination:** National and state examinations.

Maryland

3361

Health Planner
Maryland Health Resources Planning Commission
Dept. of Health and Mental Hygiene
4201 Patterson Ave.
Baltimore, MD 21215
Phone: (410)225-5141

Credential Type: License. **Requirements:** Contact licensing body for application information.

3362

Nursing Home Administrator
Board of Examiners for Nursing Home Administrators
4201 Patterson Ave., Rm. 313
Baltimore, MD 21215-2299
Phone: (410)764-4750
Fax: (410)764-5987

Credential Type: Nursing Home Administrator. **Duration of License:** Two years. **Requirements:** Bachelor's degree and specified courses and experience. Must have one year of administrator-in-training program. Renewal requires 30 hours of continuing education every two years. **Examination:** National and state examinations. **Fees:** $50 administrator-in-training fee. $65 state exam fee. $175 national exam fee. $100 license fee. $100 renewal fee.

Massachusetts

3363

Nursing Home Administrator
Board of Registration for Nursing Home Administrators
1519 Leverett Saltonstall Bldg.
100 Cambridge St.
Boston, MA 02202
Phone: (617)727-3069
Fax: (617)727-7378

Credential Type: Nursing Home Administrator. **Duration of License:** One year. **Requirements:** Bachelor's degree. Must have six months of administrator-in-training program. Renewal requires 30 hours of continuing education every two years. **Examination:** National examination. **Reciprocity:** Yes. **Fees:** $50 application fee. $165 exam fee. $100 reciprocity fee.

Michigan

3364

Nursing Home Administrator
Nursing Home Administrator Board
Dept. of Licensure and Regulation
PO Box 30018
Lansing, MI 48909
Phone: (517)373-1699
Fax: (517)373-2795

Credential Type: Nursing Home Administrator. **Duration of License:** Two years. **Requirements:** Bachelor's degree. Registered Nurse. Must have specified courses and experience. Renewal requires 36 hours of continuing education every two years. **Examination:** National and state examinations.

Minnesota

3365

Nursing Home Administrator
Board of Examiners for Nursing Home Administrators
2700 University Ave. W
St Paul, MN 55114
Phone: (612)642-0595
Fax: (612)642-0393

Credential Type: Nursing Home Administrator. **Duration of License:** One year. **Requirements:** Bachelor's degree with specified courses. Must have 400 to 500 hours of administrator-in-training program. Renewal requires 30 hours of continuing education each year. **Examination:** National and state examinations. **Fees:** $100 application fee. $125 national exam fee. $75 state exam fee. $150 license fee. $150 renewal fee.

Mississippi

3366

Nursing Home Administrator
Board of Nursing Home Administrators
Robert E. Lee Bldg., Ste. 405
239 N. Lamar St.
Jackson, MS 39201-1311
Phone: (601)359-6044

Credential Type: Nursing Home Administrator. **Duration of License:** Two years. **Authorization:** An associate's degree with specified courses and one year's experience. Must have six months of administrator-in-training program. Renewal requires 40 hours of continuing education every two years. **Requirements:** National and state examinations. **Reciprocity:** Yes. Must take state exam. **Fees:** $75 application fee. $135 national exam fee. $45 state exam fee. $335 license fee (pro-rated). $335 renewal fee.

Missouri

3367

Nursing Home Administrator
Board of Nursing Home Administrators
2701 W. Main
PO Box 1337
Jefferson City, MO 65102
Phone: (314)751-3511
Fax: (314)751-8687

Credential Type: Nursing Home Administrator. **Duration of License:** One year. **Requirements:** Meet specified education and experience requirements. Must have 300 hours of administrator-in-training program. Renewal requires 20 hours of continuing education each year. **Examination:** National and state examinations. **Fees:** $100 application fee. $150 exam fee (national and state). $50 license fee. $50 renewal fee.

Montana

3368

Nursing Home Administrator
Montana Board of Nursing Home Administrators
111 N. Jackson
Helena, MT 59620
Phone: (406)444-4288

Credential Type: License. **Duration of License:** One year. **Requirements:** 60 semester hours of college coursework. Three years of administrative experience or a one-year internship in a nursing home. **Examination:** National and state. **Fees:** $70 application fee. $65—$100 license fee. $100 renewal fee. **Governing Statute:** Montana Code Annotated 37-9-301 through 37-9-312.

Nebraska

3369

Nursing Home Administrator
Nebraska Board of Examiners in Nursing Home Administration
301 Centennial Mall S.
PO Box 95007
Lincoln, NE 68509
Phone: (402)471-2115

Credential Type: License. **Duration of License:** Two years. **Requirements:** Must have a bachelor of science degree in Health Services Administration or an associate degree in Long-term Care Administration, Allied Health or Human Services, including completion of two credit hour courses in the following areas: general administration; social gerontology; health and social service delivery systems; and a seminar on contemporary developments in aging. **Examination:** Yes. **Fees:** $100 initial examination fee. $250 initial license fee. $250 renewal fee.

3370

Safety Hygienist, Industrial
Nebraska Dept. of Labor
Div. of Safety
301 Centennial Mall S.
PO Box 95024
Lincoln, NE 68509
Phone: (402)471-2239

Credential Type: License. **Duration of License:** One year. **Requirements:** Must have a bachelor of science degree plus five years of experience, or a master's degree of science plus four years experience in an industrial hygiene field. **Examination:** Yes. **Fees:** $60 application fee. $90 examination fee. $40 renewal fee.

Nevada

3371

Health Services Administrator
Nevada State Board for Examiners for Nursing Home Administrators
1701 S. Torrey Pines Dr.
Las Vegas, NV 89102
Phone: (702)871-0005
Fax: (702)876-5993

Credential Type: License. **Duration of License:** One year. **Requirements:** Must meet necessary age and character qualifications. Completion of a course related to health care facilities. Continue training as prescribed by the Board. **Examination:**

Nevada 3372

Health Services Administrator, continued

Yes. **Fees:** $100 application fee. $150 exam fee. $200 license fee. $100 renewal fee.

3372

Nursing Home Administrator
Board of Examiners for Nursing Home Administrators
PO Box 26209
Las Vegas, NV 89126
Phone: (702)871-0005
Fax: (702)876-5993

Credential Type: Nursing Home Administrator. **Duration of License:** Two years. **Requirements:** High school diploma and one year's experience. Renewal requires 20 hours of continuing education every two years. **Examination:** National examination.

New Hampshire

3373

Nursing Home Administrator
Board of Examiners of Nursing Home Administrators
Health and Human Services
6 Hazen Dr.
Concord, NH 03301
Phone: (603)271-4728

Credential Type: Nursing Home Administrator. **Duration of License:** Two years. **Requirements:** Bachelor's degree. Nursing Home Administration (NHA) program and one year's experience. Must have one year of administrator-in-training program. Renewal requires 25 hours of continuing education every two years. **Examination:** National and state examinations. **Reciprocity:** Yes. **Fees:** $150 application fee. $130 national exam fee. $75 state exam fee. $150 renewal fee.

New Jersey

3374

Nursing Home Administrator
Nursing Home Administrators Licensing Board
CN367
Trenton, NJ 08625-0367
Phone: (609)588-7772

Credential Type: License. **Requirements:** A baccalaureate degree from an accredited institution. Attendance at 100 hours of seminars, workshops or courses in the health care field. One year of experience in a responsible administrative position or serve in an approved internship program in a long-term care facility for at least six months. 18 years of age. At least 40 hours in health-related seminars, workshops, lectures or formal courses every two years. **Examination:** Written. **Reciprocity:** Yes. **Fees:** $75 exam fee. $100 license fee. **Governing Statute:** NJSA 26:2H, 27 and 28. NJAC 8:34.

New Mexico

3375

Nursing Home Administrator
Board of Nursing Home Administrators
PO Box 25101
Santa Fe, NM 87504
Phone: (505)827-7170
Fax: (505)827-7095

Credential Type: Nursing Home Administrator. **Duration of License:** One year. **Requirements:** Bachelor's degree or hospital experience. Renewal requires 24 hours of continuing education each year. **Examination:** National examination.

New York

3376

Nursing Home Administrator
Board of Examiners of Nursing Home Administrators
New York Dept. of Health
Corning Tower, ESP, Rm. 1931
Albany, NY 12237-0754
Phone: (518)474-3042

Credential Type: Nursing Home Administrator. **Duration of License:** Two years. **Requirements:** Bachelor's degree with specified courses and experience. Must have nine months of administrator-in-training program. Renewal requires 72 hours of continuing education every two years. **Examination:** National examination.

North Carolina

3377

Industrial Hygienist
American Industrial Hygiene Assn.
475 Wolf Ledges Pky.
Akron, OH 44311
Phone: (216)762-7294

Credential Type: Certification. **Duration of License:** Three years. **Requirements:** Bachelor's degree in industrial hygiene, chemistry, physics or another discipline depending upon the scientific content of the curriculum. Five years of experience in industrial hygiene. 18 years of age. Two references. **Examination:** Multiple choice. **Fees:** $60 application fee. $90 exam fee.

3378

Nursing Home Administrator
North Carolina State Board of Examiners for Nursing Home Administrators
701 Barbour Dr., Rm. 102
Raleigh, NC 27603
Phone: (919)733-6225

Credential Type: License. **Duration of License:** Two years. **Requirements:** 18 years of age. Sound physical and mental health. The equivalent of at least two years of college-level study from an accredited school. Two years of experience in a nursing home is equivalent to one year of college. Completion of an administrator-in-training period. **Examination:** National and state exams. **Fees:** $75 AIT fee. $200 license fee. $140 exam fee. $200 renewal fee.

North Dakota

3379

Nursing Home Administrator
Board of Examiners for Nursing Home Administrators
120 W. Thayer Ave.
Bismarck, ND 58502
Phone: (701)222-4867

Credential Type: Nursing Home Administrator. **Duration of License:** One year. **Requirements:** An associate's degree. Renewal requires 25 hours of continuing education every year. **Examination:** National and state examinations.

Ohio

3380

Nursing Home Administrator
Board of Examiners for Nursing Home Administrators
131 N. High St., Box 118
Columbus, OH 43266-0118
Phone: (614)466-5114
Fax: (614)752-8739

Credential Type: Nursing Home Administrator. **Duration of License:** One year. **Requirements:** Bachelor's degree with specified courses and experience. Must have three to nine months of administrator-in-training program. Renewal requires 20 hours of continuing education each year. **Examination:** National and state examinations. **Reciprocity:** Yes. **Fees:** $50 administrator-in-training fee. $150 license and exam fee. $150 renewal fee.

Oklahoma

3381

Nursing Home Administrator
Oklahoma State Board of Nursing Homes
3033 N. Walnut, Ste. 100E
Oklahoma City, OK 73105
Phone: (405)521-0991

Credential Type: License. **Duration of License:** One year. **Requirements:** High school graduate. Completion of a program in nursing home administration. 24 hours of continuing education each year. 21 years of age. **Examination:** National Association of Board of Nursing Home Administrators Examination. State Standards and Review. **Fees:** $275 exam fee. $150 application fee. $150 license fee. $150 renewal fee.

Oregon

3382

Nursing Home Administrator
Board of Examiners of Nursing Home Administrators
800 NE Oregon St.
Portland, OR 97232
Phone: (503)731-4046

Credential Type: License. **Duration of License:** One year. **Requirements:** Must have a college degree and six months of training in a nursing home; or have a license from another state and a degree if license in other state was issued after January 1, 1983; or one year of experience as administrator in a hospital with physically attached nursing home. **Examination:** Yes. **Reciprocity:** Yes. **Fees:** $100 exam fee. $100 license fee. $100 renewal fee. **Governing Statute:** ORS 678.710 to 678.990.

Pennsylvania

3383

Nursing Home Administrator
Board of Examiners of Nursing Home Administrators
PO Box 2649
Harrisburg, PA 17105-2649
Phone: (717)783-7155
Fax: (717)787-7769

Credential Type: Nursing Home Administrator. **Duration of License:** Two years. **Requirements:** An associate's degree with specified courses and experience. Renewal requires 48 hours of continuing education every two years. **Examination:** National and state examinations.

Rhode Island

3384

Nursing Home Administrator
Board of Examiners for Nursing Home Administrators
Div. of Professional Regulation
104 Cannon Bldg.
Three Capitol Hill
Providence, RI 02908-5097
Phone: (401)277-2827
Fax: (401)277-2172

Credential Type: Nursing Home Administrator. **Duration of License:** One year. **Requirements:** Bachelor's degree with specified courses and experience. **Examination:** National examination. **Fees:** $100 application fee. $50 exam fee. $50 renewal fee.

South Carolina

3385

Nursing Home Administrator
South Carolina State Board of Examiners for Nursing Home Administrators
2221 Devine St.
Columbia, SC 29211
Phone: (803)734-9186

Credential Type: License. **Duration of License:** Two years. **Requirements:** Reputable and responsible character. Sound physical and mental health. Bachelor's degree in nursing home administration or a related field. One year of experience in a nursing home or a related health care administration field. **Examination:** Yes. **Fees:** $250 license fee. $250 renewal fee. $250 emergency license.

South Dakota

3386

Nursing Home Administrator
Board of Examiners for Nursing Home Administrators
804 Western Ave. N
Sioux Falls, SD 57104-2098
Phone: (605)339-2071
Fax: (605)339-1354

Credential Type: Nursing Home Administrator. **Duration of License:** One year. **Requirements:** An associate degree with specified courses. Must have six months of administrator-in-training program. Renewal requires 20 hours of continuing education each year. **Examination:** National and state examinations. **Fees:** $100 application fee. $150 national exam fee. $50 state exam fee. $75 renewal fee.

Tennessee

3387

Nursing Home Administrator
Board of Nursing Home Administrators
Tennessee Dept. of Public Health
283 Plus Park Blvd.
Nashville, TN 37219-5407
Phone: (615)367-6280

Credential Type: Nursing Home Administrator. **Duration of License:** Two years. **Requirements:** Bachelor's degree in health care administration or public administration. Must have six to 12 months of administrator-in-training program. Renewal requires 18 hours of continuing education each year. **Examination:** National and state examinations. **Fees:** $160 application fee. $150 exam fee.

Texas

3388

Child Care Administrator
Texas Dept. of Human Services
Child Care Administrators' Licensing, W-403
PO Box 149030
Austin, TX 78714
Phone: (512)450-3255

Credential Type: License. **Duration of License:** Two years. **Requirements:** Master's or doctoral degree in social work or related area of study, and one year experience in management/supervision of child care personnel and programs; or bachelor's degree and two years experience in child

Texas

Child Care Administrator,
continued

care or closely related field and one year experience in management/supervision of child care personnel and programs; or associate degree from junior college and four years experience and at least one year experience in management/supervision of child care personnel and programs; or high school diploma or equivalent and six years experience and at least one year experience in management/supervision of child care personnel and programs. Fifteen hours of acceptable continuing education required for renewal. **Examination:** Examination in Texas law and management principles. **Fees:** $25 exam fee. $50 license fee. $50 renewal fee. **Governing Statute:** HRC 43.001, 40 TAC 85.5001.

3389

Nursing Home Administrator
Texas Board of Licensure for
 Nursing Home Administrators
4800 N. Lamar, Ste. 310
Austin, TX 78756
Phone: (512)458-1955

Credential Type: License. **Duration of License:** Two years. **Requirements:** 18 years of age. Sound physical and mental health. Bachelor's degree. Completion of a 200-hour curriculum approved by the Board in an accredited post-secondary institution. Internship of 520 hours in a licensed nursing home, completed during a minimum period of 26 weeks or equivalent college practicum served through an approved college. 24 hours of continuing education every two years for renewal. **Examination:** Texas Comprehensive Examination. Texas State Standards Examination. **Fees:** $250 application fee. $250 license fee. $250 renewal fee. **Governing Statute:** VACS 4442d, 22 TAC 243.

Utah

3390

Health Facility Administrator
Dept. of Commerce
Div. of Occupational and
 Professional Licnesing
160 E. 300 S.
PO Box 45802
Salt Lake City, UT 84145
Phone: (801)530-6628

Credential Type: License. **Duration of License:** Two years. **Requirements:** Must have a bachelor's degree in Health Care Administration or a bachelor's degree in a related field with special classes taken. Must have completed 300 clock hour practicum in a long term care facility under the supervision of a licensed administrator. **Examination:** Yes. **Fees:** $60 license fee. $30 renewal fee.

3391

Nursing Home Administrator
Div. of Occupational and
 Professional Licensing
160 E. 300 S.
PO Box 45802
Salt Lake City, UT 84145
Phone: (801)530-6621
Fax: (801)530-6511

Credential Type: Nursing Home Administrator. **Duration of License:** Two years. **Requirements:** Bachelor's degree in health care administration. Must have 300 hours of administrator-in-training program. Renewal requires 40 hours of continuing education every two years. **Examination:** National and state examinations.

Vermont

3392

Nursing Home Administrator
Board of Examiners for Nursing
 Home Administrators
Pavilion Office Bldg.
Montpelier, VT 05602
Phone: (802)828-2373

Credential Type: License. **Duration of License:** Two years. **Requirements:** 18 years of age. Good moral character. High school graduate or equivalent. Mentally and physically able to perform duties. And one of the following: Complete an approved program leading to an AA or BA in Health Care Administration; Completion of a course or training relevant to NHA; Sufficient experience or education that qualifies candidate for examination as an NHA; Licensed in another state. **Examination:** Yes. **Reciprocity:** Yes. **Fees:** $100 Initial application and exam. $100 Renewal with 40 hours of continuing education. **Governing Statute:** Title 18, VSA Sections 2051-2061.

Virginia

3393

Nursing Home Administrator
State Board of Examiners for
 Nursing Home Administrators
Dept. of Commerce
3600 W. Broad St.
Richmond, VA 23230
Phone: (804)662-9111
Fax: (804)662-9943

Credential Type: License. **Duration of License:** One year. **Requirements:** 21 years of age. A baccalaureate or higher degree in nursing home administration or in a health administration field including a 400 hour residency experience in nursing home administration; or successfully completed high school and have completed the administrator-in-training program as specified by the Board. **Examination:** National and state exams. **Fees:** $156 application fee. $188 national exam fee. $125 state exam fee. $125 annual renewal fee.

Washington

3394

Nursing Home Administrator
Board of Examiners for Nursing
 Home Administrators
PO Box 9012
Olympia, WA 98504
Phone: (206)586-6350
Fax: (206)586-7774

Credential Type: Nursing Home Administrator. **Duration of License:** One year. **Requirements:** Be at least 21 years of age. Associate's degree and/or acceptable experience. Renewal requires 54 hours of continuing education every three years. **Examination:** National and state examinations. **Reciprocity:** Yes. **Fees:** $500 application fee. $400 reciprocity fee. $380 renewal fee.

West Virginia

3395

Nursing Home Administrator
Nursing Home Administration
 Licensing Board
110 Shumate St.
Oak Hill, WV 25901
Phone: (304)348-0558

Credential Type: Nursing Home Administrator. **Duration of License:** One year. **Requirements:** Bachelor's degree in health care administration and experience. Must have one year of administrator-in-training program. Renewal requires 30 hours of continuing education each year. **Examination:** National and state examinations.

Wisconsin

3396

Nursing Home Administrator
Regulations and Licensing Dept.
Nursing Home Administrator Board
PO Box 8935
Madison, WI 53708-8935
Phone: (608)266-8609

Credential Type: License. **Duration of License:** Two years. **Requirements:** Completion of a regular course of study in nursing home administration; or attendance at specialized courses; or attandance at a program of study in the area of institutional administration. Six months to one year of experience. 18 years of age. **Examination:** National and state exams. **Reciprocity:** Yes. **Fees:** $165 application and exam fee. $50 reciprocity fee. $40 renewal fee.

Wyoming

3397

Administrator, Nursing Home
Board of Nursing Home
   Administration
Hathaway Bldg., 4th Fl.
2300 Capitol Ave.
Cheyenne, WY 82002
Phone: (307)777-6464

Credential Type: License. **Duration of License:** One year. **Requirements:** 21 years of age. Possess at least a college associate's degree. Complete six months administrator-in-training under the supervision of a licensed administrator. Pass a written state examination. Pass the national examination. Complete application and provide two letters of recommendation from professional associates within the last calendar year. **Examination:** Yes. **Fees:** $5 (actual cost) National Examination. $15 State Examination. $50 License. $50 Renewal.

Hearing Aid Dealers and Fitters

The following states grant licenses in this occupational category as of the date of publication:

Alabama	District of	Iowa	Minnesota	New Mexico	Rhode Island	Washington
Alaska	Columbia	Kansas	Mississippi	New York	South Carolina	West Virginia
Arizona	Florida	Kentucky	Missouri	North Carolina	South Dakota	Wisconsin
Arkansas	Georgia	Louisiana	Montana	North Dakota	Tennessee	Wyoming
California	Hawaii	Maine	Nebraska	Ohio	Texas	
Colorado	Idaho	Maryland	Nevada	Oklahoma	Utah	
Connecticut	Illinois	Massachusetts	New Hampshire	Oregon	Vermont	
Delaware	Indiana	Michigan	New Jersey	Pennsylvania	Virginia	

Alabama

3398

Hearing Aid Specialist
Alabama Board of Hearing Aid Dealers
Bureau of Environmental and Health Service Standards
328 State Office Bldg.
Mongomery, AL 36130
Phone: (205)242-5004

Credential Type: License. **Duration of License:** One year. **Requirements:** 19 years of age. Must hold a high school diploma or equivalent. Must not have a record of any felony convictions for crimes of moral turpitude or any contagious diseases. **Examination:** Written and practical examinations. **Fees:** $100 registration fee. $100 renewal fee. $25 examination fee.

Alaska

3399

Hearing Aid Dealer
Dept. of Commerce and Economic Development
Div. of Occupational Licensing
PO Box 110806
Juneau, AK 99811-0806
Phone: (907)465-3811
Fax: (907)465-2974

Credential Type: Hearing aid dealer license. **Duration of License:** Two years. **Requirements:** At least 18 years of age. Must maintain a current state business license. High school diploma or equivalent. Provide a surety bond of $5,000 to the State of Alaska, or a Time Certificate of Deposit, Savings Passbook, or cash in lieu of other bonding. **Exemptions:** A physician or audiologist may deal in hearing aids without being so licensed. **Fees:** $30 application fee. $60 license fee. **Governing Statute:** Alaska Statutes 08.55.

Arizona

3400

Hearing Aid Dispenser
Arizona Dept. of Health Services
Div. of Family Health Services
Hearing Aid Dispenser Licensing Program
1740 W. Adams, Rm. 310
Phoenix, AZ 85007
Phone: (602)542-1181 or (602)542

Credential Type: Hearing aid dispenser license. **Duration of License:** One year. **Requirements:** Be of good moral character. Have an education equivalent to a four-year course in an accredited high school or have continuously engaged in the practice of fitting and dispensing hearing aids for three years. Be free of contagious or infectious disease. Not have had license revoked or suspended by a state within the past two years, not be ineligible for licensure in any state due to prior revocation or suspension. Pass written and practical exam unless applying for license by reciprocity.

A person who is currently licensed in another state or jurisdiction that meets the minimum licensure requirements of Arizona may be granted a license without taking the examination.

License renewal requires eight hours of continuing education. **Examination:** Hearing Aid Dispenser Licensing Examination. **Exemptions:** Medical or osteopathic physicians licensed to practice in Arizona may treat or fit hearing aids without additional licensing. **Fees:** $50 application fee.

Credential Type: Temporary license. **Authorization:** Allows licensee to practice the fitting and dispensing of hearing aids for a period ending on the last day of the month following a scheduled examination. **Requirements:** Be of good moral character. Have an education equivalent to a four-year course in an accredited high school or have continuously engaged in the practice of fitting and dispensing hearing aids for three years. Be free of contagious or infectious disease. Not have had license revoked or suspended by a state within the past two years, not be ineligible for licensure in any state due to prior revocation or suspension.

Applicant must be supervised and trained by a licensed sponsor. If a sponsor terminates sponsorship, then the temporary license terminates when the department receives notice from the sponsor. **Fees:** $20 application fee.

Arkansas

3401

Hearing Aid Dispenser
Arkansas State Board of Hearing Aid Dispensers
10 Corporate Hill Drive, Ste. 350
Little Rock, AR 72205
Phone: (501)228-9888

Credential Type: License. **Duration of License:** One year. **Requirements:** 21 years of age. High school graduate. Pass examination given by the Board. **Examination:** Yes. **Fees:** $40 Written, oral and practical examinations. $20 Registration (one time only). $25 Temporary permit. $50 License. $50 Renewal.

Hearing Aid Dealers and Fitters

California

3402

Hearing Aid Dispenser
Hearing Aid Dispensers Examining Committee
1420 Howe Ave., Ste. 12
Sacramento, CA 95825-3233
Phone: (916)920-6377

Credential Type: Hearing Aid Dispenser License. **Duration of License:** One year. **Requirements:** Possess knowledge of hearing aid dispensing and hearing testing audiometry. **Examination:** Written and practical skills examination. **Reciprocity:** No. **Fees:** $122 application fee (includes fingerprint processing fee). $75 exam fee. $150 license fee. $200 renewal fee. **Governing Statute:** Business and Professions Code, Sect. 3300 et seq.

Colorado

3403

Hearing Aid Dealer/Dispenser
Attorney General
1525 Sherman St., 3rd Fl.
Denver, CO 80203
Phone: (303)866-5005

Credential Type: License. **Requirements:** Contact licensing body for application information.

Connecticut

3404

Hearing Aid Dealer
Div. of Medical Quality Assurance
Health Systems Regulation Bureau
Health Services Dept.
150 Washington St.
Hartford, CT 06106
Phone: (203)566-3207

Credential Type: License. **Requirements:** Contact licensing body for application information.

Delaware

3405

Hearing Aid Dispenser
Board of Examiners of Speech-Language Pathologists, Audiologists, and Hearing Aid Dispensers
Dept. of Administrative Services
Div. of Professional Regulation
Margaret O'Neill Bldg.
PO Box 1401
Dover, DE 19903
Phone: (302)739-4522

Credential Type: Hearing Aid Dispenser Licence. **Duration of License:** Two years. **Requirements:** Contact licensing body for application information. **Reciprocity:** Yes, for states, territories, and foreign countries, provinces, and states with equivalent requirements. **Fees:** $50 application fee. $70 renewal fee.

District of Columbia

3406

Hearing Aid Dispenser
Dept. of Consumer and Regulatory Affairs
Service Facility Regulation Administration
Pharmaceutical and Medical Devices Control Div.
PO Box 37200
Washington, DC 20013-7200
Phone: (202)727-7728

Alternate Information: 614 H St., NW, Rm. 1016, Washington, DC 20001

Credential Type: Registration. **Duration of License:** One year. **Requirements:** At least 18 years of age. High school diploma or equivalent. All hearing aid dispensers must submit proof of certification by the National Hearing Aid Society. **Fees:** $30 registration fee. $20 renewal fee. **Governing Statute:** D.C. Law 7-46.

Florida

3407

Hearing Aid Specialist
Board of Hearing Aid Specialists
Dept. of Professional Regulation
1940 N. Monroe St.
Tallahassee, FL 32399-0759
Phone: (904)487-1813

Credential Type: Hearing Aid Specialist License. **Duration of License:** Two years. **Requirements:** Be at least 18 years of age. Possess high school diploma or equivalent. Good moral character. Complete appropriate training. **Examination:** Florida Hearing Aid Specialist Licensing Examination, including written theory, written practical, and clinical practical sections. **Exemptions:** Licensed physicians and audiologists may fit and dispense hearing aids without additional licensing. **Reciprocity:** No. **Fees:** $325 application and examination fee. $375 renewal fee. $100 trainee registration fee. **Governing Statute:** Florida Statutes, Chapter 484, Part II.

Georgia

3408

Hearing Aid Dealer
State Board of Hearing Aid Dealers and Dispensers
Health Care Practitioners Section
Professional Examining Boards
166 Pryor St., SW
Atlanta, GA 30303
Phone: (404)656-3912

Credential Type: Hearing Aid Dealer's License. **Duration of License:** Two years. **Requirements:** Submit application and pay fees. Present evidence that applicant has established or will establish and maintain a regular office, store, or location for the dispensing of hearing aid devices or instruments. Provide evidence that a holder of a valid Georgia dispenser's license will be responsible for the dispensing of hearing aids under the dealer's license. **Fees:** $80 application fee. $80 renewal fee. **Governing Statute:** Official Code of Georgia Annotated 43-20. Rules of the Georgia State Board of Hearing Aid Dealers and Dispensers, Chap. 276.

Credential Type: Nonresident License. **Duration of License:** Two years. **Requirements:** Submit application and pay fee. Meet requirements of board. **Fees:** $80 application fee. $80 renewal fee. **Governing Statute:** Official Code of Georgia Annotated 43-20. Rules of the Georgia State Board of Hearing Aid Dealers and Dispensers, Chap. 276.

Georgia

3409

Hearing Aid Dispenser
State Board of Hearing Aid Dealers and Dispensers
Health Care Practitioners Section
Professional Examining Boards
166 Pryor St., SW
Atlanta, GA 30303
Phone: (404)656-3912

Credential Type: Hearing Aid Dispenser's License. **Duration of License:** Two years. **Requirements:** Be at least 18 years of age. Good moral character. Maintain a satisfactory relationship with and responsibility to a holder of a hearing aid dealer's license. Pass examination.

Renewal requires 12 hours of continuing education. **Examination:** Hearing Aid Dispenser's Examination. **Fees:** $80 application fee. $50 exam fee ($5 per part). $80 renewal fee. **Governing Statute:** Official Code of Georgia Annotated 43-20. Rules of the Georgia State Board of Hearing Aid Dealers and Dispensers, Chap. 276.

Credential Type: Nonresident License. **Duration of License:** Two years. **Requirements:** Must hold a current license from resident state with requirements equivalent to or higher than Georgia's. State must have reciprocal agreement with Georgia. **Examination:** No exam. **Fees:** $80 application fee. $80 renewal fee. **Governing Statute:** Official Code of Georgia Annotated 43-20. Rules of the Georgia State Board of Hearing Aid Dealers and Dispensers, Chap. 276.

3410

Hearing Aid Dispenser Apprentice
State Board of Hearing Aid Dealers and Dispensers, Health Care Practitioners Section, Professional Examining Boards
166 Pryor St., SW
Atlanta, GA 30303
Phone: (404)656-3912

Credential Type: Apprentice Dispenser's Permit. **Duration of License:** One year (non-renewable). **Requirements:** Supervising dealer must provide a statement that applicant is capable. Applicant must pass practical portion of examination. **Examination:** Hearing Aid Dispenser's Examination, practical part. **Fees:** $80 permit fee. **Governing Statute:** Official Code of Georgia Annotated 43-20. Rules of the Georgia State Board of Hearing Aid Dealers and Dispensers, Chap. 276.

Hawaii

3411

Hearing Aid Dealer and Fitter
Hawaii Board of Hearing Aid Dealers and Fitters
Dept. of Commerce and Consumer Affairs
PO Box 3469
Honolulu, HI 96801
Phone: (808)548-3086

Credential Type: License. **Duration of License:** Two years. **Requirements:** High school graduate or equivalent. **Examination:** Written and practical. **Reciprocity:** License through endorsement may be granted with current outof-state licenses in good standing and equal or higher licensing requirement fulfillment. **Fees:** $30 application fee. $65 exam fee. $50 temporary permit. $30 license fee. $20—$40 Compliance Resolution Fund fee. $100 renewal fee.

Idaho

3412

Hearing Aid Dealer
Hearing Aid Dealers and Fitters
Bureau of Occupational Licenses
1109 Main St., Ste. 220
Boise, ID 83702-5642
Phone: (208)334-3233

Credential Type: Hearing Aid Dealers and Fitters License. **Duration of License:** One year. **Requirements:** Be at least 21 years of age. Good moral character. Educational equivalent of four years of high school. Be free of contagious or infectious disease.

Renewal requires 18 contact hours of continuing education per year. **Examination:** Written and practical tests. **Reciprocity:** Yes, with states having requirements substantially equivalent to or higher than those in effect. **Fees:** $250 application/examination fee. $150 renewal fee. $250 reciprocity fee. **Governing Statute:** Idaho Code, Title 54, Chap. 29. Rules and Regulations of the Idaho State Board of Hearing Aid Dealers and Fitters.

Credential Type: Temporary permit. **Duration of License:** One year. **Requirements:** Meet basic requirements. Work under the direction and supervision of a licensed dealer or fitter. Must pass examination within one year. **Fees:** $250 temporary permit fee. **Governing Statute:** Idaho Code, Title 54, Chap. 29. Rules and Regulations of the Idaho State Board of Hearing Aid Dealers and Fitters.

3413

Hearing Aid Fitter
Hearing Aid Dealers and Fitters
Bureau of Occupational Licenses
1109 Main St., Ste. 220
Boise, ID 83702-5642
Phone: (208)334-3233

Credential Type: Hearing Aid Dealers and Fitters License. **Duration of License:** One year. **Requirements:** Be at least 21 years of age. Good moral character. Educational equivalent of four years of high school. Be free of contagious or infectious disease.

Renewal requires 18 contact hours of continuing education per year. **Examination:** Written and practical tests. **Reciprocity:** Yes, with states having requirements substantially equivalent to or higher than those in effect. **Fees:** $250 application/examination fee. $150 renewal fee. $250 reciprocity fee. **Governing Statute:** Idaho Code, Title 54, Chap. 29. Rules and Regulations of the Idaho State Board of Hearing Aid Dealers and Fitters.

Credential Type: Temporary permit. **Duration of License:** One year. **Requirements:** Meet basic requirements. Work under the direction and supervision of a licensed dealer or fitter. Must pass examination within one year. **Fees:** $250 temporary permit fee. **Governing Statute:** Idaho Code, Title 54, Chap. 29. Rules and Regulations of the Idaho State Board of Hearing Aid Dealers and Fitters.

Illinois

3414

Hearing Aid Dispenser
Illinois Dept. of Public Health
525 W. Jefferson
Springfield, IL 62761
Phone: (217)782-4733

Credential Type: Hearing Aid Dispenser License. **Duration of License:** Two years. **Requirements:** At least 18 years of age. U.S. citizen or legal alien. High school graduate or equivalent. Pass examination. Renewal requires 20 hours of continuing education. **Examination:** Hearing Aid Licensing Examination. **Reciprocity:** No. **Fees:** $75 written examination fee. $150 performance examination fee. $40 application fee. $80 initial license fee. $80 renewal fee. **Governing Statute:** Hearing Aid Consumer Protection Code 77, Illinois Administrative Code 682.

Indiana

3415

Hearing Aid Dealer
Hearing Aid Dealer Committee
Health Professions Bureau
402 W. Washington St., Rm. 041
Indianapolis, IN 46204
Phone: (317)232-2960

Credential Type: Certificate of registration to practice. **Duration of License:** Two years. **Authorization:** Provides authorization to fit and sell hearing aids. **Requirements:** Must be at least 18 years of age. Must not have been convicted of a felony. **Examination:** Board-administered examination. **Fees:** $35 administrative fee plus cost of exam. $50 license issuance fee. $40 renewal fee. **Governing Statute:** Indiana Code 25-20-1-3.

Credential Type: Student permit. **Duration of License:** One year. **Authorization:** Provides authorization to students to fit and sell hearing aids. **Requirements:** Must be at least 18 years of age. Must be employed or supervised by a registered dealer. **Fees:** $25 issuance fee. $10 renewal fee. **Governing Statute:** Indiana Code 25-20-1-5.

Iowa

3416

Hearing Aid Dealer
Board of Examiners of Hearing Aid Dealers
Dept. of Public Health
Lucas State Office Bldg.
Des Moines, IA 50319
Phone: (515)281-6762

Credential Type: License. **Duration of License:** Two years. **Examination:** Written and practical exam. **Reciprocity:** Yes. **Fees:** $50 exam fee. $130 license fee. $130 renewal fee. $35 temporary permit.

Kansas

3417

Hearing Aid Fitter and Dispenser
State Board of Hearing Aid Examiners
PO Box 252
Wichita, KS 67201-0252
Phone: (316)263-0774

Credential Type: License to fit and dispense hearing aids. **Duration of License:** One year. **Requirements:** Must be a state resident. Must be at least 18 years of age. Must have education equivalent to a four-year course in an accredited high school. Must attend courses offered by the board, or complete the education requirements of the National Hearing Aid Association or the National Manufacturers' Symposium.

Renewal requires at least two days of continuing education. **Examination:** Written and practical examination. **Fees:** $50 application fee. $50 renewal fee. **Governing Statute:** K.S.A. 74-5801 ff. K.A.R. 67-1-1 ff.

Credential Type: Temporary license. **Duration of License:** Until 30 days following the conclusion of the next exam. **Authorization:** Must work under a licensed individual. **Requirements:** Must have submitted license application and be waiting for the next examination. **Fees:** $25 temporary license fee. **Governing Statute:** K.S.A. 74-5801 ff. K.A.R. 67-1-1 ff.

Kentucky

3418

Hearing Instrument Specialist
Occupations and Professions Board
PO Box 456
Frankfort, KY 40602
Phone: (502)564-3296

Credential Type: License. **Duration of License:** One year. **Requirements:** High school diploma or equivalent. 21 years of age. U.S. citizen or legal alien. Excellent health. Completion of a 12 month apprenticeship. Ten hours of continuing education for renewal. **Examination:** Yes.

Louisiana

3419

Hearing Aid Dealer
Louisiana Board for Hearing Aid Dealers
PO Box 499
Baton Rouge, LA 70821
Phone: (504)342-0818

Credential Type: License. **Duration of License:** Permanent. **Requirements:** 21 years of age. High school diploma or equivalent. **Examination:** Written, practical and oral. **Fees:** $25 exam fee. $100 license fee

Maine

3420

Hearing Aid Dealer and Fitter
Board of Hearing Aid Dealers and Fitters
Dept. of Professional and Financial Regulation
Div. of Licensing and Enforcement
State House Station 35
Augusta, ME 04333
Phone: (207)582-8723

Credential Type: License. **Duration of License:** One year. **Requirements:** At least 18 years of age. High school graduate or equivalent. Have obtained trainee permit and received at least 30 days of training under the direct supervision of a licensed hearing aid dealer and fitter. Renewal requires continuing education. **Examination:** Board-administered examination. **Reciprocity:** Yes, with states having similar requirements. **Fees:** $100 license fee. $100 renewal fee. **Governing Statute:** 32 M.S.R.A. Chap. 23-A.

Credential Type: Temporary trainee permit. **Requirements:** At least 18 years of age. High school graduate or equivalent. Submit application with signature of a licensed hearing aid dealer and fitter who will be responsible for trainee's direct supervision. **Fees:** $50 permit fee.

Maryland

3421

Hearing Aid Dealer
Board of Examiners for Hearing Aid Dealers
Dept. of Licensing and Regulation
501 St. Paul Pl.
Baltimore, MD 21202-2272
Phone: (410)333-6322

Credential Type: License. **Duration of License:** Two years. **Requirements:** At least 18 years of age. Good character and reputation. High school graduate or equivalent. Free of any contagious or infectious diseases.

Renewal requires continuing education of 20 hours during the two-year period. **Examination:** Board-administered examination, written and practical. **Fees:** $50 application fee. $100 license fee. $100 renewal fee. **Governing Statute:** Annotated Code of Maryland, Title 8.

Massachusetts

3422

Hearing Aid Dealer/Dispenser
Attorney General
One Ashburton Pl., Rm. 2010
Boston, MA 02108
Phone: (617)727-2200

Credential Type: License. **Requirements:** Contact licensing body for application information.

Michigan

3423

Hearing Aid Dealer
Board of Hearing Aid Dealers
Bureau of Occupational &
  Professional Regulation
Dept. of Commerce
PO Box 30018
Lansing, MI 48909
Phone: (517)373-9153

Credential Type: License. **Duration of License:** Two years. **Requirements:** At least 18 years of age. High school diploma or its equivalent. Worked as a licensed hearing aid salesperson for at least two years under the direction and supervision of a licensed hearing aid dealer. Be of good moral character. Maintain a place of business. Renewal requires a simple statement in writing listing the current educational material in the hearing aid field they have studied or the educational classes they have attended during the previous year. **Examination:** Written and practical exam. **Fees:** $20 application processing fee. $100 initial exam fee ($35 per exam part). $20 exam review fee. $80 initial license fee, per year. $80 renewal fee, per year. **Governing Statute:** The Occupational Code, Act 299 of 1980, as amended.

3424

Hearing Aid Salesperson
Board of Hearing Aid Dealers
Bureau of Occupational &
  Professional Regulation
Dept. of Commerce
PO Box 30018
Lansing, MI 48909
Phone: (517)373-9153

Credential Type: License. **Duration of License:** One year. **Requirements:** At least 18 years of age. High school diploma or its equivalent. Have been a hearing aid trainee for a period of at least six months. Not have been convicted of a felony or a misdemeanor involving moral turpitude. Comply with all rules and regulations of the Board. Be of good moral character. Be employed by a hearing aid dealer. **Examination:** Written and practical exam. **Fees:** $20 application processing fee. $100 initial exam fee ($30 per exam part). $20 exam review fee. $50 initial license fee, per year. $50 renewal fee, per year. **Governing Statute:** The Occupational Code, Act 299 of 1980, as amended.

3425

Hearing Aid Trainee
Board of Hearing Aid Dealers
Bureau of Occupational &
  Professional Regulation
Dept. of Commerce
PO Box 30018
Lansing, MI 48909
Phone: (517)373-9153

Credential Type: License. **Duration of License:** One year. **Requirements:** At least 18 hears of age. Work for and under the direction of a licensed hearing aid dealer. Be of good moral character. Comply with all rules and regulations of the Board. **Fees:** $10 application processing fee. $20 initial license fee, per year. **Governing Statute:** The Occupational Code, Act 299 of 1980, as amended.

Minnesota

3426

Hearing Aid Dispenser
Dept. of Health
Bureau of Health Resources and
  Managed Care Services
Health Occupations Programs
717 Delaware St., SE
Box 9441
Minneapolis, MN 55440
Phone: (612)623-5611
Phone: (612)623-5000
Fax: (612)623-5043

Credential Type: Hearing Aid Dispenser Registration. **Duration of License:** One year. **Authorization:** Registration required to use occupational title. Permit required to sell hearing instruments. **Requirements:** Be at least 18 years of age. Have equipment certified to meet ANSI standards. Renewal of registration requires 20 contact hours of continuing education. **Examination:** Written and practical examination. **Reciprocity:** Yes, provided state has equivalent requirements. **Fees:** $93 registration fee. $50 exam fee. $93 renewal fee. $35 surcharge fee (charged to registrants through April 30, 1995). $140 annual permit fee. **Governing Statute:** Minnesota Statutes Chap. 153A. Minnesota Rules Chap. 4745.

3427

Hearing Aid Dispenser
Dept. of Health
Bureau of Health Resources and
  Managed Care Services
Health Occupations Programs
717 Delaware St., SE
Box 9441
Minneapolis, MN 55440
Phone: (612)623-5611
Phone: (612)623-5000
Fax: (612)623-5043

Credential Type: Hearing Aid Dispenser Registration. **Authorization:** Registration required to use occupational title. **Requirements:** Contact licensing body for application information. **Governing Statute:** Minnesota Statutes 214.13.

Mississippi

3428

Hearing Aid Dealer
State Dept. of Health
Professional Licensure-Hearing Aid
PO Box 1700
Jackson, MS 39215-1700
Phone: (601)987-4153

Credential Type: License. **Duration of License:** One year. **Requirements:** High school graduate or equivalent. Complete a period of supervised training of at least 90 days, but not more than nine months. **Examination:** NIHIS examination. Practical examination. Examination on Mississippi law. **Reciprocity:** Yes, based on passing appropriate examinations. **Fees:** $100 license by examination fee. $100 reciprocity fee.

Credential Type: Temporary Permit. **Duration of License:** Until 30 days after next scheduled exam. **Authorization:** May work only under the supervision of a licensed hearing aid dealer. **Requirements:** High school graduate or equivalent. **Fees:** $100 temporary permit fee.

Missouri

3429

Hearing Aid Fitter and Dealer
Council for Hearing Aid Dealers and Fitters
PO Box 1335
Jefferson City, MO 65102
Phone: (314)751-0240

Credential Type: License and Registration. **Duration of License:** One year. **Requirements:** Be at least 21 years of age. Good moral character. High school graduate or equivalent. **Examination:** Written and practical examination. **Reciprocity:** Yes, provided state has equivalent or higher requirements. **Fees:** $75 license by examination fee. $125 reciprocity fee. **Governing Statute:** Chap. 346, RSMo. Four CSR 160-1.

Credential Type: Temporary Permit. **Duration of License:** One year. **Authorization:** May work only under the supervision and training of a licensed hearing aid fitter and dealer. Temporary permits are renewable once for a period of six months. **Requirements:** Be at least 21 years of age. Good moral character. High school graduate or equivalent. **Fees:** $50 temporary permit fee. **Governing Statute:** Chap. 346, RSMo. Four CSR 160-1.

Montana

3430

Hearing Aid Dispenser
Montana Board of Hearing Aid Dispensers
111 N. Jackson
Helena, MT 59620
Phone: (406)444-5433

Credential Type: Hearing Aid Trainee License. **Requirements:** Graduation from high school or equivalent. Three years of experience in the selling, fitting, or dispensing of hearing aids in Montana, or equivalent. **Examination:** Written. **Fees:** $125 application, exam and trainee license fee. **Governing Statute:** Montana Code Annotated 37-16-401 through 37-16-413.

Credential Type: Hearing Aid Dispenser License. **Duration of License:** One year. **Requirements:** Completion of the 12-month training program. **Examination:** Written and oral. **Exemptions:** Licensed audiologists may take exam without taking the training program. **Fees:** $150 application fee. $100 license fee. $125 renewal fee. **Governing Statute:** Montana Code Annotated 37-16-401 through 37-16-413.

Nebraska

3431

Hearing Aid Instrument Dispenser and Fitter
Nebraska Board of Examiners of Hearing Aid Instrument Dispensers and Fitters
301 Centennial Mall S.
PO Box 95007
Lincoln, NE 68509
Phone: (402)471-2115

Credential Type: License. **Duration of License:** Two years. **Requirements:** 21 years of age. Must hold a high school diploma. Must be free of contagious or infectious disease. **Examination:** Yes. **Fees:** $200 license fee. $250 renewal fee.

Nevada

3432

Hearing Aid Specialist
Nevada State Board of Hearing Aid Specialists
440-B E. Sahara Ave.
Las Vegas, NV 89104
Phone: (702)732-8721

Credential Type: License. **Requirements:** Master's degree in audiology or 10 years of experience. Completion of the NHAS course. **Examination:** Yes. **Fees:** $100 application fee. $100 license fee. $10 certificate fee. $10 certificate renewal fee.

New Hampshire

3433

Hearing Aid Dealer/Dispenser
Hearing Aid Licensing
Health and Welfare Bldg.
6 Hazen Dr.
Concord, NH 03301
Phone: (603)271-1203
Phone: (603)271-4503

Credential Type: Registration. **Requirements:** Contact licensing body for application information.

New Jersey

3434

Hearing Aid Dispenser
Hearing Aid Dispensers Examining Committe
28 W. State St.
Trenton, NJ 08608
Phone: (609)292-4843

Credential Type: License. **Requirements:** 18 years of age. Successful completion of the Hearing Technology program at Camden County College; or six months of training and experience in fitting and dispensing of hearing aids under the direct supervision of a licensed dispenser; or two years of previous training and experience. Some continuing education is required. **Examination:** Written and practical. **Reciprocity:** Yes. **Fees:** $50 exam fee. $80 renewal fee. $50 temporary license fee. **Governing Statute:** NJSA 45:9A. NJAC 13:35-8.

New Mexico

3435

Hearing Aid Dispenser
Hearing Aid Advisory Board
Dept. of Regulation and Licensing
PO Box 25101
Santa Fe, NM 87504
Phone: (505)827-7164

Credential Type: License. **Duration of License:** One year. **Requirements:** Be at least 18 years of age. High school graduate or equivalent. Meet one of the following sets of requirements: (1) Certification by the American Speech, Language, and Hearing Association (ASHA). Demonstrate experience and knowledge by completing a graduate training program or appropriate work or training experience. Pass jurisprudence exam. (2) Meet the requirements for certification by the American Speech, Language, and Hearing Association (ASHA). Demonstrate experience and knowledge by completing a graduate training program or appropriate work or training experience. Pass jurisprudence exam. (3) Be a licensed physician eligible for certification or certified by the American Board of Otorhinolaryngologists (head and neck surgery). Pass jurisprudence exam. (4) Complete at least seven months of work under a trainee permit. Pass written, practical, and jurisprudence exams.

Renewal requires 20 clock hours of continuing education every two years. **Examination:** National Hearing Aid Society (NHAS) Hearing Aid Dispensers Examination. Practical Examination. Jurisprudence

Hearing Aid Dispenser, continued

examination. **Reciprocity:** Yes, provided requirements of the other state are equivalent to those of New Mexico. **Fees:** $150 application fee. $75 renewal fee.

Credential Type: Temporary Trainee Permit. **Duration of License:** One year. **Requirements:** Be at least 18 years of age. High school graduate or equivalent. Identify a qualified sponsor. Have applied for licensure by examination.

New York

3436

Hearing Aid Dealer
Dept. of State
Div. of Licensing Services
162 Washington Ave.
Albany, NY 12231
Phone: (518)474-4429

Credential Type: Registration. **Duration of License:** One year. **Requirements:** Submit application and pay fee. **Fees:** $15 application fee. $50 registration fee. $50 renewal fee. **Governing Statute:** Article 37, Section 780 et seq.

North Carolina

3437

Hearing Aid Dealer and Fitter
North Carolina State Board of
 Hearing Aid Dealers and Fitters
136 Oakwood Dr.
Winston-Salem, NC 27103
Phone: (919)722-0120

Credential Type: License. **Duration of License:** One year. **Requirements:** One year apprenticeship under the direct supervision of a licensed hearing aid dealer and fitter or five years of formal education with a major in audiology or a master's degree in audiology. 18 years of age. Three character references. **Examination:** Written. **Fees:** $105 license and exam fee. $100 renewal fee.

North Dakota

3438

Hearing Aid Dealer and Dispenser
State Board of Hearing Aid Dealers
 and Fitters
Box 931
Bismarck, ND 58502-0931
Phone: (701)223-5807

Credential Type: License. **Duration of License:** One year. **Requirements:** Be at least 18 years of age. Good moral character. High school graduate or equivalent. Must be free of contagious or infectious disease. Complete a one year training period.

Renewal requires two days of continuing education per year. **Examination:** Written and practical examinations. **Governing Statute:** North Dakota Century Code 43-33. North Dakota Articles 10-14.

Credential Type: Temporary Trainee Permit. **Duration of License:** One year. **Authorization:** Allows holder to be trained under the direct supervision of a valid license holder. **Requirements:** Issued to applicants for licensure who fulfill age, character, education, and health requirements. **Governing Statute:** North Dakota Century Code 43-33. North Dakota Articles 10-14.

Ohio

3439

Hearing Aid Dealer and Fitter
Hearing Aid Dealers and Fitters
 Licensing Board
PO Box 118
Columbus, OH 43216
Phone: (614)466-5215

Credential Type: License. **Duration of License:** One year. **Requirements:** Be at least 18 years of age. Good moral character. Free of contagious or infectious disease. **Examination:** Written and performance examination. **Fees:** $150 license fee. $112.50 renewal fee. **Governing Statute:** Ohio Revised Code, Section 4747.01 et seq. Rules of Section 4747.

Credential Type: Trainee Permit. **Duration of License:** One year. **Authorization:** Must be supervised and trained by a licensed hearing aid fitter. **Requirements:** Be at least 18 years of age. High school graduate or equivalent. Good moral character. Free of contagious or infectious disease. **Fees:** $37.50 permit fee.

Oklahoma

3440

Hearing Aid Dealer and Fitter
Oklahoma State Dept. of Health
1000 N.E. Tenth
Oklahoma City, OK 73152
Phone: (405)271-5217

Credential Type: License. **Duration of License:** One year. **Requirements:** High school diploma or GED. Knowledge of hearing loss measurement. 18 years of age. **Examination:** Hearing Aid Fitness Exam. **Fees:** $35 exam fee. $50 license fee. $50 renewal fee.

Oregon

3441

Hearing Aid Dealer
Hearing Aid Dealer Licensing
Health Div. Licensing Programs
750 Front St. NE, Ste. 200
Salem, OR 97310
Phone: (503)378-8667

Credential Type: License. **Duration of License:** One year. **Requirements:** 18 years of age. High school diploma or equivalent. Must be trained and supervised by a hearing aid dealer, or an audiologist or otolaryngologist, or licensure in another state as a hearing aid dealer. **Examination:** Yes. **Fees:** $135 exam fee. $125 license fee. $125 renewal fee. **Governing Statute:** ORS 694.015 to 694.170.

Pennsylvania

3442

Hearing Aid Dealer and Fitter
State Dept. of Health
Bureau of Quality Assurance
Hearing Aid Program
Health and Welfare Bldg., Rm. 907
Harrisburg, PA 17120
Phone: (717)787-8015

Credential Type: Hearing Aid Dealer Registration. **Duration of License:** One year. **Authorization:** A dealer registration is required of all firms owned and operated by anyone other than a hearing aid fitter. **Requirements:** Submit application and pay fee. **Fees:** $100 registration fee.

Credential Type: Hearing Aid Fitter Registration. **Duration of License:** One year. **Requirements:** Complete a six-month apprenticeship. **Examination:** Written examination. **Reciprocity:** Yes, provided state has equivalent requirements. **Fees:** $75 exam fee.

Credential Type: Apprentice Fitter Registration. **Duration of License:** One year. **Authorization:** Must be supervised and trained by a registered hearing aid fitter. **Requirements:** Must have a sponsor responsible for training and supervision. **Fees:** $25 registration fee. $50 renewal fee.

Credential Type: Temporary Registration. **Duration of License:** One year or 30 days after next scheduled exam. **Requirements:** Must have been engaged in the fitting and selling of hearing aids at an established place of business in another state for a period of two years within the past five years. Temporary registrant must take the hearing aid fitter's exam to qualify for regular registration. **Fees:** $25 temporary registration fee.

Rhode Island

3443

Hearing Aid Dealer/Fitter
Board of Hearing Aid Dealers and Fitters
Rhode Island Dept. of Business Regulation
233 Richmond St.
Providence, RI 02903
Phone: (401)277-2416

Credential Type: Hearing Aid Dealer/Fitter License. **Duration of License:** One or two years. **Requirements:** At least 21 years of age. High school graduate or equivalent. Apply for Basic Audiology course offered by the National Hearing Aid Society. Two years of experience under the supervision of a licensed hearing aid specialist. **Examination:** Written and oral examination. **Reciprocity:** No. **Fees:** $25 temporary one-year permit fee. $50 biennial renewal fee.

South Carolina

3444

Hearing Aid Dealer and Fitter
Dept. of Health and Environmental Control
Div. of Health Licensing
2600 Bull St.
Columbia, SC 29201
Phone: (803)737-7202

Alternate Information: 1777 St. Julian Pl., Ste. 402, Columbia, SC 29201

Credential Type: License and Registration. **Duration of License:** One year. **Requirements:** Be at least 21 years of age. High school graduate or equivalent. Renewal requires eight hours of continuing education per year. **Examination:** Written and practical examination. **Exemptions:** A licensed audiologist may apply for a license without examination. **Fees:** $50 license fee. $50 exam fee. $50 renewal fee.

Credential Type: Temporary Permit. **Duration of License:** One year. **Authorization:** Must be trained and supervised by a licensed hearing aid dealer. **Requirements:** Be at least 21 years of age. High school graduate or equivalent. **Fees:** $25 temporary permit fee.

South Dakota

3445

Hearing Aid Dispenser
Board of Hearing Aid Dispensers
PO Box 654
Spearfish, SD 57783-0654
Phone: (605)642-1600

Credential Type: License. **Duration of License:** One year. **Requirements:** Be at least 18 years of age. Must be a resident of South Dakota. Good moral character. High school graduate or equivalent.

Renewal requires 12 hours of approved advanced training school sessions per year. **Examination:** Written and oral examination. **Exemptions:** Licensed physicians. **Reciprocity:** Yes, with states that have equivalent or higher requirements. **Fees:** $100 license fee. $50 temporary license fee. **Governing Statute:** South Dakota Codified Laws, Chap. 36-24. Administrative Rules of South Dakota, Article 20:46.

Tennessee

3446

Hearing Aid Dispenser
Hearing Aid Dispensers Board
283 Plus Park Blvd.
Nashville, TN 37247-1010
Phone: (615)367-6207

Credential Type: License. **Duration of License:** One year. **Requirements:** 18 years old. High school graduate or equivalent. Complete 16 hours of continuing education every other year. Good moral character. **Examination:** Yes. **Reciprocity:** Yes. **Fees:** $330 Registration. $100 Examination. $35 Application.

Texas

3447

Hearing Aid Dispenser
Texas Board of Examiners in the Fitting and Dispensing of Hearing Aids
4800 N. Lamar, Ste. 150
Austin, TX 78756
Phone: (512)459-1488

Credential Type: License. **Duration of License:** One year. **Requirements:** 18 years of age. High school diploma or equivalent. 150 hours of practicum with training in specified areas, under the direct supervision of a licensed hearing aid dispenser. 10 hours of continuing education credit or re-examination required for license renewal. **Examination:** Written, oral, and practicum tests. **Fees:** $125 exam fee. $75 license fee. $195 renewal fee. **Governing Statute:** VACS 4566, 22 TAC 141.

Utah

3448

Hearing Aid Specialist
Dept. of Commerce
Div. of Occupational and Professional Licensing
160 E. 300 S.
PO Box 45802
Salt Lake City, UT 84145
Phone: (801)530-6628

Credential Type: License. **Duration of License:** Two years. **Requirements:** 18 years of age. Must be a high school graduate. **Examination:** Yes. **Fees:** $90 license fee. $60 renewal fee.

Vermont

3449

Hearing Aid Dealer/Dispenser
Secretary of State's Office
Hearing Aid Licensing
Pavillion Office Bldg.
Montpelier, VT 05602
Phone: (802)828-2191

Credential Type: License. **Requirements:** Contact licensing body for application information.

Virginia

3450

Hearing Aid Dealer and Fitter
Virginia Board for Hearing Aid Dealers and Fitters
Dept. of Commerce
3600 W. Broad St.
Richmond, VA 23230
Phone: (804)367-2194

Credential Type: License. **Requirements:** Encouraged by the Board to take the National Hearing Aid Society course. **Examination:** Yes. **Fees:** Yes.

Washington

3451

Hearing Aid Dispenser/Fitter
Dept. of Health
1300 SE Quince
Olympia, WA 98504
Phone: (206)586-6351

Credential Type: Hearing Aid Dispenser/Fitter License. **Duration of License:** One year. **Requirements:** At least 18 years of age. Post a $10,000 Surety Bond. Complete a four- hour course in AIDS education. **Examination:** Written and practical examination. **Fees:** $500 examination fee. $30 partial reexamination fee. $200 license renewal fee.

Credential Type: Hearing Aid Dispenser/Fitter Trainee License. **Duration of License:** One year. **Requirements:** At least 18 years of age. Complete a four-hour course in AIDS education. Be sponsored by a licensed Hearing Aid Dispenser/Fitter who has held a license for at least one year. **Fees:** $350 application fee. $200 fee for transfer of sponsor. $200 for extension of trainee license.

West Virginia

3452

Hearing Aid Specialist
Board of Hearing Aid Dealers
701 Jefferson Rd.
S. Charleston, WV 25309
Phone: (304)348-7886

Credential Type: License. **Duration of License:** One year. **Requirements:** U.S. citizen. 18 years old. High school diploma. After obtaining permit, trainee must take exam within six months. **Examination:** Yes. **Fees:** $65 Examination. $50 License. $40 Renewal.

Wisconsin

3453

Hearing Instrument Specialist
Regulations and Licensing Dept.
Hearing & Speech Board
PO Box 8935
Madison, WI 53708-8935
Phone: (608)266-8609

Credential Type: License. **Requirements:** High school diploma or equivalent. 18 years of age. **Examination:** Written and practical. **Reciprocity:** Yes.

Wyoming

3454

Hearing Aid Specialist
Wyoming Board of Hearing Aid Specialists
1710 Central Ave.
Cheyenne, WY 82001
Phone: (307)634-4100

Credential Type: License. **Duration of License:** One year. **Requirements:** Must have a high school diploma. Must pass a written examination. **Examination:** Yes. **Fees:** $200 Examination. $100 Temporary permit. $100 Renewal.

Heating, Air-Conditioning, and Refrigeration Mechanics

The following states grant licenses in this occupational category as of the date of publication:

Alabama	Delaware	Florida	Massachusetts	Nevada	Oklahoma	Texas
Alaska	District of	Georgia	Missouri	North Carolina	Oregon	Virginia
Connecticut	Columbia	Louisiana	Nebraska	North Dakota	Rhode Island	

Alabama

3455

Heating and Air Conditioning Contractor
Alabama State Board of Heating and Air Conditioning Contractors
421 S. McDonough St.
Montgomery, AL 36104
Phone: (205)242-5550

Credential Type: License. **Duration of License:** One year. **Requirements:** Must have knowledge of the trade. **Examination:** Written examination. **Fees:** $50 examination fee. $50 renewal fee.

3456

Heating and Air Conditioning Mechanic
Board of HVAC Contractors
421 McDonough St.
Montgomery, AL 36104
Phone: (205)261-5550

Credential Type: License. **Requirements:** Contact licensing body for application information.

Alaska

3457

Heating and Air Conditioning Mechanic
Dept. of Commerce
Div. of Occupational Licensing
PO Box D-1
Juneau, AK 99811
Phone: (907)465-2535

Credential Type: License. **Requirements:** Contact licensing body for application information.

Connecticut

3458

Heating-Cooling Apprentice
Heating, Piping, and Cooling Work Examining Board
Occupational Licensing Div.
Consumer Protection Dept.
165 Capitol Ave.
Hartford, CT 06106
Phone: (203)566-3275

Credential Type: Apprentice permit. **Duration of License:** Until next licensure examination. **Authorization:** Work may be performed only under the supervision of a licensed contractor or journeyman. **Requirements:** Be of good moral character. Have an 8th grade education or equivalent. **Governing Statute:** General Statutes of Connecticut, Chap. 393.

3459

Heating-Cooling Contractor
Heating, Piping, and Cooling Work Examining Board
Occupational Licensing Div.
Consumer Protection Dept.
165 Capitol Ave.
Hartford, CT 06106
Phone: (203)566-3275

Credential Type: Unlimited heating-cooling contractor's license (S-1). **Duration of License:** Two years. **Requirements:** Be of good moral character. Have an 8th grade education or equivalent. Must have served as an heating-cooling journeyman for not less than two years. If service was outside of state, must submit evidence that service was comparable to service in state or that applicant has education and experience and has passed an examination demonstrating competency to be an unlimited contractor. **Examination:** State licensure exam. **Reciprocity:** Yes, with selected states. **Fees:** $75 application fee. $150 license fee. **Governing Statute:** General Statutes of Connecticut, Chap. 393.

Credential Type: Limited heating-cooling contractor's license (S-3). **Duration of License:** Two years. **Authorization:** Limited to installation, repair, replacement, alteration, or maintenance of any apparatus of piping, appliances, devices, or accessories for heating systems and boilers, excluding sheet metal work, air conditioning, and refrigeration systems. May install hot, chilled, and condensed water, as well as steam piping in air conditioning systems. **Requirements:** Be of good moral character. Have an 8th grade education or equivalent. Must have served one year as a heating-cooling apprentice, plus one year as a licensed journeyman. **Examination:** State licensure exam. **Reciprocity:** Yes, with selected states. **Fees:** $75 application fee.

Heating-Cooling Contractor, continued

$150 license fee. **Governing Statute:** General Statutes of Connecticut, Chap. 393.

Credential Type: Limited heating-cooling contractor's license (S-5). **Duration of License:** Two years. **Authorization:** May perform only work limited to hot water or steam heating systems for buildings not over three stories high. Does not cover the installation or servicing of oil burners of any size. **Requirements:** Be of good moral character. Have an 8th grade education or equivalent. Must have served as a heating-cooling journeyman for not less than two years. If service was outside of state, must submit evidence that service was comparable to service in state. **Examination:** State licensure exam. **Reciprocity:** Yes, with selected states. **Fees:** $75 application fee. $150 license fee. **Governing Statute:** General Statutes of Connecticut, Chap. 393.

Credential Type: Limited heating-cooling contractor's license (S-7). **Duration of License:** Two years. **Authorization:** May perform only work limited to hot water or steam heating systems for buildings not over three stories high. May install or service oil burners handling up to five gallons per hour as well as gas piping for the work covered by this license. **Requirements:** Be of good moral character. Have an 8th grade education or equivalent. Must have served as a heating-cooling journeyman for not less than two years. If service was outside of state, must submit evidence that service was comparable to service in state. **Examination:** State licensure exam. **Reciprocity:** Yes, with selected states. **Fees:** $75 application fee. $150 license fee. **Governing Statute:** General Statutes of Connecticut, Chap. 393.

Credential Type: Limited heating-cooling contractor's license (B-1). **Duration of License:** Two years. **Authorization:** Permits the installation, service, and repair of gas or oil burners for domestic and light commercial installations consuming less than five gallons per hour. **Requirements:** Be of good moral character. Have an 8th grade education or equivalent. Must have served as a heating-cooling journeyman for not less than two years. If service was outside of state, must submit evidence that service was comparable to service in state. **Examination:** State licensure exam. **Reciprocity:** Yes, with selected states. **Fees:** $75 application fee. $150 license fee. **Governing Statute:** General Statutes of Connecticut, Chap. 393.

Credential Type: Limited heating-cooling contractor's license (B-3). **Duration of License:** Two years. **Authorization:** Permits the installation, service, and repair of any gas or oil fired burners. **Requirements:** Be of good moral character. Have an 8th grade education or equivalent. Must have served as a heating-cooling journeyman for not less than two years. If service was outside of state, must submit evidence that service was comparable to service in state. **Examination:** State licensure exam. **Reciprocity:** Yes, with selected states. **Fees:** $75 application fee. $150 license fee. **Governing Statute:** General Statutes of Connecticut, Chap. 393.

Credential Type: Limited heating-cooling contractor's license (D-1). **Duration of License:** Two years. **Authorization:** Permits the installation, service, repair, replacement, maintenance, or alteration of any warm air, air conditioning, and refrigeration system, including necessary piping and associated pumping equipment. Does not cover the installation or servicing of oil burners of any size. **Requirements:** Be of good moral character. Have an 8th grade education or equivalent. Must have served as a heating-cooling journeyman for not less than two years. If service was outside of state, must submit evidence that service was comparable to service in state. **Examination:** State licensure exam. **Reciprocity:** Yes, with selected states. **Fees:** $75 application fee. $150 license fee. **Governing Statute:** General Statutes of Connecticut, Chap. 393.

Credential Type: Limited heating-cooling contractor's license (D-3). **Duration of License:** Two years. **Authorization:** May perform only work limited to the installation, service, repair, replacement, maintenance, or alteration of all refrigeration systems included in food storage, air conditioning, and special process systems. **Requirements:** Be of good moral character. Have an 8th grade education or equivalent. Must have served as a heating-cooling journeyman for not less than two years. If service was outside of state, must submit evidence that service was comparable to service in state. **Examination:** State licensure exam. **Reciprocity:** Yes, with selected states. **Fees:** $75 application fee. $150 license fee. **Governing Statute:** General Statutes of Connecticut, Chap. 393.

Credential Type: Limited heating, piping and cooling contractor's license (G-1). **Duration of License:** Two years. **Authorization:** May perform only work limited to the installation, service, repair, replacement, maintenance, or alteration of gas piping systems and approved gas appliances, gas utilization equipment and accessories for use with LP gas. **Requirements:** Be of good moral character. Have an 8th grade education or equivalent. Must have served as a heating-cooling journeyman for not less than two years. If service was outside of state, must submit evidence that service was comparable to service in state. **Examination:** State licensure exam. **Reciprocity:** Yes, with selected states. **Fees:** $75 application fee. $150 license fee. **Governing Statute:** General Statutes of Connecticut, Chap. 393.

3460

Heating-Cooling Journeyman
Heating, Piping, and Cooling Work Examining Board
Occupational Licensing Div.
Consumer Protection Dept.
165 Capitol Ave.
Hartford, CT 06106
Phone: (203)566-3275

Credential Type: Unlimited heating-cooling journeyman's license (S-2). **Duration of License:** Two years. **Requirements:** Be of good moral character. Have an 8th grade education or equivalent. Complete a bona fide apprenticeship program, including not less than four years experience. Demonstrate competency by completing applicable state licensure examination. **Examination:** State licensure exam. **Reciprocity:** Yes, with selected states. **Fees:** $45 application fee. $150 license fee. **Governing Statute:** General Statutes of Connecticut, Chap. 393.

Credential Type: Limited heating-cooling journeyman's license (S-4). **Duration of License:** Two years. **Authorization:** Limited to installation, repair, replacement, alteration, or maintenance of any apparatus of piping, appliances, devices, or accessories for heating systems and boilers, excluding sheet metal work, air conditioning, and refrigeration systems. May install hot, chilled, and condensed water, as well as steam piping in air conditioning systems. Must be in the employ of a licensed contractor. **Requirements:** Be of good moral character. Have an 8th grade education or equivalent. Complete a bona fide apprenticeship program, including not less than four years experience. Demonstrate competency by completing applicable state licensure examination. **Examination:** State licensure exam. **Reciprocity:** Yes, with selected states. **Fees:** $45 application fee. $150 license fee. **Governing Statute:** General Statutes of Connecticut, Chap. 393.

Credential Type: Limited heating-cooling journeyman's license (S-6). **Duration of License:** Two years. **Authorization:** May perform only work limited to hot water or steam heating systems for buildings not over three stories high. Does not cover the installation or servicing of oil burners of any size. Must be in the employ of a licensed contractor. **Requirements:** Be of good moral character. Have an 8th grade

Heating, Air-Conditioning, and Refrigeration Mechanics

education or equivalent. Complete a bona fide apprenticeship program, including not less than four years experience. Demonstrate competency by completing applicable state licensure examination. **Examination:** State licensure exam. **Reciprocity:** Yes, with selected states. **Fees:** $45 application fee. $150 license fee. **Governing Statute:** General Statutes of Connecticut, Chap. 393.

Credential Type: Limited heating-cooling journeyman's license (S-8). **Duration of License:** Two years. **Authorization:** May perform only work limited to hot water or steam heating systems for buildings not over three stories high. May install or service oil burners handling up to five gallons per hour as well as gas piping for the work covered by this license. Must be in the employ of a licensed contractor. **Requirements:** Be of good moral character. Have an 8th grade education or equivalent. Complete a bona fide apprenticeship program, including not less than four years experience. Demonstrate competency by completing applicable state licensure examination. **Examination:** State licensure exam. **Reciprocity:** Yes, with selected states. **Fees:** $45 application fee. $150 license fee. **Governing Statute:** General Statutes of Connecticut, Chap. 393.

Credential Type: Limited heating-cooling journeyman's license (B-2). **Duration of License:** Two years. **Authorization:** Permits the installation, service, and repair of gas or oil burners for domestic and light commercial installations consuming less than five gallons per hour. Must be in the employ of a licensed contractor. **Requirements:** Be of good moral character. Have an 8th grade education or equivalent. Complete a bona fide apprenticeship program, including not less than four years experience. Demonstrate competency by completing applicable state licensure examination. **Examination:** State licensure exam. **Reciprocity:** Yes, with selected states. **Fees:** $45 application fee. $150 license fee. **Governing Statute:** General Statutes of Connecticut, Chap. 393.

Credential Type: Limited heating-cooling journeyman's license (B-4). **Duration of License:** Two years. **Authorization:** Permits the installation, service, and repair of any gas or oil fired burners. Must be in the employ of a licensed contractor. **Requirements:** Be of good moral character. Have an 8th grade education or equivalent. Complete a bona fide apprenticeship program, including not less than four years experience. Demonstrate competency by completing applicable state licensure examination. **Examination:** State licensure exam. **Reciprocity:** Yes, with selected states. **Fees:** $45 application fee. $150 license fee.

Governing Statute: General Statutes of Connecticut, Chap. 393.

Credential Type: Limited heating-cooling journeyman's license (D-2). **Duration of License:** Two years. **Authorization:** Permits the installation, service, repair, replacement, maintenance, or alteration of any warm air, air conditioning, and refrigeration system, including necessary piping and associated pumping equipment. Does not cover the installation or servicing of oil burners of any size. Must be in the employ of a licensed contractor. **Requirements:** Be of good moral character. Have an 8th grade education or equivalent. Complete a bona fide apprenticeship program, including not less than four years experience. Demonstrate competency by completing applicable state licensure examination. **Examination:** State licensure exam. **Reciprocity:** Yes, with selected states. **Fees:** $45 application fee. $150 license fee. **Governing Statute:** General Statutes of Connecticut, Chap. 393.

Credential Type: Limited heating-cooling journeyman's license (D-4). **Duration of License:** Two years. **Authorization:** May perform only work limited to the installation, service, repair, replacement, maintenance, or alteration of all refrigeration systems included in food storage, air conditioning, and special process systems. Must be in the employ of a licensed contractor. **Requirements:** Be of good moral character. Have an 8th grade education or equivalent. Complete a bona fide apprenticeship program, including not less than four years experience. Demonstrate competency by completing applicable state licensure examination. **Examination:** State licensure exam. **Reciprocity:** Yes, with selected states. **Fees:** $45 application fee. $150 license fee. **Governing Statute:** General Statutes of Connecticut, Chap. 393.

Credential Type: Limited heating, piping and cooling journeyman's license (G-2). **Duration of License:** Two years. **Authorization:** May perform only work limited to the installation, service, repair, replacement, maintenance, or alteration of gas piping systems and approved gas appliances, gas utilization equipment and accessories for use with LP gas. Must be in the employ of a licensed contractor. **Requirements:** Be of good moral character. Have an 8th grade education or equivalent. Complete a bona fide apprenticeship program, including not less than four years experience. Demonstrate competency by completing applicable state licensure examination. **Examination:** State licensure exam. **Reciprocity:** Yes, with selected states. **Fees:** $45 application fee. $150 license fee. **Governing Statute:** General Statutes of Connecticut, Chap. 393.

3461

Solar Apprentice

Heating, Piping, and Cooling Work Examining Board
Occupational Licensing Div.
Consumer Protection Dept.
165 Capitol Ave.
Hartford, CT 06106
Phone: (203)566-3275

Credential Type: Apprentice permit. **Duration of License:** Until next licensure examination. **Authorization:** Work may be performed only under the supervision of a licensed contractor or journeyman. **Requirements:** Be of good moral character. Have an 8th grade education or equivalent. **Governing Statute:** General Statutes of Connecticut, Chap. 393.

3462

Solar Contractor

Heating, Piping, and Cooling Work Examining Board
Occupational Licensing Div.
Consumer Protection Dept.
165 Capitol Ave.
Hartford, CT 06106
Phone: (203)566-3275

Credential Type: Solar contractor's license. **Duration of License:** Two years. **Authorization:** Covers the installation, repair, replacement, alteration, or maintenance of an active, passive, or hybrid solar hot water heating system. **Requirements:** Be of good moral character. Have an 8th grade education or equivalent. Must have served as a solar journeyman for not less than two years. If service was outside of state, must submit evidence that service was comparable to service in state or that applicant has education and experience and has passed an examination demonstrating competency to be a solar contractor.

Heating-cooling contractors and plumbing-piping contractors who were licensed before July 1, 1984, or who have installed at least six fully operational solar hot water heating systems may be granted a solar contractor's license upon completion of state licensure examination. **Examination:** State licensure exam. **Reciprocity:** Yes, with selected states. **Fees:** $75 application fee. $150 license fee. **Governing Statute:** General Statutes of Connecticut, Chap. 393.

Connecticut

3463

Solar Journeyman
Heating, Piping, and Cooling Work Examining Board
Occupational Licensing Div.
Consumer Protection Dept.
165 Capitol Ave.
Hartford, CT 06106
Phone: (203)566-3275

Credential Type: Solar journeyman's license. **Duration of License:** Two years. **Authorization:** Must work under the supervision of a licensed solar contractor. **Requirements:** Be of good moral character. Have an 8th grade education or equivalent. Complete a bona fide apprenticeship program, including not less than two years experience. Demonstrate competency by completing applicable state licensure examination.

Heating-cooling journeymen and plumbing-piping journeymen who were licensed before July 1, 1984, may be granted a solar contractor's license upon completion of state licensure examination. **Examination:** State licensure exam. **Reciprocity:** Yes, with selected states. **Fees:** $45 application fee. $150 license fee. **Governing Statute:** General Statutes of Connecticut, Chap. 393.

Delaware

3464

Heating and Air Conditioning Mechanic
State Board of Electrical Examiners
PO Box 1401
Dover, DE 19903
Phone: (302)736-4522

Credential Type: License. **Requirements:** Contact licensing body for application information.

District of Columbia

3465

Refrigeration and Air Conditioning Contractor
License and Certification Div.
Occupational and Professional Licensure Administration
Consumer and Regulatory Affairs Dept.
PO Box 37200
Washington, DC 20013-7200
Phone: (202)727-7823
Phone: (202)727-7480

Alternate Information: 614 H St., NW, Washington, DC 20001.

Credential Type: Refrigeration and Air Conditioning Contractor License. **Duration of License:** One year. **Requirements:** Business must be conducted by or employ a person holding a Master Refrigeration and Air Conditioning Mechanic Limited License. Business must be conducted from a specific location. **Fees:** $50 application fee. $20 license fee. $70 annual renewal fee. **Governing Statute:** Municipal Regulations, Title 17, Chap. 3.

3466

Refrigeration and Air Conditioning Mechanic
License and Certification Div.
Occupational and Professional Licensure Administration
Consumer and Regulatory Affairs Dept.
PO Box 37200
Washington, DC 20013-7200
Phone: (202)727-7823
Phone: (202)727-7480

Alternate Information: 614 H St., NW, Washington, DC 20001.

Credential Type: Master Refrigeration and Air Conditioning Mechanic License. **Duration of License:** One year. **Requirements:** Have been employed for at least five years in installing, maintaining, repairing, and replacing refrigerators and air conditioning systems larger than 25 compressor horsepower or the equivalent tons in refrigeration. Post $5,000 bond. **Examination:** Written and practical examination. **Fees:** $10 application fee. $10 license fee. $20 exam fee. $30 annual renewal fee. **Governing Statute:** Municipal Regulations, Title 17, Chap. 3.

Credential Type: Master Refrigeration and Air Conditioning Mechanic Limited License. **Duration of License:** One year. **Requirements:** Have been employed for at least five years in installing, maintaining, repairing, and replacing refrigerators and air conditioning systems less than 25 compressor horsepower or the equivalent tons in refrigeration. Post $5,000 bond. **Examination:** Written and practical examination. **Fees:** $10 application fee. $10 license fee. $20 exam fee. $30 annual renewal fee. **Governing Statute:** Municipal Regulations, Title 17, Chap. 3.

Florida

3467

Air Conditioning Contractor
Dept. of Professional Regulation
Construction Industry Licensing Board
PO Box 2
Jacksonville, FL 32201
Phone: (904)359-6310

Credential Type: Class A State Certified License. **Duration of License:** Two or three years. **Authorization:** Authorized to work throughout the State of Florida without taking additional examinations in this construction category. Class A air conditioning contractor services are unlimited with regard to size of unit. **Requirements:** Be at least 18 years of age. Good moral character. Meet one of the following criteria: (1) Baccalaureate degree from an accredited four-year college in the appropriate field. Have one year of proven experience or a minimum of 2000 manhours. (2) Have at least four years of active experience, either as a workman who has learned the trade by serving an apprenticeship as a skilled workman who is able to comand the rate of a mechanic in applicant's field, or as a foreman. (3) Have a combination of not less than one year of experience as a foreman and not less than three years of credits for any accredited college-level courses; or a combination of not less than one year of experience as a foreman, one year as a skilled workman, and not less than two years of credits for any accredited college-level courses; or a combination of not less than one year of experience as a foreman, two years as a skilled workman, and not less than one year of credits for any accredited college-level courses.

Pass State Certification Examination. Must have appropriate workers' compensation coverage.

An active certified Class C (no longer issued) air conditioning contractor with four years of proven experience is eligible to take the Class A air conditioning contractors' examination. An active certified Class B air conditioning contractor with one year of proven experience is eligible to take the Class A air conditioning contractors' examination. **Examination:** State Certification Examination. **Reciprocity:** Yes. Applicant must have passed a similar national, regional, state, or U.S. territorial licensing examination. **Fees:** $254 examination fee. **Governing Statute:** Florida Statutes, Chapter 489, Part I.

Credential Type: Class A State Registered License. **Duration of License:** Two or three years. **Authorization:** Allows applicant to work only in those local areas in which applicant has complied with local requirements. Class A air conditioning contractor services are unlimited with regard to size of unit. **Requirements:** Applicant must first contact county or municipality in which applicant wishes to work for occupational and competency requirements. After meeting local requirements, applicant may apply for state registration. **Governing Statute:** Florida Statutes, Chapter 489, Part I.

Credential Type: Class B State Certified License. **Duration of License:** Two or three years. **Authorization:** Authorized to work throughout the State of Florida without taking additional examinations in this construction category. Class B air conditioning contractor services are limited to 25 tons of cooling and 500,000 BTU of heating in any one system. **Requirements:** Be at least 18 years of age. Good moral character. Meet one of the following criteria: (1) Baccalaureate degree from an accredited four-year college in the appropriate field. Have one year of proven experience or a minimum of 2000 man-hours. (2) Have at least four years of active experience, either as a workman who has learned the trade by serving an apprenticeship as a skilled workman who is able to comand the rate of a mechanic in applicant's field, or as a foreman. (3) Have a combination of not less than one year of experience as a foreman and not less than three years of credits for any accredited college-level courses; or a combination of not less than one year of experience as a foreman, one year as a skilled workman, and not less than two years of credits for any accredited college-level courses; or a combination of not less than one year of experience as a foreman, two years as a skilled workman, and not less than one year of credits for any accredited college-level courses.

Pass State Certification Examination. Must have appropriate workers' compensation coverage.

An active certified Class C (no longer issued) air conditioning contractor with three years of proven experience is eligible to take the Class B air conditioning contractors' examination. **Examination:** State Certification Examination. **Reciprocity:** Yes. Applicant must have passed a similar national, regional, state, or U.S. territorial licensing examination. **Fees:** $254 examination fee. **Governing Statute:** Florida Statutes, Chapter 489, Part I.

Credential Type: Class B State Registered License. **Duration of License:** Two or three years. **Authorization:** Allows applicant to work only in those local areas in which applicant has complied with local requirements. Class B air conditioning contractor services are limited to 25 tons of cooling and 500,000 BTU of heating in any one system. **Requirements:** Applicant must first contact county or municipality in which applicant wishes to work for occupational and competency requirements. After meeting local requirements, applicant may apply for state registration. **Governing Statute:** Florida Statutes, Chapter 489, Part I.

3468

Residential Solar Water Heating Specialty Contractor
Dept. of Professional Regulation
Construction Industry Licensing Board
PO Box 2
Jacksonville, FL 32201
Phone: (904)359-6310

Credential Type: State Certified License. **Duration of License:** Two or three years. **Authorization:** Authorized to work throughout the State of Florida without taking additional examinations in this construction category. **Requirements:** Be at least 18 years of age. Good moral character. Meet one of the following criteria: (1) Baccalaureate degree from an accredited four-year college in the appropriate field. Have one year of proven experience or a minimum of 2000 man-hours. (2) Have at least four years of active experience, either as a workman who has learned the trade by serving an apprenticeship as a skilled workman who is able to comand the rate of a mechanic in applicant's field, or as a foreman. (3) Have a combination of not less than one year of experience as a foreman and not less than three years of credits for any accredited college-level courses; or a combination of not less than one year of experience as a foreman, one year as a skilled workman, and not less than two years of credits for any accredited college-level courses; or a combination of not less than one year of experience as a foreman, two years as a skilled workman, and not less than one year of credits for any accredited college-level courses.

Pass State Certification Examination. Must have appropriate workers' compensation coverage. **Examination:** State Certification Examination. **Reciprocity:** Yes. Applicant must have passed a similar national, regional, state, or U.S. territorial licensing examination. **Fees:** $254 examination fee. **Governing Statute:** Florida Statutes, Chapter 489, Part I.

Credential Type: State Registered License. **Duration of License:** Two or three years. **Authorization:** Allows applicant to work only in those local areas in which applicant has complied with local requirements. **Requirements:** Applicant must first contact county or municipality in which applicant wishes to work for occupational and competency requirements. After meeting local requirements, applicant may apply for state registration. **Governing Statute:** Florida Statutes, Chapter 489, Part I.

Georgia

3469

Conditioned Air Contractor
State Construction Industry Licensing Board
Div. of Conditioned Air Contractors
Professional Examining Boards
166 Pryor St., SW
Atlanta, GA 30303
Phone: (404)656-3939

Credential Type: Class I Conditioned Air Contractor License. **Authorization:** Restricted to 175,000 BTU of heating and five tons (60,000 BTU) of cooling. **Requirements:** Minimum of three years of primary experience gained through the direct installation of and responsibility for conditioned air systems. A maximum of one year of secondary experience or education may be substituted for the experience requirement, where secondary experience means work or training related to the installation of conditioned air systems. Submit three professional references. **Examination:** Construction Industry Licensing Board Examination for Class I Conditioned Air Contractors. **Reciprocity:** Applicant who holds a current out of state license based on passing an examination may be granted a license by endorsement, provided that applicant meets Georgia's experience requirements. **Fees:** $29 application fee. $56 exam fee. **Governing Statute:** Official Code of Georgia Annotated 43-14. Rules of the State Construction Industry Licensing Board, Chap. 121.

Credential Type: Class II Conditioned Air Contractor License. **Authorization:** Unrestrcited as to the capacity of the system. **Requirements:** Minimum of three years of primary experience gained through the di-

Louisiana 3470

Conditioned Air Contractor, continued

rect installation of and responsibility for conditioned air systems. A maximum of one year of secondary experience or education may be substituted for the experience requirement, where secondary experience means work or training related to the installation of conditioned air systems. Submit three professional references. **Examination:** Construction Industry Licensing Board Examination for Class II Conditioned Air Contractors. **Reciprocity:** Applicant who holds a current out of state license based on passing an examination may be granted a license by endorsement, provided that applicant meets Georgia's experience requirements. **Fees:** $29 application fee. $56 exam fee. **Governing Statute:** Official Code of Georgia Annotated 43-14. Rules of the State Construction Industry Licensing Board, Chap. 121.

Louisiana

3470

Heating and Air Conditioning Mechanic
Contractor's Board
PO Box 14419
Baton Rouge, LA 70898-4419
Phone: (504)765-2301

Credential Type: License. **Requirements:** Contact licensing body for application information.

Massachusetts

3471

Refrigeration Contractor
Dept. of Public Safety
Div. of Inspection
Engineering Section
One Ashburton Pl.
Boston, MA 02108
Phone: (617)727-3200

Credential Type: Contractor License. **Authorization:** Required for installing, repairing, replacing, or maintaining any refrigeration/air conditioning system 10 tons or over. **Requirements:** Must own a refrigeration contracting business and have at least four years of experience. **Examination:** Yes. **Fees:** $150 license and exam fee. **Governing Statute:** Massachusetts General Laws, Chap. 146.

3472

Refrigeration Technician
Dept. of Public Safety
Div. of Inspection
Engineering Section
One Ashburton Pl.
Boston, MA 02108
Phone: (617)727-3200

Credential Type: Technician License. **Authorization:** Required for installing, repairing, replacing, or maintaining any refrigeration/air conditioning system 10 tons or over. **Requirements:** Have at least three years of experience. **Examination:** Yes. **Fees:** $75 license and exam fee. **Governing Statute:** Massachusetts General Laws, Chap. 146.

Credential Type: Trainee License. **Authorization:** Required for installing, repairing, replacing, or maintaining any refrigeration/air conditioning system 10 tons or over. **Requirements:** Be at least 18 years of age and in a refrigeration apprenticeship program. **Examination:** No exam required. **Fees:** $20 license fee. **Governing Statute:** Massachusetts General Laws, Chap. 146.

Missouri

3473

Heating and Air Conditioning Mechanic
Div. of Professional Registration
Dept. of Economic Development
3523 N. Ten Mile Dr.
Jefferson City, MO 65102
Phone: (314)751-2334

Credential Type: License. **Requirements:** Contact licensing body for application information.

Nebraska

3474

Air Conditioning/Heating Contractor
Dept. of Building and Safety
City County Bldg.
555 S. 10th St.
Lincoln, NE 68508
Phone: (402)471-7525

Credential Type: License. **Duration of License:** One year. **Requirements:** Must have three years of experience in the field. **Examination:** Yes. **Fees:** $30 application and examination fee. $20 registration fee. $20 renewal fee.

Nevada

3475

Heating and Air Conditioning Mechanic
State Contractor's Board
70 Linden St.
Reno, NV 89502
Phone: (702)688-1141

Credential Type: License. **Requirements:** Contact licensing body for application information.

North Carolina

3476

Plumbing, Heating, and Air Conditioning Contractor
North Carolina State Board of Examiners for Plumbing, Heating and Air Conditioning Contractors
PO Box 110
Raleigh, NC 27602
Phone: (919)733-9350

Credential Type: License. **Duration of License:** One year. **Requirements:** 18 years of age. **Examination:** Yes. **Fees:** $10 exam fee. $25—$50 license fee. $25—$50 renewal fee.

3477

Refrigeration Contractor
North Carolina State Board of Refrigeration Examiners
PO Box 10553
Raleigh, NC 27605
Phone: (919)834-5484

Credential Type: License. **Duration of License:** One year. **Requirements:** Minimum of 2,000 hours of supervised field experience. 18 years of age. **Examination:** Written. **Fees:** $40 initial fee. $40 renewal fee.

North Dakota

3478

Heating and Air Conditioning Contractor
Secretary of State
Contractor's Div.
Capitol Bldg.
Bismarck, ND 58505
Phone: (701)224-2900

Credential Type: License. **Requirements:** Contact licensing body for application information.

3479

Heating and Air Conditioning Mechanic
Secretary of State
Contractor's Div.
Capitol Bldg.
Bismarck, ND 58505
Phone: (701)224-2900

Credential Type: License. **Requirements:** Contact licensing body for application information.

Oklahoma

3480

Mechanical Journeyman
Oklahoma State Health Dept.
Mechanical Div.
1000 N.E. Tenth
Oklahoma City, OK 73152
Phone: (405)271-5217

Credential Type: License. **Duration of License:** One year. **Requirements:** 19 years of age. Three years of experience as a regular apprentice. **Examination:** Journeyman Mechanical Exam. **Fees:** $25 exam fee. $25 license fee. $25 renewal fee.

Oregon

3481

Building Service Mechanic
Building Codes Agency
1535 Edgewater
Salem, OR 97310
Phone: (503)373-1268

Credential Type: License. **Requirements:** Must have four years of experience. **Examination:** Yes. **Fees:** $25 exam fee. **Governing Statute:** ORS 480.630.

Rhode Island

3482

Air Conditioning Mechanic
State Board of Pipefitter,
  Refrigeration, and Fire Protection
  Sprinkler Contractors,
  Journeypersons
Rhode Island Dept. of Labor
544 Elmwood Ave.
Providence, RI 02907
Phone: (401)457-1860

Credential Type: Air Conditioning Mechanic—Journeyperson License. **Duration of License:** One year. **Requirements:** At least 18 years of age. Four years of practical experience working as a registered apprentice for a licensed air conditioning mechanic. Alternative licensing requirements are available through the board. **Examination:** Written examination. **Reciprocity:** No. **Fees:** $30 application fee. $20 apprentice registration fee. $25 license fee.

Credential Type: Air Conditioning Mechanic—Master License. **Duration of License:** One year. **Requirements:** Hold Journeyperson's license for at least one year and complete 10,000 hours of related experience. Alternative licensing requirements are available through the board. **Examination:** Written examination. **Reciprocity:** No. **Fees:** $30 application fee. $100 All Master 1 (Contractor) "Bond" fee. $40 All Master 2 (Contractor) "Bond" fee.

3483

Refrigeration Mechanic
State Board of Pipefitter,
  Refrigeration, and Fire Protection
  Sprinkler Contractors,
  Journeypersons
Rhode Island Dept. of Labor
544 Elmwood Ave.
Providence, RI 02907
Phone: (401)457-1860

Credential Type: Refrigeration Mechanic—Journeyperson License. **Duration of License:** One year. **Requirements:** At least 18 years of age. Four years of practical experience working as a registered apprentice for a licensed refrigeration mechanic. Alternative licensing requirements are available through the board. **Examination:** Written examination. **Reciprocity:** No. **Fees:** $30 application fee. $20 apprentice registration fee. $30 license fee.

Credential Type: Refrigeration Mechanic—Master License. **Duration of License:** One year. **Requirements:** Hold Journeyperson's license for at least one year and complete 10,000 hours of related experience. Alternative licensing requirements are available through the board. **Examination:** Written examination. **Reciprocity:** No. **Fees:** $30 application fee. $100 All Master 1 (Contractor) "Bond" fee. $40 All Master 2 (Contractor) "Bond" fee.

Texas

3484

Air Conditioning & Refrigeration Contractor
Texas Dept. of Labor and Standards,
  Licensing Section
PO Box 12157
Austin, TX 78711
Phone: (512)463-2904

Credential Type: Class A License. **Duration of License:** Three years. **Authorization:** Allows holder to install, repair, and alter the type of equipment for which the license is endorsed (environmental, commercial, or both) of any size or capacity. **Requirements:** 18 years of age. Certificate of required insurance of $300,000. Three years of practical experience within the last five years; or a degree in air conditioning engineering or mechanical engineering, and one year of experience; or a combination of at least one year experience with technical education, at the rate of one month experience for each two months of education, equal to three years. **Examination:** Written or oral. **Fees:** $100 exam fee. $300 license fee. $150 renewal fee. **Governing Statute:** VACS 8861, 16 TAC 75.1.

Credential Type: Class B License. **Duration of License:** Three years. **Authorization:** Allows holder to install, repair, and alter the type of equipment for which the license is endorsed (environmental, commercial, or both) of not more than 25 tons cooling capacity and not more than 1.5 million BTU per hours output heating capacity. **Requirements:** 18 years of age. Certificate of required insurance of $100,000. Three years of practical experience within the last five years; or a degree in air conditioning engineering or mechanical engineering, and one year of experience; or a combination of at least one year experience with technical education, at the rate of one month experience for each two months of education, equal to three years. **Examination:** Written or oral. **Fees:** $100 exam fee. $150 license fee. $75 renewal fee. **Governing Statute:** VACS 8861, 16 TAC 75.1.

Virginia

3485

Heating and Air Conditioning Mechanic
State Board of Contractors
3600 W. Broad St.
Richmond, VA 23230
Phone: (804)367-8511

Credential Type: License. **Requirements:** Contact licensing body for application information.

Human Services Workers

The following states grant licenses in this occupational category as of the date of publication: Kentucky, Missouri, Montana, New Hampshire, New Jersey, North Dakota, Rhode Island, Utah, Virginia, Wisconsin, Wyoming.

Kentucky

3486

Rehabilitation Counselor
Dept. of Vocational Rehabilitation
Capital Plaza Tower
Frankfort, KY 40601
Phone: (502)564-4440

Credential Type: License. **Requirements:** Bachelor's degree in rehabilitation, guidance and/or counseling, sociology, psychology, social work, special education, or education with emphasis in vocational counseling or a related field. **Examination:** Yes.

Missouri

3487

Substance Abuse Counselor
Missouri Substance Abuse
 Counselors Certification Board
Div. of Professional Registration
3605 Missouri Blvd.
Jefferson City, MO 65102
Phone: (314)751-0018

Credential Type: Certification. **Requirements:** Contact licensing body for application information.

Montana

3488

Chemical Dependency Counselor
Montana Dept. of Institutions
Chemical Dependency Bureau
1539 11th Ave.
Helena, MT 59620
Phone: (406)444-2827

Credential Type: License. **Duration of License:** Four years. **Requirements:** 200 points based on a combination of academic preparation and work experience. Four years of approved college coursework or five years of work experience amounts to approximately 65 points. The remaining points are made up through exams. A 25-45 minute tape of a counseling session conducted by the applicant. 12 quarter hours of continuing education or equivalent every four years. **Examination:** Yes. **Fees:** $50 application and exam fee. **Governing Statute:** Montana Code Annotated 53-24-204.

New Hampshire

3489

Certified Alcohol Counselor (CAC)
Office of Alcohol & Drug Abuse
 Prevention
105 Pleasant St.
Concord, NH 03301
Phone: (603)271-6112
Fax: (603)271-6116

Credential Type: Alcohol Counselor Certificate. **Duration of License:** Two years. **Requirements:** At least 180 hours of training in substance abuse and/or counseling (6 hours must be in ethics). 24 hours must have been acquired within one year of application. Must have two years or 4,000 hours of supervised experience with alcohol clients. A minimum of 1,000 hours must be in the form of direct counseling. Must also complete a 220 hour practicum. Applicant must sign Code of Ethics and submit evaluation from a supervisor of six months, or longer, and two professional references. Oral interview will consist of case presentation prepared by applicant. Renewal requires 48 hours of continuing education. **Examination:** National Certification Examination. **Reciprocity:** Yes, with application to the National Certification Reciprocity Consortium. **Fees:** $10 application packet fee. $55 written examination fee. $90 certification processing fee. $50 biennial recertification fee. $100 reciprocity fee.

3490

Certified Alcohol and Drug Abuse Counselor (CADAC)
Office of Alcohol & Drug Abuse
 Prevention
105 Pleasant St.
Concord, NH 03301
Phone: (603)271-6112
Fax: (603)271-6116

Credential Type: Alcohol and Drug Abuse Counselor Certificate. **Duration of License:** Two years. **Requirements:** At least 270 hours of training in substance abuse and/or counseling (6 hours must be in ethics). 24 hours of training must have been acquired within one year of application. Must have three years or 6,000 hours of supervised counseling experience in alcohol and/or drug abuse. At least 2,000 hours must be spent working with alcohol clients and 2,000 hours working with drug clients. A minimum of 1,500 hours must be spent in direct counseling. A practicum of 300 hours is also required. Applicant must sign Code of Ethics and submit evaluation from a su-

New Hampshire

Certified Alcohol and Drug Abuse Counselor (CADAC), continued

pervisor of six months, or longer, and two professional references. Oral interview will consist of case presentation prepared by applicant. Renewal requires 48 hours of continuing education. **Examination:** National Certification Examination. **Reciprocity:** Yes, with application to the National Certification Reciprocity Consortium. **Fees:** $10 application packet fee. $55 written exam fee. $90 certification processing fee. $50 biennial recertification fee. $100 reciprocity fee.

3491

Certified Drug Counselor (CDC)
Office of Alcohol & Drug Abuse Prevention
105 Pleasant St.
Concord, NH 03301
Phone: (603)271-6112
Fax: (603)271-6116

Credential Type: Drug Counselor Certificate. **Duration of License:** Two years. **Requirements:** At least 180 hours of training in substance abuse and/or counseling (6 hours must be in ethics). 24 hours must have been acquired within one year of application. Must have two years or 4,000 hours of supervised experience with drug clients. A minimum of 1,000 hours must be in the form of direct counseling. Must also complete a 220 hour practicum. Applicant must sign Code of Ethics and submit evaluation from a supervisor of six months, or longer, and two professional references. Oral interview will consist of case presentation prepared by applicant. Renewal requires 48 hours of continuing education. **Examination:** National Certification Examination. **Reciprocity:** Yes, with application to the National Certification Reciprocity Consortium. **Fees:** $10 application packet fee. $55 written examination fee. $90 certification processing fee. $50 biennial recertification fee. $100 reciprocity fee.

New Jersey

3492

Drug Abuse Counselor
Alcohol and Other Drugs of Abuse Counselor Certification Board
90 Manmouth St., Ste. 1
Red Bank, NJ 07701
Phone: (201)741-3835

Credential Type: Certified Drug Counselor. **Requirements:** At least 240 clock hours of approved substance abuse training experience and 220 supervised practical training hours. At least 4,000 hours of documented supervised drug counseling experience. **Fees:** $10 orientation fee. $65 application fee.

North Dakota

3493

Addiction Counselor
State Board of Addiction Counseling Examiners
1406 Second St. NW
Mandan, ND 58554
Phone: (701)663-2321

Credential Type: Addiction Counselor License. **Duration of License:** One year. **Requirements:** Bachelor's degree plus 12 required courses. Complete at least a 9-month clinical training program, followed by one year of work experience or internship. **Examination:** Written Examination. Oral Case Presentation Examination. **Fees:** $150 license fee. $60 written exam fee. $75 oral exam fee. $75 renewal fee. **Governing Statute:** North Dakota Century Code 43-45.

Rhode Island

3494

Chemical Dependency Professional
Rhode Island Board for Certification of Chemical Dependency Professionals.
84 Broad St.
Pawtucket, RI 02860
Phone: (401)233-2215

Credential Type: Chemical Dependency Professional Certificate—Level I. **Duration of License:** Four years. **Requirements:** Must complete 140 hours of educational courses, of which 70 hours must be directly related to substance abuse. Complete 150 hours of clinical supervision. Complete 2,000 hours of work in a licensed substance abuse facility. **Examination:** Written examination. **Reciprocity:** No. **Fees:** $150 initial certification. $125 recertification.

Credential Type: Advanced Chemical Dependency Professional Certificate—Level II. **Duration of License:** Four years. **Requirements:** Complete a board approved program of additional work experience, education and supervision. **Examination:** Written and oral examination. **Reciprocity:** Yes. **Fees:** $150 initial certification. $125 recertification.

Credential Type: Chemical Dependency Supervisor—Level III. **Duration of License:** Four years. **Requirements:** Level II certification and complete a board approved program of additional work related education. **Reciprocity:** Yes. **Fees:** $150 initial certification. $125 recertification.

Utah

3495

Social Service Aide
Dept. of Commerce
Div. of Occupational and Professional Licensing
160 E. 300 S.
PO Box 45802
Salt Lake City, UT 84145
Phone: (801)530-6628

Credential Type: Social service aide license. **Duration of License:** Two years. **Requirements:** Be at least 18 years of age. Pass required examination. Have a personal interview with the examining board. **Examination:** Yes. **Fees:** $15 license fee. $10 renewal fee.

3496

Social Service Worker
Dept. of Commerce
Div. of Occupational and Professional Licensing
160 E. 300 S.
PO Box 45802
Salt Lake City, UT 84145
Phone: (801)530-6628

Credential Type: Social service worker license. **Duration of License:** Two years. **Requirements:** Bachelor's degree in social work. Pass required examination. **Examination:** Yes. **Fees:** $50 license and exam fee. $30 renewal fee.

Virginia

3497

Substance Abuse Counselor
Virginia Board of Professional Counselors
1601 Rolling Hills Dr.
Richmond, VA 23229
Phone: (804)662-9920

Credential Type: License. **Requirements:** High school diploma. Must complete 400 hours in a substance abuse education program accredited by a college or university, or an integrated program approved by the Board. Must also complete 2,000 hours of supervised experience as specified by the Board. **Examination:** Yes.

Wisconsin

3498

Rehabilitation Counselor
Bureau of Health Service Professions
Dept. of Regulation and Licensing
PO Box 8935
Madison, WI 53708
Phone: (608)266-8609

Credential Type: Certification. **Authorization:** Certification required for use of title. **Requirements:** New certification rules to be established by May 1, 1993. If applying before May 31, 1995, requirements for certification without examination are a graduate degree in professional counseling or its equivalent from an approved program. Within the past five years, meet one of the following sets of requirements: (1) With a master's degree, have at least two years of full-time supervised clinical professional counseling experience. (2) With a doctoral degree, have at least one year of full-time supervised clinical professional counseling experience. **Fees:** $39 certification fee. **Governing Statute:** 1991 Wisconsin Act 160.

Wyoming

3499

Chemical Dependency Specialist Counselor
Wyoming Mental Health Professions Licensing Board
PO Box 591
Cheyenne, WY 82003
Phone: (307)635-2816

Credential Type: License. **Duration of License:** Two years. **Requirements:** Age of majority. Hold a Masters, Educational Specialist, or Doctorate degree in the appropriate field from an accredited school. Have accumulated 3000 hours of supervised experience. Pass a nationally recommended examination accepted by the Board. **Examination:** Yes. **Fees:** $60 Application. $50 License. $50 Renewal. Additional cost for examination.

Inspectors and Compliance Officers, Except Construction

One or more occupations in this chapter require a federal license. Additionally, the following states grant licenses as of the date of publication:

Alabama	Georgia	Kentucky	Nebraska	Ohio	Texas	Wyoming
Alaska	Hawaii	Louisiana	Nevada	Oklahoma	Utah	
Arizona	Idaho	Maryland	New Jersey	Oregon	Vermont	
Arkansas	Illinois	Massachusetts	New Mexico	Rhode Island	Virginia	
Connecticut	Indiana	Michigan	New York	South Carolina	Washington	
Delaware	Iowa	Minnesota	North Carolina	South Dakota	West Virginia	
Florida	Kansas	Montana	North Dakota	Tennessee	Wisconsin	

Federal Licenses

3500

Customs Broker
U.S. Dept. of Treasury
U.S. Customs Service
Office of Public Affairs
1301 Constitution Ave., NW
Washington, DC 20229
Phone: (202)566-2041

Credential Type: Customs Broker License. **Requirements:** Must be a citizen of the United States, but may not be an officer or employee of the United States. Be at least 21 years of age. Good moral character. Establish through an examination that applicant has sufficient knowledge of Customs and related laws.

Application for license is to be submitted to the director of the district in which the applicant intends to do business. Each person granted a broker's license is concurrently issued a permit for the district through which the application was submitted without a fee. Permits for additional districts may be applied for and granted with a fee. **Examination:** Written examination. **Fees:** $300 application and examination fee. $100 additional permit fee. $125 annual user fee (per permit). **Governing Statute:** 19 CFR, Chap. 1, Part 111.

Alabama

3501

Mine Fireboss
Board of Mine Examiners
Div. of Safety and Inspection
PO Box 10444
Birmingham, AL 35202
Phone: (205)254-1275

Credential Type: License. **Requirements:** 23 years of age. Citizen of the U.S. Must have three years of practical experience. **Examination:** Written, oral, and practical examinations. **Fees:** $20 examination fee.

3502

Wrestling Medical Examiner
State Athletic Commission
50 N. Ripley St., Rm. 4121
Montgomery, AL 36132
Phone: (205)242-1380

Credential Type: License. **Duration of License:** One year. **Requirements:** Must be a licensed physician. **Fees:** $5 license fee.

Alaska

3503

Examining Physician, Boxing
Dept. of Commerce and Economic Development
Div. of Occupational Licensing
Athletic Commission
PO Box D-LIC
Juneau, AK 99811-0800
Phone: (907)465-2534
Fax: (907)465-2974

Credential Type: License. **Duration of License:** One year. **Authorization:** Only physicians licensed by the commission may be employed to perform examinations of licensees. **Fees:** $10 license fee. **Governing Statute:** Alaska Statutes 05.05 and 08.10. Professional Regulations 12 AAC 06.

Arizona

3504

Assayer
Board of Technical Registration
1951 W. Camelback, Ste. 250
Phoenix, AZ 85015
Phone: (602)255-4053

Credential Type: Registration to Practice. **Duration of License:** Three years. **Requirements:** Be of good moral character. Have at least six years education or experience, or combination of both with at least two years of experience. Pass in-training and professional examination administered by the board. **Examination:** In-training and professional examinations. **Exemptions:** The in-training exam may be waived for candidates who have a degree in chemistry, metallurgy, or other science directly related to the analysis of metals and ores. **Fees:**

$90 application fee. $200 exam fee. $126 renewal fee.

Credential Type: Registration without examination. **Requirements:** Hold a valid registration in another state, jurisdiction, territory, or country. Meet experience and education requirements similar to those of Arizona, or have been actively engaged in the profession for at least 10 years. **Fees:** $90 application fee.

3505

Assayer-in-Training
Board of Technical Registration
1951 W. Camelback, Ste. 250
Phoenix, AZ 85015
Phone: (602)255-4053

Credential Type: In-training registration. **Requirements:** Be of good moral character. To qualify for the in-training examination on the basis of education, must be a graduate of a four-year degree program of an accredited college or university, with a major in chemistry, metallurgy, or other science directly related to the analysis of metals and ores.

To qualify for the in-training examination on the basis of experience, must have at least four years of education or experience or both directly related to the practice of assaying. **Examination:** In-training examination. **Fees:** $30 application fee. $200 exam fee.

3506

Public Weighmaster
Dept. of Weights and Measures
1951 W. North Lane
Phoenix, AZ 85021
Phone: (602)255-5211

Credential Type: Public weighmaster license. **Duration of License:** One year. **Authorization:** Public weighing of any property, livestock, or commodity shall be performed only by a public weighmaster. **Requirements:** Submit application and license fee. **Fees:** $48 license fee. **Governing Statute:** Arizona Revised Statutes, Title 41, Chapter 15.

Credential Type: Limited weighmaster license. **Duration of License:** One year. **Authorization:** Authorized to act as a public weighmaster only within the scope of individual's official employment and duties in enforcing local ordinances. **Requirements:** Be a qualified officer or employee of a city, county, or the state. Submit request for license. **Fees:** No fee. **Governing Statute:** Arizona Revised Statutes, Title 41, Chapter 15.

Arkansas

3507

Boiler Inspector, State
Arkansas Dept. of Labor
Boiler Inspection Div.
10421 W. Markham
Little Rock, AR 72205
Phone: (501)682-4513

Credential Type: License. **Requirements:** Five years experience in construction, maintenance, installation and repair of high-pressure boilers and unfired pressure vessels. Furnish a bond in the sum of $2,000. **Examination:** Yes. **Fees:** No fees

3508

Clerk of Scales
Arkansas State Racing Commission
Ledbetter Bldg., Rm. G08
7th & Wolfe St.
PO Box 3076
Little Rock, AR 72203
Phone: (501)682-1467

Credential Type: License. **Duration of License:** One year. **Requirements:** Application must be approved by the Stewards. Must be qualified as to ability and integrity, and have endorsement by employer. Must be 16 years of age. Never convicted of a crime, excluding minor traffic offenses. Not be habitually intoxicated or addicted to drugs. Must not be engaged in any activity or practice which is illegal, undesirable, or detrimental to the best interest of the public and the sport of racing. **Examination:** No. **Fees:** $3 License. $3 Renewal.

3509

Greyhound Clerk of Scales
Arkansas State Racing Commission
Ledbetter Bldg., Rm. G08
7th & Wolfe St.
PO Box 3076
Little Rock, AR 72203
Phone: (501)682-1467

Credential Type: License. **Duration of License:** One year. **Requirements:** Must not be associated with any bookmaking practices which are illegal or would be detrimental to the public or the sport of racing. Never convicted of a crime. Qualified as to ability and integrity of license sought and have endorsement of employer. Not be habitually intoxicated or addicted to drugs. Declare ownership or interest in any greyhound. Application must contain no falsehoods. 16 years of age. Application approved by Director of Racing. **Examination:** No **Fees:** $3 License. $3 Renewal.

3510

Insurance Inspector (Boiler)
Arkansas Dept. of Labor
Boiler Inspector Div.
10421 W. Markham
Little Rock, AR 72202
Phone: (501)682-4513

Credential Type: License. **Requirements:** Must be employed by a company authorized to insure boilers against explosion. Meet all requirements and be approved by State Insurance Commission to insure boilers and machinery. Pass written examination and be issued a certificate of competency as a boiler inspector. **Examination:** Yes. **Fees:** $25 Written examination and initial license. $15 Renewal.

3511

Sanitarian
State Board of Sanitarians
4815 W. Markham
Little Rock, AR 72205
Phone: (501)661-2171

Credential Type: License. **Duration of License:** One year. **Requirements:** Bachelor or masters degree in Public Health or one of the natural sciences; or, Bachelors degree with at least 30 hours in natural science, plus one year in environmental sanitation. **Examination:** Yes. **Fees:** $20 Written examination. $10 Registration (first year). $20 Registration (every year thereafter).

Connecticut

3512

Clerk of Scales (Racetrack)
Connecticut Div. of Special Revenue
Russell Rd.
PO Box 11424
Newington, CT 06111-0424
Phone: (203)566-2756

Credential Type: License Registration. **Requirements:** Submit application and fingerprint card. Pay fee. **Fees:** $20 registration fee.

Connecticut

3513

Public Weigher
Weights and Measures Div.
Consumer Protection Dept.
165 Capitol Ave.
Hartford, CT 06106
Phone: (203)566-4778

Credential Type: Public Weigher's License. **Duration of License:** One year. **Requirements:** Submit application and fee. **Fees:** $20 license fee.

Delaware

3514

Breath Analyzer (Racetrack)
Delaware Harness Racing
  Commission
2320 S. DuPont Hwy.
Dover, DE 19901
Phone: (302)739-4811

Credential Type: License Registration. **Requirements:** Submit application and fingerprint card. Pay fee. **Fees:** $5 registration fee.

3515

Equipment Inspector (Racetrack)
Delaware Harness Racing
  Commission
2320 S. DuPont Hwy.
Dover, DE 19901
Phone: (302)739-4811

Credential Type: License Registration. **Requirements:** Submit application and fingerprint card. Pay fee. **Fees:** $10 registration fee.

3516

Laboratory Official (Racetrack)
Delaware Harness Racing
  Commission
2320 S. DuPont Hwy.
Dover, DE 19901
Phone: (302)739-4811

Credential Type: License Registration. **Requirements:** Submit application and fingerprint card. Pay fee. **Fees:** $5 registration fee.

3517

Paddock Inspector (Racetrack)
Delaware Harness Racing
  Commission
2320 S. DuPont Hwy.
Dover, DE 19901
Phone: (302)739-4811

Credential Type: License Registration. **Requirements:** Submit application and fingerprint card. Pay fee. **Fees:** $5 registration fee.

Florida

3518

Clerk of Scales (Racetrack)
Florida Dept. of Business
Div. of Pari-Mutuel Wagering
Licensing Section
725 S. Bronough St.
Tallahassee, FL 32399-1037
Phone: (904)488-9161

Credential Type: License Registration Code 1032. **Requirements:** Submit application and fingerprint card. Pay fee. **Fees:** $40 registration fee.

Georgia

3519

Certified Landfill Inspector
Dept. of Natural Resources
Environmental Protection Div.
205 Butler St., Ste. 1154
Atlanta, GA 30334
Phone: (404)656-4713

Credential Type: Landfill Inspector Certification. **Duration of License:** Five years. **Authorization:** Effective July 1, 1992, certification is required for all employees of the Department of Natural Resources who inspect municipal solid waste disposal facilities. **Requirements:** Complete Landfill Certification Training Course and examination. Be employed by the Georgia Department of Natural Resources and be required to conduct landfill inspections. **Examination:** Landfill Operator Certification Examination. **Reciprocity:** Yes, provided that requirements for certification do not conflict and are not of a lower standard, and that state, territory, or possession of the United States has a reciprocal agreement with Georgia. **Governing Statute:** Rules of the Georgia Department of Natural Resources, Environmental Protection Division, Chapter 391-3-4.

Hawaii

3520

Sanitarian
Hawaii State Dept. of Health,
  Sanitation Branch
591 Ala Moana Blvd.
Honolulu, HI 96813
Phone: (808)548-5397

Credential Type: License. **Duration of License:** One year. **Requirements:** Bachelor's Degree from an accredited college with a biological, physical or sanitary sciences major. **Examination:** Yes. **Exemptions:** May be granted if exam is passed in another state. **Fees:** $10 application fee. $60 exam fee. $3 renewal fee.

Idaho

3521

Environmental Health Specialist
Environmental Health Specialists
  Board of Examiners
Bureau of Occupational Licenses
1109 Main St., Ste. 220
Boise, ID 83702-5642
Phone: (208)334-3233

Credential Type: Environmental Health Specialist Certificate of Registration. **Duration of License:** One year. **Requirements:** Good moral character. Meet one of the following sets of requirements: (1) Graduate of a recognized college or university with at least a baccalaureate degree in public health, or equivalent, and have taken at least 30 credit hours in physical, biological, chemical, social, and sanitary sciences. A baccalaureate degree in environmental health, sanitary science, environmental science, or comparable degrees with a minimum of 30 quarter hours or 20 semester hours in environmental health shall be considered equivalent for purposes of licensing. (2) Graduate of a recognized college or university with at least a baccalaureate degree in public health, or equivalent; and not having taken the requisite 30 hours in physical, biological, chemical, social, and sanitary sciences, have been gainfully employed in environmental health for a period of at least 12 months prior to application. **Examination:** Yes. **Reciprocity:** Yes, with states having substantially equal requirements. **Fees:** $25 application fee. $75 exam fee. $50 renewal fee. $75 reciprocity fee. **Governing Statute:** Idaho Code, Title 54, Chap. 24. Rules of the Idaho State Environmental Health Specialists Board of Examiners.

3522

Environmental Health Specialist Trainee
Environmental Health Specialists Board of Examiners
Bureau of Occupational Licenses
1109 Main St., Ste. 220
Boise, ID 83702-5642
Phone: (208)334-3233

Credential Type: Environmental Health Specialist Trainee Certificate of Registration. **Duration of License:** Three years. **Requirements:** Good moral character. Meet one of the following sets of requirements: (1) Graduate of a recognized college or university with at least a baccalaureate degree in public health, or equivalent, and have taken at least 30 quarter hours or 20 semester hours in physical, biological, chemical, social, and sanitary sciences. A baccalaureate degree in environmental health, sanitary science, environmental science, or comparable degrees with a minimum of 30 quarter hours or 20 semester hours in environmental health shall be considered equivalent for purposes of licensing. (2) Graduate of a recognized college or university with at least a baccalaureate degree in public health, or equivalent; and not having taken the requisite 30 hours in physical, biological, chemical, social, and sanitary sciences, have been gainfully employed in environmental health for a period of at least 12 months prior to application. **Examination:** Yes. **Reciprocity:** Yes, with states having substantially equal requirements. **Fees:** $25 application fee. **Governing Statute:** Idaho Code, Title 54, Chap. 24. Rules of the Idaho State Environmental Health Specialists Board of Examiners.

Illinois

3523

Breath Analyzer Operator
Illinois Dept. of Health
Alcohol and Substance Testing
535 W. Jefferson St.
Springfield, IL 62761
Phone: (217)782-1571

Credential Type: Breath Analyzer Operator License. **Duration of License:** One year. **Requirements:** Must be employed by a law enforcement agency or the Illinois Department of Health. Complete a minimum of 32 hours of instruction. **Examination:** Breath Analysis Instrument Operator Examination. **Reciprocity:** Yes, with a valid license and equivalent hours of training. Must take a four hour written test and be tested on the instrument. **Fees:** No fee. **Governing Statute:** Illinois Vehicle Code, Section 11.501.2.

3524

Cross-Connection Control Device Inspector
Illinois Environmental Protection Agency
2200 Churchill Rd.
PO Box 19276
Springfield, IL 62794-9276
Phone: (217)782-1869

Credential Type: Cross-Connection Control Device Inspector Certificate. **Duration of License:** One year. **Requirements:** Must be licensed as a plumber in the state of Illinois. Complete four-day training course and pass examination. **Examination:** Written and performance examination. **Reciprocity:** No. **Fees:** $180 course and examination fee. **Governing Statute:** Illinois Revised Statutes 1989, Chapter 1001.

3525

Deputy Boiler Inspector
Illinois State Fire Marshal
Div. of Boiler & Pressure Vessel Safety
1035 Stevenson Drive
Springfield, IL 62703
Phone: (217)785-1010

Credential Type: Deputy Boiler Inspector Certificate. **Duration of License:** One year. **Requirements:** Must have at least five years experience in the construction, maintenance, repair or operation of high pressure boilers and unfired pressure vessels. Experience may be gained in the position of mechanical engineer, steam engineer, boiler maker, or boiler inspector. **Examination:** National Board Exam for Boiler and Pressure Vessel Inspectors. **Reciprocity:** Yes, with states that require passage of the National Board of Boiler and Pressure Vessel Inspectors Exam. **Fees:** $15 examination fee. $15 application fee. $10 initial license fee. $5 renewal fee. $10 reinstatement fee. **Governing Statute:** Boiler and Pressure Vessel Safety Act—Chapter 111.

3526

Illinois County Coroner
Illinois Local Law Enforcement Officer Training Board
600 S. Second St., Ste. 300
Springfield, IL 62704
Phone: (217)782-4540

Credential Type: County Coroner Certificate. **Duration of License:** Indefinite. **Requirements:** Resident of Illinois. Live in county of office. Pass examination. Renewal requires 24 hours of continuing education per year. **Examination:** Written examination. **Reciprocity:** No. **Fees:** No fee. **Governing Statute:** Public Act 85-985.

3527

Mine Examiner
Illinois Dept. of Mines & Minerals
300 W. Jefferson St., Ste. 300
PO Box 10137
Springfield, IL 62791-0137
Phone: (217)782-6791

Credential Type: Mine Examiner Certificate. **Duration of License:** Permanent. **Requirements:** At least 21 years of age. U.S. citizen. Four years of practical underground mining experience. First Class Certificate of Competency issued by Department of Mines and Minerals. Approved first aid training and mine rescue methods course. Applicant will receive one year experiential credit for associate degree in Coal Mining Technology and two years credit for a degree in Mining Engineering. Must submit copy of degree with application. **Examination:** Written and oral examinations. **Reciprocity:** No. **Fees:** No fee. **Governing Statute:** 1989 Illinois Revised Statutes, Chapter 96 1/2.

Credential Type: Temporary Certificate. **Duration of License:** Six months or until next examination date. **Requirements:** Must have valid equivalent certificate issued by another state agency. Must submit photo copy of certificate. **Fees:** No fee. **Governing Statute:** 1989 Illinois Revised Statutes, Chapter 96 1/2.

3528

Radon Measurement Specialist
Illinois Dept. of Nuclear Safety
1035 Outer Park Drive
Springfield, IL 62704
Phone: (217)785-9900

Credential Type: Radon Measurement Specialist Certificate. **Duration of License:** Two years. **Requirements:** Complete an approved course in radon measurement.

Illinois 3529

Radon Measurement Specialist, continued

Have four years experience or A.A.S. and two years experience. **Reciprocity:** Yes, with approved course completion. **Fees:** $100 license fee. **Governing Statute:** 32 Illinois Administrative Code 420.

3529

Shaft and Slope Examiner (Construction and Mining)
Illinois Dept. of Mines and Minerals
300 W. Jefferson St., Ste. 300
PO Box 10137
Springfield, IL 62791-0137
Phone: (217)782-6791

Credential Type: Shaft and Slope Examiner Certificate. **Duration of License:** Permanent. **Requirements:** At least 18 years of age. U.S. citizen. Two years of shaft and slope underground construction experience. One year of experience requirement may be satisfied with a degree in Mining Engineering. **Examination:** Written and oral examination. **Reciprocity:** No. **Fees:** No fee. **Governing Statute:** 62 Illinois Administrative Code 220.190(w).

3530

Special Boiler Inspector (Insurance Co.)
Illinois State Fire Marshal
Div. of Boiler & Pressure Vessel Safety
1035 Stevenson Drive
Springfield, IL 62703
Phone: (217)785-1010

Credential Type: Special Boiler Inspector Certificate. **Duration of License:** One year. **Authorization:** Allows inspection of boilers and pressure vessels for authorized insurance companies. **Requirements:** Must have at least three years experience in the construction, maintenance, repair or operation of high pressure boilers and pressure vessels. **Examination:** National Board Exam for Boiler and Pressure Vessel Inspectors. **Reciprocity:** Yes, with states that require passage of the National Board of Boiler and Pressure Vessel Inspectors Exam. **Fees:** $15 examination fee. $15 application fee. $10 initial license fee. $5 renewal fee. $10 reinstatement fee. **Governing Statute:** Boiler and Pressure Vessel Safety Act—Chapter 111.

3531

State Mine Inspector (Coal Mine)
Illinois Dept. of Mines and Minerals
300 W. Jefferson St., Ste. 300
PO Box 10137
Springfield, IL 62791-0137
Phone: (217)782-6791

Credential Type: State Mine Inspector Certificate. **Duration of License:** Two years (unless actively employed as a Mine Inspector). **Requirements:** At least 30 years of age. Illinois resident. U.S. citizen. Four years of high school or equivalent education. Must have Mine Manager's Certificate of Competency. Must have 10 years experience in practical mining. At least two years of the experience requirement must be in Illinois mines. **Examination:** Written and oral examination. **Reciprocity:** No. **Fees:** No fee. **Governing Statute:** 1989 Illinois Revised Statutes, Chapter 96 1/2.

3532

State Mine Inspector (Metal Mine)
Illinois Dept. of Mines and Minerals
300 W. Jefferson St., Ste. 300
PO Box 10137
Springfield, IL 62791-0137
Phone: (217)782-6791

Credential Type: State Mine Inspector Certificate. **Duration of License:** Two years (unless actively employed as a Mine Inspector). **Requirements:** At least 30 years of age. Illinois resident for a minimum of one year. U.S. citizen. Have enough practical experience in metalliferous or mineral mining to be knowledgeable about mining operations above and below ground. **Examination:** Written and oral examination. **Reciprocity:** No. **Fees:** No fee. **Governing Statute:** 1989 Illinois Revised Statutes, Chapter 96 1/2.

Indiana

3533

Sanitarian
Sanitarian Board
Health Professions Bureau
402 W. Washington St., Rm. 041
Indianapolis, IN 46204
Phone: (317)232-2960

Credential Type: Registration permit. **Duration of License:** Two years. **Authorization:** Provides authorization to practice as an environmental health specialist. **Requirements:** Bachelor's degree or higher, with at least 30 semester hours in basic physical, chemical, biological, and sanitary science. Must have two years experience. **Examination:** Yes. **Fees:** $40 application fee. $60 exam fee. $10 permit issuance fee. $35 renewal fee. **Governing Statute:** Indiana Code 25-32. 896 Indiana Administrative Code.

Iowa

3534

Boiler Inspector
Iowa Dept. of Employment Services
Chief Boiler Inspector
1000 E. Grand Ave.
Des Moines, IA 50319
Phone: (515)281-3606

Credential Type: Commission. **Duration of License:** One year. **Requirements:** A degree in engineering plus two years of experience with high pressure boilers and pressure boilers; or an associate degree in mechanical technology plus two years of experience; or a high school diploma or equivalent plus three years of experience. **Examination:** Yes. **Reciprocity:** Yes. **Fees:** $25 National Board Commission card fee. $20 renewal fee.

3535

Radon Measurement Specialist
Bureau of Radiological Health
Iowa Dept. of Health
Lucas State Office Bldg., 3rd Fl.
Des Moines, IA 50319
Phone: (515)281-3478

Credential Type: Certificate. **Duration of License:** One year. **Requirements:** 18 years of age. Bachelor's degree in natural science, engineering or a related discipline. Three years of experience in relevant professional work. Completion of an approved radon measurement course. Enrollment in the U.S. Environmental Protection Agency's Radon Measurement Proficiency Program. **Examination:** Iowa Dept. of Public Health exam. **Fees:** $25 application fee. $100 exam fee. $250 annual certification fee.

3536

Radon Mitigation Specialist
Bureau of Radiological Health
Iowa Dept. of Public Health
Lucas State Office Bldg., 3rd Fl.
Des Moines, IA 50319
Phone: (515)281-3478

Credential Type: Credential. **Duration of License:** One year. **Requirements:** 18 years of age. Three years of relevant professional work experience. Successful completion of the U.S. E.P.A.'s Radon Contractors Proficiency Program. **Fees:** $25 application fee for state residents. $100 application fee for non-residents. $150 credential fee. $150 renewal fee. $100 program fee.

Kansas

3537

Clerk of Scales (Racetrack)
Kansas Racing Commission
3400 VanBuren
Topeka, KS 66611-2228
Phone: (913)296-5800

Credential Type: License Registration. **Requirements:** Submit application and fingerprint card. Pay fee. **Fees:** $10 registration fee.

3538

Testing Technician (Racetrack)
Kansas Racing Commission
3400 VanBuren
Topeka, KS 66611-2228
Phone: (913)296-5800

Credential Type: License Registration. **Requirements:** Submit application and fingerprint card. Pay fee. **Fees:** $10 registration fee.

Kentucky

3539

Boiler Inspector
Dept. of Housing, Building and Construction
1047 U.S. 127 South
Frankfort, KY 40601
Phone: (502)564-3626

Credential Type: License. **Requirements:** High school diploma or equivalent. Five years of experience in boiler and/or pressure vessel construction, repair, operation or maintenance inspection. **Examination:** Yes. **Fees:** $20 exam fee. $50 license fee. $25 renewal fee.

3540

Clerk of Scales (Racetrack)
Kentucky State Racing Commission
PO Box 1080
Lexington, KY 40588
Phone: (606)254-7021

Credential Type: Association Employee and Occupational License. **Requirements:** Submit application and fingerprint card. Pay fee. **Fees:** $10 license fee.

3541

Commission Chemist (Racetrack)
Kentucky State Racing Commission
PO Box 1080
Lexington, KY 40588
Phone: (606)254-7021

Credential Type: License Registration. **Requirements:** Submit application and fingerprint card. Pay fee. **Fees:** $35 registration fee.

3542

Commission Horse Identifier (Racetrack)
Kentucky State Racing Commission
PO Box 1080
Lexington, KY 40588
Phone: (606)254-7021

Credential Type: License Registration. **Requirements:** Submit application and fingerprint card. Pay fee. **Fees:** $35 registration fee.

3543

Commission Inspector (Racetrack)
Kentucky State Racing Commission
PO Box 1080
Lexington, KY 40588
Phone: (606)254-7021

Credential Type: License Registration. **Requirements:** Submit application and fingerprint card. Pay fee. **Fees:** $35 registration fee.

3544

Commission License Administrator (Racetrack)
Kentucky State Racing Commission
PO Box 1080
Lexington, KY 40588
Phone: (606)254-7021

Credential Type: License Registration. **Requirements:** Submit application and fingerprint card. Pay fee. **Fees:** $35 registration fee.

3545

Coroner
Dept. of Criminal Justice Training
Eastern Kentucky University, Stratton Bldg., Rm. 112
Richmond, KY 40475
Phone: (606)622-6165

Credential Type: License. **Duration of License:** One year. **Requirements:** 24 years of age. Must be a two-year resident of Kentucky and a one-year resident in the County in which he/she is an candidate. Successful completion of a forty-hour basic training course within one year of taking office. Must complete an 18-hour course for renewal. **Examination:** Yes.

Credential Type: Deputy Coroner License. **Duration of License:** One year. **Requirements:** Successful completion of a forty-hour basic training course within one year of taking office for certification. Must complete an 18-hour course annually. **Examination:** Yes.

3546

Mining Electrical Inspector
Dept. of Mines and Minerals
PO Box 14080
Lexington, KY 40512
Phone: (606)254-0367

Credential Type: License. **Duration of License:** One year. **Requirements:** Ten years experience in coal mines, two of which were in Kentucky mines. A bachelor's degree in mining engineering will substitute for two years of the required experience. An associate degree in mining technology will substitute for one year of experience. Must be a Kentucky resident. 16 hours of retraining annually. **Examination:** Yes. **Reciprocity:** No. **Fees:** $50 exam fee.

3547

Mining Fire Boss
Dept. of Mines and Minerals
PO Box 14080
Lexington, KY 40512
Phone: (606)254-0367

Credential Type: License. **Duration of License:** One year. **Requirements:** 21 years of age or three years of experience after 18th birthday with one year of the experience at the face of the coal. An associate degree in mine technology will count for one year experience, while a four-year

Kentucky 3548

Mining Fire Boss, continued

degree in mining engineering will count toward two year experience credit. Must be a resident of Kentucky or employed by a mine in Kentucky. 16 hours of retraining required annually. **Examination:** Yes. **Reciprocity:** No. **Fees:** $50 exam fee.

3548

Mining Inspector
Dept. of Mines and Minerals
PO Box 14080
Lexington, KY 40512
Phone: (606)254-0367

Credential Type: License. **Duration of License:** One year. **Requirements:** Must have 10 years experience in coal mines, at least two of which were in Kentucky mines, after the age of 18. A bachelor's degree in mining engineering will substitute for two years of the required work experience. An associate degree in mining technology will count for one year of the required work experience. 16 hours of re-training annually. **Examination:** Yes. **Fees:** $50 exam fee.

3549

Sanitarian, Registered
Cabinet for Human Resources
Dept. of Health Services
275 E. Main St.
Frankfort, KY 40621
Phone: (502)564-4935

Credential Type: License. **Requirements:** Bachelor's degree or higher with at least 18 semester hours or 27 quarter hours of academic training in basic physical, chemical, biological or sanitary sciences. Two years active service as a sanitarian with an approved public health agency. **Examination:** Yes. **Fees:** $30 exam fee. $12 renewal fee.

Louisiana

3550

Boiler Inspector/Director of Boiler Inspections
State Board of Boiler Examiners
Office of State Fire Marshall
Boiler Inspection Section
1033 N. Lobdell Blvd.
Baton Rouge, LA 70806
Phone: (504)925-4911

Credential Type: License. **Duration of License:** One year. **Requirements:** High school diploma or equivalent. Must maintain a valid National Board Commission. **Fees:** $40 license fee. $20 renewal fee.

3551

Motor Vehicle Inspector
Office of Motor Vehicles
PO Box 64886
Baton Rouge, LA 70896
Phone: (504)925-6277

Credential Type: Motor Vehicle Inspector License. **Duration of License:** One year. **Requirements:** Be at least 18 years of age. Hold a valid Louisiana driver's license. Attend a special training course. **Examination:** Yes. **Fees:** $5 inspector license fee. **Governing Statute:** R.S. 32:1301-1309.

3552

Sanitarian
Louisiana State Board of Examiners
  for Sanitarians
PO Box 60630
New Orleans, LA 70160
Phone: (504)568-5181

Credential Type: License. **Duration of License:** One year. **Requirements:** Bachelor's degree with required coursework in the biological sciences. Completion of the Center for Disease Control's homestudy course, "Community Hygiene." One year of field training under a supervising sanitarian. **Examination:** Written and oral. **Fees:** $15 exam fee. $10 transcript review fee. $10 renewal fee.

3553

Weighmaster
Dept. of Agriculture
Div. of Weights and Measures
PO Box 44456
Baton Rouge, LA 70804
Phone: (504)925-3780

Credential Type: License. **Duration of License:** One year. **Requirements:** Must demonstrate knowledge of and skill in operating appropriate weighing and measuring devices. **Fees:** None. **Governing Statute:** R.S. 55, Regulation 11.

Maryland

3554

Environmental Sanitarian
Environmental Sanitarian Board
Dept. of the Environment
2500 Broening Hwy.
Baltimore, MD 21224
Phone: (410)631-3168

Credential Type: Environmental Sanitarian License. **Duration of License:** Two years. **Requirements:** Meet one of the following sets of requirements: (1) B.A. or B.S. degree with 60 science credits and one math course. One year experience as a sanitarian-in-training. (2) B.A. or B.S. degree with 30 science credits and one math course. Two years experience as a sanitarian-in-training. **Examination:** Registered Sanitarian Examination. **Fees:** $50 license fee. $50 renewal fee.

3555

Mining Fire Boss
Bureau of Mines
Dept. of Natural Resources
PO Drawer C
Westernport, MD 21562
Phone: (301)689-4136

Credential Type: License. **Requirements:** Contact licensing body for application information.

3556

Post-Mortem Examiner
Post-Mortem Examiners
Dept. of Health and Mental Hygiene
4201 Patterson Ave.
Baltimore, MD 21215
Phone: (410)328-3313

Credential Type: License. **Requirements:** Contact licensing body for application information.

3557

Sanitarian-in-Training
Environmental Sanitarian Board
Dept. of the Environment
2500 Broening Hwy.
Baltimore, MD 21224
Phone: (410)631-3167

Credential Type: Sanitarian-in-Training Certificate. **Duration of License:** One or two years. **Requirements:** One year as sanitarian-in-training is required of applicants with a B.S. or B.A. degree and 60 science credits and one math course. Two years are required of applicants with a B.S. or B.A. degree and 30 science credits and one math course. **Fees:** $15 application fee.

Massachusetts

3558

Health Officer
Board of Certification of Health Officers
Div. of Registration
100 Cambridge St., 15th Fl.
Boston, MA 02202
Phone: (617)727-3069

Credential Type: Certification. **Duration of License:** One year. **Requirements:** Contact licensing body for application information. Renewal requires 12 contact hours of continuing education per year.

3559

Insurance Inspector
Dept. of Public Safety
Div. of Inspection
Engineering Section
One Ashburton Pl.
Boston, MA 02108
Phone: (617)727-3200

Credential Type: Certificate of competency. **Duration of License:** Two years. **Authorization:** Licenses are issued for inspectors of pressure vessels and amusement devices. **Requirements:** Submit application and pass examination for competency. **Examination:** Written and oral examination. **Fees:** $50 license fee. **Governing Statute:** Massachusetts General Laws, Chap. 146.

3560

Sanitarian
Board of Registration of Sanitarians
Div. of Registration
100 Cambridge St., 15th fl.
Boston, MA 02202
Phone: (617)727-1747

Credential Type: License. **Duration of License:** One year. **Requirements:** Bachelor's degree in science. Have at least one year of experience in environmental or public health. **Examination:** National examination. **Reciprocity:** Yes, if applicant meets state requirements. **Fees:** $50 application fee. $100 exam fee. $50 renewal fee. $75 reciprocity fee.

Michigan

3561

Boiler Inspector
Boiler Div.
Bureau of Construction Codes
Dept. of Labor
7150 Harris Dr.
PO Box 30015
Lansing, MI 48909
Phone: (517)322-1287

Credential Type: License. **Duration of License:** One year. **Authorization:** Must be both licensed and certified competent. **Requirements:** Must be certified competent according to the National Board of Boiler and Pressure Vessel Inspectors Inspection Code. Must be employed by a company authorized to insure against loss from explosion of boilers or by a city having an authorized boiler inspection department. **Examination:** No separate licensing examination. **Exemptions:** Boiler inspectors employed by the City of Detroit are licensed by the city. **Reciprocity:** Yes. **Fees:** $30 fee covers exam, license, and certificate of competency. $15 license renewal fee. $30 reciprocity fee. **Governing Statute:** Boiler Act, Act 290 of 1965.

Credential Type: Certification. **Duration of License:** Permanent. **Authorization:** Must be both licensed and certified competent. **Requirements:** Requirements for certification include three years of practical experience in the design, construction, or operation of high pressure boilers as a mechanical engineer, steam engineer, or boilermaker, or at least three years of inspection experience as an inspector of high pressure boilers. A credit of two years of the required experience will be given to applicants holding an engineering degree from an accredited college of engineering. **Examination:** Written certification examination of the National Board of Boiler and Pressure Vessel Inspectors. **Fees:** $30 fee covers exam, license, and certificate of competency. **Governing Statute:** Boiler Act, Act 290 of 1965.

3562

Inspector, Vehicle Emission Testing
Auto Exhaust Testing Div.
Bureau of Automotive Regulation
Dept. of State
208 N. Capitol Ave.
Lansing, MI 48918
Phone: (517)322-1460

Credential Type: Approval. **Duration of License:** Lifelong. **Examination:** Written exam. **Governing Statute:** Vehicle Emissions Inspection and Maintenance Act, Act 83 of 1980.

3563

Sanitarian
Board of Sanitarians
Bureau of Occupational & Professional Regulation
Dept. of Commerce
PO Box 30018
Lansing, MI 48909
Phone: (517)373-9153

Credential Type: Registration. **Duration of License:** Two years. **Requirements:** Graduated with a baccalaureate degree or higher from an accredited college or university in a field of environmental health. At least three years of experience as a practicing Sanitarian. A combination of education and experience which totals at least seven years. Be of good moral character. **Examination:** Written exam. **Reciprocity:** Reciprocity exists for individuals from those states with requirements substantially equivalent to Michigan's. A letter of endorsement from those states is necessary for reciprocity to be granted. **Fees:** $20 application processing fee. $90 initial exam fee. $20 exam review fee. 30 initial registration fee, per year. $30 renewal fee, per year. $30 reciprocity fee. $15 temporary registration fee. $10 annual limited registration fee. **Governing Statute:** Sanitarian's Registration Act, Act 147 of 1963, as amended.

Minnesota

3564

Environmental Health Specialist (Sanitarian)
Dept. of Health
Environmental Health Div.
Environmental Field Services Section
717 Delaware St., SE
Box 9441
Minneapolis, MN 55440
Phone: (612)627-5032
Fax: (612)623-5043

Credential Type: Registration. **Duration of License:** Two years. **Requirements:** Must have undergraduate degree in environmental health or related field. Complete one year of supervised work experience in a related field. Pass examination. **Examination:** Yes. **Fees:** Contact board for fees.

Minnesota 3565

3565

Hazardous Waste Disposal Facility Inspector
Pollution Control Agency
520 N. Lafayette Rd.
St. Paul, MN 55155
Phone: (612)296-7283

Credential Type: Type I Inspector Certification. **Duration of License:** Three years. **Authorization:** All inspectors must be certified. **Requirements:** Must have a B.S. in biological, chemical, or physical sciences. Complete at least 15 hours of training within the three years immediately prior to application. Complete at least 10 inspections of this type of facility within the past year. Complete one year of employment.

Renewal requires 18 contact hours of additional job-related training. **Examination:** Yes. **Fees:** $15 exam fee. $15 certification fee. $15 renewal fee. **Governing Statute:** Minnesota Statutes 116.41. Pollution Control Agency Rules 6 MCAR 4.6088 et seq.

3566

Non-Hazardous Waste Disposal Facility Inspector
Pollution Control Agency
520 N. Lafayette Rd.
St. Paul, MN 55155
Phone: (612)296-7283

Credential Type: Type II Inspector Certification. **Duration of License:** Three years. **Authorization:** All inspectors must be certified. Type II Certification covers sanitary, modified sanitary, and sludge landfills. **Requirements:** High school graduate or equivalent. Complete at least 15 hours of training within the three years immediately prior to application. Complete at least 10 inspections of this type of facility within the past year. Complete one year of employment.

Renewal requires 18 contact hours of additional job-related training. **Examination:** Yes. **Fees:** $15 exam fee. $15 certification fee. $15 renewal fee. **Governing Statute:** Minnesota Statutes 116.41. Pollution Control Agency Rules 6 MCAR 4.6088 et seq.

Credential Type: Type III Inspector Certification. **Duration of License:** Three years. **Authorization:** Type III Certification covers demolition waste and nonhazardous source-specific industrial waste disposal facilities. **Requirements:** Complete at least four hours of training within the three years immediately prior to application. Complete at least 10 inspections of this type of facility within the past year. Complete one year of employment.

Renewal requires six contact hours of additional job-related training. **Examination:** Yes. **Fees:** $15 exam fee. $15 certification fee. $15 renewal fee. **Governing Statute:** Minnesota Statutes 116.41. Pollution Control Agency Rules 6 MCAR 4.6088 et seq.

Credential Type: Type IV Inspector Certification. **Duration of License:** Three years. **Authorization:** Type IV Certification covers land application sites and facilities for sewage sludge or industrial-commercial sludges. **Requirements:** High school graduate or equivalent. Complete at least nine hours of training within the three years immediately prior to application. Complete at least 10 inspections of this type of facility within the past year. Complete one year of employment.

Renewal requires nine contact hours of additional job-related training. **Examination:** Yes. **Fees:** $15 exam fee. $15 certification fee. $15 renewal fee. **Governing Statute:** Minnesota Statutes 116.41. Pollution Control Agency Rules 6 MCAR 4.6088 et seq.

3567

Wastewater Disposal Facility Inspector
Pollution Control Agency
520 N. Lafayette Rd.
St. Paul, MN 55155
Phone: (612)296-7283

Credential Type: Type V Inspector Certification. **Duration of License:** Three years. **Authorization:** Type V Certification covers land application systems for industrial, commercial, or agricultural wastewaters. If three or fewer operators are employed at a facility, at least one must be certified. If 4-7 operators, then at least two must be certified. If more than eight operators, then at least three must be certified. **Requirements:** Complete at least nine hours of training within the three years immediately prior to application. Complete at least 10 inspections of this type of facility within the past year. Complete one year of employment.

Renewal requires six contact hours of additional job-related training. **Examination:** Yes. **Fees:** $15 exam fee. $15 certification fee. $15 renewal fee. **Governing Statute:** Minnesota Statutes 116.41. Pollution Control Agency Rules 6 MCAR 4.6088 et seq.

Montana

3568

Clerk of Scales (Racetrack)
State of Montana Board of Horse Racing
Dept. of Commerce
1424 9th Ave.
Helena, MT 59620
Phone: (406)444-4287

Credential Type: License Registration. **Requirements:** Submit application and fingerprint card. Pay fee. **Fees:** $20 registration fee.

3569

Identifier (Racetrack)
State of Montana Board of Horse Racing
Dept. of Commerce
1424 9th Ave.
Helena, MT 59620
Phone: (406)444-4287

Credential Type: License Registration. **Requirements:** Submit application and fingerprint card. Pay fee. **Fees:** $20 registration fee.

3570

Sanitarian
Montana Board of Sanitarians
111 N. Jackson
Helena, MT 59620
Phone: (406)444-3091

Credential Type: Registration. **Duration of License:** One year. **Requirements:** Bachelor's degree in environmental health or equivalent. **Examination:** Environmental Health Proficiency Examination. Oral interview. **Reciprocity:** Yes. **Fees:** $90 exam fee. $50 application fee. $40 renewal fee. **Governing Statute:** Montana Code Annotated 37-40-301 through 37-40-312.

3571

Underground Storage Tank Inspector
Dept. of Health and Environmental Sciences
Environmental Sciences Div.
Solid and Hazardous Wastes Bureau
836 Front St.
Helena, MT 59620
Phone: (406)444-1430

Credential Type: Underground Storage Tank Inspector License. **Duration of License: Three years (annual renewal). **Requirements:** Contact licensing body for application information. During three-year license term, 16 hours of continuing education are required for renewal. **Examination:** Yes. **Fees:** $50 exam and license fee. $25 annual renewal fee. **Governing Statute:** Montana Code Annotated 75-11.

Nebraska

3572

Boiler/Boilerhouse Inspector
Div. of Safety, Boiler Section
301 Centennial Mall S.
PO Box 95024
Lincoln, NE 68509
Phone: (402)471-4721

Credential Type: License. **Duration of License:** Two years. **Requirements:** Must have at least 10 years experience in construction, installation, repair, and inspection of boilers. **Examination:** Yes. **Fees:** $30 examination fee. $20 initial renewal fee. $10 renewal fee.

3573

Identifier-Tattooer
Nebraska Racing Commision
301 Centennial Mall S.
PO Box 95014
Lincoln, NE 68509
Phone: (402)471-4155

Credential Type: License. **Duration of License:** One year. **Requirements:** 16 years of age. A felony conviction may be grounds for denial of the license. **Fees:** $20 license fee. $20 renewal fee.

3574

Sanitarian
Nebraska Board of Registration for Sanitarians
301 Centennial Mall S.
PO Box 95007
Lincoln, NE 68509
Phone: (402)471-2115

Credential Type: License. **Duration of License:** Two years. **Requirements:** Must have a baccalaureate or higher degree from an accredited school. Must have completed at least 45 quarter or semester hours of academic work in the natural sciences. Must have worked full-time as a sanitarian for a period of not less than one year. **Examination:** Yes. **Fees:** $60 examination fee. $10 certification fee. $5 in-training certification fee. $50 renewal fee.

Nevada

3575

Health and Safety Inspectors
Nevada State Health Div.
Bureau of Health Protection Services
505 E. King St., Rm. 103
Carson City, NV 89710
Phone: (702)687-4750

Credential Type: License. **Duration of License:** One year. **Requirements:** Bachelor's degree from an accredited institution. Completion of 30 semester hours of course work in environmental health and public hygiene or related subjects. Two years of experience in this field of public health. **Examination:** Yes. **Fees:** $100 exam fee. $25 license fee. $25 renewal fee.

New Jersey

3576

Animal Control Officer
New Jersey Dept. of Health
Biological Services Progam, CN364
Trenton, NJ 08625-0364
Phone: (609)984-3400

Credential Type: Certified Animal Control Officer. **Requirements:** Completion of an approved course offered by an accredited college or university. 18 years of age. **Governing Statute:** NJSA 4:19-15. NJAC 8:23-5.

3577

Inplant Inspector
New Jersey Dept. of Community Affairs
Bureau of Technical Services
CN816
Trenton, NJ 08625-0816
Phone: (609)530-8803

Credential Type: License. **Requirements:** Five years experience as a journeyman in a skilled trade regulated by the building, electrical, fire protection or plumbing subcode; or five years experience as a building, electrical, fire protection or plumbing inspector; or five years experience as a construction contractor; or three years experience and a bachelor's degree in architecture or engineering; or a New Jersey license in architecture or engineering. One technical CEU of continuing education is required for license renewal. **Examination:** Yes. **Fees:** $30 license fee. **Governing Statute:** NJSA 52:27. NJAC 5:23-5.

3578

Public Health Officer
New Jersey Dept. of Environmental Protection
Bureau of Revenue
CN402
Trenton, NJ 08625-0402
Phone: (609)530-5760

Credential Type: License. **Requirements:** A Diplomate of the American Board of Preventative Medicine; or a doctor's or master's degree from an accredited college or university in a health-related field. Two years of experience in an administrative public health position. **Examination:** Written. **Fees:** $25 exam fee. **Governing Statute:** NJSA 26:1A. NJAC 8:7.

3579

Sanitary Inspector
New Jersey Dept. of Environmental Protection
Bureau of Revenue
CN402
Trenton, NJ 08625-0402
Phone: (609)530-5760

Credential Type: Sanitary Inspector, first grade. **Requirements:** A bachelor's degree from an accredited college or university with a minimum of 32 credits in a related field. Successful completion of a course in environmental health and law. Successful completion of an approved field training course or one year of full-time employment in a public health agency. **Examination:** Written. **Fees:** $25 exam fee. **Governing Statute:** NJSA 26:1A. NJAC 8:7.

3580

Weighmaster
New Jersey Dept. of Law and Public Safety
Office of Weights and Measures
1261 Routes 1 and 9 South
Avanel, NJ 07001
Phone: (201)815-4840

Credential Type: License. **Duration of License:** Three years. **Requirements:** 18 years of age. Experience in weighing operations and a full working knowledge of New Jersey Weights and Measures law. **Fees:** $30 certificate fee. **Governing Statute:** NJSA 51:1.

New Mexico

3581

Clerk of Scales (Racetrack)
New Mexico State Racing
 Commission
PO Box 8576, Highland Station
Albuquerque, NM 87198
Phone: (505)841-4644

Credential Type: License Registration. **Requirements:** Submit application and fingerprint card. Pay fees. **Fees:** $16 registration fee. $1 notary fee. $23 fingerprint card processing fee.

3582

Identifier (Racetrack)
New Mexico State Racing
 Commission
PO Box 8576, Highland Station
Albuquerque, NM 87198
Phone: (505)841-4644

Credential Type: License Registration. **Requirements:** Submit application and fingerprint card. Pay fees. **Fees:** $16 registration fee. $1 notary fee. $23 fingerprint card processing fee.

New York

3583

Boiler Inspector (Boiler and Pressure Vessel Inspector)
New York State Dept. of Labor
Boiler Safety Bureau
State Office Campus, Bldg. 12, Rm. 134
Albany, NY 12240-0102
Phone: (518)457-2722

Credential Type: Certificate. **Duration of License:** One year. **Requirements:** Bachelor's Degree in Mechanical Engineering plus one year of experience. Or Associate's Degree in Mechanical Technology plus two years of experience. Or High School Diploma plus three years of experience in operating boiler/pressure vessels. Must be employed by a state licensed insurance agency to work as a boiler inspector in the private sector. **Examination:** Two day exam. Math and practical questions. **Fees:** $50 exam fee. $20 license fee. **Governing Statute:** Section 204 of the New York State Labor Law.

3584

Certified Motor-Vehicle Inspector
Dept. of Motor Vehicles
Div. of Vehicle Safety Services
Empire State Plaza
Swan St. Bldg.
Albany, NY 12228
Phone: (518)474-5282

Credential Type: Certificate. **Duration of License:** Three years. **Requirements:** Graduation from a motor vehicle trade school. **Examination:** Written. **Fees:** $10 application fee. $15 certification fee. $15 renewal fee. **Governing Statute:** Section 301 of Vehicle Traffic Law.

North Carolina

3585

Boiler Inspector
Dept. of Labor
Boiler and Pressure Vessel Div.
4 W. Edenton St.
Raleigh, NC 27601
Phone: (919)733-3034

Credential Type: License. **Duration of License:** One year. **Requirements:** High school diploma or equivalent. 18 years of age. Three years of experience with boilers and pressure vessels; or an equivalent combination of education and experience. **Examination:** National exam. **Fees:** $5 certification fee. $20 exam fee. $25 renewal fee.

3586

Electrical Inspector
Dept. of Insurance
Div. of Engineering and Building Codes
PO Box 26387
Raleigh, NC 27611
Phone: (919)733-3901

Credential Type: License. **Duration of License:** One year. **Requirements:** High school diploma or equivalent. Must be presently employed by a state or local government department. At least one year of technical or trade school training, or an apprenticeship program in electrical installation and codes, or six months of work under the direct supervision of a certified building inspector. There are various alternatives to these requirements. **Examination:** 200 multiple choice questions. **Fees:** $20 initial fee. $10 renewal fee.

3587

Food Inspector
Dept. of Agriculture
Meat & Poultry Inspection Service
PO Box 27647
Raleigh, NC 27611
Phone: (919)733-4136

Credential Type: License. **Duration of License:** Permanent. **Requirements:** High school diploma. Completion of a meat and poultry inspector job training program offered through the Dept. of Agriculture. 18 years of age. **Examination:** Yes.

3588

Safety Inspection Mechanic
Dept. of Transportation
Div. of Motor Vehicles
1100 New Bern Ave.
Raleigh, NC 27697
Phone: (919)733-0133

Credential Type: License. **Duration of License:** Permanent. **Requirements:** 16 years of age. Valid driver's license. Completion of one four-hour course from an accredited school. **Examination:** Written and practical.

3589

Sanitarian
North Carolina State Board of
 Sanitarian Examiners
Rte. 8 Box 342
Taylorsville, NC 28681
Phone: (704)495-8593

Credential Type: Sanitarian Intern Registration. **Duration of License:** One year. **Requirements:** Bachelor's degree from an accredited college with a minimum of 15 semester hours in the physical and/or biological sciences. **Fees:** $35 application fee. $20 renewal fee.

Credential Type: Registered Sanitarian. **Duration of License:** One year. **Requirements:** Bachelor's degree from an accredited college with a minimum of 15 semester hours in the physical and/or biological sciences. Completion of a two year internship. **Examination:** Written and oral. **Fees:** $60 exam fee. $20 renewal fee.

Inspectors and Compliance Officers, Except Construction

North Dakota

3590

Clerk of Scales (Racetrack)
North Dakota Racing Commission
State Capitol Bldg.
Bismarck, ND 58505
Phone: (701)224-2210

Credential Type: License Registration. **Requirements:** Submit application and fingerprint card. Pay fee. **Fees:** $10 license fee. $10 duplicate license fee.

3591

Environmental Health Practitioner
State Dept. of Health and
  Consolidated Laboratories
Environmental Health Section
600 E. Blvd., Judicial Wing, 2nd Fl.
Bismarck, ND 58505
Phone: (701)224-5188

Credential Type: Environmental Health Practitioner. **Duration of License:** Two years. **Requirements:** A B.S. degree in either an accredited environmental health curriculum or in the physical, chemical, or biological sciences. Complete at least two years of work experience. **Examination:** National Environmental Health Practitioner Registry Examination (NEHA). **Reciprocity:** Yes, provided another state or country has same requirements as those of North Dakota. **Fees:** $50 application fee. $15 renewal fee.

3592

Horse Identifier (Racetrack)
North Dakota Racing Commission
State Capitol Bldg.
Bismarck, ND 58505
Phone: (701)224-2210

Credential Type: License Registration. **Requirements:** Submit application and fingerprint card. Pay fee. **Fees:** $10 license fee. $10 duplicate license fee.

3593

Weighman
Dept. of Weights and Measures
Public Service Commission
State Capitol, 12th Fl.
Bismarck, ND 58505
Phone: (701)224-2400

Credential Type: Weighman License. **Duration of License:** One year. **Authorization:** A license is required to serve as a weighman at any public market. **Requirements:** Good moral character. **Fees:** $2.50 license fee. **Governing Statute:** North Dakota Century Code, Chap. 36-21-14 et seq.

3594

Weighmaster
Dept. of Weights and Measures
Public Service Commission
State Capitol, 12th Fl.
Bismarck, ND 58505
Phone: (701)224-2400

Credential Type: Weighmaster License. **Duration of License:** Two years. **Requirements:** Good moral character. Post $1000 surety bond. **Fees:** $5 license fee. **Governing Statute:** North Dakota Century Code, Chap. 36-06-05.

Ohio

3595

Boiler Inspector
Div. of Boiler Inspection
Dept. of Industrial Relations
2323 W. 5th Ave.
PO Box 825
Columbus, OH 43266-0567
Phone: (614)644-2236

Credential Type: Boiler Inspector Certification. **Duration of License:** Three years. **Requirements:** Submit application and pass examination for competency. **Examination:** Examination for Boiler and Pressure Piping Vessel Inspector. **Fees:** $50 exam fee. **Governing Statute:** Ohio Revised Code 4104.07.

3596

Deputy Mine Inspector
Mine Examining Board
Dept. of Industrial Relations
2323 W. Fifth Ave.
PO Box 825
Columbus, OH 43216
Phone: (614)644-2234

Credential Type: License. **Duration of License:** Permanent. **Requirements:** Submit application and pay fee. Pass examination. **Examination:** Mine inspector examination. **Fees:** $10 exam fee.

3597

Identifier (Thoroughbred, Standardbred, and Quarter Horse Racing)
Ohio State Racing Commission
State Office Tower
77 S. High St., 18th Fl.
Columbus, OH 43266-0416
Phone: (614)466-2757

Credential Type: License Registration. **Requirements:** Submit application and fingerprint card. Pay fee. **Fees:** $25 registration fee.

3598

Mine Fire Boss
Mine Examining Board
Dept. of Industrial Relations
2323 W. Fifth Ave.
PO Box 825
Columbus, OH 43216
Phone: (614)644-2234

Credential Type: License. **Duration of License:** Permanent. **Requirements:** Be able to read and write English. Have at least three years of practical experience. **Examination:** Fire boss examination. **Fees:** $10 exam fee.

Oklahoma

3599

Fire Boss (Underground)
State Mining Commission
4040 N. Lincoln, Ste. 107
Oklahoma City, OK 73105
Phone: (405)521-3859

Credential Type: Certificate. **Duration of License:** Lifetime. **Authorization:** A fire boss inspects underground mines and work sites to ensure that there is no collection of mine gases. **Requirements:** A working knowledge of the occupation is necessary. State resident. Must hold a first-aid certificate. Two years of practical underground experience. **Examination:** Fire Boss Examination. **Fees:** $10 exam fee. $10 certificate fee.

Oklahoma

3600

Sanitarian-in-Training
Oklahoma State Dept. of Health
Sanitarian Advisory Council
1000 N.E. Tenth
PO Box 53551
Oklahoma City, OK 73152
Phone: (405)271-8056

Credential Type: License. **Duration of License:** One year. **Requirements:** Bachelor of Science or Bachelor of Arts degree. Two years of postgraduate, full-time experience in the field of environmental health. No felony convictions. **Examination:** Professional Entrance Exam. **Fees:** $10 license fee. $7.50 renewal fee.

3601

Sanitarian (Registered)
Oklahoma State Dept. of Health
Sanitarian Advisory Council
1000 N.E. Tenth
PO Box 53551
Oklahoma City, OK 73152
Phone: (405)271-8056

Credential Type: Certificate. **Duration of License:** One year. **Requirements:** Bachelor of Science or Bachelor of Arts degree. Two years of postgraduate, full-time experience in the field of environmental health. No felony convictions. **Examination:** Professional Entrance Exam. **Fees:** $20 certification fee. $7.50 renewal fee.

Oregon

3602

Amusement Ride Inspector
Building Codes Agency
1535 Edgewater NW
Salem, OR 97310
Phone: (503)373-1268

Credential Type: Certificate. **Requirements:** Must have two years of experience with an insurance company as an amusement ride inspector; or have two years experience inspecting amusement rides and enforcing amusement ride codes while employed by a governmental body regulating rides; or have not less than five years documented field operating maintenance experience with amusement rides and devices; or have not less than ten years documented practical experience in design, construction, matintenance, repair, field inspection and operation of amusement rides and devices as an authorized representative of a recognized manufacturer; or have a combination of training and experience deemed equivalent by the Director of the Building Codes Agency. **Fees:** $100 certification fee. **Governing Statute:** ORS 460.400.

3603

Electrical Inspector
Building Codes Agency
1535 Edgewater NW
Salem, OR 97310
Phone: (503)373-1268

Credential Type: License. **Requirements:** Must have four years of experience as a journeyman electrician, plus two years experience as a general supervising electrician with valid supervisor license; or have a degree in electrical engineering plus three years approved experience in design, inspection or supervision of electrical installations; or equivalent experience approved by the Electrical Board. **Examination:** Yes. **Fees:** $22 exam fee. **Governing Statute:** ORS 455.730 and Oregon Administrative Rules 814-22-108.

3604

Sanitarian, Registered
Sanitarians Registration Board
800 NE Oregon St.
Portland, OR 97232
Phone: (503)731-4049

Credential Type: License. **Duration of License:** Two years. **Requirements:** Bacalaureate degree with at least 45 quarter hours in science courses relating to environmental sanitation. Two years of supervised experience in environmental sanitation; or a graduate degree in public or community health from an accredited college or university and one year of supervised experience in enviromental sanitation. Continuing education required. **Examination:** Yes. **Fees:** $120 exam fee. $80 license fee. $80 renewal fee. **Governing Statute:** ORS 700.020 to 700.220.

3605

Sanitarian Trainee
Sanitarian Registration Board
800 NE Oregon St.
Portland, OR 97232
Phone: (503)731-4049

Credential Type: License. **Duration of License:** Two years. **Requirements:** Baccalaureate degree with at least 45 quarter hours in science courses relating to environmental sanitation; or have 15 quarter hours in science courses relating to environmental sanitation and five years of supervised experience in environmental sanitation. Continuing education required. **Examination:** Yes. **Fees:** $90 exam fee. $80 license fee. $80 renewal fee. **Governing Statute:** ORS 700.020 to 700.220.

3606

Water Rights Examiner, Certified
Board of Engineering Examiners
750 Front St. NE, 240
Salem, OR 97310
Phone: (503)378-4180

Credential Type: Certification. **Duration of License:** Two years. **Requirements:** Must be a currenty registered engineer or land surveyor. **Examination:** Yes. **Fees:** $20 exam fee. $5 certificate fee. $20 renewal fee. **Governing Statute:** ORS 537.797.

Rhode Island

3607

Sanitarian
State Board of Sanitarians
Div. of Professional Regulation
Rhode Island Dept. of Health
3 Capitol Hill
Providence, RI 02908
Phone: (401)277-2827

Credential Type: Sanitarian License. **Duration of License:** One year. **Requirements:** At least 21 years old. Good moral character. Foreign born must show proof of legal entry into U.S. Meet one of the following requirements: (1) Bachelor's degree in sanitary science or sanitary engineering from an accredited school; (2) Bachelor's degree with 30 semester hours of basic science and special training in sanitation; (3) Complete two years in an approved college program with 15 semester hours in basic science and special training in sanitation, plus two years experience in public health sanitation; (4) Bachelor's degree in dairy science or management with 15 semester hours in basic science. **Examination:** Written examination. **Reciprocity:** No. **Fees:** $15 application fee. $30 renewal fee.

Inspectors and Compliance Officers, Except Construction

South Carolina

3608

Sanitarian
South Carolina State Board of Examiners for Registered Sanitarians
PO Box 8793
Columbia, SC 29202
Phone: (803)254-3661

Credential Type: License. **Requirements:** A degree from a four-year, accredited college or university with a minimum of 12 semester hours in the natural sciences. **Examination:** Yes. **Fees:** $80 exam fee. $75 license fee. $20 renewal fee.

South Dakota

3609

Clerk of Scales (Greyhound Racing)
South Dakota Racing Commission
c/o 500 East Capitol
Pierre, SD 57501
Phone: (605)773-6050

Credential Type: License Registration. **Requirements:** Submit application and fingerprint card. Pay fee. **Fees:** $15 registration fee.

Tennessee

3610

Certified Public Weigher
Dept. of Agriculture
Weights and Measurements Div.
PO Box 40627
Nashville, TN 37204
Phone: (615)360-0159

Credential Type: License. **Duration of License:** One year. **Requirements:** Surety bond for $5,000. Good moral character. **Fees:** $10 Registration.

3611

Weighmaster
Dept. of Agriculture
Weights and Measures Div.
PO Box 40627
Nashville, TN 37204
Phone: (615)360-0159

Credential Type: License. **Duration of License:** One year. **Requirements:** 18 years old. **Reciprocity:** No. **Fees:** $10 Registration.

Texas

3612

Sanitarian
Texas Dept. of Health
Sanitarian Registration Program
1100 W. 49th St.
Austin, TX 78756
Phone: (512)834-6635

Credential Type: Sanitarian-in-Training License. **Duration of License:** One year. **Requirements:** Graduation with a B.A. or B.S. from a recognized college or university with at least 15 semseter hours in basic and/or natural science. **Examination:** Written. **Fees:** $5 registration fee. $10 renewal fee. **Governing Statute:** VACS 4477-3, 25 TAC 337.181.

Credential Type: Sanitarian License. **Duration of License:** One year. **Requirements:** Graduation with a B.A. or B.S. from a recognized college or university with at least 15 semester hours in basic and/or natural science. At least one year experience in the field. **Examination:** Written. **Fees:** $10 registration fee. $10 renewal fee. **Governing Statute:** VACS 4477-3, 25 TAC 337.181.

3613

Test Technician (Racetrack)
Texas Racing Commission
PO Box 12080
Austin, TX 78711
Phone: (512)794-8461

Credential Type: License Registration. **Requirements:** Submit application and fingerprint card. Pay fee. **Fees:** $20 registration fee.

Utah

3614

Fire Boss (Mining)
The Industrial Commission of Utah
160 E. 300 S.
Salt Lake City, UT 84151-0910
Phone: (801)530-6869

Credential Type: Fire Boss License. **Requirements:** Must have two years of varied underground coal mining experience and hold a U.S. Bureau of Mines First Aid Certificate or the equivalent training. One year of experience may be credited to a mining engineering graduate of an approved four-year college; or six months experience may be credited to a graduate of a two-year course in mining. **Examination:** Yes. **Fees:** $50 license fee.

3615

Sanitarian
Dept. of Commerce
Div. of Occupational and Professional Licensing
160 E. 300 S.
PO Box 45802
Salt Lake City, UT 84145
Phone: (801)530-6628

Credential Type: License. **Duration of License:** Two years. **Requirements:** Must have a bachelor's degree or higher from an accredited college including at least 45 quarter hours or 30 semester hours in environmental health, the physical and biological sciences, or their equivalents. **Examination:** Yes. **Fees:** $50 license fee. $30 renewal fee.

Vermont

3616

Clerk of Scales (Greyhound Racing)
Vermont Racing Commission
State Office Bldg.
Montpelier, VT 05602
Phone: (802)828-3429

Credential Type: License Registration. **Requirements:** Submit application and fingerprint card. Pay fee. **Fees:** $20 registration fee. $5 duplicate license.

Virginia

3617

Clerk of Scales (Racetrack)
Virginia Racing Commission
PO Box 1123
Richmond, VA 23208
Phone: (804)371-7363

Credential Type: License Registration. **Requirements:** Submit application and fingerprint card. Pay fee. **Fees:** $10 registration fee.

3618

Horse Identifier (Racetrack)
Virginia Racing Commission
PO Box 1123
Richmond, VA 23208
Phone: (804)371-7363

Credential Type: License Registration. **Requirements:** Submit application and fingerprint card. Pay fee. **Fees:** $10 registration fee.

Washington

3619

Amusement Ride Inspector
Dept. of Labor & Industries
Building & Construction Safety Inspection Services
General Administration Bldg., HC-101
Olympia, WA 98504
Phone: (206)753-6194

Credential Type: Amusement Ride Inspector Certificate. **Duration of License:** One year. **Requirements:** Meet one of the following requirements: (1) Have two years experience as an insurance company ride inspector; (2) Have two years experience as a ride inspector for a governmental body; (3) Have five years of documented field experience; (4) Have 10 years experience in design/construction of amusement ride equipment. **Fees:** $20 certificate fee.

3620

Boiler Inspector
Dept. of Labor & Industries
Building & Construction Safety Inspection Services
General Administration Bldg., HC-101
Olympia, WA 98504
Phone: (206)586-0217

Credential Type: Boiler Inspector License. **Duration of License:** permanent. **Requirements:** High school graduate. Engineering degree or approved equivalent experience. Certificate of Competency. **Examination:** Written examination. **Reciprocity:** Yes. **Fees:** $40 Certificate of Competency fee. $10 annual Commission renewal fee. $25 reciprocal commission renewal fee.

3621

Inspector (Professional Boxing/ Wrestling)
Professional Athletic Commission
2626 12th Court, GT-17
Olympia, WA 98504-8321
Phone: (206)753-3713

Credential Type: Inspector License. **Duration of License:** One year. **Requirements:** Submit application with current photo. **Fees:** No fee.

3622

Waterfront Equipment Inspector
Dept. of Labor & Industries
Div. of Industrial Safety & Health
General Administration Bldg., HC-101
Olympia, WA 98504
Phone: (206)753-6509

Credential Type: Waterfront Equipment Inspector License. **Duration of License:** Three years. **Requirements:** Submit application and resume with satisfactory record of experience and performance. Requires inspection of work performed. Must have approval of Crane Certification Board. **Fees:** No fee.

3623

Weigher (Dairy & Food)
Dept. of Agriculture
Consumer and Producer Protection
406 General Administration Bldg., AX-41
Olympia, WA 98504-0641
Phone: (206)545-2830

Credential Type: Weigher License. **Duration of License:** One year. **Requirements:** Gain experience through on-the-job training. Background investigation and inspection of work performed required. **Fees:** $5 license fee.

3624

Weighmaster
Dept. of Agriculture
Dairy & Food Div.
406 General Administration Bldg., AX-41
Olympia, WA 98504-0641
Phone: (206)545-2830

Credential Type: Weighmaster License. **Duration of License:** One year. **Requirements:** At least 21 years of age. Requires background investigation and inspection of work performed. **Examination:** Practical examination. **Fees:** $20 license fee.

West Virginia

3625

Sanitarian
Dept. of Health
Board of Registration for Sanitarians
PO Box 927
Charleston, WV 25323
Phone: (304)348-8050

Credential Type: License. **Duration of License:** One year. **Requirements:** U.S. citizen. Degree from accredited college. Attendance at state training center. Never convicted of a felony. **Examination:** Yes. **Fees:** $10 Application. $30 Examination. $10 Renewal.

3626

School Social Services and Attendance Investigator
Dept. of Education
Office of Educational Personnel Development
1900 Washington St. E
Charleston, WV 25305
Phone: (800)982-2378

Credential Type: Certification. **Duration of License:** Three or five years. **Requirements:** U.S. citizen. 18 years old. Bachelors degree, completion of approved social science and attendance program. Never convicted of a felony. **Examination:** No. **Fees:** $5 Application (for three or five year Certificate). $5 Renewal (for permanent Certificate).

Wisconsin

3627

Clerk of Scales (Racetrack)
Wisconsin Racing Board
PO Box 7975
Madison, WI 53707-7975
Phone: (608)267-3291

Credential Type: License Registration. **Requirements:** Submit application and two sets of fingerprint cards. Pay fee. **Fees:** $50 registration fee. $20 duplicate license.

Wyoming

3628

Mine Examiner
Mining Board of Wyoming
PO Box 1094
Rock Springs, WY 82901
Phone: (307)362-5222

Credential Type: License. **Requirements:** 23 years of age. Two years experience in the type of mine desired; or, one year training as a mine engineer from an accredited college and one year experience in the type of mine desired. Pass the examination. **Examination:** Yes. **Fees:** $25 License.

3629

Mine Inspector
Mining Board of Wyoming
PO Box 1094
Rock Springs, WY 82901
Phone: (307)362-5222

Credential Type: License. **Requirements:** 35 years of age. Qualified elector of the state. Good reputation and temperate habits. Have 10 years experience in addition to Mine Foreman experience, in underground mines. **Examination:** No. **Fees:** None.

Inspectors, Testers, and Graders

The following states grant licenses in this occupational category as of the date of publication:

Arkansas	Georgia	Louisiana	Mississippi	New York	Rhode Island	West Virginia
California	Idaho	Maine	Missouri	North Carolina	South Carolina	Wisconsin
Colorado	Illinois	Maryland	Montana	North Dakota	South Dakota	
Connecticut	Iowa	Massachusetts	Nevada	Ohio	Tennessee	
Delaware	Kansas	Michigan	New Hampshire	Oregon	Virginia	
Florida	Kentucky	Minnesota	New Mexico	Pennsylvania	Washington	

Arkansas

3630

Egg Grader
Arkansas Livestock and Poultry Commission
1 Natural Resources Dr.
PO Box 549
Little Rock, AR 72215
Phone: (501)225-5138

Credential Type: License. **Requirements:** Based upon evaluation of experience, education and training. Must be in good physical health. **Examination:** Yes. **Fees:** None.

3631

Milk Tester
Dept. of Health
Div. of Environmental Health Protection
4815 W. Markham St.
Little Rock, AR 72205-3867
Phone: (501)661-2616
Phone: (501)661-2000

Credential Type: License. **Duration of License:** One year. **Requirements:** Submit application and pay fee. **Examination:** Written examination. **Fees:** $10 annual license fee.

California

3632

Milk Hauler and Tester
Dept. of Food and Agriculture
Div. of Animal Industry
Milk and Dairy Foods Control Branch
1220 N St.
Sacramento, CA 94271
Phone: (916)654-0773
Fax: (916)654-1274

Credential Type: License. **Requirements:** Contact licensing body for application information.

Colorado

3633

Milk and Cream Sampler
Dept. of Health
Consumer Protection Div.
4300 Cherry Creek Dr. S.
Denver, CO 80222-1530
Phone: (303)692-3641
Phone: (303)692-2000

Credential Type: License. **Duration of License:** One year. **Requirements:** Be at least 16 years of age. Pass an evaluation for certification. **Examination:** Written examination. Practical performance test. **Fees:** $3 annual license fee.

3634

Milk and Cream Tester
Dept. of Health
Consumer Protection Div.
4300 Cherry Creek Dr. S.
Denver, CO 80222-1530
Phone: (303)692-3641
Phone: (303)692-2000

Credential Type: License. **Duration of License:** One year. **Requirements:** Be at least 16 years of age. Must have tested at least 10 samples of milk or cream under the supervision of a person holding a valid Colorado license. **Examination:** Written examination. Practical performance test. **Fees:** $3 annual license fee.

Connecticut

3635

Milk Hauler and Tester
Dept. of Agriculture
Dairy Div.
State Office Bldg.
165 Capitol Ave.
Hartford, CT 06115
Phone: (203)566-5894
Fax: (203)566-6094

Credential Type: License. **Requirements:** Contact licensing body for application information.

Delaware

3636

Milk Hauler and Tester
Div. of Public Health
Office of Food Control
Jesse Cooper Bldg.
Dover, DE 19901
Phone: (302)739-4731
Fax: (302)739-6617

Credential Type: License. **Requirements:** Contact licensing body for application information.

Florida

3637

Milk Hauler and Tester
Dept. of Agriculture and Consumer Services
Div. of Dairy Industry
3125 Conner Blvd.
Tallahassee, FL 32399-1650
Phone: (904)487-1460
Fax: (904)488-0863

Credential Type: License. **Requirements:** Contact licensing body for application information.

Georgia

3638

Milk Hauler and Tester
Dept. of Agriculture
Dairy Regulatory Div.
19 Martin Luther King Jr. Dr.
Capitol Sq.
Atlanta, GA 30334
Phone: (404)656-3625
Fax: (404)656-9380

Credential Type: License. **Requirements:** Contact licensing body for application information.

Idaho

3639

Milk Hauler and Tester
Dept. of Health and Welfare
Bureau of Preventive Medicine
450 W. State St.
Boise, ID 83720
Phone: (208)334-5930
Fax: (208)334-5694

Credential Type: License. **Requirements:** Contact licensing body for application information.

Illinois

3640

Bulk Milk Hauler/Sampler
Illinois Dept. of Public Health
Div. of Food, Drugs, and Dairies
525 W. Jefferson St.
Springfield, IL 62761
Phone: (217)785-2439

Credential Type: Bulk Milk Hauler/Sampler License. **Duration of License:** One year. **Authorization:** Allows applicant to measure and screen milk, then haul milk to dairy processing plant or transfer station from farm dairies. **Requirements:** Submit application and pay fees. Pass examination. **Examination:** Written examination. **Reciprocity:** No. **Fees:** $25 initial license fee. $25 renewal fee. **Governing Statute:** Title 77, Chapter I.

Iowa

3641

Milk Grader
Dept. of Agriculture and Land Stewardship
Dairy Products Control Bureau
Henry A. Wallace Bldg.
Des Moines, IA 50319
Phone: (515)381-3545

Credential Type: License. **Duration of License:** One year. **Requirements:** Pass written examination. Must attend the state milk grader's school every three years. **Examination:** Written examination. **Fees:** $10 annual license fee.

3642

Milkfat Tester
Dept. of Agriculture and Land Stewardship
Dairy Products Control Bureau
Henry A. Wallace Bldg.
Des Moines, IA 50319
Phone: (515)381-3545

Credential Type: License. **Duration of License:** One year. **Requirements:** Pass written examination. **Examination:** Written examination. **Fees:** $25 annual license fee.

Kansas

3643

Milk Hauler and Tester
State Board of Agriculture
Div. of Inspection-Dairy
901 S. Kansas Ave.
Topeka, KS 66612-1272
Phone: (913)296-3731
Phone: (913)296-7020
Fax: (913)296-7951

Credential Type: License. **Requirements:** Contact licensing body for application information.

Kentucky

3644

Milk Sampler - Weigher
University of Kentucky Regulatory Services
Regulatory Services Bldg., Rm. 103
Lexington, KY 40546
Phone: (606)257-2785

Credential Type: License. **Duration of License:** One year. **Requirements:** Must meet health requirements. **Examination:** Yes. **Fees:** $7 exam fee. $7 renewal fee.

3645

Milk Tester
University of Kentucky Regulatory Services
Regulatory Services Bldg., Rm. 103
Lexington, KY 40546
Phone: (606)257-2785

Credential Type: License. **Duration of License:** One year. **Requirements:** Must meet health requirements. **Examination:** Yes. **Fees:** $7 exam fee. $7 renewal fee.

Louisiana

3646

Milk and Cream Measurer/Sampler
Dairy Industry Promotion Board
Dept. of Agriculture
12055 Airline Hwy.
Baton Rouge, LA 70817
Phone: (504)925-4652

Credential Type: License. **Duration of License:** Two years. **Requirements:** Submit application and pass exams. **Examination:** Written and practical examinations. **Fees:** None. **Governing Statute:** R.S. 40:882.2. R.S.40:889.

3647

Milk and Cream Tester
Dairy Industry Promotion Board
Dept. of Agriculture
12055 Airline Hwy.
Baton Rouge, LA 70817
Phone: (504)925-4652

Credential Type: License. **Duration of License:** Two years. **Requirements:** Submit application and pass exams. **Examination:** Written and practical exams. **Fees:** None. **Governing Statute:** R.S. 40:882.2. R.S. 40:889.

Maine

3648

Milk Hauler and Tester
Dept. of Agriculture
Food and Rural Resources
Div. of Regulation, Dairy Inspection
State House Station 28
Augusta, ME 04333
Phone: (207)289-3841
Fax: (207)289-7548

Credential Type: License. **Requirements:** Contact licensing body for application information.

Maryland

3649

Milk Hauler and Tester
Dept. of Health and Mental Hygiene
Office of Food Protection and
   Consumer Health Services
4201 Patterson Ave., Rm. 515
Baltimore, MD 21215
Phone: (410)764-3579
Fax: (410)764-3591

Credential Type: License. **Requirements:** Contact licensing body for application information.

Massachusetts

3650

Milk Hauler and Tester
Dept. of Food and Agricutlure
Bureau of Dairying
100 Cambridge St.
Boston, MA 02202
Phone: (617)727-3020
Fax: (617)727-7235

Credential Type: License. **Requirements:** Contact licensing body for application information.

Michigan

3651

Butter Grader
Dairy Products Div.
Dept. of Agriculture
Ottawa Bldg., N.
PO Box 30017
Lansing, MI 48909
Phone: (517)373-1104

Credential Type: License. **Duration of License:** One year. **Requirements:** Some experience in the manufacture and grading of butter. Abide by the rules of the Department of Agriculture. **Examination:** Written and practical examination. **Governing Statute:** Butter Grading Law, Act 211 of 1955.

3652

Certified Industry Fieldperson
Dairy Products Div.
Dept. of Agriculture
Ottawa Bldg., N.
PO Box 30017
Lansing, MI 48909
Phone: (517)373-1104

Credential Type: Certification. **Duration of License:** One year. **Authorization:** All individuals conducting certified farm inspections for milk distributors or milk plant operators must be certified by the Dairy Products Division of the Department of Agriculture. **Requirements:** Appropriate experience in the field of milk sanitation and be a full-time employee of a milk plant, a producer association, or an officially designated laboratory or be employed on a consulting basis by such establishments. Abide by all rules of the Department of Agriculture. **Examination:** Practical exam. **Fees:** $10 initial exam and certificate fee. $10 renewal fee. **Governing Statute:** Fluid Milk Act, Act 233 of 1965.

3653

Milk Fat Tester
Dairy Products Div.
Dept. of Agriculture
Ottawa Bldg., N.
PO Box 30017
Lansing, MI 48909
Phone: (517)373-1104

Credential Type: License. **Duration of License:** One year. **Requirements:** Abide by the rules of the Department of Agriculture. **Examination:** Written and practical test. **Fees:** $5 initial license fee. $5 renewal fee. **Governing Statute:** Milk Fat Test Law, Act 212 of 1935, as amended.

Minnesota

3654

Milk Tester
Dept. of Agricutlure
Dairy and Livestock Div.
90 W. Plato Blvd.
St. Paul, MN 55107
Phone: (612)296-3647
Fax: (612)297-5176

Credential Type: Milk and Cream Grading and Testing License. **Requirements:** Contact licensing body for application information. **Fees:** $50 license fee. $25 renewal fee.

Mississippi

3655

Milk Hauler and Tester
Dept. of Health
Milk and Shellfish Sanitation Br.
2423 N. State St.
Jackson, MS 39215-1700
Phone: (601)960-7697
Fax: (601)960-7948

Credential Type: License. **Requirements:** Contact licensing body for application information.

Missouri

3656

Milk Hauler and Tester
State Milk Board
915-C Leslie Blvd.
Jefferson City, MO 65101
Phone: (314)751-3830
Fax: (314)751-2527

Credential Type: License. **Requirements:** Contact licensing body for application information.

Montana

3657

Milk and Cream Tester
Dept. of Livestock
Animal Health Div.
Capital Sta.
Helena, MT 59620
Phone: (406)444-2043

Credential Type: License. **Duration of License:** One year. **Examination:** Submit application and pay fee. **Exemptions:** Performance examination. **Fees:** $10 annual license fee.

3658

Milk and Cream Weigher, Grader, and Sampler
Dept. of Livestock
Animal Health Div.
Capital Sta.
Helena, MT 59620
Phone: (406)444-2043

Credential Type: License. **Duration of License:** One year. **Examination:** Submit application and pay fee. **Exemptions:** Performance examination. **Fees:** $5 annual license fee.

Nevada

3659

Milk Tester
Dept. of Human Resources
Health Div.
Bureau of Health Protection Services
505 E. King St., Rm. 103
Carson City, NV 89710
Phone: (702)687-4750

Credential Type: License. **Duration of License:** One year. **Authorization:** A license is required if testing for producer payment of either milk or cream. **Requirements:** Must have required testing equipment. **Examination:** Oral examination. **Fees:** $10 annual license fee.

New Hampshire

3660

Milk Hauler and Tester
Dairy Sanitation Program
Office of Environmental Health
Dept. of Health and Human Services
6 Hazen Dr.
Concord, NH 03301-6527
Phone: (603)271-4673
Fax: (603)271-3745

Credential Type: License. **Requirements:** Contact licensing body for application information.

New Mexico

3661

Milk Hauler and Tester
State Environmental Dept.
4131 Montgomery Blvd. NE
Albuquerque, NM 87109
Phone: (505)841-9450
Fax: (505)884-9254

Credential Type: License. **Requirements:** Contact licensing body for application information.

New York

3662

Milk Tester
Dept. of Agriculture and Markets
Div. of Milk Control
One Winners Circle
Albany, NY 12235
Phone: (518)457-1772

Credential Type: License. **Duration of License:** Five years. **Examination:** Written and practical. **Fees:** $5 application fee. $2 renewal fee. **Governing Statute:** Article four Section 56b, 57, and 57a of Agriculture and Markets Law, and Title 1, New York Consolidated Rules and Regulations, Part 6.

North Carolina

3663

Farm Bulk Milk Hauler/Sampler
Dept. of Agriculture
Food & Drug Protection Div.
PO Box 27647
Raleigh, NC 27611
Phone: (919)733-7366

Credential Type: License. **Duration of License:** One year. **Examination:** Written. **Fees:** $2 initial fee. $2 renewal fee.

3664

Milk Tester
Dept. of Agriculture
Food & Drug Protection
PO Box 27647
Raleigh, NC 27611
Phone: (919)733-7366

Credential Type: License. **Duration of License:** One year. **Requirements:** Must be familiar with the Milk Testing Law of North Carolina. **Examination:** Written and practical. **Fees:** $2 initial fee. $2 renewal fee.

3665

Petroleum Device Technician
Dept. of Agriculture
Standards Div., Measurement Section
1 W. Edenton St.
Raleigh, NC 27611
Phone: (919)733-3313

Credential Type: License. **Duration of License:** One year. **Requirements:** 18 years of age. Two letters of endorsement. One year of supervised experience with

Petroleum Device Technician, continued

liquid fuel pumps, meters and other measuring devices.

North Dakota

3666

Milk Hauler and Tester
Dept. of Agriculture
Dairy Commissioner
State Capitol
Bismarck, ND 58505
Phone: (701)224-4763
Fax: (701)224-4567

Credential Type: License. **Requirements:** Contact licensing body for application information.

Ohio

3667

Milk Hauler and Tester
Dept. of Health
Milk Program
246 High St.
Columbus, OH 43266-0118
Phone: (614)466-5550
Fax: (614)644-1909

Credential Type: License. **Requirements:** Contact licensing body for application information.

Oregon

3668

Milk Grader and/or Sampler
Oregon Dept. of Agriculture
635 Capitol NE
Salem, OR 97310
Phone: (503)378-3790

Credential Type: License. **Duration of License:** One year. **Requirements:** 18 years of age. Free of communicable disease. Must have at least three months practical experience in helping to operate pasteurization equipment or to grade milk or cream. **Examination:** Yes. **Fees:** $25 exam fee. $25 license fee. $25 renewal fee. **Governing Statute:** ORS 621.005 to 621.990.

Pennsylvania

3669

Milk Hauler and Tester
Dept. of Agriculture
Div. of Milk Sanitation
2301 N. Cameron St.
Harrisburg, PA 17120
Phone: (717)787-4316
Fax: (717)772-2780

Credential Type: License. **Requirements:** Contact licensing body for application information.

Rhode Island

3670

Milk Hauler and Tester
Dept. of Health
Div. of Food Protection
State Milk Program
3 Capitol Hill, Rm. 203
Providence, RI 02908-5097
Phone: (401)277-2749
Fax: (401)277-6548

Credential Type: License. **Requirements:** Contact licensing body for application information.

South Carolina

3671

Milk Tester
Dept. of Agriculture
Laboratory Div.
1101 Williams St.
PO Box 11280
Columbia, SC 29211
Phone: (803)737-2070

Credential Type: License. **Duration of License:** One year. **Requirements:** Complete a training course conducted by the dairy department of Clemson University. **Examination:** Written examination.

3672

Milk Weigher and Sampler
Dept. of Agriculture
Laboratory Div.
1101 Williams St.
PO Box 11280
Columbia, SC 29211
Phone: (803)737-2070

Credential Type: License. **Duration of License:** One year. **Requirements:** Submit application and pass exam. **Examination:** Written examination.

3673

Percolation Test Technician
South Carolina Board of Certification of Environmental Systems Operators
2221 Devine St., Ste. 320
Columbia, SC 29205
Phone: (803)734-9140

Credential Type: License. **Requirements:** Six months of experience in assisting and observing percolation tests under the supervision of a registered professional engineer, certified percolation test technician, or professional soil classifier. **Fees:** $48 license fee.

South Dakota

3674

Milk Hauler and Tester
Dept. of Agriculture
Div. of Regulatory Services
Office of Dairy Inspection
Anderson Bldg.
Pierre, SD 57501
Phone: (605)773-3724
Fax: (605)773-5891

Credential Type: License. **Requirements:** Contact licensing body for application information.

Tennessee

3675

Milk Sampler
Dept. of Agriculture
Ellington Agricultural Center
Div. of Quality and Standards
Box 40627, Melrose Sta.
Nashville, TN 37204
Phone: (615)360-0150

Credential Type: Samplers License. **Duration of License:** One year. **Authorization:** Every person receiving or buying milk or cream on the basis of its chemical or physical constituents must have in each milk transport tank truck, a licensed milk sampler or tester. **Requirements:** Submit application and pay fee. Demonstrate honesty and competence to do sampling work. **Examination:** Exam may be required. **Fees:** $5 annual license fee.

Inspectors, Testers, and Graders

3676

Milk Tester
Dept. of Agriculture
Ellington Agricultural Center
Div. of Quality and Standards
Box 40627, Melrose Sta.
Nashville, TN 37204
Phone: (615)360-0150

Credential Type: Testers License. **Duration of License:** One year. **Authorization:** Every person receiving or buying milk or cream on the basis of its chemical or physical constituents must be or have in their employ a licensed milk tester to make the official analysis. **Requirements:** Submit application and pay fee. Demonstrate competence by passing written exam. **Examination:** Written examination. **Fees:** $5 annual license fee.

Virginia

3677

Milk Tester
Dept. of Agriculture and Consumer Services
Div. of Dairy and Foods
PO Box 1163
Richmond, VA 23209
Phone: (804)786-8899
Fax: (804)371-7792

Credential Type: Permit. **Duration of License:** One year. **Requirements:** Pass written exam. **Examination:** Written examination. **Fees:** $1 annual permit fee.

Washington

3678

Milk Hauler and Tester
Dept. of Agriculture
Dairy and Food Div.
406 General Administration Bldg., AX-41
Olympia, WA 98504
Phone: (206)753-5043
Fax: (206)753-3700

Credential Type: License. **Requirements:** Contact licensing body for application information.

West Virginia

3679

Bulk Milk Hauler and Sampler
Dept. of Agriculture
Consumer Protection Div.
Agriculture Center
Capitol Bldg.
Charleston, WV 25305
Phone: (304)348-2201

Credential Type: License. **Duration of License:** One year. **Requirements:** Pass written examination. In addition, must obtain a permit from the state Department of Public Health, which also requires an examination. **Examination:** Written examination. **Fees:** $2 annual license fee. $1.50 exam fee.

Wisconsin

3680

Bulk Milk Weigher and Sampler
Dept. of Agriculture
Trade and Consumer Protection
Food Div.
801 W. Badger Rd.
PO Box 8911
Madison, WI 53708
Phone: (608)266-2227

Credential Type: License. **Duration of License:** Two years. **Requirements:** Submit application and pay fee. **Fees:** $40 license fee. $40 reinspection fee.

3681

Butter Grader
Dept. of Agriculture
Trade and Consumer Protection
Food Div.
801 W. Badger Rd.
PO Box 8911
Madison, WI 53708
Phone: (608)266-2227

Credential Type: License. **Duration of License:** Two years. **Requirements:** Submit application and pay fee. **Fees:** $50 license fee.

3682

Cheese Grader
Dept. of Agriculture
Trade and Consumer Protection
Food Div.
801 W. Badger Rd.
PO Box 8911
Madison, WI 53708
Phone: (608)266-2227

Credential Type: License. **Duration of License:** Two years. **Authorization:** Separate licenses are issued for graders of American cheese, Swiss cheese, and brick and Muenster cheese. **Requirements:** Submit application and pay fee. **Fees:** $50 license fee.

3683

Milk or Cream Tester
Dept. of Agriculture
Trade and Consumer Protection
Food Div.
801 W. Badger Rd.
PO Box 8911
Madison, WI 53708
Phone: (608)266-2227

Credential Type: License. **Duration of License:** Two years. **Requirements:** Submit application and pay fee. **Fees:** $50 license fee. $25 reinspection fee.

Instructors and Coaches, Sports and Physical Training

The following states grant licenses in this occupational category as of the date of publication:

Alabama	Connecticut	Idaho	Massachusetts	North Carolina	Pennsylvania	Tennessee
Alaska	Delaware	Illinois	Nebraska	North Dakota	Rhode Island	Texas
Arizona	Florida	Indiana	New Jersey	Ohio	South Carolina	Washington
California	Georgia	Kentucky	New Mexico	Oklahoma	South Dakota	West Virginia

Alabama

3684

Wrestling Trainer
State Athletic Commission
50 N. Ripley St., Rm. 4121
Montgomery, AL 36132
Phone: (205)242-1380

Credential Type: License. **Duration of License:** One year. **Fees:** $5 license fee.

Alaska

3685

Boxing Trainer
Dept. of Commerce and Economic Development
Div. of Occupational Licensing
Athletic Commission
PO Box D-LIC
Juneau, AK 99811-0800
Phone: (907)465-2534
Fax: (907)465-2974

Credential Type: License. **Duration of License:** One year. **Fees:** $10 license fee. **Governing Statute:** Alaska Statutes 05.05 and 08.10. Professional Regulations 12 AAC 06.

Arizona

3686

Trainer (Boxing)
Boxing Commission
1645 W. Jefferson, Rm. 212
Phoenix, AZ 85007
Phone: (602)542-1417

Credential Type: License. **Requirements:** Contact the commission for an application.

California

3687

Firearms Instructor
Bureau of Collection and Investigative Services
400 R St., Ste. 2001
Sacramento, CA 95814-6234
Phone: (916)445-7366

Credential Type: License. **Requirements:** Contact licensing body for application information.

3688

Trainer (Boxing, Kickboxing, or Martial Arts)
Athletic Commission
1424 Howe Ave., Ste. 33
Sacramento, CA 95814-6200
Phone: (916)920-7300

Credential Type: License. **Duration of License:** One year. **Requirements:** Submit application and pay fee. **Fees:** $25 license fee. $25 renewal fee.

Connecticut

3689

Player's Trainer (Racetrack)
Connecticut Div. of Special Revenue
Russell Rd.
PO Box 11424
Newington, CT 06111-0424
Phone: (203)566-2756

Credential Type: License Registration. **Requirements:** Submit application and fingerprint card. Pay fee. **Fees:** $5 registration fee.

Delaware

3690

Athletic Trainer
State Examining Board of Physical Therapy
Div. of Professional Regulation
O'Neill Bldg.
PO Box 1401
Dover, DE 19903
Phone: (302)739-4522

Credential Type: License. **Duration of License:** Two years. **Requirements:** Complete an approved program of education for athletic trainers. Submit two professional references. Renewal requires completion of three continuing education units (CEUs) every two years. **Examination:** National Athletic Training Association Professional Examination. **Reciprocity:** Yes, provided home state has similar requirements for licensure or registration. **Fees:** $10 application fee. $125 exam fee. $79 endorsement fee.

Credential Type: Temporary License. **Duration of License:** Varies. **Authorization:** May practice only under the direction of a licensed athletic trainer. **Requirements:** May be issued to four types of applicants: (1) Those eligible and waiting to take the examination. (2) Those requesting reciprocity. (3) Those engaged in a special project. (4) Those who have not yet completed the CEU requirements for renewal.

Florida

3691

Athletic Trainer (Racetrack)
Florida Dept. of Business
Div. of Pari-Mutuel Wagering
Licensing Section
725 S. Bronough St.
Tallahassee, FL 32399-1037
Phone: (904)488-9161

Credential Type: License Registration Code 1050. **Requirements:** Submit application and fingerprint card. Pay fee. **Fees:** $10 registration fee.

3692

Players' Trainer/Assistant (Jai-Alai)
Florida Dept. of Business
Div. of Pari-Mutuel Wagering
Licensing Section
725 S. Bronough St.
Tallahassee, FL 32399-1037
Phone: (904)488-9161

Credential Type: License Registration Code 2050. **Requirements:** Submit application and fingerprint card. Pay fee. **Fees:** $40 registration fee.

Georgia

3693

Athletic Trainer
State Board of Athletic Trainers
Health and Consumer Services Section
Professional Examining Boards
166 Pryor St., SW
Atlanta, GA 30303
Phone: (404)656-3933

Credential Type: License. **Requirements:** Contact licensing body for application information.

Idaho

3694

Athletic Trainer
Idaho State Board of Medicine
Board of Athletic Trainers
280 N. 8th St., Ste. 202
Boise, ID 83720
Phone: (208)334-2822

Credential Type: Athletic Trainer Registration. **Duration of License:** One year. **Requirements:** Good moral character. College baccalaureate degree. **Examination:** Athletic Trainer Examination, written. **Exemptions:** Examination may be waived if applicant is certified by the National Athletic Trainers Association Board of Certification. **Reciprocity:** No. **Fees:** $80 registration fee. $40 renewal fee. **Governing Statute:** Idaho Code, Title 54, Chap. 37. IDAPA 22.J.

Credential Type: Provisional Registration. **Duration of License:** One year. **Requirements:** May be issued to applicants who are actively participating in an internship program or curriculum of an institution approved by the board and under the supervision of a registered athletic trainer. **Fees:** $40 provisional registration fee. $40 renewal fee. **Governing Statute:** Idaho Code, Title 54, Chap. 37. IDAPA 22.J.

Illinois

3695

Athletic Trainer
Illinois Dept. of Professional Regulations
320 W. Washington St.
Springfield, IL 62786
Phone: (217)782-8556

Credential Type: Registration. **Duration of License:** Two years. **Requirements:** Graduate of a four-year accredited college in an Athletic Training Curriculum that meets the requirements of the NATA. Must have 800 hours of clinical experience. **Examination:** National Athletic Trainer's Association (NATA) Certification Examination for Athletic Trainers. **Reciprocity:** Yes, providing requirements in the applicant's state of registration are substantially equivalent to those of Illinois. **Fees:** $250 examination fee for NATA members. $300 examination fee for non-members of NATA. $50 initial license fee. $50 license by endorsement fee. $40 renewal fee. $40 restoration from inactive status. **Governing Statute:** The Illinois Athletic Trainers Practice Act.—Illinois Revised Statutes 1991, Chapter 111.

3696

Trainer/Second (Boxing)
Illinois Dept. of Professional Regulations
State of Illinois Ctr.
100 W. Randolph, Ste. 9-300
Chicago, IL 60601
Phone: (312)814-2719

Credential Type: Trainer License. **Duration of License:** Two years. **Requirements:** Must have knowledge of boxing, conditioning, and first aid. Pass Athletic Board Staff evaluation. Submit application and pay fee. **Examination:** Basic Safety Test. **Reciprocity:** No. **Fees:** $10 initial license fee. $10 renewal fee. **Governing Statute:** The Illinois Professional Boxing and Wrestling Act, Illinois Revised Statutes 1987, Chapter 111.

Indiana

3697

Trainer (Boxing)
Boxing Commission
Examination Administrative Div.
Professional Licensing Agency
1021 State Office Bldg.
Indianapolis, IN 46204
Phone: (317)232-3897

Credential Type: License. **Requirements:** Contact licensing body for application information.

Kentucky

3698

Athletic Trainer
Kentucky Board of Medical Licensure
310 Whittington Pky., Ste. 1B
Louisville, KY 40222
Phone: (502)429-8046

Credential Type: License. **Requirements:** Complete an athletic training curriculum of an approved and certified college or university; or hold a certificate or a degree in physical therapy; or complete at least four consecutive years beyond the secondary school level, while either an undergraduate or graduate student, as an apprentice athletic trainer at a college or university under the direct supervision of an athletic trainer approved by the board. **Examination:** Yes. **Reciprocity:** Yes. **Fees:** $75 exam fee. $25 certification fee.

Massachusetts

3699

Athletic Trainer
Board of Registration of Allied
    Health Professionals
Div. of Registration
100 Cambridge St., 15th fl.
Boston, MA 02202
Phone: (617)727-3071

Credential Type: License and certification. **Duration of License:** Two years. **Requirements:** Bachelor's degree in Sports Medicine. **Examination:** National Athletic Trainers Association (NATA) Certification Examination. **Reciprocity:** Yes, provided applicant meets Massachusetts standards. **Fees:** $50 application fee. $50 renewal fee.

Credential Type: Temporary License. **Requirements:** Contact licensing body for application information. **Fees:** $10 temporary license fee.

3700

Riding Instructor
Div. of Animal Health
Dept. of Food and Agriculture
100 Cambridge St., 21st Fl.
Boston, MA 02202
Phone: (617)727-3018

Credential Type: License. **Duration of License:** One year. **Requirements:** Demonstrate appropriate experience. **Examination:** Written examination. **Fees:** $10 application fee. $15 license fee.

3701

Trainer (Boxing)
State Boxing Commission
Dept. of Public Safety
One Ashburton Pl., Rm. 1310
Boston, MA 02108
Phone: (617)727-3296

Credential Type: License. **Requirements:** Submit application and pay fee. **Fees:** Contact commission for fee. **Governing Statute:** Annotated Laws of Massachusetts, Chap. 147.

Nebraska

3702

Athletic Trainer
Nebraska Board of Examiners in
    Athletic Training
301 Centennial Mall S.
PO Box 95007
Lincoln, NE 68509
Phone: (402)471-2115

Credential Type: License. **Duration of License:** Two years. **Requirements:** 19 years of age and must have graduated from an accredited college with completion of an athletic training program; or must have graduated from an accredited college and have completed two years of student athletic training. **Examination:** Yes. **Fees:** $300 license fee. $400 renewal fee.

New Jersey

3703

Athletic Trainer
Board of Medical Trainers
28 W. State St.
Trenton, NJ 08608
Phone: (609)292-4843

Credential Type: License. **Duration of License:** Two years. **Requirements:** High school diploma or equivalent. Graduation from an approved college or university with an athletic training curriculum. 18 years of age. No narcotic or alcohol abuse. **Examination:** Written, oral and practical exams. **Reciprocity:** Yes. **Fees:** $60 initial license fee. $60 renewal fee. **Governing Statute:** NJSA 45:9-37.

New Mexico

3704

Athletic Trainer
Athletic Trainers Board
Dept. of Regulation and Licensing
PO Box 25101
725 St. Michael's Dr.
Santa Fe, NM 87504
Phone: (505)827-7164

Credential Type: License. **Duration of License:** One year. **Requirements:** Have cardiopulmonary resuscitation (CPR) verification from the American Red Cross or American Heart Association. Complete an approved training program. **Examination:** National Athletic Trainers Association (NATA) exam or board examination. Jurisprudence examination. **Fees:** $100 exam fee. $100 license fee. $150 renewal fee. **Governing Statute:** Rules Regulations 91-1 et seq.

Credential Type: Provisional License. **Requirements:** May be issued to applicants who meet requirements for licensure and who have applied for examination. No applicant will be issued a provisional license more than twice within a three-year period. **Fees:** $100 exam fee. $100 provisional license fee.

3705

Trainer (Boxing, Wrestling, Martial Arts, and Kick Boxing)
Athletic Commission
Dept. of Regulation and Licensing
PO Box 25101
725 St. Michael's Dr.
Santa Fe, NM 87504
Phone: (505)827-7172

Credential Type: License. **Duration of License:** One year. **Requirements:** Submit application and pay fee. **Fees:** $25 license fee.

North Carolina

3706

Firearms Trainer
Private Protective Services Board
PO Box 29500
Raleigh, NC 27626
Phone: (919)779-1611

Credential Type: Certification. **Duration of License:** Two years. **Requirements:** High school diploma. One year of supervisory experience in security with a contract company or proprietary security organization; or one year of experience with a law enforcement agency. Completion of a board approved firearms training course. 18 years of age. U.S. citizen or resident alien. Good moral character. Eight hours of safety training upon renewal. **Examination:** Yes. **Fees:** $50 application fee. $25 renewal fee.

North Dakota

3707

Athletic Trainer
John Quick, Exec. Sec.
Board of Athletic Trainers
Dakota Sports Medicine
1702 S. University Dr.
Fargo, ND 58108
Phone: (701)280-3460

Credential Type: License. **Duration of License:** One year. **Requirements:** Submit application and pay fee. Must meet requirements of certification established by the National Athletic Trainers Association. **Examination:** Yes. **Governing Statute:** North Dakota Century Code, Chap. 43-39.

Ohio

3708

Athletic Trainer
Ohio Occupational Therapy, Physical Therapy, and Athletic Trainers Board
77 S. High St., 16th Fl.
Columbus, OH 43266-0317
Phone: (614)466-3774

Credential Type: License. **Duration of License:** Three years. **Requirements:** Complete an education program approved by the National Athletic Trainers Association. Renewal requires completing six continuing education units (CEUs) every three years, where 10 contact hours equals one CEU. **Examination:** National Athletic Trainers Association (NATA) certifiying examination. Ohio laws and rules examination. **Fees:** $60 license fee. $250 exam fee. $45 renewal fee. **Governing Statute:** Ohio Revised Code, Chap. 4755. Administrative Rules 4755-4001 et seq.

Oklahoma

3709

Athletic Trainer/Apprentice Athletic Trainer
State Board of Medical Licensure and Supervision
PO Box 18256
Oklahoma City, OK 73154
Phone: (405)848-6841

Credential Type: License. **Duration of License:** One year. **Requirements:** Completion of the athletic training curriculum at an accredited college or university. Two consecutive years as an apprentice athletic trainer. Three recommendations. Health certificate. **Examination:** National Athletic Trainers Association Certifying Exam. **Fees:** $100 application fee. $30 renewal fee.

Pennsylvania

3710

Athletic Trainer
State Board of Physical Therapy
PO Box 2649
Harrisburg, PA 17105-2649
Phone: (717)787-8503

Credential Type: Class A Certificate. **Duration of License:** Two years. **Authorization:** May provide therapeutic care and exercise to injured athletes in addition to functions of a Class B certificate holder. **Requirements:** Baccalaureate degree from a regionally accredited institution of higher education in the United States. Complete a board-approved athletic training educational program. **Examination:** Class A examination. **Reciprocity:** Out-of-state license holders who received their licenses from states with substantially equivalent requirements to those of Pennsylvania may qualify for a reciprocal license. License must be valid and the issuing state must extend reciprocity to licensees of Pennsylvania. **Fees:** $15 certification fee. $45 renewal fee.

Credential Type: Class B Certificate. **Duration of License:** Two years. **Authorization:** May administer injury-prevention conditioning procedures, provide emergency care, perform tests and measurements to evaluate injuries, provide physical support for athletic activity, apply cold or superficial heat in the prevention or treatment of injuries, administer normal exercise for reconditioning. **Requirements:** Meet one of the following sets of requirements: (1) Baccalaureate degree from a regionally accredited institution of higher education in the United States. Complete an athletic training educational program approved by NATA or the board. Pass examination. (2) Baccalaureate degree from a regionally accredited institution of higher education in the United States. Be certified by the NATA. **Examination:** Class B examination. **Exemptions:** NATA-certified applicants need not take examination. **Reciprocity:** Out-of-state license holders who received their licenses from states with substantially equivalent requirements to those of Pennsylvania may qualify for a reciprocal license. License must be valid and the issuing state must extend reciprocity to licensees of Pennsylvania. **Fees:** $15 certification fee. $80 exam and certification fee. $45 renewal fee.

Credential Type: Temporary License. **Duration of License:** Four months (failure of Certificate examination will immediately cancel temporary license). **Authorization:** Must work under the direct supervision of a certified athletic trainer. **Requirements:** Must meet all requirements for certification as an athletic trainer, with the exception of having passed the examination.

Rhode Island

3711

Athletic Trainer
Board of Examiners for Athletic Trainers
Div. of Professional Regulation
Rhode Island Dept. of Health
3 Capitol Hill
Providence, RI 02908
Phone: (401)277-2827

Credential Type: Athletic Trainer License. **Duration of License:** Two years. **Requirements:** Foreign born must show proof of legal entry into the U.S. Graduate from an approved four-year college program. 1800 hours of clinical experience. **Examination:** Written examination if graduated/certified before 7/31/70. **Reciprocity:** No. **Fees:** $25 application fee. $15 examination fee. $40 renewal fee.

South Carolina

3712

Boxing-Wrestling Trainer
State Athletic Commission
PO Box 2461
Columbia, SC 29202
Phone: (803)254-3661

Credential Type: License. **Requirements:** Submit application and pay fee. **Fees:** $10 license fee.

South Dakota

3713

Athletic Trainer
State Board of Medical and Osteopathic Examiners
Dept. of Commerce and Consumer Affairs
1323 S. Minnesota Ave.
Sioux Falls, SD 57105
Phone: (605)336-1965

Credential Type: Athletic Trainer Certification. **Duration of License:** One year. **Requirements:** Graduation from an approved athletic trainer program. Possess National Registry certificate. Pass interview with board.

Renewal requires completion of four continuing education units every three years. **Examination:** National Athletic Trainers

Athletic Trainer, continued

Association (NATA) examination. **Reciprocity:** Yes. **Fees:** $100 certification fee. $25 renewal fee.

Tennessee

3714

Athletic Trainer
Board of Medical Examiners
283 Plus Park Blvd.
Nashville, TN 37247-1010
Phone: (615)367-6231

Credential Type: License. **Requirements:** BA degree for high school trainer. Masters for college trainer. Must complete six hours of continuing education every two years. 1900 hours supervised experience. **Examination:** Yes. **Reciprocity:** Yes. **Fees:** $160 Application.

Texas

3715

Athletic Trainer
Texas Dept. of Health
Advisory Board of Athletic Trainers
1100 W. 49th St.
Austin, TX 78756
Phone: (512)834-6615

Credential Type: License. **Duration of License:** One year. **Requirements:** College degree meeting athletic training curriculum requirements; or a degree or certificate in physical therapy and completion of basic athletic training course, plus a two-year apprenticeship; or a degree in corrective therapy with at least a minor in physical therapy or health, plus two years apprenticeship or other requirements established by board. Completion of a CPR course. Completion of a basic Red Cross first aid course or emergency care attendant training or emergency medical technician training. A minimum of 600 hours apprenticeship per academic year for a minimum of three years. 24 hours of continuing education required every three years. **Examination:** Written and practical. **Fees:** $50 exam fee. $50 license fee. $40 renewal fee. **Governing Statute:** VACS 4512d, 25 TAC 313.

Washington

3716

Firearms Safety Instructor
Dept. of Wildlife
600 N. Capitol, GJ-11
Olympia, WA 98504-0091
Phone: (206)753-5710

Credential Type: Firearms Safety Instructor License. **Duration of License:** Indefinite. **Requirements:** Skill and knowledge of firearms safety and handling. Must submit to background investigation if not active for one year or more. **Examination:** Written examination. **Fees:** No fee.

West Virginia

3717

Athletic Trainer
Dept. of Education
Office of Educational Personnel
    Development
1900 Washington St. E
Charleston, WV 25305
Phone: (800)982-2378

Credential Type: License. **Duration of License:** One, three or five years. **Requirements:** U.S. citizen. 18 years old. Bachelors degree and completion of state approved athletic training program. Never convicted of a felony. **Examination:** Yes. **Fees:** $5 three or five year Professional Certificate. $5 for Permanent certificate.

Insulation/Asbestos Workers

The following states grant licenses in this occupational category as of the date of publication:

Alaska	Illinois	Maryland	Minnesota	Nevada	North Dakota	Texas
Arkansas	Indiana	Massachusetts	Mississippi	New Jersey	Oklahoma	
Florida	Iowa	Michigan	Montana	New York	Rhode Island	

Alaska

3718

Asbestos Removal Worker
Alaska Dept. of Labor
Labor Standards and Safety Div.
Occupational Safety and Health
PO Box 21149
Juneau, AK 99802
Phone: (907)465-4855

Credential Type: Certificate. **Duration of License:** Three years. **Requirements:** Completion of a 32-hour training program offered by a state approved training provider. Certification renewal requires an eight-hour refresher course. **Examination:** Written and practical examination given by the approved training provider. **Fees:** No fee.

Arkansas

3719

Asbestos Removal Worker
Dept. of Pollution Control and
  Ecology
8001 National Dr.
Little Rock, AR 72209
Phone: (501)562-7444

Credential Type: License. **Requirements:** Must be a licensed contractor. Proof of training in asbestos removal by Dept. of Pollution Control and Ecology. Proof of liability insurance. **Examination:** Yes. **Fees:** No fee for Practical Examination. $100 License.

Florida

3720

Asbestos Consultant
Board of Professional Engineers
Div. of Professions
Dept. of Professional Regulation
1940 N. Monroe St.
Tallahassee, FL 32399-0755
Phone: (904)488-9912

Credential Type: Asbestos Consultant License. **Duration of License:** Two years. **Requirements:** Hold a Florida professional engineer license. Complete an approved abatement project training course. Submit evidence of basic asbestos consultant responsibility in the performance of satisfactory work on 10 asbestos abatement projects within the past five years. Submit evidence of financial stability.

Renewal requires completion of two days of refresher courses per year. **Examination:** Yes. **Fees:** $200 application fee. $200 exam fee. $100 initial licensure fee. $200 renewal fee. **Governing Statute:** Florida Statutes, Chapter 455. Rules of the Board of Professional Engineers, Chapter 21H-28, F.A.C.

Illinois

3721

Asbestos Air Sampling Professional
Illinois Dept. of Public Health
Div. of Environmental Health
525 W. Jefferson St.
Springfield, IL 62761
Phone: (217)782-3517

Credential Type: Asbestos Air Sampling Professional License. **Duration of License:** One year. **Requirements:** Complete Illinois Registered National Institute of Occupational Safety & Health (NIOSH) 582 Course. Bachelor's degree in live, environmental, or physical science or engineering, or 12 months of experience in on-site air sampling for asbestos abatement projects. Plus have three months of experience in general indoor air pollution sampling. **Examination:** National Institute of Occupational Safety & Health (NIOSH) Examination. **Reciprocity:** Yes, if license was received in a state with requirements equal to or greater than those of Illinois. Must pay Illinois license fee. **Fees:** $50 initial license fee. $50 license renewal fee. $15 license reinstatement fee. $15 duplicate license fee. **Governing Statute:** Illinois Asbestos Abatements act, Illinois Revised Statutes, Chapter 122.

3722

Asbestos Management Planner
Illinois Dept. of Public Health
Div. of Environmental Health
525 W. Jefferson St.
Springfield, IL 62761
Phone: (217)782-3517

Credential Type: Asbestos Manager Planner License. **Duration of License:** One year. **Requirements:** Complete an Illinois accredited Inspector course and a Management Planner training course. Meet one of the following requirements: (1) Be an Illinois Registered Architect; (2) Be an Illinois-licensed Structural Engineer; (3) Be an Illinois professional Engineer; (4) Be a Certified Industrial Hygienist; (5) Have a bachelor's degree or higher in architecture, engineering, mathematics, or science and a minimum of six months experience inspecting buildings for asbestos-containing materials. (6) Have a bachelor's degree or higher in architecture, engineering, mathematics, or science and two years of experience in

Illinois 3723

Asbestos Management Planner, continued

asbestos inspections, instructions, project management, project design, or other asbestos management and control activities. Renewal requires one-half day refresher course for Management Planners and one-half day refresher course for Inspectors annually. **Examination:** Written examination. **Reciprocity:** Yes, if license was received in a state with requirements equal to or greater than those of Illinois. Must pay Illinois license fee. **Fees:** $50 initial license fee. $50 license renewal fee. $15 license reinstatement fee. **Governing Statute:** Illinois Asbestos Abatements act, Illinois Revised Statutes, Chapter 122.

3723

Asbestos Project Designer
Illinois Dept. of Public Health
Div. of Environmental Health
525 W. Jefferson St.
Springfield, IL 62761
Phone: (217)782-3517

Credential Type: Asbestos Project Designer License. **Duration of License:** One year. **Requirements:** Complete an Illinois accredited Inspector, Management Planner, and Contractor/Supervisor course. Must be one of the following: (1) an Illinois Registered Architect; (2) an Illinois Licensed Professional Engineer; (3) an Illinois Licensed Structural Engineer; (4) a Certified Industrial Hygienist. Renewal requires one-half day refresher course for Inspectors, one-half day refresher course for Management Planners, and a full day refresher course for Contractors/Supervisors. **Examination:** Written examination. **Reciprocity:** Yes, if license was received in a state with requirements equal to or greater than those of Illinois. Must pay Illinois license fee. **Fees:** $50 initial license fee. $50 license renewal fee. $15 license reinstatement fee. **Governing Statute:** Illinois Asbestos Abatements act, Illinois Revised Statutes, Chapter 122.

3724

Asbestos Project Manager
Illinois Dept. of Public Health
Div. of Environmental Health
525 W. Jefferson St.
Springfield, IL 62761
Phone: (217)782-3517

Credential Type: Asbestos Project Manager License. **Duration of License:** One year. **Requirements:** Complete an Illinois accredited Contractor/Supervisor course. Must have one year, on-site working experience in building construction projects or three months on-site working experience assisting the licensed project manager on asbestos abatement projects. Renewal requires a one-half day refresher course for Contractors/Supervisors annually. **Examination:** Written examination. **Reciprocity:** Yes, if license was received in a state with requirements equal to or greater than those of Illinois. Must pay Illinois license fee. **Fees:** $50 initial license fee. $50 license renewal fee. $15 license reinstatement fee. **Governing Statute:** Illinois Asbestos Abatements act, Illinois Revised Statutes, Chapter 122.

3725

Asbestos Project Supervisor
Illinois Dept. of Public Health
Div. of Environmental Health
525 W. Jefferson St.
Springfield, IL 62761
Phone: (217)782-3517

Credential Type: Asbestos Project Supervisor License. **Duration of License:** One year. **Requirements:** Complete an Illinois accredited asbestos Contractor/Supervisor training course or hold a current Illinois asbestos worker license. Renewal requires a one-half day refresher course for asbestos Contractors/Supervisors annually. **Examination:** Written examination. **Reciprocity:** Yes, if license was received in a state with requirements equal to or greater than those of Illinois. Must pay Illinois license fee. **Fees:** $50 initial license fee. $50 license renewal fee. $15 license reinstatement fee. **Governing Statute:** Illinois Asbestos Abatements act, Illinois Revised Statutes, Chapter 122.

3726

Asbestos Worker
Illinois Dept. of Public Health
Div. of Environmental Health
525 W. Jefferson St.
Springfield, IL 62761
Phone: (217)782-3517

Credential Type: Asbestos Worker License. **Duration of License:** One year. **Requirements:** At least 18 years of age. Complete an Illinois accredited Asbestos Worker or Contractor/Supervisor training course. Renewal requires an Illinois accredited one day refresher course for Asbestos Workers or Contractors/Supervisors annually. **Examination:** Written examination. **Reciprocity:** Yes, if license was received in a state with requirements equal to or greater than those of Illinois. Must pay Illinois license fee. **Fees:** $25 initial license fee. $25 license renewal fee. $15 license reinstatement fee. **Governing Statute:** Illinois Asbestos Abatements act, Illinois Revised Statutes, Chapter 122.

Indiana

3727

Asbestos Contractor
Dept. of Environmental Management
Office of Air Management
Asbestos Section
PO Box 7060
Indianapolis, IN 46202-7060
Phone: (317)232-8232

Credential Type: Accreditation. **Duration of License:** One year. **Requirements:** Submit proof of financial responsibility. Attend an approved training course. A contractor may designate an employee to take the training course. Demonstrate competence.

Renewal requires attending a refresher course. **Examination:** Training course examination. **Fees:** $150 annual accreditation fee. **Governing Statute:** 326 IAC 18-1 et seq.

3728

Asbestos Project Designer
Dept. of Environmental Management
Office of Air Management
Asbestos Section
PO Box 7060
Indianapolis, IN 46202-7060
Phone: (317)232-8232

Credential Type: Accreditation. **Duration of License:** One year. **Requirements:** Have an associate's degree or higher in architecture, industrial hygiene, engineering, building system design, or a related field of study; or be a high school graduate and have one year of experience in either planning, supervision, or cost estimation of building construction or asbestos projects, or in asbestos inspection or general building inspection. Attend an approved training course.

Renewal requires attending a refresher course. **Examination:** Training course examination. **Fees:** $100 annual accreditation fee. **Governing Statute:** 326 IAC 18-1 et seq.

3729

Asbestos Project Supervisor
Dept. of Environmental Management
Office of Air Management
Asbestos Section
PO Box 7060
Indianapolis, IN 46202-7060
Phone: (317)232-8232

Credential Type: Accreditation. **Duration of License:** One year. **Requirements:** Have at least six months experience as an asbestos project supervisor or as an asbestos worker. Attend an approved training course.

Renewal requires attending a refresher course. **Examination:** Training course examination. **Fees:** $100 annual accreditation fee. **Governing Statute:** 326 IAC 18-1 et seq.

3730

Asbestos Waste Disposal Manager
Dept. of Environmental Management
Office of Air Management
Asbestos Section
PO Box 7060
Indianapolis, IN 46202-7060
Phone: (317)232-8232

Credential Type: Accreditation. **Duration of License:** One year. **Requirements:** Attend an approved training course. Renewal requires attending a refresher course. **Examination:** Training course examination. **Fees:** $50 annual accreditation fee. **Governing Statute:** 326 IAC 18-1 et seq.

3731

Asbestos Worker
Dept. of Environmental Management
Office of Air Management
Asbestos Section
PO Box 7060
Indianapolis, IN 46202-7060
Phone: (317)232-8232

Credential Type: Accreditation. **Duration of License:** One year. **Requirements:** Attend an approved training course. Renewal requires attending a refresher course. **Examination:** Training course examination. **Fees:** $50 annual accreditation fee. **Governing Statute:** 326 IAC 18-1 et seq.

Iowa

3732

Asbestos Abatement Worker
Iowa Dept. of Employment of Services
Labor Services Div.
1000 E. Grand Ave.
Des Moines, IA 50319
Phone: (515)281-3606

Credential Type: License. **Duration of License:** One year. **Requirements:** 18 years of age. Physically capable of performing the work safely. Successful completion of the approved training course. Passing of an Asbestos physical exam. **Reciprocity:** Licenses from other states will be reviewed. **Fees:** $20 license fee. $20 renewal fee.

3733

Asbestos Management Planner
Iowa Dept. of Employment Services
Labor Services Div.
1000 E. Grand Ave.
Des Moines, IA 50319
Phone: (515)281-3606

Credential Type: License. **Duration of License:** One year. **Requirements:** 18 years of age. Physically capable of performing the work safely. Successful completion of two approved training courses. **Reciprocity:** Licenses from other states will be reviewed. **Fees:** $20 license fee. $20 renewal fee.

3734

Asbestos Project Designer
Iowa Dept. of Employment Services
Labor Services Div.
1000 E. Grand Ave.
Des Moines, IA 50319
Phone: (515)281-3606

Credential Type: License. **Duration of License:** One year. **Requirements:** 18 years of age. Physically capable of performing the work safely. Completion of one of two available courses. **Reciprocity:** Licenses from other states will be reviewed. **Fees:** $50 license fee. $50 renewal fee.

Maryland

3735

Asbestos Abatement Worker
Air Management Administration
Dept. of the Environment
2500 Broening Hwy.
Baltimore, MD 21224
Phone: (410)631-3200
Phone: (410)631-3255

Credential Type: License. **Requirements:** Contact licensing body for application information.

Massachusetts

3736

Asbestos Abatement Project Designer
Dept. of Labor and Industries
Bureau of Technical Services
100 Cambridge St., Rm. 1101
Boston, MA 02202-0003
Phone: (617)727-1932
Phone: (617)727-1933

Credential Type: Certification. **Requirements:** Have at least a bachelor's degree in industrial hygiene, occupational health, environmental science, biological science, or physical science, or be registered as an architect or engineer. Complete required training. Have at least 12 months work experience in asbestos abatement field. **Fees:** $300 certification fee. **Governing Statute:** M.G.L. c149, ss 6-6F. 453 CMR 6.01 ff.

3737

Asbestos Abatement Project Monitor
Dept. of Labor and Industries
Bureau of Technical Services
100 Cambridge St., Rm. 1101
Boston, MA 02202-0003
Phone: (617)727-1932
Phone: (617)727-1933

Credential Type: Certification. **Requirements:** Have at least an associate's or technical degree, or equivalent, or two years of college credit. Complete required training. Have at least six months work experience in a comparable occupation or two months field experience under the supervision of a certified asbestos abatement project monitor. **Fees:** $300 certification fee. **Governing Statute:** M.G.L. c149, ss 6-6F. 453 CMR 6.01 ff.

3738

Asbestos Abatement Worker
Dept. of Labor and Industries
Bureau of Technical Services
100 Cambridge St., Rm. 1101
Boston, MA 02202-0003
Phone: (617)727-1932
Phone: (617)727-1933

Credential Type: Certification. **Requirements:** Complete required training. **Fees:** $25 certification fee. **Governing Statute:** M.G.L. c149, ss 6-6F. 453 CMR 6.01 ff.

3739

Asbestos Analytical Services Provider
Dept. of Labor and Industries
Bureau of Technical Services
100 Cambridge St., Rm. 1101
Boston, MA 02202-0003
Phone: (617)727-1932
Phone: (617)727-1933

Credential Type: Certification. **Requirements:** Submit application and pay fee. Submit appropriate laboratory documentation, air sampling documentation, and bulk sampling documentation. **Fees:** $350 certification fee. **Governing Statute:** M.G.L. c149, ss 6-6F. 453 CMR 6.01 ff.

3740

Asbestos Management Planner
Dept. of Labor and Industries
Bureau of Technical Services
100 Cambridge St., Rm. 1101
Boston, MA 02202-0003
Phone: (617)727-1932
Phone: (617)727-1933

Credential Type: Certification. **Requirements:** Have at least an associate's degree or certificate in project planning, management, environmental sciences, engineering, construction, architecture, industrial hygiene, occupational health, or a related scientific field. Complete required training. Have at least six months work experience in asbestos abatement field, including experience in asbestos management. **Fees:** $300 certification fee. (If one person is applying for certification as both an Asbestos Inspector and an Asbestos Management Planner, only one $300 certification fee is required.) **Governing Statute:** M.G.L. c149, ss 6-6F. 453 CMR 6.01 ff.

3741

Asbestos Supervisor-Foreman
Dept. of Labor and Industries
Bureau of Technical Services
100 Cambridge St., Rm. 1101
Boston, MA 02202-0003
Phone: (617)727-1932
Phone: (617)727-1933

Credential Type: Certification. **Requirements:** Complete required training. **Fees:** $100 certification fee. **Governing Statute:** M.G.L. c149, ss 6-6F. 453 CMR 6.01 ff.

Michigan

3742

Asbestos Abatement Project Designer
Asbestos Licensing
Div. of Occupational Health
Dept. of Public Health
3423 N. Logan
PO Box 30195
Lansing, MI 48909
Phone: (517)335-8000

Credential Type: Accreditation. **Duration of License:** One year. **Requirements:** At least two years experience in asbestos related work or not less than five years of supervisory experience in school building operations and maintenance. Pass an Environmental Protection Agency (EPA) or state accredited Asbestos Abatement Project Designer Course or 32-hour Asbestos Abatement Contractor/Supervisor Course. Renewal requires completion of one-day refresher training course. **Examination:** Written exam. **Reciprocity:** Reciprocity may be granted if the requirements of the other state are equal to or exceed those of Michigan, and the individual submits a certificate of successful completion of training from the other state. **Fees:** $150 initial accreditation fee. $75 renewal fee. $150 reciprocity fee. **Governing Statute:** Asbestos Workers Accreditation Act, Act 440 of 1988.

3743

Asbestos Abatement Worker
Asbestos Licensing
Div. of Occupational Health
Dept. of Public Health
3423 N. Logan
PO Box 30195
Lansing, MI 48909
Phone: (517)335-8000

Credential Type: Accreditation. **Duration of License:** One year. **Requirements:** Pass an Environmental Protection Agency (EPA) or state accredited three-day Asbestos Worker Course. Renewal requires completion of one-day refresher training course. **Examination:** Written exam. **Reciprocity:** Reciprocity may be granted if the requirements of the other state are equal to or exceed those of Michigan, and the individual submits a certificate of successful completion of training from the other state. **Fees:** $25 initial accreditation fee. $25 renewal fee. $25 reciprocity fee. **Governing Statute:** Asbestos Workers Accreditation Acts, Acts 439 and 440 of 1988. Michigan Occupational Safety and Health Act, Act 154 of 1974, as amended.

3744

Asbestos Management Planner
Asbestos Licensing
Div. of Occupational Health
Dept. of Public Health
3423 N. Logan
PO Box 30195
Lansing, MI 48909
Phone: (517)335-8000

Credential Type: Accreditation. **Duration of License:** One year. **Requirements:** At least two years experience in asbestos related work or not less than five years of supervisory experience in school building operations and maintenance. Pass an Environmental Protection Agency (EPA) or state accredited three-day Asbestos Inspector Course and two-day Asbestos Management Planner Course. Renewal requires completion of one-day refresher training course. **Examination:** Written exam. **Reciprocity:** Reciprocity may be granted if the requirements of the other state are equal to or exceed those of Michigan and the individual submits a certificate of successful completion of training from the other state. **Fees:** $150 initial accreditation fee. $75 renewal fee. $150 reciprocity fee. **Governing Statute:** Asbestos Workers Accreditation Act, Act 440 of 1988.

Minnesota

3745

Asbestos Abatement Worker
Dept. of Health
Environmental Health Div.
Asbestos Abatement Unit
717 Delaware St., SE
Box 9441
Minneapolis, MN 55440
Phone: (612)627-5089
Fax: (612)623-5043

Credential Type: Worker Certification. **Requirements:** Contact licensing body for application information. **Fees:** $50 certification fee.

Mississippi

3746

Asbestos Management Planner
Dept. of Environmental Quality
Office of Pollution Control
PO Box 10385
Jackson, MS 39289-0385
Phone: (601)961-5100

Credential Type: Certification. **Duration of License:** One year. **Requirements:** Must be a registered professional engineer or licensed architect in the state. Must attend a 3-day inspector's course and a 2-day management planner course. Additional training must be taken annually for recertification. **Examination:** EPA-approved examination for management planner certification. **Exemptions:** Certification not required for federally owned buildings or small-scale, short duration activities. **Reciprocity:** No reciprocity. **Fees:** $100 license fee. $100 renewal fee.

3747

Asbestos Project Designer
Dept. of Environmental Quality
Office of Pollution Control
PO Box 10385
Jackson, MS 39289-0385
Phone: (601)961-5100

Credential Type: Certification. **Duration of License:** One year. **Requirements:** Must be a registered professional engineer or licensed architect in the state. Must attend an EPA-approved 3-day project designer course or an EPA-approved 4-day contractor/supervisor course. Refresher course must be taken after initial training. Additional training must be taken annually for recertification. **Examination:** EPA-approved examination for project designer certification or for contractor/supervisor certification. **Exemptions:** Certification not required for federally owned buildings or small-scale, short duration activities. **Reciprocity:** No reciprocity. **Fees:** $100 license fee. $100 renewal fee.

3748

Asbestos Worker
Dept. of Environmental Quality
Office of Pollution Control
PO Box 10385
Jackson, MS 39289-0385
Phone: (601)961-5100

Credential Type: Certification. **Duration of License:** One year. **Requirements:** Written approval from a physician must be submitted every three years. Must attend an EPA-approved 3-day worker training course. **Examination:** EPA-approved examination for worker certification. **Exemptions:** Certification not required for federally owned buildings. **Reciprocity:** No reciprocity. **Fees:** $25 license fee. $25 renewal fee.

Montana

3749

Asbestos Abatement Contractor/ Supervisor
Dept. of Health and Environmental Sciences
Health Services Div.
Occupational Health Bureau
1400 Broadway
Cogswell Bldg.
Helena, MT 59620
Phone: (406)444-3671

Credential Type: License and Accreditation. **Duration of License:** One year. **Requirements:** Contact licensing body for application information. Renewal requires completing a refresher course. **Fees:** $100 annual license fee. **Governing Statute:** Montana Code Annotated 75-2.

3750

Asbestos Abatement Project Designer
Dept. of Health and Environmental Sciences
Health Services Div.
Occupational Health Bureau
1400 Broadway
Cogswell Bldg.
Helena, MT 59620
Phone: (406)444-3671

Credential Type: License and Accreditation. **Duration of License:** One year. **Requirements:** Contact licensing body for application information. Renewal requires completing a refresher course. **Fees:** $200 annual license fee. **Governing Statute:** Montana Code Annotated 75-2.

3751

Asbestos Management Planner
Dept. of Health and Environmental Sciences
Health Services Div.
Occupational Health Bureau
1400 Broadway
Cogswell Bldg.
Helena, MT 59620
Phone: (406)444-3671

Credential Type: License and Accreditation. **Duration of License:** One year. **Requirements:** Contact licensing body for application information. Renewal requires completing a refresher course. **Fees:** $100 annual license fee. **Governing Statute:** Montana Code Annotated 75-2.

3752

Asbestos Worker
Dept. of Health and Environmental Sciences
Health Services Div.
Occupational Health Bureau
1400 Broadway
Cogswell Bldg.
Helena, MT 59620
Phone: (406)444-3671

Credential Type: License and Accreditation. **Duration of License:** One year. **Requirements:** Contact licensing body for application information. Renewal requires completing a refresher course. **Fees:** $25 annual license fee. **Governing Statute:** Montana Code Annotated 75-2.

Nevada

3753

Insulation Installer
Nevada State Contractors Board
70 Linden St.
Reno, NV 89502
Phone: (702)486-3500

Credential Type: License. **Requirements:** Four years of skilled experience in the field. Financial responsibility and good character. **Examination:** Yes. **Fees:** $270 application fee. $120 license fee. $120 renewal fee. $40 exam fee.

New Jersey

3754

Asbestos Employee
New Jersey Dept. of Labor
Office of Asbestos Control and Licensing
CNO54
Trenton, NJ 08625
Phone: (609)633-3760

Credential Type: License. **Duration of License:** One year. **Requirements:** Must attend a certified training course of at least 30 hours. 18 years of age. **Examination:** Written. **Fees:** $20 annual permit fee. **Governing Statute:** NJSA 34:5A-32. NJAC 12:120.

New York

3755

Asbestos Handler
New York State Dept. of Labor
Div. of Safety and Health
One Main St., Rm. 801
Brooklyn, NY 11201
Phone: (718)797-7659

Credential Type: Certificate. **Duration of License:** One year. **Requirements:** Completion of course approved by the New York State Dept. of Health. 18 years of age. **Examination:** Written. **Fees:** $25 license fee. **Governing Statute:** Section 902 of the New York State Labor Law.

North Dakota

3756

Asbestos Abatement Management Planner
State Dept. of Health and Consolidated Laboratories
Box 5520
1200 Missouri Ave.
Bismarck, ND 58502-5520
Phone: (701)224-5188

Credential Type: Asbestos Abatement Management Planner License. **Duration of License:** One year. **Requirements:** Complete an EPA-approved Asbestos Abatement Management Planner Course. Renewal requires attendance at annual refresher course. **Examination:** Written examination given as part of course. **Exemptions:** In-house non-public employees. Public employees and contractor employees disturbing less than three square feet or three line feet of asbestos-containing material. **Reciprocity:** All EPA-approved courses are recognized as acceptable. **Fees:** $25 license fee per discipline.

3757

Asbestos Abatement Project Designer
State Dept. of Health and Consolidated Laboratories
Box 5520
1200 Missouri Ave.
Bismarck, ND 58502-5520
Phone: (701)224-5188

Credential Type: Asbestos Abatement Project Designer License. **Duration of License:** One year. **Requirements:** Complete an EPA-approved Asbestos Abatement Project Designer Course. Renewal requires attendance at annual refresher course. **Examination:** Written examination given as part of course. **Exemptions:** In-house non-public employees. Public employees and contractor employees disturbing less than three square feet or three line feet of asbestos-containing material. **Reciprocity:** All EPA-approved courses are recognized as acceptable. **Fees:** $25 license fee per discipline.

3758

Asbestos Abatement Project Monitor
State Dept. of Health and Consolidated Laboratories
Box 5520
1200 Missouri Ave.
Bismarck, ND 58502-5520
Phone: (701)224-5188

Credential Type: Asbestos Abatement Project Monitor License. **Duration of License:** One year. **Requirements:** Complete an EPA-approved Asbestos Abatement Course for supervisors or project desginers. Must attend a NIOSH 582 or equivalent air sampling course. Renewal requires attendance at annual refresher course. **Examination:** Written examination given as part of course. **Exemptions:** Asbestos abatement contractors performing their own air monitoring. In-house non-public employees. **Reciprocity:** All EPA-approved courses for project designer or supervisor are recognized as acceptable. **Fees:** $25 license fee per discipline.

3759

Asbestos Abatement Supervisor
State Dept. of Health and Consolidated Laboratories
Box 5520
1200 Missouri Ave.
Bismarck, ND 58502-5520
Phone: (701)224-5188

Credential Type: Asbestos Abatement Supervisor License. **Duration of License:** One year. **Requirements:** Complete an EPA-approved Asbestos Abatement Supervisor Course. Renewal requires attendance at annual refresher course. **Examination:** Written examination given as part of course. **Exemptions:** In-house non-public employees. Public employees and contractor employees disturbing less than three square feet or three line feet of asbestos-containing material. **Reciprocity:** All EPA-approved courses are recognized as acceptable. **Fees:** $25 license fee per discipline.

3760

Asbestos Abatement Worker
State Dept. of Health and Consolidated Laboratories
Box 5520
1200 Missouri Ave.
Bismarck, ND 58502-5520
Phone: (701)224-5188

Credential Type: Asbestos Abatement Worker License. **Duration of License:** One year. **Requirements:** Complete an EPA-approved Asbestos Abatement Worker Course. Renewal requires attendance at annual refresher course. **Examination:** Written examination given as part of course. **Exemptions:** In-house non-public employees. Public employees and contractor employees disturbing less than three square feet or three line feet of asbestos-containing material. **Reciprocity:** All EPA-approved courses are recognized as acceptable. **Fees:** $25 license fee per discipline.

Oklahoma

3761

Asbestos Abatement Worker
Dept. of Labor, Asbestos Div.
4001 N. Lincoln
Oklahoma City, OK 73105
Phone: (405)528-1500

Credential Type: License. **Duration of License:** One year. **Requirements:** Completion of a 32-hour course in asbestos abatement at an accredited program. 16 hours of related, simulated work experience. Eight hours of continuing education each year. Evidence of respiratory training and equipment operation. **Examination:** Asbestos Abatement Worker Examination. **Fees:** $25 license fee. $25 renewal fee.

Rhode Island

3762

Asbestos Abatement Site Supervisor
Div. of Occupational and Radiological Health
Rhode Island Dept. of Health
3 Capitol Hill
Providence, RI 02908
Phone: (401)277-3601

Credential Type: Asbestos Abatement Site Supervisor License. **Duration of License:** Two years. **Requirements:** At least 18 years of age. Complete 40 hours of approved asbestos abatement training. **Examination:** Written examination. **Reciprocity:** No. **Fees:** $40 biennial renewal fee.

3763

Asbestos Abatement Worker
Div. of Occupational and Radiological Health
Rhode Island Dept. of Health
3 Capitol Hill
Providence, RI 02908
Phone: (401)277-3601

Credential Type: Asbestos Abatement Worker License. **Duration of License:** Two years. **Requirements:** At least 18 years of age. Complete 32 hours of approved asbestos abatement training. **Examination:** Written examination. **Reciprocity:** No. **Fees:** $20 biennial renewal fee.

Texas

3764

Air Monitoring Technician
Texas Dept. of Health
Occupational Health Div.
Asbestos Licensing Section
1100 W. 49th St.
Austin, TX 78756
Phone: (512)834-6600

Credential Type: Air Monitoring Technician License. **Duration of License:** One year. **Authorization:** License required to perform air monitoring services for an asbestos abatement project or related activity in a public building. **Requirements:** Completion of an approved training course for air monitoring technicians. Renewal requires completion of annual refresher training. Pass physical examination.

An upgraded license to perform analysis of airborne fibers in the field requires completion of the National Institute of Occupational Safety & Health No. 582 training course, or equivalent, titled "Analysis of Asbestos Dust" and current accreditation by the Asbestos Analyst Registry. **Fees:** $50 license fee. **Governing Statute:** Texas Civil Statutes, Article 4477-3a. Texas Asbestos Health Protection Rules, Section 295.

3765

Asbestos Consultant
Texas Dept. of Health
Occupational Health Div.
Asbestos Licensing Section
1100 W. 49th St.
Austin, TX 78756
Phone: (512)834-6600

Credential Type: Individual Asbestos Consultant License. **Duration of License:** One year. **Authorization:** License required to design asbestos abatement projects. **Requirements:** Must meet one of the following requirements: (1) Must be registered in Texas as an architect or professional engineer; or (2) Must be a member, with the current highest full qualifications, in a national professional organization devoted to technical proficiency in environmental or occupational health protection; or (3) Have a bachelor's degree in architecture, engineering, or physical or natural science from an accredited four-year college or university, with four years experience in areas affecting environmental or occupational health matters.

Pass physical examination. Complete one of the following training courses within the past 12 months: (1) Approved training course for abatement project designers; or (2) Modified three-day training course in sampling techniques and use of monitoring equipment; or (3) Training in asbestos building surveys; or (4) Annual refresher course, consisting of eight hours of instruction designed specifically for asbestos consultants. **Fees:** $300 license fee. **Governing Statute:** Texas Civil Statutes, Article 4477-3a. Texas Asbestos Health Protection Rules, Section 295.

3766

Asbestos Management Planner
Texas Dept. of Health
Occupational Health Div.
Asbestos Licensing Section
1100 W. 49th St.
Austin, TX 78756
Phone: (512)834-6600

Credential Type: Individual Asbestos Management Planner License. **Duration of License:** One year. **Authorization:** License required to develop an asbestos management plan. **Requirements:** Completion of Environmental Protection Agency (EPA) or state-approved inspector training courses together with the additional management planner courses of instruction within the past 12 months. Renewal requires completion of annual refresher training for management planners and inspectors. Must have an associate's degree or 60 credit hours from a college or university, or must currently be performing management plans and pass a state-administered competency test. **Examination:** Competency test. **Exemptions:** Competency test not required if applicant has an associate's degree or 60 credit hours from a college or university. **Fees:** $120 license fee. **Governing Statute:** Texas Civil Statutes, Article 4477-3a. Texas Asbestos Health Protection Rules, Section 295.

3767

Asbestos Operations and Maintenance Supervisor
Texas Dept. of Health
Occupational Health Div.
Asbestos Licensing Section
1100 W. 49th St.
Austin, TX 78756
Phone: (512)834-6600

Credential Type: Asbestos Operations and Maintenance Supervisor License (Restricted). **Duration of License:** One year. **Authorization:** Operations and maintenance activities are restricted to small-scale, short-duration work practices and engineering controls that result in the disturbance, dislodgement, or removal of asbestos in the course of performing repairs, maintenance, renovation, installation, replacement, or cleanup operations. **Requirements:** Completion within the past 12 months of an approved training course for asbestos abatement contractors and project supervisors. Renewal requires completing the annual refresher training course. Must pass physical examination. **Fees:** $90 license fee. **Governing Statute:** Texas Civil Statutes, Article 4477-3a. Texas Asbestos Health Protection Rules, Section 295.

3768

Asbestos Project Manager
Texas Dept. of Health
Occupational Health Div.
Asbestos Licensing Section
1100 W. 49th St.
Austin, TX 78756
Phone: (512)834-6600

Credential Type: Asbestos Project Manager License. **Duration of License:** One year. **Authorization:** Must be licensed and employed by a licensed asbestos consultant agency to evaluate the quality of work being done on an asbestos abatement project. **Requirements:** High school graduate or a GED certificate. Completion within the past 12 months of an approved training course for asbestos abatement contractors and project supervisors. Renewal requires completing the annual refresher training course. Must pass physical examination. **Fees:** $150 license fee. **Governing Statute:** Texas Civil Statutes, Article 4477-3a. Texas Asbestos Health Protection Rules, Section 295.

3769

Asbestos Project Supervisor
Texas Dept. of Health
Occupational Health Div.
Asbestos Licensing Section
1100 W. 49th St.
Austin, TX 78756
Phone: (512)834-6600

Credential Type: Asbestos Project Supervisor License (Restricted). **Duration of License:** One year. **Authorization:** License required to engage in supervision of an asbestos abatement project conducted in a public building. **Requirements:** Completion within the past 12 months of an approved training course for asbestos abatement contractors and project supervisors. Renewal requires completing the annual refresher training course. Must pass physical examination. Must have appropriate work experience of at least 90 days over a period of not less than 12 months and not more than 24 months. **Fees:** $300 license fee. **Governing Statute:** Texas Civil Statutes, Article 4477-3a. Texas Asbestos Health Protection Rules, Section 295.

3770

Asbestos Training Provider
Texas Dept. of Health
Occupational Health Div.
Asbestos Licensing Section
1100 W. 49th St.
Austin, TX 78756
Phone: (512)834-6600

Credential Type: Asbestos Training Provider License. **Duration of License:** One year. **Authorization:** License required to offer and conduct asbestos training for fulfillment of specific training requirements prerequisite to licensing or registration by the Texas Department of Health. **Requirements:** Instructors must meet one of the following requirements: (1) At least two years of actual hands-on experience in asbestos-related activities with training accreditation from the Environmental Protection Agency (EPA). A high school diploma. Completion of one or more teacher education courses in vocational or industrial teaching; or

(2) A college degree in natural or physical sciences or a related field. One year of actual hands-on experience in asbestos-related activities. Current accreditation in at least one EPA asbestos course; or

(3) At least three years teaching experience in Hazmat or HazWoper or EPA approved asbestos courses. Completion of one or more teacher education courses in vocational or industrial teaching from an accredited junior college or university; or

(4) Qualification on an individual basis of professional persons for the purpose of teaching their specialty; or

(5) A vocational teacher with certification from the Texas Education Agency. One year of actual hands-on experience in asbestos-related activities. Current accreditation in at least one EPA asbestos course. **Fees:** $500 license fee. **Governing Statute:** Texas Civil Statutes, Article 4477-3a. Texas Asbestos Health Protection Rules, Section 295.

3771

Asbestos Transporter
Texas Dept. of Health
Occupational Health Div.
Asbestos Licensing Section
1100 W. 49th St.
Austin, TX 78756
Phone: (512)834-6600

Credential Type: Asbestos Transporter License. **Duration of License:** One year. **Requirements:** Must have liability insurance of $1 million. Must submit a copy of emergency response plan and evidence of workers compensation insurance. **Fees:** $200 license fee. **Governing Statute:** Texas Civil Statutes, Article 4477-3a. Texas Asbestos Health Protection Rules, Section 295.

Insurance Agents and Brokers

The following states grant licenses in this occupational category as of the date of publication:

Alabama	District of	Iowa	Minnesota	New Mexico	Rhode Island	Washington
Alaska	Columbia	Kansas	Mississippi	New York	South Carolina	West Virginia
Arizona	Florida	Kentucky	Missouri	North Carolina	South Dakota	Wisconsin
Arkansas	Georgia	Louisiana	Montana	North Dakota	Tennessee	Wyoming
California	Hawaii	Maine	Nebraska	Ohio	Texas	
Colorado	Idaho	Maryland	Nevada	Oklahoma	Utah	
Connecticut	Illinois	Massachusetts	New Hampshire	Oregon	Vermont	
Delaware	Indiana	Michigan	New Jersey	Pennsylvania	Virginia	

Alabama

3772

Insurance Agent
Dept. of Insurance
135 S. Union St.
Montgomery, AL 36130
Phone: (205)269-3570

Credential Type: License. **Duration of License:** One year. **Requirements:** 19 years of age. Resident of Alabama. No felony convictions. Must complete 40 hours of Insurance Commission-approved courses of study on the general principles of insurance. **Examination:** Written examination. **Fees:** $10 examination fee. $7.50 renewal fee (per company appointment). $20 application fee.

3773

Insurance Broker
Dept. of Insurance
135 S. Union St.
Montgomery, AL 36130
Phone: (205)269-3570

Credential Type: License. **Duration of License:** One year. **Requirements:** 19 years of age. Resident of Alabama. No felony convictions. Must have served as a licensed Insurance Agent for at least three years prior to becoming an Insurance Broker. **Fees:** $50 renewal fee.

Alaska

3774

Insurance Producer
Div. of Insurance
Dept. of Commerce and Economic Development
State Office Bldg., 9th Fl.
33 Willoughby Ave.
PO Box 110805
Juneau, AK 99811-0805
Phone: (907)465-2579
Phone: (907)465-2575
Phone: (907)465-2578

Credential Type: All Lines License. **Duration of License:** Two years. **Authorization:** An insurance producer is anyone who solicits, negotiates, effects, procures, or delivers a policy of insurance, or to the extent authorized by the insurer, renews, continues, or binds a policy of insurance. **Requirements:** A $10,000 minimum bond is required if applicant is not acting solely as an agent, or receives money that is required to be received into a fiduciary account, or is acting as a broker. **Fees:** $200 resident fee. $400 non-resident fee. **Governing Statute:** Alaska Statutes, Title 21.

Credential Type: Property/Casualty Lines License. **Duration of License:** Two years. **Authorization:** An insurance producer is anyone who solicits, negotiates, effects, procures, or delivers a policy of insurance, or to the extent authorized by the insurer, renews, continues, or binds a policy of insurance. **Requirements:** A $10,000 minimum bond is required if applicant is not acting solely as an agent, or receives money that is required to be received into a fiduciary account, or is acting as a broker. **Fees:** $100 resident fee. $200 non-resident fee. **Governing Statute:** Alaska Statutes, Title 21.

Credential Type: Life Lines License. **Duration of License:** Two years. **Authorization:** An insurance producer is anyone who solicits, negotiates, effects, procures, or delivers a policy of insurance, or to the extent authorized by the insurer, renews, continues, or binds a policy of insurance. **Requirements:** A $10,000 minimum bond is required if applicant is not acting solely as an agent, or receives money that is required to be received into a fiduciary account, or is acting as a broker. **Fees:** $100 resident fee. $200 non-resident fee. **Governing Statute:** Alaska Statutes, Title 21.

Credential Type: Trainee Insurance Producer Property/Casualty Lines License. **Duration of License:** Two years. **Requirements:** Contact licensing body for application information. **Fees:** $50 resident fee. **Governing Statute:** Alaska Statutes, Title 21.

3775

Managing General Agent (Insurance)
Div. of Insurance
Dept. of Commerce and Economic Development
State Office Bldg., 9th Fl.
33 Willoughby Ave.
PO Box 110805
Juneau, AK 99811-0805
Phone: (907)465-2579
Phone: (907)465-2575
Phone: (907)465-2578

Credential Type: All Lines License. **Duration of License:** Two years. **Authorization:** A managing general agent is a person who has authority to exercise general supervision over the business of one or more admitted insurers; and who performs administrative functions normally performed by the insurer. **Requirements:** Contact li-

Alaska

Managing General Agent (Insurance), continued

censing body for application information. **Fees:** $200 resident fee. $400 non-resident fee. **Governing Statute:** Alaska Statutes, Title 21.

Credential Type: Property/Casualty Lines License. **Duration of License:** Two years. **Authorization:** An insurance producer is anyone who solicits, negotiates, effects, procures, or delivers a policy of insurance, or to the extent authorized by the insurer, renews, continues, or binds a policy of insurance. **Requirements:** Must have a physical place of business that is accessible to the public. **Fees:** $100 resident fee. $200 non-resident fee. **Governing Statute:** Alaska Statutes, Title 21.

Credential Type: Life Lines License. **Duration of License:** Two years. **Authorization:** An insurance producer is anyone who solicits, negotiates, effects, procures, or delivers a policy of insurance, or to the extent authorized by the insurer, renews, continues, or binds a policy of insurance. **Requirements:** Contact licensing body for application information. **Fees:** $100 resident fee. $200 non-resident fee. **Governing Statute:** Alaska Statutes, Title 21.

Credential Type: Trainee Managing General Agent. **Duration of License:** Two years. **Requirements:** Contact licensing body for application information. **Fees:** $100 resident fee (Life Lines or Property/Casualty). $200 non-resident fee (Life Lines or Property/Casualty). $200 resident fee (All Lines). $400 non-resident fee (All Lines). **Governing Statute:** Alaska Statutes, Title 21.

3776

Reinsurance Intermediary Broker
Div. of Insurance
Dept. of Commerce and Economic Development
State Office Bldg., 9th Fl.
33 Willoughby Ave.
PO Box 110805
Juneau, AK 99811-0805
Phone: (907)465-2579
Phone: (907)465-2575
Phone: (907)465-2578

Credential Type: Reinsurance Intermediary Broker License. **Duration of License:** Two years. **Requirements:** Contact licensing body for application information. **Fees:** $300 resident fee. $900 non-resident fee. **Governing Statute:** Alaska Statutes, Title 21.

Credential Type: Trainee License. **Duration of License:** Two years. **Requirements:** Contact licensing body for application information. **Fees:** $300 resident fee. $900 non-resident fee. **Governing Statute:** Alaska Statutes, Title 21.

3777

Reinsurance Intermediary Manager
Div. of Insurance
Dept. of Commerce and Economic Development
State Office Bldg., 9th Fl.
33 Willoughby Ave.
PO Box 110805
Juneau, AK 99811-0805
Phone: (907)465-2579
Phone: (907)465-2575
Phone: (907)465-2578

Credential Type: Reinsurance Intermediary Manager License. **Duration of License:** Two years. **Requirements:** Contact licensing body for application information. **Fees:** $300 resident fee. $900 non-resident fee. **Governing Statute:** Alaska Statutes, Title 21.

Credential Type: Trainee License. **Duration of License:** Two years. **Requirements:** Contact licensing body for application information. **Fees:** $300 resident fee. $900 non-resident fee. **Governing Statute:** Alaska Statutes, Title 21.

3778

Surplus Lines Broker
Div. of Insurance
Dept. of Commerce and Economic Development
State Office Bldg., 9th Fl.
33 Willoughby Ave.
PO Box 110805
Juneau, AK 99811-0805
Phone: (907)465-2579
Phone: (907)465-2575
Phone: (907)465-2578

Credential Type: Surplus Lines Broker License. **Duration of License:** Two years. **Requirements:** A $200,000 bond is required. **Fees:** $300 resident fee. $900 non-resident fee. **Governing Statute:** Alaska Statutes, Title 21.

Credential Type: Trainee License. **Duration of License:** Two years. **Requirements:** Contact licensing body for application information. **Fees:** $300 resident fee. $900 non-resident fee. **Governing Statute:** Alaska Statutes, Title 21.

Arizona

3779

Insurance Broker
Dept. of Insurance
Licensing Section
Abacus Towers 1100
3030 N. 3rd St.
Phoenix, AZ 85012
Phone: (602)255-5605

Credential Type: Broker's Property and Casualty License. **Duration of License:** Two years. **Requirements:** Pass security clearance with the Arizona Department of Public Safety and the Federal Bureau of Investigation. Pass appropriate exam. Post $1,000 surety bond. **Examination:** Broker's Property and Casualty Exam, Series 13-34. **Reciprocity:** Yes, if state extends similar licensing privileges to residents of Arizona. **Fees:** $75 exam fee. $35.65 license fee.

Credential Type: Surplus Lines Broker License. **Duration of License:** Two years. **Requirements:** Must hold an Agent Property and Casualty License and/or a Broker Property and Casualty License. Post $20,000 surety bond. **Fees:** $356.50 license fee.

3780

Insurance Sales Agent
Dept. of Insurance
Licensing Section
Abacus Towers 1100
3030 N. 3rd St.
Phoenix, AZ 85012
Phone: (602)255-5605

Credential Type: Agent's Life License. **Duration of License:** Two years. **Requirements:** Pass security clearance with the Arizona Department of Public Safety and the Federal Bureau of Investigation. Pass appropriate exam. **Examination:** Agent's Life Exam, Series 13-31. **Reciprocity:** Yes, if state extends similar licensing privileges to residents of Arizona. **Fees:** $53 exam fee. $35.65 license fee.

Credential Type: Agent's Disability License. **Duration of License:** Two years. **Requirements:** Pass security clearance with the Arizona Department of Public Safety and the Federal Bureau of Investigation. Pass appropriate exam. **Examination:** Agent's Disability Exam, Series 13-32. **Reciprocity:** Yes, if state extends similar licensing privileges to residents of Arizona. **Fees:** $53 exam fee. $35.65 license fee.

Credential Type: Agent's Life and Disability License. **Duration of License:** Two years. **Requirements:** Pass security clearance with the Arizona Department of Public Safety and the Federal Bureau of Investigation. Pass appropriate exam. **Examination:** Agent's Life and Disability Exam, Series 13-33. **Reciprocity:** Yes, if state extends similar licensing privileges to residents of Arizona. **Fees:** $75 exam fee. $35.65 license fee.

Credential Type: Agent's Property and Casualty License. **Duration of License:** Two years. **Requirements:** Pass security clearance with the Arizona Department of Public Safety and the Federal Bureau of Investigation. Pass appropriate exam. **Examination:** Agent's Property and Casualty Exam, Series 13-34. **Reciprocity:** Yes, if state extends similar licensing privileges to residents of Arizona. **Fees:** $75 exam fee. $35.65 license fee.

Credential Type: Variable Annuity Contracts Agent License. **Duration of License:** Two years. **Requirements:** Pass NASD exam and be affiliated with an Arizona insurance broker/dealer. **Reciprocity:** Yes, if state extends similar licensing privileges to residents of Arizona. **Fees:** $35.65 license fee.

3781

Insurance Solicitor
Dept. of Insurance
Licensing Section
Abacus Towers 1100
3030 N. 3rd St.
Phoenix, AZ 85012
Phone: (602)255-5605

Credential Type: Solicitor's Property and Casualty License. **Duration of License:** Two years. **Requirements:** Pass security clearance with the Arizona Department of Public Safety and the Federal Bureau of Investigation. Pass appropriate exam. Must not also be an insurance agent or broker. **Examination:** Solicitor's Property and Casualty Exam, Series 13-34. **Fees:** $75 exam fee. $35.65 license fee.

Credential Type: Solicitor's Life License. **Duration of License:** Two years. **Requirements:** Pass security clearance with the Arizona Department of Public Safety and the Federal Bureau of Investigation. Pass appropriate exam. Must not also be an insurance agent or broker. **Examination:** Solicitor's Life Exam, Series 13-31. **Fees:** $53 exam fee. $35.65 license fee.

Credential Type: Solicitor's Disability License. **Duration of License:** Two years. **Requirements:** Pass security clearance with the Arizona Department of Public Safety and the Federal Bureau of Investigation. Pass appropriate exam. **Examination:** Solicitor's Disability Exam, Series 13-32. **Fees:** $53 exam fee. $35.65 license fee.

Credential Type: Solicitor's Life and Disability License. **Duration of License:** Two years. **Requirements:** Pass security clearance with the Arizona Department of Public Safety and the Federal Bureau of Investigation. Pass appropriate exam. Must not also be an insurance agent or broker. **Examination:** Solicitor's Life and Disability Exam, Series 13-33. **Fees:** $75 exam fee. $35.65 license fee.

Arkansas

3782

Insurance Sales Agent
Arkansas Insurance Dept.
400 University Tower Bldg.
12th & University St.
Little Rock, AR 72204
Phone: (501)371-1421

Credential Type: License. **Requirements:** 18 years of age. Satisfy 36 hours of approved classroom instruction. Pass written examination. Resident of Arkansas. **Examination:** Yes. **Fees:** $25 Written examination. $10 Appointment (per company). $10 Renewal (per company).

California

3783

Insurance Agent
Dept. of Insurance
700 L St.
Sacramento, CA 95814
Phone: (916)322-3555
Phone: (415)557-1126

Credential Type: Resident Life Agent License. **Duration of License:** Two years. **Requirements:** Contact licensing body for application information. **Fees:** $96 license fee. $96 renewal fee.

Credential Type: Nonresident Life Agent License. **Duration of License:** Two years. **Requirements:** Contact licensing body for application information. **Fees:** $106 minimum license fee (fee based on state of residence). $106 minimum renewal fee (fee based on state of residence).

Credential Type: Fire and Casualty Agent License. **Duration of License:** Two years. **Requirements:** Be at least 18 years of age. Complete at least 40 hours of prelicensing classroom study and 12 hours of study on ethics and the insurance code. Submit an Action Notice of Appointment.

The continuing education requirement for the first year of licensure is 25 classroom hours of instruction. The requirement for subsequent years is 15 classroom hours per year. **Examination:** Yes. **Fees:** $112 license fee. $32 exam fee. $112 renewal fee.

Credential Type: Travel Insurance Agent License. **Duration of License:** Two years. **Requirements:** Contact licensing body for application information. Must be a California resident. **Fees:** $38 license fee. $38 renewal fee.

Credential Type: Motor Club Agent License. **Duration of License:** Two years. **Requirements:** Contact licensing body for application information. Must be a California resident. **Fees:** $112 license fee. $112 renewal fee.

3784

Insurance Broker
Dept. of Insurance
700 L St.
Sacramento, CA 95814
Phone: (916)322-3555
Phone: (415)557-1126

Credential Type: Surplus and/or Special Lines Broker License. **Duration of License:** Two years. **Requirements:** Contact licensing body for application information. Must be a California resident. **Fees:** $944 license fee. $944 renewal fee.

Credential Type: Fire and Casualty Broker License. **Duration of License:** Two years. **Requirements:** Be at least 18 years of age. Complete at least 40 hours of prelicensing classroom study and 12 hours of study on ethics and the insurance code. Post a $5000 broker's bond.

The continuing education requirement for the first year of licensure is 25 classroom hours of instruction. The requirement for subsequent years is 15 classroom hours per year. **Examination:** Yes. **Fees:** $112 license fee. $32 exam fee. $112 renewal fee.

Colorado

3785

Insurance Broker
Dept. of Regulatory Agencies
Div. of Insurance
303 W. Colfax, Ste. 500
Denver, CO 80204
Phone: (303)866-6248

Credential Type: Professional license. **Duration of License:** Two years. **Requirements:** Based on experience. **Reciprocity:** Yes. **Fees:** $44 life insurance (accidental

Insurance Broker, continued

and health) license fee. $34 multiple lines license fee. $69 all lines license fee.

3786

Insurance Sales Agent
Dept. of Regulatory Agencies
Div. of Insurance
303 W. Colfax, Ste. 500
Denver, CO 80204
Phone: (303)866-6248

Credential Type: Professional license. **Duration of License:** Two years. **Requirements:** Pass appropriate ASI administered examinations. **Examination:** ASI administered examinations in Life, Accidental and Health, Property, and Casualty Insurance. **Exemptions:** Individuals with CPCU or CLU designations. **Reciprocity:** Yes. **Fees:** $67 exam fee. $29 license fee. $19 appointment fee.

Connecticut

3787

Insurance Agent
Licensing and Investigations Div.
Insurance Dept.
PO Box 816
Hartford, CT 06142-0816
Phone: (203)297-3800

Credential Type: Insurance Agent License. **Requirements:** Contact licensing body for application information. **Fees:** $25 filing fee. **Governing Statute:** Connecticut General Statutes, 38a-769.

3788

Insurance Broker
Licensing and Investigations Div.
Insurance Dept.
PO Box 816
Hartford, CT 06142-0816
Phone: (203)297-3800

Credential Type: Individual Insurance Broker's License. **Duration of License:** Two years. **Requirements:** Complete educational requirements of 40 hours of approved training for each line of insurance being applied for. Pass examinations required for the lines of insurance applied for. **Examination:** Yes, for each line of insurance. **Fees:** $25 filing fee. $88 license fee.

3789

Insurance Broker (Racetrack)
Connecticut Div. of Special Revenue
Russell Rd.
PO Box 11424
Newington, CT 06111-0424
Phone: (203)566-2756

Credential Type: License Registration. **Requirements:** Submit application and fingerprint card. Pay fee. **Fees:** $5 registration fee.

3790

Insurance Consultant
Licensing and Investigations Div.
Insurance Dept.
PO Box 816
Hartford, CT 06142-0816
Phone: (203)297-3800

Credential Type: License **Requirements:** Contact licensing body for application information.

3791

Surplus Lines Broker
Licensing and Investigations Div.
Insurance Dept.
PO Box 816
Hartford, CT 06142-0816
Phone: (203)297-3800

Credential Type: License. **Requirements:** Contact licensing body for application information.

Delaware

3792

Fraternal Representative
Dept. of Insurance
841 Silver Lake Blvd.
Rodney Bldg.
Dover, DE 19901
Phone: (302)739-4251

Credential Type: Fraternal Representative License and Certificate of Authority. **Duration of License:** Permanent. **Requirements:** Must be at least 18 years of age. Be competent, trustworthy, financially responsible, and of good reputation. **Fees:** $10 application fee.

3793

Insurance Agent
Dept. of Insurance
841 Silver Lake Blvd.
Rodney Bldg.
Dover, DE 19901
Phone: (302)739-4251

Credential Type: Agent License and Certificate of Authority. **Duration of License:** Permanent. **Authorization:** Up to 14 lines of insurance may be authorized. **Requirements:** Must be at least 18 years of age. Be competent, trustworthy, financially responsible, and of good reputation. Demonstrate competency by completing qualification examination. File at least one request for appointment by an authorized insurer. Residents must furnish appropriate forms for each insurer and examination report from ASI. In addition, non-residents must provide Letter of Certification from home state or examination report from ASI. **Examination:** Yes. **Fees:** $30 application fee.

3794

Insurance Broker
Dept. of Insurance
841 Silver Lake Blvd.
Rodney Bldg.
Dover, DE 19901
Phone: (302)739-4251

Credential Type: Broker's License and Certificate of Authority. **Duration of License:** Permanent. **Authorization:** Up to 14 lines of insurance may be authorized. **Requirements:** Must be at least 18 years of age. Be competent, trustworthy, financially responsible, and of good reputation. Demonstrate competency by completing qualification examination. Have been certified as an insurance agent for at least two years. Furnish examination report from ASI. Post minimum bond of $5,000. In addition, non-residents must provide Letter of Certification from home state or examination report from ASI. **Examination:** Yes. **Fees:** $60 application fee.

3795

Insurance Consultant
Dept. of Insurance
841 Silver Lake Blvd.
Rodney Bldg.
Dover, DE 19901
Phone: (302)739-4251

Credential Type: Insurance Consultant License and Certificate of Authority. **Duration of License:** Permanent. **Requirements:** Must be at least 18 years of age. Be competent, trustworthy, financially respon-

Insurance Agents and Brokers

sible, and of good reputation. Demonstrate competency by completing qualification examination. Have held a resident broker's license for at least two years. Submit letter from an authorized insurer or licensed resident broker attesting to applicant's ability to serve as a consultant. In addition, nonresidents must provide Letter of Certification/Qualification from home state. **Examination:** Yes. **Fees:** $150 application fee.

3796

Surplus Lines Broker
Dept. of Insurance
841 Silver Lake Blvd.
Rodney Bldg.
Dover, DE 19901
Phone: (302)739-4251

Credential Type: Surplus Lines Broker's License and Certificate of Authority. **Duration of License:** Permanent. **Requirements:** Must be at least 18 years of age. Be competent, trustworthy, financially responsible, and of good reputation. Demonstrate competency by completing qualification examination. Have held a resident broker's license for at least one year. Non-residents may not be licensed as a Surplus Lines Broker. **Examination:** Yes. **Fees:** $150 application fee.

District of Columbia

3797

Fire and Casualty Insurance Agent
Insurance Commission
Dept. of Consumer and Regulatory Affairs
PO Box 37200
Washington, DC 20013-7200
Phone: (202)727-7424

Alternate Information: 614 H St., NW, Washington, DC 20001

Credential Type: Policywriting Agent License. **Duration of License:** One year. **Requirements:** Must reside or have principal place of business in the District of Columbia. Submit application and pay fee. Broker privilege may be added for additional fee and by executing bond requirement. **Examination:** Written examination of the National Testing Service. **Fees:** $50 license fee (covers up to two members). $10 license fee for each additional member. $10 broker privilege fee. $50 renewal fee.

Credential Type: Salaried Company Employee License (Sign and Solicit). **Duration of License:** One year. **Requirements:** Submit application and pay fee. No residency requirement. Broker privilege may be added for additional fee and by executing bond requirement. **Examination:** Written examination of the National Testing Service. **Fees:** $50 license fee. $50 renewal fee. $10 broker privilege fee.

3798

Fire and Casualty Insurance Broker
Insurance Commission
Dept. of Consumer and Regulatory Affairs
PO Box 37200
Washington, DC 20013-7200
Phone: (202)727-7424

Alternate Information: 614 H St., NW, Washington, DC 20001

Credential Type: Broker License. **Duration of License:** One year. **Requirements:** Must reside or have principal place of business in the District of Columbia. Must execute bond requirement. **Examination:** Written examination of the National Testing Service. **Fees:** $50 license fee. $50 renewal fee.

Credential Type: Non-Resident Broker. **Duration of License:** One year. **Requirements:** Must execute bond requirement. Must submit proof of licensure in home state with current letter of certification. **Examination:** Written examination of the National Testing Service. **Fees:** $50 license fee. $50 renewal fee.

3799

Fire and Casualty Insurance Solicitor
Insurance Commission
Dept. of Consumer and Regulatory Affairs
PO Box 37200
Washington, DC 20013-7200
Phone: (202)727-7424

Alternate Information: 614 H St., NW, Washington, DC 20001

Credential Type: Agency Solicitor License. **Duration of License:** One year. **Requirements:** Must reside or have principal place of business in the District of Columbia. Must be appointed by a licensed policywriting agent. May represent one policywriting agent only and may not hold a company solicitor's license. **Examination:** Written examination of the National Testing Service. **Fees:** $10 license fee (one company represented). $20 license fee (2 or more companies represented).

Credential Type: Salaried Company Employee License (Solicit Only). **Duration of License:** One year. **Requirements:** Must reside or have principal place of business in the District of Columbia. Submit application and pay fee. **Examination:** Written examination of the National Testing Service. **Fees:** $10 license fee (one company represented). $20 license fee (2 or more companies represented).

Credential Type: Company Solicitor License. **Duration of License:** One year. **Requirements:** Must reside or have principal place of business in the District of Columbia. Submit application and pay fee. **Examination:** Written examination of the National Testing Service. **Fees:** $10 license fee (one company represented). $20 license fee (2 or more companies represented).

Florida

3800

Insurance Agent
Dept. of Insurance
Bureau of Agent and Agency Licensing
The Capitol
Tallahassee, FL 32399-0300
Phone: (904)922-3137

Credential Type: Resident Agent License. **Duration of License:** Two years. **Authorization:** Licenses are issued for the following lines of insurance: General Lines, Life, Life (including Variable), Health, Life and Health, Life (including Variable) and Health, and Credit Life (including Credit Disability). **Requirements:** Contact licensing body for application information.

Credential Type: Nonresident Agent License. **Duration of License:** Two years. **Authorization:** Licenses are issued for the following lines of insurance: General Lines, Life, Life (including Variable), Health, Life and Health, Life (including Variable) and Health, and Credit Life (including Credit Disability). **Requirements:** Contact licensing body for application information. **Fees:** $50 application fee. $58 fingerprint processing fee. $5 license fee. $60 state appointment fee. $6 county appointment fee per county.

Georgia

3801

Insurance Agent
State Insurance Dept.
Agents Licensing Div.
Box 101208
Atlanta, GA 30392-1208
Phone: (404)656-2056
Fax: (404)656-7628

Credential Type: Resident Agent License. **Authorization:** Licenses are issued for the following lines or combinations of insurance: Life, Allied and Surety, Credit Life and Credit Allied and Surety, Variable Life, Travel, Property and Casualty, Limited Property, Limited Casualty, Limited Auto, and Limited Surety. **Requirements:** Complete a 40-hour classroom pre-licensing course. Applicants for a variable life agent license must complete an eight-hour classroom pre-licensing course, have NASD certification, and also hold a valid life agent license. Applicants for a variable annuity agent license need not take any pre-licensing course, but must have NASD certification and also hold a valid life agent license. **Examination:** ASI Examination. **Fees:** $15 application fee. $50 license fee. $90 exam fee. $10 certificate of authority fee.

Credential Type: Nonresident Agent License. **Authorization:** Licenses are issued for the following lines or combinations of insurance: Life, Allied and Surety, Credit Life and Credit Allied and Surety, Variable Life, Travel, Property and Casualty, Limited Property, Limited Casualty, Limited Auto, and Limited Surety. **Requirements:** Must hold a current valid license in home state. **Fees:** $20 license fee (minimum fee based on state of residence). $5 certificate of authority fee.

3802

Insurance Counselor
State Insurance Dept.
Agents Licensing Div.
Box 101208
Atlanta, GA 30392-1208
Phone: (404)656-2056
Fax: (404)656-7628

Credential Type: Counselor License. **Requirements:** Post appropriate bond. **Examination:** ASI Examination. **Fees:** $15 application fee. $50 license fee. $90 exam fee.

3803

Insurance Sales Agent
Commission of Insurance
Agents Licensing
West Tower, 7th Fl.
2 Martin Luther King Jr. Dr.
Atlanta, GA 30334
Phone: (404)656-2104

Credential Type: License. **Requirements:** Contact licensing body for application information.

Hawaii

3804

Insurance Salesperson
Hawaii State Dept. of Commerce and
 Consumer Affairs
Insurance Div.
PO Box 3469
Honolulu, HI 96801
Phone: (808)548-6522

Credential Type: License. **Duration of License:** Two years. **Requirements:** State resident. 18 years of age. **Examination:** Comprehensive and written. **Reciprocity:** None. **Fees:** $52—$69 exam fee. $20—$25 issuance fee. $20—$50 renewal fee.

Idaho

3805

Insurance Broker
Licensing Bureau
Dept. of Insurance
550 S. Tenth St.
Boise, ID 83720
Phone: (208)334-2250

Credential Type: Resident Broker General Lines License. **Duration of License:** Two years. **Authorization:** Covers property, casualty, motor vehicle physical damage, and surety insurance. **Requirements:** Submit broker application and post $10,000 surety bond. **Examination:** Examination for each line. **Fees:** $200 license fee. $25 exam fee for each exam. $45 fingerprint processing fee. **Governing Statute:** Idaho Code, Title 41, Chap. 10.

Credential Type: Resident Broker Life and Disability License. **Duration of License:** Two years. **Authorization:** Covers life, disability, credit life, and disability lines. **Requirements:** Submit broker application and post $10,000 surety bond. **Examination:** Examination for each line. **Fees:** $200 license fee. $25 exam fee for each exam. $45 fingerprint processing fee.

Governing Statute: Idaho Code, Title 41, Chap. 10.

Credential Type: Non-Resident Broker General Lines License. **Duration of License:** Two years. **Authorization:** Covers property, casualty, motor vehicle physical damage, and surety insurance. **Requirements:** Submit broker application and post $10,000 surety bond. Must submit current, original Letter of Certification from domicile state. **Examination:** Examination for each line. **Fees:** $200 license fee. $25 exam fee for each exam. $45 fingerprint processing fee. Additional license fee may be charged, based on the fee charged Idaho residents by applicant's state of domicile if more than Idaho's $200 license fee. **Governing Statute:** Idaho Code, Title 41, Chap. 10.

Credential Type: Non-Resident Broker Life and Disability License. **Duration of License:** Two years. **Authorization:** Covers life, disability, credit life, and disability lines. **Requirements:** Submit broker application and post $10,000 surety bond. Must submit current, original Letter of Certification from domicile state. **Examination:** Examination for each line. **Fees:** $200 license fee. $25 exam fee for each exam. $45 fingerprint processing fee. Additional license fee may be charged, based on the fee charged Idaho residents by applicant's state of domicile if more than Idaho's $40 license fee. **Governing Statute:** Idaho Code, Title 41, Chap. 10.

3806

Insurance Consultant
Licensing Bureau
Dept. of Insurance
550 S. Tenth St.
Boise, ID 83720
Phone: (208)334-2250

Credential Type: Resident Consultant General Lines License. **Duration of License:** Two years. **Authorization:** Covers property, casualty, motor vehicle physical damage, and surety insurance. **Requirements:** Be at least 25 years of age. Submit application and post $10,000 surety bond. Must have at least five years continuous experience as a licensed broker or agent or other special training. **Examination:** Examination for each line. **Fees:** $200 license fee. $25 exam fee for each exam. $45 fingerprint processing fee. **Governing Statute:** Idaho Code, Title 41, Chap. 10.

Credential Type: Resident Consultant Life and Disability License. **Duration of License:** Two years. **Authorization:** Covers life, disability, credit life, and disability lines. **Requirements:** Be at least 25 years of age. Submit application and post

Insurance Agents and Brokers

$10,000 surety bond. Must have at least five years continuous experience as a licensed broker or agent or other special training. **Examination:** Examination for each line. **Fees:** $200 license fee. $25 exam fee for each exam. $45 fingerprint processing fee. **Governing Statute:** Idaho Code, Title 41, Chap. 10.

Credential Type: Non-Resident Consultant General Lines License. **Duration of License:** Two years. **Authorization:** Covers property, casualty, motor vehicle physical damage, and surety insurance. **Requirements:** Be at least 25 years of age. Submit application and post $10,000 surety bond. Must submit current, original Letter of Certification from domicile state. Must have at least five years continuous experience as a licensed broker or agent or other special training. **Examination:** Examination for each line. **Fees:** $200 license fee. $25 exam fee for each exam. $45 fingerprint processing fee. Additional license fee may be charged, based on the fee charged Idaho residents by applicant's state of domicile if more than Idaho's $200 license fee. **Governing Statute:** Idaho Code, Title 41, Chap. 10.

Credential Type: Non-Resident Consultant Life and Disability License. **Duration of License:** Two years. **Authorization:** Covers life, disability, credit life, and disability lines. **Requirements:** Be at least 25 years of age. Submit application and post $10,000 surety bond. Must submit current, original Letter of Certification from domicile state. Must have at least five years continuous experience as a licensed broker or agent or other special training. **Examination:** Examination for each line. **Fees:** $200 license fee. $25 exam fee for each exam. $45 fingerprint processing fee. Additional license fee may be charged, based on the fee charged Idaho residents by applicant's state of domicile if more than Idaho's $40 license fee. **Governing Statute:** Idaho Code, Title 41, Chap. 10.

3807

Insurance Sales Agent
Licensing Bureau
Dept. of Insurance
550 S. Tenth St.
Boise, ID 83720
Phone: (208)334-2250

Credential Type: Resident Agent General Lines License. **Duration of License:** Two years. **Authorization:** Covers property, casualty, motor vehicle physical damage, and surety insurance. **Requirements:** Submit application. Must be recommended and employed by a sponsoring company. **Examination:** Examination for each line. **Fees:** $40 license fee. $25 exam fee for each exam. $45 fingerprint processing fee. **Governing Statute:** Idaho Code, Title 41, Chap. 10.

Credential Type: Resident Agent Life and Disability License. **Duration of License:** Two years. **Authorization:** Covers life, disability, credit life, and disability lines. **Requirements:** Submit application. Must be recommended and employed by a sponsoring company. **Examination:** Examination for each line. **Fees:** $40 license fee. $25 exam fee for each exam. $45 fingerprint processing fee. **Governing Statute:** Idaho Code, Title 41, Chap. 10.

Credential Type: Company Appointment. **Requirements:** Given to currently licensed agents to represent additional insurers. **Fees:** $10 company appointment fee. **Governing Statute:** Idaho Code, Title 41, Chap. 10.

Credential Type: Non-Resident Agent General Lines License. **Duration of License:** Two years. **Authorization:** Covers property, casualty, motor vehicle physical damage, and surety insurance. **Requirements:** Submit application. Must be recommended and employed by a sponsoring company. Must submit current, original Letter of Certification from domicile state. **Examination:** Examination for each line. **Fees:** $40 license fee. $25 exam fee for each exam. $45 fingerprint processing fee. Additional license fee may be charged, based on the fee charged Idaho residents by applicant's state of domicile if more than Idaho's $40 license fee. **Governing Statute:** Idaho Code, Title 41, Chap. 10.

Credential Type: Non-Resident Agent Life and Disability License. **Duration of License:** Two years. **Authorization:** Covers life, disability, credit life, and disability lines. **Requirements:** Submit application. Must be recommended and employed by a sponsoring company. Must submit current, original Letter of Certification from domicile state. **Examination:** Examination for each line. **Fees:** $40 license fee. $25 exam fee for each exam. $45 fingerprint processing fee. Additional license fee may be charged, based on the fee charged Idaho residents by applicant's state of domicile if more than Idaho's $40 license fee. **Governing Statute:** Idaho Code, Title 41, Chap. 10.

Illinois

3808

Insurance Producer
Illinois Dept. of Insurance
320 W. Washington
Springfield, IL 62767
Phone: (217)782-6366

Credential Type: Insurance Producer License. **Duration of License:** One year. **Requirements:** At least 18 years of age. Must have 15 hours of education per line of insurance (life, accident & health, property and/or casualty). First four renewals of license require 25 hours of continuing education for each renewal. **Examination:** Illinois Insurance Licensing Examination. **Reciprocity:** Yes, if applicant holds a valid license from another state. **Fees:** $80 examination fee. $25 application fee. $75 initial license fee. $75 renewal fee. $50 reinstatement fee. **Governing Statute:** Illinois Insurance Code, Chapter 73.

Indiana

3809

Insurance Agent
Insurance Dept.
311 W. Washington St., Ste. 300
Indianapolis, IN 46204-2787
Phone: (317)232-2385
Fax: (317)232-5251

Credential Type: License. **Requirements:** Contact licensing body for application information.

3810

Insurance Consultant
Insurance Dept.
311 W. Washington St., Ste. 300
Indianapolis, IN 46204-2787
Phone: (317)232-2385
Fax: (317)232-5251

Credential Type: License. **Requirements:** Contact licensing body for application information.

Iowa

3811

Insurance Agent
Agent Licensing Bureau
Iowa Div. of Insurance
Lucas State Office Bldg.
Des Moines, IA 50319
Phone: (515)281-4025

Credential Type: License. **Duration of License:** Three years. **Examination:** Exam is given by the Insurance Testing Corp. of St. Paul, MN. **Fees:** $68—$85 exam fee. $50 license fee. $50 reciprocity fee. $10 continuing education fee.

Kansas

3812

Insurance Agent
Agents and Brokers Div.
Insurance Dept.
420 SW 9th St.
Topeka, KS 66612-1678
Phone: (913)296-7860

Credential Type: Insurance Agents License. **Duration of License:** Permanent. **Authorization:** License must be currently contracted and certified by each company represented. **Requirements:** Must be a high school graduate or equivalent. Submit application and pay fee. Submit NASD registration if variable contract authority is desired.

Non-residents must provide certification of insurance authority from state of residence. **Fees:** $20 application fee. $10 minimum nonresident certification fee, plus additional retaliatory fee based on nonresident state's fees.

Kentucky

3813

Insurance Agent
Kentucky Dept. of Insurance
PO Box 517
Frankfort, KY 40602
Phone: (502)564-3630

Credential Type: General Lines License. **Duration of License:** Two years. **Requirements:** High school diploma or equivalent. 40 hours of pre-licensing instruction in insurance. 18 years of age. **Examination:** Yes. **Fees:** $50 exam fee. $20—$40 renewal fee.

Credential Type: Life & Health License. **Duration of License:** Two years. **Requirements:** High school diploma or equivalent. 40 hours of pre-licensing instructions in insurance. Must be sponsored by an authorized insurance company. 18 years of age. **Examination:** Yes. **Fees:** $50 exam fee. $20—$40 license fee.

3814

Insurance Consultant
Kentucky Dept. of Insurance
PO Box 517
Frankfort, KY 40602
Phone: (502)564-3630

Credential Type: License. **Requirements:** 25 years of age. Five years of actual experience as a licensed agent, or other special experience, education or training. Must secure a surety bond or deposit a cash surety bond. **Examination:** Yes.

3815

Insurance Solicitor
Kentucky Dept. of Insurance
PO Box 517
Frankfort, KY 40602
Phone: (502)564-3630

Credential Type: License. **Requirements:** High school diploma or equivalent. 40 hours of pre-licensing instruction in insurance. Must be sponsored by a licensed, resident insurance agent or licensed insurance corporation. 18 years of age. Must be a state resident at time of application. **Examination:** Yes. **Fees:** $50 exam fee. $20—$40 license fee.

Louisiana

3816

Insurance Agent
Dept. of Insurance, Commissioner's Office
PO Box 94214, Capitol Station
Baton Rouge, LA 70804-9214
Phone: (504)342-5338
Phone: (504)342-5900

Credential Type: License. **Duration of License:** Two years. **Requirements:** Must abide by applicable laws, rules and regulations. **Examination:** Written examination required for property and casualty insurance; life, health, and accident insurance; and variable annuity insurance. **Reciprocity:** Yes. **Fees:** $10—$65 license fees (varies with lines). $10—$65 renewal fees (varies with lines).

3817

Insurance Broker
Dept. of Insurance, Commissioner's Office
PO Box 94214, Capitol Station
Baton Rouge, LA 70804-9214
Phone: (504)342-5338
Phone: (504)342-5900

Credential Type: License. **Duration of License:** Two years. **Requirements:** Must abide by applicable laws, rules and regulations. **Examination:** Written examination required for property and casualty insurance; life, health, and accident insurance; and variable annuity insurance. **Reciprocity:** Yes. **Fees:** $10—$65 license fees (varies with lines). $10—$65 renewal fees (varies with lines).

3818

Insurance Solicitor
Dept. of Insurance, Commissioner's Office
PO Box 94214, Capitol Station
Baton Rouge, LA 70804-9214
Phone: (504)342-5338
Phone: (504)342-5900

Credential Type: License. **Duration of License:** Two years. **Requirements:** Must abide by applicable laws, rules and regulations. **Examination:** Written examination required for property and casualty insurance; life, health, and accident insurance; and variable annuity insurance. **Reciprocity:** Yes. **Fees:** $10—$65 license fees (varies with lines). $10—$65 renewal fees (varies with lines).

Maine

3819

Insurance Agent
Bureau of Insurance
Dept. of Professional and Financial Regulation
State House Station 34
Augusta, ME 04333
Phone: (207)582-8707
Fax: (207)582-8716

Credential Type: Resident Agent License. **Duration of License:** One or two years. **Authorization:** Licenses are issued for the following lines of insurance: Permanent General Lines, Credit Life, Permanent Life, Limited Auto, and Travel and Baggage. **Requirements:** Contact licensing body for application information. **Fees:** $15 application fee.

Credential Type: Nonresident Agent License. **Duration of License:** One or two years. **Authorization:** Licenses are issued for the following lines of insurance: Permanent General Lines, Credit Life, Permanent Life, Limited Auto, and Travel and Baggage. **Requirements:** Contact licensing body for application information. **Fees:** Fees are based on state of residence.

3820

Insurance Broker
Bureau of Insurance
Dept. of Professional and Financial Regulation
State House Station 34
Augusta, ME 04333
Phone: (207)582-8707
Fax: (207)582-8716

Credential Type: Resident Broker License. **Duration of License:** One or two years. **Authorization:** Licenses are issued for the following lines of insurance: Life-Health and/or Property-Casualty. **Requirements:** Contact licensing body for application information. Post $2500 bond per line. **Fees:** $35 license fee (one year). $70 license fee (two years).

Credential Type: Nonresident Broker License. **Duration of License:** One or two years. **Authorization:** Licenses are issued for the following lines of insurance: Life-Health and/or Property-Casualty. **Requirements:** Contact licensing body for application information. Post $2500 bond per line. **Fees:** $75 license fee (one year). $150 license fee (two years).

3821

Insurance Consultant
Bureau of Insurance
Dept. of Professional and Financial Regulation
State House Station 34
Augusta, ME 04333
Phone: (207)582-8707
Fax: (207)582-8716

Credential Type: Insurance Consultant License. **Requirements:** Contact licensing body for application information.

Maryland

3822

Insurance Adviser
Insurance Div.
Dept. of Licensing and Regulation
501 St. Paul Pl.
Baltimore, MD 21202-2272
Phone: (410)333-4057
Phone: (410)659-4055

Credential Type: Adviser's License (Life or Health Lines). **Duration of License:** Two years. **Requirements:** Have at least three years experience in the life and health field of insurance. **Examination:** Adviser's Life & Health Examination. **Exemptions:** Exam not required of Certified Life Underwriter (CLU) in good standing. **Fees:** $33 preregistered exam fee.

Credential Type: Adviser's License (Property or Casualty Lines). **Duration of License:** Two years. **Requirements:** Have at least three years experience in the property and casualty field of insurance. **Examination:** Adviser's Property and Casualty Examination. **Exemptions:** Exam not required of Chartered Property and Casualty Underwriter (CPCU) in good standing. **Fees:** $33 preregistered exam fee.

3823

Insurance Agent
Insurance Div.
Dept. of Licensing and Regulation
501 St. Paul Pl.
Baltimore, MD 21202-2272
Phone: (410)333-4057
Phone: (410)659-4055

Credential Type: Resident Agent License (Life or Health Lines). **Duration of License:** Two years. **Requirements:** Must be a Maryland resident or a resident of another state with a place of business in Maryland. Minimum of 60 hours of study, with at least 30 hours in company or individual training. Must be sponsored by a Life/Health Insurer or Agency. **Examination:** Life and/or Accident & Health Examination(s). **Exemptions:** Exam not required of Certified Life Underwriter (CLU) in good standing. **Fees:** $30 license fee. $33 preregistered exam fee (each line). $49 walk-in exam fee (each line).

Credential Type: Resident Agent License (Property or Casualty Lines). **Duration of License:** Two years. **Requirements:** Must be a Maryland resident or a resident of another state with a place of business in Maryland. Meet one of the following sets of requirements: (1) Complete a 96-hour course of study given by an approved school. (2) Show regular employment by an insurer, agent, or broker. (3) Have held a license in property or casualty for at least one year in another state or jurisdiction. **Examination:** Property and/or Casualty Examination(s). **Exemptions:** Exam not required of Chartered Property and Casualty Underwriter (CPCU) in good standing. **Fees:** $30 license fee. $33 preregistered exam fee (each line). $49 walk-in exam fee (each line).

Credential Type: Resident Agent License (All Lines). **Duration of License:** Two years. **Requirements:** Must be a Maryland resident or a resident of another state with a place of business in Maryland. Meet all of the requirements for both Life/Health and Property/Casualty lines. Must be sponsored by a Life/Health Insurer or Agency. **Examination:** All Lines Examination. **Fees:** $30 license fee. $33 preregistered exam fee.

Credential Type: Resident Agent License (Fraternal Benefit). **Duration of License:** Two years. **Requirements:** Must be a Maryland resident or a resident of another state with a place of business in Maryland. Complete at least 60 hours of study, of which 30 hours must be by company or individual training. Must be sponsored by an Insurer or Agency. **Examination:** Fraternal Benefit Examination. **Exemptions:** Exam not required of Certified Life Underwriter (CLU) in good standing. **Fees:** $30 license fee. $33 preregistered exam fee (up to two lines). $49 walk-in exam fee (up to two lines).

Credential Type: Resident Agent License (Limited Lines). **Duration of License:** Two years. **Authorization:** Licensed limited lines are Automobile, Mortgage Guaranty, Title, Boiler and Machinery, Industrial Fire, and Fidelity and Surety. **Requirements:** Must be a Maryland resident or a resident of another state with a place of business in Maryland. Meet one of the following sets of requirements: (1) Complete a 30-hour study course given by an approved school. (2) Show regular employment by an insurer, agent, or broker. (3) Have held a license in appropriate property or casualty lines for at least one year in another state or jurisdiction. **Examination:** Limited Lines Examinations. **Fees:** $30 license fee. $33 preregistered exam fee (up to two lines). $49 walk-in exam fee (up to two lines).

Credential Type: Non-resident Agent License. **Duration of License:** Two years. **Requirements:** Submit original letter of certification from home state. **Fees:** Contact commission for fees.

Maryland 3824

3824

Insurance Broker
Insurance Div.
Dept. of Licensing and Regulation
501 St. Paul Pl.
Baltimore, MD 21202-2272
Phone: (410)333-4057
Phone: (410)659-4055

Credential Type: Resident Broker License (Life or Health Lines). **Duration of License:** Two years. **Requirements:** Must be a Maryland resident or a resident of another state with a place of business in Maryland. Post $10,000 bond. Minimum of 60 hours of study, with at least 30 hours in company or individual training. Must be sponsored by a Life/Health Insurer or Agency. **Examination:** Life and/or Accident & Health Examination(s). **Exemptions:** Exam not required of Certified Life Underwriter (CLU) in good standing. **Fees:** $60 license fee. $33 preregistered exam fee (each line). $49 walk-in exam fee (each line).

Credential Type: Resident Broker License (Property or Casualty Lines). **Duration of License:** Two years. **Requirements:** Must be a Maryland resident or a resident of another state with a place of business in Maryland. Post $10,000 bond. Meet one of the following sets of requirements: (1) Complete a 96-hour course of study given by an approved school. (2) Show regular employment by an insurer, agent, or broker. (3) Have held a license in property or casualty for at least one year in another state or jurisdiction. **Examination:** Property and/or Casualty Examination(s). **Exemptions:** Exam not required of Chartered Property and Casualty Underwriter (CPCU) in good standing. **Fees:** $60 license fee. $33 preregistered exam fee (each line). $49 walk-in exam fee (each line).

Credential Type: Resident Broker License (All Lines). **Duration of License:** Two years. **Requirements:** Must be a Maryland resident or a resident of another state with a place of business in Maryland. Post $10,000 bond. Meet all of the requirements for both Life/Health and Property/Casualty lines. Must be sponsored by a Life/Health Insurer or Agency. **Examination:** All Lines Examination. **Fees:** $60 license fee. $33 preregistered exam fee.

Credential Type: Resident Broker License (Fraternal Benefit). **Duration of License:** Two years. **Requirements:** Must be a Maryland resident or a resident of another state with a place of business in Maryland. Post $10,000 bond. Complete at least 60 hours of study, of which 30 hours must be by company or individual training. Must be sponsored by an Insurer or Agency. **Examination:** Fraternal Benefit Examination. **Exemptions:** Exam not required of CLU in good standing. **Fees:** $60 license fee. $33 preregistered exam fee (up to two lines). $49 walk-in exam fee (up to two lines).

Credential Type: Resident Broker License (Limited Lines). **Duration of License:** Two years. **Authorization:** Licensed limited lines are Automobile, Mortgage Guaranty, Title, Boiler and Machinery, Industrial Fire, and Fidelity and Surety. **Requirements:** Must be a Maryland resident or a resident of another state with a place of business in Maryland. Post $10,000 bond. Meet one of the following sets of requirements: (1) Complete a 30-hour study course given by an approved school. (2) Show regular employment by an insurer, agent, or broker. (3) Have held a license in appropriate property or casualty lines for at least one year in another state or jurisdiction. **Examination:** Limited Lines Examinations. **Fees:** $60 license fee. $33 preregistered exam fee (up to two lines). $49 walk-in exam fee (up to two lines).

Credential Type: Non-resident Broker License. **Duration of License:** Two years. **Requirements:** Submit original letter of certification from home state. Post bond. **Fees:** Contact commission for fees.

Credential Type: Resident Surplus Lines Broker. **Duration of License:** Two years. **Requirements:** Must be a Licensed Resident Broker. Post $10,000 bond. **Fees:** $200 license fee.

Credential Type: Non-resident Surplus Lines Broker. **Requirements:** Must be a Licensed Broker. Submit original letter of certification from home state. Post bond. **Fees:** $200 license fee.

Massachusetts

3825

Insurance Agent
Commonwealth of Massachusetts
Div. of Insurance
280 Friend St.
Boston, MA 02114
Phone: (617)727-7189

Credential Type: Resident Agent License. **Duration of License:** Three years. **Authorization:** Licenses are issued for the following lines of insurance: Life, Accident and Health, and Property and Casualty. **Requirements:** Be at least 18 years of age. Complete an approved course of instruction or have one year of acceptable experience. Renewal requires 60 hours of continuing education during the first three years and 45 hours during subsequent three-year periods. **Examination:** ASI Examination. **Fees:** $50 license fee (minimum fee based on home state of insurance company). **Governing Statute:** Massachusetts General Laws, Chap. 175, Section 163.

Credential Type: Nonresident Agent License. **Duration of License:** Three years. **Authorization:** Licenses are issued for the following lines of insurance: Life, Accident and Health, and Property and Casualty. **Requirements:** Be at least 18 years of age. Be a licensed agent or broker in home state. Renewal requires 60 hours of continuing education during the first three years and 45 hours during subsequent three-year periods. **Fees:** $50 license fee (minimum fee based on home state). **Governing Statute:** Massachusetts General Laws, Chap. 175, Section 163.

3826

Insurance Broker
Commonwealth of Massachusetts
Div. of Insurance
280 Friend St.
Boston, MA 02114
Phone: (617)727-7189

Credential Type: Resident Broker License. **Duration of License:** Three years. **Authorization:** Licenses are issued for the following lines of insurance: Life, Accident and Health, and Property and Casualty. **Requirements:** Be at least 18 years of age. Meet one of the following sets of requirements: (1) Complete an approved course of instruction. (2) Have one year of acceptable experience. (3) Have been licensed as an agent by the Commonwealth of Massachusetts within the past 12 months.

Renewal requires 60 hours of continuing education during the first three years and 45 hours during subsequent three-year periods. **Examination:** ASI Examination. **Fees:** $200 license fee. **Governing Statute:** Massachusetts General Laws, Chap. 175, Section 166.

Credential Type: Nonresident Broker License. **Duration of License:** Three years. **Authorization:** Licenses are issued for the following lines of insurance: Life, Accident and Health, and Property and Casualty. **Requirements:** Be at least 18 years of age. Be a licensed agent or broker in home state. Renewal requires 60 hours of continuing education during the first three years and 45 hours during subsequent three-year periods. **Fees:** $200 license fee (minimum fee based on home state). **Governing Statute:** Massachusetts General Laws, Chap. 175, Section 166.

Insurance Agents and Brokers | **3831** Minnesota

Michigan

3827

Insurance Agent
Licensing Section
Insurance Bureau
Dept. of Commerce
PO Box 30220
Lansing, MI 48909
Phone: (517)373-9153

Credential Type: License. **Duration of License:** One year. **Requirements:** Be a resident of Michigan. Abide by the rules and regulations of the Michigan Insurance Bureau. **Examination:** Written exam. **Fees:** Contact bureau for fees. **Governing Statute:** Insurance Code, Act 218 of 1956, as amended.

3828

Insurance Agent, Surplus Lines
Licensing Section
Insurance Bureau
Dept. of Commerce
PO Box 30220
Lansing, MI 48909
Phone: (517)373-9153

Credential Type: License. **Duration of License:** One year. **Requirements:** Post a bond with the Michigan Insurance Bureau of $5,000 or the amount of the largest semi-annual surplus lines premium tax liability incurred in the preceding five years, whichever is greater. Have a resolution from a corporation stating that they are authorized to represent that corporation as a surplus lines agent (if the applicant will act as a surplus lines agent for that corporation). Be a Michigan licensed resident insurance agent for property and casualty and/or accident and health. Abide by the rules and regulations of the Michigan Insurance Bureau. **Examination:** Written exam. **Fees:** $10 application fee. $100 initial license fee. $100 renewal fee. **Governing Statute:** Insurance Code, Act 218 of 1956, as amended.

3829

Insurance Counselor
Licensing Section
Insurance Bureau
Dept. of Commerce
PO Box 30220
Lansing, MI 48909
Phone: (517)373-9153

Credential Type: License. **Duration of License:** One year. **Requirements:** Abide by the rules and regulations of the Michigan Insurance Bureau. **Examination:** Written exam. **Exemptions:** The examination may be partially waived for life counselors who submit with their application proof of holding the CLU, ChFC, or CFP designation; and for property and casualty counselors who submit with their application proof of holding the CPCU, CIC, or AAI designation. **Fees:** $10 application fee. $10 initial license fee. $10 renewal fee. **Governing Statute:** Insurance Code, Act 218 of 1956, as amended.

3830

Insurance Solicitor
Licensing Section
Insurance Bureau
Dept. of Commerce
PO Box 30220
Lansing, MI 48909
Phone: (517)373-9153

Credential Type: License. **Duration of License:** One year. **Requirements:** Be a resident of Michigan. Act under a written contract with the sponsoring agent or agency. Abide by the rules and regulations of the Michigan Insurance Bureau. **Examination:** Written exam. **Fees:** $10 application fee. $10 initial license fee. $10 renewal fee. **Governing Statute:** Insurance Code, Act 218 of 1956, as amended.

Minnesota

3831

Insurance Agent
Dept. of Commerce
Licensing Unit
133 E. 7th St.
St. Paul, MN 55101
Phone: (612)296-6319

Credential Type: Resident Life and Accident and Health Insurance License. **Duration of License:** One year. **Requirements:** Be at least 18 years of age. Complete at least 30 hours of classroom study in Basic Fundamentals. Complete at least 15 hours of classroom study in Life and Accident and Health.

Renewal requires 20 hours of continuing education per year. **Examination:** ASI Examination, Parts 1 and 2. **Reciprocity:** A nonresident license may be issued to an applicant who is licensed in this line in another state. **Fees:** $25 license fee. $25 renewal fee. $71 exam fee (with on-site score reporting). $41 exam fee (with regular score reporting).

Credential Type: Resident Property and Casualty Insurance License. **Duration of License:** One year. **Requirements:** Be at least 18 years of age. Complete at least 30 hours of classroom study in Basic Fundamentals. Complete at least 15 hours of classroom study in Property and Casualty.

Renewal requires 20 hours of continuing education per year. **Examination:** ASI Examination, Parts 1 and 2. **Reciprocity:** A nonresident license may be issued to an applicant who is licensed in this line in another state. **Fees:** $25 license fee. $25 renewal fee. $71 exam fee (with on-site score reporting). $41 exam fee (with regular score reporting).

Credential Type: Variable Annuity License. **Duration of License:** One year. **Requirements:** Must hold a Minnesota Life-Health-Accident license. Must have a valid Securities license.

Renewal requires 20 hours of continuing education per year. **Reciprocity:** A nonresident license may be issued to an applicant who is licensed in this line in another state. **Fees:** $25 license fee. $25 renewal fee.

Credential Type: Surplus Lines License. **Duration of License:** One year. **Requirements:** Must hold a Property-Casualty License. Post $5000 surety bond or the largest semi-annual surplus lines premium tax liability incurred by the agent, whichever is larger.

Renewal requires 20 hours of continuing education per year. **Reciprocity:** A nonresident license may be issued to an applicant who is licensed in this line in another state. **Fees:** $150 license fee. $150 renewal fee.

Credential Type: Farm Property and Liability License. **Duration of License:** One year. **Requirements:** Submit application and pay fees.

Renewal requires 20 hours of continuing education per year. **Examination:** ASI Examination, parts 1 and 2. **Reciprocity:** A nonresident license may be issued to an applicant who is licensed in this line in another state. **Fees:** $25 license fee. $25 renewal fee. $41 exam fee.

Credential Type: Title Insurance License. **Duration of License:** One year. **Requirements:** Submit application and pay fees.

Renewal requires 20 hours of continuing education per year. **Reciprocity:** A nonresident license may be issued to an applicant who is licensed in this line in another state. **Fees:** $25 license fee. $25 renewal fee.

Credential Type: Travel-Baggage Insurance License. **Duration of License:** One year. **Requirements:** Submit application and pay fees.

Renewal requires 20 hours of continuing education per year. **Reciprocity:** A nonresident license may be issued to an applicant

Insurance Agent, continued

who is licensed in this line in another state. **Fees:** $25 license fee. $25 renewal fee.

Mississippi

3832

Insurance Sales Agent
Licensing Div.
Insurance Dept.
PO Box 79
Jackson, MS 39205
Phone: (601)359-3582

Credential Type: Life, Health and Accident, or Hospital Agents License. **Duration of License:** One year. **Requirements:** Comply with 40-hour pre-licensing requirement. Variable contracts may be added to a current license in the life line of insurance by passing appropriate NASD examination and paying certificate of authority fees. **Examination:** Written examination. **Exemptions:** Credit life and health and accident agents need not take examination. **Reciprocity:** Non-resident agents may be licensed by submitting application and proof of current certification from home state and paying fees. **Fees:** $30 exam fee. $20 privilege tax license fee. $10 certificate of authority fee (local agents). $15 certificate of authority fee (general, district agent, or manager).

Credential Type: Managing General Agent License. **Duration of License:** One year. **Authorization:** Does not entitle agent or corporation to directly solicit from the public. Issued to a manager, trustee, or administrator who may serve in an administrative capacity in behalf of insurance companies listed on the application. **Requirements:** Submit application with letter of appointment from each insurance company listed on the application. **Fees:** $100 privilege tax license fee (corporation). $50 privilege tax license fee (individual).

Credential Type: Property and Casualty Agent License. **Duration of License:** One year. **Requirements:** Submit application and pay fees. **Examination:** Written examination. **Reciprocity:** Non-resident license may be issued by submitting application and paying appropriate fees. Certificates of authority are not issued to non-residents. **Fees:** $30 exam fee. $25 privilege tax license fee. $10 certificate of authority fee (local agents). $15 certificate of authority fee (general, district agent, or manager).

Credential Type: Land Title Agent License. **Duration of License:** One year. **Requirements:** Submit application and pay fees. License fee not required if already licensed as a fire and casualty agent or a practicing attorney. **Fees:** $25 privilege tax license fee. $10 certificate of authority fee (local agents). $15 certificate of authority fee (general, district agent, or manager).

Credential Type: Legal Insurance Agent License. **Duration of License:** One year. **Requirements:** Submit application and pay license fee. No certificate of authority is required. **Fees:** $10 privilege tax license fee.

3833

Insurance Solicitor
Licensing Div.
Insurance Dept.
PO Box 79
Jackson, MS 39205
Phone: (601)359-3582

Credential Type: Solicitor's License. **Duration of License:** One year. **Authorization:** Issued for full line and limited property and casualty lines. **Requirements:** Submit application and pay fees. **Examination:** Written examination. **Fees:** $30 exam fee. $25 privilege tax license fee. $2 certificate of appointment fee.

Missouri

3834

Insurance Agent
Dept. of Insurance
PO Box 690
Jefferson City, MO 65102-0690
Phone: (314)751-4126

Credential Type: Agent License. **Duration of License:** Two years. **Authorization:** Licenses are issued for the following lines or combinations of insurance: Life, Life (Vairable Contract), Accident and Health, General Casualty, Fire and Allied Lines, Title, Restricted to Credit, Restricted to Travel, Crop. **Requirements:** Complete an approved course of instruction within the past year. Applicants with CPCU and CLU designations are considerd to have met pre-licensing education requirements for relevant lines. Renewal of life-health and fire-casualty licenses requires 10 hours of continuing education every two years. **Examination:** ITC Examination. **Exemptions:** No exam required for title, credit, or travel lines. **Reciprocity:** Yes. **Fees:** $25 license fee. $25 renewal fee.

3835

Insurance Broker
Dept. of Insurance
PO Box 690
Jefferson City, MO 65102-0690
Phone: (314)751-4126

Credential Type: Broker License. **Duration of License:** Two years. **Authorization:** Licenses are issued for the following lines or combinations of insurance: Life, Life (Vairable Contract), Accident and Health, General Casualty, Fire and Allied Lines, Title, Restricted to Credit, Restricted to Travel, Crop. **Requirements:** Complete an approved course of instruction within the past year. Applicants with CPCU and CLU designations are considerd to have met pre-licensing education requirements for relevant lines. Renewal of life-health and fire-casualty licenses requires 10 hours of continuing education every two years. **Examination:** ITC Examination. **Reciprocity:** Yes. **Fees:** $100 license fee. $100 renewal fee.

Montana

3836

Insurance Agent
Montana Insurance Dept.
PO Box 4009
Helena, MT 59604
Phone: (406)444-2040

Credential Type: Agent License. **Duration of License:** One year. **Requirements:** 18 years of age. Experience or training in the type of insurance for which licensure is sought. Appointment as an agent by a licensed employer. **Examination:** Written. **Fees:** $15 exam fee. $15 license fee. $10 appointment fee. $10 renewal fee. **Governing Statute:** Montana Code Annotated 33-17-201 through 33-17-232.

3837

Insurance Solicitor
Montana Insurance Dept.
PO Box 4009
Helena, MT 59604
Phone: (406)444-2040

Credential Type: Agent License. **Duration of License:** One year. **Requirements:** 18 years of age. Experience or training in the type of insurance for which licensure is sought. Appointment as a solicitor by a licensed employer. **Examination:** Written. **Fees:** $15 exam fee. $15 license fee. $10 renewal fee. **Governing Statute:** Montana Code Annotated 33-17-201 through 33-17-232.

Insurance Agents and Brokers

Nebraska

3838

Insurance Agent
Nebraska Dept. of Insurance
941 "O" St., Ste. 400
Lincoln, NE 68508
Phone: (402)471-2201

Credential Type: License. **Duration of License:** One year. **Requirements:** Must meet a five year education requirement in insurance-related courses that are approved by the state within five years of the initial license issue date. **Examination:** Yes. **Fees:** $10 renewal fee. $15—$70 examination fee.

Nevada

3839

Insurance Agent
Nevada State Dept. of Commerce
Insurance Div.
Capitol Complex, 1665 Hot Springs Rd.
Carson City, NV 89710
Phone: (702)687-4270

Credential Type: License. **Requirements:** State residency. 18 years of age. Obtain a fingerprint card from the local police. **Examination:** Yes. **Fees:** $82 exam fee. $78 license fee. $15 Recovery Fund fee. $5 Notice of Appointment fee.

New Hampshire

3840

Insurance Agent
New Hampshire Insurance Dept.
169 Manchester St.
Concord, NH 03301
Phone: (603)271-2261

Credential Type: Insurance Agent License. **Duration of License:** One year. **Requirements:** Resident of New Hampshire or another state that honors New Hampshire licenses. Submit application and pass examination. **Examination:** Examination administered by the Insurance Testing Corporation (ITC). **Reciprocity:** Yes, with a valid license. **Fees:** $15 (per line) application fee. $10 (per line) resident license fee. $10 renewal fee. $5 express registration fee. $63 New Hampshire Laws and Regulations fee. $63 Life or Accident/Health Exam fee. $77 Life, Accident, & Health Exam fee. $77 Property & Casualty Exam Fee. $63 Physical Damage/Mechanical Breakdown Exam fee. $63 Home Warranty Exam fee. $63 Pre-Need Funeral Exam fee. $63 Title Insurance Exam fee. $63 Travel Accident/Baggage Exam fee.

3841

Insurance Broker
New Hampshire Insurance Dept.
169 Manchester St.
Concord, NH 03301
Phone: (603)271-2261

Credential Type: Insurance Broker License. **Duration of License:** Two years. **Requirements:** Good moral character. Submit application which must include the following information: age; sex; domicile; line or lines of insurance applicant will be working in; and place of business. **Examination:** Examination administered by the Insurance Testing Corporation (ITC). **Reciprocity:** Yes, with similar license, application, certificate of insurance from home state, and appropriate fees. **Fees:** $15 application fee. $30 resident license fee. $30 biennial renewal fee. $5 express registration fee. $63 New Hampshire Laws and Regulations Exam fee. $63 Life or Accident/Health Exam fee. $77 Life, Accident, & Health Exam fee. $77 Property & Casualty Exam Fee.

3842

Insurance Consultant
New Hampshire Insurance Dept.
169 Manchester St.
Concord, NH 03301
Phone: (603)271-2261

Credential Type: Insurance Consultant License. **Duration of License:** One year. **Requirements:** Good moral character. Submit application which must include the following information: age; sex; domicile; line or lines of insurance applicant will be working in; and place of business. **Examination:** Examination administered by the Insurance Testing Corporation (ITC). **Reciprocity:** Yes, with a similar license. **Fees:** $15 application fee. $30 resident license fee. $5 express registration fee. $63 New Hampshire Laws and Regulations Exam fee. $63 Life or Accident/Health Exam fee. $77 Life, Accident, & Health Exam fee. $77 Property & Casualty Exam Fee.

3843

Surplus Lines Insurance Agent
New Hampshire Insurance Dept.
169 Manchester St.
Concord, NH 03301
Phone: (603)271-2261

Credential Type: Surplus Lines Agent License. **Duration of License:** One year. **Requirements:** Submit application and pay fees. New Hampshire resident. Hold a license as a Property & Casualty Agent. **Reciprocity:** No. **Fees:** $15 application fee. $100 resident license fee. $50 annual renewal fee.

New Jersey

3844

Insurance Agent
New Jersey Dept. of Insurance
License Processing
CN327
Trenton, NJ 08625-0327
Phone: (609)292-4337

Credential Type: Insurance Producer License. **Requirements:** 18 years of age. Must reside or engage in business in the state. Completion of an approved course. No convictions for a crime involving moral turpitude. **Examination:** Written. **Reciprocity:** Yes. **Fees:** $328 application fee. **Governing Statute:** NJSA 17:22A. NJAC 11:17.

New Mexico

3845

Insurance Agent
State Dept. of Insurance
Pera Bldg., Rm. 434
PO Drawer 1269
Santa Fe, NM 87504-1269
Phone: (505)827-4500

Credential Type: Resident Agent License. **Duration of License:** One year. **Authorization:** Licenses are granted for different lines of insurance. **Requirements:** Contact licensing body for application information. Renewal requires 15 hours of continuing education, except for title insurance, which requires seven hours. **Examination:** New Mexico Insurance Examination. **Fees:** $30 license fee. $20 agent appointment fee per class. $50 exam fee per line.

Credential Type: Nonresident Agent License. **Duration of License:** One year. **Requirements:** Submit application, notice of agent or solicitor appointment, and original certificate of license state from home state

New Mexico

Insurance Agent, continued

insurance department. **Fees:** $30 license fee (for all states except AK, CA, DC, IL, MT, NJ, NV, WI, WY, which are retaliatory). $20 agent appointment fee per class.

3846

Insurance Broker
State Dept. of Insurance
Pera Bldg., Rm. 434
PO Drawer 1269
Santa Fe, NM 87504-1269
Phone: (505)827-4500

Credential Type: Resident Broker License. **Duration of License:** One year. **Requirements:** Contact licensing body for application information. **Examination:** New Mexico Insurance Examination.

Credential Type: Nonresident Broker License. **Duration of License:** One year. **Authorization:** A nonresident broker license is required if individual is in the employ of a licensed agent or insurance company licensed to transact business in New Mexico. **Requirements:** Submit application and original certificate of license state from home state insurance department. May need to post bond depending on state of residence. Renewal requires 15 hours of continuing education, except for title insurance, which requires seven hours. **Fees:** Retaliatory license fee based on state of residence.

3847

Insurance Solicitor
State Dept. of Insurance
Pera Bldg., Rm. 434
PO Drawer 1269
Santa Fe, NM 87504-1269
Phone: (505)827-4500

Credential Type: Resident Solicitor License. **Duration of License:** One year. **Authorization:** Licenses are granted for different lines of insurance. **Requirements:** Contact licensing body for application information. Renewal requires 15 hours of continuing education, except for title insurance, which requires seven hours. **Examination:** New Mexico Insurance Examination. **Fees:** $30 license fee. $20 agent appointment fee per class. $50 exam fee per line.

New York

3848

General Insurance Consultant
New York State Insurance Dept.
Licensing Unit
Agency Bldg. One
Empire State Plaza
Albany, NY 12257
Phone: (518)474-7159

Credential Type: License. **Duration of License:** One year. **Requirements:** Interest in property and casualty insurance. **Examination:** Written. **Fees:** $50 exam fee. $50—$100 license fee. $50—$100 renewal fee. **Governing Statute:** Section 2017 and 2119 of the Insurance Law.

3849

Insurance Agent, General Property and Casualty
New York State Insurance Dept.
Licensing Unit
Agency Bldg. One
Empire State Plaza
Albany, NY 12257
Phone: (518)474-6630

Credential Type: License. **Duration of License:** Two years. **Requirements:** Completion of an approved 90-hour agents and brokers insurance training course. 18 years of age. **Examination:** Property & Casualty Agent Exam. **Reciprocity:** All states for licensed non-residents. **Fees:** $22—$54 exam fee. $40 license fee. $40 renewal fee. **Governing Statute:** Section 2103 of the Insurance Law.

3850

Insurance Agent, Life Insurance, Variable Annuities, Accident and Health
New York State Insurance Dept.
Licensing Unit
Agency Bldg. One
Empire State Plaza
Albany, NY 12257
Phone: (518)474-6630

Credential Type: License. **Duration of License:** Two years. **Requirements:** Completion of an approved 40-hour life accident and health insurance training course. 18 years of age. **Examination:** Life, Accident and Health exam. **Reciprocity:** All states for licensed non-residents. **Fees:** $22—$74 exam fee. $40 license fee. $40 renewal fee plus $40 for each sub-license. **Governing Statute:** Section 2103(a) of the Insurance Law.

3851

Insurance Agent, Mortgage Guaranty
New York State Insurance Dept.
Licensing Unit
Agency Bldg. One
Empire State Plaza
Albany, NY 12257
Phone: (518)474-7159

Credential Type: License. **Requirements:** Completion of an approved 90-hour agents and brokers insurance training course. **Examination:** General Agent/Broker Exam. **Reciprocity:** All states for licensed non-residents. **Fees:** $20 exam fee. **Governing Statute:** Section 6505 of the Insurance Law.

3852

Insurance Broker
New York State Insurance Dept.
Licensing Unit
Agency Bldg. One
Empire State Plaza
Albany, NY 12257
Phone: (518)474-4570

Credential Type: License. **Duration of License:** Two years. **Requirements:** Completion of an approved 90-hour agents and brokers insurance training course. 21 years of age. **Examination:** Property & Casualty Agent exam. **Reciprocity:** All states for licensed non-residents. **Fees:** $22—$74 exam fee. $40 license fee. $40 renewal fee. **Governing Statute:** Section 2104 of the Insurance Law.

3853

Life Insurance Consultant
New York State Insurance Dept.
Licensing Unit
Agency Bldg. One
Empire State Plaza
Albany, NY 12257
Phone: (518)474-7159

Credential Type: License. **Duration of License:** One year. **Examination:** Written. **Fees:** $50 exam fee. $50 application fee plus $50 for each additional sub-license. $50 renewal fee plus $50 for each additional sub-license. **Governing Statute:** Section 2107 and 2119 of the Insurance Law.

Insurance Agents and Brokers

North Carolina

3854

Insurance Agent
Dept. of Insurance
Agent Services Div.
PO Box 26267
Raleigh, NC 27611
Phone: (919)733-7487

Credential Type: License. **Duration of License:** Permanent. **Requirements:** Attendance at an approved pre-licensing study course. 18 years of age. **Examination:** Written. **Fees:** $10 registration fee. $16 exam fee.

North Dakota

3855

Insurance Agent
Dept. of Insurance
600 E. Blvd.
Bismarck, ND 58505
Phone: (701)224-2440

Credential Type: Resident Agent License. **Duration of License:** Perpetual. **Authorization:** Licenses are issued for different lines of insurance. **Requirements:** Comply with pre-licensure requirement of eight classroom hours of education for each line of insurance, to be completed within six months of application. Must meet continuing education requirement of 15 hours per year. **Examination:** Yes. **Fees:** $10 license fee (per line). $10 appointment fee (per company).

Credential Type: Nonresident Agent License. **Authorization:** Licenses are issued for different lines of insurance. **Requirements:** Submit application and current letter of certification from home state. Must meet continuing education requirement of 15 hours per year. **Fees:** Fees are based on state of residence.

3856

Insurance Broker
Dept. of Insurance
600 E. Blvd.
Bismarck, ND 58505
Phone: (701)224-2440

Credential Type: Resident Broker License. **Duration of License:** Perpetual. **Authorization:** Licenses are issued for different lines of insurance. **Requirements:** Must have two years of experience. Post $2000 broker's bond. Must concurrently hold a license with at least one company. Must meet continuing education requirement of 15 hours per year. **Fees:** $10 license fee.

Credential Type: Nonresident Broker License. **Requirements:** Submit application and current letter of certification from home state. Must have two years of experience. Post minimum of $2000 broker's bond (may be more depending on state of residence). Must concurrently hold a nonresident license with at least one company. Must meet continuing education requirement of 15 hours per year. **Fees:** Fees are based on state of residence.

Ohio

3857

Insurance Agent
Licensing Div.
Dept. of Insurance
2100 Stella Ct.
Columbus, OH 43266-0566
Phone: (614)644-2665

Credential Type: Insurance Agent License. **Duration of License:** One year. **Authorization:** Separate licenses are issued for specific lines of insurance. **Requirements:** Pre-licensing education consisting of 40 hours of training is required for licenses in the following lines of insurance: Life, Accident and Health, Variable Annuity, Accident and Health (HMO), Multiple Lines—Property and Casualty. **Examination:** An Insurance Testing Corporation (ITC) examination is required for the following lines of insurance: Fire and Casualty; Pre-paid Dental; Fire Only; Fire Auto; Casualty (includes Surety and Accident and Health, if company is qualified); Variable Annuity; Life and Accident and Health; Title; Health Maintenance Organization (HMO); Health Care Corporation; Reciprocal Agent; Dental Care; Medical Care. **Exemptions:** No exam is required for a license in the following lines of insurance: Variable Annuity (nonresident), Accident and Health (nonresident), Life and Accident and Health (nonresident), Fraternal (nonresident), Fraternal, Special Representative, Reciprocal Attorney. **Reciprocity:** Yes, provided proof of certification is submitted. **Fees:** $10 application fee. $20 license fee. $20 renewal fee. **Governing Statute:** Ohio Revised Code 3901.01. Ohio Insurance and Administrative Code.

3858

Insurance Solicitor
Licensing Div.
Dept. of Insurance
2100 Stella Ct.
Columbus, OH 43266-0566
Phone: (614)644-2665

Credential Type: Insurance Solicitor License (Accident and Health). **Duration of License:** One year. **Requirements:** Pre-licensing education consisting of 40 hours of training is required. **Examination:** Insurance Testing Corporation (ITC) examination. **Reciprocity:** Yes, provided proof of certification is submitted. **Fees:** $10 application fee. $20 license fee. $20 renewal fee. **Governing Statute:** Ohio Revised Code 3901.01. Ohio Insurance and Administrative Code.

Credential Type: Insurance Solicitor License (Fire, Casualty, Surety, Accident and Health). **Duration of License:** One year. **Requirements:** Pre-licensing education consisting of 40 hours of training is required. **Examination:** Insurance Testing Corporation (ITC) examination. **Reciprocity:** Yes, provided proof of certification is submitted. **Fees:** $10 application fee. $20 license fee. $20 renewal fee. **Governing Statute:** Ohio Revised Code 3901.01. Ohio Insurance and Administrative Code.

Oklahoma

3859

Insurance Agent
State of Oklahoma Insurance Commission
1901 N. Walnut
PO Box 53408
Oklahoma City, OK 73152
Phone: (405)521-3916

Credential Type: License. **Duration of License:** One year. **Requirements:** 18 years of age. 18 clock hours of continuing education every three years. **Examination:** Insurance Agents Exam. **Fees:** $30—$40 exam fee. $15—$100 license fee. $15—$100 renewal fee.

Oklahoma 3860

3860

Insurance Consultant
State of Oklahoma Insurance Commission
Agents Licensing Div.
1901 N. Walnut
PO Box 53408
Oklahoma City, OK 73152
Phone: (405)521-3916

Credential Type: License. **Duration of License:** One year. **Requirements:** 18 years of age. No felony convictions. **Examination:** Insurance Consultant's Exam. **Fees:** $40 exam fee. $50 application fee. $50 renewal fee.

3861

Insurance Representative (Limited)
Oklahoma State Insurance Commission
1901 N. Walnut
PO Box 53408
Oklahoma City, OK 73152
Phone: (405)521-3916

Credential Type: License. **Duration of License:** One year. **Requirements:** 18 years of age. No felony convictions. **Examination:** Limited Insurance Representatives Exam. **Fees:** $30 exam fee. $20 application fee. $20 renewal fee.

Oregon

3862

Insurance Agent
Insurance Div.
Labor & Industries Bldg., Rm. 440
Salem, OR 97310
Phone: (503)378-4511

Credential Type: License. **Duration of License:** Two years. **Requirements:** Residence or place of business in Oregon. Good moral character. Must complete pre-licensing training: 40 hours property and casualty; 30 hours life; 12 hours health; 12 hours code. **Examination:** Yes. **Fees:** $99 Life and Health exam. $99 Property/Casualty exam. $60 license fee. $60 renewal fee. **Governing Statute:** ORS 744.005 to 744.405.

3863

Insurance Consultant
Insurance Div.
Labor & Industries Bldg., Rm. 440
Salem, OR 97310
Phone: (503)378-4511

Credential Type: License. **Duration of License:** Two years. **Requirements:** Residence or place of business in Oregon. Five years of insurance experience or equivalent educational qualifications. Must have a $5,000 bond and errors and omissions insurance with limits not less than $1 million per occurrence. **Examination:** Yes. **Fees:** $99 for Life and Health exam fee. $99 for Property/Casualty exam fee. $60 license fee. $60 renewal fee. **Governing Statute:** ORS 744.605.

3864

Non-Resident Agent
Dept. of Insurance and Finance, Insurance Div.
Labor & Industries Bldg., Rm. 440
Salem, OR 97310
Phone: (503)378-4511

Credential Type: License. **Duration of License:** Two years. **Requirements:** Cannot be a resident of Oregon or have a firm which transacts insurance business in Oregon. Must be licensed in home state for classes of insurance applying for in Oregon. The state must be one with which Oregon has a reciprocal agreement. **Fees:** $60 license fee. $60 renewal fee. **Governing Statute:** ORS 744.055.

3865

Surplus Line Agent
Insurance Div.
Labor & Industries Bldg., Rm. 440
Salem, OR 97310
Phone: (503)378-4511

Credential Type: License. **Requirements:** Must be a resident General Lines Agent and file a $50,000 bond. **Examination:** Yes. **Fees:** $81 exam fee. $60 license fee. **Governing Statute:** ORS 735.400 to 735.495.

Pennsylvania

3866

Insurance Agent
State Insurance Dept.
Div. of Agents and Brokers
1300 Strawberry Sq.
Harrisburg, PA 17120
Phone: (717)787-3840

Credential Type: Resident Agent License. **Authorization:** Licenses are issued for the following lines of insurance: Life and Health, Property, Casualty, and Miscellaneous. **Requirements:** Be at least 18 years of age. Possess requisite competence, general fitness, and integrity of character. Be able to read and write English. **Examination:** ITC Examination. **Exemptions:** No exam required for applicants with CLU or CPCU designations. Attorneys applying for title insurance license need not take exam. **Fees:** License fees are billed to sponsoring company. Exam fees vary.

Credential Type: Resident Surplus Lines Agent License. **Requirements:** Be currently licensed in Pennsylvania as a resident property and casualty broker. Post surety bond of $25,000. **Examination:** Surplus Lines Examination. **Fees:** $10 application fee. $100 license fee. $10 certification fee per certificate of eligibility.

Credential Type: Nonresident Agent License. **Requirements:** Must be licensed in home state for same lines as are being applied for. Must have qualified for license by passing a written examination or have been licensed prior to home state's requirement of a written examination. **Examination:** ITC Examination. **Exemptions:** Exam will be waived if home state grants a waiver of examination to Pennsylvania agents.

3867

Insurance Broker
State Insurance Dept.
Div. of Agents and Brokers
1300 Strawberry Sq.
Harrisburg, PA 17120
Phone: (717)787-3840

Credential Type: Resident Broker License. **Authorization:** Licenses are issued for the following lines of insurance: Life and Health, Property and Casualty. **Requirements:** Be at least 18 years of age. Possess requisite competence, general fitness, and integrity of character. Be able to read and write English. Meet one of the following sets of requirements: (1) Be currently licensed and have been continuously licensed as an agent for the past two years. (2) Be currently licensed and have been continuously licensed as a broker in another state for the past two years. **Examination:** ITC Examination. **Exemptions:** No exam required for applicants with CLU designation.

Credential Type: Nonresident Broker License. **Requirements:** Must be licensed in home state for same lines as are being applied for. Must have qualified for license by passing a written examination or have been licensed prior to home state's requirement of a written examination. **Examination:** ITC Examination. **Exemptions:** Exam will be waived if home state grants a waiver of examination to Pennsylvania brokers.

Rhode Island

3868

Insurance Agent
Office of the Insurance
 Commissioner
Insurance Div.
Rhode Island Dept. of Business
 Regulation
233 Richmond St.
Providence, RI 02903
Phone: (401)277-2223

Credential Type: Marine, Casualty, or Surety Insurance License. **Duration of License:** Three years. **Requirements:** At least 18 years of age. New Hampshire resident for casualty line. Must pass a screening by the State Police Bureau of Criminal Identification. Complete approved instruction in insurance or have at least one year experience as an underwriter, field representative, solicitor, agent, or subagent of an insurance agent or broker. Alternative requirements are available through licensing agency. **Examination:** Written examination. **Reciprocity:** Yes. **Fees:** $10 application fee. $25 license fee. $75 renewal fee.

Credential Type: Life and Health Insurance License. **Duration of License:** Three years. **Requirements:** At least 18 years of age. Must pass a screening by the State Police Bureau of Criminal Identification. Meet one of the following requirements: (1) Complete 40 hours of appropriate approved classroom study and receive certification; (2) Complete bachelor's degree in insurance from an accredited school; (3) Have CLU designation. Alternative requirements are available through licensing agency. **Examination:** Written examination. **Reciprocity:** Yes. **Fees:** $10 application fee. $25 license fee. $75 renewal fee.

3869

Insurance Broker
Office of the Insurance
 Commissioner
Insurance Div.
Rhode Island Dept. of Business
 Regulation
233 Richmond St.
Providence, RI 02903
Phone: (401)277-2223

Credential Type: Insurance Broker License. **Duration of License:** Three years. **Requirements:** At least 18 years of age. Complete approved course work which must include instruction in general casualty insurance. Pass a screening by the State Police Bureau of Criminal Identification. Brokers dealing in insurance, other than life insurance, must post $1,000 bond. **Examination:** Written examination. **Reciprocity:** Yes. **Fees:** $10 application fee. $50 license fee. $150 renewal fee.

3870

Insurance Solicitor
Office of the Insurance
 Commissioner
Insurance Div.
Rhode Island Dept. of Business
 Regulation
233 Richmond St.
Providence, RI 02903
Phone: (401)277-2223

Credential Type: Insurance Solicitor License. **Duration of License:** Three years. **Authorization:** May solicit business, quote prices, and complete applications. Not authorized to sign policies. **Requirements:** At least 18 years of age. Pass a screening by the State Police Bureau of Criminal Identification. **Reciprocity:** No. **Fees:** $10 application fee. $25 license fee. $75 renewal fee.

3871

Surplus Line Broker (Insurance)
Office of Insurance Commissioner
Insurance Div.
Rhode Island Dept. of Business
 Regulation
233 Richmond St.
Providence, RI 02903
Phone: (401)277-2223

Credential Type: Surplus Line Broker License. **Duration of License:** One year. **Requirements:** At least 18 years of age. Hold a valid insurance agent license. Post a $5,000 bond. **Reciprocity:** Yes. **Fees:** $50 license fee. $50 renewal fee.

South Carolina

3872

Insurance Agent
South Carolina Dept. of Insurance
1612 Marion St.
PO Box 100105
Columbia, SC 29201
Phone: (803)737-6110

Credential Type: License. **Requirements:** 18 years of age. Sponsored by an insurer and licensed for the lines of insurance for which the company appoints the applicant. U.S. citizenship or a properly registered alien.

South Dakota

3873

Insurance Agent
Commerce and Regulations Dept.
Insurance Div.
Insurance Bldg.
910 E. Sioux
Pierre, SD 57501
Phone: (605)773-4104
Phone: (605)773-3563
Fax: (605)773-5369

Credential Type: Agent License. **Requirements:** Contact licensing body for application information.

Tennessee

3874

Insurance Agent
Dept. of Commerce and Insurance
500 James Robertson Pky.
Nashville, TN 37219
Phone: (615)741-2693

Credential Type: License. **Duration of License:** One year. **Requirements:** 18 years old. Must have some experience. 20 hours of prelicensing education. 25 hours of continuing education per year (for the first four years). **Examination:** Yes. **Reciprocity:** Yes, except Hawaii **Fees:** $25 Examination. $50 Application. $25 Renewal.

Texas

3875

Insurance Agent
Texas Dept. of Insurance,
  Applications, MC 107-1A
PO Box 149104
Austin, TX 78714
Phone: (512)322-3503

Credential Type: License. **Duration of License:** Two years. **Requirements:** Texas residency. 18 years of age. Forty hours pre-licensing education for a Group 1 license. Study at an approved classroom insurance course; or study with an approved company or agents association school; or study with an approved correspondence course; or four years of college with a major in insurance. 15 hours continuing education per year. **Examination:** Written. **Fees:** $50—$60 application fee. $27 or more exam fee. $48 renewal fee. **Governing Statute:** Insurance Code 21.07, 21.07-1, 21.14.

Utah

3876

Insurance Agent
Utah State Insurance Dept.
3110 State Office Bldg.
Salt Lake City, UT 84114
Phone: (801)538-3855

Credential Type: Insurance agent license. **Requirements:** Must be 18 years of age. Must complete an approved state pre-license study program. Pass license examination. **Examination:** Yes. **Fees:** $61 examination-combined license fee. $55 examination-single line fee. $40 resident license fee. $30 non-resident license fee.

3877

Insurance Broker
Utah State Insurance Dept.
3110 State Office Bldg.
Salt Lake City, UT 84114
Phone: (801)538-3855

Credential Type: Insurance broker license. **Requirements:** Must be 18 years of age. Must complete an approved state pre-license study program. Pass license examination. Must have been an insurance agent in the same license class for at least two years during the three years immediately preceding the date of application or have been regularly employed for that period by an insurer in a capacity which would provide the person with comparable preparation to act as an insurance broker. **Examination:** Yes. **Fees:** $61 examination-combined license fee. $55 examination-single line fee. $40 license fee.

3878

Insurance Consultant
Utah State Insurance Dept.
3110 State Office Bldg.
Salt Lake City, UT 84114
Phone: (801)538-3855

Credential Type: Insurance consultant license. **Requirements:** Must be 18 years of age. Must complete an approved state pre-license study program. Pass license examination. Must have three years experience out of the last five years in the lines of insurance in which he or she plans to consult. **Examination:** Yes. **Fees:** $61 examination-combined license fee. $55 examination-single line fee. $40 license fee.

3879

Insurance Surplus Line Broker
Utah State Insurance Dept.
3110 State Office Bldg.
Salt Lake City, UT 84114
Phone: (801)538-3855

Credential Type: Surplus line broker's license. **Requirements:** Must be 18 years of age. Must complete an approved state pre-license study program. Pass license examination. Must have been an agent in the same license class for a period totalling not less than three years during the four years immediately preceding the date of application or have been regularly employed for that period by an insurer in a capacity which would provide the person with comparable preparation to act as an insurance surplus line broker. Must also be licensed as an insurance broker. **Examination:** Yes. **Fees:** $61 examination-combined license fee. $55 examination-single line fee. $20 surplus line broker license fee.

Vermont

3880

Insurance Agent
Dept. of Banking and Insurance
120 State St.
Montpelier, VT 05602
Phone: (802)828-3301

Credential Type: License. **Duration of License:** One year. **Requirements:** 18 years of age. Resident of, or principal place of business in Vermont. Sponsored by Insurance company. Good personal and business reputation. **Examination:** Yes. **Reciprocity:** Yes. **Fees:** $20 Application fee. $20 License fee. $20 Renewal. **Governing Statute:** Title 8, VSA Sections 4791-4793, 4800 and 4801.

3881

Insurance Broker
Dept. of Banking and Insurance
120 State St.
Montpelier, VT 05602
Phone: (802)828-3301

Credential Type: License. **Duration of License:** One year. **Requirements:** 18 years of age. Good personal and business reputation. Two years experience as an insurance agent (or comparable) within past three years. Proof of employment from employer. $5,000 surety bond. **Examination:** No. **Reciprocity:** Yes. **Fees:** $40 License. $20 Application fee. $40 Renewal. **Governing Statute:** Title 8, VSA Sections 4791-4793, 4800 and 4801.

3882

Insurance Broker, Surplus lines
Dept. of Banking and Insurance
120 State St.
Montpelier, VT 05602
Phone: (802)828-3301

Credential Type: License. **Duration of License:** One year. **Requirements:** Good personal and business reputation. Licensed in Vermont as a resident Insurance Agent or Broker. Two years experience within the past three years. Proof of employment from employer. **Examination:** No. **Reciprocity:** No. **Fees:** $20,000 Bond. $200 License. $20 Application. $200 Renewal. **Governing Statute:** Title 8, VSA Sections 4791-4793, 4800 and 4801.

3883

Insurance Consultant
Dept. of Banking and Insurance
120 State St.
Montpelier, VT 05602
Phone: (802)828-3301

Credential Type: License. **Duration of License:** One year. **Requirements:** Good personal and business reputation. Must not hold any other Insurance license in any line. Obtain prior written agreement on approved form. **Examination:** Yes. **Reciprocity:** Yes. **Fees:** $5,000 Bond. $100 License. $20 Application. $100 Renewal. **Governing Statute:** Title 8, VSA Sections 4791-4793, 4800 and 4802.

Virginia

3884

Insurance Agent
State Corporation Commission
Bureau of Insurance
PO Box 1157
Richmond, VA 23209
Phone: (804)786-3741

Credential Type: License. **Requirements:** 18 years of age. Must hold a Certificate of Qualification according to the specification of the Bureau. Must complete a 45-hour training course and submit the certification of completion along with the proper application form. **Examination:** Yes.

Washington

3885

Insurance Agent
Insurance Commission
Insurance Bldg., AQ-21
Olympia, WA 98504-0321
Phone: (206)753-7307

Credential Type: Insurance Agent License. **Duration of License:** One year. **Requirements:** At least 18 years of age. Resident of Washington or proof of licensure in home state. Submit to background investigation. Submit fingerprint card. Must post bond of $20,000 for first affiliate and $5,000 for each additional. Submit Certificate of Affiliation. Continuing education is required for renewal. **Examination:** ASI Examination. **Fees:** $25 license fee. $45 examination fee (one exam). $60 examination fee (two exams). $5 filing fee. $10 fee for each Certificate of Affiliation. $10 fee for each appointment. $25 minimum for non-resident license fee.

3886

Insurance Broker
Insurance Commission
Insurance Bldg., AQ-21
Olympia, WA 98504-0321
Phone: (206)753-7307

Credential Type: Insurance Broker License. **Duration of License:** One year. **Requirements:** At least 18 years of age. Resident of Washington or proof of licensure in home state. Submit to background investigation. Must have a minimum of two years experience in the insurance field. Submit fingerprint card. Must post bond of $20,000 for first affiliate and $5,000 for each additional. Submit Certificate of Affiliation. Continuing education is required for renewal. **Examination:** ASI Examination. **Fees:** $50 license fee. $100 examination fee. $5 filing fee. $10 fee for each Certificate of Affiliation. $50 minimum for non-resident license fee.

West Virginia

3887

Insurance Agent (Non-resident)
Insurance Commissioner
2100 Washington St. E
Charleston, WV 25305
Phone: (304)348-3354

Credential Type: License. **Requirements:** 18 years old. Must be licensed in state of domicile and provide certification for type of license applied for. **Examination:** No. **Fees:** $25 License. $25 Renewal.

3888

Insurance Agent (Resident)
Insurance Commissioner
2100 Washington St. E
Charleston, WV 25305
Phone: (304)348-3354

Credential Type: License. **Duration of License:** One year. **Requirements:** 18 years old. State resident. **Examination:** Yes. **Fees:** $25 License. $25 Renewal. Examination costs depend on site.

3889

Insurance Broker (Non-resident)
Insurance Commissioner
2100 Washington St. E
Charleston, WV 25305
Phone: (304)348-3354

Credential Type: License. **Requirements:** 18 years old. Must be licensed in state of domicile and provide certification of license applied for. **Examination:** No. **Fees:** $25 License. $25 Renewal.

3890

Insurance Solicitor
Insurance Commissioner
2100 Washington St. E
Charleston, WV 25305
Phone: (304)348-3354

Credential Type: License. **Duration of License:** One year. **Requirements:** 18 years old. State resident. **Examination:** Yes. **Fees:** $25 License. $25 Renewal. Examination fees depend on site.

Wisconsin

3891

Insurance Agent
Office of the Commissioner of Insurance
Agent Licensing Section
PO Box 7872
Madison, WI 53707-7872
Phone: (608)266-7465

Credential Type: Resident Agent License. **Duration of License:** Two years. **Authorization:** Licenses are issued for the following major lines of insurance: Life, Accident and Health, Property, and Casualty. Licenses are issued for the following limited lines of insurance: Credit Life/Credit Accident and Health, Automobile, and Title. **Requirements:** Submit application and pay fee. **Examination:** ASI Examination. **Fees:** $40 license fee (one or two lines). $80 license fee (three or four lines). $10 biennial regulation fee.

Credential Type: Nonresident Agent License. **Duration of License:** Two years. **Requirements:** Must hold a valid current license in another state and submit a letter of certification from home state. **Fees:** $40 license fee (1 or two lines). $80 license fee (3 or four lines). $30 biennial regulation fee.

Wyoming

3892

Salesperson, Insurance
State Insurance Dept.
Herschler Bldg.
122 W. 25th St.
Cheyenne, WY 82002
Phone: (307)777-7310

Credential Type: License. **Duration of License:** One year. **Requirements:** 19 years of age. Good moral character. Pass background inspection. Have an appointment from an insurance company or agent that is licensed in Wyoming. Resident of Wyoming. Pass a written examination. **Examination:** Yes. **Fees:** $58 Pre-registered examination (Casper and Cheyenne), $45 in Rock Springs. $75 Walk-in examination (Casper and Cheyenne), $45 in Rock Springs. $30 License for Life and Disability insurance. $30 License for Auto, Property and Title insurance. $10 Annual company appointment. $5 Continuing Education.

Janitors and Cleaners

The following states grant licenses in this occupational category as of the date of publication:

Arkansas	Illinois	Kentucky	New Mexico	Ohio	Texas
California	Iowa	Maryland	New York	Oregon	Virginia
Delaware	Kansas	Montana	North Dakota	South Dakota	

Arkansas

3893

Jockey Room Custodian
Arkansas State Racing Commission
Ledbetter Bldg., Rm. G08
7th & Wolfe St.
PO Box 3076
Little Rock, AR 72203
Phone: (501)682-1467

Credential Type: License. **Duration of License:** One year. **Requirements:** Application approved by the Stewards. Qualified as to ability and integrity of license sought and have the endorsement of employer. 16 years of age. Never convicted of a crime. Not be habitually addicted to drugs. Not be engaged in any activity or practice which is illegal, undesirable, or detrimental to the best interest of the public or the sport of racing. **Examination:** No **Fees:** $3 License. $3 Renewal.

3894

Receiving Barn Custodian (Racing)
Arkansas State Racing Commission
Ledbetter Bldg., Rm. G08
7th & Wolfe St.
PO Box 3076
Little Rock, AR 72203
Phone: (501)862-1467

Credential Type: License. **Duration of License:** One year. **Requirements:** Application must be approved by the Stewards. Must be qualified as to ability and integrity of license sought and have the endorsement of employer. 16 years of age. Never convicted of a crime. Not be habitually addicted to drugs or intoxicated. Must not be engaged in any activity which is illegal, undesirable or detrimental to the best interest of the public and the sport of racing. **Examination:** No **Fees:** $3 License. $3 Renewal.

California

3895

Custodian (Racetrack)
California Horse Racing Board
1010 Hurley Way, Ste. 190
Sacramento, CA 95825
Phone: (916)920-7178

Credential Type: License Registration. **Requirements:** Submit application and fingerprint card. Pay fee. **Fees:** $75 registration fee.

Delaware

3896

Maintenance Employee (Racetrack)
Delaware Harness Racing Commission
2320 S. DuPont Hwy.
Dover, DE 19901
Phone: (302)739-4811

Credential Type: License Registration. **Requirements:** Submit application and fingerprint card. Pay fee. **Fees:** $5 registration fee.

Illinois

3897

Housekeeper (Gaming)
Illinois Gaming Board
PO Box 19474
Springfield, IL 62794-9474
Phone: (217)524-0228

Credential Type: Housekeeper License. **Duration of License:** One year. **Requirements:** At least 18 years of age. U.S. citizen or legal alien as specified by the federal employment eligibility requirement. Submit application and pay fee. **Reciprocity:** No. **Fees:** $75 application fee. $50 initial license fee. $50 renewal fee. **Governing Statute:** Illinois Revised Statutes, Chapter 120.

3898

Maintenance Manager (Gaming)
Illinois Gaming Board
PO Box 19474
Springfield, IL 62794-9474
Phone: (217)524-0228

Credential Type: Maintenance Manager License. **Authorization:** Authorizes applicant to oversee the maintenance and housekeeping departments in a gaming establishment. **Requirements:** At least 18 years of age. Supervisory experience. Previous experience in maintenance preferred. U.S. citizen or legal alien as specified by the federal employment eligibility requirement. **Reciprocity:** No. **Fees:** $75 application fee. $50 initial license fee. $50 renewal fee. **Governing Statute:** Illinois Revised Statutes, Chapter 120.

3899

Maintenance Supervisor (Gaming)
Illinois Gaming Board
PO Box 19474
Springfield, IL 62794-9474
Phone: (217)524-0228

Credential Type: Maintenance Supervisor License. **Authorization:** Authorizes applicant to oversee the maintenance and cleaning of a gaming facility and its grounds. **Requirements:** At least 18 years of age. Supervisory experience. Previous experience in maintenance preferred. U.S. citizen or legal alien as specified by the federal employment eligibility requirement. **Reciprocity:** No. **Fees:** $75 application fee. $50 initial license fee. $50 renewal fee. **Governing Statute:** Illinois Revised Statutes, Chapter 120.

3900

Maintenance Worker (Gaming)
Illinois Gaming Board
PO Box 19474
Springfield, IL 62794-9474
Phone: (217)524-0228

Credential Type: Maintenance Worker License. **Authorization:** Authorizes applicant to oversee operation of the maintenance and housekeeping departments in a gaming establishment. **Requirements:** At least 18 years of age. U.S. citizen or legal alien as specified by the federal employment eligibility requirement. Strong mechanical aptitude. Previous experience preferred. **Reciprocity:** No. **Fees:** $75 application fee. $50 initial license fee. $50 renewal fee. **Governing Statute:** Illinois Revised Statutes, Chapter 120.

Iowa

3901

Janitorial Employee (Riverboat Gambling)
Iowa Racing and Gaming Commission
Lucas State Office Bldg.
Des Moines, IA 50319
Phone: (515)281-7352

Credential Type: License Registration. **Requirements:** Submit application and pay fees. **Fees:** $10 license fee.

3902

Maintenance Employee (Racetrack)
Iowa State Racing Commission
Lucas State Office Bldg.
Des Moines, IA 50319
Phone: (515)281-7352

Credential Type: License Registration. **Requirements:** Submit application and fingerprint card. Pay fee. **Fees:** $5 registration fee.

3903

Maintenance Supervisor (Riverboat Gambling)
Iowa Racing and Gaming Commission
Lucas State Office Bldg.
Des Moines, IA 50319
Phone: (515)281-7352

Credential Type: License Registration. **Requirements:** Submit application and pay fees. **Fees:** $50 license fee.

Kansas

3904

Maintenance Employee (Racetrack)
Kansas Racing Commission
3400 VanBuren
Topeka, KS 66611-2228
Phone: (913)296-5800

Credential Type: License Registration. **Requirements:** Submit application and fingerprint card. Pay fee. **Fees:** $5 registration fee.

Kentucky

3905

Jockey Room Custodian (Racetrack)
Kentucky State Racing Commission
PO Box 1080
Lexington, KY 40588
Phone: (606)254-7021

Credential Type: Association Employee and Occupational License. **Requirements:** Submit application and fingerprint card. Pay fee. **Fees:** $10 license fee.

3906

Maintenance Department Manager/ Employee (Racetrack)
Kentucky State Racing Commission
PO Box 1080
Lexington, KY 40588
Phone: (606)254-7021

Credential Type: Association Employee and Occupational License. **Requirements:** Submit application and fingerprint card. Pay fee. **Fees:** $10 license fee.

Maryland

3907

Maintenance Employee (Harness Racing)
Maryland Racing Commission
Stanbalt Bldg., 14th Fl.
501 St. Paul Place
Baltimore, MD 21202
Phone: (301)333-6267

Credential Type: License Registration. **Requirements:** Submit application, fingerprint card, and three passport size photos. Pay fee. **Fees:** $5 registration fee.

3908

Maintenance Employee (Thoroughbred Racing)
Maryland Racing Commission
Stanbalt Bldg., 14th Fl.
501 St. Paul Place
Baltimore, MD 21202
Phone: (301)333-6267

Credential Type: License Registration. **Requirements:** Submit application, fingerprint card, and three passport size photos. Pay fee. **Fees:** $5 registration fee.

Montana

3909

Jockey Room Custodian (Racetrack)
State of Montana Board of Horse Racing
Dept. of Commerce
1424 9th Ave.
Helena, MT 59620
Phone: (406)444-4287

Credential Type: License Registration. **Requirements:** Submit application and fingerprint card. Pay fee. **Fees:** $20 registration fee.

Montana

3910

Septic Tank Cleaner
Dept. of Health and Environmental Sciences
Food and Consumer Safety Bureau
1400 Broadway
Cogswell Bldg.
Helena, MT 59620
Phone: (406)444-2408

Credential Type: Septic Tank, Cesspool, and Privy Cleaner License. **Duration of License:** One year. **Requirements:** Submit application and pay fee. Disposal sites must be approved by a county health officer or sanitarian. **Fees:** $25 annual license fee. **Governing Statute:** Montana Code Annotated 37-41.

3911

Track Maintenance Worker (Racetrack)
State of Montana Board of Horse Racing
Dept. of Commerce
1424 9th Ave.
Helena, MT 59620
Phone: (406)444-4287

Credential Type: License Registration. **Requirements:** Submit application and fingerprint card. Pay fee. **Fees:** $20 registration fee.

New Mexico

3912

Janitor (Racetrack)
New Mexico State Racing Commission
PO Box 8576, Highland Station
Albuquerque, NM 87198
Phone: (505)841-4644

Credential Type: License Registration. **Requirements:** Submit application and fingerprint card. Pay fees. **Fees:** $12 registration fee. $1 notary fee. $23 fingerprint card processing fee.

3913

Jockey Room Custodian (Racetrack)
New Mexico State Racing Commission
PO Box 8576, Highland Station
Albuquerque, NM 87198
Phone: (505)841-4644

Credential Type: License Registration. **Requirements:** Submit application and fingerprint card. Pay fees. **Fees:** $16 registration fee. $1 notary fee. $23 fingerprint card processing fee.

3914

Track Maintenance Employee (Racetrack)
New Mexico State Racing Commission
PO Box 8576, Highland Station
Albuquerque, NM 87198
Phone: (505)841-4644

Credential Type: License Registration. **Requirements:** Submit application and fingerprint card. Pay fees. **Fees:** $14 registration fee. $1 notary fee. $23 fingerprint card processing fee.

New York

3915

Cleaning Services Employee (Harness or Quarter Horse Racing)
New York State Racing and Wagering Board
400 Broome St.
New York, NY 10013
Phone: (212)219-4230

Credential Type: License Registration. **Duration of License:** One year. **Requirements:** Submit application, F.B.I fingerprint card, New York state fingerprint card, and three photos. Pay fees. **Fees:** $5 registration fee. $44 New York state fingerprint card processing fee (valid for five years).

3916

Cleaning Services Employee (Thoroughbred Racing)
New York State Racing and Wagering Board
400 Broome St.
New York, NY 10013
Phone: (212)219-4230

Credential Type: License Registration. **Duration of License:** One year. **Requirements:** Submit application, F.B.I fingerprint card, New York state fingerprint card, and three photos. Pay fees. **Fees:** $5 registration fee. $44 New York state fingerprint card processing fee (valid for five years).

North Dakota

3917

Jockey Room Custodian (Racetrack)
North Dakota Racing Commission
State Capitol Bldg.
Bismarck, ND 58505
Phone: (701)224-2210

Credential Type: License Registration. **Requirements:** Submit application and fingerprint card. Pay fee. **Fees:** $10 license fee. $10 duplicate license fee.

3918

Track Maintenance (Racetrack)
North Dakota Racing Commission
State Capitol Bldg.
Bismarck, ND 58505
Phone: (701)224-2210

Credential Type: License Registration. **Requirements:** Submit application and fingerprint card. Pay fee. **Fees:** $10 license fee. $10 duplicate license fee.

Ohio

3919

Maintenance Employee (Thoroughbred, Standardbred, and Quarter Horse Racing)
Ohio State Racing Commission
State Office Tower
77 S. High St., 18th Fl.
Columbus, OH 43266-0416
Phone: (614)466-2757

Credential Type: License Registration. **Requirements:** Submit application and fingerprint card. Pay fee. **Fees:** $10 registration fee.

Oregon

3920

Maintenance Employee (Racetrack)
Oregon Racing Commission
113 State Office Bldg.
1400 SW Fifth
Portland, OR 97201
Phone: (503)229-5820

Credential Type: License Registration.
Requirements: Submit application and fingerprint card. Pay fee. **Fees:** $30 registration fee. $6 duplicate fee.

South Dakota

3921

Jockey Room Custodian (Horse Racing)
South Dakota Racing Commission
c/o 500 East Capitol
Pierre, SD 57501
Phone: (605)773-6050

Credential Type: License Registration.
Requirements: Submit application and fingerprint card. Pay fee. **Fees:** $10 registration fee.

Texas

3922

Maintenance Employee (Racetrack)
Texas Racing Commission
PO Box 12080
Austin, TX 78711
Phone: (512)794-8461

Credential Type: License Registration.
Requirements: Submit application and fingerprint card. Pay fee. **Fees:** $20 registration fee.

Virginia

3923

Jockey Room Custodian (Racetrack)
Virginia Racing Commission
PO Box 1123
Richmond, VA 23208
Phone: (804)371-7363

Credential Type: License Registration.
Requirements: Submit application and fingerprint card. Pay fee. **Fees:** $10 registration fee.

Kindergarten and Elementary School Teachers

The following states grant licenses in this occupational category as of the date of publication:

Alabama	District of Columbia	Iowa	Minnesota	New Mexico	Rhode Island	Washington
Alaska		Kansas	Mississippi	New York	South Carolina	West Virginia
Arizona	Florida	Kentucky	Missouri	North Carolina	South Dakota	Wisconsin
Arkansas	Georgia	Louisiana	Montana	North Dakota	Tennessee	Wyoming
California	Hawaii	Maine	Nebraska	Ohio	Texas	
Colorado	Idaho	Maryland	Nevada	Oklahoma	Utah	
Connecticut	Illinois	Massachusetts	New Hampshire	Oregon	Vermont	
Delaware	Indiana	Michigan	New Jersey	Pennsylvania	Virginia	

Alabama

3924

Early Childhood Education Teacher

State Dept. of Education,
Certification Officer
Montgomery, AL 36130
Phone: (205)242-9977

Credential Type: Initial Teaching Certificate. **Duration of License:** Eight years. **Requirements:** Basic program of teacher education includes two components, general and professional studies, each requiring two years of study. General studies (years one and 2) consist of 60 semester hours and must include 15 hours of humanities, 12 hours of social science which includes three hours of economics, 12 hours of natural and physical science which includes mathematics, three hours of health and physical education, and 18 hours of electives. Professional studies (years three and 4) consist of 72 semester hours and must include 12 hours of foundations of professional studies which includes three hours in survey course in exceptional child education. 30 hours of study in art, music, speech, creative drama, movement education, health education, parent education, and family life are required, as well as six hours of reading, nine hours of curriculum, teaching and media, three hours evaluation of teaching and learning, nine hours internship and three hours of electives.

Credential Type: Fifth Year Certificate. **Requirements:** Initial Certificate. Advanced professional studies program totaling 33 hours which includes 12 hours in teaching field, six hours of curriculum and teaching, 6-9 hours of foundations of professional studies which includes three hours in a general survey course in special education (if this requirement has not already been met), three hours of evaluation of teaching and learning, and three to six hours of electives.

Credential Type: Sixth Year Certificate. **Reciprocity:** Fifth Year Certificate. Advanced professional studies program totaling 33 hours which includes 12 hours in teaching field, 6-9 hours foundations of professional studies, three hours of evaluation of teaching and learning, and three to six hours of electives.

Credential Type: Seventh Year Certificate. **Requirements:** Sixth Year Certificate. Complete planned program and achieve stated objectives by completing further studies in the field of specialization and/or related fields, foundations of professional studies, and evaluation and educational research.

3925

Elementary Teacher

State Dept. of Education,
Certification Officer
Montgomery, AL 36130
Phone: (205)242-9977

Credential Type: Initial Teaching Certificate. **Duration of License:** Eight years. **Requirements:** Basic program of teacher education includes two components, general and professional studies, each requiring two years of study. General studies (years one and 2) consist of 60 semester hours and must include 15 hours of humanities, 12 hours of social science which includes three hours of economics, 12 hours of natural and physical science which includes mathematics, three hours of health and physical education, and 18 hours of electives. Professional studies (years three and 4) consist of 72 semester hours and must include 12 hours of foundations of professional studies which includes three hours in survey course in exceptional child education, 27 hours in studies in elementary school curriculum areas including health education, 12 hours curriculum and teaching, three hours evaluation of teaching and learning, six hours reading, nine hours internship, and three hours of electives.

Credential Type: Fifth Year Certificate. **Requirements:** Initial Certificate. Advanced professional studies program totaling 33 hours which includes 12 hours in teaching field, six hours of curriculum and teaching, 6-9 hours of foundations of professional studies which includes three hours in a general survey course in special education (if this requirement has not already been met), three hours of evaluation of teaching and learning, and three to six hours of electives.

Credential Type: Sixth Year Certificate. **Requirements:** Fifth Year Certificate. Advanced professional studies program totaling 33 hours which includes 12 hours in teaching field, 6-9 hours foundations of professional studies, three hours of evaluation of teaching and learning, and three to six hours of electives.

Credential Type: Seventh Year Certificate. **Requirements:** Sixth year certificate. Complete planned program and achieve stated objectives by completing further studies in the field of specialization and/or related fields, foundations of professional studies, and evaluation and educational research.

3926

Special Education Teacher
State Dept. of Education,
 Certification Officer
Montgomery, AL 36130
Phone: (205)242-9977

Credential Type: Class B Special Education Professional Certificate. **Authorization:** Exceptionalities which may be endorsed are: crippled and other health impaired, including homebound; early education for the handicapped; emotionally conflicted; gifted and talented; hearing impaired; learning disabilities; mental retardation; multihandicapped/deaf-blind; speech pathology; and visually impaired **Requirements:** Bachelor's degree from an accredited institution. Completion of a program in special education approved by the Alabama State Board of Education or the National Council for Accreditation of Teacher Education or the National Association of State Directors of Teacher Education and Certification or ICP. Recommending institution must list the exceptionality for which the applicant was trained.

Credential Type: Class A Special Education Professional Certificate. **Requirements:** Eligibility for the Class B Professional Certificate. Master's degree in special education approved by the Alabama State Board of Education.

Credential Type: Class AA Special Education Professional Certificate. **Requirements:** Eligibility for a Class A Special Education Professional Certificate endorsed in the same area in which the Class AA Certificate is desired, except as otherwise noted in the standards. Completion of a sixth year program in special education as approved by the Alabama State Board of Education.

Alaska

3927

Early Childhood Education Associate
Dept. of Education, Certification
 Analyst
Box F
Juneau, AK 99811-0500
Phone: (907)465-2810
Phone: (907)465-2831

Credential Type: Early Childhood Education Associate I Certificate—Type E. **Duration of License:** Five years. **Requirements:** Completion of 30 credits in university or college early childhood education program requiring at least 400 hours of supervised practicum experience or received approved Child Development Association (CDA) Award.

To renew certificate applicant must have current CDA credentials or six semester hours of renewal credit in early childhood education. **Fees:** $43 fingerprint card processing fee. $125 application fee. $10 endorsement fee.

Credential Type: Early Childhood Education Associate II Certificate—Type E. **Duration of License:** Five years. **Requirements:** Completion of approved Associate Degree Program in Early Childhood Education (ECE). Completion of requirements for ECE Associate I. To renew certificate applicant must have six semester hours of renewal credit in early childhood education. **Fees:** $43 fingerprint card processing fee. $125 application fee. $10 endorsement fee.

3928

Elementary or Secondary Teacher
Dept. of Education, Certification
 Analyst
PO Box F
Juneau, AK 99811-0500
Phone: (907)465-2810
Phone: (907)465-2831

Credential Type: Regular Certificate—Type A. **Duration of License:** Five years. **Requirements:** Bachelor's degree from an accredited institution. Completion of approved teacher education program, plus institutional recommendation or recommendation from certifying State Department. Completion of six semester hours within the five-year period immediately preceding the date of application.

Certificate may be renewed six months before expiration date upon application and completion of six semester hours of credit during the life of the certificate. Three of the six semester hours may be in correspondence, or by completing workshops or institutes or by travel for which nonacademic credit has been approved by the Commission of Education prior to the holding of the workshop, travel, or institute. First time renewals must complete three semester hours in Alaska studies and three semester hours in multicultural education.

Endorsements will be granted as recommended by the preparing institution and may be deleted if the individual is not under contract in the endorsed area. **Fees:** $43 fingerprint card processing fee. $125 application fee. $10 endorsement fee.

Credential Type: Temporary Certificate—Type T (For Type A). **Duration of License:** One year. **Requirements:** Meet all application requirements except the six semester hours of recency. Proof of satisfactory teaching service for at least three years. Never possessed an Alaska teacher certificate. Nonrenewable. **Fees:** $20 temporary certificate application fee.

Arizona

3929

Elementary Teacher (K-8)
Teacher Certification Unit
PO Box 25609
1535 W. Jefferson
Phoenix, AZ 85002
Phone: (602)542-4368

Credential Type: Temporary Elementary Certificate. **Duration of License:** Eight years (nonrenewable). **Requirements:** Bachelor's degree from a regionally accredited institution. Completion of an approved professional teacher education program in Elementary Education to include student teaching in grades K-8 or a bachelor's degree from a regionally accredited institution and a general studies program which includes a minor of 18 hours in a content area and 45 semester hours in elementary Professional Education including: classroom management; curriculum and instruction in Language Arts; Science, Social Science, Math, and Reading; assessment and evaluation; growing and learning theories; educational foundations ; organization and administration; plus eight hours of student teaching within grades K-8 or two years full time teaching experience at that level. Six semester hours in mathematics content for elementary school teachers. Pass Arizona Teacher Proficiency Exam (ATPE) exam.

Requirements to be satisfied prior to or during initial year of certification include a college level course or examination on the Arizona Constitution, a college level course or examination on the U.S. Constitution, one reading decoding skills course, and a reading practicum which includes decoding skills. **Examination:** Arizona Teacher Proficiency Exam.

Credential Type: Standard Elementary Certificate. **Duration of License:** Six years. **Requirements:** Qualify for the Temporary Elementary Certificate. Master's degree from a regionally accredited institution or 40 semester hours of upper division or graduate course work from a regionally accredited institution (10 hours may be State Board approved district in-service).

Credential Type: Special Subject Endorsements (Art, Music, Physical Education, and Industrial Arts). **Requirements:** Arizona Elementary or Secondary Teaching Certificate. Methods of teaching special

Arizona

Elementary Teacher (K-8), continued

subject area. 40 semester hours in special subject area.

3930

Special Education Teacher (K-12)
Teacher Certification Unit
PO Box 25609
1535 W. Jefferson
Phoenix, AZ 85002
Phone: (602)542-4368

Credential Type: Temporary Special Education Certificate. **Duration of License:** Eight years (nonrenewable). **Authorization:** Issued in the areas of learning disabled, seriously emotionally handicapped, physically handicapped, and mentally handicapped. **Requirements:** Bachelor's degree from a regionally accredited institution. Completion of a professional teacher education program in Special Education to include student teaching in the specific area of exceptionality in grades K-12 or bachelor's degree from a regionally accredited institution and 45 semester hours of upper division or graduate educational course work which includes 21 semester hours of Special Education course work as prescribed and professional education course work that includes methods of teaching Arithmetic and Reading and at least two of the following: Language Arts; Social Studies; Science. Six semester hours in mathematics content. Pass Arizona Teacher Proficiency Exam (ATPE) exam.

Requirements to be satisfied prior to or during initial year of certification include a college level course or examination on the Arizona Constitution, a college level course or examination on the U.S. Constitution, one reading decoding skills course, and a reading practicum which includes decoding skills. **Examination:** Arizona Teacher Proficiency Examination.

Credential Type: Standard Special Education Certificate. **Duration of License:** Six years. **Requirements:** Qualify for the Temporary Special Education Certificate. Master's degree from a regionally accredited institution or 40 semester hours of upper division or graduate course work from a regionally accredited institution (10 semester hours may be State Board approved district in-service credit.)

Arkansas

3931

Art Teacher (K-12)
Teacher Education and Licensure
State Dept. of Education
4 State Capitol Mall
Little Rock, AR 72201-1071
Phone: (501)682-4342

Credential Type: Art Specialist Certificate. **Duration of License:** Six years. **Requirements:** Initial Certification which includes a bachelor's degree from an approved institution and includes courses in language, mathematics, sciences, history, philosophy, literature, the arts, and health and wellness education. Completion of a degree major in a teaching field. Proficiency in oral and written communication and mathematics, with at least a grade of "C" in each course. Successful completion of an approved teacher education program from an institution that includes the following: Requiring no less than a 2.5 grade point average on a 4.0 scale to enter the program; Requiring students to obtain acceptable scores on entrance tests into teacher education that assess competency in computation, reading, and writing, as well as on exit tests in professional knowledge and the academic teaching area; Two weeks of student teaching; Professional studies component should provide competencies specified by the Arkansas Department of Education; Recommendation from the institution. Also passage of the National Teacher Examination.

In addition the Art Specialist Certificate requires 18 semester hours of professional education, including study of the school, of the learning processes, and of elementary and secondary teaching which includes a methods course in reading and six semester hours of directed teaching. Plus 24 semester hours of specialization requirements. **Examination:** National Teacher Examination.

3932

Early Childhood Special Education Teacher
Teacher Education and Licensure
State Dept. of Education
4 State Capitol Mall
Little Rock, AR 72201-1071
Phone: (501)682-4342

Credential Type: Early Childhood Special Education Certificate. **Requirements:** Bachelor or graduate degree in the field from an approved institution or bachelor's degree in an approved related field. Three semester hours each of child development, behavior management, study of the school, and principles of learning. A six semester hr. practicum in early childhood special education. An additional 18 semester hours addressing specified competencies related to teaching children with handicaps, birth through five years of age.

3933

Elementary Physical Education Teacher (K-6)
Teacher Education and Licensure
State Dept. of Education
4 State Capitol Mall
Little Rock, AR 72201-1071
Phone: (501)682-4342

Credential Type: Elementary Physical Education Specialist Certificate. **Requirements:** Initial Certification which includes a bachelor's degree from an approved institution and includes courses in language, mathematics, sciences, history, philosophy, literature, the arts, and health and wellness education. Completion of a degree major in a teaching field. Proficiency in oral and written communication and mathematics, with at least a grade of "C" in each course. Successful completion of an approved teacher education program from an institution that includes the following: Requiring no less than a 2.5 grade point average on a 4.0 scale to enter the program; Requiring students to obtain acceptable scores on entrance tests into teacher education that assess competency in computation, reading, and writing, as well as on exit tests in professional knowledge and the academic teaching area; Two weeks of student teaching; Professional studies component should provide competencies specified by the Arkansas Dept. of Education; Recommendation from the institution. Also passage of the National Teacher Examination.

In addition the P.E. Specialist Certificate requires 18 semester hours of professional education, including study of the school, of the learning processes, and of elementary teaching which includes a methods course in reading and six semester hours of directed teaching. Plus 26 semester hours of specialization requirements. **Examination:** National Teacher Examination.

3934

Elementary Reading Teacher (K-6)
Teacher Education and Licensure
State Dept. of Education
4 State Capitol Mall
Little Rock, AR 72201-1071
Phone: (501)682-4342

Credential Type: Elementary Reading Specialist Certificate. **Duration of License:**

Kindergarten and Elementary School Teachers

Six years. **Requirements:** Initial Certification which includes a bachelor's degree from an approved institution and includes courses in language, mathematics, sciences, history, philosophy, literature, the arts, and health and wellness education. Completion of a degree major in a teaching field. Proficiency in oral and written communication and mathematics, with at least a grade of "C" in each course. Successful completion of an approved teacher education program from an institution that includes the following: Requiring no less than a 2.5 grade point average on a 4.0 scale to enter the program; Requiring students to obtain acceptable scores on entrance tests into teacher education that assess competency in computation, reading, and writing, as well as on exit tests in professional knowledge and the academic teaching area; Two weeks of student teaching; Professional studies component should provide competencies specified by the Arkansas Department of Education; Recommendation from the institution. Also passage of the National Teacher Examination.

In addition the Elementary Reading Specialist Certificate requires 18 semester hours of professional education, including study of the school, of the learning processes, and of elementary teaching which includes a methods course in reading and six semester hours of directed teaching. Plus nine semester hours of specialization requirements. **Examination:** National Teacher Examination.

3935

Elementary Teacher
Teacher Education and Licensure
State Dept. of Education
4 State Capitol Mall
Little Rock, AR 72201-1071
Phone: (501)682-4342

Credential Type: Six Year Elementary Certificate. **Duration of License:** Six years. **Requirements:** Initial Certification which includes a bachelor's degree from an approved institution and includes courses in language, mathematics, sciences, history, philosophy, literature, the arts, and health and wellness education. Completion of a degree major in a teaching field. Proficiency in oral and written communication and mathematics, with at least a grade of "C" in each course. Successful completion of an approved teacher education program from an institution that includes the following: Requiring no less than a 2.5 grade point average on a 4.0 scale to enter the program; Requiring students to obtain acceptable scores on entrance tests into teacher education that assess competency in computation, reading, and writing, as well as on exit tests in professional knowledge and the academic teaching area; Two weeks of student teaching; Professional studies component should provide competencies specified by the Arkansas Department of Education; Recommendation from the institution. Also passage of the National Teacher Examination.

In addition to qualify for the Six Year Elementary Certificate applicants must fulfill Professional Requirements of 18 semester hours of elementary education which include study of the school, of the learning processes, elementary teaching that includes a methods course in reading, and six semester hours of directed teaching. Specialization Requirements include three hours public school art and craft, three hours public school music, three hours geography, three hours U.S. history, three hours U.S. government, three hours economics, three hours children's literature, six hours mathematics, three hours elementary science, and two hours elementary physical education. **Examination:** National Teacher Examination.

Credential Type: Specialist Certificate K-6. **Requirements:** Professional Requirements include 18 semester hours of professional education, including study of the school, of the learning processes, and of elementary teaching which includes a methods course in reading and six semester hours of directed teaching. Specialization Requirements include a bachelor's degree in Elementary Education of Early Childhood Education which meets requirements for standard Six Year Elementary Certificate, three hours Child Development, six hours Early Childhood Curriculum Methods and Materials, and six semester hours of practicum (successful teaching experience may cause a portion of the practicum to be waived).

3936

Middle School Teacher
Teacher Education and Licensure
State Dept. of Education
4 State Capitol Mall
Little Rock, AR 72201-1071
Phone: (501)682-4342

Credential Type: Middle School Certificate. **Authorization:** Middle School Certificates are available in the following areas: agriculture; business; English; French; Spanish; physical education; home economics; industrial arts; math; science; social studies. **Requirements:** Must hold a high school or elementary teaching certificate based on a bachelor's degree. A teacher teaching in a departmental situation shall meet one of the following requirements: Hold a secondary teaching certificate and have 18 semester hours in the field in which he/she is teaching. Plus three semester hours in human growth and development of children below adolescent age and three semester hours of elementary or middle school teaching methods ; Or hold an elementary teaching certificate and have 18 semester hours in the field in which he/she is teaching.

3937

Music Teacher (K-12)
Teacher Education and Licensure
State Dept. of Education
4 State Capitol Mall
Little Rock, AR 72201-1071
Phone: (501)682-4342

Credential Type: Music Specialist Certificate. **Duration of License:** Six years. **Requirements:** Initial Certification which includes a bachelor's degree from an approved institution and includes courses in language, mathematics, sciences, history, philosophy, literature, the arts, and health and wellness education. Completion of a degree major in a teaching field. Proficiency in oral and written communication and mathematics, with at least a grade of "C" in each course. Successful completion of an approved teacher education program from an institution that includes the following: Requiring no less than a 2.5 grade point average on a 4.0 scale to enter the program; Requiring students to obtain acceptable scores on entrance tests into teacher education that assess competency in computation, reading, and writing, as well as on exit tests in professional knowledge and the academic teaching area; Two weeks of student teaching; Professional studies component should provide competencies specified by the Arkansas Department of Education; Recommendation from the institution. Also passage of the National Teacher Examination.

In addition the Music Specialist Certificate requires 18 semester hours of professional education, including study of the school, of the learning processes, and of elementary and secondary teaching which includes a methods course in reading and six semester hours of directed teaching. Plus 24 semester hours of specialization requirements. **Examination:** National Teacher Examination.

Arkansas

3938

Physical Education Teacher (K-12)
Teacher Education and Licensure
State Dept. of Education
4 State Capitol Mall
Little Rock, AR 72201-1071
Phone: (501)682-4342

Credential Type: Physical Education Specialist. **Requirements:** Initial Certification which includes a bachelor's degree from an approved institution and includes courses in language, mathematics, sciences, history, philosophy, literature, the arts, and health and wellness education. Completion of a degree major in a teaching field. Proficiency in oral and written communication and mathematics, with at least a grade of "C" in each course. Successful completion of an approved teacher education program from an institution that includes the following: Requiring no less than a 2.5 grade point average on a 4.0 scale to enter the program; Requiring students to obtain acceptable scores on entrance tests into teacher education that assess competency in computation, reading, and writing, as well as on exit tests in professional knowledge and the academic teaching area; Two weeks of student teaching; Professional studies component should provide competencies specified by the Arkansas Department of Education; Recommendation from the institution. Also passage of the National Teacher Examination.

To qualify for P.E. Specialist an additional 32 semester hours of course work is required. Must also meet one of the following field experiences: three semester hours of the student teaching requirement must be completed at the elementary or middle school level, below 9th grade, where the cooperating teacher is certified in Elementary Physical Education; or must complete a three semester hour internship under the direct supervision from the staff of the physical education department of a college or university. Must also acquire a coaching endorsement by completing three semester hours of coaching theory. **Examination:** National Teacher Examination.

3939

Reading Specialist (K-12)
Teacher Education and Licensure
State Dept. of Education
4 State Capitol Mall
Little Rock, AR 72201-1071
Phone: (501)682-4342

Credential Type: Reading Specialist Certificate. **Duration of License:** 10 years. **Requirements:** Initial Certification which includes a bachelor's degree from an approved institution and includes courses in language, mathematics, sciences, history, philosophy, literature, the arts, and health and wellness education. Completion of a degree major in a teaching field. Proficiency in oral and written communication and mathematics, with at least a grade of "C" in each course. Successful completion of an approved teacher education program from an institution that includes the following: Requiring no less than a 2.5 grade point average on a 4.0 scale to enter the program; Requiring students to obtain acceptable scores on entrance tests into teacher education that assess competency in computation, reading, and writing, as well as on exit tests in professional knowledge and the academic teaching area; Two weeks of student teaching; Professional studies component should provide competencies specified by the Arkansas Department of Education; Recommendation from the institution. Also passage of the National Teacher Examination.

To qualify for a Reading Specialist Certificate requires an additional 18 semester hours of professional education, including study of the school, of the learning processes, and of elementary and secondary teaching which includes a methods course in reading and six semester hours of directed teaching. Plus 12 semester hours of specialization requirements. **Examination:** National Teacher Examination.

3940

Special Education Teacher
Teacher Education and Licensure
State Dept. of Education
4 State Capitol Mall
Little Rock, AR 72201-1071
Phone: (501)682-4342

Credential Type: Special Education Certificate. **Authorization:** Certificates may be issued in the following areas: Mildly handicapped K-12; Moderately/Profoundly handicapped K-12; Severely emotionally disturbed K-12. **Requirements:** The certificate should encompass present general education requirements as stipulated in "Arkansas Laws and Regulations for Certification of Teachers, Administrators, and Supervisors, Bulletin VII". All candidates must receive 15 hours of training in the following areas: Child and adolescent development, six hours; Principles of learning, three hours; Application of behavior management principles, three hours; Study of the school three hours For each of the certifiable areas, students must take a minimum of 24 semester hours in addition to the 15 basic core hours Students in preservice programs will complete appropriate field and teaching experience at both elementary and secondary levels.

California

3941

Elementary School Teacher
Commission on Teacher Credentialing
PO Box 944270
Sacramento, CA 94244-7000
Phone: (916)445-7524

Credential Type: Multiple Subjects Instruction Five Year Preliminary Credential. **Duration of License:** Five years (nonrenewable). **Authorization:** Most commonly required for elementary school teachers, however he/she may also be assigned to teach in any self-contained classroom in grades preschool, K-12, and in adult education. **Requirements:** Pass the CBEST examination. Verification of teaching or administrative experience. Official report of any examination scores. Bachelor's or higher degree except in education (unless the education degree was completed outside of California). Teacher preparation program, including student teaching completed with a grade of B or higher on a five point scale. U.S. Constitution course or examination. Subject matter confidence verified by California institution or by examination. Completion of a course in the methods of teaching reading or passage (with a score of 680) of the National Teacher Examination (NTE) "Introductions to Teaching of Reading" test. Verification of English writing proficiency through tests or written institutional recommendations. **Examination:** California Basic Education Skills Test **Fees:** $60 application fee. $30 test score recording and evaluation fee, except for CBEST.

Credential Type: One Year Preliminary Multiple Subjects Credential. **Duration of License:** One year (nonrenewable). **Authorization:** Available only to candidates prepared outside of California. **Requirements:** Pass the CBEST examination. Bachelor's or higher degree except in education (unless the education degree was completed outside of California). Teacher preparation program, including student teaching completed with a grade of B or higher on a five point scale. Verification of teaching or administrative experience. Official report of any examination scores. **Examination:** California Basic Education Skills Test **Fees:** $60 application fee. $30 test score recording and evaluation fee, except for CBEST.

Credential Type: Multiple Subjects Instruction Five Year Professional Clear Credential. **Duration of License:** Five years. **Requirements:** Five Year Preliminary Credential. Fifth year of study beyond bachelor's degree. Health education, including drug and alcohol abuse, and nutrition. Special education with concentration on mainstreaming. Computer education. Recommendation of a California college or university with an approved multiple or single subject program (unless program and fifth year is completed outside of California). Renewal requirements include planned professional growth activities of at least 150 clock hours and one-half of one year of teaching experience. **Fees:** $60 application fee. $30 test score recording and evaluation fee, except for CBEST.

Credential Type: Five Year Clear Specialist Instructional Credential. **Duration of License:** Five years. **Authorization:** Authorizes the holder to teach in the area of specialization in preschool, grades K-12, or adult classes and includes such subjects as agriculture, bilingual, cross-cultural education, health science, mathematics, and reading. **Requirements:** Valid California teaching credential which requires a bachelor's degree and a professional preparation program including student teaching. Fifth year of study beyond the bachelor's degree. Professional preparation in the specialist area. Recommendation of a California college or university with the specific approved specialist program. Out-of-state applicants who meet requirements may still be certified. Their student teaching or field work must have been completed with a grade of B on a five point scale. **Fees:** $60 application fee. $30 test score recording and evaluation fee, except for CBEST.

Credential Type: One Year Preliminary Credential for Designated Subjects. **Duration of License:** One year. **Authorization:** Authorizes the holder to teach the subject or trade designated on the credential in preschool, grades K-12, or adult classes including such areas as trade, technical, and vocational courses. **Requirements:** Valid California teaching credential which requires a bachelor's degree and a professional preparation program including student teaching. Adequate, successful, recent experience in the technical skills or subjects named on the credential, equal to five years experience. An approved program of inservice training, plus appropriate teaching experience. Course or examination covering the provisions and principals of the U.S. Constitution for full-time credentials. CBEST for adult academic subjects and special subjects driver education. Recommendation from an approved Local Educational Agency or employing California school district. **Examination:** California Basic Education Skills Test **Fees:** $60 application fee. $30 test score recording and evaluation fee, except for CBEST.

Colorado

3942

General Teacher
Teacher Certification
State Dept. of Education
201 E. Colifax
Denver, CO 80203
Phone: (303)866-6628

Credential Type: General Teacher Certificate—Type A. **Duration of License:** Five years. **Requirements:** Initial teacher certification which requires the following: Bachelor's degree. Completion of an approved program of teacher preparation from a four year, regionally accredited, degree granting institution which must include student teaching. Six semester hours of credit applicable to the certificate being sought, and/or general education, and/or child abuse, taken within the past five years from date of application. Course work in the exceptional child, covering the full range of exceptionalities, gifted through handicapped, and course work in the theory, methods, and related practice of the teaching of reading. Passage of the spelling, language, and mathematics sections of Level 19 of the California Achievement Test and oral English competence which is met by having a B— or better in a public speaking course taken from a regionally accredited college or passing an oral English panel assessment. Completed and signed appropriate application. Institutional recommendation from the school(s) where the teacher preparation work was completed. Official, original transcripts from all applicable institutions.

In addition the General Teacher Certificate requires Institutional recommendation to verify satisfactory completion of teacher preparation including: student teaching; completion of grade levels, subject areas, or service specialization; passing competency examination, meeting the Recent Credit Requirement (having earned six semester or nine quarter hours within the five years prior to the date of application for the certificate) or Renewal Credit Requirement. **Examination:** California Achievement Test Level 19 (spelling, language, and mathematics sections) **Fees:** $45 initial certification application fee. $40 fingerprint card processing fee.

Credential Type: Professional Teacher Certificate—Type B. **Duration of License:** Five years. **Requirements:** Applicants must have a master's or higher degree from a regionally accredited institution of higher education, meet all of the requirements of a Type A certificate, and have three years fulltime teaching experience. Renewable every five years with completion of the Renewal Credit Requirements. **Fees:** $45 initial certification application fee. $40 fingerprint card processing fee.

Connecticut

3943

Elementary School Teacher (PK-8)
State Dept. of Education
Teacher Certification, Chief
165 Capitol Ave.
PO Box 2219
Hartford, CT 06145
Phone: (203)566-4561

Credential Type: Initial Educator Certificate. **Requirements:** Bachelor's degree. 75 hours of general education study including English (minimum of six hours), Science, Mathematics, Social studies (minimum of six hours), and Fine arts. 30 hours of professional education study which includes Foundations of Education, Educational Psychology, Curriculum and Methods of Teaching, Guidance, and Health and Safety. Must include three semester hours in teaching developmental reading in the elementary school, three semester hours in children's literature. 6-12 semester hours of full-time student teaching or one year of successful teaching at the elementary level.

Credential Type: Provisional Educator Certificate. **Requirements:** Initial Educator Certificate. Completion of beginning educator support and assessment program, as may be available from the Connecticut Board, and one school year of successful service under the interim or initial certificates or three years of successful teaching in the area for which the certificate is being sought, in a approved school, within 10 years prior to application.

Credential Type: Professional Educator Certificate. **Requirements:** Three years of successful teaching under the Provisional Educator Certificate. 30 semester hours of course work beyond the bachelor's degree which includes a planned program at an institution of higher learning related directly to the subject(s) being taught or an individual program designed to increase the ability of the teacher to improve student learning.

Credential Type: Endorsements. **Authorization:** Endorsements may be made in any of the following classification or combinations of them: PK-K; PK-3; PK-6; and 4-8. Teaching endorsements may be extended to additional levels or fields under conditions set forth in (New)Regulations, Section

Connecticut

Elementary School Teacher (PK-8), continued

10145d-116(b). **Requirements:** Passing score on the elementary education area test of the Connecticut Board of Education. **Examination:** Connecticut Board of Education Examination.

3944

Special Subjects Teacher
State Dept. of Education
Teacher Certification, Chief
165 Capitol Ave.
PO Box 2219
Hartford, CT 06145
Phone: (203)566-4561

Credential Type: Special Subjects Initial Certificate. **Authorization:** This certificate authorizes the holder to specialize in teaching in the areas of agriculture, art, health, home economics, technology education, music, or physical education. **Requirements:** Bachelor's degree. 45 semester hours of general education which includes at least three of the following areas, in addition to the area of major specialization: English (6 hours minimum); Science; Mathematics; Social Studies, including U.S. History (6 hr. minimum); Fine Arts; and Foreign Languages. 18 semester hours of professional education which include: Foundations of Education; Educational Psychology; Curriculum and Methods of Teaching (must include three hours of Developmental Reading and three hours in English); Guidance; and Health and Safety. 6-12 semester hours of full-time student teaching in a secondary school or one successful year of teaching at the secondary level. 35 semester hours of appropriate technical courses in the special subject.

Credential Type: Provisional Special Subjects Certificate. **Requirements:** Special Subjects Initial Certificate. Completion of beginning educator support and assessment program, as may be available from the Connecticut Board, and one school year of successful service under the interim or initial certificates or three years of successful teaching in the area for which the certificate is being sought, in an approved school, within 10 years prior to application.

Credential Type: Professional Special Subjects Certificate. **Requirements:** Three years of successful teaching under the Provisional Special Subjects Certificate. 30 semester hours of course work beyond the bachelor's degree which includes a planned program at an institution of higher learning related directly to the subject(s) being taught or an individual program designed to increase the ability of the teacher to improve student learning.

Delaware

3945

Early Childhood Teacher K-3
Teacher Certification
Dept. of Public Instruction
Box 1402
Dover, DE 19903
Phone: (302)739-4688

Credential Type: Early Childhood Certificate. **Requirements:** Bachelors degree in general education from an accredited college. Complete an approved program in early childhood education or complete 48 semester hours of the following professional education courses and the specified number of semester hours: teaching of reading 6; child development 6; psychology of learning 3; early childhood or kindergarten curriculum 3; curriculum content 12; mathematics methods 3; science methods 3; social studies methods 3; language arts methods 3; clinical and/or field experience including teaching at the K-3 level 6; and teaching at the N/K level 6. Must successfully complete the Educational Testing Service Pre-Professional Skills Tests with the following minimum scores: Reading 175; Writing 172; Mathematics 175. **Examination:** Educational Testing Service Pre-Professional Skills Tests.

3946

Early Childhood Teacher (Pre-K and K)
Div. of Teacher Services
Dept. of Public Instruction
PO Box 1402
Dover, DE 19903
Phone: (302)739-4688

Credential Type: Standard Certificate. **Requirements:** Bachelor's degree. Satisfactory completion of 18 semester hours of preparation for teaching on the early childhood level which may be part of, or in addition to, the degree requirements. The following courses, or their equivalent, should be included in the course of study: Child Development; Curriculum for Early childhood Education—Foundations, Content, Methods, and Materials; The Role of the Early Childhood Teacher; and The Exceptional Child. Observation and Student Teaching or one year of successful teaching experience under supervision.

Applicants for teacher certification must file a completed application with the Director which includes official transcripts, verification of previous teaching experience, and an affidavit of previous nonteaching or technical experience when applicable. **Examination:** National Teacher Examination (communications skills test) **Reciprocity:** Applicants who have been employed for at least 27 months under a standard certificate, or are completing teacher training in an approved program at a U.S. college or university outside the District of Columbia, may apply for certification under the Interstate Agreement on Qualifications of Educational Personnel, providing their state has signed a reciprocity agreement. Must have a valid certificate and complete application procedures.

Credential Type: Provisional Certificate. **Duration of License:** 18 months. **Authorization:** Temporarily allows applicant to hold teaching position while satisfactorily completing license deficits and/or attainment of a passing score on the DCPS Teacher Content Knowledge Test. **Requirements:** Standard Certificate requirements, but allows for some licensing deficits.

3947

Elementary School Teacher
Teacher Certification
Dept. of Public Instruction
Box 1402
Dover, DE 19903
Phone: (302)739-4688

Credential Type: Elementary School Certificate. **Authorization:** Allows teaching in grades 1-6 and in state middle school grades 5-8. **Requirements:** Bachelors degree in general education from an accredited college. Complete an approved program in elementary education or complete 45 semester hours of the following professional education courses and the specified number of semester hours: teaching of reading 6; child development 3; educational psychology 3; sociology 3; curriculum content 12; mathematics methods 3; science methods 3; social studies methods 3; language arts methods 3; clinical and/or field experience which includes student teaching at appropriate level 6. Must successfully complete the Educational Testing Service Pre-Professional Skills Tests with the following minimum scores: Reading 175; Writing 172; Mathematics 175. **Examination:** Educational Testing Service Pre-Professional Skills Tests.

Credential Type: Special Subjects Endorsements. **Authorization:** Authorizes the teaching of a specific subject at the elementary level. **Requirements:** Must have an elementary teaching certificate or a bachelor's degree and 15 semester hours of professional education which includes courses in human behavior, methods and materials, and clinical and/or field experience including student teaching. Must have a major in one of the following subjects with the minimum number of semester hours as specified: Art 36; Music 36; or Physical Education 40.

3948

Teacher of Exceptional Children
Teacher Certification
Dept. of Public Instruction
Box 1402
Dover, DE 19903
Phone: (302)739-4688

Credential Type: Initial Standard Certificate. **Authorization:** Under this certificate endorsements will be granted in the following areas: Mentally Retarded; Socially and Emotionally Maladjusted; Learning Disabled; Physically Handicapped; Visually Impaired; Hearing Impaired; or Gifted. **Requirements:** Bachelor's degree in special education. Institutional recommendation. A total of 39 semester hours of course work which includes the following three semester hr. courses: Methods of Teaching Reading; Methods of Teaching Mathematics; Educational Psychology; Child Growth and Development; Behavior Problems and/or Modification Management; Survey/Introduction to the Education of Exceptional Children; Review Theories of Exceptional Children; Methods and Curriculum for Exceptional Children; and Identification, Diagnosis, and Assessment of Exceptional Children. Must also have six semester hours of student teaching in the area of endorsement. Must successfully complete the Educational Testing Service PreProfessional Skills Tests with the following minimum scores: Reading 175; Writing 172; Mathematics 175. **Examination:** Educational Testing Service Pre-Professional Skills Tests.

District of Columbia

3949

Elementary School Teacher (1-6)
Div. of Teacher Services
Dept. of Public Instruction
PO Box 1402
Dover, DE 19903
Phone: (302)739-4688

Credential Type: Standard Certificate. **Requirements:** Bachelor's degree. Completion of a course in preparation for teaching on the elementary level which may be part of or in addition to the degree requirements. The following academic semester credits are required: English 12; Geography 3; History 6; Mathematics 9; Science (biological and physical) 6; Music 2; Art 2; Health and Nutrition 3; Physical Education 3. Also the following education courses, or their equivalent, are required: The Exceptional Child; Educational Psychology; Classroom Management; Corrective or Remedial Techniques of Reading; Mathematics for Elementary Teachers; Speech and Language Development for Teachers; Development of Oral Communication Skills in Children; Materials and Methods (for teaching basic subjects taught at the elementary level). Observation and student teaching in the elementary school or one successful teaching experience at the elementary level. Passage of the communications skills portion of the National Teacher Examination.

In addition teachers of special subjects must have the following semester hr. requirements in their area of specialization: Teachers of Art 42; Teachers of Health and Physical Education 48; Teachers of Foreign Language 30; Science Resource Teachers 18; and Mathematics Resource Teachers 18.

Applicants for teacher certification must file a completed application with the Director which includes official transcriptts, verification of previous teaching experience, and an affidavit of previous nonteaching or technical experience when applicable. **Examination:** National Teacher Examination (communications skills test) **Reciprocity:** Applicants who have been employed for at least 27 months under a standard certificate, or are completing teacher training in an approved program at a U.S. college or university outside the District of Columbia, may apply for certification under the Interstate Agreement on Qualifications of Educational Personnel, providing their state has signed a reciprocity agreement. Must have a valid certificate and complete application procedures.

Credential Type: Provisional Certificate. **Duration of License:** 18 months. **Authorization:** Temporarily allows applicant to hold teaching position while satisfactorily completing license deficits and/or attainment of a passing score on the DCPS Teacher Content Knowledge Test. **Requirements:** Standard Certificate requirements, but allows for some licensing deficits.

Florida

3950

Elementary School Teacher
Bureau of Teacher Certification
Florida Education Center
325 W. Gaines, Rm. 201
Tallahassee, FL 32399
Phone: (904)488-2317

Credential Type: Professional Certificate. **Duration of License:** Five years. **Requirements:** Bachelor's degree with a major in elementary education which includes teaching reading at the elementary level or bachelor's degree with 24 semester hours in elementary education including three hours in competencies for teaching reading and materials used for teaching basic subjects. Meets professional preparation requirements. Has completed at least six semester hours or two years of full-time teaching experience at level of certification during the five years preceding application. Has obtained a minimum 2.5 grade point average in each subject shown on the certificate. Has received a passing score on the College Level Academic Skills Test (CLAST). Has received a passing score on the Professional Education Subtest of the Florida Teacher Certification Examination. Has received a passing score on an approved subject area examination for each subject or field shown on the certificate. Completes a Florida Professional Orientation Program (year long internship). Completes a general preparation plan of 45 semester hours which includes six hours, but not more than 12, in each of the following areas: arts of communication; human adjustment; biological science; physical sciences, and mathematics; social science; humanities; and applied arts. (A graduate of a standard institution shall be considered to have met the general preparation requirements.) Renewal of certificate requires six hours (or 120 staff development units) every five years. **Examination:** College Level Academic Skills Test. Professional Education Subtest of the Florida Teacher Certification Examination.

Georgia

3951

Teacher (K-12)
Div. of Teacher Education
State Dept. of Education
1452 Twin Towers East
Atlanta, GA 30334-5070
Phone: (404)656-2406

Credential Type: Initial Teaching Certificate. **Requirements:** Bachelor's degree

Teacher (K-12), continued

from an accredited institution. Teacher education program approved by the NCATE (National Council for Accreditation of Teacher Education Programs). Certification by evaluation will allow those applicants not qualifying under the approved program plan to have their credentials evaluated for possible certification. Another alternative certification program allows applicants with a fifth year or master's degree to be certified if they have completed a MED, MAT, or MALT in the same subject area as their bachelor's degree. Applicants seeking initial certification in the teaching fields of science, mathematics, and foreign languages may meet these fields' requirements through a state approved staff development program or through a summer institute sponsored by the Department of Education.

Must complete a five quarter hr. course in the Identification and Education of Children with Special Needs. Applicants wishing to teach in grades 1-8 must complete a five quarter hr. course in the Teaching of Reading. Appropriate certification tests and on-the-job assessments are required of all teacher candidates.

Hawaii

3952

Teacher (K-12)
Dept. of Education
Office of Personnel Services
PO Box 2360
Honolulu, HI 96804
Phone: (808)548-5803

Credential Type: Initial Basic Teacher Certificate. **Requirements:** Complete an institution's state approved teacher education program at the baccalaureate level. Pass the National Teacher Examination (NTE) Core Battery and Specialty Area Tests. Special majors approved for K-12 general certification include: Art, Music, Physical Education, and Reading. A college or university's state-approved academic major or program is required for the following subject matter fields for secondary certification: Agricultural Arts; Art; Business Education; Distributive Education; English; Guidance; Hawaiian Studies; Health; Health and Physical Education; Home Economics; Industrial Arts; Industrial Technical; Foreign Languages; Mathematics; Music; Office Education; Physical Education; Reading; Science; Vocational Agriculture; and Vocational Home Economics. Trade experience is required for vocational and technical programs. Majors for Special Education include: Mild/Moderate; Severe/Profound; Hearing Impaired; Visually Impaired; Orthopedically Handicapped; or DeafBlind. **Examination:** NTE Core Battery and Specialty Area Tests.

Credential Type: Basic Teacher Certificate. **Requirements:** Initial Basic Certificate. Two years of successful teaching in the public schools of Hawaii.

Credential Type: Initial Professional Teacher Certificate. **Requirements:** Complete an institution's state approved graduate teacher education program. Pass the NTE Core Battery and Specialty Area Tests. **Examination:** NTE Core Battery and Specialty Area Test.

Credential Type: Professional Teacher Certificate. **Requirements:** Initial Professional Teacher Certificate. Complete two years of successful teaching in the public schools of Hawaii.

Idaho

3953

Elementary School Teacher (1-8)
Certification Analyst
State Dept. of Education
L. B. Jordan Office Bldg.
Boise, ID 83720
Phone: (208)334-3475

Credential Type: Standard Elementary Certificate. **Duration of License:** Five years. **Requirements:** Bachelor's degree. 24 semester hours of professional requirements which include philosophical, psychological, and methodological foundations of education. Six semester hours of elementary student teaching or three years of successful teaching in an elementary school. 42 semester hours of general education which includes the following: 12 hours of English which includes composition and literature; 12 hours of Social Science which includes United States history and/or government; eight hours consisting of two or more areas of Natural Science; three hours of Fine Arts; and six hours of Fundamentals of Mathematics. Pass the NTE Battery. May be renewed upon completion of at least six semester credits of college courses within the period of validity. **Examination:** National Teachers Examination Battery.

Credential Type: Advanced Elementary Certificate. **Duration of License:** Five years. **Requirements:** Standard Elementary Certificate. Master's degree in a related area from an accredited college or university. Three years of satisfactory teaching experience. May be renewed upon completion of at least six semester credits of college courses within the period of validity.

3954

Teacher of the Exceptional Child
Certification Analyst
State Dept. of Education
L. B. Jordan Office Bldg.
Boise, ID 83720
Phone: (208)334-3475

Credential Type: Generalist (Educationally Handicapped) Endorsement. **Duration of License:** Five years. **Requirements:** Completion of a program in Elementary, Secondary, or Special Education approved by the Idaho State Board of Education or by the State Educational Agency where the program was completed. 30 semester hours of special education courses to include developmental processes; evaluation; individualization of instruction for exceptional child; instructional experience; individual and group classroom management; knowledge of and coordination with other school personnel; knowledge of state and community ancillary services; and work with parents. Valid for five years and may be renewed upon completion of at least six semester credits of college courses within the period of validity.

Credential Type: Specialized Endorsement. **Authorization:** Authorizes the holder to specialize in one of the following areas: hearing and visually impaired; physically and multiple handicapped; severe retardation; and severe behavior problems. **Requirements:** Baccalaureate degree. 30 semester hour approved program in area of endorsement.

Credential Type: Advanced Exceptional Child Certificate. **Duration of License:** Five years. **Requirements:** Must hold a Standard or Specialist Certificate. Applicants holding a Standard Exceptional Child Certificate require a master's degree with emphasis in Exceptional Child area and three years of satisfactory teaching experience in Exceptional Child area, grades N-12. Applicants holding a Specialized Endorsement require a master's degree in the area of endorsement. Valid for five years and may be renewed upon completion of at least six semester credits of college courses within the period of validity.

Credential Type: Consulting Teacher Endorsement. **Duration of License:** Five years. **Requirements:** Valid Advanced Exceptional Child Certificate. Standard Elementary or Secondary Teaching Certificate. Completion of Fifth Year or master's degree program. Three years of teaching experience. Valid for five years and may be renewed upon completion of at least six semester credits of college courses within the period of validity.

Illinois

3955

Early Childhood Teacher PK-3
Certification and Placement Section
100 N. First St.
Springfield, IL 62777
Phone: (217)782-4321

Credential Type: Early Childhood Certificate. **Duration of License:** Four years. **Requirements:** Good character. Good health. At least 19 years of age. Citizen of the U.S. Evidence of teaching experience or completion of an approved program of teacher preparation. Bachelor's degree. 78 semester hours of general education classes which include the following courses and specified semester hours: Language Arts 9; Science 7; Social Science (to include American History and/or Government) 7; Humanities (to include one hr. art and one hr.in music) 7; Health and Physical Education 3; plus approved general education electives. 32 semester hours of professional education to include the following courses and semester hours: Child growth and development with emphasis on the young child 3; History and philosophy of early childhood education 3; Instructional methods that include types of activity/learning centers, individualization, educational play, and media and their utilization in extending the child's understanding of art, music, literature, reading instruction, mathematics, natural and social science 4; Methods of teaching reading 2; Techniques and methodology of teaching language arts, mathematics, science, and social studies at the primary level 4; Development and acquisition of language in young children 2; Child family and community relations 3; Psychology, identification, and methods of teaching exceptional children 3; Pre-student teaching clinical experiences equivalent to 100 clock hours including experience with infant/toddlers, preschool/kindergarten, and primary age students;student teaching five and electives in professional education 3. Applicants who have had five semester hours of student teaching at the primary level (K-3) and who have had teaching experience are not required to take a practicum at the preschool level. Total teacher preparation program must total at least 120 semester hours All applicants must take and pass the Illinois Certification Basic Skills and Subject-Matter Knowledge Tests. **Examination:** Illinois Certification Basic Skills and Subject-Matter Knowledge Tests. **Reciprocity:** Reciprocity exists for applicants holding out-of-state teaching certificates providing their teacher preparation was comparable to that required by the state of Illinois. **Fees:** $44 per section of the Illinois Certification Test.

3956

Elementary School Teacher K-9
Certification and Placement Section
100 N. First St.
Springfield, IL 62777
Phone: (217)782-4321

Credential Type: Standard Elementary Certificate. **Duration of License:** Four years. **Requirements:** Good character. Good health. At least 19 years of age. Citizen of the U.S. Evidence of teaching experience or completion of an approved program of teacher preparation. Bachelor's degree. 78 semester hours of general education classes which include the following courses and specified semester hours: Language Arts 9; Science 7; Social Science (to include American History and/or Government) 7; Humanities (to include one hr. art and one hr. in music) 8; Mathematics 5; Health and Physical Education 3; plus approved general education electives. 16 semester hours of professional education to include the following courses and semester hours: Educational psychology (to include human growth and development) 2; Methods and techniques of teaching on the elementary level 2; History and/or philosophy of education 2; Methods of teaching reading 2; Pre-student teaching clinical experiences of 100 clock hours at the grade level or in the area of specialization; Identification of and methods of teaching exceptional children 3; plus 16 semester hours of approved professional education electives. Total teacher preparation including professional education, general education, and electives must total at least 120 semester hours Applicants with successful teaching experience at appropriate level do not need to complete pre-student teaching requirement. All applicants must take and pass the Illinois Certification Basic Skills and Subject-Matter Knowledge Tests. Renewal is possible with the passage of a State of Illinois and U.S. Constitution examination. **Examination:** Illinois Certification Basic Skills and Subject-Matter Knowledge Test. **Reciprocity:** Reciprocity exists for applicants holding out-of-state teaching certificates providing their teacher preparation was comparable to that required by the state of Illinois. **Fees:** $44 per section of the Illinois Certification Test.

3957

Teacher of the Blind and Partially Sighted
Certification and Placement Section
100 N. First St.
Springfield, IL 62777
Phone: (217)782-4321

Credential Type: Standard Special Education Certificate. **Duration of License:** Four years. **Requirements:** Good character. Good health. At least 19 years of age. Citizen of the U.S. Evidence of special education teaching experience or completion of an approved special education program of teacher preparation. Bachelor's degree. Meet specified general and professional education requirements. 32 semester hours of appropriate courses in the field including: survey of exceptional children; characteristics of the blind and partially sighted child; methods courses which includes the teaching of Braille; psychological diagnosis; and student teaching. Pass required sections of the Illinois Certification Test. **Examination:** Illinois Certification Test. **Reciprocity:** Reciprocity exists for applicants holding out-of-state teaching certificates providing their teacher preparation was comparable to that required by the state of Illinois. **Fees:** $44 per section of the Illinois Certification Test.

3958

Teacher of the Deaf and Hard of Hearing
Certification and Placement Section
100 N. First St.
Springfield, IL 62777
Phone: (217)782-4321

Credential Type: Standard Special Education Certificate. **Duration of License:** Four years. **Requirements:** Good character. Good health. At least 19 years of age. Citizen of the U.S. Evidence of special education teaching experience or completion of an approved special education program of teacher preparation. Bachelor's degree. Meet specified general and professional education requirements. 32 semester hours of appropriate courses in the field including: five hours in the psychological area; 10 hoursin the science area; 12 hours in the communications and education area; and five hours of student teaching. Pass required sections of the Illinois Certification Test. **Examination:** Illinois Certification Test. **Reciprocity:** Reciprocity exists for applicants holding out-of-state teaching certificates providing their teacher preparation was comparable to that required by the state of Illinois. **Fees:** $44 per section of the Illinois Certification Test.

3959

Teacher of the Educable Mentally Handicapped

Certification and Placement Section
100 N. First St.
Springfield, IL 62777
Phone: (217)782-4321

Credential Type: Standard Special Education Certificate. **Duration of License:** Four years. **Requirements:** Good character. Good health. At least 19 years of age. Citizen of the U.S. Evidence of special education teaching experience or completion of an approved special education program of teacher preparation. Bachelor's degree. Meet specified general and professional education requirements. 32 semester hours of appropriate courses in the field including: survey of exceptional children; characteristics; methods course; psychological diagnosis; and student teaching. Pass required sections of the Illinois Certification Test. **Examination:** Illinois Certification Test. **Reciprocity:** Reciprocity exists for applicants holding out-of-state teaching certificates providing their teacher preparation was comparable to that required by the state of Illinois. **Fees:** $44 per section of the Illinois Certification Test.

3960

Teacher of the Learning Disabled Student

Certification and Placement Section
100 N. First St.
Springfield, IL 62777
Phone: (217)782-4321

Credential Type: Standard Special Education Certificate. **Duration of License:** Four years. **Requirements:** Good character. Good health. At least 19 years of age. Citizen of the U.S. Evidence of special education teaching experience or completion of an approved special education program of teacher preparation. Bachelor's degree. Meet specified general and professional education requirements. 32 semester hours of appropriate courses in the field including: survey of exceptional children; characteristics; methods course; psychological diagnosis; and student teaching in learning disabilities. Pass required sections of the Illinois Certification Test. **Examination:** Illinois Certification Test. **Reciprocity:** Reciprocity exists for applicants holding out-of-state teaching certificates providing their teacher preparation was comparable to that required by the state of Illinois. **Fees:** $44 per section of the Illinois Certification Test.

3961

Teacher of the Physically Handicapped

Certification and Placement Section
100 N. First St.
Springfield, IL 62777
Phone: (217)782-4321

Credential Type: Standard Special Education Certificate. **Duration of License:** Four years. **Requirements:** Good character. Good health. At least 19 years of age. Citizen of the U.S. Evidence of special education teaching experience or completion of an approved special education program of teacher preparation. Bachelor's degree. Meet specified general and professional education requirements. 32 semester hours of appropriate courses in the field including: survey of exceptional children; characteristics of the physically handicapped child; methods courses which includes the teaching of Braille; psychological diagnosis; and student teaching. Pass required sections of the Illinois Certification Test. **Examination:** Illinois Certification Test. **Reciprocity:** Reciprocity exists for applicants holding out-of-state teaching certificates providing their teacher preparation was comparable to that required by the state of Illinois. **Fees:** $44 per section of the Illinois Certification Test.

3962

Teacher of the Socially-Emotionally Impaired

Certification and Placement Section
100 N. First St.
Springfield, IL 62777
Phone: (217)782-4321

Credential Type: Standard Special Education Certificate. **Duration of License:** Four years. **Requirements:** Good character. Good health. At least 19 years of age. Citizen of the U.S. Evidence of special education teaching experience or completion of an approved special education program of teacher preparation. Bachelor's degree. Meet specified general and professional education requirements. 32 semester hours of appropriate courses in the field including: survey of exceptional children; characteristics of the socially-emotionally impaired child; methods course; psychological diagnosis; and student teaching. Pass required sections of the Illinois Certification Test. **Examination:** Illinois Certification Test. **Reciprocity:** Reciprocity exists for applicants holding out-of-state teaching certificates providing their teacher preparation was comparable to that required by the state of Illinois. **Fees:** $44 per section of the Illinois Certification Test.

3963

Teacher of Special Subjects K-12

Certification and Placement Section
100 N. First St.
Springfield, IL 62777
Phone: (217)782-4321

Credential Type: Standard Special Subjects Certificate. **Duration of License:** Four years. **Requirements:** Good character. Good health. At least 19 years of age. Citizen of the U.S. Evidence of teaching experience or completion of an approved program of teacher preparation. Bachelor's degree. 42 semester hours of general education classes which include the following courses and specified semester hours: Language Arts 8; Science and/or Mathematics 6; Social Science (to include American History and/or Government) 6; Humanities 6; Health and Physical Education 3; plus additional electives in general education. 16 semester hours of professional education to include the following courses and semester hours: Educational psychology (to include human growth and development) 2; Methods and techniques of teaching in the area of specialization 2; History and/or philosophy of education 2; Pre-student teaching clinical experiences of 100 clock hours in the area of specialization; Identification of and methods of teaching exceptional children 3; plus five semester hours of approved professional education electives. Must complete one major area of specialization totaling 32 semester hours Total teacher preparation including professional education, general education, major and electives must total at least 120 semester hours Applicants with successful teaching experience at appropriate level do not need to complete pre-student teaching requirement. All applicants must take and pass the Illinois Certification Basic Skills and Subject-Matter Knowledge Tests. Renewal is possible with the passage of a State of Illinois and U.S. Constitution examination. **Examination:** Illinois Certification Basic Skills and Subject-Matter Knowledge Tests. **Reciprocity:** Reciprocity exists for applicants holding out-of-state teaching certificates providing their teacher preparation was comparable to that required by the state of Illinois. **Fees:** $44.00 per section of the Illinois Certification Test.

Credential Type: Supervisory Endorsement. **Requirements:** Standard Special Subject Certificate. Master's degree. Eight semester hours of graduate professional education courses which includes one course in supervision of personnel and one course in administration and organization of schools. Two years of appropriate teaching experience.

3964

Teacher of Speech and Language Impaired Students
Certification and Placement Section
100 N. First St.
Springfield, IL 62777
Phone: (217)782-4321

Credential Type: Standard Special Education Endorsement. **Duration of License:** Four years. **Requirements:** Good character. Good health. At least 19 years of age. Citizen of the U.S. Evidence of special education teaching experience or completion of an approved special education program of teacher preparation. Bachelor's degree. Meet specified general and professional education requirements. Master's degree and completion of a course in communicative disorders and related disciplines. Knowledge and understanding of the normal development use of speech, hearing, and language. General understanding of the public schools; general knowledge of procedures used with other educational handicaps. Knowledge and competency in application of psychological principles. Clinical practicum in communicative disorders. Pass required sections of the Illinois Certification Test. **Examination:** Illinois Certification Test. **Reciprocity:** Reciprocity exists for applicants holding out-of-state teaching certificates providing their teacher preparation was comparable to that required by the state of Illinois. **Fees:** $44 per section of the Illinois Certification Test.

3965

Teacher of the Trainable Mentally Handicapped
Certification and Placement Section
100 N. First St.
Springfield, IL 62777
Phone: (217)782-4321

Credential Type: Standard Special Education Certificate. **Duration of License:** Four years. **Requirements:** Good character. Good health. At least 19 years of age. Citizen of the U.S. Evidence of special education teaching experience or completion of an approved special education program of teacher preparation. Bachelor's degree. Meet specified general and professional education requirements. 32 semester hours of appropriate courses in the field including: survey of exceptional children; characteristics of the trainable mentally handicapped child; methods course; psychological diagnosis; and student teaching. Pass required sections of the Illinois Certification Test. **Examination:** Illinois Certification Test. **Reciprocity:** Reciprocity exists for applicants holding out-of-state teaching certificates providing their teacher preparation was comparable to that required by the state of Illinois. **Fees:** $44 per section of the Illinois Certification Test.

Indiana

3966

Elementary School Teacher (1-6)
Teacher Certification
Center for Professional Development
State House, Rm. 229
Indianapolis, IN 46204-2798
Phone: (317)232-9010

Credential Type: Standard License. **Duration of License:** Five years. **Authorization:** Authorizes the teaching of first through 6th grade and nondepartmentalized 7th and 8th grade. **Requirements:** Baccalaureate degree. An undergraduate program of 124 semester hours structured as follows: 70 hours of general education which includes language arts, science, social studies, mathematics, arts, and electives such as physical and mental health, communicative exceptionality, safety education, recreation, physical activity, and nutrition; 30 hours of professional education which includes foundations of education, educational psychology, methods and materials, specific and continuing pre-student teaching field experience, classroom management, developmental reading, educational measurement and evaluation, ethnic and disability awareness, and nine weeks of full-time student teaching; plus 24 hours of electives. Be recommended for licensing by the institution granting degree. Successfully complete the National Teachers Examination (NTE) Core Battery and the NTE Specialty Area exam in Early Childhood Education.

License may be renewed for the following five year period if continuing education requirements are completed. These may include additional graduate semester hours and certification renewal units (CRUs) granted for approved professional experiences. The Standard License may be endorsed for specific subjects (Grades 1-9) upon completion of 18 semester hours of course work in the subject and a practicum in junior high education. **Examination:** NTE Core Battery and the NTE Specialty Area Exam in Elementary Education.

Credential Type: Professionalization Endorsement. **Duration of License:** 10 years. **Requirements:** Complete five years' teaching experience in accredited schools at the level covered by the Standard License. Approved master's degree. 15 semester hours of graduate level courses.(Candidates with additional teaching areas of endorsement may professionalize these areas on completion of three semester hours of course work in subject matter area.) Be recommended for Professional Licensure by institution granting the master's degree. The Professional License may be endorsed for specific subjects (Grades 1-9) upon completion of 18 semester hours of course work in the subject and a practicum in junior high education.

3967

Primary School Teacher (K-3)
Teacher Certification
Center for Professional Development
State House, Rm. 229
Indianapolis, IN 46204-2798
Phone: (317)232-9010

Credential Type: Standard License. **Duration of License:** Five years. **Requirements:** Baccalaureate degree. Completion of undergraduate program consisting of the following semester hours: 40 hours of general education which includes language arts, science, social studies, mathematics, and arts; 30 subject matter hours; and 30 hours of professional education that includes one semester of full-time student teaching, foundations of education, educational psychology, methods and materials, classroom management, six hours of development, diagnostic and corrective reading, ethnic and disability awareness, and 24 hours of electives. Be recommended for licensing by the institution granting degree. Successfully complete the NTE Core Battery and the National Teachers Examination (NTE) Specialty Area exam in Early Childhood Education.

License may be renewed for the following five year period if continuing education requirements are completed. These may include additional graduate semester hours and certification renewal units (CRUs) granted for approved professional experiences. The Standard License may also be extended in subject area coverages upon completion of appropriate endorsement teaching minors.

Credential Type: Professionalization Endorsement. **Duration of License:** 10 years. **Requirements:** Complete five years' teaching experience in accredited schools at the level covered by the Standard License. Approved master's degree. 15 semester hours of graduate level courses.(Candidates with additional teaching areas of endorsement may professionalize these areas on completion of three semester hours of course work in subject matter area.) Be recommended for Professional Licensure by institution granting the master's degree. The Professional License may also be extended in subject area coverages upon com-

Primary School Teacher (K-3), continued

pletion of appropriate endorsement teaching minors.

Iowa

3968

Elementary School Teacher (K-6)
Board of Educational Examiners
Grimes State Office Bldg.
Des Moines, IA 50319-0147
Phone: (515)281-3245

Credential Type: Provisional Certificate. **Duration of License:** Two years. **Requirements:** Baccalaureate degree. Complete approved teacher program. Complete approved human relations component. Complete course work or evidence of competency in: structure of American education; philosophies of education; professional ethics and legal responsibilities; psychology of teaching; audiovisual/media/computer technology; evaluation techniques; human development; exceptional learner; classroom management; instructional planning; curriculum; methods of teaching; prestudent field-based experiences; and student teaching in desired subject area and grade level. Plus curriculum content courses that include: methods and materials of teaching a variety of elementary subjects; prestudent teaching experience in at least two different grades; and specialization in a single discipline or a formal interdisciplinary program of at least 12 semester hours Certificate is renewable for a second two-year term.

Credential Type: Education Certificate. **Duration of License:** Five years. **Requirements:** Provisional Certificate. Two years of successful teaching experience based on a local evaluation process. Renewable.

Credential Type: Professional Teacher's Certificate. **Duration of License:** Five years. **Requirements:** Holder of or eligible for an Education Certificate. Five years of teaching experience. Master's degree in the area of a teaching endorsement. Renewable.

3969

Prekindergarten/Kindergarten Teacher
Board of Educational Examiners
Grimes State Office Bldg.
Des Moines, IA 50319-0147
Phone: (515)281-3245

Credential Type: Provisional Certificate. **Duration of License:** Two years. **Requirements:** Baccalaureate degree. Complete approved teacher program. Complete approved human relations component. Complete course work or evidence of competency in: structure of American education; philosophies of education; professional ethics and legal responsibilities; psychology of teaching; audiovisual/media/computer technology; evaluation techniques; human development; exceptional learner; classroom management; instructional planning; curriculum; methods of teaching; prestudent field-based experiences; and student teaching in desired subject area and grade level. Plus curriculum content courses that include: methods and materials used in teaching young children; pre-student teaching experience; and specialization in a single discipline or a formal interdisciplinary program of at least 12 semester hours Certificate is renewable for a second two-year term.

Credential Type: Education Certificate. **Duration of License:** Five years. **Requirements:** Provisional Certificate. Two years of successful teaching experience based on a local evaluation process. Renewable.

Credential Type: Professional Teacher's Certificate. **Duration of License:** Five years. **Requirements:** Holder of or eligible for an Education Certificate. Five years of teaching experience. Master's degree in the area of a teaching endorsement. Renewable.

3970

Reading Specialist (K-12)
Board of Educational Examiners
Grimes State Office Bldg.
Des Moines, IA 50319-0147
Phone: (515)281-3245

Credential Type: Reading Specialist Endorsement. **Requirements:** Master's degree. Holder of or eligible for the Education Certificate and an endorsement. One year experience which includes the teaching of reading as a significant part. Complete 27 semester hours focusing on reading, including a practicum in reading.

3971

Special Education Teacher
Board of Educational Examiners
Grimes State Office Bldg.
Des Moines, IA 50319-0147
Phone: (515)281-3245

Credential Type: Special Education Endorsement. **Requirements:** Baccalaureate degree. Complete an approved teacher education program. Complete an approved human relations component. 24 semester hours in special education, as well as other specific requirements, as necessary for teaching endorsements in the areas of mental and learning disabilities, hearing and visual impairment, the physically handicapped, and early childhood-special education.

Kansas

3972

Elementary School Teacher
Certification Specialist
Kansas State Dept. of Education
Kansas State Education Bldg.
120 E. 10th St.
Topeka, KS 66612-1103
Phone: (913)296-2288

Credential Type: Elementary Certificate. **Duration of License:** Three years. **Requirements:** Bachelor's degree. Complete a state-approved teacher education program with general, professional, and field specialization components. The general component must be designed to develop the student's skills of analysis, synthesis and evaluation, competence in written and oral communication skills, understanding of and the ability to use basic mathematical properties, processes and symbols, and the study and application of modes of inquiry, plus the characteristics of the disciplines in the arts, humanities, natural sciences, and the social sciences. This component also requires the study of the historical and cultural values, customs, and social institutions of both western and non-western cultures, and both minority and majority cultures in our society. The professional component must be based on studies which include: the foundations of education; methods and materials of teaching; and supervised laboratory experiences as designed to provide competencies required in the education professions. Must also include observation and experience with school-age youth and a supervised student teaching program. The field of specialization component must be designed to produce the competencies needed to teach the subject at the designated grade fields. Minimum GPA of 2.5 on a four point scale. Pass Pre-Professional Skills Test with the following scores: 168 Reading; 168 Mathematics; 170 Writing. Pass the National Teacher Examination, Professional Knowledge portion, with a score of 642. Have recent college credit or recent accredited experience, within six years preceding application. **Examination:** Pre-Professional Skills Test. National Teacher Examination (Professional Knowledge).

Kentucky

3973

Early Childhood Teacher (K-4)
Kentucky Dept. of Education
Div. of Teacher Education and Certification
Capitol Plaza Tower, 18th Fl.
500 Mero St.
Frankfort, KY 40601
Phone: (502)564-4606

Credential Type: Provisional Certificate for Teaching in the Early Elementary Grades. **Duration of License:** Five years. **Requirements:** Complete an approved program at a four year college or university. Program must be completed within five years of application or complete six semester hours of graduate credit in that time period. Must apply for a permit from the State Board of Education to enter into a one year beginning teacher internship and complete that internship successfully. Must complete written tests designated by the State Board of Education for: general knowledge; communication skills; professional education; concepts; and knowledge in the specific teaching field of the applicant, with minimum scores in each test as set by the Board. An applicant who holds an expired teaching certificate or an applicant having completed two or more years of acceptable teaching experience outside of Kentucky, who otherwise qualifies for certification, will not be required to take the written tests or to participate in the beginning teacher internship program. Certificate may be renewed upon three years of successful teaching experience or six semester hours of graduate credit. **Examination:** Written examinations determines by the State Board of Education.

Credential Type: Kindergarten Endorsement. **Requirements:** Complete an approved program at a college or university for Kindergarten aged students. Successful teaching experience.

Credential Type: Standard Certificate (K-4). **Duration of License:** Five years. **Requirements:** Qualify for Provisional Certificate for Teaching in the Early Elementary Grades. Master's degree.

Credential Type: Temporary Certificate. **Duration of License:** One year. **Requirements:** Applicants who do not meet the recency of preparation requirement and who have not previously held a regular Kentucky teaching certificate, but who otherwise qualify for certification, may be issued a one year certificate which expires on June 30 of the next calendar year. During the life of the temporary certificate the applicant will be required to complete six semester hours of credit to renew his/her certificate in the usual manner.

3974

Middle School Teacher (5-8)
Kentucky Dept. of Education
Div. of Teacher Education and Certification
Capitol Plaza Tower, 18th Fl.
500 Mero St.
Frankfort, KY 40601
Phone: (502)564-4606

Credential Type: Provisional Certification for Teaching in the Middle Grades. **Duration of License:** Five years. **Requirements:** Complete an approved program at a four year college or university. Program must be completed within five years of application or complete six semester hours of graduate credit in that time period. Must apply for a permit from the State Board of Education to enter into a one year beginning teacher internship and complete that internship successfully. Must complete written tests designated by the State Board of Education for: general knowledge; communication skills; professional education; concepts; and knowledge in the specific teaching field of the applicant, with minimum scores in each test as set by the Board. An applicant who holds an expired teaching certificate or an applicant having completed two or more years of acceptable teaching experience outside of Kentucky, who otherwise qualifies for certification, will not be required to take the written tests or to participate in the beginning teacher internship program. Certificate may be renewed upon three years of successful teaching experience or six semester hours of graduate credit. **Examination:** Written examinations determines by the State Board of Education.

Credential Type: Middle Grade Endorsement of Early Childhood or Secondary Grades. **Requirements:** Complete an approved program at a college or university for secondary school students. Successful teaching experience.

Credential Type: Temporary Certificate. **Duration of License:** One year. **Requirements:** Applicants who do not meet the recency of preparation requirement and who have not previously held a regular Kentucky teaching certificate, but who otherwise qualify for certification, may be issued a one year certificate which expires on June 30 of the next calendar year. During the life of the temporary certificate the applicant will be required to complete six semester hours of credit to renew his/her certificate in the usual manner.

3975

Music Teacher
Kentucky Dept. of Education
Div. of Teacher Education and Certification
Capitol Plaza Tower, 18th Fl.
500 Mero St.
Frankfort, KY 40601
Phone: (502)564-4606

Credential Type: Provisional Certificate for Teaching of Music. **Duration of License:** Five years. **Requirements:** Four year program of teacher preparation including bachelor's degree. 24 semester hours of professional preparation which includes: three hours human growth and development and learning theory; two hours basic concepts concerning education; music education methods and materials appropriate for all grade levels; and a practicum. Preparation must also include 48 hours of instrumental music, 48 hours of vocal music, and 60 hours that combines instrumental and vocal music. Other courses must include music theory, harmony, ear training, comprehensive musicianship, form, analysis, orchestration, arranging, counterpoint, composition, conducting, history of music, and literature of music. Certificate is renewable.

3976

Special Education Teacher
Kentucky Dept. of Education
Div. of Teacher Education and Certification
Capitol Plaza Tower, 18th Fl.
500 Mero St.
Frankfort, KY 40601
Phone: (502)564-4606

Credential Type: Provisional Certificate for Teachers of Exceptional Children. **Duration of License:** Five years. **Requirements:** Complete program approved by the Kentucky State Plan for the Preparation Program for Certification of Professional School Personnel for learning and behavior

Kentucky 3977

Special Education Teacher, continued

disorders or trainable mentally handicapped, or hearing impaired. Qualify for a provisional teaching certificate in grades K-4 or 5-8.

Credential Type: Standard Special Education Certificate. **Duration of License:** Five years. **Requirements:** Qualify for Provisional Certificate for Teachers of Exceptional Children. Hold a master's degree consisting of 30 graduate credit hours or 24 graduate credit hours and a thesis. Nine hours should include credit from the following areas: general study of curriculum development; research methodology; advanced study in human growth and development; psychology of learning; a seminar in instruction devoted to the methods of teaching; and foundations in education, which include sociological, psychological, philosophical, and historical. 12 hours should include courses in applicant's specialization or that further develop educational background.

3977

Teacher for Gifted Education
Kentucky Dept. of Education
Div. of Teacher Education and Certification
Capitol Plaza Tower, 18th Fl.
500 Mero St.
Frankfort, KY 40601
Phone: (502)564-4606

Credential Type: Gifted Education Endorsement. **Requirements:** Classroom teaching certificate. One year of teaching experience. Complete an approved graduate level curriculum with at least nine semester hours of credit that gives emphasis to the following: nature and needs of gifted education; assessment and/or counseling of the gifted; curriculum development for the gifted; and creative studies. Three semester hours of credit in a supervised practicum for gifted education. However, with two years experience as a teacher for gifted, the practicum may be waived.

Louisiana

3978

Early Childhood Teacher (N-K)
Louisiana Dept. of Education
Box 94064
Baton Rouge, LA 70804-9064
Phone: (504)342-3490

Credential Type: Standard Certificate—Type C. **Duration of License:** Three years. **Requirements:** Baccalaureate degree, including an approved teacher education program and student teaching. Appropriate National Teacher Examination (NTE) scores. 46 general education semester hours which include: 12 hours English; 12 hours Social Studies; 12 hours Science; six hours Mathematics; and four hours health and physical education. 27 professional education hours which include: three hours history of education, introduction to education, foundations of education and/or philosophy of education; three hours educational psychology and/or principles of teaching and learning; nine hours of student teaching or practicum; and 12 hours of professional courses for teaching children under age six. 39 semester hours of specialized academic education to include 21 additional hours in the following: art; children's literature; safety and first aid; Louisiana history and/or geography; music; speech; teaching of reading; nutrition; methods and materials and/or creative activities for young children. Plus 18 hours of home economics. **Examination:** NTE.

Credential Type: Standard Certificate—Type B. **Duration of License:** Valid for life for continuous service endorsed thereon. **Requirements:** Standard Type C Certificate or equivalent. Three years of successful teaching experience.

Credential Type: Standard Certificate—Type A. **Duration of License:** Valid for life for continuous service. **Requirements:** Standard Type C or Type B Certificate or equivalent. Master's degree, or higher, from an approved institution. Five years of successful teaching in a certified field.

3979

Elementary School Teacher
Louisiana Dept. of Education
Box 94064
Baton Rouge, LA 70804-9064
Phone: (504)342-3490

Credential Type: Standard Certificate—Type C. **Duration of License:** Three years. **Requirements:** Baccalaureate degree, including an approved teacher education program and student teaching. Appropriate National Teacher Examination (NTE) scores. 46 general education semester hours which include: 12 hours of English, including grammar and composition; 12 hours of Social Studies; 12 hours of Science, including biological and physical; six hours of Mathematics; and four hours of Health and Physical Education. 30 hours of professional education which include: three hours history of education, introduction to education, foundations of education and/or philosophy of education; three hours educational psychology and/or principles of teaching and learning; nine hours of student teaching or practicum; three hours introduction to the study of exceptional children; three hours of child psychology; six hours of reading; and a three hr. reading practicum. Specialized academic education to include: three hours of children's literature; three hours of speech; two hours of nutrition education; three hours of Louisiana history and/or Louisiana geography; three hours of art for elementary students; and three hours of music. **Examination:** NTE.

Credential Type: Standard Certificate—Type B. **Duration of License:** Valid for life for continuous service endorsed thereon. **Requirements:** Standard Type C Certificate or equivalent. Three years of successful teaching experience.

Credential Type: Standard Certificate—Type A. **Duration of License:** Valid for life for continuous service. **Requirements:** Standard Type C or Type B Certificate or equivalent. Master's degree, or higher, from an approved institution. Five years of successful teaching in a certified field.

3980

Teacher of Exceptional Children
Louisiana Dept. of Education
Box 94064
Baton Rouge, LA 70804-9064
Phone: (504)342-3490

Credential Type: Standard Certificate with Mild/Moderate Impairment Endorsement. **Requirements:** Baccalaureate degree, including an approved teacher education program and student teaching. Appropriate National Teacher Examination (NTE) scores. 46 general education hours which include: 12 hours English; 12 hours Social Studies; 12 hours Science; six hours Mathematics; and four hours Physical Education. 27 professional education semester hours which include: three hours history of education; three hours educational psychology and/or principles of teaching; and student teaching in a mild/moderate classroom. For elementary level teaching: three hours of child psychology; three hours teaching of reading, and a three semester hr. practicum. For secondary level teaching: three hours adolescent psychology and six hours teaching of reading. 36 hours of specialized education which includes: six hours general knowledge; 12 hours methods and materials; nine hours management; six hours assessment and evaluation; and three hours mainstreaming practicum. Secondary level teaching also requires six hours teaching prevocational/vocational skills.

Credential Type: Standard Certificate with Severe/Profound Endorsement. **Requirements:** Baccalaureate degree, including an approved teacher education program and student teaching. Appropriate NTE scores. 46 general education semester hours which include: 12 hours English; 12 hours Social Studies; 12 hours Science; six hours Mathematics; and four hours Physical Education. 30 professional education semester hours which include: three hours history of education; three hours educational psychology and/or principles of teaching; nine hours student teaching in severe/profound classroom; and 15 hours of professional education teaching courses. 36 specialized education semester hours to include six hours general knowledge; six hours instructional strategies; three hours learning principles and classroom/behavior management; six hours assessment and evaluation; three hours methods of working with paraprofessionals; three hours parent, family and community involvement; three hours communication strategies; and six hours of electives.

Maine

3981

Elementary Teacher (K-6)
Teacher Certification
Dept. of Education
State House Station 23
Augusta, ME 04333
Phone: (207)289-5944

Credential Type: Provisional Certificate. **Duration of License:** Two years. **Requirements:** Bachelor's degree from an approved institution. Complete an approved preparation program for the education of elementary teachers which is comprised of a least 50 percent liberal arts and a distribution of six semester hours in each of the four content areas (math, English, science, social science). Or applicant may hold a bachelor's degree with a liberal arts distribution and at least six semester hours in each of the four content areas. 24 semester hours must be comprised of courses from the following list: knowledge of the learner; knowledge of the learning process; teaching exceptional children in the regular classroom; content area methods; curriculum design and program evaluation; early and ongoing experience or practicum; and one academic semester or 15 weeks of full-time student teaching. Formal recommendation of the institution where degree was granted. Pass the NTE Core Battery. Nonrenewable. **Examination:** National Teacher Examination Core Battery.

Credential Type: Conditional Certificate. **Duration of License:** Two years. **Authorization:** Authorizes an applicant to hold a paid teaching position while completing requirements for a particular position. **Requirements:** Applicants are expected to complete all requirements for desired certificate during the term of this conditional certificate. Renewable only with approval.

Credential Type: Professional Certificate. **Duration of License:** Five years. **Requirements:** Hold Provisional Certificate. Be recommended for the professional certificate from the support system, based upon the completion of a Professional Renewal Plan (PRP), including six classroom observations. Renewable.

Credential Type: Master Certificate. **Duration of License:** Five years. **Requirements:** Hold a Professional Certificate. Demonstrate exemplary professional skills. Have knowledge of current theories of effective instruction. Has made outstanding contributions to the teaching profession in curriculum design, staff development, clinical supervision of student teachers or peer observation of teachers, or educational leadership.

Maryland

3982

Early Childhood Teacher (N-3)
Dept. of Certification 18100
State Dept. of Education
200 W. Baltimore St.
Baltimore, MD 21201
Phone: (301)333-2142

Credential Type: Standard Professional Certificate. **Requirements:** Bachelor's or higher degree completed within five years preceding the issuance of the certificate or hold a bachelor's degree and complete six hours of acceptable credit within five years preceding the issuance of the certificate. Graduate from an approved teacher preparation program in Maryland or complete the specific credit count requirements for Maryland for an early childhood teacher or complete an undergraduate pre-service program produced by the National Council for Accreditation of Teacher Education (NCATE) after July 1, 1975. Must have completed a teacher education program within the past 10 years from an approved institution or hold a professional teacher's certificate from one of the states participating in the Interstate Contract Agreement and have taught for at least 27 months during the past seven years. Must pass the following tests in the National Teacher's Examinations: The Communication Skills Test of the Core Battery; The General Knowledge Test of the Core Battery; The Professional Knowledge Test of the Core Battery; and the appropriate Specialty Area Test. Must have 80 semester credit hours in the following academic content courses to include: nine hours English; nine hours social studies (6 hours history and three hours geography); three hours mathematics; six science (including three each in biological and physical science); two hours art; two hours music; and two hours physical education. Plus 26 semester hours in professional education courses to include: six hours foundations of education (including education psychology); 12 hours curriculum and methods (including reading, language arts, social studies, and creative activities); and eight hours of student teaching which includes a combination of N/K and grades 1, 2, or 3. All applicants must have three semester hours of college credit or state-approved inservice workshop credit in special education approved by the board. **Examination:** Following sections of the National Teacher's Examinations: The Communication Skills Test of the Core Battery; The General Knowledge Test of the Core Battery; The Professional Knowledge Test of the Core Battery; and the appropriate Specialty Area Test.

Credential Type: Provisional Degree Certificate. **Authorization:** Issued to applicant with bachelor's degree who fails to meet the requirements for Standard Professional Certificate. **Requirements:** Bachelor's degree. Continue working towards Standard Professional Certificate.

Credential Type: Advanced Professional Certificate. **Requirements:** Three years of successful teaching experience. Meet requirements for Standard Professional Certificate. Have relevant master's degree or complete 30 semester hours relevant to professional assignment (at least 15 hours must be a graduate level) or complete at least 30 semester hours of in-service education developed by the local school units and approved by the State Superintendent of Schools.

Credential Type: Resident Teacher Certificate. **Duration of License:** One year. **Requirements:** Bachelor's degree from an accredited institution with a concentration in a discipline appropriate to the early childhood education curriculum. Grades of "B" or better in major area of study. Must pass the following tests in the National Teacher's Examinations: The Communication Skills Test of the Core Battery; The General Knowledge Test of the Core Battery; and the appropriate Specialty Area Test. Verification by the local Superintendent of 90 clock hours of study developed according to the Maryland State Dept. of Education guidelines. Other requirements, as deemed necessary, by the State Dept. of Education. Renewable for one year.

Maryland

3983

Elementary School Teacher
Dept. of Certification 18100
State Dept. of Education
200 W. Baltimore St.
Baltimore, MD 21201
Phone: (301)333-2142

Credential Type: Standard Professional Certificate. **Requirements:** Bachelor's or higher degree completed within five years preceding the issuance of the certificate or hold a bachelor's degree and complete six hours of acceptable credit within five years preceding the issuance of the certificate. Graduate from an approved teacher preparation program in Maryland or complete the specific credit count requirements for Maryland for an elementary school teacher or complete an undergraduate pre-service program produced by the NCATE after July 1, 1975. Must have completed a teacher education program within the past 10 years from an approved institution or hold a professional teacher's certificate from one of the states participating in the Interstate Contract Agreement and have taught for at least 27 months during the past seven years. Must pass the following tests in the National Teacher's Examinations: The Communication Skills Test of the Core Battery; The General Knowledge Test of the Core Battery; The Professional Knowledge Test of the Core Battery; and the appropriate Specialty Area Test. Complete 80 semester hours of academic content courses to include: 12 hours English; 15 hours social studies (including three hours of geography and nine hours of history); 12 hours science (including three hours each in biological and physical science); six hours mathematics; two hours art; two hours music; and two hours physical education. 26 semester hours of professional education which includes: six hours foundations of education, including educational psychology; 12 hours of curriculum and methods of elementary education, consisting of the teaching of reading and other basic subjects; and eight semester hours of supervised observation and student teaching in the elementary grades. All applicants must have three semester hours of college credit or state-approved inservice workshop credit in special education approved by the board. **Examination:** Following sections of the National Teacher's Examinations: The Communication Skills Test of the Core Battery; The General Knowledge Test of the Core Battery; The Professional Knowledge Test of the Core Battery; and the appropriate Specialty Area Test.

Credential Type: Provisional Degree Certificate. **Authorization:** Issued to applicant with bachelor's degree who fails to meet the requirements for Standard Professional Certificate. **Requirements:** Bachelor's degree. Continue working towards Standard Professional Certificate.

Credential Type: Advanced Professional Certificate. **Requirements:** Three years of successful teaching experience. Meet requirements for Standard Professional Certificate. Have relevant master's degree or complete 30 semester hours relevant to professional assignment (at least 15 hours must be a graduate level) or complete at least 30 semester hours of in-service education developed by the local school units and approved by the State Superintendent of Schools.

Credential Type: Resident Teacher Certificate. **Duration of License:** One year. **Requirements:** Bachelor's degree from an accredited institution with a concentration in a discipline appropriate to the elementary education curriculum. Grades of "B" or better in major area of study. Must pass the following tests in the National Teacher's Examinations: The Communication Skills Test of the Core Battery; The General Knowledge Test of the Core Battery; and the appropriate Specialty Area Test. Verification by the local Superintendent of 90 clock hours of study developed according to the Maryland State Dept. of Education guidelines. Other requirements, as deemed necessary, by the State Dept. of Education. Renewable for one year.

Massachusetts

3984

Early Childhood Teacher (K-3)
Massachusetts Dept. of Education
1385 Hancock St.
Quincy, MA 02169
Phone: (617)770-7500

Credential Type: Teaching Certificate. **Requirements:** Satisfy the five Standards established by the Massachusetts Dept. of Education. Standard I includes 36 semester hours of course work in the following areas: stages and characteristics of normal child development; sensory, motor, social, emotional and cognitive development; learning theory in general; and basic studies of early childhood education which include reading, communication, the arts, mathematics, science, social studies, health, and physical education. Plus 21 semester hours of pre-practicum experience and, in addition, complete a successful practicum of 300 clock hours, at least half of which must be in grades K-3 and the remainder in a preschool setting. Standard II-Be able to communicate clearly, understandably, and appropriately. Standard III—Be able to design instruction to facilitate learning consistent with needs and interest of the learners. Standard IV—Be able to use results of various evaluative procedures to stress effectiveness of instruction. Standard V—Be equitable, sensitive, and responsive to all learners.

3985

Elementary School Teacher (1-6)
Massachusetts Dept. of Education
1385 Hancock St.
Quincy, MA 02169
Phone: (617)770-7500

Credential Type: Teaching Certificate. **Requirements:** Satisfy the five Standards established by the Massachusetts Dept. of Education. Standard I includes 36 semester hours of course work in basic studies of elementary education which include reading, communication, the arts, mathematics, science, social studies, health, and physical education. Concentration in one or more of these fields at a level that approximates a college minor. Plus 21 semester hours of pre-practicum experience and, in addition, complete a successful practicum of 300 clock hours at the elementary level. Standard II-Be able to communicate clearly, understandably, and appropriately. Standard III—Be able to design instruction to facilitate learning consistent with needs and interest of the learners. Standard IV—Be able to use results of various evaluative procedures to stress effectiveness of instruction. Standard V—Be equitable, sensitive, and responsive to all learners.

3986

Teacher of Children With Special Needs
Massachusetts Dept. of Education
1385 Hancock St.
Quincy, MA 02169
Phone: (617)770-7500

Credential Type: Young Children With Special Needs Endorsement. **Requirements:** Teaching Certificate. Complete a pre-practicum of 30 semester hours of course work and other related experiences plus a 300 clock hr. practicum for preschool children with special needs. Demonstrate the competencies contained in the five Standards established by the Massachusetts Dept. of Education for working with young children with special needs. Standard I-Knowledge of the following: Developmental psychology and psychology of children in general and particularly for young children. Standard II-Be able to communicate clearly, understandably, and appropriately. Standard III—Be able to design instruction to facilitate learning consistent with needs and interest of the learners. Standard IV—Be able to use results of various evaluative procedures to stress effectiveness of instruction. Standard V—Be equitable, sensitive, and responsive to all learners.

Credential Type: Children With Severe Special Needs Endorsement. **Requirements:** Teaching Certificate. Complete a pre-practicum of 30 semester hours of course work and other related experiences plus a 300 clock hr. practicum for children with severe special needs. Demonstrate the competencies contained in the five Standards established by the Massachusetts Dept. of Education for working with young children with special needs. Standard I-Knowledge of the following: Developmental psychology and psychology of children in general and particularly for children with severe special needs. Standard IIBe able to communicate clearly, understandably, and appropriately. Standard III—Be able to design instruction to facilitate learning consistent with needs and interest of the learners. Standard IV—Be able to use results of various evaluative procedures to stress effectiveness of instruction. Standard V—Be equitable, sensitive, and responsive to all learners.

Credential Type: Children With Moderate Special Needs Endorsement. **Requirements:** Teaching Certificate. Complete a pre-practicum of 30 semester hours of course work and other related experiences plus a 300 clock hr. practicum for children with moderate special needs. Demonstrate the competencies contained in the five Standards established by the Massachusetts Dept. of Education for working with young children with special needs. Standard I-Knowledge of the following: Developmental psychology and psychology of children in general and particularly for children with moderate special needs. Standard II-Be able to communicate clearly, understandably, and appropriately. Standard III—Be able to design instruction to facilitate learning consistent with needs and interest of the learners. Standard IV—Be able to use results of various evaluative procedures to stress effectiveness of instruction. Standard V—Be equitable, sensitive, and responsive to all learners.

Credential Type: Children With Special Needs Endorsement—Vision. **Requirements:** Teaching Certificate. Complete a pre-practicum of 30 semester hours of course work and other related experiences plus a 300 clock hr. practicum for children with vision impairment. Demonstrate the competencies contained in the five Standards established by the Massachusetts Dept. of Education for working with young children with special needs. Standard I-Knowledge of the following: Developmental psychology and psychology of children in general and particularly for children with vision impairment. Standard II-Be able to communicate clearly, understandably, and appropriately. Standard III—Be able to design instruction to facilitate learning consistent with needs and interest of the learners. Standard IV—Be able to use results of various evaluative procedures to stress effectiveness of instruction. Standard V—Be equitable, sensitive, and responsive to all learners.

Credential Type: Children With Special Needs—Audition. **Requirements:** Teaching Certificate with 36 semester hours in subject field. Complete a pre-practicum of 48 semester hours of course work and other related experiences plus a 300 clock hr. practicum for children with hearing impairment. Demonstrate the competencies contained in the five Standards established by the Massachusetts Dept. of Education for working with young children with special needs. Standard I-Knowledge of the following: Developmental psychology and psychology of children in general and particularly for children with hearing impairment. Standard II-Be able to communicate clearly, understandably, and appropriately. Standard III—Be able to design instruction to facilitate learning consistent with needs and interest of the learners. Standard IV—Be able to use results of various evaluative procedures to stress effectiveness of instruction. Standard V—Be equitable, sensitive, and responsive to all learners.

Credential Type: Children With Speech, Language, and Hearing Disorders Endorsement. **Requirements:** Teaching Certificate. Complete a pre-practicum of 60 semester hours of course work and other related experiences plus a 300 clock hr. practicum for children with speech, language, and hearing disorders. Demonstrate the competencies contained in the five Standards established by the Massachusetts Dept. of Education for working with young children with special needs. Standard IKnowledge of the following: Developmental psychology and psychology of children in general and particularly for children with speech, language, and hearing disorders. Standard II-Be able to communicate clearly, understandably, and appropriately. Standard III—Be able to design instruction to facilitate learning consistent with needs and interest of the learners. Standard IV—Be able to use results of various evaluative procedures to stress effectiveness of instruction. Standard V—Be equitable, sensitive, and responsive to all learners.

Credential Type: Consulting Teacher of Children With Special Needs Endorsement. **Requirements:** Classroom teaching certificate and two years of employment under the certificate. Complete a pre-practicum of 60 semester hours of course work and other related experiences plus a 300 clock hr. practicum for children with special needs. Demonstrate the competencies contained in the five Standards established by the Massachusetts Dept. of Education for working with young children with special needs. Standard I-Knowledge of the following: Developmental psychology and psychology of children in general and particularly for children with special needs. Standard II-Be able to communicate clearly, understandably, and appropriately. Standard III—Be able to design instruction to facilitate learning consistent with needs and interest of the learners. Standard IV—Be able to use results of various evaluative procedures to stress effectiveness of instruction. Standard V—Be equitable, sensitive, and responsive to all learners.

3987

Transitional Bilingual Education Teacher
Massachusetts Dept. of Education
1385 Hancock St.
Quincy, MA 02169
Phone: (617)770-7500

Credential Type: Transitional Bilingual Education Endorsement. **Requirements:** Teaching certificate. Demonstrate, through state administered test procedures, speaking and reading proficiency in a language other than English and knowledge of culture associated with other languages. **Examination:** Massachusetts state test in speaking and reading proficiency in a language other than English.

Michigan

3988

Elementary School Teacher
Teacher Preparation and Certification
Michigan Dept. of Education
Box 30008
Lansing, MI 48909
Phone: (517)373-3310

Credential Type: State Elementary Provisional Certificate. **Duration of License:** Six years. **Authorization:** Certificates issued since September 1, 1988 are valid for all subjects in grades K-5 and are valid in areas of certification (subject area majors and minors) in grades 6-8. Teachers assigned to self contained classrooms may also teach all subjects in grades 6-8. **Requirements:** Bachelor's degree and recommendation from an approved teacher training institution. Three minors of 20 semester hours each, of which two will be in substantive fields, and may include a group minor

Minnesota 3989

Elementary School Teacher, continued

of 24 semester hours, and one of which may be a combination of methods and content appropriate to elementary education. Or candidate may have a major of 30 semester hours (group majors must be 36 semester hours) and one minor of 20 semester hours in other fields relevant to elementary education. Six semester hours of teaching of reading are required plus 20 professional education requirements to include: developmental needs of preadolescents and early adolescents, including the needs of the exceptional child; structure, function and purposes of educational institutions in our society; methods and materials of elementary and middle level instruction; and at least six hours of directed teaching at the elementary level.

Credential Type: State Elementary Professional Certificate. **Authorization:** Hold a Provisional Certificate. Three years of successful teaching experience. Complete a planned program of 18 semester hours of appropriate credit subsequent to the issuance of the Provisional Certificate (not required for those holding master's degrees). Six semester hours must be in teaching of reading. Effective July 30, 1992, those eligible for an Initial Continuing Certificate will now qualify for the Professional Certificate.

Credential Type: Endorsements. **Requirements:** Elementary Provisional or Professional Certificate. Endorsements may be completed with a planned program of a minimum of 18 hours in the following areas: early childhood; bilingual language; general elementary; middle school; and areas appropriate to the secondary grades.

Minnesota 3989

Elementary School Teacher (K-6)
Teacher Licensing and Placement
State Dept. of Education
616 Capitol Square Bldg.
St. Paul, MN 55101
Phone: (612)296-2046

Credential Type: Elementary Teaching Certificate. **Requirements:** Bachelor's degree from an approved four year college or university. Complete a teacher education program, including credits in professional education for the elementary school, that meets the number of education credits prescribed by the Minnesota State Board of Teaching. Kindergarten teachers are required to include a course in early childhood education. All applicants must complete a student teacher program. Complete an approved, competency-based human relations program and pass the PPST. **Examination:** Pre-Professional Skills Test.

Credential Type: Temporary Teaching Certificate. **Duration of License:** One year. **Authorization:** Allows out-of-state teachers, who have not fulfilled the human relations program and/or PPST requirement(s) but meet all other requirements for a Minnesota teaching certificate, to hold a teaching position while satisfying these special requirements. **Requirements:** Out-of-state teaching certificate. Must satisfy PPST requirement and human relations requirement within one year. Nonrenewable.

Mississippi 3990

School Teacher
Teacher Certification
State Dept. of Education
Box 771
Jackson, MS 39205-0771
Phone: (601)359-3483

Credential Type: Provisional Certificate. **Duration of License:** One year. **Requirements:** Pass the Core Battery of the NTE and appropriate specialty area tests. Complete teacher preparation courses at an approved four year college or university. Renewable for not more than two additional one year periods. **Examination:** Core Battery of the National Teacher Examination.

Credential Type: Standard Certificate. **Duration of License:** One year. **Authorization:** Three levels of certificates will be awarded which authorize individuals to teach different grade levels. An elementary certificate will allow teaching in grades K-8, a secondary certificate will allow teaching in grades 7-12, and a special area certificate will allow teaching in grades K-12 according to endorsement. **Requirements:** Successful completion of the provisional certification period, which includes an evaluation of on-the-job performance. Demonstrate the mastery of the teaching competencies at the prescribed level. One of four classes of the standard certificate may be issued dependent on the candidate's education and experience. The classes are A, AA, AAA, and AAAA. Certificate will be extended based on the educator's successful completion of staff development requirements.

Missouri 3991

Early Childhood Teacher (K-3)
Teacher Certification
Dept. of Elementary and Secondary Education
Box 480
Jefferson City, MO 65102
Phone: (314)751-3486

Credential Type: Early Childhood Teaching Certificate. **Requirements:** Bachelor's degree. Recommendation of designated official for teacher education. Basic requirements include two courses from the following list: music, art, foreign language, western and nonwestern cultures, philosophy, literature, classical studies, theater, and drama. Must also have two courses in English composition, one in oral communication, one in American history, one in American government, one in physical or earth science, one in biology, and one college level math course. At least one of the natural science courses must have a laboratory component. Plus one course from the following list: geography, economics, sociology, anthropology, or psychology. Professional courses include 60 semester hours, 10 of which must be in foundations of teaching and 15 must be basic methods classes covering the following subjects: reading (minimum eight hours), children's literature, language arts, mathematics, science, social studies, art, music, and physical education. Must have two semester hours of field experience prior to student teaching and a minimum of nine semester hours in early childhood student teaching. Early childhood special requirements also include courses in language acquisition and development, utilizing family and community resources, curriculum methods and materials, screening, diagnosis and prescribing instruction, health, perceptual motor development, and mathematics.

3992

Elementary School Teacher (1-8)
Teacher Certification
Dept. of Elementary and Secondary Education
Box 480
Jefferson City, MO 65102
Phone: (314)751-3486

Credential Type: Elementary School Teaching Certificate. **Requirements:** Bachelor's degree. Recommendation of designated official for teacher education. Basic requirements include two courses from the following list: music, art, foreign language, western and nonwestern cultures, philosophy, literature, classical studies, theater, and drama. Must also have two courses in English composition, one in oral communication, one in American history, one in American government, one in physical or earth science, one in biology, and one college level math course. At least one of the natural science courses must have a laboratory component. Plus one course from the following list: geography, economics, sociology, anthropology, or psychology. Professional courses include 60 semester hours, 10 of which must be in foundations of teaching and 15 must be basic methods classes covering the following subjects: reading (minimum eight hours), children's literature, language arts, mathematics, science, social studies, art, music, and physical education. Must have two semester hours of field experience prior to student teaching and a minimum of five semester hours in elementary student teaching. Elementary special courses also include two additional mathematics courses appropriate to elementary level (minimum of five hours), 20 additional hours in economics, geography, health, art, music, or sociology, and 21 hours in the area of concentration.

3993

Special Education Teacher
Teacher Certification
Dept. of Elementary and Secondary Education
Box 480
Jefferson City, MO 65102
Phone: (314)751-3486

Credential Type: Special Education Certificate. **Requirements:** Bachelor's or master's degree with a complete major in an area of special education. Recommendation of the designated official for teacher education in the college or university. Minimum, overall grade point average of 2.5 on a scale of 4.0. Requirements vary according to area of specialization. Missouri certifies special education teachers in the following areas: Learning Disabled, Behaviorally Disordered, Mentally Handicapped, Orthopedically and/or Health Impaired, Blind and Partially Sighted, Severely Developmentally Disabled, Early Childhood Special Education, Deaf and Hearing Impaired, Special Reading Needs, and Speech and Language Needs.

Montana

3994

Elementary School Teacher
Teacher Certification
Office of Public Instruction
State Capitol
Helena, MT 59620
Phone: (406)444-3150

Credential Type: Class 5 Provisional Certificate. **Duration of License:** Three years. **Requirements:** Bachelor's degree. Partially completed program in elementary education. Written recommendation from college or university. Nonrenewable.

Credential Type: Class 2 Standard Certificate. **Duration of License:** Five years. **Requirements:** Bachelor's degree. Competed program in elementary education. Pass NTE Core Battery with the following minimum scores: Communication Skills 648, General Knowledge 644, and Professional Knowledge 648. Renewable upon verification of one year of successful teaching experience and six quarter credits during the valid term of the certificate. **Examination:** National Teacher Examination Core Battery.

Credential Type: Class 1 Professional Certificate. **Duration of License:** Five years. **Requirements:** Eligibility for Standard Certificate plus completion of an approved master's degree or planned fifth year program. Three years of successful teaching experience at appropriate level. Pass NTE Core Battery with the following minimum scores: Communication Skills 648, General Knowledge 644, and Professional Knowledge 648. Renewable upon verification of one year of successful teaching experience during the valid term of the certificate. Beginning with those certificates expiring in 1995, six quarter credits will also be required for renewal. **Examination:** National Teacher Examination Core Battery.

Nebraska

3995

School Teacher K-12
Teacher Certification
State Dept. of Education
301 Centennial Mall South
Box 94987
Lincoln, NE 68509-4987
Phone: (402)471-2496

Credential Type: Initial Teaching Certificate. **Requirements:** Sound mental and physical health. Good citizenship and moral character. Baccalaureate degree and approved program for preparation of teachers. Pass the PPST with the following minimum scores: reading 170; mathematics 171; writing 172. Complete an approved program of human relations skills training from a teacher training college. Complete three hours of credit in an approved course in special education, not limited to the gifted. Complete an approved program for grade level, subject field, and area for which applicant is specifically prepared to teach. At least six hours of course work must have been completed in the three years prior to application. **Examination:** Pre-Professional Skills Test.

Credential Type: Standard Teaching Certificate. **Requirements:** Initial Teaching Certificate or equivalent. Successful teaching experience within the last five years, with two years in the same school at the grade level, subject field, and area of specialization indicated on the certificate.

Credential Type: Professional Teaching Certificate. **Requirements:** Standard Teaching Certificate. Master degree or 36 semester hours or approved fifth-year program of graduate work beyond the baccalaureate degree in teaching fields endorsed upon applicant's Standard Certificate. Six semester hours of course work must have been completed in the three years prior to application.

Nevada

3996

Elementary School Teacher K-8
Nevada Dept. of Education
State Mail Room
1850 E. Sahara, Ste. 200
Las Vegas, NV 89158
Phone: (702)386-5401

Credential Type: Elementary Certificate. **Duration of License:** Five years. **Authorization:** Authorizes the teaching of grades K-8 whether self-contained or departmentalized. **Requirements:** Bachelor's degree. Completion of a state Board of Education approved program of preparation for teaching in elementary grades to include six semester hours of teaching of reading, reading skills, and phonic skills or 30 elementary professional education credit hours, eight supervised teaching semester hours, six teaching of reading method hours, and eight basic subjects method hours Renewable upon completion of an additional six semester hours of credit.

Credential Type: Limited Elementary Certificate. **Duration of License:** Five years. **Requirements:** Bachelor's degree. 18 credit hours in elementary professional education, eight semester hours in super-

Elementary School Teacher K-8, continued

vised teaching, and eight semester hours in methods of teaching the basic subjects, including the teaching of reading. Nonrenewable. Must complete requirements for Elementary Certificate to be recertified.

Credential Type: Professional Elementary Certificate. **Duration of License:** Six years with master's degree, eight years with specialist degree, and 10 years for doctor's degree. **Requirements:** Elementary Certificate or equivalent. Master's degree. Three years of elementary teaching experience in public schools. Master's degree level is renewable upon completion of six semester credit hours or equivalent. Specialist's and Doctor's degree levels are renewable upon evidence of professional growth during the term of the certificate.

Credential Type: Elementary Substitute Certificate. **Duration of License:** Five years. **Authorization:** Limited to 60 days of consecutive service, with exception of extenuating circumstances, in which case the Superintendent has the authority to extend service. **Requirements:** 62 semester credit hours from an accredited university. Six hours of elementary education credit. Renewable.

New Hampshire

3997

School Teacher K-12
Bureau of Teacher Education and Professional Standards
State Dept. of Education
101 Pleasant St.
Concord, NH 03301
Phone: (603)271-2407

Credential Type: Beginning Educator Certificate. **Duration of License:** Three years. **Requirements:** New Hampshire has four alternatives for certification. Alternative 1—Approved Program in New Hampshire. Complete a teacher education program at an approved college or university within New Hampshire. Written recommendation by designated official at preparing institution.

Alternative 2—States Other Than New Hampshire (Covers states and territories participating in the Interstate Certification Compact). Graduate of an approved collegiate program with less than three years teaching experience. Competence in the basic skills of reading, writing, and mathematics as demonstrated by one of the following: master's degree; valid teaching credential from a state requiring a basic skills competence test for educational certification; or statement from candidate's undergraduate institution verifying basic skill competence.

Alternative 3—Demonstrated Competence and Equivalent Experiences. Must have gained competencies, skills, and knowledge through experience. Must submit for Board of Examiners review a description of background, with three to five references, from persons in the area where certification is sought. Must have competence in the basic skills of reading, writing, and mathematics by one of the following: master's degree; valid teaching credential from a state requiring a basic skills competence test for educational certification; or statement from candidate's undergraduate institution verifying basic skill competence. Candidates not party to the interstate compact will be handles on an individual basis.

Alternative 4—Individualized Professional Development Plan—Under the Critical Staff Clause, a secondary teacher may be recommended for certification if he/she has a bachelor's degree and a collegiate major compatible with prospective teaching assignment.

Alternative 5—Provisional Plan. Bachelor's degree from an approved institution. Candidates who have graduated within five years preceding application must possess an overall grade point average of 2.5. Secondary teachers must have a 30 credit hour major and elementary teachers must have a four year liberal arts background, including a major. Must complete a specially designed education plan, containing both pre-service and in-service components, normally during the first year of service. Candidates who have graduated more than five years preceding application must pursue other alternatives for certification.

Credential Type: Experienced Educator Certificate. **Duration of License:** Three years. **Requirements:** Must have recommendation of the Superintendent of Schools during the life of the Beginning Educator Certificate. Must have met all requirements for previous level of certification or successfully completed an approved graduate program that extends clinical experience to a full year under supervision.

New Jersey

3998

School Teacher K-12
Office of Teacher Certification and Academic Credentials
CN 503
Trenton, NJ 08625-0503
Phone: (609)292-2079

Credential Type: Instructional Certificate. **Requirements:** Bachelor's degree from an accredited college or university. Secondary teachers must pass specialization area and elementary or nursery teachers must pass general knowledge area of the NTE. Complete an academic major in liberal arts, science or technology. Complete an approved teacher preparation program or a provisional teacher program as specified by the state's alternate route to certification.(exceptions include bilingual/ESL education, special education, and vocational education). **Examination:** National Teacher Examination (areas as required by specific endorsement) **Reciprocity:** Holders of instructional certificates completed in a state which has endorsed the Interstate Certification Compact will be qualified for New Jersey's Instructional Certificate upon successful completion of required areas of the NTE written examination.

New Mexico

3999

Elementary Teacher K-8
Director, Professional Licensing Unit
Education Bldg.
300 Don Gaspar
Santa Fe, NM 87503
Phone: (505)827-6587

Credential Type: Initial License—Level 1. **Duration of License:** Three years. **Authorization:** Classroom instruction **Requirements:** Bachelor's degree from an accredited institution. Pass the Core Battery of the NTE with the following minimum scores: 644 Communication Skills, 645 General Knowledge, and 630 Professional Knowledge. 54 semester hours of general education which includes: 12 hours of English; 12 hours of history (including American and western civilization); six hours of mathematics; six hours of government, economics, or sociology; and six hours of science which includes biology, chemistry, physics, geology, zoology or botany. 30-36 semester hours of professional education which includes completion of the State Board's approved functional areas and related competencies in professional education and a student teaching component. 24-

36 semester hours in a teaching field such as mathematics, science, language arts, reading, social studies, or other content related areas. Nonrenewable. **Examination:** Core Battery of the National Teacher Examination.

Credential Type: Initial License—Level 2. **Duration of License:** Nine years. **Authorization:** Classroom instruction **Requirements:** Meet all requirements for Level one License. Verification by local superintendent or private school officials that applicant has met State Board's prescribed teaching competencies. Renewable.

Credential Type: Initial License—Level 3-A. **Duration of License:** Nine years. **Authorization:** Advanced classroom instruction and instructional leadership **Requirements:** Meet all requirements for Level two License. Master's degree. Verification by local superintendent or private school official that applicant has met the State Board's prescribed Level 3-A competencies.

New York

4000

Early Childhood, Upper Elementary, and Early Secondary Teacher N-9
Administrator of Teacher Certification Policy
Univ. of the State of New York
State Education Dept.
Cultural Center, Rm. 5-A-11
Albany, NY 12230
Phone: (518)474-6440

Credential Type: Provisional Certificate. **Duration of License:** Five years. **Authorization:** Authorizes the teaching of grades N-6 with special subject area endorsement which may be taught in grades 7-9. **Requirements:** Baccalaureate degree with a four year program of collegiate preparation at a regionally accredited or approved higher institution. 24 semester hours of professional education courses to include six semester hoursin teaching of reading. A supervised student teaching experience. With recommendation, one full year of full-time teaching experience on the appropriate level may be substituted for student teaching. Academic concentration in subject for which certificate is issued, semester hr. requirements as follows: English 30; foreign language 24; general science 36 (must include college level study in at least two sciences); mathematics 18; and social studies 30. Note: The city of Buffalo, New York has certification standards that are exclusive of New York State.

Credential Type: Permanent Certificate. **Duration of License:** Permanent. **Requirements:** Hold a Provisional Certificate at level where certification is sought. Master's degree in or functionally related to field of teaching experience. Two years of elementary school or special subject teaching experience dependent on teaching assignment level. Note: The city of Buffalo, New York has certification standards that are exclusive of New York State.

4001

Early Childhood and Upper Elementary Teacher N-6
Administrator of Teacher Certification Policy
Univ. of the State of New York
State Education Dept.
Cultural Center, Rm. 5-A-11
Albany, NY 12230
Phone: (518)474-6440

Credential Type: Provisional Certificate. **Duration of License:** Five years. **Authorization:** Authorizes the teaching of grades N-6. **Requirements:** Baccalaureate degree with a four year program of collegiate preparation at a regionally accredited or approved higher institution. 24 semester hours of professional education courses to include six semester hoursin teaching of reading. A supervised student teaching experience. With recommendation, one full year of full-time teaching experience on the appropriate level may be substituted for student teaching. Note: The city of Buffalo, New York has certification standards that are exclusive of New York State.

Credential Type: Permanent Certificate. **Duration of License:** Permanent. **Requirements:** Hold a Provisional Certificate at level where certification is sought. Master's degree in or functionally related to field of teaching experience. Two years of elementary school teaching experience. Note: The city of Buffalo, New York has certification standards that are exclusive of New York State.

4002

Special Subjects Teacher N-12
Administrator of Teacher Certification Policy
Univ. of the State of New York
State Education Dept.
Cultural Center, Rm. 5-A-11
Albany, NY 12230
Phone: (518)474-6440

Credential Type: Provisional Special Subjects Certificate. **Duration of License:** Five years. **Authorization:** Authorizes the teaching of special subjects, outside of the regular classroom academics, according to area of specialization in grades N-12. **Requirements:** Bachelor's degree from a regionally accredited or approved institution. 12 semester hours of professional education courses. 36 semester hours in technical courses in subject for which certificate is issued. A college supervised student teaching experience. One year of approved and appropriate occupational experience for the commerce and distributive occupations only is allowable in place of student teaching. Note: The city of Buffalo, New York has certification standards that are exclusive of New York State.

Credential Type: Permanent Special Subjects Certificate. **Duration of License:** Permanent. **Requirements:** Hold a Provisional Special Subjects Certificate at level where certification is sought. Master's degree in or functionally related to field of teaching experience. Two years of special subject(s) teaching experience. Note: The city of Buffalo, New York has certification standards that are exclusive of New York State.

North Carolina

4003

Public School Teacher K-12
Certification Section
State Dept. of Public Instruction
Raleigh, NC 27603
Phone: (919)733-4125

Credential Type: Initial Certificate. **Duration of License:** Two years. **Requirements:** Bachelor's degree. Pass NTE examination. Institutional recommendation. Complete an approved teacher education program which includes basic skills required of all teachers in English and English usage, Literature, The Fine Arts, Social Studies, Mathematics, and Science, areas of specialization, and professional education. Nonrenewable. **Examination:** National Teacher Examination **Fees:** $30.00 application fee.

Credential Type: Continuing Professional Certificate. **Duration of License:** Five years. **Requirements:** Two years of successful teaching experience in North Carolina under the Initial Certificate. May be renewed anytime after January 1, prior to the certificate's expiration date, upon application and completion of 10 semester hours of appropriate college credit earned during the previous five years. Hours may also be completed by workshops or institutes for which prior credit has been approved by the Local Administrative Unit. **Fees:** $30.00 application fee.

North Carolina

Public School Teacher K-12, continued

Credential Type: Subject Endorsement. **Requirements:** Valid North Carolina teaching certificate. Endorsement will be granted in the applicant's subject of specialization (major or minor) as recommended by the preparing institution.

4004

Special Education Teacher K-12
Certification Section
State Dept. of Public Instruction
Raleigh, NC 27603
Phone: (919)733-4125

Credential Type: Special Education Certificate. **Duration of License:** Five years. **Requirements:** Complete a program of teacher preparation with a bachelor's or higher degree and specialization in the requested area of certification. Pass NTE examination. Institutional recommendation. Examinations proving competencies in area of specialization may also be required. **Examination:** National Teacher Examination. **Fees:** $30 application fee. $30 renewal fee.

North Dakota

4005

Elementary School Teacher
Director of Certification
State Dept. of Public Instruction
Bismarck, ND 58505
Phone: (701)224-2264

Credential Type: North Dakota Educator's Professional Certificate. **Duration of License:** Entrance two years, renewable for five years. **Requirements:** Bachelor's degree from an accredited college approved to offer teacher preparation. 34 semester credit hours of professional education. Overall GPA of 2.5. Renewal is possible with two years of successful teaching experience and four semester credit hours of work.

Ohio

4006

Elementary School Teacher 1-8
Teacher Education and Certification
State Dept. of Education
65 S. Front St., Rm 1012
Columbus, OH 43266-0308
Phone: (614)466-3593

Credential Type: Provisional Elementary Certificate. **Requirements:** Baccalaureate degree. Good moral character. Complete an approved program of teacher preparation including an examination. Recommendation of preparing institution. 30 semester hours of general education courses to include: the humanities; mathematics; natural sciences; and social science. 20 semester hours of course work pertaining to the elementary aged child. 30 semester hours of professional education courses and both clinical and field-based experiences designed for teaching the 1-8 level. 30 semester hours of curriculum content course work for 1-8 students that includes course work in health, language arts, mathematics, music, physical education, reading, science, social studies, and visual arts.

4007

Kindergarten and Primary Grade Teacher K-3
Teacher Education and Certification
State Dept. of Education
65 S. Front St., Rm 1012
Columbus, OH 43266-0308
Phone: (614)466-3593

Credential Type: Provisional Kindergarten and Primary Certificate. **Requirements:** Baccalaureate degree. Good moral character. Complete an approved program of teacher preparation including an examination. Recommendation of preparing institution. 30 semester hours of general education courses to include: the humanities; mathematics; natural sciences; and social science. 20 semester hours of course work pertaining to the kindergarten and/or primary aged child. 30 semester hours of professional education courses and both clinical and field-based experiences designed for teaching the K-3 level. 30 semester hours of curriculum content course work for K-3 students that includes course work in health, language arts, mathematics, music, physical education, reading, science, social studies, and visual arts.

4008

Public School Teacher K-12
Teacher Education and Certification
State Dept. of Education
65 S. Front St., Rm. 1012
Columbus, OH 43266-0308
Phone: (614)466-3593

Credential Type: Provisional All Grades Certificate. **Requirements:** Baccalaureate degree. Good moral character. Complete an approved program of teacher preparation including an examination. Recommendation of preparing institution. 30 semester hours of general education courses distributed over the humanities, mathematics, natural sciences, and social sciences. 30 professional education semester hours, both clinical and field-based, designed for teaching grades K-12. Curriculum content must include the following minimum number of course work semester hours in the area of specialization: computer science 30; dance 45; drama/theater 45; health education 30; industrial technology 45; library/media 30; foreign language 45 (more than one language 30 hours each); music 45; physical education 45; reading 30; and visual art 45.

4009

Special Education Teacher K-12
Teacher Education and Certification
State Dept. of Education
65 S. Front St., Rm. 1012
Columbus, OH 43266-0308
Phone: (614)466-3593

Credential Type: Provisional Special Education of the Handicapped Certificate. **Requirements:** Baccalaureate degree. Good moral character. Complete an approved program of teacher preparation including an examination. Recommendation of preparing institution. 30 semester hours of general education courses distributed over the humanities, mathematics, natural sciences, and social sciences. 20 semester hours of professional education courses, both clinical and fieldbased, designed for teaching grades K-12. 30 semester hours of curriculum content work including health, language arts, mathematics, music, physical education, reading, science, social studies, and visual arts. 20 semester hours of specialization courses in one of the following: developmentally handicapped; hearing handicapped; multi-handicapped; orthopedically handicapped; severe behavior handicapped; special learning disabled; and visually handicapped.

4010

Teacher of Special Subjects
Teacher Education and Certification
State Dept. of Education
65 S. Front St., Rm. 1012
Columbus, OH 43266-0308
Phone: (614)466-3593

Credential Type: Special Subjects Endorsement. **Requirements:** Baccalaureate degree. Good moral character. Complete an approved program of teacher preparation including an examination. Recommendation of preparing institution. Ohio Standard Teaching Certificate. Endorsement is possible in the following subjects with the specified number of semester credit hours: Driver Education 6; Library/Media 20; Reading 12; and Typing/Keyboarding 6. Other fields possible as approved by the State Board of Education.

Credential Type: Special Subject Validation. **Requirements:** Baccalaureate degree. Good moral character. Complete an approved program of teacher preparation including an examination. Recommendation of preparing institution. Ohio Standard Teaching Certificate which relates directly to area in which validation is sought. Validation is possible in the following subjects with 20 semester credit hours of additional course work: Adapted Physical Education; Bilingual/Multicultural Education; Gifted Education; Pre-Kindergarten; Teaching English to Speakers of Other Languages; and Early Education of Handicapped Children. Other fields possible as approved by the State Board of Education.

Oklahoma

4011

Early Childhood Teacher PK-3
Teacher Education and Certification
State Dept. of Education
2500 N. Lincoln Blvd., Rm. 211
Oklahoma City, OK 73105
Phone: (405)521-3337

Credential Type: Early Childhood General Certificate. **Duration of License:** One year. **Requirements:** Complete an approved certificate program at an accredited college or university and receive recommendation from that institution. Pass the state teacher certification test(s) in early childhood competencies. **Examination:** State teacher certification test(s). **Reciprocity:** Oklahoma recognizes some out-of-state teaching certificates.

Credential Type: Early Childhood Standard Certificate (undergraduate). **Duration of License:** Five years. **Requirements:** Complete an approved certificate program at an accredited college or university which includes a minimum of the following: a baccalaureate degree; 50 semester hours in general education; 30 semester hours in professional education; and 40 semester hours in course work pertaining to teaching the early childhood student. Pass the state certified test(s) in early childhood competencies. Successfully complete the Entry-Year Assistance Program as a licensed teacher. Complete a course of two or more semester hours in the education of the exceptional child. **Examination:** State certification test(s). **Reciprocity:** Oklahoma recognizes some out-of-state teaching certificates.

Credential Type: Provisional Level II Certificate—Early Childhood. **Duration of License:** Two years. **Requirements:** Complete approved certificate program at an accredited college or university. Baccalaureate degree. 56 semester hours in general education course work. 24 semester hours in professional education which includes field experiences and student teaching. 30 semester hours in early childhood education. Pass the state certification test(s) in early childhood education. Successfully complete the Entry-Year Assistance Program as a licensed teacher. Complete a course of two or more semester hours in the education of the exceptional child. **Examination:** State certification test(s). **Reciprocity:** Oklahoma recognizes some out-of-state teaching certificates.

Credential Type: Provisional Level I Certificate—Early Childhood. **Duration of License:** One year. **Requirements:** Complete approved certificate program at an accredited college or university. Baccalaureate degree. 56 semester hours in general education course work. 18 semester hours in professional education which includes field experiences and student teaching. 24 semester hours in early childhood education. Pass the state certification test(s) in early childhood education. Successfully complete the Entry-Year Assistance Program as a licensed teacher. Complete a course of two or more semester hours in the education of the exceptional child. **Examination:** State certification test(s). **Reciprocity:** Oklahoma recognizes some out-of-state teaching certificates.

Credential Type: Additional Certificate. **Requirements:** Certified individuals who seek additional certification must complete the following: a methods course appropriate to the second certificate sought and a developmental psychology course appropriate to the grade level of the certificate.

4012

Elementary School Teacher K-8
Teacher Education and Certification
State Dept. of Education
2500 N. Lincoln Blvd., Rm. 211
Oklahoma City, OK 73105
Phone: (405)521-3337

Credential Type: Elementary General Certificate. **Duration of License:** One year. **Requirements:** Complete an approved certificate program at an accredited college or university and receive recommendation from that institution. Pass the state teacher certification test(s) in elementary education competencies. **Examination:** State teacher certification test(s). **Reciprocity:** Oklahoma recognizes some out-of-state teaching certificates.

Credential Type: Elementary Standard Certificate (undergraduate). **Duration of License:** Five years. **Requirements:** Complete an approved certificate program at an accredited college or university which includes a minimum of the following: a baccalaureate degree; 50 semester hours in general education; 30 semester hours in professional education; and 40 semester hours in course work pertaining to teaching the elementary student. Pass the state certified test(s) in elementary education competencies. Successfully complete the Entry-Year Assistance Program as a licensed teacher. Complete a course of two or more semester hours in the education of the exceptional child. **Examination:** State certification test(s). **Reciprocity:** Oklahoma recognizes some out-of-state teaching certificates.

Credential Type: Provisional Level II Certificate—Elementary. **Duration of License:** Two years. **Requirements:** Complete approved certificate program at an accredited college or university. Baccalaureate degree. 56 semester hours in general education course work. 24 semester hours in professional education which includes field experiences and student teaching. 30 semester hours in elementary education. Pass the state certification test(s) in elementary education. Successfully complete the Entry-Year Assistance Program as a licensed teacher. Complete a course of two or more semester hours in the education of the exceptional child. **Examination:** State certification test(s). **Reciprocity:** Oklahoma recognizes some out-of-state teaching certificates.

Credential Type: Provisional Level I Certificate—Elementary. **Duration of License:** One year. **Requirements:** Complete approved certificate program at an accredited college or university. Baccalaureate degree. 56 semester hours in general

Oklahoma

Elementary School Teacher K-8, continued

education course work. 18 semester hours in professional education which includes field experiences and student teaching. 24 semester hours in elementary education. Pass the state certification test(s) in elementary education. Successfully complete the Entry-Year Assistance Program as a licensed teacher. Complete a course of two or more semester hours in the education of the exceptional child. **Examination:** State certification test(s). **Reciprocity:** Oklahoma recognizes some out-of-state teaching certificates.

Credential Type: Additional Certificate. **Requirements:** Certified individuals who seek additional certification must complete the following: a methods course appropriate to the second certificate sought and a developmental psychology course appropriate to the grade level of the certificate.

4013

Special Education Teacher N-12
Teacher Education and Certification
State Dept. of Education
2500 N. Lincoln Blvd., Rm. 211
Oklahoma City, OK 73105
Phone: (405)521-3337

Credential Type: Elementary-Secondary General Certificate. **Duration of License:** One year. **Requirements:** Complete an approved certificate program at an accredited college or university and receive recommendation from that institution. Pass the state teacher certification test(s) in special education competencies. **Examination:** State teacher certification test(s). **Reciprocity:** Oklahoma recognizes some out-of-state teaching certificates.

Credential Type: Elementary-Secondary Standard Certificate (undergraduate). **Duration of License:** Five years. **Requirements:** Complete an approved certificate program at an accredited college or university which includes a minimum of the following: a baccalaureate degree; 50 semester hours in general education; 30 semester hours in professional education; and 40 semester hours in course work pertaining to teaching special education. Pass the state certified test(s) in special education competencies. Successfully complete the Entry-Year Assistance Program as a licensed teacher. Complete a course of two or more semester hours in the education of the exceptional child. **Examination:** State certification test(s). **Reciprocity:** Oklahoma recognizes some out-of-state teaching certificates.

Credential Type: Provisional Level II Certificate—Special Education. **Duration of License:** Two years. **Requirements:** Complete approved certificate program at an accredited college or university. Baccalaureate degree. 56 semester hours in general education course work. 24 semester hours in professional education which includes field experiences and student teaching. 30 semester hours in special education. Pass the state certification test(s) in special education. Successfully complete the Entry-Year Assistance Program as a licensed teacher. Complete a course of two or more semester hours in the education of the exceptional child. **Examination:** State certification test(s). **Reciprocity:** Oklahoma recognizes some out-of-state teaching certificates.

Credential Type: Provisional Level I Certificate—Special Education. **Duration of License:** One year. **Requirements:** Complete approved certificate program at an accredited college or university. Baccalaureate degree. 56 semester hours in general education course work. 18 semester hours in professional education which includes field experiences and student teaching. 24 semester hours in special education. Pass the state certification test(s) in special education. Successfully complete the Entry-Year Assistance Program as a licensed teacher. Complete a course of two or more semester hours in the education of the exceptional child. **Examination:** State certification test(s). **Reciprocity:** Oklahoma recognizes some out-of-state teaching certificates.

Credential Type: Additional Certificate. **Requirements:** Certified individuals who seek additional certification must complete the following: a methods course appropriate to the second certificate sought and a developmental psychology course appropriate to the grade level of the certificate.

Oregon

4014

Public School Teacher K-12
Teacher Standards and Practices Commission
630 Center St. NE, Ste. 200
Salem, OR 97310-0320
Phone: (503)378-3586

Credential Type: Basic Teaching Certificate. **Duration of License:** Three years. **Requirements:** Baccalaureate degree. Complete a four year teacher program. Professional education courses must equal 36 quarter hours and include competencies in diagnostic and prescriptive techniques; methods in appropriate subject and grade level of endorsement; teaching reading; public school curriculum; foundations of education; educational psychology of individuals and groups served by public schools; classroom management; education of exceptional children and/or youth; and student teaching or internship. Complete one of the subject or special education endorsements established by the Teacher Standards and Practices Commission. One year of successful public school teaching experience within the three-year period preceding application or nine quarter hours of preparation in a teacher education institution within the past three years. Passing scores on the CBEST. Out-of-state prepared applicants may submit their passing scores on the Core Battery of the National Teacher Examination, in lieu of the CBEST. **Examination:** California Basic Educational Skills Test.

Credential Type: Standard Teaching Certificate. **Duration of License:** Five years. **Requirements:** Complete a five year teacher education program with 5th year culminating in a master's degree or complete 45 quarter hours of upper division and graduate study. Applicants prepared out-of-state must have verification of a master's degree from an approved teacher education institution. Must have two years of successful teaching experience on a Basic Teaching Certificate in Oregon schools.

Credential Type: Subject Matter Endorsements. **Requirements:** Endorsements may be added to Standard Certificates with an additional 15 quarter hours credit in the endorsement area being sought. Endorsements may be added to Basic Certificates with the specified number of quarter hr. credits as follows: Elementary 60; Agriculture 60; Art 45; Business and Office Education 48; Educational Media 24; Marketing 48; Foreign Language 48; Health Education 42; Home Economics (non-vocational) 48; Technology Education 45; Language Arts 45; Speech 24; Drama 24; Basic Mathematics 21; Advanced Mathematics 42; Music 60; Physical Education 48; Reading 21; Biology 45; Integrated Science 45; Chemistry 27; Physics 27; and Social Studies 54.

Pennsylvania

4015

Classroom Teacher K-12
Bureau of Certification
Dept. of Education
333 Market St.
Harrisburg, PA 17126-0333
Phone: (717)787-2967

Credential Type: Intern Certificate. **Duration of License:** Three years. **Require-

Kindergarten and Elementary School Teachers

ments: Non-education major baccalaureate degree. Complete appropriate professional education courses in an approved intern program. Recommendation of preparing institution. Successful completion of the required basic skills, general knowledge and subject matter tests. Qualified to hold Instructional Certificate I after completion of internship and passage of the NTE Professional Knowledge Test.

All new applicants must produce a background clearance as required in Act 34. A Pennsylvania State Police background check is required for Pennsylvania residents and an F.B.I. background check is required for out-of-state residents. Applicants may not teach without this clearance. **Examination:** NTE Communications Test; NTE General Knowledge Test; and Area of Specialization Test.

Credential Type: Instructional Certificate I—Provisional. **Duration of License:** Six years. **Requirements:** Bachelor's degree. Complete approved program of study. Recommendation by preparing institution. Successful completion of Pennsylvania Teacher Certification Testing Program. Must participate in a district developed, PDE approved plan for continuing, professional development.

All new applicants must produce a background clearance as required in Act 34. A Pennsylvania State Police background check is required for Pennsylvania residents and an F.B.I. background check is required for out-of-state residents. Applicants may not teach without this clearance **Examination:** NTE Communications Skills Test; NTE General Knowledge Test; NTE Professional Knowledge Test; and Area of Specialization Test.

Credential Type: Instructional Certificate II—Permanent. **Duration of License:** Permanent. **Requirements:** Completion of Department-approved induction plan. Three years of satisfactory teaching under Instructional Certificate I. Complete 24 semester hours of post-baccalaureate study which may be satisfied, in whole or part, through PDE approved in-service programs.

4016

Educational Specialist
Bureau of Certification
Dept. of Education
333 Market St.
Harrisburg, PA 17126-0333
Phone: (717)787-2967

Credential Type: Educational Specialist I—Provisional. **Duration of License:** Six years. **Authorization:** Authorizes holding public school positions as non-teaching professionals. **Requirements:** Bachelor's degree. Complete approved program of study. Recommendation by preparing institution.

All new applicants must produce a background clearance as required in Act 34. A Pennsylvania State Police background check is required for Pennsylvania residents and an F.B.I. background check is required for out-of-state residents. Applicants may not work in Pennsylvania public schools without this clearance.

Credential Type: Educational Specialist II—Permanent. **Duration of License:** Permanent. **Authorization:** Authorizes holding public school positions as non-teaching professionals. **Requirements:** Three years of satisfactory service in a single area while holding the Educational Specialist I Certificate. 24 semester hours of postbaccalaureate study that may be satisfied, in whole or in part, through PDE approved in-service programs.

Rhode Island

4017

Early Childhood Teacher (PK-2)
Office of Teacher Certification
State Dept. of Education
22 Hayes St.
Providence, RI 02908
Phone: (401)277-2675

Credential Type: Provisional Certificate. **Duration of License:** Three years. **Requirements:** Bachelor's degree. Complete an approved program for Early Childhood education or complete six semester hours of student teaching in early elementary and 24 semester hours of course work in the following areas: child growth and development; curriculum and methods in early childhood education; reading readiness and developmental reading; health and nutrition for the young child; child, family, and community relationships; and identification and service to special needs children. Pass the Core Battery of the NTE with minimum scores as follows: Communication Skills 657; General Knowledge 649; Professional Knowledge 648. Nonrenewable. **Examination:** Core Battery of the National Teacher Examination.

Credential Type: Professional Certificate. **Duration of License:** Five years. **Requirements:** Complete six credits while holding a Rhode Island Provisional Certificate. Three of the six credits may be inservice and the rest must be college level courses. Proof of three years of teaching experience in Rhode Island. Renewal is possible with completion of nine graduate credits (3 credits may be inservice work) and verification of continued teaching experience in early childhood or a related area.

Credential Type: Life Professional Certificate. **Duration of License:** Permanent. **Requirements:** Master's degree in early childhood, or elementary education with a concentration in early childhood, or a master's degree in any field of education with 15 semester hours of graduate work in early childhood or a master's degree in a field other than education with 21 semester hours of graduate work in early childhood. Must have six years of teaching experience in an approved setting at the early childhood level. Three years of the experience requirement must be completed in Rhode Island schools.

4018

Elementary School Teacher 1-8
Office of Teacher Certification
State Dept. of Education
22 Hayes St.
Providence, RI 02908
Phone: (401)277-2675

Credential Type: Provisional Certificate. **Duration of License:** Three years. **Authorization:** Authorizes teaching grades 1-8, except where grades seven and eight are organized on the middle school or secondary school plan. **Requirements:** Bachelor's degree. Complete an approved program for elementary teachers or six semester hours of elementary student teaching and 24 hours of semester course work in the following areas: child growth and development; methods and materials of teaching reading; math, language, arts, science, and social studies in the elementary school; the arts; identification and service to special needs children; and foundations of education. Pass the Core Battery of the NTE with minimum scores as follows: Communication Skills 657; General Knowledge 649; Professional Knowledge 648. Nonrenewable. **Examination:** Core Battery of the National Teacher Examination.

Credential Type: Professional Certificate. **Duration of License:** Five years. **Requirements:** Complete six credits while holding a Rhode Island Provisional Certificate. Three of the six credits may be inservice and the rest must be college level courses. Proof of three years of teaching experience in Rhode Island. Renewal is possible with completion of nine graduate credits (3 credits may be inservice work) and verification of continued teaching experience in elementary education or a related area.

Credential Type: Life Professional Certificate. **Duration of License:** Permanent. **Requirements:** Master's degree in elementary education or a master's degree in any

Elementary School Teacher 1-8, continued

field of education with 15 semester hours of graduate work in elementary education or a master's degree in a field other than education with 21 semester hours of graduate work in elementary education. Must have six years of teaching experience in an approved setting at the elementary level. Three years of the experience requirement must be completed in Rhode Island schools.

4019

Special Subjects Teacher PK-12
Office of Teacher Certification
State Dept. of Education
22 Hayes St.
Providence, RI 02908
Phone: (401)277-2675

Credential Type: Provisional Certificate. **Duration of License:** Three years. **Requirements:** Bachelor's degree. Complete an approved program designed for the preparation of special subject teachers or complete six semester hours of student teaching in the special subjects field at both the elementary and secondary levels and 18 semester hours of course work to include the following areas: human growth and development; foundations of education; methodology; measurement and evaluation; identification of and service to special needs students; and the teaching of reading in the content area. In some cases the student teaching requirement may be waived or reduced if the applicant has had prior experience teaching in his/her special subject field. The following list denotes the minimum number of semester hours required to be certified in each special subject area: Art 36; Dance 24; Health 24; Physical Education 24; Health and Physical Education (with equal time divided between subjects) 48; Home Economics 36; Industrial Arts 36; Library/Media 36; Music 36; Theater 24; and special subjects not listed 18. Extensions are possible for individuals who have not completed three years of teaching during the life of this certificate, all others must apply for the Professional Certificate.

Credential Type: Professional Certificate. **Duration of License:** Five years. **Requirements:** Complete six credits while under the Rhode Island Provisional Certificate. Three of the six credits may be approved in-service course work and the rest must be college credits. Three years of successful teaching in the special subjects field while under the provisional certificate in Rhode Island.

Credential Type: Life Professional Certificate. **Duration of License:** Permanent.

Requirements: Master's degree in the special subjects field in which provisional certification is held or a master's degree in any field of education and 15 semester hours of graduate level course work in the special field in which provisional certification is held, either as part of or beyond the master's degree, in education. Must have six years of teaching experience in the special field, of which three years must be in Rhode Island.

South Carolina

4020

Public School Teacher PK-12
Teacher Education and Certification
State Dept. of Education
Rutledge Bldg., Rm. 1015
Columbia, SC 29201
Phone: (803)734-8464

Credential Type: Initial Certificate. **Requirements:** Complete a State Board of Education approved teacher training program. Pass the NTE Core Battery of Professional Knowledge. Teachers of Special Subjects must pass the NTE Specialty Area Examination or South Carolina Area Examination. **Examination:** National Teacher Examination Core Battery of Professional Knowledge; National Teacher Examination Specialty Area Examination or South Carolina Area Examination (teachers of special subjects only).

Credential Type: Professional Certificate—Class III. **Requirements:** South Carolina Initial Certificate. Bachelor's degree.

Credential Type: Professional Certificate—Class II. **Requirements:** South Carolina Initial Certificate. Bachelor's degree plus 18 semester hours of graduate credit.

Credential Type: Professional Certificate—Class I. **Requirements:** South Carolina Initial Certificate. Master's degree.

Credential Type: Specialist Professional Certificate—Class I. **Requirements:** South Carolina Initial Certificate. Master's or specialist's degree consisting of 60 semester hours, of which 30 semester hours of graduate credit must be a planned program approved by the State Board of Education.

Credential Type: Advanced Professional Certificate—Class I. **Requirements:** South Carolina Initial Certificate. Doctorate from an approved program.

Credential Type: Certificate Endorsement. **Requirements:** Areas of certification may be added to professional South Carolina Teaching Credentials by completing approved programs of specific course requirements as specified by the South Carolina State Board of Education.

South Dakota

4021

Elementary School Teacher
Teacher Education and Certification
State Dept. of Education
700 Governor's Drive
Pierre, SD 57501
Phone: (605)773-3553

Credential Type: Elementary Certificate Endorsement. **Duration of License:** Five years. **Requirements:** Complete approved bachelor's degree program in elementary education. Must have completed program within the five years preceding application or must have earned six semester hours or nine quarter hours of credit pertaining to elementary education within five years preceding application. The holder of a master's degree in elementary education will be exempt from the additional credits provided the master's degree was earned within the 10 years preceding application. Elementary education program must consist of the following: 26 semester hours of education courses which includes six semester hours of student teaching; 11 semester hours of methods classes which includes language arts, social studies, computers, science, arithmetic, and a minimum of three hours of reading; nine semester hours of professional education which includes psychology of teaching, learning, child development, and the exceptional child and 32 semester hours in basic subject areas that includes composition and grammar, speech, music, art, first aid and health, U.S. government, Indian studies, geography, mathematics, physical science for elementary teachers, biological science, and American history. All of the basic subject area courses should be a minimum of two semester hours with the exceptions of composition and grammar which should be five hours, Indian studies three hours, and mathematics six hours

Renewal is possible with six semester hours of credit completed during the life of the certificate, of which three semester hours may be completed in approved workshops. The holder of a master's degree may renew without additional credits. **Fees:** $20 certification fee. $20 renewal fee.

4022

School Reading Specialist K-12
Teacher Education and Certification
State Dept. of Education
700 Governor's Drive
Pierre, SD 57501
Phone: (605)773-3553

Credential Type: Reading Specialist Certificate Endorsement. **Requirements:** Valid South Dakota elementary or secondary certificate. Complete three years of classroom teaching in which the teaching of reading was an important responsibility of the position. Must have undergraduate credit in the following: measurement and/or evaluation; child and/or adolescent psychology; psychology including such aspects as personality, cognition, and learning behaviors; and literature for children and/or adolescents. Complete a minimum of 12 semester hours in graduate level reading courses with at least one course in each of the following: foundations or survey of reading; diagnosis and correction of reading disabilities; and clinical or laboratory practicum in reading.

Tennessee

4023

Elementary School Teacher K-8
Office of Teaching Licensing
Dept. of Education
Cordell Hull Bldg.
Nashville, TN 37219-5335
Phone: (615)741-1644

Credential Type: Probationary License. **Duration of License:** One year. **Requirements:** Bachelor's degree. Complete an approved teacher education program which consists of the following: 60 quarter hours of general education which includes course work in communications, health, physical education, personal development, humanities, natural sciences, social studies, and fundamental concepts of mathematics; 36 quarter hours of professional education which includes psychological foundations of education, human growth and development, learning, measurement, evaluation, and guidance, curriculum school organization and management, audio-visual aids, education for exceptional children, materials and methods, and six quarter hours of supervised student teaching. Endorsements for K-8 teaching is possible with the additional quarter hours of study as follows: natural science 18; language arts 18; humanities 18; health 18; physical education 18; personal development 18; home and family living 18; social studies 18; and mathematics 9. Pass NTE Core Battery and required Specialty Area Test. Renewable. **Examination:** National Teacher Examination and Specialty Area Test.

Credential Type: Interim Probationary "A" Teacher's License. **Duration of License:** One year. **Requirements:** Bachelor's degree. Six quarter hours of professional education college credit. Content course work for an area of endorsement. Intention of employment by a local education agency. Renewable four times with the successful completion of nine quarter hours of applicable course work for each renewal and a statement of intention of employment with a local school system.

Credential Type: Interim Probationary "B" Teacher's License. **Duration of License:** One year. **Requirements:** Meets all state requirements for Probationary Teacher's License but lacks qualifying scores required on NTE tests. Bachelor's degree. Renewable one time.

Credential Type: Apprentice License. **Duration of License:** Three years. **Requirements:** Probationary License. Satisfactory completion of the probationary year. Renewable.

Credential Type: Professional License. **Duration of License:** 10 years. **Requirements:** Bachelor's degree. Probationary License. Three years of successful service in a Tennessee public school. Renewable.

Credential Type: Out-of-State Teacher's License. **Duration of License:** Three years. **Requirements:** Bachelor's degree and approved teacher education program. One year of successful teaching experience. Pass the NTE Core Battery and Specialty Area Tests. **Examination:** National Teacher Examination Core Battery and Specialty Area Tests.

Credential Type: Career Level I Certificate. **Duration of License:** 10 years. **Requirements:** Apprentice License. Satisfactory performance at the apprentice level with local education agency recommendation. Renewable.

Credential Type: Career Level II and III Certificates. **Duration of License:** 10 years. **Requirements:** Career Level I Certificate. Must elect to be evaluated and pass evaluation. Renewable.

4024

Special Education Teacher
Office of Teaching Licensing
Dept. of Education
Cordell Hull Bldg.
Nashville, TN 37219-5335
Phone: (615)741-1644

Credential Type: Special Education Endorsement. **Authorization:** Endorsement will be granted to teach in one of the following areas: learning disabilities; mental retardation; emotionally disturbed; socially maladjusted; gifted; and crippling and special health conditions. **Requirements:** Bachelor's degree in a special education field. Must demonstrate in early and continual student placements in supervised laboratory and field settings the competencies outlined and must be recommended for certification by a college or university whose approved program was completed.

Texas

4025

Texas Public School Teacher
Texas Education Agency
1701 N. Congress Ave.
Austin, TX 78701-1494
Phone: (512)463-8976

Credential Type: Provisional Certificate. **Authorization:** Certificate will be endorsed to teach in one of the following areas: Elementary grades 1-8; High school grades 6-12; Hearing impaired grades PK-12; Speech and language therapy grades PK-12; Special subjects (art, music, physical education, and speech communication). **Requirements:** Bachelor's degree from a college or university approved for teacher education. 60 semester hours of general education which includes: 12 hours English; three hours speech; six hours American history; three hours Political Science that covers the U.S. and Texas constitutions; 3-6 hours of natural science with lab; three hours of mathematics (college algebra or above); three hours computing and information technology (demonstration of competency also accepted); three hours fine arts; plus electives. 18 semester hours of professional development courses which includes core requirements, methodology, field experience. Core requirements must consist of studies in the following: teaching/learning processes, including measurement and evaluation of student achievement; human growth and development; knowledge and skills concerning the unique needs of special learners; legal and ethical aspects of teaching to include the recognition of an response to signs of abuse and

Texas Public School Teacher, continued

neglect in children; structure, organization and management of the American school system, with emphasis upon the state and local structure in Texas; and education computing, media, and other technologies. Methodology must include studies of the following: instructional methods and strategies that emphasize practical applications of the teaching/learning processes; curriculum organization, planning, and evaluation; basic principles and procedures of classroom management with emphasis on classroom discipline, utilizing group and individual processes, as well as different techniques and procedures adapted to the personality of the teacher; and the scope and sequence of the essential elements for all subjects required in the elementary course of study that are not included in the academic specialization when elementary options are selected. Areas of academic specialization requires 36-48 semester hours in the subject area. Field experience must consist of not fewer than 45 clock hours of pre-student teaching which shall include observation and experience at the level for which a student teaching assignment is anticipated and a six semester hours student teaching assignment. Student teaching may be waived if the applicant has taught in an accredited school as a classroom teacher for two or more years at the level at which certification is sought. Must pass the ExCET examination. **Examination:** Examination for the Certification of Educators in Texas.

Credential Type: Professional Certificate. **Requirements:** Bachelor's degree. Valid Texas provisional teacher certificate. Complete 30 semester hours of an approved graduate program in area of specialization. Three years of teaching experience.

Utah

4026

Early Childhood Education Teacher K-3
Certification and Personnel Development Section
State Board of Education
250 East 500 South St.
Salt Lake City, UT 84111
Phone: (801)538-7740

Credential Type: Basic Certificate. **Duration of License:** Four years. **Authorization:** Required for teaching kindergarten and permits assignment in grades K-3. Recommended for teaching in formal programs below kindergarten level. **Requirements:** Bachelor's degree. Complete an approved college level program in early childhood education. Applicants holding an Elementary Teaching Certificate, with two years of successful teaching experience in a full kindergarten or prekindergarten program, may be issued a concurrent Early Childhood Education Certificate.

Credential Type: Standard Certificate. **Duration of License:** Valid indefinitely with consistent employment. **Requirements:** Two years of successful teaching experience under the Basic Teaching Certificate. Recommendation from the employing school district with input from a teacher education institution. Valid indefinitely providing holder verifies appropriate employment in education of at least three years during each succeeding five year interval. May also be renewed with nine quarter hours of approved credit earned within the five year period prior to date of application if more than five years have elapsed since applicant received bachelor's or higher degree.

4027

Elementary School Teacher 1-8
Certification and Personnel Development Section
State Board of Education
250 East 500 South St.
Salt Lake City, UT 84111
Phone: (801)538-7740

Credential Type: Basic Certificate. **Duration of License:** Four years. **Authorization:** Authorizes the holder to teach all subjects 1-6. Must have subject endorsement to teach specific subjects at the 7-8 grade level. **Requirements:** Bachelor's degree. Complete an approved college level program for elementary school teachers. Recommendation of institute where preparation took place.

Credential Type: Standard Certificate. **Duration of License:** Valid indefinitely with consistent employment. **Requirements:** Two years of successful teaching experience under the Basic Teaching Certificate. Recommendation from the employing school district with input from a teacher education institution. Valid indefinitely providing holder verifies appropriate employment in education of at least three years during each succeeding five year interval. May also be renewed with nine quarter hours of approved credit earned within the five year period prior to date of application if more than five years have elapsed since applicant received bachelor's or higher degree.

4028

Special Education Teacher K-12
Certification and Personnel Development Section
State Board of Education
250 East 500 South St.
Salt Lake City, UT 84111
Phone: (801)538-7740

Credential Type: Special Education Certificate. **Requirements:** Bachelor's degree. Completion of an approved program in the specific area of endorsement. Utah issues endorsements in the following areas: Mild/moderate learning and behavior problems; Severe learning and behavior problems; Hearing handicaps; Visual handicaps.

4029

Teacher of Pupils with Communications Disorders K-12
Certification and Personnel Development Section
State Board of Education
250 East 500 South St.
Salt Lake City, UT 84111
Phone: (801)538-7740

Credential Type: Communications Disorders Certificate. **Requirements:** Bachelor's degree approved program for teaching pupils with communications disorders. Plus a master's degree or 55 quarter hours of credit earned after meeting requirements for the bachelor's degree. Recommendation of preparing institution.

Vermont

4030

Consulting Teacher or Learning Specialist
Teacher Licensure
State Dept. of Education
Montpelier, VT 05602-2703
Phone: (802)828-2445

Credential Type: Initial Certificate. **Authorization:** Holder of this is certificate is authorized to assist and share responsibility with regular and special education personnel in designing, implementing, and evaluating Individual Education Programs for handicapped students. **Requirements:** Master's degree or its equivalent in special education. Supervised advanced clinical practicum with handicapped students. Two years of educational work experience with both handicapped and nonhandicapped students. Meet specific competencies as determined by the Standards Board.

Kindergarten and Elementary School Teachers

4031

Elementary School Teacher K-6
Teacher Licensure
State Dept. of Education
Montpelier, VT 05602-2703
Phone: (802)828-2445

Credential Type: Level One: Beginning Educator's License. **Duration of License:** Two years. **Authorization:** Allows teaching of grades K-6 all subjects. May teach a single subject in grades seven and eight with a minor in that subject area. **Requirements:** Graduate from a regionally accredited or state approved four year institution or a state approved fifth year program. By July 1995, a bachelor's degree and a major in the liberal arts will be required. Must demonstrate ability to write clearly, to apply appropriate mathematical skills effectively, to speak correctly and effectively, and to respond constructively to student behavior. One semester of student teaching, or an equivalent learning experience, or completion of an approved fifth year, mentor, or internship program. Competency in teaching as specified in the following requirements: ability to identify the processes by which students learn and ability to select appropriate methods and materials to meet students' learning needs; ability to select, use, and interpret assessment processes and instruments to identify the strengths and weaknesses of individual students; ability to teach reading skills as they relate to the subject matter being taught; ability to recognize the individual learner's physical, intellectual and psychological developmental needs; ability to apply knowledge of child development, and of early and late adolescence development, to learning; ability to integrate special education students into appropriate learning situations; ability to develop students' awareness of and responsibility for personal health; ability to select and use appropriate technology within the endorsement area(s); ability to apply current state and federal laws and regulations as they apply to all children; ability to identify conditions and actions which would tend to discriminate against students on the basis of sex, race, color, creed, age, handicap, or national origin and to develop teaching strategies to overcome those conditions and actions. Renewal requires recommendation by the Local Standards Board upon completion of an approved Individual Professional Development Plan. **Reciprocity:** Reciprocity exists for persons certified to teach in a state with which Vermont has signed a reciprocal agreement. All others will be evaluated on an individual basis.

Credential Type: Level Two: Professional Educator's License. **Duration of License:** Seven years. **Requirements:** Two years of experience under a Level One License. Demonstrate the following characteristics: ability to plan instruction; ability to maintain a positive learning environment; ability to conduct learning experiences for individuals as well as groups; knowledge of content area; and interest and motivation in continuing professional development. Renewal requires nine credit hours, or the equivalent of educational development activity, per license endorsement area.

4032

Teacher of the Handicapped
Teacher Licensure
State Dept. of Education
Montpelier, VT 05602-2703
Phone: (802)828-2445

Credential Type: Level One: Beginning Educator's License. **Duration of License:** Two years. **Authorization:** Endorsements will be granted in four areas: Essential Early Education Classroom or Home Programs; Intensive Special Education Classrooms or Multihandicapped; Special Education Class Programs/Resource Teacher Programs; and Secondary Diversified Occupations Program. **Requirements:** Graduate from a regionally accredited or state approved four year institution or a state approved fifth year program. Must meet specific requirements for specific endorsement as established by the Standards Board. Must demonstrate ability to write clearly, to apply appropriate mathematical skills effectively, to speak correctly and effectively, and to respond constructively to student behavior. One semester of student teaching, or an equivalent learning experience, or completion of an approved fifth year, mentor, or internship program. Competency in teaching as specified in the following requirements: ability to identify the processes by which students learn and ability to select appropriate methods and materials to meet students' learning needs; ability to select, use, and interpret assessment processes and instruments to identify the strengths and weaknesses of individual students; ability to teach reading skills as they relate to the subject matter being taught; ability to recognize the individual learner's physical, intellectual and psychological developmental needs; ability to apply knowledge of child development, and of early and late adolescence development, to learning; ability to integrate special education students into appropriate learning situations; ability to develop students' awareness of and responsibility for personal health; ability to select and use appropriate technology within the endorsement area(s); ability to apply current state and federal laws and regulations as they apply to all children; ability to identify conditions and actions which would tend to discriminate against students on the basis of sex, race, color, creed, age, handicap, or national origin and to develop teaching strategies to overcome those conditions and actions. Renewal requires recommendation by the Local Standards Board upon completion of an approved Individual Professional Development Plan.

Credential Type: Level Two: Professional Educator's License. **Duration of License:** Seven years. **Requirements:** Two years of experience under a Level One License. Demonstrate the following characteristics: ability to plan instruction; ability to maintain a positive learning environment; ability to conduct learning experiences for individuals as well as groups; knowledge of content area; and interest and motivation in continuing professional development. Renewal requires nine credit hours, or the equivalent of educational development activity, per license endorsement area.

Virginia

4033

Early Education Teacher NK-4
Administrative Director
Office of Professional Development and Teacher Education
Dept. of Education
PO Box 6-Q
Richmond, VA 23216-2060
Phone: (804)225-2094

Credential Type: Probational Certificate. **Duration of License:** One year. **Authorization:** Authorizes candidate who has gained employment in the Virginia Public Schools, but has not yet satisfied the National Teacher Examination (NTE) requirement, to teach for a period of one year. **Requirements:** Meet BTAP (Beginning Teacher Assistance Program) competencies. 48 semester hours of general studies to include six hours each of the following: social sciences; natural sciences; mathematics; school health; and physical education. Must also include 12 semester hours of humanities, social science (including American history), and natural sciences and mathematics. Plus four semester hours of school health and physical education.

Must have 12 semester hours of professional studies including not less than three hours each of human growth and development, curriculum and instructional procedures, and foundations of education. Plus a six semester hr. student teaching experience which includes 200 clock hours in the classroom, and at least 60 percent of that time candidate must provide direct instruction.

Early Education Teacher NK-4, continued

60 semester hours of specialized courses for early education must include: reading; language arts; social science; math; science; art; music; physical education and health; and electives chosen from math and science. Must complete NTE requirements during the life of the certificate. Nonrenewable.

Credential Type: Provisional Certificate. **Duration of License:** Two years. **Authorization:** Authorizes candidates who have not yet satisfied requirements for Virginia's Beginning Teacher Assistance Program, or individuals entering the profession five or more years after their last formal study, or individuals holding a baccalaureate degree with one or more endorsements at the secondary level, or individuals failing to meet general or professional education requirements but have one or more specific endorsements to be employed in a Virginia Public School for a period of two years. **Requirements:** Pass NTE examination. Meet BTAP competencies. 48 semester hours of general studies to include six hours each of the following: social sciences; natural sciences; mathematics; school health; and physical education. Must also include 12 semester hours of humanities, social science (including American history), and natural sciences and mathematics. Plus four semester hours of school health and physical education.

Must have 12 semester hours of professional studies including not less than three hours each of human growth and development, curriculum and instructional procedures, and foundations of education. Plus a six semester hr. student teaching experience which includes 200 clock hours in the classroom, and at least 60 percent of that time candidate must provide direct instruction.

60 semester hours of specialized courses for early education must include: reading; language arts; social science; math; science; art; music; physical education and health; and electives chosen from math and science. Some allowances may be made for incomplete requirements. Must complete any requirement deficits during the life of the certificate. Nonrenewable. **Examination:** National Teacher Examination.

Credential Type: Collegiate Professional Certificate. **Duration of License:** Five years. **Requirements:** Baccalaureate degree from an accredited institution. Pass NTE examination. Meet BTAP competencies. 48 semester hours of general studies to include six hours each of the following: social sciences; natural sciences; mathematics; school health; and physical education. Must also include 12 semester hours of humanities, social science (including American history), and natural sciences and mathematics. Plus four semester hours of school health and physical education.

Must have 12 semester hours of professional studies including not less than three hours each of human growth and development, curriculum and instructional procedures, and foundations of education. Plus a six semester hr. student teaching experience which includes 200 clock hours in the classroom, and at least 60 percent of that time candidate must provide direct instruction.

60 semester hours of specialized courses for early education must include: reading; language arts; social science; math; science; art; music; physical education and health; and electives chosen from math and sciences. Renewable. **Reciprocity:** Applicants who have completed a college level teacher preparation program out-of-state may qualify for this certificate upon approval.

4034

Reading Specialist NK-12
Administrative Director
Office of Professional Development
 and Teacher Education
Dept. of Education
PO Box 6-Q
Richmond, VA 23216-2060
Phone: (804)225-2094

Credential Type: Reading Specialist Endorsement. **Requirements:** Postgraduate Professional Teaching Certificate and three years of successful classroom teaching experience. 18 semester hours of graduate courses to include: foundations or survey of reading instruction; language development; reading in content areas; organization and supervision of reading program; diagnosis and remediation of reading difficulties and a practicum. 12 semester hours of graduate or undergraduate courses to include: measurement and/or evaluation; child and/or adolescent psychology; personality and learning behavior; literature; language arts instruction; learning disabilities; contemporary issues in teaching of reading.

4035

Teacher of the Emotionally Disturbed
Administrative Director
Office of Professional Development
 and Teacher Education
Dept. of Education
PO Box 6-Q
Richmond, VA 23216-2060
Phone: (804)225-2094

Credential Type: Emotionally Disturbed Endorsement. **Requirements:** Teaching Certificate. All applicants, except those who plan to work with preschool handicapped, must complete 18 semester hours of the following core courses: psychoeducational assessment; sociocultural and vocational aspects of disabilities; modifications of curriculum and instruction; language development; current trends and legal issues; and teaching methods in remediation of academic subjects for exceptional individuals. Plus 15 semester hours that include: characteristics of emotionally disturbed; techniques of behavior management; educational programming; and student teaching.

4036

Teacher of the Hearing Impaired
Administrative Director
Office of Professional Development
 and Teacher Education
Dept. of Education
PO Box 6-Q
Richmond, VA 23216-2060
Phone: (804)225-2094

Credential Type: Hearing Impaired Endorsement. **Requirements:** Teaching Certificate. All applicants, except those who plan to work with preschool handicapped, must complete 18 semester hours of the following core courses: psychoeducational assessment; sociocultural and vocational aspects of disabilities; modifications of curriculum and instruction; language development; current trends and legal issues; and teaching methods in remediation of academic subjects for exceptional individuals. Plus 15 semester hours which includes course work in: characteristics of hearing impaired students; speech science and audiology; instructional procedures; individual and group amplification systems; and student teaching.

4037

Teacher of the Learning Disabled
Administrative Director
Office of Professional Development
  and Teacher Education
Dept. of Education
PO Box 6-Q
Richmond, VA 23216-2060
Phone: (804)225-2094

Credential Type: Learning Disabled Endorsement. **Requirements:** Teaching Certificate. All applicants, except those who plan to work with preschool handicapped, must complete 18 semester hours of the following core courses: psychoeducational assessment; sociocultural and vocational aspects of disabilities; modifications of curriculum and instruction; language development; current trends and legal issues; and teaching methods in remediation of academic subjects for exceptional individuals. Plus 15 semester hours of the following course work: characteristics of the learning disabled; techniques for diagnosis and intervention; methods of basic skills instruction; adaptation of various levels of general education; and student teaching.

4038

Teacher of the Mentally Retarded
Administrative Director
Office of Professional Development
  and Teacher Education
Dept. of Education
PO Box 6-Q
Richmond, VA 23216-2060
Phone: (804)225-2094

Credential Type: Mentally Retarded Endorsement. **Requirements:** Teaching Certificate. All applicants, except those who plan to work with preschool handicapped, must complete 18 semester hours of the following core courses: psychoeducational assessment; sociocultural and vocational aspects of disabilities; modifications of curriculum and instruction; language development; current trends and legal issues; and teaching methods in remediation of academic subjects for exceptional individuals. Plus 15 semester hours of the following courses of study: characteristics of the mentally retarded, including medical aspects; teaching methods and materials; vocational exploration; educational evaluation; and student teaching.

4039

Teacher of the Severely and Profoundly Handicapped
Administrative Director
Office of Professional Development
  and Teacher Education
Dept. of Education
PO Box 6-Q
Richmond, VA 23216-2060
Phone: (804)225-2094

Credential Type: Severely and Profoundly Handicapped Endorsement. **Requirements:** Teaching Certificate. All applicants, except those who plan to work with preschool handicapped, must complete 18 semester hours of the following core courses: psychoeducational assessment; sociocultural and vocational aspects of disabilities; modifications of curriculum and instruction; language development; current trends and legal issues; and teaching methods in remediation of academic subjects for exceptional individuals. Plus 15 semester hours of the following course work: characteristics and medical aspects of severe and profound handicaps; advanced techniques of behavior management; occupational and physical therapy techniques; social and leisure skills development; and student teaching.

4040

Teacher of Speech and Language Disorders
Administrative Director
Office of Professional Development
  and Teacher Education
Dept. of Education
PO Box 6-Q
Richmond, VA 23216-2060
Phone: (804)225-2094

Credential Type: Speech and Language Disorders Endorsement. **Requirements:** Teaching Certificate. All applicants, except those who plan to work with preschool handicapped, must complete 18 semester hours of the following core courses: psychoeducational assessment; sociocultural and vocational aspects of disabilities; modifications of curriculum and instruction; language development; current trends and legal issues; and teaching methods in remediation of academic subjects for exceptional individuals. Plus 24 semester hours of course work in the following: speech pathology; anatomy and physiology of speech and auditory mechanisms; speech and language development; and audiology; management techniques for disorders of articulation, language, fluency, voice and resonance.

4041

Teacher of the Visually Impaired
Administrative Director
Office of Professional Development
  and Teacher Education
Dept. of Education
PO Box 6-Q
Richmond, VA 23216-2060
Phone: (804)225-2094

Credential Type: Visually Impaired Endorsement. **Requirements:** Teaching Certificate. All applicants, except those who plan to work with preschool handicapped, must complete 18 semester hours of the following core courses: psychoeducational assessment; sociocultural and vocational aspects of disabilities; modifications of curriculum and instruction; language development; current trends and legal issues; and teaching methods in remediation of academic subjects for exceptional individuals. Plus 15 semester hours of course work to include: anatomy, physiology, and diseases of the eye; nature and needs; reading and writing Braille; procedures for teaching the visually impaired; and student teaching.

Washington

4042

Public School Teacher PK-12
Superintendent of Public Instruction
Professional Education and
  Certification
Old Capitol Bldg. FG-11
Seattle, WA 98504-3211
Phone: (206)753-6773

Credential Type: Initial Certificate. **Duration of License:** Four years. **Authorization:** Certificate will be endorsed for teaching in PK-3, K-8, 4-12, or K-12 grade levels. **Requirements:** 18 years of age. Good moral character. Citizen of U.S. or declaration of intent to become a citizen. Baccalaureate degree from a regionally accredited institution and completion of a state approved teacher education program. Complete a 45 quarter hr. of 30 semester hr. major in one endorsement area. Renewable for an additional three years while the holder meets requirements for a Continuing Teacher Certificate.

Credential Type: Continuing Teacher Certificate. **Duration of License:** Five years. **Requirements:** Initial Certificate. Master's degree from a regionally accredited institution. Meet experience requirement as determined by the Superintendent of Public Instruction. Be eligible for at least two endorsements. Renewable upon com-

Washington

Public School Teacher PK-12, continued

pletion of 150 clock hours of full-time teaching during the life of the certificate.

4043

Reading Resource Specialist
Superintendent of Public Instruction
Professional Education and
   Certification
Old Capitol Bldg. FG-11
Seattle, WA 98504-3211
Phone: (206)753-6773

Credential Type: Initial Educational Staff Associate Certificate. **Duration of License:** Seven years. **Authorization:** Authorizes service in primary role of assistant to the learner, the teacher, the administrator, and/or the educational program. **Requirements:** Hold a valid teaching certificate. Complete all course work (except special projects or thesis) for a master's degree with a major in the teaching of reading.

Credential Type: Continuing Educational Staff Associate Certificate. **Duration of License:** Five years. **Requirements:** Master's degree in the teaching of reading. Verification of 180 days of experience in the role. Complete a college level course which includes peer review while employed in the role. Out-of-state applicants must complete a comprehensive written examination (unless already taken as part of the master's degree). Renewable upon 150 clock hours of work in this position during the life of the certificate.

West Virginia

4044

Public School Teacher
State Dept. of Education
Certification Unit
Charleston, WV 25305
Phone: (800)982-2378

Credential Type: Professional Teaching Certificate—Three Year. **Duration of License:** Three years. **Requirements:** U.S. citizen. Good moral character. Physically, mentally, and emotionally qualified to perform the duties of a teacher. 18 years of age on or before the first day of October of the year in which the certificate is issued. Complete a state approved, four year, teacher preparation program at the college level. Must demonstrate competencies in reading, writing, mathematics, speaking and listening. Pass the National Teacher Examination (NTE) Pre-Professional Skills Test. Must complete general studies and content specialization classes as outlined by the preparing institution. Professional education component must include courses in performance assessment measurement and theory, skills, strategies and methods of designing, implementing and evaluating education.

Applicants who have successfully completed the APET alternative program for teacher certification will be granted the Professional Certificate after successful completion of the program and a support team comprehensive evaluation. **Examination:** National Teacher Examination in Pre-Professional Skills. **Reciprocity:** Reciprocity exists for those out-of-state applicants who received their certification in a state that has signed a reciprocity statement with West Virginia or in a state that has standards substantially equivalent to West Virginia. Out-of-state applicants who did not complete a content test as part of the approved program must successfully complete the West Virginia Content Test. **Fees:** $5 certification fee.

Credential Type: Alternative Program Teaching Certificate (APET). **Duration of License:** One school year (expires on June 30 of the school year in which it was issued). **Requirements:** U.S. citizen. Good moral character. Physically, mentally, and emotionally qualified to perform the duties of a teacher. 18 years of age on or before the first day of October of the year in which the certificate is issued. Must not have previously completed a state approved teacher preparation program. Bachelor's degree from an accredited institution in a discipline taught in the public schools and in a teaching specialization approved by the state board for APET. Satisfy appropriate state board approved basic skills and subject matter test requirements or complete three years of successful teaching experience within the last seven years in the area for which licensure is sought. After meeting the requirements listed above, the applicant must apply to the West Virginia Dept. of Education for a letter of eligibility which permits the individual to seek employment in a school included in an approved APET program. Once employment is secured an APET certificate will be issued. An extension of this certificate may be possible, however, the candidate is expected to undergo evaluation and progress to the Professional Certificate upon completion of this program. Note: Beginning July 1, 1994, candidates for the APET certificate must have achieved a minimum overall grade point average of 2.5 on a 4.0 scale for all college courses attempted. **Fees:** $5 certification fee.

Credential Type: Professional Certificate—Five Year. **Duration of License:** Five years. **Requirements:** Must hold a Three Year Professional Certificate. Must complete six semester hours of renewal credit subsequent to the original certificate or hold a master's degree and the MA30 salary classification or complete three years of teaching experience, one year of which must be in West Virginia, at the program level appearing on the original certificate. **Fees:** $5 certification fee.

Wisconsin

4045

Elementary School Teacher
Teacher Education, Licensing, and
   Placement
Box 7841
Madison, WI 53707-7841
Phone: (608)266-1027

Credential Type: Elementary Regular Teaching License. **Requirements:** Complete an approved program at a college or university. Recommendation from the preparing institution. Pass the PreProfessional Skills Test in Mathematics, Reading, and Writing. Must complete a minimum of 26 semester hours of professional education credits which include the following: child development, including educational psychology or psychology of learning; methods; a fulltime, full semester student teaching assignment or complete a parttime student teaching assignment plus two consecutive semesters of successful regular teaching experience under school district supervision; 12 semester credits in the teaching of reading; a course in exceptional education (minimum three semester hours); adequate preparation in environmental education; and a minor in a licensable area. Kindergarten teachers must also complete 22 semester hours in early childhood education. **Examination:** Professional Skills Test in Mathematics, Reading, and Writing.

4046

Teacher of Special Subjects
Teacher Education, Licensing, and
   Placement
Box 7841
Madison, WI 53707-7841
Phone: (608)266-1027

Credential Type: Special Subjects License. **Authorization:** Licenses are available in Technology Education, Family and Consumer Education, Business Education, Agriculture, Music, Art, and Physical Education. **Requirements:** Complete an approved program at a college or university. Recommendation from the preparing institution. Pass the PreProfessional Skills Test in Mathematics, Reading, and Writing.

Complete a 34 semester hr. teaching major in the special subject area. (Music requires a 46 semester hr. major and physical education and art require 54 semester hours) Have a minimum of 18 semester credits of professional education including: educational psychology or psychology of learning; methods of teaching; a fulltime, full semester student teaching assignment or complete a parttime student teaching assignment plus two consecutive semesters of successful regular teaching experience under school district supervision; six semester hours of teaching of reading; and a three semester hr. course or equivalent in exceptional education. **Examination:** Pre-Professional Skills Test in Mathematics, Reading, and Writing.

Wyoming

4047

Elementary School Teacher K-6
State Dept. of Education
Certification and Accreditation
Services Unit, Hathaway Bldg.
Cheyenne, WY 82002
Phone: (307)777-7291

Credential Type: Standard Teaching Certificate. **Duration of License:** Five years. **Requirements:** Bachelor's degree. Teacher preparation program. 40 semester hours in general education to include six of the following areas: English; fine arts; foreign language; health and physical education; humanities; mathematics; practical arts; psychology; science; and social studies. 24 semester hours of professional education to include: human growth and development; research; educational evaluation; methods, materials and media appropriate to field of teaching specialization; historical, philosophical, and sociological foundations of public education in the United States; understanding the purposes, administrative organization and operation of the school; recognition of exceptional children; teaching of reading; human relations, computer assisted instruction; and gifted and talented. Plus 24 semester hours of professional education in elementary methods which includes: arithmetic; science; language arts; reading; social studies; children's literature or library science for children; fine arts; health or physical education.

Credential Type: Professional Teaching Certificate. **Duration of License:** 10 years. **Requirements:** Hold or be eligible for Standard Teaching Certificate. Five years of teaching experience. Master's degree in teaching endorsement or master's degree with work in four of the following areas: area of teaching endorsement; supporting professional courses in area of teaching endorsement; educational foundations; human development or psychology; curriculum or supervision; practicum or internship or directed teaching experience.

Credential Type: Education Specialist Certificate. **Duration of License:** Five years. **Requirements:** Master's degree. Experience in K-6 setting. Valid Wyoming teacher certificate.

Credential Type: Professional Education Specialist Certificate. **Duration of License:** 10 years. **Requirements:** Master's degree. 30 semester hours of credit beyond the master's degree.

Credential Type: Special Pupil Service Endorsement. **Requirements:** Bachelor's Degree. The following endorsements may be added to a Standard Teaching Certificate, or higher teaching certificate, by completing the specified number of semester hours in the special endorsement area: Audiovisual 12; Head Teacher (Limited to attendance centers employing six or fewer teachers) 15; Library-Media 24; Library Science 15; and Instructional Media 9.

4048

School Reading Specialist
State Dept. of Education
Certification and Accreditation
Services Unit, Hathaway Bldg.
Cheyenne, WY 82002
Phone: (307)777-7291

Credential Type: Reading Specialist Endorsement. **Requirements:** Teaching certification and Education Specialist certification. 24 semester hours of graduate work, including a master's degree and the following courses of study: developmental reading instruction; diagnosis and correction of reading disabilities; measurement and evaluation; literature for children and adolescents; communications and linguistics; organization and supervision of reading programs; practicum experience; and psychology. Two years of classroom teaching or counseling or supervisory or administrative experience in a K-12 setting. Experience must also include one year as a reading teacher.

Landscape Architects

The following states grant licenses in this occupational category as of the date of publication:

Alabama	Georgia	Kentucky	Mississippi	New York	South Carolina	West Virginia
Arizona	Hawaii	Louisiana	Missouri	North Carolina	South Dakota	Wyoming
Arkansas	Idaho	Maine	Montana	Ohio	Tennessee	
California	Illinois	Maryland	Nebraska	Oklahoma	Texas	
Connecticut	Indiana	Massachusetts	Nevada	Oregon	Utah	
Delaware	Iowa	Michigan	New Jersey	Pennsylvania	Virginia	
Florida	Kansas	Minnesota	New Mexico	Rhode Island	Washington	

Alabama

4049

Landscape Architect
Board of Examiners of Landscape Architects
908 S. Hull St.
Montgomery, AL 36104
Phone: (205)262-7768

Credential Type: License. **Duration of License:** One year. **Requirements:** 19 years of age. Must hold a B.S. degree with a major in Landscape Architecture; or have no degree and eight years work experience under a licensed landscape architect. **Examination:** Written examination. **Reciprocity:** Yes. **Fees:** $85 registration fee. $250 examination fee. $50 renewal fee. $85 reciprocity fee.

4050

Landscape Horticulturist
Dept. Agricultural and Industries
Div. of Agricultural Chemistry and Plant Industry
Beard Bldg.
PO Box 3336
Montgomery, AL 36193
Phone: (205)242-2656

Credential Type: License. **Duration of License:** One year. **Requirements:** Must submit a written statement outlining training and experience in this field. **Examination:** Written examination. **Fees:** $10 examination fee. $25 renewal fee.

Arizona

4051

Landscape Architect
Board of Technical Registration
1951 W. Camelback, Ste. 250
Phoenix, AZ 85015
Phone: (602)255-4053

Credential Type: Registration to practice. **Duration of License:** Three years. **Requirements:** Be of good moral character. Have at least eight years education or experience, or combination of both with at least four years of experience. Pass in-training and professional examination administered by the board. **Examination:** Landscape architect-in-training exam: section two (design), section three (design application). Professional landscape architect exam: section one (professional practice), section four (design and implementation), section five (grading and drainage). **Exemptions:** The in-training exam may be waived for candidates who have a degree in landscape architecture. **Fees:** $90 application fee. National exam fees: $45 section 1, $56 section 2, $105 section 3, $99 section 4, $92 section 5. $126 renewal fee.

Credential Type: Registration without examination. **Requirements:** Hold a valid registration in another state, jurisdiction, territory, or country; or hold a certificate of qualification issued by the Council of Landscape Architectural Registration Board. Meet experience and education requirements similar to those of Arizona, or have been actively engaged in the profession for at least 10 years. **Fees:** $90 application fee. $126 renewal fee.

4052

Landscape Architect-in-Training
Board of Technical Registration
1951 W. Camelback, Ste. 250
Phoenix, AZ 85015
Phone: (602)255-4053

Credential Type: In-training registration. **Requirements:** Be of good moral character. To qualify for the in-training examination on the basis of education, must be a graduate of a four—or five-year landscape architectural degree program of an accredited college or university.

To qualify for the intraining examination on the basis of experience, must have at least four years of education or experience or both directly related to the practice of landscape architecture. **Examination:** Landscape architect-in-training exam: section two (design), section three (design application). **Fees:** $30 application fee. National exam fees: $56 section 2, $105 section 3.

Arkansas

4053

Landscape Architect
Arkansas State Board of Architects
1515 Bldg., Rm. 512
1515 W. 7th St.
Little Rock, AR 72202
Phone: (501)375-1310

Credential Type: License. **Requirements:** Hold a Bachelors degree in landscape architecture plus one year experience; or, Hold a degree in a field related to landscape architecture plus four years experience; or, seven years experience in landscape architecture. **Examination:** Yes. **Fees:** $50 Registration.

Landscape Architects

California

4054

Landscape Architect
State Board of Landscape Architects
400 R St., Ste. 4020
Sacramento, CA 95814
Phone: (916)445-4954
Fax: (916)324-2333

Credential Type: Landscape Architect Registration. **Duration of License:** One year. **Requirements:** Must be at least 18 years of age. No minimum degree required. Meet one of the following sets of requirements: (1) LAAB accredited LA degree and two years experience under the supervision of a LA; (2) non-accredited LA degree and three years experience under the supervision of a LA; (3) accredited architectural or civil engineering degree and four years experience under the supervision of a LA; (4) any bachelor's degree and five years experience under the supervision of a LA; (5) Associate's degree and five years experience under the supervision of a LA; (6) High school diploma and six years experience under the supervision of a LA. **Examination:** National and state examinations. **Fees:** $325 application fee for reciprocal registration. $150 annual renewal fee.

Connecticut

4055

Landscape Architect
Dept. of Consumer Protection
Board of Landscape Architects
165 Capitol Ave., Rm. G-1
Hartford, CT 06106
Phone: (203)566-4223
Fax: (203)566-7630

Credential Type: Landscape Architect Registration. **Duration of License:** One year. **Requirements:** Bachelor's degree. Must have LAAB accredited LA degree and two years experience under the supervision of a LA or have a nonaccredited LA degree and eight years experience under the supervision of a LA. **Examination:** National examination. **Fees:** $40 minimum exam administration fee. $30 application fee for reciprocal registration. $80 annual renewal fee.

Delaware

4056

Landscape Architect
Board of Landscape Architects
O'Neil Bldg., Box 1401
Dover, DE 19903
Phone: (302)739-4522
Fax: (302)739-6148

Credential Type: Landscape Architect Registration. **Duration of License:** One year. **Requirements:** Bachelor's degree. Must have an LAAB accredited LA degree or a non-accredited LA degree with eight years of experience under the supervision of an LA. Accredited Architectural or Civil Engineering degrees may be acceptable as determined by board. **Examination:** National examination. **Fees:** $10 application fee for reciprocal registration. $75 annual renewal fee.

Florida

4057

Landscape Architect
Board of Landscape Architecture
Dept of Professional Regulation
1940 N. Monroe St.
Tallahassee, FL 32399-0766
Phone: (904)488-6685

Credential Type: License by Examination. **Duration of License:** Two years. **Requirements:** Complete a professional degree program in landscape architecture, and have at least one year of practical experience in landscape architectural work; or have at least six years of actual practical experience in landscape architectural work. Each year of education is considered the equivalent to one year of experience, with a maximum credit of four years. **Examination:** Landscape Architect Registration Examination (LARE). Florida Plant Materials Examination. **Fees:** $100 application fee. $735 examination fee (LARE and Section 8). $225.00 licensure fee. $225 renewal fee. **Governing Statute:** Florida Statutes, Chapter 481, Part II. Rules of the Board of Landscape Architecture, Chapter 21-K.

Credential Type: License by Endorsement. **Duration of License:** Two years. **Requirements:** Meet basic experience and educational requirements. Have passed a substantially equivalent national, regional, state, or territorial licensing examination; or hold a valid license to practice landscape architecture issued by another state or territory of the United States with substantially identical licensure criteria. **Fees:** $150 application fee (endorsement). $337.50 licensure fee. $235 renewal fee. **Governing Statute:** Florida Statutes, Chapter 481, Part II. Rules of the Board of Landscape Architecture, Chapter 21-K.

Georgia

4058

Landscape Architect
State Board of Landscape Architects
Sciences and Professions Section
Professional Examining Boards
166 Pryor St., SW
Atlanta, GA 30303
Phone: (404)656-2281

Credential Type: Landscape Architect Certificate of Registration. **Duration of License:** Two years. **Requirements:** Be at least 18 years of age. Have at least 6.5 years of training in landscape architecture, or have a degree which requires five academic years of education from a school of landscape architecture, environmental design, or its equivalent, and 1.5 years of training in landscape architecture. **Examination:** Written examination. **Reciprocity:** Yes, based on substantially equivalent licensing requirements and reciprocity with Georgia. **Fees:** $25 application fee. $80 initial registration fee. $100 renewal fee. $80 reciprocal license fee. **Governing Statute:** Official Code of Georgia Annotated 43-23. Rules of the Georgia State Board of Landscape Architects, Chap. 310.

Credential Type: Temporary License. **Duration of License:** One year. **Authorization:** Issued for a stipulated site and project within Georgia. **Requirements:** Be at least 18 years of age. Be registered in any other state or country. Present evidence of competency to practice in Georgia. **Fees:** $50 temporary license fee. $50 temporary license renewal fee. **Governing Statute:** Official Code of Georgia Annotated 43-23. Rules of the Georgia State Board of Landscape Architects, Chap. 310.

Hawaii

4059

Architect, Landscape
Hawaii Board of Engineers, Architects, Surveyors and Landscape Architects
Dept. of Commerce and Consumer Affairs
PO Box 3469
Honolulu, HI 96801
Phone: (808)548-8542

Credential Type: License. **Duration of License:** Six months. **Requirements:** Master's Degree in landscape architecture, graduation from a four-year landscape architecture program, plus two years of experience as a landscape architect, or graduation from an approved four-year landscape architecture program plus three years of experience, or graduation from an approved four-year pre-landscape architecture or arts and science curriculum plus five years of experience, or 12 years of satisfactory experience. Three statements from landscape architects certifying experience, character and reputation. **Examination:** Given in June. **Exemptions:** Exam may be waived if applicant passed an equivalent exam in another state and holds a valid registration from that state. **Fees:** $50 application fee. $85 exam fee. $30 license fee. $15 $30 Compliance Resolution Fund fee. $30 renewal fee.

Idaho

4060

Landscape Architect
Board of Examiners of Landscape Architects
Bureau of Occupational Licenses
1109 Main St., Ste. 220
Boise, ID 83702-5642
Phone: (208)334-3233

Credential Type: Landscape Architect License. **Duration of License:** One year. **Requirements:** Be at least 18 years of age. Complete a course of study in landscape architecture and graduate from a college or school accredited by the American Society of Landscape Architects or approved by the board. Complete a combination of four years of practical experience and education. In lieu of graduation, four years of practical experience may satisfy requirement. **Examination:** Landscape Architect Registration Examination (LARE), published by the Council of Landscape Architectural Registration Boards (CLARB). Idaho plant material examination. **Reciprocity:** Yes, provided applicant has already passed LARE. **Fees:** $75 application fee. Exam fees: Section 1, $15; Section 2, $20; Section 3, $65; Section 4, $60; Section 5, $80; Section 6, $70; Section 7, $35; Section 8, $40. $75 original license fee. $75 renewal fee. **Governing Statute:** Idaho Code, Title 54, Chap. 30. Rules and Regulations of the Idaho State Board of Landscape Architects.

4061

Landscape Designer
Plant Industries Div.
Agriculture Dept.
PO Box 790
Boise, ID 83701
Phone: (208)334-2986

Credential Type: Class A License. **Duration of License:** One year. **Authorization:** Required if gross business is over $1,000 per year. Covers persons engaged in landscaping property for which licensee will furnish plants, trees, or shrubs from own nursery or by purchase or contract from other nurseries. **Requirements:** Submit application and pay fee. **Fees:** $50 license fee per outlet. **Governing Statute:** Idaho Code, Title 22, Chap. 23.

Credential Type: Class B License. **Duration of License:** One year. **Authorization:** Required if gross business is $1,000 or less per year. Covers persons engaged in landscaping property for which licensee will furnish plants, trees, or shrubs from own nursery or by purchase or contract from other nurseries. **Requirements:** Submit application and pay fee. **Fees:** $15 license fee. **Governing Statute:** Idaho Code, Title 22, Chap. 23.

Illinois

4062

Landscape Architect
Dept. of Professional Regulation
320 W. Washington St., 3rd Fl.
Springfield, IL 62786
Phone: (217)785-7564
Fax: (217)782-7645

Credential Type: Landscape Architect Registration. **Duration of License:** One year. **Requirements:** As of January 1, 1993, all candidates must have a bachelor's degree in Landscape Architecture. **Examination:** National examination. **Fees:** $100 exam administration fee. $100 application fee for reciprocal registration. $100 annual renewal fee.

Indiana

4063

Landscape Architect
Professional Licensing Agency
State Office Bldg., Rm. 1021
Indianapolis, IN 46204-2246
Phone: (317)232-2980
Fax: (317)232-2312

Credential Type: Landscape Architect Registration. **Duration of License:** One year. **Requirements:** Must be at least 18 years of age. Must have an LAAB accredited or board-approved LA degree, or eight years of experience under the supervision of an LA. **Examination:** National examination. **Fees:** $69 exam administration fee. $100 application fee for reciprocal registration. $20 annual renewal fee.

Iowa

4064

Landscape Architect
Iowa Board of Landscape Architectural Examiners
1918 SE Hulsizer
Ankeny, IA 50021
Phone: (515)281-7362

Credential Type: Registration. **Duration of License:** Two years. **Requirements:** Graduation from a college offering an accredited four-year curriculum in landscape architecture, plus a minimum of three years of practical experience. One year of experience must be under the supervision of a registered landscape architect; or graduation from a college offering a non-accredited four-year course in landscape architecture, plus a minimum of four years of practical experience. One year of experience must be under the supervision of a registered landscape architect; or a minimum of ten years of practical experience as a landscape architect. **Examination:** Uniform national examination. **Fees:** $410 exam fee. $50 registration fee. $175 renewal fee.

Kansas

4065

Landscape Architect
Board of Technical Professions
900 Jackson St., Ste. 507
Topeka, KS 66612-1214
Phone: (913)296-3053
Fax: (913)296-6729

Credential Type: Landscape Architect Registration. **Duration of License:** One year. **Requirements:** Must have a five-year LAAB accredited LA degree with one year of experience under the supervision of a LA, or a four-year nonaccredited LA degree with two years of experience under the supervision of an LA. All other candidates must have seven years of combined landscape architectural education and/or experience that meets board approval. **Examination:** National and state examinations. **Fees:** $27 exam administration fee. $372 application fee for reciprocal registration. $15 annual renewal fee.

Kentucky

4066

Landscape Architect
State Board of Examiners & Registration of Landscape Architects
160 Democrat Dr.
Frankfort, KY 40601
Phone: (502)564-3263

Credential Type: License. **Duration of License:** One year. **Requirements:** 21 years of age. High school diploma and seven years of supervised work experience, or a bachelor's degree and two years of supervised work experience. 15 hours of continuing education for renewal. **Examination:** Yes. **Reciprocity:** Yes. **Fees:** $60 renewal fee.

Louisiana

4067

Landscape Architect
Horticulture Commission
PO Box 3118
Baton Rouge, LA 70821
Phone: (504)925-7772

Credential Type: License. **Duration of License:** One year. **Requirements:** A baccalaureate degree and/or experience. **Examination:** Yes. **Reciprocity:** The commission may enter into reciprocal agreements with licensing agencies in other states. **Fees:** $150 exam fee. $35 license fee. $35 renewal fee.

4068

Landscape Contractor
Horticulture Commission
PO Box 3118
Baton Rouge, LA 70821
Phone: (504)925-7772

Credential Type: License. **Duration of License:** One year. **Examination:** Written. **Fees:** $35 exam fee. $35 license fee. $35 renewal fee.

Maine

4069

Landscape Architect
State Board for Licensing Landscape Architects
Dept. of Professional & Financial Regulation
State House Station 35
Augusta, ME 04333
Phone: (207)582-8723
Fax: (207)582-5415

Credential Type: Landscape Architect Registration. **Duration of License:** One year. **Requirements:** Must meet one of the following sets of requirements: (1) LAAB accredited LA degree and two years experience under the supervision of a LA; (2) non-accredited LA degree and three years experience under the supervision of a LA; (3) accredited architectural or civil engineering degree and four years experience under the supervision of a LA; (4) any bachelor's degree and five years experience under the supervision of a LA; (5) Associate's degree and seven years experience under the supervision of a LA. **Examination:** National examination. **Fees:** $210 exam administration fee. $300 application fee for reciprocal registration. $60 annual renewal fee.

Maryland

4070

Landscape Architect
Dept. of Licensing & Regulation
Occupational & Professional Licensing Boards
501 St. Paul Pl., Rm. 902
Baltimore, MD 21202
Phone: (301)333-6322
Fax: (301)333-1229

Credential Type: Landscape Architect Registration. **Duration of License:** One year. **Requirements:** Must be at least 18 years of age. Must have a combination of eight years of landscape architectural education and experience. **Examination:** National examination. **Fees:** $25 exam administration fee. $100 application fee for reciprocal registration. $200 annual renewal fee.

Massachusetts

4071

Landscape Architect
Board of Registration for Landscape Architects
100 Cambridge St., Rm. 1513
Boston, MA 02202
Phone: (617)727-3093

Credential Type: Landscape Architect Registration. **Duration of License:** One year. **Requirements:** Must be at least 23 years of age. Bachelor's degree in landscape architecture. Must have an LAAB accredited LA degree and two years experience under the supervision of an LA or a nonaccredited degree and six years of experience under the supervision of an LA. **Examination:** National examination. **Fees:** $60 exam administration fee. $65 application fee for reciprocal registration. $50 annual renewal fee.

Michigan

4072

Landscape Architect
Dept. of Licensing & Regulation
Board of Landscape Architects
PO Box 30018
Lansing, MI 48909
Phone: (517)335-1669
Fax: (517)373-7285

Credential Type: Landscape Architect Registration. **Duration of License:** One year. **Requirements:** Must have an LAAB accredited LA degree and three years expe-

Minnesota 4073

Landscape Architect, continued

rience under the supervision of a BLA. All other candidates are subject to board review. **Examination:** National examination. **Fees:** $30 exam administration fee. $30 application fee for reciprocal registration. $40 annual renewal fee.

Minnesota

4073

Landscape Architect
Board of Landscape Architecture & Certified Interior Design
133 E. 7th St.
St. Paul, MN 55101
Phone: (612)297-2388
Fax: (612)297-5310

Credential Type: Landscape Architect Registration. **Duration of License:** One year. **Requirements:** Must be at least 25 years of age. No minimum degree required. Meet one of the following sets of requirements: (1) LAAB accredited five-year LA degree and three years experience under the supervision of a LA; (2) LAAB accredited three-year LA degree and four years experience under the supervision of a LA; (3) Non-accredited LA degree and four years experience under the supervision of a LA; (4) accredited architectural or civil engineering degree and five years experience under the supervision of a LA; (5) any bachelor's degree and five years experience under the supervision of a LA; (6) Associate's degree and six years experience under the supervision of a LA; (7) High school diploma and eight years experience under the supervision of a LA. **Examination:** National examination. **Fees:** $20 exam administration fee. $100 application fee for reciprocal registration. $29 annual renewal fee.

Mississippi

4074

Landscape Architect
State Board of Architecture
239 N. Lamar St., Rm. 502
Jackson, MS 39201-1311
Phone: (601)359-6020
Fax: (601)359-6159

Credential Type: Landscape Architect Registration. **Duration of License:** One year. **Requirements:** Must be at least 21 years of age. Meet one of the following sets of requirements: (1) hold a professional degree from an accredited school of landscape architecture; (2) hold a high school diploma have seven years of board-approved landscape architectural experience; (3) graduate from a college or university with a degree in a curriculum other than landscape architecture and have five years of experience working in landscape architecture. **Examination:** National examination. **Fees:** $60 exam administration fee. $250 application fee for reciprocal registration. $72 annual renewal fee.

4075

Landscape Horticulturist
Dept. of Agriculture and Commerce
Div. of Plant Industry
PO Box 5207
Mississippi State, MS 39762
Phone: (601)325-3390

Credential Type: Horticulturist License. **Duration of License:** Indefinite. **Requirements:** Meet one of the following sets of requirements: (1) Graduate from a college or university with at least 15 semester hours or the equivalent in the field for which a license is requested. (2) Have at least two years of college or university training, with special training in the field for which a license is requested. (3) Be a high school graduate or equivalent and have at least one year of experience with a licensed horticulturist within the past two years. (4) If applicant is not a high school graduate, must have completed at least two years of experience with a licensed horticulturist within the past three years.

Renewal requires attending an approved training course every three years. **Examination:** Written examination in landscape gardening. **Reciprocity:** Exam may be waived if applicant is licensed in a state with standards equal to those of Mississippi and that state will honor the Mississippi Examination.

Missouri

4076

Landscape Architect
Missouri Land Architectural Council
PO Box 471
Jefferson City, MO 65102
Phone: (314)751-0877
Fax: (314)751-4176

Credential Type: Landscape Architect Registration. **Duration of License:** One year. **Requirements:** Must be at least 21 years of age. Must have a LAAB accredited LA degree and three years of experience in landscape architecture, or eight years of satisfactory training and experience in landscape architecture. **Examination:** National and state examinations. **Fees:** $50 exam administration fee. $195 application fee for reciprocal registration. $95 annual renewal fee.

Montana

4077

Landscape Architect
Montana Board of Landscape Architects
111 N. Jackson
Helena, MT 59620
Phone: (406)444-5433

Credential Type: License. **Duration of License:** One year. **Examination:** National board exam. **Fees:** $75 application fee. $380 exam fee. $35 license fee. $90 renewal fee. **Governing Statute:** Montana Code Annotated 37-66-301 through 37-66-323.

Nebraska

4078

Landscape Architect
Nebraska Board of Examiners for Landscape Architects
600 NBC Center
Lincoln, NE 68508
Phone: (402)477-9291

Credential Type: License. **Duration of License:** One year. **Requirements:** 21 years of age. Must be a graduate of a college curriculum in landscape architecture, or related field approved by the board. Must have four years of practical experience. **Examination:** Yes. **Fees:** $50 application fee. $320 examination fees. $50 certification fee. $65 renewal fee.

Nevada

4079

Landscape Architect
Nevada State Board of Landscape Architecture
PO Box 40968
Reno, NV 89504
Phone: (702)829-8117

Credential Type: License. **Duration of License:** One year. **Requirements:** Six years of education and experience in landscape architecture. **Examination:** Yes. **Fees:** $250 exam fee. $130 certificate fee. $130 renewal fee. $200 application fee.

Landscape Architects

New Jersey
4080

Landscape Architect
State Board of Architects and
 Certified Landscape Architects
1100 Raymond Blvd., Rm. 511
Newark, NJ 07102
Phone: (201)648-2378

Credential Type: Certified Landscape Architect. **Duration of License:** Two years. **Requirements:** At least a bachelor's degree in landscape architecture from an accredited college or university. At least six years of combined work and education at least two of which must be practical landscape architecture experience. Some continuing education is required. **Examination:** Yes. **Reciprocity:** Yes. **Fees:** $100 application fee. $140 license fee. $100 registration fee. $242 exam fee. **Governing Statute:** NJSA 45:3-3. NJAC 13:27.

New Mexico
4081

Landscape Architect
Board of Landscape Architects
PO Box 25101
Santa Fe, NM (505)827-7
Phone: (505)827-7095

Credential Type: Landscape Architect Registration. **Duration of License:** One year. **Requirements:** Must be at least 29 years of age. Must have a LAAB accredited baccalaureate degree in LA and three years of experience under the supervision of an LA, or a non-accredited baccalaureate degree in LA and four years of experience under the supervision of a LA. **Examination:** National examination. **Fees:** $65 exam administration fee. $200 application fee for reciprocal registration. $100 annual renewal fee.

New York
4082

Landscape Architect
State Education Dept.
Div. of Professional Licensing
 Services
Cultural Education Center
Empire State Plaza
Albany, NY 12230
Phone: (518)474-3326

Credential Type: License. **Duration of License:** Three years. **Requirements:** Bachelor's Degree in landscape architecture or 12 years of experience. 21 years of age. Three or four years of appropriate architectural experience. U.S. citizen or alien lawfully admitted for permanent residency. **Examination:** Written. **Fees:** $375 application fee. $155 renewal fee. **Governing Statute:** Title VIII Articles 130, 148 of the Education Law.

North Carolina
4083

Landscape Architect
North Carolina State Board of
 Landscape Architecture
PO Box 26852
Raleigh, NC 27611
Phone: (919)781-7259

Credential Type: License. **Duration of License:** One year. **Requirements:** Graduation from an accredited landscape architectural curriculum plus one year of practical experience; or a combination of seven years of education and experience. **Examination:** National exam. **Fees:** $75 application fee. $225 exam fee. $45 renewal fee.

Ohio
4084

Landscape Architect
Board of Landscape Architect
 Examiners
77 S. High St., 16th Fl.
Columbus, OH 43266-0303
Phone: (614)466-2316
Fax: (614)644-9048

Credential Type: Landscape Architect Registration. **Duration of License:** One year. **Requirements:** Must be at least 18 years of age. Have a baccalaureate degree in landscape architecture and one year of experience under the supervision of an LA, or have eight years of experience under the supervision of an LA. A combination of education and experience which meets board approval is also an avenue to licensure. **Examination:** National examination. **Fees:** $50 annual renewal fee.

Oklahoma
4085

Landscape Architect
Board of Governors of the Licensed
 Architects and Landscape
 Architects of Oklahoma
6901 N. Broadway, Ste. 201
Oklahoma City, OK 73116
Phone: (405)848-6596

Credential Type: License. **Duration of License:** Two years. **Requirements:** An accredited degree in landscape architecture and two years of approved training. A two-year internship under the direct supervision of a landscape architect. 21 years of age. State resident. No felony convictions. **Examination:** Uniform National Examination. **Fees:** $310 exam fee. $75 administration fee. $100 application fee. $75—$150 license fee. $150 renewal fee.

Oregon
4086

Landscape Architect
Landscape Architect Board
750 Front St. NE, Ste. 260
Salem, OR 97310
Phone: (503)378-4270

Credential Type: License. **Duration of License:** One year. **Requirements:** Must have a five year Bachelor of Landscape Architecture degree. **Examination:** Yes. **Fees:** $200 exam fee. $125 license fee. $125 renewal fee. **Governing Statute:** ORS 671.310 to 671.459 and Administrative Rules, Chapter 804.

4087

Landscape Contractor
Landscape Contractors Board
Veterans Bldg., Ste. 300
Salem, OR 97309-5052
Phone: (503)378-4621, ext. 4032

Credential Type: License. **Requirements:** Must have two years of landscape experience or one year of experience and one year of education in landscape contracting. **Examination:** Yes. **Fees:** $25 exam fee. $30 license fee. $30 renewal fee. **Governing Statute:** ORS 671.510 to 671.990.

Pennsylvania

4088

Landscape Architect
State Board of Landscape Architects
PO Box 2649
Harrisburg, PA 17105-2649
Phone: (717)783-3398
Fax: (717)787-7769

Credential Type: Landscape Architect Registration. **Duration of License:** One year. **Requirements:** Must have an accredited degree in landscape architecture and two years of post-graduate experience, or eight years of practical landscape architecture experience that has been board approved. Licensure Law allows two out of the required eight years of work experience to be under the supervision of a licensed design professional. **Examination:** National examination. **Fees:** $29 exam administration fee. $45 application fee for reciprocal registration. $63 annual renewal fee.

Rhode Island

4089

Landscape Architect
Board of Landscape Architects
83 Park St., 6th Fl.
Providence, RI 02903
Phone: (401)861-1631

Credential Type: Landscape Architect Registration. **Duration of License:** One year. **Requirements:** Must be at least 21 years of age. Must have an undergraduate degree in landscape architecture, or a related field, and two years of experience under the supervision of a LA. **Examination:** National and state examinations. **Fees:** $75 exam administration fee. $100 application fee for reciprocal registration. $40 annual renewal fee.

South Carolina

4090

Landscape Architect
Board of Registration for Landscape Architects
2221 Devine St., Ste. 222
Columbia, SC 29205-2474
Phone: (803)734-9100
Fax: (803)734-9200

Credential Type: Landscape Architect Registration. **Duration of License:** One year. **Requirements:** Must have a LAAB accredited B.S. degree in landscape architecture and two years experience under the supervision of a LA, or a non-accredited B.S. degree in landscape architecture and five years experience under the supervision of a LA. **Examination:** National examination. **Fees:** $50 exam administration fee. $125 application fee for reciprocal registration. $58 annual renewal fee.

South Dakota

4091

Landscape Architect
State Commission of Examiners
2040 W. Main, Ste. 304
Rapid City, SD 57702-2447
Phone: (605)394-2510
Fax: (605)394-2509

Credential Type: Landscape Architect Registration. **Duration of License:** One year. **Requirements:** No minimum degree required. Meet one of the following sets of requirements: (1) LAAB accredited five-year LA degree and one year experience under the supervision of a LA; (2) LAAB accredited four-year LA degree and two years experience under the supervision of a LA; (3) Non-accredited LA degree and five years experience under the supervision of a LA; (4) accredited architectural or civil engineering four-year degree and two years experience under the supervision of a LA; (5) any bachelor's degree and eight years experience under the supervision of a LA; (6) Associate's degree and eight years experience under the supervision of a LA; (7) High school diploma and 12 years experience under the supervision of a LA. **Examination:** National and state examinations. **Fees:** $5 exam administration fee. $100 application fee for reciprocal registration. $30 annual renewal fee.

Tennessee

4092

Landscape Architect
Board of Architectural and Engineering Examiners
Volunteer Plaza Bldg., 3rd Fl.
500 James Robertson Pky.
Nashville, TN 37243
Phone: (615)741-3221

Credential Type: License. **Duration of License:** One year. **Requirements:** Three years experience after graduation. Hold a professional degree from an accredited school (ASLA). Must be able to speak and write the English language. Good moral character. **Examination:** Council of Landscape Architect Registration Board (CLARB) Uniform National Examination. **Reciprocity:** Yes. **Fees:** $75 Application (plus exam costs if necessary). $100 Application (without exam). $30 Renewal.

Texas

4093

Landscape Architect
Texas Board of Architectural Examiners
8213 Shoal Creek Blvd., Ste. 107
Austin, TX 78758
Phone: (512)458-4126

Credential Type: License. **Duration of License:** One year. **Requirements:** Professional degree from a recognized school whose study of landscape architecture is accredited by Landscape Architecture Accredited Programs; or seven years or more of actual experience in the office of a licensed landscape architect. **Examination:** Landscape Architect Registration Examination (LARE). **Fees:** $10 application fee. $445 exam fee. $70 resident renewal fee. $100 non-resident renewal fee. **Governing Statute:** VACS 249c, 22 TAC 3.

Utah

4094

Landscape Architect
Dept. of Commerce
Div. of Occupational and Professional Licensing
160 E. 300 S.
PO Box 45802
Salt Lake City, UT 84145
Phone: (801)530-6628

Credential Type: License. **Duration of License:** Two years. **Requirements:** Must be a high school and college graduate holding a degree in landscape architecture; or have completed not less than eight years of practical experience under the direction of one or more landscape architects, of which at least four of the years shall be countinuous and immediately precede the filing of an application. **Examination:** Yes. **Fees:** $60 license fee. $35 renewal fee.

Landscape Architects

Virginia

4095

Landscape Architect
State Board of Certified Landscape Architects
Dept. of Commerce
3600 W. Broad St.
Richmond, VA 23230
Phone: (804)367-8514

Credential Type: Certified. **Requirements:** 18 years of age. Must have a degree in landscape architecture from an accredited program of study; or must have eight years of combined education and experience in landscape architecture acceptable to the Board. Must have three years of practical training in the offices of registered landscape architects. **Examination:** Yes. **Fees:** $40 application fee. $175 examination fee.

Washington

4096

Landscape Architect
Dept. of Licensing
PO Box 9649
Olympia, WA 98502
Phone: (206)753-6967
Fax: (206)586-0998

Credential Type: Landscape Architect Registration. **Duration of License:** One year. **Requirements:** Must be at least 18 years of age. No minimum degree required. Meet one of the following sets of requirements: (1) LAAB accredited LA degree and one year experience under the supervision of a LA; (2) non-accredited LA degree and 1.33 years experience under the supervision of a LA; (3) accredited architectural or civil engineering degree and 1.66 years experience under the supervision of a LA; (4) any bachelor's degree and 1.66 years experience under the supervision of a LA; (5) Associate's degree and 2.33 years experience under the supervision of a LA; (6) High school diploma and 2.33 years experience under the supervision of a LA. **Examination:** National and state examinations. **Fees:** $205 exam administration fee. $200 application fee for reciprocal registration. $150 annual renewal fee.

West Virginia

4097

Landscape Architect
Board of Landscape Architects
PO Box 6108
Agricultural Sciences Bldg.
West Virginia Univ.
Morgantown, WV 26506-6108
Phone: (304)293-2141

Credential Type: License. **Requirements:** 18 years old. Hold a degree in LA. Two years experience under supervision of a licensed architect. May not have had license revoked within one year prior to application. Never convicted of a felony. **Examination:** Yes. **Fees:** $40 Application. $280 Examination. $35 Renewal.

Wyoming

4098

Landscape Architect
State Board of Architects
The Barrett Bldg.
2301 Central Ave.
Cheyenne, WY 82002
Phone: (307)777-6313
Fax: (307)777-6005

Credential Type: Landscape Architect Registration. **Duration of License:** One year. **Requirements:** Must be at least 19 years of age. Meet one of the following sets of requirements: (1) LAAB accredited bachelor's or master's degree in landscape architecture and one year experience under the supervision of a LA; (2) non-accredited LA, Environmental Design, or Landscape Design degree and one year experience under the supervision of a LA. **Examination:** National examination. **Fees:** $50 exam administration fee. $100 application fee for reciprocal registration. $25 annual renewal fee.

Lawyers

The following states grant licenses in this occupational category as of the date of publication:

Alabama	District of	Iowa	Minnesota	New Mexico	Rhode Island	Washington
Alaska	Columbia	Kansas	Mississippi	New York	South Carolina	West Virginia
Arizona	Florida	Kentucky	Missouri	North Carolina	South Dakota	Wisconsin
Arkansas	Georgia	Louisiana	Montana	North Dakota	Tennessee	Wyoming
California	Hawaii	Maine	Nebraska	Ohio	Texas	
Colorado	Idaho	Maryland	Nevada	Oklahoma	Utah	
Connecticut	Illinois	Massachusetts	New Hampshire	Oregon	Vermont	
Delaware	Indiana	Michigan	New Jersey	Pennsylvania	Virginia	

Alabama

4099

Attorney
Alabama State Bar
415 Dexter Ave.
PO Box 671
Montgomery, AL 36101
Phone: (205)269-1515

Credential Type: License. **Duration of License:** One year. **Requirements:** 19 years of age. Must be a graduate of an approved law school or one of three non-accredited schools located in Alabama. **Examination:** Yes. **Fees:** $10-$100 registration fee. $185 examination fee. $385 character report.

Alaska

4100

Attorney
Alaska Bar Association
Box 100279
Anchorage, AK 99510
Phone: (907)272-7469

Credential Type: Attorney's License. **Requirements:** Graduate of a law school approved by the American Bar Association or has completed preparation in a law office. Graduate of a non-ABA-approved school may take bar exam if he or she has already passed another state's bar exam. **Examination:** Multistate Bar Examination (MBE). Multistate Professional Responsibility Examination (MPRE). **Exemptions:** If an applicant has passed a written examination in a reciprocal jurisdiction and has recently and actively been practicing law for five to seven years in one or more jurisdictions, he/she may be admitted without examination.

Fees: $700 bar examination fee. $1,000 Admission on Motion fee.

Arizona

4101

Attorney
Committee on Examinations and Character and Fitness
363 N. First Ave.
Phoenix, AZ 85003-1580
Phone: (602)252-4804

Credential Type: Attorney's License. **Requirements:** Graduate of an American Bar Association-approved law school. Graduate of a non-ABA-approved school may take bar exam if he or she has already passed another state's bar exam. Continuing education requirement mandates 15 hours every year, including two hours of ethics. **Examination:** Multistate Bar Examination (MBE). Multistate Professional Responsibility Examination (MPRE). **Fees:** $300 bar examination fee. $175 NCBE Report.

Arkansas

4102

Attorney
Arkansas Supreme Court
Justice Bldg.
Little Rock, AR 72201
Phone: (501)682-6849

Credential Type: License. **Requirements:** Graduate of an accredited law school. Successfully pass the Arkansas Bar Exam. **Examination:** Yes. **Fees:** $150 Examination (first time). $100 Examination (second time). $150 Examination (subsequent retakes). $50 License. $50 Renewal.

California

4103

Attorney
California Committee of Bar Examiners
State Bar of California
555 Franklin St.
Box 7908
San Francisco, CA 94120
Phone: (415)561-8303

Credential Type: Attorney's License. **Requirements:** Graduate of an American Bar Association-approved law school or California law school or correspondence school or has completed preparation in a law office. Graduate of a non-ABA-approved school may take bar exam if he or she has already passed another state's bar exam. **Examination:** Multistate Bar Examination (MBE). Multistate Professional Responsibility Examination (MPRE). **Fees:** $50 law student registration fee. $310 non-attorney bar examination fee. $425 attorney bar examination fee. $425 attorney examination fee. $250 application for admission (moral character review).

Colorado

4104

Attorney
Supreme Court Board and Law Examiners
600 17th St., Ste. 520-S
Denver, CO 80202
Phone: (303)893-8096

Credential Type: Attorney's License. **Requirements:** Graduate of an American Bar Association-approved law school or approved out-of-state school. Graduate of a non-ABA-approved school may take bar exam if he or she has already passed another state's bar exam. Continuing education requirement mandates 45 hours of legal education over a three-year period and includes two hours of legal ethics. **Examination:** Multistate Bar Examination (MBE). **Fees:** $200 non-attorney bar examination fee. $300 attorney bar examination fee. $400 Admission on Motion fee.

Connecticut

4105

Attorney
Connecticut Bar Examining
  Committee
Box 260430
Hartford, CT 06126-0430
Phone: (203)566-3770

Credential Type: Attorney's License. **Requirements:** Graduate of an American Bar Association-approved law school. Graduate of a non-ABA-approved school may take bar exam if he or she has already passed another state's bar exam. **Examination:** Multistate Bar Examination (MBE). Multistate Professional Responsibility Examination (MPRE). **Fees:** $110-$310 non-attorney bar examination fee. $160-$460 attorney bar examination fee. $500 Admission on Motion fee.

Delaware

4106

Attorney
Delaware Board of Bar Examiners
Box 8965
One Rodney Square
Wilmington, DE 19899
Phone: (302)651-3113

Credential Type: Attorney's License. **Requirements:** Graduate of an American Bar Association-approved law school. Must have five months' experience as a law clerk. Must attend a Delaware Supreme Court and Board of Bar Examiners preadmission session. Continuing education requirement mandates 30 hours of legal education over a two year period. **Examination:** Multistate Bar Examination (MBE). **Fees:** $250-$350 bar examination fee.

District of Columbia

4107

Attorney
D.C. Court of Appeals
500 Indiana Ave. NW, Rm. 4200
Washington, DC 20001
Phone: (202)879-2710

Credential Type: Attorney's License. **Requirements:** Graduate of an American Bar Association-approved law school. **Examination:** Multistate Bar Examination (MBE). Multistate Professional Responsibility Examination (MPRE). **Exemptions:** An attorney from an American Bar Association-approved law school, with a J.D., may be admitted without examination if he/she has attained a 133 scaled MBE score within the past 25 months and has earned a 75 scaled MPRE score. **Fees:** $143 bar examination fee. $475 Admission of Motion fee.

Florida

4108

Attorney
Florida Board of Bar Examiners
1300 E. Park Ave.
Tallahassee, FL 32399-1750
Phone: (904)487-1292

Credential Type: Attorney's License. **Requirements:** Graduate of an American Bar Association-approved law school. Graduate of a non-ABA-approved school may take bar exam if he or she has already passed another state's bar exam. Continuing education requirement mandates 30 hours of legal education over a three-year period and must include two hours of legal ethics. **Examination:** Multistate Bar Examination (MBE). Multistate Professional Responsibility Examination (MPRE). **Fees:** $60-$300 law student registration fee. $276 non-attorney bar examination fee. $828 attorney bar examination fee.

Georgia

4109

Attorney
Supreme Court of Georgia
Office of Bar Admissions
Box 38466
Atlanta, GA 30334
Phone: (404)656-3490

Credential Type: Attorney's License. **Requirements:** Graduate of an American Bar Association-approved law school or an approved Georgia law school. Continuing education requirement mandates 12 hours of legal education per year and must include one hr. of legal ethics, one hr. of professionalism, and three hours of trial study. **Examination:** Multistate Bar Examination (MBE). Multistate Professional Responsibility Examination (MPRE). **Fees:** $75 bar examination fee. $300-$600 character and fitness fees.

Hawaii

4110

Attorney
The Supreme Court of Hawaii Board
  of Examiners
The Supreme Court of Hawaii
Supreme Court Clerk
PO Box 2560
Honolulu, HI 96804
Phone: (808)548-7430

Credential Type: License. **Requirements:** U.S citizen or permanent resident. Graduation from an approved law school or fullfillment of the alternative requirement of an active practice of law in another jurisdiction. Recommendations from two attorneys in good standing in the Hawaii Bar. **Examination:** Written. **Reciprocity:** None. **Fees:** $100 application fee. $175 character check. $10 certificate of admission. Various dues and registration fees paid through the Hawaii State Board Assn.

Idaho

4111

Attorney
Idaho State Bar
204 W. State St.
PO Box 895
Boise, ID 83701
Phone: (208)342-8958

Credential Type: Attorney's License. **Requirements:** Graduate of an American Bar Association-approved law school. Graduate of a non-ABA-approved school may take bar exam if he or she has already passed another state's bar exam. Continuing education requirement mandates 30 hours of legal education during a three-year period. **Examination:** Multistate Bar Examination (MBE). Multistate Professional Responsibility Examination (MPRE). **Fees:** $10 application packet fee. $35 character and fitness fee. $350 non-attorney bar examination fee. $500 attorney bar examination fee.

Illinois

4112

Attorney
Illinois State Board of Law
   Examiners
340 First of America Ctr.
Springfield, IL 62701
Phone: (217)522-5917

Credential Type: Attorney's License. **Requirements:** Graduate of an American Bar Association-approved law school. **Examination:** Multistate Bar Examination (MBE). Multistate Professional Responsibility Examination (MPRE). **Fees:** $150 bar examination fee.

Indiana

4113

Attorney
Indiana State Board of Law
   Examiners
101 W. Ohio St., Ste. 450
Indianapolis, IN 46204
Phone: (317)232-2552

Credential Type: Attorney's License. **Requirements:** Graduate of an American Bar Association-approved law school. Must complete the following law courses and specified number of semester hours: Administrative Law and Procedure 3; Business Organizations 3; Civil Procedure 4; Commercial Law and Contracts 6; Constitutional Law 3; Criminal Law and/or Criminal Procedure 4; Evidence 3; Legal Ethics 2; Legal Research and Writing 2; Property 4; Taxation 3; and Torts 4. Continuing education requirement mandates 36 hours of legal education over a three-year period with a minimum of six hours per year. **Fees:** $225 bar examination fee. $750 Admission on Motion fee. $175 National Conference of Bar Examiners (NCBE) Report.

Iowa

4114

Lawyer
Clerk of the Iowa Supreme Court
Statehouse
Des Moines, IA 50319
Phone: (515)281-5911

Credential Type: License. **Duration of License:** One year. **Requirements:** Graduation from a reputable law school that is fully accredited by the American Bar Assn. **Examination:** Written. **Reciprocity:** Yes. **Fees:** $100 exam and background investigation fee. $25—$100 annual assessment fee. $350 reciprocity fee.

Kansas

4115

Attorney
Kansas Board of Law Examiners
Kansas Judicial Center
301 W. 10th St., Rm. 374
Topeka, KS 66612
Phone: (913)296-3229

Credential Type: Attorney's License. **Requirements:** Graduate of an American Bar Association-approved law school. Continuing education requirement mandates 12 hours of legal education annually. **Examination:** Multistate Bar Examination (MBE). Multistate Professional Responsibility Examination (MPRE). **Exemptions:** Attorneys performing temporary restricted legal services for a single employer may be admitted without examination if they meet requirements of Supreme Court Rule 706. **Fees:** $175 bar examination fee. $400 Admission on Motion fee. $175 National Conference of Bar Examiners (NCBE) Report.

Kentucky

4116

Attorney
Kentucky Board of Bar Examiners
1220 Harrodsbury, Ste. 401
Lexington, KY 40504
Phone: (606)253-2733

Credential Type: Attorney's License. **Requirements:** Graduate of an American Bar Association-approved law school. Continuing education requirement mandates 15 hours of legal education annually and must include two hours of ethics. **Examination:** Multistate Bar Examination (MBE). **Fees:** $100 bar examination fee. $350 Admission on Motion fee.

Louisiana

4117

Lawyer
Louisiana State Bar Assn.
601 St. Charles Ave.
New Orleans, LA 70130
Phone: (504)566-1600

Credential Type: License. **Duration of License:** One year. **Requirements:** 18 years of age. U.S. citizen or resident alien. Graduation from an approved law school. **Examination:** Yes. **Fees:** $100 exam fee. $40 annual Bar membership dues.

Maine

4118

Attorney
Maine Board of Bar Examiners
Box 30
Augusta, ME 04332-0330
Phone: (207)623-2464

Credential Type: Attorney's License. **Requirements:** Graduate of an American Bar Association-approved law school or preparation in a law office. Must complete a practical skills course within 18 months of admission. Graduate of a non-ABA-approved school may take bar exam if he or she has already passed another state's bar exam. **Examination:** Multistate Bar Examination (MBE). Multistate Professional Responsibility Examination (MPRE). **Fees:** $250 non-attorney bar examination fee. $350 attorney bar examination fee.

Maryland

4119

Attorney
State Board of Law Examiners
People's Resource Center, Rm. 1210
100 Community Pl.
Crownsville, MD 21032-2026
Phone: (301)514-7044

Credential Type: Attorney's License. **Requirements:** Graduate of a law school approved by the American Bar Association or an out-of-state law school. Graduate of a non-ABA-approved school may take bar exam if he or she has already passed another state's bar exam. Must complete a course on legal professionalism. **Examination:** Multistate Bar Examination (MBE). **Fees:** $215-$265 bar examination fee. $575 attorney examination fee. $175 National Conference of Bar Examiners (NCBE) Report. $400 filing fee.

Massachusetts

4120

Attorney
Massachusetts Board of Bar
   Examiners
77 Franklin St.
Boston, MA 02110
Phone: (617)482-4466

Credential Type: Attorney's License. **Requirements:** Graduate of an American Bar

Association-approved or in-state approved law school. **Examination:** Multistate Bar Examination (MBE). Multistate Professional Responsibility Examination (MPRE). **Fees:** $160 bar examination fee. $410 Admission on Motion fee. $175 attorney examination fee.

Michigan

4121

Attorney
State Board of Law Examiners
200 Washington Sq., N.
PO Box 30104
Lansing, MI 48909
Phone: (517)373-0120

Credential Type: License. **Duration of License:** Lifelong. **Requirements:** At least 18 years of age. At least two years of undergraduate studies before law school. Graduated from an approved law school. Good moral character. Intend in good faith to practice or teach in Michigan. Fingerprint card. Reside in a U.S. state, territory or the District of Columbia. Abide by the rules of the State Bar of Michigan. **Examination:** Written exam. **Reciprocity:** At least 18 years of age. At least two years of undergraduate studies before law school. Graduated from an approved law school. Good moral character. Licensed to practice law in the United States. Member in good standing of the State Bar where admitted. Intend to practice law in Michigan as a principal occupation, and maintain an office for the practice of law in Michigan. Have, after being licensed, actively practiced law as a principle occupation for three of the five years preceding the application. **Fees:** $175 initial exam fee. $25 certificate of admission fee. $400 reciprocity fee. $200 annual dues for active members of the State Bar of Michigan. **Governing Statute:** Revised Judicature Act, Act 236 of 1961,as amended.

Minnesota

4122

Attorney
Minnesota State Board of Law
 Examiners
One West Water St., Ste. 250
St. Paul, MN 55107
Phone: (612)297-1800

Credential Type: Attorney's License. **Requirements:** Graduate of an American Bar Association-approved law school. Continuing education requirement mandates 45 hours of legal education (including ethics) over a three-year period. **Examination:** Multistate Bar Examination (MBE). Multistate Professional Responsibility Examination (MPRE). **Fees:** $300 bar examination fee. $600 Admission on Motion fee. $150 additional fee for late filing.

Mississippi

4123

Attorney
Mississippi Board of Bar Admissions
Box 1449
Jackson, MS 39215
Phone: (601)359-1268

Credential Type: Attorney's License. **Requirements:** Graduate of an American Bar Association-approved law school. Continuing education requirement mandates 18 hours of legal education annually. **Examination:** Multistate Bar Examination (MBE). Multistate Professional Responsibility Examination (MPRE). **Fees:** $100 law student registration. $225-$525 bar examination fee. $500 Admission on Motion fee. $175 National Conference of Bar Examiners (NCBE) Report. $200 additional fee for late filing.

Missouri

4124

Attorney
Missouri State Board of Law
 Examiners
Box 150
Jefferson City, MO 65102
Phone: (314)751-4144

Credential Type: Attorney's License. **Requirements:** Graduate of an American Bar Association-approved law school. Graduate of a non-ABA-approved school may take bar exam if he or she has already passed another state's bar exam. Continuing education requirement mandates 15 hours of legal education per year and must include three hours of ethics every three years. Applicants newly admitted to the bar must also have an additional three hours of professionalism, ethics, or malpractice each year (all others must fulfill this requirement every three years). **Examination:** Multistate Bar Examination (MBE). Multistate Professional Responsibility Examination (MPRE). **Exemptions:** A lawyer may be admitted without examination if he/she attends The Missouri Bar Practical Skills Course (or other accredited continuing legal education program) and files a report with The Missouri Bar within 12 months of admission. **Fees:** $50 law student registration fee. $150 bar examination fee. $100 National Conference of Bar Examiners (NCBE) Report. $300 Admission on Motion fee. $150 additional fee for late filing.

Montana

4125

Attorney
Supreme Court Clerk
Justice Bldg., Rm. 323
Helena, MT 59620
Phone: (406)444-3858

Credential Type: License. **Duration of License:** One year. **Requirements:** Three successive years of study in an accredited law school. **Examination:** Montana bar exam. **Fees:** $75 application fee. $373 exam fee. $50 enrollment fee. $10 license tax. **Governing Statute:** Montana Code Annotated 37-61-201 through 37-61-215.

Nebraska

4126

Attorney
Nebraska Supreme Court
State Capitol, Rm. 2413
Lincoln, NE 68509
Phone: (402)471-3731

Credential Type: License. **Requirements:** See Nebrska Bar application process. **Examination:** Yes. **Fees:** $300 application fee. $200 examination fee. $500 background check.

Nevada

4127

Lawyer
State Bar of Nevada
201 Las Vegas Blvd. South, Ste. 200
Las Vegas, NV 89101
Phone: (702)382-2200

Credential Type: License. **Duration of License:** One year. **Requirements:** Graduation from an approved law school. **Examination:** Yes. **Fees:** $250 annual dues for active members practicing five years or more. $150 annual dues for active members practicing less than five years.

New Hampshire

4128

Attorney
Supreme Court
Supreme Court Bldg.
Concord, NH 03301
Phone: (603)271-2646

Credential Type: Attorney's License. **Requirements:** Graduate of an American Bar Association-approved law school. **Examination:** Multistate Bar Examination (MBE). Multistate Professional Responsibility Examination (MPRE). **Fees:** $210 bar examination fee.

New Jersey

4129

Attorney
Board of Bar Examiners
The Supreme Court of New Jersey, CN973
Trenton, NJ 08625-0973
Phone: (609)984-7783

Credential Type: License. **Requirements:** A Juris Doctorate degree from an approved law school and completion of a practical skills and methods course. **Examination:** Written. **Fees:** $175 application fee. **Governing Statute:** New Jersey Supreme Court Rule 1-24-1.

New Mexico

4130

Attorney
New Mexico State Board of Bar Examiners
Box 848
Santa Fe, NM 87503
Phone: (505)827-4860

Credential Type: Attorney's License. **Requirements:** Graduate of an American Bar Association-approved law school. Graduate of a non-ABA-approved school may take bar exam if he or she has already passed another state's bar exam. Continuing education requirement mandates 15 hours of legal education annually that must include one hr. of legal ethics. Applicants newly admitted to the bar must complete 10 hours of practical skills during the first two reporting years. **Examination:** Multistate Bar Examination (MBE). **Fees:** $325 non-attorney bar examination fee. $500 attorney bar examination fee. $175 National Conference of Bar Examiners (NCBE) Report. $325 filing fee. $150 late fee.

New York

4131

Lawyer (Attorney, Counselor at Law)
State Board of Law Examiners
7 Executive Center Dr.
Albany, NY 12203
Phone: (518)452-8700

Credential Type: Certificate. **Requirements:** Graduation from a School of Law approved by the American Bar Association or registered with the New York State Education Dept. 21 years of age. **Examination:** Written. **Fees:** $140 exam fee. **Governing Statute:** Sections 53, 56, 90, 460 of the Judicial Law, Article 94 Civil Practice Law and Rules.

North Carolina

4132

Attorney
North Carolina State Board of Law Examiners
PO Box 2946
Raleigh, NC 27602
Phone: (919)828-4886

Credential Type: License. **Duration of License:** Permanent. **Requirements:** 18 years of age. Graduation from an approved law school. **Examination:** Yes. **Fees:** $700 application fee.

North Dakota

4133

Attorney
State Board of Bar Examiners
Judicial Wing, 1st Fl.
600 E. Blvd. Ave.
Bismarck, ND 58505-0530
Phone: (701)224-4201

Credential Type: Attorney's License. **Requirements:** Graduate of an American Bar Association-approved law school. Continuing education requirement mandates 45 hours of legal education in a three-year period. **Examination:** Multistate Bar Examination (MBE). Multistate Professional Responsibility Examination (MPRE). **Fees:** $50 bar examination fee. $200 Admission on Motion fee. $175 attorney examination fee.

Ohio

4134

Attorney
Ohio Board of Bar Examiners
State Office Towers
30 E. Broad St.
Columbus, OH 43266-0419
Phone: (614)644-9316

Credential Type: Attorney's License. **Requirements:** Graduate of an American Bar Association-approved law school. Must have at least 10 hours of classroom instruction in legal ethics. Continuing education requirement mandates 24 hours of legal education every two years, of which two hours must include legal ethics and substance abuse. **Examination:** Multistate Bar Examination (MBE). **Fees:** $30 law student registration fee. $125 bar examination fee. $400 Admission on Motion fee. $175 National Conference of Bar Examiners (NCBE) Report (admission without exam). $95 NCBE Report (admission by examination).

Oklahoma

4135

Attorney
Board of Bar Examiners of the State of Oklahoma
1901 N. Lincoln
PO Box 53036
Oklahoma City, OK 73152
Phone: (405)542-2365

Credential Type: License. **Duration of License:** Lifetime. **Requirements:** Juris Doctor degree from an accredited law school. 12 hours of continuing legal education each year. 18 years of age. Oath of office. **Examination:** Oklahoma Bar Examination. **Fees:** $250 exam fee. $175 annual dues.

Oregon

4136

Attorney
Oregon State Bar
5200 SW Meadow Rd.
Box 1689
Lake Oswego, OR 97035-0889
Phone: (800)452-7636

Credential Type: License. **Requirements:** 18 years of age. Must be a graduate of a law school approved by the Bar. **Examination:** Yes. **Fees:** $400 examination fee. $550 if applicant is licensed in any other jurisdiction Bar membership. $226—$29 renewal fee. **Governing Statute:** ORS 9.010 to 9.665.

Pennsylvania

4137

Attorney
Pennsylvania Board of Law Examiners
674 Public Ledger Bldg.
Independence Sq.
Philadelphia, PA 19106
Phone: (215)627-3246

Credential Type: Attorney's License. **Requirements:** Graduate of an American Bar Association-approved law school or Pennsylvania law school or out-of-state law school. **Examination:** Multistate Bar Examination (MBE). **Fees:** $175 bar examination fee. $500 Admission on Motion fee.

Rhode Island

4138

Attorney
Providence County Court House
250 Benefit St.
Providence, RI 02903
Phone: (401)277-3272

Credential Type: Attorney's License. **Requirements:** Graduate of an American Bar Association-approved law school. Must complete a Rhode Island Bar Association sponsored training course prior to admission or within one year of being admitted. **Examination:** Multistate Bar Examination (MBE). Multistate Professional Responsibility Examination (MPRE). **Fees:** $200 non-attorney bar examination fee. $500 attorney bar examination fee. $300 Admission on Motion fee. $100-$200 character and fitness investigation.

South Carolina

4139

Attorney
South Carolina State Board of Law Examiners
PO Box 11330
Columbia, SC 29211
Phone: (803)734-3193

Credential Type: License. **Requirements:** Graduation from an approved law school with certain course requirements. Attend "Bridge The Gap." Meet trial experience requirements. **Examination:** Yes. **Fees:** $100 exam fee. $50 provisional application fee. $25 motions and petitions fee. $10 initial license fee.

South Dakota

4140

Attorney
South Dakota Board of Bar Examiners
State Capitol
500 E. Capitol
Pierre, SD 57501
Phone: (605)773-4898

Credential Type: Attorney's License. **Requirements:** Graduate of an American Bar Association-approved law school. **Examination:** Multistate Bar Examination (MBE). Multistate Professional Responsibility Examination (MPRE). **Fees:** $225 bar examination fee.

Tennessee

4141

Attorney
Tennessee Board of Law Examiners
L & C Tower, 10th Fl.
401 Church St.
Nashville, TN 37243-0740
Phone: (615)741-3234

Credential Type: Attorney's License. **Requirements:** Graduate of an American Bar Association-approved law school or state approved Tennessee law school. Continuing education requirement mandates 12 hours of legal education per calendar year. **Examination:** Multistate Bar Examination (MBE). **Fees:** $150 resident bar examination fee. $350 non-resident bar examination fee. $600 Admission on Motion fee. $175 National Conference of Bar Examiners (NCBE) Report (add $25 for non-resident).

Texas

4142

Attorney
Board of Law Examiners
PO Box 13486
Austin, TX 78711
Phone: (512)463-1621

Credential Type: License. **Requirements:** Graduation from a law school accredited by the American Bar Association (ABA). U.S. citizenship or permanent resident alien. 18 years of age. Pass moral character and fitness investigation. **Examination:** Texas Bar Examination. Multistate Professional Responsibility Examination. **Fees:** $125 to file Declaration of Intention to Study Law. $100 application fee. **Governing Statute:** Sec. 82.001 et seg., Tex. Gov. Code.

Utah

4143

Attorney
Utah State Bar Association
645 S. 200 E.
Salt Lake City, UT 84111-3834
Phone: (801)531-9077

Credential Type: License. **Requirements:** Must hold a law degree from an American Bar Association-approved school. **Examination:** Utah State Bar Association Examination. **Fees:** $15 application fee. $475 filing fee. $250 resident student fee. $375 non-resident student fee. $140—$225 renewal fee.

Vermont

4144

Attorney
Board of Bar Examiners
111 State St.
c/o Pavilion Bldg. Post Office
Montpelier, VT 05602
Phone: (802)828-3281

Credential Type: License. **Duration of License:** One year. **Requirements:** 18 years of age. US citizen or lawfully admitted alien. Good moral character. One of the following: graduate of approved law school and six months law office study; or four years law office study; or two years study of law in law school and two years law office study; or practiced law in another state for five years. **Examination:** Yes. **Reciprocity:** Yes. **Fees:** $10 examination application packet. $190 examination fee. $500 examination with motion. $75 license. $75 annual renewal. $25 clerkship fee (three or six month). $100 four year clerkship fee.

Virginia

4145

Lawyer
The Virginia Board of Bar
  Examiners
700 E. Main St.
Richmond, VA 23219
Phone: (804)786-7490

Credential Type: Licensed. **Requirements:** 18 years of age. Must be a resident of Virginia on or by the date specified in accord with each examination date. Must have a degree from an approved law school or have completed the approved course of office study as specified by the Board. **Examination:** Yes. **Fees:** $125 application fee.

Washington

4146

Attorney
Washington Board of Bar Examiners
500 Westin Bldg.
2001 Sixth Ave.
Seattle, WA 98121-2599
Phone: (206)448-0563

Credential Type: Attorney's License. **Requirements:** Graduate of an American Bar Association-approved law school or state approved Washington law school or state approved out-of-state law school or law office preparation. Continuing education requirement mandates 15 hours of legal education per calendar year. Newly admitted applicants are exempt from the continuing education requirement during the year they are admitted and for the following calendar year. **Fees:** $350 non-attorney bar examination fee. $580 attorney bar examination fee.

West Virginia

4147

Attorney
Board of Law Examiners
State Capitol Complex
Bldg. 1, Rm. E-400
Charleston, WV 25305
Phone: (304)348-7815

Credential Type: License. **Requirements:** Must hold an undergraduate degree and a JD. **Examination:** Yes. **Reciprocity:** Yes. **Fees:** $250 Application. $5 License.

Wisconsin

4148

Attorney
Board of Bar Examiners
119 Martin Luther King Jr. Blvd.
Madison, WI 53703-3355
Phone: (608)266-9760

Credential Type: Attorney's License. **Requirements:** Graduate of an American Bar Association-approved law school. Continuing education requirement mandates 30 hours of legal education during a two-year period. **Examination:** Multistate Bar Examination (MBE). **Fees:** $300 bar examination fee. $675 Admission on Motion fee.

Wyoming

4149

Lawyer
Board of Law Examiners
PO Box 109
Cheyenne, WY 82003
Phone: (307)632-9061

Credential Type: License. **Duration of License:** One year. **Requirements:** Graduate from an approved American Bar Association (ABA) law school. Pass the Wyoming Bar examination. Or be admitted to the Wyoming Supreme Court. **Examination:** Yes. **Fees:** $100 Examination. $112.50 to $225 Yearly dues.

Librarians

The following states grant licenses in this occupational category as of the date of publication:

Arizona	District of Columbia	Iowa	Massachusetts	Nevada	South Carolina	Washington
Arkansas		Kansas	Michigan	New Jersey	Tennessee	Wisconsin
California	Florida	Kentucky	Minnesota	New York	Texas	Wyoming
Connecticut	Georgia	Louisiana	Missouri	North Carolina	Utah	
Delaware	Hawaii	Maine	Montana	North Dakota	Vermont	
	Illinois	Maryland	Nebraska	Oklahoma	Virginia	

Arizona

4150

School Librarian
Teacher Certification Unit
PO Box 25609
1535 W. Jefferson
Phoenix, AZ 85002
Phone: (602)542-4368

Credential Type: School Librarian Endorsement. **Requirements:** Arizona Elementary, Secondary, or Special Education Certificate. 18 semester hours of upper level or graduate course work in Library Science to include literature for children or adolescents, cataloging and classification, administration and organization of school library, principles and policies of selection of book and nonprint materials, and reference.

Arkansas

4151

School Library Media Administrator
Teacher Education and Licensure
State Dept. of Education
4 State Capitol Mall
Little Rock, AR 72201-1071
Phone: (501)682-4342

Credential Type: Library Media Administrator Certificate. **Duration of License:** 10 years. **Requirements:** Master's degree plus 30 semester hours. Certified as a Library Media Specialist K-12. Minimum of four years successful experience as a classroom teacher in an accredited elementary school, secondary school and/or as a library media center Specialist in a unified school library media center (a minimum of two of the four years must have been as a Media Center Specialist).

Specialized Requirements include an additional 30 semester hours in graduate education courses including an appropriate distribution in administration, supervision and related fields.

4152

School Library Media Personnel
Teacher Education and Licensure
State Dept. of Education
4 State Capitol Mall
Little Rock, AR 72201-1071
Phone: (501)682-4342

Credential Type: Library Media Certificate K-12. **Duration of License:** Six years. **Requirements:** General Requirements include a bachelor's degree with 12 additional hours of professional education courses in the area(s) other than the level of his/her certificate. The 12 semester hours must include: study of the elementary or secondary school; study of the learning processes; teaching in the secondary school or teaching in the elementary school, including a methods course in reading. Practicum experience with equal time spent in elementary and secondary school library media centers.

Specialized Requirements specify a bachelor's degree and a teaching certificate and a practicum of three semester hours (minimum 120 clock hours) of directed experience in a unified school library media center at the same level as teacher certification (in some cases school library employment or public school teaching experience may be accepted in lieu of the practicum). 21 semester hours in basic library/media education designed to develop introductory competencies in the following areas: relation of media to instructional systems; organization and administration of media programs; evaluation, selection, and organization of media and accompanying technology; utilization of media and accompanying technology; production of media; evaluation of media programs; and leadership and professionalism.

4153

School Library Media Specialist
Teacher Education and Licensure
State Dept. of Education
4 State Capitol Mall
Little Rock, AR 72201-1071
Phone: (501)682-4342

Credential Type: Library Media Specialist Certificate. **Duration of License:** 10 years. **Requirements:** Must have current teaching certificate. For K-12 certification candidates with either an elementary or secondary teaching certificate must complete 12 additional hours in the area other than the level of the teaching certificate and an approved practicum at both the elementary and secondary levels.

Specialized Requirements include a practicum of three semester hours, a master's degree in an approved program including library science and educational media or a unified library media program offered by an accredited institution that includes 24 semester hours of the following: relation of media to instructional systems; organization and administration of media programs; evaluation, selection, and organization of media and accompanying technology; utilization of media and accompanying technology; production of media; evaluation of media programs; and leadership and professionalism.

California

4154

School Library Media Teacher
Commission on Teacher
  Credentialing
PO Box 944270
Sacramento, CA 94244-7000
Phone: (916)445-7254

Credential Type: Library Media Teacher Services Credential. **Authorization:** Authorizes the holder to assist and instruct pupils in the choice and use of library materials; to plan and coordinate school library programs with the instructional programs of a school district; to select materials for school and district libraries; to conduct a planned course of instruction for those pupils who assist in the operation of school libraries; to supervise classified personnel assigned to school library duties; and to develop procedures for and management of the school and district libraries. **Requirements:** A baccalaureate degree from a regionally accredited college or university. A valid prerequisite California teaching credential that requires a program of professional preparation including student teaching. A Commission-approved library media services program and the recommendation of the California college or university where the program was completed. An out-of-state applicant who has completed a library media services program of 30 graduate semester units approved by the appropriate state agency in the state where the program was competed and meets all other requirements may be issued a certificate. Passage of CBEST. **Examination:** California Basic Education Skills Test. **Fees:** $60 application fee. $30 test score recording and evaluation fee, except for CBEST.

Connecticut

4155

School Library Media Associate
State Dept. of Education
Teacher Certification, Chief
165 Capitol Ave.
PO Box 2219
Hartford, CT 06145
Phone: (203)566-4561

Credential Type: School Library-Media Initial Certificate. **Requirements:** Bachelor's degree. Holds or is eligible for a Connecticut teaching certificate. One year of successful teaching experience. 24 semester hours of graduate credits leading either to a master's degree or a sixth-year certificate in school-library media. (There are other routes of eligibility available.)

Credential Type: School Library-Media Provisional Certificate. **Requirements:** Evidence of meeting the general requirements for a School Library-Media Initial Certificate. Completion of beginning educator support and assessment program as may be available from the Connecticut Board and one school year of successful service under the School Library-Media Initial Certificate or three successful years in school library-media programs in a school approved by the board, within the 10 years prior to application.

Credential Type: School Library-Media Professional Certificate. **Requirements:** Three years of successful teaching under the School Library-Media Provisional Certificate. Master's degree or sixth year program in school-library media at an approved institution or master's degree in another field from an approved institution, plus 30 semester hours of graduate credit in school-library media from an approved institution.

Delaware

4156

School Library-Media Specialist
Teacher Certification
Dept. of Public Instruction
Box 1402
Dover, DE 19903
Phone: (302)739-4688

Credential Type: Library-Media Endorsement. **Requirements:** Bachelor's degree. Valid teaching certificate. Minimum of 15 semester hours of professional education that includes work in human development and methods. Complete a program in teacher education with a major in school library or complete a master's degree in school librarianship from a school accredited by the American Library Association or complete a minimum of 24 semester hours in library-media education. Must complete a six semester hr. practicum in a school library. Must have one year of successful experience in a school library-media program, plus six hours of additional courses in library science (beyond the degree or forementioned requirement of 24 hours). Must successfully complete the Educational Testing Service Pre-Professional Skills Tests with the following minimum scores: Reading 175; Writing 172; Mathematics 175. **Examination:** Educational Testing Service Pre-Professional Skills Tests.

District of Columbia

4157

Elementary School Librarian/Media Specialist
Div. of Teacher Services
Dept. of Public Instruction
PO Box 1402
Dover, DE 19903
Phone: (302)739-4688

Credential Type: Class 1 School Library/Media Specialist. **Requirements:** Master's degree. 18 semester credits in Library Science including the following: Organization and Administration of School Media Centers and their Collections; Cataloging; Selection and Utilization of Instructional Media for Children and Young People; Reference Materials; and Computer and the Media Center. In addition 15 semester hours which include the following: Educational Psychology; The Teaching of Reading; Media for Children; Classroom Management; and The Exceptional Child. Observation and student teaching or two years of successful teaching experience on the elementary level or two years of experience as a librarian.

4158

Junior High School Library/Media Specialist
Div. of Teacher Services
Dept. of Public Instruction
PO Box 1402
Dover, DE 19903
Phone: (302)739-4688

Credential Type: Class 2 School Library/Media Specialist. **Requirements:** Master's degree. 18 semester credit hours in Library Science including the following: Organization and Administration of School Media Centers and their Collections; Cataloging; Selection and Utilization of Instructional Media for Children and Young People; Reference Materials; Instructional Media-Production; and Computer and the Media Center. In addition the following 15 semester hours in education are required: Educational Psychology; The Teaching of Reading ; Classroom Management; and The Exceptional Child. Observation and student teaching or two years of successful teaching experience on the secondary level or two years of library experience.

4159

School Librarian/Media Specialist for Senior High and Career Development Centers
Div. of Teacher Services
Dept. of Public Instruction
PO Box 1402
Dover, DE 19903
Phone: (302)739-4688

Credential Type: Class 3 School Librarian/Media Specialist. **Requirements:** Master's degree. 30 semester hours in Library Science including the following: Organization and Administration of School Media Centers and their Collections; Cataloging; Selection and Utilization for Instructional Materials for Children and Young People; Reference Materials; Instructional Media-Production; and Computer and the Media Center. In addition the following 15 semester hours in education are required: Educational Psychology; The Teaching of Reading; Classroom Management; and The Exceptional Child. Observation and student teaching or two years of successful teaching experience on the secondary level or two years of library experience.

Florida

4160

School Educational Media Specialist
Bureau of Teacher Certification
Florida Education Center
325 W. Gaines, Rm. 201
Tallahassee, FL 32399
Phone: (904)488-2317

Credential Type: Educational Media Specialist Certificate. **Requirements:** Bachelor's degree with a major in educational media or a bachelor's degree with 24 hours of work in educational media that includes: nine hours Selection and utilization media; three hours Functional operation of the school media center; three hours biological control; and three hours Design and production of various types of educational media.

Georgia

4161

Librarian
State Board for the Certification of Librarians
Sciences and Professions Section
Professional Examining Boards
166 Pryor St., SW
Atlanta, GA 30303
Phone: (404)656-2281

Credential Type: Para-Professional Certificate. **Duration of License:** Two years. **Authorization:** Restricted to para-professional duties performed under the supervision of a full-time professional librarian. **Requirements:** Graduate of a four-year college. Complete at least 12 semester hours in a planned program of library science at an institution approved by a state or regional accrediting agency. **Fees:** $50 application fee. $50 renewal fee. **Governing Statute:** Official Code of Georgia Annotated 43-24. Rules of the State Board for the Certification of Librarians, Chap. 320.

Credential Type: Librarian's Professional Graduate Certificate. **Duration of License:** Two years. **Requirements:** Hold a master's degree in the field of librarianship from a library school whose program is accredited by the American Library Association. A graduate of a foreign library school must demonstrate attainments and abilities equivalent to those of a person who is a graduate of a library school whose program is accredited by the American Library Association. **Fees:** $50 application fee. $50 renewal fee. **Governing Statute:** Official Code of Georgia Annotated 43-24. Rules of the State Board for the Certification of Librarians, Chap. 320.

Credential Type: Librarian's Advanced Professional Graduate Certificate. **Duration of License:** Two years. **Authorization:** Valid for any professional position in any library. **Requirements:** Must qualify for a Librarian's Professional Graduate Certificate and complete a sixth year or more of planned graduate study in the field of librarianship from a library school whose program is accredited by the American Library Association. **Fees:** $50 application fee. $50 renewal fee. **Governing Statute:** Official Code of Georgia Annotated 43-24. Rules of the State Board for the Certification of Librarians, Chap. 320.

Credential Type: Librarian's Doctoral Certificate. **Duration of License:** Two years. **Authorization:** Valid for any professional position in any library. **Requirements:** Must qualify for a Librarian's Professional Graduate Certificate and hold an earned doctorate in the field of librarianship from a library school whose master's program is accredited by the American Library Association. **Fees:** $50 application fee. $50 renewal fee. **Governing Statute:** Official Code of Georgia Annotated 43-24. Rules of the State Board for the Certification of Librarians, Chap. 320.

Hawaii

4162

School Librarian
Dept. of Education
Office of Personnel Services
PO Box 2360
Honolulu, HI 96804
Phone: (808)548-5803

Credential Type: Initial Specialist Basic Certificate. **Requirements:** Complete a state approved teacher education program at the baccalaureate level with a major in library/media. Pass the National Teachers Examination (NTE) Core Battery and Specialty Area Test. **Examination:** NTE Core Battery and Specialty Area Test.

Credential Type: Specialist Basic Certificate. **Requirements:** Initial Specialist Basic Certificate. Complete two years of successful performance in the public schools of Hawaii.

Credential Type: Initial Specialist Professional Certificate. **Requirements:** Complete a state approved teacher education program majoring in library/media with a master's degree or equivalent five year university program. Pass the NTE Core Battery and Specialty Area Tests. **Examination:** NTE Core Battery and Specialty Area Test.

Credential Type: Specialist Professional Certificate. **Requirements:** Initial Specialist Professional Certificate. Two years of successful performance in the public schools of Hawaii.

Illinois

4163

School Media Specialist/Librarian
Certification and Placement Section
100 N. First St.
Springfield, IL 62777
Phone: (217)782-4321

Credential Type: Media Professional Endorsement—Library and Audio-visual. **Requirements:** Good character. Good health. At least 19 years of age. Citizen of the U.S. Teaching certificate. 18 semester hours of library science—media courses at the college or graduate level. Competencies in

School Media Specialist/Librarian, continued

administration, organization, reference, and selection of materials at elementary and/or secondary levels. Pass required sections of the Illinois Certification Test. **Examination:** Illinois Certification Test. **Reciprocity:** Reciprocity exists for applicants holding out-of-state certificates providing their preparation was comparable to that required by the state of Illinois. **Fees:** $44 per section of the Illinois Certification Test.

Credential Type: Media Specialist Endorsement. **Requirements:** Standard Special Certificate with Library Science-Media endorsement. 32 semester hours college level study in the field. Competencies in administration, organization, reference, and selection of materials at elementary and/or secondary levels. Pass required sections of the Illinois Certification Test. **Examination:** Illinois Certification Test. **Reciprocity:** Reciprocity exists for applicants holding out-of-state certificates providing their preparation was comparable to that required by the state of Illinois. **Fees:** $44 per section of the Illinois Certification Test.

Credential Type: Media Supervisor/Director Endorsement. **Requirements:** Supervisory or Standard Special Supervisory Endorsement or the General Supervisory Endorsement with specialization in media. **Reciprocity:** Reciprocity exists for applicants holding out-of-state certificates providing their preparation was comparable to that required by the state of Illinois. **Fees:** $44 per section of the Illinois Certification Test.

Iowa

4164

Elementary School Media Specialist (1-6)
Board of Educational Examiners
Grimes State Office Bldg.
Des Moines, IA 50319-0147
Phone: (515)281-3245

Credential Type: Elementary School Media Specialist Endorsement. **Requirements:** Baccalaureate degree. Complete an approved teacher education program. Complete an approved human relations component. 24 semester hours in school media course work, including a practicum in an elementary school media center.

4165

School Media Specialist (K-12)
Board of Educational Examiners
Grimes State Office Bldg.
Des Moines, IA 50319-0147
Phone: (515)281-3245

Credential Type: School Media Specialist Endorsement. **Requirements:** Master's degree. Complete an approved teacher education program. Complete an approved human relations component. 30 semester hours in school media course work, including a practicum in both an elementary and secondary school media center.

4166

Secondary School Media Specialist (7-12)
Board of Educational Examiners
Grimes State Office Bldg.
Des Moines, IA 50319-0147
Phone: (515)281-3245

Credential Type: Secondary School Media Specialist Endorsement. **Requirements:** Baccalaureate degree. Complete an approved teacher education program. Complete an approved human relations component. 24 semester hours in school media course work, including a practicum in a secondary school media center.

Kansas

4167

Library Media Specialist (K-12)
Certification Specialist
Kansas State Dept. of Education
Kansas State Education Bldg.
120 E. 10th St.
Topeka, KS 66612-1103
Phone: (913)296-2288

Credential Type: Library Media Endorsement. **Authorization:** Endorsements may be given for work at the elementary, secondary, or Kindergarten-12 level. **Requirements:** Successful completion of a state approved library media program with course work beyond the baccalaureate degree. Hold a valid teaching certificate. Be recommended by a teacher education institution.

Kentucky

4168

School Media Librarian (K-12)
Kentucky Dept. of Education
Div. of Teacher Education and Certification
Capitol Plaza Tower, 18th Fl.
500 Mero St.
Frankfort, KY 40601
Phone: (502)564-4606

Credential Type: Provisional Certificate for School Media Librarian. **Duration of License:** Five years. **Requirements:** Complete an approved four year college or university program for a librarian and/or school media specialist. Qualify for a teaching certificate. Bachelor's degree which includes the following studies: 25 semester hours of professional training that includes 150 clock hours of clinical and field experiences and a supervised practice in a school media center for 12 weeks; 30 semester hours of a major with studies in school media organization and administration, media classification and processing, literature by content and age level, computer applications, reference and bibliographic services, special users, media design and production; 21 semester hours in a minor or in two academic subject fields. Certificate may be renewed upon three years of successful experience or six semester hours of graduate credit.

Credential Type: Standard Certificate for School Media Librarian. **Duration of License:** Five years. **Requirements:** Eligible for Provisional Certificate for School Media Librarian. Master's degree or a 32 hr. semester hr. planned fifthyear program to include 12 hours of specialization in media library study and 12 hours of research and methodology. Certificate may be renewed upon three years of successful experience or six semester hours of graduate credit.

Louisiana

4169

School Librarian
Louisiana Dept. of Education
Box 94064
Baton Rouge, LA 70804-9064
Phone: (504)342-3490

Credential Type: Standard Certificate. **Requirements:** Elementary or secondary school teaching certificate. 21 semester hours of library courses which include: nine hours elementary and/or secondary school library materials; six hours organization, administration and interpretation of elementary and/or secondary school library services; three hours elementary and /or secondary school library practice; and three hours audiovisual education.

Maine

4170

School Library-Media Specialist (K-12)
Teacher Certification
Dept. of Education
State House Station 23
Augusta, ME 04333
Phone: (207)289-5944

Credential Type: Library-Media Specialist Certificate. **Duration of License:** Five years. **Requirements:** Hold a Maine provisional or professional level teaching certificate with a subject area endorsement. Complete an approved graduate program for the preparation of school library-media specialists or 36 graduate credit hours which include: teaching of research techniques; administration of unified library-media programs; evaluation, selection, and organization of library-media materials; prescription and provision of materials and services to classroom teachers; curriculum design and development; technology applications; cataloging and classification; children's and adolescent's literature; and teaching exceptional children. Professional requirements to include 24 semester hours in the following areas: knowledge of the learner; knowledge of the learning process; teaching exceptional students in the regular classroom; content area methods; curriculum design and methods of program evaluation; and a practicum. Renewal requires six semester hours of approved study, preferably academic study in the certificate area.

Maryland

4171

Audio-Visual/Library Associate
Dept. of Certification 18100
State Dept. of Education
200 W. Baltimore St.
Baltimore, MD 21201
Phone: (301)333-2142

Credential Type: Associate Level I Endorsement. **Requirements:** Bachelor's degree with 18 semester hours in basic media education to include introductory knowledge of educational systems and introductory knowledge of media and information systems. Practicum or two years of successful teaching or two years of successful media-related experience.

Credential Type: Educational Media Generalist Level II Endorsement. **Requirements:** Master's degree in education or 36 semester hours of equivalent graduate credit, of which 15 must be completed at one institution. Must include knowledge of educational systems and knowledge of media and information systems. Practicum or two years of successful teaching or two years of successful media-related experience.

Credential Type: Educational Media Specialist Level II Endorsement. **Requirements:** Master's degree from an accredited graduate program or an equivalent program of 36 semester hours which includes knowledge of education systems. Specialist program to develop full professional competency in a special or media related field. Practicum.

Credential Type: Educational Media Administration Level III Endorsement. **Requirements:** Master's degree in media program from an accredited institution. 15 semester hours of graduate credit, or equivalent, that includes six hours in administration an supervision, with remaining credits chosen from management, planning, research, human relations etc. Three years of successful school media program experience. Upon recommendation, two years of related successful experience may be substituted for two years of school media experience. Eligibility for Educational Media Generalist Level II Endorsement.

Massachusetts

4172

Unified Media Specialist
Massachusetts Dept. of Education
1385 Hancock St.
Quincy, MA 02169
Phone: (617)770-7500

Credential Type: Unified Media Specialist Endorsement. **Requirements:** Massachusetts teaching certificate. 30 semester hr. prepracticum. In addition, complete a 150 clock hr. practicum. Candidates previously certified as a school library or audio-visual media specialist may be certified as a unified media specialist by completing a prepracticum of 12 semester hours of course work and a 150 clock hr. practicum. Demonstrate the competencies contained in the five Standards established by the Massachusetts Dept. of Education for unified media specialists. Standard I-Knowledge of the following: general theory and methods of curriculum development; reference systems; selection, acquisition, organization and maintenance of media resources and equipment; planning and management of media programs; knowledge of federal and state laws. Standard II—Communicate clearly and appropriately. Standard III-Ability to design instruction to facilitate learning. Standard IV-Ability to use evaluative procedures to assess programs. Standard V-Be sensitive and responsive.

Michigan

4173

Library Staff Member, Public
Certification Specialist
Library of Michigan
717 W. Allegan St.
PO Box 30007
Lansing, MI 48909
Phone: (517)373-1580

Credential Type: Librarian's Permanent Professional Certification. **Duration of License:** Permanent. **Authorization:** A minimum number of librarians employed in each public library or library system must hold a personnel certificate issued by the Library of Michigan in order for the public library to qualify for state aid. There are currently seven classifications of librarian certificates. **Requirements:** Have a bachelor's degree from a college or university accredited by a regional accrediting body. Have a master's degree or its equivalent from a library school accredited by the American Library Association. Verify that four years of satisfactory professional experience in a library or libraries approved by the Library of Michigan were attained after completion of the educational requirements stated above. **Reciprocity:** No. **Fees:** No fees. **Governing Statute:** State Aid and Library System Act, Act 286 of 1965. Library Cooperative and State Aid Act, Act 89 of 1977.

Credential Type: Librarian's Professional Certification. **Duration of License:** Four years. **Authorization:** A minimum number of librarians employed in each public library or library system must hold a personnel certificate issued by the Library of Michigan in order for the public library to qualify for state aid. There are currently seven classifications of librarian certificates. **Requirements:** Have a bachelor's degree from a college or university accredited by a regional accrediting body. Have a master's degree or its equivalent from a library school accredited by the American Library Association. This certificate may be exchanged for a librarian's permanent professional certificate as soon as the experience requirement is met. **Reciprocity:** No. **Fees:** No fees. **Governing Statute:** State Aid and Library System Act, Act 286

Library Staff Member, Public, continued

of 1965. Library Cooperative and State Aid Act, Act 89 of 1977.

Credential Type: Special Professional Certification. **Duration of License:** Permanent. **Authorization:** A minimum number of librarians employed in each public library or library system must hold a personnel certificate issued by the Library of Michigan in order for the public library to qualify for state aid. There are currently seven classifications of librarian certificates. **Requirements:** Have a master's degree in a special subject field, other than library science, or have a master's degree in library science from a curriculum in a school not accredited by the American Library Association. **Reciprocity:** No. **Fees:** No fees. **Governing Statute:** State Aid and Library System Act, Act 286 of 1965. Library Cooperative and State Aid Act, Act 89 of 1977.

Credential Type: Limited Professional Certification: Class A. **Duration of License:** Permanent. **Authorization:** A minimum number of librarians employed in each public library or library system must hold a personnel certificate issued by the Library of Michigan in order for the public library to qualify for state aid. There are currently seven classifications of librarian certificates. **Requirements:** Be a college graduate with a major (24 semester hours or its equivalent) in library science, or be a college graduate enrolled in a library school accredited by the American Library Association. **Reciprocity:** No. **Fees:** No fees. **Governing Statute:** State Aid and Library System Act, Act 286 of 1965. Library Cooperative and State Aid Act, Act 89 of 1977.

Credential Type: Limited Professional Certification: Class B. **Duration of License:** Permanent. **Authorization:** A minimum number of librarians employed in each public library or library system must hold a personnel certificate issued by the Library of Michigan in order for the public library to qualify for state aid. There are currently seven classifications of librarian certificates. **Requirements:** Be a college graduate with a major (24 semester hours or its equivalent) in a subject field other than library science. **Reciprocity:** No. **Fees:** No fees. **Governing Statute:** State Aid and Library System Act, Act 286 of 1965. Library Cooperative and State Aid Act, Act 89 of 1977.

Credential Type: Library Technician's Certification. **Duration of License:** Permanent. **Authorization:** A minimum number of librarians employed in each public library or library system must hold a personnel certificate issued by the Library of Michigan in order for the public library to qualify for state aid. There are currently seven classifications of librarian certificates. **Requirements:** Have completed a two-year library technician curriculum approved by the Library of Michigan. **Reciprocity:** No. **Fees:** No fees. **Governing Statute:** State Aid and Library System Act, Act 286 of 1965. Library Cooperative and State Aid Act, Act 89 of 1977.

Credential Type: Certificate of Library Experience. **Duration of License:** Three years. **Authorization:** A minimum number of librarians employed in each public library or library system must hold a personnel certificate issued by the Library of Michigan in order for the public library to qualify for state aid. There are currently seven classifications of librarian certificates. **Requirements:** Have graduated from high school or its equivalent. Have successfully completed a Beginning Workshop approved by the Library of Michigan within two years after their appointment. **Reciprocity:** No. **Fees:** No fees. **Governing Statute:** State Aid and Library System Act, Act 286 of 1965. Library Cooperative and State Aid Act, Act 89 of 1977.

4174

School Librarian
Teacher Preparation and Certification
Michigan Dept. of Education
Box 30008
Lansing, MI 48909
Phone: (517)373-3310

Credential Type: Teacher Librarian Endorsement. **Authorization:** Valid at level of Michigan teaching certificate. **Requirements:** Valid Michigan teaching certificate. 20 semester hr. minor in Library Science which may be one of the minors presented to meet the general requirements for either the elementary or secondary provisional certificate.

Credential Type: K-12 Librarian Endorsement. **Authorization:** Valid at all grade levels. May teach at elementary or secondary levels. **Requirements:** Valid Michigan teaching certificate. 30 semester hr. major in Library Science which may be one of the majors presented to meet the general requirements for either the elementary or secondary provisional certificate.

Minnesota

4175

School Media Generalist
Teacher Licensing and Placement
State Dept. of Education
616 Capitol Square Bldg.
St. Paul, MN 55101
Phone: (612)296-2046

Credential Type: Media Generalist Endorsement. **Duration of License:** Five years. **Requirements:** Valid Minnesota teaching certificate. Two years of successful teaching experience. Completion of approved program in media and related fields of at least 36 quarter hours or equivalent. Renewable with one or more years of successful full-time experience or two or more years of successful half-time experience.

Missouri

4176

Instructional School Media Technologist
Teacher Certification
Dept. of Elementary and Secondary Education
Box 480
Jefferson City, MO 65102
Phone: (314)751-3486

Credential Type: Instructional Media Technologist Certificate. **Requirements:** Hold a valid Missouri Teacher's Certificate. Complete 18 semester hours of course work to include a class in each of the following: administration of instructional media and technology programs; selection and utilization of instructional media; graphic production; instructional design; still photography, motion picture production, or television production; and a practicum in instructional media and technology programs.

4177

School Librarian
Teacher Certification
Dept. of Elementary and Secondary Education
Box 480
Jefferson City, MO 65102
Phone: (314)751-3486

Credential Type: Librarian Certificate. **Requirements:** Hold a valid Missouri Teacher's Certificate. 18 hours of Library Science course work which includes a course in each of the following areas: cataloging; selection and acquisition; reference;

administration of school libraries; children's literature or adolescent literature; and a practicum in learning resources.

Montana

4178

School Librarian
Teacher Certification
Office of Public Instruction
State Capitol
Helena, MT 59620
Phone: (406)444-3150

Credential Type: Librarian Endorsement. **Requirements:** Endorsement will be added to a valid Montana teaching certificate after completion of an approved K-12 program in library science, from an accredited institution, with a minimum of 20 semester hours

Nebraska

4179

Educational Media Specialist (Librarian)
Nebraska Dept. of Education
PO Box 94987
Lincoln, NE 68509
Phone: (402)471-2496

Credential Type: License. **Requirements:** Must be a certified teacher with a recommendation from an accredited teachers college. **Fees:** $40 application fee.

Nevada

4180

Librarian
Nevada State Dept. of Education
Licensing Office
400 W. King St., Capitol Complex
Carson City, NV 89701
Phone: (702)687-3115

Credential Type: License. **Requirements:** Must obtain a teaching license. Bachelor's degree in library science or the equivalent. Completion all the special courses required for a teacher to serve as a library specialist. Completion of an additional eight semester hours of preparation in library science.

New Jersey

4181

Educational Media Specialist
Office of Teacher Certification and
  Academic Credentials
CN 503
Trenton, NJ 08625-0503
Phone: (609)292-2079

Credential Type: Associate Educational Media Specialist Endorsement. **Authorization:** Authorizes the holder to perform educational media services in the public schools under the supervision of a qualified supervisor. **Requirements:** Bachelor's degree. Regular New Jersey instructional certificate. Passing score in specified areas of the NTE written examination or 18 undergraduate or graduate hours of study to include: organization and retrieval of information and media resources; production of educational media; evaluation, selection, and utilization of educational media; integration of educational media through the school curriculum; and field experience in a school media program. **Examination:** National Teachers Examination (if applicant has not met the college study requirements).

Credential Type: Educational Media Specialist Endorsement. **Authorization:** Authorizes the holder to develop and coordinate educational media services in the public schools. **Requirements:** Master's degree. Regular New Jersey instructional certificate or associate educational media specialist endorsement. One year of successful teaching or experience as an associate educational media specialist. Passing score in specified areas of the NTE written examination or 30 graduate hours of study to include the following areas: organization and coordination of school media services and materials; application of learning theory in reading, listening, and viewing educational media materials; design and development of educational media programs and materials; integration of educational media through the school curriculum; evaluation, selection, and utilization of educational media; development of individual and group processes in the media program; and field experience in a school media program. **Examination:** National Teachers Examination (if applicant has not met the college study requirements).

4182

Librarian
New Jersey Dept. of Education
Office of Teacher Certification and
  Academic Credentials
3535 Quakerbridge Rd., CN503
Trenton, NJ 08625
Phone: (609)588-3100

Credential Type: Professional Librarian License. **Requirements:** 18 years of age. Master's degree in library or information science from an approved program. **Fees:** $40 application fee. **Governing Statute:** NJSA 45:8A.

New York

4183

School Media Specialist K-12
Administrator of Teacher
  Certification Policy
Univ. of the State of New York
State Education Dept.
Cultural Center, Rm. 5-A-11
Albany, NY 12230
Phone: (518)474-6440

Credential Type: School Media Specialist Provisional Certificate. **Duration of License:** Five years. **Requirements:** Bachelor's degree. 18 semester hours of study in school library media and 18 semester hoursof study in school educational communications media. 12 semester hours of professional education classes and a practicum covering both school library media and school educational communications media. One year of full-time experience, which covers the same areas of media as the required practicum, may be accepted in lieu of the practicum pending approval and recommendation of employing school district administrator. Note: The city of Buffalo, New York has certification standards that are exclusive of New York State.

Credential Type: School Media Library Specialist Provisional Certificate. **Duration of License:** Five years. **Requirements:** Bachelor's degree. 36 semester hours of study in school media which includes a minimum of 24 semester hours of courses in school library media. 12 semester hours of professional education classes and a practicum covering school library media. One year of full-time experience, which covers the same area of media as the required practicum, may be accepted in lieu of the practicum pending approval and recommendation of employing school district administrator. Note: The city of Buffalo, New York has certification standards that are exclusive of New York State.

School Media Specialist K-12, continued

Credential Type: School Media Educational Communications Specialist Provisional Certificate. **Duration of License:** Five years. **Requirements:** Bachelor's degree. 36 semester hours of study in school media which includes a minimum of 24 semester hours of courses in school educational communications media. 12 semester hours of professional education classes and a practicum covering school educational communications media. One year of fulltime experience, which covers the same area of media as the required practicum, may be accepted in lieu of the practicum pending approval and recommendation of employing school district administrator. Note: The city of Buffalo, New York has certification standards that are exclusive of New York State.

Credential Type: Permanent Certificate. **Duration of License:** Permanent. **Requirements:** Master's degree in the field of media. Must have 36 semester hours of graduate work in media which includes 15 semester hours in the area of media specialization and 15 semester hours in social and behavioral sciences. Two years of experience as a school media specialist. 12 semester hours of professional education and a college supervised practicum. Note: The city of Buffalo, New York has certification standards that are exclusive of New York State.

North Carolina

4184

Librarian
Div. of State Library
Dept. of Cultural Resources
109 E. Jones St.
Raleigh, NC 27611
Phone: (919)733-2570

Credential Type: Certification. **Duration of License:** Permanent. **Requirements:** Master's degree in library and information science from an accredited school or university. 18 years of age.

4185

School Media Personnel K-12
Certification Section
State Dept. of Public Instruction
Raleigh, NC 27603
Phone: (919)733-4125

Credential Type: Media Coordinator Certificate. **Duration of License:** Five years. **Requirements:** Hold a valid teaching certificate. Demonstrate competence in media selection, cataloging, reference, media utilization and production, curriculum, and administration. Pass the NTE. **Examination:** National Teacher Examination. **Fees:** $30 application fee. $30 renewal fee.

Credential Type: Media Specialist Certificate. **Duration of License:** Five years. **Requirements:** Master's degree or higher degree. Hold a valid teaching certificate. Completed program must include competencies in instructional development, production, and television instruction. Pass the NTE. **Examination:** National Teacher Examination. **Fees:** $30 application fee. $30 renewal fee.

North Dakota

4186

School Media Specialist
Director of Certification
State Dept. of Public Instruction
Bismarck, ND 58505
Phone: (701)224-2264

Credential Type: Media Specialist—Library Certificate. **Duration of License:** Five years. **Authorization:** Authorizes holder to work in or be in charge of public school libraries, but does not qualify holder to be in charge of an audiovisual department. **Requirements:** Bachelor's degree. Valid North Dakota Educator's Professional Certificate. One or more years of teaching experience. 16 semester hours of library science courses to include: library organization and administration; cataloging and classification; book selection and acquisition; reference material; general bibliography; literature for children or adolescents; audiovisual aids.

Credential Type: Media Specialist—Library-Audiovisual Certificate. **Duration of License:** Five years. **Authorization:** Authorizes holder to work in and/or be in charge of both public school libraries and audiovisual departments. **Requirements:** Bachelor's degree. Valid North Dakota Educator's Professional Certificate. One or more years of teaching experience. 16 semester hours of library science courses and 10 semester hours of audiovisual education.

Credential Type: Media Specialist—Audiovisual Certificate. **Duration of License:** Five years. **Authorization:** Authorizes holder to work in or be in charge of a public school audiovisual department, but does not authorize holder to be in charge of a public school library. **Requirements:** Bachelor's degree. Valid North Dakota Educator's Professional Certificate. One or more years of teaching experience. 12 semester hours of audiovisual education courses.

Credential Type: Media Director. **Duration of License:** Authorizes holder to be in charge of public school media departments, both library and audiovisual, within a school district. **Requirements:** Master's degree. Valid North Dakota Educator's Professional Certificate. One or more years of teaching experience. 16 semester hours of library science courses and 10 semester hours of audiovisual education. Plus 12 semester hours of graduate courses specifically related to media education.

Oklahoma

4187

School Service Personnel K-12
Teacher Education and Certification
State Dept. of Education
2500 N. Lincoln Blvd., Rm. 211
Oklahoma City, OK 73105
Phone: (405)521-3337

Credential Type: Standard Certificate in a School Personnel Field—Graduate. **Duration of License:** Five years. **Authorization:** Endorsement will be given to persons seeking positions in the following fields: Counselor; Library Media Specialist; Elementary School Principal; Secondary School Principal; School Superintendent; School Psychometrist; School Psychologist; SpeechLanguage Pathologist; or Reading Specialist. **Requirements:** Complete an approved certificate program at an accredited college or university which includes a minimum of the following: a baccalaureate degree; 50 semester hours in general education; 30 semester hours in professional education; and 40 semester hours in course work pertaining to the area of specialization. Pass the state certified test(s) in specialization competencies. Complete State Board graduate level course requirements.

South Carolina

4188

School Media Communication Specialist
Teacher Education and Certification
State Dept. of Education
Rutledge Bldg., Rm. 1015
Columbia, SC 29201
Phone: (803)734-8464

Credential Type: Media Communication Specialist Certificate. **Requirements:** Bachelor's degree. Complete State Board of Education approved program in media communication. Minimum score of 590 on the NTE for Media Specialist. **Examination:** National Teacher Examination for Media Specialist.

4189

School Media Specialist
Teacher Education and Certification
State Dept. of Education
Rutledge Bldg., Rm. 1015
Columbia, SC 29201
Phone: (803)734-8464

Credential Type: Media Specialist Certificate. **Requirements:** Bachelor's degree. Complete State Board of Education approved program in media. Minimum score of 590 on the NTE for LibrarianMedia Specialist. **Examination:** National Teacher Examination for Librarian-Media Specialist.

4190

School Media Supervisor
Teacher Education and Certification
State Dept. of Education
Rutledge Bldg., Rm. 1015
Columbia, SC 29201
Phone: (803)734-8464

Credential Type: Media Supervisor Certificate. **Requirements:** Master's degree. Certification as elementary or secondary supervisor. Valid South Carolina teaching credential with endorsement as a Media Specialist or Media Communication Specialist. Six graduate credit hours in supervision of school media programs and in research and evaluation of school media programs.

Tennessee

4191

School Librarian
Office of Teaching Licensing
Dept. of Education
Cordell Hull Bldg.
Nashville, TN 37219-5335
Phone: (615)741-1644

Credential Type: Professional School Personnel License. **Duration of License:** 10 years. **Requirements:** Secondary librarians must meet all requirements for a Professional Teaching Certificate endorsed in a 7-12 subject area. Elementary librarians must meet all requirements for a Professional Teaching Certificate and complete 27 quarter hours of study which includes: books and related materials for children and young people; reference materials; organization of materials; school library administration; books and related materials for adults; audio-visual materials; and principles of librarianship. Renewable.

Texas

4192

Librarian, County
Texas State Library and Archives Commisssion
Library Development Div.
PO Box 12927
Austin, TX 78711
Phone: (512)463-5466

Credential Type: Grade III License. **Duration of License:** Two years. **Requirements:** 30 semester hours at an accredited college or university; or a high school diploma or equivalent and 1,000 hours of paid or voluntary work experience in a library within the past five years, or a combination of education and experience. Three semester hours of continuing education is required for renewal. **Examination:** None. **Fees:** No fees. **Governing Statute:** VACS 1683, 13 TAC 5.

Credential Type: Grade II License. **Duration of License:** Two years. **Requirements:** Graduation from an accredited senior college or university; or 60 semester hours at an accredited college or university and 2,000 hours of paid or voluntary work experience in a library within the past five years, or a combination of education and experience. Three semester hours of continuing education required for renewal. **Examination:** None. **Fees:** No fees. **Governing Statute:** VACS 1683, 13 TAC 5.

Credential Type: Grade I License. **Duration of License:** Permanent. **Requirements:** Fifth-year or higher degree from a library school offering an ALA-approved degree in library or information science. **Examination:** None. **Fees:** No fees. **Governing Statute:** VACS 1683, 13 TAC 5.

Utah

4193

Library Media Associate K-12
Certification and Personnel Development Section
State Board of Education
250 East 500 South St.
Salt Lake City, UT 84111
Phone: (801)538-7740

Credential Type: Basic Certificate. **Duration of License:** Four years. **Authorization:** Allows service at both the elementary and secondary level, exclusive of jobs in media supervision, direction, or coordination. **Requirements:** Hold or be eligible for a Basic or Standard Teaching Certificate. Complete an approved program for the preparation of library media professionals. Demonstrate competence in computer understanding and use. Have recommendation of preparing institute or have competencies assessed by a committee of peers who hold standard library media certificates, under the direction of the Utah State Office of Education.

Credential Type: Standard Certificate. **Duration of License:** Valid indefinitely with consistent employment in media. **Authorization:** Allows service as regional media coordinator, supervisor, or director. **Requirements:** Two years of successful experience as a library media specialist. Recommendation of employing school district.

Vermont

4194

Library Media Specialist
Teacher Licensure
State Dept. of Education
Montpelier, VT 05602-2703
Phone: (802)828-2445

Credential Type: Initial License. **Authorization:** Holder of this license is authorized to professionally manage, administer, and supervise the combined print, audio-visual, and networking services, resources, and staff at the building, district, or supervisory level, and to instruct students. **Requirements:** Must hold a bachelor's degree and be working towards a graduate degree. Meet competencies for a library media position as specified by the Standards Board.

Virginia

4195

School Library Media Specialist NK-12
Administrative Director
Office of Professional Development and Teacher Education
Dept. of Education
PO Box 6-Q
Richmond, VA 23216-2060
Phone: (804)225-2094

Credential Type: Library Media Endorsement. **Requirements:** Teaching certificate. Three semester hours experience in a school library. 24 semester hours of course study to include: selection and utilization of library-media materials; production of me-

School Library Media Specialist NK-12, continued

dia and instructional materials; organization, administration, and evaluation of a library-media center; theory and management of reference and bibliography; selection of materials for children and adolescents; technical processing of materials; role of a librarymedia specialist as a resource person; clinical experience.

Washington

4196

Librarian
Washington State Library
State Library Bldg., AJ-11
Olympia, WA 98504-0111
Phone: (206)753-2914

Credential Type: Librarian License. **Duration of License:** Continuing. **Requirements:** Must meet one of the following requirements: (1) Graduate from a school of library science certified by the American Library Association; (2) Hold a bachelor's degree from a recognized institution and complete a curriculum of librarianship; (3) Hold a bachelor's degree from a recognized institution and be recommended by the person in charge of the librarianship curriculum; (4) Hold a bachelor's degree from a recognized institution and have the attainments and abilities equivalent to a library school graduate. **Fees:** $20 license fee.

4197

Library Media Specialist
Superintendent of Public Instruction
Professional Education and
   Certification
Old Capitol Bldg. FG-11
Seattle, WA 98504-3211
Phone: (206)753-6773

Credential Type: Library Media Specialist Endorsement. **Requirements:** Regular teaching certificate. Courses in media, selection, cataloging, reference, media utilization and production, curriculum and administration, with minimum of 16 semester hours Demonstrated competencies.

Wisconsin

4198

Instructional Library Media Specialist
Teacher Education, Licensing, and
   Placement
Box 7841
Madison, WI 53707-7841
Phone: (608)266-1027

Credential Type: Initial License. **Duration of License:** Five years. **Requirements:** Complete an approved program for Instructional Library Media Specialist and have institutional endorsement. Eligible to hold a Wisconsin teaching license or complete an approved program for elementary or secondary classroom teachers. Complete a student teaching assignment in an elementary or secondary library. Complete a minimum of 24 semester hours in an approved library media services program covering competency areas. Renewable, with six semester hours of professional credits or an approved equivalent, during the life of the license.

Credential Type: Regular License. **Requirements:** Eligibility to hold the Initial Instructional Library Media Specialist License. Master's degree in an approved library media services program or a total of 39 semester hours in an approved library media services program, 15 of which must be completed after the Bachelor's degree and must cover specific competency areas.

Wyoming

4199

Librarian, School
Wyoming Dept. of Education
Hathaway Bldg.
2300 Capitol Ave.
Cheyenne, WY 82002
Phone: (307)777-7292

Credential Type: License. **Duration of License:** Five years. **Requirements:** Must complete a four year teacher education program with an additional 15 hours in library science and nine hours in instructional methods. **Examination:** No. **Fees:** $20 License. $20 Renewal.

Licensed Practical Nurses

The following states grant licenses in this occupational category as of the date of publication:

Alabama	District of	Iowa	Minnesota	New Mexico	Rhode Island	Washington
Alaska	Columbia	Kansas	Mississippi	New York	South Carolina	West Virginia
Arizona	Florida	Kentucky	Missouri	North Carolina	South Dakota	Wisconsin
Arkansas	Georgia	Louisiana	Montana	North Dakota	Tennessee	Wyoming
California	Hawaii	Maine	Nebraska	Ohio	Texas	
Colorado	Idaho	Maryland	Nevada	Oklahoma	Utah	
Connecticut	Illinois	Massachusetts	New Hampshire	Oregon	Vermont	
Delaware	Indiana	Michigan	New Jersey	Pennsylvania	Virginia	

Alabama

4200

Licensed Practical Nurse
Alabama Board of Nursing
State of Alabama
Montgomery, AL 36130
Phone: (205)242-4060

Credential Type: License. **Requirements:** Must be a high school graduate or equivalent. Must have completed an approved practical nursing program of at least one year in length. **Examination:** National Council Licensure Examination for Practical Nurses (NCLEX-PN). **Reciprocity:** Yes. **Fees:** Contact board for fees.

Alaska

4201

Licensed Practical Nurse
Dept. of Commerce and Economic Development
Div. of Occupational Licensing
Board of Nursing
PO Box D
Juneau, AK 99811-0800
Phone: (907)465-2544
Fax: (907)465-2974

Credential Type: Licensed Practical Nurse License by Examination. **Duration of License:** Two years. **Requirements:** Completed a practical nursing education program accredited by the board, or one outside the state which meets the minimum requirements of the board for an accredited program, or one accredited by the National League for Nursing. Pass a written exam prescribed by the board.

Must meet continuing competency requirements for license renewal by completing two of the following three methods: 15 contact hours of board approved continuing education; 15 hours of participation in board approved professional activities; at least 320 hours of nursing practice during the past two years. **Examination:** National Council Licensing Examination. **Fees:** $30 application fee. $25 fee for National Council License Examination. $90 license fee. $90 license renewal fee. **Governing Statute:** Alaska Statutes 08.68. Professional Regulations 12 AAC 44.

Credential Type: Practical Nurse License by Endorsement. **Duration of License:** Two years. **Requirements:** Hold a current license to practice in another jurisdiction whose licensing requirements include completion of a recognized nursing education program and passing one of the following examinations: National Council Licensing Examination, State Board Test Pool (before 1982), an examination by another licensing jurisdiction before 1953.

Letter of reference from previous employer if employed within the past five years. If not employed wihtin the past five years, proof of meeting the continuing competency requirements of the board or complete a course of study approved by the board.

Graduates of foreign schools of nursing shall take the National Council Licensing Examination or have passed it elsewhere. Applicants licensed in Canada who passed the national Canadian examination may receive a license by endorsement. **Fees:** $30 application fee. $25 fee for National Council License Examination. $90 license fee. $90 license renewal fee. **Governing Statute:** Alaska Statutes 08.68. Professional Regulations 12 AAC 44.

Credential Type: Nonrenewable temporary permit. **Duration of License:** Four months or until test results are announced. **Requirements:** Must be awaiting the results of the National Council Licensing Examination or be scheduled to take the next NCLEX, or must be licensed to practice as a practical nurse in another state licensing jurisdiction. **Fees:** $30 application fee. $25 fee for National Council License Examination. $90 license fee. $20 temporary permit fee. **Governing Statute:** Alaska Statutes 08.68. Professional Regulations 12 AAC 44.

Arizona

4202

Licensed Practical Nurse
Arizona State Board of Nursing
2001 W. Camelback Rd., Ste. 350
Phoenix, AZ 85015
Phone: (602)255-5092
Fax: (602)255-5130

Credential Type: Licensed Practical Nurse License. **Requirements:** Graduate from a state approved nursing program or equivalent. Be proficient in English language as it relates to nursing. **Examination:** National Council Licensure Examination (NCLEX)-PN.

Arkansas

4203

Licensed Practical Nurse
Arkansas State Board of Nursing
University Tower Bldg., Ste. 800
1123 S. University
Little Rock, AR 72204
Phone: (501)371-2751

Credential Type: License. **Duration of License:** Two years. **Requirements:** Good moral character. 12th grade education or equivalent. Completion of the prescribed

625

Licensed Practical Nurse, continued

curriculum in an approved program for Licensed Practical Nurses. **Examination:** Yes. **Fees:** $16.50 Written and Oral Examination. $50 Endorsement. $20 License. $20 Renewal.

California

4204

Vocational Nurse
Board of Vocational Nurse and
 Psychiatric Technician Examiners
1414 K St., Ste. 103
Sacramento, CA 95814
Phone: (916)445-0793

Credential Type: Licensed Vocational Nurse. **Duration of License:** Two years. **Requirements:** Be at least 17 years of age. High school graduate or equivalent. Meet one of the following sets of requirements: (1) Graduate from a California accredited Vocational Nursing Program. (2) Graduate from an accredited Vocational Nursing Program in another state. (3) Graduate from a California approved Vocational Nursing Program. Complete 36 months of verified full-time paid work experience in medical/surgical nursing in a general acute care facility. Experience must be within past 10 years, and at least 12 months of experience must have been during the past 24 months. (4) Have equivalent education and/or experience, including a pharmacology course of at least 54 theory hours. Complete at least 51 months of paid general duty bedside nursing experience in a general acute care facility. Experience must be within past 10 years, at least half of which was within five years of application. Applicants with formal nursing education may receive credit for paid bedside nursing experience. (5) Have at least 12 months service on active duty in the medical corps of any of the armed forces rendering patient care. Must have completed a basic course of instruction in nursing while in armed forces. Military and nonmilitary experience may not be combined. Applicants qualifying with military experience need not have graduated from high school. **Examination:** Written examination. **Exemptions:** State examination will be waived if applicant is currently licensed in another state or foreign country and has passed either the NLN or NCLEX-PN exam. **Reciprocity:** Endorsement is available for anyone holding a valid license or certificate issued by any other state or foreign country. **Fees:** $50 application fee. $75 license fee. $75 renewal fee.

Colorado

4205

Licensed Practical Nurse
Colorado Board of Nursing
1560 Broadway, Ste. 670
Denver, CO 80202
Phone: (303)894-2430
Fax: (303)894-2821

Credential Type: Licensed Practical Nurse License. **Requirements:** Graduate from a state approved nursing program or equivalent. Be proficient in the English language as it relates to nursing. **Examination:** National Council Licensure Examination (NCLEX)-PN.

Connecticut

4206

Licensed Practical Nurse
Connecticut Board of Examiners for
 Nursing
150 Washington St.
Hartford, CT 06106
Phone: (203)566-1041
Fax: (203)566-8401

Credential Type: Licensed Practical Nurse License. **Requirements:** High school graduate or equivalent. Graduate of a state approved nursing program or equivalent. Work experience may be accepted in lieu of education. Good physical and mental health. Be proficient in English language as it relates to nursing.

Delaware

4207

Licensed Practical Nurse
Board of Nursing
Dept. of Administrative Services
Div. of Professional Regulation
PO Box 1401
Dover, DE 19903
Phone: (302)739-4522

Credential Type: License by examination. **Duration of License:** Two years. **Requirements:** Be a high school graduate or equivalent. Must be competent in English related to nursing. Graduate of a board-approved practical nursing education program. **Examination:** NCLEX-PN. **Exemptions:** See license by endorsement. **Reciprocity:** Holders of an out-of-state or foreign license may apply for license by endorsement. **Fees:** $30 license fee. **Governing Statute:** Delaware Code, Title 24, Chapter 19.

Credential Type: License by endorsement. **Duration of License:** Two years. **Requirements:** Hold a license from another state, territory, or foreign country that has equivalent requirements. Must have been actively employed in practical nursing for the past five years, or complete a practical nursing refresher program with an approved agency within the past year. **Examination:** No exam required for license by endorsement. **Fees:** $30 license fee. **Governing Statute:** Delaware Code, Title 24, Chapter 19.

District of Columbia

4208

Licensed Practical Nurse
DC Board of Nursing
614 H. St., NW
Washington, DC 20001
Phone: (202)727-7468
Fax: (202)727-8030

Credential Type: Licensed Practical Nurse License. **Requirements:** High school graduate or equivalent. Graduate from state approved nursing program or equivalent. Meet age requirement. Be proficient in English language as it relates to nursing. Must report criminal convictions. Board hearing may be required.

Florida

4209

Licensed Practical Nurse
Florida Board of Nursing
111 Coastline Dr. E., Ste 516
Jacksonville, FL 32202
Phone: (904)359-6331
Fax: (904)359-6323

Credential Type: Licensed Practical Nurse License. **Requirements:** Graduate from a state-approved nursing program or equivalent. Be proficient in English language as it relates to nursing. **Examination:** NCLEX-PN.

Georgia

4210

Licensed Practical Nurse
Georgia State Board of Licensed Practical Nurses
166 Pryor St., SW
Atlanta, GA 30303
Phone: (404)656-3921
Fax: (404)651-9532

Credential Type: Licensed Practical Nurse License. **Requirements:** High school graduate or equivalent. Graduate from state approved program or equivalent. Meet age requirement. Good moral character. Good physical and mental health. Be proficient in English as it relates to nursing. **Examination:** National Council Licensure Examination (NCLEX)-PN.

4211

Licensed Undergraduate Nurse
Georgia Board of Nursing
Professional Examining Boards
166 Pryor St., SW
Atlanta, GA 30303
Phone: (404)656-3943

Credential Type: Undergraduate Nurse License. **Requirements:** Contact licensing body for application information.

Hawaii

4212

Nurse, Licensed Practical
Hawaii Board of Nursing
PO Box 3469
Honolulu, HI 96801
Phone: (808)548-3086

Credential Type: License. **Duration of License:** Six months. **Requirements:** Graduation from a state-accredited nursing program in the U.S. or U.S. jurisdiction. Pass the National Council Licensure Examination (NCLEX); or pass the State Board Test Pool Exam (SBTPE); or pass another state's exam prior to inception of the SBTPE in this state. **Reciprocity:** Yes, provided applicant has been accepted for employment in Hawaii. **Fees:** $20 application fee. $15 license fee. $15—$30 Compliance Resolution Fund fee. $10 renewal fee.

Credential Type: Temporary Permit. **Requirements:** Issued to endorsement applicants who have met Hawaii's educational requirements, hold a current license in another state, have been accepted for employment in Hawaii, and have passed the SBTPE or NCLEX in another state. Exam applicants may also be granted a temporary permit.

Idaho

4213

Licensed Practical Nurse
Idaho Nursing Board
280 N. 8th St., Ste. 210
Boise, ID 83720
Phone: (208)334-3110

Credential Type: Licensed Practical Nurse License. **Requirements:** Graduate from state approved nursing program or equivalent. Good physical and mental health. Be proficient in English language as it relates to nursing. **Examination:** National Council Licensure Examination (NCLEX)-PN.

Illinois

4214

Licensed Practical Nurse
Illinois Dept. of Professional Regulation
159 N. Dearborn, 6th Fl.
Chicago, IL 60601
Phone: (312)814-4619
Fax: (312)814-1664

Credential Type: Licensed Practical Nurse License. **Requirements:** Graduate of state approved nursing program or equivalent. Good moral character. Good physical and mental health. **Examination:** National Council Licensure Examination (NCLEX)-PN.

Indiana

4215

Licensed Practical Nurse
Indiana State Board of Nursing
Health Professional Bureau
402 W. Washington St., Rm. 041
Indianapolis, IN 46204
Phone: (317)232-2960
Fax: (317)233-4236

Credential Type: Licensed Practical Nurse. **Requirements:** High school graduate or equivalent. Graduate from state approved nursing program or equivalent. Good physical and mental health. Be proficient in English language as it relates to nursing. **Examination:** English Competency Test.

Iowa

4216

Licensed Practical Nurse
Iowa Board of Nursing
State Capitol Complex
1223 East Court
Des Moines, IA 50319
Phone: (515)281-3256

Alternate Information: Executive Hills East, Des Moines, IA 50319

Credential Type: License. **Duration of License:** Three years. **Requirements:** High school diploma or equivalent, plus completion of a state-approved program in practical nursing. **Examination:** National written examination. **Fees:** $40 exam fee. $60 endorsement fee. $48 renewal fee.

Kansas

4217

Licensed Practical Nurse
Kansas Board of Nursing
Landon State Office Bldg.
900 SW Jackson, Ste. 551-S
Topeka, KS 66612-1256
Phone: (913)296-4068
Fax: (913)296-6729

Credential Type: Licensed Practical Nurse License. **Requirements:** U.S. citizen. High school graduate or equivalent. Graduate of state approved nursing program. Good physical and mental health. Be proficient in English language as it relates to nursing. No felonies or criminal record. **Examination:** National Council Licensure Examination (NCLEX)-PN.

Kentucky

4218

Nurse, Licensed Practical
Kentucky Board of Nursing
312 Whittington Rd.
Louisville, KY 40222
Phone: (502)329-7000

Credential Type: License. **Duration of License:** Two years. **Requirements:** High school diploma or equivalent. Successful completion of a program that is a minimum of nine months with theory and instruction in practical nursing from a state-approved school of practical nursing. Continuing education required. **Examination:** Yes. **Fees:** $20 administration fee. $70 application fee. $50 renewal fee.

4219

Practical Nurse and Nurse Aide Instructor
Louisiana State Dept. of Education
Teacher Certification
PO Box 94064
Baton Rouge, LA 70804
Phone: (504)342-3490

Credential Type: Certificate. **Duration of License:** One year. **Requirements:** Graduation from a licensed nursing school. Two years of experience in staff nursing or nursing education within the past four years. Continuing education requirements must be met before renewal.

Louisiana

4220

Nurse/Practical
Louisiana State Board of Practical Nurse Examiners
1408 Pere Marquette Bldg.
New Orleans, LA 70112
Phone: (504)568-6480

Credential Type: License. **Duration of License:** One year. **Requirements:** U.S. citizen or taken our first citizenship papers. Completion of an accredited training course for practical nurses. **Examination:** Yes. **Reciprocity:** Yes, if the licensees meet the requirements for practical nursing in Louisiana. **Fees:** $30 exam fee. $10 renewal fee.

Maine

4221

Licensed Practical Nurse
Maine State Board of Nursing
State House Station No. 158
Augusta, ME 04333-0158
Phone: (207)624-5275

Credential Type: Licensed Practical Nurse License. **Requirements:** High school graduate or equivalent. Graduate from state approved nursing program. Be proficient in English language as it relates to nursing.

Maryland

4222

Licensed Practical Nurse
Maryland Board of Nursing
4201 Patterson Ave.
Baltimore, MD 21215-2299
Phone: (301)764-4747
Fax: (301)764-5987

Credential Type: Practical Nurse License. **Duration of License:** One year. **Requirements:** High school graduate or equivalent. Graduate from a state approved practical nursing program. Be proficient in English language as it relates to nursing. No felonies or criminal record. **Examination:** NCLEX-PN. **Fees:** $50 exam fee. $75 endorsement fee. $25 renewal fee.

Massachusetts

4223

Licensed Practical Nurse
Board of Registration in Nursing
Leverett Saltonstall Bldg.
100 Cambridge St., Rm. 1519
Boston, MA 02202
Phone: (617)727-9962
Fax: (617)727-7378

Credential Type: Practical Nurse License. **Duration of License:** Two years. **Requirements:** High school graduate or equivalent. Graduate from state approved nursing program. Good moral character. Be proficient in English language as it relates to nursing. **Examination:** National Council Licensure Examination for Practical Nurses (NCLEX-PN). **Reciprocity:** Yes, if licensing requirements are the same as Massachusetts. **Fees:** $40 license fee. $87 exam fee. $40 renewal fee. $75 endorsement fee.

Michigan

4224

Licensed Practical Nurse
Bureau of Occupational and Professional Regulation
Michigan Dept. of Commerce
Ottawa Towers N.
611 W. Ottawa
Lansing, MI 48933
Phone: (517)373-1600
Fax: (517)373-2179

Credential Type: Licensed Practical Nurse License. **Requirements:** Graduate from state approved nursing program. Meet age requirement. Good moral character. Be proficient in English language as it relates to nursing. Felony conviction requires Board investigation.

Minnesota

4225

Licensed Practical Nurse
Minnesota Board of Nursing
2700 University Ave. W, 108
St. Paul, MN 55114
Phone: (612)642-0567
Fax: (612)642-0574

Credential Type: Licensed Practical Nurse License. **Duration of License:** Two years. **Requirements:** Graduate from state approved nursing program. Work experience may be excepted in lieu of education requirement. **Examination:** NCLEX-PN. **Reciprocity:** License by endorsement may be issued if applicant holds a valid license from another state and has passed the same examination. **Fees:** $50 exam fee. $55 endorsement fee. $35 renewal fee. **Governing Statute:** Minnesota Statutes, Sections 148.171-148.299. Minnesota Rules 6300-6399.

Mississippi

4226

Licensed Practical Nurse
Mississippi Board of Nursing
239 N. Lamar St., Ste. 401
Jackson, MS 39201-1311
Phone: (601)359-6170
Fax: (601)359-6185

Credential Type: Licensed Practical Nurse License. **Requirements:** High school graduate or equivalent. Graduate of state nursing program or equivalent program. Be proficient in English as it relates to nursing. **Examination:** National Council Licensure Examination (NCLEX)-PN.

Missouri

4227

Licensed Practical Nurse
Missouri State Board of Nursing
PO Box 656
Jefferson City, MO 65102
Phone: (314)751-0681
Fax: (314)751-4176

Credential Type: Licensed Practical Nurse License. **Requirements:** High school graduate or equivalent. Graduate of state approved nursing program or equivalent program. Meet age requirement. Good moral

Montana

4228

Licensed Practical Nurse
Montana State Board of Nursing
111 N. Jackson
Helena, MT 59620
Phone: (406)444-42071
Phone: (444)-2071-4279

Credential Type: License. **Duration of License:** One year. **Requirements:** High school diploma or equivalent. Graduation from an approved practical nursing program. **Examination:** National Council Licensing Exam. **Fees:** $35 application fee. $20 renewal fee. **Governing Statute:** Montana Code Annotated 37-8-401 through 37-8-444.

Nebraska

4229

Nurse, Licensed Practical (LPN)
Nebraska Board of Nursing
301 Centennial Mall S.
PO Box 95007
Lincoln, NE 68509
Phone: (402)471-2115

Credential Type: License. **Duration of License:** Two years. **Requirements:** 18 years of age. Must hold a high school diploma. Must have completed the basic curriculum in an accredited school of practical nursing. **Examination:** Yes. **Fees:** $60 application fee. $40 renewal fee.

Nevada

4230

Licensed Practical Nurse
Nevada State Board of Nursing
1281 Terminal Way, Rm. 116
Reno, NV 89502
Phone: (702)786-2778

Credential Type: License. **Duration of License:** One year. **Requirements:** High school diploma or equivalent. Graduation from an approved practical nursing program. **Examination:** Yes. **Fees:** $73 exam fee. $45 license fee. $50 renewal fee.

New Hampshire

4231

Licensed Practical Nurse
New Hampshire Board of Nursing
Health & Welfare Bldg.
6 Hazen Dr.
Concord, NH 03301-6527
Phone: (603)271-2323
Fax: (603)271-3745

Credential Type: Licensed Practical Nurse License. **Requirements:** Graduate from state approved nursing program or equivalent program. Good physical and mental health. Be proficient in English language as it relates to nursing. No criminal record involving moral turpitude. **Examination:** National Council Licensure Examination (NCLEX)-PN.

New Jersey

4232

Licensed Practical Nurse
New Jersey Board of Nursing
1100 Raymond Blvd., Rm. 508
Newark, NJ 07102
Phone: (201)648-2490

Credential Type: License. **Duration of License:** Two years. **Requirements:** 10th grade education or equivalent. Completion of an approved course or program in practical nursing. 18 years of age. Good moral character. **Examination:** Yes. **Reciprocity:** Yes. **Fees:** $30 exam fee. $24 biennial registration fee. **Governing Statute:** NJSA 45:11. NJAC 13:37.

New Mexico

4233

Licensed Practical Nurse
New Mexico Board of Nursing
4253 Montgomery Blvd., Ste. 130
Albuquerque, NM 87109
Phone: (505)841-8340

Credential Type: Licensed Practical Nurse License. **Requirements:** High school graduate. Graduate of state approved nursing program. Criminal record must be reviewed by Board before a license is granted.

New York

4234

Licensed Practical Nurse
State Education Dept.
Div. of Professional Licensing Services
Cultural Education Center
Empire State Plaza
Albany, NY 12230
Phone: (518)474-1593

Credential Type: License. **Duration of License:** Three years. **Requirements:** Completion of a vocational program of study in practical nursing. 17 years of age. **Examination:** Written. **Fees:** $165 application fee. $50 renewal fee. **Governing Statute:** Title VIII Articles 130, 139 of the Education Law.

North Carolina

4235

Licensed Practical Nurse
North Carolina Board of Nursing
PO Box 2129
Raleigh, NC 27602
Phone: (919)782-3211

Credential Type: License. **Duration of License:** Two years. **Requirements:** High school diploma or equivalent. Graduation from a board approved nursing program. **Examination:** National exam. **Fees:** $65 exam fee. $40 renewal fee.

North Dakota

4236

Licensed Practical Nurse
North Dakota Board of Nursing
919 S. 7th St., Ste. 504
Bismarck, ND 58504-5881
Phone: (701)224-2974
Fax: (701)224-4614

Credential Type: Licensed Practical Nurse License. **Requirements:** Graduate from state approved nursing program or equivalent nursing program. **Examination:** National Council Licensure Examination (NCLEX)-PN.

Ohio

4237

Licensed Practical Nurse
Ohio Board of Nursing
77 S. High St., 17th Fl.
Columbus, OH 43266-0316
Phone: (614)466-3947
Fax: (614)466-0388

Credential Type: Licensed Practical Nurse License. **Requirements:** Graduate from state approved nursing program. Be proficient in English language as it relates to nursing. No felony or criminal record.

Oklahoma

4238

Nurse, Licensed Practical (LPN)
Board of Nurse Registration and Nursing Education
2915 N. Classen Blvd., Ste. 524
Oklahoma City, OK 73106
Phone: (405)525-2076

Credential Type: License. **Duration of License:** Two years. **Requirements:** Completion of a 12-month, state-approved practical nurse program. Supervised clinical experience. 10th-grade education or GED equivalency. **Examination:** National Council Licensure Exam for Practical Nurses. **Fees:** $40 exam fee. $50 application and license fee. $40 renewal fee.

Oregon

4239

Nurse, Licensed Practical
Oregon State Board of Nursing
800 NE Oregon St. 25, Ste. 465
Portland, OR 97232
Phone: (503)731-4745

Credential Type: License. **Duration of License:** Two years. **Requirements:** Must be a graduate of a program preparing persons for the Licensed Practical Nursing role. **Examination:** Yes. **Fees:** $40 exam fee. $70 license fee. $44 renewal fee. **Governing Statute:** ORS 678.040, 678.050, 678.101.

Pennsylvania

4240

Licensed Practical Nurse
Pennsylvania State Board of Nursing
PO Box 2649
Harrisburg, PA 17105
Phone: (717)783-7142
Fax: (717)787-7769

Credential Type: Licensed Practical Nurse License. **Requirements:** High school graduate or equivalent. Graduate from state approved nursing program. Meet age requirement. Good moral character. Be proficient in English language as it relates to nursing. No felony or criminal record.

Rhode Island

4241

Licensed Practical Nurse
Board of Nurse Registration & Nurse Education
Cannon Health Bldg.
Three Capitol Hill, Rm. 104
Providence, RI 02908-5097
Phone: (401)277-2827
Fax: (401)277-1272

Credential Type: Licensed Practical Nurse License. **Requirements:** High school graduate or equivalent. Graduate from a state approved nursing program. Good moral character. No felony or criminal record. **Examination:** National Council Licensure Examination (NCLEX)-PN.

South Carolina

4242

Licensed Practical Nurse
South Carolina State Board of Nursing
1777 St. Julian Pl., Ste. 102
Columbia, SC 29204
Phone: (803)737-6594

Credential Type: Licensed Practical Nurse. **Requirements:** 18 years of age. Two years of high school or equivalent. Completion of a course of study in an approved school for training of practical nurses or equivalent. **Examination:** Yes. **Fees:** $65 exam fee. $25 renewal fee. $75 endorsement fee. $45 reinstatement fee.

South Dakota

4243

Licensed Practical Nurse
South Dakota Board of Nursing
3307 S. Lincoln Ave.
Sioux Falls, SD 57105-5224
Phone: (605)335-4973
Fax: (605)335-2977

Credential Type: Licensed Practical Nurse License. **Requirements:** High school graduate or equivalent. Graduate of state approved nursing program or equivalent program. Be proficient in English language as it relates to nursing. **Examination:** National Council Licensure Examination (NCLEX)-PN.

Tennessee

4244

Practical Nurse
Board of Nursing
283 Plus Park Blvd.
Nashville, TN 37247
Phone: (615)367-6232

Credential Type: License. **Requirements:** Completion of 12th grade or equivalent. Graduate of an approved school of practical nursing. Must actively engage in nursing within past five years to maintain an active license. No criminal convictions. **Examination:** National Council Licensure Examination (NCLEX-PN). **Fees:** $35 Examination. $40 Test Service.

Texas

4245

Nurse, Licensed Vocational
Texas Board of Vocational Nurse Examiners
9101 Burnet Rd., Ste. 105
Austin, TX 78758
Phone: (512)835-2071

Credential Type: License. **Duration of License:** Two years. **Requirements:** At least two years of high school education or GED equivalent, and completion of a course of not less than 12 months in an approved school of vocational nursing; or at least two years of education in an approved school of professional nursing. Proof of continuing education required for biennial renewal. **Examination:** National Council Licensure Examination (NCLEX). **Fees:** $80 application and exam fee. $20 renewal fee. **Governing Statute:** VACS 4528c, 22 TAC 235.

Utah

4246

Nurse, Licensed Practical
Dept. of Commerce
Div. of Occupational and
   Professional Licensing
160 E. 300 S.
PO Box 45802
Salt Lake City, UT 84145
Phone: (801)530-6628

Credential Type: License. **Duration of License:** Two years. **Requirements:** Must be a graduate of an approved nurse education program or the equivalent; or hold a license issued in another state. **Examination:** Yes. **Reciprocity:** Yes. **Fees:** $50 license fee. $35 renewal fee.

Vermont

4247

Licensed Practical Nurse (LPN)
Vermont State Board of Nursing
Pavilion Office Bldg.
Montpelier, VT 05602
Phone: (802)828-2396

Credential Type: License. **Duration of License:** Two years. **Requirements:** 18 years of age. Good moral character. Mentally and physically able to perform duties. High school graduate. Hold diploma from approved nursing school or equivalent. **Examination:** Yes. **Reciprocity:** Yes. **Fees:** $70 Application by examination. $20 Renewal. $25 Limited practice reinstatement. $25 Application by endorsement. **Governing Statute:** Title 26, VSA Section 1555.

Virginia

4248

Licensed Practical Nurse
Virginia Board of Nursing
1601 Rolling Hills Dr.
Richmond, VA 23229
Phone: (804)662-9909

Credential Type: Licensed. **Duration of License:** Two years. **Requirements:** Must complete a practical nursing program. **Examination:** Yes. **Reciprocity:** Yes. **Fees:** $35 application fee. $28 renewal fee.

Washington

4249

Licensed Practical Nurse
Washington State Board of Practical
   Nursing
1300 SE Quince St.
PO Box 47865
Olympia, WA 98504-7865
Phone: (206)753-2807
Fax: (206)753-1338

Credential Type: Licensed Practical Nurse License. **Requirements:** Graduate from state approved nursing program or equivalent nursing program. Meet age requirement. Good moral character. Good physical and mental health. Be proficient in English language as it relates to nursing. **Examination:** National Council Licensure Examination (NCLEX)-PN.

West Virginia

4250

Licensed Practical Nurse
Board of Examiners for Licensed
   Practical Nurses
922 Quarrier St., Ste. 506
Charleston, WV 25301
Phone: (304)348-3572

Credential Type: License. **Duration of License:** One year. **Requirements:** Graduate of an approved one year program or equivalent training in the Armed Forces. Never convicted of a felony. No addictions to any drugs. **Examination:** Yes. **Fees:** $60 Application. $35 Examination. $15 Renewal.

Wisconsin

4251

Nurse/Licensed Practical
Regulations and Licensing Dept.
Nurses Board
PO Box 8935
Madison, WI 53708-8935
Phone: (608)266-8609

Credential Type: License. **Requirements:** 10th grade education or equivalent. No arrests or convictions. Graduation from an approved, practical school of nursing. 18 years of age. **Examination:** National Boards. **Reciprocity:** Yes.

Wyoming

4252

Nurse, Licensed Practical
State Board of Nursing
Barrett Bldg., 2nd Fl.
2301 Central Ave.
Cheyenne, WY 82002
Phone: (307)777-7601

Credential Type: License. **Duration of License:** Two years. **Requirements:** Graduate from an approved practical nursing program. Pass a national licensure examination. Meet continued competency requirements. **Examination:** Yes. **Fees:** $70 Licensing by endorsement. $75 Licensing by examination. $42 Renewal.

Lobbyists

One or more occupations in this chapter require a federal license. Additionally, the following states grant licenses as of the date of publication:

Alabama	District of	Iowa	Minnesota	New Mexico	Rhode Island	Washington
Alaska	Columbia	Kansas	Mississippi	New York	South Carolina	West Virginia
Arizona	Florida	Kentucky	Missouri	North Carolina	South Dakota	Wisconsin
Arkansas	Georgia	Louisiana	Montana	North Dakota	Tennessee	Wyoming
California	Hawaii	Maine	Nebraska	Ohio	Texas	
Colorado	Idaho	Maryland	Nevada	Oklahoma	Utah	
Connecticut	Illinois	Massachusetts	New Hampshire	Oregon	Vermont	
Delaware	Indiana	Michigan	New Jersey	Pennsylvania	Virginia	

Federal Licenses

4253

Lobbyist
Office of the Clerk
Office of Records and Registration
U.S. House of Representatives
Longworth House Office Bldg., Rm. 1036
Washington, DC 20515-6612
Phone: (202)225-1300

Alternate Information: Also must register with the Secretary of the Senate, S-208 The Capitol, Washington, DC 20510-7100. Phone: (202)224-0758.

Credential Type: Lobbyist registration. **Authorization:** Applies to any person who shall engage for pay or any consideration in attempting to influence the passage or defeat of any legislation by the Congress of the United States. **Requirements:** Register with the Clerk of the House of Representatives and the Secretary of the Senate. Must furnish name and business address, employer's name and address, in whose interest individual is appearing, duration of such employment, amount being paid and by whom. Must file quarterly reports detailing expenditures. **Governing Statute:** Federal Regulation of Lobbying Act of 1946.

Alabama

4254

Lobbyist
State Ethics Commission
RSA Plaza
770 Washington Ave., Ste. 330
Montgomery, AL 36130
Phone: (205)261-2997

Credential Type: Lobbyist registration. **Duration of License:** One year. **Authorization:** For lobbying the legislature and for attempts to influence executive action on legislation. **Requirements:** The individual lobbyist must register, and the employer must certify such registration, annually or within five days after beginning lobbying activity.

Both employer and lobbyist must file monthly reports. Reports are to include information about monies expended, loans, and business relationships with members of the legislature, and types of legislation that are of interest.

In addition, lobbyists must register with the secretary of the senate and/or the clerk of the house. Separate registration is required for each house. **Governing Statute:** Chap. 25, Code of Ethics for Public Officials, Employees, Etc.

Alaska

4255

Lobbyist
Alaska Public Offices Commission
Juneau Branch Office
211 4th St., No. 114
PO Box CO
Juneau, AK 99811-0222
Phone: (907)465-4864

Alternate Information: Alaska Public Offices Commission, Anchorage Branch Office, 2221 E. Northern Lights Blvd., Rm. 128, Anchorage, AK 99508-3598. Phone: (907)276-4176.

Credential Type: Lobbyist registration. **Duration of License:** One year. **Authorization:** For lobbying activities. **Requirements:** The lobbyist must register.

Both employer and lobbyist (except for representational and volunteer lobbyists) must file reports. Lobbyist must file monthly reports wheen the legislature is in session and quarterly reports when the legislature is not in session. Employer must file quarterly reports. **Governing Statute:** Alaska Statutes, Title 24, Chap. 45, Sections .011—.181, 1976, as amended.

Arizona

4256

Lobbyist
Secretary of State
1700 W. Washington St., Ste. 700
State Capitol, W. Wing
Phoenix, AZ 85007
Phone: (602)542-4285

Credential Type: Lobbyist registration. **Duration of License:** Two years. **Authorization: For lobbying the legislature and regulatory/executive agencies. **Requirements:** The lobbyist's principal and any person who engages a lobbyist must register. Lobbyist must register before doing anything in furtherance of lobbying activity.

Principal must file monthly reports listing any single expenditure, and to whom, made in excess of $25. Principal must file annually for the preceding year reporting: the total of all expenditures incurred in lobbying activities, not including expenditures for personal lodging and travel; separate listing of special events held for legislators, including parties and dinners; separate listing of any individual expenditure exceeding $25. **Fees:** No fee. **Governing Statute:** Arizona Revised Statutes, Title 41, Chap. 7, Article 8.1, Sections 41-1231 to 41-1239.

Arkansas

4257

Lobbyist
Secretary of State
State Capitol, Rm. 206
Little Rock, AR 72201-1094
Phone: (501)682-1010

Credential Type: Lobbyist registration. **Duration of License:** One year. **Authorization:** For lobbying the legislature and regulatory/executive agencies. **Requirements:** The individual lobbyist must register within five days after beginning lobbying.

Lobbyist must file monthly reports when the general assembly is in session and quarterly lobbyist activity reports. Reports must include the total of all expenditures made or incurred by the lobbyist or on behalf of the lobbyist by his/her employer, itemized according to financial category and employers and clients. A list must be itemized when valued at $100 or more. Food, lodging, travel, or any other item given to a public servant is itemized if valued over $25. Special events need not be itemized by the individual benefiting, but the date, location, name of governmental body or groups of public officials invited, and total expenses shall be stated. **Fees:** No fee. **Governing Statute:** Initiated Act I of 1988 and 1990. The Standards of Conduct for Lobbyists and Elected Officials, effective January 1, 1989, and amended to include local officials by Act 719.

California

4258

Lobbyist
Secretary of State
Political Reform Division
PO Box 1467
Sacramento, CA 95812-1467
Phone: (916)322-5662

Credential Type: Lobbyist registration. **Duration of License:** Two years. **Authorization:** For lobbying the legislature and regulatory/executive agencies. **Requirements:** Lobbying firms, lobbyist employers, and lobbying coalitions employing in-house lobbyists must register within 10 days of becoming a lobbying firm/employer.

Lobbyists must complete and verify a "Lobbyist Certification Statement."

Lobbyists must attend an orientation course, each biannual legislative session, on the relevant ethical issues and laws relating to lobbying.

Lobbyists, employers, firms, coalitions, and persons not employing lobbyists but spending $5,000 or more in a calendar quarter to influence legislative or administrative action must file reports.

Lobbyist must file quarterly, reporting all activity expenses (payments that benefit reportable persons), including the date, name and address of payee, name and official position of reportable persons and amount benefiting each, description of consideration, and the total amount of the activity expense. Lobbyist is also required to disclose all monetary and non-monetary contributions, and independent expenditures of $100 or more made from the lobbyist's personal funds during the quarter, or from a separate account under the control of the lobbyist, to state candidates, elected state officers, their controlled committees, or committees primarily formed to support such officers or candidates, or delivered in person by the lobbyist to state candidates or elected state officers.

Employer must file quarterly reports providing the name and title of each partner, owner, officer, and emplooyee who is a lobbyist. Employer must disclose payments to lobbyists and lobbying firms; office overhead and operating expenses attributable to lobbying; compensation to employees who spend 10 percent or more of their time in lobbying activity; activity expenses, including the date, name, and address of the payee, name and official position of reportable persons, description of consideration, total amount of activity; and provide a specific description of each legislative or administrative action the employer or his/her lobbyist actively influenced or attempted to influence during the calendar quarter. Employer must disclose all monetary and non-monetary contributions and independent expenditures of $100 or more made to or on behalf of state candidates, elected state officers. Employer must also disclose payments made during a calendar quarter to lobbying coalitions.

Firms must file quarterly reports providing the name and title of each partner, owner, officer, and employee of the lobbying firm who is a lobbyist; report payments received in connection with lobbying activity including the name, address, and telephone number, and a specific description of the lobbying interests, of each person with whom the firm contracts; payments made for activity expenses, including the date, name, and address of the payee, name and official position of reportable persons, description of consideration, total amount of activity; payments made to other lobbying firms, including name, address, and telephone number of firm contracted with, name of employer or client for whom subcontractor was retained to lobby, amount paid this period, and cumulative total to date. Firm must disclose monetary and non-monetary contributions and independent expenditures of $100 or more made to or on behalf of state candidates, elected state officers, or committees supporting such candidates or officers. Firm must also disclose payments made during a calendar quarter to lobbying coalitions.

Coalitions must file quarterly lobbyist employer reports and disclose each quarter the name, address, and amount received from each member of the coalition.

Any individual, business association, organization, or group that does not employ a lobbyist but makes payments totaling $5,000 or more in a calendar quarter to influence legislative or administrative action must file quarterly reports. **Fees:** $25 registration fee. Employers, firms, and coalitions are also required to provide a recent 3-inch x 4-inch black and white photograph for each employee who is certified to lobby on their behalf. **Governing Statute:** Title nine of the Government Code: Political Reform Act of 1974, adopted by initiative June 4, 1974, as amended to January 1, 1991.

Colorado

4259

Lobbyist
Secretary of State
Elections Dept.
1560 Broadway, Ste. 200
Denver, CO 80202
Phone: (303)894-2200

Credential Type: Lobbyist registration. **Duration of License:** One year. **Authorization:** For lobbying the legislature and regulatory/executive agencies, and for efforts to influence executive action on pending legislation. **Requirements:** Lobbyist must register before engaging in lobbying activity.

Lobbyist must file monthly reports and a final cumulative annual report. Employer receiving money to be used by any person for lobbying (earmarked funds) are required to report. **Fees:** No fee. **Governing Statute:** Colorado Revised Statutes, Title 24, Article 6, Part three Regulation of Lobbyists, as amended through 1984.

Connecticut

4260

Lobbyist
State Ethics Commission
97 Elm St. (Rear)
Hartford, CT 06106
Phone: (203)566-4472

Credential Type: Lobbyist registration. **Duration of License:** One year. **Authorization:** For lobbying the legislature (including attempts to influence executive action thereon) and regulatory/executive agencies. **Requirements:** Lobbyists who receive or expend $1,000 or more in a calendar year for lobbying activities (this includes individual lobbyists and employers) must register prior to commencement of lobbying.

Both lobbyist and employer must file reports.

Reports are due by April 10, July 10, and January 10. All reports must be filed as long as lobbyist remains registered.

Monthly reports are due for those registered for legislative lobbying and are required for the months during which the general assembly is in regular session.

Reports must show receipts and expenditures incident to lobbying, plus itemized reports of each expenditure of $10 or more per person per occasion for benefit of public official, staff, or immediate family itemized by date, beneficiary, amount, and circumstances. Registrant must report payment or reimbursement of necessary fees within 30 days. **Fees:** $60 fee per calendar year. **Governing Statute:** Connecticut GSA Title 1, Chapter 10, Part II, Sections 1-91 1-101, Code of Ethics for Lobbyists, as amended through 1991.

Delaware

4261

Lobbyist
Legislative Council
Legislative Hall
Dover, DE 19901
Phone: (302)736-4114

Credential Type: Lobbyist registration. **Duration of License:** Term of legislature or until terminated. **Authorization:** For lobbying the legislature and regulatory/executive agencies. **Requirements:** Lobbyist must register before doing any lobbying.

Lobbyist must file quarterly reports detailing expenditures and identifying any member of the legislature who is the recipient of expenditures exceeding $50 in any day. **Governing Statute:** House Bill 1117, signed August 23, 1976 and effective January 1, 1977.

District of Columbia

4262

Lobbyist
Director of Campaign Finance
Office of Campaign Finance
2000 14th St., NW, Ste. 420
Washington, DC 20009
Phone: (202)939-8717

Credential Type: Lobbyist registration. **Duration of License:** One year. **Authorization:** For lobbying the legislature and regulatory/executive agencies. **Requirements:** Lobbyist (within 15 days of becoming a lobbyist) and employer must register. A separate registration must be filed for each employer. Both lobbyist and employer must file reports.

Twice yearly, lobbyist must file a sworn report with the campaign finance office covering his/her lobbying activities during the preceding six months. Lobbyist must report on total expenditures in each of five categories: office, advertising and publication, compensation to others, personal sustenance (including lodging and travel), and other. Expenditures of $50 or more must be itemized, including the names of the recipients thereof. Lobbyist must also list each legislative or executive branch official with whom he/she has had oral or written communication. A separate activity report is required for each employer for which lobbyist has registered and been active. **Fees:** No fee. **Governing Statute:** Subchapter V of the District of Columbia Campaign Finance Reform and Conflict of Interest Act, Lobbying, D.C. Code 1-1451 et seq.

Florida

4263

Lobbyist
Legislative Lobbyist Registration
111 W. Madison St., Rm. G-68
Tallahassee, FL 32399-1425
Phone: (904)488-7864

Credential Type: Legislative lobbying registration. **Duration of License:** Two years. **Authorization:** For lobbying the legislature. **Requirements:** Lobbyist must register before engaging in lobbying activities (separate registration is required for each principal represented).

Lobbyist must file semiannual expenditure reports for each principal he/she is registered to represent. Lobbyist must list all lobbying expenditures, the source of the funds, and the amount.

Lobbyist, his/her partners, firms, employers, principals, or another on their behalf who give a reportable gift between $25 and $100 to a reporting individual of the legislature must request a Gift Disclosure Report (to be filed quarterly with the Legislative Lobbyist Registration) from the Commission on Ethics (Room 2105 in the capitol). Gift disclosure reports must include a description of the gift, monetary value, name and address of the donor, name and address of the recipient, and the date it was given. **Fees:** $100 joint biennial registration fee ($50 per chamber for the first principal represented). $20 joint fee ($10 per chamber) for each additional principal. **Governing Statute:** Florida Statutes, Sections 11.045—11.062 and 112.3215, amended 1991; House Rule 13.

Credential Type: Executive branch lobbying registration. **Duration of License:** One year. **Authorization:** For lobbying regulatory/executive agencies. **Requirements:** Lobbyist must register before engaging in lobbying activities in Tallahassee (separate registration is required for each principal represented).

Lobbyist must file semiannual expenditure reports, representing each principal, listing all lobbying expenditures, the source of the funds, and the amount.

Lobbyist, his/her partners, firms, employers, principals, or another on their behalf who give a reportable gift between $25 and $100 to a reporting individual of the legislature must request a Gift Disclosure Report (to be filed quarterly with the Legislative Lobbyist Registration) from the Commission on Ethics (Room 2105 in the capitol). Gift disclosure reports must include a description of the gift, monetary value, name and address of the donor, name and address of the recipient, and the date it was given. **Fees:** $20 fee for each principal represented. **Governing Statute:** Florida Statutes, Sections 11.045—11.062 and 112.3215, amended 1991; House Rule 13.

Georgia

4264

Lobbyist
Secretary of State
110 State Capitol
Atlanta, GA 30334-1505
Phone: (404)656-2871

Credential Type: Lobbyist registration. **Duration of License:** One regular or extraordinary session of the legislature. **Authorization:** For lobbying the legislature. **Requirements:** Lobbyist must register.

No reports are required. **Fees:** $5 fee. **Governing Statute:** Georgia Code 28-7-1—28-7-5, Lobbying, 1970.

Hawaii

4265

Lobbyist
State Ethics Commission
Bishop Sq., Pacific Tower 970
1001 Bishop St.
Honolulu, HI 96813
Phone: (808)587-0460
Fax: (808)587-0470

Credential Type: Lobbyist registration. **Duration of License:** Two years. **Authorization:** For lobbying the legislature and regulatory/executive agencies. **Requirements:** Lobbyist must register within five days of becoming a lobbyist.

Lobbyist, employer, and any person who spends $275 or more in any six month period for lobbying purposes must file reports twice yearly. Reports must contain the following: name and address of each person with respect to whom expenditure was made totaling $25 or more per day and the amount; name and address of each person with respect to whom expenditure was made aggregating $150 or more in reporting period and the amount; total amount spent on lobbying during period in excess of $275; name and address of each person making contributions to the person filing the report for the purpose of lobbying in the total sum of $25 or more during the statement period and the amount or value of such contribution; subject area of reporter's involvement.

Employer report must show pro rata share of lobbyist's salary for lobbying activities. **Governing Statute:** Chapter 97, Hawaii Revised Statutes, as amended 1989.

Idaho

4266

Lobbyist
Secretary of State
State House, Rm. 205
Boise, ID 83720
Phone: (208)334-2300
Phone: (208)334-2852

Credential Type: Lobbyist registration. **Duration of License:** One year. **Authorization:** For lobbying the legislature. **Requirements:** Lobbyist must register before lobbying or within 30 days of employment, whichever is first.

Lobbyist must file annual report signed by employer and him/herself, itemizing the total expenditures in excess of $50 for a legislator or other holder of public office.

Lobbyist must file monthly (when legislature is in session) report, signed by him/herself, itemizing the total expenditures in excess of $50 for a legislator or other holder of public office.

Records must be retained for three years. **Fees:** $10 fee. **Governing Statute:** The Sunshine Law for Political Funds and Lobbyist Activity Disclosure, Sections 67-6601—67-6628, Idaho Code (relevant sections).

Illinois

4267

Lobbyist
Secretary of State
Index Dept.
111 E. Monroe St.
Springfield, IL 62756
Phone: (217)782-7017

Credential Type: Lobbyist registration. **Duration of License:** One year. **Authorization:** For lobbying the legislature, including attempts to influence the governor's action on legislation. **Requirements:** Lobbyist and employer must register before lobbyist engages in lobbying activity.

Both lobbyist and employer must file reports.

Reports must disclose all expenditures made, and itemize those of more than $25. Expenditures of $25 or less may be aggregated and reported in total amounts rather than in detail. The report must show the person or legislator to whom or for whose benefit expenditures were made. **Fees:** No fee. **Governing Statute:** Illinois Revised Statutes, 1989, Chapter 63, 171—182, Lobbyist Registration Act.

Indiana

4268

Lobbyist
Secretary of State
201 State House
Indianapolis, IN 46204
Phone: (317)232-6531

Credential Type: Lobbyist registration. **Duration of License:** One year. **Authorization:** For lobbying the legislature, including attempts to influence the governor's actions. **Requirements:** Both lobbyist and employer must register.

Both lobbyist and employer must file semi-annual activity reports. Reports must include total expenditures on lobbying, a statement of expenditures and gifts that equal $100 in one day or that together total $500 during the calendar year if made to a member, officer, or employee of the general assembly or a family member thereof, any expenditure for the benefit of all general assembly members and a list of the general subject matter of each item on which a lobbying effort was made. In the second report, amounts must be reported for that period and for the entire reporting year.

Staff time spent in preparing letters, making telephone calls, and sending facsimile messages or any other communication or lobbying activity should be pro-rated from that person's yearly salary and reported in the category "compensation to others." **Fees:** $20 fee. **Governing Statute:** Indiana Code, Title 2, Article 7, Lobbyists, Chapters 1—6, amended 1982, 1985, 1987.

Iowa

4269

Lobbyist
Secretary of the Senate or Chief Clerk of the House
State Capitol
Des Moines, IA 50319
Phone: (515)281-5307
Phone: (515)281-5381

Credential Type: Lobbyist registration. **Duration of License:** One year. **Authorization:** For lobbying the legislature. **Requirements:** Lobbyist must register separately for each body on or before engaging in lobbying activities.

Lobbyist must file monthly reports (including gifts made to regulatory/executive agencies) of the nature, amount, and date of any gift to a member, officer, or employee of the general assembly or their immediate family members, that exceeds $15 in value.

Reports must be filed separately for the house and senate. Senate gifts are reported to the secretary of the senate and house gifts to the chief clerk of the house. House and senate reports must include the monthly total of all gifts, including food, entertainment, travel, recreation, lodging, and the amount of any honorarium paid to a member, officer, or employee of the general assembly, or their immediate family.

Gifts made to regulatory/executive agency officials are reported to the secretary of state's office. (Employers must file reports when gifts are made to regulatory/executive agencies.) **Governing Statute:** Chapter 68B, Code of 1987, "Conflicts of Interest of Public Officers and Employees"; House Rules Governing Lobbyists, as amended in 1989; and Senate Rules Governing Lobbyists, as amended in 1989.

Kansas

4270

Lobbyist
Secretary of State
State Capitol, 2nd Fl.
Topeka, KS 66612
Phone: (913)296-4219

Credential Type: Lobbyist registration. **Duration of License:** One year. **Authorization:** For lobbying the legislature and regulatory/executive agencies. **Requirements:** Lobbyist must register before engaging in any lobbying activities.

Lobbyist must file reports of all expenditures made, or a statement that no expenditures in excess of $100 were made. Whenever an individual lobbyist contributes to a single special event, the lobbyist must report only the aggregate amount or value of the expenditure. **Fees:** $250 fee for an employee of a lobbying group or firm; $15 fee for all others who anticipate spending $1,000 or less on behalf of any one employer; $125 fee for all persons who anticipate spending more than $1,000 on behalf of any one employer. Upon payment, lobbyist is issued an identification tag that must be worn when lobbying in the capitol. **Governing Statute:** Kansas Statutes Annotated 46.215—46.280 (1975, as amended 1983, 1987, 1990, 1991).

Kentucky

4271

Lobbyist
Office of the Attorney General
Lobbyist Registration
Capitol Bldg., Ste. 122
Frankfort, KY 40601
Phone: (502)564-7600

Credential Type: Lobbyist registration. **Duration of License:** One legislative session. **Authorization:** For lobbying the legislature. **Requirements:** Both lobbyist and employer must register within one week after lobbyist's employment.

Both lobbyist and employer must file reports.

Lobbyist must file annual report detailing expenditures made or incurred during the session.

Employer must file annual report detailing expenditures made in connection with employment of lobbyists or promoting or opposing legislation. If the report is by a corporation, its president or treasurer must sign. **Fees:** No fee. **Governing Statute:** Kentucky Revised Statutes, 6.250—6.990.

Louisiana

4272

Lobbyist
Clerk of the House
Secretary of the Senate
State Capitol
Baton Rouge, LA 70804
Phone: (504)342-7259
Phone: (504)342-2040

Credential Type: Lobbyist registration. **Duration of License:** One year. **Authorization:** For lobbying the legislature. **Requirements:** Lobbyist must register with both the clerk of the house and secretary of the senate before engaging in lobbying activities.

No reports are required. **Fees:** $10 fee. Two photographs. **Governing Statute:** Louisiana Revised Statutes: 24:51[—55, Legislative Lobbying Registration Law, 1978.]

Maine

4273

Lobbyist
Lobbyist Registrar
Secretary of State
State Office Bldg., Rm. 221
Augusta, ME 04333
Phone: (207)289-6221

Credential Type: Lobbyist registration. **Duration of License:** One year. **Authorization:** For lobbying the legislature. **Requirements:** Lobbyist and employer must register jointly within 15 business days after commencing lobbying activities.

Lobbyist must file monthly activity reports including: restatement of registration information; compensation received; expenditures received; expenditures made; total expenditures on legislative officials and their families, scope of activities and disclosure of the names of those officials and their families on whom the lobbyist has spent more than $25 cumulative during any one month; a list of the legislation the lobbyist was supporting/opposing and a specific identification of legislation on which the lobbyist was compensated or expended more than $1,000.

Lobbyist and employer must file an annual report jointly detailing legislative actions not previously reported and summarizing all lobbying activities for the calendar year. **Fees:** $75 joint registration fee. **Governing Statute:** Maine Revised Statutes, Title 3, Chapter 15, Lobbyist Disclosure Procedures, Sections 311—326, as amended.

Maryland

4274

Lobbyist
State Ethics Commission
300 E. Joppa Rd., Ste. 301
Baltimore, MD 21204
Phone: (301)321-3636

Credential Type: Lobbyist registration. **Duration of License:** One year. **Authorization:** For lobbying the legislature and regulatory/executive agencies. **Requirements:** Any person who expends a cumulative value of $100 or more during a reporting period on one or more executive branch officials or employees for meals, beverages, special events, or gifts in connection with influencing executive action; any person who expends $2,000, including postage, in a reporting period for the express purpose of soliciting others to communicate with any official to influence any legislative or executive action; and lobbyists (any person who communicates with any legislative or executive branch official or employee, in his/her presence, for the purpose of influencing legislative action and who incurs expenses of $100 or more or who receives $500 or more as compensation) must register no later than five days after beginning lobbying activities.

Both lobbyist and employer (unless exempt due to reporting by lobbyist and meeting other requirements) must file reports twice yearly including: total expenditures for compensation; office expenses; research; publications; witnesses' names and fees related to lobbying; and expenditures for entertainment and special events, meals, and beverages provided to officials, employees, and/or their immediate families.

Reports must also include the names of officials, employees, and/or families who have benefited from any cumulative gifts of $75 or more during the reporting period. Gifts totaling less than $15 in any calendar day need not be counted towards the cumulative value of the $75 threshold. Each gift of $10 or more above the $75 cumulative value total must be itemized.

In situations where an employee or official receives $200 or more in expenses in return for appearing on a panel or giving a speech, the person's name and amount spent must be reported.

If an employer or registrant (where there is no employer) is organized and operated for the primary purpose of attempting to influence any legislative or executive action, it is required to report the name and permanent address of each person who provided at least five percent of the entity's receipts during the preceding 12 months. **Governing Statute:** Annotated Code of Maryland, Article 40A, Maryland Public Ethics Law: Title 5, Lobbying Disclosure.

Massachusetts

4275

Lobbyist
Dept. of the State Secretary
Div. of Public Records
1 Ashburton Pl., Rm. 1719
Boston, MA 02108
Phone: (617)727-2832

Credential Type: Lobbyist registration. **Duration of License:** One year. **Authorization:** For lobbying the legislature and regulatory/executive agencies and influencing the governor's actions. **Requirements:** Lobbyist must register within 10 days of employment as a legislative agent. Employer must start the registration process by notifying the state secretary within one week after employment has begun.

Both lobbyist and employer must file reports twice yearly.

Lobbyist must report all expenditures made, and must itemize each expenditure if total expenditures in any one day total $35 or more, and include amounts, payees, or beneficiaries thereof.

Employer must report all expenditures made, and whenever an employer has expended more than $50 during a reporting period, all expenditures beyond the initial $50 amount must be itemized, no matter how little the excess may have been. Employer must report the salary of the legislative agent. **Fees:** $50 initial registration fee; $25 fee per client. **Governing Statute:** Massachusetts General Laws, Chapter 3, Sections 39—50.

Michigan

4276

Lobbyist
Bureau of Elections
PO Box 20126
Lansing, MI 48901
Phone: (517)373-7655

Credential Type: Lobbyist. **Duration of License:** Ongoing. **Authorization:** For lobbying the legislature and regulatory/executive agencies. **Requirements:** Lobbyist agent (employee) must register within three days of receiving in excess of $350 in compensation or reimbursement for lobbying during any 12 month period.

Lobbyist (employer) must register within 15 days of spending in excess of $1,400 for lobbying or $350 for lobbying a single public official during any 12 month period.

Both lobbyist agent and lobbyist must file semiannual financial disclosure reports.

Financial transactions of $700 or more between a lobbyist or lobbyist agent and a public official, a member of the official's immediate family, or business must be reported.

The name and title of each public official on whose behalf more than $35 in food and beverage was purchased during any month in the reporting period or on whose behalf more than $225 in food and beverage was purchased between January one and the end of the reporting period.

The name and address of all persons employed or reimbursed for lobbying in excess of $14 in a 12 month period must be reported. **Fees:** No fee. **Governing Statute:** Michigan Statutes, MCL 4.411—4.431; R 4.411—4.471, PA 472 of 1978, PA 82 of 1986.

Minnesota

4277

Lobbyist
Minnesota State Ethical Practices Board
Centennial Bldg., 1st Fl. S.
658 Cedar St.
St. Paul, MN 55155
Phone: (612)296-5148

Credential Type: Lobbyist registration. **Duration of License:** Until terminated by lobbyist. **Authorization:** For lobbying the legislature, regulatory/executive agencies, and the metropolitan governmental unit. **Requirements:** Lobbyist must register within five days after qualifying as a lobbyist.

Both lobbyist and employer must file reports.

Lobbyist must file reports three times yearly revealing full information on lobbyist disbursement, including the name and address of any public official to whom a gift, loan, honorarium, item, or benefit (including entertainment, food and beverage, travel, and lodging) is given, when such item is equal in value to $50 or more. The source of funds in excess of $500 in any year used for lobbying must be detailed.

Employer must file annual reports including the total amount spent to influence legislative action, administrative action, and the official action of metropolitan governmental units. The category selected must include all direct payments to lobbyists in Minnesota and all expenditures for advertising, mailing, research analysis, compilation and dissemination of information, and public relations campaigns related to legislative and administrative actions or the official action of metropolitan governmental units in Minnesota. **Governing Statute:** Minnesota Statutes, Chapter 10A, Ethics in Government Act, as amended through 1991.

Mississippi

4278

Lobbyist
Secretary of State
PO Box 136
Jackson, MS 39205
Phone: (601)359-1350

Credential Type: Lobbyist registration. **Duration of License:** One year. **Authorization:** For lobbying the legislature, regulatory/executive agencies, and the local governing boards. **Requirements:** Lobbyist and employer must register jointly before engaging in any lobbying activity.

Both lobbyist and employer must file reports.

Employer must file an annual itemized, verified statement showing in detail all expenses paid, incurred, or promised in connection with legislative matters during the previous 12 months, with names of payees and amounts paid to each.

Employer/lobbyist must file an annual itemized, verified statement showing in detail all money or things of value received or expended by him/her on legislative matters, including the names and addresses of persons to whom expenditures were made, and amount paid or promised. **Fees:** $25 fee. **Governing Statute:** Mississippi Code of 1972, Chapter 7, Section 5-7-1—5-7-19.

Missouri

4279

Lobbyist
Clerk of the House
Secretary of the State
State Capitol
Jefferson City, MO 65101
Phone: (314)751-3829

Credential Type: Lobbyist registration. **Duration of License:** Until terminated. **Authorization:** For lobbying the legislature and regulatory/executive agencies. **Requirements:** Lobbyist must register with the clerk of the house and the secretary of the senate within five days after beginning lobbying.

Lobbyist must file expenditure reports twice yearly and monthly reports when the general assembly is in session. Reports must include expenditures grouped into general categories together with a list of recipients of honoraria, gifts or loans, including a service or anything of value exceeding $50 in the aggregate for any reporting period. Reports must include a separate statement of the proposed legislation or legislative action that the lobbyist supported or opposed, for each entity employing the lobbyist. **Governing Statute:** Revised Statutes of Missouri, Chapter 105, Section 105.470, Supp 1991.

Montana

4280

Lobbyist
Commissioner of Political Practices
Capitol Station
Helena, MT 59620
Phone: (406)444-2942

Credential Type: Lobbyist registration. **Duration of License:** Two years. **Authorization:** For lobbying the legislature and public officials. **Requirements:** Lobbyist must register before any lobbying is undertaken and within one week after employment begins (employer has joint obligation to assure this).

Employer (principal) must file annual and monthly reports while the legislature is in session (for months in which the principal spent $5,000 or more) including all payments made. Among reportable items are: each separate payment conferring $50 or more benefit to a public official, or $100 or more to a group of more than one official, itemizing payee and beneficiary; each contribution and membership fee of $250 or more aggregated over the period of a calendar year paid to the principal, if intended for lobbying purposes, with full address of each payer and issue area if earmarked as such; each official action during which principal and agents exerted a major effort to support/oppose along with a statement of the principal's position in such action. **Fees:** $10 fee. **Governing Statute:** Lobbyist Registration and Licensing Law, Title 5, Chapter 7, Sections 5-7-101—5-7-305, Montana Code Annotated (MCA), as amended 1991.

Nebraska

4281

Lobbyist
Clerk of the Legislature
State Capitol, Rm. 2016
Lincoln, NE 68509
Phone: (402)471-2608

Credential Type: Lobbyist registration. **Duration of License:** Two years. **Authorization:** For lobbying the legislature and regulatory/executive agencies. **Requirements:** Lobbyist must register before engaging in any lobbying activities.

Both lobbyist and employer must file reports monthly, 45 days after the legislature adjourns, and after the interim period between regular session disclosing the amounts of money received or expended, directly or indirectly, for lobbying activities.

Employer must report the names and addresses of every person from whom he/she has received more than $100 in any one month for lobbying purposes. **Fees:** $35 fee. **Governing Statute:** Nebraska Political Accountability and Disclosure Act, Revised Statutes of Nebraska 49-1401—49-14,138, as amended through 1980.

Nevada

4282

Lobbyist
Director of Legislative Counsel Bureau
Capitol Complex, Legislative Bldg.
Carson City, NV 89710
Phone: (702)687-6800

Credential Type: Lobbyist registration. **Duration of License:** Until terminated or end of legislative session, whichever occurs first. **Authorization:** For lobbying the legislature **Requirements:** Lobbyist must register within two days after lobbying begins.

Lobbyist must file monthly reports and annual reports.

Monthly reports must include total expenditures made, including expenditures made by others on behalf of the lobbyist. If the expenditures exceed $50, the report must also include a compilation of expenditures itemized in the following categories: entertainment expenditures made in connection with a party or similar event hosted by the organization represented by the registrant, gifts and loans, and other expenditures directly associated with legislative action. **Fees:** $50 fee for "paid lobbyist" (those receiving compensation for lobbying services). $5 fee for non-compensated lobbyists. **Governing Statute:** Nevada Revised Statutes, Sections 218.900—218.944, Nevada Lobbying Disclosure Act, amended 1977, 1979, 1981, 1987, 1989, and 1991.

New Hampshire

4283

Lobbyist
Secretary of State
State House
Concord, NH 03301
Phone: (603)271-3242

Credential Type: Lobbyist registration. **Duration of License:** One legislative session. **Authorization:** For lobbying the legislature. **Requirements:** Lobbyist must register before engaging in lobbying activities.

Lobbyist must file reports three times yearly listing all fees and expenditures in connection with his/her legislative employment, including who paid or charged. **Fees:** $50 fee. **Governing Statute:** New Hampshire Statutes, Chapter 15, Sections 1-7.

New Jersey

4284

Lobbyist
New Jersey Election Law
  Enforcement Commission
CN-185
Trenton, NJ 08625-0185
Phone: (609)292-8700

Credential Type: Lobbyist registration. **Duration of License:** Until terminated. **Authorization:** For lobbying the legislature, including efforts to influence the governor's action on pending legislation. For lobbying regulatory/executive agencies, including efforts to influence rulemaking. **Requirements:** Lobbyist (legislative agent) must register prior to any communication to the legislature, legislative staff, governor, governor's staff, or members of the executive branch regarding legislation or rulemaking and within 30 days of employment as an agent.

Both legislative agent and employer must file reports.

Legislative agent must file quarterly reports including particular items or general types of legislation promoted or opposed, as well as the names of the legislators and members of the governor's staff contacted regarding such legislation. Reports must include particular regulations promoted or opposed and the names of executive branch members lobbied.

Legislative agent must file annual reports of contributions, receipts, and expenditures, if sum exceeds $2,500 for the previous calendar year. Reports must include the costs of all fees, salary, retainers, allowances, or other compensation—or that pro rata share related to direct communication. Reports must detail benefits, that exceed (per individual) $25 per day or $200 per year, passed to legislators, legislative staff, the governor, the governor's staff, and members of the executive branch. Reports must contain a detailed account of expenditures exceeding $25 per day or $200 per year on behalf of a particular legislator and expenditures of $100 per event. An agent retained by more than one principal must include expenditures on behalf of all principals in report.

Employer must file annual financial reports of contributions and expenditures for lobbying during the previous calendar year. Report must include payments to all employees qualifying as "legislative agents" such as fees, allowances, retainers, salaries, or other compensation in full—or pro-rata share—related to "Communication" for the specific purpose of affecting legislation paid to the agent detailed as to amount, to whom paid, and for what purpose. **Fees:** $100 annual filing fee. **Governing Statute:** P.L. 1981, Chapter 150, Section five (amends N.J.S.A. 52:13C—18) et seq.

New Mexico

4285

Lobbyist
Secretary of State
Bureau of Elections
Lamy Bldg.
491 Old Santa Fe Trail
Santa Fe, NM 87503
Phone: (505)827-3600

Credential Type: Lobbyist registration. **Duration of License:** One regular session. **Authorization:** For lobbying regulatory/executive agencies and the legislature and for contacts with the governor urging veto or approval of legislation. **Requirements:** Lobbyist must register in the month of January prior to each regular session or before any lobbying is done.

Both lobbyist and employer must file reports at time of registration and annually itemizing any single expenditure exceeding $50. **Fees:** $25 fee. **Governing Statute:** Sections 2-11-1 through 2-11-9, New Mexico Statutes Annotated, 1978 Compilation (New Mexico Laws 1977, Chapter 261, as amended by Laws of 1991, Chapter 16).

New York

4286

Lobbyist
New York Temporary State
  Commission on Lobbying
1 Commerce Plaza
Mezzanine Level, Ste. 304
Albany, NY 12210
Phone: (518)474-7126

Credential Type: Lobbyist registration. **Duration of License:** One year. **Authorization:** For lobbying regulatory/executive agencies and the legislature, including efforts to influence executive action on pending legislation. **Requirements:** Lobbyist who reasonably anticipates expending, incurring, or receiving combined compensation and expenses for the purposes of lobbying in excess of $2,000 in the aggregate per annum must register no later than 10 days after incurring or receiving the combined compensation or expenses. A separate registration statement must be filed for each client.

Lobbyist and employer must file reports.

Lobbyist must file first periodic report by the 15th of the month following the end of the reporting period in which combined reportable compensation and expenses for all clients exceed $2,000 in the aggregate for the lobbying year; and subsequent periodic reports by the 15th day of the month following the end of each reporting period thereafter in which the combination for all clients during such reporting period exceeds $500 in the aggregate. Expenditures exceeding $75 must be itemized.

Lobbyist and employer must file annual reports, lobbyist if required to file a statement of registration or a periodic report, and employer which incurred or expended more than $2,000 for lobbying during the year. **Fees:** $50 registration fee (no fee required for subsequent statement of registration during same lobbying year). **Governing Statute:** Lobbying Act of 1981, New York Legislative Law, Chapter 1040, Laws of 1981, amended 1983 and 1987.

North Carolina

4287

Lobbyist
Secretary of State
300 N. Salisbury St.
Raleigh, NC 27603-5909
Phone: (919)733-4161

Credential Type: Lobbyist registration. **Duration of License:** Two years. **Authorization:** For lobbying the legislature. **Re-

Lobbyist, continued

quirements: Lobbyist must register before engaging in any lobbying activity.

Both lobbyist and employer must file annual reports detailing the amounts paid and to whom in each of the following categories: transportation, lodging, entertainment, food, items having cash value of more than $25, contributions.

Employer must reveal amount paid to lobbyist. **Fees:** $75 fee for each lobbyist's principal. **Governing Statute:** Chapter 740, House Bill 89.

North Dakota

4288

Lobbyist
Secretary of State
State Capitol
Bismarck, ND 58505
Phone: (701)224-2900
Phone: (701)224-3665

Credential Type: Lobbyist registration. **Duration of License:** Until December 31 of year of registration. **Authorization:** For lobbying the legislature and attempts to influence executive approval or veto thereof. **Requirements:** Lobbyist must register before commencing any lobbying activity.

Lobbyist must file annual detailed report itemizing each expenditure of $25 or more to any individual made during the legislative session or the interim. **Fees:** $10 annual fee. **Governing Statute:** North Dakota Century Code, Sections 54-05.1-01-54-05.07, Legislative Lobbying, as amended 1983.

Ohio

4289

Lobbyist
Joint Committee on Agency Rule Review
State House, basement level
Columbus, OH 43266-0604
Phone: (614)466-4086

Credential Type: Lobbyist registration. **Duration of License:** Legislative registration two years; executive registration one year. **Authorization:** For lobbying the legislature and regulatory/executive agencies. **Requirements:** Lobbyist and employer must register within 10 days after the legislative or executive agency lobbyist is engaged.

Both lobbyist and employer must file reports (employee files only updated information and expenditures not disclosed by lobbyist).

Reports must disclose expenditures made for lobbying purposes during the reporting period, and to the extent that expenditures on any single official total more than $500 for travel, lodging or honoraria, or miscellaneous expenditures of $150, in which case that individual, the total expenditure, and the legislation or executive agency decision in question must be identified.

Financial transactions between lobbyist/employer and public officer or employee, relating to business ventures not made to influence legislation, must be reported with the updated registration statements. **Fees:** No fee. **Governing Statute:** Ohio Revised Code, Sections 101.70—101.79, amended June and December 1990 (Legislative); O.R.C., Sections 121.60—121.69, enacted and amended 1990.

Oklahoma

4290

Lobbyist
Ethics Commission
State Capitol, Rm. B-2A
Oklahoma City, OK 73105
Phone: (405)521-3451

Credential Type: Lobbyist registration. **Duration of License:** Two years. **Authorization:** For lobbying the legislature, regulatory/executive agencies, and the judicial branch. **Requirements:** Lobbyist must register within five days after beginning lobbying activity.

Lobbyist must file semiannual signed and notarized reports including the type of expenditure and name of any official on whose behalf a single expenditure exceeds $41.27 and for any expenditure of $330.13 or more on any one member.

Reports are also required of any such expenditures when made by other persons on behalf of the registrant if they were made with the knowledge and consent of the registrant. **Fees:** No fee. **Governing Statute:** Title 74 O.S.1991; 4200 et seq.

Oregon

4291

Lobbyist
Oregon Government Ethics Commission
700 Pringle Pky., SE, 1st Fl.
Salem, OR 97310-1360
Phone: (503)378-5105

Credential Type: Lobbyist registration. **Duration of License:** Until terminated by lobbyist. **Authorization:** For lobbying the legislature and attempts to influence any matter subject to the veto or approval of the governor. **Requirements:** Any individual, corporation, association, organization, or other group who spends more than 16 hours during any calendar quarter lobbying, excluding travel time, or who spends in excess of $50 for the purposes of lobbying must register within three working days after lobbying activity begins.

Both lobbyist and employer must file reports.

Lobbyist must file expenditure reports (2 or three times yearly) showing moneys expended in the following categories: food, entertainment, refreshments; printing, postage, telephone; advertising, public relations, education, research; miscellaneous. Reports must itemize any expenditure made to a legislative or executive official in excess of $48 as to date, name of payee/beneficiary, purpose, and amount.

Employer must file annual report showing total moneys expended (excluding living expenses during session of legislative assembly) and itemized amounts in excess of $48 spent on legislative or executive officials if not previously reported by lobbyist. **Fees:** No fee. **Governing Statute:** Oregon Revised Statutes, Lobbying-Regulation, Sections 171.725—.790, 171.992 amended 1989.

Pennsylvania

4292

Lobbyist
Secretary of the Senate
Chief Clerk of the House
State Capitol
Harrisburg, PA 17120
Phone: (717)787-5920
Phone: (717)787-2372

Credential Type: Lobbyist registration. **Duration of License:** One year. **Authorization:** For lobbying the legislature and regulatory/executive agencies. **Requirements:** Lobbyist must register with both the secretary of the senate and the chief clerk of the house within five days of beginning lobbying activity.

Lobbyist must file sworn statements twice yearly of expenditures, together with the name and title of any official—elected or appointed—or any other state employee who has received any pecuniary benefit in excess of $150 as a result of a lobbyist's activities. **Governing Statute:** Lobbying Registration and Regulation Act, Pennsylvania Statutes, Title 46, Sections 148.1—148.9 (as amended by P.L. 212, October 7, 1976).

Rhode Island

4293

Lobbyist
Office Secretary of State
State House, Rm. 43
Providence, RI 02903
Phone: (401)277-2370

Credential Type: Lobbyist registration. **Duration of License:** One legislative session. **Authorization:** For lobbying the legislature, including attempts to influence executive approval or veto of legislation. **Requirements:** Lobbyist and employer have a joint obligation for lobbyist to register before performing any lobbying activity.

Both lobbyist and employer must file reports.

Initial report is due upon registration. Monthly and annual reports must list all compensation paid to the lobbyist for lobbying, including the total amount expended for lobbying purposes, and an itemization of any expenditures, gifts, or honoraria of $25 or more for each occurrence concerning any legislative or executive official. Reports must include the names of the persons receiving or in whose behalf such expenditures have been made, in addition to the reason, time, and place. **Fees:** $5 charge for a lobbyist badge. **Governing Statute:** Chapter 22-10 of the General Laws.

South Carolina

4294

Lobbyist
Secretary of State
Wade Hampton Office Bldg.
PO Box 11350
Columbia, SC 29211
Phone: (803)734-2158

Credential Type: Lobbyist registration. **Duration of License:** One year. **Authorization:** For lobbying the legislature and regulatory/executive agencies. **Requirements:** Lobbyist and employer must register within 15 days of employment.

Lobbyist must file reports twice yearly including all amounts expended for lobbying during the covered period. The totals must be segregated by amounts expended for office expenses, rent, utilities, supplies, and compensation of support personnel attributable to lobbying. The employer must include pro-rata share of lobbyist's salary.

The employer can comply with the reporting requirements by attaching a copy of the lobbyist's report to the employer report, if the information requested is the same. **Fees:** $50 registration fee. **Governing Statute:** South Carolina Code, 2-17-10, Lobbyists and Lobbying.

South Dakota

4295

Lobbyist
Secretary of State
500 E. Capitol
State Capitol Bldg.
Pierre, SD 57501-5077
Phone: (605)773-3537

Credential Type: Lobbyist registration. **Duration of License:** One session. **Authorization:** For lobbying the legislature. **Requirements:** Lobbyist must register within one week after employment (joint obligation of employer and lobbyist to ensure registration).

Both lobbyist and employer must file annual detailed, sworn statements of all expenses ppaid or incurred, to whom, and in what amounts. **Fees:** $25 fee per employer lobbyist represents. **Governing Statute:** South Dakota Code, Sections 2-12—2-12-14.

Tennessee

4296

Lobbyist
Registry of Election Finance
404 James Robertson Pky., Ste. 1614
Nashville, TN 37243-1360
Phone: (615)741-7959

Credential Type: Lobbyist registration. **Duration of License:** One year. **Authorization:** For lobbying the legislature and regulatory/executive agencies. **Requirements:** Lobbyist must register within five days of becoming a lobbyist.

Lobbyist must file annual sworn reports specifying: any business arrangements, with legislative and executive officials; itemization of gifts of $50 or more and political contributions of more than $100 for members of the legislative branch of government, or gifts of $25 or more and political contributions of $100 or more for members of the executive branch; an itemization of all gifts to legislators on whom more than $500 was spent. **Fees:** $25 fee per each client represented. **Governing Statute:** TCA 3-6-101—3-6-110, Lobbying, as amended 1989.

Texas

4297

Lobbyist
Texas Ethics Commission
1101 Camino La Costa
PO Box 12070
Austin, TX 78711-2070
Phone: (512)406-0100

Credential Type: Lobbyist registration. **Duration of License:** Two years. **Authorization:** For lobbying the legislature and regulatory/executive agencies. **Requirements:** Lobbyist must register within five days after making first communication requiring registration.

Lobbyist must file monthly reports listing expenditures for the following: entertainment, including but not limited to food, beverages, maintenance of a hospitality room, sporting events, theatrical and musical events, and any transportation, lodging, or admission expenses incurred in connection with the entertainment; gifts, awards, loans, or other contributions.

Expenditures exceeding $50 a day for an official must be itemized. **Fees:** $300 registration fee, unless lobbyist is employed by a 501(c)(3) or 501(c)(4) organization (in which case the registration fee is $100). **Governing Statute:** Chapter 305 of the Texas Government Code.

Utah

4298

Lobbyist
Lt. Governor
203 State Capitol
Salt Lake City, UT 84114
Phone: (801)538-1040

Credential Type: Lobbyist registration. **Duration of License:** Two years. **Authorization:** For lobbying the legislature. **Requirements:** Lobbyist must register before doing any lobbying.

Lobbyist, continued

Lobbyist must file reports. **Fees:** $25 fee. **Governing Statute:** Utah Code Annotated, Chapter 11, Sections (amended) 76-8-103; (enacted) 20-14-6.5, 36-11-101-106, 36-11-201,202, 36-11-301-303, 36-11-401-405; Lobbyist Disclosure and Regulation Act, amended 1975, 1984, 1991; Lobbyist Registration Form, revised April 1991.

Vermont

4299

Lobbyist
Secretary of State
Lobbyist Registration
Pavilion Office Bldg.
Montpelier, VT 05602
Phone: (802)828-2175
Phone: (802)828-2363

Credential Type: Lobbyist registration. **Duration of License:** One year. **Authorization:** For lobbying the legislature and regulatory/executive agencies. **Requirements:** Lobbyist must register within 48 hours of commencing lobbying activities. Employer must register within 48 hours of employing lobbyist.

Both lobbyist and employer must file disclosure reports three times yearly including the following: a total of all expenditures, to the nearest $200, made by the lobbyist or the employer to influence legislative or administrative action; an itemized list of every gift, valued more than $5, made by or on behalf of a lobbyist to or at the request of one or more legislators or administrative officials, and with respect to each gift, the date made, the nature and value of the gift, the identity of administrative officials who requested the gift and the identity of any recipients of the gift, except gifts reported by an employer; (by the employer) the total amount of pro-rated compensation, to the nearest $200 paid to the lobbyists for lobbying. **Fees:** $25 initial registration fee for lobbyist and employer. $5 fee paid by employer for each lobbyist. $5 fee paid by lobbyist for each employer. **Governing Statute:** two V.S.A. 261—268, 1990.

Virginia

4300

Lobbyist
Secretary of the Commonwealth
PO Box 1-D
Capitol Sq. - Old Finance Bldg.
Richmond, VA 23201
Phone: (804)786-2441

Credential Type: Lobbyist registration. **Duration of License:** One session of legislature. **Authorization:** For lobbying the legislature. **Requirements:** Lobbyist must register before engaging in lobbying activity if lobbying takes place in Richmond; within five days if lobbying takes place outside Richmond.

Both lobbyist and employer must file joint returns on expenditure/payments made during the session. **Fees:** $30 registration fee. **Governing Statute:** Code of Virginia, Lobbying—Chapter 2.1, Sections 30-28.01 30-28.10:1, as amended by 1984 Acts of Assembly.

Washington

4301

Lobbyist
Public Disclosure Commission
403 Evergreen Plaza FJ-42
711 Capitol Way
Olympia, WA 98504
Phone: (206)753-1111

Credential Type: Lobbyist registration. **Duration of License:** Two years. **Authorization:** For lobbying the legislature, regulatory/executive agencies, and grass-roots campaigns. **Requirements:** Lobbyist must register within 30 days of being employed as a lobbyist, or before beginning lobbying, whichever comes first.

Both lobbyist and employer must file reports.

Lobbyist must file monthly reports showing total expenditures segregated into designated categories for lobbying activities.

Employer must file annual reports of expenditures and monthly reports of contributions they give to state and local office candidates, public officials, and political committees unless those contributions are made through and reported by the lobbyist. **Governing Statute:** RCW 42.17, amended 1977, 1979.

Credential Type: Grass-roots campaign sponsor registration. **Duration of License:** Two years. **Authorization:** For grass-roots campaigns. **Requirements:** Sponsor of grass-roots campaign—when expenditures for program addressed to the public and primarily intended to influence legislation exceed $1,000 in any three month period, or $500 in any month, the sponsor must register within 30 days of becoming a sponsor and file monthly reports of receipts and expenditures until the program is terminated, unless these expenditures are reported by a registered lobbyist, candidate, or political committee. **Governing Statute:** RCW 42.17, amended 1977, 1979.

West Virginia

4302

Lobbyist
West Virginia Ethics Commission
1207 Quarrier St., 4th Fl.
Charleston, WV 25301
Phone: (304)348-0664

Credential Type: Lobbyist registration. **Duration of License:** Two years. **Authorization:** For lobbying the legislature and regulatory/executive agencies. **Requirements:** Lobbyist must register before lobbying activity begins or within 30 days after being employed as a lobbyist, whichever is first.

Lobbyist must file reports showing the total amount of all expenditures made or incurred by the lobbyist for lobbying. Reports must also show subtotals according to financial category including meals and beverages; living accommodations; advertising; travel; contributions; gifts to government officers or employees or to members of the immediate family of such persons; other expenses or services. **Fees:** $20 fee. **Governing Statute:** Chapter 6B, Article 3. Lobbyists, 1989.

Wisconsin

4303

Lobbyist
Ethics Board
44 E. Mifflin St., Ste. 601
Madison, WI 53703-2800
Phone: (608)266-8123

Credential Type: Lobbyist registration. **Duration of License:** Two years. **Authorization:** For lobbying the legislature and regulatory/executive agencies. **Requirements:** Both lobbyist and employer must register.

Both lobbyist and employer must file reports.

Lobbyist must provide report for employer with all information needed by employer to file his/her report.

Employer must file a detailed statement twice yearly of all expenses paid or obligations incurred by both employer and lobbyist for all non-exempt lobbying activities (including copy of lobbyist's report to employer). **Fees:** $100 initial registration fee. $10 authorization statement fee. $10 verified statement fee (filed by principals whose expenditures are not expected to exceed $500 in a calendar year). **Governing Statute:** Wisconsin Statutes, Chapter 13 Legislative Branch, Subchapter III—Regulation of Lobbying 13.61—13.75, Wisconsin Act 338.1989.

Wyoming

4304

Lobbyist
Legislative Service Office
213 State Capitol
Cheyenne, WY 82002
Phone: (307)777-7881

Credential Type: Lobbyist registration. **Duration of License:** Two years. **Authorization:** For lobbying the legislature. **Requirements:** Lobbyist must register before engaging in lobbying activity.

No reports required. **Fees:** Less than $5 charge for registered lobbyist pin. **Governing Statute:** Wyoming Statutes, Title 28, Chapter 7, Sections 101—104.

Manufacturers' and Wholesale Sales Representatives

The following states grant licenses in this occupational category as of the date of publication: Kentucky, Michigan, Ohio, Pennsylvania, Vermont, Virginia.

Kentucky

4305

Stable-Area Supplier (Racetrack)
Kentucky State Racing Commission
PO Box 1080
Lexington, KY 40588
Phone: (606)254-7021

Credential Type: Supplier License. **Authorization:** Authorizes work in supplying horse feed, tack, medication, and food services. **Requirements:** Submit application and fingerprint card. Pay fee. **Fees:** $25 license fee.

Michigan

4306

Residential Builder Salesperson
Residential Builders Board
Bureau of Occupational & Professional Regulation
Dept. of Commerce
PO Box 30245
Lansing, MI 48909
Phone: (517)373-9153

Credential Type: License. **Duration of License:** One year. **Requirements:** Be an employee of a licensed residential builder or residential maintenance and alteration contractor. Comply with all rules of the Residential Builders Board. **Examination:** Written exam. **Fees:** $15 application processing fee. $30 initial exam fee. $30 initial license fee. $30 renewal fee. **Governing Statute:** The Occupational Code, Act 299 of 1980, Article 24, as amended.

Ohio

4307

Supply Salesman (Thoroughbred, Standardbred, and Quarter Horse Racing)
Ohio State Racing Commission
State Office Tower
77 S. High St., 18th Fl.
Columbus, OH 43266-0416
Phone: (614)466-2757

Credential Type: License Registration. **Requirements:** Submit application and fingerprint card. Pay fee. **Fees:** $10 registration fee.

Pennsylvania

4308

Salesman (Harness Racing)
Pennsylvania State Harness Racing Commission
2301 N. Cameron St.
Harrisburg, PA 17110-9408
Phone: (717)787-5196

Credential Type: License Registration. **Duration of License:** Three years. **Requirements:** Submit application, three photos, and fingerprint card. Pay fee. **Fees:** $30 registration fee. $5 duplicate license. $33 fingerprint processing fee.

Vermont

4309

Supplier (Racetrack)
Vermont Racing Commission
State Office Bldg.
Montpelier, VT 05602
Phone: (802)828-3429

Credential Type: License Registration. **Requirements:** Submit application and fingerprint card. Pay fee. **Fees:** $2 registration fee. $2 duplicate license.

Virginia

4310

Pharmaceutical Representative (Racetrack)
Virginia Racing Commission
PO Box 1123
Richmond, VA 23208
Phone: (804)371-7363

Credential Type: License Registration. **Requirements:** Submit application and fingerprint card. Pay fee. **Fees:** $25 registration fee.

Marketing, Advertising, and Public Relations Managers and Promoters

The following states grant licenses in this occupational category as of the date of publication:

Alabama	Arkansas	Florida	Iowa	Minnesota	New Mexico	Tennessee
Alaska	California	Illinois	Maine	Missouri	North Dakota	Texas
Arizona	Connecticut	Indiana	Massachusetts	Nebraska	South Carolina	Washington

Alabama

4311

Wrestling Matchmaker
State Athletic Commission
50 N. Ripley St., Rm. 4121
Montgomery, AL 36132
Phone: (205)242-1380

Credential Type: License. **Duration of License:** One year. **Fees:** $150 license fee.

4312

Wrestling Promoter
State Athletic Commission
50 N. Ripley St., Rm. 4121
Montgomery, AL 36132
Phone: (205)242-1380

Credential Type: License. **Duration of License:** One year. **Fees:** $500 license fee.

Alaska

4313

Concert Promoter
Dept. of Commerce and Economic Development
Div. of Occupational Licensing
Concert Promoters Registration
PO Box 110806
Juneau, AK 99811-0806
Phone: (907)465-3811
Fax: (907)465-2974

Credential Type: Promoter's Certificate of Registration. **Duration of License:** Two years. **Authorization:** To engage in the business of promoting concerts. **Requirements:** Concert promoter's bond or cash deposit in the amount of $5,000. A time certificate of deposit or savings passbook can be accepted in lieu of bond. **Exemptions:** Registration not required for concerts promoted, organized, or produced by a nonprofit corporation, society, or group; or by a promoter for presentation within a municipality having a population of less than 10,000 persons. **Fees:** $30 application fee. $60 initial registration fee. **Governing Statute:** Alaska Statutes 08.92.

4314

Promoter, Boxing and Wrestling Matches
Dept. of Commerce and Economic Development
Div. of Occupational Licensing
Athletic Commission
PO Box D-LIC
Juneau, AK 99811-0800
Phone: (907)465-2534
Fax: (907)465-2974

Credential Type: License. **Duration of License:** Six months or one year. **Requirements:** File a bond of $1,000 in cities of less than 10,000 inhabitants, $2500 in cities of more than 10,000 inhabitants. Report of contest required within three days before contest is held. Submit financial statement, two letters of recommendation, and full credit report. **Governing Statute:** Alaska Statutes 05.05 and 08.10. Professional Regulations 12 AAC 06.

Arizona

4315

Matchmaker
Boxing Commission
1645 W. Jefferson, Rm. 212
Phoenix, AZ 85007
Phone: (602)542-1417

Credential Type: License. **Requirements:** Contact the commission for an application.

4316

Promoter
Boxing Commission
1645 W. Jefferson, Rm. 212
Phoenix, AZ 85007
Phone: (602)542-1417

Credential Type: License. **Requirements:** Contact the commission for an application.

Arkansas

4317

Athletic Promoter/Matchmaker
Arkansas Athletic Commission
Quawpaw Towers, Rm. 2A
Little Rock, AR 72201
Phone: (501)371-2110

Credential Type: License. **Duration of License:** One year. **Requirements:** License based on experience listed on application. License must be granted and signed by the Post Commander of a local unit of a statewide patriotic organization, chartered by a special Act of Congress. (VFW or American Legion). **Examination:** No. **Fees:** $60 License (Promoter). $60 License (Matchmaker). $35 Renewal.

California

4318

Amateur Boxing Promoter
Athletic Commission
1424 Howe Ave., Ste. 33
Sacramento, CA 95814-6200
Phone: (916)920-7300

Credential Type: License. **Duration of License:** One year. **Requirements:** Submit application and pay fee. **Fees:** $50 license fee. $50 renewal fee.

4319

Assistant Matchmaker (Boxing, Kickboxing, or Martial Arts)
Athletic Commission
1424 Howe Ave., Ste. 33
Sacramento, CA 95814-6200
Phone: (916)920-7300

Credential Type: License. **Duration of License:** One year. **Requirements:** Submit application and pay fee. **Fees:** $75 license fee. $75 renewal fee.

4320

Matchmaker (Boxing, Kickboxing, or Martial Arts)
Athletic Commission
1424 Howe Ave., Ste. 33
Sacramento, CA 95814-6200
Phone: (916)920-7300

Credential Type: License. **Duration of License:** One year. **Requirements:** Submit application and pay fee. **Fees:** $100 license fee. $100 renewal fee.

4321

Professional Athletic Promoter
Athletic Commission
1424 Howe Ave., Ste. 33
Sacramento, CA 95814-6200
Phone: (916)920-7300

Credential Type: License. **Duration of License:** One year. **Requirements:** Submit application and pay fee. **Fees:** $200 license fee. $200 renewal fee.

Connecticut

4322

Matchmaker (Boxing and Wrestling)
Athletic Div.
Consumer Protection Dept.
165 Capitol Ave.
Hartford, CT 06106
Phone: (203)566-3843

Credential Type: License. **Requirements:** Contact licensing body for application information.

4323

Promoter (Boxing and Wrestling)
Athletic Div.
Consumer Protection Dept.
165 Capitol Ave.
Hartford, CT 06106
Phone: (203)566-3843

Credential Type: License. **Requirements:** Contact licensing body for application information.

4324

Public Relations Employee (Racetrack)
Connecticut Div. of Special Revenue
Russell Rd.
PO Box 11424
Newington, CT 06111-0424
Phone: (203)566-2756

Credential Type: License Registration. **Requirements:** Submit application and fingerprint card. Pay fee. **Fees:** $5 registration fee.

4325

Publicist (Racetrack)
Connecticut Div. of Special Revenue
Russell Rd.
PO Box 11424
Newington, CT 06111-0424
Phone: (203)566-2756

Credential Type: License Registration. **Requirements:** Submit application and fingerprint card. Pay fee. **Fees:** $5 registration fee.

4326

Publicity Director (Racetrack)
Connecticut Div. of Special Revenue
Russell Rd.
PO Box 11424
Newington, CT 06111-0424
Phone: (203)566-2756

Credential Type: License Registration. **Requirements:** Submit application and fingerprint card. Pay fee. **Fees:** $5 registration fee.

Florida

4327

Horse Show Promoter (Racetrack)
Florida Dept. of Business
Div. of Pari-Mutuel Wagering
Licensing Section
725 S. Bronough St.
Tallahassee, FL 32399-1037
Phone: (904)488-9161

Credential Type: License Registration Code 1075. **Requirements:** Submit application and fingerprint card. Pay fee. **Fees:** $75 registration fee.

Illinois

4328

Associate Director of Sales/Sales Manager (Gaming Industry)
Illinois Gaming Board
PO Box 19474
Springfield, IL 62794-9474
Phone: (217)524-0228

Credential Type: Sales Director/Manager License. **Duration of License:** One year. **Requirements:** At least 18 years of age. U.S. citizen or legal alien. College degree in marketing. Minimum of five years of marketing and/or sales experience with a service industry. **Reciprocity:** No. **Fees:** $75 application fee. $50 annual renewal fee. **Governing Statute:** Illinois Revised Statutes, Chapter 120.

4329

Director of Marketing and Public Relations (Gaming)
Illinois Gaming Board
PO Box 19474
Springfield, IL 62794-9474
Phone: (217)524-0228

Credential Type: Director of Marketing License. **Duration of License:** One year.

Requirements: At least 18 years of age. College degree in marketing. Must have five or more years experience in a service related business as a marketing manager. U.S. citizen or legal alien as specified by the federal employment eligibility requirement. **Reciprocity:** No. **Fees:** $75 application/initial license fee. $50 renewal fee. **Governing Statute:** Illinois Revised Statutes, Chapter 120.

4330

Match-Maker (Boxing/Wrestling)
Illinois Dept. of Professional Regulations
State of Illinois Ctr.
100 W. Randolph, Ste. 9-300
Chicago, IL 60601
Phone: (312)814-2719

Credential Type: Registration. **Duration of License:** Lifetime. **Requirements:** Submit registration to board. Must re-register if original information changes. **Reciprocity:** No. **Governing Statute:** The Illinois Professional Boxing and Wrestling Act. Illinois Revised Statutes 1991, Chapter 111.

4331

Professional Boxing Promoter
Illinois Dept. of Professional Regulation
State of Illinois Ctr.
100 W. Randolph, Ste. 9-300
Chicago, IL 60601
Phone: (312)814-2719

Credential Type: Professional Boxing Promoter License. **Duration of License:** Two years. **Requirements:** At least 18 years of age. Good moral character. Have basic knowledge of the sport of boxing. Must appear before the State Athletic Board to prove integrity, financial stability, and knowledge of the responsibility of a boxing promoter. Must be bonded at no less than $5,000. Must place a $5,000 cashier's check or money order with the Board until the completion of six promotions. Submit application, two recent photos, and a sworn statement that applicant is not in violation of any federal, state, or local boxing laws. **Reciprocity:** No. **Fees:** $300 initial license fee. $300 renewal fee. **Governing Statute:** The Professional Boxing and Wrestling Act, Illinois Statutes 1991.

4332

Regional Sales Manager (Gaming)
Illinois Gaming Board
PO Box 19474
Springfield, IL 62794-9474
Phone: (217)524-0228

Credential Type: Regional Sales Manager License. **Duration of License:** One year. **Requirements:** At least 18 years of age. U.S. citizen or legal alien as specified by Federal employability requirement. No felony convictions. Marketing degree. Must have three to five years of marketing experience in a service based industry. **Reciprocity:** No. **Fees:** $75 application/initial license fee. $50 renewal fee. **Governing Statute:** Illinois Revised Statutes, Chapter 120.

4333

Wrestling Promoter
Illinois Dept. of Professional Regulations
State of Illinois Ctr.
100 W. Randolph, Ste. 9-300
Chicago, IL 60601
Phone: (312)814-2719

Credential Type: Wrestling Promoter Permit. **Duration of License:** Two years. **Requirements:** Good moral character. Financially stable. Post surety bond of at least $5,000. Must have proof of integrity and knowledge of the responsibilities of a wrestling promoter. Submit application with sworn statement attesting that the applicant is not currently in violation of any federal, state, or local laws governing wrestling. **Reciprocity:** No. **Fees:** $300 initial license fee. $300 renewal fee. **Governing Statute:** The Illinois Professional Boxing and Wrestling Act, Illinois Revised Statutes 1991, Chapter 111.

Indiana

4334

Matchmaker (Boxing)
Boxing Commission
Examination Administrative Div.
Professional Licensing Agency
1021 State Office Bldg.
Indianapolis, IN 46204
Phone: (317)232-3897

Credential Type: License. **Requirements:** Contact licensing body for application information.

4335

Promoter (Boxing)
Boxing Commission
Examination Administrative Div.
Professional Licensing Agency
1021 State Office Bldg.
Indianapolis, IN 46204
Phone: (317)232-3897

Credential Type: License. **Requirements:** Contact licensing body for application information.

Iowa

4336

Entertainment Director (Riverboat Gambling)
Iowa Racing and Gaming Commission
Lucas State Office Bldg.
Des Moines, IA 50319
Phone: (515)281-7352

Credential Type: License Registration. **Requirements:** Submit application and pay fees. **Fees:** $50 license fee.

Maine

4337

Amateur Boxing Promoter
Athletic Commission
Dept. of Professional and Financial Regulation
Div. of Licensing and Enforcement
State House Station 35
Augusta, ME 04333
Phone: (207)582-8723

Credential Type: License. **Duration of License:** One year. **Requirements:** Knowledge of laws and rules. Submit application and pay fee. **Fees:** No fee required. **Governing Statute:** 32 M.S.R.A. Chap. 115.

4338

Amateur Kickboxing Promoter
Athletic Commission
Dept. of Professional and Financial Regulation
Div. of Licensing and Enforcement
State House Station 35
Augusta, ME 04333
Phone: (207)582-8723

Credential Type: License. **Duration of License:** One year. **Requirements:** Knowledge of laws and rules. Submit application

Maine

Amateur Kickboxing Promoter, continued

and pay fee. **Fees:** No fee required. **Governing Statute:** 32 M.S.R.A. Chap. 115.

4339

Kickboxing Matchmaker
Athletic Commission
Dept. of Professional and Financial Regulation
Div. of Licensing and Enforcement
State House Station 35
Augusta, ME 04333
Phone: (207)582-8723

Credential Type: License. **Duration of License:** One year. **Requirements:** Knowledge of laws and rules. Submit application and pay fee. **Fees:** $20 license fee. **Governing Statute:** 32 M.S.R.A. Chap. 115.

4340

Professional Boxing Promoter
Athletic Commission
Dept. of Professional and Financial Regulation
Div. of Licensing and Enforcement
State House Station 35
Augusta, ME 04333
Phone: (207)582-8723

Credential Type: License. **Duration of License:** One year. **Requirements:** Knowledge of laws and rules. Submit application and pay fee. **Fees:** $50 to $100 (depending on location) license fee. **Governing Statute:** 32 M.S.R.A. Chap. 115.

4341

Professional Wrestling Promoter
Athletic Commission
Dept. of Professional and Financial Regulation
Div. of Licensing and Enforcement
State House Station 35
Augusta, ME 04333
Phone: (207)582-8723

Credential Type: License. **Duration of License:** One year. **Requirements:** Knowledge of laws and rules. Submit application and pay fee. **Fees:** $50 to $100 (depending on location) license fee. **Governing Statute:** 32 M.S.R.A. Chap. 115.

4342

Wrestling Matchmaker
Athletic Commission
Dept. of Professional and Financial Regulation
Div. of Licensing and Enforcement
State House Station 35
Augusta, ME 04333
Phone: (207)582-8723

Credential Type: License. **Duration of License:** One year. **Requirements:** Knowledge of laws and rules. Submit application and pay fee. **Fees:** $25 license fee. **Governing Statute:** 32 M.S.R.A. Chap. 115.

Massachusetts

4343

Matchmaker (Boxing)
State Boxing Commission
Dept. of Public Safety
One Ashburton Pl., Rm. 1310
Boston, MA 02108
Phone: (617)727-3296

Credential Type: License. **Requirements:** Submit application and pay fee. **Fees:** Contact commission for fee. **Governing Statute:** Annotated Laws of Massachusetts, Chap. 147.

Minnesota

4344

Promoter (Boxing and Kick Boxing)
Board of Boxing
133 E. 7th and Robert Sts.
St. Paul, MN 55101
Phone: (612)296-2501

Credential Type: License. **Duration of License:** One year. **Requirements:** Submit application and pay fee. **Fees:** Contact board for fees. **Governing Statute:** Minnesota Statutes, Chap. 341. Minnesota Rules 2200-2299.

Missouri

4345

Matchmaker (Boxing, Wrestling, or Karate)
Office of Athletics
Dept. of Economic Development
3605 Missouri Blvd.
PO Box 1335
Jefferson City, MO 65102
Phone: (314)751-0243

Credential Type: License. **Duration of License:** One year. **Requirements:** Application for license must be submitted no later than 10 business days prior to a professional exhibition and seven days prior to an amateur exhibition. **Fees:** $10 license fee. **Governing Statute:** four CSR 40.

4346

Promoter (Boxing, Wrestling, or Karate)
Office of Athletics
Dept. of Economic Development
3605 Missouri Blvd.
PO Box 1335
Jefferson City, MO 65102
Phone: (314)751-0243

Credential Type: License. **Duration of License:** One year. **Requirements:** Application for license must be submitted no later than 10 business days prior to a professional exhibition and seven days prior to an amateur exhibition. Must post surety bond of $2500. **Fees:** $50 professional license fee. $10 amateur license fee. $5 nonprofit (patriotic, benevelont, fraternal, or religious) license fee. **Governing Statute:** four CSR 40.

Nebraska

4347

Boxing Promoter
Nebraska Athletic Commission
301 Centennial Mall S.
PO Box 94743
Lincoln, NE 68509
Phone: (402)471-2009

Credential Type: License. **Duration of License:** One year. **Requirements:** Must be approved by the Nebraska Athletic Commision. **Fees:** $10 application fee. $100 professional license fee. $25 amateur license fee.

New Mexico

4348

Matchmaker (Boxing, Wrestling, Martial Arts, and Kick Boxing)
Athletic Commission
Dept. of Regulation and Licensing
PO Box 25101
725 St. Michael's Dr.
Santa Fe, NM 87504
Phone: (505)827-7172

Credential Type: License. **Duration of License:** One year. **Requirements:** Submit application and pay fee. **Fees:** $25 license fee.

North Dakota

4349

Boxing Promoter
North Dakota Secretary of State
600 E. Blvd. Ave.
Capitol Bldg., 1st Fl.
Bismarck, ND 58505
Phone: (701)224-4284

Credential Type: License. **Duration of License:** One year. **Requirements:** Submit application and pay fee. **Fees:** $100 license fee. (The license fee for individuals holding more than one license is the highest of the applicable license fees.)

South Carolina

4350

Boxing-Wrestling Matchmaker
State Athletic Commission
PO Box 2461
Columbia, SC 29202
Phone: (803)254-3661

Credential Type: License. **Requirements:** Submit application and pay fee. **Fees:** $20 license fee.

4351

Promoter (Boxing)
State Athletic Commission
PO Box 2461
Columbia, SC 29202
Phone: (803)254-3661

Credential Type: License. **Requirements:** Submit application and pay fee. **Fees:** $50 license fee.

Tennessee

4352

Boxing Promoter
Boxing and Racing Board
500 James Robertson Pky.
Nashville, TN 37243
Phone: (615)741-2384

Credential Type: License. **Requirements:** 18 years old. Have a $15,000 surety bond. **Examination:** Yes. **Reciprocity:** Yes. **Fees:** $25 Renewal.

Texas

4353

Boxing Matchmaker
Texas Dept. of Licensing & Regulation
PO Box 12157
Austin, TX 78711
Phone: (512)463-5522

Credential Type: License. **Requirements:** Submit application and pay fee. **Fees:** $75 license fee. **Governing Statute:** VACS 8501-1, 16 TAC 61.1.

4354

Boxing Promoter
Texas Dept. of Licensing & Regulation
PO Box 12157
Austin, TX 78711
Phone: (512)463-5522

Credential Type: License. **Authorization:** Valid only in the limits of the city for which license is granted. **Requirements:** $10,000 for broker estate if person dies from injuries. Financial statement prepared by CPA or $10,000 performance bond. Surety bond of $5,000. Insurance coverage. **Examination:** Hearing held in Austin. **Fees:** $500 minimum license fee. $300 minimum surety bond. **Governing Statute:** VACS 8501-1, 16 TAC 61.1.

Washington

4355

Matchmaker (Professional Boxing/ Wrestling)
Professional Athletic Commission
2626 12th Court, GT-17
Olympia, WA 98504-8321
Phone: (206)753-3713

Credential Type: Matchmaker License. **Duration of License:** One year. **Requirements:** Submit application with current photo. **Fees:** $40 license fee.

4356

Promoter (Professional Boxing/ Wrestling)
Professional Athletic Commission
2626 12th Court, GT-17
Olympia, WA 98504-8321
Phone: (206)753-3713

Credential Type: Promoter License. **Duration of License:** One year. **Requirements:** Submit application. Post bond of $10,000. Secure medical insurance to cover each event. **Fees:** No fee.

Material Moving Equipment Operators

The following states grant licenses in this occupational category as of the date of publication: District of Columbia, Illinois, Massachusetts, Montana, New Jersey, New York, Oklahoma, Rhode Island.

District of Columbia

4357

Operating Engineer
License and Certification Div.
Occupational and Professional Licensure Administration
Consumer and Regulatory Affairs Dept.
PO Box 37200
Washington, DC 20013-7200
Phone: (202)727-7823
Phone: (202)727-7480

Alternate Information: 614 H St., NW, Washington, DC 20001.

Credential Type: License and certification. **Duration of License:** One year. **Authorization:** Ten classes of license are issued for steam and other operating engineers. **Requirements:** Must meet appropriate experience requirements for each class of license. **Examination:** Written examination. **Fees:** $10 application fee. $5 license fee. $10 license fee. $10 exam fee. $20 annual renewal fee. **Governing Statute:** Municipal Regulations, Title 17, Chap. 4.

Illinois

4358

Electrical Hoisting Engineer (Coal Mine)
Illinois Dept. of Mines and Minerals
PO Box 10137
300 W. Jefferson St., Ste. 300
Springfield, IL 62791-0137
Phone: (217)782-6791

Credential Type: Electrical Hoisting Engineer Certificate. **Duration of License:** No expiration. **Requirements:** At least 21 years of age. U.S. citizen. Complete a training course approved by the Department. Submit 30 hour training log signed by a certified Hoisting Engineer. Have two years experience with electrical hoisting equipment. **Examination:** Written examination. **Reciprocity:** No. **Fees:** No fee. **Governing Statute:** 1989 Illinois Revised Statutes, Chapter 96 1/2.

4359

Metal Mine Hoisting Engineer
Illinois Dept. of Mines & Minerals
300 W. Jefferson St., Ste. 300
PO Box 10137
Springfield, IL 62791-0137
Phone: (217)782-6791

Credential Type: Metal Mine Hoisting Certificate. **Duration of License:** Permanent. **Requirements:** At least 21 years of age. U.S. citizen. Must have a minimum of six months experience. Requires knowledge of laws relating to signals. **Examination:** Written and oral examinations. **Reciprocity:** No. **Fees:** No fee. **Governing Statute:** 1989 Illinois Revised Statutes, Chapter 96 1/2.

Massachusetts

4360

Elevator Operator
Dept. of Public Safety
Div. of Inspection
Elevator Inspection Section
One Ashburton Pl.
Boston, MA 02108
Phone: (617)727-3200

Credential Type: License. **Requirements:** Contact licensing body for application information. **Governing Statute:** Massachusetts General Laws, Chap. 143.

4361

Hoisting Operator
Dept. of Public Safety
Div. of Inspection
Engineering Section
One Ashburton Pl.
Boston, MA 02108
Phone: (617)727-3200

Credential Type: Class A License. **Authorization:** Valid for all mechanical hoisting equipment other than steam. **Requirements:** Demonstrate practical knowledge of all working parts of electrical, wire, cable, and hydraulically operated hoisting machinery. **Examination:** Written and oral examination. **Fees:** $60 license and exam fee. **Governing Statute:** Massachusetts General Laws, Chap. 146.

Credential Type: Class B License. **Authorization:** Valid for hydraulically operated machinery as well as hoisting machinery that has an internal combustion engine with either cable or a hydraulically operated hoist. **Requirements:** Demonstrate practical knowledge of all working parts of electrical, wire, cable, and hydraulically operated hoisting machinery. **Examination:** Written and oral examinations. **Fees:** $60 license and exam fee. **Governing Statute:** Massachusetts General Laws, Chap. 146.

Credential Type: Class C License. **Authorization:** Valid for hydraulically operated machinery. **Requirements:** Demonstrate practical knowledge of all working parts of hydraulically operated hoisting machinery. **Examination:** Written and oral examinations. **Fees:** $60 license and exam fee. **Governing Statute:** Massachusetts General Laws, Chap. 146.

Montana

4362

Hoisting Engineer
Montana Safety Bureau
Div. of Worker's Compensation
5 S. Last Chance Gulch
Helena, MT 59601
Phone: (406)444-6401

Credential Type: Third Class Hoisting Engineer. **Duration of License:** One year. **Requirements:** 18 years of age. Experience with equipment in the class for which licensure is sought. **Examination:** Written. **Fees:** $12 license fee. $4 renewal fee. **Governing Statute:** Montana Code Annotated 50-76-101 through 50-76-109.

Credential Type: Second Class Hoisting Engineer. **Duration of License:** One year. **Requirements:** 18 years of age. Physical exam. Two years experience with equipment in the class for which licensure is sought. **Examination:** Written. **Fees:** $20 license fee. $4 renewal fee. **Governing Statute:** Montana Code Annotated 50-76-101 through 50-76-109.

Credential Type: First Class Hoisting Engineer. **Duration of License:** One year. **Requirements:** 18 years of age. Physical exam. Three years experience with equipment in the class for which licensure is sought. **Examination:** Written. **Fees:** $30 license fee. $4 renewal fee. **Governing Statute:** Montana Code Annotated 50-76-101 through 50-76-109.

New Jersey

4363

Long Boom Crane Operator
New Jersey Dept. of Labor
Office of Boiler and Pressure Vessel
 Compliance
CN392
Trenton, NJ 08625-0392
Phone: (609)292-2921

Credential Type: Long Boom Hoisting Engineer, Blue Seal, 7-C License. **Duration of License:** Three years. **Requirements:** 18 years of age. Six months experience as a crane operator, three of which were on long boom cranes. **Examination:** Written. **Fees:** $15 exam fee. $10 raise of grade or additional classification fee. $10 renewal fee. **Governing Statute:** NJSA 34:7. NJAC 12:90.

4364

Operating Engineer - Gold Seal
New Jersey Dept. of Labor
Office of Boiler and Pressure Vessel
 Compliance
CN392
Trenton, NJ 08625-0392
Phone: (609)292-2921

Credential Type: 1st Class Engineer, Gold Seal, 1-A, 2-A, 3-A, 8-A or 9-A. **Duration of License:** Three years. **Requirements:** A valid New Jersey 2nd grade license and one-year's subsequent experience as a chief engineer in a plant requiring supervision by a 2nd grade engineer; or a 2nd grade license and two years of subsequent experience as an operating engineer in a plant requiring supervision by a 1st grade engineer. **Examination:** Written. **Fees:** $15 exam fee. $10 raise of grade or additional classification fee. $10 renewal fee. **Governing Statute:** NJSA 34:7. NJAC 12:90.

4365

Operating Engineer - Red Seal
New Jersey Dept. of Labor
Office of Boiler and Pressure Vessel
 Compliance
CN392
Trenton, NJ 08625-0392
Phone: (609)292-2921

Credential Type: 2nd Class Engineer, Red Seal, 1-B, 2-B, 3-B, 8-B or 9-B. **Duration of License:** Three years. **Requirements:** Must hold a valid New Jersey 3rd grade license. At least one year's subsequent practical experience in the operation of equipment requiring supervision by a 2nd grade or 1st grade engineer. **Examination:** Written. **Fees:** $15 exam fee. $10 raise of grade or additional classification. $10 renewal fee. **Governing Statute:** NJSA 34:7. NJAC 12:90.

New York

4366

Crane Operator
New York State Dept. of Labor
Div. of Safety and Health
One Main St., Rm. 801
Brooklyn, NY 11201
Phone: (718)797-7659

Credential Type: Certificate. **Duration of License:** Three years. **Requirements:** Minimum of three years of experience working with cranes under the direct supervision of a certified crane operator. 21 years of age. **Examination:** Written and practical. **Fees:** $60 license fee. **Governing Statute:** Article 28D, General Business Law.

Oklahoma

4367

Hoisting Engineer (Underground)
State Mining Commission
4040 N. Lincoln, Ste. 107
Oklahoma City, OK 73105
Phone: (405)521-3859

Credential Type: Certificate. **Duration of License:** Lifetime. **Requirements:** State resident. One year of practical hoisting experience. **Examination:** Hoisting Engineer Examination. **Fees:** $10 exam fee. $10 certification fee.

Rhode Island

4368

Hoisting Engineer
State Board of Hoisting Engineers
Div. of Professional Regulation
Rhode Island Dept. of Labor
220 Elmwood Ave.
Providence, RI 02907

Credential Type: Hoisting Engineer License—Limited License A. **Duration of License:** One year. **Authorization:** Authorizes licensee to only operate equipment specified on license. **Requirements:** At least 18 years of age. Complete a three-year union apprenticeship or be self-taught. **Examination:** Written or oral examination. **Reciprocity:** No. **Fees:** $30 application fee. $35 license fee.

Credential Type: Hoisting Engineer License—Limited License B. **Duration of License:** One year. **Authorization:** Authorizes work done under the employment of one employer. **Requirements:** At least 18 years of age. Complete a three-year union apprenticeship or be self-taught. **Examination:** Written or oral examination. **Reciprocity:** No. **Fees:** $30 application fee. $35 license fee.

Credential Type: Hoisting Engineer License—Full License. **Duration of License:** One year. **Authorization:** Authorizes licensee to operate all hoisting and excavating equipment. **Requirements:** At least 18 years of age. Complete a three-year union apprenticeship or be self-taught. **Examination:** Written or oral examination. **Reciprocity:** No. **Fees:** $30 application fee. $35 license fee. $40 renewal fee.

Medical Assistants

The following states grant licenses in this occupational category as of the date of publication: Arkansas, Louisiana, Nevada, Ohio, South Dakota, Texas, Virginia.

Arkansas

4369

Dispensing Optician Assistant
Arkansas Board of Dispensing Opticians
107 Central Ave.
Searcy, AR 72143
Phone: (501)268-1673

Credential Type: License. **Requirements:** Must be working under the direct and physical supervision of a licensed Dispensing Optician. **Examination:** No. **Fees:** $50 Application. $25 License. $25 Renewal.

Louisiana

4370

Acupuncture Assistant
State Board of Medical Examiners
830 Union St., Ste. 100
New Orleans, LA 70112
Phone: (504)524-6763

Credential Type: Certificate to Practice. **Duration of License:** One year. **Authorization:** Must work under the supervision of a licensed physician. **Requirements:** Complete 36 months of training in a school or clinic of traditional Chinese acupuncture. **Fees:** $100 processing fee. $25 renewal fee. **Governing Statute:** R.S. 37:1356-1360.

Nevada

4371

Medical Laboratory Assistant
Bureau of Regulatory Health Services
505 E. King St., Rm. 202
Carson City, NV 89710
Phone: (702)687-4475

Credential Type: License. **Requirements:** High school diploma. Six months of training in laboratory procedures. **Fees:** $25 license fee. $18 renewal fee.

Ohio

4372

Medical/First Aid Employee (Thoroughbred, Standardbred, and Quarter Horse Racing)
Ohio State Racing Commission
State Office Tower
77 S. High St., 18th Fl.
Columbus, OH 43266-0416
Phone: (614)466-2757

Credential Type: License Registration. **Requirements:** Submit application and fingerprint card. Pay fee. **Fees:** $10 registration fee.

South Dakota

4373

Medical Assistant
State Board of Medical and Osteopathic Examiners
Dept. of Commerce and Consumer Affairs
1323 S. Minnesota Ave.
Sioux Falls, SD 57105
Phone: (605)336-1965

Credential Type: Medical Assistant Registration. **Duration of License:** Two years. **Requirements:** Graduation from an approved medical assistant program. **Fees:** $10 registration fee. $5 renewal fee.

Texas

4374

Medical Staff Employee (Racetrack)
Texas Racing Commission
PO Box 12080
Austin, TX 78711
Phone: (512)794-8461

Credential Type: License Registration. **Requirements:** Submit application and fingerprint card. Pay fee. **Fees:** $20 registration fee.

Virginia

4375

Medical Employee (Racetrack)
Virginia Racing Commission
PO Box 1123
Richmond, VA 23208
Phone: (804)371-7363

Credential Type: License Registration. **Requirements:** Submit application and fingerprint card. Pay fee. **Fees:** $10 registration fee.

4376

Podiatrist's Assistant
Board of Medicine
1601 Rolling Hills Dr.
Richmond, VA 23261
Phone: (804)662-9920

Credential Type: License. **Duration of License:** One year. **Requirements:** Must complete an approved and accredited course of study. **Examination:** Yes. **Fees:** $100 application fee. $25 registration fee.

Mining, Quarrying, and Tunneling Occupations

The following states grant licenses in this occupational category as of the date of publication:

Alabama	Illinois	Michigan	New Jersey	Oregon	Vermont
Arizona	Iowa	Minnesota	New York	Rhode Island	Washington
Arkansas	Kentucky	Montana	North Dakota	South Carolina	West Virginia
Connecticut	Louisiana	Nebraska	Ohio	Texas	Wyoming
Idaho	Maryland	Nevada	Oklahoma	Utah	

Alabama

4377

Coal Mine Foreman (surface)
Board of Mine Examiners
Div. of Safety and Inspection
1816 8th Ave. N.
PO Box 10444
Birmingham, AL 35202
Phone: (205)254-1275

Credential Type: License. **Duration of License:** One year. **Requirements:** 18 years of age. Must have worked under the supervision of a licensed surface coal mine foreman for at least one year. **Examination:** Written examination.

4378

Coal Mine Foreman (underground)
Board of Mine Examiners
Div. of Safety and Inspection
1816 8th Ave., N.
PO Box 10444
Birmingham, AL 35202
Phone: (205)254-1275

Credential Type: License. **Requirements:** 23 years of age and a U.S. citizen. Four years practical mining experience; or three years experience and a university degree; or an associate degree in mine technology. **Examination:** Written, oral, and practical examinations. **Fees:** $20 registration and exam fee.

4379

Mine Electrician
Board of Mine Examiners
Div. of Safety and Inspection
1816 8th Ave. N.
PO Box 10444
Birmingham, AL 35202
Phone: (205)254-1300

Credential Type: Certificate. **Duration of License:** One year. **Requirements:** One year of work experience. Must have completed 90 clock hours of course work. Renewal requires 16 hours of continuing education. **Examination:** Written examination.

4380

Mine Fireboss
Board of Mine Examiners
Div. of Safety and Inspection
PO Box 10444
Birmingham, AL 35202
Phone: (205)254-1275

Credential Type: License. **Requirements:** 23 years of age. Citizen of the U.S. Must have three years of practical experience. **Examination:** Written, oral, and practical examinations. **Fees:** $20 examination fee.

Arizona

4381

Well Driller (Water)
Arizona Dept. of Water Resources
15 S. 15th Ave.
Phoenix, AZ 85007
Phone: (602)542-1581
Fax: (602)256-0506

Credential Type: Well drilling license. **Duration of License:** One year. **Requirements:** Good moral character and reputation. Have three years experience dealing specifically with the type of drilling for which license is being applied. Demonstration of a high degree of understanding and knowledge of well drilling techniques may reduce experience requirement to not less than two years. Pass examination given by the department. **Examination:** Examination consists of sections on legal requirements, general knowledge of water wells, and specialized drilling techniques. **Fees:** $50 license fee.

Credential Type: Single well license. **Duration of License:** One year. **Authorization:** To drill a single well. **Requirements:** Submit application and pass single well examination. **Examination:** Single well examination covering abandonment techniques, minimum well construction requirements, and drilling techniques applicable to the proposed design of the well.

Arkansas

4382

Pump Installer
Waterwell Construction Commission
One Capitol Mall, Ste. 2C
Little Rock, AR 72201
Phone: (501)682-1025

Credential Type: License. **Requirements:** 18 years of age. Two years experience on-the-job training. **Examination:** Yes. **Fees:** $70 License. $70 Renewal.

4383

Waterwell Driller
Arkansas Waterwell Construction Commission
1 Capitol Mall, Ste. 22
Little Rock, AR 72201
Phone: (501)682-1025

Credential Type: License. **Duration of License:** One year. **Requirements:** 18 years of age. Two years work experience of on the job training. **Examination:** Yes. **Fees:** $70 License. $70 Renewal.

Connecticut

4384

Well Drilling Contractor
Plumbing and Piping Work Examining Board
Occupational Licensing Div.
Consumer Protection Dept.
165 Capitol Ave.
Hartford, CT 06106
Phone: (203)566-3275

Credential Type: Certificate of registration. **Requirements:** Contact licensing body for application information.

4385

Well Drilling Journeyman
Plumbing and Piping Work Examining Board
Occupational Licensing Div.
Consumer Protection Dept.
165 Capitol Ave.
Hartford, CT 06106
Phone: (203)566-3275

Credential Type: License. **Requirements:** Contact licensing body for application information.

Idaho

4386

Water Well Drilling Operator
Dept. of Water Resources
1301 N. Orchard
Statehouse Mail
Boise, ID 83706
Phone: (208)327-7900
Phone: (208)327-7956

Credential Type: Operator Permit. **Duration of License:** One year. **Requirements:** Submit application and pass examination. **Examination:** Written examination administered by the director. **Fees:** $25 license fee. $10 renewal fee. **Governing Statute:** Rules and Regulations, Water Well Driller's Licenses, Idaho Dept. of Water Resources.

4387

Water Well Drilling Supervisor
Dept. of Water Resources
1301 N. Orchard
Statehouse Mail
Boise, ID 83706
Phone: (208)327-7900
Phone: (208)327-7956

Credential Type: Well Drilling License. **Duration of License:** One year. **Requirements:** Must have been employed on a full-time basis for at least 30 months, under the supervision of a person holding a valid Idaho well driller's license. Up to 12 months of classroom study may be credited toward the experience requirement. Post bond of $5,000 to $20,000. **Examination:** Written and/or oral examination administered by the director. **Fees:** $25 license fee. $10 renewal fee. **Governing Statute:** Rules and Regulations, Water Well Driller's Licenses, Idaho Dept. of Water Resources.

Illinois

4388

Blaster
Illinois Dept. of Mines and Minerals
Land Reclamation Div.
300 W. Jefferson
PO Box 10197
Springfield, IL 62791-0197
Phone: (217)782-4970

Credential Type: Blaster Certificate. **Duration of License:** Five years. **Requirements:** Must successfully complete a blaster course which covers the material required by the state of Illinois. **Examination:** Written examination. **Reciprocity:** Yes, a six month certificate will be issued to applicants who received certification in a state with an OSMRE program. **Fees:** No fee. **Governing Statute:** Illinois Administrative Code 1850.

4389

Coal Mine Worker
Dept. of Mines and Minerals
PO Box 10137
300 W. Jefferson St., Ste. 300
Springfield, IL 62791-0137
Phone: (217)782-6791

Credential Type: First Class Worker Certificate of Competency. **Duration of License:** No expiration. **Requirements:** At least 18 years of age. U.S. citizen. An Associate degree in Coal Mining Technology and six months experience in coal mining or one complete year of experience at face of coal. First Aid and Modified Mine Rescue Training Certificate issued by the State of Illinois or a valid 5000-23 form. Submit a letter of verification from mine or mines worked that lists dates of employment and job classifications held. **Examination:** Oral examination. **Reciprocity:** No. **Fees:** $2 fee for duplicate face papers. **Governing Statute:** 1989 Illinois Revised Statutes, Chapter 96 1/2.

4390

Electrical Hoisting Engineer (Coal Mine)
Illinois Dept. of Mines and Minerals
PO Box 10137
300 W. Jefferson St., Ste. 300
Springfield, IL 62791-0137
Phone: (217)782-6791

Credential Type: Electrical Hoisting Engineer Certificate. **Duration of License:** No expiration. **Requirements:** At least 21 years of age. U.S. citizen. Complete a training course approved by the Department. Submit 30 hour training log signed by a certified Hoisting Engineer. Have two years experience with electrical hoisting equipment. **Examination:** Written examination. **Reciprocity:** No. **Fees:** No fee. **Governing Statute:** 1989 Illinois Revised Statutes, Chapter 96 1/2.

4391

Explosives Detonator and Storekeeper
Illinois Dept. of Mines and Minerals
503 E. Main St.
Benton, IL 62812-2599
Phone: (618)439-4320

Credential Type: Individual Explosives License. **Duration of License:** Three years. **Requirements:** At least 21 years of age. Good moral character. No recent felonies. Mentally and physically competent. Knowledge and experience in the handling and safe use of explosives. **Examination:** Explosives Exam 3. **Reciprocity:** No. **Fees:** $75 examination fee. $75 initial license fee. $75 renewal fee. $43 fingerprinting fee. **Governing Statute:** The Illinois Explosives Act, Illinois Administrative Code 62.

4392

Explosives Handler (Magazine)
Illinois Dept. of Mines and Minerals
503 E. Main St.
Benton, IL 62812-2599
Phone: (618)439-4320

Credential Type: Magazine License. **Duration of License:** One year. **Requirements:** Good moral character. At least 21 years of age. No recent felonies. Knowledge of explosives. **Reciprocity:** No. **Fees:** Fees range from $25 to $200 based on the amount and type of explosives. **Governing Statute:** The Illinois Explosives Act.

4393

Metal Mine Foreman
Illinois Dept. of Mines & Minerals
300 W. Jefferson St., Ste. 300
PO Box 10137
Springfield, IL 62791-0137
Phone: (217)782-6791

Credential Type: Metal Mine Foreman Certificate. **Duration of License:** Permanent. **Requirements:** At least 24 years of age. U.S. citizen. Four-year degree from an accredited engineering school and two years experience or four years experience without a degree. **Examination:** Written and oral examinations. **Reciprocity:** No. **Fees:** No fee. **Governing Statute:** 1989 Illinois Revised Statutes, Chapter 96 1/2.

4394

Metal Mine Hoisting Engineer
Illinois Dept. of Mines & Minerals
300 W. Jefferson St., Ste. 300
PO Box 10137
Springfield, IL 62791-0137
Phone: (217)782-6791

Credential Type: Metal Mine Hoisting Certificate. **Duration of License:** Permanent. **Requirements:** At least 21 years of age. U.S. citizen. Must have a minimum of six months experience. Requires knowledge of laws relating to signals. **Examination:** Written and oral examinations. **Reciprocity:** No. **Fees:** No fee. **Governing Statute:** 1989 Illinois Revised Statutes, Chapter 96 1/2.

4395

Mine Examiner
Illinois Dept. of Mines & Minerals
300 W. Jefferson St., Ste. 300
PO Box 10137
Springfield, IL 62791-0137
Phone: (217)782-6791

Credential Type: Mine Examiner Certificate. **Duration of License:** Permanent. **Requirements:** At least 21 years of age. U.S. citizen. Four years of practical underground mining experience. First Class Certificate of Competency issued by Department of Mines and Minerals. Approved first aid training and mine rescue methods course. Applicant will receive one year experiential credit for associate degree in Coal Mining Technology and two years credit for a degree in Mining Engineering. Must submit copy of degree with application. **Examination:** Written and oral examinations. **Reciprocity:** No. **Fees:** No fee. **Governing Statute:** 1989 Illinois Revised Statutes, Chapter 96 1/2.

Credential Type: Temporary Certificate. **Duration of License:** Six months or until next examination date. **Requirements:** Must have valid equivalent certificate issued by another state agency. Must submit photo copy of certificate. **Fees:** No fee. **Governing Statute:** 1989 Illinois Revised Statutes, Chapter 96 1/2.

4396

Mine Manager
Illinois Dept. of Mines & Minerals
300 W. Jefferson St., Ste. 300
PO Box 10137
Springfield, IL 62791-0137
Phone: (217)782-6791

Credential Type: Mine Manager Certificate. **Duration of License:** Permanent. **Requirements:** At least 23 years of age. U.S. citizen. Four years of practical underground mining experience. First Class Certificate of Competency issued by Department of Mines and Minerals or equivalent issued by another state. Approved first aid training and mine rescue methods course or a valid 5000-23 form. Applicant will receive one year experiential credit for associate degree in Coal Mining Technology and two years credit for a degree in Mining Engineering. **Examination:** Written and oral examinations. **Reciprocity:** No. **Fees:** No fee. **Governing Statute:** 1989 Illinois Revised Statutes, Chapter 96 1/2.

Credential Type: Temporary Certificate. **Duration of License:** Six months or until next examination date. **Requirements:** Must have valid equivalent certificate issued by another state agency. Must submit photo copy of certificate. **Fees:** No fee. **Governing Statute:** 1989 Illinois Revised Statutes, Chapter 96 1/2.

4397

Mine Rescue Station Assistant
Illinois Dept. of Mines & Minerals
300 W. Jefferson St., Ste. 300
PO Box 10137
Springfield, IL 62791-0137
Phone: (217)782-6791

Credential Type: Mine Rescue Station Assistant Certificate. **Duration of License:** Two years (unless currently employed in field which would allow a permanent certificate). **Requirements:** At least 18 years of age. U.S. citizen. Complete the equivalent of four years high school. Hold an Advanced First Aid and Mine Rescue Certificate of Competency issued by the Department of Mines and Minerals. Must have three years experience in underground gassy mines. Knowledge of department rules, mine rescue operation rules, and equipment and supplies. **Examination:** Written and oral examinations. **Reciprocity:** No. **Fees:** No fee. **Governing Statute:** 1989 Illinois Revised Statutes, Chapter 96 1/2.

Mining, Quarrying, and Tunneling Occupations

4398

Mine Rescue Station Supervisor
Illinois Dept. of Mines & Minerals
300 W. Jefferson St., Ste. 300
PO Box 10137
Springfield, IL 62791-0137
Phone: (217)782-6791

Credential Type: Mine Rescue Station Supervisor Certificate. **Duration of License:** Two years (unless currently employed in field which would allow a permanent certificate). **Requirements:** At least 18 years of age. U.S. citizen. Complete the equivalent of four years high school. Hold an Advanced First Aid and Mine Rescue Certificate of Competency issued by the Department of Mines and Minerals. Must have four years experience in underground gassy mines. Knowledge of department rules, mine rescue operation rules, and equipment and supplies. **Examination:** Written and oral examinations. **Reciprocity:** No. **Fees:** No fee. **Governing Statute:** 1989 Illinois Revised Statutes, Chapter 96 1/2.

4399

Shaft and Slope Examiner (Construction and Mining)
Illinois Dept. of Mines and Minerals
300 W. Jefferson St., Ste. 300
PO Box 10137
Springfield, IL 62791-0137
Phone: (217)782-6791

Credential Type: Shaft and Slope Examiner Certificate. **Duration of License:** Permanent. **Requirements:** At least 18 years of age. U.S. citizen. Two years of shaft and slope underground construction experience. One year of experience requirement may be satisfied with a degree in Mining Engineering. **Examination:** Written and oral examination. **Reciprocity:** No. **Fees:** No fee. **Governing Statute:** 62 Illinois Administrative Code 220.190(w).

4400

Shaft and Slope Supervisor (Construction and Mining)
Illinois Dept. of Mines and Minerals
300 W. Jefferson St., Ste. 300
PO Box 10137
Springfield, IL 62791-0137
Phone: (217)782-6791

Credential Type: Shaft and Slope Supervisor Certificate. **Duration of License:** Permanent. **Requirements:** At least 18 years of age. U.S. citizen. Three years of shaft and slope underground construction experience or 18 months of experience with a degree in Mining Engineering or Civil Engineering. Must complete a course in instruction of first aid. **Examination:** Written and oral examination. **Reciprocity:** No. **Fees:** No fee. **Governing Statute:** 62 Illinois Administrative Code 220.190(y).

4401

Shaft and Slope Worker (Construction and Mining)
Illinois Dept. of Mines and Minerals
300 W. Jefferson St., Ste. 300
PO Box 10137
Springfield, IL 62791-0137
Phone: (217)782-6791

Credential Type: Shaft and Slope Worker Certificate. **Duration of License:** Permanent. **Requirements:** At least 18 years of age. U.S. citizen. Must have six months experience in shaft and slope construction. Complete a course in first aid and modified mine rescue. **Examination:** Oral examination. **Reciprocity:** No. **Fees:** No fee. **Governing Statute:** 62 Illinois Administrative Code 220.190(y).

4402

State Mine Inspector (Coal Mine)
Illinois Dept. of Mines and Minerals
300 W. Jefferson St., Ste. 300
PO Box 10137
Springfield, IL 62791-0137
Phone: (217)782-6791

Credential Type: State Mine Inspector Certificate. **Duration of License:** Two years (unless actively employed as a Mine Inspector). **Requirements:** At least 30 years of age. Illinois resident. U.S. citizen. Four years of high school or equivalent education. Must have Mine Manager's Certificate of Competency. Must have 10 years experience in practical mining. At least two years of the experience requirement must be in Illinois mines. **Examination:** Written and oral examination. **Reciprocity:** No. **Fees:** No fee. **Governing Statute:** 1989 Illinois Revised Statutes, Chapter 96 1/2.

4403

State Mine Inspector (Metal Mine)
Illinois Dept. of Mines and Minerals
300 W. Jefferson St., Ste. 300
PO Box 10137
Springfield, IL 62791-0137
Phone: (217)782-6791

Credential Type: State Mine Inspector Certificate. **Duration of License:** Two years (unless actively employed as a Mine Inspector). **Requirements:** At least 30 years of age. Illinois resident for a minimum of one year. U.S. citizen. Have enough practical experience in metalliferous or mineral mining to be knowledgeable about mining operations above and below ground. **Examination:** Written and oral examination. **Reciprocity:** No. **Fees:** No fee. **Governing Statute:** 1989 Illinois Revised Statutes, Chapter 96 1/2.

4404

Surface Mine Supervisor
Illinois Dept. of Mines and Minerals
300 W. Jefferson St., Ste. 300
PO Box 10137
Springfield, IL 62791-0137
Phone: (217)782-6791

Credential Type: Surface Mine Supervisor Certificate. **Duration of License:** Permanent. **Requirements:** At least 18 years of age. U.S. citizen. Two years of field experience. Must pass four category examination. **Exemptions:** Written and oral examination in the following categories: (1) Overburden Stripping; (2) Drilling and Shooting; (3) Pit Coal Loading; (4) Reclamation. **Reciprocity:** No. **Fees:** No fee. **Governing Statute:** 1989 Illinois Revised Statutes, Chapter 96 1/2.

4405

Underground Shot Firer (Coal Mine)
Illinois Dept. of Mines & Minerals
300 W. Jefferson St., Ste. 300
PO Box 10137
Springfield, IL 62791-0137
Phone: (217)782-6791

Credential Type: Underground Shot Firer Certificate. **Duration of License:** Permanent. **Requirements:** At least 18 years of age. U.S. citizen. Must have First Class Certificate of Competency issued by the Department of Mines & Minerals. Must also complete eight hours of instruction from the Department **Examination:** Written and oral examination. **Reciprocity:** No. **Fees:** No fee. **Governing Statute:** 62 Illinois Administrative Code 225.80.

4406

Water Well Contractor
Illinois Dept. of Health
525 W. Jefferson
Springfield, IL 62761
Phone: (217)782-5830

Credential Type: Water Well Contractor License. **Duration of License:** One year. **Requirements:** At least 18 years of age.

Water Well Contractor, continued

U.S. citizen or declared intention to become a citizen. Must have two years experience under the supervision of a licensed well contractor. **Examination:** Water Well Contractor Licensing Examination. **Reciprocity:** No. **Fees:** $50 examination fee. $50 application/initial license fee. $25 renewal fee. **Governing Statute:** Illinois Revised Statutes 1991, Chapter 111.

4407

Water Well and Pump Installation Contractor
Illinois Dept. of Health
525 W. Jefferson
Springfield, IL 62761
Phone: (217)782-5830

Credential Type: Water Well and Pump Installation Contractor License. **Duration of License:** One year. **Requirements:** At least 18 years of age. U.S. citizen or declared intention to become a citizen. Must have two years experience under the supervision of a licensed water well and pump contractor. **Examination:** Water Well and Pump Installation Contractor Licensing Examination. **Reciprocity:** No. **Fees:** $80 examination fee. $80 application/initial license fee. $35 renewal fee. **Governing Statute:** Illinois Revised Statutes 1991, Chapter 111.

4408

Water Well Pump Installation Contractor
Illinois Dept. of Health
525 W. Jefferson
Springfield, IL 62761
Phone: (217)782-5830

Credential Type: Water Well Pump Installation Contractor License. **Duration of License:** One year. **Requirements:** At least 18 years of age. U.S. citizen or declared intention to become a citizen. Must have two years experience under the supervision of a licensed water well contractor. **Examination:** Water Well Pump Installation Contractor Licensing Examination. **Reciprocity:** No. **Fees:** $50 examination fee. $50 application/initial license fee. $25 renewal fee. **Governing Statute:** Illinois Revised Statutes 1991, Chapter 111.

Iowa

4409

Blaster
State Fire Marshal
Wallace State Office Bldg.
Des Moines, IA 50319
Phone: (515)281-8622

Credential Type: License. **Requirements:** Contact licensing body for application information.

4410

Well Driller
Dept. of Natural Resources
Licensing Bureau
Wallace State Office Bldg.
Des Moines, IA 50319
Phone: (515)281-4508

Credential Type: License. **Fees:** $30 registration fee.

Kentucky

4411

Miner
Dept. of Mines and Minerals
PO Box 14080
Lexington, KY 40512
Phone: (606)254-0367

Credential Type: License. **Duration of License:** One year. **Requirements:** Must have 48 hours in experienced miner training course. Must have pre-employment physical exam. Must have worked 90 days after 18th birthday. 16 hours of re-training per year. **Examination:** Yes.

Credential Type: Miner Trainee License. **Requirements:** Must complete a 48 hour inexperienced miner training course after reaching 18th birthday. 16 hours of retraining per year. **Examination:** Yes.

4412

Mining Blaster
Dept. of Mines and Minerals,
 Explosives and Blasting Div.
PO Box 14080
Lexington, KY 40512
Phone: (606)254-0367

Credential Type: License. **Duration of License:** One year. **Requirements:** Must have worked two years in a blasting operation under the supervision of an experienced blaster. 18 years of age. A 30-hour training course in blasting safety and techniques is recommended. **Examination:** Yes. **Reciprocity:** With Alabama, Virginia, and Indiana. **Fees:** $25 license fee. $40 exam fee. $20 renewal fee.

4413

Mining Electrical Inspector
Dept. of Mines and Minerals
PO Box 14080
Lexington, KY 40512
Phone: (606)254-0367

Credential Type: License. **Duration of License:** One year. **Requirements:** Ten years experience in coal mines, two of which were in Kentucky mines. A bachelor's degree in mining engineering will substitute for two years of the required experience. An associate degree in mining technology will substitute for one year of experience. Must be a Kentucky resident. 16 hours of retraining annually. **Examination:** Yes. **Reciprocity:** No. **Fees:** $50 exam fee.

4414

Mining Electrical Worker
Dept. of Mines and Minerals
PO Box 14080
Lexington, KY 40512
Phone: (606)254-0367

Credential Type: License. **Duration of License:** One year. **Requirements:** One year experience of electrical work on surface mines, in underground mines, mine equipment manufacturing industry or in any other industry using or manufacturing similar equipment. Retraining is required. **Examination:** Yes.

4415

Mining Emergency Medical Technician
Dept. of Mines and Minerals
PO Box 14080
Lexington, KY 40512
Phone: (606)254-0367

Credential Type: License. **Requirements:** Must have 103 hours of classroom training as required by the Cabinet for Human Resources and the Department of Mines and Minerals. Retraining required. **Examination:** Yes. **Fees:** $16 exam fee.

4416

Mining Fire Boss
Dept. of Mines and Minerals
PO Box 14080
Lexington, KY 40512
Phone: (606)254-0367

Credential Type: License. **Duration of License:** One year. **Requirements:** 21 years of age or three years of experience after 18th birthday with one year of the experience at the face of the coal. An associate degree in mine technology will count for one year experience, while a four-year degree in mining engineering will count toward two year experience credit. Must be a resident of Kentucky or employed by a mine in Kentucky. 16 hours of retraining required annually. **Examination:** Yes. **Reciprocity:** No. **Fees:** $50 exam fee.

4417

Mining Foreman
Dept. of Mines and Minerals
PO Box 14080
Lexington, KY 40512
Phone: (606)254-0367

Credential Type: License. **Duration of License:** One year. **Requirements:** Must have five years actual underground mining experience after reaching the 18th birthday, of which one year experience must have been at the face of the coal. An associate degree in mining technology or a four-year degree in mining engineering will count for two years of experience. Must be a resident of Kentucky or employed by a mine in Kentucky. 16 hours of retraining required annually. **Examination:** Yes. **Fees:** $50 exam fee.

4418

Mining Inspector
Dept. of Mines and Minerals
PO Box 14080
Lexington, KY 40512
Phone: (606)254-0367

Credential Type: License. **Duration of License:** One year. **Requirements:** Must have 10 years experience in coal mines, at least two of which were in Kentucky mines, after the age of 18. A bachelor's degree in mining engineering will substitute for two years of the required work experience. An associate degree in mining technology will count for one year of the required work experience. 16 hours of re-training annually. **Examination:** Yes. **Fees:** $50 exam fee.

4419

Mining Safety Instructor
Dept. of Mines and Minerals
PO Box 14080
Lexington, KY 40512
Phone: (606)254-0367

Credential Type: License. **Duration of License:** One year. **Requirements:** Must be a Kentucky resident. Must have 10 years of work experience in coal mines after the age of 18, of which two years must be in a Kentucky mine. A bachelor's degree in mining engineering from a recognized institution will substitute for two years of work experience. An associate degree in mining technology will count for one year of work experience. Must possess an underground mine foreman certificate and a mine safety underground mine instructor's certificate issued by the Department. 16 hours of retraining are required annually. **Examination:** Yes. **Fees:** $50 exam fee.

4420

Water Well Driller
Cabinet of Natural Resources & Environmental Protection
Div. of Water
14 Reilly Rd.
Frankfort, KY 40601
Phone: (502)564-3410

Credential Type: License. **Duration of License:** One year. **Requirements:** 18 years of age. U.S. citizen or legal alien. Two years work experience under the supervision of a certified water well driller or have other suitable experience or education. Continuing education required. **Examination:** Yes. **Fees:** $40 exam fee. $25 application fee. $100 certification fee. $100 renewal fee.

Louisiana

4421

Explosives Handler
Office of State Police
Explosives Control Unit
PO Box 66614
Baton Rouge, LA 70809
Phone: (504)925-6178

Credential Type: License. **Duration of License:** One year. **Authorization:** License is required of a person employed by a user who detonates or otherwise effects the explosion of an explosive or who is in immediate personal charge and supervision of one or more other persons engaged in such activity. **Requirements:** Submit application and pay fee. **Fees:** $10 license fee. **Governing Statute:** R.S. 40:1471.

Maryland

4422

Blaster
State Fire Marshal's Office
Dept. of Public Safety and Correctional Services
106 Old Court Rd., Ste. 300
Pikesville, MD 21208-4016
Phone: (410)764-4324
Fax: (410)764-4576

Credential Type: Blaster Permit. **Duration of License:** One year. **Requirements:** Applicant must be an employee of a company with a permit to manufacture or use explosives in the state. Must have three years of experience. (Individuals are not issued a blaster's permit.) **Fees:** $10 permit fee per blaster.

4423

Mining Fire Boss
Bureau of Mines
Dept. of Natural Resources
PO Drawer C
Westernport, MD 21562
Phone: (301)689-4136

Credential Type: License. **Requirements:** Contact licensing body for application information.

4424

Mining Foreman
Bureau of Mines
Dept. of Natural Resources
PO Drawer C
Westernport, MD 21562
Phone: (301)689-4136

Credential Type: License. **Requirements:** Contact licensing body for application information.

4425

Pump Installer
Board of Well Drillers
Dept. of the Environment
2500 Broening Hwy.
Baltimore, MD 21224
Phone: (410)631-3168

Credential Type: Pump Installer License. **Duration of License:** Two years. **Requirements:** At least three years experience installing pumps, or two years as an appren-

Pump Installer, continued

tice pump installer. Post $2000 performance bond. Have appropriate bodily injury and property damage insurance. Renewal requires 20 hours of continuing education during the previous two years. **Examination:** Licensure examination, written. **Fees:** $25 application fee. $50 license fee. **Governing Statute:** Annotated Code of Maryland, Title 26, subtitle 05.

Credential Type: Apprentice Pump Installer License. **Duration of License:** Two years. **Requirements:** At least one year of related experience. **Examination:** Licensure examination, written. **Fees:** $25 application fee. $25 license fee. **Governing Statute:** Annotated Code of Maryland, Title 26, subtitle 05.

4426

Well Driller
Board of Well Drillers
Dept. of the Environment
2500 Broening Hwy.
Baltimore, MD 21224
Phone: (410)631-3168

Credential Type: Master Well Driller License. **Duration of License:** Two years. **Authorization:** General, geotechnical, and water supply categories of licenses are issued in this class. **Requirements:** At least seven years experience of active practice of well drilling, or two years experience as a journeyman well driller in the same category. Post $5000 performance bond. Have appropriate bodily injury and property damage insurance. Renewal requires 20 hours of continuing education during the previous two years. **Examination:** Licensure examination, written. **Fees:** $25 application fee. $100 license fee. **Governing Statute:** Annotated Code of Maryland, Title 26, subtitle 05.

Credential Type: Journeyman Driller License. **Duration of License:** Two years. **Authorization:** General, geotechnical, and water supply categories of licenses are issued in this class. **Requirements:** At least five years experience of active practice of well drilling, or three years experience as an apprentice well driller in the same category. Renewal requires 20 hours of continuing education during the previous two years. **Examination:** Licensure examination, written. **Fees:** $25 application fee. $50 license fee. **Governing Statute:** Annotated Code of Maryland, Title 26, subtitle 05.

Credential Type: Apprentice Well Driller License. **Duration of License:** Two years. **Requirements:** At least one year of related experience. **Examination:** Licensure examination, written. **Fees:** $25 application fee. $25 license fee. **Governing Statute:** Annotated Code of Maryland, Title 26, subtitle 05.

Michigan

4427

Dewatering Well Contractor
Ground Water Quality Control Section
Dept. of Public Health
3423 N. Logan
PO Box 30195
Lansing, MI 48909
Phone: (517)335-8000

Credential Type: Registration. **Duration of License:** One year. **Requirements:** Completed the 10th grade or submit proof of the equivalent ability. Up to four years of work experience may be substituted for equal years of education. Two years of work experience in the dewatering well field. It is recommended that six months of this experience be obtained within the two years prior to application and under the supervision of a Michigan registered dewatering well contractor. Submit a chronological work history form. Be of sound moral character. Submit two personal reference statements, one of which must be from a Michigan registered dewatering well contractor, well drilling contractor, or pump installer. **Examination:** Oral appraisal and written exam. **Reciprocity:** Reciprocity may be granted if the other state accepts Michigan registration and has standards which are substantially the same as those of Michigan. **Fees:** $40 initial exam and registration fee (includes the registration of one drilling machine). $40 renewal fee. $40 reciprocity fee. **Governing Statute:** Public Health Code, Act 368 of 1978.

4428

Explosive Handler
Fire Marshal Div.
Dept. of State Police
7150 Harris Dr.
Lansing, MI 48913
Phone: (517)332-2521

Credential Type: License. **Duration of License:** Five years. **Requirements:** Have first obtained a temporary permit and then applied in writing for a regular license. Abide by the rules of the Department of State Police. **Fees:** $1 regular (permanent) license fee. $1 renewal fee. **Governing Statute:** Explosives Act, Act 202 of 1970.

Credential Type: Temporary License. **Duration of License:** One year. **Requirements:** At least 18 years of age. Have no felony convictions in the last five years. Must not have been judged insane or must have been restored to full mental competency (documented by a court order). **Fees:** $1 temporary license fee. $1 renewal fee. **Governing Statute:** Explosives Act, Act 202 of 1970.

4429

Pump Installer
Ground Water Quality Control Section
Dept. of Public Health
3423 N. Logan
PO Box 30195
Lansing, MI 48909
Phone: (517)335-8000

Credential Type: Registration. **Duration of License:** One year. **Requirements:** Completed the 10th grade or submit proof of the equivalent ability as indicated by the successful completion of approved short courses or written examinations. Up to four years of work experience may be substituted for equal years of education. Two years of work experience in the pump installation field. It is recommended that six months of this experience be obtained within the two years prior to application and under the supervision of a Michigan registered pump installation contractor. Submit a chronological work history form. Be of sound moral character. Submit two personal reference statements. One of the reference statements must be completed by a Michigan registered well drilling contractor or pump installer. The second statement must be completed by a person familiar with the applicant's work experience in the well and pump field. **Examination:** Oral appraisal and written exam. **Reciprocity:** Reciprocity may be granted if the other state accepts Michigan registration and has standards which are substantially the same as those of Michigan. **Fees:** $25 initial exam and registration fee. $25 renewal fee. $25 reciprocity fee. **Governing Statute:** Public Health Code, Act 368 of 1978.

4430

Well Drilling Contractor
Ground Water Quality Control Section
Dept. of Public Health
3423 N. Logan
PO Box 30195
Lansing, MI 48909
Phone: (517)335-8000

Credential Type: Registration. **Duration of License:** One year. **Requirements:** Completed the 10th grade or submit proof of the equivalent ability as indicated by the successful completion of approved short courses or written examinations. Up to four years of work experience may be substituted for equal years of education. Two years of work experience in the well drilling field. It is recommended that six months of this experience be obtained within the two years prior to application and under the supervision of a Michigan registered well drilling contractor. Submit a chronological work history form. Be of sound moral character. Submit two personal reference statements. One of the reference statements must be completed by a Michigan registered well drilling contractor or pump installer. The second statement must be completed by a person familiar with the applicant's work experience in the well and pump field. **Examination:** Oral appraisal and written exam. **Reciprocity:** Reciprocity may be granted if the other state accepts Michigan registration and has standards which are substantially the same as those of Michigan. **Fees:** $40 initial exam and registration fee (includes the registration of one drilling machine). $40 renewal fee. $40 reciprocity fee. **Governing Statute:** Public Health Code, Act 368 of 1978, as amended.

Minnesota

4431

Water Well Contractor
Dept. of Health
Environmental Health Div.
Water Supply and General
  Engineering Section
Well Management Unit
717 Delaware St., SE
Box 9441
Minneapolis, MN 55440
Phone: (612)627-5147
Phone: (612)627-5133
Fax: (612)623-5043

Credential Type: Full Contractor License. **Authorization:** Authorizes holder to construct, repair, and seal all types of wells and borings regulated by the Department of Health, with the exception of exploratory borings. **Requirements:** Complete examination and meet minimum experience requirements. **Examination:** Written examination. **Fees:** $50 application fee. $250 license fee.

Credential Type: Limited Contractor License. **Authorization:** Issued for five categories of work: (1) pump installation and repair; (2) pitless unit and adapter/well screen installation and repair; (3) well sealing; (4) construction, sealing, and repair of unconventional wells; (5) construction, sealing, and repair of dewatering wells. **Requirements:** Complete examination and meet minimum experience requirements. **Examination:** Written examination. **Fees:** $50 application fee. $50 license fee.

Montana

4432

Construction Blaster
Montana Safety Bureau
Worker's Compensation Div.
5 S. Last Chance Gulch
Helena, MT 59601
Phone: (406)444-6401

Credential Type: License. **Duration of License:** One year. **Requirements:** 18 years of age. Completion of an approved course in construction blasting. One year of experience in construction blasting. **Examination:** Yes. **Fees:** $5 application fee. $5 exam fee. $15 license fee. $10 renewal fee. **Governing Statute:** Montana Code Annotated 37-72-301 through 37-72-307.

Nebraska

4433

Pump Installer/Well Driller
Div. of Drinking Water &
  Environmental Sanitation
301 Centennial Mall S.
PO Box 95007
Lincoln, NE 68509
Phone: (402)471-2541

Credential Type: License. **Duration of License:** One year. **Requirements:** Must have been in the industry for two years. Must have $100,000 in public liability and property damage insurance. Supervisors are not required to show proof of the $100,000 in public liability and property damage insurance. **Examination:** Yes. **Fees:** $15 application fee. $150 license fee. $35 supervisor's certificate fee. $150 license renewal fee. $35 supervisor's certificate fee.

Nevada

4434

Rotary Driller
Nevada State Dept. of Conservation
  and Natural Resources
Div. of Water Resources
123 W. Nye Ln., Capitol Complex
Carson City, NV 89710
Phone: (702)687-4380

Credential Type: License. **Examination:** Yes. **Fees:** $50 filing fee. $25 renewal fee.

New Jersey

4435

Pump Installer
New Jersey Dept. of Environmental
  Protection
Div. of Water Resources
CN029
Trenton, NJ 08625-0029
Phone: (609)984-6831

Credential Type: License. **Examination:** Practical. **Fees:** $10 license fee. **Governing Statute:** NJSA 58:4A.

4436

Well Driller
Well Driller and Pump Installers
  Examining and Advisory Board
Div. of Water Resources
CN029
Trenton, NJ 08625-0029
Phone: (609)984-6831

Credential Type: Master Well Driller. **Requirements:** Journeyman license and two years of experience. **Examination:** Practical. **Reciprocity:** Yes. **Fees:** $25 license fee. **Governing Statute:** NJSA 58:4A.

Credential Type: Journeyman Well Driller. **Requirements:** Three years of practical experience. **Examination:** Practical. **Reciprocity:** Yes. **Fees:** $10 license fee. **Governing Statute:** NJSA 58:4A.

New York

4437

Blaster
New York State Dept. of Labor
Div. of Safety and Health
One Main St., Rm. 801
Brooklyn, NY 11201
Phone: (718)797-7659

Credential Type: Certificate. **Duration of License:** Three years. **Requirements:** 21 years of age. Willingness to do hazardous work. **Examination:** Written and practical. **Fees:** $60 license fee. **Governing Statute:** Article 28 of the General Business Law. Rule 39 of the Industrial Code.

North Dakota

4438

Monitoring Well Contractor
State Board of Water Well
  Contractors
900 E. Blvd.
Bismarck, ND 58505
Phone: (701)224-2754

Credential Type: Monitoring Well Contractor Certification. **Duration of License:** One year. **Requirements:** Have at least one year of experience under a certified contractor. Post $2000 surety bond. **Examination:** Written certification examination. **Fees:** $50 certification fee. $10 exam fee. $50 renewal fee. **Governing Statute:** North Dakota Century Code 43-35.

4439

Pump and Pitless Unit Contractor
State Board of Water Well
  Contractors
900 E. Blvd.
Bismarck, ND 58505
Phone: (701)224-2754

Credential Type: Pump and Pitless Unit Contractor Certification. **Duration of License:** One year. **Requirements:** Have at least one year of experience under a qualified contractor. Post $2000 surety bond. **Examination:** Written certification examination. **Fees:** $25 certification fee. $10 exam fee. $25 renewal fee. **Governing Statute:** North Dakota Century Code 43-35.

4440

Water Well Contractor
State Board of Water Well
  Contractors
900 E. Blvd.
Bismarck, ND 58505
Phone: (701)224-2754

Credential Type: Water Well Contractor Certification. **Duration of License:** One year. **Requirements:** Have at least one year of experience under a certified driller. A recognized course in water well drilling may be substituted for the experience requirement. Post $2000 surety bond. **Examination:** Written certification examination. **Fees:** $50 certification fee. $10 exam fee. $50 renewal fee. **Governing Statute:** North Dakota Century Code 43-35.

Ohio

4441

Deputy Mine Inspector
Mine Examining Board
Dept. of Industrial Relations
2323 W. Fifth Ave.
PO Box 825
Columbus, OH 43216
Phone: (614)644-2234

Credential Type: License. **Duration of License:** Permanent. **Requirements:** Submit application and pay fee. Pass examination. **Examination:** Mine inspector examination. **Fees:** $10 exam fee.

4442

Mine Electrician
Mine Examining Board
Dept. of Industrial Relations
2323 W. Fifth Ave.
PO Box 825
Columbus, OH 43216
Phone: (614)644-2234

Credential Type: License. **Duration of License:** Permanent. **Authorization:** Must remain employed to keep license. **Requirements:** Be able to read and write English. Have at least one year of practical experience. **Examination:** Mine electrician examination. **Fees:** $10 exam fee.

4443

Mine Fire Boss
Mine Examining Board
Dept. of Industrial Relations
2323 W. Fifth Ave.
PO Box 825
Columbus, OH 43216
Phone: (614)644-2234

Credential Type: License. **Duration of License:** Permanent. **Requirements:** Be able to read and write English. Have at least three years of practical experience. **Examination:** Fire boss examination. **Fees:** $10 exam fee.

4444

Mine Foreman
Mine Examining Board
Dept. of Industrial Relations
2323 W. Fifth Ave.
PO Box 825
Columbus, OH 43216
Phone: (614)644-2234

Credential Type: License. **Duration of License:** Permanent. **Authorization:** There are separate license categories for a foreman of a gaseous mine, a non-gaseous mine, and a clay mine or stripping pit. **Requirements:** Be able to read and write English. Have at least three years of practical experience. **Examination:** Mine foreman examination. **Fees:** $10 exam fee.

4445

Surface Blaster
Mine Examining Board
Dept. of Industrial Relations
2323 W. Fifth Ave.
PO Box 825
Columbus, OH 43216
Phone: (614)644-2234

Credential Type: License. **Duration of License:** Three years. **Requirements:** Submit application and pay fee. Pass examination. **Examination:** Surface blaster examination. **Fees:** $10 exam fee. $10 renewal fee.

Oklahoma

4446

Blaster, Surface
State Mining Commission
4040 N. Lincoln, Ste. 107
Oklahoma City, OK 73105
Phone: (405)521-3859

Credential Type: Certificate. **Duration of License:** Two years. **Requirements:** Completion of week-long course. An eight-hour refresher course is required every two years. 21 years of age. One year's experience with a certified blaster. No felony convictions. **Examination:** Surface Blasting Certification Exam. **Fees:** $10 certification fee (includes exam fee).

4447

Fire Boss (Underground)
State Mining Commission
4040 N. Lincoln, Ste. 107
Oklahoma City, OK 73105
Phone: (405)521-3859

Credential Type: Certificate. **Duration of License:** Lifetime. **Authorization:** A fire boss inspects underground mines and work sites to ensure that there is no collection of mine gases. **Requirements:** A working knowledge of the occupation is necessary. State resident. Must hold a first-aid certificate. Two years of practical underground experience. **Examination:** Fire Boss Examination. **Fees:** $10 exam fee. $10 certificate fee.

4448

Groundwater and Observation Water Well Driller
Oklahoma Water Resources Board
600 N. Harver
PO Box 150
Oklahoma City, OK 73101
Phone: (405)231-2500

Credential Type: License. **Duration of License:** One year. **Requirements:** High school diploma or GED. Two years of experience in water well drilling or one year of experience as a licensed operator. **Examination:** Groundwater and Observation Well Drillers Examination. **Fees:** $50 exam fee. $100 application fee. $50 license fee. $50 renewal fee.

4449

Mine Foreman (Underground)
State Mining Commission
4040 N. Lincoln, Ste. 107
Oklahoma City, OK 73105
Phone: (405)521-3859

Credential Type: Certificate. **Duration of License:** Lifetime. **Requirements:** State resident. First-aid certificate. Three years of practical underground experience. Completion of a two-year of four-year accredited mining program shall be credited one year of experience. **Examination:** Mine Foreman Certificate of Competency. **Fees:** $15 exam fee. $15 certification fee.

4450

Mine Shot Firer (Underground)
State Mining Commission
4040 N. Lincoln, Ste. 107
Oklahoma City, OK 73105
Phone: (405)521-3859

Credential Type: Certificate. **Duration of License:** Lifetime. **Requirements:** 21 years of age. First-aid certificate. No felony convictions. One year of practical underground experience. **Examination:** Shot Firer Examination. **Fees:** $10 exam fee. $10 certification fee.

4451

Monitoring Well Driller
Oklahoma Water Resources Board
600 N. Harvey
PO Box 150
Oklahoma City, OK 73101
Phone: (405)231-2500

Credential Type: License. **Duration of License:** One year. **Requirements:** 90-day, in-state residency. Two years of experience in monitoring well drilling or one year of experience as a licensed operator. **Examination:** Monitoring Well Drillers Examination. **Fees:** $50 exam fee. $100 application fee. $50 license fee. $50 renewal fee.

4452

Practical Miner (Underground)
State Mining Commission
4040 N. Lincoln, Ste. 107
Oklahoma City, OK 73105
Phone: (405)521-3859

Credential Type: Certificate. **Duration of License:** Lifetime. **Requirements:** One year of practical experience as an underground miner. State resident. First-aid certificate. **Examination:** Practical Miner Certificate of Competency. **Fees:** $5 exam fee. $5 certification fee.

4453

Pump Installer
Oklahoma Water Resources Board
600 N. Harvey
PO Box 150
Oklahoma City, OK 73101
Phone: (405)231-2500

Credential Type: License. **Duration of License:** One year. **Requirements:** 90-day residency. Two years of experience in pump installations or one year as a licensed operator. **Examination:** Pump Installers Examination. **Fees:** $50 exam fee. $100 application fee. $50 license fee. $50 renewal fee. $100 filing fee. $50 indemnity fund fee. $50 testing fee.

4454

Superintendent (Underground)
State Mining Commission
4040 N. Lincoln, Ste. 107
Oklahoma City, OK 73105
Phone: (405)521-3859

Credential Type: Certificate. **Duration of License:** Lifetime. **Requirements:** State resident. First-aid certificate. Five years of practical underground experience. **Examination:** Superintendent Examination. **Fees:** $20 exam fee. $20 certification fee.

4455

Surface Supervisor
State Mining Commission
4040 N. Lincoln, Ste. 107
Oklahoma City, OK 73105
Phone: (405)521-3859

Credential Type: Certificate. **Duration of License:** One year for coal certificate. Two years for non-coal. **Requirements:** First-aid certificate. One year of mining industry experience. **Examination:** Surface Supervisor Certification Examination. **Fees:** $5 exam fee. $5 certification fee.

Oregon

4456

Monitor Well Constructor
Water Resources Dept.
3850 Portland Rd. NE
Salem, OR 97310
Phone: (503)378-8455

Credential Type: License. **Duration of License:** One or five years. **Requirements:** 18 years of age. At least one year of experience on a minimum of 15 monitoring wells. Experience must be in monitoring well construction, alteration or abandonment. **Examination:** Yes. **Fees:** $20 exam fee. $50 license fee. $50 renewal fee for one year. $200 renewal fee for five years. **Governing Statute:** ORS 537.747.

Oregon

4457

Water Well Constructor
Water Resources Dept.
3850 Portland Rd. NE
Salem, OR 97310
Phone: (503)378-8455

Credential Type: License. **Duration of License:** One or five years. **Requirements:** 18 years of age. Must have one year or more experience operating well drilling machinery on at least 15 wells. **Examination:** Yes. **Fees:** $20 exam fee. $50 fee for one-year license. $200 fee for five-year license. $50 renewal fee for one-year license. $200 renewal fee for five-year license. **Governing Statute:** ORS 537.740 to 537.753.

Rhode Island

4458

Blaster
State Fire Marshal's Office
Rhode Island Div. of Fire Safety
1270 Mineral Spring Ave.
North Providence, RI 02904
Phone: (401)277-2335

Credential Type: Blaster License. **Duration of License:** One year. **Authorization:** Authorizes applicant to assemble, plant, and detonate charges of industrial explosives. **Requirements:** At least 21 years of age. Experience under the supervision of a licensed blaster. Must have sponsorship of a licensed blaster. Pass criminal identification check by the Bureau of State Police. **Examination:** Written examination. **Reciprocity:** No. **Fees:** $10 examination fee. $15 license fee.

4459

Pump Installer (Drinking Water Wells)
Div. of Groundwater, ISDS Section
Rhode Island Dept. of Environmental Management
291 Promenade St.
Providence, RI 02908
Phone: (401)277-2234

Credential Type: Pump Installer License. **Duration of License:** One year. **Requirements:** At least 16 years of age. Submit application with certificate of liability insurance providing $300,000 body coverage and $100,000 property coverage. Must submit proof of adequate financial resources to own and maintain necessary tools and machinery. Reexamination required after the fourth renewal of license. **Examination:** Written examination. **Exemptions:** Plumber with master license is exempt. **Reciprocity:** No. **Fees:** $200 registration fee. $100 renewal fee.

4460

Well-Drill Operator (Drinking Water Wells)
Div. of Groundwater, ISDS Section
Rhode Island Dept. of Environmental Management
291 Promenade St.
Providence, RI 02908
Phone: (401)277-2234

Credential Type: Well-Drill Operator License. **Duration of License:** One year. **Requirements:** At least 16 years of age. Submit application with certificate of liability insurance providing $300,000 body coverage and $100,000 property coverage. Must submit proof of adequate financial resources to own and maintain necessary tools and machinery. Reexamination required after the fourth renewal of license. **Examination:** Written examination. **Exemptions:** Plumber with master license is exempt. Separate licenses are required for cable tool, air rotary, mud rotary, driving and jetting, and boring and auger. **Reciprocity:** No. **Fees:** $200 registration fee. $100 renewal fee.

South Carolina

4461

Well Driller
South Carolina Board of Certification of Environmental Systems Operators
2221 Devine St., Ste. 320
Columbia, SC 29205
Phone: (803)734-9140

Credential Type: License. **Requirements:** Two years of experience under the direction of a certified water well driller. **Examination:** Yes. **Fees:** $40 license fee.

Texas

4462

Water Well Driller
Texas Water Commission
Texas Water Well Drillers Board
PO Box 13085
Austin, TX 78711
Phone: (512)371-6299

Credential Type: License. **Duration of License:** One year. **Requirements:** Texas resident for at least 90 days. Four letters of reference. Two years experience as a water well driller under the supervision of a licensed driller, or comparable well driller experience. **Examination:** Written or oral. **Fees:** $100 exam and license registration fee. $125 renewal fee. **Governing Statute:** VACS 7621e, 31 TAC 231.

Utah

4463

Fire Boss (Mining)
The Industrial Commission of Utah
160 E. 300 S.
Salt Lake City, UT 84151-0910
Phone: (801)530-6869

Credential Type: Fire Boss License. **Requirements:** Must have two years of varied underground coal mining experience and hold a U.S. Bureau of Mines First Aid Certificate or the equivalent training. One year of experience may be credited to a mining engineering graduate of an approved four-year college; or six months experience may be credited to a graduate of a two-year course in mining. **Examination:** Yes. **Fees:** $50 license fee.

4464

Mine Electrician
The Industrial Commission of Utah
160 E. 300 S.
Salt Lake City, UT 84151-0910
Phone: (801)530-6869

Credential Type: Mine Electrician License. **Requirements:** Must have at least one year of experience in performing electrical work underground in a coal mine, in the surface coal mine, in a non-coal mine, in the mine equipment manufacturing industry, or in any other industry using or manufacturing similar equipment. Must hold a U.S. Bureau of Mines First Aid Certificate or the equivalent training. **Examination:** Yes. **Fees:** $50 license fee.

4465

Mine Foreman
The Industrial Commission of Utah
160 E. 300 S.
Salt Lake City, UT 84151-0910
Phone: (801)530-6869

Credential Type: Mine Foreman License. **Requirements:** Must have four years of varied underground coal mining experience. Must be trained in mine rescue and hold a U.S. Bureau of Mines First Aid Certificate or equivalent training. Two years experience may be credited to a mining engineering graduate of an approved four-year college; or one year's experience may be credited to a graduate of a two-year course in mining technology. **Examination:** Yes. **Fees:** $50 license fee.

4466

Surface Blaster (Mining)
The Industrial Commission of Utah
160 E. 300 S.
Salt Lake City, UT 84151-0910
Phone: (801)530-6869

Credential Type: Surface Blaster. **Requirements:** Must have two years of blasting experience and hold a U.S. Bureau of Mines First Aid Certificate or the equivalent training. Must attend a forty-hour training class. **Fees:** $50 license fee.

4467

Surface Foreman
The Industrial Commission of Utah
160 E. 300 S.
Salt Lake City, UT 84151-0910
Phone: (801)530-6869

Credential Type: Surface Foreman License. **Requirements:** Must have three years of varied suface experience. Must have a U.S. Bureau of Mines First Aid Certificate or the equivalent training; or must hold an underground mine foreman certificate with three years of varied surface mining experience in any other industry that has substantially equivalent surface facilities, if the applicant has performed or is presently performing the duties normally required of a surface foreman. **Examination:** Yes. **Fees:** $50 license fee.

Vermont

4468

Blaster
Vermont State Police
Fire Investigation Unit
103 S. Main St.
Waterbury, VT 05676
Phone: (802)244-8781

Credential Type: License. **Requirements:** Vermont Explosives License. **Examination:** No. **Reciprocity:** No. **Fees:** $2 Resident. $4 Non-resident.

4469

Well Driller
Dept. of Environmental Conservation
Agency of Natural Resources
103 South Main St., 10N
Waterbury, VT 05676
Phone: (802)244-5638

Credential Type: License. **Duration of License:** Three years. **Requirements:** Make application to the Environmental Conservation Department. An investigation of applicant's experience must be conducted. **Examination:** Yes. **Reciprocity:** No. **Fees:** $60 Initial application. $30 Renewal. **Governing Statute:** Title 10, VSA Sections 1395-1402.

Washington

4470

Blaster (Explosives User)
Dept. of Labor & Industries
Div. of Industrial Safety & Health
General Administration Bldg., HC-101
Olympia, WA 98504
Phone: (206)586-2813

Credential Type: Blaster License. **Duration of License:** One year. **Requirements:** At least 21 years of age. Experience in the use of explosives. May require background investigation. Fingerprint check. **Examination:** Written examination. **Fees:** $5 license fee.

West Virginia

4471

Electrician (Mine)
Dept. of Energy
State Capitol Bldg.
Charleston, WV 25305
Phone: (304)348-3500

Credential Type: License. **Requirements:** 19 years old. One year of experience in electrical work. Eight hours of hazard training. Must obtain license legally. **Examination:** Yes. **Fees:** $15 License.

4472

Mine Foreman
Dept. of Energy
State Capitol Bldg.
Charleston, WV 25305
Phone: (304)348-3500

Credential Type: License. **Requirements:** State resident. 18 years old. Foreman—five years experience with a degree in mining. Assistant—three years experience or degree in mining. **Examination:** Yes. **Fees:** $25 License.

4473

Mine Surveyor
Dept. of Examiners of Land
  Surveyors
PO Box 925
Fayetteville, WV 25840
Phone: (304)574-2980

Credential Type: License. **Duration of License:** One year. **Requirements:** U.S. resident. 18 years old. Four years of experience under a license holder and three years of underground surveying; or completion of an accredited curriculum and two years of land surveying experience plus three years of underground surveying experience. Never convicted of a felony. **Examination:** Yes. **Fees:** $10 License. $30 Land Survey license. $20 Renewal.

4474

Miner
Dept. of Energy
State Capitol Bldg.
Charleston, WV 25305
Phone: (304)348-3500

Credential Type: License. **Requirements:** 18 years old. Six months of experience (40 hours as apprentice for surface mining, 80 hours experience as apprentice for underground). Never convicted of a felony. **Examination:** Yes. **Fees:** $5 License.

4475

Shot Firer
Dept. of Energy
State Capitol Bldg.
Charleston, WV 25305
Phone: (304)348-3500

Credential Type: License. **Requirements:** 20 years old. Two years mining experience. **Examination:** Yes. **Fees:** $5 License.

Wyoming

4476

Mine Examiner
Mining Board of Wyoming
PO Box 1094
Rock Springs, WY 82901
Phone: (307)362-5222

Credential Type: License. **Requirements:** 23 years of age. Two years experience in the type of mine desired; or, one year training as a mine engineer from an accredited college and one year experience in the type of mine desired. Pass the examination. **Examination:** Yes. **Fees:** $25 License.

4477

Mine Foreman
Mining Board of Wyoming
PO Box 1094
Rock Springs, WY 82901
Phone: (307)362-5222

Credential Type: License. **Requirements:** 23 years of age. Must have at least three years experience in the type of mine desired; or, two years of training as a mining engineer from an accredited college and one year of experience in the type of mine desired. Pass the examination. **Examination:** Yes. **Fees:** $25 License.

4478

Mine Inspector
Mining Board of Wyoming
PO Box 1094
Rock Springs, WY 82901
Phone: (307)362-5222

Credential Type: License. **Requirements:** 35 years of age. Qualified elector of the state. Good reputation and temperate habits. Have 10 years experience in addition to Mine Foreman experience, in underground mines. **Examination:** No. **Fees:** None.

Notary Publics

The following states grant licenses in this occupational category as of the date of publication:

Alabama	District of	Iowa	Minnesota	New Mexico	Rhode Island	Washington
Alaska	Columbia	Kansas	Mississippi	New York	South Carolina	West Virginia
Arizona	Florida	Kentucky	Missouri	North Carolina	South Dakota	Wisconsin
Arkansas	Georgia	Louisiana	Montana	North Dakota	Tennessee	Wyoming
California	Hawaii	Maine	Nebraska	Ohio	Texas	
Colorado	Idaho	Maryland	Nevada	Oklahoma	Utah	
Connecticut	Illinois	Massachusetts	New Hampshire	Oregon	Vermont	
Delaware	Indiana	Michigan	New Jersey	Pennsylvania	Virginia	

Alabama

4479

Notary Public
Office of Secretary of State
Statehouse Rm. 21
11 Union St.
Montgomery, AL 36130
Phone: (205)242-7210

Credential Type: Notary Public Commission. **Duration of License:** Four years. **Requirements:** At least 18 years of age. Minimum one day of residency. Endorsement by three county citizens. Must be a registered voter. Must post $10,000 bond. **Fees:** $1 commission fee.

Alaska

4480

Notary Public
Office of Lieutenant Governor
PO Box AA
Juneau, AK 99811
Phone: (907)465-3509

Credential Type: Notary Public Commission. **Duration of License:** Four years. **Requirements:** At least 19 years of age. Minimum 30 days of residency. Endorsement by local superior court clerk. Must be a registered voter. Must post $1,000 bond. **Fees:** $40 commission fee.

Arizona

4481

Notary Public
Office of Secretary of State
Capitol West Wing, 1st Fl.
Phoenix, AZ 85007
Phone: (602)543-6176

Credential Type: Notary Public Commission. **Duration of License:** Four years. **Requirements:** At least 18 years of age. Minimum seven months of residency. Must have no felonies on record. Must post $1,000 bond. **Fees:** $12.50 commission fee.

Arkansas

4482

Notary Public
Secretary of State
256 State Capitol
Little Rock, AR 72201
Phone: (501)682-1010

Credential Type: License. **Duration of License:** Eight years. **Requirements:** 18 years of age. US Citizen. Resided in precinct for at least 30 days. Must be a resident of the county in which the commission is granted. Must be able to read and write English. Must not have had a commission revoked within the past 10 years. **Examination:** No **Fees:** $10 Application.

California

4483

Notary Public
Office of Secretary of State
PO Box 942877
Sacramento, CA 94277-0001
Phone: (916)445-6507

Credential Type: Notary Public Commission. **Duration of License:** Four years. **Requirements:** At least 18 years of age. Pass examination. Must post $10,000 bond. **Examination:** State examination. **Fees:** $67 commission fee. $40 renewal fee.

Colorado

4484

Notary Public
Office of Secretary of State
1560 Broadway, Ste. 200
Denver, CO 80202
Phone: (303)894-2215

Credential Type: Notary Public Commission. **Duration of License:** Four years. **Requirements:** At least 18 years of age. U.S. citizen. Must read and write English. Must have no felonies on record. Minimum 25 days of residency. Must be a qualified elector. **Fees:** $10 commission fee.

Connecticut

4485

Notary Public
Office of Secretary of State
30 Trinity St.
Hartford, CT 06106
Phone: (203)566-5273

Credential Type: Notary Public Commission. **Duration of License:** Five years. **Requirements:** At least 18 years of age. Endorsement by town clerk and three public officials. Pass examination. **Examination:** State examination. **Fees:** $60 commission fee.

Delaware

4486

Notary Public
Office of Secretary of State
Notary Division
PO Box 793
Dover, DE 19903
Phone: (302)739-6479

Credential Type: Notary Public Commission. **Duration of License:** Two or four years. **Requirements:** At least 18 years of age. Minimum one year of residency. Must have two letters of recommendation. **Fees:** $53 commission fee (2 years). $78 commission fee (4 years).

District of Columbia

4487

Notary Public
Office of the Secretary, DC
Notary Commission &
  Authentication Sec.
717 14th St. NW, Ste. 230
Washington, DC 20005
Phone: (202)727-3117

Credential Type: Notary Public Commission. **Duration of License:** Five years. **Requirements:** At least 18 years of age. Pass examination. Must have three letters of reference. Must post $2,000 bond. **Examination:** State examination. **Fees:** $30 commission fee.

Florida

4488

Notary Public
Office of Secretary of State
Capitol Bldg., No. 2002
Tallahassee, FL 32399-0250
Phone: (904)488-7521

Credential Type: Notary Public Commission. **Duration of License:** Four years. **Requirements:** At least 18 years of age. Legal resident of Florida. Noncitizens are required to submit domicile declaration. Must have a character witness. Must post $5,000 bond. **Fees:** $35 commission fee.

Georgia

4489

Notary Public
Office of Secretary of State
Notary Division
West Tower, Ste. 816
2 Martin Luther King Dr.
Atlanta, GA 30334
Phone: (404)656-2899

Credential Type: Notary Public Commission. **Duration of License:** Four years. **Requirements:** At least 18 years of age. Endorsement by two county residents who are at least 18 years of age. Must read and write English. Must be resident of the county where appointed. Commuting nonresidents may also qualify. **Fees:** $8 commission fee.

Hawaii

4490

Notary Public
Dept. of Attorney General
425 Queen St.
Honolulu, HI 96813
Phone: (808)586-1218

Credential Type: Notary Public Commission. **Duration of License:** Four years. **Requirements:** At least 18 years of age. Pass examination. Letter of recommendation. Must post $1,000 bond. **Examination:** State examination. **Fees:** $35 commission fee. $15 renewal fee.

Idaho

4491

Notary Public
Office of Secretary of State
Statehouse
Boise, ID 83720
Phone: (208)334-2300

Credential Type: Notary Public Commission. **Duration of License:** Six years. **Requirements:** At least 18 years of age. Must be a U.S. citizen. Must read and write English. Must post $10,000 bond. **Fees:** $30 commission fee.

Illinois

4492

Notary Public
Office of Secretary of State
Index Dept.
111 E. Monroe St.
Springfield, IL 62756
Phone: (217)782-7017

Credential Type: Notary Public Commission. **Duration of License:** Four years. **Requirements:** At least 18 years of age. Minimum 30 days of residency. Must read and write English. Must post $5,000 bond. **Fees:** $10 commission.

Indiana

4493

Notary Public
Office of Secretary of State
Statehouse No. 201
Indianapolis, IN 46204
Phone: (317)232-6542

Credential Type: Notary Public Commission. **Duration of License:** Four years. **Requirements:** At least 18 years of age. Must not hold lucrative public office. Must be resident of state. Must post $5,000 bond. **Fees:** $10 commission fee.

Iowa

4494

Notary Public
Office of Secretary of State
Hoover Office Bldg., 2nd Fl.
Des Moines, IA 50319
Phone: (515)281-3677

Credential Type: Notary Public Commission. **Duration of License:** Three years (resident), one year (non-resident). **Requirements:** At least 18 years of age. Commuting non-residents from bordering state may qualify. **Fees:** $30 commission fee.

Kansas

4495

Notary Public
Office of Secretary of State
State Capitol, 2nd Fl.
Topeka, KS 66612
Phone: (913)296-2744

Credential Type: Notary Public Commission. **Duration of License:** Four years. **Requirements:** At least 18 years of age. Must read and write English. No felonies on record. No loss of professional license. Commuting non-residents may qualify. Must post $7,500 bond. **Fees:** $10 commission fee.

Kentucky

4496

Notary Public
Office of Secretary of State
Capitol Bldg.
PO Box 821
Frankfort, KY 40602-0821
Phone: (502)564-3490

Credential Type: Notary Public Commission. **Duration of License:** Four years. **Requirements:** At least 18 years of age. Minimum 30 day residency. Must have endorsement by a public official authorized by statute. Must post $1,000 bond in Jefferson County (other counties' requirements vary). **Fees:** $10 commission fee.

Louisiana

4497

Notary Public
Office of Secretary of State
PO Box 94125
Baton Rouge, LA 70804-9125
Phone: (504)342-4981

Credential Type: Notary Public Commission. **Duration of License:** Permanent. **Requirements:** At least 18 years of age. All applicants, except attorneys, must pass examination and post a $5,000 bond. Endorsement by two reputable citizens. Must be a qualified elector. **Examination:** State examination. **Fees:** $35 commission fee. $20 renewal fee.

Maine

4498

Notary Public
Office of Secretary of State
Bureau of Corporation, Elections and Commissions
Statehouse Station 101
Augusta, ME 04333
Phone: (207)289-4181
Phone: (207)289-4173

Credential Type: Notary Public Commission. **Duration of License:** Seven years. **Requirements:** At least 18 years of age. Pass examination. Must be a registered voter, elected official, municipal clerk, or registrar of voters. **Examination:** State examination. **Fees:** $25 commission fee.

Maryland

4499

Notary Public
Office of Secretary of State
Statehouse
Annapolis, MD 21401
Phone: (301)974-5520

Credential Type: Notary Public Commission. **Duration of License:** Four years. **Requirements:** At least 18 years of age. Endorsement by U.S. senator. Out-of-state residents commuting to Maryland may qualify. **Fees:** $21 commission fee.

Massachusetts

4500

Notary Public
Notary Public Office
Statehouse No. 184
Boston, MA 02133
Phone: (617)727-2795

Credential Type: Notary Public Commission. **Duration of License:** Seven years. **Requirements:** At least 18 years of age. Minimum 30 days of residency. Endorsement by elected official, judge, lawyer, and three other citizens. **Fees:** $25 commission fee.

Michigan

4501

Notary Public
Dept. of State
Office of the Great Seal
Lansing, MI 48918
Phone: (517)373-0082

Credential Type: Notary Public Commission. **Duration of License:** Four years. **Requirements:** At least 18 years of age. Endorsement by probate/circuit judge or legislator. Must post $10,000 bond. **Fees:** $3 commission fee.

Minnesota

4502

Notary Public
Dept. of Commerce
Licensing Unit
133 E. 7th St.
St. Paul, MN 55101
Phone: (612)296-6319

Credential Type: Notary Public Commission. **Duration of License:** Six years. **Requirements:** At least 18 years of age. **Fees:** $10 commission fee.

Mississippi

4503

Notary Public
Office of Secretary of State
PO Box 136
Jackson, MS 39205-0136
Phone: (601)359-1615

Credential Type: Notary Public Commission. **Duration of License:** Four years. **Requirements:** At least 18 years of age. Must be U.S. citizen and qualified elector. Must post $5,000 bond. **Fees:** $25 commission fee.

Missouri

4504

Notary Public
Office of Secretary of State
PO Box 778
Jefferson City, MO 65102
Phone: (314)751-2783
Phone: (314)751-2796

Credential Type: Notary Public Commission. **Duration of License:** Four years. **Requirements:** At least 18 years of age. U.S.

Notary Public, continued

citizen. Minimum 30 days of residency. Endorsement by two registered voters. Must read and write English. Commuting non-residents may qualify. Must post $10,000 bond. **Fees:** $15 commission fee.

Montana

4505

Notary Public
Office of Secretary of State
State Capitol
Helena, MT 59620
Phone: (406)444-5379

Credential Type: Notary Public Commission. **Duration of License:** Three years. **Requirements:** At least 18 years of age. Minimum one year residency. U.S. citizen. Must post $5,000 bond. **Fees:** $15 commission fee

Nebraska

4506

Notary Public
Nebraska Secretary of State Notary Div.
State Capitol Bldg., Rm. 345E
Lincoln, NE 68509
Phone: (402)471-2558

Credential Type: License. **Duration of License:** Four years. **Requirements:** Must be a resident of Nebraska. Must be registered to vote. Must be a U.S. citizen. 19 years of age. Must have no felony convictions. Must have 25 signatures from county residents, endorsing applicant as being trustworthy and qualified for the Notary Public position. **Fees:** $20 commission fee. $20 renewal fee.

Nevada

4507

Notary Public
Office of Secretary of State
State Capitol Complex
Carson City, NV 89710
Phone: (702)687-5115
Phone: (702)687-5203

Credential Type: Notary Public Commission. **Duration of License:** Four years. **Requirements:** At least 18 years of age. Minimum 30 days of residency. U.S. citizen. Resident alien may be approved by INS. No loss of civil rights. Must post $10,000 bond. **Fees:** $35 commission fee.

New Hampshire

4508

Notary Public
Office of Secretary of State
Statehouse, Rm. 204
Concord, NH 03301
Phone: (603)271-3242

Credential Type: Notary Public Commission. **Duration of License:** Five years. **Requirements:** At least 18 years of age. Must be a U.S. citizen and a legal resident of the state. Endorsement by two notaries and one registered voter. **Fees:** $50 commission fee.

New Jersey

4509

Notary Public
Dept. of State
Div. of Commercial Recording, Notary Sec.
CN452
Trenton, NJ 08625
Phone: (609)530-6421

Credential Type: Notary Public Commission. **Duration of License:** Five years. **Requirements:** At least 18 years of age. Endorsement by secretary of state, assistant secretary, and state senator or assemblyman. No criminal convictions involving dishonesty. Commuting non-residents may qualify for commission. **Fees:** $25 commission fee.

New Mexico

4510

Notary Public
Office of the Secretary of State
State Capitol Bldg.
Santa Fe, NM 87503
Phone: (505)827-3600

Credential Type: Notary Public Commission. **Duration of License:** Four years. **Requirements:** At least 18 years of age. Must have two character witnesses. No felonies on record. No commission revocation. Must read and write English. Must post $500 bond. **Fees:** $10 commission fee.

New York

4511

Notary Public
Div. of Licensing Services
162 Washington Ave.
Albany, NY 12231
Phone: (518)474-4429

Credential Type: Notary Public Commission. **Duration of License:** Two years. **Requirements:** At least 18 years of age. All applicants, except attorneys, must pass examination. No felonies on record. Commuting nonresidents may qualify. **Examination:** State examination. **Fees:** $20 commission fee.

North Carolina

4512

Notary Public
Secretary of State
Notary Public Div.
Legislative Office Bldg.
Raleigh, NC 27611
Phone: (919)733-3406

Credential Type: License. **Duration of License:** Five years. **Requirements:** 18 years of age. Recommendation from an elected official. High school diploma or GED. Completion of a notary public course. **Fees:** $15 application fee. $15 renewal fee.

North Dakota

4513

Notary Public
Office of Secretary of State
Capitol Bldg.
Bismarck, ND 58505
Phone: (701)224-3666

Credential Type: Notary Public Commission. **Duration of License:** Six years. **Requirements:** At least 18 years of age. Minimum 30 days of residency. U.S. citizen. Must post $7,500 bond. **Fees:** $20 commission fee.

Ohio

4514

Notary Public
Office of Governor
77 S. High St., B-1 Level
Columbus, OH 43215
Phone: (614)466-2566

Credential Type: Notary Public Commission. **Duration of License:** Five years or life for attorneys. **Requirements:** At least 18 years of age. U.S. citizen. Minimum 30 days of residency. Examination may be required. Endorsement by judge. **Fees:** $5 commission fee (non-attorney). $10 commission fee (attorney).

Oklahoma

4515

Notary Public
Office of Secretary of State
101 State Capitol Bldg.
Oklahoma City, OK 73105
Phone: (405)521-3911

Credential Type: Notary Public Commission. **Duration of License:** Four years. **Requirements:** At least 18 years of age. U.S. citizen. Must post $1,000 bond. **Fees:** $25 commission fee. $20 renewal fee.

Oregon

4516

Notary Public
Office of Secretary of State
142 State Capitol
Salem, OR 97310
Phone: (503)378-4724

Credential Type: Notary Public Commission. **Duration of License:** Four years. **Requirements:** At least 18 years of age. Pass examination. Residents of bordering states commuting to Oregon may qualify. No felonies or misdemeanors in last 10 years. No negative licensing action. **Fees:** $20 commission fee.

Pennsylvania

4517

Notary Public
Dept. of State
Commission Bureau
North Office Bldg., No. 305
Harrisburg, PA 17120
Phone: (717)787-4035

Credential Type: Notary Public Commission. **Duration of License:** Four years. **Requirements:** At least 18 years of age. U.S. citizen. Minimum one year of residency. Endorsement by state senator. Two reputable citizens must endorse application. Must post $3,000 bond. **Fees:** $40 commission fee.

Rhode Island

4518

Notary Public
Office of Secretary of State
100 N. Main St.
Providence, RI 02903
Phone: (401)277-3040

Credential Type: Notary Public Commission. **Duration of License:** Two years. **Requirements:** At least 18 years of age. Minimum one month residency. Application endorsed by Board of Canvassers. Must read, write, and speak English. Must be a qualified elector. **Fees:** $40 commission fee.

South Carolina

4519

Notary Public
Office of Secretary of State
PO Box 11350
Columbia, SC 29211
Phone: (803)734-2167

Credential Type: Notary Public Commission. **Duration of License:** 10 years. **Requirements:** At least 18 years of age. Endorsement by eight county legislators (half). Must be U.S. citizen and a registered voter. **Fees:** $25 commission fee.

South Dakota

4520

Notary Public
Office of Secretary of State
500 East Capitol
Pierre, SD 57501-5077
Phone: (605)773-5004

Credential Type: Notary Public Commission. **Duration of License:** Eight years. **Requirements:** At least 18 years of age. Must pass examination. Must post $500 Notary surety bond. **Examination:** State examination. **Fees:** $5 commission fee.

Tennessee

4521

Notary Public
Office of Secretary of State
James K. Polk Bldg., 18th Fl.
Nashville, TN 37243-0306
Phone: (615)741-3699

Credential Type: Notary Public Commission. **Duration of License:** Four years. **Requirements:** At least 18 years of age. Must be U.S. citizen. Endorsement by county commissioner(s). Must post $10,000 bond in Shelby county. All other counties require $5,000 bond. **Fees:** $7 county commission fee. $3 state commission fee.

Texas

4522

Notary Public
Office of Secretary of State
PO Box 12079
Austin, TX 78711
Phone: (512)463-5705

Credential Type: Notary Public Commission. **Duration of License:** Four years. **Requirements:** At least 18 years of age. Must be U.S. citizen. No felonies or crimes of moral turpitude convictions. Must post $2,500 bond. **Fees:** $21 commission fee.

Utah

4523

Notary Public
Div. of Corporations & Commercial Code
160 E. 300 South
PO Box 45801
Salt Lake City, UT 84145-0801
Phone: (801)530-6078

Credential Type: Notary Public Commission. **Duration of License:** Four years. **Requirements:** At least 18 years of age. Minimum 30 days of residency. Must be resident of Utah. Must read and write English. Must post $5,000 bond. **Fees:** $15 commission fee.

Vermont

4524

Notary Public
Office of Secretary of State
109 State St.
Montpelier, VT 05609-1103
Phone: (802)828-2308

Credential Type: Notary Public Commission. **Duration of License:** Four years. **Requirements:** At least 18 years of age. (Applicants under 18 may be qualified by appointing judge.) **Fees:** $15 commission fee.

Virginia

4525

Notary Public
Office of Secretary of Commonwealth
Notary Public Division
PO Box 1795
Richmond, VA 23214-1795
Phone: (804)786-2441

Credential Type: Notary Public Commission. **Duration of License:** Four years. **Requirements:** At least 18 years of age. Endorsement by state official and two registered voters. No felonies. Must read and write English. Commuting non-residents may qualify. **Fees:** $25 commission fee.

Washington

4526

Notary Public
Professional Licensing Services
PO Box 9027
Olympia, WA 98507-9027
Phone: (206)586-4575

Credential Type: Notary Public Commission. **Duration of License:** Four years. **Requirements:** At least 18 years of age. Endorsement by three residents who are 18 years of age or older. Must read and write English. Must post $10,000 bond. **Fees:** $20 commission fee.

West Virginia

4527

Notary Public
Office of Secretary of State
Capitol Bldg., No. 157-K
Charleston, WV 25305
Phone: (304)345-4000

Credential Type: Notary Public Commission. **Duration of License:** 10 years. **Requirements:** At least 18 years of age. Minimum 30 days of residency. May qualify for residency if business address is in state. Endorsement by three qualified electors. Must read and write English. **Fees:** $50 commission fee. $2 recording fee.

Wisconsin

4528

Notary Public
Office of Secretary of State
PO Box 7848
Madison, WI 53707-7848
Phone: (608)266-5594

Credential Type: Notary Public Commission. **Duration of License:** Four years or life for attorneys. **Requirements:** At least 18 years of age. Must have completed 8th grade. No convictions relating to the duties of a Notary. Must post $500 bond. **Fees:** $15 commission fee.

Wyoming

4529

Notary Public
Office of Secretary of State
The Capitol
Cheyenne, WY 82002-0020
Phone: (307)777-5342

Credential Type: Notary Commission. **Duration of License:** Four years. **Requirements:** At least 19 years of age. Must pass examination. Must read and write English. Must post $500 bond. **Examination:** State examination **Fees:** $30 commission fee.

Nuclear Medicine Technologists

The following states grant licenses in this occupational category as of the date of publication: California, Delaware, Florida, Illinois, Louisiana, Maine, Maryland, Massachusetts, New Jersey, New Mexico, Pennsylvania, Washington.

California

4530

Nuclear Medical Technologist
Dept. of Health Services
Radiological Health Branch
601 N. 7th St.
Sacramento, CA 95814-0208
Phone: (916)445-6695

Credential Type: Nuclear Medical Technologist Certification. **Duration of License:** Five years. **Requirements:** Submit application. Meet board education and experience requirements. **Examination:** State or Nuclear Medicine Technology Certification Board (NMTCB) examination. **Fees:** $75 application fee. $50 renewal fee.

Delaware

4531

Nuclear Medical Technologist
Board of Public Health
Central Billing
PO Box 637
Dover, DE 19903
Phone: (302)739-3787

Credential Type: Nuclear Medical Technologist Certification. **Duration of License:** Four years. **Requirements:** Submit application. Meet board education and experience requirements. **Examination:** State, Nuclear Medicine Technology Certification Board (NMTCB), or American Registry of Radiologic Technologists (ARRT) examination. **Fees:** $10 application fee. $10 renewal fee.

Florida

4532

Nuclear Medical Technologist
Office of Radiation control
1317 Winewood Blvd.
Tallahassee, FL 32301
Phone: (904)487-3451

Credential Type: Nuclear Medical Technologist Certification. **Duration of License:** Two years. **Requirements:** Submit application. Meet board education and experience requirements. Renewal requires 12 hours of continuing education every two years. **Examination:** State, American Registry of Clinical Radiography Technologists (ARCRT), Nuclear Medicine Technology Certification Board (NMTCB), or American Registry of Radiologic Technologists (ARRT) examination. **Fees:** $50 license by examination fee. $35 license by endorsement fee. $40 renewal fee.

Illinois

4533

Nuclear Medicine Technologist
Illinois Dept. of Nuclear Safety
1035 Outer Park Drive
Springfield, IL 62704
Phone: (217)785-9900

Credential Type: License Accreditation. **Duration of License:** Two years. **Requirements:** Must complete an approved training program. Pass examination by the American Registry of Radiologic Technologists (ARRT) or the Nuclear Medicine Technologist Certification Board (NMTCB). Renewal requires 12 contact hours per year. **Examination:** Written examination. **Reciprocity:** No. **Fees:** $45 examination fee. $40 application fee. **Governing Statute:** Illinois Administrative Code 401.

Louisiana

4534

Nuclear Medical Technologist
Louisiana State Radiologic
 Technology Board of Examiners
3108 Cleary Ave., Ste. 207
Metairie, LA 70002
Phone: (504)838-5231

Credential Type: Nuclear Medical Technologist License. **Duration of License:** Two years. **Requirements:** Submit application. Meet board education and experience requirements. **Examination:** State, Nuclear Medicine Technology Certification Board (NMTCB), or American Registry of Radiologic Technologists (ARRT) examination. **Fees:** $50 application fee. $50 renewal fee.

Maine

4535

Nuclear Medicine Technologist
Radiologic Technology Board of
 Examiners
Dept. of Professional and Financial
 Regulation
Div. of Licensing and Enforcement
State House Station 35
Augusta, ME 04333
Phone: (207)582-8723

Credential Type: Nuclear Medicine Technologist License. **Duration of License:** Two years. **Requirements:** High school graduate or equivalent. Be at least 18 years of age. Complete a course of study in nuclear medicine technology accredited by

Nuclear Medicine Technologist, continued

the Committee on Allied Health Education and Accreditation. Possess current national certification or pass the Nuclear Medicine Technologist Certification Examination. **Examination:** Nuclear Medicine Technologist Certification Examination. **Exemptions:** Exam not required if nationally certified. **Fees:** $10 application fee. $40 license fee. $40 renewal fee. $30 exam fee. **Governing Statute:** 32 M.S.R.A. Chap. 103.

Credential Type: Special Permit Nuclear Medicine Technologist. **Duration of License:** One year. **Requirements:** High school graduate or equivalent. Be at least 18 years of age. Possess current national certification as a radiographer. Board must find evidence of unavailability of sufficient licensed nuclear medical technologists in locality in which applicant intends to practice. After one year, applicant shall be eligible for examination and licensure. **Fees:** $10 application fee. $25 permit fee. **Governing Statute:** 32 M.S.R.A. Chap. 103.

Credential Type: Temporary License. **Duration of License:** 90 days or when exam results are published. **Requirements:** High school graduate or equivalent. Be at least 18 years of age. Complete or be about to complete within one month a board-approved course of study. Document availability of a licensed practitioner to provide supervision. **Fees:** $10 application fee. $10 license fee. $10 renewal fee.

Maryland

4536

Nuclear Medical Technologist
Maryland Board of Physician Quality Assurance
4201 Patterson Ave.
PO Box 2571
Baltimore, MD 21215-0002
Phone: (301)764-4777

Credential Type: Nuclear Medical Technologist License. **Duration of License:** Two years. **Requirements:** Submit application. Meet board education and experience requirements. Renewal requires 30 hours of continuing education every year. **Examination:** State or American Registry of Radiologic Technologists (ARRT) examination. **Fees:** $100 application fee. $50 renewal fee.

Massachusetts

4537

Nuclear Medical Technologist
Radiation Control Program
Dept. of Public Health
305 South St., 7th Fl.
Jamaica Plain, MA 02130
Phone: (617)727-6214

Credential Type: Nuclear Medical Technologist License. **Duration of License:** Two years. **Requirements:** Submit application. Meet board education and experience requirements. Renewal requires 30 hours of continuing education every year. **Examination:** State or American Registry of Radiologic Technologists (ARRT) examination. **Fees:** $25 application fee. $50 renewal fee.

New Jersey

4538

Nuclear Medical Technologist
New Jersey Dept. of Environmental Protection
Bureau of Revenue
CN402
Trenton, NJ 08625-0402
Phone: (609)530-5760

Credential Type: License. **Duration of License:** One year. **Requirements:** Completion of a course of study in nuclear medical technology at an accredited school. **Examination:** Yes. **Exemptions:** The department may waive the examination for applicants passing a national certification exam. **Reciprocity:** Yes. **Fees:** $40 application fee. $20 annual registration fee. **Governing Statute:** NJSA 26:D. NJAC 7:28-24.

New Mexico

4539

Nuclear Medical Technologist
Radiologic Licensing and Registration
1190 St. Francis Dr.
Santa Fe, NM 87503
Phone: (505)827-2948

Credential Type: Nuclear Medical Technologist Certificate. **Duration of License:** Two years. **Requirements:** Submit application. Meet board education and experience requirements. Renewal requires 20 hours of continuing education every year. **Examination:** State, American Registry of Clinical Radiography Technologists (ARCRT), or American Registry of Radiologic Technologists (ARRT) examination. **Fees:** $60 application fee. $50 renewal fee.

Pennsylvania

4540

Nuclear Medicine Technologist
State Board of Medicine
Bureau of Professional and Occupational Affairs
Dept. of State
Transportation and Safety Bldg., 6th Fl.
Harrisburg, PA 17120
Phone: (717)787-8503

Credential Type: Nuclear Medicine Technologist License. **Duration of License:** Two years. **Requirements:** Must be certified by the American Registry of Radiologic Technologists, or pass the ARRT examination in Nuclear Medicine Technology, or pass a course and examination in Nuclear Medicine Technology given by an accredited body recognized by the board. **Examination:** American Registry of Radiologic Technologists (ARRT) examination in Nuclear Medicine Technology or board-approved examination. **Fees:** $25 examination fee.

Washington

4541

Nuclear Medical Technologist
Department of Health
1300 SE Quince St., EY-28
PO Box 1099
Olympia, WA 98504
Phone: (206)586-6100

Credential Type: Nuclear Medical Technologist Certificate. **Duration of License:** One year. **Requirements:** Submit application. Meet board education and experience requirements. **Examination:** State or American Registry of Radiologic Technologists (ARRT) examination. **Fees:** $50 application fee. $50 renewal fee.

Nursery Workers

The following states grant licenses in this occupational category as of the date of publication: Arkansas, Idaho, Louisiana, Michigan, Montana, Rhode Island.

Arkansas

4542

Nurseryman
Arkansas State Plant Board
No. 1 Natural Resources Dr.
PO Box 1069
Little Rock, AR 72205
Phone: (501)225-1598

Credential Type: License. **Requirements:** Be of sound moral and financial character. **Examination:** No. **Fees:** $10 License. $45 Inspection.

Idaho

4543

Nursery Agent
Plant Industries Div.
Agriculture Dept.
PO Box 790
Boise, ID 83701
Phone: (208)334-2986

Credential Type: Agent's License. **Duration of License:** One year. **Requirements:** Submit application and pay fee. **Exemptions:** Agents soliciting sales only from persons licensed as florists, nurserymen, or landsacpe designers are exempt from license fees. **Fees:** $25 fee per principal respresented. **Governing Statute:** Idaho Code, Title 22, Chap. 23.

4544

Nurseryman
Plant Industries Div.
Agriculture Dept.
PO Box 790
Boise, ID 83701
Phone: (208)334-2986

Credential Type: Class A License. **Duration of License:** One year. **Authorization:** Required if gross business is over $1,000 per year. **Requirements:** Submit application and pay fee. **Fees:** $50 license fee per outlet. **Governing Statute:** Idaho Code, Title 22, Chap. 23.

Credential Type: Class B License. **Duration of License:** One year. **Authorization:** Required if gross business is $1,000 or less per year. **Requirements:** Submit application and pay fee. **Fees:** $15 license fee. **Governing Statute:** Idaho Code, Title 22, Chap. 23.

Louisiana

4545

Nursery Stock Dealer
Horticulture Commission
Plant Quarantine and Horticulture Programs
PO Box 44517, Capitol Sta.
Baton Rouge, LA 70804
Phone: (504)925-7772

Credential Type: Permit. **Duration of License:** One year. **Requirements:** Submit application and pay fee. **Fees:** $65 permit fee. $35 renewal fee. **Governing Statute:** R.S. 37:1961-1974.

Michigan

4546

Nursery Dealer
Pesticide and Plant Pest Management Div.
Dept. of Agriculture
Ottawa Bldg. N.
PO Box 30017
Lansing, MI 48909
Phone: (517)373-1104

Credential Type: License. **Duration of License:** One year. **Requirements:** Submit application and pay fee. Must sell nursery stock that is free of dangerous plant pests and that is purchased from a certified source. Abide by the rules of the Department of Agriculture. **Fees:** $50 initial license fee. $50 renewal fee. Nonresident nursery dealers are required to pay the $50 license fee. **Governing Statute:** Insect Pests and Plant Diseases Act, Act 189 of 1931, as amended.

4547

Nurseryperson (Nurseryman)
Pesticide and Plant Pest Management Div.
Dept. of Agriculture
Ottawa Bldg. N.
PO Box 30017
Lansing, MI 48909
Phone: (517)373-1104

Credential Type: License. **Duration of License:** One year. **Requirements:** Submit application and pay fee. Must have nursery stock inspected for dangerous insect pests and plant diseases and certified to be apparently free of such pests and diseases by the Department or a Department-approved inspector. **Fees:** $50 initial license fee. $50

Michigan

Nurseryperson (Nurseryman), continued

renewal fee. Nonresident nurserypersons are required to pay the $50 license fee. **Governing Statute:** Insect Pests and Plant Diseases Act, Act 189 of 1931, as amended.

4548

Plant Dealer
Pesticide and Plant Pest Management Div.
Dept. of Agriculture
Ottawa Bldg., N.
PO Box 30017
Lansing, MI 48909
Phone: (517)373-1104

Credential Type: License. **Duration of License:** One year. **Requirements:** Must sell plants that have been obtained from a Department of Agriculture certified source. Abide by the rules of the Department of Agriculture. **Fees:** $20 initial license fee. $20 renewal fee. **Governing Statute:** Insect Pests and Plant Diseases Act, Act 189 of 1931, as amended.

Montana

4549

Nurseryman
Dept. of Agriculture
Plant Industry Div.
Agriculture and Livestock Bldg.
6th and Roberts
Helena, MT 59620
Phone: (406)444-3730

Credential Type: Class A License. **Authorization:** General nursery license. **Requirements:** Submit application and pay fee. **Fees:** $50 license fee. **Governing Statute:** ARM, Title 80, Chap. 7.

Credential Type: Class B License. **Authorization:** Limited to small fruits, shrubs, and bushes. **Requirements:** Submit application and pay fee. **Fees:** $35 license fee. **Governing Statute:** ARM, Title 80, Chap. 7.

Credential Type: Class C License. **Authorization:** Limited to bulbs, perennials, and greenhouse plants. **Requirements:** Submit application and pay fee. **Fees:** $20 license fee. **Governing Statute:** Montana Code Annotated, Title 80, Chap. 7.

Rhode Island

4550

Nurseryman
Div. of Agriculture
Rhode Island Dept. of Environmental Management
22 Hayes St., Rm. 120
Providence, RI 02908
Phone: (401)277-2781

Credential Type: Nurseryman License. **Duration of License:** One year. **Requirements:** Submit application and pay fee. **Fees:** $50 license fee. $50 renewal fee.

Nursing Aides and Psychiatric Aides

The following states grant licenses in this occupational category as of the date of publication: Alaska, Arizona, Arkansas, California, Colorado, Connecticut, Iowa, Kansas, Maryland, Montana, Texas, Washington.

Alaska

4551

Nurse Aide
Dept. of Commerce and Economic Development
Div. of Occupational Licensing
Nurse Aide Registry
PO Box D
Juneau, AK 99811-0800
Phone: (907)561-2878
Fax: (907)465-2974

Credential Type: Nurse Aide Certificate. **Duration of License:** Two years. **Requirements:** Complete an approved nurse aide program. Pass an approved nurse aide competency examination. **Examination:** Yes, with written, oral, and skills components. **Fees:** $30 application fee. **Governing Statute:** Alaska Statutes 08.68. Professional Regulations 12 AAC 44.

Arizona

4552

Lay Midwife
Dept. of Health Services
Office of Maternal and Child Health
1740 W. Adams
Phoenix, AZ 85007
Phone: (602)542-1875

Credential Type: Lay midwife license. **Authorization:** To attend births and provide prenatal, postpartum, and newborn care. **Requirements:** Pass written, oral, and practical examination over a 3-day period. **Examination:** Written, oral, and practical examination. **Reciprocity:** No **Fees:** $25 application fee. $150 exam and license fee.

Arkansas

4553

Psychiatric Technician - Nurse
Arkansas State Board of Nursing
University Tower Bldg. Ste. 800
1123 S. University
Little Rock, AR 72204
Phone: (501)371-2751

Credential Type: License. **Duration of License:** Two years. **Requirements:** Good moral character. 12th grade education or equivalent. Satisfactory completion of the prescribed curriculum in a State approved program for the preparation of Psychiatric Technician Nurses. **Examination:** Yes. **Fees:** $35 Written and oral examinations. $50 Endorsement. $20 License. $20 Renewal.

California

4554

Psychiatric Technician
Board of Vocational Nurse and
  Psychiatric Technician Examiners
1414 K St., Ste. 103
Sacramento, CA 95814
Phone: (916)445-2933

Credential Type: License. **Duration of License:** Two years. **Requirements:** Be at least 18 years of age. High school graduate or equivalent. Meet one of the following sets of requirements: (1) Graduate from a California accredited program for psychiatric technicians. (2) Complete equivalent study and training consisting of 576 hours of theory and 954 hours of supervised clinical experience. The supervised clinical experience requirement may be satisfied by 31.8 months of paid work experience within the past 10 years. (3) Complete an armed forces course involving neuropsychiatric nursing and one year of verified work experience in caring for the mentally disordered and developmentally disabled. (4) Complete a California board approved equivalency course for psychiatric technicians consisting of at least 450 hours of theory instruction. Complete 18 months of paid work experience within the past 36 months. **Examination:** Written examination. **Reciprocity:** Endorsement is available for anyone holding a valid license or certificate issued by any other state or foreign country. **Fees:** $25 application fee. $90 license fee. $90 renewal fee.

Colorado

4555

Psychiatric Technician
Board of Nursing
Dept. of Regulatory Agencies
Div. of Registrations
1560 Broadway
Denver, CO 80202
Phone: (303)894-2430

Credential Type: License. **Requirements:** Contact licensing body for application information.

Connecticut

4556

Midwife
Div. of Medical Quality Assurance
Health Systems Regulation Bureau
Health Services Dept.
150 Washington St.
Hartford, CT 06106
Phone: (203)566-3207

Credential Type: License. **Requirements:** Contact licensing body for application information.

4557

Nurse Aide
Div. of Medical Quality Assurance
Health Systems Regulation Bureau
Health Services Dept.
150 Washington St.
Hartford, CT 06106
Phone: (203)566-3207

Credential Type: License. **Requirements:** Contact licensing body for application information.

Iowa

4558

Certified Nursing Assistant (Nurse Aid)
Dept. of Inspection and Appeals
Div. of Health Facilities
Lucas State Office Bldg., 3rd Fl.
Des Moines, IA 50319
Phone: (515)281-4233

Credential Type: Certificate. **Requirements:** 16 years of age. Attend 75 hours of training offered by a community college. **Examination:** Written and practical. **Fees:** $20—$50 exam fee.

Kansas

4559

Nurse Aide
Health Occupations Credentialling Bureau of Adult and Child Care
Dept. of Health and Environment
Landon State Office Bldg., Ste. 901
Topeka, KS 66612-1290
Phone: (913)296-1284

Credential Type: Nurse Aide Certificate. **Requirements:** Contact licensing body for application information. **Examination:** Written exam. **Reciprocity:** Applicant's training from another state may be endorsed only if applicant is on that state's nurse aide registry. **Fees:** $7.50 certification fee.

Maryland

4560

Midwife
Office of Regulatory Services
Dept. of Health and Mental Hygiene
4201 Patterson Ave.
Baltimore, MD 21215
Phone: (410)225-5300

Credential Type: License. **Requirements:** Contact licensing body for application information.

4561

Psychiatrist's Assistant
Licensing and Certification Div.
Dept. of Health and Mental Hygiene
4201 Patterson Ave.
Baltimore, MD 21215
Phone: (410)764-4770
Phone: (410)764-2750

Credential Type: License. **Requirements:** Contact licensing body for application information.

Montana

4562

Lay Midwife
Board of Alternative Health Care
111 N. Jackson
Helena, MT 59620
Phone: (406)444-3737

Credential Type: Direct Entry Midwife License. **Duration of License:** One year. **Requirements:** Complete an apprenticeship consisting of 100 prenatal examinations, observation of 40 births, and participation as primary birth attendant for 25 births. Minimum education may be required. **Examination:** MANA exam may be required. **Fees:** $250 application fee. $50 license fee. $300 exam fee. $300 renewal fee.

Texas

4563

Medication Aide
Texas Dept. of Health
Medication Aide Training Program
1100 W. 49th St.
Austin, TX 78756
Phone: (512)834-6618

Credential Type: License. **Duration of License:** One year. **Requirements:** 18 years of age. High school diploma or equivalent. Current employment in a facility as a nurse aide or non-licensed direct care staff person; or must have been employed in a facility for 90 days as a nurse aide or non-licensed direct care staff person. This employment must have been completed within the 12 month period preceding the first official day of the applicant's medication aide training program. Completion of a state-approved medication aide training program. Continuing education required for renewal. **Examination:** Written. **Fees:** $25 exam and permit fee. $15 renewal fee. **Governing Statute:** (512)834-6618.

4564

Midwife, Lay
Texas Dept. of Health
Bureau of Maternal and Child Health
1100 W. 49th St.
Austin, TX 78756
Phone: (512)458-7700

Credential Type: License. **Duration of License:** One year. **Authorization:** Practice restricted to normal or uncomplicated pregnancy, childbirth, and immediate care of the normal infant. **Requirements:** Annual documentation with the Midwifery Program. Current adult and infant CPR certification. Newborn screening test training or agreement with a healthy authority. Must file a copy of documentation with the local registrar of births. Mandatory education and continuing education requirements which become effective in September 1993 are yet to be developed. **Examination:** Optional. **Fees:** $50 annual documentation fee. $25 optional exam fee. **Governing Statute:** VACS 4512i, 25 TAC 37.

4565

Nurse Aide, Long Term Care
Nurse Aide Registry and Training Program
Texas Dept. of Health
1100 W. 49th St.
Austin, TX 78756
Phone: (512)458-7229

Credential Type: License. **Requirements:** Completion of a training course which includes a minimum of 75 clock hours, including 51 clock hours of classroom and skills training and 24 clock hours of clinical training under the direct supervision of a licensed nurse. A new training and competency evaluation program must be completed if an individual has not worked as a nurse aide for pay for at least one day during any 24 month period after completion of a training and competency evaluation program or a competency evaluation. **Examination:** Competency examination. **Fees:** $66 exam fee. **Governing Statute:** VACS 4414b, 25 TAC 151.

Washington

4566

Midwife
Dept. of Health
1112 SE Quince
Olympia, WA 98504
Phone: (206)753-4614

Credential Type: Midwife License. **Duration of License:** One year. **Requirements:** Certificate or diploma from a state approved school of midwifery or equivalent education and experience. Must complete a course in AIDS education. **Examination:** Written examination. **Fees:** $337.50 initial application fee. $375 examination or reexamination fee. $275 renewal fee.

4567

Nursing Assistant/Aide
Dept. of Health
1112 SE Quince
Olympia, WA 98504
Phone: (206)753-5612

Credential Type: Registration. **Duration of License:** One year. **Requirements:** Submit application and pay fees. Complete AIDS education. **Fees:** $5 application fee. $10 renewal fee.

Credential Type: Certification. **Duration of License:** One year. **Requirements:** Complete an approved training program. Complete AIDS education. **Examination:** Yes. **Fees:** $5 application fee. $10 renewal fee.

Occupational Therapists

The following states grant licenses in this occupational category as of the date of publication:

Alabama	District of	Iowa	Michigan	New Hampshire	Oregon	Utah
Alaska	Columbia	Kansas	Minnesota	New Mexico	Pennsylvania	Virginia
Arizona	Florida	Kentucky	Mississippi	New York	Rhode Island	Washington
Arkansas	Georgia	Louisiana	Missouri	North Carolina	South Carolina	West Virginia
California	Idaho	Maine	Montana	North Dakota	South Dakota	Wisconsin
Connecticut	Illinois	Maryland	Nebraska	Ohio	Tennessee	Wyoming
Delaware	Indiana	Massachusetts	Nevada	Oklahoma	Texas	

Alabama

4568

Occupational Therapist
State Board of Occupational Therapy
PO Box 4424
Montgomery, AL 36103-4424
Phone: (205)265-9654

Credential Type: License. **Duration of License:** One year. **Requirements:** Complete the academic requirements in occupational therapy in an approved program that is accredited by the committee on allied health education and accreditation of the American Medical Association in collaboration with the American Occupational Therapy Association. Be certified by the American Occupational Therapy Certification Board (AOTCB). **Fees:** $90 license fee.

Alaska

4569

Occupational Therapist
Dept. of Commerce and Economic Development
Div. of Occupational Licensing
State Physical Therapy and Occuapational Therapy Board
PO Box D
Juneau, AK 99811-0800
Phone: (907)465-2551
Fax: (907)465-2974

Credential Type: License by Credentials. **Duration of License:** Two years. **Requirements:** Certification as an Occupational Therapist by the American Occupational Therapy Certification Board (AOTCB). Complete a curriculum of occupational therapy approved by the committee of Allied Health Education and Accreditation of the American Medical Association, and the American Occupational Therapy Association. Complete six months of supervised field work.

If not AOTCB certified, pass an examination prepared by a national testing service approved by the board or an examination recognized by the American Occupational Therapy Association.

Applicant who is licensed as an occupational therapist in another state, if the requirements for licensure were substantially equal to those of Alaska, may be granted a license without examination. **Fees:** $30 application fee. $100 license fee. **Governing Statute:** Alaska Statutes 08.84. Professional Regulations 12 AAC 54.

Credential Type: License by Examination. **Duration of License:** Two years. **Requirements:** Pass the AOTCB examination. Then apply for license by credentials. **Examination:** AOTCB examination. **Fees:** $30 application fee. $100 license fee. **Governing Statute:** Alaska Statutes 08.84. Professional Regulations 12 AAC 54.

Credential Type: Temporary Permit. **Duration of License:** Eight months. **Authorization:** Allows individual to practice while awaiting next examination or completing application for licensure by credentials. **Requirements:** Completed supervised field work. **Fees:** $30 application fee. $50 temporary permit fee. **Governing Statute:** Alaska Statutes 08.84. Professional Regulations 12 AAC 54.

Credential Type: Limited Permit. **Duration of License:** 120 days. **Requirements:** Be licensed to practice occupational therapy in another state or meets requirements for certification by the American Occupational Therapy Certification Board. Has not previously been denied occupational therapy licensing by the board. **Fees:** $30 application fee. $50 limited permit fee. **Governing Statute:** Alaska Statutes 08.84. Professional Regulations 12 AAC 54.

Arizona

4570

Occupational Therapist
State Board of Occupational Therapy Examiners
1645 W. Jefferson, Rm. 424
Phoenix, AZ 85007
Phone: (602)542-6784

Credential Type: License and Registration. **Duration of License:** One year. **Authorization:** Must have a license in order to practice. **Requirements:** Be certified by the American Occupational Therapy Certification Board (AOTCB). Submit two professional recommendations. **Fees:** $100 application fee. $125 license fee. $125 renewal fee. **Governing Statute:** Arizona Revised Statutes, 32-34.

Credential Type: Limited Permit License. **Duration of License:** Four months. **Authorization:** Must work in association with a licensed occupational therapist. **Requirements:** Submit two professional recommendations. The limited permit license is generally granted to a recent graduate who is a firsttime applicant for licensure and has not taken the AOTCB exam or is awaiting exam results. **Fees:** $35 limited permit license fee (deductible from full license fee).

Arkansas

4571

Occupational Therapist
Arkansas State Medical Board
PO Box 102
Harrisburg, AR 72432
Phone: (501)455-1412

Alternate Information: State Examining Committee for Occupational Therapists, 7413 Henderson Rd., Little Rock, AR 72210

Credential Type: License. **Requirements:** 18 years of age. US citizen. Good moral character. Pass the National written examination. Completed training in an approved occupational therapy educational program. Must complete six months of supervised field work. **Examination:** Yes. **Fees:** $50 License. $10 Renewal.

California

4572

Occupational Therapist
Occupational Therapy Association of California
1414 K St., Ste. 620
Sacramento, CA 95814
Phone: (916)441-6822

Credential Type: Certification. **Authorization:** AOTCB certification required to practice. **Requirements:** California does not license occupational therapists. The state's Business and Professions Code requires that an individual be certified by the American Occupational Therapy Certification Board (AOTCB) to practice in California.

Connecticut

4573

Occupational Therapist
Div. of Medical Quality Assurance
Health Systems Regulation Bureau
Health Services Dept.
150 Washington St.
Hartford, CT 06106
Phone: (203)566-1483
Phone: (203)566-3207

Credential Type: License. **Duration of License:** Two years. **Requirements:** Have a bachelor's degree. Complete an education program accredited by the American Occupational Therapy Association, or an equivalent program in another country. Complete at least 24 weeks of supervised field work approved by the educational institution where the academic requirements were met.

Renewal requires completing 12 units of qualifying continued competency activity every two years. **Examination:** American Occupational Therapy Association certifying examination. **Reciprocity:** Yes, by endorsement, provided state has commensurate licensing standards. **Fees:** $100 application fee.

Credential Type: Temporary Permit. **Duration of License:** Until exam results are given. **Authorization:** Allows individual to practice under the supervision of a licensed occupational therapist. **Requirements:** Issued to recent graduates of an AOTA accredited program or equivalent until results of next scheduled exam are available. **Fees:** $25 temporary permit fee.

Delaware

4574

Occupational Therapist
Board of Occupational Therapy
Dept. of Administrative Services
Div. of Professional Regulation
PO Box 1401
Dover, DE 19903
Phone: (302)739-4522

Credential Type: Occupational Therapist Registration. **Requirements:** Complete an educational program in occupational therapy recognized by the board. Complete a period of supervised field work experience arranged by academic institution. **Examination:** Yes, administered by the Professional Examination Service of New York City. **Fees:** $150 registration fee. $110 renewal fee.

District of Columbia

4575

Occupational Therapist
Board of Occupational Therapy
Dept. of Consumer and Regulatory Affairs
Occupational and Professional Licensing Administration
PO Box 37200
Washington, DC 20013-7200
Phone: (202)727-7454

Alternate Information: 614 H St., NW, Washington, DC 20001

Credential Type: License. **Duration of License:** One year. **Requirements:** At least 18 years of age. Must have completed an educational program in occupational therapy at an institution accredited by the Committee on Allied Health Education and Accreditation (CAHEA) of the American Medical Association (AMA) in collaboration with the American Occupational Therapy Association (AOTA), with a concentration in a biological or physical science, psychology, or sociology and with training in activity analysis. Complete a period of six months of supervised field work experience at a CAHEA accredited institution or program.

Applicants educated outside the United States must demonstrate their education and training are substantially equivalent to a CAHEA-AMA accredited program. **Examination:** Occupational Therapy Certification Examination (AOTCB). **Reciprocity:** Yes, provided state has substantially equivalent licensure requirements and offers similar privileges to applicants from the District of Columbia. **Fees:** $20 application fee.

Florida

4576

Occupational Therapist
Board of Medicine
Occupational Therapy Council
Dept. of Professional Regulation
1940 N. Monroe St.
Tallahassee, FL 32399-0750
Phone: (904)488-0595

Credential Type: License by Examination. **Duration of License:** Two years. **Requirements:** Good moral character. Complete the academic requirements of an educational program in occupational therapy that is accredited by the American Medical Association in collaboration with the American Occupational Therapy Association. Complete a period of supervised fieldwork of at least six months.

The educational requirements may be waived for an applicant who has practiced as a state-licensed or American Occupational Therapy Associationcertified occupational therapy assistant for four years and who has completed a minimum of six months of supervised fieldwork experience.

A graduate from an occupational therapy course or school located in a foreign country may be admitted to the examination by demonstrating that his or her course of training met the same standards as Florida's.

Renewal requires 24 hours of continuing professional respiratory care education. **Examination:** American Occupational Therapy Association Examination, as administered by the Professional Examination

Georgia 4577

Occupational Therapist, continued

Services. **Fees:** $100 application fee. $50 license fee. $50 renewal fee. **Governing Statute:** Florida Statutes, Chapter 468, Part III. Florida Administrative Code, Rules 21-M.

Credential Type: License by Endorsement. **Duration of License:** Two years. **Requirements:** Meet basic experience and educational requirements. Have passed a substantially equivalent national, regional, state, or territorial licensing examination; or hold a valid license to practice occupational therapy issued by another state or territory of the United States with substantially identical licensure criteria.

Renewal requires 24 hours of continuing professional respiratory care education. **Fees:** $100 application fee. $50 license fee. $50 renewal fee. **Governing Statute:** Florida Statutes, Chapter 468, Part III. Florida Administrative Code, Rules 21-M.

Credential Type: Temporary Permit. **Duration of License:** Until next board meeting. **Requirements:** A temporary permit may be issued to an applicant who appears eligible for licensure by examination or by endorsement. **Governing Statute:** Florida Statutes, Chapter 468, Part III. Florida Administrative Code, Rules 21-M.

Georgia

4577

Occupational Therapist
State Board of Occupational Therapy
Allied Health Fields Section
Professional Examining Boards
166 Pryor St., SW
Atlanta, GA 30303
Phone: (404)656-3921

Credential Type: Occupational Therapist License. **Duration of License:** Two years. **Requirements:** Good moral character. Complete the academic requirements of an educational program in occupational therapy accredited by the American Occupational Therapy Association (AOTA) in collaboration with the American Medical Association. Comparable educational programs may be recognized by the board. Complete a minimum of six months of supervised field work. **Examination:** AOTCB Certification Examination. **Reciprocity:** License by endorsement may be granted to an applicant who holds a current license in AR, DC, IL, IA, KS, LA, NE, NY, OH, or SC. **Fees:** $60 application fee. $50 renewal fee. **Governing Statute:** Official Code of Georgia Annotated 43-28.

Idaho

4578

Occupational Therapist
Idaho State Board of Medicine
280 N. 8th St., Ste. 202
Boise, ID 83720
Phone: (208)334-2822

Credential Type: Occupational Therapist License. **Duration of License:** One year. **Requirements:** Good moral character. Graduate from an approved occupational therapy curriculum. **Examination:** Written examination. **Exemptions:** Exam may be waived if applicant if certified by the American Occupational Therapy Certification Board (AOTCB). **Reciprocity:** License by endorsement may be granted without examination if applicant holds a current, valid license from another state, territory, or district of the United States that has similar requirements. **Fees:** $80 initial license fee. $40 renewal fee. **Governing Statute:** Idaho Code, Title 54, Chap. 37. IDAPA 22.I.

Credential Type: Limited Permit. **Duration of License:** Six months. **Authorization:** Allows individual to practice only in association with and under the supervision of a licensed occupational therapist. **Requirements:** Complete application for an occupational therapist license must be filed. **Fees:** $25 permit fee. **Governing Statute:** Idaho Code, Title 54, Chap. 37. IDAPA 22.I.

Illinois

4579

Registered Occupational Therapist
Illinois Dept. of Professional Regulations
320 W. Washington St.
Springfield, IL 62786
Phone: (217)782-8556

Credential Type: Registered Occupational Therapist License. **Duration of License:** Two years. **Requirements:** Complete a four-year occupational therapy program approved by the Department of Professional Regulations that results in a baccalaureate degree or its equivalent. Minimum of six months supervised occupational therapy experience. **Examination:** American Occupational Therapy Certification Board (AOTCB) Examination. **Reciprocity:** Yes, if requirements for licensure were substantially equivalent to those of Illinois. **Fees:** $225 U.S. graduate examination fee. $375 foreign graduate examination fee. $25 initial license fee. $50 license by endorsement. $40 renewal fee. **Governing Statute:** Illinois Occupational Therapy Practice Act, Illinois Revised Statutes 1991.

Indiana

4580

Occupational Therapist
Occupational Therapy Committee
Health Professions Bureau
402 W. Washington St., Rm. 041
Indianapolis, IN 46204
Phone: (317)232-2960

Credential Type: Certificate to practice. **Duration of License:** Two years. **Requirements:** Graduate of an occupational therapy program that meets board standards; or be certified by the American Occupational Therapy Certification Board. **Examination:** Yes. **Reciprocity:** License by endorsement may be granted. **Fees:** $50 exam fee. $50 endorsement fee. $10 license issuance fee. **Governing Statute:** Indiana Code 25-23.5.

Credential Type: Temporary permit to practice. **Duration of License:** Valid until fully certified. **Authorization:** Provides temporary authorization to practice occupational therapy. **Requirements:** Must hold a valid license in another state or be waiting to take the first examination. Must have submitted application and be awaiting committee approval of a permanent certification. **Fees:** $10 temporary permit fee. **Governing Statute:** Indiana Code 25-23.5.

Iowa

4581

Occupational Therapist
Board of Physical and Occupational Therapy Examiners
Dept. of Public Health
Lucas State Office Bldg.
Des Moines, IA 50319
Phone: (515)281-6762

Credential Type: License. **Duration of License:** Two years. **Requirements:** BA or BS degree in occupational therapy from an accredited program, plus six months of supervised field experience. **Examination:** American Occupational Therapy Certification Board exam. **Fees:** $150 exam fee. $55 application fee. $55 renewal fee.

Kansas

4582

Occupational Therapist
State Board of Healing Arts
235 SW Topeka Blvd.
Topeka, KS 66603-3059
Phone: (913)296-7413

Credential Type: Occupational Therapist Registration. **Duration of License:** One year. **Requirements:** Complete an approved educational program for occupational therapists, including any program accredited by the committee on allied health education and accreditation of the American Medical Association in collaboration with the American Occupational Therapy Association, or any program equal to the program for occupational therapists at the University of Kansas School of Alllied Health.

Renewal requires completion of at least 40 contact hours of continuing education during the preceding two years. **Examination:** Certification examination for certified occupational therapist of the American Occupational Therapy Association. **Fees:** $40 application fee. $30 renewal fee. $190 board-administered exam fee. **Governing Statute:** K.S.A. 65-5401 ff. K.A.R. 100-54-1 ff.

Kentucky

4583

Occupational Therapist
Occupations and Professions Board
PO Box 456
Frankfort, KY 40602
Phone: (502)564-3296

Credential Type: Assistant License. **Duration of License:** One year. **Requirements:** Educational requirements are set by the American Occupational Therapy Certification Board. **Examination:** Yes. **Fees:** $50 renewal fee.

Credential Type: Occuapational Therapist License. **Duration of License:** One year. **Requirements:** Educational requirements are set by the American Occupational Therapy Certification Board. **Examination:** Yes. **Fees:** $50 renewal fee.

Louisiana

4584

Occupational Therapist
Louisiana State Board of Medical Examiners
830 Union St., Ste. 100
New Orleans, LA 70112
Phone: (504)524-6763

Credential Type: Occupational Therapist. **Duration of License:** One year. **Requirements:** 21 years of age. Occupational therapy degree. **Examination:** Yes. **Fees:** $80 license fee. $55 renewal fee.

4585

Occupational Therapist (School)
Louisiana State Dept. of Education, Teacher Certification
PO Box 94064
Baton Rouge, LA 70804
Phone: (504)342-3490

Credential Type: Provisional Certificate. **Duration of License:** Two years (non-renewable). **Requirements:** Must hold a temporary license to practice occupational therapy in the the state.

Credential Type: Certified Occupational Therapist (School). **Duration of License:** Five years. **Requirements:** Must hold a valid license to practice occupational therapy in the state. Completion of two years of work experience as an occupational therapist with children.

Maine

4586

Occupational Therapist
Board of Occupational Therapy Practice
State House Station 35
Augusta, ME 04333
Phone: (207)582-8723

Credential Type: License. **Duration of License:** Two years. **Requirements:** Complete the academic requirements in occupational therapy in an approved program that is accredited by the committee on allied health education and accreditation of the American Medical Association in collaboration with the American Occupational Therapy Association. Complete six months of supervised fieldwork experience arranged by the educational institution where the academic requirements were met. Be certified by the American Occupational Therapy Certification Board (AOTCB). **Examination:** AOTCB written examination. **Fees:** $100 application fee. $120 license fee. **Governing Statute:** 32 M.S.R.A. Chap. 32.

Credential Type: Temporary License. **Duration of License:** Until exam results are given. **Authorization:** Allows individual to practice under the supervision of a licensed occupational therapist. **Requirements:** Must have completed education and experience requirements for licensure and be scheduled to take AOTCB exam or be awaiting exam results. Submit two professional references. **Fees:** $100 application fee. $50 temporary license fee. **Governing Statute:** 32 M.S.R.A. Chap. 32.

Maryland

4587

Occupational Therapist
State Board of Occupational Therapy
Metro Executive Office Bldg., Rm. 312
4201 Patterson Ave.
Baltimore, MD 21215-2299
Phone: (301)764-4727

Credential Type: License. **Requirements:** Contact licensing body for application information.

Massachusetts

4588

Occupational Therapist
Board of Registration of Allied Health Professionals
Div. of Registration
100 Cambridge St., 15th fl.
Boston, MA 02202
Phone: (617)727-3071

Credential Type: License and registration. **Duration of License:** Two years. **Requirements:** Bachelor's degree in Occupational Therapy. **Examination:** American Occupational Therapy Certification Board (AOTCB) Certification Examination. **Reciprocity:** Yes, provided applicant meets Massachusetts standards. **Fees:** $50 application fee. $50 renewal fee. $50 reciprocity fee.

Credential Type: Temporary License. **Requirements:** Contact licensing body for application information. **Fees:** $10 temporary license fee.

Michigan

4589

Occupational Therapist
Bureau of Occupational &
  Professional Regulation
Dept. of Commerce
PO Box 30018
Lansing, MI 48909
Phone: (517)335-0918

Credential Type: Registration. **Requirements:** Contact licensing body for application information.

Minnesota

4590

Occupational Therapist
Dept. of Health
Bureau of Health Resources and
  Managed Care Services
Health Occupations Programs
717 Delaware St., SE
Box 9441
Minneapolis, MN 55440
Phone: (612)623-5611
Fax: (612)623-5043

Credential Type: Occupational Therapist Registration. **Authorization:** Registration required to use occupational title. **Requirements:** Contact licensing body for application information. **Governing Statute:** Minnesota Statutes 214.13.

Mississippi

4591

Occupational Therapist
State Dept. of Health
Professional Licensure
PO Box 1700
2423 N. State St.
Jackson, MS 39215-1700
Phone: (601)987-4153
Phone: (601)960-7400
Fax: (601)960-7948

Credential Type: License. **Duration of License:** One year. **Requirements:** Complete the academic requirements in occupational therapy in an approved program that is accredited by the committee on allied health education and accreditation of the American Medical Association in collaboration with the American Occupational Therapy Association. Complete six months of supervised fieldwork experience. Foreign trained applicants must complete substantially equivalent educational and fieldwork experience requirements. Be certified by the American Occupational Therapy Certification Board (AOTCB).

Renewal requires completing 10 contact hours of continuing education per year. **Examination:** AOTCB written examination. **Reciprocity:** Yes, based on passing a national exam. **Fees:** $95 application fee.

Credential Type: Limited Permit. **Duration of License:** One year. **Authorization:** May practice only under the supervision of a licensed occupational therapist. **Requirements:** Must have applied for licensure and be eligible to take the national examination. Must take the next scheduled exam.

Missouri

4592

Occupational Therapist
Dept. of Economic Development
Div. of Professional Registration
Office of Health Care Providers-
  Occupational Therapists
PO Box 471
Jefferson City, MO 65102-0471
Phone: (314)751-0877
Fax: (314)751-4176

Credential Type: Registration. **Duration of License:** One year. **Authorization:** Although anyone may practice occupational therapy in Missouri, registration is required to use the title, "Registered Occupational Therapist." **Requirements:** Be certified by the American Occupational Therapy Certification Board (AOTCB). **Fees:** $35 registration fee. $35 renewal fee. **Governing Statute:** Missouri Statutes, Rules and Regulations, Chap. 334. 4CSR 155-1.020.

Montana

4593

Occupational Therapist
Montana Board of Occupational
  Therapists
111 N. Jackson
Helena, MT 59620
Phone: (406)444-3091

Credential Type: Occupational Therapist License. **Duration of License:** One year. **Requirements:** Completion of an approved occupational therapy program. Completion of six months of supervised field work. **Examination:** American Occupational Therapy Certification Board Examination. **Fees:** $80 application fee. $80 license fee. $60 renewal fee. **Governing Statute:** Montana Code Annotated 37-24-301 through 37-24-311.

Nebraska

4594

Occupational Therapist
Nebraska Board of Occupational
  Therapy Practice
301 Centennial Mall S.
PO Box 95007
Lincoln, NE 68509
Phone: (402)471-2115

Credential Type: License. **Duration of License:** Two years. **Requirements:** Must have completed an accredited program in occupational therapy, plus six months supervised field work at an educational institution. Must be certified as a registered occupational therapist. **Examination:** Yes. **Fees:** $200 license fee. $200 renewal fee.

Nevada

4595

Occupational Therapist
Board of Occupational Therapy
PO Box 70220
Reno, NV 89570
Phone: (702)857-1700

Credential Type: License. **Duration of License:** One year. **Requirements:** Graduate from an educational program that is approved by the board and that includes a fieldwork program. Submit three professional references. An applicant who has graduated from a school in another country must submit an evaluation that states education is at least equivalent to a bachelor's degree in occupational therapy.

Renewal requires 10 hours of continuing education per year. **Examination:** American Occupational Therapy Certification Board (AOTCB) written examination. **Fees:** $250 application fee. $150 license fee. $240 renewal fee. **Governing Statute:** NAC 640A.

New Hampshire

4596

Occupational Therapist
Board of Registration in Medicine
Hazen Drive
Concord, NH 03301
Phone: (603)271-1203

Credential Type: Occupational Therapist License. **Duration of License:** One year. **Requirements:** At least 18 years of age. Good moral character. Bachelor's degree in a recognized four-year occupational therapy program approved by the Board. Must complete a minimum of six months of supervised fieldwork experience. Renewal requires 12 hours of continuing education annually. **Examination:** Examination required by Board. **Reciprocity:** No. **Fees:** $50 initial license application fee. $25 annual renewal fee.

New Mexico

4597

Occupational Therapist
Occupational Therapy Board
Dept. of Regulation and Licensing
PO Box 25101
725 St. Michael's Dr.
Santa Fe, NM 87504
Phone: (505)827-7162

Credential Type: Occupational Therapist License. **Duration of License:** One year. **Requirements:** Complete an occupational therapy educational program that is accredited by the committee on Allied Health Education and Accreditation of the American Medical Association. The program shall include at least six months of supervised field work experience. Foreign-trained occupational therapists must complete a program approved by a member association of the World Federation of Occupational Therapy. **Examination:** American Occupational Therapy Association examination. **Fees:** $75 license fee. $50 renewal fee. **Governing Statute:** Occupational Therapy Board Rules and Regulations 90-1. Occupational Therapy Licensing Law 61-12A-1 NMSA 1978 et seq.

New York

4598

Occupational Therapist
State Education Dept.
Div. of Professional Licensing Services
Cultural Education Center
Empire State Plaza
Albany, NY 12230
Phone: (518)474-5170

Credential Type: License. **Duration of License:** Three years. **Requirements:** Bachelor's or Master's Degree in occupational therapy. 21 years of age. Minimum of six months of supervised experience in occupational therapy. **Examination:** Written. **Fees:** $150 exam fee. $270 application fee. $155 renewal fee. **Governing Statute:** Title VIII Articles 130, 156 of the Education Law.

North Carolina

4599

Occupational Therapist
North Carolina Board of Occupational Therapy
PO Box 2280
Raleigh, NC 27602
Phone: (919)832-1380

Credential Type: Certification. **Duration of License:** One year. **Requirements:** Graduation from an accredited occupational therapy education program which includes six to nine months of supervised clinical work. **Examination:** National exam. **Fees:** $10 application fee. $150 exam fee. $100 license fee. $50 renewal fee.

North Dakota

4600

Occupational Therapist
State Board of Occupational Therapy Practice
1837 S. 15th St.
Fargo, ND 58103
Phone: (701)293-1817

Credential Type: License. **Requirements:** Contact licensing body for application information.

Ohio

4601

Occupational Therapist
Ohio Occupational Therapy, Physical Therapy, and Athletic Trainers Board
77 S. High St., 16th Fl.
Columbus, OH 43266-0317
Phone: (614)466-3774

Credential Type: License. **Duration of License:** Two years. **Requirements:** Complete an education program accredited by the American Occupational Therapy Association. **Examination:** American Occupational Therapy Certification Board (AOTCB) written examination. **Fees:** $75 license fee. $60 renewal fee. **Governing Statute:** Ohio Revised Code, Chap. 4755. Administrative Rules 4755-1-01 et seq.

Credential Type: Limited Permit. **Duration of License:** Until results of exam are given. **Authorization:** Allows individual to practice under the supervision of a licensed occupational therapist. **Requirements:** Must be scheduled for participation in the qualifying examination. **Fees:** $25 limited permit fee (to be credited toward license fee). **Governing Statute:** Ohio Revised Code, Chap. 4755. Administrative Rules 4755-1-01 et seq.

4602

School Occupational Therapist
Teacher Education and Certification
State Dept. of Education
65 S. Front St., Rm. 1012
Columbus, OH 43266-0308
Phone: (614)466-3593

Credential Type: Provisional Pupil Personnel Certificate—Occupational Therapy. **Requirements:** Recommendation of university official. Complete examination prescribed by the State Board of Education. Proof of education and experience in area of specialization. Baccalaureate degree and current license to practice occupational therapy in the State of Ohio. **Examination:** Examination prescribed by the State Board of Education.

Oklahoma

4603

Occupational Therapist
State Board of Medical License and Supervision
PO Box 18256
Oklahoma City, OK 73154
Phone: (405)848-6841

Credential Type: License. **Duration of License:** One year. **Requirements:** Completion of an accredited educational program in occupational therapy. Six months of supervised field work. 20 contact hours of continuing education every two years. Three recommendations are required. **Examination:** Certified Occupational Therapist Examination. **Fees:** $200 exam fee. $100 application fee. $40 renewal fee.

Oregon

4604

Occupational Therapist
Occupational Therapy Board
PO Box 231
Portland, OR 97207
Phone: (503)731-4048

Credential Type: License. **Duration of License:** One year. **Requirements:** Successful completion of four years of occupational therapy coursework and six months of supervised field work. **Examination:** Yes. **Fees:** $175 exam fee. $70 license fee.

Occupational Therapist, continued

$70 renewal fee. **Governing Statute:** ORS 675.210 to 675.340.

Pennsylvania

4605

Occupational Therapist (O.T.R.)
State Board of Occupational Therapy, Education, and Licensure
Bureau of Professional and Occupational Affairs
Dept. of State
Transportation and Safety Bldg., 6th Fl.
Harrisburg, PA 17120
Phone: (717)787-8503

Credential Type: Occupational Therapist License. **Duration of License:** Two years. **Requirements:** Good moral character. Must complete a board-approved four-year education program in occupational therapy. Complete a minimum of six months of supervised field work experience. Pass a board-approved examination.

Foreign graduates must have completed a program substantially equal to the requirements stated above. The board will accept a credentials evaluation done by the Div. of Credentialing of the American Occupational Therapy Association (AOA). Board may require up to one year of field experience for foreign graduates. **Examination:** Board-approved examination in occupational therapy.

Credential Type: Temporary License. **Duration of License:** until next examination. **Authorization:** Authorizes the practice of occupational therapy only as an assistant under the direct supervision of a licensed occupational therapist. **Requirements:** Must have completed all requirements for standard occupational therapy licensure with the exception of passage of examination.

Credential Type: Non-Resident's Temporary License. **Duration of License:** Six months. **Authorization:** Allows practice as an occupational therapist in the state of Pennsylvania for no longer than six consecutive months. **Requirements:** Must be a non-resident. Must hold an occupational therapist license from another state, District of Columbia, or territory of the United States. The licensure requirements under which the applicant received his/her license must be substantially equivalent to those required by Pennsylvania.

Rhode Island

4606

Occupational Therapist
Board of Occupational Therapy
Div. of Professional Regulation
Rhode Island Dept. of Health
3 Capitol Hill
Providence, RI 02908
Phone: (401)277-2827

Credential Type: Occupational Therapist License. **Duration of License:** Two years. **Requirements:** Good moral character. At least 18 years of age. Foreign born must show proof of legal entry into U.S. Graduate from an accredited occupational therapy program. Complete six months of supervised field experience. **Examination:** American Occupational Therapy Association (AOTA) Examination. **Reciprocity:** No. **Fees:** $50 application/license fee. $20 renewal fee.

South Carolina

4607

Occupational Therapist
South Carolina State Board of Occupational Therapy
PO Box 399
Lexington, SC 29072
Phone: (803)359-7914

Credential Type: License. **Requirements:** Completion of an accredited program in occupational therapy and six months of supervised field work. **Examination:** Yes. **Fees:** $50 application fee. $35 renewal fee.

South Dakota

4608

Occupational Therapist
State Board of Medical and Osteopathic Examiners
Dept. of Commerce and Consumer Affairs
1323 S. Minnesota Ave.
Sioux Falls, SD 57105
Phone: (605)336-1965

Credential Type: Occupational Therapy Certification and License. **Duration of License:** One year. **Requirements:** High school graduate or equivalent. Graduation from an approved occupational therapist program. Certification by the American Occupational Therapy Association (AOTA). Complete six months of supervised field work experience.

Renewal requires completing 12 continuing competency points per year. **Reciprocity:** Yes. **Fees:** $50 application and certification fee. $25 renewal fee.

Credential Type: Limited License. **Requirements:** High school graduate or equivalent. Graduation from an approved occupational therapist program. Must have been accepted to write the exam administered by the American Occupational Therapy Association (AOTA). Complete six months of supervised field work experience. **Fees:** $25 application and license fee.

Tennessee

4609

Occupational Therapist
Board of Occupational and Physical Therapy Examiners
283 Plus Park Blvd.
Nashville, TN 37247
Phone: (615)367-6243

Credential Type: License. **Duration of License:** One year. **Requirements:** 18 years old. Complete the academic requirements for an educational program in occupational therapy, accredited by the AMA or the CAHE. Must provide proof of good moral character. **Examination:** Occupational Therapy Registration examination. **Reciprocity:** Yes. **Fees:** $80 Registration. $25 Application. $80 Renewal.

Texas

4610

Occupational Therapist
Texas Advisor Board of Occupational Therapy
Texas Rehabilitation Commission
4900 N. Lamar Blvd.
Austin, TX 78751
Phone: (512)483-4072

Credential Type: Occupational Therapy License. **Duration of License:** One year. **Requirements:** Bachelor's or master's degree in occupational therapy or equivalent, and six months supervised field work. Continuing education required for renewal. **Examination:** Yes. **Fees:** $10 application fee. $70 license fee. $70 renewal fee. **Governing Statute:** VACS 8851, 40 TAC 361.1.

Utah

4611

Occupational Therapist
Dept. of Commerce
Div. of Occupational and
    Professional Licensing
160 E. 300 S.
PO Box 45802
Salt Lake City, UT 84145
Phone: (801)530-6628

Credential Type: Occupational Therapist's License. **Duration of License:** Two years. **Requirements:** Must complete an approved educational program in occupational therapy. Must complete a six-month period of supervised field work. **Examination:** Yes. **Fees:** $60 license fee. $30 renewal fee.

Virginia

4612

Occupational Therapist
State Board of Medicine
Dept. of Health Professions
6606 W. Broad St., 4th Fl.
Richmond, VA 23230-1717
Phone: (804)662-7664

Credential Type: Certification. **Duration of License:** Two years. **Requirements:** Complete the academic requirements in occupational therapy in an approved program that is accredited by the committee on allied health education and accreditation of the American Medical Association in collaboration with the American Occupational Therapy Association. Degrees from foreign occupational therapy programs are recognized. Be certified by the AOTCB. **Examination:** American Occupational Therapy Certification Board (AOTCB) written examination. **Exemptions:** An applicant who has graduated from an accredited program in occupational therapy may practice for one year after graduation or upon passing the AOTCB exam, whichever occurs sooner. **Fees:** $150 application and certification fee. $85 renewal fee. **Governing Statute:** Code of Virginia 54.1-2956. VR465-08-01.

Washington

4613

Occupational Therapist
Dept. of Health
112 SE Quince
Olympia, WA 98504
Phone: (206)753-0876

Credential Type: Occupational Therapist License. **Duration of License:** Two years. **Requirements:** Complete a four-year educational program in occupational therapy. Must complete six months of supervised field work. **Examination:** National Examination. **Fees:** $90 initial license fee. $125 renewal fee. $15 duplicate license fee.

Credential Type: Limited Permit. **Requirements:** Complete a four-year educational program in occupational therapy. Be sponsored by a licensed Occupational Therapist. **Fees:** $40 limited permit fee.

4614

School Occupational Therapist
Superintendent of Public Instruction
Professional Education and
    Certification
Old Capitol Bldg. FG-11
Seattle, WA 98504-3211
Phone: (206)753-6773

Credential Type: Initial Educational Staff Associate Certificate. **Duration of License:** Seven years. **Requirements:** Baccalaureate degree in occupational therapy. Complete all course work (with exception of special projects or thesis) for a master's degree with a major in occupational therapy. Valid Washington state license in occupational therapy.

West Virginia

4615

Occupational Therapist
Board of Occupational Therapy
PO Box 8750
S. Charleston, WV 25303
Phone: (304)744-6570

Credential Type: License. **Duration of License:** One year. **Requirements:** Graduate from an approved program in occupational therapy. Must have AOTCB certification. **Examination:** AOTCB Examination. **Fees:** $75 license fee. $25 renewal fee.

Credential Type: Limited Permit. **Duration of License:** 60 days after next scheduled exam. **Requirements:** Limited permits are available to graduates of an approved school and those who are foreign-trained, while awaiting the next AOTCB exam. **Fees:** $50 limited permit fee.

Wisconsin

4616

Occupational Therapist
Regulations and Licensing Dept.
Medical Board
PO Box 8935
Madison, WI 53708-8935
Phone: (608)266-8609

Credential Type: License. **Requirements:** Graduation from an approved or accredited school. 18 years of age. **Examination:** Yes.

Wyoming

4617

Occupational Therapist
Board of Occupational Therapy
Barrett Bldg., 3rd Fl.
2301 Central Ave.
Cheyenne, WY 82002
Phone: (307)777-6313
Phone: (307)777-6529
Phone: (307)777-7788
Fax: (307)777-6005

Credential Type: License. **Duration of License:** One year. **Requirements:** Complete the academic requirements in occupational therapy in an approved program that is accredited by the committee on allied health education and accreditation of the American Medical Association in collaboration with the American Occupational Therapy Association. Complete 24 hours of supervised fieldwork experience arranged by the educational institution where the academic requirements were met.

Renewal requires 16 contact hours of continuing education per year. **Examination:** American Occupational Therapy Certification Board (AOTCB) written examination. **Reciprocity:** Yes, by endorsement for applicants licensed in another state with equivalent requirements. **Fees:** $125 application fee. $105 license fee. $150 renewal fee. **Governing Statute:** Wyoming Statutes 33-40-101 et seq. Board Rules and Regulations.

Credential Type: Limited Permit. **Duration of License:** Six months. **Authorization:** Allows applicant to practice under the general supervision of a licensed occupational therapist. **Requirements:** May be granted to the following individuals: (1) Those whose license has been on inactive

Occupational Therapist, continued

status for more than five years. (2) Those who have failed to renew a license for more than five years. (3) Those who are awaiting certification examination results. The limited permit may be renewed once. **Fees:** $55 limited permit fee. **Governing Statute:** Wyoming Statutes 33-40-101 et seq. Board Rules and Regulations.

Occupational Therapy Assistants and Aides

The following states grant licenses in this occupational category as of the date of publication:

Alabama	District of	Iowa	Mississippi	New York	South Carolina	Wisconsin
Alaska	Columbia	Kansas	Missouri	North Carolina	South Dakota	Wyoming
Arizona	Florida	Louisiana	Montana	North Dakota	Tennessee	
Arkansas	Georgia	Maine	Nebraska	Ohio	Texas	
Connecticut	Idaho	Maryland	Nevada	Oklahoma	Utah	
Delaware	Illinois	Massachusetts	New Hampshire	Oregon	Washington	
	Indiana	Minnesota	New Mexico	Pennsylvania	West Virginia	

Alabama

4618

Occupational Therapy Assistant
State Board of Occupational Therapy
PO Box 4424
Montgomery, AL 36103-4424
Phone: (205)265-9654

Credential Type: License. **Duration of License:** One year. **Requirements:** Complete the academic requirements in occupational therapy in an approved program that is accredited by the committee on allied health education and accreditation of the American Medical Association in collaboration with the American Occupational Therapy Association. Be certified by the American Occupational Therapy Certification Board (AOTCB). **Fees:** $70 license fee.

Alaska

4619

Occupational Therapy Assistant
Dept. of Commerce and Economic Development
Div. of Occupational Licensing
State Physical Therapy and Occupational Therapy Board
PO Box D
Juneau, AK 99811-0800
Phone: (907)465-2551
Fax: (907)465-2974

Credential Type: License by Credentials. **Duration of License:** Two years. **Requirements:** Certification as an Occupational Therapy Assistant by the American Occupational Therapy Certification Board (AOTCB). Complete a curriculum of occupational therapy approved by the committee of Allied Health Education and Accreditation of the American Medical Association, and the American Occupational Therapy Association. Complete two months of supervised field work.

If not AOTCB certified, pass an examination prepared by a national testing service approved by the board or an examination recognized by the American Occupational Therapy Association.

Applicant who is licensed as an occupational therapy assistant in another state, if the requirements for licensure were substantially equal to those of Alaska, may be granted a license without examination. **Fees:** $30 application fee. $100 license fee. **Governing Statute:** Alaska Statutes 08.84. Professional Regulations 12 AAC 54.

Credential Type: License by Examination. **Duration of License:** Two years. **Requirements:** Pass the AOTCB examination. Then apply for license by credentials. **Examination:** AOTCB examination. **Fees:** $30 application fee. $100 license fee. **Governing Statute:** Alaska Statutes 08.84. Professional Regulations 12 AAC 54.

Credential Type: Temporary Permit. **Duration of License:** Eight months. **Authorization:** Allows individual to practice while awaiting next examination or completing application for licensure by credentials. **Requirements:** Completed supervised field work. **Fees:** $30 application fee. $50 temporary permit fee. **Governing Statute:** Alaska Statutes 08.84. Professional Regulations 12 AAC 54.

Credential Type: Limited Permit. **Duration of License:** 120 days. **Requirements:** Be licensed to practice occupational therapy in another state or meets requirements for certification by the American Occupational Therapy Certification Board. Has not previously been denied occupational therapy licensing by the board. **Fees:** $30 application fee. $50 limited permit fee. **Governing Statute:** Alaska Statutes 08.84. Professional Regulations 12 AAC 54.

Arizona

4620

Occupational Therapy Assistant
State Board of Occupational Therapy Examiners
1645 W. Jefferson, Rm. 424
Phoenix, AZ 85007
Phone: (602)542-6784

Credential Type: License. **Duration of License:** One year. **Authorization:** Must have a license in order to practice. **Requirements:** Be certified by the American Occupational Therapy Certification Board (AOTCB). Submit two professional recommendations. **Fees:** $100 application fee. $75 license fee. $75 renewal fee. **Governing Statute:** Arizona Revised Statutes, 32-34.

Credential Type: Limited Permit License. **Duration of License:** Four months. **Authorization:** Must work in association with a licensed occupational therapist. **Requirements:** Submit two professional recommendations. The limited permit license is generally granted to a recent graduate who is a first-time applicant for licensure and has not taken the AOTCB exam or is awaiting exam results. **Fees:** $35 limited permit license fee (deductible from full license fee).

Arkansas

4621

Occupational Therapy Assistant
Arkansas State Medical Board
PO Box 102
Harrisburg, AR 72432
Phone: (501)455-1412

Alternate Information: State Examining Committee for Occupational Therapists, 7413 Henderson Rd., Little Rock, AR 72210

Credential Type: License. **Duration of License:** One year. **Requirements:** 18 years of age. US citizen. Good moral character. Pass the National written examination. Completed training in an approved occupational therapy educational program. Must complete two months of supervised field work. **Examination:** Yes. **Fees:** $50 License. $10 Renewal.

Connecticut

4622

Occupational Therapy Assistant
Div. of Medical Quality Assurance
Health Systems Regulation Bureau
Health Services Dept.
150 Washington St.
Hartford, CT 06106
Phone: (203)566-1483
Phone: (203)566-3207

Credential Type: License. **Duration of License:** Two years. **Requirements:** Have an associate's degree. Complete an education program accredited by the American Occupational Therapy Association, or an equivalent program in another country. Complete at least eight weeks of supervised field work approved by the educational institution where the academic requirements were met.

Renewal requires completing nine units of qualifying continued competency activity every two years. **Examination:** American Occupational Therapy Association certifying examination. **Reciprocity:** Yes, by endorsement, provided state has commensurate licensing standards. **Fees:** $100 application fee.

Credential Type: Temporary Permit. **Duration of License:** Until exam results are given. **Authorization:** Allows individual to practice under the supervision of a licensed occupational therapist. **Requirements:** Issued to recent graduates of an AOTA accredited program or equivalent until results of next scheduled exam are available. **Fees:** $25 temporary permit fee.

Delaware

4623

Occupational Therapy Assistant
Board of Occupational Therapy
Dept. of Administrative Services
Div. of Professional Regulation
PO Box 1401
Dover, DE 19903
Phone: (302)739-4522

Credential Type: Occupational Therapy Assistant Certificate. **Requirements:** Complete an educational program in occupational therapy recognized by the board. Complete a period of supervised field work experience arranged by academic institution. **Examination:** Yes, administered by the Professional Examination Service of New York City. **Fees:** $60 certification fee. $40 renewal fee.

District of Columbia

4624

Occupational Therapy Assistant
Board of Occupational Therapy
Dept. of Consumer and Regulatory
 Affairs
Occupational and Professional
 Licensing Administration
PO Box 37200
Washington, DC 20013-7200
Phone: (202)727-7454

Alternate Information: 614 H St., NW, Washington, DC 20001

Credential Type: License. **Duration of License:** One year. **Requirements:** At least 18 years of age. Must have completed an educational program in occupational therapy, at the occupational therapy assistant level, at an institution accredited by the Committee on Allied Health Education and Accreditation (CAHEA) of the American Medical Association (AMA) in collaboration with the American Occupational Therapy Association (AOTA). Complete a period of two months of supervised field work experience at a CAHEA accredited institution or program.

Applicants educated outside the United States must demonstrate their education and training are substantially equivalent to a CAHEA-AMA accredited program. **Examination:** Occupational Therapy Certification Examination (AOTCB). **Reciprocity:** Yes, provided state has substantially equivalent licensure requirements and offers similar privileges to applicants from the District of Columbia. **Fees:** $20 application fee.

Florida

4625

Occupational Therapy Assistant
Board of Medicine
Occupational Therapy Council
Dept. of Professional Regulation
1940 N. Monroe St.
Tallahassee, FL 32399-0750
Phone: (904)488-0595

Credential Type: License by Examination. **Duration of License:** Two years. **Requirements:** Good moral character. Complete the academic requirements of an educational program in occupational therapy that is approved by the American Occupational Therapy Association. Complete a period of supervised fieldwork of at least two months.

Renewal requires 24 hours of continuing professional respiratory care education. **Examination:** American Occupational Therapy Association Examination, as administered by the Professional Examination Services. **Fees:** $100 application fee. $50 license fee. $50 renewal fee. **Governing Statute:** Florida Statutes, Chapter 468, Part III. Florida Administrative Code, Rules 21-M.

Credential Type: License by Endorsement. **Duration of License:** Two years. **Requirements:** Meet basic experience and educational requirements. Have passed a substantially equivalent national, regional, state, or territorial licensing examination.

Renewal requires 24 hours of continuing professional respiratory care education. **Fees:** $100 application fee. $50 license fee. $50 renewal fee. **Governing Statute:** Florida Statutes, Chapter 468, Part III. Florida Administrative Code, Rules 21-M.

Credential Type: Temporary Permit. **Duration of License:** Until next board meeting. **Requirements:** A temporary permit may be issued to an applicant who appears eligible for licensure by examination or by endorsement. **Governing Statute:** Florida Statutes, Chapter 468, Part III. Florida Administrative Code, Rules 21-M.

Occupational Therapy Assistants and Aides

Georgia

4626

Occupational Therapy Assistant
State Board of Occupational Therapy
Allied Health Fields Section
Professional Examining Boards
166 Pryor St., SW
Atlanta, GA 30303
Phone: (404)656-3921

Credential Type: Occupational Therapy Assistant License. **Duration of License:** Two years. **Requirements:** Good moral character. Complete the academic requirements of an educational program in occupational therapy accredited by the American Occupational Therapy Association (AOTA). Comparable educational programs may be recognized by the board. Complete a minimum of two months of supervised field work. **Examination:** AOTCB Certification Examination. **Reciprocity:** License by endorsement may be granted to an applicant who holds a current license in AR, DC, IL, IA, KS, LA, NE, NY, OH, or SC. **Fees:** $50 application fee. $40 renewal fee. **Governing Statute:** Official Code of Georgia Annotated 43-28.

Idaho

4627

Occupational Therapy Assistant
Idaho State Board of Medicine
280 N. 8th St., Ste. 202
Boise, ID 83720
Phone: (208)334-2822

Credential Type: Occupational Therapy Assistant License. **Duration of License:** One year. **Requirements:** Good moral character. Graduate from an approved occupational therapy assistant curriculum. **Examination:** Written examination. **Exemptions:** Exam may be waived if applicant if certified by the American Occupational Therapy Certification Board (AOTCB). **Reciprocity:** License by endorsement may be granted without examination if applicant holds a current, valid license from another state, territory, or district of the United States that has similar requirements. **Fees:** $60 initial license fee. $30 renewal fee. **Governing Statute:** Idaho Code, Title 54, Chap. 37. IDAPA 22.I.

Credential Type: Limited Permit. **Duration of License:** Six months. **Authorization:** Allows individual to practice only in association with and under the supervision of a licensed occupational therapist. **Requirements:** Complete application for an occupational therapist license must be filed. **Fees:** $25 permit fee. **Governing Statute:** Idaho Code, Title 54, Chap. 37. IDAPA 22.I.

Illinois

4628

Certified Occupational Therapy Assistant
Illinois Dept. of Professional Regulations
320 W. Washington St.
Springfield, IL 62786
Phone: (217)782-8556

Credential Type: Certified Occupational Therapy Assistant License. **Duration of License:** Two years. **Requirements:** Complete an approved two-year occupational therapy assistant program that results in an associate degree or its equivalent. **Examination:** American Occupational Therapy Certification Board (AOTCB) Examination. **Reciprocity:** Yes, if requirements for licensure were substantially equivalent to those of Illinois. **Fees:** $225 U.S. graduate examination fee. $375 foreign graduate examination fee. $25 initial license fee. $50 license by endorsement. $40 renewal fee. **Governing Statute:** Illinois Occupational Therapy Practice Act, Illinois Revised Statutes 1991.

4629

Habilitation Aide
Illinois Dept. of Public Health
Education and Training
525 W. Jefferson
Springfield, IL 62761
Phone: (217)785-5133

Credential Type: Registration. **Duration of License:** Indefinite. **Requirements:** At least 16 years of age. Complete at least eight years of grade school or equivalent. Complete a 120-155 hour training program. **Examination:** Written and manual skills competency evaluation. **Reciprocity:** Yes, if training meets Illinois standards. **Fees:** No fee. **Governing Statute:** Nursing Home Act, IRS, Chapter 111 1/2.

4630

Occupational Rehabilitation Aide
Dept. of Public Aid
Bureau of Long Term Quality Care
201 S. Grand Ave. E.
Springfield, IL 62763-0001
Phone: (217)785-0545

Credential Type: Validation. **Duration of License:** No expiration date. **Requirements:** Be at least 18 years of age. Complete 24-hour basic rehabilitation aide training program. Meet one of the following sets of requirements: (1) Be a Certified Nurse Aide. (2) Have a related associate's degree or two years of college in an approved subject. (3) Complete a 36-hour activity course. (4) Be a Developmental Disability Aide. (5) Be a Basic Child Care or Habilitation Aide. **Fees:** No fees. **Governing Statute:** 89 Ill. Adm. Code, CHap. I 147.200.

Indiana

4631

Occupational Therapy Assistant
Occupational Therapy Committee
Health Professions Bureau
402 W. Washington St., Rm. 041
Indianapolis, IN 46204
Phone: (317)232-2960

Credential Type: Certificate to practice. **Duration of License:** Two years. **Requirements:** Graduate of an occupational therapy assistant program that meets board standards; or be certified by the American Occupational Therapy Certification Board. **Examination:** Yes. **Reciprocity:** License by endorsement may be granted. **Fees:** $50 exam fee. $50 endorsement fee. $10 license issuance fee. **Governing Statute:** Indiana Code 25-23.5.

Credential Type: Temporary permit to practice. **Duration of License:** Valid until fully certified. **Authorization:** Provides temporary authorization to practice as an occupational therapy assistant. **Requirements:** Must hold a valid license in another state or be waiting to take the first examination. Must have submitted application and be awaiting committee approval of a permanent certification. **Fees:** $10 temporary permit fee. **Governing Statute:** Indiana Code 25-23.5.

Iowa

4632

Occupational Therapy Assistant
Board of Physical and Occupational Therapy Examiners
Dept. of Public Health
Lucas State Office Bldg.
Des Moines, IA 50319
Phone: (515)281-6762

Credential Type: License. **Duration of License:** Two years. **Requirements:** Completion of an occupational therapy assistant program approved by the American Occupational Therapy Assn., plus two months supervised field experience. **Examination:**

Occupational Therapy Assistant, continued

American Occupational Therapy Certification Board exam. **Fees:** $150 exam fee. $45 application fee. $45 renewal fee.

Kansas

4633

Occupational Therapy Assistant
State Board of Healing Arts
235 SW Topeka Blvd.
Topeka, KS 66603-3059
Phone: (913)296-7413

Credential Type: Occupational Therapy Assistant Registration. **Duration of License:** One year. **Requirements:** Complete an approved educational program for occupational therapy assistants, including any program accredited by the committee on allied health education and accreditation of the American Medical Association in collaboration with the American Occupational Therapy Association, or any program equal to the program for occupational therapy assistants at Barton County Community College.

Renewal requires completion of at least 40 contact hours of continuing education during the preceding two years. **Examination:** Certification examination for certified occupational therapy assistant of the American Occupational Therapy Association. **Fees:** $40 application fee. $30 renewal fee. $190 board-administered exam fee. **Governing Statute:** K.S.A. 65-5401 ff. K.A.R. 100-54-1 ff.

Louisiana

4634

Occupational Therapy Assistant
Louisiana State Board of Medical Examiners
830 Union St., Ste. 100
New Orleans, LA 70112
Phone: (504)524-6763

Credential Type: Occupational Therapy Assistant. **Duration of License:** One year. **Requirements:** 21 years of age. Occupational assistant degree. **Examination:** Yes. **Fees:** $25 license fee.

Maine

4635

Occupational Therapy Assistant
Board of Occupational Therapy Practice
State House Station 35
Augusta, ME 04333
Phone: (207)582-8723

Credential Type: License. **Duration of License:** Two years. **Requirements:** Complete the academic requirements in occupational therapy in an approved program that is accredited by the committee on allied health education and accreditation of the American Medical Association in collaboration with the American Occupational Therapy Association. Complete two months of supervised fieldwork experience arranged by the educational institution where the academic requirements were met. Be certified by the American Occupational Therapy Certification Board (AOTCB). **Examination:** AOTCB written examination. **Fees:** $100 application fee. $120 license fee. **Governing Statute:** 32 M.S.R.A. Chap. 32.

Credential Type: Temporary License. **Duration of License:** Until exam results are given. **Authorization:** Allows individual to practice under the supervision of a licensed occupational therapist. **Requirements:** Must have completed education and experience requirements for licensure and be scheduled to take AOTCB exam or be awaiting exam results. Submit two professional references. **Fees:** $100 application fee. $50 temporary license fee. **Governing Statute:** 32 M.S.R.A. Chap. 32.

Maryland

4636

Occupational Therapist Assistant
Board of Occupational Therapy
Dept. of Health and Mental Hygiene
4201 Patterson Ave.
Baltimore, MD 21215
Phone: (410)764-4747

Credential Type: License. **Requirements:** Contact licensing body for application information.

Massachusetts

4637

Occupational Therapy Assistant
Board of Registration of Allied Health Professionals
Div. of Registration
100 Cambridge St., 15th fl.
Boston, MA 02202
Phone: (617)727-3071

Credential Type: License and certification. **Duration of License:** Two years. **Requirements:** Associate's degree in Occupational Therapy. **Examination:** AOTCB Certification Examination. **Reciprocity:** Yes, provided applicant meets Massachusetts standards. **Fees:** $50 application fee. $50 renewal fee.

Credential Type: Temporary License. **Requirements:** Contact licensing body for application information. **Fees:** $10 temporary license fee.

Minnesota

4638

Occupational Therapy Assistant
Dept. of Health
Bureau of Health Resources and Managed Care Services
Health Occupations Programs
717 Delaware St., SE
Box 9441
Minneapolis, MN 55440
Phone: (612)623-5611
Fax: (612)623-5043

Credential Type: Occupational Therapy Assistant Registration. **Authorization:** Registration required to use occupational title. **Requirements:** Contact licensing body for application information. **Governing Statute:** Minnesota Statutes 214.13.

Mississippi

4639

Occupational Therapy Assistant
State Dept. of Health
Professional Licensure
PO Box 1700
2423 N. State St.
Jackson, MS 39215-1700
Phone: (601)987-4153
Phone: (601)960-7400
Fax: (601)960-7948

Credential Type: License. **Duration of License:** One year. **Requirements:** Complete the academic requirements in occupational therapy in an approved program that is accredited by the committee on allied health education and accreditation of the American Medical Association in collaboration with the American Occupational Therapy Association. Complete two months of supervised fieldwork experience. Foreign trained applicants must complete substantially equivalent educational and fieldwork experience requirements. Be certified by the American Occupational Therapy Certification Board (AOTCB).

Renewal requires completing 10 contact hours of continuing education per year. **Examination:** AOTCB written examination. **Reciprocity:** Yes, based on passing a national exam. **Fees:** $75 application fee.

Credential Type: Limited Permit. **Duration of License:** One year. **Requirements:** Must have applied for licensure and be eligible to take the national examination. Must take the next scheduled exam.

Missouri

4640

Occupational Therapy Assistant
Dept. of Economic Development
Div. of Professional Registration
Office of Health Care Providers-
  Occupational Therapists
PO Box 471
Jefferson City, MO 65102-0471
Phone: (314)751-0877
Fax: (314)751-4176

Credential Type: Registration. **Duration of License:** One year. **Authorization:** Although anyone may practice occupational therapy in Missouri, registration is required to use the title, "Certified Occupational Therapist Assistant." **Requirements:** Be certified by the American Occupational Therapy Certification Board (AOTCB). **Fees:** $25 registration fee. $25 renewal fee. **Governing Statute:** Missouri Statutes, Rules and Regulations, Chap. 334. 4CSR 155-1.020.

Montana

4641

Occupational Therapy Assistant
Montana Board of Occupational
  Therapists
111 N. Jackson
Helena, MT 59620
Phone: (406)444-3091

Credential Type: Occupational Therapy Assistant License. **Duration of License:** One year. **Requirements:** Completion of an approved occupational therapy assistant program. Completion of two months of supervised field work. **Examination:** American Occupational Therapy Certification Board Examination. **Fees:** $80 application fee. $80 license fee. $60 renewal fee. **Governing Statute:** Montana Code Annotated 37-24-301 through 37-24-311.

Nebraska

4642

Occupational Therapist Assistant
Nebraska Board of Occupational
  Therapy Practice
301 Centennial Mall S.
PO Box 95007
Lincoln, NE 68509
Phone: (402)471-2115

Credential Type: License. **Duration of License:** Two years. **Requirements:** Must have completed an accredited program in occupational therapy, plus six months supervised field work at an educational institution. Must be certified as a registered occupational therapist or assistant. **Examination:** Yes. **Fees:** $200 license fee. $200 renewal fee.

Nevada

4643

Occupational Therapy Assistant
Board of Occupational Therapy
PO Box 70220
Reno, NV 89570
Phone: (702)857-1700

Credential Type: License. **Duration of License:** One year. **Authorization:** Must work under the direct supervision of a licensed occupational therapist. **Requirements:** Graduate from an educational program that is approved by the board and that includes a fieldwork program. Submit three professional references. An applicant who has graduated from a school in another country must submit an evaluation that states education is at least equivalent to a bachelor's degree in occupational therapy.

Renewal requires 10 hours of continuing education per year. **Examination:** American Occupational Therapy Certification Board (AOTCB) written examination. **Fees:** $175 application fee. $100 license fee. $180 renewal fee. **Governing Statute:** NAC 640A.

New Hampshire

4644

Occupational Therapist Assistant
Board of Registration in Medicine
Hazen Drive
Concord, NH 03301
Phone: (603)271-1203

Credential Type: Occupational Therapist Assistant License. **Duration of License:** One year. **Requirements:** At least 18 years of age. Good moral character. Bachelor's degree. Complete the academic requirements of an occupational therapy program approved by the Board. Must complete a minimum of two months of supervised fieldwork experience. Renewal requires 12 hours of continuing education annually. **Examination:** Examination required by Board. **Reciprocity:** No. **Fees:** $50 initial license application fee. $25 annual renewal fee.

New Mexico

4645

Occupational Therapy Assistant
Occupational Therapy Board
Dept. of Regulation and Licensing
PO Box 25101
725 St. Michael's Dr.
Santa Fe, NM 87504
Phone: (505)827-7162

Credential Type: Certified Occupational Therapy Assistant License. **Duration of License:** One year. **Requirements:** Complete an occupational therapy educational program that is accredited by the committee on Allied Health Education and Accreditation of the American Medical Association. The program shall include at least two months of supervised field work experience. Foreign-trained occupational therapists must complete a program approved by a member association of the World Federation of Occupational Therapy. **Examination:** American Occupational Therapy Association examination. **Fees:** $75 license fee. $30 renewal fee. **Governing Statute:** Occupational Therapy Board Rules and Regulations 90-1. Occupational Therapy Licensing Law 61-12A-1 NMSA 1978 et seq.

New York

4646

Occupational Therapy Assistant
State Education Dept.
Div. of Professional Licensing Services
Cultural Education Center
Empire State Plaza
Albany, NY 12230
Phone: (518)474-5170

Credential Type: Certificate. **Duration of License:** Three years. **Requirements:** Associate's Degree or post-secondary schooling as occupational therapy assistant. **Fees:** $95 application fee. $50 renewal fee. **Governing Statute:** Title VIII Articles 130, 156 of the Education Law.

North Carolina

4647

Occupational Therapist Assistant
North Carolina Board of Occupational Therapy
PO Box 2280
Raleigh, NC 27602
Phone: (919)832-1380

Credential Type: Certification. **Duration of License:** One year. **Requirements:** Graduation from an accredited occupational therapy assistant educational program. A clinical internship must be completed as part of the program. Two character references. **Examination:** National exam. **Fees:** $10 application fee. $150 exam fee. $100 license fee. $50 renewal fee.

North Dakota

4648

Occupational Therapy Assistant
State Board of Occupational Therapy Practice
1837 S. 15th St.
Fargo, ND 58103
Phone: (701)293-1817

Credential Type: License. **Requirements:** Contact licensing body for application information.

Ohio

4649

Occupational Therapy Assistant
Ohio Occupational Therapy, Physical Therapy, and Athletic Trainers Board
77 S. High St., 16th Fl.
Columbus, OH 43266-0317
Phone: (614)466-3774

Credential Type: License. **Duration of License:** Two years. **Authorization:** Must work under the supervision of a licensed occupational therapist. **Requirements:** Complete an education program accredited by the American Occupational Therapy Association. **Examination:** American Occupational Therapy Certification Board (AOTCB) written examination. **Fees:** $75 license fee. $60 renewal fee. **Governing Statute:** Ohio Revised Code, Chap. 4755. Administrative Rules 4755-1-01 et seq.

Credential Type: Limited Permit. **Duration of License:** Until results of exam are given. **Authorization:** Allows individual to practice under the supervision of a licensed occupational therapist. **Requirements:** Must be scheduled for participation in the qualifying examination. **Fees:** $25 limited permit fee (to be credited toward license fee). **Governing Statute:** Ohio Revised Code, Chap. 4755. Administrative Rules 4755-1-01 et seq.

Oklahoma

4650

Occupational Therapy Assistant
State Board of Medical License and Supervision
PO Box 18256
Oklahoma City, OK 73154
Phone: (405)848-6841

Credential Type: License. **Duration of License:** One year. **Requirements:** Completion of an approved program in occupational therapy. Two months of supervised field work. 20 contact hours of continuing education every two years. Three recommendations are required. **Examination:** Certified Occupational Therapy Assistant Examination. **Fees:** $200 exam fee. $100 application fee. $40 renewal fee.

Oregon

4651

Occupational Therapy Assistant
Occuaptional Therapy Board
PO Box 231
Portland, OR 97207
Phone: (503)731-4048

Credential Type: License. **Duration of License:** One year. **Requirements:** 18 years of age. Successful completion of a two-year course. Completion of two months of supervised field work. **Examination:** Yes. **Fees:** $175 exam fee. $50 license fee. $60 renewal fee. **Governing Statute:** ORS 675.210 to 675.340.

Pennsylvania

4652

Certified Occupational Therapy Assistant (C.O.T.A.)
State Board of Occupational Therapy Education and Licensure
Bureau of Professional and Occupational Affairs
Dept. of State
Transportation and Safety Bldg., 6th Fl.
Harrisburg, PA 17120
Phone: (717)787-8503

Credential Type: Certified Occupational Therapy Assistant License. **Duration of License:** Two years. **Requirements:** Good moral character. Must complete a board-approved two-year education program in occupational therapy. Complete a minimum of two months of supervised field work experience. Pass a board-approved examination.

Foreign graduates must have completed a program substantially equal to the requirements stated above. The board will accept a credentials evaluation done by the Div. of Credentialing of the American Occupational Therapy Association (AOA). Board may require up to one year of field experience for foreign graduates. **Examination:** Board-approved examination in occupational therapy.

South Carolina

4653

Occupational Therapy Assistant
South Carolina State Board of Occupational Therapy
PO Box 399
Lexington, SC 29072
Phone: (803)359-7914

Credential Type: Certificate. **Requirements:** Completion of an accredited program. **Examination:** Yes. **Fees:** $50 application fee. $25 renewal fee.

South Dakota

4654

Occupational Therapy Assistant
State Board of Medical and Osteopathic Examiners
Dept. of Commerce and Consumer Affairs
1323 S. Minnesota Ave.
Sioux Falls, SD 57105
Phone: (605)336-1965

Credential Type: Occupational Therapy Assistant License. **Duration of License:** One year. **Requirements:** High school graduate or equivalent. Graduation from an approved occupational therapy assistant program. Certification by the American Occupational Therapy Association (AOTA). Complete two months of supervised field work experience.

Renewal requires completing 12 continuing competency points per year. **Fees:** $50 application and certification fee. $25 renewal fee.

Credential Type: Limited License. **Requirements:** High school graduate or equivalent. Graduation from an approved occupational therapy assistant program. Must have been accepted to write the exam administered by the American Occupational Therapy Association (AOTA). Complete six months of supervised field work experience. **Fees:** $25 application and license fee.

Tennessee

4655

Occupational Therapy Assistant
Board of Occupational and Physical Therapy Examiners
283 Plus Park Blvd.
Nashville, TN 37243
Phone: (615)367-6225

Credential Type: License. **Duration of License:** One year. **Requirements:** 18 years old. Complete all educational requirements for a program in desired line of work. School must be accredited by the AMA or CAHEA. Proof of good moral character. **Examination:** Occupational Therapy Registration examination. **Reciprocity:** Yes. **Fees:** $65 Registration. $20 Application. $65 Renewal.

Texas

4656

Occupational Therapy Assistant
Texas Advisor Board of Occupational Therapy
Texas Rehabilitation Commission
4900 N. Lamar Blvd.
Austin, TX 78751
Phone: (512)483-4072

Credential Type: Occupational Therapy Assistant. **Duration of License:** One year. **Requirements:** Associate degree or certificate in occupational therapy and two months supervised field work. Continuing education required for renewal. **Examination:** Yes. **Fees:** $10 application fee. $50 license fee. $50 renewal fee. **Governing Statute:** VACS 8851, 40 TAC 361.1.

Utah

4657

Occupational Therapy Assistant
Dept. of Commerce
Div. of Occupational and Professional Licensing
160 E. 300 S.
PO Box 45802
Salt Lake City, UT 84145
Phone: (801)530-6628

Credential Type: Occupational Therapy Assistant's License. **Duration of License:** Two years. **Requirements:** Must complete an approved educational program in occupationl therapy. Must complete a two-month period of supervised field work. **Examination:** Yes. **Fees:** $60 license fee. $30 renewal fee.

Washington

4658

Occupational Therapist Assistant
Dept. of Health
112 SE Quince
Olympia, WA 98504
Phone: (206)753-0876

Credential Type: Occupational Therapist Assistant License. **Duration of License:** Two years. **Requirements:** Complete a four-year educational program in occupational therapy. Complete two months of supervised field work. **Fees:** $90 initial license fee. $125 renewal fee. $15 duplicate license fee.

West Virginia

4659

Occupational Therapy Assistant
Board of Occupational Therapy
1545 Mt. Vernon Rd.
Charleston, WV 25314
Phone: (304)346-5836

Credential Type: License. **Duration of License:** One year. **Requirements:** Graduate from an approved program in occupational therapy. Must have AOTCB certification. **Examination:** AOTCB Examination. **Fees:** $50 license fee. $15 renewal fee.

Credential Type: Limited Permit. **Duration of License:** 60 days after next scheduled exam. **Requirements:** Limited permits are available to graduates of an approved school and those who are foreign-trainined, while awaiting the next AOTCB exam. **Fees:** $50 limited permit fee.

Wisconsin

4660

Occupational Therapy Assistant
Regulations and Licensing Dept.
Medical Board
PO Box 8935
Madison, WI 53708-8935
Phone: (608)266-8609

Credential Type: License. **Requirements:** Graduation from an approved or accredited school. 18 years of age. **Examination:** Yes.

Wyoming

Occupational Therapy Assistant
Board of Occupational Therapy
Barrett Bldg., 3rd Fl.
2301 Central Ave.
Cheyenne, WY 82002
Phone: (307)777-6313
Phone: (307)777-6529
Phone: (307)777-7788
Fax: (307)777-6005

Credential Type: License. **Duration of License:** One year. **Requirements:** Complete the academic requirements in occupational therapy in an approved program that is accredited by the committee on allied health education and accreditation of the American Medical Association in collaboration with the American Occupational Therapy Association. Complete 24 hours of supervised fieldwork experience arranged by the educational institution where the academic requirements were met.

Renewal requires 16 contact hours of continuing education per year. **Examination:** American Occupational Therapy Certification Board (AOTCB) written examination. **Reciprocity:** Yes, by endorsement for applicants licensed in another state with equivalent requirements. **Fees:** $125 application fee. $50 license fee. $100 renewal fee. **Governing Statute:** Wyoming Statutes 33-40-101 et seq. Board Rules and Regulations.

Optometrists

The following states grant licenses in this occupational category as of the date of publication:

Alabama	District of	Iowa	Minnesota	New Mexico	Rhode Island	Washington
Alaska	Columbia	Kansas	Mississippi	New York	South Carolina	West Virginia
Arizona	Florida	Kentucky	Missouri	North Carolina	South Dakota	Wisconsin
Arkansas	Georgia	Louisiana	Montana	North Dakota	Tennessee	Wyoming
California	Hawaii	Maine	Nebraska	Ohio	Texas	
Colorado	Idaho	Maryland	Nevada	Oklahoma	Utah	
Connecticut	Illinois	Massachusetts	New Hampshire	Oregon	Vermont	
Delaware	Indiana	Michigan	New Jersey	Pennsylvania	Virginia	

Alabama

4662

Optometrist
Alabama Board of Optometry
PO Box 448
Attalla, AL 35954
Phone: (205)538-9903

Credential Type: License. **Duration of License:** One year. **Requirements:** 21 years of age. Must be a high school graduate. Must have a minimum of three years of pre-optometry at an accredited college. Must have completed a course of study in an accredited school of optometry. **Examination:** Yes. **Fees:** $100 examination fee. $112 renewal fee.

Alaska

4663

Optometrist
Dept. of Commerce and Economic
   Development
Div. of Occupational Licensing
Board of Examiners in Optometry
PO Box D-LIC
Juneau, AK 99811-0800
Phone: (907)465-2534

Credential Type: License to practice. **Duration of License:** Two years. **Requirements:** Visual acuity of a standard of at least 20/40 in at least one eye as corrected. Not afflicted with a contagious or infectious disease. Equivalent to four years of high school. Graduate of a recognized school or college of optometry.

Pass appropriate written, oral, and practical exams.

An average of 12 hours per year of continuing education courses or seminars are required for renewal of license. **Examination:** All parts of written exam offered by the National Board of Examiners in Optometry. "Treatment and Management of Ocular Disease" written exam offered by the International Association of Boards of Examiners in Optometry. Practical exam. Oral exam. **Exemptions:** Written exam may be waived if applicant holds a current license by examination in any state or a province of Canada and has been established in practice for at least three years, or shows evidence of having passed the written portion of the NBEO exam. **Fees:** $30 application fee. $50 exam or reexamination fee. $100 license fee. $100 biennial renewal fee. **Governing Statute:** Alaska Statutes 08.72. Professional Regulations 12 AAC 48.

Credential Type: Pharmaceutical Agent License Endorsement. **Duration of License:** Two years. **Requirements:** Pass current NBEO exam or section 9, "Ocular Pharmacology," of the former NBEO exam. If applicable, meet continuing education requirements. **Fees:** $20 license fee. $20 biennial renewal fee. **Governing Statute:** Alaska Statutes 08.72. Professional Regulations 12 AAC 48.

Arizona

4664

Optometrist
Board of Optometry
1645 W. Jefferson, Rm. 410
Phoenix, AZ 85007
Phone: (602)542-3095

Credential Type: License to practice optometry. **Duration of License:** Two years. **Requirements:** Graduate from a college or university, having taken courses teaching the profession of optometry, that is accredited by a nationally accepted accrediting body on optometric education. Pass optometric examination. **Examination:** Optometric examination. **Reciprocity:** Yes. **Fees:** $150 application fee. $300 license fee.

Arkansas

4665

Optometrist
State Board of Optometry
PO Box 512
Searcy, AR 72143
Phone: (501)268-4351

Credential Type: License. **Requirements:** Be a graduate of an approved school of Optometry. **Examination:** Yes. **Fees:** $100 Written examination (National and State Boards).

California

4666

Optometrist
Board of Optometry
400 R St., Ste. 3130
Sacramento, CA 95814-6200
Phone: (916)323-8720

Credential Type: License and Registration. **Duration of License:** One year. **Requirements:** Doctor of Optometry degree. **Examination:** National Board of Examiners in Optometry Examination, Parts 1 and 2. California license examination. **Reciprocity:** No. **Fees:** $275 exam fee. $150 renewal fee.

Colorado

4667

Optometrist
Board of Optometric Examiners
Dept. of Regulatory Agencies
Div. of Registrations
1560 Broadway, Ste. 1310
Denver, CO 80202
Phone: (303)894-7755

Credential Type: Optometrist license. **Requirements:** Be at least 21 years of age. Graduate with a degree of doctor of optometry from an approved school or college of optometry. Not be addicted to the use of any controlled substance, nor have habitual intemperance in the use of alcoholic liquors. Submit proof of financial responsibility. **Examination:** National Board of Examiners in Optometry (NBEO) examination. Treatment and Management of Ocular Diseases (TMOD) examination of the International Association of Boards of Examiners in Optometry. Colorado State Board of Optometric Examiners Licensing Examination. **Fees:** $218 application fee. **Governing Statute:** Colorado Statutes Title 12, Article 40.

Credential Type: Certificate for use of pharmaceutical agents. **Authorization:** Covers topically applied mydriatics, miotics, cycloplegics, and anesthetics. **Requirements:** Complete at least 60 classroom hours of study in ocular pharmacology, clinical pharmacology, therapeutic, and anterior segment disease, Complete at least 60 hours of approved supervised clinical training. Complete a course in cardiopulmonary resuscitation (CPR). **Governing Statute:** Colorado Statutes Title 12, Article 40.

Connecticut

4668

Optometrist
Dept. of Health Services
Div. of Medical Quality Assurance
150 Washington St.
Hartford, CT 06106
Phone: (203)566-1039

Credential Type: Optometry License. **Duration of License:** One year. **Requirements:** High school graduate or equivalent. Graduate from an accredited college or school of optometry. **Examination:** National Board of Examiners in Optometry (NBOE) written and Clinical Skills/VRICS examinations. **Reciprocity:** Yes, provided home state maintains equal standards and extends similar privileges of reciprocity to Connecticut. **Fees:** $450 application fee. $375 renewal fee.

Delaware

4669

Optometrist
Board of Examiners in Optometry
Dept. of Administrative Services
Div. of Professional Regulation
PO Box 1401
Dover, DE 19903
Phone: (302)739-4522

Credential Type: Optometrist License. **Duration of License:** Two years. **Requirements:** Complete two years of pre-optometry study and four years of study in an optometry college. Complete 6-month internship. **Examination:** National Board Examination and Clinical Skills Examination. **Reciprocity:** Yes, with states, territories, and foreign countries, provinces, and states having equivalent or greater requirements. **Fees:** $75 application fee. $200 renewal fee.

District of Columbia

4670

Optometrist
Board of Optometry
Occupational and Professional Licensure Administration
Consumer and Regulatory Affairs Dept.
PO Box 37200
Washington, DC 20013-7200
Phone: (202)727-7823
Phone: (202)727-7454
Phone: (202)727-7480

Alternate Information: 614 H St., NW, Washington, DC 20001

Credential Type: Optometrist License. **Duration of License:** Two years. **Requirements:** Be at least 18 years of age. Must have a doctoral degree in optometry from an institution accredited at the time of the degree by the Council on Optometric Education of the American Optometric Association. Applicants educated in a foreign country must possess a doctoral degree in optometry and demonstrate that education and training are equivalent to the board's requirements.

Renewal requires 24 hours of continuing education during the past two years. **Examination:** National Board of Examiners in Optometry examination. Boardadministered practical examination. **Fees:** $80 application and license fee.

Florida

4671

Optometrist
Board of Optometry
Dept. of Professional Regulation
1940 N. Monroe St.
Tallahassee, FL 32399
Phone: (904)922-4971

Credential Type: Licensed Optometrist. **Duration of License:** Two years. **Requirements:** Be at least 18 years of age. Good moral character. Graduate from an accredited school or college of optometry approved by the board.

Renewal requires 28 clock hours of continuing education. **Examination:** National Board of Examiners in Optometry (NBEO) examination. Parts I and II of the state examination for licensure. **Fees:** $325 exam fee. $140 initial license fee. $220 renewal fee. **Governing Statute:** Florida Statutes, Chapter 463. Florida Administrative Code, Rules 21-Q.

Credential Type: Certified Optometrist. **Duration of License:** Two years. **Authorization:** Certification is required to administer and prescribe topical ocular pharmaceutical agents. **Requirements:** Be a licensd optometrist. Complete at least 110 hours of board-approved transcript quality coursework and clinical training in general and ocular pharmacology conducted by an accredited institution. Complete at least one year of supervised experience in differential diagnosis of eye diseases or disorders, either in an academic or clinical setting or as part of optometric training.

Renewal requires 28 clock hours of continuing education, of which at least six hours must be in approved transcript quality coursework in ocular pharmacology. **Examination:** Certified Optometrist Examination testing knowledge of general and ocular pharmacology. **Fees:** $100 certification fee. $250 certification exam fee. $80 renewal fee. **Governing Statute:** Florida Statutes, Chapter 463. Florida Administrative Code, Rules 21-Q.

Georgia

4672

Optometrist
State Board of Examiners in Optometry
Health Care Practitioners Section
Professional Examining Boards
166 Pryor St., SW
Atlanta, GA 30303
Phone: (404)656-3912

Credential Type: Optometrist Certificate of Registration. **Duration of License:** Two years. **Requirements:** Be at least 21 years of age. Good moral character. High school graduate or equivalent. Complete at least two years of preoptometry college work in a college of arts and sciences approved by the board. Hold a certificate of graduation from an accredited college or university teaching optometry with a required course of study of at least three school years. **Examination:** National Board Examination. Board-administered clinical examination. **Reciprocity:** Yes. **Fees:** $325 application fee. $175 exam fee. $150 registration fee. $150 renewal fee. **Governing Statute:** Official Code of Georgia Annotated 43-30. Rules of the Georgia State Board of Examiners in Optometry, Chap. 430.

Hawaii

4673

Optometrist
Hawaii Board of Optometry
1010 Richards St.
PO Box 3469
Honolulu, HI 96801
Phone: (808)548-7471

Credential Type: License. **Duration of License:** Six months. **Requirements:** Graduation from an approved optometry college. **Examination:** National Board of Examiners in Optometry exam. Hawaii board's written and practical exams. **Fees:** $15 application fee. $50 exam fee. $25 license fee. $25 $50 Compliance Resolution Fund fee. $50 renewal fee.

Idaho

4674

Optometrist
State Board of Optometry
Bureau of Occupational Licenses
1109 Main St., Ste. 220
Boise, ID 83702-5642
Phone: (208)334-3233

Credential Type: Optometrist License. **Duration of License:** One year. **Requirements:** Be at least 21 years of age. Good moral character. Graduate of an accredited college or university of optometry. **Examination:** National Board of Examiners in Optometry Examination, written and practical.

Renewal requires 12 hours of post-graduate optometric education courses or meetings per year. **Reciprocity:** With states that afford like privileges and rights to optometrists licensed in Idaho. Applicant must have practiced for four of the five years preceding application and must intend to reside in Idaho. **Fees:** $100 application fee. $40 renewal fee. $30 annual optometry fund fee. **Governing Statute:** Idaho Code, Title 54, Chap. 15. Rules of the Idaho State Board of Optometry.

Illinois

4675

Optometrist
Dept. of Professional Regulations
320 W. Washington St.
Springfield, IL 62786
Phone: (217)782-8556

Credential Type: Optometry License. **Duration of License:** Two years. **Requirements:** Graduate from an accredited college or school of optometry. Renewal requires 24 hours of continuing education every two years. Must apply for certification to use topical ocular pharmaceutical (TOP) agents. **Examination:** National Board Examination, Parts I-III. **Reciprocity:** Yes, with states that have similar licensing requirements. **Fees:** $200 application fee (by examination). $200 application fee (by endorsement). $130 TOP certification fee. $200 renewal fee. $50 TOP renewal fee. **Governing Statute:** Illinois Revised Statute 1991, Chap. 111, 3901-3929. 68 IAC 1320.

Indiana

4676

Optometrist
Optometry Board
Health Professions Bureau
401 W. Washington St., Rm. 041
Indianapolis, IN 46204
Phone: (317)232-2960

Credential Type: Optometry License. **Duration of License:** Two years. **Requirements:** Complete two years of premedical or pre-optometry education. Grdauate of an accredited optometry school. **Examination:** Written national exam (NBEO). Board-administered clinical exam. Written jurisprudence exam. **Fees:** $100 application/examination fee. $10 license issuance fee. **Governing Statute:** Indiana Code 25-24. 852 Indiana Administrative Code.

Iowa

4677

Optometrist
Board of Optometry Examiners
Dept. of Public Health
Lucas State Office Bldg.
Des Moines, IA 50319
Phone: (515)281-6762

Credential Type: License. **Duration of License:** Two years. **Requirements:** Graduation from an accredited school or college of optometry. **Examination:** National Board of Examiners of Optometry exam. International Assn. of Boards of Examiners in Optometry exam on "Treatment and Management of Ocular Disease." Written and practical clinical exams of the Iowa State Board of Optometry Examiners. **Fees:** $250 application fee. $120 renewal fee.

Kansas

4678

Optometrist
Board of Optometry Examiners
403 W. Lyman Rd.
Topeka, KS 66608-1969
Phone: (913)235-6550

Credential Type: License. **Duration of License:** One year. **Requirements:** Optometry degree from an accredited school of optometry. Renewal requires 20 hours of continuing education. **Examination:** National Board exam, three parts, including clinical skills. **Fees:** $150 exam fee. $25 license fee. $110 renewal fee.

Kentucky

4679

Optometrist
Kentucky Board of Optometric
  Examiners
1000 W. Main St.
Georgetown, KY 40324
Phone: (502)863-5816

Credential Type: License. **Duration of License:** One year. **Requirements:** Minimum of three years of college, with four years of graduate school with 12 semester hours in general and ocular pharmacology. 18 years of age. Continuing education required. **Examination:** Yes. **Fees:** $200 exam fee. $125 renewal fee.

Louisiana

4680

Optometrist
Louisiana State Board of Optometry
  Examiners
PO Box 46431
Baton Rouge, LA 70895
Phone: (504)925-1740

Credential Type: License. **Duration of License:** One year. **Requirements:** High school diploma or equivalent. Complete pre-optometry college credits. Graduation from an accredited school of optometry. **Examination:** Written, oral and practical. **Fees:** $100 application fee. $150 license fee. $100 renewal fee.

Maine

4681

Optometrist
State Board of Optometry
Dept. of Professional and Financial
  Regulation
3 Mulliken Ct.
Augusta, ME 04330
Phone: (207)289-2535

Credential Type: License. **Duration of License:** One year. **Requirements:** Bachelor's degree and graduation from an approved optometric college. **Examination:** National Board of Examiners in Optometry Examination. State practical examination. **Reciprocity:** Yes. **Fees:** $100 license fee. $100 renewal fee. $100 exam fee. $25 fee for each auxiliary office. **Governing Statute:** 32 M.S.R.A.

Maryland

4682

Optometrist
Board of Examiners in Optometry
Dept. of Health and Mental Hygiene
4201 Patterson Ave., Rm. 317
Baltimore, MD 21215-2299
Phone: (410)764-4725

Credential Type: License. **Duration of License:** Two years. **Requirements:** Doctor of Optometry degree and completion of a four-year postgraduate program. **Examination:** National Board of Examiners in Optometry Examination (NBEO). Maryland Licensure Examination. **Exemptions:** Optometrists licensed in another state are exempt from the NBEO examination. **Fees:** $100 exam fee. $100 renewal fee. **Governing Statute:** Annotated Code of Maryland, Title 11. Code of Maryland Regulations, Title 11, Subtitle 28.

Credential Type: Limited License. **Duration of License:** One year. **Authorization:** May be issued to allow an out-of-state licensed optometrist to participate in postgraduate teaching, research, or training programs at an institution in Maryland. **Requirements:** Must be licensed in another state and be eligible to sit for the Maryland examination. **Governing Statute:** Annotated Code of Maryland, Title 11. Code of Maryland Regulations, Title 11, Subtitle 28.

Massachusetts

4683

Optometrist
Board of Registration of Optometry
Div. of Registration
100 Cambridge St., 15th fl.
Boston, MA 02202
Phone: (617)727-1817

Credential Type: License. **Duration of License:** One year. **Requirements:** Graduation from an approved Optometric school with an O.D. degree. **Examination:** North East Region Clinical Optometric Assessments Testing Service examination (NERCOATS). **Reciprocity:** Yes, with states that grant reciprocity to Massachusetts. **Fees:** $750 exam fee. $50 license fee. $25 renewal fee.

Michigan

4684

Ocularist
Ocularist Regulation
Bureau of Occupational &
  Professional Regulation
Dept. of Commerce
PO Box 30018
Lansing, MI 48909
Phone: (517)373-7902

Credential Type: Certification. **Duration of License:** One year. **Authorization:** All persons who design and fabricate ocular prosthetic appliances; fit ocular prosthetic appliances; or perform the necessary procedures to provide an ocular prosthetic service for patients in an ocularist's office or laboratory in Michigan must be certified by the Department of Commerce. **Requirements:** At least 18 years of age. High school diploma or equivalent. Be of good moral character. Completed at least five years of apprenticeship training under an ocularist in Michigan; have completed a prescribed course in ocularist training programs in a college, teaching facility, or university approved by the Department; or have been principally engaged in the practice of ocularism outside of this state for at least five years and been employed by an ocularist, optometrist, or physician for at least one year in Michigan. **Exemptions:** Licensed optometrists and physicians are exempt from the certification. **Fees:** $15 application processing fee. $20 initial certificate fee. $20 renewal fee. **Governing Statute:** Occupational Code, Act 299 of 1980, as amended. License Fee Act, Act 152 of 1979, as amended.

Credential Type: Apprentice Certification. **Duration of License:** One year. **Requirements:** At least 18 years of age. High school diploma or equivalent. Be of good moral character. Furnish the Department with a statement from an ocularist that he/she is receiving training under the ocularist's direct supervision. **Fees:** $15 application processing fee. $10 initial certification fee. $10 renewal fee. **Governing Statute:** Occupational Code, Act 299 of 1980, as amended. License Fee Act, Act 152 of 1979, as amended.

4685

Optometrist
Board of Optometry
Bureau of Occupational & Professional Regulation
Michigan Dept. of Commerce
PO Box 30018
Lansing, MI 48909
Phone: (517)373-7902

Credential Type: License. ** Two years. **Requirements:** At least 18 years of age. High school diploma or equivalent. Graduated from a university, school, or college offering a six-year course of study in optometry approved by the Board. Submit a transcript of college credits with the application. Be of good moral character. Working knowledge of the English language. Abide by the rules and regulations of the Board. Renewal requires at least 24 hours of continuing education during the current two-year licensing period. **Examination:** Michigan written and practical exam, National written exam. **Reciprocity:** Licensed optometrists from other states may be licensed in Michigan without examination if the home state requirements are substantially equivalent to those of Michigan and they have passed an equivalent examination. **Fees:** $20 application processing fee. $200 initial exam fee ($50 per exam part). $20 exam review fee. $40 initial license fee, per year. $40 renewal fee, per year. $100 reciprocity fee. **Governing Statute:** Public Health Code, Act 368 of 1978, as amended.

Minnesota

4686

Optometrist
State Board of Optometry
2700 University Ave. W., Ste. 103
St. Paul, MN 55114-1087
Phone: (612)642-0594

Credential Type: Optometry License. **Duration of License:** One year. **Requirements:** Graduate from an accredited college or school of optometry. Renewal requires 45 clock hours of academic or non-academic education within a three-year compliance period. **Examination:** National Board of Examiners in Optometry (NBOE) Examinations, Part I (Basic Science), Part II (Clinical Science), and Part III (Patient Care). State law examination. **Reciprocity:** Yes, provided applicant has practiced for at least three years. **Fees:** $12 license issuance fee. $90 annual license fee. $75 reciprocity fee. **Governing Statute:** Minnesota Statutes, Sections 148.52-148.62. Minnesota Rules 6500-6599.

Mississippi

4687

Optometrist
State Board of Optometry
PO Box 688
McComb, MS 39648
Phone: (601)684-6241

Credential Type: License. **Requirements:** Contact licensing body for application information.

Missouri

4688

Optometrist
State Board of Optometry
Div. of Professional Registration
3605 Missouri Blvd.
PO Box 423
Jefferson City, MO 65102
Phone: (314)751-0814

Credential Type: Certificate of registration. **Duration of License:** One year. **Requirements:** Be at least 21 years of age. Good moral character. Graduation from a board-approved school of optometry. Renewal requires eight hours of continuing education per year. **Examination:** National Board of Examiners in Optometry (NBEO) written examination. Clinical Skills/VRICS examination of the NBEO. Missouri law examination. **Reciprocity:** Yes, provided requirements in the applicant's state, territory, country, or province were, at the date of licensure, substantially equal to the requirements then in force in this state. **Fees:** $50 application fee. $100 license fee. $75 renewal fee. **Governing Statute:** Chap. 336, RSMo, Rules and Regulations.

Montana

4689

Optometrist
Montana Board of Optomotrists
111 N. Jackson
Helena, MT 59620
Phone: (406)444-5436

Credential Type: Certificate of Registration. **Duration of License:** One year. **Requirements:** 18 years of age. Graduation from an accredited high school. Graduation from an accredited school of optometry. **Examination:** Written, oral and practical exams. **Reciprocity:** Yes, provided state offers equal privileges to applicants from Montana. **Fees:** $150 exam fee. $125 license fee. $100 renewal fee. $250 reciprocity fee. **Governing Statute:** Montana Code Annotated 37-10-301 through 37-10-313.

Nebraska

4690

Optometrist
Nebraska Board of Examiners in Optometry
301 Centennial Mall S.
PO Box 95007
Lincoln, NE 68509
Phone: (402)471-2115

Credential Type: License. **Duration of License:** Two years. **Requirements:** 19 years of age. Must be a graduate of an accredited school of optometry. **Examination:** Yes. **Fees:** $300 initial fee. $300 renewal fee.

Nevada

4691

Optometrist
Nevada State Board of Optometry
PO Box 1687
Carson City, NV 89702
Phone: (702)883-8367

Credential Type: License. **Duration of License:** One year. **Requirements:** Graduation from an approved school of optometry. 18 hours of continuing education each year. **Examination:** Yes. **Fees:** $100 exam fee. $25 license fee. $250 renewal fee.

New Hampshire

4692

Optometrist
Board of Registration in Optometry
6 Hazen Dr.
Concord, NH 03301
Phone: (603)271-2428

Credential Type: Optometry License. **Duration of License:** One year. **Requirements:** Graduate from an accredited college or school of optometry. Renewal requires 15 hours of continuing education. **Examination:** National Board Examinations and NERCOATS. **Reciprocity:** Yes, with states that have similar licensing requirements and that reciprocate in kind. **Fees:** $150 application fee. $100 renewal fee.

New Jersey

4693

Optometrist
State Board of Optometrists
1100 Raymond Blvd., Rm. 501
Newark, NJ 07102
Phone: (201)648-2012

Credential Type: License. **Duration of License:** Two years. **Requirements:** 21 years of age. Doctor of Optometry degree from an accredited school or college of optometry. Good moral character. **Examination:** Written and clinical exams. **Reciprocity:** Yes. **Fees:** $225 exam fee. $100 license fee. $100 biennial registration fee. **Governing Statute:** NJSA 45:12. NJAC 13:38.

New Mexico

4694

Optometrist
Optometry Board
Dept. of Regulation and Licensing
PO Box 25101
725 St. Michael's Dr.
Santa Fe, NM 87504
Phone: (505)827-7170

Credential Type: License. **Duration of License:** One year. **Requirements:** Complete an approved undergraduate pre-optometry curriculum and a four-year accredited degree program at an approved school or college of optometry.

Renewal requires 16 hours of continuing education per year. **Examination:** State optometry examination. **Reciprocity:** Yes. **Fees:** $100 exam fee. $125 license fee. $100 renewal fee. **Governing Statute:** 61-2-1 et seq. NMSA 1978. Rules of the State Board of Examiners in Optometry.

New York

4695

Optometrist
State Education Dept.
Div. of Professional Licensing Services
Cultural Education Center
Empire State Plaza
Albany, NY 12230
Phone: (518)474-3326

Credential Type: License. **Duration of License:** Three years. **Requirements:** Associate's or Bachelor's Degree plus degree in optometry. 21 years of age. **Examination:** Written and practical. **Fees:** $430 application fee. $210 renewal fee. **Governing Statute:** Title VIII Articles 130, 143 of the Education Law.

North Carolina

4696

Optometrist
North Carolina State Board of Optometry
PO Box 609
Wallace, NC 28466
Phone: (919)285-3160

Credential Type: License. **Duration of License:** One year. **Requirements:** Graduation from a board accredited graduate school of optometry with a minimum of two years of pre-optometry undergraduate study. **Examination:** Written, oral and clinical. **Fees:** $1,080 exam fee. $165 renewal fee.

North Dakota

4697

Optometrist
State Board of Optometry
45 Eighth St.
Dickinson, ND 58601
Phone: (701)225-9333

Credential Type: Optometrist License. **Duration of License:** One year. **Requirements:** Complete four years of college and be a graduate from a four-year program of an accredited optometry school. **Examination:** National Board of Examiners in Optometry (NBEO) examination, all parts. North Dakota State Board Examination. **Reciprocity:** Yes. **Fees:** $175 license fee.

Ohio

4698

Optometrist
State Board of Optometry
77 S. High St., 16th Fl.
Columbus, OH 43266-0318
Phone: (614)466-5115
Fax: (614)644-8112

Credential Type: Optometry License. **Requirements:** Graduate from an accredited college or school of optometry. Must have completed CPR training. Effective May 17, 1992, all candidates for licensure must qualify for Therapeutic Pharmaceutical Agents Certification. **Examination:** National Board of Examiners in Optometry (NBOE) Basic Science, Clinical Science, TMOD, and Clinical Skills/VRICS Examinations. **Fees:** $110 license fee.

Oklahoma

4699

Optometrist (O.D.)
Board of Examiners in Optometry
Box 719
Bristow, OK 74010
Phone: (405)367-6780

Credential Type: License. **Duration of License:** One year. **Requirements:** Doctor of Optometry degree. 12 hours of continuing education each year. 21 years of age. **Examination:** Examination required by Board of Examiners in Optometry. **Fees:** $100 exam fee. $25 license fee. $60 renewal fee.

Oregon

4700

Optometrist
Oregon Board of Optometry
695 Summer St. NE
Salem, OR 97310
Phone: (503)373-7721

Credential Type: License. **Duration of License:** One year. **Requirements:** Graduation from a School of Optometry which maintains a standard of four school years. Completion of coursework in pharmacology, as it pertains to optometry. **Examination:** Yes. **Fees:** $50 exam fee. $10 license fee. $80 renewal fee. **Governing Statute:** ORS 683.010 to 683.990.

Pennsylvania

4701

Optometrist
State Board of Optometrical Examiners
Dept. of State
PO Box 2649
Harrisburg, PA 17120
Phone: (717)787-8503

Credential Type: Optometrist License. **Duration of License:** Two years. **Requirements:** At least 21 years of age. Good moral character and free from addiction to alcohol, narcotics, or other habit-forming drugs. Graduate from a school of optometry which is accredited by the Council on Optometric Education of the American Optometric Association or submit credentials to an approved school for evaluation and make up deficiencies. Renewal requires 24 hours of continuing education every two years. **Examination:** State examination. **Exemptions:** Optometrists employed in Federal Service (i.e., medical service of the U.S. armed forces, U.S. Public Health Services, or the Veteran's Administration) are exempt from licensure while performing official duties. **Reciprocity:** Reciprocity exists with graduates of optometric schools from others states, subject to board approval. **Fees:** $25 application fee.

Rhode Island

4702

Optometrist
Board of Examiners in Optometry
Div. of Professional Regulation
Dept. of Health
3 Capitol Hill
Providence, RI 02908
Phone: (401)277-2827

Credential Type: License. **Duration of License:** One year. **Requirements:** Be at least 18 years or older. Complete two years of college and be a graduate of an accredited, approved school of optometry. Serve full-time board-approved internship under the supervision of a physician. Board certification requires completion of 96 hours of postgraduate instruction under a board-certified opthalmologist and pasisng an additional exam. **Examination:** American Optometric Association (AOA) written and practical examinations. State practical examination. **Reciprocity:** Yes. **Fees:** $40 application fee. $45 renewal fee.

South Carolina

4703

Optometrist
South Carolina Board of Examiners of Optometry
PO Box 769
Easley, SC 29641
Phone: (803)859-3233

Credential Type: License. **Requirements:** Two years at an accredited college or university. Graduation from an accredited, four-year school of optometry. **Examination:** Yes. **Fees:** $200 exam fee. $90 renewal fee. $25 certificate fee.

South Dakota

4704

Optometrist
Board of Examiners in Optometry
PO Box 370
Sturgis, SD 57785-0370
Phone: (605)347-2666

Credential Type: Optometry License. **Duration of License:** One year. **Requirements:** Possess a Doctor of Optometry degree. **Examination:** National Board Examination. **Reciprocity:** Yes, with states having equal educational requirements and granting similar reciprocity. **Fees:** $125 exam fee. $175 renewal fee.

Tennessee

4705

Optometrist
Board of Optometry
283 Plus Park Blvd.
Nashville, TN 37243
Phone: (615)367-6225

Credential Type: License. **Requirements:** Over 21 years old. Graduate of an accredited school of optometry. 15 hours of continuing education annually. Good moral character. **Examination:** National Board examination, International Boards of Examinations (IAB) in Optometry. **Fees:** $175 Registration. $100 Application.

Texas

4706

Optometrist
Texas Optometry Board
9101 Burnet Rd., Ste. 214
Austin, TX 78758
Phone: (512)835-1938

Credential Type: License. **Duration of License:** One year. **Requirements:** 21 years of age. High school graduation. Graduation from a reputable college or university of optometry, acceptable to the Board, whose term of instruction shall not be less than six terms of eight months each. Twelve hours of continuing education per year for renewal of license. **Examination:** National written examination. Practical examination. **Fees:** $55 exam fee. $40 license fee. $135 renewal fee. **Governing Statute:** VACS 4552, 22 TAC 273.

Utah

4707

Optometrist
Dept. of Commerce
Div. of Occupational and Professional Licensing
160 E. 300 S.
PO Box 45802
Salt Lake City, UT 84145
Phone: (801)530-6628

Credential Type: License. **Duration of License:** Two years. **Requirements:** Must be a graduate of an approved College of Optometry. **Examination:** Yes. **Fees:** $75 license fee. $50 renewal fee.

Vermont

4708

Optometrist
State Board of Examiners in Optometry
Pavilion Office Bldg.
Montpelier, VT 05602
Phone: (802)828-2390

Credential Type: License. **Duration of License:** Two years. **Requirements:** An adult of good moral character. Graduate from an approved school of optometry; or, licensed in other states which have equivalent requirements. **Examination:** Yes. **Reciprocity:** Yes. **Fees:** $75 Exam fee. $20 Renewal. $50 Licensing through Reciprocity. **Governing Statute:** Title 26, VSA Sections 1691-1696.

Virginia

4709

Optometrist
Board of Optometery
1601 Rolling Hills Dr.
Richmond, VA 23229
Phone: (804)662-9920

Credential Type: License. **Duration of License:** Two years. **Requirements:** Must submit an application. Must submit transcripts as specified by the Board. Must be a graduate of an approved school of optometry. **Examination:** Yes. **Fees:** $100 examination fee. $200 renewal fee.

Washington

4710

Optometrist
Dept. of Health
1112 SE Quince
Olympia, WA 98504
Phone: (206)753-4614

Credential Type: License. **Duration of License:** Two years. **Requirements:** Graduate from an accredited college of optometry. Complete four hours of AIDS education. Renewal requires 50 hours of continuing education every two years. **Examination:** Written, oral, and practical examinations. **Fees:** $100 application fee. $250 exam fee. $160 renewal fee.

West Virginia

4711

Optometrist
Board of Optometry
PO Box 710
St. Albans, WV 25177
Phone: (304)624-5836

Credential Type: License. **Duration of License:** One year. **Requirements:** U.S. citizen. Graduate from a school of optometry. 21 years old. Never convicted of a felony. **Examination:** Yes. **Fees:** $200 Application and examination. $75 License. $30 Renewal.

Wisconsin

4712

Optometrist
Regulations and Licensing Dept.
Optometry Board
PO Box 8935
Madison, WI 53708-8935
Phone: (608)266-8609

Credential Type: Optometrist License. **Requirements:** Graduation from an approved and accredited school of optometry. 18 years of age. **Examination:** Written and practical exams. **Reciprocity:** Yes.

Credential Type: Optometrist/Diagnostic Pharmaceutical Agents (DPA) License. **Requirements:** 60 hours of general and ocular pharmacology. At least 30 of the hours must be in ocular pharmacology. **Examination:** Clinical Pharmacology portion of the National Boards.

Credential Type: Optometrist/TPA Certified. **Requirements:** DPA certification. Completion of a 100-hour, board-approved TPA course or IAB.

Wyoming

4713

Optometrist
State Board of Optometry
PO Box 400
Newcastle, WY 82701
Phone: (307)746-2371

Credential Type: License. **Duration of License:** One year. **Requirements:** Graduate from an approved school of optometry. Pass the National Board Licensing Examination. Pass the state examination. **Examination:** Yes. **Fees:** $100 License. $100 Renewal.

Personnel, Training, and Labor Relations Specialists and Managers

The following states grant licenses in this occupational category as of the date of publication: Alaska, Arkansas, District of Columbia, Illinois, Maryland, Michigan, Minnesota, Nebraska, New Jersey, North Dakota, Oklahoma, Oregon, Tennessee.

Alaska

4714

Employment Agency Operator
Alaska Dept. of Labor
Labor Standards and Safety Div.
Wage and Hour Administration
PO Box 107021
Anchorage, AK 99510
Phone: (907)264-2435

Credential Type: Permit. **Duration of License:** One year. **Authorization:** Permit required to operate an employment agency. **Requirements:** A bond of $10,000 must be furnished to the Dept. of Labor. **Fees:** $10 permit fee. $10 renewal fee.

Arkansas

4715

Employment Agency Counselor
Arkansas Dept of Labor
Private Employment Agency Div.
10421 W. Markham
Little Rock, AR 72205
Phone: (501)682-4505

Credential Type: License. **Duration of License:** One year. **Requirements:** U.S. citizen. Good moral character. Not have had a license suspended or revoked within the past two years. Able to demonstrate business integrity. File a written application and have two letters of character reference from persons of reputed business integrity. **Examination:** Yes. **Fees:** $5 Written examination. $10 Temporary license. $20 License. $20 Renewal.

4716

Employment Agency Manager
Arkansas Dept. of Labor
Private Employment Agency Div.
10421 W. Markham
Little Rock, AR 72205
Phone: (501)682-4505

Credential Type: License. **Duration of License:** One year. **Requirements:** US citizen. Good moral character. 21 years of age. Not have had a license suspended or revoked within the past two years. Completed 12th grade or equivalent and possess a satisfactory level of intellectual competency, judgement, and responsibility. Demonstrate business integrity and financial responsibility. File a written application and provide two character references from persons of reputed business. **Examination:** Yes. **Fees:** $5 Written examination. $10 Temporary license. $25 License. $25 Renewal.

4717

Employment Agent
Arkansas Dept. of Labor
Private Employment Agency Div.
10421 W. Markham
Little Rock, AR 72205
Phone: (501)682-4505

Credential Type: License. **Duration of License:** One year. **Requirements:** US citizen. Good moral character. 21 years of age. Not have had a license suspended or revoked within past two years. Completed 12th grade and possess a satisfactory level of intellectual competency, judgement, and financial responsibility. File a $5,000 bond. Present a copy of all forms and fee schedules to be used in the business. Get an approved location of business. **Examination:** Yes. **Fees:** $5 Written examination. $100 Temporary license. $250 Renewal.

District of Columbia

4718

Employment Counselor
License and Certification Div.
Occupational and Professional Licensure Administration
Consumer and Regulatory Affairs Dept.
PO Box 37200
Washington, DC 20013-7200
Phone: (202)727-7823
Phone: (202)727-7480

Alternate Information: 614 H St., NW, Washington, DC 20001 **Requirements:** Contact licensing body for application information.

Illinois

4719

Human Resource Manager (Gaming)
Illinois Gaming Board
PO Box 19474
Springfield, IL 62794-9474
Phone: (217)524-0228

Credential Type: Human Resource Manager License. **Duration of License:** One year. **Requirements:** At least 18 years of age. U.S. citizen or legal alien as specified by the federal employment eligibility requirement. Four-year college degree in Human Resources. Between five and seven years experience as a generalist in a medium-size company. **Reciprocity:** No. **Fees:** $75 application/initial license fee.

Illinois

Human Resource Manager (Gaming), continued

$50 renewal fee. **Governing Statute:** Illinois Revised Statutes, Chapter 120.

4720

Private Employment Agency Counselor
Illinois Dept. of Labor
310 S. Michigan Ave., 10th Fl.
Chicago, IL 60604
Phone: (312)793-2810

Credential Type: Private Employment Agency Counselor License. **Duration of License:** One year. **Requirements:** Submit application on appropriate forms. Be employed by a licensed employment agency. Pass examination within 90 days of application. Pay fee. **Examination:** Written examination. **Reciprocity:** No. **Fees:** $50 examination/90 day permit fee. $50 application fee. $25 renewal fee. **Governing Statute:** Illinois Revised Statutes, Chapter 111.

Maryland

4721

Employment Counselor
Commissioner of Labor and Industry
Dept. of Licensing and Regulation
501 St. Paul Pl.
Baltimore, MD 21202-2272
Phone: (410)333-4211

Credential Type: License. **Duration of License:** Duration of agency employment. **Requirements:** Pass background investigation into character and integrity. **Fees:** $5 license fee.

Michigan

4722

Employment Agency Manager
Employment Agency Board
Bureau of Occupational & Professional Regulation
Dept. of Commerce
PO Box 30018
Lansing, MI 48909
Phone: (517)373-9153

Credential Type: License. **Duration of License:** One year. **Requirements:** Submit an application and a credit report. Abide by the rules and regulations of the Employment Agency Board. Be of good moral character. **Examination:** Written exam.

Fees: $15 application fee. $50 exam fee. $30 license fee. $30 renewal fee. **Governing Statute:** The Occupational Code, Act 299 of 1980, as amended.

Minnesota

4723

Employment Agency Manager
Dept. of Labor and Industry
Labor Standards Div.
443 Lafayette Rd.
St. Paul, MN 55155
Phone: (612)296-2342

Credential Type: Manager License. **Requirements:** Be employed by an employment agency. Pass one-hour exam. **Examination:** Yes. **Fees:** Contact board for license and exam fees. **Governing Statute:** Minnesota Statutes, Chap. 175-178, 181-184, and 326. Minnesota Rules 5200-5499.

4724

Employment Counselor
Dept. of Labor and Industry
Labor Standards Div.
443 Lafayette Rd.
St. Paul, MN 55155
Phone: (612)296-2342

Credential Type: Counselor License. **Requirements:** Be employed by an employment agency. Pass one-hour exam. **Examination:** Yes. **Fees:** Contact board for license and exam fees. **Governing Statute:** Minnesota Statutes, Chap. 175-178, 181-184, and 326. Minnesota Rules 5200-5499.

Nebraska

4725

Employment Agent
Nebraska Dept. of Labor
1313 Farnam St., 3rd Fl.
Omaha, NE 68102
Phone: (402)595-3095

Credential Type: License. **Duration of License:** One year. **Requirements:** No person with financial interest or managerial control of an agency may have been convicted of a felony. **Fees:** $150 plus $10,000 surety bond license fee. $150 renewal fee.

New Jersey

4726

Director of Student Personnel Services
Office of Teacher Certification and Academic Credentials
CN 503
Trenton, NJ 08625-0503
Phone: (609)292-2079

Credential Type: Director of Student Personnel Services Endorsement. **Authorization:** Authorizes candidate to hold the following positions: director, administrator, or supervisor of guidance and personnel services of a school system, including the supervision of the various special services in a given school district. **Requirements:** Bachelor's degree from an accredited institution. Regular New Jersey student personnel services (counseling) endorsement or its equivalent. Three years of successful experience in school student personnel work. Passing score in specified areas of the NTE written examination or 40 post-baccalaureate semester hours to include courses in the following: 18 hours in guidance including principles of guidance, individual analysis, organization and administration of guidance programs, job analysis, research, seminar in guidance, counseling, group methods in guidance, student personnel work, occupational and educational information, placement, vocational education and a practicum; 10 hours of psychology (exclusive of introductory courses) including psychology of physical and mental growth, child and adolescent psychology, tests and measurements, psychology of parent and child relationships, mental hygiene, statistics, mental abnormalities and defects; 12 hours consisting of one course in each sociology, administration and curriculum, and supervision of instruction. **Examination:** National Teachers Examination (if applicant has not met the college study requirements).

4727

Employment Agency Operator
Div. of Consumer Affairs
Private Employment Agency Section
1100 Raymond Blvd., Rm. 518
Newark, NJ 07102
Phone: (201)648-2882

Credential Type: License. **Requirements:** High school diploma or equivalent. Six months of related experience. **Examination:** Written. **Fees:** $15 license fee. **Governing Statute:** NJSA 34:8. NJAC 13:45B.

North Dakota

4728

Employment Agent
Dept. of Labor
600 E. Blvd.
Bismarck, ND 58505
Phone: (701)224-2660

Credential Type: License. **Duration of License:** One year. **Authorization:** There are three classes of licenses covering different types of occupations. **Requirements:** Post $5000 surety bond. Must file schedule of fees to be charged. **Fees:** $200 license fee. **Governing Statute:** North Dakota Century Code, Chap. 34-13.

Oklahoma

4729

School Service Personnel K-12
Teacher Education and Certification
State Dept. of Education
2500 N. Lincoln Blvd., Rm. 211
Oklahoma City, OK 73105
Phone: (405)521-3337

Credential Type: Standard Certificate in a School Personnel Field—Graduate. **Duration of License:** Five years. **Authorization:** Endorsement will be given to persons seeking positions in the following fields: Counselor; Library Media Specialist; Elementary School Principal; Secondary School Principal; School Superintendent; School Psychometrist; School Psychologist; SpeechLanguage Pathologist; or Reading Specialist. **Requirements:** Complete an approved certificate program at an accredited college or university which includes a minimum of the following: a baccalaureate degree; 50 semester hours in general education; 30 semester hours in professional education; and 40 semester hours in course work pertaining to the area of specialization. Pass the state certified test(s) in specialization competencies. Complete State Board graduate level course requirements.

Oregon

4730

Private Employment Agent
Bureau of Labor & Industries,
  Licensing Office
800 NE Oregon St. 32, Ste. 1160
Portland, OR 97232
Phone: (503)731-4074, ext. 230

Credential Type: License. **Duration of License:** One year. **Requirements:** 18 years of age. One year of experience in an employment agency or the equivalent. Must not have had a license as a Private Employment Agent denied or revoked within three years. Financial responsibility. **Examination:** Yes. **Fees:** $50 exam fee. $250 license fee. $250 renewal fee. **Governing Statute:** ORS 658.005 to 658.245.

Tennessee

4731

Personnel Consultant
Personnel Recruiting Services Board
500 James Robertson Pky., 2nd Fl.
Nashville, TN 37243
Phone: (615)741-4700

Credential Type: License. **Duration of License:** Two years. **Requirements:** 18 years old. Narrative of qualifications. Agency license requires a financial statement. **Examination:** Yes. **Fees:** $10 Registration. $40 Examination. $35 Application. $35 Renewal.

4732

Personnel Service Manager
Personnel Recruiting Services Board
500 James Robertson Pky., 2nd Fl.
Nashville, TN 37243
Phone: (615)741-4700

Credential Type: License. **Duration of License:** Two years. **Requirements:** 18 years old. Narrative of qualifications. Agency license requires a financial statement. **Examination:** Yes. **Fees:** $20 Registration. $50 Examination. $75 Application.

Pest Controllers and Assistants

The following states grant licenses in this occupational category as of the date of publication:

Alabama	District of	Iowa	Minnesota	New Mexico	Rhode Island	Washington
Alaska	Columbia	Kansas	Mississippi	New York	South Carolina	West Virginia
Arizona	Florida	Kentucky	Missouri	North Carolina	South Dakota	Wisconsin
Arkansas	Georgia	Louisiana	Montana	North Dakota	Tennessee	Wyoming
California	Hawaii	Maine	Nebraska	Ohio	Texas	
Colorado	Idaho	Maryland	Nevada	Oklahoma	Utah	
Connecticut	Illinois	Massachusetts	New Hampshire	Oregon	Vermont	
Delaware	Indiana	Michigan	New Jersey	Pennsylvania	Virginia	

Alabama

4733

Pest Control Operator and Fumigator
Dept. of Agriculture
Div. of Agricultural Chemistry and Plant Industry
Beard Bldg.
PO Box 3336
Montgomery, AL 36193
Phone: (205)242-2656

Credential Type: License. **Duration of License:** One year. **Requirements:** Must have either a college degree in Entomology or one year of work experience under a licensed supervisor in the field of pest control. **Examination:** Written examination. **Fees:** $10 examination fee. $50 renewal fee.

Alaska

4734

Commercial Pesticide Applicator
Alaska Dept. of Environmental Conservation
Div. of Environmental Health
500 S. Alaska St., Ste. A
Palmer, AK 99645
Phone: (907)745-3236

Credential Type: Commercial Applicator License. **Duration of License:** Three years. **Requirements:** Complete an approved training session or correspondence course, or pass a written or oral exam administered by the Dept. of Environmental Conservation. License renewal requires completion of a continuing education class and passing a written or oral exam. **Examination:** Written or oral exam administered by the Dept. of Environmental Conservation. **Fees:** No fee.

4735

Private Pesticide Applicator
Alaska Dept. of Environmental Conservation
Div. of Environmental Health
500 S. Alaska St., Ste. A
Palmer, AK 99645
Phone: (907)745-3236

Credential Type: Private Applicator License. **Duration of License:** Three years. **Requirements:** Complete an approved training session or correspondence course, or pass a written or oral exam administered by the Dept. of Environmental Conservation. License renewal requires completion of a continuing education class and passing a written or oral exam. **Examination:** Written or oral exam administered by the Dept. of Environmental Conservation. **Fees:** No fee.

4736

Wood Preservative Applicator
Alaska Dept. of Environmental Conservation
Div. of Environmental Health
500 S. Alaska St., Ste. A
Palmer, AK 99645
Phone: (907)745-3236

Credential Type: Wood Preservative Applicator License. **Duration of License:** Three years. **Requirements:** Complete an approved training session or correspondence course, or pass a written or oral exam administered by the Dept. of Environmental Conservation. License renewal requires completion of a continuing education class and passing a written or oral exam. **Examination:** Written or oral exam administered by the Dept. of Environmental Conservation. **Fees:** No fee.

Arizona

4737

Agricultural Pest Control Advisor
Environmental Services Div.
Dept. of Agriculture
PO Box 1586
Mesa, AZ 85211
Phone: (602)833-5442

Credential Type: License. **Duration of License:** One year. **Requirements:** One year agriculture-related experience. Six hours continuing education for annual renewal. **Examination:** Written exam on laws and rules and any specific areas of expertise. **Fees:** $50 license fee.

4738

Custom Applicator of Pesticides
Environmental Services Div.
Dept. of Agriculture
PO Box 1586
Mesa, AZ 85211
Phone: (602)833-5442

Credential Type: Custom Applicator License. **Authorization:** Application of pesticides for hire or by aircraft **Requirements:** If by air, Commercial Applicator Certification, FAA certification. Proof of financial responsibility. **Examination:** Custom Applicator CORE written exam. **Fees:** $100 license fee.

Pest Controllers and Assistants

4739

Pest Control Advisor
Structural Pest Control Commission
1150 S. Priest, Ste. 4
Tempe, AZ 85281
Phone: (602)255-3664

Credential Type: Pest control advisor's license. **Duration of License:** One year. **Requirements:** Pass written examination. Provide proof of financial responsibility or $100,000 surety bond. Complete at least 12 hours of accredited continuing education classes every two years for license renewal. **Examination:** Written examination. **Fees:** $35 license fee. $35 renewal fee.

4740

Structural Pesticide Applicator
Structural Pest Control Commission
1150 S. Priest, Ste. 4
Tempe, AZ 85281
Phone: (602)255-3664

Credential Type: Structural pesticide applicator certificate. **Duration of License:** One year. **Authorization:** All structural pesticide applicators must be both registered and certified in order to apply pesticides. **Requirements:** An employee of a business licensee who applies pesticides must register with the commission within 30 working days of beginning employment. Each employee who is not certified must be trained by the business licensee and work under the direct supervision of a qualifying party or certified applicator.

For certification, pass a two-part examination covering core information and specific categories in which applicant will be working. Complete 12 hours of continuing education every two years for certification renewal. **Examination:** Two-part examination. **Fees:** $30 application fee. $20 certificate renewal fee. $5 registration fee. $3 registration renewal fee.

Arkansas

4741

Agricultural Consultant
Arkansas State Plant Board
1 Natural Resources Dr.
PO Box 1069
Little Rock, AR 72203
Phone: (501)225-1598

Credential Type: License. **Requirements:** Masters or Phd from an accredited college or university in an appropriate discipline. Pass a written examination given by the board. Three years experience waives the test; or, a Bachelor's degree from an accredited school and one year experience and pass the exam given by the board; or, completed two years of training with an accredited school, three years of experience and passes the written examination given by the board. **Examination:** Written examination. **Fees:** $50 License fee.

4742

Commercial Applicator
Arkansas State Plant Board
PO Box 1069
Little Rock, AR 72203
Phone: (501)225-1598

Credential Type: License. **Requirements:** Must show proof of financial responsibility. Must have knowledge of various pesticides and their usage, and be fully aware of all regulations concerning the application of seeds, fertilizers and pesticides. **Examination:** Yes. **Fees:** $25 Written Examination. $75 Application. $15 Equipment, per article. $25 Pilots license.

4743

Custom Applicator
Arkansas State Plant Board
1 Natural Resources Dr.
PO Box 1069
Little Rock, AR 72203
Phone: (501)225-1598

Credential Type: License. **Requirements:** Must have a pilots license with two years experience and 500 hours of agricultural related flying. Proof of financial responsibility. File spray reports within seven days of spraying. **Examination:** Yes. **Fees:** $25 Written examination. $10 License. $25 Pilot license. $25 Operator in charge.

4744

Pest Exterminator
Arkansas State Plant Board
PO Box 1069
Little Rock, AR 72203
Phone: (501)225-1598

Credential Type: License. **Requirements:** Must have two years of college work with one course in entomology; or, must have served under a licensed agent for one year prior to taking the exam. **Examination:** Yes. **Fees:** $75 Written examination, plus $50 for each additional category. $100 License, plus $75 for each additional category or up to a maximum of $200.

4745

Seed Treatment Commercial Applicator
Arkansas State Plant Board
PO Box 1069
Little Rock, AR 72203
Phone: (501)225-1598

Credential Type: License. **Requirements:** Must pass the written examination. **Examination:** Yes. **Fees:** $10 License.

California

4746

Agricultural Pest Control Adviser
California Environmental Protection Agency
Dept. of Pesticide Regulation
1220 N St.
PO Box 942871
Sacramento, CA 94271-0001
Phone: (916)654-0606
Fax: (916)654-1427

Credential Type: Agricultural Pest Control Adviser (APCA) License. **Duration of License:** One year. **Authorization:** License is required for any individual who offers a recommendation on any agricultural use. **Requirements:** Meet one of the following sets of requirements: (1) Have a bachelors degree in agricultural sciences, biological science, or pest management. (2) Have completed at least 60 semester hours (90 quarter hours) of college level curriculum in agricultural sciences, biological science, or pest management. Complete 24 months of technical experience as an assistant to an APCA or equivalent.

At least 40 hours of continuing education are required every two years for renewal. **Examination:** Laws and Regulations Examination. At least one category examination. **Fees:** $50 application fee. $30 annual renewal fee.

4747

Pesticide Applicator
Structural Pest Control Board
1422 Howe Ave., Ste. 3
Sacramento, CA 95825-3280
Phone: (916)924-2291

Credential Type: Applicator Registration. **Duration of License:** Three years. **Requirements:** Submit application and pay fee. Pass examination. Reexamination is required at end of three-year registration period. **Examination:** Applicator examination. **Fees:** $10 exam fee. **Governing Statute:** Structural Pest Control Act, Busi-

California

Pesticide Applicator, continued

ness and Professions Code 8500 et seq., Div. 3, Chap. 14. California Code of Regulations, Title 16, Div. 19.

4748

Pesticide Dealer
California Environmental Protection Agency
Dept. of Pesticide Regulation
1220 N St.
PO Box 942871
Sacramento, CA 94271-0001
Phone: (916)654-0606
Fax: (916)654-1427

Credential Type: Pesticide Dealer License. **Duration of License:** One year. **Requirements:** Each location must have a person who is responsible for the dealership who holds a Designated Agent License, Agricultural Pest Control Adviser License, Pest Control Aircraft Pilot Certificate, or a Qualified Applicator License. **Fees:** $100 annual license fee for principal office. $50 annual license fee for each branch location.

Credential Type: Designated Agent License. **Duration of License:** One year. **Authorization:** Required of any person who is responsible for supervising the operations conducted by a licensed pesticide dealer. **Requirements:** Submit application and pay fee. Pass exam on the sale and use of pesticides and dealer responsibilities. **Examination:** Written exam. **Fees:** $15 application fee. $15 renewal fee.

4749

Qualified Pesticide Applicator
California Environmental Protection Agency
Dept. of Pesticide Regulation
1220 N St.
PO Box 942871
Sacramento, CA 94271-0001
Phone: (916)654-0606
Fax: (916)654-1427

Credential Type: Qualified Applicator License. **Duration of License:** One year. **Authorization:** There are 12 categories of licensure. License is required for the individual who is responsible for the safe and legal operations of a pest control business and for any individual who uses or supervises the use of restricted use pesticides for any purpose other than that of a private applicator. **Requirements:** Demonstrate competency by passing appropriate examinations.

At least 20 hours of continuing education are required every two years for renewal. **Examination:** Laws and Regulations Examination. At least one category examination. **Fees:** $40 application fee. $30 annual renewal fee.

Credential Type: Qualified Applicator Certificate. **Duration of License:** One year. **Authorization:** There are 13 categories of certification. Required of any person who uses or supervises the use of restricted use pesticides for any purpose other than that of a private applicator. Also required of any individual in the business of landscape maintenance who performs pest control incidentally to that business. **Requirements:** Demonstrate competency by passing appropriate examinations.

At least 20 hours of continuing education are required every two years for renewal. **Examination:** Laws and Regulations Examination. At least one category examination. **Fees:** $25 application fee. $15 annual renewal fee.

4750

Structural Pest Control Field Representative
Structural Pest Control Board
1422 Howe Ave., Ste. 3
Sacramento, CA 95825-3280
Phone: (916)924-2291

Credential Type: Field Representative License. **Duration of License:** Three years. **Authorization:** Licenses granted in four branches: fumigation, general pest, termite, and roof restoration. **Requirements:** Must have training and experience in the branch(es) applied for. **Examination:** Separate examinations for fumigation, general pest, termite, and roof restoration. **Fees:** $10 exam fee (per branch). $30 license fee. **Governing Statute:** Structural Pest Control Act, Business and Professions Code 8500 et seq., Div. 3, Chap. 14. California Code of Regulations, Title 16, Div. 19.

4751

Structural Pest Control Operator
Structural Pest Control Board
1422 Howe Ave., Ste. 3
Sacramento, CA 95825-3280
Phone: (916)924-2291

Credential Type: Operator License. **Duration of License:** Three years. **Authorization:** Licenses granted in four branches: fumigation, general pest, termite, and roof restoration. **Requirements:** Must have been licensed as a field representative for at least one year in the branch applied for, or have equivalent training and experience. **Examination:** Separate examinations for fumigation, general pest, termite, and roof restoration. **Fees:** $25 exam fee (per branch). $150 license fee. **Governing Statute:** Structural Pest Control Act, Business and Professions Code 8500 et seq., Div. 3, Chap. 14. California Code of Regulations, Title 16, Div. 19.

Colorado

4752

Commercial Pesticide Applicator
Dept. of Agriculture
Div. of Plant Industry
Pesticide Applicator Section
700 Kipling St., Ste. 4000
Lakewood, CO 80215-5894
Phone: (303)239-4139
Phone: (303)239-4140

Credential Type: Commercial Applicator License. **Duration of License:** One year. **Authorization:** Required of any business or individual who applies pesticides commercially (i.e., receives compensation). **Requirements:** Must employ at least one qualified supervisor who is licensed in the class or subclass of application being performed. Provide proof of insurance. **Fees:** $250 license fee.

Credential Type: Limited Commercial Applicator Registration. **Duration of License:** One year. **Authorization:** Must register if applying restricted use pesticides. **Requirements:** Must employ at least one qualified supervisor who is licensed in the class or subclass of application being performed. **Fees:** $50 registration fee.

4753

Pesticide Operator
Dept. of Agriculture
Div. of Plant Industry
Pesticide Applicator Section
700 Kipling St., Ste. 4000
Lakewood, CO 80215-5894
Phone: (303)239-4139
Phone: (303)239-4140

Credential Type: Certified Operator License. **Duration of License:** Three years. **Authorization:** Required of an individual who used restricted use pesticides without on-site supervision of a qualified supervisor. **Requirements:** Demonstrate competency by passing appropriate examinations. **Examination:** General exam plus appropriate category examinations. **Reciprocity:** Yes. **Fees:** $75 license fee.

4754

Pesticide Supervisor
Dept. of Agriculture
Div. of Plant Industry
Pesticide Applicator Section
700 Kipling St., Ste. 4000
Lakewood, CO 80215-5894
Phone: (303)239-4139
Phone: (303)239-4140

Credential Type: Qualified Supervisor License. **Duration of License:** Three years. **Authorization:** Required of any individual in the employ of a commercial, limited commercial, or public applicator; who, without supervision, evaluates pest problems or recommends pest controls, or who mixes, loads, or applies any pesticides, or sells any application services, or operates devices, or supervises others in these functions. **Requirements:** Demonstrate competency by passing appropriate examinations. Experience requirements vary with category. **Examination:** General exam plus appropriate category examinations. **Fees:** $75 license fee.

4755

Public Pesticide Applicator
Dept. of Agriculture
Div. of Plant Industry
Pesticide Applicator Section
700 Kipling St., Ste. 4000
Lakewood, CO 80215-5894
Phone: (303)239-4139
Phone: (303)239-4140

Credential Type: Public Applicator Registration. **Duration of License:** One year. **Authorization:** Must register if applying restricted use pesticides. **Requirements:** Must employ at least one qualified supervisor who is licensed in the class or subclass of application being performed. **Fees:** $50 registration fee.

Connecticut

4756

Commercial Pesticide Applicator
Environmental Protection Dept.
165 Capitol Ave.
Hartford, CT 06106
Phone: (203)566-2110

Credential Type: Supervisory Certification. **Duration of License:** Five years. **Authorization:** Supervisory certification required for commercial applicators who are responsible for deciding whether or not pesticides are to be employed, how they are to be mixed, where they are to be employed, what pesticides are to be used, etc. **Requirements:** Must be at least 18 years of age. Submit application and pay fee. Pass examination. **Examination:** Yes. **Governing Statute:** General Statutes of Connecticut, Chap. 441.

Credential Type: Operational Certification. **Authorization:** Operational certification required for commercial applicators who actively use pesticides in other than a supervisory capacity. **Requirements:** Must be at least 18 years of age. Submit application and pay fee. Pass examination. **Examination:** Yes. **Governing Statute:** General Statutes of Connecticut, Chap. 441.

4757

Pesticide Dealer
Dept. of Environmental Protection
Pesticide Control Section
165 Capitol Ave.
Hartford, CT 06106
Phone: (203)566-2110
Phone: (203)566-5148
Fax: (203)566-4924

Credential Type: Private Dealer License. **Duration of License:** One year. **Requirements:** Demonstrate competency by passing appropriate examination. **Examination:** Written examination. **Fees:** $25 exam fee. $30 annual license fee. **Governing Statute:** General Statutes of Connecticut, Chap. 441.

4758

Private Pesticide Applicator
Dept. of Environmental Protection
Pesticide Control Section
165 Capitol Ave.
Hartford, CT 06106
Phone: (203)566-2110
Fax: (203)566-4924

Credential Type: Private Applicator Certification. **Duration of License:** Varies. **Authorization:** There are 13 categories of certification. **Requirements:** Demonstrate competency by passing appropriate examinations. **Examination:** Private Applicator Pesticide Examination. **Fees:** $5 exam fee (per category). $5 per year certification fee (total amount varies from $5-$25 based on first letter of last name). **Governing Statute:** General Statutes of Connecticut, Chap. 441.

Delaware

4759

Commercial Pesticide Applicator
Dept. of Agriculture
Pesticide Section
2320 S. duPont Hwy.
Dover, DE 19901
Phone: (302)739-4811
Fax: (302)697-6287

Credential Type: Commercial Applicator Certification. **Duration of License:** Three years. **Requirements:** Submit application and pass examination. Recertification requires 26 hours of continuing education as specified by the department for each category. **Examination:** Core examination and category examination(s). **Governing Statute:** Delaware Pesticide Law.

4760

Private Pesticide Applicator
Dept. of Agriculture
Pesticide Section
2320 S. duPont Hwy.
Dover, DE 19901
Phone: (302)739-4811
Fax: (302)697-6287

Credential Type: Private Applicator Certification. **Duration of License:** Three years. **Authorization:** May apply restricted-use pesticides only to land that is owned or rented by certified individual or employer. **Requirements:** Submit application and pass examination. Available only to producers of an agricultural commodity. Recertification requires three hours of continuing education. **Examination:** Core examination. **Governing Statute:** Delaware Pesticide Law.

District of Columbia

4761

Commercial Pesticide Applicator
Dept. of Consumer and Regulatory Affairs
Environmental Control Div.
2100 Martin Luther King, Jr. Ave., SE, Ste. 203
Washington, DC 20020
Phone: (202)404-1167

Credential Type: Commercial Applicator Certification. **Duration of License:** Three years. **Authorization:** There are eight categories of certification. **Requirements:** Meet one of the following sets of requirements: (1) Complete one year of experience as a full-time registered employee engaged

Commercial Pesticide Applicator, continued

in those categories for which certification is sought. (2) Have a degree or certification from an accredited college or university with acceptable specialized training. (3) Have a combination of training and experience of at least one year.

Recertification requires completing at least one refresher training course every three years. **Examination:** Examinations on general standards and specific categories. **Reciprocity:** Yes. **Governing Statute:** District of Columbia Municipal Regulations, Title 20, Chaps. 10-13.

Credential Type: Commercial Applicator License. **Duration of License:** One year. **Authorization:** License authorizes purchase and use of restricted use pesticides for which competency has been demonstrated. **Requirements:** A license will be issued upon meeting the requirements for certification. **Reciprocity:** Yes. **Fees:** $50 annual license fee. **Governing Statute:** District of Columbia Municipal Regulations, Title 20, Chaps. 10-13.

4762

Pesticide Dealer

Dept. of Consumer and Regulatory Affairs
Environmental Control Div.
2100 Martin Luther King Jr. Ave. SE, Ste. 203
Washington, DC 20020
Phone: (202)404-1167

Credential Type: Dealer Registration and License. **Duration of License:** One year. **Requirements:** Submit application and pay fee. **Fees:** $25 license fee. **Governing Statute:** District of Columbia Municipal Regulations, Title 20, Chaps. 10-13.

4763

Pesticide Employee

Dept. of Consumer and Regulatory Affairs
Environmental Control Div.
2100 Martin Luther King, Jr. Ave., SE, Ste. 203
Washington, DC 20020
Phone: (202)404-1167

Credential Type: Registration. **Authorization:** Authorizes application of pesticides under the direct supervision of a licensed certified applicator. **Requirements:** Must be able to read and comprehend written instructions. Must be capable of properly handling and applying a given pesticide. **Governing Statute:** District of Columbia Municipal Regulations, Title 20, Chaps. 10-13.

4764

Pesticide Operator

Dept. of Consumer and Regulatory Affairs
Environmental Control Div.
2100 Martin Luther King, Jr. Ave., SE, Ste. 203
Washington, DC 20020
Phone: (202)404-1167

Credential Type: Pesticide Operator License. **Duration of License:** One year. **Requirements:** Application must specify the categories or subcategories of pest control activity in which the business may lawfully engage. Must furnish evidence of financial responsibility in the form of liability insurance. **Fees:** $100 license fee. **Governing Statute:** District of Columbia Municipal Regulations, Title 20, Chaps. 10-13.

4765

Private Pesticide Applicator

Dept. of Consumer and Regulatory Affairs
Environmental Control Div.
2100 Martin Luther King, Jr. Ave., SE, Ste. 203
Washington, DC 20020
Phone: (202)404-1167

Credential Type: Private Applicator Certification. **Duration of License:** Three years. **Requirements:** Demonstrate competency by passing an examination and performing a labeling exercise. Recertification requires completing at least one refresher training course every three years. **Examination:** Written examination. **Reciprocity:** Yes. **Governing Statute:** District of Columbia Municipal Regulations, Title 20, Chaps. 10-13.

Credential Type: Private Applicator License. **Duration of License:** One year. **Authorization:** License authorizes purchase and use of restricted use pesticides for which competency has been demonstrated. **Requirements:** A license will be issued upon meeting the requirements for certification. **Reciprocity:** Yes. **Fees:** No fee. **Governing Statute:** District of Columbia Municipal Regulations, Title 20, Chaps. 10-13.

4766

Public Pesticide Applicator

Dept. of Consumer and Regulatory Affairs
Environmental Control Div.
2100 Martin Luther King, Jr. Ave., SE, Ste. 203
Washington, DC 20020
Phone: (202)404-1167

Credential Type: Public Applicator Certification. **Duration of License:** Three years. **Authorization:** There are eight categories of certification. **Requirements:** Meet one of the following sets of requirements: (1) Complete one year of experience as a full-time registered employee engaged in those categories for which certification is sought. (2) Have a degree or certification from an accredited college or university with acceptable specialized training. (3) Have a combination of training and experience of at least one year.

Recertification requires completing at least one refresher training course every three years. **Examination:** Examinations on general standards and specific categories. **Reciprocity:** Yes. **Governing Statute:** District of Columbia Municipal Regulations, Title 20, Chaps. 10-13.

Credential Type: Public Applicator License. **Duration of License:** One year. **Authorization:** License authorizes purchase and use of restricted use pesticides for which competency has been demonstrated. **Requirements:** A license will be issued upon meeting the requirements for certification. **Reciprocity:** Yes. **Fees:** No fee. **Governing Statute:** District of Columbia Municipal Regulations, Title 20, Chaps. 10-13.

Florida

4767

Commercial Applicator

Dept. of Agriculture and Consumer Services
Bureau of Pesticides
3125 Conner Blvd. MD-1
Tallahassee, FL 32399-1650
Phone: (904)488-6838

Credential Type: Certification and Restricted Use Pesticide License. **Duration of License:** Four years. **Authorization:** There are 15 license categories that correspond to specific certifying examinations. **Requirements:** Demonstrate competency by passing appropriate certifying examination. Recertification requires completion of a recertification program or retesting. Aerial category applicants must have a valid pilot's license, submit proof of insurance, and post a $25,000 surety bond. **Examination:** Certification examination in appropriate category. **Fees:** $75 license fee. **Governing Statute:** Florida Statutes, Chap. 487. FAC 5E-2 and 5E-9.

4768

Pest Control Operator
Dept. of Agriculture and Consumer Services
Div. of Agricultural Environmental Services
Bureau of Entomology and Pest Control
PO Box 210
Jacksonville, FL 32231
Phone: (904)798-4609

Credential Type: Pest Control Operator Certificate. **Requirements:** Be at least 18 years of age. Meet one of the following sets of requirements: (1) Complete at least three years of employment as a service employee of a licensee in the appropriate category. At least one year of employment must have been in Florida for the year immediately preceding application. Be a high shcool graduate or equivalent. Must have completed, under the supervision of a certified operator, at least 15 jobs in each category for which certification is sought. (2) Have a degree with advanced training or a major in entomology, botany, agronomy, or horticulture from a recognized college or university. Complete one year of employment as a service employee of a licensee in the appropriate category. (3) Have a two-year degree in horticultural technology or the equivalent, with advanced training of at least 20 semester hours (30 quarter hours) in horticulture. Complete one year of employment as a service employee of a licensee in the appropriate category. (4) Have a two-year degree in general pest control technology or the equivalent, with advanced training of at least 20 semester hours (30 quarter hours) in entomology. Complete one year of employment as a service employee of a licensee that performs pest control. (5) Complete 24 semester hours (36 quarter hours) in entomology, pest control technology, and related subjects. Complete one year of employment as a service employee of a licensee that performs pest control in the category of general household pest, termite, and fumigation. Such an applicant is qualified only for the examination in the categories of general household pest control, termite and other wood-destroying organisms pest control, and fumigation. (6) Complete 24 semester hours (36 quarter hours) in entomology. Complete one year of employment as a service employee of a licensee that performs pest control in the category of lawn and ornamental pest control. Such an applicant is qualified only for the examination in the category of lawn and ornamental pest control. **Examination:** Examinations in appropriate categories. **Fees:** $150 exam fee (per category). **Governing Statute:** Florida Statutes, Chap. 482. Florida Administrative Code, Chap. 10D-55.

Credential Type: Special Identification Card-Fumigation. **Requirements:** Have participated in a minimum of 15 fumigation operations. **Examination:** Special Identification Card Examination. **Fees:** $100 exam fee. **Governing Statute:** Florida Statutes, Chap. 482. Florida Administrative Code, Chap. 10D-55.

4769

Pesticide Dealer
Dept. of Agriculture and Consumer Services
Bureau of Pesticides
3125 Conner Blvd. MD-1
Tallahassee, FL 32399-1650
Phone: (904)488-6838

Credential Type: Pesticide Dealer License. **Duration of License:** One year. **Requirements:** Submit application. There are no training or experience requirements. **Fees:** No fee. **Governing Statute:** Florida Statutes, Chap. 487. FAC 5E-2 and 5E-9.

4770

Private Applicator
Dept. of Agriculture and Consumer Services
Bureau of Pesticides
3125 Conner Blvd. MD-1
Tallahassee, FL 32399-1650
Phone: (904)488-6838

Credential Type: Certification and Restricted Use Pesticide License. **Duration of License:** Four years. **Authorization:** There are 15 license categories that correspond to specific certifying examinations. **Requirements:** Demonstrate competency by passing appropriate certifying examination. Recertification requires completion of a recertification program or retesting. Aerial category applicants must have a valid pilot's license, submit proof of insurance, and post a $25,000 surety bond. **Examination:** Certification examination in appropriate category. **Fees:** $30 license fee. **Governing Statute:** Florida Statutes, Chap. 487. FAC 5E-2 and 5E-9.

4771

Public Applicator
Dept. of Agriculture and Consumer Services
Bureau of PEsticides
3125 Conner Blvd. MD-1
Tallahassee, FL 32399-1650
Phone: (904)488-6838

Credential Type: Certification and Restricted Use Pesticide License. **Duration of License:** Four years. **Authorization:** There are 15 license categories that correspond to specific certifying examinations. **Requirements:** Demonstrate competency by passing appropriate certifying examination. Recertification requires completion of a recertification program or retesting. Aerial category applicants must have a valid pilot's license. **Examination:** Certification examination in appropriate category. **Fees:** $30 license fee. **Governing Statute:** Florida Statutes, Chap. 487. FAC 5E-2 and 5E-9.

Georgia

4772

Commercial Pesticide Applicator (Certified Operator)
Dept. of Agriculture
Pesticides Div.
Agriculture Bldg.
Capitol Sq.
Atlanta, GA 30334
Phone: (404)656-4958
Fax: (404)656-9380

Credential Type: Certification for Restricted Use Pesticides (Certified Operator). **Duration of License:** Five years. **Authorization:** Each licensed pesticide contractor must designate a Certified Operator to be in charge of and actively participate in providing adequate personal supervision in the pest control operations of each office. **Requirements:** Meet one of the following sets of requirements: (1) Complete two years of actual service experience in the categories for which certification is sought. Specialized category training under university or college supervision may be substituted for practical experience at the ratio of one year of training for one-fourth year of experience. (2) Bachelor's degree from a recognized college or university with advanced training or a major in entomology, sanitary or public health engineering, or related subjects, and one year of actual service experience in the categories for which certification is sought. General Standards Examination and at least one category examination.

Georgia

4773
Commercial Pesticide Applicator (Certified Operator), continued

Recertification requires completion of 26 hours of training every five years and passing a written exam. **Examination:** General Standards Examination and at least one category examination. **Fees:** $25 certification fee. **Governing Statute:** Official Code of Georgia Annotated, Title 2, Chap. 7, Article 3. Rules of the Structural Pest Control Commission, Chap. 620-3.

4773

Pesticide Contractor
Dept. of Agriculture
Pesticides Div.
Agriculture Bldg.
Capitol Sq.
Atlanta, GA 30334
Phone: (404)656-4958
Fax: (404)656-9380

Credential Type: Pesticide Contractor License. **Duration of License:** Two years. **Authorization:** Each licensed pesticide contractor must designate a Certified Operator to be in charge of and actively participate in providing adequate personal supervision in the pest control operations of each office. **Requirements:** Submit application containing information regarding qualifications and proposed operations. Submit proof of financial responsibility. **Fees:** $50 license fee. $90 research fee. **Governing Statute:** Official Code of Georgia Annotated, Title 2, Chap. 7, Article 3. Rules of the Structural Pest Control Commission, Chap. 620-3.

4774

Pesticide Employee
Dept. of Agriculture
Pesticides Div.
Agriculture Bldg.
Capitol Sq.
Atlanta, GA 30334
Phone: (404)656-4958
Fax: (404)656-9380

Credential Type: Pesticide Employee Registration. **Duration of License:** Two years. **Authorization:** Must be registered to solicit business and perform pest control work. **Requirements:** Complete 10 hours of approved classroom training. Complete 70 hours of on-the-job experience under the constant personal supervision of a certified operator or currently registered employee.

Renewal requires completing 13 hours of approved training every two years. **Examination:** Written examination on classsroom training. **Fees:** $10 registration fee. $10 renewal fee. **Governing Statute:** Official Code of Georgia Annotated, Title 2, Chap. 7, Article 3. Rules of the Structural Pest Control Commission, Chap. 620-3.

Hawaii

4775

Fumigator Operator
Hawaii Pest Control Board
1010 Richards St.
PO Box 3469
Honolulu, HI 96801
Phone: (808)548-7462

Credential Type: Fumigator Operator License. **Duration of License:** Two years. **Requirements:** At least two experience certifications of at least two years. Job report indicating at least 100 jobs. Certification under the Hawaii pesticides law as a commercial applicator. **Examination:** Given six times per year. **Fees:** $25 application fee. $25 exam fee. $25 license fee. $25-$50 Compliance Resolution Fund fee. $100 renewal fee.

4776

Pest Control Field Representative
Hawaii Pest Control Board
1010 Richards St.
PO Box 3469
Honolulu, HI 96801
Phone: (808)548-7462

Credential Type: Pest Control Field Representative License. **Duration of License:** Two years. **Requirements:** At least two experience certifications of at least six months. A list of at least 25 jobs during the six-month experience period. Submit the employing firm's Responsible Managing Employee (RME) statement that RME will be responsible for applicant's acts, conduct, representations, etc. **Examination:** Given six times per year. **Fees:** $15 application fee. $25 exam fee. $15 license fee. $25-$50 Compliance Resolution Fund fee. $100 renewal fee.

4777

Pest Control Operator
Hawaii Pest Control Board
1010 Richards St.
PO Box 3469
Honolulu, HI 96801
Phone: (808)548-7462

Credential Type: Pest Control Operator License. **Duration of License:** Two years. **Requirements:** Two years of experience, one of which was in a supervisory capacity. Participated in at least 100 jobs during the two-year period. Certification under the Hawaii pesticides law as a commercial applicator. **Examination:** Given six times per year. **Fees:** $25 application fee. $25 exam fee. $25 license fee. $25—$50 Compliance Resolution Fund fee. $100 renewal fee.

Idaho

4778

Commercial Applicator
Pesticide Enforcement Bureau
Plant Industries Div.
Agriculture Dept.
PO Box 790
2270 Old Penitentiary Rd.
Boise, ID 83701
Phone: (208)334-3243

Credential Type: Commercial Applicator License. **Duration of License:** One year. **Authorization:** A Commercial Applicator owns or operates a business engaged in applying pesticides to the land or property of others for hire. Must be licensed regardless of whether general use or restricted use pesticides are applied. May make recommendations in those categories for which licensed. **Requirements:** Submit application and pass examination. Provide written proof of financial responsibility. Must recertify every five years either by taking 40 approved recertification credit hours with a maximum of 15 hours in any one year, or by passing a recertification exam in each category for which recertification is sought. **Examination:** Written exam for Commercial Applicator covering categories that pertain to type of work being done. **Reciprocity:** With Montana, Wyoming, Utah, Oregon, and Washington only. **Fees:** $50 license fee. $50 renewal fee. $25 fee per piece of application equipment to be licensed. **Governing Statute:** Idaho Pesticide Law. Idaho Pesticide Use Rules and Regulations.

4779

Commercial Operator
Pesticide Enforcement Bureau
Plant Industries Div.
Agriculture Dept.
PO Box 790
2270 Old Penitentiary Rd.
Boise, ID 83701
Phone: (208)334-3243

Credential Type: Commercial Operator License. **Duration of License:** One year. **Authorization:** A Commercial Operator works for a Commerical Applicator and can only be licensed in the categories that the Commercial Applicator is licensed in. May not make recommendations without being licensed as a Pest Control Consultant. **Requirements:** Submit application and pass examination. Must work for a licensed Commercial Applicator. Must recertify every five years either by taking 40 approved recertification credit hours with a maximum of 15 hours in any one year, or by passing a recertification exam in each category for which recertification is sought. **Examination:** Written exam for Commercial Operator covering categories that pertain to type of work being done. **Reciprocity:** With Montana, Wyoming, Utah, Oregon, and Washington only. **Fees:** $40 license fee. $40 renewal fee. **Governing Statute:** Idaho Pesticide Law. Idaho Pesticide Use Rules and Regulations.

4780

Limited Applicator
Pesticide Enforcement Bureau
Plant Industries Div.
Agriculture Dept.
PO Box 790
2270 Old Penitentiary Rd.
Boise, ID 83701
Phone: (208)334-3243

Credential Type: Limited Applicator License. **Duration of License:** One year. **Authorization:** A Limited Applicator does not offer his or her services to the public for hire and is generally not directly involved in agricultural commodity production. May use or supervise the use of restricted use pesticides only on land owned or rented by himself or the agency or company that employs him. May make recommendations in those categories for which licensed. **Requirements:** Submit application and pass examination. Must recertify every five years either by taking 40 approved recertification credit hours with a maximum of 15 hours in any one year, or by passing a recertification exam in each category for which recertification is sought. **Examination:** Written exam for Limited Applicator covering categories that pertain to type of work being done. **Reciprocity:** With Montana, Wyoming, Utah, Oregon, and Washington only. **Fees:** $50 license fee. $50 renewal fee. **Governing Statute:** Idaho Pesticide Law. Idaho Pesticide Use Rules and Regulations.

4781

Mixer-Loader
Pesticide Enforcement Bureau
Plant Industries Div.
Agriculture Dept.
PO Box 790
2270 Old Penitentiary Rd.
Boise, ID 83701
Phone: (208)334-3243

Credential Type: Mixer-Loader License. **Duration of License:** One year. **Authorization:** A Mixer-Loader works for a Commerical Applicator in the mixing and loading of pesticides to prepare for, but not actually make, applications. **Requirements:** Must work for a licensed Commercial Applicator. Receive department-approved mixer-loader training or pass with a minimu score of 60 percent the department's mixer-loader examination **Examination:** Written exam for Mixer-Loader. **Reciprocity:** With Montana, Wyoming, Utah, Oregon, and Washington only. **Fees:** No fee. **Governing Statute:** Idaho Pesticide Law. Idaho Pesticide Use Rules and Regulations.

4782

Pest Control Consultant
Pesticide Enforcement Bureau
Plant Industries Div.
Agriculture Dept.
PO Box 790
2270 Old Penitentiary Rd.
Boise, ID 83701
Phone: (208)334-3243

Credential Type: Pest Control Consultant License. **Duration of License:** One year. **Authorization:** A Pest Control Consultant may make recommendations or give technical advice concerning the use of pesticides for agricultural purposes. License does not permit holder to apply pesticides. **Requirements:** Submit application and pass examination. Must recertify every five years either by taking 40 approved recertification credit hours with a maximum of 15 hours in any one year, or by passing a recertification exam in each category for which recertification is sought. **Examination:** Written exam for Pest Control Consultant or for all categories that pertain to agricultural pesticides. **Reciprocity:** With Montana, Wyoming, Utah, Oregon, and Washington only. **Fees:** $50 license fee. $50 renewal fee. **Governing Statute:** Idaho Pesticide Law. Idaho Pesticide Use Rules and Regulations.

4783

Pesticide Dealer
Pesticide Enforcement Bureau
Plant Industries Div.
Agriculture Dept.
PO Box 790
2270 Old Penitentiary Rd.
Boise, ID 83701
Phone: (208)334-3243

Credential Type: Pesticide Dealer License. **Duration of License:** One year. **Authorization:** Each outlet in the state that distributes limited use pesticides must have a licensed Pesticide Dealer. A Licensed Pesticide Dealer may not make recommendations or give technical advice unless also certified as a Pest Control Consultant, Commercial Applicator, or Limited Applicator. **Requirements:** Submit application and pass examination. Must recertify every five years either by taking 40 approved recertification credit hours with a maximum of 15 hours in any one year, or by passing a recertification exam in each category for which recertification is sought. **Examination:** Written exam for Pest Control Consultant or for all categories that pertain to the type(s) of restricted use pesticides sold. **Reciprocity:** With Montana, Wyoming, Utah, Oregon, and Washington only. **Fees:** $50 license fee. $50 renewal fee. **Governing Statute:** Idaho Pesticide Law. Idaho Pesticide Use Rules and Regulations.

4784

Private Applicator
Pesticide Enforcement Bureau
Plant Industries Div.
Agriculture Dept.
PO Box 790
2270 Old Penitentiary Rd.
Boise, ID 83701
Phone: (208)334-3243

Credential Type: Private Applicator License. **Duration of License:** Five years. **Authorization:** A Private Applicator is any individual growing agricultural commodities who uses or supervises the use of restricted pesticides on his or her own land or on land rented by him or his supervisor. A Private Applicator may not apply pesticides to the land or property of others for hire. **Requirements:** Attend a University of Idaho Cooperative Extension Service Private Applicator training session or pass examination with a minimum score of 70 percent. Must recertify every five years either by taking 15 approved recertification credit hours with a maximum of six hours in any one year, or by passing a private applicator recertification exam during or after the 5th year of the recertification period. **Examina-**

Private Applicator, continued

tion: Written exam for Private Applicator. **Reciprocity:** With Montana, Wyoming, Utah, Oregon, and Washington only. **Fees:** $25 license fee. $25 renewal fee. **Governing Statute:** Idaho Pesticide Law. Idaho Pesticide Use Rules and Regulations.

Illinois

4785

Commercial Pesticide Applicator
Illinois Dept. of Agriculture
Bureau of Environmental Programs
PO Box 19281
State Fairgrounds
Springfield, IL 62794-9281
Phone: (217)785-2427

Credential Type: Commercial Pesticide Applicator License. **Duration of License:** One year. **Authorization:** Authorizes applicant to sell the services of applying pesticides on a customer's property. May sell, buy, and apply pesticides. **Requirements:** At least 16 years of age. Illinois resident. Must carry insurance coverage of $50,000 per person and $100,000 bodily injury liability. Training preferred. Must retake examination every three years. **Examination:** General Standard Pesticide Examination. Category (Specialty) Examination. **Reciprocity:** Yes, with a valid Pesticide license from a state immediately adjacent to Illinois. **Fees:** $50 initial license fee. $50 renewal fee. **Governing Statute:** Illinois Revised Statutes, Chapter 5.

4786

Commercial Pesticide Applicator For Private Company (Not For Hire)
Illinois Dept. of Agriculture
Bureau of Environmental Programs
PO Box 19281
State Fairgrounds
Springfield, IL 62794-9281
Phone: (217)785-2427

Credential Type: Commercial Pesticide Applicator (Not For Hire) License. **Duration of License:** One year. **Authorization:** Authorizes applicant to purchase, handle, and use pesticides only in the maintenance of the property of the company for which he/she is employed. **Requirements:** At least 16 years of age. Illinois resident. Training preferred. Must retake examination every three years. **Examination:** General Standard Pesticide Examination. Category (Specialty) Examination. **Reciprocity:** Yes, with a valid Pesticide license from a state immediately adjacent to Illinois. **Fees:** No fee. **Governing Statute:** Illinois Revised Statutes, Chapter 5.

4787

Commercial Pesticide Operator
Illinois Dept. of Agriculture
Bureau of Environmental Programs
PO Box 19281
State Fairgrounds
Springfield, IL 62794-9281
Phone: (217)785-2427

Credential Type: Commercial Pesticide Operator License. **Duration of License:** One year. **Authorization:** Authorizes applicant to use pesticides at the job site under the supervision of a licensed Commercial Pesticide Applicator. **Requirements:** At least 16 years of age. Illinois resident. Training preferred. Can only be licensed when employed to work with a licensed Pesticide Applicator. Must retake examination every three years. **Examination:** General Standard Pesticide Examination. **Reciprocity:** Yes, with a valid Pesticide license from a state immediately adjacent to Illinois. **Fees:** $20 initial license fee. $20 renewal fee. **Governing Statute:** Illinois Revised Statutes, Chapter 5.

4788

Commercial Pesticide Operator For Private Company (Not For Hire)
Illinois Dept. of Agriculture
Bureau of Environmental Programs
PO Box 19281
State Fairgrounds
Springfield, IL 62794-9281
Phone: (217)785-2427

Credential Type: Commercial Pesticide Operator (Not For Hire) License. **Duration of License:** One year. **Authorization:** Authorizes applicant, employed by a private company, to use pesticides in the maintenance of company owned property, under the supervision of a licensed Pesticide Applicator. **Requirements:** At least 16 years of age. Illinois resident. Can only be licensed when employed to work with a licensed Pesticide Applicator. Must retake examination every three years. **Examination:** General Standard Pesticide Examination. **Reciprocity:** Yes, with a valid Pesticide license from a state immediately adjacent to Illinois. **Fees:** No fee. **Governing Statute:** Illinois Revised Statutes, Chapter 5.

4789

Pesticide Dealer
Illinois Dept. of Agriculture
Bureau of Environmental Programs
PO Box 19281
State Fairgrounds
Springfield, IL 62794-9281
Phone: (217)785-2427

Credential Type: Pesticide Dealer License. **Duration of License:** One year. **Authorization:** Authorizes applicant to sell Restricted Use Pesticides. **Requirements:** At least 16 years of age. Illinois resident. Must retake examination every three years. **Examination:** Pesticide Dealer Examination. **Reciprocity:** Yes, with a valid Pesticide license from a state immediately adjacent to Illinois. **Fees:** $200 initial license fee. $200 renewal fee. **Governing Statute:** Illinois Revised Statutes, Chapter 5.

4790

Private Pesticide Applicator
Illinois Dept. of Agriculture
Bureau of Environmental Programs
PO Box 19281
State Fairgrounds
Springfield, IL 62794-9281
Phone: (217)785-2427

Credential Type: Private Pesticide Applicator License. **Duration of License:** Three years. **Authorization:** Authorizes applicant to use pesticides to produce an agricultural commodity on his/her own property. **Requirements:** At least 16 years of age. Illinois resident. Training preferred. Must retake examination every three years. **Examination:** Private Pesticide Applicators Examination. Private Grain Fumigation Category Examination (if applicant intends to fumigate his/her grain bin). **Reciprocity:** Yes, with a valid Pesticide license from a state immediately adjacent to Illinois. **Fees:** $10 initial license fee. $10 renewal fee. **Governing Statute:** Illinois Revised Statutes, Chapter 5.

4791

Public Pesticide Applicator
Illinois Dept. of Agriculture
Bureau of Environmental Programs
PO Box 19281
State Fairgrounds
Springfield, IL 62794-9281
Phone: (217)785-2427

Credential Type: Public Pesticide Applicator License. **Duration of License:** One year. **Authorization:** Authorizes applicant to purchase, store, handle, and use pesticides for the governmental organization for which he/she is employed. **Requirements:** At least 16 years of age. Illinois resident. Training preferred. Must retake examination every three years. **Examination:** General Standard Pesticide Examination. Category (Specialty) Examination. **Reciprocity:** Yes, with a valid Pesticide license from a state immediately adjacent to Illinois. **Fees:** No fee. **Governing Statute:** Illinois Revised Statutes, Chapter 5.

4792

Public Pesticide Operator

Illinois Dept. of Agriculture
Bureau of Environmental Programs
PO Box 19281
State Fairgrounds
Springfield, IL 62794-9281
Phone: (217)785-2427

Credential Type: Public Pesticide Operator License. **Duration of License:** One year. **Authorization:** Authorizes applicant, who works for a governmental organization, to use pesticides on that organization's property under the supervision of a licensed Pesticide Applicator. **Requirements:** At least 16 years of age. Illinois resident. Can only be licensed when employed to work with a licensed Pesticide Applicator. Must retake examination every three years. **Examination:** General Standard Pesticide Examination. **Reciprocity:** Yes, with a valid Pesticide license from a state immediately adjacent to Illinois. **Fees:** No fee. **Governing Statute:** Illinois Revised Statutes, Chapter 5.

4793

Structural Pest Control Technician (General Use)

Illinois Dept. of Public Health
525 W. Jefferson
Springfield, IL 62761
Phone: (217)782-4674

Credential Type: General Use Pest Control Technician Certificate. **Duration of License:** Three years. **Requirements:** High school graduate or GED certificate. Application must be filed 30 days prior to examination date. Must attend at least one recertification seminar before renewing certificate. **Examination:** General Standards Examination. **Reciprocity:** No. **Fees:** $40 examination fee. $40 reexamination fee. **Governing Statute:** Structural Pest Control Act, Chapter 111 1/2.

4794

Structural Pest Control Technician (Restricted Use)

Illinois Dept. of Public Health
525 W. Jefferson
Springfield, IL 62761
Phone: (217)782-4674

Credential Type: Restricted Use Pest Control Technician Certificate. **Duration of License:** Three years. **Requirements:** High school graduate or GED certificate. Meet one of the following requirements: (1) Have six months experience in structural pest control; (2) Have 16 semester hours credit in entomology or related fields; (3) Complete a structural pest control course approved by the Department of Public Health. Application must be filed 30 days prior to examination date. Must attend at least one recertification seminar before renewing certificate. **Examination:** General Standards Examination. Sub-category (Restricted Use Pesticides) Examination. **Reciprocity:** No. **Fees:** $40 examination fee. $40 reexamination fee. **Governing Statute:** Structural Pest Control Act, Chapter 111 1/2.

Indiana

4795

Commercial Pesticide Applicator

Office of the Indiana State Chemist
 and Seed Commissioner
Dept. of Biochemistry
Purdue Univ.
W. Lafayette, IN 47907
Phone: (317)494-1594

Credential Type: Certification. **Duration of License:** Four years. **Authorization:** There are 11 categories of certification. **Requirements:** Demonstrate competency by passing appropriate examinations. **Examination:** Core (General Standard) and appropriate category-specific examinations. **Governing Statute:** IC 15-3-3.6. IAC Title 355 and 357.

Credential Type: License (For Hire). **Duration of License:** One year. **Authorization:** License required of certified individuals in the employ of a licensed pesticide operator (business) who has assumed direct responsibility for the use or supervision of the use of pesticides by the firm. **Requirements:** Must first obtain certification by passing appropriate examinations. Additional requirements for the structural pest control category are the following: (1) Complete one year of active experience as a registered technician in Indiana or another state having a comparable technician program. (2) Complete an advanced training program.

Meet one of the following sets of requirements for the turf pest control category: (1) Complete 90 days of active employment as a registered technician for a single licensed business in this category. (2) Complete two years of active employment within the past four years as a licensed (not for hire) or public applicator in this category. (3) Complete a formal two-year turf program or related program following high school. (4) Complete two years of active employment within the past four years as a licensed applicator for hire in agricultural plant pest control, ornamental pest control, or right-of-way pest control. **Fees:** $30 license fee. $30 renewal fee. **Governing Statute:** IC 15-3-3.6. IAC Title 355 and 357.

Credential Type: License (Not For Hire). **Duration of License:** One year. **Authorization:** License required of certified individuals whose duties as an employee of a non-public employer include the use or supervision of the use of restricted-use pesticides only on the premises of, and only on the property of, the employer. **Requirements:** Must first obtain certification by passing appropriate examinations.

Meet one of the following sets of requirements for the turf pest control category: (1) Complete 90 days of active employment as a registered technician for a single licensed business or public agency in this category. (2) Complete two years of active employment within the past four years as an applicator of pesticides to turf. (3) Complete a formal two-year turf program or related program following high school. (4) Complete two years of active employment within the past four years as an applicator of pesticides in agricultural plant pest control, ornamental pest control, or right-of-way pest control. **Fees:** $30 license fee. $30 renewal fee. **Governing Statute:** IC 15-3-3.6. IAC Title 355 and 357.

4796

Pesticide Consultant

Office of the Indiana State Chemist
 and Seed Commissioner
Dept. of Biochemistry
Purdue Univ.
W. Lafayette, IN 47907
Phone: (317)494-1594

Credential Type: Registration. **Duration of License:** One year. **Requirements:** Must submit proof to the state chemist that applicant is qualified to make recommendations and offer advice concerning the use of pesticides. **Exemptions:** No fee required of governmental employees. **Fees:** $30 annual

Indiana 4797

Pesticide Consultant, continued

registration fee. **Governing Statute:** IC 15-3-3.6. IAC Title 355 and 357.

4797

Pesticide Technician
Office of the Indiana State Chemist and Seed Commissioner
Dept. of Biochemistry
Purdue Univ.
W. Lafayette, IN 47907
Phone: (317)494-1594

Credential Type: Registration. **Duration of License:** One year. **Authorization:** Registration of technicians is required in the categories of structural pest control and turf pest control. **Requirements:** Supervising licensed applicator must submit application. For the structural pest control category, applicant must complete a 20-day training program. Upon completion of the training program, the applicant must complete a workbook provided by the state chemist.

For the turf pest control category, applicant must complete a 14-day training program. Upon completion of the training program, the applicant must pass an exam designated by the state chemist. **Examination:** Examination required for turf pest control category. **Fees:** $25 registration fee (structural pest control). $30 registration fee (turf pest control). **Governing Statute:** IC 15-3-3.6. IAC Title 355 and 357.

4798

Private Pesticide Applicator
Office of the Indiana State Chemist and Seed Commissioner
Dept. of Biochemistry
Purdue Univ.
W. Lafayette, IN 47907
Phone: (317)494-1594

Credential Type: Certification. **Duration of License:** Four years. **Authorization:** Certification is required to obtain a permit to use a restricted-use pesticide. There are two categories of certification for private applicators, Production Agriculture and Fumigation. **Requirements:** Certification is obtained by participating in an approved procedure, including the following: (1) Training by the Indiana Cooperative Extension Service. (2) Home-study programmed instruction. (3) Closed book examination, either the Private Applicator Examination or the Commercial Core Examination. **Examination:** Private Applicator Examination or the Commercial Core Examination. **Fees:** $10 certification fee. **Governing Statute:** IC 15-3-3.6. IAC Title 355 and 357.

4799

Public Pesticide Applicator
Office of the Indiana State Chemist and Seed Commissioner
Dept. of Biochemistry
Purdue Univ.
W. Lafayette, IN 47907
Phone: (317)494-1594

Credential Type: Certification. **Duration of License:** Four years. **Authorization:** There are 11 categories of certification. **Requirements:** Demonstrate competency by passing appropriate examinations. **Examination:** Core (General Standard) and appropriate category-specific examinations. **Governing Statute:** IC 15-3-3.6. IAC Title 355 and 357.

Credential Type: License. **Duration of License:** One year. **Authorization:** License required of a certified individual whose duties as an employee of government include the use or supervision of the use of restricted use pesticides. **Requirements:** Must first obtain certification by passing appropriate examinations.

Meet one of the following sets of requirements for the turf pest control category: (1) Complete 90 days of active employment as a registered technician for a single licensed business or public agency in this category. (2) Complete two years of active employment within the past four years as an applicator of pesticides to turf. (3) Complete a formal two-year turf program or related program following high school. (4) Complete two years of active employment within the past four years as an applicator of pesticides in agricultural plant pest control, ornamental pest control, or right-of-way pest control. **Governing Statute:** IC 15-3-3.6. IAC Title 355 and 357.

Iowa

4800

Pesticide Applicator
Dept. of Agriculture and Land Stewardship
Pesticide Bureau
Wallace State Office Bldg.
Des Moines, IA 50319
Phone: (515)281-8591

Credential Type: Certificate. **Duration of License:** One year. **Requirements:** An applicant must study the "Iowa Core Manual" and at least 18 other manuals and pass exams administered by the Dept. of Agriculture. **Examination:** Yes. **Reciprocity:** Reciprocity with some states. **Fees:** $30 certification fee.

Kansas

4801

Commercial Pesticide Applicator
State Board of Agriculture
Div. of Plant Health
901 S. Kansas Ave.
Topeka, KS 66612
Phone: (913)296-2263

Credential Type: Commercial Applicator Certification. **Duration of License:** Three years. **Authorization:** There are 10 categories of certification. The owner or one or more applicator employees of every licensed pesticide business must have commercial certification in each category in which the business is licensed. **Requirements:** Be at least 18 years of age. Demonstrate competency by passing appropriate examinations. Recertification requires retesting or attending recertification training. **Examination:** General examination and appropriate category examinations. **Fees:** $35 application fee per category. $25 exam fee per category. No fee for general exam.

4802

Pesticide Dealer
State Board of Agriculture
Div. of Plant Health
901 S. Kansas Ave.
Topeka, KS 66612
Phone: (913)296-2263

Credential Type: Pesticide Dealer Registration. **Duration of License:** One year. **Authorization:** Each location that sells general or restricted use pesticides must register as a pesticide dealer. **Requirements:** Submit application and pay fee. **Fees:** $15 annual registration fee.

4803

Private Pesticide Applicator
State Board of Agriculture
Div. of Plant Health
901 S. Kansas Ave.
Topeka, KS 66612
Phone: (913)296-2263

Credential Type: Private Applicator Certification. **Duration of License:** Five years. **Authorization:** Authorizes individual to apply or supervise the application of restricted use pesticides for (1) the purpose of producing any agricultural commodity on property owned or rented by the individual

Pest Controllers and Assistants

or his/her employer, or on the property of another for no compensation other than the trading of personal services; and (2) for the purpose of controlling ornamental shrubbery or turf pests on property owned or rented by the individual and that is used as the individual's residence. **Requirements:** Pass examination and pay fee. Recertification requires retesting. **Examination:** Private applicator examination. **Fees:** $10 certification fee.

Kentucky

4804

Pesticide Applicator
Dept. of Agriculture
Div. of Pesticides
700 Capital Plaza Tower
Frankfort, KY 40601
Phone: (502)564-7274

Credential Type: License. **Duration of License:** One year. **Requirements:** 18 years of age. Continuing education required. **Examination:** Yes. **Fees:** $25 license fee.

4805

Pesticide Dealer
Dept. of Agriculture
Div. of Pesticides
700 Capital Plaza Tower
Frankfort, KY 40601
Phone: (502)564-7274

Credential Type: License. **Duration of License:** One year. **Requirements:** 18 years of age. Continuing education required. **Examination:** Yes. **Fees:** $25 certification fee. $5 license fee.

4806

Pesticide Exterminator
Dept. of Agriculture
Div. of Pesticides
700 Capital Plaza Tower
Frankfort, KY 40601
Phone: (502)564-7274

Credential Type: License. **Requirements:** Must have two years experience with a pest control company, or a degree in entomology. 18 years of age. Must be familiar with the laws and regulations set forth by the Kentucky Dept. of Agriculture. Must be able to identify specimens. **Examination:** Yes. **Fees:** $50 exam fee.

Louisiana

4807

Agricultural Consultant
Dept. of Agriculture
Agricultural and Environmental Programs
PO Box 44153, Capitol Sta.
Baton Rouge, LA 70804
Phone: (504)342-7011

Credential Type: Certification. **Duration of License:** One year followed by three-year renewal periods. **Requirements:** Have at least a bachelor's degree from an accredited university. Have worked for a minimum of four crop seasons. **Examination:** Certification examination. **Fees:** $5 certification fee. $5 exam fee. **Governing Statute:** R.S. 3:3246.

Credential Type: License. **Duration of License:** One year. **Authorization:** All agricultural consultants operating as a business and charging a fee must be licensed. **Requirements:** Must be or must employ a certified agricultural consultant. All field checkers must be registered with the Department. **Fees:** $25 license fee. $25 annual renewal fee. $5 per field scout.]GOV R.S. 3:3246.

4808

Commercial Pesticide Applicator
Dept. of Agriculture
Agricultural and Environmental Programs
PO Box 44153, Capitol Sta.
Baton Rouge, LA 70804
Phone: (504)342-7011
Phone: (504)925-3763

Credential Type: Commercial Applicator Cerification. **Duration of License:** One year, followed by three-year renewal periods. **Requirements:** Be at least 18 years of age. **Examination:** Certification examination. **Fees:** $5 exam fee (in Baton Rouge). $15 exam fee (at a district office). $5 certification fee. **Governing Statute:** R.S. 3:3242.

Credential Type: Non-fee Commercial Applicator Certification. **Duration of License:** One year, followed by three-year renewal periods. **Requirements:** Be at least 18 years of age. Submit application and pass exam. Have at least two years of experience. **Examination:** Certification examination. **Fees:** $5 exam fee (in Baton Rouge). $15 exam fee (at a district office). $5 certification fee. **Governing Statute:** R.S. 3:3242.

4809

Pest Control Operator
Louisiana Dept. of Agriculture and Forestry
Structural Pest Control Commission
PO Box 3596
Baton Rouge, LA 70821
Phone: (504)925-3764

Credential Type: License. **Duration of License:** Indefinite. **Requirements:** Four years of experience; or a degree in entomology; or a bachelor's degree from an accredited university with at least 12 semester hours of coursework in entomology and at least one year of experience as a registered technician. **Examination:** Yes. **Fees:** $50 exam fee.

4810

Pesticide Dealer
Dept. of Agriculture—Pesticides
PO Box 44153, Capitol Sta.
Baton Rouge, LA 70804
Phone: (504)925-3796

Credential Type: Pesticide Dealer License. **Duration of License:** One year. **Authorization:** A dealer license is required for each location at which restricted-use pesticides are sold. **Requirements:** Each person employed by a pesticide dealer and who sells restricted-use pesticides must be a certified pesticide salesperson. Dealer must keep records on hand covering two years. **Fees:** $25 license fee. **Governing Statute:** R.S. 3:3245.

4811

Pesticide Salesperson
Dept. of Agriculture—Salesperson Certification
PO Box Box 44153, Capitol Sta.
Baton Rouge, LA 70804
Phone: (504)925-3796
Phone: (504)342-7011

Credential Type: Pesticide Salesperson Certification. **Duration of License:** Three years. **Requirements:** Submit application and pass exam. **Examination:** Certification examination. **Fees:** $5 exam fee. **Governing Statute:** R.S. 3:3244.

4812

Private Pesticide Applicator
Dept. of Agriculture
Agricultural and Environmental Programs
PO Box 44153, Capitol Sta.
Baton Rouge, LA 70804
Phone: (504)342-7011
Phone: (504)925-3763

Credential Type: Private Applicator Certification. **Duration of License:** Three years. **Requirements:** Submit application and pass exam. **Examination:** Certification examination. **Fees:** None.

Maine

4813

Commercial Pesticide Applicator
Dept. of Agriculture
Food and Rural Resources
Board of Pesticides Control
State House Station 28
Augusta, ME 04333
Phone: (207)287-2731

Credential Type: Commercial Applicator/ Master Certification. **Duration of License:** Five years. **Authorization:** There are 11 categories of certification. Master certification is required for at least one person who is responsible for major pest control decisions, establishing policies, and employee training. **Requirements:** Demonstrate competency by passing appropriate examinations. Meet one of the following sets of requirements: (1) Complete two years or growing seasons working under the supervision of a licensed commercial applicator. (2) Be licensed for at least one year as a commercial applicator. (3) Complete 25 college credit hours of appropriate courses or 40 hours of equivalent training.

Recertification requires retesting or attending recertification training. **Examination:** General examination and appropriate category examinations. **Fees:** $10 exam fee per category.

Credential Type: Commercial Applicator/ Master License. **Duration of License:** One year. **Requirements:** License will be issued upon receiving certification. Must have appropriate insurance coverage. **Reciprocity:** Yes. **Fees:** $20 annual license fee.

Credential Type: Commercial Applicator/ Operator Certification. **Duration of License:** Five years. **Authorization:** There are 11 categories of certification. Operator certification is required for individuals who apply or direct the application of pesticides according to the instructions of the master applicator. **Requirements:** Demonstrate competency by passing appropriate examinations. Recertification requires retesting or attending recertification training. **Examination:** General examination and appropriate category examinations. **Fees:** $10 exam fee per category.

4814

Government Pesticide Supervisor
Dept. of Agriculture
Food and Rural Resources
Board of Pesticides Control
State House Station 28
Augusta, ME 04333
Phone: (207)287-2731

Credential Type: Government Pesticide Supervisor Certification. **Duration of License:** Five years. **Authorization:** There are 11 categories of certification. **Requirements:** Demonstrate competency by passing appropriate examinations.

Recertification requires retesting or attending recertification training. **Examination:** General examination and appropriate category examinations. **Fees:** No fees.

Credential Type: Government Pesticide Supervisor License. **Duration of License:** One year. **Requirements:** License will be issued upon receiving certification. **Reciprocity:** Yes. **Fees:** No fees.

4815

Pesticide Dealer
Dept. of Agriculture
Food and Rural Resources
Board of Pesticides Control
State House Station 28
Augusta, ME 04333
Phone: (207)287-2731

Credential Type: Pesticide Dealer Certification. **Duration of License:** Five years. **Requirements:** Demonstrate competency by passing appropriate examination.

Recertification requires retesting or attending recertification training. **Examination:** Dealer examination. **Fees:** $10 exam fee.

Credential Type: Pesticide Dealer License. **Duration of License:** One year. **Requirements:** License will be issued upon receiving certification and proper reports. **Reciprocity:** Yes. **Fees:** $20 license fee per location. $20 fee per salesperson operating outside location.

4816

Private Pesticide Applicator
Dept. of Agriculture
Food and Rural Resources
Board of Pesticides Control
State House Station 28
Augusta, ME 04333
Phone: (207)287-2731

Credential Type: Private Applicator Certification. **Duration of License:** Three years. **Authorization:** Applies to any person who uses or supervises the use of any restricted use pesticide for the purposes of producing any agricultural commodity on property owned by the individual or the individual's employer, or on the property of another for no compensation other than the trading of personal services. **Requirements:** Demonstrate competency by passing appropriate examinations. Recertification requires retesting or attending recertification training. **Examination:** General examination and appropriate commodity examination.

Credential Type: Private Applicator License. **Duration of License:** Three years. **Requirements:** License will be issued upon receiving certification. **Reciprocity:** Yes. **Fees:** $6 license fee.

Maryland

4817

Commercial Pesticide Applicator
Pesticide Regulation Section
Dept. of Agriculture
50 Harry S. Truman Pky.
Annapolis, MD 21401
Phone: (410)841-5710

Credential Type: Commercial Pesticide Certificate. **Duration of License:** One year. **Requirements:** Bachelor's degree in a biological field of study. Have at least one year of experience working for a licensed business. Renewal requires attendance at one recertification session. **Examination:** Industrial, Institutional, Structural, and Health Related Examination. **Reciprocity:** Yes. **Fees:** $50 certification fee. $100 business license fee.

4818

Pest Control Consultant
Pesticide Regulation Section
Dept. of Agriculture
50 Harry S. Truman Pky.
Annapolis, MD 21401
Phone: (410)841-5710

Credential Type: Pest Control Consultant License and Certificate. **Duration of License: One year. **Requirements:** Bachelor's degree in a biological field of study, or at least one year of experience under the supervision of a certified applicator or consultant in the appropriate category. Proof of insurance required for license. Certificate renewal requires attendance at one recertification session. **Examination:** Varies with category of operation. **Fees:** $50 certificate fee. $100 license fee.

4819

Pest Control Operator
Pesticide Regulation Section
Dept. of Agriculture
50 Harry S. Truman Pky.
Annapolis, MD 21401
Phone: (410)841-5710

Credential Type: Commercial Pesticide Business License. **Duration of License:** One year. **Authorization:** Required for any business applying general or restricted use pesticides. **Requirements:** Must have at least one certified employee in each category for which services are provided. Must maintain general liability insurance. Must designate a certified commercial applicator for each place of business. **Fees:** $100 license fee. $100 renewal fee.

4820

Public Agency Applicator
Pesticide Regulation Section
Dept. of Agriculture
50 Harry S. Truman Pky.
Annapolis, MD 21401
Phone: (410)841-5710

Credential Type: Public Agency Applicator License. **Duration of License:** One year. **Requirements:** Bachelor's degree in a biological field of study. Have at least one year of experience working for a licensed business. Renewal requires attendance at one recertification session. **Examination:** Industrial, Institutional, Structural, and Health Related Examination. **Fees:** No fees.

Massachusetts

4821

Commercial Pesticide Applicator
Dept. of Food and Agriculture
Pesticide Bureau
Licensing and Certification
100 Cambridge St., 21st Fl.
Boston, MA 02202
Phone: (617)727-3020

Credential Type: Commercial Applicator Certification. **Authorization:** There are 20 categories of commercial certification. **Requirements:** Demonstrate competency by passing appropriate exams. **Examination:** Core examination and appropriate category examinations. **Fees:** $25 exam fee (per exam).

4822

Pesticide Applicator
Dept. of Food and Agriculture
Pesticide Bureau
Licensing and Certification
100 Cambridge St., 21st Fl.
Boston, MA 02202
Phone: (617)727-3020

Credential Type: Applicator License. **Requirements:** Demonstrate competency by passing appropriate exam. **Examination:** Core examination. **Fees:** $25 exam fee.

4823

Pesticide Dealer
Dept. of Food and Agriculture
Pesticide Bureau
Licensing and Certification
100 Cambridge St., 21st Fl.
Boston, MA 02202
Phone: (617)727-3020

Credential Type: Dealer License. **Requirements:** Demonstrate competency by passing appropriate exams. **Examination:** Core examination. Dealer examination. **Fees:** $25 exam fee (per exam).

4824

Private Pesticide Applicator
Dept. of Food and Agriculture
Pesticide Bureau
Licensing and Certification
100 Cambridge St., 21st Fl.
Boston, MA 02202
Phone: (617)727-3020

Credential Type: Private Applicator Certification. **Authorization:** There are nine categories of private certification. **Requirements:** Demonstrate competency by passing appropriate exams. **Examination:** Core examination and appropriate category examinations. **Fees:** $25 exam fee (per exam).

Michigan

4825

Pesticide Applicator, Aerial
Pesticide and Plant Pest Management Div.
Dept. of Agriculture
Ottawa Bldg., N.
PO Box 30017
Lansing, MI 48909
Phone: (517)373-1104

Credential Type: Certification. **Duration of License:** Three years. **Requirements:** Be a certified commercial pesticide applicator or private pesticide applicator. At least three years of experience with no fewer than 200 hours of agricultural aerial application under the supervision of a commercial aerial pesticide applicator; or have completed an approved aerial applicator training program. Renewal requires participation in a self-regulating application flight efficiency clinic sponsored or recognized by the Michigan Cooperative Extension Service and approved by the Department; or retake the certification examinations and submit to an aircraft, equipment, and spray operations inspection by the Department. **Examination:** Written exam. **Reciprocity:** Michigan may grant reciprocity to persons holding certificates issued by other states or Federal agencies if these states or agencies have an approved certification plan and if their requirements equal or exceed the requirements of their state. Currently, these states include Indiana, Ohio, and Wisconsin. **Fees:** $50 initial exam and certificate fee. Renewal fee is same as initial fee. **Governing Statute:** Michigan Pesticide Control Act, Act 171 of 1976, as amended.

4826

Pesticide Applicator, Commercial
Pesticide and Plant Pest Management Div.
Dept. of Agriculture
Ottawa Bldg., N.
PO Box 30017
Lansing, MI 48909
Phone: (517)373-1104

Credential Type: Certification. **Duration of License:** Three years. **Authorization:** May be certified in one or more categories of pesticide application. **Requirements:** At

Michigan

Pesticide Applicator, Commercial, continued

least 18 years of age. Pass an exam in each category or subcategory of application applied for, plus a general "Core" exam. An additional exam is required for those who will use fumigant pesticides or will apply pesticides by aircraft. **Examination:** Written exam. **Reciprocity:** Michigan may grant reciprocity to persons holding certificates issued by other states or Federal agencies if these states or agencies have an approved certification plan and if their requirements equal or exceed the requirements of their state. Currently, these states include Indiana, Ohio, and Wisconsin. **Fees:** $50 initial exam and certificate fee. Renewal fee is same as initial fee. **Governing Statute:** Michigan Pesticide Control Act, Act 171 of 1976, as amended.

4827

Pesticide Applicator, Private

Pesticide and Plant Pest Management Div.
Dept. of Agriculture
Ottawa Bldg., N.
PO Box 30017
Lansing, MI 48909
Phone: (517)373-1104

Credential Type: Certification. **Duration of License:** Three years. **Authorization:** Persons who apply restricted use pesticides for an agricultural purpose on their own property, on an employer's property, or on the property of another person without receiving compensation must be certified as a private pesticide applicator by the Department of Agriculture. **Requirements:** Pass an examination administered by the Department with a score of at least 70 percent. **Examination:** Written exam. **Reciprocity:** Michigan may grant reciprocity to persons holding certificates issued by other states or Federal agencies if these states or agencies have an approved certification plan and if their requirements equal or exceed the requirements of their state. Currently, these states include Indiana, Ohio, and Wisconsin. **Fees:** $10 initial exam and certificate fee. Renewal fee is same as initial fee. **Governing Statute:** Michigan Pesticide Control Act, Act 171 of 1976, as amended.

4828

Pesticide Applicator, Registered

Pesticide and Plant Pest Management Div.
Dept. of Agriculture
Ottawa Bldg., N.
PO Box 30017
Lansing, MI 48909
Phone: (517)373-1104

Credential Type: Registration. **Duration of License:** Three years. **Authorization:** Persons who apply pesticides as a scheduled and required work assignment in the course of their employment on the property of another person must be designated as a registered pesticide applicator by the Department of Agriculture. **Requirements:** Completed an approved training program. Have either a valid temporary registration certificate or a valid registration card from the Department. Renewal requires completion of a refresher training program during the current registration period. **Examination:** Written exam. **Reciprocity:** Michigan may grant reciprocity to persons holding certificates issued by other states or Federal agencies if these states or agencies have an approved certification plan and if their requirements equal or exceed the requirements of their state. Currently, these states include Indiana, Ohio, and Wisconsin. **Fees:** $10 initial exam and certificate fee. Renewal fee is same as initial fee. **Governing Statute:** Michigan Pesticide Control Act, Act 171 of 1976, as amended.

4829

Pesticide Dealer, Restricted Use

Pesticide and Plant Pest Management Div.
Dept. of Agriculture
Ottawa Bldg., N.
PO Box 30017
Lansing, MI 48909
Phone: (517)373-1104

Credential Type: License. **Duration of License:** One year. **Requirements:** Be in charge of the business location. Abide by the rules put into effect by the Department of Agriculture. **Examination:** Written exam. **Fees:** $50 initial exam and license fee. $50 renewal fee. **Governing Statute:** Michigan Pesticide Control Act, Act 171 of 1976, as amended.

Minnesota

4830

Commercial Pesticide Applicator

Dept. of Agriculture
Agronomy Services Div.
Pesticide Registration Unit
90 W. Plato Blvd.
St. Paul, MN 55155
Phone: (612)297-2530

Credential Type: Commercial Pesticide Applicator License. **Duration of License:** One year. **Authorization:** A person may not apply a pesticide for hire without a commercial applicator license for the appropriate use categories. **Requirements:** Submit application. Pass examination. Pay fee. Provide evidence of financial responsibility.

Aerial applicators must meet additional requirements. An aquatic category endorsement is required to apply pesticides on or into surface waters. **Examination:** Written examination. **Exemptions:** A licensed structural pest control applicator need not also have a commercial applicator license. **Fees:** $50 application fee. **Governing Statute:** Minnesota Statutes, Chap. 18B.

4831

Non-Commercial Pesticide Applicator

Dept. of Agriculture
Agronomy Services Div.
Pesticide Registration Unit
90 W. Plato Blvd.
St. Paul, MN 55155
Phone: (612)297-2530

Credential Type: Non-Commercial Pesticide Applicator License. **Duration of License:** One year. **Authorization:** A person may not use a restricted use pesticide without a license for the appropriate use categories. **Requirements:** Submit application. Pass examination. Pay fee.

An aquatic category endorsement is required to apply pesticides on or into surface waters. **Examination:** Written examination. **Exemptions:** A licensed structural pest control applicator, licensed commercial applicator, or certified private applicator need not also have a non-commercial applicator license. **Fees:** $50 application fee. $10 application fee (government employees only). **Governing Statute:** Minnesota Statutes, Chap. 18B.

Credential Type: Private Applicator Certification. **Duration of License:** Three years. **Authorization:** Required for use of a restricted use pesticide in the production of an agricultural commodity as a traditional exchange of services without financial compenstion, or on a site owned, rented, or managed by the individual or the individual's employees. **Requirements:** Meet established certification requirements, including a prescribed training program. Pass examination. **Examination:** Written examination. **Exemptions:** A licensed commercial or noncommercial applicator need not obtain private applicator certification. **Fees:** $10 application fee. **Governing Statute:** Minnesota Statutes, Chap. 18B.

4832

Pesticide Dealer
Dept. of Agriculture
Agronomy Services Div.
Pesticide Registration Unit
90 W. Plato Blvd.
St. Paul, MN 55155
Phone: (612)297-2530

Credential Type: Pesticide Dealer License. **Duration of License:** One year. **Requirements:** Submit application. Pass examination. Pay fee. **Examination:** Written examination. **Fees:** $50 license fee. $50 renewal fee. **Governing Statute:** Minnesota Statutes, Chap. 18B.

4833

Structural Pest Control Applicator
Dept. of Agriculture
Agronomy Services Div.
Pesticide Registration Unit
90 W. Plato Blvd.
St. Paul, MN 55155
Phone: (612)297-2530

Credential Type: Master Structural Pest Control License. **Duration of License:** One year. **Requirements:** Have at least two years experience as a licensed journeyman in this state or a state with equivalent requirements. Provide evidence of financial responsibility (not required if an employee of a licensed individual). **Examination:** Written examination. **Fees:** $100 business license fee. $50 employee license fee. **Governing Statute:** Minnesota Statutes, Chap. 18B.

Credential Type: Journeyman Structural Pest Control License. **Duration of License:** One year. **Requirements:** Demonstrate qualifications in the practical selection and application of pesticides. Be engaged as an employee of a person licensed as a master under a structural pest control license. **Examination:** Written examination. **Fees:** $100 business license fee. $50 employee license fee. **Governing Statute:** Minnesota Statutes, Chap. 18B.

Credential Type: Structural Pest Control License—Fumigator. **Duration of License:** One year. **Requirements:** Must be licensed as a master or journeyman. Demonstrate knowledge the practical selection and application of pesticides. Provide evidence of financial responsibility (not required if an employee of a licensed individual). **Examination:** Written examination. **Fees:** $100 business license fee. $50 employee license fee. **Governing Statute:** Minnesota Statutes, Chap. 18B.

Mississippi

4834

Pest Control Operator
Dept. of Agriculture and Commerce
Div. of Plant Industry
PO Box 5207
Mississippi State, MS 39762
Phone: (601)325-3390

Credential Type: Pest Control Operator License. **Duration of License:** Three years. **Authorization:** There are seven categories for which licenses are issued. Entomologists (pest control) and pathologists (plant disease) must obtain a license in order to advertise and receive a fee for performing professional services. **Requirements:** Meet one of the following sets of requirements: (1) Graduate from a college or university with at least 15 semester hours or the equivalent in the category for which a license is requested. (2) Have at least two years of college or university training, with special training in the category for which a license is requested. (3) Be a high school graduate or equivalent and have at least four years of experience with a licensed operator within the past six years.

Renewal requires attending an approved training course every three years. **Examination:** Appropriate category examinations. **Reciprocity:** Exam may be waived if applicant is licensed in a state with standards equal to those of Mississippi and that state will honor the Mississippi Examination.

Credential Type: Pest Control Permit. **Duration of License:** Three years. **Authorization:** Each branch office must have at least one licensee or permit holder for each category for which business is advertised and performed. **Requirements:** Must be an employee of a licensed operator. Renewal requires attending an approved training course every three years. **Examination:** Written examination. **Reciprocity:** Exam may be waived if applicant is licensed in a state with standards equal to those of Mississippi and that state will honor the Mississippi Examination.

4835

Pest Control Technician
Dept. of Agriculture and Commerce
Div. of Plant Industry
PO Box 5207
Mississippi State, MS 39762
Phone: (601)325-3390

Credential Type: Registration. **Duration of License:** Three years. **Authorization:** A registered technician identification card is required of all license holders, permit holders, owners, or employees of a pest control business. **Requirements:** Complete a training program of at least eight classroom hours for general pesticide use and eight classroom hours for each category for which registration is sought. Receive at least 40 hours of on-the-job training for each category for which registration is sought. **Fees:** $1 registration fee.

4836

Pesticide Dealer
Dept. of Agriculture and Commerce
Div. of Plant Industry
PO Box 5207
Mississippi State, MS 39762
Phone: (601)325-3390

Credential Type: Pesticide Dealer License. **Duration of License:** One year. **Authorization:** Each location or outlet must be licensed. **Requirements:** Demonstrate competence in the use and handling of pesticides by passing examination. **Examination:** Written examination. **Reciprocity:** Exam may be waived if applicant is licensed in a state with standards equal to those of Mississippi and that state will honor the Mississippi Examination.

4837

Pesticide Operator - Weed Control
Dept. of Agriculture and Commerce
Div. of Plant Industry
PO Box 5207
Mississippi State, MS 39762
Phone: (601)325-3390

Credential Type: Weed Control License. **Duration of License:** Three years. **Authorization:** There are five categories of weed control licenses. **Requirements:** Meet one of the following sets of requirements: (1) Graduate from a college or university with at least 15 semester hours or the equivalent in weed control. (2) Have at least two years of college or university training, with special training in weed control. (3) Be a high school graduate or equivalent and have at least one year of experience with a licensed operator within the past two years. (4) If

Pesticide Operator - Weed Control, continued

applicant is not a high school graduate, must have completed at least two years of experience with a licensed operator within the past three years.

Renewal requires attending an approved training course every three years. **Examination:** Written examination in appropriate categories. **Reciprocity:** Exam may be waived if applicant is licensed in a state with standards equal to those of Mississippi and that state will honor the Mississippi Examination.

Credential Type: Weed Control Permit. **Duration of License:** Three years. **Authorization:** Each branch office must have at least one licensee or permit holder for each category for which business is advertised and performed. **Requirements:** Must be an employee of a licensed operator. Renewal requires attending an approved training course every three years. **Examination:** Written examination. **Reciprocity:** Exam may be waived if applicant is licensed in a state with standards equal to those of Mississippi and that state will honor the Mississippi Examination.

Missouri

4838

Commercial Pesticide Applicator
Dept. of Agriculture
Div. of Plant Industries
Bureau of Pesticide Control
PO Box 630
Jefferson City, MO 65102
Phone: (314)751-2462

Credential Type: Certified Commercial Applicator License. **Duration of License:** One year. **Authorization:** There are 11 categories of certification. License required of individuals who use, supervise the use of, or determine the need for the use of any pesticide on the lands of another as a service to the public in exchange for a fee or compensation. **Requirements:** Demonstrate competency by passing appropriate exams. For the structural pest control category, must also meet one of the following sets of requirements: (1) Associate's degree or higher in agriculture, biology, chemistry, or entomology from an accredited college or university. (2) Have at least one year of qualifying experience within the past three years as an applicator in the appropriate subcategory. (3) Have a combination of education and experience that includes completion of an approved correspondence course within the past three years and at least six months of qualifying experience within the past three years as an applicator in the appropriate subcategory. **Examination:** Certification examination. Licensing examination. **Fees:** $50 annual license fee. **Governing Statute:** Section 281, RSMo. Two CSR 70-25.

4839

Noncommercial Pesticide Applicator
Dept. of Agriculture
Div. of Plant Industries
Bureau of Pesticide Control
PO Box 630
Jefferson City, MO 65102
Phone: (314)751-2462

Credential Type: Certified Noncommercial Applicator License. **Duration of License:** One year. **Authorization:** There are 11 categories of certification. License required of individuals who use, supervise the use of, or determine the need for the use of any pesticide only on the lands owned or rented by them or their employers. **Requirements:** Demonstrate competency by passing appropriate exams. **Examination:** Certification examination. Licensing examination. **Fees:** $25 licene fee. **Governing Statute:** Section 281, RSMo. Two CSR 70-25.

4840

Pesticide Dealer
Dept. of Agriculture
Div. of Plant Industries
Bureau of Pesticide Control
PO Box 630
Jefferson City, MO 65102
Phone: (314)751-2462

Credential Type: Pesticide Dealer License. **Duration of License:** One year. **Authorization:** License is required for each location or outlet. **Requirements:** Demonstrate knowledge of the laws and regulations governing the use and sale of pesticides. **Fees:** $25 license fee. **Governing Statute:** Section 281, RSMo. Two CSR 70-25.

4841

Pesticide Technician
Dept. of Agriculture
Div. of Plant Industries
Bureau of Pesticide Control
PO Box 630
Jefferson City, MO 65102
Phone: (314)751-2462

Credential Type: Pesticide Technician License. **Authorization:** License required of individuals under the direct supervision of certified commercial applicators in the categories or subcategories of ornamental and turf pest control, general structural pest control, or termite pest control. **Requirements:** Complete an approved training program within the past year of at least 10 hours of classroom training and 30 hours of on-the-job practical training. **Governing Statute:** Section 281, RSMo. Two CSR 70-25.

4842

Private Pesticide Applicator
Dept. of Agriculture
Div. of Plant Industries
Bureau of Pesticide Control
PO Box 630
Jefferson City, MO 65102
Phone: (314)751-2462

Credential Type: Certified Private Applicator License. **Duration of License:** Five years. **Authorization:** License required of individuals who use or supervise the use of restricted use pesticides for the purpose of producing any agricultural commodity on property owned or rented by them or their employer, or on the property of another without compensation. **Requirements:** Complete an approved training program. **Governing Statute:** Section 281, RSMo. Two CSR 70-25.

4843

Public Pesticide Operator
Dept. of Agriculture
Div. of Plant Industries
Bureau of Pesticide Control
PO Box 630
Jefferson City, MO 65102
Phone: (314)751-2462

Credential Type: Certified Public Operator License. **Duration of License:** Three years. **Authorization:** There are 11 categories of certification. License required of individuals who use or supervise the use of restricted use pesticides as employees of federal, state, county, or local governmental agencies. License is valid only when functioning as an employee of the agency. **Requirements:** Demonstrate competency by passing appropriate exams. For the structural pest control category, must also meet one of the following sets of requirements: (1) Associate's degree or higher in agriculture, biology, chemistry, or entomology from an accredited college or university. (2) Have at least one year of qualifying experience within the past three years as an applicator in the appropriate subcategory. (3) Have a combination of education and experience that includes completion of an approved correspondence course within the past three years and at least six months of qualifying experience within the past three years as an applicator in the appropriate subcategory. **Examination:** Certification examination. Licensing examination. **Governing Statute:** Section 281, RSMo. Two CSR 70-25.

Montana

4844

Commercial Pesticide Applicator
Dept. of Agriculture
Agricultural and Biological Sciences Div.
PO Box 200201
Helena, MT 59620-0201
Phone: (406)444-2944

Credential Type: Commercial Applicator License. **Duration of License:** One year. **Requirements:** Submit application and pay fee. Meet liability requirements. Pass examination. **Examination:** Written examination. **Fees:** $45 annual license fee.

4845

Governmental Pesticide Applicator
Dept. of Agriculture
Agricultural and Biological Sciences Div.
PO Box 200201
Helena, MT 59620-0201
Phone: (406)444-2944

Credential Type: Governmental Applicator License. **Duration of License:** One year. **Requirements:** Submit application and pay fee. Pass examination. **Examination:** Written examination. **Fees:** $50 annual license fee.

4846

Noncommercial Pesticide Applicator
Dept. of Agriculture
Agricultural and Biological Sciences Div.
PO Box 200201
Helena, MT 59620-0201
Phone: (406)444-2944

Credential Type: Noncommercial Applicator License. **Duration of License:** One year. **Requirements:** Submit application and pay fee. Pass examination. **Examination:** Written examination. **Fees:** $45 annual license fee.

4847

Pesticide Dealer
Dept. of Agriculture
Agricultural and Biological Sciences Div.
PO Box 200201
Helena, MT 59620-0201
Phone: (406)444-2944

Credential Type: Pesticide Dealer License. **Duration of License:** One year. **Requirements:** Submit application and pay fee. Pass examination. **Examination:** Written examination. **Fees:** $45 annual license fee.

Nebraska

4848

Exterminator
Environmental Protection Agency
100 Centennial Mall N.
Lincoln, NE 68508
Phone: (402)437-5080

Credential Type: Certificate. **Duration of License:** Three years. **Examination:** Yes.

Nevada

4849

Commercial Pesticide Applicator
Dept. of Agriculture
PO Box 11100
Reno, NV 89510-1100
Phone: (702)688-1180
Fax: (702)688-1178

Credential Type: Pest Control Operating License. **Duration of License:** One year. **Authorization:** License required of any individual or organization who conducts pest control for hire, or who advertises or solicits such services. **Requirements:** Meet one of the following sets of requirements: (1) Complete two years of pesticide application experience. (2) Complete six months of practical experience in pesticide application, or related pest control, and at least 16 college credit hours in biological sciences, of which at least eight hours are directly related to the field of pest control.

In addition, must have appropriate insurance. **Examination:** General examination and appropriate category examinations. **Fees:** $50 business license fee. $10 operator license fee (per operator). **Governing Statute:** Nevada Revised Statutes, Chap. 555. Nevada Administrative Code, Chap. 555.

New Hampshire

4850

Pesticide Applicator
New Hampshire Dept. of Agriculture
Division of Pesticide Control
10 Ferry St., Caller Box 2042
Concord, NH 03302-2042
Phone: (603)271-3550

Credential Type: Pesticide Applicator License—Supervisory Level Commercial For-Hire. **Duration of License:** One year. **Requirements:** Commercial business, employing or owned by applicant, must be registered. Applicant must meet Board requirements of five years of education and practical experience. Have mandatory levels of liability insurance coverage as defined in Statutes. **Examination:** Written and oral examination in both general aspects and category of endeavor. **Reciprocity:** No. **Fees:** $5.00 examination (commercial and dealer) fee per category. $20 commercial applicator license. $20 dealer license. $33 annual fee per pesticide registered.

Credential Type: Pesticide Applicator License—Supervisory Level Commercial Not-For-Hire or Operational Level Commercial Not-For-Hire or Operational Level Commercial For-Hire. **Duration of License:** One year. **Requirements:** Commercial business, employing or owned by applicant, must be registered. Applicant must meet Board requirements of five years of education and practical experience. Have mandatory levels of liability insurance coverage as defined in Statutes. **Examination:** Written examination in both general aspects and category of endeavor. **Reciprocity:** No. **Fees:** $5.00 examination (commercial and dealer) fee per category. $20 commercial applicator license. $20 dealer license. $33 annual fee per pesticide registered.

Credential Type: Pesticide Applicator Restricted Use Private Permit. **Requirements:** Submit application. Pass examination. **Examination:** Written examination in both general aspects and commodity of endeavor. **Fees:** No fee for private permits. $33 annual fee per pesticide registered.

New Jersey

4851

Pesticide Applicator - Commercial
New Jersey Dept. of Environmental Protection
Pesticide Control Program
CN411
Trenton, NJ 08625-0411
Phone: (609)530-4070

Credential Type: License. **Requirements:** 18 years of age. **Examination:** Yes. **Reciprocity:** Yes. **Fees:** $30 registration fee. **Governing Statute:** NJSA 13:1F. NJAC 7:30-6.

4852

Pesticide Applicator - Private
New Jersey Dept. of Environmental Protection
Pesticide Control Program
CN411
Trenton, NJ 08625-0411
Phone: (609)530-4070

Credential Type: License. **Requirements:** 18 years of age. **Examination:** Yes. **Reciprocity:** Yes. **Governing Statute:** NJSA 13:1F. NJAC 7:30-8.

4853

Pesticide Dealer
New Jersey Dept. of Environmental Protection
Pesticide Control Program
CN411
Trenton, NJ 08625-0411
Phone: (609)530-4070

Credential Type: License. **Requirements:** 18 years of age. **Examination:** Yes. **Reciprocity:** Yes. **Fees:** $30 registration fee. **Governing Statute:** NJSA 13:1F. NJAC 7:30-3.

4854

Pesticide Operator
New Jersey Dept. of Environmental Protection
Pesticide Control Program
CN411
Trenton, NJ 08625-0411
Phone: (609)530-4070

Credential Type: Commercial Pesticide Operator. **Requirements:** 18 years of age. Must obtain training from a registered pesticide applicator. **Fees:** $5 registration fee. **Governing Statute:** NJSA 13-1F. NJAC 7:30-5.

Credential Type: Private Pesticide Operator. **Requirements:** 16 years of age. Must obtain training from a registered pesticide applicator. **Governing Statute:** NJSA 13-1F. NJAC 7:30-5.

New Mexico

4855

Commercial Pesticide Applicator
Dept. of Agriculture
Div. of Agricultural and Environmental Services
Box 30005, Dept. 3AQ
Las Cruces, NM 88003-0005
Phone: (505)646-2133

Credential Type: Commercial Applicator License. **Duration of License:** One year. **Authorization:** There are 17 license classifications with corresponding certification examinations. Each license category has a clearly defined scope of permitted operations. **Requirements:** Meet one of the following sets of requirements: (1) Complete two years of pesticide application experience in the category for which certification is sought. (2) Complete one year of pesticide application experience in the category for which certification is sought and not less than 20 college credit hours in biological or agricultural sciences.

In addition, equipment must pass inspection. **Examination:** Qualifying examination in appropriate category. **Fees:** $50 annual license fee. **Governing Statute:** New Mexico Statutes Annotated, Chap. 76, Article 4, Section one et seq.

4856

Noncommercial Pesticide Applicator
Dept. of Agriculture
Div. of Agricultural and Environmental Services
Box 30005, Dept. 3AQ
Las Cruces, NM 88003-0005
Phone: (505)646-2133

Credential Type: Noncommercial Applicator License. **Duration of License:** One year. **Authorization:** There are 17 license classifications with corresponding certification examinations. Each license category has a clearly defined scope of permitted operations. **Requirements:** Demonstrate competency by passing examination. **Examination:** Qualifying examination in appropriate category. **Fees:** $50 annual license fee. **Governing Statute:** New Mexico Statutes Annotated, Chap. 76, Article 4, Section one et seq.

4857

Pest Management Consultant
Dept. of Agriculture
Div. of Agricultural and Environmental Services
Box 30005, Dept. 3AQ
Las Cruces, NM 88003-0005
Phone: (505)646-2133

Credential Type: Pest Management Consultant License. **Duration of License:** One year. **Authorization:** There are 17 license classifications with corresponding certification examinations. Each license category has a clearly defined scope of permitted operations. **Requirements:** Demonstrate competency by passing examination. **Examination:** Qualifying examination in appropriate category. **Fees:** $50 annual license fee. **Governing Statute:** New Mexico Statutes Annotated, Chap. 76, Article 4, Section one et seq.

4858

Pesticide Dealer
Dept. of Agriculture
Div. of Agricultural and Environmental Services
Box 30005, Dept. 3AQ
Las Cruces, NM 88003-0005
Phone: (505)646-2133

Credential Type: Pesticide Dealer License. **Duration of License:** One year. **Authorization:** A separate license is required for each business location or outlet. **Requirements:** Submit application and pay fee. **Fees:** $35 annual license fee. **Governing Statute:** New Mexico Statutes Annotated, Chap. 76, Article 4, Section one et seq.

4859

Pesticide Operator
Dept. of Agriculture
Div. of Agricultural and Environmental Services
Box 30005, Dept. 3AQ
Las Cruces, NM 88003-0005
Phone: (505)646-2133

Credential Type: Operator License. **Duration of License:** One year. **Authorization:** An operator license is required to be an employee of a commercial pesticide applicator and to apply pesticides. **Requirements:** Demonstrate competency by passing examination. **Examination:** Qualifying examination in appropriate category. **Fees:** $25 annual license fee. **Governing Statute:**

New Mexico Statutes Annotated, Chap. 76, Article 4, Section one et seq.

4860

Private Pesticide Applicator
Dept. of Agriculture
Div. of Agricultural and
 Environmental Services
Box 30005, Dept. 3AQ
Las Cruces, NM 88003-0005
Phone: (505)646-2133

Credential Type: Private Applicator Certification. **Duration of License:** Three years. **Requirements:** Demonstrate competency by passing examination. Must obtain a user permit prior to purchase and use of a restricted use pesticide. Each application involving a specific risk to the environment must first be approved. **Examination:** Qualifying examination in appropriate category. **Fees:** $5 certification fee. **Governing Statute:** New Mexico Statutes Annotated, Chap. 76, Article 4, Section one et seq.

4861

Public Pest Management Consultant
Dept. of Agriculture
Div. of Agricultural and
 Environmental Services
Box 30005, Dept. 3AQ
Las Cruces, NM 88003-0005
Phone: (505)646-2133

Credential Type: Public Pest Management Consultant License. **Duration of License:** One year. **Authorization:** There are 17 license classifications with corresponding certification examinations. Each license category has a clearly defined scope of permitted operations. A public pest management consultant is an individual employed by a governmental agency or municipality. This license is valid only when acting in that capacity. **Requirements:** Demonstrate competency by passing examination. **Examination:** Qualifying examination in appropriate category. **Fees:** No license fee. **Governing Statute:** New Mexico Statutes Annotated, Chap. 76, Article 4, Section one et seq.

New York

4862

Pesticide Applicator
Dept. of Environmental Conservation
Bureau of Pesticide Regulation
50 Wolf Rd., Rm. 404
Albany, NY 12233-7254
Phone: (518)457-7482

Credential Type: License. **Requirements:** Contact licensing body for application information.

4863

Pesticide Dealer
Dept. of Environmental Conservation
Bureau of Pesticide Regulation
50 Wolf Rd., Rm. 404
Albany, NY 12233-7254
Phone: (518)457-7482

Credential Type: License. **Requirements:** Contact licensing body for application information.

North Carolina

4864

Aerial Pesticide Applicator
Dept. of Agriculture
Pesticide Section
PO Box 27647
Raleigh, NC 27611
Phone: (919)733-3556

Credential Type: License. **Duration of License:** One year. **Requirements:** Applicants must meet the requirements of the Federal Aviation Administration to operate the equipment, 125 hours of flying experience and one year of flying experience as a pilot in the field of aerial pesticide application. 18 years of age. Four credit hours of continuing education is required every two years. **Examination:** Written. **Fees:** $25 license fee. $10 plane inspection fee. $35 renewal fee.

4865

Certified Structural Pest Control Applicator
Dept. of Agriculture
Structural Pest Control Div.
PO Box 27647
Raleigh, NC 27611
Phone: (919)733-6100

Credential Type: Certification. **Duration of License:** One year. **Requirements:** Must be familiar with the appropriate study materials. 18 years of age. **Examination:** Multiple choice. **Fees:** $10 exam fee. $30 certification fee. $30 renewal fee.

4866

Ground Pesticide Applicator
Dept. of Agriculture
Food & Drug Protection Div.
PO Box 27647
Raleigh, NC 27611
Phone: (919)733-3556

Credential Type: License. **Duration of License:** One year. **Requirements:** 18 years of age. Sufficient knowledge of the laws and regulations governing the use and application of pesticides. Some continuing education is required. **Examination:** Written. **Fees:** $25 license fee. $25 renewal fee.

4867

Licensed Structural Pest Control Operator
Dept. of Agriculture
Structural Pest Control Div.
PO Box 27647
Raleigh, NC 27611
Phone: (919)733-6100

Credential Type: License. **Duration of License:** One year. **Requirements:** Must be previously certified in the phase or phases in which the licensing is desired, plus two years of experience. Specialized or formal training may be substituted for practical experience. 18 years of age. Liability insurance. **Examination:** Yes. **Fees:** $25 exam fee per phase. $100 license fee for first phase, $50 for each additional phase.

4868

Pesticide Consultant
Dept. of Agriculture
Pesticide Section
PO Box 27647
Raleigh, NC 27611
Phone: (919)733-3556

Credential Type: License. **Duration of License:** One year. **Requirements:** 18 years of age. Knowledge of pesticides. Three to 10 hours of continuing education every five years. **Examination:** Written. **Fees:** $25 license fee. $25 renewal fee.

4869

Pesticide Dealer
Dept. of Agriculture
Pesticide Section
PO Box 27647
Raleigh, NC 27611
Phone: (919)733-3556

Credential Type: License. **Duration of License:** One year. **Requirements:** 18 years of age. Knowledge of pesticides. Five hours of continuing education every five years. **Examination:** Written. **Fees:** $25 license fee. $25 renewal fee.

North Dakota

4870

Commercial Pesticide Applicator
Dept. of Agriculture
Pesticide Div.
600 E. Blvd., 6th Fl.
Bismarck, ND 58505-0020
Phone: (701)224-4756

Credential Type: Commercial Applicator Certification. **Duration of License:** Three years. **Authorization:** There are 12 categories of certification. **Requirements:** Be at least 18 years of age. Demonstrate competency by passing appropriate examinations. Recertification requires retesting or attending recertification training. **Examination:** Core examination and appropriate category examinations. **Governing Statute:** North Dakota Century Code 4-35.

4871

Pesticide Dealer
Dept. of Agriculture
Pesticide Div.
600 E. Blvd., 6th Fl.
Bismarck, ND 58505-0020
Phone: (701)224-4756

Credential Type: Pesticide Dealer Certification. **Duration of License:** Three years. **Authorization:** There are 12 categories of certification. **Requirements:** Be at least 18 years of age. Demonstrate competency by passing appropriate examinations. Recertification requires retesting or attending recertification training. **Examination:** Core examination and appropriate category examinations. **Governing Statute:** North Dakota Century Code 4-35.

4872

Private Pesticide Applicator
Dept. of Agriculture
Pesticide Div.
600 E. Blvd., 6th Fl.
Bismarck, ND 58505-0020
Phone: (701)224-4756

Credential Type: Private Applicator Certification. **Duration of License:** Five years. **Requirements:** Be at least 18 years of age. Meet one of the following sets of requirements: (1) Attend an approved educational seminar and pass an exam. (2) Complete a course of self-instruction and pass an exam at the North Dakota's state university extension office. (3) Complete a take-home self-study program and pass an exam. (4) Pass the pesticide dealer or commercial applicator certification exam. **Examination:** Choice of examinations. **Governing Statute:** North Dakota Century Code 4-35.

Ohio

4873

Custom Applicator
Dept. of Agriculture
Div. of Plant Industry
Pesticide Regulation
8995 E. Main St.
Reynoldsburg, OH 43068-3399
Phone: (614)866-6361

Credential Type: Custom Applicator Certification. **Duration of License:** Three years. **Authorization:** Required of individuals or businesses that apply either general or restricted use pesticides to the property of another. There are 11 categories of certification. **Requirements:** Demonstrate competency by passing appropriate examinations. License must be renewed each year to maintain certification. Recertification requires retesting or attending recertification training. **Examination:** Core examination and appropriate category examinations. **Fees:** No fee in addition to license fee.

Credential Type: Custom Applicator License. **Duration of License:** One year. **Authorization:** Required of individuals or businesses that apply either general or restricted use pesticides to the property of another. **Requirements:** License will be issued upon receiving certification. Must carry proper amount of liability insurance. **Fees:** $100 annual license fee.

4874

Custom Operator
Dept. of Agriculture
Div. of Plant Industry
Pesticide Regulation
8995 E. Main St.
Reynoldsburg, OH 43068-3399
Phone: (614)866-6361

Credential Type: Custom Operator Certification. **Duration of License:** Three years. **Authorization:** Required of individuals employed or directly supervised by a Custom Applicator. Custom Operators may directly supervise activities in the field. There are 11 categories of certification. **Requirements:** Demonstrate competency by passing appropriate examinations. License must be renewed each year to maintain certification. Recertification requires retesting or attending recertification training. **Examination:** Core examination and appropriate category examinations. **Fees:** No fee in addition to license fee.

Credential Type: Custom Operator License. **Duration of License:** One year. **Authorization:** Required of individuals employed or directly supervised by a Custom Applicator. Custom Operators may directly supervise activities in the field. There are 11 categories of certification. **Requirements:** License will be issued upon receiving certification. **Fees:** $30 annual license fee.

4875

Limited Commercial Applicator
Dept. of Agriculture
Div. of Plant Industry
Pesticide Regulation
8995 E. Main St.
Reynoldsburg, OH 43068-3399
Phone: (614)866-6361

Credential Type: Limited Commercial Applicator Certification. **Duration of License:** Three years. **Authorization:** Required of individuals other than private applicators who limit their pesticide application activities to their own property or that of their employers. There are 11 categories of certification. **Requirements:** Demonstrate competency by passing appropriate examinations. License must be renewed each year to maintain certification. Recertification requires retesting or attending recertification training. **Examination:** Core examination and appropriate category examinations. **Fees:** No fee in addition to license fee.

Credential Type: Limited Commercial Applicator License. **Duration of License:** One year. **Authorization:** Required of individuals other than private applicators who limit their pesticide application activities to their own property or that of their employers. **Requirements:** License will be issued upon receiving certification. **Fees:** $50 annual license fee.

4876

Pesticide Dealer
Dept. of Agriculture
Div. of Plant Industry
Pesticide Regulation
8995 E. Main St.
Reynoldsburg, OH 43068-3399
Phone: (614)866-6361

Credential Type: Pesticide Dealer License. **Duration of License:** One year. **Requirements:** Submit application and pay fee. **Fees:** $25 annual license fee.

4877

Public Operator
Dept. of Agriculture
Div. of Plant Industry
Pesticide Regulation
8995 E. Main St.
Reynoldsburg, OH 43068-3399
Phone: (614)866-6361

Credential Type: Public Operator Certification. **Duration of License:** Three years. **Authorization:** Required of an individual who applies or supervises the application of general or restricted-use pesticides while acting as a governmental employee. **Requirements:** Demonstrate competency by passing appropriate examinations. License must be renewed each year to maintain certification. Recertification requires retesting or attending recertification training. **Examination:** Core examination and appropriate category examinations. **Fees:** No fee in addition to license fee.

Credential Type: Public Operator License. **Duration of License:** One year. **Authorization:** Required of an individual who applies or supervises the application of general or restricted-use pesticides while acting as a governmental employee. **Requirements:** License will be issued upon receiving certification. **Fees:** $20 annual license fee.

Oklahoma

4878

Pesticide Applicator, Commercial (Certified)
Oklahoma Dept. of Agriculture
2800 N. Lincoln
Oklahoma City, OK 73105
Phone: (405)521-3864

Credential Type: License. **Duration of License:** One year. **Requirements:** Certified applicator license. Five to 20 hours of continuing education. **Examination:** General Certification Exam. "Category" Exam. **Fees:** $20 exam fee for each category. $50 license, certification and registration fee. $50 renewal fee.

4879

Pesticide Applicator, Non-Commercial (Certified)
Oklahoma Dept. of Agriculture
2800 N. Lincoln
Oklahoma City, OK 73105
Phone: (405)521-3864

Credential Type: License. **Duration of License:** One year. **Requirements:** Certified applicator license. Five to 20 hours of continuing education each year. **Examination:** General Certification Exam. "Category" Exam. **Fees:** $20 exam fee for each category. $20 license fee. $20 renewal fee.

Oregon

4880

Pesticide Applicator
Oregon Dept. of Agriculture
635 Capitol NE
Salem, OR 97310
Phone: (503)378-3776

Credential Type: Commercial License. **Duration of License:** One year. **Requirements:** 18 years of age. **Examination:** Yes. **Fees:** $15 license fee. $15 renewal fee. **Governing Statute:** ORS 634.006 to 634.992.

Credential Type: Private License. **Duration of License:** Five years. **Requirements:** 18 years of age. **Examination:** Yes. **Fees:** $25 license fee. $25 renewal fee. **Governing Statute:** ORS 634.006 to 634.992.

Credential Type: Public License. **Duration of License:** One year. **Requirements:** 18 years of age. **Examination:** Yes. **Fees:** $10 license fee. $10 renewal fee. **Governing Statute:** ORS 634.006 to 634.992.

4881

Pesticide Consultant
Oregond Dept. of Agriculture
635 Capitol NE
Salem, OR 97310
Phone: (503)378-3776

Credential Type: License. **Duration of License:** One year. **Requirements:** 18 years of age. **Examination:** Yes. **Fees:** $15 license fee. $15 renewal fee. **Governing Statute:** ORS 634.006 to 634.992.

Pennsylvania

4882

Commercial Pesticide Applicator
Dept. of Agriculture
Bureau of Plant Industry
2301 N. Cameron St.
Harrisburg, PA 17110-9408
Phone: (717)787-4392

Credential Type: Commercial Applicator Certification. **Duration of License:** One year. **Authorization:** There are 23 specialty categories. **Requirements:** Demonstrate competency by passing appropriate category examinations. Recertification requires completing appropriate training every three years. **Examination:** Written core examination and examinations for each category. **Fees:** $30 annual certification fee. $50 core exam fee. $10 category exam fee (per category). **Governing Statute:** seven Pa. Code, Chaps. 75, 128, and 129.

4883

Pest Management Consultant
Dept. of Agriculture
Bureau of Plant Industry
2301 N. Cameron St.
Harrisburg, PA 17110-9408
Phone: (717)787-4392

Credential Type: Pest Management Consultant License. **Duration of License:** One year. **Authorization:** There are 23 specialty categories. **Requirements:** Demonstrate competency by passing examination. **Examination:** Written examination. **Fees:** $25 annual license fee. No exam fee. **Governing Statute:** seven Pa. Code, Chaps. 75, 128, and 129.

Pennsylvania

4884

Pesticide Technician
Dept. of Agriculture
Bureau of Plant Industry
2301 N. Cameron St.
Harrisburg, PA 17110-9408
Phone: (717)787-4392

Credential Type: Registration. **Duration of License:** One year. **Requirements:** Complete an appropriate training program under the direction of a certified applicator with at least one year of experience. **Fees:** $20 annual registration fee. **Governing Statute:** seven Pa. Code, Chaps. 75, 128, and 129.

4885

Private Pesticide Applicator
Dept. of Agriculture
Bureau of Plant Industry
2301 N. Cameron St.
Harrisburg, PA 17110-9408
Phone: (717)787-4392

Credential Type: Private Applicator Permit. **Duration of License:** Three years. **Requirements:** Demonstrate competency by passing examination. Recertification requires completing appropriate training every three years. **Examination:** Written examination. **Fees:** $10 triennial permit fee. No exam fee. **Governing Statute:** seven Pa. Code, Chaps. 75, 128, and 129.

4886

Public Pesticide Applicator
Dept. of Agriculture
Bureau of Plant Industry
2301 N. Cameron St.
Harrisburg, PA 17110-9408
Phone: (717)787-4392

Credential Type: Public Applicator Certification. **Duration of License:** Three years. **Authorization:** There are 23 specialty categories. **Requirements:** Demonstrate competency by passing appropriate category examinations. Recertification requires completing appropriate training every three years. **Examination:** Written core examination and examinations for each category. **Fees:** $10 triennial certification fee. $50 core exam fee. $10 category exam fee (per category). **Governing Statute:** seven Pa. Code, Chaps. 75, 128, and 129.

Rhode Island

4887

Pesticide Applicator
Div. of Agriculture
Rhode Island Dept. of Environmental Management
22 Hayes St.
Providence, RI 02908
Phone: (401)277-2781

Credential Type: Pesticide Applicator Private Certificate. **Duration of License:** One year. **Requirements:** At least 18 years of age. Complete a URI/DEM sponsored 16-hour training in the general use of pesticides. **Examination:** Written examination. **Reciprocity:** Yes. **Fees:** $20 certificate fee. $20 renewal fee.

Credential Type: Pesticide Applicator Commercial License. **Duration of License:** One year. **Requirements:** At least 18 years of age. Complete a URI/DEM sponsored 16-hour training in the general use of pesticides. **Examination:** Written examination. **Reciprocity:** Yes. **Fees:** $30 license fee. $30 renewal fee.

Credential Type: Pesticide Applicator Commercial Certificate. **Duration of License:** One year. **Requirements:** At least 18 years of age. Complete a URI/DEM sponsored 16-hour training in the general use of pesticides. Complete eight hours of training on the safe use of pesticides. **Examination:** Written examination. **Reciprocity:** Yes. **Fees:** $45 certificate fee. $45 renewal fee.

Credential Type: Pesticide Applicator Dealer License. **Duration of License:** One year. **Requirements:** At least 18 years of age. Must have a fixed distribution center. Complete the URI/DEM sponsored core training program. **Examination:** Written examination. **Reciprocity:** Yes. **Fees:** $30 license fee. $30 renewal fee.

South Carolina

4888

Commercial Pesticide Applicator
Dept. of Fertilizer and Pesticide Control
Regulatory and Public Service Programs
256 Poole Agricultural Center
Clemson Univ.
Clemson, SC 29634-0394
Phone: (803)656-2527
Fax: (803)656-3219

Credential Type: Commercial Applicator Certification and License. **Duration of License:** Three years. **Authorization:** There are 12 categories of certification and licensure. Applies to any person who uses any pesticides for hire or compensation. **Requirements:** Be at least 18 years of age. Demonstrate minimum financial responsibility of $5000 for property damage and public liability. Demonstrate competency by passing appropriate examinations. **Examination:** General examination and appropriate category examinations. **Fees:** $25 basic license fee. $5 license fee per additional category.

4889

Noncommercial Pesticide Applicator
Dept. of Fertilizer and Pesticide Control
Regulatory and Public Service Programs
256 Poole Agricultural Center
Clemson Univ.
Clemson, SC 29634-0394
Phone: (803)656-2527
Fax: (803)656-3219

Credential Type: Noncommercial Applicator Certification and License. **Duration of License:** One year. **Authorization:** There are 12 categories of certification and licensure. Applies to any person working as an individual or as an employee of a firm or government agency who uses or demonstrates the use of any restricted use pesticide, and who does not qualify as a private applicator nor require a commercial applicator's license. **Requirements:** Be at least 18 years of age. Demonstrate competency by passing appropriate examinations. **Examination:** General examination and appropriate category examinations. **Fees:** No fees.

4890

Pesticide Dealer
Dept. of Fertilizer and Pesticide Control
Regulatory and Public Service Programs
256 Poole Agricultural Center
Clemson Univ.
Clemson, SC 29634-0394
Phone: (803)656-2527
Fax: (803)656-3219

Credential Type: Pesticide Dealer License. **Duration of License:** One year. **Authorization:** There shall be a separate licensed individual for each location that sells restricted use pesticides. **Requirements:** Be at least 18 years of age. Pass written exam. **Examination:** Written examination. **Fees:** $25 annual license fee.

4891

Private Pesticide Applicator
Dept. of Fertilizer and Pesticide Control
Regulatory and Public Service Programs
256 Poole Agricultural Center
Clemson Univ.
Clemson, SC 29634-0394
Phone: (803)656-2527
Fax: (803)656-3219

Credential Type: Private Applicator Certification and License. **Duration of License:** One year. **Authorization:** Applies to any person who uses or supervises the use of any restricted use pesticide for the purposes of producing any agricultural commodity on property owned by the individual or the individual's employer, or on the property of another for no compensation other than the trading of personal services. **Requirements:** Be at least 15 years of age. Complete a prescribed training program dealing with pesticides. **Fees:** $1 annual license fee.

South Dakota

4892

Commercial Pesticide Applicator
Dept. of Agriculture
Office of Agronomy Services
Anderson Bldg.
Pierre, SD 57501-3185
Phone: (605)773-4032

Credential Type: Commercial Applicator Certification. **Duration of License:** Two years. **Authorization:** There are 16 categories of certification. **Requirements:** Demonstrate competency by passing appropriate examinations. License must be renewed each year to maintain certification. Recertification requires retesting or attending recertification training. **Examination:** Core examination and appropriate category examinations. **Fees:** No fee in addition to license fee.

Credential Type: Commercial Applicator License. **Duration of License:** One year. **Requirements:** License will be issued upon receiving certification. **Fees:** $25 annual license fee.

4893

Pesticide Dealer
Dept. of Agriculture
Office of Agronomy Services
Anderson Bldg.
Pierre, SD 57501-3185
Phone: (605)773-4032

Credential Type: Pesticide Dealer License. **Duration of License:** Two years. **Requirements:** Submit application and pay fee. Pass pesticide dealer's open-book examination. Renewal requires retesting or attending a certification shortcourse. **Examination:** Written examination.

4894

Private Pesticide Applicator
Dept. of Agriculture
Office of Agronomy Services
Anderson Bldg.
Pierre, SD 57501-3185
Phone: (605)773-4032

Credential Type: Private Applicator Certification. **Duration of License:** Two years. **Requirements:** Complete an approved training course or a home study course. **Fees:** No fee in addition to license fee.

Credential Type: Private Applicator License. **Duration of License:** One year. **Requirements:** License will be issued upon receiving certification. **Fees:** $25 annual license fee.

Tennessee

4895

Pest Control Operator
Dept. of Agriculture
PO Box 40627, Melrose Sta.
Nashville, TN 37204
Phone: (615)360-0130

Credential Type: License. **Duration of License:** One year. **Requirements:** Degree in entomology or related field, or two years experience under licensed operator. 10 points of continuing education every five years in each category. **Examination:** Yes. **Fees:** $25 Examination. $5 Application. $5 Renewal.

Texas

4896

Pesticide Applicator
Texas Dept. of Agriculture,
Certification and Training
PO Box 12847
Austin, TX 78711
Phone: (512)475-1621

Credential Type: Structural Pest Control License. **Requirements:** One year experience under supervision of a licensed applicator, including six months experience as a licensed technician; or a degree in biological sciences from an accredited college or university; or technical field experience from previous occupation. **Examination:** Written. **Fees:** $30 examination fee. $66 certified applicator license fee. $18 apprentice fee. **Governing Statute:** Agriculture Code 76.105, VACS 135b-6, 22 TAC 593.

Credential Type: Agricultural Pest Control License. **Duration of License:** One year. **Requirements:** One year experience under supervision of a licensed applicator, including six months experience as a licensed technician; or a degree in biological sciences from an accredited college or university; or technical field experience from previous occupation. **Examination:** Written. **Fees:** $10 examination fee for each category. $150 license fee. $150 renewal fee. **Governing Statute:** Agriculture Code 76.105, VACS 135b-6, 22 TAC 593.

4897

Structural Pest Control Technician
Texas Dept. of Agriculture,
Certification and Training
PO Box 12847
Austin, TX 78711
Phone: (512)475-1621

Credential Type: Technician License. **Requirements:** At least 16 years of age. Complete specialized training. Be employed by a licensed business. **Examination:** Written. **Fees:** $30 examination fee. $36 technician license fee. $18 apprentice fee. **Governing Statute:** Agriculture Code 76.105, VACS 135b-6, 22 TAC 593.

Utah

4898

Commercial Pesticide Applicator
Dept. of Agriculture
Div. of Plant Industry
350 N. Redwood Rd.
Salt Lake City, UT 84116
Phone: (801)538-7188
Fax: (801)538-7126

Credential Type: Commercial Applicator Certification. **Duration of License:** Three years. **Authorization:** There are 11 categories of certification. Applies to any person who uses any pesticides for hire or compensation. **Requirements:** Demonstrate competency by passing appropriate examinations. Recertification requires retesting or attending recertification training. **Examination:** General examination and appropriate category examinations. **Governing Statute:** Utah Pesticide Control Act, Title 4, Chap. 14. Rules and Regulations R68-7.

Credential Type: Commercial Applicator License. **Duration of License:** One year. **Authorization:** Applies to any person who uses any pesticides for hire or compensation. **Requirements:** License will be issued upon receiving certification. **Fees:** $10 annual license fee. **Governing Statute:** Utah Pesticide Control Act, Title 4, Chap. 14. Rules and Regulations R68-7.

4899

Noncommercial Pesticide Applicator
Dept. of Agriculture
Div. of Plant Industry
350 N. Redwood Rd.
Salt Lake City, UT 84116
Phone: (801)538-7188
Fax: (801)538-7126

Credential Type: Noncommercial Applicator Certification. **Duration of License:** Three years. **Authorization:** There are 11 categories of certification. Applies to any person working as an individual or as an employee of a firm or government agency who uses or demonstrates the use of any restricted use pesticide, and who does not qualify as a private applicator or a commercial applicator. **Requirements:** Demonstrate competency by passing appropriate examinations. Recertification requires retesting or attending recertification training. **Examination:** General examination and appropriate category examinations. **Governing Statute:** Utah Pesticide Control Act, Title 4, Chap. 14. Rules and Regulations R68-7.

Credential Type: Noncommercial Applicator License. **Duration of License:** One year. **Authorization:** Applies to any person working as an individual or as an employee of a firm or government agency who uses or demonstrates the use of any restricted use pesticide, and who does not qualify as a private applicator nor require a commercial applicator's license. **Requirements:** License will be issued upon receiving certification. **Fees:** No license fee. **Governing Statute:** Utah Pesticide Control Act, Title 4, Chap. 14. Rules and Regulations R68-7.

4900

Pesticide Dealer
Dept. of Agriculture
Div. of Plant Industry
350 N. Redwood Rd.
Salt Lake City, UT 84116
Phone: (801)538-7188
Fax: (801)538-7126

Credential Type: Pesticide Dealer License. **Duration of License:** One year. **Authorization:** Each location that sells restricted use pesticides must register as a pesticide dealer. **Requirements:** Submit application and pay fee. **Fees:** $10 annual license fee. **Governing Statute:** Utah Pesticide Control Act, Title 4, Chap. 14. Rules and Regulations R68-7.

4901

Private Pesticide Applicator
Dept. of Agriculture
Div. of Plant Industry
350 N. Redwood Rd.
Salt Lake City, UT 84116
Phone: (801)538-7188
Fax: (801)538-7126

Credential Type: Private Applicator Certification. **Duration of License:** Three years. **Authorization:** There are 11 categories of certification. Applies to any person who uses or supervised the use of any restricted use pesticide for the purposes of producing any agricultural commodity on property owned by the individual or the individual's employer, or on the property of another for no compensation other than the trading of personal services. **Requirements:** Meet one of the following sets of requirements: (1) Complete an approved training course. (2) Complete an approved self-study workbook. (3) Pass an approved written exam.

Recertification requires retesting or attending recertification training. **Examination:** Exam may be required. **Fees:** No fee. **Governing Statute:** Utah Pesticide Control Act, Title 4, Chap. 14. Rules and Regulations R68-7.

Vermont

4902

Pesticide Applicator—Commercial
Vermont Dept. of Agriculture
Plant Industry Div.
116 State St.
Montpelier, VT 05602
Phone: (802)828-2431

Credential Type: License. **Duration of License:** One year. **Requirements:** Must be knowledgeable about the safe and effective use of pesticides. Self study materials are available. **Examination:** Yes. 75 percent or better. 11 different categories. Exams good for five years. **Reciprocity:** Yes. **Fees:** $20 Company license (annual). $10 Individual certification/category (annual).

Virginia

4903

Pesticide Applicator
Office of Pesticide Management
Dept. of Agriculture and Consumer Service
PO Box 1163
Richmond, VA 23209
Phone: (804)371-6560
Phone: (804)371-0152

Credential Type: License. **Requirements:** Contact licensing body for application information.

4904

Pesticide Dealer
Office of Pesticide Management
Dept. of Agriculture and Consumer Service
PO Box 1163
Richmond, VA 23209
Phone: (804)371-6560
Phone: (804)371-0152

Credential Type: License. **Requirements:** Contact licensing body for application information.

Washington

4905

Commercial Pest Control Consultant

Dept. of Agriculture
Pesticide Management
Plant Services
406 General Administration Bldg., AX-41
Olympia, WA 98504-0641
Phone: (206)753-5064

Credential Type: Commercial Pest Control Consultant License. **Duration of License:** One year. **Requirements:** Submit application. Meet experience and education requirements. Background investigation required of applicants with previous violations. Recertification required periodically. **Examination:** Written examination. **Fees:** $30 license fee. $5 surcharge.

4906

Commercial Pest Control Operator/Consultant

Dept. of Agriculture
Pesticide Management
Plant Services
406 General Administration Bldg., AX-41
Olympia, WA 98504-0641
Phone: (206)753-5064

Credential Type: Commercial Pest Control Operator License. **Duration of License:** One year. **Requirements:** Submit application. Meet experience and education requirements. Background investigation required of applicants with previous violations. Recertification required periodically. **Examination:** Written examination. **Fees:** $15 license fee. $5 surcharge.

4907

Commercial Pesticide Applicator

Dept. of Agriculture
Pesticide Management & Plant Services
406 General Administration Bldg., AX-41
Olympia, WA 98504-0641
Phone: (206)753-5064

Credential Type: Commercial Pesticide Applicator License. **Duration of License:** Two years. **Authorization:** Authorizes application of pesticides as a business to the property of a client. **Requirements:** Submit application and pay fee. Meet insurance requirements. Background investigation may be required if previous pesticide law violation exists. Recertification requirements must be met for renewal. **Examination:** Written examination. **Fees:** $125 commercial license fee. $5 surcharge.

4908

Private Commercial Pesticide Applicator

Dept. of Agriculture
Pesticide Management & Plant Services
406 General Administration Bldg., AX-41
Olympia, WA 98504-0641
Phone: (206)753-5064

Credential Type: Private Commercial Pesticide Applicator License. **Duration of License:** Five years. **Authorization:** Authorizes application of pesticides on lands owned by licensee or his/her employer. Not valid for lands used to produce an agricultural commodity. **Requirements:** Submit application and pay fee. Recertification requirements must be met for renewal. **Examination:** Written examination. **Fees:** $50 license fee. $5 surcharge.

4909

Public Pesticide Consultant

Dept. of Agriculture
Pesticide Management & Plant Services
406 General Administration Bldg., AX-41
Olympia, WA 98504-0641
Phone: (206)753-5064

Credential Type: Public Pesticide Consultant License. **Duration of License:** One year. **Authorization:** Issued to government agency employees to supply technical advice, supervision, aid, or to make recommendations for pesticide use as part of their employment with a government agency. **Requirements:** Submit application and pay fee. Background investigation may be required if previous pesticide violation exists. Recertification requirements must be met for renewal. **Examination:** Written examination. **Fees:** $15 license fee. $5 surcharge.

4910

Public Pesticide Operator

Dept. of Agriculture
Pesticide Management & Plant Services
406 General Administration Bldg., AX-41
Olympia, WA 98504-0641
Phone: (206)753-5064

Credential Type: Public Pesticide Operator License. **Duration of License:** One year. **Authorization:** Issued to government agency employees to apply pesticides as part of their job related duties. **Requirements:** Submit application and pay fee. Background investigation may be required if previous pesticide violation exists. Recertification requirements must be met for renewal. **Examination:** Written examination. **Fees:** $15 license fee. $5 surcharge.

West Virginia

4911

Pesticide Applicator

Dept. of Agriculture
Pesticides Div.
Guthrie Ctr.
State Capitol Complex
Charleston, WV 25305
Phone: (304)348-2209

Credential Type: License. **Duration of License:** One year. **Requirements:** Must not violate any state laws governing pesticide use. **Examination:** Yes. **Fees:** $1 License ($50 Business license). $1 Renewal.

Wisconsin

4912

Pesticide Applicator

Dept. of Agriculture, Trade, and Consumer Protection
Applicator Certification and Licensing
801 W. Badger Rd.
PO Box 8911
Madison, WI 53708
Phone: (608)266-0197

Credential Type: Certification and License. **Requirements:** Contact licensing body for application information.

Wisconsin

4913

Pesticide Dealer
Dept. of Agriculture, Trade and Consumer Protection
Applicator Certification and Licensing
801 W. Badger Rd.
PO Box 8911
Madison, WI 53708
Phone: (608)266-0197

Credential Type: License. **Requirements:** Contact licensing body for application information.

Wyoming

4914

Commercial Pesticide Applicator
Dept. of Agriculture
Licensing and Registrations Section
2219 Carey Ave.
Cheyenne, WY 82002-0100
Phone: (307)777-7321
Phone: (307)777-6573

Credential Type: Certified Commercial Applicator License. **Duration of License:** Two years. **Requirements:** Demonstrate competency by passing appropriate examination. In addition, must have appropriate insurance. Recertification requires completing 24 hours of training every two years. **Examination:** General examination and appropriate category examinations. **Fees:** $10 license fee per category, to a maximum of $50. **Governing Statute:** Wyoming Environmental Pesticide Control Act of 1973 (35-7). Rules and Regulations.

4915

Pesticide Dealer
Dept. of Agriculture
Licensing and Registrations Section
2219 Carey Ave.
Cheyenne, WY 82002-0100
Phone: (307)777-7321
Phone: (307)777-6573

Credential Type: Registration and License. **Duration of License:** One year. **Requirements:** Submit application and register principal business location. **Fees:** No fees. **Governing Statute:** Wyoming Environmental Pesticide Control Act of 1973 (35-7). Rules and Regulations.

4916

Private Pesticide Applicator
Dept. of Agriculture
Licensing and Registrations Section
2219 Carey Ave.
Cheyenne, WY 82002-0100
Phone: (307)777-7321
Phone: (307)777-6573

Credential Type: Certified Private Applicator License. **Duration of License:** Five years. **Authorization:** There are three licensing options: (1) General license covering any restricted-use pesticide. (2) A license limited to a specific commodity or site. (3) A license limited to a single restricted-use product. **Requirements:** Demonstrate competency by meeting one of the following requirements: (1) Complete an approved training course. (2) Complete a program instruction workbook. (3) Pass a written or oral examination.

Recertification requires completing a refresher training course every five years. **Fees:** No fees. **Governing Statute:** Wyoming Environmental Pesticide Control Act of 1973 (35-7). Rules and Regulations.

Pharmacists

The following states grant licenses in this occupational category as of the date of publication:

Alabama	District of	Iowa	Minnesota	New Mexico	Rhode Island	Washington
Alaska	Columbia	Kansas	Mississippi	New York	South Carolina	West Virginia
Arizona	Florida	Kentucky	Missouri	North Carolina	South Dakota	Wisconsin
Arkansas	Georgia	Louisiana	Montana	North Dakota	Tennessee	Wyoming
California	Hawaii	Maine	Nebraska	Ohio	Texas	
Colorado	Idaho	Maryland	Nevada	Oklahoma	Utah	
Connecticut	Illinois	Massachusetts	New Hampshire	Oregon	Vermont	
Delaware	Indiana	Michigan	New Jersey	Pennsylvania	Virginia	

Alabama

4917

Pharmacist
Alabama State Board of Pharmacy
1 Perimeter Park S., Ste. 425 S.
Birmingham, AL 35243
Phone: (205)967-0130

Credential Type: License. **Duration of License:** One year. **Requirements:** 19 years of age. Must hold a degree in pharmacy. Must have completed 1500 supervised training hours in a recognized pharmacy. **Examination:** Yes. **Fees:** $210 examination fee. $60 license fee. $60 renewal fee.

Alaska

4918

Pharmacist
Board of Pharmacy
PO Box D
Juneau, AK 99811-0800
Phone: (907)465-3811

Credential Type: Pharmacist License. **Duration of License:** Two years. **Requirements:** Good moral character. Graduate from an accredited first professional degree program of a college of pharmacy. Have 1500 hours of prior practical experience, 160 hours of which must be completed after graduation.

An average of 15 credit hours per year of continuing education sponsored by American Council on Pharmaceutical Education (ACPE)-approved providers is required for renewal. **Examination:** National Association of Boards of Pharmacy Licensure Examination (NABPLEX). **Reciprocity:** Yes. License by transfer granted to holders of a license in good standing from another state, provided that applicant passes a jurisprudence examination. **Fees:** $30 application fee. $150 exam fee. $180 initial license fee. $180 renewal fee. $210 license transfer fee.

Credential Type: Temporary Permit. **Requirements:** Issued to qualified licensure transfer applicants.

4919

Pharmacy Intern
Board of Pharmacy
PO Box D
Juneau, AK 99811-0800
Phone: (907)465-3811

Credential Type: Pharmacy Intern Registration. **Duration of License:** Intern duration. **Requirements:** Submit application and pay fees. **Fees:** $20 registration fee. $20 annual renewal fee.

Arizona

4920

Pharmacist
Board of Pharmacy
5060 N. 19th Ave., Ste.101
Phoenix, AZ 85015
Phone: (602)255-5125

Credential Type: Pharmacist License. **Duration of License:** Two years. **Requirements:** Good moral character. Graduate from an accredited first professional degree program of a college of pharmacy. Have 1500 hours of prior practical experience acquired in either hospital pharmacy or retail pharmacy licensed by the board. No more than 500 hours of practical experience may apply in any pharmacy specialty other than a retail or hospital pharmacy. Foreign graduates who are Foreign Pharmacy Graduate Examination Commission (FPGEC)-certified, pass board examination, and meet practical experience requirements may be licensed.

Renewal requires completion of 3.0 continuing education units of professional education activities sponsored by American Council on Pharmaceutical Education (ACPE) or board-approved providers. At least 0.3 continuing education units (CEUs) must be pharmacy law subjects. **Examination:** National Association of Boards of Pharmacy Licensure Examination (NABPLEX). **Reciprocity:** Yes. License by transfer granted to holders of a license in good standing from another state with requirements equivalent to those of Arizona. Must pass an examination in jurisprudence. Must have held a valid pharmacist license for at least one year to be eligible. **Fees:** $200 exam fee. $20 initial license fee. $100 renewal fee. $300 license transfer fee.

4921

Pharmacy Intern
Board of Pharmacy
5060 N. 19th Ave., Ste.101
Phoenix, AZ 85015
Phone: (602)255-5125

Credential Type: Pharmacy Intern Registration. **Duration of License:** Six years maximum. **Requirements:** Submit application and pay fees. **Reciprocity:** $10 initial registration fee. $10 biennial registration.

Arkansas

4922

Pharmacist
Arkansas State Board of Pharmacy
320 W. Capitol, Ste. 807
Little Rock, AR 72201
Phone: (501)371-3050

Credential Type: License. **Duration of License:** One year. **Requirements:** 21 years of age. US citizen. Good moral character and temperate habits. Graduate of an accredited school or college of pharmacy. Serve 12 months with a minimum of 2000 hours of practical experience in training under approved conditions. Minimum of six months of this one year requirement must be obtained after graduation. **Examination:** Yes. **Fees:** $175 Written examination. $10 Certification. $50 License. $50 Renewal.

4923

Pharmacist Intern
Arkansas State Board of Pharmacy
320 W. Capitol, Ste. 802
Little Rock, AR 72201
Phone: (501)371-3050

Credential Type: License. **Requirements:** Must be a student of an accredited school or college of pharmacy. Must successfully complete the first professional year of a two or three year program; or, complete the second professional year of a four year program of study. **Examination:** No **Fees:** $20 Registration.

California

4924

Pharmacist
Board of Pharmacy
400 "R" St., Ste. 4070
Sacramento, CA 95814
Phone: (916)445-5014

Credential Type: Pharmacist License. **Duration of License:** Two years. **Requirements:** Good moral character. 18 years of age. Graduate from an accredited first professional degree program of a college of pharmacy. Have 1500 hours of prior practical experience in both hospital and retail settings. 1000 hours are required before sitting for examination. Passing grade on state licensure examination. Foreign graduates who are Foreign Pharmacy Graduate Examination Commission (FPGEC) certified and pass the state board examination may be licensed. Renewal requires 30 hours of approved continuing pharmaceutical education every two years. All continuing education must be American Council on Pharmaceutical Education (ACPE)-approved, recognized by the Accreditation Evaluation Service (AES), or approved directly by the Board. **Examination:** California State Licensure Examination. **Reciprocity:** No. **Fees:** $155 exam fee. $115 initial license fee. $115 renewal fee.

4925

Pharmacy Intern
Board of Pharmacy
400 "R" St., Ste. 4070
Sacramento, CA 95814
Phone: (916)445-5014

Credential Type: Pharmacy Intern Registration. **Duration of License:** Five years. **Requirements:** Submit application and pay fees. **Fees:** $65 initial registration fee.

Colorado

4926

Pharmacist
Board of Pharmacy
1560 Broadway, Ste. 4070
Denver, CO 80202-5146
Phone: (303)894-7750

Credential Type: Pharmacist License. **Duration of License:** Two years. **Requirements:** Good moral character. 21 years of age. Graduate from an accredited first professional degree program of a college of pharmacy. Have 1800 hours of prior practical experience. Intern registration required for experience validation. Foreign graduates who are Foreign Pharmacy Graduate Examination Commission (FPGEC)-certified, pass board examination, and meet practical experience requirements may be licensed. **Examination:** National Association of Boards of Pharmacy Licensure Examination (NABPLEX). **Reciprocity:** Yes. License by transfer granted to holders of a license in good standing from another state with requirements equivalent to those of Colorado. Must have held a valid pharmacist license for at least one year to be eligible. **Fees:** $228 exam fee. $190 license renewal fee. $160 license transfer fee.

4927

Pharmacy Intern
Board of Pharmacy
1560 Broadway, Ste. 4070
Denver, CO 80202-5146
Phone: (303)894-7750

Credential Type: Pharmacy Intern Registration. **Duration of License:** One year. **Requirements:** Submit application and pay fee. **Fees:** $41 initial registration fee.

Connecticut

4928

Pharmacist
Board of Pharmacy
State Office Bldg., Rm. G-1A
Hartford, CT 06106
Phone: (203)566-3917

Credential Type: Pharmacist License. **Duration of License:** One year. **Requirements:** Good moral character. 21 years of age. Graduate from an accredited first professional degree program of a college of pharmacy. **Examination:** National Association of Boards of Pharmacy Licensure Examination (NABPLEX). **Reciprocity:** Yes. License by transfer granted to holders of a license in good standing from another state with requirements equivalent to those of Connecticut. Must have held a valid pharmacist license for at least one year to be eligible. Must pass math examination. **Fees:** $100 exam fee. $30 license renewal fee. $100 license transfer fee.

4929

Pharmacy Intern
Board of Pharmacy
State Office Bldg., Rm. G-1A
Hartford, CT 06106
Phone: (203)566-3917

Credential Type: Pharmacist Intern Registration. **Duration of License:** Intern duration. **Requirements:** Submit application and pay fee. **Fees:** $30 initial registration fee.

Delaware

4930

Pharmacist
Board of Pharmacy
Cooper Bldg.
Federal & Water Sts.
Dover, DE 19901
Phone: (302)739-4708

Credential Type: Pharmacist License. **Duration of License:** Two years. **Requirements:** Good moral character. 21 years of age. Graduate from an accredited first professional degree program of a college of pharmacy. Have 1500 hours of prior practical experience. Foreign graduates who are Foreign Pharmacy Graduate Examination Commission (FPGEC) certified, pass board examination, and meet practical experience requirements may be licensed.

Renewal requires 30 hours of continuing pharmaceutical education every two years. **Examination:** National Association of Boards of Pharmacy Licensure Examination (NABPLEX). **Reciprocity:** Yes. License by transfer granted to holders of a license in good standing from another state with requirements equivalent to those of Delaware. Must pass jurisprudence examination. **Fees:** $200 exam fee. $50 renewal fee. $150 license transfer fee.

4931

Pharmacy Intern
Board of Pharmacy
Cooper Bldg.
Federal & Water Sts.
Dover, DE 19901
Phone: (302)739-4708

Credential Type: Pharmacy Intern Registration. **Duration of License:** 2.5 years maximum. **Requirements:** Submit application and pay fees. **Fees:** $5 initial registration fee. $5 biennial renewal fee.

District of Columbia

4932

Pharmacist
Board of Pharmacy
614 H St. NW, Rm. 923
Washington, DC 20001
Phone: (202)727-7468

Credential Type: Pharmacist License. **Duration of License:** Two years. **Requirements:** Good moral character. 18 years of age. Graduate from an accredited first professional degree program of a college of pharmacy. Have 1500 hours of prior practical experience. Intern registration required for experience validation. Foreign graduates who are Foreign Pharmacy Graduate Examination Commission (FPGEC) certified and pass the state board examination may be licensed. **Examination:** National Association of Boards of Pharmacy Licensure Examination (NABPLEX). Federal Drug Law Examination (FDLE). **Reciprocity:** Yes. License by transfer granted to holders of a license in good standing from another state with requirements equivalent to those of the District of Columbia. Must pass jurisprudence examination. **Fees:** $60 examination fee. $20 initial license fee. $95 renewal fee. $80 license transfer fee.

4933

Pharmacy Intern
Board of Pharmacy
614 H St. NW, Rm. 923
Washington, DC 20001
Phone: (202)727-7468

Credential Type: Pharmacist Intern Registration. **Duration of License:** Intern duration. **Requirements:** Submit application and pay fee. **Fees:** $28 initial registration fee.

Florida

4934

Pharmacist
Board of Pharmacy
Northwood Center
1940 N. Monroe, Ste. 60
Tallahassee, FL 32399-0775
Phone: (904)488-7546

Credential Type: Pharmacist License. **Duration of License:** Two years. **Requirements:** Good moral character. 18 years of age. Graduate from an accredited first professional degree program of a college of pharmacy. Must have 2080 hours of prior practical experience in either hospital pharmacy or retail pharmacy licensed by the board or complete a board-approved 1500 hour internship program. Intern registration required for experience validation. Foreign graduates who are Foreign Pharmacy Graduate Examination Commission (FPGEC) certified, pass board examination, and meet practical experience requirements may be licensed upon completing a test of spoken English.

Renewal requires 15 hours of professional continuing education per year. **Examination:** National Association of Boards of Pharmacy Licensure Examination (NABPLEX). **Fees:** $250 exam fee. $105 initial certificate fee. $140 renewal fee. $105 license transfer fee.

4935

Pharmacy Intern
Board of Pharmacy
Northwood Center
1940 N. Monroe, Ste. 60
Tallahassee, FL 32399-0775
Phone: (904)488-7546

Credential Type: Pharmacy Intern Registration. **Duration of License:** Intern duration. **Requirements:** Submit application.

Georgia

4936

Nuclear Pharmacist
State Board of Pharmacy
Health Care Practitioners Section
Professional Examining Boards
166 Pryor St., SW
Atlanta, GA 30303
Phone: (404)656-3912

Credential Type: Nuclear Pharmacist License. **Requirements:** Contact licensing body for application information.

4937

Pharmacist
Board of Pharmacy
166 Pryor St. SW
Atlanta, GA 30303
Phone: (404)656-3912

Credential Type: Pharmacist License. **Duration of License:** Two years. **Requirements:** Good moral character. 18 years of age. Graduate from an accredited first professional degree program of a college of pharmacy. Have 1500 hours of prior practical experience. Foreign graduates who are Foreign Pharmacy Graduate Examination Commission (FPGEC) certified and pass the state board examination may be licensed.

Renewal requires 30 hours (3.0 continuing education units) of pharmaceutical education every two years. **Examination:** National Association of Boards of Pharmacy Licensure Examination (NABPLEX). **Reciprocity:** Yes. License by transfer granted to holders of a license in good standing from another state with requirements equivalent to those of Georgia. Must pass an examination in jurisprudence. Must have held a valid pharmacist license for at least one year to be eligible. **Fees:** $75 applica-

Georgia | 4938

Pharmacist, continued

tion fee. $150 exam fee. $70 license renewal fee. $300 license transfer fee.

4938

Pharmacy Intern
Board of Pharmacy
166 Pryor St. SW
Atlanta, GA 30303
Phone: (404)656-3912

Credential Type: Pharmacist Intern Registration. **Duration of License:** Five years. **Requirements:** Submit application and pay fee. **Fees:** $25 initial registration fee.

Hawaii

4939

Pharmacist
Hawaii Board of Pharmacy
1010 Richards St.
PO Box 3469
Honolulu, HI 96801
Phone: (808)548-3086

Credential Type: License. **Duration of License:** Six months. **Requirements:** Degree from a school of pharmacy. At least 2,000 hours of practical experience under the supervision of a licensed U.S. registered pharmacist in a U.S. pharmacy. Separate requirements for foreign pharmacy school graduates. Temporary licenses available. **Examination:** NABPLEX exam. FDLE exam. State Jurisprudence exam. **Reciprocity:** Board will review applications. **Fees:** $15 application fee. $225 exam fee. $30 temporary license fee. $15 license fee. $20 Compliance Resolution Fund fee. $35 renewal fee.

Idaho

4940

Pharmacist
Board of Pharmacy
280 N. 8th St., Ste. 204
Boise, ID 83720
Phone: (208)334-2356

Credential Type: Pharmacist License. **Duration of License:** One year. **Requirements:** Good moral character. Age of majority. Graduate from an accredited first professional degree program of a college of pharmacy. Have 1500 hours of prior practical experience. Intern registration required for experience validation. Foreign graduates who are Foreign Pharmacy Graduate Examination Commission (FPGEC)-certified and pass the state board examination may be licensed.

Renewal requires 15 hours (1.5 continuing education units (CEUs)) of approved continuing pharmacy education programs each year. A minimum of 10 hours (1.0 CEU) must be in American Council on Pharmaceutical Education (ACPE)-approved education and a minimum of one hour (0.1 CEU) must be in pharmacy laws. **Examination:** National Association of Boards of Pharmacy Licensure Examination (NABPLEX). **Reciprocity:** Yes. License by transfer granted to holders of a license in good standing from another state with requirements equivalent to those of Idaho. Must pass an examination in jurisprudence. **Fees:** $225 exam fee. $75 license renewal fee. $25 controlled substances permit fee. $250 license transfer fee.

4941

Pharmacy Intern
Board of Pharmacy
280 N. 8th St., Ste. 204
Boise, ID 83720
Phone: (208)334-2356

Credential Type: Pharmacy Intern Registration. **Duration of License:** One year. **Requirements:** Submit application and pay fees. **Fees:** $10 initial registration fee. $10 renewal fee.

Illinois

4942

Pharmacist
Board of Pharmacy
Dept. of Professional Regulation
320 W. Washington St., 3rd Fl.
Springfield, IL 62786
Phone: (217)782-0556

Credential Type: Pharmacist License. **Duration of License:** Two years. **Requirements:** Good moral character. 21 years of age. Graduate from an accredited first professional degree program of a college of pharmacy. 400 hour internship required in conjunction with academic credit (ie; externship, clerkship, clinical rotation). Foreign graduates who have five years of education, are Foreign Pharmacy Graduate Examination Commission (FPGEC) certified, pass board examination, and meet practical experience requirements may be licensed.

Renewal requires 30 hours (3.0 continuing education unit (CEUs)) of pharmacy continuing education from American Council on Pharmaceutical Education (ACPE)-approved educators every two years. **Examination:** National Association of Boards of Pharmacy Licensure Examination (NABPLEX). Federal Drug Law Examination (FDLE). **Reciprocity:** Yes. License by transfer granted to holders of a license in good standing from another state. Must have a baccalaureate degree in pharmacy or PharmD from a college whose degree program is accredited by ACPE and approved by the Department of Professional Regulation. **Fees:** $326.10 exam fee. $75 initial license fee. $150 renewal fee. $200 license transfer fee.

Credential Type: Temporary Permit. **Requirements:** Issued to qualified licensure transfer applicants.

4943

Pharmacy Intern
Board of Pharmacy
Dept. of Professional Regulation
320 W. Washington St., 3rd Fl.
Springfield, IL 62786
Phone: (217)782-0556

Credential Type: Pharmacy Intern Registration. **Duration of License:** One year. **Requirements:** Submit application and pay fees. **Fees:** $40 initial registration fee. $25 renewal fee.

Indiana

4944

Pharmacist
Board of Pharmacy
Health Professionals Bureau
402 W. Washington St., Rm. 041
Indianapolis, IN 46204
Phone: (317)232-2960

Credential Type: Pharmacist License. **Duration of License:** Two years. **Requirements:** Good moral character. 18 years of age. Graduate from an accredited first professional degree program of a college of pharmacy. Have 1040 hours of prior practical experience in either hospital pharmacy or retail pharmacy licensed by the board. Some of the experience requirement must be fulfilled after graduation. State structured internship program No. "H" required. Intern registration required for experience validation.

Renewal requires 30 hours of continuing approved pharmacy education every two years. **Examination:** National Association of Boards of Pharmacy Licensure Examination (NABPLEX). Federal Drug Law Examination (FDLE). **Reciprocity:** Yes. License by transfer granted to holders of a license in good standing from another state with requirements equivalent to those of

Indiana. Must pass an examination in jurisprudence. If license was held less than one year, wet lab required. **Fees:** $25 examination fee. $50 renewal fee. $150 license trasfer fee.

4945

Pharmacy Intern
Board of Pharmacy
Health Professionals Bureau
402 W. Washington St., Rm. 041
Indianapolis, IN 46204
Phone: (317)232-2960

Credential Type: Pharmacy Intern Registration. **Duration of License:** Six years. **Requirements:** Submit application and pay fee. **Fees:** $10 initial registration fee.

Iowa

4946

Pharmacist
Board of Pharmacy Examiners
Executive Hills West
1209 E. Court
Des Moines, IA 50319
Phone: (515)281-8630

Credential Type: License. **Duration of License:** Two years. **Requirements:** Graduation from an accredited colledge or school of pharmacy. 30 hours of continuing education every two years. **Examination:** Written. **Fees:** $310 exam fee (includes license). $100 renewal fee.

Kansas

4947

Pharmacist
Board of Pharmacy
Landon State Office Bldg., Rm. 513
900 Jackson
Topeka, KS 66612
Phone: (913)296-4056

Credential Type: Pharmacist License. **Duration of License:** One year. **Requirements:** Good moral character. Legal age. Graduate from an accredited first professional degree program of a college of pharmacy. Have 1500 hours (1 year) of prior practical experience. Intern registration required for experience validation. Foreign graduates who are Foreign Pharmacy Graduate Examination Commission (FPGEC)-certified, pass board examination, and meet practical experience requirements may be licensed. Foreign students who do not have FPGEC certification may request education evaluation.

Renewal requires 15 hours (1.5 continuing education unit (CEUs)) of approved continuing pharmaceutical education per year. **Examination:** National Association of Boards of Pharmacy Licensure Examination (NABPLEX). Federal Drug Law Examination (FDLE). **Reciprocity:** Yes. License by transfer granted to holders of a license in good standing from another state with requirements equivalent to those of Kansas. Must pass an examination in jurisprudence. Must have held valid pharmacy license for one year if required by state of original licensure. **Fees:** $250 exam fee. $75 renewal fee. $250 license transfer fee.

4948

Pharmacy Intern
Board of Pharmacy
Landon State Office Bldg., Rm. 513
900 Jackson
Topeka, KS 66612
Phone: (913)296-4056

Credential Type: Pharmacy Intern Registration. **Duration of License:** Five years. **Requirements:** Submit application and pay fee. **Fees:** $25 initial registration fee.

Kentucky

4949

Pharmacist
Kentucky Board of Pharmacy
1228 U.S. 127 South
Frankfort, KY 40601
Phone: (502)564-3833

Credential Type: License. **Duration of License:** One year. **Requirements:** Graduation from an approved, five-year college of pharmacy or must have an entry level doctor of pharmacy degree. Completion of a 1,500 hour internship. U.S. citizen. 18 years of age. Continuing education required. **Examination:** Yes. **Fees:** $150 exam fee. $70 renewal fee.

Louisiana

4950

Pharmacist
Louisiana Board of Pharmacy
5615 Corporate Blvd., Ste. 8-E
Baton Rouge, LA 70808
Phone: (504)925-6496

Credential Type: License. **Duration of License:** One year. **Requirements:** 21 years of age. U.S. citizen. B.S. degree from an accredited and approved college of pharmacy. One year of practical experience. **Examination:** Yes. **Fees:** $75 license fee.

Maine

4951

Pharmacist
Dept. of Professional & Financial Regulation
Div. of Licensing & Enforcement
Commission of Pharmacy
State House Station No. 35
Augusta, ME 04333
Phone: (207)582-8723

Credential Type: Pharmacist License. **Duration of License:** One year. **Requirements:** Good moral character. 21 years of age. U.S. citizenship. Graduate from an accredited first professional degree program of a college of pharmacy. Have 1500 hours of prior practical experience.

Renewal requires 15 hours of approved continuing pharmaceutical education each year. **Examination:** National Association of Boards of Pharmacy Licensure Examination (NABPLEX). **Reciprocity:** Yes. License by transfer granted to holders of a license in good standing from another state with requirements equivalent to those of Maine. Must pass an examination in jurisprudence. May be required to pass oral examination. **Fees:** $200 exam fee. $60 license renewal fee. $150 license transfer fee.

Maryland

4952

Pharmacist
Board of Pharmacy
4201 Patterson Ave.
Baltimore, MD 21215-2299
Phone: (301)764-4755

Credential Type: Pharmacist License. **Duration of License:** Two years. **Requirements:** Good moral character, temperate habits, and professional demeanor. 18 years of age. Graduate from an accredited first professional degree program of a college of pharmacy. Have 1500 hours of prior practical experience. Foreign graduates who are Foreign Pharmacy Graduate Examination Commission (FPGEC) certified and pass board examination may be licensed. **Examination:** National Association of Boards of Pharmacy Licensure Examination (NABPLEX). Federal Drug Law Examination (FDLE). **Reciprocity:** License by transfer granted to holders of a license in good standing from another state with requirements equivalent to those of Mary-

Pharmacist, continued

land. Must have 520 hours of practical experience after graduation. **Fees:** $240 exam fee. $10 initial license fee. $50 renewal fee. $150 license transfer fee.

Massachusetts

4953

Pharmacist
Board of Pharmacy
100 Cambridge St., Rm 1514
Boston, MA 02202
Phone: (617)727-7390

Credential Type: Pharmacist License. **Duration of License:** Two years. **Requirements:** Good moral character. 18 years of age. Graduate from an accredited first professional degree program of a college of pharmacy. Have 1500 hours of prior practical experience.

Renewal requires 30 hours of continuing pharmaceutical education every two years. Two hours of this requirement must be in Pharmacy Law, five hours in live programs, and no more than 10 hours may be credited through correspondence courses. **Examination:** National Association of Boards of Pharmacy Licensure Examination (NABPLEX). **Reciprocity:** Yes. License by transfer granted to holders of a license in good standing from another state with requirements equivalent to those of Massachusetts. **Fees:** $302 exam fee. $75 initial license fee. $75 renewal fee. $100 license transfer fee.

Michigan

4954

Pharmacist
Board of Pharmacy
611 W. Ottawa, 4th Fl.
PO Box 30018
Lansing, MI 48909
Phone: (517)373-0620

Credential Type: Pharmacist License. **Duration of License:** Two years. **Requirements:** Good moral character. 18 years of age. Graduate from an accredited first professional degree program of a college of pharmacy. Have 1000 hours of prior practical experience. Intern registration required for experience validation. Foreign students must pass Foreign Pharmacy Graduate Equivalency Examination (FPGEE), an English test, and meet internship requirements to be licensed.

Renewal requires 30 hours of approved continuing pharmaceutical education every two years. **Examination:** National Association of Boards of Pharmacy Licensure Examination (NABPLEX). **Reciprocity:** Yes. License by transfer granted to holders of a license in good standing from another state with requirements equivalent to those of Michigan. Must pass an examination in jurisprudence. **Fees:** $244 exam fee. $20.00 license renewal fee. $60 controlled substances permit fee. $100 controlled substances permit biennial renewal. $60 license transfer fee.

Credential Type: Temporary License. **Duration of License:** One year. **Requirements:** Issued to applicant working on updating lapsed Pharmacist License. Non-renewable.

Credential Type: Limited License. **Requirements:** Issued to foreign graduates wishing to gain internship hours. Must pass FPGEE test and pass English examination. **Examination:** FPGEE exam. English exam.

4955

Pharmacy Intern
Board of Pharmacy
611 W. Ottawa, 4th Fl.
PO Box 30018
Lansing, MI 48909
Phone: (517)373-0620

Credential Type: Pharmacy Intern Registration. **Duration of License:** One year. **Requirements:** Submit application and pay fees. **Fees:** $35 initial registration. $15 annual renewal.

Minnesota

4956

Pharmacist
Board of Pharmacy
2700 University Ave. W., No. 107
St. Paul, MN 55114-1079
Phone: (612)642-0541

Credential Type: Pharmacist License. **Duration of License:** One year. **Requirements:** Good moral character. 21 years of age. Graduate from an accredited first professional degree program of a college of pharmacy. Have 1500 hours of prior practical experience in either hospital pharmacy or retail pharmacy licensed by the board. Pass internship competency examination. Foreign graduates who are Foreign Pharmacy Graduate Examination Commission (FPGEC) certified, pass board examination, and meet practical experience requirements may be licensed.

Renewal requires 30 hours of accredited continuing pharmaceutical education every two years. **Examination:** National Association of Boards of Pharmacy Licensure Examination (NABPLEX). Federal Drug Law Examination (FDLE). **Reciprocity:** Yes. License by transfer granted to holders of a license in good standing from another state with requirements equivalent to those of Minnesota. Must pass an examination in jurisprudence. Must have held a valid pharmacist license for at least one year to be eligible. **Fees:** $200 exam fee. $65 initial license fee. $65 renewal fee. $165 license transfer fee.

4957

Pharmacy Intern
Board of Pharmacy
2700 University Ave. W., No. 107
St. Paul, MN 55114-1079
Phone: (612)642-0541

Credential Type: Pharmacy Intern License. **Duration of License:** Intern duration. **Requirements:** Submit application and pay fee. **Fees:** $20 initial registration fee.

Mississippi

4958

Pharmacist
Board of Pharmacy
C & F Plaza, Ste. 1165
2310 Hwy. 80 W.
Jackson, MS 39204
Phone: (601)354-6750

Credential Type: Pharmacist License. **Duration of License:** Two years. **Requirements:** Good moral character. Graduate from an accredited first professional degree program of a college of pharmacy. Have 1500 hours of prior practical experience in either hospital pharmacy or retail pharmacy licensed by the board. Board may approve special externship or internship program.

Renewal requires 20 hours (2.0 CEUs) of approved continuing education every two years. **Examination:** National Association of Boards of Pharmacy Licensure Examination (NABPLEX). **Reciprocity:** Yes. License by transfer granted to holders of a license in good standing from another state with requirements equivalent to those of Mississippi. Must pass an examination in jurisprudence. May be required to take oral examination. **Fees:** $175 exam fee. $70 initial license fee. $70 renewal fee. $70 license transfer fee.

4959

Pharmacy Intern
Board of Pharmacy
C & F Plaza, Ste. 1165
2310 Hwy. 80 W.
Jackson, MS 39204
Phone: (601)354-6750

Credential Type: Pharmacy Intern Registration. **Duration of License:** Four years or until licensed as a pharmacist. **Requirements:** Submit application and pay fee. **Fees:** $50 initial registration fee.

Missouri

4960

Pharmacist
Board of Pharmacy
PO Box 625
Jefferson City, MO 65102
Phone: (314)751-0091

Credential Type: Pharmacist License. **Duration of License:** One year. **Requirements:** Good moral character. 21 years of age. Graduate from an accredited first professional degree program of a college of pharmacy. Have 1500 hours of prior practical experience. Foreign graduates must have five years of education, pay filing fee, pass a test of spoken English, pass the Foreign Pharmacy Graduate Equivalency Examination (FPGEE) examination, and meet practical experience requirements. Foreign graduates must also submit a notarized Foreign Pharmacy Graduate Examination Commission (FPGEC) certificate, two photos, and proof of U.S. citizenship or visa.

Renewal requires 10 hours (1.0 continuing education unit (CEUs)) of continuing pharmaceutical education each year. **Examination:** National Association of Boards of Pharmacy Licensure Examination (NABPLEX). Federal Drug Law Examination (FDLE). **Reciprocity:** Yes. License by transfer granted to holders of a license in good standing from another state with requirements equivalent to those of Missouri. Must pass an examination in jurisprudence. Must have held a valid pharmacist license for at least one year to be eligible. **Fees:** $275 exam fee. $60 license renewal fee. $50 foreign graduate filing fee. $350 license transfer fee.

4961

Pharmacy Intern
Board of Pharmacy
PO Box 625
Jefferson City, MO 65102
Phone: (314)751-0091

Credential Type: Pharmacy Intern Registration. **Duration of License:** Five years. **Requirements:** Submit application.

Montana

4962

Pharmacist
Montana Board of Pharmacy
111 N. Jackson
Helena, MT 59620
Phone: (406)444-5436

Credential Type: License. **Duration of License:** One year. **Requirements:** Graduation from an accredited school of pharmacy. Completion of 1,500 hours of internship. **Examination:** NABPLEX examination. Jurisprudence examination. **Fees:** $175 exam fee. $60 license fee. $40 intern registration fee. $55 renewal fee. **Governing Statute:** Montana Code Annotated 37-7-301 through 37-7-324.

Nebraska

4963

Pharmacist
Nebraska Board of Examiners in Pharmacy
301 Centennial Mall S.
PO Box 95007
Lincoln, NE 68509
Phone: (402)471-2115

Credential Type: License. **Duration of License:** One year. **Requirements:** 21 years of age. Must be a graduate of an accredited school of pharmacy recognized by the board. Must have proof of internship under a licensed pharmacist. **Examination:** Yes. **Fees:** $150 initial pharmacist fee. $200 initial pharmacy fee. $150 establishment fee. $75 pharmacy renewal fee. $102 pharmacist renewal fee.

Nevada

4964

Pharmacist
Nevada State Board of Pharmacy
1201 Terminal Way, Ste. 212
Reno, NV 89502
Phone: (702)322-0691

Credential Type: License. **Requirements:** Degree in pharmacy from an accredited school. 1,500 hours of internship. **Examination:** State and national exams. **Fees:** $40 application fee. $150 exam fee. $100 license fee. $100 renewal fee.

Credential Type: Pharmaceutical Technician License. **Requirements:** 18 years of age. High school degree or equivalent. Must have a job with a supervising pharmacist. **Fees:** $10 registration fee.

New Hampshire

4965

Pharmacist
Board of Pharmacy
Health & Human Services Bldg.
6 Hazen Dr.
Concord, NH 03301
Phone: (603)271-2350

Credential Type: Pharmacist License. **Duration of License:** One year. **Requirements:** Good moral character, temperate habits, and professional demeanor. 18 years of age. Graduate from an accredited first professional degree program of a college of pharmacy. Have 1500 hours of prior practical experience in either a hospital pharmacy or retail pharmacy approved by board. Special internship and externship programs may be approved by board. Pass examination.

Renewal requires 15 hours (1.5 continuing education units (CEUs)) of continuing education with a minimum of five hours (0.5 CEU) of didactic education. **Examination:** National Association of Boards of Pharmacy Licensure Examination (NABPLEX). **Reciprocity:** Yes. License by transfer granted to holders of a license in good standing from another state with requirements equivalent to those of New Hampshire. Must pass an examination in jurisprudence. Must hold a baccalaureate in pharmacy or PharmD from a college accredited by the American Council on Pharmaceutical Education (ACPE) and approved by the board. Must show proof of passing NABPLEX examination. **Fees:** $200 exam fee. $40 license renewal fee. $200 license transfer fee.

New Jersey

4966

Pharmacist
Board of Pharmacy
1100 Raymond Blvd.
Newark, NJ 07102
Phone: (201)648-2433

Credential Type: Registered Pharmacist. **Duration of License:** Two years. **Requirements:** 21 years of age. Bachelor of Science degree from an approved school or college of pharmacy. Good moral character. 1,000 hours of experience as a registered intern or extern under a certified preceptor. **Examination:** Written and practical exam. **Reciprocity:** Yes. **Fees:** $125 exam fee. $80 biennial registration fee. **Governing Statute:** NJSA 45:14. NJAC 13:39.

New Mexico

4967

Pharmacist
Board of Pharmacy
University Towers
1650 University Blvd. N.E., Ste. 400B
Albuquerque, NM 87102
Phone: (505)841-9102

Credential Type: Pharmacist License. **Duration of License:** One year. **Requirements:** Good moral character, temperate habits, and professional demeanor. Age of majority. Graduate from an accredited first professional degree program of a college of pharmacy. Have 1500 hours of prior practical experience. Special internship and externship programs may be approved by board. Intern registration required for experience validation. Foreign applicants must have graduated from an American Council on Pharmaceutical Education (ACPE)-accredited school.

Renewal requires 15 hours (1.5 continuing education units (CEUs)) of continuing education that is ACPE accredited each year. **Examination:** National Association of Boards of Pharmacy Licensure Examination (NABPLEX). **Reciprocity:** Yes. License by transfer granted to holders of a license in good standing from another state with requirements equivalent to those of New Mexico. Must pass an examination in jurisprudence. Must hold a baccalaureate in pharmacy or PharmD from a college accredited by the ACPE and approved by the board. **Fees:** $200 exam fee. $20 initial license fee. $35 inactive license renewal fee (resident). $100 active license renewal fee (resident and non-resident). $60 controlled substances permit. $200 license transfer fee.

4968

Pharmacy Intern
Board of Pharmacy
University Towers
1650 University Blvd. N.E., Ste. 400B
Albuquerque, NM 87102
Phone: (505)841-9102

Credential Type: Pharmacy Intern Registration. **Duration of License:** Intern duration. **Requirements:** Submit application and pay fees. **Fees:** $15 initial registration fee. $10 annual renewal fee.

New York

4969

Pharmacist
State Education Dept.
Div. of Professional Licensing Services
Cultural Education Center
Empire State Plaza
Albany, NY 12230
Phone: (518)474-3826

Credential Type: License. **Duration of License:** Three years. **Requirements:** Bachelor's Degree in pharmacy. 21 years of age. U.S. citizen or alien lawfully admitted for permanent residency. Six-months of supervised experience in pharmacy practice. **Examination:** Written, practical and professional law. **Fees:** $330 application fee. $155 renewal fee. **Governing Statute:** Title VIII Articles 130, 137 of the Education Law.

North Carolina

4970

Pharmacist
North Carolina Board of Pharmacy
PO Box H
Carrboro, NC 27510
Phone: (919)942-4454

Credential Type: License. **Duration of License:** One year. **Requirements:** Bachelor's or pharmacy degree from an accredited school or pharmacy. At least 1,500 hours of clinical work and up to a one-year internship, under the direct supervision of an approved pharmacist. Two references. **Examination:** Theoretical and practical. **Fees:** $250 exam fee. $65 renewal fee.

North Dakota

4971

Pharmacist
Board of Pharmacy
PO Box 1354
Bismarck, ND 58502-1354
Phone: (701)258-1535

Credential Type: Pharmacist License. **Duration of License:** One year. **Requirements:** Good moral character. 18 years of age. Graduate from an accredited first professional degree program of a college of pharmacy. Have 1500 hours of prior practical experience. Special internships and externships may be board approved. Intern registration required for experience validation. Foreign graduates who are Foreign Pharmacy Graduate Examination Commission (FPGEC) certified, pass board examination, and meet practical experience requirements may be licensed. **Examination:** National Association of Boards of Pharmacy Licensure Examination (NABPLEX). Federal Drug Law Examination (FDLE). **Reciprocity:** Yes. License by transfer granted to holders of a license in good standing from another state with requirements equivalent to those of North Dakota. Must pass an examination in jurisprudence. **Fees:** $245 exam fee. $25 initial license fee. $150 renewal fee. $150 license transfer fee.

4972

Pharmacy Intern
Board of Pharmacy
PO Box 1354
Bismarck, ND 58502-1354
Phone: (701)258-1535

Credential Type: Pharmacy Intern Registration. **Duration of License:** One year. **Requirements:** Submit application and pay fees. **Fees:** $10 initial registration fee (pre-pharmacy student). $100 annual registration fee (professional pharmacy internship).

Ohio

4973

Pharmacist
Board of Pharmacy
77 S. High St., 17th Fl.
Columbus, OH 43266-0320
Phone: (614)466-4143

Credential Type: Pharmacist License. **Duration of License:** One year. **Requirements:** Good moral character. 18 years of age. Graduate from an accredited first professional degree program of a college of pharmacy. Have 1500 hours of prior practical experience in either a hospital pharmacy or retail pharmacy licensed by the board. Board may approve up to 300 hours of practical experience for training received on a site other than a pharmacy. Intern registration required for experience validation. Foreign graduates who are Foreign Pharmacy Graduate Examination Commission (FPGEC) certified, pass board examination, pass test of spoken English, and meet practical experience requirements may be licensed.

Renewal requires 4.5 continuing education units (CEUs) of approved continuing pharmaceutical education every three years. **Examination:** National Association of Boards of Pharmacy Licensure Examination (NABPLEX). **Reciprocity:** Yes. License by transfer granted to holders of a license in good standing from another state at the discretion of the Board. **Fees:** $110 exam fee. $50 license renewal fee. $225 license transfer fee.

4974

Pharmacy Intern
Board of Pharmacy
77 S. High St., 17th Fl.
Columbus, OH 43266-0320
Phone: (614)466-4143

Credential Type: Pharmacy Intern Registration. **Duration of License:** One year. **Requirements:** Submit application and pay fees. **Fees:** $10 initial registration fee. $10 annual renewal fee.

Oklahoma

4975

Pharmacist
Oklahoma State Board of Pharmacy
4545 Lincoln Blvd., Ste. 112
Oklahoma City, OK 73105
Phone: (405)521-3815

Credential Type: License. **Duration of License:** One year. **Requirements:** Bachelor's degree in pharmacy from an accredited school or college. 1,500 hours of experience. 15 clock hours of continuing education through an accredited program. **Examination:** Pharmacist Registrant Examination. **Fees:** $100 license fee (plus cost of exam). $50 renewal fee. $30 intern license.

Oregon

4976

Pharmacist
Oregon Board of Pharmacy
800 NE Oregon St., Ste. 425
Portland, OR 97232
Phone: (503)731-4032

Credential Type: License. **Duration of License:** One year. **Requirements:** 18 years of age. Good moral character. Complete requirements for the first professional undergraduate degree as certified by an approved school or college of pharmacy. Complete an internship or other approved program. 15 hours of continuing education each year. **Examination:** Yes. **Fees:** $200 exam fee. $75 license fee. $75 renewal fee. **Governing Statute:** ORS 689.225 to 689.285.

4977

Pharmacy Intern
Oregon Board of Pharmacy
800 NE Oregon St., Ste. 425
Portland, OR 97232
Phone: (503)731-4032

Credential Type: License. **Duration of License:** Three years. **Requirements:** Complete the junior or third academic year of a course of study at an approved college or pharmacy. **Examination:** No. **Fees:** $30 license fee. $30 renewal fee. **Governing Statute:** ORS 689.245.

Pennsylvania

4978

Pharmacist
Board of Pharmacy
Transportation & Safety Bldg., 6th Fl.
PO Box 2649
Harrisburg, PA 17105-2649
Phone: (717)783-7157

Credential Type: Pharmacist License. **Duration of License:** Two years. **Requirements:** Good moral character. 21 years of age. Graduate from an accredited first professional degree program of a college of pharmacy. Have 1500 hours of prior practical experience in either a hospital pharmacy or retail pharmacy licensed by the board. Special internship and externship programs may be approved by the board. Internship registration required for experience validation. Foreign graduates must be Foreign Pharmacy Graduate Examination Commission (FPGEC) certified and pass state board examination to be licensed. **Examination:** National Association of Boards of Pharmacy Licensure Examination (NABPLEX). Federal Drug Law Examination (FDLE). **Reciprocity:** Yes. License by transfer granted to holders of a license in good standing from another state with requirements equivalent to those of Pennsylvania. Must pass an examination in jurisprudence. FDLE required of applicants licensed after April 1, 1983. **Fees:** $198.75 exam fee. $25 initial license fee. $120 renewal fee. $25 license transfer application fee. $73.75 license transfer fee.

4979

Pharmacy Intern
Board of Pharmacy
Transportation & Safety Bldg., 6th Fl.
PO Box 2649
Harrisburg, PA 17105-2649
Phone: (717)783-7157

Credential Type: Pharmacy Intern Registration. **Duration of License:** Six years. **Requirements:** Submit application and pay fee. **Fees:** $35 initial registration fee.

Rhode Island

4980

Pharmacist
Board of Pharmacy
3 Capitol Hill, Rm. 304
Providence, RI 02908
Phone: (401)277-2837

Credential Type: Pharmacist License. **Duration of License:** One year. **Requirements:** Good moral character. 18 years of age. Graduate from an accredited first professional degree program of a college of pharmacy. Have 1500 hours of prior practical experience in either a hospital pharmacy or retail pharmacy approved by board. Foreign graduates must pass Foreign Pharmacy Graduate Equivalency Examination (FPGEE) examination, a test of English, and meet internship requirements.

Renewal requires 15 hours (1.5 continuing education units (CEUs)) of approved continuing education each year, with a minimum of five hours of participation in live programs. **Examination:** National Association of Boards of Pharmacy Licensure Examination (NABPLEX). **Reciprocity:** Yes. License by transfer granted to holders of a license in good standing from another state with requirements equivalent to those of Rhode Island. Must pass an examination in jurisprudence. Must have full Foreign Pharmacy Graduate Examination Commission

Pharmacist, continued

(FPGEC) Certification or hold a baccalaureate in pharmacy or PharmD from a college accredited by the American Council on Pharmaceutical Education (ACPE) and approved by the board. **Fees:** $100 exam fee. $50 license renewal fee. $100 license transfer fee.

4981

Pharmacy Intern
Board of Pharmacy
3 Capitol Hill, Rm. 304
Providence, RI 02908
Phone: (401)277-2837

Credential Type: Pharmacy Intern Registration. **Duration of License:** One year. **Requirements:** Submit application and pay fees. **Fees:** $10 initial registration fee. $10 renewal fee.

South Carolina

4982

Pharmacist
South Carolina State Board of
 Pharmacy
PO Box 11927
Columbia, SC 29211
Phone: (803)734-1010

Credential Type: Pharmacist License. **Requirements:** Graduation from an approved school of pharmacy, plus 1,500 hours of experience as a pharmacy intern. **Examination:** Yes. **Fees:** $220 exam fee. $50 renewal fee.

Credential Type: Pharmacy Intern. **Requirements:** Acceptance to an approved school of pharmacy.

South Dakota

4983

Pharmacist
Board of Pharmacy
PO Box 518
Pierre, SD 57501-0518
Phone: (605)224-2338

Credential Type: Pharmacist License. **Duration of License:** One year. **Requirements:** Good moral character. 18 years of age. Physical examination. Graduate from an accredited first professional degree program of a college of pharmacy. Have 1500 hours of prior practical experience. Foreign graduates must be Foreign Pharmacy Graduate Examination Commission (FPGEC) certified and pass state board examination to be licensed.

Renewal requires 12 hours of approved continuing education annually. **Examination:** National Association of Boards of Pharmacy Licensure Examination (NABPLEX). **Reciprocity:** Yes. License by transfer granted to holders of a license in good standing from another state with requirements equivalent to those of South Dakota. Must have held pharmacy license for a minimum of one year, when that is a requirement of original state of licensure. **Fees:** $150 exam fee. $35 initial license fee. $35 renewal fee. $150 license transfer fee.

4984

Pharmacy Intern
Board of Pharmacy
PO Box 518
Pierre, SD 57501-0518
Phone: (605)224-2338

Credential Type: Pharmacy Intern Registration. **Duration of License:** Duration of work experience. **Requirements:** Submit application and pay fee. **Fees:** $10 registration fee.

Tennessee

4985

Pharmacist
Board of Pharmacy
Volunteer Plaza Bldg., 2nd Fl.
500 James Robertson Pky.
Nashville, TN 37243
Phone: (615)741-2718

Credential Type: License. **Requirements:** 21 years old. 1500 hours internship. Graduate of an accredited pharmacy college (B.S. or Pharm.D). 15 hours of continuing education for renewal. **Examination:** National licensing examination (NABPLEX). **Reciprocity:** Yes, except California and Florida. **Fees:** $68 Registration. $200 Examination. $68 Application.

Texas

4986

Pharmacist
Texas State Board of Pharmacy
8505 Cross Park, Ste. 110
Austin, TX 78754
Phone: (512)832-0661

Credential Type: License. **Duration of License:** One year. **Requirements:** Graduation from an accredited college of pharmacy. Internship of 1,500 hours in Board-approved internship program. Twelve hours of Board-approved continuing education per year for annual license renewal. **Examination:** National Association of Boards of Pharmacy Licensing Examination (NABPLEX). Texas jurisprudence examination. **Fees:** $250 exam fee. $45.50—$119.75 initial license fee (prorated). $86 renewal fee. **Governing Statute:** VACS 4542a-1, 22 TAC Part xv.

Utah

4987

Pharmacist and Pharmacy Intern
Dept. of Commerce
Div. of Occupational and
 Professional Licensing
160 E. 300 S.
PO Box 45802
Salt Lake City, UT 84145
Phone: (801)530-6628

Credential Type: License. **Duration of License:** Two years. **Requirements:** 21 years of age. Must have completed pre-professional college training and one quarter of 15 hours of training in professional pharmacy courses. **Examination:** Yes. **Fees:** $20 license fee. $15 renewal fee.

Credential Type: Pharmacist. **Duration of License:** Two years. **Requirements:** Must meet above requirements and be a graduate of an approved college of pharmacy. Must complete an internship. **Examination:** Yes. **Fees:** $90 license fee. $60 renewal fee. $90 controlled substance license fee. $50 controlled substance renewal fee.

Vermont

4988

Pharmacist
Board of Pharmacy
Pavilion Office Bldg.
Montpelier, VT 05602
Phone: (802)828-2363

Credential Type: License. **Duration of License:** Two years. **Requirements:** 18 years of age. Good moral character. Graduate of an approved school or college of Pharmacology. **Examination:** Yes. **Reciprocity:** Yes. **Fees:** $40 Application fee. $145 Exam fee. $30 Renewal. $2 Late fee. **Governing Statute:** Title 26, VSA Sections 2021-2064.

Virginia

4989

Pharmacist
Board of Pharmacy
1601 Rolling Hills Dr.
Richmond, VA 23229
Phone: (804)662-9911

Credential Type: License. **Duration of License:** One year. **Requirements:** Must have a professional degree from an approved school of pharmacy. Must have at least six months of practical experience in a pharmacy. **Examination:** Yes. **Fees:** $300 application fee. $20 renewal fee.

Washington

4990

Pharmacist
Board of Pharmacy
Dept. of Health
1300 Quince St. SE
Mail Stop EY-20
Olympia, WA 98504
Phone: (206)753-6834

Credential Type: Pharmacist License. **Duration of License:** One year. **Requirements:** Good moral character. 18 years of age. Graduate from an accredited first professional degree program of a college of pharmacy. Have 1500 hours of prior practical experience in either a hospital pharmacy or retail pharmacy approved by board. Special internship and externship programs may be approved by board. Internship registration required for experience validation. Foreign graduates must be Foreign Pharmacy Graduate Examination Commission (FPGEC) certified and pass state board examination to be licensed.

Renewal requires 15 hours (1.5 continuing education units (CEUs)) of professional continuing education annually. **Examination:** National Association of Boards of Pharmacy Licensure Examination (NABPLEX). Federal Drug Law Examination (FDLE). **Reciprocity:** Yes. License by transfer granted to holders of a license in good standing from another state with requirements equivalent to those of Washington. Must pass an examination in jurisprudence. **Fees:** $200 exam and license fee. $100 initial license fee. $105 renewal fee. $250 license transfer fee.

4991

Pharmacy Intern
Board of Pharmacy
Dept. of Health
1300 Quince St. SE
Mail Stop EY-20
Olympia, WA 98504
Phone: (206)753-6834

Credential Type: Pharmacy Intern Registration. **Duration of License:** One year. **Requirements:** Submit application and pay fees. **Fees:** $15 initial registration fee. $15 renewal fee.

4992

Pharmacy Preceptor
Dept. of Health
Board of Pharmacy
1300 SE Quince, EY-20
Olympia, WA 98504
Phone: (206)753-6834

Credential Type: Certification. **Duration of License:** Five years. **Authorization:** Required to ensure that preceptors are qualified to instruct pharmacy interns. **Requirements:** Be at least 19 years of age. Must be a United States citizen or registered alien. Have a B.S. in pharmacy and one year of practice. Must be employed in a Class A pharmacy. Recertification requires 15 hours of continuing education per year. **Fees:** No fees.

West Virginia

4993

Pharmacist
Board of Pharmacy
236 Capitol St.
Charleston, WV 25301
Phone: (304)348-0558

Credential Type: License. **Duration of License:** One year. **Requirements:** U.S. citizen. 18 years old. Graduate of an approved school. Nine months of internship (out of school). Never convicted of a felony. **Examination:** Yes. **Fees:** $255 Examination. $150 National Association of Boards of Pharmacy Licensure Examination (NABPLEX). $30 Renewal.

Wisconsin

4994

Pharmacist
Regulations and Licensing Dept.
Pharmacy Board
PO Box 8935
Madison, WI 53708-8935
Phone: (608)266-8609

Credential Type: License. **Requirements:** High school diploma. B.S. degree in pharmacy from an approved school. One year internship. 18 years of age. **Examination:** Written and practical exams. **Reciprocity:** Yes.

Wyoming

4995

Pharmacist
State Board of Pharmacy
1720 S. Poplar St., Ste. 5
Casper, WY 82601
Phone: (307)234-0294

Credential Type: License. **Duration of License:** One year. **Requirements:** U.S. citizen. Attained the age of majority. Complete a degree in pharmacy from an accredited college. Complete a 1500 hour internship program. Pass the examination. **Examination:** Yes. **Fees:** $200 License examination. $35 Renewal.

Photographers and Camera Operators

The following states grant licenses in this occupational category as of the date of publication: California, Connecticut, Delaware, Kansas, Kentucky, Montana, New Mexico, North Dakota, Ohio, South Dakota, Vermont, Virginia, Wisconsin.

California

4996

Photofinish Operator (Racetrack)
California Horse Racing Board
1010 Hurley Way, Ste. 190
Sacramento, CA 95825
Phone: (916)920-7178

Credential Type: License Registration.
Requirements: Submit application and fingerprint card. Pay fee. **Fees:** $75 registration fee.

4997

Video Operator (Racetrack)
California Horse Racing Board
1010 Hurley Way, Ste. 190
Sacramento, CA 95825
Phone: (916)920-7178

Credential Type: License Registration.
Requirements: Submit application and fingerprint card. Pay fee. **Fees:** $75 registration fee.

Connecticut

4998

Cameraman (Racetrack)
Connecticut Div. of Special Revenue
Russell Rd.
PO Box 11424
Newington, CT 06111-0424
Phone: (203)566-2756

Credential Type: License Registration.
Requirements: Submit application and fingerprint card. Pay fee. **Fees:** $5 registration fee.

4999

Photo Finish Operator (Racetrack)
Connecticut Div. of Special Revenue
Russell Rd.
PO Box 11424
Newington, CT 06111-0424
Phone: (203)566-2756

Credential Type: License Registration.
Requirements: Submit application and fingerprint card. Pay fee. **Fees:** $5 registration fee.

5000

Photographer (Racetrack)
Connecticut Div. of Special Revenue
Russell Rd.
PO Box 11424
Newington, CT 06111-0424
Phone: (203)566-2756

Credential Type: License Registration.
Requirements: Submit application and fingerprint card. Pay fee. **Fees:** $5 registration fee.

5001

T.V. Tech Cameraman (Racetrack)
Connecticut Div. of Special Revenue
Russell Rd.
PO Box 11424
Newington, CT 06111-0424
Phone: (203)566-2756

Credential Type: License Registration.
Requirements: Submit application and fingerprint card. Pay fee. **Fees:** $5 registration fee.

Delaware

5002

Photographer Assistant (Racetrack)
Delaware Harness Racing
   Commission
2320 S. DuPont Hwy.
Dover, DE 19901
Phone: (302)739-4811

Credential Type: License Registration.
Requirements: Submit application and fingerprint card. Pay fee. **Fees:** $5 registration fee.

5003

Photographer (Racetrack)
Delaware Harness Racing
   Commission
2320 S. DuPont Hwy.
Dover, DE 19901
Phone: (302)739-4811

Credential Type: License Registration.
Requirements: Submit application and fingerprint card. Pay fee. **Fees:** $15 registration fee.

Kansas

5004

Photo Finish Operator (Racetrack)
Kansas Racing Commission
3400 VanBuren
Topeka, KS 66611-2228
Phone: (913)296-5800

Credential Type: License Registration.
Requirements: Submit application and fingerprint card. Pay fee. **Fees:** $10 registration fee.

Photographers and Camera Operators

5005

Video Operator (Racetrack)
Kansas Racing Commission
3400 VanBuren
Topeka, KS 66611-2228
Phone: (913)296-5800

Credential Type: License Registration. **Requirements:** Submit application and fingerprint card. Pay fee. **Fees:** $10 registration fee.

Kentucky

5006

Film Patrol/Video Tape Operator and Projectionist (Racetrack)
Kentucky State Racing Commission
PO Box 1080
Lexington, KY 40588
Phone: (606)254-7021

Credential Type: Association Employee and Occupational License. **Requirements:** Submit application and fingerprint card. Pay fee. **Fees:** $10 license fee.

5007

Photo Finish Operator (Racetrack)
Kentucky State Racing Commission
PO Box 1080
Lexington, KY 40588
Phone: (606)254-7021

Credential Type: Association Employee and Occupational License. **Requirements:** Submit application and fingerprint card. Pay fee. **Fees:** $10 license fee.

Montana

5008

Photo Employee (Racetrack)
State of Montana Board of Horse Racing
Dept. of Commerce
1424 9th Ave.
Helena, MT 59620
Phone: (406)444-4287

Credential Type: License Registration. **Requirements:** Submit application and fingerprint card. Pay fee. **Fees:** $20 registration fee.

5009

Photo Manager (Racetrack)
State of Montana Board of Horse Racing
Dept. of Commerce
1424 9th Ave.
Helena, MT 59620
Phone: (406)444-4287

Credential Type: License Registration. **Requirements:** Submit application and fingerprint card. Pay fee. **Fees:** $20 registration fee.

New Mexico

5010

Film Employee (Racetrack)
New Mexico State Racing Commission
PO Box 8576, Highland Station
Albuquerque, NM 87198
Phone: (505)841-4644

Credential Type: License Registration. **Requirements:** Submit application and fingerprint card. Pay fees. **Fees:** $14 registration fee. $1 notary fee. $23 fingerprint card processing fee.

5011

Photo Employee (Racetrack)
New Mexico State Racing Commission
PO Box 8576, Highland Station
Albuquerque, NM 87198
Phone: (505)841-4644

Credential Type: License Registration. **Requirements:** Submit application and fingerprint card. Pay fees. **Fees:** $13 registration fee. $1 notary fee. $23 fingerprint card processing fee.

5012

Photo Operator (Racetrack)
New Mexico State Racing Commission
PO Box 8576, Highland Station
Albuquerque, NM 87198
Phone: (505)841-4644

Credential Type: License Registration. **Requirements:** Submit application and fingerprint card. Pay fees. **Fees:** $14 registration fee. $1 notary fee. $23 fingerprint card processing fee.

5013

Photographer (Racetrack Win Circle)
New Mexico State Racing Commission
PO Box 8576, Highland Station
Albuquerque, NM 87198
Phone: (505)841-4644

Credential Type: License Registration. **Requirements:** Submit application and fingerprint card. Pay fees. **Fees:** $21 registration fee. $1 notary fee. $23 fingerprint card processing fee.

North Dakota

5014

Photo Employee (Racetrack)
North Dakota Racing Commission
State Capitol Bldg.
Bismarck, ND 58505
Phone: (701)224-2210

Credential Type: License Registration. **Requirements:** Submit application and fingerprint card. Pay fee. **Fees:** $10 license fee. $10 duplicate license fee.

5015

Photo Manager (Racetrack)
North Dakota Racing Commission
State Capitol Bldg.
Bismarck, ND 58505
Phone: (701)224-2210

Credential Type: License Registration. **Requirements:** Submit application and fingerprint card. Pay fee. **Fees:** $10 license fee. $10 duplicate license fee.

Ohio

5016

Photographer (Thoroughbred and Quarter Horse Racing)
Ohio State Racing Commission
State Office Tower
77 S. High St., 18th Fl.
Columbus, OH 43266-0416
Phone: (614)466-2757

Credential Type: License Registration. **Requirements:** Submit application and fingerprint card. Pay fee. **Fees:** $25 registration fee.

South Dakota

5017

Photo Finish Employee (Horse Racing)
South Dakota Racing Commission
c/o 500 East Capitol
Pierre, SD 57501
Phone: (605)773-6050

Credential Type: License Registration. **Requirements:** Submit application and fingerprint card. Pay fee. **Fees:** $15 registration fee.

5018

Photographer (Horse Racing)
South Dakota Racing Commission
c/o 500 East Capitol
Pierre, SD 57501
Phone: (605)773-6050

Credential Type: License Registration. **Requirements:** Submit application and fingerprint card. Pay fee. **Fees:** $15 registration fee.

Vermont

5019

Photographer, Itinerant
Secretary of State Licensing and Registration
Pavilion Office Bldg.
Montpelier, VT 05602
Phone: (802)828-2363

Credential Type: License. **Duration of License:** One year. **Requirements:** Make application to Secretary of State. Local licenses may be required. **Examination:** No. **Reciprocity:** No. **Fees:** $10 Annual fee. **Governing Statute:** Title 32, VSA Sections 9002-9008.

Virginia

5020

Photo-Finish Camera Operator (Racetrack)
Virginia Racing Commission
PO Box 1123
Richmond, VA 23208
Phone: (804)371-7363

Credential Type: License Registration. **Requirements:** Submit application and fingerprint card. Pay fee. **Fees:** $10 registration fee.

5021

Video Patrol Personnel (Racetrack)
Virginia Racing Commission
PO Box 1123
Richmond, VA 23208
Phone: (804)371-7363

Credential Type: License Registration. **Requirements:** Submit application and fingerprint card. Pay fee. **Fees:** $10 registration fee.

Wisconsin

5022

Film Patrol Employee (Racetrack)
Wisconsin Racing Board
PO Box 7975
Madison, WI 53707-7975
Phone: (608)267-3291

Credential Type: License Registration. **Requirements:** Submit application and two sets of fingerprint cards. Pay fee. **Fees:** $50 registration fee. $20 duplicate license.

5023

Photo Finish Employee (Racetrack)
Wisconsin Racing Board
PO Box 7975
Madison, WI 53707-7975
Phone: (608)267-3291

Credential Type: License Registration. **Requirements:** Submit application and two sets of fingerprint cards. Pay fee. **Fees:** $50 registration fee. $20 duplicate license.

Physical and Corrective Therapy Assistants and Aides

The following states grant licenses in this occupational category as of the date of publication:

Alabama	Florida	Kansas	Nebraska	Ohio	South Carolina	Virginia
Alaska	Georgia	Maine	New Hampshire	Oklahoma	Tennessee	West Virginia
Arkansas	Idaho	Maryland	New York	Oregon	Texas	
California	Illinois	Massachusetts	North Carolina	Pennsylvania	Utah	
Delaware	Indiana	Mississippi	North Dakota	Rhode Island	Vermont	

Alabama

5024

Physical Therapist Assistant
Alabama State Board of Physical Therapy
777 S. Lawrence St., Ste. 220
Montgomery, AL 36104
Phone: (205)242-4064

Credential Type: License. **Duration of License:** One year. **Requirements:** Must ba a graduate of an approved program of physical therapy. **Examination:** Written examination. **Reciprocity:** Yes. **Fees:** $85 application fee. $95 examination fee. $40 renewal fee.

Alaska

5025

Physical Therapy Assistant
Dept. of Commerce and Economic Development
Div. of Occupational Licensing
State Physical Therapy and Occuapational Therapy Board
PO Box D
Juneau, AK 99811-0800
Phone: (907)465-2551
Fax: (907)465-2974

Credential Type: License by Credentials. **Duration of License:** Two years. **Requirements:** Applicant who is licensed as a physical therapy assistant in another state, if the requirements for licensure were substantially equal to those of Alaska, may be granted a license without examination. Have graduated from a school of physical therapy approved by the Council on Medical Education and Hospitals of the American Medical Association, or the American Physical Therapy Association. Submit scores from a National Physical Therapy examination directly from the American Physical Therapy Association or the Professional Examination Services. Have worked in physical therapy at least 300 hours in a given 15-month period within the 48 months immediately preceding the date of application. Submit professional reference from supervising physical therapist, physician, dean of physical therapy school, or instructor. **Fees:** $30 application fee. $100 license fee. **Governing Statute:** Alaska Statutes 08.84. Professional Regulations 12 AAC 54.

Credential Type: License by Examination. **Duration of License:** Two years. **Requirements:** Pass the National Physical Therapy examination. Have graduated from a school of physical therapy approved by the Council on Medical Education and Hospitals of the American Medical Association, or the American Physical Therapy Association. Submit professional reference from supervising physical therapist, physician, dean of physical therapy school, or instructor. **Examination:** National Physical Therapy examination. **Fees:** $30 application fee. $100 license fee. $80 examination fee. **Governing Statute:** Alaska Statutes 08.84. Professional Regulations 12 AAC 54.

Credential Type: Temporary Permit. **Duration of License:** Eight months. **Authorization:** Allows individual to practice while awaiting next examination or completing application for licensure by credentials. **Requirements:** Have graduated from a school of physical therapy approved by the Council on Medical Education and Hospitals of the American Medical Association, or the American Physical Therapy Association. Submit professional reference from supervising physical therapist, physician, dean of physical therapy school, or instructor. **Fees:** $30 application fee. $50 temporary permit fee. **Governing Statute:** Alaska Statutes 08.84. Professional Regulations 12 AAC 54.

Credential Type: Limited Permit. **Duration of License:** 120 days. **Requirements:** Be licensed to practice physical therapy in another state. Has not been previously denied a physical therapy license in the state. **Fees:** $30 application fee. $50 limited permit fee. **Governing Statute:** Alaska Statutes 08.84. Professional Regulations 12 AAC 54.

Arkansas

5026

Physical Therapist Assistant
Arkansas State Medical Board
PO Box 102
Harrisburg, AR 72432
Phone: (501)578-2448

Credential Type: License. **Duration of License:** One year. **Requirements:** Must be a graduate of college level associates degree (AA) program approved by the American Physical Therapy Association. **Examination:** Yes. **Fees:** $95 Examination, application and original license. $80 Repeat examinations. $10 Renewal. $5 Temporary permit.

5027

Therapy Technician (Masseur/Masseuse)
Arkansas State Board of Therapy Technology
2001 Laurel St.
Pine Bluff, AR 71601
Phone: (501)534-4734

Credential Type: License. **Requirements:** Graduate of an accredited school of therapy technology. **Examination:** Yes. **Fees:** $15

Therapy Technician (Masseur/Masseuse), continued

Written, oral and practical examinations. $50 Application (original license). $15 Renewal.

California

5028

Physical Therapist Assistant
Physical Therapy Examining Committee
1434 Howe Ave., Ste. 92
Sacramento, CA 95825-3291
Phone: (916)920-6373

Credential Type: License. **Requirements:** Meet one of the following sets of requirements: (1) Complete a training program in an approved physical therapist assistant school. (2) Receive military training, including completion of a basic hospital corps-member course and a formal physical therapist assistant course that includes a minimum of 550 hours of technical courses relating to physical therapy and 350 hours of supervised clinical experience. (3) Complete a combination of 30 semester units of training and 36 months of full-time work experience in physical therapy. (4) Complete 60 months of full-time work experience in physical therapy. (5) Complete any other acceptable combination of education, training, and experience. **Examination:** Written examination. **Fees:** $30 application fee. $50 fingerprint fee. $140 exam fee. $80 license fee. **Governing Statute:** Business and Professions Code, Chap. 5.7, Section 2655.

Delaware

5029

Physical Therapist Assistant
State Examining Board of Physical Therapy
Div. of Professional Regulation
O'Neill Bldg.
PO Box 1401
Dover, DE 19903
Phone: (302)739-4522

Credential Type: License. **Duration of License:** Two years. **Requirements:** Complete an approved program of education in physical therapy. Submit two professional references. Renewal requires completion of three continuing education units (CEUs) every two years. **Examination:** National Physical Therapists Examination. **Reciprocity:** Yes, provided home state has similar requirements for licensure or registration. **Fees:** $10 application fee. $125 exam fee. $79 endorsement fee.

Credential Type: Temporary License. **Duration of License:** Varies. **Authorization:** May practice only under the direction of a licensed physical therapist. **Requirements:** May be issued to four types of applicants: (1) Those eligible and waiting to take the examination. (2) Those requesting reciprocity. (3) Those engaged in a special project. (4) Those who have not yet completed the CEU requirements for renewal.

Florida

5030

Physical Therapist Assistant
Board of Physical Therapy Practice
Dept. of Professional Regulation
1940 N. Monroe St.
Tallahassee, FL 32399-0750
Phone: (904)487-3372

Credential Type: Physical Therapist Assistant License. **Duration of License:** Two years. **Requirements:** Be at least 18 years of age. Good moral character. Have an associate's degree, or equivalent, for physical therapis assistants from a course approved by the American Physical Therapy Association. Foreign graduates must have credentials equivalent to the associate's degree. **Examination:** Written examination. **Exemptions:** A license without examination may be issued to an applicant who has passed an examination before a similar, lawful, authorized examining board in physical therapy in another state, the District of Columbia, territory, or foreign country, if their standards are as high as those maintained in Florida. **Reciprocity:** The holder of a valid license in another state may be licensed to practice without examination, provided that state's licensing requirements are substantially equivalent to Florida's. **Fees:** $100 application fee (examination). $170 application fee (endorsement). $55 license fee. $55 renewal fee. **Governing Statute:** Florida Statutes, Chapter 486. Florida Administrative Code, Rules 21-MM.

Credential Type: Temporary Permit. **Duration of License:** One year maximum. **Requirements:** A temporary permit may be issued to an applicant who appears eligible for license by examination or endorsement. **Governing Statute:** Florida Statutes, Chapter 486. Florida Administrative Code, Rules 21-MM.

Georgia

5031

Therapeutic Recreation Technician
State Board of Recreation Examiners
Allied Health Fields Section
Professional Examining Boards
166 Pryor St., SW
Atlanta, GA 30303
Phone: (404)656-3921

Credential Type: Therapeutic Recreation Technician License. **Duration of License:** Two years. **Authorization:** Licensee must work under the supervision of a therapeutic recreation specialist or master therapeutic recreation specialist. **Requirements:** Meet one of the following criteria: (1) Baccalaureate degree in recreation from an accredited college or university. (2) Baccalaureate degree in a related field from an accredited college or university. Either six months of supervised work experience in therapeutic recreation, or five quarter hours or three semester hours in approved therapeutic recreation topics. (3) Associate degree in therapeutic recreation from an accredited college or university. (4) Associate degree in recreation from an accredited college or university. Either six months of supervised work experience in therapeutic recreation, or five quarter hours or three semester hours in approved therapeutic recreation topics. (5) Associate degree in a related field. Either one year of supervised work experience in therapeutic recreation, or 10 quarter hours or six semester hours in approved therapeutic recreation topics. (6) High school diploma or equivalency certificate. One year of supervised work experience in therapeutic recreation. Five continuing professional development units in approved therapeutic recreation topics. **Examination:** Therapeutic Recreation Technician License Examination. **Reciprocity:** No. **Fees:** $20 application fee. $40 exam fee. $50 renewal fee. **Governing Statute:** Official Code of Georgia Annotated 43-41.

Idaho

5032

Physical Therapy Assistant
Idaho State Board of Medicine
280 N. 8th St., Ste. 202
Boise, ID 83720
Phone: (208)334-2822

Credential Type: Certificate of registration. **Duration of License:** One year. **Requirements:** Good moral character. Graduate from an approved physical therapy assistant curriculum. **Examination:** Written examination. **Reciprocity:** License by endorsement may be granted without examination if applicant holds a current, valid license from another state, territory, or district of the United States that has similar requirements. **Fees:** Contact board for fees. **Governing Statute:** Idaho Code, Title 54, Chap. 37. IDAPA 22.E.

Credential Type: Temporary Registration. **Requirements:** Complete application for physical therapy assistant registration. Have personal interview with member of the board or designated individual. **Fees:** Contact board for fees. **Governing Statute:** Idaho Code, Title 54, Chap. 37. IDAPA 22.E.

Illinois

5033

Physical Rehabilitation Aide
Dept. of Public Aid
Bureau of Long Term Quality Care
201 S. Grand Ave. E.
Springfield, IL 62763-0001
Phone: (217)785-0545

Credential Type: Validation. **Duration of License:** No expiration date. **Requirements:** Be at least 18 years of age. Complete 24-hour basic rehabilitation aide training program. Meet one of the following sets of requirements: (1) Be a Certified Nurse Aide. (2) Complete one year of education in a curriculum leading to credentials as a Registered Nurse or Licensed Practical Nurse. (3) Be a Developmental Disability Aide. (4) Be a Basic Child Care or Habilitation Aide. **Fees:** No fees. **Governing Statute:** 89 Ill. Adm. Code, CHap. I 147.200.

5034

Physical Therapist Assistant
Illinois Dept. of Professional
 Regulations
320 W. Washington St.
Springfield, IL 62786
Phone: (217)782-8556

Credential Type: Physical Therapist Assistant License. **Duration of License:** Two years. **Requirements:** At least 18 years of age. Good moral character. Must graduate from a two-year, college level, physical therapy program approved by the Illinois Department of Professional Regulations. **Examination:** Physical Therapist Assistant Examination. **Reciprocity:** Yes, with current licensure in another state that has substantially equivalent requirements to those of Illinois. **Fees:** $134.40 examination fee. $25 initial license fee. $25 license by endorsement fee. $60 renewal fee. **Governing Statute:** The Illinois Physical Therapy Act, Illinois Revised Statutes 1991, Chapter 111.

Indiana

5035

Physical Therapist Assistant
Physical Therapy Committee
Health Professions Bureau
402 W. Washington St., Rm. 041
Indianapolis, IN 46204
Phone: (317)232-2960

Credential Type: Certificate to practice. **Duration of License:** Two years. **Requirements:** Graduation from a physical therapist's assistant program that is approved by the committee. **Examination:** Written examination. **Reciprocity:** License by endorsement may be granted. **Fees:** $50 exam fee. $50 endorsement fee. **Governing Statute:** Indiana Code 25-22.5.

Credential Type: Temporary certificate to practice. **Duration of License:** Expires when applicant becomes licensed or certified. **Authorization:** Provides temporary authorization to practice as a physical therapist's assistant under the supervision of a licensed physical therapist. **Requirements:** Graduation from a physical therapist's assistant program that is approved by the committee. Must have submitted application and received committee approval to take examination. **Fees:** $10 temporary permit fee. **Governing Statute:** Indiana Code 25-27-1-8.

Kansas

5036

Physical Therapy Assistant
State Board of Healing Arts
235 SW Topeka Blvd.
Topeka, KS 66603-3059
Phone: (913)296-7413

Credential Type: Physical Therapy Assistant Registration. **Duration of License:** Two years. **Requirements:** Graduation from high school. Complete an approved educational program for physical therapy assistants.

Renewal requires completion of at least 40 contact hours of continuing education during the preceding two years. **Examination:** Board-administered examination, or examination of the American Registry of Physical Therapists. **Fees:** $40 application fee. $30 renewal fee. $100 exam fee. **Governing Statute:** K.S.A. 65-2901 ff. K.A.R. 100-34-1 ff.

Credential Type: Temporary permit. **Duration of License:** Until exam results are recorded or license issued. **Requirements:** Issued to applicants who have met the qualifications for licensure, except passage of required examination, and who must wait for completion of next examination. Must have paid appropriate license fees. **Fees:** $15 temporary permit fee. **Governing Statute:** K.S.A. 65-2901 ff. K.A.R. 100-34-1 ff.

Maine

5037

Physical Therapist Assistant
Board of Examiners in Physical
 Therapy
Dept. of Professional and Financial
 Regulation
Div. of Licensing and Enforcement
State House Station 35
Augusta, ME 04333
Phone: (207)582-8723

Credential Type: License. **Requirements:** Contact licensing body for application information.

Maryland

5038

Physical Therapy Assistant
Board of Physical Therapy
 Examiners
4201 Patterson Ave., 316
Baltimore, MD 21215-2299
Phone: (410)764-4752

Credential Type: Physical Therapy Assistant License. **Duration of License:** Two years. **Requirements:** Graduate of an approved two-year educational program with an Associate degree with a major in physical therapy. **Examination:** National Licensing Examination for Physical Therapy Assistants. **Fees:** $125 application fee. $130 exam fee. $180 renewal fee.

Massachusetts

5039

Physical Therapist Assistant
Board of Registration of Allied
 Health Professionals
Div. of Registration
100 Cambridge St., 15th fl.
Boston, MA 02202
Phone: (617)727-3071

Credential Type: License. **Duration of License:** Two years. **Requirements:** Asso-

Physical Therapist Assistant, continued

ciate's degree and graduate of an approved training program. **Examination:** National Physical Therapy Examination (NPTE). **Reciprocity:** Yes, provided applicant meets Massachusetts standards. **Fees:** $179 license and examination fee. $50 renewal fee. $80 reciprocity fee.

Mississippi

5040

Physical Therapist Assistant
State Dept. of Health
Professional Licensure
PO Box 1700
2423 N. State St.
Jackson, MS 39215-1700
Phone: (601)987-4153
Phone: (601)960-7400
Fax: (601)960-7948

Credential Type: License. **Requirements:** Complete an approved physical therapist assistant program. Foreign education applicants must obtain a credential evaluation stating that applicant's education is substantially equivalent to an accredited physical therapy educational program. **Examination:** National Physical Therapist Examination. **Reciprocity:** Yes, based on passing a national exam. **Fees:** $100 application fee.

Credential Type: Temporary License. **Duration of License:** 60 days. **Requirements:** Must have applied for licensure and be eligible to take the national examination. Must take the next scheduled exam.

Nebraska

5041

Physical Therapist Assistant
Nebraska Board of Examiners in
  Physical Therapy
301 Centennial Mall St.
PO Box 95007
Lincoln, NE 68509
Phone: (402)471-2115

Credential Type: Certification. **Duration of License:** Two years. **Requirements:** 19 years of age. Must be a high school graduate. Must have graduated from an accredited school of physical therapy. **Examination:** Yes. **Fees:** $150 certification fee. $150 renewal fee.

New Hampshire

5042

Physical Therapist Assistant
Board of Registration in Medicine
Health and Human Services Building
6 Hazen Drive
Concord, Ne 03301
Phone: (603)271-1203

Credential Type: Physical Therapist Assistant License. **Duration of License:** One year. **Requirements:** Good moral character. Complete a Board-approved program in physical therapy in an accredited school. **Examination:** Examination as required by Board. **Reciprocity:** No. **Fees:** $25 license/application fee. $110 examination fee. $25 annual renewal fee.

New York

5043

Physical Therapy Assistant
State Education Dept.
Div. of Professional Licensing
  Services
Cultural Education Center
Empire State Plaza
Albany, NY 12230
Phone: (518)474-3279

Credential Type: License. **Duration of License:** Three years. **Requirements:** Associate's Degree or equivalent in a physical therapy assistant program. 18 years of age. **Examination:** Written. **Fees:** $95 application fee. $50 renewal fee. **Governing Statute:** Title VIII Articles 130, 136 of the Education Law.

North Carolina

5044

Physical Therapist Assistant
North Carolina State Examining
  Committee of Physical Therapy
2426 Tryon Rd.
Durham, NC 27705
Phone: (919)489-7814

Credential Type: License. **Duration of License:** One year. **Requirements:** High school diploma and completion of an accredited two-year program leading to an associate degree in physical therapy. **Examination:** Written. **Fees:** $50 application fee. $70 exam fee. $65 endorsement fee. $25 renewal fee.

North Dakota

5045

Physical Therapist Assistant
State Examining Committee of
  Physical Therapists
PO Box 69
Grafton, ND 58237
Phone: (701)352-0125

Credential Type: Registration. **Duration of License:** One year. **Requirements:** Graduate from a physical therapist assistant program approved by the American Physical Therapy Association, or from a comparable program in another country.

Renewal requires 25 contact hours of continuing education every two years. **Examination:** National examination. **Reciprocity:** Yes, provided state has substantially equal requirements and applicant has passed a recognized national examination. **Fees:** $50 application fee. $125 exam fee. **Governing Statute:** North Dakota Century Code 43-26. Administrative Rules, Title 61.5.

Credential Type: Temporary Registration. **Duration of License:** Three months. **Requirements:** Must have applied for registration and be eligible to take the national examination. **Governing Statute:** North Dakota Century Code 43-26. Administrative Rules, Title 61.5.

Ohio

5046

Physical Therapist Assistant
Ohio Occupational Therapy, Physical
  Therapy, and Athletic Trainers
  Board
77 S. High St., 16th Fl.
Columbus, OH 43266-0317
Phone: (614)466-3774

Credential Type: License. **Duration of License:** Two years. **Authorization:** Must work under the supervision of a licensed physical therapist. **Requirements:** Be at least 18 years of age. Complete a two-year physical therapist assistants program approved by the board. **Examination:** Written examination. Examination on state laws and rules. **Fees:** $75 license fee. $60 renewal fee. **Governing Statute:** Ohio Revised Code, Chap. 4755. Administrative Rules 4755-2101 et seq.

Oklahoma

5047

Physical Therapy Assistant
State Board of Medical Licensure
 and Supervision
PO Box 18256
Oklahoma City, OK 73154
Phone: (405)848-6841

Credential Type: License. **Duration of License:** One year. **Requirements:** Graduation from an approved program for physical therapy assistants. Three recommendations. **Examination:** American Physical Therapy Association Examination. **Fees:** $100 exam fee. $35 application fee. $25 renewal fee.

Oregon

5048

Massage Technician
Oregon Board of Massage
 Technicians
800 N. Oregon, 4th Fl.
Portland, OR 97232
Phone: (503)731-4064

Credential Type: License. **Duration of License:** Two years. **Requirements:** Must meet certain education requirements. Must have current first and cardio pulmonary resuscitation training. **Examination:** Yes. **Fees:** $80 exam fee. $100 license fee. $100 renewal fee. **Governing Statute:** ORS 687.011 to 687.991.

5049

Physical Therapist Assistant
Oregon State Physical Therapist
 Licensing Board
800 NE Oregon St., Ste. 407
Portland, OR 97232
Phone: (503)731-4047

Credential Type: License. **Duration of License:** One year. **Requirements:** 18 years of age. Graduation from an approved school for physical therapist assistants. **Examination:** Yes. **Fees:** $100 exam fee. $75 license fee. $35 renewal fee. **Governing Statute:** ORS 688.010 to 688.235.

Pennsylvania

5050

Physical Therapist Assistant
State Board of Physical Therapy
PO Box 2649
Harrisburg, PA 17105-2649
Phone: (717)787-8503

Credential Type: Physical Therapist Assistant Registration. **Duration of License:** Two years. **Authorization:** Must work under the direct supervision of a licensed physical therapist. **Requirements:** Apply for registration within 30 days from date of employment. **Fees:** $5 registration fee.

Rhode Island

5051

Physical Therapy Assistant
Board of Physical Therapy
Div. of Professional Regulation
Rhode Island Dept. of Health
3 Capitol Hill
Providence, RI 02908
Phone: (401)277-2827

Credential Type: Physical Therapy Assistant License. **Duration of License:** Two years. **Requirements:** Good moral character. At least 18 years of age. Foreign born must show proof of legal entry into U.S. Graduate from an accredited training program for physical therapy assistants that is approved by the board. Alternative requirements are available from the board. **Examination:** National examination by the American Physical Therapy Association or the Assessment Systems Inc. **Reciprocity:** Yes. **Fees:** $75 application fee. $30 renewal fee.

South Carolina

5052

Physical Therapist Assistant
South Carolina State Board of
 Physical Therapy Examiners
PO Box 11594
Columbia, SC 29211
Phone: (803)734-3184

Credential Type: Physical Therapy Assistant. **Requirements:** High school education or equivalent. Completion of an approved course of study for physical therapist assistants. **Examination:** Yes. **Fees:** $130 license fee. $30 renewal fee. $120 license by endorsement fee.

Tennessee

5053

Physical Therapy Assistant
Board of Occupational and Physical
 Therapists
283 Plus Park Blvd.
Nashville, TN 37247
Phone: (615)367-6243

Credential Type: License. **Duration of License:** Renewable every June 30 of odd-numbered year. **Requirements:** 18 years old. Approved assistant physical therapist program. Good moral character. **Examination:** Yes. **Reciprocity:** Yes. **Fees:** $60 Registration. $95 Examination. $25 Application. $50 Renewal.

Texas

5054

Physical Therapist Assistant
Texas State Board of Physical
 Therapy Examiners
3001 S. Lamar, Ste. 101
Austin, TX 78704
Phone: (512)443-8202

Credential Type: Physical Therapist Assistant License. **Duration of License:** One year. **Requirements:** Completion of an accredited physical therapist assistant program. **Examination:** Written. **Fees:** $60 application fee. $90 exam fee. $65 renewal fee. **Governing Statute:** VACS 4512e, 22 TAC 329.

Utah

5055

Massage Technician
Dept. of Commerce
Div. of Occupational and
 Professional Licensing
160 E. 300 S.
PO Box 45802
Salt Lake City, UT 84145
Phone: (801)530-6628

Credential Type: License. **Duration of License:** One year. **Requirements:** 18 years of age. Must not have been convicted of a felony within five years. Must present a diploma or credentials of up to 1,000 hours of study of massage. **Examination:** Yes. **Fees:** $75 license fee. $50 renewal fee.

Vermont

5056

Physical Therapist Assistant
Physical Therapist Registration
Pavilion Office Bldg.
Montpelier, VT 05602
Phone: (802)828-2363
Phone: (802)828-2390

Credential Type: License. **Duration of License:** Two years. **Requirements:** Good moral character. Graduate from an American Medical Association (AMA) or American Physical Therapy Association (APTA) approved program. **Examination:** Yes. **Reciprocity:** Yes. **Fees:** $125 Physical Therapist Assistant Exam. $35 Endorsement. $8 Renewal. **Governing Statute:** Title 26, VSA Sections 2151-2157.

Virginia

5057

Physical Therapist's Assistant
Virginia Board of Medicine
1601 Rolling Hills Dr.
Richmond, VA 23229
Phone: (804)662-9920

Credential Type: License. **Requirements:** 18 years of age. Must be a graduate of a two year college program for physical therapy assistants approved by the Board. **Examination:** Yes. **Fees:** $85 application fee.

West Virginia

5058

Physical Therapy Assistant
Board of Physical Therapy
Rt. 1, Box 306
Lost Creek, WV 26385
Phone: (304)745-4161

Credential Type: License. **Requirements:** 18 years old. Two year college level program approved by the American Physical Therapy Association (APTA), or foreign equivalent. **Examination:** Yes. **Fees:** $55 Application and License. $80 Examination. $25 Renewal.

Physical Therapists

The following states grant licenses in this occupational category as of the date of publication:

Alabama	District of	Iowa	Minnesota	New Mexico	Rhode Island	Washington
Alaska	Columbia	Kansas	Mississippi	New York	South Carolina	West Virginia
Arizona	Florida	Kentucky	Missouri	North Carolina	South Dakota	Wisconsin
Arkansas	Georgia	Louisiana	Montana	North Dakota	Tennessee	Wyoming
California	Hawaii	Maine	Nebraska	Ohio	Texas	
Colorado	Idaho	Maryland	Nevada	Oklahoma	Utah	
Connecticut	Illinois	Massachusetts	New Hampshire	Oregon	Vermont	
Delaware	Indiana	Michigan	New Jersey	Pennsylvania	Virginia	

Alabama

5059

Physical Therapist
Alabama State Board of Physical Therapy
777 S. Lawrence St., Ste. 220
Montgomery, AL 36104
Phone: (205)242-4064

Credential Type: License. **Duration of License:** One year. **Requirements:** Must be graduate of an approved program of physical therapy. **Examination:** Written examination. **Reciprocity:** Yes. **Fees:** $85 application fee. $105 examination fee. $60 renewal fee.

Alaska

5060

Physical Therapist
Dept. of Commerce and Economic Development
Div. of Occupational Licensing
State Physical Therapy and Occuapational Therapy Board
PO Box D
Juneau, AK 99811-0800
Phone: (907)465-2551
Fax: (907)465-2974

Credential Type: License by Credentials. **Duration of License:** Two years. **Requirements:** Applicant who is licensed as a physical therapist in another state, if the requirements for licensure were substantially equal to those of Alaska, may be granted a license without examination. Have graduated from a school of physical therapy approved by the Council on Medical Education and Hospitals of the American Medical Association, or the American Physical Therapy Association. Submit scores from a National Physical Therapy examination directly from the American Physical Therapy Association or the Professional Examination Services. Have worked in physical therapy at least 300 hours in a given 15-month period within the 48 months immediately preceding the date of application. Submit professional reference from supervising physical therapist, physician, dean of physical therapy school, or instructor. **Fees:** $30 application fee. $100 license fee. **Governing Statute:** Alaska Statutes 08.84. Professional Regulations 12 AAC 54.

Credential Type: License by Examination. **Duration of License:** Two years. **Requirements:** Pass the National Physical Therapy examination. Have graduated from a school of physical therapy approved by the Council on Medical Education and Hospitals of the American Medical Association, or the American Physical Therapy Association. Submit professional reference from supervising physical therapist, physician, dean of physical therapy school, or instructor. **Examination:** National Physical Therapy examination. **Fees:** $30 application fee. $100 license fee. $90 examination fee. **Governing Statute:** Alaska Statutes 08.84. Professional Regulations 12 AAC 54.

Credential Type: Temporary Permit. **Duration of License:** Eight months. **Authorization:** Allows individual to practice while awaiting next examination or completing application for licensure by credentials. **Requirements:** Have graduated from a school of physical therapy approved by the Council on Medical Education and Hospitals of the American Medical Association, or the American Physical Therapy Association. Submit professional reference from supervising physical therapist, physician, dean of physical therapy school, or instructor. **Fees:** $30 application fee. $50 temporary permit fee. **Governing Statute:** Alaska Statutes 08.84. Professional Regulations 12 AAC 54.

Credential Type: Limited Permit. **Duration of License:** 120 days. **Requirements:** Be licensed to practice physical therapy in another state. Has not been previously denied a physical therapy license in the state. **Fees:** $30 application fee. $50 limited permit fee. **Governing Statute:** Alaska Statutes 08.84. Professional Regulations 12 AAC 54.

Arizona

5061

Physical Therapist
Arizona State Board of Physical Therapy Examiners
1645 W. Jefferson, Rm. 410
Phoenix, AZ 85007
Phone: (602)542-3095

Credential Type: Physical therapist license. **Duration of License:** Two years. **Requirements:** Good moral character. Complete an accredited physical therapy education program. Pass a board-conducted examination. **Examination:** Board-conducted examination. **Fees:** $100 application fee. $125 examination fee. $75 renewal fee. **Governing Statute:** Arizona Revised Statutes, Title 32, Chapter 19.

Credential Type: License by endorsement. **Duration of License:** Two years. **Requirements:** Hold an active physical therapist license issued by a state or territory having licensing requirements similar to those of Arizona. Has graduated from an accredited physical therapy education program. If applicant has not practiced physical therapy in the past five years, applicant must demonstrate competency in the practice of physical therapy, or serve an internship, or take remedial courses as determined by the

Physical Therapist, continued

board. **Fees:** $100 application fee. $75 renewal fee. **Governing Statute:** Arizona Revised Statutes, Title 32, Chapter 19.

Credential Type: Temporary license. **Duration of License:** 120 days. **Requirements:** Must be seeking licensure in Arizona. Be a graduate of an accredited physical therapy education program and be currently licensed in another state. **Fees:** $100 application fee. $75 renewal fee. **Governing Statute:** Arizona Revised Statutes, Title 32, Chapter 19.

Arkansas

5062

Physical Therapist
Arkansas State Medical Board
PO Box 102
Harrisburg, AR 72432
Phone: (501)578-2448

Credential Type: License. **Duration of License:** One year. **Requirements:** Must be a graduate of an accredited school of physical therapy. **Examination:** Yes. **Fees:** $100 Written, oral and practical examinations plus application and original license. $85 Repeat examination. $10 Renewal. $5 Temporary permit.

California

5063

Physical Therapist
Physical Therapy Examining Committee
1434 Howe Ave., Ste. 92
Sacramento, CA 95825-3291
Phone: (916)920-6373

Credential Type: License. **Requirements:** Complete an approved physical therapist program. **Examination:** Written examination. **Fees:** $30 application fee (U.S. trained). $60 application fee (foreign educated). $50 fingerprint fee. $140 exam fee. $80 license fee. **Governing Statute:** Business and Professions Code, Chap. 5.7, Section 2655.

Colorado

5064

Physical Therapist
Physical Therapy Licensure
Dept. of Regulatory Agencies
Div. of Registrations
1560 Broadway, Ste. 670
Denver, CO 80202
Phone: (303)894-2440

Credential Type: License by Examination. **Requirements:** Must complete an approved physical therapy program accredited by the American Physical Therapy Association, or an equivalent program approved by the Director. Applicants educated outside the United States must provide evidence of having received appropriate education and training; and must hold an active, valid license or other authorization to practice physical therapy from an appropriate authority in the country where the foreign-trained applicant is practicing or has practiced. **Examination:** State-administered written examination. **Governing Statute:** Colorado Revised Statutes, Title 12, Article 41.

Credential Type: License by Endorsement. **Requirements:** Must possess an active, valid license in good standing from another state or territory of the United States. Must have graduated from an accredited program within the past two years and passed an examination substantially equivalent to Colorado's examination; or have practiced as a registered or licensed physical therapist for at least two of the five previous years; or, if applicant has not practiced for at least two of the five previous years, must have passed an examination substantially equivalent to Colorado's examination and have demonstrated competency by completing an internship; if applicant has not passed such an examination, then applicant must pass state exam and complete internship. **Fees:** $94 application fee. **Governing Statute:** Colorado Revised Statutes, Title 12, Article 41.

Credential Type: Temporary Permit. **Duration of License:** Until examination. **Authorization:** May be issued to an applicant for licensure by examination. Authorizes practice under the personal and responsible supervision and direction of a licensed physical therapist. **Requirements:** Must be qualified to take examination. **Governing Statute:** Colorado Revised Statutes, Title 12, Article 41.

Credential Type: Temporary License. **Duration of License:** Four months. **Authorization:** May be issued to an applicant for licensure by endorsement. **Requirements:** Must have submitted application for state license and hold an active, valid license from another state or territory of the United States. **Governing Statute:** Colorado Revised Statutes, Title 12, Article 41.

Connecticut

5065

Masseur (Racetrack)
Connecticut Div. of Special Revenue
Russell Rd.
PO Box 11424
Newington, CT 06111-0424
Phone: (203)566-2756

Credential Type: License Registration. **Requirements:** Submit application and fingerprint card. Pay fee. **Fees:** $5 registration fee.

5066

Physical Therapist
Div. of Medical Quality Assurance
Health Systems Regulation Bureau
Health Services Dept.
150 Washington St.
Hartford, CT 06106
Phone: (203)566-3207

Credential Type: License. **Requirements:** Contact licensing body for application information.

Delaware

5067

Masseuse/Masseur
Committee on Massage and Bodywork Practitioners
Dept. of Administrative Services
Div. of Professional Regulation
PO Box 1401
Dover, DE 19903
Phone: (302)739-4522

Credential Type: License. **Requirements:** APP

5068

Physical Therapist
State Examining Board of Physical Therapy
Div. of Professional Regulation
O'Neill Bldg.
PO Box 1401
Dover, DE 19903
Phone: (302)739-4522

Credential Type: License. **Duration of License:** Two years. **Requirements:** Complete an approved program of education in physical therapy. Submit two professional references. Renewal requires completion of three continuing education units (CEUs) every two years. **Examination:** National Physical Therapists Examination. **Reciprocity:** Yes, provided home state has similar requirements for licensure or registration. **Fees:** $10 application fee. $125 exam fee. $79 endorsement fee.

Credential Type: Temporary License. **Duration of License:** Varies. **Authorization:** May practice only under the direction of a licensed physical therapist. **Requirements:** May be issued to four types of applicants: (1) Those eligible and waiting to take the examination. (2) Those requesting reciprocity. (3) Those engaged in a special project. (4) Those who have not yet completed the CEU requirements for renewal.

District of Columbia

5069

Physical Therapist
Board of Physical Therapy
Dept. of Consumer and Regulatory Affairs
Occupational and Professional Licensing Administration
PO Box 37200
Washington, DC 20013-7200
Phone: (202)727-7454

Credential Type: License. **Requirements:** Contact licensing body for application information.

Florida

5070

Personal Massage Therapist
Florida Board of Massage
Dept. of Professional Regulation
1940 N. Monroe St.
Tallahassee, FL 32399-0774
Phone: (904)488-6021

Credential Type: Personal Therapist License. **Duration of License:** Two years. **Requirements:** Be at least 16 years of age or posses a high school diploma or GED. Complete either a course of study at a board-approved massage school, or a board-approved apprenticeship program with a minimum of 500 classroom hours. **Examination:** Written and practical state examination. **Reciprocity:** License may be granted by endorsement. **Fees:** $175 license and examination fee. $100 renewal fee. $175 license by endorsement fee. **Governing Statute:** Florida Statutes, Chapter 480.

5071

Physical Therapist
Board of Physical Therapy Practice
Dept. of Professional Regulation
1940 N. Monroe St.
Tallahassee, FL 32399-0750
Phone: (904)487-3372

Credential Type: Physical Therapist License. **Duration of License:** Two years. **Requirements:** Be at least 18 years of age. Good moral character. Have a bachelor's degree, or equivalent, in physical therapy from a course approved by the American Physical Therapy Association. Foreign graduates must have credentials equivalent to the bachelor's degree. **Examination:** Written examination. **Exemptions:** A license without examination may be issued to an applicant who has passed an examination before a similar, lawful, authorized examining board in physical therapy in another state, the District of Columbia, territory, or foreign country, if their standards are as high as those maintained in Florida. **Fees:** $100 application fee (examination). $175 application fee (endorsement). $55 license fee. $55 renewal fee. **Governing Statute:** Florida Statutes, Chapter 486. Florida Administrative Code, Rules 21-MM.

Credential Type: Temporary Permit. **Duration of License:** One year maximum. **Requirements:** A temporary permit may be issued to an applicant who appears eligible for license by examination or endorsement. **Governing Statute:** Florida Statutes, Chapter 486. Florida Administrative Code, Rules 21-MM.

Georgia

5072

Physical Therapist
State Board of Physical Therapy
State Examining Boards
166 Pryor St., SW
Atlanta, GA 30303
Phone: (404)656-3921

Credential Type: License. **Requirements:** Contact licensing body for application information.

Hawaii

5073

Massage Therapist
Hawaii Board of Massage
Dept. of Commerce and Consumer Affairs
PO Box 3469
Honolulu, HI 96801
Phone: (808)548-8590

Credential Type: License. **Duration of License:** Six months. **Requirements:** Completion of 150 hours of study from a licensed institution. Completion of 420 apprenticeship training hours. **Examination:** Given four times per year. **Fees:** $25 application fee. $60 exam fee. $25 license fee. $15 $30 Compliance Resolution Fund fee. $25 renewal fee.

Credential Type: Apprentice Permit. **Authorization:** Must work under the supervision of a licensed massage therapist.

5074

Physical Therapist
Hawaii Board of Physical Therapy
1010 Richards St.
PO Box 3469
Honolulu, HI 96801
Phone: (808)548-8590

Credential Type: License. **Duration of License:** Six months. **Requirements:** Graduation from an accredited institution. **Examination:** Professional Examination Services or Assessment Systems, Inc. exam. **Fees:** $50 application fee. $150 exam fee. $30 license fee. $50 renewal fee. $30 temporary license fee. $15—$30 Compliance Resolution Fund fee.

Idaho

5075

Physical Therapist
Idaho State Board of Medicine
280 N. 8th St., Ste. 202
Boise, ID 83720
Phone: (208)334-2822

Credential Type: Certificate of registration. **Duration of License:** One year. **Requirements:** Good moral character. Graduate from an approved physical therapy curriculum. **Examination:** Written examination. **Reciprocity:** License by endorsement may be granted without examination if applicant holds a current, valid license from another state, territory, or district of the United States that has similar requirements. **Fees:** Contact board for fees. **Governing Statute:** Idaho Code, Title 54, Chap. 37. IDAPA 22.E.

Credential Type: Temporary Registration. **Requirements:** Complete application for physical therapist registration. Have personal interview with member of the board or designated individual. **Fees:** Contact board for fees. **Governing Statute:** Idaho Code, Title 54, Chap. 37. IDAPA 22.E.

Illinois

5076

Physical Therapist
Illinois Dept. of Professional
 Regulations
320 W. Washington St.
Springfield, IL 62786
Phone: (217)782-8556

Credential Type: Physical Therapist License. **Duration of License:** Two years. **Requirements:** At least 18 years of age. Good moral character. Must graduate from a physical therapy program approved by the Illinois Department of Professional Regulations. **Examination:** Physical Therapy Examination. **Reciprocity:** Yes, with current licensure in another state that has substantially equivalent requirements to those of Illinois. **Fees:** $144.70 examination fee. $25 initial license fee. $25 license by endorsement fee. $60 renewal fee. **Governing Statute:** The Illinois Physical Therapy Act, Illinois Revised Statutes 1991, Chapter 111.

Indiana

5077

Physical Therapist
Physical Therapy Committee
Health Professions Bureau
402 W. Washington St., Rm. 041
Indianapolis, IN 46204
Phone: (317)232-2960

Credential Type: License to practice. **Duration of License:** Two years. **Requirements:** Graduation from a physical therapy program that is approved by the committee. **Examination:** Written examination. **Reciprocity:** License by endorsement may be granted. **Fees:** $50 exam fee plus cost of exam. $50 endorsement fee. **Governing Statute:** Indiana Code 25-27.

Credential Type: Temporary license to practice. **Duration of License:** Expires when applicant becomes licensed. **Authorization:** Provides authorization to practice as a physical therapist under the supervision of a licensed physical therapist. **Requirements:** Graduation from a school or program approved by the committee. Must have submitted application and received approval from committee to take examination. **Fees:** $10 temporary permit fee. **Governing Statute:** Indiana Code 25-27-1-8.

Iowa

5078

Physical Therapist
Board of Physical and Occupational
 Therapy Examiners
Dept. of Public Health
Lucas State Office Bldg.
Des Moines, IA 50319
Phone: (515)281-6762

Credential Type: License. **Duration of License:** Two years. **Requirements:** Graduation from an accredited program. **Examination:** National Physical Therapy License Examination. Oral interview. **Reciprocity:** Physical therapists licensed in other states may apply for a license in Iowa through Interstate Endorsement. **Fees:** $55 application fee. $100 exam fee. $55 renewal fee.

Kansas

5079

Physical Therapist
State Board of Healing Arts
235 SW Topeka Blvd.
Topeka, KS 66603-3059
Phone: (913)296-7413

Credential Type: Physical Therapist Registration. **Duration of License:** Two years. **Requirements:** Complete an approved educational program for physical therapists.

Renewal requires completion of at least 40 contact hours of continuing education during the preceding two years. **Examination:** Board-administered examination, or examination of the American Registry of Physical Therapists. **Fees:** $40 application fee. $30 renewal fee. $115 exam fee. **Governing Statute:** K.S.A. 65-2901 ff. K.A.R. 100-34-1 ff.

Credential Type: Temporary permit. **Duration of License:** Until exam results are recorded or license issued. **Requirements:** Issued to applicants who have met the qualifications for licensure, except passage of required examination, and who must wait for completion of next examination. Must have paid appropriate license fees. **Fees:** $15 temporary permit fee. **Governing Statute:** K.S.A. 65-2901 ff. K.A.R. 100-34-1 ff.

Kentucky

5080

Physical Therapist
Kentucky State Board of Physical
 Therapy
400 Sherburn Ln., Ste. 248
Louisville, KY 40207
Phone: (502)588-4687

Credential Type: Physical Therapist Assistant License. **Requirements:** Completion of all didactic and clinical portions of an accredited associate degree level program in physical therapy. **Examination:** Yes.

Credential Type: Physical Therapist License. **Requirements:** Bachelor's degree in physical therapy from an accredited and approved program. **Examination:** Yes.

Louisiana

5081

Physical Therapist (School)
Louisiana State Dept. of Education
Teacher Certification
PO Box 94064
Baton Rouge, LA 70804
Phone: (504)342-3490

Credential Type: Provisional License. **Duration of License:** Two years (non-renewable). **Requirements:** Must hold a temporary license to practice physical therapy.

Credential Type: Certificate. **Duration of License:** Five years. **Requirements:** Must hold a valid state license to practice physical therapy. Two years of work experience as a physical therapist.

Maine

5082

Physical Therapist
Board of Examiners in Physical Therapy
Dept. of Professional and Financial Regulation
Div. of Licensing and Enforcement
State House Station 35
Augusta, ME 04333
Phone: (207)582-8723

Credential Type: License. **Requirements:** Contact licensing body for application information.

Maryland

5083

Physical Therapist
Board of Physical Therapy Examiners
4201 Patterson Ave., 316
Baltimore, MD 21215-2299
Phone: (410)764-4752

Credential Type: Physical Therapist License. **Duration of License:** Two years. **Requirements:** Graduate of a physical therapy program with a Bachelor's degree from an approved college or university. **Examination:** National Licensing Examination for Physical Therapists. **Fees:** $125 application fee. $150 exam fee. $200 renewal fee.

Massachusetts

5084

Physical Therapist
Board of Registration of Allied Health Professionals
Div. of Registration
100 Cambridge St., 15th fl.
Boston, MA 02202
Phone: (617)727-3071

Credential Type: License. **Duration of License:** Two years. **Requirements:** Postbaccalaureate degree and graduate of an approved training program. **Examination:** National Physical Therapy Examination (NPTE). **Reciprocity:** Yes, provided applicant meets Massachusetts standards. **Fees:** $189 license and examination fee. $25 renewal fee. $80 reciprocity fee.

Michigan

5085

Physical Therapist
Board of Physical Therapy
Bureau of Occupational & Professional Regulation
Dept. of Commerce
PO Box 30018
Lansing, MI 48909
Phone: (517)373-7902

Credential Type: License. **Duration of License:** Two years. **Requirements:** At least 18 years of age. Graduated from a program in physical therapy at a Board-approved school. Be of good moral character. Working knowledge of the English language. Abide by the rules and regulations of the Board. **Examination:** Written exam and Michigan Jurisprudence exam. **Reciprocity:** Licensed physical therapists from other states may be licensed in Michigan without examination if they meet the educational requirements of the Board and if they have passed an examination approved by the Board. However, applicants are still required to take and pass the Michigan Jurisprudence examination. **Fees:** $20 application processing fee. $115 initial exam fee ($100 National exam, $25 Jurisprudence exam). $20 exam review fee. $25 initial license fee, per year. $25 renewal license fee, per year. $70 reciprocity fee. $20 temporary license fee. $25 limited license fee, per year. **Governing Statute:** Public Health Code, Act 368 of 1978, as amended.

Minnesota

5086

Physical Therapist
Physical Therapy Advisory Council
State Board of Medical Practice
2700 University Ave. W., Ste. 106
St. Paul, MN 55114-1080
Phone: (612)642-0538
Fax: (612)642-0393

Credential Type: Registration. **Duration of License:** One year. **Requirements:** Complete an approved program of education in physical therapy.

Renewal requires completing 20 contact hours of continuing education every two years. **Examination:** National Physical Therapy Examination. **Reciprocity:** Yes, based on passing a national exam. **Fees:** $75 application fee. $35 registration fee. $110 exam fee. $35 renewal fee. **Governing Statute:** Minnesota Statutes 148.65 et seq. Board of Medical Practice Rules, Chaps. 5600 and 5601.

Credential Type: Temporary Permit. **Duration of License:** 90 days after next exam or board meeting. **Requirements:** Must meet all registration requirements. **Fees:** $10 temporary permit fee. **Governing Statute:** Minnesota Statutes 148.65 et seq. Board of Medical Practice Rules, Chaps. 5600 and 5601.

Mississippi

5087

Physical Therapist
State Dept. of Health
Professional Licensure
PO Box 1700
2423 N. State St.
Jackson, MS 39215-1700
Phone: (601)987-4153
Phone: (601)960-7400
Fax: (601)960-7948

Credential Type: License. **Requirements:** Complete an approved physical therapist program. Foreign education applicants must obtain a credential evaluation stating that applicant's education is substantially equivalent to an accredited physical therapy educational program. **Examination:** National Physical Therapist Examination. **Reciprocity:** Yes, based on passing a national exam. **Fees:** $100 application fee.

Credential Type: Temporary License. **Duration of License:** 60 days. **Requirements:** Must have applied for licensure and be eligible to take the national examination. Must take the next scheduled exam.

Missouri

Physical Therapist
State Board of Registration for the Healing Arts
Div. of Professional Registration
3605 Missouri Blvd.
PO Box 4
Jefferson City, MO 65102
Phone: (314)751-0098

Credential Type: License and registration. **Duration of License:** Permanent license and one year registration. **Requirements:** High school graduate. Complete a board-approved or American Medical Association accredited program of physical therapy education with a physical therapy degree that is the equivalent of a bachelor's degree. **Examination:** Written examination. **Reciprocity:** Yes, provideed applicant has fulfilled all scholastic and other requirements for licensure in Missouri. A foreign-educated physical therapist must present proof of eligibility for membership in the American Physical Therapy Association, including state licensure. **Fees:** $100 exam fee. $100 reciprocity license fee. $10 renewal fee. **Governing Statute:** Missouri Statutes, Rules and Regulations, Chap. 334.

Credential Type: Temporary license. **Duration of License:** Six months. **Requirements:** May be issued without examination at the discretion of the board. **Fees:** $10 temporary license fee. **Governing Statute:** Missouri Statutes, Rules and Regulations, Chap. 334.

Montana

Physical Therapist
Montana Board of Physical Therapy Examiners
111 N. Jackson
Helena, MT 59620
Phone: (406)444-3745

Credential Type: License. **Duration of License:** One year. **Requirements:** 18 years of age. Graduation from an accredited school of physical therapy. **Examination:** Written. **Fees:** $150 exam fee. $30 license fee. $50 renewal fee. **Governing Statute:** Montana Code Annotated 37-11-301 through 37-11-322.

Nebraska

Massage Therapist
Nebraska Board of Examiners in Massage Therapy
301 Centennial Mall S.
PO Box 95007
Lincoln, NE 68509
Phone: (402)471-2115

Credential Type: License. **Duration of License:** Two years. **Requirements:** 19 years of age. Must be a resident of Nebraska. Must be a graduate from an approved school of massage therapy. **Examination:** Yes. **Fees:** $200 examination fee. $200 establishment license fee. $150 massage school license fee. $150 license examination renewal fee. $150 massage establishment license renewal fee. $300 massage school license renewal fee.

Physical Therapist
Nebraska Board of Examiners in Physical Therapy
301 Centennial Mall S.
PO Box 95007
Lincoln, NE 68509
Phone: (402)471-2115

Credential Type: License. **Duration of License:** Two years. **Requirements:** 19 years of age. Must be a high school graduate. Must have graduated from an accredited school of physical therapy. **Examination:** Yes. **Fees:** $300 physical therapist license fee. $100 renewal fee.

Nevada

Physical Therapist
Nevada State Board of Physical Therapy Examiners
PO Box 81467
Las Vegas, NV 89180-1467
Phone: (702)876-5535

Credential Type: License. **Requirements:** Completion of a curriculum of physical therapy approved by the Board. **Examination:** State Board exam. **Fees:** $300 application fee. $40 fingerprint card. $150 renewal fee.

Credential Type: Physical Therapist Assistant License. **Requirements:** 18 years of age. High school diploma from an approved school. Completion of a curriculum for physical therapist's assistant approved by the Board. **Examination:** State Board exam. **Fees:** $200 application fee. $40 fingerprint card. $100 renewal fee.

New Hampshire

Massage Practitioner
Bureau of Health Facilities
Health and Human Services Bldg.
6 Hazen Drive
Concord, NH 03301
Phone: (603)271-4592
Fax: (603)271-3745

Credential Type: Massage Practitioner License. **Duration of License:** Two years. **Requirements:** At least 18 years of age. Good moral character. Must have no record of conviction of sexually related crime or crime involving moral turpitude in the last 10 years prior to application. Submit a signed health certificate, which has been dated within 90 days of application, stating that applicant is in good physical and mental health. Complete a 750 hour course of study in specific content area. **Examination:** State examination. **Fees:** $100 application fee. $50 biennial renewal fee.

Physical Therapist
Board of Registration in Medicine
Health and Human Services Building
6 Hazen Drive
Concord, Ne 03301
Phone: (603)271-1203

Credential Type: Physical Therapist I License. **Duration of License:** One year. **Requirements:** At least 18 years of age. Good moral character. Complete a Board-approved program in physical therapy at an accredited school. **Examination:** Examination as required by Board. **Reciprocity:** No. **Fees:** $50 license/application fee. $125 examination fee. $25 annual renewal fee.

Credential Type: Physical Therapist II License. **Duration of License:** One year. **Requirements:** Hold a Physical Therapist I License and complete 60 more hours of continuing education in the Physical Therapy field. Renewal requires 20 hours of continuing education annually. **Reciprocity:** No. **Fees:** $50 license/application fee. $25 annual renewal.

New Jersey

5095

Physical Therapist
Board of Physical Therapists
1100 Raymond Blvd., Rm. 513
Newark, NJ 07102
Phone: (201)648-4033

Credential Type: Physical Therapist Assistant License. **Requirements:** Graduation from an accredited program for the education and training of physical therapist assistants. **Examination:** Written. **Reciprocity:** Yes. **Fees:** $60 registration fee. $110 exam fee. $100 license fee. $60 renewal fee. **Governing Statute:** NJSA 45:9-37. NJAC 13:39A.

Credential Type: Physical Therapist. **Requirements:** Graduation from an accredited program for the education and training of physical therapists. **Examination:** Written. **Reciprocity:** Yes. **Fees:** $60 registration fee. $125 exam fee. $100 license fee. $60 renewal fee. **Governing Statute:** NJSA 45:9-37. NJAC 13:39A.

New Mexico

5096

Massage Therapist
Massage Therapy Board
Dept. of Regulation and Licensing
PO Box 25101
Santa Fe, NM 87504
Phone: (505)827-7113

Credential Type: Massage Therapist License. **Duration of License:** Two years. **Requirements:** Be at least 18 years of age. Meet one of the following sets of requirements: (1) Complete an approved training program consisting of a minimum of 650 hours of supervised in-class massage therapy instruction, of which at least 100 hours are in anatomy and physiology and 250 hours are in basic massage therapy and related hands-on modalities. (2) Applicants with less than 650 hours of education may combine education and experience. Complete at least 300 hours of supervised in-class massage therapy instruction in an approved training program. Combined classroom hours and alternative qualifying experience must equal at least 100 hours in anatomy and physiology and 250 hours in basic massage therapy and related hands-on modalities. In addition, complete 350 hours of alternative qualifying experience, such as professional experience, apprenticeship training, clinical internship, or a previous health career. **Examination:** Written, practical, and jurisprudence examinations. **Fees:** $25 application fee. $100 license fee. $100 exam fee. **Governing Statute:** 61-12C-1 et seq. NMSA 1978. New Mexico Board of Massage Therapy Rules, Rule 92-1 et seq.

Credential Type: Provisional License. **Duration of License:** Expires 30 days after next scheduled exam. **Authorization:** Must work under direct supervision of a licensed massage therapist. **Requirements:** Must have submitted application and examination fee. Must be sponosred by a licensed massage therapist. **Governing Statute:** 61-12C-1 et seq. NMSA 1978. New Mexico Board of Massage Therapy Rules, Rule 92-1 et seq.

5097

Massage Therapy Instructor
Massage Therapy Board
Dept. of Regulation and Licensing
PO Box 25101
Santa Fe, NM 87504
Phone: (505)827-7113

Credential Type: Massage Therapy Instructor Registration. **Requirements:** Must be a licensed massage therapist in New Mexico. Complete at least two years experience in massage therapy. **Fees:** $10 registration fee. **Governing Statute:** 61-12C-1 et seq. NMSA 1978. New Mexico Board of Massage Therapy Rules, Rule 92-1 et seq.

5098

Physical Therapist
Physical Therapists' Licensing Board
Regulation and Licensing Dept.
PO Box 25101
725 St. Michael's Dr.
Santa Fe, NM 87504-5101
Phone: (505)827-7162

Credential Type: License. **Requirements:** Contact licensing body for application information.

New York

5099

Masseur/Masseuse
State Education Dept.
Div. of Professional Licensing
  Services
Cultural Education Center
Empire State Plaza
Albany, NY 12230
Phone: (518)474-5170

Credential Type: License. **Duration of License:** Three years. **Requirements:** High school diploma. Graduation from an approved school of massage. 18 years of age. U.S. citizen or an alien lawfully admitted for permanent residency. **Examination:** Written. **Fees:** $165 application fee. $50 renewal fee. **Governing Statute:** Title VIII Articles 130, 155 of the Education Law.

5100

Physical Therapist
State Education Dept.
Div. of Professional Licensing
  Services
Cultural Education Center
Empire State Plaza
Albany, NY 12230
Phone: (518)474-3279

Credential Type: License. **Duration of License:** Three years. **Requirements:** Bachelor's Degree in physical therapy or a Bachelor's Degree in a field of science plus a Master's Degree in physical therapy. 18 years of age. **Examination:** Written and practical. **Fees:** $330 application fee. $155 renewal fee. **Governing Statute:** Title VIII Articles 130, 136 of the Education Law.

North Carolina

5101

Physical Therapist
North Carolina State Examining
  Committee of Physical Therapy
2426 Tryon Rd.
Durham, NC 27705
Phone: (919)489-7814

Credential Type: License. **Duration of License:** One year. **Requirements:** Bachelor's degree in physical therapy or completion of a certificate program for students who held a bachelor's degree in another subject. **Examination:** Written. **Fees:** $65 application fee. $75 exam fee. $75 endorsement fee. $25 renewal fee.

North Dakota

5102

Massage Therapist
State Board of Massage
22 Fremont Dr. SW
Fargo, ND 58103
Phone: (701)235-9208

Credential Type: Registration. **Duration of License:** One year. **Requirements:** Graduate from a massage school accredited by the AMTA. **Examination:** State board examination. **Fees:** $150 registration fee. **Governing Statute:** North Dakota Century Code 43-21-01 et seq.

North Dakota

5103

Physical Therapist
State Examining Committee of Physical Therapists
PO Box 69
Grafton, ND 58237
Phone: (701)352-0125

Credential Type: Registration. **Duration of License:** One year. **Requirements:** Graduate from a physical therapist program approved by the American Physical Therapy Association.

Renewal requires 25 contact hours of continuing education every two years. **Examination:** National examination. **Reciprocity:** Yes, provided state has substantially equal requirements and applicant has passed a recognized national examination. **Fees:** $100 application fee. $125 exam fee. **Governing Statute:** North Dakota Century Code 43-26. Administrative Rules, Title 61.5.

Credential Type: Temporary Registration. **Duration of License:** Three months. **Requirements:** Must have applied for registration and be eligible to take the national examination. **Governing Statute:** North Dakota Century Code 43-26. Administrative Rules, Title 61.5.

Ohio

5104

Masseur/Masseuse
State Medical Board of Ohio
77 S. High St., 17th Fl.
Columbus, OH 43266-0315
Phone: (614)466-3934

Credential Type: Massage License. **Requirements:** High school graduate or equivalent. Complete a course of instruction at an approved school of massage of at least one year (600 clock hours). **Examination:** Basic Science Examination and appropriate limited branch portions of examination. **Fees:** $100 exam fee.

5105

Physical Therapist
Ohio Occupational Therapy, Physical Therapy, and Athletic Trainers Board
77 S. High St., 16th Fl.
Columbus, OH 43266-0317
Phone: (614)466-3774

Credential Type: License. **Duration of License:** Two years. **Requirements:** Be at least 18 years of age. Complete an education program approved by the board that includes at least 60 semester hours of general coursework and adequate instruction in courses as found in an accredited physical therapy program offered by a college or university. Complete all clinical education curriculum requirements.

Renewal requires 24 continuing units every two years. **Examination:** Written examination. Examination on state laws and rules. **Reciprocity:** Yes, by endorsement, provided state has substantially equal requirements and applicant has passed a recognized national examination. Must also take Ohio laws and rules exam. **Fees:** $75 license fee. $60 renewal fee. **Governing Statute:** Ohio Revised Code, Chap. 4755. Administrative Rules 4755-2101 et seq.

5106

School Physical Therapist
Teacher Education and Certification
State Dept. of Education
65 S. Front St., Rm. 1012
Columbus, OH 43266-0308
Phone: (614)466-3593

Credential Type: Provisional Pupil Personnel Certificate—Physical Therapy. **Requirements:** Recommendation of university official. Complete examination prescribed by the State Board of Education. Proof of education and experience in area of specialization. Baccalaureate degree and current license to practice physical therapy in the state of Ohio. **Examination:** Examination prescribed by the State Board of Education.

Oklahoma

5107

Physical Therapist
State Board of Medical Licensure and Supervision
PO Box 18256
Oklahoma City, OK 73154
Phone: (405)848-6841

Credential Type: License. **Duration of License:** One year. **Requirements:** Graduation from an approved school of physical therapy. Three recommendations. **Examination:** American Physical Therapy Association Examination. **Fees:** $150 exam fee. $50 application fee. $50 renewal fee.

Oregon

5108

Physical Therapist
Oregon State Physical Therapist Licensing Board
800 NE Oregon St., Ste. 407
Portland, OR 97232
Phone: (503)731-4047

Credential Type: License. **Duration of License:** One year. **Requirements:** 18 years of age. Graduation from an approved school of physical therapy. **Examination:** Yes. **Fees:** $100 exam fee. $75 license fee. $35 Renewal fee. **Governing Statute:** ORS 688.010 to 688.235.

Pennsylvania

5109

Licensed Physical Therapist (L.P.T.)
State Board of Physical Therapy
PO Box 2649
Harrisburg, PA 17105-2649
Phone: (717)787-8503

Credential Type: Physical Therapist License. **Duration of License:** Two years. **Requirements:** At least 20 years of age. Good moral character. Free from alcohol or drug addiction. Has not been convicted of a felony or has met board restrictions for previous offenders. Complete a board-approved educational program in physical therapy from an accredited institution that will award a baccalaureate degree upon completion. In addition, foreign graduates may be required to complete up to one year of supervised clinical training. **Examination:** State examination. **Reciprocity:** Out-of-state license holders who received their licenses from states with substantially equivalent requirements to those of Pennsylvania may qualify for a reciprocal license. License must be valid and the issuing state must extend reciprocity to licensees of Pennsylvania. **Fees:** $10 application fee. $95 examination fee.

Credential Type: Temporary License. **Duration of License:** Six months (Failure of examination will immediately cancel license.). **Authorization:** Allows temporary practice of physical therapy under the direct supervision of an on-site, licensed physical therapist who has been in practice for at least two years. **Requirements:** Must meet all requirements for licensure as a physical therapist, with the exception of having passed the examination.

Rhode Island

5110

Massage Therapist
Div. of Professional Regulation
Rhode Island Dept. of Health
3 Capitol Hill
Providence, RI 02908
Phone: (401)277-2827

Credential Type: Massage Therapist License. **Duration of License:** One year. **Requirements:** At least 18 years of age. Foreign born must show proof of legal entry into U.S. Graduate from a school approved by the American Massage Therapy Association or complete 1,000 hours of training in an approved program. **Reciprocity:** Yes. **Fees:** $25 license/application fee. $10 renewal fee.

5111

Physical Therapist
Board of Physical Therapy
Div. of Professional Regulation
Rhode Island Dept. of Health
3 Capitol Hill
Providence, RI 02908
Phone: (401)277-2827

Credential Type: Physical Therapist License. **Duration of License:** Two years. **Requirements:** Good moral character. At least 18 years of age. Foreign born must show proof of legal entry into U.S. Graduate from a physical therapy program that is approved by the board. **Examination:** Written examination. **Reciprocity:** Yes. **Fees:** $100 application fee. $30 renewal fee.

South Carolina

5112

Physical Therapist
South Carolina State Board of Physical Therapy Examiners
PO Box 11594
Columbia, SC 29211
Phone: (803)734-3184

Credential Type: Physical Therapist License. **Requirements:** High school education or equivalent. Graduation from an approved school of physical therapy. **Examination:** Yes. **Reciprocity:** Yes. **Fees:** $150 license fee. $35 renewal fee. $120 license by endorsement fee.

South Dakota

5113

Physical Therapist
State Board of Medical and Osteopathic Examiners
Dept. of Commerce and Consumer Affairs
1323 S. Minnesota Ave.
Sioux Falls, SD 57105
Phone: (605)336-1965

Credential Type: Physical Therapy Certification. **Duration of License:** One year. **Requirements:** High school graduate or equivalent. Graduation from an approved physical therapist program. Foreign trained physical therapists must have their education evaluated by an appropriate agency. **Reciprocity:** Yes. **Fees:** $150 application and certification fee. $25 renewal fee. $60 reciprocity fee.

Tennessee

5114

Physical Therapist
Board of Occupational and Physical Therapy Examiners
283 Plus Park Blvd.
Nashville, TN 37247
Phone: (615)367-6243

Credential Type: License. **Duration of License:** Renewable every June 30 of odd-numbered year. **Requirements:** 18 years old. Approved physical therapy academic program. Good moral character. **Examination:** Yes. **Reciprocity:** Yes, with restrictions. **Fees:** $60 Registration. $100 Examination. $35 Application. $50 Renewal.

Texas

5115

Massage Therapist
Massage Therapy Registration Program
Texas Dept. of Health
1100 W. 49th St.
Austin, TX 78756
Phone: (512)834-6616

Credential Type: License. **Duration of License:** One year. **Requirements:** Completion of a 300-hour course of instruction at a Texas Department of Health-registered massage therapy school; or completion of a 300-hour course of instruction by a Texas Department of Health-registered massage therapy instructor; or a combination of above. **Examination:** Written and practical. **Fees:** $53 application fee. $24 annual registration fee. **Governing Statute:** VACS 4512k, 25 TAC 141.

5116

Physical Therapist
Texas State Board of Physical Therapy Examiners
3001 S. Lamar, Ste. 101
Austin, TX 78704
Phone: (512)443-8202

Credential Type: Physical Therapist License. **Duration of License:** One year. **Requirements:** Completion of accredited curriculum in physical therapy education and 60 semester credits from a recognized college. **Examination:** Written. **Fees:** $60 application fee. $100 exam fee. $75 renewal fee. **Governing Statute:** VACS 4512e, 22 TAC 329.

Utah

5117

Physical Therapist
Dept. of Commerce
Div. of Occupational and Professional Licensing
160 E. 300 S.
PO Box 45802
Salt Lake City, UT 84145
Phone: (801)530-6628

Credential Type: License. **Duration of License:** Two years. **Requirements:** Must be a graduate of an approved school of physical therapy. **Examination:** Yes. **Fees:** $60 exam fee. $30 renewal fee.

Vermont

5118

Physical Therapist
Physical Therapist Registration
Pavilion Office Bldg.
Montpelier, VT 05602
Phone: (802)828-2363
Phone: (802)828-2390

Credential Type: License. **Duration of License:** Two years. **Requirements:** Good moral character. Graduate from an AMA or APTA approved program. **Examination:** Yes. **Reciprocity:** Yes. **Fees:** $125 Physical Therapist exam. $35 Endorsement. $8 Renewal. **Governing Statute:** Title 26, VSA Sections 2151-2157.

Virginia

5119

Physical Therapist
Virginia Board of Medicine
1601 Rolling Hills Dr.
Richmond, VA 23229
Phone: (804)662-9920

Credential Type: License. **Requirements:** 18 years of age. Must be a graduate of a school of physical therapy approved by the American Physical Therapy Association; or be a graduate of a school outside of the United States acceptable to the Board. **Examination:** Yes.

Washington

5120

Masseur/Masseuse/Massage Practitioner
Dept. of Health
Professional Licensing Services
1112 SE Quince
Olympia, WA 98504
Phone: (206)586-6351

Credential Type: Massage Practitioner License. **Duration of License:** One year. **Requirements:** At least 18 years of age. Complete a 500 hour course in a board approved massage school or complete a 500 hour approved apprenticeship program. Must have current first aid and CPR card and complete a four hour course in AIDS education. **Examination:** Written, oral, and practical examination. **Fees:** $80 (prorated) initial license fee. $60 written examination fee. $80 practical examination fee. $70 renewal fee.

5121

Physical Therapist
Dept. of Health
112 SE Quince
Olympia, WA 98504
Phone: (206)753-0876

Credential Type: Physical Therapist Certificate. **Duration of License:** One year. **Requirements:** At least 18 years of age. Baccalaureate degree in physical therapy from an approved school. **Examination:** Written examination. **Reciprocity:** Yes. **Fees:** $100 initial certificate fee. $90 examination fee. $70 renewal fee. $100 reciprocal certificate fee. $15 duplicate certificate fee.

5122

School Physical Therapist
Superintendent of Public Instruction
Professional Education and Certification
Old Capitol Bldg. FG-11
Seattle, WA 98504-3211
Phone: (206)753-6773

Credential Type: Initial Educational Staff Associate Certificate. **Duration of License:** Seven years. **Requirements:** Baccalaureate degree in physical therapy. Complete all course work (with exception of special projects or thesis) for a master's degree with a major in physical therapy. Valid Washington state license in physical therapy.

West Virginia

5123

Physical Therapist
Board of Physical Therapy
Rt. 1, Box 306
Lost Creek, WV 26385
Phone: (304)745-4161

Credential Type: License. **Duration of License:** One year. **Requirements:** U.S. citizen. 18 years old. Graduate of a recognized school of pharmacy. Nine months of internship, non-concurrent with school year. Never convicted of a felony. **Examination:** Yes. **Fees:** $255 Examination. $150 NABPLEX Examination. $30 Renewal

Wisconsin

5124

Physical Therapist
Regulations and Licensing Dept.
Medical Board
PO Box 8935
Madison, WI 53708-8935
Phone: (608)266-8609

Credential Type: License. **Requirements:** Graduation from an approved or accredited school of physical therapy. 18 years of age. **Examination:** Written.

Wyoming

5125

Physical Therapist
Wyoming State Board of Physical Therapy
Meridan Rte., Box 112
Cheyenne, WY 82009
Phone: (307)632-0391

Credential Type: License. **Duration of License:** One year. **Requirements:** Completion of an approved program of study. Good moral character. Pass the examination given by the Professional Examination Service. **Examination:** Yes. **Fees:** $190 Examinations. $50 License. $25 Renewal.

Physician Assistants

The following states grant licenses in this occupational category as of the date of publication:

Alabama	District of	Iowa	Minnesota	New Mexico	Rhode Island	Washington
Alaska	Columbia	Kansas	Mississippi	New York	South Carolina	West Virginia
Arizona	Florida	Kentucky	Missouri	North Carolina	South Dakota	Wisconsin
Arkansas	Georgia	Louisiana	Montana	North Dakota	Tennessee	Wyoming
California	Hawaii	Maine	Nebraska	Ohio	Texas	
Colorado	Idaho	Maryland	Nevada	Oklahoma	Utah	
Connecticut	Illinois	Massachusetts	New Hampshire	Oregon	Vermont	
Delaware	Indiana	Michigan	New Jersey	Pennsylvania	Virginia	

Alabama

5126

Physician's Assistant
Alabama Board of Medical
 Examiners
PO Box 946
Montgomery, AL 36102
Phone: (205)242-4116

Credential Type: Certificate. **Duration of License:** One year. **Requirements:** Successful completion of a training program sponsored by a four-year medical college or university. **Examination:** Board-administered examination. Written National Commission on Certification of Physician's Assistants examination. **Fees:** $200 application fee. $50 renewal fee.

5127

Surgeon's Assistant
Alabama Board of Medical
 Examiners
PO Box 946
Mongomery, AL 36102
Phone: (205)242-4116

Credential Type: Certificate. **Duration of License:** One year. **Requirements:** Must have successfully completed a training program at a four-year medical college. **Examination:** Yes. **Fees:** $200 application fee. $50 renewal fee.

Alaska

5128

Physician's Assistant
Alaska Div. of Occupational
 Licensing
3601 C St., No. 722
Anchorage, AK 99503
Phone: (907)561-2878

Credential Type: Physician's Assistant License. **Requirements:** Graduation from accredited PA program and current National Commission on Certification of Physician Assistants (NCCPA) certificate. Application must be made by supervising physician and PA, including plan of collaboration.

Arizona

5129

Physician's Assistant
Arizona Joint Board on Regulation of
 Physician's Assistants
1990 W. Camelback Rd., Ste. 401
Phoenix, AZ 85015
Phone: (602)255-3751

Credential Type: Physician's Assistant License. **Requirements:** Graduation from accredited PA program and National Commission on Certification of Physician Assistants (NCCPA) examination within six years preceding application. Interview, physical examination, mental evaluation, and oral competency examination may be required. PA applies for certification. Application, which includes job description, must be filed by physician to approve PA position. **Examination:** National Commission on Certification of Physician Assistants (NCCPA) examination.

Arkansas

5130

Physician's Assistant
Arkansas State Medical Board
PO Box 102
Harrisburg, AR 72432
Phone: (501)578-2448

Credential Type: Physician's Assistant License. **Requirements:** Graduation from accredited PA program and National Commission on Certification of Physician Assistants (NCCPA) examination; or current RN or LPN license and completion of a one year PA program in a board-approved hospital. Application must be made by PA and employing physician. Certificate is not valid for work with other physicians. **Examination:** National Commission on Certification of Physician Assistants (NCCPA) examination.

California

5131

Physician's Assistant
California Physician Assistant
 Examining Committee
Medical Board of California
1424 Howe Ave., No. 35
Sacramento, CA 95825
Phone: (916)924-2626

Credential Type: Physician's Assistant License. **Requirements:** Graduation from accredited primary care PA program. PA must apply for license and physician must apply for approval to supervise. **Examination:** National Commission on Certification of Physician Assistants (NCCPA) examination.

Colorado

5132

Physician's Assistant
Colorado Board of Medical
 Examiners
1560 Sherman St., Ste. 1300
Denver, CO 80202
Phone: (303)894-7690

Credential Type: Physician's Assistant License. **Requirements:** Graduation from accredited PA program or its equivalent. Application must be made by PA. Supervising physician must register with the board. **Examination:** National Commission on Certification of Physician Assistants (NCCPA) examination.

Connecticut

5133

Physician's Assistant
Connecticut Div. of Medical Quality
 Assurance
150 Washignton St.
Hartford, CT 06106
Phone: (203)566-7398

Credential Type: Physician's Assistant License. **Requirements:** Graduation from accredited PA program. Bachelor's degree and 60 hours of pharmacology education. **Examination:** National Commission on Certification of Physician Assistants (NCCPA) examination.

Delaware

5134

Physician's Assistant
Delaware Board of Medical Practice
O'Neil Bldg., 2nd Fl.
Federal & Court Systems
Dover, DE 19903
Phone: (302)739-4522

Credential Type: Physician's Assistant License. **Requirements:** Graduation from accredited PA program. **Examination:** National Commission on Certification of Physician Assistants (NCCPA) examination.

District of Columbia

5135

Physician's Assistant
District of Columbia Board of
 Medicine
605 G St. NW, Rm. 202-LL
Washington, DC 20001
Phone: (202)727-9794

Credential Type: Physician's Assistant. **Requirements:** Graduation from accredited PA program. License application must be made by PA. Job description, registration, and approval are handled separately. **Examination:** National Commission on Certification of Physician Assistants (NCCPA) examination.

Florida

5136

Physician's Assistant
Florida Board of Medicine
1940 N. Monroe St.
Tallahassee, FL 32399
Phone: (904)488-0595

Credential Type: Physician's Assistant. **Requirements:** Graduation from accredited PA program. Application must be made by PA and includes information about supervising physician. **Examination:** National Commission on Certification of Physician Assistants (NCCPA) examination.

5137

Physician's Assistant (Racetrack)
Florida Dept. of Business
Div. of Pari-Mutuel Wagering
Licensing Section
725 S. Bronough St.
Tallahassee, FL 32399-1037
Phone: (904)488-9161

Credential Type: License Registration Code 1016. **Requirements:** Must have a Health and Rehabilitative Services (HRS) license or a Department of Professional Regulation (DPR) license. Submit application and fingerprint card. Pay fee. **Fees:** $40 registration fee.

Georgia

5138

Physician's Assistant
Georgia Composite State Board of
 Medical Examiners
166 Pryor St. SW
Atlanta, GA 30303
Phone: (404)656-3913

Credential Type: Physician's Assistant License. **Requirements:** Graduation from accredited PA program. Interview may be required. PA applies for certification. Physician applies for approval to supervise and provides job description. **Examination:** National Commission on Certification of Physician Assistants (NCCPA) examination.

Hawaii

5139

Physician Assistant
Hawaii Board of Medical Examiners
1010 Richards St.
PO Box 3469
Honolulu, HI 96801
Phone: (808)548-4392

Credential Type: License. **Duration of License:** Six months. **Requirements:** Successful completion of the AMA-approved physician assistant training program. **Examination:** National certifying exam. **Fees:** $20 application fee. $25 license fee. $25—$50 Compliance Resolution Fund fee. $15 renewal fee.

Idaho

5140

Physician's Assistant
Idaho State Board of Medicine
280 N. 8th St., Ste. 202
Boise, ID 83720
Phone: (208)334-2822

Credential Type: Physician's Assistant License. **Requirements:** Graduation from accredited PA program. Baccalaureate degree. Application must be made by PA and physician and include job description, interview, and on-site inspection. **Examination:** National Commission on Certification of Physician Assistants (NCCPA) examination.

Illinois

5141

Physician's Assistant
Illinois Dept. of Professional
  Regulation
320 W. Washington St.
Springfield, IL 62786
Phone: (217)785-0820

Credential Type: Physician's Assistant License. **Requirements:** NCCPA examination. No person holding MD degree may apply. PA must apply for license. Physician must file notice of supervision. Renewal requires National Commission on Certification of Physician Assistants (NCCPA) certificate. **Examination:** National Commission on Certification of Physician Assistants (NCCPA) examination.

Indiana

5142

Physician's Assistant
Indiana Health Professions Service
  Bureau
Medical Licensing Board
One American Square, Ste. 1020
Indianapolis, IN 46282
Phone: (317)232-2960

Credential Type: Physician's Assistant License. **Requirements:** Graduation from accredited two-year PA program and a current National Commission on Certification of Physician Assistants (NCCPA) certificate. Application must be made by supervising physician and PA, including a job description.

Iowa

5143

Physician Assistant
Board of Physician Assistant
  Examiners
Dept. of Public Health
Lucas State Office Bldg.
Des Moines, IA 50319
Phone: (515)281-6762

Credential Type: License. **Duration of License:** Two years. **Requirements:** An applicant must have a minimum of 60 hours of undergraduate training prior to entering training to become a physician assistant. It is strongly recommended that a person also have health care experience of some sort. Most approved physician assistant programs award a bachelor's degree plus a certificate upon graduation. **Examination:** National Commission of Certification of Physician Assistants written and practical exam. **Fees:** $345 exam fee. $50 registration fee. $5 re-registration fee. $100 license fee. $100 renewal fee.

Kansas

5144

Physician's Assistant
Kansas State Board of Healing Arts
235 SW Topeka Blvd.
Topeka, KS 66603
Phone: (913)296-7413

Credential Type: Physician's Assistant. **Requirements:** Graduation from an accredited PA program or military experience that meets requirements of the medical board. Application is made by PA and must include the designation of the supervising physician. **Examination:** National Commission on Certification of Physician Assistants (NCCPA) examination.

Kentucky

5145

Physician Assistant
Kentucky Board of Medical
  Licensure
310 Whittington Pky., Ste. 1 B
Louisville, KY 40222
Phone: (502)429-8046

Credential Type: License. **Requirements:** Graduation from a program accredited by the Committee on Allied Health Education and the American Medical Association. Continuing education required. **Examination:** Yes.

Louisiana

5146

Physician's Assistant
Louisiana State Board of Medical
  Examiners
830 Union St., Ste. 100
New Orleans, LA 70112
Phone: (504)524-6763

Credential Type: License. **Duration of License:** One year. **Requirements:** 21 years of age. Graduation from an appointed physician assistant program. **Examination:** Yes. **Fees:** $155 exam fee. $25 renewal fee.

Maine

5147

Osteopathic Physician's Assistant
Board of Osteopathic Examiners
State House Station 142
Augusta, ME 04333
Phone: (207)289-2480

Credential Type: Osteopathic Physician's Assistant License. **Requirements:** Graduation from accredited PA program or passage of National Commission on Certification of Physician Assistants (NCCPA) examination and three years' experience. Application must be made by PA for certificate of qualification and by PA and physician for certificate of registration.

5148

Physician's Assistant
Maine Board of Registration in
  Medicine
State House Station 137
Augusta, ME 04333
Phone: (207)289-3601

Credential Type: Physician's Assistant. **Requirements:** Graduation from accredited PA program or current National Commission on Certification of Physician Assistants (NCCPA) certificate. Application must be made by PA for certificate of qualification and by PA and physician for certificate of registration.

Maryland

5149

Physician's Assistant
Maryland State Board of Physician
  Quality Assurance
4201 Patterson Ave.
Baltimore, MD 21215
Phone: (301)764-4777

Credential Type: Physician's Assistant License. **Requirements:** Graduation from accredited PA program. Application must be made by PA for certification and by physician for approval to supervise. Job description and interview required. **Examination:** National Commission on Certification of Physician Assistants (NCCPA) examination.

Massachusetts

5150

Physician's Assistant
Massachusetts Board of PA
　Registration
Div. of Registration
100 Cambridge St., Rm. 1609
Boston, MA 02202
Phone: (617)727-1753

Credential Type: Physician's Assistant License. **Requirements:** Graduation from accredited PA program. Physician must make application to medical board for approval to supervise. PA must make application to PA board for registration. Both boards require a list of duties to be performed by PA. **Examination:** National Commission on Certification of Physician Assistants (NCCPA) examination.

Michigan

5151

Physician's Assistant
Task Force on Physician's Assistants
Bureau of Occupational &
　Professional Regulation
Michigan Dept. of Commerce
PO Box 30018
Lansing, MI 48909
Phone: (517)373-7902

Credential Type: License. **Duration of License:** Two years. **Requirements:** At least 18 years of age. Be of good moral character. Graduate of an approved physician's assistant program or have equivalent education, training, and experience as prescribed by the Task Force. Working knowledge of the English language. Abide by the rules and regulations of the Task Force. **Examination:** The National Commission on Certification of Physician's Assistants (NCCPA) exam. **Reciprocity:** Reciprocity may be granted if a physician's assistant is legally recognized in another state which has requirements substantially equivalent to those of Michigan. **Fees:** $30 application processing fee. $350 initial exam fee (paid directly to NCCPA). $25 initial license fee, per year. $25 renewal fee, per year. $55 reciprocity fee. $35 temporary license fee. $25 limited license fee, per year. **Governing Statute:** Public Health Code, Act 368 of 1978, as amended.

Minnesota

5152

Physician Assistant
Board of Medical Practice
2700 University Ave. W., Ste. 106
St. Paul, MN 55114
Phone: (612)642-0538

Credential Type: Physician Assistant Registration. **Duration of License:** One year. **Requirements:** Graduation from program approved by board. Complete board-approved examination. PA must apply for registration. PA and supervising physician must apply jointly for approval of their practice agreement. PAs who have passed NCCPA examination, and have completed seven years' experience by August 1987, will be allowed to register. **Examination:** Yes. **Fees:** $100 registration fee. $30 supervisory agreement fee. $20 renewal fee. **Governing Statute:** Minnesota Statutes, Chap. 146-148, 319A. Minnesota Rules 5600-5615.

Mississippi

5153

Physician's Assistant
Mississippi State Board of Medical
　Licensure
2688-D Insurance Center Dr.
Jackson, MS 39216
Phone: (601)354-6645

Credential Type: Physician's Assistant. **Requirements:** Apply to physician for employment. Follow board guidelines.

Missouri

5154

Physician's Assistant
Missouri Board of Healing Arts
PO Box 4
Jefferson City, MO 65102
Phone: (314)751-0098

Credential Type: Physician's Assistant License. **Requirements:** Graduation from accredited PA program or hold a current National Commission on Certification of Physicians Assistants (NCCPA) certificate.

Montana

5155

Physician's Assistant
Montana Board of Medical
　Examiners
111 N. Jackson
Helena, MT 59620
Phone: (406)444-4284

Credential Type: Registration. **Duration of License:** One year. **Requirements:** Graduation from an approved physician's assistant program. Certification by the National Commission on Physician's Assistants. A utilization plan naming a licensed physician who will serve as a supervisor, and the duties to be performed by the assistant. Proof of insurability. **Examination:** National board exam. **Fees:** $50 application fee. $35 renewal fee. **Governing Statute:** Montana Code Annotated 37-20-101 through 37-20-303.

Nebraska

5156

Physician's Assistant
Nebraska Bureau of Examining
　Boards Physician Assistant
　Commitee
301 Centennial Mall S.
PO Box 95007
Lincoln, NE 68509
Phone: (402)471-2115

Credential Type: License. **Duration of License:** One year. **Requirements:** Must be a graduate of an accredited physician's assistant program. **Examination:** Yes. **Fees:** $50 application fee. $30 renewal fee.

Nevada

5157

Physician Assistant
Nevada State Board of Medical
　Examiners
PO Box 7238
Reno, NV 89510
Phone: (702)688-2559

Credential Type: License. **Duration of License:** Two years. **Requirements:** Graduation from an approved physician assistant program. Certification by the National Commission for Certification of Physicians' Assistants. **Examination:** State Board exam. **Fees:** $125 application fee. $100 registration fee.

New Hampshire

5158

Physician's Assistant
New Hampshire Board of Registration in Medicine
Health and Welfare Bldg.
6 Hazen Dr.
Concord, NH 03301
Phone: (603)271-1203

Credential Type: Physician's Assistant. **Requirements:** Graduation from accredited PA program and current National Commission on Certification of Physicians Assistants (NCCPA) certificate. Application must be made by PA and supervising physician. Interview required.

New Jersey

5159

Physician's Assistant
Division of Consumer Affairs
1207 Raymond Blvd.
Newark, NJ 07102
Phone: (609)292-4843
Phone: (201)504-6200

Credential Type: Physician's Assistant License. **Requirements:** Graduation from accredited PA program. PA must apply for license. **Examination:** National Commission on Certification of Physician Assistants (NCCPA) examination.

New Mexico

5160

Osteopathic Physician's Assistant
Board of Osteopathic Medical Examiners
PO Box 25101
Santa Fe, NM 87504
Phone: (505)827-7171

Credential Type: Osteopathic Physician's Assistant. **Requirements:** Graduation from accredited PA program. Current National Commission on Certification of Physician Assistants (NCCPA) certificate. PA must apply for registration and supervising physician must apply for approval.

5161

Physician's Assistant
New Mexico State Board of Medical Examiners
PO Box 20001
Lamy Bldg., 2nd Fl.
Santa Fe, NM 87504
Phone: (505)827-7363
Phone: (505)827-7317

Credential Type: Physician's Assistant Registration. **Duration of License:** One year. **Requirements:** Current NCCPA certificate and bachelor's degree in science, or two years' work experience as a certified PA. PA must apply for registration and supervising physician must apply for approval. **Fees:** $100 application fee. $25 renewal fee.

New York

5162

Physician's Assistant
State Education Dept.
Div. of Professional Licensing Services
Cultural Education Center
Empire State Plaza
Albany, NY 12230
Phone: (518)474-3279

Credential Type: License. **Duration of License:** Three years. **Requirements:** High school diploma. Completion of an approved program or training for physician's assistant or passing of the national certifying exam. **Examination:** Written and practical. **Fees:** $300 exam fee. $115 application fee. $45 renewal fee. **Governing Statute:** Title VIII Articles 130, 131-B of the Education Law.

North Carolina

5163

Physician's Assistant
North Carolina State Board of Medical Examiners
PO Box 26808
Raleigh, NC 27611
Phone: (919)876-3885

Credential Type: Registration. **Duration of License:** One year. **Requirements:** Completion of a two-year approved physician's assistant training program from an approved college. 18 years of age. Three recommendations. **Fees:** $100 application fee.

North Dakota

5164

Physician's Assistant
North Dakota State Board of Medical Examiners
418 E. Broadway, Ste. 12
Bismarck, ND 58501
Phone: (701)223-9485

Credential Type: Physician's Assistant License. **Requirements:** Pass examination. Application must be made by supervising physician and include a copy of the contract and a list of specific tasks to be delegated. **Examination:** National Commission on Certification of Physician Assistants (NCCPA) examination.

Ohio

5165

Physician's Assistant
Ohio State Medical Board
77 S. High St., 17th Fl.
Columbus, OH 43266
Phone: (614)466-3934

Credential Type: Physician's Assistant License. **Requirements:** Current National Commission on Certification of Physician Assistants (NCCPA) certificate. PA must apply for registration and supervising physician must apply for approval.

Oklahoma

5166

Physician's Assistant
Oklahoma State Board of Medical Licensure and Supervision
PO Box 18256
Oklahoma City, OK 73154
Phone: (405)848-2189

Credential Type: Physician's Assistant License. **Requirements:** Graduation from accredited PA program. Application must be made by PA and physician. Must include job description.

Oregon

5167

Physician Assistant
Oregon Board of Medical Examiners
620 Crown Plaza
1500 SW 1st Ave.
Portland, OR 97201
Phone: (503)229-5770

Credential Type: License. **Duration of License:** Two years. **Requirements:** Graduation from an approved physical assistant program. Must have the consent of a physician who will act as superviser. **Examination:** Yes. **Fees:** $175 license fee. $120 renewal fee. **Governing Statute:** ORS 677.495 to 677.550.

Pennsylvania

5168

Physician's Assistant
Pennsylvania State Board of Medicine
PO Box 2649
Harrisburg, PA 17105
Phone: (717)787-2381

Credential Type: Physician's Assistant License. **Requirements:** Graduation from accredited PA program. PA must apply for state certification. Supervising physician must register with board. Current NCCPA certificate required for renewal. **Examination:** National Commission on Certification of Physician Assistants (NCCPA) examination.

Rhode Island

5169

Physician's Assistant
Rhode Island Board of Registration for Physician Assistants
Health Dept.
Div. of Professional Regulation
75 Davis St.
Providence, RI 02908
Phone: (401)277-2827

Credential Type: Physician's Assistant License. **Requirements:** Graduation from accredited PA program. PA must apply for certificate of registration. No person holding an MD degree may apply. **Examination:** National Commission on Certification of Physician Assistants (NCCPA) examination.

South Carolina

5170

Physician's Assistant
South Carolina State Board of Medical Examiners
PO Box 12245
Columbia, SC 29211
Phone: (803)734-8901

Credential Type: Physician's Assistant License. **Requirements:** Graduation from accredited PA program. Current National Commission on Certification of Physician Assistants (NCCPA) certificate. Application must be made by PA and supervising physician. Interview and job description required.

South Dakota

5171

Physician's Assistant
South Dakota State Board of Medical and Osteopathic Examiners
1323 S. Minnesota Ave.
Sioux Falls, SD 57105
Phone: (605)336-1965

Credential Type: Physician's Assistant License. **Requirements:** Graduation from an accredited PA program. PA must apply for state certification, present job description, and appear for interview. Physician may be interviewed in person or by phone. **Examination:** National Commission on Certification of Physician Assistants (NCCPA) examination.

Tennessee

5172

Physician Assistant
Board of Medical Examiners
Committee on Physician Assistants
283 Plus Park Blvd.
Nashville, TN 37247
Phone: (615)367-6250

Credential Type: License. **Duration of License:** Two years. **Requirements:** Graduate of a physicians assistant training program. **Examination:** National Commission on the Certification of Physician Assistants. **Reciprocity:** Yes. **Fees:** $120 Registration. $60 Application.

Texas

5173

Physician's Assistant
Texas State Board of Medical Examiners
PO Box 13562, Capitol Station
Austin, TX 78711
Phone: (512)834-7728

Credential Type: Physician's Assistant License. **Requirements:** Graduation from accredited PA program. Application must be made by physician for approval to supervise.

Utah

5174

Physician Assistant
Dept. of Commerce
Div. of Occupational and Professional Licensing
160 E. 300 S.
PO Box 45802
Salt Lake City, UT 84145
Phone: (801)530-6628

Credential Type: License. **Duration of License:** Two years. **Requirements:** Must be a graduate of a physician assistant educational program approved by the Board Second Division. **Examination:** Yes. **Fees:** $100 license fee. $50 renewal fee. $30 change protocol only fee. $10 change physician only fee.

Vermont

5175

Physician's Assistant
Secretary of State
Licensing and Registration
Pavilion Office Bldg.
Montpelier, VT 05602
Phone: (802)828-2363

Credential Type: License. **Duration of License:** Two years. **Requirements:** High school education. One of the following: two years training in a school of nursing and one year training under a licensed physician; or, one year training in a medical school and one year experience under a licensed physician: or, two years training or experience under a licensed physician; or, successful completion of an acceptable program. **Examination:** No. Evaluation made by applicant and physician. **Reciprocity:** Yes. **Fees:** $50 Application. $15 Renewal. **Governing Statute:** Title 26, VSA Sections 1725-1729.

Virginia

5176

Physician's Assistant
Board of Medicine
1601 Rolling Hills Dr.
Richmond, VA 23229-5005
Phone: (804)662-9920

Credential Type: License. **Duration of License:** One year. **Requirements:** Must complete a course of study for physician's assistants approved and accredited by the Committee on Allied Health Education and Accreditation of the American Medical Association or other accrediting agencies approved by the Board. **Examination:** Yes. **Fees:** $50 application fee. $100 registration fee.

Washington

5177

Osteopathic Physician's Assistant
Washington Board of Osteopathic Medicine and Surgery
1300 Quince St., MS:EY-23
Olympia, WA 98504
Phone: (206)586-8438

Credential Type: Osteopathic Physician's Assistant License. **Requirements:** Graduation from a board-approved PA program. Must have current National Commission on Certification of Physician Assistants (NCCPA) certificate for Rx privileges.

5178

Physician's Assistant
Washington Board of Medical Examiners
1300 Quince St., MS:EY-25
Olympia, WA 98504
Phone: (206)753-2844

Credential Type: Physician's Assistant License. **Requirements:** Graduation from accredited PA program. Pass examination. Application must be made jointly by PA and physician. Must hold current NCCPA certification for Rx privileges. **Examination:** National Commission on Certification of Physician Assistants (NCCPA) examination.

West Virginia

5179

Physician Assistant
Board of Medicine
3412 Chesterfield Ave., SE
Charleston, WV 25304
Phone: (304)348-2921

Alternate Information: 100 Dee Dr., Charleston, WV 25311

Credential Type: License. **Duration of License:** One year. **Requirements:** Graduate of an approved physician assistant program. Never convicted of a felony. **Examination:** Yes. **Fees:** $50 Application. $5 Renewal.

Wisconsin

5180

Physician's Assistant
Wisconsin Medical Examining Board
PO Box 8935
Madison, WI 53708
Phone: (608)266-2811

Credential Type: Physician's Assistant License. **Requirements:** Graduation from an accredited PA program. PA must apply for state certification. **Examination:** National Commission on Certification of Physician Assistants (NCCPA) examination.

Wyoming

5181

Physician Assistant
State Board of Medical Examiners
Barrett Bldg.
2301 Central Ave.
Cheyenne, WY 82002
Phone: (307)777-6463

Credential Type: License. **Duration of License:** One year. **Requirements:** Graduate from an approved program of study. Complete a proficiency examination. Provide a written protocol. Appear for a personal interview. **Examination:** Yes. **Fees:** $25 Application. $10 Sponsor. $5 Renewal.

Physicians

One or more occupations in this chapter require a federal license. Additionally, the following states grant licenses as of the date of publication:

Alabama	District of	Iowa	Minnesota	New Mexico	Rhode Island	Washington
Alaska	Columbia	Kansas	Mississippi	New York	South Carolina	West Virginia
Arizona	Florida	Kentucky	Missouri	North Carolina	South Dakota	Wisconsin
Arkansas	Georgia	Louisiana	Montana	North Dakota	Tennessee	Wyoming
California	Hawaii	Maine	Nebraska	Ohio	Texas	
Colorado	Idaho	Maryland	Nevada	Oklahoma	Utah	
Connecticut	Illinois	Massachusetts	New Hampshire	Oregon	Vermont	
Delaware	Indiana	Michigan	New Jersey	Pennsylvania	Virginia	

Federal Licenses

5182

Ship's Doctor
U.S. Dept. of Transportation
U.S. Coast Guard
2100 Second St., SW
Washington, DC 20593
Phone: (202)267-0218

Credential Type: Medical Doctor License. **Duration of License:** Five years. **Authorization:** License may contain restrictions as to vessel type, tonnage, means of propulsion, horsepower, or water upon which service is authorized. **Requirements:** Must hold or apply for a merchant mariner's document. Must hold a valid license as physician or surgeon issued by a state or territory of the United States, Puerto Rico, or the District of Columbia. **Governing Statute:** 46 CFR Chap. 1, Part 10.

Alabama

5183

Doctor of Medicine of Osteopathy
Board of Medical Examiners
PO Box 946
Montgomery, AL 36102
Phone: (205)242-4116

Credential Type: License. **Duration of License:** One year. **Requirements:** Must have three letters of recommendation, two from medical practitioners. Must be a medical school graduate with one year of internship. **Examination:** Written examination. **Fees:** $175 registration fee. $400 examination fee. $50 renewal fee. $50 controlled substance certificate.

5184

Physician
Alabama State Board of Medical Examiners
PO Box 946
Montgomery, AL 36102
Phone: (205)242-4116

Credential Type: License by examination. **Duration of License:** One year. **Requirements:** Graduates of U.S., Canadian, and international medical schools must have one year of graduate medical education to take FLEX and to be licensed. Accepts endorsement of National Boards without further examination. **Examination:** Federation Licensing Examination (FLEX) or National Board Certifying Examination. A single United States Medical Licensing Examination has been established to replace these exams. **Fees:** $175 application fee. $400 FLEX fee (Parts I or II or both). $75 annual renewal fee.

Credential Type: License by endorsement. **Duration of License:** One year. **Requirements:** Hold out-of-state license or National Board Certificate or Licentiate of the Medical Council of Canada. Some candidates must appear for oral exam.

Graduates of international medical schools must hold Educational Commission for Foreign Medical Graduates (ECFMG) Certificate. School must be state-approved if graduated after February 9, 1988. Must appear for oral exam. **Reciprocity:** Endorses licenses granted by all states except Florida. **Fees:** $175 application fee. $175 license fee. $75 annual renewal fee.

5185

Wrestling Medical Examiner
State Athletic Commission
50 N. Ripley St., Rm. 4121
Montgomery, AL 36132
Phone: (205)242-1380

Credential Type: License. **Duration of License:** One year. **Requirements:** Must be a licensed physician. **Fees:** $5 license fee.

Alaska

5186

Examining Physician, Boxing
Dept. of Commerce and Economic Development
Div. of Occupational Licensing
Athletic Commission
PO Box D-LIC
Juneau, AK 99811-0800
Phone: (907)465-2534
Fax: (907)465-2974

Credential Type: License. **Duration of License:** One year. **Authorization:** Only physicians licensed by the commission may be employed to perform examinations of licensees. **Fees:** $10 license fee. **Governing Statute:** Alaska Statutes 05.05 and 08.10. Professional Regulations 12 AAC 06.

5187

Naturopath
Dept. of Commerce and Economic Development
Div. of Occupational Licensing
PO Box D-LIC
Juneau, AK 99811-0800
Phone: (907)465-2580

Credential Type: License to practice naturopathy. **Duration of License:** Two years. **Authorization:** A person who practices naturopathy may not give, prescribe, or recommend a prescription drug, a controlled substance, or a poison; may not engage in surgery; may not use the word "physician" in the person's title. **Requirements:** Degree from an accredited four-year college or university. Degree from a school of naturopathy that required four years attendance. Pass the Naturopathic Physicians Licensing Examination sponsored by the American Association of Naturopathic Physicians. **Examination:** Naturopathic Physicians Licensing Examination. **Reciprocity:** Yes. **Fees:** $30 application fee. $100 license fee. $100 license renewal fee. **Governing Statute:** Alaska Statutes 08.45.

5188

Osteopathic Physician (D.O.)
Licensing Examiner
Dept. of Commerce and Economic Development
Div. of Occupational Licensing
PO Box D
Juneau, AK 99811-0800
Phone: (907)465-2541

Credential Type: License to practice. **Duration of License:** Two years. **Authorization:** Unlimited practice. **Requirements:** Graduation from osteopathic college approved by state medical board. One year internship in American Osteopathic Association (AOA)- or American Medical Association (AMA)-approved hospital. Renewal requires 17 hours per year of continuing medical education. **Examination:** Federation Licensing Examination (FLEX). **Exemptions:** National Board Certificate accepted for licensure by endorsement. **Reciprocity:** No reciprocity; endorsement. **Fees:** $400 license fee. $50 application fee. $500 FLEX exam fee. $400 biennial renewal fee (active). $200 biennial renewal fee (inactive).

Credential Type: Temporary permit. **Duration of License:** Until board meets. **Requirements:** Submit application for license by endorsement. **Fees:** $50 permit fee.

Credential Type: Locum tenens permit. **Authorization:** To substitute for an Alaskan physician. **Fees:** $100 permit fee.

5189

Physician
Licensing Div. of Occupational Licensing
Alaska Board of Medical Examiners
3601 C St., No. 722
Anchorage, AK 99503
Phone: (907)561-2878

Credential Type: License by examination. **Duration of License:** Two years. **Requirements:** Graduates of U.S., Canadian, and international medical schools must have one year of graduate medical education to take FLEX and to be licensed. Accepts endorsement of National Boards without further examination.

Renewal requires 17 credit hours of continuing medical education (CME) during each year of the previous licensing period. Licensee must submit a Certificate of Compliance as proof that he/she has met the CME requirements. **Examination:** Federation Licensing Examination (FLEX) or National Board Certifying Examination. A single United States Medical Licensing Examination has been established to replace these exams. **Fees:** $50 application fee. $500 FLEX fee. $400 biennial renewal fee.

Credential Type: License by endorsement. **Duration of License:** Two years. **Requirements:** Hold out-of-state license or National Board Certificate or Licentiate of the Medical Council of Canada. All candidates must appear for interview.

Graduates of international medical schools must hold Educational Commission for Foreign Medical Graduates (ECFMG) Certificate or be licensed by exam in another state. Must appear for interview. **Reciprocity:** Endorses all licenses granted by other states. **Fees:** $50 application fee. $400 license fee. $400 biennial renewal fee.

Arizona

5190

Attending Physician
Boxing Commission
1645 W. Jefferson, Rm. 212
Phoenix, AZ 85007
Phone: (602)542-1417

Credential Type: License. **Requirements:** Contact the commission for an application.

5191

Doctor of Naturopathic Medicine (Naturopathic Physician)
Naturopathic Physicians Board of Medical Examiners
1645 W. Jefferson, Rm. 410
Phoenix, AZ 85007
Phone: (602)542-3095
Fax: (602)542-3093

Credential Type: Physicians license to practice as a doctor of naturopathic medicine. **Duration of License:** One year. **Requirements:** Be a graduate of a board-approved school of naturopathic medicine. Complete a board-approved internship, preceptorship, or clinical training program in naturopathic medicine. Have a good moral and professional reputation. Not be guilty of any act of unprofessional conduct.

Not have had a license to practice any profession refused, revoked, or suspended by any other state, district, or territory of the United States or another country for reasons which relate to applicant's ability to skillfully and safely practice as a physician in Arizona.

Pass appropriate examinations. **Examination:** Written examination conducted by the board that may also include oral, clinical, or laboratory sections. NPLEX Clinical Section examinations plus the NPLEX Minor Surgery and Homeopathy examinations. Jurisprudence examination conducted by the Arizona board. **Fees:** $300 application fee. $23 fingerprint fee. $325 fee for full written and clinical practical examination. $175 fee for endorsement of another licensing examination. $50 initial license fee. $250 annual registration fee. **Governing Statute:** Arizona Revised Statutes, Title 32, Chapter 14.

Credential Type: License by endorsement. **Duration of License:** One year. **Requirements:** Be licensed to practice as a doctor of naturopathic medicine by another state, district, or territory of the United States or another country which require a written examination that is substantially equivalent to the written examination required by Arizona.

Be actively engaged for at least three years immediately preceding application in one or more of the following: (1) active practice as a doctor of naturopathic medicine, or (2) a boardapproved internship, preceptorship, or clinical training program in naturopathic medicine, or (3) postgraduate training in naturopathic medicine deemed by the board to be equivalent to an approved clinical training program, or (4) the resident study of naturopathic medicine at a board-approved school of naturopathic medicine.

Arizona

Doctor of Naturopathic Medicine (Naturopathic Physician), continued

Pass an oral examination. **Examination:** Oral examination. Jurisprudence examination conducted by the Arizona board. Clinical practical examination conducted by the Arizona board. **Fees:** $300 application fee. $23 fingerprint fee. $175 examination fee. $50 license fee. **Governing Statute:** Arizona Revised Statutes, Title 32, Chapter 14.

5192

Homeopathic Physician
Arizona Board of Homeopathic Medical Examiners
1645 W. Jefferson, Rm. 410
Phoenix, AZ 85007
Phone: (602)542-3095

Credential Type: License to practice medicine as a homeopathic physician. **Duration of License:** One year. **Requirements:** Be of good moral character. Have a doctor of medicine degree from a board-approved college or university or hold a current license to practice medicine issued by another state. Has not had a license to practice medicine refused, revoked, suspended, or restricted by any state, territory, district, or country for reasons that relate to applicant's ability to competently and safely practice medicine. Has not enggaged in any unprofessional conduct.

Submit professional references from three physicians. Have a degree of doctor of medicine in homeopathy from a homeopathic college or other board-approved educational institution, or complete a board-approved postgraduate course. Serve a board-approved internship or preceptorship.

Pass an appropriate examination. **Examination** may be waived by the board if applicant has practiced primarily homeopathic medicine for the part three years, submits three professional references, and holds a valid medical degree from a board-approved educational institution; or if applicant holds a current license to practice homeopathic medicine issued by another state and holds a valid medical degree from a board-approved educational institution. **Examination:** Written examination. **Fees:** $250 application and examination fee. $100 initial license fee. $250 annual registration fee. **Governing Statute:** Arizona Revised Statutes, Title 32, Chapter 29.

5193

Osteopathic Physician
Arizona Board of Osteopathic Examiners in Medicine and Surgery
1830 W. Colter, Ste. 104
Phoenix, AZ 85015
Phone: (602)255-1747
Fax: (602)255-1756

Credential Type: License to practice. **Duration of License:** One year, then two years. **Authorization:** To practice medicine and surgery as an osteopathic doctor and surgeon. **Requirements:** Be a citizen of the United States or resident alien. Good moral character. Graduate of a board approved school of osteopathic medicine. Complete a board approved internship of at least one year, or an approved residency, or the equivalent as determined by the board.

Pass an examination approved by the board or possess a currently active license to practice as an osteopathic physician and surgeon issued by another state or territory whose standards are comparable to Arizona's. **Examination:** Federation licensing examination (FLEX) or the examination by the National Board of Osteopathic Examiners (NBOE). **Exemptions:** The exam may be waived if the applicant has already taken then exam within the past seven years, or has been continuously engaged in osteopathic practice and training since initial licensure. **Fees:** $300 application fee. $100 initial one-year license fee/ $400 biennial renewal fee.

5194

Physician
Arizona Board of Medical Examiners
2001 W. Camelback Rd., Ste. 300
Phoenix, AZ 85015
Phone: (602)255-3751

Credential Type: License by examination. **Duration of License:** One year. **Requirements:** Graduates of U.S. and Canadian medical schools must have one year of graduate medical education to take FLEX and to be licensed. Graduates of international medical schools must have three years of graduate medical education or complete three years as a clinical instructor (in an assistant professor or higher position) at a U.S. medical school to be eligible to take FLEX and to be licensed. Accepts endorsement of National Boards without further examination.

Renewal requires 20 credit hours of continuing medical education (CME) annually. Licensee may be called upon to demonstrate competencies related to the CME requirement prior to renewal. **Examination:** Federation Licensing Examination (FLEX) or National Board Certifying Examination. A single United States Medical Licensing Examination has been established to replace these exams. **Fees:** $550 FLEX fee (Parts I or II or both). $175 annual renewal fee.

Credential Type: License by endorsement. **Duration of License:** One year. **Requirements:** Hold National Board Certificate or Licentiate of the Medical Council of Canada. Some candidates must appear for interview.

Graduates of international medical schools must hold Educational Commission for Foreign Medical Graduates (ECFMG) Certificate. School must be state-approved. Some candidates must appear for interview. **Fees:** $450 license fee. $175 annual renewal fee.

Arkansas

5195

Osteopathic Physician (D.O.)
State Medical Board
PO Box 102
Harrisburg, AR 72432
Phone: (501)578-2448

Credential Type: License to practice. **Duration of License:** One year. **Authorization:** Unlimited practice. **Requirements:** Graduate of an American Osteopathic Association (AOA)-approved osteopathic college. One year internship in AOA-approved hospital. **Examination:** Federation Licensing Examination (FLEX). **Exemptions:** National Board Certificate accepted for licensure by endorsement. **Reciprocity:** Extended to all states, except Florida. **Fees:** $400 FLEX examination fee. $400 National Board Certificate endorsement fee. $250 (minimum) reciprocal license fee. $25 annual registration fee.

Credential Type: Temporary Permit. **Duration of License:** Until board meets. **Requirements:** Submit application. **Fees:** $50 temporary permit fee.

5196

Physician/Surgeon
Arkansas State Medical Board
PO Box 102
Harrisburg, AR 72432
Phone: (501)578-2448

Credential Type: License. **Requirements:** US Citizen. Graduate of a class A American or Canadian medical school. Must serve internship or residency in a hospital approved by the Council of Medical Education; or, graduate of an osteopathic school approved by the American Osteopathic Association; or, if not already a member of a medical society, two letters of recommendation from physicians who are members of County Medical Societies. Endorsement from the National Board. **Examination:** Yes. **Fees:** $225 Application for examination. $50 Temporary permit.

California

5197

Osteopathic Physician (D.O.)
Board of Osteopathic Examiners
921 11th St., Ste. 1201
Sacramento, CA 95814
Phone: (916)322-4306

Credential Type: License to practice. **Duration of License:** One year. **Authorization:** Unlimited practice **Requirements:** Graduation from osteopathic college approved by the American Osteopathic Association (AOA) and the State Board. One year internship in AOA– or American Medical Association (AMA)-approved hospital. Applicants completing their year of postgraduate training on or after July 1, 1990 must include four months of general medicine in their one year internship program. Minimum score of 75 percent on the State Board examination. Renewal requires 50 hours of AOA or Board approved continuing medical education annually. Twenty hours of the required continuing medical education must be in category 1-A. **Examination:** State Board written oral and practical examination. **Exemptions:** National Board Certificate accepted for licensure endorsement. **Reciprocity:** Granted to licensees of other states who hold unlimited licenses in good standing and have passed examinations recognized and approved by the State Board of California. Oral and clinical examination required. **Fees:** $175 annual renewal fee (active). $150 annual renewal fee (inactive).

5198

Physician
Medical Board of California
1426 Howe Ave., Ste. 54
Sacramento, CA 95825-3236
Phone: (916)924-2626

Credential Type: License by examination. **Duration of License:** Two years. **Requirements:** Graduates of U.S., Canadian, and international medical schools must have one year of graduate medical education to be licensed. Accepts endorsement of National Boards without further examination. Renewal requires 100 credit hours of approved continuing medical education (CME) during the four years immediately preceding renewal. Licensee may be audited by the Board to assure compliance. **Examination:** Federation Licensing Examination (FLEX) or National Board Certifying Examination. A single United States Medical Licensing Examination has been established to replace these exams. **Fees:** $625 FLEX fee (Part I). $675 FLEX fee (Part II). $800 FLEX fee (Both parts). $255 biennial renewal fee.

Credential Type: License by endorsement. **Duration of License:** Two years. **Requirements:** Hold National Board Certificate. Some candidates must appear for oral exam.

Graduates of international medical schools must hold Educational Commission for Foreign Medical Graduates (ECFMG) Certificate. School must be state-approved. Must appear for oral exam. Must take written exam if medical school was not completed within four years of application. **Fees:** $675 license fee. $255 biennial renewal fee.

5199

School Health Services Associate
Commission on Teacher
  Credentialing
PO Box 944270
Sacramento, CA 94244-7000
Phone: (916)445-7254

Credential Type: Health Services Credential. **Authorization:** Authorizes the holder to perform, in preschool, grades 1-12, and adult classes, the health service designated on the credential, (Services such as audiometrist, occupational therapist, or physical therapist are not deemed health services.) Authorized services are school nurse, physician, dentist, dental hygienist, and optometrist. **Requirements:** Valid license, certificate, or registration appropriate to the health service to be designated, issued by the California agency and authorized by law to license, certify, or register persons to practice that health service in California. Additional requirements as may be prescribed by the Commission. For school nurses, a bachelor's degree, an approved program of preparation in school nursing, and two years of successful experience as a school nurse is also required. A preliminary School Nurse Services Credential (valid for five years) requires only a bachelor's degree and a valid California registered nurse license. **Fees:** $60 application fee. $30 test score recording and evaluation fee, except for CBEST.

Colorado

5200

Osteopathic Physician (D.O.)
Board of Medical Examiners
1560 Broadway, Ste. 775
Denver, CO 80202
Phone: (303)894-7690

Credential Type: License to practice. **Duration of License:** Two years. **Authorization:** Unlimited practice. **Requirements:** Graduation from an osteopathic college approved by state medical board. One year internship in American Osteopathic Association (AOA)– or American Medical Association (AMA)-approved hospital. **Examination:** Federation Licensing Examination (FLEX). **Exemptions:** National Board Certificate accepted for licensure by endorsement. **Reciprocity:** Granted to licensees of all states, except Florida. **Fees:** $659 FLEX examination fee. $329 reciprocal license fee. $289 biennial renewal fee.

5201

Physician
Board of Medical Examiners
1560 Broadway, Ste. 1300
Denver, CO 80202-5140
Phone: (303)894-7719

Credential Type: License by examination. **Duration of License:** Two years. **Requirements:** Graduates of U.S. and Canadian medical schools may sit for FLEX examination upon being accepted to, or during the first year of, accredited residency training. However, one year of graduate medical education is required before taking Component II and to be licensed. Graduates of international medical schools must have one year of graduate medical education to take FLEX and to be licensed. Accepts endorsement of National Boards without further examination. **Examination:** Federation Licensing Examination (FLEX) or National Board Certifying Examination. A single United States Medical Licensing Examination has been established to replace these exams. **Fees:** $659 FLEX fee (Parts I or II or both). $271 biennial renewal fee.

Credential Type: License by endorsement. **Duration of License:** Two years. **Requirements:** Hold out-of-state license or National Board Certificate.

Graduates of international medical schools must pass Educational Commission for Foreign Medical Graduates examination. **Reciprocity:** Endorses all licenses granted by other states. **Fees:** $329 license fee. $271 biennial renewal fee.

Connecticut

5202

Doctor (Racetrack)
Connecticut Div. of Special Revenue
Russell Rd.
PO Box 11424
Newington, CT 06111-0424
Phone: (203)566-2756

Credential Type: License Registration. **Requirements:** Submit application and fingerprint card. Pay fee. **Fees:** $5 registration fee.

5203

Homeopathic Physician
Div. of Medical Quality Assurance
Health Systems Regulation Bureau
Health Services Dept.
150 Washington St.
Hartford, CT 06106
Phone: (203)566-3207

Credential Type: License. **Requirements:** Contact licensing body for application information.

5204

Naturopathic Physician
Div. of Medical Quality Assurance
Health Systems Regulation Bureau
Health Services Dept.
150 Washington St.
Hartford, CT 06106
Phone: (203)566-3207

Credential Type: License. **Requirements:** Contact licensing body for application information.

5205

Osteopathic Physician (D.O.)
Dept. of Health Services
Div. of Medical Quality Assurance
150 Washington St.
Hartford, CT 06106
Phone: (203)566-1039

Credential Type: License to practice. **Duration of License:** One year. **Authorization:** Unlimited practice. **Requirements:** Two years of college level courses which include chemistry, physics, and general biology. Graduation from an approved osteopathic college. One year rotating internship or training program approved by the American Osteopathic Association (AOA) or the Accreditation Council for Graduate Medical Education (ACGME). **Examination:** Federation Licensing Examination (FLEX). **Exemptions:** National Board Certificate accepted for licensure by endorsement. **Reciprocity:** None. **Fees:** $225 annual renewal fee. $150 National Board endorsement fee.

5206

Physician
Connecticut Dept. of Health Services
Medical Quality Assurance
150 Washington St.
Hartford, CT 06106
Phone: (203)566-3207

Credential Type: License by examination. **Duration of License:** One year. **Requirements:** Graduates of U.S., Canadian, and international medical schools must have two years of graduate medical education to take FLEX and to be licensed. Accepts endorsement of National Boards without further examination. **Examination:** Federation Licensing Examination (FLEX) or National Board Certifying Examination. A single United States Medical Licensing Examination has been established to replace these exams. **Fees:** $450 FLEX fee (Parts I or II or both). $100 Flex partial retest fee (If previously taken in Connecticut). $450 annual renewal fee.

Credential Type: License by endorsement. **Duration of License:** One year. **Requirements:** Hold out-of-state license or National Board Certificate or Licentiate of the Medical Council of Canada. U.S. residency training or approved two-year postgraduate training in the U.S. or abroad.

Graduates of international medical schools must hold Educational Commission for Foreign Medical Graduates (ECFMG) Certificate. School must be state-approved. **Reciprocity:** Endorses all licenses granted by other states. **Fees:** $150 license fee. $450 annual renewal fee.

Delaware

5207

Osteopathic Physician (D.O.)
Board of Medical Practice
Margaret O'Neil Bldg.
PO Box 1401
Dover, DE 19903
Phone: (302)739-4522

Credential Type: License to practice. **Duration of License:** Two years. **Authorization:** Unlimited practice. **Requirements:** Graduation from osteopathic college approved by the American Osteopathic Association (AOA). One year internship in AOA- or American Medical Association (AMA)-approved hospital. Renewal requires 40 hours of continuing medical education every two years. **Examination:** Federation Licensing Examination (FLEX). **Exemptions:** National Board Certificate accepted for licensure by endorsement. **Reciprocity:** Granted to licensees of all states and the District of Columbia. Diploma must be based on National Board or FLEX examination. Two interviews required. **Fees:** $150 National Board Certificate endorsement fee. $600 FLEX examination fee. $150 reciprocal license fee. $70 biennial renewal fee.

5208

Physician
Board of Medical Practice
O'Neill Bldg.
PO Box 1401
Dover, DE 19903
Phone: (302)739-4522

Credential Type: License by examination. **Duration of License:** Two years. **Requirements:** Graduates of U.S., Canadian, and international medical schools must have one year of graduate medical education to take FLEX and three years to be licensed. Accepts endorsement of National Boards without further examination.

Renewal requires 40 credit hours, per registration period, of continuing medical education (CME) in Category I courses. **Examination:** Federation Licensing Examination (FLEX) or National Board Certifying Examination. A single United States Medical Licensing Examination has been established to replace these exams. **Fees:** $300 FLEX fee (Part I or Part II). $600 FLEX fee (Both parts). $110 biennial renewal fee.

Credential Type: License by endorsement. **Duration of License:** Two years. **Requirements:** Hold out-of-state license or National Board Certificate or Licentiate of the Medical Council of Canada. All candidates must appear for interview.

Graduates of international medical schools must hold Educational Commission for Foreign Medical Graduates (ECFMG) Certificate. Must appear for two interviews. **Reciprocity:** Endorses all licenses granted by other states. **Fees:** $150 license fee. $110 biennial renewal fee.

District of Columbia

5209

Osteopathic Physician (D.O.)
Board of Medicine
605 G St. NW, Rm. LL202
Washington, DC 20001
Phone: (202)727-5365

Credential Type: License to practice. **Duration of License:** Two years. **Authorization:** Unlimited practice. **Requirements:** Osteopathic degree from a registered college. One year internship. **Examination:** Federation Licensing Examination (FLEX). **Exemptions:** National Board Certificate accepted for licensure by endorsement. **Reciprocity:** Granted to licensees of other states with requirements equal to those of the District of Columbia. **Fees:** $337 application/FLEX examination fee. $20 license fee. $180 reciprocity application fee. $120 biennial renewal fee.

5210

Physician
Board of Medicine
605 G St. NW, Rm. LL202
Washington, DC 20001
Phone: (202)727-5365

Credential Type: License by examination. **Duration of License:** Two years. **Requirements:** Graduates of U.S. and Canadian medical schools must have one year of graduate medical education to take FLEX and to be licensed. Graduates of international medical schools must have three years of graduate medical education to take FLEX and to be licensed. Accepts endorsement of National Boards without further examination. **Examination:** Federation Licensing Examination (FLEX) or National Board Certifying Examination. A single United States Medical Licensing Examination has been established to replace these exams. **Fees:** $202 FLEX fee (Part I). $252 FLEX fee (Part II). $377 FLEX fee (Both parts). $120 biennial renewal fee.

Credential Type: License by endorsement. **Duration of License:** Two years. **Requirements:** Hold National Board Certificate or Licentiate of the Medical Council of Canada.

Graduates of international medical schools must hold Educational Commission for Foreign Medical Graduates (ECFMG) Certificate. School must be state-approved. **Fees:** $180 license fee. $120 biennial renewal fee.

Florida

5211

Doctor (Racetrack)
Florida Dept. of Business
Div. of Pari-Mutuel Wagering
Licensing Section
725 S. Bronough St.
Tallahassee, FL 32399-1037
Phone: (904)488-9161

Credential Type: License Registration Code 1015. **Requirements:** Must have Department of Professional Regulation (DPR) license. Submit application and fingerprint card. Pay fee. **Fees:** $40 registration fee.

5212

Osteopathic Physician (D.O.)
Board of Osteopathic Medical
  Examiners
1940 N. Monroe St.
Tallahassee, FL 32399-0775
Phone: (904)488-7546

Credential Type: License to practice. **Duration of License:** Two years. **Authorization:** Unlimited practice. **Requirements:** Graduation from osteopathic college approved by American Osteopathic Association (AOA). One year internship in AOA-approved hospital. Renewal requires 40 hours of continuing medical education every two years. Five hours of the required 40 hours of continuing medical education must be in risk management and 30 must be osteopathic related. **Examination:** Florida Board examination. **Exemptions:** National Board Certificate accepted for licensure by endorsement. **Reciprocity:** Granted to licensees of other states who have passed all parts of the National Board examination or have passed an examination deemed similar or more difficult than the Florida Board examination. Federation Licensing Examination (FLEX) not acceptable. **Fees:** $200 examination fee. $200 reciprocal license fee. $250 biennial renewal fee.

5213

Physician
Board of Medical Examiners
1940 N. Monroe St.
Tallahassee, FL 32399
Phone: (904)488-7546

Credential Type: License by examination. **Duration of License:** Two years. **Requirements:** Graduates of U.S., Canadian, and international medical schools must have one year of graduate medical education to take FLEX and to be licensed. Accepts endorsement of National Boards without further examination.

Renewal requires 40 hours of continuing medical education (CME) every two years and at least five of those hours must deal with risk management. **Examination:** Federation Licensing Examination (FLEX) or National Board Certifying Examination. A single United States Medical Licensing Examination has been established to replace these exams. **Fees:** $1,000 FLEX fee (Parts I or II or both), also includes $400 application fee. $350 biennial renewal fee.

Credential Type: License by endorsement. **Duration of License:** Two years. **Requirements:** Hold National Board Certificate. Some candidates must appear for interview.

Graduates of international medical schools must hold Educational Commission for Foreign Medical Graduates (ECFMG) Certificate. Supervised clinical training received in the U.S. after November 28, 1984, must be done in a hospital accredited by the Liaison Committee on Medical Education (LCME) or a residency training program accredited by the Accreditation Council for Graduate Medical Education (ACGME). Some candidates must appear for an interview. **Fees:** $450 license fee. $350 biennial renewal fee.

Georgia

5214

Osteopathic Physician (D.O.)
State Board of Medical Examiners
166 Pryor St. SW
Atlanta, GA 30303
Phone: (404)656-3913

Credential Type: License to practice. **Duration of License:** Two years. **Authorization:** Unlimited practice. **Requirements:** Graduation from a board approved osteopathic college. One year internship or residency training program in American Osteopathic Association (AOA)- or American Medical Association (AMA)-approved hospital. **Examination:** Federation Licensing Examination (FLEX). **Exemptions:** National Board Certificate accepted for licensure by endorsement. **Reciprocity:** Granted to licensees from other states which have equal requirements for licensing and reciprocate with Georgia licensees. Applicants must have obtained their license after July 1, 1963 and must have passed an examination to qualify for licensure. **Fees:** $500 FLEX examination fee. $300 reciprocal license fee. $100 temporary reciprocal license fee. $75 biennial license renewal fee.

Georgia 5215

5215

Physician
Composite State Board of Medical Examiners
166 Pryor St. SW, Rm. 424
Atlanta, GA 30303
Phone: (404)656-3913

Credential Type: License by examination. **Duration of License:** Two years. **Requirements:** Graduates of U.S. and Canadian medical schools must have one year of graduate medical education to take FLEX and to be licensed. Graduates of international medical schools must have three years of graduate medical education to take FLEX and to be licensed. Accepts endorsement of National Boards without further examination.

Renewal requires 40 credit hours of CME per registration period. **Examination:** Federation Licensing Examination (FLEX) or National Board Certifying Examination. A single United States Medical Licensing Examination has been established to replace these exams. **Fees:** $355 FLEX fee (Part I). $410 FLEX fee (Part II). $555 FLEX fee (Both parts). $75 biennial renewal fee.

Credential Type: License by endorsement. **Duration of License:** Two years. **Requirements:** Hold out-of-state license or National Board Certificate or Licentiate of the Medical Council of Canada. Some candidates must appear for interview.

Graduates of international medical schools must hold Educational Commission for Foreign Medical Graduates (ECFMG) Certificate. School must be state-approved. Some candidates must appear for interview. **Reciprocity:** Endorses licenses granted by other states with the exceptions of Arizona, California, Connecticut, Florida, Hawaii, Illinois, New Hampshire, New York, Wisconsin, and Wyoming. **Fees:** $300 license fee. $75 biennial renewal fee.

Hawaii

5216

Naturopath
Hawaii Board of Naturopathy
PO Box 3469
Honolulu, HI 96801
Phone: (808)548-8542

Credential Type: License. **Duration of License:** Six months. **Requirements:** Graduation from an accredited naturopathy school. **Examination:** NPLEX core exam. Homeopathy exam. **Fees:** $25 application fee. $250 exam fee. $50 license fee. $25 $50 Compliance Resolution Fund fee. $100 renewal fee.

5217

Osteopathic Physician and Surgeon
Hawaii Board of Osteopathic Examiners
1010 Richards St.
PO Box 3469
Honolulu, HI 96801
Phone: (808)548-3952

Credential Type: License. **Duration of License:** Six months. **Requirements:** Graduation from an accredited osteopathic medical school. Served a one-year internship in an osteopathic hospital facility. **Examination:** Established by FLEX. **Fees:** $50 application fee. $200 license fee. $20—$40 Compliance Resolution Fund fee. $40 renewal fee.

5218

Physician, MD
Hawaii Board of Medical Examiners
1010 Richards St.
PO Box 3469
Honolulu, HI 96801
Phone: (808)548-4392

Credential Type: License. **Requirements:** Graduation from an accredited medical school program. At least a one-year residency in an accredited program. Submit proof that license(s) is(are) in good standing. Different requirements for foreign medical school graduates. **Examination:** National Board exam or Federation Licensing Exam (FLEX). **Reciprocity:** None. **Fees:** $465 exam fee. $50 application fee. $75 license fee. $25 $50 Compliance Resolution Fund fee. $75 renewal fee.

Idaho

5219

Osteopathic Physician (D.O.)
State Board of Medicine
280 N. 8th
State House, No. 202
Boise, ID 83720
Phone: (208)334-2822

Credential Type: License to practice. **Duration of License:** One year. **Authorization:** Unlimited practice **Requirements:** Graduation from an American Osteopathic Association (AOA)-approved osteopathic college. One year internship in AOA- or American Medical Association (AMA)-approved hospital. **Examination:** Federation Licensing Examination (FLEX). **Exemptions:** National Board Certificate accepted for licensure by endorsement. **Reciprocity:** Granted to licensees of other states with unlimited practice, who graduated after 1963 and have passed written examination as a condition of licensure. **Fees:** $245 Flex examination fee. $275 reciprocal license fee. $90 annual renewal fee. $60 inactive license fee. $275 National Board Certificate endorsement fee.

Credential Type: Temporary license. **Requirements:** Submit application for license without written examination. **Fees:** $100 temporary license fee.

5220

Physician
State Board of Medicine
Statehouse, No. 202
280 N. 8th St.
Boise, ID 83720
Phone: (208)334-2822

Credential Type: License by examination. **Duration of License:** One year. **Requirements:** Graduates of U.S. and Canadian medical schools must have one year of graduate medical education to take FLEX and to be licensed. Graduates of international medical schools must have three years of graduate medical education to take FLEX and to be licensed. Accepts endorsement of National Boards without further examination. **Examination:** Federation Licensing Examination (FLEX) or National Board Certifying Examination. A single United States Medical Licensing Examination has been established to replace these exams. **Fees:** $365 FLEX fee (Both parts). $90 annual renewal fee.

Credential Type: License by endorsement. **Duration of License:** One year. **Requirements:** Hold out-of-state license or National Board Certificate or Licentiate of the Medical Council of Canada. All candidates must appear and some will be interviewed.

Graduates of international medical schools must hold Educational Commission for Foreign Medical Graduates (ECFMG) Certificate. School must be state-approved. Must appear for oral exam and/or interview. **Reciprocity:** Endorses all licenses granted by other states. Florida licensees must have taken examination before 1969 to qualify. **Fees:** $275 license fee. $90 annual renewal fee.

Illinois

5221

Osteopathic Physician (D.O.)
Dept. of Professional Regulation
Medical Application Unit Health
 Services
320 W. Washington
Springfield, IL 62786
Phone: (217)782-8556

Credential Type: License to practice. **Duration of License:** Three years. **Authorization:** Unlimited practice. **Requirements:** Graduation from a Board-approved professional college. One year internship in state-approved hospital for applicants entering the program on or before December 31, 1987. Applicants entering the program on or after January 1, 1988 are required to have a two year hospital internship. **Examination:** Federation Licensing Examination (FLEX). **Exemptions:** National Board Certificate accepted for licensure by endorsement. **Reciprocity:** Granted on individual basis. **Fees:** $282.20 FLEX examination fee. $179.20 FLEX component I reexamination fee. $204.45 FLEX component II reexamination fee. $300 triennial license renewal (instate). $600 triennial license fee (out-of-state address). **Governing Statute:** Medical Practice Act.

Credential Type: Temporary Certificate. **Authorization:** Allows participation in special training/residency programs or temporary status as a visiting professor. Non-practicing physicians may hold temporary certificates which have provisions for reactivating licenses to active standings. **Requirements:** File application for temporary certificate. **Fees:** $100 temporary certificate fee (training/residency). $200 temporary certificate fee (visiting professor certificate). **Governing Statute:** Medical Practice Act.

5222

Physician
Dept. of Professional Regulations
Illinois Board of Medical Examiners
320 W. Washington, 3rd Fl.
Springfield, IL 62786
Phone: (217)782-8556

Credential Type: License by examination. **Duration of License:** Three years. **Requirements:** Graduates of U.S. and Canadian medical schools must have four months of graduate medical education to take FLEX and two years to be licensed. Accepts endorsement of National Boards without further examination. Renewal requires proof of continuing medical education (CME) during the three years prior to renewal. This requirement does not pertain to licensees renewing for the first time. **Examination:** Federation Licensing Examination (FLEX) or National Board Certifying Examination. A single United States Medical Licensing Examination has been established to replace these exams. **Fees:** $300 FLEX fee (Part I). $356 FLEX fee (Part II). $506 FLEX fee (Both parts). $300 triennial renewal fee (Resident). $600 triennial renewal fee (Nonresident).

Credential Type: License by endorsement. **Duration of License:** Three years. **Requirements:** Hold out-of-state license or National Board Certificate or Licentiate of the Medical Council of Canada. Some candidates must appear for interview.

Graduates of international medical schools must pass Educational Commission for Foreign Medical Graduates (ECFMG) or pass VQE or Foreign Medical Graduate Examination in Medical Sciences (FMGEMS). Must have completed six years of post-secondary course study that includes two academic years of liberal arts instruction, two academic years of basic sciences and two academic years in clinical sciences. Some candidates must appear for interview. **Reciprocity:** Applicants will be considered on an individual basis. **Fees:** $300 license fee. $300 triennial renewal fee (Resident). $600 triennial renewal fee (Nonresident).

5223

Physician (Boxing/Wrestling)
Illinois Dept. of Professional
 Regulations
State of Illinois Ctr.
100 W. Randolph, Ste. 9-300
Chicago, IL 60601
Phone: (312)814-2719

Credential Type: Registration. **Duration of License:** Lifetime. **Requirements:** Submit registration to board. Must re-register if original information changes. **Reciprocity:** No. **Governing Statute:** The Illinois Professional Boxing and Wrestling Act. Illinois Revised Statutes 1991, Chapter 111.

Indiana

5224

Attending Physician (Boxing)
Boxing Commission
Examination Administrative Div.
Professional Licensing Agency
1021 State Office Bldg.
Indianapolis, IN 46204
Phone: (317)232-3897

Credential Type: License. **Requirements:** Contact licensing body for application information.

5225

Osteopathic Physician (D.O.)
Medical Licensing Board
1 American Square, Ste. 1020
PO Box 82067
Indianapolis, IN 46282
Phone: (317)232-2960

Credential Type: License to practice. **Duration of License:** Two years. **Authorization:** Unlimited. **Requirements:** Graduate from a recognized college. One year internship in American Osteopathic Association (AOA)– or American Medical Association (AMA)-approved hospital. **Examination:** Federation Licensing Examination (FLEX). **Exemptions:** National Board Certificate accepted for licensure by endorsement. **Reciprocity:** Granted to licensees of states with unlimited licenses who have passed National Board exams or written examinations equal to those required by Indiana. **Fees:** $265 FLEX examination fee (Component I). $315 FLEX examination fee (Component II). $440 FLEX examination fee (both components). $200 reciprocal license fee. $50 biennial license renewal fee.

Credential Type: Temporary License. **Authorization:** Allows postdoctoral training or issued to graduate awaiting next examination period. **Requirements:** File application. **Fees:** $50 temporary license (postdoctoral training). $10 temporary license (graduate awaiting exam).

5226

Physician
Indiana Health Professions Bureau
One American Square, Ste. 1020
PO Box 82067
Indianapolis, IN 46282-0004
Phone: (317)232-2960

Credential Type: License by examination. **Duration of License:** Two years. **Requirements:** Graduates of U.S. and Canadian

Physician, continued

medical schools may sit for FLEX upon being accepted to, or during the first year of, accredited residency training. One year of graduate medical education is required to be licensed. Graduates of international medical schools must have two years of graduate medical education to take FLEX and to be licensed. Accepts endorsement of National Boards without further examination. **Examination:** Federation Licensing Examination (FLEX) or National Board Certifying Examination. A single United States Medical Licensing Examination has been established to replace these exams. **Fees:** $295 FLEX fee (Part I). $350 FLEX fee (Part II). $495 FLEX fee (Both parts). $50 biennial renewal fee.

Credential Type: License by endorsement. **Duration of License:** Two years. **Requirements:** Hold out-of-state license or National Board Certificate or Licentiate of the Medical Council of Canada. Some candidates must appear for interview.

Graduates of international medical schools must hold Educational Commission for Foreign Medical Graduates (ECFMG) Certificate. School must be state-approved. Some candidates must appear for interview. **Reciprocity:** Endorses all licenses granted by other states. Florida licensees must have taken examination before January 1969 to qualify. **Fees:** $200 license fee. $50 biennial renewal fee.

Iowa

5227

Doctor of Medicine
Iowa Board of Medical Examiners
Executive Hills West
1209 East Court
Des Moines, IA 50319
Phone: (515)281-5171

Credential Type: License. **Duration of License:** Two years. **Requirements:** Graduation from an approved college of medicine and surgery, plus one year of postgraduate training in an approved hospital. **Examination:** Federation Licensing Examination (FLEX). **Reciprocity:** Yes. **Fees:** $500 exam fee. $150 renewal fee. $300 endorsement fee for reciprocity.

5228

Doctor of Osteopathic Medicine
Iowa Board of Medical Examiners
Executive Hills West
1209 East Court
Des Moines, IA 50319
Phone: (515)281-5171

Credential Type: License. **Duration of License:** Two years. **Requirements:** Graduation from an approved college of osteopathic medicine and surgery, plus one year of post-graduate training. **Examination:** Federation Licensing Examination (FLEX). **Reciprocity:** Yes. **Fees:** $500 exam fee. $150 renewal fee. $300 endorsement fee for reciprocity.

Kansas

5229

Osteopathic Physician (D.O.)
Board of Healing Arts
235 SW Topeka Blvd.
Topeka, KS 66603
Phone: (913)296-7413

Credential Type: License to practice. **Duration of License:** One year. **Authorization:** Unlimited practice. **Requirements:** Graduation from an American Osteopathic Association (AOA)-approved osteopathic college. One year internship in AOA– or Board-approved hospital. Renewal requires 150 hours of continuing medical education every three years. **Examination:** Federation Licensing Examination (FLEX). **Exemptions:** National Board Certificate accepted for licensure by endorsement. **Fees:** $460 FLEX examination fee. $150 annual license renewal fee.

Credential Type: License by endorsement. **Requirements:** Osteopathic License from another jurisdiction. National Boards or FLEX or state exam taken prior to FLEX. **Fees:** $150 endorsement fee.

Credential Type: Temporary permit. **Authorization:** Allows postgraduate work. **Requirements:** Submit application for temporary permit. **Fees:** $25 temporary permit fee.

5230

Physician
State Board of Healing Arts
235 SW Topeka Blvd.
Topeka, KS 66603
Phone: (913)296-7413

Credential Type: License by examination. **Duration of License:** One year. **Requirements:** Graduates of U.S., Canadian, and international medical schools must have one year of graduate medical education to take Federation Licensing Examination (FLEX) and to be licensed. Accepts endorsement of National Boards without further examination.

Renewal for Doctors of Medicine and Surgery requires 150 credit hours of continuing medical education (CME) during the three years prior to renewal. American Medical Association (AMA) PRA certificates, equivalent specialty society certificates or residency in a postgraduate training program can all be used to satisfy this requirement. **Examination:** Federation Licensing Examination (FLEX) or National Board Certifying Examination. A single United States Medical Licensing Examination has been established to replace these exams. **Fees:** $275 FLEX fee (Part I). $345 FLEX fee (Part II). $525 FLEX fee (Both parts). $150 license fee. $150 annual renewal fee.

Credential Type: License by endorsement. **Duration of License:** One year. **Requirements:** Hold out-of-state license or National Board Certificate or Licentiate of the Medical Council of Canada. Some candidates must appear for interview. U.S. residency training required. Professional experience abroad or in the U.S. may be substituted for U.S. residency training with approval.

Graduates of international medical schools must hold Educational Commission for Foreign Medical Graduates (ECFMG) Certificate. School must be state-approved. Some candidates must appear for interview. **Reciprocity:** Endorses all licenses granted by other states. **Fees:** $150 license fee. $150 annual renewal fee.

Kentucky

5231

Osteopathic Physician (D.O.)
Kentucky Board of Medical
  Licensure
The Mall Office Center
400 Sherburn Ln., Ste. 222
Louisville, KY 40207
Phone: (502)896-1516

Credential Type: License to practice. **Duration of License:** One year. **Authorization:** Unlimited practice. **Requirements:** Graduation from an American Osteopathic Association (AOA)-approved osteopathic college. One year internship in AOA– or American Medical Association (AMA)-approved hospital. **Examination:** Federation Licensing Examination (FLEX). State examination in osteopathic principles and practice. **Exemptions:** National Board Certificate accepted for licensure by endorsement. **Fees:** $65 annual renewal fee. $450 FLEX examination fee.

Credential Type: Temporary permit. **Requirements:** Hold unlimited license in another state. **Fees:** $50 temporary permit fee.

Credential Type: License by endorsement. **Requirements:** Credential approved by board. **Fees:** $150 endorsement fee.

5232

Physician
Board of Medical Licensure
400 Sherburn Ln., Rm. 222
Louisville, KY 40207
Phone: (502)896-1516

Credential Type: License by examination. **Duration of License:** One year. **Requirements:** Graduates of U.S. and Canadian medical schools may sit for FLEX examination upon being accepted to, or during the first year of, accredited residency training. One year of graduate medical education is required to be licensed. Graduates of international medical schools must have two years of graduate medical education to take FLEX and to be licensed. Accepts endorsement of National Boards without further examination. **Examination:** Federation Licensing Examination (FLEX) or National Board Certifying Examination. A single United States Medical Licensing Examination has been established to replace these exams. **Fees:** $225 FLEX fee (Part I). $275 FLEX fee (Part II). $450 FLEX fee (Both parts). $65 annual renewal fee.

Credential Type: License by endorsement. **Duration of License:** One year. **Requirements:** Hold out-of-state license or National Board Certificate or Licentiate of the Medical Council of Canada.

Graduates of international medical schools must hold Educational Commission for Foreign Medical Graduates (ECFMG) Certificate. School must be state-approved. **Reciprocity:** Endorses all licenses granted by other states. **Fees:** $150 license fee. $65 annual renewal fee.

Louisiana

5233

Osteopathic Physician (D.O.)
Board of Medical Examiners
830 Union St., Ste. 100
New Orleans, LA 70112
Phone: (504)524-6763

Credential Type: License to practice. **Duration of License:** One year. **Authorization:** Unlimited for graduates of approved schools after June 1, 1971. **Requirements:** Graduation from a Board approved osteopathic school. **Examination:** Federation Licensing Examination (FLEX). **Reciprocity:** Granted to licensees of all states with licenses issued after June 1, 1971 and based on passage of FLEX examination. **Fees:** $200 FLEX examination fee. $200 reciprocal license fee.

5234

Physician
Louisiana State Board of Medical Examiners
830 Union St., Ste. 100
New Orleans, LA 70112
Phone: (504)524-6763

Credential Type: License by examination. **Duration of License:** One year. **Requirements:** Accepts endorsement of National Boards without further examination. **Examination:** Federation Licensing Examination (FLEX) or National Board Certifying Examination. A single United States Medical Licensing Examination has been established to replace these exams. **Fees:** $240 FLEX fee (Part II). $465 FLEX fee (both parts), also includes $100 application fee. $100 annual renewal fee.

Credential Type: License by endorsement. **Duration of License:** One year. **Requirements:** Hold out-of-state license or National Board Certificate or, if applicant graduated medical school on or before December 21, 1986, National Board (NB) or state board exam. All candidates must appear for interview.

Graduates of international medical schools must hold Educational Commission for Foreign Medical Graduates (ECFMG) Certificate or be American specialty board certified or pass the VQE. Must appear for interview. **Reciprocity:** Endorses licenses granted by all states with the exceptions of Florida and Hawaii. International medical graduates who were issued licenses based on the passage of FLEX may also qualify. **Fees:** $200 license fee. $100 annual renewal fee.

Maine

5235

Osteopathic Physician (D.O.)
Board of Osteopathic Examination & Registration
2 Bangor St.
Augusta, ME 04330
Phone: (207)289-2480

Credential Type: License to practice. **Duration of License:** One year. **Authorization:** Unlimited practice. **Requirements:** Thirty-six months of professional study leading to a D.O. degree. One year internship approved by the American Osteopathic Association (AOA) or the Accreditation Council for Graduate Medical Education (ACGME). Renewal requires 50 hours of continuing medical education per year. Twenty of the required continuing medical education hours must be osteopathic. **Examination:** Federation Licensing Examination (FLEX). State examination on osteopathic principals and practice. **Exemptions:** National Board Certificate accepted on individual basis for licensure by endorsement. **Reciprocity:** Granted to licensees of all states with equivalent education requirements. Must have Board approval. **Fees:** $125 state examination fee. $465 FLEX examination fee. $125 reciprocal license fee. $150 annual license renewal fee.

Credential Type: Temporary license. **Authorization:** Allows temporary practice by interns, residents, camp physicians, and substitute physicians (locum tenens). **Requirements:** Submit application for temporary license. **Fees:** $150 temporary license fee.

5236

Physician
Maine Board of Registration in Medicine
2 Bangor St.
State House Station 137
Augusta, ME 04333
Phone: (207)289-2480

Credential Type: License by examination. **Duration of License:** Two years. **Requirements:** Graduates of U.S. and Canadian medical schools must have two years of graduate medical education to take FLEX and to be licensed. Graduates of international medical schools must have three years of graduate medical education to take FLEX and to be licensed. Accepts endorsement of National Boards without further examination.

Renewal requires proof of 100 credit hours of continuing medical education (CME) during the two years prior to renewal. Forty of the required hours must be in American Medical Association (AMA) Category I. **Examination:** Federation Licensing Examination (FLEX) or National Board Certifying Examination. A single United States Medical Licensing Examination has been established to replace these exams. **Fees:** $100 FLEX fee (Additional charges will be made for oral examination and cost of FLEX). $100 biennial fee.

Maryland

Physician, continued

Credential Type: License by endorsement. **Duration of License:** Two years. **Requirements:** Hold out-of-state license or National Board Certificate or Licentiate of the Medical Council of Canada. All candidates must appear for oral exam.

Graduates of international medical schools must hold Educational Commission for Foreign Medical Graduates (ECFMG) Certificate or be certified by American specialty board or pass VQE. Must appear for oral exam. **Reciprocity:** Endorses all licenses granted by other states. **Fees:** $125 license fee. $100 biennial fee.

Maryland

5237

Osteopathic Physician (D.O.)
Board of Physician Quality Assurance
4201 Patterson Ave.
Baltimore, MD 21215
Phone: (301)764-4777

Credential Type: License to practice. **Duration of License:** Two years. **Authorization:** Unlimited practice. **Requirements:** Graduation from an American Osteopathic Association (AOA)-approved school. One year internship in an AOA-approved program. Renewal requires 100 hours of continuing medical education every two years. Minimum of 40 hours of the required continuing medical education must be in Category I. **Examination:** Federation Licensing Examination (New FLEX). **Exemptions:** National Board Certificate accepted for licensure by endorsement. **Reciprocity:** Granted to out-of-state unlimited license holders with licenses issued in states extending reciprocity to Maryland. **Fees:** $300 New FLEX examination fee (Component I). $370 New FLEX examination fee (Component II). $560 New FLEX examination fee (both components). $200 biennial license renewal fee.

Credential Type: Limited permit. **Duration of License:** One year. **Authorization:** Allows one year of post-graduate teaching. **Requirements:** Submit application for limited permit. **Fees:** $5 limited license fee.

5238

Physician
Board of Physician Quality Assurance
4201 Patterson Ave.
Baltimore, MD 21215
Phone: (301)764-4777

Credential Type: License by examination. **Duration of License:** Two years. **Requirements:** Graduates of U.S., Canadian, and international medical schools must have one year of approved graduate medical education to take Federation Licensing Examination (FLEX) and to be licensed. Graduates of medical schools deemed "unapproved" or "new" must have three years (2 years of same specialty) of graduate medical education to sit for examination. Accepts endorsement of National Boards without further examination.

Renewal requires 100 credit hours of approved continuing medical education (CME) in the two years preceding renewal. **Examination:** Federation Licensing Examination (FLEX) or National Board Certifying Examination. A single United States Medical Licensing Examination has been established to replace these exams. **Fees:** $220 FLEX fee (Part I). $280 FLEX fee (Part II). $435 FLEX fee (Both parts). $90 biennial renewal fee. *Graduates of foreign medical schools must add $25 to all fees, excluding renewal fee.

Credential Type: License by endorsement. **Duration of License:** Two years. **Requirements:** Hold out-of-state license or National Board Certificate or Licentiate of the Medical Council of Canada.

Graduates of international medical schools must hold Educational Commission for Foreign Medical Graduates (ECFMG) Certificate. School must be state-approved or applicant must have three years of U.S. training, two of which must be in the same specialty. **Reciprocity:** Accepts all licenses granted by other states which are endorsed by the National Board, FLEX, Licentiate of the Medical Council of Canada (LMCC), or state medical board examination prior to January 1972. **Fees:** $200 license fee (Add $25 if graduate of a foreign medical school). $90 biennial renewal fee.

Massachusetts

5239

Osteopathic Physician (D.O.)
Board of Registration in Medicine
10 West St.
Boston, MA 02111
Phone: (617)727-1788

Credential Type: License to practice. **Duration of License:** Two years. **Authorization:** Unlimited. (Some licenses may be restricted to specialty.) **Requirements:** Must be a graduate of a four-year legally charted medical school. Each year of medical school must contain no less than 32 weeks of instruction. One year internship in American Osteopathic Association (AOA)- or American Medical Association (AMA)-approved hospital. Renewal requires 100 hours of continuing medical education every two years. Physicians who treat Medicare patients must agree to charge no more than the allowed Medicare specified fees before being granted or renewing their licenses. **Examination:** Federation Licensing Examination (FLEX). **Exemptions:** National Board Certificate accepted as endorsement by statute. **Reciprocity:** Granted to licensees from other states with examination standards deemed equivalent to Massachusetts. **Fees:** $300 reciprocal license fee. $300 National Board Certificate endorsement fee. $150 biennial license renewal fee.

Credential Type: Limited license. **Authorization:** Allows practice for fellows, interns, and medical officers. **Requirements:** Submit application for limited license. **Fees:** $50 limited license fee.

Credential Type: Temporary permit. **Duration of License:** Eight months maximum. **Authorization:** Allows a physician to substitute for another, to get continuing medical education credits, or to accept a faculty appointment in a teaching hospital. **Requirements:** Submit application for temporary permit. **Fees:** $150 temporary permit fee.

5240

Physician
Massachusetts Board of Registration in Medicine
10 West St., 3rd Fl.
Boston, MA 02111
Phone: (617)727-1788

Credential Type: License by examination. **Duration of License:** Two years. **Requirements:** Graduates of U.S., Canadian, and international medical schools must have one year of graduate medical education to take FLEX and to be licensed. Accepts endorsement of National Boards without further examination.

Renewal requires 100 credit hours of approved continuing medical education (CME) during the two years preceding renewal. At least 40 of the required 100 hours must be in American Medical Association (AMA) Category I courses. In lieu of the required 100 hours, a licensee may enroll in an approved residency program or Board approved CME program to satisfy CME requirement. All licensees must complete a minimum of 10 credit hours in risk management during the two years preceding renewal. **Examination:** Federation Licensing Examination (FLEX) or National Board Certifying Examination. A single United States Medical Licensing Examination has been established to replace these exams. **Fees:** $200 FLEX fee (Part I). $300 FLEX fee (Part II). $440 FLEX fee (Both parts). $150 biennial renewal fee.

Credential Type: License by endorsement. **Duration of License:** Two years. **Requirements:** Hold out-of-state license or National Board Certificate or Licentiate of the Medical Council of Canada with a valid Canadian provincial license. Some candidates must appear for interview.

Graduates of international medical schools must hold Educational Commission for Foreign Medical Graduates (ECFMG) Certificate or be certified by American specialty board or pass VQE. Must appear for oral exam. **Reciprocity:** Endorses licenses obtained by written examination from other states. National Board Diplomate is acceptable. Florida State Boards are not endorsed without the basic science portion of the examination. **Fees:** $150 license fee. $150 biennial renewal fee.

5241

Physician (Boxing)
State Boxing Commission
Dept. of Public Safety
One Ashburton Pl., Rm. 1310
Boston, MA 02108
Phone: (617)727-3296

Credential Type: License. **Requirements:** Must be a licensed physician with at least three years experience as a medical practitioner. **Fees:** Contact commission for fee. **Governing Statute:** Annotated Laws of Massachusetts, Chap. 147.

Michigan

5242

Medical Training Student (Postgraduate)
Board of Medicine
Bureau of Occupational & Professional Regulation
Dept. of Commerce
PO Box 30192
Lansing, MI 48909
Phone: (517)373-9153

Credential Type: Educational Limited License. **Duration of License:** One year for a maximum of five years. **Authorization:** A person engaging in post-graduate medical training in an approved hospital or institution must obtain an educational limited license from the Board of Medicine of the Department of Commerce. **Requirements:** At least 18 years of age. Be of good moral character. Completed a minimum of 60 semester hours of general study in an accredited college or university. Completed the requirements for a degree in medicine as defined by the Board's rules. Working knowledge of the English language. Comply with the rules and regulations of the Board. **Examination:** Exam. **Fees:** $80 initial license fee. $30 renewal fee. **Governing Statute:** Public Health Code, Act 368 of 1978, as amended.

5243

Osteopathic Physician (D.O.)
Board of Osteopathic Medicine and Surgery
PO Box 30018
Lansing, MI 48909
Phone: (517)373-6650

Credential Type: License to practice. **Duration of License:** Three years. **Authorization:** Unlimited practice. **Requirements:** Graduate of four-year recognized osteopathic hospital. One year internship in American Osteopathic Association (AOA)-approved hospital. Renewal requires 150 hours of continuing medical education every three years. **Examination:** State examination. **Exemptions:** National Board Certificate and certified copy of grades accepted for licensure by endorsement. **Reciprocity:** Granted to licensees from all states with equivalent licensing requirements. **Fees:** $240 examination fee. $45 partial reexamination fee. $150 complete reexamination fee. $90 reciprocal license fee. $120 triennial renewal fee.

Credential Type: Limited license. **Authorization:** Allows practice by interns and residents. **Requirements:** Submit limited license application. **Fees:** $80 limited license fee.

Credential Type: Controlled substance license. **Duration of License:** Three years. **Requirements:** Submit application. **Fees:** $150 license fee. $150 triennial renewal fee.

5244

Physician
Michigan Board of Medicine
611 W. Ottawa St.
PO Box 30018
Lansing, MI 48909
Phone: (517)373-0680

Credential Type: License by examination. **Duration of License:** Three years. **Requirements:** Graduates of U.S., Canadian, and international medical schools must have one year of graduate medical education to take FLEX and two years to be licensed. Accepts endorsement of National Boards without further examination.

Renewal requires 150 credit hours of continuing medical education (CME). **Examination:** Federation Licensing Examination (FLEX) or National Board Certifying Examination. A single United States Medical Licensing Examination has been established to replace these exams. **Fees:** $309 FLEX fee (Part I). $359 FLEX fee (Part II). $539 FLEX fee (Both parts). $120 triennial renewal fee.

Credential Type: License by endorsement. **Duration of License:** Three years. **Requirements:** Hold approved out-of-state license or National Board Certificate or State Board.

Graduates of international medical schools must hold Educational Commission for Foreign Medical Graduates (ECFMG) Certificate. Must have completed specified basic science courses and clinical clerkships in hospitals that are board approved. **Reciprocity:** Endorses out-of-state licenses from states whose standards are substantially equivalent to Michigan's. **Fees:** $90 license fee. $120 triennial renewal fee.

Minnesota

5245

Osteopathic Physician (D.O.)
Board of Medical Examiners
2700 University Ave. W, Rm. 106
St. Paul, MN 551143-108
Phone: (612)642-0538

Credential Type: License to practice. **Duration of License:** One year. **Authorization:** Unlimited. **Requirements:** Gradua-

Minnesota 5246

Osteopathic Physician (D.O.), continued

tion with degree from an osteopathic hospital recognized by the State Board. One year internship or other approved graduate training. Renewal requires 75 continuing medical education hours every three years. **Examination:** Federation Licensing Examination (FLEX). **Exemptions:** National Board Certificate accepted for license by endorsement if grade average is 75 percent or above. **Reciprocity:** Granted to licensees of other states with similar board examinations. Examination grade must be at least 75 percent. **Fees:** $740 FLEX examination fee. $200 National Board Certificate endorsement fee. $200 reciprocal license fee. $115 annual renewal fee.

Credential Type: Temporary permit. **Duration of License:** Until board meets. **Authorization:** Allows practice by persons seeking reciprocal license or by diplomates of National Boards. **Requirements:** Submit application for temporary permit. **Fees:** $60 temporary permit fee.

5246

Physician
Board of Medical Examiners
2700 University Ave. W., No. 106
St. Paul, MN 55114-1080
Phone: (612)642-0538

Credential Type: License by examination. **Duration of License:** One year. **Requirements:** Graduates of U.S., Canadian, and international medical schools may sit for FLEX examination upon being accepted to, or during the first year of, accredited residency training. One year of graduate medical education is required to be licensed. Accepts endorsement of National Boards without further examination.

Licensees are required to complete 75 hours of continuing medical education (CME) credits every three years. **Examination:** Federation Licensing Examination (FLEX) or National Board Certifying Examination. A single United States Medical Licensing Examination has been established to replace these exams. **Fees:** $200 application fee. $250 FLEX fee (Part I). $300 FLEX fee (Part II). $425 FLEX fee (Both parts). $115 annual renewal fee.

Credential Type: License by endorsement. **Duration of License:** One year. **Requirements:** Hold out-of-state license or National Board Certificate or Licentiate of the Medical Council of Canada. All candidates must appear for interview.

Graduates of international medical schools must hold Educational Commission for Foreign Medical Graduates (ECFMG) Certificate. School must be state-approved. Must appear for interview. **Reciprocity:** Endorses all licenses granted by other states. **Fees:** $200 license fee. $115 annual renewal fee.

Mississippi

5247

Osteopathic Physician (D.O.)
State Board of Medical Licensure
2688-D Insurance Center Dr.
Jackson, MS 39216
Phone: (601)354-6645

Credential Type: License to practice. **Duration of License:** One year. **Authorization:** Unlimited. **Requirements:** Graduate with diploma from a school that is American Osteopathic Association (AOA)-approved. One year internship is required for all applicants after July 1, 1981. **Examination:** Federation Licensing Examination (FLEX). Special Purpose Examination (SPEX). **Exemptions:** National Board Certificate accepted for license by endorsement. **Reciprocity:** Granted to licensees from all states with requirements equivalent to Mississippi. **Fees:** $500 FLEX examination fee. $375 SPEX examination fee. $500 reciprocal license fee. $75 annual renewal fee.

5248

Physician
Mississippi State Board of Medical Licensure
2688-D Insurance Center Dr.
Jackson, MS 39216
Phone: (601)354-6645

Credential Type: License by examination. **Duration of License:** One year. **Requirements:** Graduates of U.S. and Canadian medical schools must have one year of graduate medical education to be licensed. Graduates of international medical schools must have three years of graduate medical education to take FLEX and to be licensed. Accepts endorsement of National Boards without further examination. **Examination:** Federation Licensing Examination (FLEX) or National Board Certifying Examination. A single United States Medical Licensing Examination has been established to replace these exams. **Fees:** $325 FLEX fee (Part I). $375 FLEX fee (Part II). $500 FLEX fee (Both parts). $75 annual renewal fee.

Credential Type: License by endorsement. **Duration of License:** One year. **Requirements:** Hold out-of-state license or National Board Certificate or Licentiate of the Medical Council of Canada. All candidates must appear for interview.

Graduates of international medical schools must hold Educational Commission for Foreign Medical Graduates (ECFMG) Certificate. School must be state-approved. Must appear for interview. **Reciprocity:** Endorses licenses from other states that are based on passage of the FLEX or National Board written examinations taken after March 8, 1973. **Fees:** $500 license fee. $75 annual renewal fee.

Missouri

5249

Osteopathic Physician (D.O.)
State Board of Registration for the Healing Arts
PO Box 4
Jefferson City, MO 65102
Phone: (314)751-0098

Credential Type: License to practice. **Duration of License:** One year. **Authorization:** Unlimited practice. **Requirements:** Graduation from an American Osteopathic Association (AOA)-approved college. One year internship. Renewal requires 25 hours of continuing medical education each year. **Examination:** Federation Licensing Examination (FLEX). **Exemptions:** National Board Certificate accepted for licensure by endorsement. **Reciprocity:** Granted to licensees from other states that have reciprocity with Missouri. Must have Board approval. **Fees:** $450 National Board Certificate endorsement fee. $450 reciprocal license fee. $30 annual renewal fee.

5250

Physician
Missouri State Board of Registration for the Healing Arts
3605 Missouri Blvd.
Jefferson City, MO 65109
Phone: (314)751-0098

Credential Type: License by examination. **Duration of License:** One year. **Requirements:** Graduates of U.S. and Canadian medical schools must have one year of graduate medical education to take Federation Licensing Examination (FLEX) and to be licensed. Graduates of international medical schools must have three years of graduate medical education to take FLEX and to be licensed. Accepts endorsement of National Boards without further examination.

Licensees are required to complete 75 hours of continuing medical education

(CME) credits every three years. **Examination:** Federation Licensing Examination (FLEX) or National Board Certifying Examination. A single United States Medical Licensing Examination has been established to replace these exams. **Fees:** $250 FLEX fee (Part I). $300 FLEX fee (Part II). $450 FLEX fee (Both parts). $75 annual renewal fee.

Credential Type: License by endorsement. **Duration of License:** One year. **Requirements:** Hold out-of-state license or National Board Certificate. Some candidates must appear.

Graduates of international medical schools must hold Educational Commission for Foreign Medical Graduates (ECFMG) Certificate. **Reciprocity:** Endorses all licenses granted by other states. **Fees:** $450 license fee. $75 annual renewal fee.

Montana

5251

Naturopathic Physician
Board of Alternative Health Care
111 N. Jackson
Helena, MT 59620
Phone: (406)444-3737

Credential Type: License. **Duration of License:** One year. **Requirements:** Graduation from an approved naturopathic medical college that has a minimum four-year, full-time resident program of academic and clinical study. Complete a clinical practicum while in school. **Examination:** NPLEX—Basic Sciences, Clinical Sciences, and minor surgery and homeopathic add-ons. **Reciprocity:** Yes. **Fees:** $300 application fee. $200 license fee. $350 renewal fee.

5252

Osteopathic Physician (D.O.)
Board of Medical Examiners
Professional and Occupational
  Licensing
1424 9th Ave.
Helena, MT 59620
Phone: (406)444-4284

Credential Type: License to practice. **Duration of License:** One year. **Authorization:** Unlimited practice. **Requirements:** Graduation from American Osteopathic Association (AOA)-approved college. One year internship approved by the AOA, American Medical Association (AMA), or State Board. **Examination:** Federation Licensing Examination (FLEX). **Exemptions:** National Board Certificate accepted for licensure by endorsement. **Reciprocity:** Granted to licensees from other states with requirements similar to Montana. Must have graduated after 1955. **Fees:** $240 FLEX examination fee (Component I). $290 FLEX examination fee (Component II). $465 FLEX examination fee (both components). $200 license application fee. $20 National Board Certificate endorsement fee. $15 DO annual board fee (resident). $7.50 DO annual board fee (non-resident). $125 annual composite board fee (active). $50 annual composite board fee (inactive).

5253

Physician
Montana Board of Medical
  Examiners
111 N. Jackson
Helena, MT 59620
Phone: (406)444-4284

Credential Type: License. **Duration of License:** One year. **Requirements:** Graduation from an approved medical school. Completion of a one-year internship or equivalent. **Examination:** FLEX exam. **Fees:** $200 application fee. $465 exam fee. $125 renewal fee. **Governing Statute:** Montana Code Annotated 37-3-301 through 37-3-328.

Nebraska

5254

Osteopath
Bureau of Examining Boards in
  Medicine and Surgery
301 Centennial Mall S.
PO Box 95007
Lincoln, NE 68509
Phone: (402)471-2115

Credential Type: License. **Duration of License:** Two years. **Requirements:** Must be a high school graduate and a graduate of an accredited school of osteopathy. **Examination:** Yes. **Fees:** $200 initial fee. $40 renewal fee.

5255

Physician/Surgeon
Nebraska Board of Examiners in
  Medicine and Surgery
301 Centennial Mall S.
PO Box 95007
Lincoln, NE 68509
Phone: (402)471-2115

Credential Type: License. **Duration of License:** Two years. **Requirements:** Must be a graduate of an accredited school of medicine, present proof that he/she has served at least one year of graduate medical education approved by the board. **Examination:** Yes. **Fees:** $200 application for license fee. $475 examination fee. $90 license to supervise physician assistant fee. $100 renewal fee. $30 license to supervise physician assistant renewal fee.

Nevada

5256

Osteopathic Physician (D.O.)
Board of Osteopathic Examiners
1198 Sweetwater Dr.
Reno, NV 89509
Phone: (702)826-8383

Credential Type: License to practice. **Duration of License:** One year. **Authorization:** Unlimited practice. **Requirements:** Diploma from an osteopathic college that requires 36 months of actual attendance and offers courses specified by statute. One year of an American Osteopathic Association (AOA)-approved internship or three years of American Medical Association (AMA)-approved postgraduate training. Renewal requires 35 continuing medical education hours per year. **Examination:** State examination. **Exemptions:** National Board Certificate accepted for license by endorsement. **Reciprocity:** Granted to holders of licenses issued by out-of-state DO boards and most composite boards. **Fees:** $200 examination fee. $200 reciprocal license fee. $100 annual registration fee.

5257

Physician
Nevada State Board of Medical
  Examiners
PO Box 7238
Reno, NV 89510
Phone: (702)688-2559

Credential Type: License. **Duration of License:** Two years. **Requirements:** Completion of a doctor of medicine program at an approved medical school. Three years of post-graduate training. **Examination:** Yes. **Fees:** $250 application fee. $400 registration fee.

New Hampshire

5258

Osteopathic Physician (D.O.)
Board of Registration in Medicine
Health and Welfare Bldg.
Hazen Dr.
Concord, NH 03301
Phone: (603)271-1203

Credential Type: License to practice. **Duration of License:** One year. **Authorization:** Unlimited practice. **Requirements:** Osteopathic degree from a college approved by the American Osteopathic Association (AOA). Two years of approved postgraduate training. 150 hours of continuing medical education is required every three years. **Examination:** State examination **Exemptions:** National Board Certificate accepted for licensure by endorsement. **Reciprocity:** None. **Fees:** $150 examination fee. $150 National Board Certificate endorsement fee. $50 annual renewal fee.

5259

Physician
Board of Registration in Medicine
Health & Welfare Bldg.
6 Hazen Dr.
Concord, NH 03301
Phone: (603)271-1203

Credential Type: License by examination. **Duration of License:** Two years. **Requirements:** Graduates of U.S., Canadian, and international medical schools must have two years of graduate medical education to take FLEX and to be licensed. Accepts endorsement of National Boards without further examination.

Licensees are required to complete 150 hours of continuing medical education (CME) credits every three years. **Examination:** Federation Licensing Examination (FLEX) or National Board Certifying Examination. A single United States Medical Licensing Examination has been established to replace these exams. **Fees:** $150 annual renewal fee.

Credential Type: License by endorsement. **Duration of License:** Two years. **Requirements:** Hold approved out-of-state license or National Board Certificate or Licentiate of the Medical Council of Canada. All candidates must appear for interview.

Graduates of international medical schools must hold Educational Commission for Foreign Medical Graduates (ECFMG) Certificate. Must appear for full board interview. **Reciprocity:** Applicants will be considered on an individual basis. Must be prepared to set up practice in New Hampshire within 18 months and must stay in practice for at least one year. **Fees:** $150 annual renewal fee.

New Jersey

5260

Osteopathic Physician (D.O.)
Board of Medical Examiners
28 W. State St.
Trenton, NJ 08608
Phone: (609)292-4843

Credential Type: License to practice. **Duration of License:** Two years. **Authorization:** Unlimited practice. **Requirements:** Graduation from a four-year osteopathic college. One year internship or specialty residency in a hospital approved by the board. **Examination:** Federation Licensing Examination (FLEX). **Exemptions:** National Board Certificate accepted for license by endorsement. **Reciprocity:** Granted to licensees from other states with board approval. State licensing examinations can not be accepted if taken after December 31, 1972. **Fees:** $425 FLEX examination fee (both components). $250 FLEX examination fee (Component I). $300 FLEX examination fee (Component II). $225 National Board Certificate endorsement fee. $160 biennial renewal fee.

5261

Physician
Board of Medical Examiners
28 W. State St., Rm. 914
Trenton, NJ 08608
Phone: (609)292-4843

Credential Type: License. **Duration of License:** Two years. **Requirements:** 21 years of age. Completion of at least two years of university level education including at least one course in biology, chemistry and physics. Doctor of Medicine or Doctor of Osteopathic degree from an approved medical school. Completion of a one-year internship at an approved hospital. **Examination:** FLEX exam. **Reciprocity:** Yes. **Fees:** $30 certificate fee. $425 exam fee. $225 license fee. $160 biennial registration fee. **Governing Statute:** NJSA 45:9. NJAC 13:35.

New Mexico

5262

Osteopathic Physician (D.O.)
Board of Osteopathic Medical Examiners
PO Box 25101
Santa Fe, NM 87504
Phone: (505)827-7171

Credential Type: License to practice. **Duration of License:** One year. **Authorization:** Unlimited practice. **Requirements:** Graduation from an osteopathic school that meets the statutory requirements of the state. One year internship in an American Osteopathic Association (AOA)- or American Medical Association (AMA)-approved hospital program. Renewal requires 75 hours of Category I continuing medical education every three years or 150 hours of general continuing medical education every three years. **Examination:** Federation Licensing Examination (FLEX). **Exemptions:** National Board Certificate accepted for license by endorsement. **Reciprocity:** Granted to licensees of all states. **Fees:** $355 FLEX examination fee. $255 National Board Certificate endorsement fee. $255 reciprocal license fee. $100 annual license fee.

5263

Physician
Board of Medical Examiners
LAMY Bldg., Rm. 129
491 Old Santa Fe Trail
PO Box 20001
Santa Fe, NM 87504
Phone: (505)827-7363

Credential Type: License by examination. **Duration of License:** Three years. **Requirements:** Graduates of U.S. and Canadian medical schools must have one year of graduate medical education to take FLEX and to be licensed. Graduates of international medical schools must have two years of graduate medical education to take FLEX and to be licensed. Accepts endorsement of National Boards without further examination.

Renewal requires 75 credit hours of American Medical Association (AMA) Category one CME. In lieu of continuing medical education (CME) requirements, the Board will accept the passage of FLEX Component II with a score of 75, certification or recertification by specialty board, or the AMA/PRA, American Academy of Family Physicians (AAFP) Certificate. **Examination:** Federation Licensing Examination (FLEX) or National Board Certifying Examination. A single United States Medical

Licensing Examination has been established to replace these exams. **Fees:** $290 FLEX fee (Part I). $340 FLEX fee (Part II). $500 FLEX fee (Both parts). $70 triennial renewal fee.

Credential Type: License by endorsement. **Duration of License:** Three years. **Requirements:** Hold out-of-state license or National Board Certificate or Licentiate of the Medical Council of Canada. All candidates must complete orientation course.

Graduates of international medical schools must hold Educational Commission for Foreign Medical Graduates (ECFMG) Certificate. Must have completed supervised clinical training in a hospital affiliated with an LCME accredited medical school or completed Accreditation Council for Graduate Medical Education (ACGME) accredited residency training. Must appear for interview and orientation. **Reciprocity:** Endorses all licenses granted by other states. **Fees:** $350 license fee. $70 triennial renewal fee.

New York

5264

Osteopathic Physician (D.O.)
State Board for Medicine
Cultural Education Center
Empire State Plaza
Albany, NY 12230
Phone: (518)474-3841

Credential Type: License to practice. **Duration of License:** Three years. **Authorization:** Unlimited practice. **Requirements:** Must complete an osteopathic program of not less than 32 months. School must be American Osteopathic Association (AOA)-approved or registered with the Regents of the University of the State of New York. Must complete one year of postgraduate training. **Examination:** Federation Licensing Examination (FLEX). **Exemptions:** National Board Certificate accepted for license by endorsement. **Fees:** $500 FLEX examination fee. $175 reexamination fee. $240 triennial renewal fee. $100 limited permit fee (for residents).

Credential Type: License by endorsement. **Requirements:** Valid out-of-state license. Passing FLEX scores. **Examination:** Federation Licensing Examination (FLEX). **Fees:** $375 endorsement fee.

5265

Physician
State Education Dept.
Div. of Professional Licensing Services
Cultural Education Center
Empire State Plaza
Albany, NY 12230
Phone: (518)474-3826

Credential Type: License. **Duration of License:** Three years. **Requirements:** Premedical undergraduate degree and four years of medical school. 21 years of age. Completion of one to three years of satisfactory hospital training depending upon education. U.S. citizen or alien lawfully admitted for permanent residency. **Examination:** National Board Examination or Federation Licensing Examination. **Fees:** $500 application fee. $240 renewal fee. **Governing Statute:** Title VIII Articles 130, 131 of the Education Law.

North Carolina

5266

Medical Doctor
North Carolina State Board of Medical Examiners
PO Box 26808
Raleigh, NC 27611
Phone: (919)876-3885

Credential Type: License. **Duration of License:** Two years. **Requirements:** Completion of four years of medical school and one year as a resident-in-training. Three letters of recommendations. **Examination:** FLEX exam. **Fees:** $615 exam fee. $25 resident-in-training fee. $50 renewal fee.

5267

Osteopath
North Carolina State Board of Medical Examiners
PO Box 26808
Raleigh, NC 27611
Phone: (919)876-3885

Credential Type: License. **Duration of License:** Two years. **Requirements:** Completion of four years of medical school at an accredited school of osteopathic medicine. One year as a resident-in-training. Three recommendations. 18 years of age. **Examination:** FLEX exam. **Fees:** $615 exam fee. $25 resident-in-training fee. $50 renewal fee.

North Dakota

5268

Osteopathic Physician (D.O.)
Board of Medical Examiners
418 E. Broadway, Ste. C10
Bismarck, ND 58501
Phone: (701)223-9485

Credential Type: License to practice. **Duration of License:** One year. **Authorization:** Unlimited practice. **Requirements:** Graduation from a board-approved osteopathic college. Complete a one year internship in an approved hospital. **Examination:** State examination. **Reciprocity:** Granted to licensees of all states if their licenses were obtained by passing examination. Requires board approval. **Fees:** $60 annual registration fee.

5269

Physician
Board of Medical Examiners
418 E. Broadway Ave., Ste. 12
Bismarck, ND 58501
Phone: (701)223-9485

Credential Type: License by examination. **Duration of License:** One year. **Requirements:** Graduates of U.S., Canadian, and international medical schools must have one year of graduate medical education to take Federation Licensing Examination (FLEX) and to be licensed. Accepts endorsement of National Boards without further examination. **Examination:** Federation Licensing Examination (FLEX) or National Board Certifying Examination. A single United States Medical Licensing Examination has been established to replace these exams. **Fees:** $75 annual renewal fee.

Credential Type: License by endorsement. **Duration of License:** One year. **Requirements:** Hold out-of-state license or National Board Certificate or Licentiate of the Medical Council of Canada or State Board exam prior to FLEX. Some candidates must appear for interview and/or oral exam.

Graduates of international medical schools must hold Educational Commission for Foreign Medical Graduates (ECFMG) Certificate or be certified by American specialty board. Must have three years of postgraduate training in the U.S. or Canada. School must be state-approved. Must appear for interview. **Reciprocity:** Endorses licenses granted by other states. Florida licensees must have passed North Dakota written examination before 1968 or FLEX after June 1969. **Fees:** $200 license fee. $75 annual renewal fee.

Ohio

5270

Doctor (Thoroughbred, Standardbred, and Quarter Horse Racing)
Ohio State Racing Commission
State Office Tower
77 S. High St., 18th Fl.
Columbus, OH 43266-0416
Phone: (614)466-2757

Credential Type: License Registration. **Requirements:** Submit application and fingerprint card. Pay fee. **Fees:** $25 registration fee.

5271

Osteopathic Physician (D.O.)
State Medical Board
77 S. High St., 17th Fl.
Columbus, OH 43215
Phone: (614)466-3934

Credential Type: License to practice. **Duration of License:** Two years. **Authorization:** Unlimited practice. **Requirements:** Graduation from an osteopathic college approved by the American Osteopathic Association (AOA). One year internship at an AOA- or American Medical Association (AMA)-approved hospital. Renewal requires 100 hours of continuing medical education every two years. Forty of the required continuing medical education hours must be in category I. **Examination:** Federation Licensing Examination (FLEX). **Exemptions:** National Board Certificate accepted for license by endorsement. **Fees:** $365 FLEX examination fee. $175 National Board Certificate endorsement. $160 biennial renewal fee.

Credential Type: License by endorsement. **Requirements:** Submit application for endorsement. Meet board requirements. **Fees:** $175 endorsement fee.

Credential Type: Temporary Certificate. **Authorization:** Allows practice for interns, residents, and fellows. **Requirements:** Submit application for temporary certificate. **Fees:** $10 certificate fee. $10 renewal fee.

5272

Physician
Ohio State Medical Board
77 S. High St., 17th Fl.
Columbia, OH 43266-0315
Phone: (614)466-3934

Credential Type: License by examination. **Duration of License:** Two years. **Requirements:** Graduates of U.S. medical schools must have one year of graduate medical education to take FLEX and to be licensed. Graduates of international medical schools must have two years of graduate medical education to take Federation Licensing Examination (FLEX) and to be licensed. Accepts endorsement of National Boards without further examination.

Renewal requires 100 hours of continuing medical education (CME). **Examination:** Federation Licensing Examination (FLEX) or National Board Certifying Examination. A single United States Medical Licensing Examination has been established to replace these exams. **Fees:** $220 FLEX fee (Part I). $275 FLEX fee (Part II). $430 FLEX fee (both parts). $100 biennial renewal fee.

Credential Type: License by endorsement. **Duration of License:** Two years. **Requirements:** Hold out-of-state license or National Board Certificate or Licentiate of the Medical Council of Canada. Some candidates must appear. U.S. residency training required. Professional experience abroad or in the U.S. may be substituted for U.S. residency training with approval.

Graduates of international medical schools must hold Educational Commission for Foreign Medical Graduates (ECFMG) Certificate. School must be state-approved. **Reciprocity:** Endorses licenses granted by other states. Applicants for reciprocal licenses will be considered on an individual basis. Only licenses based on passage of the FLEX or National Board written examinations taken after February 10, 1982 will be considered. **Fees:** $185 license fee. $100 biennial renewal fee.

Oklahoma

5273

Osteopathic Physician (D.O.)
State Board of Osteopathic Examiners
4848 N. Lincoln, Ste. 100
Oklahoma City, OK 73105
Phone: (405)528-8625

Credential Type: License. **Duration of License:** One year. **Requirements:** Doctor of Osteopathy degree. One-year internship or the equivalent in an approved hospital. 16 hours of continuing education each year. 21 years of age. No criminal convictions. **Examination:** National Osteopathic Medical Exam or the Oklahoma Osteopathic Exam. **Fees:** $200 exam fee. $200 application fee. $100 license fee. $100 renewal fee.

5274

Physician/Surgeon (M.D.)
State Board of Medical Licensure and Supervision
PO Box 18256
Oklahoma City, OK 73154
Phone: (405)848-6841

Credential Type: License. **Duration of License:** One year. **Requirements:** Doctor of Medicine degree. One year of supervised clinical experience. **Examination:** National Board Exam or Federal Licensing Exam. **Fees:** $420 exam fee. $350 application fee. $50 license fee. $100 renewal fee.

Oregon

5275

Naturopathic Physician
Board of Naturopathic Examiners
800 NE Oregon St.
Salem, OR 97232
Phone: (503)731-4045

Credential Type: License. **Duration of License:** Two years. **Requirements:** Two years of liberal arts or science study. Graduation from an approved naturopathic college. **Examination:** Yes. **Fees:** $350 exam fee. $150 license fee. $375 renewal fee. **Governing Statute:** ORS 685.020.

5276

Osteopathic Physician
Oregon Board of Medical Examiners
620 Crown Plaza
1500 SW 1st Ave.
Portland, OR 97201
Phone: (503)229-5770

Credential Type: License. **Duration of License:** Two years. **Requirements:** Graduation from an approved medical/osteopathic school. Completion of a one-year approved internship/residency training. **Examination:** Yes. **Fees:** $465 exam fee. $270 filing fee. $330 renewal fee. **Governing Statute:** ORS 677.010 to 677.990.

5277

Physician
Oregon Board of Medical Examiners
620 Crown Plaza
1500 SW 1st St.
Portland, OR 97201
Phone: (503)229-5770

Credential Type: License. **Duration of License:** Two years. **Requirements:** Graduation from an approved medical/osteopathic school. Completion of a one-year approved internship/residency training. **Examination:** Yes. **Fees:** $465 exam fee. $270 filing fee. $330 renewal fee. **Governing Statute:** ORS 677.010 to 677.990.

Pennsylvania

5278

Osteopathic Physician (D.O.)
State Board of Osteopathic Medicine
PO Box 2649
Harrisburg, PA 17105
Phone: (717)783-4858

Credential Type: License to practice. **Duration of License:** Two years. **Authorization:** Unrestricted practice. **Requirements:** Graduation from osteopathic hospital which meets statutory requirements. One year of rotating internship that meets with board approval. **Examination:** State examination. Osteopathic manipulative therapy examination. **Exemptions:** National Board Certificate or Federation Licensing Examination (FLEX) accepted for license by endorsement providing the applicant holds a valid license in another state and meets board requirements. **Reciprocity:** Granted to licensees of other states that have requirements equal to Pennsylvania. Must not have previously failed Pennsylvania licensing exam. Practical examination in osteopathic manipulative therapy required. **Fees:** $220 state examination fee. $75 biennial renewal fee.

5279

Physician
Pennsylvania State Board of Medicine
PO Box 2649
Harrisburg, PA 17105
Phone: (717)783-4858

Credential Type: License by examination. **Duration of License:** Two years. **Requirements:** Must have two years of graduate medical education to be licensed. (Only one year of graduate medical education is required for applicants with U.S. training prior to July 1, 1987.) Accepts endorsement of National Boards without further examination. **Examination:** Federation Licensing Examination (FLEX) or National Board Certifying Examination. A single United States Medical Licensing Examination has been established to replace these exams. **Fees:** $275 FLEX fee (Part I). $330 FLEX fee (Part II). $485 FLEX fee (both parts). $25 biennial renewal fee.

Credential Type: License by endorsement. **Duration of License:** Two years. **Requirements:** Hold out-of-state license or National Board Certificate or Licentiate of the Medical Council of Canada.

Graduates of international medical schools must hold Educational Commission for Foreign Medical Graduates (ECFMG) Certificate. **Reciprocity:** Endorses licenses granted by other states. **Fees:** $20 license fee. $25 biennial renewal fee.

Rhode Island

5280

Osteopathic Physician (D.O.)
Board of Medical Licensure and Discipline
205 Cannon Bldg.
3 Capitol Hill
Providence, RI 02908-5097
Phone: (401)277-3855

Credential Type: License to practice. **Duration of License:** One year. **Authorization:** Unlimited practice. **Requirements:** Graduate of a board-approved osteopathic hospital. Complete one year of board-approved postgraduate training. Renewal requires 75 hours of continuing medical education every three years. **Examination:** Federation Licensing Examination (FLEX). Osteopathic theory and practice examination. **Exemptions:** National Board Certificate accepted for license by endorsement with board approval. **Reciprocity:** Granted to licensees from other states with requirements equal to Rhode Island. Personal interview required. **Fees:** $350 reciprocal license fee. $350 examination fee.

Credential Type: Temporary permit. **Authorization:** Allows practice by interns, residents, and hospital officers. **Requirements:** Submit application for temporary permit. **Fees:** $25 permit fee.

5281

Physician
Rhode Island Board of Medicine and Discipline
Joseph E. Cannon Bldg., Rm. 205
3 Capitol Hill
Providence, RI 02908-5097
Phone: (401)277-3855

Credential Type: License by examination. **Duration of License:** One year. **Requirements:** Graduates of U.S. medical schools must have one year of graduate medical education to take Federation Licensing Examination (FLEX) and to be licensed. Graduates of international medical schools must have three years of graduate medical education to take FLEX and to be licensed. Accepts endorsement of National Boards without further examination.

Licensees are required to complete 60 hours of CME every three years. **Examination:** Federation Licensing Examination (FLEX) or National Board Certifying Examination. A single United States Medical Licensing Examination has been established to replace these exams. **Fees:** $350 FLEX fee (Parts I or II or both). $235 annual renewal fee.

Credential Type: License by endorsement. **Duration of License:** One year. **Requirements:** Hold approved out-of-state license or National Board Certificate or Licentiate of the Medical Council of Canada. All candidates must appear for interview.

Graduates of international medical schools must hold Educational Commission for Foreign Medical Graduates (ECFMG) Certificate. Must have three years of postgraduate training in the U.S. or Canada. School must be state-approved. Must have completed supervised clinical training in a hospital affiliated with a Liaison Committee on Medical Education (LCME)-accredited medical school or completed Accreditation Council for Graduate Medical Education (ACGME)-accredited residency training. Must appear for interview. **Reciprocity:** Out-of-state licenses will be considered for endorsement on an individual basis. **Fees:** $350 license fee. $235 annual renewal fee.

South Carolina

5282

Osteopathic Physician (D.O.)
State Board of Medical Examiners
1220 Pickers
PO Box 12245
Columbia, SC 29221
Phone: (803)734-8901

Credential Type: License to practice. **Duration of License:** One year. **Authorization:** Unlimited practice. **Requirements:** Graduation from an American Osteopathic Association (AOA)-approved osteopathic school. One year approved internship. **Examination:** Federation Licensing Examination (FLEX). **Exemptions:** National Board Certificate accepted for licensure by endorsement. **Fees:** $600 FLEX examination fee. $75 temporary license fee. $80 annual renewal fee. $500 license endorsement fee.

5283

Physician/Surgeon
South Carolina State Board of
  Medical Examiners
1220 Pickens St.
Columbia, SC 29201
Phone: (803)734-8901

Credential Type: Physician License. **Requirements:** Generally, graduation from an approved medical school. Other requirements are very specific. **Examination:** Federation Licensing Examination (FLEX). SPEX examination. **Fees:** $1,100 exam fee. $80 re-registration fee.

Credential Type: Physician's Assistant License. **Requirements:** An application submitted by a physician with whom the assistant will work and who will assume responsibility for the assistant's performance. Completion of a certified assistant's training program. **Fees:** $75 application and examination fee. $25 re-registration fee.

South Dakota

5284

Osteopathic Physician (D.O.)
Board of Medical and Osteopathic
  Examiners
1323 S. Minnesota Ave.
Sioux Falls, SD 57105
Phone: (605)336-1965

Credential Type: License to practice. **Duration of License:** One year. **Authorization:** Unlimited practice. **Requirements:** Graduation from an American Osteopathic Association (AOA)-approved osteopathic college. One year internship in AOA—or American Medical Association (AMA)-approved hospital. All applicants entering their postgraduate training after July 1, 1987 are required to complete an approved residency. **Examination:** Federation Licensing Examination (FLEX). **Exemptions:** National Board Certificate accepted for licensure by endorsement. **Reciprocity:** Reciprocity exists with Colorado, Georgia, Idaho, Illinois, Indiana, Iowa, Kansas, Kentucky, Massachusetts, Minnesota, Missouri, New Jersey, New York, North Dakota, Ohio, Oregon, Rhode Island, South Carolina, Virginia, Wisconsin, and Wyoming. Texas applicants are included when their license is based on passage of FLEX. All others will be considered individually. **Fees:** $550 FLEX examination fee (both components). $275 FLEX examination fee (Component I or II). $200 National Board Certificate endorsement fee. $200 reciprocal license fee. $50 Locum tenens certificate fee.

5285

Physician
South Dakota Dept. of Medical
  Examiners
1323 S. Minnesota Ave.
Sioux Falls, SD 57105
Phone: (605)336-1965

Credential Type: License by examination. **Duration of License:** One year. **Requirements:** Graduates of U.S., Canadian, and international medical schools may sit for FLEX examination upon being accepted to, or during the first year of, accredited residency training. Two years of graduate medical education is required to be licensed. Accepts endorsement of National Boards without further examination. **Examination:** Federation Licensing Examination (FLEX) or National Board Certifying Examination. A single United States Medical Licensing Examination has been established to replace these exams. **Fees:** $275 FLEX fee (Part I or Part II). $550 FLEX fee (Both parts). $50 annual renewal fee.

Credential Type: License by endorsement. **Duration of License:** One year. **Requirements:** Hold approved out-of-state license or National Board Certificate or Licentiate of the Medical Council of Canada. All candidates must appear for interview.

Graduates of international medical schools must hold Educational Commission for Foreign Medical Graduates (ECFMG) Certificate. School must be state-approved. Must appear for interview. **Reciprocity:** Endorses licenses granted by other states. **Fees:** $200 license fee. $50 annual renewal fee.

Tennessee

5286

Osteopathic Physician
Board of Osteopathic Examination
283 Plus Park Blvd.
Nashville, TN 37247
Phone: (615)367-6393

Credential Type: License. **Requirements:** 18 years old. Graduate of osteopathic school of medicine. 16 hours of CME for renewal. **Examination:** National Board of Osteopathic Medical Examiners or Tennessee State Board examination. **Reciprocity:** Yes. **Fees:** $60 Registration. $200 Examination. $50 Application.

5287

Physician
Board of Medical Examiners
283 Plus Park Blvd.
Nashville, TN 37247
Phone: (615)367-6231

Credential Type: License. **Requirements:** Graduate of an accredited medical school and residency training. Letters of reference. **Examination:** FLEX or National Board. **Reciprocity:** Yes. **Fees:** $24 Registration. $415 Examination. $175 Application. $45 Renewal.

Texas

5288

Osteopathic Physician (D.O.)
State Board of Medical Examiners
PO Box 13562
Capitol Station
Austin, TX 78711
Phone: (512)452-1078

Credential Type: License to practice. **Duration of License:** One year. **Authorization:** Unlimited practice. **Requirements:** DO or MD degree from an approved college. One year internship. **Examination:** Federation Licensing Examination (FLEX). Medical jurisprudence examination. **Exemptions:** National Board Certificate accepted (as of 1991) for licensure by endorsement. **Reciprocity:** Granted to licensees from all states. Medical jurisprudence examination is required. In some cases, Special Purpose Examination (SPEX) may also be required. **Fees:** $500 examination fee. $500 reciprocal license fee. $50 temporary license fee. $25 intern registration fee. $92 annual renewal fee.

5289

Physician
Texas State Board of Medical Examiners
1812 Centre Creek Dr., Ste. 300
Austin, TX 78754
Phone: (512)834-7728

Credential Type: License. **Duration of License:** One year. **Requirements:** 21 years of age. 60 semester hours of premedical college courses. Graduation from an approved medical school or college. One-year program of graduate medical training approved by the Board. **Examination:** Federation Licensing Examination (FLEX). Texas jurisprudence examination. Additional exams or interviews may be required. **Fees:** $900 application and exam fee. $200 intern and resident permit fee. $400 renewal fee. **Governing Statute:** VACS 4495b, 22 TAC 163.

Utah

5290

Osteopathic Physician and Surgeon
Div. of Occupaional and Professional Licensing
160 E. 300 S.
PO Box 45802
Salt Lake City, UT 84145
Phone: (801)530-6628

Credential Type: License. **Duration of License:** Two years. **Requirements:** Must complete at least two years of college work. Must graduate from a college of osteopathic medicine. Must complete 12 months of hospital training or approved postgraduate training or hospital residence training. **Examination:** Yes. **Fees:** $150 license fee. $100 renewal fee. $90 controlled substance license fee. $50 controlled substance renewal fee.

5291

Physician and Surgeon
Dept. of Commerce
Div. of Occupational and Professional Licensing
160 E. 300 S.
PO Box 45802
Salt Lake City, UT 84145
Phone: (801)530-6628

Credential Type: License. **Duration of License:** Two years. **Requirements:** Must have completed two years of general study in a college or university. Must hold a degree of doctor of medicine from a school which is approved by the Division. Must have completed 12 months of hospital training or hospital residency training. **Examination:** Yes. **Fees:** $100 license fee. $75 renewal fee. $90 controlled substance license fee. $50 controlled substance license renewal fee.

Vermont

5292

Osteopath
Board of Osteopathic Examination and Registration
Pavilion Office Bldg.
Montpelier, VT 05602
Phone: (802)828-2363

Credential Type: License. **Duration of License:** Two years. **Requirements:** 18 years of age. Good moral character. Two years of college. Four year course in osteopathic medicine. One year internship in a hospital. Pass either a state or national exam. Deemed eligible to take the state exam. **Examination:** Yes. **Reciprocity:** Yes. **Fees:** $25 Exam. $5 Recording fee. $4 Renewal (non-resident). $6 Renewal (resident). **Governing Statute:** Title 26, VSA Sections 1831-1836.

5293

Physician/Surgeon
State Board of Medical Examiners
Pavilion Office Bldg.
Montpelier, VT 05602
Phone: (802)828-2363

Credential Type: License. **Duration of License:** Two years. **Requirements:** Age of Majority. High school graduate. Good moral character. Two year course of study in a college of arts and sciences. Graduate of an accredited medical college. Successful completion of FLEX or National Board of Medical Examiners Exam. Letters of reference as to moral character and professional competence from Chief of Staff and two others from hospital last affiliated with. Demonstrate competency in reading, writing and speaking the English language. Personal Interview. **Examination:** Yes. **Reciprocity:** Yes. **Fees:** $475 Federation Licensing Examination. $105 License Application. $100 Renewal. **Governing Statute:** Title 26, VSA Sections 1391-1400.

Virginia

5294

Osteopathic Physician (D.O.)
Board of Medicine
1601 Rolling Hills Dr.
Richmond, VA 23233-5005
Phone: (804)662-9908

Credential Type: License to practice. **Duration of License:** Two years. **Authorization:** Unlimited practice. **Requirements:** Graduation from an American Osteopathic Association (AOA)-approved osteopathic college. One year internship approved by the AOA or American Medical Association (AMA). **Examination:** Federation Licensing Examination (FLEX). **Exemptions:** National Board Certificate accepted for licensure by endorsement. **Reciprocity:** Granted to licensees from states with requirements equivalent to Virginia. **Fees:** $550 FLEX examination fee (both components). $275 FLEX examination fee (Component I or II). $300 reciprocal license fee. $125 biennial renewal fee.

5295

Physician
Board of Medicine
1601 Rolling Hills Dr.
Richmond, VA 23261-5005
Phone: (804)662-9920

Credential Type: License. **Duration of License:** One year. **Requirements:** Graduation from an approved school of medicine or school of osteopathy. Completion of an approved one-year residency at a hospital in the U.S. or Canada. 18 years of age. **Examination:** Yes. **Fees:** $500 exam fee.

Washington

5296

Naturopath
Dept. of Health
1112 SE Quince
Olympia, WA 98504
Phone: (206)753-4614

Credential Type: Naturopath Certificate. **Duration of License:** One year. **Requirements:** Graduate of an approved school. Submit to background investigation. Renewal requires 20 continuing education hours annually. **Examination:** Written examination. **Reciprocity:** Yes. **Fees:** $550 examination fee. $300 partial examination fee (Basic Science portion). $550 renewal fee. $50 certificate fee. $50 duplicate certificate fee. $550 application for reciprocity fee.

Washington

5297

Osteopathic Physician (D.O.)
Board of Osteopathic Medicine and Surgery
1300 Quince St.
MS:EY-23
Olympia, WA 98504
Phone: (206)586-8438

Credential Type: License to practice. **Duration of License:** One year. **Authorization:** Unlimited practice. **Requirements:** Graduation from an osteopathic college approved by the American Osteopathic Association (AOA). One year internship in AOA- or American Medical Association (AMA)-approved hospital. Renewal requires 150 hours of continuing medical education every three years. Sixty hours of the continuing medical education requirement must be in Category I courses. **Examination:** Federation Licensing Examination (FLEX). Osteopathic Principles and Practices examination (OPP). **Exemptions:** National Board Certificate accepted for licensure by endorsement. **Reciprocity:** None. **Fees:** $600 license/examination fee (FLEX and OPP). $100 OPP examination fee. $400 National Board Certificate endorsement fee. $300 annual renewal fee.

5298

Physician
Washington Dept. of Health
Medical Services Unit
1300 Quince St., EY-25
Olympia, WA 98504
Phone: (206)586-8438

Credential Type: License by examination. **Duration of License:** One year. **Requirements:** Graduates of U.S., Canadian, and international medical schools must have two years of graduate medical education to take FLEX and to be licensed. Accepts endorsement of National Boards without further examination.

Licensees are required to complete 150 hours of continuing medical education (CME) every three years. In lieu of the CME requirement, the Board will accept recertification by a specialty board or Certificates of American Medical Association (AMA)/PRA, American Academy of Family Physicians (AAFP), American College of Obstetricians and Gynecologists (ACOG) etc. **Examination:** Federation Licensing Examination (FLEX) or National Board Certifying Examination. A single United States Medical Licensing Examination has been established to replace these exams. **Fees:** $295 FLEX fee (Part I). $320 FLEX fee (Part II). $600 FLEX fee (Both parts). $240 annual renewal fee. Add $25 to all fees if initial application.

Credential Type: License by endorsement. **Duration of License:** One year. **Requirements:** Hold approved out-of-state license or National Board Certificate or Licentiate of the Medical Council of Canada completed after 1969. Some candidates must appear for interview.

Graduates of international medical schools must hold Educational Commission for Foreign Medical Graduates (ECFMG) Certificate. **Reciprocity:** Endorses licenses granted by other states. **Fees:** $300 license fee (Add $25 if initial application). $240 annual renewal fee.

West Virginia

5299

Medical Doctor
Board of Medicine
3412 Chesterfield Ave.
Charleston, WV 25304
Phone: (304)348-2921

Alternate Information: 100 Dee Dr., Charleston, WV 25311

Credential Type: License. **Duration of License:** Two years. **Requirements:** Graduation from an approved medical school. One year postgraduate training. Pass exam (75 percent). Never convicted of a felony. **Examination:** Yes. **Fees:** $200 Application. $500 Examination. $200 Renewal (Active), $50 Renewal (Inactive).

5300

Osteopathic Physician
Board of Osteopathy
334 Penco Rd.
Weirton, WV 26062
Phone: (304)723-4638

Credential Type: License. **Duration of License:** Two years. **Requirements:** 18 years old. Graduate of approved osteopathic school. One year in an approved hospital. Never convicted of a felony. **Examination:** Yes. **Reciprocity:** Yes. **Fees:** $100 Reciprocity. $200 National Boards. $55 Renewal.

Wisconsin

5301

Medical Doctor/Doctor of Osteopathy
Regulations and Licensing Dept.
Medical Board
PO Box 8935
Madison, WI 53708-8935
Phone: (608)266-8609

Credential Type: License. **Requirements:** Graduation from a medical school. Completion of a one-year internship. 18 years of age. **Examination:** Federation Licensing Examination (FLEX) or NBME. **Reciprocity:** Yes.

5302

Osteopathic Physician (D.O.)
Medical Examining Board
1400 E. Washington Ave.
Madison, WI 53702
Phone: (608)266-2811

Credential Type: License to practice. **Duration of License:** Two years. **Authorization:** Unlimited practice. **Requirements:** Graduation from an approved osteopathic college. One year internship in an approved hospital. Renewal requires 30 hours of Category I continuing medical education every two years. **Examination:** Federation Licensing Examination (FLEX). **Exemptions:** National Board Certificates accepted for licensure by endorsement. **Fees:** $405 FLEX examination fee. $40 National Board Certificate endorsement fee. $82 biennial renewal fee.

Credential Type: License by endorsement. **Duration of License:** Until next examination. **Authorization:** Granted to applicants awaiting oral examination. **Requirements:** Valid license from other state. Meet board approval. Oral examination required. Written examination required if licensed before 1972. **Requirements:** Submit temporary license application. **Fees:** $50 endorsement fee. Temporary License. **Fees:** $10 temporary license fee (if more than 30 days to examination).

Wyoming

5303

Physician, Medical and Osteopath
State Board of Medical Examiners
Barrett Bldg.
2301 Central Ave.
Cheyenne, WY 82002
Phone: (307)777-6463

Credential Type: License. **Duration of License:** One year. **Requirements:** Graduate from an approved school. One year internship; or, one year postgraduate training. Pass a written exam. Appear for a personal interview. **Examination:** Yes. **Fees:** $100 Licence. $40 Renewal. $25 Temporary permit.

Plumbers and Pipefitters

The following states grant licenses in this occupational category as of the date of publication:

Alabama	District of	Illinois	Massachusetts	New Hampshire	Oregon	Utah
Alaska	Columbia	Indiana	Michigan	New Jersey	Rhode Island	Vermont
Arkansas	Florida	Kentucky	Minnesota	New Mexico	South Carolina	Washington
Colorado	Georgia	Louisiana	Montana	North Carolina	South Dakota	
Connecticut	Hawaii	Maine	Nebraska	North Dakota	Tennessee	
	Idaho	Maryland	Nevada	Oklahoma	Texas	

Alabama

5304

Apprentice Gas Fitter
Alabama Plumbers and Gas Fitters Examiners Board
11 W. Oxmoor Rd., Ste. 104
Birmingham, AL 35209
Phone: (205)945-4857

Credential Type: Registration. **Duration of License:** One year. **Requirements:** 16 years of age. Must possess sufficient education and experience. **Fees:** $15 registration and card fee.

5305

Apprentice Plumber
Alabama Plumbers and Gas Fitters Examiners Board
11 W. Oxmoor Rd., Ste. 104
Birmingham, AL 35209
Phone: (205)945-4857

Credential Type: Registration. **Duration of License:** One year. **Requirements:** 16 years of age. Must possess sufficient education and experience. **Fees:** $15 registration and card fee.

5306

Journeyman Gas Fitter
Alabama Plumbers and Gas Fitters Examiners Board
11 W. Oxmoor Rd., Ste. 104
Birmingham, AL 35209
Phone: (205)945-4857

Credential Type: Certificate. **Duration of License:** One year. **Requirements:** 16 years of age. Must possess sufficient education and experience. Must have an apprentice card. **Examination:** Written Journeyman Gas Fitter Examination. **Fees:** $50 exam fee. $50 card fee.

5307

Journeyman Plumber
Alabama Plumbers and Gas Fitters Examiners Board
11 W. Oxmoor Rd., Ste. 104
Birmingham, AL 35209
Phone: (205)945-4857

Credential Type: Certificate. **Duration of License:** One year. **Requirements:** 16 years of age. Must possess sufficient education and experience. Must have an apprentice card. **Examination:** Written Journeyman Plumber Examination. **Fees:** $50 exam fee. $50 card fee.

5308

Master Gas Fitter
Alabama Plumbers and Gas Fitters Examiners Board
11 W. Oxmoor Rd., Ste. 104
Birmingham, AL 35209
Phone: (205)945-4857

Credential Type: Certificate. **Duration of License:** One year. **Requirements:** 16 years of age. Must possess sufficient education and experience. Must have a journeyman's card. **Examination:** Written Master Gas Fitter Examination. **Fees:** $100 exam fee. $75 card fee.

5309

Master Plumber
Alabama Plumbers and Gas Fitters Examiners Board
11 W. Oxmoor Rd., Ste. 104
Birmingham, AL 35209
Phone: (205)945-4857

Credential Type: Certificate. **Duration of License:** One year. **Requirements:** 16 years of age. Must possess sufficient education and experience. Must have a journeyman's card. **Examination:** Written Master Plumber Examination. **Fees:** $100 exam fee. $75 card fee.

5310

Plumber and/or Gas Fitter
Alabama Plumers and Gas Fitters Examiners Board
11 West Oxmoor Rd.
Birmingham, AL 35209
Phone: (205)945-4857

Credential Type: Certificate. **Duration of License:** One year. **Requirements:** 16 years of age. Must posses sufficient education and experience. **Examination:** Yes. **Fees:** $50 journeyman exam fee. $50 journeyman card fee. $100 master exam fee. $75 master card fee.

Alaska

5311

Plumber
Alaska Dept. of Labor
Div. of Labor Standards and Safety
Mechanical Inspection
PO Box 107021
Anchorage, AK 99510
Phone: (907)283-3778

Alternate Information: PO Box 21149, Juneau, AK 99802, (907)465-4871

Credential Type: Plumber Journeyworker Certificate. **Duration of License:** One or three years. **Requirements:** Four years or 8,000 hours of experience. Accredited apprenticeship or classroom training may be substituted for some of the work experience required. Submit letter of experience from prior employer or union. **Examination:** Yes. **Fees:** $40 annual license fee, or $75 triennial license fee.

Credential Type: Plumber Restricted Certificate. **Duration of License:** One or three years. **Requirements:** Two years or 4,000 hours of experience. Accredited apprenticeship or classroom training may be substituted for some of the work experience required. Submit letter of experience from prior employer or union. **Examination:** Yes. **Fees:** $40 annual license fee, or $75 triennial license fee.

Credential Type: Plumber Trainee Certificate. **Duration of License:** One or three years. **Requirements:** Submit letter attesting applicant will be working under a certified plumber. **Fees:** $40 annual license fee, or $75 triennial license fee.

Arkansas

5312

Gas Fitter
Arkansas Dept. of Health
Div. of Plumbing and Natural Gas
4815 W. Markham
Little Rock, AR 72201
Phone: (501)661-2642

Credential Type: License. **Requirements:** Served two years as a Registered Gas Fitter Trainee. **Examination:** Yes. **Fees:** $75 Written and practical examinations. $75 License.

5313

Gas Fitter Supervisor
Arkansas Dept. of Health
Div. of Plumbing and Natural Gas
4815 W. Markham
Little Rock, AR 72201
Phone: (501)661-2642

Credential Type: License. **Duration of License:** One year. **Requirements:** Minimum of six years of gas fitting experience. One full year as a licensed gas fitter. **Examination:** Yes. **Fees:** $125 Written and practical examination. $200 License. $200 Renewal.

5314

Gas Fitter Trainee
Arkansas Dept. of Health
Div. of Plumbing and Natural Gas
4815 W. Markham
Little Rock, AR 72201
Phone: (501)661-2642

Credential Type: License. **Duration of License:** One year. **Requirements:** Must have secured a training agreement from an employer who is or employs licensed gas fitters. **Examination:** No **Fees:** $25 License. $25 Renewal.

5315

Hospital Maintenance Plumber
Arkansas Dept. of Health
Div. of Plumbing and Natural Gas
4815 W. Markham St.
Little Rock, AR 72201
Phone: (501)661-2642

Credential Type: License. **Duration of License:** One year. **Requirements:** Must have a four year training period. State Committee of Plumbing Examiners may waive experience based on other evidence. **Examination:** Yes. **Fees:** $75 Written and practical examinations. $37.50 License. $37.50 Renewal.

5316

Hospital Maintenance Plumber Trainee
Arkansas Dept. of Health
Div. of Plumbing and Natural Gas
4815 W. Markham
Little Rock, AR 72201
Phone: (501)661-2642

Credential Type: License. **Duration of License:** One year. **Requirements:** Must have a signed training agreement from an employer who is licensed. Must serve a training period of four years. The State Committee of Plumbing Examiners may waive the experience requirement. **Examination:** No **Fees:** $25 Registration. $25 Renewal.

5317

Hospital Maintenance Plumbing Supervisor
Arkansas Dept. of Health
Div. of Plumbing and Natural Gas
4815 W. Markham
Little Rock, AR 72201
Phone: (501)661-2642

Credential Type: License. **Duration of License:** One year. **Requirements:** Must have a minimum of six years hospital maintenance plumbing experience or its equivalent. One year of the six must have been as a licensed hospital maintenance plumber. **Examination:** Yes. **Fees:** $125 Written and practical examinations. $100 License. $100 Renewal.

5318

Journeyman Plumber
Arkansas Dept. of Health
Div. of Plumbing and Natural Gas
4815 W. Markham St.
Little Rock, AR 72201
Phone: (501)661-2642

Credential Type: License. **Duration of License:** One year. **Requirements:** Provide evidence of completion of apprenticeship training; or, five years experience in plumbing. Graduates of trade school courses in plumbing will be given credit toward the five year experience requirement. **Examination:** Yes. **Fees:** $75 Written and Practical Examination. $75 License. $75 Renewal.

5319

Limited Plumber
Arkansas Dept. of Health
Div. of Plumbing and Natural Gas
4815 W. Markham
Little Rock, AR 72201
Phone: (501)661-2642

Credential Type: License. **Duration of License:** One year. **Requirements:** Show proof of apprenticeship training; or, minimum of five years experience in plumbing. Trade school graduates (or correspondence schools) will be given credit toward the experience requirement. **Examination:** Yes. **Fees:** $50 Written and practical examination. $50 License. $ percent0 Renewal.

Arkansas 5320

5320

Limited Plumber Assistant
Arkansas Dept. of Health
Div. of Plumbing and Natural Gas
4815 W. MArkham
Little Rock, AR 72201
Phone: (501)661-2642

Credential Type: License. **Duration of License:** One year. **Requirements:** Qualifications determined from application. **Examination:** Yes. **Fees:** $25 Written and practical examination. $25 License. $25 Renewal.

5321

Master Plumber
Arkansas Dept. of Health
Div. of Plumbing and Natural Gas
4815 W. Markham St.
Little Rock, AR 72201
Phone: (501)661-2642

Credential Type: License. **Duration of License:** One year. **Requirements:** Must have six years of experience. One full year of experience as a licensed journeyman plumber. **Examination:** Yes. **Fees:** $125 Written and Practical examination. $200 License. $200 Renewal.

5322

Plumber Apprentice
Arkansas Dept. of Health
Div. of Plumbing and Natural Gas
4815 W. Markham St.
Little Rock, AR 72201
Phone: (501)661-2642

Credential Type: License. **Duration of License:** One year. **Requirements:** Must have a signed agreement from an employer who is licensed, or employs licensed plumbers. **Examination:** No **Fees:** $25 License. $25 Renewal.

5323

Pump Installer
Waterwell Construction Commission
One Capitol Mall, Ste. 2C
Little Rock, AR 72201
Phone: (501)682-1025

Credential Type: License. **Requirements:** 18 years of age. Two years experience on-the-job training. **Examination:** Yes. **Fees:** $70 License. $70 Renewal.

5324

Special Gas Fitter
Arkansas Dept of Health
Div. of Plumbing and Natural Gas
4815 W. Markham St.
Little Rock, AR 72201
Phone: (501)661-2642

Credential Type: License. **Requirements:** Must complete gas filler apprentice training; or, a minimum of five years experience at the trade. Trade school or correspondence courses can substitute for part of the five years experience. **Examination:** Yes. **Fees:** $75 Written examination. $75 License. $75 Renewal.

Colorado

5325

Journeyman Plumber
Examining Board of Plumbers
Dept. of Regulatory Agencies
Div. of Registrations
1390 Logan St., Ste 400
Denver, CO 80203-2390
Phone: (303)894-2319

Credential Type: Journeyman Plumber's license. **Duration of License:** One year. **Requirements:** Have at least 6800 hours of practical experience. School courses in plumbing work from an accredited trade school or community college counts as one hour for every six hours of training or experience up to a maximum of one year. Military experience or training in plumbing counts as one month for every six months of training or experience up to a maximum of one year. The maximum credit allowed for plumbing maintenance work is two years. **Examination:** Board administered journeyman plumber's examination, written and practical sections. **Fees:** $39 exam fee. $39 permit fee. $69 license fee. **Governing Statute:** Colorado Statutes Title 12, Article 58.

Credential Type: License by endorsement. **Duration of License:** One year. **Requirements:** Hold a current license from another state for at least six months. Complete a state approved apprenticeship program or 6800 hours of practical experience or its equivalent. Complete a comparable state plumbing examination based on the Uniform Plumbing Code currently adopted by the Colorado Examining Board of Plumbers. **Fees:** $39 permit fee. $69 license fee. **Governing Statute:** Colorado Statutes Title 12, Article 58.

5326

Master Plumber
Examining Board of Plumbers
Dept. of Regulatory Agencies
Div. of Registrations
1390 Logan St., Ste. 400
Denver, CO 80203-2390
Phone: (303)894-2319

Credential Type: Master Plumber's license. **Duration of License:** One year. **Requirements:** Have at least five years of practical experience. School courses in plumbing work from an accredited trade school or community college counts as one hour for every six hours of training or experience up to a maximum of one year. Military experience or training in plumbing counts as one month for every six months of training or experience up to a maximum of one year. The maximum credit allowed for plumbing maintenance work is two years. **Examination:** Board administered master plumber's examination, written only. **Fees:** $59 exam fee. $109 license fee. **Governing Statute:** Colorado Statutes Title 12, Article 58.

Credential Type: License by endorsement. **Duration of License:** One year. **Requirements:** Hold a current license from another state for at least six months. Complete a state approved apprenticeship program or five years of practical experience or its equivalent. Complete a comparable state plumbing examination based on the Uniform Plumbing Code currently adopted by the Colorado Examining Board of Plumbers. **Fees:** $59 permit fee. $109 license fee. **Governing Statute:** Colorado Statutes Title 12, Article 58.

5327

Plumber Apprentice
Examining Board of Plumbers
Dept. of Regulatory Agencies
Div. of Registrations
1390 Logan St., Ste. 400
Denver, CO 80203-2390
Phone: (303)894-2319

Credential Type: Apprentice registration. **Duration of License:** One year. **Authorization:** Anyone working for a plumbing contractor must register within 30 days of hire. **Fees:** $14 registration fee. **Governing Statute:** Colorado Statutes Title 12, Article 58.

Plumbers and Pipefitters

5328

Residential Plumber
Examining Board of Plumbers
Dept. of Regulatory Agencies
Div. of Registrations
1390 Logan St., Ste. 400
Denver, CO 80203-2390
Phone: (303)894-2319

Credential Type: Residential Plumber's license. **Duration of License:** One year. **Requirements:** Have at least 3400 hours of practical experience. School courses in plumbing work from an accredited trade school or community college counts as one hour for every six hours of training or experience up to a maximum of one year. Military experience or training in plumbing counts as one month for every six months of training or experience up to a maximum of one year. The maximum credit allowed for plumbing maintenance work is one year. **Examination:** Board administered residential plumber's examination, written and practical sections. **Fees:** $34 exam fee. $34 permit fee. $59 license fee. **Governing Statute:** Colorado Statutes Title 12, Article 58.

Credential Type: License by endorsement. **Duration of License:** One year. **Requirements:** Hold a current license from another state for at least six months. Complete a state approved apprenticeship program or 3400 hours of practical experience or its equivalent. Complete a comparable state plumbing examination based on the Uniform Plumbing Code currently adopted by the Colorado Examining Board of Plumbers. **Fees:** $34 permit fee. $59 license fee. **Governing Statute:** Colorado Statutes Title 12, Article 58.

Connecticut

5329

Fire Protection Sprinkler Apprentice
Fire Protection Sprinkler Systems Work Board
Occupational Licensing Div.
Consumer Protection Dept.
165 Capitol Ave.
Hartford, CT 06106
Phone: (203)566-3275

Credential Type: Apprentice permit. **Duration of License:** Until next licensure examination. **Authorization:** Work may be performed only under the supervision of a licensed contractor or journeyman. **Requirements:** Be of good moral character. Have an 8th grade education or equivalent. **Governing Statute:** General Statutes of Connecticut, Chap. 393.

5330

Fire Protection Sprinkler Contractor
Fire Protection Sprinkler Systems Work Board
Occupational Licensing Div.
Consumer Protection Dept.
165 Capitol Ave.
Hartford, CT 06106
Phone: (203)566-3275

Credential Type: Unlimited fire protection sprinkler contractor license (F-1). **Duration of License:** Two years. **Requirements:** Be of good moral character. Have an 8th grade education or equivalent. Must have served at least two years as a F-2 journeyman or have equivalent experience. **Examination:** State licensure exam. **Reciprocity:** Yes, with selected states. **Fees:** $75 application fee. $150 license fee. **Governing Statute:** General Statutes of Connecticut, Chap. 393.

Credential Type: Limited fire protection sprinkler contractor license (F-3). **Duration of License:** Two years. **Authorization:** Limited to work involving foam extinguishing systems, special hazard systems, halon, and other liquid or gas fire suppression systems. **Requirements:** Be of good moral character. Have an 8th grade education or equivalent. Must have served at least two years as a F-4 journeyman or have equivalent experience. **Examination:** State licensure exam. **Reciprocity:** Yes, with selected states. **Fees:** $75 application fee. $150 license fee. **Governing Statute:** General Statutes of Connecticut, Chap. 393.

5331

Fire Protection Sprinkler Journeyman
Fire Protection Sprinkler Systems Work Board
Occupational Licensing Div.
Consumer Protection Dept.
165 Capitol Ave.
Hartford, CT 06106
Phone: (203)566-3275

Credential Type: Unlimited fire protection sprinkler journeyman's license (F-2). **Duration of License:** Two years. **Authorization:** Must be in the employ of a licensed contractor. **Requirements:** Be of good moral character. Have an 8th grade education or equivalent. Complete a four-year fire protection sprinkler apprentice program or have equivalent experience. **Examination:** State licensure exam. **Reciprocity:** Yes, with selected states. **Fees:** $45 application fee. $120 license fee. **Governing Statute:** General Statutes of Connecticut, Chap. 393.

Credential Type: Limited fire protection sprinkler journeyman's license (F-4). **Duration of License:** Two years. **Authorization:** Limited to work involving foam extinguishing systems, special hazard systems, halon, and other liquid or gas fire suppression systems. Must be in the employ of a licensed contractor. **Requirements:** Be of good moral character. Have an 8th grade education or equivalent. Complete a three-year fire protection non-sprinkler apprentice program or have equivalent experience. **Examination:** State licensure exam. **Reciprocity:** Yes, with selected states. **Fees:** $45 application fee. $120 license fee. **Governing Statute:** General Statutes of Connecticut, Chap. 393.

5332

Irrigation Contractor
Plumbing and Piping Work Examining Board
Occupational Licensing Div.
Consumer Protection Dept.
165 Capitol Ave.
Hartford, CT 06106
Phone: (203)566-3275

Credential Type: Irrigation contractor's license. **Duration of License:** Two years. **Requirements:** Be of good moral character. Have an 8th grade education or equivalent. Have requisite skill and pass appropriate state licensure examination. **Examination:** State licensure exam. **Reciprocity:** Yes, with selected states. **Fees:** $75 application fee. $150 license fee. **Governing Statute:** General Statutes of Connecticut, Chap. 393.

5333

Plumber, Journeyman
Plumber's Examining Board
Dept. of Labor and Industry
120 State St.
Montpelier, VT 05602
Phone: (802)828-2108

Credential Type: License. **Requirements:** Successful completion of apprenticeship program and certification from Vermont State Apprenticeship Council; or, training and experience acceptable to the Board. **Examination:** Yes. **Reciprocity:** Yes. (New Hampshire only). **Fees:** $5 Exam with license fee. **Governing Statute:** Title 26, VSA Sections 2192-2195.

Connecticut

5334

Plumbing-Piping Apprentice
Plumbing and Piping Work Examining Board
Occupational Licensing Div.
Consumer Protection Dept.
165 Capitol Ave.
Hartford, CT 06106
Phone: (203)566-3275

Credential Type: Apprentice permit. **Duration of License:** Until next licensure examination. **Authorization:** Work may be performed only under the supervision of a licensed contractor or journeyman. **Requirements:** Be of good moral character. Have an 8th grade education or equivalent. **Governing Statute:** General Statutes of Connecticut, Chap. 393.

5335

Plumbing-Piping Contractor
Plumbing and Piping Work Examining Board
Occupational Licensing Div.
Consumer Protection Dept.
165 Capitol Ave.
Hartford, CT 06106
Phone: (203)566-3275

Credential Type: Unlimited plumbing-piping contractor's license (P-1). **Duration of License:** Two years. **Requirements:** Be of good moral character. Have an 8th grade education or equivalent. Must have served as an plumbing-piping journeyman for not less than two years. If service was outside of state, must submit evidence that service was comparable to service in state or that applicant has education and experience and has passed an examination demonstrating competency to be an unlimited contractor. **Examination:** State licensure exam. **Reciprocity:** Yes, with selected states. **Fees:** $75 application fee. $150 license fee. **Governing Statute:** General Statutes of Connecticut, Chap. 393.

Credential Type: Contractor license—limited to gasoline station tanks and pumping equipment (P-9). **Duration of License:** Two years. **Authorization:** Limited to installation, repair, replacement, alteration, or maintenance of piping for gasoline tanks and related pumping equipment. **Requirements:** Be of good moral character. Have an 8th grade education or equivalent. Must have served one year as a plumbing-piping apprentice, plus one year as a licensed journeyman. **Examination:** State licensure exam. **Reciprocity:** Yes, with selected states. **Fees:** $75 application fee. $150 license fee. **Governing Statute:** General Statutes of Connecticut, Chap. 393.

Credential Type: Limited plumbing-piping contractor's license (J-1). **Duration of License:** Two years. **Authorization:** May perform only work limited to domestic water pumps and water conditioning. **Requirements:** Be of good moral character. Have an 8th grade education or equivalent. Must have served as a plumbing-piping journeyman for not less than two years. If service was outside of state, must submit evidence that service was comparable to service in state. **Examination:** State licensure exam. **Reciprocity:** Yes, with selected states. **Fees:** $75 application fee. $150 license fee. **Governing Statute:** General Statutes of Connecticut, Chap. 393.

Credential Type: Limited plumbing-piping contractor's license (W-9). **Duration of License:** Two years. **Authorization:** May perform only work limited to sewer and storm lines, from a point outside of a structure to the point of utility responsibility. **Requirements:** Be of good moral character. Have an 8th grade education or equivalent. Must have served as a plumbing-piping journeyman for not less than six months. **Examination:** State licensure exam. **Reciprocity:** Yes, with selected states. **Fees:** $75 application fee. $150 license fee. **Governing Statute:** General Statutes of Connecticut, Chap. 393.

Credential Type: Contractor license—limited to water, sewer, and storm lines (P-7). **Duration of License:** Two years. **Authorization:** Permits the installation, repair, replacement, alteration, or maintenance of piping limited to water, sewer, and storm lines from the point of utility reponsibility to a point immediately inside a structure. **Requirements:** Be of good moral character. Have an 8th grade education or equivalent. Must have served as a plumbing-piping apprentice for not less than one year, plus one year as a licensed journeyman. **Examination:** State licensure exam. **Reciprocity:** Yes, with selected states. **Fees:** $75 application fee. $150 license fee. **Governing Statute:** General Statutes of Connecticut, Chap. 393.

Credential Type: Contractor license—limited to lawn sprinkler lines (J-3). **Duration of License:** Two years. **Authorization:** Permits the installation, repair, replacement, alteration, or maintenance of lawn sprinkler systems. **Requirements:** Be of good moral character. Have an 8th grade education or equivalent. Must have served as a plumbing-piping apprentice for not less than one year, plus one year as a licensed journeyman.

5336

Plumbing-Piping Journeyman
Plumbing and Piping Work Examining Board
Occupational Licensing Div.
Consumer Protection Dept.
165 Capitol Ave.
Hartford, CT 06106
Phone: (203)566-3275

Credential Type: Unlimited plumbing-piping journeyman's license (P-2). **Duration of License:** Two years. **Authorization:** Must be in the employ of a licensed contractor. **Requirements:** Be of good moral character. Have an 8th grade education or equivalent. Complete a bona fide apprenticeship program, including not less than four years experience. Demonstrate competency by completing applicable state licensure examination. **Examination:** State licensure exam. **Reciprocity:** Yes, with selected states. **Fees:** $45 application fee. $150 license fee. **Governing Statute:** General Statutes of Connecticut, Chap. 393.

Credential Type: Journeyman license—limited to gasoline station tanks and pumping equipment (P-8). **Duration of License:** Two years. **Authorization:** Limited to installation, repair, replacement, alteration, or maintenance of piping for gasoline tanks and related pumping equipment. Must be in the employ of a licensed contractor. **Requirements:** Be of good moral character. Have an 8th grade education or equivalent. Complete a bona fide apprenticeship program, including not less than four years experience. Demonstrate competency by completing applicable state licensure examination. **Examination:** State licensure exam. **Reciprocity:** Yes, with selected states. **Fees:** $45 application fee. $120 license fee. **Governing Statute:** General Statutes of Connecticut, Chap. 393.

Credential Type: Limited plumbing-piping journeyman's license (J-2). **Duration of License:** Two years. **Authorization:** May perform only work limited to domestic water pumps and water conditioning. Must be in the employ of a licensed contractor. **Requirements:** Be of good moral character. Have an 8th grade education or equivalent. Complete a bona fide apprenticeship program, including not less than four years experience. Demonstrate competency by completing applicable state licensure examination. **Examination:** State licensure exam. **Reciprocity:** Yes, with selected states. **Fees:** $45 application fee. $120 license fee. **Governing Statute:** General Statutes of Connecticut, Chap. 393.

Credential Type: Journeyman's license—limited to drain laying (W-8). **Duration of License:** Two years. **Authorization:** May perform only work limited to sewer and storm lines, from a point outside of a structure to the point of utility responsibility. Must be in the employ of a licensed contractor. **Requirements:** Be of good moral character. Have an 8th grade education or equivalent. Must have served six months as an apprentice. **Examination:** State licensure exam. **Reciprocity:** Yes, with selected states. **Fees:** $45 application fee. $120 license fee. **Governing Statute:** General Statutes of Connecticut, Chap. 393.

Credential Type: Journeyman license—limited to water, sewer, and storm lines (P-6). **Duration of License:** Two years. **Authorization:** Permits the installation, repair, replacement, alteration, or maintenance of piping limited to water, sewer, and storm lines from the point of utility reponsibility to a point immediately inside a structure. Must be in the employ of a licensed contractor. **Requirements:** Be of good moral character. Have an 8th grade education or equivalent. Must have served one year as an apprentice. **Examination:** State licensure exam. **Reciprocity:** Yes, with selected states. **Fees:** $45 application fee. $120 license fee. **Governing Statute:** General Statutes of Connecticut, Chap. 393.

Credential Type: Journeyman license—limited to lawn sprinkler lines (J-3). **Duration of License:** Two years. **Authorization:** Permits the installation, repair, replacement, alteration, or maintenance of lawn sprinkler systems. Must be in the employ of a licensed contractor. **Requirements:** Be of good moral character. Have an 8th grade education or equivalent. Must have served one year as an apprentice.

District of Columbia

5337

Gasfitter
License and Certification Div.
Occupational and Professional Licensure Administration
Consumer and Regulatory Affairs Dept.
PO Box 37200
Washington, DC 20013-7200
Phone: (202)727-7823
Phone: (202)727-7480

Alternate Information: 614 H St., NW, Washington, DC 20001

Credential Type: Master Gasfitter License. **Requirements:** Contact licensing body for application information.

5338

Plumber
License and Certification Div.
Occupational and Professional Licensure Administration
Consumer and Regulatory Affairs Dept.
PO Box 37200
Washington, DC 20013-7200
Phone: (202)727-7823
Phone: (202)727-7480

Alternate Information: 614 H St., NW, Washington, DC 20001 **Requirements:** Contact licensing body for application information.

5339

Plumbing Contractor
License and Certification Div.
Occupational and Professional Licensure Administration
Consumer and Regulatory Affairs Dept.
PO Box 37200
Washington, DC 20013-7200
Phone: (202)727-7823
Phone: (202)727-7480

Alternate Information: 614 H St., NW, Washington, DC 20001 **Requirements:** Contact licensing body for application information.

Florida

5340

Plumbing Contractor
Dept. of Professional Regulation
Construction Industry Licensing Board
PO Box 2
Jacksonville, FL 32201
Phone: (904)359-6310

Credential Type: State Certified License. **Duration of License:** Two or three years. **Authorization:** Authorized to work throughout the State of Florida without taking additional examinations in this construction category. **Requirements:** Be at least 18 years of age. Good moral character. Meet one of the following criteria: (1) Baccalaureate degree from an accredited four-year college in the appropriate field. Have one year of proven experience or a minimum of 2000 man-hours. (2) Have at least four years of active experience, either as a workman who has learned the trade by serving an apprenticeship as a skilled workman who is able to comand the rate of a mechanic in applicant's field, or as a foreman. (3) Have a combination of not less than one year of experience as a foreman and not less than three years of credits for any accredited college-level courses; or a combination of not less than one year of experience as a foreman, one year as a skilled workman, and not less than two years of credits for any accredited college-level courses; or a combination of not less than one year of experience as a foreman, two years as a skilled workman, and not less than one year of credits for any accredited college-level courses.

Pass State Certification Examination. Must have appropriate workers' compensation coverage. **Examination:** State Certification Examination. **Reciprocity:** Yes. Applicant must have passed a similar national, regional, state, or U.S. territorial licensing examination. **Fees:** $254 examination fee. **Governing Statute:** Florida Statutes, Chapter 489, Part I.

Credential Type: State Registered License. **Duration of License:** Two or three years. **Authorization:** Allows applicant to work only in those local areas in which applicant has complied with local requirements. **Requirements:** Applicant must first contact county or municipality in which applicant wishes to work for occupational and competency requirements. After meeting local requirements, applicant may apply for state registration. **Governing Statute:** Florida Statutes, Chapter 489, Part I.

Georgia

5341

Journeyman Plumber
State Construction Industry Licensing Board
Div. of Master Plumbers and Journeyman Plumbers
Professional Examining Boards
166 Pryor St., SW
Atlanta, GA 30303
Phone: (404)656-3939

Credential Type: Statewide Journeyman Plumber License. **Requirements:** Minimum of three years experience in plumbing work. Completion of a diploma program of a technical school in engineering technology may be credited as no more than two years of experience. Completion of a certificate program of a vocational-technical school may be credited as no more than one year of experience. **Examination:** Construction Industry Licensing Board Examination for Journeyman Plumbers. **Reciprocity:** Applicant who holds a current out of state license based on passing an examination may be granted a license by endorsement, provided that applicant meets Geor-

Georgia

Journeyman Plumber, continued

gia's experience requirements. **Fees:** $29 application fee. $56 exam fee. **Governing Statute:** Official Code of Georgia Annotated 43-14. Rules of the State Construction Industry Licensing Board, Chap. 121.

5342

Master Plumber
State Construction Industry Licensing Board
Div. of Master Plumbers and Journeyman Plumbers
Professional Examining Boards
166 Pryor St., SW
Atlanta, GA 30303
Phone: (404)656-3939

Credential Type: Class I Master Plumber License. **Authorization:** Restricted to plumbing involving single-family dwellings, one-level dwellings designed for not more than two families, and commercial structures not to exceed 10,000 square feet in area. **Requirements:** Minimum of five years experience in plumbing work. At least two years must be primary experience gained through the direct installation of plumbing systems. Secondary experience means work experience gained while engaged in work or training related to the installation of plumbing. Completion of a diploma program of a technical school in engineering technology may be credited as no more than two years of secondary experience. Completion of a certificate program of a vocational-technical school may be credited as no more than one year of secondary experience. **Examination:** Construction Industry Licensing Board Examination for Class I Master Plumbers. **Reciprocity:** Applicant who holds a current out of state license based on passing an examination may be granted a license by endorsement, provided that applicant meets Georgia's experience requirements. **Fees:** $29 application fee. $56 exam fee. **Governing Statute:** Official Code of Georgia Annotated 43-14. Rules of the State Construction Industry Licensing Board, Chap. 121.

Credential Type: Class II Master Plumber License. **Authorization:** Unrestricted as to plumbing. **Requirements:** Minimum of five years experience in plumbing work. At least two years must be primary experience gained through the direct installation of plumbing systems. Secondary experience means work experience gained while engaged in work or training related to the installation of plumbing. Completion of a diploma program of a technical school in engineering technology may be credited as no more than two years of secondary experience. Completion of a certificate program of a vocational-technical school may be credited as no more than one year of secondary experience. **Examination:** Construction Industry Licensing Board Examination for Class II Master Plumbers. **Reciprocity:** Applicant who holds a current out of state license based on passing an examination may be granted a license by endorsement, provided that applicant meets Georgia's experience requirements. **Fees:** $29 application fee. $56 exam fee. **Governing Statute:** Official Code of Georgia Annotated 43-14. Rules of the State Construction Industry Licensing Board, Chap. 121.

Hawaii

5343

Plumber
Hawaii Board of Electricians and Plumbers
1010 Richards St.
PO Box 3469
Honolulu, HI 96801
Phone: (808)548-3952

Credential Type: Journeyman Plumber License. **Duration of License:** Six months. **Requirements:** At least five years of experience and not less than 10,000 hours as a journeyman or master plumber's helper or apprentice plumber. **Examination:** Written. **Fees:** $15 application fee. $35 exam fee. $10 license fee. $10 renewal fee. $15—$30 Compliance Resolution Fund fee.

Credential Type: Master Plumber License. **Duration of License:** Six months. **Requirements:** At least two years as a journeyman plumber; or at least two years as a licensed master plumber in a county, state or country with equivalent requirements. **Examination:** Written. **Fees:** $15 application fee. $35 exam fee. $10 license fee. $10 renewal fee. $15—$30 Compliance Resolution Fund fee.

Idaho

5344

Journeyman Plumber
Plumbing Administration
Dept. of Labor and Industrial Services
277 N. 6th
State House Mail
Boise, ID 83720
Phone: (208)334-3442
Phone: (208)334-3950
Fax: (208)334-2683

Credential Type: Journeyman Plumber's License (Certificate of Competency). **Duration of License:** One year. **Requirements:** Complete at least four years experience as an apprentice under the constant on-the-job supervision of a qualified journeyman plumber. A license from another jurisdiction may be accepted as proof of experience. Complete a related training class of four years duration. **Examination:** Written and practical examination. **Reciprocity:** Washington, Oregon, and Montana only. **Fees:** $22.50 application fee. $35 exam fee. $15 license fee. $7.50 renewal fee. **Governing Statute:** Idaho Code, Title 54, Chap. 26.

5345

Plumber Apprentice
Plumbing Administration
Dept. of Labor and Industrial Services
277 N. 6th
State House Mail
Boise, ID 83720
Phone: (208)334-3442
Phone: (208)334-3950
Fax: (208)334-2683

Credential Type: Apprentice Registration. **Duration of License:** One year. **Requirements:** Be at least 16 years of age. Apprenticeship consists of four years work under the supervision of a licensed journeyman plumber. During this period must be enrolled in a related training class. **Fees:** $5 yearly registration fee. **Governing Statute:** Idaho Code, Title 54, Chap. 26.

5346

Plumbing Contractor
Plumbing Administration
Dept. of Labor and Industrial
   Services
277 N. 6th
State House Mail
Boise, ID 83720
Phone: (208)334-3442
Phone: (208)334-3950
Fax: (208)334-2683

Credential Type: Plumbing Contractor's License (Certificate of Competency). **Duration of License:** One year. **Requirements:** Complete 2.5 years experience as a licensed journeyman plumber. **Examination:** Written and practical examination. **Reciprocity:** No. **Fees:** $22.50 application fee. $35 exam fee. $75 license fee. $37.50 renewal fee. **Governing Statute:** Idaho Code, Title 54, Chap. 26.

Illinois

5347

Apprentice Plumber
Illinois Dept. of Public Health
525 W. Jefferson
Springfield, IL 62761
Phone: (217)782-5830

Credential Type: Apprentice Plumber License. **Duration of License:** One year. **Requirements:** At least 16 years of age. Must be sponsored by a licensed Illinois plumber. Submit application and pay fee. **Reciprocity:** No. **Fees:** $15 initial license fee. $10 renewal fee. **Governing Statute:** Illinois Plumbing License Law 1991, Illinois Revised Statutes, Chapter 111.

5348

Plumber
Illinois Dept. of Public Health
525 W. Jefferson
Springfield, IL 62761
Phone: (217)782-5830

Credential Type: Plumber License. **Duration of License:** One year. **Requirements:** Must be, or in the process of becoming, a U.S. citizen. Illinois resident. Two years of high school or equivalent. Must have completed an approved course of instruction in plumbing or have four years of licensed apprenticeship as a plumber. **Examination:** Plumbing License Examination. **Reciprocity:** Yes, with current licensure in another state that has substantially equivalent requirements to those of Illinois. Must take and pass Illinois examination. **Fees:** $50 exam filing fee (resident). $55 exam filing fee (nonresident). $25 initial license fee. $25 renewal fee. **Governing Statute:** Illinois Plumbing License Law 1991, Illinois Revised Statutes, Chapter 111.

5349

Water Well and Pump Installation Contractor
Illinois Dept. of Health
525 W. Jefferson
Springfield, IL 62761
Phone: (217)782-5830

Credential Type: Water Well and Pump Installation Contractor License. **Duration of License:** One year. **Requirements:** At least 18 years of age. U.S. citizen or declared intention to become a citizen. Must have two years experience under the supervision of a licensed water well and pump contractor. **Examination:** Water Well and Pump Installation Contractor Licensing Examination. **Reciprocity:** No. **Fees:** $80 examination fee. $80 application/initial license fee. $35 renewal fee. **Governing Statute:** Illinois Revised Statutes 1991, Chapter 111.

5350

Water Well Pump Installation Contractor
Illinois Dept. of Health
525 W. Jefferson
Springfield, IL 62761
Phone: (217)782-5830

Credential Type: Water Well Pump Installation Contractor License. **Duration of License:** One year. **Requirements:** At least 18 years of age. U.S. citizen or declared intention to become a citizen. Must have two years experience under the supervision of a licensed water well contractor. **Examination:** Water Well Pump Installation Contractor Licensing Examination. **Reciprocity:** No. **Fees:** $50 examination fee. $50 application/initial license fee. $25 renewal fee. **Governing Statute:** Illinois Revised Statutes 1991, Chapter 111.

Indiana

5351

Plumber
Licensing Division
Professional Licensing Agency
1021 State Office Bldg.
100 N. Senate Ave.
Indianapolis, IN 46204
Phone: (317)232-5955

Credential Type: License. **Requirements:** Contact licensing body for application information.

5352

Plumber Contractor
Licensing Division
Professional Licensing Agency
1021 State Office Bldg.
100 N. Senate Ave.
Indianapolis, IN 46204
Phone: (317)232-5955

Credential Type: License. **Requirements:** Contact licensing body for application information.

Kentucky

5353

Plumber
Dept. of Housing, Building &
   Construction
1047 U.S. 127 South
Frankfort, KY 40601
Phone: (502)564-3580

Credential Type: Jouneyman License. **Duration of License:** One year. **Requirements:** U.S. citizen or legal alien. 18 years of age. Two consecutive years experience as an apprentice under the supervision of a master or journeyman plumber. **Examination:** Yes. **Fees:** $50 exam fee. $40 renewal fee.

Credential Type: Master License. **Duration of License:** One year. **Requirements:** U.S. citizen or legal alien. 18 years of age. Must have possessed a journeyman license for two years and been actively employed in plumbing in two or the last five years. **Examination:** Yes. **Fees:** $150 exam fee. $250 renewal fee.

Louisiana

5354

Fire Protection Sprinkler Contractor
Office of the State Fire Marshal
1033 N. Lobdell Blvd.
Baton Rouge, LA 70806
Phone: (504)925-4911

Credential Type: Permit. **Duration of License:** One year. **Requirements:** Complete competency test and document past year's work. **Examination:** Competency test. **Fees:** $100 permit fee. **Governing Statute:** R.S. 40:1625 et seq.

5355

Plumber
State Plumbing Board
512 Colonial Bank Bldg.
2714 Canal St.
New Orleans, LA 70119
Phone: (504)568-4900

Credential Type: Journeyman Plumber's License. **Duration of License:** One year. **Requirements:** Complete five years (8000 hours) in the trade of plumbing. **Examination:** Written and manual examination. **Fees:** $30 license fee. $75 exam fee. $30 annual renewal fee. **Governing Statute:** R.S. 37:1365-1378.

Credential Type: Temporary Permit. **Requirements:** Issued to applicants who are considered eligible for the examination and are waiting for the next scheduled exam. **Fees:** $50 temporary permit fee. **Governing Statute:** R.S. 37:1365-1378.

Maine

5356

Oil Burner Technician
Oil and Solid Fuel Board
Dept. of Professional and Financial Regulation
Div. of Licensing and Enforcement
State House Station 35
Augusta, ME 04333
Phone: (207)582-8723

Credential Type: Master License. **Duration of License:** Two years. **Authorization:** Issued with designations for different categories of oil burners. **Requirements:** Complete four years of licensed practical experience. **Examination:** Yes. **Fees:** $10 application fee. $100 license fee. $150 renewal fee. Exam fee to be determined. $25 license upgrade fee. **Governing Statute:** 32 M.S.R.A. Chap. 33.

Credential Type: Journeyman License. **Duration of License:** Two years. **Authorization:** Issued with designations for different categories of oil burners. Must work under the supervision or in the employ of a Master Oil Burner Technician. **Requirements:** Complete at least one year of licensed practical experience; or complete six months of licensed practical experience and an oil burner technician course of at least 160 hours of study, of which at least 75 hours are made up of laboratory work. **Examination:** Yes. **Fees:** $10 application fee. $50 license fee. $75 renewal fee. Exam fee to be determined. $25 license upgrade fee. **Governing Statute:** 32 M.S.R.A. Chap. 33.

Credential Type: Apprentice License. **Authorization:** Permitted to work under the direct supervision of a journeyman. **Requirements:** Issued without examination upon payment of fee and signature of responsible master. **Fees:** $10 application fee. $20 license fee. $25 renewal fee. **Governing Statute:** 32 M.S.R.A. Chap. 33.

5357

Plumber
Plumbers' Examining Board
Dept. of Professional and Financial Regulation
Div. of Licensing and Enforcement
State House Station 35
Augusta, ME 04333
Phone: (207)582-8723

Credential Type: Journeyman License. **Duration of License:** Two years. **Requirements:** Meet one of the following sets of requirements: (1) Have at least two years (4000 hours) of work in the field of plumbing installations as a trainee plumber under the supervision of a master plumber, and pass journeyman's examination. (2) Have at least one year (2000 hours) of work in the field of plumbing installations as a journeyman-in-training under the supervision of a master plumber, provided the work experience was obtained within four years of the date the journeyman-in-training license was issued. **Examination:** Journeyman's examination. **Fees:** $25 application fee. $75 license fee. **Governing Statute:** 32 M.S.R.A. Chap. 49.

Credential Type: Journeyman-in-Training License. **Duration of License:** Two years. **Requirements:** Complete one academic year of instruction in plumbing at a Maine technical college, and pass journeyman's examination. **Examination:** Journeyman's examination. **Fees:** $25 application fee. $8 license fee. **Governing Statute:** 32 M.S.R.A. Chap. 49.

Credential Type: Master Plumber License. **Duration of License:** Two years. **Requirements:** Have at least one year (2000 hours) of work in the field of plumbing installations as a journeyman plumber or at least four years (8000 hours) of work in the field of plumbing installations as a trainee plumber under the supervision of a master plumber. Pass master's examination. **Examination:** Master's examination. **Fees:** $25 application fee. $150 license fee. **Governing Statute:** 32 M.S.R.A. Chap. 49.

Credential Type: Trainee License. **Duration of License:** Two years. **Requirements:** Submit application and provide evidence of employment by a master plumber who will assist applicant as a plumber's trainee. Application should be submitted within 10 business days of employment. **Fees:** $25 application fee. $40 license fee. **Governing Statute:** 32 M.S.R.A. Chap. 49.

5358

Solid Fuel Burner Technician
Oil and Solid Fuel Board
Dept. of Professional and Financial Regulation
Div. of Licensing and Enforcement
State House Station 35
Augusta, ME 04333
Phone: (207)582-8723

Credential Type: Master License. **Duration of License:** Two years. **Authorization:** Issued with designations for different categories of oil burners. **Requirements:** Complete two years of licensed practical experience; or have a master oil burner technician's license and present evidence of knowledge of solid fuel burning equipment; or have a bachelor's degree in engineering and present evidence of knowledge of solid fuel burning equipment. **Examination:** Yes. **Fees:** $10 application fee. $100 license fee. $150 renewal fee. Exam fee to be determined. $25 license upgrade fee. **Governing Statute:** 32 M.S.R.A. Chap. 33.

Plumbers and Pipefitters | Massachusetts

Maryland

5359

Plumber
State Board of Plumbing
Dept. of Licensing and Regulation
501 St. Paul Pl.
Baltimore, MD 21202-2272
Phone: (410)333-6322

Credential Type: Journey Plumber License. **Duration of License:** Two years. **Requirements:** Have held an apprentice license or equivalent for at least four years, during which applicant shall have completed at least 7500 hours of training in providing plumbing services under the direction of a licensed master plumber. The board may allow up to 1500 hours of accredited, approved school study to apply toward the experience requirement. **Examination:** Journey plumber examination. **Reciprocity:** Yes. **Fees:** $10 application fee. $50 license fee.

Credential Type: Master Plumber License. **Duration of License:** Two years. **Requirements:** Have held a journey plumber license or equivalent for at least two years, during which applicant shall have completed at least 3750 hours of training in providing plumbing services under the direction of a licensed master plumber. **Examination:** Master plumber examination. **Reciprocity:** Yes. **Fees:** $25 application fee. $100 license fee.

Credential Type: Apprentice Plumber License. **Duration of License:** Two years. **Authorization:** May work only under the direction and control of a licensed master plumber. **Requirements:** Submit application and pay fee. Must be in the employ of a licensed master plumber. **Fees:** $15 application fee.

5360

Pump Installer
Board of Well Drillers
Dept. of the Environment
2500 Broening Hwy.
Baltimore, MD 21224
Phone: (410)631-3168

Credential Type: Pump Installer License. **Duration of License:** Two years. **Requirements:** At least three years experience installing pumps, or two years as an apprentice pump installer. Post $2000 performance bond. Have appropriate bodily injury and property damage insurance. Renewal requires 20 hours of continuing education during the previous two years. **Examination:** Licensure examination, written. **Fees:** $25 application fee. $50 license fee. **Governing Statute:** Annotated Code of Maryland, Title 26, subtitle 05.

Credential Type: Apprentice Pump Installer License. **Duration of License:** Two years. **Requirements:** At least one year of related experience. **Examination:** Licensure examination, written. **Fees:** $25 application fee. $25 license fee. **Governing Statute:** Annotated Code of Maryland, Title 26, subtitle 05.

5361

Water Conditioner Installer
Board of Well Drillers
Dept. of the Environment
2500 Broening Hwy.
Baltimore, MD 21224
Phone: (410)631-3168

Credential Type: Water Conditioner Installer License. **Duration of License:** Two years. **Requirements:** At least three years experience installing water conditioning equipment, or two years as an apprentice water conditioner installer. Post $2000 performance bond. Have appropriate bodily injury and property damage insurance. Renewal requires 20 hours of continuing education during the previous two years. **Examination:** Licensure examination, written. **Fees:** $25 application fee. $50 license fee. **Governing Statute:** Annotated Code of Maryland, Title 26, subtitle 05.

Credential Type: Apprentice Water Conditioner Installer License. **Duration of License:** Two years. **Requirements:** At least one year of related experience. **Examination:** Licensure examination, written. **Fees:** $25 application fee. $25 license fee. **Governing Statute:** Annotated Code of Maryland, Title 26, subtitle 05.

Massachusetts

5362

Gas Fitter
Board of Registration of Plumbers
  and Gas Fitters
Div. of Registration
100 Cambridge St., 15th Fl.
Boston, MA 02202
Phone: (617)727-9952

Credential Type: Master Gas Fitter License. **Requirements:** Contact licensing body for application information. **Examination:** Yes. **Governing Statute:** Annotated Laws of Massachusetts, Chap. 142.

Credential Type: Journeyman Gas Fitter License. **Requirements:** Contact licensing body for application information. **Examination:** Yes. **Governing Statute:** Annotated Laws of Massachusetts, Chap. 142.

5363

Liquefied Petroleum Gas Installer
Board of Registration of Plumbers
  and Gas Fitters
Div. of Registration
100 Cambridge St., 15th Fl.
Boston, MA 02202
Phone: (617)727-9952

Credential Type: Liquefied Petroleum Gas Installer License. **Requirements:** Contact licensing body for application information. **Examination:** Yes. **Governing Statute:** Annotated Laws of Massachusetts, Chap. 142.

Credential Type: Limited Liquefied Petroleum Gas Installer License. **Requirements:** Contact licensing body for application information. **Examination:** Yes. **Governing Statute:** Annotated Laws of Massachusetts, Chap. 142.

5364

Oil Burner Technician
Dept. of Public Safety
Div. of Inspection
Engineering Section
One Ashburton Pl.
Boston, MA 02108
Phone: (617)727-3200

Credential Type: Group 1 Certificate—Unrestricted Power Burners. **Requirements:** Have five to seven years of experience plus classroom instruction. Must demonstrate thorough knowledge of field, including safety devices and automatic, pneumatic, and electronic controls. Knowledge of pipefitting and heating. Must demonstrate proficiency in the two lower grades of certification. **Examination:** Written and oral examination. **Fees:** $60 license and exam fee. **Governing Statute:** Massachusetts General Laws, Chap. 146.

Credential Type: Group 2 Certificate—Power Burners 1 and 2 Oil. **Requirements:** Be at least 18 years of age. Have attended at least 26 weeks of classroom instruction. Have obtained apprentice license to learn how to clean boilers and install equipment. Demonstrate knowledge of oil burners, safety devices, and electrical and electronic controls. Demonstrate knowledge of testing equipment. Must be proficient in the Group 3 certification grade. **Examination:** Written and oral examinations. **Fees:** $60 license and exam fee. **Governing Statute:** Massachusetts General Laws, Chap. 146.

Massachusetts 5365

Oil Burner Technician, continued

Credential Type: Group 3 Certificate—Gravity Feed. **Requirements:** Demonstrate knowledge of sleeve burner and pot type burners. Show proficiency in use of small hand tools and in the cleaning of stoves, burners, and chimneys. Be able to handle wicks, water heating devices, and side arm heaters. **Examination:** Written and oral examinations. **Fees:** $60 license and exam fee. **Governing Statute:** Massachusetts General Laws, Chap. 146.

Credential Type: Apprentice Certificate. **Requirements:** Must be employed by a person certified at a higher grade. **Examination:** No exam required. **Fees:** $10 license fee. **Governing Statute:** Massachusetts General Laws, Chap. 146.

5365

Pipefitter
Dept. of Public Safety
Div. of Inspection
Engineering Section
One Ashburton Pl.
Boston, MA 02108
Phone: (617)727-3200

Credential Type: Master Pipefitter License. **Requirements:** Must own a business and have at least four years of experience. **Examination:** Yes. **Fees:** $75 license and exam fee. **Governing Statute:** Massachusetts General Laws, Chap. 146.

Credential Type: Journeyman Pipefitter License. **Requirements:** Have at least three years of experience. **Fees:** $50 license and exam fee. **Governing Statute:** Massachusetts General Laws, Chap. 146.

Credential Type: Apprentice Pipefitter License. **Requirements:** Must work under the direct supervision of a licensed master or journeyman pipefitter. **Examination:** No exam required. **Fees:** $20 license fee. **Governing Statute:** Massachusetts General Laws, Chap. 146.

5366

Plumber
Board of Registration of Plumbers
  and Gas Fitters
Div. of Registration
100 Cambridge St., 15th Fl.
Boston, MA 02202
Phone: (617)727-9952

Credential Type: Master Plumber License. **Requirements:** Contact licensing body for application information. **Examination:** Yes. **Governing Statute:** Annotated Laws of Massachusetts, Chap. 142.

Credential Type: Journeyman Plumber License. **Requirements:** Contact licensing body for application information. **Examination:** Yes. **Governing Statute:** Annotated Laws of Massachusetts, Chap. 142.

Michigan

5367

Plumber, Journeyperson
Board of Plumbing
Plumbing Div.
Dept. of Labor
7150 Harris Dr.
PO Box 30015
Lansing, MI 48909
Phone: (517)322-1287

Credential Type: License. **Duration of License:** One year. **Requirements:** At least 19 years old. Furnish a notarized statement from present or former employers indicating that they have had at least three years of experience as an apprentice in the practical installation of plumbing under the supervision of a master plumber. Applicants who are attending or who are graduates of a recognized trade school may receive up to one year of credit towards the required three years of apprenticeship. **Examination:** Oral, written, and practical exam. **Reciprocity:** Licensed journeyperson plumbers from another state may be licensed in Michigan without examination if the Board determines the requirements of the other state are equivalent to those of Michigan. (The Board of Plumbing has a reciprocity agreement with the state of Indiana.) **Fees:** $45 initial examination and license fee. $20 renewal license fee. $20 reciprocity fee. **Governing Statute:** Plumbing Act, Act 266 of 1929, as amended.

5368

Plumber, Master
Board of Plumbing
Plumbing Div.
Dept. of Labor
7150 Harris Dr.
PO Box 30015
Lansing, MI 48909
Phone: (517)322-1287

Credential Type: License. **Duration of License:** One year. **Requirements:** At least 21 years old. Be on record with the Board of Plumbing office as having had two years of experience as a Michigan licensed journeyperson plumber. **Examination:** Oral, written, and practical exam. **Fees:** $125 initial examination and license fee. $75 renewal license fee. $50 Homeowner construction lien fund assessment. $75 reciprocity fee. **Governing Statute:** Plumbing Act, Act 266 of 1929, as amended.

5369

Pump Installer
Ground Water Quality Control
  Section
Dept. of Public Health
3423 N. Logan
PO Box 30195
Lansing, MI 48909
Phone: (517)335-8000

Credential Type: Registration. **Duration of License:** One year. **Requirements:** Completed the 10th grade or submit proof of the equivalent ability as indicated by the successful completion of approved short courses or written examinations. Up to four years of work experience may be substituted for equal years of education. Two years of work experience in the pump installation field. It is recommended that six months of this experience be obtained within the two years prior to application and under the supervision of a Michigan registered pump installation contractor. Submit a chronological work history form. Be of sound moral character. Submit two personal reference statements. One of the reference statements must be completed by a Michigan registered well drilling contractor or pump installer. The second statement must be completed by a person familiar with the applicant's work experience in the well and pump field. **Examination:** Oral appraisal and written exam. **Reciprocity:** Reciprocity may be granted if the other state accepts Michigan registration and has standards which are substantially the same as those of Michigan. **Fees:** $25 initial exam and registration fee. $25 renewal fee. $25 reciprocity fee. **Governing Statute:** Public Health Code, Act 368 of 1978.

Minnesota

5370

Plumber
Dept. of Health
Environmental Health Div.
Water Supply and General
  Engineering Section
Plumbing Program
717 Delaware St., SE
Box 9441
Minneapolis, MN 55440
Phone: (612)627-5117
Phone: (612)627-5133
Fax: (612)623-5043

Credential Type: Journeyman Plumber License. **Duration of License:** One year. **Authorization:** Plumbers working in communities with a population of 5000 or more must be licensed by the state. **Requirements:** Complete four years of experience. **Examination:** Written examination. **Fees:** $45 license fee. $30 exam fee.

Credential Type: Master Plumber License. **Duration of License:** One year. **Requirements:** Complete five years of experience. **Examination:** Written examination. **Fees:** $80 license fee. $30 exam fee. $40 bond filing fee.

Credential Type: Apprentice Registration. **Duration of License:** One year. **Requirements:** Submit application and pay fee. **Fees:** $15 registration fee.

5371

Water Conditioning Contractor
Dept. of Health
Environmental Health Div.
Water Supply and General
  Engineering Section
Plumbing Program
717 Delaware St., SE
Box 9441
Minneapolis, MN 55440
Phone: (612)627-5117
Phone: (612)627-5133
Fax: (612)623-5043

Credential Type: Contractor License. **Duration of License:** One year. **Authorization:** License required if working in community with a population of 5000 or more. **Requirements:** Submit application and pass examination. **Examination:** Written examination. **Fees:** $50 license fee. $30 exam fee. $40 bond filing fee.

5372

Water Conditioning Installer
Dept. of Health
Environmental Health Div.
Water Supply and General
  Engineering Section
Plumbing Program
717 Delaware St., SE
Box 9441
Minneapolis, MN 55440
Phone: (612)627-5117
Phone: (612)627-5133
Fax: (612)623-5043

Credential Type: Installer License. **Duration of License:** One year. **Authorization:** License required if working in community with a population of 5000 or more. **Requirements:** Submit application and pass examination. **Examination:** Written examination. **Fees:** $30 license fee. $30 exam fee.

Montana

5373

Plumber
Montana Board of Plumbers
1218 E. 6th Ave.
Helena, MT 59620
Phone: (406)444-4390

Credential Type: Journeyworker Plumber. **Duration of License:** One year. **Requirements:** Completion of an approved plumber apprenticeship program, or four years of plumbing experience. **Examination:** Written and practical exam. **Fees:** $30 application fee. $95 exam fee. $85 license fee. $85 renewal fee. **Governing Statute:** Montana Code Annotated 37-69-301 through 37-69-324.

Credential Type: Master Plumber. **Duration of License:** One year. **Requirements:** Four years of experience as a journeyworker plumber. Three years of experience in supervising plumbing projects. **Examination:** Written and practical exam. **Fees:** $30 application fee. $95 exam fee. $85 license fee. $85 renewal fee. **Governing Statute:** Montana Code Annotated 37-69-301 through 37-69-324.

Nebraska

5374

Fire Protection Sprinkler System Contractor
Lincoln Bureau of Fire Prevention
555 S. 10th St.
Lincoln, NE 68508
Phone: (402)471-7791

Credential Type: License. **Duration of License:** One year. **Requirements:** Must have four years experience as an apprentice in order to take the journeyman's exam. Applicants for a contractors exam must have at least one year of experience as a journeyman. **Examination:** Yes. **Fees:** $15 examination fee. Registration fees vary. $50 contractor renewal fee. $5 journeyman renewal fee.

5375

Plumber (Journeyman)
Lincoln City Codes Administration
555 S 10th St.
Lincoln, NE 68508
Phone: (402)471-7525

Credential Type: License. **Duration of License:** One year. **Requirements:** An apprentice plumber must have at least four years experience before applying for a journeyman's license. A journeyman is also required to hold a journeyman's license for at least one year before applying for a master's license. **Examination:** Yes. **Fees:** $5 apprentice license fee. $30 journeyman's examination and license fees. $30 master's examination and license fees. $10 journeyman's renewal fee. $50 master's renewal fee.

5376

Pump Installer/Well Driller
Div. of Drinking Water &
  Environmental Sanitation
301 Centennial Mall S.
PO Box 95007
Lincoln, NE 68509
Phone: (402)471-2541

Credential Type: License. **Duration of License:** One year. **Requirements:** Must have been in the industry for two years. Must have $100,000 in public liability and property damage insurance. Supervisors are not required to show proof of the $100,000 in public liability and property damage insurance. **Examination:** Yes. **Fees:** $15 application fee. $150 license fee. $35 supervisor's certificate fee. $150 license renewal fee. $35 supervisor's certificate fee.

Nevada

5377

Plumber/Pipefitter
Nevada State Contractors Board
70 Linden St.
Reno, NV 89502
Phone: (702)688-1141

Credential Type: License. **Requirements:** Four years of skilled experience in the licensed field. Financial responsibility and good character. **Examination:** Yes. **Fees:** $270 application fee. $120 license fee. $120 renewal fee. $40 exam fee.

New Hampshire

5378

Plumber
Plumbers' Licensing Board
105 Loudon Rd., Bldg. 3
Concord, NH 03301
Phone: (603)271-3267

Credential Type: Journeyman Plumber License. **Duration of License:** One year. **Requirements:** U.S. citizen. Successfully complete an acceptable apprenticeship program in plumbing and present certificate of completion. **Examination:** Examination as required by Board. **Reciprocity:** Yes, if reciprocal agreement exists between New Hampshire and applicant's state. **Fees:** $30 initial license fee. $30 annual renewal fee.

Credential Type: Master Plumber License. **Duration of License:** One year. **Requirements:** Hold a Journeyman Plumber License for at least six months. **Examination:** Examination as required by Board. **Reciprocity:** Yes, with states having a reciprocal agreement with New Hampshire. Qualifications for out-of-state license must be equal to or hire than those of New Hampshire. **Fees:** $125 initial license fee. $125 annual license renewal fee.

New Jersey

5379

Plumber
Board of Examiners of Master Plumbers
1100 Raymond Blvd., Rm. 503
Newark, NJ 07102
Phone: (201)648-3310

Credential Type: Master Plumber's License. **Duration of License:** Two years. **Requirements:** 21 years of age. Five years experience in the plumbing industry, with at least three years as a journeyman plumber; or a bachelor's degree in engineering from an accredited college and one year of practical work experience. **Examination:** Written. **Reciprocity:** Yes. **Fees:** $100 exam fee. $100 biennial registration fee. **Governing Statute:** NJSA 45:14C-1. NJAC 13:32-1.

5380

Pump Installer
New Jersey Dept. of Environmental Protection
Div. of Water Resources
CN029
Trenton, NJ 08625-0029
Phone: (609)984-6831

Credential Type: License. **Examination:** Practical. **Fees:** $10 license fee. **Governing Statute:** NJSA 58:4A.

New Mexico

5381

Journeyman Gas Fitter
Construction Industries Div.
Dept. of Regulation and Licensing
PO Box 25101
725 St. Michael's Dr.
Santa Fe, NM 87504
Phone: (505)827-7030
Fax: (505)827-7045

Credential Type: Journeyman Gas Fitter Certificate of Competence. **Duration of License:** One year. **Authorization:** Must be employed by a properly licensed contractor. **Requirements:** Be at least 18 years of age. Complete at least two years of approved experience or a course in the trade approved by the vocational educational division of the state department of public education. **Examination:** Mechanical Journeyman Examination. **Fees:** $25 exam fee. $25 renewal fee. **Governing Statute:** Construction Industries Division Rules and Regulations. New Mexico Construction Industries Licensing Act, Chapter 60.

5382

Journeyman Pipe Fitter
Construction Industries Div.
Dept. of Regulation and Licensing
PO Box 25101
725 St. Michael's Dr.
Santa Fe, NM 87504
Phone: (505)827-7030
Fax: (505)827-7045

Credential Type: Journeyman Pipe Fitter Certificate of Competence. **Duration of License:** One year. **Authorization:** Must be employed by a properly licensed contractor. **Requirements:** Be at least 18 years of age. Complete at least two years of approved experience or a course in the trade approved by the vocational educational division of the state department of public education. **Examination:** Mechanical Journeyman Examination. **Fees:** $25 exam fee. $25 renewal fee. **Governing Statute:** Construction Industries Division Rules and Regulations. New Mexico Construction Industries Licensing Act, Chapter 60.

5383

Journeyman Plumber
Construction Industries Div.
Dept. of Regulation and Licensing
PO Box 25101
725 St. Michael's Dr.
Santa Fe, NM 87504
Phone: (505)827-7030
Fax: (505)827-7045

Credential Type: Journeyman Plumber Certificate of Competence. **Duration of License:** One year. **Authorization:** Must be employed by a properly licensed contractor. **Requirements:** Be at least 18 years of age. Complete at least two years of approved experience or a course in the trade approved by the vocational educational division of the state department of public education. **Examination:** Mechanical Journeyman Examination. **Fees:** $25 exam fee. $25 renewal fee. **Governing Statute:** Construction Industries Division Rules and Regulations. New Mexico Construction Industries Licensing Act, Chapter 60.

North Carolina

5384

Plumbing, Heating, and Air Conditioning Contractor
North Carolina State Board of Examiners for Plumbing, Heating and Air Conditioning Contractors
PO Box 110
Raleigh, NC 27602
Phone: (919)733-9350

Credential Type: License. **Duration of License:** One year. **Requirements:** 18 years of age. **Examination:** Yes. **Fees:** $10 exam fee. $25—$50 license fee. $25—$50 renewal fee.

North Dakota

5385

Plumber
State Plumbing Board
204 W. Thayer Ave.
Bismarck, ND 58501
Phone: (701)224-4651

Credential Type: Master Plumber License. **Duration of License:** One year. **Requirements:** Be at least 21 years of age. Complete at least two years of experience (3500 hours) as a journeyman plumber. Renewal requires at least two credit hours of continuing education per year. **Examination:** Master Plumber Examination. **Reciprocity:** Yes, but must take examination. Agreements with Minnesota, Montana, and South Dakota. **Fees:** $50 exam fee. $150 license fee. $150 renewal fee. **Governing Statute:** North Dakota Century Code 43-18-01 et seq.

Credential Type: Journeyman Plumber License. **Duration of License:** One year. **Requirements:** Meet one of the following sets of requirements: (1) Complete at least four years of experience (7600 hours) as an apprentice plumber under a licensed master plumber. (2) For applicants working where a state license is not required, complete five years (9500 hours) of work experience. Pass journeyman examination screening test prior to sitting for examination. Renewal requires at least two credit hours of continuing education per year. **Examination:** Journeyman Plumber Examination. **Reciprocity:** Yes, but must take examination. Agreements with Minnesota, Montana, and South Dakota. **Fees:** $50 exam fee. $60 license fee. $60 renewal fee. **Governing Statute:** North Dakota Century Code 43-18-01 et seq.

Credential Type: Apprentice Registration. **Duration of License:** Four years. **Authorization:** Must work under a licensed master plumber until completion of 5700 hours of training. After completing 5700 hours, an apprentice may work alone if employed by a licensed master plumber, or be self-employed if working in cities of 1000 population or less or in a rural area. **Requirements:** Be at least 18 years of age. Must register within 30 days of beginning apprenticeship. Apprenticeship lasts for four years (7600 hours). Must purchase Plumbing Code Book and Study Guide ($35). **Fees:** $20 registration fee (1st year, up to 1700 hours). $30 registration fee (2nd year, 1701-3800 hours). $40 registration fee (3rd year, 3801-5700 hours). $50 registration fee (4th year, 57017600 hours). **Governing Statute:** North Dakota Century Code 43-18-01 et seq.

Credential Type: Temporary Permit. **Duration of License:** Until end of calendar year. **Authorization:** Issued for master plumber or journeyman plumber, or both. **Requirements:** Furnish evidence of qualifications. Must have paid examination fee and submitted application for licensure. **Governing Statute:** North Dakota Century Code 43-18-15.

5386

Pump and Pitless Unit Contractor
State Board of Water Well
  Contractors
900 E. Blvd.
Bismarck, ND 58505
Phone: (701)224-2754

Credential Type: Pump and Pitless Unit Contractor Certification. **Duration of License:** One year. **Requirements:** Have at least one year of experience under a qualified contractor. Post $2000 surety bond. **Examination:** Written certification examination. **Fees:** $25 certification fee. $10 exam fee. $25 renewal fee. **Governing Statute:** North Dakota Century Code 43-35.

5387

Sewer and Water Contractor
State Plumbing Board
204 W. Thayer Ave.
Bismarck, ND 58501
Phone: (701)224-4651

Credential Type: Sewer and Water Contractor License. **Duration of License:** One year. **Requirements:** Complete at least one year (1700 hours) of experience as an installer in this state. **Examination:** Written examination. **Reciprocity:** Yes, but must take examination. **Fees:** $100 license and exam fee. $100 renewal fee. **Governing Statute:** North Dakota Century Code 43-18.2-01 et seq.

5388

Sewer and Water Installer
State Plumbing Board
204 W. Thayer Ave.
Bismarck, ND 58501
Phone: (701)224-4651

Credential Type: Sewer and Water Installer License. **Duration of License:** One year. **Requirements:** Complete at least two years (3400 hours) of experience as an apprentice building sewer and water installer in this state. **Examination:** Written examination. **Reciprocity:** Yes, but must take examination. **Fees:** $25 license and exam fee. $25 renewal fee. **Governing Statute:** North Dakota Century Code 43-18.2-01 et seq.

Credential Type: Apprentice Sewer and Water Installer License. **Duration of License:** Two years with annual renewal. **Authorization:** Must work under the supervision of a licensed building sewer and water installer. **Requirements:** Submit application. Apprenticeship lasts two years (3400 hours). **Fees:** No fee. **Governing Statute:** North Dakota Century Code 43-18.2-01 et seq.

5389

Water Conditioning Contractor
State Plumbing Board
204 W. Thayer Ave.
Bismarck, ND 58501
Phone: (701)224-4651

Credential Type: Water Conditioning Contractor License and Registration. **Duration of License:** One year. **Requirements:** Be at least 21 years of age. Complete at least one year (1900 hours) of experience as a licensed water conditioning installer. **Examination:** Written examination. **Reciprocity:** Yes, but must take examination. **Fees:** $40 license and exam fee. $40 renewal fee. **Governing Statute:** North Dakota Century Code 43-18.1-01 et seq.

5390

Water Conditioning Installer
State Plumbing Board
204 W. Thayer Ave.
Bismarck, ND 58501
Phone: (701)224-4651

Credential Type: Water Conditioning Installer License and Registration. **Duration of License:** One year. **Requirements:** Meet one of the following sets of requirements: (1) Complete at least one year (1700 hours) of experience as an apprentice water conditioning installer under a licensed water conditioning contractor. (2) Graduate from the plumbing course of an accredited trade school with at least a 9-month (1020 hour) course in plumbing. **Examination:** Written examination. **Reciprocity:** Yes, but must take examination. **Fees:** $20 license and exam fee. $20 renewal fee. **Governing Statute:** North Dakota Century Code 43-18.1-01 et seq.

Credential Type: Apprentice Water Conditioning Installer License. **Authorization:** Must work under the direct supervision of a licensed water conditioning contractor or installer. **Requirements:** Submit application. Apprenticeship lasts one year (1700 hours). **Fees:** No fee. **Governing Statute:**

Oklahoma 5391

Water Conditioning Installer, continued

North Dakota Century Code 43-18.1-01 et seq.

Oklahoma

5391

Plumber, Journeyman
Oklahoma State Dept. of Health
1000 N.E. 10th, Rm. 806
Oklahoma City, OK 73152
Phone: (405)271-5217

Credential Type: License. **Duration of License:** One year. **Requirements:** Three-year internship as a plumber's apprentice. Classroom training may be substituted for half of the required internship. 19 years of age. **Examination:** Journeyman Plumber Examination. **Fees:** $25 exam fee. $15 license fee. $15 renewal fee.

5392

Plumbing Contractor
Oklahoma State Health Dept.
1000 N.E. Tenth, Rm. 806
Oklahoma City, OK 73152
Phone: (405)271-5217

Credential Type: License. **Duration of License:** One year. **Requirements:** 20 years of age. Four years of experience in the plumbing trade. **Examination:** Plumbing Contractor Examination. **Fees:** $50 exam fee. $50 license fee. $50 renewal fee.

5393

Pump Installer
Oklahoma Water Resources Board
600 N. Harvey
PO Box 150
Oklahoma City, OK 73101
Phone: (405)231-2500

Credential Type: License. **Duration of License:** One year. **Requirements:** 90-day residency. Two years of experience in pump installations or one year as a licensed operator. **Examination:** Pump Installers Examination. **Fees:** $50 exam fee. $100 application fee. $50 license fee. $50 renewal fee. $100 filing fee. $50 indemnity fund fee. $50 testing fee.

Oregon

5394

Liquified Petroleum Gas (LPG) Fitter
Office of State Fire Marshall
4760 Portland Rd. NE
Salem, OR 97305
Phone: (503)378-2848

Credential Type: License. **Duration of License:** One year. **Requirements:** Must be employed by a licensed LPG Installer. **Examination:** Yes. **Fees:** $5 license fee. $5 renewal fee. **Governing Statute:** ORS 480.410 to 480.460.

5395

Plumber
Building Codes Agency
1535 Edgewater NW
Salem, OR 97310
Phone: (503)373-1268

Credential Type: License. **Duration of License:** One year. **Requirements:** Complete a four-year apprenticeship program and pass the exams, or have four years experience as journeyman plumber in another state. **Examination:** Yes. **Fees:** $100 exam fee. $50 license fee. $50 renewal fee. **Governing Statute:** ORS 693.010 to 693.

5396

Plumbing Contractor
Building Codes Agency
1535 Edgewater NW
Salem, OR 97310
Phone: (503)373-1268

Credential Type: License. **Examination:** Yes. **Fees:** $150 license fee. $150 renewal fee. **Governing Statute:** ORS 693.135.

5397

Steamfitter/Pipefitter
Buiding Codes Agency
1535 Edgewater Dr. NW
Salem, OR 97310
Phone: (503)373-1268

Credential Type: License. **Requirements:** Must have four years of experience. **Examination:** Yes. **Fees:** $25 exam fee. **Governing Statute:** ORS 480-630.

Rhode Island

5398

Fire Extinguisher Installer/Servicer
State Fire Marshal's Office
Rhode Island Div. of Fire Safety
1270 Mineral Spring Ave.
North Providence, RI 02904
Phone: (401)277-2335

Credential Type: Fire Extinguisher Installer/Servicer Apprentice Permit. **Duration of License:** One year. **Requirements:** Have at least six months of experience working on fixed fire extinguisher systems, or four months of experience on portable fire extinguishers, under the supervision of an employer holding a certificate of registration. **Reciprocity:** No. **Fees:** $5 apprentice permit fee.

Credential Type: Fire Extinguisher Installer/Servicer Journeyperson License. **Duration of License:** One year. **Requirements:** Have a minimum of one year working with fire extinguishers. Pass examination. **Examination:** Written examination for each class of fire extinguisher. **Reciprocity:** No. **Fees:** $10 examination fee. $10 portable extinguisher license fee. $10 fixed system license fee. $10 hydrostatic testing license fee. $10 annual renewal fee.

5399

Fire Protection Sprinkler Fitter
State Board of Pipefitter,
  Refrigeration, and Fire Protection
  Sprinkler Contractors &
  Journeypersons
Rhode Island Dept. of Labor
544 Elmwood Ave.
Providence, RI 02907
Phone: (401)457-1860

Credential Type: Fire Protection Sprinkler Fitter Journeyperson License. **Duration of License:** One year. **Requirements:** At least 18 years of age. Four years of practical experience as an apprentice working for a licensed fire protection sprinkler fitter. Must register with the board as an apprentice before beginning training. Contact board for alternative licensing requirements. **Examination:** Written examination. **Reciprocity:** No. **Fees:** $30 application fee. $20 apprentice registration. $25 license fee.

Credential Type: Fire Protection Sprinkler Fitter Master License. **Duration of License:** One year. **Requirements:** Hold Journeyperson's License for at least one year. Complete 10,000 hours of related experience. Contact board for alternative licensing requirements. **Examination:** Written examination. **Reciprocity:** No. **Fees:**

$30 application fee. $100 All Master 1 (Contractor) "Bond" fee. $40 All Master 2 (Contractor) "Bond" fee.

5400

Oil Burnerperson
State Board of Examiners of Electricians
Div. of Professional Regulation
Rhode Island Dept. of Labor
220 Elmwood Ave.
Providence, RI 02907
Phone: (401)457-1860

Credential Type: Oil Burnerperson—Journeyperson License (Cert. F). **Duration of License:** One year. **Requirements:** Complete 6,000 hours of practical experience as an apprentice to a licensed oil burner contractor. Apprentices must register with licensing agency before beginning training. **Examination:** Written examination. **Reciprocity:** No. **Fees:** $30 application fee. $20 apprentice registration fee. $30 license fee.

Credential Type: Oil Burnerperson—Master (Contractor) License (Cert. E). **Duration of License:** One year. **Requirements:** Hold journeyperson's license for at least one year. Complete 10,000 hours of related experience. **Examination:** Written examination. **Reciprocity:** No. **Fees:** $30 application fee. $100 license fee.

5401

Pipefitter
State Board of Pipefitter, Refrigeration, and Fire Protection Sprinkler Contractors, Journeypersons
Rhode Island Dept. of Labor
544 Elmwood Ave.
Providence, RI 02907
Phone: (401)457-1860

Credential Type: Pipefitter Journeyperson License. **Duration of License:** One year. **Requirements:** At least 18 years of age. Four years of practical experience as an apprentice working for a licensed pipefitter. Must register with the board as an apprentice before beginning training. Contact board for alternative licensing requirements. **Examination:** Written examination. **Reciprocity:** No. **Fees:** $30 application fee. $20 apprentice registration. $30 license fee.

Credential Type: Pipefitter Master License. **Duration of License:** One year. **Requirements:** Hold Journeyperson's License for at least one year. Complete 10,000 hours of related experience. Contact board for alternative licensing require-

ments. **Examination:** Written examination. **Reciprocity:** No. **Fees:** $30 application fee. $100 All Master 1 (Contractor) "Bond" license fee. $40 All Master 2 (Contractor) "Bond" license fee.

5402

Plumber
State Board of Plumbing Examiners
Div. of Professional Regulation
Rhode Island Dept. of Health
3 Capitol Hill
Providence, RI 02908
Phone: (401)277-2827

Credential Type: Journeyperson Plumber License. **Duration of License:** One year. **Requirements:** Foreign born must show proof of legal entry into U.S. Complete a registered apprenticeship for four years or complete two years of trade school or college study in plumbing or sanitary engineering and a two-year registered apprenticeship. **Examination:** Written examination. **Reciprocity:** No. **Fees:** $5 apprentice registration. $50 examination fee. $10 license renewal fee.

Credential Type: Master Plumber License. **Duration of License:** One year. **Requirements:** Hold Journeyperson Plumber License for at least one year. Post a $3,000 bond. **Examination:** Written examination. **Reciprocity:** No. **Fees:** $100 examination fee. $35 license renewal fee.

5403

Pump Installer (Drinking Water Wells)
Div. of Groundwater, ISDS Section
Rhode Island Dept. of Environmental Management
291 Promenade St.
Providence, RI 02908
Phone: (401)277-2234

Credential Type: Pump Installer License. **Duration of License:** One year. **Requirements:** At least 16 years of age. Submit application with certificate of liability insurance providing $300,000 body coverage and $100,000 property coverage. Must submit proof of adequate financial resources to own and maintain necessary tools and machinery. Reexamination required after the fourth renewal of license. **Examination:** Written examination. **Exemptions:** Plumber with master license is exempt. **Reciprocity:** No. **Fees:** $200 registration fee. $100 renewal fee.

South Carolina

5404

Fire Protection Contractor
South Carolina State Licensing Board for Contractors
PO Box 5737
Columbia, SC 29250
Phone: (803)734-8954

Credential Type: Fire Protection Contractor License. **Requirements:** Approved financial statement showing net worth. **Examination:** Yes. **Fees:** $250 license fee.

South Dakota

5405

Appliance Installation Plumbing Contractor
State Plumbing Commission
222 E. Capitol
PO Box 807
Pierre, SD 57501
Phone: (605)773-3429
Phone: (605)224-4374

Credential Type: Appliance Installation Plumbing Contractor License. **Duration of License:** One year. **Requirements:** Have at least one year experience as an appliance plumbing installer in South Dakota. **Examination:** Written examination. **Reciprocity:** Yes, provided state has same qualifications as South Dakota. **Fees:** $110 license and exam fee. $60 renewal fee. $50 temporary license fee. **Governing Statute:** South Dakota Codified Laws, Chap. 36-25. Administrative Rules of South Dakota, Article 20:53.

5406

Appliance Plumbing Installer
State Plumbing Commission
222 E. Capitol
PO Box 807
Pierre, SD 57501
Phone: (605)773-3429
Phone: (605)224-4374

Credential Type: Appliance Plumbing Installer's License. **Duration of License:** One year. **Requirements:** Have at least two years experience as an appliance plumbing installer apprentice in South Dakota. **Examination:** Written examination. **Reciprocity:** Yes, provided state has same qualifications as South Dakota. **Fees:** $40 license and exam fee. $30 renewal fee. **Governing Statute:** South Dakota Codified Laws, Chap. 36-25. Administrative Rules of South Dakota, Article 20:53.

Appliance Plumbing Installer, continued

Credential Type: Appliance Plumbing Installer Apprentice License. **Duration of License:** Two years with annual renewal. **Authorization:** Must work under the supervision of a licensed installer. **Requirements:** Submit appplication and name of supervising installer. **Fees:** No fee for first two years. $30 renewal fee in third year. **Governing Statute:** South Dakota Codified Laws, Chap. 36-25. Administrative Rules of South Dakota, Article 20:53.

5407

Manufactured and Mobile Home Installation Plumbing Contractor

State Plumbing Commission
222 E. Capitol
PO Box 807
Pierre, SD 57501
Phone: (605)773-3429
Phone: (605)224-4374

Credential Type: Manufactured and Mobile Home Installation Plumbing Contractor License. **Duration of License:** One year. **Requirements:** Have at least one year experience as a manufactured and mobile home plumbing installer in South Dakota. **Examination:** Written examination. **Exemptions:** Manufactured and mobile home licenses not required of licensed plumbing contractors, plumbers, or plumber apprentices. **Reciprocity:** Yes, provided state has same qualifications as South Dakota. **Fees:** $110 license and exam fee. $60 renewal fee. **Governing Statute:** South Dakota Codified Laws, Chap. 36-25. Administrative Rules of South Dakota, Article 20:53.

5408

Manufactured and Mobile Home Plumbing Installer

State Plumbing Commission
222 E. Capitol
PO Box 807
Pierre, SD 57501
Phone: (605)773-3429
Phone: (605)224-4374

Credential Type: Manufactured and Mobile Home Plumbing Installer's License. **Duration of License:** One year. **Requirements:** Have at least two years experience as a manufactured and mobile home plumbing installer apprentice in South Dakota. **Examination:** Written examination. **Exemptions:** Manufactured and mobile home licenses not required of licensed plumbing contractors, plumbers, or plumber apprentices. **Reciprocity:** Yes, provided state has same qualifications as South Dakota. **Fees:** $40 license and exam fee. $30 renewal fee. **Governing Statute:** South Dakota Codified Laws, Chap. 36-25. Administrative Rules of South Dakota, Article 20:53.

Credential Type: Manufactured and Mobile Home Plumbing Installer Apprentice License. **Duration of License:** Two years with annual renewal. **Authorization:** Must work under the supervision of a licensed installer. **Requirements:** Submit appplication and name of supervising installer. **Fees:** No fee for first two years. $30 renewal fee in third year. **Governing Statute:** South Dakota Codified Laws, Chap. 36-25. Administrative Rules of South Dakota, Article 20:53.

5409

Plumber

State Plumbing Commission
222 E. Capitol
PO Box 807
Pierre, SD 57501
Phone: (605)773-3429
Phone: (605)224-4374

Credential Type: Plumber's License. **Duration of License:** One year. **Requirements:** Meet one of the following sets of requirements: (1) Complete at least four years of experience (1900 hour per year) as an apprentice plumber. (2) Graduate from an accredited trade school with at least a 9-month, 1020-hour program in plumbing and complete at least three years of experience (1900 hour per year) as an apprentice plumber. (3) Graduate from a three-year association apprenticeship training program in plumbing with at least three years of experience (1900 hour per year) as an apprentice plumber. **Examination:** Plumber's examination. **Reciprocity:** Yes, provided state has same qualifications as South Dakota. **Fees:** $60 license and exam fee. $50 renewal fee. **Governing Statute:** South Dakota Codified Laws, Chap. 36-25. Administrative Rules of South Dakota, Article 20:53.

Credential Type: Plumber's Apprentice License. **Duration of License:** Four years with annual renewal. **Authorization:** Must work under the supervision of a licensed plumber for the first three years (5700 hours) of apprenticeship. **Requirements:** Submit appplication and name of supervising plumber. **Fees:** No fee for first three years. $50 renewal fee in fourth year. **Governing Statute:** South Dakota Codified Laws, Chap. 36-25. Administrative Rules of South Dakota, Article 20:53.

5410

Plumbing Contractor

State Plumbing Commission
222 E. Capitol
PO Box 807
Pierre, SD 57501
Phone: (605)773-3429
Phone: (605)224-4374

Credential Type: Plumbing Contractor License. **Duration of License:** One year. **Requirements:** Complete at least six years of experience (1900 hour per year) as a plumbing contractor, plumber, or apprentice plumber, with at least two of those years as a plumbing contractor or plumber. **Examination:** Plumbing contractor examination. **Reciprocity:** Yes, provided state has same qualifications as South Dakota. **Fees:** $200 license and exam fee. $150 renewal fee. **Governing Statute:** South Dakota Codified Laws, Chap. 36-25. Administrative Rules of South Dakota, Article 20:53.

5411

Sewage and Water Installation Plumbing Contractor

State Plumbing Commission
222 E. Capitol
PO Box 807
Pierre, SD 57501
Phone: (605)773-3429
Phone: (605)224-4374

Credential Type: Sewage and Water Installation Plumbing Contractor License. **Duration of License:** One year. **Requirements:** Have at least one year experience as a sewage and water plumbing installer in South Dakota. **Examination:** Written examination. **Reciprocity:** Yes, provided state has same qualifications as South Dakota. **Fees:** $170 license and exam fee. $120 renewal fee. **Governing Statute:** South Dakota Codified Laws, Chap. 36-25. Administrative Rules of South Dakota, Article 20:53.

5412

Sewage and Water Plumbing Installer

State Plumbing Commission
222 E. Capitol
PO Box 807
Pierre, SD 57501
Phone: (605)773-3429
Phone: (605)224-4374

Credential Type: Sewage and Water Plumbing Installer's License. **Duration of License:** One year. **Requirements:** Have at least two years experience as a sewage and water plumbing installer apprentice in South Dakota. **Examination:** Written examination. **Reciprocity:** Yes, provided state has same qualifications as South Dakota. **Fees:** $60 license and exam fee. $30 renewal fee. **Governing Statute:** South Dakota Codified Laws, Chap. 36-25. Administrative Rules of South Dakota, Article 20:53.

Credential Type: Sewage and Water Plumbing Installer Apprentice License. **Duration of License:** Two years with annual renewal. **Authorization:** Must work under the supervision of a licensed installer. **Requirements:** Submit appplication and name of supervising installer. **Fees:** No fee for first two years. $30 renewal fee in third year. **Governing Statute:** South Dakota Codified Laws, Chap. 36-25. Administrative Rules of South Dakota, Article 20:53.

5413

Water Conditioning Plumbing Installer
State Plumbing Commission
222 E. Capitol
PO Box 807
Pierre, SD 57501
Phone: (605)773-3429
Phone: (605)224-4374

Credential Type: Water Conditioning Plumbing Installer's License. **Duration of License:** One year. **Requirements:** Submit application and pay fees. Demonstrate qualifications. **Examination:** Written examination. **Exemptions:** Water conditioning licenses not required of licensed plumbing contractors, plumbers, or plumber apprentices. **Reciprocity:** Yes, provided state has same qualifications as South Dakota. **Fees:** $40 license and exam fee. $30 renewal fee. $50 temporary license fee. **Governing Statute:** South Dakota Codified Laws, Chap. 36-25. Administrative Rules of South Dakota, Article 20:53.

Credential Type: Water Conditioning Plumbing Installer Apprentice License. **Duration of License:** Two years with annual renewal. **Authorization:** Must work under the supervision of a licensed installer for the first two years (3800 hours) of apprenticeship. **Requirements:** Submit appplication and name of supervising installer. **Exemptions:** Water conditioning licenses not required of licensed plumbing contractors, plumbers, or plumber apprentices. **Fees:** No fee for first two years. $30 renewal fee in third year. **Governing Statute:** South Dakota Codified Laws, Chap. 36-25. Administrative Rules of South Dakota, Article 20:53.

5414

Water Conditioning and Treatment Plumbing Contractor
State Plumbing Commission
222 E. Capitol
PO Box 807
Pierre, SD 57501
Phone: (605)773-3429
Phone: (605)224-4374

Credential Type: Water Conditioning and Treatment Plumbing Contractor License. **Duration of License:** One year. **Requirements:** Submit application and pay fees. Demonstrate qualifications. **Examination:** Written examination. **Exemptions:** Water conditioning licenses not required of licensed plumbing contractors, plumbers, or plumber apprentices. **Reciprocity:** Yes, provided state has same qualifications as South Dakota. **Fees:** $110 license and exam fee. $60 renewal fee. $50 temporary license fee. **Governing Statute:** South Dakota Codified Laws, Chap. 36-25. Administrative Rules of South Dakota, Article 20:53.

Tennessee

5415

Fire Protection Sprinkler System Contractor
Dept. of Commerce and Insurance
Div. of Fire Prevention and Engineering
500 James Robertson Pky., 3rd Fl.
Nashville, TN 37243
Phone: (615)741-7190

Credential Type: License. **Requirements:** 18 years old. Must have Responsible Managing Employee on staff. Must have $10,000 surety bond. Complete application. **Fees:** $500 Registration. $100 Application. $100 Renewal (if not filed in time).

5416

Fire Protection Sprinkler System Contractor/Responsible Managing Employee (RME)
Dept. of Commerce and Insurance
Div. of Fire Prevention and Engineering
500 James Robertson Pky., 3rd Fl.
Nashville, TN 37243
Phone: (615)741-7190

Credential Type: License. **Requirements:** 18 years old. Licensed architect or engineer in Tennessee, or complete NICET 'Level III'. Complete application. **Examination:** Yes. **Fees:** $200 Registration. $25 Application. Renewal fees apply. Examination fees will be levied when taking the NICET.

Texas

5417

Fire Alarm System Contractor
Texas State Fire Marshal, Div. 30
1110 San Jacinto
Austin, TX 78701-1998
Phone: (512)322-3550

Credential Type: Superintendent license and registration. **Duration of License:** Two years. **Requirements:** Must obtain certificate of registration and be or employ a licensed individual. Registration requires certificate of liability insurance ($100,000/$300,000). License requires proof of registration in Texas as a professional engineer or successful completion of an examination. **Examination:** NICET examination at level II for fire alarm planning superintendent license. Exam by state fire marshal on rules and regulations or technical information. **Fees:** $500 registration fee. $1000 registration renewal fee. $20 exam fee. $100 license fee. $200 license renewal fee. **Governing Statute:** Insurance Code 5.43-1,2,3; 37 TAC 521, 531, 541.

Credential Type: Technician license. **Duration of License:** Two years. **Requirements:** Contact licensing body for application information. **Examination:** Exam by state fire marshal on rules and regulations or technical information. **Fees:** $20 exam fee. $100 license fee. $200 license renewal fee. **Governing Statute:** Insurance Code 5.43-1,2,3; 37 TAC 521, 531, 541.

5418

Fire Extinguisher System Contractor
Texas State Fire Marshal, Div. 30
1110 San Jacinto
Austin, TX 78701-1998
Phone: (512)322-3550

Credential Type: License and registration. **Duration of License:** Two years. **Authorization:** Various classes of registration certificates and licenses are issued. License and registration. **Requirements:** Must obtain certificate of registration and be or employ a licensed individual. Registration requires certificate of liability insurance ($100,000/$300,000). License requires proof of registration in Texas as a professional engineer or successful completion of an examination. **Examination:** NICET examination at level III for fire extinguisher license, Type PL. Exam by state fire marshal on rules and regulations or technical

Texas 5419

Fire Extinguisher System Contractor, continued

information. **Fees:** $450 registration fee (Types A,B,PL). $600 registration renewal fee. $250 registration fee (Type C). $300 registration renewal fee (Type C). $20 exam fee. $50 license fee (Types A,B,PL). $100 license renewal fee (Types A,B,PL). **Governing Statute:** Insurance Code 5.43-1,2,3; 37 TAC 521, 531, 541.

5419

Fire Protection Sprinkler System Contractor
Texas State Fire Marshal, Div. 30
1110 San Jacinto
Austin, TX 78701-1998
Phone: (512)322-3550

Credential Type: License and registration. **Duration of License:** Two years. **Requirements:** Must obtain certificate of registration and be or employ a licensed individual. Registration requires certificate of liability insurance ($100,000/$300,000). License requires proof of registration in Texas as a professional engineer or successful completion of an examination. **Examination:** NICET examination at level III for RME automatic sprinkler system license. Exam by state fire marshal on rules and regulations or technical information. **Fees:** $50 application fee. $900 registration fee. $1800 registration renewal fee. $50 exam fee. $175 license (RME) fee. $350 license renewal fee. **Governing Statute:** Insurance Code 5.43-1,2,3; 37 TAC 521, 531, 541.

5420

Irrigator
Texas Board of Irrigators
PO Box 12337
Austin, TX 78711
Phone: (512)463-7990

Credential Type: License. **Duration of License:** One year. **Examination:** Yes. **Fees:** $75 exam fee. $85 renewal fee. **Governing Statute:** VACS 9751, 31 TAC 421.1.

5421

Plumber
Texas State Board of Plumbing Examiners
PO Box 4200
Austin, TX 78756
Phone: (512)458-2145

Credential Type: Journeyman License. **Duration of License:** One year. **Requirements:** 17 years of age. Combination of work experience and/or technical training equaling 6,000 hours. **Examination:** Written and mechanical. **Fees:** $50 exam fee. $50 license fee. $50 renewal fee. **Governing Statute:** VACS 6243-101, 22 TAC 361.

Credential Type: Master License. **Duration of License:** One year. **Requirements:** 18 years of age. Possession of a journeyman's license for 12 months. High school graduate or equivalent. **Examination:** Written and mechanical. **Fees:** $75 exam fee. $75 license fee. $75 renewal fee. **Governing Statute:** VACS 6243-101, 22 TAC 361.

Utah

5422

Plumber
Dept. of Commerce
Div. of Occupational and Professional Licensing
160 E. 300 S.
PO Box 45802
Salt Lake City, UT 84145
Phone: (801)530-6628

Credential Type: License. **Requirements:** A journeyman must produce satisfactory evidence of successful completion of the equivalent of at least four years of full-time training and instruction as a licensed apprentice plumber under supervision of a licensed journeyman plumber and in accourdance with a planned program of training approved by the Division. **Examination:** Yes. **Fees:** $100 license fee. $75 renewal fee.

Vermont

5423

Plumber, Master
Plumber's Examining Board
Dept. of Labor and Industry
120 State St.
Montpelier, VT 05602
Phone: (802)828-2108

Credential Type: License. **Requirements:** Journeyman's license for six months: or, experience acceptable to the Board. **Examination:** Yes, given monthly. **Reciprocity:** Yes. (New Hampshire only). **Fees:** $25 License. **Governing Statute:** Title 26, VSA Sections 2191, 2193-2195.

Washington

5424

Journeyman Plumber
Dept. of Labor & Industries
Building & Construction Safety Inspection Services
General Administration Bldg., HC-101
Olympia, WA 98504
Phone: (206)753-5022

Credential Type: Journeyman Plumber Certificate. **Duration of License:** Two years. **Requirements:** Must have 6,000 hours of work experience or a valid license from another state. Notarized affidavit of work experience required. **Examination:** Written examination. **Reciprocity:** Yes. **Fees:** $100 examination fee. $80 initial certificate fee. $80 renewal fee.

Podiatrists

The following states grant licenses in this occupational category as of the date of publication:

Alabama	District of	Iowa	Minnesota	New Mexico	Rhode Island	Washington
Alaska	Columbia	Kansas	Mississippi	New York	South Carolina	West Virginia
Arizona	Florida	Kentucky	Missouri	North Carolina	South Dakota	Wisconsin
Arkansas	Georgia	Louisiana	Montana	North Dakota	Tennessee	Wyoming
California	Hawaii	Maine	Nebraska	Ohio	Texas	
Colorado	Idaho	Maryland	Nevada	Oklahoma	Utah	
Connecticut	Illinois	Massachusetts	New Hampshire	Oregon	Vermont	
Delaware	Indiana	Michigan	New Jersey	Pennsylvania	Virginia	

Alabama

5425

Podiatrist
Alabama State Board of Podiatry
5220 Meadow Brook Rd.
Birmingham, AL 35242
Phone: (205)995-8537

Credential Type: License. **Duration of License:** One year. **Requirements:** 21 years of age and a U.S. citizen. Must be a graduate of a recognized college of podiatry. Must have completed a one-year postgraduate training program. **Examination:** Yes. **Fees:** Contact board for fees.

Alaska

5426

Podiatrist
State Medical Board
PO Box D-LIC
Juneau, AK 99811-0800
Phone: (907)465-2541

Credential Type: License to practice. **Duration of License:** Two years. **Requirements:** Must have podiatry diploma. One year of podiatric residency. **Examination:** National Boards. **Fees:** $450 application/examination fee. $400 renewal fee.

Arizona

5427

Podiatrist
State Board of Podiatry Examiners
1645 W. Jefferson, Rm. 410
Phoenix, AZ 85007
Phone: (602)542-3095

Credential Type: License to practice. **Duration of License:** One year. **Requirements:** Must have podiatry diploma. One year of podiatric residency. **Examination:** Written and oral state exam. **Fees:** $200 examination fee. $200 renewal fee. $100 provisional license fee.

Arkansas

5428

Podiatrist
Arkansas State Podiatry Examining Board
6105 Lee St.
Little Rock, AR 72205
Phone: (501)664-8888

Credential Type: License. **Requirements:** Must have three years college in pre-podiatry. Must be a graduate of an approved podiatry college. **Examination:** Yes. **Fees:** Written, oral and practical examinations—costs not to exceed $200.

California

5429

Podiatrist
Dept. of Consumer Affairs
Board of Podiatric Medicine
1420 Howe Ave., Ste. 8
Sacramento, CA 95825-3229
Phone: (916)920-6347

Credential Type: License to practice. **Duration of License:** Two years. **Requirements:** Must have podiatry diploma. One year of podiatric residency. **Examination:** National Boards. Oral and clinical state examination. **Fees:** $1,667 license fee. $60 limited license fee. $800 renewal fee.

Colorado

5430

Podiatrist
Dept. of Regulatory Agencies
Colorado Podiatry Board
1560 Broadway, Ste. 1300
Denver, CO 80202-5140
Phone: (303)894-7721

Credential Type: License to practice. **Duration of License:** One year. **Requirements:** Must have podiatry diploma. One year of podiatric residency. **Examination:** National Boards. Podiatric Medical Licensure Examination (PM Lexis). **Fees:** $509 application/examination fee. $314 renewal fee.

Connecticut

5431

Podiatrist
Podiatry Licensure
Dept. of Health Services
150 Washington St.
Hartford, CT 06106
Phone: (203)566-1031

Credential Type: License to practice. **Duration of License:** One year. **Requirements:** Podiatric College Training. **Examination:** National Boards. Podiatric Medical Licensure Examination (PM Lexis). State law, oral, and practical state examinations. **Fees:** $300 application/examination fee. $150 renewal fee. $450 licensure by endorsement fee.

Delaware

5432

Podiatrist
Board of Podiatry
Margaret O'Neill Bldg.
PO Box 1401
Dover, DE 19720
Phone: (302)736-4522

Credential Type: License to practice. **Duration of License:** Two years. **Requirements:** Must have podiatry diploma. One year of post-graduate training. **Examination:** National Boards. Podiatric Medical Licensure Examination (PM Lexis). **Fees:** $175 examination fee. $290 renewal fee.

District of Columbia

5433

Podiatrist
License and Certification Div.
Occupational and Professional Licensure Administration
Consumer and Regulatory Affairs Dept.
PO Box 37200
Washington, DC 20013-7200
Phone: (202)727-7823
Phone: (202)727-7480

Credential Type: License to practice. **Requirements:** Contact licensing body for requirements.

Florida

5434

Podiatrist
Board of Podiatric Medicine
Dept. of Professional Regulations
1940 N. Monroe St.
Tallahassee, FL 32301
Phone: (904)487-1814

Credential Type: License to practice. **Duration of License:** Two years. **Requirements:** Podiatric college certification. Complete one year of postgraduate training or five years of practice. **Examination:** Written state examination. **Fees:** $350 examination fee. $250 renewal fee.

Georgia

5435

Podiatrist
State Board of Podiatry Examiners
166 Pryor St. SW
Atlanta, GA 30303
Phone: (404)656-3912

Credential Type: License to practice. **Duration of License:** Two years. **Requirements:** Must have podiatry diploma. One year of podiatric residency. **Examination:** Written and practical state examinations. **Fees:** $150 examination fee. $80 renewal fee.

Hawaii

5436

Podiatrist
Board of Medical Examiners
PO Box 3469
Honolulu, HI 96801
Phone: (808)548-4100

Credential Type: License to practice. **Duration of License:** Two years. **Requirements:** Must have podiatry diploma. One year of podiatric residency. **Examination:** National Boards. Podiatric Medical Licensure Practical Examination (PM Lexis). **Fees:** $250 application fee. $50 license fee. $130 renewal fee.

Idaho

5437

Podiatrist
Bureau of Occupational Licenses
1109 Main St., Ste. 220
Boise, ID 83702-5642
Phone: (208)334-3233

Credential Type: License to practice. **Duration of License:** One year. **Requirements:** Must have podiatry diploma. One year of podiatric residency. **Examination:** National Boards. Podiatric Medical Licensure Examination (PM Lexis). **Fees:** $400 license with examination fee. $200 license without examination fee. $100 renewal fee.

Illinois

5438

Podiatrist
Dept. of Professional Regulation
Licensure Maintenance Unit
320 W. Washington, 3rd Floor
Springfield, IL 62786
Phone: (217)785-0842

Credential Type: License to practice. **Duration of License:** One year. **Requirements:** Podiatric college certification. One year of post-graduate training. **Examination:** National Boards. Podiatric Medical Licensure Examination (PM Lexis). **Fees:** $250 license fee. $305.50 examination fee. $100 renewal fee.

Indiana

5439

Podiatrist
Committee of Podiatric Medical Examiners
One American Square, Ste. 1020
PO Box 82067
Indianapolis, IN 46282
Phone: (317)232-2960

Credential Type: License to practice. **Duration of License:** Two years. **Requirements:** Must have podiatry diploma. **Examination:** National Boards. Podiatric Medical Licensure Examination (PM Lexis). **Fees:** $250 examination fee. $50 renewal fee. $200 endorsement fee.

Podiatrists | 5448 Minnesota

Iowa

5440

Podiatrist
Board of Podiatry Examiners
Dept. of Public Health
Lucas State Office Bldg.
Des Moines, IA 50319
Phone: (515)281-6762

Credential Type: License. **Duration of License:** Two years. **Requirements:** High school graduation. Two years of education from a recognized college or university. Graduation from a four-year school of podiatry. **Examination:** National board exam. State exam. **Reciprocity:** Yes, if the applicant meets Iowa's requirements. **Fees:** $100 application fee. $250 exam fee. $140 renewal fee. $100 reciprocity fee.

Kansas

5441

Podiatrist
State Board of Healing Arts
235 S. Topeka Blvd.
Topeka, KS 66603
Phone: (913)296-7413

Credential Type: License to practice. **Duration of License:** One year. **Requirements:** Must have podiatry diploma. One year of podiatric residency. **Examination:** National Boards. Podiatric Medical Licensure Examination (PM Lexis). Oral state examination. **Fees:** $320 application/examination fee. $150 renewal fee. $150 endorsement fee. $25 limited license fee.

Kentucky

5442

Podiatrist
Kentucky Board of Podiatry
110 N. Hubbard Ln.
Louisville, KY 40207
Phone: (502)897-2047

Credential Type: License. **Duration of License:** One year. **Requirements:** 18 years of age. Kentucky resident. Graduate of an approved school or college of podiatry. **Examination:** Yes. **Fees:** $200 exam fee. $100 renewal fee.

Louisiana

5443

Podiatrist
Louisiana Board of Medical
 Examiners
830 Union St., Ste. 100
New Orleans, LA 70112
Phone: (504)524-6763

Credential Type: License. **Duration of License:** One year. **Requirements:** 21 years of age. U.S. citizen. Graduation from an approved school or college of podiatry. **Examination:** Yes. **Reciprocity:** Yes. **Fees:** $50 exam fee. $10 processing fee. $2 issuing fee. $25 renewal fee.

Maine

5444

Podiatrist
State Board of Podiatric Examiners
State House Station 137
Augusta, ME 04333
Phone: (207)289-3601

Credential Type: License to practice. **Duration of License:** Two years. **Requirements:** Must have podiatry diploma. **Examination:** National Boards. Oral state examination. **Fees:** $100 examination fee. $100 renewal fee.

Maryland

5445

Podiatrist
State Board of Podiatric Medicine
4201 Patterson Ave.
Baltimore, MD 21515-2299
Phone: (301)764-4785

Credential Type: License to practice. **Duration of License:** Two years. **Requirements:** Podiatric college certification. One year of podiatric residency. **Examination:** National Boards. Written state examination. **Fees:** $300 examination fee. $50 renewal fee.

Massachusetts

5446

Podiatrist
Board of Registration in Podiatry
100 Cambridge St., 15th Floor
Boston, MA 02202
Phone: (617)727-1817

Credential Type: License to practice. **Duration of License:** One year. **Requirements:** Podiatric college certification. One year of post-graduate training. **Examination:** National Boards. Podiatric Medical Licensure Examination (PM Lexis). **Fees:** $345 examination fee. $50 application fee. $50 renewal fee.

Michigan

5447

Podiatrist
Board of Podiatric Medicine &
 Surgery
Dept. of Licensure & Regulations
PO Box 30018
Lansing, MI 48915
Phone: (517)373-3596

Credential Type: License to practice. **Duration of License:** Three years. **Requirements:** Podiatric college certification. One year of post-graduate training. **Examination:** National Boards. Podiatric Medical Licensure Examination (PM Lexis). **Fees:** $230 examination fee. $150 renewal fee. $25 limited license fee.

Minnesota

5448

Podiatrist
Board of Podiatric Medicine
2700 University Ave. W., Ste. 101
St. Paul, MN 55114
Phone: (612)642-0588

Credential Type: License to practice. **Duration of License:** One year. **Requirements:** Podiatric college certification. One year of post-graduate training. **Examination:** National Boards. Podiatric Medical Licensure Examination (PM Lexis) parts two & 3. **Fees:** $250 examination fee. $200 license fee. $200 renewal fee.

Mississippi

5449

Podiatrist
State Board of Podiatry
2688-D Insurance Center Dr.
Jackson, MS 39216
Phone: (601)354-6645

Credential Type: License to practice. **Duration of License:** One year. **Requirements:** Must have podiatry diploma. One year of podiatric residency. **Examination:** National Boards. **Fees:** $250 application fee. $40 renewal fee.

Missouri

5450

Podiatrist
State Board of Podiatry
PO Box 423
Jefferson City, MO 65102
Phone: (314)751-0873

Credential Type: License to practice. **Duration of License:** One year. **Requirements:** Must have podiatry diploma. **Examination:** National Boards. Podiatric Medical Licensure Examination (PM Lexis). **Fees:** $300 application/examination fee. $150 renewal fee.

Montana

5451

Podiatrist
Montana Board of Medical
  Examiners
111 N. Jackson
Helena, MT 59620
Phone: (406)444-4284

Credential Type: License. **Duration of License:** One year. **Requirements:** Graduation from an accredited school of podiatry. One year of post-graduate training or equivalent. **Examination:** National board exam. **Fees:** $50 application fee. $35 exam fee. $25 renewal fee. **Governing Statute:** Montana Code Annotated 36-6-301 through 37-6-312.

Nebraska

5452

Podiatrist
Nebraska Board of Examiners in
  Podiatry
301 Centennial Mall S.
PO Box 95007
Lincoln, NE 68509
Phone: (402)471-2115

Credential Type: License. **Duration of License:** Two years. **Requirements:** Must be a high school graduate. Must be a graduate of a school of podiatry or chiropody. Twenty-four hours of continuing eductation are required biennially. **Examination:** Yes. **Fees:** $250 initial fee. $250 renewal fee.

Nevada

5453

Podiatrist
Nevada State Board of Podiatry
2413 S. Eastern, Ste. 142
Las Vegas, NV 89104
Phone: (702)687-4475

Credential Type: License. **Duration of License:** One year. **Requirements:** Graduation from an accredited four-year college of podiatric medicine. **Examination:** State Board exam. National Board exams. **Fees:** $600 license fee.

New Hampshire

5454

Podiatrist
Board of Registration in Podiatry
6 Hazen Drive
Concord, NH 03301
Phone: (603)271-1203

Credential Type: License to practice. **Duration of License:** One year. **Requirements:** Podiatric college certification. **Examination:** National boards. Podiatric Medical Licensure Examination (PM Lexis). Oral state examination. **Fees:** $150 application fee. $250 examination fee. $25 renewal fee.

New Jersey

5455

Podiatrist
State Board of Medical Examiners
28 W. State St., Rm. 914
Trenton, NJ 08608
Phone: (609)292-4843

Credential Type: License. **Duration of License:** Two years. **Requirements:** 21 years of age. High school diploma or equivalent. Completion of two years of approved college or university credits. Doctorate of Podiatry degree from an approved college. Completion of a one-year internship at a licensed clinic, hospital or institution. Good moral character. **Examination:** Written. **Reciprocity:** Yes. **Fees:** $150 exam fee. $120 biennial registration fee. **Governing Statute:** NJSA 45:5. NJAC 13:35.

New Mexico

5456

Podiatrist
Board of Medical Examiners
PO Box 25101
Santa Fe, NM 87504
Phone: (505)827-7177

Credential Type: License to practice. **Duration of License:** One year. **Requirements:** Must have podiatry diploma. **Examination:** National Boards. Podiatric Medical Licensure Examination (PM Lexis). **Fees:** $400 examination fee. $125 renewal fee. $25 wall license fee.

New York

5457

Podiatrist
State Education Dept.
Div. of Professional Licensing
  Services
Cultural Education Center
Empire State Plaza
Albany, NY 12230
Phone: (518)474-3279

Credential Type: License. **Duration of License:** Three years. **Requirements:** Bachelor's Degree plus degree of Doctor of Podiatric Medicine. 21 years of age. 50 hours of approved continuing education prior to renewal. **Examination:** Written and practical. **Fees:** $225 exam fee. $430 application fee. $210 renewal fee. **Governing Statute:** Title VIII Articles 130, 141 of the Education Law.

North Carolina

5458

Podiatrist
The Board of Podiatry Examiners of the State of North Carolina
PO Box 1088
Raleigh, NC 27602
Phone: (919)829-4989

Credential Type: License. **Duration of License:** One year. **Requirements:** Two years of instruction at a college or university and graduation from an accredited college of podiatric medicine. 25 hours of continuing education each year. **Examination:** Written, oral and practical. **Fees:** $200 license and exam fee. $125 renewal fee.

North Dakota

5459

Podiatrist
Board of Podiatry Examiners
PO Box 1980
Jamestown, ND 58401
Phone: (701)252-0120

Credential Type: License to practice. **Duration of License:** One year. **Requirements:** Must have podiatry diploma. **Examination:** National Boards. Written, oral, and practical state examinations. **Fees:** $150 renewal fee. $250 surcharge fee for first two years.

Ohio

5460

Podiatrist
State Medical Board
77 South High St.
Columbus, OH 43266-0315
Phone: (614)466-3934

Credential Type: License to practice. **Duration of License:** Two years. **Requirements:** Must have podiatry diploma. **Examination:** National Boards. Podiatric Medical Licensure Examination (PM Lexis). **Fees:** $185 application fee. $160 renewal fee.

Oklahoma

5461

Podiatrist
Oklahoma State Board of Podiatry
PO Box 18256
Oklahoma City, OK 73152
Phone: (405)848-6841

Credential Type: License. **Duration of License:** One year. **Requirements:** Doctor of Podiatric Medicine degree. Clinical rotation in practice settings. 30 hours of continuing education each year. 30-day training period. 21 years of age. Free of infectious disease. **Fees:** $200 exam fee. $200 application fee. $75 renewal fee.

Oregon

5462

Podiatrist
Oregon Board of Medical Examiners
620 Crown Plaza
1500 SW 1st Ave.
Portland, OR 97201
Phone: (503)229-5770

Credential Type: License. **Duration of License:** Two years. **Requirements:** Graduation from an approved Podiatric school. Completion of one-year approved residency training. **Examination:** Yes. **Fees:** $250 license fee. $320 renewal fee. **Governing Statute:** ORS 677.010 to 677.990.

Pennsylvania

5463

Podiatrist
State Board of Podiatry
PO Box 2649
Harrisburg, PA 17105
Phone: (717)783-7134

Credential Type: License to practice. **Duration of License:** Two years. **Requirements:** Podiatric college certification. **Examination:** National Boards. Podiatric Medical Licensure Examination (PM Lexis). **Fees:** $303.75 examination fee. $105 renewal fee.

Rhode Island

5464

Podiatrist
Board of Examiners of Podiatry
104 Cannon Bldg.
3 Capitol Hill
Providence, RI 02908
Phone: (401)277-2827

Credential Type: License to practice. **Duration of License:** Two years. **Requirements:** Podiatric college certification. Eight months to one year of postgraduate training. **Examination:** National Boards. Podiatric Medical Licensure Examination (PM Lexis). **Fees:** $250 application fee. $150 renewal fee.

South Carolina

5465

Podiatrist
South Carolina State Board of Podiatry Examiners
119 Sumner St.
Greenville, SC 29601
Phone: (803)225-8131

Credential Type: License. **Requirements:** Four years of high school, plus three years of pre-podiatry training at a recognized college. Graduation from a recognized four-year college of podiatric medicine. One year of postgraduate residency or preceptorship. **Examination:** Yes. **Fees:** $400 license fee. $60 renewal fee.

South Dakota

5466

Podiatrist
Board of Podiatry
808 S. Minnesota Ave.
Sioux Falls, SD 57104
Phone: (605)336-7753

Credential Type: License to practice. **Duration of License:** One year. **Requirements:** Must have podiatry diploma. **Examination:** National Boards. Written state examination.

Tennessee

5467

Podiatrist
Board of Registration in Podiatry
283 Plus Park Blvd.
Nashville, TN 37243
Phone: (615)367-6291

Credential Type: License. **Requirements:** 18 years old. One year residency, or two years preceptorship. D.P.M. degree. 15 hours of continuing education per renewal period. **Examination:** Yes. **Fees:** $180 Registration. $300 Examination. $100 Application.

Texas

5468

Podiatrist
Texas State Board of Podiatry
  Examiners
3420 Executive Center Dr., Ste. 305
Austin, TX 78731
Phone: (512)794-0145

Credential Type: License. **Duration of License:** One year. **Requirements:** 21 years of age. Completion of 90 semester hours of college courses. Graduation from a bona fide reputable school of podiatry or chiropody consisting of at least four terms of eight months each. Training in CPR. Any other training required by the Board. 15 hours of continuing education required for license renewal. **Examination:** National Base Examination. Oral examination on laws and board rules. **Fees:** $500 exam fee. $200 renewal fee. **Governing Statute:** VACS 4567, 22 TAC 371.

Utah

5469

Podiatrist
Dept. of Commerce
Div. of Occupational and Professionl
  Licensing
160 E. 300 S.
PO Box 45802
Salt Lake City, UT 84145
Phone: (801)530-6628

Credential Type: License. **Requirements:** Must complete either two years of college study in a recognized college of liberal arts or sciences and earn a doctor of podiatry degree in an approved three-year program; or one year of college study in a recognized college of liberal arts or sciences, and earn a degree of doctor of podiatry in an approved four-year program. **Examination:** Yes. **Fees:** $70 license fee. $55 renewal fee. $90 controlled substance license fee. $50 controlled substance license renewal fee.

Vermont

5470

Podiatrist
State Board of Medical Practice
Pavilion Office Bldg.
Montpelier, VT 05602
Phone: (802)828-2363

Credential Type: License. **Requirements:** 18 years of age. Good moral character. Graduate from a legally incorporated school of podiatry. Completion of an accredited four year course of study in the U.S. **Examination:** Yes. **Fees:** $75 License. $5 Recording fee. There is no renewal fee. **Governing Statute:** Title 26, VSA Sections 361-369.

Virginia

5471

Podiatrist
Board of Medicine
1601 Rolling Hills Dr.
Richmond, VA 23229-5005
Phone: (804)662-9924
Phone: (804)662-9927

Credential Type: License to practice. **Duration of License:** Two years. **Requirements:** Podiatric college certification. One year of podiatric residency. **Examination:** National Boards. Podiatric Medical Licensure Examination (PM Lexis). **Fees:** $250 examination fee. $125 renewal fee.

Washington

5472

Podiatrist
State Board
Podiatry Section
1300 Quince St., MS-EY-23
Olympia, WA 98504
Phone: (206)586-5962

Credential Type: License to practice. **Duration of License:** One year. **Requirements:** Podiatric college certification. Continuing medical education (CME) AIDS Certification. **Examination:** National Boards. Podiatric Medical Licensure Examination (PM Lexis). **Fees:** $500 examination fee. $650 renewal fee. $400 endorsement fee.

West Virginia

5473

Podiatrist
State Board of Medicine
3412 Chesterfield Ave.
Charleston, WV 25304
Phone: (304)348-2921

Alternate Information: 100 Dee Dr., Charleston, WV 25311

Credential Type: License. **Duration of License:** Two years. **Requirements:** Graduate from an approved school of podiatry. Never convicted of a felony. **Examination:** Yes. **Fees:** $200 Application. $250 Examination. $200 Active renewal. $50 Inactive renewal.

Wisconsin

5474

Podiatrist
Regulations and Licensing Dept.
Medical Board
PO Box 8935
Madison, WI 53708-8935
Phone: (608)266-8609

Credential Type: License. **Requirements:** Diploma from a school of podiatric medicine. 18 years of age. **Examination:** National Boards and an oral exam.

Wyoming

5475

Podiatrist
State Board of Podiatry
PO Box 6019
Cheyenne, WY 82003
Phone: (307)634-2781

Credential Type: License. **Duration of License:** One year. **Requirements:** 21 years of age. Complete three years of college. Graduate from a four-year approved school of podiatry. Pass the oral and written state examinations. Pass the National Board examination. **Examination:** Yes. **Fees:** $100 Examinations. $100 Renewal.

Police, Detectives, and Special Agents

The following states grant licenses in this occupational category as of the date of publication: Alabama, Arkansas, Illinois, Kentucky, Maryland, Michigan, Minnesota, Nebraska, North Carolina, North Dakota, Texas, Wyoming.

Alabama

5476

Law Enforcement Personnel
Alabama Peace Officers
Standards & Training Commission
472 S. Lawrence St., Ste. 202
Montgomery, AL 36104
Phone: (205)242-4045

Credential Type: License. **Duration of License:** Varies. **Authorization:** Any person with the power to arrest must be a licensed law enforcement officer. **Requirements:** 19 years of age. Citizen of the U.S. No felony convictions. Must be a high school graduate or equivalent.

Licensing procedure begins when applicant has obtained employment. Within first nine months of employment, applicant must complete one of the Alabama-certified regional departmental law enforcement training academies, which range from seven to 16 weeks of training. **Examination:** Yes, during academy training.

Arkansas

5477

State Trooper
Arkansas State Police
3 Natural Resources Dr.
PO Box 5901
Little Rock, AR 72215
Phone: (501)224-3101

Credential Type: License. **Requirements:** Arkansas Resident. US Citizen. Must be fingerprinted. Never convicted of a felony, class A misdemeanor or crime. Good moral character. High school graduate or equivalent. Have a current valid Arkansas drivers license. Have visual acuity of 20/70 uncorrected; corrected to 20/20 in each eye. Pass a department physical and psychological test. **Examination:** Yes. **Fees:** None

Illinois

5478

Accident Reconstruction Specialist
Illinois Law Enforcement Officers
  Training Board
600 S. Second St., Ste. 300
Springfield, IL 62704
Phone: (217)782-4540

Credential Type: Accident Reconstruction Specialist Certificate. **Duration of License:** Lifetime. **Requirements:** At least 21 years of age. Complete the following training programs from schools certified by the Illinois Local Governmental Law Enforcement Officers Training Board: (1) On Scene Accident Investigation; (2) Technical Accident Investigation; (3) Vehicle Dynamics; (4) Accident Reconstruction. Complete one year of experience as an accident investigator prior to completing Accident Reconstruction course. **Examination:** Comprehensive Accident Reconstruction Specialist Exam. **Reciprocity:** No. **Governing Statute:** Illinois Revised Statutes, Chapter 85.

5479

Electronic Criminal Surveillance Officer
Illinois Local Governmental Law
  Enforcement Officer Training
  Board
600 S. Second St., Ste. 300
Springfield, IL 62704
Phone: (217)782-4540

Credential Type: Level I Certificate. **Duration of License:** Three years. **Requirements:** U.S. citizen. Resident of county where employed. Complete a 10 week basic law enforcement recruitment course. Complete 120 hours of series course work in electronic criminal surveillance. Renewal requires 20 hours of continuing education annually. **Examination:** Written examination. **Reciprocity:** No. **Fees:** No fee. **Governing Statute:** Public Act 85-1203.

Credential Type: Level II Certificate. **Duration of License:** Three years. **Requirements:** Hold a Level I Certificate. Complete 80 additional hours of series course work in electronic criminal surveillance. **Examination:** Written examination. **Reciprocity:** No. **Fees:** No fee. **Governing Statute:** Public Act 85-1203

Credential Type: Level III Certificate. **Duration of License:** Three years. **Requirements:** Hold a Level II Certificate. Complete 40 additional hours of series course work in electronic criminal surveillance. **Examination:** Written examination. **Reciprocity:** No. **Fees:** No fee. **Governing Statute:** Public Act 85-1203

5480

Illinois County Sheriff
Illinois Local Law Enforcement
 Officer Training Board
600 S. Second St., Ste. 300
Springfield, IL 62704
Phone: (217)782-4540

Credential Type: County Sheriff Certificate. **Duration of License:** Indefinite. **Requirements:** Illinois resident. Live in county of office. Pass examination. Renewal requires 20 hours of continuing education per year. **Examination:** Written examination. **Reciprocity:** No. **Fees:** No fee. **Governing Statute:** Public Act 85-985.

5481

Law Enforcement Officer
Illinois Local Law Enforcement
 Training Board
600 S. Second St., Ste. 300
Springfield, IL 62704
Phone: (217)782-4540

Credential Type: Law Enforcement Certificate. **Duration of License:** Lifetime. **Requirements:** At least 21 years of age. Residency is a requirement in some departments. High school graduate or equivalent. Some departments may require college credits. **Examination:** Law Enforcement Certification Examination. **Reciprocity:** Yes. **Fees:** No fee. **Governing Statute:** Illinois Police Training Act, Illinois Revised Statutes, Chapter 85.

Kentucky

5482

Police Officer
Dept. of Criminal Justice Training
Eastern Kentucky University, Stratton
 Bldg., Rm. 112
Richmond, KY 40475
Phone: (606)622-6165

Credential Type: License. **Requirements:** High school graduate or GED. Completion of 400 hours of basic training approved by the Kentucky Law Enforcement Council within the first year of employment. 21 years of age. 40 hours of continuing education required annually.

Maryland

5483

Police Officer
Police Training Commission
Dept. of Public Safety and
 Correctional Service
3085 Hernwood Rd.
Woodstock, MD 21163
Phone: (301)442-2700

Credential Type: Police Officer Certification. **Duration of License:** Three years. **Requirements:** High school graduate or equivalent. Complete police academy training. **Reciprocity:** Yes. **Fees:** No fees.

Michigan

5484

Railroad Police Officer
Private Security and Investigation
 Section
Dept. of State Police
General Office Bldg.
7150 Harris Dr.
Lansing, MI 48913
Phone: (517)332-2521

Credential Type: Commission. **Duration of License:** Lifelong. **Requirements:** At least 18 years of age. Be a United States citizen. Complete at least 200 hours of police training offered by the Michigan Law Enforcement Officers Training Council. High school education or its equivalent. Be examined by a licensed physician and meet specific physical standards. Be of good moral character and have no prior felony conviction. Submit a photograph and three letters of character reference. Pass fingerprint check and background investigation. File a $1,000 surety bond with the county clerk where the oath of office was taken. **Examination:** Exam. **Fees:** $2 commission fee. **Governing Statute:** Railroad Police Act, Act 114 of 1941, as amended.

Minnesota

5485

Peace Officer
Board of Peace Officer Standards and
 Training
1600 University Ave., Ste. 200
St. Paul, MN 55104
Phone: (612)643-3060

Credential Type: Peace Officer License. **Duration of License:** Three years. **Requirements:** Must be a citizen of the United States and possess a Minnesota driver's license. No history of felony conviction or serious misconduct. Complete academic and skills pre-service education. Pass medical examination, a job-related test of physical strength and agility, a psychological evaluation, and an oral interview prior to appointment in a law enforcement agency. Must be appointed to a law enforcement agency prior to receiving license. **Examination:** Peace Officer Licensing Examination. **Reciprocity:** Yes. Training and experience will be evaluated to determine elgibility to take licensing examination. **Fees:** $40 exam fee. $15 license fee. **Governing Statute:** Minnesota Statutes, Chap. 214 and 367; Sections 382.28, 626.84-626.88. Minnesota Rules 6700-6700.2704.

Credential Type: Part-Time Peace Officer License. **Duration of License:** Three years. **Requirements:** Must be a citizen of the United States and possess a Minnesota driver's license. No history of felony conviction or serious misconduct. Complete approved training in first-aid and firearms. Pass medical examination and a psychological evaluation. **Examination:** Part-Time Peace Officer Licensing Examination. **Reciprocity:** Yes. Training and experience will be evaluated to determine elgibility to take licensing examination. **Fees:** $12.50 exam fee. $7.50 license fee. **Governing Statute:** Minnesota Statutes, Chap. 214 and 367; Sections 382.28, 626.84-626.88. Minnesota Rules 6700-6700.2704.

Nebraska

5486

Law Enforcement Officer
Nebraska Crime Commission
Rte. 3, PO Box 50
Grand Island, NE 68801
Phone: (308)381-5700

Credential Type: License. **Requirements:** 21 years of age. Must have a high school diploma. Must be a citizen of the United States. Must pass a criminal history check. Must hold a drivers license. Must have vision correctable to 20/30. Must have normal hearing in both ears. Must not have been convicted of driving while intoxicated in the two years immediately preceding admission. **Examination:** Yes.

North Carolina

5487

Sworn Police Officer
Dept. of Justice
Criminal Justice Standards Div.
PO Box 149
Raleigh, NC 27602
Phone: (919)733-2530

Credential Type: Certification. **Duration of License:** Permanent. **Requirements:** 20 years of age. High school diploma or GED. Completion of an accredited course or a 113 hour pre-service training course. A probationary certificate is issued, which is valid for one year, in which officers who attended the pre-service training must complete the remaining 256 hours of training. Once the basic training requirements are met and the probationary service period is completed, the officer is issued a continuing general certification. **Examination:** Written and practical.

North Dakota

5488

Peace Officer
Peace Officers Standards and Training Board
Criminal Justice Training and Statistics Div.
Office of the Attorney General
600 E. Boulevard Ave.
Bismarck, ND 58505
Phone: (701)224-3404

Credential Type: License. **Duration of License:** Three years. **Requirements:** Good moral character. High school graduate or equivalent. Pass medical and psychological exam. Complete an approved training program. **Examination:** Written examination. **Governing Statute:** North Dakota Century Code, Chap. 12-63.

Credential Type: Limited License. **Duration of License:** Until next available training session. **Authorization:** Limited to the jurisdiction in which individual is employed. **Requirements:** Must complete educational, medical, and psychogigal requirements and be qualified to carry a sidearm.

Texas

5489

Law Enforcement Officer
Commission on Law Enforcement Officer Standards and Education
1033 La Posada, Ste. 240
Austin, TX 78752
Phone: (512)450-0188

Credential Type: License. **Requirements:** U.S. citizenship. 21 years of age. High school diploma or equivalent. Completion of training operated or approved by the Commission. Weapons proficiency training. **Examination:** Written. Demonstration of weapons proficiency. **Governing Statute:** Ch. 415 Gov. Code.

Wyoming

5490

Law Enforcement Officer
Wyoming Highway Patrol
Safety and Training Div.
PO Box 1708
Cheyenne, WY 82002-9019
Phone: (307)777-7301

Credential Type: License. **Requirements:** U.S. citizen. Must be the age of majority. High school graduate. Undergo a background check. Must be free of physical, medical and emotional problems. Pass an oral interview. Must attend a Commission-approved academy for basic training. **Examination:** Yes. **Fees:** None.

5491

Law Enforcement Officer (Highway Patrol Officer)
Wyoming Highway Patrol
Safety and Training Div.
PO Box 1708
Cheyenne, WY 82002-9019
Phone: (307)777-4301

Credential Type: License. **Requirements:** U.S. citizen. 23 years of age. High school graduate. Minimum of 20/70 visual acuity in each eye, and be correctable to 20/20 in each eye. Must be free of mental, physical and emotional problems. Pass an oral interview. Pass a background check. Pass all required examinations (contact Board for details). **Examination:** Yes. **Fees:** None.

Polygraph Examiners and Assistants

The following states grant licenses in this occupational category as of the date of publication:

Alabama	**Indiana**	**Massachusetts**	**Nevada**	**Oregon**	**Utah**
Arizona	**Iowa**	**Michigan**	**New Mexico**	**South Carolina**	**Vermont**
Arkansas	**Kentucky**	**Mississippi**	**North Carolina**	**South Dakota**	**Virginia**
Georgia	**Louisiana**	**Montana**	**North Dakota**	**Tennessee**	**West Virginia**
Illinois	**Maine**	**Nebraska**	**Oklahoma**	**Texas**	

Alabama

5492

Polygraph Examiner
Polygraph Examiners Board
500 Dexter Ave., Rm. 404
Montgomery, AL 36102-1511
Phone: (205)242-4068

Credential Type: License. **Duration of License:** One year. **Requirements:** 21 years of age and a U.S. citizen. Must never have been convicted of a felony. Must have four years of college or five years investigative experience. Must have gone to an approved polygraph school. Must have worked under a licensed polygraph examiner for a period of six to 12 months. **Examination:** Written, oral, and practical examinations. **Fees:** $150 application fee. $150 license fee. $100 internship license fee. $125 renewal fee.

Arizona

5493

Polygraph Examiner
Dept. of Public Safety
PO Box 6328
Phoenix, AZ 85005
Phone: (602)223-2361

Credential Type: Polygraph examiner license. **Duration of License:** One year. **Requirements:** At least 18 years of age. No felony convictions. Complete a course of polygraph instruction in an approved school and be certified by that school after graduating.

Meet one of the following requirements: (1) have a baccalaureate degree from an accredited college or university, or (2) be a high school graduate with five years experience as a licensed private investigator or law enforcement officer commissioned by the federal government or by a state, county, or municipal government, or (3) pass an oral and written examination conducted by the department.

Submit a $5000 surety bond with application. **Examination:** Optional oral and written examination conducted by the department. **Reciprocity:** Yes. **Fees:** $50 application fee, plus cost of fingerprint processing. $50 license fee. $35 renewal fee. **Governing Statute:** Arizona Revised Statutes, Title 32, Chapter 27.

5494

Polygraph Examiner Intern
Dept. of Public Safety
PO Box 6328
Phoenix, AZ 85005
Phone: (602)223-2361

Credential Type: Polygraph examiner intern license. **Duration of License:** Six months. **Authorization:** May administer polygraph examinations, but must consult with supervisory examiner at least once a month concerning progress and expertise. **Requirements:** Complete a course in polygraphy in an approved school. **Fees:** $50 application fee, plus cost of fingerprint processing. $25 intern license fee. **Governing Statute:** Arizona Revised Statutes, Title 32, Chapter 27.

Arkansas

5495

Polygraph Examiner
Arkansas State Police
3 Natural Resources Dr.
PO Box 5901
Little Rock, AR 72215
Phone: (501)224-3101

Credential Type: License. **Requirements:** Must be registered with the Circuit Clerk. 21 years of age. Must be a US citizen. Must have character references. Must not have been convicted of a felony or a misdemeanor involving moral turpitude. Must have a baccalaureate degree from a college or university or five years active investigative experience. Must be a graduate of polygraph examiners course and six months internship training. **Examination:** Yes. **Fees:** $1000 Surety Bond. $20 Written examination. $60 License. $25 Renewal.

Georgia

5496

Polygraph Examiner
State Board of Polygraph Examiners
Businesses and Occupations Section
Professional Examining Boards
166 Pryor St., SW
Atlanta, GA 30303
Phone: (404)656-2282

Credential Type: Polygraph Examiner License. **Requirements:** Meet one of the following sets of requirements: (1) Bachelor's degree with at least one course in physical science and one in psychology; or (2) two years of college, with at least one course in physical science and one in psychology, and two years experience as an investigator with a government agency; or (3) High school diploma or equivalent and five years experience as an investigator with a government agency.

Complete a formal training course of at least six months duration in the use of poolygraph. Complete an internship of at least six months duration.

Submit evidence of either $25,000 professional liability insurance, or a surety bond of $10,000, or an audited financial statement showing a net worth of at least $50,000. **Examination:** Polygraph, specifics and hypothetical. **Reciprocity:** Yes, with states that have similar licensing requirements. **Fees:** $50 exam fee. $300 license fee. **Governing Statute:** Georgia Polygraph Examiners Act.

5497

Polygraph Examiner, Intern
State Board of Polygraph Examiners
Businesses and Occupations Section
Professional Examining Boards
166 Pryor St., SW
Atlanta, GA 30303
Phone: (404)656-2282

Credential Type: Intern License. **Requirements:** Meet one of the following sets of requirements: (1) Bachelor's degree with at least one course in physical science and one in psychology; or (2) two years of college, with at least one course in physical science and one in psychology, and two years experience as an investigator with a government agency; or (3) High school diploma or equivalent and five years experience as an investigator with a government agency. **Examination:** Polygraph, specifics and hypothetical. **Reciprocity:** Yes, with states that have similar licensing requirements. **Fees:** $50 application fee. $50 exam fee. **Governing Statute:** Georgia Polygraph Examiners Act.

Illinois

5498

Detection of Deception Examiner (Lie Detector Operator)
Illinois Dept. of Professional Regulations
320 W. Washington St.
Springfield, IL 62786
Phone: (217)782-8556

Credential Type: Detection of Deception Trainee License. **Duration of License:** One year. **Requirements:** Good moral character. Bachelor's degree from an accredited university. Submit application on appropriate forms. **Fees:** No fee. **Governing Statute:** The Detection of Deception Examiners Act, Illinois Revised Statutes 1991, Chapter 111.

Credential Type: Detection of Deception Examiner License. **Duration of License:** Two years. **Requirements:** Good moral character. Bachelor's degree from an accredited university. Complete six month study program in detection of deception under approved instructors. **Examination:** Professional Committee Exam (two parts). **Reciprocity:** Yes, with substantially equivalent training. **Fees:** $99.50 examination fee. $25 initial license fee. $50 license by endorsement fee. $180 renewal fee. **Governing Statute:** The Detection of Deception Examiners Act, Illinois Revised Statutes 1991, Chapter 111.

Indiana

5499

Polygraph Examiner
Polygraph Certification
Indiana State Police
Government Center N.
100 N. Senate Ave., Rm. 312
Indianapolis, IN 46204
Phone: (317)232-8263

Credential Type: Certification. **Requirements:** Contact licensing body for application information.

Iowa

5500

Polygraph Examiner
Div. of Administrative Services
Dept. of Public Safety
Wallace State Office Bldg.
Des Moines, IA 50319
Phone: (515)281-8422

Credential Type: License. **Duration of License:** Two years. **Requirements:** 18 years of age. U.S. citizenship. No convictions for an aggravated misdemeanor or a felony. An applicant should submit pictures and fingerprints along with a completed application. Applicant must be approved for a $5,000 surety bond.

Kentucky

5501

Polygraph Examiner
Kentucky State Police - Polygraph Unit
1250 Louisville Rd.
Frankfort, KY 40601
Phone: (502)564-7110

Credential Type: License. **Duration of License:** One year. **Requirements:** High school diploma or equivalent. Graduation from an examiner training school recognized by the regulatory agency. 18 years of age. Must have more than one year experience as a polygraph examiner. Continuing education required. **Examination:** Yes. **Fees:** $50 application fee. $40 renewal fee.

Credential Type: Polygraph Intern License. **Duration of License:** One year. **Requirements:** High school diploma or GED. Graduation from an examiner training school recognized by the regulatory agency. 18 years of age. Resident of Kentucky. Applicant may have less than one year work experience as an examiner. **Examination:** Yes. **Fees:** $50 application fee. $40 renewal fee.

Louisiana

5502

Polygraphist
State of Louisiana Polygraph Board
PO Box 7972
Alexandria, LA 71306
Phone: (318)484-4202

Credential Type: Certificate. **Duration of License:** One year. **Requirements:** No felony convictions or crimes involving moral turpitude. High school diploma. Graduation from a satisfactory polygraph course. **Examination:** Yes. **Reciprocity:** Yes, with the discretion of the board. **Fees:** $25 application fee. $50 renewal fee. $100 certificate fee.

5503

Voice Stress Analyst
Louisiana Stress Analysis Board
1414 W. Hall Ave.
Slidel, LA 70160
Phone: (504)944-3371
Phone: (504)643-4503

Credential Type: Certification. **Duration of License:** One year. **Requirements:** Complete required internship program. Contact board for additional requirements.

Voice Stress Analyst, continued

Fees: $75 certification fee. $50 renewal fee. **Governing Statute:** R.S. 37:2861-2887.

Maine

5504

Polygraph Examiner
Dept. of Public Safety
State House Station 42
Augusta, ME 04333
Phone: (207)624-7068

Credential Type: Polygraph Examiners License. **Duration of License:** Two years. **Requirements:** Be at least 21 years of age. No conviction of a crime involving moral turpitude. High school graduate or equivalent. Graduate from an approved polygraph examiner's course. Complete an internship of at least six months. **Examination:** Written and practical examination. **Reciprocity:** Yes, provided requirements in home state are substantially equivalent and home state grants similar reciprocity to license holders in Maine. **Fees:** $100 license fee. $50 renewal fee. $50 exam fee. **Governing Statute:** 32 M.S.R.A. 7151 through 7169.

Credential Type: Intern License. **Duration of License:** One year. **Authorization:** Must conduct examinations under the supervision of a sponsor. **Requirements:** Be at least 21 years of age. No conviction of a crime involving moral turpitude. High school graduate or equivalent. Graduate from an approved polygraph examiner's course. Must have as a sponsor a licensed polygraph examiner. **Fees:** $100 license fee. $25 renewal or extension fee. **Governing Statute:** 32 M.S.R.A. 7151 through 7169.

Massachusetts

5505

Polygraph Examiner
Dept. of Public Safety
One Ashburton Pl.
McCormac Bldg.
Boston, MA 02108
Phone: (617)727-3692

Credential Type: License. **Requirements:** Contact licensing body for application information.

Michigan

5506

Forensic Polygraph Examiner
Forensic Polygraph Examiners' Licensing Board
Bureau of Occupational & Professional Regulation
Dept. of Commerce
PO Box 30018
Lansing, MI 48909
Phone: (517)373-9153

Credential Type: Examiner License. **Duration of License:** One year. **Requirements:** At least 18 years of age. Be a United States citizen and have resided in Michigan for at least six continuous calendar months immediately prior to the date of application. Not have been convicted of a felony; a misdemeanor punishable by more than one year imprisonment; or any crime involving moral turpitude. Have at least a bachelor's degree which is suitable for and related to specialization as an examiner. Complete an approved internship training program or satisfy the Board that they have the training or experience equivalent to that which would be acquired in the internship training program. Provide two completed fingerprint cards along with other identifying information. Pass a background investigation. Comply with the Forensic Polygraph Examiners' Act and the rules of the Board. **Examination:** Written and oral exam. **Reciprocity:** A Michigan examiner's license may be granted to an applicant who is licensed by another state or territory of the United States if: 1. The requirements for licensing of examiners in that state or territory are substantially equivalent to those of Michigan. 2. Any differing or additional requirements for licensing of examiners in Michigan are fulfilled by the applicant. 3. The other state or territory grants similar reciprocity to licensed examiners of Michigan. **Fees:** $50 initial exam fee. $25 initial license fee (public examiner). $100 initial license fee (private examiner). $200 initial license fee for non-residents for one year. $25 renewal fee (public examiner). $50 renewal fee (private examiner). $200 renewal fee for non-residents for one year. $25 reciprocity fee (public examiner). $100 reciprocity fee (private examiner). **Governing Statute:** Forensic Polygraph Examiners Act, Act 295 of 1972, as amended.

Credential Type: Intern License. **Duration of License:** Six months. **Requirements:** At least 18 years of age. Be a United States citizen and have resided in Michigan for at least six continuous calendar months immediately prior to the date of application. Not have been convicted of a felony; a misdemeanor punishable by more than one year imprisonment; or any crime involving moral turpitude. Have at least a bachelor's degree which is suitable for and related to specialization as an examiner. Complete an approved internship training program or satisfy the Board that they have the training or experience equivalent to that which would be acquired in the internship training program. Provide two completed fingerprint cards along with other identifying information. Pass a background investigation. Comply with the Forensic Polygraph Examiners' Act and the rules of the Board. **Examination:** Written and oral exam. **Fees:** $50 initial exam fee. $25 initial license fee. $25 renewal fee. **Governing Statute:** Forensic Polygraph Examiners Act, Act 295 of 1972, as amended.

Credential Type: Temporary License. **Duration of License:** 10 days. **Fees:** $100 initial temporary license fee. $100 temporary license renewal fee. **Governing Statute:** Forensic Polygraph Examiners Act, Act 295 of 1972, as amended.

Mississippi

5507

Polygraph Examiner
Board of Polygraph Examiners
PO Box 958
Jackson, MS 39205
Phone: (601)987-4202

Credential Type: License. **Requirements:** Contact licensing body for application information.

Montana

5508

Polygraph Examiner
Montana Board of Polygraph Examiners
111 N. Jackson
Helena, MT 59620
Phone: (406)444-5433

Credential Type: License. **Duration of License:** One year. **Requirements:** 18 years of age. U.S. citizenship. High school graduation or equivalent. Completion of a course in polygraph instruction. **Examination:** Written. **Fees:** $125 application and license fee. $10 exam fee. $100 renewal fee. **Governing Statute:** Montana Code Annotated 37-62-201 through 37-62-213.

Nebraska

5509

Polygraph Examiner
Nebraska Secretary of State
State Capitol Bldg., Ste. 2300
Lincoln, NE 68509
Phone: (402)471-2554

Credential Type: License. **Duration of License:** One year. **Requirements:** 21 years of age. Must complete a course at an accredited polygraph school. **Examination:** Yes. **Fees:** $50 testing and license fees. $25 renewal fee.

Nevada

5510

Polygraph Examiner
Office of the Attorney General
Private Investigator's Licensing Board
Capitol Complex
Carson City, NV 89710
Phone: (702)687-3535

Credential Type: License. **Requirements:** Contact licensing body for application information.

New Mexico

5511

Polygraph Examiner
Polygraph Examiners Bureau
Dept. of Regulation and Licensing
PO Box 25101
725 St. Michael's Dr.
Santa Fe, NM 87504
Phone: (505)827-7172

Credential Type: Polygraph Examiner License. **Duration of License:** One year. **Authorization:** A new licensee must serve six months in a provisional status with an assigned sponsor. **Requirements:** Complete at least two years of college. Graduate from an approved polygraph school. **Examination:** Local written examination. **Reciprocity:** No. **Fees:** $100 license fee. $50 exam fee. $100 renewal fee.

North Carolina

5512

Polygraph Examiner
Private Protective Services Board
PO Box 29500
Raleigh, NC 27626
Phone: (919)779-1611

Credential Type: Certification. **Duration of License:** One year. **Requirements:** High school diploma. Completion of an approved school of polygraph evaluation. One year of polygraph experience with the past three years or completion of six months of supervised training. 18 years of age. **Examination:** Written and oral exam. **Fees:** $150 application fee. $150 license fee. $50 recovery fund fee. $150 trainee permit fee. $150 renewal fee.

North Dakota

5513

Polygraph Operator
Licensing Div.
North Dakota Attorney General
600 E. Blvd., 1st Fl.
Bismarck, ND 58505
Phone: (701)224-2219

Credential Type: Detection of Deception Examiner License. **Duration of License:** One year. **Requirements:** Complete an approved polygraph examiner's course. Complete at least six months of internship training, including at least 25 examination records selected and inspected by the supervising examiner. **Examination:** Yes. **Reciprocity:** Yes, if laws are equal to or greater than North Dakota law. **Fees:** $35 license fee. $50 exam fee. $25 internship license. $25 renewal fee.

Oklahoma

5514

Polygraph Examiner
State of Oklahoma Board of
  Polygraph Examiners
Cimarron Station
PO Box 11476
Oklahoma City, OK 73136
Phone: (405)946-7230

Credential Type: License. **Duration of License:** One year. **Requirements:** Bachelors degree or high school diploma and five consecutive years of investigative experience. Six-month internship program. Six hours of continuing education per year. State resident. 21 years of age. Investigative experience. **Examination:** State of Oklahoma Board of Polygraph Examiners Exam. **Fees:** $50 exam fee. $100 license fee.

5515

Polygraph Intern
State of Oklahoma Board of
  Polygraph Examiners
Cimarron Station
PO Box 11476
Oklahoma City, OK 73136
Phone: (405)425-2778

Credential Type: License. **Duration of License:** One year. **Requirements:** A bachelor's degree or a high school diploma and five consecutive years of investigative experience. Six-month internship program. Six hours of continuing education each year. State resident. 21 years of age. No felony convictions. Investigative experience. **Examination:** State of Oklahoma Board of Polygraph Examiners Exam. **Fees:** $50 exam fee. $100 license fee.

Oregon

5516

Polygraph Examiner
Board on Public Safety Standards
  and Training
550 N. Monmouth Ave.
Monmouth, OR 97361
Phone: (503)378-2100
Fax: (503)838-8907

Credential Type: Polygraph Examiners License. **Duration of License:** One year. **Requirements:** Be at least 18 years of age. Citizen of the United States. Have a bachelor's degree from an accredited college or university, or be a high school graduate with at least five years of active investigative experience. Graduate from an approved polygraph examiners course and complete at least 200 examinations, or have worked as a polygraph examiner for a governmental agency in Oregon for five years and complete 200 examinations. **Examination:** Board administered examination. **Reciprocity:** Yes, provided requirements in home state are substantially equivalent and home state grants similar reciprocity to license holders in Oregon. **Fees:** $50 license fee. $50 renewal fee. $50 exam fee. $33 fingerprint fee. **Governing Statute:** ORS, Chap. 703.

Credential Type: Trainee License. **Requirements:** Be at least 18 years of age. Citizen of the United States. Graduate from an approved polygraph examiners course. **Fees:** $35 trainee license fee. $35 renewal

South Carolina

Polygraph Examiner, continued

fee. $33 fingerprint fee. **Governing Statute:** ORS, Chap. 703.

South Carolina

5517

Polygraph Examiner
State Law Enforcement Div.,
   Regulatory Services
PO Box 21398
Columbia, SC 29221
Phone: (803)737-9073

Credential Type: Polygraph Examiner License. **Requirements:** 21 years of age. U.S. citizen. No felony convictions or misdemeanors involving moral turpitude. Bachelor's degree from an accredited college, a high school diploma with five consecutive years of active investigative experience immediately preceding application. Graduation from an approved polygraph examiner's course. Six- or 12-month internship. $5,000 surety bond or insurance. **Examination:** Yes. **Fees:** $50 license fee. $50 renewal fee.

Credential Type: Polygraph Examiner Intern. **Requirements:** Application and fee payment. **Fees:** $25 license fee. $25 renewal fee.

South Dakota

5518

Polygraph Examiner
Law Enforcement Standards and
   Training Commission
Div. of Criminal Investigation
Rol Kebach Criminal Justice
   Training Center
Pierre, SD 57501-5050
Phone: (605)773-3584

Credential Type: Polygraph Examiners License. **Duration of License:** One year. **Requirements:** Be at least 21 years of age. Meet one of the following sets of requirements: (1) Complete at least 240 hours of study in the use of a polygraph in the detection of deception at a school certified by the American Polygraph Association. (2) If applicant has not attended an APA-accredited school, submit documentation of course requirements and grades from school attended, and records indicating competency in the use of a polygraph. **Reciprocity:** Yes, provided requirements in home state are substantially equivalent, applicant has at least six months working experience, and home state grants similar reciprocity to li-

cense holders in South Dakota. **Fees:** $25 license fee. $25 renewal fee. **Governing Statute:** SDCL 36-30. Polygraph Rules and Regulations, Sections 2:01:10:01 et seq.

Tennessee

5519

Polygraph Operator
Board for Control for Polygraph
   Examiners
500 James Robertson Pky., 2nd Fl.
Nashville, TN 37243
Phone: (615)741-0697

Credential Type: License. **Duration of License:** One year. **Requirements:** 21 years old. B.A. degree or two years college and five years criminal or counterintelligence (investigative) work and graduation from polygraph school. 12 hours of continuing education per renewal period. US citizen, no felony or misdemeanor convictions. **Examination:** Yes. **Reciprocity:** No. **Fees:** $500 Registration. $100 Application. $500 Renewal.

Texas

5520

Polygraph Examiner
Polygraph Examiner Board
PO Box 4087
Austin, TX 78773
Phone: (512)465-2058

Credential Type: Intern Permit. **Duration of License:** One year. **Requirements:** Bachelor's degree from an accredited college; or five consecutive years of active investigative experience. Sponsorship by a licensed examiner. **Examination:** Yes. **Fees:** $300 license fee. $150 renewal fee. **Governing Statute:** VACS 4413(29cc), 22 TAC 391.

Credential Type: Examiner License. **Duration of License:** One year. **Requirements:** 5,000 surety bond or insurance policy. Bachelor's degree from an accredited college, or five consecutive years of active investigative experience. Graduation from an approved polygraph examiners course and six months of internship training, or 12 months of internship training in lieu of polygraph examiners course. **Examination:** Yes. **Fees:** $500 license fee. $400 annual renewal fee. **Governing Statute:** VACS 4413(29cc), 22 TAC 391.

Utah

5521

Polygraph Examiner
Office of Regulatory Licensing
4501 S. 2700 W.
Salt Lake City, UT 84119
Phone: (801)965-4484

Credential Type: License. **Requirements:** Must hold a bachelor's degree from an accredited college or a high school diploma and at least four years of investigative experience; or a combination of experience and college study equal to four years, completion of an approved formal training course at an examiners school, and a minimum of one year as a licensed intern. **Examination:** Yes. **Fees:** $20 intern fee. $20 examiner fee.

Vermont

5522

Polygraph Examiner
Commission of Public Safety
Vermont State Police Headquarters
Waterbury State Complex
103 South Main St.
Waterbury, VT 05676
Phone: (802)244-8781

Credential Type: License. **Duration of License:** One year. **Requirements:** Integrity, honesty, truthfulness. Never convicted of a felony or misdemeanor involving moral turpitude. Graduate of an approved polygraphers; exam. Completed six months of internship training. **Examination:** Yes. **Reciprocity:** Yes. **Fees:** $15 License. $15 Renewal. $10 Intern registration. **Governing Statute:** Title 26, VSA Sections 2901-2910.

Virginia

5523

Polygraph Examiner
Dept. of Commerce
Polygraph Examiners
3600 W. Broad St.
Richmond, VA 23230
Phone: (804)367-8534

Credential Type: License. **Duration of License:** One year. **Requirements:** Must have a high school diploma and a minimum of five years experience acceptable to the Department; or an associate degree from an accredited college with three years of experience; or a bachelor's degree. Must complete training from a polygraph school and six months as a licensed intern examiner. **Examination:** Yes. **Fees:** $125 application fee. $100 renewal fee.

West Virginia

5524

Polygraph Examiner
Dept. of Labor
1800 Washington St. E
Charleston, WV 25305
Phone: (304)348-7890

Credential Type: License. **Duration of License:** One year. **Requirements:** 18 years old. Baccalaureate degree. Graduate from an accredited school of polygraphy. Honorable discharge from the armed services. **Examination:** Yes. **Fees:** $100 Application. $100 Renewal.

Power Plant Systems Operators and Managers

One or more occupations in this chapter require a federal license. Additionally, the following states grant licenses as of the date of publication: District of Columbia, Maryland, Massachusetts, Montana, New Jersey, Ohio.

Federal Licenses

5525

Nuclear Facility Operator
Nuclear Regulatory Commission
Washington, DC 20555
Phone: (301)492-7000
Fax: (301)492-1672

Credential Type: Operator License. **Duration of License:** Six years. **Authorization:** To manipulate a control of a nuclear facility. **Requirements:** Pass a medical exam at least every two years. Pass a written exam and operating test. Must be employed by a licensed facility. Complete facility licensee's requirements to be licensed as an operator, including an NRC-approved training program that includes five significant control manipulations that affect reactivity or power level. Simulated control manipulations may be accepted for a facility that has not completed pre-operational testing and initial startup test program.

To maintain active status, licensee shall perform the functions of an operator on a minimum of seven eight-hour or five 12-hour shifts per calendar quarter. For test and research purposes, licensee shall perform the functions of an operator for a minimum of four hours per calendar quarter.

Renewal requires completion of an approved requalification program and passing of a comprehensive requalification exam and an annual operating test. **Examination:** Written exam and operating test. **Exemptions:** Any or all of the requirements for a written exam and operating test may be waived based on experience and past performance. **Governing Statute:** 10 CFR Ch. 1, Part 55.

Credential Type: Senior Operator License. **Duration of License:** Six years. **Authorization:** To manipulate a control of a nuclear facility. To direct the licensed activities of licensed operators. **Requirements:** Pass a medical exam at least every two years. Pass a written exam and operating test. Must be employed by a licensed facility. Licensed operators applying for a senior operator license must submit certification of successful operation of the controls of the facility as a licensed operator.

To maintain active status, licensee shall perform the functions of a senior operator on a minimum of seven eight-hour or five 12-hour shifts per calendar quarter. For test and research purposes, licensee shall perform the functions of a senior operator for a minimum of four hours per calendar quarter.

Renewal requires completion of an approved requalification program and passing of a comprehensive requalification exam and an annual operating test. **Examination:** Written exam and operating test. **Exemptions:** Any or all of the requirements for a written exam and operating test may be waived based on experience and past performance. **Governing Statute:** 10 CFR Ch. 1, Part 55.

Credential Type: Conditional License. **Requirements:** May be issued when an applicant's medical condition does not meet minimum standards. **Governing Statute:** 10 CFR Ch. 1, Part 55.

District of Columbia

5526

Steam Engineer
License and Certification Div.
Occupational and Professional Licensure Administration
Consumer and Regulatory Affairs Dept.
PO Box 37200
Washington, DC 20013-7200
Phone: (202)727-7823
Phone: (202)727-7480

Alternate Information: 614 H St., NW, Washington, DC 20001.

Credential Type: License and certification. **Duration of License:** One year. **Authorization:** Ten classes of license are issued for steam and other operating engineers. **Requirements:** Must meet appropriate experience requirements for each class of license. **Examination:** Written examination. **Fees:** $10 application fee. $5 license fee. $10 exam fee. $20 annual renewal fee. **Governing Statute:** Municipal Regulations, Title 17, Chap. 4.

Maryland

5527

Stationary Engineer
Board of Examining Engineers
Dept. of Licensing and Regulation
501 St. Paul Pl.
Baltimore, MD 21202-2272
Phone: (410)333-6322

Credential Type: First Grade Stationary Engineer Certificate and License. **Duration of License:** Two years. **Authorization:** Authorizes holder to take charge of any plant machinery. **Requirements:** Be at least 21 years of age. Meet one of the following sets of requirements: (1) Hold a second grade stationary engineer license for at least one year. Be employed for at least 12 months (1750 working hours) in the operation of high pressure boilers. (2) Have five or more years operating experience in a plant that generates a minimum of 17,250 pounds of steam per hour. (3) Have a degree in mechanical engineering from an accredited college or university, and six months or more of practical experience. (4) Hold a valid marine engineer's certificate or a chief petty officer's certificate from the U.S. Navy, with steam boiler engineering training. **Examination:** Board-administered examination. **Fees:** $20 application fee. $15 certificate fee. $30 renewal fee. **Governing Statute:** Public Local Laws of Maryland, Article 4. Code of Maryland Regulations, Title 09, Subtitle 17.

Credential Type: Second Grade Stationary Engineer Certificate and License. **Duration of License:** Two years. **Authorization:** Authorizes holder to take charge of any plant machinery from one to 500 horsepower. **Requirements:** Be at least 21 years of age. Meet one of the following sets of requirements: (1) Be employed for at least 24 months (3,500 working hours) in a power plant under the direct supervision of a licensed first grade stationary engineer. (2) Be employed as a third grade stationary engineer for at least one year. (3) Hold a valid marine engineer's certificate or a chief petty officer's certificate from the U.S. Navy. **Examination:** Board-administered examination. **Fees:** $15 application fee. $15 certificate fee. $30 renewal fee. **Governing Statute:** Public Local Laws of Maryland, Article 4. Code of Maryland Regulations, Title 09, Subtitle 17.

Credential Type: Third Grade Stationary Engineer Certificate and License. **Duration of License:** Two years. **Authorization:** Authorizes holder to take charge of any plant machinery from one to 30 horsepower. **Requirements:** Be at least 21 years of age. Show experience in the operation of or working around a plant or machinery. **Examination:** Board-administered examination. **Fees:** $10 application fee. $15 certificate fee. $30 renewal fee. **Governing Statute:** Public Local Laws of Maryland, Article 4. Code of Maryland Regulations, Title 09, Subtitle 17.

Credential Type: Fourth Grade Stationary Engineer Certificate and License. **Duration of License:** Two years. **Authorization:** Authorizes holder to take charge of any hoisting or portable plant machinery. **Requirements:** Be at least 21 years of age. Show experience in the operation of or working around a plant or machinery. **Examination:** Board-administered examination. **Fees:** $10 application fee. $15 certificate fee. $30 renewal fee. **Governing Statute:** Public Local Laws of Maryland, Article 4. Code of Maryland Regulations, Title 09, Subtitle 17.

Massachusetts

5528

Nuclear Power Plant Engineer
Dept. of Public Safety
Div. of Inspection
Engineering Section
One Ashburton Pl.
Boston, MA 02108
Phone: (617)727-3200

Credential Type: Senior Supervising Engineer License. **Requirements:** Must be a United States citizen. Have been employed for at least two years in a steam power plant. Have held and used a Massachusetts First Class Engineer's License or a Nuclear Power Plant Operating Engineer's License for at least two years. One or more years of attendance at a recognized full time school of nuclear power plant engineering may be substituted for an equivalent year of experience as a nuclear power plant operating engineer. **Examination:** Written and oral examination. **Fees:** $130 license fee. $35 exam fee. **Governing Statute:** Massachusetts General Laws, Chap. 146.

Credential Type: Operating Engineer License. **Requirements:** Must be a United States citizen. Meet one of the following sets of requirements: (1) Have been employed for at least 1.5 years in a steam power plant. Have held and used a Massachusetts Second Class Engineer's License or an Assistant Nuclear Power Plant Operator's License for at least 1.5 years. One or more years of attendance at a recognized full time school of nuclear power plant engineering may be substituted for an equivalent year of experience as a nuclear power plant operating engineer. (2) Bachelor of Science degree in engineering and one year of employment in connection with the operation of a steam plant. **Examination:** Written and oral examination. **Fees:** $60 license fee. $35 exam fee. **Governing Statute:** Massachusetts General Laws, Chap. 146.

5529

Nuclear Power Plant Operator
Dept. of Public Safety
Div. of Inspection
Engineering Section
One Ashburton Pl.
Boston, MA 02108
Phone: (617)727-3200

Credential Type: Assistant Operator License. **Requirements:** Have been employed in a steam power plant as a fireman, water tender, control room assistant, or as a designated assistant to the engineer in charge for at least one year. **Examination:** Written and oral examination. **Fees:** $60 license fee. $35 exam fee. **Governing Statute:** Massachusetts General Laws, Chap. 146.

5530

Stationary Engineer
Dept. of Public Safety
Div. of Inspection
Engineering Section
One Ashburton Pl.
Boston, MA 02108
Phone: (617)727-3200

Credential Type: First Class Engineer License. **Duration of License:** Two years. **Requirements:** Meet one of the following sets of requirements: (1) Complete three years of employment as an engineer in charge of a steam plant. (2) Have held and used a Second Class Engineer's License for 1.5 years. (3) Have been employed as an assistant engineer in a first class plant for 1.5 years. (4) Have held and used an equivalent license in the U.S. merchant marine for at least three years. (5) Have held and used an equivalent license issued by another state for at least three years. **Examination:** Written and oral examination. **Fees:** $60 license and exam fee. **Governing Statute:** Massachusetts General Laws, Chap. 146.

Credential Type: Second Class Engineer License. **Duration of License:** Two years. **Requirements:** Be a United States citizen or have declared intention to become one. Meet one of the following sets of requirements: (1) Have at least two years of related work experience. (2) Have held and used an equivalent license in the U.S. merchant marine. (3) Have held and used an equivalent license issued by another state for at least one year. (4) Have been licensed to operate a first class plant for at least two years. (5) Have served a three-year apprenticeship to a machinist or boiler making trade and have one year of employment in a steam plant. (6) Bachelor of Science degree in engineering and one year of employment in a steam

Montana 5531

Stationary Engineer, continued

plant. **Examination:** Written and oral examinations. **Fees:** $50 license and exam fee. **Governing Statute:** Massachusetts General Laws, Chap. 146.

Credential Type: Third Class Engineer License. **Requirements:** Be a United States citizen or have declared intention to become one. Meet one of the following sets of requirements: (1) Have at least 1.5 years of related work experience. (2) Have held and used an equivalent license in the U.S. merchant marine. (3) Used a current Third Class Steam License issued by another state for at least one year. (4) Held and used a First Class Fireman's license for at least one year. **Examination:** Written and oral examination. **Fees:** $60 license and exam fee. **Governing Statute:** Massachusetts General Laws, Chap. 146.

Credential Type: Fourth Class Engineer License. **Requirements:** Contact licensing body for application information. **Examination:** Written and oral examinations. **Fees:** $50 license and exam fee. **Governing Statute:** Massachusetts General Laws, Chap. 146.

Credential Type: Portable Class Engineer License. **Requirements:** Contact licensing body for application information. **Examination:** Written and oral examinations. **Fees:** $25 license and exam fee. **Governing Statute:** Massachusetts General Laws, Chap. 146.

Montana

5531

Stationary Engineer
Montana Safety Bureau, Worker's Compensation Div.
5 South Last Chance Gulch
Helena, MT 59601
Phone: (406)444-6401

Credential Type: Low-Pressure Engineer. **Duration of License:** One year. **Requirements:** 18 years of age. Three months of experience with steam boilers less than 15 pounds per square inch and water boilers less than 50 pounds per square inch. **Examination:** Written. **Fees:** $8 license fee. $4 renewal fee. **Governing Statute:** Montana Code Annotated 50-74-301 through 50-74-317.

Credential Type: Third-Class Engineer. **Duration of License:** One year. **Requirements:** 18 years of age. Six months of experience with steam boilers less than 100 pounds per square inch, and water boilers less than 160 pounds per square inch and 350 degrees F. **Examination:** Written.

Fees: $12 license fee. $4 renewal fee. **Governing Statute:** Montana Code Annotated 50-74-301 through 50-74-317.

Credential Type: Second-Class Engineer. **Duration of License:** One year. **Requirements:** 18 years of age. Two years of experience with steam boilers less than 250 pounds per square inch, and water boilers less than 375 pounds per square inch and 450 degrees F. **Examination:** Written. **Fees:** $20 license fee. $4 renewal fee. **Governing Statute:** Montana Code Annotated 50-74-301 through 50-74-317.

Credential Type: First-Class Engineer. **Duration of License:** One year. **Requirements:** 18 years of age. Three years of experience with all types of boilers. **Examination:** Written. **Fees:** $30 license fee. $4 renewal fee. **Governing Statute:** Montana Code Annotated 50-74-301 through 50-74-317.

Credential Type: Traction Engineer. **Duration of License:** One year. **Authorization:** For non-stationary boilers only. **Requirements:** 18 years of age. Six months of experience with traction engines. **Examination:** Written. **Fees:** $12 license fee. $4 renewal fee. **Governing Statute:** Montana Code Annotated 50-74-301 through 50-74-317.

New Jersey

5532

Nuclear Engineer - Blue Seal
New Jersey Dept. of Labor
Div. of Workplace Standards
CN392
Trenton, NJ 08625-0392
Phone: (609)292-2921

Credential Type: 3rd Class Nuclear Engineer, Blue Seal, 3-C. **Duration of License:** Three years. **Requirements:** 18 years of age. Must hold certification from the U.S. Nuclear Commission certifying qualification to operate nuclear power equipment. **Examination:** Written. **Fees:** $15 exam fee. $10 raise of grade or additional classification. $10 renewal fee. **Governing Statute:** NJSA 34:7. NJAC 12:90.

5533

Refrigeration Engineer - Blue Seal
New Jersey Dept. of Labor
Office of Boiler and Pressure Vessel Compliance
CN392
Trenton, NJ 08625-0392
Phone: (609)292-2921

Credential Type: 3rd Class Refrigeration Engineer, Blue Seal, 2-C License. **Duration of License:** Three years. **Requirements:** Six months as an assistant to an operator of a flammable or toxic refrigeration system; or three months as an operator of a flammable or toxic refrigeration system; or three months as an assistant, provided the applicant is given intensive training and the chief engineer verifies such training; or six months as an operator of a nontoxic refrigeration system of at least 250 tons capacity and three months as an assistant to a licensed operator of a flammable or toxic refrigeration system; or six months as an operator of a nontoxic system of at least 250 tons capacity and satisfactory proof of completion of sufficient education in the operation of a flammable or toxic refrigeration system in an educational program approved by the New Jersey Dept. of Education. **Examination:** Written. **Fees:** $15 exam fee. $10 raise of grade or additional classification fee. $10 renewal fee. **Governing Statute:** NJSA 34:7. NJAC 12:90.

5534

Steam Engineer - Blue Seal
New Jersey Dept. of Labor
Office of Boiler and Pressure Vessel Compliance
CN392
Trenton, NJ 08625-0392
Phone: (609)292-2921

Credential Type: 3rd Class Steam Engingeer, Blue Seal, 1-C or 8-C. **Duration of License:** Three years. **Requirements:** Must have a valid New Jersey High Pressure Boiler Operator-in-charge license. At least six months subsequent experience in the operation of equipment requiring supervision by a 3rd class steam engineer, or as an assistant in the operation of equipment requiring a 3rd class license for shift operations. 18 years of age. **Examination:** Written. **Fees:** $15 exam fee. $10 raise of grade or additional classification fee. $10 renewal fee. **Governing Statute:** NJSA 34:7. NJAC 12:90.

Ohio

5535

Steam Engineer
Div. of Examiners of Steam Engineers
Dept. of Industrial Relations
2323 W. 5th Ave.
PO Box 825
Columbus, OH 43266-0567
Phone: (614)644-2248

Credential Type: Steam Engineer License. **Duration of License:** One year. **Requirements:** Submit application and pass examination for competency. **Examination:** Steam Engineer Examination. **Fees:** $50 license and exam fee. $25 renewal fee. **Governing Statute:** Ohio Revised Code 4739.05.

Precision Instrument Repairers

The following states grant licenses in this occupational category as of the date of publication: Arizona, Connecticut, Illinois, New Jersey, North Carolina, Tennessee, Vermont.

Arizona

5536

Registered Serviceman (Weights and Measures)
Dept. of Weights and Measures
1951 W. North Lane
Phoenix, AZ 85021
Phone: (602)255-5211

Credential Type: Registered serviceman license. **Duration of License:** One year. **Requirements:** Have a thorough working knowledge of all appropriate weights and measures laws, orders, rules, and regulation. Have possession of, or available for use, appropriate weights and testing equipment. Submit application and license fee. **Fees:** $4.80 license fee. **Governing Statute:** Arizona Revised Statutes, Title 41, Chapter 15.

Connecticut

5537

Dealer/Repairer, Weighing and Measuring Devices
Weights and Measures Div.
Dept. of Consumer Protection
165 Capitol Ave.
State Office Bldg.
Hartford, CT 06106
Phone: (203)566-4778

Credential Type: Repairman Registration. **Duration of License:** One year. **Authorization:** To service, install, or repair weighing or measuring devices. **Requirements:** Submit application and fee. **Fees:** $10 registration fee. **Governing Statute:** Connecticut General Statutes, Section 43-47.

Credential Type: Dealer Registration. **Duration of License:** One year. **Authorization:** Required for dealer employing repairmen. **Requirements:** Submit application and fee. **Fees:** $25 registration fee. **Governing Statute:** Connecticut General Statutes, Section 43-47.

Illinois

5538

Registered Serviceperson (Weighing & Measuring Devices)
Illinois Dept. of Agriculture
Div. of Consumer Services
PO Box 19281
Springfield, IL 62794-9281
Phone: (217)782-3817

Credential Type: Serviceperson Registration. **Duration of License:** One year. **Authorization:** Allows applicant to sell, install, service, recondition and/or repair weighing or measuring devices used in trade or commerce. **Requirements:** Submit application and pay fee. **Examination:** Written examination. **Reciprocity:** Yes, with those applicants who have successfully passed the examination given by the state of Missouri. **Fees:** $5 application/initial registration fee. $5 renewal fee.

New Jersey

5539

Weighing or Measuring Mechanic
New Jersey Dept. of Law and Public Safety
Office of Weights and Measures
1261 Routes 1 and 9 South
Avanel, NJ 07001
Phone: (201)815-4840

Credential Type: License. **Examination:** Yes. **Governing Statute:** NJSA 51:1.

North Carolina

5540

Scale Technician
Dept. of Agriculture
Standards Div., Measurement Section
1 W. Edenton St.
Raleigh, NC 27611
Phone: (919)733-3313

Credential Type: Registration. **Duration of License:** One year. **Requirements:** Must be knowledgeable of the laws governing weights and measurements.

Tennessee

5541

Service Technician
Dept of Agriculture
Weights and Measures Div.
PO Box 40627
Nashville, TN 37204
Phone: (615)360-0159

Credential Type: License. **Requirements:** References required. Have officially calibrated equipment, re-calibrated every two years. **Reciprocity:** No. **Fees:** $10 Registration.

Vermont

5542

Dealer, Repairer Weighing and Measuring Devices
Dept. Of Agriculture
Div. of Weights and Measures
116 State St.
Montpelier, VT 05602
Phone: (802)828-2463

Credential Type: License. **Duration of License:** One year. **Requirements:** Adequate experience to demonstrate competency. Have adequate testing equipment. **Examination:** No. **Reciprocity:** No. **Fees:** $6 License. $4 Renewal. **Governing Statute:** Title 9, VSA Sections 2725-2729.

Preschool Workers

The following states grant licenses in this occupational category as of the date of publication:

Alabama	Colorado	Indiana	Maryland	Ohio	Utah
Alaska	Delaware	Iowa	New York	Oklahoma	Virginia
Arkansas	Illinois	Louisiana	North Carolina	Rhode Island	

Alabama

5543

Early Childhood Education Teacher

State Dept. of Education, Certification Officer
Montgomery, AL 36130
Phone: (205)242-9977

Credential Type: Initial Teaching Certificate. **Duration of License:** Eight years. **Requirements:** Basic program of teacher education includes two components, general and professional studies, each requiring two years of study. General studies (years one and 2) consist of 60 semester hours and must include 15 hours of humanities, 12 hours of social science which includes three hours of economics, 12 hours of natural and physical science which includes mathematics, three hours of health and physical education, and 18 hours of electives. Professional studies (years three and 4) consist of 72 semester hours and must include 12 hours of foundations of professional studies which includes three hours in survey course in exceptional child education. 30 hours of study in art, music, speech, creative drama, movement education, health education, parent education, and family life are required, as well as six hours of reading, nine hours of curriculum, teaching and media, three hours evaluation of teaching and learning, nine hours internship and three hours of electives.

Credential Type: Fifth Year Certificate. **Requirements:** Initial Certificate. Advanced professional studies program totaling 33 hours which includes 12 hours in teaching field, six hours of curriculum and teaching, 6-9 hours of foundations of professional studies which includes three hours in a general survey course in special education (if this requirement has not already been met), three hours of evaluation of teaching and learning, and three to six hours of electives.

Credential Type: Sixth Year Certificate. **Reciprocity:** Fifth Year Certificate. Advanced professional studies program totaling 33 hours which includes 12 hours in teaching field, 6-9 hours foundations of professional studies, three hours of evaluation of teaching and learning, and three to six hours of electives.

Credential Type: Seventh Year Certificate. **Requirements:** Sixth Year Certificate. Complete planned program and achieve stated objectives by completing further studies in the field of specialization and/or related fields, foundations of professional studies, and evaluation and educational research.

Alaska

5544

Child Care Provider (Center)

Dept. of Health and Social Services
Div. of Family and Youth Services
PO Box H-05
Juneau, AK 99811-0630
Phone: (907)465-2145

Credential Type: Child Caregiver License. **Duration of License:** Two years. **Authorization:** Required of persons working in a child care center as care givers. **Requirements:** Be at least 18 years of age. Have at least 12 hours inservice training per year. Submit three character references. Applicants must submit verification they do not have tuberculosis and must be free of serious physical and mental problems. **Fees:** No fee

5545

Early Childhood Education Associate

Dept. of Education, Certification Analyst
Box F
Juneau, AK 99811-0500
Phone: (907)465-2810
Phone: (907)465-2831

Credential Type: Early Childhood Education Associate I Certificate—Type E. **Duration of License:** Five years. **Requirements:** Completion of 30 credits in university or college early childhood education program requiring at least 400 hours of supervised practicum experience or received approved Child Development Association (CDA) Award.

To renew certificate applicant must have current CDA credentials or six semester hours of renewal credit in early childhood education. **Fees:** $43 fingerprint card processing fee. $125 application fee. $10 endorsement fee.

Credential Type: Early Childhood Education Associate II Certificate—Type E. **Duration of License:** Five years. **Requirements:** Completion of approved Associate Degree Program in Early Childhood Education (ECE). Completion of requirements for ECE Associate I. To renew certificate applicant must have six semester hours of renewal credit in early childhood education. **Fees:** $43 fingerprint card processing fee. $125 application fee. $10 endorsement fee.

Arkansas

5546

Early Childhood Special Education Teacher
Teacher Education and Licensure
State Dept. of Education
4 State Capitol Mall
Little Rock, AR 72201-1071
Phone: (501)682-4342

Credential Type: Early Childhood Special Education Certificate. **Requirements:** Bachelor or graduate degree in the field from an approved institution or bachelor's degree in an approved related field. Three semester hours each of child development, behavior management, study of the school, and principles of learning. A six semester hr. practicum in early childhood special education. An additional 18 semester hours addressing specified competencies related to teaching children with handicaps, birth through five years of age.

Colorado

5547

Child Health Associate
Board of Medical Examiners
Dept. of Regulatory Agencies
Div. of Registrations
1560 Broadway, Ste. 1300
Denver, CO 80202
Phone: (303)894-7690

Credential Type: License. **Requirements:** Contact licensing body for application information.

Delaware

5548

Early Childhood Teacher (Pre-K and K)
Div. of Teacher Services
Dept. of Public Instruction
PO Box 1402
Dover, DE 19903
Phone: (302)739-4688

Credential Type: Standard Certificate. **Requirements:** Bachelor's degree. Satisfactory completion of 18 semester hours of preparation for teaching on the early childhood level which may be part of, or in addition to, the degree requirements. The following courses, or their equivalent, should be included in the course of study: Child Development; Curriculum for Early childhood Education—Foundations, Content, Methods, and Materials; The Role of the Early Childhood Teacher; and The Exceptional Child. Observation and Student Teaching or one year of successful teaching experience under supervision.

Applicants for teacher certification must file a completed application with the Director which includes official transcripts, verification of previous teaching experience, and an affidavit of previous nonteaching or technical experience when applicable. **Examination:** National Teacher Examination (communications skills test) **Reciprocity:** Applicants who have been employed for at least 27 months under a standard certificate, or are completing teacher training in an approved program at a U.S. college or university outside the District of Columbia, may apply for certification under the Interstate Agreement on Qualifications of Educational Personnel, providing their state has signed a reciprocity agreement. Must have a valid certificate and complete application procedures.

Credential Type: Provisional Certificate. **Duration of License:** 18 months. **Authorization:** Temporarily allows applicant to hold teaching position while satisfactorily completing license deficits and/or attainment of a passing score on the DCPS Teacher Content Knowledge Test. **Requirements:** Standard Certificate requirements, but allows for some licensing deficits.

Illinois

5549

Child Care Aide
Illinois Dept. of Public Health
Education and Training
525 W. Jefferson
Springfield, IL 62761
Phone: (217)785-5133

Credential Type: Registration. **Duration of License:** Indefinite. **Requirements:** At least 16 years of age. Complete at least eight years of grade school or equivalent. Complete a 120-155 hour training program. **Examination:** Written and manual skills competency evaluation. **Reciprocity:** Yes, if training meets Illinois standards. **Fees:** No fee. **Governing Statute:** Nursing Home Act, IRS, Chapter 111 1/2.

5550

Early Childhood Teacher PK-3
Certification and Placement Section
100 N. First St.
Springfield, IL 62777
Phone: (217)782-4321

Credential Type: Early Childhood Certificate. **Duration of License:** Four years. **Requirements:** Good character. Good health. At least 19 years of age. Citizen of the U.S. Evidence of teaching experience or completion of an approved program of teacher preparation. Bachelor's degree. 78 semester hours of general education classes which include the following courses and specified semester hours: Language Arts 9; Science 7; Social Science (to include American History and/or Government) 7; Humanities (to include one hr. art and one hr.in music) 7; Health and Physical Education 3; plus approved general education electives. 32 semester hours of professional education to include the following courses and semester hours: Child growth and development with emphasis on the young child 3; History and philosophy of early childhood education 3; Instructional methods that include types of activity/learning centers, individualization, educational play, and media and their utilization in extending the child's understanding of art, music, literature, reading instruction, mathematics, natural and social science 4; Methods of teaching reading 2; Techniques and methodology of teaching language arts, mathematics, science, and social studies at the primary level 4; Development and acquisition of language in young children 2; Child family and community relations 3; Psychology, identification, and methods of teaching exceptional children 3; Pre-student teaching clinical experiences equivalent to 100 clock hours including experience with infant/toddlers, preschool/kindergarten, and primary age students;student teaching five and electives in professional education 3. Applicants who have had five semester hours of student teaching at the primary level (K-3) and who have had teaching experience are not required to take a practicum at the preschool level. Total teacher preparation program must total at least 120 semester hours All applicants must take and pass the Illinois Certification Basic Skills and Subject-Matter Knowledge Tests. **Examination:** Illinois Certification Basic Skills and Subject-Matter Knowledge Tests. **Reciprocity:** Reciprocity exists for applicants holding out-of-state teaching certificates providing their teacher preparation was comparable to that required by the state of Illinois. **Fees:** $44 per section of the Illinois Certification Test.

Indiana

Early Childhood Teacher (Pre-K)
Teacher Certification
Center for Professional Development
State House, Rm. 229
Indianapolis, IN 46204-2798
Phone: (317)232-9010

Credential Type: Standard License. **Duration of License:** Five years. **Requirements:** Baccalaureate degree. Complete a 124 semester hr. program structured as follows: 40 hours general education which includes language arts, children's literature, science, mathematics and art; 24 hours in subject matter; and 40 hours of professional education which includes nine weeks of student teaching, human growth and learning (infancy to age 8), laboratory experiences with individual children and parents, curricula with reading readiness, ethnic, cultural, and disability awareness, and 20 semester hours of electives. Be recommended for licensing by the institution granting degree. Successfully complete the National Teachers Examination (NTE) Core Battery and the ITTP Specialty Area exam in Early Childhood Education.

License may be renewed for the following five year period if continuing education requirements are completed. These may include additional graduate semester hours and certification renewal units (CRUs) granted for approved professional experiences. The Standard License may also be extended in subject area coverages upon completion of appropriate endorsement teaching minors. **Examination:** NTE Core Battery. ITTP Specialty Area Exam in Early Childhood Education.

Credential Type: Professionalization Endorsement. **Duration of License:** 10 years. **Requirements:** Complete five years' teaching experience in accredited schools at the level covered by the Standard License. Approved master's degree. 15 semester hours of graduate level courses. (Candidates with additional teaching areas of endorsement may professionalize these areas on completion of three semester hours of course work in subject matter area.) Be recommended for Professional Licensure by institution granting the master's degree. The Professional License may also be extended in subject area coverages upon completion of appropriate endorsement teaching minors.

Iowa

Prekindergarten/Kindergarten Teacher
Board of Educational Examiners
Grimes State Office Bldg.
Des Moines, IA 50319-0147
Phone: (515)281-3245

Credential Type: Provisional Certificate. **Duration of License:** Two years. **Requirements:** Baccalaureate degree. Complete approved teacher program. Complete approved human relations component. Complete course work or evidence of competency in: structure of American education; philosophies of education; professional ethics and legal responsibilities; psychology of teaching; audiovisual/media/computer technology; evaluation techniques; human development; exceptional learner; classroom management; instructional planning; curriculum; methods of teaching; prestudent field-based experiences; and student teaching in desired subject area and grade level. Plus curriculum content courses that include: methods and materials used in teaching young children; pre-student teaching experience; and specialization in a single discipline or a formal interdisciplinary program of at least 12 semester hours Certificate is renewable for a second two-year term.

Credential Type: Education Certificate. **Duration of License:** Five years. **Requirements:** Provisional Certificate. Two years of successful teaching experience based on a local evaluation process. Renewable.

Credential Type: Professional Teacher's Certificate. **Duration of License:** Five years. **Requirements:** Holder of or eligible for an Education Certificate. Fiveyears of teaching experience. Master's degree in the area of a teaching endorsement. Renewable.

Louisiana

Early Childhood Teacher (N-K)
Louisiana Dept. of Education
Box 94064
Baton Rouge, LA 70804-9064
Phone: (504)342-3490

Credential Type: Standard Certificate—Type C. **Duration of License:** Three years. **Requirements:** Baccalaureate degree, including an approved teacher education program and student teaching. Appropriate National Teacher Examination (NTE) scores. 46 general education semester hours which include: 12 hours English; 12 hours Social Studies; 12 hours Science; six hours Mathematics; and four hours health and physical education. 27 professional education hours which include: three hourshistory of education, introduction to education, foundations of education and/or philosophy of education; three hours educational psychology and/or principles of teaching and learning; nine hours of student teaching or practicum; and 12 hours of professional courses for teaching children under age six. 39 semester hours of specialized academic education to include 21 additional hours in the following: art; children's literature; safety and first aid; Louisiana history and/or geography; music; speech; teaching of reading; nutrition; methods and materials and/or creative activities for young children. Plus 18 hours of home economics. **Examination:** NTE.

Credential Type: Standard Certificate—Type B. **Duration of License:** Valid for life for continuous service endorsed thereon. **Requirements:** Standard Type C Certificate or equivalent. Three years of successful teaching experience.

Credential Type: Standard Certificate—Type A. **Duration of License:** Valid for life for continuous service. **Requirements:** Standard Type C or Type B Certificate or equivalent. Master's degree, or higher, from an approved institution. Fiveyears of successful teaching in a certified field.

Maryland

Early Childhood Teacher (N-3)
Dept. of Certification 18100
State Dept. of Education
200 W. Baltimore St.
Baltimore, MD 21201
Phone: (301)333-2142

Credential Type: Standard Professional Certificate. **Requirements:** Bachelor's or higher degree completed within five years preceding the issuance of the certificate or hold a bachelor's degree and complete six hours of acceptable credit within five years preceding the issuance of the certificate. Graduate from an approved teacher preparation program in Maryland or complete the specific credit count requirements for Maryland for an early childhood teacher or complete an undergraduate pre-service program produced by the National Council for Accreditation of Teacher Education (NCATE) after July 1, 1975. Must have completed a teacher education program within the past 10 years from an approved institution or hold a professional teacher's certificate from one of the states participating in the Interstate Contract Agreement and have taught for at least 27 months during the past seven years. Must pass the following tests in the National Teacher's Examinations: The Communication Skills Test of the Core Battery; The General Knowledge Test of the Core Battery; The Professional Knowledge Test of the Core Battery; and the appropriate Specialty Area Test. Must have 80 semester credit hours in the following academic content courses to include: nine hours English; nine hours social studies (6 hours history and three hours geography); three hours mathematics; six science (including three each in biological and physical science); two hours art; two hours music; and two hours physical education. Plus 26 semester hours in professional education courses to include: six hours foundations of education (including education psychology); 12 hours curriculum and methods (including reading, language arts, social studies, and creative activities); and eight hours of student teaching which includes a combination of N/K and grades 1, 2, or 3. All applicants must have three semester hours of college credit or state-approved inservice workshop credit in special education approved by the board. **Examination:** Following sections of the National Teacher's Examinations: The Communication Skills Test of the Core Battery; The General Knowledge Test of the Core Battery; The Professional Knowledge Test of the Core Battery; and the appropriate Specialty Area Test.

Credential Type: Provisional Degree Certificate. **Authorization:** Issued to applicant with bachelor's degree who fails to meet the requirements for Standard Professional Certificate. **Requirements:** Bachelor's degree. Continue working towards Standard Professional Certificate.

Credential Type: Advanced Professional Certificate. **Requirements:** Three years of successful teaching experience. Meet requirements for Standard Professional Certificate. Have relevant master's degree or complete 30 semester hours relevant to professional assignment (at least 15 hours must be a graduate level) or complete at least 30 semester hours of in-service education developed by the local school units and approved by the State Superintendent of Schools.

Credential Type: Resident Teacher Certificate. **Duration of License:** One year. **Requirements:** Bachelor's degree from an accredited institution with a concentration in a discipline appropriate to the early childhood education curriculum. Grades of "B" or better in major area of study. Must pass the following tests in the National Teacher's Examinations: The Communication Skills Test of the Core Battery; The General Knowledge Test of the Core Battery; and the appropriate Specialty Area Test. Verification by the local Superintendent of 90 clock hours of study developed according to the Maryland State Dept. of Education guidelines. Other requirements, as deemed necessary, by the State Dept. of Education. Renewable for one year.

5555

Family Day Care Provider
Child Care Administration
Dept. of Human Resources
2701 N. Charles St., 5th Fl.
Baltimore, MD 21218
Phone: (410)554-0400

Credential Type: Registration. **Duration of License:** Two years. **Requirements:** Must be at least 18 years of age. Attend an orientation session. Submit to background check. Meet one of the following sets of requirements: (1) Complete three clock hours of approved training in child development, age-appropriate activities, or the operation of a family day care home. (2) Request permission to substitute experience for training, based on having been a registered provider for the previous four years with no record of suspensions or revocations or a history of repeated violations.

Renewal requires completion of at least six clock hours of approved training within the past two years. **Governing Statute:** Annotated Code of Maryland, Title 07, Subtitle 04.

New York

5556

Early Childhood and Upper Elementary Teacher N-6
Administrator of Teacher Certification Policy
Univ. of the State of New York
State Education Dept.
Cultural Center, Rm. 5-A-11
Albany, NY 12230
Phone: (518)474-6440

Credential Type: Provisional Certificate. **Duration of License:** Five years. **Authorization:** Authorizes the teaching of grades N-6. **Requirements:** Baccalaureate degree with a four year program of collegiate preparation at a regionally accredited or approved higher institution. 24 semester hours of professional education courses to include six semester hoursin teaching of reading. A supervised student teaching experience. With recommendation, one full year of full-time teaching experience on the appropriate level may be substituted for student teaching. Note: The city of Buffalo, New York has certification standards that are exclusive of New York State.

Credential Type: Permanent Certificate. **Duration of License:** Permanent. **Requirements:** Hold a Provisional Certificate at level where certification is sought. Master's degree in or functionally related to field of teaching experience. Two years of elementary school teaching experience. Note: The city of Buffalo, New York has certification standards that are exclusive of New York State.

North Carolina

5557

Center Day Care Teacher/Caregiver
Dept. of Human Resources
Child Day Care Section
701 Barbour Dr.
Raleigh, NC 27603
Phone: (919)733-4801

Credential Type: Registration. **Duration of License:** Two years. **Requirements:** High school diploma or GED, plus one year of experience in a child day care center or 20 additional hours of training within the first six months of employment. 18 years of age. Valid driver's license. Some continuing education is required. Good moral character and physical health.

5558

Home Day Care Teacher/Caregiver
Dept. of Human Resources
Child Day Care Section
701 Barbour Dr.
Raleigh, NC 27603
Phone: (919)733-4801

Credential Type: Registration. **Duration of License:** Two years. **Requirements:** High school diploma or 18 years of age. Basic first-aid skills. Valid driver's license. Good moral character and physical health.

Ohio

5559

Pre-Kindergarten Teacher
Teacher Education and Certification
State Dept. of Education
65 S. Front St., Rm. 1012
Columbus, OH 43266-0308
Phone: (614)466-3593

Credential Type: Provisional Pre-Kindergarten Certificate. **Requirements:** Bacca-

Pre-Kindergarten Teacher, continued

laureate degree. Good moral character. Complete an approved program of teacher preparation including an examination. Recommendation of preparing institution. 30 semester hours of general education courses to include: the humanities; mathematics; natural sciences; and social science. 20 semester hours of course work pertaining to the Pre-K child. 30 semester hours of professional education courses and both clinical and field-based experiences designed for teaching the Pre-K level. 30 semester hours of curriculum content course work for Pre-K students which includes communication arts, concept development, creative arts, physical development, and social development.

Oklahoma

5560

Early Childhood Teacher PK-3
Teacher Education and Certification
State Dept. of Education
2500 N. Lincoln Blvd., Rm. 211
Oklahoma City, OK 73105
Phone: (405)521-3337

Credential Type: Early Childhood General Certificate. **Duration of License:** One year. **Requirements:** Complete an approved certificate program at an accredited college or university and receive recommendation from that institution. Pass the state teacher certification test(s) in early childhood competencies. **Examination:** State teacher certification test(s). **Reciprocity:** Oklahoma recognizes some out-of-state teaching certificates.

Credential Type: Early Childhood Standard Certificate (undergraduate). **Duration of License:** Five years. **Requirements:** Complete an approved certificate program at an accredited college or university which includes a minimum of the following: a baccalaureate degree; 50 semester hours in general education; 30 semester hours in professional education; and 40 semester hours in course work pertaining to teaching the early childhood student. Pass the state certified test(s) in early childhood competencies. Successfully complete the Entry-Year Assistance Program as a licensed teacher. Complete a course of two or more semester hours in the education of the exceptional child. **Examination:** State certification test(s). **Reciprocity:** Oklahoma recognizes some out-of-state teaching certificates.

Credential Type: Provisional Level II Certificate—Early Childhood. **Duration of License:** Two years. **Requirements:** Complete approved certificate program at an accredited college or university. Baccalaureate degree. 56 semester hours in general education course work. 24 semester hours in professional education which includes field experiences and student teaching. 30 semester hours in early childhood education. Pass the state certification test(s) in early childhood education. Successfully complete the Entry-Year Assistance Program as a licensed teacher. Complete a course of two or more semester hours in the education of the exceptional child. **Examination:** State certification test(s). **Reciprocity:** Oklahoma recognizes some out-of-state teaching certificates.

Credential Type: Provisional Level I Certificate—Early Childhood. **Duration of License:** One year. **Requirements:** Complete approved certificate program at an accredited college or university. Baccalaureate degree. 56 semester hours in general education course work. 18 semester hours in professional education which includes field experiences and student teaching. 24 semester hours in early childhood education. Pass the state certification test(s) in early childhood education. Successfully complete the Entry-Year Assistance Program as a licensed teacher. Complete a course of two or more semester hours in the education of the exceptional child. **Examination:** State certification test(s). **Reciprocity:** Oklahoma recognizes some out-of-state teaching certificates.

Credential Type: Additional Certificate. **Requirements:** Certified individuals who seek additional certification must complete the following: a methods course appropriate to the second certificate sought and a developmental psychology course appropriate to the grade level of the certificate.

Rhode Island

5561

Early Childhood Teacher (PK-2)
Office of Teacher Certification
State Dept. of Education
22 Hayes St.
Providence, RI 02908
Phone: (401)277-2675

Credential Type: Provisional Certificate. **Duration of License:** Three years. **Requirements:** Bachelor's degree. Complete an approved program for Early Childhood education or complete six semester hours of student teaching in early elementary and 24 semester hours of course work in the following areas: child growth and development; curriculum and methods in early childhood education; reading readiness and developmental reading; health and nutrition for the young child; child, family, and community relationships; and identification and service to special needs children. Pass the Core Battery of the NTE with minimum scores as follows: Communication Skills 657; General Knowledge 649; Professional Knowledge 648. Nonrenewable. **Examination:** Core Battery of the National Teacher Examination.

Credential Type: Professional Certificate. **Duration of License:** Five years. **Requirements:** Complete six credits while holding a Rhode Island Provisional Certificate. Three of the six credits may be inservice and the rest must be college level courses. Proof of three years of teaching experience in Rhode Island. Renewal is possible with completion of nine graduate credits (3 credits may be inservice work) and verification of continued teaching experience in early childhood or a related area.

Credential Type: Life Professional Certificate. **Duration of License:** Permanent. **Requirements:** Master's degree in early childhood, or elementary education with a concentration in early childhood, or a master's degree in any field of education with 15 semester hours of graduate work in early childhood or a master's degree in a field other than education with 21 semester hours of graduate work in early childhood. Must have six years of teaching experience in an approved setting at the early childhood level. Three years of the experience requirement must be completed in Rhode Island schools.

5562

Family Day Care Provider
Rhode Island Dept. of Children,
 Youth, and Families
610 Mt. Pleasant Ave.
Providence, RI 02908
Phone: (401)457-4536

Credential Type: Family Day Care Provider License. **Duration of License:** One year. **Authorization:** Allows licensee to provide care for four to six children within a 24-hour period in a family day care home. May care for seven to eight children with an additional adult assistant. **Requirements:** At least 21 years of age. Resident of Rhode Island. Submit application with background information and medical statement. Show evidence of having been fingerprinted by state or local police. Pass screening by Child Abuse and Neglected Tracking System (CANTS). Day care facility must be inspected and recertified every two years. **Examination:** None. **Reciprocity:** No. **Fees:** No fee.

Preschool Workers

5563

Family Group Day Care Provider
Rhode Island Dept. of Children,
  Youth, and Families
610 Mt. Pleasant Ave.
Providence, RI 02908
Phone: (401)457-4536

Credential Type: Family Group Day Care Provider License. **Duration of License:** One year. **Authorization:** Allows licensee to provide care and/or treatment of nine to 12 children within a 24-hour period in a family day care home. **Requirements:** At least 21 years of age. Resident of Rhode Island. Must hold an associate or higher degree from an accredited child development or early childhood education program, or have a Child Development Associate certificate (CDA) in family day care. Submit application with background information and medical statement. Show evidence of having been fingerprinted by state or local police. Pass screening by Child Abuse and Neglected Tracking System (CANTS). Day care facility must be inspected and recertified every two years. Alternative requirements are available through the licensing agency. **Examination:** None. **Reciprocity:** No. **Fees:** No fee.

Utah

5564

Preschool Special Education Teacher
Certification and Personnel
  Development Section
State Board of Education
250 East 500 South St.
Salt Lake City, UT 84111
Phone: (801)538-7740

Credential Type: Preschool Special Education Certificate. **Requirements:** Bachelor's degree. Complete an approved program for teaching preschool children with handicaps which addresses newly adopted early childhood handicaps and special education endorsement competencies.

Virginia

5565

Early Education Teacher NK-4
Administrative Director
Office of Professional Development
  and Teacher Education
Dept. of Education
PO Box 6-Q
Richmond, VA 23216-2060
Phone: (804)225-2094

Credential Type: Probational Certificate. **Duration of License:** One year. **Authorization:** Authorizes candidate who has gained employment in the Virginia Public Schools, but has not yet satisfied the National Teacher Examination (NTE) requirement, to teach for a period of one year. **Requirements:** Meet BTAP (Beginning Teacher Assistance Program) competencies. 48 semester hours of general studies to include six hours each of the following: social sciences; natural sciences; mathematics; school health; and physical education. Must also include 12 semester hours of humanities, social science (including American history), and natural sciences and mathematics. Plus four semester hours of school health and physical education.

Must have 12 semester hours of professional studies including not less than three hours each of human growth and development, curriculum and instructional procedures, and foundations of education. Plus a six semester hr. student teaching experience which includes 200 clock hours in the classroom, and at least 60 percent of that time candidate must provide direct instruction.

60 semester hours of specialized courses for early education must include: reading; language arts; social science; math; science; art; music; physical education and health; and electives chosen from math and science. Must complete NTE requirements during the life of the certificate. Nonrenewable.

Credential Type: Provisional Certificate. **Duration of License:** Two years. **Authorization:** Authorizes candidates who have not yet satisfied requirements for Virginia's Beginning Teacher Assistance Program, or individuals entering the profession five or more years after their last formal study, or individuals holding a baccalaureate degree with one or more endorsements at the secondary level, or individuals failing to meet general or professional education requirements but have one or more specific endorsements to be employed in a Virginia Public School for a period of two years. **Requirements:** Pass NTE examination. Meet BTAP competencies. 48 semester hours of general studies to include six hours each of the following: social sciences; natural sciences; mathematics; school health; and physical education. Must also include 12 semester hours of humanities, social science (including American history), and natural sciences and mathematics. Plus four semester hours of school health and physical education.

Must have 12 semester hours of professional studies including not less than three hours each of human growth and development, curriculum and instructional procedures, and foundations of education. Plus a six semester hr. student teaching experience which includes 200 clock hours in the classroom, and at least 60 percent of that time candidate must provide direct instruction.

60 semester hours of specialized courses for early education must include: reading; language arts; social science; math; science; art; music; physical education and health; and electives chosen from math and science. Some allowances may be made for incomplete requirements. Must complete any requirement deficits during the life of the certificate. Nonrenewable. **Examination:** National Teacher Examination.

Credential Type: Collegiate Professional Certificate. **Duration of License:** Five years. **Requirements:** Baccalaureate degree from an accredited institution. Pass NTE examination. Meet BTAP competencies. 48 semester hours of general studies to include six hours each of the following: social sciences; natural sciences; mathematics; school health; and physical education. Must also include 12 semester hours of humanities, social science (including American history), and natural sciences and mathematics. Plus four semester hours of school health and physical education.

Must have 12 semester hours of professional studies including not less than three hours each of human growth and development, curriculum and instructional procedures, and foundations of education. Plus a six semester hr. student teaching experience which includes 200 clock hours in the classroom, and at least 60 percent of that time candidate must provide direct instruction.

60 semester hours of specialized courses for early education must include: reading; language arts; social science; math; science; art; music; physical education and health; and electives chosen from math and sciences. Renewable. **Reciprocity:** Applicants who have completed a college level teacher preparation program out-of-state may qualify for this certificate upon approval.

5566

Preschool Teacher of the Handicapped
Administrative Director
Office of Professional Development
 and Teacher Education
Dept. of Education
PO Box 6-Q
Richmond, VA 23216-2060
Phone: (804)225-2094

Credential Type: Preschool Handicapped Endorsement. **Requirements:** Collegiate Professional Teaching Certificate. Minimum of two years experience as an elementary or special education teacher. Complete 30 semester hours of upper or graduate level work in specialized area. Complete a minimum student teaching assignment of six semester hours in area of specialization.

5567

Reading Specialist NK-12
Administrative Director
Office of Professional Development
 and Teacher Education
Dept. of Education
PO Box 6-Q
Richmond, VA 23216-2060
Phone: (804)225-2094

Credential Type: Reading Specialist Endorsement. **Requirements:** Postgraduate Professional Teaching Certificate and three years of successful classroom teaching experience. 18 semester hours of graduate courses to include: foundations or survey of reading instruction; language development; reading in content areas; organization and supervision of reading program; diagnosis and remediation of reading difficulties and a practicum. 12 semester hours of graduate or undergraduate courses to include: measurement and/or evaluation; child and/or adolescent psychology; personality and learning behavior; literature; language arts instruction; learning disabilities; contemporary issues in teaching of reading.

Professional Engineers

The following states grant licenses in this occupational category as of the date of publication:

Alabama	District of	Iowa	Minnesota	New Mexico	Rhode Island	Washington
Alaska	Columbia	Kansas	Mississippi	New York	South Carolina	West Virginia
Arizona	Florida	Kentucky	Missouri	North Carolina	South Dakota	Wisconsin
Arkansas	Georgia	Louisiana	Montana	North Dakota	Tennessee	Wyoming
California	Hawaii	Maine	Nebraska	Ohio	Texas	
Colorado	Idaho	Maryland	Nevada	Oklahoma	Utah	
Connecticut	Illinois	Massachusetts	New Hampshire	Oregon	Vermont	
Delaware	Indiana	Michigan	New Jersey	Pennsylvania	Virginia	

Alabama

5568

Engineer-in-Training
Alabama State Board of Registration
  for Professional Engineers and
  Land Surveyors
301 Interstate Park Dr.
Montgomery, AL 36130-1001
Phone: (205)242-5568

Credential Type: License. **Duration of License:** One year. **Requirements:** Must be a graduate of an accredited engineering program, or a graduate of an unapproved program with two years of satisfactory experience, or a graduate of an approved engineering technology or related science curriculum with four years of satisfactory experience. Must be a resident of Alabama. **Examination:** Fundamentals of Engineering Examination. **Fees:** $30 application fee. $5 renewal fee.

5569

Professional Engineer
Alabama State Board of Rgistration
  for Professional Engineers and
  Land Surveyors
750 Washington Ave., Ste. 212
Montgomery, AL 36130-1001
Phone: (205)242-5568

Credential Type: License. **Duration of License:** One year. **Requirements:** Must be a resident of Alabama. Must be a graduate of a an approved school of engineering and have four years of apprenticeship, or a graduate from an unapproved engineering curriculum and have six years of apprenticeship, or a graduate in an approved engineering technology or related science curriculum and have eight years of experience. Non-college graduates may apply for registration after completing twelve years of apprenticeship. **Examination:** Fundamentals of Engineering Examination. Principles and Practices of Engineering Examination. **Fees:** $25 application fee. $25 examination fee.

Alaska

5570

Professional Engineer
Dept. of Commerce and Economic
  Development
Div. of Occupational Licensing
State Board of Registration for
  Architects, Engineers and Land
  Surveyors
PO Box D
Juneau, AK 99811-0800
Phone: (907)465-2540

Credential Type: Certificate of registration. **Duration of License:** Two years. **Requirements:** Good character and reputation. Five references, including three from engineers.

To be eligible for fundamentals fo engineering exam, applicant must have completed at least 75 percent of the required credit hours leading to an undergraduate degree in an engineering curriculum accredited by ABET, or submit evidence that applicant has met the education and experience requirements for engineer-in-training, as follows: combination of four years education and experience with a B.S. degree in engineering, or combination of five years education and experience with some course work or a B.S. degree in engineering technology, or combination of six years education and experience with course work in non-ABET engineering technology or no engineering education.

To be eligible for the professional engineering exam, applicant must have passed the fundamentals of engineering exam and submit evidence that applicant has met the education and experience requirements for professional engineer, as follows: combination of eight years education and experience with ABET accredited B.S. degree in engineering, or combination of 10 years education and experience with course work in ABET accredited engineering or engineering technology curriculum, or combination of 12 years education and experience with course work in non-ABET accredited engineering technology program or no engineering education. **Examination:** Fundamentals of engineering exam (engineer-in-training). Principles and practices of engineering exam (professional engineer). **Exemptions:** Engineers with 20 years experience need not take the fundamentals of engineering exam. **Reciprocity:** Yes. **Fees:** $30 application fee. $130 application fee for license by comity. $100 registration fee. $100 biennial renewal fee. $50 fee for having exam proctored out of state. $50 for fundamentals of engineering or engineer in training exam. $100 for principles and practices of engineering (PE) exam. **Governing Statute:** Alaska Statutes 08.48. Professional Regulations 12 AAC 36.

Arizona

5571

Engineer
Board of Technical Registration
1951 W. Camelback, Ste. 250
Phoenix, AZ 85015
Phone: (602)255-4053

Credential Type: Registration to Practice. **Duration of License:** Three years. **Requirements:** Be of good moral character. Have at least eight years education or expe-

841

Engineer, continued

rience, or combination of both with at least four years of experience. Pass in-training and professional examination administered by the board. **Examination:** In-training and professional (Principles and Practices) examinations. **Exemptions:** The in-training exam may be waived for candidates who have a degree in engineering. **Fees:** $90 application fee. $70 exam fee. $200 geological and geophysical engineer exam fee. $190 structural engineer exam fee for Parts I and II. $126 renewal fee.

Credential Type: Registration without examination. **Requirements:** Hold a valid registration in another state, jurisdiction, territory, or country; or hold a certificate of qualification issued by the National Council of Examiners for Engineers and Surveyors. Meet experience and education requirements similar to those of Arizona, or have been actively engaged in the profession for at least 10 years. **Fees:** $90 application fee. $126 renewal fee.

5572

Engineer-in-Training
Board of Technical Registration
1951 W. Camelback, Ste. 250
Phoenix, AZ 85015
Phone: (602)255-4053

Credential Type: In-training registration. **Requirements:** Be of good moral character. To qualify for the in-training examination on the basis of education, must be a graduate of a four-year engineering program of an accredited college or university.

To qualify for the in-training examination on the basis of experience, must have at least four years of education or experience or both directly related to the practice of engineering. **Examination:** In-training examination. **Fees:** $30 application fee. $50 exam fee.

Arkansas

5573

Engineer
Arkansas Board of Registration for
  Professional Engineers and Land
  Surveyors
TCB Bldg., Ste. 700
PO Box 2541
Little Rock, AR 72203
Phone: (501)371-2517

Credential Type: License. **Duration of License:** One year. **Requirements:** Graduate of an accredited engineering curriculum of four years and four years of experience in engineering and pass the examination; or, eight years of progressive experience in engineering work accepted by the Board and pass the examination. **Examination:** Yes. **Fees:** $60 Written examination. $35 Application. $20 Renewal.

5574

Engineer in Training
Arkansas State Board of Registration
  for Professional Engineers and
  Land Surveyors
TCB Bldg., Ste. 700
PO Box 2541
Little Rock, AR 72203
Phone: (501)371-2517

Credential Type: License. **Duration of License:** One year. **Requirements:** Graduate of an approved engineering curriculum of four years; or, four years of progressive experience in engineering work acceptable to the board and pass an examination. **Examination:** Yes. **Fees:** $10 Application. $20 Written examination. $5 Renewal.

California

5575

Engineer-in-Training
Board of Registration for
  Professional Engineers and Land
  Surveyors
PO Box 349002
Sacramento, CA 95825-9002
Phone: (916)920-7466

Credential Type: Engineer-in-Training Certification. **Requirements:** Complete at least three years of college in a board-approved engineering curriculum, or have three years of engineering-related experience. **Examination:** Fundamentals of Engineering Examination. **Fees:** $60 certification fee. **Governing Statute:** California Code of Regulations, Title 16, Chap. 5, Sections 400-471.

5576

General Engineering Contractor
California State License Board
9835 Goethe Rd.
PO Box 26000
Sacramento, CA 95826
Phone: (916)366-5153
Phone: (916)327-9707
Phone: (800)321-CSLB

Credential Type: Contractor's license. **Duration of License:** Two years. **Authorization:** Covers contractors whose principal contracting business is in connection with fixed works requiring specialized engineering knowledge and skill. **Requirements:** Must have at least four years experience within the past 10 years as a journeyman, foreman, supervising employee, or contractor in the class applied for. More than $2,500 worth of operating capital, proof of workers' compensation insurance coverage, file a Contractors Bond or cash deposit in the amount of $5,000 (except for Swimming Pool classification which requires $10,000) for the Responsible Managing Employee or the Responsible Managing Officer. **Examination:** Law and Business examination and second test covering the specific trade or certification area that the contractor is applying for. **Reciprocity:** California and Arizona honor each other's licensing qualifications as long as applicants pass Arizona's Business Management Exam and California's Business and Law Exam. Also reciprocity with Nevada and Utah. **Fees:** $150 application processing fee (plus $50 fee for each additional classification). $150 initial license fee. $200 renewal fee. **Governing Statute:** Business and Professions Code, Sections 7065-7068 and the Board Rule 816 (California Administrative Code).

5577

Professional Engineer
Board of Registration for
  Professional Engineers and Land
  Surveyors
PO Box 349002
Sacramento, CA 95825-9002
Phone: (916)920-7466

Credential Type: Professional Engineer Registration. **Duration of License:** Four years following initial period of one year. **Requirements:** Be certified as an Engineer-in-Training by meeting one of the following sets of requirements: (1) Pass the Fundamentals of Engineering Examination in California or another state. (2) Have a B.S. degree in engineering from a board approved engineering curriculum and 15 years of qualifying experience. (3) Be a graduate from a non-approved engineering curriculum and have 17 years of qualifying experience.

Complete six years of qualifying experience or a combination of education and experience. **Examination:** Principles and Practice of Engineering. Take-home test on California engineering laws and board rules. **Fees:** $175 registration fee. $160 renewal fee. **Governing Statute:** Business and Professions Code, Chap. 7, Div. 3, Sections 67006799. California Code of Regulations, Title 16, Chap. 5, Sections 400-471.

Credential Type: Civil Engineer Registration. **Duration of License:** Four years following initial period of one year. **Requirements:** Meet all requirements for Professional Engineer Registration and pass special tests on seismic principles and on engineering surveying principles. **Examination:** Principles and Practice of Engineering. Take-home test on California engineering laws and board rules. Proctored tests on seismic principles and on engineering surveying principles. **Fees:** $175 registration fee. $160 renewal fee. **Governing Statute:** Business and Professions Code, Chap. 7, Div. 3, Sections 67006799. California Code of Regulations, Title 16, Chap. 5, Sections 400-471.

Colorado

5578

Engineer-in-Training
Board of Registration for
 Professional Engineers and
 Professional Land Surveyors
Dept. of Regulatory Agencies
Div. of Registrations
1560 Broadway, Ste. 1370
Denver, CO 80202
Phone: (303)894-7788

Credential Type: Engineer-in-Training Registration. **Requirements:** Must provide documentation of technical competence. Must meet one of the following sets of requirements:

(1) Must have graduated from a board-approved engineering curriculum of four or more years, or have senior status in a board-approved engineering curriculum of four or more years.

(2) Must have six years of progressive engineering experience, of which educational study may be a part. Must have graduated from a board-approved engineering technology curriculum of four or more years.

(3) Must have graduated from an engineering curriculum of four or more years not approved by the board or from a related science curriculum of four or more years. Must have four years of progressive engineering experience, of which educational study may be a part.

(4) Be a high school graduate or equivalent. Must have six years of progressive engineering experience, of which educational study may be a part. **Examination:** Fundamentals of engineering examination. **Reciprocity:** Yes, if applicant is licensed in good standing in another jurisdiction requiring qualifications substantially equivalent to Colorado's. **Fees:** License, renewal, and exam fees. **Governing Statute:** Colorado Revised Statutes, Title 12, Article 25.

5579

Professional Engineer
Board of Registration for
 Professional Engineers and
 Professional Land Surveyors
Dept. of Regulatory Agencies
Div. of Registrations
1560 Broadway, Ste. 1370
Denver, CO 80202
Phone: (303)894-7788

Credential Type: Professional Engineer License. **Requirements:** Must meet one of the following sets of requirements:

(1) Must have graduated from a board-approved engineering curriculum of four or more years. Must have eight years of progressive engineering experience, of which educational study may be a part. Must have been enrolled as an engineer-in-training in the state of Colorado.

(2) Must have graduated from a board-approved engineering technology curriculum of four or more years. Must have 10 years of progressive engineering experience, of which educational study may be a part. Must have been enrolled as an engineer-in-training in the state of Colorado.

(3) Must have graduated from an engineering curriculum of four or more years not approved by the board or from a related science curriculum of four or more years. Must have 10 years of progressive engineering experience, of which educational study may be a part. Must have been enrolled as an engineer-in-training in the state of Colorado.

(4) Must have graduated from an engineering curriculum of four or more years or from a related science curriculum of four or more years. Must have 20 years of progressive engineering experience, of which educational study may be a part. Must have been enrolled as an engineer-in-training in the state of Colorado.

(5) Must have 12 years of progressive engineering experience, of which educational study may be a part. Must have been enrolled as an engineer-in-training in the state of Colorado. **Examination:** Principles and practices of engineering examination. **Reciprocity:** Yes, if applicant is licensed in good standing in another jurisdiction requiring qualifications substantially equivalent to Colorado's. **Fees:** License, renewal, and exam fees. **Governing Statute:** Colorado Revised Statutes, Title 12, Article 25.

Connecticut

5580

Engineer-in-Training
Board of Professional Engineers &
 Land Surveyors
Professional Licensing Div.
Consumer Protection Dept.
165 Capitol Ave.
Hartford, CT 06106
Phone: (203)566-1814

Credential Type: Engineer-in-Training License. **Duration of License:** 10 years. **Requirements:** Graduate from an approved course in engineering. In lieu of graduation the board may accept six years active practice in engineering work. Pass the Fundamentals of Engineering Examination. **Examination:** Fundamentals of Engineering Examination of the National Council of Examiners for Engineering and Surveying (NCEES). **Reciprocity:** Yes. **Fees:** $38 application fee. **Governing Statute:** General Statutes of Connecticut, Chap. 391.

5581

Professional Engineer
Board of Professional Engineers &
 Land Surveyors
Professional Licensing Div.
Consumer Protection Dept.
165 Capitol Ave.
Hartford, CT 06106
Phone: (203)566-1814

Credential Type: Professional Engineer's License. **Duration of License:** One year. **Requirements:** Graduate from an approved course in engineering in a board approved school or college. At least four years active practice in engineering work. In lieu of graduation the board may accept six years active practice in engineering work. **Examination:** Fundamentals of Engineering Examination and Principles and Practice of Engineering Examination of the National Council of Examiners for Engineering and Surveying (NCEES). **Exemptions:** Written exam may be waived if applicant has 20 years or more of engineering practice. Fundamentals examination may be waived if applicant has completed an approved course in engineering and has at least eight years of engineering experience. **Reciprocity:** Yes. **Fees:** $150 application fee (professional engineer license or combined professional engineer and land surveyor license). $225 annual renewal fee. **Governing Statute:** General Statutes of Connecticut, Chap. 391.

Delaware

5582

Engineer-in-Training
Delaware Association of Professional Engineers
2005 Concord Pike
Wilmington, DE 19803
Phone: (302)656-7311
Fax: (302)656-9410

Credential Type: Engineer-in-Training Certification. **Requirements:** Meet one of the following sets of requirements: (1) Graduation with a baccalaureate degree in engineering from a curriculum accredited by the Accreditation Board for Engineering and Technology (ABET) or the Canadian Engineering Accreditation Board (CEAB). (2) Graduation from a non-ABET accredited engineering, engineering technology, or science related to engineering curriculum. (3) Be 45 years of age or more with 20 years of professional experience in engineering. **Examination:** Fundamentals of Engineering Examination. **Fees:** $10 application fee. $50 Fundamentals of Engineering Examination fee.

5583

Professional Engineer
Delaware Association of Professional Engineers
2005 Concord Pike
Wilmington, DE 19803
Phone: (302)656-7311
Fax: (302)656-9410

Credential Type: Professional Engineer Registration. **Duration of License:** Two years. **Requirements:** Meet one of the following sets of requirements: (1) Graduation with a baccalaureate degree in engineering from a curriculum accredited by the Accreditation Board for Engineering and Technology (ABET) or the Canadian Engineering Accreditation Board (CEAB). Have four years of acceptable professional engineering experience. (2) Graduation from a non-ABET accredited engineering, engineering technology, or science related to engineering curriculum. Have eight years of acceptable professional engineering experience. (3) Be 45 years of age or more. Have 20 years of professional experience in engineering. **Examination:** Fundamentals of Engineering Examination. Principles and Practice of Engineering. **Reciprocity:** Yes, based on passing comparable examinations. **Fees:** $75 application fee. $36 registration fee (per two years). $36 renewal fee. $50 Fundamentals of Engineering Examination fee. $100 Principles and Practice of Engineering Examination fee. **Governing Statute:** Delaware Code, Title 24, Chap. 28.

District of Columbia

5584

Professional Engineer
Board of Registration for Professional Engineers
614 H St., NW, Rm. 923
Washington, DC 20001
Phone: (202)727-7468

Credential Type: Professional Engineer Registration. **Requirements:** Contact licensing body for application information.

Florida

5585

Professional Engineer
Board of Professional Engineers
Div. of Professions
Dept. of Professional Regulation
1940 N. Monroe St.
Tallahassee, FL 32399-0755
Phone: (904)488-9912

Credential Type: License by Examination. **Duration of License:** Two years. **Requirements:** Good moral character. Meet one of the following sets of requirements: (1) Graduate from an approved engineering curriculum of four years or more. At least four years of active engineering experience. (2) Graduate of an approved engineering technology curriculum of four years or more, prior to July 1, 1979. At least four years of active engineering experience. **Examination:** National Council of Engineering Examiners (NCEE) examination. Part 1—Engineering Fundamentals. Part 2—Professional Practice and Principles. **Fees:** $100 application fee (graduate of a board-approved program). $125 application fee (graduate of a program requiring board inquiry concerning approval). $70 exam fee (both parts). $75 initial registration and licensure fee. $80 renewal fee. **Governing Statute:** Florida Statutes, Chapter 471.

Credential Type: License by Endorsement. **Duration of License:** Two years. **Requirements:** Meet one of the following sets of requirements: (1) Have passed a substantially equivalent national, regional, state, or territorial licensing examination. Have at least four years of active engineering experience. (2) Hold a valid license to practice engineering issued by another state or territory of the United States. Criteria for issuance must have been substantially identical to Florida's. (3) Part one of the examination shall be deemed passed if applicant has held a valid professional engineer's license in another state for at least 15 years, and has at least 20 years of continuous professional engineering experience. (4) Parts one and two of the examination shall be deemed passed if applicant has held a valid professional engineer's license in another state for at least 25 years, and has at least 30 years of continuous professional engineering experience. **Fees:** $75 license by endorsement fee. $80 renewal fee. **Governing Statute:** Florida Statutes, Chapter 471. Rules of the Board of Professional Engineers, Chapter 21H, F.A.C.

Georgia

5586

Engineer-in-Training
State Board of Professional Engineers and Land Surveyors
Professional Examining Boards
166 Pryor St., SW
Atlanta, GA 30303
Phone: (404)656-3926

Credential Type: Engineer-in-Training Certificate. **Duration of License:** Two years. **Requirements:** Meet one of the following sets of requirements: (1) Graduate in an engineering curriculum of not less than four years from a board-approved school or college; or (2) Graduate in an engineering curriculum of not less than four years or in a curriculum of four or more years in engineering technology or related science from a board-approved school or college; or (3) Have not less than eight years of experience in engineering work. **Examination:** Fundamentals of Engineering. **Fees:** $20 exam application fee. $60 exam fee (Fundamentals of Engineering). **Governing Statute:** Official Code of Georgia Annotated 43-15.

5587

Professional Engineer
State Board of Professional Engineers and Land Surveyors
Professional Examining Boards
166 Pryor St., SW
Atlanta, GA 30303
Phone: (404)656-3926

Credential Type: Certificate of Registration. **Duration of License:** Two years. **Requirements:** Meet one of the following sets of requirements: (1) Obtain certification as an engineer-in-training. Graduate in an engineering curriculum of not less than four years from a board approved school or college. Have at least four years of experience in engineering work. (2) Obtain certifica-

Professional Engineers

tion as an engineer-in-training. Graduate in an engineering curriculum of not less than four years or in a curriculum of four or more years in engineering technology or related science from a board-approved school or college. Have at least seven years of experience in engineering work. (3) Obtain certification as an engineer-in-training by having not less than eight years of experience in engineering work. Have at least seven additional years of experience in engineering work. (4) Graduate in an engineering curriculum of not less than four years from a board-approved school or college. Have at least 16 years of experience in engineering work. **Examination:** Principles and Practices of Engineering. **Reciprocity:** Registration by comity may be granted to any individual who holds a certificate of qualification or registration issued by authority of the National Council of Engineering Examiners or of any state, territory, or possession of the United States, provided that the requirements do not conflict with Georgia's and are not of a lower standard. **Fees:** $30 exam application fee. $100 exam fee (Principles and Practices, Group I and II). $90 exam fee (Principles and Practices, Structural I). $50 renewal fee. $70 application fee for comity. $50 temporary permit fee. **Governing Statute:** Official Code of Georgia Annotated 43-15.

Hawaii

5588

Engineer, Professional
Hawaii Board of Engineers,
 Architects, Surveyors and
 Landscape Architects
Dept. of Commerce and Consumer
 Affairs
PO Box 3469
Honolulu, HI 96801
Phone: (808)548-8452

Credential Type: License. **Duration of License:** Six months. **Requirements:** Master's Degree in engineering, graduation from a four-year engineering curriculum and three years of engineering experience; or Master's Degree in engineering and four years of experience; or graduation from a four-year engineering curriculum and four years of experience; or graduation from a four-year engineering technology or arts and science curriculum and eight years of experience; or 12 years of engineering experience. Three letters of recommendation from professional engineers certifying experience and reputation. Applicants taking the EIT Exam only have a different set of requirements. **Examination:** Four exams. **Exemptions:** Parts of the NCEE exam may be waived if an equivalent has been passed in another state and a current license is held. **Fees:** $50 application fee. $275 exam fee. $30 license fee. $15 $30 Compliance Resolution Fund fee. $30 renewal fee.

Idaho

5589

Engineer-in-Training
Board of Registration of Professional
 Engineers and Professional Land
 Surveyors
600 S. Orchard, Ste. A
Boise, ID 83705-1242
Phone: (208)334-3860

Credential Type: Certificate of Registration. **Duration of License:** One year. **Requirements:** Meet one of the following sets of requirements: (1) Graduation from an approved engineering curriculum of four years or more from a board-approved college or university, or be in the last two semesters of such a course of study. (2) In lieu of graduation from an approved engineering curriculum, demonstrate equivalent knowledge and skill. Complete at least four years of progressive experience demonstrating competency to enroll as an engineer-in-training. **Examination:** Engineering Fundamentals. **Reciprocity:** Yes. **Fees:** Contact board for fees. **Governing Statute:** Idaho Code, Title 54, Chap. 12.

5590

Professional Engineer
Board of Registration of Professional
 Engineers and Professional Land
 Surveyors
600 S. Orchard, Ste. A
Boise, ID 83705-1242
Phone: (208)334-3860

Credential Type: Certificate of Registration. **Duration of License:** One year. **Requirements:** Meet one of the following sets of requirements: (1) Graduation from an approved engineering curriculum of four years or more from a board-approved college or university. Complete four years of progressive experience demonstrating competency to practice professional engineering. One year of graduate study in engineering may be credited as one year of experience. (2) In lieu of graduation from an approved engineering curriculum, demonstrate equivalent knowledge and skill by passing a fundamentals of engineering examination. Complete at least eight years of progressive experience demonstrating competency to practice professional engineering. **Examination:** Engineering Fundamentals. Principles and Practice of Engineering. **Reciprocity:** Yes. **Fees:** Contact board for fees. **Governing Statute:** Idaho Code, Title 54, Chap. 12.

Illinois

5591

Engineer
Illinois Dept. of Professional
 Regulation
320 W. Washington St.
Springfield, IL 62786
Phone: (217)782-8556

Credential Type: Intern Engineer License. **Duration of License:** Indefinite. **Requirements:** Must complete a bachelor's degree in a four-year approved engineering curriculum or complete a bachelor's degree in basic engineering, or a related science, and have four years of progressive engineering experience after graduation. **Examination:** National Council of Examiners for Engineering and Surveying (NCESS) Examination—Part I. **Reciprocity:** No. **Fees:** $68.60 examination fee. $20 license fee. **Governing Statute:** The Professional Engineering Practice Act of 1989, Illinois Revised Statutes 1991, Chapter 111.

Credential Type: Professional Engineer License. **Duration of License:** Two years. **Requirements:** Complete an approved engineering curriculum of four or more years and have an additional four years of approved engineering experience, or complete a bachelor's degree in basic engineering and have eight years of progressive engineering experience after graduation. **Examination:** National Council of Examiners for Engineering and Surveying (NCESS) Examination—Parts I and II. **Reciprocity:** Yes, providing the requirements for licensure were substantially equivalent to those of Illinois. **Fees:** $68.60 Part I examination fee. $99.50 Part II examination fee. $120.10 Parts I and II examination fee. $25 initial license fee. $40 license by endorsement fee. $40 renewal fee. **Governing Statute:** The Professional Engineering Practice Act of 1989, Illinois Revised Statutes 1991, Chapter 111.

5592

Structural Engineer
Illinois Dept. of Professional
 Regulation
320 W. Washington St.
Springfield, IL 62786
Phone: (217)782-8556

Credential Type: Structural Engineer License. **Duration of License:** Two years. **Requirements:** Good moral character.

Indiana

Structural Engineer, continued

Meet one of the following sets of requirements: (1) Hold a Bachelor of Science degree in Engineering that includes a minimum of 18 semester hours of courses in structural analysis and design, plus four years experience under the supervision of a licensed Structural Engineer; (2) Complete a four-year college degree in a related field, plus eight years of experience under the direct supervision of a licensed Structural Engineer. Two years of the experience requirement (one or two) must be in a position of being in charge and responsible for resulting work. **Examination:** National Council Examiners for Engineering and Surveying (NCEES) Examination. **Reciprocity:** Yes, considered on an individual basis. **Fees:** $68.60 Fundamental Engineering examination fee. $78.90 Structural I examination fee. $99.50 Structural II examination fee. $99.50 Fundamental of Engineering & Structural I examination fee. $120.10 Fundamental of Engineering & Structural II examination fee. $130.40 Structural I & II examination fee. $151.00 Fundamental of Engineering, Structural I and II examination fee. $25 initial license fee. $40 license by endorsement fee. $40 renewal fee. **Governing Statute:** The Structural Engineering License Act of 1989, Illinois Revised Statutes 1991, Chapter 111.

Indiana

5593

Engineer
State Board of Registration for Professional Engineers and Land Surveyors
Professional Licensing Agency
1021 State Office Bldg.
100 N. Senate Ave.
Indianapolis, IN 46204
Phone: (317)232-2980

Credential Type: License. **Requirements:** Contact licensing body for application information.

5594

Engineer-in-Training
State Board of Registration for Professional Engineers and Land Surveyors
Professional Licensing Agency
1021 State Office Bldg.
100 N. Senate Ave.
Indianapolis, IN 46204
Phone: (317)232-2980

Credential Type: Engineer-in-Training. **Requirements:** Contact licensing body for application information.

Iowa

5595

Engineer, Registered
Engineer and Land Surveying Examining Board
1918 SE Hulsizer
Ankeny, IA 50021
Phone: (515)281-7360

Credential Type: License. **Duration of License:** Two years. **Requirements:** College degree in engineering and four years of practical experience. **Examination:** Fundamentals of Engineering. Principles and Practices of Engineering.

Kansas

5596

Engineer-in-Training
State Board of Technical Professions
LSOB, 900 SW Jackson, Rm. 507
Topeka, KS 66612-1257
Phone: (913)296-3053

Credential Type: Engineer-in-Training Certificate. **Duration of License:** Two years. **Requirements:** Must be a resident of Kansas. Meet one of the following sets of requirements: (1) Graduate of an accredited engineering curriculum with MS or Ph.D. in engineering. (2) Graduate of an accredited engineering curriculum. (3) Graduate of a nonaccredited engineering curriculum with MS or Ph.D. in engineering. (4) Graduate of a non-accredited engineering curriculum, including one year of experience. (5) Graduate of a board-approved related science curriculum with MS or Ph.D. in engineering, including 1.5 years of experience. (6) Graduate of an accredited four-year technology program, including four years of experience. (7) Graduate of a non-accredited four-year technology program, including five years of experience. (8) Graduate of a board-approved related science curriculum, including five years of experience. (9) Graduate of a two-year technology program, including six years of experience. (10) A non-graduate with eight years of experience. **Examination:** Fundamentals of Engineering. **Fees:** Contact board for fees.

5597

Professional Engineer
State Board of Technical Professions
LSOB, 900 SW Jackson, Rm. 507
Topeka, KS 66612-1257
Phone: (913)296-3053

Credential Type: Professional Engineer License. **Duration of License:** Two years. **Requirements:** Must be a resident of Kansas. Meet one of the following sets of requirements: (1) Graduate of an accredited engineering curriculum with MS or Ph.D. in engineering, plus three years of additional experience. (2) Graduate of an accredited engineering curriculum, plus four years of additional experience. (3) Graduate of a non-accredited engineering curriculum with MS or Ph.D. in engineering, plus four years of additional experience. (4) Graduate of a non-accredited engineering curriculum, including one year of experience, plus four years of additional experience. (5) Graduate of a board-approved related science curriculum with MS or Ph.D. in engineering, including 1.5 years of experience, plus four years of additional experience. (6) Graduate of an accredited four-year technology program, including four years of experience, plus four years of additional experience. (7) Graduate of a non-accredited four-year technology program, including five years of experience, plus four years of additional experience. (8) Graduate of a board-approved related science curriculum, including five years of experience, plus four years of additional experience. (9) Graduate of a two-year technology program, including six years of experience, plus four years of additional experience. (10) A non-graduate with 12 years of experience. **Examination:** Fundamentals of Engineering. Principles and Practices of Engineering. **Reciprocity:** Yes, provided applicant would have met Kansas standards on the date applicant was granted license in home state. **Fees:** Contact board for fees.

Kentucky

5598

Engineer, Professional
Kentucky State Board of Registration for Professional Engineers and Land Surveyors
160 Democrat Dr.
Frankfort, KY 40601
Phone: (502)564-2680

Credential Type: License. **Duration of License:** Two years. **Requirements:** Bachelor's degree from an accredited school of engineering. Four years of satisfactory engineering experience. **Examination:** Yes. **Reciprocity:** Yes. **Fees:** $30 application fee. $130 exam fee. $10 registration fee. $80 renewal fee.

Louisiana

5599

Engineer/Land Surveyor
State Board of Registration for Professional Engineers and Land Surveyors
1055 Saint Charles Ave., Ste. 415
New Orleans, LA 70130
Phone: (504)568-8450

Credential Type: License. **Duration of License:** Two years. **Requirements:** Bachelor's degree in engineering. A minimum of four years of acceptable engineering experience. **Examination:** Written, practical and oral exam. **Fees:** $50 exam fee. $25 license fee. $25 renewal fee.

Maine

5600

Engineer-in-Training
State Board of Registration for Professional Engineers
State House Station 92
Augusta, ME 04333
Phone: (207)289-3236

Credential Type: Engineer-in-Training Certification. **Duration of License:** One year. **Requirements:** Meet one of the following sets of requirements: (1) Have a B.S. degree in engineering or engineering technology from an approved curriculum. (2) High school graduate with eight years of qualifying experience. **Reciprocity:** Yes, based on passing a comparable written examination. **Fees:** $10 application fee. $25 exam fee for Fundamental of Engineering Examination. $20 certification fee. **Governing Statute:** Title 32, Chap. 19, Revised Statutes of 1964.

5601

Professional Engineer
State Board of Registration for Professional Engineers
State House Station 92
Augusta, ME 04333
Phone: (207)289-3236

Credential Type: Professional Engineer Registration. **Duration of License:** One year. **Requirements:** Meet one of the following sets of requirements: (1) Have a B.S. degree in engineering from an approved curriculum and four years of qualifying experience. (2) High school graduate with 12 years of qualifying experience. (3) Complete 15 years of lawful practice. **Examination:** Fundamentals of Engineering Examination. Principles and Practice of Engineering. **Reciprocity:** Yes, based on passing comparable written examinations. **Fees:** $10 application fee. $25 exam fee for Fundamentals of Engineering Examination. $75 exam fee for Principles and Practice of Engineering Examination. $20 registration fee. **Governing Statute:** Title 32, Chap. 19, Revised Statutes of 1964.

Maryland

5602

Engineer-in-Training
Board of Registration for Professional Engineers
Dept. of Licensing and Regulation
501 St. Paul Pl.
Baltimore, MD 21202-2272
Phone: (410)333-6322

Credential Type: Certification. **Requirements:** Contact licensing body for application information. **Examination:** Fundamentals of Engineering Examination. **Fees:** Contact board for fees. **Governing Statute:** Annotated Code of Maryland, Title 14. Code of Maryland Regulations, Title 09, Subtitle 23.

5603

Professional Engineer
Board of Registration for Professional Engineers
Dept. of Licensing and Regulation
501 St. Paul Pl.
Baltimore, MD 21202-2272
Phone: (410)333-6322

Credential Type: License and Registration. **Duration of License:** Two years. **Requirements:** Meet one of the following sets of requirements: (1) Graduate from a college or university upon completion of at least a four-year curriculum in engineering that is approved by the board. Complete at least four years of experience in engineering. Graduate study in engineering may count toward fulfillment of up to one year of the experience requirement. Pass examinations. (2) Graduate from a college or university upon completion of at least a four-year curriculum in engineering that is not approved by the board. Complete at least eight years of experience in engineering. Pass examinations. (3) Have at least 12 years of work experience in engineering, with at least five years of responsible charge experience. Undergraduate study in land surveying may count toward fulfillment of the experience requirement. Pass principles and practices examination. **Examination:** Fundamentals of Engineering Examination. Principles and Practices of Engineering Examination. **Fees:** $20 license fee. $65 fundamentals exam fee. $65 principles and practices exam fee. **Governing Statute:** Annotated Code of Maryland, Title 14. Code of Maryland Regulations, Title 09, Subtitle 23.

Credential Type: Temporary Permit. **Duration of License:** One year. **Authorization:** Allows a non-resident professional engineer to perform a specific job in Maryland, requiring one year or less, without Maryland registration. **Requirements:** Have a license or registration in good standing in another state. Must not have a place of business in Maryland, except for a temporary office set up exclusively for the specific job. **Governing Statute:** Annotated Code of Maryland, Title 14. Code of Maryland Regulations, Title 09, Subtitle 23.

Massachusetts

5604

Professional Engineer
Board of Professional Engineers and Land Surveyors
100 Cambridge St., Rm. 1512
Boston, MA 02202
Phone: (617)727-3055
Phone: (617)727-9956
Phone: (617)727-9957

Credential Type: Professional Engineer Registration. **Requirements:** Meet one of the following sets of requirements: (1) An ABET accredited B.S. degree in engineering and four years of qualifying experience. (2) Graduation from a non-accredited engineering curriculum or related science, or a B.S. degree in engineering technology, and eight years of acceptable engineering practice. (3) Twelve years of acceptable engi-

Michigan

Professional Engineer, continued

neering practice, including at least five years in responsible charge of engineering work. Credit may be allowed for completion of up to three years of an approved engineering curriculum. **Examination:** Fundamentals of Engineering Examination. Principles and Practice of Engineering. **Reciprocity:** Registration may be granted to applicants registered in another state who meet Massachusetts requirements. **Fees:** $60 application fee. **Governing Statute:** General Laws, Chap. 112, Section 81.

Michigan

5605

Engineer, Licensed Professional
Board of Professional Engineers
Bureau of Occupational & Professional Regulation
Dept. of Commerce
PO Box 30018
Lansing, MI 48909
Phone: (517)373-9153

Credential Type: License. **Duration of License:** Two years. **Requirements:** Minimum of eight years of acceptable experience in engineering. An acceptable bachelor's degree in engineering which may be substituted for four years of the required experience. Applicants with an acceptable master's or doctor's degree in engineering may be granted one additional year of experience credit for each degree. Up to six years of experience credit may be given for education. Submit at least five reference statements (three of the references must be licensed professional engineers, having personal knowledge of the applicant's engineering experience.) Abide by the rules and regulations of the Board. Be of good moral character. **Examination:** Written exam. **Reciprocity:** A licensed professional engineer from another state may be licensed in Michigan, if the applicant meets Michigan's requirements for licensure and has passed the two-part, 16-hour written exam in the state where originally licensed. **Fees:** $30 application processing fee. $50 exam fee (Part I). $80 exam fee (Part II). $20 initial license fee, per year. $20 renewal fee, per year. $30 reciprocity fee. **Governing Statute:** The Occupational Code, Act 299 of 1980, Article 20.

Minnesota

5606

Engineer
Board of Architecture, Engineering, Land Surveying, and Landscape Architecture
133 7th St. E., 3rd Fl.
St. Paul, MN 55101-2333
Phone: (612)296-2388

Credential Type: Professional Engineer License. **Duration of License:** Two years. **Requirements:** Bachelor of science degree from an approved engineering program. Complete four years of qualifying engineering experience subsequent to graduation. **Examination:** Fundamentals of Engineering Examination. Principles and Practice of Engineering Examination. **Reciprocity:** Yes, based on comity, provided out-of-state applicant received original license based on requirements equal to or greater than Minnesota requirements at the time of original licensure. Must also pass 4-hour exam on Minnesota land surveying law and procedures. **Fees:** $30 exam fee (Fundamentals). $70 exam fee (Principles and Practice). $58 renewal fee. $100 comity application fee. **Governing Statute:** Minnesota Statutes, 326.02-326.15, 326.53, 609.03. Minnesota Rules 1800.0200 to 1805.1600.

5607

Engineer-in-Training
Board of Architecture, Engineering, Land Surveying, and Landscape Architecture
133 7th St. E., 3rd Fl.
St. Paul, MN 55101-2333
Phone: (612)296-2388

Credential Type: Engineer-in-Training License. **Duration of License:** Two years. **Requirements:** Be a graduating senior or hold a bachelor of science degree from an approved engineering program (degrees from engineering technology programs are not acceptable). **Examination:** Fundamentals of Engineering Examination. **Reciprocity:** Yes, based on comity, provided out-of-state applicant received original license based on requirements equal to or greater than Minnesota requirements at the time of original licensure. Must also pass four-hour exam on Minnesota land surveying law and procedures. **Fees:** $30 exam fee (Fundamentals). $58 renewal fee. $100 comity application fee. **Governing Statute:** Minnesota Statutes 326.02-326.15; 326.53; 609.03. Minnesota Rules 1800.0200 to 1805.1600.

Mississippi

5608

Professional Engineer
State Board of Registration for Professional Engineers and Land Surveyors
PO Box 3
Jackson, MS 39205
Phone: (601)359-6160

Credential Type: Professional Engineer Registration. **Requirements:** Must be a state resident. Meet one of the following sets of requirements: (1) An ABET accredited B.S. degree in engineering and four years of qualifying experience. (2) Eight years of qualifying experience or a combination of experience and education. **Examination:** Fundamentals of Engineering Examination. Principles and Practice of Engineering. **Fees:** $25 application fee for Fundamentals of Engineering Examination. $75 application fee for Principles and Practice of Engineering Examination.

Missouri

5609

Engineer-in-Training
State Board of Registration for Architects, Professional Engineers, and Land Surveyors
3605 Missouri Blvd.
PO Box 184
Jefferson City, MO 65102-0184
Phone: (314)751-0047

Credential Type: Engineer-in-Training Registration. **Duration of License:** One year. **Requirements:** Contact licensing body for application information. **Examination:** Fundamentals of Engineering Examination. **Reciprocity:** Yes, based on passing comparable written examinations. **Fees:** $20 Application fee. $30 renewal fee. **Governing Statute:** Missouri Revised Statutes, Chap. 327. 4 CSR 30 (Rules of the Board).

5610

Professional Engineer
State Board of Registration for Architects, Professional Engineers, and Land Surveyors
3605 Missouri Blvd.
PO Box 184
Jefferson City, MO 65102-0184
Phone: (314)751-0047

Credential Type: Professional Engineer Registration. **Duration of License:** One year. **Requirements:** Be at least 21 years of age. Have a B.S. degree in engineering from an accredited school of engineering and four years of qualifying experience. One year of postgraduate study and each year of teaching engineering subjects may be credited toward the experience requirement. **Examination:** Fundamentals of Engineering Examination. Principles and Practice of Engineering. **Reciprocity:** Yes, based on passing comparable written examinations. **Fees:** $100 application fee. $30 renewal fee. **Governing Statute:** Missouri Revised Statutes, Chap. 327. Four CSR 30 (Rules of the Board).

Montana

5611

Engineer
Montana Board of Professional
 Engineers and Land Surveyors
111 N. Jackson
Helena, MT 59620
Phone: (406)444-4285

Credential Type: Professional Engineer. **Duration of License:** Two years. **Requirements:** Graduation from an approved engineering or engineering technology program, or the equivalent. Four years of experience on engineering projects. **Examination:** Written. **Fees:** $100 application and exam fee. $40 renewal fee. **Governing Statute:** Montana Code Annotated 37-67-301 through 37-67-332.

5612

Engineer-in-Training
Montana Board of Professional
 Engineers and Land Surveyors
111 N. Jackson
Helena, MT 59620
Phone: (406)444-4285

Credential Type: Engineer-in-Training. **Requirements:** Graduation from an approved engineering or engineering technology program, or the equivalent. **Examination:** Written. **Fees:** $40 application and exam fee. **Governing Statute:** Montana Code Annotated 37-67-301 through 37-67-332.

Nebraska

5613

Engineer
Nebraska Board of Examiners for
 Professional Engineers and
 Architects
301 Centennial Mall S.
PO Box 94751
Lincoln, NE 68509
Phone: (402)471-2021

Credential Type: License. **Duration of License:** One year. **Requirements:** 24 years of age. Must be a graduate of an accredited four-year engineering school. Must have completed four years of work experience in a reasonable position. **Examination:** Yes. **Fees:** $200 examination fees. $30 renewal fee.

Nevada

5614

Engineer
Nevada State Board of Registered
 Professional Engineers and Land
 Surveyors
1755 E. Plumb Ln., Ste. 135
Reno, NV 89502
Phone: (702)688-1231

Credential Type: License. **Requirements:** Bachelor's degree in engineering from an accredited engineering program. Four years of approved engineering work experience under a registered professional engineer. **Examination:** Yes. **Fees:** $200 application fee.

New Hampshire

5615

Professional Engineer
Joint Board of Engineers, Architects,
 Land Surveyors & Natural
 Scientists
57 Regional Drive
Concord, NH 03301
Phone: (603)271-2219

Credential Type: Professional Engineer License. **Duration of License:** Two years. **Requirements:** Good professional character. U.S. citizen. Graduate of college or engineering school. Eight years, or more, of experience and education in engineering. **Examination:** Engineering examination. **Reciprocity:** Yes, with approval. **Fees:** $50 application/license fee. $50 biennial renewal fee.

New Jersey

5616

Engineer-In-Training
State Board of Professional
 Engineers and Land Surveyors
1100 Raymond Blvd., Rm. 317
Newark, NJ 07102
Phone: (201)648-2660

Credential Type: Certificate. **Requirements:** Graduation from an approved, four-year curriculum in engineering or a related science. **Examination:** Written. **Fees:** $25 application fee. $45 examination fee. **Governing Statute:** NJSA 45:8. NJAC 13:40.

5617

Professional Engineer
State Board of Professional
 Engineers and Land Surveyors
1100 Raymond Blvd., Rm. 317
Newark, NJ 07102
Phone: (201)648-2660

Credential Type: License. **Duration of License:** Two years. **Requirements:** Graduation from an approved curriculum in engineering of four years or more plus four years of experience; or graduation from an approved science or engineering technology curriculum of four years or more plus six years of experience. Educational degree can be substituted for one or two years of experience. Must be able to speak and write the English language. **Examination:** Written. **Fees:** $60 application fee. $100 exam fee. $30 biennial registration fee. **Governing Statute:** NJSA 45:8-27. NJAC 13:40-1.

New Mexico

5618

Engineer Intern
Engineers and Surveyors Board
440 Cerrillos Rd., Ste. A
Santa Fe, NM 87501
Phone: (505)827-7316

Credential Type: Engineer Intern Registration and Certification. **Duration of License:** Indefinite. **Requirements:** Meet one of the following sets of requirements: (1) Graduate of a four-year board-approved engineering curriculum. (2) Graduate of an unapproved engineering or related science curriculum. Complete four years of post-degree engineering experience. **Examination:** Fundamentals of Engineering Examination. **Reciprocity:** Yes, provided that applicant was registered under qualifications comparable to or exceeding New Mexico's

Engineer Intern, continued

at the time of initial registration. **Fees:** $65 application and exam fee. $65 additional exam fee. $15 certification fee. **Governing Statute:** New Mexico Engineering and Surveying Practice Act, Sections 61-23-1 through 61-23-32 NMSA (1978). Rules 89-1 and 89-2.

5619

Professional Engineer
Engineers and Surveyors Board
440 Cerrillos Rd., Ste. A
Santa Fe, NM 87501
Phone: (505)827-7316

Credential Type: Professional Engineer Registration. **Duration of License:** One year. **Requirements:** Meet one of the following sets of requirements: (1) Graduate of a four-year board-approved engineering curriculum. Complete four years of post-degree engineering experience. (2) Graduate of an unapproved engineering or related science curriculum. Complete eight years of post-degree engineering experience. **Examination:** Principles and Practice of Engineering. **Reciprocity:** Yes, provided that applicant was registered under qualifications comparable to or exceeding New Mexico's at the time of initial registration. **Fees:** $100 application fee. $65 exam fee. $40 registration fee. $40 renewal fee. **Governing Statute:** New Mexico Engineering and Surveying Practice Act, Sections 61-23-1 through 61-23-32 NMSA (1978). Rules 89-1 and 89-2.

New York

5620

Engineer, Professional
State Education Dept.
Div. of Professional Licensing Services
Cultural Education Center
Empire State Plaza
Albany, NY 12230
Phone: (518)474-3833

Credential Type: License. **Duration of License:** Three years. **Requirements:** Bachelor's Degree in engineering program approved by the licensing agency. **Examination:** National examination.

North Carolina

5621

Engineer-in-Training
North Carolina State Board of Registration for Professional Engineers and Land Surveyors
3620 Six Forks Rd.
Raleigh, NC 27609
Phone: (919)781-9499

Credential Type: Engineer-in Training. **Requirements:** For students within three years of graduation, or engineering graduates who have graduated within the previous two years from an accredited curriculum.

5622

Professional Engineer
North Carolina State Board of Registration for Professional Engineers and Land Surveyors
3620 Six Forks Rd.
Raleigh, NC 27609
Phone: (919)781-9499

Credential Type: Professional Engineer License. **Duration of License:** One year. **Requirements:** High school diploma or equivalent. Eight years of progressive engineering experience under the supervision of a registered professional engineer before qualifying for Exam I. Upon passing Exam I and a minimum of 12 years of experience the applicant is eligible to take Exam II. Experience requirements vary depending on the applicant's educational level. 18 years of age. **Examination:** Two eight-hour national exams. **Fees:** $100 application and exam fee. $3 professional engineering application kit fee. $30 renewal fee.

North Dakota

5623

Professional Engineer
State Board of Registration for Professional Engineers and Land Surveyors
Box 1357
Bismarck, ND 58502-1357
Phone: (701)258-0786

Credential Type: Professional Engineer Registration. **Duration of License:** One year. **Requirements:** Bachelor's of science degree in engineering and four years of experience. **Examination:** Fundamentals of Engineering. Principles and Practice of Land Engineering. **Reciprocity:** Yes, with all 50 states. **Fees:** $85 exam fee. $27.50 registration fee. $27.50 renewal fee.

Ohio

5624

Engineer-in-Training
State Board of Registration for Professional Engineers and Land Surveyors
77 S. High St., 16th Fl.
Columbus, OH 43266-0314
Phone: (614)466-8948
Fax: (614)644-9048

Credential Type: Engineer-in-Training Certification. **Duration of License:** One year. **Requirements:** Be a recent graduate, a student who is a candidate for graduation, or complete four or more years of the curriculum of a recognized college of engineering. **Examination:** Fundamentals of Engineering Examination. **Reciprocity:** Yes, based on passing comparable written examinations. **Fees:** $25 application fee. $16 renewal fee. **Governing Statute:** Chap. 4733, R.C. Registration Laws. Chap. 4733, A.C. Board Rules.

5625

Professional Engineer
State Board of Registration for Professional Engineers and Land Surveyors
77 S. High St., 16th Fl
Columbus, OH 43266-0314
Phone: (614)466-8948
Fax: (614)644-9048

Credential Type: Professional Engineer Registration. **Duration of License:** One year. **Requirements:** Meet one of the following sets of requirements: (1) Have a B.S. degree in engineering from an accredited school of engineering and four years of qualifying experience. (2) Complete four or more academic years from a non-approved college curriculum in engineering, engineering technology, or a related science. Have eight years of qualifying experience. **Examination:** Fundamentals of Engineering Examination. Principles and Practice of Engineering. **Reciprocity:** Yes, based on passing comparable written examinations. **Fees:** $25 application fee. $30 registration fee. $16 renewal fee. $105 reciprocity fee. **Governing Statute:** Chap. 4733, R.C. Registration Laws. Chap. 4733, A.C. Board Rules.

Oklahoma

5626

Engineer Intern
Oklahoma State Board of Registration for Professional Engineers and Land Surveyors
201 N.E. 27th St., Ste. 120
Oklahoma City, OK 73105
Phone: (405)521-2874

Credential Type: Registration. **Duration of License:** Two years. **Requirements:** Degree in engineering or other science-related curriculum. State resident. **Examination:** Fundamentals of Engineering. **Fees:** $20 exam fee. $15 application fee. $20 renewal fee.

5627

Engineer, Registered Professional
Oklahoma State Board of Registration for Professional Engineers and Land Surveyors
201 N.E. 27th St., Ste. 120
Oklahoma City, OK 73105
Phone: (405)521-2874

Credential Type: Registration. **Duration of License:** Two years. **Requirements:** Degree in engineering or other science-related area, or a long-established practice. State resident. **Examination:** Principles and Practice of Engineering. **Fees:** $50 exam fee. $50 application fee. $50 renewal fee.

Oregon

5628

Engineer, Professional
Oregon State Board of Engineering Examiners
750 Front St. NE, Ste. 240
Salem, OR 97310
Phone: (503)378-4180

Credential Type: License. **Duration of License:** Two years. **Requirements:** Eight years of experience or a bachelor of science degree in engineering and four years of experience. **Examination:** Yes. **Fees:** $80 exam fee. $5 certificate fee. $40 renewal fee. **Governing Statute:** ORS 672.002 to 672.325.

Pennsylvania

5629

Professional Engineer
State Registration Board for Professional Engineers and Professional Land Surveyors
Bureau of Professional and Occupational Affairs
Dept. of State
Transportation and Safety Bldg., 6th Fl.
Harrisburg, PA 17120
Phone: (717)787-8503

Credential Type: Professional Engineer License. **Duration of License:** Two years. **Requirements:** At least 25 years of age. Good moral character and repute. Able to speak and write the English language. Graduate from an approved four-year engineering school, or complete at least eight years of progressive experience in engineering which approximates the education received in a four-year engineering course. Complete an engineering fundamentals examination and become certified as an engineer-in-training. As an engineer-in-training, the applicant must have an additional four years progressive experience in engineering, or the teaching of engineering, under the supervision of a professional engineer. Must also pass examination in engineering principles and practices. **Examination:** State examination.

Rhode Island

5630

Engineer
State Board of Registration for Professional Engineers
Rhode Island Dept. of Business Regulation
233 Richmond St.
Providence, RI 02903
Phone: (401)277-2565

Credential Type: Professional Engineer License. **Duration of License:** Two years. **Requirements:** Graduate from an ABET accredited Engineering program. Hold a NCESS certificate. Minimum four years experience in engineering. Alternative licensing requirements are available through the board. **Examination:** National Council of Examiners for Engineering and Surveying (NCESS) Professional Examination. **Reciprocity:** Yes. **Fees:** $100 application fee. $250 license renewal fee.

5631

Engineer-In-Training
State Board of Registration for Professional Engineers
Rhode Island State Dept. of Business Regulation
233 Richmond St.
Providence, RI 02903
Phone: (401)277-2565

Credential Type: Engineer-In-Training Certificate. **Duration of License:** 12 years. **Requirements:** Graduate from an engineering program accredited by the Accreditation Board for Engineering and Technology, Inc. (ABET). Alternative licensing requirements are available through the board. **Examination:** National Council of Examiners for Engineering and Surveying (NCEES) Examination "fundamentals" section. **Reciprocity:** Yes. **Fees:** $100 application fee. $40 engineer-in-training certificate fee.

South Carolina

5632

Engineer
South Carolina Board of Registration for Engineers and Land Surveyors
PO Drawer 50408
Columbia, SC 29250
Phone: (803)734-9166

Credential Type: Professional Engineer License. **Duration of License:** One year. **Requirements:** Graduation from an approved four-year, engineering curriculum, plus four years of experience in engineering work; or graduation from a non-approved curriculum, plus eight years of experience. **Examination:** Yes. **Fees:** $50 application fee. $45 renewal fee.

5633

Engineer-In-Training
South Carolina Board of Registration for Engineers and Land Surveyors
PO Drawer 50408
Columbia, SC 29250
Phone: (803)734-9166

Credential Type: Engineer-in-Training Certificate. **Requirements:** Graduation from an approved, four-year engineering curriculum; or graduation from a non-approved, four-year engineering curriculum plus four years of experience. **Examination:** Yes. **Fees:** $35 certificate fee.

South Dakota

5634

Engineer-in-Training
Commission of Engineering, Architectural, and Land Surveying Examiners
2040 W. Main St., Ste. 304
Rapid City, SD 57702-2447
Phone: (605)394-2510

Credential Type: Engineer-in-Training Certification. **Duration of License:** Unlimited. **Requirements:** Be in the senior year of an ABET engineering school. **Examination:** Fundamentals of Engineering. **Reciprocity:** Yes, if state had equal requirements at time of certification. **Fees:** $35 exam fee.

5635

Professional Engineer
Commission of Engineering, Architectural, and Land Surveying Examiners
2040 W. Main St., Ste. 304
Rapid City, SD 57702-2447
Phone: (605)394-2510

Credential Type: Registration. **Duration of License:** Two years. **Requirements:** Meet one of the following sets of requirements: (1) Have a five-year ABET engineering M.S. or Ph.D. degree and three years experience. (2) Have a four-year ABET engineering B.S. degree and four years experience. (3) Have a four-year ABET technology B.S. degree and five years experience. (4) Complete a four-year non-ABET engineering program and six years experience. (5) Have two years of a related vocational-technical curriculum and nine years experience. (6) No schooling and 12 years experience. **Examination:** Principles and Practice of Engineering. **Reciprocity:** Yes, if state had equal requirements at time of registration. **Fees:** $100 application fee. $70 exam fee. $60 renewal fee.

Tennessee

5636

Engineer
Board of Architectural and Engineering Examiners
Volunteer Plaza Bldg., 3rd Fl.
500 James Robertson Pky.
Nashville, TN 37243
Phone: (615)741-3221

Credential Type: License. **Requirements:** Four years experience after graduation with Accreditation. Minimum of eight years with engineering related science degree. **Examination:** National Council of Engineering Examining Services (NCEES) Fundamentals of Engineering; NCEES Principles and Practice of Engineering. **Reciprocity:** Yes, if state meets Tennessee requirements. **Fees:** $165 Application. $100 If no examination is required.

Texas

5637

Engineer
State Board of Registration for Professional Engineers
PO Drawer 18329
Austin, TX 78760
Phone: (512)440-7723

Credential Type: Engineer License. **Duration of License:** One year. **Requirements:** Graduation from a four-year, approved curriculum in engineering and an additional four years or more of experience in the active practice of engineering work; or graduation from a four-year curriculum in engineering or related science and an additional eight years or more of active practice in engineering work. **Examination:** Fundamentals of Engineering. Principles and Practices of Engineering. **Fees:** $50 registration fee. $100 exam fee. $75 renewal fee. **Governing Statute:** VACS 3271a, 22 TAC 131.

5638

Engineer-In-Training
State Board of Registration for Professional Engineers
PO Drawer 18329
Austin, TX 78760
Phone: (512)440-7723

Credential Type: Engineer-in-Training. **Requirements:** Graduation from an engineering or related science curriculum. **Examination:** Fundamentals of Engineering. **Governing Statute:** VACS 3271a, 22 TAC 131.

Utah

5639

Engineer
Dept. of Commerce
Div. of Occupational and Professional Licensing
160 E. 300 S.
PO Box 45802
Salt Lake City, UT 84145
Phone: (801)530-6628

Credential Type: Engineer License. **Requirements:** Must hold an Engineer-in-Training certificate and have four years of engineering experience. **Examination:** Yes. **Fees:** $100 license fee. $30 renewal fee.

5640

Engineer-in-Training
Dept. of Commerce
Div. of Occupational and Professional Licensing
160 E. 300 S.
PO Box 45802
Salt Lake City, UT 84145
Phone: (801)530-6628

Credential Type: Certificate. **Requirements:** To qualify for the Engineer-in-Training Certificate, one must be a graduate of an approved engineering curriculum; or without graduation from an approved engineering curriculum, have four years of satisfactory experience. **Examination:** Yes. **Fees:** $30 Engineer-in-Training certificate fee.

Vermont

5641

Engineer-in-training
Board of Professional Engineering
Pavilion Office Bldg.
Montpelier, VT 05602
Phone: (802)828-2372

Credential Type: License. **Duration of License:** 12 years. **Requirements:** Good moral character and reputation. **Examination:** Yes. **Reciprocity:** Yes. **Fees:** $25 Application fee. $40 Exam fee. $5 Replacement of license. **Governing Statute:** Title 26, VSA Sections 1161-1194.

5642

Engineer, Professional
Board of Professional Engineering
Pavilion Office Bldg.
Montpelier, VT 05602
Phone: (802)828-2372

Credential Type: License. **Duration of License:** Two years. **Requirements:** Graduate of four year engineering program and four years of practice; or 12 years approved practice; or 20 years approved practice with 10 years in responsible charge; or registered in another state. **Examination:** Yes. **Reciprocity:** Yes. **Fees:** $100 Exam. $20 Renewal. $50 Application for initial license. $25 Late renewal penalty. $5 Replacement of lost license. $25 Additional specialty certification. **Governing Statute:** Title 26, VSA Sections 1161-1194.

Virginia

5643

Engineer
State Board of Architects,
 Professional Engineers, Land
 Surveyors & Certified Landscape
 Architects
3600 W. Broad St.
Richmond, VA 23230
Phone: (804)367-8514

Credential Type: License. **Requirements:** Must submit three references. Must have college degrees in engineering with four or more years of work experience **Examination:** Yes. **Reciprocity:** Yes. **Fees:** $40 application fee. $180 exam fee.

Washington

5644

Engineer
Board of Registration for
 Professional Engineers and Land
 Surveyors
Dept. of Licensing
Professional Licensing Services
PO Box 9649
Olympia, WA 98507-9649
Phone: (206)753-6966
Phone: (206)753-3634

Credential Type: Engineer License. **Duration of License:** Two years. **Requirements:** Graduate an approved engineering school and have four years experience or have eight years of engineering experience. **Examination:** Written examination. **Reciprocity:** Yes. **Fees:** $100 initial license fee. $90 renewal fee. $90 examination retake fee. $100 reciprocal license fee.

5645

Engineer-in-Training
Board of Registration for
 Professional Engineers and Land
 Surveyors
Dept. of Licensing
PO Box 9649
Olympia, WA 98507-9649
Phone: (206)753-6966
Phone: (206)753-3634

Credential Type: Engineer-in-Training License. **Duration of License:** Indefinite. **Requirements:** Graduate from an approved engineering school or have four years of engineering experience. **Examination:** Written examination. **Fees:** $50 license fee. $50 examination retake fee.

West Virginia

5646

Engineer
State Board of Registration for
 Professional Engineers
608 Union Bldg.
Charleston, WV 25301
Phone: (304)348-3554

Credential Type: License. **Duration of License:** One year. **Requirements:** State resident. Graduate of Board approved curricula. Four years experience. Never convicted of a felony. **Examination:** Yes. **Fees:** $25 Application. $25 License.

Wisconsin

5647

Designer
Regulations and Licensing Dept.
Architects & Engineers Board
PO Box 8935
Madison, WI 53708-8935
Phone: (608)266-8609

Credential Type: License. **Authorization:** Covers designers of engineering and related systems. **Requirements:** Eight years of experience with credit allowed for education or apprenticeship. **Examination:** Yes. **Exemptions:** Applicants with 12 years of experience and who are at least 35 years of age are exempt from the exam. **Reciprocity:** Yes.

5648

Engineer
Regulations and Licensing Dept.
Architects & Engineers Board
PO Box 8935
Madison, WI 53708-8935
Phone: (608)266-8609

Credential Type: Engineer License. **Requirements:** Accreditation Board for Engineering and Technology (ABET) degree and four years of experience; or eight years of experience with credit allowed for education. **Examination:** Written. **Exemptions:** Applicants with an ABET degree or equivalent with eight years of experience are exempt from the exam. **Reciprocity:** Yes.

5649

Engineer-in-Training
Regulations and Licensing Dept.
Architects & Engineers Board
PO Box 8935
Madison, WI 53708-8935
Phone: (608)266-8609

Credential Type: Engineer-in-training. **Requirements:** Contact licensing body for application information.

Wyoming

5650

Engineer, Professional
State Board for Professional
 Engineers and Land Surveyors
Herschler Bldg., Rm. 4135 E.
122 W. 25th St.
Cheyenne, WY 82002
Phone: (307)777-6155

Credential Type: License. **Duration of License:** Two years. **Requirements:** Engineer—Must be a Registered Engineer in training, must be actively engaged in education and/or experience for at least an additional four years beyond that required for an engineer in training, pass a written examination or qualify by reciprocity. Engineer in Training—Must hold a bachelors of science degree in an engineering curriculum, pass a written examination; or, have eight years of education and/or experience in engineering work and pass the examination. **Examination:** Yes. **Reciprocity:** Yes. **Fees:** $75 Engineer license. $30 Engineer in Training License. $25 UW student. $70 Examination for Engineer, $45 for Engineer in Training. $45 Renewal.

Property and Real Estate Managers

The following states grant licenses in this occupational category as of the date of publication: District of Columbia, Florida, Hawaii, Oregon, South Carolina, South Dakota.

District of Columbia

5651

Property Manager
License and Certification Div.
Occupational and Professional Licensure Administration
Consumer and Regulatory Affairs Dept.
PO Box 37200
Washington, DC 20013-7200
Phone: (202)727-7823
Phone: (202)727-7480

Alternate Information: 614 H St., NW, Washington, DC 20001.

Credential Type: License. **Duration of License:** Two years. **Requirements:** Submit application and pay fee. Renewal requires 12 hours of continuing education. **Examination:** Written examination. **Exemptions:** If applicant was actively engaged in the practice of property management in the District of Columbia for four years, a license may be granted without examination. **Fees:** $50 application fee. $130 license fee. $160 renewal fee. $60 fund fee. **Governing Statute:** Municipal Regulations, Title 17, Chap. 26.

Florida

5652

Condominium Manager
Dept. of Professional Regulation
Div. of Real Estate
PO Box 1900
Orlando, FL 32802-1900
Phone: (407)423-6071

Credential Type: Condominium Manager License. **Requirements:** Contact licensing body for application information.

Hawaii

5653

Condominium Managing Agent
Hawaii Real Estate Commission
Dept. of Commerce and Consumer Affairs
PO Box 3469
Honolulu, HI 96801
Phone: (808)548-4100
Phone: (808)548-3201

Credential Type: License. **Requirements:** Hawaii real estate broker license. Business or trade name approved under the real estate broker license. Fidelity bond. **Fees:** $25 registration fee. $15—$30 Compliance Resolution Fund fee.

Oregon

5654

Real Estate Property Manager
Oregon Real Estate Agency
158 12th St. NE
Salem, OR 97310
Phone: (503)378-4170

Credential Type: License. **Duration of License:** Two years. **Requirements:** 18 years of age. Successful completion of required courses. **Examination:** Yes. **Fees:** $50 exam fee. $150 license fee. $150 renewal fee. **Governing Statute:** ORS 696.020.

South Carolina

5655

Real Estate Property Manager
South Carolina Real Estate Commission
1201 Main St., Ste. 1500
Columbia, SC 29201
Phone: (803)737-0700

Credential Type: License. **Requirements:** 21 years of age. State resident. Thirty hours of real estate property management instruction in an accredited college or approved school. A degree in real estate from an accredited college, or a law degree, or three years of equivalent experience in property management activities. **Examination:** Yes. **Fees:** $50 license fee.

South Dakota

5656

Real Estate Property Manager
South Dakota Real Estate Commission
PO Box 490
Pierre, SD 57501-0490
Phone: (605)773-3600
Phone: (605)773-3150

Credential Type: Real Estate Property Manager License. **Duration of License:** Two years. **Requirements:** Submit application and pay fees. **Examination:** State-administered property manager's examination. **Fees:** $100 application and license fee. $80 renewal fee.

Psychologists

The following states grant licenses in this occupational category as of the date of publication:

Alabama	District of	Iowa	Minnesota	New Mexico	Rhode Island	Washington
Alaska	Columbia	Kansas	Mississippi	New York	South Carolina	West Virginia
Arizona	Florida	Kentucky	Missouri	North Carolina	South Dakota	Wisconsin
Arkansas	Georgia	Louisiana	Montana	North Dakota	Tennessee	Wyoming
California	Hawaii	Maine	Nebraska	Ohio	Texas	
Colorado	Idaho	Maryland	Nevada	Oklahoma	Utah	
Connecticut	Illinois	Massachusetts	New Hampshire	Oregon	Vermont	
Delaware	Indiana	Michigan	New Jersey	Pennsylvania	Virginia	

Alabama

5657

Psychologist
Alabama Board of Examiners in Psychology
821 S. Perry St.
Montgomery, AL 36101-0098
Phone: (205)242-4127

Credential Type: License. **Duration of License:** One year. **Requirements:** 21 years of age. Must hold a doctorate degree in psychology from an accredited institution. **Examination:** Yes. **Fees:** $150 registration fee. $150 examination fee. $100 renewal fee. $50 continuing education fee.

5658

School Psychometrist
State Dept. of Education
Montgomery, AL 36130
Phone: (205)242-9977

Credential Type: Class A School Psychometrist Professional Certificate. **Requirements:** Eligibility for a Class B Professional Certificate. Two years appropriate professional experience, one of which must be in teaching. Master's degree in school psychometry approved by the Alabama State Board of Education or the National Council for Accreditation of Teacher Education or the National Association of State Directors of Teacher Education and Certification or ICP.

Credential Type: Class AA School Psychologist and Psychometrist Professional Certificate. **Requirements:** Eligibility for Class A School Psychometrist Professional Certificate. Completion of a sixth year program approved by the Alabama State Board of Education.

Alaska

5659

Psychological Associate
Dept. of Commerce and Economic Development
Div. of Occupational Licensing
Board of Psychologists and Psychological Associate Examiners
PO Box 110806
Juneau, AK 99811-0806
Phone: (907)465-2551

Credential Type: Psychological Associate license. **Requirements:** Masters degree. Three years of post-degree experience in supervision. **Examination:** Examination for Professional Practice in Psychology (EPPP) and Law/Ethics. **Governing Statute:** AS 08.86 Assoc AS 08.86.162 Psy AS 08.86.130.

5660

Psychologist
Dept. of Commerce and Economic Development
Div. of Occupational Licensing
Board of Psychologists and Psychological Associate Examiners
PO Box 110806
Juneau, AK 99811-0806
Phone: (907)465-2551

Credential Type: Psychologist license. **Requirements:** Doctorate degree. One year of post-doctoral experience in supervision. Certification by American Board of Professional Psychology qualifies candidate for EPPP exam. **Examination:** Examination for Professional Practice in Psychology (EPPP) and Law/Ethics. **Governing Statute:** AS 08.86 Assoc AS 08.86.162 Psy AS 08.86.130.

Arizona

5661

Psychologist
Arizona Board of Psychological Examiners
1645 W. Jefferson, Rm. 410
Phoenix, AZ 85007
Phone: (602)542-3095

Credential Type: Psychologist license. **Duration of License:** Two years. **Requirements:** Doctorate degree. Certification by American Board of Professional Psychology qualifies candidate for EPPP exam. Renewal requires 60 continuing education Units. **Examination:** Examination for Professional Practice in Psychology (EPPP). **Governing Statute:** Arizona REV.STAT.ANN. 32-2061.

5662

School Psychologist
Teacher Certification Unit
PO Box 25609
1535 W. Jefferson
Phoenix, AZ 85002
Phone: (602)542-4368

Credential Type: School Psychologist Certificate. **Duration of License:** Six years. **Requirements:** Master's or higher degree from a regionally accredited institution. 60 graduate semester hours. Completion of an approved program in school psychology from a regionally accredited institution or written verification that a diploma in psychology was granted by the American Board of Professional Psychology. Internship of 1,000 clock hours in school psychology within a program accredited by the American Psychological Association (APA) or the National Association of School Psychologists (NASP).

Arizona

5663

School Psychometrist (K-12)
Teacher Certification Unit
PO Box 25609
1535 W. Jefferson
Phoenix, AZ 85002
Phone: (602)542-4368

Credential Type: School Psychometrist Certificate (K-12). **Duration of License:** Six years. **Requirements:** Master's or higher degree from a regionally accredited institution. 30 graduate semester hours. Completion of a school psychology program accredited by the American Psychological Association (APA) or National Association of School Psychologists (NASP) or a school psychology program from a regionally accredited institution. Practicum of 100 clock hours in school psychometry in a school psychology program accredited by APA or NASP.

Arkansas

5664

Psychological Examiner
Arkansas Board of Examiners in Psychology
1515 Bldg. Ste. 315
1515 W. 7th St.
Little Rock, AR 72202
Phone: (501)682-6167

Credential Type: License. **Requirements:** Masters degree in Psychology or closely related field. Serve an internship under a licensed examiner of at least 500 hours. **Examination:** Yes. **Fees:** $130 Written examination. $50 Application. $50 License. $80 Renewal.

5665

Psychologist
Arkansas Board of Examiners in Psychology
1515 Bldg. Ste. 315
1515 W. 7th St.
Little Rock, AR 72202
Phone: (501)682-6167

Credential Type: License. **Duration of License:** One year. **Requirements:** Doctoral degree in Psychology or a closely related field. 2000 hours of internship experience. **Examination:** Yes. **Fees:** $130 Written examination. $50 Application. $50 License. $80 Renewal.

California

5666

Educational Psychologist
Board of Behavioral Science Examiners
400 R St., Ste. 3150
Sacramento, CA 95814-6200
Phone: (916)445-4933

Credential Type: License. **Requirements:** Contact licensing body for application information.

5667

Psychological Assistant
Medical Board of Psychology
Board of Psychology
1426 Howe Ave., Ste. 54
Sacramento, CA 95825-3236
Phone: (916)920-6383

Credential Type: Psychological Assistant license. **Requirements:** Masters degree. **Governing Statute:** CAL. Bus. & Prof. Code Section 2900 (West).

5668

Psychologist
Medical Board of Psychology
Board of Psychology
1426 Howe Ave., Ste. 54
Sacramento, CA 95825-3236
Phone: (916)920-6383

Credential Type: Psychologist license. **Requirements:** Doctorate degree. One year of post-doctoral experience. Two years of experience in supervision. **Examination:** Examination for Professional Practice in Psychology (EPPP) and Oral. **Governing Statute:** CAL. Bus. & Prof. Code Section 2900 (West).

Colorado

5669

Psychologist
Colorado State Board of Psychologist Examiners
1560 Broadway, Ste. 1340
Denver, CO 80202
Phone: (303)866-3248

Credential Type: Psychologist license. **Requirements:** Doctorate degree. 12 months of experience (1,500 hours). 75 hours of experience in supervision. Certification by American Board of Professional Psychology qualifies candidate for endorsement Licensure. **Examination:** Examination for Professional Practice in Psychology (EPPP), Oral, and Jurisprudence (clinical & counseling areas). **Governing Statute:** COLO.REV.STAT. 12-43-101, et.seq.

5670

School Special Service Associate
Teacher Certification
State Dept. of Education
201 E. Colifax
Denver, CO 80203
Phone: (303)866-6628

Credential Type: Special Service Certificate—Type E. **Duration of License:** Five years. **Authorization:** Authorizes service in specialized areas including Audiology, Therapy, Nursing, Psychology, Social Work, and Speech Corrections. **Requirements:** Bachelor's degree. Must complete a program in one of the following Special Service endorsement areas: Audiologist, Occupational Therapist, Peripatology, Physical Therapist, School Nurse, School Psychologist, School Social Worker, or Speech Correctionist/Language Specialist. Passage of the spelling, language, and mathematics sections of Level 19 of the California Achievement Test and oral English competence which is met by having a B—or better in a public speaking course taken from a regionally accredited college or passing an oral English panel assessment. Official, original transcripts from all applicable institutions. **Examination:** California Achievement Test Level 19 (spelling, language, and mathematics sections) **Fees:** $45 initial certification application fee. $40 fingerprint card processing fee.

Connecticut

5671

Psychologist
Connecticut Psychology Licensure
150 Washington St.
Hartford, CT 06106
Phone: (203)566-1039

Credential Type: Psychologist license. **Requirements:** Doctorate degree. Two years of experience, one of which must be post-doctoral. Certification by American Board of Professional Psychology waives the Examination for Professional Practice in Psychology (EPPP) exam. **Examination:** EPPP and Connecticut Jurisprudence. **Governing Statute:** CONN GEN. STAT. ch. 383, 20-186-20-195.

Delaware

5672

Psychological Assistant
Delaware Board of Examiners of Psychologists
Margaret O'Neil Bldg.
PO Box 1401
Dover, DE 19903
Phone: (302)739-4521

Credential Type: Psychological Assistant license. **Duration of License:** Two years. **Authorization:** Must work under the direct supervision of a licensed psychologist. **Requirements:** Masters degree in a mental health related field. Renewal requires 20 hours of continuing education. **Governing Statute:** DEL. CODE ANN. Title 24/Chapter 35.

5673

Psychologist
Delaware Board of Examiners of Psychologists
Margaret O'Neil Bldg.
PO Box 1401
Dover, DE 19903
Phone: (302)739-4521

Credential Type: Psychologist license. **Duration of License:** Two years. **Requirements:** Doctorate degree. Two years of post-doctoral experience in supervision (3,000 hours). Renewal requires 40 hours of continuing education. **Examination:** Examination for Professional Practice in Psychology (EPPP). **Governing Statute:** DEL. CODE ANN. Title 24/Chapter 35.

District of Columbia

5674

Psychologist
District of Columbia Board of Psychology
614 H St., NW, Rm. 923
Washington, DC 20001
Phone: (202)727-7468

Credential Type: Psychologist license. **Duration of License:** Two years. **Requirements:** Doctoral degree. Two years of post-doctoral experience (4,000 hours of psychological practice). Renewal requires 15 hours of continuing education per year, 30 hours within two year licensing cycle. **Examination:** Examination for Professional Practice in Psychology (EPPP) and District objective exam on Health Occupations Revision Act, Ethics and D.C. Laws which regulate practice. **Governing Statute:** D.C. Law 6-99 (District of Columbia Health Occupation Revision Act of 1985).

Florida

5675

Psychologist
Florida Board of Psychological Examiners
1940 N. Monroe St., Ste. 412
Tallahassee, FL 32399-0788
Phone: (904)922-6728

Credential Type: Psychologist license. **Duration of License:** Two years. **Requirements:** Doctoral degree. Two years of experience in supervision, one of which must be at the post-doctoral level. Renewal requires 40 hours of continuing education. **Examination:** Examination for Professional Practice in Psychology (EPPP) and Jurisprudence. **Governing Statute:** Chapter 490, Florida Statutes.

Georgia

5676

Psychologist
Georgia Board of Exam. of Psychologists
166 Pryor St., SW
Atlanta, GA 30303
Phone: (404)656-3989

Credential Type: Psychologist license. **Requirements:** Doctorate degree. Two years of experience in supervision (1 year internship). One year of post-doctoral experience. Renewal requires 40 hours of continuing education (including three hours of Ethics). Certification by American Board of Professional Psychology waives Examination for Professional Practice in Psychology (EPPP) exam (written). **Examination:** EPPP and Oral. **Governing Statute:** GA. CODE Title 43, Chapter 39.

5677

School Service Associate
Div. of Teacher Education
State Dept. of Education
1452 Twin Towers East
Atlanta, GA 30334-5070
Phone: (404)656-2406

Credential Type: School Service Certificate. **Authorization:** Authorizes the holder to administer school services in one of the following occupations: Audiologist, Media Specialist, School Counselor, School Nutrition Director, School Psychometrist, School Psychologist, School Social Worker/Visiting Teacher, or Speech and Language Pathologist. **Requirements:** Bachelor's degree is required for Nutrition Director, Speech/ Language Pathologist and Media Specialist. Master's degree and sixth year program is required for Psychologist. All other occupations require a master's degree or fifth year program. Media Specialist requires Initial Teaching Certificate. A staff development program in the Identification and Education of Children with Special Needs and a certification test is required at the master's degree level in the field of School Counseling. Three years of acceptable school experience are required of in the fields of nutrition and counseling.

Hawaii

5678

Psychologist
Hawaii Board of Psychology
1010 Richards St.
PO Box 3469
Honolulu, HI 96801
Phone: (808)548-7697

Credential Type: License. **Duration of License:** Six months. **Requirements:** Doctoral Degree in psychology or educational psychology from an approved program. At least a one-year internship under a licensed psychologist's supervision or two years of experience in supervised work. **Examination:** Examination for Professional Practice of Psychology. State jurisprudence exam. Oral interview. **Exemptions:** There is licensure through exam waiver. **Fees:** $50 application fee. $150 exam fee. $30 temporary permit fee. $30 license fee. $25—$50 Compliance Resolution Fund fee. $50 renewal fee.

Idaho

5679

Psychologist
Idaho Board of Psychologists Examiners
2417 Bank Dr., No. 312
Boise, ID 83705
Phone: (208)334-3233

Credential Type: Psychologist license. **Requirements:** Doctorate degree. Two years of experience in supervision. Renewal requires 20 hours of continuing education. **Examination:** Examination for Professional Practice in Psychology (EPPP). **Governing Statute:** IDAHO CODE Section 54-23.

Idaho

5680

School Psychological Examiner
Certification Analyst
State Dept. of Education
L. B. Jordan Office Bldg.
Boise, ID 83720
Phone: (208)334-3475

Credential Type: Psychological Examiner Endorsement. **Requirements:** Master's degree in Education or Psychology. Completion of State Board of Education approved by Psychological Examiner training program. Completion of a 200 clock-hour internship under supervision of the training institution and a certified school psychologist. Nonrenewable.

5681

School Psychologist
Certification Analyst
State Dept. of Education
L. B. Jordan Office Bldg.
Boise, ID 83720
Phone: (208)334-3475

Credential Type: License. **Duration of License:** Five years. **Requirements:** Master's degree program of 30 semester hours in education or psychology, plus 30 hours in school psychology. 60 semester hours in master's degree program in School Psychology or 60 semester hours in School Psychology Specialist program which did not require a master's degree. Laboratory experience. A 300 clock-hour internship. Certificate may be renewed upon completion of at least six semester credits of college courses within the period of validity.

Illinois

5682

Licensed Clinical Psychologist
Clinical Psychologists Licensing and Disciplinary Committee
320 W. Washington St.
Springfield, IL 62786
Phone: (217)785-0872

Credential Type: Licensed Clinical Psychologist license. **Requirements:** Doctorate degree. Two years of satisfactory supervised experience in clinical or counseling psychology, at least one of which is postdoctoral. Certification by American Board of Professional Psychology waives EPPP exam. **Examination:** Examination for Professional Practice in Psychology (EPPP). **Governing Statute:** ILL.REV.STAT. 1989 ch. 111, par 5351-5379, Inclusive.

5683

School Psychologist
Certification and Placement Section
100 N. First St.
Springfield, IL 62777
Phone: (217)782-4321

Credential Type: School Psychologist Certificate. **Requirements:** Good character. Good health. At least 19 years of age. Citizen of the U.S. Teaching certificate. Master's or higher degree in psychology or educational psychology with specialization in school psychology. Must have a minimum of 60 semester hours of course work, field experiences, and internship at the graduate level. Required academic work may be completed through titled courses, seminars, or practica. Graduate credit may also be earned for academic course work in related fields (ie; special education and educational psychology). Applicants must complete the following semester hours of course work: Educational Foundations 3; Psychological Foundations 9; Professional School Psychology 2; Assessment (Ages 0-21) 8; Intervention (from two of the following: Behavior Management/Modification, Counseling and/or Psychotherapeutic Methods, and Consultation) 6; Statistics, Measurement, and Research 3; Field Experience (to include a minimum of 250 clock hours in a school setting and/or child study center) 2; and a Supervised Internship (full school year and at least 1200 clock hours) 4.

Must have at least one year of supervised professional psychological experience with children of school age, preferably in a school setting and under the supervision of an individual qualified as a supervising psychologist. Must have proficiency in individual psychological examination of children including educational diagnostic techniques including; ability to plan and carry out a diagnosis adequate for each particular case; ability to handle staff conferences, interpret data, and write adequate reports; and have proficiency in counseling and other functions that may be needed to supplement the psychological assessment of children. Must have ability and willingness to work according to the high standards and competencies that comply with the code of ethics or recognized professional associations. Must pass required sections of the Illinois Certification Test. **Examination:** Illinois Certification Test. **Fees:** $44 per section of the Illinois Certification Test.

Indiana

5684

Psychologist
Indiana State Psychology Board
Health Profession Bureau
402 W. Washington St., Rm. 041
Indianapolis, IN 46204
Phone: (317)232-2960

Credential Type: Psychologist license. **Duration of License:** Two years. **Requirements:** Doctorate degree. **Examination:** Examination for Professional Practice in Psychology (EPPP). **Fees:** $50 application fee. $135 EPPP fee. $50 license issuance fee. **Governing Statute:** IND. CODE 25-33.

Credential Type: Endorsement as a health service provider. **Requirements:** Doctorate degree. Two years of experience in supervision: one year in internship and one year post-doctoral. **Examination:** Oral Jurisprudence. **Fees:** $50 application fee. $50 license issuance fee. **Governing Statute:** IND. CODE 25-33.

Iowa

5685

Health Service Provider in Psychology
Board of Psychology Examiners
Dept. of Public Health
Lucas State Office Bldg.
Des Moines, IA 50319
Phone: (515)281-6762

Credential Type: License. **Duration of License:** Two years. **Requirements:** A certified health service provider in psychology is licensed to practice psychology and has a doctoral degree in psychology or, prior to July 1, 1984, was licensed at the doctoral level with a degree in psychology or its equivalent or, prior to January 1, 1985, received a doctoral degree equivalent to a doctoral degree in psychology, and has at least two years of clinical experience in a recognized health service setting. **Fees:** $140 application fee. $40 renewal fee.

5686

Psychologist
Board of Psychology Examiners
Dept. of Public Health
Lucas State Office Bldg.
Des Moines, IA 50319
Phone: (515)281-6762

Credential Type: License. **Duration of License:** Two years. **Requirements:** An applicant must have a doctorate in psychology from an accredited institution, plus one year of supervised professional experience. **Examination:** Examination for Professional Practice in Psychology. **Reciprocity:** Yes. **Fees:** $150 exam fee. $100 application fee. $140 renewal fee.

Kansas

5687

Psychologist
Behavioral Science Regulatory Board
900 Jackson, Rm. 855-S
Topeka, KS 66612
Phone: (913)296-3240

Credential Type: Psychologist license. **Duration of License:** Two years. **Requirements:** Doctorate degree. Two years of post-doctoral experience. Renewal requires 100 hours of continuing education. **Examination:** Examination for Professional Practice in Psychology (EPPP). **Governing Statute:** KAN. STAT. ANN. 74-53.

Kentucky

5688

Psychological Associate
State Board of Psychology
PO Box 456
Frankfort, KY 40602-0456
Phone: (502)564-3296

Credential Type: Psychological Associate license. **Requirements:** Masters degree. **Examination:** Examination for Professional Practice in Psychology (EPPP). **Governing Statute:** Kentucky Revised Statute 319.

5689

Psychologist
State Board of Psychology
PO Box 456
Frankfort, KY 40602-0456
Phone: (502)564-3296

Credential Type: Psychologist license. **Requirements:** Doctorate degree. One year of pre-doctoral or post-doctoral experience. Certification by American Board of Professional Psychology qualifies candidate for oral exam. **Examination:** Examination for Professional Practice in Psychology (EPPP) and structured oral exam in specialty area. **Governing Statute:** Kentucky Revised Statute 319.

5690

School Psychologist
Kentucky Dept. of Education
Div. of Teacher Education and Certification
Capitol Plaza Tower, 18th Fl.
500 Mero St.
Frankfort, KY 40601
Phone: (502)564-4606

Credential Type: Provisional Certificate for School Psychologist. **Duration of License:** One year. **Authorization:** This temporary certificate allows an applicant to work as a school psychologist while completing requirements for a Standard Certificate in school psychology. **Requirements:** One year of supervised internship experience. Master's degree. Complete 48 semester hours of a 60 semester hours program that includes the following professional requirements: 12 hours psychological foundations, nine hours education foundations, 15 hours assessment and intervention which includes preparation in referral and assessment of students who experience problems of learning and adjustment, and preparation in planning and implementing direct and indirect interventions including counseling, instructional and behavioral management, and consultant and other prevention approaches; three hours of professional school psychology which includes the history and foundation of school psychology, legal and ethical issues, professional issues and standards, and roles and functions of the school psychologist; and nine hours of research, evaluation, and statistics. Pass the National Teacher Examination Specialty Exam 40 with a score of 630. **Examination:** National Teacher Examination Specialty Exam 40.

Credential Type: Standard Certificate for School Psychologist. **Duration of License:** Five years. **Requirements:** One year of supervised internship experience. Master's degree of at least 60 semester hours which include the following professional requirements: 12 hours psychological foundations, nine hours education foundations, 15 hours assessment and intervention which includes preparation in referral and assessment of students who experience problems of learning and adjustment, and preparation in planning and implementing direct and indirect interventions including counseling, instructional and behavioral management, and consultant and other prevention approaches; three hours of professional school psychology which includes the history and foundation of school psychology, legal and ethical issues, professional issues and standards, and roles and functions of the school psychologist; and nine hours of research, evaluation, and statistics. Pass the National Teacher Examination Specialty Exam 40 with a score of 630. Certificate may be renewed with three years experience as a school psychologist which includes attendance and participation in 72 hours of continuing professional development. **Examination:** National Teacher Examination Specialty Exam 40.

Louisiana

5691

Psychologist
Louisiana State Board of Examiners of Psychologists
11853 Bricksome Ave., Ste. B
Baton Rouge, LA 70816
Phone: (504)293-2238

Credential Type: License. **Duration of License:** One year. **Requirements:** 21 years of age. Doctoral degree with a major in psychology. Two years of experience under a licensed psychologist. **Examination:** Written and oral. **Fees:** $195 exam fee. $150 application fee. $200 renewal fee.

5692

Psychologist Assistant (School)
Louisiana State Dept. of Education, Teacher Certification
PO Box 94064
Baton Rouge, LA 70804
Phone: (504)342-5840

Credential Type: License. **Duration of License:** Three years. **Requirements:** Master's degree in psychology, educational psychology or school psychology from an accredited college or university with the required course work. Six semester hours of supervised experience.

5693

School Psychologist
Louisiana State Dept. of Education, Teacher Certification
PO Box 94064
Baton Rouge, LA 70804
Phone: (504)342-5840

Credential Type: Provisional Certificate. **Duration of License:** One year. **Requirements:** Completed academic preparation in a school of psychology.

Credential Type: Standard Certificate. **Duration of License:** Five years. **Requirements:** Completion of a school psychology training program in Louisiana. **Reciprocity:** Yes.

Maine

5694

Psychological Examiner
Maine Board of Examiners of
 Psychologists
State House Station 35
Augusta, ME 04333
Phone: (207)582-8723

Credential Type: Psychological Examiner license. **Requirements:** Masters degree. Two years of experience in supervision. **Examination:** Examination for Professional Practice in Psychology (EPPP) and Oral (Law/Ethics). **Governing Statute:** 32 M.R.S.A. Chapter 56.

5695

Psychologist
Maine Board of Examiners of
 Psychologists
State House Station 35
Augusta, ME 04333
Phone: (207)582-8723

Credential Type: Psychologist license. **Duration of License:** Two years. **Requirements:** Doctorate degree. Two years of experience in supervision. Renewal requires 40 hours of continuing education. **Examination:** Examination for Professional Practice in Psychology (EPPP) and Oral. **Governing Statute:** 32 M.R.S.A. Chapter 56.

Maryland

5696

Psychologist
Board of Examiners of Psychologists
4201 Patterson Ave., Rm. 311
Baltimore, MD 21215-2299
Phone: (301)764-4787

Credential Type: Psychologist license. **Duration of License:** One year. **Requirements:** Doctorate degree. Two years of experience, one year of which must be postdoctoral. Renewal requires 30 hours of continuing education. **Examination:** Examination for Professional Practice in Psychology (EPPP) and State Essay (pass 3.0). **Governing Statute:** Annotated Code of Maryland, Health Occupation Title 18.

Massachusetts

5697

Psychologist
Div. of Registration
Board of Registration of
 Psychologists
100 Cambridge St.
Boston, MA 02202
Phone: (617)727-9925

Credential Type: Psychologist license. **Duration of License:** Two years. **Requirements:** Doctorate degree. Two years of experience in supervision. Renewal requires 20 hours of continuing education. Certification by American Board of Professional Psychology qualifies candidate for Examination for Professional Practice in Psychology (EPPP) exam. **Examination:** EPPP. **Governing Statute:** MASS.ANN.LAWS. CH. 112 & 118.

5698

School Psychologist
Massachusetts Dept. of Education
1385 Hancock St.
Quincy, MA 02169
Phone: (617)770-7500

Credential Type: School Psychologist Endorsement. **Requirements:** 60 semester hours of graduate level course work. Complete a successful double practicum of 600 clock hours Two-thirds must be in a school setting an one-third may be in a clinical, supervised setting. Demonstrate the competencies contained in the four Standards established by the Massachusetts Dept. of Education for school psychologists. Standard I-Knowledge of the following: developmental psychology; psychology of learning; principles of behavior; psychological abnormality and normality; diagnosis and treatment of learning and behavioral disorders; individual and group measures of human functioning; major theories of counseling and psychotherapy; issues that relate to a school psychologist's effectiveness in schools; major theories and techniques of consultation; recent developments in fields of education and psychology. Standard II-Communicate clearly and appropriately. Standard III-Ability to design and implement diagnostic procedures, plans, educational prescriptions, psycho-educational strategies, and intervention. Standard IV-Be equitable, sensitive, and responsive to students, families, teachers, administrators, and the community.

Michigan

5699

Psychologist
Board of Psychology
Bureau of Occupational &
 Professional Regulation
Dept. of Commerce
PO Box 30018
Lansing, MI 48909
Phone: (517)373-7902

Credential Type: License. **Duration of License:** Two years. **Requirements:** Hold a doctorate degree in psychology, or a closely related field, from a Board-approved college or university. Completed a 2,000-hour internship. Two years of postdoctoral experience in the practice of psychology, in an organized health care setting. Be of good moral character. Working knowledge of the English language. Completed courses in assessment and treatment. Completed courses in three of the four (4) areas: biological basis of behavior, cognitive effect, social basis of behavior, and individual differences. Comply with all the rules and regulations of the Board. **Examination:** Board administered written exam. **Fees:** $50 application processing fee. $115 initial exam fee. $20 exam review fee. $40 initial license fee, per year. Renewal fee, per year is same as initial fee. **Governing Statute:** Public Health Code, Act 368 of 1978, as amended.

Credential Type: Limited License. **Duration of License:** Two years. **Requirements:** Master's degree in psychology from a Board-approved college or university. Completed a 500-hour practicum. One year of supervised postgraduate experience in a health care setting. Supervision must be provided by a licensed psychologist or other approved personnel. Completed a course in assessment and treatment. **Examination:** Board administered written exam. **Fees:** $50 application processing fee. $115 initial exam fee. $20 exam review fee. $30 initial license fee, per year. **Governing Statute:** Public Health Code, Act 368 of 1978, as amended.

5700

School Psychologist
Policy, State Plan, and Monitoring Program
Special Education Services
Michigan Dept. of Education
PO Box 30008
Lansing, MI 48909
Phone: (517)373-3324

Credential Type: School Psychologist Approval. **Duration of License:** Permanent. **Requirements:** At least a master's degree in school psychology or its equivalent. Completed a minimum of 45 graduate semester hours in school psychology or related areas. Completed not less than 500 clock hours of supervised internship with school age persons under the supervision of an approved school psychologist training institution.

School psychologists must obtain approval from Special Education Services of the Michigan Department of Education. Meet the Department's competency requirements. Completed one year of work experience as a school psychologist with temporary approval, while under the direction of a fully approved school psychologist. Approval is permanent as long as the school psychologist is employed by a school. **Fees:** $125 in-state, $175 out-of-state application fee. **Governing Statute:** Public Health Code, Act 368 of 1978, as amended.

Minnesota

5701

Psychological Practitioner
Board of Psychology
2700 University Ave. W., Rm. 101
St. Paul, MN 55114-1095
Phone: (612)642-0587

Credential Type: Psychological Practitioner License. **Duration of License:** Two years. **Requirements:** At least a master's degree with a major in psychology. No employment requirements. **Examination:** EPPP, oral, and written jurisprudence examinations. **Fees:** $160 exam fee. $250 license fee. $250 renewal fee. **Governing Statute:** Minnesota Statutes 148.88-98. Minnesota Rules 7200-7299.

5702

Psychologist
Board of Psychology
2700 University Ave. W., Rm. 101
St. Paul, MN 55114-1095
Phone: (612)642-0587

Credential Type: Psychologist License. **Duration of License:** Two years. **Requirements:** At least a master's degree with a major in psychology. Complete two years of supervised post-graduate experience. Certification by American Board of Professional Psychology qualifies candidate for EPPP exam. **Examination:** EPPP, oral, and written jurisprudence examinations. **Fees:** $160 exam fee. $250 license fee. $250 renewal fee. **Governing Statute:** Minnesota Statutes 148.88-98. Minnesota Rules 7200-7299.

Mississippi

5703

Psychologist
Mississippi State Board of Psychological Examiners
812 N. President St.
Jackson, MS 39202
Phone: (601)353-8871

Credential Type: Psychologist license. **Requirements:** Doctorate degree. One year internship. **Examination:** Examination for Professional Practice in Psychology (EPPP) and Oral. **Governing Statute:** MISS. CODE ANN 73-31-1.

Credential Type: Certificate to perform Civil Commitment Evaluations. **Requirements:** Specialization in Clinical or Counseling Psychology. Licensure as Psychologist. **Examination:** Jurisprudence and Performance. **Governing Statute:** MISS. CODE ANN 73-31-1.

Missouri

5704

Psychologist
State Committee of Psychologists
PO Box 153
Jefferson City, MO 65102
Phone: (314)751-0099

Credential Type: Psychologist license. **Requirements:** Doctorate degree and one year of experience or Masters Degree and three years of experience. **Examination:** Examination for Professional Practice in Psychology (EPPP). **Governing Statute:** 337.010-090 RSMo (Cum. Supp. 1990).

Montana

5705

Psychologist
Montana Board of Psychologists
111 N. Jackson
Helena, MT 59620
Phone: (406)444-5436

Credential Type: License. **Duration of License:** One year. **Requirements:** 18 years of age. A doctoral degree in clinical psychology from an accredited institution or equivalent. Two years of experience in the practice, research, or teaching of psychology, one year of which is postdoctoral. **Examination:** Written and oral exam. **Fees:** $110 application fee. $150 exam fee. $110 renewal fee. **Governing Statute:** Montana Code Annotated 37-17-301 through 37-17-313.

5706

School Psychologist
Teacher Certification
Office of Public Instruction
State Capitol
Helena, MT 59620
Phone: (406)444-3150

Credential Type: Class 6 Specialist Certificate. **Duration of License:** Five years. **Requirements:** Master's degree in school psychology, or equivalent related areas, to include specific courses in education, psychological methods and techniques. Renewable with verification of one year of successful specialist experience and six graduate quarter credits during the valid term of the certificate.

Nebraska

5707

Psychologist
Nebraska Board of Examiners of Psychologists
301 Centennial Mall S.
Lincoln, NE 68509
Phone: (402)471-2115

Credential Type: License. **Duration of License:** Two years. **Requirements:** Must have a doctoral degree in psychology from an institution accredited by the American Psychological Association. 21 years of age. **Examination:** Yes. **Fees:** $400 application fee. $300 clinical psychology certification fee. $300 license renewal fee. $325 license and clinical certification renewal fees.

Nebraska

5708

School Psychologist
Teacher Certification
State Dept. of Education
301 Centennial Mall South
Box 94987
Lincoln, NE 68509-4987
Phone: (402)471-2496

Credential Type: Initial Special Services Certificate. **Duration of License:** Three years. **Requirements:** Accredited training in psychology from an institute of higher education and submit official transcripts. Pass the PPST with the following minimum scores: reading 170; mathematics 171; writing 172. **Examination:** Pre-Professional Skills Test.

Credential Type: Advanced Special Services Certificate. **Duration of License:** Seven years. **Requirements:** Baccalaureate degree from an approved, accredited institution. Completion of degree level course of study in psychology plus 60 semester hours in an approved program beyond the baccalaureate degree. Six semester hours of credit within the past three years or a valid, regular, approved license for practicing nursing in Nebraska. Renewal is possible with two years of successful service within the past seven years or six semester hours of college credit in area of service within the immediate past three years.

Nevada

5709

Psychologist
Nevada State Board of Psychological
 Examiners
427 Ridge St.
Reno, NV 89502
Phone: (702)324-7729

Credential Type: License. **Duration of License:** Two years. **Requirements:** Doctoral degree or the equivalent from an approved college or university. Completion of two years of supervised experience under a licensed psychologist. **Examination:** State Board exam. **Fees:** $100 application fee. $135 exam fee. $25 license fee. $300 renewal fee.

5710

School Psychologist
Nevada State Dept. of Education
Licensing Office
400 W. King St., Capitol Complex
Carson City, NV 89701
Phone: (702)687-3115

Credential Type: License. **Requirements:** Graduate degree from an accredited institution. Completion of an internship, or a school psychologist certificate issued by the National School Psychology Certification Board, or completion of a program for preparation as a school psychologist approved by the State Board of Education. Completion of required coursework. **Fees:** $84 license fee. $50 license fee.

New Hampshire

5711

Psychologist
New Hampshire Board of Examiners
 of Psychologists
105 Pleasant St., Box 457
Concord, NH 03301
Phone: (603)226-2599

Credential Type: Psychologist license. **Duration of License:** One year. **Requirements:** Doctorate degree. One year internship. One year of post-doctoral experience. Renewal requires 20 hours of continuing education. Certification by American Board of Professional Psychology waives Examination for Professional Practice in Psychology (EPPP) exam, but candidate must fill out application forms. **Examination:** EPPP and four essay questions to be sent in with application form. **Governing Statute:** N.H.Rev.Stat.Ann. 330-A:1.

New Jersey

5712

Psychologist
State Board of Psychological
 Examiners
1100 Raymond Blvd.
Newark, NJ 07102
Phone: (201)648-2792

Credential Type: License. **Duration of License:** Two years. **Requirements:** A degree of Doctor of Philosophy in psychology from an accredited educational institution or a doctoral degree in a closely allied field. At least two years of full-time professional employment, at least one of which is post-doctoral. Other education and experience combinations also are acceptable. 21 years of age. Good moral character. **Examination:** Written and oral exams. **Reciprocity:** Yes. **Fees:** $75 application fee. $275 exam fee. $140 biennial registration fee. $50 temporary permit fee. **Governing Statute:** NJSA 45-14B. NJAC 13:42.

New Mexico

5713

Psychological Associate
New Mexico Board of Psychological
 Examiners
PO Box 25101
Santa Fe, NM 87504
Phone: (505)827-7163

Credential Type: Psychological Associate license. **Duration of License:** Three years. **Requirements:** Masters degree. Five years. years of experience. One year of experience in supervision within last five years. Renewal requires 36 hours continuing education. **Examination:** Examination for Professional Practice in Psychology (EPPP) and Oral. **Governing Statute:** N.M. STAT. ANN. 61-9-1.

5714

Psychologist
New Mexico Board of Psychological
 Examiners
PO Box 25101
Santa Fe, NM 87504
Phone: (505)827-7163

Credential Type: Psychologist license. **Duration of License:** Three years. **Requirements:** Doctorate degree. Two years of post-doctoral experience in supervision. Renewal requires 60 hours of continuing education. Certification by American Board of Professional Psychology qualifies candidate for EPPP exam. **Examination:** Examination for Professional Practice in Psychology (EPPP) and Oral. **Governing Statute:** N.M. STAT. ANN. 61-9-1.

New York

5715

Psychologist
State Education Dept.
Div. of Professional Licensing Services
Cultural Education Center
Empire State Plaza
Albany, NY 12230
Phone: (518)474-3696

Credential Type: License. **Duration of License:** Three years. **Requirements:** Doctoral Degree in psychology and two years of supervised experience. 21 years of age. **Examination:** Written. **Fees:** $325 application fee. $155 renewal fee. **Governing Statute:** Title VIII Articles 130, 153 of the Education Law.

North Carolina

5716

Practicing Psychologist
North Carolina State Board of Examiners for Practicing Psychologists
Appalachian State University
Boone, NC 28608
Phone: (704)262-2258

Credential Type: License. **Duration of License:** One year. **Requirements:** Doctorate degree based on a planned and directed program of study in psychology from an accredited college or university. Two years of supervised experience or post-doctoral work. Three references. **Examination:** National and state exams. **Fees:** $50 application fee. $110 exam fee. $30 renewal fee.

5717

Psychological Associate
North Carolina State Board of Examiners for Practicing Psychologists
Appalachian State University
Boone, NC 28608
Phone: (704)262-2258

Credential Type: License. **Duration of License:** One year. **Requirements:** Master's degree in psychology from an accredited university or college. Three references. **Examination:** National and state exams. **Fees:** $50 application fee. $110 exam fee. $30 renewal fee.

5718

Psychological Stress Evaluator (PSE)
Private Protective Services Board
PO Box 29500
Raleigh, NC 27626
Phone: (919)779-1611

Credential Type: License. **Duration of License:** One year. **Requirements:** High school diploma. Completion of a course of instruction at an approved PSE school. 18 years of age. **Fees:** $150 application fee. $150 license fee. $50 recovery fund fee. $150 renewal fee.

5719

School Psychologist
Certification Section
State Dept. of Public Instruction
Raleigh, NC 27603
Phone: (919)733-4125

Credential Type: School Psychologist Level II Certificate. **Duration of License:** Five years. **Requirements:** Sixth-year degree in school psychology from an accredited institution. Pass the NTE. Institutional recommendation. **Examination:** National Teachers Examination. **Fees:** $30 application fee. $30 renewal fee.

Credential Type: School Psychologist Level III Certificate. **Duration of License:** Five years. **Requirements:** Doctoral degree in school psychology from an accredited institution. Pass the NTE. Institutional recommendation. **Examination:** National Teacher Examination. **Fees:** $30 application fee. $30 renewal fee.

North Dakota

5720

Psychologist
North Dakota Board of Psychologist Examiners
1406 2nd St., NW
Mandan, ND 58554
Phone: (701)663-2321

Credential Type: Psychologist license. **Requirements:** Doctorate degree. One year internship is required to provide therapy or counseling. Certification by American Board of Professional Psychology allows licensure without any examinations. **Examination:** Examination for Professional Practice in Psychology (EPPP), Oral Jurisprudence, and Ethics. **Governing Statute:** N.D. CENT. CODE 43-32-02.

Ohio

5721

Psychologist
State Board of Psychology
77 S. High St., 18th Fl.
Columbus, OH 43266-0321
Phone: (614)466-8808
Fax: (614)644-8112

Credential Type: Psychologist license. **Requirements:** Doctoral degree. Two years of experience in supervision, one year of which must be post-doctoral experience. Certification by American Board of Professional Psychology waives Examination for Professional Practice in Psychology (EPPP) exam. **Examination:** EPPP and Oral. **Governing Statute:** OHIO REV. CODE ANN. Ch. 4732 (effective 9/22/72).

5722

School Psychologist
State Board of Psychology
77 S. High St., 18th Fl.
Columbus, OH 43266-0321
Phone: (614)466-8808
Fax: (614)644-8112

Credential Type: School Psychologist license. **Requirements:** Masters degree in School Psychology. Four years of experience, one of which must be supervised. Certification by American Board of Professional Psychology in School Psychology waives SP exam. **Examination:** National Teacher Examination (NTE)-SPSA objective, written, and oral. **Governing Statute:** OHIO REV. CODE ANN. Ch. 4732 (effective 9/22/72).

Oklahoma

5723

Psychologist
State Board of Examiners of Psychologists
PO Box 53551
Oklahoma City, OK 73152
Phone: (405)271-6118

Credential Type: License. **Duration of License:** One year. **Requirements:** Doctoral degree from an accredited university in a psychology program. One-year, full-time internship. 20 hours of continuing education per year. 21 years of age. **Examination:** Examination for the Professional Practice in Psychology and an oral exam. **Fees:** $335 license fee. $130 renewal fee.

Oklahoma

5724

School Service Personnel K-12
Teacher Education and Certification
State Dept. of Education
2500 N. Lincoln Blvd., Rm. 211
Oklahoma City, OK 73105
Phone: (405)521-3337

Credential Type: Standard Certificate in a School Personnel Field—Graduate. **Duration of License:** Five years. **Authorization:** Endorsement will be given to persons seeking positions in the following fields: Counselor; Library Media Specialist; Elementary School Principal; Secondary School Principal; School Superintendent; School Psychometrist; School Psychologist; SpeechLanguage Pathologist; or Reading Specialist. **Requirements:** Complete an approved certificate program at an accredited college or university which includes a minimum of the following: a baccalaureate degree; 50 semester hours in general education; 30 semester hours in professional education; and 40 semester hours in course work pertaining to the area of specialization. Pass the state certified test(s) in specialization competencies. Complete State Board graduate level course requirements.

Oregon

5725

Psychologist
State Board of Psychologist
 Examiners
895 Summer St. NE
Salem, OR 97310
Phone: (503)378-4154

Credential Type: License. **Duration of License:** One year. **Requirements:** Doctorate in psychology. Two years of supervised work experience. **Examination:** Yes. **Fees:** $140 exam fee. $50 license fee. $100 renewal fee. **Governing Statute:** ORS 675.010 to 675.150.

5726

Psychologist Associate
State Board of Psychologist
 Examiners
895 Summer St. NE
Salem, OR (503)378-4
Phone: (503)378-4154

Credential Type: License. **Duration of License:** One year. **Requirements:** Master's degree in psychology or equivalent. One-year fulltime internship. Three years of supervised experience. **Examination:** Yes. **Fees:** $140 exam fee. $50 license fee. $100 renewal fee. **Governing Statute:** ORS 657.010 to 657.150.

5727

School Psychologist
Teacher Standards and Practices
 Commission
630 Center St. NE, Ste. 200
Salem, OR 97310-0320
Phone: (503)378-3586

Credential Type: Basic Personnel Service Certificate—Psychologist Endorsement. **Duration of License:** Three years. **Requirements:** Master's degree from an approved teacher education institution. Evidence of recent public school personnel service experience. Passing scores on the CBEST. Out-of-state prepared applicants may submit their passing scores on the Core Battery of the National Teacher Examination, in lieu of the CBEST. Completion of a 75 quarter hr. graduate program in educational psychology, including a clinical practicum. Completion of full-time public school practicum for nine weeks under the direct supervision of a certified school psychologist. **Examination:** California Basic Education Skills Test.

Credential Type: Standard Personnel Service Certificate—Psychologist Endorsement. **Duration of License:** Five years. **Requirements:** Two years of successful experience as a school psychologist in Oregon public schools while holding a basic school psychologist endorsement.

Pennsylvania

5728

Psychologist
Pennsylvania State Board of
 Psychology
PO Box 2649
Harrisburg, PA 17105-2649
Phone: (717)783-7155

Credential Type: Psychologist license. **Requirements:** Doctorate degree. Two years of experience in supervision (1 year may be pre-doctoral internship), minimum of 3,000 hours: one year/1,500 hours under licensed psychologist pre-doctoral internship; one year/1,500 hours under licensed professional postdoctoral; experience commenced after March 23, 1991 must be under licensed psychologist postdoctoral; or

Masters Degree. Three years of post-masters experience in supervision with 3,500 hours under a licensed psychologist. **Examination:** Examination for Professional Practice in Psychology (EPPP) & PPLE (Pennsylvania Law Examination). **Governing Statute:** 63 P.S., Section 1201 et. seq.

Rhode Island

5729

Psychologist
Rhode Island Board of Psychology
104 Cannon Bldg, 3 Capitol Hill
Providence, RI 02908-5097
Phone: (401)277-2827
Fax: (401)277-1272

Credential Type: Psychologist license. **Duration of License:** Two years. **Requirements:** Doctorate degree. Two years of experience, at least one of which must be post-doctoral in supervision. Renewal requires 40 hours of continuing education. Certification by American Board of Professional Psychology waives Examination for Professional Practice in Psychology (EPPP) exam. **Examination:** EPPP and Oral. **Governing Statute:** R.I. GEN. LAWS 5-44-1.

South Carolina

5730

Psychologist
South Carolina State Board of
 Examiners in Psychology
PO Box 11477
Columbia, SC 29211
Phone: (803)253-4050

Credential Type: License. **Duration of License:** One year. **Requirements:** Doctorate degree in psychology or a closely allied field from an accredited educational institution, plus two years of supervised professional experience under a licensed psychologist. **Examination:** Yes. **Fees:** $200 application fee. $195 exam fee. $100 renewal fee.

South Dakota

5731

Psychologist
South Dakota Board of Examiners in
 Psychology
PO Box 654
Spearfish, SD 57783-0654
Phone: (605)642-1600

Credential Type: Psychologist license. **Requirements:** Doctorate degree. 1800 hours of experience within two consecutive calendar years pre-doctoral internship. One year of post-doctoral experience in supervision. Certification by American Board of Professional Psychology qualifies candidate for Examination for Professional Practice in Psychology (EPPP) exam. **Examination:** EPPP and Oral (AASPB Code & SD Law). **Governing Statute:** S.D. COFIFIED LAWS ANN. 36-27A.

Tennessee

5732

Psychologist
Board of Examiners in Psychology
283 Plus Park Blvd.
Nashville, TN 37247
Phone: (615)367-1010

Credential Type: License. **Requirements:** One year full time, two years part time internship at psychologist level. Doctorate degree for Psychologist, Masters degree for Psychological Examiner. **Examination:** Yes. **Reciprocity:** Only written scores on exams. **Fees:** $175 Examination. $50 Application.

Texas

5733

Psychologist
Texas State Board of Examiners of Psychologists
9101 Burnet Rd., Ste. 212
Austin, TX 78758
Phone: (512)835-2036

Credential Type: Psychological Associate Certification. **Duration of License:** One year. **Requirements:** Master's degree of 42 semester hours based on a program of primarily psychological studies. 450 clock hours of experience under licensed psychologist. **Examination:** Examination for Professional Practice in Psychology (EPPP). Texas jurisprudence examination. **Fees:** $235 exam fee. $150 application fee. $70 renewal fee. **Governing Statute:** VACS 4512c, 22 TAC 461.

Credential Type: Psychologist Certification. **Duration of License:** One year. **Requirements:** 18 years of age. Doctoral degree in psychology, received on or after January 1, 1979, from a regionally accredited institution; or doctoral degree in psychology, or the equivalent in both subject matter and training, received before January 1, 1979, from a regionally accredited institution. **Examination:** Examination for Professional Practice in Psychology (EPPP). Texas jurisprudence examination. Oral examination on practical issues. **Fees:** $535 exam fee. $300 application fee. $65 renewal fee. **Governing Statute:** VACS 4512c, 22 TAC 461.

Credential Type: Psychologist License. **Duration of License:** One year. **Requirements:** 18 years of age. Doctoral degree in psychology, received on or after January 1, 1979, from a regionally accredited institution; or doctoral degree in psychology, or the equivalent in both subject matter and training, received before January 1, 1979, from a regionally accredited institution. **Examination:** Examination for Professional Practice in Psychology (EPPP). Texas jurisprudence examination. Oral examination on practical issues. **Fees:** $535 exam fee. $140 application fee. $160 renewal fee. $200 professional fee. **Governing Statute:** VACS 4512c, 22 TAC 461.

Utah

5734

Psychologist
Dept. of Commerce
Div. of Occupational and Professional Licensing
160 E. 300 S.
PO Box 45802
Salt Lake City, UT 84145
Phone: (801)530-6628

Credential Type: License. **Duration of License:** Two years. **Requirements:** Must have a doctorate degree in psychology. Must have two years experience in psychological services. **Examination:** Yes. **Fees:** $140 license fee. $80 renewal fee.

5735

School Psychologist
Teacher Certification
250 E. 500 S.
Salt Lake City, UT 84111
Phone: (801)538-7740

Credential Type: Cetificate. **Requirements:** Must hold a valid Basic or Standard School Psychologist Certificate issued by the Utah State Board of Education upon completion of a master's degree in this area. **Fees:** $10 renewal fee.

Vermont

5736

Psychologist, Doctorate
State Board of Psychological Examiners
Pavilion Office Bldg.
Montpelier, VT 05602
Phone: (802)828-2373

Credential Type: License. **Duration of License:** Two years. **Requirements:** 18 years of age. Resident of Vermont, or in regular practice in Vermont. Doctorate in Psychology from an accredited school or equivalent (i.e. Ph.D. in a closely related field). Two years fulltime experience in practicing psychology after doctorate work is completed. **Examination:** Yes. **Reciprocity:** No. **Fees:** $25 Application. $150 Exam. $20 Renewal. **Governing Statute:** Title 26, VSA Sections 3010-3017.

5737

Psychologist, Master
State Board of Psychological Examiners
Pavilion Office Bldg.
Montpelier, VT 05602
Phone: (802)828-2373

Credential Type: License. **Duration of License:** Two years. **Requirements:** 18 years of age. Resident of, or in regular practice in Vermont. Master's degree in Psychology from an accredited school or equivalent. Two full-time years in practicing psychology, three of which must be post-master's, under the supervision of a licensed practicing psychologist or a person qualified to obtain a license. **Examination:** Yes. **Reciprocity:** No. **Fees:** $25 Application. $150 Exam. $20 Initial license. $20 Renewal. **Governing Statute:** Title 26, VSA Sections 3010-3017.

Virginia

5738

Psychologist
Virginia Board of Psychology
1601 Rolling Hills Dr.
Richmond, VA 23229
Phone: (804)662-9920

Credential Type: Psychologist License. **Duration of License:** Two years. **Requirements:** Doctrate degree in psychology. Must have two years of postdoctoral experience under supervision. Must complete a one year internship for a specialty in clinical services. **Examination:** Yes. **Fees:**

Virginia 5739

Psychologist, continued

$150 application fee. $150 renewal fee. $325 examination fee.

Credential Type: Clinical psychologist license. **Duration of License:** Two years. **Requirements:** Doctorate degree in clinical psychology. Must have two years of clinical experience under supervision. Must complete a one year internship. **Examination:** Yes. **Fees:** $350 application fee. $80 renewal fee. $350 examination.

Credential Type: School psychologist license. **Duration of License:** Two years. **Requirements:** Must hold at least a master's degree with courses and training in school psychology as specified by the board. **Examination:** Yes. **Fees:** $150 application fee. $150 renewal fee. $325 examination fee.

5739

School Psychologist
Administrative Director
Office of Professional Development and Teacher Education
Dept. of Education
PO Box 6-Q
Richmond, VA 23216-2060
Phone: (804)225-2094

Credential Type: Psychologist Endorsement. **Requirements:** Master's degree in school psychology, or equivalent, consisting of 60 graduate semester hours. Graduate course work with the following specified number of semester hours: assessment/evaluation 12; intervention techniques 6; psychological foundations 15; school organization 6; measurement and research 6; electives 3; and a full-time supervised internship 12.

Washington

5740

Hypnotherapist
Dept. of Health
1112 SE Quince
Olympia, WA 98504
Phone: (206)753-6936

Credential Type: Hypnotherapist License. **Duration of License:** Two years. **Requirements:** Complete a four-hour course in AIDS education. Submit application and pay fee. **Fees:** $78.50 application fee. $73.50 renewal fee. $42 duplicate license fee. $50 registration verification fee.

5741

Psychologist
Washington State Examining Board of Psychology
1300 Quince St., SE, E4-21
Olympia, WA 98504
Phone: (206)753-3095

Credential Type: Psychologist license. **Duration of License:** Three years. **Requirements:** Doctorate degree. One year of post-doctoral experience in supervision. Renewal requires 150 hours of continuing education. Certification by American Board of Professional Psychology qualifies candidate for EPPP exam. **Examination:** Examination for Professional Practice in Psychology (EPPP) and Oral. **Governing Statute:** WASH. REV. CODE 18.83.005.

5742

School Psychologist
Superintendent of Public Instruction
Professional Education and Certification
Old Capitol Bldg. FG-11
Seattle, WA 98504-3211
Phone: (206)753-6773

Credential Type: Initial Educational Staff Associate Certificate. **Duration of License:** Seven years. **Authorization:** Authorizes service in primary role of assistant to the learner, the teacher, the administrator, and/or the educational program. **Requirements:** Complete all course work (except special projects or thesis) for a master's degree with a major in psychology.

Credential Type: Continuing Educational Staff Associate Certificate. **Duration of License:** Five years. **Requirements:** Master's degree in psychology. Verification of 180 days of experience in the role. Complete a college level course which includes peer review while employed in the role. Out-of-state applicants must complete a comprehensive written examination (unless already taken as part of the master's degree). Renewable upon 150 clock hours of work in this position during the life of the certificate.

West Virginia

5743

Psychologist
Board of Examiners of Psychologists
306 Student Services Ctr.
West Virginia Univ.
Morgantown, WV 26506
Phone: (304)366-2070

Alternate Information: 200 Gaston Ave., Fairmont, WV 26554

Credential Type: License. **Duration of License:** Two years. **Requirements:** PhD or Masters in Psychology. One year post-doctorate, or five years post-Masters experience. Never convicted of a felony. **Examination:** Yes. **Fees:** $50 Application. $210 Examination. $30 Renewal.

5744

School Psychologist
Dept. of Education
Office of Educational Personnel Development
1900 Washington St. E
Charleston, WV 25305
Phone: (800)982-2378

Credential Type: Certification. **Requirements:** U.S. citizen. 18 years old. Masters degree and completion of approved educational preparatory program. Never convicted of a felony. **Examination:** Yes. **Fees:** $5 Application. $5 Renewal.

Wisconsin

5745

Psychologist
Regulations and Licensing Dept.
Psychology Board
PO Box 8935
Madison, WI 53708-8935
Phone: (608)266-8609

Credential Type: License. **Requirements:** Doctorate degree in psychology or equivalent in academic training, plus 3,000 hours of experience with 1,500 of those hours in post-doctorate work; or a master's degree in psychology and 6,000 hours of experience. 18 years of age. **Examination:** Written and oral exams.

Credential Type: School Psychology/Private Practice License. **Requirements:** Must hold a regular license as a school psychologist from the Department of Public Instruction. **Examination:** Written and oral exams.

Wyoming

5746

Psychologist
State Board of Psychology
1001 W. 31st St.
Cheyenne, WY 82001
Phone: (307)634-6883

Credential Type: License. **Duration of License:** One year. **Requirements:** 21 years of age. Good moral character. Be a Wyoming resident. Complete a program of 2000 hours which includes a practicum or internship appropriate for the field of Psychology. Be a recipient of a doctoral degree that is primarily psychological from an accredited institution. Pass the examination in professional practice of psychology; or, hold a license from another state with a passing examination score in Wyoming. **Examination:** Yes. **Reciprocity:** Yes. **Fees:** $110 Examination. $60 Temporary Registration. $40 Renewal.

5747

School Psychologist
State Dept. of Education
Certification and Accreditation Services Unit, Hathaway Bldg.
Cheyenne, WY 82002
Phone: (307)777-7291

Credential Type: School Psychologist Endorsement. **Requirements:** Education Specialist teacher certification. 60 semester hours of graduate work including a master's degree and the following courses of study: social management; exceptional child or special education; educational psychology; developmental psychology; clinical psychology; testing; counseling; consultation methods; behavior management; cultural diversity; statistics and program evaluation; professional school psychology; and practicum experience in school psychology. One year, full-time internship in school psychology (500 clock hours per semester) or two years of school psychology experience in a K-12 setting.

Racetrack Occupations

The following states grant licenses in this occupational category as of the date of publication:

Arizona	Florida	Louisiana	Montana	North Dakota	South Dakota	Wisconsin
Arkansas	Idaho	Maryland	Nebraska	Ohio	Tennessee	Wyoming
California	Illinois	Massachusetts	Nevada	Oklahoma	Texas	
Colorado	Iowa	Michigan	New Jersey	Oregon	Vermont	
Connecticut	Kansas	Minnesota	New Mexico	Pennsylvania	Virginia	
Delaware	Kentucky	Missouri	New York	Rhode Island	Washington	

Arizona

5748

Apprentice Jockey
Arizona Dept. of Racing
Investigations and Licensing Div.
800 W. Washington, Rm. 515
Phoenix, AZ 85007
Phone: (602)542-5151

Credential Type: Jockey apprentice certificate. **Duration of License:** Three years. **Requirements:** At least 16 years of age. Not have been convicted of a felony or any crime involving moral turpitude within the last five years. If applicant has not been previously licensed as a jockey apprentice in Arizona or in another recognized racing association state with pari-mutuel wagering, then application will be reviewed by the Board of Stewards. **Fees:** $75 license fee.

5749

Authorized Agent
Arizona Dept. of Racing
Investigations and Licensing Div.
800 W. Washington, Rm. 515
Phoenix, AZ 85007
Phone: (602)542-5151

Credential Type: Authorized agent license. **Duration of License:** Three years. **Requirements:** At least 16 years of age. Not have been convicted of a felony or any crime involving moral turpitude within the last five years. Application must be signed by the principal(s) and clearly set forth the powers of the agent. **Fees:** $36 license fee if not licensed in another category. $5 license fee if licensed in another category.

5750

Concession Employee
Arizona Dept. of Racing
Investigations and Licensing Div.
800 W. Washington, Rm. 515
Phoenix, AZ 85007
Phone: (602)542-5151

Credential Type: Concession employee license. **Duration of License:** One or three years. **Requirements:** At least 16 years of age. Not have been convicted of a felony or any crime involving moral turpitude within the last five years. **Fees:** $15 license fee (3 years). $7 license fee (1 year).

5751

Cool-out (Racetrack)
Arizona Dept. of Racing
Investigations and Licensing Div.
800 W. Washington, Rm. 515
Phoenix, AZ 85007
Phone: (602)542-5151

Credential Type: Cool-out license. **Duration of License:** One or three years. **Requirements:** At least 16 years of age. Not have been convicted of a felony or any crime involving moral turpitude within the last five years. **Fees:** $15 license fee (3 years). $7 license fee (1 year).

5752

Exercise Rider (Racetrack)
Arizona Dept. of Racing
Investigations and Licensing Div.
800 W. Washington, Rm. 515
Phoenix, AZ 85007
Phone: (602)542-5151

Credential Type: Exercise rider license. **Duration of License:** Three years. **Requirements:** At least 16 years of age. Not have been convicted of a felony or any crime involving moral turpitude within the last five years. If applicant has not been previously licensed in this category in Arizona or in another recognized racing association state with pari-mutuel wagering, then applicant must be screened and approved by the Board of Stewards. **Fees:** $15 license fee.

5753

Groom (Racetrack)
Arizona Dept. of Racing
Investigations and Licensing Div.
800 W. Washington, Rm. 515
Phoenix, AZ 85007
Phone: (602)542-5151

Credential Type: Groom license. **Duration of License:** Three years. **Requirements:** At least 16 years of age. Not have been convicted of a felony or any crime involving moral turpitude within the last five years. **Fees:** $15 license fee.

5754

Jockey
Arizona Dept. of Racing
Investigations and Licensing Div.
800 W. Washington, Rm. 515
Phoenix, AZ 85007
Phone: (602)542-5151

Credential Type: Jockey license. **Duration of License:** Three years. **Requirements:** At least 16 years of age. Not have been convicted of a felony or any crime involving moral turpitude within the last five years. If applicant has not been previously licensed as a jockey in Arizona or in another recognized racing association state with pari-mutuel wagering, then application will be reviewed by the Board of Stewards. **Fees:** $75 license fee.

5755

Jockey Agent
Arizona Dept. of Racing
Investigations and Licensing Div.
800 W. Washington, Rm. 515
Phoenix, AZ 85007
Phone: (602)542-5151

Credential Type: Jockey agent license. **Duration of License:** Three years. **Requirements:** At least 16 years of age. Not have been convicted of a felony or any crime involving moral turpitude within the last five years. Must be accompanied by the jockey(s) the applicant represents. No jockey agent may represent more than two jockeys and one apprentice jockey at any one time. A jockey agent cannot be licensed in more than one category at any track. **Fees:** $75 license fee.

5756

Lead-out (Racetrack)
Arizona Dept. of Racing
Investigations and Licensing Div.
800 W. Washington, Rm. 515
Phoenix, AZ 85007
Phone: (602)542-5151

Credential Type: Lead-out license. **Duration of License:** One or three years. **Requirements:** At least 16 years of age. Not have been convicted of a felony or any crime involving moral turpitude within the last five years. **Fees:** $15 license fee (3 years). $7 license fee (1 year).

5757

Lessee
Arizona Dept. of Racing
Investigations and Licensing Div.
800 W. Washington, Rm. 515
Phoenix, AZ 85007
Phone: (602)542-5151

Credential Type: Lessee license. **Duration of License:** Three years. **Authorization:** Any person who does not own but is leasing a horse or greyhound. **Requirements:** At least 16 years of age. Not have been convicted of a felony or any crime involving moral turpitude within the last five years. **Exemptions:** A person currently licensed as an owner is not required to obtain a lessee license. **Fees:** $36 license fee.

5758

Lessor
Arizona Dept. of Racing
Investigations and Licensing Div.
800 W. Washington, Rm. 515
Phoenix, AZ 85007
Phone: (602)542-5151

Credential Type: Lessor license. **Duration of License:** Three years. **Authorization:** Any person not licensed as an owner who leases a horse or greyhound to another individual. **Requirements:** At least 16 years of age. Not have been convicted of a felony or any crime involving moral turpitude within the last five years. **Exemptions:** A person currently licensed as an owner is not required to obtain a lessor license. **Fees:** $36 license fee.

5759

Mutuel Clerk
Arizona Dept. of Racing
Investigations and Licensing Div.
800 W. Washington, Rm. 515
Phoenix, AZ 85007
Phone: (602)542-5151

Credential Type: Mutuel clerk license. **Duration of License:** One or three years. **Authorization:** Mutuel employees must be licensed for each type of track at which they are employed. **Requirements:** At least 18 years of age. Not have been convicted of a felony or any crime involving moral turpitude within the last five years. **Fees:** $15 license fee (3 years). $7 license fee (1 year).

5760

Outrider (Racetrack)
Arizona Dept. of Racing
Investigations and Licensing Div.
800 W. Washington, Rm. 515
Phoenix, AZ 85007
Phone: (602)542-5151

Credential Type: Outrider license. **Duration of License:** Three years. **Requirements:** At least 16 years of age. Not have been convicted of a felony or any crime involving moral turpitude within the last five years. If applicant has not been previously licensed in this category in Arizona or in another recognized racing association state with pari-mutuel wagering, then applicant must be screened and approved by the Board of Stewards. **Fees:** $15 license fee.

5761

Owner
Arizona Dept. of Racing
Investigations and Licensing Div.
800 W. Washington, Rm. 515
Phoenix, AZ 85007
Phone: (602)542-5151

Credential Type: Owner license. **Duration of License:** Three years. **Requirements:** Any owner under 18 years of age must have a parent or guardian sign the license application assuming full financial responsibility for the applicant. Not have been convicted of a felony or any crime involving moral turpitude within the last five years. Animal registration papers must be on file or in their trainer's file registered in the Racing Secretary's office of the track before being licensed. **Fees:** $36 license fee.

5762

Pony Rider (Racetrack)
Arizona Dept. of Racing
Investigations and Licensing Div.
800 W. Washington, Rm. 515
Phoenix, AZ 85007
Phone: (602)542-5151

Credential Type: Pony rider license. **Duration of License:** Three years. **Requirements:** At least 16 years of age. Not have been convicted of a felony or any crime involving moral turpitude within the last five years. If applicant has not been previously licensed in this category in Arizona or in another recognized racing association state with pari-mutuel wagering, then applicant must be screened and approved by the Board of Stewards. **Fees:** $15 license fee.

5763

Track Official
Arizona Dept. of Racing
Investigations and Licensing Div.
800 W. Washington, Rm. 515
Phoenix, AZ 85007
Phone: (602)542-5151

Credential Type: Track official license. **Duration of License:** Three years. **Authorization:** A track official license allows the license holder to serve in any of the following positions without additional licensing: director of racing, mutuel manager, clerk of the scales, track veterinarian, jockey room custodian, mechanical lure operator, track superintendent, handicapper, kennel master, patrol judge, starter, timer, announcer, chief of security, chart writer, racing secretary, paddock judge, horsemen's bookkeeper. One person may serve in more than

Arizona 5764

Track Official, continued

one official position with the consent and approval of the department. **Requirements:** At least 16 years of age. Not have been convicted of a felony or any crime involving moral turpitude within the last five years. **Fees:** $36 license fee.

5764

Track Veterinarian
Arizona Dept. of Racing
Investigations and Licensing Div.
800 W. Washington, Rm. 515
Phoenix, AZ 85007
Phone: (602)542-5151

Credential Type: Veterinarian license. **Duration of License:** Three years. **Requirements:** At least 16 years of age. Not have been convicted of a felony or any crime involving moral turpitude within the last five years. May not own, lease, or train horses or greyhounds at the track at which applicant would practice. Application will be referred to the Arizona Department of Racing Veterinarian for review. **Exemptions:** A holder of a track official license may serve as a track veterinarian without additional licensing. **Fees:** $36 license fee.

5765

Trainer (Racetrack)
Arizona Dept. of Racing
Investigations and Licensing Div.
800 W. Washington, Rm. 515
Phoenix, AZ 85007
Phone: (602)542-5151

Credential Type: Trainer license. **Duration of License:** Three years. **Requirements:** At least 18 years of age. Not have been convicted of a felony or any crime involving moral turpitude within the last five years. If applicant has not been previously licensed as a trainer in Arizona or in another recognized racing association state with pari-mutuel wagering, then applicant must pass a written and practical examination administered by the Board of Stewards. Animal registration papers must be on file in the Racing Secretary's office of the track before being licensed. **Examination:** Written and practical examination administered by the Board of Stewards (new trainer license applications only). **Fees:** $36 license fee.

Credential Type: Assistant trainer license. **Duration of License:** Three years. **Requirements:** At least 18 years of age. Not have been convicted of a felony or any crime involving moral turpitude within the last five years. If applicant has not been previously licensed as a trainer in Arizona or in another recognized racing association state with pari-mutuel wagering, then applicant must pass a written examination administered by the Board of Stewards. **Examination:** Written examination administered by the Board of Stewards (new license applications only). **Fees:** $36 license fee. $5 administrative fee if applicant is already licensed as a trainer.

Arkansas

5766

Clerk of Scales
Arkansas State Racing Commission
Ledbetter Bldg., Rm. G08
7th & Wolfe St.
PO Box 3076
Little Rock, AR 72203
Phone: (501)682-1467

Credential Type: License. **Duration of License:** One year. **Requirements:** Application must be approved by the Stewards. Must be qualified as to ability and integrity, and have endorsement by employer. Must be 16 years of age. Never convicted of a crime, excluding minor traffic offenses. Not be habitually intoxicated or addicted to drugs. Must not be engaged in any activity or practice which is illegal, undesirable, or detrimental to the best interest of the public and the sport of racing. **Examination:** No. **Fees:** $3 License. $3 Renewal.

5767

Commission Clocker
Arkansas State Racing Commission
Ledbetter Bldg., Rm. G08
7th & Wolfe St.
PO Box 3076
Little Rock, AR 72203
Phone: (501)682-1467

Credential Type: License. **Duration of License:** One year. **Requirements:** Application must be approved by the Stewards. Must be qualified as to ability and integrity, and have endorsement by employer. Must be 16 years of age. Never convicted of a crime, excluding minor traffic offenses. Not be habitually intoxicated or addicted to drugs. Must not be engaged in any activity or practice which is illegal, undesirable, or detrimental to the best interest of the public and the sport of racing. **Examination:** No. **Fees:** $3 License. $3 Renewal.

5768

Commission Veterinarian
Arkansas State Racing Commission
Ledbetter Bldg., Rm. G08
7th & Wolfe St.
PO Box 3076
Little Rock, AR 72203
Phone: (501)682-1467

Credential Type: License. **Duration of License:** One year. **Requirements:** Must meet all requirements and be licensed to practice veterinary medicine in the state of Arkansas. **Examination:** Yes. **Fees:** $100 Written, oral and practical examinations. $35 Temporary permit. $90 National Board Examination. $10 Commission license. $10 Renewal.

5769

Equine Dentist
Arkansas State Racing Commission
Ledbetter Bldg., Rm. G08
7th & Wolfe St.
PO Box 3076
Little Rock, AR 72203
Phone: (501)682-1467

Credential Type: License. **Duration of License:** One year. **Requirements:** Must be registered with the Arkansas State Veterinary Board (yet does not have to be a veterinarian). Application approved by the Stewards. **Fees:** $10 License. $10 Renewal.

5770

Farrier (Horse Racing)
Arkansas State Racing Commission
Ledbetter Bldg., Rm. G08
7th & Wolfe St.
PO Box 3076
Little Rock, AR 72203
Phone: (501)682-1467

Credential Type: License. **Duration of License:** One year. **Requirements:** Application must be approved by the Stewards. **Examination:** Yes. **Fees:** $3 License. $3 Renewal.

5771

Greyhound Clerk of Scales
Arkansas State Racing Commission
Ledbetter Bldg., Rm. G08
7th & Wolfe St.
PO Box 3076
Little Rock, AR 72203
Phone: (501)682-1467

Credential Type: License. **Duration of License:** One year. **Requirements:** Must not be associated with any bookmaking practices which are illegal or would be detrimental to the public or the sport of racing. Never convicted of a crime. Qualified as to ability and integrity of license sought and have endorsement of employer. Not be habitually intoxicated or addicted to drugs. Declare ownership or interest in any greyhound. Application must contain no falsehoods. 16 years of age. Application approved by Director of Racing. **Examination:** No **Fees:** $3 License. $3 Renewal.

5772

Greyhound Commission Judge
Arkansas State Racing Commission
Ledbetter Bldg., Rm. G08
7th & Wolfe St.
PO Box 3076
Little Rock, AR 72203
Phone: (501)682-1467

Credential Type: License. **Duration of License:** One year. **Requirements:** Must not be associated with any bookmaking practices which are illegal or would be detrimental to the public or the sport of racing. Never convicted of a crime. Qualified as to ability and integrity of license sought and have endorsement of employer. Not be habitually intoxicated or addicted to drugs. Declare ownership or interest in any greyhound. Application must contain no falsehoods. 16 years of age. Application approved by Director of Racing. **Examination:** No **Fees:** $3 License. $3 Renewal.

5773

Greyhound Commission Veterinarian
Arkansas State Racing Commission
Ledbetter Bldg., Rm. G08
7th & Wolfe St.
PO Box 3076
Little Rock, AR 72203
Phone: (501)682-1467

Credential Type: License. **Duration of License:** One year. **Requirements:** Meet all requirement of veterinarian in Arkansas. **Examination:** Yes. **Fees:** $100 Written oral and practical examinations. $35 Temporary permit. $90 National Board Examination. $10 Commission license. $10 Renewal.

5774

Greyhound Kennel Manager (Racing)
Arkansas State Racing Commission
Ledbetter Bldg., Rm. G08
7th & Wolfe St.
PO Box 3076
Little Rock, AR 72203
Phone: (501)682-1467

Credential Type: License. **Duration of License:** One year. **Requirements:** Must not be associated with any bookmaking practices which are illegal or would be detrimental to the public or the sport of racing. Never convicted of a crime. Qualified as to ability and integrity of license sought and have endorsement of employer. Not be habitually intoxicated or addicted to drugs. Declare ownership or interest in any greyhound. Application must contain no falsehoods. 16 years of age. Application approved by Director of Racing. **Examination:** No **Fees:** $3 License. $3 Renewal.

5775

Greyhound Lead-Out (Racing)
Arkansas State Racing Commission
Ledbetter Bldg., Rm. G08
7th & Wolfe St.
PO Box 3076
Little Rock, AR 72203
Phone: (501)682-1467

Credential Type: License. **Duration of License:** One year. **Requirements:** Must not be associated with any bookmaking practices which are illegal or would be detrimental to the public or the sport of racing. Never convicted of a crime. Qualified as to ability and integrity of license sought and have endorsement of employer. Not be habitually intoxicated or addicted to drugs. Declare ownership or interest in any greyhound. Application must contain no falsehoods. 16 years of age. Application approved by Director of Racing. **Examination:** No **Fees:** $3 License. $3 Renewal.

5776

Greyhound Mutuels Director
Arkansas State Racing Commission
Ledbetter Bldg., Rm. G08
7th & Wolfe St.
PO Box 3076
Little Rock, AR 72203
Phone: (501)682-1467

Credential Type: License. **Duration of License:** One year. **Requirements:** Must not be associated with any bookmaking practices which are illegal or would be detrimental to the public or the sport of racing. Never convicted of a crime. Qualified as to ability and integrity of license sought and have endorsement of employer. Not be habitually intoxicated or addicted to drugs. Declare ownership or interest in any greyhound. Application must contain no falsehoods. 16 years of age. Application approved by Director of Racing. **Examination:** No **Fees:** $3 License. $3 Renewal.

5777

Greyhound Paddock Judge
Arkansas State Racing Commission
Ledbetter Bldg., Rm. G08
7th & Wolfe St.
PO Box 3076
Little Rock, AR 72203
Phone: (501)682-1467

Credential Type: License. **Duration of License:** One year. **Requirements:** Must not be associated with any bookmaking practices which are illegal or would be detrimental to the public or the sport of racing. Never convicted of a crime. Qualified as to ability and integrity of license sought and have endorsement of employer. Not be habitually intoxicated or addicted to drugs. Declare ownership or interest in any greyhound. Application must contain no falsehoods. 16 years of age. Application approved by Director of Racing. **Examination:** No **Fees:** $3 License. $3 Renewal.

5778

Greyhound Presiding Judge
Arkansas State Racing Commission
Ledbetter Bldg., Rm. G08
7th & Wolfe St.
PO Box 3076
Little Rock, AR 72203
Phone: (501)682-1467

Credential Type: License. **Duration of License:** One year. **Requirements:** Must not be associated with any bookmaking practices which are illegal or would be detrimental to the public or the sport of racing.

Greyhound Presiding Judge, continued

Never convicted of a crime. Qualified as to ability and integrity of license sought and have endorsement of employer. Not be habitually intoxicated or addicted to drugs. Declare ownership or interest in any greyhound. Application must contain no falsehoods. 16 years of age. Application approved by Director of Racing. **Examination:** No **Fees:** $3 License. $3 Renewal.

5779

Greyhound Racing Director
Arkansas State Racing Commission
Ledbetter Bldg., Rm. G08
7th & Wolfe St.
PO Box 3076
Little Rock, AR 72203
Phone: (501)682-1467

Credential Type: License. **Duration of License:** One year. **Requirements:** Must not be associated with any bookmaking practices which are illegal or would be detrimental to the public or the sport of racing. Never convicted of a crime. Qualified as to ability and integrity of license sought and have endorsement of employer. Not be habitually intoxicated or addicted to drugs. Declare ownership or interest in any greyhound. Application must contain no falsehoods. 16 years of age. Application approved by Director of Racing. **Examination:** No **Fees:** $3 License. $3 Renewal.

5780

Greyhound Racing Secretary
Arkansas State Racing Commission
Ledbetter Bldg., Rm. G08
7th & Wolfe St.
PO Box 3076
Little Rock, AR 72203
Phone: (501)682-1467

Credential Type: License. **Duration of License:** One year. **Requirements:** Must not be associated with any bookmaking practices which are illegal or would be detrimental to the public or the sport of racing. Never convicted of a crime. Qualified as to ability and integrity of license sought and have endorsement of employer. Not be habitually intoxicated or addicted to drugs. Declare ownership or interest in any greyhound. Application must contain no falsehoods. 16 years of age. Application approved by Director of Racing. **Examination:** No **Fees:** $3 License. $3 Renewal.

5781

Greyhound Starter
Arkansas State Racing Commission
Ledbetter Bldg., Rm. G08
7th & Wolfe St.
PO Box 3076
Little Rock, AR 72203
Phone: (501)682-1467

Credential Type: License. **Duration of License:** One year. **Requirements:** Must not be associated with any bookmaking practices which are illegal or would be detrimental to the public or the sport of racing. Never convicted of a crime. Qualified as to ability and integrity of license sought and have endorsement of employer. Not be habitually intoxicated or addicted to drugs. Declare ownership or interest in any greyhound. Application must contain no falsehoods. 16 years of age. Application approved by Director of Racing. **Examination:** No **Fees:** $3 License. $3 Renewal.

5782

Greyhound Trainer Assistant (Racing)
Arkansas State Racing Commission
Ledbetter Bldg., Rm. G08
7th & Wolfe St.
PO Box 3076
Little Rock, AR 72203
Phone: (501)682-1467

Credential Type: License. **Duration of License:** One year. **Requirements:** Must not be associated with any bookmaking practices which are illegal or would be detrimental to the public or the sport of racing. Never convicted of a crime. Qualified as to ability and integrity of license sought and have endorsement of employer. Not be habitually intoxicated or addicted to drugs. Declare ownership or interest in any greyhound. Application must contain no falsehoods. 16 years of age. Application approved by Director of Racing. **Examination:** No **Fees:** $15 License. $15 Renewal.

5783

Greyhound Trainer (Racing)
Arkansas State Racing Commission
Ledbetter Bldg., Rm. G08
7th & Wolfe St.
PO Box 3076
Little Rock, AR 72203
Phone: (501)682-1467

Credential Type: License. **Duration of License:** One year. **Requirements:** Must not be associated with any bookmaking practices which are illegal or would be detrimental to the public or the sport of racing. Never convicted of a crime. Qualified as to ability and integrity of license sought and have endorsement of employer. Not be habitually intoxicated or addicted to drugs. Declare ownership or interest in any greyhound. Application must contain no falsehoods. 16 years of age. Application approved by Director of Racing. **Examination:** No **Fees:** $15 License. $15 Renewal.

5784

Handicapper
Arkansas State Racing Commission
Ledbetter Bldg., Rm. G08
7th & Wolfe St.
PO Box 3076
Little Rock, AR 72203
Phone: (501)682-1467

Credential Type: License. **Duration of License:** One year. **Requirements:** Application must be approved by the Stewards. Qualified as to ability of license sought and have the endorsement of the employer. Never convicted of a crime. Not be habitually intoxicated or addicted to drugs. Must not be engaged in any activity or practice which is illegal, undesirable or detrimental to the best interest of the public or the sport of racing. **Examination:** No **Fees:** $3 License. $3 Renewal.

5785

Horse Exerciser (Racing)
Arkansas State Racing Commission
Ledbetter Bldg., Rm. G08
7th & Wolfe St.
PO Box 3076
Little Rock, AR 72203
Phone: (501)682-1467

Credential Type: License. **Duration of License:** One year. **Requirements:** Application must be approved by the Stewards. Must be qualified as to ability and integrity of license sought and have the endorsement of the employer. Must be 16 years of age. Never convicted of a crime. Must not be habitually intoxicated or addicted to drugs. Must not be engaged in any activity or practice which is illegal, undesirable, or detrimental to the best interest of the public and the sport of racing. **Examination:** Yes. **Fees:** $3 License. $3 Renewal.

5786

Horse Race Starter
Arkansas State Racing Commission
Ledbetter Bldg., Rm. G08
7th & Wolfe St.
PO Box 3076
Little Rock, AR 72203
Phone: (501)682-1467

Credential Type: License. **Duration of License:** One year. **Requirements:** Application must be approved by the Stewards. Must be qualified as to ability and integrity of license sought and have the endorsement of the employer. Must be 16 years of age. Never convicted of a crime. Must not be habitually intoxicated or addicted to drugs. Must not be engaged in any activity or practice which is illegal, undesirable, or detrimental to the best interest of the public and the sport of racing. **Examination:** No **Fees:** $3 License. $3 Renewal.

5787

Horse Trainer Assistant (Racing)
Arkansas State Racing Commission
Ledbetter Bldg., Rm. G08
7th & Wolfe St.
PO Box 3076
Little Rock, AR 72203
Phone: (501)682-1467

Credential Type: License. **Duration of License:** One year. **Requirements:** Application must be approved by the Stewards. **Examination:** Yes. **Fees:** $15 License. $15 Renewal.

5788

Horse Trainer (Racing)
Arkansas State Racing Commission
Ledbetter Bldg., Rm. G08
7th & Wolfe St.
PO Box 3076
Little Rock, AR 72203
Phone: (501)682-1467

Credential Type: License. **Requirements:** Application must be approved by the Stewards. **Examination:** Yes, unless valid license is currently held from another racing jurisdiction and is in good standing with all jurisdictions. **Fees:** $15 License. $15 Renewal.

5789

Jockey
Arkansas State Racing Commission
Ledbetter Bldg., Rm. G08
7th & Wolfe St.
PO Box 3076
Little Rock, AR 72203
Phone: (501)682-1467

Credential Type: License. **Duration of License:** One year. **Requirements:** 18 years of age. Must not be an owner of any horse racing in Arkansas. Application must be approved by the Stewards. **Examination:** No **Fees:** $15 License. $15 Renewal.

5790

Jockey Agent
Arkansas State Racing Commission
Ledbetter Bldg., Rm. G08
7th & Wolfe St.
PO Box 3076
Little Rock, AR 72203
Phone: (501)682-1467

Credential Type: License. **Duration of License:** One year. **Requirements:** Application must be approved by the Stewards. **Examination:** No **Fees:** $15 License. $15 Renewal.

5791

Jockey Apprentice
Arkansas Sate Racing Commission
Ledbetter Bldg., Rm. G08
7th & Wolfe St.
PO Box 3076
Little Rock, AR 72203
Phone: (501)682-1467

Credential Type: License. **Duration of License:** One year. **Requirements:** Between ages of 18 and 25. Provide evidence of date of birth. Not have been licensed as a jockey in any country. Be bound to an owner or trainer for no less than three years, but no longer than five years. Proof of at least two years service with a racing stable. Application approved by the Stewards. **Examination:** No **Fees:** $15 License. $15 Renewal.

5792

Jockey Room Custodian
Arkansas State Racing Commission
Ledbetter Bldg., Rm. G08
7th & Wolfe St.
PO Box 3076
Little Rock, AR 72203
Phone: (501)682-1467

Credential Type: License. **Duration of License:** One year. **Requirements:** Application approved by the Stewards. Qualified as to ability and integrity of license sought and have the endorsement of employer. 16 years of age. Never convicted of a crime. Not be habitually addicted to drugs. Not be engaged in any activity or practice which is illegal, undesirable, or detrimental to the best interest of the public or the sport of racing. **Examination:** No **Fees:** $3 License. $3 Renewal.

5793

Lead Pony Rider (Racing)
Arkansas State Racing Commission
Ledbetter Bldg., Rm. G08
7th & Wolfe St.
PO Box 3076
Little Rock, AR 72203
Phone: (501)682-1467

Credential Type: License. **Duration of License:** One year. **Requirements:** Application approved by the Stewards. Qualified as to ability and integrity of license sought and have the endorsement of employer. 16 years of age. Never convicted of a crime. Not be habitually addicted to drugs. Not be engaged in any activity or practice which is illegal, undesirable, or detrimental to the best interest of the public or the sport of racing. **Examination:** No **Fees:** $3 License. $3 Renewal.

5794

Paddock Judge
Arkansas State Racing Commission
Ledbetter Bldg., Rm. G08
7th & Wolfe St.
PO Box 3076
Little Rock, AR 72203
Phone: (501)268-4351

Credential Type: License. **Duration of License:** One year. **Requirements:** Applications must be approved by the Stewards. Must be qualified as to ability and integrity of license sought. Must be 16 years of age. Must have endorsement of employer. Never convicted of a crime. Must not be habitually intoxicated or addicted to drugs. Must not be engaged in any activity or

Paddock Judge, continued

practice which is illegal or undesirable, or detrimental to the best interest of the public or the sport of racing. **Examination:** No **Fees:** $3 License. $3 Renewal.

5795

Pari-Mutuel Ticket Cashier
Arkansas State Racing Commission
Ledbetter Bldg., Rm. G08
7th & Wolfe St.
PO Box 3076
Little Rock, AR 72203
Phone: (501)682-1467

Credential Type: License. **Duration of License:** One year. **Requirements:** Applications must be approved by the Stewards. Must be qualified as to ability and integrity of license sought. Must be 16 years of age. Must have endorsement of employer. Never convicted of a crime. Must not be habitually intoxicated or addicted to drugs. Must not be engaged in any activity or practice which is illegal or undesirable, or detrimental to the best interest of the public or the sport of racing. **Examination:** No **Fees:** $3 License. $3 Renewal.

5796

Pari-Mutuel Ticket Checker
Arkansas State Racing Commission
Ledbetter Bldg., Rm. G08
7th & Wolfe St.
PO Box 3076
Little Rock, AR 72203
Phone: (501)682-1467

Credential Type: License. **Duration of License:** One year. **Requirements:** Applications must be approved by the Stewards. Must be qualified as to ability and integrity of license sought. Must be 16 years of age. Must have endorsement of employer. Never convicted of a crime. Must not be habitually intoxicated or addicted to drugs. Must not be engaged in any activity or practice which is illegal or undesirable, or detrimental to the best interest of the public or the sport of racing. **Examination:** No **Fees:** $3 License. $3 Renewal.

5797

Pari-Mutuel Ticket Seller
Arkansas State Racing Commission
Ledbetter Bldg., Rm. G08
7th & Wolfe St.
PO Box 3076
Little Rock, AR 72203
Phone: (501)682-1467

Credential Type: License. **Duration of License:** One year. **Requirements:** Applications must be approved by the Stewards. Must be qualified as to ability and integrity of license sought. Must be 16 years of age. Must have endorsement of employer. Never convicted of a crime. Must not be habitually intoxicated or addicted to drugs. Must not be engaged in any activity or practice which is illegal or undesirable, or detrimental to the best interest of the public or the sport of racing. **Examination:** No **Fees:** $3 License. $3 renewal.

5798

Patrol Judge
Arkansas State Racing Commission
Ledbetter Bldg., Rm. G08
7th & Wolfe St.
PO Box 3076
Little Rock, AR 72203
Phone: (501)682-1467

Credential Type: License. **Duration of License:** One year. **Requirements:** Applications must be approved by the Stewards. Must be qualified as to ability and integrity of license sought. Must be 16 years of age. Must have endorsement of employer. Never convicted of a crime. Must not be habitually intoxicated or addicted to drugs. Must not be engaged in any activity or practice which is illegal or undesirable, or detrimental to the best interest of the public or the sport of racing. **Examination:** No **Fees:** $3 License. $3 Renewal.

5799

Placing Judge
Arkansas State Racing Commission
Ledbetter Bldg., Rm. G08
7th & Wolfe St.
PO Box 3076
Little Rock, AR 72203
Phone: (501)682-1467

Credential Type: License. **Duration of License:** One year. **Requirements:** Application must be approved by the Stewards. Must be qualified as to ability and integrity of license sought and have the endorsement of employer. 16 years of age. Never convicted of a crime. Not be habitually addicted to drugs or intoxicated. Must not be engaged in any activity which is illegal, undesirable or detrimental to the best interest of the public and the sport of racing. **Examination:** No **Fees:** $3 License. $3 Renewal.

5800

Racetrack Steward
Arkansas State Racing Commission
Ledbetter Bldg., Rm. G08
7th & Wolfe St.
PO Box 3076
Little Rock, AR 72203
Phone: (501)682-1467

Credential Type: License. **Requirements:** Must have held a position related to race meeting prior to application; duration must be at least 60 days during the last three years. **Examination:** No **Fees:** None

5801

Racing Agent
Arkansas State Racing Commission
Ledbetter Bldg., Rm. G08
7th & Wolfe St.
PO Box 3076
Little Rock, AR 72203
Phone: (501)682-1467

Credential Type: License. **Duration of License:** One year. **Requirements:** Meet all requirements listed in the Arkansas State Racing Commission Rules and Regulations. Must be approved by the Stewards. **Examination:** No **Fees:** $5 License (per owner or trainer represented per year).

5802

Racing Secretary
Arkansas State Racing Commission
Ledbetter Bldg., Rm. G08
7th & Wolfe St.
PO Box 3076
Little Rock, AR 72203
Phone: (501)682-1467

Credential Type: License. **Duration of License:** One year. **Requirements:** Application must be approved by the Stewards. Must be qualified as to ability and integrity of license sought and have the endorsement of employer. 16 years of age. Never convicted of a crime. Not be habitually addicted to drugs or intoxicated. Must not be engaged in any activity which is illegal, undesirable or detrimental to the best interest of the public and the sport of racing. **Examination:** No **Fees:** $3 License. $3 Renewal.

Racetrack Occupations

5803

Receiving Barn Custodian (Racing)
Arkansas State Racing Commission
Ledbetter Bldg., Rm. G08
7th & Wolfe St.
PO Box 3076
Little Rock, AR 72203
Phone: (501)862-1467

Credential Type: License. **Duration of License:** One year. **Requirements:** Application must be approved by the Stewards. Must be qualified as to ability and integrity of license sought and have the endorsement of employer. 16 years of age. Never convicted of a crime. Not be habitually addicted to drugs or intoxicated. Must not be engaged in any activity which is illegal, undesirable or detrimental to the best interest of the public and the sport of racing. **Examination:** No **Fees:** $3 License. $3 Renewal.

5804

Stable Attendant (Racing)
Arkansas State Racing Commission
Ledbetter Bldg., Rm. G08
7th & Wolfe St.
PO Box 3076
Little Rock, AR 72203
Phone: (501)682-1467

Credential Type: License. **Duration of License:** One year. **Requirements:** Application must be approved by the Stewards. Must be qualified as to ability and integrity of license sought and have the endorsement of employer. 16 years of age. Never convicted of a crime. Not be habitually addicted to drugs or intoxicated. Must not be engaged in any activity which is illegal, undesirable or detrimental to the best interest of the public and the sport of racing. **Examination:** No **Fees:** $3 License. $3 Renewal.

5805

Track Superintendent
Arkansas State Racing Commission
Ledbetter Bldg., Rm. G08
7th & Wolfe St.
PO Box 3076
Little Rock, AR 72203
Phone: (501)682-1467

Credential Type: License. **Duration of License:** One year. **Requirements:** Application must be approved by the Stewards. Must be qualified as to ability and integrity of license sought and have the endorsement of employer. 16 years of age. Never convicted of a crime. Not be habitually addicted to drugs or intoxicated. Must not be engaged in any activity which is illegal, undesirable or detrimental to the best interest of the public and the sport of racing. **Examination:** No **Fees:** $3 License. $3 Renewal.

California

5806

Announcer (Racetrack)
California Horse Racing Board
1010 Hurley Way, Ste. 190
Sacramento, CA 95825
Phone: (916)920-7178

Credential Type: License Registration. **Requirements:** Submit application and fingerprint card. Pay fee. **Fees:** $75 registration fee.

5807

Apprentice Jockey (Racetrack)
California Horse Racing Board
1010 Hurley Way, Ste. 190
Sacramento, CA 95825
Phone: (916)920-7178

Credential Type: License Registration. **Requirements:** Submit application and fingerprint card. Pay fee. **Fees:** $150 registration fee.

5808

Assistant Manager (Racetrack)
California Horse Racing Board
1010 Hurley Way, Ste. 190
Sacramento, CA 95825
Phone: (916)920-7178

Credential Type: License Registration. **Requirements:** Submit application and fingerprint card. Pay fee. **Fees:** $75 registration fee.

5809

Assistant to a Racing Official, Official, or Manager (Racetrack)
California Horse Racing Board
1010 Hurley Way, Ste. 190
Sacramento, CA 95825
Phone: (916)920-7178

Credential Type: License Registration. **Requirements:** Submit application and fingerprint card. Pay fee. **Fees:** $75 registration fee.

5810

Assistant Starter (Racetrack)
California Horse Racing Board
1010 Hurley Way, Ste. 190
Sacramento, CA 95825
Phone: (916)920-7178

Credential Type: License Registration. **Requirements:** Submit application and fingerprint card. Pay fee. **Fees:** $75 registration fee.

5811

Assistant Trainer (Racetrack)
California Horse Racing Board
1010 Hurley Way, Ste. 190
Sacramento, CA 95825
Phone: (916)920-7178

Credential Type: License Registration. **Requirements:** Submit application and fingerprint card. Pay fee. **Fees:** $150 registration fee.

5812

Assistant to the Veterinarian (Racetrack)
California Horse Racing Board
1010 Hurley Way, Ste. 190
Sacramento, CA 95825
Phone: (916)920-7178

Credential Type: License Registration. **Requirements:** Submit application and fingerprint card. Pay fee. **Fees:** $75 registration fee.

5813

Bloodstock Agent (Racetrack)
California Horse Racing Board
1010 Hurley Way, Ste. 190
Sacramento, CA 95825
Phone: (916)920-7178

Credential Type: License Registration. **Requirements:** Submit application and fingerprint card. Pay fee. **Fees:** $150 registration fee.

5814

Clerical Employee (Racetrack)
California Horse Racing Board
1010 Hurley Way, Ste. 190
Sacramento, CA 95825
Phone: (916)920-7178

Credential Type: License Registration. **Requirements:** Submit application and fin-

Clerical Employee (Racetrack), continued

gerprint card. Pay fee. **Fees:** $75 registration fee.

5815

Colors Attendant (Racetrack)
California Horse Racing Board
1010 Hurley Way, Ste. 190
Sacramento, CA 95825
Phone: (916)920-7178

Credential Type: License Registration. **Requirements:** Submit application and fingerprint card. Pay fee. **Fees:** $75 registration fee.

5816

Custodian (Racetrack)
California Horse Racing Board
1010 Hurley Way, Ste. 190
Sacramento, CA 95825
Phone: (916)920-7178

Credential Type: License Registration. **Requirements:** Submit application and fingerprint card. Pay fee. **Fees:** $75 registration fee.

5817

Driver (Racetrack)
California Horse Racing Board
1010 Hurley Way, Ste. 190
Sacramento, CA 95825
Phone: (916)920-7178

Credential Type: License Registration. **Requirements:** Submit application and fingerprint card. Pay fee. **Fees:** $150 registration fee.

5818

Exercise Rider (Racetrack)
California Horse Racing Board
1010 Hurley Way, Ste. 190
Sacramento, CA 95825
Phone: (916)920-7178

Credential Type: License Registration. **Requirements:** Submit application and fingerprint card. Pay fee. **Fees:** $75 registration fee.

5819

Flagman (Racetrack)
California Horse Racing Board
1010 Hurley Way, Ste. 190
Sacramento, CA 95825
Phone: (916)920-7178

Credential Type: License Registration. **Requirements:** Submit application and fingerprint card. Pay fee. **Fees:** $75 registration fee.

5820

Food Service Person (Racetrack)
California Horse Racing Board
1010 Hurley Way, Ste. 190
Sacramento, CA 95825
Phone: (916)920-7178

Credential Type: License Registration. **Requirements:** Submit application and fingerprint card. Pay fee. **Fees:** $75 registration fee.

5821

Groom or Stable Employee (Racetrack)
California Horse Racing Board
1010 Hurley Way, Ste. 190
Sacramento, CA 95825
Phone: (916)920-7178

Credential Type: License Registration. **Requirements:** Submit application and fingerprint card. Pay fee. **Fees:** $35 registration fee. $20 annual renewal fee.

5822

Horse Owner by Open Claim (Racetrack)
California Horse Racing Board
1010 Hurley Way, Ste. 190
Sacramento, CA 95825
Phone: (916)920-7178

Credential Type: License Registration. **Requirements:** Submit application and fingerprint card. Pay fee. **Fees:** $250 registration fee.

5823

Horse Owner (Racetrack)
California Horse Racing Board
1010 Hurley Way, Ste. 190
Sacramento, CA 95825
Phone: (916)920-7178

Credential Type: License Registration. **Requirements:** Submit application and fingerprint card. Pay fee. **Fees:** $150 registration fee.

5824

Horseshoer (Racetrack)
California Horse Racing Board
1010 Hurley Way, Ste. 190
Sacramento, CA 95825
Phone: (916)920-7178

Credential Type: License Registration. **Requirements:** Submit application and fingerprint card. Pay fee. **Fees:** $75 registration fee.

5825

Jockey Agent (Racetrack)
California Horse Racing Board
1010 Hurley Way, Ste. 190
Sacramento, CA 95825
Phone: (916)920-7178

Credential Type: License Registration. **Requirements:** Submit application and fingerprint card. Pay fee. **Fees:** $150 registration fee.

5826

Jockey (Racetrack)
California Horse Racing Board
1010 Hurley Way, Ste. 190
Sacramento, CA 95825
Phone: (916)920-7178

Credential Type: License Registration. **Requirements:** Submit application and fingerprint card. Pay fee. **Fees:** $150 registration fee.

5827

Jockey Room/Driver's Room Attendant (Racetrack)
California Horse Racing Board
1010 Hurley Way, Ste. 190
Sacramento, CA 95825
Phone: (916)920-7178

Credential Type: License Registration. **Requirements:** Submit application and fingerprint card. Pay fee. **Fees:** $75 registration fee.

5828

Marshal (Racetrack)
California Horse Racing Board
1010 Hurley Way, Ste. 190
Sacramento, CA 95825
Phone: (916)920-7178

Credential Type: License Registration.
Requirements: Submit application and fingerprint card. Pay fee. **Fees:** $75 registration fee.

5829

Officer, Director, or Partner of a Racing Association (Racetrack)
California Horse Racing Board
1010 Hurley Way, Ste. 190
Sacramento, CA 95825
Phone: (916)920-7178

Credential Type: License Registration.
Requirements: Submit application and fingerprint card. Pay fee. **Fees:** $200 registration fee.

5830

Official and Manager of a Racing Association (Racetrack)
California Horse Racing Board
1010 Hurley Way, Ste. 190
Sacramento, CA 95825
Phone: (916)920-7178

Credential Type: License Registration.
Requirements: Submit application and fingerprint card. Pay fee. **Fees:** $150 registration fee.

5831

Outrider (Racetrack)
California Horse Racing Board
1010 Hurley Way, Ste. 190
Sacramento, CA 95825
Phone: (916)920-7178

Credential Type: License Registration.
Requirements: Submit application and fingerprint card. Pay fee. **Fees:** $75 registration fee.

5832

Paddock Attendant (Racetrack)
California Horse Racing Board
1010 Hurley Way, Ste. 190
Sacramento, CA 95825
Phone: (916)920-7178

Credential Type: License Registration.
Requirements: Submit application and fingerprint card. Pay fee. **Fees:** $75 registration fee.

5833

Parimutuel Employee (Racetrack)
California Horse Racing Board
1010 Hurley Way, Ste. 190
Sacramento, CA 95825
Phone: (916)920-7178

Credential Type: License Registration.
Requirements: Submit application and fingerprint card. Pay fee. **Fees:** $75 registration fee.

5834

Photofinish Operator (Racetrack)
California Horse Racing Board
1010 Hurley Way, Ste. 190
Sacramento, CA 95825
Phone: (916)920-7178

Credential Type: License Registration.
Requirements: Submit application and fingerprint card. Pay fee. **Fees:** $75 registration fee.

5835

Pony Rider (Racetrack)
California Horse Racing Board
1010 Hurley Way, Ste. 190
Sacramento, CA 95825
Phone: (916)920-7178

Credential Type: License Registration.
Requirements: Submit application and fingerprint card. Pay fee. **Fees:** $75 registration fee.

5836

Racing Official (Racetrack)
California Horse Racing Board
1010 Hurley Way, Ste. 190
Sacramento, CA 95825
Phone: (916)920-7178

Credential Type: License Registration.
Requirements: Submit application and fingerprint card. Pay fee. **Fees:** $150 registration fee.

5837

Satellite Facility Supervisor (Racetrack)
California Horse Racing Board
1010 Hurley Way, Ste. 190
Sacramento, CA 95825
Phone: (916)920-7178

Credential Type: License Registration.
Requirements: Submit application and fingerprint card. Pay fee. **Fees:** $150 registration fee.

5838

Security Guard (Racetrack)
California Horse Racing Board
1010 Hurley Way, Ste. 190
Sacramento, CA 95825
Phone: (916)920-7178

Credential Type: License Registration.
Requirements: Submit application and fingerprint card. Pay fee. **Fees:** $75 registration fee.

5839

Security Investigator (Racetrack)
California Horse Racing Board
1010 Hurley Way, Ste. 190
Sacramento, CA 95825
Phone: (916)920-7178

Credential Type: License Registration.
Requirements: Submit application and fingerprint card. Pay fee. **Fees:** $75 registration fee.

5840

Security Officer (Racetrack)
California Horse Racing Board
1010 Hurley Way, Ste. 190
Sacramento, CA 95825
Phone: (916)920-7178

Credential Type: License Registration.
Requirements: Submit application and fingerprint card. Pay fee. **Fees:** $75 registration fee.

5841

Stable Agent (Racetrack)
California Horse Racing Board
1010 Hurley Way, Ste. 190
Sacramento, CA 95825
Phone: (916)920-7178

Credential Type: License Registration.
Requirements: Submit application and fin-

California

Stable Agent (Racetrack), continued

gerprint card. Pay fee. **Fees:** $75 registration fee.

5842

Stable Foreman (Racetrack)
California Horse Racing Board
1010 Hurley Way, Ste. 190
Sacramento, CA 95825
Phone: (916)920-7178

Credential Type: License Registration. **Requirements:** Submit application and fingerprint card. Pay fee. **Fees:** $75 registration fee.

5843

Starting Gate Driver (Racetrack)
California Horse Racing Board
1010 Hurley Way, Ste. 190
Sacramento, CA 95825
Phone: (916)920-7178

Credential Type: License Registration. **Requirements:** Submit application and fingerprint card. Pay fee. **Fees:** $75 registration fee.

5844

Steward (Racetrack)
California Horse Racing Board
1010 Hurley Way, Ste. 190
Sacramento, CA 95825
Phone: (916)920-7178

Credential Type: License Registration. **Requirements:** Submit application and fingerprint card. Pay fee. **Fees:** $150 registration fee.

5845

Steward's Aid (Racetrack)
California Horse Racing Board
1010 Hurley Way, Ste. 190
Sacramento, CA 95825
Phone: (916)920-7178

Credential Type: License Registration. **Requirements:** Submit application and fingerprint card. Pay fee. **Fees:** $75 registration fee.

5846

Superintendent (Racetrack)
California Horse Racing Board
1010 Hurley Way, Ste. 190
Sacramento, CA 95825
Phone: (916)920-7178

Credential Type: License Registration. **Requirements:** Submit application and fingerprint card. Pay fee. **Fees:** $75 registration fee.

5847

Totalisator Technician (Racetrack)
California Horse Racing Board
1010 Hurley Way, Ste. 190
Sacramento, CA 95825
Phone: (916)920-7178

Credential Type: License Registration. **Requirements:** Submit application and fingerprint card. Pay fee. **Fees:** $75 registration fee.

5848

Trainer (Racetrack)
California Horse Racing Board
1010 Hurley Way, Ste. 190
Sacramento, CA 95825
Phone: (916)920-7178

Credential Type: License Registration. **Requirements:** Submit application and fingerprint card. Pay fee. **Fees:** $150 registration fee.

5849

Valet (Racetrack)
California Horse Racing Board
1010 Hurley Way, Ste. 190
Sacramento, CA 95825
Phone: (916)920-7178

Credential Type: License Registration. **Requirements:** Submit application and fingerprint card. Pay fee. **Fees:** $75 registration fee.

5850

Vendor (Racetrack)
California Horse Racing Board
1010 Hurley Way, Ste. 190
Sacramento, CA 95825
Phone: (916)920-7178

Credential Type: License Registration. **Requirements:** Submit application and fingerprint card. Pay fee. **Fees:** $75 registration fee.

5851

Veterinarian (Racetrack)
California Horse Racing Board
1010 Hurley Way, Ste. 190
Sacramento, CA 95825
Phone: (916)920-7178

Credential Type: License Registration. **Requirements:** Submit application and fingerprint card. Pay fee. **Fees:** $150 registration fee.

5852

Video Operator (Racetrack)
California Horse Racing Board
1010 Hurley Way, Ste. 190
Sacramento, CA 95825
Phone: (916)920-7178

Credential Type: License Registration. **Requirements:** Submit application and fingerprint card. Pay fee. **Fees:** $75 registration fee.

Colorado

5853

Apprentice Jockey (Horse)
Colorado Racing Commission
Dept. of Regulatory Agencies
1560 Broadway, Ste. 1540
Denver, CO 80202
Phone: (303)894-2990
Fax: (303)894-7580

Credential Type: Apprentice Jockey License. **Requirements:** Submit application and pay fee. **Fees:** $44 license fee.

5854

Assistant Starter (Horse)
Colorado Racing Commission
Dept. of Regulatory Agencies
1560 Broadway, Ste. 1540
Denver, CO 80202
Phone: (303)894-2990
Fax: (303)894-7580

Credential Type: Assistant Starter License. **Requirements:** Submit application and pay fee. **Fees:** $24 license fee.

5855

Assistant Trainer (Greyhound Racing)
Colorado Racing Commission
Dept. of Regulatory Agencies
1560 Broadway, Ste. 1540
Denver, CO 80202
Phone: (303)894-2990
Fax: (303)894-7580

Credential Type: Assistant Trainer License. **Duration of License:** Three years. **Requirements:** Submit application, pay fees, and pass examination. **Examination:** Assistant Trainer's Test. **Fees:** $33 application/exam/license fee.

5856

Assistant Trainer (Horse Racing)
Colorado Racing Commission
Dept. of Regulatory Agencies
1560 Broadway, Ste. 1540
Denver, CO 80202
Phone: (303)894-2990
Fax: (303)894-7580

Credential Type: Assistant Trainer License. **Duration of License:** Three years. **Requirements:** Submit application, pay fees, and pass examination. **Examination:** Assistant Trainer's Test. **Fees:** $59 application/exam/license fee.

5857

Authorized Agent (Greyhound)
Colorado Racing Commission
Dept. of Regulatory Agencies
1560 Broadway, Ste. 1540
Denver, CO 80202
Phone: (303)894-2990
Fax: (303)894-7580

Credential Type: Authorized Agent License. **Duration of License:** Three years. **Requirements:** Submit application and pay fee. **Fees:** $44 license fee.

5858

Authorized Agent (Horse)
Colorado Racing Commission
Dept. of Regulatory Agencies
1560 Broadway, Ste. 1540
Denver, CO 80202
Phone: (303)894-2990
Fax: (303)894-7580

Credential Type: Authorized Agent License. **Requirements:** Submit application and pay fee. **Fees:** $24 license fee.

5859

Exercise Person (Horse Racing)
Colorado Racing Commission
Dept. of Regulatory Agencies
1560 Broadway, Ste. 1540
Denver, CO 80202
Phone: (303)894-2990
Fax: (303)894-7580

Credential Type: Exercise Person License. **Requirements:** Submit application and pay fee. **Fees:** $24 license fee.

5860

Groom (Greyhound Racing)
Colorado Racing Commission
Dept. of Regulatory Agencies
1560 Broadway, Ste. 1540
Denver, CO 80202
Phone: (303)894-2990
Fax: (303)894-7580

Credential Type: Groom License. **Requirements:** Submit application and pay fee. **Fees:** $24 license fee.

5861

Groom (Horse Racing)
Colorado Racing Commission
Dept. of Regulatory Agencies
1560 Broadway, Ste. 1540
Denver, CO 80202
Phone: (303)894-2990
Fax: (303)894-7580

Credential Type: Groom License. **Requirements:** Submit application and pay fee. **Fees:** $24 license fee.

5862

Jockey Agent (Horse)
Colorado Racing Commission
Dept. of Regulatory Agencies
1560 Broadway, Ste. 1540
Denver, CO 80202
Phone: (303)894-2990
Fax: (303)894-7580

Credential Type: Jockey Agent License. **Requirements:** Submit application and pay fee. **Fees:** $44 license fee.

5863

Jockey (Horse)
Colorado Racing Commission
Dept. of Regulatory Agencies
1560 Broadway, Ste. 1540
Denver, CO 80202
Phone: (303)894-2990
Fax: (303)894-7580

Credential Type: Jockey License. **Requirements:** Submit application and pay fee. **Fees:** $44 license fee.

5864

Kennel Helper (Greyhound Racing)
Colorado Racing Commission
Dept. of Regulatory Agencies
1560 Broadway, Ste. 1540
Denver, CO 80202
Phone: (303)894-2990
Fax: (303)894-7580

Credential Type: Kennel Helper License. **Duration of License:** Three years. **Requirements:** Submit application and pay fee. **Fees:** $24 license fee.

5865

Mutuel Employee (Greyhound)
Colorado Racing Commission
Dept. of Regulatory Agencies
1560 Broadway, Ste. 1540
Denver, CO 80202
Phone: (303)894-2990
Fax: (303)894-7580

Credential Type: Mutuel Employee License. **Duration of License:** Three years. **Requirements:** Submit application and pay fee. **Fees:** $29 license fee.

5866

Mutuel Employee (Horse)
Colorado Racing Commission
Dept. of Regulatory Agencies
1560 Broadway, Ste. 1540
Denver, CO 80202
Phone: (303)894-2990
Fax: (303)894-7580

Credential Type: Mutuel Employee License. **Duration of License:** Three years. **Requirements:** Submit application and pay fee. **Fees:** $29 license fee.

5867

Owner (Greyhound)
Colorado Racing Commission
Dept. of Regulatory Agencies
1560 Broadway, Ste. 1540
Denver, CO 80202
Phone: (303)894-2990
Fax: (303)894-7580

Credential Type: Owner License. **Duration of License:** Three years. **Requirements:** Submit application and pay fee. **Fees:** $44 license fee.

5868

Owner (Horse)
Colorado Racing Commission
Dept. of Regulatory Agencies
1560 Broadway, Ste. 1540
Denver, CO 80202
Phone: (303)894-2990
Fax: (303)894-7580

Credential Type: Owner License. **Duration of License:** Three years. **Requirements:** Submit application and pay fee. **Fees:** $44 license fee.

5869

Owner/Trainer (Greyhound)
Colorado Racing Commission
Dept. of Regulatory Agencies
1560 Broadway, Ste. 1540
Denver, CO 80202
Phone: (303)894-2990
Fax: (303)894-7580

Credential Type: Owner/Trainer License. **Duration of License:** Three years. **Requirements:** Submit application, pay fees, and pass examination. **Examination:** Trainer's Test. **Reciprocity:** Yes. **Fees:** $79 application/exam/license fee.

5870

Owner/Trainer (Horse)
Colorado Racing Commission
Dept. of Regulatory Agencies
1560 Broadway, Ste. 1540
Denver, CO 80202
Phone: (303)894-2990
Fax: (303)894-7580

Credential Type: Owner/Trainer License. **Duration of License:** Three years. **Requirements:** Submit application, pay fees, and pass examination. **Examination:** Trainer's Test. **Fees:** $79 application/exam/license fee.

5871

Plater (Horse Racing)
Colorado Racing Commission
Dept. of Regulatory Agencies
1560 Broadway, Ste. 1540
Denver, CO 80202
Phone: (303)894-2990
Fax: (303)894-7580

Credential Type: Plater License. **Duration of License:** Three years. **Requirements:** Submit application and pay fee. **Fees:** $59 license fee.

5872

Pony Person (Racing)
Colorado Racing Commission
Dept. of Regulatory Agencies
1560 Broadway, Ste. 1540
Denver, CO 80202
Phone: (303)894-2990
Fax: (303)894-7580

Credential Type: Pony Person License. **Duration of License:** Three years. **Requirements:** Submit application and pay fee. **Fees:** $24 license fee.

5873

Racing Official (Greyhound)
Colorado Racing Commission
Dept. of Regulatory Agencies
1560 Broadway, Ste. 1540
Denver, CO 80202
Phone: (303)894-2990
Fax: (303)894-7580

Credential Type: Steward/Judge, Racing Official License. **Duration of License:** Three years. **Requirements:** Submit application, pay fees, and pass examination. **Examination:** Steward/Judge Exam. **Fees:** $44 application/exam/license fee.

5874

Racing Official (Horse)
Colorado Racing Commission
Dept. of Regulatory Agencies
1560 Broadway, Ste. 1540
Denver, CO 80202
Phone: (303)894-2990
Fax: (303)894-7580

Credential Type: Steward/Judge, Racing Official License. **Duration of License:** Three years. **Requirements:** Submit application, pay fees, and pass examination. **Examination:** Steward/Judge Exam. **Fees:** $44 application/exam/license fee.

5875

Track Veterinarian (Horse)
Colorado Racing Commission
Dept. of Regulatory Agencies
1560 Broadway, Ste. 1540
Denver, CO 80202
Phone: (303)894-2990
Fax: (303)894-7580

Credential Type: Track Veterinarian License. **Duration of License:** Three years. **Requirements:** Submit application and pay fee. **Fees:** $59 license fee.

5876

Trainer (Greyhound Racing)
Colorado Racing Commission
Dept. of Regulatory Agencies
1560 Broadway, Ste. 1540
Denver, CO 80202
Phone: (303)894-2990
Fax: (303)894-7580

Credential Type: Trainer License. **Duration of License:** Three years. **Requirements:** Submit application, pay fees, and pass examination. **Examination:** Trainer's Test. **Reciprocity:** Yes. **Fees:** $59 application/exam/license fee.

5877

Trainer (Horse Racing)
Colorado Racing Commission
Dept. of Regulatory Agencies
1560 Broadway, Ste. 1540
Denver, CO 80202
Phone: (303)894-2990
Fax: (303)894-7580

Credential Type: Trainer License. **Duration of License:** Three years. **Requirements:** Submit application, pay fees, and pass examination. **Examination:** Trainer's Test. **Fees:** $59 application/exam/license fee.

5878

Valet (Horse)
Colorado Racing Commission
Dept. of Regulatory Agencies
1560 Broadway, Ste. 1540
Denver, CO 80202
Phone: (303)894-2990
Fax: (303)894-7580

Credential Type: Valet License. **Duration of License:** Three years. **Requirements:** Submit application and pay fee. **Fees:** $29 license fee.

Connecticut

5879

Administrator (Racetrack)
Connecticut Div. of Special Revenue
Russell Rd.
PO Box 11424
Newington, CT 06111-0424
Phone: (203)566-2756

Credential Type: License Registration.
Requirements: Submit application and fingerprint card. Pay fee. **Fees:** $5 registration fee.

5880

Announcer (Racetrack)
Connecticut Div. of Special Revenue
Russell Rd.
PO Box 11424
Newington, CT 06111-0424
Phone: (203)566-2756

Credential Type: License Registration.
Requirements: Submit application and fingerprint card. Pay fee. **Fees:** $5 registration fee.

5881

Assistant Announcer (Racetrack)
Connecticut Div. of Special Revenue
Russell Rd.
PO Box 11424
Newington, CT 06111-0424
Phone: (203)566-2756

Credential Type: License Registration.
Requirements: Submit application and fingerprint card. Pay fee. **Fees:** $5 registration fee.

5882

Assistant Controller (Racetrack)
Connecticut Div. of Special Revenue
Russell Rd.
PO Box 11424
Newington, CT 06111-0424
Phone: (203)566-2756

Credential Type: License Registration.
Requirements: Submit application and fingerprint card. Pay fee. **Fees:** $5 registration fee.

5883

Assistant Director of Security (Racetrack)
Connecticut Div. of Special Revenue
Russell Rd.
PO Box 11424
Newington, CT 06111-0424
Phone: (203)566-2756

Credential Type: License Registration.
Requirements: Submit application and fingerprint card. Pay fee. **Fees:** $20 registration fee.

5884

Assistant General Manager (Racetrack)
Connecticut Div. of Special Revenue
Russell Rd.
PO Box 11424
Newington, CT 06111-0424
Phone: (203)566-2756

Credential Type: License Registration.
Requirements: Submit application and fingerprint card. Pay fee. **Fees:** $20 registration fee.

5885

Assistant Manager (Racetrack)
Connecticut Div. of Special Revenue
Russell Rd.
PO Box 11424
Newington, CT 06111-0424
Phone: (203)566-2756

Credential Type: License Registration.
Requirements: Submit application and fingerprint card. Pay fee. **Fees:** $5-$20 registration fee.

5886

Assistant Operations Manager (Racetrack)
Connecticut Div. of Special Revenue
Russell Rd.
PO Box 11424
Newington, CT 06111-0424
Phone: (203)566-2756

Credential Type: License Registration.
Requirements: Submit application and fingerprint card. Pay fee. **Fees:** $5 registration fee.

5887

Assistant Plant Superintendent (Racetrack)
Connecticut Div. of Special Revenue
Russell Rd.
PO Box 11424
Newington, CT 06111-0424
Phone: (203)566-2756

Credential Type: License Registration.
Requirements: Submit application and fingerprint card. Pay fee. **Fees:** $5 registration fee.

5888

Assistant Player's Manager (Racetrack)
Connecticut Div. of Special Revenue
Russell Rd.
PO Box 11424
Newington, CT 06111-0424
Phone: (203)566-2756

Credential Type: License Registration.
Requirements: Submit application and fingerprint card. Pay fee. **Fees:** $20 registration fee.

5889

Assistant Racing Secretary (Racetrack)
Connecticut Div. of Special Revenue
Russell Rd.
PO Box 11424
Newington, CT 06111-0424
Phone: (203)566-2756

Credential Type: License Registration.
Requirements: Submit application and fingerprint card. Pay fee. **Fees:** $20 registration fee.

5890

Assistant Starter (Racetrack)
Connecticut Div. of Special Revenue
Russell Rd.
PO Box 11424
Newington, CT 06111-0424
Phone: (203)566-2756

Credential Type: License Registration.
Requirements: Submit application and fingerprint card. Pay fee. **Fees:** $20 registration fee.

5891

Assistant Trainer (Racetrack)
Connecticut Div. of Special Revenue
Russell Rd.
PO Box 11424
Newington, CT 06111-0424
Phone: (203)566-2756

Credential Type: License Registration.
Requirements: Submit application and fingerprint card. Pay fee. **Fees:** $20 registration fee.

5892

Authorized Agent (Greyhound Track)
Connecticut Div. of Special Revenue
Russell Rd.
PO Box 11424
Newington, CT 06111-0424
Phone: (203)566-2756

Credential Type: License Registration.
Requirements: Submit application and fingerprint card. Pay fee. **Fees:** $5 registration fee.

5893

Ball Boy (Racetrack)
Connecticut Div. of Special Revenue
Russell Rd.
PO Box 11424
Newington, CT 06111-0424
Phone: (203)566-2756

Credential Type: License Registration.
Requirements: Submit application and fingerprint card. Pay fee. **Fees:** $5 registration fee.

5894

Ball Repairer (Racetrack)
Connecticut Div. of Special Revenue
Russell Rd.
PO Box 11424
Newington, CT 06111-0424
Phone: (203)566-2756

Credential Type: License Registration.
Requirements: Submit application and fingerprint card. Pay fee. **Fees:** $5 registration fee.

5895

Ballmaker (Racetrack)
Connecticut Div. of Special Revenue
Russell Rd.
PO Box 11424
Newington, CT 06111-0424
Phone: (203)566-2756

Credential Type: License Registration.
Requirements: Submit application and fingerprint card. Pay fee. **Fees:** $5 registration fee.

5896

Bench Technician (Racetrack)
Connecticut Div. of Special Revenue
Russell Rd.
PO Box 11424
Newington, CT 06111-0424
Phone: (203)566-2756

Credential Type: License Registration.
Requirements: Submit application and fingerprint card. Pay fee. **Fees:** $5 registration fee.

5897

Box Office Employee (Racetrack)
Connecticut Div. of Special Revenue
Russell Rd.
PO Box 11424
Newington, CT 06111-0424
Phone: (203)566-2756

Credential Type: License Registration.
Requirements: Submit application and fingerprint card. Pay fee. **Fees:** $5 registration fee.

5898

Brakeman (Racetrack)
Connecticut Div. of Special Revenue
Russell Rd.
PO Box 11424
Newington, CT 06111-0424
Phone: (203)566-2756

Credential Type: License Registration.
Requirements: Submit application and fingerprint card. Pay fee. **Fees:** $5 registration fee.

5899

Budget Analyst (Racetrack)
Connecticut Div. of Special Revenue
Russel Rd.
PO Box 11424
Newington, CT 06111-0424
Phone: (203)566-2756

Credential Type: License Registration.
Requirements: Submit application and fingerprint card. Pay fee. **Fees:** $5 registration fee.

5900

Business Agent (Racetrack)
Connecticut Div. of Special Revenue
Russell Rd.
PO Box 11424
Newington, CT 06111-0424
Phone: (203)566-2756

Credential Type: License Registration.
Requirements: Submit application and fingerprint card. Pay fee. **Fees:** $5 registration fee.

5901

Cameraman (Racetrack)
Connecticut Div. of Special Revenue
Russell Rd.
PO Box 11424
Newington, CT 06111-0424
Phone: (203)566-2756

Credential Type: License Registration.
Requirements: Submit application and fingerprint card. Pay fee. **Fees:** $5 registration fee.

5902

Cesta Maker (Racetrack)
Connecticut Div. of Special Revenue
Russell Rd.
PO Box 11424
Newington, CT 06111-0424
Phone: (203)566-2756

Credential Type: License Registration.
Requirements: Submit application and fingerprint card. Pay fee. **Fees:** $5 registration fee.

Racetrack Occupations — Connecticut

5903
Chart Writer (Racetrack)
Connecticut Div. of Special Revenue
Russell Rd.
PO Box 11424
Newington, CT 06111-0424
Phone: (203)566-2756

Credential Type: License Registration.
Requirements: Submit application and fingerprint card. Pay fee. **Fees:** $20 registration fee.

5904
Clerk of Scales (Racetrack)
Connecticut Div. of Special Revenue
Russell Rd.
PO Box 11424
Newington, CT 06111-0424
Phone: (203)566-2756

Credential Type: License Registration.
Requirements: Submit application and fingerprint card. Pay fee. **Fees:** $20 registration fee.

5905
Computer Analyst (Racetrack)
Connecticut Div. of Special Revenue
Russell Rd.
PO Box 11424
Newington, CT 06111-0424
Phone: (203)566-2756

Credential Type: License Registration.
Requirements: Submit application and fingerprint card. Pay fee. **Fees:** $5 registration fee.

5906
Computer Operator (Racetrack)
Connecticut Div. of Special Revenue
Russell Rd.
PO Box 11424
Newington, CT 06111-0424
Phone: (203)566-2756

Credential Type: License Registration.
Requirements: Submit application and fingerprint card. Pay fee. **Fees:** $5 registration fee.

5907
Concession Employee (Racetrack)
Connecticut Div. of Special Revenue
Russell Rd.
PO Box 11424
Newington, CT 06111-0424
Phone: (203)566-2756

Credential Type: License Registration.
Requirements: Submit application and fingerprint card. Pay fee. **Fees:** $5 registration fee.

5908
Concessionaire II (Racetrack)
Connecticut Div. of Special Revenue
Russell Rd.
PO Box 11424
Newington, CT 06111-0424
Phone: (203)566-2756

Credential Type: License Registration.
Requirements: Submit application and fingerprint card. Pay fee. **Fees:** $100 registration fee.

5909
Corporation Director II (Racetrack)
Connecticut Div. of Special Revenue
Russell Rd.
PO Box 11424
Newington, CT 06111-0424
Phone: (203)566-2756

Credential Type: License Registration.
Requirements: Submit application and fingerprint card. Pay fee. **Fees:** $20 registration fee.

5910
Corporation Officer II (Racetrack)
Connecticut Div. of Special Revenue
Russell Rd.
PO Box 11424
Newington, CT 06111-0424
Phone: (203)566-2756

Credential Type: License Registration.
Requirements: Submit application and fingerprint card. Pay fee. **Fees:** $20 registration fee.

5911
Courier (Racetrack)
Connecticut Div. of Special Revenue
Russell Rd.
PO Box 11424
Newington, CT 06111-0424
Phone: (203)566-2756

Credential Type: License Registration.
Requirements: Submit application and fingerprint card. Pay fee. **Fees:** $5 registration fee.

5912
Customer Service Employee (Racetrack)
Connecticut Div. of Special Revenue
Russell Rd.
PO Box 11424
Newington, CT 06111-0424
Phone: (203)566-2756

Credential Type: License Registration.
Requirements: Submit application and fingerprint card. Pay fee. **Fees:** $5 registration fee.

5913
Deputy Judge (Racetrack)
Connecticut Div. of Special Revenue
Russell Rd.
PO Box 11424
Newington, CT 06111-0424
Phone: (203)566-2756

Credential Type: License Registration.
Requirements: Submit application and fingerprint card. Pay fee. **Fees:** $20 registration fee.

5914
Director of Security (Racetrack)
Connecticut Div. of Special Revenue
Russell Rd.
PO Box 11424
Newington, CT 06111-0424
Phone: (203)566-2756

Credential Type: License Registration.
Requirements: Submit application and fingerprint card. Pay fee. **Fees:** $20 registration fee.

5915

Doctor (Racetrack)
Connecticut Div. of Special Revenue
Russell Rd.
PO Box 11424
Newington, CT 06111-0424
Phone: (203)566-2756

Credential Type: License Registration.
Requirements: Submit application and fingerprint card. Pay fee. **Fees:** $5 registration fee.

5916

Dog Owner (Racetrack)
Connecticut Div. of Special Revenue
Russell Rd.
PO Box 11424
Newington, CT 06111-0424
Phone: (203)566-2756

Credential Type: License Registration.
Requirements: Submit application and fingerprint card. Pay fee. **Fees:** $20 registration fee.

5917

Electrician (Racetrack)
Connecticut Div. of Special Revenue
Russell Rd.
PO Box 11424
Newington, CT 06111-0424
Phone: (203)566-2756

Credential Type: License Registration.
Requirements: Submit application and fingerprint card. Pay fee. **Fees:** $5 registration fee.

5918

Facility Supervisor (Racetrack)
Connecticut Div. of Special Revenue
Russell Rd.
PO Box 11424
Newington, CT 06111-0424
Phone: (203)566-2756

Credential Type: License Registration.
Requirements: Submit application and fingerprint card. Pay fee. **Fees:** $20 registration fee.

5919

Field Service Manager (Racetrack)
Connecticut Div. of Special Revenue
Russell Rd.
PO Box 11424
Newington, CT 06111-0424
Phone: (203)566-2756

Credential Type: License Registration.
Requirements: Submit application and fingerprint card. Pay fee. **Fees:** $5 registration fee.

5920

Field Technician (Racetrack)
Connecticut Div. of Special Revenue
Russell Rd.
PO Box 11424
Newington, CT 06111-0424
Phone: (203)566-2756

Credential Type: License Registration.
Requirements: Submit application and fingerprint card. Pay fee. **Fees:** $5 registration fee.

5921

General Manager II (Racetrack)
Connecticut Div. of Special Revenue
Russell Rd.
PO Box 11424
Newington, CT 06111-0424
Phone: (203)566-2756

Credential Type: License Registration.
Requirements: Submit application and fingerprint card. Pay fee. **Fees:** $20 registration fee.

5922

General Partner II (Racetrack)
Connecticut Div. of Special Revenue
Russell Rd.
PO Box 11424
Newington, CT 06111-0424
Phone: (203)566-2756

Credential Type: License Registration.
Requirements: Submit application and fingerprint card. Pay fee. **Fees:** $20 registration fee.

5923

Group Sales Person (Racetrack)
Connecticut Div. of Special Revenue
Russell Rd.
PO Box 11424
Newington, CT 06111-0424
Phone: (203)566-2756

Credential Type: License Registration.
Requirements: Submit application and fingerprint card. Pay fee. **Fees:** $5 registration fee.

5924

Handicapper (Racetrack)
Connecticut Div. of Special Revenue
Russell Rd.
PO Box 11424
Newington, CT 06111-0424
Phone: (203)566-2756

Credential Type: License Registration.
Requirements: Submit application and fingerprint card. Pay fee. **Fees:** $5 registration fee.

5925

Harness Driver (Racetrack)
Connecticut Div. of Special Revenue
Russell Rd.
PO Box 11424
Newington, CT 06111-0424
Phone: (203)566-2756

Credential Type: License Registration.
Requirements: Submit application and fingerprint card. Pay fee. **Fees:** $5 registration fee.

5926

Instructor (Racetrack)
Connecticut Div. of Special Revenue
Russell Rd.
PO Box 11424
Newington, CT 06111-0424
Phone: (203)566-2756

Credential Type: License Registration.
Requirements: Submit application and fingerprint card. Pay fee. **Fees:** $5 registration fee.

5927

Insurance Broker (Racetrack)
Connecticut Div. of Special Revenue
Russell Rd.
PO Box 11424
Newington, CT 06111-0424
Phone: (203)566-2756

Credential Type: License Registration.
Requirements: Submit application and fingerprint card. Pay fee. **Fees:** $5 registration fee.

5928

Insurance Investigator (Racetrack)
Connecticut Div. of Special Revenue
Russell Rd.
PO Box 11424
Newington, CT 06111-0424
Phone: (203)566-2756

Credential Type: License Registration.
Requirements: Submit application and fingerprint card. Pay fee. **Fees:** $5 registration fee.

5929

Internal Auditor (Racetrack)
Connecticut Div. of Special Revenue
Russell Rd.
PO Box 11424
Newington, CT 06111-0424
Phone: (203)566-2756

Credential Type: License Registration.
Requirements: Submit application and fingerprint card. Pay fee. **Fees:** $5 registration fee.

5930

Jockey (Racetrack)
Connecticut Div. of Special Revenue
Russell Rd.
PO Box 11424
Newington, CT 06111-0424
Phone: (203)566-2756

Credential Type: License Registration.
Requirements: Submit application and fingerprint card. Pay fee. **Fees:** $5 registration fee.

5931

Judge (Racetrack)
Connecticut Div. of Special Revenue
Russell Rd.
PO Box 11424
Newington, CT 06111-0424
Phone: (203)566-2756

Credential Type: License Registration.
Requirements: Submit application and fingerprint card. Pay fee. **Fees:** $20 registration fee.

5932

Kennel Helper (Racetrack)
Connecticut Div. of Special Revenue
Russell Rd.
PO Box 11424
Newington, CT 06111-0424
Phone: (203)566-2756

Credential Type: License Registration.
Requirements: Submit application and fingerprint card. Pay fee. **Fees:** $5 registration fee.

5933

Kennel Master (Racetrack)
Connecticut Div. of Special Revenue
Russell Rd.
PO Box 11424
Newington, CT 06111-0424
Phone: (203)566-2756

Credential Type: License Registration.
Requirements: Submit application and fingerprint card. Pay fee. **Fees:** $20 registration fee.

5934

Laundry Employee (Racetrack)
Connecticut Div. of Special Revenue
Russell Rd.
PO Box 11424
Newington, CT 06111-0424
Phone: (203)566-2756

Credential Type: License Registration.
Requirements: Submit application and fingerprint card. Pay fee. **Fees:** $5 registration fee.

5935

Lure Operator (Racetrack)
Connecticut Div. of Special Revenue
Russell Rd.
PO Box 11424
Newington, CT 06111-0424
Phone: (203)566-2756

Credential Type: License Registration.
Requirements: Submit application and fingerprint card. Pay fee. **Fees:** $20 registration fee.

5936

Maintenance Employee (Racetrack)
Connecticut Div. of Special Revenue
Russell Rd.
PO Box 11424
Newington, CT 06111-0424
Phone: (203)566-2756

Credential Type: License Registration.
Requirements: Submit application and fingerprint card. Pay fee. **Fees:** $5 registration fee.

5937

Masseur (Racetrack)
Connecticut Div. of Special Revenue
Russell Rd.
PO Box 11424
Newington, CT 06111-0424
Phone: (203)566-2756

Credential Type: License Registration.
Requirements: Submit application and fingerprint card. Pay fee. **Fees:** $5 registration fee.

5938

Mutuel Employee (Racetrack)
Connecticut Div. of Special Revenue
Russell Rd.
PO Box 11424
Newington, CT 06111-0424
Phone: (203)566-2756

Credential Type: License Registration.
Requirements: Submit application and fingerprint card. Pay fee. **Fees:** $10 registration fee.

5939

Mutuel Manager and Assistant Mutuel Manager (Racetrack)
Connecticut Div. of Special Revenue
Russell Rd.
PO Box 11424
Newington, CT 06111-0424
Phone: (203)566-2756

Credential Type: License Registration.
Requirements: Submit application and fingerprint card. Pay fee. **Fees:** $20 registration fee.

5940

Newsstand Operator (Racetrack)
Connecticut Div. of Special Revenue
Russell Rd.
PO Box 11424
Newington, CT 06111-0424
Phone: (203)566-2756

Credential Type: License Registration.
Requirements: Submit application and fingerprint card. Pay fee. **Fees:** $5 registration fee.

5941

Nurse (Racetrack)
Connecticut Div. of Special Revenue
Russell Rd.
PO Box 11424
Newington, CT 06111-0424
Phone: (203)566-2756

Credential Type: License Registration.
Requirements: Submit application and fingerprint card. Pay fee. **Fees:** $5 registration fee.

5942

Office Employee (Racetrack)
Connecticut Div. of Special Revenue
Russell Rd.
PO Box 11424
Newington, CT 06111-0424
Phone: (203)566-2756

Credential Type: License Registration.
Requirements: Submit application and fingerprint card. Pay fee. **Fees:** $5 registration fee.

5943

Office Secretary (Racetrack)
Connecticut Div. of Special Revenue
Russell Rd.
PO Box 11424
Newington, CT 06111-0424
Phone: (203)566-2756

Credential Type: License Registration.
Requirements: Submit application and fingerprint card. Pay fee. **Fees:** $5 registration fee.

5944

Official (Racetrack)
Connecticut Div. of Special Revenue
Russell Rd.
PO Box 11424
Newington, CT 06111-0424
Phone: (203)566-2756

Credential Type: License Registration.
Requirements: Submit application and fingerprint card. Pay fee. **Fees:** $20 registration fee.

5945

Operators Manager (Racetrack)
Connecticut Div. of Special Revenue
Russell Rd.
PO Box 11424
Newington, CT 06111-0424
Phone: (203)566-2756

Credential Type: License Registration.
Requirements: Submit application and fingerprint card. Pay fee. **Fees:** $5 registration fee.

5946

Paddock Judge (Racetrack)
Connecticut Div. of Special Revenue
Russell Rd.
PO Box 11424
Newington, CT 06111-0424
Phone: (203)566-2756

Credential Type: License Registration.
Requirements: Submit application and fingerprint card. Pay fee. **Fees:** $20 registration fee.

5947

Parking Attendant (Racetrack)
Connecticut Div. of Special Revenue
Russell Rd.
PO Box 11424
Newington, CT 06111-0424
Phone: (203)566-2756

Credential Type: License Registration.
Requirements: Submit application and fingerprint card. Pay fee. **Fees:** $5 registration fee.

5948

Patrol Judge (Racetrack)
Connecticut Div. of Special Revenue
Russell Rd.
PO Box 11424
Newington, CT 06111-0424
Phone: (203)566-2756

Credential Type: License Registration.
Requirements: Submit application and fingerprint card. Pay fee. **Fees:** $20 registration fee.

5949

Photo Finish Operator (Racetrack)
Connecticut Div. of Special Revenue
Russell Rd.
PO Box 11424
Newington, CT 06111-0424
Phone: (203)566-2756

Credential Type: License Registration.
Requirements: Submit application and fingerprint card. Pay fee. **Fees:** $5 registration fee.

5950

Photographer (Racetrack)
Connecticut Div. of Special Revenue
Russell Rd.
PO Box 11424
Newington, CT 06111-0424
Phone: (203)566-2756

Credential Type: License Registration.
Requirements: Submit application and fingerprint card. Pay fee. **Fees:** $5 registration fee.

Racetrack Occupations

5951

Player Attendant (Racetrack)
Connecticut Div. of Special Revenue
Russell Rd.
PO Box 11424
Newington, CT 06111-0424
Phone: (203)566-2756

Credential Type: License Registration.
Requirements: Submit application and fingerprint card. Pay fee. **Fees:** $5 registration fee.

5952

Player Judge (Racetrack)
Connecticut Div. of Special Revenue
Russell Rd.
PO Box 11424
Newington, CT 06111-0424
Phone: (203)566-2756

Credential Type: License Registration.
Requirements: Submit application and fingerprint card. Pay fee. **Fees:** $20 registration fee.

5953

Player Manager II (Racetrack)
Connecticut Div. of Special Revenue
Russell Rd.
PO Box 11424
Newington, CT 06111-0424
Phone: (203)566-2756

Credential Type: License Registration.
Requirements: Submit application and fingerprint card. Pay fee. **Fees:** $20 registration fee.

5954

Player's Trainer (Racetrack)
Connecticut Div. of Special Revenue
Russell Rd.
PO Box 11424
Newington, CT 06111-0424
Phone: (203)566-2756

Credential Type: License Registration.
Requirements: Submit application and fingerprint card. Pay fee. **Fees:** $5 registration fee.

5955

Promoter (Racetrack)
Connecticut Div. of Special Revenue
Russell Rd.
PO Box 11424
Newington, CT 06111-0424
Phone: (203)566-2756

Credential Type: License Registration.
Requirements: Submit application and fingerprint card. Pay fee. **Fees:** $5 registration fee.

5956

Proprietor (Racetrack)
Connecticut Div. of Special Revenue
Russell Rd.
PO Box 11424
Newington, CT 06111-0424
Phone: (203)566-2756

Credential Type: License Registration.
Requirements: Submit application and fingerprint card. Pay fee. **Fees:** $5 registration fee.

5957

Public Director (Racetrack)
Connecticut Div. of Special Revenue
Russell Rd.
PO Box 11424
Newington, CT 06111-0424
Phone: (203)566-2756

Credential Type: License Registration.
Requirements: Submit application and fingerprint card. Pay fee. **Fees:** $5 registration fee.

5958

Public Relations Employee (Racetrack)
Connecticut Div. of Special Revenue
Russell Rd.
PO Box 11424
Newington, CT 06111-0424
Phone: (203)566-2756

Credential Type: License Registration.
Requirements: Submit application and fingerprint card. Pay fee. **Fees:** $5 registration fee.

5959

Publicist (Racetrack)
Connecticut Div. of Special Revenue
Russell Rd.
PO Box 11424
Newington, CT 06111-0424
Phone: (203)566-2756

Credential Type: License Registration.
Requirements: Submit application and fingerprint card. Pay fee. **Fees:** $5 registration fee.

5960

Publicity Director (Racetrack)
Connecticut Div. of Special Revenue
Russell Rd.
PO Box 11424
Newington, CT 06111-0424
Phone: (203)566-2756

Credential Type: License Registration.
Requirements: Submit application and fingerprint card. Pay fee. **Fees:** $5 registration fee.

5961

Race Control Employee (Racetrack)
Connecticut Div. of Special Revenue
Russell Rd.
PO Box 11424
Newington, CT 06111-0424
Phone: (203)566-2756

Credential Type: License Registration.
Requirements: Submit application and fingerprint card. Pay fee. **Fees:** $5 registration fee.

5962

Racing Secretary (Racetrack)
Connecticut Div. of Special Revenue
Russell Rd.
PO Box 11424
Newington, CT 06111-0424
Phone: (203)566-2756

Credential Type: License Registration.
Requirements: Submit application and fingerprint card. Pay fee. **Fees:** $20 registration fee.

5963

Registered Nurse (Racetrack)
Connecticut Div. of Special Revenue
Russell Rd.
PO Box 11424
Newington, CT 06111-0424
Phone: (203)566-2756

Credential Type: License Registration.
Requirements: Submit application and fingerprint card. Pay fee. **Fees:** $5 registration fee.

5964

Security Employee (Racetrack)
Connecticut Div. of Special Revenue
Russell Rd.
PO Box 11424
Newington, CT 06111-0424
Phone: (203)566-2756

Credential Type: License Registration.
Requirements: Submit application and fingerprint card. Pay fee. **Fees:** $5 registration fee.

5965

Sportswriter (Racetrack)
Connecticut Div. of Special Revenue
Russell Rd.
PO Box 11424
Newington, CT 06111-0424
Phone: (203)566-2756

Credential Type: License Registration.
Requirements: Submit application and fingerprint card. Pay fee. **Fees:** $5 registration fee.

5966

Starter (Racetrack)
Connecticut Div. of Special Revenue
Russell Rd.
PO Box 11424
Newington, CT 06111-0424
Phone: (203)566-2756

Credential Type: License Registration.
Requirements: Submit application and fingerprint card. Pay fee. **Fees:** $20 registration fee.

5967

Statistician (Racetrack)
Connecticut Div. of Special Revenue
Russell Rd.
PO Box 11424
Newington, CT 06111-0424
Phone: (203)566-2756

Credential Type: License Registration.
Requirements: Submit application and fingerprint card. Pay fee. **Fees:** $20 registration fee.

5968

Storekeeper (Racetrack)
Connecticut Div. of Special Revenue
Russell Rd.
PO Box 11424
Newington, CT 06111-0424
Phone: (203)566-2756

Credential Type: License Registration.
Requirements: Submit application and fingerprint card. Pay fee. **Fees:** $5 registration fee.

5969

Superintendent (Racetrack)
Connecticut Div. of Special Revenue
Russell Rd.
PO Box 11424
Newington, CT 06111-0424
Phone: (203)566-2756

Credential Type: License Registration.
Requirements: Submit application and fingerprint card. Pay fee. **Fees:** $5 registration fee.

5970

Supplier (Racetrack)
Connecticut Div. of Special Revenue
Russell Rd.
PO Box 11424
Newington, CT 06111-0424
Phone: (203)566-2756

Credential Type: License Registration.
Requirements: Submit application and fingerprint card. Pay fee. **Fees:** $5 registration fee.

5971

Telephone Operator (Racetrack)
Connecticut Div. of Special Revenue
Russell Rd.
PO Box 11424
Newington, CT 06111-0424
Phone: (203)566-2756

Credential Type: License Registration.
Requirements: Submit application and fingerprint card. Pay fee. **Fees:** $5 registration fee.

5972

Tote Technician (Racetrack)
Connecticut Div. of Special Revenue
Russell Rd.
PO Box 11424
Newington, CT 06111-0424
Phone: (203)566-2756

Credential Type: License Registration.
Requirements: Submit application and fingerprint card. Pay fee. **Fees:** $5 registration fee.

5973

Trainer (Racetrack)
Connecticut Div. of Special Revenue
Russell Rd.
PO Box 11424
Newington, CT 06111-0424
Phone: (203)566-2756

Credential Type: License Registration.
Requirements: Submit application and fingerprint card. Pay fee. **Fees:** $20 registration fee.

5974

Treasurer (Racetrack)
Connecticut Div. of Special Revenue
Russell Rd.
PO Box 11424
Newington, CT 06111-0424
Phone: (203)566-2756

Credential Type: License Registration.
Requirements: Submit application and fingerprint card. Pay fee. **Fees:** $5 registration fee.

5975

T.V. Tech Cameraman (Racetrack)
Connecticut Div. of Special Revenue
Russell Rd.
PO Box 11424
Newington, CT 06111-0424
Phone: (203)566-2756

Credential Type: License Registration.
Requirements: Submit application and fingerprint card. Pay fee. **Fees:** $5 registration fee.

5976

Usher (Racetrack)
Connecticut Div. of Special Revenue
Russell Rd.
PO Box 11424
Newington, CT 06111-0424
Phone: (203)566-2756

Credential Type: License Registration.
Requirements: Submit application and fingerprint card. Pay fee. **Fees:** $5 registration fee.

5977

Veterinarian (Racetrack)
Connecticut Div. of Special Revenue
Russell Rd.
PO Box 11424
Newington, CT 06111-0424
Phone: (203)566-2756

Credential Type: License Registration.
Requirements: Submit application and fingerprint card. Pay fee. **Fees:** $20 registration fee.

Delaware

5978

Admission Employee (Racetrack)
Delaware Harness Racing
   Commission
2320 S. DuPont Hwy.
Dover, DE 19901
Phone: (302)739-4811

Credential Type: License Registration.
Requirements: Submit application and fingerprint card. Pay fee. **Fees:** $5 registration fee.

5979

Assistant Racing Secretary (Racetrack)
Delaware Harness Racing
   Commission
2320 S. DuPont Hwy.
Dover, DE 19901
Phone: (302)739-4811

Credential Type: License Registration.
Requirements: Submit application and fingerprint card. Pay fee. **Fees:** $10 registration fee.

5980

Associate Judge (Racetrack)
Delaware Harness Racing
   Commission
2320 S. DuPont Hwy.
Dover, DE 19901
Phone: (302)739-4811

Credential Type: License Registration.
Requirements: Submit application and fingerprint card. Pay fee. **Fees:** $15 registration fee.

5981

Breath Analyzer (Racetrack)
Delaware Harness Racing
   Commission
2320 S. DuPont Hwy.
Dover, DE 19901
Phone: (302)739-4811

Credential Type: License Registration.
Requirements: Submit application and fingerprint card. Pay fee. **Fees:** $5 registration fee.

5982

Clerk of the Course (Racetrack)
Delaware Harness Racing
   Commission
2320 S. DuPont Hwy.
Dover, DE 19901
Phone: (302)739-4811

Credential Type: License Registration.
Requirements: Submit application and fingerprint card. Pay fee. **Fees:** $15 registration fee.

5983

Concession Stand Employee (Racetrack)
Delaware Harness Racing
   Commission
2320 S. DuPont Hwy.
Dover, DE 19901
Phone: (302)739-4811

Credential Type: License Registration.
Requirements: Submit application and fingerprint card. Pay fee. **Fees:** $5 registration fee.

5984

Equipment Inspector (Racetrack)
Delaware Harness Racing
   Commission
2320 S. DuPont Hwy.
Dover, DE 19901
Phone: (302)739-4811

Credential Type: License Registration.
Requirements: Submit application and fingerprint card. Pay fee. **Fees:** $10 registration fee.

5985

General Paddock Employee (Racetrack)
Delaware Harness Racing
   Commission
2320 S. DuPont Hwy.
Dover, DE 19901
Phone: (302)739-4811

Credential Type: License Registration.
Requirements: Submit application and fingerprint card. Pay fee. **Fees:** $5 registration fee.

5986

Groom (Racetrack)
Delaware Harness Racing
   Commission
2320 S. DuPont Hwy.
Dover, DE 19901
Phone: (302)739-4811

Credential Type: License Registration.
Requirements: Submit application and fingerprint card. Pay fee. **Fees:** $5 registration fee.

5987

Horse Driver (Racetrack)
Delaware Harness Racing
  Commission
2320 S. DuPont Hwy.
Dover, DE 19901
Phone: (302)739-4811

Credential Type: License Registration.
Requirements: Submit application and fingerprint card. Pay fee. **Fees:** $10 registration fee.

5988

Horse Owner (Racetrack)
Delaware Harness Racing
  Commission
2320 S. DuPont Hwy.
Dover, DE 19901
Phone: (302)739-4811

Credential Type: License Registration.
Requirements: Submit application and fingerprint card. Pay fee. **Fees:** $10 registration fee.

5989

Horse Trainer (Racetrack)
Delaware Harness Racing
  Commission
2320 S. DuPont Hwy.
Dover, DE 19901
Phone: (302)739-4811

Credential Type: License Registration.
Requirements: Submit application and fingerprint card. Pay fee. **Fees:** $10 registration fee.

5990

Laboratory Official (Racetrack)
Delaware Harness Racing
  Commission
2320 S. DuPont Hwy.
Dover, DE 19901
Phone: (302)739-4811

Credential Type: License Registration.
Requirements: Submit application and fingerprint card. Pay fee. **Fees:** $5 registration fee.

5991

Maintenance Employee (Racetrack)
Delaware Harness Racing
  Commission
2320 S. DuPont Hwy.
Dover, DE 19901
Phone: (302)739-4811

Credential Type: License Registration.
Requirements: Submit application and fingerprint card. Pay fee. **Fees:** $5 registration fee.

5992

Mutuel Employee (Racetrack)
Delaware Harness Racing
  Commission
2320 S. DuPont Hwy.
Dover, DE 19901
Phone: (302)739-4811

Credential Type: License Registration.
Requirements: Submit application and fingerprint card. Pay fee. **Fees:** $5 registration fee.

5993

Paddock Inspector (Racetrack)
Delaware Harness Racing
  Commission
2320 S. DuPont Hwy.
Dover, DE 19901
Phone: (302)739-4811

Credential Type: License Registration.
Requirements: Submit application and fingerprint card. Pay fee. **Fees:** $5 registration fee.

5994

Paddock Judge (Racetrack)
Delaware Harness Racing
  Commission
2320 S. DuPont Hwy.
Dover, DE 19901
Phone: (302)739-4811

Credential Type: License Registration.
Requirements: Submit application and fingerprint card. Pay fee. **Fees:** $10 registration fee.

5995

Parking Lot Attendant (Racetrack)
Delaware Harness Racing
  Commission
2320 S. DuPont Hwy.
Dover, DE 19901
Phone: (302)739-4811

Credential Type: License Registration.
Requirements: Submit application and fingerprint card. Pay fee. **Fees:** $5 registration fee.

5996

Patrol Judge (Racetrack)
Delaware Harness Racing
  Commission
2320 S. DuPont Hwy.
Dover, DE 19901
Phone: (302)739-4811

Credential Type: License Registration.
Requirements: Submit application and fingerprint card. Pay fee. **Fees:** $10 registration fee.

5997

Photographer Assistant (Racetrack)
Delaware Harness Racing
  Commission
2320 S. DuPont Hwy.
Dover, DE 19901
Phone: (302)739-4811

Credential Type: License Registration.
Requirements: Submit application and fingerprint card. Pay fee. **Fees:** $5 registration fee.

5998

Photographer (Racetrack)
Delaware Harness Racing
  Commission
2320 S. DuPont Hwy.
Dover, DE 19901
Phone: (302)739-4811

Credential Type: License Registration.
Requirements: Submit application and fingerprint card. Pay fee. **Fees:** $15 registration fee.

5999

Presiding Judge (Racetrack)
Delaware Harness Racing
  Commission
2320 S. DuPont Hwy.
Dover, DE 19901
Phone: (302)739-4811

Credential Type: License Registration.
Requirements: Submit application and fingerprint card. Pay fee. **Fees:** $20 registration fee.

6000

Program Director (Racetrack)
Delaware Harness Racing
  Commission
2320 S. DuPont Hwy.
Dover, DE 19901
Phone: (302)739-4811

Credential Type: License Registration.
Requirements: Submit application and fingerprint card. Pay fee. **Fees:** $5 registration fee.

6001

Racing Secretary (Racetrack)
Delaware Harness Racing
  Commission
2320 S. DuPont Hwy.
Dover, DE 19901
Phone: (302)739-4811

Credential Type: License Registration.
Requirements: Submit application and fingerprint card. Pay fee. **Fees:** $20 registration fee.

6002

Security Employee (Racetrack)
Delaware Harness Racing
  Commission
2320 S. DuPont Hwy.
Dover, DE 19901
Phone: (302)739-4811

Credential Type: License Registration.
Requirements: Submit application and fingerprint card. Pay fee. **Fees:** $5 registration fee.

6003

Starter (Racetrack)
Delaware Harness Racing
  Commission
2320 S. DuPont Hwy.
Dover, DE 19901
Phone: (302)739-4811

Credential Type: License Registration.
Requirements: Submit application and fingerprint card. Pay fee. **Fees:** $15 registration fee.

6004

State Steward (Racetrack)
Delaware Harness Racing
  Commission
2320 S. DuPont Hwy.
Dover, DE 19901
Phone: (302)739-4811

Credential Type: License Registration.
Requirements: Submit application and fingerprint card. Pay fee. **Fees:** $15 registration fee.

6005

Thoroughbred Jockey (Racetrack)
Delaware Thoroughbred Racing
  Commission
820 French St., 3rd Level
Wilmington, DE 19801
Phone: (302)577-3288

Credential Type: License Registration.
Requirements: Contact licensing body for application information.

6006

Thoroughbred Owner (Racetrack)
Delaware Thoroughbred Racing
  Commission
820 French St., 3rd Level
Wilmington, DE 19801
Phone: (302)577-3288

Credential Type: License Registration.
Requirements: Contact licensing body for application information.

6007

Thoroughbred Racing Official (Racetrack)
Delaware Thoroughbred Racing
  Commission
820 French St., 3rd Level
Wilmington, DE 19801
Phone: (302)577-3288

Credential Type: License Registration.
Requirements: Contact licensing body for application information.

6008

Thoroughbred Racing Personnel (Racetrack)
Delaware Thoroughbred Racing
  Commission
820 French St., 3rd Level
Wilmington, DE 19801
Phone: (302)577-3288

Credential Type: License Registration.
Requirements: Contact licensing body for application information.

6009

Thoroughbred Trainer (Racetrack)
Delaware Thoroughbred Racing
  Commission
820 French St., 3rd Level
Wilmington, DE 19801
Phone: (302)577-3288

Credential Type: License Registration.
Requirements: Contact licensing body for application information.

6010

Timer (Racetrack)
Delaware Harness Racing
  Commission
2320 S. DuPont Hwy.
Dover, DE 19901
Phone: (302)739-4811

Credential Type: License Registration.
Requirements: Submit application and fingerprint card. Pay fee. **Fees:** $5 registration fee.

Delaware

6011

Totalizator (Racetrack)
Delaware Harness Racing
  Commission
2320 S. DuPont Hwy.
Dover, DE 19901
Phone: (302)739-4811

Credential Type: License Registration.
Requirements: Submit application and fingerprint card. Pay fee. **Fees:** $5 registration fee.

6012

Vendor Employee (Racetrack)
Delaware Harness Racing
  Commission
2320 S. DuPont Hwy.
Dover, DE 19901
Phone: (302)739-4811

Credential Type: License Registration.
Requirements: Submit application and fingerprint card. Pay fee. **Fees:** $5 registration fee.

6013

Vendor (Racetrack)
Delaware Harness Racing
  Commission
2320 S. DuPont Hwy.
Dover, DE 19901
Phone: (302)739-4811

Credential Type: License Registration.
Requirements: Submit application and fingerprint card. Pay fee. **Fees:** $15 registration fee.

6014

Veterinarian Assistant (Racetrack)
Delaware Harness Racing
  Commission
2320 S. DuPont Hwy.
Dover, DE 19901
Phone: (302)739-4811

Credential Type: License Registration.
Requirements: Submit application and fingerprint card. Pay fee. **Fees:** $5 registration fee.

6015

Veterinarian (Racetrack)
Delaware Harness Racing
  Commission
2320 S. DuPont Hwy.
Dover, DE 19901
Phone: (302)739-4811

Credential Type: License Registration.
Requirements: Submit application and fingerprint card. Pay fee. **Fees:** $15 registration fee.

Florida

6016

Agent, Jockey (Racetrack)
Florida Dept. of Business
Div. of Pari-Mutuel Wagering
Licensing Section
725 S. Bronough St.
Tallahassee, FL 32399-1037
Phone: (904)488-9161

Credential Type: License Registration Code 1054. **Requirements:** Submit application and fingerprint card. Pay fee. **Fees:** $40 registration fee.

6017

Alternate Racing/Game Official (Racetrack)
Florida Dept. of Business
Div. of Pari-Mutuel Wagering
Licensing Section
725 S. Bronough St.
Tallahassee, FL 32399-1037
Phone: (904)488-9161

Credential Type: License Registration Code 1067. **Requirements:** Submit application and fingerprint card. Pay fee. **Fees:** $10 registration fee.

6018

Announcer (Racetrack)
Florida Dept. of Business
Div. of Pari-Mutuel Wagering
Licensing Section
725 S. Bronough St.
Tallahassee, FL 32399-1037
Phone: (904)488-9161

Credential Type: License Registration Code 1006. **Requirements:** Submit application and fingerprint card. Pay fee. **Fees:** $40 registration fee.

6019

Association Manager/Supervisor (Racetrack)
Florida Dept. of Business
Div. of Pari-Mutuel Wagering
Licensing Section
725 S. Bronough St.
Tallahassee, FL 32399-1037
Phone: (904)488-9161

Credential Type: License Registration Code 1005. **Authorization:** Authorizes work in the following positions: admissions manager, chief of security, concession manager or owner, general manager, mutuels manager, parking director, public relations director, plant superintendent, and track superintendent. **Requirements:** Submit application and fingerprint card. Pay fee. **Fees:** $40 registration fee.

6020

Association Officer/Director/ Manager (Racetrack)
Florida Dept. of Business
Div. of Pari-Mutuel Wagering
Licensing Section
725 S. Bronough St.
Tallahassee, FL 32399-1037
Phone: (904)488-9161

Credential Type: License Registration Code 1066. **Requirements:** Submit application and fingerprint card. Pay fee. **Fees:** $40 registration fee.

6021

Athletic Trainer (Racetrack)
Florida Dept. of Business
Div. of Pari-Mutuel Wagering
Licensing Section
725 S. Bronough St.
Tallahassee, FL 32399-1037
Phone: (904)488-9161

Credential Type: License Registration Code 1050. **Requirements:** Submit application and fingerprint card. Pay fee. **Fees:** $10 registration fee.

6022

Authorized Agent (Racetrack)
Florida Dept. of Business
Div. of Pari-Mutuel Wagering
Licensing Section
725 S. Bronough St.
Tallahassee, FL 32399-1037
Phone: (904)488-9161

Credential Type: License Registration Code 1047. **Requirements:** Submit application and fingerprint card. Pay fee. **Fees:** $40 registration fee.

6023

Blacksmith/Plater (Racetrack)
Florida Dept. of Business
Div. of Pari-Mutuel Wagering
Licensing Section
725 S. Bronough St.
Tallahassee, FL 32399-1037
Phone: (904)488-9161

Credential Type: License Registration Code 1055. **Requirements:** Submit application and fingerprint card. Pay fee. **Fees:** $10 registration fee.

6024

Chart Writer (Racetrack)
Florida Dept. of Business
Div. of Pari-Mutuel Wagering
Licensing Section
725 S. Bronough St.
Tallahassee, FL 32399-1037
Phone: (904)488-9161

Credential Type: License Registration Code 1032. **Requirements:** Submit application and fingerprint card. Pay fee. **Fees:** $40 registration fee.

6025

Clerk of Scales (Racetrack)
Florida Dept. of Business
Div. of Pari-Mutuel Wagering
Licensing Section
725 S. Bronough St.
Tallahassee, FL 32399-1037
Phone: (904)488-9161

Credential Type: License Registration Code 1032. **Requirements:** Submit application and fingerprint card. Pay fee. **Fees:** $40 registration fee.

6026

Comptroller (Racetrack)
Florida Dept. of Business
Div. of Pari-Mutuel Wagering
Licensing Section
725 S. Bronough St.
Tallahassee, FL 32399-1037
Phone: (904)488-9161

Credential Type: License Registration Code 1008. **Requirements:** Submit application and fingerprint card. Pay fee. **Fees:** $40 registration fee.

6027

Concession Employee (Racetrack)
Florida Dept. of Business
Div. of Pari-Mutuel Wagering
Licensing Section
725 S. Bronough St.
Tallahassee, FL 32399-1037
Phone: (904)488-9161

Credential Type: License Registration Code 1003. **Authorization:** Authorizes work in the following positions: admission employee, calculator, clerical help, concession employee, security guard, maintenance employee, mutuel employee, parking employee, public relations staff, switchboard operator, track/fronton employee, head lead out, lead out, kennel master, ball boy, ball maker, and cesta maker. **Requirements:** Submit application and fingerprint card. Pay fee. **Fees:** $10 registration fee.

6028

Concession Manager/Supervisor (Racetrack)
Florida Dept. of Business
Div. of Pari-Mutuel Wagering
Licensing Section
725 S. Bronough St.
Tallahassee, FL 32399-1037
Phone: (904)488-9161

Credential Type: License Registration Code 1005. **Authorization:** Authorizes work in the following positions: admissions manager, chief of security, concession manager or owner, general manager, mutuels manager, parking director, public relations director, plant superintendent, and track superintendent. **Requirements:** Submit application and fingerprint card. Pay fee. **Fees:** $40 registration fee.

6029

Contractual Concessionaire (Racetrack)
Florida Dept. of Business
Div. of Pari-Mutuel Wagering
Licensing Section
725 S. Bronough St.
Tallahassee, FL 32399-1037
Phone: (904)488-9161

Credential Type: License Registration Code 1025. **Requirements:** Submit application and fingerprint card. Pay fee. **Fees:** $150 registration fee.

6030

Doctor (Racetrack)
Florida Dept. of Business
Div. of Pari-Mutuel Wagering
Licensing Section
725 S. Bronough St.
Tallahassee, FL 32399-1037
Phone: (904)488-9161

Credential Type: License Registration Code 1015. **Requirements:** Must have Department of Professional Regulation (DPR) license. Submit application and fingerprint card. Pay fee. **Fees:** $40 registration fee.

6031

Entry Clerk (Racetrack)
Florida Dept. of Business
Div. of Pari-Mutuel Wagering
Licensing Section
725 S. Bronough St.
Tallahassee, FL 32399-1037
Phone: (904)488-9161

Credential Type: License Registration Code 1032. **Requirements:** Submit application and fingerprint card. Pay fee. **Fees:** $40 registration fee.

6032

Exercise Person (Racetrack)
Florida Dept. of Business
Div. of Pari-Mutuel Wagering
Licensing Section
725 S. Bronough St.
Tallahassee, FL 32399-1037
Phone: (904)488-9161

Credential Type: License Registration Code 1053. **Requirements:** Submit application and fingerprint card. Pay fee. **Fees:** $10 registration fee.

6033

General Employee (Racetrack)
Florida Dept. of Business
Div. of Pari-Mutuel Wagering
Licensing Section
725 S. Bronough St.
Tallahassee, FL 32399-1037
Phone: (904)488-9161

Credential Type: License Registration Code 1003. **Authorization:** Authorizes work in the following positions: admission employee, calculator, clerical help, concession employee, security guard, maintenance employee, mutuel employee, parking employee, public relations staff, switchboard operator, track/fronton employee, head lead out, lead out, kennel master, ball boy, ball maker, and cesta maker. **Requirements:** Submit application and fingerprint card. Pay fee. **Fees:** $10 registration fee.

6034

Greyhound Judge (Racetrack)
Florida Dept. of Business
Div. of Pari-Mutuel Wagering
Licensing Section
725 S. Bronough St.
Tallahassee, FL 32399-1037
Phone: (904)488-9161

Credential Type: License Registration Code 6035. **Requirements:** Submit application and fingerprint card. Pay fee. **Fees:** $40 registration fee.

6035

Greyhound Owner (Racetrack)
Florida Dept. of Business
Div. of Pari-Mutuel Wagering
Licensing Section
725 S. Bronough St.
Tallahassee, FL 32399-1037
Phone: (904)488-9161

Credential Type: License Registration Code 6049. **Requirements:** Submit application and fingerprint card. Pay fee. **Fees:** $40 registration fee.

6036

Greyhound Trainer/Assistant (Racetrack)
Florida Dept. of Business
Div. of Pari-Mutuel Wagering
Licensing Section
725 S. Bronough St.
Tallahassee, FL 32399-1037
Phone: (904)488-9161

Credential Type: License Registration Code 6050. **Requirements:** Submit application and fingerprint card. Pay fee. **Fees:** $40 registration fee.

6037

Handicapper (Racetrack)
Florida Dept. of Business
Div. of Pari-Mutuel Wagering
Licensing Section
725 S. Bronough St.
Tallahassee, FL 32399-1037
Phone: (904)488-9161

Credential Type: License Registration Code 1017. **Requirements:** Submit application and fingerprint card. Pay fee. **Fees:** $10 registration fee.

6038

Harness Driver (Racetrack)
Florida Dept. of Business
Div. of Pari-Mutuel Wagering
Licensing Section
725 S. Bronough St.
Tallahassee, FL 32399-1037
Phone: (904)488-9161

Credential Type: License Registration Code 4027. **Requirements:** Submit application and fingerprint card. Pay fee. **Fees:** $40 registration fee.

6039

Harness Owner (Racetrack)
Florida Dept. of Business
Div. of Pari-Mutuel Wagering
Licensing Section
725 S. Bronough St.
Tallahassee, FL 32399-1037
Phone: (904)488-9161

Credential Type: License Registration Code 4049. **Requirements:** Submit application and fingerprint card. Pay fee. **Fees:** $40 registration fee.

6040

Harness Trainer/Assistant (Racetrack)
Florida Dept. of Business
Div. of Pari-Mutuel Wagering
Licensing Section
725 S. Bronough St.
Tallahassee, FL 32399-1037
Phone: (904)488-9161

Credential Type: License Registration Code 4050. **Requirements:** Submit application and fingerprint card. Pay fee. **Fees:** $40 registration fee.

6041

Horse Identifier (Racetrack)
Florida Dept. of Business
Div. of Pari-Mutuel Wagering
Licensing Section
725 S. Bronough St.
Tallahassee, FL 32399-1037
Phone: (904)488-9161

Credential Type: License Registration Code 1033. **Requirements:** Submit application and fingerprint card. Pay fee. **Fees:** $40 registration fee.

6042

Horse Show Promoter (Racetrack)
Florida Dept. of Business
Div. of Pari-Mutuel Wagering
Licensing Section
725 S. Bronough St.
Tallahassee, FL 32399-1037
Phone: (904)488-9161

Credential Type: License Registration Code 1075. **Requirements:** Submit application and fingerprint card. Pay fee. **Fees:** $75 registration fee.

6043

Horsemen's Bookkeeper (Racetrack)
Florida Dept. of Business
Div. of Pari-Mutuel Wagering
Licensing Section
725 S. Bronough St.
Tallahassee, FL 32399-1037
Phone: (904)488-9161

Credential Type: License Registration Code 1018. **Requirements:** Submit application and fingerprint card. Pay fee. **Fees:** $40 registration fee.

6044

Jockey/Apprentice Jockey (Racetrack)
Florida Dept. of Business
Div. of Pari-Mutuel Wagering
Licensing Section
725 S. Bronough St.
Tallahassee, FL 32399-1037
Phone: (904)488-9161

Credential Type: License Registration Code 1028. **Requirements:** Submit application and fingerprint card. Pay fee. **Fees:** $40 registration fee.

6045

Lure Operator (Racetrack)
Florida Dept. of Business
Div. of Pari-Mutuel Wagering
Licensing Section
725 S. Bronough St.
Tallahassee, FL 32399-1037
Phone: (904)488-9161

Credential Type: License Registration Code 6065. **Requirements:** Submit application and fingerprint card. Pay fee. **Fees:** $40 registration fee.

6046

Nurse (Racetrack)
Florida Dept. of Business
Div. of Pari-Mutuel Wagering
Licensing Section
725 S. Bronough St.
Tallahassee, FL 32399-1037
Phone: (904)488-9161

Credential Type: License Registration Code 1019. **Requirements:** Must have a Department of Professional Regulation (DPR) license. Submit application and fingerprint card. Pay fee. **Fees:** $40 registration fee.

6047

Paddock/Patrol/Placing Judge (Racetrack)
Florida Dept. of Business
Div. of Pari-Mutuel Wagering
Licensing Section
725 S. Bronough St.
Tallahassee, FL 32399-1037
Phone: (904)488-9161

Credential Type: License Registration Code 1035. **Requirements:** Submit application and fingerprint card. Pay fee. **Fees:** $40 registration fee.

6048

Paramedic/EMT (Racetrack)
Florida Dept. of Business
Div. of Pari-Mutuel Wagering
Licensing Section
725 S. Bronough St.
Tallahassee, FL 32399-1037
Phone: (904)488-9161

Credential Type: License Registration Code 1016. **Requirements:** Must have a Health and Rehabilitative Services (HRS) license or a Department of Professional Regulation (DPR) license. Submit application and fingerprint card. Pay fee. **Fees:** $40 registration fee.

6049

Physician's Assistant (Racetrack)
Florida Dept. of Business
Div. of Pari-Mutuel Wagering
Licensing Section
725 S. Bronough St.
Tallahassee, FL 32399-1037
Phone: (904)488-9161

Credential Type: License Registration Code 1016. **Requirements:** Must have a Health and Rehabilitative Services (HRS) license or a Department of Professional Regulation (DPR) license. Submit application and fingerprint card. Pay fee. **Fees:** $40 registration fee.

6050

Players' Trainer/Assistant (Jai-Alai)
Florida Dept. of Business
Div. of Pari-Mutuel Wagering
Licensing Section
725 S. Bronough St.
Tallahassee, FL 32399-1037
Phone: (904)488-9161

Credential Type: License Registration Code 2050. **Requirements:** Submit application and fingerprint card. Pay fee. **Fees:** $40 registration fee.

6051

Quarter Horse Owner (Racetrack)
Florida Dept. of Business
Div. of Pari-Mutuel Wagering
Licensing Section
725 S. Bronough St.
Tallahassee, FL 32399-1037
Phone: (904)488-9161

Credential Type: License Registration Code 5049. **Requirements:** Submit application and fingerprint card. Pay fee. **Fees:** $40 registration fee.

6052

Quarter Horse Trainer/Assistant (Racetrack)
Florida Dept. of Business
Div. of Pari-Mutuel Wagering
Licensing Section
725 S. Bronough St.
Tallahassee, FL 32399-1037
Phone: (904)488-9161

Credential Type: License Registration Code 5050. **Requirements:** Submit application and fingerprint card. Pay fee. **Fees:** $40 registration fee.

6053

Racing Secretary, Assistant (Racetrack)
Florida Dept. of Business
Div. of Pari-Mutuel Wagering
Licensing Section
725 S. Bronough St.
Tallahassee, FL 32399-1037
Phone: (904)488-9161

Credential Type: License Registration Code 1042. **Requirements:** Submit application and fingerprint card. Pay fee. **Fees:** $40 registration fee.

6054

Racing Secretary (Racetrack)
Florida Dept. of Business
Div. of Pari-Mutuel Wagering
Licensing Section
725 S. Bronough St.
Tallahassee, FL 32399-1037
Phone: (904)488-9161

Credential Type: License Registration Code 1042. **Requirements:** Submit application and fingerprint card. Pay fee. **Fees:** $40 registration fee.

6055

Stable Agent (Racetrack)
Florida Dept. of Business
Div. of Pari-Mutuel Wagering
Licensing Section
725 S. Bronough St.
Tallahassee, FL 32399-1037
Phone: (904)488-9161

Credential Type: License Registration Code 1068. **Requirements:** Submit application and fingerprint card. Pay fee. **Fees:** $10 registration fee.

Florida

6056

Stable/Kennel Helper (Racetrack)
Florida Dept. of Business
Div. of Pari-Mutuel Wagering
Licensing Section
725 S. Bronough St.
Tallahassee, FL 32399-1037
Phone: (904)488-9161

Credential Type: License Registration Code 1056. **Authorization:** Authorizes work in the following positions: groom, horse clipper, hot walker, pony rider, outrider, kennel help, and similar positions. **Requirements:** Submit application and fingerprint card. Pay fee. **Fees:** $10 registration fee.

6057

Starter (Racetrack)
Florida Dept. of Business
Div. of Pari-Mutuel Wagering
Licensing Section
725 S. Bronough St.
Tallahassee, FL 32399-1037
Phone: (904)488-9161

Credential Type: License Registration Code 1044. **Requirements:** Submit application and fingerprint card. Pay fee. **Fees:** $40 registration fee.

6058

Steward (Racetrack)
Florida Dept. of Business
Div. of Pari-Mutuel Wagering
Licensing Section
725 S. Bronough St.
Tallahassee, FL 32399-1037
Phone: (904)488-9161

Credential Type: License Registration Code 1045. **Requirements:** Submit application and fingerprint card. Pay fee. **Fees:** $40 registration fee.

6059

Thoroughbred Owner (Racetrack)
Florida Dept. of Business
Div. of Pari-Mutuel Wagering
Licensing Section
725 S. Bronough St.
Tallahassee, FL 32399-1037
Phone: (904)488-9161

Credential Type: License Registration Code 3049. **Requirements:** Submit application and fingerprint card. Pay fee. **Fees:** $40 registration fee.

6060

Thoroughbred Trainer/Assistant (Racetrack)
Florida Dept. of Business
Div. of Pari-Mutuel Wagering
Licensing Section
725 S. Bronough St.
Tallahassee, FL 32399-1037
Phone: (904)488-9161

Credential Type: License Registration Code 3050. **Requirements:** Submit application and fingerprint card. Pay fee. **Fees:** $40 registration fee.

6061

Tote Employee (Racetrack)
Florida Dept. of Business
Div. of Pari-Mutuel Wagering
Licensing Section
725 S. Bronough St.
Tallahassee, FL 32399-1037
Phone: (904)488-9161

Credential Type: License Registration Code 1001. **Requirements:** Submit application and fingerprint card. Pay fee. **Fees:** $4 registration fee.

6062

Tote Owner/Operator (Racetrack)
Florida Dept. of Business
Div. of Pari-Mutuel Wagering
Licensing Section
725 S. Bronough St.
Tallahassee, FL 32399-1037
Phone: (904)488-9161

Credential Type: License Registration Code 1022. **Requirements:** Submit application and fingerprint card. Pay fee. **Fees:** $25 registration fee.

6063

Vendor (Racetrack)
Florida Dept. of Business
Div. of Pari-Mutuel Wagering
Licensing Section
725 S. Bronough St.
Tallahassee, FL 32399-1037
Phone: (904)488-9161

Credential Type: License Registration Code 1069. **Requirements:** Submit application and fingerprint card. Pay fee. **Fees:** $10 registration fee.

6064

Vendor Representative/Salesman (Racetrack)
Florida Dept. of Business
Div. of Pari-Mutuel Wagering
Licensing Section
725 S. Bronough St.
Tallahassee, FL 32399-1037
Phone: (904)488-9161

Credential Type: License Registration Code 1070. **Requirements:** Submit application and fingerprint card. Pay fee. **Fees:** $10 registration fee.

6065

Veterinarian Assistant (Racetrack)
Florida Dept. of Business
Div. of Pari-Mutuel Wagering
Licensing Section
725 S. Bronough St.
Tallahassee, FL 32399-1037
Phone: (904)488-9161

Credential Type: License Registration Code 1061. **Requirements:** Submit application and fingerprint card. Pay fee. **Fees:** $10 registration fee.

6066

Veterinarian (Racetrack)
Florida Dept. of Business
Div. of Pari-Mutuel Wagering
Licensing Section
725 S. Bronough St.
Tallahassee, FL 32399-1037
Phone: (904)488-9161

Credential Type: License Registration Code 1046. **Requirements:** Must have a Department of Professional Regulation (DPR) license. Submit application and fingerprint card. Pay fee. **Fees:** $40 registration fee.

Idaho

6067

Apprentice Jockey (Racetrack)
Idaho State Horse Racing Commission
6133 Corporal Lane
Boise, ID 83704
Phone: (208)327-7105

Credential Type: License Registration. **Requirements:** Submit application and fingerprint card. Pay fee. **Fees:** $20 registration fee.

6068

Assistant Trainer (Racetrack)
Idaho State Horse Racing
  Commission
6133 Corporal Lane
Boise, ID 83704
Phone: (208)327-7105

Credential Type: License Registration.
Requirements: Submit application and fingerprint card. Pay fee. **Fees:** $20 registration fee.

6069

Concession Employee (Racetrack)
Idaho State Horse Racing
  Commission
6133 Corporal Lane
Boise, ID 83704
Phone: (208)327-7105

Credential Type: License Registration.
Requirements: Submit application and fingerprint card. Pay fee. **Fees:** $10 registration fee.

6070

Concessionaire (Racetrack)
Idaho State Horse Racing
  Commission
6133 Corporal Lane
Boise, ID 83704
Phone: (208)327-7105

Credential Type: License Registration.
Requirements: Submit application and fingerprint card. Pay fee. **Fees:** $20 registration fee.

6071

Donated Concession Employee (Racetrack)
Idaho State Horse Racing
  Commission
6133 Corporal Lane
Boise, ID 83704
Phone: (208)327-7105

Credential Type: License Registration.
Requirements: Submit application and fingerprint card. Pay fee. **Fees:** $1 registration fee.

6072

Exercise Boy/Girl (Racetrack)
Idaho State Horse Racing
  Commission
6133 Corporal Lane
Boise, ID 83704
Phone: (208)327-7105

Credential Type: License Registration.
Requirements: Submit application and fingerprint card. Pay fee. **Fees:** $10 registration fee.

6073

Groom (Racetrack)
Idaho State Horse Racing
  Commission
6133 Corporal Lane
Boise, ID 83704
Phone: (208)327-7105

Credential Type: License Registration.
Requirements: Submit application and fingerprint card. Pay fee. **Fees:** $10 registration fee.

6074

Jockey Agent (Racetrack)
Idaho State Horse Racing
  Commission
6133 Corporal Lane
Boise, ID 83704
Phone: (208)327-7105

Credential Type: License Registration.
Requirements: Submit application and fingerprint card. Pay fee. **Fees:** $25 registration fee.

6075

Jockey (Racetrack)
Idaho State Horse Racing
  Commission
6133 Corporal Lane
Boise, ID 83704
Phone: (208)327-7105

Credential Type: License Registration.
Requirements: Submit application and fingerprint card. Pay fee. **Fees:** $20 registration fee.

6076

Kennel Employee (Racetrack)
Idaho State Horse Racing
  Commission
6133 Corporal Lane
Boise, ID 83704
Phone: (208)327-7105

Credential Type: License Registration.
Requirements: Submit application and fingerprint card. Pay fee. **Fees:** $20 registration fee.

6077

Mutuel Employee (Racetrack)
Idaho State Horse Racing
  Commission
6133 Corporal Lane
Boise, ID 83704
Phone: (208)327-7105

Credential Type: License Registration.
Requirements: Submit application and fingerprint card. Pay fee. **Fees:** $10 registration fee.

6078

Official (Racetrack)
Idaho State Horse Racing
  Commission
6133 Corporal Lane
Boise, ID 83704
Phone: (208)327-7105

Credential Type: License Registration.
Requirements: Submit application and fingerprint card. Pay fee. **Fees:** $25 registration fee.

6079

Owner (Racetrack)
Idaho State Horse Racing
  Commission
6133 Corporal Lane
Boise, ID 83704
Phone: (208)327-7105

Credential Type: License Registration.
Requirements: Submit application and fingerprint card. Pay fee. **Fees:** $25 registration fee.

6080

Plater (Racetrack)
Idaho State Horse Racing
 Commission
6133 Corporal Lane
Boise, ID 83704
Phone: (208)327-7105

Credential Type: License Registration.
Requirements: Submit application and fingerprint card. Pay fee. **Fees:** $25 registration fee.

6081

Pony Boy/Girl (Racetrack)
Idaho State Horse Racing
 Commission
6133 Corporal Lane
Boise, ID 83704
Phone: (208)327-7105

Credential Type: License Registration.
Requirements: Submit application and fingerprint card. Pay fee. **Fees:** $10 registration fee.

6082

Stable Employee (Racetrack)
Idaho State Horse Racing
 Commission
6133 Corporal Lane
Boise, ID 83704
Phone: (208)327-7105

Credential Type: License Registration.
Requirements: Submit application and fingerprint card. Pay fee. **Fees:** $20 registration fee.

6083

Trainer (Racetrack)
Idaho State Horse Racing
 Commission
6133 Corporal Lane
Boise, ID 83704
Phone: (208)327-7105

Credential Type: License Registration.
Requirements: Submit application and fingerprint card. Pay fee. **Fees:** $25 registration fee.

6084

Veterinarian (Racetrack)
Idaho State Horse Racing
 Commission
6133 Corporal Lane
Boise, ID 83704
Phone: (208)327-7105

Credential Type: License Registration.
Requirements: Submit application and fingerprint card. Pay fee. **Fees:** $30 registration fee.

Illinois

6085

Animal Health Technician (Racetrack)
Illinois Racing Board
100 W. Randolph St., Ste. 11-100
Chicago, IL 60601
Phone: (312)814-2600

Credential Type: License Registration.
Requirements: Submit application and fingerprint card. Pay fee. **Fees:** $15 registration fee. $2 photo fee. $10 fingerprint card fee.

6086

Apprentice Blacksmith (Racetrack)
Illinois Racing Board
100 W. Randolph St., Ste. 11-100
Chicago, IL 60601
Phone: (312)814-2600

Credential Type: License Registration.
Requirements: Submit application and fingerprint card. Pay fee. **Fees:** $25 registration fee. $2 photo fee. $10 fingerprint card fee.

6087

Apprentice Jockey (Racetrack)
Illinois Racing Board
100 W. Randolph St., Ste. 11-100
Chicago, IL 60601
Phone: (312)814-2600

Credential Type: License Registration.
Requirements: Submit application and fingerprint card. Pay fee. **Fees:** $25 registration fee. $2 photo fee. $10 fingerprint card fee.

6088

Assistant Starter (Racetrack)
Illinois Racing Board
100 W. Randolph St., Ste. 11-100
Chicago, IL 60601
Phone: (312)814-2600

Credential Type: License Registration.
Requirements: Submit application and fingerprint card. Pay fee. **Fees:** $5 registration fee. $2 photo fee. $10 fingerprint card fee.

6089

Assistant Trainer (Racetrack)
Illinois Racing Board
100 W. Randolph St., Ste. 11-100
Chicago, IL 60601
Phone: (312)814-2600

Credential Type: License Registration.
Requirements: Submit application and fingerprint card. Pay fee. **Fees:** $15 registration fee. $2 photo fee. $10 fingerprint card fee.

6090

Authorized Agent (Racetrack)
Illinois Racing Board
100 W. Randolph St., Ste. 11-100
Chicago, IL 60601
Phone: (312)814-2600

Credential Type: License Registration.
Requirements: Submit application and fingerprint card. Pay fee. **Fees:** $25 registration fee. $2 photo fee. $10 fingerprint card fee.

6091

Blacksmith (Racetrack)
Illinois Racing Board
100 W. Randolph St., Ste. 11-100
Chicago, IL 60601
Phone: (312)814-2600

Credential Type: License Registration.
Requirements: Submit application and fingerprint card. Pay fee. **Fees:** $25 registration fee. $2 photo fee. $10 fingerprint card fee.

6092

Driver (Racetrack)
Illinois Racing Board
100 W. Randolph St., Ste. 11-100
Chicago, IL 60601
Phone: (312)814-2600

Credential Type: License Registration.
Requirements: Submit application and fin-

Racetrack Occupations 6104 Illinois

gerprint card. Pay fee. **Fees:** $25 registration fee. $2 photo fee. $10 fingerprint card fee.

6093

Driver-Trainer (Racetrack)
Illinois Racing Board
100 W. Randolph St., Ste. 11-100
Chicago, IL 60601
Phone: (312)814-2600

Credential Type: License Registration.
Requirements: Submit application and fingerprint card. Pay fee. **Fees:** $25 registration fee. $2 photo fee. $10 fingerprint card fee.

6094

Exercise Person (Racetrack)
Illinois Racing Board
100 W. Randolph St., Ste. 11-100
Chicago, IL 60601
Phone: (312)814-2600

Credential Type: License Registration.
Requirements: Submit application and fingerprint card. Pay fee. **Fees:** $10 registration fee. $2 photo fee. $10 fingerprint card fee.

6095

Foreman (Racetrack)
Illinois Racing Board
100 W. Randolph St., Ste. 11-100
Chicago, IL 60601
Phone: (312)814-2600

Credential Type: License Registration.
Requirements: Submit application and fingerprint card. Pay fee. **Fees:** $10 registration fee. $2 photo fee. $10 fingerprint card fee.

6096

Groom (Racetrack)
Illinois Racing Board
100 W. Randolph St., Ste. 11-100
Chicago, IL 60601
Phone: (312)814-2600

Credential Type: License Registration.
Requirements: Submit application and fingerprint card. Pay fee. **Fees:** $5 registration fee. $2 photo fee. $10 fingerprint card fee.

6097

Hotwalker (Racetrack)
Illinois Racing Board
100 W. Randolph St., Ste. 11-100
Chicago, IL 60601
Phone: (312)814-2600

Credential Type: License Registration.
Requirements: Submit application and fingerprint card. Pay fee. **Fees:** $5 registration fee. $2 photo fee. $10 fingerprint card fee.

6098

Intertrack Employee (Racetrack)
Illinois Racing Board
100 W. Randolph St., Ste. 11-100
Chicago, IL 60601
Phone: (312)814-2600

Credential Type: License Registration.
Requirements: Submit application and fingerprint card. Pay fee. **Fees:** $25 registration fee. $2 photo fee. $10 fingerprint card fee.

6099

Jockey Agent (Racetrack)
Illinois Racing Board
100 W. Randolph St., Ste. 11-100
Chicago, IL 60601
Phone: (312)814-2600

Credential Type: License Registration.
Requirements: Submit application and fingerprint card. Pay fee. **Fees:** $25 registration fee. $2 photo fee. $10 fingerprint card fee.

6100

Jockey (Racetrack)
Illinois Racing Board
100 W. Randolph St., Ste. 11-100
Chicago, IL 60601
Phone: (312)814-2600

Credential Type: License Registration.
Requirements: Submit application and fingerprint card. Pay fee. **Fees:** $25 registration fee. $2 photo fee. $10 fingerprint card fee.

6101

Owner-Assistant Trainer (Racetrack)
Illinois Racing Board
100 W. Randolph St., Ste. 11-100
Chicago, IL 60601
Phone: (312)814-2600

Credential Type: License Registration.
Requirements: Submit application and fingerprint card. Pay fee. **Fees:** $25 registration fee. $2 photo fee. $10 fingerprint card fee.

6102

Owner-Driver (Racetrack)
Illinois Racing Board
100 W. Randolph St., Ste. 11-100
Chicago, IL 60601
Phone: (312)814-2600

Credential Type: License Registration.
Requirements: Submit application and fingerprint card. Pay fee. **Fees:** $25 registration fee. $2 photo fee. $10 fingerprint card fee.

6103

Owner-Driver-Trainer (Racetrack)
Illinois Racing Board
100 W. Randolph St., Ste. 11-100
Chicago, IL 60601
Phone: (312)814-2600

Credential Type: License Registration.
Requirements: Submit application and fingerprint card. Pay fee. **Fees:** $25 registration fee. $2 photo fee. $10 fingerprint card fee.

6104

Owner (Racetrack)
Illinois Racing Board
100 W. Randolph St., Ste. 11-100
Chicago, IL 60601
Phone: (312)814-2600

Credential Type: License Registration.
Requirements: Submit application and fingerprint card. Pay fee. **Fees:** $25 registration fee. $2 photo fee. $10 fingerprint card fee.

Illinois 6105

6105

Owner-Trainer (Racetrack)
Illinois Racing Board
100 W. Randolph St., Ste. 11-100
Chicago, IL 60601
Phone: (312)814-2600

Credential Type: License Registration.
Requirements: Submit application and fingerprint card. Pay fee. **Fees:** $25 registration fee. $2 photo fee. $10 fingerprint card fee.

6106

Pony Person (Racetrack)
Illinois Racing Board
100 W. Randolph St., Ste. 11-100
Chicago, IL 60601
Phone: (312)814-2600

Credential Type: License Registration.
Requirements: Submit application and fingerprint card. Pay fee. **Fees:** $10 registration fee. $2 photo fee. $10 fingerprint card fee.

6107

Race Track Employee (Racetrack)
Illinois Racing Board
100 W. Randolph St., Ste. 11-100
Chicago, IL 60601
Phone: (312)814-2600

Credential Type: License Registration.
Requirements: Submit application and fingerprint card. Pay fee. **Fees:** $5 registration fee. $2 photo fee. $10 fingerprint card fee.

6108

Racing Official (Racetrack)
Illinois Racing Board
100 W. Randolph St., Ste. 11-100
Chicago, IL 60601
Phone: (312)814-2600

Credential Type: License Registration.
Requirements: Submit application and fingerprint card. Pay fee. **Fees:** $25 registration fee. $2 photo fee. $10 fingerprint card fee.

6109

Starter (Racetrack)
Illinois Racing Board
100 W. Randolph St., Ste. 11-100
Chicago, IL 60601
Phone: (312)814-2600

Credential Type: License Registration.
Requirements: Submit application and fingerprint card. Pay fee. **Fees:** $25 registration fee. $2 photo fee. $10 fingerprint card fee.

6110

Steward (Racetrack)
Illinois Racing Board
100 W. Randolph St., Ste. 11-100
Chicago, IL 60601
Phone: (312)814-2600

Credential Type: License Registration.
Requirements: Submit application and fingerprint card. Pay fee. **Fees:** $25 registration fee. $2 photo fee. $10 fingerprint card fee.

6111

Totalizator Employee (Racetrack)
Illinois Racing Board
100 W. Randolph St., Ste. 11-100
Chicago, IL 60601
Phone: (312)814-2600

Credential Type: License Registration.
Requirements: Submit application and fingerprint card. Pay fee. **Fees:** $25 registration fee. $2 photo fee. $10 fingerprint card fee.

6112

Trainer (Racetrack)
Illinois Racing Board
100 W. Randolph St., Ste. 11-100
Chicago, IL 60601
Phone: (312)814-2600

Credential Type: License Registration.
Requirements: Submit application and fingerprint card. Pay fee. **Fees:** $25 registration fee. $2 photo fee. $10 fingerprint card fee.

6113

Valet (Racetrack)
Illinois Racing Board
100 W. Randolph St., Ste. 11-100
Chicago, IL 60601
Phone: (312)814-2600

Credential Type: License Registration.
Requirements: Submit application and fingerprint card. Pay fee. **Fees:** $10 registration fee. $2 photo fee. $10 fingerprint card fee.

6114

Vendor (Racetrack)
Illinois Racing Board
100 W. Randolph St., Ste. 11-100
Chicago, IL 60601
Phone: (312)814-2600

Credential Type: License Registration.
Requirements: Submit application and fingerprint card. Pay fee. **Fees:** $25 registration fee. $2 photo fee. $10 fingerprint card fee.

6115

Vendor's Helper (Racetrack)
Illinois Racing Board
100 W. Randolph St., Ste. 11-100
Chicago, IL 60601
Phone: (312)814-2600

Credential Type: License Registration.
Requirements: Submit application and fingerprint card. Pay fee. **Fees:** $10 registration fee. $2 photo fee. $10 fingerprint card fee.

6116

Veterinarian Assistant (Racetrack)
Illinois Racing Board
100 W. Randolph St., Ste. 11-100
Chicago, IL 60601
Phone: (312)814-2600

Credential Type: License Registration.
Requirements: Submit application and fingerprint card. Pay fee. **Fees:** $15 registration fee. $2 photo fee. $10 fingerprint card fee.

6117

Veterinarian (Racetrack)
Illinois Racing Board
100 W. Randolph St., Ste. 11-100
Chicago, IL 60601
Phone: (312)814-2600

Credential Type: License Registration.
Requirements: Submit application and fingerprint card. Pay fee. **Fees:** $25 registration fee. $2 photo fee. $10 fingerprint card fee.

Iowa

6118

Administrator (Racetrack)
Iowa State Racing Commission
Lucas State Office Bldg.
Des Moines, IA 50319
Phone: (515)281-7352

Credential Type: License Registration.
Requirements: Submit application and fingerprint card. Pay fee. **Fees:** $5 registration fee.

6119

Announcer (Racetrack)
Iowa State Racing Commission
Lucas State Office Bldg.
Des Moines, IA 50319
Phone: (515)281-7352

Credential Type: License Registration.
Requirements: Submit application and fingerprint card. Pay fee. **Fees:** $10 registration fee.

6120

Apprentice Jockey (Racetrack)
Iowa State Racing Commission
Lucas State Office Bldg.
Des Moines, IA 50319
Phone: (515)281-7352

Credential Type: License Registration.
Requirements: Submit application and fingerprint card. Pay fee. **Fees:** $10 registration fee.

6121

Assistant Manager (Racetrack)
Iowa State Racing Commission
Lucas State Office Bldg.
Des Moines, IA 50319
Phone: (515)281-7352

Credential Type: License Registration.
Requirements: Submit application and fingerprint card. Pay fee. **Fees:** $20 registration fee.

6122

Assistant Racing Secretary (Racetrack)
Iowa State Racing Commission
Lucas State Office Bldg.
Des Moines, IA 50319
Phone: (515)281-7352

Credential Type: License Registration.
Requirements: Submit application and fingerprint card. Pay fee. **Fees:** $10 registration fee.

6123

Assistant Trainer (Racetrack)
Iowa State Racing Commission
Lucas State Office Bldg.
Des Moines, IA 50319
Phone: (515)281-7352

Credential Type: License Registration.
Requirements: Submit application and fingerprint card. Pay fee. **Fees:** $10 registration fee.

6124

Authorized Agent (Racetrack)
Iowa State Racing Commission
Lucas State Office Bldg.
Des Moines, IA 50319
Phone: (515)281-7352

Credential Type: License Registration.
Requirements: Submit application and fingerprint card. Pay fee. **Fees:** $10 registration fee.

6125

Chart Writer (Racetrack)
Iowa State Racing Commission
Lucas State Office Bldg.
Des Moines, IA 50319
Phone: (515)281-7352

Credential Type: License Registration.
Requirements: Submit application and fingerprint card. Pay fee. **Fees:** $10 registration fee.

6126

Concession Employee (Racetrack)
Iowa State Racing Commission
Lucas State Office Bldg.
Des Moines, IA 50319
Phone: (515)281-7352

Credential Type: License Registration.
Requirements: Submit application and fingerprint card. Pay fee. **Fees:** $5 registration fee.

6127

Concession Operator (Racetrack)
Iowa State Racing Commission
Lucas State Office Bldg.
Des Moines, IA 50319
Phone: (515)281-7352

Credential Type: License Registration.
Requirements: Submit application and fingerprint card. Pay fee. **Fees:** $20 registration fee.

6128

Corporate Director/Officer (Racetrack)
Iowa State Racing Commission
Lucas State Office Bldg.
Des Moines, IA 50319
Phone: (515)281-7352

Credential Type: License Registration.
Requirements: Submit application and fingerprint card. Pay fee. **Fees:** $10 registration fee.

6129

Driver/Jockey (Racetrack)
Iowa State Racing Commission
Lucas State Office Bldg.
Des Moines, IA 50319
Phone: (515)281-7352

Credential Type: License Registration.
Requirements: Submit application and fingerprint card. Pay fee. **Fees:** $10 registration fee.

6130

Exercise Rider (Racetrack)
Iowa State Racing Commission
Lucas State Office Bldg.
Des Moines, IA 50319
Phone: (515)281-7352

Credential Type: License Registration.
Requirements: Submit application and fingerprint card. Pay fee. **Fees:** $5 registration fee.

6131

Groom (Racetrack)
Iowa State Racing Commission
Lucas State Office Bldg.
Des Moines, IA 50319
Phone: (515)281-7352

Credential Type: License Registration.
Requirements: Submit application and fingerprint card. Pay fee. **Fees:** $5 registration fee.

6132

Jockey Agent (Racetrack)
Iowa State Racing Commission
Lucas State Office Bldg.
Des Moines, IA 50319
Phone: (515)281-7352

Credential Type: License Registration.
Requirements: Submit application and fingerprint card. Pay fee. **Fees:** $10 registration fee.

6133

Kennel Helper (Racetrack)
Iowa State Racing Commission
Lucas State Office Bldg.
Des Moines, IA 50319
Phone: (515)281-7352

Credential Type: License Registration.
Requirements: Submit application and fingerprint card. Pay fee. **Fees:** $5 registration fee.

6134

Kennel Owner (Racetrack)
Iowa State Racing Commission
Lucas State Office Bldg.
Des Moines, IA 50319
Phone: (515)281-7352

Credential Type: License Registration.
Requirements: Submit application and fingerprint card. Pay fee. **Fees:** $20 registration fee.

6135

Lead Out (Racetrack)
Iowa State Racing Commission
Lucas State Office Bldg.
Des Moines, IA 50319
Phone: (515)281-7352

Credential Type: License Registration.
Requirements: Submit application and fingerprint card. Pay fee. **Fees:** $5 registration fee.

6136

Maintenance Employee (Racetrack)
Iowa State Racing Commission
Lucas State Office Bldg.
Des Moines, IA 50319
Phone: (515)281-7352

Credential Type: License Registration.
Requirements: Submit application and fingerprint card. Pay fee. **Fees:** $5 registration fee.

6137

Manager (Racetrack)
Iowa State Racing Commission
Lucas State Office Bldg.
Des Moines, IA 50319
Phone: (515)281-7352

Credential Type: License Registration.
Requirements: Submit application and fingerprint card. Pay fee. **Fees:** $20 registration fee.

6138

Mutuel Employee (Racetrack)
Iowa State Racing Commission
Lucas State Office Bldg.
Des Moines, IA 50319
Phone: (515)281-7352

Credential Type: License Registration.
Requirements: Submit application and fingerprint card. Pay fee. **Fees:** $5 registration fee.

6139

Mutuels Manager (Racetrack)
Iowa State Racing Commission
Lucas State Office Bldg.
Des Moines, IA 50319
Phone: (515)281-7352

Credential Type: License Registration.
Requirements: Submit application and fingerprint card. Pay fee. **Fees:** $20 registration fee.

6140

Official (Racetrack)
Iowa State Racing Commission
Lucas State Office Bldg.
Des Moines, IA 50319
Phone: (515)281-7352

Credential Type: License Registration.
Requirements: Submit application and fingerprint card. Pay fee. **Fees:** $10 registration fee.

6141

Outrider (Racetrack)
Iowa State Racing Commission
Lucas State Office Bldg.
Des Moines, IA 50319
Phone: (515)281-7352

Credential Type: License Registration.
Requirements: Submit application and fingerprint card. Pay fee. **Fees:** $10 registration fee.

6142

Owner (Racetrack)
Iowa State Racing Commission
Lucas State Office Bldg.
Des Moines, IA 50319
Phone: (515)281-7352

Credential Type: License Registration.
Requirements: Submit application and fingerprint card. Pay fee. **Fees:** $10 registration fee.

6143

Owner-Trainer-Driver (Racetrack)
Iowa State Racing Commission
Lucas State Office Bldg.
Des Moines, IA 50319
Phone: (515)281-7352

Credential Type: License Registration.
Requirements: Submit application and fingerprint card. Pay fee. **Fees:** $20 registration fee.

6144

Owner-Trainer (Racetrack)
Iowa State Racing Commission
Lucas State Office Bldg.
Des Moines, IA 50319
Phone: (515)281-7352

Credential Type: License Registration.
Requirements: Submit application and fingerprint card. Pay fee. **Fees:** $20 registration fee.

6145

Parking/Admissions Employee
Iowa State Racing Commission
Lucas State Office Bldg.
Des Moines, IA 50319
Phone: (515)281-7352

Credential Type: License Registration.
Requirements: Submit application and fingerprint card. Pay fee. **Fees:** $5 registration fee.

6146

Racing Secretary (Racetrack)
Iowa State Racing Commission
Lucas State Office Bldg.
Des Moines, IA 50319
Phone: (515)281-7352

Credential Type: License Registration.
Requirements: Submit application and fingerprint card. Pay fee. **Fees:** $20 registration fee.

6147

Security Employee (Racetrack)
Iowa State Racing Commission
Lucas State Office Bldg.
Des Moines, IA 50319
Phone: (515)281-7352

Credential Type: License Registration.
Requirements: Submit application and fingerprint card. Pay fee. **Fees:** $5 registration fee.

6148

Track Superintendent (Racetrack)
Iowa State Racing Commission
Lucas State Office Bldg.
Des Moines, IA 50319
Phone: (515)281-7352

Credential Type: License Registration.
Requirements: Submit application and fingerprint card. Pay fee. **Fees:** $10 registration fee.

6149

Trainer (Racetrack)
Iowa State Racing Commission
Lucas State Office Bldg.
Des Moines, IA 50319
Phone: (515)281-7352

Credential Type: License Registration.
Requirements: Submit application and fingerprint card. Pay fee. **Fees:** $10 registration fee.

6150

Veterinarian (Racetrack)
Iowa State Racing Commission
Lucas State Office Bldg.
Des Moines, IA 50319
Phone: (515)281-7352

Credential Type: License Registration.
Requirements: Submit application and fingerprint card. Pay fee. **Fees:** $10 registration fee.

Kansas

6151

Administrative Support Employee (Racetrack)
Kansas Racing Commission
3400 VanBuren
Topeka, KS 66611-2228
Phone: (913)296-5800

Credential Type: License Registration.
Requirements: Submit application and fingerprint card. Pay fee. **Fees:** $5 registration fee.

6152

Administrator (Racetrack)
Kansas Racing Commission
3400 VanBuren
Topeka, KS 66611-2228
Phone: (913)296-5800

Credential Type: License Registration.
Requirements: Submit application and fingerprint card. Pay fee. **Fees:** $20 registration fee.

6153

Announcer (Racetrack)
Kansas Racing Commission
3400 VanBuren
Topeka, KS 66611-2228
Phone: (913)296-5800

Credential Type: License Registration.
Requirements: Submit application and fingerprint card. Pay fee. **Fees:** $5 registration fee.

6154

Apprentice Jockey (Racetrack)
Kansas Racing Commission
3400 VanBuren
Topeka, KS 66611-2228
Phone: (913)296-5800

Credential Type: License Registration.
Requirements: Submit application and fingerprint card. Pay fee. **Fees:** $10 registration fee.

6155

Assistant Manager (Racetrack)
Kansas Racing Commission
3400 VanBuren
Topeka, KS 66611-2228
Phone: (913)296-5800

Credential Type: License Registration.
Requirements: Submit application and fingerprint card. Pay fee. **Fees:** $20 registration fee.

6156

Assistant Racing Secretary (Racetrack)
Kansas Racing Commission
3400 VanBuren
Topeka, KS 66611-2228
Phone: (913)296-5800

Credential Type: License Registration.
Requirements: Submit application and fingerprint card. Pay fee. **Fees:** $10 registration fee.

6157

Assistant Starter (Racetrack)
Kansas Racing Commission
3400 VanBuren
Topeka, KS 66611-2228
Phone: (913)296-5800

Credential Type: License Registration.
Requirements: Submit application and fingerprint card. Pay fee. **Fees:** $5 registration fee.

6158

Assistant Trainer (Racetrack)
Kansas Racing Commission
3400 VanBuren
Topeka, KS 66611-2228
Phone: (913)296-5800

Credential Type: License Registration.
Requirements: Submit application and fingerprint card. Pay fee. **Fees:** $10 registration fee.

6159

Authorized Agent (Racetrack)
Kansas Racing Commission
3400 VanBuren
Topeka, KS 66611-2228
Phone: (913)296-5800

Credential Type: License Registration.
Requirements: Submit application and fin-

Kansas 6160

Authorized Agent (Racetrack), continued

gerprint card. Pay fee. **Fees:** $10 registration fee.

6160

Blacksmith (Racetrack)
Kansas Racing Commission
3400 VanBuren
Topeka, KS 66611-2228
Phone: (913)296-5800

Credential Type: License Registration.
Requirements: Submit application and fingerprint card. Pay fee. **Fees:** $10 registration fee.

6161

Bloodstock Agent (Racetrack)
Kansas Racing Commission
3400 VanBuren
Topeka, KS 66611-2228
Phone: (913)296-5800

Credential Type: License Registration.
Requirements: Submit application and fingerprint card. Pay fee. **Fees:** $10 registration fee.

6162

Brakeman (Racetrack)
Kansas Racing Commission
3400 VanBuren
Topeka, KS 66611-2228
Phone: (913)296-5800

Credential Type: License Registration.
Requirements: Submit application and fingerprint card. Pay fee. **Fees:** $10 registration fee.

6163

Chart Writer (Racetrack)
Kansas Racing Commission
3400 VanBuren
Topeka, KS 66611-2228
Phone: (913)296-5800

Credential Type: License Registration.
Requirements: Submit application and fingerprint card. Pay fee. **Fees:** $10 registration fee.

6164

Clerk of Scales (Racetrack)
Kansas Racing Commission
3400 VanBuren
Topeka, KS 66611-2228
Phone: (913)296-5800

Credential Type: License Registration.
Requirements: Submit application and fingerprint card. Pay fee. **Fees:** $10 registration fee.

6165

Colors Attendant (Racetrack)
Kansas Racing Commission
3400 VanBuren
Topeka, KS 66611-2228
Phone: (913)296-5800

Credential Type: License Registration.
Requirements: Submit application and fingerprint card. Pay fee. **Fees:** $5 registration fee.

6166

Concession Employee (Racetrack)
Kansas Racing Commission
3400 VanBuren
Topeka, KS 66611-2228
Phone: (913)296-5800

Credential Type: License Registration.
Requirements: Submit application and fingerprint card. Pay fee. **Fees:** $5 registration fee.

6167

Concession Operator (Racetrack)
Kansas Racing Commission
3400 VanBuren
Topeka, KS 66611-2228
Phone: (913)296-5800

Credential Type: License Registration.
Requirements: Submit application and fingerprint card. Pay fee. **Fees:** $10 registration fee.

6168

Director of Racing (Racetrack)
Kansas Racing Commission
3400 VanBuren
Topeka, KS 66611-2228
Phone: (913)296-5800

Credential Type: License Registration.
Requirements: Submit application and fingerprint card. Pay fee. **Fees:** $20 registration fee.

6169

Director of Security (Racetrack)
Kansas Racing Commission
3400 VanBuren
Topeka, KS 66611-2228
Phone: (913)296-5800

Credential Type: License Registration.
Requirements: Submit application and fingerprint card. Pay fee. **Fees:** $20 registration fee.

6170

Driver (Racetrack)
Kansas Racing Commission
3400 VanBuren
Topeka, KS 66611-2228
Phone: (913)296-5800

Credential Type: License Registration.
Requirements: Submit application and fingerprint card. Pay fee. **Fees:** $10 registration fee.

6171

Emergency Medical Technician (Racetrack)
Kansas Racing Commission
3400 VanBuren
Topeka, KS 66611-2228
Phone: (913)296-5800

Credential Type: License Registration.
Requirements: Submit application and fingerprint card. Pay fee. **Fees:** $5 registration fee.

6172

Exercise Person (Racetrack)
Kansas Racing Commission
3400 VanBuren
Topeka, KS 66611-2228
Phone: (913)296-5800

Credential Type: License Registration.
Requirements: Submit application and fingerprint card. Pay fee. **Fees:** $5 registration fee.

6173

Farrier (Racetrack)
Kansas Racing Commission
3400 VanBuren
Topeka, KS 66611-2228
Phone: (913)296-5800

Credential Type: License Registration.
Requirements: Submit application and fin-

gerprint card. Pay fee. **Fees:** $10 registration fee.

6174

Flagman (Racetrack)
Kansas Racing Commission
3400 VanBuren
Topeka, KS 66611-2228
Phone: (913)296-5800

Credential Type: License Registration. **Requirements:** Submit application and fingerprint card. Pay fee. **Fees:** $10 registration fee.

6175

Groom/Hot Walker (Racetrack)
Kansas Racing Commission
3400 VanBuren
Topeka, KS 66611-2228
Phone: (913)296-5800

Credential Type: License Registration. **Requirements:** Submit application and fingerprint card. Pay fee. **Fees:** $5 registration fee.

6176

Horsemen's Bookkeeper (Racetrack)
Kansas Racing Commission
3400 VanBuren
Topeka, KS 66611-2228
Phone: (913)296-5800

Credential Type: License Registration. **Requirements:** Submit application and fingerprint card. Pay fee. **Fees:** $10 registration fee.

6177

Identifier (Racetrack)
Kansas Racing Commission
3400 VanBuren
Topeka, KS 66611-2228
Phone: (913)296-5800

Credential Type: License Registration. **Requirements:** Submit application and fingerprint card. Pay fee. **Fees:** $10 registration fee.

6178

Jockey Agent (Racetrack)
Kansas Racing Commission
3400 VanBuren
Topeka, KS 66611-2228
Phone: (913)296-5800

Credential Type: License Registration. **Requirements:** Submit application and fingerprint card. Pay fee. **Fees:** $10 registration fee.

6179

Jockey (Racetrack)
Kansas Racing Commission
3400 VanBuren
Topeka, KS 66611-2228
Phone: (913)296-5800

Credential Type: License Registration. **Requirements:** Submit application and fingerprint card. Pay fee. **Fees:** $10 registration fee.

6180

Jockey Room Attendant (Racetrack)
Kansas Racing Commission
3400 VanBuren
Topeka, KS 66611-2228
Phone: (913)296-5800

Credential Type: License Registration. **Requirements:** Submit application and fingerprint card. Pay fee. **Fees:** $5 registration fee.

6181

Kennel Helper (Racetrack)
Kansas Racing Commission
3400 VanBuren
Topeka, KS 66611-2228
Phone: (913)296-5800

Credential Type: License Registration. **Requirements:** Submit application and fingerprint card. Pay fee. **Fees:** $5 registration fee.

6182

Kennel Master (Racetrack)
Kansas Racing Commission
3400 VanBuren
Topeka, KS 66611-2228
Phone: (913)296-5800

Credential Type: License Registration. **Requirements:** Submit application and fingerprint card. Pay fee. **Fees:** $20 registration fee.

6183

Kennel Owner (Racetrack)
Kansas Racing Commission
3400 VanBuren
Topeka, KS 66611-2228
Phone: (913)296-5800

Credential Type: License Registration. **Requirements:** Submit application and fingerprint card. Pay fee. **Fees:** $20 registration fee.

6184

Lead Out (Racetrack)
Kansas Racing Commission
3400 VanBuren
Topeka, KS 66611-2228
Phone: (913)296-5800

Credential Type: License Registration. **Requirements:** Submit application and fingerprint card. Pay fee. **Fees:** $5 registration fee.

6185

Lure Operator (Racetrack)
Kansas Racing Commission
3400 VanBuren
Topeka, KS 66611-2228
Phone: (913)296-5800

Credential Type: License Registration. **Requirements:** Submit application and fingerprint card. Pay fee. **Fees:** $10 registration fee.

6186

Maintenance Employee (Racetrack)
Kansas Racing Commission
3400 VanBuren
Topeka, KS 66611-2228
Phone: (913)296-5800

Credential Type: License Registration. **Requirements:** Submit application and fingerprint card. Pay fee. **Fees:** $5 registration fee.

Kansas 6187

6187
Managing Owner (Racetrack)
Kansas Racing Commission
3400 VanBuren
Topeka, KS 66611-2228
Phone: (913)296-5800

Credential Type: License Registration.
Requirements: Submit application and fingerprint card. Pay fee. **Fees:** $5 registration fee.

6188
Mutuel Employee (Racetrack)
Kansas Racing Commission
3400 VanBuren
Topeka, KS 66611-2228
Phone: (913)296-5800

Credential Type: License Registration.
Requirements: Submit application and fingerprint card. Pay fee. **Fees:** $5 registration fee.

6189
Official (Racetrack)
Kansas Racing Commission
3400 VanBuren
Topeka, KS 66611-2228
Phone: (913)296-5800

Credential Type: License Registration.
Requirements: Submit application and fingerprint card. Pay fee. **Fees:** $10 registration fee.

6190
Outrider (Racetrack)
Kansas Racing Commission
3400 VanBuren
Topeka, KS 66611-2228
Phone: (913)296-5800

Credential Type: License Registration.
Requirements: Submit application and fingerprint card. Pay fee. **Fees:** $10 registration fee.

6191
Owner By Open Claim (Racetrack)
Kansas Racing Commission
3400 VanBuren
Topeka, KS 66611-2228
Phone: (913)296-5800

Credential Type: License Registration.
Requirements: Submit application and fingerprint card. Pay fee. **Fees:** $10 registration fee.

6192
Owner (Racetrack)
Kansas Racing Commission
3400 VanBuren
Topeka, KS 66611-2228
Phone: (913)296-5800

Credential Type: License Registration.
Requirements: Submit application and fingerprint card. Pay fee. **Fees:** $10 registration fee.

6193
Paddock Attendant (Racetrack)
Kansas Racing Commission
3400 VanBuren
Topeka, KS 66611-2228
Phone: (913)296-5800

Credential Type: License Registration.
Requirements: Submit application and fingerprint card. Pay fee. **Fees:** $5 registration fee.

6194
Paddock Judge (Racetrack)
Kansas Racing Commission
3400 VanBuren
Topeka, KS 66611-2228
Phone: (913)296-5800

Credential Type: License Registration.
Requirements: Submit application and fingerprint card. Pay fee. **Fees:** $10 registration fee.

6195
Parking Attendant (Racetrack)
Kansas Racing Commission
3400 VanBuren
Topeka, KS 66611-2228
Phone: (913)296-5800

Credential Type: License Registration.
Requirements: Submit application and fingerprint card. Pay fee. **Fees:** $5 registration fee.

6196
Patrol Judge (Racetrack)
Kansas Racing Commission
3400 VanBuren
Topeka, KS 66611-2228
Phone: (913)296-5800

Credential Type: License Registration.
Requirements: Submit application and fingerprint card. Pay fee. **Fees:** $10 registration fee.

6197
Photo Finish Operator (Racetrack)
Kansas Racing Commission
3400 VanBuren
Topeka, KS 66611-2228
Phone: (913)296-5800

Credential Type: License Registration.
Requirements: Submit application and fingerprint card. Pay fee. **Fees:** $10 registration fee.

6198
Plater (Racetrack)
Kansas Racing Commission
3400 VanBuren
Topeka, KS 66611-2228
Phone: (913)296-5800

Credential Type: License Registration.
Requirements: Submit application and fingerprint card. Pay fee. **Fees:** $10 registration fee.

6199
Pony Person (Racetrack)
Kansas Racing Commission
3400 VanBuren
Topeka, KS 66611-2228
Phone: (913)296-5800

Credential Type: License Registration.
Requirements: Submit application and fingerprint card. Pay fee. **Fees:** $5 registration fee.

6200
Practicing Veterinarian Assistant (Racetrack)
Kansas Racing Commission
3400 VanBuren
Topeka, KS 66611-2228
Phone: (913)296-5800

Credential Type: License Registration.
Requirements: Submit application and fingerprint card. Pay fee. **Fees:** $5 registration fee.

6201
Practicing Veterinarian (Racetrack)
Kansas Racing Commission
3400 VanBuren
Topeka, KS 66611-2228
Phone: (913)296-5800

Credential Type: License Registration.
Requirements: Submit application and fin-

Racetrack Occupations

Kansas

gerprint card. Pay fee. **Fees:** $10 registration fee.

6202

Program Manager (Racetrack)
Kansas Racing Commission
3400 VanBuren
Topeka, KS 66611-2228
Phone: (913)296-5800

Credential Type: License Registration.
Requirements: Submit application and fingerprint card. Pay fee. **Fees:** $20 registration fee.

6203

Promotion Manager (Racetrack)
Kansas Racing Commission
3400 VanBuren
Topeka, KS 66611-2228
Phone: (913)296-5800

Credential Type: License Registration.
Requirements: Submit application and fingerprint card. Pay fee. **Fees:** $20 registration fee.

6204

Racing Secretary (Racetrack)
Kansas Racing Commission
3400 VanBuren
Topeka, KS 66611-2228
Phone: (913)296-5800

Credential Type: License Registration.
Requirements: Submit application and fingerprint card. Pay fee. **Fees:** $20 registration fee.

6205

Security Employee (Racetrack)
Kansas Racing Commission
3400 VanBuren
Topeka, KS 66611-2228
Phone: (913)296-5800

Credential Type: License Registration.
Requirements: Submit application and fingerprint card. Pay fee. **Fees:** $5 registration fee.

6206

Selection Sheet Operator (Racetrack)
Kansas Racing Commission
3400 VanBuren
Topeka, KS 66611-2228
Phone: (913)296-5800

Credential Type: License Registration.
Requirements: Submit application and fingerprint card. Pay fee. **Fees:** $10 registration fee.

6207

Stable Trainer/Agent (Racetrack)
Kansas Racing Commission
3400 VanBuren
Topeka, KS 66611-2228
Phone: (913)296-5800

Credential Type: License Registration.
Requirements: Submit application and fingerprint card. Pay fee. **Fees:** $10 registration fee.

6208

Starter (Racetrack)
Kansas Racing Commission
3400 VanBuren
Topeka, KS 66611-2228
Phone: (913)296-5800

Credential Type: License Registration.
Requirements: Submit application and fingerprint card. Pay fee. **Fees:** $10 registration fee.

6209

Supervisor of Mutuels (Racetrack)
Kansas Racing Commission
3400 VanBuren
Topeka, KS 66611-2228
Phone: (913)296-5800

Credential Type: License Registration.
Requirements: Submit application and fingerprint card. Pay fee. **Fees:** $20 registration fee.

6210

Testing Technician (Racetrack)
Kansas Racing Commission
3400 VanBuren
Topeka, KS 66611-2228
Phone: (913)296-5800

Credential Type: License Registration.
Requirements: Submit application and fingerprint card. Pay fee. **Fees:** $10 registration fee.

6211

Timer (Racetrack)
Kansas Racing Commission
3400 VanBuren
Topeka, KS 66611-2228
Phone: (913)296-5800

Credential Type: License Registration.
Requirements: Submit application and fingerprint card. Pay fee. **Fees:** $10 registration fee.

6212

Totalisator Employee (Racetrack)
Kansas Racing Commission
3400 VanBuren
Topeka, KS 66611-2228
Phone: (913)296-5800

Credential Type: License Registration.
Requirements: Submit application and fingerprint card. Pay fee. **Fees:** $5 registration fee.

6213

Track Superintendent (Racetrack)
Kansas Racing Commission
3400 VanBuren
Topeka, KS 66611-2228
Phone: (913)296-5800

Credential Type: License Registration.
Requirements: Submit application and fingerprint card. Pay fee. **Fees:** $10 registration fee.

6214

Trainer (Racetrack)
Kansas Racing Commission
3400 VanBuren
Topeka, KS 66611-2228
Phone: (913)296-5800

Credential Type: License Registration.
Requirements: Submit application and fingerprint card. Pay fee. **Fees:** $10 registration fee.

Kansas

6215

Valet (Racetrack)
Kansas Racing Commission
3400 VanBuren
Topeka, KS 66611-2228
Phone: (913)296-5800

Credential Type: License Registration.
Requirements: Submit application and fingerprint card. Pay fee. **Fees:** $5 registration fee.

6216

Video Operator (Racetrack)
Kansas Racing Commission
3400 VanBuren
Topeka, KS 66611-2228
Phone: (913)296-5800

Credential Type: License Registration.
Requirements: Submit application and fingerprint card. Pay fee. **Fees:** $10 registration fee.

Kentucky

6217

Admission Department Manager/ Employee(Racetrack)
Kentucky State Racing Commission
PO Box 1080
Lexington, KY 40588
Phone: (606)254-7021

Credential Type: Association Employee and Occupational License. **Requirements:** Submit application and fingerprint card. Pay fee. **Fees:** $10 license fee.

6218

Assistant Trainer (Racetrack)
Kentucky State Racing Commission
PO Box 1080
Lexington, KY 40588
Phone: (606)254-7021

Credential Type: License Registration.
Requirements: Submit application and fingerprint card. Pay fee. **Fees:** $35 registration fee.

6219

Blacksmith (Racetrack)
Kentucky State Racing Commission
PO Box 1080
Lexington, KY 40588
Phone: (606)254-7021

Credential Type: License Registration.
Requirements: Submit application and fingerprint card. Pay fee. **Fees:** $35 registration fee.

6220

Carpenter (Racetrack)
Kentucky State Racing Commission
PO Box 1080
Lexington, KY 40588
Phone: (606)254-7021

Credential Type: Association Employee and Occupational License. **Requirements:** Submit application and fingerprint card. Pay fee. **Fees:** $10 license fee.

6221

Clerk of Scales (Racetrack)
Kentucky State Racing Commission
PO Box 1080
Lexington, KY 40588
Phone: (606)254-7021

Credential Type: Association Employee and Occupational License. **Requirements:** Submit application and fingerprint card. Pay fee. **Fees:** $10 license fee.

6222

Commission Chemist (Racetrack)
Kentucky State Racing Commission
PO Box 1080
Lexington, KY 40588
Phone: (606)254-7021

Credential Type: License Registration.
Requirements: Submit application and fingerprint card. Pay fee. **Fees:** $35 registration fee.

6223

Commission Director of Security (Racetrack)
Kentucky State Racing Commission
PO Box 1080
Lexington, KY 40588
Phone: (606)254-7021

Credential Type: License Registration.
Requirements: Submit application and fingerprint card. Pay fee. **Fees:** $35 registration fee.

6224

Commission Horse Identifier (Racetrack)
Kentucky State Racing Commission
PO Box 1080
Lexington, KY 40588
Phone: (606)254-7021

Credential Type: License Registration.
Requirements: Submit application and fingerprint card. Pay fee. **Fees:** $35 registration fee.

6225

Commission Inspector (Racetrack)
Kentucky State Racing Commission
PO Box 1080
Lexington, KY 40588
Phone: (606)254-7021

Credential Type: License Registration.
Requirements: Submit application and fingerprint card. Pay fee. **Fees:** $35 registration fee.

6226

Commission License Administrator (Racetrack)
Kentucky State Racing Commission
PO Box 1080
Lexington, KY 40588
Phone: (606)254-7021

Credential Type: License Registration.
Requirements: Submit application and fingerprint card. Pay fee. **Fees:** $35 registration fee.

6227

Commission Supervisor of Pari-Mutuel Betting (Racetrack)
Kentucky State Racing Commission
PO Box 1080
Lexington, KY 40588
Phone: (606)254-7021

Credential Type: License Registration.
Requirements: Submit application and fingerprint card. Pay fee. **Fees:** $35 registration fee.

6228

Commission Veterinarian (Racetrack)
Kentucky State Racing Commission
PO Box 1080
Lexington, KY 40588
Phone: (606)254-7021

Credential Type: License Registration. **Requirements:** Submit application and fingerprint card. Pay fee. **Fees:** $35 registration fee.

6229

Concessions Manager/Employee (Racetrack)
Kentucky State Racing Commission
PO Box 1080
Lexington, KY 40588
Phone: (606)254-7021

Credential Type: Association Employee and Occupational License. **Requirements:** Submit application and fingerprint card. Pay fee. **Fees:** $10 license fee.

6230

Dental Technician (Racetrack)
Kentucky State Racing Commission
PO Box 1080
Lexington, KY 40588
Phone: (606)254-7021

Credential Type: License Registration. **Requirements:** Submit application and fingerprint card. Pay fee. **Fees:** $35 registration fee.

6231

Director of Racing (Racetrack)
Kentucky State Racing Commission
PO Box 1080
Lexington, KY 40588
Phone: (606)254-7021

Credential Type: License Registration. **Requirements:** Submit application and fingerprint card. Pay fee. **Fees:** $35 registration fee.

6232

Entry Clerk (Racetrack)
Kentucky State Racing Commission
PO Box 1080
Lexington, KY 40588
Phone: (606)254-7021

Credential Type: Association Employee and Occupational License. **Requirements:** Submit application and fingerprint card. Pay fee. **Fees:** $10 license fee.

6233

Farm Manager/Agent (Racetrack)
Kentucky State Racing Commission
PO Box 1080
Lexington, KY 40588
Phone: (606)254-7021

Credential Type: License Registration. **Requirements:** Submit application and fingerprint card. Pay fee. **Fees:** $35 registration fee.

6234

Farrier/Apprentice Farrier (Racetrack)
Kentucky State Racing Commission
PO Box 1080
Lexington, KY 40588
Phone: (606)254-7021

Credential Type: Farrier/Apprentice Farrier License. **Requirements:** Submit application and fingerprint card. Pay fee. **Fees:** $35 license fee.

6235

Film Patrol/Video Tape Operator and Projectionist (Racetrack)
Kentucky State Racing Commission
PO Box 1080
Lexington, KY 40588
Phone: (606)254-7021

Credential Type: Association Employee and Occupational License. **Requirements:** Submit application and fingerprint card. Pay fee. **Fees:** $10 license fee.

6236

Flagman (Racetrack)
Kentucky State Racing Commission
PO Box 1080
Lexington, KY 40588
Phone: (606)254-7021

Credential Type: Association Employee and Occupational License. **Requirements:** Submit application and fingerprint card. Pay fee. **Fees:** $10 license fee.

6237

Groundsman (Racetrack)
Kentucky State Racing Commission
PO Box 1080
Lexington, KY 40588
Phone: (606)254-7021

Credential Type: Association Employee and Occupational License. **Requirements:** Submit application and fingerprint card. Pay fee. **Fees:** $10 license fee.

6238

Jockey Agent (Racetrack)
Kentucky State Racing Commission
PO Box 1080
Lexington, KY 40588
Phone: (606)254-7021

Credential Type: License Registration. **Requirements:** Submit application and fingerprint card. Pay fee. **Fees:** $45 license fee.

6239

Jockey Apprentice (Racetrack)
Kentucky State Racing Commission
PO Box 1080
Lexington, KY 40588
Phone: (606)254-7021

Credential Type: License Registration. **Requirements:** Submit application and fingerprint card. Pay fee. **Fees:** $25 registration fee.

6240

Jockey (Racetrack)
Kentucky State Racing Commission
PO Box 1080
Lexington, KY 40588
Phone: (606)254-7021

Credential Type: License Registration. **Requirements:** Submit application and fingerprint card. Pay fee. **Fees:** $35 registration fee.

6241

Jockey Room Custodian (Racetrack)
Kentucky State Racing Commission
PO Box 1080
Lexington, KY 40588
Phone: (606)254-7021

Credential Type: Association Employee and Occupational License. **Requirements:**

Kentucky 6242

Jockey Room Custodian (Racetrack), continued

Submit application and fingerprint card. Pay fee. **Fees:** $10 license fee.

6242

Maintenance Department Manager/Employee (Racetrack)
Kentucky State Racing Commission
PO Box 1080
Lexington, KY 40588
Phone: (606)254-7021

Credential Type: Association Employee and Occupational License. **Requirements:** Submit application and fingerprint card. Pay fee. **Fees:** $10 license fee.

6243

Mechanic (Racetrack)
Kentucky State Racing Commission
PO Box 1080
Lexington, KY 40588
Phone: (606)254-7021

Credential Type: Association Employee and Occupational License. **Requirements:** Submit application and fingerprint card. Pay fee. **Fees:** $10 license fee.

6244

Mutuel Department Employee (Racetrack)
Kentucky State Racing Commission
PO Box 1080
Lexington, KY 40588
Phone: (606)254-7021

Credential Type: Mutuel Department Employee License. **Authorization:** Authorizes work in the following positions: manger, calculator, sheet writer, supervisor, ticket checker, ticket seller, ticket cashier, messenger, runner, outbook clerk, program clerk, porter, information and change clerk, boardman, ticket room and money room clerk, or totalizator employee. **Requirements:** Submit application and fingerprint card. Pay fee. **Fees:** $5 license fee.

6245

Outrider (Racetrack)
Kentucky State Racing Commission
PO Box 1080
Lexington, KY 40588
Phone: (606)254-7021

Credential Type: Association Employee and Occupational License. **Requirements:** Submit application and fingerprint card. Pay fee. **Fees:** $10 license fee.

6246

Owner (Racetrack)
Kentucky State Racing Commission
PO Box 1080
Lexington, KY 40588
Phone: (606)254-7021

Credential Type: Owner License. **Requirements:** Submit application and fingerprint card. Pay fee. **Fees:** $35 license fee.

6247

Paddock Judge (Racetrack)
Kentucky State Racing Commission
PO Box 1080
Lexington, KY 40588
Phone: (606)254-7021

Credential Type: License Registration. **Requirements:** Submit application and fingerprint card. Pay fee. **Fees:** $35 registration fee.

6248

Parking Manager/Employee (Racetrack)
Kentucky State Racing Commission
PO Box 1080
Lexington, KY 40588
Phone: (606)254-7021

Credential Type: Association Employee and Occupational License. **Requirements:** Submit application and fingerprint card. Pay fee. **Fees:** $10 license fee.

6249

Patrol Judge (Racetrack)
Kentucky State Racing Commission
PO Box 1080
Lexington, KY 40588
Phone: (606)254-7021

Credential Type: License Registration. **Requirements:** Submit application and fingerprint card. Pay fee. **Fees:** $35 registration fee.

6250

Photo Finish Operator (Racetrack)
Kentucky State Racing Commission
PO Box 1080
Lexington, KY 40588
Phone: (606)254-7021

Credential Type: Association Employee and Occupational License. **Requirements:** Submit application and fingerprint card. Pay fee. **Fees:** $10 license fee.

6251

Placing Judge (Racetrack)
Kentucky State Racing Commission
PO Box 1080
Lexington, KY 40588
Phone: (606)254-7021

Credential Type: License Registration. **Requirements:** Submit application and fingerprint card. Pay fee. **Fees:** $35 registration fee.

6252

Racing Department Employee (Racetrack)
Kentucky State Racing Commission
PO Box 1080
Lexington, KY 40588
Phone: (606)254-7021

Credential Type: License Registration. **Requirements:** Submit application and fingerprint card. Pay fee. **Fees:** $35 registration fee.

6253

Racing Official (Racetrack)
Kentucky State Racing Commission
PO Box 1080
Lexington, KY 40588
Phone: (606)254-7021

Credential Type: License Registration. **Requirements:** Submit application and fingerprint card. Pay fee. **Fees:** $35 registration fee.

6254

Racing Secretary/Assistant Racing Secretary (Racetrack)
Kentucky State Racing Commission
PO Box 1080
Lexington, KY 40588
Phone: (606)254-7021

Credential Type: License Registration. **Requirements:** Submit application and fin-

Racetrack Occupations

gerprint card. Pay fee. **Fees:** $35 registration fee.

6255

Security Department Employee (Racetrack)
Kentucky State Racing Commission
PO Box 1080
Lexington, KY 40588
Phone: (606)254-7021

Credential Type: Association Employee and Occupational License. **Authorization:** Authorizes work in the following positions: police chief, detective, policeman, watchman, fireman, and ambulance driver/attendant. **Requirements:** Submit application and fingerprint card. Pay fee. **Fees:** $10 license fee.

6256

Stable-Area Supplier (Racetrack)
Kentucky State Racing Commission
PO Box 1080
Lexington, KY 40588
Phone: (606)254-7021

Credential Type: Supplier License. **Authorization:** Authorizes work in supplying horse feed, tack, medication, and food services. **Requirements:** Submit application and fingerprint card. Pay fee. **Fees:** $25 license fee.

6257

Stable Employee (Racetrack)
Kentucky State Racing Commission
PO Box 1080
Lexington, KY 40588
Phone: (606)254-7021

Credential Type: Stable Employee License. **Authorization:** Authorizes work in the following positions: foreman, exercise boy, groom, hotwalker, watchman, or pony boy. **Requirements:** Submit application and fingerprint card. Pay fee. **Fees:** $5 license fee.

6258

Starter/Assistant Starter (Racetrack)
Kentucky State Racing Commission
PO Box 1080
Lexington, KY 40588
Phone: (606)254-7021

Credential Type: License Registration. **Requirements:** Submit application and fingerprint card. Pay fee. **Fees:** $35 registration fee.

6259

Steward (Racetrack)
Kentucky State Racing Commission
PO Box 1080
Lexington, KY 40588
Phone: (606)254-7021

Credential Type: License Registration. **Requirements:** Submit application and fingerprint card. Pay fee. **Fees:** $35 registration fee.

6260

Testing Laboratory Employee (Racetrack)
Kentucky State Racing Commission
PO Box 1080
Lexington, KY 40588
Phone: (606)254-7021

Credential Type: License Registration. **Requirements:** Submit application and fingerprint card. Pay fee. **Fees:** $35 registration fee.

6261

Timer (Racetrack)
Kentucky State Racing Commission
PO Box 1080
Lexington, KY 40588
Phone: (606)254-7021

Credential Type: License Registration. **Requirements:** Submit application and fingerprint card. Pay fee. **Fees:** $35 registration fee.

6262

Track Superintendent (Racetrack)
Kentucky State Racing Commission
PO Box 1080
Lexington, KY 40588
Phone: (606)254-7021

Credential Type: Association Employee and Occupational License. **Requirements:** Submit application and fingerprint card. Pay fee. **Fees:** $10 license fee.

6263

Trainer (Racetrack)
Kentucky State Racing Commission
PO Box 1080
Lexington, KY 40588
Phone: (606)254-7021

Credential Type: License Registration. **Requirements:** Submit application and fingerprint card. Pay fee. **Fees:** $35 registration fee.

6264

Valet (Racetrack)
Kentucky State Racing Commission
PO Box 1080
Lexington, KY 40588
Phone: (606)254-7021

Credential Type: Association Employee and Occupational License. **Requirements:** Submit application and fingerprint card. Pay fee. **Fees:** $10 license fee.

6265

Veterinarian Assistant (Racetrack)
Kentucky State Racing Commission
PO Box 1080
Lexington, KY 40588
Phone: (606)254-7021

Credential Type: License Registration. **Requirements:** Submit application and fingerprint card. Pay fee. **Fees:** $25 registration fee.

6266

Veterinarian (Racetrack)
Kentucky State Racing Commission
PO Box 1080
Lexington, KY 40588
Phone: (606)254-7021

Credential Type: License Registration. **Requirements:** Submit application and fingerprint card. Pay fee. **Fees:** $35 registration fee.

Louisiana

6267

Assistant Starter (Racetrack)
Louisiana State Racing Commission
320 N. Carrollton Ave., Ste. 2-B
New Orleans, LA 70119-5111
Phone: (504)483-4000

Credential Type: License Registration. **Duration of License:** One year. **Require-**

Assistant Starter (Racetrack), continued

ments: At least 18 years of age. Abide by state rules and regulations. Submit application and pay fees. **Fees:** $25 registration fee.

6268

Exercise Rider (Racetrack)
Louisiana State Racing Commission
320 N. Carrollton Ave., Ste. 2-B
New Orleans, LA 70119-5111
Phone: (504)483-4000

Credential Type: License Registration. **Duration of License:** One year initial license. **Requirements:** At least 18 years of age or 16 years of age with permit. Abide by state rules and regulations. Submit application and pay fees. **Fees:** $25 registration fee. $75 three year renewal fee.

6269

Groom (Racetrack)
Louisiana State Racing Commission
320 N. Carrollton Ave., Ste. 2-B
New Orleans, LA 70119-5111
Phone: (504)483-4000

Credential Type: License Registration. **Duration of License:** One year. **Requirements:** At least 18 years of age. Abide by state rules and regulations. Submit application and pay fees. **Fees:** $12.50 registration fee.

6270

Hot Walker (Racetrack)
Louisiana State Racing Commission
320 N. Carrollton Ave., Ste. 2-B
New Orleans, LA 70119-5111
Phone: (504)483-4000

Credential Type: License Registration. **Duration of License:** One year. **Requirements:** At least 18 years of age. Abide by state rules and regulations. Submit application and pay fees. **Fees:** $12.50 registration fee.

6271

Jockey
Louisiana State Racing Commission
320 N. Carrollton Ave., Ste. 2-B
New Orleans, LA 70119
Phone: (504)483-4000

Credential Type: Apprentice Jockey Certificate. **Duration of License:** One year. **Requirements:** 18 years of age, or 16 years of age with a permit. Approval by the stewards. **Fees:** $25 certificate fee.

Credential Type: Jockey License. **Duration of License:** One or three years. **Requirements:** 18 years of age, or 16 years of age with a permit. Approval by the stewards. **Fees:** $25 license fee for one year license. $75 license fee for three year license.

6272

Jockey Agent
Louisiana State Racing Commission
320 N. Carrollton Ave., Ste 2-B
New Orleans, LA 70119
Phone: (504)483-4000

Credential Type: License. **Duration of License:** One or three years. **Requirements:** 18 years of age. **Examination:** Yes. **Fees:** $25 license fee for one year. $75 license fee for three years.

6273

Jockey Room Custodian (Racetrack)
Louisiana State Racing Commission
320 N. Carrollton Ave., Ste. 2-B
New Orleans, LA 70119-5111
Phone: (504)483-4000

Credential Type: License Registration. **Duration of License:** One year. **Requirements:** At least 18 years of age. Abide by state rules and regulations. Submit application. **Fees:** $25 registration fee.

6274

Mutuel Employee (Racetrack)
Louisiana State Racing Commission
320 N. Carrollton Ave., Ste. 2-B
New Orleans, LA 70119-5111
Phone: (504)483-4000

Credential Type: License Registration. **Duration of License:** One year. **Requirements:** At least 18 years of age. Abide by state rules and regulations. Submit application and pay fees. **Fees:** $25 registration fee.

6275

Outrider (Racetrack)
Louisiana State Racing Commission
320 N. Carrollton Ave., Ste. 2-B
New Orleans, LA 70119-5111
Phone: (504)483-4000

Credential Type: License Registration. **Duration of License:** One year. **Requirements:** At least 18 years of age. Abide by state rules and regulations. Submit application and pay fees. **Fees:** $25 registration fee.

6276

Plater (Racetrack)
Louisiana State Racing Commission
320 N. Carrollton Ave., Ste. 2-B
New Orleans, LA 70119-5111
Phone: (504)483-4000

Credential Type: License Registration. **Duration of License:** One year. **Requirements:** At least 18 years of age. Abide by state rules and regulations. May be required to demonstrate horseshoeing ability. Submit application and pay fees. **Fees:** $25 registration fee.

6277

Pony Boy/Pony Girl (Racetrack)
Louisiana State Racing Commission
320 N. Carrollton Ave., Ste. 2-B
New Orleans, LA 70119-5111
Phone: (504)483-4000

Credential Type: License Registration. **Duration of License:** One year. **Requirements:** At least 18 years of age. Abide by state rules and regulations. Submit application and pay fees. **Fees:** $25 registration fee.

6278

Racehorse Owner
Louisiana State Racing Commission
320 N. Carrollton Ave., Ste. 2-B
New Orleans, LA 70119
Phone: (504)483-4000

Credential Type: License. **Duration of License:** One or three years. **Requirements:** 18 years of age. Own horses. Financially responsible. **Fees:** $25 license fee for one year license. $75 license fee for three year license.

6279

Racehorse Trainer
Louisiana State Racing Commission
320 N. Carrollton Ave., Ste. 2-B
New Orleans, LA 70119
Phone: (504)483-4000

Credential Type: y. **Duration of License:** One or three years. **Requirements:** 18 years of age. Two years of racing experience. Two recommendations. **Examination:** Yes. **Fees:** $25 one-year license fee. $75 three-year license fee.

6280

Racehorse Veterinarian
Louisiana State Racing Commission
320 N. Carrollton Ave., Ste. 2-B
New Orleans, LA 70119
Phone: (504)483-4000

Credential Type: License. **Duration of License:** One or three years. **Requirements:** 18 years of age. Licensed under the Louisiana Veterinary Board. **Fees:** $100 one-year license fee. $300 three-year license fee.

6281

Racetrack Employee
Louisiana State Racing Commission
320 N. Carrollton Ave., Ste. 2-B
New Orleans, LA 70119-5111
Phone: (504)483-4000

Credential Type: License Registration. **Duration of License:** One year. **Authorization:** Covers all racetrack employees not specifically mentioned, such as bartenders, waiters, and parking lot attendants. **Requirements:** At least 18 years of age. Abide by state rules and regulations. Submit application and pay fees. **Fees:** Contact Commission for fees.

6282

Racetrack Vendor
Louisiana State Racing Commission
320 N. Carrollton Ave., Ste. 2-B
New Orleans, LA 70119
Phone: (504)483-4000

Credential Type: License. **Duration of License:** One year. **Requirements:** 18 years of age. Must be approved by the racing association where the applicant intends to conduct business. **Fees:** $25 license fee.

6283

Stable Foreman (Racetrack)
Louisiana State Racing Commission
320 N. Carrollton Ave., Ste. 2-B
New Orleans, LA 70119-5111
Phone: (504)483-4000

Credential Type: License Registration. **Duration of License:** One year. **Requirements:** At least 18 years of age. Abide by state rules and regulations. Submit application and pay fees. **Fees:** $25 registration fee.

6284

Steward (Racetrack)
Louisiana State Racing Commission
320 N. Carrollton Ave., Ste. 2-B
New Orleans, LA 70119-5111
Phone: (504)483-4000

Credential Type: License Registration. **Duration of License:** One year. **Requirements:** At least 18 years of age. Abide by state rules and regulations. Submit application and pay fees. **Examination:** Written examination. **Fees:** Contact Commission for fees.

6285

Valet (Racetrack)
Louisiana State Racing Commission
320 N. Carrollton Ave., Ste. 2-B
New Orleans, LA 70119-5111
Phone: (504)483-4000

Credential Type: License Registration. **Duration of License:** One year. **Requirements:** At least 18 years of age. Abide by state rules and regulations. Submit application and pay fees. **Fees:** $25 registration fee.

Maryland

6286

Assistant Trainer (Thoroughbred Racing)
Maryland Racing Commission
Stanbalt Bldg., 14th Fl.
501 St. Paul Place
Baltimore, MD 21202
Phone: (301)333-6267

Credential Type: License Registration. **Requirements:** Submit application, fingerprint card, and three passport size photos. Pay fee. **Fees:** $25 registration fee.

6287

Caterer (Harness Racing)
Maryland Racing Commission
Stanbalt Bldg., 14th Fl.
501 St. Paul Place
Baltimore, MD 21202
Phone: (301)333-6267

Credential Type: License Registration. **Requirements:** Submit application, fingerprint card, and three passport size photos. Pay fee. **Fees:** $5 registration fee.

6288

Caterer (Thoroughbred Racing)
Maryland Racing Commission
Stanbalt Bldg., 14th Fl.
501 St. Paul Place
Baltimore, MD 21202
Phone: (301)333-6267

Credential Type: License Registration. **Requirements:** Submit application, fingerprint card, and three passport size photos. Pay fee. **Fees:** $5 registration fee.

6289

Driver (Harness Racing)
Maryland Racing Commission
Stanbalt Bldg., 14th Fl.
501 St. Paul Place
Baltimore, MD 21202
Phone: (301)333-6267

Credential Type: License Registration. **Requirements:** Submit application, fingerprint card, and three passport size photos. Pay fee. **Fees:** $25 registration fee.

6290

Farrier (Harness Racing)
Maryland Racing Commission
Stanbalt Bldg., 14th Fl.
501 St. Paul Place
Baltimore, MD 21202
Phone: (301)333-6267

Credential Type: License Registration. **Requirements:** Submit application, fingerprint card, and three passport size photos. Pay fee. **Fees:** $10 registration fee.

6291

Farrier (Thoroughbred Racing)
Maryland Racing Commission
Stanbalt Bldg., 14th Fl.
501 St. Paul Place
Baltimore, MD 21202
Phone: (301)333-6267

Credential Type: License Registration.
Requirements: Submit application, fingerprint card, and three passport size photos. Pay fee. **Fees:** $10 registration fee.

6292

Jockey Agent (Thoroughbred Racing)
Maryland Racing Commission
Stanbalt Bldg., 14th Fl.
501 St. Paul Place
Baltimore, MD 21202
Phone: (301)333-6267

Credential Type: License Registration.
Requirements: Submit application, fingerprint card, and three passport size photos. Pay fee. **Fees:** $25 registration fee.

6293

Jockey/Apprentice Jockey (Thoroughbred Racing)
Maryland Racing Commission
Stanbalt Bldg., 14th Fl.
501 St. Paul Place
Baltimore, MD 21202
Phone: (301)333-6267

Credential Type: License Registration.
Requirements: Submit application, fingerprint card, and three passport size photos. Pay fee. **Fees:** $25 registration fee.

6294

Maintenance Employee (Harness Racing)
Maryland Racing Commission
Stanbalt Bldg., 14th Fl.
501 St. Paul Place
Baltimore, MD 21202
Phone: (301)333-6267

Credential Type: License Registration.
Requirements: Submit application, fingerprint card, and three passport size photos. Pay fee. **Fees:** $5 registration fee.

6295

Maintenance Employee (Thoroughbred Racing)
Maryland Racing Commission
Stanbalt Bldg., 14th Fl.
501 St. Paul Place
Baltimore, MD 21202
Phone: (301)333-6267

Credential Type: License Registration.
Requirements: Submit application, fingerprint card, and three passport size photos. Pay fee. **Fees:** $5 registration fee.

6296

Owner (Harness Racing)
Maryland Racing Commission
Stanbalt Bldg., 14th Fl.
501 St. Paul Place
Baltimore, MD 21202
Phone: (301)333-6267

Credential Type: License Registration.
Requirements: Submit application, fingerprint card, and three passport size photos. Pay fee. **Fees:** $50 original registration fee. $25 renewal fee.

6297

Owner (Thoroughbred Racing)
Maryland Racing Commission
Stanbalt Bldg., 14th Fl.
501 St. Paul Place
Baltimore, MD 21202
Phone: (301)333-6267

Credential Type: License Registration.
Requirements: Submit application, fingerprint card, and three passport size photos. Pay fees. **Fees:** $50 original license registration fee. $150 Maryland Jockey Fund fee. $25 renewal fee.

6298

Pari-Mutuel Employee (Harness Racing)
Maryland Racing Commission
Stanbalt Bldg., 14th Fl.
501 St. Paul Place
Baltimore, MD 21202
Phone: (301)333-6267

Credential Type: License Registration.
Requirements: Submit application, fingerprint card, and three passport size photos. Pay fee. **Fees:** $5 registration fee.

6299

Pari-Mutuel Employee (Thoroughbred Racing)
Maryland Racing Commission
Stanbalt Bldg., 14th Fl.
501 St. Paul Place
Baltimore, MD 21202
Phone: (301)333-6267

Credential Type: License Registration.
Requirements: Submit application, fingerprint card, and three passport size photos. Pay fee. **Fees:** $5 registration fee.

6300

Stable Employee (Harness Racing)
Maryland Racing Commission
Stanbalt Bldg., 14th Fl.
501 St. Paul Place
Baltimore, MD 21202
Phone: (301)333-6267

Credential Type: License Registration.
Requirements: Submit application, fingerprint card, and three passport size photos. Pay fee. **Fees:** $5 registration fee.

6301

Stable Employee (Thoroughbred Racing)
Maryland Racing Commission
Stanbalt Bldg., 14th Fl.
501 St. Paul Place
Baltimore, MD 21202
Phone: (301)333-6267

Credential Type: License Registration.
Requirements: Submit application, fingerprint card, and three passport size photos. Pay fee. **Fees:** $5 registration fee.

6302

Track Employee (Harness Racing)
Maryland Racing Commission
Stanbalt Bldg., 14th Fl.
501 St. Paul Place
Baltimore, MD 21202
Phone: (301)333-6267

Credential Type: License Registration.
Requirements: Submit application, fingerprint card, and three passport size photos. Pay fee. **Fees:** $5 registration fee.

Racetrack Occupations

6303

Track Employee (Thoroughbred Racing)
Maryland Racing Commission
Stanbalt Bldg., 14th Fl.
501 St. Paul Place
Baltimore, MD 21202
Phone: (301)333-6267

Credential Type: License Registration.
Requirements: Submit application, fingerprint card, and three passport size photos. Pay fee. **Fees:** $5 registration fee.

6304

Trainer (Harness Racing)
Maryland Racing Commission
Stanbalt Bldg., 14th Fl.
501 St. Paul Place
Baltimore, MD 21202
Phone: (301)333-6267

Credential Type: License Registration.
Requirements: Submit application, fingerprint card, and three passport size photos. Pay fee. **Fees:** $25 registration fee.

6305

Trainer (Thoroughbred Racing)
Maryland Racing Commission
Stanbalt Bldg., 14th Fl.
501 St. Paul Place
Baltimore, MD 21202
Phone: (301)333-6267

Credential Type: License Registration.
Requirements: Submit application, fingerprint card, and three passport size photos. Pay fee. **Fees:** $50 original registration fee. $25 renewal fee.

6306

Vendor (Harness Racing)
Maryland Racing Commission
Stanbalt Bldg., 14th Fl.
501 St. Paul Place
Baltimore, MD 21202
Phone: (301)333-6267

Credential Type: License Registration.
Requirements: Submit application, fingerprint card, and three passport size photos. Pay fee. **Fees:** $5 registration fee.

6307

Vendor (Thoroughbred Racing)
Maryland Racing Commission
Stanbalt Bldg., 14th Fl.
501 St. Paul Place
Baltimore, MD 21202
Phone: (301)333-6267

Credential Type: License Registration.
Requirements: Submit application, fingerprint card, and three passport size photos. Pay fee. **Fees:** $25 registration fee.

6308

Veterinarian (Harness Racing)
Maryland Racing Commission
Stanbalt Bldg., 14th Fl.
501 St. Paul Place
Baltimore, MD 21202
Phone: (301)333-6267

Credential Type: License Registration.
Requirements: Submit application, fingerprint card, and three passport size photos. Pay fee. **Fees:** $25 registration fee.

6309

Veterinarian (Thoroughbred Racing)
Maryland Racing Commission
Stanbalt Bldg., 14th Fl.
501 St. Paul Place
Baltimore, MD 21202
Phone: (301)333-6267

Credential Type: License Registration.
Requirements: Submit application, fingerprint card, and three passport size photos. Pay fee. **Fees:** $25 registration fee.

Massachusetts

6310

Blacksmith (Racetrack)
Massachusetts State Racing Commission
1 Ashburton Place, Rm. 1313
Boston, MA 02108
Phone: (617)727-2581

Credential Type: License Registration.
Requirements: Submit application and fingerprint card. Pay fee. **Fees:** $20 registration fee.

6311

Greyhound Assistant Trainer (Racetrack)
Massachusetts State Racing Commission
1 Ashburton Place, Rm. 1313
Boston, MA 02108
Phone: (617)727-2581

Credential Type: License Registration.
Requirements: Submit application and fingerprint card. Pay fee. **Fees:** $20 registration fee.

6312

Greyhound Authorized Agent (Racetrack)
Massachusetts State Racing Commission
1 Ashburton Place, Rm. 1313
Boston, MA 02108
Phone: (617)727-2581

Credential Type: License Registration.
Requirements: Submit application and fingerprint card. Pay fee. **Fees:** $20 registration fee.

6313

Greyhound Owner (Racetrack)
Massachusetts State Racing Commission
1 Ashburton Place, Rm. 1313
Boston, MA 02108
Phone: (617)727-2581

Credential Type: License Registration.
Requirements: Submit application and fingerprint card. Pay fee. **Fees:** $25 registration fee.

6314

Greyhound Trainer (Racetrack)
Massachusetts State Racing Commission
1 Ashburton Place, Rm. 1313
Boston, MA 02108
Phone: (617)727-2581

Credential Type: License Registration.
Requirements: Submit application and fingerprint card. Pay fee. **Fees:** $25 registration fee.

Massachusetts

6315

Jockey Agent (Racetrack)
Massachusetts State Racing
   Commission
1 Ashburton Place, Rm. 1313
Boston, MA 02108
Phone: (617)727-2581

Credential Type: License Registration.
Requirements: Submit application and fingerprint card. Pay fee. **Fees:** $50 registration fee.

6316

Jockey Apprentice (Racetrack)
Massachusetts State Racing
   Commission
1 Ashburton Place, Rm. 1313
Boston, MA 02108
Phone: (617)727-2581

Credential Type: License Registration.
Requirements: Submit application and fingerprint card. Pay fee. **Fees:** $50 registration fee.

6317

Jockey (Racetrack)
Massachusetts State Racing
   Commission
1 Ashburton Place, Rm. 1313
Boston, MA 02108
Phone: (617)727-2581

Credential Type: License Registration.
Requirements: Submit application and fingerprint card. Pay fee. **Fees:** $50 registration fee.

6318

Outrider (Racetrack)
Massachusetts State Racing
   Commission
1 Ashburton Place, Rm. 1313
Boston, MA 02108
Phone: (617)727-2581

Credential Type: License Registration.
Requirements: Submit application and fingerprint card. Pay fee. **Fees:** $10 registration fee.

6319

Racing Official (Racetrack)
Massachusetts State Racing
   Commission
1 Ashburton Place, Rm. 1313
Boston, MA 02108
Phone: (617)727-2581

Credential Type: License Registration.
Requirements: Submit application and fingerprint card. Pay fee. **Fees:** $20 registration fee.

6320

Stable Employee (Racetrack)
Massachusetts State Racing
   Commission
1 Ashburton Place, Rm. 1313
Boston, MA 02108
Phone: (617)727-2581

Credential Type: License Registration.
Requirements: Submit application and fingerprint card. Pay fee. **Fees:** $5 registration fee.

6321

Thoroughbred Owner (Racetrack)
Massachusetts State Racing
   Commission
1 Ashburton Place, Rm. 1313
Boston, MA 02108
Phone: (617)727-2581

Credential Type: License Registration.
Requirements: Submit application and fingerprint card. Pay fee. **Fees:** $25 registration fee.

6322

Thoroughbred Trainer (Racetrack)
Massachusetts State Racing
   Commission
1 Ashburton Place, Rm. 1313
Boston, MA 02108
Phone: (617)727-2581

Credential Type: License Registration.
Requirements: Submit application and fingerprint card. Pay fee. **Fees:** $25 registration fee.

6323

Valet (Racetrack)
Massachusetts State Racing
   Commission
1 Ashburton Place, Rm. 1313
Boston, MA 02108
Phone: (617)727-2581

Credential Type: License Registration.
Requirements: Submit application and fingerprint card. Pay fee. **Fees:** $10 registration fee.

6324

Vendor (Racetrack)
Massachusetts State Racing
   Commission
1 Ashburton Place, Rm. 1313
Boston, MA 02108
Phone: (617)727-2581

Credential Type: License Registration.
Requirements: Submit application and fingerprint card. Pay fee. **Fees:** $10 registration fee.

6325

Veterinarian (Racetrack)
Massachusetts State Racing
   Commission
1 Ashburton Place, Rm. 1313
Boston, MA 02108
Phone: (617)727-2581

Credential Type: License Registration.
Requirements: Submit application and fingerprint card. Pay fee. **Fees:** $50 registration fee.

Michigan

6326

Assistant Trainer (Racetrack)
Michigan Office of Racing
   Commissioner
37650 Professional Center Dr.
Livonia, MI 48154-1114
Phone: (313)462-2400

Credential Type: License Registration.
Requirements: Submit application and fingerprint card. Pay fee. **Fees:** $20 registration fee. $5 duplicate license fee.

Racetrack Occupations

Michigan

6327
Association/Track Employee (Racetrack)
Michigan Office of Racing Commissioner
37650 Professional Center Dr.
Livonia, MI 48154-1114
Phone: (313)462-2400

Credential Type: License Registration.
Requirements: Submit application and fingerprint card. Pay fee. **Fees:** $10 registration fee. $5 duplicate license fee.

6328
Authorized Agent (Racetrack)
Michigan Office of Racing Commissioner
37650 Professional Center Dr.
Livonia, MI 48154-1114
Phone: (313)462-2400

Credential Type: License Registration.
Requirements: Submit application and fingerprint card. Pay fee. **Fees:** $10 registration fee. $5 duplicate license fee.

6329
Blacksmith (Racetrack)
Michigan Office of Racing Commissioner
37650 Professional Center Dr.
Livonia, MI 48154-1114
Phone: (313)462-2400

Credential Type: License Registration.
Requirements: Submit application and fingerprint card. Pay fee. **Fees:** $20 registration fee. $5 duplicate license fee.

6330
Driver (Racetrack)
Michigan Office of Racing Commissioner
37650 Professional Center Dr.
Livonia, MI 48154-1114
Phone: (313)462-2400

Credential Type: License Registration.
Requirements: Submit application and fingerprint card. Pay fee. **Fees:** $20 registration fee. $5 duplicate license fee.

6331
Driver-Trainer (Racetrack)
Michigan Office of Racing Commissioner
37650 Professional Center Dr.
Livonia, MI 48154-1114
Phone: (313)462-2400

Credential Type: License Registration.
Requirements: Submit application and fingerprint card. Pay fee. **Fees:** $40 registration fee.

6332
Farrier (Racetrack)
Michigan Office of Racing Commissioner
37650 Professional Center Dr.
Livonia, MI 48154-1114
Phone: (313)462-2400

Credential Type: License Registration.
Requirements: Submit application and fingerprint card. Pay fee. **Fees:** $20 registration fee. $5 duplicate license fee.

6333
Groom (Racetrack)
Michigan Office of Racing Commissioner
37650 Professional Center Dr.
Livonia, MI 48154-1114
Phone: (313)462-2400

Credential Type: License Registration.
Requirements: Submit application and fingerprint card. Pay fee. **Fees:** $10 registration fee. $5 duplicate license fee.

6334
Jockey Agent (Racetrack)
Michigan Office of Racing Commissioner
37650 Professional Center Dr.
Livonia, MI 48154-1114
Phone: (313)462-2400

Credential Type: License Registration.
Requirements: Submit application and fingerprint card. Pay fee. **Fees:** $20 registration fee. $5 duplicate license fee.

6335
Jockey/Apprentice Jockey (Racetrack)
Michigan Office of Racing Commissioner
37650 Professional Center Dr.
Livonia, MI 48154-1114
Phone: (313)462-2400

Credential Type: License Registration.
Requirements: Submit application and fingerprint card. Pay fee. **Fees:** $20 registration fee. $5 duplicate license fee.

6336
Owner (Racetrack)
Michigan Office of Racing Commissioner
37650 Professional Center Dr.
Livonia, MI 48154-1114
Phone: (313)462-2400

Credential Type: License Registration.
Requirements: Submit application and fingerprint card. Pay fee. **Fees:** $20 registration fee. $5 duplicate license fee.

6337
Plater (Racetrack)
Michigan Office of Racing Commissioner
37650 Professional Center Dr.
Livonia, MI 48154-1114
Phone: (313)462-2400

Credential Type: License Registration.
Requirements: Submit application and fingerprint card. Pay fee. **Fees:** $20 registration fee. $5 duplicate license fee.

6338
Racing Official (Racetrack)
Michigan Office of Racing Commissioner
37650 Professional Center Dr.
Livonia, MI 48154-1114
Phone: (313)462-2400

Credential Type: License Registration.
Requirements: Submit application and fingerprint card. Pay fee. **Fees:** $20 registration fee. $5 duplicate license fee.

Michigan

6339

Stable Helper (Racetrack)
Michigan Office of Racing
   Commissioner
37650 Professional Center Dr.
Livonia, MI 48154-1114
Phone: (313)462-2400

Credential Type: License Registration.
Requirements: Submit application and fingerprint card. Pay fee. **Fees:** $10 registration fee. $5 duplicate license fee.

6340

Trainer (Racetrack)
Michigan Office of Racing
   Commissioner
37650 Professional Center Dr.
Livonia, MI 48154-1114
Phone: (313)462-2400

Credential Type: License Registration.
Requirements: Submit application and fingerprint card. Pay fee. **Fees:** $20 registration fee. $5 duplicate license fee.

6341

Vendor (Racetrack)
Michigan Office of Racing
   Commissioner
37650 Professional Center Dr.
Livonia, MI 48154-1114
Phone: (313)462-2400

Credential Type: License Registration.
Requirements: Submit application and fingerprint card. Pay fee. **Fees:** $20 registration fee. $5 duplicate license fee.

6342

Veterinarian (Racetrack)
Michigan Office of Racing
   Commissioner
37650 Professional Center Dr.
Livonia, MI 48154-1114
Phone: (313)462-2400

Credential Type: License Registration.
Requirements: Submit application and fingerprint card. Pay fee. **Fees:** $20 registration fee. $5 duplicate license fee.

Minnesota

6343

Bloodstock Agent (Racetrack)
Minnesota Racing Commission
11000 W. 78th St., Ste. 201
Eden Prairie, MN 55344
Phone: (612)341-7555

Credential Type: License Registration.
Requirements: Submit application and fingerprint card. Pay fee. **Fees:** $100 registration fee.

6344

Concession/Vendor Employee (Racetrack)
Minnesota Racing Commission
11000 W. 78th St., Ste. 201
Eden Prairie, MN 55344
Phone: (612)341-7555

Credential Type: License Registration.
Requirements: Submit application and fingerprint card. Pay fee. **Fees:** $10 registration fee.

6345

Concessionaire/Vendor (Racetrack)
Minnesota Racing Commission
11000 W. 78th St., Ste. 201
Eden Prairie, MN 55344
Phone: (612)341-7555

Credential Type: License Registration.
Requirements: Submit application and fingerprint card. Pay fee. **Fees:** $100 registration fee.

6346

Driver (Racetrack)
Minnesota Racing Commission
11000 W. 78th St., Ste. 201
Eden Prairie, MN 55344
Phone: (612)341-7555

Credential Type: License Registration.
Requirements: Submit application and fingerprint card. Pay fee. **Fees:** $25 registration fee.

6347

Equine Dentist (Racetrack)
Minnesota Racing Commission
11000 W. 78th St., Ste. 201
Eden Prairie, MN 55344
Phone: (612)341-7555

Credential Type: License Registration.
Requirements: Submit application and fingerprint card. Pay fee. **Fees:** $25 registration fee.

6348

Exercise Rider (Racetrack)
Minnesota Racing Commission
11000 W. 78th St., Ste. 201
Eden Prairie, MN 55344
Phone: (612)341-7555

Credential Type: License Registration.
Requirements: Submit application and fingerprint card. Pay fee. **Fees:** $15 registration fee.

6349

Farrier (Racetrack)
Minnesota Racing Commission
11000 W. 78th St., Ste. 201
Eden Prairie, MN 55344
Phone: (612)341-7555

Credential Type: License Registration.
Requirements: Submit application and fingerprint card. Pay fee. **Fees:** $25 registration fee.

6350

Farrier's Assistant (Racetrack)
Minnesota Racing Commission
11000 W. 78th St., Ste. 201
Eden Prairie, MN 55344
Phone: (612)341-7555

Credential Type: License Registration.
Requirements: Submit application and fingerprint card. Pay fee. **Fees:** $10 registration fee.

6351

Gate Crew (Racetrack)
Minnesota Racing Commission
11000 W. 78th St., Ste. 201
Eden Prairie, MN 55344
Phone: (612)341-7555

Credential Type: License Registration.
Requirements: Submit application and fingerprint card. Pay fee. **Fees:** $10 registration fee.

Racetrack Occupations — Minnesota

6352
Groom/Hotwalker (Racetrack)
Minnesota Racing Commission
11000 W. 78th St., Ste. 201
Eden Prairie, MN 55344
Phone: (612)341-7555

Credential Type: License Registration.
Requirements: Submit application and fingerprint card. Pay fee. **Fees:** $5 registration fee.

6353
Horsemen's Bookkeeper (Racetrack)
Minnesota Racing Commission
11000 W. 78th St., Ste. 201
Eden Prairie, MN 55344
Phone: (612)341-7555

Credential Type: License Registration.
Requirements: Submit application and fingerprint card. Pay fee. **Fees:** $25 registration fee.

6354
Jockey Agent (Racetrack)
Minnesota Racing Commission
11000 W. 78th St., Ste. 201
Eden Prairie, MN 55344
Phone: (612)341-7555

Credential Type: License Registration.
Requirements: Submit application and fingerprint card. Pay fee. **Fees:** $25 registration fee.

6355
Jockey Apprentice (Racetrack)
Minnesota Racing Commission
11000 W. 78th St., Ste. 201
Eden Prairie, MN 55344
Phone: (612)341-7555

Credential Type: License Registration.
Requirements: Submit application and fingerprint card. Pay fee. **Fees:** $25 registration fee.

6356
Jockey (Racetrack)
Minnesota Racing Commission
11000 W. 78th St., Ste. 201
Eden Prairie, MN 55344
Phone: (612)341-7555

Credential Type: License Registration.
Requirements: Submit application and fingerprint card. Pay fee. **Fees:** $25 registration fee.

6357
Owner (Racetrack)
Minnesota Racing Commission
11000 W. 78th St., Ste. 201
Eden Prairie, MN 55344
Phone: (612)341-7555

Credential Type: License Registration.
Requirements: Submit application and fingerprint card. Pay fee. **Fees:** $25 registration fee.

6358
Pari-Mutuel Clerk (Racetrack)
Minnesota Racing Commission
11000 W. 78th St., Ste. 201
Eden Prairie, MN 55344
Phone: (612)341-7555

Credential Type: License Registration.
Requirements: Submit application and fingerprint card. Pay fee. **Fees:** $10 registration fee.

6359
Pony Rider (Racetrack)
Minnesota Racing Commission
11000 W. 78th St., Ste. 201
Eden Prairie, MN 55344
Phone: (612)341-7555

Credential Type: License Registration.
Requirements: Submit application and fingerprint card. Pay fee. **Fees:** $10 registration fee.

6360
Racing Official (Racetrack)
Minnesota Racing Commission
11000 W. 78th St., Ste. 201
Eden Prairie, MN 55344
Phone: (612)341-7555

Credential Type: License Registration.
Requirements: Submit application and fingerprint card. Pay fee. **Fees:** $25 registration fee.

6361
Security Officer (Racetrack)
Minnesota Racing Commission
11000 W. 78th St., Ste. 201
Eden Prairie, MN 55344
Phone: (612)341-7555

Credential Type: License Registration.
Requirements: Submit application and fingerprint card. Pay fee. **Fees:** $25 registration fee.

6362
Stable Foreman (Racetrack)
Minnesota Racing Commission
11000 W. 78th St., Ste. 201
Eden Prairie, MN 55344
Phone: (612)341-7555

Credential Type: License Registration.
Requirements: Submit application and fingerprint card. Pay fee. **Fees:** $5 registration fee.

6363
Trainer Assistant (Racetrack)
Minnesota Racing Commission
11000 W. 78th St., Ste. 201
Eden Prairie, MN 55344
Phone: (612)341-7555

Credential Type: License Registration.
Requirements: Submit application and fingerprint card. Pay fee. **Fees:** $15 registration fee.

6364
Trainer (Racetrack)
Minnesota Racing Commission
11000 W. 78th St., Ste. 201
Eden Prairie, MN 55344
Phone: (612)341-7555

Credential Type: License Registration.
Requirements: Submit application and fingerprint card. Pay fee. **Fees:** $25 registration fee.

6365
Valet (Racetrack)
Minnesota Racing Commission
11000 W. 78th St., Ste. 201
Eden Prairie, MN 55344
Phone: (612)341-7555

Credential Type: License Registration.
Requirements: Submit application and fingerprint card. Pay fee. **Fees:** $5 registration fee.

6366

Veterinarian (Racetrack)
Minnesota Racing Commission
11000 W. 78th St., Ste. 201
Eden Prairie, MN 55344
Phone: (612)341-7555

Credential Type: License Registration.
Requirements: Submit application and fingerprint card. Pay fee. **Fees:** $100 registration fee.

6367

Veterinary Assistant (Racetrack)
Minnesota Racing Commission
11000 W. 78th St., Ste. 201
Eden Prairie, MN 55344
Phone: (612)341-7555

Credential Type: License Registration.
Requirements: Submit application and fingerprint card. Pay fee. **Fees:** $25 registration fee.

Missouri

6368

Assistant Trainer (Racetrack)
Missouri Horse Racing Commission
PO Box 754
Jefferson City, MO 65102
Phone: (314)751-3565

Credential Type: License Registration.
Requirements: Submit application and fingerprint card. Pay fee. **Fees:** $20 registration fee. $4 duplicate registration fee.

6369

Association Employee (Racetrack)
Missouri Horse Racing Commission
PO Box 754
Jefferson City, MO 65102
Phone: (314)751-3565

Credential Type: License Registration.
Requirements: Submit application and fingerprint card. Pay fee. **Fees:** $5 registration fee. $4 duplicate registration fee.

6370

Concession Employee (Racetrack)
Missouri Horse Racing Commission
PO Box 754
Jefferson City, MO 65102
Phone: (314)751-3565

Credential Type: License Registration.
Requirements: Submit application and fingerprint card. Pay fee. **Fees:** $5 registration fee. $4 duplicate registration fee.

6371

Driver (Racetrack)
Missouri Horse Racing Commission
PO Box 754
Jefferson City, MO 65102
Phone: (314)751-3565

Credential Type: License Registration.
Requirements: Submit application and fingerprint card. Pay fee. **Fees:** $50 registration fee. $4 duplicate registration fee.

6372

Exercise Rider (Racetrack)
Missouri Horse Racing Commission
PO Box 754
Jefferson City, MO 65102
Phone: (314)751-3565

Credential Type: License Registration.
Requirements: Submit application and fingerprint card. Pay fee. **Fees:** $15 registration fee. $4 duplicate registration fee.

6373

Farrier Assistant (Racetrack)
Missouri Horse Racing Commission
PO Box 754
Jefferson City, MO 65102
Phone: (314)751-3565

Credential Type: License Registration.
Requirements: Submit application and fingerprint card. Pay fee. **Fees:** $10 registration fee. $4 duplicate registration fee.

6374

Farrier (Racetrack)
Missouri Horse Racing Commission
PO Box 754
Jefferson City, MO 65102
Phone: (314)751-3565

Credential Type: License Registration.
Requirements: Submit application and fingerprint card. Pay fee. **Fees:** $50 registration fee. $4 duplicate registration fee.

6375

Jockey Agent (Racetrack)
Missouri Horse Racing Commission
PO Box 754
Jefferson City, MO 65102
Phone: (314)751-3565

Credential Type: License Registration.
Requirements: Submit application and fingerprint card. Pay fee. **Fees:** $25 registration fee. $4 duplicate registration fee.

6376

Jockey (Racetrack)
Missouri Horse Racing Commission
PO Box 754
Jefferson City, MO 65102
Phone: (314)751-3565

Credential Type: License Registration.
Requirements: Submit application and fingerprint card. Pay fee. **Fees:** $25 registration fee. $4 duplicate registration fee.

6377

Mutuel Employee (Racetrack)
Missouri Horse Racing Commission
PO Box 754
Jefferson City, MO 65102
Phone: (314)751-3565

Credential Type: License Registration.
Requirements: Submit application and fingerprint card. Pay fee. **Fees:** $10 registration fee. $4 duplicate registration fee.

6378

Official (Racetrack)
Missouri Horse Racing Commission
PO Box 754
Jefferson City, MO 65102
Phone: (314)751-3565

Credential Type: License Registration.
Requirements: Submit application and fingerprint card. Pay fee. **Fees:** $10 registration fee. $4 duplicate registration fee.

6379

Owner-Trainer (Racetrack)
Missouri Horse Racing Commission
PO Box 754
Jefferson City, MO 65102
Phone: (314)751-3565

Credential Type: License Registration.
Requirements: Submit application and fingerprint card. Pay fee. **Fees:** $25 registration fee. $4 duplicate registration fee.

6380

Stable Employee (Racetrack)
Missouri Horse Racing Commission
PO Box 754
Jefferson City, MO 65102
Phone: (314)751-3565

Credential Type: License Registration.
Requirements: Submit application and fingerprint card. Pay fee. **Fees:** $5 registration fee. $4 duplicate registration fee.

6381

Vendor (Racetrack)
Missouri Horse Racing Commission
PO Box 754
Jefferson City, MO 65102
Phone: (314)751-3565

Credential Type: License Registration.
Requirements: Submit application and fingerprint card. Pay fee. **Fees:** $50 registration fee. $4 duplicate registration fee.

6382

Veterinarian Assistant (Racetrack)
Missouri Horse Racing Commission
PO Box 754
Jefferson City, MO 65102
Phone: (314)751-3565

Credential Type: License Registration.
Requirements: Submit application and fingerprint card. Pay fee. **Fees:** $10 registration fee. $4 duplicate registration fee.

6383

Veterinarian (Racetrack)
Missouri Horse Racing Commission
PO Box 754
Jefferson City, MO 65102
Phone: (314)751-3565

Credential Type: License Registration.
Requirements: Submit application and fingerprint card. Pay fee. **Fees:** $50 registration fee. $4 duplicate registration fee.

Montana

6384

Announcer (Racetrack)
State of Montana Board of Horse Racing
Dept. of Commerce
1424 9th Ave.
Helena, MT 59620
Phone: (406)444-4287

Credential Type: License Registration.
Requirements: Submit application and fingerprint card. Pay fee. **Fees:** $20 registration fee.

6385

Assistant Trainer (Racetrack)
State of Montana Board of Horse Racing
Dept. of Commerce
1424 9th Ave.
Helena, MT 59620
Phone: (406)444-4287

Credential Type: License Registration.
Requirements: Submit application and fingerprint card. Pay fee. **Fees:** $30 registration fee.

6386

Auditor (Racetrack)
State of Montana Board of Horse Racing
Dept. of Commerce
1424 9th Ave.
Helena, MT 59620
Phone: (406)444-4287

Credential Type: License Registration.
Requirements: Submit application and fingerprint card. Pay fee. **Fees:** $20 registration fee.

6387

Authorized Agent (Racetrack)
State of Montana Board of Horse Racing
Dept. of Commerce
1424 9th Ave.
Helena, MT 59620
Phone: (406)444-4287

Credential Type: License Registration.
Requirements: Submit application and fingerprint card. Pay fee. **Fees:** $20 registration fee.

6388

Calculator Operator (Racetrack)
State of Montana Board of Horse Racing
Dept. of Commerce
1424 9th Ave.
Helena, MT 59620
Phone: (406)444-4287

Credential Type: License Registration.
Requirements: Submit application and fingerprint card. Pay fee. **Fees:** $20 registration fee.

6389

Chief of Security (Racetrack)
State of Montana Board of Horse Racing
Dept. of Commerce
1424 9th Ave.
Helena, MT 59620
Phone: (406)444-4287

Credential Type: License Registration.
Requirements: Submit application and fingerprint card. Pay fee. **Fees:** $20 registration fee.

6390

Clerk of Scales (Racetrack)
State of Montana Board of Horse Racing
Dept. of Commerce
1424 9th Ave.
Helena, MT 59620
Phone: (406)444-4287

Credential Type: License Registration.
Requirements: Submit application and fingerprint card. Pay fee. **Fees:** $20 registration fee.

6391

Director of Racing (Racetrack)
State of Montana Board of Horse Racing
Dept. of Commerce
1424 9th Ave.
Helena, MT 59620
Phone: (406)444-4287

Credential Type: License Registration.
Requirements: Submit application and fingerprint card. Pay fee. **Fees:** $20 registration fee.

6392

Director at Simulcast Facility (Racetrack)
State of Montana Board of Horse Racing
Dept. of Commerce
1424 9th Ave.
Helena, MT 59620
Phone: (406)444-4287

Credential Type: License Registration.
Requirements: Submit application and fingerprint card. Pay fee. **Fees:** $35 registration fee.

6393

Director of Simulcast Network (Racetrack)
State of Montana Board of Horse Racing
Dept. of Commerce
1424 9th Ave.
Helena, MT 59620
Phone: (406)444-4287

Credential Type: License Registration.
Requirements: Submit application and fingerprint card. Pay fee. **Fees:** $35 registration fee.

6394

Exercise Person (Racetrack)
State of Montana Board of Horse Racing
Dept. of Commerce
1424 9th Ave.
Helena, MT 59620
Phone: (406)444-4287

Credential Type: License Registration.
Requirements: Submit application and fingerprint card. Pay fee. **Fees:** $20 registration fee.

6395

Gate Attendant (Racetrack)
State of Montana Board of Horse Racing
Dept. of Commerce
1424 9th Ave.
Helena, MT 59620
Phone: (406)444-4287

Credential Type: License Registration.
Requirements: Submit application and fingerprint card. Pay fee. **Fees:** $20 registration fee.

6396

Groom (Racetrack)
State of Montana Board of Horse Racing
Dept. of Commerce
1424 9th Ave.
Helena, MT 59620
Phone: (406)444-4287

Credential Type: License Registration.
Requirements: Submit application and fingerprint card. Pay fee. **Fees:** $20 registration fee.

6397

Handicapper (Racetrack)
State of Montana Board of Horse Racing
Dept. of Commerce
1424 9th Ave.
Helena, MT 59620
Phone: (406)444-4287

Credential Type: License Registration.
Requirements: Submit application and fingerprint card. Pay fee. **Fees:** $20 registration fee.

6398

Horsemen's Bookkeeper (Racetrack)
State of Montana Board of Horse Racing
Dept. of Commerce
1424 9th Ave.
Helena, MT 59620
Phone: (406)444-4287

Credential Type: License Registration.
Requirements: Submit application and fingerprint card. Pay fee. **Fees:** $20 registration fee.

6399

Hot Walker (Racetrack)
State of Montana Board of Horse Racing
Dept. of Commerce
1424 9th Ave.
Helena, MT 59620
Phone: (406)444-4287

Credential Type: License Registration.
Requirements: Submit application and fingerprint card. Pay fee. **Fees:** $20 registration fee.

6400

Identifier (Racetrack)
State of Montana Board of Horse Racing
Dept. of Commerce
1424 9th Ave.
Helena, MT 59620
Phone: (406)444-4287

Credential Type: License Registration.
Requirements: Submit application and fingerprint card. Pay fee. **Fees:** $20 registration fee.

6401

Jockey Agent (Racetrack)
State of Montana Board of Horse Racing
Dept. of Commerce
1424 9th Ave.
Helena, MT 59620
Phone: (406)444-4287

Credential Type: License Registration.
Requirements: Submit application and fingerprint card. Pay fee. **Fees:** $30 registration fee.

6402

Jockey Apprentice (Racetrack)
State of Montana Board of Horse Racing
Dept. of Commerce
1424 9th Ave.
Helena, MT 59620
Phone: (406)444-4287

Credential Type: License Registration.
Requirements: Submit application and fingerprint card. Pay fee. **Fees:** $30 registration fee.

6403

Jockey (Racetrack)
State of Montana Board of Horse Racing
Dept. of Commerce
1424 9th Ave.
Helena, MT 59620
Phone: (406)444-4287

Credential Type: License Registration.
Requirements: Submit application and fingerprint card. Pay fee. **Fees:** $20 registration fee.

6404
Jockey Room Custodian (Racetrack)
State of Montana Board of Horse Racing
Dept. of Commerce
1424 9th Ave.
Helena, MT 59620
Phone: (406)444-4287

Credential Type: License Registration.
Requirements: Submit application and fingerprint card. Pay fee. **Fees:** $20 registration fee.

6405
Office Worker (Racetrack)
State of Montana Board of Horse Racing
Dept. of Commerce
1424 9th Ave.
Helena, MT 59620
Phone: (406)444-4287

Credential Type: License Registration.
Requirements: Submit application and fingerprint card. Pay fee. **Fees:** $20 registration fee.

6406
Outrider (Racetrack)
State of Montana Board of Horse Racing
Dept. of Commerce
1424 9th Ave.
Helena, MT 59620
Phone: (406)444-4287

Credential Type: License Registration.
Requirements: Submit application and fingerprint card. Pay fee. **Fees:** $20 registration fee.

6407
Owner (Racetrack)
State of Montana Board of Horse Racing
Dept. of Commerce
1424 9th Ave.
Helena, MT 59620
Phone: (406)444-4287

Credential Type: License Registration.
Requirements: Submit application and fingerprint card. Pay fee. **Fees:** $30 registration fee.

6408
Paddock Judge (Racetrack)
State of Montana Board of Horse Racing
Dept. of Commerce
1424 9th Ave.
Helena, MT 59620
Phone: (406)444-4287

Credential Type: License Registration.
Requirements: Submit application and fingerprint card. Pay fee. **Fees:** $20 registration fee.

6409
Parimutuel Employees (Racetrack)
State of Montana Board of Horse Racing
Dept. of Commerce
1424 9th Ave.
Helena, MT 59620
Phone: (406)444-4287

Credential Type: License Registration.
Authorization: Authorizes work at live race meets and simulcast races. **Requirements:** Submit application and fingerprint card. Pay fee. **Fees:** $10 registration fee.

6410
Parimutuel Manager (Racetrack)
State of Montana Board of Horse Racing
Dept. of Commerce
1424 9th Ave.
Helena, MT 59620
Phone: (406)444-4287

Credential Type: License Registration.
Requirements: Submit application and fingerprint card. Pay fee. **Fees:** $30 registration fee.

6411
Parimutuel Manager at Simulcast Network (Racetrack)
State of Montana Board of Horse Racing
Dept. of Commerce
1424 9th Ave.
Helena, MT 59620
Phone: (406)444-4287

Credential Type: License Registration.
Requirements: Submit application and fingerprint card. Pay fee. **Fees:** $30 registration fee.

6412
Patrol Judge (Racetrack)
State of Montana Board of Horse Racing
Dept. of Commerce
1424 9th Ave.
Helena, MT 59620
Phone: (406)444-4287

Credential Type: License Registration.
Requirements: Submit application and fingerprint card. Pay fee. **Fees:** $20 registration fee.

6413
Photo Employee (Racetrack)
State of Montana Board of Horse Racing
Dept. of Commerce
1424 9th Ave.
Helena, MT 59620
Phone: (406)444-4287

Credential Type: License Registration.
Requirements: Submit application and fingerprint card. Pay fee. **Fees:** $20 registration fee.

6414
Photo Manager (Racetrack)
State of Montana Board of Horse Racing
Dept. of Commerce
1424 9th Ave.
Helena, MT 59620
Phone: (406)444-4287

Credential Type: License Registration.
Requirements: Submit application and fingerprint card. Pay fee. **Fees:** $20 registration fee.

6415
Placing Judge (Racetrack)
State of Montana Board of Horse Racing
Dept. of Commerce
1424 9th Ave.
Helena, MT 59620
Phone: (406)444-4287

Credential Type: License Registration.
Requirements: Submit application and fingerprint card. Pay fee. **Fees:** $20 registration fee.

6416

Plater (Racetrack)
State of Montana Board of Horse Racing
Dept. of Commerce
1424 9th Ave.
Helena, MT 59620
Phone: (406)444-4287

Credential Type: License Registration.
Requirements: Submit application and fingerprint card. Pay fee. **Fees:** $30 registration fee.

6417

Pony Person (Racetrack)
State of Montana Board of Horse Racing
Dept. of Commerce
1424 9th Ave.
Helena, MT 59620
Phone: (406)444-4287

Credential Type: License Registration.
Requirements: Submit application and fingerprint card. Pay fee. **Fees:** $20 registration fee.

6418

Practicing Veterinarian (Racetrack)
State of Montana Board of Horse Racing
Dept. of Commerce
1424 9th Ave.
Helena, MT 59620
Phone: (406)444-4287

Credential Type: License Registration.
Requirements: Submit application and fingerprint card. Pay fee. **Fees:** $30 registration fee.

6419

Program Employee (Racetrack)
State of Montana Board of Horse Racing
Dept. of Commerce
1424 9th Ave.
Helena, MT 59620
Phone: (406)444-4287

Credential Type: License Registration.
Requirements: Submit application and fingerprint card. Pay fee. **Fees:** $20 registration fee.

6420

Program Manager (Racetrack)
State of Montana Board of Horse Racing
Dept. of Commerce
1424 9th Ave.
Helena, MT 59620
Phone: (406)444-4287

Credential Type: License Registration.
Requirements: Submit application and fingerprint card. Pay fee. **Fees:** $30 registration fee.

6421

Racing Secretary Assistant (Racetrack)
State of Montana Board of Horse Racing
Dept. of Commerce
1424 9th Ave.
Helena, MT 59620
Phone: (406)444-4287

Credential Type: License Registration.
Requirements: Submit application and fingerprint card. Pay fee. **Fees:** $20 registration fee.

6422

Racing Secretary (Racetrack)
State of Montana Board of Horse Racing
Dept. of Commerce
1424 9th Ave.
Helena, MT 59620
Phone: (406)444-4287

Credential Type: License Registration.
Requirements: Submit application and fingerprint card. Pay fee. **Fees:** $30 registration fee.

6423

Security Staff Person (Racetrack)
State of Montana Board of Horse Racing
Dept. of Commerce
1424 9th Ave.
Helena, MT 59620
Phone: (406)444-4287

Credential Type: License Registration.
Requirements: Submit application and fingerprint card. Pay fee. **Fees:** $20 registration fee.

6424

Stable Foreman (Racetrack)
State of Montana Board of Horse Racing
Dept. of Commerce
1424 9th Ave.
Helena, MT 59620
Phone: (406)444-4287

Credential Type: License Registration.
Requirements: Submit application and fingerprint card. Pay fee. **Fees:** $20 registration fee.

6425

Stable Superintendent (Racetrack)
State of Montana Board of Horse Racing
Dept. of Commerce
1424 9th Ave.
Helena, MT 59620
Phone: (406)444-4287

Credential Type: License Registration.
Requirements: Submit application and fingerprint card. Pay fee. **Fees:** $20 registration fee.

6426

Starter Assistant (Racetrack)
State of Montana Board of Horse Racing
Dept. of Commerce
1424 9th Ave.
Helena, MT 59620
Phone: (406)444-4287

Credential Type: License Registration.
Requirements: Submit application and fingerprint card. Pay fee. **Fees:** $20 registration fee.

6427

Starter (Racetrack)
State of Montana Board of Horse Racing
Dept. of Commerce
1424 9th Ave.
Helena, MT 59620
Phone: (406)444-4287

Credential Type: License Registration.
Requirements: Submit application and fingerprint card. Pay fee. **Fees:** $20 registration fee.

6428

Steward (Racetrack)
State of Montana Board of Horse Racing
Dept. of Commerce
1424 9th Ave.
Helena, MT 59620
Phone: (406)444-4287

Credential Type: License Registration.
Requirements: Submit application and fingerprint card. Pay fee. **Fees:** $20 registration fee.

6429

Timer (Racetrack)
State of Montana Board of Horse Racing
Dept. of Commerce
1424 9th Ave.
Helena, MT 59620
Phone: (406)444-4287

Credential Type: License Registration.
Requirements: Submit application and fingerprint card. Pay fee. **Fees:** $20 registration fee.

6430

Tip Sheet Seller (Racetrack)
State of Montana Board of Horse Racing
Dept. of Commerce
1424 9th Ave.
Helena, MT 59620
Phone: (406)444-4287

Credential Type: License Registration.
Requirements: Submit application and fingerprint card. Pay fee. **Fees:** $20 registration fee.

6431

Tote Employee (Racetrack)
State of Montana Board of Horse Racing
Dept. of Commerce
1424 9th Ave.
Helena, MT 59620
Phone: (406)444-4287

Credential Type: License Registration.
Requirements: Submit application and fingerprint card. Pay fee. **Fees:** $20 registration fee.

6432

Track Maintenance Worker (Racetrack)
State of Montana Board of Horse Racing
Dept. of Commerce
1424 9th Ave.
Helena, MT 59620
Phone: (406)444-4287

Credential Type: License Registration.
Requirements: Submit application and fingerprint card. Pay fee. **Fees:** $20 registration fee.

6433

Track Superintendent (Racetrack)
State of Montana Board of Horse Racing
Dept. of Commerce
1424 9th Ave.
Helena, MT 59620
Phone: (406)444-4287

Credential Type: License Registration.
Requirements: Submit application and fingerprint card. Pay fee. **Fees:** $20 registration fee.

6434

Track Veterinarian (Racetrack)
State of Montana Board of Horse Racing
Dept. of Commerce
1424 9th Ave.
Helena, MT 59620
Phone: (406)444-4287

Credential Type: License Registration.
Requirements: Submit application and fingerprint card. Pay fee. **Fees:** $30 registration fee.

6435

Trainer (Racetrack)
State of Montana Board of Horse Racing
Dept. of Commerce
1424 9th Ave.
Helena, MT 59620
Phone: (406)444-4287

Credential Type: License Registration.
Requirements: Submit application and fingerprint card. Pay fee. **Fees:** $30 registration fee.

6436

Valet (Racetrack)
State of Montana Board of Horse Racing
Dept. of Commerce
1424 9th Ave.
Helena, MT 59620
Phone: (406)444-4287

Credential Type: License Registration.
Requirements: Submit application and fingerprint card. Pay fee. **Fees:** $20 registration fee.

6437

Veterinarian Assistant (Racetrack)
State of Montana Board of Horse Racing
Dept. of Commerce
1424 9th Ave.
Helena, MT 59620
Phone: (406)444-4287

Credential Type: License Registration.
Requirements: Submit application and fingerprint card. Pay fee. **Fees:** $20 registration fee.

6438

Watchman (Racetrack)
State of Montana Board of Horse Racing
Dept. of Commerce
1424 9th Ave.
Helena, MT 59620
Phone: (406)444-4287

Credential Type: License Registration.
Requirements: Submit application and fingerprint card. Pay fee. **Fees:** $20 registration fee.

Nebraska

6439

Admissions Employee (Racetrack)
Nebraska Racing Commission
PO Box 95014
301 Centennial Mall S.
Lincoln, NE 68509
Phone: (402)471-4155

Credential Type: License Registration. **Duration of License:** One year. **Requirements:** At least 16 years of age. No felony convictions. Secure employment and submit application completed and signed by management. Pay fees. **Fees:** $10 license fee. $10 renewal fee.

6440

Apprentice Jockey (Racetrack)
Nebraska Racing Commission
PO Box 95014
301 Centennial Mall S.
Lincoln, NE 68509
Phone: (402)471-4155

Credential Type: License Registration. **Duration of License:** One year. **Requirements:** At least 16 years of age. No felony convictions. Secure employment and submit application completed and signed by management. Pay fees. **Examination:** Tested by Board of Stewards. **Fees:** $25 license fee. $25 renewal fee.

6441

Assistant Starter (Racetrack)
Nebraska Racing Commission
PO Box 95014
301 Centennial Mall S.
Lincoln, NE 68509
Phone: (402)471-4155

Credential Type: License Registration. **Duration of License:** One year. **Requirements:** At least 16 years of age. No felony convictions. Secure employment and submit application completed and signed by management. Pay fees. **Examination:** Tested by Board of Stewards. **Fees:** $10 license fee. $10 renewal fee.

6442

Assistant Trainer (Racetrack)
Nebraska Racing Commission
PO Box 95014
301 Centennial Mall S.
Lincoln, NE 68509
Phone: (402)471-4155

Credential Type: License Registration. **Duration of License:** One year. **Requirements:** At least 16 years of age. No felony convictions. Secure employment and submit application completed and signed by management. Pay fees. **Examination:** Tested by Board of Stewards. **Fees:** $20 license fee. $20 renewal fee.

6443

Concessions Employee (Racetrack)
Nebraska Racing Commission
PO Box 95014
301 Centennial Mall S.
Lincoln, NE 68509
Phone: (402)471-4155

Credential Type: License Registration. **Duration of License:** One year. **Requirements:** At least 16 years of age. No felony convictions. Secure employment and submit application completed and signed by management. Pay fees. **Fees:** $10 license fee. $10 renewal fee.

6444

Exercise Rider (Racetrack)
Nebraska Racing Commission
PO Box 95014
301 Centennial Mall S.
Lincoln, NE 68509
Phone: (402)471-4155

Credential Type: License Registration. **Duration of License:** One year. **Requirements:** At least 16 years of age. No felony convictions. Secure employment and submit application completed and signed by management. Pay fees. **Examination:** Tested by Board of Stewards. **Fees:** $20 license fee. $20 renewal fee.

6445

Groom
Nebraska Racing Commision
PO Box 95014
Lincoln, NE 68509
Phone: (402)471-2577

Credential Type: License. **Duration of License:** One year. **Requirements:** 16 years of age. **Fees:** $10 license fee. $10 renewal fee.

6446

Horse Owner (Racing)
Nebraska Racing Commision
301 Centennial Mall S.
PO Box 68509
Lincoln, NE 68509
Phone: (402)471-4155

Credential Type: License. **Duration of License:** One year. **Requirements:** 16 years of age. Must be able to show ownership documents to identify any horse to be raced. **Fees:** $15 license. $15 renewal fee.

6447

Horseshoer (Racetrack)
Nebraska Racing Commission
PO Box 95014
301 Centennial Mall S.
Lincoln, NE 68509
Phone: (402)471-4155

Credential Type: License Registration. **Duration of License:** One year. **Requirements:** At least 16 years of age. No felony convictions. Secure employment and submit application completed and signed by management. Pay fees. **Examination:** Tested by Board of Stewards. **Fees:** $20 license fee. $20 renewal fee.

6448

Identifier-Tattooer
Nebraska Racing Commision
301 Centennial Mall S.
PO Box 95014
Lincoln, NE 68509
Phone: (402)471-4155

Credential Type: License. **Duration of License:** One year. **Requirements:** 16 years of age. A felony conviction may be grounds for denial of the license. **Fees:** $20 license fee. $20 renewal fee.

6449

Jockey
Nebraska Racing Commission
301 Centennial Mall S.
PO Box 95014
Lincoln, NE 68509
Phone: (402)471-2577

Credential Type: License. **Duration of License:** One year. **Requirements:** 16 years of age. **Examination:** Yes. **Fees:** $25 license fee. $25 renewal fee.

6450

Jockey Agents (Racetrack)
Nebraska Racing Commission
PO Box 95014
301 Centennial Mall S.
Lincoln, NE 68509
Phone: (402)471-4155

Credential Type: License Registration. **Duration of License:** One year. **Requirements:** At least 16 years of age. No felony convictions. Secure employment and submit application completed and signed by management. Pay fees. **Examination:** Tested by Board of Stewards. **Fees:** $15 (per rider) license fee. $15 (per rider) renewal fee.

6451

Mutuel Employee (Racetrack)
Nebraska Racing Commission
PO Box 95014
301 Centennial Mall S.
Lincoln, NE 68509
Phone: (402)471-4155

Credential Type: License Registration. **Duration of License:** One year. **Requirements:** At least 16 years of age. No felony convictions. Secure employment and submit application completed and signed by management. Pay fees. **Fees:** $15 license fee. $15 renewal fee.

6452

Official (Racetrack)
Nebraska Racing Commission
PO Box 95014
301 Centennial Mall S.
Lincoln, NE 68509
Phone: (402)471-4155

Credential Type: License Registration. **Duration of License:** One year. **Requirements:** At least 16 years of age. No felony convictions. Secure employment and submit application completed and signed by management. Pay fees. **Fees:** $20 license fee. $20 renewal fee.

6453

Pony Person (Racetrack)
Nebraska Racing Commission
PO Box 95014
301 Centennial Mall S.
Lincoln, NE 68509
Phone: (402)471-4155

Credential Type: License Registration. **Duration of License:** One year. **Requirements:** At least 16 years of age. No felony convictions. Secure employment and submit application completed and signed by management. Pay fees. **Examination:** Tested by Board of Stewards. **Fees:** $20 license fee. $20 renewal fee.

6454

Security Guard (Racetrack)
Nebraska Racing Commission
PO Box 95014
301 Centennial Mall S.
Lincoln, NE 68509
Phone: (402)471-4155

Credential Type: License Registration. **Duration of License:** One year. **Requirements:** At least 16 years of age. No felony convictions. Secure employment and submit application completed and signed by management. Pay fees. **Fees:** $10 license fee. $10 renewal fee.

6455

Stable Foreman (Racetrack)
Nebraska Racing Commission
PO Box 95014
301 Centennial Mall S.
Lincoln, NE 68509
Phone: (402)471-4155

Credential Type: License Registration. **Duration of License:** One year. **Requirements:** At least 16 years of age. No felony convictions. Secure employment and submit application completed and signed by management. Pay fees. **Fees:** $20 license fee. $20 renewal fee.

6456

Trainer (Race Horse)
Nebraska Racing Commission
PO Box 95014
301 Centennial Mall S.
Lincoln, NE 68509
Phone: (402)471-2477

Credential Type: License. **Duration of License:** One year. **Requirements:** 16 years of age. Must be approved by the Board of Stewards. A felony conviction may be grounds for denial of license. **Examination:** Yes. **Fees:** $25 license fee. $25 renewal fee.

6457

Valet (Racetrack)
Nebraska Racing Commission
PO Box 95014
301 Centennial Mall S.
Lincoln, NE 68509
Phone: (402)471-4155

Credential Type: License Registration. **Duration of License:** One year. **Requirements:** At least 16 years of age. No felony convictions. Secure employment and submit application completed and signed by management. Pay fees. **Fees:** $20 license fee. $20 renewal fee.

6458

Veterinarian's Assistant (Racetrack)
Nebraska Racing Commission
PO Box 95014
301 Centennial Mall S.
Lincoln, NE 68509
Phone: (402)471-4155

Credential Type: License Registration. **Duration of License:** One year. **Requirements:** At least 16 years of age. No felony convictions. Secure employment and submit application completed and signed by management. Pay fees. **Fees:** $10 license fee. $10 renewal fee.

Nevada

6459

Assistant Trainer (Racetrack)
Nevada Racing Commission
4820 Alpine Ct., Ste. 203
Las Vegas, NV 89107
Phone: (702)486-7619

Credential Type: License Registration. **Requirements:** Submit application and fingerprint card. Pay fee. **Fees:** $20 registration fee.

6460

Association Racing Official (Racetrack)
Nevada Racing Commission
4820 Alpine Ct., Ste. 203
Las Vegas, NV 89107
Phone: (702)486-7619

Credential Type: License Registration. **Requirements:** Submit application and fingerprint card. Pay fee. **Fees:** $25 registration fee.

6461

Authorized Agent (Racetrack)
Nevada Racing Commission
4820 Alpine Ct., Ste. 203
Las Vegas, NV 89107
Phone: (702)486-7619

Credential Type: License Registration. **Requirements:** Submit application and fingerprint card. Pay fee. **Fees:** $25 registration fee.

6462

Concession Employee (Racetrack)
Nevada Racing Commission
4820 Alpine Ct., Ste. 203
Las Vegas, NV 89107
Phone: (702)486-7619

Credential Type: License Registration. **Requirements:** Submit application and fingerprint card. Pay fee. **Fees:** $10 registration fee.

6463

Kennel Helper (Racetrack)
Nevada Racing Commission
4820 Alpine Ct., Ste. 203
Las Vegas, NV 89107
Phone: (702)486-7619

Credential Type: License Registration. **Requirements:** Submit application and fingerprint card. Pay fee. **Fees:** $10 registration fee.

6464

Lead Out (Racetrack)
Nevada Racing Commission
4820 Alpine Ct., Ste. 203
Las Vegas, NV 89107
Phone: (702)486-7619

Credential Type: License Registration. **Requirements:** Submit application and fingerprint card. Pay fee. **Fees:** $15 registration fee.

6465

Mutuel Employee (Racetrack)
Nevada Racing Commission
4820 Alpine Ct., Ste. 203
Las Vegas, NV 89107
Phone: (702)486-7619

Credential Type: License Registration. **Requirements:** Submit application and fingerprint card. Pay fee. **Fees:** $20 registration fee.

6466

Owner (Racetrack)
Nevada Racing Commission
4820 Alpine Ct., Ste. 203
Las Vegas, NV 89107
Phone: (702)486-7619

Credential Type: License Registration. **Requirements:** Submit application and fingerprint card. Pay fee. **Fees:** $25 registration fee.

6467

Owner-Trainer (Racetrack)
Nevada Racing Commission
4820 Alpine Ct., Ste. 203
Las Vegas, NV 89107
Phone: (702)486-7619

Credential Type: License Registration. **Requirements:** Submit application and fingerprint card. Pay fee. **Fees:** $45 registration fee.

6468

Security Employee (Racetrack)
Nevada Racing Commission
4820 Alpine Ct., Ste. 203
Las Vegas, NV 89107
Phone: (702)486-7619

Credential Type: License Registration. **Requirements:** Submit application and fingerprint card. Pay fee. **Fees:** $20 registration fee.

6469

Trainer (Racetrack)
Nevada Racing Commission
4820 Alpine Ct., Ste. 203
Las Vegas, NV 89107
Phone: (702)486-7619

Credential Type: License Registration. **Requirements:** Submit application and fingerprint card. Pay fee. **Fees:** $35 registration fee.

New Jersey

6470

Authorized Agent (Racetrack)
New Jersey Racing Commission
200 Woolverton St.
Trenton, NJ 08625-0088
Phone: (609)292-0613

Credential Type: License Registration. **Requirements:** At least 18 years of age or 16 years of age with working papers. U.S. citizen or valid immigration card. No drug convictions. No convictions of crimes involving moral turpitude. Submit application and fingerprint card. Pay fees. **Fees:** $29 application fee. $25 registration fee.

6471

Clocker (Racetrack)
New Jersey Racing Commission
200 Woolverton St.
Trenton, NJ 08625-0088
Phone: (609)292-0613

Credential Type: License Registration. **Requirements:** At least 18 years of age or 16 years of age with working papers. U.S. citizen or valid immigration card. No drug convictions. No convictions of crimes involving moral turpitude. Submit application and fingerprint card. Pay fees. **Fees:** $14 application fee. $5 registration fee.

6472

Groom
New Jersey Racing Commission
CN088
Trenton, NJ 08625-0088
Phone: (609)292-0613

Credential Type: License. **Requirements:** 16 years of age. U.S. citizen or valid immigration card. **Fees:** $5 license fee. **Governing Statute:** NJSA 5:5. NJAC 13:70-4.

6473

Harness Race Driver
New Jersey Racing Commission
200 Woolverton St., CN088
Trenton, NJ 08625-0613
Phone: (609)292-0613

Credential Type: License. **Requirements:** Requirements are based on the class of license requested. U.S citizen or valid immigration card. 16 years of age. **Examination:** Written. **Fees:** $50 license fee. **Governing Statute:** NJSA 5:5. NJAC 13:71-7.

6474

Jockey
New Jersey Racing Commission
200 Woolverton St., CN088
Trenton, NJ 08625-0088
Phone: (609)292-0613

Credential Type: License. **Requirements:** 16 years of age with working papers. Good moral character. U.S. citizen or valid immigration card. **Fees:** $25 license fee. **Governing Statute:** NJSA 5:5. NJAC 13:70-9.

6475

Pari-mutuel Employee (Racetrack)
New Jersey Racing Commission
200 Woolverton St.
Trenton, NJ 08625-0088
Phone: (609)292-0613

Credential Type: License Registration. **Requirements:** At least 18 years of age or 16 years of age with working papers. U.S. citizen or valid immigration card. No drug convictions. No convictions of crimes involving moral turpitude. Submit application and fingerprint card. Pay fees. **Fees:** $29 application fee. $15 registration fee.

6476

Plater (Racetrack)
New Jersey Racing Commission
200 Woolverton St.
Trenton, NJ 08625-0088
Phone: (609)292-0613

Credential Type: License Registration. **Requirements:** At least 18 years of age or 16 years of age with working papers. U.S. citizen or valid immigration card. No drug convictions. No convictions of crimes involving moral turpitude. Submit application and fingerprint card. Pay fees. **Fees:** $29 registration fee. $15 registration fee.

6477

Race Horse Owner
New Jersey Racing Commission
200 Woolverton St., CN088
Trenton, NJ 08625-0088
Phone: (609)292-0613

Credential Type: License. **Requirements:** U.S. citizen or legal resident. Good moral character. **Fees:** $50 license fee. **Governing Statute:** NJSA 5:5. NJAC 13:71-7. NJAC 13:70-21.

6478

Starter (Racetrack)
New Jersey Racing Commission
200 Woolverton St.
Trenton, NJ 08625-0088
Phone: (609)292-0613

Credential Type: License Registration. **Requirements:** At least 18 years of age or 16 years of age with working papers. U.S. citizen or valid immigration card. No drug convictions. No convictions of crimes involving moral turpitude. Submit application and fingerprint card. Pay fees. **Fees:** $14 application fee. $5 registration fee.

6479

Timer (Racetrack)
New Jersey Racing Commission
200 Woolverton St.
Trenton, NJ 08625-0088
Phone: (609)292-0613

Credential Type: License Registration. **Requirements:** At least 18 years of age or 16 years of age with working papers. U.S. citizen or valid immigration card. No drug convictions. No convictions of crimes involving moral turpitude. Submit application and fingerprint card. Pay fees. **Fees:** $14 application fee. $5 registration fee.

6480

Valet (Racetrack)
New Jersey Racing Commission
200 Woolverton St.
Trenton, NJ 08625-0088
Phone: (609)292-0613

Credential Type: License Registration. **Requirements:** At least 18 years of age or 16 years of age with working papers. U.S. citizen or valid immigration card. No drug convictions. No convictions of crimes involving moral turpitude. Submit application and fingerprint card. Pay fees. **Fees:** $29 application fee. $15 registration fee.

6481

Vendor (Racetrack)
New Jersey Racing Commission
200 Woolverton St.
Trenton, NJ 08625-0088
Phone: (609)292-0613

Credential Type: License Registration. **Requirements:** At least 18 years of age or 16 years of age with working papers. U.S. citizen or valid immigration card. No drug convictions. No convictions of crimes involving moral turpitude. Submit application and fingerprint card. Pay fees. **Fees:** $29 application fee. $25 registration fee.

New Mexico

6482

Admissions Gateman (Racetrack)
New Mexico State Racing Commission
PO Box 8576, Highland Station
Albuquerque, NM 87198
Phone: (505)841-4644

Credential Type: License Registration. **Requirements:** Submit application and fingerprint card. Pay fees. **Fees:** $13 registration fee. $1 notary fee. $23 fingerprint card processing fee.

6483

Admissions Ticket Seller (Racetrack)
New Mexico State Racing Commission
PO Box 8576, Highland Station
Albuquerque, NM 87198
Phone: (505)841-4644

Credential Type: License Registration. **Requirements:** Submit application and fingerprint card. Pay fees. **Fees:** $13 registration fee. $1 notary fee. $23 fingerprint card processing fee.

6484

Announcer (Racetrack)
New Mexico State Racing Commission
PO Box 8576, Highland Station
Albuquerque, NM 87198
Phone: (505)841-4644

Credential Type: License Registration. **Requirements:** Submit application and fingerprint card. Pay fees. **Fees:** $14 registration fee. $1 notary fee. $23 fingerprint card processing fee.

6485

Assistant Racing Secretary (Racetrack)
New Mexico State Racing Commission
PO Box 8576, Highland Station
Albuquerque, NM 87198
Phone: (505)841-4644

Credential Type: License Registration. **Requirements:** Submit application and fingerprint card. Pay fees. **Fees:** $16 registration fee. $1 notary fee. $23 fingerprint card processing fee.

6486

Authorized Agent (Racetrack)
New Mexico State Racing Commission
PO Box 8576, Highland Station
Albuquerque, NM 87198
Phone: (505)841-4644

Credential Type: License Registration. **Requirements:** Submit application and fingerprint card. Pay fees. **Fees:** $21 registration fee. $1 notary fee. $23 fingerprint card processing fee.

6487

Clerk of Scales (Racetrack)
New Mexico State Racing
  Commission
PO Box 8576, Highland Station
Albuquerque, NM 87198
Phone: (505)841-4644

Credential Type: License Registration.
Requirements: Submit application and fingerprint card. Pay fees. **Fees:** $16 registration fee. $1 notary fee. $23 fingerprint card processing fee.

6488

Clocker (Racetrack)
New Mexico State Racing
  Commission
PO Box 8576, Highland Station
Albuquerque, NM 87198
Phone: (505)841-4644

Credential Type: License Registration.
Requirements: Submit application and fingerprint card. Pay fees. **Fees:** $16 registration fee. $1 notary fee. $23 fingerprint card processing fee.

6489

Concession Employee (Racetrack)
New Mexico State Racing
  Commission
PO Box 8576, Highland Station
Albuquerque, NM 87198
Phone: (505)841-4644

Credential Type: License Registration.
Requirements: Submit application and fingerprint card. Pay fees. **Fees:** $14 registration fee. $1 notary fee. $23 fingerprint card processing fee.

6490

Concession Operator (Racetrack)
New Mexico State Racing
  Commission
PO Box 8576, Highland Station
Albuquerque, NM 87198
Phone: (505)841-4644

Credential Type: License Registration.
Requirements: Submit application and fingerprint card. Pay fees. **Fees:** $61 registration fee. $1 notary fee. $23 fingerprint card processing fee.

6491

Director of Racing (Racetrack)
New Mexico State Racing
  Commission
PO Box 8576, Highland Station
Albuquerque, NM 87198
Phone: (505)841-4644

Credential Type: License Registration.
Requirements: Submit application and fingerprint card. Pay fees. **Fees:** $21 registration fee. $1 notary fee. $23 fingerprint card processing fee.

6492

Electrician (Racetrack)
New Mexico State Racing
  Commission
PO Box 8576, Highland Station
Albuquerque, NM 87198
Phone: (505)841-4644

Credential Type: License Registration.
Requirements: Submit application and fingerprint card. Pay fees. **Fees:** $14 registration fee. $1 notary fee. $23 fingerprint card processing fee.

6493

Exercise Boy (Racetrack)
New Mexico State Racing
  Commission
PO Box 8576, Highland Station
Albuquerque, NM 87198
Phone: (505)841-4644

Credential Type: License Registration.
Requirements: Submit application and fingerprint card. Pay fees. **Fees:** $16 registration fee. $1 notary fee. $23 fingerprint card processing fee.

6494

Film Employee (Racetrack)
New Mexico State Racing
  Commission
PO Box 8576, Highland Station
Albuquerque, NM 87198
Phone: (505)841-4644

Credential Type: License Registration.
Requirements: Submit application and fingerprint card. Pay fees. **Fees:** $14 registration fee. $1 notary fee. $23 fingerprint card processing fee.

6495

General Manager (Racetrack)
New Mexico State Racing
  Commission
PO Box 8576, Highland Station
Albuquerque, NM 87198
Phone: (505)841-4644

Credential Type: License Registration.
Requirements: Submit application and fingerprint card. Pay fees. **Fees:** $21 registration fee. $1 notary fee. $23 fingerprint card processing fee.

6496

Groom (Racetrack)
New Mexico State Racing
  Commission
PO Box 8576, Highland Station
Albuquerque, NM 87198
Phone: (505)841-4644

Credential Type: License Registration.
Requirements: Submit application and fingerprint card. Pay fees. **Fees:** $12 registration fee. $1 notary fee. $23 fingerprint card processing fee.

6497

Horsemen's Bookkeeper (Racetrack)
New Mexico State Racing
  Commission
PO Box 8576, Highland Station
Albuquerque, NM 87198
Phone: (505)841-4644

Credential Type: License Registration.
Requirements: Submit application and fingerprint card. Pay fees. **Fees:** $16 registration fee. $1 notary fee. $23 fingerprint card processing fee.

6498

Identifier (Racetrack)
New Mexico State Racing
  Commission
PO Box 8576, Highland Station
Albuquerque, NM 87198
Phone: (505)841-4644

Credential Type: License Registration.
Requirements: Submit application and fingerprint card. Pay fees. **Fees:** $16 registration fee. $1 notary fee. $23 fingerprint card processing fee.

Racetrack Occupations — New Mexico

6499

Janitor (Racetrack)
New Mexico State Racing Commission
PO Box 8576, Highland Station
Albuquerque, NM 87198
Phone: (505)841-4644

Credential Type: License Registration. **Requirements:** Submit application and fingerprint card. Pay fees. **Fees:** $12 registration fee. $1 notary fee. $23 fingerprint card processing fee.

6500

Jockey Agent (Racetrack)
New Mexico State Racing Commission
PO Box 8576, Highland Station
Albuquerque, NM 87198
Phone: (505)841-4644

Credential Type: License Registration. **Requirements:** Submit application and fingerprint card. Pay fees. **Fees:** $21 registration fee. $1 notary fee. $23 fingerprint card processing fee.

6501

Jockey Apprentice (Racetrack)
New Mexico State Racing Commission
PO Box 8576, Highland Station
Albuquerque, NM 87198
Phone: (505)841-4644

Credential Type: License Registration. **Requirements:** Submit application and fingerprint card. Pay fees. **Fees:** $16 registration fee. $1 notary fee. $23 fingerprint card processing fee.

6502

Jockey (Racetrack)
New Mexico State Racing Commission
PO Box 8576, Highland Station
Albuquerque, NM 87198
Phone: (505)841-4644

Credential Type: License Registration. **Duration of License:** Three years. **Requirements:** Submit application and fingerprint card. Pay fees. **Fees:** $105.50 registration fee. $1 notary fee. $23 fingerprint card processing fee.

6503

Jockey Room Custodian (Racetrack)
New Mexico State Racing Commission
PO Box 8576, Highland Station
Albuquerque, NM 87198
Phone: (505)841-4644

Credential Type: License Registration. **Requirements:** Submit application and fingerprint card. Pay fees. **Fees:** $16 registration fee. $1 notary fee. $23 fingerprint card processing fee.

6504

Jockey Valet (Racetrack)
New Mexico State Racing Commission
PO Box 8576, Highland Station
Albuquerque, NM 87198
Phone: (505)841-4644

Credential Type: License Registration. **Requirements:** Submit application and fingerprint card. Pay fees. **Fees:** $14 registration fee. $1 notary fee. $23 fingerprint card processing fee.

6505

Laborer (Racetrack)
New Mexico State Racing Commission
PO Box 8576, Highland Station
Albuquerque, NM 87198
Phone: (505)841-4644

Credential Type: License Registration. **Requirements:** Submit application and fingerprint card. Pay fees. **Fees:** $13 registration fee. $1 notary fee. $23 fingerprint card processing fee.

6506

Office Worker (Racetrack)
New Mexico State Racing Commission
PO Box 8576, Highland Station
Albuquerque, NM 87198
Phone: (505)841-4644

Credential Type: License Registration. **Requirements:** Submit application and fingerprint card. Pay fees. **Fees:** $13 registration fee. $1 notary fee. $23 fingerprint card processing fee.

6507

Outrider (Racetrack)
New Mexico State Racing Commission
PO Box 8576, Highland Station
Albuquerque, NM 87198
Phone: (505)841-4644

Credential Type: License Registration. **Requirements:** Submit application and fingerprint card. Pay fees. **Fees:** $16 registration fee. $1 notary fee. $23 fingerprint card processing fee.

6508

Owner (Racetrack)
New Mexico State Racing Commission
PO Box 8576, Highland Station
Albuquerque, NM 87198
Phone: (505)841-4644

Credential Type: License Registration. **Duration of License:** Three years. **Requirements:** Submit application and fingerprint card. Pay fees. **Fees:** $105.50 registration fee. $1 notary fee. $23 fingerprint card processing fee.

6509

Paddock Judge (Racetrack)
New Mexico State Racing Commission
PO Box 8576, Highland Station
Albuquerque, NM 87198
Phone: (505)841-4644

Credential Type: License Registration. **Requirements:** Submit application and fingerprint card. Pay fees. **Fees:** $16 registration fee. $1 notary fee. $23 fingerprint card processing fee.

6510

Pari-Mutuel Employee (Racetrack)
New Mexico State Racing Commission
PO Box 8576, Highland Station
Albuquerque, NM 87198
Phone: (505)841-4644

Credential Type: License Registration. **Requirements:** Submit application and fingerprint card. Pay fees. **Fees:** $14 registration fee. $1 notary fee. $23 fingerprint card processing fee.

New Mexico 6511

6511

Pari-Mutuel Manager (Racetrack)
New Mexico State Racing
  Commission
PO Box 8576, Highland Station
Albuquerque, NM 87198
Phone: (505)841-4644

Credential Type: License Registration.
Requirements: Submit application and fingerprint card. Pay fees. **Fees:** $21 registration fee. $1 notary fee. $23 fingerprint card processing fee.

6512

Photo Employee (Racetrack)
New Mexico State Racing
  Commission
PO Box 8576, Highland Station
Albuquerque, NM 87198
Phone: (505)841-4644

Credential Type: License Registration.
Requirements: Submit application and fingerprint card. Pay fees. **Fees:** $13 registration fee. $1 notary fee. $23 fingerprint card processing fee.

6513

Photo Operator (Racetrack)
New Mexico State Racing
  Commission
PO Box 8576, Highland Station
Albuquerque, NM 87198
Phone: (505)841-4644

Credential Type: License Registration.
Requirements: Submit application and fingerprint card. Pay fees. **Fees:** $14 registration fee. $1 notary fee. $23 fingerprint card processing fee.

6514

Photographer (Racetrack Win Circle)
New Mexico State Racing
  Commission
PO Box 8576, Highland Station
Albuquerque, NM 87198
Phone: (505)841-4644

Credential Type: License Registration.
Requirements: Submit application and fingerprint card. Pay fees. **Fees:** $21 registration fee. $1 notary fee. $23 fingerprint card processing fee.

6515

Placing Judge (Racetrack)
New Mexico State Racing
  Commission
PO Box 8576, Highland Station
Albuquerque, NM 87198
Phone: (505)841-4644

Credential Type: License Registration.
Requirements: Submit application and fingerprint card. Pay fees. **Fees:** $16 registration fee. $1 notary fee. $23 fingerprint card processing fee.

6516

Plater (Racetrack)
New Mexico State Racing
  Commission
PO Box 8576, Highland Station
Albuquerque, NM 87198
Phone: (505)841-4644

Credential Type: License Registration.
Requirements: Submit application and fingerprint card. Pay fees. **Fees:** $21 registration fee. $1 notary fee. $23 fingerprint card processing fee.

6517

Pony Boy (Racetrack)
New Mexico State Racing
  Commission
PO Box 8576, Highland Station
Albuquerque, NM 87198
Phone: (505)841-4644

Credential Type: License Registration.
Requirements: Submit application and fingerprint card. Pay fees. **Fees:** $16 registration fee. $1 notary fee. $23 fingerprint card processing fee.

6518

Practicing Veterinarian (Racetrack)
New Mexico State Racing
  Commission
PO Box 8576, Highland Station
Albuquerque, NM 87198
Phone: (505)841-4644

Credential Type: License Registration.
Duration of License: Three years. **Requirements:** Submit application and fingerprint card. Pay fees. **Fees:** $105.50 registration fee. $1 notary fee. $23 fingerprint card processing fee.

6519

Racing Secretary (Racetrack)
New Mexico State Racing
  Commission
PO Box 8576, Highland Station
Albuquerque, NM 87198
Phone: (505)841-4644

Credential Type: License Registration.
Requirements: Submit application and fingerprint card. Pay fees. **Fees:** $21 registration fee. $1 notary fee. $23 fingerprint card processing fee.

6520

Security Chief (Racetrack)
New Mexico State Racing
  Commission
PO Box 8576, Highland Station
Albuquerque, NM 87198
Phone: (505)841-4644

Credential Type: License Registration.
Requirements: Submit application and fingerprint card. Pay fees. **Fees:** $16 registration fee. $1 notary fee. $23 fingerprint card processing fee.

6521

Security Staff Employee (Racetrack)
New Mexico State Racing
  Commission
PO Box 8576, Highland Station
Albuquerque, NM 87198
Phone: (505)841-4644

Credential Type: License Registration.
Requirements: Submit application and fingerprint card. Pay fees. **Fees:** $14 registration fee. $1 notary fee. $23 fingerprint card processing fee.

6522

Simulcast Company Employee (Racetrack)
New Mexico State Racing
  Commission
PO Box 8576, Highland Station
Albuquerque, NM 87198
Phone: (505)841-4644

Credential Type: License Registration.
Requirements: Submit application and fingerprint card. Pay fees. **Fees:** $14 registration fee. $1 notary fee. $23 fingerprint card processing fee.

Racetrack Occupations

6523

Simulcast Operator (Racetrack)
New Mexico State Racing
  Commission
PO Box 8576, Highland Station
Albuquerque, NM 87198
Phone: (505)841-4644

Credential Type: License Registration.
Requirements: Submit application and fingerprint card. Pay fees. **Fees:** $111 registration fee. $1 notary fee. $23 fingerprint card processing fee.

6524

Stable Area Gateman (Racetrack)
New Mexico State Racing
  Commission
PO Box 8576, Highland Station
Albuquerque, NM 87198
Phone: (505)841-4644

Credential Type: License Registration.
Requirements: Submit application and fingerprint card. Pay fees. **Fees:** $13 registration fee. $1 notary fee. $23 fingerprint card processing fee.

6525

Stable Foreman (Racetrack)
New Mexico State Racing
  Commission
PO Box 8576, Highland Station
Albuquerque, NM 87198
Phone: (505)841-4644

Credential Type: License Registration.
Requirements: Submit application and fingerprint card. Pay fees. **Fees:** $16 registration fee. $1 notary fee. $23 fingerprint card processing fee.

6526

Stable Superintendent (Racetrack)
New Mexico State Racing
  Commission
PO Box 8576, Highland Station
Albuquerque, NM 87198
Phone: (505)841-4644

Credential Type: License Registration.
Requirements: Submit application and fingerprint card. Pay fees. **Fees:** $16 registration fee. $1 notary fee. $23 fingerprint card processing fee.

6527

Starter Assistant (Racetrack)
New Mexico State Racing
  Commission
PO Box 8576, Highland Station
Albuquerque, NM 87198
Phone: (505)841-4644

Credential Type: License Registration.
Requirements: Submit application and fingerprint card. Pay fees. **Fees:** $14 registration fee. $1 notary fee. $23 fingerprint card processing fee.

6528

Starter (Racetrack)
New Mexico State Racing
  Commission
PO Box 8576, Highland Station
Albuquerque, NM 87198
Phone: (505)841-4644

Credential Type: License Registration.
Requirements: Submit application and fingerprint card. Pay fees. **Fees:** $21 registration fee. $1 notary fee. $23 fingerprint card processing fee.

6529

State Auditor (Racetrack)
New Mexico State Racing
  Commission
PO Box 8576, Highland Station
Albuquerque, NM 87198
Phone: (505)841-4644

Credential Type: License Registration.
Requirements: Submit application and fingerprint card. Pay fees. **Fees:** $21 registration fee. $1 notary fee. $23 fingerprint card processing fee.

6530

Timer (Racetrack)
New Mexico State Racing
  Commission
PO Box 8576, Highland Station
Albuquerque, NM 87198
Phone: (505)841-4644

Credential Type: License Registration.
Requirements: Submit application and fingerprint card. Pay fees. **Fees:** $16 registration fee. $1 notary fee. $23 fingerprint card processing fee.

6531

Totalisator Operator (Racetrack)
New Mexico State Racing
  Commission
PO Box 8576, Highland Station
Albuquerque, NM 87198
Phone: (505)841-4644

Credential Type: License Registration.
Requirements: Submit application and fingerprint card. Pay fees. **Fees:** $14 registration fee. $1 notary fee. $23 fingerprint card processing fee.

6532

Track Maintenance Employee (Racetrack)
New Mexico State Racing
  Commission
PO Box 8576, Highland Station
Albuquerque, NM 87198
Phone: (505)841-4644

Credential Type: License Registration.
Requirements: Submit application and fingerprint card. Pay fees. **Fees:** $14 registration fee. $1 notary fee. $23 fingerprint card processing fee.

6533

Track Steward (Racetrack)
New Mexico State Racing
  Commission
PO Box 8576, Highland Station
Albuquerque, NM 87198
Phone: (505)841-4644

Credential Type: License Registration.
Requirements: Submit application and fingerprint card. Pay fees. **Fees:** $21 registration fee. $1 notary fee. $23 fingerprint card processing fee.

6534

Track Superintendent (Racetrack)
New Mexico State Racing
  Commission
PO Box 8576, Highland Station
Albuquerque, NM 87198
Phone: (505)841-4644

Credential Type: License Registration.
Requirements: Submit application and fingerprint card. Pay fees. **Fees:** $16 registration fee. $1 notary fee. $23 fingerprint card processing fee.

New Mexico

6535

Track Veterinarian (Racetrack)
New Mexico State Racing
  Commission
PO Box 8576, Highland Station
Albuquerque, NM 87198
Phone: (505)841-4644

Credential Type: License Registration. **Duration of License:** Three years. **Requirements:** Submit application and fingerprint card. Pay fees. **Fees:** $105.50 registration fee. $1 notary fee. $23 fingerprint card processing fee.

6536

Trainer Assistant (Racetrack)
New Mexico State Racing
  Commission
PO Box 8576, Highland Station
Albuquerque, NM 87198
Phone: (505)841-4644

Credential Type: License Registration. **Requirements:** Submit application and fingerprint card. Pay fees. **Fees:** $21 registration fee. $1 notary fee. $23 fingerprint card processing fee.

6537

Trainer (Racetrack)
New Mexico State Racing
  Commission
PO Box 8576, Highland Station
Albuquerque, NM 87198
Phone: (505)841-4644

Credential Type: License Registration. **Duration of License:** Three years. **Requirements:** Submit application and fingerprint card. Pay fees. **Fees:** $105.50 registration fee. $1 notary fee. $23 fingerprint card processing fee.

6538

Veterinarian Assistant (Racetrack)
New Mexico State Racing
  Commission
PO Box 8576, Highland Station
Albuquerque, NM 87198
Phone: (505)841-4644

Credential Type: License Registration. **Requirements:** Submit application and fingerprint card. Pay fees. **Fees:** $14 registration fee. $1 notary fee. $23 fingerprint card processing fee.

6539

Watchman (Racetrack)
New Mexico State Racing
  Commission
PO Box 8576, Highland Station
Albuquerque, NM 87198
Phone: (505)841-4644

Credential Type: License Registration. **Requirements:** Submit application and fingerprint card. Pay fees. **Fees:** $13 registration fee. $1 notary fee. $23 fingerprint card processing fee.

New York

6540

Assistant Trainer (Thoroughbred Racing)
New York State Racing and
  Wagering Board
400 Broome St.
New York, NY 10013
Phone: (212)219-4230

Credential Type: License Registration. **Duration of License:** One year. **Requirements:** Submit application, F.B.I fingerprint card, New York state fingerprint card, and three photos. Pay fees. **Fees:** $30 registration fee. $44 New York state fingerprint card processing fee (valid for five years).

6541

Authorized Agent (Thoroughbred Racing)
New York State Racing and
  Wagering Board
400 Broome St.
New York, NY 10013
Phone: (212)219-4230

Credential Type: License Registration. **Duration of License:** One year. **Requirements:** Submit application, F.B.I fingerprint card, New York state fingerprint card, and three photos. Pay fees. **Fees:** $5 registration fee. $44 New York state fingerprint card processing fee (valid for five years).

6542

Cleaning Services Employee (Harness or Quarter Horse Racing)
New York State Racing and
  Wagering Board
400 Broome St.
New York, NY 10013
Phone: (212)219-4230

Credential Type: License Registration. **Duration of License:** One year. **Requirements:** Submit application, F.B.I fingerprint card, New York state fingerprint card, and three photos. Pay fees. **Fees:** $5 registration fee. $44 New York state fingerprint card processing fee (valid for five years).

6543

Cleaning Services Employee (Thoroughbred Racing)
New York State Racing and
  Wagering Board
400 Broome St.
New York, NY 10013
Phone: (212)219-4230

Credential Type: License Registration. **Duration of License:** One year. **Requirements:** Submit application, F.B.I fingerprint card, New York state fingerprint card, and three photos. Pay fees. **Fees:** $5 registration fee. $44 New York state fingerprint card processing fee (valid for five years).

6544

Driver (Harness or Quarter Horse Racing)
New York State Racing and
  Wagering Board
400 Broome St.
New York, NY 10013
Phone: (212)219-4230

Credential Type: License Registration. **Duration of License:** One year. **Requirements:** Submit application, F.B.I fingerprint card, New York state fingerprint card, and three photos. Pay fees. **Fees:** $20 registration fee. $44 New York state fingerprint card processing fee (valid for five years).

Racetrack Occupations

6545

Farrier (Harness or Quarter Horse Racing)
New York State Racing and Wagering Board
400 Broome St.
New York, NY 10013
Phone: (212)219-4230

Credential Type: License Registration. **Duration of License:** One year. **Requirements:** Submit application, F.B.I fingerprint card, New York state fingerprint card, and three photos. Pay fees. **Fees:** $20 registration fee. $44 New York state fingerprint card processing fee (valid for five years).

6546

Farrier (Thoroughbred Racing)
New York State Racing and Wagering Board
400 Broome St.
New York, NY 10013
Phone: (212)219-4230

Credential Type: License Registration. **Duration of License:** One year. **Requirements:** Submit application, F.B.I fingerprint card, New York state fingerprint card, and three photos. Pay fees. **Fees:** $20 registration fee. $44 New York state fingerprint card processing fee (valid for five years).

6547

Food Services Employee (Harness or Quarter Horse Racing)
New York State Racing and Wagering Board
400 Broome St.
New York, NY 10013
Phone: (212)219-4230

Credential Type: License Registration. **Duration of License:** One year. **Requirements:** Submit application, F.B.I fingerprint card, New York state fingerprint card, and three photos. Pay fees. **Fees:** $5 registration fee. $44 New York state fingerprint card processing fee (valid for five years).

6548

Food Services Employee (Thoroughbred Racing)
New York State Racing and Wagering Board
400 Broome St.
New York, NY 10013
Phone: (212)219-4230

Credential Type: License Registration. **Duration of License:** One year. **Requirements:** Submit application, F.B.I fingerprint card, New York state fingerprint card, and three photos. Pay fees. **Fees:** $5 registration fee. $44 New York state fingerprint card processing fee (valid for five years).

6549

General Service Employee (Harness or Quarter Horse Racing)
New York State Racing and Wagering Board
400 Broome St.
New York, NY 10013
Phone: (212)219-4230

Credential Type: License Registration. **Duration of License:** One year. **Requirements:** Submit application, F.B.I fingerprint card, New York state fingerprint card, and three photos. Pay fees. **Fees:** $30 registration fee. $44 New York state fingerprint card processing fee (valid for five years).

6550

General Service Employee (Thoroughbred Racing)
New York State Racing and Wagering Board
400 Broome St.
New York, NY 10013
Phone: (212)219-4230

Credential Type: License Registration. **Duration of License:** One year. **Requirements:** Submit application, F.B.I fingerprint card, New York state fingerprint card, and three photos. Pay fees. **Fees:** $10 registration fee. $44 New York state fingerprint card processing fee (valid for five years).

6551

Groom (Harness or Quarter Horse Racing)
New York State Racing and Wagering Board
400 Broome St.
New York, NY 10013
Phone: (212)219-4230

Credential Type: License Registration. **Duration of License:** One year. **Requirements:** Submit application, F.B.I fingerprint card, New York state fingerprint card, and three photos. Pay fees. **Fees:** $5 registration fee. $44 New York state fingerprint card processing fee (valid for five years).

6552

Jockey Agent (Thoroughbred Racing)
New York State Racing and Wagering Board
400 Broome St.
New York, NY 10013
Phone: (212)219-4230

Credential Type: License Registration. **Duration of License:** One year. **Requirements:** Submit application, F.B.I fingerprint card, New York state fingerprint card, and three photos. Pay fees. **Fees:** $20 registration fee. $44 New York state fingerprint card processing fee (valid for five years).

6553

Jockey/Apprentice Jockey (Thoroughbred Racing)
New York State Racing and Wagering Board
400 Broome St.
New York, NY 10013
Phone: (212)219-4230

Credential Type: License Registration. **Duration of License:** One year. **Requirements:** Submit application, F.B.I fingerprint card, New York state fingerprint card, and three photos. Pay fees. **Fees:** $50 registration fee. $44 New York state fingerprint card processing fee (valid for five years).

6554

Mutuel Employee (Harness or Quarter Horse Racing)
New York State Racing and Wagering Board
400 Broome St.
New York, NY 10013
Phone: (212)219-4230

Credential Type: License Registration. **Duration of License:** One year. **Requirements:** Submit application, F.B.I fingerprint card, New York state fingerprint card, and three photos. Pay fees. **Fees:** $10 registration fee. $44 New York state fingerprint card processing fee (valid for five years).

6555

Mutuel Employee (Thoroughbred Racing)
New York State Racing and
 Wagering Board
400 Broome St.
New York, NY 10013
Phone: (212)219-4230

Credential Type: License Registration. **Duration of License:** One year. **Requirements:** Submit application, F.B.I fingerprint card, New York state fingerprint card, and three photos. Pay fees. **Fees:** $10 registration fee. $44 New York state fingerprint card processing fee (valid for five years).

6556

Owner (Harness or Quarter Horse Racing)
New York State Racing and
 Wagering Board
400 Broome St.
New York, NY 10013
Phone: (212)219-4230

Credential Type: License Registration. **Duration of License:** One year. **Requirements:** Submit application, F.B.I fingerprint card, New York state fingerprint card, and three photos. Pay fees. **Fees:** $100 original registration fee. $50 annual renewal fee. $44 New York state fingerprint card processing fee (valid for five years).

6557

Owner (Thoroughbred Racing)
New York State Racing and
 Wagering Board
400 Broome St.
New York, NY 10013
Phone: (212)219-4230

Credential Type: License Registration. **Duration of License:** One year. **Requirements:** Submit application, F.B.I fingerprint card, New York state fingerprint card, and three photos. Pay fees. **Fees:** $100 original registration fee. $50 annual renewal. $44 New York state fingerprint card processing fee (valid for five years).

6558

Racing Official (Thoroughbred Racing)
New York State Racing and
 Wagering Board
400 Broome St.
New York, NY 10013
Phone: (212)219-4230

Credential Type: License Registration. **Duration of License:** One year. **Requirements:** Submit application, F.B.I fingerprint card, New York state fingerprint card, and three photos. Pay fees. **Fees:** $10 registration fee. $44 New York state fingerprint card processing fee (valid for five years).

6559

Security Employee (Harness or Quarter Horse Racing)
New York State Racing and
 Wagering Board
400 Broome St.
New York, NY 10013
Phone: (212)219-4230

Credential Type: License Registration. **Duration of License:** One year. **Requirements:** Submit application, F.B.I fingerprint card, New York state fingerprint card, and three photos. Pay fees. **Fees:** $10 registration fee. $44 New York state fingerprint card processing fee (valid for five years).

6560

Security Employee (Thoroughbred Racing)
New York State Racing and
 Wagering Board
400 Broome St.
New York, NY 10013
Phone: (212)219-4230

Credential Type: License Registration. **Duration of License:** One year. **Requirements:** Submit application, F.B.I fingerprint card, New York state fingerprint card, and three photos. Pay fees. **Fees:** $10 registration fee. $44 New York state fingerprint card processing fee (valid for five years).

6561

Simulcast Employee (Harness or Quarter Horse Racing)
New York State Racing and
 Wagering Board
400 Broome St.
New York, NY 10013
Phone: (212)219-4230

Credential Type: License Registration. **Duration of License:** One year. **Requirements:** Submit application, F.B.I fingerprint card, New York state fingerprint card, and three photos. Pay fees. **Fees:** $10 registration fee. $44 New York state fingerprint card processing fee (valid for five years).

6562

Simulcast Employee (Thoroughbred Racing)
New York State Racing and
 Wagering Board
400 Broome St.
New York, NY 10013
Phone: (212)219-4230

Credential Type: License Registration. **Duration of License:** One year. **Requirements:** Submit application, F.B.I fingerprint card, New York state fingerprint card, and three photos. Pay fees. **Fees:** $30 registration fee. $44 New York state fingerprint card processing fee (valid for five years).

6563

Stable Worker (Thoroughbred Racing)
New York State Racing and
 Wagering Board
400 Broome St.
New York, NY 10013
Phone: (212)219-4230

Credential Type: License Registration. **Duration of License:** One year. **Requirements:** Submit application, F.B.I fingerprint card, New York state fingerprint card, and three photos. Pay fees. **Fees:** $5 registration fee. $44 New York state fingerprint card processing fee (valid for five years).

6564

Track Manager (Harness or Quarter Horse Racing)
New York State Racing and Wagering Board
400 Broome St.
New York, NY 10013
Phone: (212)219-4230

Credential Type: License Registration. **Duration of License:** One year. **Requirements:** Submit application, F.B.I fingerprint card, New York state fingerprint card, and three photos. Pay fees. **Fees:** $20 registration fee. $44 New York state fingerprint card processing fee (valid for five years).

6565

Track Manager (Thoroughbred Racing)
New York State Racing and Wagering Board
400 Broome St.
New York, NY 10013
Phone: (212)219-4230

Credential Type: License Registration. **Duration of License:** One year. **Requirements:** Submit application, F.B.I fingerprint card, New York state fingerprint card, and three photos. Pay fees. **Fees:** $20 registration fee. $44 New York state fingerprint card processing fee (valid for five years).

6566

Trainer/Assistant Trainer (Harness or Quarter Horse Racing)
New York State Racing and Wagering Board
400 Broome St.
New York, NY 10013
Phone: (212)219-4230

Credential Type: License Registration. **Duration of License:** One year. **Requirements:** Submit application, F.B.I fingerprint card, New York state fingerprint card, and three photos. Pay fees. **Fees:** $20 registration fee. $44 New York state fingerprint card processing fee (valid for five years).

6567

Trainer (Thoroughbred Racing)
New York State Racing and Wagering Board
400 Broome St.
New York, NY 10013
Phone: (212)219-4230

Credential Type: License Registration. **Duration of License:** One year. **Requirements:** Submit application, F.B.I fingerprint card, New York state fingerprint card, and three photos. Pay fees. **Fees:** $30 registration fee. $44 New York state fingerprint card processing fee (valid for five years).

6568

Veterinarian (Harness or Quarter Horse Racing)
New York State Racing and Wagering Board
400 Broome St.
New York, NY 10013
Phone: (212)219-4230

Credential Type: License Registration. **Duration of License:** One year. **Requirements:** Submit application, F.B.I fingerprint card, New York state fingerprint card, and three photos. Pay fees. **Fees:** $20 registration fee. $44 New York state fingerprint card processing fee (valid for five years).

6569

Veterinarian (Thoroughbred Racing)
New York State Racing and Wagering Board
400 Broome St.
New York, NY 10013
Phone: (212)219-4230

Credential Type: License Registration. **Duration of License:** One year. **Requirements:** Submit application, F.B.I fingerprint card, New York state fingerprint card, and three photos. Pay fees. **Fees:** $30 registration fee. $44 New York state fingerprint card processing fee (valid for five years).

North Dakota

6570

Announcer (Racetrack)
North Dakota Racing Commission
State Capitol Bldg.
Bismarck, ND 58505
Phone: (701)224-2210

Credential Type: License Registration. **Requirements:** Submit application and fingerprint card. Pay fee. **Fees:** $10 license fee. $10 duplicate license fee.

6571

Assistant Veterinarian (Racetrack)
North Dakota Racing Commission
State Capitol Bldg.
Bismarck, ND 58505
Phone: (701)224-2210

Credential Type: License Registration. **Requirements:** Submit application and fingerprint card. Pay fee. **Fees:** $25 license fee. $10 duplicate license fee.

6572

Association Veterinarian (Racetrack)
North Dakota Racing Commission
State Capitol Bldg.
Bismarck, ND 58505
Phone: (701)224-2210

Credential Type: License Registration. **Requirements:** Submit application and fingerprint card. Pay fee. **Fees:** $100 license fee. $10 duplicate license fee.

6573

Attendant (Racetrack)
North Dakota Racing Commission
State Capitol Bldg.
Bismarck, ND 58505
Phone: (701)224-2210

Credential Type: License Registration. **Requirements:** Submit application and fingerprint card. Pay fee. **Fees:** $10 license fee. $10 duplicate license fee.

6574

Auditor (Racetrack)
North Dakota Racing Commission
State Capitol Bldg.
Bismarck, ND 58505
Phone: (701)224-2210

Credential Type: License Registration. **Requirements:** Submit application and fingerprint card. Pay fee. **Fees:** $10 license fee. $10 duplicate license fee.

6575

Authorized Agent (Racetrack)
North Dakota Racing Commission
State Capitol Bldg.
Bismarck, ND 58505
Phone: (701)224-2210

Credential Type: License Registration. **Requirements:** Submit application and fin-

North Dakota

Authorized Agent (Racetrack), continued

gerprint card. Pay fee. **Fees:** $25 license fee. $10 duplicate license fee.

6576

Calculator Operator (Racetrack)
North Dakota Racing Commission
State Capitol Bldg.
Bismarck, ND 58505
Phone: (701)224-2210

Credential Type: License Registration.
Requirements: Submit application and fingerprint card. Pay fee. **Fees:** $10 license fee. $10 duplicate license fee.

6577

Chief of Security (Racetrack)
North Dakota Racing Commission
State Capitol Bldg.
Bismarck, ND 58505
Phone: (701)224-2210

Credential Type: License Registration.
Requirements: Submit application and fingerprint card. Pay fee. **Fees:** $10 license fee. $10 duplicate license fee.

6578

Clerk of Scales (Racetrack)
North Dakota Racing Commission
State Capitol Bldg.
Bismarck, ND 58505
Phone: (701)224-2210

Credential Type: License Registration.
Requirements: Submit application and fingerprint card. Pay fee. **Fees:** $10 license fee. $10 duplicate license fee.

6579

Director of Racing (Racetrack)
North Dakota Racing Commission
State Capitol Bldg.
Bismarck, ND 58505
Phone: (701)224-2210

Credential Type: License Registration.
Requirements: Submit application and fingerprint card. Pay fee. **Fees:** $10 license fee. $10 duplicate license fee.

6580

Exercise Person (Racetrack)
North Dakota Racing Commission
State Capitol Bldg.
Bismarck, ND 58505
Phone: (701)224-2210

Credential Type: License Registration.
Requirements: Submit application and fingerprint card. Pay fee. **Fees:** $10 license fee. $10 duplicate license fee.

6581

Gate Admission Seller (Racetrack)
North Dakota Racing Commission
State Capitol Bldg.
Bismarck, ND 58505
Phone: (701)224-2210

Credential Type: License Registration.
Requirements: Submit application and fingerprint card. Pay fee. **Fees:** $10 license fee. $10 duplicate license fee.

6582

Gate Attendant (Racetrack)
North Dakota Racing Commission
State Capitol Bldg.
Bismarck, ND 58505
Phone: (701)224-2210

Credential Type: License Registration.
Requirements: Submit application and fingerprint card. Pay fee. **Fees:** $10 license fee. $10 duplicate license fee.

6583

Groom (Racetrack)
North Dakota Racing Commission
State Capitol Bldg.
Bismarck, ND 58505
Phone: (701)224-2210

Credential Type: License Registration.
Requirements: Submit application and fingerprint card. Pay fee. **Fees:** $10 license fee. $10 duplicate license fee.

6584

Handicapper (Racetrack)
North Dakota Racing Commission
State Capitol Bldg.
Bismarck, ND 58505
Phone: (701)224-2210

Credential Type: License Registration.
Requirements: Submit application and fingerprint card. Pay fee. **Fees:** $10 license fee. $10 duplicate license fee.

6585

Horse Identifier (Racetrack)
North Dakota Racing Commission
State Capitol Bldg.
Bismarck, ND 58505
Phone: (701)224-2210

Credential Type: License Registration.
Requirements: Submit application and fingerprint card. Pay fee. **Fees:** $10 license fee. $10 duplicate license fee.

6586

Hot Walker (Racetrack)
North Dakota Racing Commission
State Capitol Bldg.
Bismarck, ND 58505
Phone: (701)224-2210

Credential Type: License Registration.
Requirements: Submit application and fingerprint card. Pay fee. **Fees:** $10 license fee. $10 duplicate license fee.

6587

Jockey Agent (Racetrack)
North Dakota Racing Commission
State Capitol Bldg.
Bismarck, ND 58505
Phone: (701)224-2210

Credential Type: License Registration.
Requirements: Submit application and fingerprint card. Pay fee. **Fees:** $25 license fee. $10 duplicate license fee.

6588

Jockey Apprentice (Racetrack)
North Dakota Racing Commission
State Capitol Bldg.
Bismarck, ND 58505
Phone: (701)224-2210

Credential Type: License Registration.
Requirements: Submit application and fingerprint card. Pay fee. **Fees:** $25 license fee. $10 duplicate license fee.

6589

Jockey-Driver (Racetrack)
North Dakota Racing Commission
State Capitol Bldg.
Bismarck, ND 58505
Phone: (701)224-2210

Credential Type: License Registration.
Requirements: Submit application and fingerprint card. Pay fee. **Fees:** $100 license fee. $10 duplicate license fee.

Racetrack Occupations

North Dakota

6590

Jockey Room Custodian (Racetrack)
North Dakota Racing Commission
State Capitol Bldg.
Bismarck, ND 58505
Phone: (701)224-2210

Credential Type: License Registration.
Requirements: Submit application and fingerprint card. Pay fee. **Fees:** $10 license fee. $10 duplicate license fee.

6591

Office Worker (Racetrack)
North Dakota Racing Commission
State Capitol Bldg.
Bismarck, ND 58505
Phone: (701)224-2210

Credential Type: License Registration.
Requirements: Submit application and fingerprint card. Pay fee. **Fees:** $10 license fee. $10 duplicate license fee.

6592

Outrider (Racetrack)
North Dakota Racing Commission
State Capitol Bldg.
Bismarck, ND 58505
Phone: (701)224-2210

Credential Type: License Registration.
Requirements: Submit application and fingerprint card. Pay fee. **Fees:** $10 license fee. $10 duplicate license fee.

6593

Owner (Racetrack)
North Dakota Racing Commission
State Capitol Bldg.
Bismarck, ND 58505
Phone: (701)224-2210

Credential Type: License Registration.
Requirements: Submit application and fingerprint card. Pay fee. **Fees:** $25 license fee. $5 additional fee for each horse owned over three horses in number. $10 duplicate license fee.

6594

Owner-Trainer (Racetrack)
North Dakota Racing Commission
State Capitol Bldg.
Bismarck, ND 58505
Phone: (701)224-2210

Credential Type: License Registration.
Requirements: Submit application and fingerprint card. Pay fee. **Fees:** $50 license fee. $5 additional fee for each horse owned over three horses in number. $10 duplicate license fee.

6595

Paddock Judge (Racetrack)
North Dakota Racing Commission
State Capitol Bldg.
Bismarck, ND 58505
Phone: (701)224-2210

Credential Type: License Registration.
Requirements: Submit application and fingerprint card. Pay fee. **Fees:** $10 license fee. $10 duplicate license fee.

6596

Pari-Mutuel Employee (Racetrack)
North Dakota Racing Commission
State Capitol Bldg.
Bismarck, ND 58505
Phone: (701)224-2210

Credential Type: License Registration.
Requirements: Submit application and fingerprint card. Pay fee. **Fees:** $10 license fee. $10 duplicate license fee.

6597

Pari-Mutuel Manager (Racetrack)
North Dakota Racing Commission
State Capitol Bldg.
Bismarck, ND 58505
Phone: (701)224-2210

Credential Type: License Registration.
Requirements: Submit application and fingerprint card. Pay fee. **Fees:** $10 license fee. $10 duplicate license fee.

6598

Patrol Judge (Racetrack)
North Dakota Racing Commission
State Capitol Bldg.
Bismarck, ND 58505
Phone: (701)224-2210

Credential Type: License Registration.
Requirements: Submit application and fingerprint card. Pay fee. **Fees:** $10 license fee. $10 duplicate license fee.

6599

Photo Employee (Racetrack)
North Dakota Racing Commission
State Capitol Bldg.
Bismarck, ND 58505
Phone: (701)224-2210

Credential Type: License Registration.
Requirements: Submit application and fingerprint card. Pay fee. **Fees:** $10 license fee. $10 duplicate license fee.

6600

Photo Manager (Racetrack)
North Dakota Racing Commission
State Capitol Bldg.
Bismarck, ND 58505
Phone: (701)224-2210

Credential Type: License Registration.
Requirements: Submit application and fingerprint card. Pay fee. **Fees:** $10 license fee. $10 duplicate license fee.

6601

Placing Judge (Racetrack)
North Dakota Racing Commission
State Capitol Bldg.
Bismarck, ND 58505
Phone: (701)224-2210

Credential Type: License Registration.
Requirements: Submit application and fingerprint card. Pay fee. **Fees:** $10 license fee. $10 duplicate license fee.

6602

Pony Person (Racetrack)
North Dakota Racing Commission
State Capitol Bldg.
Bismarck, ND 58505
Phone: (701)224-2210

Credential Type: License Registration.
Requirements: Submit application and fingerprint card. Pay fee. **Fees:** $10 license fee. $10 duplicate license fee.

6603

Racing Secretary Assistant (Racetrack)
North Dakota Racing Commission
State Capitol Bldg.
Bismarck, ND 58505
Phone: (701)224-2210

Credential Type: License Registration.
Requirements: Submit application and fingerprint card. Pay fee. **Fees:** $10 license fee. $10 duplicate license fee.

6604

Racing Secretary (Racetrack)
North Dakota Racing Commission
State Capitol Bldg.
Bismarck, ND 58505
Phone: (701)224-2210

Credential Type: License Registration.
Requirements: Submit application and fingerprint card. Pay fee. **Fees:** $25 license fee. $10 duplicate license fee.

6605

Security Employee (Racetrack)
North Dakota Racing Commission
State Capitol Bldg.
Bismarck, ND 58505
Phone: (701)224-2210

Credential Type: License Registration.
Requirements: Submit application and fingerprint card. Pay fee. **Fees:** $10 license fee. $10 duplicate license fee.

6606

Stable Foreman (Racetrack)
North Dakota Racing Commission
State Capitol Bldg.
Bismarck, ND 58505
Phone: (701)224-2210

Credential Type: License Registration.
Requirements: Submit application and fingerprint card. Pay fee. **Fees:** $10 license fee. $10 duplicate license fee.

6607

Starter (Racetrack)
North Dakota Racing Commission
State Capitol Bldg.
Bismarck, ND 58505
Phone: (701)224-2210

Credential Type: License Registration.
Requirements: Submit application and fingerprint card. Pay fee. **Fees:** $10 license fee. $10 duplicate license fee.

6608

Steward (Racetrack)
North Dakota Racing Commission
State Capitol Bldg.
Bismarck, ND 58505
Phone: (701)224-2210

Credential Type: License Registration.
Requirements: Submit application and fingerprint card. Pay fee. **Fees:** $25 license fee. $10 duplicate license fee.

6609

Timer (Racetrack)
North Dakota Racing Commission
State Capitol Bldg.
Bismarck, ND 58505
Phone: (701)224-2210

Credential Type: License Registration.
Requirements: Submit application and fingerprint card. Pay fee. **Fees:** $10 license fee. $10 duplicate license fee.

6610

Tip Sheet Seller (Racetrack)
North Dakota Racing Commission
State Capitol Bldg.
Bismarck, ND 58505
Phone: (701)224-2210

Credential Type: License Registration.
Requirements: Submit application and fingerprint card. Pay fee. **Fees:** $10 license fee. $10 duplicate license fee.

6611

Totalizer Operator (Racetrack)
North Dakota Racing Commission
State Capitol Bldg.
Bismarck, ND 58505
Phone: (701)224-2210

Credential Type: License Registration.
Requirements: Submit application and fingerprint card. Pay fee. **Fees:** $10 license fee. $10 duplicate license fee.

6612

Track Maintenance (Racetrack)
North Dakota Racing Commission
State Capitol Bldg.
Bismarck, ND 58505
Phone: (701)224-2210

Credential Type: License Registration.
Requirements: Submit application and fingerprint card. Pay fee. **Fees:** $10 license fee. $10 duplicate license fee.

6613

Track Superintendent (Racetrack)
North Dakota Racing Commission
State Capitol Bldg.
Bismarck, ND 58505
Phone: (701)224-2210

Credential Type: License Registration.
Requirements: Submit application and fingerprint card. Pay fee. **Fees:** $10 license fee. $10 duplicate license fee.

6614

Trainer (Racetrack)
North Dakota Racing Commission
State Capitol Bldg.
Bismarck, ND 58505
Phone: (701)224-2210

Credential Type: License Registration.
Requirements: Submit application and fingerprint card. Pay fee. **Fees:** $25 license fee. $10 duplicate license fee.

6615

Valet (Racetrack)
North Dakota Racing Commission
State Capitol Bldg.
Bismarck, ND 58505
Phone: (701)224-2210

Credential Type: License Registration.
Requirements: Submit application and fingerprint card. Pay fee. **Fees:** $10 license fee. $10 duplicate license fee.

Ohio

6616

Admission Employee (Thoroughbred, Standardbred, and Quarter Horse Racing)
Ohio State Racing Commission
State Office Tower
77 S. High St., 18th Fl.
Columbus, OH 43266-0416
Phone: (614)466-2757

Credential Type: License Registration.
Requirements: Submit application and fingerprint card. Pay fee. **Fees:** $10 registration fee.

6617

Apprentice Jockey (Thoroughbred and Quarter Horse Racing)
Ohio State Racing Commission
State Office Tower
77 S. High St., 18th Fl.
Columbus, OH 43266-0416
Phone: (614)466-2757

Credential Type: License Registration.
Requirements: Submit application and fingerprint card. Pay fee. **Fees:** $25 registration fee.

6618

Assistant Racing Secretary (Thoroughbred, Standardbred, and Quarter Horse Racing)
Ohio State Racing Commission
State Office Tower
77 S. High St., 18th Fl.
Columbus, OH 43266-0416
Phone: (614)466-2757

Credential Type: License Registration.
Requirements: Submit application and fingerprint card. Pay fee. **Fees:** $25 registration fee.

6619

Assistant Starter (Thoroughbred, Standardbred, and Quarter Horse Racing)
Ohio State Racing Commission
State Office Tower
77 S. High St., 18th Fl.
Columbus, OH 43266-0416
Phone: (614)466-2757

Credential Type: License Registration.
Requirements: Submit application and fingerprint card. Pay fee. **Fees:** $25 registration fee.

6620

Assistant Trainer (Thoroughbred, Standardbred, and Quarter Horse Racing)
Ohio State Racing Commission
State Office Tower
77 S. High St., 18th Fl.
Columbus, OH 43266-0416
Phone: (614)466-2757

Credential Type: License Registration.
Requirements: Submit application and fingerprint card. Pay fee. **Fees:** $25 registration fee.

6621

Authorized Agent (Thoroughbred, Standardbred, and Quarter Horse Racing)
Ohio State Racing Commission
State Office Tower
77 S. High St., 18th Fl.
Columbus, OH 43266-0416
Phone: (614)466-2757

Credential Type: License Registration.
Requirements: Submit application and fingerprint card. Pay fee. **Fees:** $25 registration fee.

6622

Chief of Security (Thoroughbred, Standardbred, and Quarter Horse Racing)
Ohio State Racing Commission
State Office Tower
77 S. High St., 18th Fl.
Columbus, OH 43266-0416
Phone: (614)466-2757

Credential Type: License Registration.
Requirements: Submit application and fingerprint card. Pay fee. **Fees:** $25 registration fee.

6623

Clerical Worker (Thoroughbred, Standardbred, and Quarter Horse Racing)
Ohio State Racing Commission
State Office Tower
77 S. High St., 18th Fl.
Columbus, OH 43266-0416
Phone: (614)466-2757

Credential Type: License Registration.
Requirements: Submit application and fingerprint card. Pay fee. **Fees:** $10 registration fee.

6624

Clerk of Course (Thoroughbred, Standardbred, and Quarter Horse Racing)
Ohio State Racing Commission
State Office Tower
77 S. High St., 18th Fl.
Columbus, OH 43266-0416
Phone: (614)466-2757

Credential Type: License Registration.
Requirements: Submit application and fingerprint card. Pay fee. **Fees:** $25 registration fee.

6625

Concession Employee (Thoroughbred, Standardbred, and Quarter Horse Racing)
Ohio State Racing Commission
State Office Tower
77 S. High St., 18th Fl.
Columbus, OH 43266-0416
Phone: (614)466-2757

Credential Type: License Registration.
Requirements: Submit application and fingerprint card. Pay fee. **Fees:** $10 registration fee.

6626

Concession Manager (Thoroughbred, Standardbred, and Quarter Horse Racing)
Ohio State Racing Commission
State Office Tower
77 S. High St., 18th Fl.
Columbus, OH 43266-0416
Phone: (614)466-2757

Credential Type: License Registration.
Requirements: Submit application and fingerprint card. Pay fee. **Fees:** $25 registration fee.

6627

Doctor (Thoroughbred, Standardbred, and Quarter Horse Racing)
Ohio State Racing Commission
State Office Tower
77 S. High St., 18th Fl.
Columbus, OH 43266-0416
Phone: (614)466-2757

Credential Type: License Registration.
Requirements: Submit application and fingerprint card. Pay fee. **Fees:** $25 registration fee.

6628

Driver/Trainer (Standardbred Racing)
Ohio State Racing Commission
State Office Tower
77 S. High St., 18th Fl.
Columbus, OH 43266-0416
Phone: (614)466-2757

Credential Type: License Registration. **Requirements:** Submit application and fingerprint card. Pay fee. **Fees:** $25 registration fee.

6629

Equine Tooth Dresser (Thoroughbred, Standardbred, and Quarter Horse Racing)
Ohio State Racing Commission
State Office Tower
77 S. High St., 18th Fl.
Columbus, OH 43266-0416
Phone: (614)466-2757

Credential Type: License Registration. **Requirements:** Submit application and fingerprint card. Pay fee. **Fees:** $25 registration fee.

6630

Exercise Boy/Girl (Thoroughbred and Quarter Horse Racing)
Ohio State Racing Commission
State Office Tower
77 S. High St., 18th Fl.
Columbus, OH 43266-0416
Phone: (614)466-2757

Credential Type: License Registration. **Requirements:** Submit application and fingerprint card. Pay fee. **Fees:** $10 registration fee.

6631

General Manager (Thoroughbred, Standardbred, and Quarter Horse Racing)
Ohio State Racing Commission
State Office Tower
77 S. High St., 18th Fl.
Columbus, OH 43266-0416
Phone: (614)466-2757

Credential Type: License Registration. **Requirements:** Submit application and fingerprint card. Pay fee. **Fees:** $25 registration fee.

6632

Groom (Thoroughbred, Standardbred, and Quarter Horse Racing)
Ohio State Racing Commission
State Office Tower
77 S. High St., 18th Fl.
Columbus, OH 43266-0416
Phone: (614)466-2757

Credential Type: License Registration. **Requirements:** Submit application and fingerprint card. Pay fee. **Fees:** $10 registration fee.

6633

Horsemen's Bookkeeper (Thoroughbred, Standardbred, and Quarter Horse Racing)
Ohio State Racing Commission
State Office Tower
77 S. High St., 18th Fl.
Columbus, OH 43266-0416
Phone: (614)466-2757

Credential Type: License Registration. **Requirements:** Submit application and fingerprint card. Pay fee. **Fees:** $25 registration fee.

6634

Horseshoer (Thoroughbred, Standardbred, and Quarter Horse Racing)
Ohio State Racing Commission
State Office Tower
77 S. High St., 18th Fl.
Columbus, OH 43266-0416
Phone: (614)466-2757

Credential Type: License Registration. **Requirements:** Submit application and fingerprint card. Pay fee. **Fees:** $25 registration fee.

6635

Identifier (Thoroughbred, Standardbred, and Quarter Horse Racing)
Ohio State Racing Commission
State Office Tower
77 S. High St., 18th Fl.
Columbus, OH 43266-0416
Phone: (614)466-2757

Credential Type: License Registration. **Requirements:** Submit application and fingerprint card. Pay fee. **Fees:** $25 registration fee.

6636

Jockey Agent (Thoroughbred and Quarter Horse Racing)
Ohio State Racing Commission
State Office Tower
77 S. High St., 18th Fl.
Columbus, OH 43266-0416
Phone: (614)466-2757

Credential Type: License Registration. **Requirements:** Submit application and fingerprint card. Pay fee. **Fees:** $25 registration fee.

6637

Jockey (Thoroughbred and Quarter Horse Racing)
Ohio State Racing Commission
State Office Tower
77 S. High St., 18th Fl.
Columbus, OH 43266-0416
Phone: (614)466-2757

Credential Type: License Registration. **Requirements:** Submit application and fingerprint card. Pay fee. **Fees:** $25 registration fee.

6638

Judge (Standardbred Racing)
Ohio State Racing Commission
State Office Tower
77 S. High St., 18th Fl.
Columbus, OH 43266-0416
Phone: (614)466-2757

Credential Type: License Registration. **Requirements:** Submit application and fingerprint card. Pay fee. **Fees:** $25 registration fee.

6639

Maintenance Employee (Thoroughbred, Standardbred, and Quarter Horse Racing)
Ohio State Racing Commission
State Office Tower
77 S. High St., 18th Fl.
Columbus, OH 43266-0416
Phone: (614)466-2757

Credential Type: License Registration. **Requirements:** Submit application and fingerprint card. Pay fee. **Fees:** $10 registration fee.

Racetrack Occupations

6640

Medical/First Aid Employee (Thoroughbred, Standardbred, and Quarter Horse Racing)
Ohio State Racing Commission
State Office Tower
77 S. High St., 18th Fl.
Columbus, OH 43266-0416
Phone: (614)466-2757

Credential Type: License Registration. **Requirements:** Submit application and fingerprint card. Pay fee. **Fees:** $10 registration fee.

6641

Mutuel Employee (Thoroughbred, Standardbred, and Quarter Horse Racing)
Ohio State Racing Commission
State Office Tower
77 S. High St., 18th Fl.
Columbus, OH 43266-0416
Phone: (614)466-2757

Credential Type: License Registration. **Requirements:** Submit application and fingerprint card. Pay fee. **Fees:** $10 registration fee.

6642

Mutuel Manager (Thoroughbred, Standardbred, and Quarter Horse Racing)
Ohio State Racing Commission
State Office Tower
77 S. High St., 18th Fl.
Columbus, OH 43266-0416
Phone: (614)466-2757

Credential Type: License Registration. **Requirements:** Submit application and fingerprint card. Pay fee. **Fees:** $25 registration fee.

6643

Outrider (Thoroughbred, Standardbred, and Quarter Horse Racing)
Ohio State Racing Commission
State Office Tower
77 S. High St., 18th Fl.
Columbus, OH 43266-0416
Phone: (614)466-2757

Credential Type: License Registration. **Requirements:** Submit application and fingerprint card. Pay fee. **Fees:** $10 registration fee.

6644

Owner (Thoroughbred, Standardbred, and Quarter Horse Racing)
Ohio State Racing Commission
State Office Tower
77 S. High St., 18th Fl.
Columbus, OH 43266-0416
Phone: (614)466-2757

Credential Type: License Registration. **Requirements:** Submit application and fingerprint card. Pay fee. **Fees:** $25 registration fee.

6645

Paddock Judge (Thoroughbred, Standardbred, and Quarter Horse Racing)
Ohio State Racing Commission
State Office Tower
77 S. High St., 18th Fl.
Columbus, OH 43266-0416
Phone: (614)466-2757

Credential Type: License Registration. **Requirements:** Submit application and fingerprint card. Pay fee. **Fees:** $25 registration fee.

6646

Parking Lot Employee (Thoroughbred and Quarter Horse Racing)
Ohio State Racing Commission
State Office Tower
77 S. High St., 18th Fl.
Columbus, OH 43266-0416
Phone: (614)466-2757

Credential Type: License Registration. **Requirements:** Submit application and fingerprint card. Pay fee. **Fees:** $10 registration fee.

6647

Patrol Judge (Thoroughbred and Quarter Horse Racing)
Ohio State Racing Commission
State Office Tower
77 S. High St., 18th Fl.
Columbus, OH 43266-0416
Phone: (614)466-2757

Credential Type: License Registration. **Requirements:** Submit application and fingerprint card. Pay fee. **Fees:** $25 registration fee.

6648

Photographer (Thoroughbred and Quarter Horse Racing)
Ohio State Racing Commission
State Office Tower
77 S. High St., 18th Fl.
Columbus, OH 43266-0416
Phone: (614)466-2757

Credential Type: License Registration. **Requirements:** Submit application and fingerprint card. Pay fee. **Fees:** $25 registration fee.

6649

Placing Judge (Thoroughbred and Quarter Horse Racing)
Ohio State Racing Commission
State Office Tower
77 S. High St., 18th Fl.
Columbus, OH 43266-0416
Phone: (614)466-2757

Credential Type: License Registration. **Requirements:** Submit application and fingerprint card. Pay fee. **Fees:** $25 registration fee.

6650

Porter (Thoroughbred and Quarter Horse Racing)
Ohio State Racing Commission
State Office Tower
77 S. High St., 18th Fl.
Columbus, OH 43266-0416
Phone: (614)466-2757

Credential Type: License Registration. **Requirements:** Submit application and fingerprint card. Pay fee. **Fees:** $10 registration fee.

6651

Racing Secretary (Thoroughbred, Standardbred, and Quarter Horse Racing)
Ohio State Racing Commission
State Office Tower
77 S. High St., 18th Fl.
Columbus, OH 43266-0416
Phone: (614)466-2757

Credential Type: License Registration. **Requirements:** Submit application and fingerprint card. Pay fee. **Fees:** $25 registration fee.

6652

Security Employee (Thoroughbred, Standardbred, and Quarter Horse Racing)
Ohio State Racing Commission
State Office Tower
77 S. High St., 18th Fl.
Columbus, OH 43266-0416
Phone: (614)466-2757

Credential Type: License Registration. **Requirements:** Submit application and fingerprint card. Pay fee. **Fees:** $10 registration fee.

6653

Starter (Thoroughbred, Standardbred, and Quarter Horse Racing)
Ohio State Racing Commission
State Office Tower
77 S. High St., 18th Fl.
Columbus, OH 43266-0416
Phone: (614)466-2757

Credential Type: License Registration. **Requirements:** Submit application and fingerprint card. Pay fee. **Fees:** $25 registration fee.

6654

Steward (Thoroughbred and Quarter Horse Racing)
Ohio State Racing Commission
State Office Tower
77 S. High St., 18th Fl.
Columbus, OH 43266-0416
Phone: (614)466-2757

Credential Type: License Registration. **Requirements:** Submit application and fingerprint card. Pay fee. **Fees:** $25 registration fee.

6655

Supply Salesman (Thoroughbred, Standardbred, and Quarter Horse Racing)
Ohio State Racing Commission
State Office Tower
77 S. High St., 18th Fl.
Columbus, OH 43266-0416
Phone: (614)466-2757

Credential Type: License Registration. **Requirements:** Submit application and fingerprint card. Pay fee. **Fees:** $10 registration fee.

6656

Telephone Operator (Thoroughbred, Standardbred, and Quarter Horse Racing)
Ohio State Racing Commission
State Office Tower
77 S. High St., 18th Fl.
Columbus, OH 43266-0416
Phone: (614)466-2757

Credential Type: License Registration. **Requirements:** Submit application and fingerprint card. Pay fee. **Fees:** $10 registration fee.

6657

Timer (Thoroughbred, Standardbred, and Quarter Horse Racing)
Ohio State Racing Commission
State Office Tower
77 S. High St., 18th Fl.
Columbus, OH 43266-0416
Phone: (614)466-2757

Credential Type: License Registration. **Requirements:** Submit application and fingerprint card. Pay fee. **Fees:** $10 registration fee.

6658

Trainer (Thoroughbred, Standardbred, and Quarter Horse Racing)
Ohio State Racing Commission
State Office Tower
77 S. High St., 18th Fl.
Columbus, OH 43266-0416
Phone: (614)466-2757

Credential Type: License Registration. **Requirements:** Submit application and fingerprint card. Pay fee. **Fees:** $25 registration fee.

6659

Valet (Thoroughbred and Quarter Horse Racing)
Ohio State Racing Commission
State Office Tower
77 S. High St., 18th Fl.
Columbus, OH 43266-0416
Phone: (614)466-2757

Credential Type: License Registration. **Requirements:** Submit application and fingerprint card. Pay fee. **Fees:** $10 registration fee.

6660

Veterinarian (Thoroughbred, Standardbred, and Quarter Horse Racing)
Ohio State Racing Commission
State Office Tower
77 S. High St., 18th Fl.
Columbus, OH 43266-0416
Phone: (614)466-2757

Credential Type: License Registration. **Requirements:** Submit application and fingerprint card. Pay fee. **Fees:** $25 registration fee.

6661

Veterinarian's Assistant (Thoroughbred, Standardbred, and Quarter Horse Racing)
Ohio State Racing Commission
State Office Tower
77 S. High St., 18th Fl.
Columbus, OH 43266-0416
Phone: (614)466-2757

Credential Type: License Registration. **Requirements:** Submit application and fingerprint card. Pay fee. **Fees:** $10 registration fee.

Oklahoma

6662

Administrative Employee (Racetrack)
Oklahoma Horse Racing Commission
6501 N. Broadway, Ste. 180
Oklahoma City, OK 73116
Phone: (405)848-0404

Credential Type: License Registration. **Duration of License:** One year. **Requirements:** Submit application and fingerprint card. Pay fee. **Fees:** $25 registration fee. $25 annual renewal.

6663

Apprentice Jockey (Racetrack)
Oklahoma Horse Racing Commission
6501 N. Broadway, Ste. 180
Oklahoma City, OK 73116
Phone: (405)848-0404

Credential Type: License Registration. **Duration of License:** One year. **Requirements:** Submit application and fingerprint card. Pay fee. **Fees:** $50 registration fee. $50 annual renewal. $120 triennial renewal.

6664

Assistant Trainer (Racetrack)
Oklahoma Horse Racing Commission
6501 N. Broadway, Ste. 180
Oklahoma City, OK 73116
Phone: (405)848-0404

Credential Type: License Registration. **Duration of License:** One year. **Requirements:** Submit application and fingerprint card. Pay fee. **Fees:** $50 registration fee. $50 annual renewal.

6665

Authorized Agent (Racetrack)
Oklahoma Horse Racing Commission
6501 N. Broadway, Ste. 180
Oklahoma City, OK 73116
Phone: (405)848-0404

Credential Type: License Registration. **Duration of License:** One year. **Requirements:** Submit application and fingerprint card. Pay fee. **Fees:** $50 registration fee. $50 annual renewal.

6666

Blacksmith (Racetrack)
Oklahoma Horse Racing Commission
6501 N. Broadway, Ste. 180
Oklahoma City, OK 73116
Phone: (405)848-0404

Credential Type: License Registration. **Duration of License:** One year. **Requirements:** Submit application and fingerprint card. Pay fee. **Fees:** $50 registration fee. $50 annual renewal. $120 triennial renewal.

6667

Bloodstock Agent (Racetrack)
Oklahoma Horse Racing Commission
6501 N. Broadway, Ste. 180
Oklahoma City, OK 73116
Phone: (405)848-0404

Credential Type: License Registration. **Duration of License:** One year. **Requirements:** Submit application and fingerprint card. Pay fee. **Fees:** 50 registration fee. $50 annual renewal.

6668

Concession Employee (Racetrack)
Oklahoma Horse Racing Commission
6501 N. Broadway, Ste. 180
Oklahoma City, OK 73116
Phone: (405)848-0404

Credential Type: License Registration. **Duration of License:** One year. **Requirements:** Submit application and fingerprint card. Pay fee. **Fees:** $25 registration fee. $25 annual renewal.

6669

Exercise Person (Racetrack)
Oklahoma Horse Racing Commission
6501 N. Broadway, Ste. 180
Oklahoma City, OK 73116
Phone: (405)848-0404

Credential Type: License Registration. **Duration of License:** One year. **Requirements:** Submit application and fingerprint card. Pay fee. **Fees:** $25 registration fee. $25 annual renewal.

6670

General Services Employee (Racetrack)
Oklahoma Horse Racing Commission
6501 N. Broadway, Ste. 180
Oklahoma City, OK 73116
Phone: (405)848-0404

Credential Type: License Registration. **Duration of License:** One year. **Requirements:** Submit application and fingerprint card. Pay fee. **Fees:** $25 registration fee. $25 annual renewal.

6671

Groom (Racetrack)
Oklahoma Horse Racing Commission
6501 N. Broadway, Ste. 180
Oklahoma City, OK 73116
Phone: (405)848-0404

Credential Type: License Registration. **Duration of License:** One year. **Requirements:** Submit application and fingerprint card. Pay fee. **Fees:** $25 registration fee. $25 annual renewal.

6672

Horse Industry Representative (Racetrack)
Oklahoma Horse Racing Commission
6501 N. Broadway, Ste. 180
Oklahoma City, OK 73116
Phone: (405)848-0404

Credential Type: License Registration. **Duration of License:** One year. **Requirements:** Submit application and fingerprint card. Pay fee. **Fees:** $25 registration fee. $25 annual renewal.

6673

Jockey Agent (Racetrack)
Oklahoma Horse Racing Commission
6501 N. Broadway, Ste. 180
Oklahoma City, OK 73116
Phone: (405)848-0404

Credential Type: License Registration. **Duration of License:** One year. **Requirements:** Submit application and fingerprint card. Pay fee. **Fees:** $50 registration fee. $50 annual renewal.

6674

Jockey (Racetrack)
Oklahoma Horse Racing Commission
6501 N. Broadway, Ste. 180
Oklahoma City, OK 73116
Phone: (405)848-0404

Credential Type: License Registration. **Duration of License:** One year. **Requirements:** Submit application and fingerprint card. Pay fee. **Fees:** $50 registration fee. $50 annual renewal. $120 triennial renewal.

6675

License Clerk (Racetrack)
Oklahoma Horse Racing Commission
6501 N. Broadway, Ste. 180
Oklahoma City, OK 73116
Phone: (405)848-0404

Credential Type: License Registration. **Duration of License:** One year. **Requirements:** Submit application and fingerprint card. Pay fee. **Fees:** $25 registration fee. $25 annual renewal.

6676

Mutuel Employee (Racetrack)
Oklahoma Horse Racing Commission
6501 N. Broadway, Ste. 180
Oklahoma City, OK 73116
Phone: (405)848-0404

Credential Type: License Registration. **Duration of License:** One year. **Requirements:** Submit application and fingerprint card. Pay fee. **Fees:** $25 registration fee. $25 annual renewal.

6677

Outrider (Racetrack)
Oklahoma Horse Racing Commission
6501 N. Broadway, Ste. 180
Oklahoma City, OK 73116
Phone: (405)848-0404

Credential Type: License Registration. **Duration of License:** One year. **Requirements:** Submit application and fingerprint card. Pay fee. **Fees:** $25 registration fee. $25 annual renewal.

6678

Owner/Assistant Trainer (Racetrack)
Oklahoma Horse Racing Commission
6501 N. Broadway, Ste. 180
Oklahoma City, OK 73116
Phone: (405)848-0404

Credential Type: License Registration. **Duration of License:** One year. **Requirements:** Submit application and fingerprint card. Pay fee. **Fees:** $50 registration fee. $50 annual renewal.

6679

Owner By Open Claim (Racetrack)
Oklahoma Horse Racing Commission
6501 N. Broadway, Ste. 180
Oklahoma City, OK 73116
Phone: (405)848-0404

Credential Type: License Registration. **Duration of License:** One year. **Requirements:** Submit application and fingerprint card. Pay fee. **Fees:** $50 registration fee. $50 annual renewal.

6680

Owner (Racetrack)
Oklahoma Horse Racing Commission
6501 N. Broadway, Ste. 180
Oklahoma City, OK 73116
Phone: (405)848-0404

Credential Type: License Registration. **Duration of License:** One year. **Requirements:** Submit application and fingerprint card. Pay fee. **Fees:** $50 registration fee. $50 annual renewal. $120 triennial renewal.

6681

Owner/Trainer (Racetrack)
Oklahoma Horse Racing Commission
6501 N. Broadway, Ste. 180
Oklahoma City, OK 73116
Phone: (405)848-0404

Credential Type: License Registration. **Duration of License:** One year. **Requirements:** Submit application and fingerprint card. Pay fee. **Fees:** $50 registration fee. $50 annual renewal. $120 triennial renewal.

6682

Pony Rider (Racetrack)
Oklahoma Horse Racing Commission
6501 N. Broadway, Ste. 180
Oklahoma City, OK 73116
Phone: (405)848-0404

Credential Type: License Registration. **Duration of License:** One year. **Requirements:** Submit application and fingerprint card. Pay fee. **Fees:** $25 registration fee. $25 annual renewal.

6683

Racehorse Trainer
Oklahoma Horse Racing Commission
6501 N. Broadway, Ste. 180
Oklahoma City, OK 73116
Phone: (405)848-0404

Credential Type: License. **Duration of License:** One and three years. **Requirements:** 18 years of age. **Examination:** Oklahoma Horse Racing Commission Trainers Examination. **Fees:** $50 exam fee. $50 application fee. $50 renewal fee.

6684

Racehorse Trainer, Assistant
Oklahoma Horse Racing Commission
6501 N. Broadway, Ste. 180
Oklahoma City, OK 73116
Phone: (405)848-0404

Credential Type: License. **Duration of License:** One year. **Requirements:** 18 years of age. **Examination:** Oklahoma Horse Racing Commission Trainers Exam. **Fees:** $50 exam fee. $50 application fee. $50 renewal fee.

6685

Racing Official (Racetrack)
Oklahoma Horse Racing Commission
6501 N. Broadway, Ste. 180
Oklahoma City, OK 73116
Phone: (405)848-0404

Credential Type: License Registration. **Duration of License:** One year. **Requirements:** Submit application and fingerprint card. Pay fee. **Fees:** $50 registration fee. $50 annual renewal.

6686

Security Employee (Racetrack)
Oklahoma Horse Racing Commission
6501 N. Broadway, Ste. 180
Oklahoma City, OK 73116
Phone: (405)848-0404

Credential Type: License Registration. **Duration of License:** One year. **Requirements:** Submit application and fingerprint card. Pay fee. **Fees:** $25 registration fee. $25 annual renewal.

6687

Track Manager (Racetrack)
Oklahoma Horse Racing Commission
6501 N. Broadway, Ste. 180
Oklahoma City, OK 73116
Phone: (405)848-0404

Credential Type: License Registration. **Duration of License:** One year. **Requirements:** Submit application and fingerprint card. Pay fee. **Fees:** $50 registration fee. $50 annual renewal.

6688

Trainer (Racetrack)
Oklahoma Horse Racing Commission
6501 N. Broadway, Ste. 180
Oklahoma City, OK 73116
Phone: (405)848-0404

Credential Type: License Registration. **Duration of License:** One year. **Requirements:** Submit application and fingerprint card. Pay fee. **Fees:** $50 registration fee. $50 annual renewal. $120 triennial renewal.

6689

Valet (Racetrack)
Oklahoma Horse Racing Commission
6501 N. Broadway, Ste. 180
Oklahoma City, OK 73116
Phone: (405)848-0404

Credential Type: License Registration. **Duration of License:** One year. **Requirements:** Submit application and fingerprint card. Pay fee. **Fees:** $25 registration fee. $25 annual renewal.

6690

Vendor Employee (Racetrack)
Oklahoma Horse Racing Commission
6501 N. Broadway, Ste. 180
Oklahoma City, OK 73116
Phone: (405)848-0404

Credential Type: License Registration. **Duration of License:** One year. **Requirements:** Submit application and fingerprint card. Pay fee. **Fees:** $25 registration fee. $25 annual renewal.

6691

Vendor (Racetrack)
Oklahoma Horse Racing Commission
6501 N. Broadway, Ste. 180
Oklahoma City, OK 73116
Phone: (405)848-0404

Credential Type: License Registration. **Duration of License:** One year. **Requirements:** Submit application and fingerprint card. Pay fee. **Fees:** $50 registration fee. $50 annual renewal.

6692

Veterinarian Assistant (Racetrack)
Oklahoma Horse Racing Commission
6501 N. Broadway, Ste. 180
Oklahoma City, OK 73116
Phone: (405)848-0404

Credential Type: License Registration. **Duration of License:** One year. **Requirements:** Submit application and fingerprint card. Pay fee. **Fees:** $25 registration fee. $25 annual renewal.

6693

Veterinarian (Racetrack)
Oklahoma Horse Racing Commission
6501 N. Broadway, Ste. 180
Oklahoma City, OK 73116
Phone: (405)848-0404

Credential Type: License Registration. **Duration of License:** One year. **Requirements:** Submit application and fingerprint card. Pay fee. **Fees:** $50 registration fee. $50 annual renewal. $120 triennial renewal fee.

Oregon

6694

Apprentice Jockey (Racetrack)
Oregon Racing Commission
113 State Office Bldg.
1400 SW Fifth
Portland, OR 97201
Phone: (503)229-5820

Credential Type: License Registration. **Requirements:** Submit application and fingerprint card. Pay fee . **Fees:** $30 registration fee. $6 duplicate fee.

6695

Assistant Trainer (Racetrack)
Oregon Racing Commission
113 State Office Bldg.
1400 SW Fifth
Portland, OR 97201
Phone: (503)229-5820

Credential Type: License Registration. **Requirements:** Submit application and fingerprint card. Pay fee. **Fees:** $30 registration fee. $6 duplicate fee.

6696

Association Employee (Racetrack)
Oregon Racing Commission
113 State Office Bldg.
1400 SW Fifth
Portland, OR 97201
Phone: (503)229-5820

Credential Type: License Registration. **Requirements:** Submit application and fingerprint card. Pay fee. **Fees:** $30 registration fee. $6 duplicate fee.

6697

Concessions Employee (Racetrack)
Oregon Racing Commission
113 State Office Bldg.
1400 SW Fifth
Portland, OR 97201
Phone: (503)229-5820

Credential Type: License Registration. **Requirements:** Submit application and fingerprint card. Pay fee. **Fees:** $30 registration fee. $6 duplicate fee.

6698

Exercise Person (Racetrack)
Oregon Racing Commission
113 State Office Bldg.
1400 SW Fifth
Portland, OR 97201
Phone: (503)229-5820

Credential Type: License Registration. **Requirements:** Submit application and fingerprint card. Pay fee. **Fees:** $30 registration fee. $6 duplicate fee.

6699

Groom/Hot Walker (Racetrack)
Oregon Racing Commission
113 State Office Bldg.
1400 SW Fifth
Portland, OR 97201
Phone: (503)229-5820

Credential Type: License Registration. **Requirements:** Submit application and fingerprint card. Pay fee. **Fees:** $30 registration fee. $6 duplicate fee.

6700

Horseshoer/Plater (Racetrack)
Oregon Racing Commission
113 State Office Bldg.
1400 SW Fifth
Portland, OR 97201
Phone: (503)229-5820

Credential Type: License Registration.
Requirements: Submit application and fingerprint card. Pay fee. **Fees:** $30 registration fee. $6 duplicate fee.

6701

Jockey Agent (Racetrack)
Oregon Racing Commission
113 State Office Bldg.
1400 SW Fifth
Portland, OR 97201
Phone: (503)229-5820

Credential Type: License Registration.
Requirements: Submit application and fingerprint card. Pay fee. **Fees:** $30 registration fee. $6 duplicate fee.

6702

Jockey (Racetrack)
Oregon Racing Commission
113 State Office Bldg.
1400 SW Fifth
Portland, OR 97201
Phone: (503)229-5820

Credential Type: License Registration.
Requirements: Submit application and fingerprint card. Pay fee. **Fees:** $30 registration fee. $6 duplicate fee.

6703

Kennel Employee (Racetrack)
Oregon Racing Commission
113 State Office Bldg.
1400 SW Fifth
Portland, OR 97201
Phone: (503)229-5820

Credential Type: License Registration.
Requirements: Submit application and fingerprint card. Pay fee. **Fees:** $30 registration fee. $6 duplicate fee.

6704

Lead Out (Racetrack)
Oregon Racing Commission
113 State Office Bldg.
1400 SW Fifth
Portland, OR 97201
Phone: (503)229-5820

Credential Type: License Registration.
Requirements: Submit application and fingerprint card. Pay fee. **Fees:** $30 registration fee. $6 duplicate fee.

6705

Maintenance Employee (Racetrack)
Oregon Racing Commission
113 State Office Bldg.
1400 SW Fifth
Portland, OR 97201
Phone: (503)229-5820

Credential Type: License Registration.
Requirements: Submit application and fingerprint card. Pay fee. **Fees:** $30 registration fee. $6 duplicate fee.

6706

Official (Racetrack)
Oregon Racing Commission
113 State Office Bldg.
1400 SW Fifth
Portland, OR 97201
Phone: (503)229-5820

Credential Type: License Registration.
Requirements: Submit application and fingerprint card. Pay fee. **Fees:** $30 registration fee. $6 duplicate fee.

6707

Owner (Racetrack)
Oregon Racing Commission
113 State Office Bldg.
1400 SW Fifth
Portland, OR 97201
Phone: (503)229-5820

Credential Type: License Registration.
Requirements: Submit application and fingerprint card. Pay fee. **Fees:** $30 registration fee. $6 duplicate fee.

6708

Pari-Mutuel Employee (Racetrack)
Oregon Racing Commission
113 State Office Bldg.
1400 SW Fifth
Portland, OR 97201
Phone: (503)229-5820

Credential Type: License Registration.
Requirements: Submit application and fingerprint card. Pay fee. **Fees:** $30 registration fee. $6 duplicate fee.

6709

Pony Person (Racetrack)
Oregon Racing Commission
113 State Office Bldg.
1400 SW Fifth
Portland, OR 97201
Phone: (503)229-5820

Credential Type: License Registration.
Requirements: Submit application and fingerprint card. Pay fee. **Fees:** $30 registration fee. $6 duplicate fee.

6710

Starter/Assistant Starter (Racetrack)
Oregon Racing Commission
113 State Office Bldg.
1400 SW Fifth
Portland, OR 97201
Phone: (503)229-5820

Credential Type: License Registration.
Requirements: Submit application and fingerprint card. Pay fee. **Fees:** $30 registration fee. $6 duplicate fee.

6711

Timer (Racetrack)
Oregon Racing Commission
113 State Office Bldg.
1400 SW Fifth
Portland, OR 97201
Phone: (503)229-5820

Credential Type: License Registration.
Requirements: Submit application and fingerprint card. Pay fee. **Fees:** $30 registration fee. $6 duplicate fee.

6712

Trainer (Racetrack)
Oregon Racing Commission
113 State Office Bldg.
1400 SW Fifth
Portland, OR 97201
Phone: (503)229-5820

Credential Type: License Registration.
Requirements: Submit application and fingerprint card. Pay fee. **Fees:** $30 registration fee. $6 duplicate fee.

6713

Valet (Racetrack)
Oregon Racing Commission
113 State Office Bldg.
1400 SW Fifth
Portland, OR 97201
Phone: (503)229-5820

Credential Type: License Registration.
Requirements: Submit application and fingerprint card. Pay fee. **Fees:** $30 registration fee. $6 duplicate fee.

6714

Veterinarian (Racetrack)
Oregon Racing Commission
113 State Office Bldg.
1400 SW Fifth
Portland, OR 97201
Phone: (503)229-5820

Credential Type: License Registration.
Requirements: Submit application and fingerprint card. Pay fee. **Fees:** $30 registration fee. $6 duplicate fee.

Pennsylvania

6715

Apprentice Jockey (Horse Racing)
Pennsylvania State Horse Racing Commission
2301 N. Cameron St., Rm. 306, 4th Fl.
Harrisburg, PA 17110-9408
Phone: (717)787-1942

Credential Type: License Registration.
Duration of License: Three years. **Requirements:** Submit application, two photos, and fingerprint card. Pay fee. **Fees:** $30 registration fee. $2 duplicate license.

6716

Assistant Trainer (Horse Racing)
Pennsylvania State Horse Racing Commission
2301 N. Cameron St., Rm. 306, 4th Fl.
Harrisburg, PA 17110-9408
Phone: (717)787-1942

Credential Type: License Registration.
Duration of License: Three years. **Requirements:** Submit application, two photos, and fingerprint card. Pay fee. **Fees:** $30 registration fee. $2 duplicate license.

6717

Association Employee (Harness Racing)
Pennsylvania State Harness Racing Commission
2301 N. Cameron St.
Harrisburg, PA 17110-9408
Phone: (717)787-5196

Credential Type: License Registration.
Duration of License: Three years. **Requirements:** Submit application, three photos, and fingerprint card. Pay fee. **Fees:** $15 registration fee. $5 duplicate license. $33 fingerprint processing fee.

6718

Authorized Agent (Horse Racing)
Pennsylvania State Horse Racing Commission
2301 N. Cameron St., Rm. 306, 4th Fl.
Harrisburg, PA 17110-9408
Phone: (717)787-1942

Credential Type: License Registration.
Duration of License: Three years. **Requirements:** Submit application, two photos, and fingerprint card. Pay fee. **Fees:** $30 registration fee. $2 duplicate license.

6719

Blacksmith (Harness Racing)
Pennsylvania State Harness Racing Commission
2301 N. Cameron St.
Harrisburg, PA 17110-9408
Phone: (717)787-5196

Credential Type: License Registration.
Duration of License: Three years. **Requirements:** Submit application, three photos, and fingerprint card. Pay fee. **Fees:** $30 registration fee. $5 duplicate license. $33 fingerprint processing fee.

6720

Concession Employee (Harness Racing)
Pennsylvania State Harness Racing Commission
2301 N. Cameron St.
Harrisburg, PA 17110-9408
Phone: (717)787-5196

Credential Type: License Registration.
Duration of License: Three years. **Requirements:** Submit application, three photos, and fingerprint card. Pay fee. **Fees:** $15 registration fee. $5 duplicate license. $33 fingerprint processing fee.

6721

Driver/Groom (Harness Racing)
Pennsylvania State Harness Racing Commission
2301 N. Cameron St.
Harrisburg, PA 17110-9408
Phone: (717)787-5196

Credential Type: License Registration.
Duration of License: Three years. **Requirements:** Submit application, three photos, and fingerprint card. Pay fee. **Fees:** $45 registration fee. $5 duplicate license. $33 fingerprint processing fee.

6722

Driver (Harness Racing)
Pennsylvania State Harness Racing Commission
2301 N. Cameron St.
Harrisburg, PA 17110-9408
Phone: (717)787-5196

Credential Type: License Registration.
Duration of License: Three years. **Requirements:** Submit application, three photos, and fingerprint card. Pay fee. **Fees:** $30 registration fee. $5 duplicate license. $33 fingerprint processing fee.

6723

Driver/Trainer/Groom (Harness Racing)
Pennsylvania State Harness Racing Commission
2301 N. Cameron St.
Harrisburg, PA 17110-9408
Phone: (717)787-5196

Credential Type: License Registration.
Duration of License: Three years. **Requirements:** Submit application, three photos, and fingerprint card. Pay fee. **Fees:** $75 registration fee. $5 duplicate license. $33 fingerprint processing fee.

6724

Driver/Trainer (Harness Racing)
Pennsylvania State Harness Racing Commission
2301 N. Cameron St.
Harrisburg, PA 17110-9408
Phone: (717)787-5196

Credential Type: License Registration. **Duration of License:** Three years. **Requirements:** Submit application, three photos, and fingerprint card. Pay fee. **Fees:** $60 registration fee. $5 duplicate license. $33 fingerprint processing fee.

6725

Farrier (Horse Racing)
Pennsylvania State Horse Racing Commission
2301 N. Cameron St., Rm. 306, 4th Fl.
Harrisburg, PA 17110-9408
Phone: (717)787-1942

Credential Type: License Registration. **Duration of License:** Three years. **Requirements:** Submit application, two photos, and fingerprint card. Pay fee. **Fees:** $45 registration fee. $2 duplicate license.

6726

Groom (Harness Racing)
Pennsylvania State Harness Racing Commission
2301 N. Cameron St.
Harrisburg, PA 17110-9408
Phone: (717)787-5196

Credential Type: License Registration. **Duration of License:** Three years. **Requirements:** Submit application, three photos, and fingerprint card. Pay fee. **Fees:** $15 registration fee. $5 duplicate license. $33 fingerprint processing fee.

6727

Jockey Agent (Horse Racing)
Pennsylvania State Horse Racing Commission
2301 N. Cameron St., Rm. 306, 4th Fl.
Harrisburg, PA 17110-9408
Phone: (717)787-1942

Credential Type: License Registration. **Duration of License:** Three years. **Requirements:** Submit application, two photos, and fingerprint card. Pay fee. **Fees:** $30 registration fee. $2 duplicate license.

6728

Jockey (Horse Racing)
Pennsylvania State Horse Racing Commission
2301 N. Cameron St., Rm. 306, 4th Fl.
Harrisburg, PA 17110-9408
Phone: (717)787-1942

Credential Type: License Registration. **Duration of License:** Three years. **Requirements:** Submit application, two photos, and fingerprint card. Pay fee. **Fees:** $30 registration fee. $2 duplicate license.

6729

Official (Horse Racing)
Pennsylvania State Horse Racing Commission
2301 N. Cameron St., Rm. 306, 4th Fl.
Harrisburg, PA 17110-9408
Phone: (717)787-1942

Credential Type: License Registration. **Duration of License:** Three years. **Requirements:** Submit application, two photos, and fingerprint card. Pay fee. **Fees:** $30 registration fee. $2 duplicate license.

6730

Officials (Harness Racing)
Pennsylvania State Harness Racing Commission
2301 N. Cameron St.
Harrisburg, PA 17110-9408
Phone: (717)787-5196

Credential Type: License Registration. **Duration of License:** Three years. **Requirements:** Submit application, three photos, and fingerprint card. Pay fee. **Fees:** $60 registration fee. $5 duplicate license. $33 fingerprint processing fee.

6731

Owner/Driver/Groom (Harness Racing)
Pennsylvania State Harness Racing Commission
2301 N. Cameron St.
Harrisburg, PA 17110-9408
Phone: (717)787-5196

Credential Type: License Registration. **Duration of License:** Three years. **Requirements:** Submit application, three photos, and fingerprint card. Pay fee. **Fees:** $75 registration fee. $5 duplicate license. $33 fingerprint processing fee.

6732

Owner/Driver (Harness Racing)
Pennsylvania State Harness Racing Commission
2301 N. Cameron St.
Harrisburg, PA 17110-9408
Phone: (717)787-5196

Credential Type: License Registration. **Duration of License:** Three years. **Requirements:** Submit application, three photos, and fingerprint card. Pay fee. **Fees:** $60 registration fee. $5 duplicate license. $33 fingerprint processing fee.

6733

Owner/Groom (Harness Racing)
Pennsylvania State Harness Racing Commission
2301 N. Cameron St.
Harrisburg, PA 17110-9408
Phone: (717)787-5196

Credential Type: License Registration. **Duration of License:** Three years. **Requirements:** Submit application, three photos, and fingerprint card. Pay fee. **Fees:** $60 registration fee. $5 duplicate license. $33 fingerprint processing fee.

6734

Owner (Harness Racing)
Pennsylvania State Harness Racing Commission
2301 N. Cameron St.
Harrisburg, PA 17110-9408
Phone: (717)787-5196

Credential Type: License Registration. **Duration of License:** Three years. **Requirements:** Submit application, three photos, and fingerprint card. Pay fee. **Fees:** $60 registration fee. $5 duplicate license. $33 fingerprint processing fee.

6735

Owner (Horse Racing)
Pennsylvania State Horse Racing Commission
2301 N. Cameron St., Rm. 306, 4th Fl.
Harrisburg, PA 17110-9408
Phone: (717)787-1942

Credential Type: License Registration. **Duration of License:** Three years. **Requirements:** Submit application, two photos, and fingerprint card. Pay fee. **Fees:** $75 registration fee. $2 duplicate license.

Racetrack Occupations

Pennsylvania

6736

Owner/Trainer/Driver/Groom (Harness Racing)
Pennsylvania State Harness Racing Commission
2301 N. Cameron St.
Harrisburg, PA 17110-9408
Phone: (717)787-5196

Credential Type: License Registration. **Duration of License:** Three years. **Requirements:** Submit application, three photos, and fingerprint card. Pay fee. **Fees:** $75 registration fee. $5 duplicate license. $33 fingerprint processing fee.

6737

Owner/Trainer/Driver (Harness Racing)
Pennsylvania State Harness Racing Commission
2301 N. Cameron St.
Harrisburg, PA 17110-9408
Phone: (717)787-5196

Credential Type: License Registration. **Duration of License:** Three years. **Requirements:** Submit application, three photos, and fingerprint card. Pay fee. **Fees:** $60 registration fee. $5 duplicate license. $33 fingerprint processing fee.

6738

Owner/Trainer/Groom (Harness Racing)
Pennsylvania State Harness Racing Commission
2301 N. Cameron St.
Harrisburg, PA 17110-9408
Phone: (717)787-5196

Credential Type: License Registration. **Duration of License:** Three years. **Requirements:** Submit application, three photos, and fingerprint card. Pay fee. **Fees:** $75 registration fee. $5 duplicate license. $33 fingerprint processing fee.

6739

Owner/Trainer (Harness Racing)
Pennsylvania State Harness Racing Commission
2301 N. Cameron St.
Harrisburg, PA 17110-9408
Phone: (717)787-5196

Credential Type: License Registration. **Duration of License:** Three years. **Requirements:** Submit application, three photos, and fingerprint card. Pay fee. **Fees:** $60 registration fee. $5 duplicate license. $33 fingerprint processing fee.

6740

Pari-Mutuel Employee (Harness Racing)
Pennsylvania State Harness Racing Commission
2301 N. Cameron St.
Harrisburg, PA 17110-9408
Phone: (717)787-5196

Credential Type: License Registration. **Duration of License:** Three years. **Requirements:** Submit application, three photos, and fingerprint card. Pay fee. **Fees:** $30 registration fee. $5 duplicate license. $33 fingerprint processing fee.

6741

Pari-Mutuel Employee (Horse Racing)
Pennsylvania State Horse Racing Commission
2301 N. Cameron St., Rm. 306, 4th Fl.
Harrisburg, PA 17110-9408
Phone: (717)787-1942

Credential Type: License Registration. **Duration of License:** Three years. **Requirements:** Submit application, two photos, and fingerprint card. Pay fee. **Fees:** $15 registration fee. $2 duplicate license.

6742

Salesman (Harness Racing)
Pennsylvania State Harness Racing Commission
2301 N. Cameron St.
Harrisburg, PA 17110-9408
Phone: (717)787-5196

Credential Type: License Registration. **Duration of License:** Three years. **Requirements:** Submit application, three photos, and fingerprint card. Pay fee. **Fees:** $30 registration fee. $5 duplicate license. $33 fingerprint processing fee.

6743

Stable Employee (Horse Racing)
Pennsylvania State Horse Racing Commission
2301 N. Cameron St., Rm. 306, 4th Fl.
Harrisburg, PA 17110-9408
Phone: (717)787-1942

Credential Type: License Registration. **Duration of License:** Three years. **Requirements:** Submit application, two photos, and fingerprint card. Pay fee. **Fees:** $15 registration fee. $2 duplicate license.

6744

Track Employee (Horse Racing)
Pennsylvania State Horse Racing Commission
2301 N. Cameron St., Rm. 306, 4th Fl.
Harrisburg, PA 17110-9408
Phone: (717)787-1942

Credential Type: License Registration. **Duration of License:** Three years. **Requirements:** Submit application, two photos, and fingerprint card. Pay fee. **Fees:** $15 registration fee. $2 duplicate license.

6745

Track Manager (Harness Racing)
Pennsylvania State Harness Racing Commission
2301 N. Cameron St.
Harrisburg, PA 17110-9408
Phone: (717)787-5196

Credential Type: License Registration. **Duration of License:** Three years. **Requirements:** Submit application, three photos, and fingerprint card. Pay fee. **Fees:** $30 registration fee. $5 duplicate license. $33 fingerprint processing fee.

6746

Trainer/Groom (Harness Racing)
Pennsylvania State Harness Racing Commission
2301 N. Cameron St.
Harrisburg, PA 17110-9408
Phone: (717)787-5196

Credential Type: License Registration. **Duration of License:** Three years. **Requirements:** Submit application, three photos, and fingerprint card. Pay fee. **Fees:** $45 registration fee. $5 duplicate license. $33 fingerprint processing fee.

6747

Trainer (Harness Racing)
Pennsylvania State Harness Racing Commission
2301 N. Cameron St.
Harrisburg, PA 17110-9408
Phone: (717)787-5196

Credential Type: License Registration. **Duration of License:** Three years. **Requirements:** Submit application, three photos, and fingerprint card. Pay fee. **Fees:** $30 registration fee. $5 duplicate license. $33 fingerprint processing fee.

6748

Trainer (Horse Racing)
Pennsylvania State Horse Racing Commission
2301 N. Cameron St., Rm. 306, 4th Fl.
Harrisburg, PA 17110-9408
Phone: (717)787-1942

Credential Type: License Registration. **Duration of License:** Three years. **Requirements:** Submit application, two photos, and fingerprint card. Pay fee. **Fees:** $45 registration fee. $2 duplicate license.

6749

Vendor Employee (Horse Racing)
Pennsylvania State Horse Racing Commission
2301 N. Cameron St., Rm. 306, 4th Fl.
Harrisburg, PA 17110-9408
Phone: (717)787-1942

Credential Type: License Registration. **Duration of License:** Three years. **Requirements:** Submit application, two photos, and fingerprint card. Pay fee. **Fees:** $15 registration fee. $2 duplicate license.

6750

Vendor (Horse Racing)
Pennsylvania State Horse Racing Commission
2301 N. Cameron St., Rm. 306, 4th Fl.
Harrisburg, PA 17110-9408
Phone: (717)787-1942

Credential Type: License Registration. **Duration of License:** Three years. **Requirements:** Submit application, two photos, and fingerprint card. Pay fee. **Fees:** $45 registration fee. $2 duplicate license.

6751

Veterinarian (Harness Racing)
Pennsylvania State Harness Racing Commission
2301 N. Cameron St.
Harrisburg, PA 17110-9408
Phone: (717)787-5196

Credential Type: License Registration. **Duration of License:** Three years. **Requirements:** Submit application, three photos, and fingerprint card. Pay fee. **Fees:** $60 registration fee. $5 duplicate license. $33 fingerprint processing fee.

6752

Veterinarian (Horse Racing)
Pennsylvania State Horse Racing Commission
2301 N. Cameron St., Rm. 306, 4th Fl.
Harrisburg, PA 17110-9408
Phone: (717)787-1942

Credential Type: License Registration. **Duration of License:** Three years. **Requirements:** Submit application, two photos, and fingerprint card. Pay fee. **Fees:** $45 registration fee. $2 duplicate license.

Rhode Island

6753

Concessionaire Employee (Racetrack)
Rhode Island Dept. of Business Regulations
Div. of Racing & Athletics
233 Richmond St., Ste. 234
Providence, RI 02903-4234
Phone: (401)277-6541

Credential Type: License Registration. **Duration of License:** Three years. **Requirements:** Submit application and fingerprint card. Pay fee. **Fees:** $5 registration fee.

6754

Kennel Employee (Racetrack)
Rhode Island Dept. of Business Regulations
Div. of Racing & Athletics
233 Richmond St., Ste. 234
Providence, RI 02903-4234
Phone: (401)277-6541

Credential Type: License Registration. **Duration of License:** Three years. **Requirements:** Submit application and fingerprint card. Pay fee. **Fees:** $5 registration fee.

6755

Lead Out (Racetrack)
Rhode Island Dept. of Business Regulations
Div. of Racing & Athletics
233 Richmond St., Ste. 234
Providence, RI 02903-4234
Phone: (401)277-6541

Credential Type: License Registration. **Duration of License:** Three years. **Requirements:** Submit application and fingerprint card. Pay fee. **Fees:** $5 registration fee.

6756

Management Employee (Racetrack)
Rhode Island Dept. of Business Regulations
Div. of Racing & Athletics
233 Richmond St., Ste. 234
Providence, RI 02903-4234
Phone: (401)277-6541

Credential Type: License Registration. **Duration of License:** Three years. **Requirements:** Submit application and fingerprint card. Pay fee. **Fees:** $5 registration fee.

6757

Owners (Racetrack)
Rhode Island Dept. of Business Regulations
Div. of Racing & Athletics
233 Richmond St., Ste. 234
Providence, RI 02903-4234
Phone: (401)277-6541

Credential Type: License Registration. **Duration of License:** Three years. **Requirements:** Submit application and fingerprint card. Pay fee. **Fees:** $75 registration fee.

6758

Pari-Mutuel Employee (Racetrack)
Rhode Island Dept. of Business Regulations
Div. of Racing & Athletics
233 Richmond St., Ste. 234
Providence, RI 02903-4234
Phone: (401)277-6541

Credential Type: License Registration. **Duration of License:** Three years. **Requirements:** Submit application and fin-

gerprint card. Pay fee. **Fees:** $5 registration fee.

6759

Trainer (Racetrack)
Rhode Island Dept. of Business Regulations
Div. of Racing & Athletics
233 Richmond St., Ste. 234
Providence, RI 02903-4234
Phone: (401)277-6541

Credential Type: License Registration. **Duration of License:** Three years. **Requirements:** Submit application and fingerprint card. Pay fee. **Fees:** $20 registration fee.

6760

Vendor Employee (Racetrack)
Rhode Island Dept. of Business Regulations
Div. of Racing & Athletics
233 Richmond St., Ste. 234
Providence, RI 02903-4234
Phone: (401)277-6541

Credential Type: License Registration. **Duration of License:** Three years. **Requirements:** Submit application and fingerprint card. Pay fee. **Fees:** $5 registration fee.

South Dakota

6761

Announcer (Horse Racing)
South Dakota Racing Commission
c/o 500 East Capitol
Pierre, SD 57501
Phone: (605)773-6050

Credential Type: License Registration. **Requirements:** Submit application and fingerprint card. Pay fee. **Fees:** $10 registration fee.

6762

Apprentice Jockey (Horse Racing)
South Dakota Racing Commission
c/o 500 East Capitol
Pierre, SD 57501
Phone: (605)773-6050

Credential Type: License Registration. **Requirements:** Submit application and fingerprint card. Pay fee. **Fees:** $25 registration fee.

6763

Assistant Starter (Horse Racing)
South Dakota Racing Commission
c/o 500 East Capitol
Pierre, SD 57501
Phone: (605)773-6050

Credential Type: License Registration. **Requirements:** Submit application and fingerprint card. Pay fee. **Fees:** $10 registration fee.

6764

Assistant Trainer (Greyhound Racing)
South Dakota Racing Commission
c/o 500 East Capitol
Pierre, SD 57501
Phone: (605)773-6050

Credential Type: License Registration. **Requirements:** Submit application and fingerprint card. Pay fee. **Fees:** $15 registration fee.

6765

Associate Judge (Greyhound Racing)
South Dakota Racing Commission
c/o 500 East Capitol
Pierre, SD 57501
Phone: (605)773-6050

Credential Type: License Registration. **Requirements:** Submit application and fingerprint card. Pay fee. **Fees:** $15 registration fee.

6766

Association Employee (Greyhound Racing)
South Dakota Racing Commission
c/o 500 East Capitol
Pierre, SD 57501
Phone: (605)773-6050

Credential Type: License Registration. **Requirements:** Submit application and fingerprint card. Pay fee. **Fees:** $10 registration fee.

6767

Authorized Agent (Greyhound Racing)
South Dakota Racing Commission
c/o 500 East Capitol
Pierre, SD 57501
Phone: (605)773-6050

Credential Type: License Registration. **Requirements:** Submit application and fingerprint card. Pay fee. **Fees:** $15 registration fee.

6768

Authorized Agent (Horse Racing)
South Dakota Racing Commission
c/o 500 East Capitol
Pierre, SD 57501
Phone: (605)773-6050

Credential Type: License Registration. **Requirements:** Submit application and fingerprint card. Pay fee. **Fees:** $15 registration fee.

6769

Bookkeeper (Horse Racing)
South Dakota Racing Commission
c/o 500 East Capitol
Pierre, SD 57501
Phone: (605)773-6050

Credential Type: License Registration. **Requirements:** Submit application and fingerprint card. Pay fee. **Fees:** $15 registration fee.

6770

Chart Writer (Greyhound Racing)
South Dakota Racing Commission
c/o 500 East Capitol
Pierre, SD 57501
Phone: (605)773-6050

Credential Type: License Registration. **Requirements:** Submit application and fingerprint card. Pay fee. **Fees:** $15 registration fee.

6771

Clerk of Scales (Greyhound Racing)
South Dakota Racing Commission
c/o 500 East Capitol
Pierre, SD 57501
Phone: (605)773-6050

Credential Type: License Registration. **Requirements:** Submit application and fin-

Clerk of Scales (Greyhound Racing), continued

gerprint card. Pay fee. **Fees:** $15 registration fee.

6772

Concession Employee (Greyhound Racing)
South Dakota Racing Commission
c/o 500 East Capitol
Pierre, SD 57501
Phone: (605)773-6050

Credential Type: License Registration.
Requirements: Submit application and fingerprint card. Pay fee. **Fees:** $7.50 registration fee.

6773

Concession Employee (Horse Racing)
South Dakota Racing Commission
c/o 500 East Capitol
Pierre, SD 57501
Phone: (605)773-6050

Credential Type: License Registration.
Requirements: Submit application and fingerprint card. Pay fee. **Fees:** $10 registration fee.

6774

Concession Operator (Horse Racing)
South Dakota Racing Commission
c/o 500 East Capitol
Pierre, SD 57501
Phone: (605)773-6050

Credential Type: License Registration.
Requirements: Submit application and fingerprint card. Pay fee. **Fees:** $10 registration fee.

6775

Entry Clerk (Horse Racing)
South Dakota Racing Commission
c/o 500 East Capitol
Pierre, SD 57501
Phone: (605)773-6050

Credential Type: License Registration.
Requirements: Submit application and fingerprint card. Pay fee. **Fees:** $10 registration fee.

6776

Exercise Rider (Horse Racing)
South Dakota Racing Commission
c/o 500 East Capitol
Pierre, SD 57501
Phone: (605)773-6050

Credential Type: License Registration.
Requirements: Submit application and fingerprint card. Pay fee. **Fees:** $10 registration fee.

6777

Gateman (Horse Racing)
South Dakota Racing Commission
c/o 500 East Capitol
Pierre, SD 57501
Phone: (605)773-6050

Credential Type: License Registration.
Requirements: Submit application and fingerprint card. Pay fee. **Fees:** $10 registration fee.

6778

Groom (Horse Racing)
South Dakota Racing Commission
c/o 500 East Capitol
Pierre, SD 57501
Phone: (605)773-6050

Credential Type: License Registration.
Requirements: Submit application and fingerprint card. Pay fee. **Fees:** $10 registration fee.

6779

Jockey Agent (Horse Racing)
South Dakota Racing Commission
c/o 500 East Capitol
Pierre, SD 57501
Phone: (605)773-6050

Credential Type: License Registration.
Requirements: Submit application and fingerprint card. Pay fee. **Fees:** $20 registration fee.

6780

Jockey (Horse Racing)
South Dakota Racing Commission
c/o 500 East Capitol
Pierre, SD 57501
Phone: (605)773-6050

Credential Type: License Registration.
Requirements: Submit application and fingerprint card. Pay fee. **Fees:** $25 registration fee.

6781

Jockey Room Custodian (Horse Racing)
South Dakota Racing Commission
c/o 500 East Capitol
Pierre, SD 57501
Phone: (605)773-6050

Credential Type: License Registration.
Requirements: Submit application and fingerprint card. Pay fee. **Fees:** $10 registration fee.

6782

Kennel Helper (Greyhound Racing)
South Dakota Racing Commission
c/o 500 East Capitol
Pierre, SD 57501
Phone: (605)773-6050

Credential Type: License Registration.
Requirements: Submit application and fingerprint card. Pay fee. **Fees:** $7.50 registration fee.

6783

Kennel Master (Greyhound Racing)
South Dakota Racing Commission
c/o 500 East Capitol
Pierre, SD 57501
Phone: (605)773-6050

Credential Type: License Registration.
Requirements: Submit application and fingerprint card. Pay fee. **Fees:** $15 registration fee.

6784

Kennel Operator (Greyhound Racing)
South Dakota Racing Commission
c/o 500 East Capitol
Pierre, SD 57501
Phone: (605)773-6050

Credential Type: License Registration.
Requirements: Submit application and fingerprint card. Pay fee. **Fees:** $15 registration fee.

6785

Kennel Owner (Greyhound Racing)
South Dakota Racing Commission
c/o 500 East Capitol
Pierre, SD 57501
Phone: (605)773-6050

Credential Type: License Registration.
Requirements: Submit application and fingerprint card. Pay fee. **Fees:** $15 registration fee.

6786

Lead Out (Greyhound Racing)
South Dakota Racing Commission
c/o 500 East Capitol
Pierre, SD 57501
Phone: (605)773-6050

Credential Type: License Registration.
Requirements: Submit application and fingerprint card. Pay fee. **Fees:** $7.50 registration fee.

6787

Lure Operator (Greyhound Racing)
South Dakota Racing Commission
c/o 500 East Capitol
Pierre, SD 57501
Phone: (605)773-6050

Credential Type: License Registration.
Requirements: Submit application and fingerprint card. Pay fee. **Fees:** $15 registration fee.

6788

Mutuel Employee (Greyhound Racing)
South Dakota Racing Commission
c/o 500 East Capitol
Pierre, SD 57501
Phone: (605)773-6050

Credential Type: License Registration.
Requirements: Submit application and fingerprint card. Pay fee. **Fees:** $10 registration fee.

6789

Mutuel Employee (Horse Racing)
South Dakota Racing Commission
c/o 500 East Capitol
Pierre, SD 57501
Phone: (605)773-6050

Credential Type: License Registration.
Requirements: Submit application and fingerprint card. Pay fee. **Fees:** $7 registration fee.

6790

Mutuel Operator (Horse Racing)
South Dakota Racing Commission
c/o 500 East Capitol
Pierre, SD 57501
Phone: (605)773-6050

Credential Type: License Registration.
Requirements: Submit application and fingerprint card. Pay fee. **Fees:** $15 registration fee.

6791

Official (Horse Racing)
South Dakota Racing Commission
c/o 500 East Capitol
Pierre, SD 57501
Phone: (605)773-6050

Credential Type: License Registration.
Requirements: Submit application and fingerprint card. Pay fee. **Fees:** $15 registration fee.

6792

Outrider (Horse Racing)
South Dakota Racing Commission
c/o 500 East Capitol
Pierre, SD 57501
Phone: (605)773-6050

Credential Type: License Registration.
Requirements: Submit application and fingerprint card. Pay fee. **Fees:** $10 registration fee.

6793

Owner (Horse Racing)
South Dakota Racing Commission
c/o 500 East Capitol
Pierre, SD 57501
Phone: (605)773-6050

Credential Type: License Registration.
Requirements: Submit application and fingerprint card. Pay fee. **Fees:** $25 registration fee.

6794

Owner/Trainer (Greyhound Racing)
South Dakota Racing Commission
c/o 500 East Capitol
Pierre, SD 57501
Phone: (605)773-6050

Credential Type: License Registration.
Requirements: Submit application and fingerprint card. Pay fee. **Fees:** $25 registration fee.

6795

Owner/Trainer (Horse Racing)
South Dakota Racing Commission
c/o 500 East Capitol
Pierre, SD 57501
Phone: (605)773-6050

Credential Type: License Registration.
Requirements: Submit application and fingerprint card. Pay fee. **Fees:** $40 registration fee.

6796

Paddock Judge (Greyhound Racing)
South Dakota Racing Commission
c/o 500 East Capitol
Pierre, SD 57501
Phone: (605)773-6050

Credential Type: License Registration.
Requirements: Submit application and fingerprint card. Pay fee. **Fees:** $15 registration fee.

6797

Parking Lot Employee (Horse Racing)
South Dakota Racing Commission
c/o 500 East Capitol
Pierre, SD 57501
Phone: (605)773-6050

Credential Type: License Registration.
Requirements: Submit application and fingerprint card. Pay fee. **Fees:** $10 registration fee.

6798

Photo Finish Employee (Horse Racing)
South Dakota Racing Commission
c/o 500 East Capitol
Pierre, SD 57501
Phone: (605)773-6050

Credential Type: License Registration.
Requirements: Submit application and fingerprint card. Pay fee. **Fees:** $15 registration fee.

6799

Photographer (Horse Racing)
South Dakota Racing Commission
c/o 500 East Capitol
Pierre, SD 57501
Phone: (605)773-6050

Credential Type: License Registration.
Requirements: Submit application and fingerprint card. Pay fee. **Fees:** $15 registration fee.

6800

Plater (Horse Racing)
South Dakota Racing Commission
c/o 500 East Capitol
Pierre, SD 57501
Phone: (605)773-6050

Credential Type: License Registration.
Requirements: Submit application and fingerprint card. Pay fee. **Fees:** $10 registration fee.

6801

Pony Rider (Horse Racing)
South Dakota Racing Commission
c/o 500 East Capitol
Pierre, SD 57501
Phone: (605)773-6050

Credential Type: License Registration.
Requirements: Submit application and fingerprint card. Pay fee. **Fees:** $10 registration fee.

6802

Presiding Judge (Greyhound Racing)
South Dakota Racing Commission
c/o 500 East Capitol
Pierre, SD 57501
Phone: (605)773-6050

Credential Type: License Registration.
Requirements: Submit application and fingerprint card. Pay fee. **Fees:** $15 registration fee.

6803

Programmer (Horse Racing)
South Dakota Racing Commission
c/o 500 East Capitol
Pierre, SD 57501
Phone: (605)773-6050

Credential Type: License Registration.
Requirements: Submit application and fingerprint card. Pay fee. **Fees:** $10 registration fee.

6804

Racing Secretary (Greyhound Racing)
South Dakota Racing Commission
c/o 500 East Capitol
Pierre, SD 57501
Phone: (605)773-6050

Credential Type: License Registration.
Requirements: Submit application and fingerprint card. Pay fee. **Fees:** $15 registration fee.

6805

Security Employee (Horse Racing)
South Dakota Racing Commission
c/o 500 East Capitol
Pierre, SD 57501
Phone: (605)773-6050

Credential Type: License Registration.
Requirements: Submit application and fingerprint card. Pay fee. **Fees:** $10 registration fee.

6806

Starter (Greyhound Racing)
South Dakota Racing Commission
c/o 500 East Capitol
Pierre, SD 57501
Phone: (605)773-6050

Credential Type: License Registration.
Requirements: Submit application and fingerprint card. Pay fee. **Fees:** $15 registration fee.

6807

Starter (Horse Racing)
South Dakota Racing Commission
c/o 500 East Capitol
Pierre, SD 57501
Phone: (605)773-6050

Credential Type: License Registration.
Requirements: Submit application and fingerprint card. Pay fee. **Fees:** $15 registration fee.

6808

Tattooer (Horse Racing)
South Dakota Racing Commission
c/o 500 East Capitol
Pierre, SD 57501
Phone: (605)773-6050

Credential Type: License Registration.
Requirements: Submit application and fingerprint card. Pay fee. **Fees:** $10 registration fee.

6809

Timer (Greyhound Racing)
South Dakota Racing Commission
c/o 500 East Capitol
Pierre, SD 57501
Phone: (605)773-6050

Credential Type: License Registration.
Requirements: Submit application and fingerprint card. Pay fee. **Fees:** $15 registration fee.

6810

Trainer (Greyhound Racing)
South Dakota Racing Commission
c/o 500 East Capitol
Pierre, SD 57501
Phone: (605)773-6050

Credential Type: License Registration.
Requirements: Submit application and fingerprint card. Pay fee. **Fees:** $15 registration fee.

6811

Trainer (Horse Racing)
South Dakota Racing Commission
c/o 500 East Capitol
Pierre, SD 57501
Phone: (605)773-6050

Credential Type: License Registration.
Requirements: Submit application and fingerprint card. Pay fee. **Fees:** $25 registration fee.

6812

True Owner (Greyhound Racing)
South Dakota Racing Commission
c/o 500 East Capitol
Pierre, SD 57501
Phone: (605)773-6050

Credential Type: License Registration.
Requirements: Submit application and fingerprint card. Pay fee. **Fees:** $15 registration fee.

6813

Valet (Horse Racing)
South Dakota Racing Commission
c/o 500 East Capitol
Pierre, SD 57501
Phone: (605)773-6050

Credential Type: License Registration.
Requirements: Submit application and fingerprint card. Pay fee. **Fees:** $10 registration fee.

6814

Veterinarian Assistant (Horse Racing)
South Dakota Racing Commission
c/o 500 East Capitol
Pierre, SD 57501
Phone: (605)773-6050

Credential Type: License Registration.
Requirements: Submit application and fingerprint card. Pay fee. **Fees:** $10 registration fee.

6815

Veterinarian (Horse Racing)
South Dakota Racing Commission
c/o 500 East Capitol
Pierre, SD 57501
Phone: (605)773-6050

Credential Type: License Registration.
Requirements: Submit application and fingerprint card. Pay fee. **Fees:** $25 registration fee.

Tennessee

6816

Assistant Trainer (Racetrack)
Tennessee State Racing Commission
500 James Robertson Pky., 2nd Fl.
Nashville, TN 37243
Phone: (615)741-1952

Credential Type: License Registration.
Requirements: Submit application and fingerprint card. Pay fee. **Fees:** $20 registration fee.

6817

Association Employee (Racetrack)
Tennessee State Racing Commission
500 James Robertson Pky., 2nd Fl.
Nashville, TN 37243
Phone: (615)741-1952

Credential Type: License Registration.
Requirements: Submit application and fingerprint card. Pay fee. **Fees:** $10 registration fee.

6818

Concession Employee (Racetrack)
Tennessee State Racing Commission
500 James Robertson Pky., 2nd Fl.
Nashville, TN 37243
Phone: (615)741-1952

Credential Type: License Registration.
Requirements: Submit application and fingerprint card. Pay fee. **Fees:** $10 registration fee.

6819

Driver/Jockey (Racetrack)
Tennessee State Racing Commission
500 James Robertson Pky., 2nd Fl.
Nashville, TN 37243
Phone: (615)741-1952

Credential Type: License Registration.
Requirements: Submit application and fingerprint card. Pay fee. **Fees:** $25 registration fee.

6820

Exercise Rider (Racetrack)
Tennessee State Racing Commission
500 James Robertson Pky., 2nd Fl.
Nashville, TN 37243
Phone: (615)741-1952

Credential Type: License Registration.
Requirements: Submit application and fingerprint card. Pay fee. **Fees:** $15 registration fee.

6821

Farrier Assistant (Racetrack)
Tennessee State Racing Commission
500 James Robertson Pky., 2nd Fl.
Nashville, TN 37243
Phone: (615)741-1952

Credential Type: License Registration.
Requirements: Submit application and fingerprint card. Pay fee. **Fees:** $10 registration fee.

6822

Farrier (Racetrack)
Tennessee State Racing Commission
500 James Robertson Pky., 2nd Fl.
Nashville, TN 37243
Phone: (615)741-1952

Credential Type: License Registration.
Requirements: Submit application and fingerprint card. Pay fee. **Fees:** $50 registration fee.

6823

Jockey Agent (Racetrack)
Tennessee State Racing Commission
500 James Robertson Pky., 2nd Fl.
Nashville, TN 37243
Phone: (615)741-1952

Credential Type: License Registration.
Requirements: Submit application and fingerprint card. Pay fee. **Fees:** $25 registration fee.

6824

Mutuel Employee (Racetrack)
Tennessee State Racing Commission
500 James Robertson Pky., 2nd Fl.
Nashville, TN 37243
Phone: (615)741-1952

Credential Type: License Registration.
Requirements: Submit application and fingerprint card. Pay fee. **Fees:** $10 registration fee.

Tennessee

6825

Official (Racetrack)
Tennessee State Racing Commission
500 James Robertson Pky., 2nd Fl.
Nashville, TN 37243
Phone: (615)741-1952

Credential Type: License Registration.
Requirements: Submit application and fingerprint card. Pay fee. **Fees:** $10 registration fee.

6826

Owner (Racetrack)
Tennessee State Racing Commission
500 James Robertson Pky., 2nd Fl.
Nashville, TN 37243
Phone: (615)741-1952

Credential Type: License Registration.
Requirements: Submit application and fingerprint card. Pay fee. **Fees:** $25 registration fee.

6827

Stable Employee (Racetrack)
Tennessee State Racing Commission
500 James Robertson Pky., 2nd Fl.
Nashville, TN 37243
Phone: (615)741-1952

Credential Type: License Registration.
Requirements: Submit application and fingerprint card. Pay fee. **Fees:** $10 registration fee.

6828

Trainer/Driver (Racetrack)
Tennessee State Racing Commission
500 James Robertson Pky., 2nd Fl.
Nashville, TN 37243
Phone: (615)741-1952

Credential Type: License Registration.
Requirements: Submit application and fingerprint card. Pay fee. **Fees:** $25 registration fee.

6829

Trainer (Racetrack)
Tennessee State Racing Commission
500 James Robertson Pky., 2nd Fl.
Nashville, TN 37243
Phone: (615)741-1952

Credential Type: License Registration.
Requirements: Submit application and fingerprint card. Pay fee. **Fees:** $25 registration fee.

6830

Vendor Employee (Racetrack)
Tennessee State Racing Commission
500 James Robertson Pky., 2nd Fl.
Nashville, TN 37243
Phone: (615)741-1952

Credential Type: License Registration.
Requirements: Submit application and fingerprint card. Pay fee. **Fees:** $10 registration fee.

6831

Vendor (Racetrack)
Tennessee State Racing Commission
500 James Robertson Pky., 2nd Fl.
Nashville, TN 37243
Phone: (615)741-1952

Credential Type: License Registration.
Requirements: Submit application and fingerprint card. Pay fee. **Fees:** $50 registration fee.

6832

Veterinarian Assistant (Racetrack)
Tennessee State Racing Commission
500 James Robertson Pky., 2nd Fl.
Nashville, TN 37243
Phone: (615)741-1952

Credential Type: License Registration.
Requirements: Submit application and fingerprint card. Pay fee. **Fees:** $10 registration fee.

6833

Veterinarian (Racetrack)
Tennessee State Racing Commission
500 James Robertson Pky., 2nd Fl.
Nashville, TN 37243
Phone: (615)741-1952

Credential Type: License Registration.
Requirements: Submit application and fingerprint card. Pay fee. **Fees:** $50 registration fee.

Texas

6834

Admission Person (Racetrack)
Texas Racing Commission
PO Box 12080
Austin, TX 78711
Phone: (512)794-8461

Credential Type: License Registration.
Requirements: Submit application and fingerprint card. Pay fee. **Fees:** $20 registration fee.

6835

Announcer (Racetrack)
Texas Racing Commission
PO Box 12080
Austin, TX 78711
Phone: (512)794-8461

Credential Type: License Registration.
Requirements: Submit application and fingerprint card. Pay fee. **Fees:** $20 registration fee.

6836

Apprentice Jockey (Racetrack)
Texas Racing Commission
PO Box 12080
Austin, TX 78711
Phone: (512)794-8461

Credential Type: License Registration.
Requirements: Submit application and fingerprint card. Pay fee. **Fees:** $65 registration fee.

6837

Assistant Starter (Racetrack)
Texas Racing Commission
PO Box 12080
Austin, TX 78711
Phone: (512)794-8461

Credential Type: License Registration.
Requirements: Submit application and fingerprint card. Pay fee. **Fees:** $20 registration fee.

6838

Assistant Trainer/Owner (Racetrack)
Texas Racing Commission
PO Box 12080
Austin, TX 78711
Phone: (512)794-8461

Credential Type: License Registration.
Requirements: Submit application and fingerprint card. Pay fee. **Fees:** $75 registration fee.

6839

Assistant Trainer (Racetrack)
Texas Racing Commission
PO Box 12080
Austin, TX 78711
Phone: (512)794-8461

Credential Type: License Registration.
Requirements: Submit application and fingerprint card. Pay fee. **Fees:** $75 registration fee.

6840

Association Employee (Racetrack)
Texas Racing Commission
PO Box 12080
Austin, TX 78711
Phone: (512)794-8461

Credential Type: License Registration.
Requirements: Submit application and fingerprint card. Pay fee. **Fees:** $20 registration fee.

6841

Association Judge (Racetrack)
Texas Racing Commission
PO Box 12080
Austin, TX 78711
Phone: (512)794-8461

Credential Type: License Registration.
Requirements: Submit application and fingerprint card. Pay fee. **Fees:** $65 registration fee.

6842

Association Office Staff Worker (Racetrack)
Texas Racing Commission
PO Box 12080
Austin, TX 78711
Phone: (512)794-8461

Credential Type: License Registration.
Requirements: Submit application and fingerprint card. Pay fee. **Fees:** $20 registration fee.

6843

Association Officer/Director (Racetrack)
Texas Racing Commission
PO Box 12080
Austin, TX 78711
Phone: (512)794-8461

Credential Type: License Registration.
Requirements: Submit application and fingerprint card. Pay fee. **Fees:** $75 registration fee.

6844

Authorized Agent (Racetrack)
Texas Racing Commission
PO Box 12080
Austin, TX 78711
Phone: (512)794-8461

Credential Type: License Registration.
Requirements: Submit application and fingerprint card. Pay fee. **Fees:** $10 registration fee.

6845

Box Person (Racetrack)
Texas Racing Commission
PO Box 12080
Austin, TX 78711
Phone: (512)794-8461

Credential Type: License Registration.
Requirements: Submit application and fingerprint card. Pay fee. **Fees:** $20 registration fee.

6846

Chaplain (Racetrack)
Texas Racing Commission
PO Box 12080
Austin, TX 78711
Phone: (512)794-8461

Credential Type: License Registration.
Requirements: Submit application and fingerprint card. Pay fee. **Fees:** $20 registration fee.

6847

Chart Writer (Racetrack)
Texas Racing Commission
PO Box 12080
Austin, TX 78711
Phone: (512)794-8461

Credential Type: License Registration.
Requirements: Submit application and fingerprint card. Pay fee. **Fees:** $20 registration fee.

6848

Concessionaire Employee (Racetrack)
Texas Racing Commission
PO Box 12080
Austin, TX 78711
Phone: (512)794-8461

Credential Type: License Registration.
Requirements: Submit application and fingerprint card. Pay fee. **Fees:** $20 registration fee.

6849

Concessionaire (Racetrack)
Texas Racing Commission
PO Box 12080
Austin, TX 78711
Phone: (512)794-8461

Credential Type: License Registration.
Requirements: Submit application and fingerprint card. Pay fee. **Fees:** $75 registration fee.

6850

Cool Out (Racetrack)
Texas Racing Commission
PO Box 12080
Austin, TX 78711
Phone: (512)794-8461

Credential Type: License Registration.
Requirements: Submit application and fingerprint card. Pay fee. **Fees:** $20 registration fee.

6851

Entry Clerk (Racetrack)
Texas Racing Commission
PO Box 12080
Austin, TX 78711
Phone: (512)794-8461

Credential Type: License Registration.
Requirements: Submit application and fingerprint card. Pay fee. **Fees:** $20 registration fee.

6852

Exercise Rider (Racetrack)
Texas Racing Commission
PO Box 12080
Austin, TX 78711
Phone: (512)794-8461

Credential Type: License Registration.
Requirements: Submit application and fin-

Texas 6853

Exercise Rider (Racetrack), continued

gerprint card. Pay fee. **Fees:** $20 registration fee.

6853

Farrier/Plater/Blacksmith (Racetrack)
Texas Racing Commission
PO Box 12080
Austin, TX 78711
Phone: (512)794-8461

Credential Type: License Registration.
Requirements: Submit application and fingerprint card. Pay fee. **Fees:** $65 registration fee.

6854

Food Service Employee (Racetrack)
Texas Racing Commission
PO Box 12080
Austin, TX 78711
Phone: (512)794-8461

Credential Type: License Registration.
Requirements: Submit application and fingerprint card. Pay fee. **Fees:** $20 registration fee.

6855

Groom (Racetrack)
Texas Racing Commission
PO Box 12080
Austin, TX 78711
Phone: (512)794-8461

Credential Type: License Registration.
Requirements: Submit application and fingerprint card. Pay fee. **Fees:** $20 registration fee.

6856

Horse Owner (Racetrack)
Texas Racing Commission
PO Box 12080
Austin, TX 78711
Phone: (512)794-8461

Credential Type: License Registration.
Requirements: Submit application and fingerprint card. Pay fee. **Fees:** $75 registration fee.

6857

Jockey Agent (Racetrack)
Texas Racing Commission
PO Box 12080
Austin, TX 78711
Phone: (512)794-8461

Credential Type: License Registration.
Requirements: Submit application and fingerprint card. Pay fee. **Fees:** $75 registration fee.

6858

Jockey (Racetrack)
Texas Racing Commission
PO Box 12080
Austin, TX 78711
Phone: (512)794-8461

Credential Type: License Registration.
Requirements: Submit application and fingerprint card. Pay fee. **Fees:** $75 registration fee.

6859

Kennel Helper (Racetrack)
Texas Racing Commission
PO Box 12080
Austin, TX 78711
Phone: (512)794-8461

Credential Type: License Registration.
Requirements: Submit application and fingerprint card. Pay fee. **Fees:** $20 registration fee.

6860

Kennel Owner (Racetrack)
Texas Racing Commission
PO Box 12080
Austin, TX 78711
Phone: (512)794-8461

Credential Type: License Registration.
Requirements: Submit application and fingerprint card. Pay fee. **Fees:** $75 registration fee.

6861

Kennel Owner/Trainer (Racetrack)
Texas Racing Commission
PO Box 12080
Austin, TX 78711
Phone: (512)794-8461

Credential Type: License Registration.
Requirements: Submit application and fingerprint card. Pay fee. **Fees:** $75 registration fee.

6862

Lead Out (Racetrack)
Texas Racing Commission
PO Box 12080
Austin, TX 78711
Phone: (512)794-8461

Credential Type: License Registration.
Requirements: Submit application and fingerprint card. Pay fee. **Fees:** $20 registration fee.

6863

Maintenance Employee (Racetrack)
Texas Racing Commission
PO Box 12080
Austin, TX 78711
Phone: (512)794-8461

Credential Type: License Registration.
Requirements: Submit application and fingerprint card. Pay fee. **Fees:** $20 registration fee.

6864

Medical Staff Employee (Racetrack)
Texas Racing Commission
PO Box 12080
Austin, TX 78711
Phone: (512)794-8461

Credential Type: License Registration.
Requirements: Submit application and fingerprint card. Pay fee. **Fees:** $20 registration fee.

6865

Mutuel Clerk (Racetrack)
Texas Racing Commission
PO Box 12080
Austin, TX 78711
Phone: (512)794-8461

Credential Type: License Registration.
Requirements: Submit application and fingerprint card. Pay fee. **Fees:** $20 registration fee.

6866

Mutuel Employee (Racetrack)
Texas Racing Commission
PO Box 12080
Austin, TX 78711
Phone: (512)794-8461

Credential Type: License Registration.
Requirements: Submit application and fin-

Racetrack Occupations

gerprint card. Pay fee. **Fees:** $20 registration fee.

6867

Official (Racetrack)
Texas Racing Commission
PO Box 12080
Austin, TX 78711
Phone: (512)794-8461

Credential Type: License Registration.
Requirements: Submit application and fingerprint card. Pay fee. **Fees:** $75 registration fee.

6868

Outrider (Racetrack)
Texas Racing Commission
PO Box 12080
Austin, TX 78711
Phone: (512)794-8461

Credential Type: License Registration.
Requirements: Submit application and fingerprint card. Pay fee. **Fees:** $20 registration fee.

6869

Parking Attendant (Racetrack)
Texas Racing Commission
PO Box 12080
Austin, TX 78711
Phone: (512)794-8461

Credential Type: License Registration.
Requirements: Submit application and fingerprint card. Pay fee. **Fees:** $20 registration fee.

6870

Pony Person (Racetrack)
Texas Racing Commission
PO Box 12080
Austin, TX 78711
Phone: (512)794-8461

Credential Type: License Registration.
Requirements: Submit application and fingerprint card. Pay fee. **Fees:** $20 registration fee.

6871

Security Officer (Racetrack)
Texas Racing Commission
PO Box 12080
Austin, TX 78711
Phone: (512)794-8461

Credential Type: License Registration.
Requirements: Submit application and fingerprint card. Pay fee. **Fees:** $20 registration fee.

6872

Stable Foreman (Racetrack)
Texas Racing Commission
PO Box 12080
Austin, TX 78711
Phone: (512)794-8461

Credential Type: License Registration.
Requirements: Submit application and fingerprint card. Pay fee. **Fees:** $50 registration fee.

6873

Tattooer (Racetrack)
Texas Racing Commission
PO Box 12080
Austin, TX 78711
Phone: (512)794-8461

Credential Type: License Registration.
Requirements: Submit application and fingerprint card. Pay fee. **Fees:** $75 registration fee.

6874

Test Technician (Racetrack)
Texas Racing Commission
PO Box 12080
Austin, TX 78711
Phone: (512)794-8461

Credential Type: License Registration.
Requirements: Submit application and fingerprint card. Pay fee. **Fees:** $20 registration fee.

6875

Tooth Floater (Racetrack)
Texas Racing Commission
PO Box 12080
Austin, TX 78711
Phone: (512)794-8461

Credential Type: License Registration.
Requirements: Submit application and fingerprint card. Pay fee. **Fees:** $75 registration fee.

6876

Tote Technician (Racetrack)
Texas Racing Commission
PO Box 12080
Austin, TX 78711
Phone: (512)794-8461

Credential Type: License Registration.
Requirements: Submit application and fingerprint card. Pay fee. **Fees:** $20 registration fee.

6877

Trainer (Racetrack)
Texas Racing Commission
PO Box 12080
Austin, TX 78711
Phone: (512)794-8461

Credential Type: License Registration.
Requirements: Submit application and fingerprint card. Pay fee. **Fees:** $75 registration fee.

6878

Valet (Racetrack)
Texas Racing Commission
PO Box 12080
Austin, TX 78711
Phone: (512)794-8461

Credential Type: License Registration.
Requirements: Submit application and fingerprint card. Pay fee. **Fees:** $20 registration fee.

6879

Vendor Employee (Racetrack)
Texas Racing Commission
PO Box 12080
Austin, TX 78711
Phone: (512)794-8461

Credential Type: License Registration.
Requirements: Submit application and fingerprint card. Pay fee. **Fees:** $20 registration fee.

6880

Vendor (Racetrack)
Texas Racing Commission
PO Box 12080
Austin, TX 78711
Phone: (512)794-8461

Credential Type: License Registration.
Requirements: Submit application and fingerprint card. Pay fee. **Fees:** $75 registration fee.

Texas

6881

Veterinarian Assistant (Racetrack)
Texas Racing Commission
PO Box 12080
Austin, TX 78711
Phone: (512)794-8461

Credential Type: License Registration.
Requirements: Submit application and fingerprint card. Pay fee. **Fees:** $20 registration fee.

6882

Veterinarian (Racetrack)
Texas Racing Commission
PO Box 12080
Austin, TX 78711
Phone: (512)794-8461

Credential Type: License Registration.
Requirements: Submit application and fingerprint card. Pay fee. **Fees:** $75 registration fee.

Vermont

6883

Assistant Trainer (Greyhound Racing)
Vermont Racing Commission
State Office Bldg.
Montpelier, VT 05602
Phone: (802)828-3429

Credential Type: License Registration.
Requirements: Submit application and fingerprint card. Pay fee. **Fees:** $20 registration fee. $5 duplicate license.

6884

Association Official (Greyhound Racing)
Vermont Racing Commission
State Office Bldg.
Montpelier, VT 05602
Phone: (802)828-3429

Credential Type: License Registration.
Requirements: Submit application and fingerprint card. Pay fee. **Fees:** $20 registration fee. $5 duplicate license.

6885

Authorized Agent (Greyhound Racing)
Vermont Racing Commission
State Office Bldg.
Montpelier, VT 05602
Phone: (802)828-3429

Credential Type: License Registration.
Requirements: Submit application and fingerprint card. Pay fee. **Fees:** $20 registration fee. $5 duplicate license.

6886

Authorized Agent (Racetrack)
Vermont Racing Commission
State Office Bldg.
Montpelier, VT 05602
Phone: (802)828-3429

Credential Type: License Registration.
Requirements: Submit application and fingerprint card. Pay fee. **Fees:** $5 registration fee. $2 duplicate license.

6887

Blacksmith (Racetrack)
Vermont Racing Commission
State Office Bldg.
Montpelier, VT 05602
Phone: (802)828-3429

Credential Type: License Registration.
Requirements: Submit application and fingerprint card. Pay fee. **Fees:** $2 registration fee. $2 duplicate license.

6888

Chart Writer (Greyhound Racing)
Vermont Racing Commission
State Office Bldg.
Montpelier, VT 05602
Phone: (802)828-3429

Credential Type: License Registration.
Requirements: Submit application and fingerprint card. Pay fee. **Fees:** $20 registration fee. $5 duplicate license.

6889

Clerk of Scales (Greyhound Racing)
Vermont Racing Commission
State Office Bldg.
Montpelier, VT 05602
Phone: (802)828-3429

Credential Type: License Registration.
Requirements: Submit application and fingerprint card. Pay fee. **Fees:** $20 registration fee. $5 duplicate license.

6890

Concession Employee (Greyhound Racing)
Vermont Racing Commission
State Office Bldg.
Montpelier, VT 05602
Phone: (802)828-3429

Credential Type: License Registration.
Requirements: Submit application and fingerprint card. Pay fee. **Fees:** $5 registration fee. $5 duplicate license.

6891

Concession Employee (Racetrack)
Vermont Racing Commission
State Office Bldg.
Montpelier, VT 05602
Phone: (802)828-3429

Credential Type: License Registration.
Requirements: Submit application and fingerprint card. Pay fee. **Fees:** $2 registration fee. $2 duplicate license.

6892

Director of Racing (Greyhound Racing)
Vermont Racing Commission
State Office Bldg.
Montpelier, VT 05602
Phone: (802)828-3429

Credential Type: License Registration.
Requirements: Submit application and fingerprint card. Pay fee. **Fees:** $20 registration fee. $5 duplicate license.

6893

Exercise Boy (Racetrack)
Vermont Racing Commission
State Office Bldg.
Montpelier, VT 05602
Phone: (802)828-3429

Credential Type: License Registration.
Requirements: Submit application and fingerprint card. Pay fee. **Fees:** $2 registration fee. $2 duplicate license.

Racetrack Occupations — Vermont

6894

Foreman (Racetrack)
Vermont Racing Commission
State Office Bldg.
Montpelier, VT 05602
Phone: (802)828-3429

Credential Type: License Registration.
Requirements: Submit application and fingerprint card. Pay fee. **Fees:** $2 registration fee. $2 duplicate license.

6895

Groom (Racetrack)
Vermont Racing Commission
State Office Bldg.
Montpelier, VT 05602
Phone: (802)828-3429

Credential Type: License Registration.
Requirements: Submit application and fingerprint card. Pay fee. **Fees:** $2 registration fee. $2 duplicate license.

6896

Hot Walker (Racetrack)
Vermont Racing Commission
State Office Bldg.
Montpelier, VT 05602
Phone: (802)828-3429

Credential Type: License Registration.
Requirements: Submit application and fingerprint card. Pay fee. **Fees:** $2 registration fee. $2 duplicate license.

6897

Jockey Agent (Racetrack)
Vermont Racing Commission
State Office Bldg.
Montpelier, VT 05602
Phone: (802)828-3429

Credential Type: License Registration.
Requirements: Submit application and fingerprint card. Pay fee. **Fees:** $5 registration fee. $2 duplicate license.

6898

Jockey Apprentice (Racetrack)
Vermont Racing Commission
State Office Bldg.
Montpelier, VT 05602
Phone: (802)828-3429

Credential Type: License Registration.
Requirements: Submit application and fingerprint card. Pay fee. **Fees:** $5 registration fee. $2 duplicate license.

6899

Jockey (Racetrack)
Vermont Racing Commission
State Office Bldg.
Montpelier, VT 05602
Phone: (802)828-3429

Credential Type: License Registration.
Requirements: Submit application and fingerprint card. Pay fee. **Fees:** $5 registration fee. $2 duplicate license.

6900

Judge (Greyhound Racing)
Vermont Racing Commission
State Office Bldg.
Montpelier, VT 05602
Phone: (802)828-3429

Credential Type: License Registration.
Requirements: Submit application and fingerprint card. Pay fee. **Fees:** $20 registration fee. $5 duplicate license.

6901

Kennel Helper (Greyhound Racing)
Vermont Racing Commission
State Office Bldg.
Montpelier, VT 05602
Phone: (802)828-3429

Credential Type: License Registration.
Requirements: Submit application and fingerprint card. Pay fee. **Fees:** $5 registration fee. $5 duplicate license.

6902

Kennel Master (Greyhound Racing)
Vermont Racing Commission
State Office Bldg.
Montpelier, VT 05602
Phone: (802)828-3429

Credential Type: License Registration.
Requirements: Submit application and fingerprint card. Pay fee. **Fees:** $20 registration fee. $5 duplicate license.

6903

Official (Racetrack)
Vermont Racing Commission
State Office Bldg.
Montpelier, VT 05602
Phone: (802)828-3429

Credential Type: License Registration.
Requirements: Submit application and fingerprint card. Pay fee. **Fees:** $5 registration fee. $2 duplicate license.

6904

Operator of Mechanical Lure (Greyhound Racing)
Vermont Racing Commission
State Office Bldg.
Montpelier, VT 05602
Phone: (802)828-3429

Credential Type: License Registration.
Requirements: Submit application and fingerprint card. Pay fee. **Fees:** $20 registration fee. $5 duplicate license.

6905

Outrider (Racetrack)
Vermont Racing Commission
State Office Bldg.
Montpelier, VT 05602
Phone: (802)828-3429

Credential Type: License Registration.
Requirements: Submit application and fingerprint card. Pay fee. **Fees:** $20 registration fee. $2 duplicate license.

6906

Owner (Greyhound Racing)
Vermont Racing Commission
State Office Bldg.
Montpelier, VT 05602
Phone: (802)828-3429

Credential Type: License Registration.
Requirements: Submit application and fingerprint card. Pay fee. **Fees:** $20 registration fee. $5 duplicate license.

6907

Owner (Harness Racing)
Vermont Racing Commission
State Office Bldg.
Montpelier, VT 05602
Phone: (802)828-3429

Credential Type: License Registration.
Requirements: Submit application and fingerprint card. Pay fee. **Fees:** $5 registration fee. $2 duplicate license.

6908

Paddock Judge (Greyhound Racing)
Vermont Racing Commission
State Office Bldg.
Montpelier, VT 05602
Phone: (802)828-3429

Credential Type: License Registration.
Requirements: Submit application and fingerprint card. Pay fee. **Fees:** $20 registration fee. $5 duplicate license.

6909

Pari-Mutuel Employee (Greyhound Racing)
Vermont Racing Commission
State Office Bldg.
Montpelier, VT 05602
Phone: (802)828-3429

Credential Type: License Registration.
Requirements: Submit application and fingerprint card. Pay fee. **Fees:** $10 registration fee. $5 duplicate license.

6910

Pari-Mutuel Employee (Racetrack)
Vermont Racing Commission
State Office Bldg.
Montpelier, VT 05602
Phone: (802)828-3429

Credential Type: License Registration.
Requirements: Submit application and fingerprint card. Pay fee. **Fees:** $5 registration fee. $2 duplicate license.

6911

Patrol Judge (Greyhound Racing)
Vermont Racing Commission
State Office Bldg.
Montpelier, VT 05602
Phone: (802)828-3429

Credential Type: License Registration.
Requirements: Submit application and fingerprint card. Pay fee. **Fees:** $20 registration fee. $5 duplicate license.

6912

Pony Boy (Racetrack)
Vermont Racing Commission
State Office Bldg.
Montpelier, VT 05602
Phone: (802)828-3429

Credential Type: License Registration.
Requirements: Submit application and fingerprint card. Pay fee. **Fees:** $2 registration fee. $2 duplicate license.

6913

Racing Secretary (Greyhound Racing)
Vermont Racing Commission
State Office Bldg.
Montpelier, VT 05602
Phone: (802)828-3429

Credential Type: License Registration.
Requirements: Submit application and fingerprint card. Pay fee. **Fees:** $20 registration fee. $5 duplicate license.

6914

Starter (Greyhound Racing)
Vermont Racing Commission
State Office Bldg.
Montpelier, VT 05602
Phone: (802)828-3429

Credential Type: License Registration.
Requirements: Submit application and fingerprint card. Pay fee. **Fees:** $20 registration fee. $5 duplicate license.

6915

Supplier (Racetrack)
Vermont Racing Commission
State Office Bldg.
Montpelier, VT 05602
Phone: (802)828-3429

Credential Type: License Registration.
Requirements: Submit application and fingerprint card. Pay fee. **Fees:** $2 registration fee. $2 duplicate license.

6916

Timer (Greyhound Racing)
Vermont Racing Commission
State Office Bldg.
Montpelier, VT 05602
Phone: (802)828-3429

Credential Type: License Registration.
Requirements: Submit application and fingerprint card. Pay fee. **Fees:** $20 registration fee. $5 duplicate license.

6917

Track Service Employee (Racetrack)
Vermont Racing Commission
State Office Bldg.
Montpelier, VT 05602
Phone: (802)828-3429

Credential Type: License Registration.
Requirements: Submit application and fingerprint card. Pay fee. **Fees:** $2 registration fee. $2 duplicate license.

6918

Trainer/Driver (Harness Racing)
Vermont Racing Commission
State Office Bldg.
Montpelier, VT 05602
Phone: (802)828-3429

Credential Type: License Registration.
Requirements: Submit application and fingerprint card. Pay fee. **Fees:** $5 registration fee. $2 duplicate license.

6919

Trainer (Greyhound Racing)
Vermont Racing Commission
State Office Bldg.
Montpelier, VT 05602
Phone: (802)828-3429

Credential Type: License Registration.
Requirements: Submit application and fingerprint card. Pay fee. **Fees:** $20 registration fee. $5 duplicate license.

6920

Trainer (Thoroughbred Racing)
Vermont Racing Commission
State Office Bldg.
Montpelier, VT 05602
Phone: (802)828-3429

Credential Type: License Registration.
Requirements: Submit application and fingerprint card. Pay fee. **Fees:** $5 registration fee. $2 duplicate license.

6921

Valet (Racetrack)
Vermont Racing Commission
State Office Bldg.
Montpelier, VT 05602
Phone: (802)828-3429

Credential Type: License Registration.
Requirements: Submit application and fin-

gerprint card. Pay fee. **Fees:** $2 registration fee. $2 duplicate license.

6922

Vendor (Racetrack)
Vermont Racing Commission
State Office Bldg.
Montpelier, VT 05602
Phone: (802)828-3429

Credential Type: License Registration.
Requirements: Submit application and fingerprint card. Pay fee. **Fees:** $2 registration fee. $2 duplicate license.

6923

Veterinarian (Greyhound Racing)
Vermont Racing Commission
State Office Bldg.
Montpelier, VT 05602
Phone: (802)828-3429

Credential Type: License Registration.
Requirements: Submit application and fingerprint card. Pay fee. **Fees:** $20 registration fee. $5 duplicate license.

6924

Veterinarian (Racetrack)
Vermont Racing Commission
State Office Bldg.
Montpelier, VT 05602
Phone: (802)828-3429

Credential Type: License Registration.
Requirements: Submit application and fingerprint card. Pay fee. **Fees:** $5 registration fee. $2 duplicate license.

Virginia

6925

Administrative Employee (Racetrack)
Virginia Racing Commission
PO Box 1123
Richmond, VA 23208
Phone: (804)371-7363

Credential Type: License Registration.
Requirements: Submit application and fingerprint card. Pay fee. **Fees:** $10 registration fee.

6926

Apprentice Jockey (Racetrack)
Virginia Racing Commission
PO Box 1123
Richmond, VA 23208
Phone: (804)371-7363

Credential Type: License Registration.
Requirements: Submit application and fingerprint card. Pay fee. **Fees:** $10 registration fee.

6927

Assistant General Manager (Racetrack)
Virginia Racing Commission
PO Box 1123
Richmond, VA 23208
Phone: (804)371-7363

Credential Type: License Registration.
Requirements: Submit application and fingerprint card. Pay fee. **Fees:** $10 registration fee.

6928

Assistant Racing Secretary (Racetrack)
Virginia Racing Commission
PO Box 1123
Richmond, VA 23208
Phone: (804)371-7363

Credential Type: License Registration.
Requirements: Submit application and fingerprint card. Pay fee. **Fees:** $10 registration fee.

6929

Assistant Starter (Racetrack)
Virginia Racing Commission
PO Box 1123
Richmond, VA 23208
Phone: (804)371-7363

Credential Type: License Registration.
Requirements: Submit application and fingerprint card. Pay fee. **Fees:** $5 registration fee.

6930

Assistant Trainer (Racetrack)
Virginia Racing Commission
PO Box 1123
Richmond, VA 23208
Phone: (804)371-7363

Credential Type: License Registration.
Requirements: Submit application and fingerprint card. Pay fee. **Fees:** $10 registration fee.

6931

Authorized Agent (Racetrack)
Virginia Racing Commission
PO Box 1123
Richmond, VA 23208
Phone: (804)371-7363

Credential Type: License Registration.
Requirements: Submit application and fingerprint card. Pay fee. **Fees:** $10 registration fee.

6932

Bloodstock Agent (Racetrack)
Virginia Racing Commission
PO Box 1123
Richmond, VA 23208
Phone: (804)371-7363

Credential Type: License Registration.
Requirements: Submit application and fingerprint card. Pay fee. **Fees:** $10 registration fee.

6933

Claims Clerk (Racetrack)
Virginia Racing Commission
PO Box 1123
Richmond, VA 23208
Phone: (804)371-7363

Credential Type: License Registration.
Requirements: Submit application and fingerprint card. Pay fee. **Fees:** $10 registration fee.

6934

Clerk of Course (Racetrack)
Virginia Racing Commission
PO Box 1123
Richmond, VA 23208
Phone: (804)371-7363

Credential Type: License Registration.
Requirements: Submit application and fingerprint card. Pay fee. **Fees:** $10 registration fee.

6935

Clerk of Scales (Racetrack)
Virginia Racing Commission
PO Box 1123
Richmond, VA 23208
Phone: (804)371-7363

Credential Type: License Registration.
Requirements: Submit application and fingerprint card. Pay fee. **Fees:** $10 registration fee.

6936

Clocker (Racetrack)
Virginia Racing Commission
PO Box 1123
Richmond, VA 23208
Phone: (804)371-7363

Credential Type: License Registration.
Requirements: Submit application and fingerprint card. Pay fee. **Fees:** $10 registration fee.

6937

Concessionaire/Vendor Employee (Racetrack)
Virginia Racing Commission
PO Box 1123
Richmond, VA 23208
Phone: (804)371-7363

Credential Type: License Registration.
Requirements: Submit application and fingerprint card. Pay fee. **Fees:** $5 registration fee.

6938

Concessionaire/Vendor (Racetrack)
Virginia Racing Commission
PO Box 1123
Richmond, VA 23208
Phone: (804)371-7363

Credential Type: License Registration.
Requirements: Submit application and fingerprint card. Pay fee. **Fees:** $25 registration fee.

6939

Director of Security (Racetrack)
Virginia Racing Commission
PO Box 1123
Richmond, VA 23208
Phone: (804)371-7363

Credential Type: License Registration.
Requirements: Submit application and fingerprint card. Pay fee. **Fees:** $10 registration fee.

6940

Driver (Racetrack)
Virginia Racing Commission
PO Box 1123
Richmond, VA 23208
Phone: (804)371-7363

Credential Type: License Registration.
Requirements: Submit application and fingerprint card. Pay fee. **Fees:** $10 registration fee.

6941

Entry Clerk (Racetrack)
Virginia Racing Commission
PO Box 1123
Richmond, VA 23208
Phone: (804)371-7363

Credential Type: License Registration.
Requirements: Submit application and fingerprint card. Pay fee. **Fees:** $10 registration fee.

6942

Exercise Rider (Racetrack)
Virginia Racing Commission
PO Box 1123
Richmond, VA 23208
Phone: (804)371-7363

Credential Type: License Registration.
Requirements: Submit application and fingerprint card. Pay fee. **Fees:** $10 registration fee.

6943

Farrier (Racetrack)
Virginia Racing Commission
PO Box 1123
Richmond, VA 23208
Phone: (804)371-7363

Credential Type: License Registration.
Requirements: Submit application and fingerprint card. Pay fee. **Fees:** $10 registration fee.

6944

Foreman (Racetrack)
Virginia Racing Commission
PO Box 1123
Richmond, VA 23208
Phone: (804)371-7363

Credential Type: License Registration.
Requirements: Submit application and fingerprint card. Pay fee. **Fees:** $10 registration fee.

6945

Gap Attendant (Racetrack)
Virginia Racing Commission
PO Box 1123
Richmond, VA 23208
Phone: (804)371-7363

Credential Type: License Registration.
Requirements: Submit application and fingerprint card. Pay fee. **Fees:** $10 registration fee.

6946

General Manager (Racetrack)
Virginia Racing Commission
PO Box 1123
Richmond, VA 23208
Phone: (804)371-7363

Credential Type: License Registration.
Requirements: Submit application and fingerprint card. Pay fee. **Fees:** $10 registration fee.

6947

Groom/Hotwalker (Racetrack)
Virginia Racing Commission
PO Box 1123
Richmond, VA 23208
Phone: (804)371-7363

Credential Type: License Registration.
Requirements: Submit application and fingerprint card. Pay fee. **Fees:** $5 registration fee.

6948

Horse Identifier (Racetrack)
Virginia Racing Commission
PO Box 1123
Richmond, VA 23208
Phone: (804)371-7363

Credential Type: License Registration.
Requirements: Submit application and fingerprint card. Pay fee. **Fees:** $10 registration fee.

6949

Horse Owner (Racetrack)
Virginia Racing Commission
PO Box 1123
Richmond, VA 23208
Phone: (804)371-7363

Credential Type: License Registration.
Requirements: Submit application and fingerprint card. Pay fee. **Fees:** $10 registration fee.

6950

Horsemen's Bookkeeper (Racetrack)
Virginia Racing Commission
PO Box 1123
Richmond, VA 23208
Phone: (804)371-7363

Credential Type: License Registration.
Requirements: Submit application and fingerprint card. Pay fee. **Fees:** $10 registration fee.

6951

Jockey Agent (Racetrack)
Virginia Racing Commission
PO Box 1123
Richmond, VA 23208
Phone: (804)371-7363

Credential Type: License Registration.
Requirements: Submit application and fingerprint card. Pay fee. **Fees:** $10 registration fee.

6952

Jockey (Racetrack)
Virginia Racing Commission
PO Box 1123
Richmond, VA 23208
Phone: (804)371-7363

Credential Type: License Registration.
Requirements: Submit application and fingerprint card. Pay fee. **Fees:** $10 registration fee.

6953

Jockey Room Custodian (Racetrack)
Virginia Racing Commission
PO Box 1123
Richmond, VA 23208
Phone: (804)371-7363

Credential Type: License Registration.
Requirements: Submit application and fingerprint card. Pay fee. **Fees:** $10 registration fee.

6954

Marketing Employee (Racetrack)
Virginia Racing Commission
PO Box 1123
Richmond, VA 23208
Phone: (804)371-7363

Credential Type: License Registration.
Requirements: Submit application and fingerprint card. Pay fee. **Fees:** $10 registration fee.

6955

Medical Employee (Racetrack)
Virginia Racing Commission
PO Box 1123
Richmond, VA 23208
Phone: (804)371-7363

Credential Type: License Registration.
Requirements: Submit application and fingerprint card. Pay fee. **Fees:** $10 registration fee.

6956

Mutuel Clerk (Racetrack)
Virginia Racing Commission
PO Box 1123
Richmond, VA 23208
Phone: (804)371-7363

Credential Type: License Registration.
Requirements: Submit application and fingerprint card. Pay fee. **Fees:** $10 registration fee.

6957

Mutuel Manager (Racetrack)
Virginia Racing Commission
PO Box 1123
Richmond, VA 23208
Phone: (804)371-7363

Credential Type: License Registration.
Requirements: Submit application and fingerprint card. Pay fee. **Fees:** $10 registration fee.

6958

Nightwatchman (Racetrack)
Virginia Racing Commission
PO Box 1123
Richmond, VA 23208
Phone: (804)371-7363

Credential Type: License Registration.
Requirements: Submit application and fingerprint card. Pay fee. **Fees:** $10 registration fee.

6959

Operations Employee (Racetrack)
Virginia Racing Commission
PO Box 1123
Richmond, VA 23208
Phone: (804)371-7363

Credential Type: License Registration.
Requirements: Submit application and fingerprint card. Pay fee. **Fees:** $10 registration fee.

6960

Outrider (Racetrack)
Virginia Racing Commission
PO Box 1123
Richmond, VA 23208
Phone: (804)371-7363

Credential Type: License Registration.
Requirements: Submit application and fingerprint card. Pay fee. **Fees:** $10 registration fee.

6961

Paddock Judge (Racetrack)
Virginia Racing Commission
PO Box 1123
Richmond, VA 23208
Phone: (804)371-7363

Credential Type: License Registration.
Requirements: Submit application and fingerprint card. Pay fee. **Fees:** $10 registration fee.

6962

Patrol Judge (Racetrack)
Virginia Racing Commission
PO Box 1123
Richmond, VA 23208
Phone: (804)371-7363

Credential Type: License Registration.
Requirements: Submit application and fingerprint card. Pay fee. **Fees:** $10 registration fee.

6963

Pharmaceutical Representative (Racetrack)
Virginia Racing Commission
PO Box 1123
Richmond, VA 23208
Phone: (804)371-7363

Credential Type: License Registration.
Requirements: Submit application and fingerprint card. Pay fee. **Fees:** $25 registration fee.

6964

Photo-Finish Camera Operator (Racetrack)
Virginia Racing Commission
PO Box 1123
Richmond, VA 23208
Phone: (804)371-7363

Credential Type: License Registration.
Requirements: Submit application and fingerprint card. Pay fee. **Fees:** $10 registration fee.

6965

Placing Judge (Racetrack)
Virginia Racing Commission
PO Box 1123
Richmond, VA 23208
Phone: (804)371-7363

Credential Type: License Registration.
Requirements: Submit application and fingerprint card. Pay fee. **Fees:** $10 registration fee.

6966

Plant Employee (Racetrack)
Virginia Racing Commission
PO Box 1123
Richmond, VA 23208
Phone: (804)371-7363

Credential Type: License Registration.
Requirements: Submit application and fingerprint card. Pay fee. **Fees:** $10 registration fee.

6967

Pony Rider (Racetrack)
Virginia Racing Commission
PO Box 1123
Richmond, VA 23208
Phone: (804)371-7363

Credential Type: License Registration.
Requirements: Submit application and fingerprint card. Pay fee. **Fees:** $10 registration fee.

6968

Program Director (Racetrack)
Virginia Racing Commission
PO Box 1123
Richmond, VA 23208
Phone: (804)371-7363

Credential Type: License Registration.
Requirements: Submit application and fingerprint card. Pay fee. **Fees:** $10 registration fee.

6969

Racing Secretary (Racetrack)
Virginia Racing Commission
PO Box 1123
Richmond, VA 23208
Phone: (804)371-7363

Credential Type: License Registration.
Requirements: Submit application and fingerprint card. Pay fee. **Fees:** $10 registration fee.

6970

Security Officer (Racetrack)
Virginia Racing Commission
PO Box 1123
Richmond, VA 23208
Phone: (804)371-7363

Credential Type: License Registration.
Requirements: Submit application and fingerprint card. Pay fee. **Fees:** $10 registration fee.

6971

Staff Employee (Racetrack)
Virginia Racing Commission
PO Box 1123
Richmond, VA 23208
Phone: (804)371-7363

Credential Type: License Registration.
Requirements: Submit application and fingerprint card. Pay fee. **Fees:** $10 registration fee.

6972

Stall Superintendent (Racetrack)
Virginia Racing Commission
PO Box 1123
Richmond, VA 23208
Phone: (804)371-7363

Credential Type: License Registration.
Requirements: Submit application and fingerprint card. Pay fee. **Fees:** $10 registration fee.

6973

Starter (Racetrack)
Virginia Racing Commission
PO Box 1123
Richmond, VA 23208
Phone: (804)371-7363

Credential Type: License Registration.
Requirements: Submit application and fingerprint card. Pay fee. **Fees:** $10 registration fee.

6974

Timer (Racetrack)
Virginia Racing Commission
PO Box 1123
Richmond, VA 23208
Phone: (804)371-7363

Credential Type: License Registration.
Requirements: Submit application and fingerprint card. Pay fee. **Fees:** $10 registration fee.

6975

Track Superintendent (Racetrack)
Virginia Racing Commission
PO Box 1123
Richmond, VA 23208
Phone: (804)371-7363

Credential Type: License Registration.
Requirements: Submit application and fingerprint card. Pay fee. **Fees:** $10 registration fee.

6976

Trainer (Racetrack)
Virginia Racing Commission
PO Box 1123
Richmond, VA 23208
Phone: (804)371-7363

Credential Type: License Registration.
Requirements: Submit application and fingerprint card. Pay fee. **Fees:** $10 registration fee.

6977

Valet (Racetrack)
Virginia Racing Commission
PO Box 1123
Richmond, VA 23208
Phone: (804)371-7363

Credential Type: License Registration. **Requirements:** Submit application and fingerprint card. Pay fee. **Fees:** $5 registration fee.

6978

Veterinarian (Racetrack)
Virginia Racing Commission
PO Box 1123
Richmond, VA 23208
Phone: (804)371-7363

Credential Type: License Registration. **Requirements:** Submit application and fingerprint card. Pay fee. **Fees:** $10 registration fee.

6979

Video Patrol Personnel (Racetrack)
Virginia Racing Commission
PO Box 1123
Richmond, VA 23208
Phone: (804)371-7363

Credential Type: License Registration. **Requirements:** Submit application and fingerprint card. Pay fee. **Fees:** $10 registration fee.

Washington

6980

Authorized Agent (Racetrack)
Washington Horse Racing
  Commission
3700 Martin Way, Ste. 101
Olympia, WA 98506
Phone: (206)459-6462

Credential Type: License Registration. **Duration of License:** One year. **Requirements:** Submit application and fingerprint card. Pay fee. **Fees:** $5 registration fee. $5 duplicate license fee.

6981

Dentist (Racetrack)
Washington Horse Racing
  Commission
3700 Martin Way, Ste. 101
Olympia, WA 98506
Phone: (206)459-6462

Credential Type: License Registration. **Duration of License:** One year. **Requirements:** Submit application and fingerprint card. Pay fee. **Fees:** $15 registration fee. $5 duplicate license fee.

6982

General Employee (Racetrack)
Washington Horse Racing
  Commission
3700 Martin Way, Ste. 101
Olympia, WA 98506
Phone: (206)459-6462

Credential Type: Occupational License Registration. **Duration of License:** One year. **Authorization:** Authorizes general racetrack jobs such as groom, vendor employee, concessions employee etc. **Requirements:** Submit application and fingerprint card. Pay fee. **Fees:** $5 registration fee. $5 duplicate license fee.

6983

Horse Owner (Racetrack)
Washington Horse Racing
  Commission
3700 Martin Way, Ste. 101
Olympia, WA 98506
Phone: (206)459-6462

Credential Type: License Registration. **Duration of License:** One year. **Requirements:** Submit application and fingerprint card. Pay fee. **Fees:** $15 registration fee. $5 duplicate license fee.

6984

Jockey Agent (Racetrack)
Washington Horse Racing
  Commission
3700 Martin Way, Ste. 101
Olympia, WA 98506
Phone: (206)459-6462

Credential Type: License Registration. **Duration of License:** One year. **Requirements:** Submit application and fingerprint card. Pay fee. **Fees:** $5 registration fee. $5 duplicate license fee.

6985

Jockey (Racetrack)
Washington Horse Racing
  Commission
3700 Martin Way, Ste. 101
Olympia, WA 98506
Phone: (206)459-6462

Credential Type: License Registration. **Duration of License:** One year. **Requirements:** Submit application and fingerprint card. Pay fee. **Fees:** $15 registration fee. $5 duplicate license fee.

6986

Owner/Trainer (Racetrack)
Washington Horse Racing
  Commission
3700 Martin Way, Ste. 101
Olympia, WA 98506
Phone: (206)459-6462

Credential Type: License Registration. **Duration of License:** One year. **Requirements:** Submit application and fingerprint card. Pay fee. **Fees:** $30 registration fee. $5 duplicate license fee.

6987

Plater (Racetrack)
Washington Horse Racing
  Commission
3700 Martin Way, Ste. 101
Olympia, WA 98506
Phone: (206)459-6462

Credential Type: License Registration. **Duration of License:** One year. **Requirements:** Submit application and fingerprint card. Pay fee. **Fees:** $10 registration fee. $5 duplicate license.

6988

Trainer (Racetrack)
Washington Horse Racing
  Commission
3700 Martin Way, Ste. 101
Olympia, WA 98506
Phone: (206)459-6462

Credential Type: License Registration. **Duration of License:** One year. **Requirements:** Submit application and fingerprint card. Pay fee. **Fees:** $15 registration fee. $5 duplicate license fee.

Washington

6989

Veterinarian (Racetrack)
Washington Horse Racing Commission
3700 Martin Way, Ste. 101
Olympia, WA 98506
Phone: (206)459-6462

Credential Type: License Registration. **Duration of License:** One year. **Requirements:** Submit application and fingerprint card. Pay fee. **Fees:** $15 registration fee. $5 duplicate license fee.

Wisconsin

6990

Announcer (Racetrack)
Wisconsin Racing Board
PO Box 7975
Madison, WI 53707-7975
Phone: (608)267-3291

Credential Type: License Registration. **Requirements:** Submit application and two sets of fingerprint cards. Pay fee. **Fees:** $50 registration fee. $20 duplicate license.

6991

Assistant Racing Secretary (Racetrack)
Wisconsin Racing Board
PO Box 7975
Madison, WI 53707-7975
Phone: (608)267-3291

Credential Type: License Registration. **Requirements:** Submit application and two sets of fingerprint cards. Pay fee. **Fees:** $20 registration fee. $20 duplicate license.

6992

Assistant Trainer (Dog Racing)
Wisconsin Racing Board
PO Box 7975
Madison, WI 53707-7975
Phone: (608)267-3291

Credential Type: License Registration. **Requirements:** Submit application and two sets of fingerprint cards. Pay fee. **Fees:** $20 registration fee. $20 duplicate license.

6993

Association Steward (Racetrack)
Wisconsin Racing Board
PO Box 7975
Madison, WI 53707-7975
Phone: (608)267-3291

Credential Type: License Registration. **Requirements:** Submit application and two sets of fingerprint cards. Pay fee. **Fees:** $50 registration fee. $20 duplicate license.

6994

Authorized Agent (Dog Racing)
Wisconsin Racing Board
PO Box 7975
Madison, WI 53707-7975
Phone: (608)267-3291

Credential Type: License Registration. **Requirements:** Submit application and two sets of fingerprint cards. Pay fee. **Fees:** $25 registration fee. $20 duplicate license.

6995

Chartwriter (Racetrack)
Wisconsin Racing Board
PO Box 7975
Madison, WI 53707-7975
Phone: (608)267-3291

Credential Type: License Registration. **Requirements:** Submit application and two sets of fingerprint cards. Pay fee. **Fees:** $50 registration fee. $20 duplicate license.

6996

Clerk of Scales (Racetrack)
Wisconsin Racing Board
PO Box 7975
Madison, WI 53707-7975
Phone: (608)267-3291

Credential Type: License Registration. **Requirements:** Submit application and two sets of fingerprint cards. Pay fee. **Fees:** $50 registration fee. $20 duplicate license.

6997

Concession Employee (Racetrack)
Wisconsin Racing Board
PO Box 7975
Madison, WI 53707-7975
Phone: (608)267-3291

Credential Type: License Registration. **Requirements:** Submit application and two sets of fingerprint cards. Pay fee. **Fees:** $20 registration fee. $20 duplicate license.

6998

Concession Owner (Racetrack)
Wisconsin Racing Board
PO Box 7975
Madison, WI 53707-7975
Phone: (608)267-3291

Credential Type: License Registration. **Requirements:** Submit application and two sets of fingerprint cards. Pay fee. **Fees:** $100 registration fee. $20 duplicate license.

6999

Director of Racing (Racetrack)
Wisconsin Racing Board
PO Box 7975
Madison, WI 53707-7975
Phone: (608)267-3291

Credential Type: License Registration. **Requirements:** Submit application and two sets of fingerprint cards. Pay fee. **Fees:** $50 registration fee. $20 duplicate license.

7000

Dog Owner (Racetrack)
Wisconsin Racing Board
PO Box 7975
Madison, WI 53707-7975
Phone: (608)267-3291

Credential Type: License Registration. **Requirements:** Submit application and two sets of fingerprint cards. Pay fee. **Fees:** $40 registration fee. $20 duplicate license.

7001

Film Patrol Employee (Racetrack)
Wisconsin Racing Board
PO Box 7975
Madison, WI 53707-7975
Phone: (608)267-3291

Credential Type: License Registration. **Requirements:** Submit application and two sets of fingerprint cards. Pay fee. **Fees:** $50 registration fee. $20 duplicate license.

7002

General Manager/Assistant General Manager (Racetrack)
Wisconsin Racing Board
PO Box 7975
Madison, WI 53707-7975
Phone: (608)267-3291

Credential Type: License Registration. **Requirements:** Submit application and

Racetrack Occupations — Wisconsin

two sets of fingerprint cards. Pay fee. **Fees:** $100 registration fee. $20 duplicate license.

7003

Kennel Helper (Dog Racing)
Wisconsin Racing Board
PO Box 7975
Madison, WI 53707-7975
Phone: (608)267-3291

Credential Type: License Registration.
Requirements: Submit application and two sets of fingerprint cards. Pay fee. **Fees:** $20 registration fee. $20 duplicate license.

7004

Kennel Master (Racetrack)
Wisconsin Racing Board
PO Box 7975
Madison, WI 53707-7975
Phone: (608)267-3291

Credential Type: License Registration.
Requirements: Submit application and two sets of fingerprint cards. Pay fee. **Fees:** $20 registration fee. $20 duplicate license.

7005

Kennel Operator (Racetrack)
Wisconsin Racing Board
PO Box 7975
Madison, WI 53707-7975
Phone: (608)267-3291

Credential Type: License Registration.
Requirements: Submit application and two sets of fingerprint cards. Pay fee. **Fees:** $80 registration fee. $20 duplicate license.

7006

Kennel Owner (Dog Racing)
Wisconsin Racing Board
PO Box 7975
Madison, WI 53707-7975
Phone: (608)267-3291

Credential Type: License Registration.
Requirements: Submit application and two sets of fingerprint cards. Pay fee. **Fees:** $750 registration fee. $20 duplicate license.

7007

Lead Out (Racetrack)
Wisconsin Racing Board
PO Box 7975
Madison, WI 53707-7975
Phone: (608)267-3291

Credential Type: License Registration.
Requirements: Submit application and two sets of fingerprint cards. Pay fee. **Fees:** $20 registration fee. $20 duplicate license.

7008

Lure Operator (Racetrack)
Wisconsin Racing Board
PO Box 7975
Madison, WI 53707-7975
Phone: (608)267-3291

Credential Type: License Registration.
Requirements: Submit application and two sets of fingerprint cards. Pay fee. **Fees:** $50 registration fee. $20 duplicate license.

7009

Mutuel Employee (Racetrack)
Wisconsin Racing Board
PO Box 7975
Madison, WI 53707-7975
Phone: (608)267-3291

Credential Type: License Registration.
Requirements: Submit application and two sets of fingerprint cards. Pay fee. **Fees:** $20 registration fee. $20 duplicate license.

7010

Mutuel Manager (Racetrack)
Wisconsin Racing Board
PO Box 7975
Madison, WI 53707-7975
Phone: (608)267-3291

Credential Type: License Registration.
Requirements: Submit application and two sets of fingerprint cards. Pay fee. **Fees:** $50 registration fee. $20 duplicate license.

7011

Owner/Trainer (Dog Racing)
Wisconsin Racing Board
PO Box 7975
Madison, WI 53707-7975
Phone: (608)267-3291

Credential Type: License Registration.
Requirements: Submit application and two sets of fingerprint cards. Pay fee. **Fees:** $50 registration fee. $20 duplicate license.

7012

Paddock Judge (Racetrack)
Wisconsin Racing Board
PO Box 7975
Madison, WI 53707-7975
Phone: (608)267-3291

Credential Type: License Registration.
Requirements: Submit application and two sets of fingerprint cards. Pay fee. **Fees:** $50 registration fee. $20 duplicate license.

7013

Photo Finish Employee (Racetrack)
Wisconsin Racing Board
PO Box 7975
Madison, WI 53707-7975
Phone: (608)267-3291

Credential Type: License Registration.
Requirements: Submit application and two sets of fingerprint cards. Pay fee. **Fees:** $50 registration fee. $20 duplicate license.

7014

Practicing Veterinarian (Racetrack)
Wisconsin Racing Board
PO Box 7975
Madison, WI 53707-7975
Phone: (608)267-3291

Credential Type: License Registration.
Requirements: Submit application and two sets of fingerprint cards. Pay fee. **Fees:** $100 registration fee. $20 duplicate license.

7015

Racing Secretary (Racetrack)
Wisconsin Racing Board
PO Box 7975
Madison, WI 53707-7975
Phone: (608)267-3291

Credential Type: License Registration.
Requirements: Submit application and two sets of fingerprint cards. Pay fee. **Fees:** $50 registration fee. $20 duplicate license.

7016

Security Employee (Racetrack)
Wisconsin Racing Board
PO Box 7975
Madison, WI 53707-7975
Phone: (608)267-3291

Credential Type: License Registration.
Requirements: Submit application and two sets of fingerprint cards. Pay fee. **Fees:** $20 registration fee. $20 duplicate license.

7017

Timer (Racetrack)
Wisconsin Racing Board
PO Box 7975
Madison, WI 53707-7975
Phone: (608)267-3291

Credential Type: License Registration.
Requirements: Submit application and two sets of fingerprint cards. Pay fee. **Fees:** $20 registration fee. $20 duplicate license.

7018

Tip Sheet Employee (Racetrack)
Wisconsin Racing Board
PO Box 7975
Madison, WI 53707-7975
Phone: (608)267-3291

Credential Type: License Registration.
Requirements: Submit application and two sets of fingerprint cards. Pay fee. **Fees:** $20 registration fee. $20 duplicate license.

7019

Totalizator Employee (Racetrack)
Wisconsin Racing Board
PO Box 7975
Madison, WI 53707-7975
Phone: (608)267-3291

Credential Type: License Registration.
Requirements: Submit application and two sets of fingerprint cards. Pay fee. **Fees:** $25 registration fee. $20 duplicate license.

7020

Totalizator Operator (Racetrack)
Wisconsin Racing Board
PO Box 7975
Madison, WI 53707-7975
Phone: (608)267-3291

Credential Type: License Registration.
Requirements: Submit application and two sets of fingerprint cards. Pay fee. **Fees:** $50 registration fee. $20 duplicate license.

7021

Track Superintendent (Racetrack)
Wisconsin Racing Board
PO Box 7975
Madison, WI 53707-7975
Phone: (608)267-3291

Credential Type: License Registration.
Requirements: Submit application and two sets of fingerprint cards. Pay fee. **Fees:** $50 registration fee. $20 duplicate license.

7022

Trainer (Dog Racing)
Wisconsin Racing Board
PO Box 7975
Madison, WI 53707-7975
Phone: (608)267-3291

Credential Type: License Registration.
Requirements: Submit application and two sets of fingerprint cards. Pay fee. **Fees:** $50 registration fee. $20 duplicate license.

Wyoming

7023

Agent (Racetrack)
Wyoming State Pari-Mutuel Commission
Barrett Bldg., 3rd Fl.
Cheyenne, WY 82002
Phone: (307)777-5887

Credential Type: License Registration.
Requirements: Submit application and fingerprint card. Pay fee. **Fees:** $20 registration fee. $10 duplicate license.

7024

Assistant Starter (Racetrack)
Wyoming State Pari-Mutuel Commission
Barrett Bldg., 3rd Fl.
Cheyenne, WY 82002
Phone: (307)777-5887

Credential Type: License Registration.
Requirements: Submit application and fingerprint card. Pay fee. **Fees:** $10 registration fee. $10 duplicate license.

7025

Concession Employee (Racetrack)
Wyoming State Pari-Mutuel Commission
Barrett Bldg., 3rd Fl.
Cheyenne, WY 82002
Phone: (307)777-5887

Credential Type: License Registration.
Requirements: Submit application and fingerprint card. Pay fee. **Fees:** $10 registration fee. $10 duplicate license.

7026

Concession Operator (Racetrack)
Wyoming State Pari-Mutuel Commission
Barrett Bldg., 3rd Fl.
Cheyenne, WY 82002
Phone: (307)777-5887

Credential Type: License Registration.
Requirements: Submit application and fingerprint card. Pay fee. **Fees:** $20 registration fee. $10 duplicate license.

7027

Exerciser (Racetrack)
Wyoming State Pari-Mutuel Commission
Barrett Bldg., 3rd Fl.
Cheyenne, WY 82002
Phone: (307)777-5887

Credential Type: License Registration.
Requirements: Submit application and fingerprint card. Pay fee. **Fees:** $20 registration fee. $10 duplicate license.

7028

Groom (Racetrack)
Wyoming State Pari-Mutuel Commission
Barrett Bldg., 3rd Fl.
Cheyenne, WY 82002
Phone: (307)777-5887

Credential Type: License Registration.
Requirements: Submit application and fingerprint card. Pay fee. **Fees:** $10 registration fee. $10 duplicate license.

7029

Horsemen's Bookkeeper (Racetrack)
Wyoming State Pari-Mutuel Commission
Barrett Bldg., 3rd Fl.
Cheyenne, WY 82002
Phone: (307)777-5887

Credential Type: License Registration.
Requirements: Submit application and fingerprint card. Pay fee. **Fees:** $20 registration fee. $10 duplicate license.

Racetrack Occupations

7030

Jockey/Apprentice Jockey (Racetrack)
Wyoming State Pari-Mutuel Commission
Barrett Bldg., 3rd Fl.
Cheyenne, WY 82002
Phone: (307)777-5887

Credential Type: License Registration.
Requirements: Submit application and fingerprint card. Pay fee. **Fees:** $20 registration fee. $10 duplicate license.

7031

Jockey Runner (Racetrack)
Wyoming State Pari-Mutuel Commission
Barrett Bldg., 3rd Fl.
Cheyenne, WY 82002
Phone: (307)777-5887

Credential Type: License Registration.
Requirements: Submit application and fingerprint card. Pay fee. **Fees:** $10 registration fee. $10 duplicate license.

7032

Mutuel Employee (Racetrack)
Wyoming State Pari-Mutuel Commission
Barrett Bldg., 3rd Fl.
Cheyenne, WY 82002
Phone: (307)777-5887

Credential Type: License Registration.
Requirements: Submit application and fingerprint card. Pay fee. **Fees:** $10 registration fee. $10 duplicate license.

7033

Mutuel Official (Racetrack)
Wyoming State Pari-Mutuel Commission
Barrett Bldg., 3rd Fl.
Cheyenne, WY 82002
Phone: (307)777-5887

Credential Type: License Registration.
Requirements: Submit application and fingerprint card. Pay fee. **Fees:** $20 registration fee. $10 duplicate license.

7034

Outrider (Racetrack)
Wyoming State Pari-Mutuel Commission
Barrett Bldg., 3rd Fl.
Cheyenne, WY 82002
Phone: (307)777-5887

Credential Type: License Registration.
Requirements: Submit application and fingerprint card. Pay fee. **Fees:** $20 registration fee. $10 duplicate license.

7035

Owner (Racetrack)
Wyoming State Pari-Mutuel Commission
Barrett Bldg., 3rd Fl.
Cheyenne, WY 82002
Phone: (307)777-5887

Credential Type: License Registration.
Requirements: Submit application and fingerprint card. Pay fee. **Fees:** $20 registration fee. $10 duplicate license.

7036

Permittee Employee (Racetrack)
Wyoming State Pari-Mutuel Commission
Barrett Bldg., 3rd Fl.
Cheyenne, WY 82002
Phone: (307)777-5887

Credential Type: License Registration.
Requirements: Submit application and fingerprint card. Pay fee. **Fees:** $10 registration fee. $10 duplicate license.

7037

Permittee Official (Racetrack)
Wyoming State Pari-Mutuel Commission
Barrett Bldg., 3rd Fl.
Cheyenne, WY 82002
Phone: (307)777-5887

Credential Type: License Registration.
Requirements: Submit application and fingerprint card. Pay fee. **Fees:** $20 registration fee. $10 duplicate license.

7038

Plater (Racetrack)
Wyoming State Pari-Mutuel Commission
Barrett Bldg., 3rd Fl.
Cheyenne, WY 82002
Phone: (307)777-5887

Credential Type: License Registration.
Requirements: Submit application and fingerprint card. Pay fee. **Fees:** $20 registration fee. $10 duplicate license.

7039

Pony Rider (Racetrack)
Wyoming State Pari-Mutuel Commission
Barrett Bldg., 3rd Fl.
Cheyenne, WY 82002
Phone: (307)777-5887

Credential Type: License Registration.
Requirements: Submit application and fingerprint card. Pay fee. **Fees:** $20 registration fee. $10 duplicate license.

7040

Racing Secretary (Racetrack)
Wyoming State Pari-Mutuel Commission
Barrett Bldg., 3rd Fl.
Cheyenne, WY 82002
Phone: (307)777-5887

Credential Type: License Registration.
Requirements: Submit application and fingerprint card. Pay fee. **Fees:** $20 registration fee. $10 duplicate license.

7041

Roper (Racetrack)
Wyoming State Pari-Mutuel Commission
Barrett Bldg., 3rd Fl.
Cheyenne, WY 82002
Phone: (307)777-5887

Credential Type: License Registration.
Requirements: Submit application and fingerprint card. Pay fee. **Fees:** $20 registration fee. $10 duplicate license.

7042

Security Employee (Racetrack)
Wyoming State Pari-Mutuel
 Commission
Barrett Bldg., 3rd Fl.
Cheyenne, WY 82002
Phone: (307)777-5887

Credential Type: License Registration.
Requirements: Submit application and fingerprint card. Pay fee. **Fees:** $10 registration fee. $10 duplicate license.

7043

Trainer/Assistant Trainer (Racetrack)
Wyoming State Pari-Mutuel
 Commission
Barrett Bldg., 3rd Fl.
Cheyenne, WY 82002
Phone: (307)777-5887

Credential Type: License Registration.
Requirements: Submit application and fingerprint card. Pay fee. **Fees:** $20 registration fee. $10 duplicate license.

7044

Veterinarian Assistant (Racetrack)
Wyoming State Pari-Mutuel
 Commission
Barrett Bldg., 3rd Fl.
Cheyenne, WY 82002
Phone: (307)777-5887

Credential Type: License Registration.
Requirements: Submit application and fingerprint card. Pay fee. **Fees:** $20 registration fee. $10 duplicate license.

7045

Veterinarian (Racetrack)
Wyoming State Pari-Mutuel
 Commission
Barrett Bldg., 3rd Fl.
Cheyenne, WY 82002
Phone: (307)777-5887

Credential Type: License Registration.
Requirements: Submit application and fingerprint card. Pay fee. **Fees:** $20 registration fee. $10 duplicate license.

Radio, T.V., and Other Announcers and Newscasters

The following states grant licenses in this occupational category as of the date of publication:

Alabama	California	Illinois	Missouri	North Dakota	Washington
Arizona	Connecticut	Iowa	Montana	South Carolina	Wisconsin
Arkansas	Florida	Kansas	New Mexico	South Dakota	

Alabama

7046

Wrestling Announcer
State Athletic Commission
50 N. Ripley St., Rm. 4121
Montgomery, AL 36132
Phone: (205)242-1380

Credential Type: License. **Duration of License:** One year. **Fees:** $5 license fee.

Arizona

7047

Announcer
Boxing Commission
1645 W. Jefferson, Rm. 212
Phoenix, AZ 85007
Phone: (602)542-1417

Credential Type: License. **Requirements:** Contact the commission for an application.

Arkansas

7048

Ring Announcer
Arkansas Athletic Commission
Quawpaw Towers, Rm. 2A
Little Rock, AR 72201
Phone: (501)371-2110

Credential Type: License. **Duration of License:** One year. **Requirements:** License must be granted locally by either the VFW or the American Legion. **Examination:** No **Fees:** $10 License. $10 Renewal.

California

7049

Announcer (Boxing, Kickboxing, or Martial Arts)
Athletic Commission
1424 Howe Ave., Ste. 33
Sacramento, CA 95814-6200
Phone: (916)920-7300

Credential Type: License. **Duration of License:** One year. **Requirements:** Submit application and pay fee. **Fees:** $25 license fee. $25 renewal fee.

7050

Announcer (Racetrack)
California Horse Racing Board
1010 Hurley Way, Ste. 190
Sacramento, CA 95825
Phone: (916)920-7178

Credential Type: License Registration. **Requirements:** Submit application and fingerprint card. Pay fee. **Fees:** $75 registration fee.

Connecticut

7051

Announcer (Boxing and Wrestling)
Athletic Div.
Consumer Protection Dept.
165 Capitol Ave.
Hartford, CT 06106
Phone: (203)566-3843

Credential Type: License. **Requirements:** Contact licensing body for application information.

7052

Announcer (Racetrack)
Connecticut Div. of Special Revenue
Russell Rd.
PO Box 11424
Newington, CT 06111-0424
Phone: (203)566-2756

Credential Type: License Registration. **Requirements:** Submit application and fingerprint card. Pay fee. **Fees:** $5 registration fee.

7053

Assistant Announcer (Racetrack)
Connecticut Div. of Special Revenue
Russell Rd.
PO Box 11424
Newington, CT 06111-0424
Phone: (203)566-2756

Credential Type: License Registration. **Requirements:** Submit application and fingerprint card. Pay fee. **Fees:** $5 registration fee.

Florida

7054

Announcer (Racetrack)
Florida Dept. of Business
Div. of Pari-Mutuel Wagering
Licensing Section
725 S. Bronough St.
Tallahassee, FL 32399-1037
Phone: (904)488-9161

Credential Type: License Registration Code 1006. **Requirements:** Submit application and fingerprint card. Pay fee. **Fees:** $40 registration fee.

Illinois

7055

Announcer (Boxing/Wrestling)
Illinois Dept. of Professional
  Regulations
State of Illinois Ctr.
100 W. Randolph, Ste. 9-300
Chicago, IL 60601
Phone: (312)814-2719

Credential Type: Registration. **Duration of License:** Lifetime. **Requirements:** Submit registration to board. Must re-register if original information changes. **Reciprocity:** No. **Governing Statute:** The Illinois Professional Boxing and Wrestling Act. Illinois Revised Statutes 1991, Chapter 111.

Iowa

7056

Announcer (Racetrack)
Iowa State Racing Commission
Lucas State Office Bldg.
Des Moines, IA 50319
Phone: (515)281-7352

Credential Type: License Registration. **Requirements:** Submit application and fingerprint card. Pay fee. **Fees:** $10 registration fee.

Kansas

7057

Announcer (Racetrack)
Kansas Racing Commission
3400 VanBuren
Topeka, KS 66611-2228
Phone: (913)296-5800

Credential Type: License Registration. **Requirements:** Submit application and fingerprint card. Pay fee. **Fees:** $5 registration fee.

Missouri

7058

Announcer (Boxing, Wrestling, or Karate)
Office of Athletics
Dept. of Economic Development
3605 Missouri Blvd.
PO Box 1335
Jefferson City, MO 65102
Phone: (314)751-0243

Credential Type: License. **Duration of License:** One year. **Requirements:** Application for license must be submitted no later than 10 business days prior to a professional exhibition and seven days prior to an amateur exhibition. **Fees:** $10 license fee. **Governing Statute:** four CSR 40.

Montana

7059

Announcer (Racetrack)
State of Montana Board of Horse
  Racing
Dept. of Commerce
1424 9th Ave.
Helena, MT 59620
Phone: (406)444-4287

Credential Type: License Registration. **Requirements:** Submit application and fingerprint card. Pay fee. **Fees:** $20 registration fee.

New Mexico

7060

Announcer (Racetrack)
New Mexico State Racing
  Commission
PO Box 8576, Highland Station
Albuquerque, NM 87198
Phone: (505)841-4644

Credential Type: License Registration. **Requirements:** Submit application and fingerprint card. Pay fees. **Fees:** $14 registration fee. $1 notary fee. $23 fingerprint card processing fee.

North Dakota

7061

Announcer (Racetrack)
North Dakota Racing Commission
State Capitol Bldg.
Bismarck, ND 58505
Phone: (701)224-2210

Credential Type: License Registration. **Requirements:** Submit application and fingerprint card. Pay fee. **Fees:** $10 license fee. $10 duplicate license fee.

South Carolina

7062

Boxing-Wrestling Announcer
State Athletic Commission
PO Box 2461
Columbia, SC 29202
Phone: (803)254-3661

Credential Type: License. **Requirements:** Submit application and pay fee. **Fees:** $10 license fee.

South Dakota

7063

Announcer (Horse Racing)
South Dakota Racing Commission
c/o 500 East Capitol
Pierre, SD 57501
Phone: (605)773-6050

Credential Type: License Registration. **Requirements:** Submit application and fingerprint card. Pay fee. **Fees:** $10 registration fee.

Washington

7064

Announcer/Timekeeper (Professional Boxing & Wrestling)
Boxing Commission
414 12th Ave., PH-21
Olympia, WA 98504-8321
Phone: (206)753-3713

Credential Type: Announcer/Timekeeper License. **Duration of License:** One year. **Requirements:** Submit application with current photo. **Fees:** No fee.

Wisconsin

7065

Announcer (Racetrack)
Wisconsin Racing Board
PO Box 7975
Madison, WI 53707-7975
Phone: (608)267-3291

Credential Type: License Registration. **Requirements:** Submit application and two sets of fingerprint cards. Pay fee. **Fees:** $50 registration fee. $20 duplicate license.

Radiologic Technologists

The following states grant licenses in this occupational category as of the date of publication:

Arizona	Hawaii	Kentucky	Massachusetts	New Mexico	Tennessee	Washington
California	Illinois	Louisiana	Montana	New York	Texas	West Virginia
Delaware	Indiana	Maine	Nebraska	Oregon	Utah	Wyoming
Florida	Iowa	Maryland	New Jersey	Pennsylvania	Vermont	

Arizona

7066

Practical Technologist in Podiatry
Medical Radiologic Technology
  Board of Examiners
4814 S. 40th St.
Phoenix, AZ 85040
Phone: (602)255-4845

Credential Type: Practical Technologist in Podiatry Certificate. **Duration of License:** Two years. **Requirements:** Pass the Arizona State written Podiatric Exam and after clinicals have been completed, films must be graded by the Podiatric Film Review Committee. **Examination:** Arizona State written Podiatric Exam. **Exemptions:** Licensed practitioners defined as Medical Doctors, Doctors of Osteopathy, Dentists, Doctors of Chiropractic, Doctors of Naturopathy, and Podiatric Physicians. **Reciprocity:** None. **Fees:** $60 application and license fee. $60 Podiatric Written Exam fee.

7067

Practical Technologist in Radiology
Medical Radiologic Technology
  Board of Examiners
4814 S. 40th St.
Phoenix, AZ 85040
Phone: (602)255-4845

Credential Type: Practical Technologist in Radiology Certificate. **Duration of License:** Two years. **Requirements:** Pass American Registry of Radiologic Technologists Limited Scope examination. If a technologist has not practiced within the last three years, applicant must also pass the Arizona State Practical Technologist in Radiology Refresher Examination. **Examination:** American Registry of Radiologic Technologists Limited Scope examination **Exemptions:** Licensed practitioners defined as Medical Doctors, Doctors of Osteopathy, Dentists, Doctors of Chiropractic, Doctors of Naturopathy, and Podiatric Physicians. **Reciprocity:** None. **Fees:** $60 application and license fee. $60 refresher exam fee. $25 Limited Scope exam fee.

7068

Radiation Therapy Technologist
Medical Radiologic Technology
  Board of Examiners
4814 S. 40th St.
Phoenix, AZ 85040
Phone: (602)255-4845

Credential Type: Radiation Therapy Technologist Certificate. **Duration of License:** Two years. **Requirements:** Pass American Registry of Radiologic Technologists Therapy examination. If a technologist has not practiced within the last three years, applicant must also pass the Arizona State Radiation Therapist Refresher examination. **Examination:** American Registry of Radiologic Technologists Therapy examination. **Exemptions:** Licensed practitioners defined as Medical Doctors, Doctors of Osteopathy, Dentists, Doctors of Chiropractic, Doctors of Naturopathy, and Podiatric Physicians. **Reciprocity:** None. **Fees:** $60 application and license fee. $60 refresher exam fee.

7069

Radiologic Technologist
Medical Radiologic Technology
  Board of Examiners
4814 S. 40th St.
Phoenix, AZ 85040
Phone: (602)255-4845

Credential Type: Radiologic Technologist Certificate. **Duration of License:** Two years. **Requirements:** Pass American Registry of Radiologic Technologists Radiography examination. If a technologist has not practiced within the last three years, applicant must also pass the Arizona State Radiologic Technologist Refresher examination. **Examination:** American Registry of Radiologic Technologists Radiography Examination. **Exemptions:** Licensed practitioners defined as Medical Doctors, Doctors of Osteopathy, Dentists, Doctors of Chiropractic, Doctors of Naturopathy, and Podiatric Physicians. **Reciprocity:** None. **Fees:** $60 application and license fee. $60 refresher exam fee.

California

7070

Radiation Therapy Technologist
Dept. of Health Services
Radiological Health Branch
601 N. 7th St.
Sacramento, CA 95814-0208
Phone: (916)445-6695

Credential Type: Radiation Therapy Technologist Certification. **Duration of License:** Two years. **Requirements:** Submit application. Meet board education and experience requirements. **Examination:** State or Nuclear Medicine Technology Certification Board (NMTCB) examination. **Fees:** $30.50 application fee. $29 renewal fee.

Radiologic Technologists

7071

Radiologic Technologist
Dept. of Health Services
Radiological Health Branch
601 N. 7th St.
Sacramento, CA 95814-0208
Phone: (916)445-6695

Credential Type: Radiologic Technologist Certificate. **Duration of License:** Two years. **Requirements:** Submit application. Meet board education and experience requirements. **Examination:** State or Nuclear Medicine Technology Certification Board (NMTCB) examination. **Fees:** $30.50 application fee. $29 renewal fee.

Credential Type: Limited Radiologic Technologist Certification. **Duration of License:** Two years. **Authorization:** Authorizes the holder to do radiological work in the following areas: Chest; Extremities; Skull; Dermatology; Therapy; Leg; Genitourinary; Musculoskeletal; Photofluorographic; Dental; Podiatric. **Requirements:** Must have board approved training and experience. **Fees:** $30.50 application fee. $29 renewal fee.

Delaware

7072

Radiation Therapy Technologist
Board of Public Health
Central Billing
PO Box 637
Dover, DE 19903
Phone: (302)739-3787

Credential Type: Radiation Therapy Technologist Certification. **Duration of License:** Four years. **Requirements:** Submit application. Meet board education and experience requirements. **Examination:** State, Nuclear Medicine Technology Certification Board (NMTCB), or American Registry of Radiologic Technologists (ARRT) examination. **Fees:** $10 application fee. $10 renewal fee.

7073

Radiologic Technician
Board of Public Health
Central Billing
PO Box 637
Dover, DE 19903
Phone: (302)739-3787

Credential Type: Radiologic Technician Certification. **Duration of License:** Four years. **Requirements:** Submit application. Meet board education and experience requirements. **Examination:** State, Nuclear Medicine Technology Certification Board (NMTCB), or American Registry of Radiologic Technologists (ARRT) examination. **Fees:** $10 application fee. $10 renewal fee.

Florida

7074

Dental Radiographer
Board of Dentistry
Dept. of Professional Regulation
1940 N. Monroe St.
Tallahassee, FL 32399-0765
Phone: (904)488-6015

Credential Type: Dental Radiographer Certificate. **Duration of License:** Two years. **Authorization:** Certificate required for dental assistants to position and expose dental radiographic films, unless they have graduated from a board-approved dental assisting program or school. **Requirements:** Dental assistant may be certified as a dental readiographer by completing at least three months of continuous on-the-job training through assisting in the positioning and exposing of dental radiographic film under the direct supervision of a Florida licensed dentist. Complete a board-approved course in dental radiography within 12 months after completing on-the-job training. **Fees:** $20 certification fee. **Governing Statute:** Florida Statutes, Chapter 455 and 466. Florida Administrative Code, Rule 21-G.

7075

Radiation Therapy Technologist
Office of Radiation control
1317 Winewood Blvd.
Tallahassee, FL 32301
Phone: (904)487-3451

Credential Type: Radiation Therapy Technologist Certification. **Duration of License:** Two years. **Requirements:** Submit application. Meet board education and experience requirements. Renewal requires 12 hours of continuing education every two years. **Examination:** State, American Registry of Clinical Radiography Technologists (ARCRT), Nuclear Medicine Technology Certification Board (NMTCB), or American Registry of Radiologic Technologists (ARRT) examination. **Fees:** $50 license by examination fee. $35 license by endorsement fee. $40 renewal fee.

7076

Radiologic Technologist
Office of Radiation Control
1317 Winewood Blvd.
Tallahassee, FL 32301
Phone: (904)487-3451

Credential Type: Radiologic Technologist Certification. **Duration of License:** Two years. **Requirements:** Submit application. Meet board education and experience requirements. Renewal requires 12 hours of continuing education every two years. **Examination:** State, American Registry of Clinical Radiography Technologists (ARCRT), Nuclear Medicine Technology Certification Board (NMTCB), or American Registry of Radiologic Technologists (ARRT) examination. **Fees:** $50 license by examination fee. $35 license by endorsement fee. $40 renewal fee.

Credential Type: Limited Radiologic Technologist Certification. **Duration of License:** Two years. **Authorization:** Authorizes holder to do Basic and Podiatric radiological procedures. **Requirements:** Submit application. Meet board education and experience requirements. Renewal requires 12 hours of continuing education every two years. **Examination:** Board approved examination. **Fees:** $50 license by examination fee. $35 license by endorsement fee. $40 renewal fee.

Hawaii

7077

Radiologic Technologist
Hawaii Board of Radiologic Technologists
Dept. of Health
591 Ala Moana Blvd.
Honolulu, HI 96813
Phone: (808)548-3075

Credential Type: License. **Requirements:** High school diploma or equivalent. Completion of an accredited radiologic technology training program. **Examination:** Written. **Fees:** $10 application fee.

Illinois

7078

Industrial Radiographer
Illinois Dept. of Nuclear Safety
1035 Outer Drive
Springfield, IL 62704
Phone: (217)785-9900

Credential Type: Industrial Radiographer Certificate. **Duration of License:** Five

Illinois

Industrial Radiographer, continued

years. **Requirements:** Complete an approved training program in Industrial Radiography. **Examination:** Certified Industrial Radiographer State Examination. **Reciprocity:** Yes, with other states who have examinations and standards substantially equivalent to those of Illinois. **Fees:** $60 examination fee. $30 application fee. **Governing Statute:** 32 Illinois Administrative Code.

7079

Medical Radiographer
Illinois Dept. of Nuclear Safety
1035 Outer Drive
Springfield, IL 62704
Phone: (217)785-9900

Credential Type: Medical Radiographer Accreditation. **Duration of License:** Two years. **Requirements:** Complete an approved training program in Medical Radiography. Must have 12 contact hours of continuing education annually. **Examination:** Written examination. **Reciprocity:** No. **Fees:** $45 examination fee. $40 application fee. **Governing Statute:** 32 Illinois Administrative Code 401.

Credential Type: Limited Medical Radiographer Accreditation. **Duration of License:** Two years. **Authorization:** Limited to specific parts of the body for diagnostic purposes. **Requirements:** Must be trained by a supervising physician or employer. **Examination:** Written examination. **Reciprocity:** No. **Fees:** $30 examination fee. $40 application fee. **Governing Statute:** 32 Illinois Administrative Code 401.

7080

Radiation Therapist
Illinois Dept. of Nuclear Safety
1035 Outer Drive
Springfield, IL 62704
Phone: (217)785-9900

Credential Type: Radiation Therapy Accreditation. **Duration of License:** Two years. **Authorization:** Allows work with radiation only under the supervision of a licensed practitioner. **Requirements:** Complete an approved training program in Radiation Therapy. Must complete 12 contact hours of continuing education per year. **Examination:** Written examination. **Reciprocity:** No. **Fees:** $45 examination fee. $40 application fee. **Governing Statute:** 32 Illinois Administrative Code 401.

7081

Radiation Therapy Technologist
Div. of Radiologic Technology Certification
Dept. of Nuclear Safety
1035 Outer Park Dr.
PO Box 1964
Springfield, IL 62704
Phone: (217)785-9900

Credential Type: Radiation Therapy License. **Duration of License:** Two years. **Requirements:** Submit application. Meet board education and experience requirements. Renewal requires 12 hours of continuing education every year. **Examination:** State or American Registry of Radiologic Technologists (ARRT) examination. **Fees:** $40 application fee. $40 renewal fee.

7082

Radiologic Technologist
Div. of Radiologic Technology Certification
Dept. of Nuclear Safety
1035 Outer Park Dr.
PO Box 1964
Springfield, IL 62704
Phone: (217)785-9900

Credential Type: Radiologic Technologist License. **Duration of License:** Two years. **Requirements:** Submit application. Meet board education and experience requirements. Renewal requires 12 hours of continuing education every year. **Examination:** State or American Registry of Radiologic Technologists (ARRT) examination. **Fees:** $40 application fee. $40 renewal fee.

Credential Type: Limited Radiologic Technologist License. **Duration of License:** Two years. **Authorization:** Authorizes holder to do radiological work in the following areas: Chest; Extremity; Skull and Sinus; Spine. **Requirements:** Submit application. Meet board education and experience requirements. Renewal requires 12 hours of continuing education every year. **Examination:** Board approved examination. **Fees:** $40 application fee. $40 renewal fee.

Indiana

7083

Radiologic Technologist
Radiological Health Division
Indiana State Board of Health
1330 W. Michigan St.
PO Box 1964
Indianapolis, IN 46206
Phone: (317)633-0146

Credential Type: Radiologic Technologist License. **Duration of License:** Two years. **Requirements:** Submit application. Meet board education and experience requirements. **Examination:** State or American Registry of Radiologic Technologists (ARRT) examination. **Fees:** $30 application fee. $30 renewal fee.

Credential Type: Limited Radiologic Technologist License. **Authorization:** Authorizes holder to do radiological work in the following areas: Chest; Chiropractic; Podiatric; Dental or Limited General. **Examination:** Board approved examination. **Fees:** $30 application fee. $30 renewal fee.

Iowa

7084

Radiographer
Bureau of Radiological Health
Iowa Dept. of Health
Lucas State Office Bldg., 3rd Fl.
Des Moines, IA 50319
Phone: (515)281-3478

Credential Type: General Diagnostic Radiographer License. **Duration of License:** One year. **Requirements:** 18 years of age. High school education. Completion of an approved, two-year, full-time program. **Examination:** American Registry of Radiologic Technologists exam. **Reciprocity:** Applicants licensed in other states may get an Iowa license if the other state's requirements are equal to Iowa's. **Fees:** $25 exam fee. $45 permit-to-practice fee. $35 renewal fee.

Credential Type: Limited Diagnostic Radiographer License. **Duration of License:** One year. **Requirements:** 18 years of age. High school education. Complete a three to four month program. **Examination:** American Registry of Radiologic Technologists exam. **Reciprocity:** Applicants licensed in other states may get an Iowa license if the other state's requirements are equal to Iowa's. **Fees:** $35 exam fee. $45 permit-to-practice fee. $35 renewal fee.

Kentucky

7085

Radiation Operator
Div. of Community Safety
275 E. Main St.
Frankfort, KY 40621
Phone: (502)564-3700

Credential Type: General Certified License. **Duration of License:** Two years. **Requirements:** High school diploma or GED. Completion of a 24 month course of study in medical, osteopathic, or chiropractic radiography approved by the regulatory agency. 18 years of age. Continuing education required. **Examination:** Yes. **Fees:** $35 exam fee. $50 registration fee. $30 renewal fee.

Credential Type: Limited Certified License. **Duration of License:** Two years. **Requirements:** High school diploma or GED. Completion of a limited course of study in medical, osteopathic or chiropractic radiography approved by the regulatory agency. 18 years of age. **Examination:** Yes. **Fees:** $30 exam fee. $50 registration fee. $30 renewal fee.

Louisiana

7086

Radiation Therapy Technologist
Louisiana State Radiologic
    Technology Board of Examiners
3108 Cleary Ave., Ste. 207
Metairie, LA 70002
Phone: (504)838-5231

Credential Type: Radiation Therapy Technologist License. **Duration of License:** Two years. **Requirements:** Submit application. Meet board education and experience requirements. **Examination:** State, Nuclear Medicine Technology Certification Board (NMTCB), or American Registry of Radiologic Technologists (ARRT) examination. **Fees:** $50 application fee. $50 renewal fee.

7087

Radiologic Technologist
Louisiana State Radiologic
    Technology Board of Examiners
3108 Cleary Ave., Ste. 207
Metairie, LA 70002
Phone: (504)838-5231

Credential Type: Radiologic Technologist License. **Duration of License:** Two years. **Requirements:** Submit application. Meet board education and experience requirements. **Examination:** State, Nuclear Medicine Technology Certification Board (NMTCB), or American Registry of Radiologic Technologists (ARRT) examination. **Fees:** $50 application fee. $50 renewal fee.

Maine

7088

Radiation Therapy Technologist
Radiologic Technology Board of
    Examiners
Dept. of Professional and Financial
    Regulation
Div. of Licensing and Enforcement
State House Station 35
Augusta, ME 04333
Phone: (207)582-8723

Credential Type: Radiation Therapy Technologist License. **Duration of License:** Two years. **Requirements:** High school graduate or equivalent. Be at least 18 years of age. Complete a course of study in radiography and radiation therapy technology accredited by the Committee on Allied Health Education and Accreditation. Possess current national certification or pass an examination approved by the board to practice as a radiation therapy technologist. **Examination:** Radiation therapy technologist examination. **Exemptions:** Exam not required if nationally certified. **Fees:** $10 application fee. $40 license fee. $40 renewal fee. $30 exam fee. **Governing Statute:** 32 M.S.R.A. Chap. 103.

Credential Type: Temporary License. **Duration of License:** 90 days or when exam results are published. **Requirements:** High school graduate or equivalent. Be at least 18 years of age. Complete or be about to complete within one month a board-approved course of study. Document availability of a licensed practitioner to provide supervision. **Fees:** $10 application fee. $10 license fee. $10 renewal fee.

7089

Radiographer
Radiologic Technology Board of
    Examiners
Dept. of Professional and Financial
    Regulation
Div. of Licensing and Enforcement
State House Station 35
Augusta, ME 04333
Phone: (207)582-8723

Credential Type: Radiographer License. **Duration of License:** Two years. **Requirements:** High school graduate or equivalent. Be at least 18 years of age. Complete a course of study in radiography accredited by the Committee on Allied Health Education and Accreditation. Possess current national certification or pass the examination of the American Registry of Radiologic Technologists. **Examination:** American Registry of Radiologic Technologists Examination. **Exemptions:** Exam not required if nationally certified. **Fees:** $10 application fee. $40 license fee. $40 renewal fee. $30 exam fee. **Governing Statute:** 32 M.S.R.A. Chap. 103.

Credential Type: Limited Radiographer License. **Duration of License:** Two years. **Authorization:** Categories include skull, spine, chest, extremities, and podiatry. **Requirements:** High school graduate or equivalent. Be at least 18 years of age. Complete academic core requirements of a board-approved course of study. Clinical practicum obtained from a board-approved clinical site for each category of license requested. **Examination:** Limited radiographer's examination for appropriate category, written and practical. **Fees:** $10 application fee. $40 license fee. $40 renewal fee. $30 exam fee. **Governing Statute:** 32 M.S.R.A. Chap. 103.

Credential Type: Temporary License. **Duration of License:** 90 days or when exam results are published. **Requirements:** High school graduate or equivalent. Be at least 18 years of age. Complete or be about to complete within one month a board-approved course of study. Document availability of a licensed practitioner to provide supervision. **Fees:** $10 application fee. $10 license fee. $10 renewal fee.

Maryland

7090

Radiation Therapy Technologist
Maryland Board of Physician Quality
    Assurance
4201 Patterson Ave.
PO Box 2571
Baltimore, MD 21215-0002
Phone: (301)764-4777

Credential Type: Radiation Therapy Technologist License. **Duration of License:** Two years. **Requirements:** Submit application. Meet board education and experience requirements. Renewal requires 30 hours of continuing education every year. **Examination:** State or American Registry of Radiologic Technologists (ARRT) examination. **Fees:** $100 application fee. $50 renewal fee.

Maryland

7091

Radiologic Technologist
Maryland Board of Physician Quality Assurance
4201 Patterson Ave.
PO Box 2571
Baltimore, MD 21215-0002
Phone: (301)764-4777

Credential Type: Radiologic Technologist License. **Duration of License:** Two years. **Requirements:** Submit application. Meet board education and experience requirements. Renewal requires 30 hours of continuing education every year. **Examination:** State or American Registry of Radiologic Technologists (ARRT) examination. **Fees:** $100 application fee. $50 renewal fee.

Massachusetts

7092

Radiation Therapy Technologist
Radiation Control Program
Dept. of Public Health
305 South St., 7th Fl.
Jamaica Plain, MA 02130
Phone: (617)727-6214

Credential Type: Radiation Therapy Technologist License. **Duration of License:** Two years. **Requirements:** Submit application. Meet board education and experience requirements. Renewal requires 30 hours of continuing education every year. **Examination:** State or American Registry of Radiologic Technologists (ARRT) examination. **Fees:** $25 application fee. $50 renewal fee.

7093

Radiologic Technologist
Radiation Control Program
Dept. of Public Health
305 South St., 7th Fl.
Jamaica Plain, MA 02130
Phone: (617)727-6214

Credential Type: Radiologic Technologist License. **Duration of License:** Two years. **Requirements:** Submit application. Meet board education and experience requirements. Renewal requires 30 hours of continuing education every year. **Examination:** State or American Registry of Radiologic Technologists (ARRT) examination. **Fees:** $25 application fee. $50 renewal fee.

Montana

7094

Radiologic Technologist
Montana Board of Radiologic Technologists
111 N. Jackson
Helena, MT 59620
Phone: (406)444-4288

Credential Type: License. **Duration of License:** One year. **Requirements:** 18 years of age. Completion of a two-year radiologic technology program. **Examination:** National board exam. **Fees:** $60 application fee. $65 exam fee. $35 license fee. $25 renewal fee. **Governing Statute:** Montana Code Annotated 37-14-301 through 37-14-323.

Nebraska

7095

Radiologic Technologist
Nebraska Dept. of Health
Radiological Health Div.
301 Centennial Mall S.
PO Box 95007
Lincoln, NE 68509
Phone: (402)471-2168

Credential Type: License. **Duration of License:** One year. **Requirements:** Must successfully complete an agency approved two year training course in radiological technology, or be certified by the American Registry of Radiologic Technologists. **Fees:** $30 initial fee. $25 renewal fee.

New Jersey

7096

Chest X-Ray Technologist
New Jersey Dept. of Environmental Protection
Bureau of Revenue
CN402
Trenton, NJ 08625-0402
Phone: (609)530-5760

Credential Type: License. **Requirements:** 18 years of age. High school diploma. Completion of the basic approved curriculum for chest radiology or its equivalent. **Examination:** Yes. **Fees:** $30 exam fee. $30 application fee. **Governing Statute:** NJSA 26:2D. NJAC 28-19.

7097

Dental X-Ray Technologist
New Jersey Dept. of Environmental Protection
Bureau of Revenue
CN402
Trenton, NJ 08625-0402
Phone: (609)530-5760

Credential Type: License. **Duration of License:** Two years. **Requirements:** High school diploma. Completion of a curriculum for dental radiology or its equivalent. 18 years of age. **Examination:** Yes. **Fees:** $30 exam fee. $20 biennial registration fee. $30 application fee. **Governing Statute:** NJSA 26-2D. NJAC 7:28-19.

7098

Diagnostic X-Ray Technologist
New Jersey Dept. of Environmental Protection
Bureau of Revenue
CN402
Trenton, NJ 08625
Phone: (609)530-5760

Credential Type: License. **Requirements:** 18 years of age. High school diploma or equivalent. Completion of an approved 24-month course in diagnostic X-ray technology or its equivalent. **Examination:** Yes. **Reciprocity:** Yes. **Fees:** $30 exam fee. $30 application fee. **Governing Statute:** NJSA 26-2D. NJAC 7:28-19.

7099

Orthopedic X-Ray Technologist
New Jersey Dept. of Environmental Protection
Bureau of Revenue
CN402
Trenton, NJ 08625-0402
Phone: (609)530-5760

Credential Type: License. **Duration of License:** Two years. **Requirements:** High school diploma or equivalent. Completion of an approved curriculum for orthopedic radiography or its equivalent. 18 years of age. **Examination:** Yes. **Fees:** $30 exam fee. $20 biennial registration fee. $30 application fee. **Governing Statute:** NJSA 26-2D. NJAC 7:28-19.

Radiologic Technologists

7100

Radiation Therapy Technologist
New Jersey Dept. of Environmental Protection
Bureau of Revenue
CN402
Trenton, NJ 08625
Phone: (609)530-5760

Credential Type: License. **Requirements:** 18 years of age. High school diploma or equivalent. Completion of an approved 24-month course of study in radiation therapy technology. **Examination:** Written. **Reciprocity:** Yes. **Fees:** $30 application fee. $30 exam fee. **Governing Statute:** NJSA 26:2D. NJAC 7:28-19.

7101

Urologic X-ray Technologist
New Jersey Dept. of Environmental Protection
Bureau of Revenue
CN402
Trenton, NJ 08625-0402
Phone: (609)530-5760

Credential Type: License. **Duration of License:** Two years. **Requirements:** 18 years of age. High school diploma. Satisfactory completion of a curriculum for urologic radiography or its equivalent as approved by the Radiologic Technology Board of Examiners. **Examination:** Yes. **Fees:** $30 exam fee. $20 biennial registration fee. $30 application fee. **Governing Statute:** NJSA 26-2D. NJAC 7:28-19.

New Mexico

7102

Radiation Therapy Technologist
Radiologic Licensing and Registration
1190 St. Francis Dr.
Santa Fe, NM 87503
Phone: (505)827-2948

Credential Type: Radiation Therapy Technologist Certificate. **Duration of License:** Two years. **Requirements:** Submit application. Meet board education and experience requirements. Renewal requires 20 hours of continuing education every year. **Examination:** State, American Registry of Clinical Radiography Technologists (ARCRT), or American Registry of Radiologic Technologists (ARRT) examination. **Fees:** $60 application fee. $50 renewal fee.

7103

Radiologic Technologist
Radiologic Licensing and Registration
1190 St. Francis Dr.
Santa Fe, NM 87503
Phone: (505)827-2948

Credential Type: Radiologic Technologist Certificate. **Duration of License:** Two years. **Requirements:** Submit application. Meet board education and experience requirements. Renewal requires 20 hours of continuing education every year. **Examination:** State, American Registry of Clinical Radiography Technologists (ARCRT), or American Registry of Radiologic Technologists (ARRT) examination. **Fees:** $60 application fee. $50 renewal fee.

Credential Type: Limited Radiologic Technologist Certificate. **Duration of License:** Two years. **Authorization:** Authorizes holder to do radiological work in the following areas: Thorax; Extremities; Dental. **Requirements:** Must have board approved training and experience. **Fees:** $25 application fee. $30 renewal fee.

New York

7104

Radiologic Technologist/ Radiotherapy Technologist
New York State Dept. of Health
Bureau of Environmental Radiation Protection
2 University Pl., Rm. 325
Albany, NY 12203
Phone: (518)458-6482

Credential Type: License. **Duration of License:** One and two years. **Requirements:** High school diploma plus an approved radiologic or radiotherapy course given by a hospital or school. 18 years of age. **Examination:** Written. **Fees:** $20 application fee. $15—$30 license fee. $30 renewal fee. **Governing Statute:** Article 35 of the Public Health Law.

Oregon

7105

Radiologic Technologist
Board of Radiologic Technology
800 NE Oregon St. 21, Ste. 407
Portland, OR 97232
Phone: (503)731-4088

Credential Type: Full License. **Duration of License:** Two years. **Requirements:** Current certification by the American Registry of Radiologic Technologists; or completion of an approved two-year program. **Examination:** Yes. **Fees:** $20 exam fee. $70 license fee. $70 renewal fee. **Governing Statute:** ORS 688.405 to 688.605.

Credential Type: Limited Permit. **Duration of License:** Two years. **Requirements:** Completion of a board-approved course in radiation use/safety, positioning/techniques. Completion of a practical experience requirement. **Examination:** Yes. **Fees:** $20 exam fee per category. $70 license fee. $70 renewal fee. **Governing Statute:** ORS 688.405 to 688.605.

Pennsylvania

7106

Radiation Therapy Technologist
State Board of Medicine
Bureau of Professional and Occupational Affairs
Dept. of State
Transportation and Safety Bldg., 6th Fl.
Harrisburg, PA 17120
Phone: (717)787-8503

Credential Type: Radiation Therapy Technologist License. **Duration of License:** Two years. **Requirements:** Must be certified by the American Registry of Radiologic Technologists, or pass the ARRT examination in Radiation Therapy, or pass a course and examination in Radiation Therapy given by an accredited body recognized by the board. **Examination:** American Registry of Radiologic Technologists (ARRT) examination in Radiation Therapy or board-approved examination. **Fees:** $25 examination fee.

7107

Radiologic Technologist
State Board of Medicine
Bureau of Professional and Occupational Affairs
Dept. of State
Transportation and Safety Bldg., 6th Fl.
Harrisburg, PA 17120
Phone: (717)787-8503

Credential Type: Radiologic Technologist License. **Duration of License:** Two years. **Requirements:** Must be certified by the American Registry of Radiologic Technologists, or pass the ARRT examination in Radiography, or pass a course and examination in Radiography given by an accredited body recognized by the board. **Examination:** American Registry of Radiologic

Tennessee 7108

Radiologic Technologist,
continued

Technologists (ARRT) examination in Radiography or board-approved examination. **Fees:** $25 examination fee.

Tennessee

7108

Radiation Therapy Technologist
Tennessee Board of Medical
 Examiners
283 Plus Park Blvd.
Nashville, TN 37219
Phone: (615)367-6231

Credential Type: Radiation Therapy Technologist Certificate. **Requirements:** Submit application. Meet board education and experience requirements. **Examination:** State, American Registry of Clinical Radiography Technologists (ARCRT), or American Registry of Radiologic Technologists (ARRT) examination.

7109

Radiologic Technologist
Tennessee Board of Medical
 Examiners
283 Plus Park Blvd.
Nashville, TN 37219
Phone: (615)367-6231

Credential Type: Radiologic Technologist Certificate. **Requirements:** Submit application. Meet board education and experience requirements. **Examination:** State, American Registry of Clinical Radiography Technologists (ARCRT), or American Registry of Radiologic Technologists (ARRT) examination.

Credential Type: Limited Radiologic Technologist Certificate. **Authorization:** Authorizes holder to do radiological work in the areas of Chest or Extremities. **Requirements:** Submit application. Meet board education and experience requirements. **Examination:** Board approved examination.

Texas

7110

Medical Radiologic Technician
Texas Medical Radiologic
 Technologist Program
Texas Dept. of Health
1100 W. 49th St.
Austin, TX 78756
Phone: (512)834-6617

Credential Type: License. **Duration of License:** Two years. **Requirements:** Successful completion of an approved course of study or program of radiologic technology, or the equivalent as determined by nationally established guidelines, or as determined by the advisory board on an individual basis. **Examination:** MRT examination. LMRT examination. **Fees:** $20 application fee. $30 certification fee. $30 renewal fee. **Governing Statute:** VACS 4512m, 25 TAC 143.

Utah

7111

Radiology Technologist
Dept. of Commerce
Div. of Occupational and
 Professional Licensing
160 E. 300 S.
PO Box 45802
Salt Lake City, UT 84145
Phone: (801)530-6628

Credential Type: License. **Requirements:** Must be a graduate from a program in radiology technology or the equivalent approved by the Division. **Examination:** Yes.

Vermont

7112

Radiological Technologist
Board of Radiological Technology
Pavilion Office Bldg.
Montpelier, VT 05602
Phone: (802)828-2372

Credential Type: License. **Duration of License:** Two years. **Requirements:** 18 years of age. Good moral character. High school graduate or equivalent. Graduate from an accredited school of Radiological Technology. **Examination:** Yes. **Reciprocity:** Yes. **Fees:** $25 Application. $5 Initial license. $10 Renewal. $10 Late renewal. $10 Reinstatement of revoked or lapsed license. $5 Replacement of lost license. $40 Examination. **Governing Statute:** Title 26, VSA Sections 2801-2833.

7113

Radiological Technologist, Limited
Board of Radiological Technology
Pavilion Office Bldg.
Montpelier, VT 05602
Phone: (802)828-2372

Credential Type: License. **Duration of License:** Two years. **Authorization:** Authorized to x-ray only the chest and extremities. **Requirements:** 18 years of age. Good moral character. High school graduate or equivalent. **Examination:** Yes. **Reciprocity:** Yes. **Fees:** $25 Application. $5 Initial license. $10 Renewal. $40 Examination. **Governing Statute:** Title 26, VSA Sections 2801-2833.

Washington

7114

Radiation Therapy Technologist
Department of Health
1300 SE Quince St., EY-28
PO Box 1099
Olympia, WA 98504
Phone: (206)586-6100

Credential Type: Radiation Therapy Technologist Certificate. **Duration of License:** One year. **Requirements:** Submit application. Meet board education and experience requirements. **Examination:** State or American Registry of Radiologic Technologists (ARRT) examination. **Fees:** $50 application fee. $50 renewal fee.

7115

Radiologic Technologist
Department of Health
1300 SE Quince St., EY-28
PO Box 1099
Olympia, WA 98504
Phone: (206)586-6100

Credential Type: Radiologic Technologist Certificate. **Duration of License:** One year. **Requirements:** Submit application. Meet board education and experience requirements. **Examination:** State or American Registry of Radiologic Technologists (ARRT) examination. **Fees:** $50 application fee. $50 renewal fee.

Credential Type: Limited Radiologic Technologist Certificate. **Duration of License:** One year. **Requirements:** Submit application. Meet board education and experience requirements. **Examination:** State or ARRT examination. **Fees:** $50 application fee. $50 renewal fee.

West Virginia

7116

Radiologic Technician
Board of Examiners for Radiologic
 Technology
500 N. Valley Dr., Ste. 303
Beckley, WV 25801
Phone: (304)348-0662

Credential Type: License. **Duration of License:** One year. **Requirements:** High school diploma. 24 month course of approved study. Never convicted of a felony. **Examination:** Yes. **Fees:** $15 Examination. $30 License. $20 Renewal.

Wyoming

7117

Radiation Technician
Wyoming Board of Radiologic
 Technologists
5102 Hickory Pl.
Cheyenne, WY 82009
Phone: (307)634-6785

Credential Type: License. **Duration of License:** One year. **Requirements:** 18 years of age. Pass a written examination given by the Board. **Examination:** Yes. **Fees:** $20 License. $20 Renewal. $25 Special license. $10 Temporary license.

7118

Radiologic Technologist
Wyoming Board of Radiologic
 Technologists
5102 Hickory Pl.
Cheyenne, WY 82009
Phone: (307)634-6785

Credential Type: License. **Duration of License:** Two years. **Requirements:** 18 years of age. Must have completed a Joint Review Committee in Radiologic Technology course at an approved school. Pass a written examination given by the American Registry of Radiologic Technologists in cooperation with the Board. **Examination:** Yes. **Fees:** $35 License. $35 Renewal. $25 Special license. $10 Temporary license.

Real Estate Agents, Brokers, and Appraisers

The following states grant licenses in this occupational category as of the date of publication:

Alabama	District of	Iowa	Minnesota	New Mexico	Rhode Island	Washington
Alaska	Columbia	Kansas	Mississippi	New York	South Carolina	West Virginia
Arizona	Florida	Kentucky	Missouri	North Carolina	South Dakota	Wisconsin
Arkansas	Georgia	Louisiana	Montana	North Dakota	Tennessee	Wyoming
California	Hawaii	Maine	Nebraska	Ohio	Texas	
Colorado	Idaho	Maryland	Nevada	Oklahoma	Utah	
Connecticut	Illinois	Massachusetts	New Hampshire	Oregon	Vermont	
Delaware	Indiana	Michigan	New Jersey	Pennsylvania	Virginia	

Alabama

7119

Real Estate Appraiser
Alabama Real Estate Commission
Real Estate Appraisal Board
State Capitol
Montgomery, AL 36130
Phone: (205)242-8747

Credential Type: Real Estate Appraiser License. **Duration of License:** One year. **Authorization:** Authorizes holder to provide real estate appraisal services in federally-related transactions in connection with non-complex one-to-four-unit residential properties having a transaction value of less than $1 million; complex one-to-four-unit residential properties of less than $250,000; and commercial properties of less than $250,000. **Requirements:** Complete 75 classroom hours in approved courses, 15 hours of which must be related to standards of professional practice. **Examination:** Licensing Examination. **Fees:** $100 exam fee. $325 application and license fee. $200 renewal fee.

Credential Type: Residential Real Estate Appraiser Certificate. **Duration of License:** One year. **Authorization:** Authorizes holder to provide real estate appraisal services in federally-related transactions in connection with one-to-four-unit residential properties without regard to value; and commercial properties of less than $250,000. **Requirements:** Complete 105 classroom hours in approved courses, 15 hours of which must be related to standards of professional practice. Complete at least 2000 hours of appraisal work over at least two calendar years (24 months). **Examination:** Residential Appraiser Certification Examination. **Fees:** $100 exam fee. $325 application and license fee. $200 renewal fee.

Credential Type: General Real Estate Appraiser Certificate. **Duration of License:** One year. **Authorization:** Authorizes holder to provide real estate appraisal services in federally-related transactions with all types of property without regard to value. **Requirements:** Complete 165 classroom hours in approved courses, 15 hours of which must be related to standards of professional practice. Complete at least 2000 hours of appraisal work over at least two calendar years (24 months), 1000 hours of which must have been in non-residential real property appraisal work. **Examination:** General Appraiser Certification Examination. **Fees:** $100 exam fee. $325 application and license fee. $200 renewal fee.

7120

Real Estate Broker
Alabama Real Estate Commission
State Capitol
Montgomery, AL 36130
Phone: (205)242-5544

Credential Type: License. **Duration of License:** Two years. **Requirements:** 19 years of age and a U.S. citizen. Must hold a high school diploma. Must either have held an active real estate broker's or salesman's license in Alabama for at least 24 months of the 36-month period immediately preceding the date of application and complete the Alabama Real Estate Commission-approved 45-hour course, "Principles of Real Estate"; or must have completed at least 15 semester hours in real estate coursework approved by the Commission.

Renewal requires 12 clock hours of continuing education. **Examination:** Written examination. **Fees:** $75 examination fee. $35 license fee. $30 recovery fund fee. $70 renewal fee. $25 transfer fee.

7121

Real Estate Salesperson
Alabama Real Estate Commission
State Capitol
Montgomery, AL 36130
Phone: (205)242-5544

Credential Type: License. **Duration of License:** Two years. **Requirements:** 19 years of age and U.S. citizen. Must have a high school diploma. Must pass the Alabama Real Estate Commission "Principles of Real Estate" course. **Examination:** Written examination. **Fees:** $75 examination fee. $25 license fee. $30 recovery fee. $50 renewal fee. $25 transfer fee.

7122

Real Estate Time-Share Seller
Alabama Real Estate Commission
State Capitol
Montgomery, AL 36130
Phone: (205)242-5545

Credential Type: License. **Duration of License:** One year. **Requirements:** 19 years of age and a citizen of the U.S. No formal course work or education is required, but applicant must be both knowledgeable and competent. **Examination:** Written examination. **Fees:** $50 license fee. $75 examination fee. $50 renewal fee. $50 transfer fee.

Alaska

7123

Associate Real Estate Broker
Dept. of Commerce and Economic Development
Div. of Occupational Licensing
Real Estate Commission
PO Box D
Juneau, AK 99811-0800
Phone: (907)465-2534
Fax: (907)465-2974

Credential Type: Associate Real Estate Broker License. **Duration of License:** Two years. **Requirements:** Pass real estate brokers examination within six months prior to application. Complete 15 hours of commission approved education. Must have at least 24 months of active and continuous experience as a licensed real estate salesperson. Must be employed by a licensed real estate broker as an associate real estate broker. License renewal requires 20 hours of commission approved continuing education. **Examination:** Real estate brokers examination. **Fees:** $40 examination fee. $125 license fee. $125 license renewal fee. **Governing Statute:** Alaska Statutes 08.88. Professional Regulations 12 AAC 64.

7124

General Real Estate Appraiser
Dept. of Commerce and Economic Development
Board of Certified Real Estate Appraisers
PO Box 110806
Juneau, AK 99811-0806
Phone: (907)465-2542
Fax: (907)465-2974

Credential Type: General Real Estate Appraiser Certificate by Examination. **Duration of License:** Two years. **Requirements:** Completed 150 or more classroom hours of instruction in subjects related to real estate appraisal from an appraisal organization or academic institution approved by the board. Completed 15 classroom hours of instruction related to standards of professional practice as a real estate appraiser. Within seven years immediately preceding application have four years experience in real property appraisal or three years experience as a registered trainee. Complete an examination prescribed by the board. No conviction of a crime involving moral turpitude.

Renewal requires 40 classroom hours of instruction in board approved courses or seminars. **Examination:** National Uniform Appraiser Examination endorsed by the Appraiser Qualifications Board of The Appraisal Foundation, or similar nationally administered examination which has provisions for examination review. **Fees:** $30 application fee. $300 certification fee. $25 federal registry fee. **Governing Statute:** Alaska Statutes 08.87. Professional Regulations 12 AAC 70.

Credential Type: General Real Estate Appraiser Certificate by Endorsement. **Duration of License:** Two years. **Requirements:** Must have been certified in another state that has certification requirements substantially equivalent. Not be the subject of an unresolved complaint or disciplinary action. Not failed the examination for certification in Alaska. Not had certification revoked or suspended in any state. Submitted proof of 40 hours of continuing education in real estate appraisal that was obtained within three years immediately preceding application. Pass an examination that may be prescribed by the board relating to appraisal matters unique to Alaska.

Renewal requires 40 classroom hours of instruction in board approved courses or seminars. **Examination:** Board may require examination on appraisal matters unique to Alaska. **Fees:** $30 application fee. $300 certification fee. $25 federal registry fee. **Governing Statute:** Alaska Statutes 08.87. Professional Regulations 12 AAC 70.

7125

Limited Real Estate Appraiser
Dept. of Commerce and Economic Development
Board of Certified Real Estate Appraisers
PO Box 110806
Juneau, AK 99811-0806
Phone: (907)465-2542
Fax: (907)465-2974

Credential Type: Limited Real Estate Appraiser Certificate. **Duration of License:** Two years. **Authorization:** Issued for the purpose of appraising property in a sparsely settled area of the state or when the cost of an appraisal by a certified appraiser would be unreasonably high with regard to the value of the property. The appraisal must be consistent with federal law. The transaction value of the residential property being appraised must not exceed $1 million. The transaction of the nonrersidential or commercial property being appraised must not exceed $250,000. May not charge an appraisal fee. **Requirements:** Within five years immediately preceding application have two years experience in real property appraisal or one year experience as a registered trainee. Must be a permanent full-time employee of, and perform the appraisal service for, a financial institution with offices in Alaska. **Governing Statute:** Alaska Statutes 08.87. Professional Regulations 12 AAC 70.

7126

Real Estate Appraiser Trainee
Dept. of Commerce and Economic Development
Board of Certified Real Estate Appraisers
PO Box 110806
Juneau, AK 99811-0806
Phone: (907)465-2542
Fax: (907)465-2974

Credential Type: Registered Trainee Certificate. **Requirements:** Must be employed by or under the direct supervision of a certified real estate appraiser. Completed at least 30 classroom hours of course in subjects related to real estate apprisal from a board approved organization or academic institution. **Fees:** $25 registration fee. $30 application fee. **Governing Statute:** Alaska Statutes 08.87. Professional Regulations 12 AAC 70.

7127

Real Estate Broker
Dept. of Commerce and Economic Development
Div. of Occupational Licensing
Real Estate Commission
PO Box D
Juneau, AK 99811-0800
Phone: (907)465-2534
Fax: (907)465-2974

Credential Type: Real Estate Broker License. **Duration of License:** Two years. **Requirements:** Pass real estate brokers examination within six months prior to application. Complete 15 hours of commission approved education. Must have at least 24 months of active and continuous experience as a licensed real estate salesperson. Must own a real estate business or be employed as a real estate broker. License renewal requires 20 hours of commission approved continuing education. **Examination:** Real estate brokers examination. **Fees:** $40 examination fee. $125 license fee. $125 license renewal fee. **Governing Statute:** Alaska Statutes 08.88. Professional Regulations 12 AAC 64.

7128

Real Estate Instructor
Dept. of Commerce and Economic Development
Div. of Occupational Licensing
Real Estate Commission
PO Box D
Juneau, AK 99811-0800
Phone: (907)465-2534
Fax: (907)465-2974

Credential Type: Approved Real Estate Instructor. **Duration of License:** Two years. **Requirements:** A bachelor's degree, two years experience as a real estate broker, and 30 contact hours of experience teaching adults; or a bachelor's degree, three years experience as an associate real estate broker, and 30 contact hours of experience teaching adults; or five years experience as a real estate licensee and 60 contact hours of experience teaching adults; or a juris doctorate or equivalent degree from an accredited law school and three years experience in the areas of proposesd instruction; or three years experience in a specialized area related to real estate that is the proposed area of instruction, and 30 contact hours of experience teaching adults; or another combination of experience and education that the commision finds sufficient.

Successful completion of an instructor workshop sponsored by the National Association of Real Estate License Law Officials or the National Association of Realtors may be substituted for 30 contact hours of teaching experience. **Fees:** $100 instructor approval fee. **Governing Statute:** Alaska Statutes 08.88. Professional Regulations 12 AAC 64.

Credential Type: Temporary Real Estate Instructor Approval. **Duration of License:** Five days. **Requirements:** Currently certified by a nationally recognized organization that requires similar instructor standards or have sufficient experience in the specific area of real estate to be covered by that course. **Fees:** $50 temporary instructor approval **Governing Statute:** Alaska Statutes 08.88. Professional Regulations 12 AAC 64.

7129

Real Estate Salesperson
Dept. of Commerce and Economic Development
Div. of Occupational Licensing
Real Estate Commission
PO Box D
Juneau, AK 99811-0800
Phone: (907)465-2534
Fax: (907)465-2974

Credential Type: Real Estate Salesperson License. **Duration of License:** Two years. **Requirements:** At least 19 years of age. Pass real estate salesperson examination within six months prior to application. Complete 20 hours of commission approved education. Must be employed by a licensed real estate broker. **Examination:** Real estate salesperson examination. **Fees:** $40 examination fee. $125 license fee. $125 license renewal fee. **Governing Statute:** Alaska Statutes 08.88. Professional Regulations 12 AAC 64.

Credential Type: License by Endorsement. **Duration of License:** Two years. **Requirements:** Hold a valid active real estate license issued by another state. Pass the portion of the real estate salesperson examination which examines on Alaska law. At least 19 years of age. Must be employed by a licensed real estate broker. License renewal requires 20 hours of commission approved continuing education. **Examination:** Real estate salesperson examination (partial). **Fees:** $40 examination fee. $125 license fee. $125 license renewal fee. **Governing Statute:** Alaska Statutes 08.88. Professional Regulations 12 AAC 64.

7130

Residential Real Estate Appraiser
Dept. of Commerce and Economic Development
Board of Certified Real Estate Appraisers
PO Box 110806
Juneau, AK 99811-0806
Phone: (907)465-2542
Fax: (907)465-2974

Credential Type: Residential Real Estate Appraiser Certificate by Examination. **Duration of License:** Two years. **Requirements:** Completed 60 classroom hours of instruction in subjects related to residential real estate appraisal from an appraisal organization or academic institution approved by the board. Completed 15 classroom hours of instruction related to standards of professional practice as a real estate appraiser. Within five years immediately preceding application have three years experience in real property appraisal or two years experience as a registered trainee. Complete an examination prescribed by the board. No conviction of a crime involving moral turpitude.

Renewal requires 40 classroom hours of instruction in board approved courses or seminars. **Examination:** National Uniform Appraiser Examination endorsed by the Appraiser Qualifications Board of The Appraisal Foundation, or similar nationally administered examination which has provisions for examination review. **Fees:** $30 application fee. $300 certification fee. $25 federal registry fee. **Governing Statute:** Alaska Statutes 08.87. Professional Regulations 12 AAC 70.

Credential Type: Residential Real Estate Appraiser Certificate by Endorsement. **Duration of License:** Two years. **Requirements:** Must have been certified in another state that has certification requirements substantially equivalent. Not be the subject of an unresolved complaint or disciplinary action. Not failed the examination for certification in Alaska. Not had certification revoked or suspended in any state. Submitted proof of 40 hours of continuing education in real estate appraisal that was obtained within three years immediately preceding application. Pass an examination that may be prescribed by the board relating to appraisal matters unique to Alaska.

Renewal requires 40 classroom hours of instruction in board approved courses or seminars. **Examination:** Board may require examination on appraisal matters unique to Alaska. **Fees:** $30 application fee. $300 certification fee. $25 federal registry fee. **Governing Statute:** Alaska Statutes 08.87. Professional Regulations 12 AAC 70.

Arizona

7131

Campground Membership Broker and Salesperson
Dept. of Real Estate
202 E. Earll Dr., No. 400
Phoenix, AZ 85012
Phone: (602)279-2909

Credential Type: License. **Requirements:** Contact licensing body for application information.

Real Estate Agents, Brokers, and Appraisers

7132

Cemetery Broker and Salesperson
Dept. of Real Estate
202 E. Earll Dr., 400
Phoenix, AZ 85012
Phone: (602)279-2909

Credential Type: License. **Requirements:** Contact licensing body for application information.

7133

Manufactured Home Dealer/Broker
Dept. of Building and Fire Safety
1540 W. Van Buren
Phoenix, AZ 85007
Phone: (602)255-4072

Credential Type: License. **Requirements:** Contact licensing body for application information. **Fees:** $40 application fee. $23 background investigation fee.

7134

Manufactured Home Salesperson
Dept. of Building and Fire Safety
1540 W. Van Buren
Phoenix, AZ 85007
Phone: (602)255-4072

Requirements: Contact licensing body for application information. **Fees:** $40 application fee. $23 background investigation fee.

7135

Real Estate Appraiser
Arizona Board of Appraisal
1700 W. Washington, Ste. 133
Phoenix, AZ 85007
Phone: (602)542-1539
Fax: (602)542-1598

Credential Type: Real Estate Appraiser License. **Duration of License:** Two years. **Authorization:** Authorizes holder to provide real estate appraisal services in federally-related transactions in connection with non-complex one-to-four-unit residential properties having a transaction value of less than $1 million; complex one-to-four-unit residential properties of less than $250,000; and commercial properties of less than $250,000. **Requirements:** Complete 75 classroom hours in approved courses. Complete at least 2000 hours of appraisal work over any period of time. Ten continuing education classroom hours of instruction in courses or seminars for each year during the period preceding the renewal. **Examination:** Licensing Examination. **Fees:** $400 application and license fee. **Governing Statute:** Arizona Revised Statutes Chap. 36, Title 32. Arizona Board of Appraisal Rules.

Credential Type: Residential Real Estate Appraiser Certificate. **Duration of License:** Two years. **Authorization:** Authorizes holder to provide real estate appraisal services in federally-related transactions in connection with one-to-four-unit residential properties without regard to value; and commercial properties of less than $250,000. **Requirements:** Complete 105 classroom hours in approved courses. Equivalent of two years appraisal experience. Ten continuing education classroom hours of instruction in courses or seminars for each year during the period preceding the renewal. **Examination:** Residential Appraiser Certification Examination. **Fees:** $400 application and license fee. **Governing Statute:** Arizona Revised Statutes Chap. 36, Title 32. Arizona Board of Appraisal Rules.

Credential Type: General Real Estate Appraiser Certificate. **Duration of License:** Two years. **Authorization:** Authorizes holder to provide real estate appraisal services in federally-related transactions with all types of property without regard to value. **Requirements:** Complete 165 classroom hours in approved courses. Equivalent of two years appraisal experience. Ten continuing education classroom hours of instruction in courses or seminars for each year during the period preceding the renewal. **Examination:** General Appraiser Certification Examination. **Fees:** $400 application and license fee. **Governing Statute:** Arizona Revised Statutes Chap. 36, Title 32. Arizona Board of Appraisal Rules.

7136

Real Estate Broker
Dept. of Real Estate
202 E. Earll Dr., 400
Phoenix, AZ 85012
Phone: (602)255-4345

Credential Type: Real Estate Broker License. **Duration of License:** Two years. **Requirements:** Complete 180 classroom hours of real estate education, plus six hours within 90 days of licensure. Must have three years of real estate sales experience within the five years preceding application. Renewal requires 24 hours of continuing education. **Examination:** ASI Examination. **Reciprocity:** Yes. **Fees:** $85 exam fee. $125 original license fee. $125 renewal fee.

7137

Real Estate Sales Agent
Dept. of Real Estate
202 E. Earll Dr., 400
Phoenix, AZ 85012
Phone: (602)255-4345

Credential Type: Real Estate Agent License. **Duration of License:** Two years. **Requirements:** Complete 90 classroom hours of real estate education, plus six hours within 90 days of licensure. Renewal requires 24 hours of continuing education. **Examination:** ASI Examination. **Reciprocity:** Yes. **Fees:** $41 exam fee. $60 original license fee. $60 renewal fee.

Arkansas

7138

Real Estate Appraiser
Arkansas Real Estate Commission
612 Summit St.
Little Rock, AR 72201-4740
Phone: (501)682-2732
Fax: (501)376-4041

Credential Type: Real Estate Appraiser License. **Authorization:** Authorizes holder to provide real estate appraisal services in federally-related transactions in connection with non-complex one-to-four-unit residential properties having a transaction value of less than $1 million; complex one-to-four-unit residential properties of less than $250,000; and commercial properties of less than $250,000. **Requirements:** Complete 75 classroom hours in approved courses. Complete at least 2000 hours of appraisal work over any period of time. **Examination:** Licensing Examination.

Credential Type: Residential Real Estate Appraiser Certificate. **Authorization:** Authorizes holder to provide real estate appraisal services in federally-related transactions in connection with one-to-four-unit residential properties without regard to value; and commercial properties of less than $250,000. **Requirements:** Complete 105 classroom hours in approved courses. Complete at least 2000 hours of appraisal work over at least two calendar years (24 months). **Examination:** Residential Appraiser Certification Examination.

Credential Type: General Real Estate Appraiser Certificate. **Authorization:** Authorizes holder to provide real estate appraisal services in federally-related transactions with all types of property without regard to value. **Requirements:** Complete 165 classroom hours in approved courses. Complete at least 2000 hours of appraisal work over at least two calendar years (24 months),

Arkansas

Real Estate Appraiser, continued

1000 hours of which must have been in non-residential real property appraisal work. **Examination:** General Appraiser Certification Examination.

7139

Real Estate Broker
Arkansas Real Estate Commission
612 Summit St.
Little Rock, AR 72201-4740
Phone: (501)682-2732

Credential Type: License. **Duration of License:** One year. **Requirements:** 18 years of age. 30 classroom hours in Principles of Real Estate and 24 months ow experience as a bondable salesman/broker. **Examination:** Yes. **Fees:** $31.50 Written examination. $35 Application. $40 License. $40 Renewal. $25 Recovery fund (if not paid when Agent license was issued).

7140

Real Estate Sales Agent
Arkansas Real Estate Commission
612 Summit St.
Little Rock, AR 72201-4740
Phone: (501)682-2732

Credential Type: License. **Duration of License:** One year. **Requirements:** 18 years of age. Successful completion of at least 30 classroom hours in Principles of Real Estate. Pass the State Salesman Exam. **Fees:** $31.50 Written examination. $35 Application. $20 License. $25 Recovery Fund.

California

7141

Cemetery Broker
Cemetery Board
1434 Howe Ave., Ste. 88
Sacramento, CA 95825-3218
Phone: (916)920-6078

Credential Type: License. **Requirements:** Contact licensing body for application information.

7142

Cemetery Sales Agent
Cemetery Board
1434 Howe Ave., Ste. 88
Sacramento, CA 95825-3218
Phone: (916)920-6078

Credential Type: License. **Requirements:** Contact licensing body for application information.

7143

Real Estate Appraiser
Office of Real Estate Appraisers
PO Box 942874
Sacramento, CA 94274-0001
Phone: (916)653-0045

Credential Type: Real Estate Appraiser License. **Authorization:** Authorizes holder to provide real estate appraisal services in federally-related transactions in connection with non-complex one-to-four-unit residential properties having a transaction value of less than $1 million; complex one-to-four-unit residential properties of less than $250,000; and commercial properties of less than $250,000. **Requirements:** Complete 75 classroom hours in approved courses. Complete at least 2000 hours of appraisal work over any period of time. **Examination:** Licensing Examination. **Fees:** $200 application fee. $50 exam fee.

Credential Type: Residential Real Estate Appraiser Certificate. **Authorization:** Authorizes holder to provide real estate appraisal services in federally-related transactions in connection with one-to-four-unit residential properties without regard to value; and commercial properties of less than $250,000. **Requirements:** Complete 105 classroom hours in approved courses. Complete at least 2000 hours of appraisal work over at least two calendar years (24 months). **Examination:** Residential Appraiser Certification Examination. **Fees:** $200 application fee. $100 exam fee.

Credential Type: General Real Estate Appraiser Certificate. **Authorization:** Authorizes holder to provide real estate appraisal services in federally-related transactions with all types of property without regard to value. **Requirements:** Complete 165 classroom hours in approved courses. Complete at least 2000 hours of appraisal work over at least two calendar years (24 months), 1000 hours of which must have been in non-residential real property appraisal work. **Examination:** General Appraiser Certification Examination. **Fees:** $200 application fee. $100 exam fee.

7144

Real Estate Broker
Dept. of Real Estate
185 Berry St., Rm. 3400
San Francisco, CA 94107
Phone: (415)904-5900

Credential Type: Real Estate Broker License. **Duration of License:** Four years. **Requirements:** Complete 270 classroom hours of real estate education and related credits, plus 90 hours within 18 months of licensure. Must have two years of real estate sales experience within the five years preceding application. Renewal requires 45 hours of continuing education. **Examination:** California Agency/Staff Examination. **Reciprocity:** Yes. **Fees:** $50 exam fee. $165 original license fee. $165 renewal fee.

7145

Real Estate Sales Agent
Dept. of Real Estate
185 Berry St., Rm. 3400
San Francisco, CA 94107
Phone: (415)904-5900

Credential Type: Real Estate Agent License. **Duration of License:** Four years. **Requirements:** Complete 45 hours of real estate education, plus 90 hours within 18 months of licensure. First renewal requires six hours of continuing education. Each subsequent renewal requires 45 hours of continuing education. **Examination:** California Agency/Staff Examination. **Reciprocity:** Yes. **Fees:** $25 exam fee. $120 original license fee. $120 renewal fee.

Colorado

7146

Manufactured Housing Dealer
Manufactured Housing Licensing Board
Dept. of Regulatory Agencies
Div. of Registrations
1560 Broadway, Ste. 1370
Denver, CO 80202
Phone: (303)894-7802

Credential Type: Manufactured Housing Dealership License. **Duration of License:** One year. **Requirements:** Submit application, pay fees, and pass exam. **Examination:** Board administered Manufactured Housing Dealer Exam. **Fees:** $284 exam fee. $684 license fee. $784 renewal fee. $500 recovery fund fee.

Real Estate Agents, Brokers, and Appraisers | 7151 Connecticut

7147

Manufactured Housing Salesperson
Manufactured Housing Licensing Board
Dept. of Regulatory Agencies
Div. of Registrations
1560 Broadway, Ste. 1370
Denver, CO 80202
Phone: (303)894-7802

Credential Type: Manufactured Housing Salesperson License. **Duration of License:** One year. **Requirements:** Submit application, pay fees, and pass exam. **Examination:** Board administered Manufactured Housing Salesperson Exam. **Fees:** $134 exam fee. $234 license fee. $259 renewal fee. $25 recovery fund fee.

7148

Real Estate Appraiser
Board of Real Estate Appraisers
1776 Logan, 4th Fl.
Denver, CO 80203
Phone: (303)894-2166

Credential Type: Real Estate Appraiser License. **Duration of License:** Original license expires on December 31 of the year of issue. Thereafter, duration is three years. **Authorization:** Authorizes holder to provide real estate appraisal services in federally-related transactions in connection with non-complex one-to-four-unit residential properties having a transaction value of less than $1 million; complex one-to-four-unit residential properties of less than $250,000; and commercial properties of less than $250,000. **Requirements:** Complete 95 classroom hours in approved courses. Complete at least 2000 hours of appraisal work. **Examination:** Licensing Examination. **Fees:** $75 exam fee. $111 application and initial licensure fee. $333 renewal fee (includes $25/year Federal Registry fee).

Credential Type: Residential Real Estate Appraiser Certificate. **Duration of License:** Original certificate expires on December 31 of the year of issue. Thereafter, duration is three years. **Authorization:** Authorizes holder to provide real estate appraisal services in federally-related transactions in connection with one-to-four-unit residential properties without regard to value; and commercial properties of less than $250,000. **Requirements:** Complete 105 classroom hours in approved courses. Complete at least 2000 hours of appraisal work. **Examination:** Residential Appraiser Certification Examination. **Fees:** $75 exam fee. $119 application and initial licensure fee. $360 renewal fee (includes $25/year Federal Registry fee).

Credential Type: General Real Estate Appraiser Certificate. **Duration of License:** Original certificate expires on December 31 of the year of issue. Thereafter, duration is three years. **Authorization:** Authorizes holder to provide real estate appraisal services in federally-related transactions with all types of property without regard to value. **Requirements:** Complete 165 classroom hours in approved courses. Complete at least 3000 hours of appraisal workover at least three calendar years (36 months), 1000 hours of which must have been in non-residential real property appraisal work. **Examination:** General Appraiser Certification Examination. **Fees:** $75 exam fee. $119 application and initial licensure fee. $360 renewal fee (includes $25/year Federal Registry fee).

Credential Type: Real Estate Appraiser Registration. **Duration of License:** Original certificate expires on December 31 of the year of issue. Thereafter, duration is three years. **Authorization:** Entry/apprentice level. **Requirements:** Complete 55 classroom hours in approved courses. **Examination:** Real Estate Appraiser Registration Examination. **Fees:** $75 exam fee. $77 application and initial licensure fee. $228 renewal fee (no Federal Registry fee).

7149

Real Estate Broker
Dept. of Regulatory Agencies
Div. of Real Estate
1776 Logan St., 4th Fl.
Denver, CO 80203
Phone: (303)894-2166

Credential Type: Real Estate Broker License. **Duration of License:** Three years. **Requirements:** Complete 120 classroom hours of real estate education. Must have two years of real estate sales experience. Renewal requires 24 hours of continuing education. **Examination:** ASI Examination. **Reciprocity:** No. **Fees:** $72 exam fee. $129 original license fee. $214 renewal fee.

7150

Real Estate Sales Agent
Dept. of Regulatory Agencies
Div. of Real Estate
1776 Logan St., 4th Fl.
Denver, CO 80203
Phone: (303)894-2166

Credential Type: Real Estate Agent License. **Duration of License:** Three years. **Requirements:** Complete 72 classroom hours of real estate education. Renewal requires 24 hours of continuing education. **Examination:** ASI Examination. **Reciprocity:** No. **Fees:** $72 exam fee. $105 original license fee. $169 renewal fee.

Connecticut

7151

General Real Estate Appraiser
Real Estate Div.
Consumer Protection Dept.
165 Capitol Ave.
Hartford, CT 06106
Phone: (203)566-5130

Credential Type: General Appraiser's License. **Duration of License:** One year. **Authorization:** Does not cover federally related transactions. **Requirements:** Have been actively engaged for at least two years as a licensed residential appraiser under the supervision of an appraiser licensed or certified, other than a residential appraiser; or have been actively engaged for at least four years as a real estate appraiser trainee under the supervision of an appraiser licensed or certified, other than a residential appraiser; or if applicant has been actively engaged as a licensed residential appraiser for less than two years, have any combination of such experience as a licensed residential appraiser and a real estate appraiser trainee totalling at least four years.

Complete courses approved by the commission in residential real estate appraisal and income-producing real estate appraisal of at least 60 classroom hours. Complete an additional course prescribed by the commission of at least 60 classroom hours.

In lieu of the above requirements, applicant may demonstrate equivalent experience and education as determined by the commission.

Renewal requires 12 hours of continuing education every two years. **Examination:** Written exam. **Fees:** $40 application fee. $225 renewal fee. $8 continuing education processing fee (every other year). **Governing Statute:** General Statutes of Connecticut, Chap. 392.

Credential Type: Certified Real Estate Appraiser License. **Duration of License:** One year. **Authorization:** Includes federally related transactions. **Requirements:** Must have suitable experience in real estate appraisal and classroom education as prescribed by the Appraiser Qualifications Board (AQB) of the Appraisal Foundation. **Examination:** Written exam. **Fees:** $60 application fee. $300 renewal fee. $8 continuing education processing fee. **Governing Statute:** General Statutes of Connecticut, Chap. 392.

Connecticut

7152

Real Estate Broker
Real Estate Div.
Consumer Protection Dept.
165 Capitol Ave.
Hartford, CT 06106
Phone: (203)566-5130

Credential Type: Real Estate Broker's License. **Duration of License:** One year. **Requirements:** Have been actively engaged for at least two years as a licensed real estate salesperson under the supervision of a licenses real estate broker in Connecticut. Complete a course approved by the real estate commission in real estate principles and practices of at least 30 classroom hours. Complete a course approved by the real estate commission in real estate appraisal of at least 30 classroom hours. Complete an additional course prescribed by the real estate commission of at least 30 classroom hours.

Nonresident applicants who are from a state or jurisdiction that does not have a reciprocal agreement with Connecticut must demonstrate equivalent experience and education before taking the Brokers Examination. Non-resident applicants from non-reciprocal states must hold a current license and submit three letters of recommendation from persons who have known the applicant for at least three years. **Examination:** Brokers Exam. **Exemptions:** Applicants from states with a reciprocal agreement with Connecticut may obtain a license without examination by submitting a completed application, paying appropriate fees, and holding a current license from their state. **Reciprocity:** Connecticut has reciprocity agreements with Illinois, Massachusetts, Nebraska, New Jersey, New York, North Carolina, Oklahoma, and Rhode Island. **Fees:** $60 application fee. $55 exam fee. $450 initial license fee. $300 license renewal fee. **Governing Statute:** General Statutes of Connecticut, Chap. 392.

7153

Real Estate Salesperson
Real Estate Div.
Consumer Protection Dept.
165 Capitol Ave.
Hartford, CT 06106
Phone: (203)566-5130

Credential Type: Real Estate Salesperson's License. **Duration of License:** One year. **Requirements:** Successfully complete a course approved by the real estate commission in real estate principles and practices consisting of at least 30 classroom hours, or demonstrate equivalent experience or education. **Examination:** Salespersons Exam. **Exemptions:** Applicants from states with a reciprocal agreement with Connecticut may obtain a license without examination by submitting a completed application, paying appropriate fees, and holding a current license from their state. **Reciprocity:** Connecticut has reciprocity agreements with Illinois, Massachusetts, Nebraska, New Jersey, New York, North Carolina, Oklahoma, and Rhode Island. **Fees:** $40 application fee. $55 exam fee. $225 annual license fee. **Governing Statute:** General Statutes of Connecticut, Chap. 392.

7154

Residential Real Estate Appraiser
Real Estate Div.
Consumer Protection Dept.
165 Capitol Ave.
Hartford, CT 06106
Phone: (203)566-5130

Credential Type: Residential Appraiser's License. **Duration of License:** One year. **Requirements:** Have been actively engaged for at least two years as a real estate appraiser trainee under the supervision of an appraiser licensed or certified in this state or another state with similar licensing requirements.

Complete a course approved by the commission in residential real estate appraisal of at least 30 classroom hours. Complete an additional course prescribed by the commission of at least 30 classroom hours.

In lieu of the above requirements, applicant may demonstrate equivalent experience and education as determined by the commission.

Renewal requires 12 hours of continuing education every two years. **Examination:** Written exam. **Fees:** $40 application fee. $225 renewal fee. $8 continuing education processing fee (every other year). **Governing Statute:** General Statutes of Connecticut, Chap. 392.

Credential Type: Certified Residential Appraiser License. **Duration of License:** One year. **Authorization:** Includes federally related transactions. **Requirements:** Must complete commission approved courses of at least 75 classroom hours of study. Must meet the experience requirements established by the Appraiser Qualifications Board (AQB) of the Appraisal Foundation. **Examination:** Written exam. **Fees:** $60 application fee. $300 renewal fee. $8 continuing education processing fee. **Governing Statute:** General Statutes of Connecticut, Chap. 392.

Delaware

7155

Real Estate Broker
Dept. of Administrative Services
O'Neil Bldg.
PO Box 1401
Dover, DE 19902
Phone: (302)739-4522

Credential Type: Real Estate Broker License. **Requirements:** Complete 168 classroom hours of real estate education within the year preceding application. Must have five years of sales experience. Renewal requires 15 hours of continuing education every two years.

7156

Real Estate Sales Agent
Dept. of Administrative Services
O'Neil Bldg.
PO Box 1401
Dover, DE 19902
Phone: (302)739-4522

Credential Type: Real Estate Agent License. **Requirements:** Complete 93 classroom hours of real estate education within the year preceding application. Renewal requires 15 hours of continuing education every two years.

District of Columbia

7157

Real Estate Appraiser
Dept. of Consumer & Regulatory Affairs
Licensing and Certification Div.
PO Box 37200
Washington, DC 20013-7200
Phone: (202)727-7823
Phone: (202)727-7824

Credential Type: Real Estate Appraiser License. **Duration of License:** Two years. **Authorization:** Authorizes holder to provide real estate appraisal services in federally-related transactions in connection with non-complex one-to-four-unit residential properties having a transaction value of less than $1 million; complex one-to-four-unit residential properties of less than $250,000; and commercial properties of less than $250,000. **Requirements:** Complete 75 classroom hours in approved courses. Complete at least 2000 hours of appraisal work over any period of time. **Examination:** Licensing Examination. **Fees:** Fees not set. Contact licensing division.

Credential Type: Residential Real Estate Appraiser Certificate. **Duration of License:** Two years. **Authorization:** Authorizes holder to provide real estate appraisal services in federally-related transactions in connection with one-to-four-unit residential properties without regard to value; and commercial properties of less than $250,000. **Requirements:** Complete 105 classroom hours in approved courses. Complete at least 2000 hours of appraisal work over at least two calendar years (24 months). **Examination:** Residential Appraiser Certification Examination. **Fees:** Fees not set. Contact licensing division.

Credential Type: General Real Estate Appraiser Certificate. **Duration of License:** Two years. **Authorization:** Authorizes holder to provide real estate appraisal services in federally-related transactions with all types of property without regard to value. **Requirements:** Complete 165 classroom hours in approved courses. Complete at least 2000 hours of appraisal work over at least two calendar years (24 months), 1000 hours of which must have been in non-residential real property appraisal work. **Examination:** General Appraiser Certification Examination. **Fees:** Fees not set. Contact licensing division.

7158

Real Estate Broker
Dept. of Consumer & Regulatory Affairs
614 H St., NW, Rm. 923
PO Box 37200
Washington, DC 20013-7200
Phone: (202)727-7468

Credential Type: Real Estate Broker License. **Duration of License:** Two years. **Requirements:** Complete 180 classroom hours of real estate education. Must have two years of real estate sales experience within the two years preceding application. Renewal requires 12 hours of continuing education. **Examination:** ASI Examination. **Reciprocity:** Yes. **Fees:** $19.95 exam fee. $150 original license fee. $160 renewal fee.

7159

Real Estate Sales Agent
Dept. of Consumer & Regulatory Affairs
614 H St., NW, Rm. 923
PO Box 37200
Washington, DC 20013-7200
Phone: (202)727-7468

Credential Type: Real Estate Agent License. **Duration of License:** Two years. **Requirements:** Complete 45 classroom hours of real estate education. Renewal requires 12 hours of continuing education. **Examination:** ASI Examination. **Reciprocity:** Yes. **Fees:** $19.95 exam fee. $150 original license fee. $100 renewal fee.

Florida

7160

Cemetery Lot Salesperson
Dept. of Professional Regulation
Div. of Real Estate
PO Box 1900
Orlando, FL 32802-1900
Phone: (407)423-6071

Credential Type: Cemetery Lot Sales License. **Requirements:** Contact licensing body for application information.

7161

Real Estate Appraiser
Florida Real Estate Appraisal Board
Hurston North Tower
400 W. Robinson St., Rm. 309
Orlando, FL 32801-1772
Phone: (407)423-6053

Credential Type: Registered Appraiser. **Duration of License:** One year. **Requirements:** Be at least 18 years of age. Possess high school diploma or equivalent. Complete 75 classroom hours of approved education, or equivalent.

Renewal requires 30 hours of continuing education. **Reciprocity:** No. **Fees:** $50 application fee. $35 renewal fee. $25 federal registry fee. **Governing Statute:** Florida Statutes, Chapter 475, Part II. Florida Administrative Code, Rules 21-V.

Credential Type: Licensed Appraiser. **Duration of License:** One year. **Requirements:** Be at least 18 years of age. Possess high school diploma or equivalent. Complete 75 classroom hours of approved education, or equivalent. Complete two years of experience.

Renewal requires 30 hours of continuing education. **Examination:** 100-question statte licensure examination. **Reciprocity:** No. **Fees:** $110 application and examination fee. $35 renewal fee. $25 federal registry fee. **Governing Statute:** Florida Statutes, Chapter 475, Part II. Florida Administrative Code, Rules 21-V.

Credential Type: Certified Residential Appraiser. **Duration of License:** One year. **Requirements:** Be at least 18 years of age. Possess high school diploma or equivalent. Complete 105 classroom hours of approved education, or equivalent. Complete two years of experience.

Renewal requires 30 hours of continuing education. **Examination:** 100-question state residential certification examination. **Reciprocity:** No. **Fees:** $110 application and examination fee. $35 renewal fee. $25 federal registry fee. **Governing Statute:** Florida Statutes, Chapter 475, Part II. Florida Administrative Code, Rules 21-V.

Credential Type: Certified General Appraiser. **Duration of License:** One year. **Requirements:** Be at least 18 years of age. Possess high school diploma or equivalent. Complete 165 classroom hours of approved education, or equivalent. Complete two years of experience, of which half must be in non-residential appraisal work.

Renewal requires 30 hours of continuing education. **Examination:** 100-question state residential certification examination. **Fees:** $110 application and examination fee. $35 renewal fee. $25 federal registry fee. **Governing Statute:** Florida Statutes, Chapter 475, Part II. Florida Administrative Code, Rules 21-V.

7162

Real Estate Broker
Florida Real Estate Commission
Hurston North Tower
400 W. Robinson St., Rm. 309
Orlando, FL 32801-1772
Phone: (407)423-6053

Credential Type: Real Estate Broker License. **Duration of License:** Two years. **Requirements:** Be at least 18 years of age. Possess high school diploma or equivalent. Good moral character. Complete 135 classroom hours of education courses for brokers.

Renewal requires 14 hours of continuing education. Newly licensed brokers must complete 60 hours of commission-approved post-licensure education by the time of their first renewal. **Examination:** 100-question examination. **Reciprocity:** No. **Fees:** $65 application and examination fee. $60 renewal fee. **Governing Statute:** Florida Statutes, Chapter 475, Part I. Florida Administrative Code, Rules 21-V.

Florida

7163

Real Estate Instructor
Florida Real Estate Commission
Hurston North Tower
400 W. Robinson St., Rm. 309
Orlando, FL 32801-1772
Phone: (407)423-6053

Credential Type: Real Estate Instructor License. **Duration of License:** Two years. **Requirements:** Contact licensing body for application information. **Reciprocity:** No. **Fees:** $50 license fee. $50 renewal fee. **Governing Statute:** Florida Statutes, Chapter 475, Part I. Florida Administrative Code, Rules 21-V.

7164

Real Estate Salesperson
Florida Real Estate Commission
Hurston North Tower
400 W. Robinson St., Rm. 309
Orlando, FL 32801-1772
Phone: (407)423-6053

Credential Type: Real Estate Salesperson License. **Duration of License:** Two years. **Requirements:** Be at least 18 years of age. Possess high school diploma or equivalent. Good moral character. Complete up to 63 classroom hours of education courses for salespersons.

Renewal requires 14 hours of continuing education. Newly licensed salespersons must complete 45 hours of commission-approved post-licensure education by the time of their first renewal. **Examination:** 100-question examination. **Reciprocity:** No. **Fees:** $65 application and examination fee. $50 renewal fee. **Governing Statute:** Florida Statutes, Chapter 475, Part I. Florida Administrative Code, Rules 21-V.

7165

Time-Share Agent
Dept. of Professional Regulation
Div. of Real Estate
PO Box 1900
Orlando, FL 32802-1900
Phone: (407)423-6071

Credential Type: Time-Share Agent License. **Requirements:** Contact licensing body for application information.

Georgia

7166

Real Estate Appraiser
Georgia Real Estate Appraisers Board
Sussex Pl., Ste. 500
148 International Blvd., N.E.
Atlanta, GA 30303-1734
Phone: (404)656-3916

Credential Type: Real Estate Appraiser License. **Duration of License:** One year. **Authorization:** Authorizes holder to provide real estate appraisal services in federally-related transactions in connection with non-complex one-to-four-unit residential properties having a transaction value of less than $1 million; complex one-to-four-unit residential properties of less than $250,000; and commercial properties of less than $250,000. **Requirements:** Be at least 18 years of age. High school graduate or equivalent. Complete 75 classroom hours in approved courses. Complete at least 2000 hours of appraisal work. Renewal requires 10 hours of continuing education per year. **Examination:** Licensing Examination. **Fees:** $150 fee if applying within three months of taking the exam or $275 fee if applying after three months but within 12 months after taking exam. $105 renewal fee. **Governing Statute:** O.C.G.A. 43-39A-1 et seq. Rules and Regulations.

Credential Type: Residential Real Estate Appraiser Certificate. **Duration of License:** One year. **Authorization:** Authorizes holder to provide real estate appraisal services in federally-related transactions in connection with one-to-four-unit residential properties without regard to value; and commercial properties of less than $250,000. **Requirements:** Be at least 18 years of age. High school graduate or equivalent. Complete 105 classroom hours in approved courses. Complete at least 2000 hours of appraisal work over at least two calendar years (24 months), including at least 500 hours of property appraisal experience in complex 1-4 unit residential real property appraisal work. Renewal requires 10 hours of continuing education per year. **Examination:** Residential Appraiser Certification Examination. **Fees:** $150 fee if applying within three months of taking the exam or $275 fee if applying after three months but within 12 months after taking exam. $105 renewal fee. **Governing Statute:** O.C.G.A. 43-39A-1 et seq. Rules and Regulations.

Credential Type: General Real Estate Appraiser Certificate. **Duration of License:** One year. **Authorization:** Authorizes holder to provide real estate appraisal services in federally-related transactions with all types of property without regard to value. **Requirements:** Be at least 18 years of age. High school graduate or equivalent. Complete 165 classroom hours in approved courses. Complete at least 2000 hours of appraisal work over at least two calendar years (24 months), 1000 hours of which must have been in non-residential real property appraisal work. Renewal requires 10 hours of continuing education per year. **Examination:** General Appraiser Certification Examination. **Fees:** $150 fee if applying within three months of taking the exam or $275 fee if applying after three months but within 12 months after taking exam. $105 renewal fee. **Governing Statute:** O.C.G.A. 43-39A-1 et seq. Rules and Regulations.

Credential Type: Real Estate Appraiser Registration. **Authorization:** Authorizes holder to provide real estate appraisal services except for use in federally-related transactions. **Requirements:** Be at least 18 years of age. High school graduate or equivalent. Complete 75 classroom hours in approved courses. Renewal requires 10 hours of continuing education per year. **Examination:** No exam required. **Fees:** $125 application and registration fee. $105 renewal fee. **Governing Statute:** O.C.G.A. 43-39A-1 et seq. Rules and Regulations.

7167

Real Estate Broker
Real Estate Commission
Sussex Place, Ste. 500
148 International Blvd. N.E.
Atlanta, GA 30303-1734
Phone: (404)656-3916

Credential Type: Real Estate Broker License. **Duration of License:** Four years. **Requirements:** Complete 135 classroom hours of real estate education. Must have three years of real estate sales experience. All persons licensed after Dec. 31, 1979, must have six hours of continuing education annually for license renewal. **Examination:** AMP Examination. **Reciprocity:** Yes, with selected states. **Fees:** $23.50 exam fee. $235 original license fee. $160 renewal fee.

7168

Real Estate Sales Agent
Real Estate Commission
Sussex Place, Ste. 500
148 International Blvd. N.E.
Atlanta, GA 30303-1734
Phone: (404)656-3916

Credential Type: Real Estate Agent License. **Duration of License:** Four years.

Requirements: Complete 75 classroom hours of real estate education. All persons licensed after Dec. 31, 1979, must have six hours of continuing education annually for license renewal. **Examination:** AMP Examination. **Reciprocity:** Yes, with selected states. **Fees:** $23.50 exam fee. $165 original license fee. $90 renewal fee.

Hawaii

7169

Real Estate Appraiser
Hawaii Real Estate Commission
Dept. of Commerce and Consumer Affairs
PO Box 3469
Honolulu, HI 96801
Phone: (808)548-4100
Phone: (808)548-7464

Credential Type: Real Estate Appraiser License. **Authorization:** Authorizes holder to provide real estate appraisal services in federally-related transactions in connection with non-complex one-to-four-unit residential properties having a transaction value of less than $1 million; complex one-to-four-unit residential properties of less than $250,000; and commercial properties of less than $250,000. **Requirements:** Complete 75 classroom hours in approved courses. Complete at least 2000 hours of appraisal work over any period of time. **Examination:** Licensing Examination.

Credential Type: Residential Real Estate Appraiser Certificate. **Authorization:** Authorizes holder to provide real estate appraisal services in federally-related transactions in connection with one-to-four-unit residential properties without regard to value; and commercial properties of less than $250,000. **Requirements:** Complete 105 classroom hours in approved courses. Complete at least 2000 hours of appraisal work over at least two calendar years (24 months). **Examination:** Residential Appraiser Certification Examination.

Credential Type: General Real Estate Appraiser Certificate. **Authorization:** Authorizes holder to provide real estate appraisal services in federally-related transactions with all types of property without regard to value. **Requirements:** Complete 165 classroom hours in approved courses. Complete at least 2000 hours of appraisal work over at least two calendar years (24 months), 1000 hours of which must have been in non-residential real property appraisal work. **Examination:** General Appraiser Certification Examination.

7170

Real Estate Broker
Hawaii Real Estate Commission
828 Fort St. Mall 600
PO Box 3469
Honolulu, HI 96801
Phone: (808)548-4100

Credential Type: License. **Duration of License:** Two years. **Requirements:** Hawaii salesperson license. At least two years of full-time experience as a Hawaii salesperson with at least 10 real estate transactions, including three executed listings and three executed sales contracts that have closed escrow or commercial, industrial or management equivalents. Submit an "Experience Certificate." Pass an accredited broker course or have a qualifying waiver. **Examination:** Given monthly. **Reciprocity:** None. **Fees:** $10 application fee. $30 exam fee. $30 license fee. $50 recovery fund fee. $20—$40 Compliance Resolution Fund fee. $20—$40 education fund fee. $80 renewal fund fee.

7171

Real Estate Salesman
Hawaii Real Estate Commission
828 Fort St. Mall 600
PO Box 3469
Honolulu, HI 96801
Phone: (808)548-4100

Credential Type: License. **Duration of License:** Two years. **Requirements:** 18 years of age. Completion of an accredited salesman course. **Examination:** Given monthly. **Exemptions:** Educational waivers may be granted. **Reciprocity:** None. **Fees:** $30 license fee. $50 Recovery Fund fee. $20—$40 Compliance Resolution Fund fee. $20—$40 Education Fund fee. $30 renewal fee.

Idaho

7172

Associate Real Estate Broker
Real Estate Commission
633 N. 4th St.
State House Mail
Boise, ID 83720-6000
Phone: (208)334-3285

Credential Type: Associate Real Estate Broker's License. **Duration of License:** Two years. **Authorization:** Individual has qualified as a real estate broker and is licensed under and associated with a broker. May directly or indirectly represent said broker in the performance of acts a broker is licensed to perform. **Requirements:** Must be at least 18 years of age. Must not have had a license as a real estate salesperson revoked or refused within the past two years. Must not have been convicted of any felony or misdemeanor involving moral turpitude within the past five years.

Be a high school graduate or equivalent. Complete 90 classroom hours required of real estate salespersons, including 45 hours of Real Estate Essentials and 45 hours of Real Estate Practice. Complete an additional 90 classroom hours, including 30 hours of Brokerage Management, 30 hours of Real Estate Law, and two electives of at least 20 hours each in separate subjects.

Complete two years active real estate sales experience within the past five years.

Renewal requires 12 hours of continuing education. **Examination:** Salesperson Examination, written. **Reciprocity:** A nonresident broker in good standing may be licensed as a nonresident broker by written reciprocal agreement. **Fees:** $50 exam fee if preregistered. $60 exam fee if walk-in. $160 license fee. **Governing Statute:** Idaho Code, Title 54, Chap. 20.

7173

General Real Estate Appraiser, Certified
Certified Real Estate Appraiser Board
Bureau of Occupational Licenses
1109 Main St., Ste. 220
Boise, ID 83702-5642
Phone: (208)334-3233

Credential Type: General Real Estate Appraiser Certification. **Duration of License:** Three years. **Authorization:** Applies to the appraisal of all types of real property. **Requirements:** Must have a college degree or equivalent. Complete at least 165 classroom hours of courses in subjects related to real estate appraisal approved by the board, including the following: At least 50 classroom hours of study relating to the basic principles of real estate appraising and at least 15 but not more than 20 classroom hours of studies within the past five years specifically relating to Uniform Standards of Professional Appraisal Practice and the Code of Ethics and provisions of the State Act; and at least 100 classroom hours of advanced study in real estate appraisal topics. The educational requirement of 165 classroom hours may be fulfilled as part of the college degree program.

Must have at least three years of practical experience in real estate appraising.

Renewal requires the equivalent of 15 classroom hours of continuing education per year during the period preceding renewal. **Examination:** Yes. **Reciprocity:**

General Real Estate Appraiser, Certified, continued

Yes, provided state has reciprocity agreement and substantially equivalent requirements. **Fees:** $200 application fee. $200 exam fee. $100 original certification fee. $275 certification renewal fee. $200 reciprocity application fee. **Governing Statute:** Idaho Code, Title 54, Chap. 41. Idaho State Certified Real Estate Appraiser Board Rules.

7174

Manufactured Home Broker
Manufactured Home Advisory Board
Dept. of Labor and Industrial
 Services
277 N. 6th
Statehouse Mail
Boise, ID 83720
Phone: (208)334-3950
Fax: (208)334-2683

Credential Type: Manufactured Home Broker License. **Duration of License:** One year. **Requirements:** Submit application and pay fee. Post $20,000 bond with department. **Fees:** $250 license fee. **Governing Statute:** Idaho Code, Title 44, Chapt. 21.

7175

Manufactured Home Dealer
Manufactured Home Advisory Board
Dept. of Labor and Industrial
 Services
277 N. 6th
Statehouse Mail
Boise, ID 83720
Phone: (208)334-3950
Fax: (208)334-2683

Credential Type: Manufactured Home Dealer License. **Duration of License:** One year. **Requirements:** Submit application and pay fee. Post $20,000 bond with department. **Fees:** $250 license fee. **Governing Statute:** Idaho Code, Title 44, Chapt. 21.

7176

Manufactured Home Salesperson
Manufactured Home Advisory Board
Dept. of Labor and Industrial
 Services
277 N. 6th
Statehouse Mail
Boise, ID 83720
Phone: (208)334-3950
Fax: (208)334-2683

Credential Type: Manufactured Home Salesperson License. **Duration of License:** One year. **Requirements:** Submit application and pay fee. **Fees:** $25 license fee. **Governing Statute:** Idaho Code, Title 44, Chapt. 21.

7177

Real Estate Broker
Real Estate Commission
633 N. 4th St.
State House Mail
Boise, ID 83720-6000
Phone: (208)334-3285

Credential Type: Real Estate Broker's License. **Duration of License:** Two years. **Requirements:** Must be at least 18 years of age. Must not have had a license as a real estate salesperson revoked or refused within the past two years. Must not have been convicted of any felony or misdemeanor involving moral turpitude within the past five years.

Be a high school graduate or equivalent. Complete 90 classroom hours required of real estate salespersons, including 45 hours of Real Estate Essentials and 45 hours of Real Estate Practice. Complete an additional 90 classroom hours, including 30 hours of Brokerage Management, 30 hours of Real Estate Law, and two electives of at least 20 hours each in separate subjects.

Complete two years active real estate sales experience within the past five years.

Renewal requires 12 hours of continuing education. **Examination:** Salesperson Examination, written. **Reciprocity:** A nonresident broker in good standing may be licensed as a nonresident broker by written reciprocal agreement. **Fees:** $50 exam fee if preregistered. $60 exam fee if walk-in. $160 license fee. **Governing Statute:** Idaho Code, Title 54, Chap. 20.

7178

Real Estate Salesperson
Real Estate Commission
633 N. 4th St.
State House Mail
Boise, ID 83720-6000
Phone: (208)334-3285

Credential Type: Real Estate Salesperson License. **Duration of License:** Two years. **Authorization:** Must be licensed under and associated with a licensed real estate broker or be a member of a real estate firm. **Requirements:** Must be at least 18 years of age. Must not have had a license as a real estate salesperson revoked or refused within the past two years. Must not have been convicted of any felony or misdemeanor involving moral turpitude within the past five years.

Be a high school graduate or equivalent. Complete 90 classroom hours, including 45 hours of Real Estate Essentials and 45 hours of Real Estate Practice.

Renewal requires 12 hours of continuing education. **Examination:** Salesperson Examination, written. **Reciprocity:** A nonresident salesperson in good standing may be licensed as a nonresident salesperson by written reciprocal agreement. **Fees:** $50 exam fee if preregistered. $60 exam fee if walk-in. $160 license fee. **Governing Statute:** Idaho Code, Title 54, Chap. 20.

7179

Residential Real Estate Appraiser, Licensed
Certified Real Estate Appraiser Board
Bureau of Occupational Licenses
1109 Main St., Ste. 220
Boise, ID 83702-5642
Phone: (208)334-3233

Credential Type: Residential Real Estate Appraiser License. **Duration of License:** Three years. **Authorization:** Limited to the appraisal of residential real estate. May appraise 1-4 family residential real estate units. **Requirements:** Must have an Associate College Degree or equivalent. Complete at least 75 classroom hours of courses in subjects related to real estate appraisal approved by the board, including the following: At least 50 classroom hours of study relating to the basic principles of real estate appraising and at least 15 but not more than 20 classroom hours of studies within the past five years specifically relating to Uniform Standards of Professional Appraisal Practice and the Code of Ethics and provisions of the State Act. The educational requirement of 75 classroom hours may be fulfilled as part of the Associate College Degree program.

Must have at least two years of practical experience in real estate appraising.

Renewal requires the equivalent of 15 classroom hours of continuing education per year during the period preceding renewal. **Examination:** Yes. **Reciprocity:** Yes, provided state has reciprocity agreement and substantially equivalent requirements. **Fees:** $200 application fee. $200 exam fee. $100 original license fee. $275 license renewal fee. $200 reciprocity application fee. **Governing Statute:** Idaho Code, Title 54, Chap. 41. Idaho State Certified Real Estate Appraiser Board Rules.

Illinois

7180

Real Estate Broker
Dept. of Professional Regulation
320 W. Washington St.
Springfield, IL 62786
Phone: (217)785-0891

Credential Type: Real Estate Broker License. **Requirements:** Complete 90 classroom hours of real estate education. Must have one year of real estate sales experience within the three years preceding application.

7181

Real Estate Sales Agent
Dept. of Professional Regulation
320 W. Washington St.
Springfield, IL 62786
Phone: (217)785-0891

Credential Type: Real Estate Agent License. **Requirements:** Complete 30 classroom hours of real estate education.

Indiana

7182

Real Estate Appraiser
Real Estate Appraiser Licensure and Certification Board
Professional Licensing Agency
State Government Center N.
100 N. Senate Ave., Rm. 1021
Indianapolis, IN 46204-2246
Phone: (317)232-2980

Credential Type: Real Estate Appraiser License. **Duration of License:** Two years. **Authorization:** Authorizes holder to provide real estate appraisal services in federally-related transactions in connection with non-complex one-to-four-unit residential properties having a transaction value of less than $1 million; complex one-to-four-unit residential properties of less than $250,000; and commercial properties of less than $250,000. **Requirements:** Complete 75 classroom hours in approved courses. Complete at least 2000 hours of appraisal work over at least two calendar years (24 months) during the preceding five years prior to filing application. Renewal requires 20 classroom hours of continuing education. **Examination:** Licensing Examination. **Fees:** $100 application fee. $65 exam fee. $150 license fee. $150 renewal fee.

Credential Type: Residential Real Estate Appraiser Certificate. **Duration of License:** Two years. **Authorization:** Authorizes holder to provide real estate appraisal services in federally-related transactions in connection with one-to-four-unit residential properties without regard to value; and commercial properties of less than $250,000. **Requirements:** Complete 105 classroom hours in approved courses. Complete at least 2000 hours of appraisal work over at least two calendar years (24 months) during the preceding five years prior to filing application. Renewal requires 20 classroom hours of continuing education. **Examination:** Residential Appraiser Certification Examination. **Fees:** $100 application fee. $65 exam fee. $150 certification fee. $150 renewal fee.

Credential Type: General Real Estate Appraiser Certificate. **Duration of License:** Two years. **Authorization:** Authorizes holder to provide real estate appraisal services in federally-related transactions with all types of property without regard to value. **Requirements:** Complete 165 classroom hours in approved courses. Complete at least 2000 hours of appraisal work, 1000 hours of which must have been in non-residential real property appraisal work, over at least two calendar years (24 months) during the preceding five years prior to filing application. Renewal requires 20 classroom hours of continuing education. **Examination:** General Appraiser Certification Examination. **Fees:** $100 application fee. $65 exam fee. $150 certification fee $150 renewal fee.

Credential Type: Temporary Permit. **Duration of License:** 30 days. **Authorization:** Issued only for one or more appraising assignments requiring no more than 30 days. **Requirements:** Must be licensed or certified in another state. **Fees:** $10 application fee.

7183

Real Estate Broker
Professional Licensing Agency
1021 Government Center N.
100 N. Senate Ave.
Indianapolis, IN 46204
Phone: (317)232-2980

Credential Type: Real Estate Broker License. **Requirements:** Complete 108 classroom hours of real estate education. Must have one year of real estate sales experience.

7184

Real Estate Sales Agent
Professional Licensing Agency
1021 Government Center N.
100 N. Senate Ave.
Indianapolis, IN 46204
Phone: (317)232-2980

Credential Type: Real Estate Agent License. **Requirements:** Complete 54 classroom hours of real estate education.

Iowa

7185

Real Estate Appraiser
Iowa Real Estate Commission
1918 SE Hulsizer
Ankeny, IA 50021
Phone: (515)281-7361

Credential Type: Real Estate Appraiser License. **Requirements:** Satisfy the criteria for certification issued by the Board. **Examination:** Uniform State Certification Exam. **Reciprocity:** Agreements with IL, KS, MN, MO, NE, ND, OK, and SD.

7186

Real Estate Broker
Iowa Real Estate Commission
1918 SE Hulsizer
Ankeny, IA 50021
Phone: (515)281-7361

Credential Type: Real Estate Broker License. **Duration of License:** Three years. **Requirements:** 18 years of age. Completion of a 60 hour pre-license education course and 24 months of experience as a real estate salesperson. **Examination:** Written. **Reciprocity:** Agreements with IL, KS, MN, MO, NE, ND, OK, and SD. **Fees:** $19 exam fee. $120 license fee. $120 renewal fee.

Iowa

7187

Real Estate Salesperson
Iowa Real Estate Commission
1918 SE Hulsizer
Ankeny, IA 50021
Phone: (515)281-7361

Credential Type: Real Estate Salesperson License. **Duration of License:** Three years. **Requirements:** 18 years of age. Completion of a commission-approved, 30 contact-hour course in real estate. **Examination:** Written. **Reciprocity:** Agreements with IL, KS, MN, MO, NE, ND, OK, and SD. **Fees:** $19 exam fee. $75 license fee. $75 renewal fee.

Kansas

7188

Real Estate Appraiser
Real Estate Appraisal Board
Landon State Office Bldg.
900 Jackson, Rm. 501
Topeka, KS 66612-1220
Phone: (913)296-0706

Credential Type: Real Estate Appraiser License. **Duration of License:** One year. **Authorization:** Authorizes holder to provide real estate appraisal services in federally-related transactions in connection with non-complex one-to-four-unit residential properties having a transaction value of less than $1 million; complex one-to-four-unit residential properties of less than $250,000; and commercial properties of less than $250,000. **Requirements:** Complete 75 classroom hours in approved courses. Complete at least 2000 hours of appraisal work over any period of time. Renewal requires 10 classroom hours of continuing education instruction. **Examination:** Licensing Examination. **Fees:** $50 application fee. $200 original licensure fee. $200 license renewal fee. **Governing Statute:** Kansas Statutes Annotated 58-4104 et seq. Rules and Regulations 117-1-1 ff.

Credential Type: Residential Real Estate Appraiser Certificate. **Duration of License:** One year. **Authorization:** Authorizes holder to provide real estate appraisal services in federally-related transactions in connection with one-to-four-unit residential properties without regard to value; and commercial properties of less than $250,000. **Requirements:** Complete 105 classroom hours in approved courses. Complete at least 2000 hours of appraisal work over at least two calendar years (24 months). Renewal requires 10 classroom hours of continuing education instruction. **Examination:** Residential Appraiser Certification Examination. **Fees:** $50 application fee. $200 original certification fee. $200 certificate renewal fee. **Governing Statute:** Kansas Statutes Annotated 58-4104 et seq. Rules and Regulations 117-1-1 ff.

Credential Type: General Real Estate Appraiser Certificate. **Duration of License:** One year. **Authorization:** Authorizes holder to provide real estate appraisal services in federally-related transactions with all types of property without regard to value. **Requirements:** Complete 165 classroom hours in approved courses. Complete at least 2000 hours of appraisal work over at least two calendar years (24 months). Renewal requires 10 classroom hours of continuing education instruction. **Examination:** General Appraiser Certification Examination. **Fees:** $50 application fee. $200 original certification fee. $200 certificate renewal fee. **Governing Statute:** Kansas Statutes Annotated 58-4104 et seq. Rules and Regulations 117-1-1 ff.

Credential Type: Temporary Permit. **Requirements:** Must be licensed or certified in another state. **Fees:** $50 fee. **Governing Statute:** Kansas Statutes Annotated 58-4104 et seq. Rules and Regulations 117-1-1 ff.

7189

Real Estate Broker
Real Estate Commission
Landon State Office Bldg., Rm. 501
900 Jackson St.
Topeka, KS 66612-1220
Phone: (913)296-3411

Credential Type: Real Estate Broker License. **Duration of License:** Two years. **Requirements:** Complete 54 classroom hours of real estate education. Must have two years of real estate sales experience. **Examination:** ASI Examination. **Reciprocity:** No. **Fees:** $23.25 exam fee. $100 original license fee. $100 renewal fee.

7190

Real Estate Sales Agent
Real Estate Commission
Landon State Office Bldg., Rm. 501
900 Jackson St.
Topeka, KS 66612-1220
Phone: (913)296-3411

Credential Type: Real Estate Agent License. **Duration of License:** Two years. **Requirements:** Complete 30 classroom hours of real estate education. First renewal requires 30 hours of continuing education and 12 hours for each subsequent renewal. **Examination:** ASI Examination. **Reciprocity:** No. **Fees:** $23.25 exam fee. $60 original license fee. $60 renewal fee.

Kentucky

7191

Real Estate Appraiser
Kentucky Real Estate Appraisers Board
10200 Linn Station Rd., Ste. 201
Louisville, KY 40223
Phone: (502)425-4273

Credential Type: Certified General License. **Duration of License:** One year. **Requirements:** High school diploma or GED. Completion of 165 classroom hours of courses related to real estate appraisal which shall include 15 hours of the Uniform Standards of Professional Appraisal Practice (USPAP). 18 years of age. Continuing education required. **Examination:** Yes. **Fees:** $200 renewal fee.

Credential Type: Certified Residential License. **Duration of License:** One year. **Requirements:** High school diploma or GED. Completion of 105 classroom hours of courses in subjects related to real estate appraisal which shall include 15 classroom hours of the USPAP. After January 1, 1994, the educational credits will increase to 165 classroom hours. 18 years of age. Continuing education required. **Examination:** Yes. **Fees:** $200 exam fee. $200 renewal fee.

Credential Type: Licensed Appraiser. **Duration of License:** One year. **Requirements:** High school diploma or GED. Completion of 75 classroom hours of courses in subjects related to real estate appraisal which shall include 15 classroom hours of the USPAP. 18 years of age. Continuing education required. **Examination:** Yes. **Fees:** $200 exam fee. $200 renewal fee.

7192

Real Estate Broker
Kentucky Real Estate Commission
10200 Linn Station Rd., Ste. 201
Louisville, KY 40223
Phone: (502)425-4273

Credential Type: License. **Duration of License:** One year. **Requirements:** 18 years of age. High school diploma or GED. 21 credit hours, 12 of which must be in real estate, from an accredited college or university, or 336 clock hours from an approved private school. Resident of Kentucky. Two years work experience as a real estate sales associate. Continuing education required. **Examination:** Yes. **Fees:** $50 exam fee. $30 renewal fee. $30 Education, Research and Recovery Fund fee.

7193

Real Estate Sales Associate
Kentucky Real Estate Commission
10200 Linn Station Rd., Ste. 201
Louisville, KY 40223
Phone: (502)425-4273

Credential Type: License. **Duration of License:** One year. **Requirements:** High school graduate or GED. Completion of six credit hours or 96 classroom hours of instruction in real estate courses from an accredited college, university or a commission-approved proprietary school. 18 years of age. Resident of Kentucky. **Examination:** Yes. **Fees:** $50 exam fee. $30 renewal fee. $30 Educational, Research and Recovery Fund fee.

Louisiana

7194

Manufactured Housing Dealer
Office of the State Fire Marshal
1033 N. Lobdell Blvd.
Baton Rouge, LA 70806
Phone: (504)925-4911

Credential Type: License. **Duration of License:** One year. **Requirements:** Must have served for one year as a salesperson or have purchased an existing licensed dealership. **Fees:** $100 license fee. $25 branch fee.

7195

Manufactured Housing Salesman
Office of the State Fire Marshal
1033 N. Lobdell Blvd.
Baton Rouge, LA 70806
Phone: (504)925-4911

Credential Type: License. **Duration of License:** One year. **Requirements:** Must complete 30 days of employment by a licensed dealer. Be at least 18 years of age. **Fees:** $50 license fee.

7196

Real Estate Appraiser
Real Estate Appraisal Subcommittee
9071 Interline Ave.
PO Box 14785
Baton Rouge, LA 70898-4785
Phone: (504)925-4771

Credential Type: Residential Real Estate Appraiser Certificate. **Authorization:** Authorizes holder to provide real estate appraisal services in federally-related transactions in connection with one-to-four-unit residential properties without regard to value; and commercial properties of less than $250,000. **Requirements:** Complete 105 classroom hours in approved courses. Complete at least 2000 hours of appraisal work over at least two calendar years (24 months) within the five years preceding the filing of the experience credit application (Note: Experience requirement can be completed within three years after passing the exam). **Examination:** Residential Appraiser Certification Examination. **Fees:** $200 initial certificate fee. $20 research and education fund fee. $25 processing fee. **Governing Statute:** Louisiana Revised Statutes, Title 37, Chap. 51.

Credential Type: General Real Estate Appraiser Certificate. **Authorization:** Authorizes holder to provide real estate appraisal services in federally-related transactions with all types of property without regard to value. **Requirements:** Complete 165 classroom hours in approved courses. Complete at least 3000 hours of appraisal work over at least three calendar years (36 months) within the five years preceding the filing of the experience credit application (Note: Experience requirement can be completed within three years after passing the exam). **Examination:** General Appraiser Certification Examination. **Fees:** $200 initial certificate fee. $20 research and education fund fee. $25 processing fee. **Governing Statute:** Louisiana Revised Statutes, Title 37, Chap. 51.

7197

Real Estate Broker
Real Estate Commission
PO Box 14785
Baton Rouge, LA 70898
Phone: (504)925-4800

Credential Type: License. **Duration of License:** Two years. **Requirements:** 18 years of age. High school diploma or equivalent. Completion of necessary education requirements. **Examination:** Written. **Fees:** $261 license and examination fee.

7198

Real Estate Salesperson
Real Estate Commission
PO Box 14785
Baton Rouge, LA 70898
Phone: (504)925-4800

Credential Type: License. **Duration of License:** Two years. **Requirements:** 18 years of age. High school diploma or equivalent. Completion of necessary education requirements. **Examination:** Written. **Fees:** $111 license and examination fee.

7199

Timeshare Interest Salesperson
Real Estate Commission
Dept. of Economic Development
PO Box 14785
Baton Rouge, LA 70808
Free: 800-821-4529

Credential Type: Registration. **Duration of License:** Two years. **Requirements:** Be at least 18 years of age. High school graduate or equivalent. Submit application. **Governing Statute:** R.S. 37:1430-1465. R.S. 9:1131.111131.27.

Maine

7200

Manufactured Home Dealer
Dept. of Professional and Financial
  Regulation
Div. of Licensing and Enforcement
Manufactured Housing Board
State House Station 35
Augusta, ME 04333
Phone: (207)582-8723

Credential Type: License. **Duration of License:** Two years. **Requirements:** Submit application and pay fee. **Fees:** $200 license fee. $5 per additional location.

7201

Real Estate Appraiser
Dept. of Professional and Financial
  Regulation
Div. of Licensing and Enforcement
Board of Real Estate Appraisers
State House Station 35
Augusta, ME 04333
Phone: (207)582-8723

Credential Type: Certified General Appraiser. **Duration of License:** Two years. **Requirements:** Complete 165 classroom hours of appraisal training. Have appraisal experience for at least two of the previous five years. Must hold an active appraiser license to become certified. **Examination:** General Appraiser Examination. **Reciprocity:** With CT, NH, and NY. (RI and MA are in the works.) **Fees:** $125 application fee. $125 exam fee. $300 license fee. **Governing Statute:** 32 M.S.R.A. Chap. 123.

Credential Type: Certified Residential Appraiser. **Duration of License:** Two years. **Requirements:** Complete 105 classroom hours of appraisal training. Have appraisal experience for at least two of the previous five years. Must hold an active appraiser license to become certified. **Ex-**

Maine 7202

Real Estate Appraiser, continued

amination: Residential Appraiser Examination. **Reciprocity:** With CT, NH, and NY. (RI and MA are in the works.) **Fees:** $125 application fee. $125 exam fee. $300 license fee. **Governing Statute:** 32 M.S.R.A. Chap. 123.

Credential Type: Licensed Real Estate Appraiser. **Duration of License:** Two years. **Requirements:** Complete 75 classroom hours of appraisal training. **Examination:** Appraisers Examination. **Reciprocity:** With CT, NH, and NY. (RI and MA are in the works.) **Fees:** $125 application fee. $125 exam fee. $250 license fee. **Governing Statute:** 32 M.S.R.A. Chap. 123.

7202

Real Estate Associate Broker
Maine Real Estate Commission
Dept. of Professional and Financial Regulation
Div. of Licensing and Enforcement
State House Station 35
Augusta, ME 04333
Phone: (207)582-8727

Credential Type: License. **Duration of License:** Two years. **Requirements:** Contact licensing body for application information. There are three methods of qualification. **Reciprocity:** Yes. **Fees:** $80 license fee. $80 renewal fee. $50 exam fee.

7203

Real Estate Broker
Maine Real Estate Commission
Dept. of Professional and Financial Regulation
Div. of Licensing and Enforcement
State House Station 35
Augusta, ME 04333
Phone: (207)582-8727

Credential Type: License. **Duration of License:** Two years. **Requirements:** Complete "Role of the Designated Broker" course. Complete at least one year of practice as a full-time Associate Broker in the year immediately preceding application, or one year of practice as a Sales Agent. **Examination:** No exam. **Reciprocity:** Yes. **Fees:** $90 license fee. $90 renewal fee.

7204

Real Estate Sales Agent
Maine Real Estate Commission
Dept. of Professional and Financial Regulation
Div. of Licensing and Enforcement
State House Station 35
Augusta, ME 04333
Phone: (207)582-8727

Credential Type: License. **Duration of License:** Two years. **Authorization:** License is not renewable, but may be extended for one year due to extenuating circumstances. **Requirements:** Complete "Introduction to Real Estate" course, or pass the commission's Sales Agent Examination. **Examination:** Sales Agent Examination. **Exemptions:** Exam not required if course is successfully completed. **Fees:** $60 license fee. $50 exam fee.

7205

Time-Share Agent
Dept. of Professional & Financial Regulation
State House Station No. 35
Augusta, ME 04333
Phone: (207)582-8727

Credential Type: Time-Share Agent License. **Requirements:** Contact licensing body for application information.

Maryland

7206

Real Estate Appraiser
Real Estate Appraisers Commission
Dept. of Licensing and Regulation
501 St. Paul Pl., 9th Fl. S.
Baltimore, MD 21202-2272
Phone: (410)333-6590
Fax: (410)333-1229

Credential Type: Real Estate Appraiser License. **Duration of License:** Three years. **Authorization:** Authorizes holder to provide real estate appraisal services in federally-related transactions in connection with non-complex one-to-four-unit residential properties having a transaction value of less than $1 million; complex one-to-four-unit residential properties of less than $250,000; and commercial properties of less than $250,000. **Requirements:** Complete 75 classroom hours in approved courses. Complete at least 2000 hours of appraisal work over any period of time. **Examination:** Licensing Examination. **Exemptions:** Waiver of examination may be granted to out-of-state licensed real estate appraisers. **Fees:** $150 application and exam fee. $75 Federal Fund Registry fee.

Credential Type: Provisional Real Estate Appraiser License. **Duration of License:** Expires 12-31-93. **Authorization:** A transitional license that allows the holder to complete either the educational or experience requirement for licensure. **Requirements:** Complete either 75 classroom hours in approved courses, or at least 2000 hours of appraisal work over any period of time. **Examination:** Licensing Examination. **Exemptions:** Waiver of examination may be granted to out-of-state licensed real estate appraisers. **Fees:** $150 application and exam fee. $75 Federal Fund Registry fee.

Credential Type: Residential Real Estate Appraiser Certificate. **Duration of License:** Three years. **Authorization:** Authorizes holder to provide real estate appraisal services in federally-related transactions in connection with one-to-four-unit residential properties without regard to value; and commercial properties of less than $250,000. **Requirements:** Complete 105 classroom hours in approved courses. Complete at least 2000 hours of appraisal work over at least two calendar years (24 months). **Examination:** Residential Appraiser Certification Examination. **Exemptions:** Waiver of examination may be granted to out-of-state licensed real estate appraisers. **Fees:** $250 application and exam fee. $75 Federal Fund Registry fee.

Credential Type: General Real Estate Appraiser Certificate. **Duration of License:** Three years. **Authorization:** Authorizes holder to provide real estate appraisal services in federally-related transactions with all types of property without regard to value. **Requirements:** Complete 165 classroom hours in approved courses. Complete at least 2000 hours of appraisal work over at least two calendar years (24 months), 1000 hours of which must have been in non-residential real property appraisal work. **Examination:** General Appraiser Certification Examination. **Exemptions:** Waiver of examination may be granted to out-of-state licensed real estate appraisers. **Fees:** $250 application and exam fee. $75 Federal Fund Registry fee.

Credential Type: Temporary Permit. **Duration of License:** Six months. **Authorization:** Issued only for a particular assignment. **Requirements:** Must be licensed or certified in another state. Must be appraising property in Maryland. Business in Maryland must be of a temporary nature. **Fees:** No fee.

7207

Real Estate Associate Broker
Real Estate Commission
Dept. of Licensing and Regulation
501 St. Paul Pl.
Baltimore, MD 21202-2272
Phone: (410)333-6230

Credential Type: License. **Requirements:** Contact licensing body for application information.

7208

Real Estate Broker
Real Estate Commission
501 St. Paul Place, 8th Fl.
Baltimore, MD 21202
Phone: (301)333-6230

Credential Type: Real Estate Broker License. **Duration of License:** Two years. **Requirements:** Complete 180 classroom hours of real estate education. Must have three years of real estate sales experience. Renewal requires 12 hours of continuing education. **Examination:** ASI Examination. **Reciprocity:** No. **Fees:** $25 exam fee. $95 original license fee. $95 renewal fee.

7209

Real Estate Sales Agent
Real Estate Commission
501 St. Paul Place, 8th Fl.
Baltimore, MD 21202
Phone: (301)333-6230

Credential Type: Real Estate Agent License. **Duration of License:** Two years. **Requirements:** Complete 45 classroom hours of real estate education. Renewal requires 12 hours of continuing education. **Examination:** ASI Examination. **Reciprocity:** No. **Fees:** $25 exam fee. $45 original license fee. $45 renewal fee.

Massachusetts

7210

Real Estate Appraiser
Real Estate Appraisal Board
100 Cambridge St., Rm. 1518
Boston, MA 02202
Phone: (617)727-1738

Credential Type: Real Estate Appraiser License. **Duration of License:** Three years. **Authorization:** Authorizes holder to provide real estate appraisal services in federally-related transactions in connection with non-complex one-to-four-unit residential properties having a transaction value of less than $1 million; complex one-to-four-unit residential properties of less than $250,000; and commercial properties of less than $250,000. **Requirements:** Complete 75 classroom hours in approved courses. Complete at least 2000 hours of appraisal work over any period of time. **Examination:** Licensing Examination. **Fees:** $150 application fee. $435 license fee. $435 renewal fee.

Credential Type: Residential Real Estate Appraiser Certificate. **Duration of License:** Three years. **Authorization:** Authorizes holder to provide real estate appraisal services in federally-related transactions in connection with one-to-four-unit residential properties without regard to value; and commercial properties of less than $250,000. **Requirements:** Complete 105 classroom hours in approved courses. Complete at least 2000 hours of appraisal work over at least two calendar years (24 months). **Examination:** Residential Appraiser Certification Examination. **Fees:** $150 application fee. $435 license fee. $435 renewal fee.

Credential Type: General Real Estate Appraiser Certificate. **Duration of License:** Three years. **Authorization:** Authorizes holder to provide real estate appraisal services in federally-related transactions with all types of property without regard to value. **Requirements:** Complete 165 classroom hours in approved courses. Complete at least 2000 hours of appraisal work over at least two calendar years (24 months), 1000 hours of which must have been in non-residential real property appraisal work. **Examination:** General Appraiser Certification Examination. **Fees:** $250 application and exam fee. $75 Federal Fund Registry fee. **Governing Statute:** $150 application fee. $435 license fee. $435 renewal fee.

7211

Real Estate Broker
Board of Registration of Real Estate
   Brokers & Salesmen
Real Estate Board
100 Cambridge St., Rm. 1518
Boston, MA 02202
Phone: (617)727-2373

Credential Type: Real Estate Broker License. **Duration of License:** Two years. **Requirements:** Complete 54 classroom hours of real estate education. Must have one year of real estate sales experience. **Examination:** ASI Examination. **Reciprocity:** Yes. **Fees:** $63 exam fee. $90 original license fee. $90 renewal fee.

7212

Real Estate Sales Agent
Board of Registration of Real Estate
   Brokers & Salesmen
Real Estate Board
100 Cambridge St., Rm. 1518
Boston, MA 02202
Phone: (617)727-2373

Credential Type: Real Estate Agent License. **Duration of License:** Two years. **Requirements:** Complete 24 classroom hours of real estate education. **Examination:** ASI Examination. **Reciprocity:** Yes. **Fees:** $48 exam fee. $60 original license fee. $60 renewal fee.

Michigan

7213

Assessor
State Assessors Board
Dept. of Treasury
Treasury Bldg.
Lansing, MI 48922
Phone: (517)373-3200

Credential Type: Class I Certification. **Duration of License:** Two years. **Authorization:** Can assess residential property, land improvements on residential property, all types of land, and timber. **Requirements:** Knowledge and understanding of the assessing profession. Apply for certification within 180 days after passing the written exam. Prepare and submit for approval an appraisal record card (based on data obtained from the applicant's field of work), according to instructions provided in the Assessors Manual (which is published by the State Tax Commission). Comply with all rules of the State Assessors Board. Renewal requires attendance of renewal seminar. **Examination:** Written exam. **Fees:** $25 initial exam fee. $35 initial regular certification fee. $35 conditional certification fee. $35 provisional certification fee. $50 renewal regular certification fee. **Governing Statute:** Assessment, Levy and Collection of Taxes Act, Act 206 of 1893, as amended.

Credential Type: Class II Certification. **Duration of License:** Two years. **Authorization:** Can assess residential property, land improvements on residential property, all types of land, and timber. Can assess small commercial properties and general-purpose industrial properties. **Requirements:** Knowledge and understanding of the assessing profession. Apply for certification within 180 days after passing the written exam. Prepare and submit for approval an appraisal record card (based on data obtained from the applicant's field of

Assessor, continued

work), according to instructions provided in the Assessors Manual (which is published by the State Tax Commission). Comply with all rules of the State Assessors Board. Renewal requires attendance of renewal seminar. **Examination:** Written exam. **Fees:** $25 initial exam fee. $35 initial regular certification fee. $35 conditional certification fee. $35 provisional certification fee. $50 renewal regular certification fee. **Governing Statute:** Assessment, Levy and Collection of Taxes Act, Act 206 of 1893, as amended.

Credential Type: Class III Certification. **Duration of License:** Two years. **Authorization:** Can assess residential property, land improvements on residential property, all types of land, and timber. Can assess small commercial properties and general-purpose industrial properties. Can assess large and difficult-to-evaluate properties of all types, such as regional shopping centers, industrial complexes and heavy manufacturing facilities, concentrated downtown areas, and condominium and apartment complexes. **Requirements:** Knowledge and understanding of the assessing profession. Meet all Class I and II requirements. Two years experience in assessment administration. Apply for certification within 180 days after passing the written exam. Prepare and submit for approval an appraisal record card (based on data obtained from the applicant's field of work), according to instructions provided in the Assessors Manual (which is published by the State Tax Commission). Comply with all rules of the State Assessors Board. Renewal requires attendance of renewal seminar and six-hour appraisal seminar conducted by an assessment or appraisal association. **Examination:** Written exam. **Fees:** $25 initial exam fee. $35 initial regular certification fee. $35 conditional certification fee. $35 provisional certification fee. $95 renewal regular certification fee. **Governing Statute:** Assessment, Levy and Collection of Taxes Act, Act 206 of 1893, as amended.

Credential Type: Class IV Certification. **Duration of License:** Two years. **Authorization:** Can assess residential property, land improvements on residential property, all types of land, and timber. Can assess small commercial properties and general-purpose industrial properties. Can assess large and difficult-to-evaluate properties of all types, such as regional shopping centers, industrial complexes and heavy manufacturing facilities, concentrated downtown areas, and condominium and apartment complexes. Can administer and formulate policies for assessment offices which do the more complex evaluations. **Requirements:** Knowledge and understanding of the assessing profession. Meet all Class I, II and III requirements. Three years experience in assessment administration. Apply for certification within 180 days after passing the written or oral exam. Prepare and submit for approval an appraisal record card (based on data obtained from the applicant's field of work), according to instructions provided in the Assessors Manual (which is published by the State Tax Commission). Comply with all rules of the State Assessors Board. Renewal requires attendance of renewal seminar and six-hour appraisal seminar conducted by an assessment or appraisal association. **Examination:** Written and oral exam. **Fees:** $25 initial exam fee. $35 initial regular certification fee. $35 conditional certification fee. $35 provisional certification fee. $95 renewal regular certification fee. **Governing Statute:** Assessment, Levy and Collection of Taxes Act, Act 206 of 1893, as amended.

7214

Mobile Home Dealer
Mobile Home and Land Resources Div.
Dept. of Commerce
PO Box 30222
Lansing, MI 48909
Phone: (517)373-9153

Credential Type: License. **Duration of License:** One year. **Requirements:** At least 18 years old. Post a $10,000 surety bond for each location at which a business is being conducted. Establish a consumer deposit escrow account or a consumer deposit bond or deposit cash or other securities with a financial institution for the protection of consumer deposits. Comply with all rules and regulations of the Mobile Home and Land Resources Division pertaining to licensure, the business of mobile home sales, and mobile home installation and repair if applicable. **Fees:** $150 initial license fee. $150 renewal fee. **Governing Statute:** Mobile Home Commission Act, Act 96 of 1987, as amended.

7215

Mobile Home Lessor
Mobile Home and Land Resources Div.
Dept. of Commerce
PO Box 30222
Lansing, MI 48909
Phone: (517)373-9153

Credential Type: License. **Duration of License:** One year. **Requirements:** Post a $10,000 surety bond for each mobile home lessor location. **Fees:** $150 initial license fee. $150 renewal fee. **Governing Statute:** Mobile Home Commission Act, Act 96 of 1987, as amended.

7216

Real Estate Appraiser
Board of Real Estate Appraisers
Bureau of Occupational & Professional Regulation
Dept. of Commerce
PO Box 30243
Lansing, MI 48909
Phone: (517)373-9153

Credential Type: Real Estate Appraiser Certification. **Duration of License:** One year. **Authorization:** A person who appraises real property of any type or value, including appraisals required for federally related transactions, must become a certified real estate appraiser through the Department of Commerce. **Requirements:** At least 2,000 hours of Department-approved work experience in appraising real property, at least 1,000 of these hours must have been in appraising nonresidential real property. Completed a minimum of 165 clock hours of approved classroom courses emphasizing all types and values of real property appraisals. With 90 hours relating to the appraisal of nonresidential real property, an applicant may apply the 75 clock hours used to obtain licensure as a state licensed real estate appraiser toward the requirement of 165 clock hours. Be of good moral character. Abide by the rules and regulations of the Department. **Examination:** Written exam. **Reciprocity:** A certified real estate appraiser from another state may be certified or licensed in Michigan without examination, if the requirements of the home state are at least equal to those of Michigan. **Fees:** $25 application fee. $175 license fee. $175 renewal fee. **Governing Statute:** The Occupational Code, Act 299 of 1980, as amended. Michigan Public Act 268 of 1990. Michigan Public Act 269 of 1990.

Credential Type: Real Estate Appraiser License. **Duration of License:** One year. **Authorization:** A person who appraises residential real property and any other property (less than $1,000,000 in value or 1-to-4 unit, single family) involving a federally related transaction must become a licensed real estate appraiser through the Department of Commerce. **Requirements:** At least 2,000 hours of Department-approved work experience in appraising residential real property. Completed a minimum of 75 clock hours of approved classroom courses emphasizing the appraisal of residential real property. Be of good moral character. Abide by the rules and regulations of the Department. **Examination:** Written exam. **Reciprocity:** A licensed real estate appraiser from another state may be certified or licensed in Michigan without examination, if the requirements of the home state are at least equal to those of Michigan. **Fees:** $25 application fee. $175 license fee. $175 renewal fee. **Governing Statute:** The Occupational Code, Act 299 of 1980, as amended. Michigan Public Act 268 of 1990. Michigan Public Act 269 of 1990.

7217

Real Estate Broker
Dept. of Commerce
Board of Real Estate Brokers & Salespersons
PO Box 30243
Lansing, MI 48909
Phone: (517)373-0490

Credential Type: Real Estate Broker License. **Duration of License:** One year. **Requirements:** Complete 130 classroom hours of real estate education. Must have three years of real estate sales experience. Renewal requires six hours of continuing education. **Examination:** AMP Examination. **Fees:** $18 exam fee. $38 original license fee. $18 renewal fee.

7218

Real Estate Sales Agent
Dept. of Commerce
Board of Real Estate Brokers & Salespersons
PO Box 30243
Lansing, MI 48909
Phone: (517)373-0490

Credential Type: Real Estate Agent License. **Duration of License:** One year. **Requirements:** Complete 40 classroom hours of real estate education. Renewal requires six hours of continuing education. **Examination:** AMP Examination. **Fees:** $18 exam fee. $23 original license fee. $13 renewal fee.

Minnesota

7219

Assessor
Dept. of Revenue
Board of Assessors
Mail Station 3340
St. Paul, MN 55146-3340
Phone: (612)296-0209

Credential Type: Certified Assessor License. **Duration of License:** One year. **Authorization:** All persons engaged in valuing or classifying property must be licensed within three years of being employed. **Requirements:** Complete one year of experience working in an assessor's office or alternate experience. Complete three week-long training courses.

Renewal requires earning four Continuing Educational Units (CEUs) every four years. **Examination:** Yes, given at conclusion of courses. **Fees:** $30 license fee. **Governing Statute:** Minnesota Statutes 270.41-270.53. Board of Assessors' Rules.

Credential Type: Certified Assessor Specialist License. **Duration of License:** One year. **Authorization:** All persons engaged in valuing or classifying property must be licensed within three years of being employed. **Requirements:** Complete two years of experience working in an assessor's office or alternate experience. Complete five weeks of training courses.

Renewal requires earning four Continuing Educational Units (CEUs) every four years. **Examination:** Yes, given at conclusion of courses. **Fees:** $40 license fee. **Governing Statute:** Minnesota Statutes 270.41-270.53. Board of Assessors' Rules.

Credential Type: Accredited Assessor License. **Duration of License:** One year. **Authorization:** All persons engaged in valuing or classifying property must be licensed within three years of being employed. **Requirements:** Complete three years of experience working as a trainee or certified assessor in an assessor's office or alternate experience. Complete five weeks of training courses. Complete a demonstration narrative appraisal.

Renewal requires earning five Continuing Educational Units (CEUs) every four years. **Examination:** Yes, given at conclusion of courses. **Fees:** $50 license fee. **Governing Statute:** Minnesota Statutes 270.41-270.53. Board of Assessors' Rules.

Credential Type: Senior Accredited Assessor License. **Duration of License:** One year. **Authorization:** All persons engaged in valuing or classifying property must be licensed within three years of being employed. **Requirements:** Complete five years of experience working in an assessor's office or alternate experience. Complete five weeks of training courses. Complete a second demonstration narrative appraisal or obtain sufficient points to achieve the designation vie the Contract Alternative Point System.

Renewal requires earning five Continuing Educational Units (CEUs) every four years. **Examination:** Yes, given at conclusion of courses. **Fees:** $75 license fee. **Governing Statute:** Minnesota Statutes 270.41-270.53. Board of Assessors' Rules.

7220

Real Estate Appraiser
Dept. of Commerce
Licensing Unit
133 E. 7th St.
St. Paul, MN 55101
Phone: (612)296-6319

Credential Type: State Real Property Appraiser License. **Authorization:** May appraise residential or agricultural property when a net income capitalization analysis is not required. This license classification does not meet federal certification criteria. **Requirements:** Complete a 15-hour Professional Standards and Ethics course. **Fees:** $50 license fee. $25 renewal fee.

Credential Type: Certified Federal Residential Real Property Appraiser License. **Authorization:** May appraise one to four residential units without regard to transaction value or complexity. May do appraisals involving federal transactions. **Requirements:** Contact licensing body for application information.

Credential Type: Certified Federal General Real Property Appraiser License. **Authorization:** May appraise all types of real property. May do appraisals involving federal transactions. **Requirements:** Contact licensing body for application information.

7221

Real Estate Broker
Dept. of Commerce
Licensing Unit
133 E. 7th St.
St. Paul, MN 55101
Phone: (612)296-6319

Credential Type: Real Estate Broker License. **Duration of License:** One year. **Requirements:** Have at least two years experience as a licensed real estate salesperson. Complete the educational requirements for a salesperson license. Complete a 30-hour real estate broker course within six months prior to application.

Renewal requires meeting a continuing education requirement that will be assigned to each licensee. **Examination:** Real Estate Broker Examination. **Reciprocity:** Yes. **Fees:** Contact board for fees. **Governing Statute:** Minnesota Statutes, Chap. 82 and 83. Real Estate Rules.

Minnesota 7222

7222

Real Estate Salesperson
Dept. of Commerce
Licensing Unit
133 E. 7th St.
St. Paul, MN 55101
Phone: (612)296-6319

Credential Type: Real Estate Salesperson License. **Duration of License:** One year. **Requirements:** Complete real estate Courses I, II, and III. Only Course I must be completed before taking examination. Courses II and III must be completed within one year of taking the examination. License application must be submitted within one year of taking the examination.

Additional education of 30 hours is required in the first year after licensing, after which the salesperson is assigned a continuing education requirement. **Examination:** Salesperson Examination. **Reciprocity:** Yes. **Fees:** Contact board for fees. **Governing Statute:** Minnesota Statutes, Chap. 82 and 83. Real Estate Rules.

Mississippi

7223

Real Estate Appraiser
Mississippi Real Estate Appraiser
  Licensing and Certification Board
1920 Dunbarton Dr.
Jackson, MS 39216-5087
Phone: (601)987-3969

Credential Type: Real Estate Appraiser License. **Duration of License:** Two years. **Authorization:** Authorizes holder to provide real estate appraisal services in federally-related transactions in connection with non-complex one-to-four-unit residential properties having a transaction value of less than $1 million; complex one-to-four-unit residential properties of less than $250,000; and commercial properties of less than $250,000. **Requirements:** Complete 75 classroom hours in approved courses. Score 75 percent on exam. Be trustworthy and competent. **Examination:** Licensing Examination. **Fees:** $175 exam fee. $250 license fee. **Governing Statute:** Mississippi Real Estate Appraiser Licensing and Certification Act of 1990, Sect. 73-34-1 through 73-34-63.

Credential Type: Residential Real Estate Appraiser Certificate. **Duration of License:** Two years. **Authorization:** Authorizes holder to provide real estate appraisal services in federally-related transactions in connection with one-to-four-unit residential properties without regard to value; and commercial properties of less than $250,000. **Requirements:** Complete 105 classroom hours in approved courses. Complete at least two years of real property appraisal work. Score 75 percent on exam. **Examination:** Residential Appraiser Certification Examination. **Fees:** $175 exam fee. $275 certification fee. **Governing Statute:** Mississippi Real Estate Appraiser Licensing and Certification Act of 1990, Sect. 73-34-1 through 73-34-63.

Credential Type: General Real Estate Appraiser Certificate. **Duration of License:** Two years. **Authorization:** Authorizes holder to provide real estate appraisal services in federally-related transactions with all types of property without regard to value. **Requirements:** Complete 165 classroom hours in approved courses. Have at least two years of experience in real property appraisal. Score 75 percent on exam. **Examination:** General Appraiser Certification Examination. **Fees:** $175 exam fee. $300 certification fee. **Governing Statute:** Mississippi Real Estate Appraiser Licensing and Certification Act of 1990, Sect. 73-34-1 through 73-34-63.

Credential Type: Timberland Real Estate Appraiser Certificate. **Duration of License:** Two years. **Requirements:** Complete 75 classroom hours in approved courses. Have at least two years of experience in real property appraisal. Score 75 percent on exam. **Examination:** Timberland Appraiser Certification Examination. **Fees:** $175 exam fee. $300 certification fee. **Governing Statute:** Mississippi Real Estate Appraiser Licensing and Certification Act of 1990, Sect. 73-34-1 through 73-34-63.

7224

Real Estate Broker
Real Estate Commission
1920 Dunbarton Dr.
Jackson, MS 39216-5087
Phone: (601)987-3969

Credential Type: Resident Broker's License. **Duration of License:** One year initially, followed by two year renewal periods. **Requirements:** Be at least 21 years of age. Citizen of the United States and resident of Mississippi at time of application. Have held a license as a real estate sales person for 12 months immediately prior to making application. Complete one of the following real estate education programs: (1) Complete four three-semester-hour courses in real estate that are acceptable for credit toward a degree at a college or university. (2) Complete a minimum of 120 classroom hours of real estate education as provided by the Mississippi Realtors Institute. (3) Complete 90 classroom hours of real estate education as provided by the Mississippi Realtors Institute and 30 hours provided through an approved professionally designated program. (4) Complete 90 classroom hours of real estate education as provided by the Mississippi Realtors Institute and one three-semester-hour college course in real estate.

Applicants who have not held an active real estate salesperson's license for at least 12 months prior to application must complete one of the following real estate education programs: (1) Minimum of five three-semester-hour courses in real estate that are accceptable for credit toward a degree at a college or university. (2) Complete a minimum of 150 classroom hours of real estate education as provided by the Mississippi Realtors Institute. (3) Complete 120 classroom hours of real estate education as provided by the Mississippi Realtors Institute and 30 hours provided through an approved professionally designated program. (4) Complete 120 classroom hours of real estate education as provided by the Mississippi Realtors Institute and one three-semester-hour college course in real estate.

Renewal requires eight clock hours of continuing education. **Examination:** Written broker's examination. **Fees:** $100 license fee (first year). $80 biennial renewal fee.

Credential Type: Nonresident Broker's License. **Duration of License:** One year initially, followed by two year renewal periods. **Requirements:** Must either be a licensed broker in another state, or be affiliated with a resident or nonresident broker in Mississippi, or be a nonresident who applies for a broker's license and will maintain an office in Mississippi. Must meet all qualifications required of a resident broker, except for residency. **Examination:** Written broker's examination. **Fees:** $100 license fee (first year). $80 biennial renewal fee.

7225

Real Estate Salesperson
Real Estate Commission
1920 Dunbarton Dr.
Jackson, MS 39216-5087
Phone: (601)987-3969

Credential Type: Resident Salesperson License. **Duration of License:** One year initially, followed by two year renewal periods. **Requirements:** Be at least 18 years of age. Citizen of the United States and resident of Mississippi at time of application. Complete at least two three-semester-hour courses in real estate that are acceptable for credit toward a degree at a college or university; or complete a minimum of 60 classroom hours of real estate education as provided by the Mississippi Realtors Institute.

Renewal requires eight clock hours of continuing education. **Examination:** Written salesperson's examination. **Fees:** $80 license fee (first year). $60 biennial renewal fee.

Credential Type: Nonresident Salesperson License. **Duration of License:** One year initially, followed by two year renewal periods. **Requirements:** Must meet all qualifications required of a resident salesperson, except for residency. **Examination:** Written salesperson's examination. **Fees:** $80 license fee (first year). $60 biennial renewal fee.

Missouri

7226

Real Estate Appraiser
Real Estate Appraisers Commission
Div. of Professional Registration
3605 Missouri Blvd.
PO Box 202
Jefferson City, MO 65102
Phone: (314)751-0038

Credential Type: Certified General Real Estate Appraiser. **Duration of License:** Three years. **Requirements:** Complete at least two years (2000 hours) of real estate appraisal experience, of which at least half is in non-residential work. Experience must have been acquired within the five-year period immediately preceding application. Complete at least 165 classroom hours of appraisal instruction.

Renewal requires 30 hours of continuing education during the three-year license period. **Examination:** Written examination. **Reciprocity:** Yes, provided state extends similar reciprocity to Missouri. Board may also issue a non-resident certificate. **Fees:** $125 application fee. $250 license fee. $250 annual renewal fee. **Governing Statute:** 4 CSR 245.

Credential Type: Certified Residential Real Estate Appraiser. **Duration of License:** Three years. **Requirements:** Complete at least two years (2000 hours) of real estate appraisal experience. Experience must have been acquired within the five-year period immediately preceding application. Complete at least 75 classroom hours of appraisal instruction.

Renewal requires 30 hours of continuing education during the three-year license period. **Examination:** Written examination. **Reciprocity:** Yes, provided state extends similar reciprocity to Missouri. Board may also issue a non-resident certificate. **Fees:** $125 application fee. $225 license fee. $225 annual renewal fee. **Governing Statute:** 4 CSR 245.

Credential Type: Licensed Real Estate Appraiser. **Duration of License:** Three years. **Requirements:** Contact licensing body for application information. **Examination:** Written examination. **Reciprocity:** Yes, provided state extends similar reciprocity to Missouri. Board may also issue a non-resident license. **Fees:** $125 application fee. $200 license fee. $200 annual renewal fee. **Governing Statute:** 4 CSR 245.

Credential Type: Temporary License. **Duration of License:** 18 months. **Requirements:** May be issued to a non-resident appraiser conducting an appraisal that is part of a federally-related transaction, the appraiser's business is of a temporary nature, and the appraiser registers with the commission. **Fees:** $350 temporary license fee. **Governing Statute:** 4 CSR 245.

7227

Real Estate Broker
Real Estate Commission
PO Box 1339
Jefferson City, MO 65102
Phone: (314)751-2628

Credential Type: Real Estate Broker License. **Duration of License:** Two years. **Requirements:** Complete 108 classroom hours of real estate education, or have one year of real estate sales experience. Renewal requires 12 hours of continuing education. **Examination:** AMP Examination. **Reciprocity:** Yes. **Fees:** $18.50 exam fee. $20 original license fee. $20 renewal fee.

7228

Real Estate Sales Agent
Real Estate Commission
PO Box 1339
Jefferson City, MO 65102
Phone: (314)751-2628

Credential Type: Real Estate Agent License. **Duration of License:** Two years. **Requirements:** Complete 60 classroom hours of real estate education. Renewal requires 12 hours of continuing education. **Examination:** AMP Examination. **Reciprocity:** Yes. **Fees:** $18.50 exam fee. $10 original license fee. $10 renewal fee.

Montana

7229

Real Estate Appraiser
Dept. of Commerce
Public Safety Div.
111 N. Jackson
Helena, MT 59620-0407
Phone: (406)444-4294

Credential Type: Real Estate Appraiser License. **Duration of License:** Three years. **Authorization:** Authorizes holder to provide real estate appraisal services in federally-related transactions in connection with non-complex one-to-four-unit residential properties having a transaction value of less than $1 million; complex one-to-four-unit residential properties of less than $250,000; and commercial properties of less than $250,000. **Requirements:** Complete 75 classroom hours in approved courses. Complete at least 2000 hours of appraisal work. **Examination:** Licensing Examination. **Reciprocity:** Yes, provded state has equal requirements and offers same privileges to applicants from Montana. **Fees:** $75 exam fee. $450 license fee. $450 renewal fee. $25 federal registry fee. **Governing Statute:** Montana Code Annotated 37-54-101 et seq. Administrative Rules of Montana 8.57.101 et seq.

Credential Type: Residential Real Estate Appraiser Certificate. **Duration of License:** Three years. **Authorization:** Authorizes holder to provide real estate appraisal services in federally-related transactions in connection with one-to-four-unit residential properties without regard to value; and commercial properties of less than $250,000. **Requirements:** Complete 105 classroom hours in approved courses (after January 1, 1994, at least 165 hours). Complete at least 2000 hours of appraisal work. **Examination:** Residential Appraiser Certification Examination. **Reciprocity:** Yes, provded state has equal requirements and offers same privileges to applicants from Montana. **Fees:** $75 exam fee. $450 license fee. $450 renewal fee. $25 federal registry fee. **Governing Statute:** Montana Code Annotated 37-54-101 et seq. Administrative Rules of Montana 8.57.101 et seq.

Credential Type: General Real Estate Appraiser Certificate. **Duration of License:** Three years. **Authorization:** Authorizes holder to provide real estate appraisal services in federally-related transactions with all types of property without regard to value. **Requirements:** Complete 165 classroom hours in approved courses. Complete at least 2000 hours of appraisal work, 1000 hours of which must have been in non-residential real property appraisal work. **Examination:** General Appraiser Certifi-

Real Estate Appraiser, continued

cation Examination. **Reciprocity:** Yes, provded state has equal requirements and offers same privileges to applicants from Montana. **Fees:** $75 exam fee. $450 license fee. $450 renewal fee. $25 federal registry fee. **Governing Statute:** Montana Code Annotated 37-54-101 et seq. Administrative Rules of Montana 8.57.101 et seq.

Credential Type: Agricultural Real Estate Appraiser Certificate. **Duration of License:** Three years. **Requirements:** Complete 165 classroom hours in approved courses. Complete at least 2000 hours of appraisal work, 1000 hours of which must have been in agricultural real estate appraisal work. **Examination:** Agricultural Appraiser Certification Examination. **Reciprocity:** Yes, provded state has equal requirements and offers same privileges to applicants from Montana. **Fees:** $75 exam fee. $450 license fee. $450 renewal fee. $25 federal registry fee. **Governing Statute:** Montana Code Annotated 37-54-101 et seq. Administrative Rules of Montana 8.57.101 et seq.

Credential Type: Temporary Permit. **Authorization:** Issued only for a particular assignment. **Requirements:** Must be licensed or certified in another state. **Fees:** $150 fee. **Governing Statute:** Montana Code Annotated 37-54-101 et seq. Administrative Rules of Montana 8.57.101 et seq.

7230

Real Estate Broker
Montana Board of Realty Regulation
111 N. Jackson
Helena, MT 59620
Phone: (406)444-2961

Credential Type: Real Estate Broker. **Duration of License:** One year. **Requirements:** 18 years of age. High school diploma or equivalent. Two years of experience as a licensed real estate salesperson or equivalent. Completion of an additional 60 hours of approved real estate courses. **Examination:** Written. **Fees:**. $35 exam fee. $50 license fee. $60 renewal fee. **Governing Statute:** Montana Code Annotated 37-51-301 through 37-51-323.

7231

Real Estate Salesperson
Montana Board of Realty Regulation
111 N. Jackson
Helena, MT 59620
Phone: (406)444-2961

Credential Type: Real Estate Salesperson. **Duration of License:** One year. **Requirements:** 18 years of age. Two years of high school or equivalent. Completion of 60 hours of approved real estate courses. A statement from a licensed broker certifying that the broker will supervise and train the applicant. **Examination:** Written. **Fees:** $35 exam fee. $25 license fee. $30 renewal fee. **Governing Statute:** Montana Code Annotated 37-51-301 through 37-51-323.

7232

Timeshare Broker
Board of Real Estate
Professional and Occupational
 Licensing Bureau
111 N. Jackson
Helena, MT 59620
Phone: (406)444-2961

Credential Type: Timeshare Broker License. **Duration of License:** One year. **Requirements:** Contact licensing body for application information. **Examination:** Written. **Fees:** $35 exam fee. $35 license fee. $35 renewal fee. **Governing Statute:** Montana Code Annotated 37-53.

7233

Timeshare Salesperson
Board of Real Estate
Professional and Occupational
 Licensing Bureau
111 N. Jackson
Helena, MT 59620
Phone: (406)444-2961

Credential Type: Timeshare Salesperson License. **Duration of License:** One year. **Requirements:** Contact licensing body for application information. **Examination:** Written. **Fees:** $35 exam fee. $15 license fee. $15 renewal fee. **Governing Statute:** Montana Code Annotated 37-53.

Nebraska

7234

Real Estate Appraiser
Real Estate Appraiser Board
301 Centennial Mall S.
PO Box 94963
Lincoln, NE 68509-4963
Phone: (402)471-9015

Credential Type: Real Estate Appraiser License. **Duration of License:** One year. **Authorization:** Authorizes holder to provide real estate appraisal services in federally-related transactions in connection with non-complex one-to-four-unit residential properties having a transaction value of less than $1 million; complex one-to-four-unit residential properties of less than $250,000; and commercial properties of less than $250,000. **Requirements:** Complete 75 classroom hours in approved courses. Complete at least 2000 hours of appraisal work over at least two calendar years (24 months). Submit three appraisal reports. Renewal requires 20 classroom hours of continuing education. **Examination:** Licensing Examination. **Fees:** $100 application fee. $200 license fee. $25 Federal Registry fee. $225 renewal fee.

Credential Type: Real Estate Appraiser Certificate. **Duration of License:** One year. **Authorization:** Authorizes holder to provide real estate appraisal services in federally-related transactions in connection with one-to-four-unit residential properties without regard to value; and commercial properties of less than $250,000. **Requirements:** Complete 165 classroom hours in approved courses. Complete at least 2000 hours of appraisal work over at least two calendar years (24 months), 1000 hours of which must have been in non-residential real property appraisal work. Submit three appraisal reports. Renewal requires 20 classroom hours of continuing education. **Examination:** Residential Appraiser Certification Examination. **Fees:** $100 application fee. $300 certification fee. $25 Federal Fund Registry fee. $325 renewal fee.

Credential Type: Real Estate Appraiser Registration. **Duration of License:** One year. **Authorization:** Authorizes holder to perform appraisals in any time of transaction except those that are federally related. **Requirements:** Complete 75 class hours in approved subjects related to real estate appraisal, 15 of which must be related to standards of professional practice. **Examination:** Registration Examination. **Fees:** $100 registration fee.

7235

Real Estate Salesperson/Broker
Nebraska Real Estate Commission
301 Centennial Mall S.
PO Box 94667
Lincoln, NE 68509
Phone: (402)471-2004

Credential Type: License. **Duration of License:** One year. **Requirements:** 19 years of age. Must be a high school graduate. Salespersons must successfully complete two courses, not less than 30 hours each, of approved real estate education. Brokers must complete four courses, not less than 30 hours each, or must show proof of two years of full-time experience, or its part-time equivalent, in licensed sales activity, and successfully complete two courses, not less than 30 hours each. **Exam-**

Real Estate Agents, Brokers, and Appraisers

ination: Yes. **Fees:** $125 application and examination fees for salesperson and broker. $85 salesperson renewal fee. $60 broker renewal fee.

Nevada

7236

Real Estate Agent
Nevada Real Estate Div.
1665 Hot Springs Rd., Capitol Complex
Carson City, NV 89710
Phone: (702)687-4280

Credential Type: Real Estate Salesperson License. **Duration of License:** Two years. **Requirements:** 90 hours of classroom instruction in real estate principles, principles and law at an approved school. **Examination:** State and national exams. **Fees:** $55 exam fee. $100 license fee. $40 Recovery Fund fee. $100 renewal fee.

Credential Type: Real Estate Broker/Salesperson License. **Requirements:** 64 college semester units combining real estate, business, economics, and other college level courses. Active full-time experience may be counted toward completion of the 24 required credits in real estate and business. **Examination:** State and national exams. **Fees:** $55 exam fee. $130 license fee. $40 Recovery Fund fee. $130 renewal fee.

Credential Type: Real Estate Broker License. **Requirements:** Submission of a personal financial statement. Active engagement as a full-time licensed real estate broker/salesperson for at least two of the four years immediately prior to the issuance of the broker's license. **Examination:** State and national exams. **Fees:** $55 exam fee. $130 license fee. $40 Recovery Fund fee. $130 renewal fee.

7237

Real Estate Appraiser
Nevada Real Estate Div.
2501 E. Sahara Ave.
Las Vegas, NV 89158
Phone: (702)486-4033

Credential Type: Licensed Residential Real Estate Appraiser. **Duration of License:** Two years. **Requirements:** Completion of 75 hours of approved instruction. Two years, or 2,400 hours, of active, full-time appraising experience within the five-year period immediately preceding the date of application. **Examination:** Yes. **Fees:** $55 exam fee. $100 application fee. $250 license fee.

Credential Type: Certified Residential Real Estate Appraiser. **Duration of License:** Two years. **Requirements:** Completion of 120 hours of approved instruction. Two years, or 2,400 hours, of active, full-time appraising experience within the five-year period immediately preceding the date of application. 500 hours of complex residential appraising. **Examination:** Yes. **Fees:** $55 exam fee. $100 application fee. $250 license fee.

Credential Type: Certified General Property Appraiser. **Duration of License:** Two years. **Requirements:** Completion of 165 hours of approved instruction. Three years, or 3,600 hours, of active, full-time appraising experience within the five-year period immediately preceding the date of application. 1,000 hours of nonresidential property appraising. **Examination:** Yes. **Fees:** $55 exam fee. $100 application fee. $350 license fee.

New Hampshire

7238

Real Estate Broker
Real Estate Commission
Spaulding Bldg.
State Office Park S.
95 Pleasant St.
Concord, NH 03301
Phone: (603)271-2701

Credential Type: Real Estate Broker License. **Requirements:** Must have one year of real estate sales experience within the 10 years preceding application. Renewal requires three hours of continuing education every two years.

7239

Real Estate Sales Agent
Real Estate Commission
Spaulding Bldg.
State Office Park S.
95 Pleasant St.
Concord, NH 03301
Phone: (603)271-2701

Credential Type: Real Estate Agent License. **Requirements:** Renewal requires three hours of continuing education every two years. Contact board for additional requirements.

New Jersey

7240

Cemetery Salesperson
New Jersey Cemetery Board
CN040
Trenton, NJ 08625-0040
Phone: (609)292-5892

Credential Type: License. **Duration of License:** Two years. **Requirements:** 21 years of age. State resident. No criminal convictions for crimes of moral turpitude. **Fees:** $25 exam fee. $30 license fee. $20 renewal fee. **Governing Statute:** NJSA 8A-9.

7241

Real Estate Appraiser
Dept. of Law and Public Safety
Div. of Consumer Affairs
State Board of Real Estate Appraisers
124 Halsey St., 6th Fl.
Newark, NJ 07102
Phone: (201)504-6480

Credential Type: Residential Real Estate Appraiser License. **Duration of License:** Two years. **Authorization:** Authorizes holder to provide real estate appraisal services in federally-related transactions in connection with non-complex one-to-four-unit residential properties having a transaction value of less than $1 million; complex one-to-four-unit residential properties of less than $250,000; and commercial properties of less than $250,000. **Requirements:** Complete 75 classroom hours in approved courses. Complete at least 2000 hours of appraisal work over any period of time. **Examination:** Licensing Examination. **Reciprocity:** Yes, provided state has equal criteria. **Fees:** $160 registration fee. $160 renewal fee. $125 reciprocity fee.

Credential Type: Residential Real Estate Appraiser Certificate. **Duration of License:** Two years. **Authorization:** Authorizes holder to provide real estate appraisal services in federally-related transactions in connection with one-to-four-unit residential properties without regard to value; and commercial properties of less than $250,000. **Requirements:** Complete 105 classroom hours in approved courses. Complete at least 2000 hours of appraisal work over at least two calendar years (24 months). **Examination:** Residential Appraiser Certification Examination. **Reciprocity:** Yes, provided state has equal criteria. **Fees:** $200 certification fee. $200 renewal fee. $125 reciprocity fee.

New Jersey

Real Estate Appraiser, continued

Credential Type: General Real Estate Appraiser Certificate. **Duration of License:** Two years. **Authorization:** Authorizes holder to provide real estate appraisal services in federally-related transactions with all types of property without regard to value. **Requirements:** Complete 165 classroom hours in approved courses. Complete at least 2000 hours of appraisal work over at least two calendar years (24 months), 1000 hours of which must have been in non-residential real property appraisal work. **Examination:** General Appraiser Certification Examination. **Reciprocity:** Yes, provided state has equal criteria. **Fees:** $240 certification fee. $240 renewal fee. $125 reciprocity fee.

7242

Real Estate Broker
New Jersey Real Estate Commission
20 W. State St., 10 Fl.
Trenton, NJ 08625-0325
Phone: (609)292-7055

Credential Type: License. **Requirements:** 18 years of age. The equivalent of a 12th grade education. Completion of an approved 90-hour real estate brokers' course. Must work as a licensed real estate salesperson for the equivalent of two full years of full-time employment. **Examination:** Written. **Reciprocity:** Yes. **Fees:** $10 application fee. $16—$31 exam fee. $50 license fee. $10 guarantee fund. **Governing Statute:** NJSA 45:15. NJAC 11:5.

7243

Real Estate Instructor
New Jersey Real Estate Commission
20 W. State St., 10th Fl.
Trenton, NJ 08625-0325
Phone: (609)292-7055

Credential Type: License. **Requirements:** 18 years of age. A member of the faculty of an accredited college or university and have previously taught at least one course in real estate or a related subject; or have actively practiced as a licensed attorney at law in New Jersey for at least three years and have substantial experience in real estate; or hold a recent bachelor's degree in real estate; or hold a bachelor's degree and possess at least 15 credits in real estate or a related subject, and hold a teaching certificate; or be a New Jersey licensed real estate broker with five years of experience as a New Jersey licensee; or otherwise possess the competency to effectively teach real estate subjects. Good moral character.

7244

Real Estate Salesperson
New Jersey Real Estate Commission
20 W. State St., 10th Fl.
Trenton, NJ 08625-0325
Phone: (609)292-7055

Credential Type: License. **Requirements:** 18 years of age. Equivalent of a 12th grade education. Completion of a 75 hour course in real estate subjects at an approved school. **Examination:** Written. **Fees:** $10 application fee. $16—$31 exam fee. $25 license fee. $8 criminal history record fee. $5 guarantee fund fee. **Governing Statute:** NJSA 45:15. NJAC 11:5.

New Mexico

7245

Manufactured Housing Associate Broker
Manufactured Housing Div.
Dept. of Regulation and Licensing
PO Box 25101
725 St. Michael's Dr.
Santa Fe, NM 87504
Phone: (505)827-7070

Credential Type: Associate Broker License. **Requirements:** Submit application and pay fee. **Fees:** $50 license fee.

7246

Manufactured Housing Broker
Manufactured Housing Div.
Dept. of Regulation and Licensing
PO Box 25101
725 St. Michael's Dr.
Santa Fe, NM 87504
Phone: (505)827-7070

Credential Type: Broker License. **Requirements:** Submit application and pay fee. **Fees:** $200 license fee.

7247

Manufactured Housing Salesperson
Manufactured Housing Div.
Dept. of Regulation and Licensing
PO Box 25101
725 St. Michael's Dr.
Santa Fe, NM 87504
Phone: (505)827-7070

Credential Type: Salesperson License. **Requirements:** Submit application and pay fee. **Fees:** $50 license fee.

7248

Real Estate Appraiser
Real Estate Appraisal Board
Dept. of Regulation and Licensing
1650 University Blvd. NE, Ste. 490
Albuquerque, NM 87102
Phone: (505)841-9120

Credential Type: Registered Appraiser. **Duration of License:** One year. **Requirements:** Complete 60 classroom hours in basic appraisal courses, including 15 hours in Standards of Professional Practice. Each course must be at least 15 hours and include an exam. **Examination:** No exam required. **Reciprocity:** Currently available only for Colorado licensees. **Fees:** $100 license fee. $100 renewal fee.

Credential Type: State Licensed Appraiser. **Duration of License:** One year. **Requirements:** Complete 75 classroom hours in basic appraisal courses, including 15 hours in Standards of Professional Practice. Each course must be at least 15 hours and include an exam. Have at least 2000 hours of appraisal experience. **Examination:** State examination. National examination administered by the National Assessment Institute. **Reciprocity:** Currently available only for Colorado licensees. **Fees:** $200 license fee. $100 exam fee. $100 renewal fee.

Credential Type: Residential Appraiser Certificate. **Duration of License:** One year. **Requirements:** Complete 105 classroom hours in basic appraisal courses, including 15 hours in Standards of Professional Practice. Each course must be at least 15 hours and include an exam. Have at least 2000 hours of appraisal experience. **Examination:** State examination. National examination administered by the National Assessment Institute. **Reciprocity:** Currently available only for Colorado licensees. **Fees:** $200 license fee. $100 exam fee. $100 renewal fee.

Credential Type: General Appraiser Certificate. **Duration of License:** One year. **Requirements:** Complete 165 classroom hours in basic appraisal courses, including 15 hours in Standards of Professional Practice. Each course must be at least 15 hours and include an exam. Have at least 2000 hours of appraisal experience, of which at least 1000 hours must be in non-residential appraisal. **Examination:** State examination. National examination administered by the National Assessment Institute. **Reciprocity:** Currently available only for Colorado licensees. **Fees:** $250 certificate fee. $100 exam fee. $150 renewal fee.

7249

Real Estate Broker
Real Estate Commission
1650 University Blvd. N.E., Ste. 490
Albuquerque, NM 87102-1733
Phone: (505)841-9120

Credential Type: Real Estate Broker License. **Duration of License:** One year. **Requirements:** Complete 150 hours of real estate curriculum, including 30 hours of real estate law, 30 hours of real estate practice and principles, 30 hours of real estate appraisal, 30 hours of real estate finance, and 30 hours of elective real estate courses. **Examination:** National Assessment Institute broker's examination, state and national parts. **Reciprocity:** No. **Fees:** $60 license fee. $60 exam fee. $60 renewal fee.

7250

Real Estate Salesperson
Real Estate Commission
1650 University Blvd. N.E., Ste. 490
Albuquerque, NM 87102-1733
Phone: (505)841-9120

Credential Type: Real Estate Salesperson License. **Duration of License:** One year. **Requirements:** Complete 60 hours of real estate curriculum, including 30 hours of real estate law and 30 hours of real estate practice and principles. **Examination:** National Assessment Institute salesperson's examination, state and national parts. **Fees:** $60 license fee. $60 exam fee. $60 renewal fee.

New York

7251

Real Estate Appraiser
Licensing Services Div.
Dept. of State
162 Washington Ave.
Albany, NY 12231
Phone: (518)474-4429
Phone: (518)474-4664

Credential Type: Real Estate Appraiser License. **Authorization:** Authorizes holder to provide real estate appraisal services in federally-related transactions in connection with non-complex one-to-four-unit residential properties having a transaction value of less than $1 million; complex one-to-four-unit residential properties of less than $250,000; and commercial properties of less than $250,000. **Requirements:** Be at least 18 years of age. Complete 75 classroom hours in approved courses, 15 hours of which must be related to standards of professional practice. Complete at least two years of appraisal work. **Examination:** Licensing Examination. **Fees:** $300 application fee (includes $50 federal registry fee).

Credential Type: Residential Real Estate Appraiser Certificate. **Authorization:** Authorizes holder to provide real estate appraisal services in federally-related transactions in connection with one-to-four-unit residential properties without regard to value; and commercial properties of less than $250,000. **Requirements:** Be at least 18 years of age. Complete 105 classroom hours in approved courses, 15 hours of which must be related to standards of professional practice. Complete at least two years of appraisal work. **Examination:** Residential Appraiser Certification Examination. **Fees:** $300 application fee (includes $50 federal registry fee).

Credential Type: General Real Estate Appraiser Certificate. **Authorization:** Authorizes holder to provide real estate appraisal services in federally-related transactions with all types of property without regard to value. **Requirements:** Be at least 18 years of age. Complete 165 classroom hours in approved courses, 15 hours of which must be related to standards of professional practice. Complete at least two years of appraisal work. **Examination:** General Appraiser Certification Examination. **Fees:** $300 application fee (includes $50 federal registry fee).

7252

Real Estate Broker
New York State Dept. of State
Div. of Licensing Services
162 Washington Ave.
Albany, NY 12231
Phone: (518)474-2650

Credential Type: License. **Duration of License:** Two years. **Requirements:** Must have one year of experience as a real estate salesperson. Must complete 1,750 working hours under the supervision of a licensed, real estate broker. Completion of a 90-hour, approved broker qualifying class. There is a continuing education requirement every four years. 19 years of age. **Examination:** Written. **Fees:** $15 exam fee. $150 application fee. $150 renewal fee. **Governing Statute:** Article 12-A of the Real Property Law.

7253

Real Estate Salesperson
New York State Dept. of State
Div. of Licensing Services
162 Washington Ave.
Albany, NY 12231
Phone: (518)474-2650

Credential Type: License. **Duration of License:** Two years. **Requirements:** Completion of a 45-hour, approved course. There is a continuing education requirement every four years. 18 years of age. Must be sponsored by a licensed real estate broker. **Examination:** Written. **Fees:** $15 exam fee. $50 application fee. $50 renewal fee. **Governing Statute:** Article 12-A of the Real Property Law.

North Carolina

7254

Cemetery Broker
Dept. of Commerce
Cemetery Commission
430 N. Salisbury St.
Raleigh, NC 27611
Phone: (919)733-4919

Credential Type: License. **Duration of License:** One year. **Requirements:** 18 years of age. State resident for one year. **Fees:** $200 application fee. $100 license fee. $100 renewal fee.

7255

Cemetery Salesperson
Dept. of Commerce
Cemetery Commission
430 N. Salisbury St.
Raleigh, NC 27611
Phone: (919)733-4915

Credential Type: License. **Duration of License:** One year. **Fees:** $25 application and license fee. $10 renewal fee.

7256

Real Estate Appraiser
North Carolina Real Estate Commission
Real Estate Appraisal Board
1313 Navaho Dr.
PO Box 17100
Raleigh, NC 27619
Phone: (919)733-9580

Credential Type: Real Estate Appraiser License. **Duration of License:** One year. **Authorization:** Authorizes holder to pro-

North Carolina

Real Estate Appraiser, continued

vide real estate appraisal services in federally-related transactions in connection with non-complex one-to-four-unit residential properties having a transaction value of less than $1 million; complex one-to-four-unit residential properties of less than $250,000; and commercial properties of less than $250,000. **Requirements:** Complete 90 classroom hours in approved courses within the five year period preceding the date of application. Complete at least 2000 hours of appraisal work over any period of time. Renewal requires 10 classroom hours of continuing education. **Examination:** Licensing Examination. **Fees:** $150 application fee. $100 renewal fee. **Governing Statute:** General Statutes of North Carolina, 93A-70 et seq. North Carolina Administrative Code, Subchapter 58D, Title 21.

Credential Type: Residential Real Estate Appraiser Certificate. **Duration of License:** One year. **Authorization:** Authorizes holder to provide real estate appraisal services in federally-related transactions in connection with one-to-four-unit residential properties without regard to value; and commercial properties of less than $250,000. **Requirements:** Complete 120 classroom hours in approved courses. Complete at least 2000 hours of appraisal work over at least two calendar years (24 months). All qualifying education and experience must have been acquired within the five year period preceding the date of application. Renewal requires 10 classroom hours of continuing education. **Examination:** Residential Appraiser Certification Examination. **Fees:** $150 application fee. $100 renewal fee. **Governing Statute:** General Statutes of North Carolina, 93A-70 et seq. North Carolina Administrative Code, Subchapter 58D, Title 21.

Credential Type: General Real Estate Appraiser Certificate. **Duration of License:** One year. **Authorization:** Authorizes holder to provide real estate appraisal services in federally-related transactions with all types of property without regard to value. **Requirements:** Complete 180 classroom hours in approved courses. Complete at least 2000 hours of appraisal work over at least two calendar years (24 months), 1000 hours of which must have been in non-residential real property appraisal work. All qualifying education and experience must have been acquired within the five year period preceding the date of application. Renewal requires 10 classroom hours of continuing education. **Examination:** General Appraiser Certification Examination. **Fees:** $150 application fee. $100 renewal fee. **Governing Statute:** General Statutes of North Carolina, 93A-70 et seq. North Carolina Administrative Code, Subchapter 58D, Title 21.

Credential Type: Temporary Permit. **Authorization:** Issued only for a particular assignment. **Requirements:** Must be licensed or certified in another state. **Governing Statute:** General Statutes of North Carolina, 93A-70 et seq. North Carolina Administrative Code, Subchapter 58D, Title 21.

7257

Real Estate Broker
North Carolina Real Estate
    Commission
PO Box 17100
Raleigh, NC 27619
Phone: (919)733-9580

Credential Type: License. **Duration of License:** One year. **Requirements:** Completion of 120 hours of classroom instruction within the past five years from an approved course. Licensed real estate salespersons with two years of experience in the past five years also are eligible to take the broker's examination. 18 years of age. **Examination:** Written. **Fees:** $30 initial fee. $20 renewal fee.

7258

Real Estate Salesperson
North Carolina Real Estate
    Commission
PO Box 17100
Raleigh, NC 27619
Phone: (919)733-9580

Credential Type: License. **Duration of License:** One year. **Requirements:** 18 years of age. Good moral character. Must pass the Fundamentals of Real Estate course within the past five years. **Examination:** Written. **Fees:** $30 initial fee. $20 renewal fee.

North Dakota

7259

Real Estate Appraiser
Real Estate Appraiser Qualifications
    and Ethics Board
PO Box 1336
Bismarck, ND 58502-1336
Phone: (701)222-1051

Credential Type: Real Estate Appraiser License. **Duration of License:** One year. **Authorization:** Authorizes holder to provide real estate appraisal services in federally-related transactions in connection with non-complex one-to-four-unit residential properties having a transaction value of less than $1 million; complex one-to-four-unit residential properties of less than $250,000; and commercial properties of less than $250,000. **Requirements:** Be at least 18 years of age. High school graduate or equivalent. Possess good character. Complete at least a 15-hour Uniform Standards of Professional Appraisal Practice (USPAP) Class. Complete 75 classroom hours in approved courses. Complete at least 2000 hours of appraisal work over at least two calendar years (24 months). **Examination:** Licensing Examination. **Fees:** $200 annual fee. $50 "one time" out-of-state resident application fee.

Credential Type: General Real Estate Appraiser Certificate. **Duration of License:** One year. **Authorization:** Authorizes holder to provide real estate appraisal services in federally-related transactions with all types of property without regard to value. **Requirements:** Be at least 18 years of age. High school graduate or equivalent. Possess good character. Complete at least a 15-hour Uniform Standards of Professional Appraisal Practice (USPAP) Class. Complete 165 classroom hours in approved courses. Complete at least 2000 hours of appraisal work over at least two calendar years (24 months), 1000 hours of which must have been in non-residential real property appraisal work. **Examination:** General Appraiser Certification Examination. **Fees:** $200 annual fee. $50 "one time" out of state resident application fee.

Credential Type: Apprentice Appraiser Permit. **Duration of License:** One year. **Requirements:** Complete 15 hours of education related to the Uniform Standards of Professional Appraisal Practice (USPAP). **Fees:** $200 annual permit fee.

7260

Real Estate Broker
Real Estate Commission
314 E. Thayer Ave.
PO Box 727
Bismarck, ND 58502
Phone: (701)224-2749

Credential Type: Real Estate Broker License. **Duration of License:** One year. **Requirements:** Complete 120 classroom hours of real estate education. Must have two years of real estate sales experience. Renewal requires 24 hours of continuing education every three years. **Examination:** ASI Examination. **Reciprocity:** No. **Fees:** $20 exam fee. $50 original license fee. $50 renewal fee.

7261

Real Estate Sales Agent
Real Estate Commission
314 E. Thayer Ave.
PO Box 727
Bismarck, ND 58502
Phone: (701)224-2749

Credential Type: Real Estate Agent License. **Duration of License:** One year. **Requirements:** Complete 30 classroom hours or real estate education prior to sitting for examination. Renewal requires 24 hours of continuing education every three years. **Examination:** ASI Examination. **Reciprocity:** No. **Fees:** $20 exam fee. $40 original license fee. $40 renewal fee.

Ohio

7262

Real Estate Appraiser
Real Estate Appraisal Board
Div. of Real Estate
77 S. High St., 20th Fl.
Columbus, OH 43266-0547
Phone: (614)466-4100

Credential Type: Residential Real Estate Appraiser License (State Licensed). **Authorization:** Authorizes holder to provide real estate appraisal services in federally-related transactions in connection with non-complex one-to-four-unit residential properties having a transaction value of less than $1 million; complex one-to-four-unit residential properties of less than $250,000; and commercial properties of less than $250,000. **Requirements:** Complete 75 classroom hours in approved courses. Complete at least 2000 hours of appraisal work over a two-year period of time. **Examination:** Licensing Examination. **Fees:** $125 application fee. $35 exam fee. $125 license fee (includes $25 federal registry fee).

Credential Type: General Real Estate Appraiser Certificate (State Certified). **Authorization:** Authorizes holder to provide real estate appraisal services in federally-related transactions with all types of property without regard to value. **Requirements:** Complete 165 classroom hours in approved courses. Complete at least 2000 hours of appraisal work over at least two calendar years (24 months), 1000 hours of which must have been in non-residential real property appraisal work. **Examination:** General Appraiser Certification Examination. **Fees:** $125 application fee. $35 exam fee. $125 certification fee (includes $25 federal registry fee).

7263

Real Estate Broker
Div. of Real Estate
77 S. High St.
Columbus, OH 43266-0547
Phone: (614)466-4100

Credential Type: Real Estate Broker License. **Duration of License:** One year. **Requirements:** Education requirement varies with year of licensure. Contact board for specific education requirements. Must have two years of real estate sales experience within the five years preceding application. Renewal requires 30 hours of continuing education every three years. **Examination:** Agency/Staff Examination. **Reciprocity:** Yes. **Fees:** $59 exam fee. $34 license renewal fee.

7264

Real Estate Sales Agent
Div. of Real Estate
77 S. High St.
Columbus, OH 43266-0547
Phone: (614)466-4100

Credential Type: Real Estate Agent License. **Duration of License:** One year. **Requirements:** Complete 120 classroom hours of real estate education, plus 10 hours within one year of licensure. Renewal requires 30 hours of continuing education every three years. **Examination:** Agency/Staff Examination. **Reciprocity:** Yes. **Fees:** $39 exam fee. $24 license renewal fee.

Oklahoma

7265

Real Estate Agent (Sales Associate)
Oklahoma Real Estate Commission
4040 N. Lincoln
Oklahoma City, OK 73105
Phone: (405)521-3387

Credential Type: License. **Duration of License:** Three years. **Requirements:** Completion of "Real Estate Principles" course. 21 clock hours of continuing education every three years. 18 years of age. **Examination:** Real Estate Sales Associate Pre-License Examination. **Fees:** $40 exam fee. $40 application fee. $75 license fee. $15 education and recovery fund.

7266

Real Estate Appraiser
Oklahoma Insurance Commission
1901 N. Walnut
Oklahoma City, OK 73105
Phone: (405)521-2828

Credential Type: Certificate. **Duration of License:** One year. **Requirements:** 30 hours of continuing education each year. Two years of experience in real property appraisal. **Examination:** Certified Real Estate Appraisal I. Certified Real Estate Appraisal II. **Fees:** $150 exam fee. $150 certification fee. $150 renewal fee.

7267

Real Estate Broker
Oklahoma Real Estate Commission
4040 N. Lincoln
Oklahoma City, OK 73105
Phone: (405)521-3387

Credential Type: License. **Duration of License:** Three years. **Requirements:** Completion of a real estate practices course or three equivalent college credit hours. 21 clock hours of continuing education every three years. 18 years of age. Completion of a one-year licensure as a sales associate. No felony convictions. **Examination:** Real Estate Broker Pre-Licensing Examination. **Fees:** $50 exam fee. $50 application fee. $120 license fee. $120 renewal fee.

Oregon

7268

Escrow Agent
Oregon Real Estate Agency
158 12th St. NE
Salem, OR 97310
Phone: (503)378-4170

Credential Type: License. **Duration of License:** One year. **Requirements:** Escrow experience. Must provide current financial statements. **Examination:** No. **Fees:** $200 license fee. $200 renewal fee. **Governing Statute:** ORS Chapter 696.

7269

Real Estate Appraiser
Secretary of State, Office of
    Appraiser Certification
325 13th St. NE, Ste. 301
Salem, OR 97310
Phone: (503)373-1505

Credential Type: License. **Duration of License:** One year. **Requirements:** 18

Oregon 7270

Real Estate Appraiser, continued

years of age. Must have approval of qualifications by Appraiser Certification and Licensure Board. **Examination:** Yes. **Fees:** $50 exam fee. $75 application fee. $525 license fee. $425 renewal fee. **Governing Statute:** ORS 674.000.

7270

Real Estate Broker
Oregon Real Estate Agency
158 12th St. NE
Salem, OR 97310
Phone: (503)378-4170

Credential Type: License. **Duration of License:** Two years. **Requirements:** 18 years of age. Successful completion of required courses. Must furnish proof of three years experience as a licensed real estate salesperson or have real estate experience and/or education approved by the Real Estate Board. **Examination:** Yes. **Fees:** $50 exam fee. $150 license fee. $150 renewal fee. **Governing Statute:** ORS 696.020.

7271

Real Estate Salesperson
Oregon Real Estate Agency
158 12th St. NE
Salem, OR 97310
Phone: (503)378-4170

Credential Type: License. **Duration of License:** Two years. **Requirements:** 18 years of age. Successful completion of required courses. Successful completion of the salesperson's license exam or successful completion of the Real Estate Agency competency challenge exams in all three required course areas. **Examination:** Yes. **Fees:** $50 exam fee. $105 license fee. $105 renewal fee. **Governing Statute:** ORS 696.020.

Pennsylvania

7272

Real Estate Appraiser
State Board of Certified Real Estate Appraisers
Dept. of State
Bureau of Professional & Occupational Affairs
619 Transportation & Safety Bldg.
Harrisburg, PA 17120
Phone: (717)783-7226
Fax: (717)787-7769

Credential Type: Residential Real Estate Appraiser Certificate. **Duration of License:** Two years. **Authorization:** Authorizes holder to provide real estate appraisal services in federally-related transactions in connection with one-to-four-unit residential properties without regard to value; and commercial properties of less than $250,000. **Requirements:** Complete 105 classroom hours in approved courses. Complete at least 2000 hours of appraisal work over at least two calendar years (24 months). Renewal requires 20 classroom hours of continuing education. **Examination:** Residential Appraiser Certification Examination. **Fees:** $55 application fee. $35 re-application fee. $50 exam fee. $45 initial certification fee (if certified before 6/30/93).

Credential Type: General Real Estate Appraiser Certificate. **Duration of License:** Two years. **Authorization:** Authorizes holder to provide real estate appraisal services in federally-related transactions with all types of property without regard to value. **Requirements:** Complete 165 classroom hours in approved courses. Complete at least 2000 hours of appraisal work over at least two calendar years (24 months), 1000 hours of which must be in commercial property appraisal. Renewal requires 20 classroom hours of continuing education. **Examination:** General Appraiser Certification Examination. **Fees:** $55 application fee. $35 re-application fee. $50 exam fee. $45 initial certification fee (if certified before June 30, 1993).

7273

Real Estate Auctioneer
Real Estate Commission
Transportation and Safety Bldg., Rm. 611
PO Box 2649
Harrisburg, PA 17105-2649
Phone: (717)783-3658

Credential Type: Real Estate Auctioneer License. **Requirements:** Contact licensing body for application information.

7274

Real Estate Broker
Real Estate Commission
Transportation and Safety Bldg., Rm. 611
PO Box 2649
Harrisburg, PA 17105-2649
Phone: (717)783-3658

Credential Type: Real Estate Broker License. **Duration of License:** Two years. **Requirements:** Complete 300 classroom hours of real estate education. Must have three years of real estate sales experience or 200 points from point system based on number of transactions completed. Renewal requires 14 hours of continuing education. **Examination:** ASI Examination. **Reciprocity:** Yes. **Fees:** $15 exam fee. $45 original license fee. $34.50 renewal fee.

7275

Real Estate Sales Agent
Real Estate Commission
Transportation and Safety Bldg., Rm. 611
PO Box 2649
Harrisburg, PA 17105-2649
Phone: (717)783-3658

Credential Type: Real Estate Agent License. **Duration of License:** Two years. **Requirements:** Complete 60 classroom hours of real estate education. Renewal requires 14 hours of continuing education. **Examination:** ASI Examination. **Reciprocity:** Yes. **Fees:** $15 exam fee. $15 original license fee. $34.50 renewal fee.

Rhode Island

7276

Real Estate Appraiser
Dept. of Business Regulation
Licensing and Consumer Protection
Real Estate Appraiser Section
233 Richmond St., Ste. 230
Providence, RI 02903-4230
Phone: (401)277-2262
Phone: (401)277-2255

Credential Type: Real Estate Appraiser License. **Duration of License:** One year. **Authorization:** Authorizes holder to provide real estate appraisal services in federally-related transactions in connection with non-complex one-to-four-unit residential properties having a transaction value of less than $1 million; complex one-to-four-unit residential properties of less than $250,000; and commercial properties of less than $250,000. **Requirements:** Complete 75 classroom hours in approved courses. Complete at least 2000 hours of appraisal work during the five years immediately preceding the applicant's application. Renewal requires 20 classroom hours of instruction in courses or seminars from a dulylicenses real estate school. **Examination:** Licensing Examination. **Fees:** $150 application fee. $200 out-of-state resident application fee. $75 exam fee. $150 license fee (per year). **Governing Statute:** Rhode Island General Laws, Section 5-20.7-1 et seq. Rules and Regulations.

Credential Type: Residential Real Estate Appraiser Certificate. **Duration of License:** One year. **Authorization:** Authorizes holder to provide real estate appraisal services in federally-related transactions in connection with one-to-four-unit residential properties without regard to value; and commercial properties of less than $250,000. **Requirements:** Complete 105 classroom hours in approved courses. Complete at least 2000 hours of appraisal work during the five years immediately preceding the applicant's application. Renewal requires 20 classroom hours of instruction in courses or seminars from a dulylicenses real estate school. **Examination:** Residential Appraiser Certification Examination. **Fees:** $150 application fee. $200 out-of-state resident application fee. $75 exam fee. $150 certification fee (per year). **Governing Statute:** Rhode Island General Laws, Section 5-20.7-1 et seq. Rules and Regulations.

Credential Type: General Real Estate Appraiser Certificate. **Authorization:** Authorizes holder to provide real estate appraisal services in federally-related transactions with all types of property without regard to value. **Requirements:** Complete 165 classroom hours in approved courses. Complete at least 2000 hours of appraisal work during the five years immediately preceding the applicant's application. Renewal requires 20 classroom hours of instruction in courses or seminars from a dulylicenses real estate school. **Examination:** General Appraiser Certification Examination. **Fees:** $150 application fee. $200 out-of-state resident application fee. $75 exam fee. $150 certification fee (per year). **Governing Statute:** Rhode Island General Laws, Section 5-20.7-1 et seq. Rules and Regulations.

Credential Type: Temporary Practice License/Certificate. **Duration of License:** 90 days. **Authorization:** Limited to the appraisal of redsidential property with a transaction value of less than $1,000. Must work directly under a certified appraiser. **Requirements:** Current certification/license as an appraiser in another state. Complete 75 classroom hours in approved courses. **Fees:** $50 temporary practice license or certificate fee (90 days). $50 temporary 30-day renewal fee (maximum 3). **Governing Statute:** Rhode Island General Laws, Section 5-20.7-1 et seq. Rules and Regulations.

South Carolina

7277

Manufactured Housing Representative
State Board of Manufactured Housing
1201 Main St., Ste. 820
AT&T Bldg.
Columbia, SC 29201
Phone: (803)737-0567

Credential Type: License. **Requirements:** Contact licensing body for application information. **Fees:** $20 license fee.

7278

Manufactured Housing Retail Dealer
State Board of Manufactured Housing
1201 Main St., Ste. 820
AT&T Bldg.
Columbia, SC 29201
Phone: (803)737-0567

Credential Type: License. **Requirements:** Contact licensing body for application information. **Fees:** $25 license fee.

7279

Manufactured Housing Salesperson
State Board of Manufactured Housing
1201 Main St., Ste. 820
AT&T Bldg.
Columbia, SC 29201
Phone: (803)737-0567

Credential Type: License. **Requirements:** Contact licensing body for application information. **Fees:** $10 license fee.

7280

Real Estate Appraiser
Real Estate Appraisers Board
Capitol Center, AT&T Bldg.
1201 Main St., Ste. 1530
Columbia, SC 29201
Phone: (803)737-0898

Credential Type: State Licensed Real Estate Appraiser. **Duration of License:** One year. **Authorization:** Authorizes holder to provide real estate appraisal services in federally-related transactions in connection with non-complex one-to-four-unit residential properties having a transaction value of less than $1 million; complex one-to-four-unit residential properties of less than $250,000; and commercial properties of less than $250,000. **Requirements:** Be at least 18 years of age. Complete 75 classroom hours in approved courses. Complete at least 2000 hours of appraisal work over at least two calendar years (24 months). Renewal requires 10 classroom hours of continuing education. **Examination:** Licensing Examination. **Fees:** $100 exam fee.

Credential Type: State Certified Real Estate Appraiser. **Duration of License:** One year. **Authorization:** Authorizes holder to provide real estate appraisal services in any type of transaction without regard to value. **Requirements:** Be at least 18 years of age. Complete 165 classroom hours in approved courses. Complete at least 2000 hours of appraisal work over at least two calendar years (24 months), 1000 hours of which must have been in non-residential real property appraisal work. Renewal requires 10 classroom hours of continuing education. **Examination:** Certification Examination. **Fees:** $100 exam fee.

Credential Type: State Registered Real Estate Appraiser. **Duration of License:** One year. **Authorization:** Authorizes holder to engage in any type of real estate appraisal activity which does not involve a federally-related transaction. **Requirements:** Must hold a real estate broker-in-charge, broker, or salesperson license. Re-

South Carolina 7281

Real Estate Appraiser, continued

newal requires 10 classroom hours of continuing education.

7281

Real Estate Broker
South Carolina Real Estate
  Commission
1201 Main St., Ste. 1500
Columbia, SC 29201
Phone: (803)737-0700

Credential Type: License. **Requirements:** Three years of experience as a licensed real estate salesman immediately preceding the broker application, plus 90 hours of real estate instruction in an accredited college or a bachelor's degree with a real estate major, a law degree, or five years of experience in business activities related to real estate. 21 years of age. **Examination:** Yes. **Fees:** $50 license fee.

7282

Real Estate Salesman
South Carolina Real Estate
  Commission
1201 Main St., Ste. 1500
Columbia, SC 29201
Phone: (803)737-0700

Credential Type: Salesman One License. **Requirements:** 18 years of age. State resident. Thirty hours of real estate instruction in an accredited college or an approved school. **Examination:** Yes. **Fees:** $50 license fee.

Credential Type: Salesman License. **Requirements:** 18 years of age. State resident. Sixty hours of real estate instruction in an accredited college or an approved school, plus one year of real estate sales experience, six credit hours in real estate or related subjects at an accredited college, or a law degree. **Examination:** Yes. **Fees:** $50 license fee.

South Dakota

7283

Real Estate Appraiser
Dept. of Commerce and Regulation
Office of the Secretary
910 E. Sioux Ave.
Pierre, SD 57501-3940
Phone: (605)773-3178
Fax: (605)773-5369

Credential Type: Real Estate Appraiser License. **Duration of License:** One year. **Authorization:** Authorizes holder to provide real estate appraisal services in federally-related transactions in connection with non-complex one-to-four-unit residential properties having a transaction value of less than $1 million; complex one-to-four-unit residential properties of less than $250,000; and commercial properties of less than $250,000. **Requirements:** Complete 75 classroom hours in approved courses. Complete at least 2000 hours of appraisal work over at least two calendar years (24 months). **Examination:** Licensing Examination. **Fees:** $35 application fee. $125 annual fee. $25 Federal Registry fee. **Governing Statute:** Administrative Rules of South Dakota, Article 20:14.

Credential Type: General Real Estate Appraiser Certificate. **Authorization:** Authorizes holder to provide real estate appraisal services in federally-related transactions with all types of property without regard to value. **Requirements:** Complete 165 classroom hours in approved courses. Complete at least 2000 hours of appraisal work over at least two calendar years (24 months), 1000 hours of which must have been in non-residential real property appraisal work. **Examination:** General Appraiser Certification Examination. **Fees:** $50 application fee. $150 annual fee. $25 Federal Registry fee. **Governing Statute:** Administrative Rules of South Dakota, Article 20:14.

Credential Type: Temporary License. **Duration of License:** Six months. **Authorization:** Authorizes holder to appraise real estate involving a federally related transaction. **Requirements:** Must be licensed or certified or transitionally licensed in another state. **Fees:** $200 license fee. **Governing Statute:** Administrative Rules of South Dakota, Article 20:14.

7284

Real Estate Auctioneer
South Dakota Real Estate
  Commission
PO Box 490
Pierre, SD 57501-0490
Phone: (605)773-3600
Phone: (605)773-3150

Credential Type: Real Estate Auctioneer License. **Duration of License:** Two years. **Requirements:** Submit application and pay fees. **Examination:** State-administered auctioneer's examination. **Exemptions:** Real estate brokers do not need an auctioneer's license. **Fees:** $100 application and license fee. $80 renewal fee.

7285

Real Estate Broker
Real Estate Commission
212 E. Capitol
PO Box 490
Pierre, SD 57501-0490
Phone: (605)773-3600

Credential Type: Real Estate Broker License. **Duration of License:** Two years. **Requirements:** Complete 90 classroom hours of real estate education. Must have two years of real estate sales experience. Renewal requires 24 hours of continuing education. **Examination:** ASI Examination. **Reciprocity:** Yes. **Fees:** $31 exam fee. $100 original license fee. $80 renewal fee.

7286

Real Estate Sales Agent
Real Estate Commission
212 E. Capitol
PO Box 490
Pierre, SD 57501-0490
Phone: (605)773-3600

Credential Type: Real Estate Agent License. **Duration of License:** Two years. **Requirements:** Complete 30 classroom hours of real estate education. Renewal requires 24 hours of continuing education. **Examination:** ASI Examination. **Reciprocity:** Yes. **Fees:** $31 exam fee. $100 original license fee. $60 renewal fee.

Tennessee

7287

Real Estate Affiliate Broker
Real Estate Commission
500 James Robertson Pky., Ste. 180
Nashville, TN 37243
Phone: (615)741-2273
Phone: (800)342-4031

Credential Type: License. **Requirements:** 18 years old. Experience as an affiliate broker. Education requirements apply, please check with the Board. 16 hours of continuing education every two years. **Examination:** Yes. **Reciprocity:** Yes, Arkansas, Georgia, Kentucky, North Carolina, Missouri, Oklahoma, Virginia, West Virginia **Fees:** $77 Examination. $80 Application.

7288

Real Estate Appraiser
Dept. of Commerce & Insurance
Real Estate Appraiser Commission
500 James Robertson Pky.
Nashville, TN 37243-1166
Phone: (615)741-1831

Credential Type: Real Estate Appraiser License. **Duration of License:** Two years. **Authorization:** Authorizes holder to provide real estate appraisal services in federally-related transactions in connection with non-complex one-to-four-unit residential properties having a transaction value of less than $1 million; complex one-to-four-unit residential properties of less than $250,000; and commercial properties of less than $250,000. **Requirements:** High school graduate or equivalent. Complete 75 classroom hours in approved courses. Complete at least 2000 hours of appraisal work over at least two calendar years (24 months). **Examination:** Licensing Examination. **Fees:** $100 application fee. $200 licensure fee. $50 Federal Registry fee. $200 renewal fee.

Credential Type: Residential Real Estate Appraiser Certificate. **Duration of License:** Two years. **Authorization:** Authorizes holder to provide real estate appraisal services in federally-related transactions in connection with one-to-four-unit residential properties without regard to value; and commercial properties of less than $250,000. **Requirements:** High school graduate or equivalent. Complete 105 classroom hours in approved courses. Complete at least 2000 hours of appraisal work over at least two calendar years (24 months). **Examination:** Residential Appraiser Certification Examination. **Fees:** $100 application fee. $200 certification fee. $50 Federal Registry fee. $200 renewal fee.

Credential Type: General Real Estate Appraiser Certificate. **Duration of License:** Two years. **Authorization:** Authorizes holder to provide real estate appraisal services in federally-related transactions with all types of property without regard to value. **Requirements:** High school graduate or equivalent. Complete 165 classroom hours in approved courses. Complete at least 2000 hours of appraisal work over at least two calendar years (24 months), 1000 hours of which must have been in non-residential real property appraisal work. **Examination:** General Appraiser Certification Examination. **Fees:** $100 application fee. $200 certification fee. $50 Federal Registry fee. $200 renewal fee.

Credential Type: Trainee Registration. **Duration of License:** Two years. **Authorization:** A licensed or certified appraiser must review and sign all appraisals. **Requirements:** High school graduate or equivalent. May sit for trainee examination after completing 75 hours of approved education. A registered may wait and sit for a licensing or certification examination after meeting the experience requirements instead of taking the trainee examination. **Examination:** Trainee examination (not mandatory). **Fees:** $50 registration fee. $50 renewal fee.

7289

Real Estate Broker
Real Estate Commission
500 James Robertson Pky., Ste. 180
Volunteer Plaza
Nashville, TN 37243-1151
Phone: (615)741-2273

Credential Type: Real Estate Broker License. **Requirements:** Complete 120 classroom hours of real estate education. Must have three years of real estate sales experience. **Examination:** ASI Examination. **Reciprocity:** Yes. **Fees:** $77 exam fee. $80 original license fee. $40 renewal fee.

7290

Real Estate Sales Agent
Real Estate Commission
500 James Robertson Pky., Ste. 180
Volunteer Plaza
Nashville, TN 37243-1151
Phone: (615)741-2273

Credential Type: Real Estate Agent License. **Requirements:** Complete 60 classroom hours of real estate education. Renewal requires 16 hours of continuing education every two years. **Examination:** ASI Examination. **Reciprocity:** Yes. **Fees:** $77 exam fee. $80 original license fee. $40 renewal fee.

7291

Time-Share Agent
Real Estate Commission
500 James Robertson Pky., Ste. 180
Volunteer Plaza
Nashville, TN 37243-1151
Phone: (615)741-2273

Credential Type: Time-Share Agent License. **Requirements:** Contact licensing body for application information.

Texas

7292

Real Estate Appraiser
Appraiser Licensing and Certification Board
PO Box 12188
Austin, TX 78711-2188
Phone: (512)465-3950
Fax: (512)465-3998

Credential Type: Real Estate Appraiser License. **Duration of License:** Two years. **Authorization:** Authorizes holder to provide real estate appraisal services in federally-related transactions in connection with non-complex one-to-four-unit residential properties having a transaction value of less than $1 million; complex one-to-four-unit residential properties of less than $250,000; and commercial properties of less than $250,000. **Requirements:** Complete 75 classroom hours in approved courses. Complete at least 2000 hours of appraisal work over any period of time. **Examination:** Licensing Examination. **Fees:** $125 application and license fee. $50 exam fee. $100 renewal fee. $50 federal registry fee.

Credential Type: Residential Real Estate Appraiser Certificate. **Duration of License:** Two years. **Authorization:** Authorizes holder to provide real estate appraisal services in federally-related transactions in connection with one-to-four-unit residential properties without regard to value; and commercial properties of less than $250,000. **Requirements:** Complete 105 classroom hours in approved courses. Complete at least 2000 hours of appraisal work over at least two calendar years (24 months). **Examination:** Residential Appraiser Certification Examination. **Fees:** $125 application and license fee. $50 exam fee. $100 renewal fee. $50 federal registry fee.

Credential Type: General Real Estate Appraiser Certificate. **Duration of License:** Two years. **Authorization:** Authorizes holder to provide real estate appraisal services in federally-related transactions with all types of property without regard to value. **Requirements:** Complete 165 classroom hours in approved courses. Complete at least 2000 hours of appraisal work over at least two calendar years (24 months), 1000 hours of which must have been in non-residential real property appraisal work. **Examination:** General Appraiser Certification Examination. **Fees:** $125 application and license fee. $50 exam fee. $100 renewal fee. $50 federal registry fee.

Credential Type: Temporary Registration. **Duration of License:** 60 days. **Authorization:** May appraise only "federally related

Texas 7293

Real Estate Appraiser, continued

transactions". Issued only for a particular assignment. **Requirements:** Must be licensed or certified in another state.

7293

Real Estate Broker
Texas Real Estate Commission
PO Box 12188
Austin, TX 78711
Phone: (512)459-6544

Credential Type: Broker License. **Duration of License:** One year. **Requirements:** U.S. citizen or legal alien. Texas resident for at least 60 days. 18 years of age. At least two years active experience as a sales agent, and 60 semester hours, or equivalent classroom hours, in core real estate or acceptable courses. Completion of 15 classroom hours of acceptable continuing education per two year renewal. **Examination:** Written. **Fees:** $25 exam fee. $100 application fee. $100 renewal fee. **Governing Statute:** VACS 6573a, 22 TAC 535.

7294

Real Estate Inspector
Texas Real Estate Commission
PO Box 12188
Austin, TX 78711
Phone: (512)459-6544

Credential Type: Apprentice License. **Requirements:** 18 years of age. U.S. citizen or legal alien. Texas resident for at least 60 days. Sponsorship by an unrestricted inspector. Must be registered with a sponsoring inspector for 90 days. Must perform 25 inspections under direct supervision of an inspector. **Examination:** Written. **Fees:** $100 exam fee. $75 application fee. $125 renewal fee. **Governing Statute:** Section 23, 6573a, VTCS.

Credential Type: Inspector-in-Training License. **Requirements:** 18 years of age. U.S. citizen or legal alien. Texas resident for at least 60 days. Sponsorship by an unrestricted inspector. Completion of 90 days of approved apprenticeship. Completion of 90 classroom hours in core real estate inspection courses and pass an examination. Work as an inspector-in-training for a minimum of 12 months. Perform a minimum of 175 inspections. Must have four hours core real estate inspection courses annually for license renewal. **Examination:** Written. **Fees:** $100 exam fee. $125 application fee. $175 renewal fee. **Governing Statute:** Section 23, 6573a, VTCS.

Credential Type: Restricted Inspector License. **Requirements:** 18 years of age. U.S. citizen or legal alien. Texas resident for at least 60 days. Sponsorship by an unrestricted inspector. Must satisfy requirements of inspector-in-training. 75 additional inspections in the preceding year. Additional 38 hours core real estate inspection courses. Must have eight hours core real estate inspection courses annually for license renewal. **Examination:** Written. **Fees:** $100 exam fee. $150 application fee. $200 renewal fee. **Governing Statute:** Section 23, 6573a, VTCS.

Credential Type: Unrestricted Inspector License. **Requirements:** 18 years of age. U.S. citizen or legal alien. Texas resident for at least 60 days. Sponsorship by an unrestricted inspector. Must satisfy requirements of restricted inspector. 125 additional inspections. Must have eight hours core real estate inspection courses annually for license renewal. **Examination:** Written. **Fees:** $100 exam fee. $150 application fee. $200 renewal fee. **Governing Statute:** Section 23, 6573a, VTCS.

7295

Real Estate Sales Agent
Texas Real Estate Commission
PO Box 12188
Austin, TX 78711
Phone: (512)459-6544

Credential Type: Agent License. **Duration of License:** One year. **Requirements:** U.S. citizen or legal alien. Texas resident for at least 60 days. 18 years of age. Sponsorship by a broker. Completion of 12 semester hours or equivalent classroom hours in core real estate courses from an accredited college or school. Two semester hours or 30 classroom hours required for annual renewals until a total of 18 semester hours or 270 classroom hours are attained. Thereafter 15 classroom hours of continuing education required per two-year renewal period. **Examination:** Written. **Fees:** $25 exam fee. $50 application fee. $50 renewal fee. **Governing Statute:** VACS 6573a, 22 TAC 535.

Utah

7296

Real Estate Appraiser
Dept. of Commerce
Div. of Real Estate
Heber M. Wells Bldg.
160 E. 300 S.
PO Box 45806
Salt Lake City, UT 84145-0806
Phone: (801)530-6747

Credential Type: Real Estate Appraiser Registration. **Duration of License:** Two years. **Authorization:** Authorizes holder to provide real estate appraisal services in federally-related transactions in connection with non-complex one-to-four-unit residential properties having a transaction value of less than $1 million; complex one-to-four-unit residential properties of less than $250,000; and commercial properties of less than $250,000. **Requirements:** Complete 75 classroom hours in approved courses. **Examination:** No exam **Fees:** $200 registration fee.

Credential Type: Residential Real Estate Appraiser Certificate. **Duration of License:** Two years. **Authorization:** Authorizes holder to provide real estate appraisal services in federally-related transactions in connection with one-to-four-unit residential properties without regard to value; and commercial properties of less than $250,000. **Requirements:** Complete 120 classroom hours in approved courses. Complete at least 2000 hours of appraisal work over at least two calendar years (24 months). Renewal requires 20 continuing education hours. **Examination:** Residential Appraiser Certification Examination. **Fees:** $250 certification fee.

Credential Type: General Real Estate Appraiser Certificate. **Duration of License:** Two years. **Authorization:** Authorizes holder to provide real estate appraisal services in federally-related transactions with all types of property without regard to value. **Requirements:** Complete 165 classroom hours in approved courses. Complete at least 2000 hours of appraisal work over at least two calendar years (24 months). Renewal requires 20 continuing education hours. **Examination:** General Appraiser Certification Examination. **Fees:** $250 certification fee.

7297

Real Estate Broker
Div. of Real Estate
160 E. 300 S., 4th Fl.
PO Box 45802
Salt Lake City, UT 84145-0802
Phone: (801)530-6747

Credential Type: Real Estate Broker's License. **Duration of License:** Two years. **Requirements:** Must have at least three years of active full-time experience as a licensed real estate person in Utah. Must complete at least 30 hours Broker/Advanced Appraisal, 30 hours Broker/Advanced Finance, 30 hours Broker/Advanced Real Estate Law, and 30 hours Brokerage Management. **Examination:** Yes. **Fees:** $35 exam fee. $86 license fee. $86 renewal fee.

7298

Real Estate Salesperson
Div. of Real Estate
160 E. 300 S., 4th Fl.
PO Box 45802
Salt Lake City, UT 84145-0802
Phone: (801)530-6747

Credential Type: Real Estate Salesperson's License. **Duration of License:** Two years. **Requirements:** Must complete at least 90 classroom hours of approved study, or an eight-hour credited university course in elementary principles and practeces of real estate. **Examination:** Yes. **Fees:** $25 exam fee. $74 renewal fee.

Vermont

7299

Real Estate Appraiser
Board of Real Estate Appraisers
Office of Professional Regulation
109 State St.
Montpelier, VT 05609-1106
Phone: (802)828-2363
Phone: (802)828-2191

Credential Type: Real Estate Appraiser License. **Duration of License:** Two years. **Authorization:** Authorizes holder to provide real estate appraisal services in federally-related transactions in connection with non-complex one-to-four-unit residential properties having a transaction value of less than $1 million; complex one-to-four-unit residential properties of less than $250,000; and commercial properties of less than $250,000. **Requirements:** Complete 75 classroom hours in approved courses. Complete 2000 hours of appraisal work. Ten continuing education classroom hours of instruction in courses or seminars for each year during the period preceding the renewal. **Examination:** Licensing Examination. **Fees:** $125 application fee. $60 license fee. $25 Federal Fund Registry fee. $225 biennial renewal fee. **Governing Statute:** Real Estate Appraiser Law, Title 26, Chap. 69.

Credential Type: Residential Real Estate Appraiser Certificate. **Duration of License:** Two years. **Authorization:** Authorizes holder to provide real estate appraisal services in federally-related transactions in connection with one-to-four-unit residential properties without regard to value; and commercial properties of less than $250,000. **Requirements:** Complete 105 classroom hours in approved courses. Equivalent of two years appraisal experience. Ten continuing education classroom hours of instruction in courses or seminars for each year during the period preceding the renewal. **Examination:** Residential Appraiser Certification Examination. **Fees:** $125 application fee. $60 license fee. $25 Federal Fund Registry fee. $225 biennial renewal fee. **Governing Statute:** Real Estate Appraiser Law, Title 26, Chap. 69.

Credential Type: General Real Estate Appraiser Certificate. **Duration of License:** Two years. **Authorization:** Authorizes holder to provide real estate appraisal services in federally-related transactions with all types of property without regard to value. **Requirements:** Complete 165 classroom hours in approved courses. Equivalent of two years appraisal experience. Ten continuing education classroom hours of instruction in courses or seminars for each year during the period preceding the renewal. **Examination:** General Appraiser Certification Examination. **Fees:** $125 application fee. $60 license fee. $25 Federal Fund Registry fee. $225 biennial renewal fee. **Governing Statute:** Real Estate Appraiser Law, Title 26, Chap. 69.

Credential Type: Temporary License. **Authorization:** Issued only for a particular assignment. **Requirements:** Must be licensed or certified in another state. **Fees:** $50 temporary license fee. **Governing Statute:** Real Estate Appraiser Law, Title 26, Chap. 69.

7300

Real Estate Broker
Vermont Real Estate Commission
Pavilion Office Bldg.
Montpelier, VT 05602
Phone: (802)828-3228

Credential Type: License. **Duration of License:** Two years. **Requirements:** 18 years of age. One year of experience, which includes six transactions under supervision of a licensed broker. An approved eight hour pre-licensing course. An approved course of instruction can replace the one year of experience (24 college-level courses). **Examination:** Yes. **Reciprocity:** No. **Fees:** $51.50 Exam. $25 License. $50 Renewal. **Governing Statute:** Title 26, VSA Sections 2211 and 2291-2296.

7301

Real Estate Salesperson (Agent)
Vermont Real Estate Commission
Pavilion Office Bldg.
Montpelier, VT 05602
Phone: (802)828-3228

Credential Type: License. **Duration of License:** Two years. **Requirements:** 18 years of age. **Examination:** Yes. **Reciprocity:** No. **Fees:** $51.50 Exam. $25 License. $50 Renewal. **Governing Statute:** Title 26, VSA Sections 2211 and 2291-2296.

Virginia

7302

Real Estate Appraiser
Virginia Real Estate Appraiser Board
Dept. of Commerce
3600 W. Broad St.
Richmond, VA 23230
Phone: (804)367-8552

Credential Type: Real Estate Appraiser. **Requirements:** 18 years of age. Must have 75 classroom hours of courses in subjects related to real estate appraisal. Must have a minimum of two calendar years and 2,000 hours of experience as an appraiser. **Examination:** Yes. **Fees:** $15 exam fee.

7303

Real Estate Appraiser
Real Estate Appraiser Board
Dept. of Commerce
3600 W. Broad St.
Richmond, VA 23230
Phone: (804)367-2039

Credential Type: Real Estate Appraiser License. **Duration of License:** Two years. **Authorization:** Authorizes holder to provide real estate appraisal services in federally-related transactions in connection with non-complex one-to-four-unit residential properties having a transaction value of less than $1 million; complex one-to-four-unit residential properties of less than $250,000; and commercial properties of less than $250,000. **Requirements:** Complete 75

Virginia 7304

Real Estate Appraiser, continued

classroom hours in approved courses. Complete at least 2000 hours of appraisal work over at least two calendar years (24 months). Renewal requires 20 classroom hours of continuing education. **Examination:** Licensing Examination. State Rules and Regulations Examination. **Fees:** $120 application fee. $165 renewal fee. $50 National Registry fee. $95 exam fee. **Governing Statute:** Code of Virginia, Chap. 20.1, Title 54.1. Real Estate Appraiser Board Regulations.

Credential Type: Residential Real Estate Appraiser Certificate. **Duration of License:** Two years. **Authorization:** Authorizes holder to provide real estate appraisal services in federally-related transactions in connection with one-to-four-unit residential properties without regard to value; and commercial properties of less than $250,000. **Requirements:** Complete 105 classroom hours in approved courses. Complete at least 2000 hours of appraisal work over at least two calendar years (24 months). Renewal requires 20 classroom hours of continuing education. **Examination:** Residential Appraiser Certification Examination. **Fees:** $120 application fee. $165 renewal fee. $50 National Registry fee. $95 exam fee. **Governing Statute:** Code of Virginia, Chap. 20.1, Title 54.1. Real Estate Appraiser Board Regulations.

Credential Type: General Real Estate Appraiser Certificate. **Duration of License:** Two years. **Authorization:** Authorizes holder to provide real estate appraisal services in federally-related transactions with all types of property without regard to value. **Requirements:** Complete 165 classroom hours in approved courses. Complete at least 2000 hours of appraisal work over at least two calendar years (24 months), 1000 hours of which must have been in non-residential real property appraisal work. Renewal requires 20 classroom hours of continuing education. **Examination:** General Appraiser Certification Examination. **Exemptions:** Waiver of examination may be granted to out-of-state licensed real estate appraisers. **Fees:** $120 application fee. $165 renewal fee. $50 National Registry fee. $95 exam fee. **Governing Statute:** Code of Virginia, Chap. 20.1, Title 54.1. Real Estate Appraiser Board Regulations.

Credential Type: Temporary Permit. **Authorization:** Issued only for a particular assignment. **Requirements:** Must be licensed or certified in another state. **Fees:** $120 application fee. **Governing Statute:** Code of Virginia, Chap. 20.1, Title 54.1. Real Estate Appraiser Board Regulations.

7304

Real Estate Broker
Virginia Real Estate Board
Dept. of Commerce
3600 W. Broad St.
Richmond, VA 23230
Phone: (804)367-8552

Credential Type: Real Estate Broker License. **Duration of License:** Two years. **Requirements:** Must have been employed as a real estate sales person for 36 of 48 months prior to making exam application. Must have the specific broker-related courses. **Examination:** Yes. **Fees:** $50 license fee. $50 renewal fee. $15 exam fee.

7305

Real Estate Salesperson
Virginia Real Estate Board
Dept. of Commerce
3600 W. Broad St.
Richmond, VA 23230
Phone: (804)367-8552

Credential Type: Real Estate Salesperson License. **Duration of License:** Two years. **Requirements:** Must have completed three semester hours in Principles of Real Estate. **Examination:** Yes. **Fees:** $30 license fee. $30 renewal fee. $15 exam fee.

Washington

7306

Campground Lot Salesperson
Dept. of Licensing
PO Box 9015
Olympia, WA 98504
Phone: (206)753-6974

Credential Type: Campground Lot Sales License. **Requirements:** Contact licensing body for application information.

7307

Cemetery Lot Salesperson
Dept. of Licensing
PO Box 9015
Olympia, WA 98504
Phone: (206)753-6974

Credential Type: Cemetery Lot Sales License. **Requirements:** Contact licensing body for application information.

7308

Escrow Agent
Dept. of Licensing
Professional Licensing Services
Real Estate
2424 Bristol Court SW
Olympia, WA 98504
Phone: (206)753-6974

Credential Type: Escrow Agent License. **Duration of License:** One year. **Requirements:** Maintain office in Washington state. Submit to background investigation. Must post $200,000 fidelity bond. Must submit to trust account and record-keeping audits. **Fees:** $345 initial license fee. $345 renewal fee. $25 duplicate license and transfer fee.

7309

Land Development Representative
Dept.of Licensing
Professional Licensing Services - Real Estate
2424 Bristol Ct. SW
Olympia, WA 98504
Phone: (206)853-2250

Credential Type: License. **Duration of License:** One year. **Authorization:** Allows the holder to disseminate information, contact purchasers, and transport purchasers to land developments for a real estate broker or land developer. **Requirements:** Be at least 18 years of age. Resident of Washington. Must work under the supervision of a licensed real estate broker. **Fees:** $25 license fee.

7310

Real Estate Appraiser
Dept. of Licensing
Appraiser Sect.
PO Box 9021
Olympia, WA 98507-9021
Phone: (206)753-1062

Credential Type: Residential Real Estate Appraiser Certificate/75 Classification. **Duration of License:** Two years. **Authorization:** Authorizes holder to provide real estate appraisal services in federally-related transactions in connection with non-complex one-to-four-unit residential properties having a transaction value of less than $1 million; complex one-to-four-unit residential properties of less than $250,000; and commercial properties of less than $250,000. **Requirements:** Complete 75 classroom hours in approved courses. Complete at least 3000 hours of appraisal work over at least two calendar years (24 months) within the five years immediately preceding filing of application. Renewal requires 20 classroom hours of continuing education. **Examination:** Residential Appraiser Certification Examination. **Fees:** $175 application fee. $75 exam fee. $100 original certification fee. $275 certification renewal fee. **Governing Statute:** 18.140 RCW, Certified Real Estate Appraiser Act. Chap. 308125 WAC.

Credential Type: Residential Real Estate Appraiser Certificate/105 Classification. **Duration of License:** Two years. **Authorization:** Authorizes holder to provide real estate appraisal services in federally-related transactions in connection with one-to-four-unit residential properties without regard to value; and commercial properties of less than $250,000. **Requirements:** Complete 105 classroom hours in approved courses. Complete at least 3000 hours of appraisal work over at least two calendar years (24 months) within the five years immediately preceding filing of application. Renewal requires 20 classroom hours of continuing education. **Examination:** Residential Appraiser Certification Examination. **Fees:** $175 application fee. $75 exam fee. $100 original certification fee. $275 certification renewal fee. **Governing Statute:** 18.140 RCW, Certified Real Estate Appraiser Act. Chap. 308125 WAC.

Credential Type: General Real Estate Appraiser Certificate. **Duration of License:** Two years. **Authorization:** Authorizes holder to provide real estate appraisal services in federally-related transactions with all types of property without regard to value. **Requirements:** Complete 165 classroom hours in approved courses. Complete at least 3000 hours of appraisal work, 1500 hours of which must have been in non-residential real property appraisal work, over at least two calendar years (24 months) within the five years immediately preceding filing of application. Renewal requires 20 classroom hours of continuing education. **Examination:** General Appraiser Certification Examination. **Fees:** $175 application fee. $75 exam fee. $100 original certification fee. $275 certification renewal fee. **Governing Statute:** 18.140 RCW, Certified Real Estate Appraiser Act. Chap. 308125 WAC.

Credential Type: Temporary Permit. **Duration of License:** 90 days. **Requirements:** Must be licensed or certified in another state. **Fees:** $150 temporary permit fee. **Governing Statute:** 18.140 RCW, Certified Real Estate Appraiser Act. Chap. 308125 WAC.

7311

Real Estate Broker
Dept. of Licensing
PO Box 9015
Olympia, WA 98504
Phone: (206)753-6974

Credential Type: Real Estate Broker License. **Duration of License:** Two years. **Requirements:** Complete 120 classroom hours of real estate education within the five years preceding application. Must have two years of real estate sales experience during the past five years. Renewal requires 30 hours of continuing education. **Examination:** ASI/Agency Examination. **Reciprocity:** Yes. **Fees:** $85 exam fee. $160 original license fee. $160 renewal fee.

7312

Real Estate Sales Agent
Dept. of Licensing
PO Box 9015
Olympia, WA 98504
Phone: (206)753-6974

Credential Type: Real Estate Agent License. **Duration of License:** Two years. **Requirements:** Complete 30 classroom hours of real estate education within the five years preceding application. Renewal requires 30 hours of continuing education. **Examination:** ASI/Agency Examination. **Reciprocity:** Yes. **Fees:** $85 exam fee. $100 original license fee. $100 renewal fee.

West Virginia

7313

Real Estate Appraiser
Real Estate Appraiser Licensing & Certification Board
814 Virginia St., E., Ste. 212
Charleston, WV 25301-2826
Phone: (304)558-3919
Fax: (304)558-3983

Credential Type: Real Estate Appraiser License. **Duration of License:** One year. **Authorization:** Authorizes holder to provide real estate appraisal services in federally-related transactions in connection with non-complex one-to-four-unit residential properties having a transaction value of less than $1 million; complex one-to-four-unit residential properties of less than $250,000; and commercial properties of less than $250,000. **Requirements:** Complete 75 classroom hours in approved courses. Complete at least 2000 hours of appraisal work over at least two calendar years (24 months). **Examination:** Licensing Examination. **Fees:** $100 application and exam fee. $325 annual license fee.

Credential Type: Residential Real Estate Appraiser Certificate. **Duration of License:** One year. **Authorization:** Authorizes holder to provide real estate appraisal services in federally-related transactions in connection with one-to-four-unit residential properties without regard to value; and commercial properties of less than $250,000. **Requirements:** Complete 105 classroom hours in approved courses. Complete at least 2000 hours of appraisal work over at least two calendar years (24 months). **Examination:** Residential Appraiser Certification Examination. **Fees:** $100 application and exam fee. $325 annual residential certification fee.

Credential Type: General Real Estate Appraiser Certificate. **Duration of License:** One year. **Authorization:** Authorizes holder to provide real estate appraisal services in federally-related transactions with all types of property without regard to value. **Requirements:** Complete 165 classroom hours in approved courses. Complete at least 2000 hours of appraisal work over at least two calendar years (24 months), 1000 hours of which must have been in non-residential real property appraisal work. **Examination:** General Appraiser Certification Examination. **Fees:** $100 application and exam fee. $525 annual general certification fee.

7314

Real Estate Broker
Real Estate Commission
1033 Quarrier St., Ste. 400
Charleston, WV 25301
Phone: (304)348-3555

Credential Type: License. **Duration of License:** One year. **Requirements:** U.S. citizen. 18 years old. High school education and 180 clock hours in approved courses. Two years as licensed real estate salesman. **Examination:** Yes. **Fees:** $50 Examination. $50 License. $50 Renewal.

7315

Real Estate Salesperson
Real Estate Commission
1033 Quarrier St., Ste. 400
Charleston, WV 25301
Phone: (304)348-3555

Credential Type: License. **Duration of License:** One year. **Requirements:** 18 years old. High school education and 90 hours in approved courses. Never convicted of a felony. **Examination:** Yes. **Fees:** $25 Examination. $25 License. $25 Renewal.

Wisconsin

7316

Real Estate Appraiser
Regulations and Licensing Dept.
Real Estate Appraisers Board
PO Box 8935
Madison, WI 53708-8935
Phone: (608)266-8609

Credential Type: Certified General Appraiser. **Requirements:** 2,000 hours of education, including 15 hours of Standards of Practice. 2,000 hours of experience in a minimum of two years. **Examination:** AQB-approved general certification exam. **Reciprocity:** Yes.

Credential Type: Certified Residential Appraiser. **Requirements:** 120 hours of education, including 15 hours of Standards of Practice. 2,000 hours of experience in a minimum of two years. **Examination:** AQB-approved residential exam. **Reciprocity:** Yes.

7317

Real Estate Broker
Regulations and Licensing Dept.
Real Estate Board
PO Box 8935
Madison, WI 53708-8935
Phone: (608)266-8609

Credential Type: License. **Requirements:** Must have passed the real estate salesperson exam. 36 hours of real estate courses or 20 semester credits of real estate courses at an institution of higher learning. Members of the Wisconsin Bar also qualify. 18 years of age. **Examination:** Written. **Reciprocity:** Some licenses may be accepted by the board.

7318

Real Estate Salesperson
Regulations and Licensing Dept.
Real Estate Board
PO Box 8935
Madison, WI 53708-8935
Phone: (608)266-8609

Credential Type: License. **Requirements:** 72 hours of real estate courses in real property law and principles of real estate, or 10 semester credits of real estate courses at an institution of higher learning. 18 years of age. **Examination:** Written. **Reciprocity:** Licensees from other states only need to take a portion of the written exam.

7319

Real Estate Timeshare Salesperson
Regulations and Licensing Dept.
Real Estate Board
PO Box 8935
Madison, WI 53708-8935
Phone: (608)266-8609

Credential Type: License. **Requirements:** Contact licensing body for application information.

Wyoming

7320

Real Estate Appraiser
Certified Real Estate Appraiser Board
Barrett Bldg., 2nd Fl.
Cheyenne, WY 82002
Phone: (307)777-7142

Credential Type: Residential Real Estate Appraiser Certificate. **Authorization:** Authorizes holder to provide real estate appraisal services in federally-related transactions in connection with one-to-four-unit residential properties without regard to value; and commercial properties of less than $250,000. **Requirements:** Complete 105 classroom hours in approved courses. Complete at least 2000 hours of appraisal work over at least two calendar years (24 months) within the five years preceding the filing of application. Minimum of 120 supportable and documented residential appraisal reports. **Examination:** Residential Appraiser Certification Examination.

Credential Type: General Real Estate Appraiser Certificate. **Authorization:** Authorizes holder to provide real estate appraisal services in federally-related transactions with all types of property without regard to value. **Requirements:** Complete 165 classroom hours in approved courses. Complete at least 2000 hours of appraisal work over at least two calendar years (24 months) within the five years preceding the filing of application. Minimum of 30 non-residential appraisal reports. **Examination:** General Appraiser Certification Examination.

Credential Type: Trainee Permit. **Requirements:** Complete 30 hours in approved courses.

7321

Real Estate Broker
Real Estate Commission
2301 Central Ave., 2nd Fl.
Cheyenne, WY 82002
Phone: (307)777-7141

Credential Type: Real Estate Broker License. **Duration of License:** Three years. **Requirements:** Complete 36 classroom hours of real estate education. Must have two years of real estate sales experience. Renewal requires 45 hours of continuing education. **Examination:** ASI Examination. **Reciprocity:** Yes. **Fees:** $40 exam fee. $50 original license fee. $150 renewal fee.

7322

Real Estate Sales Agent
Real Estate Commission
2301 Central Ave., 2nd Fl.
Cheyenne, WY 82002
Phone: (307)777-7141

Credential Type: Real Estate Agent License. **Duration of License:** Three years. **Requirements:** Complete 30 classroom hours of real estate education. Renewal requires 45 hours of continuing education. **Examination:** ASI Examination. **Reciprocity:** Yes. **Fees:** $40 exam fee. $50 original license fee. $150 renewal fee.

7323

Salesperson, Real Estate
Wyoming Real Estate Commission
Barrett Bldg.
2301 Central Ave.
Cheyenne, WY 82002
Phone: (307)777-7141

Credential Type: License. **Duration of License:** Three years. **Requirements:** Must be of legal age. Must have 30 hours of pre-licensing education from an approved school. Must be sponsored by a licensed broker. Must pass a written examination or meet total reciprocal agreement requirements. **Examination:** Yes. **Reciprocity:** Yes. **Fees:** $40 Examination. $100 Renewal.

Registered Nurses

One or more occupations in this chapter require a federal license. Additionally, the following states grant licenses as of the date of publication:

Alabama	District of	Iowa	Minnesota	New Mexico	Rhode Island	Washington
Alaska	Columbia	Kansas	Mississippi	New York	South Carolina	West Virginia
Arizona	Florida	Kentucky	Missouri	North Carolina	South Dakota	Wisconsin
Arkansas	Georgia	Louisiana	Montana	North Dakota	Tennessee	Wyoming
California	Hawaii	Maine	Nebraska	Ohio	Texas	
Colorado	Idaho	Maryland	Nevada	Oklahoma	Utah	
Connecticut	Illinois	Massachusetts	New Hampshire	Oregon	Vermont	
Delaware	Indiana	Michigan	New Jersey	Pennsylvania	Virginia	

Federal Licenses

7324

Ship's Nurse
U.S. Dept. of Transportation
U.S. Coast Guard
2100 Second St., SW
Washington, DC 20593
Phone: (202)267-0218

Credential Type: Nurse's License. **Duration of License:** Five years. **Authorization:** License may contain restrictions as to vessel type, tonnage, means of propulsion, horsepower, or water upon which service is authorized. **Requirements:** Must hold or apply for a merchant mariner's document. Must hold a valid license as a registered nurse issued by a state or territory of the United States, Puerto Rico, or the District of Columbia. **Governing Statute:** 46 CFR Chap. 1, Part 10.

Alabama

7325

Nurse Anesthetist
Alabama Board of Nursing
Montgomery, AL 36130-4601
Phone: (205)242-4060

Credential Type: License. **Requirements:** Current licensure as a registered nurse in Alabama. Graduate of a school of anesthesia. Must be currently certified as a registered nurse anesthetist by the Council on Certification/Recertification of Nurse Anesthetists.

7326

Nurse Midwife
Alabama Board of Nursing
State of Alabama
Montgomery, AL 36130-4601
Phone: (205)242-4060

Credential Type: License. **Duration of License:** Two years. **Requirements:** Must be a graduate from an approved nurse midwife program. Must be certified by the American College of Nurse-Midwifes. Must be registered as a registered professional nurse. Must submit the name of a duly licensed physician sponsor actively engaged in the practice of obstetrics and gynecology. **Examination:** Yes. **Fees:** Yes, periodically changing.

7327

Nurse Practitioner
Alabama Board of Nursing
State of Alabama
Montgomery, AL 36130-4601
Phone: (205)242-4060

Credential Type: License. **Requirements:** Must be currently registered as a nurse in Alabama. Must hold a B.S. degree in nursing prior to enrollment in a nurse practitioner program. Must be a graduate of a recognized post-basic program of study and clinical experience. Must hold a certification as a nurse practitioner in the appropriate area of practice.

7328

Registered Nurse
Alabama Board of Nursing
State of Alabama
Montgomery, AL 36130
Phone: (205)242-4060

Credential Type: License. **Requirements:** Must be a high school graduate. Must be a graduate of an approved registered nurse program. Must have completed either a two-year Associate degree program, two-or three-year diploma program, or a four-year degree program in nursing. **Examination:** National Council Licensure Examination for Registered Nurses (NCLEX-RN). **Fees:** Yes, periodically changing.

Alaska

7329

Advanced Nurse Practitioner
Dept. of Commerce and Economic
   Development
Div. of Occupational Licensing
Board of Nursing
PO Box 110806
Juneau, AK 99811-0806
Phone: (907)465-2544
Fax: (907)465-2974

Credential Type: Advanced Nurse Practitioner Authorization. **Duration of License:** Two years. **Authorization:** To perform acts of medical diagnosis and the prescription of medical, therapeutic, or corrective measures. **Requirements:** Possess a current Alaska registered nurse license. Complete a one-year formal academic program preparing a registered nurse for an expanded role in health care delivery. Program must include didactic and clinical expedrience leading to a certificate, diploma, or degree. Pass a national certifying exami-

Advanced Nurse Practitioner, continued

nation in a specialty area offered by a board approved national certifying body. Document current certification or recertification, if applicable, or fulfill board's requirements of 30 contact hours every two years. Submit a written plan which outlines procedures for consultation and referral with other health care professionals and includes a method for quality assurance. **Fees:** $30 application fee. $25 authorization fee. **Governing Statute:** Alaska Statutes 08.68. Professional Regulations 12 AAC 44.

Credential Type: Nonrenewable temporary permit. **Duration of License:** Four months or until test or certification results are announced. **Requirements:** Be currently certified as an advanced nurse practitioner in another state or jurisdiction; or has been accepted to take the next specialty board examination or is awaiting certification results. **Fees:** $30 application fee. $25 authorization fee. $20 temporary permit fee. **Governing Statute:** Alaska Statutes 08.68. Professional Regulations 12 AAC 44.

7330

Registered Nurse
Dept. of Commerce and Economic Development
Div. of Occupational Licensing
Board of Nursing
PO Box D
Juneau, AK 99811-0800
Phone: (907)465-2544
Fax: (907)465-2974

Credential Type: Registered Nurse License by Examination. **Duration of License:** Two years. **Requirements:** Completed a registered nursing education program accredited by the board, or one outside the state which meets the minimum requirements of the board for an accredited program, or one accredited by the National League for Nursing. Pass a written exam prescribed by the board.

Must meet continuing competency requirements for license renewal by completing two of the following three methods: 15 contact hours of board approved continuing education; 15 hours of participation in board approved professional activities; at least 320 hours of nursing practice during the past two years. **Examination:** National Council Licensing Examination. **Fees:** $30 application fee. $25 fee for National Council License Examination. $90 license fee. $90 license renewal fee. **Governing Statute:** Alaska Statutes 08.68. Professional Regulations 12 AAC 44.

Credential Type: Registered Nurse License by Endorsement. **Duration of License:** Two years. **Requirements:** Hold a current license to practice in another jurisdiction whose licensing requirements include completion of a recognized nursing education program and passing one of the following examinations: National Council Licensing Examination, State Board Test Pool (before 1982), an examination by another licensing jurisdiction before 1953.

Letter of reference from previous employer if employed within the past five years. If not employed wihtin the past five years, proof of meeting the continuing competency requirements of the board or complete a course of study approved by the board.

Graduates of foreign schools of nursing shall take the National Council Licensing Examination or have passed it elsewhere. Applicants licensed in Canada who passed the national Canadian examination may receive a license by endorsement. **Fees:** $30 application fee. $25 fee for National Council License Examination. $90 license fee. $90 license renewal fee. **Governing Statute:** Alaska Statutes 08.68. Professional Regulations 12 AAC 44.

Credential Type: Nonrenewable temporary permit. **Duration of License:** Four months or until test results are announced. **Requirements:** Must be awaiting the results of the National Council Licensing Examination or be scheduled to take the next NCLEX, or must be licensed to practice as a registered nurse in another state licensing jurisdiction. **Fees:** $30 application fee. $25 fee for National Council License Examination. $90 license fee. $20 temporary permit fee. **Governing Statute:** Alaska Statutes 08.68. Professional Regulations 12 AAC 44.

7331

Registered Nurse Anesthetist
Dept. of Commerce and Economic Development
Div. of Occupational Licensing
Board of Nursing
PO Box D
Juneau, AK 99811-0800
Phone: (907)465-2544
Fax: (907)465-2974

Credential Type: Registered Nurse Anesthetist Authorization. **Duration of License:** Two years. **Authorization:** To select and administer anesthetics and give anesthesia care. **Requirements:** Possess a current Alaska registered nurse license. Complete an educational program prescribed by a school of anesthesia accredited by a nationally recognized accrediting agency. Pass the National Certifying Examination and maintain current recertification. Submit written practice guidelines which outline procedures for collaboration and quality assurance. **Examination:** National Certifying Examination. **Fees:** $30 application fee. $25 authorization fee. **Governing Statute:** Alaska Statutes 08.68. Professional Regulations 12 AAC 44.

Credential Type: Nonrenewable temporary permit. **Duration of License:** Until test results are announced. **Authorization:** To practice only under the medical director or an anesthesia service. **Requirements:** Have been accepted to take the next scheduled examination or be awaiting the results of the examination. **Fees:** $30 application fee. $25 authorization fee. $20 temporary permit fee. **Governing Statute:** Alaska Statutes 08.68. Professional Regulations 12 AAC 44.

Arizona

7332

Registered Nurse
Arizona State Board of Nursing
2001 W. Camelback Rd., Ste. 350
Phoenix, AZ 85015
Phone: (602)255-5092
Fax: (602)255-5130

Credential Type: Registered Nurse License. **Requirements:** High school graduate or equivalent. Graduate from a state approved nursing program or New York Regents external degree program. Be proficient in English language as it relates to nursing. **Examination:** National Council Licensure Examination (NCLEX)-RN.

Arkansas

7333

Certified Registered Nurse Anesthetist
Arkansas State Board of Nursing
University Tower Bldg.
1123 S. University
Little Rock, AR 72204
Phone: (501)371-2751

Credential Type: License. **Duration of License:** Two years. **Requirements:** Completion, beyond General Nursing preparation, of a formal accredited education program. Current certification from the Council on Certification of Nurses Anesthetists. **Examination:** Yes. **Fees:** $25 License. $10 Renewal.

7334

Licensed Nurse Midwife
Arkansas State Board of Nursing
University Tower Bldg., Ste. 800
1123 S. University
Little Rock, AR 72204
Phone: (501)371-2751

Credential Type: License. **Duration of License:** Two years. **Requirements:** Possess an active license as a registered nurse. Show proof of certification by the ACNW. Possess an agreement with a consulting physician licensed in Arkansas who has obstetrical privileges in a hospital. Possess written protocols evaluated by criteria approved by the Board. **Examination:** Yes. **Fees:** $25 License. $10 Renewal.

7335

Registered Nurse
Arkansas State Board of Nursing
University Tower Bldg. Ste. 800
1123 S. University
Little Rock, AR 72204
Phone: (501)371-2751

Credential Type: License. **Duration of License:** Two years. **Requirements:** Good moral character. 12th grade education or equivalent. Satisfactory completion of an approved professional nursing education program. **Examination:** Yes. **Fees:** $41.50 plus $40 National for written, oral and practical examinations.

7336

Registered Nurse Practitioner
Arkansas State Board of Nursing
University Tower Bldg. Ste. 800
1123 S. University
Little Rock, AR 72204
Phone: (501)371-2751

Credential Type: License. **Duration of License:** Two years. **Requirements:** Possess the general requirements of a Registered nurse. Possess educational qualifications beyond that required to be licensed as a Registered Nurse. **Examination:** Yes. **Fees:** $25 License. $10 Renewal.

California

7337

Nurse Anesthetist
Board of Registered Nursing
400 R St., Ste. 4030
Sacramento, CA 95814
Phone: (916)322-3350

Alternate Information: PO Box 944210, Sacramento, CA 94244-2100

Credential Type: Nurse Anesthetist Certification. **Duration of License:** Two years. **Requirements:** Must be a licensed Registered Nurse in California. Must be eligible for certification by the Council on Certification of Nurse Anesthetists. **Examination:** Council on Certification of Nurse Anesthetists examination. **Fees:** $75 certification fee. $50 renewal fee.

7338

Nurse Midwife
Board of Registered Nursing
400 R St., Ste. 4030
Sacramento, CA 95814
Phone: (916)322-3350

Alternate Information: PO Box 944210, Sacramento, CA 94244-2100

Credential Type: Nurse Midwife Certification. **Duration of License:** Two years. **Requirements:** Must be a licensed Registered Nurse in California. Meet one of the following sets of requirements: (1) Complete a nurse-midwifery program that conforms to board standards (no degree required). (2) If applicant has graduated from a nurse-midwifery program not meeting board standards, then applicant must show evidence that deficiencies in the program have been corrected or take specific courses that meet board standards. (3) Be certified by a national or state organization whose standards are satisfactory to the board. (4) Successfully challenge the curriculum of a nurse-midwifery educational program that meets board standards, and provide verification of clinical competency in management of normal labor and delivery by a certified nurse-midwife and by a physician. (5) Have advanced training and practice in Maternal and Child Care that partially fulfills the requirements for certification, and remediate the deficiencies in a nurse-midwifery program that meets board standards. (6) Have advanced training and practice in Maternal and Child Care that partially fulfills the requirements for certification; pass a nurse-midwifery examination satisfactory to the board; and provide verification of clinical competency in management of normal labor and delivery by a certified nurse-midwife and by a physician. **Examination:** Nurse-midwifery examination (if required). **Reciprocity:** Yes, if applicant meets certification requirements. **Fees:** $75 certification fee. $100 exam fee. $50 renewal fee.

7339

Nurse Practitioner
Board of Registered Nursing
400 R St., Ste. 4030
Sacramento, CA 95814
Phone: (916)322-3350

Alternate Information: PO Box 944210, Sacramento, CA 94244-2100

Credential Type: Nurse Practitioner Certification. **Duration of License:** Two years. **Requirements:** Must be a licensed Registered Nurse in California. Meet one of the following sets of requirements: (1) Complete a Nurse Practitioner Program that conforms to board standards (no degree required). (2) Be certified by a national or state organization whose standards are equivalent to California's. (3) If applicant has not completed a course that meets board standards, then applicant must provide verification of clinical experience and of clinical competency as well as documentation of courses completed. **Examination:** No exam. **Reciprocity:** Yes, if applicant meets certification requirements. **Fees:** $75 certification fee.

7340

Psychiatric-Mental Health Nurse
Board of Registered Nursing
400 R St., Ste. 4030
Sacramento, CA 95814
Phone: (916)322-3350

Alternate Information: PO Box 944210, Sacramento, CA 94244-2100

Credential Type: Psychiatric-Mental Health Nurse Certification. **Duration of License:** Two years. **Requirements:** Must be a licensed Registered Nurse in California. Have a Master's degree in Psychiatric-Mental Health Nursing. Complete two years of supervised experience in providing psychiatric-mental health counseling services after receiving Master's degree. **Reciprocity:** Yes, if applicant meets certification requirements. **Fees:** No fees.

California

7341

Registered Nurse
Board of Registered Nursing
400 R St., Ste. 4030
Sacramento, CA 95814
Phone: (916)322-3350

Alternate Information: PO Box 944210, Sacramento, CA 94244-2100

Credential Type: Registered Nurse License. **Duration of License:** Two years. **Requirements:** Complete a RN program that conforms to board requirements (no degree required). **Examination:** National Council Licensure Examination for Registered Nurses NCLEX-RN. **Reciprocity:** Yes, if applicant meets California requirements. **Fees:** $102 application fee (includes fingerprint fee). $40 exam fee. $80 renewal fee.

Credential Type: Interim Permit. **Duration of License:** Until next examination. **Authorization:** Allows applicants to work under direct supervision until their first examination in the United States. **Requirements:** Must have completed nursing program and be scheduled for the examination. **Fees:** $30 interim permit fee.

Credential Type: Temporary License. **Duration of License:** Six months. **Authorization:** Allows applicant for license by endorsement to practice pending issuance of a permanent license. **Requirements:** Must submit application for license by endorsement. **Fees:** $30 temporary license fee.

7342

School Health Services Associate
Commission on Teacher Credentialing
PO Box 944270
Sacramento, CA 94244-7000
Phone: (916)445-7254

Credential Type: Health Services Credential. **Authorization:** Authorizes the holder to perform, in preschool, grades 1-12, and adult classes, the health service designated on the credential, (Services such as audiometrist, occupational therapist, or physical therapist are not deemed health services.) Authorized services are school nurse, physician, dentist, dental hygienist, and optometrist. **Requirements:** Valid license, certificate, or registration appropriate to the health service to be designated, issued by the California agency and authorized by law to license, certify, or register persons to practice that health service in California. Additional requirements as may be prescribed by the Commission. For school nurses, a bachelor's degree, an approved program of preparation in school nursing, and two years of successful experience as a school nurse is also required. A preliminary School Nurse Services Credential (valid for five years) requires only a bachelor's degree and a valid California registered nurse license. **Fees:** $60 application fee. $30 test score recording and evaluation fee, except for CBEST.

Colorado

7343

Registered Nurse
Colorado Board of Nursing
1560 Broadway, Ste. 670
Denver, CO 80202
Phone: (303)894-2430
Fax: (303)894-2821

Credential Type: Registered Nurse License. **Requirements:** Graduate from a state approved nursing program or New York Regents external degree program or any equivalent nursing program. Be proficient in English language as it relates to nursing. **Examination:** National Council Licensure Examination (NCLEX)-RN.

7344

School Special Service Associate
Teacher Certification
State Dept. of Education
201 E. Colifax
Denver, CO 80203
Phone: (303)866-6628

Credential Type: Special Service Certificate—Type E. **Duration of License:** Five years. **Authorization:** Authorizes service in specialized areas including Audiology, Therapy, Nursing, Psychology, Social Work, and Speech Corrections. **Requirements:** Bachelor's degree. Must complete a program in one of the following Special Service endorsement areas: Audiologist, Occupational Therapist, Peripatology, Physical Therapist, School Nurse, School Psychologist, School Social Worker, or Speech Correctionist/Language Specialist. Passage of the spelling, language, and mathematics sections of Level 19 of the California Achievement Test and oral English competence which is met by having a B—or better in a public speaking course taken from a regionally accredited college or passing an oral English panel assessment. Official, original transcripts from all applicable institutions. **Examination:** California Achievement Test Level 19 (spelling, language, and mathematics sections) **Fees:** $45 initial certification application fee. $40 fingerprint card processing fee.

Connecticut

7345

Nurse Midwife
Div. of Medical Quality Assurance
Health Systems Regulation Bureau
Health Services Dept.
150 Washington St.
Hartford, CT 06106
Phone: (203)566-3207

Credential Type: License. **Requirements:** Contact licensing body for application information.

7346

Nurse (Racetrack)
Connecticut Div. of Special Revenue
Russell Rd.
PO Box 11424
Newington, CT 06111-0424
Phone: (203)566-2756

Credential Type: License Registration. **Requirements:** Submit application and fingerprint card. Pay fee. **Fees:** $5 registration fee.

7347

Registered Nurse
Connecticut Board of Examiners for Nursing
150 Washington St.
Hartford, CT 06106
Phone: (203)566-1041
Fax: (203)566-8401

Credential Type: Registered Nurse License. **Requirements:** High school graduate or equivalent. Graduate from a state approved nursing program or New York Regents external degree program. Experience may be accepted in lieu of education. Good physical and mental health. Be proficient in English language as it relates to nursing.

7348

Registered Nurse (Racetrack)
Connecticut Div. of Special Revenue
Russell Rd.
PO Box 11424
Newington, CT 06111-0424
Phone: (203)566-2756

Credential Type: License Registration. **Requirements:** Submit application and fingerprint card. Pay fee. **Fees:** $5 registration fee.

Delaware

7349

Registered Nurse
Board of Nursing
Dept. of Administrative Services
Div. of Professional Regulation
PO Box 1401
Dover, DE 19903
Phone: (302)739-4522

Credential Type: License by examination. **Duration of License:** Two years. **Requirements:** Be a high school graduate or equivalent. Must be competent in English related to nursing. Graduate of a board-approved nursing education program that is authorized to prepare persons for licensure as a registered nurse. **Examination:** NCLEX-RN. **Exemptions:** See license by endorsement. **Reciprocity:** Holders of an out-of-state or foreign license may apply for license by endorsement. **Fees:** $30 license fee. **Governing Statute:** Delaware Code, Title 24, Chapter 19.

Credential Type: License by endorsement. **Duration of License:** Two years. **Requirements:** Hold a license from another state, territory, or foreign country that has equivalent requirements. Must have been actively employed in professional nursing for the past five years, or complete a professional nursing refresher program with an approved agency within the past year. **Examination:** No exam required for license by endorsement. **Fees:** $30 license fee. **Governing Statute:** Delaware Code, Title 24, Chapter 19.

District of Columbia

7350

Nurse Midwife
License and Certification Div.
Occupational and Professional Licensure Administration
Consumer and Regulatory Affairs Dept.
PO Box 37200
Washington, DC 20013-7200
Phone: (202)727-7823
Phone: (202)727-7480

Alternate Information: 614 H St. NW, Washington, DC 20001

Credential Type: Certification. **Duration of License:** Two years. **Authorization:** May practice only in collaboration with an obstetrician-gynecologist, unless directly employed or practicing in a hospital health maintenance organization, ambulatory surgical facility, or other similar facility or agency licensed in the District of Columbia that requires at least a general collaboration. **Requirements:** Complete a nurse-midwifery educational program approved by the American College of Nurse-Midwives (ACNM). Must have assisted at least 20 women during their pregnancies, and have observed an additional 20 women during their intrapartum periods. Must either be certified or awaiting certification as a nurse-midwife by the ACNM. **Examination:** ACNM examination. **Fees:** $41 application fee. $28 certification fee. $28 renewal fee. **Governing Statute:** Municipal Regulations, Title 17, Chap. 58.

7351

Registered Nurse
DC Board of Nursing
614 H. St., NW
Washington, DC 20001
Phone: (202)727-7468
Fax: (202)727-8030

Credential Type: Registered Nurse License. **Requirements:** High school graduate or equivalent. Graduate of a state approved nursing program or equivalent. Meet age requirement. Be proficient in English language as it relates to nursing. Must report criminal convictions. Board hearing may be required.

Florida

7352

Nurse (Racetrack)
Florida Dept. of Business
Div. of Pari-Mutuel Wagering
Licensing Section
725 S. Bronough St.
Tallahassee, FL 32399-1037
Phone: (904)488-9161

Credential Type: License Registration Code 1019. **Requirements:** Must have a Department of Professional Regulation (DPR) license. Submit application and fingerprint card. Pay fee. **Fees:** $40 registration fee.

7353

Registered Nurse
Florida Board of Nursing
111 Coastline Dr. E., Ste. 516
Jacksonville, FL 32202
Phone: (904)359-6331
Fax: (904)359-6323

Credential Type: Registered Nurse License. **Requirements:** High school graduate or equivalent. Graduate from a state-approved nursing program or New York Regents external degree program. Be proficient in English language as it relates to nursing. **Examination:** NCLEX-RN.

Georgia

7354

Registered Nurse
Georgia Board of Nursing
166 Pryor St. SW
Atlanta, GA 30303
Phone: (404)656-3921
Fax: (404)651-9532

Credential Type: Registered Nurse License. **Requirements:** Graduate from a state approved nursing program or New York Regents external degree program. Be proficient in English language as it relates to nursing. **Examination:** National Council Licensure Examination (NCLEX)-RN.

Hawaii

7355

Nurse, Registered
Hawaii Board of Nursing
1010 Richards St.
PO Box 3469
Honolulu, HI 96801
Phone: (808)548-3086

Credential Type: License. **Duration of License:** Six months. **Requirements:** Graduation from a state-accredited nursing program in the U.S. or U.S. jurisdiction. Pass the National Council Licensure Examination (NCLEX); or pass the State Board Test Pool Exam (SBTPE); or pass another state's exam prior to inception of the SBTPE in this state. **Reciprocity:** Yes, provided applicant has been accepted for employment in Hawaii. **Fees:** $20 application fee. $15 license fee. $15—$30 Compliance Resolution Fund fee. $10 renewal fee.

Credential Type: Temporary Permit. **Requirements:** Issued to endorsement applicants who have met Hawaii's educational requirements, hold a current license in another state, have been accepted for employment in Hawaii, and have passed the SBTPE or NCLEX in another state.

Exam applicants may also be granted a temporary permit.

Idaho

7356

Certified Registered Nurse Anesthetist
Nursing Board
280 N. 8th St., Ste. 210
Boise, ID 83720-7000
Phone: (208)334-3110

Credential Type: Nurse Anesthetist Certificate. **Duration of License:** Two years. **Requirements:** Must hold a current license in good standing as a professional (registered) nurse in Idaho. Must be a graduate of a nationally accredited nurse anesthetist program. Must pass a qualifying examination administered by a nationally organized group and have current initial certification or current recertification from the national group. Must have been employed in nursing within five years of application. **Examination:** American Association of Nurse Anesthetists Examination. **Fees:** $25 initial registration fee. $15 renewal fee. **Governing Statute:** Idaho Code, Title 54, Chap. 14.

7357

Nurse Practitioner
Nursing Board
280 N. 8th St., Ste. 210
Boise, ID 83720-7000
Phone: (208)334-3110

Credential Type: Nurse Practitioner Certificate. **Duration of License:** Two years. **Requirements:** Must hold a current license in good standing as a professional (registered) nurse in Idaho. Must have a baccalaureate degree in nursing from an approved nursing education program. Must complete a nurse practitioner program accredited by the National League for Nursing or the American Nurses Association or its equivalent. Must have proficiency in the functions to be undertaken, as evidenced by a statement from a physician, nurse practitioner preceptor, or other supervisory person or peer from last place of employment. **Examination:** Certification examination administered by the American Nurses Credentialing Center (ANCC), National Certification Board of Pediatric Nurse Practitioners and Nurses (NCBPNP/N), National Certification Corporation for the Obstetric, Gynecologic, and Neonatal Nursing Specialties (NCC), or the American College of Nurse Midwives Council. **Fees:** $75 application fee. $25 renewal fee. **Governing Statute:** Idaho Code, Title 54, Chap. 14.

7358

Registered Nurse
Nursing Board
280 N. 8th St., Ste. 210
Boise, ID 83720-7000
Phone: (208)334-3110

Credential Type: Professional Nurse License. **Duration of License:** Two years. **Requirements:** Must be a graduate of an approved professional nursing education program. **Examination:** National Council Licensure Examination for Registered Nurses (NCLEX-RN). The State Board Test Pool Examination is also accepted but is no longer administered. **Reciprocity:** Applicants are eligible for interstate endorsement if they have graduated from a nationally accredited education program, have passed a board-approved licensure examination, and have a license in good standing in another state. **Fees:** $75 license fee by examination or endorsement. $45 renewal fee. $40 exam fee. $15 temporary license fee (in addition to license fee). **Governing Statute:** Idaho Code, Title 54, Chap. 14.

7359

School Nurse
Certification Analyst
State Dept. of Education
L. B. Jordan Office Bldg.
Boise, ID 83720
Phone: (208)334-3475

Credential Type: School Nurse Endorsement. **Duration of License:** Five years. **Requirements:** Bachelor's degree in nursing from an accredited institution or work completed in an accredited institution. Two years of clinical experience in either a school or public health setting. Hold valid registered nurse license.

Illinois

7360

Registered Nurse
Illinois Dept. of Professional Regulation
159 N. Dearborn, 6th Fl.
Chicago, IL 60601
Phone: (312)814-4619
Fax: (312)814-1664

Credential Type: Registered Nurse License. **Requirements:** Graduate from state approved nursing program. Good moral character. Good physical and mental health. Be proficient in English as it relates to nursing. **Examination:** National Council Licensure Examination (NCLEX)-RN.

Indiana

7361

Nurse Midwife
Nursing Board
Health Professions Bureau
402 W. Washington St., Rm. 041
Indianapolis, IN 46204
Phone: (317)232-2960

Credential Type: Certificate to practice. **Duration of License:** Two years. **Requirements:** Graduate of a program in nurse-midwifery approved by the American College of Nurse-Midwives and National Certification by the American College of Nurse-Midwives. Must hold a current license as a Registered Nurse in any state. **Fees:** $100 fee. **Governing Statute:** Indiana Code 25-22.5-5-5.

7362

Registered Nurse
Indiana State Board of Nursing
Health Professional Bureau
402 W. Washington St., Rm. 041
Indianapolis, IN 46204
Phone: (317)232-2960
Fax: (317)233-4236

Credential Type: Registered Nurse License. **Requirements:** High school graduate or equivalent. Graduate from a state approved nursing program or New York Regents external degree program or any other equivalent nursing program. Good physical and mental health. Be proficient in English language as it relates to nursing. No felonies or criminal record.

Iowa

7363

Advanced Registered Nurse Practitioner
Iowa Board of Nursing
State Capitol Complex
1223 East Court
Des Moines, IA 50319
Phone: (515)281-3256

Alternate Information: Executive Hills East, Des Moines, IA 50319

Credential Type: Advanced Registered Nurse Practitioner. **Duration of License:** Three years. **Requirements:** Registered nurse license. Completion of a 12-18 month certification program, or a master's degree

Registered Nurses

program. **Examination:** Written exam. **Reciprocity:** Yes. **Fees:** $12 license fee. $36 renewal fee.

7364

Registered Nurse
Iowa Board of Nursing
State Capitol Complex
1223 East Court
Des Moines, IA 50319
Phone: (515)281-3256

Alternate Information: Executive Hills East, Des Moines, IA 50319

Credential Type: Registered Nurse License. **Duration of License:** Three years. **Requirements:** Graduation from an approved school of nursing. **Examination:** National exam. **Fees:** $45 exam fee. $60 endoresement fee. $48 renewal fee.

Kansas

7365

Registered Nurse
Kansas Board of Nursing
Landon State Office Bldg.
900 SW Jackson, Ste. 551-S
Topeka, KS 66612-1256
Phone: (913)296-4068
Fax: (913)296-6729

Credential Type: Registered Nurse License. **Requirements:** U.S. citizen. High school graduate or equivalent. Graduate of state approved nursing program. Good physical and mental health. Be proficient in English language as it relates to nursing. No felonies or criminal record. **Examination:** National Council Licensure Examination (NCLEX)-RN.

7366

School Nurse
Certification Specialist
Kansas State Dept. of Education
Kansas State Education Bldg.
120 E. 10th St.
Topeka, KS 66612-1103
Phone: (913)296-2288

Credential Type: School Nurse Endorsement. **Authorization:** Endorsement will allow work at the elementary or secondary level. **Requirements:** Licensed in Kansas as a registered professional nurse. Complete a state approved school nurse program and recommendation by a teacher education institution or one year of successful experience as a registered nurse or completion of a practicum in school nursing.

Kentucky

7367

Nurse Anesthetist
Kentucky Board of Nursing
312 Whittington Pky., Ste. 300
Louisville, KY 40222
Phone: (502)329-7000

Credential Type: License. **Duration of License:** Two years. **Requirements:** Completion of an approved registered nursing program. Completion of an organized post-basic program of study and clinical experience recognized by the regulatory agency. Must seek registration as an Advanced Registered Nurse Practitioner. 30 contact hours are required for renewal. **Examination:** Yes. **Fees:** $70 registration fee. $45 renewal fee.

7368

Nurse, Clinical Specialist
Kentucky Board of Nursing
312 Whittington Pky., Ste. 300
Louisville, KY 40222
Phone: (502)329-7000

Credential Type: License. **Duration of License:** Two years. **Requirements:** Successful completion of a Board-approved registered nursing program. Completion of an organized post-basic program of study and clinical experience at the graduate level. Must have a current, active RN license in Kentucky and be certified as a clinical nurse specialist. Continuing education required. **Examination:** Yes. **Fees:** $70 initial registration fee. $45 renewal fee.

7369

Nurse, Midwife
Kentucky Board of Nursing
312 Whittington Pky., Ste. 300
Louisville, KY 40222
Phone: (502)329-7000

Credential Type: License. **Duration of License:** Two years. **Requirements:** Successful completion of an approved program of registered nursing. Completion of an organized post-basic program of study and clinical experience recognized by the regulatory agency. Must have an active RN license and be certified as a nurse-midwife by the American College of Nurse-Midwives. Must seek registration as an advanced registered nurse practitioner. Continuing education required. **Examination:** Yes. **Fees:** $70 registration fee. $45 renewal fee.

7370

Nurse Practitioner
Kentucky Board of Nursing
312 Whittington Pky., Ste. 300
Louisville, KY 40222
Phone: (502)329-7000

Credential Type: License. **Duration of License:** Two years. **Requirements:** Successful completion of an approved program of registered nursing. Completion of an organized post-basic program of study and clinical experience recognized by the regulatory agency. Must have a current, active RN license in Kentucky and be certified as a nurse practitioner by the appropriate national nursing organization. Continuing education required. **Examination:** Yes. **Fees:** $70 registration fee. $45 renewal fee.

7371

Nurse, Registered
Kentucky Board of Nursing
312 Whittington Pky., Ste. 300
Louisville, KY 40222
Phone: (502)329-7000

Credential Type: License. **Duration of License:** Two years. **Requirements:** High school degree or equivalent. Successful completion of the basic curriculum in a state board-approved school of nursing that is at least two academic years in length. Continuing education required, including two hours of AIDS education. **Examination:** Yes. **Fees:** $70 application fee. $40 exam fee. $50 renewal fee.

Louisiana

7372

Nurse/Registered
Louisiana State Board of Nursing
907 Pere Marquette Bldg.
150 Barrone St.
New Orleans, LA 70112
Phone: (504)568-5464

Credential Type: License. **Duration of License:** One year. **Requirements:** Completion of the required educational program. **Examination:** Written. **Reciprocity:** Yes, if the applicant meets the requirements of the state. **Fees:** $70 exam fee. $25 license fee. $25 renewal fee. $50 fee for licensure by endorsement.

Louisiana

7373

Nurse (School)
Louisiana State Dept. of Education
Teacher Certification
PO Box 94064
Baton Rouge, LA 70804
Phone: (504)342-3490

Credential Type: Type C License. **Duration of License:** Three years. **Requirements:** Must hold a current license as a registered professional nurse in the state. A minimum of two years of experience as a registered nurse.

Credential Type: Type B License. **Duration of License:** Five years. **Requirements:** Must hold a current license as a registered professional nurse in the state. A minimum of three years of experience as a Type C school nurse. Completion of at least six semester hours of related courses at an accredited college or university.

Credential Type: Type A License. **Duration of License:** Permanent. **Requirements:** Must hold a current license as a registered professional nurse in the state. Baccalaureate degree in nursing or a health-related field from an accredited college or university. A minimum of five years of experience as a Type B school nurse.

Maine

7374

Registered Nurse
Maine State Board of Nursing
State House Station No. 158
Augusta, ME 04333-0158
Phone: (207)624-5275

Credential Type: Registered Nurse License. **Requirements:** High school graduate or equivalent. Graduate from state approved nursing program. Be proficient in English language as it relates to nursing.

Maryland

7375

Registered Nurse
Maryland Board of Nursing
4201 Patterson Ave.
Baltimore, MD 21215-2299
Phone: (410)764-4747
Fax: (410)764-5987

Credential Type: Registered Nurse License. **Duration of License:** One year. **Requirements:** High school graduate or equivalent. Graduate from a state approved registered nursing program or New York Regents external degree program or any other equivalent nursing program. Be proficient in English language as it relates to nursing. No felonies or criminal record. **Examination:** NCLEX-RN. **Fees:** $50 exam fee. $75 endorsement fee. $25 renewal fee.

Massachusetts

7376

Nurse Anesthetist
Board of Registration in Nursing
Leverett Saltonstall Bldg.
100 Cambridge St., Rm. 1519
Boston, MA 02202
Phone: (617)727-9961
Phone: (617)727-9962
Fax: (617)727-7378

Credential Type: Expanded Role Authorization. **Duration of License:** Two years. **Requirements:** Must be a Registered Nurse in Massachusetts to receive authorization for this expanded role. Not a separate license. **Fees:** $60 authorization fee.

7377

Nurse Midwife
Board of Registration in Nursing
Leverett Saltonstall Bldg.
100 Cambridge St., Rm. 1519
Boston, MA 02202
Phone: (617)727-9961
Phone: (617)727-9962
Fax: (617)727-7378

Credential Type: Expanded Role Authorization. **Duration of License:** Two years. **Requirements:** Must be a Registered Nurse in Massachusetts to receive authorization for this expanded role. Not a separate license. **Fees:** $60 authorization fee.

7378

Nurse Practitioner
Board of Registration in Nursing
Leverett Saltonstall Bldg.
100 Cambridge St., Rm. 1519
Boston, MA 02202
Phone: (617)727-9961
Phone: (617)727-9962
Fax: (617)727-7378

Credential Type: Expanded Role Authorization. **Duration of License:** Two years. **Requirements:** Must be a Registered Nurse in Massachusetts to receive authorization for this expanded role. Not a separate license. **Fees:** $60 authorization fee.

7379

Psychiatric Nurse
Board of Registration in Nursing
Leverett Saltonstall Bldg.
100 Cambridge St., Rm. 1519
Boston, MA 02202
Phone: (617)727-9961
Phone: (617)727-9962
Fax: (617)727-7378

Credential Type: Expanded Role Authorization. **Duration of License:** Two years. **Requirements:** Must be a Registered Nurse in Massachusetts to receive authorization for this expanded role. Not a separate license. **Fees:** $60 authorization fee.

7380

Registered Nurse
Board of Registration in Nursing
Leverett Saltonstall Bldg.
100 Cambridge St., Rm. 1519
Boston, MA 02202
Phone: (617)727-9961
Phone: (617)727-9962
Fax: (617)727-7378

Credential Type: Registered Nurse License. **Duration of License:** Two years. **Requirements:** High school graduate or equivalent. Graduate from a state approved nursing program or New York Regents external degree program. Good moral character. Be proficient in English language as it relates to nursing. **Examination:** National Council Licensure Examination for Registered Nurses (NCLEX-RN). **Reciprocity:** Yes, if licensing requirements are the same as Massachusetts. Foreign graduates must have CGFNS certificate. **Fees:** $40 license fee. $87 exam fee. $40 renewal fee. $75 endorsement fee.

Michigan

7381

Nurse, School
Teacher
Administrator Preparation and
    Certification Services
Dept. of Education
PO Box 30008
Lansing, MI 48909
Phone: (517)373-3324

Credential Type: Professional School Nurse Certification. **Duration of License:** Permanent. **Requirements:** Maintain a valid Michigan registered nurse license. Three years of experience as a school nurse. Bachelor's degree in nursing or a related health field. **Reciprocity:** All out-of-state applicants are evaluated according to Michigan requirements. Out-of-state applicants should apply directly through their Michigan employing school district. **Fees:** No fees. **Governing Statute:** Nursing Act, Act 187 of 1972.

Credential Type: Interim School Nurse Certificate. **Duration of License:** Two years. **Requirements:** Maintain a valid Michigan registered nurse license. Be recommended by an employing school district. May be renewed for a two year period upon the request of an employing school district and upon completion of eight semester hours of course work since the issuance of the original interim certificate in a planned program at a teacher education or nursing education institution. **Fees:** No fees. **Governing Statute:** Nursing Act, Act 187 of 1972.

Credential Type: Standard School Nurse Certificate. **Duration of License:** Three years. **Requirements:** Maintain a valid Michigan registered nurse license. Be recommended by an employing school district. Two years of experience in a public health or school nursing practice. Completed 15 semester hours of credit in a nursing or related health education program after having received the interim school nurse certificate, unless the applicant has earned a bachelor's degree in nursing or a health related field.

May be renewed for two additional three year periods upon the recommendation of an employing school district. The first renewal also requires completion of a total of 24 semester hours of course work since the issuance of the interim school nurse certificate, and the second renewal requires 36 semester hours of course work. This course work is not required if the holder has a bachelor's degree in nursing or a related health field. **Fees:** No fees. **Governing Statute:** Nursing Act, Act 187 of 1972.

7382

Registered Nurse
Bureau of Occupational and
    Professional Regulation
Michigan Dept. of Commerce
Ottawa Towers N.
611 W. Ottawa
Lansing, MI 48933
Phone: (517)373-1600
Fax: (517)373-2179

Credential Type: Registered Nurse License. **Requirements:** Graduate from state approved nursing school or New York Regents external degree program. Good moral character. Be proficient in English language as it relates to nursing. Felony conviction requires Board investigation.

Minnesota

7383

Registered Nurse
Minnesota Board of Nursing
2700 University Ave. W, 108
St. Paul, MN 55114
Phone: (612)642-0567
Fax: (612)642-0574

Credential Type: Registered Nurse License. **Duration of License:** Two years. **Requirements:** Graduate from state approved nursing program. **Examination:** NCLEX-RN. **Reciprocity:** License by endorsement may be issued if applicant holds a valid license from another state and has passed the same examination. **Fees:** $75 exam fee. $55 endorsement fee. $35 renewal fee. **Governing Statute:** Minnesota Statutes, Sections 148.171-148.299. Minnesota Rules 6300-6399.

Mississippi

7384

Registered Nurse
Mississippi Board of Nursing
239 N. Lamar St., Ste. 401
Jackson, MS 39201-1311
Phone: (601)359-6170
Fax: (601)359-6185

Credential Type: Registered Nurse License. **Requirements:** Graduate from state approved nursing program or New York Regents external degree program. Be proficient in English language as it relates to nursing. **Examination:** National Council Licensure Examination (NCLEX)-RN.

Missouri

7385

Registered Nurse
Missouri State Board of Nursing
PO Box 656
Jefferson City, MO 65102
Phone: (314)751-0681
Fax: (314)751-4176

Credential Type: Registered Nurse License. **Requirements:** High school graduate or equivalent. Graduate from state approved nursing program or New York Regents external degree program. Meet age requirement. Good moral character. Be proficient in English language as it relates to nursing.

Montana

7386

Nurse Anesthetist
Montana State Board of Nursing
111 N. Jackson
Helena, MT 59620
Phone: (406)444-2071
Phone: (406)444-4279

Credential Type: License. **Duration of License:** One year. **Requirements:** Complete one academic year beyond the professional nursing program, with four months of didactic and five months perceptorship. Must be a Registered Professional Nurse. Must maintain national certification for renewal. **Examination:** National certifying examination from a board-approved national certifying body. **Fees:** $25 license fee. $10 renewal fee. **Governing Statute:** Montana Code Annotated 37-8-401 through 37-8-444.

7387

Nurse Midwife
Montana State Board of Nursing
111 N. Jackson
Helena, MT 59620
Phone: (406)444-2071
Phone: (406)444-4279

Credential Type: License. **Duration of License:** One year. **Requirements:** Complete one academic year beyond the professional nursing program, with four months of didactic and five months perceptorship. Must be a Registered Professional Nurse. Must maintain national certification for renewal. **Examination:** National certifying examination from a board-approved national certifying body. **Fees:** $25 license fee. $10 renewal fee. **Governing Statute:** Montana Code Annotated 37-8-401 through 37-8-444.

7388

Nurse Practitioner
Montana State Board of Nursing
111 N. Jackson
Helena, MT 59620
Phone: (406)444-2071
Phone: (406)444-4279

Credential Type: License. **Duration of License:** One year. **Requirements:** Complete one academic year beyond the professional nursing program, with four months of didactic and five months perceptorship. Must be a Registered Professional Nurse. Must maintain national certification for renewal. **Examination:** National certifying

Montana

Nurse Practitioner, continued

examination from a board-approved national certifying body. **Fees:** $25 license fee. $10 renewal fee. **Governing Statute:** Montana Code Annotated 37-8-401 through 37-8-444.

7389

Registered Professional Nurse
Montana State Board of Nursing
111 N. Jackson
Helena, MT 59620
Phone: (406)444-2071
Phone: (406)444-4279

Credential Type: License. **Duration of License:** One year. **Requirements:** High school diploma or equivalent. Graduation from an approved professional nursing program. **Examination:** National Council Licensing Exam. **Fees:** $35 application fee. $20 renewal fee. **Governing Statute:** Montana Code Annotated 37-8-401 through 37-8-444.

Nebraska

7390

Midwife (Nurse)
Nebraska Bureau of Examining Boards Council of Certified Nurse Widwifery
301 Centennial Mall S.
PO Box 95007
Lincoln, NE 68509
Phone: (402)471-2115

Credential Type: License. **Duration of License:** Two years. **Requirements:** Must be a licensed registered nurse and have completed a nurse midwifery program. **Examination:** Yes. **Fees:** $50 initial fee. $30 renewal fee.

7391

Nurse Practitioner (Anesthetist)
Nebraska Bureau of Examining Boards Advisory Council
301 Centennial Mall S.
PO Box 95007
Lincoln, NE 68509
Phone: (402)471-2115

Credential Type: License. **Duration of License:** Two years. **Requirements:** Must be a licensed nurse practitioner who has completed the required courses in a school of nurse anesthesia. **Examination:** Yes. **Fees:** $50 initial fee. $30 renewal fee.

7392

Nurse, Registered Professional (RN)
Nebraska Board of Nursing
301 Centennial Mall S.
PO Box 95007
Lincoln, NE 68509
Phone: (402)471-2115

Credential Type: Registration. **Duration of License:** Two years. **Requirements:** Must have a high school diploma. Must have completed the basic curriculum for nurses in an accredited school of professional nursing. **Examination:** Yes. **Fees:** $75 application fee. $40 renewal fee.

7393

School Nurse
Teacher Certification
State Dept. of Education
301 Centennial Mall South
Box 94987
Lincoln, NE 68509-4987
Phone: (402)471-2496

Credential Type: Initial Special Services Certificate. **Duration of License:** Three years. **Requirements:** Accredited nursing training from an institute of higher education and submit official transcripts. Pass the PPST with the following minimum scores: reading 170; mathematics 171; writing 172. **Examination:** Pre-Professional Skills Test.

Credential Type: Advanced Special Services Certificate. **Duration of License:** Seven years. **Requirements:** Baccalaureate degree from an approved, accredited institution. Completion of degree level course of study in nursing. Six semester hours of credit within the past three years or a valid, regular, approved license for practicing nursing in Nebraska. Renewal is possible with two years of successful service within the past seven years or six semester hours of college credit in area of service within the immediate past three years.

Nevada

7394

Nurse Practitioner
Nevada State Board of Nursing
1281 Terminal Way, Rm. 116
Reno, NV 89502
Phone: (702)786-2778

Credential Type: Nurse Practitioner License. **Requirements:** Bachelor's degree in nursing (a master's degree will be required after June 1992). Registered nurse license. Completion of an approved program in a specialty area. **Fees:** $60 application and license fee. $60 prescribing application fee. $30 renewal fee.

7395

Registered Nurse
Nevada State Board of Nursing
1281 Terminal Way, Rm. 116
Reno, NV 89502
Phone: (702)786-2778

Credential Type: Registered Nurse License. **Duration of License:** Two years. **Requirements:** Graduation from an approved school of professional nursing. **Examination:** Yes. **Fees:** $73 exam fee. $65 license fee. $50 renewal fee.

New Hampshire

7396

Registered Nurse
New Hampshire Board of Nursing
Health & Welfare Bldg.
6 Hazen Dr.
Concord, NH 03301-6527
Phone: (603)271-2323
Fax: (603)271-3745

Credential Type: Registered Nurse License. **Requirements:** Graduate of state approved nursing program or New York Regents external degree program. Good physical and mental health. Be proficient in English language as it relates to nursing. No criminal record involving moral turpitude. **Examination:** National Council Licensure Examination (NCLEX)-RN.

New Jersey

7397

Midwife
Board of Medical Examiners
28 W. State St.
Trenton, NJ 08608
Phone: (609)292-4843

Credential Type: Certified Nurse-Midwife. **Duration of License:** Two years. **Requirements:** Graduation from a legally-chartered and approved school of Nurse-midwifery. Two years of obstetrical clinical experience in a licensed health care facility. 18 years of age. Must hold a current registration as a professional nurse in New Jersey. **Examination:** Yes. **Fees:** $120 biennial registration fee. **Governing Statute:** NJSA 45:10. NJAC 13:35.

7398

Registered Nurse
New Jersey Board of Nursing
PO Box 45010
Newark, NJ 07101
Phone: (201)648-2570
Fax: (201)648-6061

Credential Type: Registered Nurse License. **Requirements:** High school graduate or equivalent. Graduate of a state approved nursing program or New York Regents external degree program or any other equivalent nursing program. Meet age requirement. Good moral character. Be proficient in English language as it relates to nursing. No felony or criminal record. **Examination:** National Council Licensure Examination (NCLEX)-RN.

New Mexico

7399

Registered Nurse
New Mexico Board of Nursing
4253 Montgomery Blvd., Ste. 130
Albuquerque, NM 87109
Phone: (505)841-8340

Credential Type: Registered Nurse License. **Requirements:** High school graduate or equivalent. Graduate of state approved nursing program or New York Regents external degree program. Be proficient in English language as it relates to nursing. Felonies must be reviewed by Board before license can be granted.

New York

7400

Certified Nurse - Midwife
State Education Dept. of Health
Bureau of Reproductive Health
Empire State Plaza
Tower Bldg., Rm. 821
Albany, NY 12230
Phone: (518)474-8661

Credential Type: License. **Duration of License:** Three years. **Requirements:** Two to four year training to become a professional nurse. Associate's or Bachelor's Degree issued at a nursing college. One to two years of basic nurse-midwifery training. Master's Degree, or combined RN/Master in Science and Nursing curriculum. **Examination:** National Certification Examination by the American College of Nurse-Midwives. **Reciprocity:** Reciprocity is given to any other state on examinations, but applicant must meet filing requirements in New York State. **Fees:** $300 exam fee. $30 nurse's license fee. **Governing Statute:** State of New York Public Health Law, Title III, Section 2560. New York State of Codes, Rules and Regulations, Title 10, Chapter 1, Part 20.

7401

Nurse Practitioner
State Education Dept.
Office of the Professions
Cultural Education Center
Albany, NY 12230
Phone: (518)474-3843

Credential Type: Certificate. **Duration of License:** Three years. **Requirements:** Diploma or Master's Degree in one or more nurse practitioner specialties. At least three semester hours in pharmacology. Must have a practice agreement with a collaborating physician. **Fees:** $30 registration fee. $50 application fee per specialty. $30 renewal fee. **Governing Statute:** Title VIII Articles 130, 139 of the Education Law.

7402

Registered Professional Nurse
State Education Dept.
Div. of Professional Licensing Services
Cultural Education Center
Empire State Plaza
Albany, NY 12230
Phone: (518)474-1593

Credential Type: License. **Duration of License:** Three years. **Requirements:** Diploma or degree in professional nursing. 18 years of age. **Examination:** Written. **Fees:** $165 application fee. $50 renewal fee. **Governing Statute:** Title VIII Articles 130, 139 of the Education Law.

North Carolina

7403

Nurse Practitioner
North Carolina State Board of Medical Examiners
PO Box 26808
Raleigh, NC 27611
Phone: (919)876-3885

Credential Type: Registration. **Duration of License:** One year. **Requirements:** Must be a registered nurse in addition to completing an approved nurse practitioner's program. 18 years of age. Three recommendations. **Fees:** $50 application fee.

7404

Registered Nurse
North Carolina Board of Nursing
PO Box 2129
Raleigh, NC 27609
Phone: (919)782-3211

Credential Type: License. **Duration of License:** Two years. **Requirements:** High school diploma or equivalent. Associate degree from an approved junior or community college; or a diploma from an approved school of nursing; or a bachelor's degree from an approved school of nursing. **Examination:** National. **Fees:** $75 exam fee. $40 renewal fee.

North Dakota

7405

Registered Nurse
North Dakota Board of Nursing
919 S. 7th St., Ste. 504
Bismarck, ND 58504-5881
Phone: (701)224-2974
Fax: (701)224-4614

Credential Type: Registered Nurse License. **Requirements:** Graduate from state approved nursing program or New York Regents external degree program. **Examination:** National Council Licensure Examination (NCLEX)-RN.

Ohio

7406

Registered Nurse
Ohio Board of Nursing
77 S. High St., 17th Fl.
Columbus, OH 43266-0316
Phone: (614)466-3947
Fax: (614)466-0388

Credential Type: Registered Nurse License. **Requirements:** Graduate of state approved nursing program or New York Regents external degree program. Be proficient in English language as it relates to nursing. No felony or criminal record.

7407

School Nurse
Teacher Education and Certification
State Dept. of Education
65 S. Front St., Rm. 1012
Columbus, OH 43266-0308
Phone: (614)466-3593

Credential Type: Provisional School Nurse. **Authorization:** Valid for providing

Oklahoma 7408

School Nurse, continued

school health services. **Requirements:** Baccalaureate degree. Good moral character. Complete an approved program of course work distributed over educational foundations and school health services, including a practicum. Successfully complete a state approved examination. Recommendation of the conferring institution. Current license to practice as a registered nurse in the state of Ohio. **Examination:** State approved examination proving competency.

Oklahoma

7408

Nurse Anesthetist (CRNA)
Council for Certification of Nurse Anesthetist
216 Higgins Rd.
Park Ridge, IL 60068
Phone: (708)692-7050

Credential Type: Certificate. **Duration of License:** Two years. **Requirements:** Graduation from a state-approved school of nursing and a nationally accredited school of nurse anesthesiology. Supervised clinical experience in health facilities. Registered nurse license. 40 hours of continuing education in anesthesiology every two years. **Examination:** Certifying Exam for Nurse Anesthetist. **Fees:** $350 exam fee. $30 renewal fee.

7409

Nurse - Midwife (CNM)
American College of Nurse - Midwives
1522 K St. NW, Ste. 1000
Washington, DC 20005
Phone: (202)459-1321

Credential Type: Certificate. **Duration of License:** Lifetime. **Requirements:** Completion of an accredited certification program of nurse midwifery or a master's degree. Supervised clinical experience. Five continuing education units (CEUs) or 50 contact hours over a five-year period. Registered nurse license. **Examination:** American College of Nurse—Midwives National Certification Exam. **Fees:** $385 exam fee. $50 application fee.

7410

Nurse Practitioner
Board of Nurse Registration and Nursing Education
2415 N. Classen
Oklahoma City, OK 73106
Phone: (405)525-2076

Credential Type: Certificate. **Duration of License:** Lifetime. **Requirements:** Approved nurse practitioner program. A five-month internship under the tutorship of another practitioner or physician. Registered nurse license. **Examination:** Varies depending upon certifying board. **Fees:** $50 exam fee. $50 application fee.

7411

Nurse Registered
Oklahoma Board of Nurse Registration and Nursing Education
2916 N. Classen
Oklahoma City, OK 73106
Phone: (405)525-2076

Credential Type: License. **Duration of License:** Two years. **Requirements:** Degree in nursing from a state-approved school. Supervised clinical experience. High school diploma or equivalent. **Examination:** National Council Licensure Examination for Registered Nurses. **Fees:** $95 exam fee. $55 application and license fee. $40 renewal fee.

Oregon

7412

Nurse, Registered
Oregon State Board of Nursing
800 NE Oregon St. 25, Ste. 465
Portland, OR 97232
Phone: (503)731-4745

Credential Type: License. **Duration of License:** One year. **Requirements:** Must be a graduate of the program preparing persons for the Registered Nursing role. **Examination:** Yes. **Fees:** $40 exam fee. $70 license fee. $44 renewal fee. **Governing Statute:** ORS 678.040, 678.050, 678.101.

Pennsylvania

7413

Midwife
State Board of Medicine
Bureau of Professional and Occupational Affairs
Dept. of State
Transportation and Safety Bldg., 6th Fl.
Harrisburg, PA 17120
Phone: (717)787-8503

Credential Type: Midwife License. **Duration of License:** Two years. **Requirements:** Legal age. Good moral character. Free from alcohol or drug addiction. Has not been convicted of a felony or has met board restrictions for previous offenders. Be licensed as a registered nurse in Pennsylvania. Successfully complete an approved midwifery program. Pass the ACNM examination. **Examination:** The American College of Nurse-Midwives examination. **Fees:** $20 initial license fee. $25 biennial renewal fee.

7414

Registered Nurse
Pennsylvania State Board of Nursing
PO Box 2649
Harrisburg, PA 17105
Phone: (717)783-7142
Fax: (717)787-7769

Credential Type: Registered Nurse License. **Requirements:** High school graduate or equivalent. Graduate from state approved nursing program or New York Regents external degree program. Good moral character. Be proficient in English language as it relates to nursing. No felony or criminal record.

Rhode Island

7415

Registered Nurse
Board of Nurse Registration & Nurse Education
Cannon Health Bldg.
Three Capitol Hill, Rm. 104
Providence, RI 02908-5097
Phone: (401)277-2827
Fax: (401)277-1272

Credential Type: Registered Nurse License. **Requirements:** High school graduate or equivalent. Graduate of state approved nursing program or New York Regents external degree program. Good moral character. No felony or criminal rec-

Registered Nurses

ord. **Examination:** National Council Licensure Examination (NCLEX)-RN.

South Carolina

7416

Registered Nurse
South Carolina State Board of Nursing
1777 St. Julian Pl., Ste. 102
Columbia, SC 29204
Phone: (803)737-6594

Credential Type: Registered Nurse. **Requirements:** 18 years of age. High school education or equivalent. Completion of a course of study in an accredited school of nursing. **Examination:** Yes. **Fees:** $45 exam fee. $25 renewal fee. $75 endorsement fee. $45 reinstatement fee.

South Dakota

7417

Registered Nurse
South Dakota Board of Nursing
3307 S. Lincoln Ave.
Sioux Falls, SD 57105-5224
Phone: (605)335-4973
Fax: (605)335-2977

Credential Type: Registered Nurse License. **Requirements:** High school graduate or equivalent. Graduate from a state approved nursing program or New York Regents external degree program. Be proficient in English language as it relates to nursing. **Examination:** National Council Licensure Examination (NCLEX)-RN.

7418

Registered Nurse Anesthetist
South Dakota Board of Nursing
3307 S. Lincoln Ave.
Sioux Falls, SD 57105-5224
Phone: (605)335-4973
Fax: (605)335-2977

Credential Type: Certification. **Duration of License:** Two years. **Requirements:** Complete an approved program of nurse anesthesia accredited by the Council on Accreditation of Nurse Anesthesia Educational Programs/Schools. Must be a licensed registered nurse. **Examination:** Board-approved examination. **Fees:** $50 certification fee. $15 renewal fee. $15 temporary permit fee. **Governing Statute:** South Dakota Codified Laws, Chap. 36-9. Administrative Rules of South Dakota, Article 20:48.

Tennessee

7419

Registered Nurse
Board of Nursing
283 Plus Park Blvd.
Nashville, TN 37247
Phone: (615)367-6232

Credential Type: License. **Requirements:** High school graduate or equivalent. Completion of a course of study at an approved nursing school. Good physical and mental health. Must have actively practiced within the past five years. No convictions of a crime. **Examination:** National Council of State Boards of Nursing Licensure (NCLEXRN). **Fees:** $55 Examination. $40 Test Service, includes permit.

Texas

7420

Nurse, Registered
Texas State Board of Nurse Examiners
9101 Burnet Rd., Ste. 104
Austin, TX 78758
Phone: (512)835-4880

Credential Type: License. **Duration of License:** One year. **Requirements:** Graduation from an accredited program of professional nursing education. **Examination:** National Council Licensure Examination for Registered Nurses (NCLEX-RN). **Fees:** $200 exam fee. $50 renewal fee. **Governing Statute:** VACS 4518, 22 TAC 217.

Utah

7421

Nurse Anesthetist
Dept. of Commerce
Div. of Occupational and Professional Licensing
160 E. 300 S.
PO Box 45802
Salt Lake City, UT 84145
Phone: (801)530-6628

Credential Type: License. **Duration of License:** Two years. **Requirements:** Must be a registered nurse in Utah. Must have completed a nurse anesthetist program recognized by the Board. **Examination:** Yes. **Fees:** $50 license fee. $35 renewal fee.

7422

Nurse Midwife, Certified
Div. of Occupaional and Professional Licnesing
160 E. 300 S.
PO Box 45802
Salt Lake City, UT 84145
Phone: (801)530-6628

Credential Type: Certificate. **Duration of License:** Two years. **Requirements:** Must be a registered nurse in Utah. Must complete an approved nurse midwifery education program. **Examination:** Yes. **Fees:** $75 license fee. $35 renewal fee.

7423

Nurse Practitioner
Dept. of Commerce
Div. of Occupational and Professional Licensing
160 E. 300 W.
PO Box 45802
Salt Lake City, UT 84145
Phone: (801)530-6628

Credential Type: License. **Duration of License:** Two years. **Requirements:** Must have at least a bachelor's degree in nursing. Must be a registered nurse in Utah and complete a nurse practitioner program. **Fees:** $50 original fee. $35 renewal fee.

7424

Nurse, Registered
Dept. of Commerce
Div. of Occupational and Professional Licensing
160 E. 300 S.
PO Box 45802
Salt Lake City, UT 84145
Phone: (801)530-6628

Credential Type: License. **Duration of License:** Two years. **Requirements:** Must have completed a state-accredited and approved registered nursing education program; or hold a current license in another state. **Examination:** Yes. **Reciprocity:** Yes. **Fees:** $50 license fee. $35 renewal fee.

7425

Nurse, Specialist
Dept. of Commerce
Div. of Occupational and
 Professional Licensing
160 E. 300 S.
PO Box 45802
Salt Lake City, UT 84145
Phone: (801)530-6628

Credential Type: License. **Duration of License:** Two years. **Requirements:** Must be a registered nurse in Utah. Must hold a master's degree in nursing specialty. **Fees:** $50 license fee. $35 renewal fee.

Vermont

7426

Registered Nurse (RN)
Vermont State Board of Nursing
Pavilion Office Bldg.
Montpelier, VT 05602
Phone: (802)828-2396

Credential Type: License. **Duration of License:** Two years. **Requirements:** Good moral character. High school graduate. Mentally and physically able to perform duties. Graduate of an approved nursing program. **Examination:** Yes. **Reciprocity:** Yes. **Fees:** $70 Application by Examination. $25 Application by endorsement. $20 Renewal. $25 Limited practice reinstatement. $35 Nurse practitioner (additional fee). **Governing Statute:** Title 26, VSA Section 1554.

Virginia

7427

Registered Nurse
Virginia Board of Nursing
1601 Rolling Hills Dr.
Richmond, VA 23229
Phone: (804)662-9909

Credential Type: License. **Duration of License:** Two years. **Requirements:** Must complete an accredited professional nursing program. **Examination:** Yes. **Fees:** $45 application fee. $28 renewal fee.

Washington

7428

Registered Nurse
Washington State Board of Nursing
Dept. of Health
1300 Quince St., MS EY-27
Olympia, WA 98504
Phone: (206)753-2686
Fax: (206)586-5935

Credential Type: Registered Nurse License. **Requirements:** Graduate of state approved nursing program or New York Regents external degree program. Good moral character. Good physical and mental health. No criminal record relating to substance abuse or patient care. **Examination:** National Council Licensure Examination (NCLEX)-RN.

7429

School Nurse
Superintendent of Public Instruction
Professional Education and
 Certification
Old Capitol Bldg. FG-11
Seattle, WA 98504-3211
Phone: (206)753-6773

Credential Type: Initial Educational Staff Associate Certificate. **Duration of License:** Seven years. **Requirements:** Baccalaureate degree in nursing. Complete 15 quarter hours of related postbaccalaureate work. Valid Washington state license in nursing.

West Virginia

7430

Nurse Anesthetist
Board of Examiners for Registered
 Professional Nurses
922 Quarrier St., Ste. 309
Charleston, WV 25301
Phone: (304)348-3596

Credential Type: License. **Requirements:** Registered as a professional nurse. Complete an approved educational program. Never convicted of a felony. **Examination:** Yes. **Fees:** None.

7431

Nurse, Midwife
Board of Examiners for Registered
 Professional Nurses
922 Quarrier St., Ste. 309
Charleston, WV 25301
Phone: (304)348-3596

Credential Type: License. **Duration of License:** One year. **Requirements:** Registered professional nurse. Graduate of an approved educational program. Certified by the American College of Nurse Midwives. Never convicted of a felony. **Examination:** Yes. **Fees:** $20 Application. $10 Renewal.

7432

Registered Nurse
Board of Examiners for Registered
 Professional Nurses
922 Quarrier St., Ste. 309
Charleston, WV 25301
Phone: (304)348-3596

Credential Type: License. **Duration of License:** One year. **Requirements:** 18 years old. High school diploma. Graduate of accredited registered professional nursing program and hold a diploma from an accredited school. Never convicted of a felony. **Examination:** Yes. **Fees:** $76.50 Application, exam and license. $10 Renewal.

Wisconsin

7433

Nurse/Midwife
Regulations and Licensing Dept.
Nurses Board
PO Box 8935
Madison, WI 53708-8935
Phone: (608)266-8609

Credential Type: License. **Requirements:** Completion of an approved program in nurse-midwifery. Current licensure as a registered nurse in Wisconsin. Certification as a nurse-midwife from the American College of Nurse-Midwives.

7434

Nurse/Registered
Regulations and Licensing Dept.
Nurses Board
PO Box 8935
Madison, WI 53708-8935
Phone: (608)266-8609

Credential Type: License. **Requirements:** High school graduation or equivalent. No arrests or convictions. Graduation from an approved, professional school of nursing. **Examination:** National Boards. **Reciprocity:** Yes.

Wyoming

7435

Nurse Practitioner
State Board of Nursing
Barrett Bldg., 2nd Fl.
2301 Central Ave.
Cheyenne, WY 82002
Phone: (307)777-7601

Credential Type: License. **Duration of License:** Two years. **Requirements:** Must graduate from a one-year postgraduate nursing program or be certified by a national agency. **Examination:** No. **Fees:** $100 Initial Advance Practitioner Recognition. $80 License. $50 Renewal.

7436

Nurse, Registered
State Board of Nursing
Barrett Bldg., 2nd Fl.
2301 Central Ave.
Cheyenne, WY 82002
Phone: (307)777-7601

Credential Type: License. **Duration of License:** Two years. **Requirements:** Graduate from a state-approved nursing program. Pass a national examination. Meet continued competency requirements. **Examination:** Yes. **Reciprocity:** Yes. **Fees:** $50 Licensing by endorsement (out of state). $75 Licensing by examination. $50 Renewal.

7437

School Nurse
State Dept. of Education
Certification and Accreditation Services Unit, Hathaway Bldg.
Cheyenne, WY 82002
Phone: (307)777-7291

Credential Type: School Nurse Endorsement. **Requirements:** Bachelor's degree in nursing. Hold Wyoming state nursing license. 12 semester hours of professional education.

Respiratory Therapists

The following states grant licenses in this occupational category as of the date of publication:

Arizona	Idaho	Louisiana	Mississippi	New Hampshire	Oregon	Utah
Arkansas	Indiana	Maine	Missouri	New Jersey	Rhode Island	Virginia
California	Iowa	Maryland	Montana	New Mexico	South Carolina	Washington
Connecticut	Kansas	Massachusetts	Nebraska	North Dakota	Tennessee	Wisconsin
Florida	Kentucky	Minnesota	Nevada	Ohio	Texas	

Arizona

7438

Respiratory Care Practitioner
Board of Respiratory Care Examiners
1645 W. Jefferson, Rm. 420
Phoenix, AZ 85007
Phone: (602)542-5995

Credential Type: License. **Duration of License:** Two years. **Requirements:** National Board for Respiratory Care (NBRC) entry level credential. Renewal requires 20 hours of continuing education. **Fees:** $100 application fee. $65 license fee. $65 renewal fee.

Arkansas

7439

Respiratory Care Practitioner
State Medical Board
2100 Riverfront Dr., Ste. 200
Little Rock, AR 72202-1748
Phone: (501)324-9410
Fax: (501)324-9413

Credential Type: License. **Duration of License:** One year. **Requirements:** National Board for Respiratory Care (NBRC) entry level certificate. Renewal requires six hours of continuing education. **Fees:** $150 initial license fee. $5 renewal fee. $35 temporary license fee.

California

7440

Respiratory Care Practitioner
Respiratory Care Examining Committee
1426 Howe Ave., Ste. 48
Sacramento, CA 95825-3234
Phone: (916)924-2314
Fax: (916)924-4887

Credential Type: License. **Duration of License:** Two years. **Requirements:** National Board for Respiratory Care (NBRC) entry level credential. Renewal requires 15 hours of continuing education. **Examination:** State administered NBRC equivalency examination. **Fees:** $50 application fee. $90 examination fee. $50 fingerprint processing fee. $150 initial license fee. $150 renewal fee.

Connecticut

7441

Respiratory Care Practitioner
Dept. of Health Services
RCP Certification
150 Washington St.
Hartford, CT 06106
Phone: (203)566-1039

Credential Type: Certificate. **Duration of License:** permanent. **Requirements:** National Board for Respiratory Care (NBRC) entry level credential. **Fees:** $83 certificate fee.

Florida

7442

Respiratory Care Practitioner
Advisory Council on Respiratory Care
Dept. of Professional Regulation
Northwood Center
1940 N. Monroe St., FL 32399-0789
Phone: (904)487-3372

Credential Type: License. **Duration of License:** Two years. **Requirements:** National Board for Respiratory Care (NBRC) entry level credential. Renewal requires 24 hours of continuing education. **Examination:** State administered NBRC equivalency examination. **Fees:** $140 application with examination fee. $40 application without examination fee. $37 renewal fee.

7443

Respiratory Therapist
Board of Medicine
Council on Respiratory Care
Dept. of Professional Regulation
1940 N. Monroe St.
Tallahassee, FL 32399-0750
Phone: (904)488-0595

Credential Type: Respiratory Therapist Registration. **Duration of License:** Two years. **Requirements:** Be at least 18 years of age. Possess a high school diploma or graduate equivalency diploma. Meet one of the following sets of requirements: (1) Complete a training program for respiratory therapists approved by the Committee on Allied Health Education and Accreditation of the American Medical Association, or the equivalent. (2) Be a currently Registered Respiratory Therapist registered by the National Board for Respiratory Care, or the equivalent. **Fees:** $40 application fee.

Respiratory Therapists

$35 certification fee. $35 renewal fee. **Governing Statute:** Florida Statutes, Chapter 468, Part V. Florida Administrative Code, Rules 21-M.

Credential Type: License by Endorsement. **Duration of License:** Two years. **Requirements:** Be a currently Registered Respiratory Therapist registered by the National Board for Respiratory Care, or the equivalent; or have been granted registration to deliver respiratory care services in another state or country. **Fees:** $40 application fee. $35 certification fee. $35 renewal fee. **Governing Statute:** Florida Statutes, Chapter 468, Part III. Florida Administrative Code, Rules 21-M.

Credential Type: Temporary certificate. **Duration of License:** One year maximum. **Requirements:** A temporary certificate may be issued to an applicant who appears to be eligible for registration. **Governing Statute:** Florida Statutes, Chapter 468, Part III. Florida Administrative Code, Rules 21-M.

7444

Respiratory Therapy Technician
Board of Medicine
Council on Respiratory Care
Dept. of Professional Regulation
1940 N. Monroe St.
Tallahassee, FL 32399-0750
Phone: (904)488-0595

Credential Type: Certification by Examination. **Duration of License:** Two years. **Requirements:** Be at least 18 years of age. Possess a high school diploma or graduate equivalency diploma. Meet one of the following sets of requirements: (1) Complete a training program for respiratory therapy technicians or respiratory therapists approved by the Committee on Allied Health Education and Accreditation of the American Medical Association, or the equivalent. (2) Be a currently Certified Respiratory Therapy Technician certified by the National Board for Respiratory Care, or the equivalent. (3) Be a currently Registered Respiratory Therapist registered by the National Board for Respiratory Care, or the equivalent. **Examination:** National Board for Respiratory Care entry-level examination for respiratory therapy technicians, or equivalent. **Fees:** $40 application fee. $100 examination fee. $35 certification fee. $35 renewal fee. **Governing Statute:** Florida Statutes, Chapter 468, Part V. Florida Administrative Code, Rules 21-M.

Credential Type: License by Endorsement. **Duration of License:** Two years. **Requirements:** Be a currently Certified Respiratory Therapy Technician certified by the National Board for Respiratory Care, or the equivalent; or have been granted certification, registration, or other authority to deliver respiratory care services in another state or country. **Fees:** $40 application fee. $35 certification fee. $35 renewal fee. **Governing Statute:** Florida Statutes, Chapter 468, Part III. Florida Administrative Code, Rules 21-M.

Credential Type: Temporary certificate. **Duration of License:** One year maximum. **Requirements:** A temporary certificate may be issued to an applicant who appears to be eligible for certification. **Governing Statute:** Florida Statutes, Chapter 468, Part III. Florida Administrative Code, Rules 21-M.

Idaho

7445

Respiratory Therapist
Idaho State Board of Medicine
280 N. 8th St., Ste. 202
Boise, ID 83720
Phone: (208)334-2822

Credential Type: Respiratory Therapist License. **Duration of License:** One year. **Requirements:** Good moral character. Have passed the National Board for Respiratory Care entry level examination and been a certified respiratory therapist and/or have completed the National Board for Respiratory Care written registry and clinical simulation examinations and have been a registered respiratory therapist. **Fees:** Contact board for fees. **Governing Statute:** Idaho Code, Title 54, Chap. 37. IDAPA 22.K.

Credential Type: Temporary Permit. **Duration of License:** One year. **Authorization:** Allows individual to practice and perform respiratory care only under the supervision of a licensed respiratory care practitioner or a licensed physician. **Requirements:** May be issued to any person who has successfully completed an approved respiratory therapy program, and/or the National Board for Respiratory Care entry level examination, and/or the National Board for Respiratory Care written registry and clinical simulations examination. **Fees:** Contact board for fees. **Governing Statute:** Idaho Code, Title 54, Chap. 37. IDAPA 22.K.

Indiana

7446

Respiratory Care Practitioner
Respiratory Care Committee
Health Professions Bureau
402 W. Washington St., Rm. 041
Indianapolis, IN 46204
Phone: (317)232-2960

Credential Type: Certificate to practice. **Duration of License:** Two years. **Requirements:** Graduate of a respiratory care program that meets board standards; or be certified by the National Board of Respiratory Care, or have three years of continuous experience in the field of respiratory care. **Reciprocity:** License by endorsement may be granted. **Fees:** $50 exam fee. $50 endorsement fee. $50 experience verification fee. $10 license issuance fee. **Governing Statute:** Indiana Code 25-34.5.

Iowa

7447

Certified Respiratory Therapy Technician
Respiratory Care Office
Dept. of Public Health
Lucas State Office Bldg.
Des Moines, IA 50319
Phone: (515)281-6762

Credential Type: Certified Respiratory Therapy Technician License. **Duration of License:** Two years. **Requirements:** Certificate of completion from an accredited respiratory therapy training program, or at least two years of experience. One year of education. 30 hours of continuing education every two years. **Fees:** $25 application fee. $50 renewal fee.

7448

Registered Respiratory Therapist
Respiratory Care Office
Dept. of Public Health
Lucas State Office Bldg.
Des Moines, IA 50319
Phone: (515)281-6762

Credential Type: Registered Respiratory Therapist. **Duration of License:** Two years. **Requirements:** Certificate of completion from an accredited respiratory therapy training program, or at least two years of experience. Two years of education. 30 hours of continuing education every two years. **Examination:** Clinical exam. **Fees:** $25 application fee. $90 exam fee. $50 renewal fee.

Kansas

7449

Respiratory Care Practitioner
Board of Healing Arts
235 S. Topeka Blvd.
Topeka, KS 66603
Phone: (913)296-7413
Fax: (913)296-0852

Credential Type: License Registration. **Duration of License:** One year. **Requirements:** National Board for Respiratory Care (NBRC) entry level credential. Renewal requires 30 hours of continuing education every two years. **Fees:** $40 application fee. $40 renewal fee. $15 temporary registration fee. $15 special permit fee.

7450

Respiratory Therapist
State Board of Healing Arts
235 SW Topeka Blvd.
Topeka, KS 66603-3059
Phone: (913)296-7413

Credential Type: Respiratory Therapist Registration. **Duration of License:** One year. **Requirements:** Complete an approved educational program for respiratory therapists, including any program accredited by the committee on allied health education and accreditation of the American Medical Association in collaboration with the Joint Review Committee for Respiratory Therapy Education, or any program equal to the program for respiratory therapy technicians at the University of Kansas School of Allied Health.

Renewal requires completion of at least 30 contact hours of continuing education during the preceding two years. **Examination:** Certification examination for entry-level respiratory therapy practitioners of the National Board for Respiratory Care. **Fees:** $40 application fee. $30 renewal fee. $190 board-administered exam fee. **Governing Statute:** K.S.A. 65-5501 ff. K.A.R. 100-55-1 ff.

Credential Type: Temporary permit. **Duration of License:** Until exam results are recorded or license issued. **Requirements:** Issued to applicants who have met the qualifications for licensure, except passage of required examination, and who must wait for completion of next examination. Must have paid appropriate license fees. **Fees:** $15 temporary permit fee. **Governing Statute:** K.S.A. 65-5501 ff. K.A.R. 100-55-1 ff.

Kentucky

7451

Respiratory Therapist
Occupations and Professions Board
PO Box 456
Frankfort, KY 40602
Phone: (502)564-3296

Credential Type: License. **Duration of License:** Two years. **Requirements:** Completion of an accredited training program. 18 years of age. **Examination:** Yes. **Fees:** $100 initial fee. $50 renewal fee.

Louisiana

7452

Certified Respiratory Therapist Technician
Respiratory Licensure Clerk
State Board of Medical Examiners
830 Union St., Ste. 100
New Orleans, LA 70112-1499
Phone: (504)568-8566
Fax: (504)568-8893

Credential Type: License. **Duration of License:** One year. **Requirements:** National Board for Respiratory Care (NBRC) entry level credential. **Fees:** $50 initial license fee. $17 license renewal fee. $17 temporary permit fee. $17 reciprocal license fee.

7453

Registered Respiratory Therapist
Respiratory Licensure Clerk
State Board of Medical Examiners
830 Union St., Ste. 100
New Orleans, LA 70112-1499
Phone: (504)568-8566
Fax: (504)568-8893

Credential Type: License. **Duration of License:** One year. **Requirements:** National Board for Respiratory Care (NBRC) entry level credential. **Fees:** $75 initial license fee. $25 license renewal fee. $25 temporary permit. $25 reciprocal license.

Maine

7454

Respiratory Care Practitioner
Div. of Licensing and Enforcement
Board of Respiratory Care
  Practitioners
State House Station 35
Augusta, ME 04333
Phone: (207)582-8723

Credential Type: License. **Duration of License:** Two years. **Requirements:** National Board for Respiratory Care (NBRC) entry level credential. Renewal requires 30 hours of continuing education. **Fees:** $135 initial license fee. $135 renewal fee. $20 temporary license fee.

Maryland

7455

Respiratory Care Practitioner
Dept. of Health & Mental Hygiene
Physicians Board for Quality
  Assurance
4201 Patterson Ave.
PO Box 2571
Baltimore, MD 21215-0095
Phone: (410)764-4777
Fax: (410)764-5987

Credential Type: Certificate. **Duration of License:** Two years. **Requirements:** National Board for Respiratory Care (NBRC) entry level credential. Renewal requires 16 hours of continuing education. **Fees:** $75 initial certificate fee. $60 renewal fee.

Massachusetts

7456

Respiratory Care Practitioner
Board of Respiratory Care
Div. of Registration
Saltonstall Bldg., Rm. 1513
100 Cambridge St.
Boston, MA 02202
Phone: (617)727-3090

Credential Type: License. **Duration of License:** Two years. **Requirements:** Complete a respiratory care program with a bachelor's or associate's degree or certificate. Be certified by the National Board of Respiratory Care (NBRC). Renewal requires 15 hours of continuing education. **Examination:** National Board of Respiratory Care (NBRC) Examination. **Fees:** $125 application fee. $75 initial license fee. $75 renewal fee.

Minnesota

7457

Respiratory Care Practitioner
Dept. of Health
Bureau of Health Resources and Managed Care Services
Health Occupations Programs
717 Delaware St., SE
Box 9441
Minneapolis, MN 55440
Phone: (612)623-5611
Fax: (612)623-5043

Credential Type: Respiratory Care Practitioner Registration. **Authorization:** Registration required to use occupational title. **Requirements:** Contact licensing body for application information. **Governing Statute:** Minnesota Statutes 214.13.

Mississippi

7458

Respiratory Care Practitioner
State Dept. of Health
Special Licensure
PO Box 1700
Jackson, MS 39215-1700
Phone: (601)960-7769

Credential Type: License. **Duration of License:** Two years. **Requirements:** Submit application and pay fees as determined by board.

Missouri

7459

Respiratory Care Practitioner
Office of Health Care Providers
PO Box 471
Jefferson City, MO 65102-0471
Phone: (314)751-0877

Credential Type: Respiratory Care Practitioner Registration. **Duration of License:** One year. **Requirements:** Must be certified by the National Board for Respiratory Care (NBRC) to be registered. **Fees:** $35 registration fee. $35 renewal fee. **Governing Statute:** Missouri Statutes, Rules and Regulations, Chap. 334. 4 CSR 155-1.010.

7460

Respiratory Care Technician
Office of Health Care Providers
PO Box 471
Jefferson City, MO 65102-0471
Phone: (314)751-0877

Credential Type: Respiratory Care Technician Certification and Registration. **Duration of License:** One year. **Requirements:** Must be certified by the National Board for Respiratory Care (NBRC) to be registered. **Fees:** $25 registration fee. $25 renewal fee. **Governing Statute:** Missouri Statutes, Rules and Regulations, Chap. 334. 4 CSR 155-1.010.

7461

Respiratory Therapist
Office of Health Care Providers
PO Box 471
Jefferson City, MO 65102-0471
Phone: (314)751-0877

Credential Type: Respiratory Therapist Registration. **Duration of License:** One year. **Requirements:** Must be certified by the National Board for Respiratory Care (NBRC) to be registered. **Fees:** $35 registration fee. $35 renewal fee. **Governing Statute:** Missouri Statutes, Rules and Regulations, Chap. 334. 4 CSR 155-1.010.

Montana

7462

Respiratory Care Practitioner
Board of Respiratory Care Practitioners
111 N. Jackson
Helena, MT 59620-0407
Phone: (406)444-3091

Credential Type: License. **Duration of License:** One year. **Requirements:** National Board for Respiratory Care (NBRC) entry level certificate. Renewal requires 15 hours of continuing education. **Fees:** $60 initial license fee. $40 annual renewal fee. $60 temporary permit.

Nebraska

7463

Respiratory Care Practitioner
Nebraska Board of Examiners in Respiratory Care Practice
301 Centennial Mall S.
PO Box 95007
Lincoln, NE 68509
Phone: (402)471-2115

Credential Type: License. **Duration of License:** Two years. **Requirements:** 19 years of age. Must have a high school diploma. Must complete an approved respiratory care training program. **Examination:** Yes. **Fees:** $250 initial fee. $150 renewal fee.

Nevada

7464

Respiratory Therapist
Bureau of Regulatory Health Services
505 E. King St., Rm. 202
Carson City, NV 89710
Phone: (702)687-4475

Credential Type: Blood-Gas Technologist License. **Requirements:** Applicants may qualify for licensing by obtaining credentials from a national certifying board.

Credential Type: Blood-Gas Technician License. **Requirements:** Completion of a one—or two-year program from an approved school of respiratory therapy or cardiopulmonary technology, or completion of an equivalent course of training in the theory and practice of the determination of blood gases.

New Hampshire

7465

Respiratory Care Practitioner
Board of Registration & Medicine
Health and Welfare Bldg.
6 Hazen Drive
Concord, NH 03301
Phone: (603)271-1203

Credential Type: License. **Duration of License:** One year. **Requirements:** National Board for Respiratory Care (NBRC) entry level credential. Renewal requires 10 hours of continuing education. **Fees:** $50 application fee. $25 renewal fee.

New Jersey

7466

Respiratory Care Practitioner
Dept. of Law and Public Safety
Div. of Consumer Affairs
State Board of Respiratory Care
PO Box 45031
Newark, NJ 07101
Phone: (201)648-2709
Fax: (201)648-3538

Credential Type: License. **Duration of License:** Two years or permanent. **Requirements:** National Board for Respiratory Care (NBRC) entry level credential. **Fees:** $125 application fee. $180 permanent license. $45 temporary license fee. $180 renewal fee.

New Mexico

7467

Respiratory Care Practitioner
Respiratory Care Advisory Board
Dept. of Regulation and Licensing
PO Box 25101
725 St. Michael's Dr.
Santa Fe, NM 87504
Phone: (505)827-7170

Credential Type: Respiratory Care Practitioner License. **Duration of License:** Two years. **Requirements:** Good moral character. Complete an approved respiratory care training and educational program. Pass examination leading to CRTT or RRT credential from the National Board for Respiratory Care (NBRC). Renewal requires 20 hours of continuing education. **Examination:** National Board for Respiratory Care examination. **Reciprocity:** Yes, provided state has educational and training requirements at least equal to those established for licensure in New Mexico. **Fees:** $125 application fee. $105 renewal fee.

Credential Type: Temporary Permit. **Duration of License:** One year. **Authorization:** Valid only for the performance of respiratory care under the direct supervision of the supervisor who signed the application. **Requirements:** Granted to respiratory care externs enrolled in a recognized program or to non-licensed graduates of an approved respiratory care program. **Fees:** $25 temporary permit fee.

North Dakota

7468

Certified Respiratory Care Practitioner
Respiratory Care Examining Board
Cardiopulmonary Services
St. Alexius Medical Center
900 E. Broadway
Bismarck, ND 58501
Phone: (701)223-5613

Credential Type: License. **Duration of License:** One year. **Requirements:** National Board for Respiratory Care (NBRC) entry level credential. Renewal requires 10 hours of continuing education. **Fees:** $35 annual license fee. $35 temporary license fee.

7469

Registered Respiratory Care Practitioner
Respiratory Care Examining Board
Cardiopulmonary Services
St. Alexius Medical Center
900 E. Broadway
Bismarck, ND 58501
Phone: (701)223-5613

Credential Type: License. **Duration of License:** One year. **Requirements:** National Board for Respiratory Care (NBRC) entry level credential. Renewal requires 10 hours of continuing education. **Fees:** $50 annual license fee.

Ohio

7470

Respiratory Care Practitioner
Respiratory Care Board
77 S. High St., 18th Fl.
Columbus, OH 43266-0777
Phone: (614)752-9218
Fax: (614)644-8112

Credential Type: License. **Duration of License:** One year. **Requirements:** National Board for Respiratory Care (NBRC) entry level credential. Renewal requires 18 hours of continuing education every three years. **Fees:** $40 initial license fee. $40 renewal fee. $20 temporary license fee.

Oregon

7471

Respiratory Care Practitioner
Oregon Board of Medical Examiners
620 Crown Plaza
1500 SW 1st Ave.
Portland, OR 97201
Phone: (503)229-5770

Credential Type: License. **Duration of License:** Two years. **Requirements:** 18 years of age. High school diploma or equivalent. Completion of an accredited respiratory care practitioner program. **Examination:** Yes. **Fees:** $75 exam fee. $50 application fee. $200 renewal fee. **Governing Statute:** ORS 677.861 to 677.878.

Rhode Island

7472

Respiratory Care Practitioner
Respiratory Care
Dept. of Health
Div. of Professional Regulations
3 Capitol Hill, Rm. 104
Providence, RI 02908-5097
Phone: (401)277-2827

Credential Type: License. **Duration of License:** Two years. **Requirements:** National Board for Respiratory Care (NBRC) entry level credential. **Fees:** $100 application fee. $80 renewal fee.

South Carolina

7473

Respiratory Care Practitioner
State Board of Medical Examiners
1220 Pickens St.
Columbia, SC 29201
Phone: (803)734-8901

Credential Type: Permanent License. **Requirements:** Contact licensing body for application information. **Fees:** $100 license fee.

Credential Type: Limited License. **Requirements:** Contact licensing body for application information. **Fees:** $50 license fee. $50 re-registration fee.

Respiratory Therapists

Tennessee

7474

Respiratory Therapist
Board of Medical Examiners
Council on Respiratory Care
283 Plus Park Blvd.
Nashville, TN 37247
Phone: (615)367-6393

Credential Type: License. **Duration of License:** Two years. **Requirements:** 18 years old. College transcript or certificate from an accredited college. Twelve hours continuing medical education (CME) every two years for renewal. Two letters of professional recommendation from respiratory assistant, technician or doctor. **Examination:** National Board for Respiratory Care (NBRC) examination. **Fees:** $15 Registration. $30 Application.

Texas

7475

Respiratory Care Practitioner
Texas Dept. of Health
Respiratory Care Program
1100 W. 49th St.
Austin, TX 78756
Phone: (512)834-6632

Credential Type: License. **Duration of License:** One year. **Requirements:** High school graduation or equivalent. Completion of Board-approved respiratory care educational program. Three to 12 hours of continuing education credits per year may be required for certification renewal. **Examination:** To be determined. **Fees:** $30 application fee. $30 certification fee. $30 renewal fee. **Governing Statute:** VACS 4512l, 25 TAC 123.

Utah

7476

Respiratory Care Practitioner
Dept. of Commerce
Div. of Professional Licensing
Respiratory Care
160 East 300 South
PO Box 45805
Salt Lake City, UT 84145-0805
Phone: (801)530-6633
Fax: (801)530-6511

Credential Type: License. **Duration of License:** Two years. **Requirements:** National Board for Respiratory Care (NBRC) entry level credential. **Fees:** $60 application fee.

Virginia

7477

Respiratory Care Practitioner
Dept. of Health Professions
Board of Medicine
1601 Rolling Hills Dr.
Richmond, VA 23229-5005
Phone: (804)662-9908
Fax: (804)662-9943

Credential Type: Certificate. **Duration of License:** One year. **Requirements:** National Board for Respiratory Care (NBRC) entry level credential. **Fees:** $100 initial certificate. $25 renewal.

Washington

7478

Respiratory Care Practitioner
Professional Licensing Services
Respiratory Care
1300 SE Quince St., M.S., EY-21
PO Box 47868
Olympia, WA 98504-7868
Phone: (206)586-8437
Fax: (206)586-7774

Credential Type: Certificate. **Requirements:** National Board for Respiratory Care (NBRC) entry level credential. **Fees:** $85 initial certificate fee. $100 renewal fee.

Wisconsin

7479

Respiratory Care Practitioner
Bureau of Health Professions
Respiratory Care
PO Box 8935
Madison, WI 53708
Phone: (608)266-0483

Credential Type: License. **Duration of License:** Two years. **Requirements:** National Board for Respiratory Care (NBRC) entry level credential. **Fees:** $10 application fee. $40 renewal fee.

Retail Sales Workers

The following states grant licenses in this occupational category as of the date of publication:

Alabama	District of	Iowa	Michigan	New Jersey	Pennsylvania	Virginia
Arizona	Columbia	Kansas	Minnesota	New Mexico	Rhode Island	Wisconsin
Arkansas	Florida	Kentucky	Missouri	North Carolina	South Dakota	Wyoming
California	Georgia	Louisiana	Montana	North Dakota	Tennessee	
Connecticut	Hawaii	Maine	Nebraska	Ohio	Texas	
Delaware	Idaho	Maryland	Nevada	Oklahoma	Utah	
	Illinois	Massachusetts	New Hampshire	Oregon	Vermont	

Alabama

7480

Wrestling Ticket Seller
State Athletic Commission
50 N. Ripley St., Rm. 4121
Montgomery, AL 36132
Phone: (205)242-1380

Credential Type: License. **Duration of License:** One year. **Fees:** $5 license fee.

Arizona

7481

Concession Employee
Arizona Dept. of Racing
Investigations and Licensing Div.
800 W. Washington, Rm. 515
Phoenix, AZ 85007
Phone: (602)542-5151

Credential Type: Concession employee license. **Duration of License:** One or three years. **Requirements:** At least 16 years of age. Not have been convicted of a felony or any crime involving moral turpitude within the last five years. **Fees:** $15 license fee (3 years). $7 license fee (1 year).

7482

Fur Dealer
Arizona Game and Fish Dept.
2221 W. Greenway Rd.
Phoenix, AZ 85023-4312
Phone: (602)942-3000
Fax: (602)789-3920

Credential Type: Fur dealer license. **Authorization:** To engage in the business of buying for resale any specimen of predatory, nongame, and fur-bearing mammals taken within Arizona. **Requirements:** Submit application. Keep record of transactions. Submit quarterly report to the department. **Fees:** $100 license fee. **Governing Statute:** Arizona Revised Statutes, Title 17, Chapter 2.

Arkansas

7483

Automobile Dealer, New
Arkansas Motor Vehicle Commission
1515 West 7th St., Rm. 300
Little Rock, AR 72201
Phone: (501)682-1428

Credential Type: License. **Requirements:** Must have a $25,000 Surety Bond. Must have a contract or franchise from a new car manufacturer. **Examination:** No. **Fees:** $200 Manufacturer's license fee. $50 Dealer's license. $5 Salesman's license.

7484

Automobile Dealer, Used
Office of Motor Vehicles
7th and Wolfe St.
Little Rock, AR 72203
Phone: (501)682-4689

Credential Type: License. **Requirements:** Must have place of business inspected by county or city police or sheriff's department. Must have liability insurance. Must have a $25,000 surety bond. **Examination:** No. **Fees:** $100 License.

California

7485

Vendor (Racetrack)
California Horse Racing Board
1010 Hurley Way, Ste. 190
Sacramento, CA 95825
Phone: (916)920-7178

Credential Type: License Registration. **Requirements:** Submit application and fingerprint card. Pay fee. **Fees:** $75 registration fee.

Connecticut

7486

Concession Employee (Racetrack)
Connecticut Div. of Special Revenue
Russell Rd.
PO Box 11424
Newington, CT 06111-0424
Phone: (203)566-2756

Credential Type: License Registration. **Requirements:** Submit application and fingerprint card. Pay fee. **Fees:** $5 registration fee.

7487

Concessionaire II (Racetrack)
Connecticut Div. of Special Revenue
Russell Rd.
PO Box 11424
Newington, CT 06111-0424
Phone: (203)566-2756

Credential Type: License Registration. **Requirements:** Submit application and fingerprint card. Pay fee. **Fees:** $100 registration fee.

7488

Group Sales Person (Racetrack)
Connecticut Div. of Special Revenue
Russell Rd.
PO Box 11424
Newington, CT 06111-0424
Phone: (203)566-2756

Credential Type: License Registration. **Requirements:** Submit application and fingerprint card. Pay fee. **Fees:** $5 registration fee.

7489

Newsstand Operator (Racetrack)
Connecticut Div. of Special Revenue
Russell Rd.
PO Box 11424
Newington, CT 06111-0424
Phone: (203)566-2756

Credential Type: License Registration. **Requirements:** Submit application and fingerprint card. Pay fee. **Fees:** $5 registration fee.

Delaware

7490

Concession Stand Employee (Racetrack)
Delaware Harness Racing Commission
2320 S. DuPont Hwy.
Dover, DE 19901
Phone: (302)739-4811

Credential Type: License Registration. **Requirements:** Submit application and fingerprint card. Pay fee. **Fees:** $5 registration fee.

7491

Vendor Employee (Racetrack)
Delaware Harness Racing Commission
2320 S. DuPont Hwy.
Dover, DE 19901
Phone: (302)739-4811

Credential Type: License Registration. **Requirements:** Submit application and fingerprint card. Pay fee. **Fees:** $5 registration fee.

7492

Vendor (Racetrack)
Delaware Harness Racing Commission
2320 S. DuPont Hwy.
Dover, DE 19901
Phone: (302)739-4811

Credential Type: License Registration. **Requirements:** Submit application and fingerprint card. Pay fee. **Fees:** $15 registration fee.

District of Columbia

7493

Motor Vehicle Dealer
License and Certification Div.
Occupational and Professional Licensure Administration
Consumer and Regulatory Affairs Dept.
PO Box 37200
Washington, DC 20013-7200
Phone: (202)727-7823
Phone: (202)727-7480

Alternate Information: 614 H St., NW, Washington, DC 20001

Credential Type: License. **Requirements:** Contact licensing body for application information.

7494

Motor Vehicle Salesperson
License and Certification Div.
Occupational and Professional Licensure Administration
Consumer and Regulatory Affairs Dept.
PO Box 37200
Washington, DC 20013-7200
Phone: (202)727-7823
Phone: (202)727-7480

Alternate Information: 614 H St., NW, Washington, DC 20001

Credential Type: License. **Requirements:** Contact licensing body for application information.

7495

Pawnbroker
License and Certification Div.
Occupational and Professional Licensure Administration
Consumer and Regulatory Affairs Dept.
PO Box 37200
Washington, DC 20013-7200
Phone: (202)727-7823
Phone: (202)727-7480

Alternate Information: 614 H St., NW, Washington, DC 20001 **Requirements:** Contact licensing body for application information.

Florida

7496

Concession Employee (Racetrack)
Florida Dept. of Business
Div. of Pari-Mutuel Wagering
Licensing Section
725 S. Bronough St.
Tallahassee, FL 32399-1037
Phone: (904)488-9161

Credential Type: License Registration Code 1003. **Authorization:** Authorizes work in the following positions: admission employee, calculator, clerical help, concession employee, security guard, maintenance employee, mutuel employee, parking employee, public relations staff, switchboard operator, track/fronton employee, head lead out, lead out, kennel master, ball boy, ball maker, and cesta maker. **Requirements:** Submit application and fingerprint card. Pay fee. **Fees:** $10 registration fee.

7497

Concession Manager/Supervisor (Racetrack)
Florida Dept. of Business
Div. of Pari-Mutuel Wagering
Licensing Section
725 S. Bronough St.
Tallahassee, FL 32399-1037
Phone: (904)488-9161

Credential Type: License Registration Code 1005. **Authorization:** Authorizes work in the following positions: admissions manager, chief of security, concession manager or owner, general manager, mutuels manager, parking director, public relations director, plant superintendent, and track superintendent. **Requirements:** Submit application and fingerprint card. Pay fee. **Fees:** $40 registration fee.

Florida

7498

Contractual Concessionaire (Racetrack)
Florida Dept. of Business
Div. of Pari-Mutuel Wagering
Licensing Section
725 S. Bronough St.
Tallahassee, FL 32399-1037
Phone: (904)488-9161

Credential Type: License Registration Code 1025. **Requirements:** Submit application and fingerprint card. Pay fee. **Fees:** $150 registration fee.

7499

Vendor (Racetrack)
Florida Dept. of Business
Div. of Pari-Mutuel Wagering
Licensing Section
725 S. Bronough St.
Tallahassee, FL 32399-1037
Phone: (904)488-9161

Credential Type: License Registration Code 1069. **Requirements:** Submit application and fingerprint card. Pay fee. **Fees:** $10 registration fee.

7500

Vendor Representative/Salesman (Racetrack)
Florida Dept. of Business
Div. of Pari-Mutuel Wagering
Licensing Section
725 S. Bronough St.
Tallahassee, FL 32399-1037
Phone: (904)488-9161

Credential Type: License Registration Code 1070. **Requirements:** Submit application and fingerprint card. Pay fee. **Fees:** $10 registration fee.

Georgia

7501

Salvage Yard Dealer
State Board of Registration for Used Motor Vehicle Dismantlers, Rebuilders, and Salvage Dealers
Businesses and Occupations Section
Professional Examining Boards
166 Pryor St., SW
Atlanta, GA 30303
Phone: (404)656-2282

Credential Type: License. **Requirements:** Contact licensing body for application information.

7502

Used Car Dealer
State Board of Registration of Used Car Dealers
Businesses and Occupations Section
Professional Examining Boards
166 Pryor St., SW
Atlanta, GA 30303
Phone: (404)656-2282

Credential Type: Used Car Dealer License. **Duration of License:** Two years. **Requirements:** Post $20,000 surety bond and have liability insurance in the amount of $50/100/25 or single limits of $125,000. Must have a state sales tax number and fixed place of business. Must attend a seminar. **Fees:** $170 license fee. $170 renewal fee.

Hawaii

7503

Motor Vehicle Salesperson
Hawaii Motor Vehicle Industry Licensing Board
PO Box 3469
Honolulu, HI 96801
Phone: (808)548-7462

Credential Type: License. **Duration of License:** Two years. **Fees:** $20 application fee. $15 license fee. $25—$50 Compliance Resolution Fund fee. $30 renewal fee. $20 temporary license fee.

Idaho

7504

Concession Employee (Racetrack)
Idaho State Horse Racing Commission
6133 Corporal Lane
Boise, ID 83704
Phone: (208)327-7105

Credential Type: License Registration. **Requirements:** Submit application and fingerprint card. Pay fee. **Fees:** $10 registration fee.

7505

Concessionaire (Racetrack)
Idaho State Horse Racing Commission
6133 Corporal Lane
Boise, ID 83704
Phone: (208)327-7105

Credential Type: License Registration. **Requirements:** Submit application and fingerprint card. Pay fee. **Fees:** $20 registration fee.

7506

Donated Concession Employee (Racetrack)
Idaho State Horse Racing Commission
6133 Corporal Lane
Boise, ID 83704
Phone: (208)327-7105

Credential Type: License Registration. **Requirements:** Submit application and fingerprint card. Pay fee. **Fees:** $1 registration fee.

Illinois

7507

Automotive Parts Recycler
Secretary of State
Centennial Bldg., Rm. 008
Springfield, IL 62756
Phone: (217)782-7817

Credential Type: Automotive Parts Recycler License. **Duration of License:** One year. **Requirements:** Submit application and pay fees. **Reciprocity:** No. **Fees:** $50 initial license fee. $50 renewal fee. $2 identification card fee. **Governing Statute:** Illinois Vehicle Code 95.

7508

Fish Dealer (Non-Resident)
Illinois Dept. of Conservation
524 South 2nd St.
Springfield, IL 62701-1787
Phone: (217)785-3423

Credential Type: Non-Resident Fish Dealer License. **Duration of License:** One year. **Requirements:** Submit application and pay fee. **Reciprocity:** No. **Fees:** $100 initial license fee. $100 license renewal fee. **Governing Statute:** Illinois Revised Statutes, Chapter 56.

Retail Sales Workers

7509

Fish Dealer (Resident)
Illinois Dept. of Conservation
524 South 2nd St.
Springfield, IL 62701-1787
Phone: (217)785-3423

Credential Type: Resident Retail Fish Dealer. **Duration of License:** One year. **Requirements:** Must be an Illinois resident for at least 30 days. Submit application and pay fee. **Reciprocity:** No. **Fees:** $10 initial license fee. $10 license renewal fee. **Governing Statute:** Illinois Revised Statutes, Chapter 56.

Credential Type: Resident Wholesale Fish Dealer. **Duration of License:** One year. **Requirements:** Must be an Illinois resident for at least 30 days. Submit application and pay fee. **Reciprocity:** No. **Fees:** $50 initial license fee. $50 license renewal fee. **Governing Statute:** Illinois Revised Statutes, Chapter 56.

7510

Gift Shop Manager (Gaming)
Illinois Gaming Board
PO Box 19474
Springfield, IL 62794-9474
Phone: (217)524-0228

Credential Type: Gift Shop Manager License. **Duration of License:** One year. **Requirements:** At least 18 years of age. U.S. citizen. No felony convictions. High school graduate or equivalent. **Reciprocity:** No. **Fees:** $75 application/initial license fee. $50 renewal fee. **Governing Statute:** Illinois Revised Statutes, Chapter 120.

7511

Gift Shop Salesperson (Gaming)
Illinois Gaming Board
PO Box 19474
Springfield, IL 62794-9474
Phone: (217)524-0228

Credential Type: Gift Shop Salesperson License. **Duration of License:** One year. **Requirements:** At least 18 years of age. U.S. citizen. No felony convictions. High school graduate or equivalent. Retail experience preferred. **Reciprocity:** No. **Fees:** $75 application/initial license fee. $50 renewal fee. **Governing Statute:** Illinois Revised Statutes, Chapter 120.

7512

Mussel Dealer (Resident and Non-Resident)
Illinois Dept. of Conservation
524 South 2nd St.
Springfield, IL 62701-1787
Phone: (217)785-3423

Credential Type: Resident Mussel Dealer License. **Duration of License:** One year. **Requirements:** Must be an Illinois resident for a minimum of 30 days. Submit application and pay fee. **Reciprocity:** No. **Fees:** $300 initial license fee. $300 renewal fee. **Governing Statute:** Illinois Revised Statutes, Chapter 56, Illinois Conservation Law—Fish.

Credential Type: Non-Resident Mussel Dealer License. **Duration of License:** One year. **Requirements:** Submit application and pay fee. **Reciprocity:** No. **Fees:** $2,500 initial license fee. $2,500 renewal fee. **Governing Statute:** Illinois Revised Statutes, Chapter 56, Illinois Conservation Law—Fish.

7513

New Vehicle Dealer
Secretary of State
Centennial Building, Rm. 008
Springfield, IL 62756
Phone: (217)782-7817

Credential Type: Registration. **Duration of License:** One year. **Requirements:** Submit application and pay fee. **Reciprocity:** No. **Fees:** $50 initial registration fee. $50 renewal fee. **Governing Statute:** Illinois Vehicle Code 95 1/2.

7514

Used Vehicle Dealer
Secretary of State
Centennial Bldg., Rm. 008
Springfield, IL 62756
Phone: (217)782-7817

Credential Type: Used Vehicle Dealer Registration. **Duration of License:** One year. **Requirements:** Submit application and pay fee. **Reciprocity:** No. **Fees:** $50 initial license fee. $50 renewal fee. **Governing Statute:** Illinois Vehicle Code 95 1/2 5-102.

7515

Vendor (Racetrack)
Illinois Racing Board
100 W. Randolph St., Ste. 11-100
Chicago, IL 60601
Phone: (312)814-2600

Credential Type: License Registration. **Requirements:** Submit application and fingerprint card. Pay fee. **Fees:** $25 registration fee. $2 photo fee. $10 fingerprint card fee.

7516

Vendor's Helper (Racetrack)
Illinois Racing Board
100 W. Randolph St., Ste. 11-100
Chicago, IL 60601
Phone: (312)814-2600

Credential Type: License Registration. **Requirements:** Submit application and fingerprint card. Pay fee. **Fees:** $10 registration fee. $2 photo fee. $10 fingerprint card fee.

Iowa

7517

Concession Employee (Racetrack)
Iowa State Racing Commission
Lucas State Office Bldg.
Des Moines, IA 50319
Phone: (515)281-7352

Credential Type: License Registration. **Requirements:** Submit application and fingerprint card. Pay fee. **Fees:** $5 registration fee.

7518

Concession Operator (Racetrack)
Iowa State Racing Commission
Lucas State Office Bldg.
Des Moines, IA 50319
Phone: (515)281-7352

Credential Type: License Registration. **Requirements:** Submit application and fingerprint card. Pay fee. **Fees:** $20 registration fee.

Iowa

7519

Retail Salesperson (Riverboat Gambling)
Iowa Racing and Gaming Commission
Lucas State Office Bldg.
Des Moines, IA 50319
Phone: (515)281-7352

Credential Type: License Registration. **Requirements:** Submit application and pay fees. **Fees:** $10 license fee.

Kansas

7520

Concession Employee (Racetrack)
Kansas Racing Commission
3400 VanBuren
Topeka, KS 66611-2228
Phone: (913)296-5800

Credential Type: License Registration. **Requirements:** Submit application and fingerprint card. Pay fee. **Fees:** $5 registration fee.

7521

Concession Operator (Racetrack)
Kansas Racing Commission
3400 VanBuren
Topeka, KS 66611-2228
Phone: (913)296-5800

Credential Type: License Registration. **Requirements:** Submit application and fingerprint card. Pay fee. **Fees:** $10 registration fee.

Kentucky

7522

Concessions Manager/Employee (Racetrack)
Kentucky State Racing Commission
PO Box 1080
Lexington, KY 40588
Phone: (606)254-7021

Credential Type: Association Employee and Occupational License. **Requirements:** Submit application and fingerprint card. Pay fee. **Fees:** $10 license fee.

Louisiana

7523

Explosives Dealer
Office of State Police
Explosives Control Unit
PO Box 66614
Baton Rouge, LA 70809
Phone: (504)925-6178

Credential Type: License. **Duration of License:** One year. **Authorization:** License is required of a person engaged in the wholesale or retail business of buying and selling explosives. **Requirements:** Submit application and pay fee. **Fees:** $50 license fee. **Governing Statute:** R.S. 40:1471.

7524

Motor Vehicle Salesperson
Motor Vehicle Commission
Motor Vehicle Sales Finance Div.
234 Loyola Ave., Ste. 620
New Orleans, LA 70112
Phone: (504)568-5282

Credential Type: License. **Duration of License:** One year. **Requirements:** Submit application and pay fee. **Governing Statute:** R.S. 32:1251-1260. R.S. 6:951 et seq.

7525

Racetrack Vendor
Louisiana State Racing Commission
320 N. Carrollton Ave., Ste. 2-B
New Orleans, LA 70119
Phone: (504)483-4000

Credential Type: License. **Duration of License:** One year. **Requirements:** 18 years of age. Must be approved by the racing association where the applicant intends to conduct business. **Fees:** $25 license fee.

Maine

7526

Transient Seller of Merchandise (Itinerant Vendor)
Transient Sales
Dept. of Professional and Financial Regulation
State House Station 35
Augusta, ME 04333
Phone: (207)582-8723

Credential Type: Transient Seller Registration. **Duration of License:** One year. **Authorization:** Covers persons who sell merchandise to consumers by personal or telephone contact and who do not have any permanent place of business in the state. Does not apply to persons selling exclusively by mail (except contests) or persons selling at bazaars, fairs, and similar events. **Requirements:** Submit application and pay fee. Post $10,000 surety bond. **Fees:** $15 seller's registration fee. $5 employee registration fee. **Governing Statute:** 32 M.S.R.A., Chap. 69-A.

Maryland

7527

Fur Dealer
Wildlife Div.
Dept. of Natural Resources
Tawes State Office Bldg.
Annapolis, MD 21401
Phone: (410)974-3211

Credential Type: License. **Duration of License:** One year. **Requirements:** Submit application and pay fee. Must keep record book. **Fees:** $50 resident license fee. $100 non-resident license fee.

7528

Vendor (Harness Racing)
Maryland Racing Commission
Stanbalt Bldg., 14th Fl.
501 St. Paul Place
Baltimore, MD 21202
Phone: (301)333-6267

Credential Type: License Registration. **Requirements:** Submit application, fingerprint card, and three passport size photos. Pay fee. **Fees:** $5 registration fee.

7529

Vendor (Thoroughbred Racing)
Maryland Racing Commission
Stanbalt Bldg., 14th Fl.
501 St. Paul Place
Baltimore, MD 21202
Phone: (301)333-6267

Credential Type: License Registration. **Requirements:** Submit application, fingerprint card, and three passport size photos. Pay fee. **Fees:** $25 registration fee.

Massachusetts

7530

Hawker/Peddler
Div. of Standards
One Ashburton Pl.
Boston, MA 02108
Phone: (617)727-3480

Credential Type: Hawker/Peddler License. **Duration of License:** One year. **Requirements:** Submit application. Local license also required. **Fees:** $127 license fee.

7531

Transient Vendor
Div. of Standards
One Ashburton Pl.
Boston, MA 02108
Phone: (617)727-3480

Credential Type: Transient Vendor License. **Duration of License:** One year. **Authorization:** Issued for sale of goods indoors. **Requirements:** Submit application. Local license also required.

7532

Vendor (Racetrack)
Massachusetts State Racing Commission
1 Ashburton Place, Rm. 1313
Boston, MA 02108
Phone: (617)727-2581

Credential Type: License Registration. **Requirements:** Submit application and fingerprint card. Pay fee. **Fees:** $10 registration fee.

Michigan

7533

Fur Dealer
Administrative Services Div.
Dept. of Natural Resources
Stevens T. Mason Bldg.
PO Box 30028
Lansing, MI 48909
Phone: (517)373-1220

Credential Type: License. **Duration of License:** One year. **Requirements:** Abide by the laws related to the buying and selling of raw furs, hides and pelts of fur-bearing animals and the plumage, skins or hides of protected game birds and game animals. **Fees:** $10 initial license fee for a resident. $50 initial license fee for a nonresident. Renewal fee is same as initial fee. **Governing Statute:** Fur Dealer's License Act, Act 308 of 1929.

7534

Vendor (Racetrack)
Michigan Office of Racing Commissioner
37650 Professional Center Dr.
Livonia, MI 48154-1114
Phone: (313)462-2400

Credential Type: License Registration. **Requirements:** Submit application and fingerprint card. Pay fee. **Fees:** $20 registration fee. $5 duplicate license fee.

Minnesota

7535

Concession/Vendor Employee (Racetrack)
Minnesota Racing Commission
11000 W. 78th St., Ste. 201
Eden Prairie, MN 55344
Phone: (612)341-7555

Credential Type: License Registration. **Requirements:** Submit application and fingerprint card. Pay fee. **Fees:** $10 registration fee.

7536

Concessionaire/Vendor (Racetrack)
Minnesota Racing Commission
11000 W. 78th St., Ste. 201
Eden Prairie, MN 55344
Phone: (612)341-7555

Credential Type: License Registration. **Requirements:** Submit application and fingerprint card. Pay fee. **Fees:** $100 registration fee.

Missouri

7537

Concession Employee (Racetrack)
Missouri Horse Racing Commission
PO Box 754
Jefferson City, MO 65102
Phone: (314)751-3565

Credential Type: License Registration. **Requirements:** Submit application and fingerprint card. Pay fee. **Fees:** $5 registration fee. $4 duplicate registration fee.

7538

Vendor (Racetrack)
Missouri Horse Racing Commission
PO Box 754
Jefferson City, MO 65102
Phone: (314)751-3565

Credential Type: License Registration. **Requirements:** Submit application and fingerprint card. Pay fee. **Fees:** $50 registration fee. $4 duplicate registration fee.

Montana

7539

Fur or Hide Dealer
Dept. of Fish, Wildlife, and Parks
Law Enforcement Div.
1420 E. 6th Ave.
Helena, MT 59620
Phone: (406)444-2452

Credential Type: Resident License. **Requirements:** Submit application and pay fee. **Fees:** $10 license fee. **Governing Statute:** Montana Code Annotated 87-4.

Credential Type: Nonresident License. **Requirements:** Submit application and pay fee. **Fees:** $50 license fee (minimum, based on nonresident's home state fee). **Governing Statute:** Montana Code Annotated 87-4.

Credential Type: Dealer Agent License. **Requirements:** Submit application and pay fee. **Fees:** $10 license fee. **Governing Statute:** Montana Code Annotated 87-4.

7540

Tip Sheet Seller (Racetrack)
State of Montana Board of Horse Racing
Dept. of Commerce
1424 9th Ave.
Helena, MT 59620
Phone: (406)444-4287

Credential Type: License Registration. **Requirements:** Submit application and fingerprint card. Pay fee. **Fees:** $20 registration fee.

Nebraska

7541

Concessions Employee (Racetrack)
Nebraska Racing Commission
PO Box 95014
301 Centennial Mall S.
Lincoln, NE 68509
Phone: (402)471-4155

Credential Type: License Registration. **Duration of License:** One year. **Requirements:** At least 16 years of age. No felony convictions. Secure employment and submit application completed and signed by management. Pay fees. **Fees:** $10 license fee. $10 renewal fee.

7542

Hawker (Peddler)
Lincoln City Clerk's Office
550 S. 10th St.
Lincoln, NE 68508
Phone: (402)471-7437

Credential Type: License. **Duration of License:** One year. **Requirements:** 15 years of age. Felony charges and certain misdemeanors are grounds for denial. **Fees:** $110 license fee. $110 renewal fee.

7543

Motor Vehicle Dealer
Nebraska Motor Vehicle Industry Licensing Board
301 Centennial Mall S.
PO Box 94697
Lincoln, NE 68509
Phone: (402)471-2148

Credential Type: License. **Duration of License:** One year. **Requirements:** 19 years of age. Conviction of a felony may be grounds for denial of a license. **Fees:** $140 dealer application fee. $140 renewal fee.

7544

Motorcycle Dealer
Nebraska Dept. of Motor Vehicles Industry Licensing Board
301 Centennial Mall S.
PO Box 94697
Lincoln, NE 68509
Phone: (402)471-2148

Credential Type: License. **Duration of License:** One year. **Requirements:** 19 years of age. A felony conviction may be grounds for denial of a dealer's license. **Fees:** $140 dealer application fee. $140 renewal fee.

Nevada

7545

Concession Employee (Racetrack)
Nevada Racing Commission
4820 Alpine Ct., Ste. 203
Las Vegas, NV 89107
Phone: (702)486-7619

Credential Type: License Registration. **Requirements:** Submit application and fingerprint card. Pay fee. **Fees:** $10 registration fee.

New Hampshire

7546

Itinerant Vendor
Secretary of State's Office
State House, Rm. 204
Concord, NH 03301
Phone: (603)271-3242

Credential Type: Itinerant Vendor License. **Duration of License:** One year. **Requirements:** Submit application. Post a $5,000 surety bond with the Secretary of State. **Fees:** $250 license fee. $250 annual renewal fee.

New Jersey

7547

Automobile Dealer
New Jersey Div. of Motor Vehicles
Dealer Licensing Section
135 E. State St.
Trenton, NJ 08666
Phone: (609)292-4517

Credential Type: Motor Vehicle Dealer. **Requirements:** Must maintain an established place of business. No convictions for crimes involving fraud or misrepresentation in the sale or financing of a motor vehicle. 18 years of age. **Fees:** $100 license fee. **Governing Statute:** NJSA 39-10. NJAC 13:21-15.

7548

Pawnbroker
New Jersey Dept. of Banking
Consumer Credit Bureau
CN040
Trenton, NJ 08625-0040
Phone: (609)292-5466

Credential Type: License. **Duration of License:** Two years. **Requirements:** Each applicant must demonstrate that there is sufficient insurance, bond, or cash surplus coverage to operate the business. A $1,000 bond must be filed with the board. **Fees:** $600 biennial registration fee. **Governing Statute:** NJSA 45:22. NJAC 3:16.

7549

Vendor (Racetrack)
New Jersey Racing Commission
200 Woolverton St.
Trenton, NJ 08625-0088
Phone: (609)292-0613

Credential Type: License Registration. **Requirements:** At least 18 years of age or 16 years of age with working papers. U.S. citizen or valid immigration card. No drug convictions. No convictions of crimes involving moral turpitude. Submit application and fingerprint card. Pay fees. **Fees:** $29 application fee. $25 registration fee.

New Mexico

7550

Admissions Ticket Seller (Racetrack)
New Mexico State Racing Commission
PO Box 8576, Highland Station
Albuquerque, NM 87198
Phone: (505)841-4644

Credential Type: License Registration. **Requirements:** Submit application and fingerprint card. Pay fees. **Fees:** $13 registration fee. $1 notary fee. $23 fingerprint card processing fee.

7551

Concession Employee (Racetrack)
New Mexico State Racing Commission
PO Box 8576, Highland Station
Albuquerque, NM 87198
Phone: (505)841-4644

Credential Type: License Registration. **Requirements:** Submit application and fingerprint card. Pay fees. **Fees:** $14 registration fee. $1 notary fee. $23 fingerprint card processing fee.

Retail Sales Workers

7552

Concession Operator (Racetrack)
New Mexico State Racing
   Commission
PO Box 8576, Highland Station
Albuquerque, NM 87198
Phone: (505)841-4644

Credential Type: License Registration.
Requirements: Submit application and fingerprint card. Pay fees. **Fees:** $61 registration fee. $1 notary fee. $23 fingerprint card processing fee.

North Carolina

7553

Automobile Dealer
Dept. of Transportation
Dealer Section
1100 New Bern Ave.
Raleigh, NC 27697
Phone: (919)733-2281

Credential Type: Certification. **Duration of License:** One year. **Fees:** $30 certification fee. $30 renewal fee.

7554

Automobile Salesperson
Dept. of Transportation
Dealer Section
1100 New Bern Ave.
Raleigh, NC 27697
Phone: (919)733-2281

Credential Type: License. **Duration of License:** One year. **Requirements:** Must be presently employed by an automobile dealership. **Fees:** $5 license fee. $5 renewal fee.

North Dakota

7555

Gate Admission Seller (Racetrack)
North Dakota Racing Commission
State Capitol Bldg.
Bismarck, ND 58505
Phone: (701)224-2210

Credential Type: License Registration.
Requirements: Submit application and fingerprint card. Pay fee. **Fees:** $10 license fee. $10 duplicate license fee.

7556

Tip Sheet Seller (Racetrack)
North Dakota Racing Commission
State Capitol Bldg.
Bismarck, ND 58505
Phone: (701)224-2210

Credential Type: License Registration.
Requirements: Submit application and fingerprint card. Pay fee. **Fees:** $10 license fee. $10 duplicate license fee.

7557

Transient Merchant
Attorney General's Office
State Capitol Offices
600 E. Blvd. Ave.
Bismarck, ND 58505
Phone: (701)224-2210

Credential Type: License. **Duration of License:** One year. **Requirements:** Submit application and pay fee. Post required surety bond. **Fees:** $200 license fee. **Governing Statute:** North Dakota Century Code, Chap. 51-04.

Ohio

7558

Concession Employee (Thoroughbred, Standardbred, and Quarter Horse Racing)
Ohio State Racing Commission
State Office Tower
77 S. High St., 18th Fl.
Columbus, OH 43266-0416
Phone: (614)466-2757

Credential Type: License Registration.
Requirements: Submit application and fingerprint card. Pay fee. **Fees:** $10 registration fee.

7559

Concession Manager (Thoroughbred, Standardbred, and Quarter Horse Racing)
Ohio State Racing Commission
State Office Tower
77 S. High St., 18th Fl.
Columbus, OH 43266-0416
Phone: (614)466-2757

Credential Type: License Registration.
Requirements: Submit application and fingerprint card. Pay fee. **Fees:** $25 registration fee.

7560

Pawnbroker
Dept. of Commerce
Div. of Consumer Finance
77 S. High St., 23rd Fl.
Columbus, OH 43266-0511
Phone: (614)466-2221
Fax: (614)644-8292

Credential Type: License. **Requirements:** Contact licensing body for application information.

Oklahoma

7561

Concession Employee (Racetrack)
Oklahoma Horse Racing Commission
6501 N. Broadway, Ste. 180
Oklahoma City, OK 73116
Phone: (405)848-0404

Credential Type: License Registration.
Duration of License: One year. **Requirements:** Submit application and fingerprint card. Pay fee. **Fees:** $25 registration fee. $25 annual renewal.

7562

Vendor Employee (Racetrack)
Oklahoma Horse Racing Commission
6501 N. Broadway, Ste. 180
Oklahoma City, OK 73116
Phone: (405)848-0404

Credential Type: License Registration.
Duration of License: One year. **Requirements:** Submit application and fingerprint card. Pay fee. **Fees:** $25 registration fee. $25 annual renewal.

7563

Vendor (Racetrack)
Oklahoma Horse Racing Commission
6501 N. Broadway, Ste. 180
Oklahoma City, OK 73116
Phone: (405)848-0404

Credential Type: License Registration.
Duration of License: One year. **Requirements:** Submit application and fingerprint card. Pay fee. **Fees:** $50 registration fee. $50 annual renewal.

Oregon

7564

Concessions Employee (Racetrack)
Oregon Racing Commission
113 State Office Bldg.
1400 SW Fifth
Portland, OR 97201
Phone: (503)229-5820

Credential Type: License Registration. **Requirements:** Submit application and fingerprint card. Pay fee. **Fees:** $30 registration fee. $6 duplicate fee.

Pennsylvania

7565

Concession Employee (Harness Racing)
Pennsylvania State Harness Racing Commission
2301 N. Cameron St.
Harrisburg, PA 17110-9408
Phone: (717)787-5196

Credential Type: License Registration. **Duration of License:** Three years. **Requirements:** Submit application, three photos, and fingerprint card. Pay fee. **Fees:** $15 registration fee. $5 duplicate license. $33 fingerprint processing fee.

7566

Vehicle Salesperson
State Board of Vehicle Manufacturers, Dealers, and Salespersons
Bureau of Professional and Occupational Affairs
Dept. of State
Transportation and Safety Bldg., 6th Fl.
Harrisburg, PA 17120
Phone: (717)787-8503

Credential Type: Vehicle Salesperson License. **Duration of License:** Two years. **Requirements:** Must be presently employed by a currently licensed vehicle dealer. Submit application with employer recommendation. Pay fee. Renewable. **Exemptions:** Public officers who conduct the sales of vehicles in the performance of their official duties are exempt from licensure.

7567

Vendor Employee (Horse Racing)
Pennsylvania State Horse Racing Commission
2301 N. Cameron St., Rm. 306, 4th Fl.
Harrisburg, PA 17110-9408
Phone: (717)787-1942

Credential Type: License Registration. **Duration of License:** Three years. **Requirements:** Submit application, two photos, and fingerprint card. Pay fee. **Fees:** $15 registration fee. $2 duplicate license.

7568

Vendor (Horse Racing)
Pennsylvania State Horse Racing Commission
2301 N. Cameron St., Rm. 306, 4th Fl.
Harrisburg, PA 17110-9408
Phone: (717)787-1942

Credential Type: License Registration. **Duration of License:** Three years. **Requirements:** Submit application, two photos, and fingerprint card. Pay fee. **Fees:** $45 registration fee. $2 duplicate license.

Rhode Island

7569

Concessionaire Employee (Racetrack)
Rhode Island Dept. of Business Regulations
Div. of Racing & Athletics
233 Richmond St., Ste. 234
Providence, RI 02903-4234
Phone: (401)277-6541

Credential Type: License Registration. **Duration of License:** Three years. **Requirements:** Submit application and fingerprint card. Pay fee. **Fees:** $5 registration fee.

7570

Dealer (Fish)
Office of Boat Registration and Licensing
Rhode Island Dept. of Environmental Management
22 Hayes St.
Providence, RI 02908
Phone: (401)277-3576

Credential Type: Dealer License. **Duration of License:** One year. **Authorization:** Authorizes licensee to purchase fish from commercial fishers for resale to retail outlets. **Requirements:** Submit application and pay fee. **Reciprocity:** No. **Fees:** $200 finfish dealer license fee. $200 lobster dealer license fee. $200 shellfish dealer license fee. $300 multipurpose dealer license fee.

7571

Hawker/Peddler
State of Rhode Island
Office of the General Treasurer
40 Fountain St.
Providence, RI 02903
Phone: (401)277-2287

Credential Type: Hawker/Peddler License. **Duration of License:** Three months or one year. **Requirements:** At least 18 years of age. Submit application and pay appropriate fees. Municipal license may also be required. **Reciprocity:** No. **Fees:** $50 three-month state license fee. $200 one-year state license fee. $10 three-month Providence County license fee. $30 one-year Providence County license fee. $15 one-year per county fee (except Providence County).

7572

Live Bait Seller
Office of Boat Registration and Licensing
Rhode Island Dept. of Environmental Management
22 Hayes St.
Providence, RI 02908
Phone: (401)277-3576

Credential Type: Live Bait Seller License. **Duration of License:** One year. **Authorization:** Authorizes licensee to sell minnows to individuals for use as fish bait. **Requirements:** Submit application and pay fee. **Reciprocity:** No. **Fees:** $25 license fee.

7573

Lobster Seller
Office of Boat Registration and Licensing
Rhode Island Dept. of Environmental Management
22 Hayes St., Rm. 120
Providence, RI 02908
Phone: (401)277-3576

Credential Type: Lobster Seller License. **Duration of License:** One year. **Requirements:** Submit application and pay fee. **Reciprocity:** No. **Fees:** $200 license fee.

7574

Vendor Employee (Racetrack)
Rhode Island Dept. of Business Regulations
Div. of Racing & Athletics
233 Richmond St., Ste. 234
Providence, RI 02903-4234
Phone: (401)277-6541

Credential Type: License Registration. **Duration of License:** Three years. **Requirements:** Submit application and fingerprint card. Pay fee. **Fees:** $5 registration fee.

South Dakota

7575

Concession Employee (Greyhound Racing)
South Dakota Racing Commission
c/o 500 East Capitol
Pierre, SD 57501
Phone: (605)773-6050

Credential Type: License Registration. **Requirements:** Submit application and fingerprint card. Pay fee. **Fees:** $7.50 registration fee.

7576

Concession Employee (Horse Racing)
South Dakota Racing Commission
c/o 500 East Capitol
Pierre, SD 57501
Phone: (605)773-6050

Credential Type: License Registration. **Requirements:** Submit application and fingerprint card. Pay fee. **Fees:** $10 registration fee.

7577

Concession Operator (Horse Racing)
South Dakota Racing Commission
c/o 500 East Capitol
Pierre, SD 57501
Phone: (605)773-6050

Credential Type: License Registration. **Requirements:** Submit application and fingerprint card. Pay fee. **Fees:** $10 registration fee.

Tennessee

7578

Concession Employee (Racetrack)
Tennessee State Racing Commission
500 James Robertson Pky., 2nd Fl.
Nashville, TN 37243
Phone: (615)741-1952

Credential Type: License Registration. **Requirements:** Submit application and fingerprint card. Pay fee. **Fees:** $10 registration fee.

7579

Vendor Employee (Racetrack)
Tennessee State Racing Commission
500 James Robertson Pky., 2nd Fl.
Nashville, TN 37243
Phone: (615)741-1952

Credential Type: License Registration. **Requirements:** Submit application and fingerprint card. Pay fee. **Fees:** $10 registration fee.

7580

Vendor (Racetrack)
Tennessee State Racing Commission
500 James Robertson Pky., 2nd Fl.
Nashville, TN 37243
Phone: (615)741-1952

Credential Type: License Registration. **Requirements:** Submit application and fingerprint card. Pay fee. **Fees:** $50 registration fee.

Texas

7581

Concessionaire Employee (Racetrack)
Texas Racing Commission
PO Box 12080
Austin, TX 78711
Phone: (512)794-8461

Credential Type: License Registration. **Requirements:** Submit application and fingerprint card. Pay fee. **Fees:** $20 registration fee.

7582

Concessionaire (Racetrack)
Texas Racing Commission
PO Box 12080
Austin, TX 78711
Phone: (512)794-8461

Credential Type: License Registration. **Requirements:** Submit application and fingerprint card. Pay fee. **Fees:** $75 registration fee.

7583

Pawnbroker
Consumer Credit Commission
2601 N. Lamar
Austin, TX 78705
Phone: (512)479-1288

Credential Type: License. **Duration of License:** One year. **Requirements:** Net assets of at least $150,000 for each shop to be operated. **Examination:** None. **Fees:** $500 investigation fee. $100 license fee. $100 renewal fee. **Governing Statute:** VACS 5069-51.03, seven TAC 85.1.

7584

Vendor Employee (Racetrack)
Texas Racing Commission
PO Box 12080
Austin, TX 78711
Phone: (512)794-8461

Credential Type: License Registration. **Requirements:** Submit application and fingerprint card. Pay fee. **Fees:** $20 registration fee.

7585

Vendor (Racetrack)
Texas Racing Commission
PO Box 12080
Austin, TX 78711
Phone: (512)794-8461

Credential Type: License Registration. **Requirements:** Submit application and fingerprint card. Pay fee. **Fees:** $75 registration fee.

Utah

7586

Fur Dealer
Natural Resources Dept.
Div. of Wildlife Resources
1596 W. North Temple
Salt Lake City, UT 84116
Phone: (801)533-9333

Credential Type: Registration. **Requirements:** Contact licensing body for application information.

7587

Motor Vehicle Dealer
Utah State Tax Commission
Motor Vehicle Enforcement Div.
3400 W. 2100 S.
Salt Lake City, UT 84119
Phone: (801)977-9080

Credential Type: New Motor Vehicle Dealer's License. **Requirements:** Must furnish a letter verifying franchise from the manufacturer or authorized dealer. Post $20,000 surety bond. **Fees:** $80 new motor vehicle dealer's license fee.

Credential Type: Used Motor Vehicle Dealer's License. **Requirements:** Submit application and pay fee. Post $20,000 surety bond. **Fees:** $70 used motor vehicle dealer's license fee.

Credential Type: New Motorcycle or Motor Scooter Dealer's License. **Requirements:** Must furnish a letter verifying franchise from the manufacturer or authorized dealer. Post $1,000 surety bond. **Fees:** $30 new motorcycle or scooter dealer's license fee.

Credential Type: Used Motorcycle or Motor Scooter Dealer's License. **Requirements:** Submit application and pay fee. Post $1,000 surety bond. **Fees:** $40 used motorcycle or scooter dealer's license fee.

7588

Motor Vehicle Salesperson
Motor Vehicle Enforcement Div.
3400 W. 2100 S.
Salt Lake City, UT
Phone: (801)977-9080

Credential Type: Motor Vehicle Salesperson License. **Requirements:** Submit application and pay fee. **Fees:** $30 motor vehicle salesman license fee.

Vermont

7589

Concession Employee (Greyhound Racing)
Vermont Racing Commission
State Office Bldg.
Montpelier, VT 05602
Phone: (802)828-3429

Credential Type: License Registration. **Requirements:** Submit application and fingerprint card. Pay fee. **Fees:** $5 registration fee. $5 duplicate license.

7590

Concession Employee (Racetrack)
Vermont Racing Commission
State Office Bldg.
Montpelier, VT 05602
Phone: (802)828-3429

Credential Type: License Registration. **Requirements:** Submit application and fingerprint card. Pay fee. **Fees:** $2 registration fee. $2 duplicate license.

7591

Peddler
Secretary of State Licensing and Registration
Pavilion Office Bldg.
Montpelier, VT 05602
Phone: (802)828-2363

Credential Type: License. **Requirements:** Make application to Secretary of State. Obtain local licensing. **Examination:** No. **Reciprocity:** No. **Fees:** $15 Travelling by foot. $30 If transporting by beast of burden or public conveyance. $50 Transporting goods by motor vehicle. $100 Transporting by motor vehicle over one and one-half tons. Note: All fees are half price from July 31 to December 31. **Governing Statute:** Title 32, VSA Sections 9101,9115.

7592

Vendor, Itinerant
Secretary of State
Licensing and Registration
Pavilion Office Bldg.
Montpelier, VT 05602
Phone: (802)828-2363

Credential Type: License. **Requirements:** Make application to Secretary of State. Obtain license from local town clerks. **Examination:** No. **Reciprocity:** No. **Fees:** $25 License. $500 Cash surety bond. **Governing Statute:** Title 26, VSA Sections 9101-9115.

7593

Vendor (Racetrack)
Vermont Racing Commission
State Office Bldg.
Montpelier, VT 05602
Phone: (802)828-3429

Credential Type: License Registration. **Requirements:** Submit application and fingerprint card. Pay fee. **Fees:** $2 registration fee. $2 duplicate license.

Virginia

7594

Concessionaire/Vendor Employee (Racetrack)
Virginia Racing Commission
PO Box 1123
Richmond, VA 23208
Phone: (804)371-7363

Credential Type: License Registration. **Requirements:** Submit application and fingerprint card. Pay fee. **Fees:** $5 registration fee.

7595

Concessionaire/Vendor (Racetrack)
Virginia Racing Commission
PO Box 1123
Richmond, VA 23208
Phone: (804)371-7363

Credential Type: License Registration. **Requirements:** Submit application and fingerprint card. Pay fee. **Fees:** $25 registration fee.

Wisconsin

7596

Concession Employee (Racetrack)
Wisconsin Racing Board
PO Box 7975
Madison, WI 53707-7975
Phone: (608)267-3291

Credential Type: License Registration. **Requirements:** Submit application and two sets of fingerprint cards. Pay fee. **Fees:** $20 registration fee. $20 duplicate license.

Retail Sales Workers

7597

Concession Owner (Racetrack)
Wisconsin Racing Board
PO Box 7975
Madison, WI 53707-7975
Phone: (608)267-3291

Credential Type: License Registration.
Requirements: Submit application and two sets of fingerprint cards. Pay fee. **Fees:** $100 registration fee. $20 duplicate license.

Wyoming

7598

Concession Employee (Racetrack)
Wyoming State Pari-Mutuel Commission
Barrett Bldg., 3rd Fl.
Cheyenne, WY 82002
Phone: (307)777-5887

Credential Type: License Registration.
Requirements: Submit application and fingerprint card. Pay fee. **Fees:** $10 registration fee. $10 duplicate license.

7599

Concession Operator (Racetrack)
Wyoming State Pari-Mutuel Commission
Barrett Bldg., 3rd Fl.
Cheyenne, WY 82002
Phone: (307)777-5887

Credential Type: License Registration.
Requirements: Submit application and fingerprint card. Pay fee. **Fees:** $20 registration fee. $10 duplicate license.

Science Technicians

The following states grant licenses in this occupational category as of the date of publication:
Georgia, Kentucky, Montana, New York, North Dakota, South Carolina, Texas, Utah, Washington.

Georgia

7600

Wastewater Laboratory Analyst
State Board of Water and
 Wastewater Treatment Plant
 Operators and Laboratory Analysts
Health and Consumer Services
 Section
Professional Examining Boards
166 Pryor St., SW
Atlanta, GA 30303
Phone: (404)656-3933

Credential Type: Wastewater Laboratory Analyst Certificate. **Duration of License:** Two years. **Requirements:** Meet one of the following sets of experience and education requirements: (1) Have a high school diploma or GED certificate and six months of experience; or (2) Have an accredited B.S. degree or higher in biology, chemistry, engineering, or an equivalent degree, or a current Class I Certificate in another category, and six months of experience.

Complete 27 hours of basic laboratory coursework or have an Associate degree or higher in biology, environmental science, chemistry, or an equivalent degree. Coursework may be part of a post-secondary degree program.

Renewal requires 12 hours of continuing education. **Examination:** Wastewater Laboratory Analyst Examination (written). **Fees:** $50 exam fee. **Governing Statute:** Rules of the State Board of Water and Wastewater Treatment Plant Operators and Laboratory Analysts, Chap. 750.

7601

Water Laboratory Analyst
State Board of Water and
 Wastewater Treatment Plant
 Operators and Laboratory Analysts
Health and Consumer Services
 Section
Professional Examining Boards
166 Pryor St., SW
Atlanta, GA 30303
Phone: (404)656-3933

Credential Type: Water Laboratory Analyst Certificate. **Duration of License:** Two years. **Requirements:** Meet one of the following sets of experience and education requirements: (1) Have a high school diploma or GED certificate and six months of experience; or (2) Have an accredited B.S. degree or higher in biology, chemistry, engineering, or an equivalent degree, or a current Class I Certificate in another category, and six months of experience.

Complete 27 hours of basic laboratory coursework or have an Associate degree or higher in biology, environmental science, chemistry, or an equivalent degree. Coursework may be part of a post-secondary degree program.

Renewal requires 12 hours of continuing education. **Examination:** Water Laboratory Analyst Examination (written). **Fees:** $50 exam fee. **Governing Statute:** Rules of the State Board of Water and Wastewater Treatment Plant Operators and Laboratory Analysts, Chap. 750.

Kentucky

7602

Testing Laboratory Employee (Racetrack)
Kentucky State Racing Commission
PO Box 1080
Lexington, KY 40588
Phone: (606)254-7021

Credential Type: License Registration. **Requirements:** Submit application and fingerprint card. Pay fee. **Fees:** $35 registration fee.

Montana

7603

Weather Modifier
Dept. of Natural Resources and
 Conservation
Water Resources Div.
1520 E. 6th Ave.
Helena, MT 59620
Phone: (406)444-6601

Credential Type: Weather Modification License. **Authorization:** License required for any person desiring to engage in weather modification activities. In addition, a weather modification permit is required before any activity may proceed. **Requirements:** Contact licensing body for application information. **Fees:** $100 license fee. Additional permit fee based on cost of weather modification operation. **Governing Statute:** Montana Code Annotated 85-3.

Science Technicians

New York

7604

Laboratory Technician, Milk
Dept. of Agriculture and Markets
Div. of Milk Control
One Winners Circle
Albany, NY 12235
Phone: (518)457-1772

Credential Type: License. **Duration of License:** Five years. **Examination:** Written and practical. **Fees:** $5 application fee. $2 renewal fee. **Governing Statute:** Article four Section 56b, 57, and 57a of Agriculture and Markets Law, and Title 1, New York Consolidated Rules and Regulations, Part 6.

North Dakota

7605

Weather Modifier
Weather Modification Board
State Water Commission
900 E. Blvd.
Bismarck, ND 58505
Phone: (701)224-4940

Credential Type: License. **Duration of License:** One year. **Requirements:** Demonstrate competency to the board. **Fees:** $50 license fee. **Governing Statute:** North Dakota Century Code, Chap. 61-04.1.

Credential Type: Permit. **Duration of License:** One year. **Authorization:** A permit is required for each geographical area in which weather modification activities are to be conducted. **Requirements:** Must hold a valid weather modifier license. Furnish proof of financial responsibility. Set forth a complete operational plan. Post required bond. **Fees:** $25 application fee. **Governing Statute:** North Dakota Century Code, Chap. 61-04.1.

South Carolina

7606

Percolation Test Technician
South Carolina Board of Certification of Environmental Systems Operators
2221 Devine St., Ste. 320
Columbia, SC 29205
Phone: (803)734-9140

Credential Type: License. **Requirements:** Six months of experience in assisting and observing percolation tests under the supervision of a registered professional engineer, certified percolation test technician, or professional soil classifier. **Fees:** $48 license fee.

Texas

7607

Air Monitoring Technician
Texas Dept. of Health
Occupational Health Div.
Asbestos Licensing Section
1100 W. 49th St.
Austin, TX 78756
Phone: (512)834-6600

Credential Type: Air Monitoring Technician License. **Duration of License:** One year. **Authorization:** License required to perform air monitoring services for an asbestos abatement project or related activity in a public building. **Requirements:** Completion of an approved training course for air monitoring technicians. Renewal requires completion of annual refresher training. Pass physical examination.

An upgraded license to perform analysis of airborne fibers in the field requires completion of the National Institute of Occupational Safety & Health No. 582 training course, or equivalent, titled "Analysis of Asbestos Dust" and current accreditation by the Asbestos Analyst Registry. **Fees:** $50 license fee. **Governing Statute:** Texas Civil Statutes, Article 4477-3a. Texas Asbestos Health Protection Rules, Section 295.

7608

Solid Waste Technician
Texas Water Commission
PO Box 13087
1700 N. Congress Ave.
Austin, TX 78711-3087
Phone: (512)463-7830

Credential Type: Standard Letter of Competency (Certification). **Duration of License:** Four years. **Authorization:** The owner or operator of a municipal solid waste facility is required to employ solid waste technicians holding letters of competency. **Requirements:** Letters of competency are issued for four classes, each with two different combinations of education, experience, and training credit requirements. If applicant has not graduated from high school, then additional years of experience are required. Required training credits range from a minimum of 40 hours to a maximum of 120 hours. **Examination:** Competency examination. **Governing Statute:** $40 application fee (Class A). $30 application fee (Class B). $20 application fee (Class C or D). $20 renewal fee.

Credential Type: Provisional Letter of Competency (Certification). **Duration of License:** Four years. **Requirements:** A minimum of six months of experience is required. A provisional letter of competency may be issued for each class if either the required experience or training have not been met. Provisional letters are not renewable. Applicant is expected to complete training or experience requirements within four years. **Examination:** Competency examination.

Utah

7609

Weather Modifier (Cloud Seeder)
Natural Resources Dept.
Div. of Water Resources
1636 W. North Temple, Rm. 310
Salt Lake City, UT 84116
Phone: (801)538-7230

Credential Type: Registration. **Requirements:** Contact licensing body for application information.

Washington

7610

Scientific Collector
Dept. of Wildlife
600 N. Capitol Way, GJ-11
Olympia, WA 98504-0091
Phone: (206)753-5728

Credential Type: Scientific Collector License. **Duration of License:** Life of project. **Authorization:** Allows collection of wildlife for scientific purposes. **Requirements:** Must be a citizen representative of a museum or institution. Submit application and pay fee. **Fees:** $12 license fee.

Secondary School Teachers

The following states grant licenses in this occupational category as of the date of publication:

Alabama	District of	Iowa	Minnesota	New Mexico	Rhode Island	Washington
Alaska	Columbia	Kansas	Mississippi	New York	South Carolina	West Virginia
Arizona	Florida	Kentucky	Missouri	North Carolina	South Dakota	Wisconsin
Arkansas	Georgia	Louisiana	Montana	North Dakota	Tennessee	Wyoming
California	Hawaii	Maine	Nebraska	Ohio	Texas	
Connecticut	Idaho	Maryland	Nevada	Oklahoma	Utah	
Delaware	Illinois	Massachusetts	New Hampshire	Oregon	Vermont	
	Indiana	Michigan	New Jersey	Pennsylvania	Virginia	

Alabama

7611

Elementary or Secondary Teacher
Dept. of Education, Certification
  Analyst
PO Box F
Juneau, AK 99811-0500
Phone: (907)465-2810
Phone: (907)465-2831

Credential Type: Regular Certificate—Type A. **Duration of License:** Five years. **Requirements:** Bachelor's degree from an accredited institution. Completion of approved teacher education program, plus institutional recommendation or recommendation from certifying State Department. Completion of six semester hours within the five-year period immediately preceding the date of application.

Certificate may be renewed six months before expiration date upon application and completion of six semester hours of credit during the life of the certificate. Three of the six semester hours may be in correspondence, or by completing workshops or institutes or by travel for which nonacademic credit has been approved by the Commission of Education prior to the holding of the workshop, travel, or institute. First time renewals must complete three semester hours in Alaska studies and three semester hours in multicultural education.

Endorsements will be granted as recommended by the preparing institution and may be deleted if the individual is not under contract in the endorsed area. **Fees:** $43 fingerprint card processing fee. $125 application fee. $10 endorsement fee.

Credential Type: Temporary Certificate—Type T (For Type A). **Duration of License:** One year. **Requirements:** Meet all application requirements except the six semester hours of recency. Proof of satisfactory teaching service for at least three years. Never possessed an Alaska teacher certificate. Nonrenewable. **Fees:** $20 temporary certificate application fee.

7612

High School Teacher
State Dept. of Education,
  Certification Officer
Montgomery, AL 36130
Phone: (205)242-9977

Credential Type: Initial Teaching Certificate. **Duration of License:** Eight years. **Requirements:** Basic program of teacher education includes two components, general and professional studies, each requiring two years of study. General studies (years one and 2) consist of 60 semester hours and must include 15 hours of humanities, 12 hours of social science which includes three hours of economics, 12 hours of natural and physical science which includes mathematics, three hours of health and physical education, and 18 hours of electives. Professional studies (years three and 4) consist of 72 semester hours and must include 12 hours of foundations of professional studies which includes three hours in survey course in exceptional child education, work in at least two teaching fields totaling not less than 27 semester hours, three hours teaching reading in content areas, six hours curriculum and teaching and media, three hours evaluation of teaching and learning, nine hours internship, and electives.

Credential Type: Fifth Year Certificate. **Requirements:** Advanced professional studies program totaling 33 hours which includes 12 hours in teaching field, six hours of curriculum and teaching, 6-9 hours of foundations of professional studies which includes three hours in a general survey course in special education (if this requirement has not already been met), three hours of evaluation of teaching and learning, and three to six hours of electives.

Credential Type: Sixth Year Certificate. **Reciprocity:** Basic certificate. Advanced professional studies program totaling 33 hours which includes 12 hours in teaching field, 6-9 hours foundations of professional studies, three hours of evaluation of teaching and learning, and three to six hours of electives.

Credential Type: Seventh Year Certificate. **Requirements:** Basic certificate. Sixth year certificate. Complete planned program and achieve stated objectives by completing further studies in the field of specialization and/or related fields, foundations of professional studies, and in evaluation and educational research.

7613

Middle School Teacher
State Dept. of Education,
  Certification Officer
Montgomery, AL 36130
Phone: (205)242-9977

Credential Type: Initial Teaching Certificate. **Duration of License:** Eight years. **Requirements:** Basic program of teacher education includes two components, general and professional studies, each requiring two years of study. General studies (years one and 2) consist of 60 semester hours and must include 15 hours of humanities, 12 hours of social science which includes three hours of economics, 12 hours of natural and physical science which includes mathematics, three hours of health and physical education, and 18 hours of electives. Professional studies (years three and 4) consist of 72 semester hours and must include 12 hours of foundations of professional studies which includes three hours in survey course in exceptional child education, work in at least two teaching fields totaling not less than 27 semester hours, six hours reading, nine hours curriculum and teaching, three hours evaluation of teaching and learning, nine hours internship, and electives.

Credential Type: Fifth Year Certificate. **Requirements:** Initial Certificate. Advanced professional studies program totaling 33 hours which includes 12 hours in teaching field, six hours of curriculum and teaching, 6-9 hours of foundations of professional studies which includes three hours in a general survey course in special education (if this requirement has not already been met), three hours of evaluation of teaching and learning, and three to six hours of electives.

Credential Type: Sixth Year Certificate. **Requirements:** Fifth Year Certificate. Advanced professional studies program totaling 33 hours which includes 12 hours in teaching field, 6-9 hours foundations of professional studies, three hours of evaluation of teaching and learning, and three to six hours of electives.

Credential Type: Seventh Year Certificate. **Requirements:** Sixth year certificate. Complete planned program and achieve stated objectives by completing further studies in the field of specialization and/or related fields, foundations of professional studies, and evaluation and educational research.

7614

Special Education Teacher
State Dept. of Education,
 Certification Officer
Montgomery, AL 36130
Phone: (205)242-9977

Credential Type: Class B Special Education Professional Certificate. **Authorization:** Exceptionalities which may be endorsed are: crippled and other health impaired, including homebound; early education for the handicapped; emotionally conflicted; gifted and talented; hearing impaired; learning disabilities; mental retardation; multihandicapped/deaf-blind; speech pathology; and visually impaired **Requirements:** Bachelor's degree from an accredited institution. Completion of a program in special education approved by the Alabama State Board of Education or the National Council for Accreditation of Teacher Education or the National Association of State Directors of Teacher Education and Certification or ICP. Recommending institution must list the exceptionality for which the applicant was trained.

Credential Type: Class A Special Education Professional Certificate. **Requirements:** Eligibility for the Class B Professional Certificate. Master's degree in special education approved by the Alabama State Board of Education.

Credential Type: Class AA Special Education Professional Certificate. **Requirements:** Eligibility for a Class A Special Education Professional Certificate endorsed in the same area in which the Class AA Certificate is desired, except as otherwise noted in the standards. Completion of a sixth year program in special education as approved by the Alabama State Board of Education.

Alaska

7615

School Special Services or Support Staff Member
Dept. of Education, Certification
 Analyst
Box F
Juneau, AK 99811-0500
Phone: (907)465-2810
Phone: (907)465-2831

Credential Type: Special Services Certificate—Type C. **Duration of License:** Five years. **Requirements:** Completion of a program through the bachelor's or higher degree with specialization in a supportive area which can be utilized by a school district. Verification from the college that the applicant has completed a program in specific specialization or recommendation from certifying State Department.

Certificate may be renewed six months before expiration date upon application and completion of six semester hours of credit during the life of the certificate. Three of the six semester hours may be in correspondence, or by completing workshops or institutes or by travel for which non-academic credit has been approved by the Commission of Education prior to the holding of the workshop, travel, or institute. First time renewals must complete three semester hours in Alaska studies and three semester hours in multicultural education or crosscultural communications.

Endorsements will be granted as recommended by the preparing institution and may be deleted if the individual is not under contract in the endorsed area. **Fees:** $43 fingerprint card processing fee. $125 application fee. $10 endorsement fee.

Credential Type: Temporary Certificate—Type T (For Type C). **Duration of License:** One year. **Requirements:** Meet all application requirements except the six semester hours of recency. Proof of satisfactory teaching service for at least three years. Never possessed an Alaska teacher certificate. Nonrenewable. **Fees:** $20 temporary certificate application fee.

Arizona

7616

Secondary Teacher (7-12)
Teacher Certification Unit
PO Box 25609
1535 W. Jefferson
Phoenix, AZ 85002
Phone: (602)542-4368

Credential Type: Temporary Secondary Certificate. **Duration of License:** Eight years (nonrenewable). **Requirements:** Bachelor's degree from a regionally accredited institution. Completion of a professional teacher education program in Secondary Education to include student teaching within grades 7-12 or bachelor's degree from a regionally accredited institution and a general studies program which includes 30 semester hours of Secondary Professional Education including courses which teach the following teacher education skills: classroom management; curriculum and instruction; assessment and evaluation; growing and learning theories; educational foundations; and organization and administration; plus eight semester hours of student teaching in grades 7-12 or two years full-time teaching experience at that level. Pass Arizona Teacher Proficiency Exam (ATPE) exam. Thirty semester hour major in a subject taught in Arizona high schools.

Requirements to be satisfied prior to or during initial year of certification include a college level course or examination on the Arizona Constitution, a college level course or examination on the U.S. Constitution, one reading decoding skills course, and a reading practicum which includes decoding skills. **Examination:** Arizona Teacher Proficiency Exam.

Credential Type: Standard Secondary Certificate. **Duration of License:** Six years. **Requirements:** Qualify for the Temporary Secondary Certificate. Master's degree from a regionally accredited institution or 40 semester hours of upper division or graduate course work from a regionally accredited institution (10 hours may be State Board approved district in-service credit).

Credential Type: Special Subject Endorsements (Art, Music, Physical Education, and Industrial Arts). **Requirements:** Arizona Elementary or Secondary Teaching Certificate. Methods of teaching special

Arizona 7617

Secondary Teacher (7-12), continued

subject area. 40 semester hours in special subject area.

7617

Special Education Teacher (K-12)
Teacher Certification Unit
PO Box 25609
1535 W. Jefferson
Phoenix, AZ 85002
Phone: (602)542-4368

Credential Type: Temporary Special Education Certificate. **Duration of License:** Eight years (nonrenewable). **Authorization:** Issued in the areas of learning disabled, seriously emotionally handicapped, physically handicapped, and mentally handicapped. **Requirements:** Bachelor's degree from a regionally accredited institution. Completion of a professional teacher education program in Special Education to include student teaching in the specific area of exceptionality in grades K-12 or bachelor's degree from a regionally accredited institution and 45 semester hours of upper division or graduate educational course work which includes 21 semester hours of Special Education course work as prescribed and professional education course work that includes methods of teaching Arithmetic and Reading and at least two of the following: Language Arts; Social Studies; Science. Six semester hours in mathematics content. Pass Arizona Teacher Proficiency Exam (ATPE) exam.

Requirements to be satisfied prior to or during initial year of certification include a college level course or examination on the Arizona Constitution, a college level course or examination on the U.S. Constitution, one reading decoding skills course, and a reading practicum which includes decoding skills. **Examination:** Arizona Teacher Proficiency Examination.

Credential Type: Standard Special Education Certificate. **Duration of License:** Six years. **Requirements:** Qualify for the Temporary Special Education Certificate. Master's degree from a regionally accredited institution or 40 semester hours of upper division or graduate course work from a regionally accredited institution (10 semester hours may be State Board approved district in-service credit.)

Arkansas

7618

Art Teacher (K-12)
Teacher Education and Licensure
State Dept. of Education
4 State Capitol Mall
Little Rock, AR 72201-1071
Phone: (501)682-4342

Credential Type: Art Specialist Certificate. **Duration of License:** Six years. **Requirements:** Initial Certification which includes a bachelor's degree from an approved institution and includes courses in language, mathematics, sciences, history, philosophy, literature, the arts, and health and wellness education. Completion of a degree major in a teaching field. Proficiency in oral and written communication and mathematics, with at least a grade of "C" in each course. Successful completion of an approved teacher education program from an institution that includes the following: Requiring no less than a 2.5 grade point average on a 4.0 scale to enter the program; Requiring students to obtain acceptable scores on entrance tests into teacher education that assess competency in computation, reading, and writing, as well as on exit tests in professional knowledge and the academic teaching area; Two weeks of student teaching; Professional studies component should provide competencies specified by the Arkansas Department of Education; Recommendation from the institution. Also passage of the National Teacher Examination.

In addition the Art Specialist Certificate requires 18 semester hours of professional education, including study of the school, of the learning processes, and of elementary and secondary teaching which includes a methods course in reading and six semester hours of directed teaching. Plus 24 semester hours of specialization requirements. **Examination:** National Teacher Examination.

7619

Home Economics Education Teacher
Arkansas Dept. of Education
Office of Teacher Education and Licensure
State Education Bldg., Rm. 107B
Capitol Mall 4
Little Rock, AR 72201-1071
Phone: (501)682-4344

Credential Type: License. **Requirements:** Bachelors degree in Home Economics. Meet general education requirements for a secondary teaching certificate. Have a minimum of six semester hours in related art and 32 semester hours in Technical Home Economics. Completed the following classes ; Child Development with Nursery School Observation and Participation, Methods of Teaching Home Economics, Directed Teaching in Home Economics. **Examination:** Yes. **Fees:** $30 National Teacher Examination (NTE) Professional Knowledge Core Battery Test. $45 NTE Specialty Area Test. $45 NTE Specialty Area Test renewal.

7620

Middle School Teacher
Teacher Education and Licensure
State Dept. of Education
4 State Capitol Mall
Little Rock, AR 72201-1071
Phone: (501)682-4342

Credential Type: Middle School Certificate. **Authorization:** Middle School Certificates are available in the following areas: agriculture; business; English; French; Spanish; physical education; home economics; industrial arts; math; science; social studies. **Requirements:** Must hold a high school or elementary teaching certificate based on a bachelor's degree. A teacher teaching in a departmental situation shall meet one of the following requirements: Hold a secondary teaching certificate and have 18 semester hours in the field in which he/she is teaching. Plus three semester hours in human growth and development of children below adolescent age and three semester hours of elementary or middle school teaching methods ; Or hold an elementary teaching certificate and have 18 semester hours in the field in which he/she is teaching.

7621

Music Teacher (K-12)
Teacher Education and Licensure
State Dept. of Education
4 State Capitol Mall
Little Rock, AR 72201-1071
Phone: (501)682-4342

Credential Type: Music Specialist Certificate. **Duration of License:** Six years. **Requirements:** Initial Certification which includes a bachelor's degree from an approved institution and includes courses in language, mathematics, sciences, history, philosophy, literature, the arts, and health and wellness education. Completion of a degree major in a teaching field. Proficiency in oral and written communication and mathematics, with at least a grade of "C" in each course. Successful completion of an approved teacher education program from an institution that includes the following: Requiring no less than a 2.5 grade point average on a 4.0 scale to enter the program; Requiring students to obtain acceptable scores on entrance tests into teacher education that assess competency in computation, reading, and writing, as well as on exit tests in professional knowledge and the academic teaching area; Two weeks of student teaching; Professional studies component should provide competencies specified by the Arkansas Department of Education; Recommendation from the institution. Also passage of the National Teacher Examination.

In addition the Music Specialist Certificate requires 18 semester hours of professional education, including study of the school, of the learning processes, and of elementary and secondary teaching which includes a methods course in reading and six semester hours of directed teaching. Plus 24 semester hours of specialization requirements. **Examination:** National Teacher Examination.

7622

Physical Education Teacher (K-12)
Teacher Education and Licensure
State Dept. of Education
4 State Capitol Mall
Little Rock, AR 72201-1071
Phone: (501)682-4342

Credential Type: Physical Education Specialist. **Requirements:** Initial Certification which includes a bachelor's degree from an approved institution and includes courses in language, mathematics, sciences, history, philosophy, literature, the arts, and health and wellness education. Completion of a degree major in a teaching field. Proficiency in oral and written communication and mathematics, with at least a grade of "C" in each course. Successful completion of an approved teacher education program from an institution that includes the following: Requiring no less than a 2.5 grade point average on a 4.0 scale to enter the program; Requiring students to obtain acceptable scores on entrance tests into teacher education that assess competency in computation, reading, and writing, as well as on exit tests in professional knowledge and the academic teaching area; Two weeks of student teaching; Professional studies component should provide competencies specified by the Arkansas Department of Education; Recommendation from the institution. Also passage of the National Teacher Examination.

To qualify for P.E. Specialist an additional 32 semester hours of course work is required. Must also meet one of the following field experiences: three semester hours of the student teaching requirement must be completed at the elementary or middle school level, below 9th grade, where the cooperating teacher is certified in Elementary Physical Education; or must complete a three semester hour internship under the direct supervision from the staff of the physical education department of a college or university. Must also acquire a coaching endorsement by completing three semester hours of coaching theory. **Examination:** National Teacher Examination.

7623

Reading Specialist (K-12)
Teacher Education and Licensure
State Dept. of Education
4 State Capitol Mall
Little Rock, AR 72201-1071
Phone: (501)682-4342

Credential Type: Reading Specialist Certificate. **Duration of License:** 10 years. **Requirements:** Initial Certification which includes a bachelor's degree from an approved institution and includes courses in language, mathematics, sciences, history, philosophy, literature, the arts, and health and wellness education. Completion of a degree major in a teaching field. Proficiency in oral and written communication and mathematics, with at least a grade of "C" in each course. Successful completion of an approved teacher education program from an institution that includes the following: Requiring no less than a 2.5 grade point average on a 4.0 scale to enter the program; Requiring students to obtain acceptable scores on entrance tests into teacher education that assess competency in computation, reading, and writing, as well as on exit tests in professional knowledge and the academic teaching area; Two weeks of student teaching; Professional studies component should provide competencies specified by the Arkansas Department of Education; Recommendation from the institution. Also passage of the National Teacher Examination.

To qualify for a Reading Specialist Certificate requires an additional 18 semester hours of professional education, including study of the school, of the learning processes, and of elementary and secondary teaching which includes a methods course in reading and six semester hours of directed teaching. Plus 12 semester hours of specialization requirements. **Examination:** National Teacher Examination.

7624

Secondary School Teacher
Teacher Education and Licensure
State Dept. of Education
4 State Capitol Mall
Little Rock, AR 72201-1071
Phone: (501)682-4342

Credential Type: Secondary Teacher Certificate. **Requirements:** Initial Certification which includes a bachelor's degree from an approved institution and includes courses in language, mathematics, sciences, history, philosophy, literature, the arts, and health and wellness education. Completion of a degree major in a teaching field. Proficiency in oral and written communication and mathematics, with at least a grade of "C" in each course. Successful completion of an approved teacher education program from an institution that includes the following: Requiring no less than a 2.5 grade point average on a 4.0 scale to enter the program; Requiring students to obtain acceptable scores on entrance tests into teacher education that assess competency in computation, reading, and writing, as well as on exit tests in professional knowledge and the academic teaching area; Two weeks of student teaching; Professional studies component should provide competencies specified by the Arkansas Department of Education; Recommendation from the institution. Also passage of the National Teacher Examination.

In addition to qualify for a Secondary Teacher Certificate and meet the Professional Requirements the candidate must have 18 semester hours including the study of the school, of the learning processes, and of teaching, plus six semester hours of direct teaching. **Examination:** National Teacher Examination.

Credential Type: Secondary Teacher Specialist Certificate. **Requirements:** Secondary Teacher Certificate. The following is a list of semester hour requirements by teaching field: Business education 26; Driver education 6; English 24; Foreign language 24; Health education 23; Journalism 24; Mathematics 21 (to include three hours calculus); Basic mathematics 18; Physical education 26; Coach (by endorsement) 11; Reading (by endorsement) 9; General science 24; Biological science 24; Physical science 24; Chemistry 24; Physics 24; Speech 24; Social studies 36, plus at least six semester hours in the subject he/she is assigned to teach; U.S. history 12; World history 6; Political science 6; Geography 6; Economics 3; Sociology 3; Psychology 3; Anthropology 3.

Arkansas

7625

Special Education Teacher
Teacher Education and Licensure
State Dept. of Education
4 State Capitol Mall
Little Rock, AR 72201-1071
Phone: (501)682-4342

Credential Type: Special Education Certificate. **Authorization:** Certificates may be issued in the following areas: Mildly handicapped K-12; Moderately/Profoundly handicapped K-12; Severely emotionally disturbed K-12. **Requirements:** The certificate should encompass present general education requirements as stipulated in "Arkansas Laws and Regulations for Certification of Teachers, Administrators, and Supervisors, Bulletin VII". All candidates must receive 15 hours of training in the following areas: Child and adolescent development, six hours; Principles of learning, three hours; Application of behavior management principles, three hours; Study of the school three hours For each of the certifiable areas, students must take a minimum of 24 semester hours in addition to the 15 basic core hours Students in preservice programs will complete appropriate field and teaching experience at both elementary and secondary levels.

California

7626

General Teacher
Teacher Certification
State Dept. of Education
201 E. Colifax
Denver, CO 80203
Phone: (303)866-6628

Credential Type: General Teacher Certificate—Type A. **Duration of License:** Five years. **Requirements:** Initial teacher certification which requires the following: Bachelor's degree. Completion of an approved program of teacher preparation from a four year, regionally accredited, degree granting institution which must include student teaching. Six semester hours of credit applicable to the certificate being sought, and/or general education, and/or child abuse, taken within the past five years from date of application. Course work in the exceptional child, covering the full range of exceptionalities, gifted through handicapped, and course work in the theory, methods, and related practice of the teaching of reading. Passage of the spelling, language, and mathematics sections of Level 19 of the California Achievement Test and oral English competence which is met by having a B—or better in a public speaking course taken from a regionally accredited college or passing an oral English panel assessment. Completed and signed appropriate application. Institutional recommendation from the school(s) where the teacher preparation work was completed. Official, original transcripts from all applicable institutions.

In addition the General Teacher Certificate requires Institutional recommendation to verify satisfactory completion of teacher preparation including: student teaching; completion of grade levels, subject areas, or service specialization; passing competency examination, meeting the Recent Credit Requirement (having earned six semester or nine quarter hours within the five years prior to the date of application for the certificate) or Renewal Credit Requirement. **Examination:** California Achievement Test Level 19 (spelling, language, and mathematics sections) **Fees:** $45 initial certification application fee. $40 fingerprint card processing fee.

Credential Type: Professional Teacher Certificate—Type B. **Duration of License:** Five years. **Requirements:** Applicants must have a master's or higher degree from a regionally accredited institution of higher education, meet all of the requirements of a Type A certificate, and have three years fulltime teaching experience. Renewable every five years with completion of the Renewal Credit Requirements. **Fees:** $45 initial certification application fee. $40 fingerprint card processing fee.

7627

Secondary School Teacher
Commission on Teacher
  Credentialing
PO Box 944270
Sacramento, CA 94244-7000
Phone: (916)445-7524

Credential Type: Single Subject Instruction Five Year Preliminary Credential. **Duration of License:** Five years (nonrenewable). **Authorization:** Most commonly required for secondary school teachers, however he/she may also be assigned to teach any subject in his or her authorized fields, in any grade level including preschool, grades K-12, and/or adult education. **Requirements:** Pass the CBEST examination. Verification of teaching or administrative experience. Official report of any examination scores. Bachelor's or higher degree except in education (unless the education degree was completed outside of California). Teacher preparation program, including student teaching completed with a grade of B or higher on a five point scale. U.S. Constitution course or examination. Subject matter confidence verified by California institution or by examination. Completion of a course in the methods of teaching reading or passage (with a score of 680) of the National Teacher Examination (NTE) "Introductions to Teaching of Reading" test. Verification of English writing proficiency through tests or written institutional recommendations. **Examination:** California Basic Education Skills Test **Fees:** $60 application fee. $30 test score recording and evaluation fee, except for CBEST.

Credential Type: One Year Preliminary Single Subject Credential. **Duration of License:** One year (nonrenewable). **Authorization:** Available only to candidates prepared outside of California. **Requirements:** Pass the CBEST examination. Bachelor's or higher degree except in education (unless the education degree was completed outside of California). Teacher preparation program, including student teaching completed with a grade of B or higher on a five point scale. Verification of teaching or administrative experience. Official report of any examination scores. **Examination:** California Basic Education Skills Test **Fees:** $60 application fee. $30 test score recording and evaluation fee, except for CBEST.

Credential Type: Single Subject Instruction Five Year Professional Clear Credential. **Duration of License:** Five years. **Requirements:** Five Year Preliminary Credential. Fifth year of study beyond bachelor's degree. Health education, including drug and alcohol abuse, and nutrition. Special education with concentration on mainstreaming. Computer education. Recommendation of a California college or university with an approved multiple or single subject program (unless program and fifth year is completed outside of California). Renewal requirements include planned professional growth activities of at least 150 clock hours and one-half of one year of teaching experience. **Fees:** $60 application fee. $30 test score recording and evaluation fee, except for CBEST.

Credential Type: Five Year Clear Specialist Instructional Credential. **Duration of License:** Five years. **Authorization:** Authorizes the holder to teach in the area of specialization in preschool, grades K-12, or adult classes and includes such subjects as agriculture, bilingual, cross-cultural education, health science, mathematics, and reading. **Requirements:** Valid California teaching credential which requires a bachelor's degree and a professional preparation program including student teaching. Fifth year of study beyond the bachelor's degree. Professional preparation in the specialist area. Recommendation of a California college or university with the specific approved specialist program. Out-of-state applicants who meet requirements may still be certified. Their student teaching or field work must have been completed with a grade of B on a five point scale. **Fees:** $60 application fee. $30 test score recording and evaluation fee, except for CBEST.

Credential Type: One Year Preliminary Credential for Designated Subjects. **Duration of License:** One year. **Authorization:** Authorizes the holder to teach the subject or trade designated on the credential in preschool, grades K-12, or adult classes including such areas as trade, technical, and vocational courses. **Requirements:** Valid California teaching credential which requires a bachelor's degree and a professional preparation program including student teaching. Adequate, successful, recent experience in the technical skills or subjects named on the credential, equal to five years experience. An approved program of inservice training, plus appropriate teaching experience. Course or examination covering the provisions and principals of the U.S. Constitution for full-time credentials. CBEST for adult academic subjects and special subjects driver education. Recommendation from an approved Local Educational Agency or employing California school district. **Examination:** California Basic Education Skills Test **Fees:** $60 application fee. $30 test score recording and evaluation fee, except for CBEST.

Connecticut

7628

Secondary School Teacher (7-12)
State Dept. of Education
Teacher Certification, Chief
165 Capitol Ave.
PO Box 2219
Hartford, CT 06145
Phone: (203)566-4561

Credential Type: Initial Certificate. **Requirements:** Bachelor's degree. 45 semester hours of general education which includes at least three of the following areas, in addition to the area of major specialization: English (6 hours minimum); Science; Mathematics; Social Studies, including U.S. History (6 hr. minimum); Fine Arts; and Foreign Languages. 18 semester hours of professional education which include: Foundations of Education ; Educational Psychology; Curriculum and Methods of Teaching (must include three hours of Developmental Reading and three hours in English); Guidance; and Health and Safety. 6-12 semester hours of full-time student teaching in a secondary school or one successful year of teaching at the secondary level. Some requirements are scheduled to change effective July 1, 1993.

Credential Type: Provisional Certificate. **Requirements:** Initial Certificate. Completion of beginning educator support and assessment program, as may be available from the Connecticut Board, and one school year of successful service under the interim or initial certificates or three years of successful teaching in the area for which the certificate is being sought, in a approved school, within 10 years prior to application.

Credential Type: Professional Certificate. **Requirements:** Three years of successful teaching under the Provisional Educator Certificate. 30 semester hours of course work beyond the bachelor's degree which includes a planned program at an institution of higher learning related directly to the subject(s) being taught or an individual program designed to increase the ability of the teacher to improve student learning.

Credential Type: Subject Endorsements. **Authorization:** Authorizes the holder to teach in one or more areas of specialization. **Requirements:** Pass test scores on the appropriate National Teacher Examination. Complete 18-30 semester hours of course work (subject to area of study), beyond the bachelor's degree, in the area of specialization. Requirements are scheduled to change July 1, 1993. **Examination:** National Teacher Examination.

7629

Special Subjects Teacher
State Dept. of Education
Teacher Certification, Chief
165 Capitol Ave.
PO Box 2219
Hartford, CT 06145
Phone: (203)566-4561

Credential Type: Special Subjects Initial Certificate. **Authorization:** This certificate authorizes the holder to specialize in teaching in the areas of agriculture, art, health, home economics, technology education, music, or physical education. **Requirements:** Bachelor's degree. 45 semester hours of general education which includes at least three of the following areas, in addition to the area of major specialization: English (6 hours minimum); Science; Mathematics; Social Studies, including U.S. History (6 hr. minimum); Fine Arts; and Foreign Languages. 18 semester hours of professional education which include: Foundations of Education; Educational Psychology; Curriculum and Methods of Teaching (must include three hours of Developmental Reading and three hours in English); Guidance; and Health and Safety. 6-12 semester hours of full-time student teaching in a secondary school or one successful year of teaching at the secondary level. 35 semester hours of appropriate technical courses in the special subject.

Credential Type: Provisional Special Subjects Certificate. **Requirements:** Special Subjects Initial Certificate. Completion of beginning educator support and assessment program, as may be available from the Connecticut Board, and one school year of successful service under the interim or initial certificates or three years of successful teaching in the area for which the certificate is being sought, in an approved school, within 10 years prior to application.

Credential Type: Professional Special Subjects Certificate. **Requirements:** Three years of successful teaching under the Provisional Special Subjects Certificate. 30 semester hours of course work beyond the bachelor's degree which includes a planned program at an institution of higher learning related directly to the subject(s) being taught or an individual program designed to increase the ability of the teacher to improve student learning.

Delaware

7630

Secondary School Teacher
Teacher Certification
Dept. of Public Instruction
Box 1402
Dover, DE 19903
Phone: (302)739-4688

Credential Type: Secondary School Certificate. **Authorization:** Allows teaching in grades 7-12 in the area of endorsement. **Requirements:** Bachelor's degree from an accredited college in general education. Completion of a teacher education program in the area of endorsement or 15 semester hours of professional education to include human behavior, methods and materials, and student teaching plus 30-45 hours of course work (as specified) in the area of endorsement. The following teaching fields may be endorsed after completing the specified number of semester hours: Drama 30; Art 36; English 36; Foreign Language 30; Second Foreign Language 24; Health Education 30; Home Economics 30; Mathematics 30; Music 36; Chemistry 42; Physics 45; Biology 39; Earth Science 39; General Science 36; Physical Science 42; Physical Education 40; and Social Studies 36. Must successfully complete the Educational Testing Service Pre-Professional Skills Tests with the following minimum scores: Reading 175; Writing 172; Mathematics 175. **Examination:** Educational Testing Service Pre-Professional Skills Tests.

7631

Teacher of Exceptional Children
Teacher Certification
Dept. of Public Instruction
Box 1402
Dover, DE 19903
Phone: (302)739-4688

Credential Type: Initial Standard Certificate. **Authorization:** Under this certificate endorsements will be granted in the following areas: Mentally Retarded; Socially and Emotionally Maladjusted; Learning Disabled; Physically Handicapped; Visually Impaired; Hearing Impaired; or Gifted. **Requirements:** Bachelor's degree in special education. Institutional recommendation. A total of 39 semester hours of course work which includes the following three semester hr. courses: Methods of Teaching Reading; Methods of Teaching Mathematics; Educational Psychology; Child Growth and Development; Behavior Problems and/or Modification Management; Survey/Introduction to the Education of Exceptional Children; Review Theories of Exceptional Children; Methods and Curriculum for Exceptional Children; and Identification, Diagnosis, and Assessment of Exceptional Children. Must also have six semester hours of student teaching in the area of endorsement. Must successfully complete the Educational Testing Service PreProfessional Skills Tests with the following minimum scores: Reading 175; Writing 172; Mathematics 175. **Examination:** Educational Testing Service Pre-Professional Skills Tests.

District of Columbia

7632

Secondary School Teacher (7-12)
Div. of Teacher Services
Dept. of Public Instruction
PO Box 1402
Dover, DE 19903
Phone: (302)739-4688

Credential Type: Standard Certificate. **Authorization:** Authorizes the teaching of one of the following subjects at the secondary level: Art; English; Industrial Arts; Home Economics; Physical Education; Foreign Language; Mathematics; Driver Education and Safety; or Military Science and Tactics. **Requirements:** Bachelor's degree. Satisfactory completion of a sequence of courses in preparation for teaching at the secondary level which may be part of or in addition to the degree requirements. The following general courses, or their equivalent, are required: Educational Psychology; The Exceptional Child; Classroom Management; Materials and Methods of Teaching (the area of specialization); The Teaching of Reading or Reading in the Content Area; Linguistics (Foreign Language Teachers Only). Observation and student teaching at the secondary level or one year experience teaching at the secondary level.

Applicants for teacher certification must file a completed application with the Director which includes official transcripts, verification of previous teaching experience, and an affidavit of previous non-teaching or technical experience when applicable. **Examination:** National Teacher Examination (communications skills test) **Reciprocity:** Applicants who have been employed for at least 27 months under a standard certificate, or are completing teacher training in an approved program at a U.S. college or university outside the District of Columbia, may apply for certification under the Interstate Agreement on Qualifications of Educational Personnel, providing their state has signed a reciprocity agreement. Must have a valid certificate and complete application procedures.

Credential Type: Provisional Certificate. **Duration of License:** 18 months. **Authorization:** Temporarily allows applicant to hold teaching position while satisfactorily completing license deficits and/or attainment of a passing score on the DCPS Teacher Content Knowledge Test. **Requirements:** Standard Certificate requirements, but allows for some licensing deficits.

Florida

7633

Middle School Teacher (5-9)
Bureau of Teacher Certification
Florida Education Center
325 W. Gaines, Rm. 201
Tallahassee, FL 32399
Phone: (904)488-2317

Credential Type: Professional Certificate. **Duration of License:** Five years. **Requirements:** Bachelor's degree. Satisfy the following course requirements: 18 semester hours of English, including six hours composition and grammar and six hours of literature; 12 hours of mathematics, including algebra or higher courses; 18 hours of Science, including biology, physical science, and earth science; and Social Studies, including six hours American History, a course in U.S. History, and a course in geography. Meets professional preparation requirements. Has completed at least six semester hours or two years of full-time teaching experience at level of certification during the five years preceding application. Has obtained a minimum 2.5 grade point average in each subject shown on the certificate. Has received a passing score on the College Level Academic Skills Test (CLAST). Has received a passing score on the Professional Education Subtest of the Florida Teacher Certification Examination. Has received a passing score on an approved subject area examination for each subject or field shown on the certificate. Completes a Florida Professional Orientation Program (year long internship). Completes a general preparation plan of 45 semester hours which includes six hours, but not more than 12, in each of the following areas: arts of communication; human adjustment; biological science; physical sciences, and mathematics; social science; humanities; and applied arts. (A graduate of a standard institution shall be considered to have met the general preparation requirements.) Renewal of certificate requires six hours (or 120 staff development units) every five years. **Examination:** College Level Academic Skills Test. Professional Education Subtest of the Florida Teacher Certification Examination.

7634

Secondary School Teacher (6-12)
Bureau of Teacher Certification
Florida Education Center
325 W. Gaines, Rm. 201
Tallahassee, FL 32399
Phone: (904)488-2317

Credential Type: Professional Certificate. **Authorization:** Authorizes the holder to teach one of the following subjects: English; Social Science (general); Economics; Geography; Political Science; Psychology; Sociology; Mathematics; Biology; Chemistry; Earth-Space Science; or Physics. **Requirements:** Bachelor's degree. Has an acceptable major in a single subject or meets specialization requirements in the subject. Meets professional preparation requirements. Has completed at least six semester hours or two years of full-time teaching experience at level of certification during the five years preceding application. Has obtained a minimum 2.5 grade point average in each subject shown on the certificate. Has received a passing score on the College Level Academic Skills Test (CLAST). Has received a passing score on the Professional Education Subtest of the Florida Teacher Certification Examination. Has received a passing score on an approved subject area examination for each subject or field shown on the certificate. Completes a Florida Professional Orientation Program (year long internship). Completes a general preparation plan of 45 semester hours which includes six hours, but not more than 12, in each of the following areas: arts of communication; human adjustment; biological science; physical sciences, and mathematics; social science; humanities; and applied arts. (A graduate of a standard institution shall be considered to have met the general preparation requirements.) An alternative plan for certification exists if the applicant has a bachelor's degree and at least 30 semester hours in the subject field in which he/she is seeking certification. Renewal of certificate requires six hours (or 120 staff development units) every five years. **Examination:** College Level Academic Skills Test. Professional Education Subtest of the Florida Teacher Certification Examination.

Georgia

7635

Teacher (K-12)
Div. of Teacher Education
State Dept. of Education
1452 Twin Towers East
Atlanta, GA 30334-5070
Phone: (404)656-2406

Credential Type: Initial Teaching Certificate. **Requirements:** Bachelor's degree from an accredited institution. Teacher education program approved by the NCATE (National Council for Accreditation of Teacher Education Programs). Certification by evaluation will allow those applicants not qualifying under the approved program plan to have their credentials evaluated for possible certification. Another alternative certification program allows applicants with a fifth year or master's degree to be certified if they have completed a MED, MAT, or MALT in the same subject area as their bachelor's degree. Applicants seeking initial certification in the teaching fields of science, mathematics, and foreign languages may meet these fields' requirements through a state approved staff development program or through a summer institute sponsored by the Department of Education.

Must complete a five quarter hr. course in the Identification and Education of Children with Special Needs. Applicants wishing to teach in grades 1-8 must complete a five quarter hr. course in the Teaching of Reading. Appropriate certification tests and on-the-job assessments are required of all teacher candidates.

Hawaii

7636

Teacher (K-12)
Dept. of Education
Office of Personnel Services
PO Box 2360
Honolulu, HI 96804
Phone: (808)548-5803

Credential Type: Initial Basic Teacher Certificate. **Requirements:** Complete an institution's state approved teacher education program at the baccalaureate level. Pass the National Teacher Examination (NTE) Core Battery and Specialty Area Tests. Special majors approved for K-12 general certification include: Art, Music, Physical Education, and Reading. A college or university's state-approved academic major or program is required for the following subject matter fields for secondary certification: Agricultural Arts; Art; Business Education; Distributive Education; English; Guidance; Hawaiian Studies; Health; Health and Physical Education; Home Economics; Industrial Arts; Industrial Technical; Foreign Languages; Mathematics; Music; Office Education; Physical Education; Reading; Science; Vocational Agriculture; and Vocational Home Economics. Trade experience is required for vocational and technical programs. Majors for Special Education include: Mild/Moderate; Severe/Profound; Hearing Impaired; Visually Impaired; Orthopedically Handicapped; or DeafBlind. **Examination:** NTE Core Battery and Specialty Area Tests.

Credential Type: Basic Teacher Certificate. **Requirements:** Initial Basic Certificate. Two years of successful teaching in the public schools of Hawaii.

Credential Type: Initial Professional Teacher Certificate. **Requirements:** Complete an institution's state approved graduate teacher education program. Pass the NTE Core Battery and Specialty Area Tests. **Examination:** NTE Core Battery and Specialty Area Test.

Credential Type: Professional Teacher Certificate. **Requirements:** Initial Professional Teacher Certificate. Complete two years of successful teaching in the public schools of Hawaii.

Idaho

7637

Secondary School Teacher (7-12)
Certification Analyst
State Dept. of Education
L. B. Jordan Office Bldg.
Boise, ID 83720
Phone: (208)334-3475

Credential Type: Standard Secondary Certificate. **Duration of License:** Five years. **Requirements:** Bachelor's degree. 20 semester hours of professional requirements which include philosophical, psychological, and methodological foundations of education. Six semester hours of secondary student teaching or three years of successful teaching in an elementary school. Three hours of reading in the content area. 30 hours in the major subject area and 20 hours in the minor subject area or 45 hours of preparation in a single area. Pass the NTE Battery. May be renewed upon completion of at least six semester credits of college courses within the period of validity. **Examination:** National Teachers Examination Battery.

Credential Type: Advanced Secondary Certificate. **Duration of License:** Five years. **Requirements:** Standard Secondary Certificate. Master's degree in a related area from an accredited college or university. Three years of satisfactory teaching experience. May be renewed upon completion of at least six semester credits of college courses within the period of validity.

7638

Teacher of the Exceptional Child
Certification Analyst
State Dept. of Education
L. B. Jordan Office Bldg.
Boise, ID 83720
Phone: (208)334-3475

Credential Type: Generalist (Educationally Handicapped) Endorsement. **Duration of License:** Five years. **Requirements:** Completion of a program in Elementary, Secondary, or Special Education approved by the Idaho State Board of Education or by the State Educational Agency where the program was completed. 30 semester hours of special education courses to include developmental processes; evaluation; individualization of instruction for exceptional child; instructional experience; individual and group classroom management; knowledge of and coordination with other school personnel; knowledge of state and community ancillary services; and work with parents. Valid for five years and may be renewed upon

Teacher of the Exceptional Child, continued

completion of at least six semester credits of college courses within the period of validity.

Credential Type: Specialized Endorsement. **Authorization:** Authorizes the holder to specialize in one of the following areas: hearing and visually impaired; physically and multiple handicapped; severe retardation; and severe behavior problems. **Requirements:** Baccalaureate degree. 30 semester hour approved program in area of endorsement.

Credential Type: Advanced Exceptional Child Certificate. **Duration of License:** Five years. **Requirements:** Must hold a Standard or Specialist Certificate. Applicants holding a Standard Exceptional Child Certificate require a master's degree with emphasis in Exceptional Child area and three years of satisfactory teaching experience in Exceptional Child area, grades N-12. Applicants holding a Specialized Endorsement require a master's degree in the area of endorsement. Valid for five years and may be renewed upon completion of at least six semester credits of college courses within the period of validity.

Credential Type: Consulting Teacher Endorsement. **Duration of License:** Five years. **Requirements:** Valid Advanced Exceptional Child Certificate. Standard Elementary or Secondary Teaching Certificate. Completion of Fifth Year or master's degree program. Three years of teaching experience. Valid for five years and may be renewed upon completion of at least six semester credits of college courses within the period of validity.

Illinois

7639

High School Teacher 6-12
Certification and Placement Section
100 N. First St.
Springfield, IL 62777
Phone: (217)782-4321

Credential Type: Standard High School Certificate. **Duration of License:** Four years. **Requirements:** Good character. Good health. At least 19 years of age. Citizen of the U.S. Evidence of teaching experience or completion of an approved program of teacher preparation. Bachelor's degree. 42 semester hours of general education classes which include the following courses and specified semester hours: Language Arts 8; Science and/or Mathematics 6; Social Science (to include American History and/or Government) 6; Humanities 6; Health and Physical Education 3; plus additional electives in general education. 16 semester hours of professional education to include the following courses and semester hours: Educational psychology (to include human growth and development) 2; Methods and techniques of teaching on the secondary level 2; History and/or philosophy of education 2; Pre-student teaching clinical experiences of 100 clock hours at the grade level or in the area of specialization; Identification of and methods of teaching exceptional children 3; plus five semester hours of approved professional education electives. Must complete one major area of specialization totaling 32 semester hours or three minor areas of specialization totaling 24 semester hours each. Total teacher preparation including professional education, general education, major and/or minor requirements and electives must total at least 120 semester hours Applicants with successful teaching experience at appropriate level do not need to complete pre-student teaching requirement. All applicants must take and pass the Illinois Certification Basic Skills and Subject-Matter Knowledge Tests. Renewal is possible with the passage of a State of Illinois and U.S. Constitution examination. **Examination:** Illinois Certification Basic Skills and Subject-Matter Knowledge Tests. **Reciprocity:** Reciprocity exists for applicants holding out-of-state teaching certificates providing their teacher preparation was comparable to that required by the state of Illinois. **Fees:** $44 per section of the Illinois Certification Test.

7640

Teacher of the Blind and Partially Sighted
Certification and Placement Section
100 N. First St.
Springfield, IL 62777
Phone: (217)782-4321

Credential Type: Standard Special Education Certificate. **Duration of License:** Four years. **Requirements:** Good character. Good health. At least 19 years of age. Citizen of the U.S. Evidence of special education teaching experience or completion of an approved special education program of teacher preparation. Bachelor's degree. Meet specified general and professional education requirements. 32 semester hours of appropriate courses in the field including: survey of exceptional children; characteristics of the blind and partially sighted child; methods courses which includes the teaching of Braille; psychological diagnosis; and student teaching. Pass required sections of the Illinois Certification Test. **Examination:** Illinois Certification Test. **Reciprocity:** Reciprocity exists for applicants holding out-of-state teaching certificates providing their teacher preparation was comparable to that required by the state of Illinois. **Fees:** $44 per section of the Illinois Certification Test.

7641

Teacher of the Deaf and Hard of Hearing
Certification and Placement Section
100 N. First St.
Springfield, IL 62777
Phone: (217)782-4321

Credential Type: Standard Special Education Certificate. **Duration of License:** Four years. **Requirements:** Good character. Good health. At least 19 years of age. Citizen of the U.S. Evidence of special education teaching experience or completion of an approved special education program of teacher preparation. Bachelor's degree. Meet specified general and professional education requirements. 32 semester hours of appropriate courses in the field including: five hours in the psychological area; 10 hoursin the science area; 12 hours in the communications and education area; and five hours of student teaching. Pass required sections of the Illinois Certification Test. **Examination:** Illinois Certification Test. **Reciprocity:** Reciprocity exists for applicants holding out-of-state teaching certificates providing their teacher preparation was comparable to that required by the state of Illinois. **Fees:** $44 per section of the Illinois Certification Test.

7642

Teacher of the Educable Mentally Handicapped
Certification and Placement Section
100 N. First St.
Springfield, IL 62777
Phone: (217)782-4321

Credential Type: Standard Special Education Certificate. **Duration of License:** Four years. **Requirements:** Good character. Good health. At least 19 years of age. Citizen of the U.S. Evidence of special education teaching experience or completion of an approved special education program of teacher preparation. Bachelor's degree. Meet specified general and professional education requirements. 32 semester hours of appropriate courses in the field including: survey of exceptional children; characteristics; methods course; psychological diagnosis; and student teaching. Pass required sections of the Illinois Certification Test. **Examination:** Illinois Certification Test. **Reciprocity:** Reciprocity exists for applicants holding out-of-state teaching certificates providing their teacher preparation was comparable to that required by the state of Illinois. **Fees:** $44 per section of the Illinois Certification Test.

7643

Teacher of the Learning Disabled Student
Certification and Placement Section
100 N. First St.
Springfield, IL 62777
Phone: (217)782-4321

Credential Type: Standard Special Education Certificate. **Duration of License:** Four years. **Requirements:** Good character. Good health. At least 19 years of age. Citizen of the U.S. Evidence of special education teaching experience or completion of an approved special education program of teacher preparation. Bachelor's degree. Meet specified general and professional education requirements. 32 semester hours of appropriate courses in the field including: survey of exceptional children; characteristics; methods course; psychological diagnosis; and student teaching in learning disabilities. Pass required sections of the Illinois Certification Test. **Examination:** Illinois Certification Test. **Reciprocity:** Reciprocity exists for applicants holding out-of-state teaching certificates providing their teacher preparation was comparable to that required by the state of Illinois. **Fees:** $44 per section of the Illinois Certification Test.

7644

Teacher of the Physically Handicapped
Certification and Placement Section
100 N. First St.
Springfield, IL 62777
Phone: (217)782-4321

Credential Type: Standard Special Education Certificate. **Duration of License:** Four years. **Requirements:** Good character. Good health. At least 19 years of age. Citizen of the U.S. Evidence of special education teaching experience or completion of an approved special education program of teacher preparation. Bachelor's degree. Meet specified general and professional education requirements. 32 semester hours of appropriate courses in the field including: survey of exceptional children; characteristics of the physically handicapped child; methods courses which includes the teaching of Braille; psychological diagnosis; and student teaching. Pass required sections of the Illinois Certification Test. **Examination:** Illinois Certification Test. **Reciprocity:** Reciprocity exists for applicants holding out-of-state teaching certificates providing their teacher preparation was comparable to that required by the state of Illinois. **Fees:** $44 per section of the Illinois Certification Test.

7645

Teacher of the Socially-Emotionally Impaired
Certification and Placement Section
100 N. First St.
Springfield, IL 62777
Phone: (217)782-4321

Credential Type: Standard Special Education Certificate. **Duration of License:** Four years. **Requirements:** Good character. Good health. At least 19 years of age. Citizen of the U.S. Evidence of special education teaching experience or completion of an approved special education program of teacher preparation. Bachelor's degree. Meet specified general and professional education requirements. 32 semester hours of appropriate courses in the field including: survey of exceptional children; characteristics of the socially-emotionally impaired child; methods course; psychological diagnosis; and student teaching. Pass required sections of the Illinois Certification Test. **Examination:** Illinois Certification Test. **Reciprocity:** Reciprocity exists for applicants holding out-of-state teaching certificates providing their teacher preparation was comparable to that required by the state of Illinois. **Fees:** $44 per section of the Illinois Certification Test.

7646

Teacher of Special Subjects K-12
Certification and Placement Section
100 N. First St.
Springfield, IL 62777
Phone: (217)782-4321

Credential Type: Standard Special Subjects Certificate. **Duration of License:** Four years. **Requirements:** Good character. Good health. At least 19 years of age. Citizen of the U.S. Evidence of teaching experience or completion of an approved program of teacher preparation. Bachelor's degree. 42 semester hours of general education classes which include the following courses and specified semester hours: Language Arts 8; Science and/or Mathematics 6; Social Science (to include American History and/or Government) 6; Humanities 6; Health and Physical Education 3; plus additional electives in general education. 16 semester hours of professional education to include the following courses and semester hours: Educational psychology (to include human growth and development) 2; Methods and techniques of teaching in the area of specialization 2; History and/or philosophy of education 2; Pre-student teaching clinical experiences of 100 clock hours in the area of specialization; Identification of and methods of teaching exceptional children 3; plus five semester hours of approved professional education electives. Must complete one major area of specialization totaling 32 semester hours Total teacher preparation including professional education, general education, major and electives must total at least 120 semester hours Applicants with successful teaching experience at appropriate level do not need to complete pre-student teaching requirement. All applicants must take and pass the Illinois Certification Basic Skills and Subject-Matter Knowledge Tests. Renewal is possible with the passage of a State of Illinois and U.S. Constitution examination. **Examination:** Illinois Certification Basic Skills and Subject-Matter Knowledge Tests. **Reciprocity:** Reciprocity exists for applicants holding out-of-state teaching certificates providing their teacher preparation was comparable to that required by the state of Illinois. **Fees:** $44.00 per section of the Illinois Certification Test.

Credential Type: Supervisory Endorsement. **Requirements:** Standard Special Subject Certificate. Master's degree. Eight semester hours of graduate professional education courses which includes one course in supervision of personnel and one course in administration and organization of schools. Two years of appropriate teaching experience.

7647

Teacher of Speech and Language Impaired Students
Certification and Placement Section
100 N. First St.
Springfield, IL 62777
Phone: (217)782-4321

Credential Type: Standard Special Education Endorsement. **Duration of License:** Four years. **Requirements:** Good character. Good health. At least 19 years of age. Citizen of the U.S. Evidence of special education teaching experience or completion of an approved special education program of teacher preparation. Bachelor's degree. Meet specified general and professional education requirements. Master's degree and completion of a course in communicative disorders and related disciplines. Knowledge and understanding of the normal development use of speech, hearing, and language. General understanding of the public schools; general knowledge of procedures used with other educational handicaps. Knowledge and competency in application

Illinois

Teacher of Speech and Language Impaired Students, continued

of psychological principles. Clinical practicum in communicative disorders. Pass required sections of the Illinois Certification Test. **Examination:** Illinois Certification Test. **Reciprocity:** Reciprocity exists for applicants holding out-of-state teaching certificates providing their teacher preparation was comparable to that required by the state of Illinois. **Fees:** $44 per section of the Illinois Certification Test.

7648

Teacher of the Trainable Mentally Handicapped
Certification and Placement Section
100 N. First St.
Springfield, IL 62777
Phone: (217)782-4321

Credential Type: Standard Special Education Certificate. **Duration of License:** Four years. **Requirements:** Good character. Good health. At least 19 years of age. Citizen of the U.S. Evidence of special education teaching experience or completion of an approved special education program of teacher preparation. Bachelor's degree. Meet specified general and professional education requirements. 32 semester hours of appropriate courses in the field including: survey of exceptional children; characteristics of the trainable mentally handicapped child; methods course; psychological diagnosis; and student teaching. Pass required sections of the Illinois Certification Test. **Examination:** Illinois Certification Test. **Reciprocity:** Reciprocity exists for applicants holding out-of-state teaching certificates providing their teacher preparation was comparable to that required by the state of Illinois. **Fees:** $44 per section of the Illinois Certification Test.

Indiana

7649

Junior High/Middle School Teacher
Teacher Certification
Center for Professional Development
State House, Rm. 229
Indianapolis, IN 46204-2798
Phone: (317)232-9010

Credential Type: Standard License. **Duration of License:** Five years. **Requirements:** Baccalaureate degree. Complete undergraduate program of 124 semester hours which includes: 40 hours of general education consisting of 18-22 hours of humanities; 8-12 hours of life and physical science; and 8-12 hours of social and behavioral sciences. Subject matter concentration to include a primary area of 24 semester hours and supporting area(s) of 18 semester hours Also 27 semester hours of professional education which includes: foundations of education; educational psychology; methodology and organization; special methods; sociology of education; classroom management; reading; laboratory experience and nine weeks of student teaching at appropriate level. Plus an additional 15 semester hours of electives which adds breadth and/or depth to the undergraduate experience. Recommendation for licensing by the institution granting the degree. Pass the National Teachers Examination (NTE) Core Battery and either NTE or ITTP in appropriate areas.

License may be renewed for the following five year period if continuing education requirements are completed. These may include additional graduate semester hours and certification renewal units (CRUs) granted for approved professional experiences. The Standard License may also be extended in subject area coverages upon completion of appropriate endorsement teaching minors.

Applicants holding a Standard or Professional License in Elementary Education may qualify for a Junior High/Middle School endorsement by completing 15 semester hours which include adolescent psychology and a practicum at this level, plus 18 semester hours in the primary subject area. Applicants holding a Standard or Professional License in Secondary Education may receive this endorsement by completing 15 semester hours which include: psychology and growth development from childhood to early adolescence; curriculum development and organization of junior high/middle school; methods and techniques of individualized and inter-disciplinary learning; and a practicum at grade level covered by this license. **Examination:** NTE Core Battery and either NTE or ITTP in appropriate areas.

Credential Type: Professionalization Endorsement. **Duration of License:** 10 years. **Requirements:** Complete five years' teaching experience in accredited schools at the level covered by the Standard License. Approved master's degree. 15 semester hours of graduate level courses. (Candidates with additional teaching areas of endorsement may professionalize these areas on completion of three semester hours of course work in subject matter area.) Be recommended for Professional Licensure by institution granting the master's degree. The Professional License may also be extended in subject area coverages upon completion of appropriate endorsement teaching minors.

7650

Secondary School Teacher
Teacher Certification
Center for Professional Development
State House, Rm. 229
Indianapolis, IN 46204-2798
Phone: (317)232-9010

Credential Type: Standard License. **Duration of License:** Five years. **Requirements:** Baccalaureate degree. Complete undergraduate program of 124 semester hours which includes: 40 hours of general education consisting of 18-22 hours of humanities; 8-12 hours of life and physical science; and 8-12 hours of social and behavioral sciences. Subject matter concentration to include a primary area of 36-52 semester hours and supporting area(s) of 24 semester hours Also 24 semester hours of professional education which includes: foundations of education; educational psychology; methodology and organization; special methods; sociology of education; classroom management; reading; laboratory experience and nine weeks of student teaching at appropriate level. Plus electives (no specific number required) which adds breadth and/or depth to the undergraduate experience. Recommendation for licensing by the institution granting the degree. Pass the National Teachers Examination (NTE) Core Battery and either NTE or ITTP in appropriate areas.

License may be renewed for the following five year period if continuing education requirements are completed. These may include additional graduate semester hours and certification renewal units (CRUs) granted for approved professional experiences. The Standard License may also be extended in subject area coverages upon completion of appropriate endorsement teaching minors. **Examination:** NTE Core Battery and either NTE or ITTP in appropriate areas.

Credential Type: Professionalization Endorsement. **Duration of License:** 10 years. **Requirements:** Complete five years' teaching experience in accredited schools at the level covered by the Standard License. Approved master's degree. 15 semester hours of graduate level courses. (Candidates with additional teaching areas of endorsement may professionalize these areas on completion of three semester hours of course work in subject matter area.) Be recommended for Professional Licensure by institution granting the master's degree. The Professional License may also be extended in subject area coverages upon completion of appropriate endorsement teaching minors.

Iowa

7651

Reading Specialist (K-12)
Board of Educational Examiners
Grimes State Office Bldg.
Des Moines, IA 50319-0147
Phone: (515)281-3245

Credential Type: Reading Specialist Endorsement. **Requirements:** Master's degree. Holder of or eligible for the Education Certificate and an endorsement. One year experience which includes the teaching of reading as a significant part. Complete 27 semester hours focusing on reading, including a practicum in reading.

7652

Secondary School Teacher (7-12)
Board of Educational Examiners
Grimes State Office Bldg.
Des Moines, IA 50319-0147
Phone: (515)281-3245

Credential Type: Provisional Certificate. **Duration of License:** Two years. **Requirements:** Baccalaureate degree. Complete approved teacher program. Complete approved human relations component. Complete course work or evidence of competency in: structure of American education; philosophies of education; professional ethics and legal responsibilities; psychology of teaching; audiovisual/media/computer technology; evaluation techniques; human development; exceptional learner; classroom management; instructional planning; curriculum; methods of teaching; prestudent field-based experiences; and student teaching in desired subject area and grade level. Plus 30 semester hours of a teaching major that must include the requirements for at least one subject endorsement. Certificate is renewable for a second two-year term.

Credential Type: Education Certificate. **Duration of License:** Five years. **Requirements:** Provisional Certificate. Two years of successful teaching experience based on a local evaluation process. Renewable.

Credential Type: Professional Teacher's Certificate. **Duration of License:** Five years. **Requirements:** Holder of or eligible for an Education Certificate. Five years of teaching experience. Master's degree in the area of a teaching endorsement. Renewable.

7653

Special Education Teacher
Board of Educational Examiners
Grimes State Office Bldg.
Des Moines, IA 50319-0147
Phone: (515)281-3245

Credential Type: Special Education Endorsement. **Requirements:** Baccalaureate degree. Complete an approved teacher education program. Complete an approved human relations component. 24 semester hours in special education, as well as other specific requirements, as necessary for teaching endorsements in the areas of mental and learning disabilities, hearing and visual impairment, the physically handicapped, and early childhood-special education.

7654

Teacher of English As A Second Language
Board of Educational Examiners
Grimes State Office Bldg.
Des Moines, IA 50319-0147
Phone: (515)281-3245

Credential Type: Provisional Certificate. **Duration of License:** Two years. **Requirements:** Baccalaureate degree. Complete approved teacher program. Complete approved human relations component. Complete course work or evidence of competency in: structure of American education; philosophies of education; professional ethics and legal responsibilities; psychology of teaching; audiovisual/media/computer technology; evaluation techniques; human development; exceptional learner; classroom management; instructional planning; curriculum; methods of teaching; pre-student field-based experiences; and student teaching in desired subject area and grade level. Complete 24 semester hours of course work in ESOL. Certificate is renewable for a second two-year term.

Credential Type: Education Certificate. **Duration of License:** Five years. **Requirements:** Provisional Certificate. Two years of successful teaching experience based on a local evaluation process. Renewable.

Credential Type: Professional Teacher's Certificate. **Duration of License:** Five years. **Requirements:** Holder of or eligible for an Education Certificate. Five years of teaching experience. Master's degree in the area of a teaching endorsement. Renewable.

Kansas

7655

Secondary School Teacher
Certification Specialist
Kansas State Dept. of Education
Kansas State Education Bldg.
120 E. 10th St.
Topeka, KS 66612-1103
Phone: (913)296-2288

Credential Type: Secondary Certificate. **Duration of License:** Three years. **Requirements:** Bachelor's degree. Complete a state-approved teacher education program with general, professional, and field specialization components. The general component must be designed to develop the student's skills of analysis, synthesis and evaluation, competence in written and oral communication skills, understanding of and the ability to use basic mathematical properties, processes and symbols, and the study and application of modes of inquiry, plus the characteristics of the disciplines in the arts, humanities, natural sciences, and the social sciences. This component also requires the study of the historical and cultural values, customs, and social institutions of both western and non-western cultures, and both minority and majority cultures in our society. The professional component must be based on studies which include: the foundations of education; methods and materials of teaching; and supervised laboratory experiences as designed to provide competencies required in the education professions. Must also include observation and experience with school-age youth and a supervised student teaching program. The field of specialization component must be designed to produce the competencies needed to teach the subject at the designated grade fields. Minimum GPA of 2.5 on a four point scale. Pass Pre-Professional Skills Test with the following scores: 168 Reading; 168 Mathematics; 170 Writing. Pass the National Teacher Examination, Professional Knowledge portion, with a score of 642. Have recent college credit or recent accredited experience, within six years preceding application. **Examination:** Pre-Professional Skills Test. National Teacher Examination (Professional Knowledge).

Kentucky

7656

Middle School Teacher (5-8)
Kentucky Dept. of Education
Div. of Teacher Education and Certification
Capitol Plaza Tower, 18th Fl.
500 Mero St.
Frankfort, KY 40601
Phone: (502)564-4606

Credential Type: Provisional Certification for Teaching in the Middle Grades. **Duration of License:** Five years. **Requirements:** Complete an approved program at a four year college or university. Program must be completed within five years of application or complete six semester hours of graduate credit in that time period. Must apply for a permit from the State Board of Education to enter into a one year beginning teacher internship and complete that internship successfully. Must complete written tests designated by the State Board of Education for: general knowledge; communication skills; professional education; concepts; and knowledge in the specific teaching field of the applicant, with minimum scores in each test as set by the Board. An applicant who holds an expired teaching certificate or an applicant having completed two or more years of acceptable teaching experience outside of Kentucky, who otherwise qualifies for certification, will not be required to take the written tests or to participate in the beginning teacher internship program. Certificate may be renewed upon three years of successful teaching experience or six semester hours of graduate credit. **Examination:** Written examinations determines by the State Board of Education.

Credential Type: Middle Grade Endorsement of Early Childhood or Secondary Grades. **Requirements:** Complete an approved program at a college or university for secondary school students. Successful teaching experience.

Credential Type: Temporary Certificate. **Duration of License:** One year. **Requirements:** Applicants who do not meet the recency of preparation requirement and who have not previously held a regular Kentucky teaching certificate, but who otherwise qualify for certification, may be issued a one year certificate which expires on June 30 of the next calendar year. During the life of the temporary certificate the applicant will be required to complete six semester hours of credit to renew his/her certificate in the usual manner.

7657

Music Teacher
Kentucky Dept. of Education
Div. of Teacher Education and Certification
Capitol Plaza Tower. 18th Fl.
500 Mero St.
Frankfort, KY 40601
Phone: (502)564-4606

Credential Type: Provisional Certificate for Teaching of Music. **Duration of License:** Five years. **Requirements:** Four year program of teacher preparation including bachelor's degree. 24 semester hours of professional preparation which includes: three hours human growth and development and learning theory; two hours basic concepts concerning education; music education methods and materials appropriate for all grade levels; and a practicum. Preparation must also include 48 hours of instrumental music, 48 hours of vocal music, and 60 hours that combines instrumental and vocal music. Other courses must include music theory, harmony, ear training, comprehensive musicianship, form, analysis, orchestration, arranging, counterpoint, composition, conducting, history of music, and literature of music. Certificate is renewable.

7658

Secondary School Teacher (9-12)
Kentucky Dept. of Education
Div. of Teacher Education and Certification
Capitol Plaza Tower, 18th Fl.
500 Mero St.
Frankfort, KY 40601
Phone: (502)564-4606

Credential Type: Provisional Certification for Teaching in the Secondary Grades. **Duration of License:** Five years. **Requirements:** Complete an approved program at a four year college or university. Program must be completed within five years of application or complete six semester hours of graduate credit in that time period. Must apply for a permit from the State Board of Education to enter into a one year beginning teacher internship and complete that internship successfully. Must complete written tests designated by the State Board of Education for: general knowledge; communication skills; professional education; concepts; and knowledge in the specific teaching field of the applicant, with minimum scores in each test as set by the Board. An applicant who holds an expired teaching certificate or an applicant having completed two or more years of acceptable teaching experience outside of Kentucky, who otherwise qualifies for certification, will not be required to take the written tests or to participate in the beginning teacher internship program. Certificate may be renewed upon three years of successful teaching experience or six semester hours of graduate credit. **Examination:** Written examinations determined by the State Board of Education.

Credential Type: Standard Certificate (5-8). **Duration of License:** Five years. **Requirements:** Qualify for Provisional Certification for Teaching in the Secondary Grades. Master's degree.

Credential Type: Temporary Certificate. **Duration of License:** One year. **Requirements:** Applicants who do not meet the recency of preparation requirement and who have not previously held a regular Kentucky teaching certificate, but who otherwise qualify for certification, may be issued a one year certificate which expires on June 30 of the next calendar year. During the life of the temporary certificate the applicant will be required to complete six semester hours of credit to renew his/her certificate in the usual manner.

7659

Special Education Teacher
Kentucky Dept. of Education
Div. of Teacher Education and Certification
Capitol Plaza Tower, 18th Fl.
500 Mero St.
Frankfort, KY 40601
Phone: (502)564-4606

Credential Type: Provisional Certificate for Teachers of Exceptional Children. **Duration of License:** Five years. **Requirements:** Complete program approved by the Kentucky State Plan for the Preparation Program for Certification of Professional School Personnel for learning and behavior disorders or trainable mentally handicapped, or hearing impaired. Qualify for a provisional teaching certificate in grades K-4 or 5-8.

Credential Type: Standard Special Education Certificate. **Duration of License:** Five years. **Requirements:** Qualify for Provisional Certificate for Teachers of Exceptional Children. Hold a master's degree consisting of 30 graduate credit hours or 24 graduate credit hours and a thesis. Nine hours should include credit from the following areas: general study of curriculum development; research methodology; advanced study in human growth and development; psychology of learning; a seminar in instruction devoted to the methods of teaching; and foundations in education, which include sociological, psychological, philosophical, and historical. 12 hours should include courses in applicant's specialization or that further develop educational background.

7660

Teacher for Gifted Education
Kentucky Dept. of Education
Div. of Teacher Education and Certification
Capitol Plaza Tower, 18th Fl.
500 Mero St.
Frankfort, KY 40601
Phone: (502)564-4606

Credential Type: Gifted Education Endorsement. **Requirements:** Classroom teaching certificate. One year of teaching experience. Complete an approved graduate level curriculum with at least nine semester hours of credit that gives emphasis to the following: nature and needs of gifted education; assessment and/or counseling of the gifted; curriculum development for the gifted; and creative studies. Three semester hours of credit in a supervised practicum for gifted education. However, with two years experience as a teacher for gifted, the practicum may be waived.

Louisiana

7661

Secondary School Teacher
Louisiana Dept. of Education
Box 94064
Baton Rouge, LA 70804-9064
Phone: (504)342-3490

Credential Type: Standard Certificate—Type C. **Duration of License:** Three years. **Requirements:** Baccalaureate degree, including an approved teacher education program and student teaching. Appropriate National Teacher Examination (NTE) scores. 46 general education semester hours which include: 12 hours of English, including grammar and composition; 12 hours of Social Studies; 12 hours of Science, including biological and physical; six hours of Mathematics; and four hours of Health and Physical Education. 27 professional education semester hours that include: three hours history of, introduction to, foundations of, and/or philosophy of education; three hours educational psychology and/or principles of teaching; three hours in adolescent psychology; six hours teaching of reading; and nine hours student teaching in subject field. To specialize in a subject, applicants must have the following number of semester hours: agriculture 50; business and office education 36; computer science 18; English 30; foreign language 36; home economics 42; industrial arts 48; journalism 15; mathematics 20; general science 32; biology 20; earth science 20; physics 20; social studies 33; speech 30; art 36; health 22; physical education 24; vocal music 62; and instrumental music 62. **Examination:** NTE.

Credential Type: Standard Certificate—Type B. **Duration of License:** Valid for life for continuous service endorsed thereon. **Requirements:** Standard Type C Certificate or equivalent. Three years of successful teaching experience.

Credential Type: Standard Certificate—Type A. **Duration of License:** Valid for life for continuous service. **Requirements:** Standard Type C or Type B Certificate or equivalent. Master's degree, or higher, from an approved institution. Five years of successful teaching in a certified field.

7662

Teacher of Exceptional Children
Louisiana Dept. of Education
Box 94064
Baton Rouge, LA 70804-9064
Phone: (504)342-3490

Credential Type: Standard Certificate with Mild/Moderate Impairment Endorsement. **Requirements:** Baccalaureate degree, including an approved teacher education program and student teaching. Appropriate National Teacher Examination (NTE) scores. 46 general education hours which include: 12 hours English; 12 hours Social Studies; 12 hours Science; six hours Mathematics; and four hours Physical Education. 27 professional education semester hours which include: three hours history of education; three hours educational psychology and/or principles of teaching; and student teaching in a mild/moderate classroom. For elementary level teaching: three hours of child psychology; three hours teaching of reading, and a three semester hr. practicum. For secondary level teaching: three hours adolescent psychology and six hours teaching of reading. 36 hours of specialized education which includes: six hours general knowledge; 12 hours methods and materials; nine hours management; six hours assessment and evaluation; and three hours mainstreaming practicum. Secondary level teaching also requires six hours teaching prevocational/vocational skills.

Credential Type: Standard Certificate with Severe/Profound Endorsement. **Requirements:** Baccalaureate degree, including an approved teacher education program and student teaching. Appropriate NTE scores. 46 general education semester hours which include: 12 hours English; 12 hours Social Studies; 12 hours Science; six hours Mathematics; and four hours Physical Education. 30 professional education semester hours which include: three hours history of education; three hours educational psychology and/or principles of teaching; nine hours student teaching in severe/profound classroom; and 15 hours of professional education teaching courses. 36 specialized education semester hours to include six hours general knowledge; six hours instructional strategies; three hours learning principles and classroom/behavior management; six hours assessment and evaluation; three hours methods of working with paraprofessionals; three hours parent, family and community involvement; three hours communication strategies; and six hours of electives.

Maine

7663

Secondary Teacher (7-12)
Teacher Certification
Dept. of Education
State House Station 23
Augusta, ME 04333
Phone: (207)289-5944

Credential Type: Provisional Certificate. **Duration of License:** Two years. **Authorization:** Provisional Certificate will be endorsed to allow teaching of one of the following subjects areas at the secondary level: English/Language Arts; Mathematics; Life Science; Physical Science; Social Studies. **Requirements:** Bachelor's degree from an approved institution. Complete an approved preparation program for teachers in the relevant subject area which includes a major in that subject. Or a bachelor's degree with a concentration in liberal arts and at least 36 semester hours of credit in the relevant subject area for English/language arts, mathematics, social studies, and science. 24 semester hours must be comprised of courses from the following list: knowledge of the learner; knowledge of the learning process; teaching exceptional children in the regular classroom; content area methods; curriculum design and program evaluation; early and on-going experience or practicum; and one academic semester or 15 weeks of full-time student teaching. Formal recommendation of the institution where degree was granted. Pass the NTE Core Battery. Nonrenewable. **Examination:** National Teacher Examination Core Battery.

Credential Type: Conditional Certificate. **Duration of License:** Two years. **Authorization:** Authorizes an applicant to hold a paid teaching position while completing requirements for a particular position. Re-

Secondary Teacher (7-12), continued

quirements: Applicants are expected to complete all requirements for desired certificate during the term of this conditional certificate. Renewable only with approval.

Credential Type: Professional Certificate. **Duration of License:** Five years. **Requirements:** Hold Provisional Certificate. Be recommended for the professional certificate from the support system, based upon the completion of a Professional Renewal Plan (PRP), including six classroom observations. Renewable.

Credential Type: Master Certificate. **Duration of License:** Five years. **Requirements:** Hold a Professional Certificate. Demonstrate exemplary professional skills. Have knowledge of current theories of effective instruction. Has made outstanding contributions to the teaching profession in curriculum design, staff development, clinical supervision of student teachers or peer observation of teachers, or educational leadership.

Maryland

7664

Secondary School Teacher
Dept. of Certification 18100
State Dept. of Education
200 W. Baltimore St.
Baltimore, MD 21201
Phone: (301)333-2142

Credential Type: Standard Professional Certificate. **Requirements:** Bachelor's or higher degree completed within five years preceding the issuance of the certificate or hold a bachelor's degree and complete six hours of acceptable credit within five years preceding the issuance of the certificate. Graduate from an approved teacher preparation program in Maryland or complete the specific credit count requirements for Maryland for a secondary school teacher or complete an undergraduate pre-service program produced by the NCATE after July 1, 1975. Must have completed a teacher education program within the past 10 years from an approved institution or hold a professional teacher's certificate from one of the states participating in the Interstate Contract Agreement and have taught for at least 27 months during the past seven years. Must pass the following tests in the National Teacher's Examinations: The Communication Skills Test of the Core Battery; The General Knowledge Test of the Core Battery; The Professional Knowledge Test of the Core Battery; and the appropriate Specialty Area Test. Specialize in one of the following content areas with the number of semester hours specified: agriculture 56; biology 46; business education 36; chemistry 45; earth space science 46; English 36; health education 30; home economics 36; industrial arts 36; math 30; physical science 40; physics 45; social studies 57; speech communication 30; theater 42; and any other academic subject normally offered in the secondary school 24. Plus 18 semester hours of professional education courses which include: six hours foundations of education, including educational psychology; six hours secondary education, including curriculum or principle's of secondary education; and six hours special methods in subjects to be certified, including supervised observation and student teaching. Teachers of English and social studies must have an additional three semester hours in teaching of reading. All applicants must have three semester hours of college credit or state-approved inservice workshop credit in special education approved by the board. **Examination:** Following sections of the National Teacher's Examinations: The Communication Skills Test of the Core Battery; The General Knowledge Test of the Core Battery; The Professional Knowledge Test of the Core Battery; and the appropriate Specialty Area Test.

Credential Type: Provisional Degree Certificate. **Authorization:** Issued to applicant with bachelor's degree who fails to meet the requirements for Standard Professional Certificate. **Requirements:** Bachelor's degree. Continue working towards Standard Professional Certificate.

Credential Type: Advanced Professional Certificate. **Requirements:** Three years of successful teaching experience. Meet requirements for Standard Professional Certificate. Have relevant master's degree or complete 30 semester hours relevant to professional assignment (at least 15 hours must be a graduate level) or complete at least 30 semester hours of in-service education developed by the local school units and approved by the State Superintendent of Schools.

Credential Type: Resident Teacher Certificate. **Duration of License:** One year. **Requirements:** Bachelor's degree from an accredited institution with a concentration in a discipline appropriate to the secondary education curriculum. Grades of "B" or better in major area of study. Must pass the following tests in the National Teacher's Examinations: The Communication Skills Test of the Core Battery; The General Knowledge Test of the Core Battery; and the appropriate Specialty Area Test. Verification by the local Superintendent of 90 clock hours of study developed according to the Maryland State Dept. of Education guidelines. Other requirements, as deemed necessary, by the State Dept. of Education. Renewable for one year.

Massachusetts

7665

Middle School Teacher (5-9)
Massachusetts Dept. of Education
1385 Hancock St.
Quincy, MA 02169
Phone: (617)770-7500

Credential Type: Teaching Certificate. **Requirements:** Satisfy the five Standards established by the Massachusetts Dept. of Education. Standard I includes 36 semester hours of course work in middle school subject matter which includes reading, communication, literature, mathematics, biological and physical science, social studies, the arts, health, and physical education. Plus 21 semester hours of pre-practicum experience and, in addition, complete a successful practicum of 300 clock hours at the elementary level. Standard II-Be able to communicate clearly, understandably, and appropriately. Standard III—Be able to design instruction to facilitate learning consistent with needs and interest of the learners. Standard IV—Be able to use results of various evaluative procedures to stress effectiveness of instruction. Standard V—Be equitable, sensitive, and responsive to all learners.

7666

Secondary School Teacher (9-12)
Massachusetts Dept. of Education
1385 Hancock St.
Quincy, MA 02169
Phone: (617)770-7500

Credential Type: Teaching Certificate with Teaching Fields Endorsement. **Requirements:** Satisfy the five Standards established by the Massachusetts Dept. of Education. Standard I includes 36 semester hours of course work required in field of specialization for teachers of English, speech, social studies, behavioral sciences, history, geography, mathematics and science, mathematics, general science, physics, chemistry, biology, earth science, health, physical education, home economics, business management, secretarial skills, industrial arts, dance, drama, music, art, Latin and classical humanities. (Foreign Language Teachers are required to pass an exam in reading, writing, and speaking the foreign language, plus 18 semester hours in other aspects of the language, in lieu of 36 semester hours as required of other teaching fields.) Plus 21 semester hours of prepracticum experience and, in addition, complete a successful practicum of 300 clock hours at the elementary level. Standard IIBe able to communicate clearly, understandably, and appropriately. Standard III—Be able to design instruction to facilitate learning consistent with needs and interest of the learners. Standard IV—Be able to use results of various evaluative procedures to stress effectiveness of instruction. Standard V—Be equitable, sensitive, and responsive to all learners.

7667

Teacher of Children With Special Needs
Massachusetts Dept. of Education
1385 Hancock St.
Quincy, MA 02169
Phone: (617)770-7500

Credential Type: Young Children With Special Needs Endorsement. **Requirements:** Teaching Certificate. Complete a pre-practicum of 30 semester hours of course work and other related experiences plus a 300 clock hr. practicum for preschool children with special needs. Demonstrate the competencies contained in the five Standards established by the Massachusetts Dept. of Education for working with young children with special needs. Standard I-Knowledge of the following: Developmental psychology and psychology of children in general and particularly for young children. Standard II-Be able to communicate clearly, understandably, and appropriately. Standard III—Be able to design instruction to facilitate learning consistent with needs and interest of the learners. Standard IV—Be able to use results of various evaluative procedures to stress effectiveness of instruction. Standard V—Be equitable, sensitive, and responsive to all learners.

Credential Type: Children With Severe Special Needs Endorsement. **Requirements:** Teaching Certificate. Complete a pre-practicum of 30 semester hours of course work and other related experiences plus a 300 clock hr. practicum for children with severe special needs. Demonstrate the competencies contained in the five Standards established by the Massachusetts Dept. of Education for working with young children with special needs. Standard I-Knowledge of the following: Developmental psychology and psychology of children in general and particularly for children with severe special needs. Standard IIBe able to communicate clearly, understandably, and appropriately. Standard III—Be able to design instruction to facilitate learning consistent with needs and interest of the learners. Standard IV—Be able to use results of various evaluative procedures to stress effectiveness of instruction. Standard V—Be equitable, sensitive, and responsive to all learners.

Credential Type: Children With Moderate Special Needs Endorsement. **Requirements:** Teaching Certificate. Complete a pre-practicum of 30 semester hours of course work and other related experiences plus a 300 clock hr. practicum for children with moderate special needs. Demonstrate the competencies contained in the five Standards established by the Massachusetts Dept. of Education for working with young children with special needs. Standard I-Knowledge of the following: Developmental psychology and psychology of children in general and particularly for children with moderate special needs. Standard II-Be able to communicate clearly, understandably, and appropriately. Standard III—Be able to design instruction to facilitate learning consistent with needs and interest of the learners. Standard IV—Be able to use results of various evaluative procedures to stress effectiveness of instruction. Standard V—Be equitable, sensitive, and responsive to all learners.

Credential Type: Children With Special Needs Endorsement—Vision. **Requirements:** Teaching Certificate. Complete a pre-practicum of 30 semester hours of course work and other related experiences plus a 300 clock hr. practicum for children with vision impairment. Demonstrate the competencies contained in the five Standards established by the Massachusetts Dept. of Education for working with young children with special needs. Standard I-Knowledge of the following: Developmental psychology and psychology of children in general and particularly for children with vision impairment. Standard II-Be able to communicate clearly, understandably, and appropriately. Standard III—Be able to design instruction to facilitate learning consistent with needs and interest of the learners. Standard IV—Be able to use results of various evaluative procedures to stress effectiveness of instruction. Standard V—Be equitable, sensitive, and responsive to all learners.

Credential Type: Children With Special Needs—Audition. **Requirements:** Teaching Certificate with 36 semester hours in subject field. Complete a pre-practicum of 48 semester hours of course work and other related experiences plus a 300 clock hr. practicum for children with hearing impairment. Demonstrate the competencies contained in the five Standards established by the Massachusetts Dept. of Education for working with young children with special needs. Standard I-Knowledge of the following: Developmental psychology and psychology of children in general and particularly for children with hearing impairment. Standard II-Be able to communicate clearly, understandably, and appropriately. Standard III—Be able to design instruction to facilitate learning consistent with needs and interest of the learners. Standard IV—Be able to use results of various evaluative procedures to stress effectiveness of instruction. Standard V—Be equitable, sensitive, and responsive to all learners.

Credential Type: Children With Speech, Language, and Hearing Disorders Endorsement. **Requirements:** Teaching Certificate. Complete a pre-practicum of 60 semester hours of course work and other related experiences plus a 300 clock hr. practicum for children with speech, language, and hearing disorders. Demonstrate the competencies contained in the five Standards established by the Massachusetts Dept. of Education for working with young children with special needs. Standard IKnowledge of the following: Developmental psychology and psychology of children in general and particularly for children with speech, language, and hearing disorders. Standard II-Be able to communicate clearly, understandably, and appropriately. Standard III—Be able to design instruction to facilitate learning consistent with needs and interest of the learners. Standard IV—Be able to use results of various evaluative procedures to stress effectiveness of instruction. Standard V—Be equitable, sensitive, and responsive to all learners.

Credential Type: Consulting Teacher of Children With Special Needs Endorsement. **Requirements:** Classroom teaching certificate and two years of employment under the certificate. Complete a pre-practicum of 60 semester hours of course work and other related experiences plus a 300 clock hr. practicum for children with special needs. Demonstrate the competencies contained in the five Standards established by the Massachusetts Dept. of Education for working with young children with special needs. Standard I-Knowledge of the following: Developmental psychology and psychology of children in general and particularly for children with special needs. Standard II-Be able to communicate clearly, understandably, and appropriately. Standard III—Be able to design instruction to facilitate learning consistent with needs and interest of the learners. Standard IV—Be able to use results of various evaluative procedures to stress effectiveness of instruction. Standard V—Be equitable, sensitive, and responsive to all learners.

7668

Transitional Bilingual Education Teacher
Massachusetts Dept. of Education
1385 Hancock St.
Quincy, MA 02169
Phone: (617)770-7500

Credential Type: Transitional Bilingual Education Endorsement. **Requirements:** Teaching certificate. Demonstrate, through state administered test procedures, speaking and reading proficiency in a language other than English and knowledge of culture associated with other languages. **Examination:** Massachusetts state test in speaking and reading proficiency in a language other than English.

Michigan

7669

Secondary School Teacher
Teacher Preparation and Certification
Michigan Dept. of Education
Box 30008
Lansing, MI 48909
Phone: (517)373-3310

Credential Type: State Secondary Provisional Certificate. **Duration of License:** Six years. **Authorization:** Secondary certificates issued after September 1, 1988 are valid in areas of certification (subject area majors and minors) in grades 7-12. **Requirements:** Bachelor's degree and recommendation from an approved teacher training institution. A major of 30 semester hours or a group major of 36 semester hours A minor of 20 semester hours or a group minor of 24 semester hours three semester hours of teaching or reading. 20 professional education requirements to include: developmental needs of early adolescents and adolescents, including the needs of the exceptional child; structure, function and purposes of educational institutions in our society; methods and materials of secondary level instruction; and at least six hours of directed teaching at the secondary level.

Credential Type: State Secondary Professional Certificate. **Authorization:** Hold a Provisional Certificate. Three years of successful teaching experience. Complete a planned program of 18 semester hours of appropriate credit subsequent to the issuance of the Provisional Certificate (not required for those holding master's degrees). Six semester hours must be in teaching of reading. Effective July 30, 1992, those eligible for an Initial Continuing Certificate will now qualify for the Professional Certificate.

Credential Type: Endorsements. **Requirements:** Secondary Provisional or Professional Certificate. Endorsements may be completed with a planned program of a minimum of 18 hours in the following areas: early childhood; bilingual language; general elementary; middle school; and areas appropriate to the secondary grades.

Minnesota

7670

Secondary School Teacher (7-12)
Teacher Licensing and Placement
State Dept. of Education
616 Capitol Square Bldg.
St. Paul, MN 55101
Phone: (612)296-2046

Credential Type: Secondary Teaching Certificate. **Requirements:** Bachelor's degree from an approved four year college or university. Must have a subject area major which will allow for full-time teaching and a minor for teaching in a subject 1/2 time or less. Complete a teacher education program which includes a minimum of 18 semester hours credit in professional education for secondary schools and meets the number of education credits prescribed by the Minnesota State Board of Teaching. Complete an approved, competency-based human relations program and pass the PPST. **Examination:** Pre-Professional Skills Test.

Credential Type: Temporary Teaching Certificate. **Duration of License:** One year. **Authorization:** Allows out-of-state teachers, who have not fulfilled the human relations program and/or PPST requirement(s) but meet all other requirements for a Minnesota teaching certificate, to hold a teaching position while satisfying these special requirements. **Requirements:** Out-of-state teaching certificate. Must satisfy PPST requirement and human relations requirement within one year. Nonrenewable.

Mississippi

7671

School Teacher
Teacher Certification
State Dept. of Education
Box 771
Jackson, MS 39205-0771
Phone: (601)359-3483

Credential Type: Provisional Certificate. **Duration of License:** One year. **Requirements:** Pass the Core Battery of the NTE and appropriate specialty area tests. Complete teacher preparation courses at an approved four year college or university. Renewable for not more than two additional one year periods. **Examination:** Core Battery of the National Teacher Examination.

Credential Type: Standard Certificate. **Duration of License:** One year. **Authorization:** Three levels of certificates will be awarded which authorize individuals to teach different grade levels. An elementary certificate will allow teaching in grades K-8, a secondary certificate will allow teaching in grades 7-12, and a special area certificate will allow teaching in grades K-12 according to endorsement. **Requirements:** Successful completion of the provisional certification period, which includes an evaluation of on-the-job performance. Demonstrate the mastery of the teaching competencies at the prescribed level. One of four classes of the standard certificate may be issued dependent on the candidate's education and experience. The classes are A, AA, AAA, and AAAA. Certificate will be extended based on the educator's successful completion of staff development requirements.

Missouri

7672

Middle School or Junior High Teacher 4-9
Teacher Certification
Dept. of Elementary and Secondary Education
Box 480
Jefferson City, MO 65102
Phone: (314)751-3486

Credential Type: Middle Grades Teaching Certificate. **Requirements:** Bachelor's degree. Recommendation of designated official for teacher education. Basic requirements include two courses from the following list: music, art, foreign language, western and nonwestern cultures, philosophy, literature, classical studies, theater, and drama. Must also have two courses in English composition, one in oral communication, one in American history, one in American government, one in physical or earth science, one in biology, and one college level math course. At least one of the natural science courses must have a laboratory component. Plus one course from the following list: geography, economics, sociology, anthropology, or psychology. Professional preparation must include 10 semester hours that cover the following: foundation of education; middle school-junior high philosophy; organization and curriculum; personalized teaching strategies; self-awareness and human relations; child growth and development; psychology of learning; psychology and education of the exceptional child; techniques of classroom management; tests and measurements. 15 hours of teaching methods including reading (minimum five hours), language arts, children's or adolescent literature, mathematics, science, social studies, art, music, physical education, and school health. A minimum of two semester hours of field experience prior to student teaching and a minimum of five semester hours of teaching in grades 48. Middle grades special courses also include two additional mathematics courses appropriate to elementary level (minimum of five hours), 20 additional hours in economics, geography, health, art, music, or sociology. 21 semester hours are required for subject certification in the following areas language arts, foreign language, math, science, health, social studies, speech and theater, general agriculture, general home economics, industrial arts, music, instrumental, vocal, or physical education. May be granted additional subject area certification in departmentalized grades 7-9 or K-9 when secondary subject area standards for 7-9 or K-9 have been fully set.

7673

Secondary School Teacher
Teacher Certification
Dept. of Elementary and Secondary Education
Box 480
Jefferson City, MO 65102
Phone: (314)751-3486

Credential Type: Secondary Teaching Certificate. **Requirements:** Bachelor's degree. Recommendation of designated official for teacher education. Overall grade point average of at least 2.5 on a 4.0 scale. Completion of General Education as determined by the recommending institution. Basic requirements include two courses from the following list: music, art, foreign language, western and non-western cultures, philosophy, literature, classical studies, theater, and drama. Must also have two courses in English composition, one in oral communication, one in American history, one in American government, one in physical or earth science, one in biology, and one college level math course. At least one of the natural science courses must have a laboratory component. Plus one course from the following list: geography, economics, sociology, anthropology, or psychology. Professional education requirements of 24 semester hours that includes eight hours of Pupil/Society foundations of teaching that covers adolescent growth and development, adolescent behavior management techniques, psychology of learning, adolescent interaction with others, and psychology and education of the exceptional child. In addition, must include, eight hours of School/Society courses that cover legal, historical, philosophical, and sociological foundations of education. Eight semester hours of student teaching at an appropriate level. Eight semester hours of secondary methods classes and techniques which include basic reading for secondary teachers, instructional strategies, and measurement and evaluation. The following list states the number of semester hours required for each subject to be certified to teach it at the secondary level: Allied Arts (humanistic approach to music, art, literature, and drama) 18, Art 30, Business Education 30, Driver Education 21, English 30, Foreign Language 30, General Agriculture 30, General Home Economics 30, Health 30, Industrial Arts 36, Journalism 30, Mathematic 30, Music-Instrumental 36, Music-Vocal 36, Music-Instrumental and Vocal 40, Physical Education 30, Science-Biology 30, Science-Chemistry 30, Science Physics 30, Science-Earth Science 30, Social Studies 40, and Speech and Theater 30.

7674

Special Education Teacher
Teacher Certification
Dept. of Elementary and Secondary Education
Box 480
Jefferson City, MO 65102
Phone: (314)751-3486

Credential Type: Special Education Certificate. **Requirements:** Bachelor's or master's degree with a complete major in an area of special education. Recommendation of the designated official for teacher education in the college or university. Minimum, overall grade point average of 2.5 on a scale of 4.0. Requirements vary according to area of specialization. Missouri certifies special education teachers in the following areas: Learning Disabled, Behaviorally Disordered, Mentally Handicapped, Orthopedically and/or Health Impaired, Blind and Partially Sighted, Severely Developmentally Disabled, Early Childhood Special Education, Deaf and Hearing Impaired, Special Reading Needs, and Speech and Language Needs.

Montana

7675

Junior High School Teacher
Teacher Certification
Office of Public Instruction
State Capitol
Helena, MT 59620
Phone: (406)444-3150

Credential Type: Class 5 Provisional Certificate. **Requirements:** Bachelor's degree. Partially completed program in middle grade education and written recommendation from college/university or holder of Class 5, certificate endorsed at the elementary level (grades seven and 8) or the secondary level (grades 7, 8, and 9). Nonrenewable.

Credential Type: Class 2 Standard Certificate. **Duration of License:** Five years. **Requirements:** Bachelor's degree. Competed program in middle grade education. Pass NTE Core Battery with the following minimum scores: Communication Skills 648, General Knowledge 644, and Professional Knowledge 648. Or holder of Class 2, certificate endorsed at the elementary level (grades seven and 8) or the secondary level (grades 7, 8, and 9). Renewable upon verification of one year of successful teaching experience and six quarter credits during the valid term of the certificate. **Examination:** National Teacher Examination Core Battery.

Credential Type: Class 1 Professional Certificate. **Duration of License:** Five years. **Requirements:** Eligibility for Standard Certificate plus completion of an approved master's degree or planned fifth year program. Three years of successful teaching experience at appropriate level. Pass NTE Core Battery with the following minimum scores: Communication Skills 648, General Knowledge 644, and Professional Knowledge 648. Or holder of Class 1, certificate endorsed at the elementary level (grades seven and 8) or the secondary level (grades 7, 8, and 9). Renewable upon verification of one year of successful teaching experience during the valid term of the certificate. Beginning with those certificates expiring in 1995, six quarter credits will also be required for renewal. **Examination:** National Teacher Examination Core Battery.

Montana

Secondary School Teacher
Teacher Certification
Office of Public Instruction
State Capitol
Helena, MT 59620
Phone: (406)444-3150

Credential Type: Class 5 Provisional Certificate. **Duration of License:** Three years. **Authorization:** Authorizes teaching of grades 7-12. **Requirements:** Bachelor's degree which must include the following: Major teacher preparation which includes 30 semester credits in a subject commonly taught for credit in secondary schools in Montana; six semester hours in a planned program of professional education and admittance to the secondary teacher education program of an accredited college; and written reccommendation from college or university. Nonrenewable.

Credential Type: Class 2 Standard Certificate. **Duration of License:** Five years. **Duration of License:** Five years. **Authorization:** Authorizes teaching of grades 7-12. **Authorization:** Authorizes teaching grades 7-12. **Requirements:** Completion of approved bachelor's program in secondary teacher education at an approved college or university. A 30 semester hr. teaching major and a 20 semester hr. teaching minor or a 40 semester hr. broadfield major. 16 semester hours of professional education which includes student teaching or equivalent experience. Pass NTE Core Battery with the following minimum scores: Communication Skills 648, General Knowledge 644, and Professional Knowledge 648. Renewable upon verification of one year of successful teaching experience and six quarter credits during the valid term of the certificate. **Requirements:** Eligibility for Standard Certificate plus completion of an approved master's degree or planned fifth year program. Three years of successful teaching experience at appropriate level. Pass NTE Core Battery with the following minimum scores: Communication Skills 648, General Knowledge 644, and Professional Knowledge 648. Renewable upon verification of one year of successful teaching experience during the valid term of the certificate. Beginning with those certificates expiring in 1995, six quarter credits will also be required for renewal. **Examination:** National Teacher Examination Core Battery Class 1 Professional Certificate. **Examination:** National Teacher Examination Core Battery.

Nebraska

School Teacher K-12
Teacher Certification
State Dept. of Education
301 Centennial Mall South
Box 94987
Lincoln, NE 68509-4987
Phone: (402)471-2496

Credential Type: Initial Teaching Certificate. **Requirements:** Sound mental and physical health. Good citizenship and moral character. Baccalaureate degree and approved program for preparation of teachers. Pass the PPST with the following minimum scores: reading 170; mathematics 171; writing 172. Complete an approved program of human relations skills training from a teacher training college. Complete three hours of credit in an approved course in special education, not limited to the gifted. Complete an approved program for grade level, subject field, and area for which applicant is specifically prepared to teach. At least six hours of course work must have been completed in the three years prior to application. **Examination:** Pre-Professional Skills Test.

Credential Type: Standard Teaching Certificate. **Requirements:** Initial Teaching Certificate or equivalent. Successful teaching experience within the last five years, with two years in the same school at the grade level, subject field, and area of specialization indicated on the certificate.

Credential Type: Professional Teaching Certificate. **Requirements:** Standard Teaching Certificate. Master degree or 36 semester hours or approved fifth-year program of graduate work beyond the baccalaureate degree in teaching fields endorsed upon applicant's Standard Certificate. Six semester hours of course work must have been completed in the three years prior to application.

Nevada

Secondary School Teacher
Nevada Dept. of Education
State Mail Room
1850 E. Sahara, Ste. 200
Las Vegas, NV 89158
Phone: (702)386-5401

Credential Type: Secondary Certificate. **Duration of License:** Five years. **Authorization:** Authorizes the teaching of departmentalized grades seven and eight plus all junior high schools, senior high schools and designated middle schools. Limited to applicant's subject areas of specialization. **Requirements:** Bachelor's degree and completion of an approved program of preparation for secondary school teachers which includes multicultural education. Must have teaching field major consisting of comprehensive field major of 36 semester hours or single subject major of 30 semester hours Second subject endorsement may be granted for a minor. Comprehensive field minors must consist of 24 semester hours and single subject minors of 16 semester hours Must have 22 semester hours of professional education, eight hours in supervised teaching or teaching internship, and 13 hours of methods classes in field of specialization. Renewable upon an additional six semester hours of credit.

Credential Type: Professional Secondary Certificate. **Duration of License:** Six years with master's degree, eight years with specialist degree, and 10 years for doctor's degree. **Requirements:** Secondary Certificate or its equivalent. Master's degree. Three years of teaching in the public schools. Master's degree level is renewable upon completion of six semester credit hours or equivalent. Specialist's and Doctor's degree levels are renewable upon evidence of professional growth during the term of the certificate.

Credential Type: Secondary Substitute Certificate. **Duration of License:** Five years. **Authorization:** Limited to 60 days of consecutive service, with exception of extenuating circumstances, in which case the Superintendent has the authority to extend service. **Requirements:** Complete 62 semester hours of course work at an approved college or university, plus six semester hours of secondary education course work. Renewable.

New Hampshire

School Teacher K-12
Bureau of Teacher Education and
 Professional Standards
State Dept. of Education
101 Pleasant St.
Concord, NH 03301
Phone: (603)271-2407

Credential Type: Beginning Educator Certificate. **Duration of License:** Three years. **Requirements:** New Hampshire has four alternatives for certification. Alternative 1—Approved Program in New Hampshire. Complete a teacher education program at an approved college or university within New Hampshire. Written recommendation by designated official at preparing institution.

Alternative 2—States Other Than New Hampshire (Covers states and territories participating in the Interstate Certification Compact). Graduate of an approved collegiate program with less than three years teaching experience. Competence in the basic skills of reading, writing, and mathematics as demonstrated by one of the following: master's degree; valid teaching credential from a state requiring a basic skills competence test for educational certification; or statement from candidate's undergraduate institution verifying basic skill competence.

Alternative 3—Demonstrated Competence and Equivalent Experiences. Must have gained competencies, skills, and knowledge through experience. Must submit for Board of Examiners review a description of background, with three to five references, from persons in the area where certification is sought. Must have competence in the basic skills of reading, writing, and mathematics by one of the following: master's degree; valid teaching credential from a state requiring a basic skills competence test for educational certification; or statement from candidate's undergraduate institution verifying basic skill competence. Candidates not party to the interstate compact will be handles on an individual basis.

Alternative 4—Individualized Professional Development Plan—Under the Critical Staff Clause, a secondary teacher may be recommended for certification if he/she has a bachelor's degree and a collegiate major compatible with prospective teaching assignment.

Alternative 5—Provisional Plan. Bachelor's degree from an approved institution. Candidates who have graduated within five years preceding application must possess an overall grade point average of 2.5. Secondary teachers must have a 30 credit hour major and elementary teachers must have a four year liberal arts background, including a major. Must complete a specially designed education plan, containing both preservice and in-service components, normally during the first year of service. Candidates who have graduated more than five years preceding application must pursue other alternatives for certification.

Credential Type: Experienced Educator Certificate. **Duration of License:** Three years. **Requirements:** Must have recommendation of the Superintendent of Schools during the life of the Beginning Educator Certificate. Must have met all requirements for previous level of certification or successfully completed an approved graduate program that extends clinical experience to a full year under supervision.

New Jersey

7680

School Teacher K-12
Office of Teacher Certification and Academic Credentials
CN 503
Trenton, NJ 08625-0503
Phone: (609)292-2079

Credential Type: Instructional Certificate. **Requirements:** Bachelor's degree from an accredited college or university. Secondary teachers must pass specialization area and elementary or nursery teachers must pass general knowledge area of the NTE. Complete an academic major in liberal arts, science or technology. Complete an approved teacher preparation program or a provisional teacher program as specified by the state's alternate route to certification.(exceptions include bilingual/ESL education, special education, and vocational education). **Examination:** National Teacher Examination (areas as required by specific endorsement) **Reciprocity:** Holders of instructional certificates completed in a state which has endorsed the Interstate Certification Compact will be qualified for New Jersey's Instructional Certificate upon successful completion of required areas of the NTE written examination.

New Mexico

7681

Secondary Teacher 7-12
Director, Professional Licensing Unit
Education Bldg.
300 Don Gaspar
Santa Fe, NM 87503
Phone: (505)827-6587

Credential Type: Initial License—Level 1. **Duration of License:** Three years. **Authorization:** Classroom instruction **Requirements:** Bachelor's degree from an accredited institution. Pass the Core Battery of the NTE with the following minimum scores: 644 Communication Skills, 645 General Knowledge, and 630 Professional Knowledge. 54 semester hours of general education which includes: 12 hours of English; 12 hours of history (including American and western civilization); six hours of mathematics; six hours of government, economics, or sociology; and six hours of science which includes biology, chemistry, physics, geology, zoology or botany. 30-36 semester hours of professional education which includes completion of the State Board's approved functional areas and related competencies in professional education and a student teaching component. 24-36 semester hours, 12 of which must be in upper division courses as defined by the preparing institution, in a teaching field such as mathematics, science, language arts, reading, social studies, or other specialized area. Nonrenewable. **Examination:** Core Battery of the National Teacher Examination.

Credential Type: Initial License—Level 2. **Duration of License:** Nine years. **Authorization:** Classroom instruction **Requirements:** Meet all requirements for Level one License. Verification by local superintendent or private school officials that applicant has met State Board's prescribed teaching competencies. Renewable.

Credential Type: Initial License—Level 3-A. **Duration of License:** Nine years. **Authorization:** Advanced classroom instruction and instructional leadership **Requirements:** Meet all requirements for Level two License. Master's degree. Verification by local superintendent or private school official that applicant has met the State Board's prescribed Level 3-A competencies.

New York

7682

Secondary Teacher 7-12
Administrator of Teacher Certification Policy
Univ. of the State of New York
State Education Dept.
Cultural Center, Rm. 5-A-11
Albany, NY 12230
Phone: (518)474-6440

Credential Type: Provisional Certificate. **Duration of License:** Five years. **Authorization:** Authorizes the teaching of grades 7—12 in areas of specialization. **Requirements:** Baccalaureate degree with a four year program of collegiate preparation at a regionally accredited or approved higher institution. 12 semester hours of professional education courses. College supervised student teaching experience. Academic concentration in subject for which certificate is issued with semester hours as follows: English 36; foreign language 24; mathematics 24 (must include six hours of college-level study in calculus); social studies 36; science 36 (must include 15 hours of college-level study in the science or each of the sciences for which certification is sought). With recommendation, one full year of full-time teaching experience on the appropriate level may be substituted for student teaching. Note: The city of Buffalo, New York has certification standards that are exclusive of New York State.

Secondary Teacher 7-12, continued

Credential Type: Permanent Certificate. **Duration of License:** Permanent. **Requirements:** Hold a Provisional Certificate at level where certification is sought. Master's degree in or functionally related to field of teaching experience. Two years of secondary school teaching experience. Note: The city of Buffalo, New York has certification standards that are exclusive of New York State.

7683

Special Subjects Teacher N-12
Administrator of Teacher
  Certification Policy
Univ. of the State of New York
State Education Dept.
Cultural Center, Rm. 5-A-11
Albany, NY 12230
Phone: (518)474-6440

Credential Type: Provisional Special Subjects Certificate. **Duration of License:** Five years. **Authorization:** Authorizes the teaching of special subjects, outside of the regular classroom academics, according to area of specialization in grades N-12. **Requirements:** Bachelor's degree from a regionally accredited or approved institution. 12 semester hours of professional education courses. 36 semester hours in technical courses in subject for which certificate is issued. A college supervised student teaching experience. One year of approved and appropriate occupational experience for the commerce and distributive occupations only is allowable in place of student teaching. Note: The city of Buffalo, New York has certification standards that are exclusive of New York State.

Credential Type: Permanent Special Subjects Certificate. **Duration of License:** Permanent. **Requirements:** Hold a Provisional Special Subjects Certificate at level where certification is sought. Master's degree in or functionally related to field of teaching experience. Two years of special subject(s) teaching experience. Note: The city of Buffalo, New York has certification standards that are exclusive of New York State.

North Carolina

7684

Public School Teacher K-12
Certification Section
State Dept. of Public Instruction
Raleigh, NC 27603
Phone: (919)733-4125

Credential Type: Initial Certificate. **Duration of License:** Two years. **Requirements:** Bachelor's degree. Pass NTE examination. Institutional recommendation. Complete an approved teacher education program which includes basic skills required of all teachers in English and English usage, Literature, The Fine Arts, Social Studies, Mathematics, and Science, areas of specialization, and professional education. Nonrenewable. **Examination:** National Teacher Examination **Fees:** $30.00 application fee.

Credential Type: Continuing Professional Certificate. **Duration of License:** Five years. **Requirements:** Two years of successful teaching experience in North Carolina under the Initial Certificate. May be renewed anytime after January 1, prior to the certificate's expiration date, upon application and completion of 10 semester hours of appropriate college credit earned during the previous five years. Hours may also be completed by workshops or institutes for which prior credit has been approved by the Local Administrative Unit. **Fees:** $30.00 application fee.

Credential Type: Subject Endorsement. **Requirements:** Valid North Carolina teaching certificate. Endorsement will be granted in the applicant's subject of specialization (major or minor) as recommended by the preparing institution.

7685

Special Education Teacher K-12
Certification Section
State Dept. of Public Instruction
Raleigh, NC 27603
Phone: (919)733-4125

Credential Type: Special Education Certificate. **Duration of License:** Five years. **Requirements:** Complete a program of teacher preparation with a bachelor's or higher degree and specialization in the requested area of certification. Pass NTE examination. Institutional recommendation. Examinations proving competencies in area of specialization may also be required. **Examination:** National Teacher Examination. **Fees:** $30 application fee. $30 renewal fee.

North Dakota

7686

Secondary School Teacher
Director of Certification
State Dept. of Public Instruction
Bismarck, ND 58505
Phone: (701)224-2264

Credential Type: North Dakota Educator's Professional Certificate. **Duration of License:** Entrance two years, renewable for five years. **Requirements:** Bachelor's degree from an accredited college approved to offer teacher preparation. 26 semester credit hours of professional education. Overall GPA of 2.5. Renewal is possible with two years of successful teaching experience and four semester credit hours of work.

Ohio

7687

High School Teacher 7-12
Teacher Education and Certification
State Dept. of Education
65 S. Front St., Rm. 1012
Columbus, OH 43266-0308
Phone: (614)466-3593

Credential Type: Provisional High School Certificate. **Requirements:** Baccalaureate degree. Good moral character. Complete an approved program of teacher preparation including an examination. Recommendation of preparing institution. 30 semester hours of general education courses distributed over the humanities, mathematics, natural sciences, and social sciences. 24 semester hours of professional education courses, both clinical and fieldbased, designed for teaching grades 7-12. 24 semester hours of content course work in the area of specialization. Ohio recognizes the following academic subject majors: biological science; bookkeeping and basic business; chemistry; classical language; computer science; dance; drama/theater; earth science; economics; English; general science; geography; health; history; home economics; industrial technology; journalism; library/media; mathematics; music; physical education; physics; political science; psychology/sociology; sales; speech/communications; stenography and typing/keyboarding; and visual arts.

Credential Type: High School Comprehensive Certificate. **Requirements:** Baccalaureate degree. Good moral character. Complete an approved program of teacher preparation including an examination. Recommendation of preparing institution. 30 semester hours of general educa-

Secondary School Teachers

tion courses distributed over the humanities, mathematics, natural sciences, and social sciences. 24 semester hours of professional education courses, both clinical and fieldbased, designed for teaching grades 7-12. 60 semester hours of course work in Comprehensive Certificate approved majors including: business education; communications; family life education; humanities; science; and social science.

7688

Middle School Teacher 4-9
Teacher Education and Certification
State Dept. of Education
65 S. Front St., Rm 1012
Columbus, OH 43266-0308
Phone: (614)466-3593

Credential Type: Provisional Middle Grades Certificates. **Requirements:** Baccalaureate degree. Good moral character. Complete an approved program of teacher preparation including an examination. Recommendation of preparing institution. 30 semester hours of general education courses to include: the humanities; mathematics; natural sciences; and social science. 30 semester hours of professional education courses, both clinical and field-based, designed for teaching grades 4-9. 45 semester hours of curriculum content course work to be well distributed over two of the following areas, including the minimum course work specified for each: language arts and reading 30; mathematics 20; science 20; and social studies 20.

7689

Public School Teacher K-12
Teacher Education and Certification
State Dept. of Education
65 S. Front St., Rm. 1012
Columbus, OH 43266-0308
Phone: (614)466-3593

Credential Type: Provisional All Grades Certificate. **Requirements:** Baccalaureate degree. Good moral character. Complete an approved program of teacher preparation including an examination. Recommendation of preparing institution. 30 semester hours of general education courses distributed over the humanities, mathematics, natural sciences, and social sciences. 30 professional education semester hours, both clinical and field-based, designed for teaching grades K-12. Curriculum content must include the following minimum number of course work semester hours in the area of specialization: computer science 30; dance 45; drama/theater 45; health education 30; industrial technology 45; library/media 30; foreign language 45 (more than one language 30 hours each); music 45; physical education 45; reading 30; and visual art 45.

7690

Special Education Teacher K-12
Teacher Education and Certification
State Dept. of Education
65 S. Front St., Rm. 1012
Columbus, OH 43266-0308
Phone: (614)466-3593

Credential Type: Provisional Special Education of the Handicapped Certificate. **Requirements:** Baccalaureate degree. Good moral character. Complete an approved program of teacher preparation including an examination. Recommendation of preparing institution. 30 semester hours of general education courses distributed over the humanities, mathematics, natural sciences, and social sciences. 20 semester hours of professional education courses, both clinical and fieldbased, designed for teaching grades K-12. 30 semester hours of curriculum content work including health, language arts, mathematics, music, physical education, reading, science, social studies, and visual arts. 20 semester hours of specialization courses in one of the following: developmentally handicapped; hearing handicapped; multi-handicapped; orthopedically handicapped; severe behavior handicapped; special learning disabled; and visually handicapped.

7691

Teacher of Special Subjects
Teacher Education and Certification
State Dept. of Education
65 S. Front St., Rm. 1012
Columbus, OH 43266-0308
Phone: (614)466-3593

Credential Type: Special Subjects Endorsement. **Requirements:** Baccalaureate degree. Good moral character. Complete an approved program of teacher preparation including an examination. Recommendation of preparing institution. Ohio Standard Teaching Certificate. Endorsement is possible in the following subjects with the specified number of semester credit hours: Driver Education 6; Library/Media 20; Reading 12; and Typing/Keyboarding 6. Other fields possible as approved by the State Board of Education.

Credential Type: Special Subject Validation. **Requirements:** Baccalaureate degree. Good moral character. Complete an approved program of teacher preparation including an examination. Recommendation of preparing institution. Ohio Standard Teaching Certificate which relates directly to area in which validation is sought. Validation is possible in the following subjects with 20 semester credit hours of additional course work: Adapted Physical Education; Bilingual/Multicultural Education; Gifted Education; Pre-Kindergarten; Teaching English to Speakers of Other Languages; and Early Education of Handicapped Children. Other fields possible as approved by the State Board of Education.

Oklahoma

7692

Secondary School Teacher 7-12
Teacher Education and Certification
State Dept. of Education
2500 N. Lincoln Blvd., Rm. 211
Oklahoma City, OK 73105
Phone: (405)521-3337

Credential Type: Secondary General Certificate. **Duration of License:** One year. **Requirements:** Complete an approved certificate program at an accredited college or university and receive recommendation from that institution. Pass the state teacher certification test(s) in secondary education competencies. **Examination:** State teacher certification test(s). **Reciprocity:** Oklahoma recognizes some out-of-state teaching certificates.

Credential Type: Secondary Standard Certificate (undergraduate). **Duration of License:** Five years. **Requirements:** Complete an approved certificate program at an accredited college or university which includes a minimum of the following: a baccalaureate degree; 50 semester hours in general education; 30 semester hours in professional education; and 40 semester hours in course work pertaining to teaching secondary grades. Pass the state certified test(s) in secondary education competencies. Successfully complete the Entry-Year Assistance Program as a licensed teacher. Complete a course of two or more semester hours in the education of the exceptional child. **Examination:** State certification test(s). **Reciprocity:** Oklahoma recognizes some out-of-state teaching certificates.

Credential Type: Provisional Level II Certificate—Secondary. **Duration of License:** Two years. **Requirements:** Complete approved certificate program at an accredited college or university. Baccalaureate degree. 56 semester hours in general education course work. 24 semester hours in professional education which includes field experiences and student teaching. 30 semester hours in secondary education. Pass the state certification test(s) in secondary education.

Secondary School Teacher 7-12, continued

Successfully complete the Entry-Year Assistance Program as a licensed teacher. Complete a course of two or more semester hours in the education of the exceptional child. **Examination:** State certification test(s). **Reciprocity:** Oklahoma recognizes some out-of-state teaching certificates.

Credential Type: Provisional Level I Certificate—Special Education. **Duration of License:** One year. **Requirements:** Complete approved certificate program at an accredited college or university. Baccalaureate degree. 56 semester hours in general education course work. 18 semester hours in professional education which includes field experiences and student teaching. 24 semester hours in secondary education. Pass the state certification test(s) in special education. Successfully complete the Entry-Year Assistance Program as a licensed teacher. Complete a course of two or more semester hours in the education of the exceptional child. **Examination:** State certification test(s). **Reciprocity:** Oklahoma recognizes some out-of-state teaching certificates.

Credential Type: Additional Certificate. **Requirements:** Certified individuals who seek additional certification must complete the following: a methods course appropriate to the second certificate sought and a developmental psychology course appropriate to the grade level of the certificate.

7693

Special Education Teacher N-12
Teacher Education and Certification
State Dept. of Education
2500 N. Lincoln Blvd., Rm. 211
Oklahoma City, OK 73105
Phone: (405)521-3337

Credential Type: Elementary-Secondary General Certificate. **Duration of License:** One year. **Requirements:** Complete an approved certificate program at an accredited college or university and receive recommendation from that institution. Pass the state teacher certification test(s) in special education competencies. **Examination:** State teacher certification test(s). **Reciprocity:** Oklahoma recognizes some out-of-state teaching certificates.

Credential Type: Elementary-Secondary Standard Certificate (undergraduate). **Duration of License:** Five years. **Requirements:** Complete an approved certificate program at an accredited college or university which includes a minimum of the following: a baccalaureate degree; 50 semester hours in general education; 30 semester hours in professional education; and 40 semester hours in course work pertaining to teaching special education. Pass the state certified test(s) in special education competencies. Successfully complete the Entry-Year Assistance Program as a licensed teacher. Complete a course of two or more semester hours in the education of the exceptional child. **Examination:** State certification test(s). **Reciprocity:** Oklahoma recognizes some out-of-state teaching certificates.

Credential Type: Provisional Level II Certificate—Special Education. **Duration of License:** Two years. **Requirements:** Complete approved certificate program at an accredited college or university. Baccalaureate degree. 56 semester hours in general education course work. 24 semester hours in professional education which includes field experiences and student teaching. 30 semester hours in special education. Pass the state certification test(s) in special education. Successfully complete the Entry-Year Assistance Program as a licensed teacher. Complete a course of two or more semester hours in the education of the exceptional child. **Examination:** State certification test(s). **Reciprocity:** Oklahoma recognizes some out-of-state teaching certificates.

Credential Type: Provisional Level I Certificate—Special Education. **Duration of License:** One year. **Requirements:** Complete approved certificate program at an accredited college or university. Baccalaureate degree. 56 semester hours in general education course work. 18 semester hours in professional education which includes field experiences and student teaching. 24 semester hours in special education. Pass the state certification test(s) in special education. Successfully complete the Entry-Year Assistance Program as a licensed teacher. Complete a course of two or more semester hours in the education of the exceptional child. **Examination:** State certification test(s). **Reciprocity:** Oklahoma recognizes some out-of-state teaching certificates.

Credential Type: Additional Certificate. **Requirements:** Certified individuals who seek additional certification must complete the following: a methods course appropriate to the second certificate sought and a developmental psychology course appropriate to the grade level of the certificate.

Oregon

7694

Public School Teacher K-12
Teacher Standards and Practices Commission
630 Center St. NE, Ste. 200
Salem, OR 97310-0320
Phone: (503)378-3586

Credential Type: Basic Teaching Certificate. **Duration of License:** Three years. **Requirements:** Baccalaureate degree. Complete a four year teacher program. Professional education courses must equal 36 quarter hours and include competencies in diagnostic and prescriptive techniques; methods in appropriate subject and grade level of endorsement; teaching reading; public school curriculum; foundations of education; educational psychology of individuals and groups served by public schools; classroom management; education of exceptional children and/or youth; and student teaching or internship. Complete one of the subject or special education endorsements established by the Teacher Standards and Practices Commission. One year of successful public school teaching experience within the three-year period preceding application or nine quarter hours of preparation in a teacher education institution within the past three years. Passing scores on the CBEST. Out-of-state prepared applicants may submit their passing scores on the Core Battery of the National Teacher Examination, in lieu of the CBEST. **Examination:** California Basic Educational Skills Test.

Credential Type: Standard Teaching Certificate. **Duration of License:** Five years. **Requirements:** Complete a five year teacher education program with 5th year culminating in a master's degree or complete 45 quarter hours of upper division and graduate study. Applicants prepared out-of-state must have verification of a master's degree from an approved teacher education institution. Must have two years of successful teaching experience on a Basic Teaching Certificate in Oregon schools.

Credential Type: Subject Matter Endorsements. **Requirements:** Endorsements may be added to Standard Certificates with an additional 15 quarter hours credit in the endorsement area being sought. Endorsements may be added to Basic Certificates with the specified number of quarter hr. credits as follows: Elementary 60; Agriculture 60; Art 45; Business and Office Education 48; Educational Media 24; Marketing 48; Foreign Language 48; Health Education 42; Home Economics (non-vocational) 48; Technology Education 45; Language Arts 45; Speech 24; Drama 24; Basic Mathematics 21; Advanced Mathematics 42; Music 60; Physical Education 48; Reading 21; Biology 45; Integrated Science 45; Chemistry 27; Physics 27; and Social Studies 54.

Pennsylvania

7695

Classroom Teacher K-12
Bureau of Certification
Dept. of Education
333 Market St.
Harrisburg, PA 17126-0333
Phone: (717)787-2967

Credential Type: Intern Certificate. **Duration of License:** Three years. **Requirements:** Non-education major baccalaureate degree. Complete appropriate professional education courses in an approved intern program. Recommendation of preparing institution. Successful completion of the required basic skills, general knowledge and subject matter tests. Qualified to hold Instructional Certificate I after completion of internship and passage of the NTE Professional Knowledge Test.

All new applicants must produce a background clearance as required in Act 34. A Pennsylvania State Police background check is required for Pennsylvania residents and an F.B.I. background check is required for out-of-state residents. Applicants may not teach without this clearance. **Examination:** NTE Communications Test; NTE General Knowledge Test; and Area of Specialization Test.

Credential Type: Instructional Certificate I—Provisional. **Duration of License:** Six years. **Requirements:** Bachelor's degree. Complete approved program of study. Recommendation by preparing institution. Successful completion of Pennsylvania Teacher Certification Testing Program. Must participate in a district developed, PDE approved plan for continuing, professional development.

All new applicants must produce a background clearance as required in Act 34. A Pennsylvania State Police background check is required for Pennsylvania residents and an F.B.I. background check is required for out-of-state residents. Applicants may not teach without this clearance **Examination:** NTE Communications Skills Test; NTE General Knowledge Test; NTE Professional Knowledge Test; and Area of Specialization Test.

Credential Type: Instructional Certificate II—Permanent. **Duration of License:** Permanent. **Requirements:** Completion of Department-approved induction plan. Three years of satisfactory teaching under Instructional Certificate I. Complete 24 semester hours of post-baccalaureate study which may be satisfied, in whole or part, through PDE approved in-service programs.

7696

Educational Specialist
Bureau of Certification
Dept. of Education
333 Market St.
Harrisburg, PA 17126-0333
Phone: (717)787-2967

Credential Type: Educational Specialist I—Provisional. **Duration of License:** Six years. **Authorization:** Authorizes holding public school positions as non-teaching professionals. **Requirements:** Bachelor's degree. Complete approved program of study. Recommendation by preparing institution.

All new applicants must produce a background clearance as required in Act 34. A Pennsylvania State Police background check is required for Pennsylvania residents and an F.B.I. background check is required for out-of-state residents. Applicants may not work in Pennsylvania public schools without this clearance.

Credential Type: Educational Specialist II—Permanent. **Duration of License:** Permanent. **Authorization:** Authorizes holding public school positions as non-teaching professionals. **Requirements:** Three years of satisfactory service in a single area while holding the Educational Specialist I Certificate. 24 semester hours of postbaccalaureate study that may be satisfied, in whole or in part, through PDE approved inservice programs.

Rhode Island

7697

Secondary School Teacher 7-12
Office of Teacher Certification
State Dept. of Education
22 Hayes St.
Providence, RI 02908
Phone: (401)277-2675

Credential Type: Provisional Certificate. **Duration of License:** Three years. **Requirements:** Bachelor's degree. Complete an approved program for the area of certified teaching sought or six semester hours of student teaching at the secondary level and 18 semester hours of course work in the following areas: adolescent psychology; secondary methods; measurements and evaluation; identification of and service to special needs students; teaching of reading in the content area; and foundations of education. Pass the Core Battery of the NTE with minimum scores as follows: Communication Skills 657; General Knowledge 649; Professional Knowledge 648. Semester hr. requirements for certified areas of teaching are as follows: agriculture 36; business education 36; English 30; history (which may include six hours of social studies) 30; classical language 30; foreign language (a portion of required hours may be waived upon presentation of a statement proving competency) 30; mathematics 30; general science (which must include biology, physics, and chemistry) 30; biology 30; chemistry 30; physics 30; social studies 36; and academic areas not listed 18. Nonrenewable. **Examination:** Core Battery of the National Teacher Examination.

Credential Type: Professional Certificate. **Duration of License:** Five years. **Requirements:** Three years of documented teaching experience on a Rhode Island Secondary Provisional Certificate. May be renewed upon completion of nine credits and verification of continued teaching experience as a secondary teacher. Six of the required nine credits must be on the graduate level and three of the graduate credits must be in the area in which secondary certification is held. Of the nine required credits, three may be in approved,in-service work and the rest must be done at the college level.

Credential Type: Life Professional Certificate. **Duration of License:** Permanent. **Requirements:** Master's degree in the academic field in which provisional certification is held or master's degree and 15 semester hours of graduate level work in the academic field in which provisional certification is held. Must have six years of teaching experience at the secondary level, of which three years must be in Rhode Island.

7698

Special Subjects Teacher PK-12
Office of Teacher Certification
State Dept. of Education
22 Hayes St.
Providence, RI 02908
Phone: (401)277-2675

Credential Type: Provisional Certificate. **Duration of License:** Three years. **Requirements:** Bachelor's degree. Complete an approved program designed for the preparation of special subject teachers or complete six semester hours of student teaching in the special subjects field at both the elementary and secondary levels and 18 semester hours of course work to include the following areas: human growth and development; foundations of education; methodology; measurement and evaluation; identi-

Special Subjects Teacher PK-12, continued

fication of and service to special needs students; and the teaching of reading in the content area. In some cases the student teaching requirement may be waived or reduced if the applicant has had prior experience teaching in his/her special subject field. The following list denotes the minimum number of semester hours required to be certified in each special subject area: Art 36; Dance 24; Health 24; Physical Education 24; Health and Physical Education (with equal time divided between subjects) 48; Home Economics 36; Industrial Arts 36; Library/Media 36; Music 36; Theater 24; and special subjects not listed 18. Extensions are possible for individuals who have not completed three years of teaching during the life of this certificate, all others must apply for the Professional Certificate.

Credential Type: Professional Certificate. **Duration of License:** Five years. **Requirements:** Complete six credits while under the Rhode Island Provisional Certificate. Three of the six credits may be approved in-service course work and the rest must be college credits. Three years of successful teaching in the special subjects field while under the provisional certificate in Rhode Island.

Credential Type: Life Professional Certificate. **Duration of License:** Permanent. **Requirements:** Master's degree in the special subjects field in which provisional certification is held or a master's degree in any field of education and 15 semester hours of graduate level course work in the special field in which provisional certification is held, either as part of or beyond the master's degree, in education. Must have six years of teaching experience in the special field, of which three years must be in Rhode Island.

South Carolina

7699

Public School Teacher PK-12
Teacher Education and Certification
State Dept. of Education
Rutledge Bldg., Rm. 1015
Columbia, SC 29201
Phone: (803)734-8464

Credential Type: Initial Certificate. **Requirements:** Complete a State Board of Education approved teacher training program. Pass the NTE Core Battery of Professional Knowledge. Teachers of Special Subjects must pass the NTE Specialty Area Examination or South Carolina Area Examination. **Examination:** National Teacher Examination Core Battery of Professional Knowledge; National Teacher Examination Specialty Area Examination or South Carolina Area Examination (teachers of special subjects only).

Credential Type: Professional Certificate—Class III. **Requirements:** South Carolina Initial Certificate. Bachelor's degree.

Credential Type: Professional Certificate—Class II. **Requirements:** South Carolina Initial Certificate. Bachelor's degree plus 18 semester hours of graduate credit.

Credential Type: Professional Certificate—Class I. **Requirements:** South Carolina Initial Certificate. Master's degree.

Credential Type: Specialist Professional Certificate—Class I. **Requirements:** South Carolina Initial Certificate. Master's or specialist's degree consisting of 60 semester hours, of which 30 semester hours of graduate credit must be a planned program approved by the State Board of Education.

Credential Type: Advanced Professional Certificate—Class I. **Requirements:** South Carolina Initial Certificate. Doctorate from an approved program.

Credential Type: Certificate Endorsement. **Requirements:** Areas of certification may be added to professional South Carolina Teaching Credentials by completing approved programs of specific course requirements as specified by the South Carolina State Board of Education.

South Dakota

7700

School Reading Specialist K-12
Teacher Education and Certification
State Dept. of Education
700 Governor's Drive
Pierre, SD 57501
Phone: (605)773-3553

Credential Type: Reading Specialist Certificate Endorsement. **Requirements:** Valid South Dakota elementary or secondary certificate. Complete three years of classroom teaching in which the teaching of reading was an important responsibility of the position. Must have undergraduate credit in the following: measurement and/or evaluation; child and/or adolescent psychology; psychology including such aspects as personality, cognition, and learning behaviors; and literature for children and/or adolescents. Complete a minimum of 12 semester hours in graduate level reading courses with at least one course in each of the following: foundations or survey of reading; diagnosis and correction of reading disabilities; and clinical or laboratory practicum in reading.

7701

Secondary School Teacher
Teacher Education and Certification
State Dept. of Education
700 Governor's Drive
Pierre, SD 57501
Phone: (605)773-3553

Credential Type: Secondary Certificate Endorsement. **Requirements:** Complete approved bachelor's degree program in secondary education with an approved major in an academic or special field. Must have completed program within the five years preceding application or must have earned six semester hours or nine quarter hours of credit pertaining to elementary education within five years preceding application. The holder of a master's degree in secondary education will be exempt from the additional credits provided the master's degree was earned within the 10 years preceding application. Must have a three semester hr. course in Indian studies. Secondary program must have 21 semester hours of course work which includes the following: six semester hours of student teaching at the secondary level; six semester hours of secondary school methods classes which includes three semester hours of teaching reading in the content area; and nine semester hours of professional studies which includes psychology of teaching, learning, the adolescent, and the exceptional child.

Renewal is possible with six semester hours of credit completed during the life of the certificate, of which three semester hours may be completed in approved workshops. The holder of a master's degree may renew without additional credits. **Fees:** $20 certification fee. $20 renewal fee.

Tennessee

7702

Secondary School Teacher 7-12
Office of Teaching Licensing
Dept. of Education
Cordell Hull Bldg.
Nashville, TN 37219-5335
Phone: (615)741-1644

Credential Type: Probationary License. **Duration of License:** One year. **Requirements:** Bachelor's degree. Complete an approved teacher education program which consists of the following: 60 quarter hours of general education which includes course work in communications, health, physical education, personal development, human-

Secondary School Teachers

ities, natural sciences, social studies, and fundamental concepts of mathematics; 36 quarter hours of professional education which includes psychological foundations of education, human growth and development, learning, measurement, evaluation, and guidance, curriculum school organization and management, audio-visual aids, education for exceptional children, materials and methods, and six quarter hours of supervised student teaching. Endorsements for 7-12 teaching is possible with the additional quarter hours of study as follows: business 27; distributive education 30; English 36; foreign language 36; two or more foreign languages 45; health 24; home economics 36; industrial arts 45; mathematics 27; physical education 30; science group plan 48; individual science plan (biology, chemistry, physics, earth and space) 24; history 27; geography 18; sociology 18; government 18; economics 18; psychology 18; social studies group plan (American history, European history, and choice of one other) 27; and speech 21. Pass NTE Core Battery and required Specialty Area Test. Renewable. **Examination:** National Teacher Examination and Specialty Area Test.

Credential Type: Interim Probationary "A" Teacher's License. **Duration of License:** One year. **Requirements:** Bachelor's degree. Six quarter hours of professional education college credit. Content course work for an area of endorsement. Intention of employment by a local education agency. Renewable four times with the successful completion of nine quarter hours of applicable course work for each renewal and a statement of intention of employment with a local school system.

Credential Type: Interim Probationary "B" Teacher's License. **Duration of License:** One year. **Requirements:** Meets all state requirements for Probationary Teacher's License but lacks qualifying scores required on NTE tests. Bachelor's degree. Renewable one time.

Credential Type: Apprentice License. **Duration of License:** Three years. **Requirements:** Probationary License. Satisfactory completion of the probationary year. Renewable.

Credential Type: Professional License. **Duration of License:** 10 years. **Requirements:** Bachelor's degree. Probationary License. Three years of successful service in a Tennessee public school. Renewable.

Credential Type: Out-of-State Teacher's License. **Duration of License:** Three years. **Requirements:** Bachelor's degree and approved teacher education program. One year of successful teaching experience. Pass the NTE Core Battery and Specialty Area Tests. **Examination:** National Teacher Examination Core Battery and Specialty Area Tests.

Credential Type: Career Level I Certificate. **Duration of License:** 10 years. **Requirements:** Apprentice License.Satisfactory performance at the apprentice level with local education agency recommendation. Renewable.

Credential Type: Career Level II and III Certificates. **Duration of License:** 10 years. **Requirements:** Career Level I Certificate. Must elect to be evaluated and pass evaluation. Renewable.

7703

Special Education Teacher
Office of Teaching Licensing
Dept. of Education
Cordell Hull Bldg.
Nashville, TN 37219-5335
Phone: (615)741-1644

Credential Type: Special Education Endorsement. **Authorization:** Endorsement will be granted to teach in one of the following areas: learning disabilities; mental retardation; emotionally disturbed; socially maladjusted; gifted; and crippling and special health conditions. **Requirements:** Bachelor's degree in a special education field. Must demonstrate in early and continual student placements in supervised laboratory and field settings the competencies outlined and must be recommended for certification by a college or university whose approved program was completed.

Texas

7704

Texas Public School Teacher
Texas Education Agency
1701 N. Congress Ave.
Austin, TX 78701-1494
Phone: (512)463-8976

Credential Type: Provisional Certificate. **Authorization:** Certificate will be endorsed to teach in one of the following areas: Elementary grades 1-8; High school grades 6-12; Hearing impaired grades PK-12; Speech and language therapy grades PK-12; Special subjects (art, music, physical education, and speech communication). **Requirements:** Bachelor's degree from a college or university approved for teacher education. 60 semester hours of general education which includes: 12 hours English; three hours speech; six hours American history; three hours Political Science that covers the U.S. and Texas constitutions; 3-6 hours of natural science with lab; three hours of mathematics (college algebra or above); three hours computing and information technology (demonstration of competency also accepted); three hours fine arts; plus electives. 18 semester hours of professional development courses which includes core requirements, methodology, field experience. Core requirements must consist of studies in the following: teaching/learning processes, including measurement and evaluation of student achievement; human growth and development; knowledge and skills concerning the unique needs of special learners; legal and ethical aspects of teaching to include the recognition of an response to signs of abuse and neglect in children; structure, organization and management of the American school system, with emphasis upon the state and local structure in Texas; and education computing, media, and other technologies. Methodology must include studies of the following: instructional methods and strategies that emphasize practical applications of the teaching/learning processes; curriculum organization, planning, and evaluation; basic principles and procedures of classroom management with emphasis on classroom discipline, utilizing group and individual processes, as well as different techniques and procedures adapted to the personality of the teacher; and the scope and sequence of the essential elements for all subjects required in the elementary course of study that are not included in the academic specialization when elementary options are selected. Areas of academic specialization requires 36-48 semester hours in the subject area. Field experience must consist of not fewer than 45 clock hours of pre-student teaching which shall include observation and experience at the level for which a student teaching assignment is anticipated and a six semester hours student teaching assignment. Student teaching may be waived if the applicant has taught in an accredited school as a classroom teacher for two or more years at the level at which certification is sought. Must pass the ExCET examination. **Examination:** Examination for the Certification of Educators in Texas.

Credential Type: Professional Certificate. **Requirements:** Bachelor's degree. Valid Texas provisional teacher certificate. Complete 30 semester hours of an approved graduate program in area of specialization. Three years of teaching experience.

Utah

7705

Secondary School Teacher 6-12
Certification and Personnel
  Development Section
State Board of Education
250 East 500 South St.
Salt Lake City, UT 84111
Phone: (801)538-7740

Credential Type: Basic Certificate. **Duration of License:** Four years. **Authorization:** Required for teaching at the secondary level and does not allow for teaching in an elementary self-contained classroom. **Requirements:** Bachelor's degree in an approved program for secondary school teachers. Complete a 30 semester hours subject major program and a 16 semester hr. subject minor program or a 46 hr. composite subject major program. Complete an approved program in professional education that includes: student teaching; education of the exceptional child; teaching of reading in the content area; and introduction to computers. Recommendation of the preparing institute.

Credential Type: Standard Certificate. **Duration of License:** Valid indefinitely with consistent employment. **Requirements:** Two years of successful teaching experience under the Basic Teaching Certificate. Recommendation from the employing school district with input from a teacher education institution. Valid indefinitely providing holder verifies appropriate employment in education of at least three years during each succeeding five year interval. May also be renewed with nine quarter hours of approved credit earned within the five year period prior to date of application if more than five years have elapsed since applicant received bachelor's or higher degree.

7706

Special Education Teacher K-12
Certification and Personnel
  Development Section
State Board of Education
250 East 500 South St.
Salt Lake City, UT 84111
Phone: (801)538-7740

Credential Type: Special Education Certificate. **Requirements:** Bachelor's degree. Completion of an approved program in the specific area of endorsement. Utah issues endorsements in the following areas: Mild/moderate learning and behavior problems; Severe learning and behavior problems; Hearing handicaps; Visual handicaps.

7707

Teacher of Pupils with Communications Disorders K-12
Certification and Personnel
  Development Section
State Board of Education
250 East 500 South St.
Salt Lake City, UT 84111
Phone: (801)538-7740

Credential Type: Communications Disorders Certificate. **Requirements:** Bachelor's degree approved program for teaching pupils with communications disorders. Plus a master's degree or 55 quarter hours of credit earned after meeting requirements for the bachelor's degree. Recommendation of preparing institution.

Vermont

7708

Consulting Teacher or Learning Specialist
Teacher Licensure
State Dept. of Education
Montpelier, VT 05602-2703
Phone: (802)828-2445

Credential Type: Initial Certificate. **Authorization:** Holder of this is certificate is authorized to assist and share responsibility with regular and special education personnel in designing, implementing, and evaluating Individual Education Programs for handicapped students. **Requirements:** Master's degree or its equivalent in special education. Supervised advanced clinical practicum with handicapped students. Two years of educational work experience with both handicapped and nonhandicapped students. Meet specific competencies as determined by the Standards Board.

7709

Secondary School Teacher 7-12
Teacher Licensure
State Dept. of Education
Montpelier, VT 05602-2703
Phone: (802)828-2445

Credential Type: Level One: Beginning Educator's License. **Duration of License:** Two years. **Requirements:** Graduate from a regionally accredited or state approved four year institution or a state approved fifth year program. By July 1995, a bachelor's degree and a major in the liberal arts will be required. Possession of competence appropriate to the endorsement being sought. Must demonstrate ability to write clearly, to apply appropriate mathematical skills effectively, to speak correctly and effectively, and to respond constructively to student behavior. One semester of student teaching, or an equivalent learning experience, or completion of an approved fifth year, mentor, or internship program. Competency in teaching as specified in the following requirements: ability to identify the processes by which students learn and ability to select appropriate methods and materials to meet students' learning needs; ability to select, use, and interpret assessment processes and instruments to identify the strengths and weaknesses of individual students; ability to teach reading skills as they relate to the subject matter being taught; ability to recognize the individual learner's physical, intellectual and psychological developmental needs; ability to apply knowledge of child development, and of early and late adolescence development, to learning; ability to integrate special education students into appropriate learning situations; ability to develop students' awareness of and responsibility for personal health; ability to select and use appropriate technology within the endorsement area(s); ability to apply current state and federal laws and regulations as they apply to all children; ability to identify conditions and actions which would tend to discriminate against students on the basis of sex, race, color, creed, age, handicap, or national origin and to develop teaching strategies to overcome those conditions and actions. Renewal requires recommendation by the Local Standards Board upon completion of an approved Individual Professional Development Plan. **Reciprocity:** Reciprocity exists for persons certified to teach in a state with which Vermont has signed a reciprocal agreement. All others will be evaluated on an individual basis.

Credential Type: Level Two: Professional Educator's License. **Duration of License:** Seven years. **Requirements:** Two years of experience under a Level One License. Demonstrate the following characteristics: ability to plan instruction; ability to maintain a positive learning environment; ability to conduct learning experiences for individuals as well as groups; knowledge of content area; and interest and motivation in continuing professional development. Renewal requires nine credit hours, or the equivalent of educational development activity, per license endorsement area.

7710

Teacher of the Handicapped
Teacher Licensure
State Dept. of Education
Montpelier, VT 05602-2703
Phone: (802)828-2445

Credential Type: Level One: Beginning Educator's License. **Duration of License:** Two years. **Authorization:** Endorsements will be granted in four areas: Essential Early Education Classroom or Home Programs; Intensive Special Education Classrooms or Multihandicapped; Special Education Class Programs/Resource Teacher Programs; and Secondary Diversified Occupations Program. **Requirements:** Graduate from a regionally accredited or state approved four year institution or a state approved fifth year program. Must meet specific requirements for specific endorsement as established by the Standards Board. Must demonstrate ability to write clearly, to apply appropriate mathematical skills effectively, to speak correctly and effectively, and to respond constructively to student behavior. One semester of student teaching, or an equivalent learning experience, or completion of an approved fifth year, mentor, or internship program. Competency in teaching as specified in the following requirements: ability to identify the processes by which students learn and ability to select appropriate methods and materials to meet students' learning needs; ability to select, use, and interpret assessment processes and instruments to identify the strengths and weaknesses of individual students; ability to teach reading skills as they relate to the subject matter being taught; ability to recognize the individual learner's physical, intellectual and psychological developmental needs; ability to apply knowledge of child development, and of early and late adolescence development, to learning; ability to integrate special education students into appropriate learning situations; ability to develop students' awareness of and responsibility for personal health; ability to select and use appropriate technology within the endorsement area(s); ability to apply current state and federal laws and regulations as they apply to all children; ability to identify conditions and actions which would tend to discriminate against students on the basis of sex, race, color, creed, age, handicap, or national origin and to develop teaching strategies to overcome those conditions and actions. Renewal requires recommendation by the Local Standards Board upon completion of an approved Individual Professional Development Plan.

Credential Type: Level Two: Professional Educator's License. **Duration of License:** Seven years. **Requirements:** Two years of experience under a Level One License. Demonstrate the following characteristics: ability to plan instruction; ability to maintain a positive learning environment; ability to conduct learning experiences for individuals as well as groups; knowledge of content area; and interest and motivation in continuing professional development. Renewal requires nine credit hours, or the equivalent of educational development activity, per license endorsement area.

Virginia

7711

Middle School Teacher 4-8
Administrative Director
Office of Professional Development and Teacher Education
Dept. of Education
PO Box 6-Q
Richmond, VA 23216-2060
Phone: (804)225-2094

Credential Type: Probational Certificate. **Duration of License:** One year. **Authorization:** Authorizes candidate who has gained employment in the Virginia Public Schools, but has not yet satisfied the National Teacher Examination (NTE) requirement, to teach for a period of one year. **Requirements:** Meet BTAP (Beginning Teacher Assistance Program) competencies. 48 semester hours of general studies to include six hours each of the following: social sciences; natural sciences; mathematics; school health; and physical education. Must also include 12 semester hours of humanities, social science (including American history), and natural sciences and mathematics. Plus four semester hours of school health and physical education.

Must have 12 semester hours of professional studies including not less than three hours each of human growth and development, curriculum and instructional procedures, and foundations of education. Plus a six semester hr. student teaching experience which includes 200 clock hours in the classroom, and at least 60 percent of that time candidate must provide direct instruction.

60 semester hours of specialized courses for middle grade education must include six hours each of the following: reading, language arts, social science, mathematics, science, art, music, health and physical education. Plus a total of 15 semester hours in two areas of concentration chosen from language arts, social science, math or science. Nonrenewable.

Credential Type: Provisional Certificate. **Duration of License:** Two years. **Authorization:** Authorizes candidates who have not yet satisfied requirements for Virginia's Beginning Teacher Assistance Program, or individuals entering the profession five or more years after their last formal study, or individuals holding a baccalaureate degree with one or more endorsements at the secondary level, or individuals failing to meet general or professional education requirements but have one or more specific endorsements to be employed in a Virginia Public School for a period of two years. **Requirements:** Pass NTE examination. Meet BTAP competencies. 48 semester hours of general studies to include six hours each of the following: social sciences; natural sciences; mathematics; school health; and physical education. Must also include 12 semester hours of humanities, social science (including American history), and natural sciences and mathematics. Plus four semester hours of school health and physical education.

Must have 12 semester hours of professional studies including not less than three hours each of human growth and development, curriculum and instructional procedures, and foundations of education. Plus a six semester hr. student teaching experience which includes 200 clock hours in the classroom, and at least 60 percent of that time candidate must provide direct instruction.

60 semester hours of specialized courses for middle grade education must include six hours each of the following: reading, language arts, social science, mathematics, science, art, music, health and physical education. Plus a total of 15 semester hours in two areas of concentration chosen from language arts, social science, math or science. Must complete any requirement deficits during the life of the certificate. Nonrenewable. **Examination:** National Teacher Examination.

Credential Type: Collegiate Professional Certificate. **Duration of License:** Five years. **Requirements:** Baccalaureate degree from an accredited institution. Pass NTE examination. Meet BTAP competencies. 48 semester hours of general studies to include six hours each of the following: social sciences; natural sciences; mathematics; school health; and physical education. Must also include 12 semester hours of humanities, social science (including American history), and natural sciences and mathematics. Plus four semester hours of school health and physical education.

Must have 12 semester hours of professional studies including not less than three hours each of human growth and development, curriculum and instructional procedures, and foundations of education. Plus a six semester hr. student teaching experience which includes 200 clock hours in the classroom, and at least 60 percent of that

Middle School Teacher 4-8, continued

time candidate must provide direct instruction.

60 semester hours of specialized courses for middle grade education must include six hours each of the following: reading, language arts, social science, mathematics, science, art, music, health and physical education. Plus a total of 15 semester hours in two areas of concentration chosen from language arts, social science, math or science. Must complete any requirement deficits during the life of the certificate. Renewable. **Reciprocity:** Applicants who have completed a college level teacher preparation program out-of-state may qualify for this certificate upon approval.

7712

Reading Specialist NK-12
Administrative Director
Office of Professional Development and Teacher Education
Dept. of Education
PO Box 6-Q
Richmond, VA 23216-2060
Phone: (804)225-2094

Credential Type: Reading Specialist Endorsement. **Requirements:** Postgraduate Professional Teaching Certificate and three years of successful classroom teaching experience. 18 semester hours of graduate courses to include: foundations or survey of reading instruction; language development; reading in content areas; organization and supervision of reading program; diagnosis and remediation of reading difficulties and a practicum. 12 semester hours of graduate or undergraduate courses to include: measurement and/or evaluation; child and/or adolescent psychology; personality and learning behavior; literature; language arts instruction; learning disabilities; contemporary issues in teaching of reading.

7713

Secondary School Teacher
Administrative Director
Office of Professional Development and Teacher Education
Dept. of Education
PO Box 6-Q
Richmond, VA 23216-2060
Phone: (804)225-2094

Credential Type: Probational Certificate. **Duration of License:** One year. **Authorization:** Authorizes candidate, who has gained employment in the Virginia Public Schools, but has not yet satisfied the National Teacher Examination (NTE) requirement, to teach for a period of one year. **Requirements:** Meet BTAP (Beginning Teacher Assistance Program) competencies. 48 semester hours of general studies to include six hours each of the following: social sciences; natural sciences; mathematics; school health; and physical education. Must also include 12 semester hours of humanities, social science (including American history), and natural sciences and mathematics. Plus four semester hours of school health and physical education.

Must have 12 semester hours of professional studies including not less than three hours each of human growth and development, curriculum and instructional procedures, and foundations of education. Plus a six semester hr. student teaching experience which includes 200 clock hours in the classroom, and at least 60 percent of that time candidate must provide direct instruction.

Must have an endorsement for one or more special subject fields. Endorsements must have the following specified number of semester hours to qualify: Art Education (which includes both two and three dimensional media and concepts plus art history) 33; Driver Education 6; English Education (which includes history and nature of the language, literature, composition, and speech) 36; Modern Foreign Language 36; Latin 30; English as a second language 27; Health Education 36; Physical Education 36; Mathematics (which includes calculus, algebra, geometry, computer science, programming, and language) 27; General Mathematics 18; Music Education (Vocal/Chorus) 45; Music Education (Instrumental) 45; Developmental Reading 30; Biology (also preparation in chemistry, physics, and mathematics) 24; Chemistry (also preparation in biology, physics, and mathematics) 24; Earth and Space Science (also preparation in biology, chemistry or physics, and mathematics) 24; General Science (including six hours each in biology, chemistry, and physics plus 12 hours in earth and space science) 30; Physics (also preparation in chemistry, biology, and mathematics) 24; and Social Studies (including 18 hours history, 12 hours political science, six hours geography, and six hours economics) 42. Nonrenewable.

Credential Type: Provisional Certificate. **Duration of License:** Two years. **Authorization:** Authorizes candidates who have not yet satisfied requirements for Virginia's Beginning Teacher Assistance Program, or individuals entering the profession five or more years after their last formal study, or individuals holding a baccalaureate degree with one or more endorsements at the secondary level, or individuals failing to meet general or professional education requirements but have one or more specific endorsements to be employed in a Virginia Public School for a period of two years. **Requirements:** Pass NTE examination. Meet BTAP competencies. 48 semester hours of general studies to include six hours each of the following: social sciences; natural sciences; mathematics; school health; and physical education. Must also include 12 semester hours of humanities, social science (including American history), and natural sciences and mathematics. Plus four semester hours of school health and physical education.

Must have 12 semester hours of professional studies including not less than three hours each of human growth and development, curriculum and instructional procedures, and foundations of education. Plus a six semester hr. student teaching experience which includes 200 clock hours in the classroom, and at least 60 percent of that time candidate must provide direct instruction.

Must have an endorsement for one or more special subject fields. Endorsements must have the following specified number of semester hours to qualify: Art Education (which includes both two and three dimensional media and concepts plus art history) 33; Driver Education 6; English Education (which includes history and nature of the language, literature, composition, and speech) 36; Modern Foreign Language 36; Latin 30; English as a second language 27; Health Education 36; Physical Education 36; Mathematics (which includes calculus, algebra, geometry, computer science, programming, and language) 27; General Mathematics 18; Music Education (Vocal/Chorus)45; Music Education (Instrumental) 45; Developmental Reading 30; Biology (also preparation in chemistry, physics, and mathematics) 24; Chemistry (also preparation in biology, physics, and mathematics) 24; Earth and Space Science (also preparation in biology, chemistry or physics, and mathematics) 24; General Science (including six hours each in biology, chemistry, and physics plus 12 hours in earth and space science) 30; Physics (also preparation in chemistry, biology, and mathematics) 24; and Social Studies (including 18 hours history, 12 hours political science, six hours geography, and six hours economics) 42. Must complete any requirement deficits during the life of the certificate. Nonrenewable. **Examination:** National Teacher Examination.

Credential Type: Collegiate Professional Certificate. **Duration of License:** Five years. **Requirements:** Baccalaureate degree from an accredited institution. Pass NTE examination. Meet BTAP competencies. 48 semester hours of general studies to include six hours each of the following: social sciences; natural sciences; mathematics; school health; and physical education. Must also include 12 semester hours of humanities, social science (including American history), and natural sciences and mathematics. Plus four semester hours of school health and physical education.

Must have 12 semester hours of professional studies including not less than three hours each of human growth and development, curriculum and instructional procedures, and foundations of education. Plus a six semester hr. student teaching experience which includes 200 clock hours in the classroom, and at least 60 percent of that time candidate must provide direct instruction.

Must have an endorsement for one or more special subject fields. Endorsements must have the following specified number of semester hours to qualify: Art Education (which includes both two and three dimensional media and concepts plus art history) 33; Driver Education 6; English Education (which includes history and nature of the language, literature, composition, and speech) 36; Modern Foreign Language 36; Latin 30; English as a second language 27; Health Education 36; Physical Education 36; Mathematics (which includes calculus, algebra, geometry, computer science, programming, and language) 27; General Mathematics 18; Music Education (Vocal/Chorus) 45; Music Education (Instrumental) 45; Developmental Reading 30; Biology (also preparation in chemistry, physics, and mathematics) 24; Chemistry (also preparation in biology, physics, and mathematics) 24; Earth and Space Science (also preparation in biology, chemistry or physics, and mathematics) 24; General Science (including six hours each in biology, chemistry, and physics plus 12 hours in earth and space science) 30; Physics (also preparation in chemistry, biology, and mathematics) 24; and Social Studies (including 18 hours history, 12 hours political science, six hours geography, and six hours economics) 42. Must complete any requirement deficits during the life of the certificate. Renewable. **Reciprocity:** Applicants who have completed a college level teacher preparation program out-of-state may qualify for this certificate upon approval.

7714

Teacher of the Emotionally Disturbed
Administrative Director
Office of Professional Development and Teacher Education
Dept. of Education
PO Box 6-Q
Richmond, VA 23216-2060
Phone: (804)225-2094

Credential Type: Emotionally Disturbed Endorsement. **Requirements:** Teaching Certificate. All applicants, except those who plan to work with preschool handicapped, must complete 18 semester hours of the following core courses: psychoeducational assessment; sociocultural and vocational aspects of disabilities; modifications of curriculum and instruction; language development; current trends and legal issues; and teaching methods in remediation of academic subjects for exceptional individuals. Plus 15 semester hours that include: characteristics of emotionally disturbed; techniques of behavior management; educational programming; and student teaching.

7715

Teacher of the Hearing Impaired
Administrative Director
Office of Professional Development and Teacher Education
Dept. of Education
PO Box 6-Q
Richmond, VA 23216-2060
Phone: (804)225-2094

Credential Type: Hearing Impaired Endorsement. **Requirements:** Teaching Certificate. All applicants, except those who plan to work with preschool handicapped, must complete 18 semester hours of the following core courses: psychoeducational assessment; sociocultural and vocational aspects of disabilities; modifications of curriculum and instruction; language development; current trends and legal issues; and teaching methods in remediation of academic subjects for exceptional individuals. Plus 15 semester hours which includes course work in: characteristics of hearing impaired students; speech science and audiology; instructional procedures; individual and group amplification systems; and student teaching.

7716

Teacher of the Learning Disabled
Administrative Director
Office of Professional Development and Teacher Education
Dept. of Education
PO Box 6-Q
Richmond, VA 23216-2060
Phone: (804)225-2094

Credential Type: Learning Disabled Endorsement. **Requirements:** Teaching Certificate. All applicants, except those who plan to work with preschool handicapped, must complete 18 semester hours of the following core courses: psychoeducational assessment; sociocultural and vocational aspects of disabilities; modifications of curriculum and instruction; language development; current trends and legal issues; and teaching methods in remediation of academic subjects for exceptional individuals. Plus 15 semester hours of the following course work: characteristics of the learning disabled; techniques for diagnosis and intervention; methods of basic skills instruction; adaptation of various levels of general education; and student teaching.

7717

Teacher of the Mentally Retarded
Administrative Director
Office of Professional Development and Teacher Education
Dept. of Education
PO Box 6-Q
Richmond, VA 23216-2060
Phone: (804)225-2094

Credential Type: Mentally Retarded Endorsement. **Requirements:** Teaching Certificate. All applicants, except those who plan to work with preschool handicapped, must complete 18 semester hours of the following core courses: psychoeducational assessment; sociocultural and vocational aspects of disabilities; modifications of curriculum and instruction; language development; current trends and legal issues; and teaching methods in remediation of academic subjects for exceptional individuals. Plus 15 semester hours of the following courses of study: characteristics of the mentally retarded, including medical aspects; teaching methods and materials; vocational exploration; educational evaluation; and student teaching.

Virginia

7718

Teacher of the Severely and Profoundly Handicapped
Administrative Director
Office of Professional Development
and Teacher Education
Dept. of Education
PO Box 6-Q
Richmond, VA 23216-2060
Phone: (804)225-2094

Credential Type: Severely and Profoundly Handicapped Endorsement. **Requirements:** Teaching Certificate. All applicants, except those who plan to work with preschool handicapped, must complete 18 semester hours of the following core courses: psychoeducational assessment; sociocultural and vocational aspects of disabilities; modifications of curriculum and instruction; language development; current trends and legal issues; and teaching methods in remediation of academic subjects for exceptional individuals. Plus 15 semester hours of the following course work: characteristics and medical aspects of severe and profound handicaps; advanced techniques of behavior management; occupational and physical therapy techniques; social and leisure skills development; and student teaching.

7719

Teacher of Speech and Language Disorders
Administrative Director
Office of Professional Development
and Teacher Education
Dept. of Education
PO Box 6-Q
Richmond, VA 23216-2060
Phone: (804)225-2094

Credential Type: Speech and Language Disorders Endorsement. **Requirements:** Teaching Certificate. All applicants, except those who plan to work with preschool handicapped, must complete 18 semester hours of the following core courses: psychoeducational assessment; sociocultural and vocational aspects of disabilities; modifications of curriculum and instruction; language development; current trends and legal issues; and teaching methods in remediation of academic subjects for exceptional individuals. Plus 24 semester hours of course work in the following: speech pathology; anatomy and physiology of speech and auditory mechanisms; speech and language development; and audiology; management techniques for disorders of articulation, language, fluency, voice and resonance.

7720

Teacher of the Visually Impaired
Administrative Director
Office of Professional Development
and Teacher Education
Dept. of Education
PO Box 6-Q
Richmond, VA 23216-2060
Phone: (804)225-2094

Credential Type: Visually Impaired Endorsement. **Requirements:** Teaching Certificate. All applicants, except those who plan to work with preschool handicapped, must complete 18 semester hours of the following core courses: psychoeducational assessment; sociocultural and vocational aspects of disabilities; modifications of curriculum and instruction; language development; current trends and legal issues; and teaching methods in remediation of academic subjects for exceptional individuals. Plus 15 semester hours of course work to include: anatomy, physiology, and diseases of the eye; nature and needs; reading and writing Braille; procedures for teaching the visually impaired; and student teaching.

Washington

7721

Public School Teacher PK-12
Superintendent of Public Instruction
Professional Education and
  Certification
Old Capitol Bldg. FG-11
Seattle, WA 98504-3211
Phone: (206)753-6773

Credential Type: Initial Certificate. **Duration of License:** Four years. **Authorization:** Certificate will be endorsed for teaching in PK-3, K-8, 4-12, or K-12 grade levels. **Requirements:** 18 years of age. Good moral character. Citizen of U.S. or declaration of intent to become a citizen. Baccalaureate degree from a regionally accredited institution and completion of a stateapproved teacher education program. Complete a 45 quarter hr. of 30 semester hr. major in one endorsement area. Renewable for an additional three years while the holder meets requirements for a Continuing Teacher Certificate.

Credential Type: Continuing Teacher Certificate. **Duration of License:** Five years. **Requirements:** Initial Certificate. Master's degree from a regionally accredited institution. Meet experience requirement as determined by the Superintendent of Public Instruction. Be eligible for at least two endorsements. Renewable upon completion of 150 clock hours of full-time teaching during the life of the certificate.

7722

Reading Resource Specialist
Superintendent of Public Instruction
Professional Education and
  Certification
Old Capitol Bldg. FG-11
Seattle, WA 98504-3211
Phone: (206)753-6773

Credential Type: Initial Educational Staff Associate Certificate. **Duration of License:** Seven years. **Authorization:** Authorizes service in primary role of assistant to the learner, the teacher, the administrator, and/or the educational program. **Requirements:** Hold a valid teaching certificate. Complete all course work (except special projects or thesis) for a master's degree with a major in the teaching of reading.

Credential Type: Continuing Educational Staff Associate Certificate. **Duration of License:** Five years. **Requirements:** Master's degree in the teaching of reading. Verification of 180 days of experience in the role. Complete a college level course which includes peer review while employed in the role. Out-of-state applicants must complete a comprehensive written examination (unless already taken as part of the master's degree). Renewable upon 150 clock hours of work in this position during the life of the certificate.

West Virginia

7723

Public School Teacher
State Dept. of Education
Certification Unit
Charleston, WV 25305
Phone: (800)982-2378

Credential Type: Professional Teaching Certificate—Three Year. **Duration of License:** Three years. **Requirements:** U.S. citizen. Good moral character. Physically, mentally, and emotionally qualified to perform the duties of a teacher. 18 years of age on or before the first day of October of the year in which the certificate is issued. Complete a state approved, four year, teacher preparation program at the college level. Must demonstrate competencies in reading, writing, mathematics, speaking and listening. Pass the National Teacher Examination (NTE) Pre-Professional Skills Test. Must complete general studies and content specialization classes as outlined by the preparing institution. Professional education component must include courses in performance assessment measurement and theory, skills, strategies and methods of designing, implementing and evaluating education.

Applicants who have successfully completed the APET alternative program for teacher certification will be granted the Professional Certificate after successful completion of the program and a support team comprehensive evaluation. **Examination:** National Teacher Examination in Pre-Professional Skills. **Reciprocity:** Reciprocity exists for those out-of-state applicants who received their certification in a state that has signed a reciprocity statement with West Virginia or in a state that has standards substantially equivalent to West Virginia. Out-of-state applicants who did not complete a content test as part of the approved program must successfully complete the West Virginia Content Test. **Fees:** $5 certification fee.

Credential Type: Alternative Program Teaching Certificate (APET). **Duration of License:** One school year (expires on June 30 of the school year in which it was issued). **Requirements:** U.S. citizen. Good moral character. Physically, mentally, and emotionally qualified to perform the duties of a teacher. 18 years of age on or before the first day of October of the year in which the certificate is issued. Must not have previously completed a state approved teacher preparation program. Bachelor's degree from an accredited institution in a discipline taught in the public schools and in a teaching specialization approved by the state board for APET. Satisfy appropriate state board approved basic skills and subject matter test requirements or complete three years of successful teaching experience within the last seven years in the area for which licensure is sought. After meeting the requirements listed above, the applicant must apply to the West Virginia Dept. of Education for a letter of eligibility which permits the individual to seek employment in a school included in an approved APET program. Once employment is secured an APET certificate will be issued. An extension of this certificate may be possible, however, the candidate is expected to undergo evaluation and progress to the Professional Certificate upon completion of this program. Note: Beginning July 1, 1994, candidates for the APET certificate must have achieved a minimum overall grade point average of 2.5 on a 4.0 scale for all college courses attempted. **Fees:** $5 certification fee.

Credential Type: Professional Certificate—Five Year. **Duration of License:** Five years. **Requirements:** Must hold a Three Year Professional Certificate. Must complete six semester hours of renewal credit subsequent to the original certificate or hold a master's degree and the MA30 salary classification or complete three years of teaching experience, one year of which must be in West Virginia, at the program level appearing on the original certificate. **Fees:** $5 certification fee.

Wisconsin

7724

Secondary School Teacher
Teacher Education, Licensing, and
　Placement
Box 7841
Madison, WI 53707-7841
Phone: (608)266-1027

Credential Type: Secondary Regular Teaching License. **Requirements:** Complete an approved program at a college or university. Recommendation from the preparing institution. Pass the PreProfessional Skills Test in Mathematics, Reading, and Writing. Complete a 34 semester hr. teaching major. Have a minimum of 18 semester credits of professional education including: educational psychology or psychology of learning; methods of teaching; a fulltime, full semester student teaching assignment or complete a parttime student teaching assignment plus two consecutive semesters of successful regular teaching experience under school district supervision; six semester hours of teaching of reading; a three semester hr. course or equivalent in exceptional education; plus adequate preparation in conservation of natural resources is required for licenses in science, agriculture, and social studies (with the exception of philosophy, psychology, and religious studies). **Examination:** Pre-Professional Skills Test in Mathematics, Reading, and Writing.

7725

Teacher of Special Subjects
Teacher Education, Licensing, and
　Placement
Box 7841
Madison, WI 53707-7841
Phone: (608)266-1027

Credential Type: Special Subjects License. **Authorization:** Licenses are available in Technology Education, Family and Consumer Education, Business Education, Agriculture, Music, Art, and Physical Education. **Requirements:** Complete an approved program at a college or university. Recommendation from the preparing institution. Pass the PreProfessional Skills Test in Mathematics, Reading, and Writing. Complete a 34 semester hr. teaching major in the special subject area. (Music requires a 46 semester hr. major and physical education and art require 54 semester hours) Have a minimum of 18 semester credits of professional education including: educational psychology or psychology of learning; methods of teaching; a fulltime, full semester student teaching assignment or complete a parttime student teaching assignment plus two consecutive semesters of successful regular teaching experience under school district supervision; six semester hours of teaching of reading; and a three semester hr. course or equivalent in exceptional education. **Examination:** Pre-Professional Skills Test in Mathematics, Reading, and Writing.

Wyoming

7726

Middle School Teacher 5-8
State Dept. of Education
Certification and Accreditation
Services Unit, Hathaway Bldg.
Cheyenne, WY 82002
Phone: (307)777-7291

Credential Type: Standard Teaching Certificate. **Duration of License:** Five years. **Requirements:** Bachelor's degree. Complete a program designed for instruction in the middle school or complete a program designed for instruction in the elementary or secondary grades, to include middle school courses in: human growth and development; philosophy; organizing patterns, curriculum and concepts; and guidance and counseling. 40 semester hours in general education to include six of the following areas: English; fine arts; foreign language; health and physical education; humanities; mathematics; practical arts; psychology; science; and social studies. 24 semester hours of professional education to include: human growth and development; research; educational evaluation; methods, materials and media appropriate to field of teaching specialization; historical, philosophical, and sociological foundations of public education in the United States; understanding the purposes, administrative organization and operation of the school; recognition of exceptional children; teaching of reading; human relations; computer assisted instruction; and gifted and talented.

Credential Type: Professional Teaching Certificate. **Duration of License:** 10 years. **Requirements:** Hold or be eligible for Standard Teaching Certificate. Five years of teaching experience. Master's degree in teaching endorsement or master's degree with work in four of the following areas: area of teaching endorsement; supporting professional courses in area of teaching endorsement; educational foundations; human development or psychology;

Middle School Teacher 5-8, continued

curriculum or supervision; practicum or internship or directed teaching experience.

Credential Type: Education Specialist Certificate. **Duration of License:** Five years. **Requirements:** Master's degree. Experience in grade 5-8 setting. Valid Wyoming teacher certificate.

Credential Type: Professional Education Specialist Certificate. **Duration of License:** 10 years. **Requirements:** Master's degree. 30 semester hours of credit beyond the master's degree.

Credential Type: Special Pupil Service Endorsement. **Requirements:** Bachelor's Degree. The following endorsements may be added to a Standard Teaching Certificate, or higher teaching certificate, by completing the specified number of semester hours in the special endorsement area: Audiovisual 12; Head Teacher (Limited to attendance centers employing six or fewer teachers) 15; Library-Media 24; Library Science 15; and Instructional Media 9.

7727

School Reading Specialist
State Dept. of Education
Certification and Accreditation
Services Unit, Hathaway Bldg.
Cheyenne, WY 82002
Phone: (307)777-7291

Credential Type: Reading Specialist Endorsement. **Requirements:** Teaching certification and Education Specialist certification. 24 semester hours of graduate work, including a master's degree and the following courses of study: developmental reading instruction; diagnosis and correction of reading disabilities; measurement and evaluation; literature for children and adolescents; communications and linguistics; organization and supervision of reading programs; practicum experience; and psychology. Two years of classroom teaching or counseling or supervisory or administrative experience in a K-12 setting. Experience must also include one year as a reading teacher.

7728

Secondary School Teacher 7-12
State Dept. of Education
Certification and Accreditation
Services Unit, Hathaway Bldg.
Cheyenne, WY 82002
Phone: (307)777-7291

Credential Type: Standard Teaching Certificate. **Duration of License:** Five years. **Requirements:** Bachelor's degree. Complete a program designed for instruction in the secondary grades. 40 semester hours in general education to include six of the following areas: English; fine arts; foreign language; health and physical education; humanities; mathematics; practical arts; psychology; science; and social studies. 24 semester hours of professional education to include: human growth and development; research; educational evaluation; methods, materials and media appropriate to field of teaching specialization; historical, philosophical, and sociological foundations of public education in the United States; understanding the purposes, administrative organization and operation of the school; recognition of exceptional children; teaching of reading; human relations, computer assisted instruction; and gifted and talented. Satisfy requirements for one or more of the following teaching endorsements by completing the number of semester hours as indicated: agriculture 48; art 30; business education 36; cooperative vocational education 24; driver education 12; English/language arts 36; exceptional children 24; foreign language 24; health education 12; home economics 40; industrial arts 30; mathematics 24; music 36; physical education 30; psychology 18; reading 15; science 30; social studies 36 (which includes nine semester hours distributed among any four of the major social studies areas).

Credential Type: Professional Teaching Certificate. **Duration of License:** 10 years. **Requirements:** Hold or be eligible for Standard Teaching Certificate. Five years of teaching experience. Master's degree in teaching endorsement or master's degree with work in four of the following areas: area of teaching endorsement; supporting professional courses in area of teaching endorsement; educational foundations; human development or psychology; curriculum or supervision; practicum or internship or directed teaching experience.

Credential Type: Education Specialist Certificate. **Duration of License:** Five years. **Requirements:** Master's degree. Experience in grade 7-12 setting. Valid Wyoming teacher certificate.

Credential Type: Professional Education Specialist Certificate. **Duration of License:** 10 years. **Requirements:** Master's degree. 30 semester hours of credit beyond the master's degree.

Credential Type: Special Pupil Service Endorsement. **Requirements:** Bachelor's Degree. The following endorsements may be added to a Standard Teaching Certificate, or higher teaching certificate, by completing the specified number of semester hours in the special endorsement area: Audiovisual 12; Head Teacher (Limited to attendance centers employing six or fewer teachers) 15; Library-Media 24; Library Science 15; and Instructional Media 9.

Secretaries

The following states grant licenses in this occupational category as of the date of publication: California, Connecticut, Delaware, Illinois, Iowa, Kansas, Montana, New Mexico, North Dakota, Oklahoma, Texas, Virginia.

California

7729

Assistant to a Racing Official, Official, or Manager (Racetrack)
California Horse Racing Board
1010 Hurley Way, Ste. 190
Sacramento, CA 95825
Phone: (916)920-7178

Credential Type: License Registration. **Requirements:** Submit application and fingerprint card. Pay fee. **Fees:** $75 registration fee.

Connecticut

7730

Office Employee (Racetrack)
Connecticut Div. of Special Revenue
Russell Rd.
PO Box 11424
Newington, CT 06111-0424
Phone: (203)566-2756

Credential Type: License Registration. **Requirements:** Submit application and fingerprint card. Pay fee. **Fees:** $5 registration fee.

7731

Office Secretary (Racetrack)
Connecticut Div. of Special Revenue
Russell Rd.
PO Box 11424
Newington, CT 06111-0424
Phone: (203)566-2756

Credential Type: License Registration. **Requirements:** Submit application and fingerprint card. Pay fee. **Fees:** $5 registration fee.

Delaware

7732

School Administrative Assistant
Teacher Certification
Dept. of Public Instruction
Box 1402
Dover, DE 19903
Phone: (302)739-4688

Credential Type: Administrative Assistant Endorsement. **Requirements:** Master's degree. Three years' teaching experience or experience in administration or other noneducational equivalent experience. Must have specific training, to fit responsibilities, that includes internship and/or field work.

Illinois

7733

Marketing Assistant/Secretary (Gaming)
Illinois Gaming Board
PO Box 19474
Springfield, IL 62794-9474
Phone: (217)524-0228

Credential Type: Marketing Assistant License. **Requirements:** At least 18 years of age. No felony convictions. U.S. citizen or legal alien as specified by the federal employment eligibility requirement. High school graduate or equivalent. Good moral character. Good typing skills and computer experience. **Reciprocity:** No. **Fees:** $75 application/initial license fee. $50 renewal fee. **Governing Statute:** Illinois Revised Statutes, Chapter 120.

Iowa

7734

Administrative Employee (Riverboat Gambling)
Iowa Racing and Gaming Commission
Lucas State Office Bldg.
Des Moines, IA 50319
Phone: (515)281-7352

Credential Type: License Registration. **Requirements:** Submit application and pay fees. **Fees:** $10 license fee.

Kansas

7735

Administrative Support Employee (Racetrack)
Kansas Racing Commission
3400 VanBuren
Topeka, KS 66611-2228
Phone: (913)296-5800

Credential Type: License Registration. **Requirements:** Submit application and fingerprint card. Pay fee. **Fees:** $5 registration fee.

Montana

7736

Office Worker (Racetrack)
State of Montana Board of Horse Racing
Dept. of Commerce
1424 9th Ave.
Helena, MT 59620
Phone: (406)444-4287

Credential Type: License Registration. **Requirements:** Submit application and fingerprint card. Pay fee. **Fees:** $20 registration fee.

New Mexico

7737

Office Worker (Racetrack)
New Mexico State Racing Commission
PO Box 8576, Highland Station
Albuquerque, NM 87198
Phone: (505)841-4644

Credential Type: License Registration. **Requirements:** Submit application and fingerprint card. Pay fees. **Fees:** $13 registration fee. $1 notary fee. $23 fingerprint card processing fee.

North Dakota

7738

Office Worker (Racetrack)
North Dakota Racing Commission
State Capitol Bldg.
Bismarck, ND 58505
Phone: (701)224-2210

Credential Type: License Registration. **Requirements:** Submit application and fingerprint card. Pay fee. **Fees:** $10 license fee. $10 duplicate license fee.

Oklahoma

7739

Administrative Employee (Racetrack)
Oklahoma Horse Racing Commission
6501 N. Broadway, Ste. 180
Oklahoma City, OK 73116
Phone: (405)848-0404

Credential Type: License Registration. **Duration of License:** One year. **Requirements:** Submit application and fingerprint card. Pay fee. **Fees:** $25 registration fee. $25 annual renewal.

Texas

7740

Association Office Staff Worker (Racetrack)
Texas Racing Commission
PO Box 12080
Austin, TX 78711
Phone: (512)794-8461

Credential Type: License Registration. **Requirements:** Submit application and fingerprint card. Pay fee. **Fees:** $20 registration fee.

Virginia

7741

Administrative Employee (Racetrack)
Virginia Racing Commission
PO Box 1123
Richmond, VA 23208
Phone: (804)371-7363

Credential Type: License Registration. **Requirements:** Submit application and fingerprint card. Pay fee. **Fees:** $10 registration fee.

Securities and Financial Services Sales Representatives

One or more occupations in this chapter require a federal license. Additionally, the following states grant licenses as of the date of publication:

Alabama	District of	Iowa	Minnesota	New Mexico	Rhode Island	Washington
Alaska	Columbia	Kansas	Mississippi	New York	South Carolina	West Virginia
Arizona	Florida	Kentucky	Missouri	North Carolina	South Dakota	Wisconsin
Arkansas	Georgia	Louisiana	Montana	North Dakota	Tennessee	Wyoming
California	Hawaii	Maine	Nebraska	Ohio	Texas	
Colorado	Idaho	Maryland	Nevada	Oklahoma	Utah	
Connecticut	Illinois	Massachusetts	New Hampshire	Oregon	Vermont	
Delaware	Indiana	Michigan	New Jersey	Pennsylvania	Virginia	

Federal Licenses

7742

Investment Advisor
United States Securities and
  Exchange Commission
Washington, DC 20549
Phone: (202)272-7463

Credential Type: Registration. **Requirements:** Submit Form ADV. **Fees:** $150 registration fee. **Governing Statute:** Investment Advisors Act of 1940. CFR, Title 17, Part 240 et seq.

Alabama

7743

Investment Advisor
Securities Commission
770 Washington Ave., Ste. 570
Montgomery, AL 36130
Phone: (205)242-2377

Credential Type: Investment Advisor License. **Duration of License:** One year. **Requirements:** Submit application of Form ADV. File statement of financial condition. Must maintain net capital of at least $10,000. **Examination:** Uniform Securities Agent State Law Examination (USASLE or Series 63) or the Uniform Investment Adviser Law Exam (Series 65). Appropriate examination on general or limited securities approved by the Commission. **Governing Statute:** Rules of Alabama Securities Commission, as amended.

7744

Investment Advisor Representative
Securities Commission
770 Washington Ave., Ste. 570
Montgomery, AL 36130
Phone: (205)242-2377

Credential Type: Investment Advisor Representative License. **Duration of License:** One year. **Requirements:** Submit application on Form U-4. **Examination:** Uniform Securities Agent State Law Examination (USASLE or Series 63) or the Uniform Investment Adviser Law Exam (Series 65). Appropriate examination on general or limited securities. approved by the Commission. **Governing Statute:** Rules of Alabama Securities Commission, as amended.

7745

Securities Agent
Securities Commission
770 Washington Ave., Ste. 570
Montgomery, AL 36130
Phone: (205)242-2984

Credential Type: Securities Agent License. **Duration of License:** One year. **Requirements:** Submit application on Form U-4. **Examination:** Uniform Securities Agent State Law Examination (USASLE) of the National Association of Securities Dealers (NASD). Appropriate qualification examination of the NASD. **Governing Statute:** Rules of Alabama Securities Commission, as amended.

7746

Securities Dealer
Securities Commission
770 Washington Ave., Ste. 570
Montgomery, AL 36130
Phone: (205)242-2391

Credential Type: Securities Broker-Dealer License. **Duration of License:** One year. **Requirements:** Submit application on Form BD. File statement of financial condition. Must maintain net capital of at least $50,000. **Examination:** Uniform Securities Agent State Law Examination (USASLE) of the National Association of Securities Dealers (NASD). Appropriate qualification examination of the NASD. **Governing Statute:** Rules of Alabama Securities Commission, as amended.

Alaska

7747

Investment Advisor
Dept. of Commerce and Economic
  Development
Div. of Banking, Securities, and
  Corporations
PO Box 110807
Juneau, AK 998811-080
Phone: (907)465-2521

Credential Type: Investment Advisor License. **Duration of License:** One year. **Requirements:** Good repute. Must have adequate training and meet knowledge and experience standards. File statement of financial condition. Submit application on appropriate forms. **Examination:** Appropriate securities examination. **Fees:** $75 initial registration fee. $75 annual renewal fee. **Governing Statute:** Administrative Code, Title 3—Commerce, Chapter 08 Securities.

Alaska

7748

Securities Agent
Dept. of Commerce and Economic Development
Div. of Banking, Securities, and Corporations
PO Box 110807
Juneau, AK 998811-080
Phone: (907)465-2521

Credential Type: Securities Agent License. **Duration of License:** One year. **Requirements:** Good repute. Must have adequate training and meet knowledge and experience standards. Submit application on appropriate forms. **Examination:** Appropriate securities examination. **Fees:** $75 initial registration fee. $75 annual renewal fee. **Governing Statute:** Administrative Code, Title 3—Commerce, Chapter 08 Securities.

7749

Securities Broker-Dealer
Dept. of Commerce and Economic Development
Div. of Banking, Securities, and Corporations
PO Box 110807
Juneau, AK 998811-080
Phone: (907)465-2521

Credential Type: Securities Broker-Dealer License. **Duration of License:** One year. **Requirements:** Good repute. Must have adequate training and meet knowledge and experience standards. File statement of financial condition. Submit application on appropriate forms. **Examination:** Appropriate securities examination. **Fees:** $200 initial registration fee. $200 annual renewal fee. **Governing Statute:** Administrative Code, Title 3—Commerce, Chapter 08 Securities.

Arizona

7750

Securities Dealer
Corporation Commission
Securities Div.
1200 W. Washington St., Ste. 201
Phoenix, AZ 85007
Phone: (602)542-4242

Credential Type: Securities Dealers License. **Duration of License:** One year. **Requirements:** Submit application on appropriate forms. File statement of financial condition. Bond (not to exceed $25,000) may be required. **Fees:** $300 annual registration fee. **Governing Statute:** Arizona Revised Statutes, Title 44, Chapter 12.

7751

Securities Salesperson
Securities Div.
Arizona Corporation Commission
1200 W. Washington
PO Box 6019
Phoenix, AZ 85007
Phone: (602)542-4242
Fax: (602)542-3583

Credential Type: NASD member security salesperson registration. **Duration of License:** One year. **Requirements:** For NASD members, registration is handled through the CRD System. Forms U-4 and U-5 should be sent to NASAA/NASD Central Registration Depository, 9513 Key West Ave., Rockville, MD 20850. For more information call CRD Communication Center, (301)738-6500. **Fees:** $40 fee payable to NASD

Credential Type: Non-NASD member security salesperson registration. **Duration of License:** One year. **Requirements:** Submit form U-4, USASLE Series 63 results, fingerprints, and affidavit. Demonstrate business experience by passing appropriate examination. **Examination:** Yes. **Fees:** $40 registration fee. $23 fingerprint processing fee. $40 renewal fee.

Arkansas

7752

Investment Advisor
Securities Dept.
Heritage West Bldg., 3rd Fl.
201 E. Markham
Little Rock, AR 72201
Phone: (501)324-9260
Fax: (501)324-9268

Credential Type: Investment Advisor License. **Duration of License:** One year. **Requirements:** Submit application on appropriate forms with consent to service of process. File statement of financial condition and business history. Must maintain net capital of at least $12,500. Must post corporate surety bond in the amount of $50,000. **Examination:** Written examination as determined by securities commissioner. **Fees:** $300 filing/registration fee. $300 annual renewal fee. $50 investment advisor representative filing fee. **Governing Statute:** Arkansas Code of 1987, Arkansas Securities Act, Title 23, Chapter 42.

7753

Securities Agent
Securities Dept.
Heritage West Bldg., 3rd Fl.
201 E. Markham
Little Rock, AR 72201
Phone: (501)324-9260
Fax: (501)324-9268

Credential Type: Securities Agent License. **Duration of License:** One year. **Requirements:** Submit application on appropriate forms with consent to service of process. Must post a corporate surety bond in the amount of $25,000. **Examination:** Written examination as required by securities commissioner. **Fees:** $50 filing/registration fee. $50 annual renewal fee. **Governing Statute:** Arkansas Code of 1987, Arkansas Securities Act, Title 23, Chapter 42.

7754

Securities Broker-Dealer
Securities Dept.
Heritage West Bldg., 3rd Fl.
201 E. Markham
Little Rock, AR 72201
Phone: (501)324-9260
Fax: (501)324-9268

Credential Type: Securities Broker-Dealer License. **Duration of License:** One year. **Requirements:** Submit application on appropriate forms with consent to service of process. File statement of financial condition and business history. Must maintain net capital of at least $25,000. Must post a corporate surety bond in the amount of $100,000. **Examination:** Written examination as determined by securities commissioner. **Fees:** $300 filing/registration fee. $300 annual renewal fee. **Governing Statute:** Arkansas Code of 1987, Arkansas Securities Act, Title 23, Chapter 42.

7755

Securities Broker-Dealer Agent
Arkansas Securities Dept.
Heritage W. Bldg., Ste. 300
201 W. Markham
Little Rock, AR 72201
Phone: (501)371-1011

Credential Type: License. **Requirements:** Must be bonded. Submit an audited financial statement. Registered in resident state. **Examination:** No **Fees:** $300 Arkansas initial registration and license. $300 Renewal.

California

7756

Investment Adviser
Dept. of Corporations
3700 Wilshire Blvd., Ste. 600
Los Angeles, CA 90010
Phone: (213)736-2495
Phone: (213)736-2741

Credential Type: License and Registration. **Requirements:** Submit application and consent to service of process. May be licensed by notification if already registered under the Securities Exchange Act of 1934 and a member of the New York Stock Exchange, American Stock Exchange, Pacific Stock Exchange, or National Association of Securities Dealers and has not had a previous certificate or license denied or revoked in California.

Examination must have been passed within two years prior to application unless appicant has been actively and continuously engaged in some aspect of the securities business. No examination is required if applicant has been engaged as a portfolio manager or securities analyst for three of the past five years. **Examination:** Any one of the following: General Securities Examination for Principals or Registered Representatives as administered by the NASD, NYSE, Pacific Stock Exchange, or SEC; or an examination required to become a Chartered Financial Analyst or Chartered Investment Counselor; or the SECO/NASD Nonmember General Securities Examination. **Fees:** $125 filing fee. **Governing Statute:** Corporate Securities Law of 1968.

7757

Securities Broker-Dealer
Dept. of Corporations
3700 Wilshire Blvd., Ste. 600
Los Angeles, CA 90010
Phone: (213)736-2495
Phone: (213)736-2741

Credential Type: License and Registration. **Requirements:** Submit application and consent to service of process. May be licensed by notification if already registered under the Securities Exchange Act of 1934 and a member of the New York Stock Exchange, American Stock Exchange, Pacific Stock Exchange, or National Association of Securities Dealers and has not had a previous certificate or license denied or revoked in California. **Examination:** Series 63 Uniform Securities Agent State Law Examination of the NASD. **Fees:** $300 filing fee. **Governing Statute:** Corporate Securities Law of 1968.

Colorado

7758

Securities Broker-Dealer
Dept. of Regulatory Agencies
Div. of Securities
1580 Lincoln St., No. 420
Denver, CO 80203-1506
Phone: (303)894-2320

Credential Type: Securities Broker-Dealer License. **Duration of License:** One year. **Requirements:** Submit application on appropriate forms with consent to service of process. Pay license fee. **Examination:** Written examination as determined by securities commissioner. **Governing Statute:** Colorado Securities Act.

7759

Securities Sales Representative
Dept. of Regulatory Agencies
Div. of Securities
1580 Lincoln St., No. 420
Denver, CO 80203-1506
Phone: (303)894-2320

Credential Type: Securities Sales Representative License. **Duration of License:** One year. **Requirements:** Submit application on appropriate forms with consent to service of process. Must be employed, or otherwise engaged, by a licensed broker-dealer or issuer. **Examination:** Written examination as determined by securities commissioner. **Fees:** $25 (maximum) annual license fee. **Governing Statute:** Colorado Securities Act.

Connecticut

7760

Investment Advisor
Dept. of Banking
Securities and Business Investments Div.
44 Capitol Ave.
Hartford, CT 06106
Phone: (203)566-4560

Credential Type: Investment Advisor License. **Duration of License:** One year. **Requirements:** Application for registration, with consent to service of process, must be submitted under oath to verify that the facts contained therein are true to the applicant's knowledge. Photograph and statement of financial condition must accompany application. **Fees:** $250 initial registration fee. $150 annual renewal fee. **Governing Statute:** Connecticut Uniform Securities Act.

7761

Investment Advisor Agent
Dept. of Banking
Securities and Business Investments Div.
44 Capitol Ave.
Hartford, CT 06106
Phone: (203)566-4560

Credential Type: Investment Advisor Agent License. **Duration of License:** One year. **Requirements:** Application for registration, with consent to service of process, must be submitted under oath to verify that the facts contained therein are true to the applicant's knowledge. Photograph must accompany application. **Fees:** $50 initial registration fee. $50 registration transfer fee. $40 annual renewal fee. **Governing Statute:** Connecticut Uniform Securities Act.

7762

Securities Agent
Dept. of Banking
Securities and Business Investments Div.
44 Capitol Ave.
Hartford, CT 06106
Phone: (203)566-4560

Credential Type: Securities Agent License. **Duration of License:** One year. **Requirements:** Application for registration, with consent to service of process, must be submitted under oath to verify that the facts contained therein are true to the applicant's knowledge. Photograph must accompany application. **Fees:** $50 initial registration fee. $50 registration transfer fee. $40 annual renewal fee. **Governing Statute:** Connecticut Uniform Securities Act.

7763

Securities Broker-Dealer
Dept. of Banking
Securities and Business Investments Div.
44 Capitol Ave.
Hartford, CT 06106
Phone: (203)566-4560

Credential Type: Securities Broker-Dealer License. **Duration of License:** One year. **Requirements:** Application for registration, with consent to service of process, must be submitted under oath to verify that the facts contained therein are true to the applicant's knowledge. Photograph and statement of financial condition must accompany application. **Fees:** $250 initial registration fee. $150 annual renewal fee.

Securities Broker-Dealer, continued

Governing Statute: Connecticut Uniform Securities Act.

Delaware

7764

Investment Advisor
Dept. of Justice
Div. of Securities
State Office Bldg., 8th Fl.
820 N. French St.
Wilmington, DE 19801
Phone: (302)577-2515

Credential Type: Investment Advisor License. **Duration of License:** One year. **Requirements:** Submit application on appropriate forms, with consent to service of process, including such information as: business history; proposed method of doing business; statement of financial condition; and information on any misdemeanor injunction or conviction involving any aspect of securities, or any conviction of a felony. May be required to post surety bonds up to $100,000. **Fees:** $150 initial filing fee. $150 annual renewal fee. **Governing Statute:** Delaware Code Annotated, Title 6, Chapter 73.

7765

Securities Agent
Dept. of Justice
Div. of Securities
State Office Bldg., 8th Fl.
820 N. French St.
Wilmington, DE 19801
Phone: (302)577-2515

Credential Type: Securities Agent License. **Duration of License:** One year. **Requirements:** Submit application on appropriate forms, with consent to service of process, including such information as: business history; proposed method of doing business; statement of financial condition; and information on any misdemeanor injunction or conviction involving any aspect of securities, or any conviction of a felony. May be required to post surety bonds up to $25,000. **Fees:** $30 initial filing fee. $30 annual renewal fee. $30 registration transfer fee. **Governing Statute:** Delaware Code Annotated, Title 6, Chapter 73.

7766

Securities Broker-Dealer
Dept. of Justice
Div. of Securities
State Office Bldg., 8th Fl.
820 N. French St.
Wilmington, DE 19801
Phone: (302)577-2515

Credential Type: Securities Broker-Dealer License. **Duration of License:** One year. **Requirements:** Submit application, with consent to service of process, on appropriate forms including such information as: business history; proposed method of doing business; statement of financial condition; and information on any misdemeanor injunction or conviction involving any aspect of securities, or any conviction of a felony. Must maintain net capital of at least $25,000. May be required to post surety bonds up to $100,000. **Fees:** $150 initial filing fee. $150 annual renewal fee. **Governing Statute:** Delaware Code Annotated, Title 6, Chapter 73.

District of Columbia

7767

Securities Agent
Public Service Commission
Div. of Securities
450 5th St. NW, Ste. 821
Washington, DC 20001
Phone: (202)626-5105

Credential Type: Securities Agent License. **Duration of License:** One year. **Requirements:** Submit application with consent to service of process on appropriate forms. May be required to post surety bond up to $25,000. **Governing Statute:** District of Columbia Securities Act.

7768

Securities Broker-Dealer
Public Service Commission
Div. of Securities
450 5th St. NW, Ste. 821
Washington, DC 20001
Phone: (202)626-5105

Credential Type: Broker-Dealer License. **Duration of License:** One year. **Requirements:** Submit application with consent to service of process on appropriate forms including such information as: business history; proposed method of doing business; statement of financial condition; details of any disciplinary action taken against applicant by a securities exchange or association in the last 10 years; and information on any misdemeanor injunction or conviction involving any aspect of securities, or any conviction of a felony. Must maintain net capital of at least $25,000. May be required to post surety bond up to $25,000. **Governing Statute:** District of Columbia Securities Act.

Florida

7769

Investment Advisor
Dept. of Banking and Finance
Div. of Securities and Investor Protection
Bureau of Registration
Plaza Level, The Capitol
Tallahassee, FL 32399-0350
Phone: (904)488-9530

Credential Type: Investment Advisor License. **Duration of License:** One year. **Requirements:** Submit Uniform Application for Investment Advisor Registration (Form ADV) and Uniform Application for Securities Industry Registration or Transfer (Form U-4). Submit notarized affidavit attesting to applicant's knowledge of the Florida Securities Act. Present proof that, in the two years prior to application, the applicant has passed a national level securities examination approved by the Securities and Exchange Commission or has been registered with a national securities association or stock exchange affiliated with the Securities and Exchange Commission. **Governing Statute:** Florida Securities and Investor Protection Act.

7770

Mortgage Broker
Dept. of Professional Regulation
Div. of Real Estate
PO Box 1900
Orlando, FL 32802-1900
Phone: (407)423-6071

Credential Type: Mortgage Broker License. **Requirements:** Contact licensing body for application information.

Securities and Financial Services Sales Representatives

7771

Securities Associated Person
Dept. of Banking and Finance
Div. of Securities and Investor Protection
Bureau of Registration
Plaza Level, The Capitol
Tallahassee, FL 32399-0350
Phone: (904)488-9530

Credential Type: Securities Associated Person License. **Duration of License:** One year. **Requirements:** Submit Uniform Application for Securities Industry Registration (Form U-4) and Florida Fingerprint Card (Form FL921250Z). Submit notarized affidavit attesting to applicant's knowledge of the Florida Securities Act. Present proof that, in the two years prior to application, the applicant has passed a national level securities examination approved by the Securities and Exchange Commission or has been registered with a national securities association or stock exchange affiliated with the Securities and Exchange Commission. **Fees:** $33 processing fee. **Governing Statute:** Florida Securities and Investor Protection Act.

7772

Securities Dealer
Dept. of Banking and Finance
Div. of Securities and Investor Protection
Bureau of Registration
Plaza Level, The Capitol
Tallahassee, FL 32399-0350
Phone: (904)488-9530

Credential Type: Securities Broker-Dealer License. **Duration of License:** One year. **Requirements:** Submit Uniform Application for Broker-Dealer Registration (Form BD) and Uniform Application for Securities Industry Registration or Transfer (Form U-4). Must have proof of insurance coverage by the Securities Investor Protection Corporation. Submit notarized affidavit attesting to applicant's knowledge of the Florida Securities Act. Present proof that, in the two years prior to application, the applicant has passed a national level securities examination approved by the Securities and Exchange Commission or has been registered with a national securities association or stock exchange affiliated with the Securities and Exchange Commission. **Governing Statute:** Florida Securities and Investor Protection Act.

7773

Securities Issuer/Dealer
Dept. of Banking and Finance
Div. of Securities and Investor Protection
Bureau of Registration
Plaza Level, The Capitol
Tallahassee, FL 32399-0350
Phone: (904)488-9530

Credential Type: Securities Issuer/Dealer License. **Duration of License:** One year. **Requirements:** Submit Uniform Application for Broker-Dealer Registration (Form BD) and Uniform Application for Securities Industry Registration or Transfer (Form U-4). File Issuer/Dealer Compliance Form DA-5-9179. Submit notarized affidavit attesting to applicant's knowledge of the Florida Securities Act. Present proof that, in the two years prior to application, the applicant has passed a national level securities examination approved by the Securities and Exchange Commission or has been registered with a national securities association or stock exchange affiliated with the Securities and Exchange Commission. **Governing Statute:** Florida Securities and Investor Protection Act.

Georgia

7774

Securities General Dealer
Office of Secretary of State
Business Services and Regulation
West Tower, Ste. 315
2 Martin Luther King Jr. Dr.
Atlanta, GA 30334-1530
Phone: (404)656-2895

Credential Type: Securities General Dealer License. **Requirements:** Submit application on appropriate forms. Must designate at least one principal who is registered with the National Association of Securities Dealers (NASD) and meets examination requirements to supervise Georgia sales. Must be a member in good standing of the National Association of Securities Dealers, Inc. or be registered with the U.S. Securities and Exchange Commission under the Securities Act of 1934. Must be in compliance with the net capital rules of the U.S. Securities and Exchange Commission or a national securities exchange. **Examination:** Georgia Securities Law Examination or the NASD Series 63 Uniform Securities Agent State Law Examination and a general principal's examination. **Governing Statute:** Official Code of Georgia, Title 10, Chapter 5.

7775

Securities Limited Dealer
Office of Secretary of State
Business Services and Regulation
West Tower, Ste 315
2 Martin Luther King Jr. Dr.
Atlanta, GA 30334-1530
Phone: (404)656-2895

Credential Type: Securities Limited Dealer License. **Requirements:** Submit application on appropriate forms. Must designate at least one principal, who has met examination requirements, to supervise Georgia sales. Must have $15,000 in net worth and not less than $15,000 in liquid assets or be in compliance with the net capital rules of the U.S. Securities and Exchange Commission or is a member of a national securities exchange and is in compliance with its net capital rules. Proof of registration as a NASD principal or pass one of the following National Association of Securities Dealers (NASD) examinations: Series 26, Series 39, Series 53, or Series 54. **Examination:** Georgia Securities Law Examination or the NASD Series 63 Uniform Securities Agent State Law Examination and a general principal's examination. **Governing Statute:** Official Code of Georgia, Title 10, Chapter 5.

7776

Securities Salesman
Office of Secretary of State
Business Services and Regulation
West Tower, Ste. 315
2 Martin Luther King Jr. Dr.
Atlanta, GA 30334-1530
Phone: (404)656-2895

Credential Type: Securities Salesman License. **Authorization:** May sell securities for only one issuer, dealer, or limited dealer at a time. **Requirements:** Submit application on appropriate forms. **Examination:** Georgia Securities Law Examination or the National Association of Securities Dealers (NASD) Series 63 Uniform Securities Agent State Law Examination. The North American Securities Administrators Association (NASAA) real estate securities examination or one of the following NASD examinations: Series 1; Series 2; Series 6; Series 7; Series 22; or Series 52 . **Governing Statute:** Official Code of Georgia, Title 10, Chapter 5.

Credential Type: Limited Securities Salesman License. **Authorization:** May sell securities for only one issuer, dealer, or limited dealer at a time. **Requirements:** Submit application on appropriate forms. **Examination:** As required by Commis-

Hawaii

Securities Salesman, continued

sioner. **Governing Statute:** Official Code of Georgia, Title 10, Chapter 5.

Hawaii

7777

Investment Advisor
Hawaii Dept. of Commerce and Consumer Affairs
Business Registration Div.
1010 Richards St.
PO Box 40
Honolulu, HI 96813
Phone: (808)548-2021

Credential Type: License. **Duration of License:** Two years. **Requirements:** Submit the following: Consent to Service of Process; Corporate or Individual Acknowledgement; Corporate Resolution (if applicable); $5,000 or $50,000 bond; financial statements; Errors and Omission Insurance. **Examination:** Written. **Fees:** $100 registration fee. $250 exam fee. $100 renewal fee.

7778

Investment Advisor Representative
Hawaii Dept. of Commerce and Consumer Affairs
Securities Compliance Branch
Business Registration Div.
1010 Richards St.
PO Box 40
Honolulu, HI 96813
Phone: (808)548-5317

Credential Type: License. **Requirements:** Designated as a representative by a registered investment advisor. **Examination:** Written and/or oral exam. **Fees:** $25 registration fee. $50 exam fee. $25 renewal fee.

7779

Securities Dealer
Dept. of Commerce and Consumer Affairs
Business Registration Div.
PO Box 40
Honolulu, HI 96810
Phone: (808)582-2744

Credential Type: Broker-Dealer License. **Duration of License:** Two years. **Requirements:** At least 19 years of age. Good repute. Sufficient training and experience as determined by Commissioner. Submit application on appropriate forms with consent to service of process. File statement of financial condition. Must maintain a minimum net capital of $5,000. Must post $5,000 bond (or equivalent cash or securities in lieu of bond) within 30 days of filing. **Examination:** Examination as required by Commissioner. **Fees:** $100 filing fee. **Governing Statute:** Hawaii Administrative Rules, Title 16, Chapter 38.

7780

Securities Salesperson
Dept. of Commerce and Consumer Affairs
Business Registration Div.
PO Box 40
Honolulu, HI 96810
Phone: (808)582-2744

Credential Type: Securities Salesperson License. **Duration of License:** Two years. **Requirements:** Good repute. Must be appointed by a registered dealer or issuer. May only be registered with one dealer or issuer at a time. Submit application on appropriate forms with consent to service of process. Pass examinations with a score of at least 70 percent. **Examination:** New York Stock Exchange general securities examination (Part I). Uniform Securities Agent State Law Examination (USASLE) administered by the National Association of Securities Dealers (Part II). **Fees:** $50 examination fee (Part I). $50 reexamination fee (Part I). $25 registration fee. **Governing Statute:** Hawaii Administrative Rules, Title 16, Chapter 38.

Idaho

7781

Investment Adviser
Dept. of Finance
Securities Bureau
700 W. State St.
Boise, ID 83720-2700
Phone: (208)334-3313
Phone: (208)334-3684

Credential Type: Investment Adviser License. **Requirements:** Submit application. Applications are reviewed for background, employment, education, disciplinary history, exam scores, and licensing status in other states. **Governing Statute:** Idaho Securities Act.

7782

Investment Adviser Agent
Dept. of Finance
Securities Bureau
700 W. State St.
Boise, ID 83720-2700
Phone: (208)334-3313
Phone: (208)334-3684

Credential Type: Investment Adviser Agent Registration. **Requirements:** Submit application. Applications are reviewed for background, employment, education, disciplinary history, exam scores, and licensing status in other states. **Governing Statute:** Idaho Securities Act.

7783

Securities Broker-Dealer
Dept. of Finance
Securities Bureau
700 W. State St.
Boise, ID 83720-2700
Phone: (208)334-3313
Phone: (208)334-3684

Credential Type: Broker-Dealer License. **Requirements:** Submit application. Applications are approved through the national computer on-line system, Central Registration Depository (CRD). Applications are reviewed for background, employment, education, disciplinary history, exam scores, and licensing status in other states. **Governing Statute:** Idaho Securities Act.

7784

Securities Salesperson
Dept. of Finance
Securities Bureau
700 W. State St.
Boise, ID 83720-2700
Phone: (208)334-3313
Phone: (208)334-3684

Credential Type: Securities Salesperson License. **Requirements:** Submit application. Applications are approved through the national computer on-line system, Central Registration Depository (CRD). Applications are reviewed for background, employment, education, disciplinary history, exam scores, and licensing status in other states. **Governing Statute:** Idaho Securities Act.

Illinois

7785

Investment Advisor
Secretary of State
Securities Dept.
900 S. Spring St.
Springfield, IL 62704
Phone: (217)785-4929

Credential Type: Registration. **Duration of License:** One year. **Requirements:** Be at least 18 years of age. Meet one of the following sets of requirements: (1) Be a Chartered Financial Analyst (CFA). (2) Be a Chartered Investment Counselor (CIC). (3) Be a Chartered Financial Consultant (ChFC). (4) Be a Certified Financial Planner (CFP) and pass Series 65 Exam (Uniform Investment Advisor Law Exam) or Series 2 or Series 7. (5) Be a General Securities Representative and pass Series 65 Exam. **Examination:** NASD Examinations, Series 65, Series 2 and/or Series 7. **Reciprocity:** No. **Fees:** $200 application fee. $200 renewal fee. **Governing Statute:** Ill. Rev. Stat., Chap. 121-1/2, sect. 137.8D.

7786

Securities Dealer
Secretary of State
Securities Dept.
900 S. Spring St.
Springfield, IL 62704
Phone: (217)785-4929

Credential Type: Registration. **Duration of License:** One year. **Requirements:** Be at least 18 years of age. Principals must demonstrate understanding of laws and regulations of the Securities and Exchange Commission (SEC), NASD, and each state where registered. Meet minimum net capital requirements. **Examination:** NASD Examinations, Series 24 and 63. **Reciprocity:** No. **Fees:** $300 application fee. $300 renewal fee. **Governing Statute:** Ill. Rev. Stat., Chap. 121-1/2, sect. 137.8B.

7787

Securities Salesperson
Secretary of State
Securities Dept.
900 S. Spring St.
Springfield, IL 62704
Phone: (217)785-4929

Credential Type: Registration. **Duration of License:** One year. **Requirements:** Be at least 18 years of age. Must demonstrate understanding of laws and regulations of the NASD and each state where registered. **Examination:** NASD Examinations, Series 7 and 63. **Reciprocity:** No. **Fees:** $50 application fee. $50 renewal fee. **Governing Statute:** Ill. Rev. Stat., Chap. 121-1/2, sect. 137.8C.

Indiana

7788

Investment Advisor
Secretary of State
Securities Div.
302 W. Washington St., Rm. E-111
Indianapolis, IN 46204
Phone: (317)232-6681

Credential Type: Registration. **Requirements:** Contact licensing body for application information.

7789

Securities Broker-Dealer
Secretary of State
Securities Div.
302 W. Washington St., Rm. E-111
Indianapolis, IN 46204
Phone: (317)232-6681

Credential Type: Registration. **Requirements:** Contact licensing body for application information.

7790

Securities Sales Agent
Secretary of State
Securities Div.
302 W. Washington St., Rm. E-111
Indianapolis, IN 46204
Phone: (317)232-6681

Credential Type: Registration. **Requirements:** Contact licensing body for application information.

Iowa

7791

Securities Agent
Office of Commissioner of Insurance
Securities Bureau
Lucas State Office Bldg.
Des Moines, IA 50319
Phone: (515)281-4441

Credential Type: Securities Agent License. **Duration of License:** One year. **Requirements:** Submit application with consent to service of process on appropriate forms including such information as: business history; proposed method of doing business; statement of financial condition; and information on any misdemeanor injunction or conviction involving any aspect of securities, or any conviction of a felony. **Fees:** $30 filing fee. **Governing Statute:** Code of Iowa, 1989, Uniform Securities Act.

7792

Securities Broker-Dealer
Office of Commissioner of Insurance
Securities Bureau
Lucas State Office Bldg.
Des Moines, IA 50319
Phone: (515)281-4441

Credential Type: Securities Broker-Dealer License. **Duration of License:** One year. **Requirements:** Submit application with consent to service of process on appropriate forms including such information as: business history; proposed method of doing business; statement of financial condition; and information on any misdemeanor injunction or conviction involving any aspect of securities, or any conviction of a felony. May be required to post bond. **Fees:** $200 filing fee. **Governing Statute:** Code of Iowa, 1989, Uniform Securities Act.

Kansas

7793

Investment Advisor
Office of Securities Commissioner
618 S. Kansas Ave., 2nd Fl.
Topeka, KS 66603-3804
Phone: (913)296-3307

Credential Type: Investment Advisor License. **Duration of License:** One year. **Requirements:** Good character and reputation. Adequate knowledge of the securities business and financially responsible. Submit application on appropriate forms. May be required to post a bond of not less than $5,000 and not more than $25,000. **Examination:** Written examination as determined by Commissioner. **Fees:** $300 (maximum) registration fee. $300 (maximum) renewal fee. **Governing Statute:** Kansas Securities Act.

7794

Securities Agent
Office of Securities Commissioner
618 S. Kansas Ave., 2nd Fl.
Topeka, KS 66603-3804
Phone: (913)296-3307

Credential Type: Securities Agent License. **Duration of License:** One year. Re-

Kansas

Securities Agent, continued

quirements: Good character and reputation. Adequate knowledge of the securities business and financially responsible. Submit application on appropriate forms. May be required to post a bond of not less than $5,000 and not more than $25,000. **Examination:** Written examination as determined by Commissioner. **Fees:** $50 (maximum) registration fee. $50 (maximum) renewal fee. **Governing Statute:** Kansas Securities Act.

7795

Securities Broker-Dealer
Office of Securities Commissioner
618 S. Kansas Ave., 2nd Fl.
Topeka, KS 66603-3804
Phone: (913)296-3307

Credential Type: Securities Broker-Dealer License. **Duration of License:** One year. **Requirements:** Good character and reputation. Adequate knowledge of the securities business and financially responsible. Submit application on appropriate forms. May be required to post a bond of not less than $5,000 and not more than $25,000. **Fees:** $300 (maximum) registration fee. $300 (maximum) renewal fee. **Governing Statute:** Kansas Securities Act.

Kentucky

7796

Securities Agent
Dept. of Financial Institutions
911 Leawood Dr.
Frankfort, KY 40601
Phone: (502)564-2180

Credential Type: License. **Duration of License:** One year. **Requirements:** High school diploma or GED. 18 years of age. **Examination:** Yes. **Fees:** $50 initial fee. $50 renewal fee.

7797

Securities Broker/Dealer
Dept. of Financial Institutions
911 Leawood Dr.
Frankfort, KY 40601
Phone: (502)564-2180

Credential Type: License. **Duration of License:** One year. **Requirements:** Must be knowledgeable of the Kentucky Securities Act and rules and regulations promulgated there-under. 18 years of age. **Fees:** $120 initial filing fee. $120 renewal fee.

Louisiana

7798

Investment Advisor
Securities Commission
Energy Center, Ste. 2250
1100 Poydras St.
New Orleans, LA 70163
Phone: (504)568-5515

Credential Type: Investment Advisor License. **Duration of License:** One year. **Requirements:** Submit application, verified under oath, on appropriate forms. File a statement of financial condition. **Fees:** $150 original license fee. $150 annual renewal fee. **Governing Statute:** Louisiana Securities Law, Laws 1985, Act 722.

7799

Securities Dealer
Securities Commission
Energy Center, Ste. 2250
1100 Poydras St.
New Orleans, LA 70163
Phone: (504)568-5515

Credential Type: Securities Broker-Dealer License. **Duration of License:** One year. **Requirements:** Submit application, verified under oath, on appropriate forms. File a certified statement of financial condition. Each principal under applicant must pass a written securities examination as determined by the Commissioner. Must post surety bond, not to exceed $10,000. **Examination:** Written securities examination as determined by Commissioner. **Fees:** $250 original license fee. $250 annual renewal fee. **Governing Statute:** Louisiana Securities Law, Laws 1985, Act 722.

7800

Securities Salesman
Securities Commission
Energy Center, Ste. 2250
1100 Poydras St.
New Orleans, LA 70163
Phone: (504)568-5515

Credential Type: Securities Salesman License. **Duration of License:** One year. **Requirements:** Submit application, verified under oath, on appropriate forms. Provide the names of three personal references. **Examination:** Written securities examination as determined by Commissioner. **Fees:** $60 original license fee. $60 annual renewal fee. **Governing Statute:** Louisiana Securities Law, Laws 1985, Act 722.

Maine

7801

Investment Advisor
Dept. of Professional and Financial Regulation
Bureau of Banking
Securities Div.
State House Station 121
Augusta, ME 04333
Phone: (207)582-8760

Credential Type: Investment Advisor License. **Duration of License:** One year. **Requirements:** Submit application on appropriate forms with a consent to service of process. Application may not be necessary if applicant has filed a complete and current registration with the U.S. Securities and Exchange Commission, or other national registration depository system, that can be accessed by the administrator. **Examination:** Securities examination as determined by the administrator. **Fees:** $50 initial fee. $35 annual renewal fee. **Governing Statute:** Maine Revised Statutes Annotated, Title 32, Chapter 105.

7802

Securities Broker-Dealer
Dept. of Professional and Financial Regulation
Bureau of Banking
Securities Div.
State House Station 121
Augusta, ME 04333
Phone: (207)582-8760

Credential Type: Securities-Broker Dealer License. **Duration of License:** One year. **Requirements:** Submit application on appropriate forms with a consent to service of process. Application may not be necessary if applicant has filed a complete and current registration with the U.S. Securities and Exchange Commission, or other national registration depository system, that can be accessed by the administrator. **Examination:** Securities examination as determined by the administrator. **Fees:** $100 initial fee. $100 annual renewal fee. **Governing Statute:** Maine Revised Statutes Annotated, Title 32, Chapter 105.

Securities and Financial Services Sales Representatives

7803

Securities Sales Representatives
Dept. of Professional and Financial Regulation
Bureau of Banking
Securities Div.
State House Station 121
Augusta, ME 04333
Phone: (207)582-8760

Credential Type: Securities Sales Representative License. **Duration of License:** One year. **Requirements:** Submit application on appropriate forms with a consent to service of process. Application may not be necessary if applicant has filed a complete and current registration with the U.S. Securities and Exchange Commission, or other national registration depository system, that can be accessed by the administrator. **Examination:** Securities examination as determined by the administrator. **Fees:** $40 initial fee. $40 annual renewal fee. **Governing Statute:** Maine Revised Statutes Annotated, Title 32, Chapter 105.

Maryland

7804

Investment Adviser
Securities Div.
Attorney General's Office
200 St. Paul Pl.
Baltimore, MD 21202
Phone: (410)576-6360

Credential Type: Registration. **Duration of License:** One year. **Requirements:** Submit application on appropriate forms, including federal Form ADV and Maryland Investment Adviser Certification Form. Bond is also required. **Examination:** Yes. **Fees:** $300 registration fee. $300 renewal fee.

7805

Investment Adviser Representative
Securities Div.
Attorney General's Office
200 St. Paul Pl.
Baltimore, MD 21202
Phone: (410)576-6360

Credential Type: Registration. **Duration of License:** One year. **Requirements:** If applicant is not a registered agent in this state for a registered broker-dealer that is also a registered investment adviser in this state, then applicant must submit application on appropriate forms, including federal Form U-4 and Maryland Investment Adviser Certification Form. If applicant is a registered agent in this state for a registered broker-dealer that is also a registered investment adviser in this state, then applicant must submit name and CRD number and copy of Maryland Investment Adviser Certification Form. **Examination:** Yes, if not a registered securities sales agent for a registered broker-dealer that is also a registered investment adviser. **Fees:** $50 registration fee. $50 renewal fee.

7806

Mortgage Broker
Commissioner of Consumer Credit
Dept. of Licensing and Regulation
501 St. Paul Pl.
Baltimore, MD 21202-2272
Phone: (410)333-6330

Credential Type: Mortgage Lenders License. **Duration of License:** One year. **Requirements:** Must show five years of employment history. Must be examined once every three years or as needed. **Examination:** Maryland Mortgage Lenders/Brokers Examination. **Fees:** $500 license fee. $100 investigation fee. $500 renewal fee.

7807

Securities Broker-Dealer
Securities Div.
Attorney General's Office
200 St. Paul Pl.
Baltimore, MD 21202
Phone: (410)576-6360

Credential Type: Registration. **Requirements:** Submit form BD and pay fees directly to the Central Registration Depository (CRD) of the National Association of Securities Dealers (NASD). Forms are available from the state Securities Division. **Fees:** $250 registration fee. $250 renewal fee.

7808

Securities Sales Agent
Securities Div.
Attorney General's Office
200 St. Paul Pl.
Baltimore, MD 21202
Phone: (410)576-6360

Credential Type: Registration. **Requirements:** Submit form U-4 and pay fees directly to the Central Registration Depository (CRD) of the National Association of Securities Dealers (NASD). Forms are available from the state Securities Division. **Fees:** $35 registration fee. $35 renewal fee.

Massachusetts

7809

Securities Agent
Securities Div.
Office of the Secretary of State
One Ashburton Pl., 17th Fl.
Boston, MA 02108
Phone: (617)727-3548

Credential Type: Registration. **Duration of License:** One year. **Requirements:** Applications are submitted by the employing broker-dealer subsequent to the approval of the broker-dealer's registration in Massachusetts. Applications are to be filed directly with the NASD Central Registration Depository, P.O. Box 3744, Washington, DC 20013. **Examination:** Uniform Securities Agent State Law Examination (USASLE). Other applicable examinations may be required.

7810

Securities Broker-Dealer
Securities Div.
Office of the Secretary of State
One Ashburton Pl., 17th Fl.
Boston, MA 02108
Phone: (617)727-3548

Credential Type: Registration. **Duration of License:** One year. **Requirements:** Submit application directly with the Secretary of State's office, including Form BD, statement of financial condition, auditor's report, proof of National Association of Securities Dealers (NASD) registration, proof of SEC registration, and Form ACF. When seeking broker-dealer registration, applicant should only file an application for one principal agent. Subsequent agent registrations are filed through the Central Registration Depository of the NASD.

7811

Securities Issuer-Agent
Securities Div.
Office of the Secretary of State
One Ashburton Pl., 17th Fl.
Boston, MA 02108
Phone: (617)727-3548

Credential Type: Registration. **Duration of License:** One year. **Requirements:** Agents are registered by filing forms U-4(i) and ACF(i), accompanied by the application to register securities. **Fees:** $40 filing fee.

Michigan

7812

Investment Advisor
Corporation and Securities Bureau
Dept. of Commerce
6546 Mercantile Way
PO Box 30222
Lansing, MI 48909
Phone: (517)373-9153

Credential Type: Registration. **Duration of License:** One year. **Requirements:** Abide by the rules promulgated under the Michigan Uniform Securities Act. **Fees:** $150 initial registration fee. $150 renewal fee. **Governing Statute:** Michigan Uniform Securities Act, Act 265 of 1964, as amended.

7813

Residential Mortgage Broker
Dept. of Commerce
Board of Real Estate Brokers & Salespersons
PO Box 30243
Lansing, MI 48909
Phone: (517)373-0490

Credential Type: Residential Mortgage Broker License. **Requirements:** Contact licensing body for application information.

7814

Securities Agent
Corporation and Securities Bureau
Dept. of Commerce
6546 Mercantile Way
PO Box 30222
Lansing, MI 48909
Phone: (517)373-9153

Credential Type: Registration. **Duration of License:** One year. **Requirements:** At least 18 years old. Submit fingerprint cards. Comply with the rules and regulations of the Bureau. **Examination:** The Uniform State Securities Law Examination. **Fees:** $30 initial registration fee. $60 exam fee (paid to the National Association of Securities Dealers, Inc.). $30 renewal fee. **Governing Statute:** Michigan Uniform Securities Act, Act 265 of 1964, as amended.

7815

Securities Broker-Dealer
Corporation and Securities Bureau
Dept. of Commerce
6546 Mercantile Way
PO Box 30222
Lansing, MI 48909
Phone: (517)373-9153

Credential Type: Registration. **Duration of License:** One year. **Requirements:** File an application for registration which, as of its effective date, is complete in all material respects and contains no misleading or false statements with respect to any material facts. Comply with all provisions of the Michigan Uniform Securities Act. Have not been convicted of any misdemeanor involving moral turpitude or any felony. Not have been permanently or temporarily enjoined by any court of competent jurisdiction from engaging in or continuing any conduct or practice involving any aspect of the securities business. Not have been the subject of an order by the securities administrator of any other state or by the Securities and Exchange Commission (S.E.C.) denying or revoking registration as a broker-dealer, agent, or investment advisor, or the subject of a United States Post Office fraud order. Not have been the subject of an order of the Bureau denying, suspending, or revoking registration as a broker-dealer, agent, or investment advisor. Not have engaged in dishonest or unethical business practices. Supervise securities agents reasonably at all times. Not be insolvent, either in the sense that liabilities exceed assets or in the sense that obligations cannot be met as they mature. Submit a $10,000 bond on the Bureau's form if the broker-dealer's net capital is $50,000 or less. **Fees:** $250 initial registration fee. $250 renewal fee. **Governing Statute:** Michigan Uniform Securities Act, Act 265 of 1964, as amended.

Minnesota

7816

Investment Advisor
Dept. of Commerce
133 E. Seventh St.
St. Paul, MN 55101
Phone: (612)296-4026

Credential Type: Investment Advisor License. **Duration of License:** One year. **Requirements:** Submit application on appropriate forms with a consent to service of process. Application must include proposed method of doing business, financial condition, plus qualifications and experience of applicant and any partner, officer, director, or controlling person with which applicant is affiliated. Minimum capital may be required. May be required to post surety bonds in amounts up to $25,000. **Examination:** Written and/or oral examination as determined by Commissioner. **Governing Statute:** Minnesota Statutes, Regulation of Securities.

7817

Securities Agent
Dept. of Commerce
133 E. Seventh St.
St. Paul, MN 55101
Phone: (612)296-4026

Credential Type: Securities Agent License. **Duration of License:** One year. **Requirements:** Submit application on appropriate forms with a consent to service of process. Application must include proposed method of doing business, financial condition, plus qualifications and experience. May be required to post surety bonds in amounts up to $25,000. **Examination:** Written and/or oral examination as determined by Commissioner. **Governing Statute:** Minnesota Statutes, Regulation of Securities.

7818

Securities Broker-Dealer
Dept. of Commerce
133 E. Seventh St.
St. Paul, MN 55101
Phone: (612)296-4026

Credential Type: Securities Broker-Dealer License. **Duration of License:** One year. **Requirements:** Submit application on appropriate forms with a consent to service of process. Application must include proposed method of doing business, financial condition, plus qualifications and experience of applicant and any partner, officer, director, or controlling person with which applicant is affiliated. Minimum capital may be required. May be required to post surety bonds in amounts up to $25,000. **Examination:** Written and/or oral examination as determined by Commissioner. **Governing Statute:** Minnesota Statutes, Regulation of Securities.

Mississippi

7819

Investment Advisor
Office of Secretary of State
Securities Div.
PO Box 136
Jackson, MS 39205
Phone: (601)359-6371

Credential Type: Investment Advisor License. **Duration of License:** One year. **Requirements:** Submit application on appropriate forms with a consent to service of process. Application must include proposed method of doing business, financial condition, plus qualifications and experience of applicant and any partner, officer, director, or controlling person with which applicant is affiliated. Minimum capital may be required. May be required to post surety bonds in amounts up to $30,000. **Fees:** $200 initial license/filing fee. $200 annual renewal. **Governing Statute:** Mississippi Securities Act.

7820

Securities Agent
Office of Secretary of State
Securities Div.
PO Box 136
Jackson, MS 39205
Phone: (601)359-6371

Credential Type: Securities Agent License. **Duration of License:** One year. **Requirements:** Submit application on appropriate forms with a consent to service of process. Application must include proposed method of doing business, financial condition, plus qualifications and experience. May be required to post surety bonds in amounts up to $30,000. **Fees:** $50 initial license/filing fee. $50 annual renewal. **Governing Statute:** Mississippi Securities Act.

7821

Securities Broker-Dealer
Office of Secretary of State
Securities Div.
PO Box 136
Jackson, MS 39205
Phone: (601)359-6371

Credential Type: Securities Broker-Dealer License. **Duration of License:** One year. **Requirements:** Submit application on appropriate forms with a consent to service of process. Application must include proposed method of doing business, financial condition, plus qualifications and experience of applicant and any partner, officer, director, or controlling person with which applicant is affiliated. Minimum capital may be required. May be required to post surety bonds in amounts up to $30,000. **Fees:** $200 initial license/filing fee. $200 annual renewal. **Governing Statute:** Mississippi Securities Act.

Missouri

7822

Investment Advisor
Office of the Secretary of State
Securities Div.
PO Box 1276
Jefferson City, MO 65101
Phone: (314)751-4136

Credential Type: Investment Advisor License. **Duration of License:** One year. **Requirements:** Submit application on appropriate forms with a consent to service of process. Application must include proposed method of doing business, financial condition, qualifications and experience, and report of any felony or any misdemeanor or injunction involving the securities business. Minimum capital may be required. May be required to post surety bonds in amounts up to $25,000. **Fees:** $200 initial registration/filing fee. $100 annual renewal fee. **Governing Statute:** Missouri Uniform Securities Act.

7823

Securities Agent
Office of the Secretary of State
Securities Div.
PO Box 1276
Jefferson City, MO 65101
Phone: (314)751-4136

Credential Type: Securities Agent License. **Duration of License:** One year. **Requirements:** Submit application on appropriate forms with a consent to service of process. Application must include proposed method of doing business, financial condition, qualifications and experience, and report of any felony or any misdemeanor or injunction involving the securities business. May be required to post surety bonds in amounts up to $25,000. **Fees:** $50 initial registration/filing fee. $50 annual renewal fee. **Governing Statute:** Missouri Uniform Securities Act.

7824

Securities Broker-Dealer
Office of the Secretary of State
Securities Div.
PO Box 1276
Jefferson City, MO 65101
Phone: (314)751-4136

Credential Type: Securities Broker-Dealer License. **Duration of License:** One year. **Requirements:** Submit application on appropriate forms with a consent to service of process. Application must include proposed method of doing business, financial condition, qualifications and experience, and report of any felony or any misdemeanor or injunction involving the securities business. Minimum capital may be required. May be required to post surety bonds in amounts up to $25,000. May be required to carry fidelity bonds covering employees, officers, and partners in amounts up to $250,000. **Fees:** $200 initial registration/filing fee. $100 annual renewal fee. **Governing Statute:** Missouri Uniform Securities Act.

Montana

7825

Investment Advisor
State Auditor's Office
Securities Div.
PO Box 4009
Helena, MT 59604
Phone: (406)444-2040

Credential Type: Investment Advisor License. **Duration of License:** One year. **Requirements:** Submit application on appropriate forms. **Examination:** Securities examination as determined by Commissioner. **Fees:** $200 original registration. $200 annual renewal. **Governing Statute:** Montana Code Annotated, Securities Act of Montana, Title 30, Chapter 10.

7826

Investment Advisor Representative
State Auditor's Office
Securities Div.
PO Box 4009
Helena, MT 59604
Phone: (406)444-2040

Credential Type: Investment Advisor Representative License. **Duration of License:** One year. **Requirements:** Submit application on appropriate forms. Registration is only valid while applicant is associated with the registered investment advisor named on application. **Fees:** $50 original

Montana

Investment Advisor Representative, continued

registration. $50 annual renewal. $50 transfer fee. **Governing Statute:** Montana Code Annotated, Securities Act of Montana, Title 30, Chapter 10.

7827

Securities Broker-Dealer
State Auditor's Office
Securities Div.
PO Box 4009
Helena, MT 59604
Phone: (406)444-2040

Credential Type: Securities Broker-Dealer License. **Duration of License:** One year. **Requirements:** Submit application on appropriate forms. Renewal requires filing a statement of financial condition, unless the applicant is a member of the National Association of Securities Dealers (NASD). **Examination:** Securities examination as determined by Commissioner. **Fees:** $200 original registration. $200 annual renewal. **Governing Statute:** Montana Code Annotated, Securities Act of Montana, Title 30, Chapter 10.

7828

Securities Salesman
State Auditor's Office
Securities Div.
PO Box 4009
Helena, MT 59604
Phone: (406)444-2040

Credential Type: Securities Salesman License. **Duration of License:** One year. **Requirements:** Submit application on appropriate forms. Registration is only valid while applicant is associated with the issuer or registered broker-dealer named on application. Salesmen who are not in compliance with the financial responsibility requirements of the Securities Exchange Act of 1934 may be required to post a surety bond. **Fees:** $50 original registration. $50 annual renewal. $50 transfer fee. **Governing Statute:** Montana Code Annotated, Securities Act of Montana, Title 30, Chapter 10.

Nebraska

7829

Investment Advisor
Dept. of Banking and Finance
Bureau of Securities
PO Box 95006
Lincoln, NE 68509
Phone: (402)471-3445

Credential Type: Investment Advisor License. **Duration of License:** One year. **Requirements:** Submit application on "Application for Registration as Investment Advisor" (Form ADV). Complete a Schedule D form for each person employed by the applicant who will be advising clients on investments. File statement of financial condition. Submit names and addresses of at least four personal references. **Examination:** Securities examination as required by the director. **Fees:** $200 initial registration fee. $200 annual renewal fee. **Governing Statute:** Revised Statutes of Nebraska, Securities Act of Nebraska.

7830

Securities Agent
Dept. of Banking and Finance
Bureau of Securities
PO Box 95006
Lincoln, NE 68509
Phone: (402)471-3445

Credential Type: Securities Agent License. **Duration of License:** One year. **Requirements:** Submit application on appropriate forms with a consent to service of process. Application must include proposed method of doing business, financial condition, qualifications and experience, and report of any felony or any misdemeanor or injunction involving the securities business. Must be associated with a registered broker-dealer or issuer-dealer named in application. **Examination:** Securities examination as required by the director. **Fees:** $40 initial registration fee. $40 annual renewal fee. **Governing Statute:** Revised Statutes of Nebraska, Securities Act of Nebraska.

7831

Securities Broker-Dealer
Dept. of Banking and Finance
Bureau of Securities
PO Box 95006
Lincoln, NE 68509
Phone: (402)471-3445

Credential Type: Securities Broker-Dealer License. **Duration of License:** One year. **Requirements:** Submit application on appropriate forms with a consent to service of process. Application must include proposed method of doing business, financial condition, qualifications and experience, and report of any felony or any misdemeanor or injunction involving the securities business. Must maintain net capital of at least $25,000 or post a surety bond of $25,000. **Examination:** Securities examination as required by the director. **Fees:** $250 initial registration fee. $250 annual renewal fee. **Governing Statute:** Revised Statutes of Nebraska, Securities Act of Nebraska.

Nevada

7832

Investment Advisor
Dept. of State
Securities Div.
1771 Flamingo Rd., Ste. 212B
Las Vegas, NV 89158
Phone: (702)687-5203
Fax: (702)486-6408

Credential Type: Investment Advisor License. **Duration of License:** One year. **Requirements:** Submit application on appropriate forms with a consent to service of process. An application does not need to be filed if applicant maintains a current registration with the Securities and Exchange Commission, or other self-regulatory organization, that can be accessed through a central depository system. **Examination:** Written and/or oral examination as determined by the administrator. **Fees:** $150 initial license fee. $150 annual renewal fee. **Governing Statute:** Nevada Revised Statutes, Uniform Securities Act.

7833

Securities Broker-Dealer
Dept. of State
Securities Div.
1771 Flamingo Rd., Ste. 212B
Las Vegas, NV 89158
Phone: (702)687-5203
Fax: (702)486-6408

Credential Type: Securities Broker-Dealer License. **Duration of License:** One year. **Requirements:** Submit application on appropriate forms with a consent to service of process. An application does not need to be filed if applicant maintains a current registration with the Securities and Exchange Commission, or other self-regulatory organization, that can be accessed through a central depository system. **Examination:** Written and/or oral examination as determined by the administrator.

Fees: $150 initial license fee. $150 annual renewal fee. **Governing Statute:** Nevada Revised Statutes, Uniform Securities Act.

7834

Securities Sales Representative
Dept. of State
Securities Div.
1771 Flamingo Rd., Ste. 212B
Las Vegas, NV 89158
Phone: (702)687-5203
Fax: (702)486-6408

Credential Type: Securities Sales Representative License. **Duration of License:** One year. **Requirements:** Submit application on appropriate forms with a consent to service of process. An application does not need to be filed if applicant maintains a current registration with the Securities and Exchange Commission, or other self-regulatory organization, that can be accessed through a central depository system. **Examination:** Written and/or oral examination as determined by the administrator. **Fees:** $55 initial license fee. $55 annual renewal fee. **Governing Statute:** Nevada Revised Statutes, Uniform Securities Act.

New Hampshire

7835

Investment Advisor
Office of Securities Regulation
Dept. of State
Business Services and Regulation Div.
Bureau of Securities
State House Rm. 204
107 N. Main St.
Concord, NH 03301-4989
Phone: (603)271-1463

Credential Type: Investment Advisor License. **Duration of License:** One year. **Requirements:** Submit application on appropriate forms with consent to service of process. Minimum net capital may be required. Surety bonds of at least $25,000 are required. A deposit of cash or securities may be accepted in lieu of bond requirement. **Examination:** Written and/or oral examination as determined by the secretary of state. **Governing Statute:** Uniform Securities Act.

7836

Nondepository First Mortgage Banker
New Hampshire Banking Dept.
169 Manchester St.
Concord, Ne 03301
Phone: (603)271-3561

Credential Type: Nondepository First Mortgage Banker License. **Duration of License:** One year. **Requirements:** Submit application. Must show net worth of $100,000 minimum or post surety bond in that amount. Principal place of business must be located within New Hampshire. License must be posted in each place of business. **Reciprocity:** No. **Fees:** $250 application fee per office location. $250 renewal fee per office location.

7837

Securities Agent
Office of Securities Regulation
Dept. of State
Business Services and Regulation Div.
Bureau of Securities
State House Rm. 204
107 N. Main St.
Concord, NH 03301-4989
Phone: (603)271-1463

Credential Type: Securities Agent License. **Duration of License:** One year. **Requirements:** Submit application on appropriate forms with consent to service of process. Surety bonds of at least $25,000 are required. A deposit of cash or securities may be accepted in lieu of bond requirement. **Examination:** Written and/or oral examination as determined by the secretary of state. **Governing Statute:** Uniform Securities Act.

7838

Securities Broker-Dealer
Office of Securities Regulation
Dept. of State
Business Services and Regulation Div.
Bureau of Securities
State House Rm. 204
107 N. Main St.
Concord, NH 03301-4989
Phone: (603)271-1463

Credential Type: Securities Broker-Dealer License. **Duration of License:** One year. **Requirements:** Submit application on appropriate forms with consent to service of process. Minimum net capital may be required. Surety bonds of at least $25,000 are required. A deposit of cash or securities may be accepted in lieu of bond requirement. **Examination:** Written and/or oral examination as determined by the secretary of state. **Governing Statute:** Uniform Securities Act.

New Jersey

7839

Investment Advisor
New Jersey Dept. of Law and Public Safety
Bureau of Securities
2 Gateway Center, 8th Fl.
Newark, NJ 07102
Phone: (201)648-2040

Credential Type: Registration. **Requirements:** $25,000 in net capital or a surety bond may be required. **Examination:** Written. **Fees:** $100 application fee. $50 exam fee. **Governing Statute:** NJSA 49:3-29(g). NJAC 13:47A-2.1.

7840

Mortgage Banker/Broker
New Jersey Dept. of Banking
Div. of Consumer Complaints
Legal and Economic Research
CN040
Trenton, NJ 08625
Phone: (609)292-5340

Credential Type: License. **Duration of License:** Two years. **Requirements:** Must maintain a place of business in New Jersey. Must be bonded prior to doing business. Good moral character. **Examination:** Written and/or oral exam. **Fees:** $200 application fee. $800 biennial license. **Governing Statute:** NJSA 17:11B. NJAC 3:38-1.

7841

Securities Agent
New Jersey Dept. of Law and Public Safety
Bureau of Securities
2 Gateway Center, 8th Fl.
Newark, NJ 07102
Phone: (201)648-2040

Credential Type: Registration. **Requirements:** Must be employed by a registered broker-dealer or qualified issuer. **Examination:** Yes. **Fees:** $60 registration fee. $50 application for examination fee. **Governing Statute:** NJSA 49:3-49(b). NJAC 13:47A-3.1.

New Jersey

7842

Securities Broker-Dealer
New Jersey Dept. of Law and Public Safety
Bureau of Securities
2 Gateway Center, 8th Fl.
Newark, NJ 07102
Phone: (201)648-2040

Credential Type: License. **Requirements:** Must have a minimum amount of net capital or post a surety bond. **Examination:** Yes. **Fees:** $500 application fee. $50 exam fee. **Governing Statute:** NJSA 49:-49(c). NJAC 13:47A-1.1.

7843

Securities Issuer
New Jersey Dept. of Law and Public Safety
Bureau of Securities
2 Gateway Center, 8th Fl.
Newark, NJ 07102
Phone: (201)648-2040

Credential Type: Registration. **Fees:** $100 application fee. **Governing Statute:** NJSA 49:3-56(d). NJAC 13:47A-6.1.

New Mexico

7844

Investment Advisor
Regulation & Licensing Dept.
Securities Div.
PO Box 25101
Santa Fe, NM 87504
Phone: (505)827-7140

Credential Type: Investment Advisor License. **Duration of License:** One year. **Requirements:** Submit application on appropriate forms with a consent to service of process. An application does not need to be filed if applicant maintains a current registration with the Securities and Exchange Commission, or other self-regulatory organization, that can be accessed through a central depository system. Must maintain a minimum net worth as determined by the director. Renewal requires an annual report of financial condition. **Examination:** Written and/or oral examination as determined by director. **Fees:** $300 initial license fee. $300 annual renewal fee. **Governing Statute:** New Mexico Securities Act of 1986.

7845

Investment Advisor Representative
Regulation & Licensing Dept.
Securities Div.
PO Box 25101
Santa Fe, NM 87504
Phone: (505)827-7140

Credential Type: Investment Advisor Representative License. **Duration of License:** One year. **Requirements:** Submit application on appropriate forms with a consent to service of process. An application does not need to be filed if applicant maintains a current registration with the Securities and Exchange Commission, or other self-regulatory organization, that can be accessed through a central depository system. Renewal requires an annual report of financial condition. **Examination:** Written and/or oral examination as determined by director. **Fees:** $35 initial license fee. $35 annual renewal fee. **Governing Statute:** New Mexico Securities Act of 1986.

7846

Securities Broker-Dealer
Regulation & Licensing Dept.
Securities Div.
PO Box 25101
Santa Fe, NM 87504
Phone: (505)827-7140

Credential Type: Securities Broker-Dealer License. **Duration of License:** One year. **Requirements:** Submit application on appropriate forms with a consent to service of process. An application does not need to be filed if applicant maintains a current registration with the Securities and Exchange Commission, or other self-regulatory organization, that can be accessed through a central depository system. Must maintain a minimum net capital as determined by director. Renewal requires an annual report of financial condition. **Examination:** Written and/or oral examination as determined by director. **Fees:** $300 initial license fee. $300 annual renewal fee. **Governing Statute:** New Mexico Securities Act of 1986.

7847

Securities Sales Representative
Regulation & Licensing Dept.
Securities Div.
PO Box 25101
Santa Fe, NM 87504
Phone: (505)827-7140

Credential Type: Securities Sales Representative License. **Duration of License:** One year. **Requirements:** Submit application on appropriate forms with a consent to service of process. An application does not need to be filed if applicant maintains a current registration with the Securities and Exchange Commission, or other self-regulatory organization, that can be accessed through a central depository system. Renewal requires an annual report of financial condition. **Examination:** Written and/or oral examination as determined by director. **Fees:** $35 initial license fee. $35 annual renewal fee. **Governing Statute:** New Mexico Securities Act of 1986.

New York

7848

Investment Advisor
Dept. of Law
Bureau of Investor Protection and Securities
Two World Trade Center
New York, NY 10047
Phone: (212)416-8200
Fax: (212)341-2816

Credential Type: Investment Advisor License. **Duration of License:** One year. **Requirements:** Complete and file a copy of the Investment Advisor Statement (Form NY-ADV-1) with the Department of Law. Should information on the original application change, an amendment must be submitted on Form NY-ADV-2 and a supplemental statement fee paid. A financial statement is required for renewal. **Fees:** $200 filing fee. $200 annual renewal fee. $50 supplemental statement fee. **Governing Statute:** Official Compilation Codes, Rules and Regulations of the State of New York, Title 13, Chapter II.

7849

Securities Broker Dealer
Dept. of Law
Bureau of Investor Protection and Securities
Two World Trade Center
New York, NY 10047
Phone: (212)416-8200
Fax: (212)341-2816

Credential Type: Securities Broker-Dealer. **Duration of License:** One year. **Requirements:** National Association of Securities Dealers (NASD) members may file for licensing through the Central Registration Depository (CRD) by submitting Form BD or Form BDW. Non-NASD members must file Form M-1 or Form BD with the Department of Law of the State of New York. **Fees:** $200 filing fee (NASD member). $800 filing fee (Non-NASD member). **Governing Statute:** Official Compilation Codes, Rules and Regulations of the State of New York, Title 13, Chapter II.

7850

Securities Salesperson
Dept. of Law
Bureau of Investor Protection and Securities
Two World Trade Center
New York, NY 10047
Phone: (212)416-8200
Fax: (212)341-2816

Credential Type: Securities Salesperson License. **Duration of License:** One year. **Requirements:** National Association of Securities Dealers (NASD) members may file for licensing through the Central Registration Depository (CRD) by submitting Form BD or Form BDW. Non-NASD members must file Form U-4 or Form U-5 with the Department of Law of the State of New York. **Fees:** $45 filing fee (NASD member). $100 filing fee (Non-NASD member). $25 annual renewal fee (NASD member). **Governing Statute:** Official Compilation Codes, Rules and Regulations of the State of New York, Title 13, Chapter II.

North Carolina

7851

Investment Advisor
Dept. of State
Securities Div.
300 North Salisbury St., Ste. 404
Raleigh, NC 27603
Phone: (919)733-3924

Credential Type: Investment Advisor License. **Duration of License:** One year. **Requirements:** Must submit application on appropriate forms to the Administrator with a consent to service of process. May be required to post surety bonds in amounts up to $100,000. May be required to maintain a net capital of up to $100,000. **Fees:** $200 initial license/filing fee. $200 annual renewal fee. **Governing Statute:** General Statutes of North Carolina, North Carolina Securities Act.

7852

Investment Advisor Representative
Dept. of State
Securities Div.
300 North Salisbury St., Ste. 404
Raleigh, NC 27603
Phone: (919)733-3924

Credential Type: Investment Advisor Representative License. **Duration of License:** One year. **Requirements:** Must submit application on appropriate forms to the Administrator with a consent to service of process. **Fees:** $45 initial license/filing fee. $45 annual renewal fee. **Governing Statute:** General Statutes of North Carolina, North Carolina Securities Act.

7853

Securities Dealer
Dept. of State
Securities Div.
300 North Salisbury St., Ste. 404
Raleigh, NC 27603
Phone: (919)733-3924

Credential Type: Securities Broker-Dealer License. **Duration of License:** One year. **Requirements:** Must be registered as a dealer with the Securities and Exchange Commission under the Securities Exchange Act of 1934. Must submit application on appropriate forms to the Administrator with a consent to service of process. May be required to post surety bonds in amounts up to $100,000. **Fees:** $200 initial license/filing fee. $200 annual renewal fee. **Governing Statute:** General Statutes of North Carolina, North Carolina Securities Act.

7854

Securities Salesperson
Dept. of State
Securities Div.
300 North Salisbury St., Ste. 404
Raleigh, NC 27603
Phone: (919)733-3924

Credential Type: Securities Salesperson License. **Duration of License:** One year. **Requirements:** Must submit application on appropriate forms to the Administrator with a consent to service of process. May be required to post surety bonds in amounts up to $10,000. **Fees:** $55 initial license/filing fee. $55 annual renewal fee. **Governing Statute:** General Statutes of North Carolina, North Carolina Securities Act.

North Dakota

7855

Investment Adviser
Office of Securities Commissioner
5th Fl., State Capitol
600 E. Blvd.
Bismarck, ND 58505
Phone: (701)224-2910

Credential Type: Registration. **Duration of License:** One year. **Requirements:** Be at least 18 years of age. Submit application, written consent to service of process, and financial statement. Bond may also be required. **Fees:** $100 registration fee. **Governing Statute:** Securities Act of 1951.

7856

Investment Adviser Representative
Office of Securities Commissioner
5th Fl., State Capitol
600 E. Blvd.
Bismarck, ND 58505
Phone: (701)224-2910

Credential Type: Registration. **Duration of License:** One year. **Requirements:** Be at least 18 years of age. Must be employed by a registered investment adviser. **Fees:** $35 registration fee. **Governing Statute:** Securities Act of 1951.

7857

Oil and Gas Broker
State Securities Commission
600 E. Blvd.
Bismarck, ND 58505
Phone: (701)224-2910

Credential Type: Registration. **Duration of License:** One year. **Requirements:** Post required bond. **Fees:** $50 registration fee. $10 renewal fee. **Governing Statute:** North Dakota Century Code, Chap. 43-22.

7858

Securities Dealer
Office of Securities Commissioner
5th Fl., State Capitol
600 E. Blvd.
Bismarck, ND 58505
Phone: (701)224-2910

Credential Type: Registration. **Duration of License:** One year. **Requirements:** Be at least 18 years of age. Submit application, written consent to service of process, and financial statement. Bond may also be required. **Fees:** $200 registration fee. **Governing Statute:** Securities Act of 1951.

North Dakota

7859

Securities Salesperson
Office of Securities Commissioner
5th Fl., State Capitol
600 E. Blvd.
Bismarck, ND 58505
Phone: (701)224-2910

Credential Type: Registration. **Duration of License:** One year. **Requirements:** Be at least 18 years of age. **Examination:** Written examination. **Fees:** $50 registration fee. **Governing Statute:** Securities Act of 1951.

Ohio

7860

Securities Dealer
Dept. of Commerce
Div. of Securities
77 S. High St., 22nd Fl.
Columbus, OH 43266-0548
Phone: (614)644-7381

Credential Type: License. **Duration of License:** One year. **Requirements:** Submit application and irrevocable consent to service of process. **Examination:** Written examination. **Fees:** $75 exam fee. Prorated license fee: $30 per salesperson, with a minimum fee of $150 and a maximum fee of $5,000. **Governing Statute:** Ohio Revised Code, Title 17 (Securities Act).

7861

Securities Salesperson
Dept. of Commerce
Div. of Securities
77 S. High St., 22nd Fl.
Columbus, OH 43266-0548
Phone: (614)644-7381

Credential Type: License. **Duration of License:** One year. **Requirements:** Must be employed by a licensed securities dealer. **Examination:** Written examination. **Fees:** $50 license fee. $50 exam fee. $50 renewal fee. **Governing Statute:** Ohio Revised Code, Title 17 (Securities Act).

Oklahoma

7862

Broker-Dealer, Principal
Oklahoma Securities Commission, Licensing Div.
Will Rogers Memorial Office Bldg.
PO Box 5359
Oklahoma City, OK 73126
Phone: (405)521-2451

Credential Type: License. **Duration of License:** One year. **Authorization:** A broker-dealer principal is an individual who owns, manages, or operates a broker-dealership. **Requirements:** No felony convictions. **Examination:** Investement-Company Variable Contract Product, General Securities Examination and General Securities Principle Examination. **Fees:** $175 exam fee. $50 license fee. $50 renewal fee.

7863

Investment Advisor
Dept. of Securities
PO Box 53595
Oklahoma City, OK 73102
Phone: (405)235-0230

Credential Type: Investment Advisor License. **Duration of License:** One year. **Requirements:** Submit application on appropriate forms with a consent to service of process. Application must include proposed method of doing business, financial condition, qualifications and experience, and report of any felony or any misdemeanor or injunction involving the securities business. May be required to post surety bonds in amounts up to $25,000. **Governing Statute:** Oklahoma Statutes, Title 71.

7864

Investment Advisor Representative
Dept. of Securities
PO Box 53595
Oklahoma City, OK 73102
Phone: (405)235-0230

Credential Type: Investment Advisor Representative License. **Duration of License:** One year. **Requirements:** Submit application on appropriate forms with a consent to service of process. Application must include proposed method of doing business, financial condition, qualifications and experience, and report of any felony or any misdemeanor or injunction involving the securities business. May be required to post surety bonds in amounts up to $10,000. **Governing Statute:** Oklahoma Statutes, Title 71.

7865

Issuer Agent
Oklahoma Securities Commission, Licensing Div.
Will Rogers Memorial Office Bldg.
PO Box 5259
Oklahoma City, OK 73126
Phone: (405)521-2451

Credential Type: License. **Duration of License:** One year. **Requirements:** No felony convictions or securities law violations. **Examination:** Issuer Agent Examination. Uniform State Law Examination. **Fees:** $100 exam fee. $50 license fee. $50 renewal fee.

7866

Securities Agent
Dept. of Securities
PO Box 53595
Oklahoma City, OK 73102
Phone: (405)235-0230

Credential Type: Securities Agent License. **Duration of License:** One year. **Requirements:** Submit application on appropriate forms with a consent to service of process. Application must include proposed method of doing business, financial condition, qualifications and experience, and report of any felony or any misdemeanor or injunction involving the securities business. May be required to post surety bonds in amounts up to $10,000. **Governing Statute:** Oklahoma Statutes, Title 71.

7867

Securities Broker-Dealer
Dept. of Securities
PO Box 53595
Oklahoma City, Ok 73102
Phone: (405)235-0230

Credential Type: Securities Broker-Dealer License. **Duration of License:** One year. **Requirements:** Submit application on appropriate forms with a consent to service of process. Application must include proposed method of doing business, financial condition, qualifications and experience, and report of any felony or any misdemeanor or injunction involving the securities business. May be required to post surety bonds in amounts up to $25,000. **Governing Statute:** Oklahoma Statutes, Title 71.

Securities and Financial Services Sales Representatives

Oregon

7868

Debt Consolidation Agent
Div. of Finance and Corporate Securities
21 Labor & Industries Bldg.
Salem, OR 97310
Phone: (503)378-4140

Credential Type: License. **Duration of License:** Two years. **Requirements:** Must file and maintain with the Director of the Department of Insurance and Finance the following information: the name and address of the person engaging in business as a debt consolidating agency, the name and address of the debt consolidating agency, any assumed names or business names used by the debt consolidating agency, the names of persons who act as agents in the business of the debt consolidating agency, the names of persons who are agents of the debt consolidating agency for purposes of services of legal process, or an appointment of the director as agent for the debt consolidating agency for the service of process. If a person has been convicted for a criminal offense, an essential element of which is fraud, information relating to the circumstances of the conviction as required by the director. Telephone numbers of the business and all offices, all office locations, name of trust account, account number, and name and address of financial institution where account is located. If registration is for a non-profit debt consolidating business, copy of $10,000 fidelity bond; or if registration if for a for-profit debt consolidating business, copy of $10,000 surety bond payable to Department of Insurance and Finance. **Fees:** $200 license fee. $200 renewal fee. **Governing Statute:** ORS 697.602 to 697.992 and Oregon Administrative Rules, Chapter 441-800 to 441-910.

7869

Investment Adviser
Dept. of Insurance and Finance, Corporate Securities Section
Labor & Industries Bldg.
Salem, OR 97310
Phone: (503)378-4387

Credential Type: License. **Duration of License:** One year. **Requirements:** May be required to pass an examination on knowledge of the Oregon securities law and the securities business. Must file a $10,000 corporate surety bond. **Examination:** None required. **Fees:** $15 license fee. $15 renewal fee. **Governing Statute:** ORS Chapter 59.

7870

Mortgage Broker
Dept. of Insurance and Finance
Corporate Securities Section
Labor & Industries Bldg.
Salem, OR 97310
Phone: (503)378-4387

Credential Type: License. **Duration of License:** One year. **Examination:** File a $10,000 corporate Surety Bond (General Mortgage Broker only). **Fees:** $15 license fee. $15 renewal fee. **Governing Statute:** ORS Chapter 59.

7871

Securities Broker/Dealer
Dept. of Insurance and Finance
Corporate Securities Section
Labor & Industries Bldg.
Salem, OR 97310
Phone: (503)378-4387

Credential Type: License. **Duration of License:** One year. **Requirements:** Complete application form BD and file with Central Registration Depository in Rockville, Maryland. Must file a $10,000 Oregon surety bond. **Examination:** Yes. **Fees:** $60 exam fee. $100 license fee. $50 renewal fee. **Governing Statute:** ORS Chapter 59.

7872

Securities Salesperson
Dept. of Insurance and Finance
Corporate Securities Section
Labor & Industries Bldg.
Salem, OR 97310
Phone: (503)378-4387

Credential Type: License. **Duration of License:** One year. **Requirements:** Complete and file application form with the Central Registration Depository in Rockville, Maryland. Must be employed by a company dealing with stocks or bonds. **Examination:** Yes. **Fees:** $60 exam fee. $15 license fee. $15 renewal fee. **Governing Statute:** ORS Chapter 59.

Pennsylvania

7873

Investment Adviser
Securities Commission
Eastgate Office Bldg.
1010 N. Seventh St., 2nd Fl.
Harrisburg, PA 17102-1410
Phone: (717)787-5675

Credential Type: Registration. **Duration of License:** One year. **Requirements:** Submit application on appropriate forms, including Form ADV. Submit statement of financial condition. Meet net capital requirements. For the two years prior to application, or for three of the past five years, applicant must have acceptable experience in securities, banking, finance, or a related business. **Examination:** NASD, SEC, or NYSE securities examination for registered representatives or supervisors. Uniform Investment Adviser Law Examination of the NASD, Series 65. **Fees:** $200 initial filing fee. $200 renewal filing fee. **Governing Statute:** Pennsylvania Securities Act of 1972, P.L. 1280. 70 P.S. 1-301 et seq.

7874

Investment Adviser Representative (Associated Person)
Securities Commission
Eastgate Office Bldg.
1010 N. Seventh St., 2nd Fl.
Harrisburg, PA 17102-1410
Phone: (717)787-5675

Credential Type: Registration. **Duration of License:** One year. **Requirements:** For the two years prior to application, or for three of the past five years, applicant must have acceptable experience in securities, banking, finance, or a related business. **Examination:** NASD, SEC, or NYSE securities examination for registered representatives or supervisors. Uniform Investment Adviser Law Examination of the NASD, Series 65. **Fees:** $50 initial filing fee. $50 renewal filing fee. **Governing Statute:** Pennsylvania Securities Act of 1972, P.L. 1280. 70 P.S. 1-301 et seq.

Pennsylvania

7875

Mortgage Broker
Real Estate Commission
Transportation and Safety Bldg., Rm. 611
PO Box 2649
Harrisburg, PA 17105-2649
Phone: (717)783-3658

Credential Type: Mortgage Broker License. **Requirements:** Contact licensing body for application information.

7876

Securities Broker-Dealer
Securities Commission
Eastgate Office Bldg.
1010 N. Seventh St., 2nd Fl.
Harrisburg, PA 17102-1410
Phone: (717)787-5675

Credential Type: Registration. **Duration of License:** One year. **Requirements:** Submit application on appropriate forms, including Form BD. Submit statement of financial condition. Maintain net capital of $25,000. **Fees:** $250 initial filing fee. $250 renewal filing fee. **Governing Statute:** Pennsylvania Securities Act of 1972, P.L. 1280. 70 P.S. 1-301 et seq.

7877

Securities Sales Agent
Securities Commission
Eastgate Office Bldg.
1010 N. Seventh St., 2nd Fl.
Harrisburg, PA 17102-1410
Phone: (717)787-5675

Credential Type: Registration. **Duration of License:** One year. **Requirements:** Submit application on appropriate forms, including Form U-4. Must be employed by a registered broker-dealer. **Examination:** NASD, SEC, or NYSE securities examination for principals or registered representatives. Uniform Securities Agent State Law Examination (USASLE), Series 63. **Fees:** $50 initial filing fee. $50 renewal filing fee. **Governing Statute:** Pennsylvania Securities Act of 1972, P.L. 1280. 70 P.S. 1-301 et seq.

Rhode Island

7878

Investment Adviser
Dept. of Business Regulation
Securities Div.
233 Richmond St., Ste. 232
Providence, RI 02903-4232
Phone: (401)277-3048

Credential Type: License. **Duration of License:** One year. **Requirements:** Submit application and consent to service of process. **Fees:** $250 license fee. $250 renewal fee. **Governing Statute:** General Laws of Rhode Island, 1956 as amended, Sect. 7-11-101 et seq.

7879

Investment Adviser Representative
Dept. of Business Regulation
Securities Div.
233 Richmond St., Ste. 232
Providence, RI 02903-4232
Phone: (401)277-3048

Credential Type: License. **Duration of License:** One year. **Requirements:** Submit application and consent to service of process. Must be employed by a licensed investment adviser. **Fees:** $50 license fee. $50 renewal fee. **Governing Statute:** General Laws of Rhode Island, 1956 as amended, Sect. 7-11-101 et seq.

7880

Money and Mortgage Broker
Div. of Banking
Rhode Island Dept. of Business Regulation
233 Richmond St.
Providence, RI 02903
Phone: (401)277-2405

Credential Type: Money and Mortgage Broker License. **Duration of License:** One year. **Requirements:** Must have at least five years experience in a licensed lending institution as a loan officer. Submit application and pay fee. **Reciprocity:** No. **Fees:** $150 application fee. $300 license fee. $300 annual renewal fee. $25 annual report fee (required). $25 power of attorney fee. $500 (or more per diem) annual state audit fee.

7881

Securities Broker-Dealer
Dept. of Business Regulation
Securities Div.
233 Richmond St., Ste. 232
Providence, RI 02903-4232
Phone: (401)277-3048

Credential Type: License. **Duration of License:** One year. **Requirements:** Submit application and consent to service of process. **Fees:** $250 license fee. $250 renewal fee. **Governing Statute:** General Laws of Rhode Island, 1956 as amended, Sect. 7-11-101 et seq.

7882

Securities Sales Representative
Dept. of Business Regulation
Securities Div.
233 Richmond St., Ste. 232
Providence, RI 02903-4232
Phone: (401)277-3048

Credential Type: License. **Duration of License:** One year. **Requirements:** Submit application and consent to service of process. Must be employed by a licensed broker-dealer. **Fees:** $50 license fee. $50 renewal fee. **Governing Statute:** General Laws of Rhode Island, 1956 as amended, Sect. 7-11-101 et seq.

South Carolina

7883

Investment Advisor
Dept. of State
Securities Div.
1205 Pendleton St.
Edgar Brown Bldg., Ste. 501
Columbia, SC 29201
Phone: (803)734-1087

Credential Type: Investment Advisor License. **Duration of License:** Two years (as of June 30, 1993). **Requirements:** Submit application on appropriate forms with a consent to service of process. Application must include proposed method of doing business, financial condition, qualifications and experience, and report of any felony or any misdemeanor or injunction involving the securities business. May be required to maintain a minimum capital not to exceed $10,000. Must post surety bond in amounts up to $50,000. **Fees:** $400 initial license fee. $400 registration fee. **Governing Statute:** Code of Laws of South Carolina, Uniform Securities Act.

Securities and Financial Services Sales Representatives

7884

Investment Advisor Representative
Dept. of State
Securities Div.
1205 Pendleton St.
Edgar Brown Bldg., Ste. 501
Columbia, SC 29201
Phone: (803)734-1087

Credential Type: Investment Advisor Representative License. **Duration of License:** Two years (as of June 30, 1993). **Requirements:** Submit application on appropriate forms with a consent to service of process. Application must include proposed method of doing business, financial condition, qualifications and experience, and report of any felony or any misdemeanor or injunction involving the securities business. Must post surety bond in amounts up to $10,000. **Fees:** $100 initial license fee. $100 registration fee. **Governing Statute:** Code of Laws of South Carolina, Uniform Securities Act.

7885

Securities Agent
Dept. of State
Securities Div.
1205 Pendleton St.
Edgar Brown Bldg., Ste. 501
Columbia, SC 29201
Phone: (803)734-1087

Credential Type: Securities Agent License. **Duration of License:** Two years (as of June 30, 1993). **Requirements:** Submit application on appropriate forms with a consent to service of process. Application must include proposed method of doing business, financial condition, qualifications and experience, and report of any felony or any misdemeanor or injunction involving the securities business. Must post surety bond in amounts up to $10,000. **Fees:** $100 initial license fee. $100 registration fee. **Governing Statute:** Code of Laws of South Carolina, Uniform Securities Act.

7886

Securities Broker-Dealer
Dept. of State
Securities Div.
1205 Pendleton St.
Edgar Brown Bldg., Ste. 501
Columbia, SC 29201
Phone: (803)734-1087

Credential Type: Securities Broker-Dealer License. **Duration of License:** Two years. **Requirements:** Submit application on appropriate forms with a consent to service of process. Application must include proposed method of doing business, financial condition, qualifications and experience, and report of any felony or any misdemeanor or injunction involving the securities business. May be required to maintain a minimum capital not to exceed $10,000. Must post surety bond of $50,000. No bond is required if applicant is a member of the NASD or the Securities Investor Corporation. **Fees:** $400 initial license fee. $400 registration fee. **Governing Statute:** Code of Laws of South Carolina, Uniform Securities Act.

South Dakota

7887

Investment Advisor
Dept. of Commerce and Regulation
Div. of Securities
500 E. Capitol
Pierre, SD 57501-3940
Phone: (605)773-4013

Credential Type: Investment Advisor License. **Duration of License:** One year. **Requirements:** Submit application on appropriate forms with consent to service of process. Application must include proposed method of doing business, financial condition, qualifications and experience, and report of any felony or any misdemeanor or injunction involving the securities business. May be required to post surety bonds in amounts up to $25,000. **Fees:** $100 initial license/filing fee. $100 annual renewal fee. **Governing Statute:** South Dakota Codified Laws, Uniform Securities Act, Part II, Regulations of the Director of Securities.

7888

Investment Advisor Representative
Dept. of Commerce and Regulation
Div. of Securities
500 E. Capitol
Pierre, SD 57501-3940
Phone: (605)773-4013

Credential Type: Investment Advisor Representative License. **Duration of License:** One year. **Requirements:** Submit application on appropriate forms with consent to service of process. Application must include proposed method of doing business, financial condition, qualifications and experience, and report of any felony or any misdemeanor or injunction involving the securities business. **Fees:** $50 initial license/filing fee. $50 annual renewal fee. **Governing Statute:** South Dakota Codified Laws, Uniform Securities Act, Part II, Regulations of the Director of Securities.

7889

Mortgage Broker
South Dakota Real Estate Commission
PO Box 490
Pierre, SD 57501-0490
Phone: (605)773-3600
Phone: (605)773-3150

Credential Type: Mortgage Broker License. **Duration of License:** Two years. **Requirements:** Submit application and pay fees. **Examination:** State-administered mortgage broker examination. **Exemptions:** Real estate brokers do not need a mortgage broker license. **Fees:** $100 application and license fee. $80 renewal fee.

7890

Securities Agent
Dept. of Commerce and Regulation
Div. of Securities
500 E. Capitol
Pierre, SD 57501-3940
Phone: (605)773-4013

Credential Type: Securities Agent License. **Duration of License:** One year. **Requirements:** Submit application on appropriate forms with consent to service of process. Application must include proposed method of doing business, financial condition, qualifications and experience, and report of any felony or any misdemeanor or injunction involving the securities business. Must post surety bonds of at least $5,000. Pass examination with a score of at least 70 percent. **Examination:** Uniform Securities Agent Law Examination. **Fees:** $125 initial license/filing fee. $125 annual renewal fee. **Governing Statute:** South Dakota Codified Laws, Uniform Securities Act, Part II, Regulations of the Director of Securities.

7891

Securities Broker-Dealer
Dept. of Commerce and Regulation
Div. of Securities
500 E. Capitol
Pierre, SD 57501-3940
Phone: (605)773-4013

Credential Type: Securities Broker-Dealer License. **Duration of License:** One year. **Requirements:** Submit application of appropriate forms with consent to service of process. Application must include proposed method of doing business, financial condition, qualifications and experience, and report of any felony or any misdemeanor or injunction involving the securities business. Must maintain net capital of

Securities Broker-Dealer, continued

at least $15,000. Must post surety bonds in amounts up to $25,000 as determined by director.

Broker-dealer must designate one employee who will act as a supervisor and be licensed as an agent for the broker dealer. This employee must pass one of the following exams with a score of at least 80 percent: Securities and Exchange Commission Organization/National Association of Securities Dealers Nonmember General Securities Examination (series two); National Association of Securities Dealers General Securities Principal Examination (series 24); or the Municipal Securities Principal Examination (series 53). **Examination:** Written securities examination as prescribed by director. **Fees:** $150 initial license/filing fee. $150 annual renewal fee. **Governing Statute:** South Dakota Codified Laws, Uniform Securities Act, Part II, Regulations of the Director of Securities.

Tennessee

7892

Investment Advisor
Dept. of Commerce and Insurance
Securities Div.
500 James Robertson Pky.
Volunteer Plaza, 6th Fl., Ste. 680
Nashville, TN 37243-0584
Phone: (615)741-5911

Credential Type: Investment Advisor License. **Duration of License:** One year. **Requirements:** Submit application on appropriate Form ADV. File statement of financial condition. May be required to post surety bonds in amounts up to $10,000. Maintain net capital of at least $15,000. **Fees:** $200 initial license/filing fee. $200 annual renewal fee. **Governing Statute:** Tennessee Code Annotated, Tennessee Securities Act of 1980, Chapter 2, Part 1.

7893

Securities Agent
Dept. of Commerce and Insurance
Securities Div.
500 James Robertson Pky.
Volunteer Plaza, 6th Fl., Ste. 680
Nashville, TN 37243-0584
Phone: (615)741-5911

Credential Type: Securities Agent License. **Duration of License:** One year. **Requirements:** Submit application on appropriate forms with consent to service of process. Application must include proposed method of doing business, financial condition, qualifications and experience, and report of any felony or any misdemeanor or injunction involving the securities business. May be required to post surety bonds in amounts up to $10,000. **Examination:** The Uniform Securities Agent State Law Examination (USASLE). An examination administered by the NASD, New York Stock Exchange or the SEC on general knowledge of securities principles. **Fees:** $50 initial license/filing fee. $50 annual renewal fee. **Governing Statute:** Tennessee Code Annotated, Tennessee Securities Act of 1980, Chapter 2, Part 1.

7894

Securities Broker-Dealer
Dept. of Commerce and Insurance
Securities Div.
500 James Robertson Pky.
Volunteer Plaza, 6th Fl., Ste. 680
Nashville, TN 37243-0584
Phone: (615)741-5911

Credential Type: Securities Broker-Dealer License. **Duration of License:** One year. **Requirements:** All eligible applicants must apply for initial registration in Tennessee through the Central Registration Depository (CRD) system on Form BD. Must concurrently file a Form BD with the Securities Div. of Tennessee along with a statement of financial condition. Must show evidence that a principal's examination was taken and passed by a designated principal of the applicant. May be required to post surety bonds in amounts up to $10,000. Must maintain net capital as determined by Commissioner. **Fees:** $200 initial license/filing fee. $200 annual renewal fee. **Governing Statute:** Tennessee Code Annotated, Tennessee Securities Act of 1980, Chapter 2, Part 1.

Texas

7895

Investment Advisor
State Securities Board
PO Box 13167, Capitol Station
Austin, TX 78711-3167
Phone: (512)474-2233

Credential Type: Investment Advisor License. **Requirements:** Submit a sworn application on appropriate forms. File statement of financial condition. **Examination:** National Association of Securities Dealers (NASD) examination on general securities principles or approved equivalent. Uniform Securities Agent State Law Examination (USASLE) or approved equivalent. **Governing Statute:** Texas Administrative Code, Title 7, Part VII.

7896

Securities Agent
State Securities Board
PO Box 13167, Capitol Station
Austin, TX 78711-3167
Phone: (512)474-2233

Credential Type: Securities Agent License. **Requirements:** Submit a sworn application on appropriate forms. Members of the National Association of Securities Dealers Inc. (NASD) may file for licensing through the Central Registration Depository (CRD). Pass examination with a score of at least 70 percent. **Examination:** National Association of Securities Dealers (NASD) examination on general securities principles or approved equivalent. Uniform Securities Agent State Law Examination (USASLE) or approved equivalent. **Governing Statute:** Texas Administrative Code, Title 7, Part VII.

7897

Securities Dealer
State Securities Board
PO Box 13167, Capitol Station
Austin, TX 78711-3167
Phone: (512)474-2233

Credential Type: Securities Broker-Dealer License. **Requirements:** Submit a sworn application on appropriate forms. Members of the National Association of Securities Dealers Inc. (NASD) may file for licensing through the Central Registration Depository (CRD). File a statement of financial condition. Pass examination with a score of at least 70 percent. **Examination:** National Association of Securities Dealers (NASD) examination on general securities principles or approved equivalent. Uniform Securities Agent State Law Examination (USASLE) or approved equivalent. **Governing Statute:** Texas Administrative Code, Title 7, Part VII.

7898

Securities Salesman
State Securities Board
PO Box 13167, Capitol Station
Austin, TX 78711-3167
Phone: (512)474-2233

Credential Type: Securities Salesman License. **Requirements:** Submit a sworn application on appropriate forms. **Examination:** National Association of Securities Dealers (NASD) examination on general securities principles or approved equivalent. Uniform Securities Agent State Law Examination (USASLE) or approved equivalent. **Governing Statute:** Texas Administrative Code, Title 7, Part VII.

Utah

7899

Investment Adviser
Dept. of Commerce
Div. of Securities
160 E. 300 S.
Salt Lake City, UT 84111
Phone: (801)530-6600

Credential Type: Investment adviser license. **Requirements:** File with the division the following forms: SEC Form ADV (Uniform Application for Investment Adviser Registration), NASAA Form U-2 (Uniform Consent to Service of Process), Division Form 45BIA (Corporate Indemnity Bond of Investment Adviser) if applicant will have custody of client funds or securities, and National Association of Securities Dealers (NASD) Form U-4 (Uniform Application for Securities Industry Registration or Transfer) for the designated official and each agent to be registered with the division.

The designated official and each agent must pass the Series 65, Uniform Investment Adviser Exam.

An out-of-state investment adviser with a branch office in Utah must have a certificate of authority to do business in Utah. **Examination:** Series 65, Uniform Investment Adviser Exam. **Fees:** $75 registration fee for firm and designated official. $20 registration fee for each agent.

7900

Securities Agent
Dept. of Commerce
Div. of Securities
160 E. 300 S.
Salt Lake City, UT 84111
Phone: (801)530-6600

Credential Type: Securities agent license. **Requirements:** Must work for a registered securities broker-dealer. Pass the Series 63, Uniform Securities Agent State Law Examination and any other exams required by the SEC or the NASD. **Examination:** Uniform Securities Agent State Law Examination. **Fees:** $20 registration fee.

7901

Securities Broker-Dealer
Dept. of Commerce
Div. of Securities
160 E. 300 S.
Salt Lake City, UT 84111
Phone: (801)530-6600

Credential Type: Broker-Dealer license. **Requirements:** Must be a member of the National Association of Securities Dealers (NASD). File SEC Form BD and Utah form U-4 with the CRD. Principal officer and each agent must pass appropriate examinations required by the SEC or the NASD, including the Series 63, Uniform Securities Agent State Law Examination. File with the division a certificate of authority to do business in Utah, unless applicant will not have an office in Utah. **Examination:** Uniform Securities Agent State Law Examination. **Fees:** $75 registration fee.

Vermont

7902

Securities Broker-Dealer
Dept. of Banking, Insurance, and Securities
89 Main St., Drawer 20
Montpelier, VT 05620-3101
Phone: (802)828-3420

Credential Type: Securities Broker-Dealer License. **Duration of License:** One year. **Requirements:** Submit a sworn application on appropriate forms with consent to service of process. May be required to post surety bonds in amounts up to $25,000. **Fees:** $250 initial license/filing fee. $250 annual renewal fee. **Governing Statute:** Vermont Statutes Annotated, Securities Act, Title 9, Part 5, Chapter 131.

7903

Securities Sales Representative
Dept. of Banking, Insurance, and Securities
89 Main St., Drawer 20
Montpelier, VT 05620-3101
Phone: (802)828-3420

Credential Type: Securities Sales Representative License. **Duration of License:** One year. **Requirements:** Application must be filed with a registered broker-dealer. Must file evidence of good character and adequate identification. **Examination:** Examination as required by Commissioner. **Fees:** $45 initial license/filing fee. $45 annual renewal fee. **Governing Statute:** Vermont Statutes Annotated, Securities Act, Title 9, Part 5, Chapter 131.

Virginia

7904

Investment Advisor
State Corporation
Div. of Securities and Retail Franchising
PO Box 1197
Richmond, VA 23209
Phone: (804)371-2684

Credential Type: Investment Advisor License. **Duration of License:** One year. **Requirements:** Good character and repute. Submit application on appropriate forms. Maintain net capital of $25,000 or post surety bond in the amount of $25,000. **Examination:** Written examination as determined by the Commissioner. **Fees:** $200 initial license/filing fee. $200 annual renewal fee. **Governing Statute:** Code of Virginia, Securities Act, Chapter 5.

7905

Investment Advisor Representative
State Corporation
Div. of Securities and Retail Franchising
PO Box 1197
Richmond, VA 23209
Phone: (804)371-2684

Credential Type: Investment Advisor Representative License. **Duration of License:** One year. **Requirements:** Good character and repute. Submit application on appropriate forms. **Examination:** Written examination as determined by the Commissioner. **Fees:** $30-$50 initial license/filing fee. $30-50 annual renewal fee. **Governing Statute:** Code of Virginia, Securities Act, Chapter 5.

7906

Securities Agent
State Corporation
Div. of Securities and Retail Franchising
PO Box 1197
Richmond, VA 23209
Phone: (804)371-2684

Credential Type: Securities Agent License. **Duration of License:** One year. **Requirements:** Good character and repute. Submit application on appropriate forms. **Examination:** Written examination as determined by the Commissioner. **Fees:** $30-$50 initial license/filing fee. $30-50 annual

Securities Agent, continued

renewal fee. **Governing Statute:** Code of Virginia, Securities Act, Chapter 5.

7907

Securities Broker-Dealer
State Corporation
Div. of Securities and Retail Franchising
PO Box 1197
Richmond, VA 23209
Phone: (804)371-2684

Credential Type: Securities Broker-Dealer License. **Duration of License:** One year. **Requirements:** Good character and repute. Submit application on appropriate forms. Maintain net capital of $25,000 or post surety bond in the amount of $25,000. **Examination:** Written examination as determined by the Commissioner. **Fees:** $200 initial license/filing fee. $200 annual renewal fee. **Governing Statute:** Code of Virginia, Securities Act, Chapter 5.

Washington

7908

Commodity Broker-Dealer
Dept. of Licensing
Business License Services - Securities
405 Black Lake Blvd.
Olympia, WA 98504
Phone: (206)753-6928

Credential Type: Registration. **Duration of License:** One year. **Requirements:** Submit to legal and financial review. **Fees:** $200 registration fee. $100 renewal fee.

7909

Debt Adjuster
Dept. of Licensing
Professional Licensing Service
1112 SE Quince
Olympia, WA 98504
Phone: (206)596-4567

Credential Type: Debt Adjuster License. **Duration of License:** One year. **Requirements:** At least 18 years of age. Resident of Washington state for a minimum of one year. Submit to background investigation. **Examination:** Written examination. **Fees:** $500 investigation fee. $300 examination or reexamination fee. $15 duplicate license fee. $500 renewal fee.

7910

Investment Advisor
Dept. of Licensing
Securities Div.
PO Box 9033
Olympia, WA 98507-9033
Phone: (206)753-6928
Fax: (206)586-5068

Credential Type: Investment Advisor License. **Duration of License:** One year. **Requirements:** Submit application on appropriate forms with a consent to service of process. Application must include proposed method of doing business, financial condition, qualifications and experience, and report of any felony or any misdemeanor or injunction involving the securities business. Minimum net capital may be required. **Examination:** Written examination as prescribed by the director. **Governing Statute:** 1989 Revised Code of Washington, The Securities Act of Washington.

7911

Investment Advisor Salesperson
Dept. of Licensing
Securities Div.
PO Box 9033
Olympia, WA 98507-9033
Phone: (206)753-6928
Fax: (206)586-5068

Credential Type: Investment Advisor Salesperson License. **Duration of License:** One year. **Requirements:** Submit application on appropriate forms with a consent to service of process. Application must include proposed method of doing business, financial condition, qualifications and experience, and report of any felony or any misdemeanor or injunction involving the securities business. **Examination:** Written examination as prescribed by the director. **Governing Statute:** 1989 Revised Code of Washington, The Securities Act of Washington.

7912

Securities Broker-Dealer
Dept. of Licensing
Securities Div.
PO Box 9033
Olympia, WA 98507-9033
Phone: (206)753-6928
Fax: (206)586-5068

Credential Type: Securities Broker-Dealer License. **Duration of License:** One year. **Requirements:** Submit application on appropriate forms with a consent to service of process. Application must include proposed method of doing business, financial condition, qualifications and experience, and report of any felony or any misdemeanor or injunction involving the securities business. Minimum net capital may be required. **Examination:** Written examination as prescribed by the director. **Governing Statute:** 1989 Revised Code of Washington, The Securities Act of Washington.

7913

Securities Salesperson
Dept. of Licensing
Securities Div.
PO Box 9033
Olympia, WA 98507-9033
Phone: (206)753-6928
Fax: (206)586-5068

Credential Type: Securities Salesperson License. **Duration of License:** One year. **Requirements:** Submit application on appropriate forms with a consent to service of process. Application must include proposed method of doing business, financial condition, qualifications and experience, and report of any felony or any misdemeanor or injunction involving the securities business. **Examination:** Written examination as prescribed by the director. **Governing Statute:** 1989 Revised Code of Washington, The Securities Act of Washington.

West Virginia

7914

Investment Advisor
State Auditor's Office
Security Div.
Rm. W-118, State Capitol
Charleston, WV 25305
Phone: (304)558-2257

Credential Type: Investment Advisor License. **Duration of License:** One year. **Requirements:** Submit application on appropriate forms with a consent to service of process. Application must include proposed method of doing business, financial condition, qualifications and experience, and report of any felony or any misdemeanor or injunction involving the securities business. If net capital is below $25,000, applicant may be required to post a surety bond in amounts up to $10,000. **Fees:** $100 initial license/filing fee. $100 renewal fee. **Governing Statute:** Code of West Virginia, Chapter 32—Uniform Securities Act, Article 2.

Securities and Financial Services Sales Representatives

7915

Securities Agent
State Auditor's Office
Security Div.
Rm. W-118, State Capitol
Charleston, WV 25305
Phone: (304)558-2257

Credential Type: Securities Agent License. **Duration of License:** One year. **Requirements:** Submit application on appropriate forms with a consent to service of process. Application must include proposed method of doing business, financial condition, qualifications and experience, and report of any felony or any misdemeanor or injunction involving the securities business. **Fees:** $30 initial license/filing fee. $30 renewal fee. **Governing Statute:** Code of West Virginia, Chapter 32—Uniform Securities Act, Article 2.

7916

Securities Broker-Dealer
State Auditor's Office
Security Div.
Rm. W-118, State Capitol
Charleston, WV 25305
Phone: (304)558-2257

Credential Type: Securities Broker-Dealer License. **Duration of License:** One year. **Requirements:** Submit application on appropriate forms with a consent to service of process. Application must include proposed method of doing business, financial condition, qualifications and experience, and report of any felony or any misdemeanor or injunction involving the securities business. If net capital is below $25,000, applicant may be required to post a surety bond in amounts up to $10,000. **Fees:** $150 initial license/filing fee. $150 renewal fee. **Governing Statute:** Code of West Virginia, Chapter 32—Uniform Securities Act, Article 2.

Wisconsin

7917

Investment Advisor
Office of Commissioner of Securities
101 E. Wilson St.
Madison, WI 53702
Phone: (608)266-1064

Credential Type: Investment Advisor License. **Duration of License:** One year. **Requirements:** Submit application on appropriate forms with a consent to service of process. Application must include proposed method of doing business, financial condition, qualifications and experience, and report of any felony or any misdemeanor or injunction involving the securities business. Minimum net capital or furnishing of surety bonds may be required. **Examination:** Written examination as required by Commissioner. **Governing Statute:** Wisconsin Statutes, Uniform Securities Act, Subchapter III.

7918

Loan Originator
Regulations and Licensing Dept.
Mortgage Banking Board
PO Box 8935
Madison, WI 53708-8935
Phone: (608)266-8609

Credential Type: License. **Requirements:** 18 years of age.

7919

Mortgage Banker
Regulations and Licensing Dept.
Mortgage Banking Board
PO Box 8935
Madison, WI 53708-8935
Phone: (608)266-8609

Credential Type: License. **Requirements:** 18 years of age.

7920

Securities Agent
Office of Commissioner of Securities
101 E. Wilson St.
Madison, WI 53702
Phone: (608)266-1064

Credential Type: Securities Agent License. **Duration of License:** One year. **Requirements:** Submit application on appropriate forms with a consent to service of process. Application must include proposed method of doing business, financial condition, qualifications and experience, and report of any felony or any misdemeanor or injunction involving the securities business. **Examination:** Written examination as required by Commissioner. **Governing Statute:** Wisconsin Statutes, Uniform Securities Act, Subchapter III.

7921

Securities Broker-Dealer
Office of Commissioner of Securities
101 E. Wilson St.
Madison, WI 53702
Phone: (608)266-1064

Credential Type: Securities Broker-Dealer License. **Duration of License:** One year. **Requirements:** Submit application on appropriate forms with a consent to service of process. Application must include proposed method of doing business, financial condition, qualifications and experience, and report of any felony or any misdemeanor or injunction involving the securities business. Minimum net capital or furnishing of surety bonds may be required. **Examination:** Written examination as required by Commissioner. **Governing Statute:** Wisconsin Statutes, Uniform Securities Act, Subchapter III.

Wyoming

7922

Securities Agent
Office of Secretary of State
Securities Div.
State Capitol Bldg.
Cheyenne, WY 82002
Phone: (307)777-7370

Credential Type: Securities Agent License. **Duration of License:** One year. **Requirements:** Submit application on appropriate forms with a consent to service of process. Application must include proposed method of doing business, financial condition, qualifications and experience, and report of any felony or any misdemeanor or injunction involving the securities business. Minimum net capital may be required. **Examination:** Examination as required by secretary of state. **Fees:** $20 initial license/filing fee. $20 annual renewal fee. **Governing Statute:** Wyoming Statutes 1977, Uniform Securities Act.

7923

Securities Broker-Dealer
Office of Secretary of State
Securities Div.
State Capitol Bldg.
Cheyenne, WY 82002
Phone: (307)777-7370

Credential Type: Securities Broker-Dealer License. **Duration of License:** One year. **Requirements:** Submit application on appropriate forms with a consent to service of process. Application must include proposed method of doing business, finan-

Securities Broker-Dealer, continued

cial condition, qualifications and experience, and report of any felony or any misdemeanor or injunction involving the securities business. Minimum net capital may be required. Applicants with net capital under $25,000 may be required to post surety bonds in amounts up to $10,000. **Examination:** Examination as required by secretary of state. **Fees:** $100 initial license/filing fee. $100 annual renewal fee. **Governing Statute:** Wyoming Statutes 1977, Uniform Securities Act.

Services Sales Representatives

The following states grant licenses in this occupational category as of the date of publication:

Colorado	District of	Illinois	Maryland	North Carolina	Rhode Island	Washington
Connecticut	Columbia	Iowa	Michigan	North Dakota	Utah	Wisconsin
	Idaho	Maine	New Jersey	Oklahoma	Vermont	

Colorado

7924

Solicitor
Dept. of Law
Office of the Attorney General
State Services Bldg.
1525 Sherman St., 5th Fl.
Denver, CO 80203
Phone: (303)866-4500
Phone: (303)866-3611
Fax: (303)866-5691

Credential Type: Solicitor certificate of registration. **Duration of License:** Three years. **Requirements:** Submit application and pay fees. **Governing Statute:** Colorado Revised Statutes, Title 12, Chapter 14, Colorado Fair Debt Collection Practices Act. Collection Agency Board Rules.

Connecticut

7925

Antenna Service Dealer
Board of Television and Radio
  Service Examiners
Occupational Licensing Div.
Consumer Protection Dept.
165 Capitol Ave.
Hartford, CT 06106
Phone: (203)566-3275

Credential Type: Certified Master Antenna Service Dealer License. **Authorization:** Restricted to contracting to install, repair, and maintain all types of television antenna systems for the public and other dealers in the trade. **Requirements:** Must pass examination and employ licensed certified antenna technicians. **Examination:** Board examination. **Governing Statute:** Connecticut Statutes, Chap. 394. State Board of Television and Radio Service Examiners Administrative Regulations.

Credential Type: Certified Service Dealer License. **Authorization:** Restricted to contracting to install, repair, and maintain individual systems, primarily used in the home, for the public and other dealers in the trade. **Requirements:** Must pass examination. **Examination:** Board examination. **Governing Statute:** Connecticut Statutes, Chap. 394. State Board of Television and Radio Service Examiners Administrative Regulations.

7926

Home Improvement Salesperson
Occupational Licensing Div.
Consumer Protection Dept.
165 Capitol Ave.
Hartford, CT 06106
Phone: (203)566-3275

Credential Type: Certificate of registration. **Duration of License:** One year. **Requirements:** Submit application and pay fee. **Fees:** $60 application fee. $60 renewal fee. $40 guaranty fund fee. **Governing Statute:** General Statutes of Connecticut, Chap. 400.

7927

Radio Electronics Service Dealer
Board of Television and Radio
  Service Examiners
Occupational Licensing Div.
Consumer Protection Dept.
165 Capitol Ave.
Hartford, CT 06106
Phone: (203)566-3275

Credential Type: Certified Radio Electronics Service Dealer License. **Requirements:** Must pass examinations and have an established place of business. **Examination:** Board examinations. **Governing Statute:** Connecticut Statutes, Chap. 394. State Board of Television and Radio Service Examiners Administrative Regulations.

7928

Television Electronics Service Dealer
Board of Television and Radio
  Service Examiners
Occupational Licensing Div.
Consumer Protection Dept.
165 Capitol Ave.
Hartford, CT 06106
Phone: (203)566-3275

Credential Type: Service Dealer Certified Electronics Technician Owner Unrestricted License. **Requirements:** Must pass examinations and have an established place of business. **Examination:** Black and white TV, color TV, practical, and oral examinations. **Governing Statute:** Connecticut Statutes, Chap. 394. State Board of Television and Radio Service Examiners Administrative Regulations.

District of Columbia

7929

Charitable Solicitor
License and Certification Div.
Occupational and Professional Licensure Administration
Consumer and Regulatory Affairs Dept.
PO Box 37200
Washington, DC 20013-7200
Phone: (202)727-7823
Phone: (202)727-7480

Alternate Information: 614 H St., NW, Washington, DC 20001

Credential Type: Registration. **Requirements:** Contact licensing body for application information.

7930

Home Improvement Salesman
License and Certification Div.
Occupational and Professional Licensure Administration
Consumer and Regulatory Affairs Dept.
PO Box 37200
Washington, DC 20013-7200
Phone: (202)727-7823
Phone: (202)727-7480

Alternate Information: 614 H St., NW, Washington, DC 20001 **Requirements:** Contact licensing body for application information.

7931

Security Alarm Agent
License and Certification Div.
Occupational and Professional Licensure Administration
Consumer and Regulatory Affairs Dept.
PO Box 37200
Washington, DC 20013-7200
Phone: (202)727-7823
Phone: (202)727-7480

Alternate Information: 614 H St., NW, Washington, DC 20001 **Requirements:** Contact licensing body for application information.

7932

Security Alarm Dealer
License and Certification Div.
Occupational and Professional Licensure Administration
Consumer and Regulatory Affairs Dept.
PO Box 37200
Washington, DC 20013-7200
Phone: (202)727-7823
Phone: (202)727-7480

Alternate Information: 614 H St., NW, Washington, DC 20001 **Requirements:** Contact licensing body for application information.

Idaho

7933

Manufactured Home Service Company
Manufactured Home Advisory Board
Dept. of Labor and Industrial Services
277 N. 6th
Statehouse Mail
Boise, ID 83720
Phone: (208)334-3950
Fax: (208)334-2683

Credential Type: Manufactured Home Manufacturer License. **Duration of License:** One year. **Requirements:** Submit application and pay fee. Post $5,000 bond with department. **Fees:** $125 license fee. **Governing Statute:** Idaho Code, Title 44, Chapt. 21.

Illinois

7934

Associate Director of Sales/Sales Manager (Gaming Industry)
Illinois Gaming Board
PO Box 19474
Springfield, IL 62794-9474
Phone: (217)524-0228

Credential Type: Sales Director/Manager License. **Duration of License:** One year. **Requirements:** At least 18 years of age. U.S. citizen or legal alien. College degree in marketing. Minimum of five years of marketing and/or sales experience with a service industry. **Reciprocity:** No. **Fees:** $75 application fee. $50 annual renewal fee. **Governing Statute:** Illinois Revised Statutes, Chapter 120.

7935

Fire Equipment Distributor
Illinois State Fire Marshal
1035 Stevenson Drive
Springfield, IL 62703
Phone: (217)785-1010

Credential Type: Class A License. **Duration of License:** One year. **Requirements:** Maintain $300,000 in liability insurance. Own or have access to proper testing equipment. Submit application and pay fee. **Reciprocity:** No. **Fees:** $100 initial license fee. $100 renewal fee. **Governing Statute:** Public Act 85-1434, Illinois Administrative Code Part 250.

Credential Type: Class B License. **Duration of License:** One year. **Requirements:** Maintain $300,000 in liability insurance. Own or have access to proper testing equipment. Submit application and pay fee. **Reciprocity:** No. **Fees:** $200 initial license fee. $200 renewal fee. **Governing Statute:** Public Act 85-1434, Illinois Administrative Code Part 250.

Credential Type: Class C License. **Duration of License:** One year. **Requirements:** Maintain $300,000 in liability insurance. Own or have access to proper testing equipment. Submit application and pay fee. **Reciprocity:** No. **Fees:** $300 initial license fee. $300 renewal fee. **Governing Statute:** Public Act 85-1434, Illinois Administrative Code Part 250.

7936

Ring Lessor (Boxing/Wrestling)
Illinois Dept. of Professional Regulations
State of Illinois Ctr.
100 W. Randolph, Ste. 9-300
Chicago, IL 60601
Phone: (312)814-2719

Credential Type: Registration. **Duration of License:** Lifetime. **Requirements:** Submit registration to board. Must re-register if original information changes. **Reciprocity:** No. **Governing Statute:** The Illinois Professional Boxing and Wrestling Act. Illinois Revised Statutes 1991, Chapter 111.

Iowa

7937

Outside Sales Representative (Riverboat Gambling)
Iowa Racing and Gaming Commission
Lucas State Office Bldg.
Des Moines, IA 50319
Phone: (515)281-7352

Credential Type: License Registration. **Requirements:** Submit application and pay fees. **Fees:** $10 license fee.

7938

Service Representative (Riverboat Gambling)
Iowa Racing and Gaming Commission
Lucas State Office Bldg.
Des Moines, IA 50319
Phone: (515)281-7352

Credential Type: License Registration. **Requirements:** Submit application and pay fees. **Fees:** $10 license fee.

Maine

7939

Commercial Co-Venturer
Registrar of Charitable Organizations
Dept. of Professional and Financial Regulation
State House Station 35
Augusta, ME 04333
Phone: (207)582-8723

Credential Type: Commercial Co-Venturer Registration. **Duration of License:** One year. **Authorization:** Covers individual who conduct, promote, underwrite, arrange, or sponsor a sale, performance, or event of any kind which is advertised in conjunction with the name of any charitable organization. **Requirements:** Submit application and pay fee. Post $10,000 surety bond. Submit annual reports. **Exemptions:** Licensed auctioneers. **Fees:** $100 application fee. **Governing Statute:** 9 M.S.R.A., Chap. 385.

7940

Professional Fundraising Counsel
Registrar of Charitable Organizations
Dept. of Professional and Financial Regulation
State House Station 35
Augusta, ME 04333
Phone: (207)582-8723

Credential Type: Professional Fundraising Counsel Registration. **Duration of License:** One year. **Requirements:** Submit application and pay fee. Post $10,000 surety bond. Submit annual reports. **Fees:** $100 application fee. **Governing Statute:** 9 M.S.R.A., Chap. 385.

7941

Professional Solicitor (Fundraiser)
Registrar of Charitable Organizations
Dept. of Professional and Financial Regulation
State House Station 35
Augusta, ME 04333
Phone: (207)582-8723

Credential Type: Professional Solicitor Registration. **Duration of License:** One year. **Requirements:** Submit application and pay fee. Post $10,000 surety bond. Submit annual reports. **Fees:** $100 application fee. **Governing Statute:** 9 M.S.R.A., Chap. 385.

Maryland

7942

Fundraising Counsel
Secretary of State
Charitable Div.
State House
Annapolis, MD 21401
Phone: (410)974-5534

Credential Type: Registration. **Duration of License:** One year. **Authorization:** Registration required for an individual to act as a fundraising counsel for a charitable organization. **Requirements:** Submit application, copy of contract with charitable organization, and pay fee. **Fees:** $100 registration fee. $100 renewal fee. **Governing Statute:** Annotated Code of Maryland, Article 41, Section 3-201 et seq.

7943

Home Improvement Salesperson
Home Improvement Commission
Dept. of Licensing and Regulation
501 St. Paul Pl.
Baltimore, MD 21202-2272
Phone: (410)333-6309

Credential Type: License. **Duration of License:** Two years. **Requirements:** Submit application, pay fees, and pass examination. **Examination:** Salesperson Examination of the National Assessment Institute, written. **Fees:** $10 exam fee. $75 license fee. **Governing Statute:** Annotated Code of Maryland, Article 56. Code of Maryland Regulations, Title 09, Subtitle 08.

7944

Professional Solicitor
Secretary of State
Charitable Div.
State House
Annapolis, MD 21401
Phone: (410)974-5534

Credential Type: Registration. **Duration of License:** One year. **Authorization:** Registration required for an individual to act as a professional solicitor for a charitable organization. **Requirements:** Submit application, copy of contract with charitable organization, and pay fee. Post surety bond of $25,000. **Fees:** $200 registration fee. $200 renewal fee. **Governing Statute:** Annotated Code of Maryland, Article 41, Section 3-201 et seq.

Michigan

7945

Fundraiser, Professional
Consumer Protection and Charitable Trust Div.
Charitable Trust Section
Dept. of Attorney General
670 Law Bldg.
Lansing, MI 48913
Phone: (517)373-1110

Credential Type: License. **Duration of License:** One year. **Requirements:** File an application and a $10,000 bond with the Department of Attorney General. **Governing Statute:** Charitable Organizations and Solicitations Act, Act 169 of 1975, as amended.

Michigan

7946

Funeral Goods or Services (Prepaid), Contract Seller of
Prepaid Funeral Regulation
Bureau of Occupational & Professional Regulation
Dept. of Commerce
PO Box 30018
Lansing, MI 48909
Phone: (517)373-9153

Credential Type: Registration. **Duration of License:** Three years. **Requirements:** Complete an application for registration. Submit information regarding the seller's escrow agent(s). (An escrow agent holds, invests, and disburses principal and income from the funds received under a prepaid funeral contract.) Abide by the rules and regulations of the Department. **Fees:** $120 initial registration fee. $30 renewal fee. **Governing Statute:** Prepaid Funeral Contract Funding Act, Act 255 of 1986.

7947

Solicitor, Professional
Consumer Protection and Charitable Trust Div.
Charitable Trust Section
Dept. of Attorney General
670 Law Bldg.
Lansing, MI 48913
Phone: (517)373-1110

Credential Type: Registration. **Duration of License:** One year. **Requirements:** Applicants for registration must comply with the statute and rules promulgated by the Department of Attorney General. **Governing Statute:** Charitable Organizations and Solicitations Act, Act 169 of 1975, as amended.

New Jersey

7948

Home Repair Salesperson
New Jersey Dept. of Banking
Div. of Consumer Complaints
Legal and Economic Research
CN040
Trenton, NJ 08625-0040
Phone: (609)292-5340

Credential Type: License. **Duration of License:** Two years. **Requirements:** Must be in the employ of a licensed home repair contractor. **Fees:** $50 biennial license fee. **Governing Statute:** NJSA 17:16C-62. NJAC 3:19-1.1.

North Carolina

7949

Professional Solicitor
Dept. of Human Resources
Licensing Section
Charitable Solicitation Branch
701 Barbour Dr.
Raleigh, NC 27603
Phone: (919)733-4510

Credential Type: Certification. **Duration of License:** One year. **Fees:** $100 license and application fee. $100 renewal fee. $20,000 surety bond.

North Dakota

7950

Professional Fundraiser
Secretary of State
600 E. Blvd.
Bismarck, ND 58505
Phone: (701)224-2900

Credential Type: Registration. **Duration of License:** One year. **Requirements:** Submit application and pay fee. **Fees:** $100 registration fee. **Governing Statute:** North Dakota Century Code, Chap. 50-22.

Oklahoma

7951

Burglar Alarm Service and Installation Company Salesman
Oklahoma State Dept. of Health
Occupational Licensing Service
1000 N.E. Tenth
PO Box 53551
Oklahoma City, OK 73152
Phone: (405)271-5217

Credential Type: License. **Duration of License:** One year. **Requirements:** Security verification clearance. No felony convictions. **Examination:** Burglar Alarm Service and Installation Company Salesman Examination. **Fees:** $25 application fee. $25 renewal fee.

7952

Fire Alarm Service and Installation Company Salesman
Oklahoma State Dept. of Health
Occupational Licensing Service
1000 N.E. Tenth
PO Box 53551
Oklahoma City, OK 73152
Phone: (405)271-5217

Credential Type: License. **Duration of License:** One year. **Requirements:** Experience in the fire alarm industry. Security verification clearance. No felony convictions. **Examination:** Fire Alarm Service and Installation Company Salesman Examination. **Fees:** $25 exam fee. $25 application fee. $25 renewal fee.

Rhode Island

7953

Burglar and Hold-up Alarm Agent
Div. of Licensing and Consumer Protection
Rhode Island Dept. of Business Regulation.
23 Richmond St.
Providence, RI 02903
Phone: (401)277-3857

Credential Type: Burglar/Hold-up Alarm Agent License. **Duration of License:** Two years. **Requirements:** At least 18 years of age. Be employed by a license alarm business. F.B.I. fingerprint review. Submit application and pay fees. **Reciprocity:** No. **Fees:** $25 application fee. $5 biennial renewal fee. $23 F.B.I. fingerprint review fee.

Utah

7954

Pre-Need Contract Agent
Dept. of Commerce
Div. of Occupational and Professional Licensing
160 E. 300 S.
PO Box 45802
Salt Lake City, UT 84145
Phone: (801)530-6628

Credential Type: License. **Duration of License:** One year. **Authorization:** To accept funds for pre-arranged funeral plans. **Requirements:** Submit application and pay fee. **Fees:** $40 license fee. $25 renewal fee.

Vermont

7955

Installer/Seller Lightning Rods and Fire Detection Systems
Electrician's Licensing Board
Dept. of Labor and Industry
120 State St.
Montpelier, VT 05602
Phone: (802)828-2107

Credential Type: License. **Requirements:** To Install: Equipment must be approved. To Sell: Deemed qualified by State Fire Marshal. **Examination:** Installers: Yes. Sellers: No. **Reciprocity:** No. **Fees:** $10 Installers (annually). $5 Sellers (annually). **Governing Statute:** Title 9, VSA Sections 3201-3205.

Washington

7956

Franchise Broker/Dealer
Dept. of Licensing
Business License Services - Securities
405 Black Lake Blvd.
Olympia, WA 98504
Phone: (206)753-6924

Credential Type: Franchise Broker/Dealer License. **Duration of License:** One year. **Requirements:** At least 18 years of age. Submit application and pay fee. **Fees:** $50 initial license fee. $25 renewal fee.

Wisconsin

7957

Loan Solicitor
Regulations and Licensing Dept.
Mortgage Banking Board
PO Box 8935
Madison, WI 53708-8935
Phone: (608)266-8609

Credential Type: License. **Requirements:** 18 years of age.

Social Workers

The following states grant licenses in this occupational category as of the date of publication:

Alabama	District of	Iowa	Minnesota	New Mexico	Rhode Island	Washington
Alaska	Columbia	Kansas	Mississippi	New York	South Carolina	West Virginia
Arizona	Florida	Kentucky	Missouri	North Carolina	South Dakota	Wisconsin
Arkansas	Georgia	Louisiana	Montana	North Dakota	Tennessee	Wyoming
California	Hawaii	Maine	Nebraska	Ohio	Texas	
Colorado	Idaho	Maryland	Nevada	Oklahoma	Utah	
Connecticut	Illinois	Massachusetts	New Hampshire	Oregon	Vermont	
Delaware	Indiana	Michigan	New Jersey	Pennsylvania	Virginia	

Alabama

7958

Social Worker
Alabama State Board of Social Work Examiners
100 Commerece St., Ste. 403
Montgomery, AL 36104
Phone: (205)242-5860

Credential Type: License. **Duration of License:** One year. **Requirements:** 19 years of age. College graduate with a major in social work from a university accredited by the Council on Social Work Education. A Master's Degree in social work is desirable. **Examination:** Social work licensing examination. **Fees:** $75 registration fee. $90 examination fee. $50 renewal fee. $10 license reprint fee.

Alaska

7959

Clinical Social Worker
Dept. of Commerce and Economic Development
Div. of Occupational Licensing
Board of Clinical Social Work Examiners
PO Box D-LIC
Juneau, AK 99811-0800
Phone: (907)465-2551
Fax: (907)465-2974

Credential Type: License by Credentials. **Duration of License:** Two years. **Requirements:** Hold a current license to practice clinical social work in another jurisdiction that has equal or more stringent requirements for licensure. Not be the subject of an unresolved complaint or disciplinary action. Not failed the examination in Alaska. Not had a license to practice clinical social work revoked in another state or jurisdiction. Submit proof of continued competency.

License renewal requires 45 contact hours of continuing education earned during the previous licensing period. **Exemptions:** Anyone who practices clinical social work as an employee of a federal, state, or local government or of a private nonprofit organization that is exempt from federal income tax. **Fees:** $30 application fee. $300 license fee. **Governing Statute:** Alaska Statutes 08.95.

Credential Type: License by Examination. **Duration of License:** Two years. **Requirements:** Master's degree or doctoral degree in social work from a college or university accredited by the Council on Social Work Education. Completed within past 10 years either two years continuous full-time employment in postgraduate clinical social work, or 3,000 hours of less than full-time employment in a period of not less than two years in postgraduate clinical social work. At least 100 hours of employment must have been under the supervision of a licensed clinical social worker, licensed psychologist, or licensed psychiatrist. Be in good professional standing. Provide three professional references. Complete examination.

License renewal requires 45 contact hours of continuing education earned during the previous licensing period. **Examination:** Clinical Examination. **Exemptions:** Anyone who practices clinical social work as an employee of a federal, state, or local government or of a private nonprofit organization that is exempt from federal income tax. **Fees:** $90 exam fee. $30 application fee. $300 license fee. **Governing Statute:** Alaska Statutes 08.95.

Arizona

7960

Social Worker
Board of Behavioral Health Examiners
1645 W. Jefferson
Phoenix, AZ 85007
Phone: (602)542-1882

Credential Type: Independent Social Worker Certificate. **Duration of License:** Two years. **Authorization:** Voluntary certification by state board is not required by law to practice. **Requirements:** Master's degree or higher in social work. At least two years of supervised professional experience. Pass approved examination. Renewal requires 40 clock hours of continuing education. **Examination:** Yes. **Fees:** $90 exam fee. $200 certification fee. $200 renewal fee.

Credential Type: Master Social Worker Certificate. **Duration of License:** Two years. **Authorization:** Voluntary certification by state board is not required by law to practice. **Requirements:** Master's degree or higher in social work. Pass approved examination. Renewal requires 40 clock hours of continuing education. **Examination:** Yes. **Fees:** $90 exam fee. $200 certification fee. $200 renewal fee.

Credential Type: Baccalaureate Social Worker Certificate. **Duration of License:** Two years. **Authorization:** Voluntary certification by state board is not required by law to practice. **Requirements:** Bachelor's degree in social work. Pass approved examination. Renewal requires 40 clock hours of continuing education. **Examination:** Yes. **Fees:** $90 exam fee. $200 certification fee. $200 renewal fee.

Arkansas

7961

Licensed Certified Social Worker
Social Work Licensing Board
PO Box 250381
Hillcrest Station
Little Rock, AR 72225
Phone: (501)372-5071

Credential Type: License. **Duration of License:** Two years. **Requirements:** Masters degree in social work. Pass written examination. Two years post-masters work experience under supervision of a licensed Certified Social Worker. **Examination:** Yes. **Fees:** $50 Written Examination. $50 Application and license. $40 Renewal.

7962

Licensed Master Social Worker
Social Work Licensing Board
PO Box 250381
Hillcrest Station
Little Rock, AR 72225
Phone: (501)372-5071

Credential Type: License. **Duration of License:** Two years. **Requirements:** Masters degree in Social Work. Pass written examination. **Examination:** Yes. **Fees:** $50 Written Examination. $50 Application and license. $40 Renewal.

7963

Licensed Social Worker
Social Work Licensing Board
PO Box 250381
Hillcrest Station
Little Rock, AR 72225
Phone: (501)372-5071

Credential Type: License. **Duration of License:** Two years. **Requirements:** Bachelors degree in social work. Pass written examination. **Examination:** Yes. **Fees:** $50 Written examination. $50 Application and license. $40 Renewal.

California

7964

Social Worker
Board of Behavioral Science Examiners
Dept. of Consumer Affairs
400 R St., Ste. 3150
Sacramento, CA 95814-6240
Phone: (916)445-4933

Credential Type: Clinical Social Worker (LCSW) License. **Duration of License:** Two years. **Requirements:** Master's degree in social work. Two years experience. **Examination:** State written and oral examination. **Reciprocity:** No.

Colorado

7965

Licensed Clinical Social Worker
Board of Social Work Examiners
Dept. of Regulatory Agencies
Div. of Registrations
1560 Broadway, Ste. 1340
Denver, CO 80202
Phone: (303)894-7766

Credential Type: Clinical Social Worker License. **Requirements:** Master's or doctoral education and training in social work. Certification by the Academy of Certified Social Workers fulfills education requirement.

Complete one year of postdoctoral practice in applied psychotherapy under supervision, consisting of at least 1680 hours reasonably distributed over 12 months. The teaching of applied psychotherapy or clinical social work may count up to 560 hours of postdoctoral practice under supervision and up to 16 hours of supervision, provided teaching was supervised by an approved supervisor.

Or complete two years of post-master's practice in applied psychotherapy under supervision, consisting of at least 3360 hours reasonably distributed over 24 months. The teaching of applied psychotherapy or clinical social work may count up to 1120 hours of postdoctoral practice under supervision and up to 32 hours of supervision, provided teaching was supervised by an approved supervisor. **Examination:** American Association of State Social Work Boards (AASSWB) Advanced Examination. **Fees:** $174 application fee. $90 exam fee.

Credential Type: License by endorsement. **Requirements:** Be at least 21 years of age. Hold a current license to practice social work from another state. Applicant may not be subject to any injunction, malpractice judgment or claim, complaint, investigation, or disciplinary proceeding. Meet similar requirements regarding education and supervised practice as are required for a Colorado license. **Fees:** $174 application fee.

7966

School Special Service Associate
Teacher Certification
State Dept. of Education
201 E. Colifax
Denver, CO 80203
Phone: (303)866-6628

Credential Type: Special Service Certificate—Type E. **Duration of License:** Five years. **Authorization:** Authorizes service in specialized areas including Audiology, Therapy, Nursing, Psychology, Social Work, and Speech Corrections. **Requirements:** Bachelor's degree. Must complete a program in one of the following Special Service endorsement areas: Audiologist, Occupational Therapist, Peripatology, Physical Therapist, School Nurse, School Psychologist, School Social Worker, or Speech Correctionist/Language Specialist. Passage of the spelling, language, and mathematics sections of Level 19 of the California Achievement Test and oral English competence which is met by having a B—or better in a public speaking course taken from a regionally accredited college or passing an oral English panel assessment. Official, original transcripts from all applicable institutions. **Examination:** California Achievement Test Level 19 (spelling, language, and mathematics sections) **Fees:** $45 initial certification application fee. $40 fingerprint card processing fee.

Connecticut

7967

Social Worker
Dept. of Health Services
Div. of Medical Quality Assurance
Social Work Certification
150 Washington St.
Hartford, CT 06106
Phone: (203)566-1039

Credential Type: Certified Independent Social Worker (CISW) Certificate. **Requirements:** Master's degree in social work. Two years experience. **Examination:** State examination.

Delaware

7968

Licensed Clinical Social Worker
Board of Social Work Examiners
Dept. of Administrative Services
Div. of Professional Regulation
PO Box 1401
Dover, DE 19903
Phone: (302)739-4522

Credential Type: Clinical Social Worker License. **Duration of License:** Two years. **Requirements:** Master's of Social Work degree. Two years of post-degree experience and 3200 hours of supervision. **Examination:** AASSWB—Clinical level only. **Reciprocity:** Yes, with those states that license at the clinical level. **Fees:** $50 application fee. $90 examination fee. $130 license and renewal fee.

District of Columbia

7969

Social Worker
D.C. Board of Social Work
Dept. of Consumer & Regulatory Affairs
Occupational & Professional Licensing Administration
614 H St. NW, Rm. 904
Washington, DC 20001
Phone: (202)727-7454

Credential Type: Independent Clinical Social Worker (LICSW) License. **Duration of License:** One year. **Requirements:** Master's degree in social work. Two years experience. **Examination:** State examination. **Reciprocity:** Yes.

Credential Type: Independent Social Worker (LISW) License. **Requirements:** Master's degree in social work. Two years experience. **Examination:** State examination. **Reciprocity:** Yes.

Credential Type: Graduate Social Worker (LGSW) License. **Requirements:** Master's degree in social work. **Examination:** State examination. **Reciprocity:** Yes.

Florida

7970

Clinical Social Worker
Board of Clinical Social Work, Marriage and Family Therapy, and Mental Health Counseling
Dept. of Professional Regulation
1940 N. Monroe St.
Tallahassee, FL 32399-0750
Phone: (904)487-2520

Credential Type: Clinical Social Worker License. **Duration of License:** Two years. **Requirements:** A master's or doctoral degree in social work from an accredited graduate school of social work. The applicant's graduate program must have emphasized direct clinical patient or client health care services. Have at least three years of clinical social work experience, two years of which were completed after receiving graduate degree, under the supervision of a licensed clinical social worker or equivalent.

Renewal requires 30 hours of approved continuing education credit. **Examination:** Laws and rules examination. Clinical Level examination developed by the American Association of State Social Work Boards (AASSWB). **Reciprocity:** License may be granted by endorsement if applicant holds a valid license to practice from another state and has actively practiced for three of the past five years. Must meet basic educational and experience requirements. Must pass Florida laws and rules examination. **Fees:** $250 application and examination fee. $150 license by endorsement fee. $50 renewal fee. **Governing Statute:** Florida Statutes, Chapter 491. Florida Administrative Code, Rules 21-CC.

7971

Master Social Worker
Board of Clinical Social Work, Marriage and Family Therapy, and Mental Health Counseling
Dept. of Professional Regulation
1940 N. Monroe St.
Tallahassee, FL 32399-0750
Phone: (904)487-2520

Credential Type: Master Social Worker Certificate. **Duration of License:** Two years. **Requirements:** A master's or doctoral degree in social work from an accredited graduate school of social work. The applicant's graduate program must have emphasized clinical practice or administration. Have at least three years of experience including clinical services or administration, two years of which were completed after receiving a master's degree, under the supervision of a licensed clinical social worker or equivalent.

Applicant holding a graduate degree from an institution located outside the United States may apply for certification if the degree has been evaluated as equivalent to a degree from a school accredited by the Council on Social Work Education.

Renewal requires 30 hours of approved continuing education credit. **Examination:** Laws and rules examination. Clinical Level examination developed by the American Association of State Social Work Boards (AASSWB). **Reciprocity:** License may be granted by endorsement if applicant holds a valid license to practice from another state and has actively practiced for three of the past five years. Must meet basic educational and experience requirements. Must pass Florida laws and rules examination. **Fees:** $250 application and examination fee. $150 license by endorsement fee. $50 renewal fee. **Governing Statute:** Florida Statutes, Chapter 491. Florida Administrative Code, Rules 21-CC.

Georgia

7972

Clinical Social Worker
Composite Board of Professional Counselors, Social Workers, and Marriage and Family Therapists
Health and Consumer Services Section
Professional Examining Boards
166 Pryor St., SW
Atlanta, GA 30303
Phone: (404)656-3933

Credential Type: Clinical Social Work License. **Duration of License:** Two years. **Requirements:** Have a master's or doctorate degree in social work from a college or university accredited by the Council on Social Work Education. Complete a practicum or internship and meet board's experience requirements. **Examination:** American Association of State Social Work Boards (AASSWB) Examination, Advanced Level. **Fees:** $100 application fee. $90 exam fee. $100 renewal fee.

7973

Master Social Worker
Composite Board of Professional Counselors, Social Workers, and Marriage and Family Therapists
Health and Consumer Services Section
Professional Examining Boards
166 Pryor St., SW
Atlanta, GA 30303
Phone: (404)656-3933

Credential Type: Master's Social Work License. **Duration of License:** Two years. **Requirements:** Master's degree in social from a college or university accredited by the Council on Social Work Education. Complete a practicum or internship. **Examination:** American Association of State Social Work Boards (AASSWB) Examination, Intermediate Level. **Fees:** $100 application fee. $90 exam fee. $100 renewal fee.

7974

School Service Associate
Div. of Teacher Education
State Dept. of Education
1452 Twin Towers East
Atlanta, GA 30334-5070
Phone: (404)656-2406

Credential Type: School Service Certificate. **Authorization:** Authorizes the holder to administer school services in one of the following occupations: Audiologist, Media Specialist, School Counselor, School Nutrition Director, School Psychometrist, School Psychologist, School Social Worker/Visiting Teacher, or Speech and Language Pathologist. **Requirements:** Bachelor's degree is required for Nutrition Director, Speech/ Language Pathologist and Media Specialist. Master's degree and sixth year program is required for Psychologist. All other occupations require a master's degree or fifth year program. Media Specialist requires Initial Teaching Certificate. A staff development program in the Identification and Education of Children with Special Needs and a certification test is required at the master's degree level in the field of School Counseling. Three years of acceptable school experience are required of in the fields of nutrition and counseling.

Hawaii

7975

Social Worker
Board of Social Work
3442 Waialae
Honolulu, HI 96816
Phone: (808)586-2690

Credential Type: Registered Social Worker (RSW) License Registration. **Requirements:** Master's degree in social work. **Examination:** No exam required.

Idaho

7976

Certified Social Worker
Board of Social Work Examiners
Bureau of Occupational Licenses
1109 Main St., Ste. 220
Boise, ID 83702-5642
Phone: (208)334-3233

Credential Type: Certified Social Worker License. **Duration of License:** One year. **Requirements:** Good moral character. Master's degree in social work. **Examination:** Certified Social Workers Examination. **Reciprocity:** Yes. **Fees:** $25 application and original license fee. $45 license by endorsement fee. $25 renewal fee. **Governing Statute:** Idaho Code, Title 54, Chap. 32. Rules of the Idaho State Board of Social Work Examiners.

Credential Type: Certified Social Worker Licensed for Private and Independent Practice. **Duration of License:** One year. **Requirements:** Good moral character. Master's degree in social work. Complete two years experience. **Examination:** No additional exam beyond CSW Exam. **Reciprocity:** No. **Fees:** $25 application and original license fee. $45 license by endorsement fee. $40 renewal fee. **Governing Statute:** Idaho Code, Title 54, Chap. 32. Rules of the Idaho State Board of Social Work Examiners.

7977

School Social Worker
Certification Analyst
State Dept. of Education
L. B. Jordan Office Bldg.
Boise, ID 83720
Phone: (208)334-3475

Credential Type: School Social Worker Endorsement. **Duration of License:** Five years. **Requirements:** Master's degree in social work from an approved program or master's degree in guidance counseling, sociology, or psychology plus graduate work in social work education totaling 30 semester hours Certificate may be renewed upon completion of at least six semester credits of college courses within the period of validity.

7978

Social Worker
Board of Social Work Examiners
Bureau of Occupational Licenses
1109 Main St., Ste. 220
Boise, ID 83702-5642
Phone: (208)334-3233

Credential Type: Social Worker License. **Duration of License:** One year. **Requirements:** Good moral character. Bachelor's degree in social work. **Examination:** Yes. **Reciprocity:** Yes. **Fees:** $25 application and original license fee. $45 license by endorsement fee. $25 renewal fee. **Governing Statute:** Idaho Code, Title 54, Chap. 32. Rules of the Idaho State Board of Social Work Examiners.

Illinois

7979

Clinical Social Worker
Illinois Dept. of Professional Regulations
320 W. Washington St.
Springfield, IL 62786
Phone: (217)782-8556

Credential Type: Clinical Social Worker License. **Duration of License:** Two years. **Requirements:** Good moral character. Master's degree in social work and completion of 3,000 hours of satisfactory supervised clinical experience, or a doctorate in social work and completion of 2,000 hours of satisfactory supervised clinical experience. Renewal requires 30 hours of continuing education every two years (effective November 1993). **Examination:** American Association of the State Social Work Boards (AASSWB) Examination. **Reciprocity:** Yes, considered on an individual basis. **Fees:** $90 examination fee. $50 initial license fee. $200 license by endorsement fee. $60 renewal fee. **Governing Statute:** The Clinical Social Work and Social Work Practice Act, Illinois Revised Statutes 1991.

Illinois

7980

Social Worker
Illinois Dept. of Professional Regulations
320 W. Washington St.
Springfield, IL 62786
Phone: (217)782-8556

Credential Type: Social Worker License. **Duration of License:** Two years. **Requirements:** Good moral character. Master's degree in social work, or bachelor's degree in social work and three years of supervised professional experience. Renewal requires 30 hours of continuing education every two years (effective November 1993). **Examination:** American Association of the State Social Work Boards (AASSWB) Examination. **Reciprocity:** Yes, considered on an individual basis. **Fees:** $90 examination fee. $50 initial license fee. $200 license by endorsement fee. $60 renewal fee. **Governing Statute:** The Clinical Social Work and Social Work Practice Act, Illinois Revised Statutes 1991.

Indiana

7981

Social Worker
Health Professions Bureau
402 W. Washington St., Ste. 41
Indianapolis, IN 46204-2739
Phone: (317)232-2960

Credential Type: Clinical Social Worker License. **Duration of License:** Two years. **Requirements:** Master's degree in social work. Two years experience. **Examination:** State examination. **Reciprocity:** Yes.

Credential Type: Social Worker License. **Requirements:** Master's or bachelor's degree in social work. Two years experience. **Examination:** State examination. **Reciprocity:** Yes.

Iowa

7982

Social Worker
Board of Social Workers Examiners
Dept. of Public Health
Lucas State Office Bldg.
Des Moines, IA 50319
Phone: (515)281-6762

Credential Type: License. **Duration of License:** Two years. **Requirements:** Master's degree or doctoral degree in social work from an accredited college or university. Two years of experience in the practice of social work. **Examination:** Written. **Fees:** $115 exam fee. $100 application fee. $120 renewal fee.

Kansas

7983

Licensed Baccalaureate Social Worker
Behavioral Sciences Regulatory Board
900 Jackson, Rm. 651-S
Topeka, KS 66612-1263
Phone: (913)296-3240

Credential Type: Baccalaureate Social Worker License. **Duration of License:** Two years. **Requirements:** Have a baccalaureate degree from an accredited college or university that includes completion of a social work program recognized and approved by the board. Submit three written references, two of which must be from social workers licensed at a higher level.

Renewal requires 60 clock hours of continuing education. **Examination:** State social worker examination, or ASI Level A examination. **Fees:** $90 application fee. $90 renewal fee. $125 exam fee. **Governing Statute:** K.S.A. 1991 Supp. 65-6301 ff.

Credential Type: Temporary permit. **Duration of License:** Until exam results are recorded or license issued. **Authorization:** Must work under the supervision of a licensed social worker. **Requirements:** Issued to applicants who have met the qualifications for licensure, except passage of required examination, and who must wait for completion of next examination. Must have paid appropriate license fees. **Fees:** $15 temporary permit fee. **Governing Statute:** K.S.A. 1991 Supp. 65-6301 ff.

7984

Licensed Master Social Worker
Behavioral Sciences Regulatory Board
900 Jackson, Rm. 651-S
Topeka, KS 66612-1263
Phone: (913)296-3240

Credential Type: Master Social Worker License. **Duration of License:** Two years. **Requirements:** Have a master's degree from an accredited college or university that includes completion of a social work program recognized and approved by the board. Submit three written references, two of which must be from social workers licensed at a higher level.

Renewal requires 60 clock hours of continuing education. **Examination:** State social worker examination, ASI Level B examination, or Academy of Certified Social Workers (ACSW) examination. **Fees:** $95 application fee. $95 renewal fee. $125 exam fee. **Governing Statute:** K.S.A. 1991 Supp. 65-6301 ff.

Credential Type: Temporary permit. **Duration of License:** Until exam results are recorded or license issued. **Authorization:** Must work under the supervision of a licensed social worker. **Requirements:** Issued to applicants who have met the qualifications for licensure, except passage of required examination, and who must wait for completion of next examination. Must have paid appropriate license fees. **Fees:** $15 temporary permit fee. **Governing Statute:** K.S.A. 1991 Supp. 65-6301 ff.

7985

Licensed Specialist Clinical Social Worker
Behavioral Sciences Regulatory Board
900 Jackson, Rm. 651-S
Topeka, KS 66612-1263
Phone: (913)296-3240

Credential Type: Specialist Clinical Social Worker License. **Duration of License:** Two years. **Requirements:** Have a master's or doctor's degree from an accredited college or university that includes completion of a social work program recognized and approved by the board. Have two years of full-time post-master's or post-doctoral experience under the supervision of a licensed social worker in the appropriate specialty. Submit three written references, two of which must be from social workers licensed at a higher level.

Renewal requires 60 clock hours of continuing education. **Examination:** State specialist clinical social worker examination. **Fees:** $100 application fee. $100 renewal fee. $125 exam fee. **Governing Statute:** K.S.A. 1991 Supp. 65-6301 ff.

Credential Type: Temporary permit. **Duration of License:** Until exam results are recorded or license issued. **Authorization:** Must work under the supervision of a licensed social worker. **Requirements:** Issued to applicants who have met the qualifications for licensure, except passage of required examination, and who must wait for completion of next examination. Must have paid appropriate license fees. **Fees:** $15 temporary permit fee. **Governing Statute:** K.S.A. 1991 Supp. 65-6301 ff.

Kentucky

7986

Social Worker
Occuapations and Professions Board
PO Box 456
Frankfort, KY 40602
Phone: (502)564-3296

Credential Type: Bachelor License. **Duration of License:** Three years. **Requirements:** Bachelor's degree in social work or social welfare program approved by the regulatory agency; or a bachelor's degree in another field, two years experience in a social work capacity and completion of courses equivalent to a social work/social welfare program approved by the regulatory agency. 18 years of age. **Examination:** Yes. **Fees:** $45 renewal fee.

Credential Type: Certified License. **Duration of License:** Three years. **Requirements:** Master's or doctorate degree in social work from and approved educational institution. 18 years of age. **Examination:** Yes. **Fees:** $60 renewal fee.

Credential Type: Independent Practice License. **Duration of License:** Three years. **Requirements:** Master's degree plus two years of full-time experience consisting of at least 30 hours per week; or a master's degree plus three years of part-time experience consisting of at least 20 hours per week. 18 years of age. **Examination:** Yes. **Fees:** $75 renewal fee.

Louisiana

7987

Social Work
Louisiana State Board of Certified Social Work Examiners
PO Box 345
Prairieville, LA 70769
Phone: (504)673-3010

Credential Type: Board Certified Social Worker (BCSW) Certificate. **Duration of License:** One year. **Requirements:** Master's degree in social work. Resident of Louisiana. Two years experience. Renewal requires continuing education. **Examination:** State examination. **Reciprocity:** Yes.

Maine

7988

Licensed Clinical Social Worker
State Board of Social Worker Licensure
State House Station 35
Augusta, ME 04333
Phone: (207)582-8723

Credential Type: Licensed Clinical Social Worker License. **Duration of License:** Two years. **Requirements:** A valid LMSW Conditional II License. Complete a clinical internship of 3200 hours experience in not less than two years nor more than four years, while licensed as a LMSW Conditional II in a clinical setting.

Renewal requires continuing education. **Examination:** Yes. **Fees:** $25 application fee. $125 license fee. $90 exam fee. **Governing Statute:** 32 M.S.R.A. Chap. 83.

7989

Licensed Master Social Worker
State Board of Social Worker Licensure
State House Station 35
Augusta, ME 04333
Phone: (207)582-8723

Credential Type: Conditional I License. **Duration of License:** 15 months or 90 days after passing exam. **Authorization:** Temporary license issued to approved exam candidates only. **Requirements:** A master of social work degree and transcript from a CSWE accredited educational institution.

Application must have been approved by the board. **Fees:** $25 application fee. $25 license fee. **Governing Statute:** 32 M.S.R.A. Chap. 83.

Credential Type: Conditional II License. **Duration of License:** Two years. **Authorization:** Issued for internship. **Requirements:** Valid Conditional I license. Pass examination. **Examination:** Yes. **Fees:** $25 application fee. $25 license fee. $90 exam fee. **Governing Statute:** 32 M.S.R.A. Chap. 83.

Credential Type: Licensed Master Social Worker License. **Duration of License:** Two years. **Requirements:** Valid Conditional I license. A MSW degree and transcript from an accredited educational institution. Pass examination. Renewal requires continuing education. **Examination:** Yes. **Fees:** $25 application fee. $75 license fee. $90 exam fee. **Governing Statute:** 32 M.S.R.A. Chap. 83.

7990

Licensed Social Worker
State Board of Social Worker Licensure
State House Station 35
Augusta, ME 04333
Phone: (207)582-8723

Credential Type: Conditional I License. **Duration of License:** 15 months or 90 days after passing exam. **Authorization:** Temporary license issued to approved exam candidates only. **Requirements:** A bachelor of social work degree and transcript from a CSWE accredited educational institution; or a BA/BS degree and transcript plus 96 hours of consultation provided by a Licensed Clinical Social Worker, a Clinical Social Worker-IP, a Licensed Master Social Worker, or a Licensed Social Worker with a BSW degree who has completed the required LSW consultation. This consultation must be concurrent with 3200 hours of social work employment of a duration of at least two years and not more than four years.

Application must have been approved by the board. **Fees:** $25 application fee. $25 license fee. **Governing Statute:** 32 M.S.R.A. Chap. 83.

Credential Type: Conditional II License. **Duration of License:** Two years. **Authorization:** Issued for internship. **Requirements:** A BA/BS degree and evidence of employment or of intent to employ in social work. **Fees:** $25 application fee. $25 license fee. **Governing Statute:** 32 M.S.R.A. Chap. 83.

Credential Type: Licensed Social Worker License. **Requirements:** A valid LSW Conditional II license confirming completion or required experience and consultation, or a valid Conditional I license. Renewal requires continuing education. **Examination:** Yes. **Fees:** $25 application fee. $50 license fee. $90 exam fee. **Governing Statute:** 32 M.S.R.A. Chap. 83.

Maryland

7991

Certified Social Worker
Board of Social Work Examiners
Dept. of Health and Mental Hygiene
4201 Patterson Ave.
Baltimore, MD 21215
Phone: (410)764-4788

Credential Type: License and Certification. **Duration of License:** Two years. **Requirements:** Master's degree in social work from a program accredited by the Council on Social Work Education. Com-

Certified Social Worker, continued

plete two years of supervised employment consisting of 3000 hours of work under a Licensed Certified Social Worker. **Fees:** $50 license fee.

7992

Graduate Social Worker
Board of Social Work Examiners
Dept. of Health and Mental Hygiene
4201 Patterson Ave.
Baltimore, MD 21215
Phone: (410)764-4788

Credential Type: Graduate Social Worker License. **Duration of License:** Two years. **Requirements:** Master's degree in social work from a program accredited by the Council on Social Work Education. **Examination:** Intermediate examination. **Fees:** $50 application fee.

7993

Social Worker
State Board of Social Work
 Examiners
4201 Patterson Ave.
Baltimore, MD 21215-2299
Phone: (410)764-4788

Credential Type: Certified Social Worker (LCSW) License. **Duration of License:** Two years. **Requirements:** Master's degree in social work. Two years experience. Renewal requires continuing education. **Examination:** State examination. **Reciprocity:** Yes.

Credential Type: Graduate Social Worker (LGSW) License. **Requirements:** Master's degree in social work. Renewal requires continuing education. **Examination:** State examination. **Reciprocity:** Yes.

Credential Type: Social Work Associate (LSW) License. **Requirements:** Bachelor's degree in social work. Renewal requires continuing education. **Examination:** State examination. **Reciprocity:** Yes.

7994

Social Worker Associate
Board of Social Work Examiners
Dept. of Health and Mental Hygiene
4201 Patterson Ave.
Baltimore, MD 21215
Phone: (410)764-4788

Credential Type: Social Work Associate License. **Duration of License:** Two years. **Requirements:** Baccalaureate degree in social work from a program accredited by the Council on Social Work Education. **Examination:** Basic examination. **Fees:** $20 application fee.

Massachusetts

7995

Social Worker
Board of Registration of Social
 Workers
100 Cambridge St.
Boston, MA 02202
Phone: (617)727-3074

Credential Type: Independent Clinical Social Worker (ICSW) License. **Duration of License:** Two years. **Requirements:** Master's degree in social work. Two years experience. Renewal requires continuing education. **Examination:** State examination. **Reciprocity:** Yes.

Credential Type: Certified Social Worker (LCSW) License. **Requirements:** Master's degree in social work. Renewal requires continuing education. **Examination:** State examination. **Reciprocity:** Yes.

Credential Type: Social Worker (LSW) License. **Requirements:** Bachelor's degree in social work. Two years experience. Renewal requires continuing education. **Examination:** State examination. **Reciprocity:** Yes.

Credential Type: Social Work Associate (LSWA) License. **Requirements:** Associate's or Bachelor's degree in social science. Renewal requires continuing education. **Examination:** State examination. **Fees:** Yes.

Michigan

7996

Parole/Probation Officer, State
Corrections Commission
Dept. of Corrections
Grandview Plaza Bldg.
PO Box 30003
Lansing, MI 48909
Phone: (517)335-1426

Credential Type: Certification. **Duration of License:** Valid until employment is terminated from the Department of Corrections. **Authorization:** All persons employed as a State Parole/Probation Officer must be certified by the Corrections Commission of the Michigan Department of Corrections. **Requirements:** At least a bachelor's degree in criminal justice, correctional administration, criminology, psychology, social work, counseling and guidance, or other related discipline approved by the Department. Be of good moral character. Reside in the county or a contiguous county of the worksite county. Provide employment and/or personal references. Submit to a background investigation. Pass an oral interview. Complete six months of satisfactory employment. **Examination:** Michigan civil service examination for the entry-level Parole/Probation Officer (College Trainee IV). **Fees:** No fees. **Governing Statute:** Public Act 232 of 1953, as amended.

7997

Social Work Technician
Board of Examiners of Social
 Workers
Bureau of Occupational &
 Professional Regulation
Dept. of Commerce
PO Box 30018
Lansing, MI 48909
Phone: (517)373-9153

Credential Type: Registration. **Duration of License:** Two years. **Requirements:** Be of good moral character. Have had at least one year of social work experience acceptable to the Board or have successfully completed two years of college. Be employed in the practice of social work. (This requirement shall be waived if the person has the equivalent of 2,000 hours of voluntary service with recognized agencies or has received an associate degree in social work which includes supervised instructional field experience from an accredited college.) Comply with all rules and regulations of the Board of Examiners of Social Workers and the Department. **Reciprocity:** Reciprocity may be granted. However, applicants are evaluated separately according to their individual credentials. **Fees:** $15 application processing fee. $15 initial registration fee, per year. $15 renewal fee, per year. $30 reciprocity fee. **Governing Statute:** The Occupational Code, Act 299 of 1980, as amended.

7998

Social Worker
Board of Examiners of Social
 Workers
PO Box 30018
Lansing, MI 48909
Phone: (517)373-1653

Credential Type: Certified Social Worker (CSW) Certificate. **Duration of License:** Two years. **Requirements:** Master's degree in social worker. Two years experience. **Examination:** No exam required. **Reciprocity:** Yes.

Credential Type: Social Worker (SW) License. **Duration of License:** Two years. **Requirements:** Bachelor's or Master's degree in social work. Requires current employment. Two years experience. **Examination:** No exam required. **Reciprocity:** Yes.

Credential Type: Social Worker Technician (SWT) License. **Requirements:** Minimum two years of college level courses or one year of experience in social work. Requires current employment. **Examination:** No exam required. **Reciprocity:** Yes.

Minnesota
7999

Social Worker
Board of Social Work
2700 University Ave. W., Ste. 225
St. Paul, MN 55114
Phone: (612)643-2580

Credential Type: Independent Clinical Social Worker (LCSW) License. **Requirements:** Master's degree in social work. Two years experience. Renewal requires continuing education. **Examination:** State examination. **Reciprocity:** Yes.

Credential Type: Independent Social Worker (LISW) License. **Requirements:** Master's degree in social work. Two years experience. Renewal requires continuing education. **Examination:** State examination. **Reciprocity:** Yes.

Credential Type: Graduate Social Worker (LGSW) License. **Requirements:** Master's degree in social work. Renewal requires continuing education. **Examination:** State examination. **Reciprocity:** Yes.

Credential Type: Social Worker (LSW) License. **Requirements:** Bachelor's degree in social work. Renewal requires continuing education. **Examination:** State examination. **Reciprocity:** Yes.

Mississippi
8000

Social Worker
State Board of Health
Social Work Advisory Council
PO Box 1700
Jackson, MS 39215-1700
Phone: (601)987-4154

Credential Type: Certified Social Worker (LCSW) License. **Duration of License:** One year. **Requirements:** Master's degree in social work. Two years experience. **Examination:** State examination. **Reciprocity:** Yes.

Credential Type: Master Social Worker (LMSW) License. **Requirements:** Master's degree in social work. **Examination:** State examination. **Reciprocity:** Yes.

Credential Type: Social Worker (LSW). **Requirements:** Bachelor's degree in social work. **Examination:** State examination. **Reciprocity:** Yes.

Missouri
8001

Social Worker
Advisory Committee for Licensed Clinical Social Workers
Div. of Professional Registration
PO Box 85
3605 Missouri Blvd.
Jefferson City, MO 65102
Phone: (314)751-0885

Credential Type: Clinical Social Worker (LCSW) License. **Duration of License:** Two years. **Requirements:** Master's degree in social work. Two years experience. **Reciprocity:** Yes.

Montana
8002

Social Worker
Montana Board of Social Work Examiners and Professional Counselors
111 N. Jackson
Helena, MT 59620
Phone: (406)444-4285

Credential Type: License. **Duration of License:** One year. **Requirements:** A graduate degree in social work from an accredited program. 3,000 hours of post-graduate practice in psychotherapy. **Examination:** National board exam. **Fees:** $75 application fee. $75 exam fee. $120 license fee. $120 renewal fee. **Governing Statute:** Montana Code Annotated 37-22-301 through 37-22-312.

Nebraska
8003

Social Worker (Master)
Nebraska Board of Examiners in Social Work
301 Centennial Mall S.
PO Box 95007
Lincoln, NE 68509
Phone: (402)471-2115

Credential Type: Certificate. **Duration of License:** Two years. **Requirements:** Applicants for master of Social Work positions must have completed the desired degree level, must have 3,000 hours of supervised experience under a Certified Master Social Worker. A Certified Social Worker must be engaged in the practice of social work for at least 1,000 hours in a nursing home or actually engaged in the practice of social work in a nursing home at least 20 hours per week for at least three of the past seven years prior to application. **Examination:** Yes. **Fees:** $100 certified social work fee. $150 certified master social worker fee. $90 certified social worker renewal fee. $125 certified master social worker renewal fee.

Nevada
8004

Social Worker
State of Nevada Board of Examiners for Social Workers
PO Box 9779
Reno, NV 89507
Phone: (702)784-1555

Credential Type: Associate in Social Work License. **Requirements:** This category is for employees hired between July 1, 1988 and December 31, 1991 by public employers. Applicants must hold a bachelor's degree in a required field. **Examination:** Yes. **Fees:** $25 application fee. $50 license fee. $100 exam fee.

Credential Type: Social Worker License. **Requirements:** Must hold a bachelor's or master's degree in social work from an accredited program. **Examination:** Yes. **Fees:** $25 application fee. $50 license fee. $100 exam fee.

Credential Type: Independent or Clinical Social Worker License. **Requirements:** Must hold a master's or doctorate degree in social work from an accredited program. Completion of 3,000 hours of supervised, post-graduate social work. **Examination:** Yes. **Reciprocity:** Yes. **Fees:** $25 application fee. $100 license fee. $100 exam fee.

New Hampshire

Clinical Social Worker
Board of Examiners of Psychologists
PO Box 457
105 Pleasant St.
Concord, NH 03301
Phone: (603)226-2599

Credential Type: Clinical Social Worker Certificate. **Duration of License:** One year. **Requirements:** Complete a two year master's degree program or hold a doctoral degree in Social Work from a school accredited by the Council on Social Work Education. Must have at least two years (3,000 hours) of paid, supervised clinical experience after receiving master's degree. Meet requirements to be listed in Registers (have ACSW or be licensed in another state). Renewal requires 20 hours of continuing education annually. **Examination:** AASSWB examination (clinical level). **Reciprocity:** Yes, providing that standards of licensing state are equal to or higher than those of New Hampshire. **Fees:** $125 application fee. $60 annual renewal fee.

New Jersey

Social Worker
Board of Social Work Examiners
PO Box 45033
Newark, NJ 07101
Phone: (201)504-6495

Credential Type: Clinical Social Worker (LCSW) License. **Duration of License:** Two years. **Requirements:** Master's degree in social work. Two years experience. Renewal requires continuing education. **Examination:** State examination. **Reciprocity:** Yes.

Credential Type: Social Worker (LSW) License. **Requirements:** Master's degree in social work. Renewal requires continuing education. **Examination:** State examination. **Reciprocity:** Yes.

Credential Type: Certified Social Worker (CSW) Certificate. **Requirements:** Bachelor's degree in social work. Renewal requires continuing education. **Reciprocity:** Yes.

New Mexico

Social Worker
Board of Social Work Examiners
PO Box 25101
Santa Fe, NM 87504
Phone: (505)827-7167

Credential Type: Independent Social Worker (LISW) License. **Duration of License:** One year. **Requirements:** Master's degree in social work. Two years experience. Renewal requires continuing education. **Examination:** State examination. **Reciprocity:** Yes.

Credential Type: Master Social Worker (LMSW) License. **Requirements:** Master's in social work. Renewal requires continuing education. **Examination:** State examination. **Reciprocity:** Yes.

Credential Type: Baccalaureate Social Worker (LBSW) License. **Requirements:** Bachelor's degree in social work. **Examination:** State examination.

New York

Certified Social Worker
State Education Dept.
Div. of Professional Licensing Services
Cultural Education Center
Empire State Plaza
Albany, NY 12230
Phone: (518)474-3326

Credential Type: License. **Duration of License:** Three years. **Requirements:** Bachelor's Degree plus Master's Degree or equivalent in social work. 21 years of age. **Examination:** Level B or C examination administered by the American Association of State Boards of Social Work. **Fees:** $325 license fee. $155 renewal fee. **Governing Statute:** Title VIII Articles 130, 154 of the Education Law.

North Carolina

Social Worker
Certification Board for Social Work
PO Box 1043
Asheboro, NC 27204
Phone: (919)625-1679

Credential Type: Certified Social Work Manager (CSWM) Certificate. **Duration of License:** Two years. **Requirements:** Master's degree in social work. Two years experience. Renewal requires continuing education. **Examination:** State examination. **Reciprocity:** Yes.

Credential Type: Certified Clinical Social Worker (CCSW) Certificate. **Requirements:** Master's degree in social work. Two years experience. Renewal requires continuing education. **Examination:** State examination. **Reciprocity:** Yes.

Credential Type: Certified Master Social Worker (CMSW) Certificate. **Requirements:** Master's degree in social work. Renewal requires continuing education. **Examination:** State examination. **Reciprocity:** Yes.

Credential Type: Certified Social Worker (CSW) Certificate. **Requirements:** Bachelor's degree in social work. Renewal requires continuing education. **Examination:** State examination. **Reciprocity:** Yes.

North Dakota

Social Worker
Board of Social Work Examiners
PO Box 6145
Bismarck, ND 58502
Phone: (701)222-0255

Credential Type: Independent Practice License. **Duration of License:** Two years. **Requirements:** Master's degree in social work. Three years experience. Renewal requires continuing education. **Examination:** State examination. **Reciprocity:** Yes.

Credential Type: Certified Social Worker (LCSW) License. **Requirements:** Master's degree in social work. Renewal requires continuing education. **Examination:** State examination. **Reciprocity:** Yes.

Credential Type: Social Worker (LSW) License. **Requirements:** Bachelor's degree in social work. Renewal requires continuing education. **Examination:** State examination. **Reciprocity:** Yes.

Ohio

School Social Worker
Teacher Education and Certification
State Dept. of Education
65 S. Front St., Rm. 1012
Columbus, OH 43266-0308
Phone: (614)466-3593

Credential Type: Provisional Pupil Personnel Certificate—Social Work. **Requirements:** Recommendation of university official. Complete examination prescribed by the State Board of Education. Proof of education and experience in area of specialization. One year of satisfactory experience in a school or school district under a standard certificate. Master's degree with 20 semester hours of graduate course work in the areas of education and psychology of normal and exceptional children, pupil personnel services, and counseling with practical application to programs and practices in schools. Graduate level social work practicum of at least 10 weeks in an approved school or school district or Master of Social Work degree with 12 semester hours of graduate course. **Examination:** Examination prescribed by the State Board of Education.

8012

Social Worker
Counselor & Social Worker Board
77 S. High St., 16th Fl.
Columbus, OH 43266-0340
Phone: (614)466-0912

Credential Type: Independent Social Worker (LISW) License. **Duration of License:** Two years. **Requirements:** Master's degree in social work. Two years experience. Renewal requires continuing education. **Examination:** State examination. **Reciprocity:** Yes.

Credential Type: Social Worker (LSW) License. **Requirements:** Master's or bachelor's degree in social work. Renewal requires continuing education. **Examination:** State examination. **Reciprocity:** Yes.

Credential Type: Registered Social Work Assistant (RSWA) License Registration. **Requirements:** Associate's degree in social work. Renewal requires continuing education. **Reciprocity:** Yes.

Oklahoma

8013

Licensed Social Worker
Oklahoma State Board of Licensed Social Workers
4145 NW 61st Terr.
Oklahoma City, OK 73112
Phone: (405)946-7230

Credential Type: License. **Duration of License:** One year. **Requirements:** Doctoral or master's degree in social work from an accredited program. Two years of experience in the practice of social work under the professional supervision of a Licensed Social Worker. **Examination:** Advanced exam. **Fees:** $90 exam fee. $50 application fee. $50 renewal fee. **Governing Statute:** Social Workers Licensing Act (H.B. 1910, 1980 Oklahoma Legislature).

8014

Licensed Social Worker Associate
Oklahoma State Board of Licensed Social Workers
4145 NW 61st Terr.
Oklahoma City, OK 73112
Phone: (405)946-7230

Credential Type: License. **Duration of License:** One year. **Requirements:** Degree in social work from an accredited program. Two years of experience in the practice of social work under a Licensed Social Worker. **Examination:** Dependent upon area of specialization. **Fees:** $90 exam fee. $50 application fee. $40 renewal fee. **Governing Statute:** Social Workers Licensing Act (H.B. 1910, 1980 Oklahoma Legislature).

8015

Licensed Social Worker with Specialty Certification
Oklahoma State Board of Licensed Social Workers
4145 NW 61st Terr.
Oklahoma City, OK 73112
Phone: (405)946-7230

Credential Type: License. **Duration of License:** One year. **Requirements:** Doctoral or master's degree in social work from an accredited program. Two years of experience in the practice of social work under professional supervision. 12 clock hours of continuing education each year. **Examination:** Clinical Licensing Examination. **Fees:** $90 exam fee. $50 application fee. $50 renewal fee. **Governing Statute:** Social Workers Licensing Act (H.B. 1910, 1980 Oklahoma Legislature.)

Oregon

8016

Clinical Social Worker
State Board of Clinical Social Workers
895 Summer St. NE
Salem, OR 97310
Phone: (503)378-5735

Credential Type: License. **Duration of License:** One year. **Requirements:** Must have a Master's or Doctoral degree in social work from a college accredited by the Council on Social Work Education. Must complete two years full-time post-masters LCSW supervised experience in the field of clinical social work. Must document minimum of 100 hours of LCSW supervision. **Examination:** Yes. **Fees:** $150 license fee. $55 renewal fee. **Governing Statute:** ORS 675.510 to 675.610.

Pennsylvania

8017

Social Worker
State Board of Social Work Examiners
PO Box 2649
Harrisburg, PA 17105-2649
Phone: (717)783-1389

Credential Type: Social Worker (LSW) License. **Duration of License:** Two years. **Requirements:** Master's degree in social work. **Examination:** State examination. **Reciprocity:** Yes.

Credential Type: Provisional Social Worker License. **Requirements:** Bachelor's degree. Must be enrolled in a master's level program of social work. Three years experience. **Examination:** State examination. **Reciprocity:** Yes.

Rhode Island

8018

Social Worker
Board of Certification of Social Workers
Rhode Island Dept. of Human Services
600 New London Ave.
Cranston, RI 02920
Phone: (401)464-2421

Credential Type: Certified Social Worker Certificate. **Duration of License:** One year. **Requirements:** Master's degree from a school accredited by the Council on Social Work Education. Merit public trust. **Examination:** American Association of State Social Work Board (AASWB) Intermediate Level Examination. **Reciprocity:** Yes. **Fees:** $50 application fee. $25 renewal fee.

Credential Type: Certified Independent Social Worker Certificate. **Duration of License:** One year. **Requirements:** Meet requirements for Certified Social Worker Certificate. Complete two years or 3,000 hours of direct post-MSW clinical practice under the supervision of a licensed clinical social worker. **Reciprocity:** Yes. **Fees:** $50 application fee. $25 renewal fee.

South Carolina

8019

Social Worker
South Carolina State Board of Social Work Examiners
PO Box 1083
Columbia, SC 29202
Phone: (803)254-3661

Credential Type: Licensed Independent Social Worker. **Requirements:** Resident of, or employed in, South Carolina. Doctorate degree from an accredited school of social work. **Examination:** Yes. **Fees:** $50 license fee.

Credential Type: Licensed Master Social Worker. **Requirements:** Resident of, or employed in, South Carolina. Master's degree from an accredited school of social work. **Examination:** Yes. **Fees:** $45 license fee.

Credential Type: Licensed Baccalaureate Social Worker. **Requirements:** Resident of, or employed in, South Carolina. Baccalaureate degree from an accredited school of social work. **Examination:** Yes. **Fees:** $40 license fee.

South Dakota

8020

Social Worker
Dept. of Commerce and Consumer Affairs
Board of Social Work Examiners
PO Box 654
Spearfish, SD 57783-0654
Phone: (605)642-1600

Credential Type: Independent Practice (CSW-PIP) Certificate. **Duration of License:** Two years. **Requirements:** Master's degree in social work. Two years experience. Renewal requires continuing education. **Examination:** State examination. **Reciprocity:** Yes.

Credential Type: Certified Social Worker (CSW) Certificate. **Requirements:** Master's degree in social work. Renewal requires continuing education. **Examination:** State examination. **Reciprocity:** Yes.

Credential Type: Social Worker (SW) License. **Requirements:** Bachelor's degree in social work. Renewal requires continuing education. **Examination:** State examination. **Reciprocity:** Yes.

Credential Type: Social Work Associate (SWA) License. **Requirements:** Bachelor's or Associate's degree in social work. Renewal requires continuing education. **Examination:** State examination. **Reciprocity:** Yes.

Tennessee

8021

Social Worker
Board of Social Workers Certification and Licensure
283 Plus Park Blvd.
Nashville, TN 37243
Phone: (615)367-6207

Credential Type: License. **Requirements:** 18 years old. Masters in Social Work. Pass the exam. Good moral character. **Examination:** American Association of State Social Worker Board (AASSWB) approved examination, Licensed Clinical Social Worker (LCSW) examination. **Reciprocity:** Yes, with Board approval. **Fees:** $35 Registration. $50 Examination. $20 Application (CMSW), $55 Application (LCSW).

Texas

8022

Social Worker
Texas Dept. of Human Services
Social Work Certification Program, W-403
PO Box 149030
Austin, TX 78714
Phone: (512)450-3255

Credential Type: Certified Social Worker. **Requirements:** Doctoral or master's degree in social work or social welfare from approved, accredited graduate school. **Examination:** Written. **Fees:** $105 application and exam fee. $35 certification fee. $35 renewal fee. **Governing Statute:** Human Resources Code 50.001, 40 TAC 85.6001.

Credential Type: Social Worker License. **Requirements:** Bachelor's degree in social work, social welfare, or equivalent. **Examination:** Written. **Fees:** $105 for application and exam fee. $25 certification fee. $25 renewal fee. **Governing Statute:** Human Resources Code 50.001, 40 TAC 85.6001.

Credential Type: Social Work Associate License. **Requirements:** Bachelor's degree and experience specified by the Board; or associate degree and experience specified by the Board; or high school diploma and experience specified by the Board. **Examination:** Written. **Fees:** $105 application and exam fee. $15 certification fee. $15 renewal fee. **Governing Statute:** Human Resources Code 50.001, 40 TAC 85.6001.

Utah

8023

Certified Social Worker
Dept. of Commerce
Div. of Occupational and Professional Licensing
160 E. 300 S.
PO Box 45802
Salt Lake City, UT 84145
Phone: (801)530-6628

Credential Type: Certified social worker license. **Duration of License:** Two years. **Requirements:** Master's degree in social work. Pass required examination. **Examination:** Yes. **Fees:** $60 license and exam fee. $40 renewal fee.

8024

Clinical Social Worker
Dept. of Commerce
Div. of Occupational and Professional Licensing
160 E. 300 S.
PO Box 45802
Salt Lake City, UT 84145
Phone: (801)530-6628

Credential Type: Clinical social worker license. **Duration of License:** Two years. **Requirements:** Must have a graduate degree in social work and two years of clinical work. Pass required examination. **Examination:** Yes. **Fees:** $60 license fee. $40 renewal fee.

8025

School Social Worker
Teachers Certification
250 E. 500 S.
Salt Lake City, UT 84111
Phone: (801)538-7740

Credential Type: Certificate. **Requirements:** Must hold a valid Basic or Standard School Social Worker Certificate issued by the Board of Education upon completion of a master's degree. **Fees:** $10 renewal fee.

Vermont

8026

Clinical Social Worker
Secretary of State
Pavilion Office Bldg.
Montpelier, VT 05602
Phone: (802)828-2373

Credential Type: License. **Duration of License:** Six months. **Requirements:** Masters from approved social work education program. Two years post masters experience with a licensed physician in U.S. or Canada. Names and addresses of three references. **Examination:** Yes. **Reciprocity:** Yes. **Fees:** Yes. Contact Secretary of State Office. **Governing Statute:** Title 21, VSA Chapter 61, Section 3205.

Virginia

8027

School Social Worker
Administrative Director
Office of Professional Development
    and Teacher Education
Dept. of Education
PO Box 6-Q
Richmond, VA 23216-2060
Phone: (804)225-2094

Credential Type: Social Worker Endorsement. **Requirements:** Master's degree from an accredited graduate school in social work. Complete a supervised practicum or field experience in an education agency through an approved program, or complete at least one year of full-time successful experience as a school social worker. Must complete at least six graduate semester hours in the areas of education foundations, curriculum, or administration.

8028

Social Worker
Virginia Board of Social Work
1601 Rolling Hills Dr.
Richmond, VA 23229
Phone: (804)662-9920

Credential Type: License. **Requirements:** Must provide three letters of recommendation. A bachelor's degree in social work. Two years of full-time post graduate experience. **Examination:** Yes. **Fees:** $65 application fee. $85 examination fee.

Washington

8029

School Social Worker
Superintendent of Public Instruction
Professional Education and
    Certification
Old Capitol Bldg. FG-11
Seattle, WA 98504-3211
Phone: (206)753-6773

Credential Type: Initial Educational Staff Associate Certificate. **Duration of License:** Seven years. **Authorization:** Authorizes service in primary role of assistant to the learner, the teacher, the administrator, and/or the educational program. **Requirements:** Complete all course work (except special projects or thesis) for a master's degree with a major in social work.

Credential Type: Continuing Educational Staff Associate Certificate. **Duration of License:** Five years. **Requirements:** Master's degree in social work. Verification of 180 days of experience in the role. Complete a college level course which includes peer review while employed in the role. Out-of-state applicants must complete a comprehensive written examination (unless already taken as part of the master's degree). Renewable upon 150 clock hours of work in this position during the life of the certificate.

8030

Social Worker
Social Work Certification Advisory
    Committee
Dept. of Health
Professional Licensing Service
1300 SE Quince St, EY-22
Olympia, WA 98504
Phone: (206)753-1761

Credential Type: Certified Social Worker Certificate. **Duration of License:** Two years. **Requirements:** Master's degree in social work. Two years experience. **Examination:** State examination. **Reciprocity:** Yes.

West Virginia

8031

Social Worker
Board of Social Work Examiners
PO Box 5477
Charleston, WV 25323
Phone: (304)845-9897
Phone: (304)343-6141

Credential Type: License. **Duration of License:** Two years. **Requirements:** For a regular license, must have a Bachelors or Masters degree in social work. For a temporary license, must have a degree from an accredited college, or associate degree in social work, or 60 hours of college credits and two years experience as a social worker. **Examination:** Yes. **Fees:** $70 Examination. $25 Renewal.

Wisconsin

8032

Social Worker
Bureau of Health Service Professions
Dept. of Regulation and Licensing
PO Box 8935
Madison, WI 53708
Phone: (608)266-8609

Credential Type: Social Worker Certification. **Duration of License:** Two years. **Authorization:** Certification required for use of title. **Requirements:** New certification rules to be established by May 1, 1993. If applying before May 31, 1995, requirements for certification without examination are a bachelor's degree in social work and employment as a social worker. **Fees:** $39 certification fee. **Governing Statute:** 1991 Wisconsin Act 160.

Credential Type: Advanced Social Worker Certification. **Duration of License:** Two years. **Authorization:** Certification required for use of title. **Requirements:** New certification rules to be established by May 1, 1993. If applying before May 31, 1995, requirements for certification without examination are a graduate degree in social work or a related human services program. **Fees:** $39 certification fee. **Governing Statute:** 1991 Wisconsin Act 160.

Credential Type: Independent Social Worker Certification. **Duration of License:** Two years. **Authorization:** Certification required for use of title. **Requirements:** New certification rules to be established by May 1, 1993. If applying before May 31, 1995, requirements for certification without examination are a graduate degree in social work or a related human services program and at least two years of full-time super-

Social Worker, continued

vised social work practice. **Fees:** $39 certification fee. **Governing Statute:** 1991 Wisconsin Act 160.

Credential Type: Independent Clinical Social Worker Certification. **Duration of License:** Two years. **Authorization:** Certification required for use of title. **Requirements:** New certification rules to be established by May 1, 1993. If applying before May 31, 1995, requirements for certification without examination are a graduate degree in social work or a related human services program and at least two years of full-time supervised clinical social work practice. **Fees:** $39 certification fee. **Governing Statute:** 1991 Wisconsin Act 160.

Wyoming

8033

School Social Worker
State Dept. of Education
Certification and Accreditation
Services Unit, Hathaway Bldg.
Cheyenne, WY 82002
Phone: (307)777-7291

Credential Type: Social Worker Endorsement. **Requirements:** Bachelor's degree in social work. 12 semester hours of professional education.

8034

Social Worker
Wyoming Mental Health Professions
 Licensing Board
PO Box 591
Cheyenne, WY 82003
Phone: (307)635-2816

Credential Type: License. **Duration of License:** Two years. **Requirements:** Age of majority. Hold a Masters, Educational Specialist, or Doctorate degree in the appropriate field from an accredited school. Have accumulated 3000 hours of supervised experience. Pass a nationally recommended examination accepted by the Board. **Examination:** Yes. **Fees:** $60 Application. $50 License. $50 Renewal. Additional cost for examination.

Speech-Language Pathologists and Audiologists

The following states grant licenses in this occupational category as of the date of publication:

Alabama	Florida	Kentucky	Missouri	North Carolina	South Carolina	West Virginia
Alaska	Georgia	Louisiana	Montana	North Dakota	Tennessee	Wisconsin
Arkansas	Hawaii	Maine	Nebraska	Ohio	Texas	Wyoming
California	Idaho	Maryland	Nevada	Oklahoma	Utah	
Colorado	Illinois	Massachusetts	New Jersey	Oregon	Vermont	
Connecticut	Indiana	Minnesota	New Mexico	Pennsylvania	Virginia	
Delaware	Iowa	Mississippi	New York	Rhode Island	Washington	

Alabama

8035

Audiologist
ABESPA
PO Box 20833
Montgomery, AL 36120-0833
Phone: (205)834-2415

Credential Type: License. **Duration of License:** One year. **Requirements:** Must hold a master's degree in Audiology. Must have worked nine months under a licensed supervisor. **Examination:** Yes. **Fees:** $50 application fee. $50 licensure fee.

8036

Speech Pathologist
ABESPA
PO Box 20833
Montgomery, AL 36120-0833
Phone: (205)834-2415

Credential Type: License. **Duration of License:** One year. **Requirements:** Must hold a master's degree in speech pathology. Must have worked nine months under a licensed supervisor. **Examination:** Yes. **Fees:** $50 application fee. $50 license fee. $50 renewal fee.

Alaska

8037

Audiologist
Dept. of Commerce
PO Box D-LIC
Juneau, AK 9981-0800
Phone: (907)465-3035

Credential Type: Audiologist license. **Duration of License:** Two years. **Requirements:** Master's degree in audiology. Complete at least 300 clock hours of supervised clinical experience within the training institution or in one of its cooperating programs. Complete or be in the process of completing a Clinical Fellowship Year consisting of at least nine months of full-time professional experience. Pass the National Examination in Audiology. **Examination:** National Examination in Audiology. **Reciprocity:** Granted to applicants who meet American Speech-Language-Hearing Association (ASHA) CCC qualifications for licensure. **Fees:** $30 application fee. $60 renewal fee.

Credential Type: Temporary Audiologist License. **Requirements:** Must have a current Audiologist License issued by another state with equivalent requirements. Must have applied for Alaska's Audiologist License. **Fees:** $20 temporary license fee.

Arkansas

8038

Audiologist
Arkansas Board of Examiners in
  Speech Pathology and Audiology
PO Box 250345
Little Rock, AR 72225-0345
Phone: (501)371-6070

Credential Type: License. **Duration of License:** One year. **Requirements:** Possess a Master's in Audiology. Nine months of experience paid and supervised. Score at least 600 on the National Teacher Examination (NTE) Audiology Examination. **Examination:** Yes. **Fees:** $25 Application. $40 License. $25 Renewal.

8039

Speech Pathologist
Arkansas Board of Examiners in
  Speech Pathology and Audiology
PO Box 250345
Little Rock, AR 72225-0345
Phone: (501)371-6070

Credential Type: License. **Duration of License:** One year. **Requirements:** Masters degree in Speech Pathology. Nine months of supervised, paid experience. Must score 600 on National Teacher Examination (NTE) Speech Pathology Test. **Examination:** Yes. **Fees:** $25 Application. $40 License. $25 Renewal.

California

8040

Audiologist
Speech Pathology and Audiology
  Examining Committee
Board of Medical Quality Assurance
1430 Howe Ave.
Sacramento, CA 95825
Phone: (916)920-6388

Credential Type: Audiologist license. **Duration of License:** Two years. **Requirements:** Have a master's degree or equivalent with major emphasis in audiology or hearing science. Complete at least 300 clock hours of supervised clinical experience within the training institution or in one of its cooperating programs. Complete a Clinical Fellowship Year consisting of at least nine months of full-time professional experience. Pass the National Examination in Audiology. **Examination:** National Examination in Audiology. **Fees:** $35 application fee. $25 initial license. $19 fingerprint fee. $60 renewal fee.

California

Audiologist, continued

Credential Type: Temporary Audiologist license. **Duration of License:** 90 days. **Requirements:** Must be certified by the American Speech-Language-Hearing Association (ASHA) or currently licensed by a state other than California or have a postgraduate professional experience plan approved by Committee.

8041

School Clinical-Rehabilitative Associate
Commission on Teacher Credentialing
PO Box 944270
Sacramento, CA 94244-7000
Phone: (916)445-7254

Credential Type: Clinical-Rehabilitative Credential. **Authorization:** Authorizes the holder to perform clinical services at all grade levels in language, speech, and hearing; audiology; language, speech, hearing, and audiology; orientation and mobility; or language, speech, and hearing including special class authorization to teach aphasic children. **Requirements:** One post-baccalaureate year or its equivalent. Such specialized and professional preparation as may be required. Recommendation of a California institution with an approved program. **Fees:** $60 application fee. $30 test score recording and evaluation fee, except for CBEST.

8042

Speech-Language Pathologist
Speech Pathology and Audiology Examining Committee
Board of Medical Quality Assurance
1430 Howe Ave.
Sacramento, CA 95825
Phone: (916)920-6388

Credential Type: Speech-Language Pathologist license. **Duration of License:** Two years. **Requirements:** Have a master's degree or equivalent with major emphasis in speech-language pathology or speech-language science. Complete at least 300 clock hours of supervised clinical experience within the training institution or in one of its cooperating programs. Complete a Clinical Fellowship Year consisting of at least nine months of full-time professional experience. Pass the National Examination in Speech-Language Pathology. **Examination:** National Examination in Speech-Language Pathology. **Fees:** $35 application fee. $25 initial license. $19 fingerprint fee. $60 renewal fee.

Credential Type: Temporary Speech-Language Pathologist license. **Duration of License:** 90 days. **Requirements:** Must be certified by the American Speech-Language-Hearing Association (ASHA) or currently licensed by a state other than California or have a postgraduate professional experience plan approved by Committee.

Colorado

8043

School Special Service Associate
Teacher Certification
State Dept. of Education
201 E. Colifax
Denver, CO 80203
Phone: (303)866-6628

Credential Type: Special Service Certificate—Type E. **Duration of License:** Five years. **Authorization:** Authorizes service in specialized areas including Audiology, Therapy, Nursing, Psychology, Social Work, and Speech Corrections. **Requirements:** Bachelor's degree. Must complete a program in one of the following Special Service endorsement areas: Audiologist, Occupational Therapist, Peripatology, Physical Therapist, School Nurse, School Psychologist, School Social Worker, or Speech Correctionist/Language Specialist. Passage of the spelling, language, and mathematics sections of Level 19 of the California Achievement Test and oral English competence which is met by having a B—or better in a public speaking course taken from a regionally accredited college or passing an oral English panel assessment. Official, original transcripts from all applicable institutions. **Examination:** California Achievement Test Level 19 (spelling, language, and mathematics sections) **Fees:** $45 initial certification application fee. $40 fingerprint card processing fee.

Connecticut

8044

Audiologist
Speech Pathology & Audiology Licensing
Dept. of Health Services
Div. of Medical Quality Assurance
150 Washington St.
Hartford, CT 06106
Phone: (203)566-1039

Credential Type: Audiologist license. **Duration of License:** One year. **Requirements:** Have a master's degree or equivalent with major emphasis in audiology or hearing science. Complete at least 275 clock hours of supervised clinical experience within the training institution or in one of its cooperating programs. Complete a Clinical Fellowship Year consisting of at least nine months of full-time professional experience. Pass the National Examination in Audiology. **Examination:** National Examination in Audiology. **Exemptions:** Exam may be waived if certified by the American Speech-Language-Hearing Association (ASHA) or licensed by a state with equivalent standards. **Fees:** $75 application fee. $45 renewal fee.

8045

Speech-Language Pathologist
Speech Pathology & Audiology Licensing
Dept. of Health Services
Div. of Medical Quality Assurance
150 Washington St.
Hartford, CT 06106
Phone: (203)566-1039

Credential Type: Speech-Language Pathologist license. **Duration of License:** One year. **Requirements:** Have a master's degree or equivalent with major emphasis in speech-language pathology or speech-language science. Complete at least 275 clock hours of supervised clinical experience within the training institution or in one of its cooperating programs. Complete a Clinical Fellowship Year consisting of at least nine months of full-time professional experience. Pass the National Examination in Speech-Language Pathology. **Examination:** National Examination in Speech-Language Pathology. **Exemptions:** Exam may be waived if certified by the American Speech-Language-Hearing Association (ASHA) or licensed by a state with equivalent standards. **Fees:** $75 application fee. $45 renewal fee.

Delaware

8046

Audiologist
Board of Audiologists, Speech Pathologists, and Hearing Aid Dealers
O'Neal Bldg.
PO Box 1401
Dover, DE 19903
Phone: (302)736-4522

Credential Type: Audiologist license. **Duration of License:** Two years. **Requirements:** Have a master's degree or equivalent with major emphasis in audiology or hearing science. Complete at least 300 clock hours of supervised clinical experience within the training institution or in one of its cooperating programs. Complete a Clinical Fellowship Year consisting of at least nine months of full-time professional experience. Pass the National Examination in Audiology.

Renewal requires 20 continuing education hours every two years. **Examination:** National Examination in Audiology. **Exemptions:** Exam may be waived if certified by the American Speech-Language-Hearing Association (ASHA) or licensed by a state with equivalent standards. **Fees:** $50 application fee. $50 license fee. $40 examination fee. $70 renewal fee.

8047

Speech-Language Pathologist
Board of Audiologists, Speech Pathologists, and Hearing Aid Dealers
O'Neal Bldg.
PO Box 1401
Dover, DE 19903
Phone: (302)736-4522

Credential Type: Speech-Language Pathologist license. **Duration of License:** Two years. **Requirements:** Have a master's degree or equivalent with major emphasis in speech-language pathology or speech-language science. Complete at least 300 clock hours of supervised clinical experience within the training institution or in one of its cooperating programs. Complete a Clinical Fellowship Year consisting of at least nine months of full-time professional experience. Pass the National Examination in Speech-Language Pathology.

Renewal requires 20 continuing education hours every two years. **Examination:** National Examination in Speech-Language Pathology. **Exemptions:** Exam may be waived if certified by the American Speech-Language-Hearing Association (ASHA) or licensed by a state with equivalent standards. **Fees:** $50 application fee. $50 license fee. $40 examination fee. $70 renewal fee.

Florida

8048

Audiologist
Board of Speech-Language, Pathology and Audiology
Dept. of Professional Regulation
Northwood Center
1940 N. Monroe St.
Tallahassee, FL 32399-0782
Phone: (904)488-8595

Credential Type: Audiologist license. **Duration of License:** Two years. **Authorization:** License covers dispensing hearing aids. **Requirements:** Have a master's degree or equivalent with major emphasis in audiology or hearing science. Complete at least 300 clock hours of supervised clinical experience within the training institution or in one of its cooperating programs. Complete a Clinical Fellowship Year consisting of at least nine months of full-time professional experience. Pass the National Examination in Audiology.

Renewal requires 20 continuing education hours every two years. **Examination:** National Examination in Audiology. **Reciprocity:** Granted to applicants who are certified by the American Speech-Language-Hearing Association (ASHA) or who hold licenses from states that have equivalent requirements.

8049

Speech-Language Pathologist
Board of Speech-Language, Pathology and Audiology
Dept. of Professional Regulation
Northwood Center
1940 N. Monroe St.
Tallahassee, FL 32399-0782
Phone: (904)488-8595

Credential Type: Speech-Language Pathologist license. **Duration of License:** Two years. **Requirements:** Have a master's degree or equivalent with major emphasis in speech-language pathology or speech-language science. Complete at least 300 clock hours of supervised clinical experience within the training institution or in one of its cooperating programs. Complete a Clinical Fellowship Year consisting of at least nine months of full-time professional experience. Pass the National Examination in Speech-Language Pathology.

Renewal requires 20 continuing education hours every two years. **Examination:** National Examination in Speech-Language Pathology. **Reciprocity:** Granted to applicants who are certified by the American Speech-Language-Hearing Association (ASHA) or who hold licenses from states that have equivalent requirements.

Georgia

8050

Audiologist
Board of Examiners for Speech Pathology and Audiology
166 Pryor St. SW
Atlanta, GA 30303
Phone: (404)656-6719

Credential Type: Audiologist license. **Duration of License:** Two years. **Requirements:** Have a master's degree or equivalent with major emphasis in audiology or hearing science. Complete at least 300 clock hours of supervised clinical experience within the training institution or in one of its cooperating programs. Complete a Clinical Fellowship Year consisting of at least nine months of full-time professional experience. Pass the National Examination in Audiology.

Renewal requires 25 continuing education hours every two years. **Examination:** National Examination in Audiology. **Exemptions:** Exam may be waived if certified by the American Speech-Language-Hearing Association (ASHA) or licensed by a state with equivalent standards. **Fees:** $110 application fee. $50 examination fee. $60 renewal fee. $30 inactive status fee. $100 reinstatement fee.

8051

School Service Associate
Div. of Teacher Education
State Dept. of Education
1452 Twin Towers East
Atlanta, GA 30334-5070
Phone: (404)656-2406

Credential Type: School Service Certificate. **Authorization:** Authorizes the holder to administer school services in one of the following occupations: Audiologist, Media Specialist, School Counselor, School Nutrition Director, School Psychometrist, School Psychologist, School Social Worker/Visiting Teacher, or Speech and Language Pathologist. **Requirements:** Bachelor's degree is required for Nutrition Director, Speech/ Language Pathologist and Media Specialist. Master's degree and sixth year program is required for Psychologist. All other occupations require a master's degree or fifth year program. Media Specialist requires Initial Teaching Certificate. A staff development program in the Identification and Education of Children with Special Needs and a certification test is

Georgia

School Service Associate, continued

required at the master's degree level in the field of School Counseling. Three years of acceptable school experience are required of in the fields of nutrition and counseling.

8052

Speech-Language Pathologist
Board of Examiners for Speech
  Pathology and Audiology
166 Pryor St. SW
Atlanta, GA 30303
Phone: (404)656-6719

Credential Type: Speech-Language Pathologist license. **Duration of License:** Two years. **Requirements:** Have a master's degree or equivalent with major emphasis in speech-language pathology or speech-language science. Complete at least 300 clock hours of supervised clinical experience within the training institution or in one of its cooperating programs. Complete a Clinical Fellowship Year consisting of at least nine months of full-time professional experience. Pass the National Examination in Speech-Language Pathology.

Renewal requires 20 continuing education hours every two years. **Examination:** National Examination in Speech-Language Pathology. **Exemptions:** Exam may be waived if certified by the American Speech-Language-Hearing Association (ASHA) or licensed by a state with equivalent standards. **Fees:** $110 application fee. $50 examination fee. $60 renewal fee. $30 inactive status fee. $100 reinstatement fee.

Hawaii

8053

Speech Pathologist or Audiologist
Hawaii Board of Speech Pathology
  and Audiology
1010 Richards St.
PO Box 3469
Honolulu, HI 96801
Phone: (808)548-8542

Credential Type: License. **Duration of License:** Two years. **Requirements:** The American Speech-Language-Hearing Assn. Certificate of Clinical Competence which requires a master's degree or equivalent, a nine-month internship and passing a national written exam; or 300 hours of supervised clinical experience as a trainer, a master's degree or equivalent, nine months of full-time professional experience under the supervision of a licensed practitioner, passing the National Teachers Examination.

Examination: Yes. **Exemptions:** Exemptions for licensed physicians or surgeons, licensed hearing aid dealers, and college speech pathology or audiology trainees fulfilling clinical experience requirements. **Fees:** $25 application fee. $50 license fee. $15 Compliance Resolution Fund fee. $25 renewal fee.

Idaho

8054

School Audiologist
Certification Analyst
State Dept. of Education
L. B. Jordan Office Bldg.
Boise, ID 83720
Phone: (208)334-3475

Credential Type: Audiology Endorsement. **Duration of License:** Five years. **Requirements:** Complete state approved program in audiology. Master's degree in speech language pathology. 60 semester hours of appropriate courses. 300 clock-hours of supervised clinical experience. Certificate may be renewed upon completion of at least six semester credits of college courses within the period of validity.

8055

Standard Communications Disorders School Specialist
Certification Analyst
State Dept. of Education
L. B. Jordan Office Bldg.
Boise, ID 83720
Phone: (208)334-3475

Credential Type: Standard Communication Disorders Specialist Endorsement. **Duration of License:** Five years. **Requirements:** Complete state approved program in speech pathology and audiology. Master's degree in speech language pathology. 60 semester hours of appropriate courses. 300 clock-hours of supervised clinical experience. Certificate may be renewed upon completion of at least six semester credits of college courses within the period of validity.

Illinois

8056

Audiologist
Board of Speech-Language,
  Pathology, and Audiology
Dept. of Professional Regulation
320 W. Washington, 3rd Fl.
Springfield, IL 62786
Phone: (217)785-8556

Credential Type: Audiologist license. **Duration of License:** Two years. **Requirements:** Have a master's degree or equivalent with major emphasis in audiology or hearing science. Complete at least 300 clock hours of supervised clinical experience within the training institution or in one of its cooperating programs. Complete a Clinical Fellowship Year consisting of at least nine months of full-time professional experience. Pass the National Examination in Audiology. **Examination:** National Examination in Audiology. **Exemptions:** Exam may be waived if certified by the American Speech-Language-Hearing Association (ASHA) or licensed by a state with equivalent standards. **Fees:** $90 application fee. $50 renewal fee.

8057

Speech-Language Pathologist
Board of Speech-Language,
  Pathology, and Audiology
Dept. of Professional Regulation
320 W. Washington, 3rd Fl.
Springfield, IL 62786
Phone: (217)785-8556

Credential Type: Speech-Language Pathologist license. **Duration of License:** Two years. **Requirements:** Have a master's degree or equivalent with major emphasis in speech-language pathology or speech-language science. Complete at least 300 clock hours of supervised clinical experience within the training institution or in one of its cooperating programs. Complete a Clinical Fellowship Year consisting of at least nine months of full-time professional experience. Pass the National Examination in Speech-Language Pathology. **Examination:** National Examination in Speech-Language Pathology. **Exemptions:** Exam may be waived if certified by the American Speech-Language-Hearing Association (ASHA) or licensed by a state with equivalent standards. **Fees:** $90 application fee. $50 renewal fee.

Speech-Language Pathologists and Audiologists

8058

Teacher of the Deaf and Hard of Hearing
Certification and Placement Section
100 N. First St.
Springfield, IL 62777
Phone: (217)782-4321

Credential Type: Standard Special Education Certificate. **Duration of License:** Four years. **Requirements:** Good character. Good health. At least 19 years of age. Citizen of the U.S. Evidence of special education teaching experience or completion of an approved special education program of teacher preparation. Bachelor's degree. Meet specified general and professional education requirements. 32 semester hours of appropriate courses in the field including: five hours in the psychological area; 10 hours in the science area; 12 hours in the communications and education area; and five hours of student teaching. Pass required sections of the Illinois Certification Test. **Examination:** Illinois Certification Test. **Reciprocity:** Reciprocity exists for applicants holding out-of-state teaching certificates providing their teacher preparation was comparable to that required by the state of Illinois. **Fees:** $44 per section of the Illinois Certification Test.

8059

Teacher of Speech and Language Impaired Students
Certification and Placement Section
100 N. First St.
Springfield, IL 62777
Phone: (217)782-4321

Credential Type: Standard Special Education Endorsement. **Duration of License:** Four years. **Requirements:** Good character. Good health. At least 19 years of age. Citizen of the U.S. Evidence of special education teaching experience or completion of an approved special education program of teacher preparation. Bachelor's degree. Meet specified general and professional education requirements. Master's degree and completion of a course in communicative disorders and related disciplines. Knowledge and understanding of the normal development use of speech, hearing, and language. General understanding of the public schools; general knowledge of procedures used with other educational handicaps. Knowledge and competency in application of psychological principles. Clinical practicum in communicative disorders. Pass required sections of the Illinois Certification Test. **Examination:** Illinois Certification Test. **Reciprocity:** Reciprocity exists for applicants holding out-of-state teaching certificates providing their teacher preparation was comparable to that required by the state of Illinois. **Fees:** $44 per section of the Illinois Certification Test.

Indiana

8060

Audiologist
Board of Examiners of Speech
 Pathology and Audiology
1 American Sq., Ste. 1020
PO Box 82067
Indianapolis, IN 46282
Phone: (317)232-2960

Credential Type: Audiologist license. **Duration of License:** Two years. **Authorization:** License covers dispensing hearing aids. **Requirements:** Have a master's degree or equivalent with major emphasis in audiology or hearing science. Complete at least 300 clock hours of supervised clinical experience within the training institution or in one of its cooperating programs. Complete a Clinical Fellowship Year consisting of at least nine months of full-time professional experience. Pass the National Examination in Audiology.

Renewal requires 36 continuing education hours every two years. **Examination:** National Examination in Audiology. **Exemptions:** Exam may be waived if certified by the American Speech-Language-Hearing Association (ASHA) or licensed by a state with equivalent standards. **Fees:** $25 application fee. $20 license fee. $30 renewal fee.

8061

Speech-Language Pathologist
Board of Examiners of Speech
 Pathology and Audiology
1 American Sq., Ste. 1020
PO Box 82067
Indianapolis, IN 46282
Phone: (317)232-2960

Credential Type: Speech-Language Pathologist license. **Duration of License:** Two years. **Requirements:** Have a master's degree or equivalent with major emphasis in speech-language pathology or speech-language science. Complete at least 300 clock hours of supervised clinical experience within the training institution or in one of its cooperating programs. Complete a Clinical Fellowship Year consisting of at least nine months of full-time professional experience. Pass the National Examination in Speech-Language Pathology.

Renewal requires 36 continuing education hours every two years. **Examination:** National Examination in Speech-Language Pathology. **Exemptions:** Exam may be waived if certified by the American Speech-Language-Hearing Association (ASHA) or licensed by a state with equivalent standards. **Fees:** $25 application fee. $20 license fee. $30 renewal fee.

Iowa

8062

Audiologist/Speech Pathologist
Iowa State Board of Speech
 Pathology and Audiology
 Examiners
Lucas State Office Bldg.
Des Moines, IA 50319
Phone: (515)281-5596

Credential Type: License. **Duration of License:** Two years. **Requirements:** A master's degree or equivalent from an accredited college with a major in speech pathology and/or audiology, no less that 300 hours of supervised clinical training by an accredited college, plus nine months of supervised clinical experience (within one year) with a temporary license. **Examination:** National Teachers Examination in Speech-Language or Audiology. **Reciprocity:** Yes. **Fees:** $105 application fee. $80 renewal fee.

Kentucky

8063

Audiologist
Board of Examiners of Speech
 Pathologists and Audiologists
PO Box 456
Frankfort, KY 40602
Phone: (502)564-3296

Credential Type: Audiologist license. **Duration of License:** One year. **Requirements:** Have a master's degree or equivalent with major emphasis in audiology or hearing science. Complete at least 300 clock hours of supervised clinical experience within the training institution or in one of its cooperating programs. Complete a Clinical Fellowship Year consisting of at least nine months of full-time professional experience. Pass the National Examination in Audiology.

Renewal requires 15 continuing education hours every year. (Dual license holders require 25 hours each year.) **Examination:** National Examination in Audiology. **Exemptions:** Exam may be waived if certified by the American Speech-Language-Hearing Association (ASHA) or licensed by a state with equivalent standards. **Fees:** $25

Audiologist, continued

application fee. $50 license fee. $25 renewal fee.

8064

Speech-Language Pathologist
Board of Examiners of Speech
 Pathologists and Audiologists
PO Box 456
Frankfort, KY 40602
Phone: (502)564-3296

Credential Type: Speech-Language Pathologist license. **Duration of License:** One year. **Requirements:** Have a master's degree or equivalent with major emphasis in speech-language pathology or speech-language science. Complete at least 300 clock hours of supervised clinical experience within the training institution or in one of its cooperating programs. Complete a Clinical Fellowship Year consisting of at least nine months of full-time professional experience. Pass the National Examination in Speech-Language Pathology.

Renewal requires 15 continuing education hours every year. (Dual license holders require 25 hours each year.) **Examination:** National Examination in Speech-Language Pathology. **Exemptions:** Exam may be waived if certified by the American Speech-Language-Hearing Association (ASHA) or licensed by a state with equivalent standards. **Fees:** $25 application fee. $50 license fee. $25 renewal fee.

Louisiana

8065

Audiologist (School)
Louisiana State Dept. of Education
Teacher Certification
PO Box 94064
Baton Rouge, LA 70804
Phone: (504)342-3490

Credential Type: Provisional Audiologist License. **Duration of License:** Three years. **Requirements:** Master's degree in audiology or equivalent.

Credential Type: Qualified Audiologist License. **Duration of License:** Valid provided the holder maintains current Louisiana licensure as an audiologist. **Requirements:** Licensed as an audiologist in Louisiana.

8066

Speech Pathologist
Louisiana State Dept. of Education
Teacher Certification
PO Box 94064
Baton Rouge, LA 70804
Phone: (504)342-3490

Credential Type: Provisional License. **Duration of License:** Three years (non-renewable). **Requirements:** Master's degree in speech pathology or equivalent.

Credential Type: Qualified License. **Duration of License:** Unlimited. **Requirements:** Speech pathologist license. Type B or Type A Louisiana Certificate as a speech, language, and hearing specialist.

Maine

8067

Audiologist
Board of Examiners on Speech
 Pathology and Audiology
Div. of Licensing and Enforcement
State House Station 35
Augusta, ME 04333
Phone: (207)582-8723

Credential Type: Audiologist license. **Duration of License:** Two years. **Requirements:** Have a master's degree or equivalent with major emphasis in audiology or hearing science. Complete at least 300 clock hours of supervised clinical experience within the training institution or in one of its cooperating programs. Complete a Clinical Fellowship Year consisting of at least nine months of full-time professional experience. Pass the National Examination in Audiology.

Renewal requires 50 continuing education hours every two years. **Examination:** National Examination in Audiology **Exemptions:** Exam may be waived if certified by the American Speech-Language-Hearing Association (ASHA) or licensed by a U.S. jurisdiction with equivalent standards. **Fees:** $25 application fee. $50 license fee. $80 renewal fee.

Credential Type: Temporary Audiologist license. **Duration of License:** Valid for 60 days in one calendar year. **Authorization:** Authorizes practice for up to 60 days in one calendar year. **Requirements:** ASHA-certified or hold license issued by a U.S. jurisdiction with standards equivalent to that of Maine or be qualified to begin postgraduate professional experience. **Fees:** $40 temporary license.

8068

Speech-Language Pathologist
Board of Examiners on Speech
 Pathology and Audiology
Div. of Licensing and Enforcement
State House Station 35
Augusta, ME 04333
Phone: (207)582-8723

Credential Type: Speech-Language Pathologist license. **Duration of License:** Two years. **Requirements:** Have a master's degree or equivalent with major emphasis in speech-language pathology or speech-language science. Complete at least 300 clock hours of supervised clinical experience within the training institution or in one of its cooperating programs. Complete a Clinical Fellowship Year consisting of at least nine months of full-time professional experience. Pass the National Examination in Speech-Language Pathology.

Renewal requires 50 continuing education hours every two years. **Examination:** National Examination in Speech-Language Pathology. **Exemptions:** Exam may be waived if certified by the American Speech-Language-Hearing Association (ASHA) or licensed by a U.S. jurisdiction with equivalent standards. **Fees:** $25 application fee. $50 license fee. $80 renewal fee.

Credential Type: Temporary Speech-Language Pathologist license. **Duration of License:** Valid for 60 days in one calendar year. **Authorization:** Authorizes practice for up to 60 days in one calendar year. **Requirements:** American Speech-Language-Hearing Association-certified or hold license issued by a U.S. jurisdiction with standards equivalent to that of Maine or be qualified to begin postgraduate professional experience. **Fees:** $40 temporary license.

Maryland

8069

Audiologist
Boards of Examiners for Speech
 Pathologists and Audiologists
4201 Patterson Ave.
3rd Floor
Baltimore, MD 21215-2299
Phone: (410)764-4725

Credential Type: Audiologist license. **Duration of License:** Two years. **Requirements:** Have a master's degree or equivalent with major emphasis in audiology or hearing science. Complete at least 300 clock hours of supervised clinical experience within the training institution or in one of its cooperating programs. Complete a

Clinical Fellowship Year consisting of at least nine months of full-time professional experience. Pass the National Examination in Audiology.

Renewal requires 20 continuing education hours every two years. **Examination:** National Examination in Audiology. **Exemptions:** Exam may be waived if ASHA-certified or licensed by a U.S. jurisdiction with equivalent standards. **Fees:** $100 application and license fee. $50 renewal fee.

Credential Type: Limited Audiologist license. **Requirements:** Hold license in another state with equivalent standards and file for Maryland license or be qualified to begin postgraduate professional experience. **Fees:** $100 application and limited license fee. $25 renewal fee.

8070

Speech-Language Pathologist
Boards of Examiners for Speech Pathologists and Audiologists
4201 Patterson Ave.
3rd Floor
Baltimore, MD 21215-2299
Phone: (410)764-4725

Credential Type: Speech-Language Pathologist license. **Duration of License:** Two years. **Requirements:** Have a master's degree or equivalent with major emphasis in speech-language pathology or speech-language science. Complete at least 300 clock hours of supervised clinical experience within the training institution or in one of its cooperating programs. Complete a Clinical Fellowship Year consisting of at least nine months of full-time professional experience. Pass the National Examination in Speech-Language Pathology.

Renewal requires 20 continuing education hours every two years. **Examination:** National Examination in Speech-Language Pathology. **Exemptions:** Exam may be waived if ASHA-certified or licensed by a U.S. jurisdiction with equivalent standards. **Fees:** $100 application and license fee. $50 renewal fee.

Credential Type: Limited Speech-Language Pathologist license. **Requirements:** Hold license in another state with equivalent standards and file for Maryland license or be qualified to begin postgraduate professional experience. **Fees:** $100 application and limited license fee. $25 renewal fee.

Massachusetts

8071

Audiologist
Board of Registration for Speech-Language Pathology and Audiology
100 Cambridge St., 15th Fl.
Boston, MA 02202
Phone: (617)727-1747

Credential Type: Audiologist license. **Duration of License:** Two years. **Authorization:** License covers dispensing hearing aids. **Requirements:** Have a master's degree or equivalent with major emphasis in audiology or hearing science. Complete at least 300 clock hours of supervised clinical experience within the training institution or in one of its cooperating programs. Complete a Clinical Fellowship Year consisting of at least nine months of full-time professional experience. Pass the National Examination in Audiology.

Continuing education may be required for renewal subject to Board's discretion. **Examination:** National Examination in Audiology. **Exemptions:** Exam may be waived if certified by the American Speech-Language-Hearing Association (ASHA) or licensed by a U.S. jurisdiction with equivalent standards. **Fees:** $50 application fee. $50 renewal fee.

8072

Speech-Language Pathologist
Board of Registration for Speech-Language Pathology and Audiology
100 Cambridge St., 15th Fl.
Boston, MA 02202
Phone: (617)727-1747

Credential Type: Speech-Language Pathologist license. **Duration of License:** Two years. **Requirements:** Have a master's degree or equivalent with major emphasis in speech-language pathology or speech-language science. Complete at least 300 clock hours of supervised clinical experience within the training institution or in one of its cooperating programs. Complete a Clinical Fellowship Year consisting of at least nine months of full-time professional experience. Pass the National Examination in Speech-Language Pathology.

Continuing education may be required for renewal subject to Board's discretion. **Examination:** National Examination in Speech-Language Pathology. **Exemptions:** Exam may be waived if certified by the American Speech-Language-Hearing Association (ASHA) or licensed by a U.S. jurisdiction with equivalent standards. **Fees:** $50 application fee. $50 renewal fee.

Minnesota

8073

Audiologist
Dept. of Health
Bureau of Health Resources and Managed Care Services
Health Occupations Programs
717 Delaware St., SE
Box 9441
Minneapolis, MN 55440
Phone: (612)623-5611
Phone: (612)623-5000
Fax: (612)623-5043

Alternate Information: Speech-Language Pathologist and Audiologist Advisory Council, c/o Health Occupations Programs.

Credential Type: Audiologist Registration. **Authorization:** Registration required to use occupational title. **Requirements:** Contact licensing body for application information. **Governing Statute:** Minnesota Statutes 214.13.

8074

Speech-Language Pathologist
Dept. of Health
Bureau of Health Resources and Managed Care Services
Health Occupations Programs
717 Delaware St., SE
Box 9441
Minneapolis, MN 55440
Phone: (612)623-5611
Phone: (612)623-5000
Fax: (612)623-5043

Alternate Information: Speech-Language Pathologist and Audiologist Advisory Council, c/o Health Occupations Programs.

Credential Type: Speech-Language Pathologist Registration. **Authorization:** Registration required to use occupational title. **Requirements:** Contact licensing body for application information. **Governing Statute:** Minnesota Statutes 214.13.

Mississippi

8075

Audiologist
Council of Advisors in Speech
  Pathology and Audiology
Dept. of Health
Child Care & Special Licensure
PO Box 1700
Jackson, MS 39215-1700
Phone: (601)960-7504

Credential Type: Audiologist license. **Duration of License:** One year. **Requirements:** Have a master's degree or equivalent with major emphasis in audiology or hearing science. Complete at least 300 clock hours of supervised clinical experience within the training institution or in one of its cooperating programs. Complete a Clinical Fellowship Year consisting of at least nine months of full-time professional experience. Pass the National Examination in Audiology.

Renewal requires 10 continuing education hours every year. **Examination:** National Examination in Audiology. **Fees:** $50 application fee. $50 renewal fee.

Credential Type: Temporary Audiologist license. **Requirements:** Certified by the American Speech-Language-Hearing Association (ASHA) or hold license issued by a state with standards equivalent to that of Mississippi or be qualified to begin postgraduate professional experience. **Fees:** $50 temporary license. $25 temporary license renewal.

8076

Speech-Language Pathologist
Council of Advisors in Speech
  Pathology and Audiology
Dept. of Health
Child Care & Special Licensure
PO Box 1700
Jackson, MS 39215-1700
Phone: (601)960-7504

Credential Type: Speech-Language Pathologist license. **Duration of License:** One year. **Requirements:** Have a master's degree or equivalent with major emphasis in speech-language pathology or speech-language science. Complete at least 300 clock hours of supervised clinical experience within the training institution or in one of its cooperating programs. Complete a Clinical Fellowship Year consisting of at least nine months of full-time professional experience. Pass the National Examination in Speech-Language Pathology.

Renewal requires 10 continuing education hours every year. **Examination:** National Examination in Speech-Language Pathology. **Fees:** $50 application fee. $50 renewal fee.

Credential Type: Temporary Speech-Language Pathologist license. **Requirements:** Certified by the American Speech-Language-Hearing Association (ASHA) or hold license issued by a state with standards equivalent to that of Mississippi or be qualified to begin postgraduate professional experience. **Fees:** $50 temporary license. $25 temporary license renewal.

Missouri

8077

Audiologist
Committee of Speech Pathology and
  Clinical Audiology
PO Box 4
Jefferson City, MO 65102
Phone: (314)751-00098

Credential Type: Audiologist license. **Duration of License:** One year. **Requirements:** Have a master's degree or equivalent with major emphasis in audiology or hearing science. Complete at least 275 clock hours of supervised clinical experience within the training institution or in one of its cooperating programs. Complete a Clinical Fellowship Year consisting of at least nine months of full-time professional experience. Pass the National Examination in Audiology. **Examination:** National Examination in Audiology. **Exemptions:** Exam may be waived if certified by the American Speech-Language-Hearing Association (ASHA). **Reciprocity:** Persons licensed in another state may practice while application is pending. **Fees:** $50 initial license fee. $25 renewal fee. $25 reinstatement fee.

8078

Speech-Language Pathologist
Committee of Speech Pathology and
  Clinical Audiology
PO Box 4
Jefferson City, MO 65102
Phone: (314)751-00098

Credential Type: Speech-Language Pathologist license. **Duration of License:** One year. **Requirements:** Have a master's degree or equivalent with major emphasis in speech-language pathology or speech-language science. Complete at least 275 clock hours of supervised clinical experience within the training institution or in one of its cooperating programs. Complete a Clinical Fellowship Year consisting of at least nine months of full-time professional experience. Pass the National Examination in Speech-Language Pathology. **Examination:** National Examination in Speech-Language Pathology. **Exemptions:** Exam may be waived if certified by the American Speech-Language-Hearing Association (ASHA). **Reciprocity:** Persons licensed in another state may practice while application is pending. **Fees:** $50 initial license fee. $25 renewal fee. $25 reinstatement fee.

Montana

8079

Audiologist
Montana Board of Speech
  Pathologists and Audiologists
111 N. Jackson
Helena, MT 59620
Phone: (406)444-4236

Credential Type: License. **Duration of License:** One year. **Requirements:** Completion of 90 quarter hours of approved coursework in audiology. Completion of 300 hours of supervised clinical experience. **Examination:** Written. **Fees:** $40 application fee. $25 license fee. $25 renewal fee. **Governing Statute:** Montana Code Annotated 37-15-301 through 37-15-323.

8080

Speech Pathologist
Montana Board of Speech
  Pathologists and Audiologists
111 N. Jackson
Helena, MT 59620
Phone: (406)444-3091

Credential Type: License. **Duration of License:** One year. **Requirements:** Completion of 90 quarter hours of approved coursework in speech pathology. Completion of 300 hours of supervised clinical experience. **Examination:** Written. **Fees:** $40 application fee. $25 license fee. $25 renewal fee. **Governing Statute:** Montana Code Annotated 37-15-301 through 37-15-323.

Speech-Language Pathologists and Audiologists

Nebraska

8081

Speech-Language Pathologist/ Audiologist
Nebraska Board of Examiners in Audiology and Speech-Language Pathology
301 Centennial Mall S.
PO Box 95007
Lincoln, NE 68509
Phone: (402)471-2115

Credential Type: License. **Duration of License:** Two years. **Requirements:** Must hold a master's degree or its equivalent from an approved academic program. Must have at least nine calendar months of full-time experience, or 18 months of part-time professional experience. **Examination:** Yes. **Fees:** $150 license fee. $150 renewal fee.

Nevada

8082

Speech Pathologist/Audiologist
Board of Examiners for Audiology and Speech Pathology
University of Nevada-Reno
Reno, NV 89557
Phone: (702)784-4887

Credential Type: License. **Duration of License:** One year. **Requirements:** Master's degree in speech pathology or audiology. Certificate of Clinical Competence from the American Speech-Language-Hearing Association. **Examination:** Yes. **Fees:** $50 application fee. $25 license fee. $25 renewal fee.

New Jersey

8083

Audiologist/Speech Pathologist
New Jersey Audiology and Speech Pathology Advisory Committee
1100 Raymond Blvd., Rm. 500
Newark, NJ 07102
Phone: (609)648-3571

Credential Type: License. **Duration of License:** Two years. **Requirements:** Master's degree in audiology or speech pathology from an accredited college or university and completion of an approved clinical internship program. **Examination:** Written. **Reciprocity:** Yes. **Fees:** $10 application fee. $100 renewal fee. **Governing Statute:** NJSA 45:3B. NJAC 13:44C.

New Mexico

8084

Audiologist
Speech-Language Pathology and Audiology Advisory Board
PO Box 25101
Santa Fe, NM 87504-1388
Phone: (505)827-7164

Credential Type: Audiologist license. **Duration of License:** One year. **Requirements:** Have a master's degree or equivalent with major emphasis in audiology or hearing science. Complete at least 300 clock hours of supervised clinical experience within the training institution or in one of its cooperating programs. Complete a Clinical Fellowship Year consisting of at least nine months of full-time professional experience. Pass the National Examination in Audiology.

Renewal requires 20 continuing education hours every two years. **Examination:** National Examination in Audiology. **Exemptions:** Exam may be waived if certified by the American Speech-Language-Hearing Association (ASHA) or licensed by a state with equivalent standards. **Fees:** $50 application fee. $50 license fee. $50 renewal fee.

8085

Speech-Language Pathologist
Speech-Language Pathology and Audiology Advisory Board
PO Box 25101
Santa Fe, NM 87504-1388
Phone: (505)827-7164

Credential Type: Speech-Language Pathologist license. **Duration of License:** One year. **Requirements:** Have a master's degree or equivalent with major emphasis in speech-language pathology or speech-language science. Complete at least 275 clock hours of supervised clinical experience within the training institution or in one of its cooperating programs. Complete a Clinical Fellowship Year consisting of at least nine months of full-time professional experience. Pass the National Examination in Speech-Language Pathology.

Renewal requires 20 continuing education hours every two years. **Examination:** National Examination in Speech-Pathology. **Exemptions:** Exam may be waived if certified by the American Speech-Language-Hearing Association (ASHA) or licensed by a state with equivalent standards. **Fees:** $50 application fee. $50 license fee. $50 renewal fee.

New York

8086

Audiologist
State Education Dept.
Div. of Professional Licensing Services
Cultural Education Center
Empire State Plaza
Albany, NY 12230
Phone: (518)474-3279

Credential Type: License. **Duration of License:** Three years. **Requirements:** Master's Degree in Audiology. Nine months of supervised experience in audiology. 21 years of age. **Examination:** National Teacher Examination in Audiology. **Fees:** $35 exam fee. $270 license fee. $155 renewal fee. **Governing Statute:** Title VIII Articles 130, 159 of the Education Law.

8087

Speech-Language Pathologist
State Education Dept.
Div. of Professional Licensing Services
Cultural Education Center
Empire State Plaza
Albany, NY 12230
Phone: (518)474-3279

Credential Type: License. **Duration of License:** Three years. **Requirements:** Bachelor's Degree or Master's Degree in speech pathology. 21 years of age. At least nine months of paid, supervised experience in speech pathology. **Examination:** Written. **Fees:** $35 exam fee. $270 application fee. $155 renewal fee. **Governing Statute:** Title VIII Articles 130, 159 of the Education Law.

North Carolina

8088

Audiologist
North Carolina State Board of Examiners for Speech and Language Pathologist and Audiologist
PO Box 5545
Greensboro, NC 27435
Phone: (919)272-1828

Credential Type: License. **Duration of License:** One year. **Requirements:** Master's degree in audiology from a board-accredited college. 300 clock hours of supervised, direct clinical experience and nine months of full-time supervised profes-

North Carolina

Audiologist, continued

sional experience. 18 years of age. **Examination:** Written. **Fees:** $30 application fee. $25 exam fee. $40 license fee. $40 renewal fee.

8089

Speech and Language Pathologist
North Carolina State Board of Examiners for Speech and Language Pathologist and Audiologist
PO Box 5545
Greensboro, NC 27435
Phone: (919)272-1828

Credential Type: License. **Duration of License:** One year. **Requirements:** Master's degree in speech and language pathology from a board accredited college or university. 300 clock hours of supervised clinical experience and nine months of full-time professional experience. 18 years of age. **Examination:** National written exam. **Fees:** $30 application fee. $25 exam fee. $40 license fee. $40 renewal fee.

North Dakota

8090

Audiologist
Board of Examiners on Audiology and Speech-Language Pathology
Box 8158 UND
Grand Forks, ND 58202-8158
Phone: (701)777-4421

Credential Type: Audiologist license. **Duration of License:** One year. **Requirements:** Have a master's degree or equivalent with major emphasis in audiology or hearing science. Complete at least 300 clock hours of supervised clinical experience within the training institution or in one of its cooperating programs. Pass the National Examination in Audiology.

Renewal requires 10 continuing education hours every year. **Examination:** National Examination in Audiology. **Exemptions:** Exam may be waived if certified by the American Speech-Language-Hearing Association (ASHA) or licensed by a state with equivalent standards. **Fees:** $75 application and license fee. $30 renewal fee. $75 reinstatement fee.

8091

School Speech Therapist
Director of Certification
State Dept. of Public Instruction
Bismarck, ND 58505
Phone: (701)224-2264

Credential Type: Speech Clinician I Credential. **Requirements:** Valid North Dakota Educator's Professional Certificate. Special education credential in speech correction awarded on completion of the following 30 semester hours of specialized course work: six hours of credit distributed in phonetics, anatomy and physiology of the speech mechanism, psychology of speech, voice, science, and semantics; 12 hours of credit in professional speech correction and speech pathology; three hours of credit in audiology; a 200 clock hr. clinical practicum which represents actual work with major types of speech defects at varying levels in addition to observation periods and assistance with scheduling routine and other non-corrective activities; nine semester hours of credit electives in allied fields which must include courses in child psychology and mental hygiene. Applicant's personal speech habits in both voice and diction must meet an acceptable standard, as well as personal characteristics acceptable in a teacher of children. Must adhere to the Professional Code of Ethics of the American Speech and Hearing Association.

8092

Speech-Language Pathologist
Board of Examiners on Audiology and Speech-Language Pathology
Box 8158 UND
Grand Forks, ND 58202-8158
Phone: (701)777-4421

Credential Type: Speech-Language Pathologist license. **Duration of License:** One year. **Requirements:** Have a master's degree or equivalent with major emphasis in speech-language pathology or speech-language science. Complete at least 300 clock hours of supervised clinical experience within the training institution or in one of its cooperating programs. Pass the National Examination in Speech-Language Pathology.

Renewal requires 10 continuing education hours every year. **Examination:** National Examination in Speech-Language Pathology. **Exemptions:** Exam may be waived if certified by the American Speech-Language-Hearing Association (ASHA) or licensed by a state with equivalent standards. **Fees:** $75 application and license fee. $30 renewal fee. $75 reinstatement fee.

Ohio

8093

Audiologist
Board of Speech Pathology and Audiology
77 S. High St., 16th Fl.
Columbus, OH 43266
Phone: (614)466-3145

Credential Type: Audiologist license. **Duration of License:** One year. **Requirements:** Have a master's degree or equivalent with major emphasis in audiology or hearing science. Clinical practicum and post graduate professional experience. Pass the National Examination in Audiology. **Examination:** National Examination in Audiology. **Exemptions:** Exam and/or educational requirements may be waived if certified by the American Speech-Language-Hearing Association (ASHA) or licensed by a state with equivalent standards. **Reciprocity:** Granted to licensed audiologists from other states whose standards are considered equivalent to those of Ohio. Each applicant's case will be considered individually. **Fees:** $25 application fee. $50 license fee. $60 dual license fee. $40 renewal fee.

8094

School Audiologist
Teacher Education and Certification
State Dept. of Education
65 S. Front St., Rm. 1012
Columbus, OH 43266-0308
Phone: (614)466-3593

Credential Type: Provisional Pupil Personnel Certificate—Audiology. **Requirements:** Recommendation of university official. Complete examination prescribed by the State Board of Education. Proof of education and experience in area of specialization. Master's degree. Course work and field-based experience well distributed over communication skills, hearing sciences, and related fields. **Examination:** Examination prescribed by the State Board of Education.

8095

School Speech-Language Pathologist
Teacher Education and Certification
State Dept. of Education
65 S. Front St., Rm. 1012
Columbus, OH 43266-0308
Phone: (614)466-3593

Credential Type: Provisional Pupil Personnel Certificate—Speech/Language Pathology. **Requirements:** Recommendation of university official. Complete examination prescribed by the State Board of Education. Proof of education and experience in area of specialization. Master's degree. Course work and field based experiences well distributed over communication, education and related fields. **Examination:** Examination prescribed by the State Board of Education.

8096

Speech-Language Pathologist
Board of Speech Pathology and Audiology
77 S. High St., 16th Fl.
Columbus, OH 43266
Phone: (614)466-3145

Credential Type: Speech-Language Pathologist license. **Duration of License:** One year. **Requirements:** Have a master's degree or equivalent with major emphasis in speech-language pathology or speech-language science. Pass the National Examination in Speech-Language Pathology. **Examination:** National Examination in Speech-Language Pathology. **Exemptions:** Exam and/or educational requirements may be waived if certified by the American Speech-Language-Hearing Association (ASHA) or licensed by a state with equivalent standards. **Reciprocity:** Granted to licensed speech-language pathologists from other states whose standards are considered equivalent to those of Ohio. Each applicant's case will be considered individually. **Fees:** $25 application fee. $50 license fee. $60 dual license fee. $40 renewal fee.

Oklahoma

8097

Audiologist
State Board of Examiners of Speech Pathology-Audiology
PO Box 53592, State Capitol Station
Oklahoma City, OK 73105
Phone: (405)521-6131

Credential Type: License. **Duration of License:** One year. **Requirements:** Master's degree with emphasis in speech pathology or audiology. Internship is required for Oklahoma license unless national certification is obtained prior to application for licensure. **Examination:** ASHA Audiological Examination. **Fees:** $45 exam fee. $50 application fee. $25 renewal fee.

8098

School Service Personnel K-12
Teacher Education and Certification
State Dept. of Education
2500 N. Lincoln Blvd., Rm. 211
Oklahoma City, OK 73105
Phone: (405)521-3337

Credential Type: Standard Certificate in a School Personnel Field—Graduate. **Duration of License:** Five years. **Authorization:** Endorsement will be given to persons seeking positions in the following fields: Counselor; Library Media Specialist; Elementary School Principal; Secondary School Principal; School Superintendent; School Psychometrist; School Psychologist; SpeechLanguage Pathologist; or Reading Specialist. **Requirements:** Complete an approved certificate program at an accredited college or university which includes a minimum of the following: a baccalaureate degree; 50 semester hours in general education; 30 semester hours in professional education; and 40 semester hours in course work pertaining to the area of specialization. Pass the state certified test(s) in specialization competencies. Complete State Board graduate level course requirements.

8099

Speech Pathologist
State Board of Examiners of Speech Pathology-Audiology
State Capitol Sta.
PO Box 53592
Oklahoma City, OK 73105
Phone: (405)521-6131

Credential Type: License. **Duration of License:** One year. **Requirements:** Master's degree with an emphasis in speech pathology or audiology. Supervised clinical training in communication disorders. Internship. **Examination:** National Teacher Examination in Speech Pathology. **Fees:** $45 exam fee. $50 license fee. $25 renewal fee.

Oregon

8100

Audiologist
Board of Examiners for Speech Pathology and Audiology
State Office Bldg.
800 NE Oregon Ave.
Portland, OR 97232
Phone: (503)731-4050

Credential Type: License. **Duration of License:** One year. **Requirements:** Must have a Master's degree in Audiolgy. Must complete nine months of full time professional employment after receiving Master's degree. **Examination:** Yes. **Fees:** $30 application fee. $65 examination fee. $35 license fee. $35 renewal fee. **Governing Statute:** ORS 681.205 to 681.991.

8101

Speech Pathologist
Board of Examiners for Speech Pathology and Audiology
800 NE Oregon
Portland, OR 97232
Phone: (503)229-5390

Credential Type: License. **Duration of License:** One year. **Requirements:** Must have a Master's degree in Speech Pathology and complete nine months of full-time professional employment. **Examination:** Yes. **Fees:** $65 exam fee. $30 application fee. $35 license fee. $35 renewal fee. **Governing Statute:** ORS 681.205 to 681.991.

Pennsylvania

8102

Audiologist
Board of Examiners in Speech-Language and Hearing
Bureau of Professional and Occupational Affairs
PO Box 2649
Harrisburg, PA 17105-2649
Phone: (717)783-7156

Credential Type: Audiologist license. **Duration of License:** Two years. **Requirements:** Have a master's degree or equiva-

Audiologist, continued

lent with major emphasis in audiology or hearing science. Complete at least 275 clock hours of supervised clinical experience within the training institution or in one of its cooperating programs. Complete a Clinical Fellowship Year consisting of at least nine months of full-time professional experience. Pass the National Examination in Audiology. **Examination:** National Examination in Audiology. **Exemptions:** Exam and some educational requirements may be waived if certified by the American Speech-Language-Hearing Association (ASHA) or licensed by a state with equivalent standards. **Fees:** $20 license fee. $46 renewal fee.

8103

Speech-Language Pathologist
Board of Examiners in Speech-Language and Hearing
Bureau of Professional and Occupational Affairs
PO Box 2649
Harrisburg, PA 17105-2649
Phone: (717)783-7156

Credential Type: Speech-Language Pathologist license. **Duration of License:** Two years. **Requirements:** Have a master's degree or equivalent with major emphasis in speech-language pathology or speech-language science. Complete at least 275 clock hours of supervised clinical experience within the training institution or in one of its cooperating programs. Complete a Clinical Fellowship Year consisting of at least nine months of full-time professional experience. Pass the National Examination in Speech-Language Pathology. **Examination:** National Examination in Speech-Language Pathology. **Exemptions:** Exam and some educational requirements may be waived if certified by the American Speech-Language-Hearing Association (ASHA) or licensed by a state with equivalent standards. **Fees:** $20 license fee. $46 renewal fee.

Rhode Island

8104

Audiologist
Board of Examiners for Speech Pathology & Audiology
Dept. of Professional Regulation
Cannon Bldg., Rm. 104
3 Capitol Hill
Providence, RI 02908
Phone: (401)277-2827

Credential Type: Audiologist license. **Duration of License:** One year. **Requirements:** Have a master's degree or equivalent with major emphasis in audiology or hearing science. Complete at least 300 clock hours of supervised clinical experience within the training institution or in one of its cooperating programs. Complete a Clinical Fellowship Year consisting of at least nine months of full-time professional experience. Pass the National Examination in Audiology. **Examination:** National Examination in Audiology. **Exemptions:** Exam may be waived if certified by the American Speech-Language-Hearing Association (ASHA) or licensed by a state with equivalent standards. **Fees:** $25 application fee. $10 renewal fee.

8105

Speech-Language Pathologist
Board of Examiners for Speech Pathology & Audiology
Dept. of Professional Regulation
Cannon Bldg., Rm. 104
3 Capitol Hill
Providence, RI 02908
Phone: (401)277-2827

Credential Type: Speech-Language Pathologist license. **Duration of License:** One year. **Requirements:** Have a master's degree or equivalent with major emphasis in speech-language pathology or speech-language science. Complete at least 300 clock hours of supervised clinical experience within the training institution or in one of its cooperating programs. Complete a Clinical Fellowship Year consisting of at least nine months of full-time professional experience. Pass the National Examination in Speech-Language Pathology. **Examination:** National Examination in Speech-Language Pathology. **Exemptions:** Exam may be waived if certified by the American Speech-Language-Hearing Association (ASHA) or licensed by a state with equivalent standards. **Fees:** $25 application fee. $10 renewal fee.

South Carolina

8106

Speech Pathologist/Audiologist
South Carolina State Board of Examiners for Speech Pathology and Audiology
PO Box 11876
Columbia, SC 29211
Phone: (803)772-0260

Credential Type: License. **Requirements:** Master's degree in speech pathology or audiology from an approved school or equivalent, plus the completion of approved program of studies. **Examination:** Yes. **Fees:** $35 application fee. $35 license fee. $10 reorder fee.

Tennessee

8107

Audiologist
State Board of Examiners for Speech Pathology and Audiology
283 Plus Park Blvd.
Nashville, TN 37247-1010
Phone: (615)367-6243

Credential Type: License. **Duration of License:** One year. **Requirements:** 18 years old. Masters degree in area of study. Good moral character. **Examination:** American Speech-Language Hearing Association (ASHA) certified or having taken the National Teacher Examination (NTE) in speech pathology or audiology (minimum score 600). **Reciprocity:** Yes, with proof of license. **Fees:** $105 Registration. $50 Application. $45 Renewal.

8108

Speech Pathologist
Board of Examiners for Speech Pathology and Audiology
283 Plus Park Blvd.
Nashville, TN 37247
Phone: (615)367-6243

Credential Type: License. **Duration of License:** One year. **Requirements:** 18 years old. Masters degree in area of interest. Pass the examination. Good moral character. **Examination:** ASHA certification or National Teacher Examination in speech pathology (minimum score 600). **Reciprocity:** Yes, with Board approval. **Fees:** $105 Registration. $50 Application. $45 Renewal.

Texas

8109

Audiologist
Committee of Examiners for Speech-
  Language Pathology and
  Audiology
1100 W. 49th
Austin, TX 78756-3183
Phone: (512)458-7502

Credential Type: Audiologist license. **Duration of License:** One year. **Requirements:** Have a master's degree or equivalent with major emphasis in audiology or hearing science. Complete at least 300 clock hours of supervised clinical experience within the training institution or in one of its cooperating programs. Complete a Clinical Fellowship Year consisting of at least nine months of full-time professional experience. Pass the National Examination in Audiology.

Renewal requires 10 clock hours of continuing education per year or 16 clock hours for a dual license. **Examination:** National Examination in Audiology. **Exemptions:** Exam may be waived if certified by the American Speech-Language-Hearing Association (ASHA) or licensed by a state with equivalent standards. **Fees:** $30 application fee. $30 license fee. $48 dual license fee. $48 dual license fee. $30 renewal fee.

8110

Speech-Language Pathologist
Committee of Examiners for Speech-
  Language Pathology and
  Audiology
1100 W. 49th St.
Austin, TX 78756-3183
Phone: (512)458-7502

Credential Type: Speech-Language Pathologist license. **Duration of License:** One year. **Requirements:** Have a master's degree or equivalent with major emphasis in speech-language pathology or speech-language science. Complete at least 300 clock hours of supervised clinical experience within the training institution or in one of its cooperating programs. Complete a Clinical Fellowship Year consisting of at least nine months of full-time professional experience. Pass the National Examination in Speech-Language Pathology.

Renewal requires 10 clock hours of continuing education per year or 16 clock hours for a dual license. **Examination:** National Examination in Speech-Language Pathology. **Exemptions:** Exam may be waived if certified by the American Speech-Language-Hearing Association (ASHA) or licensed by a state with equivalent standards. **Fees:** $30 application fee. $30 license fee. $48 dual license fee. $48 dual license fee. $30 renewal fee.

Utah

8111

Speech Pathologist and Audiologist
Dept. of Commerce
Div. of Occupational and
  Professional Licensing
160 E. 300 S.
PO Box 45802
Salt Lake City, UT 84145
Phone: (801)530-6628

Credential Type: License. **Duration of License:** Two years. **Requirements:** Must have a master's or doctoral degree or the equivalent in the area of speech pathology, speech science, or audiology from an accredited college. Must be in compliance with the regulations of conduct and codes of ethics set out in the profession of speech pathology and audiology. Must provide verification from either a licensed speech therapist or audiologist, or an ASHA-certified speech therapist or audiologist, or completion of at least one year of direct clinical experience in treatment and management of patients. **Examination:** Yes. **Fees:** $50 examination fee. $30 renewal fee.

Vermont

8112

School Audiologist
Teacher Licensure
State Dept. of Education
Montpelier, VT 05602-2703
Phone: (802)828-2445

Credential Type: Initial License. **Requirements:** Master's degree or its equivalent in audiology. Supervised clinical experience of 300 clock hours Meet specific competencies as determined by the Standards Board.

8113

School Speech and Language Pathologist
Teacher Licensure
State Dept. of Education
Montpelier, VT 05602-2703
Phone: (802)828-2445

Credential Type: Initial Certificate. **Authorization:** Holder is authorized to diagnose speech/language disorders and to assist regular and special education personnel in designing, implementing, and evaluating individual education programs for the areas of language, hearing, articulation, fluency, and voice. **Requirements:** Master's degree or its equivalent in speech/language pathology. Supervised clinical experience of 300 clock hours Meet specific competencies as specified by the Standards Board.

Virginia

8114

Speech Pathologist and Audiologist
Dept. of Commerce
3600 W. Broad St.
Richmond, VA 23230
Phone: (804)367-2194

Credential Type: License. **Requirements:** Must have completed a college program approved by the Board with 60 semester hours in specified courses. Must have completed 300 hours of supervised clinical experience. **Examination:** Yes.

8115

Teacher of the Hearing Impaired
Administrative Director
Office of Professional Development
  and Teacher Education
Dept. of Education
PO Box 6-Q
Richmond, VA 23216-2060
Phone: (804)225-2094

Credential Type: Hearing Impaired Endorsement. **Requirements:** Teaching Certificate. All applicants, except those who plan to work with preschool handicapped, must complete 18 semester hours of the following core courses: psychoeducational assessment; sociocultural and vocational aspects of disabilities; modifications of curriculum and instruction; language development; current trends and legal issues; and teaching methods in remediation of academic subjects for exceptional individuals. Plus 15 semester hours which includes course work in: characteristics of hearing impaired students; speech science and audiology; instructional procedures; individual and group amplification systems; and student teaching.

Virginia

8116

Teacher of Speech and Language Disorders
Administrative Director
Office of Professional Development
  and Teacher Education
Dept. of Education
PO Box 6-Q
Richmond, VA 23216-2060
Phone: (804)225-2094

Credential Type: Speech and Language Disorders Endorsement. **Requirements:** Teaching Certificate. All applicants, except those who plan to work with preschool handicapped, must complete 18 semester hours of the following core courses: psychoeducational assessment; sociocultural and vocational aspects of disabilities; modifications of curriculum and instruction; language development; current trends and legal issues; and teaching methods in remediation of academic subjects for exceptional individuals. Plus 24 semester hours of course work in the following: speech pathology; anatomy and physiology of speech and auditory mechanisms; speech and language development; and audiology; management techniques for disorders of articulation, language, fluency, voice and resonance.

Washington

8117

School Communications Disorders Specialist
Superintendent of Public Instruction
Professional Education and
  Certification
Old Capitol Bldg. FG-11
Seattle, WA 98504-3211
Phone: (206)753-6773

Credential Type: Initial Educational Staff Associate Certificate. **Duration of License:** Seven years. **Authorization:** Authorizes service in primary role of assistant to the learner, the teacher, the administrator, and/or the educational program. **Requirements:** Complete all course work (except special projects or thesis) for a master's degree with a major in communications disorders.

Credential Type: Continuing Educational Staff Associate Certificate. **Duration of License:** Five years. **Requirements:** Master's degree in communications disorders. Verification of 180 days of experience in the role. Complete a college level course which includes peer review while employed in the role. Out-of-state applicants must complete a comprehensive written examination (unless already taken as part of the master's degree). Renewable upon 150 clock hours of work in this position during the life of the certificate.

West Virginia

8118

Education Audiologist
Dept. of Education
Office of Educational Personnel
  Development
1900 Washington St. E
Charleston, WV 25305
Phone: (800)982-2378

Credential Type: Certification. **Duration of License:** Three or five years. **Requirements:** U.S. citizen. 18 years old. Bachelors degree and completion of approved program. Never convicted of a felony. **Examination:** Yes. **Fees:** $5 for Professional Certificate (three or five year). $5 for Permanent Certificate.

8119

Speech Language Pathologist
Dept. of Education
Office of Educational Personnel
  Development
1900 Washington St. E
Charleston, WV 25305
Phone: (800)982-2378

Credential Type: Certification. **Duration of License:** Three or five years. **Requirements:** U.S. citizen. 18 years old. Masters degree and completion of approved program. Never convicted of a felony. **Examination:** Yes. **Fees:** $5 for three or five year Certification $5 for Permanent Certification.

Wisconsin

8120

Audiologist
Regulations and Licensing Dept.
Hearing & Speech Board
PO Box 8935
Madison, WI 53708-8935
Phone: (608)266-8609

Credential Type: License. **Requirements:** High school diploma or equivalent. 18 years of age. **Examination:** Written and practical.

8121

Speech Pathologist
Regulations and Licensing Dept.
Hearing & Speech Board
PO Box 8935
Madison, WI 53708-8935
Phone: (608)266-8609

Credential Type: License. **Requirements:** 18 years of age.

Wyoming

8122

Audiologist, Speech Pathologist
State Board of Examiners for Speech
  Pathologists and Audiologists
2008 Gregg Ave.
Worland, WY 82401
Phone: (307)347-2955

Credential Type: License. **Duration of License:** One year. **Requirements:** Completion of a Masters degree in speech pathology or audiology at an accredited university. Completion of a one year clinical fellowship (nine months of which is full time employment). Pass a national examination. **Examination:** Yes. **Fees:** $25 Application. $50 License. $25 Renewal.

8123

School Audiologist
State Dept. of Education
Certification and Accreditation
Services Unit, Hathaway Bldg.
Cheyenne, WY 82002
Phone: (307)777-7291

Credential Type: Audiologist Endorsement. **Requirements:** Master's degree in audiology.

8124

School Speech Pathologist
State Dept. of Education
Certification and Accreditation
Services Unit, Hathaway Bldg.
Cheyenne, WY 82002
Phone: (307)777-7291

Credential Type: Speech Pathologist Endorsement. **Requirements:** Bachelor's degree in speech pathology or communicative disorders. 12 semester hours of professional education.

Stenographers and Court Reporters

The following states grant licenses in this occupational category as of the date of publication:

Alabama	District of	Indiana	Michigan	New Hampshire	Pennsylvania	West Virginia
Alaska	Columbia	Iowa	Minnesota	New Jersey	Rhode Island	Wisconsin
Arizona	Florida	Kansas	Mississippi	New Mexico	South Carolina	
Arkansas	Georgia	Kentucky	Missouri	New York	Tennessee	
California	Hawaii	Louisiana	Montana	North Carolina	Texas	
Colorado	Idaho	Maine	Nebraska	Oklahoma	Utah	
	Illinois	Massachusetts	Nevada	Oregon	Washington	

Alabama

8125

Certified Shorthand Reporter
CSR Chairperson
PO Box 70
Opelika, AL 36801
Phone: (205)749-1020

Credential Type: Shorthand Reporter Certificate. **Authorization:** Certification is voluntary, with legislation pending for mandatory certification. **Requirements:** Pass required state examinations. **Exemptions:** Will grant the voluntary certificate to tested Registered Professional Reporters.

Alaska

8126

Certified Shorthand Reporter
CSR Board
2550 Denali St., No. 1505
Anchorage, AK 99503
Phone: (907)258-7100

Credential Type: Shorthand Reporter Certificate. **Requirements:** Pass required state examinations. Must be a Notary Public.

Arizona

8127

Certified Court Reporter
Management Plus
655 N. Alvernon, No. 108
Tucson, AZ 85711
Phone: (602)325-1055

Credential Type: Court Reporter Certificate. **Authorization:** Notary is not required but is necessary to swear in witnesses. **Requirements:** Pass court test. Examination requires 200 wpm and ability to transcribe with 98.5 percent accuracy.

Arkansas

8128

Certified Court Reporter
Board of Certified Court Reporter
  Examiners
Arkansas Supreme Court
Justice Bldg.
Little Rock, AR 72201
Phone: (501)682-6844

Credential Type: License. **Duration of License:** One year. **Requirements:** 18 years of age. Demonstrate the ability to make a verbatim record of court proceedings. Pass Certified Court Reporter Exam. **Examination:** Yes. **Fees:** $50 Written, oral and practical exams Application and retake if required. $20 Renewal.

California

8129

Certified Shorthand Reporter
Dept. of Consumer Affairs
CSR Board
400 "R" St., No. 2070
Sacramento, CA 95814
Phone: (916)445-5101

Credential Type: Shorthand Reporter Certificate. **Requirements:** 18 years of age. High school graduate or approved equivalent. Good moral character. Must have one of the following: one year of experience in shorthand or machine writing and transcription; a verified certificate which proves completion of an approved program in court reporting; a National Court Reporters Association Registered Professional Reporter (RPR) Certificate or Certificate of Merit; a passing grade on the California state hearing reporters examination; or a valid certified shorthand reporters certificate issued outside of the state of California.

Pass the CSR examination. The English section of the exam is written and requires a score of 70 percent to pass. The Professional Practice section is also a written exam covering legal, medical, and professional practice topics and requires a minimum score of 75 percent. The Reporting and Transcribing portion of the exam includes a 4-voice, 2,000 word dictation at 200 wpm and requires 97.5 percent accuracy to pass. The transcript must be totally typewritten. All three sections of the examination must be successfully passed within a three year period or all sections must be taken again. **Examination:** Certified Shorthand Reporter Examination. **Fees:** $40 examination fee.

Colorado

8130

Certified Shorthand Reporter
Human Resources Office
Colorado Judicial Dept.
1301 Pennsylvania St., Ste. 300
Denver, CO 80203
Phone: (303)837-3695

Credential Type: Permit to practice. **Requirements:** Pass examination with the same standards as the examination for the National Registered Professional Reporter Certificate. Must be a notary. **Examination:** Colorado Shorthand Reporters examination. **Fees:** None.

District of Columbia

8131

Certified Shorthand Reporter
CSR Contact Person
2404 Belle Haven Meadows Ct.
Alexandria, VA 22306
Phone: (703)768-8122

Credential Type: Shorthand Reporter Certificate. **Requirements:** Pass required state examinations. Notary is required to swear in witnesses.

Florida

8132

Certified Shorthand Reporter
Court Reporters Certification
  Program
Supreme Court of Florida
500 N. Duvall
Tallahassee, FL 32399-1900
Phone: (904)488-8628

Credential Type: Shorthand Reporter Certificate. **Requirements:** Must pass CSR examination. **Examination:** Certified Shorthand Reporter Examination. **Reciprocity:** Conditional reciprocity.

8133

Registered Professional Reporter
Court Reporters Certification
  Program
Supreme Court of Florida
500 N. Duvall
Tallahassee, FL 32399-1900
Phone: (904)488-8628

Credential Type: Registered Professional Reporter Certificate. **Requirements:** Must pass Written Knowledge Test (WKT) and Skills portion of the RPR examination. Must pass Florida written examination on court rules. **Examination:** Registered Professional Reporter Examination. **Reciprocity:** Conditional reciprocity.

Georgia

8134

Certified Shorthand Reporter
Board of Court Reporting
Clerk of the Board
244 Washington St. SW, Ste. 550
Atlanta, GA 30334
Phone: (404)656-6422

Credential Type: Shorthand Reporter Certificate "A". **Requirements:** 18 years of age. Good moral character. High school degree or GED. Pass CSR examination. An "A" Certificate requires taking Q & A at 225 wpm, Jury Charge at 200 wpm, Literary at 180 wpm and a written examination. **Examination:** Certified Shorthand Reporter Examination. **Fees:** $50 examination fee. $25 certificate fee.

8135

Registered Professional Reporter
Board of Court Reporting
Clerk of the Board
244 Washington St. SW, Ste. 550
Atlanta, GA 30334
Phone: (404)656-6422

Credential Type: Registered Professional Reporter Certificate "B". **Requirements:** 18 years of age. Good moral character. High school degree or GED. Must pass Written Knowledge Test (WKT) and Skills portion of the RPR examination. A "B" Certificate requires taking Q & A at 190 wpm, Jury Charge at 180 wpm, Literary at 160 wpm, and a basic written examination. **Examination:** Registered Professional Reporter Examination. **Fees:** $50 examination fee. $25 certificate fee.

Hawaii

8136

Shorthand Reporter
Hawaii Board of Certified Shorthand
  Reporters
PO Box 619
Honolulu, HI 96809
Phone: (808)548-2802

Credential Type: License. **Duration of License:** One year. **Requirements:** High school graduate or equivalent. **Examination:** Yes. **Fees:** $50 application, exam and license fee. $50 renewal fee.

Idaho

8137

Certified Shorthand Reporter
Idaho CSR Board
650 W. State, B-83
PO Box 1265
Boise, ID 83701
Phone: (208)334-2517

Credential Type: Shorthand Reporter Certificate. **Requirements:** High school graduate or GED. Must pass CSR examination. Literary/Medical portion of exam requires 160 wpm, Jury Charge or Legal Argument requires 180 wpm, and Q & A requires 200 wpm. Exam also includes a written section. **Examination:** Certified Shorthand Reporter Examination. **Fees:** $25 application fee. $25 examination fee.

Illinois

8138

Certified Shorthand Reporter
Dept. of Professional Regulation
320 W. Washington St., 3rd. Fl.
Springfield, IL 62786
Phone: (217)785-7564

Credential Type: Shorthand Reporter Certificate. **Requirements:** Pass CSR examination. Preliminary portion of the test may be waived if applicant presents a Registered Professional Reporter (RPR) Certificate from the National Court Reporters Association (NCRA) or an Affidavit of Ability from a shorthand reporting school. Must score at least 74 on Written Knowledge test. Dictation Exam requires general dictation at 200 wpm for five minutes and testimony in two voices for five minutes at 225 wpm. Both dictation tests require 95 percent accuracy. Exams may be retaken on approval. No computers allowed. **Examination:** Certified Shorthand Reporter Examination. **Reciprocity:** Reciprocity exists with states that have substantially equivalent requirements. **Fees:** $116.95 Preliminary examination fee. $116.95 Written and Dictation examination fee. $183.90 examination fee (all parts).

Indiana

8139

Certified Shorthand Reporter
ISRA President
PO Box 1103
Michigan City, IN 46340
Phone: (219)873-7008

Credential Type: Shorthand Reporter Certificate. **Authorization:** CSR legislation is pending. **Requirements:** Pass required state CSR examinations. Must be a notary. **Examination:** State CSR examinations.

Iowa

8140

Certified Shorthand Reporter
Iowa Board of Examiners of
 Shorthand Reporters
State Capitol — Iowa Supreme
 Court
Des Moines, IA 50319
Phone: (515)281-5911
Phone: (515)286-3720

Alternate Information: 405C Polk County Courthouse, Des Moines, IA 50309

Credential Type: License. **Duration of License:** One year. **Requirements:** High school diploma or equivalent. Completion of 120 quarter credit hours in a shorthand reporting course. Shorthand speed of 225 words per minute. **Examination:** Written and practical. **Fees:** $25 exam fee. $10 license fee.

Kansas

8141

Certified Shorthand Reporter
Secretary
Shawnee County Courthouse
4th Div. District Court
Topeka, KS 66603
Phone: (913)291-4302

Credential Type: Shorthand Reporter Certificate. **Requirements:** Must have two years of experience or hold a Registered Professional Reporter (RPR) Certificate from the National Court Reporters Association (NCRA) (or Certificate of Merit) or be a graduate from an approved court recording course or be a CSR in another state. Pass CSR examination which requires 2-voice dictation at 225 wpm, 1-voice solid matter dictation at 200 wpm, and 2-voice medical testimony at 180 wpm with 95 percent accuracy. **Examination:** Certified Shorthand Reporter Examination. **Fees:** $35 examination fee.

Kentucky

8142

Certified Shorthand Reporter
CSR Contact Person
111 Holt Lane
Frankfort, KY 40601
Phone: (502)223-7279

Credential Type: Shorthand Reporter Certificate. **Requirements:** Pass required state examinations. Must be a notary. **Examination:** State examinations.

Louisiana

8143

Shorthand Reporter (Certified)
Board of Examiners of Certified
 Shorthand Reporters
325 Loyola Ave., Ste. 306
New Orleans, LA 70112
Phone: (504)523-4306

Credential Type: License. **Duration of License:** One year. **Examination:** Written and verbal exams. **Fees:** $30 initial fee. $85 exam fee. $75 renewal fee.

Maine

8144

Certified Shorthand Reporter
MCRA
U.S. District Ct.
202 Harlow St., Rm. 360
Bangor, ME 04401
Phone: (207)945-0223

Credential Type: Shorthand Reporter Certificate. **Requirements:** Pass State Officials Exam. **Examination:** State Officials Exam.

Massachusetts

8145

Certified Shorthand Reporter
CSR Contact Person
MCRA
13 Short St.
Reading, MA 01867-1014
Phone: (617)342-7305

Credential Type: Shorthand Reporter Certificate. **Authorization:** Mandatory certification for reporters in state courts. Voluntary certification for freelancers. **Requirements:** Pass CSR examination. Must be a notary to swear in witnesses. **Examination:** CSR Examination.

Michigan

8146

Certified Shorthand Reporter
Court Reporting Board of Review
State Court Admin. Office
PO Box 30048
Lansing, MI 48909
Phone: (517)373-9525

Credential Type: Shorthand Reporter Certificate. **Requirements:** Over 18 years of age. Michigan resident. Graduate of an accredited court reporting program. No felony sentence for two years. Pass CSR examination. **Examination:** CSR examination, consistsing of 125-question Written Knowledge Examination and skills examination. Skills portion of exam requires Literary dictation at 180 wpm, Jury Charge 200 wpm, and Q & A 225 wpm. **Fees:** $60 examination fee.

Minnesota

8147

Certified Shorthand Reporter
MCRA
PO Box 433
Stillwater, MN 55082
Phone: (612)430-2776

Credential Type: Shorthand Reporter Certificate. **Authorization:** Legislation is in process. **Requirements:** Pass required state examinations. **Examination:** State examinations.

Mississippi

8148

Certified Shorthand Reporter
CSR Contact Person
PO Box 1384
Biloxi, MS 39533
Phone: (601)374-5066

Credential Type: Shorthand Reporter Certificate. **Authorization:** Voluntary certification with legislation in process for mandatory certification. **Requirements:** High school graduate or GED. One year experience. Must have letter from a CSR or a diploma from a school accredited by the National Court Reporters Association (NCRA) or have a CSR certificate from another state or be a Registered Professional Reporter (RPR) from another state.

Certified Shorthand Reporter, continued

Must pass written knowledge and skills tests. Must be a Notary. **Examination:** Mississippi Written Knowledge and Skills Test. **Reciprocity:** Granted to RPRs from other states on skills only. Granted to CSRs from other states after taking the Written Knowledge Test. **Fees:** $20 skills test fee. $20 written knowledge test. $40 both parts.

Missouri

8149

Certified Court Reporter
CCR Contact Person
PO Box 150
Jefferson City, MO 65102
Phone: (314)751-4144

Credential Type: Court Reporter Certificate. **Authorization:** Certification is mandatory for Official Court Reporters. **Requirements:** One year residency requirement or be a Missouri Certified Shorthand Reporter. Pass Certified Court Reporter (CCR) examination. Thirty days prior to examination students must present proof from an accredited instructor that they have passed a 200 wpm Q & A with 95 percent accuracy. Examination consists of Q & A at 225 wpm, Jury Charge at 180 wpm, Medical Q & A at 200 wpm, and a written knowledge examination. Must be a Notary. **Examination:** Certified Court Reporter Examination. **Fees:** $25 application fee.

8150

Certified Shorthand Reporter
CSR Contact Person
PO Box 405
Cabool, MO 65689
Phone: (417)962-4520

Credential Type: Shorthand Reporter Certificate. **Authorization:** Voluntary CSR for freelancers. Certified Court Reporter (CCR) is mandatory for Official Court Reporters. **Requirements:** Pass required CSR examinations. **Examination:** Certified Shorthand Reporter Examination. **Fees:** $25 application fee.

Montana

8151

Certified Shorthand Reporter
CSR Contact Person
Jeffries Court Reporting
690 SW Higgins
Lewis & Clark Bldg.
Missoula, MT 59801
Phone: (406)721-1143

Credential Type: Shorthand Reporter Certificate. **Requirements:** CSR requirements are being developed. Must be a notary.

Nebraska

8152

Court Reporter
National Court Reporters Association
8224 Old Courthouse Rd.
Vienna, VA 22182
Phone: (703)474-5314

Credential Type: Certificate. **Requirements:** Must be registered with the National Shorthand Reporters Association. **Examination:** Yes. **Fees:** $75 examination fee. $175 membership fee.

Nevada

8153

Shorthand Reporter
Nevada Certified Shorthand
  Reporters Board
PO Box 237
Las Vegas, NV 89125
Phone: (702)384-1663

Credential Type: License. **Duration of License:** One year. **Requirements:** Proof of satisfactory completion of a court reporting program, or a copy of a current license from another state, or a copy of a Registered Professional Reporter certificate from the National Shorthand Reporters Association, or one year of work experience as a shorthand reporter in a non-certifying state. **Examination:** Yes. **Fees:** $35 exam and application fee. $50 certificate fee. $50 renewal fee.

New Hampshire

8154

Certified Shorthand Reporter
CSR Board
235A Black Brook Rd.
Goffstown, NH 03045
Phone: (603)669-7410

Credential Type: Shorthand Reporter Certificate. **Requirements:** Pass CSR examination which requires Q & A dictation at 225 wpm, Jury Charge at 200 wpm, and Literary at 180 wpm. No computer transcription allowed. Notary is not required but is advised. **Examination:** Certified Shorthand Reporter Examination. **Reciprocity:** Granted to Registered Professional Reporters (RPR)s and CSRs from other states who have passed examinations equivalent to those of New Hampshire.

New Jersey

8155

Court Reporter
Board of Shorthand Reporting
1100 Raymond Blvd., Rm. 509
Newark, NJ 07102
Phone: (201)648-3697

Credential Type: Certified Shorthand Reporter. **Duration of License:** Two years. **Requirements:** High school diploma or equivalent. 18 years of age. State residency. **Examination:** Yes. **Fees:** $75 exam fee. $50 biennial registration fee. **Governing Statute:** NJSA 45:15B. NJAC 13:43.

New Mexico

8156

Certified Shorthand Reporter
Board Governing Recording of
  Judicial Proceedings
State Supreme Court Bldg.
237 Don Gaspar
Santa Fe, NM 87503
Phone: (505)827-4834

Credential Type: Shorthand Reporter Certificate. **Requirements:** Pass CSR examination. Written Knowledge portion of test requires 80 percent accuracy. Skills portion requires Q & A dictation at 225 wpm, expert testimony at 200 wpm, and literary material at 180 wpm. All skills tests are for five minutes and require 95 percent accuracy. **Examination:** Certified Shorthand Reporter Examination. **Reciprocity:** Granted to Registered Professional Reporters (RPR)s and CSRs from other states who have passed equivalent examinations or hold a Certificate of Proficiency and/or Certificate of Merit from the National Court Reporters Association (NCRA). Must have three years experience in court reporting in the four years immediately prior to application. **Fees:** $50 oral examination fee. $50 written examination fee. $75 oral and written examination fee. $50 reciprocal certificate fee.

New York

8157

Certified Shorthand Reporter
State Education Dept.
Div. of Professional Licensing Services
Cultural Education Center
Empire State Plaza
Albany, NY 12230
Phone: (518)474-5170

Credential Type: License. **Duration of License:** Three years. **Requirements:** High school diploma plus completion of approved course in shorthand reporting. Three years of satisfactory experience with post-secondary training. 21 years of age. **Examination:** Written and practical. **Fees:** $165 license fee. $50 renewal fee. **Governing Statute:** Title VIII Articles 130, 151 of the Education Law.

North Carolina

8158

Certified Shorthand Reporter
Board of Examiners for Court Reporting Standards and Testing
PO Box 2448
Raleigh, NC 27602
Phone: (919)733-7107

Credential Type: Shorthand Reporter Certificate. **Authorization:** Required for work in the General Court of Justice and Superior or District Court Division. **Requirements:** Must pass CSR examination. Must pass Written Knowledge portion of exam with 75 percent accuracy. Skills portion requires Literary dictation at 160 wpm, Jury Charge at 180 wpm, and Q & A at 200 wpm. Each portion of Skills test requires 95 percent accuracy to pass. If either portion of exam is failed, both portions must be taken again. **Examination:** Certified Shorthand Reporter Examination. **Fees:** None.

8159

Registered Professional Reporter
Board of Examiners for Court Reporting Standards and Testing
PO Box 2448
Raleigh, NC 27602
Phone: (919)733-7107

Credential Type: Shorthand Reporter Certificate. **Authorization:** Allows one year of conditional employment in the General Court of Justice and Superior or District Court Division. **Requirements:** Must pass RPR examination. **Examination:** Registered Professional Reporter Examination. **Fees:** None.

Oklahoma

8160

Shorthand Reporter, Certified
Board of Examiners Official Shorthand Reporters
1915 N. Stiles
Oklahoma City, OK 73132
Phone: (405)557-7600

Credential Type: License. **Duration of License:** Two years. **Requirements:** Attend a court reporting school. No criminal convictions. **Examination:** Certified Shorthand Reporter Test. **Fees:** $75—$150 exam fee. $75—$150 application fee. $75 renewal fee.

Oregon

8161

Shorthand Reporter, Certified
Bureau of Labor & Industries
800 NE Oregon St. No. 32, Ste. 1160
Portland, OR 97201
Phone: (503)731-4074

Credential Type: Certification. **Duration of License:** Two years. **Requirements:** High school diploma or GED. Must be a person who has not, within the past five years, had a shorthand reporter's license, registration or certificate denied, suspended or revoked. **Examination:** Yes. **Fees:** $50 exam fee. $100 certificate fee. $100 renewal fee. **Governing Statute:** ORS 703.400 to 703.414 and 703.860.

Pennsylvania

8162

Certified Court Reporter
CCR Contact Person
2846 N. 2nd St.
Harrisburg, PA 17110
Phone: (717)255-2839

Credential Type: Court Reporter Certificate. **Requirements:** Legislation is pending.

Rhode Island

8163

Certified Shorthand Reporter
Court Administrator
Superior Court
250 Benefit St.
Providence, RI 02903
Phone: (401)277-3215

Credential Type: Shorthand Reporter Certificate. **Requirements:** Must pass court skills test. Freelancers are required to be notaries; officials are not. **Examination:** Court skills test.

South Carolina

8164

Certified Shorthand Reporter
CSR Contact Person
142 George Addy Rd.
Little Mountain, SC 29075
Phone: (803)345-6587

Credential Type: Shorthand Reporter Certificate. **Requirements:** Pass CSR examination. English Knowledge written exam requires 86 percent accuracy. Skills test requires Jury Charge dictation at 200 wpm and Testimony at 225 wpm. Freelancers are required to be Notaries (Officials are not). **Examination:** Certified Shorthand Reporter Examination. **Exemptions:** Examination may be waived for Registered Professional Reporters (RPR)s and CMs.

Tennessee

8165

Certified Shorthand Reporter
CSR Board
PO Box 447
Chattanooga, TN 37401
Phone: (615)756-0221

Credential Type: Shorthand Reporter Certificate. **Authorization:** Certification is voluntary. **Requirements:** Pass required examinations or be a Registered Professional Reporter (RPR). **Reciprocity:** Granted to RPRs or individuals from other states who have passed testing equivalent to Tennessee's.

Texas

8166

Certified Shorthand Reporter
Court Reporters Certification Board
PO Box 13131
Austin, TX 78711-3131
Phone: (512)463-1630
Fax: (512)463-1117

Credential Type: Shorthand Reporters Certificate. **Duration of License:** Two years. **Requirements:** Pass CSR examination. Part A of exam consists of 2-voice, five minute, dictation of Q & A at 225 wpm, five minutes of Jury Charge at 200 wpm, and five minutes of literary materials at 180 wpm. Each portion of Part A must be passed with a minimum of 95 percent. Part B is a written examination that must be passed with a minimum of 75 percent. **Examination:** Certified Shorthand Reporter Examination. **Fees:** $85 application fee. $75 examination fee (both parts). $50 written examination fee only. $75 oral examination fee only. $100 certification biennial renewal fee.

8167

Court Reporter
Court Reporters Certification Board
PO Box 13131
Austin, TX 78711
Phone: (512)463-1630

Credential Type: License. **Duration of License:** Two years. **Requirements:** Certification in either written shorthand, machine shorthand, oral stenography, or any other method authorized by Supreme Court of Texas. Experience, education, or training sufficient to allow applicant to fulfill the responsibilities of a court reporter. **Examination:** Oral and written. **Fees:** $85 application fee. $75 exam fee. $100 renewal fee. **Governing Statute:** Government Code 52.001.

Utah

8168

Certified Shorthand Reporter
Dept. of Commerce
Div. of Occupational and
   Professional Licensing
160 E. 300 S.
PO Box 45802
Salt Lake City, UT 84145
Phone: (801)530-6628

Credential Type: License. **Duration of License:** One year. **Requirements:** 18 years of age. **Examination:** Yes. **Fees:** $35 license fee. $25 renewal fee.

Washington

8169

Certified Shorthand Reporter
Dept. of Licensing
PO Box 9649
Olympia, WA 98504
Phone: (206)753-1061

Credential Type: Shorthand Reporter Certificate. **Requirements:** CSR examination. Skills examination requires five minute Testimony dictation at 200 wpm with 95 percent accuracy. **Examination:** Certified Shorthand Reporter Exam. **Fees:** $125 examination fee.

Credential Type: Temporary Certified Shorthand Reporter Certificate. **Duration of License:** One year. **Requirements:** Must be out-of-state CSR, or Registered Professional Reporter (RPR), or graduate of a court reporting school.

West Virginia

8170

Certified Shorthand Reporter
Deputy Director
Administrative Office E-402
State Capitol
Charleston, WV 25305
Phone: (304)348-0145

Credential Type: Shorthand Reporter Certificate. **Authorization:** Certification mandatory of Official Court Reporters, voluntary for freelancers. **Requirements:** Pass CSR examination. Must pass five minute dictation with 95 percent accuracy in each of the following: Medical at 160 wpm; Jury Charge at 180 wpm; and Q & A at 200 wpm. Written Knowledge Exam requires 70 percent accuracy. **Examination:** Certified Shorthand Reporter Examination. **Reciprocity:** Granted to tested Registered Professional Reporters (RPR)s. **Fees:** $25 examination fee.

Wisconsin

8171

Registered Professional Reporter
Court Management Asst.
Supreme Court of Wisconsin
Director of State Courts
110 E. Main St., Ste. 430
Madison, WI 53703
Phone: (608)266-3501

Credential Type: Preofessional Reporter Certificate. **Requirements:** Must pass National Court Reporters Association (NCRA) Registered Professional Reporter (RPR) examination. **Examination:** NCRA Registered Professional Reporter Examination.

Surveyors

The following states grant licenses in this occupational category as of the date of publication:

Alabama	Florida	Kentucky	Missouri	North Carolina	South Dakota	Wisconsin
Alaska	Georgia	Louisiana	Montana	North Dakota	Tennessee	Wyoming
Arizona	Hawaii	Maine	Nebraska	Ohio	Texas	
Arkansas	Idaho	Maryland	Nevada	Oklahoma	Utah	
California	Illinois	Massachusetts	New Hampshire	Oregon	Vermont	
Colorado	Indiana	Michigan	New Jersey	Pennsylvania	Virginia	
Connecticut	Iowa	Minnesota	New Mexico	Rhode Island	Washington	
Delaware	Kansas	Mississippi	New York	South Carolina	West Virginia	

Alabama

8172

Land Surveyor
Alabama State Board of Registration for Professional Engineers and Land Surveyors
301 Interstate Park Dr.
Montgomery, AL 36130-1001
Phone: (205)242-5568

Credential Type: License. **Duration of License:** One year. **Requirements:** Must be a college graduate in civil or mining engineering and must have completed two to four years of apprenticeship under the supervision of a registered land surveyor; or be a non-college graduate who has completed eight years of apprenticeship. **Examination:** 16-hour written examination. **Fees:** $25 application fee. $25 registration fee. $25 renewal fee.

Alaska

8173

Land Surveyor
Dept. of Commerce and Economic Development
Div. of Occupational Licensing
State Board of Registration for Architects, Engineers and Land Surveyors
PO Box D
Juneau, AK 99811-0800
Phone: (907)465-2540

Credential Type: Certificate of registration. **Duration of License:** Two years. **Requirements:** Good character and reputation. Five references, including three from land surveyors. To be eligible for fundamentals of land surveying exam, applicant must have at least four years experience. To be elibigle for the professional land surveyor exam, applicant must have passed the fundamentals of land surveying exam and submit evidence that applicant has the appropriate combination of eight years education and experience. **Examination:** Fundamentals of land surveying exam (land surveyor-intraining). NCEE principles and practices of land surveying. Alaska land surveying exam. **Reciprocity:** Yes. **Fees:** $30 application fee. $130 application fee for license by comity. $100 registration fee. $100 biennial renewal fee. $50 fee for having exam proctored out of state. $50 fundamentals of land surveying. $50 NCEE principles and practices of land surveying sections. $40 NCEE principles and practices of land surveying, Part IIA. $35 Alaska land surveying exam. **Governing Statute:** Alaska Statutes 08.48. Professional Regulations 12 AAC 36.

Arizona

8174

Land Surveyor
Board of Technical Registration
1951 W. Camelback, Ste. 250
Phoenix, AZ 85015
Phone: (602)255-4053

Credential Type: Registration to practice. **Duration of License:** Three years. **Requirements:** Be of good moral character. Have at least six years education or experience, or combination of both with at least two years of experience. Pass in-training and professional examination administered by the board. **Examination:** Land surveyor-in-training exam (fundamentals). Professional land surveyor exam: principles and practices, public domain, and Arizona surveying methods and legal principles. **Exemptions:** The in-training exam may be waived for candidates who have a degree in land surveying. **Fees:** $90 application fee. National exam fees: $50 fundamentals, $50 principles and practices, $50 public domain. $120 local exam fee (Arizona surveying methods and legal principles). $126 renewal fee.

Credential Type: Registration without examination. **Requirements:** Hold a valid registration in another state, jurisdiction, territory, or country. Meet experience and education requirements similar to those of Arizona, or have been actively engaged in the profession for at least 10 years. **Fees:** $90 application fee. $126 renewal fee.

8175

Land Surveyor-in-Training
Board of Technical Registration
1951 W. Camelback, Ste. 250
Phoenix, AZ 85015
Phone: (602)255-4053

Credential Type: In-training registration. **Requirements:** Be of good moral character. To qualify for the in-training examination on the basis of education, must be a graduate of a four-year land surveying degree program of an accredited college or university.

To qualify for the in-training examination on the basis of experience, must have at least four years of education or experience or both directly related to the practice of land surveying. **Examination:** Land surveyor-in-training examination (fundamentals). **Fees:** $30 application fee. $50 exam fee.

Arkansas

8176

Land Surveyor
Arkansas State Board of Registration for Professional Engineers and Land Surveyors
TCB Bldg., Ste. 700
PO Box 2541
North Little Rock, AR 72203
Phone: (501)371-2517

Credential Type: License. **Duration of License:** One year. **Requirements:** 21 years of age. Graduate of an approved engineering curriculum plus two years of land surveying experience; or, Graduate of a two year surveying technology curriculum plus two years of land surveying experience; or, six years of progressive land surveying experience and pass an examination. **Examination:** Yes. **Fees:** $40 Written examination. $35 Application. $15 Renewal.

8177

Land Surveyor in Training
Arkansas State Board of Registration for Professional Engineers and Land Surveyors
TCB Bldg., Ste. 700
PO Box 2541
North Little Rock, AR 72203
Phone: (501)371-2517

Credential Type: License. **Duration of License:** One year. **Requirements:** Graduate of an approved engineering curriculum; or, graduate of a two year surveying technology curriculum; or, four years experience and pass an examination. **Examination:** Yes. **Fees:** $27.50 Written examination. $10 Application. $5 Renewal.

California

8178

Professional Land Surveyor
Board of Registration for Professional Engineers and Land Surveyors
PO Box 349002
Sacramento, CA 95825-9002
Phone: (916)920-7466

Credential Type: Professional Land Surveyor Registration. **Duration of License:** Four years following initial period of one year. **Requirements:** Complete six years of full-time surveying experience or a combination of surveying education and experience. Submit four professional references. **Examination:** Fundamentals of Land Surveying Examination. Principles and Practice of Land Surveying. **Exemptions:** The Fundamentals of Land Surveying Examination may be waived for the following: Registered Professional Engineers, Certified Engineers-in-Training, graduates of an approved four-year land surveying curriculum with 15 years of experience, and graduates of an non-approved land surveying curriculum with 17 years of experience. **Fees:** $175 registration fee. $115 renewal fee. **Governing Statute:** Business and Professions Code, Chap. 15, Div. 3, Sections 8700 et seq. and Chap. 7, Div. 3. California Code of Regulations, Title 16, Chap. 5, Sections 400-471.

Colorado

8179

Land Surveyor-in-Training
Board of Registration for Professional Engineers and Professional Land Surveyors
Dept. of Regulatory Agencies
Div. of Registrations
1560 Broadway, Ste. 1370
Denver, CO 80202
Phone: (303)894-7788

Credential Type: Land Surveyor-in-Training Certificate. **Requirements:** Be a high school graduate or equivalent. Have two or more years of progressive land surveying experience, of which a maximum of one year of educational credit may be substituted. **Examination:** Fundamentals of surveying examination. **Reciprocity:** Yes, if applicant is licensed in good standing in another jurisdiction requiring qualifications substantially equivalent to Colorado's. **Fees:** License, renewal, and exam fees. **Governing Statute:** Colorado Revised Statutes, Title 12, Article 25.

8180

Professional Land Surveyor
Board of Registration for Professional Engineers and Professional Land Surveyors
Dept. of Regulatory Agencies
Div. of Registrations
1560 Broadway, Ste. 1370
Denver, CO 80202
Phone: (303)894-7788

Credential Type: Professional Surveyor License. **Requirements:** Must provide documentation of technical competence. Must meet one of the following sets of requirements:

(1) Be a high school graduate or equivalent. Have six years of progressive land surveying experience, of which educational study may be a part and of which two years were under supervision of a professional land surveyor or exempted federal employee. Have been certified as a surveyor-in-training in Colorado.

(2) Have graduated from a board-approved surveying curriculum of four or more years. Have two years of progressive land surveying experience, of which educational study may be a part and of which two years were under supervision of a professional land surveyor or exempted federal employee. Have been certified as a surveyor-in-training in Colorado. **Examination:** Principles and practices of surveying examination. Legal aspects of surveying examination. **Reciprocity:** Yes, if applicant is licensed in good standing in another jurisdiction requiring qualifications substantially equivalent to Colorado's. **Fees:** License, renewal, and exam fees. **Governing Statute:** Colorado Revised Statutes, Title 12, Article 25.

Connecticut

8181

Land Surveyor
Board of Professional Engineers & Land Surveyors
Professional Licensing Div.
Consumer Protection Dept.
165 Capitol Ave.
Hartford, CT 06106
Phone: (203)566-1814

Credential Type: Land Surveyor's License. **Duration of License:** One year. **Requirements:** Graduate from a school or college approved by the board and complete an approved course in surveying. At least three years active practice in land surveying. In lieu of graduation board may accept six or more years of experience in surveying work. **Examination:** Fundamentals of Land Surveying Examination and Principles and Practice of Land Surveying of the National Council of Examiners for Engineering and Surveying (NCEES). **Exemptions:** Written exam may be waived for applicants with at least 16 years of practice in surveying work, at least 10 of which shall have been in land surveying. **Reciprocity:** Yes. **Fees:** $150 application fee (land surveyor license or combined land surveyor and professional engineer license). $225 annual renewal fee. **Governing Statute:** General Statutes of Connecticut, Chap. 391.

Surveyors | 8185 Georgia

8182

Land Surveyor-in-Training
Board of Professional Engineers & Land Surveyors
Professional Licensing Div.
Consumer Protection Dept.
165 Capitol Ave.
Hartford, CT 06106
Phone: (203)566-1814

Credential Type: Surveyor-in-training license. **Duration of License:** 10 years. **Requirements:** Graduate of a school or college approved by the board, or be scheduled to graduate within three months; or have six years experience in surveying work. Pass Fundamentals of Land Surveying Examination. **Examination:** Fundamentals of Land Surveying Examination of the National Council of Examiners for Engineering and Surveying (NCEES). **Reciprocity:** Yes. **Fees:** $32 application fee. **Governing Statute:** General Statutes of Connecticut, Chap. 391.

Delaware

8183

Land Surveyor
Registration for Professional Land Surveyors
Dept. of Administrative Services
Div. of Professional Regulation
PO Box 1401
Dover, DE 19903
Phone: (302)739-4522

Credential Type: Land surveyor certificate of registration. **Duration of License:** Two years. **Requirements:** Be at least 23 years of age. Good character and reputation. Complete appropriate examination. Provide at least five references, of which three are from professional land surveyors. Meet at least one of the following requirements:

(1) Graduate of a surveying curriculum of four years or more. Have at least three years of combined office and field experience in responsible charge of land surveying projects under the direct supervision of a professional land surveyor. Experience may not be concurrent with education; or

(2) Graduate of a surveying or related science curriculum of four years or more. Have at least five years of combined office and field experience in responsible charge of land surveying projects under the direct supervision of a professional land surveyor. Experience may not be concurrent with education; or

(3) Complete a 32 semester hour, or its academic equivalent, course of study in surveying or surveying-related subjects. Have at least six years of combined office and field experience in responsible charge of land surveying projects under the direct supervision of a professional land surveyor; or

(4) Have at least 10 years of combined office and field experience in responsible charge of land surveying projects under the direct supervision of a professional land surveyor. **Examination:** Fundamentals of land surveying. Principles and practices of land surveying. **Reciprocity:** Yes, provided that the requirements for licensure or registration are equal to or greater than those of Deleware. Applicant must complete examination administered by the board. **Fees:** $159 application and initial license fee. $149 renewal fee.

Florida

8184

Professional Land Surveyor
Board of Professional Land Surveyors Board
Dept. of Professional Regulation
1940 N. Monroe St.
Tallahassee, FL 32399-0750
Phone: (904)488-9912

Credential Type: License by Examination. **Duration of License:** Two years. **Requirements:** Good moral character. Meet one of the following sets of requirements: (1) Graduate of an approved course of study in land surveying from a college or university recognized by the board. Course of study must include at least 32 semester hours or academic equivalent in the science of land surveying or in board-approved land-survey-related courses. At least four years of experience as a subordinate to a professional land surveyor in the active practice of land surveying, which experience was in responsible charge of accuracy and correctness.

(2) Graduate of a four-year course of study, other than land surveying, from an accredited college or university. Course of study in disciplines other than land surveying must include at least 32 semester hours or academic equivalent, 25 hours of which shall be in land surveying or related subjects. At least six years of experience as a subordinate to a professional land surveyor in the active practice of land surveying, five years of which were in responsible charge of accuracy and correctness.

(3) Successfully complete a 32-semester-hour, or its academic equivalent, course of study in land surveying or in board-approved, land-survey-related courses at an accredited college or university. At least six years of experience as a subordinate to a professional land surveyor in the active practice of land surveying, five years of which were in responsible charge of accuracy and correctness. Must have begun work experience prior to October 1, 1988.

(4) High school graduate. At least eight years of experience as a subordinate to a professional land surveyor in the active practice of land surveying, six years of which were in responsible charge of accuracy and correctness. Must have begun work experience prior to October 1, 1988.

(5) At least 10 years of active duty in the military service of the United States, with a Military Occupational Specialty classification of 82 and a minimum skill level of 40, six years of which were in responsible charge of accuracy and correctness.

Renewal requires at least 24 hours of continuing education per biennial period. **Examination:** National Council of Engineering Examiners (NCEE) examination. Part 1—Land Surveying Fundamentals. Part 2—Professional Practice and Principles. **Fees:** $200 application and examination fee. $125 initial licensure fee. $200 renewal fee. **Governing Statute:** Florida Statutes, Chapter 472. Rules of the Board of Professional Land Surveyors, Chapter 21HH, F.A.C.

Credential Type: License by Endorsement. **Duration of License:** Two years. **Requirements:** Meet one of the following sets of requirements: (1) Have passed a substantially equivalent national, regional, state, or territorial licensing examination. Meet the experience requirements of a License by Examination. (2) Hold a valid license to practice engineering issued by another state or territory of the United States. Criteria for issuance must have been substantially identical to Florida's.

Renewal requires at least 24 hours of continuing education per biennial period. **Fees:** $100 registration by endorsement fee. **Governing Statute:** Florida Statutes, Chapter 472. Rules of the Board of Professional Land Surveyors, Chapter 21HH, F.A.C.

Georgia

8185

Land Surveyor
State Board of Professional Engineers and Land Surveyors
Professional Examining Boards
166 Pryor St., SW
Atlanta, GA 30303
Phone: (404)656-3926

Credential Type: Certificate of Registration. **Duration of License:** Two years. **Requirements:** Meet one of the following sets

1155

Georgia 8186

Land Surveyor, continued

of requirements: (1) Certification as a land surveyor-in-training by having a bachelor's degree in a board-approved curriculum, with a minimum of 15 quarter hours or equivalent in land surveying subjects. Have at least four years of combined office and field experience in land surveying, with a minimum of three years of responsible charge experience under the supervision of a registered land surveyor. (2) Certification as a land surveyor-in-training by having an associate degree or equivalent in a board-approved curriculum, with a minimum of 15 quarter hours or equivalent in land surveying subjects, and two years combined office and field experience in land surveying. Acquire at least four additional years of combined office and field experience in land surveying, with a minimum total of four years of responsible charge experience under the supervision of a registered land surveyor. (3) Certification as a land surveyor-in-training by having a high school diploma or equivalent, completing course of study necessary for land surveying, and having at least four years experience in land surveying. Acquire an additional four years of experience, with a total of at least six years of responsible charge experience under the supervision of a registered land surveyor. **Examination:** Principles and Practices of Land Surveying. **Reciprocity:** Registration by comity may be granted to any individual who holds a certificate of registration issued by a state, territory, or possession of the United States, provided it was obtained by qualifications similar to Georgia's and applicant passes a written examination on the relevant laws of Georgia. **Fees:** $30 exam application fee. $105 exam fee (Parts II and III). $90 exam fee (Part II, Principles and Practices only). $55 exam fee (Part III, Georgia Law only). $50 renewal fee. $70 application fee for comity. **Governing Statute:** Official Code of Georgia Annotated 43-15.

8186

Land Surveyor-in-Training
State Board of Professional
   Engineers and Land Surveyors
Professional Examining Boards
166 Pryor St., SW
Atlanta, GA 30303
Phone: (404)656-3926

Credential Type: Land Surveyor-in-Training Certificate. **Duration of License:** Two years. **Requirements:** Meet one of the following sets of requirements: (1) Bachelor's degree in a board-approved curriculum, with a minimum of 15 quarter hours or equivalent in land surveying subjects. (2) Associate degree or equivalent in a board-approved curriculum, with a minimum of 15 quarter hours or equivalent in land surveying subjects. Have two years combined office and field experience in land surveying. (3) High school diploma or equivalent. Complete course of study necessary for land surveying. Have at least four years experience in land surveying. **Examination:** Fundamentals of Land Surveying. **Fees:** $25 exam application fee. $82.50 exam fee (Fundamentals of Land Surveying). **Governing Statute:** Official Code of Georgia Annotated 43-15.

Hawaii

8187

Land Surveyor
Hawaii Board of Engineers,
   Architects, Surveyors and
   Landscape Architects
Dept. of Commerce and Consumer
   Affairs
PO Box 3469
Honolulu, HI 96801
Phone: (808)548-8542

Credential Type: License. **Duration of License:** Six months. **Requirements:** Graduation from a four-year geoscience, civil engineering or general engineering curriculum, plus three years of experience; or graduation from a four-year arts and science curriculum plus seven years of experience; or graduation from a two-year civil engineering technology curriculum plus seven years of experience; or 11 years of land surveying experience. Three letters of recommendation from professional land surveyors. Separate requirements for applicants taking the FLS exam only. **Examination:** Five exams. **Exemptions:** Parts of the NCEE exam may be waived if passed in another state. **Fees:** $50 application fee. $205 exam fee. $30 license fee. $15 $30 Compliance Resolution Fund fee. $30 renewal fee.

Idaho

8188

Land Surveyor-in-Training
Board of Registration of Professional
   Engineers and Professional Land
   Surveyors
600 S. Orchard, Ste. A
Boise, ID 83705-1242
Phone: (208)334-3860

Credential Type: Certificate of Registration. **Duration of License:** One year. **Requirements:** Meet one of the following sets of requirements: (1) Graduation from an approved land surveying curriculum of four years or more from a board-approved college or university. (2) Complete two years of approved formal education in a school or college above high school level of at least 60 semester hours. Complete at least three years of combined office and field experience. (3) Demonstrate equivalent knowledge and skill to that of a graduate from an approved land surveying curriculum. Complete at least four years of combined office and field experience. **Examination:** Land Surveying Fundamentals. **Fees:** Contact board for fees. **Governing Statute:** Idaho Code, Title 54, Chap. 12.

8189

Professional Land Surveyor
Board of Registration of Professional
   Engineers and Professional Land
   Surveyors
600 S. Orchard, Ste. A
Boise, ID 83705-1242
Phone: (208)334-3860

Credential Type: Certificate of Registration. **Duration of License:** One year. **Requirements:** Meet one of the following sets of requirements: (1) Graduation from an approved land surveying curriculum of four years or more from a board-approved college or university. Complete four years of combined office and field experience, with at least two years of progressive experience in responsible charge of surveying work. (2) Complete two years of approved formal education in a school or college above high school level of at least 60 semester hours. Pass a fundamentals of land surveying examination. Complete at least six years of combined office and field experience, with at least two years of progressive experience in responsible charge of surveying work. (3) In lieu of graduation from an approved land surveying curriculum, demonstrate equivalent knowledge and skill by passing a fundamentals of land surveying examination. Complete at least eight years of combined office and field experience, with at least three years of progressive experience in responsible charge of surveying work. **Examination:** Land Surveying Fundamentals. Principles and Practice of Land Surveying. **Fees:** Contact board for fees. **Governing Statute:** Idaho Code, Title 54, Chap. 12.

Surveyors — Maine

Illinois

8190

Land Surveyor
Illinois Dept. of Professional Regulations
320 W. Washingtion St.
Springfield, IL 62786
Phone: (217)782-8556

Credential Type: Land Surveyor-In-Training License. **Duration of License:** 10 years (no renewal). **Requirements:** Good moral character. Bachelor's degree in land surveying or a related degree in science which includes a minimum of 24 semester hours in land surveying. **Examination:** National Council of Examiners for Engineering and Surveying (NCEES) Fundamentals of Land Surveying Examination. **Reciprocity:** No. **Fees:** $76.30 examination fee. $20 license fee. **Governing Statute:** Illinois Professional Land Surveyor Act of 1989, Illinois Revised Statutes 1991, Chapter 111.

Credential Type: Professional Land Surveyor License. **Duration of License:** Two years. **Requirements:** Good moral character. U.S. citizen or legal alien. Bachelor's degree in land surveying or a related degree in science which includes a minimum of 24 semester hours in land surveying. Hold a Land Surveyor-In-Training License and have a minimum of four years experience in responsible charge. Pass examinations. **Examination:** National Council of Examiners for Engineering and Surveying (NCEES) Fundamentals of Land Survey Examination. NCEES Principles and Practice of Land Surveying Examination. National Council of Engineering Public Domain Examination. Illinois State Specific Jurisdiction Examination. **Reciprocity:** Yes, considered on an individual basis. **Fees:** $189.65 examination fee (all four exams). $25 initial license fee. $50 license by endorsement fee. $40 renewal fee. **Governing Statute:** Illinois Professional Land Surveyor Act of 1989, Illinois Revised Statutes 1991, Chapter 111.

Indiana

8191

Land Surveyor
State Board of Registration for Professional Engineers and Land Surveyors
Professional Licensing Agency
1021 State Office Bldg.
100 N. Senate Ave.
Indianapolis, IN 46204
Phone: (317)232-2980

Credential Type: License. **Requirements:** Contact licensing body for application information.

Iowa

8192

Land Surveyor
Engineering and Land Surveying Examining Board
1918 SE Hulsizer
Ankeny, IA 50021
Phone: (515)281-5602

Credential Type: License. **Duration of License:** Two years. **Requirements:** A minimum or two years of post-secondary education that includes courses in mathematics and the physical sciences, plus four years of acceptable experience as a land surveyor-in-training. **Examination:** Land Surveyor Practice exam.

Kansas

8193

Land Surveyor
State Board of Technical Professions
LSOB, 900 SW Jackson, Rm. 507
Topeka, KS 66612-1257
Phone: (913)296-3053

Credential Type: Professional Land Surveyor License. **Duration of License:** Two years. **Requirements:** Must be a resident of Kansas. Meet one of the following sets of requirements: (1) Graduate of an accredited four-year engineering or surveying curriculum, plus two years of additional experience. (2) Graduate of an accredited two-year surveying curriculum, plus two years of additional experience. (3) Non-graduate with some acceptable college credits up to four years, plus four years of experience. (4) Non-graduate plus four years of experience. **Examination:** Fundamentals of Land Surveying. Principles and Practices of Land Surveying. **Fees:** Contact board for fees.

Kentucky

8194

Land Surveyor
Kentucky State Board of Registration for Professional Engineers and Land Surveyors
160 Democrate Dr.
Frankfort, KY 40601
Phone: (502)564-2680

Credential Type: License. **Duration of License:** Two years. **Requirements:** A bachelor's degree and four years of work experience. Applicants with no degree need eight years of work experience. **Examination:** Yes. **Reciprocity:** Yes. **Fees:** $120 exam fee. $40 registration fee. $30 application fee. $80 renewal fee.

Louisiana

8195

Land Surveyor
State Board of Registration for Professional Engineers and Land Surveyors
1055 Saint Charles Ave., Ste. 415
New Orleans, LA 70130
Phone: (504)568-8450

Credential Type: License. **Duration of License:** Two years. **Requirements:** Bachelor's degree in land surveying. A minimum of four years of acceptable land surveying experience. **Examination:** Written, practical and oral exam. **Fees:** $50 exam fee. $25 license fee. $25 renewal fee.

Maine

8196

Land Surveyor
Board of Licensure for Professional Land Surveyors
Dept. of Professional and Financial Regulation
Div. of Licensing and Enforcement
State House Station 35
Augusta, ME 04333
Phone: (207)582-8723

Credential Type: Professional Land Surveyor License. **Duration of License:** Two years. **Requirements:** Meet one of the following sets of requirements: (1) Hold a valid Maine license as a Land-Surveyor-in-Training. Complete two years of experience. Pass Principles and Practices examination. (2) Hold a license as a Land Surveyor-in-Training from another state issued on comparable qualifications. Complete

Land Surveyor, continued

two years of experience after Land Surveyor-in-Training license was issued. Pass Principles and Practices examination. (3) Hold a license as a Land Surveyor from another state issued on comparable qualifications. Complete two years of experience after Land Surveyor license was issued. Pass Principles and Practices examination. **Examination:** Principles and Practices of Land Surveying. **Fees:** $50 application fee. $150 exam fee. $140 license fee. $140 renewal fee. **Governing Statute:** 32 M.S.R.A. Chap 121.

Credential Type: Land Surveyor-in-Training License. **Duration of License:** Two years. **Requirements:** Demonstrate mastery of the fundamentals of land surveying by successfully passing the Fundamentals of Land Surveying Examination and submitting evidence of at least seven years of experience. Completion of a core curriculum counts toward one year of the experience requirement. Completion of a core curriculum and an associate's degree in equivalent to five years of the experience requirement. A baccalaureate degree is equivalent to seven years of the experience requirement. **Examination:** Fundamentals of Land Surveying. **Fees:** $50 application fee. $75 exam fee. $75 license fee. $75 renewal fee.

Maryland

8197

Land Surveyor
Board of Registration for
 Professional Land Surveyors
Dept. of Licensing and Regulation
501 St. Paul Pl.
Baltimore, MD 21202-2272
Phone: (410)333-6322

Credential Type: Licensed Land Surveyor. **Duration of License:** Two years. **Requirements:** Meet one of the following sets of requirements: (1) Graduate from a college or university upon completion of at least a four-year curriculum in engineering or land surveying that is approved by the board. Complete at least four years of experience in land surveying. Graduate study in land surveying may count toward fulfillment of up to one year of the experience requirement. Pass examinations. (2) Graduate from a college or university upon completion of at least a four-year curriculum in engineering or land surveying that is not approved by the board. Complete at least six years of experience in land surveying. Graduate study in land surveying may count toward fulfillment of up to one year of the experience requirement. Pass examinations. (3) Have at least 12 years of experience in land surveying. Undergraduate study in land surveying may count toward fulfillment of up to one year of the experience requirement. Pass principles and practices examination. **Examination:** Fundamentals of Land Surveying. Principles and Practices of Land Surveying. **Fees:** $105 license fee. **Governing Statute:** Annotated Code of Maryland, Title 15. Code of Maryland Regulations, Title 09, Subtitle 13.

Credential Type: Limited License. **Duration of License:** One year. **Authorization:** Valid only for the specific job for which it is issued. **Requirements:** May be issued to an individual who is licensed to practice land surveying in another state, does not have a place of business in this state and is not a resident of this state. **Fees:** $25 application fee. **Governing Statute:** Annotated Code of Maryland, Title 15. Code of Maryland Regulations, Title 09, Subtitle 13.

Credential Type: Temporary License. **Duration of License:** 30 days or until license application has been considered. **Authorization:** Allows applicant to practice land surveying while license application is being considered. **Requirements:** May be issued to an individual who is licensed to practice land surveying in another state, does not have a place of business in this state and is not a resident of this state. **Fees:** $25 application fee. **Governing Statute:** *ST2 Annotated Code of Maryland, Title 15. Code of Maryland Regulations, Title 09, Subtitle 13.

Massachusetts

8198

Land Surveyor
Board of Registration of Engineers
 and Land Surveyors
Div. of Registration
100 Cambridge St., 15th Fl.
Boston, MA 02202
Phone: (617)727-9957

Credential Type: License. **Requirements:** Contact licensing body for application information.

Michigan

8199

Land Surveyor
Board of Land Surveyors
Bureau of Occupational &
 Professional Regulation
Dept. of Commerce
PO Box 30018
Lansing, MI 48909
Phone: (517)373-9153

Credential Type: License. **Duration of License:** Two years. **Requirements:** Minimum of eight years of practical experience in land surveying. Acceptable bachelor's degree in land surveying. The bachelor's degree is equivalent to four years of experience credit. Up to five years of experience credit may be given for education. Submit at least five reference statements (three of the references must be registered land surveyors, who have personal knowledge of the applicant's land surveying experience). Abide by the rules and regulations of the Board. Be of good moral character. **Examination:** Two written exams. **Reciprocity:** A licensed land surveyor from another state may be licensed in Michigan if the requirements for licensure in that state are not lower than those of Michigan. **Fees:** $30 application processing fee. $110 initial examination fee ($55 Part I, $45 Part 2a, $40 Part 2b). $50 initial license fee, per year. $50 renewal fee, per year. $30 reciprocity fee. **Governing Statute:** The Occupational Code, Act 299 of 1980, Article 20, as amended.

Minnesota

8200

Land Surveyor
Board of Architecture, Engineering,
 Land Surveying, and Landscape
 Architecture
133 7th St. E., 3rd Fl.
St. Paul, MN 55101-2333
Phone: (612)296-2388

Credential Type: Land Surveyor License. **Duration of License:** Two years. **Requirements:** Bachelor of science degree with at least 16 quarter credits of surveying coursework. Complete three or four years of land surveying experience, depending on type of degree earned. **Examination:** Fundamentals of Land Surveying Examination. Principles and Practice of Land Surveying Examination. **Reciprocity:** Yes, based on comity, provided out-of-state applicant received original license based on requirements equal to or greater than Minnesota requirements at the time of original licen-

Surveyors

sure. Must also pass 4-hour exam on Minnesota land surveying law and procedures. **Fees:** $32.50 exam fee (Fundamentals). $100 exam fee (Principles and Practice). $58 renewal fee. $100 comity application fee. **Governing Statute:** Minnesota Statutes, 326.02-326.15, 326.53, 609.03. Minnesota Rules 1800.0200 to 1805.1600.

Credential Type: Land Surveyor-in-Training License. **Duration of License:** Two years. **Requirements:** Bachelor of science degree with at least 16 quarter credits of surveying coursework. **Examination:** Fundamentals of Land Surveying Examination. **Reciprocity:** Yes, based on comity, provided out-of-state applicant received original license based on requirements equal to or greater than Minnesota requirements at the time of original licensure. Must also pass 4-hour exam on Minnesota land surveying law and procedures. **Fees:** $32.50 exam fee (Fundamentals). $58 renewal fee. $100 comity application fee. **Governing Statute:** Minnesota Statutes, 326.02-326.15, 326.53, 609.03. Minnesota Rules 1800.0200 to 1805.1600.

Mississippi

8201

Professional Land Surveyor
State Board of Registration for Professional Engineers and Land Surveyors
PO Box 3
Jackson, MS 39205
Phone: (601)359-6160

Credential Type: Professional Land Surveyor Registration. **Requirements:** Must be a state resident. Meet one of the following sets of requirements: (1) Complete an approved curriculum of two years or more (64 semester hours) and three years of qualifying surveying experience. (2) Seven years of qualifying experience or a combination of experience and education. **Examination:** Fundamentals of Land Surveying Examination. Principles and Practice of Land Surveying. **Fees:** $25 application fee for Fundamentals of Land Surveying Examination. $75 application fee for Principles and Practice of Land Surveying Examination.

Missouri

8202

Professional Land Surveyor
State Board of Registration for Architects, Professional Engineers, and Land Surveyors
3605 Missouri Blvd.
PO Box 184
Jefferson City, MO 65102-0184
Phone: (314)751-0047

Credential Type: Professional Land Surveyor Registration. **Duration of License:** One year. **Requirements:** Meet one of the following sets of requirements: (1) Complete the land surveyor-in-training program. (2) Have a B.S. degree in engineering from an accredited school of engineering and two years of land surveying experience. (3) Complete at least four years of college level engineering and science courses. (4) Be a high school graduate with eight years combined work experience and higher education. (5) Complete at least three years of field work and one year of office work. **Examination:** Fundamentals of Land Surveying Examination. Principles and Practice of Land Surveying. **Reciprocity:** Yes, based on passing comparable written examinations. **Fees:** $100 application fee. $30 renewal fee. **Governing Statute:** Missouri Revised Statutes, Chap. 327. Four CSR 30 (Rules of the Board).

Credential Type: Land Surveyor-in-Training Registration. **Duration of License:** One year. **Requirements:** Contact licensing body for application information. **Examination:** Fundamentals of Land Surveying Examination. **Reciprocity:** Yes, based on passing comparable written examinations. **Fees:** $20 application fee. $30 renewal fee. **Governing Statute:** Missouri Revised Statutes, Chap. 327. Four CSR 30 (Rules of the Board).

Montana

8203

Land Surveyor
Montana Board of Professional Engineers and Land Surveyors
111 N. Jackson
Helena, MT 59620
Phone: (406)444-4285

Credential Type: Land Surveyor-in-Training Registration. **Requirements:** Complete 90 quarter hours of approved coursework or equivalent. **Examination:** Written. **Fees:** $50 application and exam fee. **Governing Statute:** Montana Code Annotated 37-67-301 through 37-67-332.

Credential Type: Land Surveyor Registration. **Duration of License:** Two years. **Requirements:** Bachelor's degree in civil engineering or equivalent. Four years of progressive experience on surveying projects. Renewal requires 520 hours per year of practice, formal course work, or other approved study. **Examination:** Written. **Fees:** $80 application and exam fee. $40 renewal fee. **Governing Statute:** Montana Code Annotated 37-67-301 through 37-67-332.

Nebraska

8204

Land Surveyor
Nebraska Board of Examiners for Land Surveyors
555 N. Cotner Blvd., Lower Level
Lincoln, NE 68505
Phone: (402)471-2266

Credential Type: License. **Duration of License:** Two years. **Requirements:** Must have 16 years of surveying experience, three being of a responsable position. Credit may be given for education that has been approved by the board, plus an additional two years of practice in a responsable position. **Fees:** $100 application fee. $100 renewal fee.

Nevada

8205

Surveyor
State Board of Registered Professional Engineers and Land Surveyors
1755 E. Plumb Ln., Ste. 135
Reno, NV 89502
Phone: (702)688-1231

Credential Type: License. **Requirements:** Four years of college and four years of experience in land surveying, or eight years of experience under a registered land surveyor, or an equivalent combination of education and experience. **Examination:** Yes. **Fees:** $200 application fee.

New Hampshire

8206

Land Surveyor
Joint Board of Engineers, Architects, Land Surveyors, & Natural Scientists
57 Regional Drive
Concord, NH 03301
Phone: (603)271-2219

Credential Type: Land Surveyor License. **Duration of License:** Two years. **Requirements:** U.S. citizen. New Hampshire resident. Complete one college level course in land surveying or gain experience in land surveying work as a land surveyor-in-training under the supervision of a licensed land surveyor. Must have at least six years of accumulated experience/education in land surveying work. Renewal requires five continuing education credits annually up to age 65. After age 65, two continuing education credits are required annually. **Examination:** Examination as required by Board. **Reciprocity:** Yes. **Fees:** $15 application fee. $65 examination fee. $50 biennial renewal fee.

New Jersey

8207

Surveyor
State Board of Professional Engineers and Land Surveyors
1100 Raymond Blvd., Rm. 317
Newark, NJ 07102
Phone: (201)648-2660

Credential Type: License. **Duration of License:** Two years. **Requirements:** Graduation from an approved college with a four year curriculum in surveying. Three years of land surveying experience of a character satisfactory to the board. Must speak and write English. **Examination:** Written. **Fees:** $60 application fee. $145 exam fee. $30 biennial registration fee. **Governing Statute:** NJSA 45:8-27. NJAC 13:40-1.

New Mexico

8208

Land Surveyor
Engineers and Surveyors Board
440 Cerrillos Rd., Ste. A
Santa Fe, NM 87501
Phone: (505)827-7316

Credential Type: Professional Surveyor Registration. **Duration of License:** One year. **Requirements:** Graduate of a board-approved surveying curriculum of at least 45 semester hours. Complete eight years of acceptable surveying experience. **Examination:** Principles and Practice of Surveying, Parts I and IIA (national) and Part IIB (state). **Reciprocity:** Yes, provided that applicant was registered under qualifications comparable to or exceeding New Mexico's at the time of initial registration. **Fees:** $75 application fee. $80 exam fee. $40 registration fee. $40 renewal fee. **Governing Statute:** New Mexico Engineering and Surveying Practice Act, Sections 61-23-1 through 61-23-32 NMSA (1978). Rules 89-1 and 89-2.

8209

Surveyor Intern
Engineers and Surveyors Board
440 Cerrillos Rd., Ste. A
Santa Fe, NM 87501
Phone: (505)827-7316

Credential Type: Surveyor Intern Registration and Certification. **Duration of License:** Indefinite. **Requirements:** Graduate of a board-approved surveying curriculum of at least 45 semester hours. Complete four years of acceptable surveying experience. **Examination:** Fundamentals of Surveying Examination. **Reciprocity:** Yes, provided that applicant was registered under qualifications comparable to or exceeding New Mexico's at the time of initial registration. **Fees:** $75 application fee. $65 exam fee. $15 certification fee. $40 renewal fee. **Governing Statute:** New Mexico Engineering and Surveying Practice Act, Sections 61-23-1 through 61-23-32 NMSA (1978). Rules 89-1 and 89-2.

New York

8210

Land Surveyor
State Education Dept.
Div. of Professional Licensing Services
Cultural Education Center
Empire State Plaza
Albany, NY 12230
Phone: (518)474-3833

Credential Type: License. **Duration of License:** Three years. **Requirements:** Bachelor's Degree in land surveying program approved by the licensing agency. Four years of land surveying experience. 21 years of age. U.S. citizen or alien lawfully admitted for permanent residency. **Examination:** Written. **Fees:** $430 application fee. $210 renewal fee. **Governing Statute:** Title VIII Articles 130, 145 of the Educational Law.

North Carolina

8211

Land Surveyor
North Carolina State Board of Registration for Professional Engineers and Land Surveyors
3620 Six Forks Rd.
Raleigh, NC 27607
Phone: (919)781-9499

Credential Type: License. **Duration of License:** One year. **Requirements:** 18 years of age. High school diploma or equivalent. Four years of progressive practical land surveying experience, with two of the years under a practicing registered land surveyor, before qualifying for Exam I. After successful completion of Exam I, and with six years of experience, in which four are under a registered land surveyor, the applicant is eligible to take Exam II. **Examination:** Two exams. **Fees:** $100 application and exam fee. $3 land surveyor kit fee. $30 renewal fee.

North Dakota

8212

Land Surveyor
State Board of Registration for Professional Engineers and Land Surveyors
Box 1357
Bismarck, ND 58502-1357
Phone: (701)258-0786

Credential Type: Professional Land Surveyor License. **Duration of License:** One year. **Requirements:** Complete a combination of eight years of education and experience. **Examination:** Fundamentals of Land Surveying. Principles and Practice of Land Surveying. **Reciprocity:** Yes, with all 50 states. **Fees:** $110 exam fee. $27.50 renewal fee.

Ohio

8213

Professional Land Surveyor
State Board of Registration for Professional Engineers and Land Surveyors
77 S. High St., 16th Fl
Columbus, OH 43266-0314
Phone: (614)466-8948
Fax: (614)644-9048

Credential Type: Professional Land Surveyor Registration. **Duration of License:** One year. **Requirements:** Meet one of the following sets of requirements: (1) Graduate from an approved curriculum in surveying of four years or more, and complete four additional years of acceptable surveying office and field work. (2) Graduate from an approved curriculum in civil engineering of four years or more, including at least 24 quarter hours of approved surveying courses. Complete four additional years of acceptable surveying office and field work. **Examination:** Fundamentals of Land Surveying Examination. Principles and Practice of Land Surveying. **Reciprocity:** Yes, based on passing comparable written examinations. **Fees:** $25 application fee. $30 registration fee. $16 renewal fee. **Governing Statute:** Chap. 4733, R.C. Registration Laws. Chap. 4733, A.C. Board Rules.

Credential Type: Land Surveyor-in-Training Certification. **Duration of License:** One year. **Requirements:** Meet one of the following sets of requirements: (1) Be a recent graduate, a student who is a candidate for graduation, or complete four or more years of the curriculum of a recognized college of engineering and surveying. (2) Have four or more years of practical experience in engineering and surveying, with at least one year in land surveying. **Examination:** Fundamentals of Land Surveying Examination. **Reciprocity:** Yes, based on passing comparable written examinations. **Fees:** $25 application fee. $16 renewal fee. **Governing Statute:** Chap. 4733, R.C. Registration Laws. Chap. 4733, A.C. Board Rules.

Oklahoma

8214

Land Surveyor (Intern)
Oklahoma State Board of Registration for Professional Engineers and Land Surveyors
201 N.E. 27th St., Ste. 120
Oklahoma City, OK 73105
Phone: (405)521-2874

Credential Type: Registration. **Duration of License:** Two years. **Requirements:** Graduation from ABET accredited land surveying curriculum, civil engineering degree or long-established practice. State resident. **Examination:** Fundamentals of Land Surveying. **Fees:** $27.50 exam fee. $15 application fee. $20 renewal fee.

8215

Land Surveyor, Registered
Oklahoma State Board of Registration for Professional Engineers and Land Surveyors
201 N.E. 27th St., Ste. 120
Oklahoma City, OK 73105
Phone: (405)521-2875

Credential Type: Registration. **Duration of License:** Two years. **Requirements:** Graduation from ABET accredited land surveying curriculum, civil engineering degree or long-established practice. State resident. **Examination:** Fundamentals of Land Surveying. Principles of Land Surveying. Public Domain. Oklahoma Examination. **Fees:** $117.50 total exam fee. $50 application fee. $50 renewal fee.

Oregon

8216

Land Surveyor, Professional
Oregon State Board of Engineering Examiners
750 Front St. NE, Ste. 240
Salem, OR 97310
Phone: (503)378-41080

Credential Type: Certificate. **Duration of License:** Two years. **Requirements:** Eight years of experience, or a board approved bachelor of science degree in surveying and four years of experience. **Examination:** Yes. **Fees:** $80 exam fee. $5 certificate fee. $40 renewal fee. **Governing Statute:** ORS 672.002 to 672.325.

Pennsylvania

8217

Professional Land Surveyor
State Registration Board for Professional Engineers and Professional Land Surveyors
Bureau of Professional and Occupational Affairs
Dept. of State
Transportation and Safety Bldg., 6th Fl.
Harrisburg, PA 17120
Phone: (717)787-8503

Credential Type: Professional Land Surveyor License. **Duration of License:** Two years. **Requirements:** At least 21 years of age. Good moral character and repute. Able to speak and write the English language. Meet one of the following requirements: (1) Graduate of an approved four-year school of civil engineering with a minimum of 10 credit hours in surveying; (2) Complete six or more years of progressive experience in surveying which approximates the education received in a four-year school of civil engineering; (3) Earn an associates degree in an approved surveying technology curriculum. Pass a fundamentals examination in land surveying and become certified as a surveyor-in-training. As a surveyor-in-training, the applicant must have an additional four years progressive experience in land surveying, or the teaching of land surveying, under the supervision of a professional land surveyor. Must also pass examination in principles and practices of land surveying. **Examination:** State examination.

Rhode Island

8218

Land Surveyor
State Board of Registration for Professional Land Surveyors
Charles Orms Bldg.
10 Orms St.
Providence, RI 02904
Phone: (401)277-2038

Credential Type: Land Surveyor-In-Training Certificate. **Duration of License:** Two years. **Requirements:** Graduate from an accredited four-year curriculum in land surveying. Alternative requirements available through board. **Examination:** National Council of Engineering Examiners and Surveyors (NCEES) Examination, fundamentals section. **Reciprocity:** Yes. **Fees:** $100 application fee. $100 examination fee. $125 renewal fee.

Credential Type: Professional Land Surveyor Certificate. **Duration of License:** Two years. **Requirements:** Meet all requirements for Land Surveyor-In-Training Certificate. Complete four years of combined office and field experience in land surveying projects under professional supervision. Alternative requirements available through board. **Examination:** State written examination and National Council of Engineering Examiners and Surveyors (NCEES) Examination. **Reciprocity:** Yes. **Fees:** $100 application fee. $100 examination fee. $125 renewal

South Carolina

8219

Surveyor, Land
South Carolina State Board of
   Registration for Engineers and
   Land Surveyors
PO Drawer 50408
Columbia, SC 29250
Phone: (803)734-9166

Credential Type: Registered Land Surveyor. **Requirements:** Bachelor's degree in land surveying, civil engineering, or equivalent, plus two years of experience under a practicing, registered land surveyor; or an associate degree in engineering technology or land surveying, plus four years of experience under a practicing, registered land surveyor. **Examination:** Yes. **Fees:** $50 application fee. $45 renewal fee.

Credential Type: Land Surveyor-in-Training—Certificate. **Requirements:** Bachelor's degree in land surveying, civil engineering or equivalent, plus one year of experience under a practicing, registered land surveyor; or an associate degree in engineering technology or land surveying, plus two years of experience under a practicing, registered land surveyor. **Examination:** Yes. **Fees:** $50 certificate fee.

South Dakota

8220

Land Surveyor
Commission of Engineering,
   Architectural, and Land Surveying
   Examiners
2040 W. Main St., Ste. 304
Rapid City, SD 57702-2447
Phone: (605)394-2510

Credential Type: Registration. **Duration of License:** Two years. **Requirements:** Meet one of the following sets of requirements: (1) Have a 4year ABET engineering or surveying degree and three years experience. (2) Have a four-year ABET technology degree and three years experience. (3) Have two years of a related vocational-technical curriculum and six years experience. (4) No schooling and 10 years experience. **Examination:** Principles and Practice of Land Surveying. South Dakota takehome examination. **Reciprocity:** Yes, if state had equal requirements at time of registration. **Fees:** $100 application fee. $70 exam fee. $60 renewal fee.

8221

Land Surveyor-in-Training
Commission of Engineering,
   Architectural, and Land Surveying
   Examiners
2040 W. Main St., Ste. 304
Rapid City, SD 57702-2447
Phone: (605)394-2510

Credential Type: Land Surveyor-in-Training Certification. **Duration of License:** Unlimited. **Requirements:** Meet one of the following sets of requirements: (1) Have an ABET engineering or surveying degree. (2) Complete a vocationaltechnical program and have two years surveying experience. **Examination:** Fundamentals of Land Surveying. **Reciprocity:** Yes, if state had equal requirements at time of certification. **Fees:** $55 exam fee.

Tennessee

8222

Land Surveyor
Board of Examiners for Land
   Surveying
500 James Robertson Pky., 2nd Fl.
Nashville, TN 37243
Phone: (615)741-3611

Credential Type: License. **Duration of License:** One year. **Requirements:** Six years experience, including three years as a party chief. Pass exams. **Examination:** Yes. **Reciprocity:** No. **Fees:** $30 Registration. $55 Examination. $55 Application. $60 Renewal.

Texas

8223

Land Surveyor
Texas Board of Land Surveying
7701 N. Lamar, Ste. 400
Austin, TX 78752
Phone: (512)452-9427

Credential Type: Land Surveyor License. **Duration of License:** One year. **Requirements:** Possession of valid surveyor-in-training certificate. Two years as a surveyor-in-training. **Examination:** Written. **Fees:** $100 application fee. $100 examination fee. $50 renewal fee. **Governing Statute:** VACS 5282c, 22 TAC 661.

Credential Type: Surveyor-in-Training License. **Requirements:** Bachelor of science degree in surveying; or bachelor of science degree, including 32 semester hours in subjects relating to land surveying, plus one year surveying experience; or associate degree in land surveying from approved institution, plus two years experience; or 32 semester hours or equivalent in subjects relating to land surveying, plus two years surveying experience; or graduation from an accredited high school, plus six years surveying experience, and proof of self-education in surveying field. **Governing Statute:** VACS 5282c, 22 TAC 661.

Utah

8224

Land Surveyor
Dept. of Commerce
Div. of Occupational and
   Professional Licensing
160 E. 300 S.
PO Box 45802
Salt Lake City, UT 84145
Phone: (801)530-6628

Credential Type: Land Surveyor License. **Duration of License:** Two years. **Requirements:** Must hold a current land surveyor-in-training certificate. Must complete four years or more of experience on land surveying projects. **Examination:** Yes. **Fees:** $100 license fee. $30 renewal fee.

8225

Land Surveyor-in-Training
Dept. of Commerce
Div. of Occupational and
   Professional Licensing
160 E. 300 S.
PO Box 45802
Salt Lake City, UT 84145
Phone: (801)530-6628

Credential Type: Land Surveyor-in-Training License. **Duration of License:** Two years. **Requirements:** Must be a graduate from a land surveying curriculum of two years or more approved by the board; or graduate in a related field with a four-year curriculum that includes at least 32 quarter hours, or equivalent semester hours of surveying courses including courses in writing legal descriptions, the public land survey system, and surveying field techniques; or complete four years or more experience in land surveying work satisfactory to the Board. **Examination:** Yes. **Fees:** $30 Land Surveyor-in-Training fee. $100 license fee. $30 renewal fee.

Vermont

8226

Surveyor, Land
Board of Registration for Land
 Surveyors
Pavilion Office Bldg.
Montpelier, VT 05602
Phone: (802)828-2373

Credential Type: License. **Duration of License:** Two years. **Requirements:** Comity or endorsement, licensed in another state that has equivalent or better requirements than Vermont; or, graduate from an accredited four-year curriculum in surveying and have at least 24 months of experience; or, complete 30 hours of formal instruction and have 36 months of experience and pass an examination given by the board; or, complete four or more years of supervised experience and pass an examination given by the board. **Examination:** Yes. **Reciprocity:** Yes. **Fees:** $185 Examination. $50 License application (not to exceed). $10 Certificate. $20 Renewal. **Governing Statute:** Title 26, VSA Sections 2591-2598.

Virginia

8227

Land Surveyor
State Board of Architects,
 Professional Engineers, Land
 Surveyors & Certified Landscape
 Architects
3600 W. Broad St.
Richmond, VA 23230
Phone: (804)367-8514

Credential Type: License. **Requirements:** 18 years of age. Must have six years of practical experience or a combination of six years of formal education and practical experience acceptable to the Board. **Examination:** Yes. **Fees:** $40 application fee. $80 examination fee.

Washington

8228

Surveyor
Board of Registration for
 Professional Engineers and Land
 Surveyors
Dept. of Licensing
Professional Licensing Services
PO Box 9649
Olympia, WA 98507-9649
Phone: (206)753-6966
Phone: (206)753-3634

Credential Type: Surveyor License. **Duration of License:** Two years. **Requirements:** Must complete six years of land surveying experience or hold a college degree and complete two years of experience. **Examination:** Written examination. **Reciprocity:** Yes. **Fees:** $100 initial license fee. $40 FLS examination fee. $60 PPLS examination fee. $50 examination retake fee. $100 reciprocal license fee. $70 renewal fee.

West Virginia

8229

Land Surveyor
Board of Examiners of Land
 Surveyors
PO Box 925
Fayetteville, WV 25840
Phone: (304)574-2980

Credential Type: License. **Requirements:** U.S. resident. 18 years old. Four years of land surveying experience or completion of an accredited curriculum with two years experience. Never convicted of a felony. **Examination:** Yes. **Fees:** $70 License and Exam. $30 Renewal.

8230

Mine Surveyor
Dept. of Examiners of Land
 Surveyors
PO Box 925
Fayetteville, WV 25840
Phone: (304)574-2980

Credential Type: License. **Duration of License:** One year. **Requirements:** U.S. resident. 18 years old. Four years of experience under a license holder and three years of underground surveying; or completion of an accredited curriculum and two years of land surveying experience plus three years of underground surveying experience. Never convicted of a felony. **Examination:** Yes. **Fees:** $10 License. $30 Land Survey license. $20 Renewal.

Wisconsin

8231

Land Surveyors
Regulations and Licensing Dept.
Architects & Engineers Board
PO Box 8935
Madison, WI 53708-8935
Phone: (608)266-8609

Credential Type: License. **Requirements:** Completion of an approved two-year course and two years of experience; or six years of experience with credit allowed for education or apprenticeship. **Examination:** Yes. **Exemptions:** Applicants with 20 years of experience and who are at least 45 years of age are exempt from the exam. **Reciprocity:** Yes.

Wyoming

8232

Surveyor, Professional
State Board for Professional Land
 Surveyors
Herschler Bldg., Rm. 4135 E.
Cheyenne, WY 82002
Phone: (307)777-6155

Credential Type: License. **Duration of License:** Two years. **Requirements:** Pass a written examination. Pass the Wyoming take-home examinations. Registered as a Surveyor in Training and actively engaged in education, and experience for four years beyond that required to be a Surveyor in training. Any applicant license elsewhere may be considered for registration based on experience. **Examination:** Yes. **Reciprocity:** Yes. **Fees:** $30 Fundamentals of Land Surveying. $75 Land Surveying. $45 per part of examination (4 parts). $45 Renewal.

Tax Examiners, Collectors, and Revenue Agents

The following states grant licenses in this occupational category as of the date of publication: California, Kentucky, Michigan, Minnesota, Oregon, Texas.

California

8233

Tax Interviewer
Tax Preparers Program
400 R St., Ste. 3140
Sacramento, CA 95814-6200
Phone: (916)324-4977

Credential Type: Registration. **Duration of License:** One year. **Authorization:** Unregistered persons may not conduct a tax practice or hire tax interviewers. **Requirements:** Be at least 18 years of age. High school graduate or equivalent. Be employed by a registered tax preparer. Meet one of the following sets of requirements: (1) Complete 60 hours of approved instruction within the previous 18 months. (2) Have been a paid preparer for federal and state personal income tax returns for others for at least an average of 15 hours per week during two tax seasons within the last four years. (3) Have been a paid preparer for federal and state personal income tax returns for others for at least an average of eight hours per week during four tax seasons within the last six years.

Renewal requires 20 hours of continuing education. **Exemptions:** Any persons regulated by the State Board of Accountancy. Any person who is a member of the State Bar of California. Any person who is authorized to practice before the Internal Revenue Service. **Fees:** $50 registration fee. **Governing Statute:** Tax Preparer Act, Business and Professions Code 9891.

8234

Tax Preparer
Tax Preparers Program
400 R St., Ste. 3140
Sacramento, CA 95814-6200
Phone: (916)324-4977

Credential Type: Registration. **Duration of License:** One year. **Authorization:** Unregistered persons may not conduct a tax practice or hire tax interviewers. **Requirements:** Be at least 18 years of age. High school graduate or equivalent. Post $2000 surety bond for individual preparer and for each employed tax interviewer, not to exceed $50,000. Meet one of the following sets of requirements: (1) Complete 60 hours of approved instruction within the previous 18 months. (2) Have been a paid preparer for federal and state personal income tax returns for others for at least an average of 15 hours per week during two tax seasons within the last four years. (3) Have been a paid preparer for federal and state personal income tax returns for others for at least an average of eight hours per week during four tax seasons within the last six years.

A registered tax interviewer may register as a tax preparer by filing an application, posting a $2000 surety bond, and paying the $50 registration fee. Proof of continuing education must also be furnished.

Renewal requires 20 hours of continuing education. **Exemptions:** Any persons regulated by the State Board of Accountancy. Any person who is a member of the State Bar of California. Any person who is authorized to practice before the Internal Revenue Service. **Fees:** $50 registration fee. $10 registration fee for each additional location. **Governing Statute:** Tax Preparer Act, Business and Professions Code 9891.

Kentucky

8235

Property Valuation Administrator
Kentucky Revenue Cabinet
Dept. of Property Taxation
592 E. Main St.
Frankfort, KY 40620
Phone: (502)564-6730

Credential Type: License. **Requirements:** 24 years of age. Citizen of Kentucky for two years and one year in the county and district in which he/she is a candidate preceding the election. Continuing education required.

Michigan

8236

Assessor
State Assessors Board
Dept. of Treasury
Treasury Bldg.
Lansing, MI 48922
Phone: (517)373-3200

Credential Type: Class I Certification. **Duration of License:** Two years. **Authorization:** Can assess residential property, land improvements on residential property, all types of land, and timber. **Requirements:** Knowledge and understanding of the assessing profession. Apply for certification within 180 days after passing the written exam. Prepare and submit for approval an appraisal record card (based on data obtained from the applicant's field of work), according to instructions provided in the Assessors Manual (which is published by the State Tax Commission). Comply with all rules of the State Assessors Board. Renewal requires attendance of renewal seminar. **Examination:** Written

Tax Examiners, Collectors, and Revenue Agents

exam. **Fees:** $25 initial exam fee. $35 initial regular certification fee. $35 conditional certification fee. $35 provisional certification fee. $50 renewal regular certification fee. **Governing Statute:** Assessment, Levy and Collection of Taxes Act, Act 206 of 1893, as amended.

Credential Type: Class II Certification. **Duration of License:** Two years. **Authorization:** Can assess residential property, land improvements on residential property, all types of land, and timber. Can assess small commercial properties and general-purpose industrial properties. **Requirements:** Knowledge and understanding of the assessing profession. Apply for certification within 180 days after passing the written exam. Prepare and submit for approval an appraisal record card (based on data obtained from the applicant's field of work), according to instructions provided in the Assessors Manual (which is published by the State Tax Commission). Comply with all rules of the State Assessors Board. Renewal requires attendance of renewal seminar. **Examination:** Written exam. **Fees:** $25 initial exam fee. $35 initial regular certification fee. $35 conditional certification fee. $35 provisional certification fee. $50 renewal regular certification fee. **Governing Statute:** Assessment, Levy and Collection of Taxes Act, Act 206 of 1893, as amended.

Credential Type: Class III Certification. **Duration of License:** Two years. **Authorization:** Can assess residential property, land improvements on residential property, all types of land, and timber. Can assess small commercial properties and general-purpose industrial properties. Can assess large and difficult-to-evaluate properties of all types, such as regional shopping centers, industrial complexes and heavy manufacturing facilities, concentrated downtown areas, and condominium and apartment complexes. **Requirements:** Knowledge and understanding of the assessing profession. Meet all Class I and II requirements. Two years experience in assessment administration. Apply for certification within 180 days after passing the written exam. Prepare and submit for approval an appraisal record card (based on data obtained from the applicant's field of work), according to instructions provided in the Assessors Manual (which is published by the State Tax Commission). Comply with all rules of the State Assessors Board. Renewal requires attendance of renewal seminar and six-hour appraisal seminar conducted by an assessment or appraisal association. **Examination:** Written exam. **Fees:** $25 initial exam fee. $35 initial regular certification fee. $35 conditional certification fee. $35 provisional certification fee. $95 renewal regular certification fee. **Governing Statute:** Assessment, Levy and Collection of Taxes Act, Act 206 of 1893, as amended.

Credential Type: Class IV Certification. **Duration of License:** Two years. **Authorization:** Can assess residential property, land improvements on residential property, all types of land, and timber. Can assess small commercial properties and general-purpose industrial properties. Can assess large and difficult-to-evaluate properties of all types, such as regional shopping centers, industrial complexes and heavy manufacturing facilities, concentrated downtown areas, and condominium and apartment complexes. Can administer and formulate policies for assessment offices which do the more complex evaluations. **Requirements:** Knowledge and understanding of the assessing profession. Meet all Class I, II and III requirements. Three years experience in assessment administration. Apply for certification within 180 days after passing the written or oral exam. Prepare and submit for approval an appraisal record card (based on data obtained from the applicant's field of work), according to instructions provided in the Assessors Manual (which is published by the State Tax Commission). Comply with all rules of the State Assessors Board. Renewal requires attendance of renewal seminar and six-hour appraisal seminar conducted by an assessment or appraisal association. **Examination:** Written and oral exam. **Fees:** $25 initial exam fee. $35 initial regular certification fee. $35 conditional certification fee. $35 provisional certification fee. $95 renewal regular certification fee. **Governing Statute:** Assessment, Levy and Collection of Taxes Act, Act 206 of 1893, as amended.

8237

Personal Property Examiner
State Tax Commission
Dept. of Treasury
Treasury Bldg.
Lansing, MI 48922
Phone: (517)373-3200

Credential Type: Certification. **Duration of License:** Three years. **Requirements:** Be employed by a governmental assessing agency or equalization department. Pass a written examination or have at least three years of experience in auditing and assessing of personal property within Michigan. One year of college education in a curriculum related to accounting and/or auditing may be substituted for six months of experience. Education, however, may not be substituted for more than 24 months of experience. Submit a recent photograph. Comply with all rules of the State Tax Commission. **Examination:** Written exam. **Fees:** $25 initial exam fee. $25 initial certification fee. $10 renewal fee. **Governing Statute:** Assessment, Levy and Collection of Taxes Act, Act 206 of 1893, as amended.

Minnesota

8238

Assessor
Dept. of Revenue
Board of Assessors
Mail Station 3340
St. Paul, MN 55146-3340
Phone: (612)296-0209

Credential Type: Certified Assessor License. **Duration of License:** One year. **Authorization:** All persons engaged in valuing or classifying property must be licensed within three years of being employed. **Requirements:** Complete one year of experience working in an assessor's office or alternate experience. Complete three week-long training courses.

Renewal requires earning four Continuing Educational Units (CEUs) every four years. **Examination:** Yes, given at conclusion of courses. **Fees:** $30 license fee. **Governing Statute:** Minnesota Statutes 270.41-270.53. Board of Assessors' Rules.

Credential Type: Certified Assessor Specialist License. **Duration of License:** One year. **Authorization:** All persons engaged in valuing or classifying property must be licensed within three years of being employed. **Requirements:** Complete two years of experience working in an assessor's office or alternate experience. Complete five weeks of training courses.

Renewal requires earning four Continuing Educational Units (CEUs) every four years. **Examination:** Yes, given at conclusion of courses. **Fees:** $40 license fee. **Governing Statute:** Minnesota Statutes 270.41-270.53. Board of Assessors' Rules.

Credential Type: Accredited Assessor License. **Duration of License:** One year. **Authorization:** All persons engaged in valuing or classifying property must be licensed within three years of being employed. **Requirements:** Complete three years of experience working as a trainee or certified assessor in an assessor's office or alternate experience. Complete five weeks of training courses. Complete a demonstration narrative appraisal.

Renewal requires earning five Continuing Educational Units (CEUs) every four years. **Examination:** Yes, given at conclusion of courses. **Fees:** $50 license fee. **Governing Statute:** Minnesota Statutes 270.41-270.53. Board of Assessors' Rules.

Assessor, continued

Credential Type: Senior Accredited Assessor License. **Duration of License:** One year. **Authorization:** All persons engaged in valuing or classifying property must be licensed within three years of being employed. **Requirements:** Complete five years of experience working in an assessor's office or alternate experience. Complete five weeks of training courses. Complete a second demonstration narrative appraisal or obtain sufficient points to achieve the designation vie the Contract Alternative Point System.

Renewal requires earning five Continuing Educational Units (CEUs) every four years. **Examination:** Yes, given at conclusion of courses. **Fees:** $75 license fee. **Governing Statute:** Minnesota Statutes 270.41-270.53. Board of Assessors' Rules.

Oregon

8239

Tax Consultant
State Board of Tax Service
  Examiners
158 12th St. NE
Salem, OR 97310
Phone: (503)378-4034

Credential Type: License. **Duration of License:** One year. **Requirements:** Must have two years of tax preparer or equivalent experience. **Examination:** Yes. **Fees:** $60 exam fee. $60 license fee. $60 renewal fee. **Governing Statute:** ORS 673.605 to 673.990 and Oregon Administrative Rules, Chapter 800.

8240

Tax Preparer
State Board of Tax Service
  Examiners
158 12th St. NE
Salem, OR 97310
Phone: (503)378-4034

Credential Type: License. **Duration of License:** One year. **Requirements:** 18 years of age. High school diploma or GED. Successful completion of a board-approved, 80-class-hour course on basic tax law. **Examination:** Yes. **Fees:** $40 exam fee. $45 license fee. $45 renewal fee. **Governing Statute:** ORS 673.605 to 673.990 and Oregon Administrative Rules, Chapter 800.

Texas

8241

Tax Professional—Appraiser
Board of Tax Professional Examiners
Bldg. B, Ste. 140
4301 W. Bank Dr.
Austin, TX 78746
Phone: (512)329-7982

Credential Type: Registration. **Duration of License:** One year. **Requirements:** High school diploma or equivalent. Must be active in property tax field for which application is made. Texas resident. 18 years of age. **Fees:** $50 application fee. $35 registration fee. $35 renewal fee. **Governing Statute:** VACS 8885, 22 TAC 623.

Credential Type: Certification. **Duration of License:** One year. **Requirements:** Appraisers need five years of experience, must take eight specified courses and conduct on demonstration appraisal. **Examination:** Two examinations. **Fees:** $50 application fee. $35 registration fee. $35 renewal fee. **Governing Statute:** VACS 8885, 22 TAC 623.

8242

Tax Professional—Assessor-Collector
Board of Tax Professional Examiners
Bldg. B, Ste. 140
4301 W. Bank Dr.
Austin, TX 78746
Phone: (512)329-7982

Credential Type: Registration. **Duration of License:** One year. **Requirements:** High school diploma or equivalent. Must be active in property tax field for which application is made. Texas resident. 18 years of age. **Fees:** $50 application fee. $35 registration fee. $35 renewal fee. **Governing Statute:** VACS 8885, 22 TAC 623.

Credential Type: Certification. **Duration of License:** One year. **Requirements:** Assessors need five years of experience and must take eight specified courses. Collectors need three years of experience and must take six specified courses. **Examination:** Two examinations. **Fees:** $50 application fee. $35 registration fee. $35 renewal fee. **Governing Statute:** VACS 8885, 22 TAC 623.

8243

Tax Professional—Collector
Board of Tax Professional Examiners
Bldg. B, Ste. 140
4301 W. Bank Dr.
Austin, TX 78746
Phone: (512)329-7982

Credential Type: Registration. **Duration of License:** One year. **Requirements:** High school diploma or equivalent. Must be active in property tax field for which application is made. Texas resident. 18 years of age. **Fees:** $50 application fee. $35 registration fee. $35 renewal fee. **Governing Statute:** VACS 8885, 22 TAC 623.

Credential Type: Certification. **Duration of License:** One year. **Requirements:** Collectors need three years of experience and must take six specified courses. **Examination:** Yes. **Fees:** $50 application fee. $35 registration fee. $35 renewal fee. **Governing Statute:** VACS 8885, 22 TAC 623.

Taxi Drivers and Chauffeurs

The following states grant licenses in this occupational category as of the date of publication: Arkansas, Hawaii, Iowa, Maryland, Michigan, Nebraska, Nevada, New York, North Carolina, Oklahoma, Oregon, Rhode Island.

Arkansas

8244

Chauffeur
Dept. of Finance and Administration
Div. of Revenues
Ledbetter Bldg., Rm. 215
7th & Wolfe St.
Little Rock, AR 72203
Phone: (501)371-1741

Credential Type: License. **Duration of License:** Two or four years. **Requirements:** 18 years of age. Must surrender any other valid operators licenses upon issuance of chauffeur's license. **Examination:** Yes. **Fees:** $11 two year license. $21 four year license. **Governing Statute:** 359.673-014.

8245

Drivers, Commercial
Office of Driver Services
7th & Wolfe St., Rm. 125-A
Little Rock, AR 72203
Phone: (501)682-7100

Credential Type: License. **Duration of License:** Four years. **Requirements:** Pass physical. Class A—18 years of age. Class B and C 16 years of age. **Examination:** Yes. **Fees:** $35 Regular license. $20 School Bus Operator only. $62.25 four year commercial driver's license.

Hawaii

8246

Motor Vehicle Operator, Taxicab Driver
City and County Motor Vehicle Licensing Div., Motor Vehicle Branch
1455 S. Beretania St.
Honolulu, HI 96814
Phone: (808)973-2730

Credential Type: License. **Requirements:** 18 years of age. Character Reference Certificate. Type 3 driver's license. One year of driving experience. Letter of employment from a taxi company or present business license. Certificate of health. Criminal record check. Submit a traffic abstract. **Examination:** Written and oral. **Fees:** $120 permit fee. $50 license fee. $1 certificate fee.

Iowa

8247

Taxi Driver
Office of Driver Services
Dept. of Transportation
100 Euclid Ave.
Park Fair Mall
Des Moines, IA 50306
Phone: (515)237-3153

Alternate Information: 5268 2nd Ave., NW, Des Moines, IA 50313

Credential Type: License. **Duration of License:** Two or four years. **Requirements:** Chauffer's license, Class D endorsement 3. Most large cities require a special operator's license issued by the local city government. **Examination:** Vision and driving exam. **Fees:** $16 or $32 license fee.

Maryland

8248

Cab Driver
Motor Vehicle Administration
Dept. of Transportation
6601 Ritchie Hwy.
Glen Burnie, MD 21062
Phone: (301)768-7254
Phone: (301)768-7275

Credential Type: License. **Requirements:** Contact licensing body for application information.

Michigan

8249

Chauffeur
Bureau of Driver and Vehicles Records
Dept. of State
7064 Crowner Dr.
Lansing, MI 48918
Phone: (517)322-1460

Credential Type: License. **Duration of License:** Two or four years. **Authorization:** All persons employed to operate a motor vehicle as a public or common carrier of persons or property on Michigan highways must be licensed as a chauffeur by the Department of State. **Requirements:** At least 18 years of age. Must not have a physical or mental condition which may interfere with the reasonable operation of a motor vehicle. Must not be a habitual drunkard or addicted to a controlled substance. **Examination:** Written, vision, and practical exam. **Fees:** $5 (one year), $20 (four years) initial exam and license fee. $25 behind-the-wheel road test fee. $10 (two years), $20 (four years) renewal exam

Michigan

Chauffeur, continued

and license fee. **Governing Statute:** Michigan Vehicle Code, Act 300 of 1949, as amended.

8250

Motor Carrier of Passengers for Hire
Intercity Div.
Bureau of Urban and Public Transportation
Dept. of Transportation
PO Box 30050
Lansing, MI 48909
Phone: (517)373-2090

Credential Type: Certificate of authority. **Duration of License:** One year. **Requirements:** Demonstrate financial responsibility. Have a good safety record and submit a list of equipment (vehicle roster) to be used. Have motor bus(es) inspected by the Department. Submit a paid, one-year certificate of insurance with specific personal injury protection coverage and property damage coverage with a combined single limit of at least $5 million as well as $1 million Michigan basic no-fault coverage. Abide by the rules of the Department. **Examination:** Written exam. **Reciprocity:** Informal reciprocity for safety inspections of vehicles for certain states and provinces is accepted. Check with the Michigan Department of Transportation for the current list. **Fees:** $300 initial application and certificate of authority fee. $25 (times the number of motor buses used) renewal certificate of authority fee. **Governing Statute:** Motor Bus Transportation Act, Act 432 of 1982, as amended.

Nebraska

8251

Commercial Driver
Nebraska Dept. of Motor Vehicles
301 Centennial Mall S.
PO Box 94789
Lincoln, NE 68509
Phone: (402)471-2281

Credential Type: License. **Duration of License:** Four years. **Requirements:** 18 years of age for class "A". 16 years of age for class "B" or "C". Class "A" "B" and "C" must be 21 years of age if driving across state lines. **Examination:** Yes. **Fees:** $40 license fee. $5 change of class fee. $40 renewal fee. $5 endorsement fee.

8252

Taxi Driver/Chauffeur
Lincoln City Clerk's Office
555 S. 10th St.
Lincoln, NE 68508
Phone: (402)471-7437

Credential Type: License. **Duration of License:** One year. **Requirements:** 18 years of age. Must hold a valid driver's license. Must pass a criminal history check. **Fees:** $5 application fee. $10 renewal fee.

Nevada

8253

Taxi Driver
Dept. of Motor Vehicles
Driver's License Div.
305 Galletti Way
Reno, NV 89512
Phone: (702)688-2404

Credential Type: Class B Commercial Driver's License. **Examination:** Written, vision and driving exams. **Fees:** $85 exam fee. $85 license fee. $1 photo fee.

New York

8254

Chauffer
New York State Dept. of Motor Vehicles
Office of Communications
Empire State Plaza
Albany, NY 12228
Phone: (518)474-0877

Credential Type: License. **Duration of License:** Four years. **Requirements:** Pre-licensing course required. 18 years of age. Must hold a Class 4 license or equivalent out-of-state license. **Examination:** Vision, written and road tests. **Fees:** $9 application fee. $33.50—$41.50 license fee. $33.50 renewal fee. **Governing Statute:** Article 19 of the Vehicle and Traffic Law.

North Carolina

8255

Domestic Chauffeur
Dept. of Transportation
Driver's License Section
1100 New Bern Ave.
Raleigh, NC 27697
Phone: (919)733-4241

Credential Type: Class "C" Driver's License. **Duration of License:** Four years. **Requirements:** 18 years of age. **Examination:** Written, vision and practical exams. **Fees:** $10 initial fee. $10 renewal fee.

8256

Taxicab Driver
Dept. of Transportation
Driver's License Section
1100 New Bern Ave.
Raleigh, NC 27697
Phone: (919)733-4241

Credential Type: License. **Duration of License:** Four years. **Requirements:** 18 years of age. **Examination:** Written, vision and driving exams. **Fees:** $10 initial fee. $10 renewal fee.

Oklahoma

8257

Chauffeur
Oklahoma Dept. of Public Safety
3600 N. Martin Luther King Ave.
PO Box 11415
Oklahoma City, OK 73136
Phone: (405)425-2424

Credential Type: License. **Duration of License:** Four years. **Requirements:** State resident. 18 years of age. **Examination:** Driver's License Examination. **Fees:** $15 exam fee. $25 driver's license fee. $22 renewal fee.

Oregon

8258

Commercial Driver
Motor Vehicles Div.
1905 Lana Ave. NE
Salem, OR 97314
Phone: (503)299-9999

Credential Type: Commercial driver license. **Duration of License:** Three to five years. **Requirements:** 18 years of age and at least one year of driving experience.

Must have a valid medical certificate which is approved by the federal and state government for meeting medical qualifications for commercial motor vehicle operators.

Pass required knowledge tests and drive test. **Examination:** Knowledge and drive tests. Separate knowledge tests are given for the following endorsements: hazardous materials, tank, passenger, and doubles/triples. **Fees:** $3 fee for each knowldge exam. $56 for each skills test given by DMV representative. $33 for each skills test given by a certified third party tester. $25 or $31.25 license fee, depending on previous license expiration date. $13 instruction permit fee. $20.25 renewal fee. $27.25 renewal fee with motorcycle endorsement. **Governing Statute:** ORS Chapter 807.

Rhode Island

8259

Chauffeur
Div. of Motor Vehicles
Rhode Island Dept. of Motor Vehicles
2 Capitol Hill
Providence, RI 02903
Phone: (401)277-3427

Credential Type: Chauffeur License—Class I. **Duration of License:** Five years. **Authorization:** Authorizes applicant to operate any vehicle carrying up to 15 passengers with the exception of school buses. School bus drivers require a specialized license. **Requirements:** At least 18 years of age. Resident of Rhode Island. A minimum of one year of driving experience. Complete CPR course (new or renewal). **Examination:** Written, road, and eye examinations (each eye must test at least 20/40). **Reciprocity:** Yes. **Fees:** $5 written examination fee. $12 Rhode Island two-year driver's license fee. $30 Rhode Island five-year driver's license fee. $2 transfer fee to chauffeur's license.

Credential Type: Chauffeur License—Class II. **Duration of License:** Five years. **Authorization:** Authorizes applicant to operate any vehicle weighing between five and 13 tons, except school buses. **Requirements:** At least 18 years of age. Resident of Rhode Island. A minimum of one year of driving experience. Complete CPR course (new or renewal). **Examination:** Written, road, and eye examinations (each eye must test at least 20/40). **Reciprocity:** Yes. **Fees:** $5 written examination fee. $12 Rhode Island two-year driver's license fee. $30 Rhode Island five-year driver's license fee. $2 transfer fee to chauffeur's license.

Taxidermists

The following states grant licenses in this occupational category as of the date of publication:
Arizona, Idaho, Illinois, Maryland, Michigan, Montana, North Carolina, North Dakota, Washington.

Arizona

8260

Taxidermist
Arizona Game and Fish Dept.
2221 W. Greenway Rd.
Phoenix, AZ 85023-4312
Phone: (602)942-3000
Fax: (602)789-3920

Credential Type: Taxidermist license. **Authorization:** To engage in the business of a taxidermist for hire. **Requirements:** Submit application. Keep a register of persons who furnish raw and unmounted specimens. File a quarterly report in English with the department. **Fees:** $50 license fee. **Governing Statute:** Arizona Revised Statutes, Title 17, Chapter 2.

Idaho

8261

Taxidermist
License Office
Administration Bureau
Fish and Game Dept.
PO Box 25
600 S. Walnut
Boise, ID 83707
Phone: (208)334-3717

Credential Type: License. **Requirements:** Contact licensing body for application information.

Illinois

8262

Fur Tanner or Dyer
Illinois Dept. of Conservation
524 South 2nd St.
Springfield, IL 62701-1787
Phone: (217)785-3423

Credential Type: Fur Tanner or Dyer License. **Duration of License:** One year. **Requirements:** Must be an Illinois resident for at least 30 days. Submit application and pay fee. **Reciprocity:** No. **Fees:** $25 initial license fee. $25 renewal fee. **Governing Statute:** Illinois Revised Statutes, Chapter 61.

8263

Taxidermist
Illinois Dept. of Conservation
524 South 2nd St.
Springfield, IL 62701-1787
Phone: (217)785-3423

Credential Type: Taxidermist License. **Duration of License:** One year. **Requirements:** Must be an Illinois resident for at least one year. Submit application and pay fee. **Reciprocity:** No. **Fees:** $25 license fee (per site). $25 license renewal fee (per site). **Governing Statute:** Illinois Revised Statutes, Chapter 61, Illinois Conservation Law—Wildlife.

Maryland

8264

Taxidermist
Wildlife Div.
Dept. of Natural Resources
Tawes State Office Bldg.
Annapolis, MD 21401
Phone: (410)296-2230

Credential Type: Taxidermist License. **Duration of License:** One year. **Requirements:** Supply sample mount for evaluation. Maintain up-to-date log books. **Examination:** Taxidermy test. **Fees:** $50 license and test fee.

Michigan

8265

Fur Processor
Administrative Services Div.
Dept. of Natural Resources
Stevens T. Mason Bldg.
PO Box 30028
Lansing, MI 48909
Phone: (517)373-1220

Credential Type: License. **Duration of License:** One year. **Requirements:** Abide by the laws related to the custom tanning or dressing of raw furs. **Fees:** $5 initial license fee. $5 renewal fee. **Governing Statute:** Fur Dealer's License Act, Act 308 of 1929.

Taxidermists

8266

Taxidermist
Administrative Services Div.
Dept. of Natural Resources
Stevens T. Mason Bldg.
PO Box 30028
Lansing, MI 48909
Phone: (517)373-1220

Credential Type: Permit. **Duration of License:** One year. **Requirements:** Applicants for permits must comply with State game and fish laws and the rules put into effect by the Department of Natural Resources. **Fees:** $15 initial permit fee. $15 renewal fee. **Governing Statute:** The Wildlife Conservation Act, Act 256 of 1988.

Montana

8267

Taxidermist
Dept. of Fish, Wildlife, and Parks
Law Enforcement Div.
1420 E. 6th Ave.
Helena, MT 59620
Phone: (406)444-2452

Credential Type: Taxidermist License. **Requirements:** Submit application and pay fee. **Fees:** $15 license fee. **Governing Statute:** Montana Code Annotated 87-4.

North Carolina

8268

Taxidermist
Dept. of Natural Resources and
   Community Developement
License Section
512 N. Salisbury St.
Raleigh, NC 27611
Phone: (919)733-7896

Credential Type: License. **Duration of License:** One year. **Requirements:** Contact licensing body for application information.

North Dakota

8269

Taxidermist
Game and Fish Dept.
100 N. Bismarck Expy.
Bismarck, ND 58501
Phone: (701)221-6305

Credential Type: Taxidermist License. **Duration of License:** One year. **Requirements:** Submit application and pay fee. Must maintain records.

Washington

8270

Taxidermist
Dept. of Wildlife
600 N. Capitol Way, GJ-11
Olympia, WA 98504-0091
Phone: (206)753-5700

Credential Type: Taxidermist License. **Duration of License:** One year. **Requirements:** Submit application and pay fee. **Fees:** $180 license fee.

Telephone, Telegraph, and Teletype Operators

One or more occupations in this chapter require a federal license. Additionally, the following states grant licenses as of the date of publication: Connecticut, Ohio.

Federal Contacts

Federal Communications Commission
1919 M St., NW
Washington, DC 20554
Phone: (202)632-7240
Fax: (202)632-0160

Regional Offices

Federal Communications Commission
6721 W. Raspberry Rd.
Anchorage, AK 99502
Phone: (907)243-2153

Federal Communications Commission
PO Box 6
Douglas, AZ 85608
Phone: (602)364-8414

Federal Communications Commission
Cerritos Corporate Tower, Rm. 660
18000 Studebaker Rd.
Cerritos, CA 90701
Phone: (213)809-2096

Federal Communications Commission
PO Box 311
Livermore, CA 94551-0311
Phone: (415)447-3614

Federal Communications Commission
4542 Ruffner St., Rm. 370
San Diego, CA 92111-2216
Phone: (619)557-5478

Federal Communications Commission
424 Customhouse
555 Battery St.
San Francisco, CA 94111
Phone: (415)705-1101

Federal Communications Commission
165 S. Union Blvd., Ste. 860
Lakewood, CO 80228
Phone: (303)969-6497

Federal Communications Commission
PO Box 1730
Vero Beach, FL 32961-1730
Phone: (407)778-3755

Federal Communications Commission
Rochester Bldg., Rm. 310
8390 N.W. 53rd St.
Miami, FL 33166
Phone: (305)526-7420

Federal Communications Commission
2203 N. Lois Ave., Rm. 1215
Tampa, FL 33607-2356
Phone: (813)228-2872

Federal Communications Commission
Massell Bldg., Rm. 440
1365 Peachtree St., N.E.
Atlanta, GA 30309
Phone: (404)347-2631

Federal Communications Commission
PO Box 85
Powder Springs, GA 30073
Phone: (404)943-5420

Federal Communications Commission
PO Box 1030
Waipahu, HI 96797
Phone: (808)677-3318

Federal Communications Commission
Park Ridge Office Center, Rm. 306
1550 Northwest Hwy.
Park Ridge, IL 60068
Phone: (312)353-0195

Federal Communications Commission
800 W. Commerce Rd., Rm. 505
New Orleans, LA 70123
Phone: (504)589-2095

Federal Communications Commission
PO Box 470
Belfast, ME 04915
Phone: (207)338-4088

Federal Communications Commission
1017 Federal Bldg.
31 Hopkins Plaza
Baltimore, MD 21201
Phone: (301)962-2729

Federal Communications Commission
PO Box 250
Columbia, MD 21045
Phone: (301)725-3474

Federal Communications Commission
NFPA Bldg.
1 Batterymarch Pk.
Quincy, MA 02169
Phone: (617)770-4023

Federal Communications Commission
PO Box 89
Allegan, MI 49010
Phone: (616)673-2063

Federal Communications Commission
24897 Hathaway St.
Farmington Hills, MI 48335-1552
Phone: (313)226-6078

Federal Communications Commission
693 Federal Bldg. & US Courthouse
316 N. Robert St.
St. Paul, MN 55101
Phone: (612)290-3819

Federal Communications Commission
Brywood Office Tower, Rm. 320
8800 E. 63rd St.
Kansas City, MO 64133
Phone: (816)926-5111

Federal Communications Commission
PO Box 1588
Grand Island, NE 68802
Phone: (308)382-4296

Federal Communications Commission
1307 Federal Bldg.
111 W. Huron St.
Buffalo, NY 14202
Phone: (716)846-4511

Federal Communications Commission
201 Varick St.
New York, NY 10014-4870
Phone: (212)620-3437

Federal Communications Commission
1782 Federal Office Bldg.
1220 SW 3rd Ave.
Portland, OR 97204
Phone: (503)326-4114

Federal Communications Commission
One Oxford Valley Office Bldg., Rm. 404
2300 E. Lincoln Hwy.
Langhorne, PA 19047
Phone: (215)752-1324

Federal Communications Commission
747 Federal Bldg.
Hato Rey, PR 00918-2251
Phone: (809)766-5567

Federal Communications Commission
9330 LBJ Expressway, Rm. 1170
Dallas, TX 75243
Phone: (214)767-4827

Federal Communications Commission
1225 N. Loop W., Rm. 900
Houston, TX 77008
Phone: (713)229-2748

Federal Communications Commission
PO Box 632
Kingsville, TX 78363-0632
Phone: (512)592-2531

Federal Communications Commission
1200 Communications Circle
Virginia Beach, VA 23455-3725
Phone: (804)441-6472

Federal Communications Commission
One Newport, Rm. 414
3605 132nd Ave., SE
Bellevue, WA 98006
Phone: (206)764-3324

Federal Communications Commission
1330 Loomis Trail Rd.
Custer, WA 98240
Phone: (206)354-4892

Federal Licenses

8271

Marine Radio Operator

Credential Type: Marine Radio Operator Permit. **Duration of License:** Five years. **Authorization:** Required to operate radiotelephone stations aboard certain vessels that sail the Great Lakes. Also required to operate radiotelephone stations aboard vessels of more than 300 gross tons and vessels which carry more than six passengers for hire in the open sea or any tidewater area of the United States. Also required to operate certain aviation radiotelephone stations and certain coast radiotelephone stations. **Requirements:** Must be a legal resident of the United States, or otherwise be eligible for employment in the United States. Be able to receive and transmit spoken messages in English. Pass a written examination covering basic radio law and operating procedures. **Examination:** Written examination. **Governing Statute:** 47 CFR, Part 13.

8272

Radiotelegraph Operator

Credential Type: First Class Radiotelegraph Operator Certificate. **Duration of License:** Five years. **Authorization:** Required only for those who serve as the chief radio operator on a United States passenger ship. Conveys all of the operating authority of a Second Class Certificate. **Requirements:** Must be at least 21 years old. Have at least one year of experience in sending and receiving public correspondence by radiotelegraph at ship stations, coast stations, or both. Must be a legal resident of the United States, or otherwise be eligible for employment in the United States. Be able to receive and transmit spoken messages in English. Pass a Morse code examination. Pass a written examination covering basic radio law and operating procedures. **Examination:** Morse Code examination. Written examination. **Governing Statute:** 47 CFR, Part 13.

Credential Type: Second Class Radiotelegraph Operator Certificate. **Duration of License:** Five years. **Authorization:** Authorizes the holder to operate, repair, and maintain ship and coast radiotelegraph stations in the maritime services. Confers all of the operating authority of the Third Class Certificate and the General Radiotelephone Operator License. **Requirements:** Must be a legal resident of the United States, or otherwise be eligible for employment in the United States. Be able to receive and transmit spoken messages in English. Pass a Morse code examination. Pass a written examination covering basic radio law and operating procedures. **Examination:** Morse Code examination. Written examination. **Governing Statute:** 47 CFR, Part 13.

Credential Type: Third Class Radiotelegraph Operator Certificate. **Duration of License:** Five years. **Authorization:** Authorizes the operation of certain coast radiotelegraph stations. Confers all of the operating authority of the Restricted Radiotelephone Operator Permit and the Marine Radio Operator Permit. **Requirements:** Must be a legal resident of the United States, or otherwise be eligible for employment in the United States. Be able to receive and transmit spoken messages in English. Pass a Morse code examination. Pass a written examination covering basic radio law and operating procedures. **Examination:** Morse Code examination. Written examination. **Governing Statute:** 47 CFR, Part 13.

Credential Type: Ship Radar Endorsement. **Authorization:** Authorizes holder to repair, maintain, or internally adjust ship radar equipment. Endorsement placed only on General Radiotelephone Operator License or on First or Second Class Radiotelegraph Operator Certificate. **Requirements:** Pass a written examination covering special rules applicable to ship radar stations and the technical fundamentals of radar and radar maintenance techniques. **Examination:** Written examination. **Governing Statute:** 47 CFR, Part 13.

Credential Type: Six Months Service Endorsement. **Authorization:** Required on the Radiotelegraph Operator Certificate of anyone who serves as the sole radio operator aboard large U.S. cargo ships sailing on the high seas. **Requirements:** Must hold a Radio Officer's License issued by the U.S. Coast Guard at the time the endorsement is requested. Must have been employed as a radio operator on U.S. ships for at least six months, during which time the ships were in service and applicant held a First or Second Class Radiotelegraph Operator's Certificate. **Governing Statute:** 47 CFR, Part 13.

8273

Radiotelephone Operator

Credential Type: Restricted Radiotelephone Operator Permit. **Duration of License:** Lifetime. **Authorization:** Authorized to operate most aircraft and aeronautical ground stations, marine radiotelephone stations aboard pleasure craft subject to limitations. Also may operate, repair, and maintain any kind of AM, FM, TV, or international broadcast station. May act as chief engineer or chief operator of a broadcast station. **Requirements:** Must be a legal resident of the United States, or otherwise be eligible for employment in the United States, or hold an aircraft pilot certificate valid in the United States, or hold an FCC radio station license in applicant's own name.

Be able to speak and hear. Be able to keep at least a rough written log, and be familiar with provisions of applicable treaties, laws, and rules. **Examination:** No examination required. **Governing Statute:** 47 CFR, Part 13.

Credential Type: General Radiotelephone Operator License. **Duration of License:** Lifetime. **Authorization:** Required to adjust, maintain, or internally repair FCC licensed radiotelephone transmitters in the aviation, maritime, and international fixed public radio services. Conveys the same operating authority as a Marine Radio Operator Permit. Required to operate any maritime land radio station or compulsorily equipped ship radiotelephone station operating with more than 1500 watts of peak envelope power. Required to operate voluntarily equipped ship and aeronautical (including aircraft) stations with more than 1000 watts of peak envelope power. **Requirements:** Must be a legal resident of the United States, or otherwise be eligible for employment in the United States. Be able to receive and transmit spoken messages in English. Pass a written examination covering basic radio law, operating procedures, electronics fundamentals, and techniques

Radiotelephone Operator, continued

required to repair and maintain radio transmitters and receivers. **Examination:** Written examination. **Governing Statute:** 47 CFR, Part 13.

Credential Type: Ship Radar Endorsement. **Authorization:** Authorizes holder to repair, maintain, or internally adjust ship radar equipment. Endorsement placed only on General Radiotelephone Operator License or on First or Second Class Radiotelegraph Operator Certificate. **Requirements:** Pass a written examination covering special rules applicable to ship radar stations and the technical fundamentals of radar and radar maintenance techniques. **Examination:** Written examination. **Governing Statute:** 47 CFR, Part 13.

Connecticut

8274

Telephone Operator (Racetrack)
Connecticut Div. of Special Revenue
Russell Rd.
PO Box 11424
Newington, CT 06111-0424
Phone: (203)566-2756

Credential Type: License Registration. **Requirements:** Submit application and fingerprint card. Pay fee. **Fees:** $5 registration fee.

Ohio

8275

Telephone Operator (Thoroughbred, Standardbred, and Quarter Horse Racing)
Ohio State Racing Commission
State Office Tower
77 S. High St., 18th Fl.
Columbus, OH 43266-0416
Phone: (614)466-2757

Credential Type: License Registration. **Requirements:** Submit application and fingerprint card. Pay fee. **Fees:** $10 registration fee.

Truckdrivers

The following states grant licenses in this occupational category as of the date of publication:

Arkansas	Georgia	Kansas	Mississippi	New Hampshire	Ohio	Texas
California	Hawaii	Maine	Missouri	New Mexico	Oregon	Utah
Connecticut	Idaho	Maryland	Montana	New York	Pennsylvania	Washington
Delaware	Illinois	Massachusetts	Nebraska	North Carolina	Rhode Island	West Virginia
Florida	Iowa	Michigan	Nevada	North Dakota	South Dakota	Wisconsin

Arkansas

8276

Drivers, Commercial
Office of Driver Services
7th & Wolfe St., Rm. 125-A
Little Rock, AR 72203
Phone: (501)682-7100

Credential Type: License. **Duration of License:** Four years. **Requirements:** Pass physical. Class A—18 years of age. Class B and C 16 years of age. **Examination:** Yes. **Fees:** $35 Regular license. $20 School Bus Operator only. $62.25 four year commercial driver's license.

8277

Liquefied Petroleum Gas Truck Driver
The Liquefied Petroleum Gas Board
1421 W. Sixth St.
Little ROck, AR 72201
Phone: (501)371-1008

Credential Type: License. **Duration of License:** One year. **Requirements:** Show proof of training (at least 30 days). Employed by a dealer who is authorized to engage in the liquefied petroleum gas business in the state. **Examination:** Yes. **Fees:** $5 License. $5 Renewal.

California

8278

Milk Hauler and Tester
Dept. of Food and Agriculture
Div. of Animal Industry
Milk and Dairy Foods Control Branch
1220 N St.
Sacramento, CA 94271
Phone: (916)654-0773
Fax: (916)654-1274

Credential Type: License. **Requirements:** Contact licensing body for application information.

Connecticut

8279

Milk Hauler and Tester
Dept. of Agriculture
Dairy Div.
State Office Bldg.
165 Capitol Ave.
Hartford, CT 06115
Phone: (203)566-5894
Fax: (203)566-6094

Credential Type: License. **Requirements:** Contact licensing body for application information.

Delaware

8280

Milk Hauler and Tester
Div. of Public Health
Office of Food Control
Jesse Cooper Bldg.
Dover, DE 19901
Phone: (302)739-4731
Fax: (302)739-6617

Credential Type: License. **Requirements:** Contact licensing body for application information.

Florida

8281

Milk Hauler and Tester
Dept. of Agriculture and Consumer Services
Div. of Dairy Industry
3125 Conner Blvd.
Tallahassee, FL 32399-1650
Phone: (904)487-1460
Fax: (904)488-0863

Credential Type: License. **Requirements:** Contact licensing body for application information.

Georgia

8282

Milk Hauler and Tester
Dept. of Agriculture
Dairy Regulatory Div.
19 Martin Luther King Jr. Dr.
Capitol Sq.
Atlanta, GA 30334
Phone: (404)656-3625
Fax: (404)656-9380

Credential Type: License. **Requirements:** Contact licensing body for application information.

Hawaii

8283

Motor Vehicle Operator, Truck Driver
City and County Motor Vehicle Licensing Div., Motor Vehicle Branch
1455 S. Beretania St.
Honolulu, HI 96814
Phone: (808)973-2730

Credential Type: License. **Requirements:** 18 years of age. Type 5,6 or seven driver's license, depending upon truck. Type 3 automobile driver's license. Certificate of health. **Examination:** Road test. **Fees:** $3 permit fee. $3 upgrade fee.

Idaho

8284

Milk Hauler and Tester
Dept. of Health and Welfare
Bureau of Preventive Medicine
450 W. State St.
Boise, ID 83720
Phone: (208)334-5930
Fax: (208)334-5694

Credential Type: License. **Requirements:** Contact licensing body for application information.

Illinois

8285

Bulk Milk Hauler/Sampler
Illinois Dept. of Public Health
Div. of Food, Drugs, and Dairies
525 W. Jefferson St.
Springfield, IL 62761
Phone: (217)785-2439

Credential Type: Bulk Milk Hauler/Sampler License. **Duration of License:** One year. **Authorization:** Allows applicant to measure and screen milk, then haul milk to dairy processing plant or transfer station from farm dairies. **Requirements:** Submit application and pay fees. Pass examination. **Examination:** Written examination. **Reciprocity:** No. **Fees:** $25 initial license fee. $25 renewal fee. **Governing Statute:** Title 77, Chapter I.

8286

Commercial Driver (Truck or Bus)
Secretary of State
2701 S. Dirksen Parkway
Springfield, IL 62723
Phone: (217)782-0560

Credential Type: Commercial Driver License. **Duration of License:** Four years. **Authorization:** Allows applicant to operate a truck or bus that is over 26,000 pounds. **Requirements:** Must be at least 18 years of age to drive for-hire or within the state of Illinois. Must be at least 21 years of age to transport passengers or for interstate driving. **Examination:** Written and performance tests. **Reciprocity:** Yes, with a valid commercial license from another jurisdiction. **Fees:** $40 examination fee. $40 initial license fee. $40 renewal fee. **Governing Statute:** Chapter 95 1/2, Section 6-500, Illinois Vehicle Code.

8287

Transporter (Motor Vehicles)
Secretary of State
Centennial Bldg., Rm. 008
Springfield, IL 62756
Phone: (217)782-7817

Credential Type: Transporter License. **Duration of License:** One year. **Requirements:** Submit application and pay fee. **Reciprocity:** No. **Fees:** $36 Master License fee. $10 duplicate license fee. **Governing Statute:** Illinois Vehicle Code 95 1/2 5-201.

Iowa

8288

Farm Bulk Milk Hauler
Dairy Products Control Bureau
Iowa Dept. of Agriculture and Land Stewardship
Wallace State Office Bldg.
Des Moines, IA 50319
Phone: (515)281-3545

Credential Type: License. **Duration of License:** One year. **Requirements:** 16 years of age. **Examination:** Yes. **Fees:** $3 license fee. $3 renewal fee.

8289

Milk Hauler
Dept. of Agriculture and Land Stewardship
Dairy Products Control Bureau
Henry A. Wallace Bldg.
Des Moines, IA 50319
Phone: (515)381-3545

Credential Type: License. **Duration of License:** One year. **Requirements:** Submit application and pay fee. **Fees:** $10 annual license fee.

8290

Tractor-Trailer Truck Driver
Office of Driver Services
Dept. of Transportation
Park Fair Mall
100 Euclid Ave.
Des Moines, IA 50306
Phone: (515)237-3153

Alternate Information: 5268 2nd Ave., NW, Des Moines, IA 50313

Credential Type: License. **Duration of License:** Two or four years. **Requirements:** A Commercial Driver's License (CDL) is necessary to drive a truck in Iowa and the applicant must be at least 18 years of age. The U.S. Dept. of Transportation establishes minimum qualifications for truck drivers engaged in interstate commerce. **Examination:** Written, driving and vision exams. **Exemptions:** The driving test is waived for new Iowa residents who possess a CDL from their former state. **Fees:** $16 or $32 license fee.

Truckdrivers

Kansas

8291

Milk Hauler and Tester
State Board of Agriculture
Div. of Inspection-Dairy
901 S. Kansas Ave.
Topeka, KS 66612-1272
Phone: (913)296-3731
Phone: (913)296-7020
Fax: (913)296-7951

Credential Type: License. **Requirements:** Contact licensing body for application information.

Maine

8292

Milk Hauler and Tester
Dept. of Agriculture
Food and Rural Resources
Div. of Regulation, Dairy Inspection
State House Station 28
Augusta, ME 04333
Phone: (207)289-3841
Fax: (207)289-7548

Credential Type: License. **Requirements:** Contact licensing body for application information.

Maryland

8293

Certified Hazardous Waste Driver
Hazardous and Solid Waste Div.
Dept. of the Environment
2500 Broening Hwy.
Baltimore, MD 21224
Phone: (410)631-3343

Credential Type: License. **Requirements:** Contact licensing body for application information.

8294

Hauler
Motor Vehicle Administration
Dept. of Transportation
6601 Ritchie Hwy.
Glen Burnie, MD 21062
Phone: (301)787-2971

Credential Type: License. **Requirements:** Contact licensing body for application information.

8295

Hazardous Waste Hauler
Hazardous and Solid Waste Div.
Dept. of the Environment
2500 Broening Hwy.
Baltimore, MD 21224
Phone: (410)631-3343

Credential Type: License. **Requirements:** Contact licensing body for application information.

8296

Milk Hauler and Tester
Dept. of Health and Mental Hygiene
Office of Food Protection and Consumer Health Services
4201 Patterson Ave., Rm. 515
Baltimore, MD 21215
Phone: (410)764-3579
Fax: (410)764-3591

Credential Type: License. **Requirements:** Contact licensing body for application information.

Massachusetts

8297

Milk Hauler and Tester
Dept. of Food and Agricutlure
Bureau of Dairying
100 Cambridge St.
Boston, MA 02202
Phone: (617)727-3020
Fax: (617)727-7235

Credential Type: License. **Requirements:** Contact licensing body for application information.

Michigan

8298

Farm Bulk Milk Pickup Tank Operator
Dairy Products Div.
Dept. of Agriculture
Ottawa Bldg., N.
PO Box 30017
Lansing, MI 48909
Phone: (517)373-1104

Credential Type: License. **Duration of License:** One year. **Requirements:** Abide by the rules of the Department of Agriculture. **Examination:** Written and practical exam. **Fees:** $10 initial exam and license fee. $10 renewal fee. **Governing Statute:** Manufacturing Milk Act, Act 222 of 1913, as amended.

8299

Liquid Industrial Waste Remover
Waste Management Div.
Dept. of Natural Resources
Stevens T. Mason Bldg.
PO Box 30241
Lansing, MI 48909
Phone: (517)373-1220

Credential Type: License. **Duration of License:** One year. **Authorization:** Any person who transports liquid industrial waste from the premises of another must be licensed by the Department of Natural Resources. **Requirements:** Post a surety bond in the amount of $15,000 if a Michigan resident and $30,000 if a non-resident. **Fees:** $100 initial license fee. This fee is waived if a business license, issued under the authority of the Hazardous Waste Act (Public Act 64 of 1979, as amended) is obtained. $10 initial license fee for each vehicle. Renewal fee is same as initial fee. **Governing Statute:** Liquid Industrial Waste Act, Act 136 of 1969.

8300

Motor Carrier Driver
Motor Carrier Div.
Dept. of State Police
300 N. Clippert
Lansing, MI 48913
Phone: (517)332-2521

Credential Type: Certification. **Duration of License:** Three years after ending employment with the carrier. **Requirements:** At least 18 years old (or 21 years old when transporting hazardous materials). Have a currently valid Michigan chauffeur's or operator's license with proper endorsements. Be familiar with the methods and procedures for securing cargo in or on the motor vehicle which the person drives. Pass a background investigation of character and driving record. Be able to read and speak the English language. Abide by all rules and regulations of the Michigan State Police. **Examination:** Written exam, road test, and physical exam. **Exemptions:** Drivers of lightweight vehicles or combination farm vehicles are exempt from some of the above stated requirements. Contact the Michigan State Police for more information. **Governing Statute:** Motor Carrier Safety Rules, Act 181 of 1963, as amended.

Michigan 8301

8301

Truck Driver
Bureau of Driver and Vehicles
  Records
Dept. of State
7064 Crowner Dr.
Lansing, MI 48918
Phone: (517)322-1460

Credential Type: Chauffeur's License. **Duration of License:** Two or four years. **Authorization:** A "Group A" designation is required to drive combination vehicles with a trailer exceeding a gross vehicle weight rating (GVWR) of 10,000 pounds. A "Group B" designation is required to drive single vehicles with GVWR in excess of 26,000 pounds whose trailer or trailers do not exceed 10,000 pounds. A "Group C" designation is required for smaller vehicles carrying hazardous materials. Commercial vehicle "endorsement(s)" are required in conjunction with group designations for multiple trailers, tank vehicles, vehicles carrying hazardous materials, tank trucks transporting hazardous materials.

Applicants for a vehicle group designation or endorsement must not be listed on the national driver register or on a commercial driver license information system in the U.S. Department of Transportation as having been convicted of or incurred a bond forfeiture in relation to any offenses specified in section 205 (a) of the National Driver Register Act of 1982. Must not have had a six-point conviction in the two years prior to application. **Requirements:** Be at least 18 years of age. Must not have a physical or mental condition which may interfere with the reasonable operation of a motor vehicle. Must not be a habitual drunkard or addicted to a controlled substance. **Examination:** Written, vision, and practical exam. Vehicle group designation exam and road test. **Fees:** $5 (one year), $20 (four years) initial exam and license fee. $25 behind-the-wheel road test fee. $10 (two years), $20 (four years) renewal exam and license fee. $20 vehicle group designation initial examination and license fee (one to four years). $60 behind-the-wheel road test. **Governing Statute:** Michigan Vehicle Code, Act 300 of 1949, as amended.

8302

Water Hauler
Dept. of Public Health
Div. of Water Supply
3423 N. Logan
PO Box 30195
Lansing, MI 48909
Phone: (517)335-8000

Credential Type: License. **Duration of License:** One year. **Requirements:** Submit to an inspection of the water source, water transportation equipment, and operation and disinfection procedures to be used. **Reciprocity:** Licensed water haulers from other states may be licensed in Michigan if the issuing state has licensing requirements comparable to Michigan's. **Governing Statute:** Safe Water Drinking Act, Act 399 of 1976.

Mississippi

8303

Milk Hauler and Tester
Dept. of Health
Milk and Shellfish Sanitation Br.
2423 N. State St.
Jackson, MS 39215-1700
Phone: (601)960-7697
Fax: (601)960-7948

Credential Type: License. **Requirements:** Contact licensing body for application information.

Missouri

8304

Milk Hauler and Tester
State Milk Board
915-C Leslie Blvd.
Jefferson City, MO 65101
Phone: (314)751-3830
Fax: (314)751-2527

Credential Type: License. **Requirements:** Contact licensing body for application information.

Montana

8305

Truck Driver
Montana Driver Services Bureau
303 Roberts
Helena, MT 59620
Phone: (406)444-3292

Credential Type: Type 1 License. **Duration of License:** Four years. **Authorization:** Can operate anywhere in the United States. **Requirements:** A medical certificate. 21 years of age. **Examination:** Written and practical exams. **Fees:** $12 license fee. $12 endorsement fee. $24 renewal fee. **Governing Statute:** Montana Code Annotated 61-5-101 through 61-5-213.

Credential Type: Type 2 License. **Duration of License:** Four years. **Authorization:** Can operate only in Montana. **Requirements:** A medical certificate. 18 years of age. **Examination:** Written and practical exams. **Fees:** $12 license fee. $6 endorsement fee. $18 renewal fee. **Governing Statute:** Montana Code Annotated 61-5-101 through 61-5-213.

Nebraska

8306

Commercial Driver
Nebraska Dept. of Motor Vehicles
301 Centennial Mall S.
PO Box 94789
Lincoln, NE 68509
Phone: (402)471-2281

Credential Type: License. **Duration of License:** Four years. **Requirements:** 18 years of age for class "A". 16 years of age for class "B" or "C". Class "A" "B" and "C" must be 21 years of age if driving across state lines. **Examination:** Yes. **Fees:** $40 license fee. $5 change of class fee. $40 renewal fee. $5 endorsement fee.

Nevada

8307

Milk Hauler
Dept. of Human Resources
Health Div.
Bureau of Health Protection Services
505 E. King St., Rm. 103
Carson City, NV 89710
Phone: (702)687-4750

Credential Type: License. **Duration of License:** One year. **Requirements:** Pass written examination and equipment inspection. **Examination:** Written examination. **Fees:** $20 annual license fee.

8308

Trucker
Dept. of Motor Vehicles
Driver's License Div.
305 Galletti Way
Reno, NV 89512
Phone: (702)688-2404

Credential Type: Local Truck Driver. **Examination:** Written, vision, driving and medical exams. **Fees:** $85 exam and license fee. $1 photo fee. $14 fee for each additional endorsement.

Credential Type: Long Haul Truck Driver. **Examination:** Written, vision, driving and medical exams. **Fees:** $85 exam and license fee. $1 photo fee. $14 fee for each additional endorsement.

New Hampshire

8309

Milk Hauler and Tester
Dairy Sanitation Program
Office of Environmental Health
Dept. of Health and Human Services
6 Hazen Dr.
Concord, NH 03301-6527
Phone: (603)271-4673
Fax: (603)271-3745

Credential Type: License. **Requirements:** Contact licensing body for application information.

New Mexico

8310

Milk Hauler and Tester
State Environmental Dept.
4131 Montgomery Blvd. NE
Albuquerque, NM 87109
Phone: (505)841-9450
Fax: (505)884-9254

Credential Type: License. **Requirements:** Contact licensing body for application information.

New York

8311

Truck Driver, Heavy or Tractor Trailer
New York State Dept. of Motor Vehicles
Office of Communications
Empire State Plaza
Albany, NY 12228
Phone: (518)474-0877

Credential Type: License. **Duration of License:** Four years. **Requirements:** Pre-licensing course required. Written and road testing, and course requirement, waived if out-of-state domestic license is surrendered for reciprocity. 18 years of age. **Examination:** Written, road and vision tests. **Fees:** $20 course fee. $9 application fee. $33.50—$37.50 license fee. **Governing Statute:** Article 19 of the Vehicle and Traffic Law.

North Carolina

8312

Farm Bulk Milk Hauler/Sampler
Dept. of Agriculture
Food & Drug Protection Div.
PO Box 27647
Raleigh, NC 27611
Phone: (919)733-7366

Credential Type: License. **Duration of License:** One year. **Examination:** Written. **Fees:** $2 initial fee. $2 renewal fee.

8313

Truck Driver
Dept. of Transportation
Driver's License Section
1100 New Bern Ave.
Raleigh, NC 27697
Phone: (919)733-4241

Credential Type: License. **Duration of License:** Four years. **Requirements:** 18 years of age. **Fees:** $15 initial fee. $15 renewal fee.

North Dakota

8314

Milk Hauler and Tester
Dept. of Agriculture
Dairy Commissioner
State Capitol
Bismarck, ND 58505
Phone: (701)224-4763
Fax: (701)224-4567

Credential Type: License. **Requirements:** Contact licensing body for application information.

8315

Truck Driver (Commercial)
Transportation Dept.
Drivers License Div.
608 E. Blvd. Ave.
Bismarck, ND 58505-0700
Phone: (701)224-2600

Credential Type: License. **Duration of License:** Two years. **Authorization:** There are three classes of licenses and five types of endorsements. **Requirements:** Must be a state resident. Must meet requirements of the Commercial Motor Vehicle Safety Act. **Examination:** Knowledge and skills test. Additional written exam required for endorsement as a hazardous materials driver. **Fees:** $5 exam fee. $3 endorsement fee. **Governing Statute:** North Dakota Century Code, Chap. 39-06.2.

Ohio

8316

Milk Hauler and Tester
Dept. of Health
Milk Program
246 High St.
Columbus, OH 43266-0118
Phone: (614)466-5550
Fax: (614)644-1909

Credential Type: License. **Requirements:** Contact licensing body for application information.

Oregon

8317

Commercial Driver
Motor Vehicles Div.
1905 Lana Ave. NE
Salem, OR 97314
Phone: (503)299-9999

Credential Type: Commercial driver license. **Duration of License:** Three to five years. **Requirements:** 18 years of age and at least one year of driving experience. Must have a valid medical certificate which is approved by the federal and state government for meeting medical qualifications for commercial motor vehicle operators.

Pass required knowledge tests and drive test. **Examination:** Knowledge and drive tests. Separate knowledge tests are given for the following endorsements: hazardous materials, tank, passenger, and doubles/triples. **Fees:** $3 fee for each knowldge exam. $56 for each skills test given by DMV representative. $33 for each skills test given by a certified third party tester. $25 or $31.25 license fee, depending on previous license expiration date. $13 instruction permit fee. $20.25 renewal fee. $27.25 renewal fee with motorcycle endorsement. **Governing Statute:** ORS Chapter 807.

8318

Liquified Petroleum Gas (LPG) Truck Equipment Operator
Office of State Fire Marshall
4760 Portland Rd. NE
Salem, OR 97305
Phone: (503)378-2848

Credential Type: License. **Duration of License:** One year. **Requirements:** Must be employed by a licensed LPG Installer. **Examination:** Yes. **Fees:** $5 license fee. $5 renewal fee. **Governing Statute:** ORS 480.410 to 480.460.

Pennsylvania

8319

Milk Hauler and Tester
Dept. of Agriculture
Div. of Milk Sanitation
2301 N. Cameron St.
Harrisburg, PA 17120
Phone: (717)787-4316
Fax: (717)772-2780

Credential Type: License. **Requirements:** Contact licensing body for application information.

Rhode Island

8320

Commercial Driver
Div. of Motor Vehicles
Rhode Island Dept. of Transportation
2 Capitol Hill
Providence, RI 02903
Phone: (401)277-3427

Credential Type: Commercial Driver's License (CDL)—Class A. **Duration of License:** Five years. **Authorization:** Authorizes applicant to drive a commercial vehicle of 13 tons, or more, carrying over five tons. **Requirements:** At least 18 years of age. Resident of Rhode Island. A minimum of one year of driving experience. Submit application and pay fees. **Examination:** Written, road, and eye examinations (each eye must test at least 20/40). **Reciprocity:** Yes. **Fees:** $10 CDL examination fee (per exam). $100 CDL application fee. $25 CDL road test fee. $10 CDL license fee.

Credential Type: Commercial Driver's License (CDL)—Class B. **Duration of License:** Five years. **Authorization:** Authorizes applicant to drive a commercial vehicle of 13 tons, or more, but not carrying more than five tons. **Requirements:** At least 18 years of age. Resident of Rhode Island. A minimum of one year of driving experience. Submit application and pay fees. **Examination:** Written, road, and eye examinations (each eye must test at least 20/40). **Reciprocity:** Yes. **Fees:** $10 CDL examination fee (per exam). $100 CDL application fee. $25 CDL road test fee. $10 CDL license fee.

Credential Type: Commercial Driver's License (CDL)—Class C. **Duration of License:** Five years. **Authorization:** Authorizes applicant to drive a commercial vehicle not meeting Class A or B standards or carrying hazardous material or over 15 passengers, except school buses. **Requirements:** At least 18 years of age. Resident of Rhode Island. A minimum of one year of driving experience. Proper endorsements required for particular type of vehicle ("H" for hazardous material, "P" for passengers, "N" for tank vehicle, and "T" for double or triple trailers). Submit proper applications and pay fees. **Examination:** Written, road, and eye examinations (each eye must test at least 20/40). **Reciprocity:** Yes. **Fees:** $10 CDL examination fee (per exam). $100 CDL application fee. $25 CDL road test fee. $10 CDL license fee.

8321

Milk Hauler and Tester
Dept. of Health
Div. of Food Protection
State Milk Program
3 Capitol Hill, Rm. 203
Providence, RI 02908-5097
Phone: (401)277-2749
Fax: (401)277-6548

Credential Type: License. **Requirements:** Contact licensing body for application information.

South Dakota

8322

Milk Hauler and Tester
Dept. of Agriculture
Div. of Regulatory Services
Office of Dairy Inspection
Anderson Bldg.
Pierre, SD 57501
Phone: (605)773-3724
Fax: (605)773-5891

Credential Type: License. **Requirements:** Contact licensing body for application information.

8323

Truck Driver
Dept. of Commerce and Regulation
Driver Licensing Program
State Capitol
Pierre, SD 57501
Phone: (605)773-3105

Credential Type: Commercial Drivers License. **Duration of License:** Four years. **Authorization:** Required to drive the following types of trucks: (1) single vehicle with a gross vehicle weight rating (GVWR) of more than 26,000 pounds. (2) trailer with a GVWR of more than 10,000 pounds, if the gross combination weight rating is more than 26,000. (3) any size vehicle which requires hazardous materials placards. **Requirements:** Be at least 18 years of age. Resident of South Dakota. The following endorsements are available with additional testing: double-triple trailers, tank vehicles, hazardous materials, and combination tank and hazardous materials. **Examination:** Knowledge and skills test. **Fees:** $25 license fee (knowledge and skills test). $15 license fee (knowledge test only). $5 endorsement fee (per endorsement).

Texas

8324

Asbestos Transporter
Texas Dept. of Health
Occupational Health Div.
Asbestos Licensing Section
1100 W. 49th St.
Austin, TX 78756
Phone: (512)834-6600

Credential Type: Asbestos Transporter License. **Duration of License:** One year. **Requirements:** Must have liability insurance of $1 million. Must submit a copy of emergency response plan and evidence of workers compensation insurance. **Fees:** $200 license fee. **Governing Statute:** Texas Civil Statutes, Article 4477-3a. Texas Asbestos Health Protection Rules, Section 295.

Utah

8325

Driving Occupations
Dept. of Public Safety
Drivers License Div.
4501 S. 2700 W.
PO Box 30560
Salt Lake City, UT 84130-0560
Phone: (801)965-4406

Credential Type: Commercial Driver's License. **Authorization:** CDL required for the following Commercial Motor Vehicles: single vehicle of more than 26,000 pounds; trailer of more than 10,000 pounds if gross combination weight rating is more than 26,000 pounds; vehicle designed to transport more than 15 persons (including driver); any size vehicle requiring hazardous materials placards; any size vehicle used as a school bus. **Requirements:** Submit application, pay fees, and pass tests. **Examination:** Knowledge, skills, and driving tests. **Fees:** Contact department or any local motor vehicle testing station for fees.

Washington

8326

Milk Hauler and Tester
Dept. of Agriculture
Dairy and Food Div.
406 General Administration Bldg., AX-41
Olympia, WA 98504
Phone: (206)753-5043
Fax: (206)753-3700

Credential Type: License. **Requirements:** Contact licensing body for application information.

8327

Tow Truck Operator
Dept. of Licensing
Vehicle Services-Dealers
Highways-Licenses Bldg., PB-01
Olympia, WA 98504-8001
Phone: (206)753-6954

Credential Type: Tow Truck Operator License. **Duration of License:** One year. **Requirements:** Must submit fee schedule and certificate of insurance coverage. Must carry $10,000 liability-bodily injury/property insurance and $50,000 legal liability of vehicle. Must post $5,000 Surety bond. Inspection of tow truck and facility required. Additional storage spaces must be licensed and insured. **Fees:** $100 initial license fee. $50 fee per truck.

West Virginia

8328

Bulk Milk Hauler and Sampler
Dept. of Agriculture
Consumer Protection Div.
Agriculture Center
Capitol Bldg.
Charleston, WV 25305
Phone: (304)348-2201

Credential Type: License. **Duration of License:** One year. **Requirements:** Pass written examination. In addition, must obtain a permit from the state Department of Public Health, which also requires an examination. **Examination:** Written examination. **Fees:** $2 annual license fee. $1.50 exam fee.

Wisconsin

8329

Milk Distributor
Dept. of Agriculture
Trade and Consumer Protection
Food Div.
801 W. Badger Rd.
PO Box 8911
Madison, WI 53708
Phone: (608)266-2227

Credential Type: License. **Duration of License:** One year. **Requirements:** Submit application and pay fee. **Fees:** $50 license fee. $20 reinspection fee.

Ushers, Lobby Attendants, and Ticket Takers

The following states grant licenses in this occupational category as of the date of publication: Alabama, California, Connecticut, Delaware, Iowa, Montana, Nebraska, New Mexico, North Dakota, Ohio, Texas.

Alabama

8330

Wrestling Ticket Taker
State Athletic Commission
50 N. Ripley St., Rm. 4121
Montgomery, AL 36132
Phone: (205)242-1380

Credential Type: License. **Duration of License:** One year. **Fees:** $5 license fee.

California

8331

Box Office Employee (Boxing, Kickboxing, or Martial Arts)
Athletic Commission
1424 Howe Ave., Ste. 33
Sacramento, CA 95814-6200
Phone: (916)920-7300

Credential Type: License. **Duration of License:** One year. **Requirements:** Submit application and pay fee. **Fees:** $25 license fee. $25 renewal fee.

8332

Ticket Seller (Boxing, Kickboxing, or Martial Arts)
Athletic Commission
1424 Howe Ave., Ste. 33
Sacramento, CA 95814-6200
Phone: (916)920-7300

Credential Type: License. **Duration of License:** One year. **Requirements:** Submit application and pay fee. **Fees:** $25 license fee. $25 renewal fee.

8333

Ticket Taker (Boxing, Kickboxing, or Martial Arts)
Athletic Commission
1424 Howe Ave., Ste. 33
Sacramento, CA 95814-6200
Phone: (916)920-7300

Credential Type: License. **Duration of License:** One year. **Requirements:** Submit application and pay fee. **Fees:** $25 license fee. $25 renewal fee.

Connecticut

8334

Box Office Employee (Racetrack)
Connecticut Div. of Special Revenue
Russell Rd.
PO Box 11424
Newington, CT 06111-0424
Phone: (203)566-2756

Credential Type: License Registration. **Requirements:** Submit application and fingerprint card. Pay fee. **Fees:** $5 registration fee.

8335

Usher (Racetrack)
Connecticut Div. of Special Revenue
Russell Rd.
PO Box 11424
Newington, CT 06111-0424
Phone: (203)566-2756

Credential Type: License Registration. **Requirements:** Submit application and fingerprint card. Pay fee. **Fees:** $5 registration fee.

Delaware

8336

Admission Employee (Racetrack)
Delaware Harness Racing Commission
2320 S. DuPont Hwy.
Dover, DE 19901
Phone: (302)739-4811

Credential Type: License Registration. **Requirements:** Submit application and fingerprint card. Pay fee. **Fees:** $5 registration fee.

Iowa

8337

Parking/Admissions Employee
Iowa State Racing Commission
Lucas State Office Bldg.
Des Moines, IA 50319
Phone: (515)281-7352

Credential Type: License Registration. **Requirements:** Submit application and fingerprint card. Pay fee. **Fees:** $5 registration fee.

Montana

8338

Gate Attendant (Racetrack)
State of Montana Board of Horse Racing
Dept. of Commerce
1424 9th Ave.
Helena, MT 59620
Phone: (406)444-4287

Credential Type: License Registration. **Requirements:** Submit application and fin-

Ushers, Lobby Attendants, and Ticket Takers

gerprint card. Pay fee. **Fees:** $20 registration fee.

Nebraska

8339

Admissions Employee (Racetrack)
Nebraska Racing Commission
PO Box 95014
301 Centennial Mall S.
Lincoln, NE 68509
Phone: (402)471-4155

Credential Type: License Registration. **Duration of License:** One year. **Requirements:** At least 16 years of age. No felony convictions. Secure employment and submit application completed and signed by management. Pay fees. **Fees:** $10 license fee. $10 renewal fee.

New Mexico

8340

Admissions Gateman (Racetrack)
New Mexico State Racing
  Commission
PO Box 8576, Highland Station
Albuquerque, NM 87198
Phone: (505)841-4644

Credential Type: License Registration. **Requirements:** Submit application and fingerprint card. Pay fees. **Fees:** $13 registration fee. $1 notary fee. $23 fingerprint card processing fee.

8341

Admissions Ticket Seller (Racetrack)
New Mexico State Racing
  Commission
PO Box 8576, Highland Station
Albuquerque, NM 87198
Phone: (505)841-4644

Credential Type: License Registration. **Requirements:** Submit application and fingerprint card. Pay fees. **Fees:** $13 registration fee. $1 notary fee. $23 fingerprint card processing fee.

North Dakota

8342

Gate Admission Seller (Racetrack)
North Dakota Racing Commission
State Capitol Bldg.
Bismarck, ND 58505
Phone: (701)224-2210

Credential Type: License Registration. **Requirements:** Submit application and fingerprint card. Pay fee. **Fees:** $10 license fee. $10 duplicate license fee.

8343

Gate Attendant (Racetrack)
North Dakota Racing Commission
State Capitol Bldg.
Bismarck, ND 58505
Phone: (701)224-2210

Credential Type: License Registration. **Requirements:** Submit application and fingerprint card. Pay fee. **Fees:** $10 license fee. $10 duplicate license fee.

Ohio

8344

Admission Employee (Thoroughbred, Standardbred, and Quarter Horse Racing)
Ohio State Racing Commission
State Office Tower
77 S. High St., 18th Fl.
Columbus, OH 43266-0416
Phone: (614)466-2757

Credential Type: License Registration. **Requirements:** Submit application and fingerprint card. Pay fee. **Fees:** $10 registration fee.

Texas

8345

Admission Person (Racetrack)
Texas Racing Commission
PO Box 12080
Austin, TX 78711
Phone: (512)794-8461

Credential Type: License Registration. **Requirements:** Submit application and fingerprint card. Pay fee. **Fees:** $20 registration fee.

Veterinarians

The following states grant licenses in this occupational category as of the date of publication:

Alabama	District of	Iowa	Minnesota	New Mexico	Rhode Island	Washington
Alaska	Columbia	Kansas	Mississippi	New York	South Carolina	West Virginia
Arizona	Florida	Kentucky	Missouri	North Carolina	South Dakota	Wisconsin
Arkansas	Georgia	Louisiana	Montana	North Dakota	Tennessee	Wyoming
California	Hawaii	Maine	Nebraska	Ohio	Texas	
Colorado	Idaho	Maryland	Nevada	Oklahoma	Utah	
Connecticut	Illinois	Massachusetts	New Hampshire	Oregon	Vermont	
Delaware	Indiana	Michigan	New Jersey	Pennsylvania	Virginia	

Alabama

8346

Veterinarian
Alabama State Board of Veterinary Medical Examiners
PO Box 1767
Decatur, AL 35602
Phone: (205)353-3544

Credential Type: License. **Duration of License:** One year. **Requirements:** Must be a college graduate of an approved veterinary medicine program. Must have completed a six month internship under an approved licensed veterinarian. **Examination:** National Board Examination and Clinical Competency Test. **Fees:** $50 application fee. $100 examinaton fee. $75 Competency Test fee. $25 license renewal fee. $70 inspection and renewal fee.

Alaska

8347

Veterinarian
Dept. of Commerce and Economic Development
Div. of Occupational Licensing
PO Box D
Juneau, AK 99811-0800
Phone: (907)465-3035
Fax: (907)465-2974

Credential Type: License to practice. **Duration of License:** Two years. **Requirements:** Graduation from an accredited school of veterinary medicine. ECFVG certificate required for foreign graduates. **Examination:** National Board Examination. Clinical Competency Test. State examination. **Reciprocity:** None. **Fees:** $30 application fee. $100 National Board Examination fee. $75 Clinical Competency Test fee. $75 state written examination fee. $100 license fee. $100 biennial renewal fee. $50 temporary license fee. $50 temporary permit fee.

Arizona

8348

Track Veterinarian
Arizona Dept. of Racing
Investigations and Licensing Div.
800 W. Washington, Rm. 515
Phoenix, AZ 85007
Phone: (602)542-5151

Credential Type: Veterinarian license. **Duration of License:** Three years. **Requirements:** At least 16 years of age. Not have been convicted of a felony or any crime involving moral turpitude within the last five years. May not own, lease, or train horses or greyhounds at the track at which applicant would practice. Application will be referred to the Arizona Department of Racing Veterinarian for review. **Exemptions:** A holder of a track official license may serve as a track veterinarian without additional licensing. **Fees:** $36 license fee.

8349

Veterinarian
Veterinary Board
1645 W. Jefferson, Rm. 410
Phoenix, AZ 85007
Phone: (602)542-3093
Phone: (602)542-3095

Credential Type: License to practice. **Duration of License:** Two years. **Requirements:** Graduation from a recognized veterinary college. Certificate of good moral character. ECFVG certificate required for foreign graduates. **Examination:** State written and oral examinations. National examination. Clinical competency test. **Fees:** $300 application/examination fee. $200 maximum license fee. $200 maximum biennial registration fee. $75 temporary permit fee. **Governing Statute:** Practice law.

Credential Type: License by endorsement. **Duration of License:** Two years. **Requirements:** Must have active license from another state. Must have previously passed National Board Examination (NBE) with equivalent Arizona score. Must have been engaged in practice of veterinary medicine for three of the preceding five years or six of the preceding 10 years. Graduate of an American Veterinary Medical Association (AVMA)-accredited veterinary college. Must have no disciplinary action taken against license. **Examination:** State written exam. Clinical Competency Test. **Fees:** $750 license fee. **Governing Statute:** Practice law.

Arkansas

8350

Commission Veterinarian
Arkansas State Racing Commission
Ledbetter Bldg., Rm. G08
7th & Wolfe St.
PO Box 3076
Little Rock, AR 72203
Phone: (501)682-1467

Credential Type: License. **Duration of License:** One year. **Requirements:** Must meet all requirements and be licensed to practice veterinary medicine in the state of Arkansas. **Examination:** Yes. **Fees:** $100 Written, oral and practical examinations. $35 Temporary permit. $90 National Board

Examination. $10 Commission license. $10 Renewal.

8351

Equine Dentist
Arkansas State Racing Commission
Ledbetter Bldg., Rm. G08
7th & Wolfe St.
PO Box 3076
Little Rock, AR 72203
Phone: (501)682-1467

Credential Type: License. **Duration of License:** One year. **Requirements:** Must be registered with the Arkansas State Veterinary Board (yet does not have to be a veterinarian). Application approved by the Stewards. **Fees:** $10 License. $10 Renewal.

8352

Greyhound Commission Veterinarian
Arkansas State Racing Commission
Ledbetter Bldg., Rm. G08
7th & Wolfe St.
PO Box 3076
Little Rock, AR 72203
Phone: (501)682-1467

Credential Type: License. **Duration of License:** One year. **Requirements:** Meet all requirement of veterinarian in Arkansas. **Examination:** Yes. **Fees:** $100 Written oral and practical examinations. $35 Temporary permit. $90 National Board Examination. $10 Commission license. $10 Renewal.

8353

Veterinarian
Veterinary Medical Examination Board
1 Natural Resources Dr.
PO Box 5497
Little Rock, AR 72215
Phone: (501)224-2836

Credential Type: License. **Requirements:** 21 years of age. US citizen. Good moral character. Graduate of an accredited Veterinary College. Satisfactory completion of the National Boards. Satisfactory completion of the CCT Examination. **Examination:** Yes. **Fees:** $100 Written, oral and practical examinations. $35 Temporary permit. $125 National Board Examination. $100 CCT Examination.

California

8354

Veterinarian
Board of Examiners in Veterinary Medicine
1420 Howe Ave., Ste. 6
Sacramento, CA 95825
Phone: (916)920-7662

Credential Type: License to practice. **Duration of License:** Two years. **Requirements:** Must have diploma from a recognized veterinary school. **Examination:** National Examination. Clinical Competency Test. State Board Examination. **Fees:** $100 National Examination fee. $80 Clinical Competency Test fee. $100 State Board Examination fee. $150 biennial license registration fee. **Governing Statute:** Business and Professions Code, Chapter 11, Veterinary Medicine, Article 1. Sections 4800 through 4917.

Credential Type: License by endorsement. **Requirements:** Graduate of an American Veterinary Medical Association (AVMA) accredited veterinary college. Hold a valid license in one or more states. Must have no disciplinary action taken against license. Must have passed the National Board Examination and a written state board exam in the state in which license was issued. Four years of continuous practice in veterinary medicine immediately preceding application. **Examination:** National Board Examination. State written exam. **Fees:** $150 biennial license registration fee. **Governing Statute:** Business and Professions Code, Chapter 11, Veterinary Medicine, Article 1. Sections 4800 through 4917.

8355

Veterinarian (Racetrack)
California Horse Racing Board
1010 Hurley Way, Ste. 190
Sacramento, CA 95825
Phone: (916)920-7178

Credential Type: License Registration. **Requirements:** Submit application and fingerprint card. Pay fee. **Fees:** $150 registration fee.

Colorado

8356

Track Veterinarian (Horse)
Colorado Racing Commission
Dept. of Regulatory Agencies
1560 Broadway, Ste. 1540
Denver, CO 80202
Phone: (303)894-2990
Fax: (303)894-7580

Credential Type: Track Veterinarian License. **Duration of License:** Three years. **Requirements:** Submit application and pay fee. **Fees:** $59 license fee.

8357

Veterinarian
Veterinary Medical Examining Board
1560 Broadway, Ste. 1310
Denver, CO 80222-5146
Phone: (303)894-7755

Credential Type: License to practice. **Requirements:** 21 years of age. Good moral character. Must have a diploma from a school of veterinary medicine recognized by the American Veterinary Medical Association (AVMA) or hold a Certificate of Competence issued by the ECFVG. Renewal requires 16 hours of continuing education each year. **Examination:** State board examination. **Reciprocity:** Applicants considered on an individual basis. **Governing Statute:** Practice act.

Connecticut

8358

Veterinarian
Board of Veterinary Medicine
150 Washington St.
Hartford, CT 06106
Phone: (203)566-1039

Credential Type: License to practice. **Requirements:** Must hold a diploma from an approved college of veterinary medicine. ECFVG certificate required for foreign graduates. **Examination:** State board examination. **Fees:** $450 license fee. $450 registration fee. **Governing Statute:** Chapter 384, General Statutes.

Credential Type: License by endorsement. **Requirements:** Hold a license to practice veterinary medicine in a state with requirements equal to those required by the state of Connecticut. **Fees:** $450 endorsement fee. **Governing Statute:** Chapter 384, General Statutes.

Connecticut

8359

Veterinarian (Racetrack)
Connecticut Div. of Special Revenue
Russell Rd.
PO Box 11424
Newington, CT 06111-0424
Phone: (203)566-2756

Credential Type: License Registration. **Requirements:** Submit application and fingerprint card. Pay fee. **Fees:** $20 registration fee.

Delaware

8360

Veterinarian
Board of Veterinary Medicine
O'Neil Bldg.
PO Box 1401
Dover, DE 19903-1401
Phone: (302)739-4522

Credential Type: License to practice. **Duration of License:** Two years. **Requirements:** Must hold a diploma from a recognized veterinary school. Must produce two letters of recommendation. ECFVG certificate required for foreign graduates. **Examination:** National Board Examination. **Reciprocity:** Applicants considered on an individual basis. **Fees:** $150 license fee. $120 biennial registration fee. **Governing Statute:** Title 24—Chapter 33, Laws of Delaware.

8361

Veterinarian (Racetrack)
Delaware Harness Racing
 Commission
2320 S. DuPont Hwy.
Dover, DE 19901
Phone: (302)739-4811

Credential Type: License Registration. **Requirements:** Submit application and fingerprint card. Pay fee. **Fees:** $15 registration fee.

District of Columbia

8362

Veterinarian
Board of Veterinary Examiners
614 H St. NW, Rm. 923
Washington, DC 20001
Phone: (202)727-7468
Fax: (202)727-8030

Credential Type: License to practice. **Duration of License:** One or two years. **Requirements:** Must have diploma and degree in veterinary medicine. Two character references. National Board Exams must be passed with a minimum total converted score of 75. Foreign students must produce notarized copy of ECFVG certificate. **Examination:** National Board Examination. **Fees:** $20 examination/application fee. $100 examination fee. $70 new license fee (2 year). $20 new license fee (1 year). $100 biennial renewal fee. **Governing Statute:** Law 4-171. D.C. Code, TITLE 2, CHAP, 27, Sections 2721-2738.

Credential Type: License by endorsement. **Duration of License:** One or two years. **Requirements:** Must be a licensed veterinarian in good standing. License must be issued in a state which has standards equal to those of the District of Columbia and admits veterinarians licensed in D.C. without examination. **Fees:** $80 application to waive examination fee. $70 new license fee (2 year). $20 new license fee (1 year). **Governing Statute:** Law 4-171. D.C. Code, TITLE 2, CHAP, 27, Sections 2721-2738.

Florida

8363

Veterinarian
Board of Veterinary Medicine
1940 N. Monroe St.
Tallahassee, FL 32399-0787
Phone: (904)487-1820

Credential Type: License to practice. **Duration of License:** Two years. **Requirements:** Graduate from American Veterinary Medical Association (AVMA) accredited school or pass ECFVG Clinical Proficiency Examination. **Examination:** National Board Examination. Clinical Competency Test. State laws and rules examination. **Fees:** $135 National Board Examination fee. $100 Clinical Competency Test fee. $100 application fee. $200 initial licensure fee. $75 state laws and rules examination fee. $260 biennial registration fee. $250 endorsement fee. **Governing Statute:** Chapter 474, Florida Statutes (Veterinary Medical Practice Act).

Credential Type: Temporary permit. **Duration of License:** 90 days. **Authorization:** Authorizes treatment of only one owner's animals. **Requirements:** Licensed veterinarian from another state. **Governing Statute:** Chapter 474, Florida Statutes (Veterinary Medical Practice Act).

8364

Veterinarian (Racetrack)
Florida Dept. of Business
Div. of Pari-Mutuel Wagering
Licensing Section
725 S. Bronough St.
Tallahassee, FL 32399-1037
Phone: (904)488-9161

Credential Type: License Registration Code 1046. **Requirements:** Must have a Department of Professional Regulation (DPR) license. Submit application and fingerprint card. Pay fee. **Fees:** $40 registration fee.

Georgia

8365

Veterinarian
State Examining Boards/Health Care
 Practitioners Section
166 Pryor St. SW
Atlanta, GA 30303
Phone: (404)656-3900

Credential Type: License to practice. **Requirements:** Graduate of an accredited college of veterinary medicine. **Examination:** National Board Examination. State Board Examination. Clinical Competency Test. **Reciprocity:** None. **Fees:** $25 application fee. $50 State Board Examination fee. $100 National Board Examination fee. $75 Clinical Competency Test fee. $25 faculty license. $15 temporary license. **Governing Statute:** Chapter 43-50, Veterinary Practice Act.

Hawaii

8366

Veterinarian
Hawaii Board of Veterinary
 Examiners
1010 Richards St.
PO Box 3469
Honolulu, HI 96801
Phone: (808)548-7461

Credential Type: License. **Duration of License:** Two years. **Requirements:** 18 years of age. Graduation from an American

Veterinary Medical Assn.-accredited veterinary college, or graduation from a foreign veterinary college plus an American Veterinary Medical Assn. Educational Commission for Foreign Veterinary Graduates certificate. **Examination:** Clinical Competency Test. National Board exam. State Board exam. **Fees:** $100 application fee. $100 exam fee. $100 license fee. $20—$40 Compliance Resolution Fund fee. $100 renewal fee.

Idaho

8367

Veterinarian
Board of Veterinary Medicine
PO Box 7249
Boise, ID 83707
Phone: (208)344-3962

Credential Type: License to practice. **Duration of License:** One year. **Requirements:** 21 years of age. Graduation from an approved veterinarian college. **Examination:** National Board Examination. **Reciprocity:** None. **Fees:** $150 application/original license fee. $75 temporary permit fee. $75 annual renewal fee. **Governing Statute:** Title 54, Chapter 21:Title 67, Chapter 26.

8368

Veterinarian (Racetrack)
Idaho State Horse Racing
   Commission
6133 Corporal Lane
Boise, ID 83704
Phone: (208)327-7105

Credential Type: License Registration. **Requirements:** Submit application and fingerprint card. Pay fee. **Fees:** $30 registration fee.

Illinois

8369

Veterinarian
Veterinary Licensing and
   Disciplinary Board
Dept. of Professional Regulation
320 W. Washington
Springfield, IL 62786
Phone: (217)782-8556
Fax: (217)782-7645

Credential Type: License to practice. **Duration of License:** Two years. **Requirements:** Must have two years pre-veterinary training and graduate from a four-year veterinary college. Renewal requires 20 clock hours of continuing education. **Examination:** National Board Examination. Clinical Competency Test. **Fees:** $153 National Board Examination fee. $127.25 Clinical Competency Test fee. $230.25 fee to take both examinations. $25 license fee. $30 biennial renewal fee. **Governing Statute:** State of Illinois, The Veterinary Medicine and Surgery Practice Act III.

Credential Type: License by endorsement. **Requirements:** Hold a license, in good standing, to practice veterinary medicine in another state. State of issue must have requirements substantially equivalent to those of Illinois. **Fees:** $100 endorsement application fee. $25 license fee. $30 biennial renewal fee. **Governing Statute:** State of Illinois, The Veterinary Medicine and Surgery Practice Act III.

8370

Veterinarian (Racetrack)
Illinois Racing Board
100 W. Randolph St., Ste. 11-100
Chicago, IL 60601
Phone: (312)814-2600

Credential Type: License Registration. **Requirements:** Submit application and fingerprint card. Pay fee. **Fees:** $25 registration fee. $2 photo fee. $10 fingerprint card fee.

Indiana

8371

Veterinarian
Health Professions Bureau
402 W. Washington St., Rm. 041
Indianapolis, IN 46204
Phone: (317)233-4407
Fax: (317)233-4236

Credential Type: License to practice. **Duration of License:** Two years. **Requirements:** Be a graduate of, or be in the final term of, an approved college program in veterinary medicine. Non-graduates must produce a letter of recommendation from the preparing institution. ECFVG certificate required for foreign graduates. **Examination:** National Board Examination. Clinical Competency Test. State oral and practical examination. **Fees:** $135 National Board Examination fee. $110 Clinical Competency Test fee. $210 NBE & CCT examination fee. $100 oral and practical examination fee. $310 National Board Examination NBE, CCT, oral and practical examination fee. $50 biennial license renewal fee. **Governing Statute:** New Veterinary Practice Act.

Iowa

8372

Veterinarian
Iowa Board of Veterinary Medicine
Public Health Dept.
Wallace State Office Bldg., 2nd Fl.
Des Moines, IA 50319
Phone: (515)281-6762

Credential Type: License. **Duration of License:** Three years. **Requirements:** At least two years of preveterinary education and four years of veterinary medicine to get a doctorate degree. **Examination:** National Board Examination. Clinical Competency Test. Iowa Board Exam. **Fees:** $245 exam fee. $45 renewal fee.

8373

Veterinarian (Racetrack)
Iowa State Racing Commission
Lucas State Office Bldg.
Des Moines, IA 50319
Phone: (515)281-7352

Credential Type: License Registration. **Requirements:** Submit application and fingerprint card. Pay fee. **Fees:** $10 registration fee.

Kansas

8374

Practicing Veterinarian (Racetrack)
Kansas Racing Commission
3400 VanBuren
Topeka, KS 66611-2228
Phone: (913)296-5800

Credential Type: License Registration. **Requirements:** Submit application and fingerprint card. Pay fee. **Fees:** $10 registration fee.

8375

Veterinarian
Kansas Board of Veterinary
   Examiners
North Star Route
Lakin, KS 67860
Phone: (316)355-6358

Credential Type: License to practice. **Duration of License:** One year. **Requirements:** Good moral character. Graduate of an approved school of veterinary medicine. License renewal requires 20 hours of continuing education credit per year. **Examination:** National Board Examination. Clinical Competency Test. State written

Kentucky 8376

Veterinarian, continued

examination. **Fees:** $250 examination fee for all tests. $100 examination fee for state written test only. $20 biennial license renewal fee. **Governing Statute:** Chapter 47, Article 8, of Kansas Statutes Annotated.

Kentucky

8376

Commission Veterinarian (Racetrack)
Kentucky State Racing Commission
PO Box 1080
Lexington, KY 40588
Phone: (606)254-7021

Credential Type: License Registration. **Requirements:** Submit application and fingerprint card. Pay fee. **Fees:** $35 registration fee.

8377

Veterinarian
Kentucky Board of Veterinary Examiners
PO Box 456
Frankfurt, KY 40602
Phone: (502)564-3296
Fax: (502)564-4818

Credential Type: License to practice. **Duration of License:** One year. **Requirements:** 18 years of age. Good moral character. Graduate of a recognized veterinary college. **Examination:** National Board Examination. Clinical Competency Test. State written practical examination. **Fees:** $25 registration fee. **Governing Statute:** Chapter 321 of Kentucky Revised Statutes.

Credential Type: License by endorsement. **Requirements:** Reciprocity exists with Michigan, Missouri, and West Virginia. Licensees from other states will be considered if state of issuance has standards substantially equivalent to those of Kentucky and extends reciprocity to Kentucky licensees. **Fees:** $25 registration fee. **Governing Statute:** Chapter 321 of Kentucky Revised Statutes.

8378

Veterinarian (Racetrack)
Kentucky State Racing Commission
PO Box 1080
Lexington, KY 40588
Phone: (606)254-7021

Credential Type: License Registration. **Requirements:** Submit application and fingerprint card. Pay fee. **Fees:** $35 registration fee.

Louisiana

8379

Racehorse Veterinarian
Louisiana State Racing Commission
320 N. Carrollton Ave., Ste. 2-B
New Orleans, LA 70119
Phone: (504)483-4000

Credential Type: License. **Duration of License:** One or three years. **Requirements:** 18 years of age. Licensed under the Louisiana Veterinary Board. **Fees:** $100 one-year license fee. $300 three-year license fee.

8380

Veterinarian
Veterinary Board
PO Box 15191
Baton Rouge, LA 70895-5194
Phone: (504)924-6354

Credential Type: License to practice. **Duration of License:** One year. **Requirements:** 21 years of age. Good moral character. U.S. citizen or applicant for U.S. citizenship. Graduate of a veterinary college accredited by the American Veterinarian Medical Association (AVMA). ECFVG certificate required for foreign graduates. **Examination:** National Board Examination. Clinical Competency Test. Veterinary Technology National Examination. State examination. **Fees:** $150 National Board Examination fee. $125 Clinical Competency Test fee. $240 examination fee for National Board Examination (NBE) & CCT. $125 Veterinary Technology National Examination. $125 original registration fee. $75 annual renewal fee. **Governing Statute:** Louisiana Revised Statute Chapter 37;1511-58.

Maine

8381

Veterinarian
Dept. of Professional and Financial Regulation
Div. of Licensing and Enforcement
State House Station 35
Augusta, ME 04333
Phone: (207)582-8723
Fax: (207)582-5415

Credential Type: License to practice. **Duration of License:** One year. **Requirements:** U.S. citizen or applicant for U.S. citizenship. Graduate of an accredited veterinary college. ECFVG certificate required for foreign graduates. **Examination:** State examination. **Reciprocity:** None **Fees:** $100 license fee. $25 annual registration fee. **Governing Statute:** Maine Statutes.

Maryland

8382

Veterinarian
State Board of Veterinary Medical Examiners
50 Harry S. Truman Pky.
Annapolis, MD 21401
Phone: (301)841-5862
Fax: (301)841-5914

Credential Type: License to practice. **Duration of License:** One year. **Requirements:** Graduation from an accredited veterinary college. **Examination:** State examination. **Fees:** $75 license fee. $40 annual registration fee. **Governing Statute:** Agriculture Article Section 2-307, Maryland Annotated Code.

Credential Type: License by endorsement. **Requirements:** Hold a license from another state or is a graduate of a school accredited by American Veterinarian Medical Association (AVMA). Must have practiced veterinary medicine or taught clinical veterinary medicine actively for the five years preceding application. Must have passed a Board approved examination. **Governing Statute:** Agriculture Article Section 2-307, Maryland Annotated Code.

8383

Veterinarian (Harness Racing)
Maryland Racing Commission
Stanbalt Bldg., 14th Fl.
501 St. Paul Place
Baltimore, MD 21202
Phone: (301)333-6267

Credential Type: License Registration. **Requirements:** Submit application, fingerprint card, and three passport size photos. Pay fee. **Fees:** $25 registration fee.

8384

Veterinarian (Thoroughbred Racing)
Maryland Racing Commission
Stanbalt Bldg., 14th Fl.
501 St. Paul Place
Baltimore, MD 21202
Phone: (301)333-6267

Credential Type: License Registration. **Requirements:** Submit application, fingerprint card, and three passport size photos. Pay fee. **Fees:** $25 registration fee.

Massachusetts

8385

Veterinarian
Board of Registration in Veterinary Medicine
Cambridge St., Rm. 1516
Boston, MA 02202
Phone: (617)727-3080

Credential Type: License to practice. **Duration of License:** One year. **Requirements:** Good moral character. Graduate of an accredited veterinary school. ECFVG certificate required for foreign graduates. **Examination:** National Board Examination. Clinical Competency Test. **Fees:** $75 annual registration fee. **Governing Statute:** Practice Act.

Credential Type: Temporary License. **Requirements:** Must be a graduate of an approved school of veterinary medicine. Must have passed the Board's Jurisprudence Examination and either the National Board Examination or the Clinical Competency Test. **Governing Statute:** Practice Act.

8386

Veterinarian (Racetrack)
Massachusetts State Racing Commission
1 Ashburton Place, Rm. 1313
Boston, MA 02108
Phone: (617)727-2581

Credential Type: License Registration. **Requirements:** Submit application and fingerprint card. Pay fee. **Fees:** $50 registration fee.

Michigan

8387

Veterinarian
State Board of Veterinary Medicine
Dept. of Commerce
611 W. Ottawa
PO Box 30018
Lansing, MI 48909
Phone: (517)373-3596
Fax: (517)373-2179

Credential Type: License to practice. **Duration of License:** Two years. **Requirements:** Graduate of an approved veterinary college or is within 14 months of completing course work leading to a DVM degree. ECFVG certificate required for foreign graduates. **Examination:** National Board Examination. Clinical Competency Test. **Fees:** $285 examination fee. $25 temporary license fee. $50 biennial renewal fee. **Governing Statute:** Public Health Code, Act 368, Articles 1, 7, and 15.

Credential Type: License by endorsement. **Requirements:** Must hold a license in good standing from another state. Must have been engaged in the active practice of veterinary medicine for two years prior to application. **Examination:** National Board Examination. Clinical Competency Test. **Fees:** $45 endorsement fee. **Governing Statute:** Public Health Code, Act 368, Articles 1, 7, and 15.

8388

Veterinarian (Racetrack)
Michigan Office of Racing Commissioner
37650 Professional Center Dr.
Livonia, MI 48154-1114
Phone: (313)462-2400

Credential Type: License Registration. **Requirements:** Submit application and fingerprint card. Pay fee. **Fees:** $20 registration fee. $5 duplicate license fee.

Minnesota

8389

Equine Dentist (Racetrack)
Minnesota Racing Commission
11000 W. 78th St., Ste. 201
Eden Prairie, MN 55344
Phone: (612)341-7555

Credential Type: License Registration. **Requirements:** Submit application and fingerprint card. Pay fee. **Fees:** $25 registration fee.

8390

Veterinarian
Board of Veterinary Medicine
2700 University Ave. W., Rm. 102
St. Paul, MN 55114
Phone: (612)642-0597

Credential Type: License to practice. **Duration of License:** One year. **Requirements:** 18 years of age. Doctor of Veterinary Medicine from an accredited veterinary college. ECFVG certificate required for graduates of non-accredited colleges. Notarized letters of recommendation from two veterinarians and three other adults. **Examination:** National Board Examination. Clinical Competency Test. State examination. **Reciprocity:** None. **Fees:** $125 National Board Examination fee. $90 Clinical Competency Test fee. $35 State Board exam. $40 annual registration fee. **Governing Statute:** Minnesota Statutes 1961, sections 156.01 through 156.14 as amended by Minnesota session laws 965 chapter 204.

8391

Veterinarian (Racetrack)
Minnesota Racing Commission
11000 W. 78th St., Ste. 201
Eden Prairie, MN 55344
Phone: (612)341-7555

Credential Type: License Registration. **Requirements:** Submit application and fingerprint card. Pay fee. **Fees:** $100 registration fee.

Mississippi

8392

Veterinarian
Board of Veterinary Medicine
209 S. Lafayette St.
Starkville, MS 39759
Phone: (601)324-0235

Credential Type: License to practice. **Duration of License:** One year. **Requirements:** 21 years of age. Good moral character. Citizen of the U.S. or resident alien of Mississippi. Graduate of a veterinary school accredited by the American Veterinarian Medical Association (AVMA). NationalBoard EXamination (NBE) and CCT must be taken within five years of the State Boards. Renewal requires continuing eduction credits. **Examination:** National Board Examination. Clinical Competency Test. State Board examination. **Fees:** $50 examination fee. $100 maximum (variable) annual renewal fee. **Gov-

Missouri 8393

Veterinarian, continued

erning Statute: The Veterinary Practice Law (Sections 73-39-1 to 73-39-7).

Missouri

8393

Veterinarian
Veterinary Medical Board
PO Box 633
Jefferson City, MO 65102
Phone: (314)751-0031

Credential Type: License to practice. **Duration of License:** One year. **Requirements:** Graduate of a veterinary college accredited by, or having standards and requirements equal to, the American Veterinarian Medical Association (AVMA). ECFVG certificate required for foreign graduates. **Examination:** National Board Examination. Clinical Competency Test. **Fees:** $275 examination fee. $50 annual registration fee. **Governing Statute:** Original practice act.

Credential Type: License by endorsement. **Duration of License:** One year. **Requirements:** Must have license from another state with comparable standards to practice veterinary medicine. **Reciprocity:** $150 endorsement fee. **Governing Statute:** Original practice act.

8394

Veterinarian (Racetrack)
Missouri Horse Racing Commission
PO Box 754
Jefferson City, MO 65102
Phone: (314)751-3565

Credential Type: License Registration. **Requirements:** Submit application and fingerprint card. Pay fee. **Fees:** $50 registration fee. $4 duplicate registration fee.

Montana

8395

Practicing Veterinarian (Racetrack)
State of Montana Board of Horse Racing
Dept. of Commerce
1424 9th Ave.
Helena, MT 59620
Phone: (406)444-4287

Credential Type: License Registration. **Requirements:** Submit application and fingerprint card. Pay fee. **Fees:** $30 registration fee.

8396

Track Veterinarian (Racetrack)
State of Montana Board of Horse Racing
Dept. of Commerce
1424 9th Ave.
Helena, MT 59620
Phone: (406)444-4287

Credential Type: License Registration. **Requirements:** Submit application and fingerprint card. Pay fee. **Fees:** $30 registration fee.

8397

Veterinarian
Montana Board of Veterinary Medicine
111 N. Jackson
Helena, MT 59620
Phone: (406)444-5436

Credential Type: License. **Duration of License:** One year. **Requirements:** Graduation from an approved school of veterinary medicine. **Examination:** National board and clinical competency examinations. Practical and oral exams. **Fees:** $75 exam fee. $25 renewal fee. **Governing Statute:** Montana Code Annotated 37-18-301 through 37-18-502.

Nebraska

8398

Veterinarian
Nebraska Board of Examiners in Veterinary Medicine and Surgery
301 Centennial Mall S.
PO Box 95007
Lincoln, NE 68509
Phone: (402)471-2115
Fax: (402)471-0383

Credential Type: License. **Duration of License:** Two years. **Requirements:** 21 years of age. Must be a graduate of an accredited veterinary school. **Examination:** Yes. **Fees:** $75 examination fee. $50 reciprocity fee. $30 renewal fee.

Nevada

8399

Veterinarian
Nevada State Board of Veterinary Medical Examiners
1005 Terminal Way, Ste. 246
Reno, NV 89502
Phone: (702)322-9422

Credential Type: License. **Duration of License:** One year. **Requirements:** Completion of a four-year veterinary medicine program at an approved school with coursework emphasizing the area of specialization. **Examination:** Yes. **Fees:** $200 exam and license fee. $130 renewal fee.

New Hampshire

8400

Veterinarian
Board of Veterinary Medicine
Caller Box 2042
Concord, NH 03302-2042
Phone: (603)271-3706

Credential Type: License to practice. **Duration of License:** One year. **Requirements:** 18 years of age. Good moral character. Graduate of an accredited veterinary college. ECFVG certificate required for foreign graduates. Renewal requires 12 credit hours of continuing education annually. **Examination:** National Board Examination. Clinical Competency Test. **Fees:** $100 initial license fee. $85 annual registration fee. **Governing Statute:** Practice law.

Credential Type: License by endorsement. **Requirements:** Reciprocity will be extended to individual licensees at the discretion of the Board. Oral examination and CCT required. Must have graduated from an accredited school and completed five years of continuous practice. **Examination:** Oral state examination. Clinical Competency Test. **Governing Statute:** Practice law.

New Jersey

8401

Veterinarian
Board of Veterinary Medical Examiners
1100 Raymond Blvd., Rm. 513
Newark, NJ 07102
Phone: (201)648-2841

Credential Type: License. **Duration of License:** Two years. **Requirements:** Doctoral degree in veterinary medicine from a

Veterinarians

veterinary college or university. **Examination:** Written and practical exam. **Reciprocity:** Yes. **Fees:** $50 credential review. $125 exam fee. $120 biennial registration fee. **Governing Statute:** NJSA 45:16. NJAC 13:4.

New Mexico

8402

Practicing Veterinarian (Racetrack)
New Mexico State Racing Commission
PO Box 8576, Highland Station
Albuquerque, NM 87198
Phone: (505)841-4644

Credential Type: License Registration. **Duration of License:** Three years. **Requirements:** Submit application and fingerprint card. Pay fees. **Fees:** $105.50 registration fee. $1 notary fee. $23 fingerprint card processing fee.

8403

Track Veterinarian (Racetrack)
New Mexico State Racing Commission
PO Box 8576, Highland Station
Albuquerque, NM 87198
Phone: (505)841-4644

Credential Type: License Registration. **Duration of License:** Three years. **Requirements:** Submit application and fingerprint card. Pay fees. **Fees:** $105.50 registration fee. $1 notary fee. $23 fingerprint card processing fee.

8404

Veterinarian
Board of Veterinary Examiners
1650 University Blvd. NE
Albuquerque, NM 87102
Phone: (505)841-9112

Credential Type: License to practice. **Duration of License:** One year. **Requirements:** 21 years of age. U.S. citizen or filed for U.S. citizenship. Good moral character. Pass National Board Examination (NBE) or CCT within six years preceding application. ECFVG and a one year internship in New Mexico are required for foreign graduates. Renewal requires 15 hours of continuing education annually. **Examination:** National Board Examination. Clinical Competency Test. **Fees:** $100 application fee. $75 annual registration fee. **Governing Statute:** New Mexico 1978 annotated Chapter 61:Professional and Occupational Licenses—Pamphlet 97:Medical Services Providers 612-1 through 61-1-19—Article 14 Veterinary Medicine 61-14-1 through 61-14-19.

Credential Type: License by endorsement. **Duration of License:** One year. **Requirements:** Licensees from other states will qualify if they have five years of clinical practice and are approved by the Board. **Governing Statute:** New Mexico 1978 annotated Chapter 61:Professional and Occupational Licenses—Pamphlet 97:Medical Services Providers 612-1 through 61-1-19—Article 14 Veterinary Medicine 61-14-1 through 61-14-19.

New York

8405

Veterinarian
State Education Dept.
Div. of Professional Licensing Services
Cultural Education Center
Empire State Plaza
Albany, NY 12230
Phone: (518)474-3827

Credential Type: License. **Duration of License:** Three years. **Requirements:** Doctoral Degree in veterinary medicine with at least 60 college level, pre-veterinary credits. 21 years of age. U.S. citizen or alien lawfully admitted for permanent residency. **Examination:** Written and practical. **Fees:** $470 application fee. $210 renewal fee. **Governing Statute:** Title VIII Articles 130, 135 of the Education Law.

8406

Veterinarian (Harness or Quarter Horse Racing)
New York State Racing and Wagering Board
400 Broome St.
New York, NY 10013
Phone: (212)219-4230

Credential Type: License Registration. **Duration of License:** One year. **Requirements:** Submit application, F.B.I fingerprint card, New York state fingerprint card, and three photos. Pay fees. **Fees:** $20 registration fee. $44 New York state fingerprint card processing fee (valid for five years).

8407

Veterinarian (Thoroughbred Racing)
New York State Racing and Wagering Board
400 Broome St.
New York, NY 10013
Phone: (212)219-4230

Credential Type: License Registration. **Duration of License:** One year. **Requirements:** Submit application, F.B.I fingerprint card, New York state fingerprint card, and three photos. Pay fees. **Fees:** $30 registration fee. $44 New York state fingerprint card processing fee (valid for five years).

North Carolina

8408

Veterinarian
Veterinary Medical Board
PO Box 12587
Raleigh, NC 27605
Phone: (919)733-7689

Credential Type: License. **Duration of License:** One year. **Requirements:** Veterinary degree from an accredited college or university. 15 hours of continuing education required upon renewal. **Examination:** Written and clinical competency exams. **Fees:** $345 exam fee. $25 renewal fee.

North Dakota

8409

Association Veterinarian (Racetrack)
North Dakota Racing Commission
State Capitol Bldg.
Bismarck, ND 58505
Phone: (701)224-2210

Credential Type: License Registration. **Requirements:** Submit application and fingerprint card. Pay fee. **Fees:** $100 license fee. $10 duplicate license fee.

8410

Veterinarian
Veterinary Medical Examining Board
Board of Animal Health
600 E. Blvd., J-Wing, 1st Fl.
Bismarck, ND 58505-0390
Phone: (701)224-2655
Fax: (701)224-3000

Credential Type: License to practice. **Duration of License:** One year. **Require-

Ohio

Veterinarian, continued

ments: Graduate of a veterinary college approved by the Board. ECFVG Certificate required for foreign graduates. **Examination:** State examination. **Reciprocity:** None. **Fees:** $50 initial license fee. $25 annual renewal fee. **Governing Statute:** NDCC 43-29-01 through 43-29-18.

Ohio

8411

Equine Tooth Dresser (Thoroughbred, Standardbred, and Quarter Horse Racing)
Ohio State Racing Commission
State Office Tower
77 S. High St., 18th Fl.
Columbus, OH 43266-0416
Phone: (614)466-2757

Credential Type: License Registration. **Requirements:** Submit application and fingerprint card. Pay fee. **Fees:** $25 registration fee.

8412

Veterinarian
Veterinary Medical Board
77th S. High St., 16th Fl.
Columbus, OH 43266-0116
Phone: (614)644-5281

Credential Type: License to practice. **Duration of License:** Two years. **Requirements:** Graduate of an approved American Veterinary Medical Association (AVMA) veterinary school or approved equivalent program. Three letters of reference. Renewal requires 10 hours of continuing education annually. **Examination:** National Board Examination. Clinical Competency Test. **Fees:** $250 full licensure fee. $125 biennial renewal fee. **Governing Statute:** Ohio Revised Code Chapter 4741 and Ohio Administrative Code Chapter 474-1.

Credential Type: Temporary Permit. **Duration of License:** Valid until examination. **Requirements:** A temporary permit may be granted, with approval, to those individuals who have met all qualifications for licensure except passage of the National Board Examination (NBE) and/or Clinical Competency Test (CCT). **Fees:** $75 temporary permit fee. **Governing Statute:** Ohio Revised Code Chapter 4741 and Ohio Administrative Code Chapter 474-1.

Credential Type: License by endorsement. **Duration of License:** Two years. **Requirements:** Valid license from another state that has requirements equal to Ohio. Graduate of an approved school. Must have practiced veterinary medicine actively for the five years preceding application. **Examination:** National Board Examination. Clinical Competency Test. **Governing Statute:** Ohio Revised Code Chapter 4741 and Ohio Administrative Code Chapter 474-1.

8413

Veterinarian (Thoroughbred, Standardbred, and Quarter Horse Racing)
Ohio State Racing Commission
State Office Tower
77 S. High St., 18th Fl.
Columbus, OH 43266-0416
Phone: (614)466-2757

Credential Type: License Registration. **Requirements:** Submit application and fingerprint card. Pay fee. **Fees:** $25 registration fee.

Oklahoma

8414

Veterinarian
Oklahoma Board of Veterinary Medicine Examiners
PO Box 18256
Oklahoma City, OK 73154
Phone: (405)848-6841

Credential Type: License. **Duration of License:** One year. **Requirements:** A Doctor of Veterinary Medicine degree. 20 hours of continuing education each year. Three recommendations. 21 years of age. **Examination:** National Board Exam. Clinical Competency Test. Oklahoma State Board Examination. **Fees:** $475 exam fees. $50 renewal fee.

8415

Veterinarian (Racetrack)
Oklahoma Horse Racing Commission
6501 N. Broadway, Ste. 180
Oklahoma City, OK 73116
Phone: (405)848-0404

Credential Type: License Registration. **Duration of License:** One year. **Requirements:** Submit application and fingerprint card. Pay fee. **Fees:** $50 registration fee. $50 annual renewal. $120 triennial renewal fee.

Oregon

8416

Veterinarian
Oregon State Veterinary Medical Examining Board
800 NE Oregon
PO Box 14450
Portland, OR 97214
Phone: (503)731-4051

Credential Type: License. **Duration of License:** One year. **Requirements:** Graduation from a veterinary college or department of a university or college. Completion of at least one year in active practice in another state or have served at least six months' probation in the State of Oregon. **Examination:** Yes. **Fees:** $60 exam fee. $75 renewal fee. **Governing Statute:** ORS 686.

8417

Veterinarian (Racetrack)
Oregon Racing Commission
113 State Office Bldg.
1400 SW Fifth
Portland, OR 97201
Phone: (503)229-5820

Credential Type: License Registration. **Requirements:** Submit application and fingerprint card. Pay fee. **Fees:** $30 registration fee. $6 duplicate fee.

Pennsylvania

8418

Veterinarian
Board of Veterinary Medicine
PO Box 2649
Harrisburg, PA 17105-2649
Phone: (717)783-1389
Fax: (717)787-7769

Credential Type: License to practice. **Duration of License:** Two years. **Requirements:** Graduate from a recognized veterinary college. ECFVG certificate required for foreign graduates. **Examination:** National Board Examination. Clinical Competency Test. Pennsylvania Veterinary Legal Practice Examination. **Fees:** $261.25 complete examination fee. $37.50 PVLPE examination only. $83 biennial fee. **Governing Statute:** Act 54.

Veterinarians

8419

Veterinarian (Harness Racing)
Pennsylvania State Harness Racing Commission
2301 N. Cameron St.
Harrisburg, PA 17110-9408
Phone: (717)787-5196

Credential Type: License Registration. **Duration of License:** Three years. **Requirements:** Submit application, three photos, and fingerprint card. Pay fee. **Fees:** $60 registration fee. $5 duplicate license. $33 fingerprint processing fee.

8420

Veterinarian (Horse Racing)
Pennsylvania State Horse Racing Commission
2301 N. Cameron St., Rm. 306, 4th Fl.
Harrisburg, PA 17110-9408
Phone: (717)787-1942

Credential Type: License Registration. **Duration of License:** Three years. **Requirements:** Submit application, two photos, and fingerprint card. Pay fee. **Fees:** $45 registration fee. $2 duplicate license.

Rhode Island

8421

Veterinarian
Div. of Professional Regulation
Dept. of Health
3 Capitol Hill, Rm. 104
Providence, RI 02908
Phone: (401)277-2827
Fax: (401)277-1272

Credential Type: License to practice. **Duration of License:** Two years. **Requirements:** Graduate of a school approved and accredited by the American Veterinarian Medical Association (AVMA). ECFVG certificate required for foreign graduates. **Examination:** State examination. **Fees:** $20 application fee. $200 initial license fee. $200 biennial renewal fee. **Governing Statute:** Title 5, Chapter 24, General Laws.

Credential Type: License by endorsement. **Requirements:** Hold a valid veterinary license by examination issued in another state or the District of Columbia. Meet the qualifications required by Rhode Island for the practice of veterinary medicine. **Governing Statute:** Title 5, Chapter 24, General Laws.

South Carolina

8422

Veterinarian
South Carolina State Board of Veterinary Medical Examiners
PO Box 210786
Columbia, SC 29221
Phone: (803)772-8411

Credential Type: Veterinarian License. **Requirements:** Graduation from an approved school or college of veterinary medicine. **Examination:** Yes. **Fees:** $100 exam fee. $40 renewal fee.

South Dakota

8423

Veterinarian
Veterinary Board
422 S. Forte St.
Pierre, SD 57501
Phone: (605)773-3321
Fax: (605)773-5459

Credential Type: License to practice. **Duration of License:** One year. **Requirements:** 18 years of age. Citizen of the U.S. Graduate of an approved school of veterinary medicine. Must intend to practice veterinary medicine within the state of South Dakota. **Examination:** National Board Examination. **Fees:** $75 initial license fee. $50 reciprocal license fee. $25 annual renewal fee. **Governing Statute:** SDCL 36-12-12.

8424

Veterinarian (Horse Racing)
South Dakota Racing Commission
c/o 500 East Capitol
Pierre, SD 57501
Phone: (605)773-6050

Credential Type: License Registration. **Requirements:** Submit application and fingerprint card. Pay fee. **Fees:** $25 registration fee.

Tennessee

8425

Veterinarian
Board of Veterinary Medicine
283 Plus Park Blvd.
Nashville, TN 37243
Phone: (615)367-6225

Credential Type: License. **Duration of License:** One year. **Requirements:** Graduate of an accredited veterinary medicine school. D.V.M. degree from accredited college. 20 hours of continuing education per year for renewal. **Examination:** National Board Examination and State Board. **Fees:** $95 Registration. $25 Examination (State), $100 (National). $25 Application, per exam.

8426

Veterinarian (Racetrack)
Tennessee State Racing Commission
500 James Robertson Pky., 2nd Fl.
Nashville, TN 37243
Phone: (615)741-1952

Credential Type: License Registration. **Requirements:** Submit application and fingerprint card. Pay fee. **Fees:** $50 registration fee.

Texas

8427

Veterinarian
Texas Board of Veterinary Medical Examiners
1946 S. Interregional Hwy., Ste. 306
Austin, TX 78704
Phone: (512)447-1183

Credential Type: License. **Duration of License:** One year. **Requirements:** Graduation from a school or college of veterinary medicine approved by the American Veterinary Medical Association (AVMA) or the Board. **Examination:** Written and/or practical. **Fees:** $500 exam fee ($300 if only State Board exam is taken). $300 registration fee. $300 renewal fee. **Governing Statute:** VACS 8890, 22 TAC 571.

8428

Veterinarian (Racetrack)
Texas Racing Commission
PO Box 12080
Austin, TX 78711
Phone: (512)794-8461

Credential Type: License Registration. **Requirements:** Submit application and fingerprint card. Pay fee. **Fees:** $75 registration fee.

Utah

8429

Veterinarian
Dept. of Commerce
Div. of Occupational and Professional Licensing
160 E. 300 S.
PO Box 5802
Salt Lake City, UT 84145
Phone: (801)530-6628

Credential Type: License. **Duration of License:** Two years. **Requirements:** Must be a graduate from an approved veterinary college. Must practice veterinary medicine for at least six months under the supervision of a veterinarian licensed to practice in Utah; or participation in veterinary investigational, educational or sanitary control work of such nature equivalent to at least six month's veterinary medicine practice; or have practiced as a licensed veterinarian in another state or territory of the United States and currently hold a valid license in that state or territory; or have practiced as a veterinarian while an employee of the U.S. government, or the state or political subdivision for six months. **Examination:** Yes. **Reciprocity:** Yes. **Fees:** $25 examination and license fee. $20 renewal fee. $10 controlled substance license and renewal fee.

Vermont

8430

Veterinarian
State Veterinary Board
Pavilion Office Bldg.
Montpelier, VT 05602
Phone: (802)828-2363

Credential Type: License. **Duration of License:** Two years. **Requirements:** Graduate of a recognized veterinarian college approved by the American Veterinary Medical Association (AVMA); or, by endorsement, five years of licensed practice in another state. **Examination:** Yes. **Reciprocity:** To be determined by Board. **Fees:** $50 Application. $50 Licensure without Examination. $25 Temporary license. $10 License renewal. $10 Late renewal. $10 Replacement license. **Governing Statute:** Title 26, VSA Sections 2401-2432.

8431

Veterinarian (Greyhound Racing)
Vermont Racing Commission
State Office Bldg.
Montpelier, VT 05602
Phone: (802)828-3429

Credential Type: License Registration. **Requirements:** Submit application and fingerprint card. Pay fee. **Fees:** $20 registration fee. $5 duplicate license.

8432

Veterinarian (Racetrack)
Vermont Racing Commission
State Office Bldg.
Montpelier, VT 05602
Phone: (802)828-3429

Credential Type: License Registration. **Requirements:** Submit application and fingerprint card. Pay fee. **Fees:** $5 registration fee. $2 duplicate license.

Virginia

8433

Veterinarian
Virginia Board of Veterinary Medicine
1601 Rolling Hills Dr.
Richmond, VA 23229
Phone: (804)662-9920

Credential Type: License. **Duration of License:** One year. **Requirements:** 18 years of age. A degree in veterinary medicine approved by the Board. **Examination:** Yes. **Fees:** $125 examination fee. $125 renewal fee.

8434

Veterinarian (Racetrack)
Virginia Racing Commission
PO Box 1123
Richmond, VA 23208
Phone: (804)371-7363

Credential Type: License Registration. **Requirements:** Submit application and fingerprint card. Pay fee. **Fees:** $10 registration fee.

Washington

8435

Dentist (Racetrack)
Washington Horse Racing Commission
3700 Martin Way, Ste. 101
Olympia, WA 98506
Phone: (206)459-6462

Credential Type: License Registration. **Duration of License:** One year. **Requirements:** Submit application and fingerprint card. Pay fee. **Fees:** $15 registration fee. $5 duplicate license fee.

8436

Veterinarian
Veterinary Board of Governors
1300 SE Quince
Olympia, WA 98504
Phone: (206)586-6355
Phone: (206)586-6350

Credential Type: License to practice. **Requirements:** 18 years of age. Good moral character. Graduate of an accredited veterinary college. ECFVG certificate required for foreign graduates. **Examination:** State examination. National Board Examination. Clinical Competency Test. **Fees:** $225 state examination/initial license fee. $150 National Board Examination fee. $130 Clinical Competency Test fee. $140 renewal fee. **Governing Statute:** Chapter 18.92 Revised Code of Washington and Chapter 246-933 Washington Administrative Code.

8437

Veterinarian (Racetrack)
Washington Horse Racing Commission
3700 Martin Way, Ste. 101
Olympia, WA 98506
Phone: (206)459-6462

Credential Type: License Registration. **Duration of License:** One year. **Requirements:** Submit application and fingerprint card. Pay fee. **Fees:** $15 registration fee. $5 duplicate license fee.

West Virginia

8438

Veterinarian
Board of Veterinary Medicine
712 MacCorkle Ave.
Charleston, WV 25303
Phone: (304)744-4721

Credential Type: License. **Duration of License:** One year. **Requirements:** U.S. citizen. 18 years old. Graduate of accredited school, or foreign school with certification. Some specialty areas within veterinary medicine may require special exams, fees, etc. Never convicted of a felony. **Examination:** Yes. **Fees:** $50 Application. $25 Renewal.

Wisconsin

8439

Practicing Veterinarian (Racetrack)
Wisconsin Racing Board
PO Box 7975
Madison, WI 53707-7975
Phone: (608)267-3291

Credential Type: License Registration. **Requirements:** Submit application and two sets of fingerprint cards. Pay fee. **Fees:** $100 registration fee. $20 duplicate license.

8440

Veterinarian
Regulations and Licensing Dept.
Veterinary Board
PO Box 8935
Madison, WI 53708-8935
Phone: (608)266-8609

Credential Type: License. **Requirements:** Graduation from an approved veterinary college. 18 years of age. **Examination:** Written and practical. **Reciprocity:** Yes.

Wyoming

8441

Veterinarian
Wyoming Board of Veterinarian Medicine
Herschler Bldg., 3rd Fl. E.
Cheyenne, WY 82002
Phone: (307)777-7515

Credential Type: License. **Duration of License:** One year. **Requirements:** Complete a four year veterinary medicine program at an approved college of veterinary medicine. Pass the state examinations. **Examination:** Yes. **Fees:** $100 License. $10 Renewal.

8442

Veterinarian (Racetrack)
Wyoming State Pari-Mutuel Commission
Barrett Bldg., 3rd Fl.
Cheyenne, WY 82002
Phone: (307)777-5887

Credential Type: License Registration. **Requirements:** Submit application and fingerprint card. Pay fee. **Fees:** $20 registration fee. $10 duplicate license.

Visual Artists

The following states grant licenses in this occupational category as of the date of publication: Delaware, Hawaii, Iowa, Louisiana, Rhode Island, Texas.

Delaware

8443

Tattoo Artist
Committee on Massage and
 Bodywork Practitioners
Dept. of Administrative Services
Div. of Professional Regulation
PO Box 1401
Dover, DE 19903
Phone: (302)739-4522

Credential Type: License. **Requirements:** Contact licensing body for application information.

Hawaii

8444

Tattoo Artist
Hawaii State Dept. of Health,
 Sanitation Branch
591 Ala Moana Blvd.
Honolulu, HI 96813
Phone: (808)548-5397

Credential Type: License. **Duration of License:** One year. **Requirements:** Passing of a physical exam which includes a chest x-ray or TB skin test and a blood test for syphilis. **Examination:** Written. **Exemptions:** Licensed physicians are exempt. **Fees:** $75 exam fee. $7.50 renewal fee.

Iowa

8445

Tattoo Artist
Iowa Dept. of Public Health
Tattoo Permit Program
Lucas State Office Bldg.
Des Moines, IA 50319
Phone: (515)281-6762

Credential Type: License. **Duration of License:** One year. **Fees:** $60 application fee. $60 renewal fee. **Governing Statute:** Chapter 22 of the Code of Iowa.

Louisiana

8446

Art Therapist (School)
Louisiana State Dept. of Education
PO Box 94064
Baton Rouge, LA 70804
Phone: (504)342-3490

Credential Type: License. **Requirements:** Completion of an accredited art therapy degree program and registration by the American Art Therapy Association.

8447

Artist (School)
Louisiana State Dept. of Education
Teacher Certification
PO Box 94064
Baton Rouge, LA 70804
Phone: (504)342-3490

Credential Type: License. **Duration of License:** One year. **Requirements:** Written indication that the applicant will be employed once certified. Substantive evidence of artistic and/or creative accomplishment over an extended period of time. Some evidence of substantial professional recognition.

Rhode Island

8448

Tattoo Artist
Div. of Professional Regulation
Rhode Island Dept. of Health
3 Capitol Hill
Providence, RI 02908
Phone: (401)277-2827

Credential Type: Tattoo Artist License. **Duration of License:** One year. **Requirements:** At least 18 years of age. Good moral character. Foreign born must show proof of legal entry into U.S. Ability to demonstrate antiseptic tattooing technique. **Examination:** Practical examination. **Reciprocity:** No. **Fees:** $50 license fee. $50 renewal fee.

Texas

8449

Tattooer (Racetrack)
Texas Racing Commission
PO Box 12080
Austin, TX 78711
Phone: (512)794-8461

Credential Type: License Registration. **Requirements:** Submit application and fingerprint card. Pay fee. **Fees:** $75 registration fee.

Water Transportation Occupations

One or more occupations in this chapter require a federal license. Additionally, the following states grant licenses as of the date of publication:

Alabama	Florida	Iowa	Michigan	Rhode Island
Alaska	Hawaii	Maine	New Jersey	Vermont
Delaware	Illinois	Maryland	Oregon	Washington

Federal Contacts

U.S. Dept. of Transportation
2100 Second St., SW
Washington, DC 20593
Phone: (202)267-0218

Regional Offices

U.S. Coast Guard/Marine Safety Office (REC)
222 W. 7th Ave., No. 17
Anchorage, AK 99513-7565
Phone: (907)271-5137

U.S. Coast Guard/Marine Safety Office (REC)
2760 Sherwood Ln., Ste. 2A
Juneau, AK 99801-8545
Phone: (907)568-7309

U.S. Coast Guard/Marine Safety Office (REC)
Bldg. 14, Rm. 109
Coast Guard Island
Alameda, CA 94501-5100
Phone: (415)437-3092

U.S. Coast Guard/Marine Safety Office (REC)
165 N. Pico Ave.
Long Beach, CA 90802-1096
Phone: (213)499-5530

U.S. Coast Guard/Marine Safety Office (REC)
155 S. Miami Ave.
Miami, FL 33130-1609
Phone: (305)536-6548

U.S. Coast Guard/Marine Safety Office (REC)
433 Ala Mona Blvd., Rm. 1
Honolulu, HI 96813-4909
Phone: (808)541-2072

U.S. Coast Guard/Marine Safety Office (REC)
1440 Canal St.
New Orleans, LA 70112-2711
Phone: (504)589-6183

U.S. Coast Guard/Marine Safety Office (REC)
U.S. Custom House
40 S. Gay St.
Baltimore, MD 21202-4022
Phone: (301)962-5133

U.S. Coast Guard/Marine Safety Office (REC)
455 Commercial St.
Boston, MA 02109-1045
Phone: (617)223-3040

U.S. Coast Guard/Marine Safety Office (REC)
210 Tucker Blvd., Ste. 1128
St. Louis, MO 63101-1952
Phone: (314)425-4657

U.S. Coast Guard/Marine Inspection Office (REC)
Battery Park Bldg., Ste. 1128
New York, NY 10004-1466
Phone: (212)668-7492

U.S. Coast Guard/Marine Safety Office (REC)
Federal Bldg., Rm. 101
234 Summit St.
Toledo, OH 43604-1590
Phone: (419)259-6394

U.S. Coast Guard/Marine Safety Office (REC)
6767 N. Basin Ave.
Portland, OR 97217-3992
Phone: (503)240-9346

U.S. Coast Guard/Marine Safety Office (REC)
196 Tradd St.
Charleston, SC 29401-1899
Phone: (803)724-7693

U.S. Coast Guard/Marine Safety Office (REC)
200 Jefferson Ave., Ste. 1301
Memphis, TN 38103-2300
Phone: (901)544-3297

U.S. Coast Guard/Marine Safety Office (REC)
8876 Gulf Fwy., Ste. 210
Houston, TX 77017-6595
Phone: (713)947-0044

U.S. Coast Guard/Marine Safety Office (REC)
1519 Alaskan Way S.
Seattle, WA 98134-1192
Phone: (202)286-5510

Federal Licenses

8450

Assistant Engineer

Credential Type: First Assistant Engineer License. **Duration of License:** Five years. **Authorization:** License may contain restrictions as to vessel type, tonnage, means of propulsion, horsepower, or water upon which service is authorized. **Requirements:** Necessary qualifications are age (21 years with exceptions for some license restrictions), experience (varies with license restrictions), character references and recommendations, physical examination, citizenship, and training. Must pass professional examination. Must speak, read, and write English.

May not have been convicted of a violation of the dangerous drug laws of the United States within the past three years, and up to 10 yearrs depending on the gravity of the conviction.

Must have at least three months of qualifying service on vessels of appropriate tonnage or horsepower within the past three years. **Examination:** Professional exam. **Governing Statute:** 46 CFR Chap. 1, Part 10.

Credential Type: Second Assistant Engineer License. **Duration of License:** Five years. **Authorization:** License may contain restrictions as to vessel type, tonnage, means of propulsion, horsepower, or water upon which service is authorized. **Requirements:** Necessary qualifications are age (21 years with exceptions for some license restrictions), experience (varies with license

Assistant Engineer, continued

restrictions), character references and recommendations, physical examination, citizenship, and training. Must pass professional examination. Must speak, read, and write English.

May not have been convicted of a violation of the dangerous drug laws of the United States within the past three years, and up to 10 years depending on the gravity of the conviction.

Must have at least three months of qualifying service on vessels of appropriate tonnage or horsepower within the past three years. **Examination:** Professional examination. **Governing Statute:** 46 CFR Chap. 1, Part 10.

Credential Type: Third Assistant Engineer License. **Duration of License:** Five years. **Authorization:** License may contain restrictions as to vessel type, tonnage, means of propulsion, horsepower, or water upon which service is authorized. **Requirements:** Necessary qualifications are age (21 years with exceptions for some license restrictions), experience (varies with license restrictions), character references and recommendations, physical examination, citizenship, and training. Must pass professional examination. Must speak, read, and write English.

May not have been convicted of a violation of the dangerous drug laws of the United States within the passt three years, and up to 10 years depending on the gravity of the conviction.

Must have at least three months of qualifying service on vessels of appropriate tonnage or horsepower within the past three years. **Examination:** Professional examination. **Governing Statute:** 46 CFR Chap. 1, Part 10.

Credential Type: Assistant Engineer (Limited) License. **Duration of License:** Five years. **Authorization:** License may contain restrictions as to vessel type, tonnage, means of propulsion, horsepower, or water upon which service is authorized. **Requirements:** Necessary qualifications are age (21 years with exceptions for some license restrictions), experience (varies with license restrictions), character references and recommendations, physical examination, citizenship, and training. Must pass professional examination. Must speak, read, and write English.

May not have been convicted of a violation of the dangerous drug laws of the United States within the past three years, and up to 10 years depending on the gravity of the conviction.

Must have at least three months of qualifying service on vessels of appropriate tonnage or horsepower within the past three years. **Examination:** Professional examination. **Governing Statute:** 46 CFR Chap. 1, Part 10.

Credential Type: Assistant Engineer (Uninspected Fishing Vessels) License. **Duration of License:** Five years. **Authorization:** License may contain restrictions as to vessel type, tonnage, means of propulsion, horsepower, or water upon which service is authorized. **Requirements:** Necessary qualifications are age (21 years with exceptions for some license restrictions), experience (varies with license restrictions), character references and recommendations, physical examination, citizenship, and training. Must pass professional examination. Must speak, read, and write English.

May not have been convicted of a violation of the dangerous drug laws of the United States within the past three years, and up to 10 years depending on the gravity of the conviction.

Must have at least three months of qualifying service on vessels of appropriate tonnage or horsepower within the past three years. **Examination:** Professional examination. **Governing Statute:** 46 CFR Chap. 1, Part 10.

8451

Ballast Control Operator

Credential Type: Ballast Control Operator License. **Duration of License:** Five years. **Authorization:** License may contain restrictions as to vessel type, tonnage, means of propulsion, horsepower, or water upon which service is authorized. **Requirements:** Necessary qualifications are age (21 years with exceptions for some license restrictions), experience (varies with license restrictions), character references and recommendations, physical examination, citizenship, and training. Must pass professional examination. Must speak, read, and write English.

May not have been convicted of a violation of the dangerous drug laws of the United States within the past three years, and up to 10 years dependingg on the gravity of the conviction.

Must have at least one year of employment assigned to a Mobile Offshore Drilling Unit, or a degree in engineering or engineering technology with at least 28 days of service on a Mobile Offshore Drilling Unit. **Examination:** Professional examination. **Governing Statute:** 46 CFR Chap. 1, Part 10.

8452

Barge Supervisor

Credential Type: Barge Supervisor License. **Duration of License:** Five years. **Authorization:** License may contain restrictions as to vessel type, tonnage, means of propulsion, horsepower, or water upon which service is authorized. **Requirements:** Necessary qualifications are age (21 years with exceptions for some license restrictions), experience (varies with license restrictions), character references and recommendations, physical examination, citizenship, and training. Must pass professional examination. Must speak, read, and write English.

May not have been convicted of a violation of the dangerous drug laws of the United States within the past three yeears, and up to 10 years depending on the gravity of the conviction.

Must have at least three years of employment assigned to a Mobile Offshore Drilling Unit, or a degree in engineering or engineering technology with at least 168 days of service on a Mobile Offshore Drilling Unit. **Examination:** Professional examination. **Governing Statute:** 46 CFR Chap. 1, Part 10.

8453

Chief Engineer

Credential Type: Chief Engineer License. **Duration of License:** Five years. **Authorization:** License may contain restrictions as to vessel type, tonnage, means of propulsion, horsepower, or water upon which service is authorized. **Requirements:** Necessary qualifications are age (21 years with exceptions for some license restrictions), experience (varies with license restrictions), character references and recommendations, physical examination, citizenship, and training. Must pass professional examination. Must speak, read, and write English.

May not have been convicted of a violation of the dangerous drug laws of the Uniteed States within the past three years, and up to 10 years depending on the gravity of the conviction.

Must have at least three months of qualifying service on vessels of appropriate tonnage or horsepower within the past three years. **Examination:** Professional examination. **Governing Statute:** 46 CFR Chap. 1, Part 10.

Credential Type: Chief Engineer (Limited) License. **Duration of License:** Five years. **Authorization:** License may contain restrictions as to vessel type, tonnage, means of propulsion, horsepower, or water upon which service is authorized. **Requirements:** Necessary qualifications are age (21 years with exceptions for some license restrictions), experience (varies with license restrictions), character references and recommendations, physical examination, citizenship, and training. Must pass professional examination. Must speak, read, and write English.

May not have been convicted of a violation of the dangerous drug laws of the United States within the ppast three years, and up to 10 years depending on the gravity of the conviction.

Must have at least three months of qualifying service on vessels of appropriate tonnage or horsepower within the past three years. **Examination:** Professional examination. **Governing Statute:** 46 CFR Chap. 1, Part 10.

Credential Type: Chief Engineer (Uninspected Fishing Vessels) License. **Duration of License:** Five years. **Authorization:** License may contain restrictions as to vessel type, tonnage, means of propulsion, horsepower, or water upon which service is authorized. **Requirements:** Necessary qualifications are age (21 years with exceptions for some license restrictions), experience (varies with license restrictions), character references and recommendations, physical examination, citizenship, and training. Must pass professional examination. Must speak, read, and write English.

May not have been convicted of a violation of the dangerous drug laws of the United States within the past three years, and up to 10 years depending on the gravity of the conviction.

Must have at least three months of qualifying service on vessels of appropriate tonnage or horsepower within the past three years. **Examination:** Professional examination. **Governing Statute:** 46 CFR Chap. 1, Part 10.

8454

Designated Duty Engineer

Credential Type: Designated Duty Engineer License. **Duration of License:** Five years. **Authorization:** License may contain restrictions as to vessel type, tonnage, means of propulsion, horsepower, or water upon which service is authorized. **Requirements:** Necessary qualifications are age (21 years with exceptions for some license restrictions), experience (varies with license restrictions), character references and recommendations, physical examination, citizenship, and training. Must pass professional examination. Must speak, read, and write English.

May not have been convicted of a violation of the dangerous drug laws of the United States within the past three years, and up to 10 years depending on the gravity of the conviction.

Must have at least three months of qualifying service on vessels of appropriate tonnage or horsepower within the past three years. **Examination:** Professional examination. **Governing Statute:** 46 CFR Chap. 1, Part 10.

8455

Lifeboatman

Credential Type: Lifeboatman Certificate. **Duration of License:** Five years. **Authorization:** License may contain restrictions as to vessel type, tonnage, means of propulsion, horsepower, or water upon which service is authorized. **Requirements:** Must speak and understand English. Must meet one of the following requirements: (1) At least one year of sea service in the deck department, or at least two years of sea service in other departments; (2) Graduation from an approved schoolship; (3) Complete basic training as a cadet of the U.S. Merchant Marine Cadet Corps; (4) Complete three years of training at the U.S. Naval Academy or the U.S. Coast Guard Academy with at least two training cruises; (5) Complete an approved training course served aboard a training vessel; (6) Complete an approved training course including a minimum of 30 hours actual lifeboat training, provided that applicant has at least three months service at sea. **Examination:** Oral or written examination. Practical examination. **Governing Statute:** 46 CFR Chap. 1, Part 12.

8456

Master

Credential Type: Master's License. **Duration of License:** Five years. **Authorization:** License may contain restrictions as to vessel type, tonnage, means of propulsion, horsepower, or water upon which service is authorized. **Requirements:** Necessary qualifications are age (21 years with exceptions for some license restrictions), experience (varies with license restrictions), character references and recommendations, physical examination, citizenship, and training. Must pass professional examination. Must speak, read, and write English.

May not have been convicted of a violation of the dangerous drug laws of the United States within the past three years, and up to 10 years depending on tthe gravity of the conviction.

Must have at least three months of qualifying service on vessels of appropriate tonnage or horsepower within the past three years. **Examination:** Professional examination. **Governing Statute:** 46 CFR Chap. 1, Part 10.

8457

Mate

Credential Type: Mate's License. **Duration of License:** Five years. **Authorization:** License may contain restrictions as to vessel type, tonnage, means of propulsion, horsepower, or water upon which service is authorized. Licenses may be issued for first, second, and third mates. **Requirements:** Necessary qualifications are age (21 years with exceptions for some license restrictions), experience (varies with license restrictions), character references and recommendations, physical examination, citizenship, and training. Must pass professional examination. Must speak, read, and write English.

May not have been convicted of a violation of the dangerous drug laws of the United States within the past three years, and up to 10 years depending on the gravity of the conviction.

Must have at least three months of qualifying service on vessels of appropriate tonnage or horsepower within the past three years. **Examination:** Professional examination. **Governing Statute:** 46 CFR Chap. 1, Part 10.

8458

Merchant Mariner

Credential Type: Merchant Mariner's Document. **Duration of License:** Five years. **Authorization:** License may contain restrictions as to vessel type, tonnage, means of propulsion, horsepower, or water upon which service is authorized. Required of every person employed in a rating other than able seaman or qualified member of the engine department on a vessel that requires certificated personnel. **Requirements:** Varies with endorsement. Must have commitment of employment as a member of the crew of a United States merchant vessel or transcript of sea service in the U.S. Navy, Coast Guard, Military Sea Transportation Service, or Army Transportation Corps. **Governing Statute:** 46 CFR Chap. 1, Part 12.

8459

Offshore Installation Manager

Credential Type: Offshore Installation Manager License. **Duration of License:** Five years. **Authorization:** License may contain restrictions as to vessel type, tonnage, means of propulsion, horsepower, or water upon which service is authorized. **Requirements:** Necessary qualifications are age (21 years with exceptions for some license restrictions), experience (varies with license restrictions), character references and recommendations, physical examination, citizenship, and training. Must pass professional examination. Must speak, read, and write English.

May not have been convicted of a violation of the dangerous drug laws of the United States within the past three years, and up to 10 years depending on the gravity of the conviction.

Must have at least four years of employment assigned to a Mobile Offshore Drilling Unit, or a degree in engineering or engineering technology with at least 168 days of service on a Mobile Offshore Drilling Unit. **Examination:** Professional examination. **Governing Statute:** 46 CFR Chap. 1, Part 10.

8460

Operator of Uninspected Passenger Vessel

Credential Type: Operator of Uninspected Passenger Vessel License. **Duration of License:** Five years. **Authorization:** License may contain restrictions as to vessel type, tonnage, means of propulsion, horsepower, or water upon which service is authorized. **Requirements:** Necessary qualifications are age (21 years with exceptions for some license restrictions), experience (varies with license restrictions), character references and recommendations, physical examination, citizenship, and training. Must pass professional examination. Must speak, read, and write English.

May not have been convicted of a violation of the dangerous drug laws of the United States within the past three years, and up to 10 years depending on the gravity of the conviction.

Must have at least three months of qualifying service on vessels of appropriate tonnage or horsepower within the past three years. **Examination:** Professional examination. **Governing Statute:** 46 CFR Chap. 1, Part 10.

8461

Operator of Uninspected Towing Vessel

Credential Type: Operator of Uninspected Towing Vessel License. **Duration of License:** Five years. **Authorization:** License may contain restrictions as to vessel type, tonnage, means of propulsion, horsepower, or water upon which service is authorized. **Requirements:** Necessary qualifications are age (21 years with exceptions for some license restrictions), experience (varies with license restrictions), character references and recommendations, physical examination, citizenship, and training. Must pass professional examination. Must speak, read, and write English.

May not have been convicted of a violation of the dangerous drug laws of the United States within the past three years, and up to 10 years depending on the gravity of the conviction.

Must have at least three months of qualifying service on vessels of appropriate tonnage or horsepower within the past three years. **Examination:** Professional examination. **Governing Statute:** 46 CFR Chap. 1, Part 10.

8462

Pilot (Ship)

Credential Type: First Class Pilot License. **Duration of License:** Five years. **Authorization:** License may contain restrictions as to vessel type, tonnage, means of propulsion, horsepower, or water upon which service is authorized. **Requirements:** Necessary qualifications are age (21 years with exceptions for some license restrictions), experience (varies with license restrictions), character references and recommendations, physical examination, citizenship, and training. Must speak, read, and write English. Pass appropriate examination. **Examination:** Pilot's examination. **Exemptions:** A licensed master, mate, or operator of uninspected towing vessels may apply for an endorsement as first class pilot for a specific route or routes in lieu of applying for a first class pilot's license. **Governing Statute:** 46 CFR Chap. 1, Part 10.

8463

Purser

Credential Type: Chief Purser License. **Duration of License:** Five years. **Authorization:** License may contain restrictions as to vessel type, tonnage, means of propulsion, horsepower, or water upon which service is authorized. **Requirements:** Necessary qualifications are age (21 years with exceptions for some license restrictions), two years of experience (varies with license restrictions), character references and recommendations, physical examination, citizenship, and training. Must speak, read, and write English. **Governing Statute:** 46 CFR Chap. 1, Part 10.

Credential Type: Purser License. **Duration of License:** Five years. **Authorization:** License may contain restrictions as to vessel type, tonnage, means of propulsion, horsepower, or water upon which service is authorized. **Requirements:** Necessary qualifications are age (21 years with exceptions for some license restrictions), one year of experience (varies with license restrictions), character references and recommendations, physical examination, citizenship, and training. Must speak, read, and write English. **Governing Statute:** 46 CFR Chap. 1, Part 10.

Credential Type: Senior Assistant Purser License. **Duration of License:** Five years. **Authorization:** License may contain restrictions as to vessel type, tonnage, means of propulsion, horsepower, or water upon which service is authorized. **Requirements:** Necessary qualifications are age (21 years with exceptions for some license restrictions), six months of experience (varies with license restrictions), character references and recommendations, physical examination, citizenship, and training. Must speak, read, and write English. **Governing Statute:** 46 CFR Chap. 1, Part 10.

Credential Type: Junior Assistant Purser License. **Duration of License:** Five years. **Authorization:** License may contain restrictions as to vessel type, tonnage, means of propulsion, horsepower, or water upon which service is authorized. **Requirements:** Necessary qualifications are age (21 years with exceptions for some license restrictions), character references and recommendations, physical examination, citizenship, and training. Must speak, read, and write English. No previous experience required. **Governing Statute:** 46 CFR Chap. 1, Part 10.

8464

Qualified Member of the Engine Department

Credential Type: Qualified Member of the Engine Department Certificate. **Duration of License:** Five years. **Authorization:** License may contain restrictions as to vessel type, tonnage, means of propulsion, horsepower, or water upon which service is authorized. Includes any person below the rating of licensed officer and above the rating of coal passer or wiper, such as oiler, watertender, fireman, deck engineer, refrigerator engineer, junior engineer, electrician, and machinist. **Requirements:** Must speak and understand English. Pass physical examination. Have at least six months of service in a rating at least equal to a wiper or coal passer. Approved training programs may be substituted for required service at sea. **Examination:** Oral or written examination. **Governing Statute:** 46 CFR Chap. 1, Part 12.

8465

Radar Observer

Credential Type: Radar Observer License. **Duration of License:** Five years. **Authorization:** License may contain restrictions as to vessel type, tonnage, means of propulsion, horsepower, or water upon which service is authorized. **Requirements:** Necessary qualifications are age (21 years with exceptions for some license restrictions), experience (varies with license restrictions), character references and recommendations, physical examination, citizenship, and training. Must speak, read, and write English.

May not have been convicted of a violation of the dangerous drug laws of the United States within the past three years, and up to 10 years depending on the gravity of the conviction.

Must complete an approved course in radar observation, or demonstrate competency by passing a written examination. **Governing Statute:** 46 CFR Chap. 1, Part 10.

8466

Radio Officer

Credential Type: Radio Officer License. **Duration of License:** Five years. **Authorization:** License may contain restrictions as to vessel type, tonnage, means of propulsion, horsepower, or water upon which service is authorized. **Requirements:** Necessary qualifications are age (21 years with exceptions for some license restrictions), experience (varies with license restrictions), character references and recommendations, physical examination, citizenship, and training. Must speak, read, and write English. Must hold a first or second class radiotelegraph operator license issued by the Federal Communications Commission. **Governing Statute:** 46 CFR Chap. 1, Part 10.

8467

Seaman

Credential Type: Able Seaman Certificate—Any Waters, Unlimited. **Duration of License:** Five years. **Authorization:** License may contain restrictions as to vessel type, tonnage, means of propulsion, horsepower, or water upon which service is authorized. **Requirements:** Necessary qualifications are 18 years of age, three years of experience, character references and recommendations, physical examination, citizenship, and training. Must speak, read, and write English. Pass examination demonstrating ability. **Examination:** Oral or written examination. Practical examination. **Governing Statute:** 46 CFR Chap. 1, Part 12.

Credential Type: Able Seaman Certificate—Limited. **Duration of License:** Five years. **Authorization:** License may contain restrictions as to vessel type, tonnage, means of propulsion, horsepower, or water upon which service is authorized. **Requirements:** Necessary qualifications are 18 years of age, 18 months of experience, character references and recommendations, physical examination, citizenship, and training. Must speak, read, and write English. Pass examination demonstrating ability. **Examination:** Oral or written examination. Practical examination. **Governing Statute:** 46 CFR Chap. 1, Part 12.

Credential Type: Able Seaman Certificate—Special. **Duration of License:** Five years. **Authorization:** License may contain restrictions as to vessel type, tonnage, means of propulsion, horsepower, or water upon which service is authorized. **Requirements:** Necessary qualifications are 18 years of age, one year of experience, character references and recommendations, physical examination, citizenship, and training. Must speak, read, and write English. Pass examination demonstrating ability. **Examination:** Oral or written examination. Practical examination. **Governing Statute:** 46 CFR Chap. 1, Part 12.

Credential Type: Able Seaman Certificate—Special (Offshore Supply Vessel). **Duration of License:** Five years. **Authorization:** License may contain restrictions as to vessel type, tonnage, means of propulsion, horsepower, or water upon which service is authorized. **Requirements:** Necessary qualifications are 18 years of age, 6 months of experience, character references and recommendations, physical examination, citizenship, and training. Must speak, read, and write English. Pass examination demonstrating ability. **Examination:** Oral or written examination. Practical examination. **Governing Statute:** 46 CFR Chap. 1, Part 12.

8468

Ship's Doctor

Credential Type: Medical Doctor License. **Duration of License:** Five years. **Authorization:** License may contain restrictions as to vessel type, tonnage, means of propulsion, horsepower, or water upon which service is authorized. **Requirements:** Must hold or apply for a merchant mariner's document. Must hold a valid license as physician or surgeon issued by a state or territory of the United States, Puerto Rico, or the District of Columbia. **Governing Statute:** 46 CFR Chap. 1, Part 10.

8469

Ship's Nurse

Credential Type: Nurse's License. **Duration of License:** Five years. **Authorization:** License may contain restrictions as to vessel type, tonnage, means of propulsion, horsepower, or water upon which service is authorized. **Requirements:** Must hold or apply for a merchant mariner's document. Must hold a valid license as a registered nurse issued by a state or territory of the United States, Puerto Rico, or the District of Columbia. **Governing Statute:** 46 CFR Chap. 1, Part 10.

8470

Tankerman

Credential Type: Tankerman Certificate. **Duration of License:** Five years. **Authorization:** License may contain restrictions as to vessel type, tonnage, means of propulsion, horsepower, or water upon which service is authorized. **Requirements:** Must speak and understand English. Pass physical examination. Must be trained in and capable of performing the necessary operations on tank vessels that relate to the handling of cargo. **Governing Statute:** 46 CFR Chap. 1, Part 12.

Alabama

8471

Bar Pilot

State Pilotage Commission
PO Box 273
Mobile, AL 36601
Phone: (205)432-2639

Credential Type: License. **Duration of License:** One year. **Requirements:** 18 years of age and no older than 35. Must have recieved specialized training. Must have 365 days service under supervision of

Alabama 8472

Bar Pilot, continued

a senior pilot. Must have three years sea duty. **Examination:** Yes. **Fees:** $25 license fee.

8472

Harbor Pilot
State Pilotage Commission
PO Box 273
Mobile, AL 36601
Phone: (205)432-2639

Credential Type: License. **Requirements:** Must be a U.S. citizen. 21 years of age. Must be licensed by the U.S. Coast Guard.

Alaska

8473

Crewmember (fishing boat)
Alaska Dept. of Revenue
Fish & Game Licensing Section
PO Box 2-5525
Juneau, AK 99802-5525
Phone: (907)465-2376

Alternate Information: License available through most vendors who issue sport fishing licenses.
Credential Type: Crewmember License. **Duration of License:** One year. **Authorization:** Required of all people working on a commercial fishing vessel. **Fees:** $30 resident license fee. $90 nonresident license fee.

8474

Marine Pilot
Dept. of Commerce and Economic Development
Div. of Occupational Licensing
PO Box D
Juneau, AK 99811-0800
Phone: (907)465-3035

Credential Type: Deputy Pilot License. **Duration of License:** Two years. **Authorization:** Non-fishing commercial vessels navigating the inside waters of Alaska are required to be under the control of licensed pilots. Deputy pilot is limited to ships of 20,000 gross tons or less. **Requirements:** Must be at least 25 years old, a United States citizen, and a member of a recognized pilot association. Complete a board established training program. Experience as a ship master or officer. First class pilot endorsement on USCG license (without tonnage restriction) for the pilotage regiona for which licensure is sought.

License renewal requires a physical examination and proof of continuing competency. **Examination:** Written and oral exam administered by the Board of Marine Pilots. **Fees:** $30 application fee. $100 exam fee. $180 license fee.

Credential Type: Marine Pilot License. **Duration of License:** Two years. **Authorization:** Non-fishing commercial vessels navigating the inside waters of Alaska are required to be under the control of licensed pilots. **Requirements:** Must be at least 25 years old, a United States citizen, and a member of a recognized pilot association. Three years experience as a deputy marine pilot.

License renewal requires a physical examination and proof of continuing competency. **Examination:** Written and oral exam administered by the Board of Marine Pilots. **Fees:** $30 application fee. $100 exam fee. $180 license fee.

8475

Vessel Agent
Dept. of Commerce and Economic Development
Div. of Occupational Licensing
PO Box D
Juneau, AK 99811-0800
Phone: (907)465-3035

Credential Type: Vessel Agent License. **Duration of License:** Two years. **Authorization:** Anyone who acts on behalf of the owner or operator of a vessel, and who has actual or apparent authority for the purpose of securing pilotage services. **Requirements:** Submit notarized application and fee. **Fees:** $60 license fee.

Delaware

8476

River Pilot
Board of Pilot Commissioners
Dept. of Administrative Services
Div. of Professional Regulation
PO Box 1401
Dover, DE 19903
Phone: (302)739-4522

Credential Type: River Pilot License. **Requirements:** Contact licensing body for application information.

Florida

8477

Ship's Pilot
Board of Pilot Commissioners
Dept. of Professional Regulation
1940 N. Monroe St.
Tallahassee, FL 32399-0773
Phone: (904)488-0698

Credential Type: State Pilot License. **Duration of License:** Two years. **Requirements:** Be at least 21 years of age. Complete 12 years of formal education or equivalent. Be in good physical and mental health. Complete three years of service as a deputy pilot or apprentice pilot or other maritime experience satisfactory to the board.

Renewal requires maintaining Coast Guard license and radar certification. **Examination:** State Pilot Examination. Written examination given as openings in ports are declared. **Reciprocity:** No. **Fees:** $100 examination fee. $200 renewal fee. **Governing Statute:** Florida Statutes, Chapter 310. Florida Administrative Code, Rules 21-SS.

Credential Type: Deputy Pilot Certificate. **Duration of License:** Two years. **Requirements:** Be at least 21 years of age. Complete 12 years of formal education or equivalent. Be in good physical and mental health. Complete three years of service as a deputy pilot or apprentice pilot or other maritime experience satisfactory to the board.

Renewal requires maintaining Coast Guard license and radar certification. **Examination:** Deputy Pilot Examination. Written examination given as openings in ports are declared. **Reciprocity:** No. **Fees:** $100 examination fee. $100 renewal fee. **Governing Statute:** Florida Statutes, Chapter 310. Florida Administrative Code, Rules 21-SS.

Hawaii

8478

Commercial Marine License
Hawaii State Dept. of Land and Natural Resources
Div. of Aquatic Resources
1151 Punchbowl St., Rm. 300
Honolulu, HI 96813
Phone: (808)548-4001

Credential Type: License. **Duration of License:** One year. **Authorization:** Required of all fishers engaged in taking marine life for commercial purposes. **Fees:** $25 annual fee for residents. $50 annual fee for nonresidents.

Illinois

8479

Engineer (Riverboat Gambling)
Illinois Gaming Board
PO Box 19474
Springfield, IL 62794-9474
Phone: (217)524-0228

Credential Type: Engineer License (Riverboat). **Duration of License:** One year. **Requirements:** At least 18 years of age. Additional license by U.S. Coast Guard required. Extensive experience in Maritime engineering. Renewal requires recertification every five years. **Examination:** U.S. Coast Guard Chief Engineer Examination. **Reciprocity:** No. **Fees:** $385 examination fee. $75 application fee. $50 initial license fee. $50 renewal fee. **Governing Statute:** Illinois Revised Statutes, Chapter 120.

8480

First Mate (Gaming)
Illinois Gaming Board
PO Box 19474
Springfield, IL 62794-9474
Phone: (217)534-0228

Credential Type: First Mate License. **Duration of License:** One year. **Requirements:** At least 18 years of age. Knowledge and experience in Maritime field. Must have U.S. Coast Guard license. Renewal requires reexamination every five years. **Examination:** Mate (tonnage rating) examination. **Reciprocity:** No. **Fees:** $385 examination fee. $75 application fee. $50 initial license fee. $50 renewal fee. **Governing Statute:** Illinois Revised Statutes, Chapter 120.

8481

Passenger Boat/Charter Boat Operator
Illinois Dept. of Conservation
524 South 2nd St.
Springfield, IL 62701-1787
Phone: (217)785-3423

Credential Type: Boat Operator License. **Duration of License:** One year. **Requirements:** Submit application and pay fee. **Reciprocity:** No. **Fees:** $50 license fee (per boat). **Governing Statute:** Illinois Revised Statutes, Article VII, Chapter 95.

8482

Riverboat Senior Master/Captain (Gaming)
Illinois Gaming Board
PO Box 19474
Springfield, IL 62794-9474
Phone: (217)524-0228

Credential Type: Senior Master/Captain License. **Duration of License:** One year. **Requirements:** At least 18 years of age. Must have the appropriate U.S. Coast Guard's Pilots License. Must have experience as a Pilot in maritime areas. **Examination:** Master Examination (exam varies dependent on tonnage). **Reciprocity:** No. **Fees:** $385 examination fee. $75 application fee. $50 initial license fee. $50 renewal fee. **Governing Statute:** Illinois Revised Statutes, Chapter 120.

Iowa

8483

Boat Pilot (Riverboat Gambling)
Iowa Racing and Gaming Commission
Lucas State Office Bldg.
Des Moines, IA 50319
Phone: (515)281-7352

Credential Type: License Registration. **Requirements:** Submit application and pay fees. **Fees:** $50 license fee.

8484

Captain (Riverboat Gambling)
Iowa Racing and Gaming Commission
Lucas State Office Bldg.
Des Moines, IA 50319
Phone: (515)281-7352

Credential Type: License Registration. **Requirements:** Submit application and pay fees. **Fees:** $50 license fee.

8485

Deck Hand (Riverboat Gambling)
Iowa Racing and Gaming Commission
Lucas State Office Bldg.
Des Moines, IA 50319
Phone: (515)281-7352

Credential Type: License Registration. **Requirements:** Submit application and pay fees. **Fees:** $10 license fee.

Maine

8486

Ship's Pilot
Maine State Pilotage Commission
Dept. of Professional and Financial Regulation
Div. of Licensing and Enforcement
State House Station 35
Augusta, ME 04333
Phone: (207)582-8723

Credential Type: Pilot's License. **Duration of License:** One year. **Requirements:** Must be a citizen of the United States and a resident of the State of Maine. Must hold a federal first class pilot's endorsement covering the coastal waters of Maine. Must satisfy the commission that the applicant has or will have the proper means available for boarding and leaving vessels. **Exemptions:** Exempt vessels include fishing vessels and vessels powered by sail. **Fees:** $100 application fee. $10 license fee. $10 renewal fee. **Governing Statute:** 32 M.S.R.A. Chap. 1, Subchap. 3.

Maryland

8487

Ship's Pilot
Board of Examiners of Maryland Pilots
Dept. of Licensing and Regulation
501 St. Paul Pl.
Baltimore, MD 21202-2272
Phone: (410)333-6322

Credential Type: Unlimited Licensed Pilot. **Duration of License:** Two years. **Requirements:** Serve for at least three years as a limited licensed pilot. Demonstrate sufficient ability, skill, and experience based on the recommendation of the Qualification Committee, length of time applicant has piloted vessels, number of vessels piloted, pilotage routes, other licenses, and other pertinent factors. **Fees:** $300 license fee. **Governing Statute:** Annotated Code of Maryland, Title 11. Code of Maryland Regulations, Title 09, Subtitle 26.

Credential Type: Limited Licensed Pilot, 34-foot-draft. **Duration of License:** Two years. **Requirements:** A limited licensed pilot holding a license to pilot vessels not exceeding 28 feet draught may apply for a license to pilot vessels not exceeding 34 feet draught. Demonstrate sufficient ability, skill, and experience based on the recommendations of the Qualification Committee, length of time pilot has piloted 28-feet-draught vessels, number of vessels piloted, pilotage routes, and other pertinent factors.

Michigan — 8488

Ship's Pilot, continued

Fees: $300 license fee. **Governing Statute:** Annotated Code of Maryland, Title 11. Code of Maryland Regulations, Title 09, Subtitle 26.

Credential Type: Limited Licensed Pilot, 28-foot-draft. **Duration of License:** Two years. **Requirements:** Serve as an apprentice pilot for at least two years under the supervision of an unlimited licensed pilot. Demonstrate sufficient ability, skill, and experience based on the recommendations of the Qualification Committee and the supervising licensed pilots, other licenses, and the apprentice's training program, including length of time apprentice has piloted vessels, number of vessels piloted, pilotage routes, and other pertinent factors. **Fees:** $200 license fee. **Governing Statute:** Annotated Code of Maryland, Title 11. Code of Maryland Regulations, Title 09, Subtitle 26.

Credential Type: Apprentice Pilot License. **Duration of License:** Two years. **Requirements:** Pass physical examination. Meet one of the following sets of requirements: (1) Graduation from a four year course of study at an accredited maritime institution. Possess a valid license from the U.S. Coast Guard as a third mate or greater grade, of steam and motor vessels of any gross tons upon ocean. (2) Possess a valid license from the U.S. Coast Guard as a master of steam and motor vessels of any gross tons upon ocean. The license must include an appropriate radar endorsement. **Governing Statute:** Annotated Code of Maryland, Title 11. Code of Maryland Regulations, Title 09, Subtitle 26.

Michigan

8488

Operator of Vessels Carrying Passengers for Hire (Charter Boat Operator)
Administrative Services Div.
Dept. of Natural Resources
Stevens T. Mason Bldg.
PO Box 30028
Lansing, MI 48909
Phone: (517)373-1220

Credential Type: Registration. **Duration of License:** One year. **Requirements:** Have vessel(s) and equipment which meet safety standards as evidenced by a certificate of inspection which is issued by the Department. Minimum of $50,000 liability insurance for each passenger. Be a licensed ship pilot or employ a licensed ship pilot. Comply with the State law and the rules and regulations of the Department. **Examination:** Vessel inspection. **Reciprocity:** There is a reciprocity agreement with the State of Indiana. **Fees:** $250 initial certificate of inspection fee (varies according to the overall length of the vessel). $100 renewal certificate of inspection fee. $45 application fee for vessel's certificate of number. $45 renewal fee for vessel's certificate of number. $150 drydock boat inspection fee (required every six years). $100 reciprocity fee. **Governing Statute:** Vessels Carrying Passengers for Hire Act, Act 244 of 1986, as amended. Marine Safety Act, Act 303 of 1967, as amended.

8489

Pilot, Ship
Law Enforcement Div.
Dept. of Natural Resources
PO Box 30028
Lansing, MI 48909
Phone: (517)373-1220

Credential Type: License. **Duration of License:** Three years. **Authorization:** All persons who pilot passenger, cargo, excursion, or charter boats on the inland waters of the State must be licensed by the Department of Natural Resources. **Requirements:** At least 18 years of age. At least one year of experience on the type of vessel for which a license is being applied. Be in good physical condition and have good vision. Have not been convicted of a marine law violation in the past five years. Have not been convicted of violations of narcotics laws. **Examination:** Written exam. **Exemptions:** A person who holds a valid United States Coast Guard Pilot's license is not required to be licensed by the Department. **Fees:** $5 initial exam and license fee. $5 renewal fee. **Governing Statute:** Vessels Carrying Passengers for Hire Act, Act 228 of 1965.

New Jersey

8490

Harbor Pilot
U.S. Coast Guard
Regional Exam Center
Battery Park
New York, NY 10004-1466
Phone: (212)668-6395

Credential Type: Deputy Pilot License. **Requirements:** 18 years of age. Must serve four years as an apprentice, at least three of which shall be consecutive as a listed apprentice, boat keeper or assistant boat keeper. Must post a $500 surety bond. **Examination:** Yes. **Governing Statute:** NJSA 12:8.

Credential Type: Branch Pilot License. **Requirements:** 18 years of age. Must serve two years as a licensed deputy pilot. Must post a $500 surety bond. **Examination:** Yes. **Governing Statute:** NJSA 12:8.

Oregon

8491

Pilot (River or Bar)
Board of Maritime Pilots
800 NE Oregon St. 15, Ste. 507
Portland, OR 97232
Phone: (503)731-4044

Credential Type: License. **Duration of License:** One year. **Requirements:** U.S. citizenship. 18 years of age. At least six months of experience piloting ocean going vessels in the area for which application is made. Must have a federal license from the Coast Guard. **Examination:** Yes. **Fees:** $1,250 license fee. $1,250 renewal fee. **Governing Statute:** ORS 776.015 to 776.991.

Rhode Island

8492

Ship Pilot
State Pilotage Commission
Div. of Coastal Resources
Rhode Island Dept. of Environmental Management
22 Hayes St., Rm. 113
Providence, RI 02908
Phone: (401)277-3429

Credential Type: Ship Pilot License. **Duration of License:** Five years. **Requirements:** U.S. citizen. U.S. Coast Guard Master's license for unlimited tonnage, any ocean. Federal first class pilot's license for the waters of the state where application is made. Member of random drug testing program. Annual physical examination. $25,000 insurance recommended. **Examination:** Written examination. **Reciprocity:** Reciprocity exists only with New York for Block Island Sound and Long Island Sound. **Fees:** $100 license fee. $20 renewal fee.

Vermont

8493

Pilot, Ships
US Coast Guard
Marine Safety Office
447 Commercial St.
Boston, MA 01209
Phone: (617)565-9040

Credential Type: License. **Requirements:** 21 years of age. U.S. citizen. Written application. Pass physical. First aid and CPR certificates. Three years on vessels, one year of which shall be as a Licensed Operator. Radar Observer Certificate. **Examination:** Yes. **Fees:** Master's license (inland steam or motor vessel of not more than 500 gross tons). School fees for radar observer and firefighting certificates and for First Aid and CPR courses.

Washington

8494

Vessel Pilot
Dept. of Transportation
Transportation Bldg., KF-01
Olympia, WA 98504-5201
Phone: (206)464-7818

Credential Type: Vessel Pilot License. **Duration of License:** Five years. **Authorization:** State license required to pilot vessels in certain Washington waters. **Requirements:** U.S. citizen. Washington state resident. At least 25 years of age and under 70 years of age. Hold U.S. Government Masters license, a 1st class U.S. pilotage endorsement for Puget Sound and connecting inland waters or Grays Harbor and must have two years experience as a master pilot. Complete 100 "Familiarization Trips" in pilotage district. Annual physical examination required. **Examination:** Written and oral examination.

Water and Wastewater Treatment Plant Operators

The following states grant licenses in this occupational category as of the date of publication:

Alaska	Indiana	Massachusetts	Montana	North Carolina	South Dakota
Arizona	Iowa	Michigan	Nebraska	North Dakota	Vermont
Arkansas	Kentucky	Minnesota	New Hampshire	Oklahoma	Virginia
Georgia	Louisiana	Mississippi	New Jersey	Rhode Island	Washington
Illinois	Maryland	Missouri	New York	South Carolina	

Alaska

8495

Wastewater Collection System Operator
Dept. of Environmental Conservation
Facility Construction and Operation
410 Willoughby Ave.
Juneau, AK 99801-1795
Phone: (907)465-5140
Fax: (907)465-5177

Credential Type: Operator-in-Training certificate. **Duration of License:** Three years. **Requirements:** High school education or equivalent. Three months operating experience or completion of basic training course approved by the department. **Fees:** $10 application fee.

Credential Type: Level 1 operator certificate. **Duration of License:** Three years. **Authorization:** A complex point system is used to determine the level of a collection system. **Requirements:** High school education or equivalent. One year operating experience. Pass certification exam. **Examination:** State certification examination. **Fees:** $10 application fee. $15 examination fee. $30 certificate renewal fee.

Credential Type: Level 2 operator certificate. **Duration of License:** Three years. **Authorization:** A complex point system is used to determine the level of a collection system. **Requirements:** High school education or equivalent. Four years operating experience. Pass certification exam. **Examination:** State certification examination. **Fees:** $10 application fee. $15 examination fee. $30 certificate renewal fee.

Credential Type: Level 3 operator certificate. **Duration of License:** Three years. **Authorization:** A complex point system is used to determine the level of a collection system. **Requirements:** High school education or equivalent. Six years operating experience. Education and experience substitutions are allowed. Pass certification exam. **Examination:** State certification examination. **Fees:** $10 application fee. $15 examination fee. $30 certificate renewal fee.

Credential Type: Level 4 operator certificate. **Duration of License:** Three years. **Authorization:** A complex point system is used to determine the level of a collection system. **Requirements:** High school education or equivalent. Eight years operating experience. Education and experience substitutions are allowed. Pass certification exam. **Examination:** State certification examination. **Fees:** $10 application fee. $15 examination fee. $30 certificate renewal fee.

8496

Wastewater Treatment Plant Operator
Dept. of Environmental Conservation
Facility Construction and Operation
410 Willoughby Ave.
Juneau, AK 99801-1795
Phone: (907)465-5140
Fax: (907)465-5177

Credential Type: Operator-in-Training certificate. **Duration of License:** Three years. **Requirements:** High school education or equivalent. Three months operating experience or completion of basic training course approved by the department. **Fees:** $10 application fee.

Credential Type: Level 1 operator certificate. **Duration of License:** Three years. **Authorization:** A complex point system is used to determine the level of a treatment system. **Requirements:** High school education or equivalent. One year operating experience. Pass certification exam. **Examination:** State certification examination. **Fees:** $10 application fee. $15 examination fee. $30 certificate renewal fee.

Credential Type: Level 2 operator certificate. **Duration of License:** Three years. **Authorization:** A complex point system is used to determine the level of a treatment system. **Requirements:** High school education or equivalent. Three years operating experience. Pass certification exam. **Examination:** State certification examination. **Fees:** $10 application fee. $15 examination fee. $30 certificate renewal fee.

Credential Type: Level 3 operator certificate. **Duration of License:** Three years. **Authorization:** A complex point system is used to determine the level of a treatment system. **Requirements:** Two years of postsecondary education or equivalent. Four years operating experience. Two years of responsible charge experience. Education and experience substitutions are allowed. Pass certification exam. **Examination:** State certification examination. **Fees:** $10 application fee. $15 examination fee. $30 certificate renewal fee.

Credential Type: Level 4 operator certificate. **Duration of License:** Three years. **Authorization:** A complex point system is used to determine the level of a treatment system. **Requirements:** Four years of postsecondary education or equivalent. Four years operating experience. Two years of responsible charge experience. Education and experience substitutions are allowed. Pass certification exam. **Examination:** State certification examination. **Fees:** $10 application fee. $15 examination fee. $30 certificate renewal fee.

Credential Type: Conditional Level 3 operator certificate. **Duration of License:** One year. **Authorization:** A complex point system is used to determine the level of a treatment system. Valid only for the system the applicant is operating at the time of application. **Requirements:** Issued to a Level 2 operator to allow individual to accumulate responsible charge experience. Must meet Level 3 education and operating experience requirements. **Fees:** $10 application fee. $30 certificate renewal fee.

8497

Water Distribution System Operator
Dept. of Environmental Conservation
Facility Construction and Operation
410 Willoughby Ave.
Juneau, AK 99801-1795
Phone: (907)465-5140
Fax: (907)465-5177

Credential Type: Operator-in-Training certificate. **Duration of License:** Three years. **Requirements:** High school education or equivalent. Three months operating experience or completion of basic training course approved by the department. **Fees:** $10 application fee.

Credential Type: Level 1 operator certificate. **Duration of License:** Three years. **Authorization:** A complex point system is used to determine the level of a distribution system. **Requirements:** High school education or equivalent. One year operating experience. Pass certification exam. **Examination:** State certification examination. **Fees:** $10 application fee. $15 examination fee. $30 certificate renewal fee.

Credential Type: Level 2 operator certificate. **Duration of License:** Three years. **Authorization:** A complex point system is used to determine the level of a distribution system. **Requirements:** High school education or equivalent. Four years operating experience. Pass certification exam. **Examination:** State certification examination. **Fees:** $10 application fee. $15 examination fee. $30 certificate renewal fee.

Credential Type: Level 3 operator certificate. **Duration of License:** Three years. **Authorization:** A complex point system is used to determine the level of a distribution system. **Requirements:** High school education or equivalent. Six years operating experience. Education and experience substitutions are allowed. Pass certification exam. **Examination:** State certification examination. **Fees:** $10 application fee. $15 examination fee. $30 certificate renewal fee.

Credential Type: Level 4 operator certificate. **Duration of License:** Three years. **Authorization:** A complex point system is used to determine the level of a distribution system. **Requirements:** High school education or equivalent. Eight years operating experience. Education and experience sub-stitutions are allowed. Pass certification exam. **Examination:** State certification examination. **Fees:** $10 application fee. $15 examination fee. $30 certificate renewal fee.

8498

Water Treatment Plant Operator
Dept. of Environmental Conservation
Facility Construction and Operation
410 Willoughby Ave.
Juneau, AK 99801-1795
Phone: (907)465-5140
Fax: (907)465-5177

Credential Type: Operator-in-Training certificate. **Duration of License:** Three years. **Requirements:** High school education or equivalent. Three months operating experience or completion of basic training course approved by the department. **Fees:** $10 application fee.

Credential Type: Level 1 operator certificate. **Duration of License:** Three years. **Authorization:** A complex point system is used to determine the level of a treatment system. **Requirements:** High school education or equivalent. One year operating experience. Pass certification exam. **Examination:** State certification examination. **Fees:** $10 application fee. $15 examination fee. $30 certificate renewal fee.

Credential Type: Level 2 operator certificate. **Duration of License:** Three years. **Authorization:** A complex point system is used to determine the level of a treatment system. **Requirements:** High school education or equivalent. Three years operating experience. Pass certification exam. **Examination:** State certification examination. **Fees:** $10 application fee. $15 examination fee. $30 certificate renewal fee.

Credential Type: Level 3 operator certificate. **Duration of License:** Three years. **Authorization:** A complex point system is used to determine the level of a treatment system. **Requirements:** Two years of post-secondary education or equivalent. Four years operating experience. Two years of responsible charge experience. Education and experience substitutions are allowed. Pass certification exam. **Examination:** State certification examination. **Fees:** $10 application fee. $15 examination fee. $30 certificate renewal fee.

Credential Type: Level 4 operator certificate. **Duration of License:** Three years. **Authorization:** A complex point system is used to determine the level of a treatment system. **Requirements:** Four years of post-secondary education or equivalent. Four years operating experience. Two years of responsible charge experience. Education and experience substitutions are allowed. Pass certification exam. **Examination:** State certification examination. **Fees:** $10 application fee. $15 examination fee. $30 certificate renewal fee.

Credential Type: Conditional Level 3 operator certificate. **Duration of License:** One year. **Authorization:** A complex point system is used to determine the level of a treatment system. Valid only for the system the applicant is operating at the time of application. **Requirements:** Issued to a Level 2 operator to allow individual to accumulate responsible charge experience. Must meet Level 3 education and operating experience requirements. **Fees:** $10 application fee. $30 certificate renewal fee.

Arizona

8499

Wastewater Treatment Plant Operator
Dept. of Environmental Quality
Office of Water Quality
3033 N. Central Ave.
Phoenix, AZ 85012
Phone: (602)257-4627 or (602)207

Credential Type: Grade one operator certificate. **Duration of License:** Three years. **Authorization:** Includes stabilization ponds serving fewer than 2000 persons and any wastewater treatment facility not designated grades 2,3, or 4. **Requirements:** No minimum education or experience requirements. Pass examination. **Examination:** Written exam administered by the department. **Reciprocity:** Yes. **Fees:** $10 exam fee. $15 reciprocity fee. $15 certification fee. $15 renewal fee.

Credential Type: Grade two operator certificate. **Duration of License:** Three years. **Authorization:** Includes stabilization ponds serving more than 2000 persons; all aerated lagoons; and all facilities employing biological treatment or trickling filters designed to serve a population of less than 5000 persons. **Requirements:** At least two years of qualifying experience, including one year of operational experience as a Grade one certified operator; or high school graduation or the equivalent and one year of qualifying experience as a Grade one certified operator; or two years of postsecondary education in a related technical field and one year of qualifying experience, including six months as a certified Grade one operator; or a bachelor's degree in a qualifying discipline (engineering, biological or chemical sciences, or a closely related technical or scientific discipline) and six months of qualifying experience. Pass examination. **Examination:** Written exam

Wastewater Treatment Plant Operator, continued

administered by the department. **Reciprocity:** Yes. **Fees:** $10 exam fee. $15 reciprocity fee. $15 certification fee. $15 renewal fee.

Credential Type: Grade three operator certificate. **Duration of License:** Three years. **Authorization:** Includes all facilities employing biological treatment designed to serve a population of 5000-25,000 persons; facilities employing trickling filters designed to serve a population of 500025,000 persons; and variations of activated sludge requiring specialized knowledge serving any population up to 20,000 persons. **Requirements:** At least four years of qualifying experience, including two years of operational experience as a Grade two certified operator; or high school graduation or the equivalent and two years of qualifying experience as a Grade two certified operator; or two years of postsecondary education in a related technical field and six months of qualifying experience as a certified Grade two operator; or a bachelor's degree in a qualifying discipline (engineering, biological or chemical sciences, or a closely related technical or scientific discipline) and one year of qualifying experience, including six months as a certified Grade two operator. Pass examination. **Examination:** Written exam administered by the department. **Reciprocity:** Yes. **Fees:** $25 exam fee. $15 reciprocity fee. $15 certification fee. $15 renewal fee.

Credential Type: Grade four operator certificate. **Duration of License:** Three years. **Authorization:** Includes all facilities employing biological treatment designed to serve a population greater than 20,000 persons; facilities employing trickling filters designed to serve a population greater than 25,000 persons. **Requirements:** High school graduation or the equivalent and three years of qualifying experience, including one year of operational experience as a Grade three certified operator; or two years of post-secondary education in a related technical field and two years and six months of qualifying experience, including one year as a certified Grade three operator; or a bachelor's degree in a qualifying discipline (engineering, biological or chemical sciences, or a closely related technical or scientific discipline) and one year of qualifying experience as a certified Grade three operator. Pass examination. **Examination:** Written exam administered by the department. **Reciprocity:** Yes. **Fees:** $25 exam fee. $15 reciprocity fee. $15 certification fee. $15 renewal fee.

8500

Water Collection Systems Operator
Dept. of Environmental Quality
Office of Water Quality
3033 N. Central Ave.
Phoenix, AZ 85012
Phone: (602)257-4627 or (602)207

Credential Type: Grade one operator certificate. **Duration of License:** Three years. **Authorization:** Includes stabilization ponds serving fewer than 2000 persons and any wastewater treatment facility not designated grades 2,3, or 4. **Requirements:** No minimum education or experience requirements. Pass examination. **Examination:** Written exam administered by the department. **Reciprocity:** Yes. **Fees:** $10 exam fee. $15 reciprocity fee. $15 certification fee. $15 renewal fee.

Credential Type: Grade two operator certificate. **Duration of License:** Three years. **Authorization:** Includes stabilization ponds serving more than 2000 persons; all aerated lagoons; and all facilities employing biological treatment or trickling filters designed to serve a population of less than 5000 persons. **Requirements:** At least two years of qualifying experience, including one year of operational experience as a Grade one certified operator; or high school graduation or the equivalent and one year of qualifying experience as a Grade one certified operator; or two years of postsecondary education in a related technical field and one year of qualifying experience, including six months as a certified Grade one operator; or a bachelor's degree in a qualifying discipline (engineering, biological or chemical sciences, or a closely related technical or scientific discipline) and six months of qualifying experience. Pass examination. **Examination:** Written exam administered by the department. **Reciprocity:** Yes. **Fees:** $10 exam fee. $15 reciprocity fee. $15 certification fee. $15 renewal fee.

Credential Type: Grade three operator certificate. **Duration of License:** Three years. **Authorization:** Includes all facilities employing biological treatment designed to serve a population of 5000-25,000 persons; facilities employing trickling filters designed to serve a population of 500025,000 persons; and variations of activated sludge requiring specialized knowledge serving any population up to 20,000 persons. **Requirements:** At least four years of qualifying experience, including two years of operational experience as a Grade two certified operator; or high school graduation or the equivalent and two years of qualifying experience as a Grade two certified operator; or two years of postsecondary education in a related technical field and six months of qualifying experience as a certified Grade two operator; or a bachelor's degree in a qualifying discipline (engineering, biological or chemical sciences, or a closely related technical or scientific discipline) and one year of qualifying experience, including six months as a certified Grade two operator. Pass examination. **Examination:** Written exam administered by the department. **Reciprocity:** Yes. **Fees:** $25 exam fee. $15 reciprocity fee. $15 certification fee. $15 renewal fee.

Credential Type: Grade four operator certificate. **Duration of License:** Three years. **Authorization:** Includes all facilities employing biological treatment designed to serve a population greater than 20,000 persons; facilities employing trickling filters designed to serve a population greater than 25,000 persons. **Requirements:** High school graduation or the equivalent and three years of qualifying experience, including one year of operational experience as a Grade three certified operator; or two years of post-secondary education in a related technical field and two years and six months of qualifying experience, including one year as a certified Grade three operator; or a bachelor's degree in a qualifying discipline (engineering, biological or chemical sciences, or a closely related technical or scientific discipline) and one year of qualifying experience as a certified Grade three operator. Pass examination. **Examination:** Written exam administered by the department. **Reciprocity:** Yes. **Fees:** $25 exam fee. $15 reciprocity fee. $15 certification fee. $15 renewal fee.

8501

Water Distribution Systems Operator
Dept. of Environmental Quality
Office of Water Quality
3033 N. Central Ave.
Phoenix, AZ 85012
Phone: (602)257-4627
Phone: (602)207-2300

Credential Type: Grade one operator certificate. **Duration of License:** Three years. **Authorization:** Includes stabilization ponds serving fewer than 2000 persons and any wastewater treatment facility not designated grades 2,3, or 4. **Requirements:** No minimum education or experience requirements. Pass examination. **Examination:** Written exam administered by the department. **Reciprocity:** Yes. **Fees:** $10 exam fee. $15 reciprocity fee. $15 certification fee. $15 renewal fee.

Credential Type: Grade two operator certificate. **Duration of License:** Three years. **Authorization:** Includes stabilization

Water and Wastewater Treatment Plant Operators — Arizona — 8502

ponds serving more than 2000 persons; all aerated lagoons; and all facilities employing biological treatment or trickling filters designed to serve a population of less than 5000 persons. **Requirements:** At least two years of qualifying experience, including one year of operational experience as a Grade one certified operator; or high school graduation or the equivalent and one year of qualifying experience as a Grade one certified operator; or two years of postsecondary education in a related technical field and one year of qualifying experience, including six months as a certified Grade one operator; or a bachelor's degree in a qualifying discipline (engineering, biological or chemical sciences, or a closely related technical or scientific discipline) and six months of qualifying experience. Pass examination. **Examination:** Written exam administered by the department. **Reciprocity:** Yes. **Fees:** $10 exam fee. $15 reciprocity fee. $15 certification fee. $15 renewal fee.

Credential Type: Grade three operator certificate. **Duration of License:** Three years. **Authorization:** Includes all facilities employing biological treatment designed to serve a population of 5000-25,000 persons; facilities employing trickling filters designed to serve a population of 500025,000 persons; and variations of activated sludge requiring specialized knowledge serving any population up to 20,000 persons. **Requirements:** At least four years of qualifying experience, including two years of operational experience as a Grade two certified operator; or high school graduation or the equivalent and two years of qualifying experience as a Grade two certified operator; or two years of postsecondary education in a related technical field and six months of qualifying experience as a certified Grade two operator; or a bachelor's degree in a qualifying discipline (engineering, biological or chemical sciences, or a closely related technical or scientific discipline) and one year of qualifying experience, including six months as a certified Grade two operator. Pass examination. **Examination:** Written exam administered by the department. **Reciprocity:** Yes. **Fees:** $25 exam fee. $15 reciprocity fee. $15 certification fee. $15 renewal fee.

Credential Type: Grade four operator certificate. **Duration of License:** Three years. **Authorization:** Includes all facilities employing biological treatment designed to serve a population greater than 20,000 persons; facilities employing trickling filters designed to serve a population greater than 25,000 persons. **Requirements:** High school graduation or the equivalent and three years of qualifying experience, including one year of operational experience as a Grade three certified operator; or two years of post-secondary education in a related technical field and two years and six months of qualifying experience, including one year as a certified Grade three operator; or a bachelor's degree in a qualifying discipline (engineering, biological or chemical sciences, or a closely related technical or scientific discipline) and one year of qualifying experience as a certified Grade three operator. Pass examination. **Examination:** Written exam administered by the department. **Reciprocity:** Yes. **Fees:** $25 exam fee. $15 reciprocity fee. $15 certification fee. $15 renewal fee.

8502

Water Treatment Plant Operator
Dept. of Environmental Quality
Office of Water Quality
3033 N. Central Ave.
Phoenix, AZ 85012
Phone: (602)257-4627 or (602)207

Credential Type: Grade one operator certificate. **Duration of License:** Three years. **Authorization:** Includes stabilization ponds serving fewer than 2000 persons and any wastewater treatment facility not designated grades 2,3, or 4. **Requirements:** No minimum education or experience requirements. Pass examination. **Examination:** Written exam administered by the department. **Reciprocity:** Yes. **Fees:** $10 exam fee. $15 reciprocity fee. $15 certification fee. $15 renewal fee.

Credential Type: Grade two operator certificate. **Duration of License:** Three years. **Authorization:** Includes stabilization ponds serving more than 2000 persons; all aerated lagoons; and all facilities employing biological treatment or trickling filters designed to serve a population of less than 5000 persons. **Requirements:** At least two years of qualifying experience, including one year of operational experience as a Grade one certified operator; or high school graduation or the equivalent and one year of qualifying experience as a Grade one certified operator; or two years of postsecondary education in a related technical field and one year of qualifying experience, including six months as a certified Grade one operator; or a bachelor's degree in a qualifying discipline (engineering, biological or chemical sciences, or a closely related technical or scientific discipline) and six months of qualifying experience. Pass examination. **Examination:** Written exam administered by the department. **Reciprocity:** Yes. **Fees:** $10 exam fee. $15 reciprocity fee. $15 certification fee. $15 renewal fee.

Credential Type: Grade three operator certificate. **Duration of License:** Three years. **Authorization:** Includes all facilities employing biological treatment designed to serve a population of 5000-25,000 persons; facilities employing trickling filters designed to serve a population of 500025,000 persons; and variations of activated sludge requiring specialized knowledge serving any population up to 20,000 persons. **Requirements:** At least four years of qualifying experience, including two years of operational experience as a Grade two certified operator; or high school graduation or the equivalent and two years of qualifying experience as a Grade two certified operator; or two years of postsecondary education in a related technical field and six months of qualifying experience as a certified Grade two operator; or a bachelor's degree in a qualifying discipline (engineering, biological or chemical sciences, or a closely related technical or scientific discipline) and one year of qualifying experience, including six months as a certified Grade two operator. Pass examination. **Examination:** Written exam administered by the department. **Reciprocity:** Yes. **Fees:** $25 exam fee. $15 reciprocity fee. $15 certification fee. $15 renewal fee.

Credential Type: Grade four operator certificate. **Duration of License:** Three years. **Authorization:** Includes all facilities employing biological treatment designed to serve a population greater than 20,000 persons; facilities employing trickling filters designed to serve a population greater than 25,000 persons. **Requirements:** High school graduation or the equivalent and three years of qualifying experience, including one year of operational experience as a Grade three certified operator; or two years of post-secondary education in a related technical field and two years and six months of qualifying experience, including one year as a certified Grade three operator; or a bachelor's degree in a qualifying discipline (engineering, biological or chemical sciences, or a closely related technical or scientific discipline) and one year of qualifying experience as a certified Grade three operator. Pass examination. **Examination:** Written exam administered by the department. **Reciprocity:** Yes. **Fees:** $25 exam fee. $15 reciprocity fee. $15 certification fee. $15 renewal fee.

Arkansas

8503

Wastewater Treatment Plant Operator
Dept. of Pollution Control and Ecology
8001 National Dr.
PO Box 9583
Little Rock, AR 72209
Phone: (501)562-7444

Credential Type: License. **Duration of License:** One year. **Requirements:** High school graduate or equivalent. Satisfactory completion of 40 to 200 hours of approved training. Completion of one to six years of progressive work experience. Satisfactory completion of written examination for each classification. **Examination:** Yes. **Fees:** $20 Written examination. $10 License. $10 Renewal.

8504

Water Supply Operator
Arkansas Dept. of Health
Div. of Engineering
4815 W. Markham
Little Rock, AR 72201
Phone: (501)661-2651

Credential Type: License. **Duration of License:** Two years. **Requirements:** Completion of required supply training course. Satisfactory work experience as determined from application. **Examination:** Yes. **Fees:** $25 Written examination. $10 License. $10 Renewal.

Georgia

8505

Public Water Supply System Operator
State Board of Water and Wastewater Treatment Plant Operators and Laboratory Analysts
Health and Consumer Services Section
Professional Examining Boards
166 Pryor St., SW
Atlanta, GA 30303
Phone: (404)656-3933

Credential Type: Class I Certificate. **Duration of License:** Two years. **Requirements:** Must hold a Class II Certificate. Meet one of the following sets of experience and education requirements: (1) Have a high school diploma or GED certificate and three years of experience; or (2) Have an accredited B.S. degree or higher in biology, chemistry, engineering, or an equivalent degree, or a current Class I Certificate in another category, and two years of experience.

Renewal requires 18 hours of continuing education. **Examination:** Class I Water Treatment System Operator Examination (written). **Fees:** $50 exam fee. **Governing Statute:** Rules of the State Board of Water and Wastewater Treatment Plant Operators and Laboratory Analysts, Chap. 750.

Credential Type: Class II Certificate. **Duration of License:** Two years. **Requirements:** Must hold a Class III Certificate. Meet one of the following sets of experience and education requirements: (1) Have a high school diploma or GED certificate and two years of experience; or (2) Have an accredited B.S. degree or higher in biology, chemistry, engineering, or an equivalent degree, or a current Class I Certificate in another category, and one year of experience.

Must complete 48 hours of advanced water operator coursework, 12 of which must be laboratory coursework. Coursework may be part of a post-secondary degree program.

Renewal requires 12 hours of continuing education. **Examination:** Class II Water Treatment System Operator Examination (written). **Fees:** $50 exam fee. **Governing Statute:** Rules of the State Board of Water and Wastewater Treatment Plant Operators and Laboratory Analysts, Chap. 750.

Credential Type: Class III Certificate. **Duration of License:** Two years. **Requirements:** Must hold a Class III Certificate. Meet one of the following sets of experience and education requirements: (1) Have a high school diploma or GED certificate and six months of experience; or (2) Have an accredited B.S. degree or higher in biology, chemistry, engineering, or an equivalent degree, or a current Class I Certificate in another category, and six months of experience.

Must complete 27 hours of basic water operator coursework. Coursework may be part of a post-secondary degree program.

Renewal requires six hours of continuing education. **Examination:** Class III Water Treatment System Operator Examination (written). **Fees:** $50 exam fee. **Governing Statute:** Rules of the State Board of Water and Wastewater Treatment Plant Operators and Laboratory Analysts, Chap. 750.

8506

Wastewater Collection System Operator
State Board of Water and Wastewater Treatment Plant Operators and Laboratory Analysts
Health and Consumer Services Section
Professional Examining Boards
166 Pryor St., SW
Atlanta, GA 30303
Phone: (404)656-3933

Credential Type: Wastewater Collection System Operator Certificate. **Duration of License:** Two years. **Requirements:** Meet one of the following sets of experience and education requirements: (1) Have a high school diploma or GED certificate and six months of experience; or (2) Have an accredited B.S. degree or higher in biology, chemistry, engineering, or an equivalent degree, or a current Class I Certificate in another category, and six months of experience.

Complete 27 hours of wastewater collection coursework. Coursework may be part of a post-secondary degree program.

Renewal requires six hours of continuing education. **Examination:** Wastewater Collection System Operator Examination (written). **Fees:** $50 exam fee. **Governing Statute:** Rules of the State Board of Water and Wastewater Treatment Plant Operators and Laboratory Analysts, Chap. 750.

8507

Wastewater Treatment System Operator
State Board of Water and Wastewater Treatment Plant Operators and Laboratory Analysts
Health and Consumer Services Section
Professional Examining Boards
166 Pryor St., SW
Atlanta, GA 30303
Phone: (404)656-3933

Credential Type: Class I Certificate. **Duration of License:** Two years. **Requirements:** Must hold a Class II Certificate. Meet one of the following sets of experience and education requirements: (1) Have a high school diploma or GED certificate and three years of experience; or (2) Have an accredited B.S. degree or higher in biology, chemistry, engineering, or an equivalent degree, or a current Class I Certificate in another category, and two years of experience.

Renewal requires 18 hours of continuing education. **Examination:** Class I Wastewater Treatment System Operator Examination (written). **Exemptions:** Any person who was operating an industrial wastewater treatment plant on or before July 1, 1991, may continue to operate that wastewater treatment plant until July 1, 1996, without attaining certification. **Fees:** $50 exam fee. **Governing Statute:** Rules of the State Board of Water and Wastewater Treatment Plant Operators and Laboratory Analysts, Chap. 750.

Credential Type: Class II Certificate. **Duration of License:** Two years. **Requirements:** Must hold a Class III Certificate. Meet one of the following sets of experience and education requirements: (1) Have a high school diploma or GED certificate and two years of experience; or (2) Have an accredited B.S. degree or higher in biology, chemistry, engineering, or an equivalent degree, or a current Class I Certificate in another category, and one year of experience.

Complete 48 hours of advanced wastewater operator coursework, 12 of which must be laboratory coursework. Coursework may be part of a post-secondary degree program.

Renewal requires 12 hours of continuing education. **Examination:** Class II Wastewater Treatment System Operator Examination (written). **Exemptions:** Any person who was operating an industrial wastewater treatment plant on or before July 1, 1991, may continue to operate that wastewater treatment plant until July 1, 1996, without attaining certification. **Fees:** $50 exam fee. **Governing Statute:** Rules of the State Board of Water and Wastewater Treatment Plant Operators and Laboratory Analysts, Chap. 750.

Credential Type: Class III Certificate. **Duration of License:** Two years. **Requirements:** Meet one of the following sets of experience and education requirements: (1) Have a high school diploma or GED certificate and six months of experience; or (2) Have an accredited B.S. degree or higher in biology, chemistry, engineering, or an equivalent degree, or a current Class I Certificate in another category, and six months of experience.

Complete 27 hours of basic wastewater operator coursework. Coursework may be part of a post-secondary degree program.

Renewal requires six hours of continuing education. **Examination:** Class III Wastewater Treatment System Operator Examination (written). **Exemptions:** Any person who was operating an industrial wastewater treatment plant on or before July 1, 1991, may continue to operate that wastewater treatment plant until July 1, 1996, without attaining certification. **Fees:** $50 exam fee.

Governing Statute: Rules of the State Board of Water and Wastewater Treatment Plant Operators and Laboratory Analysts, Chap. 750.

Credential Type: Industrial Certificate. **Duration of License:** Two years. **Requirements:** Meet one of the following sets of experience and education requirements: (1) Have a high school diploma or GED certificate and six months of experience; or (2) Have an accredited B.S. degree or higher in biology, chemistry, engineering, or an equivalent degree, or a current Class I Certificate in another category, and six months of experience.

Complete 27 hours of wastewater operator coursework. Coursework may be part of a post-secondary degree program.

Renewal requires 12 hours of continuing education. **Examination:** Industrial Wastewater Treatment System Operator Examination (written). **Exemptions:** Any person who was operating an industrial wastewater treatment plant on or before July 1, 1991, may continue to operate that wastewater treatment plant until July 1, 1996, without attaining certification. **Fees:** $50 exam fee. **Governing Statute:** Rules of the State Board of Water and Wastewater Treatment Plant Operators and Laboratory Analysts, Chap. 750.

8508

Water Distribution System Operator
State Board of Water and Wastewater Treatment Plant Operators and Laboratory Analysts
Health and Consumer Services Section
Professional Examining Boards
166 Pryor St., SW
Atlanta, GA 30303
Phone: (404)656-3933

Credential Type: Water Distribution System Operator Certificate. **Duration of License:** Two years. **Requirements:** Meet one of the following sets of experience and education requirements: (1) Have a high school diploma or GED certificate and six months of experience; or (2) Have an accredited B.S. degree or higher in biology, chemistry, engineering, or an equivalent degree, or a current Class I Certificate in another category, and six months of experience.

Complete 27 hours of water distribution coursework. Coursework may be part of a postsecondary degree program.

Renewal requires six hours of continuing education. **Examination:** Water Distribution System Operator Examination (written). **Fees:** $50 exam fee. **Governing Statute:** Rules of the State Board of Water and Wastewater Treatment Plant Operators and Laboratory Analysts, Chap. 750.

Illinois

8509

Distribution System Operator (Water Supply)
Illinois Environmental Agency
2200 Churchill Rd.
PO Box 19276
Springfield, IL 62794-9276
Phone: (217)782-9470

Credential Type: Class D Certificate. **Duration of License:** Three years. **Requirements:** High school graduate and six months training or hands-on experience, or grammar school graduate and one year training or experience. Must have working knowledge of chemical, biological, and physical sciences essential to the practical mechanics of pumpage, storage, and distribution. **Examination:** Public Water Supplies Operator Certification Exam. **Reciprocity:** Yes, on an individual basis. **Fees:** $10 examination fee. $30 application fee. $10 renewal fee. $10 reinstatement fee. **Governing Statute:** Chapter 111 1/2, Illinois Revised Statutes and Illinois Administration Code 680.

8510

Wastewater Treatment Plant Operator
Illinois Environmental Protection Agency
2200 Churchill Rd.
PO Box 19276
Springfield, IL 62794-9276
Phone: (217)782-9720

Credential Type: Class 1 Certificate. **Duration of License:** Indefinite. **Requirements:** High school graduate or equivalent. Eight years of Wastewater Operator experience. In some cases training and/or education may be accepted to reduce amount of experience required. **Examination:** Written examination. **Reciprocity:** Yes. Each applicant's qualifications will be reviewed. **Fees:** No fee. **Governing Statute:** Illinois Environmental Protection Act, Section 13.

Credential Type: Class 2 Certificate. **Duration of License:** Indefinite. **Requirements:** High school graduate or equivalent. Six years of Wastewater Operator experience. In some cases training and/or education may be accepted to reduce amount of experience required. **Examination:** Written examination. **Reciprocity:** Yes. Each

Illinois

Wastewater Treatment Plant Operator, continued

applicant's qualifications will be reviewed. **Fees:** No fee. **Governing Statute:** Illinois Environmental Protection Act, Section 13.

Credential Type: Class 3 Certificate. **Duration of License:** Indefinite. **Requirements:** High school graduate or equivalent. Three years of Wastewater Operator experience. In some cases training and/or education may be accepted to reduce amount of experience required. **Examination:** Written examination. **Reciprocity:** Yes. Each applicant's qualifications will be reviewed. **Fees:** No fee. **Governing Statute:** Illinois Environmental Protection Act, Section 13.

Credential Type: Class 4 Certificate. **Duration of License:** Indefinite. **Requirements:** High school graduate or equivalent. One year of Wastewater Operator experience. In some cases training and/or education may be accepted to reduce amount of experience required. **Examination:** Written examination. **Reciprocity:** Yes. Each applicant's qualifications will be reviewed. **Fees:** No fee. **Governing Statute:** Illinois Environmental Protection Act, Section 13.

Credential Type: Class K (Industrial). **Duration of License:** Indefinite. **Requirements:** Submit application. **Examination:** Written examination. **Reciprocity:** Yes. Each applicant's qualifications will be reviewed. **Fees:** No fee. **Governing Statute:** Illinois Environmental Protection Act, Section 13.

Credential Type: Advanced Operator-In-Training Certificate. **Duration of License:** Indefinite. **Requirements:** High school graduate or equivalent. Three years of Wastewater Operator experience. In some cases training and/or education may be accepted to reduce amount of experience required. **Examination:** Written examination. **Reciprocity:** Yes. Each applicant's qualifications will be reviewed. **Fees:** No fee. **Governing Statute:** Illinois Environmental Protection Act, Section 13.

Credential Type: Intermediate Operator-In-Training Certificate. **Duration of License:** Indefinite. **Requirements:** One year of Wastewater Operator experience. In some cases training and/or education may be accepted to reduce amount of experience required. **Examination:** Written examination. **Reciprocity:** Yes. Each applicant's qualifications will be reviewed. **Fees:** No fee. **Governing Statute:** Illinois Environmental Protection Act, Section 13.

8511

Water Supply Operator
Illinois Environmental Protection Agency
2200 Churchill Rd.
PO Box 19276
Springfield, IL 62794-9276
Phone: (217)782-9470

Credential Type: Class A License. **Duration of License:** Three years. **Requirements:** Must be a high school graduate with three years of acceptable training/experience or a grammar school graduate with four years of acceptable training/experience. Have a working knowledge of chemical, biological, and physical science as they pertain to the practical mechanics of water treatment or distribution. Must have the ability to maintain the functions of a water treatment plant. **Examination:** Public Water Supplies Operator Certification Examination. **Reciprocity:** Yes, will be considered on a case to case basis. **Fees:** $10 examination fee. $30 application/initial license fee. $10 renewal fee. **Governing Statute:** Illinois Revised Statutes, Chapter 111 1/2.

Credential Type: Class B License. **Duration of License:** Three years. **Requirements:** Must be a high school graduate with three years of acceptable training/experience or a grammar school graduate with four years of acceptable training/experience. Have a working knowledge of chemical, biological, and physical science as they pertain to the practical mechanics of water treatment or distribution. Must have the ability to maintain the functions of a water treatment plant. **Examination:** Public Water Supplies Operator Certification Examination. **Reciprocity:** Yes, will be considered on a case to case basis. **Fees:** $10 examination fee. $30 application/initial license fee. $10 renewal fee. **Governing Statute:** Illinois Revised Statutes, Chapter 111 1/2.

Credential Type: Class C License. **Duration of License:** Three years. **Requirements:** Must be a high school graduate with one year of acceptable training/experience or a grammar school graduate with two years of acceptable training/experience. Have a working knowledge of chemical, biological, and physical science as they pertain to the practical mechanics of water treatment or distribution. Must have the ability to maintain the functions of a water treatment plant. **Examination:** Public Water Supplies Operator Certification Examination. **Reciprocity:** Yes, will be considered on a case to case basis. **Fees:** $10 examination fee. $30 application/initial license fee. $10 renewal fee. **Governing Statute:** Illinois Revised Statutes, Chapter 111 1/2.

Indiana

8512

Wastewater Treatment Plant Operator
Office of Water Management
Dept. of Environmental Management
PO Box 7060
Indianapolis, IN 46202-7060
Phone: (317)232-8666
Phone: (317)233-3555

Credential Type: Operator Certification. **Duration of License:** Two years. **Authorization:** There are 11 classes of operator certification. **Requirements:** Meet education and experience requirements for the appropriate class of certification. The educational requirement ranges from a minimum of high school graduate or equivalent to college graduate. The experience requirement ranges from one year to five years. Except for the three lowest classes, continuing education of either 10 or 20 hours every two years is required for recertification. **Examination:** Certification examination. **Fees:** $30 exam fee. **Governing Statute:** IC 13-1-6.

Iowa

8513

Wastewater Lagoon Operator
Dept. of Natural Resources
Licensing Bureau
Wallace State Office Bldg.
Des Moines, IA 50319
Phone: (515)281-4508

Credential Type: Grade I Certification. **Duration of License:** Two years. **Requirements:** High school graduate or equivalent. One year of experience. **Examination:** Written examination. **Fees:** $36 certification fee. $20 exam fee. $24 renewal fee.

Credential Type: Grade II Certification. **Duration of License:** Two years. **Requirements:** High school graduate or equivalent. Three years of experience. **Examination:** Written examination. **Fees:** $36 certification fee. $20 exam fee. $24 renewal fee.

Water and Wastewater Treatment Plant Operators

8514

Wastewater Treatment Operator
Dept. of Natural Resources
Licensing Bureau
Wallace State Office Bldg.
Des Moines, IA 50319
Phone: (515)281-4508

Credential Type: Grade I Certification. **Duration of License:** Two years. **Requirements:** High school graduate or equivalent. One year of experience. **Examination:** Written examination. **Fees:** $36 certification fee. $20 exam fee. $24 renewal fee.

Credential Type: Grade II Certification. **Duration of License:** Two years. **Requirements:** High school graduate or equivalent. Three years of experience. **Examination:** Written examination. **Fees:** $36 certification fee. $20 exam fee. $24 renewal fee.

Credential Type: Grade III Certification. **Duration of License:** Two years. **Requirements:** Two years of post-high school education. Four years of experience. **Examination:** Written examination. **Fees:** $36 certification fee. $20 exam fee. $24 renewal fee.

Credential Type: Grade IV Certification. **Duration of License:** Two years. **Requirements:** Four years of post-high school education. Four years of experience, with one year of supervisory experience in a Grade III or IV treatment plant. **Examination:** Written examination. **Fees:** $36 certification fee. $20 exam fee. $24 renewal fee.

8515

Water Distribution Operator
Dept. of Natural Resources
Licensing Bureau
Wallace State Office Bldg.
Des Moines, IA 50319
Phone: (515)281-4508

Credential Type: Grade I Certification. **Duration of License:** Two years. **Requirements:** High school graduate or equivalent. One year of experience. **Examination:** Written examination. **Fees:** $36 certification fee. $20 exam fee. $24 renewal fee.

Credential Type: Grade II Certification. **Duration of License:** Two years. **Requirements:** High school graduate or equivalent. Three years of experience. **Examination:** Written examination. **Fees:** $36 certification fee. $20 exam fee. $24 renewal fee.

Credential Type: Grade III Certification. **Duration of License:** Two years. **Requirements:** Two years of post-high school education. Four years of experience. **Examination:** Written examination. **Fees:** $36 certification fee. $20 exam fee. $24 renewal fee.

Credential Type: Grade I-R. **Duration of License:** Two years. **Authorization:** Restricted to facilities serving towns with less than 250 population. **Requirements:** High school graduate or equivalent. One year of experience. **Examination:** No exam required. **Fees:** $36 certification fee. $24 renewal fee.

8516

Water Treatment Operator
Dept. of Natural Resources
Licensing Bureau
Wallace State Office Bldg.
Des Moines, IA 50319
Phone: (515)281-4508

Credential Type: Grade I Certification. **Duration of License:** Two years. **Requirements:** High school graduate or equivalent. One year of experience. **Examination:** Written examination. **Fees:** $36 certification fee. $20 exam fee. $24 renewal fee.

Credential Type: Grade II Certification. **Duration of License:** Two years. **Requirements:** High school graduate or equivalent. Three years of experience. **Examination:** Written examination. **Fees:** $36 certification fee. $20 exam fee. $24 renewal fee.

Credential Type: Grade III Certification. **Duration of License:** Two years. **Requirements:** Two years of post-high school education. Four years of experience. **Examination:** Written examination. **Fees:** $36 certification fee. $20 exam fee. $24 renewal fee.

Credential Type: Grade IV Certification. **Duration of License:** Two years. **Requirements:** Four years of post-high school education. Four years of experience, with one year of supervisory experience in a Grade III or IV treatment plant. **Examination:** Written examination. **Fees:** $36 certification fee. $20 exam fee. $24 renewal fee.

Kentucky

8517

Drinking Water Treatment and Distribution System Operator
Natural Resources & Environmental Protection Cabinet
127 Annex Bldg.
1049 U.S. 127, Ste. 2
Frankfort, KY 40601
Phone: (502)564-3358

Credential Type: License. **Duration of License:** Two years. **Requirements:** High school diploma. College degree for the largest plants and distribution systems. Work experience is required. Twelve hours of continuing education per renewal. **Examination:** Yes. **Fees:** $30 exam fee. $20 renewal fee.

8518

Wastewater Treatment Operator
Cabinet of Natural Resources & Environmental Protection
Kentucky Div. of Water
127 Annex Bldg.
1049 U.S. 127 South, Ste. 2
Frankfort, KY 40601
Phone: (502)564-3358

Credential Type: License. **Duration of License:** Two years. **Requirements:** High school diploma or GED required as a minimum for any type plant operation, however, the larger plants require a college degree. Work experience is required. Continuing education is required. **Examination:** Yes. **Fees:** $30 exam fee. $20 renewal fee.

Louisiana

8519

Water and Wastewater Facility Operator
Office of Preventive and Public Health Services
Operator Certification and Training Unit
PO Box 60630
New Orleans, LA 70160
Phone: (504)568-5108

Credential Type: Certification. **Duration of License:** Two years. **Authorization:** A certified operator is required for facilities serving more than 500 people. **Requirements:** Contact Operator Certification and Training Unit for requirements. **Governing Statute:** R.S. 40:1141-1151.

Maryland

8520

Industrial Wastewater Treatment Superintendent
Water Quality Program
Dept. of the Environment
2500 Broening Hwy.
Baltimore, MD 21224
Phone: (410)631-3609

Credential Type: License. **Requirements:** Contact licensing body for application information.

Maryland 8521

8521

Sewage Treatment Plant Superintendent
STP Inspections
Dept. of the Environment
2500 Broening Hwy.
Baltimore, MD 21224
Phone: (410)631-3632

Credential Type: License **Requirements:** Contact licensing body for application information.

Massachusetts

8522

Drinking Water Supply Facility Operator
Board of Certification of Operators of Drinking Water Supply Facilities
Div. of Registration
100 Cambridge St., 15th fl.
Boston, MA 02202
Phone: (617)727-3070

Credential Type: Grade VSS Certification. **Duration of License:** Two years. **Authorization:** Required of operators of very small systems (VSS) serving a population of 25-499 (2500-49,900 gallons per day). **Requirements:** Meet one of the following sets of requirements: (1) At least six months operating experience of a very small water system (VSS) or higher grade drinking water facility. (2) six contact hours of on-the-job training or 0.6 Continuing Education Units in the operation of a very small water system (VSS) or higher grade drinking water facility. **Examination:** Yes. **Fees:** Contact board for fees. **Governing Statute:** 236 CMR 2.00.

Credential Type: Grade I Distribution Certification. **Duration of License:** Two years. **Authorization:** Required of operators of Class 1D, 1T, or 1C systems serving a population of 500-1,999 (50,000-199,900 gallons per day). **Requirements:** Meet one of the following sets of requirements: (1) Produce educational qualifications and experience satisfactory to the board, and demonstrate ability to operate a drinking water supply facility with limited supervision. (2) four years of high school education or equivalent. Six months full-time experience in a drinking water supply facility. (3) two years of high school education or equivalent. One year full-time experience in a drinking water supply facility. (4) eight years of education. Three years full-time experience in a drinking water supply facility. **Examination:** Yes. **Fees:** Contact board for fees. **Governing Statute:** 236 CMR 2.00.

Credential Type: Grade I Treatment Certification. **Duration of License:** Two years. **Authorization:** Required of operators of Class 1D, 1T, or 1C systems serving a population of 500-1,999 (50,000-999,900 gallons per day). **Requirements:** Meet one of the following sets of requirements: (1) Produce educational qualifications and experience satisfactory to the board, and demonstrate ability to operate a drinking water supply facility with limited supervision. (2) four years of high school education or equivalent. Six months full-time experience in a drinking water supply facility. (3) two years of high school education or equivalent. One year full-time experience in a drinking water supply facility. (4) eight years of education. Three years full-time experience in a drinking water supply facility. **Examination:** Yes. **Fees:** Contact board for fees. **Governing Statute:** 236 CMR 2.00.

Credential Type: Grade II Distribution Certification. **Duration of License:** Two years. **Authorization:** Required of operators of Class 2D, 2T, or 2C systems serving a population of 2000-24,999 (200,000-2.499 million gallons per day). **Requirements:** Meet one of the following sets of requirements: (1) Possess a Grade I Certificate with continous full-time employment in the distribution of a drinking water supply for one additional year after certification. (2) four years of high school education or equivalent. Two years full-time experience in the distribution of a drinking water supply. **Examination:** Yes. **Fees:** Contact board for fees. **Governing Statute:** 236 CMR 2.00.

Credential Type: Grade II Treatment Certification. **Duration of License:** Two years. **Authorization:** Required of operators of Class 2D, 2T, or 2C systems serving a population of 2000-24,999 (200,000-2.499 million gallons per day). **Requirements:** Meet one of the following sets of requirements: (1) Possess a Grade I Certificate with continous full-time employment in the treatment of a drinking water supply for one additional year after certification. (2) four years of high school education or equivalent. Two years full-time experience in the treatment of a drinking water supply. **Examination:** Yes. **Fees:** Contact board for fees. **Governing Statute:** 236 CMR 2.00.

Credential Type: Grade III Distribution Certification. **Duration of License:** Two years. **Authorization:** Required of operators of Class 3D, 3T, or 3C systems serving a population of 10,000-49,999 (1-4.999 million gallons per day), or any system requiring the removal of volatile organic contaminants. **Requirements:** Meet one of the following sets of requirements: (1) Possess a Grade II Certificate with continous full-time employment in the distribution of a drinking water supply for two additional years after certification. (2) four years of high school education or equivalent. Four years full-time experience in the distribution of a drinking water supply. (3) two years of college with courses in the physical or biological sciences. Two years full-time experience in a drinking water supply facility with direct responsibility for a particular distribution operation. (4) Bachelor's degree with courses in the physical or biological sciences. One year full-time experience in a drinking water supply facility with direct responsibility for a particular distribution operation. **Examination:** Yes. **Fees:** Contact board for fees. **Governing Statute:** 236 CMR 2.00.

Credential Type: Grade III Treatment Certification. **Duration of License:** Two years. **Authorization:** Required of operators of Class 3D, 3T, or 3C systems serving a population of 10,000-49,999 (1-4.999 million gallons per day), or any system requiring the removal of volatile organic contaminants. **Requirements:** Meet one of the following sets of requirements: (1) Possess a Grade II Certificate with continous full-time employment in the treatment of a drinking water supply for two additional years after certification. (2) four years of high school education or equivalent. Four years full-time experience in the treatment of a drinking water supply. (3) two years of college with courses in the physical or biological sciences. Two years full-time experience in the treatment of a drinking water supply facility with direct responsibility for a particular treatment operation. (4) Bachelor's degree with courses in the physical or biological sciences. One year full-time experience in the treatment of a drinking water supply facility with direct responsibility for a particular treatment operation. **Examination:** Yes. **Fees:** Contact board for fees. **Governing Statute:** 236 CMR 2.00.

Credential Type: Grade IV Distribution Certification. **Duration of License:** Two years. **Authorization:** Required of operators of Class 4D, 4T, or 4C systems serving a population of 25,000 or more (over 2.5 million gallons per day). **Requirements:** Meet one of the following sets of requirements: (1) Possess a Grade III Certificate with continous full-time employment in the distribution of a drinking water supply for one additional year after certification. (2) four years of college with courses in the physical or biological sciences. Three years full-time experience in a drinking water supply facility with direct responsibility for a particular distribution operation. (3) Bachelor's degree with courses in the physical or biological sciences. Two years full-time experience in a drinking water supply facility with direct responsibility for a particular distribution operation. **Examination:** Yes. **Fees:** Contact board for fees. **Governing Statute:** 236 CMR 2.00.

Credential Type: Grade IV Treatment Certification. **Duration of License:** Two years. **Authorization:** Required of operators of Class 4D, 4T, or 4C systems serving a population of 25,000 or more (over 2.5 million gallons per day). **Requirements:** Meet one of the following sets of requirements: (1) Possess a Grade III Certificate with continous full-time employment in the treatment of a drinking water supply for one additional year after certification. (2) four years of college with courses in the physical or biological sciences. Three years full-time experience in the treatment of a drinking water supply facility with direct responsibility for a particular treatment operation. (4) Bachelor's degree with courses in the physical or biological sciences. Two years full-time experience in the treatment of a drinking water supply facility with direct responsibility for a particular treatment operation. **Examination:** Yes. **Fees:** Contact board for fees. **Governing Statute:** 236 CMR 2.00.

8523

Waste Water Treatment Facility Operator
Board of Certification of Waste Water Treatment Facility Operators
Div. of Water Pollution Control
Dept. of Environmental Protection
One Winter St., 7th Fl.
Boston, MA 02108
Phone: (617)292-5673

Credential Type: License. **Requirements:** Contact licensing body for application information.

Michigan

8524

Wastewater Treatment Facility Operator, Industrial and Commercial
Planning and Special Programs Section
Surface Water Quality Div.
Dept. of Natural Resources
PO Box 30028
Lansing, MI 48909
Phone: (517)373-1220

Credential Type: Class 1 Certification. **Duration of License:** Five years. **Requirements:** Be able to read and write. Understand the principles and problems associated with management of the treatment process and facilities. Be able to perform arithmetic calculations as required to operate facilities and prepare reports. Have six months of experience. **Examination:** Written exam. **Governing Statute:** Water Resources Commission Act, Act 245 of 1929.

Credential Type: Class 2 Certification. **Duration of License:** Five years. **Requirements:** Equivalent of a high school education, including the equivalent of high school chemistry. Understand the principles and problems associated with management of the treatment process and facilities. Be able to perform arithmetic calculations as required to operate facilities and prepare reports. Have six months of experience. **Examination:** Written exam. **Governing Statute:** Water Resources Commission Act, Act 245 of 1929.

Credential Type: Class 3 Certification. **Duration of License:** Five years. **Requirements:** Equivalent of two years of college education in engineering, chemistry, biological sciences, or an allied field. Graduation from high school and at least four courses in post-high school level chemistry or biological sciences or both may be considered to be equivalent. Understand the principles and problems associated with management of the treatment process and facilities. Have six months of experience. **Examination:** Written exam. **Governing Statute:** Water Resources Commission Act, Act 245 of 1929.

8525

Water Distribution System Operator
Div. of Water Supply
Dept. of Public Health
3423 N. Logan St.
PO Box 30195
Lansing, MI 48909
Phone: (517)335-8000

Credential Type: Certification. **Authorization:** There are four levels of certification, based on population served. S-1 (population greater than 20,000); S-2 (4,000 to 20,000); S-3 (1,000 to 4,000); S-4 (less than 1,000). **Requirements:** Meet the education and experience qualifications for the specific class certificate. Some education may be substituted for experience. Submit the names of four personal references, other than relatives. Certified water distribution system operators may be required to obtain additional education or training as a condition for maintaining certification. **Examination:** Written exam. **Reciprocity:** Reciprocity may be granted if the certification requirements of another state under which a certificate is issued are comparable to the requirements of the Michigan Department of Public Health. **Fees:** No fees. **Governing Statute:** Safe Drinking Water Act, Act 399 of 1976.

8526

Water Treatment Plant Operator
Div. of Water Supply
Dept. of Public Health
3423 N. Logan St.
PO Box 30195
Lansing, MI 48909
Phone: (517)335-8000

Credential Type: Certification. **Duration of License:** Certificate becomes inactive automatically if the holder has not been employed by, or working with, public water supplies for five years or if the address of the certificate holder is unknown to the Department for two years. **Requirements:** Meet the minimum educational and experience qualifications for the specific class certificate. Some education may be substituted for experience. The minimum education and experience qualifications for each class may be requested directly from the Department of Public Health. Submit the names of four personal references, other than relatives. Certified water treatment plant operators may be required to obtain additional education or training as a condition for maintaining certification. **Examination:** Written exam. **Reciprocity:** Reciprocity may be granted if the certification requirements of another state under which a certificate is issued are comparable to the requirements of the Michigan Department of Public Health. **Governing Statute:** Safe Drinking Water Act, Act 399 of 1976.

Minnesota

8527

Public Water Supply Operator
Dept. of Health
Environmental Health Div.
Water Supply and General Engineering Section
Public Water Supply Unit
717 Delaware St., SE
Box 9441
Minneapolis, MN 55440
Phone: (612)627-5125
Phone: (612)627-5128
Fax: (612)623-5043

Alternate Information: Water Operator Certification Council, PO Box 59040, Minneapolis, MN 55454-0040.

Public Water Supply Operator, continued

Credential Type: Operator Certification. **Duration of License:** Three years. **Authorization:** Operators of municipal or other community water supply systems must be certified by the state. **Requirements:** Pass certification exam. Complete mandatory training program. **Examination:** Certification examination. **Fees:** $15 certification exam fee. $15 certification fee. $15 renewal fee.

8528

Wastewater Disposal Facility Operator
Pollution Control Agency
520 N. Lafayette Rd.
St. Paul, MN 55155
Phone: (612)296-7283

Credential Type: Type V Operator Certification. **Duration of License:** Three years. **Authorization:** Type V Certification covers land application systems for industrial, commercial, or agricultural wastewaters. If three or fewer operators are employed at a facility, at least one must be certified. If 4-7 operators, then at least two must be certified. If more than eight operators, then at least three must be certified. **Requirements:** Complete at least nine hours of training within the three years immediately prior to application. Have at least one season of acceptable experience.

Renewal requires six contact hours of additional job-related training. **Examination:** Yes. **Fees:** $15 exam fee. $15 certification fee. $15 renewal fee. **Governing Statute:** Minnesota Statutes 116.41. Pollution Control Agency Rules 6 MCAR 4.6088 et seq.

Mississippi

8529

Wastewater Facility Operator
Dept. of Environmental Quality
Office of Pollution Control
PO Box 10385
Jackson, MS 39289-0385
Phone: (601)961-5100

Credential Type: Class IV Certificate. **Duration of License:** Three years. **Authorization:** Treatment plant operators must be certified at a level equivalent to or higher than the treatment facility classification. Required of operators of trickling filter treatment facilities serving a population greater than 30,000 and operators of activated sludge treatment facilities serving a population greater than 20,000. **Requirements:** Meet one of the following sets of requirements: (1) Must have at least a bachelor's degree in engineering, biological sciences, mathematics, chemistry, or physics from an accredited college or university. Must have at least one year of expericnes. (2) High school graduate or equivalent and have at least nine years experience in a Class IV or Class III wastewater facility, of which one year must have been in a Class IV plant.

Eight weeks of classroom instruction may be substituted for one year of experience. Four weeks of Commission or Association sponsored classroom instruction may be substituted for one year of experience. Each year of college completed in the appropriate subjects may be substituted for two years of experience.

Renewal requires 48 hours of continuing education credit. **Examination:** Wastewater Operator's Examination. **Exemptions:** Operators of industrial wastewater facilities. **Reciprocity:** Reciprocal agreements with AL, AK, AR, LA, OK, TN, TX. **Fees:** $50 certification and exam fee. $30 renewal fee.

Credential Type: Class III Certificate. **Duration of License:** Three years. **Authorization:** Treatment plant operators must be certified at a level equivalent to or higher than the treatment facility classification. Required of operators of aerated lagoon treatment facilities serving a population of 5,000 or greater; operators of trickling filter treatment facilities serving a population of 3,000 to 30,000; and operators of activated sludge treatment facilities serving a population of 1,000 to 20,000. **Requirements:** Meet one of the following sets of requirements: (1) High school graduate or equivalent and have at least three years experience in a Class IV, III, or II wastewater facility, of which one year must have been in a Class III or IV plant. (2) Have at least six years experience in a Class IV, III, or II facility, of which one year must have been in a Class III or IV plant.

Eight weeks of classroom instruction may be substituted for one year of experience. Four weeks of Commission or Association sponsored classroom instruction may be substituted for one year of experience. Each year of college completed in the appropriate subjects may be substituted for two years of experience.

Renewal requires 48 hours of continuing education credit. **Examination:** Wastewater Operator's Examination. **Exemptions:** Operators of industrial wastewater facilities. **Reciprocity:** Reciprocal agreements with AL, AK, AR, LA, OK, TN, TX. **Fees:** $50 certification and exam fee. $30 renewal fee.

Credential Type: Class II Certificate. **Duration of License:** Three years. **Authorization:** Treatment plant operators must be certified at a level equivalent to or higher than the treatment facility classification. Required of operators of waste stabilization lagoon facilities serving a population of 5,000 or more; operators of aerated lagoon treatment facilities serving a population of less than 5,000; operators of trickling filter treatment facilities serving a population of less than 3,000; and operators of activated sludge treatment facilities serving a population of less than 1,000. **Requirements:** Meet one of the following sets of requirements: (1) High school graduate or equivalent and have at least one year experience in a Class IV, III, or II wastewater facility. (2) Have at least three years experience in a Class IV, III, or II facility.

Eight weeks of classroom instruction may be substituted for one year of experience. Four weeks of Commission or Association sponsored classroom instruction may be substituted for one year of experience. Each year of college completed in the appropriate subjects may be substituted for two years of experience.

Renewal requires 48 hours of continuing education credit. **Examination:** Wastewater Operator's Examination. **Exemptions:** Operators of industrial wastewater facilities. **Reciprocity:** Reciprocal agreements with AL, AK, AR, LA, OK, TN, TX. **Fees:** $50 certification and exam fee. $30 renewal fee.

Credential Type: Class I Certificate. **Duration of License:** Three years. **Authorization:** Treatment plant operators must be certified at a level equivalent to or higher than the treatment facility classification. Required of operators of waste stabilization lagoon facilities serving a population of less than 5,000 and all operators of septic tank-sand filter facilities. **Requirements:** Meet one of the following sets of requirements: (1) Have at least one year experience in a wastewater facility.

Eight weeks of classroom instruction may be substituted for one year of experience. Four weeks of Commission or Association sponsored classroom instruction may be substituted for one year of experience. Each year of college completed in the appropriate subjects may be substituted for two years of experience.

Renewal requires 48 hours of continuing education credit. **Examination:** Wastewater Operator's Examination. **Exemptions:** Operators of industrial wastewater facilities. **Reciprocity:** Reciprocal agreements with AL, AK, AR, LA, OK, TN, TX. **Fees:** $50 certification and exam fee. $30 renewal fee.

Missouri

8530

Wastewater Operator
Dept. of Natural Resources
Environmental Quality Div.
Operator Certification
PO Box 176
205 Jefferson St.
Jefferson City, MO 65102-0176
Phone: (314)751-1600
Phone: (314)751-5331

Credential Type: Certificate of Competency. **Duration of License:** Three years. **Requirements:** Must be at least 16 years of age. Certificates are issued for four levels. Meet the following requirements for each level: (1) Level A Certification requires six years of in-plant actual operating experience, two years of which may be equivalent educational or training experience. (2) Level B Certification requires four years of in-plant actual operating experience, one year of which may be equivalent educational or training experience. (3) Level C Certification requires two years of in-plant actual operating experience, one year of which may be equivalent educational or training experience. (4) Level D Certification requires one year of in-plant actual operating experience, all of which may be equivalent educational or training experience. **Examination:** Written examination. **Reciprocity:** Yes, provided applicant has actual operating experience, has obtained employment with a Missouri wastewater treatment system, and is licensed or certified from a state with equal or greater requirements. Must apply for reciprocity within 120 days of beginning employment. **Fees:** $20 application fee. $25 certification fee. $45 renewal fee. $40 reciprocity application fee. $25 reciprocity certification fee. **Governing Statute:** 10 CSR 20-9.030.

8531

Water Supply Operator
Dept. of Natural Resources
Environmental Quality Div.
Operator Certification
PO Box 176
205 Jefferson St.
Jefferson City, MO 65102-0176
Phone: (314)751-1600
Phone: (314)751-5331

Credential Type: Certificate of Competency. **Duration of License:** Three years. **Requirements:** Must be at least 16 years of age. Certificates are issued for five levels. Meet the following requirements for each level: (1) Level A Certification requires six years of water system experience, two years of which may be equivalent educational or training experience. (2) Level B Certification requires four years of water system experience, one year of which may be equivalent educational or training experience. (3) Level C Certification requires two years of water system experience, one year of which may be equivalent educational or training experience. (4) Level D Certification requires one year of water system experience, all of which may be equivalent educational or training experience. (5) Level E Certification has no education or experience requirement. **Examination:** Written examination. **Reciprocity:** Yes, provided applicant has actual operating experience, has obtained employment with a Missouri wastewater treatment system, and is licensed or certified from a state with equal or greater requirements. Must apply for reciprocity within 120 days of beginning employment. **Fees:** $20 exam fee. $25 certification fee. $45 renewal fee. $40 reciprocity application fee. $25 reciprocity certification fee. **Governing Statute:** 10 CSR 60-14.020.

Montana

8532

Water and Sewage Plant Operator
Montana Dept. of Health and
 Environmental Sciences
Cogswell Bldg., Rm. A206
Helena, MT 59620
Phone: (406)444-2691

Credential Type: Class 1 Certificate. **Duration of License:** One year. **Requirements:** Two years of experience. Renewal requires 10 hours of continuing education every two years. **Examination:** Written. **Fees:** $5 exam fee. $27 certificate fee. $27 renewal fee. **Governing Statute:** Montana Code Annotated 37-42-301 through 37-42-322.

Credential Type: Class 2 Certificate. **Duration of License:** One year. **Requirements:** 18 months of experience. Renewal requires five hours of continuing education every two years. **Examination:** Written. **Fees:** $5 exam fee. $22 certificate fee. $22 renewal fee. **Governing Statute:** Montana Code Annotated 37-42-301 through 37-42-322.

Credential Type: Class 3 Certificate. **Duration of License:** One year. **Requirements:** One year of experience. Renewal requires five hours of continuing education every two years. **Examination:** Written. **Fees:** $5 exam fee. $17 certificate fee. $17 renewal fee. **Governing Statute:** Montana Code Annotated 37-42-301 through 37-42-322.

Credential Type: Class 4 Certificate. **Duration of License:** One year. **Requirements:** Six months of experience. Renewal requires five hours of continuing education every two years. **Examination:** Written. **Fees:** $5 exam fee. $12 certificate fee. $12 renewal fee. **Governing Statute:** Montana Code Annotated 37-42-301 through 37-42-322.

Credential Type: Class 5 Certificate. **Duration of License:** One year. **Requirements:** No experience necessary. **Examination:** Written. **Fees:** $5 exam fee. $10 certificate fee. $10 renewal fee. **Governing Statute:** Montana Code Annotated 37-42-301 through 37-42-322.

Nebraska

8533

**Water Operators/Water Treatment
 Plant Operators**
Div. of Drinking Water and
 Environmental Sanitation
301 Centennial Mall S.
PO Box 95007
Lincoln, NE 68509
Phone: (402)471-2541

Credential Type: Certificate. **Duration of License:** Three years. **Requirements:** Must pass a correspondence course. **Examination:** Yes. **Fees:** $10 certification fee. $40 class fee. $10 renewal fee.

New Hampshire

8534

**Wastewater Treatment Plant
 Operator**
Dept. of Environmental Services
Water Supply & Pollution Control
PO Box 95
6 Hazen Drive
Concord, NH 03301
Phone: (603)271-3503

Credential Type: Operator-In-Training (O-I-T) Certificate. **Duration of License:** Two years. **Requirements:** Good physical condition. Good moral character. High school graduate. **Examination:** Grade I examination. **Reciprocity:** Reciprocal applications are reviewed on an individual basis. **Fees:** $50 application fee. $50 renewal fee.

Credential Type: Operator Certificate—Grade I. **Duration of License:** Two years. **Requirements:** Good physical condition. Good moral character. High school graduate. One year of experience. **Examination:** Grade I examination. **Reciprocity:** Reciprocal applications are reviewed on an indi-

New Hampshire 8535

Wastewater Treatment Plant Operator, continued

vidual basis. **Fees:** $50 application fee. $50 renewal fee.

Credential Type: Operator Certificate—Grade II. **Duration of License:** Two years. **Requirements:** Good physical condition. Good moral character. High school graduate. Three years of experience. Interview required. **Examination:** Grade II examination. **Reciprocity:** Reciprocal applications are reviewed on an individual basis. **Fees:** $50 application fee. $50 renewal fee.

Credential Type: Operator Certificate—Grade III. **Duration of License:** Two years. **Requirements:** Good physical condition. Good moral character. High school graduate. Two years of college level courses. Four years of experience. Interview required. **Examination:** Grade III examination. **Reciprocity:** Reciprocal applications are reviewed on an individual basis. **Fees:** $50 application fee. $50 renewal fee.

Credential Type: Operator Certificate—Grade IV. **Duration of License:** Two years. **Requirements:** Good physical condition. Good moral character. High school graduate. Two years of college level courses. Fiveyears of experience. Interview required. **Examination:** Grade IV examination. **Reciprocity:** Reciprocal applications are reviewed on an individual basis. **Fees:** $50 application fee. $50 renewal fee.

8535

Water Distribution System Operator

Water Supply and Pollution Control
Health & Human Services Bldg.
6 Hazen Drive
PO Box 95
Concord, NH 03302-0095
Phone: (603)271-3139
Fax: (603)271-2867

Credential Type: Operator Certificate—Grade I-A. **Duration of License:** Two years. **Requirements:** Good physical condition. U.S. citizen. New Hampshire resident. **Examination:** Written and/or oral examination. **Reciprocity:** Yes. **Fees:** $25 application fee. $40 biennial renewal fee.

Credential Type: Operator Certificate—Grade I. **Duration of License:** Two years. **Requirements:** Good physical condition. U.S. citizen. New Hampshire resident. High school graduate. One year experience. **Examination:** Written and/or oral examination. **Reciprocity:** Yes. **Fees:** $25 application fee. $40 biennial renewal fee.

Credential Type: Operator Certificate—Grade II. **Duration of License:** Two years. **Requirements:** Good physical condition. U.S. citizen. New Hampshire resident. High school graduate. Three years experience. **Examination:** Written and/or oral examination. **Reciprocity:** Yes. **Fees:** $25 application fee. $40 biennial renewal fee.

Credential Type: Operator Certificate—Grade III. **Duration of License:** Two years. **Requirements:** Good physical condition. U.S. citizen. New Hampshire resident. High school graduate. Two years of college level courses. Four years experience. **Examination:** Written and/or oral examination. **Reciprocity:** Yes. **Fees:** $25 application fee. $40 biennial renewal fee.

Credential Type: Operator Certificate—Grade IV. **Duration of License:** Two years. **Requirements:** Good physical condition. U.S. citizen. New Hampshire resident. High school graduate. Four years of college level courses. Six years experience. **Examination:** Written and/or oral examination. **Reciprocity:** Yes. **Fees:** $25 application fee. $40 biennial renewal fee.

8536

Water Treatment Plant Operator

Water Supply and Pollution Control
Health & Human Services Bldg.
6 Hazen Drive
PO Box 95
Concord, NH 03302-0095
Phone: (603)271-3139

Credential Type: Operator Certificate—Grade I-A. **Duration of License:** Two years. **Requirements:** Good physical condition. U.S. citizen. New Hampshire resident. **Examination:** Written and/or oral examination. **Reciprocity:** Yes. **Fees:** $25 application fee. $40 biennial renewal fee.

Credential Type: Operator Certificate—Grade I. **Duration of License:** Two years. **Requirements:** Good physical condition. U.S. citizen. New Hampshire resident. High school graduate. One year experience. **Examination:** Written and/or oral examination. **Reciprocity:** Yes. **Fees:** $25 application fee. $40 biennial renewal fee.

Credential Type: Operator Certificate—Grade II. **Duration of License:** Two years. **Requirements:** Good physical condition. U.S. citizen. New Hampshire resident. High school graduate. Three years experience. **Examination:** Written and/or oral examination. **Reciprocity:** Yes. **Fees:** $25 application fee. $40 biennial renewal fee.

Credential Type: Operator Certificate—Grade III. **Duration of License:** Two years. **Requirements:** Good physical condition. U.S. citizen. New Hampshire resident. High school graduate. Two years of college level courses. Four years experience. **Examination:** Written and/or oral examination. **Reciprocity:** Yes. **Fees:** $25 application fee. $40 biennial renewal fee.

Credential Type: Operator Certificate—Grade IV. **Duration of License:** Two years. **Requirements:** Good physical condition. U.S. citizen. New Hampshire resident. High school graduate. Four years of college level courses. Six years experience. **Examination:** Written and/or oral examination. **Reciprocity:** Yes. **Fees:** $25 application fee. $40 biennial renewal fee.

New Jersey

8537

Wastewater System Operator

New Jersey Dept. of Environmental Protection
Bureau of Revenue
CN402
Trenton, NJ 08625-0402
Phone: (609)530-5760

Credential Type: Classification 1. **Duration of License:** One year. **Requirements:** High school diploma or equivalent. One year of experience. **Examination:** Written and/or oral exam. **Reciprocity:** Yes. **Fees:** $35 application fee. $25 license fee. $20 registration fee. **Governing Statute:** NJSA 58:11. NJAC 7:10-13.

Credential Type: Classification 2. **Duration of License:** One year. **Requirements:** High school diploma or equivalent and three years of experience; or an associate degree and two years of experience; or a bacheor's degree and 18 months of experience. **Examination:** Written and/or oral exam. **Reciprocity:** Yes. **Fees:** $35 application fee. $25 license fee. $20 registration fee. **Governing Statute:** NJSA 58:11. NJAC 7:10-13.

Credential Type: Classification 3. **Duration of License:** One year. **Requirements:** High school diploma or equivalent and six years of experience; or an associate degree and four years of experience; or a bachelor degree and three years of experience. **Examination:** Written and/or oral exam. **Reciprocity:** Yes. **Fees:** $35 application fee. $25 license fee. $20 registration fee. **Governing Statute:** NJSA 58:11. NJAC 7:10-13.

Credential Type: Classification 4. **Duration of License:** One year. **Requirements:** High school diploma or equivalent and 10 years of experience; or an associate degree and seven years of experience; or a bachelor degree and five years of experience. **Examination:** one year. **Reciprocity:** Yes.

Fees: $35 application fee. $25 license fee. $20 registration fee. **Governing Statute:** NJSA 58:11. NJAC 7:10-13.

New York

8538

Wastewater Treatment Plant Operator
New York State Dept. of Environmental Conservation
Div. of Water
Bureau of Wastewater Facilities Operation
50 Wolf Rd.
Albany, NY 12233
Phone: (518)457-5968

Credential Type: Certificate. **Requirements:** Bachelor of Science Degree, or Associate's Degree plus five years of experience, or high school diploma plus 10 years of experience. Completion of an approved course by the Dept. of Environmental Conservation. **Examination:** Written. **Reciprocity:** Certified operators from other states my apply to have their qualifications reviewed. **Fees:** $15 exam fee. **Governing Statute:** Environmental Conservation Law six NYCRR, Chapter 10, Part 650.

8539

Water-Treatment Plant Operator
New York State Dept. of Health
Bureau of Public Water Supply Protection
2 University Pl., Rm. 406
Albany, NY 12203
Phone: (518)458-6731

Credential Type: Certificate. **Requirements:** If water system serves 1,000 persons or more, applicant must have a high school diploma. Completion of a course in water treatment. Six months to 10 years of experience, usually as an assistant operator or lesser level operator, depending on the size of the water system. **Governing Statute:** Section 225 of the Public Health Law.

North Carolina

8540

Wastewater Treatment Plant Operator
Dept. of Natural Resources and Community Development
Certification Commission
PO Box 27687
Raleigh, NC 27611
Phone: (919)733-5083

Credential Type: Certification. **Duration of License:** One year. **Requirements:** Eighth-grade education. Two years of acceptable experience with wastewater treatment operations or three years of experience in a wastewater treatment plant. **Examination:** Written. **Fees:** $25 exam and certification fee. $5 renewal fee.

8541

Water Treatment Facility Operator
North Carolina Water Treatment Facility Operators Certification Board
Environmental Health Section
PO Box 2091
Raleigh, NC 27611
Phone: (919)733-0379

Credential Type: Certification. **Duration of License:** Permanent. **Requirements:** High school diploma or equivalent. Six months of acceptable experience or completion of an approved C-Well school program. **Examination:** Written. **Fees:** $20 exam and certification. $10 annually.

North Dakota

8542

Sanitary Pumper (Cesspool Cleaner)
State Dept. of Health and Consolidated Laboratories
Div. of Water Quality
Box 5520
Bismarck, ND 58502-5520
Phone: (701)224-5210

Credential Type: License. **Duration of License:** One year. **Requirements:** Must have sufficient knowledge of sanitation and underlying principles regarding operation of cesspools and other means of treatment. **Exemptions:** Licensed plumbers are not required to obtain this license. **Fees:** $50 resident fee per complete unit plus $15 per additional unit. $100 nonresident fee per complete unit plus $50 per additional unit. $15 renewal fee per unit (resident and nonresident).

8543

Wastewater System Operator
State Dept. of Health and Consolidated Laboratories
Environmental Health Section
Water Supply and Control Div.
1200 Missouri Ave.
Bismarck, ND 58505
Phone: (701)224-2354

Credential Type: Certification. **Duration of License:** One year. **Authorization:** As of July 1, 1994, operators of systems serving 25 or more persons must be certified. **Requirements:** Contact licensing body for application information. **Examination:** Yes. **Governing Statute:** North Dakota Century Code, Chap. 23-26.

8544

Water Distribution System Operator
State Dept. of Health and Consolidated Laboratories
Environmental Health Section
Water Supply and Control Div.
1200 Missouri Ave.
Bismarck, ND 58505
Phone: (701)224-2354

Credential Type: Certification. **Duration of License:** One year. **Authorization:** As of July 1, 1994, operators of systems serving 25 or more persons must be certified. **Requirements:** Contact licensing body for application information. **Examination:** Yes. **Governing Statute:** North Dakota Century Code, Chap. 23-26.

Oklahoma

8545

Waste Water Operator
Oklahoma State Dept. of Health
1000 N.E. Tenth
PO Box 53551
Oklahoma City, OK 73152
Phone: (405)271-4281

Credential Type: Certificate. **Duration of License:** One year. **Requirements:** 12 to 100 hours of related subject training. Four hours of continuing education each year. 18 years of age. Reading and writing ability. **Examination:** Waste Water Operator Examination. **Fees:** $30 application fee. $20 renewal fee.

Oklahoma

8546

Water Operator
Oklahoma State Dept. of Health
1000 N.E. Tenth
PO Box 53551
Oklahoma City, OK 73152
Phone: (405)271-4281

Credential Type: Certificate. **Duration of License:** One year. **Requirements:** 12 to 100 hours of related subject training. Four hours of continuing education each year. 18 years of age. Reading and writing ability. **Examination:** Water Operator Examination. **Fees:** $30 application fee. $20 renewal fee.

Rhode Island

8547

Wastewater Treatment Facility Operator
Board of Certification of Operators of Wastewater Treatment Facilities
Rhode Island Dept. of Environmental Management
291 Promenade St.
Providence, RI 02908
Phone: (401)277-3961

Credential Type: Grade I—Operator Certificate. **Duration of License:** Two years. **Requirements:** High school graduate or equivalent. Complete one year of active employment in a wastewater treatment facility. **Examination:** Written examination. **Reciprocity:** Yes. **Fees:** $10 application fee. $10 renewal fee. $5 examination fee.

Credential Type: Grade II—Operations/Shift Supervisor Certificate. **Duration of License:** Two years. **Requirements:** Complete one year of employment as a Grade I Operator. **Reciprocity:** Yes. **Fees:** $10 application fee. $10 renewal fee.

Credential Type: Grade III Certificate. **Duration of License:** Two years. **Requirements:** Bachelor's or Master's degree in science, engineering, or related field. Complete two years supervision of Grade II facility. **Reciprocity:** Yes. **Fees:** $10 application fee. $10 renewal fee.

Credential Type: Grade IV Certificate. **Duration of License:** Two years. **Requirements:** Qualify for Grade III Certificate. Have three years experience supervising a Grade III facility. **Reciprocity:** Yes. **Fees:** $10 application fee. $10 renewal fee.

8548

Water Treatment Plant Operator
Advisory Committee for Certification of Operators of Water Supply Treatment Facilities
Div. of Drinking Water Quality
Rhode Island Dept. of Health
3 Capitol Hill
Providence, RI 02908
Phone: (401)277-6867

Credential Type: Class VSS Facility Certificate. **Duration of License:** Permanent. **Requirements:** Must have six months of experience operating a very small water system or higher grade facility. **Examination:** Written examination. **Reciprocity:** Yes.

Credential Type: Grade I Treatment Certificate. **Duration of License:** Permanent. **Requirements:** Have adequate educational requirements as determined by the Advisory Committee. Demonstrate ability to operate water supply facility with limited supervision. **Examination:** Written examination. **Reciprocity:** Yes.

Credential Type: Grade II Treatment Certificate. **Duration of License:** Permanent. **Requirements:** Hold Grade I Certificate. Full time employment in drinking water treatment for at least one year after certification. **Examination:** Written examination. **Reciprocity:** Yes.

Credential Type: Grade III Treatment Certificate. **Duration of License:** Permanent. **Requirements:** Hold Grade II Certificate. Full time employment in drinking water treatment Grade II for at least two years after certification. **Reciprocity:** Yes.

Credential Type: Grade IV Treatment Certificate. **Duration of License:** Permanent. **Requirements:** Hold Grade III Certificate. Full time employment in drinking water treatment Grade III for at least one year after certification. **Reciprocity:** Yes.

South Carolina

8549

Wastewater Treatment Plant Operator
South Carolina Certification of Environmental Systems Operators
2221 Devine St., Ste. 320
Columbia, SC 29205
Phone: (803)734-9140

Credential Type: Class A Certificate. **Requirements:** Hold B certificate, pass A level examination, plus four years of experience as an operator of a water or wastewater treatment facility or equivalent. **Fees:** $22 license fee.

Credential Type: Class B Certificate. **Requirements:** Hold C certificate, pass B level examination, plus three years of experience as an operator of a water or wastewater treatment facility or equivalent. **Fees:** $22 license fee.

Credential Type: Class C Certificate. **Requirements:** Hold D certificate, pass C level examination, plus two years of experience as an operator of a water or wastewater treatment facility or equivalent. **Fees:** $22 license fee.

Credential Type: Class D Certificate. **Requirements:** Hold Trainee permit, pass D level examination, plus one year of experience as an operator of a water or wastewater treatment facility. **Fees:** $22 license fee.

Credential Type: Trainee License. **Requirements:** Complete application and pay fee.

South Dakota

8550

Wastewater Collection System Operator
Board of Operator Certification
Office of Drinking Water
523 E. Capitol Ave.
Foss Bldg.
Pierre, SD 57501-3181
Phone: (605)773-4208

Credential Type: Class IV Certification. **Duration of License:** One year. **Authorization:** A class IV system serves a population of more than 50,000. **Requirements:** Meet one of the following sets of requirements: (1) Complete four years of college majoring in environmental engineering, environmental sciences, or related fields. Have four years of experience, including at least two years of direct responsible charge experience, in a Class III or higher facility. (2) Graduate from high school. Have 12 years of experience, including at least eight years of direct responsible charge experience, in a Class III or higher facility. Renewal requires completing 10 contact hours of continuing education every four years. **Examination:** Class IV Certification Examination. **Fees:** $10 exam fee. $6 renewal fee.

Credential Type: Class III Certification. **Duration of License:** One year. **Authorization:** A Class III system serves a population from 15,001 to 50,000. **Requirements:** Meet one of the following sets of requirements: (1) Complete two years of college majoring in environmental engineering, environmental sciences, or related fields. Have four years of experience, including at least two years of direct responsible charge experience, in a Class II or higher facility. (2) Graduate from high school. Have eight years of experience, including at least four years of direct responsible charge experience, in a Class II or higher facility. Renewal requires completing 10 contact hours of continuing education every four years. **Examination:** Class III Certification Examination. **Fees:** $9 exam fee. $5 renewal fee.

Credential Type: Class II Certification. **Duration of License:** One year. **Authorization:** A class II system serves a population from 1501 to 15,000. **Requirements:** Graduate from high school. Have three years of experience in a Class I facility, or two years in a Class II or higher facility. Renewal requires completing 10 contact hours of continuing education every four years. **Examination:** Class II Certification Examination. **Fees:** $7 exam fee. $4 renewal fee.

Credential Type: Class I Certification. **Duration of License:** One year. **Authorization:** A class I system serves a population not more than 1500. **Requirements:** Graduate from high school. Have one year of experience. Renewal requires completing 10 contact hours of continuing education every four years. **Examination:** Class I Certification Examination. **Fees:** $5 exam fee. $3 renewal fee.

8551

Wastewater Treatment Plant Operator
Board of Operator Certification
Office of Drinking Water
523 E. Capitol Ave.
Foss Bldg.
Pierre, SD 57501-3181
Phone: (605)773-4208

Credential Type: Class IV Certification. **Duration of License:** One year. **Authorization:** A class IV plant is rated over 75 points. **Requirements:** Meet one of the following sets of requirements: (1) Complete four years of college majoring in environmental engineering, environmental sciences, or related fields. Have four years of experience, including at least two years of direct responsible charge experience, in a Class III or higher facility. (2) Graduate from high school. Have 12 years of experience, including at least eight years of direct responsible charge experience, in a Class III or higher facility. Renewal requires completing 10 contact hours of continuing education every four years. **Examination:** Class IV Certification Examination. **Fees:** $10 exam fee. $6 renewal fee.

Credential Type: Class III Certification. **Duration of License:** One year. **Authorization:** A class III plant is rated from 56 to 75 points. **Requirements:** Meet one of the following sets of requirements: (1) Complete two years of college majoring in environmental engineering, environmental sciences, or related fields. Have four years of experience, including at least two years of direct responsible charge experience, in a Class II or higher facility. (2) Graduate from high school. Have eight years of experience, in a Class II or higher facility. Renewal requires completing 10 contact hours of continuing education every four years. **Examination:** Class III Certification Examination. **Fees:** $9 exam fee. $5 renewal fee.

Credential Type: Class II Certification. **Duration of License:** One year. **Authorization:** A class II plant is rated from 31 to 55 points. **Requirements:** Graduate from high school. Have three years of experience in a Class I facility, or two years in a Class II or higher facility. Renewal requires completing 10 contact hours of continuing education every four years. **Examination:** Class II Certification Examination. **Fees:** $7 exam fee. $4 renewal fee.

Credential Type: Class I Certification. **Duration of License:** One year. **Authorization:** A class I plant is rated at 30 points or less. **Requirements:** Graduate from high school. Have one year of experience. Renewal requires completing 10 contact hours of continuing education every four years. **Examination:** Class I Certification Examination. **Fees:** $5 exam fee. $3 renewal fee.

8552

Water Distribution System Operator
Board of Operator Certification
Office of Drinking Water
523 E. Capitol Ave.
Foss Bldg.
Pierre, SD 57501-3181
Phone: (605)773-4208

Credential Type: Class IV Certification. **Duration of License:** One year. **Authorization:** A class IV system serves a population of more than 50,000. **Requirements:** Meet one of the following sets of requirements: (1) Complete four years of college majoring in environmental engineering, environmental sciences, or related fields. Have four years of experience, including at least two years of direct responsible charge experience, in a Class III or higher facility. (2) Graduate from high school. Have 12 years of experience, including at least eight years of direct responsible charge experience, in a Class III or higher facility. Renewal requires completing 10 contact hours of continuing education every four years. **Examination:** Class IV Certification Examination. **Fees:** $10 exam fee. $6 renewal fee.

Credential Type: Class III Certification. **Duration of License:** One year. **Requirements:** Meet one of the following sets of requirements: (1) Complete two years of college majoring in environmental engineering, environmental sciences, or related fields. Have four years of experience, including at least two years of direct responsible charge experience, in a Class II or higher facility. (2) Graduate from high school. Have eight years of experience, including at least four years of direct responsible charge experience, in a Class II or higher facility. Renewal requires completing 10 contact hours of continuing education every four years. **Examination:** Class III Certification Examination.

Credential Type: Class II Certification. **Duration of License:** One year. **Authorization:** A class II system serves a population from 1501 to 15,000. **Requirements:** Graduate from high school. Have three years of experience in a Class I facility, or two years in a Class II or higher facility. Renewal requires completing 10 contact hours of continuing education every four years. **Examination:** Class II Certification examination. **Fees:** $7 exam fee. $4 renewal fee.

Credential Type: Class I Certification. **Duration of License:** One year. **Authorization:** A class I system serves a population not more than 1500. **Requirements:** Graduate from high school. Have one year of experience. Renewal requires completing 10 contact hours of continuing education every four years. **Examination:** Class I Certification Examination. **Fees:** $5 exam fee. $3 renewal fee.

8553

Water Treatment Plant Operator
Board of Operator Certification
Office of Drinking Water
523 E. Capitol Ave.
Foss Bldg.
Pierre, SD 57501-3181
Phone: (605)773-4208

Credential Type: Class IV Certification. **Duration of License:** One year. **Authorization:** A class IV plant is rated over 75 points. **Requirements:** Meet one of the following sets of requirements: (1) Complete four years of college majoring in environmental sciences, or related fields. Have four years of

Vermont 8554

Water Treatment Plant Operator, continued

experience, including at least two years of direct responsible charge experience, in a Class III or higher facility. (2) Graduate from high school. Have 12 years of experience, including at least eight years of direct responsible charge experience, in a Class III or higher facility. Renewal requires completing 10 contact hours of continuing education every four years. **Examination:** Class IV Certification Examination. **Fees:** $10 exam fee. $6 renewal fee.

Credential Type: Class III Certification. **Duration of License:** One year. **Authorization:** A class III plant is rated from 56 to 75 points. **Requirements:** Meet one of the following sets of requirements: (1) Complete two years of college majoring in environmental engineering, environmental sciences, or related fields. Have four years of experience, including at least two years of direct responsible charge experience, in a Class II or higher facility. (2) Graduate from high school. Have eight years of experience, including at least four years of direct responsible charge experience, in a Class II or higher facility. Renewal requires completing 10 contact hours of continuing education every four years. **Examination:** Class III Certification Examination. **Fees:** $9 exam fee. $5 renewal fee.

Credential Type: Class II Certification. **Duration of License:** One year. **Authorization:** A class II plant is rated from 31 to 55 points. **Requirements:** Graduate from high school. Have three years of experience in a Class I facility, or two years in a Class II or higher facility. Renewal requires completing 10 contact hours of continuing education every four years. **Examination:** Class II Certification Examination. **Fees:** $7 exam fee. $4 renewal fee.

Credential Type: Class I Certification. **Duration of License:** One year. **Authorization:** A class I plant is rated at 30 points or less. **Requirements:** Graduate from high school. Have one year of experience. Renewal requires completing 10 contact hours of continuing education every four years. **Examination:** Class I Certification Examination. **Fees:** $5 exam fee. $3 renewal fee.

Vermont

8554

Wastewater Treatment Plant Operator
Dept. of Environmental Conservation and Environmental Engineering
Agency of Natural Resources
Public Facilities Division
Bldg. 9 South
103 South Main St.
Waterbury, VT 05676
Phone: (802)244-8744

Credential Type: License. **Duration of License:** Five years. **Requirements:** Satisfactory physical condition. Read and write the English language. Note: There are five levels of water treatment plant operator certificates, each requiring progressively higher levels of education. An exam is associated with each level. **Examination:** Yes. **Reciprocity:** Yes. **Fees:** $60 license. **Governing Statute:** Title 10, VSA Sections 1263-1265.

8555

Water Treatment Plant Operator
Div. of Environmental Health
60 Main St.
PO Box 70
Burlington, VT 05402
Phone: (802)863-7200

Credential Type: License. **Duration of License:** All permits are conditional until further notice. **Requirements:** Requirements are currently being developed by the Secretary of Human Services. **Reciprocity:** Yes. **Fees:** None. **Governing Statute:** Required by law as of 1989.

Virginia

8556

Water Treatment Plant Operator
Certification of Water and Waste-Water Operations
Dept. of Commerce
3600 W. Broad St.
Richmond, VA 23230
Phone: (804)367-8534

Credential Type: License. **Duration of License:** Two years. **Requirements:** Must hold a bachelor's degree in physical, biological, or chemical science or engineering with five quarter hours in water and/or waste-water treatment, and two years of experience as an operator of treatment plants; or hold a high school diploma; or no education required, hold a Class II license and have at least five years experience in a water or waste-water plant. **Examination:** Yes. **Fees:** $50 application fee. $30 renewal fee.

Washington

8557

Wastewater Treatment Plant Operator
Dept. of Ecology
St. Martin's Campus
Olympia-Lacey, WA 98504-8711
Phone: (206)438-7043

Credential Type: Waste Treatment Plant Operator License. **Duration of License:** One year. **Requirements:** Complete minimum education and training requirements. Submit to background investigation. Renewal requires continuing education and training. **Examination:** Written examination. **Fees:** $50 initial license fee. $30 renewal fee.

8558

Water Works Operator
Dept. of Health
112 SE Quince
Olympia, WA 98504
Phone: (206)753-7433

Credential Type: Water Works Operator License. **Duration of License:** One year. **Requirements:** Meet minimum education and experience requirements. Renewal requires recommendation from Certification Board and evidence of professional growth. **Examination:** Written examination. **Fees:** $20 initial license fee. $10 renewal fee.

Wholesale and Retail Buyers and Merchandise Managers

The following states grant licenses in this occupational category as of the date of publication: Idaho, Illinois, Louisiana, New Jersey, Rhode Island, Washington.

Idaho

8559

Fur Buyer
License Office
Administration Bureau
Fish and Game Dept.
PO Box 25
600 S. Walnut
Boise, ID 83707
Phone: (208)334-3717

Credential Type: License. **Requirements:** Contact licensing body for application information.

Illinois

8560

Fur Buyer (Non-Resident)
Illinois Dept. of Conservation
524 South 2nd St.
Springfield, IL 62701-1787
Phone: (217)785-3423

Credential Type: Non-Resident Fur Buyer License. **Duration of License:** One year. **Requirements:** Submit application and pay fee. **Reciprocity:** No. **Fees:** $250 initial license fee. $250 renewal fee. **Governing Statute:** Illinois Revised Statutes, Chapter 61.

8561

Fur Buyer (Resident)
Illinois Dept. of Conservation
524 South 2nd St.
Springfield, IL 62701-1787
Phone: (217)785-3423

Credential Type: Retail Fur Buyer License. **Duration of License:** One year. **Requirements:** Must be a resident of Illinois for at least 30 days. Submit application and pay fee. **Reciprocity:** No. **Fees:** $25 initial license fee. $25 renewal fee. **Governing Statute:** Illinois Revised Statutes, Chapter 61.

Credential Type: Wholesale Fur Buyer License. **Duration of License:** One year. **Requirements:** Must be a resident of Illinois for at least 30 days. Submit application and pay fee. **Reciprocity:** No. **Fees:** $125 initial license fee. $125 renewal fee. **Governing Statute:** Illinois Revised Statutes, Chapter 61.

8562

Out-Of-State Salvage Vehicle Buyer
Secretary of State
Centennial Building, Rm. 008
Springfield, IL 62756
Phone: (217)782-7817

Credential Type: Registration. **Duration of License:** One year. **Requirements:** Submit application and pay fee. **Reciprocity:** Yes, if applicant has a valid salvage license from his/her home state. **Fees:** $5 ID card fee. $100 initial license fee. $100 renewal fee. **Governing Statute:** Illinois Vehicle Code 95 1/2 5-302.

8563

Timber Buyer
Illinois Dept. of Commerce
Div. of Forest Resources
600 N. Grand Ave. W.
PO Box 19225
Springfield, IL 62794-9225
Phone: (217)782-2361

Credential Type: Timber Buyer License. **Duration of License:** One year. **Requirements:** Must post bond of between $500 to $10,000, as determined by the Department. Submit application and pay fee. **Reciprocity:** No. **Fees:** $30 initial license fee. $30 renewal fee. **Governing Statute:** Illinois Revised Statutes 1989, 17 Illinois Administrative Code, Chapter I.

Louisiana

8564

Wholesale Florist
Horticulture Commission
PO Box 3118
Baton Rouge, LA 70821
Phone: (504)925-7772

Credential Type: License. **Duration of License:** One year. **Examination:** Written. **Fees:** $35 exam fee. $35 license fee. $35 renewal fee.

New Jersey

8565

Milk Dealer
New Jersey Dept. of Agriculture
Div. of Dairy Industry
CN332
Trenton, NJ 08625-0332
Phone: (609)292-5646

Credential Type: License. **Fees:** License fees vary depending upon the amount of milk sold and processed. **Governing Statute:** NJSA 4-12A. NJAC 2:52.

1223

Rhode Island

8566

Wholesale Fur Buyer
Office of Boat Registration and Licensing
Rhode Island Dept. of Environmental Management
22 Hayes
Providence, RI 02908
Phone: (401)277-3576

Credential Type: Wholesale Fur Buyer License. **Duration of License:** One year. **Requirements:** Submit application and pay fee. **Reciprocity:** No. **Fees:** $10 resident license fee. $30 nonresident license fee.

Washington

8567

Broker (Agriculture)
Dept. of Agriculture
406 General Administration Bldg., AX-41
Olympia, WA 98504-0641
Phone: (206)753-5053

Credential Type: Agricultural Broker License. **Duration of License:** One year. **Authorization:** Allows arrangement of sales only. **Requirements:** Submit application and pay fee. **Fees:** $220 license fee.

8568

Cash Buyer (Agricultural)
Dept. Of Agriculture
Livestock Services Division
406 General Administration Bldg., AX-41
Olympia, WA 98504-0641
Phone: (206)753-5053

Credential Type: Cash Buyer License. **Duration of License:** One year. **Authorization:** Allows individual to purchase with cash or currency (no checks) agricultural products other than livestock, hay, grain, or straw for resale. **Requirements:** Submit application and pay fee. **Fees:** $70 license fee.

Appendix 1
Occupations Rarely Licensed

This appendix lists occupations licensed in less than six states. Refer to the Master List of Professions and Occupations if you are unsure of the appropriate job title.

8569

Abstracter [Minnesota]
Board of Abstracters
3200 Main St., Ste. 330
Coon Rapids, MN 55433
Phone: (612)427-6831

Credential Type: License. **Requirements:** Submit application and pay fees. Pass examination. **Examination:** Yes. **Fees:** $50 license fee. $25 exam fee. $40 renewal fee. **Governing Statute:** Minnesota Statutes, Section 386.63. Minnesota Rules 1001-1009.

8570

Abstracter [Nebraska]
Abstracters Board of Examiners
PO Box 94944
301 Central Mall S.
Lincoln, NE 68509
Phone: (402)471-2383

Credential Type: License. **Duration of License:** One year. **Requirements:** Must have one year of land title experience. Completion of three hours of approved professionial development credits is required every two years. **Examination:** Yes. **Fees:** $50 examination fee. $50 application fee. $50 authority renewal fee. $30 registration renweal fee.

8571

Abstracter of Title [South Dakota]
South Dakota Abstractors Board of Examiners
PO Box 187
Kennebec, SD 57544-0187
Phone: (605)869-2269

Credential Type: Certificate of Registration. **Duration of License:** Two years. **Requirements:** Submit application and pass examination. Post bond in amount based on local population. **Examination:** Written examination. **Fees:** $350 registration fee ($250 in some counties). $10 exam fee. $350 renewal fee ($250 in some counties). **Governing Statute:** South Dakota Codified Laws, Chap. 36-13. Administrative Rules of South Dakota, Article 20:36.

8572

Abstractor [North Dakota]
Abstractors' Board of Examiners
Office of the Secretary
PO Box 715
Jamestown, ND 58402-0715
Phone: (701)252-4870

Credential Type: Certificate of Registration. **Duration of License:** One year. **Requirements:** High school graduation and one year of experience is recommended but not required. **Examination:** Certificate of Registration Examination. **Fees:** $75 exam and license fee. $10 renewal fee.

8573

Abstractor [Arkansas]
Abstractors Board of Examiners
4006 Royal Forest Dr.
Pine Bluff, AR 71603
Phone: (501)535-6148
Phone: (501)536-4943

Credential Type: License. **Duration of License:** One year. **Requirements:** At least one year experience under supervision of licensed abstractor. Pass the abstractors examination. Associated with or employed by a licensed abstract company. **Examination:** Written examination. **Fees:** $25 exam fee. $10 License fee. $10 Renewal (annual).

8574

Accident Reconstruction Specialist [Illinois]
Illinois Law Enforcement Officers Training Board
600 S. Second St., Ste. 300
Springfield, IL 62704
Phone: (217)782-4540

Credential Type: Accident Reconstruction Specialist Certificate. **Duration of License:** Lifetime. **Requirements:** At least 21 years of age. Complete the following training programs from schools certified by the Illinois Local Governmental Law Enforcement Officers Training Board: (1) On Scene Accident Investigation; (2) Technical Accident Investigation; (3) Vehicle Dynamics; (4) Accident Reconstruction. Complete one year of experience as an accident investigator prior to completing Accident Reconstruction course. **Examination:** Comprehensive Accident Reconstruction Specialist Exam. **Reciprocity:** No. **Governing Statute:** Illinois Revised Statutes, Chapter 85.

8575

Adoption Investigator [Iowa]
Dept. of Inspections and Appeals
Lucas State Office Bldg.
Des Moines, IA 50319
Phone: (515)281-6377

Credential Type: License. **Duration of License:** Three years. **Requirements:** Graduation from a four-year accredited college plus three years of full-time adoption experience; or graduation from four-year accredited college with a bachelor's degree in social work, plus two years of full-time adoption experience; or a master's degree in social work plus one year of full-time adoption experience.

8576

Air School Instructor [Maryland]
State Aviation Administration
Dept. of Transportation
PO Box 8766
BWI Airport
Baltimore, MD 21240
Phone: (410)859-7100

Credential Type: License. **Requirements:** Contact licensing body for application information.

8577

Airport Manager [Michigan]
Safety and Services Div.
Bureau of Aeronautics
Dept. of Transportation
Capitol City Airport
Lansing, MI 48906
Phone: (517)373-2090

Credential Type: License. **Duration of License:** One year. **Requirements:** Abide by the rules and regulations of the Commission. **Examination:** Written exam. **Fees:** No fees. **Governing Statute:** Aeronautics Code, Act 327 of 1945, as amended.

8578

Amusement Ride Inspector [Washington]
Dept. of Labor & Industries
Building & Construction Safety Inspection Services
General Administration Bldg., HC-101
Olympia, WA 98504
Phone: (206)753-6194

Credential Type: Amusement Ride Inspector Certificate. **Duration of License:** One year. **Requirements:** Meet one of the following requirements: (1) Have two years experience as an insurance company ride inspector; (2) Have two years experience as a ride inspector for a governmental body; (3) Have five years of documented field experience; (4) Have 10 years experience in design/construction of amusement ride equipment. **Fees:** $20 certificate fee.

8579

Amusement Ride Inspector [Oregon]
Building Codes Agency
1535 Edgewater NW
Salem, OR 97310
Phone: (503)373-1268

Credential Type: Certificate. **Requirements:** Must have two years of experience with an insurance company as an amusement ride inspector; or have two years experience inspecting amusement rides and enforcing amusement ride codes while employed by a governmental body regulating rides; or have not less than five years documented field operating maintenance experience with amusement rides and devices; or have not less than ten years documented practical experience in design, construction, matintenance, repair, field inspection and operation of amusement rides and devices as an authorized representative of a recognized manufacturer; or have a combination of training and experience deemed equivalent by the Director of the Building Codes Agency. **Fees:** $100 certification fee. **Governing Statute:** ORS 460.400.

8580

Animal Breeder (Fur Bearing) [Illinois]
Illinois Dept. of Conservation
524 S. Second St.
Springfield, IL 62701-1787
Phone: (217)785-3423

Credential Type: Animal Breeder License. **Duration of License:** One year. **Requirements:** Must be Illinois resident for at least 30 days. Submit application and pay fee. **Reciprocity:** No. **Fees:** $25 initial license fee. $25 renewal fee. **Governing Statute:** Illinois Revised Statutes, Chapter 61. Illinois Conservation Law-Wildlife.

8581

Animal Control Officer [New Jersey]
New Jersey Dept. of Health
Biological Services Progam, CN364
Trenton, NJ 08625-0364
Phone: (609)984-3400

Credential Type: Certified Animal Control Officer. **Requirements:** Completion of an approved course offered by an accredited college or university. 18 years of age. **Governing Statute:** NJSA 4:19-15. NJAC 8:23-5.

8582

Aquaculturist [Illinois]
Illinois Dept. of Conservation
524 S. Second St.
Springfield, IL 62701-1787
Phone: (217)785-3423

Credential Type: Aquaculturist License. **Duration of License:** One year. **Authorization:** Allows licensee to engage in breeding, hatching, propagating, or raising aquatic life. **Requirements:** Must be a resident of the state of Illinois for at least 30 days. Work site will be inspected by Agency Culturist. Submit application and pay fee. **Reciprocity:** No. **Fees:** $50 initial license fee. $50 renewal fee. **Governing Statute:** Illinois Revised Statutes, Chapter 56. Illinois Conservation Law—Fish.

8583

Artificial Inseminator [Colorado]
Board of Veterinary Medicine
Dept. of Regulatory Agencies
Div. of Registrations
1560 Broadway, Ste. 1340
Denver, CO 80202
Phone: (303)894-7755

Credential Type: License. **Requirements:** Contact licensing body for application information.

8584

Artificial Inseminator of Animals [Wyoming]
Board of Veterinary Medicine
Herschler Bldg., 3rd Fl.
122 W. 25th St.
Cheyenne, WY 82002
Phone: (307)777-7515

Credential Type: License. **Duration of License:** One year. **Requirements:** Good moral character. Graduate from an approved course in artificial insemination of animals. **Examination:** Yes. **Fees:** $10 Application. $5 Renewal. $7.50 Renewal (non-resident).

8585

Assayer [Arizona]
Board of Technical Registration
1951 W. Camelback, Ste. 250
Phoenix, AZ 85015
Phone: (602)255-4053

Credential Type: Registration to Practice. **Duration of License:** Three years. **Requirements:** Be of good moral character. Have at least six years education or experience, or combination of both with at least two years of experience. Pass in-training and professional examination administered by the board. **Examination:** In-training and professional examinations. **Exemptions:** The in-training exam may be waived for candidates who have a degree in chemistry, metallurgy, or other science directly related to the analysis of metals and ores. **Fees:** $90 application fee. $200 exam fee. $126 renewal fee.

Credential Type: Registration without examination. **Requirements:** Hold a valid registration in another state, jurisdiction, territory, or country. Meet experience and education requirements similar to those of Arizona, or have been actively engaged in the profession for at least 10 years. **Fees:** $90 application fee.

8586

Assayer-in-Training [Arizona]
Board of Technical Registration
1951 W. Camelback, Ste. 250
Phoenix, AZ 85015
Phone: (602)255-4053

Credential Type: In-training registration. **Requirements:** Be of good moral character. To qualify for the in-training examination on the basis of education, must be a graduate of a four-year degree program of an accredited college or university, with a major in chemistry, metallurgy, or other science directly related to the analysis of metals and ores.

To qualify for the in-training examination on the basis of experience, must have at least four years of education or experience or both directly related to the practice of assaying. **Examination:** In-training examination. **Fees:** $30 application fee. $200 exam fee.

8587

Auto Repossessor [District of Columbia]
License and Certification Div.
Occupational and Professional Licensure Administration
Consumer and Regulatory Affairs Dept.
PO Box 37200
Washington, DC 20013-7200
Phone: (202)727-7823
Phone: (202)727-7480

Alternate Information: 614 H St., NW, Washington, DC 20001 **Requirements:** Contact licensing body for application information.

8588

Bedding and Upholstered Furniture Repairer/Renovator [Louisiana]
Dept of Health and Human Resources
Bedding and Upholstered Furniture Inspection Unit
PO Box 60630
New Orleans, LA 70160
Phone: (504)568-5184

Credential Type: Repairer or Renovator License. **Duration of License:** One year. **Requirements:** Submit application and pay fee. **Fees:** $15 license fee. $15 renewal fee. **Governing Statute:** R.S. 40, Pt. VI 1191-1208.

8589

Bedding and Upholstered Furniture Sterilizer [Louisiana]
Dept. of Health and Human Resources
Bedding and Upholstered Furniture Inspection Unit
PO Box 60630
New Orleans, LA 70160
Phone: (504)568-5184

Credential Type: Sterilizer License. **Duration of License:** One year. **Requirements:** Submit application and pay fee. **Governing Statute:** R.S. 40, Pt. VI 1191-1208.

8590

Bingo Game Manager [Washington]
Washington State Gambling Commission
4511 Woodview Dr. SE, QB-11
Olympia, WA 98504-8121
Phone: (206)438-7654

Credential Type: Bingo Game Manager License. **Duration of License:** One year. **Requirements:** Submit to personal and criminal background investigation. Submit application and pay fee. **Fees:** $150 initial license fee. $75 renewal fee.

8591

Breath Analyzer Operator [Illinois]
Illinois Dept. of Health
Alcohol and Substance Testing
535 W. Jefferson St.
Springfield, IL 62761
Phone: (217)782-1571

Credential Type: Breath Analyzer Operator License. **Duration of License:** One year. **Requirements:** Must be employed by a law enforcement agency or the Illinois Department of Health. Complete a minimum of 32 hours of instruction. **Examination:** Breath Analysis Instrument Operator Examination. **Reciprocity:** Yes, with a valid license and equivalent hours of training. Must take a four hour written test and be tested on the instrument. **Fees:** No fee. **Governing Statute:** Illinois Vehicle Code, Section 11.501.2.

8592

Breeder, Game Fish [Michigan]
Administrative Services Div.
Dept. of Natural Resources
Stevens T. Mason Bldg.
PO Box 30028
Lansing, MI 48909
Phone: (517)373-1220

Credential Type: License. **Duration of License:** One year. **Requirements:** Must comply with laws regarding game fish breeders and rules put into effect by the Department of Natural Resources. **Fees:** $5 initial license fee. $5 renewal fee. **Governing Statute:** Fish Breeders Act, Act 196 of 1958.

8593

Breeder, Wild Animals and Birds [Michigan]
Wildlife Div.
Dept. of Natural Resources
Stevens T. Mason Bldg.
PO Box 30028
Lansing, MI 48909
Phone: (517)373-1220

Credential Type: License. **Duration of License:** Three years. **Requirements:** Have obtained wildlife in a lawful manner, as evidenced by a receipted invoice or other document. Provide humane and sanitary conditions for wildlife. Provide pens, cages, or enclosures of sufficient size to prevent the crowding of wildlife. Provide wildlife with food and water. Submit pens and wildlife to an inspection by a conservation officer. Comply with the Game Breeder's Law and the rules of the Department of Natural Resources. **Fees:** $45 minimum—$150 maximum initial license fee (which is based either on the size of the area or on the number of animals enclosed). Same renewal fee as initial fee. **Governing Statute:** The Game Breeders Law, Act 191 of 1929, as amended.

8594

Bricklayer [Nevada]
Nevada State Contractors Board
70 Linden St.
Reno, NV 89502
Phone: (702)688-1141

Credential Type: License. **Requirements:** Four years of experience in the field. Financial responsibility and good moral character. **Examination:** Yes. **Fees:** $270 application fee. $40 exam fee. $120 license fee. $120 renewal fee.

8595

Broker (Agriculture) [Washington]
Dept. of Agriculture
406 General Administration Bldg., AX-41
Olympia, WA 98504-0641
Phone: (206)753-5053

Credential Type: Agricultural Broker License. **Duration of License:** One year. **Authorization:** Allows arrangement of sales only. **Requirements:** Submit application and pay fee. **Fees:** $220 license fee.

8596

Butter Grader [Michigan]
Dairy Products Div.
Dept. of Agriculture
Ottawa Bldg., N.
PO Box 30017
Lansing, MI 48909
Phone: (517)373-1104

Credential Type: License. **Duration of License:** One year. **Requirements:** Some experience in the manufacture and grading of butter. Abide by the rules of the Department of Agriculture. **Examination:** Written and practical examination. **Governing Statute:** Butter Grading Law, Act 211 of 1955.

8597

Butter Grader [Wisconsin]
Dept. of Agriculture
Trade and Consumer Protection
Food Div.
801 W. Badger Rd.
PO Box 8911
Madison, WI 53708
Phone: (608)266-2227

Credential Type: License. **Duration of License:** Two years. **Requirements:** Submit application and pay fee. **Fees:** $50 license fee.

8598

Cardiac Technician [Georgia]
Composite State Board of Medical Examiners
Professional Examining Boards
166 Pryor St., SW
Atlanta, GA 30303
Phone: (404)656-3913

Credential Type: Cardiac Technician Certificate. **Duration of License:** Two years. **Requirements:** Complete 450 hours of approved training. ACLS certification. **Examination:** Cardiac Technician Examination. **Fees:** $50 application/exam fee. $50 renewal fee.

8599

Carpenter [Nevada]
Nevada State Contractors Board
1800 Industrial Rd.
Las Vegas, NV 89158
Phone: (702)486-3500

Credential Type: License. **Requirements:** Four years of work experience in the field. Financial responsibility and good character. **Examination:** Yes. **Fees:** $270 application fee. $40 exam fee. $120 license fee. $120 renewal fee.

8600

Carpenter (Racetrack) [Kentucky]
Kentucky State Racing Commission
PO Box 1080
Lexington, KY 40588
Phone: (606)254-7021

Credential Type: Association Employee and Occupational License. **Requirements:** Submit application and fingerprint card. Pay fee. **Fees:** $10 license fee.

8601

Cash Buyer (Agricultural) [Washington]
Dept. Of Agriculture
Livestock Services Division
406 General Administration Bldg., AX-41
Olympia, WA 98504-0641
Phone: (206)753-5053

Credential Type: Cash Buyer License. **Duration of License:** One year. **Authorization:** Allows individual to purchase with cash or currency (no checks) agricultural products other than livestock, hay, grain, or straw for resale. **Requirements:** Submit application and pay fee. **Fees:** $70 license fee.

8602

Cement Mason [Nevada]
Nevada State Contractors Board
70 Linden St.
Reno, NV 89502
Phone: (702)688-1141

Credential Type: License. **Requirements:** Four years of skilled experience in the field. Financial responsibility and good character. **Examination:** Yes. **Fees:** $270 application fee. $40 exam fee. $120 license fee. $120 renewal fee.

8603

Certified Mobile Laser Operator [New York]
New York State Dept. of Labor
Div. of Safety and Health
Radiological Health Unit
One Main St., Rm. 813
Brooklyn, NY 11201
Phone: (718)797-7642

Credential Type: Certificate. **Duration of License:** Three years. **Requirements:**

Completion of a 20-hour laser training course or one year of on-the-job training. **Examination:** Written. **Fees:** $60 license fee. $600 registration fee for each mobile or permanent installation laser. **Governing Statute:** Industrial Code, Rule 50 of the New York State Labor Law.

8604

Chaplain (Racetrack) [Texas]
Texas Racing Commission
PO Box 12080
Austin, TX 78711
Phone: (512)794-8461

Credential Type: License Registration. **Requirements:** Submit application and fingerprint card. Pay fee. **Fees:** $20 registration fee.

8605

Cheese Grader [Wisconsin]
Dept. of Agriculture
Trade and Consumer Protection
Food Div.
801 W. Badger Rd.
PO Box 8911
Madison, WI 53708
Phone: (608)266-2227

Credential Type: License. **Duration of License:** Two years. **Authorization:** Separate licenses are issued for graders of American cheese, Swiss cheese, and brick and Muenster cheese. **Requirements:** Submit application and pay fee. **Fees:** $50 license fee.

8606

Chef/Executive Kitchen Manager (Gaming) [Illinois]
Illinois Gaming Board
PO Box 19474
Springfield, IL 62794-9474
Phone: (217)524-0228

Credential Type: Chef/Executive Kitchen Manager License. **Duration of License:** One year. **Requirements:** At least 18 years of age. U.S. citizen and Illinois resident. No felony convictions. Four to five years experience as a Sous Chef. **Reciprocity:** No. **Fees:** $75 application and license fee. $50 renewal fee. **Governing Statute:** Illinois Revised Statutes, Chapter 120.

8607

Commission Chemist (Racetrack) [Kentucky]
Kentucky State Racing Commission
PO Box 1080
Lexington, KY 40588
Phone: (606)254-7021

Credential Type: License Registration. **Requirements:** Submit application and fingerprint card. Pay fee. **Fees:** $35 registration fee.

8608

Community College Teacher [Arizona]
Community College Board of Directors
Century Plaza, Ste. 1220
3225 N. Central
Phoenix, AZ 85012
Phone: (602)255-5582

Credential Type: Regular certificate. **Duration of License:** Permanent. **Requirements:** Master's degree or higher earned degree with a minimum of 24 semester hours of upper division and/or graduate credit in the discipline to be taught. Take the specified Arizona Community College Course.

For occupational teaching fields only, a Bachelor's degree with a minimum of 64 semester hours and a minimum of three years of directly-related occupational experience in the field to be taught; or an Associate's degree with a minimum of 64 semester hours and a minimum of five years of directly-related occupational experience in the field to be taught. Take the specified Arizona Community College Course. **Reciprocity:** None. **Fees:** $100 certification fee.

Credential Type: Special certificate. **Duration of License:** Two years, then six years. **Authorization:** Part-time teaching only. **Requirements:** Bachelor's degree or higher earned degree in the field to be taught. For occupational teaching fields only, a minimum of five years of directly-related occupational experience in the field to be taught; or hold a regular Arizona license or certificate in the field to be taught. Take the specified Arizona Community College Course. **Reciprocity:** None. **Fees:** $50 certification fee.

Credential Type: Honorary certificate. **Duration of License:** One year. **Requirements:** May be granted to a renowned person who does not necessarily meet the requirements for certification. **Fees:** $20 certification fee.

Credential Type: Provisional certificate. **Duration of License:** Two years (nonrenewable). **Requirements:** Meet minimum requirements of a regular certificate, but does not meet the Arizona Community College Course requirement. **Fees:** $40 certification fee.

Credential Type: District specific certificate. **Duration of License:** Two years, then six years. **Authorization:** To teach part-time except under exceptional circumstances only in the district originating the request for certification. **Requirements:** Must meet Arizona Community College Course requirement prior to first renewal. **Fees:** $50 certification fee.

Credential Type: Intern teaching certificate. **Duration of License:** One semester or six months (nonrenewable). **Requirements:** Hold or be a candidate for a Master's degree in an academic field. For an occupational field, hold or be a candidate for a Bachelor's degree. Be recommended for and admitted to an intern program recognized by the board. **Fees:** $10 certification fee.

8609

Community Planner, Professional [Michigan]
Board of Registration for Professional Community Planners
Bureau of Occupational & Professional Regulation
Dept. of Commerce
PO Box 30018
Lansing, MI 48909
Phone: (517)373-9153

Credential Type: Registration. **Duration of License:** Two years. **Requirements:** Have at least six years of planning experience in the type of work necessary to the preparation or implementation of comprehensive community plans. A minimum of two years of planning experience in the United States is mandatory. Education may be substituted for planning experiences as follows: (A) Doctorate or master's degree in planning, four years experience credit. (B) Bachelor's degree in planning, three years experience credit. (C) Doctorate or master's degree in a related field including architecture, landscape architecture, civil engineering, sociology, economics, geography, political science, or public administration, three years experience credit. (D) Any other degree in a related field, two years experience credit. Comply with all rules and regulations of the Board. **Examination:** American Institute of Certified Planners examination. Michigan Jurisprudence Exam. **Exemptions:** Applicants who have previously passed the AICP examination

Community Planner, Professional [Michigan], continued

may waive Part I of the Michigan exam. **Reciprocity:** Reciprocity may be granted. Applicants must be registered in their home state and meet Michigan requirements. If the examination given in their home state is not equivalent to that of Michigan, the applicant will be required to successfully pass the Michigan examination. **Fees:** $30 application processing fee. $100 initial exam fee. $50 initial registration fee, per year. $50 renewal fee, per year. $30 reciprocity fee. **Governing Statute:** The Occupational Code, Act 299 of 1980, Article 23, as amended.

8610

Computer Analyst (Racetrack) [Connecticut]
Connecticut Div. of Special Revenue
Russell Rd.
PO Box 11424
Newington, CT 06111-0424
Phone: (203)566-2756

Credential Type: License Registration. **Requirements:** Submit application and fingerprint card. Pay fee. **Fees:** $5 registration fee.

8611

Computer Operator (Racetrack) [Connecticut]
Connecticut Div. of Special Revenue
Russell Rd.
PO Box 11424
Newington, CT 06111-0424
Phone: (203)566-2756

Credential Type: License Registration. **Requirements:** Submit application and fingerprint card. Pay fee. **Fees:** $5 registration fee.

8612

Computer Programmer (Gaming) [Illinois]
Illinois Gaming Board
PO Box 19474
Springfield, IL 62794-9474
Phone: (217)524-0228

Credential Type: Computer Programmer License. **Duration of License:** One year. **Requirements:** At least 18 years of age. U.S. citizen and resident of Illinois. No felony convictions. High school graduate or equivalent. Good computer skills. **Reciprocity:** No. **Fees:** $75 application and initial license fee. $50 renewal fee.

8613

Concert Promoter [Alaska]
Dept. of Commerce and Economic Development
Div. of Occupational Licensing
Concert Promoters Registration
PO Box 110806
Juneau, AK 99811-0806
Phone: (907)465-3811
Fax: (907)465-2974

Credential Type: Promoter's Certificate of Registration. **Duration of License:** Two years. **Authorization:** To engage in the business of promoting concerts. **Requirements:** Concert promoter's bond or cash deposit in the amount of $5,000. A time certificate of deposit or savings passbook can be accepted in lieu of bond. **Exemptions:** Registration not required for concerts promoted, organized, or produced by a nonprofit corporation, society, or group; or by a promoter for presentation within a municipality having a population of less than 10,000 persons. **Fees:** $30 application fee. $60 initial registration fee. **Governing Statute:** Alaska Statutes 08.92.

8614

Concrete Technician [Massachusetts]
Board of Building Regulations and Standards
One Ashburton Pl., Rm. 1301
Boston, MA 02108
Phone: (617)727-3200

Credential Type: Class A Field Concrete Technician License. **Duration of License:** Two years. **Requirements:** Knowledge and ability to perform the following ASTM Standard Test Procedures: Sampling fresh concrete; test for slump; making and curing test specimens in the field; test for air content pressure and volumetric methods; test for weight per cubic foot (density); storage and transportation of test cylinders. **Examination:** Class A Field Concrete Technician examination, includes five performance tests. **Fees:** $50 examination fee. $50 license fee.

8615

Condominium Hotel Operator [Hawaii]
Hawaii Real Estate Commission
Dept. of Commerce and Consumer Affairs
PO Box 3469
Honolulu, HI 96801
Phone: (808)548-4100
Phone: (808)548-7464

Credential Type: License. **Duration of License:** One year. **Requirements:** Hawaii real estate broker license. Provide evidence of a fidelity bond. **Fees:** $25 application fee. $25 license fee. $25 renewal fee. $20—$40 Compliance Resolution Fund fee.

8616

Cook (Gaming) [Illinois]
Illinois Gaming Board
PO Box 19474
Springfield, IL 62749-9474
Phone: (217)524-0228

Credential Type: Cook License. **Duration of License:** One year. **Requirements:** At least 18 years of age. U.S. citizen or legal alien as specified by the federal employment eligibility requirement. One to two years of general restaurant experience. Submit application and pay fee. **Reciprocity:** No. **Fees:** $75 application and initial license fee. $50 renewal fee. **Governing Statute:** Illinois Revised Statutes, Chapter 120.

8617

Coroner [Kentucky]
Dept. of Criminal Justice Training
Eastern Kentucky University, Stratton Bldg., Rm. 112
Richmond, KY 40475
Phone: (606)622-6165

Credential Type: License. **Duration of License:** One year. **Requirements:** 24 years of age. Must be a two-year resident of Kentucky and a one-year resident in the County in which he/she is an candidate. Successful completion of a forty-hour basic training course within one year of taking office. Must complete an 18-hour course for renewal. **Examination:** Yes.

Credential Type: Deputy Coroner License. **Duration of License:** One year. **Requirements:** Successful completion of a forty-hour basic training course within one year of taking office for certification. Must complete an 18-hour course annually. **Examination:** Yes.

8618

Correctional Officer [Maryland]
Correctional Training Commission
Dept. of Public Safety and
 Correctional Service
3085 Hernwood Rd.
Woodstock, MD 21163
Phone: (301)442-2700

Credential Type: Certification. **Duration of License:** Valid for term of employment. **Requirements:** High school graduate or equivalent. Complete entry-level training program. **Reciprocity:** Yes, with states having comparable training programs. **Fees:** No fees.

8619

Correctional Officer, State [Michigan]
Correctional Officers' Training
 Council
DeMarse Corrections Academy
Dept. of Corrections
715 W. Willow - Main Bldg.
Lansing, MI 48913
Phone: (517)335-1426

Credential Type: Certification. **Duration of License:** One year. **Requirements:** High school diploma or equivalent. At least 18 years of age. At least 15 semester or 23 term credits from an accredited postsecondary educational institution. These credits must be in one or more of the following areas of study: Corrections (MCOTC certified program preferred), Criminal Justice, Sociology, Psychology, Educational Psychology, Family Relations, and Guidance and Counseling. Pass an oral interview. Negative results on a drug screening test. Submit to a background investigation. Provide employment and/or personal references. Be willing to work in direct contact with convicted felons and to participate in training and use of firearms. Renewal requires completion of 40 hours of mandated training. **Examination:** Michigan Civil Service Examination. **Fees:** No fees. **Governing Statute:** Correctional Officers' Training Act, Act 415 of 1982. Correctional Officers' Training Act, Act 44 of 1984. Correctional Officers' Training Act, Act four of 1989.

8620

Counterintelligence Licensee [North Carolina]
Private Protective Services Board
PO Box 29500
Raleigh, NC 27626
Phone: (919)779-1611

Credential Type: License. **Duration of License:** One year. **Requirements:** High school diploma. Three years of experience within the past five years in counterintelligence or completion of a board approved school in counterintelligence. 18 years of age. **Fees:** $150 application fee. $150 license fee. $50 recovery fund fee. $150 renewal fee.

8621

County Corrections Officer [Illinois]
Illinois Local Law Enforcement
 Officer Training Board
600 S. Second St., Ste. 300
Springfield, IL 62704
Phone: (217)782-4540

Credential Type: County Corrections Officer Certificate. **Duration of License:** Indefinite. **Requirements:** At least 18 years of age. High school graduate or equivalent. Successfully complete Basic Recruit Training in an approved Academy. Must reside within county of application. **Examination:** Written examination. **Reciprocity:** Yes. **Fees:** No fee. **Governing Statute:** Illinois Police Training Act, Illinois Revised Statutes, Chapter 85.

8622

Cross-Connection Control Device Inspector [Illinois]
Illinois Environmental Protection
 Agency
2200 Churchill Rd.
PO Box 19276
Springfield, IL 62794-9276
Phone: (217)782-1869

Credential Type: Cross-Connection Control Device Inspector Certificate. **Duration of License:** One year. **Requirements:** Must be licensed as a plumber in the state of Illinois. Complete four-day training course and pass examination. **Examination:** Written and performance examination. **Reciprocity:** No. **Fees:** $180 course and examination fee. **Governing Statute:** Illinois Revised Statutes 1989, Chapter 1001.

8623

Dairy Technician [Washington]
Dept. of Agriculture
Dairy & Food Division
406 General Administration Bldg.,
 AX-41
Olympia, WA 98504-0641
Phone: (206)753-5043
Fax: (206)753-3700

Credential Type: Dairy Technician License. **Duration of License:** Two years. **Requirements:** Submit to background investigation and inspection of work performed. Must have experience acquired through on-the-job training. **Examination:** Written and practical examination. **Fees:** $10 initial license fee. $5 renewal fee.

8624

Dance Therapist [District of Columbia]
License and Certification Div.
Occupational and Professional
 Licensure Administration
Consumer and Regulatory Affairs
 Dept.
PO Box 37200
Washington, DC 20013-7200
Phone: (202)727-7823
Phone: (202)727-7480

Credential Type: License. **Requirements:** Contact licensing body for application information.

8625

Dance Therapist (School) [Louisiana]
Louisiana State Dept. of Education
PO Box 90464
Baton Rouge, LA 70804
Phone: (504)342-3490

Credential Type: Master's Level License. **Requirements:** Master's degree in Dance Therapy. Six hours of special education. Registration by the American Dance Therapy Association.

Credential Type: Bachelor's Level License. **Requirements:** Bachelor's degree in Dance Therapy. Practical experience for two semesters in both a clinical and school setting. Registration by the American Dance Therapy Association.

8626

Debt Consolidation Agent [Oregon]
Div. of Finance and Corporate Securities
21 Labor & Industries Bldg.
Salem, OR 97310
Phone: (503)378-4140

Credential Type: License. **Duration of License:** Two years. **Requirements:** Must file and maintain with the Director of the Department of Insurance and Finance the following information: the name and address of the person engaging in business as a debt consolidating agency, the name and address of the debt consolidating agency, any assumed names or business names used by the debt consolidating agency, the names of persons who act as agents in the business of the debt consolidating agency, the names of persons who are agents of the debt consolidating agency for purposes of services of legal process, or an appointment of the director as agent for the debt consolidating agency for the service of process. If a person has been convicted for a criminal offense, an essential element of which is fraud, information relating to the circumstances of the conviction as required by the director. Telephone numbers of the business and all offices, all office locations, name of trust account, account number, and name and address of financial institution where account is located. If registration is for a non-profit debt consolidating business, copy of $10,000 fidelity bond; or if registration if for a for-profit debt consolidating business, copy of $10,000 surety bond payable to Department of Insurance and Finance. **Fees:** $200 license fee. $200 renewal fee. **Governing Statute:** ORS 697.602 to 697.992 and Oregon Administrative Rules, Chapter 441-800 to 441-910.

8627

Direct Disposer [Florida]
Board of Funeral Directors and Embalmers
Dept. of Professional Regulation
1940 N. Monroe St.
Tallahassee, FL 32399-0754
Phone: (904)488-8690

Credential Type: Direct Disposers License. **Duration of License:** Two years. **Requirements:** Be at least 18 years of age. Possess a high school diploma or equivalent. **Examination:** Objective examination. State laws and rules examination. **Reciprocity:** License may be granted by endorsement. **Fees:** $200 objective examination fee. $110 laws and rules examination fee. $200 renewal fee. $160 license by endorsement fee. **Governing Statute:** Florida Statutes, Chapter 470.

8628

Dishwasher/Kitchen Utility Helper (Gaming) [Illinois]
Illinois Gaming Board
PO Box 19474
Springfield, IL 62794-9474
Phone: (217)524-0228

Credential Type: Dishwasher/Utility License. **Duration of License:** One year. **Requirements:** At least 18 years of age. U.S. citizen or legal alien as specified by Federal employability requirement. Submit application and pay fee. **Reciprocity:** No. **Fees:** $75 application/initial license fee. $50 renewal fee. **Governing Statute:** Illinois Revised Statutes, Chapter 120.

8629

Drug Auctioneer [Rhode Island]
State Board of Pharmacy
Div. of Drug Control
Rhode Island Dept. of Health
3 Capitol Hill
Providence, RI 02908
Phone: (401)277-2837

Credential Type: Drug Auctioneer License. **Duration of License:** New license must be obtained for each auction. **Requirements:** Good moral character. Foreign born must show proof of legal entry into the U.S. Must be familiar with pharmaceutics. No addiction to alcohol or controlled substances. No felony convictions or violations of any drug statutes. **Reciprocity:** No. **Fees:** $75 license fee.

8630

Drug Researcher [Rhode Island]
Div. of Drug Control
Rhode Island Dept. of Health
3 Capitol Hill, Rm. 304
Providence, RI 02908
Phone: (401)277-2837

Credential Type: Controlled Substance License. **Duration of License:** One year. **Requirements:** Foreign born must show proof of legal entry into the U.S. Must be physician or hold professional rank in a college or university. Submit curriculum vitae and protocols for research design or program. **Reciprocity:** No. **Fees:** $50 controlled substance license fee.

8631

Egg Grader [Arkansas]
Arkansas Livestock and Poultry Commission
1 Natural Resources Dr.
PO Box 549
Little Rock, AR 72215
Phone: (501)225-5138

Credential Type: License. **Requirements:** Based upon evaluation of experience, education and training. Must be in good physical health. **Examination:** Yes. **Fees:** None.

8632

Electric Sign Installer [Rhode Island]
Board of Examiners of Electricians
Div. of Professional Regulation
Rhode Island Dept. of Labor
220 Elmwood Ave.
Providence, RI 02907
Phone: (401)457-1860

Credential Type: Journeyperson License (Cert CF). **Duration of License:** One year. **Requirements:** At least 18 years of age. Complete a 6,000 hour registered apprenticeship under the supervision of a licensed electrician. **Examination:** Written examination. **Reciprocity:** No. **Fees:** $30 application fee. $10 apprentice registration fee. $30 Journeyperson (Cert CF) license fee.

Credential Type: Master Contractor License (Cert SCF). **Duration of License:** One year. **Requirements:** Hold journeyperson's license for at least one year or complete 10,000 hours of equivalent experience. Alternative requirements are available by contacting the board. **Examination:** Written examination. **Reciprocity:** No. **Fees:** $30 application fee. $100 master contractor (Cert SCF) license fee.

8633

Electronic Criminal Surveillance Officer [Illinois]
Illinois Local Governmental Law Enforcement Officer Training Board
600 S. Second St., Ste. 300
Springfield, IL 62704
Phone: (217)782-4540

Credential Type: Level I Certificate. **Duration of License:** Three years. **Requirements:** U.S. citizen. Resident of county where employed. Complete a 10 week basic law enforcement recruitment course. Complete 120 hours of series course work in electronic criminal surveillance. Renewal requires 20 hours of continuing education annually. **Examination:** Written examination. **Reciprocity:** No. **Fees:** No fee. **Governing Statute:** Public Act 85-1203.

Credential Type: Level II Certificate. **Duration of License:** Three years. **Requirements:** Hold a Level I Certificate. Complete 80 additional hours of series course work in electronic criminal surveillance. **Examination:** Written examination. **Reciprocity:** No. **Fees:** No fee. **Governing Statute:** Public Act 85-1203

Credential Type: Level III Certificate. **Duration of License:** Three years. **Requirements:** Hold a Level II Certificate. Complete 40 additional hours of series course work in electronic criminal surveillance. **Examination:** Written examination. **Reciprocity:** No. **Fees:** No fee. **Governing Statute:** Public Act 85-1203

8634

Elevator Operator [Massachusetts]
Dept. of Public Safety
Div. of Inspection
Elevator Inspection Section
One Ashburton Pl.
Boston, MA 02108
Phone: (617)727-3200

Credential Type: License. **Requirements:** Contact licensing body for application information. **Governing Statute:** Massachusetts General Laws, Chap. 143.

8635

Entertainer (Riverboat Gambling) [Iowa]
Iowa Racing and Gaming Commission
Lucas State Office Bldg.
Des Moines, IA 50319
Phone: (515)281-7352

Credential Type: License Registration. **Requirements:** Submit application and pay fees. **Fees:** $10 license fee.

8636

Escrow Agent [Washington]
Dept. of Licensing
Professional Licensing Services
Real Estate
2424 Bristol Court SW
Olympia, WA 98504
Phone: (206)753-6974

Credential Type: Escrow Agent License. **Duration of License:** One year. **Requirements:** Maintain office in Washington state. Submit to background investigation. Must post $200,000 fidelity bond. Must submit to trust account and record-keeping audits. **Fees:** $345 initial license fee. $345 renewal fee. $25 duplicate license and transfer fee.

8637

Escrow Agent [Oregon]
Oregon Real Estate Agency
158 12th St. NE
Salem, OR 97310
Phone: (503)378-4170

Credential Type: License. **Duration of License:** One year. **Requirements:** Escrow experience. Must provide current financial statements. **Examination:** No. **Fees:** $200 license fee. $200 renewal fee. **Governing Statute:** ORS Chapter 696.

8638

Euthanasia Technician [Nevada]
Board of Veterinary Medical Examiners
Executive Plaza
1005 Terminal Way, Ste. 246
Reno, NV 89502
Phone: (702)322-9422
Fax: (702)322-1926

Credential Type: Euthanasia Technician Certificate. **Requirements:** Pass examination. **Examination:** State examination. **Fees:** $200 application/examination fee. **Governing Statute:** Practice law.

8639

Farm Labor Contractor [Maryland]
Div. of Labor and Industry
Dept. of Licensing and Regulation
501 St. Paul Pl.
Baltimore, MD 21202-2272
Phone: (410)333-4192

Credential Type: License. **Duration of License:** One year. **Authorization:** A grower must verify that a farm labor contractor is licensed before using the contractor's services. **Requirements:** Submit application and pay fee. **Fees:** $25 application fee.

8640

Farm Labor Contractor [Oregon]
Bureau of Labor and Industries, Licensing Unit
State Office Bldg., Ste. 1160
800 NE Oregon St., 32
Portland, OR 97232
Phone: (503)731-4074, ext. 229

Credential Type: License. **Duration of License:** One year. **Requirements:** Must provide a Farm Labor Contractor Corporate Surety Bond, complete Certification of Compliance (FF-137), and provide Certificate of Insurance for vehicles. **Examination:** Yes. **Fees:** $20 license fee. $20 renewal fee. **Governing Statute:** ORS 658.405 to 658-503.

8641

Farm Labor Contractor [Nebraska]
Nebraska Dept. of Labor
1313 Farnam St., 3rd Fl.
Omaha, NE 68102
Phone: (402)595-3095

Credential Type: License. **Duration of License:** One year. **Requirements:** Must secure a surety bond for the amount of not less than $5,000. Contractors must be registered with the state. **Fees:** $750 license fee. $750 renewal fee.

8642

Fire Fighter Training Instructor [Michigan]
Fire Fighters Training Council
Fire Marshall Div.
Dept. of State Police
7150 Harris Dr.
Lansing, MI 48913
Phone: (517)332-2521

Credential Type: Fire Fighter Training Instructor Certification. **Duration of License:** Lifelong. **Authorization:** All persons employed as a fire fighter training instructor must be certified by the Fire Fighters Training Council of the Michigan Department of State Police. **Requirements:** Minimum of five years experience in fire suppression service. Certification as a Fire Fighter I. Have received one positive evaluation and recommendation by a Fire Fighters Training Council representative, while a provisional instructor. Completed the Fire Fighters Training Council Basic Instructional Methodological (16 hour) Course, or its equivalent. **Fees:** No fees. **Governing Statute:** Fire Fighters Training Council Act of 1966, Act 291 of 1966, as amended.

Firearms 8643

Fire Fighter Training Instructor [Michigan], continued

Credential Type: Associate Instructor Certification. **Duration of License:** Lifelong. **Authorization:** All persons employed as a fire fighter training instructor must be certified by the Fire Fighters Training Council of the Michigan Department of State Police. **Requirements:** Have a minimum of three years experience in the specialized area or subject to be taught. Have received the recommendation and approval of a certified fire service instructor or recognized authority in the area to be taught. Abide by the rules of the Fire Fighters Training Council. **Fees:** No fees. **Governing Statute:** Fire Fighters Training Council Act of 1966, Act 291 of 1966, as amended.

Credential Type: Provisional Instructor Certification. **Duration of License:** Lifelong. **Authorization:** All persons employed as a fire fighter training instructor must be certified by the Fire Fighters Training Council of the Michigan Department of State Police. **Requirements:** Have a minimum of three years experience in fire suppression service. Have successfully completed the Fire Fighters Training Council Fire Fighter I curriculum. Have received the recommendation and approval of their fire chief or governing municipality official. Abide by the rules of the Fire Fighters Training Council. **Fees:** No fees. **Governing Statute:** Fire Fighters Training Council Act of 1966, Act 291 of 1966, as amended.

Credential Type: Fire Instructor Advisor Certification. **Duration of License:** Lifelong. **Authorization:** All persons employed as a fire fighter training instructor must be certified by the Fire Fighters Training Council of the Michigan Department of State Police. **Requirements:** Have certification as a Fire Fighter II and Fire Fighter Training Instructor. Have instructed in a minimum of five (5) Fire Fighters Training Council recognized programs. Have received three positive evaluations and recommendations by Fire Fighters Training Council representatives, while a Fire Fighter Training Instructor. Have completed the Fire Fighters Training Council Advanced Instructional Methodological Course, or its equivalent. **Fees:** No fees. **Governing Statute:** Fire Fighters Training Council Act of 1966, Act 291 of 1966, as amended.

Credential Type: Fire Training Administrator Certification. **Duration of License:** Lifelong. **Authorization:** All persons employed as a fire fighter training instructor must be certified by the Fire Fighters Training Council of the Michigan Department of State Police. **Requirements:** Have certification as a Fire Fighter II and a Fire Instructor Advisor. Have managed, supervised, or instructed in a minimum of 10 Fire Fighters Training Council recognized programs. **Fees:** No fees. **Governing Statute:** Fire Fighters Training Council Act of 1966, Act 291 of 1966, as amended.

8643

Firearms Instructor [California]
Bureau of Collection and
  Investigative Services
400 R St., Ste. 2001
Sacramento, CA 95814-6234
Phone: (916)445-7366

Credential Type: License. **Requirements:** Contact licensing body for application information.

8644

Firearms Safety Instructor [Washington]
Dept. of Wildlife
600 N. Capitol, GJ-11
Olympia, WA 98504-0091
Phone: (206)753-5710

Credential Type: Firearms Safety Instructor License. **Duration of License:** Indefinite. **Requirements:** Skill and knowledge of firearms safety and handling. Must submit to background investigation if not active for one year or more. **Examination:** Written examination. **Fees:** No fee.

8645

Firearms Trainer [North Carolina]
Private Protective Services Board
PO Box 29500
Raleigh, NC 27626
Phone: (919)779-1611

Credential Type: Certification. **Duration of License:** Two years. **Requirements:** High school diploma. One year of supervisory experience in security with a contract company or proprietary security organization; or one year of experience with a law enforcement agency. Completion of a board approved firearms training course. 18 years of age. U.S. citizen or resident alien. Good moral character. Eight hours of safety training upon renewal. **Examination:** Yes. **Fees:** $50 application fee. $25 renewal fee.

8646

Fireworks Shooter [Rhode Island]
State Fire Marshal's Office
Rhode Island Div. of Fire Safety
1270 Mineral Spring Ave.
North Providence, RI 02904
Phone: (401)277-2335

Credential Type: Fireworks Shooter License. **Duration of License:** One year. **Requirements:** At least 18 years of age. Must be sponsored by a licensed fireworks shooter. Must have at least three years of on-the-job training under the supervision of a licensed shooter. Pass State Police Bureau of Criminal Identification screening and psychiatric examination. Must carry liability insurance in amount required by local authority. **Examination:** Oral examination. **Reciprocity:** No. **Fees:** $10 examination fee. $10 license fee.

8647

Flight Instructor (Ultralight Aircraft) [Louisiana]
Dept. of Transportation and
  Development
PO Box 94245
Baton Rouge, LA 70804-7437
Phone: (504)342-7437

Credential Type: Instructor License. **Duration of License:** Two years. **Requirements:** Contact board for requirements. **Examination:** Written examination. **Fees:** $15 license fee.

8648

Floor and Carpet Layer [Nevada]
Nevada State Contractors Board
70 Linden St.
Reno, NV 89502
Phone: (702)688-1141

Credential Type: License. **Requirements:** Four years of skilled experience in the field. Finacial responsibility and good character. **Examination:** Yes. **Fees:** $270 application fee. $120 license fee. $120 renewal fee. $40 exam fee.

8649

Florist [Idaho]
Plant Industries Div.
Agriculture Dept.
PO Box 790
Boise, ID 83701
Phone: (208)334-2986

Credential Type: Class A License. **Duration of License:** One year. **Authorization:**

Required if gross business is over $1,000 per year. **Requirements:** Submit application and pay fee. **Fees:** $50 license fee per outlet. **Governing Statute:** Idaho Code, Title 22, Chap. 23.

Credential Type: Class B License. **Duration of License:** One year. **Authorization:** Required if gross business is $1,000 or less per year. **Requirements:** Submit application and pay fee. **Fees:** $15 license fee. **Governing Statute:** Idaho Code, Title 22, Chap. 23.

8650

Forest Labor Contractor   [Oregon]
Bureau of Labor and Industries
State Office Bldg., Ste. 1160
800 NE Oregon St., 32
Portland, OR 97232
Phone: (503)731-4074

Credential Type: License. **Duration of License:** One year. **Requirements:** Must provide a Farm Labor Contractor Corporate Surety Bond, complete Certification of Compliance (FF-137), provide Certificate of Insurance for vehicles and Worker's Compensation insurance. **Examination:** Yes. **Fees:** $100 license fee. $100 renewal fee. **Governing Statute:** ORS 658.405 to 658.503.

8651

Forest Products Operator [Maryland]
Forestry Div.
Dept. of Natural Resources
Tawes State Office Bldg.
Annapolis, MD 21401
Phone: (410)974-3776

Credential Type: License. **Duration of License:** One year. **Requirements:** Submit application and pay fee. Submit annual harvest disclosure. **Fees:** $10 license fee.

8652

Franchise Broker/Dealer [Washington]
Dept. of Licensing
Business License Services - Securities
405 Black Lake Blvd.
Olympia, WA 98504
Phone: (206)753-6924

Credential Type: Franchise Broker/Dealer License. **Duration of License:** One year. **Requirements:** At least 18 years of age. Submit application and pay fee. **Fees:** $50 initial license fee. $25 renewal fee.

8653

Funeral Goods or Services (Prepaid), Contract Seller of [Michigan]
Prepaid Funeral Regulation
Bureau of Occupational & Professional Regulation
Dept. of Commerce
PO Box 30018
Lansing, MI 48909
Phone: (517)373-9153

Credential Type: Registration. **Duration of License:** Three years. **Requirements:** Complete an application for registration. Submit information regarding the seller's escrow agent(s). (An escrow agent holds, invests, and disburses principal and income from the funds received under a prepaid funeral contract.) Abide by the rules and regulations of the Department. **Fees:** $120 initial registration fee. $30 renewal fee. **Governing Statute:** Prepaid Funeral Contract Funding Act, Act 255 of 1986.

8654

Fur Buyer   [Idaho]
License Office
Administration Bureau
Fish and Game Dept.
PO Box 25
600 S. Walnut
Boise, ID 83707
Phone: (208)334-3717

Credential Type: License. **Requirements:** Contact licensing body for application information.

8655

Fur Buyer (Non-Resident) [Illinois]
Illinois Dept. of Conservation
524 South 2nd St.
Springfield, IL 62701-1787
Phone: (217)785-3423

Credential Type: Non-Resident Fur Buyer License. **Duration of License:** One year. **Requirements:** Submit application and pay fee. **Reciprocity:** No. **Fees:** $250 initial license fee. $250 renewal fee. **Governing Statute:** Illinois Revised Statutes, Chapter 61.

8656

Fur Buyer (Resident)   [Illinois]
Illinois Dept. of Conservation
524 South 2nd St.
Springfield, IL 62701-1787
Phone: (217)785-3423

Credential Type: Retail Fur Buyer License. **Duration of License:** One year. **Requirements:** Must be a resident of Illinois for at least 30 days. Submit application and pay fee. **Reciprocity:** No. **Fees:** $25 initial license fee. $25 renewal fee. **Governing Statute:** Illinois Revised Statutes, Chapter 61.

Credential Type: Wholesale Fur Buyer License. **Duration of License:** One year. **Requirements:** Must be a resident of Illinois for at least 30 days. Submit application and pay fee. **Reciprocity:** No. **Fees:** $125 initial license fee. $125 renewal fee. **Governing Statute:** Illinois Revised Statutes, Chapter 61.

8657

Fur Dealer   [Maryland]
Wildlife Div.
Dept. of Natural Resources
Tawes State Office Bldg.
Annapolis, MD 21401
Phone: (410)974-3211

Credential Type: License. **Duration of License:** One year. **Requirements:** Submit application and pay fee. Must keep record book. **Fees:** $50 resident license fee. $100 non-resident license fee.

8658

Fur Dealer   [Michigan]
Administrative Services Div.
Dept. of Natural Resources
Stevens T. Mason Bldg.
PO Box 30028
Lansing, MI 48909
Phone: (517)373-1220

Credential Type: License. **Duration of License:** One year. **Requirements:** Abide by the laws related to the buying and selling of raw furs, hides and pelts of fur-bearing animals and the plumage, skins or hides of protected game birds and game animals. **Fees:** $10 initial license fee for a resident. $50 initial license fee for a nonresident. Renewal fee is same as initial fee. **Governing Statute:** Fur Dealer's License Act, Act 308 of 1929.

8659

Fur Dealer [Arizona]
Arizona Game and Fish Dept.
2221 W. Greenway Rd.
Phoenix, AZ 85023-4312
Phone: (602)942-3000
Fax: (602)789-3920

Credential Type: Fur dealer license. **Authorization:** To engage in the business of buying for resale any specimen of predatory, nongame, and fur-bearing mammals taken within Arizona. **Requirements:** Submit application. Keep record of transactions. Submit quarterly report to the department. **Fees:** $100 license fee. **Governing Statute:** Arizona Revised Statutes, Title 17, Chapter 2.

8660

Fur Dealer [Utah]
Natural Resources Dept.
Div. of Wildlife Resources
1596 W. North Temple
Salt Lake City, UT 84116
Phone: (801)533-9333

Credential Type: Registration. **Requirements:** Contact licensing body for application information.

8661

Fur or Hide Dealer [Montana]
Dept. of Fish, Wildlife, and Parks
Law Enforcement Div.
1420 E. 6th Ave.
Helena, MT 59620
Phone: (406)444-2452

Credential Type: Resident License. **Requirements:** Submit application and pay fee. **Fees:** $10 license fee. **Governing Statute:** Montana Code Annotated 87-4.

Credential Type: Nonresident License. **Requirements:** Submit application and pay fee. **Fees:** $50 license fee (minimum, based on nonresident's home state fee). **Governing Statute:** Montana Code Annotated 87-4.

Credential Type: Dealer Agent License. **Requirements:** Submit application and pay fee. **Fees:** $10 license fee. **Governing Statute:** Montana Code Annotated 87-4.

8662

Fur Processor [Michigan]
Administrative Services Div.
Dept. of Natural Resources
Stevens T. Mason Bldg.
PO Box 30028
Lansing, MI 48909
Phone: (517)373-1220

Credential Type: License. **Duration of License:** One year. **Requirements:** Abide by the laws related to the custom tanning or dressing of raw furs. **Fees:** $5 initial license fee. $5 renewal fee. **Governing Statute:** Fur Dealer's License Act, Act 308 of 1929.

8663

Fur Tanner or Dyer [Illinois]
Illinois Dept. of Conservation
524 South 2nd St.
Springfield, IL 62701-1787
Phone: (217)785-3423

Credential Type: Fur Tanner or Dyer License. **Duration of License:** One year. **Requirements:** Must be an Illinois resident for at least 30 days. Submit application and pay fee. **Reciprocity:** No. **Fees:** $25 initial license fee. $25 renewal fee. **Governing Statute:** Illinois Revised Statutes, Chapter 61.

8664

Geoduck Diver [Washington]
Dept. of Fisheries
115 General Administration Bldg., AX-11
Olympia, WA 98504-0611
Phone: (206)753-6590

Credential Type: Geoduck Diver License. **Duration of License:** One year. **Requirements:** At least 16 years of age. Submit application and pay fee. **Fees:** $100 resident license fee. $200 non-resident license fee.

8665

Geophysicist [California]
Board of Registration for Geologists and Geophysicists
400 R St., Ste. 4060
Sacramento, CA 95814-6200
Phone: (916)445-1920

Credential Type: License and Registration. **Duration of License:** Two years. **Requirements:** Have a B.A. or B.S. in Geophysics. Have at least five years of experience. **Examination:** Geophysicist examination. **Reciprocity:** No. **Fees:** $100 application and registration fee.

8666

Glazier [Nevada]
Nevada State Contractors Board
70 Linden St.
Reno, NV 89502
Phone: (702)688-1141

Credential Type: License. **Requirements:** Four years of skilled experience in the licensed fields. Financial responsibility and good character. **Examination:** Yes. **Fees:** $270 application fee. $120 license fee. $120 renewal fee. $40 exam fee.

8668

Guard Dog Service Employee [North Carolina]
Private Protective Services Board
PO Box 29500
Raleigh, NC 27626
Phone: (919)779-1611

Credential Type: License. **Duration of License:** One year. **Requirements:** High school diploma. Two years of experience performing guard dog functions within the past five years as a supervisor with a contract security company, proprietary security organization, law enforcement agency. 18 years of age. **Fees:** $150 application fee. $150 license fee. $50 recovery fund fee. $150 renewal fee.

8669

Guide Dog Instructor [California]
Board of Guide Dogs for the Blind
830 K St., Rm. 222
Sacramento, CA 95814
Phone: (916)445-9041

Credential Type: License. **Requirements:** Must complete a three-year apprenticeship. **Fees:** $75 license fee.

8670

Guide (Tourist) [District of Columbia]
License and Certification Div.
Occupational and Professional Licensure Administration
Consumer and Regulatory Affairs Dept.
PO Box 37200
Washington, DC 20013-7200
Phone: (202)727-7823
Phone: (202)727-7480

Alternate Information: 614 H St., NW, Washington, DC 20001 **Requirements:** Contact licensing body for application information.

8671

Home Health Aide [Kansas]
Health Occupations Credentialling
Bureau of Adult and Child Care
Dept. of Health and Environment
Landon State Office Bldg., Ste. 901
Topeka, KS 66612-1290
Phone: (913)296-1284

Credential Type: Home Health Aide Certificate. **Requirements:** Contact licensing body for application information. **Examination:** Written exam. **Fees:** $2.50 certification fee.

8672

Home Health Aide [Illinois]
Illinois Dept. of Health
Health Care Facilities & Programs
525 W. Jefferson
Springfield, IL 62761
Phone: (217)782-7412

Credential Type: Registration. **Duration of License:** Indefinite. **Requirements:** Complete an approved training program for Home Health Aides. **Examination:** Written examination. **Reciprocity:** Yes, providing state and federal standards have been met. **Fees:** No fee. **Governing Statute:** Home Health Agency Licensing Act, Title 77, chapter I.

8673

Home Health Aide [Texas]
Texas Dept. of Health
Health Facility Licensure and Certification Div.
1100 W. 49th St.
Austin, TX 78756
Phone: (512)458-7240

Credential Type: License. **Requirements:** Nursing school dean or director vouches for individual's competence; or previous work experience; or completed training program prior to August 1990; or satisfactory completion of a training program and/or competency evaluation. **Examination:** Competency evaluation. **Fees:** No fees. **Governing Statute:** Health & Safety Code, Ch. 142, 25 TAC 115.

8674

Hypnotherapist [Washington]
Dept. of Health
1112 SE Quince
Olympia, WA 98504
Phone: (206)753-6936

Credential Type: Hypnotherapist License. **Duration of License:** Two years. **Requirements:** Complete a four-hour course in AIDS education. Submit application and pay fee. **Fees:** $78.50 application fee. $73.50 renewal fee. $42 duplicate license fee. $50 registration verification fee.

8675

Illinois County Coroner [Illinois]
Illinois Local Law Enforcement Officer Training Board
600 S. Second St., Ste. 300
Springfield, IL 62704
Phone: (217)782-4540

Credential Type: County Coroner Certificate. **Duration of License:** Indefinite. **Requirements:** Resident of Illinois. Live in county of office. Pass examination. Renewal requires 24 hours of continuing education per year. **Examination:** Written examination. **Reciprocity:** No. **Fees:** No fee. **Governing Statute:** Public Act 85-985.

8676

Inspector, Vehicle Emission Testing [Michigan]
Auto Exhaust Testing Div.
Bureau of Automotive Regulation
Dept. of State
208 N. Capitol Ave.
Lansing, MI 48918
Phone: (517)322-1460

Credential Type: Approval. **Duration of License:** Lifelong. **Examination:** Written exam. **Governing Statute:** Vehicle Emissions Inspection and Maintenance Act, Act 83 of 1980.

8677

Installer/Seller Lightning Rods and Fire Detection Systems [Vermont]
Electrician's Licensing Board
Dept. of Labor and Industry
120 State St.
Montpelier, VT 05602
Phone: (802)828-2107

Credential Type: License. **Requirements:** To Install: Equipment must be approved. To Sell: Deemed qualified by State Fire Marshal. **Examination:** Installers: Yes. Sellers: No. **Reciprocity:** No. **Fees:** $10 Installers (annually). $5 Sellers (annually). **Governing Statute:** Title 9, VSA Sections 3201-3205.

8678

Insurance Investigator (Racetrack) [Connecticut]
Connecticut Div. of Special Revenue
Russell Rd.
PO Box 11424
Newington, CT 06111-0424
Phone: (203)566-2756

Credential Type: License Registration. **Requirements:** Submit application and fingerprint card. Pay fee. **Fees:** $5 registration fee.

8679

Interpreter for the Deaf [Texas]
Texas Commission for the Deaf and Hearing Impaired
PO Box 12904
Austin, TX 78711
Phone: (512)444-3323

Credential Type: License. **Duration of License:** One year. **Requirements:** 18 years of age. Formal post-secondary educa-

Interpreter for the Deaf [Texas], continued

tion, or experience. **Examination:** Written and practical. **Fees:** $10 license fee. $20—$60 evaluation fee. $25 annual maintenance fee. **Governing Statute:** Human Resources Code 81.007.

8680

Interpreter for the Deaf [Nebraska]
Nebraska Commission for the Hearing Impaired
4600 Valley Rd.
Lincoln, NE 68501
Phone: (402)471-3593

Credential Type: License. **Examination:** Yes. **Fees:** $30 application fee. $520 examination fees. $24-$150 renewal fee.

8681

Invention Developer [Illinois]
Secretary of State
Index Dept.
111 E. Monroe St.
Springfield, IL 62756
Phone: (217)782-7017

Credential Type: Registration. **Duration of License:** Permanent (as long as bond is in force). **Requirements:** Must post a $25,000 surety bond. Submit application. **Reciprocity:** No. **Fees:** No fee. **Governing Statute:** Illinois Revised Statutes, Chapter 29.

8682

Jailer [North Carolina]
Dept. of Justice
Attorney General's Office
Training and Standards Div.
Raleigh, NC 27602
Phone: (919)733-9236

Credential Type: Certification. **Duration of License:** Permanent. **Requirements:** High school diploma. 120 hours of training in a jailer certification course. 21 years of age. Good physical health. **Examination:** Written.

8683

Journeyman Pipeline Welder [New Mexico]
Construction Industries Div.
Dept. of Regulation and Licensing
PO Box 25101
725 St. Michael's Dr.
Santa Fe, NM 87504
Phone: (505)827-7030
Fax: (505)827-7045

Credential Type: Journeyman Pipeline Welder Certificate of Competence. **Duration of License:** One year. **Authorization:** Must be employed by a properly licensed contractor. **Requirements:** Be at least 18 years of age. Complete at least two years of approved experience or a course in the trade approved by the vocational educational division of the state department of public education. **Examination:** Yes. **Fees:** $25 exam fee. $25 renewal fee. **Governing Statute:** Construction Industries Division Rules and Regulations. New Mexico Construction Industries Licensing Act, Chapter 60.

8684

Journeyman Sheet Metal Worker [New Mexico]
Construction Industries Div.
Dept. of Regulation and Licensing
PO Box 25101
725 St. Michael's Dr.
Santa Fe, NM 87504
Phone: (505)827-7030
Fax: (505)827-7045

Credential Type: Journeyman Sheet Metal Worker Certificate of Competence. **Duration of License:** One year. **Authorization:** Must be employed by a properly licensed contractor. **Requirements:** Be at least 18 years of age. Complete at least two years of approved experience or a course in the trade approved by the vocational educational division of the state department of public education. **Examination:** Mechanical Journeyman Examination. **Fees:** $25 exam fee. $25 renewal fee. **Governing Statute:** Construction Industries Division Rules and Regulations. New Mexico Construction Industries Licensing Act, Chapter 60.

8685

Kitchen Employee (Riverboat Gambling) [Iowa]
Iowa Racing and Gaming Commission
Lucas State Office Bldg.
Des Moines, IA 50319
Phone: (515)281-7352

Credential Type: License Registration. **Requirements:** Submit application and pay fees. **Fees:** $10 license fee.

8686

Land Development Representative [Washington]
Dept.of Licensing
Professional Licensing Services - Real Estate
2424 Bristol Ct. SW
Olympia, WA 98504
Phone: (206)853-2250

Credential Type: License. **Duration of License:** One year. **Authorization:** Allows the holder to disseminate information, contact purchasers, and transport purchasers to land developments for a real estate broker or land developer. **Requirements:** Be at least 18 years of age. Resident of Washington. Must work under the supervision of a licensed real estate broker. **Fees:** $25 license fee.

8687

Lead Hazard Abatement Contractor [Rhode Island]
Office of Environmental Health Risk Assessment
Rhode Island Dept. of Health
3 Capitol Hill
Providence, RI 02908
Phone: (401)277-1417

Credential Type: Lead Hazard Abatement Contractor. **Requirements:** Submit application. Contact licensing agency for additional requirements. **Examination:** Written and practical examinations.

8688

Lead Hazard Abatement Site Supervisor [Rhode Island]
Office of Environmental Health Risk Assessment
Rhode Island Dept. of Health
3 Capitol Hill
Providence, RI 02908
Phone: (401)277-1417

Credential Type: Lead Hazard Abatement Site Supervisor. **Requirements:** Submit application. Contact licensing agency for additional requirements. **Examination:** Written and practical examinations.

8689

Lead Hazard Abatement Worker [Rhode Island]
Office of Environmental Health Risk Assessment
Rhode Island Dept. of Health
3 Capitol Hill
Providence, RI 02908
Phone: (401)277-1417

Credential Type: Lead Hazard Abatement Worker. **Requirements:** Submit application. Contact licensing agency for additional requirements. **Examination:** Written and practical examinations.

8690

Lifeguard [Rhode Island]
Div. of Parks and Recreation
Rhode Island Dept. of Environmental Management
2321 Hartford Ave.
Johnston, RI 02919
Phone: (401)277-2632

Credential Type: Lifeguard License—I Surf. **Duration of License:** One year. **Authorization:** Authorized to lifeguard in beach areas with surf conditions. **Requirements:** At least 16 years of age. Must successfully complete the following: (1) 27-hour-course in lifeguard skills; (2) 6-hour course in cardiopulmonary resuscitation; (3) 8-hour course in first aid. State employment requires physical examination. **Examination:** Practical examination. Proficiency test in surf conditions. **Reciprocity:** No. **Fees:** $10 license fee. $10 renewal fee.

Credential Type: Lifeguard License—II Non-Surf. **Duration of License:** One year. **Authorization:** Authorized to lifeguard in beach areas without surf conditions. **Requirements:** At least 16 years of age. Must successfully complete the following: (1) 27-hour-course in lifeguard skills; (2) 6-hour course in cardiopulmonary resuscitation; (3) 8-hour course in first aid. State employment requires physical examination. **Examination:** Practical examination. Proficiency test under non-surf conditions. **Reciprocity:** No. **Fees:** $10 license fee. $10 renewal fee.

Credential Type: Lifeguard License—III Pool. **Duration of License:** One year. **Authorization:** Authorized to lifeguard in pools only. **Requirements:** At least 16 years of age. Must successfully complete the following: (1) 27-hour-course in lifeguard skills; (2) 6-hour course in cardiopulmonary resuscitation; (3) 8-hour course in first aid. State employment requires physical examination. **Examination:** Practical examination. **Reciprocity:** No. **Fees:** $10 license fee. $10 renewal fee.

8691

Liquefied Petroleum Gas Appliance Servicer [Arkansas]
The Liquefied Petroleum Gas Board
1421 W. Sixth St.
Little Rock, AR 72201
Phone: (501)371-1008

Credential Type: License. **Duration of License:** One year. **Requirements:** Proof of training of no less than 30 days. Employed by a dealer who has been authorized to engage in the liquefied petroleum gas business in the state. **Examination:** Yes. **Fees:** $5 License. $5 Renewal.

8692

Liquefied Petroleum Gas Safety Supervisor [Arkansas]
The Liquefied Petroleum Gas Board
1421 W. Sixth St.
Little Rock, AR 72201
Phone: (501)371-1008

Credential Type: License. **Duration of License:** One year. **Requirements:** Employed by a class one permit holder. Have thorough knowledge of liquefied petroleum gases and the National Fire Protection Association Pamphlet 58 and the State Liquefied Petroleum Gas Code. **Examination:** Yes. **Fees:** $5 License. $5 Renewal.

8693

Live Bait Seller [Rhode Island]
Office of Boat Registration and Licensing
Rhode Island Dept. of Environmental Management
22 Hayes St.
Providence, RI 02908
Phone: (401)277-3576

Credential Type: Live Bait Seller License. **Duration of License:** One year. **Authorization:** Authorizes licensee to sell minnows to individuals for use as fish bait. **Requirements:** Submit application and pay fee. **Reciprocity:** No. **Fees:** $25 license fee.

8694

Lobster Seller [Rhode Island]
Office of Boat Registration and Licensing
Rhode Island Dept. of Environmental Management
22 Hayes St., Rm. 120
Providence, RI 02908
Phone: (401)277-3576

Credential Type: Lobster Seller License. **Duration of License:** One year. **Requirements:** Submit application and pay fee. **Reciprocity:** No. **Fees:** $200 license fee.

8695

Locksmith [California]
Bureau of Collection and Investigative Services
400 R St., Ste. 2001
Sacramento, CA 95814-6234
Phone: (916)445-7366

Credential Type: Locksmith Permit. **Duration of License:** Two years. **Requirements:** Be at least 18 years of age. Must not have been convicted of a crime constituting grounds for denial. **Fees:** $55 application and permit fee. $42 renewal fee. $27 fingerprint fee. **Governing Statute:** Business and Professions Code, Sect. 6980.

8696

Manager, Milk Gathering Plant [New York]
Dept. of Agriculture and Markets
Div. of Milk Control
One Winners Circle
Albany, NY 12235
Phone: (518)457-1772

Credential Type: License. **Duration of License:** Five years. **Examination:** Writ-

Manager, Milk Gathering Plant [New York], continued

ten and practical. **Fees:** $5 application fee. $2 renewal fee. **Governing Statute:** Article four Section 56b, 57, and 57a of Agriculture and Markets Law, and Title 1, New York Consolidated Rules and Regulations, Part 6.

8697

Massage Therapy Instructor [New Mexico]
Massage Therapy Board
Dept. of Regulation and Licensing
PO Box 25101
Santa Fe, NM 87504
Phone: (505)827-7113

Credential Type: Massage Therapy Instructor Registration. **Requirements:** Must be a licensed massage therapist in New Mexico. Complete at least two years experience in massage therapy. **Fees:** $10 registration fee. **Governing Statute:** 61-12C-1 et seq. NMSA 1978. New Mexico Board of Massage Therapy Rules, Rule 92-1 et seq.

8698

Master Therapeutic Recreation Specialist [Georgia]
State Board of Recreation Examiners
Allied Health Fields Section
Professional Examining Boards
166 Pryor St., SW
Atlanta, GA 30303
Phone: (404)656-3921

Credential Type: Master Therapeutic Recreation Specialist License. **Duration of License:** Two years. **Authorization:** May supervise and administer the practice of therapeutic recreation. **Requirements:** Meet one of the following criteria: (1) Have both a master's degree and a baccalaureate degree in therapeutic recreation from an accredited college or university. Have two years full-time experience in therapeutic recreation. (2) Have a master's degree in therapeutic recreation and a baccalaureate degree in recreation from an accredited college or university. Have three years full-time experience in therapeutic recreation. (3) Have a master's degree in recreation and a baccalaureate degree in therapeutic recreation from an accredited college or university. Have four years full-time experience in therapeutic recreation. (4) Have a master's degree in therapeutic recreation and a baccalaureate degree in a related field from an accredited college or university. Have five years full-time experience in therapeutic recreation. (5) Have a master's degree in a related field and a baccalaureate degree in therapeutic recreation from an accredited college or university. Have six years full-time experience in therapeutic recreation. (6) Have a master's degree in therapeutic recreation and a baccalaureate degree in a non-related field from an accredited college or university. Have seven years full-time experience in therapeutic recreation. (7) Have a baccalaureate degree in therapeutic recreation from an accredited college or university. Have seven years full-time experience in therapeutic recreation. Have 20 quarter hours or 12 semester hours of graduate work in approved therapeutic recreation topics. **Examination:** Master Therapeutic Recreation Specialist License Examination. **Reciprocity:** No. **Fees:** $20 application fee. $40 exam fee. $100 renewal fee. **Governing Statute:** Official Code of Georgia Annotated 43-41.

8699

Medical Training Student (Postgraduate) [Michigan]
Board of Medicine
Bureau of Occupational & Professional Regulation
Dept. of Commerce
PO Box 30192
Lansing, MI 48909
Phone: (517)373-9153

Credential Type: Educational Limited License. **Duration of License:** One year for a maximum of five years. **Authorization:** A person engaging in post-graduate medical training in an approved hospital or institution must obtain an educational limited license from the Board of Medicine of the Department of Commerce. **Requirements:** At least 18 years of age. Be of good moral character. Completed a minimum of 60 semester hours of general study in an accredited college or university. Completed the requirements for a degree in medicine as defined by the Board's rules. Working knowledge of the English language. Comply with the rules and regulations of the Board. **Examination:** Exam. **Fees:** $80 initial license fee. $30 renewal fee. **Governing Statute:** Public Health Code, Act 368 of 1978, as amended.

8700

M.I.S. Manager/Technical Supports Systems Operator (Gaming) [Illinois]
Illinois Gaming Board
PO Box 19474
Springfield, IL 62794-9474
Phone: (217)524-0228

Credential Type: M.I.S. Manager License. **Duration of License:** One year. **Requirements:** At least 18 years of age. No felony convictions. High school graduate or equivalent. Computer experience. **Reciprocity:** No. **Fees:** $75 application/initial license fee. $50 renewal fee. **Governing Statute:** Illinois Revised Statutes, Chapter 120.

8701

Motor Vehicle Dismantler [Georgia]
State Board of Registration for Used Motor Vehicle Dismantlers, Rebuilders, and Salvage Dealers
Businesses and Occupations Section
Professional Examining Boards
166 Pryor St., SW
Atlanta, GA 30303
Phone: (404)656-3900

Credential Type: Motor Vehicle Dismantler License. **Requirements:** Submit application and pay fees. Post a $10,000 surety bond and have liability insurance in the amount of $50/100/25 or single limits of $125,000. Must have a state sales tax number and fixed place of business. **Fees:** $175 application fee.

8702

Music Therapist (School) [Louisiana]
Louisiana State Dept. of Education
PO Box 94064
Baton Rouge, LA 70804
Phone: (504)342-3490

Credential Type: License. **Requirements:** Completion of an accredited Music Therapy degree program. Applicant must be registered by the National Association of Music Therapy.

8703

Nuisance Wildlife Control Operator [Illinois]
Illinois Dept. of Conservation
524 South 2nd St.
Springfield, IL 62706
Phone: (217)785-6834

Credential Type: License Permit. **Duration of License:** One year. **Requirements:** At least 18 years of age. Submit application. **Examination:** Written examination. **Reciprocity:** No. **Fees:** No fee. **Governing Statute:** Illinois Revised Statutes, Chapter 61, Illinois Administrative Code, Part 525.

8704

Nursing Home Activity Director [Iowa]
Div. of Health Facilities
Dept. of Inspection and Appeals
Lucas State Office Bldg., 3rd Fl.
Des Moines, IA 50319
Phone: (515)281-4233

Credential Type: Certificate. **Requirements:** 16 years of age and completion of a 42-hour workshop. **Examination:** Written. **Fees:** $100 workshop fee.

8705

Oil and Gas Wellhead Welder [North Dakota]
Oil and Gas Div.
Industrial Commission
600 E. Blvd.
Bismarck, ND 58505
Phone: (701)224-3722

Credential Type: Certification. **Duration of License:** Three years. **Authorization:** No person may weld on an oil and gas wellhead unless certified. **Requirements:** Pass performance test. **Examination:** Performance test of the American Society of Mechanical Engineers, Section 9, Position 6-G. **Fees:** $25 certification fee. **Governing Statute:** North Dakota Century Code, Chap. 38-08-22.

8706

Optician Technician [New Jersey]
Board of Examiners of Ophthalmic Dispensers and Ophthalmic Technicians
1100 Raymond Blvd., Rm. 501
Newark, NJ 07102
Phone: (201)648-2840

Credential Type: License. **Duration of License:** Two years. **Requirements:** 16 years of age. Must serve 12 months as an apprentice technician. **Examination:** Written. **Fees:** $75 exam fee. $50 license fee. $130 renewal fee. $50 apprentice permit. **Governing Statute:** NJSA 52:17B-41. NJAC 13:33.

8707

Orthopist [New Jersey]
State Orthoptic Commission
28 W. State St.
Trenton, NJ 08608
Phone: (609)292-4843

Credential Type: License. **Duration of License:** Two years. **Requirements:** High school diploma or equivalent. Completion of two years of college at an approved school. Completion of a course of orthoptics at an approved college or institution. Six months of clinical training in a hospital or optometric or medical institution. 21 years of age. Good moral character. **Fees:** $25 license fee. $20 biennial registration fee. **Governing Statute:** NJSA 45:12A. NJAC 13:35.

8708

Out-Of-State Salvage Vehicle Buyer [Illinois]
Secretary of State
Centennial Building, Rm. 008
Springfield, IL 62756
Phone: (217)782-7817

Credential Type: Registration. **Duration of License:** One year. **Requirements:** Submit application and pay fee. **Reciprocity:** Yes, if applicant has a valid salvage license from his/her home state. **Fees:** $5 ID card fee. $100 initial license fee. $100 renewal fee. **Governing Statute:** Illinois Vehicle Code 95 1/2 5-302.

8709

Painter [Alaska]
Alaska Dept. of Labor
Labor Standards and Safety Div.
Occupational Health and Safety
PO Box 107022
Anchorage, AK 99510
Phone: (907)264-2599

Credential Type: License. **Duration of License:** Three years. **Authorization:** All people working with hazardous paints (excluding waterbased latex paints) on a commercial basis must be licensed, effective May 15, 1989. **Requirements:** Complete a 16-hour course offered by a state approved training vendor. **Examination:** Written exam given by approved training vendor. **Fees:** $100 certification fee. $100 renewal fee.

8710

Painter/Paperhanger [Nevada]
Nevada State Contractors Board
70 Linden St.
Reno, NV 89502
Phone: (702)688-1141

Credential Type: License. **Requirements:** Four years of skilled experience in the field. Financial responsibility and good character. **Examination:** Yes. **Fees:** $270 application fee. $120 license fee. $120 renewal fee. $40 exam fee.

8711

Parole/Probation Officer, State [Michigan]
Corrections Commission
Dept. of Corrections
Grandview Plaza Bldg.
PO Box 30003
Lansing, MI 48909
Phone: (517)335-1426

Credential Type: Certification. **Duration of License:** Valid until employment is terminated from the Department of Corrections. **Authorization:** All persons employed as a State Parole/Probation Officer must be certified by the Corrections Commission of the Michigan Department of Corrections. **Requirements:** At least a bachelor's degree in criminal justice, correctional administration, criminology, psychology, social work, counseling and guidance, or other related discipline approved by the Department. Be of good moral character. Reside in the county or a contiguous county of the worksite county. Provide employment and/or personal references. Submit to a background investigation. Pass an oral interview. Complete six months of satisfactory employment. **Examination:** Michigan civil service examination for the entry-level Parole/Probation Officer (College Trainee IV). **Fees:** No fees. **Governing Statute:** Public Act 232 of 1953, as amended.

8712

Pasteurizer Operator [Oregon]
Oregon Dept. of Agriculture
635 Capitol NE
Salem, OR 97310
Phone: (503)378-3790

Credential Type: License. **Duration of License:** Two years. **Requirements:** 18 years of age. Must be free of communicable

Pasteurizer Operator [Oregon], continued

diseases. Must have six months experience helping to operate pasteurization equipment or to grade milk and cream. **Examination:** Yes. **Fees:** $50 exam fee. $50 license fee. $50 renewal fee. **Governing Statute:** ORS 621.005 to 621.990.

8713

Pastoral Counselor [New Hampshire]
Board of Examiners of Psychologists
PO Box 457, 105 Pleasant St.
Concord, NH 03301
Phone: (603)226-2599

Credential Type: Pastoral Counselor Certificate. **Duration of License:** One year. **Requirements:** Complete college undergraduate degree. Hold a graduate degree from an accredited theological school. Hold a Doctoral degree in pastoral counseling. Complete at least 12 weeks of full-time clinical pastoral education in an accredited clinical center. Must have 125 hours of counseling experience that has been supervised by at least two different supervisors. Oral interview required with the certifying committee to evaluate clinical competence. Renewal requires 20 hours of continuing education annually. **Reciprocity:** Yes, provided the applicant's state has standards equal to or higher than those of New Hampshire. **Fees:** $100 initial license/application fee. $60 annual renewal fee.

8714

Pastoral Counselor [Maine]
Board of Counseling Professionals Licensure
Dept. of Professional and Financial Regulation
Div. of Licensing and Enforcement
State House Station 35
Augusta, ME 04333
Phone: (207)582-8723

Credential Type: Licensed Pastoral Counselor. **Duration of License:** Two years. **Requirements:** Educational requirements include a Master of Divinity degree or its equivalent, with a core curriculum in the field of counseling and human relations, and clinical pastoral education consisting of a 400-contact-hour internship in a supervised ministry. In addition, two years of experience after receiving a degree are required, consisting of at least 1000 hours of direct clinical contact. Applicant must also complete 200 hours of supervision. **Examination:** One of the following: a board-approved examination, the National Counselors Examination (NCE), the Certified Clinical Mental Health Counselors Examination, the Examination in Marriage and Family Therapy, or the National Psychological Examination. **Fees:** $40 application fee. $200 license fee. $200 renewal fee. **Governing Statute:** 32 M.S.R.A. Chap. 119.

Credential Type: Conditional License. **Duration of License:** Two years. **Requirements:** Meet all requirements for licensure, except for supervised experience. **Governing Statute:** 32 M.S.R.A. Chap. 119.

Credential Type: Registered Pastoral Counselor. **Duration of License:** Two years. **Authorization:** Registration is required of individuals who are not licensed and who practice counseling. **Requirements:** Be at least 18 years of age. Good moral character. Adhere to Code of Ethics. Complete registration form and pay fee. **Fees:** $50 registration fee. $50 renewal fee. **Governing Statute:** 32 M.S.R.A. Chap. 119.

8715

Petroleum Device Technician [North Carolina]
Dept. of Agriculture
Standards Div., Measurement Section
1 W. Edenton St.
Raleigh, NC 27611
Phone: (919)733-3313

Credential Type: License. **Duration of License:** One year. **Requirements:** 18 years of age. Two letters of endorsement. One year of supervised experience with liquid fuel pumps, meters and other measuring devices.

8716

Pharmacy Preceptor [Washington]
Dept. of Health
Board of Pharmacy
1300 SE Quince, EY-20
Olympia, WA 98504
Phone: (206)753-6834

Credential Type: Certification. **Duration of License:** Five years. **Authorization:** Required to ensure that preceptors are qualified to instruct pharmacy interns. **Requirements:** Be at least 19 years of age. Must be a United States citizen or registered alien. Have a B.S. in pharmacy and one year of practice. Must be employed in a Class A pharmacy. Recertification requires 15 hours of continuing education per year. **Fees:** No fees.

8717

Pharmacy Technician [Washington]
Board of Pharmacy
Dept. of Health
1300 Quince St. SE
Mail Stop EY-20
Olympia, WA 98504
Phone: (206)753-6834

Credential Type: Pharmacy Technician License. **Requirements:** Submit application.

8718

Pharmacy Technician [Rhode Island]
Board of Pharmacy
3 Capitol Hill, Rm. 304
Providence, RI 02908
Phone: (401)277-2837

Credential Type: Pharmacy Technician License. **Requirements:** Submit application.

8719

Pharmacy Technician [Minnesota]
Board of Pharmacy
2700 University Ave. W., No. 107
St. Paul, MN 55114-1079
Phone: (612)642-0541

Credential Type: Pharmacy Technician License. **Requirements:** Submit application.

8720

Pharmacy Technician [Illinois]
Dept. of Professional Regulation
320 W. Washington St., 3rd Fl.
Springfield, IL 62786
Phone: (217)782-0556

Credential Type: Pharmacy Technician License. **Requirements:** Submit application.

8721

Photographer, Itinerant [Vermont]
Secretary of State Licensing and Registration
Pavilion Office Bldg.
Montpelier, VT 05602
Phone: (802)828-2363

Credential Type: License. **Duration of License:** One year. **Requirements:** Make

Appendix 1: Occupations Rarely Licensed

application to Secretary of State. Local licenses may be required. **Examination:** No. **Reciprocity:** No. **Fees:** $10 Annual fee. **Governing Statute:** Title 32, VSA Sections 9002-9008.

8722

Plans Examiner [Oregon]
Building Codes Agency
1535 Edgewater NW
Salem, OR 97310
Phone: (503)373-1268

Credential Type: License. **Requirements:** Combination of training and experience in building design and plans examination for building code compliance. At least one year of the required experience or education must have been within the last five years, or the applicant must have had relevant alternative experience or training during the past five years. **Examination:** Yes. **Fees:** $22 exam fee. **Governing Statute:** ORS 455.730 and Oregon Administrative Rule 814-03-025(A).

8723

Plans Examiner [Ohio]
Board of Building Standards
Dept. of Industrial Relations
2323 W. 5th Ave.
PO Box 825
Columbus, OH 43266-0567
Phone: (614)644-2613

Credential Type: Class II Plans Examiner Certification. **Duration of License:** Three years. **Requirements:** Hold an Ohio Registration as an architect or engineer. Have five years of experience in building design and construction or building inspection with a certified building department. (Experience related to 1, 2, or 3-family structures does not count.) **Fees:** $30 certification fee.

Credential Type: Class II Trainee Certification. **Duration of License:** Three years. **Authorization:** Must work under the direct supervision of a Class II certified individual. **Requirements:** Be a graduate architect or engineer from an accredited university. **Fees:** $30 certification fee.

8724

Plasterer/Drywall Installer [Nevada]
Nevada State Contractors Board
70 Linden St.
Reno, NV 89502
Phone: (702)688-1141

Credential Type: License. **Requirements:** Four years of skilled experience in the field. Financial responsibility and good character. **Examination:** Yes. **Fees:** $270 application fee. $120 license fee. $120 renewal fee. $40 exam fee.

8725

Porter (Riverboat Gambling) [Iowa]
Iowa Racing and Gaming Commission
Lucas State Office Bldg.
Des Moines, IA 50319
Phone: (515)281-7352

Credential Type: License Registration. **Requirements:** Submit application and pay fees. **Fees:** $10 license fee.

8726

Porter (Thoroughbred and Quarter Horse Racing) [Ohio]
Ohio State Racing Commission
State Office Tower
77 S. High St., 18th Fl.
Columbus, OH 43266-0416
Phone: (614)466-2757

Credential Type: License Registration. **Requirements:** Submit application and fingerprint card. Pay fee. **Fees:** $10 registration fee.

8727

Post-Mortem Examiner [Maryland]
Post-Mortem Examiners
Dept. of Health and Mental Hygiene
4201 Patterson Ave.
Baltimore, MD 21215
Phone: (410)328-3313

Credential Type: License. **Requirements:** Contact licensing body for application information.

8728

Powder-Actuated Tool Operator [Washington]
Dept. of Labor & Industries
Div. of Industrial Safety & Health
General Administration Bldg., HC-101
Olympia, WA 98504
Phone: (206)753-6381

Credential Type: Powder-Actuated Tool Operator License. **Duration of License:** Three years. **Requirements:** At least 18 years of age. Receive training from a qualified instructor. Must be able to read and understand the manufacturer's instruction manual. Must be able to distinguish colors. Permit card required and must be carried at all times while on the job. **Examination:** Written and practical examination. **Fees:** No fee.

8729

Pre-Need Contract Agent [Utah]
Dept. of Commerce
Div. of Occupational and Professional Licensing
160 E. 300 S.
PO Box 45802
Salt Lake City, UT 84145
Phone: (801)530-6628

Credential Type: License. **Duration of License:** One year. **Authorization:** To accept funds for pre-arranged funeral plans. **Requirements:** Submit application and pay fee. **Fees:** $40 license fee. $25 renewal fee.

8730

Precision Tank Tester [Vermont]
Agency of Natural Resources
Dept. of Environmental Conservation
103 S. Main St.
Waterbury, VT 05676
Phone: (802)244-8702

Credential Type: License. **Requirements:** Submit proof of training on each piece of equipment; certificates issued only for equipment trained on. **Examination:** No. **Reciprocity:** No. **Fees:** $50 (not to exceed) Annually. Fee subject to change. **Governing Statute:** Title 10, VSA Chapter 10, Section 1936.

8731

Preserve Area Operator [Illinois]
Illinois Dept. of Conservation
524 South 2nd St.
Springfield, IL 62701-1787
Phone: (217)785-3423

Credential Type: Preserve Area Operator License. **Duration of License:** One year. **Authorization:** Allows applicant to operate a preserve for breeding and hunting of game birds. **Requirements:** Must be an Illinois resident for at least 30 days. Submit application and pay fee. **Reciprocity:** No. **Fees:** $100 initial license fee. $100 renewal fee. **Governing Statute:** Illinois Revised Statutes, Chapter 61, Illinois Conservation Law—Wildlife.

8732

Property Valuation Administrator [Kentucky]
Kentucky Revenue Cabinet
Dept. of Property Taxation
592 E. Main St.
Frankfort, KY 40620
Phone: (502)564-6730

Credential Type: License. **Requirements:** 24 years of age. Citizen of Kentucky for two years and one year in the county and district in which he/she is a candidate preceding the election. Continuing education required.

8733

Prosthetist [Rhode Island]
Div. of Professional Regulation
Rhode Island Dept. of Health
3 Capitol Hill
Providence, RI 02908
Phone: (401)277-2827

Credential Type: Prosthetist License. **Duration of License:** One year. **Requirements:** Good moral character. Foreign born must show proof of legal entry into U.S. Bachelor's degree in orthotics and/or prosthetics from a program accredited by the American Board for Certification in Orthotics and Prosthetics (ABC). One year (1,900 hours) of experience in the field. **Examination:** American Board for Certification in Orthotics and Prosthetics (ABC) written and clinical examination. **Reciprocity:** No. **Fees:** $100 application fee. $25 renewal fee.

8734

Purchasing Manager/Agent (Gaming) [Illinois]
Illinois Gaming Board
PO Box 19474
Springfield, IL 62794-9474
Phone: (217)524-0228

Credential Type: Purchasing Manager/Agent License. **Duration of License:** One year. **Requirements:** At least 21 years of age. High school graduate or equivalent. No felony convictions. One year experience in purchasing. **Reciprocity:** No. **Fees:** $75 application/initial license fee. $50 renewal fee. **Governing Statute:** Illinois Revised Statutes, Chapter 120.

8735

Pyrotechnic Operator [Washington]
Dept. of Community Development
Fire Protection Services Division
Ninth and Columbia Bldg., GH-51
Olympia, WA 98504-4151
Phone: (206)493-2660

Credential Type: Pyrotechnic Operator License. **Duration of License:** One year. **Requirements:** At least 18 years of age. Submit to background investigation and inspection of work performed. Must have training and verified experience in pyrotechnics. Continuing education is required to keep abreast of new pyrotechnic techniques. **Examination:** Written examination. **Fees:** $10 license fee.

8736

Pyrotechnic Operator [Rhode Island]
State Fire Marshal's Office
Rhode Island Div. of Fire Safety
1270 Mineral Spring Ave.
North Providence, RI 02904
Phone: (401)277-2335

Credential Type: Pyrotechnic Operator License. **Duration of License:** One year. **Requirements:** At least 18 years of age. Have a licensed pyrotechnic operator sponsor. At least three years of training with a licensed operator. Pass psychiatric examination. Pass screening by the State Police Bureau of Criminal Identification. Must carry liability insurance in the amount required by local authority. **Examination:** Written examination. **Reciprocity:** No. **Fees:** $10 examination fee. $10 license fee.

8737

Railroad Police Officer [Michigan]
Private Security and Investigation Section
Dept. of State Police
General Office Bldg.
7150 Harris Dr.
Lansing, MI 48913
Phone: (517)332-2521

Credential Type: Commission. **Duration of License:** Lifelong. **Requirements:** At least 18 years of age. Be a United States citizen. Complete at least 200 hours of police training offered by the Michigan Law Enforcement Officers Training Council. High school education or its equivalent. Be examined by a licensed physician and meet specific physical standards. Be of good moral character and have no prior felony conviction. Submit a photograph and three letters of character reference. Pass fingerprint check and background investigation. File a $1,000 surety bond with the county clerk where the oath of office was taken. **Examination:** Exam. **Fees:** $2 commission fee. **Governing Statute:** Railroad Police Act, Act 114 of 1941, as amended.

8738

Real Estate Auctioneer [South Dakota]
South Dakota Real Estate Commission
PO Box 490
Pierre, SD 57501-0490
Phone: (605)773-3600
Phone: (605)773-3150

Credential Type: Real Estate Auctioneer License. **Duration of License:** Two years. **Requirements:** Submit application and pay fees. **Examination:** State-administered auctioneer's examination. **Exemptions:** Real estate brokers do not need an auctioneer's license. **Fees:** $100 application and license fee. $80 renewal fee.

8739

Real Estate Auctioneer [Pennsylvania]
Real Estate Commission
Transportation and Safety Bldg., Rm. 611
PO Box 2649
Harrisburg, PA 17105-2649
Phone: (717)783-3658

Credential Type: Real Estate Auctioneer License. **Requirements:** Contact licensing body for application information.

8740

Rebuilder of Salvage Vehicles [Illinois]
Secretary of State
Centennial Bldg., Rm. 008
Springfield, IL 62756
Phone: (217)782-7817

Credential Type: Rebuilder License. **Duration of License:** One year. **Authorization:** Allows holder to restore vehicles for which a salvage certificate has been issued. **Requirements:** Submit application and pay fees. Requires ID card. **Reciprocity:** No. **Fees:** $50 initial license fee. $50 renewal fee. $2 ID card fee. **Governing Statute:** Illinois Vehicle Code 95 1/2 5-301.

8741

Recreation Administrator [Georgia]
State Board of Recreation Examiners
Allied Health Fields Section
Professional Examining Boards
166 Pryor St., SW
Atlanta, GA 30303
Phone: (404)656-3921

Credential Type: Recreation Administrator License. **Duration of License:** Two years. **Authorization:** A recreation administrator is the executive head or management level position administering a permanent full-time recreation or park program. **Requirements:** Meet one of the following criteria: (1) Have a baccalaureate degree in recreation from an accredited college or university. Have 12 months full-time recreation experience. (2) Have a baccalaureate degree in a related field from an accredited college or university. Have 24 months full-time recreation experience. (3) Have a baccalaureate degree from an accredited college or university. Have 36 months full-time recreation experience. (4) Have 10 or more years full-time recreation or park specialty experience in an administrative or management capacity normally requiring the possession of a baccalaureate degree. **Examination:** Recreation Administrator License Examination. **Reciprocity:** No. **Fees:** $20 application fee. $40 exam fee. $100 renewal fee. **Governing Statute:** Official Code of Georgia Annotated 43-41.

8742

Recreation Leader [Georgia]
State Board of Recreation Examiners
Allied Health Fields Section
Professional Examining Boards
166 Pryor St., SW
Atlanta, GA 30303
Phone: (404)656-3921

Credential Type: Recreation Leader License. **Duration of License:** Two years. **Authorization:** A recreation leader implements recreation activities under the supervision of a recreation administrator or supervisor. **Requirements:** Meet one of the following criteria: (1) Have an associate degree in recreation. (2) Have 90 quarter hours or 60 semester hours from an accredited college or university. Either 12 months part-time recreation experience or six months full-time recreation experience. (3) High school diploma or equivalency certificate. Either 24 months part-time recreation experience or 12 months full-time recreation experience. **Examination:** Recreation Leader License Examination. **Reciprocity:** No. **Fees:** $20 application fee. $40 exam fee. $50 renewal fee. **Governing Statute:** Official Code of Georgia Annotated 43-41.

8743

Recreation Supervisor [Georgia]
State Board of Recreation Examiners
Allied Health Fields Section
Professional Examining Boards
166 Pryor St., SW
Atlanta, GA 30303
Phone: (404)656-3921

Credential Type: Recreation Supervisor License. **Duration of License:** Two years. **Authorization:** A recreation supervisor is responsible for the planning, organizing, and supervising of a part of a program administered by a recreation administrator. **Requirements:** Meet one of the following criteria: (1) Have a baccalaureate degree in recreation from an accredited college or university. (2) Have a baccalaureate degree in a related field from an accredited college or university. Have 12 months full-time recreation experience. (3) Have a baccalaureate degree from an accredited college or university. Have 24 months full-time recreation experience. (4) Have four years full-time recreation or park specialty experience in an administrative or management capacity normally requiring the possession of a baccalaureate degree. (5) Be enrolled in an accredited university or college and expect to graduate within six months and otherwise satisfy the board's requirements. Examination results will then be released upon graduation. **Examination:** Recreation Supervisor License Examination. **Reciprocity:** No. **Fees:** $20 application fee. $40 exam fee. $75 renewal fee. **Governing Statute:** Official Code of Georgia Annotated 43-41.

8744

Recreation Therapist [District of Columbia]
License and Certification Div.
Occupational and Professional
  Licensure Administration
Consumer and Regulatory Affairs
  Dept.
PO Box 37200
Washington, DC 20013-7200
Phone: (202)727-7823
Phone: (202)727-7480

Credential Type: License. **Requirements:** Contact licensing body for application information.

8745

Recreational Therapist [Utah]
Dept. of Commerce
Div. of Occupational and
  Professional Licensing
160 E. 300 S.
PO Box 45802
Salt Lake City, UT 84145
Phone: (801)530-6628

Credential Type: Technician's License. **Duration of License:** Two years. **Requirements:** Must be a high school graduate. Must have two years full-time paid experience in the therapeutic recreation field, or 200 clock hours in service training in therapeutics, or an approved combination of the two. **Examination:** Yes. **Fees:** $60 license fee. $30 renewal fee.

Credential Type: Specialist's License. **Duration of License:** Two years. **Requirements:** Must have a bachelor's degree from an accredited college with an emphasis in therapeutic recreation; or a major in recreation with one year of experience in the therapeutic recreation field; or a major in a related field and two years of experience in the therapeutic recreation field; or have a master's degree from an accredited college. **Fees:** $30 license fee. $25 renewal fee.

8746

Regulated Shooting Area Operator [Maryland]
Wildlife Div.
Dept. of Natural Resources
Tawes State Office Bldg.
Annapolis, MD 21401
Phone: (410)974-3195

Credential Type: Commercial License. **Duration of License:** One year. **Requirements:** Must include aerial photo and tax map with application. Area must include a minimum of 200 acres for upland game birds and 50 acres for "flighted" mallard ducks. **Fees:** $100 license fee.

Credential Type: Non-commercial License. **Duration of License:** One year. **Requirements:** Must include aerial photo and tax map with application. Area must include a minimum of 200 acres for upland game birds and 50 acres for "flighted" mallard ducks. **Fees:** $100 license fee.

8747

Repossession Company Operator [California]
Bureau of Collection and Investigative Services
400 R St., Ste. 2001
Sacramento, CA 95814-6234
Phone: (916)445-7366

Credential Type: Repossession Company Operator License. **Requirements:** At least one year or 2000 hours of compensated experience as an employee of a licensed repossession agency in California during the past five years, or in recovering personal property sold under a security agreement in California. **Examination:** Written examination. **Fees:** $750 license application fee. $27 fingerprint processing fee.

Credential Type: Qualified Manager Certificate. **Authorization:** Required of the person who is in active charge of the business. **Requirements:** Be at least 18 years of age. At least one year or 2000 hours of compensated experience as an employee of a licensed repossession agency in California during the past five years, or in recovering personal property sold under a security agreement in California. **Examination:** Written examination. **Fees:** $250 application and qualification certificate fee. $27 fingerprint processing fee.

8748

Repossessor [Nevada]
Office of the Attorney General
Private Investigator's Licensing Board
198 S. Carson St.
Carson City, NV 89710
Phone: (702)687-5534

Credential Type: License. **Duration of License:** One year. **Requirements:** Five years of applicable experience. $200,000 of liability insurance. **Examination:** Yes. **Fees:** $16.50 application fee. $100 exam fee. $50 abeyance fee. $360 license fee. $360 renewal fee. $750 investigation deposit.

8749

Reptile/Amphibian Catcher, Commercial [Michigan]
Fisheries Div.
Dept. of Natural Resources
Stevens T. Mason Bldg.
PO Box 30028
Lansing, MI 48909
Phone: (517)373-1220

Credential Type: License. **Duration of License:** One year. **Requirements:** Must provide a record of their catch by species on a monthly basis to the Department. **Fees:** $150 initial license fee. $150 renewal fee. **Governing Statute:** Michigan Sports Fishing Law, Act 165 of 1929, as amended.

8750

Research Animal Dealer [Michigan]
Animal Industry Div.
Dept. of Agriculture
Ottawa Bldg., N.
PO Box 30017
Lansing, MI 48909
Phone: (517)373-1104

Credential Type: License. **Duration of License:** Lifelong. **Requirements:** Be of good moral character. Never have been convicted of cruelty to animals or a violation of this Act. Pass an inspection of premises. Conduct business in a permanent structure or building. Abide by the rules put into effect by the Department of Agriculture. **Fees:** $25 initial license fee. **Governing Statute:** Animals for Research Act, Act 224 of 1969.

8751

Retail Florist [Louisiana]
Horticulture Commission
PO Box 3118
Baton Rouge, LA 70821
Phone: (504)925-7772

Credential Type: License. **Duration of License:** One year. **Examination:** Written and practical. **Fees:** $100 exam fee. $35 license fee. $35 renewal fee.

8752

Riding Instructor [Massachusetts]
Div. of Animal Health
Dept. of Food and Agriculture
100 Cambridge St., 21st Fl.
Boston, MA 02202
Phone: (617)727-3018

Credential Type: License. **Duration of License:** One year. **Requirements:** Demonstrate appropriate experience. **Examination:** Written examination. **Fees:** $10 application fee. $15 license fee.

8753

Roofer [Nevada]
Nevada State Contractors Board
1800 Industrial Rd.
Las Vegas, NV 89158
Phone: (702)486-3500

Credential Type: License. **Requirements:** Four years of skilled experience in the field. Financial responsibility and good character. **Examination:** Yes. **Fees:** $270 application fee. $120 license fee. $120 renewal fee. $40 exam fee.

8754

Salvage Pool Operator [Georgia]
State Board of Registration for Used Motor Vehicle Dismantlers, Rebuilders, and Salvage Dealers
Businesses and Occupations Section
Professional Examining Boards
166 Pryor St., SW
Atlanta, GA 30303
Phone: (404)656-2282

Credential Type: License. **Requirements:** Contact licensing body for application information.

8755

Salvage Yard Dealer [Georgia]
State Board of Registration for Used Motor Vehicle Dismantlers, Rebuilders, and Salvage Dealers
Businesses and Occupations Section
Professional Examining Boards
166 Pryor St., SW
Atlanta, GA 30303
Phone: (404)656-2282

Credential Type: License. **Requirements:** Contact licensing body for application information.

8756

School Social Services and Attendance Investigator [West Virginia]
Dept. of Education
Office of Educational Personnel Development
1900 Washington St. E
Charleston, WV 25305
Phone: (800)982-2378

Credential Type: Certification. **Duration of License:** Three or five years. **Requirements:** U.S. citizen. 18 years old. Bachelors degree, completion of approved social science and attendance program. Never convicted of a felony. **Examination:** No. **Fees:** $5 Application (for three or five year Certificate). $5 Renewal (for permanent Certificate).

8757

Scientific Collector [Washington]
Dept. of Wildlife
600 N. Capitol Way, GJ-11
Olympia, WA 98504-0091
Phone: (206)753-5728

Credential Type: Scientific Collector License. **Duration of License:** Life of project. **Authorization:** Allows collection of wildlife for scientific purposes. **Requirements:** Must be a citizen representative of a museum or institution. Submit application and pay fee. **Fees:** $12 license fee.

8758

Scrap Processor [Illinois]
Secretary of State
Centennial Bldg., Rm. 008
Springfield, IL 62756
Phone: (217)782-7817

Credential Type: Scrap Processor License. **Duration of License:** One year. **Requirements:** Submit application and pay fee. ID card required. **Reciprocity:** No. **Fees:** $50 initial license fee. $50 renewal fee. $2 ID card fee. **Governing Statute:** Illinois Vehicle Code 95 1/2 5-301.

8759

Sheep Dealer [Iowa]
Dept. of Agriculture and Land Stewardship
Sheep Bureau
Wallace State Office Bldg.
Des Moines, IA 50319
Phone: (515)281-5736

Credential Type: License. **Duration of License:** One year. **Requirements:** An applicant must file an application with the Dept. of Agriculture. **Fees:** $5 license fee. $5 renewal fee.

8760

Shellfish Diver [Washington]
Dept. of Fisheries
115 General Administration Bldg., ACC
Olympia, WA 98504-0611
Phone: (206)753-6590

Credential Type: Shellfish Diver License. **Duration of License:** One year. **Authorization:** Allows harvesting of shellfish other than clams. **Requirements:** At least 16 years of age. Submit application and pay fee. **Fees:** $50 resident license fee. $100 non-resident license fee.

8761

Slot Mechanic (Gaming) [Illinois]
Illinois Gaming Board
PO Box 19474
Springfield, IL 62794-9474
Phone: (217)524-0228

Credential Type: Slot Mechanic License. **Duration of License:** One year. **Requirements:** At least 21 years of age. U.S. citizen or legal alien as specified by Federal employability requirement. No felony convictions. High school graduate or equivalent. Knowledge of electronics and computer functions. At least six months experience in casino slot operations or one year in microprocessing video machines. **Reciprocity:** No. **Fees:** $75 application/initial license fee. $50 renewal fee. **Governing Statute:** Illinois Revised Statutes, Chapter 120.

8762

Slot Technician (Gaming) [Illinois]
Illinois Gaming Board
PO Box 19474
Springfield, IL 62794-9474
Phone: (217)524-0228

Credential Type: Slot Technician License. **Duration of License:** One year. **Requirements:** At least 21 years of age. U.S. citizen or legal alien as specified by Federal employability requirement. No felony convictions. High school graduate or equivalent. Knowledge of electronics and computer functions. At least six months experience in casino slot department operations or one year microprocessing video machines. **Reciprocity:** No. **Fees:** $75 application/initial license fee. $50 renewal fee. **Governing Statute:** Illinois Revised Statutes, Chapter 120.

8763

Sous Chef (Gaming) [Illinois]
Illinois Gaming Board
PO Box 19474
Springfield, IL 62794-9474
Phone: (217)524-0228

Credential Type: Sous Chef License. **Duration of License:** One year. **Requirements:** At least 18 years of age. U.S. citizen and Illinois resident. No felony convictions. Three or more years experience as a Sous Chef in a gourmet restaurant. **Reciprocity:** No. **Fees:** $75 application and license fee. $50 renewal fee. **Governing Statute:** Illinois Revised Statutes, Chapter 120.

8764

Sportswriter (Racetrack) [Connecticut]
Connecticut Div. of Special Revenue
Russell Rd.
PO Box 11424
Newington, CT 06111-0424
Phone: (203)566-2756

Credential Type: License Registration. **Requirements:** Submit application and fingerprint card. Pay fee. **Fees:** $5 registration fee.

8765

Statistician (Racetrack) [Connecticut]
Connecticut Div. of Special Revenue
Russell Rd.
PO Box 11424
Newington, CT 06111-0424
Phone: (203)566-2756

Credential Type: License Registration. **Requirements:** Submit application and fingerprint card. Pay fee. **Fees:** $20 registration fee.

8766

Swimming Pool Operator [Nebraska]
Div. of Drinking Water and Enviromental Sanitation
301 Centennial Mall S.
PO Box 95007
Lincoln, NE 68509
Phone: (402)471-2541

Credential Type: Certificate. **Duration of License:** Four years. **Requirements:** Must attend a swimming pool operator's training clinic. **Examination:** Yes. **Fees:** $9 certification and examination fees.

8767

Swimming Pool Operator [Illinois]
Illinois Dept. of Public Health
525 W. Jefferson St.
Springfield, IL 62761
Phone: (217)782-5830

Credential Type: Swimming Pool Operator Certificate. **Duration of License:** Indefinite. **Requirements:** Knowledge of swimming pool and bathing beach code. Submit application. **Examination:** Written examination. **Reciprocity:** No. **Fees:** No fee.

8768

Tattoo Artist [Delaware]
Committee on Massage and Bodywork Practitioners
Dept. of Administrative Services
Div. of Professional Regulation
PO Box 1401
Dover, DE 19903
Phone: (302)739-4522

Credential Type: License. **Requirements:** Contact licensing body for application information.

8769

Tattoo Artist [Iowa]
Iowa Dept. of Public Health
Tattoo Permit Program
Lucas State Office Bldg.
Des Moines, IA 50319
Phone: (515)281-6762

Credential Type: License. **Duration of License:** One year. **Fees:** $60 application fee. $60 renewal fee. **Governing Statute:** Chapter 22 of the Code of Iowa.

8770

Tattoo Artist [Hawaii]
Hawaii State Dept. of Health, Sanitation Branch
591 Ala Moana Blvd.
Honolulu, HI 96813
Phone: (808)548-5397

Credential Type: License. **Duration of License:** One year. **Requirements:** Passing of a physical exam which includes a chest x-ray or TB skin test and a blood test for syphilis. **Examination:** Written. **Exemptions:** Licensed physicians are exempt. **Fees:** $75 exam fee. $7.50 renewal fee.

8771

Tattoo Artist [Rhode Island]
Div. of Professional Regulation
Rhode Island Dept. of Health
3 Capitol Hill
Providence, RI 02908
Phone: (401)277-2827

Credential Type: Tattoo Artist License. **Duration of License:** One year. **Requirements:** At least 18 years of age. Good moral character. Foreign born must show proof of legal entry into U.S. Ability to demonstrate antiseptic tattooing technique. **Examination:** Practical examination. **Reciprocity:** No. **Fees:** $50 license fee. $50 renewal fee.

8772

Tattooer (Horse Racing) [South Dakota]
South Dakota Racing Commission
c/o 500 East Capitol
Pierre, SD 57501
Phone: (605)773-6050

Credential Type: License Registration. **Requirements:** Submit application and fingerprint card. Pay fee. **Fees:** $10 registration fee.

8773

Tattooer (Racetrack) [Texas]
Texas Racing Commission
PO Box 12080
Austin, TX 78711
Phone: (512)794-8461

Credential Type: License Registration. **Requirements:** Submit application and fingerprint card. Pay fee. **Fees:** $75 registration fee.

8774

Tax Preparer [Oregon]
State Board of Tax Service Examiners
158 12th St. NE
Salem, OR 97310
Phone: (503)378-4034

Credential Type: License. **Duration of License:** One year. **Requirements:** 18 years of age. High school diploma or GED. Successful completion of a board-approved, 80-class-hour course on basic tax law. **Examination:** Yes. **Fees:** $40 exam fee. $45 license fee. $45 renewal fee. **Governing Statute:** ORS 673.605 to 673.990 and Oregon Administrative Rules, Chapter 800.

8775

Tax Professional—Appraiser [Texas]
Board of Tax Professional Examiners
Bldg. B, Ste. 140
4301 W. Bank Dr.
Austin, TX 78746
Phone: (512)329-7982

Credential Type: Registration. **Duration of License:** One year. **Requirements:** High school diploma or equivalent. Must be active in property tax field for which application is made. Texas resident. 18 years of age. **Fees:** $50 application fee. $35 registration fee. $35 renewal fee. **Governing Statute:** VACS 8885, 22 TAC 623.

Credential Type: Certification. **Duration of License:** One year. **Requirements:** Appraisers need five years of experience, must take eight specified courses and conduct on demonstration appraisal. **Examination:** Two examinations. **Fees:** $50 application fee. $35 registration fee. $35 renewal fee. **Governing Statute:** VACS 8885, 22 TAC 623.

8776

Tax Professional—Assessor-Collector [Texas]
Board of Tax Professional Examiners
Bldg. B, Ste. 140
4301 W. Bank Dr.
Austin, TX 78746
Phone: (512)329-7982

Credential Type: Registration. **Duration of License:** One year. **Requirements:** High school diploma or equivalent. Must be active in property tax field for which application is made. Texas resident. 18 years of age. **Fees:** $50 application fee. $35 registration fee. $35 renewal fee. **Governing Statute:** VACS 8885, 22 TAC 623.

Credential Type: Certification. **Duration of License:** One year. **Requirements:** Assessors need five years of experience and must take eight specified courses. Collectors need three years of experience and must take six specified courses. **Examination:** Two examinations. **Fees:** $50 application fee. $35 registration fee. $35 renewal fee. **Governing Statute:** VACS 8885, 22 TAC 623.

8777

Tax Professional—Collector [Texas]
Board of Tax Professional Examiners
Bldg. B, Ste. 140
4301 W. Bank Dr.
Austin, TX 78746
Phone: (512)329-7982

Credential Type: Registration. **Duration of License:** One year. **Requirements:** High school diploma or equivalent. Must be active in property tax field for which application is made. Texas resident. 18 years of age. **Fees:** $50 application fee. $35 registration fee. $35 renewal fee. **Governing Statute:** VACS 8885, 22 TAC 623.

Credential Type: Certification. **Duration of License:** One year. **Requirements:** Collectors need three years of experience and must take six specified courses. **Examination:** Yes. **Fees:** $50 application fee. $35 registration fee. $35 renewal fee. **Governing Statute:** VACS 8885, 22 TAC 623.

8778

Taxidermist [Idaho]
License Office
Administration Bureau
Fish and Game Dept.
PO Box 25
600 S. Walnut
Boise, ID 83707
Phone: (208)334-3717

Credential Type: License. **Requirements:** Contact licensing body for application information.

8779

Therapeutic Recreation Specialist [Georgia]
State Board of Recreation Examiners
Allied Health Fields Section
Professional Examining Boards
166 Pryor St., SW
Atlanta, GA 30303
Phone: (404)656-3921

Credential Type: Therapeutic Recreation Specialist License. **Duration of License:** Two years. **Authorization:** May supervise and implement the practice of therapeutic recreation. **Requirements:** Meet one of the following criteria: (1) Have either a master's degree and a baccalaureate degree with a major in therapeutic recreation or a major in recreation with an emphasis in therapeutic recreation from an accredited college or university. (2) Have a baccalaureate degree with a major in recreation from an accredited college or university. Have either one year of professionally supervised work experience in therapeutic recreation and five quarter hours or three semester hours in therapeutic recreation content courses, or six months professionally supervised work experience in therapeutic recreation and 10 quarter hours or six semester hours in therapeutic recreation content courses. (3) Be enrolled in an accredited university or college and expect to graduate within six months and otherwise satisfy the board's requirements. Examination results will then be released upon graduation. **Examination:** Therapeutic Recreation Specialist License Examination. **Reciprocity:** No. **Fees:** $20 application fee. $40 exam fee. $75 renewal fee. **Governing Statute:** Official Code of Georgia Annotated 43-41.

8780

Therapeutic Recreation Technician [Georgia]
State Board of Recreation Examiners
Allied Health Fields Section
Professional Examining Boards
166 Pryor St., SW
Atlanta, GA 30303
Phone: (404)656-3921

Credential Type: Therapeutic Recreation Technician License. **Duration of License:** Two years. **Authorization:** Licensee must work under the supervision of a therapeutic recreation specialist or master therapeutic recreation specialist. **Requirements:** Meet one of the following criteria: (1) Baccalaureate degree in recreation from an accredited college or university. (2) Baccalaureate degree in a related field from an accredited college or university. Either six months of supervised work experience in therapeutic recreation, or five quarter hours or three semester hours in approved therapeutic recreation topics. (3) Associate degree in therapeutic recreation from an accredited college or university. (4) Associate degree in recreation from an accredited college or university. Either six months of supervised work experience in therapeutic recreation, or five quarter hours or three semester hours in approved therapeutic recreation topics. (5) Associate degree in a related field. Either one year of supervised work experience in therapeutic recreation, or 10 quarter hours or six semester hours in approved therapeutic recreation topics. (6) High school diploma or equivalency certificate. One year of supervised work experience in therapeutic recreation. Five continuing professional development units in approved therapeutic recreation topics. **Examination:** Therapeutic Recreation Technician License Examination. **Reciprocity:** No. **Fees:** $20 application fee. $40 exam fee. $50 renewal fee. **Governing Statute:** Official Code of Georgia Annotated 43-41.

8781

Timber Buyer [Illinois]
Illinois Dept. of Commerce
Div. of Forest Resources
600 N. Grand Ave. W.
PO Box 19225
Springfield, IL 62794-9225
Phone: (217)782-2361

Credential Type: Timber Buyer License. **Duration of License:** One year. **Requirements:** Must post bond of between $500 to $10,000, as determined by the Department. Submit application and pay fee. **Reciprocity:** No. **Fees:** $30 initial license fee. $30 renewal fee. **Governing Statute:** Illinois

Timber Buyer [Illinois], continued

Revised Statutes 1989, 17 Illinois Administrative Code, Chapter I.

8782

Tooth Floater (Racetrack) [Texas]
Texas Racing Commission
PO Box 12080
Austin, TX 78711
Phone: (512)794-8461

Credential Type: License Registration. **Requirements:** Submit application and fingerprint card. Pay fee. **Fees:** $75 registration fee.

8783

Travel Agent [Rhode Island]
Div. of Licensing and Consumer Protection, Travel Section
Rhode Island Dept. of Business Regulation
233 Richmond St.
Providence, RI 02903
Phone: (401)277-3154

Credential Type: Travel Agent License. **Duration of License:** One year. **Requirements:** At least 18 years of age. Have reputation for honesty and fair dealing. Complete a six-month registered apprenticeship at a licensed travel agency. **Examination:** Written examination. **Reciprocity:** No. **Fees:** $5 apprentice registration fee. $10 examination fee. $10 license fee.

8784

University or College Instructor (Teacher Training) [Alaska]
Dept. of Education, Certification Analyst
Box F
Juneau, AK 99811-0500
Phone: (907)465-2810
Phone: (907)465-2831

Credential Type: University Certificate—Type U. **Duration of License:** Five years. **Requirements:** Employed in a teaching position in an approved teacher training program in Alaska. Eligible to possess a Type A certificate or approved by the teacher training program.

Renewable any number of times upon evidence of satisfactory completion of 50 clock hours of K-12 teaching during the life of the certificate. **Fees:** $43 fingerprint card processing fee. $125 application fee. $10 endorsement fee.

8785

Urban Planner [New Jersey]
Board of Professional Planners
1100 Raymond Blvd.
Newark, NJ 07102
Phone: (201)648-2465

Credential Type: Licensed Professional Planner. **Duration of License:** Two years. **Requirements:** A graduate degree in professional planning from an accredited college or university and three years experience in the full-time practice of professional planning; or an undergraduate degree from an accredited college or university in a curriculum offering a major or option comprising a minimum of 21 credit hours in recognized planning subjects, and four years experience in the full-time practice of professional planning; or graduation from high school and at least 12 years of professional planning experience. **Examination:** Yes. **Reciprocity:** Yes. **Fees:** $25 application fee. $175 exam fee. $150 license fee. $65 biennial registration fee. **Governing Statute:** NJSA 45:14A. NJAC 13:41.

Credential Type: Training Certificate. **Requirements:** Graduation in an approved course in planning of four years or more from a school or college approved by the board; or at least four years of experience in the active practice of planning. **Examination:** Yes. **Governing Statute:** NJSA 45:14A. NJAC 13:41.

8786

Vehicle Auctioneer [Illinois]
Secretary of State
Centennial Bldg., Rm. 008
Springfield, IL 62756
Phone: (217)782-7817

Credential Type: Vehicle Auctioneer License. **Duration of License:** One year. **Requirements:** Submit application and pay fee. Requires ID cards. **Reciprocity:** No. **Fees:** $50 initial license fee. $50 renewal fee. **Governing Statute:** Illinois Vehicle Code 95 1/2 5-701.

8787

Vision Screening Technician [Illinois]
Illinois Dept. of Public Health
Div. of Health Assessment and Screening
525 W. Jefferson
Springfield, IL 62761
Phone: (217)782-5830

Credential Type: Vision Screening Technician Certificate. **Duration of License:** Three years. **Requirements:** At least 18 years of age. High school graduate or equivalent. Must complete a four-day vision training course sponsored by the Department of Public Health. **Examination:** Vision Training Course Final Examination. **Reciprocity:** No. **Fees:** $50 application fee. **Governing Statute:** Public Act 81-174, Administrative Code, Chapter I.

8788

Water Rights Examiner, Certified [Oregon]
Board of Engineering Examiners
750 Front St. NE, 240
Salem, OR 97310
Phone: (503)378-4180

Credential Type: Certification. **Duration of License:** Two years. **Requirements:** Must be a currenty registered engineer or land surveyor. **Examination:** Yes. **Fees:** $20 exam fee. $5 certificate fee. $20 renewal fee. **Governing Statute:** ORS 537.797.

8789

Weather Modifier [Montana]
Dept. of Natural Resources and Conservation
Water Resources Div.
1520 E. 6th Ave.
Helena, MT 59620
Phone: (406)444-6601

Credential Type: Weather Modification License. **Authorization:** License required for any person desiring to engage in weather modification activities. In addition, a weather modification permit is required before any activity may proceed. **Requirements:** Contact licensing body for application information. **Fees:** $100 license fee. Additional permit fee based on cost of weather modification operation. **Governing Statute:** Montana Code Annotated 85-3.

8790

Weather Modifier [North Dakota]
Weather Modification Board
State Water Commission
900 E. Blvd.
Bismarck, ND 58505
Phone: (701)224-4940

Credential Type: License. **Duration of License:** One year. **Requirements:** Demonstrate competency to the board. **Fees:** $50 license fee. **Governing Statute:** North Dakota Century Code, Chap. 61-04.1.

Credential Type: Permit. **Duration of License:** One year. **Authorization:** A permit is required for each geographical area in which weather modification activities are to be conducted. **Requirements:** Must hold a valid weather modifier license. Furnish proof of financial responsibility. Set forth a complete operational plan. Post required bond. **Fees:** $25 application fee. **Governing Statute:** North Dakota Century Code, Chap. 61-04.1.

8791

Weather Modifier (Cloud Seeder) [Utah]
Natural Resources Dept.
Div. of Water Resources
1636 W. North Temple, Rm. 310
Salt Lake City, UT 84116
Phone: (801)538-7230

Credential Type: Registration. **Requirements:** Contact licensing body for application information.

8792

Welder [Idaho]
Welder Licensing
370 Benjamin Lane
Boise, ID 83707
Phone: (208)377-2100

Credential Type: Welder Certification. **Requirements:** Must demonstrate competency by passing a welder certification examination. **Examination:** Welder Certification Examination. **Fees:** Fees vary; contact board.

8793

Welder [New York]
New York State Dept. of Transportation
State Office Bldg. Campus
Bldg. 5, 6th Fl.
Albany, NY 12232
Phone: (518)457-7161

Credential Type: Certificate. **Duration of License:** Three years. **Examination:** Practical. **Reciprocity:** None. **Governing Statute:** New York State Steel Construction Manual as part of New York State Dept. of Transportation Standard Specifications for Construction and Materials.

8794

Welder, Combination [Arkansas]
Pulaski Vocational Technical School
3000 W. Scenic Rd.
North Little Rock, AR 72118
Phone: (501)771-1000

Credential Type: License. **Requirements:** Must be able to weld a plate of steel 3/8 inches thick and seven inches long in particular type of welding. **Examination:** Yes. **Fees:** $25 Written and practical examination. $25 License. $25 Renewal.

8795

Whitewater Rafting Guide [Maryland]
Park Service
Dept. of Natural Resources
Tawes State Office Bldg.
Annapolis, MD 21401
Phone: (301)826-8450

Credential Type: License. **Requirements:** Contact licensing body for application information.

8796

Whitewater Rafting Operator [Maryland]
Park Service
Dept. of Natural Resources
Tawes State Office Bldg.
Annapolis, MD 21401
Phone: (301)826-8450

Credential Type: License **Requirements:** Contact licensing body for application information.

8797

Wholesale Florist [Louisiana]
Horticulture Commission
PO Box 3118
Baton Rouge, LA 70821
Phone: (504)925-7772

Credential Type: License. **Duration of License:** One year. **Examination:** Written. **Fees:** $35 exam fee. $35 license fee. $35 renewal fee.

8798

Wholesale Fur Buyer [Rhode Island]
Office of Boat Registration and Licensing
Rhode Island Dept. of Environmental Management
22 Hayes
Providence, RI 02908
Phone: (401)277-3576

Credential Type: Wholesale Fur Buyer License. **Duration of License:** One year. **Requirements:** Submit application and pay fee. **Reciprocity:** No. **Fees:** $10 resident license fee. $30 nonresident license fee.

8799

Wild Game and Bird Breeder [Illinois]
Illinois Dept. of Conservation
524 South 2nd St.
Springfield, IL 62701-1787
Phone: (217)785-3423

Credential Type: Class A (Non-Commercial) License. **Duration of License:** One year. **Requirements:** Must be an Illinois resident for at least 30 days. Submit application and pay fee. **Reciprocity:** No. **Fees:** $10 initial license fee. $10 renewal fee. **Governing Statute:** Illinois Revised Statutes, Chapter 61.

Credential Type: Class B (Commercial) License. **Duration of License:** One year. **Requirements:** Must be an Illinois resident for at least 30 days. Submit application and pay fee. **Reciprocity:** No. **Fees:** $20 initial license fee. $20 renewal fee. **Governing Statute:** Illinois Revised Statutes, Chapter 61.

8800

Wildlife Exhibitor [Maryland]
Wildlife Div.
Dept. of Natural Resources
Tawes State Office Bldg.
Annapolis, MD 21401
Phone: (410)296-2230

Credential Type: Exhibitor License. **Duration of License:** Varies. **Requirements:** Submit application with copies of appropriate federal permits. **Fees:** No fee.

8801

Wildlife Exhibitor (Animals and Birds) [Michigan]
Wildlife Div.
Dept. of Natural Resources
Stevens T. Mason Bldg.
PO Box 30028
Lansing, MI 48909
Phone: (517)373-1220

Credential Type: License. **Duration of License:** One year. **Requirements:** Have obtained animals and birds in a lawful manner, as evidenced by a receipted invoice or other document. Confine animals and birds in pens or fenced areas which meet the department's minimum specifications. Provide humane and sanitary conditions. Provide water and food. Submit to an inspection of pens and surrounding premises by a Department officer. Comply with the rules of the Department of Natural Resources. **Fees:** $15 initial permit fee. $15 renewal fee. **Governing Statute:** Game Law, Act 286 of 1929, as amended.

8802

Wildlife Propagator [Rhode Island]
Office of Boat Registration and Licensing
Rhode Island Dept. of Environmental Management
22 Hayes St.
Providence, RI 02908
Phone: (401)277-3576

Credential Type: Wildlife Propagator License. **Duration of License:** One year. **Requirements:** Premises must be inspected for suitability of facility for work with species permitted. Submit application and pay fee. **Reciprocity:** No. **Fees:** $5 non-commercial license. $25 commercial license.

Appendix 2
State Licensing Information Sources

This appendix contains selected information sources for each state, including State Occupational Information Coordinating Committees, state licensing agencies, and labor departments.

Alabama

Alabama Occupational Information Coordinating Committee
Alabama Center for Commerce, Rm. 364
401 Adams Ave.
PO Box 5690
Montgomery, AL 36103-5690
Phone: (205)242-2990
Fax: (205)242-5515
Dr. Mary Louise Simms, Dir.

Alaska

Alaska Department of Labor
Research and Analysis Section
PO Box 25501
Juneau, AK 99802
Phone: (907)465-4518
Fax: (907)465-2102
Ms. Brynn Keith, Exec. Dir.

Alaska State Department of Commerce and Economic Development
Division of Occupational Licensing
PO Box 110806
Juneau, AK 99811
Phone: (907)465-2534

Arizona

Arizona State Department of Administration
State Boards Office
1645 W. Jefferson St., Rm. 410
Phoenix, AZ 85007
Phone: (602)542-3095

Arizona State Occupational Information Coordinating Committee
1789 W. Jefferson St., 1st Fl. North
PO Box 6123, Site Code 897J
Phoenix, AZ 85005-6123
Phone: (602)542-6466
Fax: (602)542-6474
Dan Anderson, Exec. Dir.

Arkansas

Arkansas Occupational Information Coordinating Committee
Arkansas Employment Security Division
PO Box 2981
Little Rock, AR 72203
Phone: (501)682-3159
Fax: (501)682-3713
Mr. C. Coy Cozart, Exec. Dir.

California

California Occupational Information Coordinating Committee
1116 9th St., Lower Level
PO Box 944222
Sacramento, CA 94244-2220
Phone: (916)323-6544
Sigurd Brivkalns, Exec. Dir.

California State and Consumer Services Agency
Department of Consumer Affairs
400 R St., Ste. 3000
Sacramento, CA 95814
Phone: (916)445-1591

Colorado

Colorado Occupational Information Coordinating Committee
State Board Community College
1391 Speer Blvd., Ste. 600
Denver, CO 80204-2554
Phone: (303)866-4488
James L. Harris, Dir.

Colorado State Department of Regulatory Agencies
1560 Broadway
Denver, CO 80202
Phone: (303)894-7855

Connecticut

Connecticut Occupational Information Coordinating Committee
Connecticut Department of Education
25 Industrial Park Rd.
Middletown, CT 06457
Phone: (203)638-4042

Connecticut State Department of Consumer Protection
Division of Licensing and Administration
State Office Bldg.
165 Capitol Ave.
Hartford, CT 06106
Phone: (203)566-7177

Delaware

Delaware Office of Occupational and Labor Market Information
Department of Labor
University Office Plaza
PO Box 9029
Newark, DE 19714-9029
Phone: (302)368-6963
Fax: (302)368-6748
Dr. James K. McFadden, Exec. Dir.

Delaware State Department of Administrative Services
Division of Professional Regulations
Margaret O'Neill Bldg.
PO Box 1401
Dover, DE 19903
Phone: (302)739-4522

District of Columbia

District of Columbia Department of Consumer and Regulatory Affairs
Occupational and Professional Licensing Administration
614 H St. NW
Washington, DC 20001
Phone: (202)727-7480

District of Columbia Occupational Information Coordinating Committee
Department of Employment Services
500 C St., NW, Rm. 215
Washington, DC 20001
Phone: (202)639-1090
Fax: (202)639-1765
Etta Williams, Exec. Dir.

National Occupational Information Coordinating Committee
2100 M St., NW, Ste. 156
Washington, DC 20037
Phone: (202)653-5665
Fax: (202)653-2123
Juliette Lester, Exec. Dir.

Florida

Florida Bureau of Labor Market Information
Department of Labor and Employment Security
Hartman Bldg., Ste. 200
2012 Capitol Circle SE
Tallahassee, FL 32399-0673
Phone: (904)488-1048
Fax: (904)488-2558
Garry L. Breedlove, Mgr.

Florida State Department of Professional Regulation
1940 N. Monroe St.
Tallahassee, FL 32399-0750
Phone: (904)487-2252

Georgia

Georgia Occupational Information Coordinating Committee
Georgia Department of Labor
Sussex Place
148 International Blvd.
Atlanta, GA 30303-1751
Phone: (404)656-9639
Fax: (404)651-9568
Richard Jenkins, Exec. Dir.

Georgia Secretary of State Professional Examining Boards
166 Pryor St. SW
Atlanta, GA 30303
Phone: (404)656-3900

Hawaii

Hawaii State Department of Commerce and Consumer Affairs
Division of Professional and Vocational Licensing
PO Box 3469
Honolulu, HI 96801
Phone: (808)586-2691

Hawaii State Occupational Information Coordinating Committee
830 Punchbowl St., Rm. 315
Honolulu, HI 96813-5080
Phone: (808)586-8750
Fax: (808)586-9099
Patrick A. Stanley, Exec. Dir.

Idaho

Idaho Occupational Information Coordinating Committee
Len B. Jordan Bldg., Rm. 301
650 W. State St.
Boise, ID 83720
Phone: (208)334-3705
Fax: (208)334-2365
Charles R. Mollerup, Dir.

Idaho State Board of Occupational Licenses
1109 Main St.
Boise, ID 83702
Phone: (208)334-3233

Illinois

Illinois Occupational Information Coordinating Committee
217 E. Monroe, Ste. 203
Springfield, IL 62706
Phone: (217)785-0789
Fax: (217)785-6184
Mr. Jan Staggs, Exec. Dir.

Illinois State Department of Registration and Education
Division of Licensing and Testing
320 W. Washington St.
Springfield, IL 62786
Phone: (217)785-0800

Indiana

Indiana Occupational Information Coordinating Committee
309 W. Washington St., Rm. 309
Indianapolis, IN 46204
Phone: (317)232-8528
Fax: (317)233-4824
Linda Piper, Exec. Dir.

Indiana Professional Licensing Agency
IGCS, Rm. E034
302 W. Washington St.
Indianapolis, IN 46204
Phone: (317)232-2980

Iowa

Iowa Occupational Information Coordinating Committee
Iowa Department of Economic Development
200 E. Grand Ave.
Des Moines, IA 50309
Phone: (515)242-4890
Fax: (515)242-4859
Penelope Shenk, Act. Exec. Dir.

Iowa State Department of Commerce
Professional Licensing and Regulation Division
1918 SE Hulsizer Ave.
Ankney, IA 50021
Phone: (515)281-5596

Kansas

Kansas Occupational Information Coordinating Committee
401 Topeka Ave.
Topeka, KS 66603
Phone: (913)296-2387
Fax: (913)296-2119
Randall Williams, Dir.

Kentucky

Kentucky Occupational Information Coordinating Committee
Capital Plaza Tower, 3rd Fl.
Frankfort, KY 40601
Phone: (502)564-4258
Fax: (502)564-3044
Don Sullivan, Info. Liaison-Mgr.

Kentucky State Finance and Administration Cabinet
Occupations and Professions Division
PO Box 456
Frankfort, KY 40602
Phone: (502)564-3296

Louisiana

Louisiana Occupational Information Coordinating Committee
PO Box 94094
Baton Rouge, LA 70804-9094
Phone: (504)342-5149
Fax: (504)342-5115
Priscilla R. Engolia, Act. Dir.

Louisiana State Department of Health and Hospitals
Licensing and Certifications
PO Box 3767
Baton Rouge, LA 70821-3767
Phone: (504)342-0138

Maine

Maine Occupational Information Coordinating Committee
State House Sta. 71
Augusta, ME 04333
Phone: (207)624-6200
Fax: (207)624-6206
Denis Fortier, Act. Exec. Dir.

Maine State Department of Professional and Financial Regulation
Division of Licensing and Enforcement
State House Station 35
Augusta, ME 04333
Phone: (207)582-8723

Maryland

Maryland State Department of Licensing and Regulation
Division of Occupational and Professional Licensing
501 St. Paul Pl., 9th Fl.
Baltimore, MD 21202
Phone: (410)333-6200

Maryland State Occupational Information Coordinating Committee
State Department of Employment and Training
1100 N. Eutaw St., Rm. 205
Baltimore, MD 21201
Phone: (410)333-5478
Fax: (410)333-5304
Jasmin M. Duckett, Dir.

Massachusetts

Massachusetts Occupational Information Coordinating Committee
Massachusetts Division of Employment Security
C.F. Hurley Bldg., 2nd Fl.
Government Center
Boston, MA 02114
Phone: (617)727-6718
Fax: (617)727-8014
Robert Vinson, Dir.

Massachusetts State Executive Office of Consumer Affairs and Business Regulation
Division of Registration
100 Cambridge St.
Boston, MA 02202
Phone: (617)727-3074

Michigan

Michigan Occupational Information Coordinating Committee
Victor Office Center, 3rd Fl.
201 N. Washington Sq.
Box 30015
Lansing, MI 48909
Phone: (517)373-0363
Fax: (517)335-5822
Robert Sherer, Exec. Coordinator

Michigan State Department of Licensing and Regulation
PO Box 30018
Lansing, MI 48909
Phone: (517)373-1870

Minnesota

Minnesota Occupational Information Coordinating Committee
Department of Jobs and Training
390 N. Robert St.
St. Paul, MN 55101
Phone: (612)296-2072
Fax: (612)296-0994
John Cosgrove, Dir.

Minnesota State Department of Commerce
133 E. 7th St.
St. Paul, MN 55101
Phone: (612)296-4026

Mississippi

Mississippi State Board of Medical Licensure
2688-D Insurance Center Dr.
Jackson, MD 39216
Phone: (601)354-6645

Mississippi State Occupational Information Coordinating Committee
301 W. Pearl St.
Jackson, MS 39203-3089
Phone: (601)949-2240
Fax: (601)949-2291
Liz Barnett, Dir.

Missouri

Missouri Occupational Information Coordinating Committee
421 E. Dunklin St.
Jefferson City, MO 65101
Phone: (314)751-3800
Fax: (314)751-7973
Kay Raithel, Dir.

Missouri State Department of Professional Registration
3605 Missouri Blvd.
Jefferson City, MO 65102
Phone: (314)751-0293

Montana

Montana Occupational Information Coordinating Committee
1327 Lockey St., 2nd Fl.
PO Box 1728
Helena, MT 59624
Phone: (406)444-2741
Fax: (406)444-2638
Robert N. Arnold, Pro. Mgr.

Montana State Department of Commerce
Bureau of Professional and Occupational Licensing
111 N. Jackson
PO Box 200513
Helena, MT 59620
Phone: (406)444-3737

Nebraska

Nebraska Occupational Information Coordinating Committee
State House Sta.
PO Box 94600
Lincoln, NE 68509-4600
Phone: (402)471-4845
Floyd Colon, Admin.

Nebraska State Bureau of Examining Boards
Department of Health
301 Centennial Mall S.
Lincoln, NE 68509
Phone: (402)471-2115

Nevada

Nevada Occupational Information Coordinating Committee
1923 N. Carson St., Ste. 211
Carson City, NV 89710
Phone: (702)687-4577
Fax: (702)687-4119
Valorie Hopkins, Dir.

New Hampshire

New Hampshire State Occupational Information Coordinating Committee
64B Old Suncook Rd.
Concord, NH 03301
Phone: (603)228-3349
Fax: (603)228-3209
Victor P. Racicot, Dir.

New Jersey

New Jersey Occupational Information Coordinating Committee
609 Labor & Industry Bldg., CN 056
Trenton, NJ 08625-0056
Phone: (609)292-2682
Fax: (609)292-6692
Laurence H. Seidel, Staff Dir.

New Jersey State Department of Law and Public Safety
Division of Consumer Affairs
375 W. State St., 2nd Fl., CN152
Trenton, NJ 08625
Phone: (609)292-4670

New Mexico

New Mexico Occupational Information Coordinating Committee
401 Broadway, NE
Tiwa Bldg.
PO Box 1928
Albuquerque, NM 87103-1928
Phone: (505)841-8455

New Mexico State Department of Regulation and Licensing
PO Box 25101
Santa Fe, NM 87504
Phone: (505)827-7000

New York

New York Education Department
Division of Professional Licensing Services
Cultural Education Center
Albany, NY 12230
Phone: (518)474-3817

New York State Occupational Information Coordinating Committee
Department of Labor
Research & Statistics Division
State Campus, Bldg. 12, Rm. 400
Albany, NY 12240
Phone: (518)457-6182
Fax: (518)457-0620
David Nyhan, Exec. Dir.

North Carolina

North Carolina Occupational Information Coordinating Committee
1311 St. Mary's St., Ste. 250
PO Box 27625
Raleigh, NC 27611
Phone: (919)733-6700
Nancy H. MacCormac, Exec. Dir.

North Dakota

North Dakota State Licensing Department
Office of the Attorney General
600 E. Blvd.
State Capitol, 1st Fl.
Bismarck, ND 58505
Phone: (701)224-2210

North Dakota State Occupational Information Coordinating Committee
1720 Burnt Boat Dr.
PO Box 1537
Bismarck, ND 58502-1537
Phone: (701)224-2733
Fax: (701)258-9826
Dan R. Marrs, Coordinator

Ohio

Ohio Occupational Information Coordinating Committee
Division of Labor Market Information
Ohio Bureau of Employment Services
1160 Dublin Rd., Bldg. A
Columbus, OH 43215
Phone: (614)752-6863
Fax: (614)481-8543
Mark Schaff, Dir.

Ohio State Department of Commerce
Division of Licensing
77 S. High St., 23rd Fl.
Columbus, OH 43266-0546
Phone: (614)466-4130

Oklahoma

Oklahoma Occupational Information Coordinating Committee
Oklahoma Department of Vocational and Technical Education
1500 W. 7th Ave.
Stillwater, OK 74074
Phone: (405)743-5198
Fax: (405)743-6808
Curtis Shumaker, Exec. Dir.

Oregon

Oregon Occupational Information Coordinating Committee
875 Union St., NE
Salem, OR 97311
Phone: (503)378-5490
Fax: (503)373-7515

Oregon State Department of Insurance and Finance
21 Labor and Industries Bldg.
Salem, OR 97310
Phone: (503)378-4100

Pennsylvania

Pennsylvania Occupational Information Coordinating Committee
Pennsylvania Department of Labor and Industry
1224 Labor and Industry Bldg.
Harrisburg, PA 17120
Phone: (717)787-8646
Phone: (717)787-8647
Fax: (717)772-2168
Fritz J. Fichtner Jr., Dir.

Pennsylvania State Department
Bureau of Professional and Occupational Affairs
Transportation and Safety Bldg., Rm. 618
Harrisburg, PA 17120
Phone: (717)787-8503

Rhode Island

Rhode Island Occupational Information Coordinating Committee
22 Hayes St., Rm. 133
Providence, RI 02908
Phone: (401)272-0830
Mildred Nichols, Dir.

Rhode Island State Department of Labor
Division of Professional Regulation
220 Elmwood Ave.
Providence, RI 02907
Phone: (401)457-1860

South Carolina

South Carolina Occupational Information Coordinating Committee
1550 Gadsden St.
PO Box 995
Columbia, SC 29202
Phone: (803)737-2733
Fax: (803)737-2642
Carol Kososki, Dir.

South Dakota

South Dakota Occupational Information Coordinating Committee
South Dakota Department of Labor
420 S. Roosevelt St.
PO Box 4730
Aberdeen, SD 57402-4730
Phone: (605)622-2314
Phillip George, Dir.

South Dakota State Department of Commerce and Regulation
Professional and Occupational License Division
910 E. Sioux
Pierre, SD 57501
Phone: (605)773-3177

Tennessee

Tennessee Occupational Information Coordinating Committee
Volunteer Plaza, 11th Fl.
500 James Robertson Pky.
Nashville, TN 37219
Phone: (615)741-6451
Fax: (615)741-3203
Chrystal Partridge, Exec. Dir.

Tennessee State Department of Commerce and Insurance
Regulatory Boards
500 James Robertson Pkwy., 2nd Fl.
Volunteer Plaza
Nashville, TN 37243-0572
Phone: (615)741-3449

Texas

Texas Occupational Information Coordinating Committee
Texas Employment Commission Bldg., Ste. 205
3520 Executive Center Dr.
Austin, TX 78731
Phone: (512)502-3750
Fax: (512)502-3763
Richard Froeschle, Dir.

Texas State Department of Licensing and Regulation
PO Box 12157
Austin, TX 78711
Phone: (512)463-5520

Utah

Utah Occupational Information Coordinating Committee
c/o Utah Department of Employment Security
140 E. 300 S.
PO Box 11249
Salt Lake City, UT 84147
Phone: (801)536-7806
Phone: (801)536-7861
Fax: (801)536-7420
Tammy Stewart, Dir.

Utah State Department of Business Regulation
Division of Occupational and Professional Licensing
PO Box 45802
Salt Lake City, UT 84145-0801
Phone: (801)530-6628

Vermont

Vermont Occupational Information Coordinating Committee
5 Green Mountin Dr.
PO Box 488
Montpelier, VT 05601-0488
Phone: (802)229-0311
Fax: (802)828-4022
Tom Douse, Dir.

Vermont Secretary of State
Division of Licensing and Registration
Pavilion Office Bldg.
109 State St.
Montpelier, VT 05602
Phone: (802)828-2363

Virginia

Virginia Occupational Information Coordinating Committee
Virginia Employment Commission
703 E. Main St.
PO Box 1358
Richmond, VA 23211
Phone: (804)786-7496
Fax: (804)786-7844
Dolores A. Esser, Exec. Dir.

Virginia State Department of Social Services
Division of Licensing Programs
730 E. Broad St.
Richmond, VA 23219-1849
Phone: (804)692-1787

Washington

Washington Occupational Information Coordinating Committee
c/o Employment Security Department
PO Box 9046
Olympia, WA 98507-9046
Phone: (206)438-4803
Fax: (206)438-3215
A.T. Woodhouse, Dir.

Washington State Department of Licensing
Business and Professions Division
12th & Franklin
Olympia, WA 98504
Phone: (206)753-6918

West Virginia

West Virginia Occupational Information Coordinating Committee
One Dunbar Plaza, Ste. E
Dunbar, WV 25064
Phone: (304)293-5314
Fax: (304)766-7846
George McGuire, Exec. Dir.

Wisconsin

Wisconsin Occupational Information Coordinating Committee
Division of Employment & Training Policy
201 E. Washington Ave.
PO Box 7972
Madison, WI 53707
Phone: (608)266-8012
Fax: (608)267-0330
Sue Gleason, Dir.

Wisconsin State Department of Regulation and Licensing
PO Box 8935
Madison, WI 53708-8935
Phone: (608)266-8609

Wyoming

Wyoming Occupational Information Coordinating Committee
100 W. Midwest
PO Box 2760
Casper, WY 82602
Phone: (307)265-7017
Michael E. Paris, Exec. Dir.

Geographic Index

This index lists actual license names issued by federal or state agencies. Federal licenses are listed first followed by state licenses.

Federal Licenses

Air-Traffic Control-Tower Operator   329
Aircraft Dispatcher   330
Aircraft Mechanic   331
Aircraft Repairer   332
Airline Transport Pilot (Airplanes)   334
Airline Transport Pilot (Rotorcrfaft and Helicopters)   335
Assistant Engineer   8450
Ballast Control Operator   8451
Barge Supervisor   8452
Chief Engineer   8453
Commercial Pilot, Airplanes   336
Commercial Pilot, Airships   337
Commercial Pilot, Free Balloons   338
Commercial Pilot, Gliders   339
Commercial Pilot, Rotorcraft (Helicopters and Gyrocraft)   340
Customs Broker   3500
Designated Duty Engineer   8454
Flight Engineer   341
Flight Instructor   188, 342
Flight Navigator   343
Investment Advisor   7742
Lifeboatman   8455
Lobbyist   4253
Marine Radio Operator   8271
Master   8456
Mate   8457
Merchant Mariner   8458
Nuclear Facility Operator   5525
Ocean Freight Forwarder   1723
Offshore Installation Manager   8459
Operator of Uninspected Passenger Vessel   8460
Operator of Uninspected Towing Vessel   8461
Parachute Rigger   333
Pilot (Ship)   8462
Private Pilot, Airplanes   344
Private Pilot, Airships   345
Private Pilot, Balloons   346
Private Pilot, Gliders   347
Private Pilot, Rotorcraft (Helicopters and Gyrocraft)   348
Purser   8463

Qualified Member of the Engine Department   8464
Radar Observer   8465
Radio Officer   8466
Radiotelegraph Operator   8272
Radiotelephone Operator   8273
Seaman   8467
Ship's Doctor   5182, 8468
Ship's Nurse   7324, 8469
Student and Recreational Pilot, Airplanes   349
Student and Recreational Pilot, Gliders and Balloons   350
Student and Recreational Pilot, Rotorcraft (Helicopters and Gyroplanes)   351
Tankerman   8470

State Licenses

Alabama

Administrator of Vocational Education   2421
Apprentice Gas Fitter   5304
Apprentice Plumber   5305
Architect   716
Attorney   4099
Auctioneer   1208
Audiologist   8035
Bar Pilot   8471
Certified Public Accountant   1
Certified Shorthand Reporter   8125
Chiropractor (Doctor of Chiropractic)   1631
Coal Mine Foreman (surface)   1527, 4377
Coal Mine Foreman (underground)   1528, 4378
Cosmetologist   1259
Cosmetology Instructor   189, 1260
Counselor   2045
Dental Hygienist   2191
Dentist   2252
Dietitian   2362
Doctor of Medicine of Osteopathy   5183

Early Childhood Education Teacher   3924, 5543
Elementary or Secondary Teacher   7611
Elementary Teacher   3925
Embalmer   2895
Emergency Medical Technician   2671
Engineer-in-Training   5568
Fire Fighter   2798
Forester   2873
Funeral Director   2896
Gas Fitter; Apprentice   5304
Gas Fitter; Journeyman   5306
Gas Fitter; Master   5308
General Contractor   1838
Geologist   3232
Guidance Counselor   2046
Harbor Pilot   8472
Hearing Aid Specialist   3398
Heating and Air Conditioning Contractor   1839, 3455
Heating and Air Conditioning Mechanic   3456
High School Teacher   7612
Insurance Agent   3772
Insurance Broker   3773
Interior Designer   2313
Investment Advisor   7743
Investment Advisor Representative   7744
Journeyman Gas Fitter   5306
Journeyman Plumber   5307
Land Surveyor   8172
Landscape Architect   4049
Landscape Horticulturist   311, 4050
Landscape Planter   3109
Law Enforcement Personnel   5476
Licensed Practical Nurse   4200
Lobbyist   4254
Master Gas Fitter   5308
Master Plumber   5309
Middle School Teacher   7613
Mine Electrician   2546, 4379
Mine Fireboss   3501, 4380
Notary Public   4479
Nurse Anesthetist   7325
Nurse Midwife   7326
Nurse Practitioner   7327
Nursing Home Administrator   3335

Alabama, continued

Nutritionist 2363
Occupational Therapist 4568
Occupational Therapy Assistant 4618
Optometrist 4662
Osteopathy; Doctor of Medicine of 5183
Pest Control Operator and Fumigator 4733
Pharmacist 4917
Physical Therapist 5059
Physical Therapist Assistant 5024
Physician 5184
Physician's Assistant 5126
Pilot; Bar 8471
Pilot; Harbor 8472
Plumber and/or Gas Fitter 5310
Plumber; Apprentice 5305
Plumber; Journeyman 5307
Plumber; Master 5309
Podiatrist 5425
Polygraph Examiner 5492
Professional Engineer 5569
Professional Wrestler 767
Psychologist 5657
Real Estate Appraiser 7119
Real Estate Broker 7120
Real Estate Salesperson 7121
Real Estate Time-Share Seller 7122
Registered Nurse 7328
School Bus Driver 1598
School Counselor 2047
School Principal 2422
School Psychometrist 5658
School Superintendent 2423, 3128
School Supervisor 2424
Securities Agent 7745
Securities Dealer 7746
Social Worker 7958
Special Education Teacher 3926, 7614
Speech Pathologist 8036
Surgeon's Assistant 5127
Tree Surgeon 2874
Veterinarian 8346
Veterinarian Technician 357
Wrestling Announcer 7046
Wrestling Director 3129
Wrestling Judge 768
Wrestling Manager 769
Wrestling Matchmaker 4311
Wrestling Medical Examiner 3502, 5185
Wrestling Promoter 4312
Wrestling Referee 770
Wrestling Second (Substitute) 771
Wrestling Ticket Seller 7480
Wrestling Ticket Taker 8330
Wrestling Time Keeper 772
Wrestling Trainer 3684

Alaska

Acupuncturist (L.Ac.); Licensed 71
Advanced Nurse Practitioner 7329
Architect 717
Asbestos Abatement Contractor 1840
Asbestos Removal Worker 3718
Assistant Guide Outfitter (hunting) 2805
Associate Real Estate Broker 7123
Attorney 4100
Audiologist 8037
Bail Bond Person 1245
Barber 1261
Barber Instructor 190, 1262
Boiler Operator 1585
Boxer 773
Boxing Manager 774
Boxing Referee 775
Boxing Second 776
Boxing Trainer 3685
Broker; Reinsurance Intermediary 3776
Certified Public Accountant 2
Certified Shorthand Reporter 8126
Child Care Administrator (Center) 3336
Child Care Provider (Center) 5544
Chiropractor 1632
Clinical Social Worker 7959
Collection Agency Operator 97
Commercial Pesticide Applicator 4734
Concert Promoter 4313, 8613
Construction Contractor, General 1841
Construction Contractor, Mechanical 1842
Construction Contractor, Specialty 1843
Cosmetologist 1263
Cosmetologist Instructor 191, 1264
Crewmember (fishing boat) 8473
Dental Hygienist 2192
Dentist 2253
Early Childhood Education Associate 3927, 5545
Electrical Administrator 1756, 1844, 2547
Electrician Journeyman 2548
Electrician Lineman 2549
Electrician Maintenance 2550
Electrician Residential 2551
Electrician Trainee 2552
Elementary or Secondary Teacher 3928
Embalmer 2897
Emergency Medical Technician 2672
Employment Agency Operator 4714
Examining Physician, Boxing 3503, 5186
Explosives Handler 3318
Funeral Director 2898
General Real Estate Appraiser 7124
Geologist; Professional 3233
Guide Outfitter (hunting) 2806
Hairdresser 1265
Hairdresser Instructor 192, 1266
Hearing Aid Dealer 3399
Heating and Air Conditioning Mechanic 3457
Independent Insurance Adjuster 98
Insurance Producer 3774
Investment Advisor 7747
Land Surveyor 8173
Licensed Acupuncturist (L.Ac.) 71
Licensed Practical Nurse 4201
Limited Real Estate Appraiser 7125
Lobbyist 4255
Manager; Reinsurance Intermediary 3777
Managing General Agent (Insurance) 3775
Marine Pilot 8474
Mechanical Administrator - Dry Chemical Fire Protection Category 1757
Mechanical Administrator - Heating, Cooling, and Process Piping Category 1758
Mechanical Administrator - HVAC/Sheet Metal Category 1759
Mechanical Administrator - Mechanical Systems Temperature Control Category 1760
Mechanical Administrator - Plumbing Category 1761
Mechanical Administrator - Refrigeration Category 1762
Mechanical Administrator - Residential HVAC Category 1763
Mechanical Administrator - Residential Plumbing and Hydronic Heating Category 1764
Mechanical Administrator - Sprinkler System Fire Protection Category 1765
Mobile Intensive Care Paramedic 2673
Naturopath 5187
Notary Public 4480
Nurse Aide 4551
Nurse Practitioner; Advanced 7329
Nursing Home Administrator 3337
Occupational Therapist 4569
Occupational Therapy Assistant 4619
Optician 2398
Optometrist 4663
Osteopathic Physician (D.O.) 5188
Outfitter (hunting); Assistant Guide 2805
Painter 8709
Paramedic; Mobile Intensive Care 2673
Pesticide Applicator; Commercial 4734
Pharmacist 4918
Pharmacy Intern 4919
Physical Therapist 5060
Physical Therapy Assistant 5025
Physician 5189
Physician's Assistant 5128
Plumber 5311
Podiatrist 5426
Private Pesticide Applicator 4735
Professional Engineer 5570
Professional Geologist 3233
Professional Wrestler 777
Promoter, Boxing and Wrestling Matches 4314
Psychological Associate 5659
Psychologist 5660
Real Estate Appraiser; General 7124
Real Estate Appraiser; Limited 7125
Real Estate Appraiser; Residential 7130
Real Estate Appraiser Trainee 7126
Real Estate Broker 7127
Real Estate Broker; Associate 7123
Real Estate Instructor 193, 7128

Real Estate Salesperson 7129
Registered Nurse 7330
Registered Nurse Anesthetist 7331
Reinsurance Intermediary Broker 3776
Reinsurance Intermediary Manager 3777
Residential Real Estate Appraiser 7130
School Administrator 2425
School Special Services or Support Staff Member 7615
Securities Agent 7748
Securities Broker-Dealer 7749
Security Guard 3252
Surplus Lines Broker 3778
University or College Instructor (Teacher Training) 8784
Vessel Agent 8475
Veterinarian 8347
Vocational Education Teacher 194
Wastewater Collection System Operator 8495
Wastewater Treatment Plant Operator 8496
Water Distribution System Operator 8497
Water Treatment Plant Operator 8498
Wood Preservative Applicator 4736

Arizona

Adult Care Home Manager 3338
Aesthetic Instructor 195, 1267
Aesthetician 1268
Agricultural Aircraft Pilot 352
Agricultural Pest Control Advisor 4737
Announcer 7047
Apprentice Jockey 778, 5748
Architect 718
Assayer 3504, 8585
Assayer-in-Training 3505, 8586
Attending Physician 5190
Attorney 4101
Authorized Agent 779, 5749
Bail Bond Agent 1246
Barber 1269
Barber Instructor 196, 1270
Boxer 780
Boxing Judge 781
Campground Membership Broker and Salesperson 7131
Cemetery Broker and Salesperson 7132
Certified Court Reporter 8127
Certified Public Accountant 3
Chiropractor 1633
Community College Teacher 8608
Concession Employee 5750, 7481
Cool-out (Racetrack) 358, 5751
Cosmetologist 1271
Cosmetology Instructor 1272
Custom Applicator of Pesticides 4738
Dental Assistant 2183
Dental Hygienist 2193
Dentist 2254
Denturist 2243
Doctor of Naturopathic Medicine (Naturopathic Physician) 5191
Elementary Teacher (K-8) 3929

Embalmer 2899
Emergency Medical Technician 2674
Engineer 5571
Engineer-in-Training 5572
Exercise Rider (Racetrack) 359, 5752
Fishing Guide 2807
Funeral Director 2900
Fur Dealer 7482, 8659
General Contractor 1845
Geologist 3234
Geologist-in-Training 3235
Groom (Racetrack) 360, 5753
Guidance Counselor 2048
Guide (Hunting/Fishing) 2808
Hearing Aid Dispenser 3400
Homeopathic Physician 5192
Insurance Adjuster 99
Insurance Broker 3779
Insurance Sales Agent 3780
Insurance Solicitor 3781
Jockey 782, 5754
Jockey Agent 783, 5755
Land Surveyor 8174
Land Surveyor-in-Training 8175
Landscape Architect 4051
Landscape Architect-in-Training 4052
Lay Midwife 4552
Lead-out (Racetrack) 361, 5756
Lessee 5757
Lessor 5758
Licensed Practical Nurse 4202
Lobbyist 4256
Manufactured Home Dealer/Broker 7133
Manufactured Home Installer 1846
Manufactured Home Salesperson 7134
Marriage and Family Therapist 2049
Matchmaker 4315
Mutuel Clerk 5759
Nail Technician 1273
Nail Technology Instructor 197, 1274
Naturopathic Medicine (Naturopathic Physician); Doctor of 5191
Notary Public 4481
Nursing Care Institution Administrator 3339
Occupational Therapist 4570
Occupational Therapy Assistant 4620
Optician 2399
Optometrist 4664
Osteopathic Physician 5193
Outrider (Racetrack) 362, 5760
Owner 5761
Paramedic 2675
Pest Control Advisor 4739
Pesticide Applicator; Structural 4740
Pesticides; Custom Applicator of 4738
Pharmacist 4920
Pharmacy Intern 4921
Physical Therapist 5061
Physician 5194
Physician; Attending 5190
Physician; Homeopathic 5192
Physician's Assistant 5129
Pilot; Agricultural Aircraft 352
Podiatrist 5427
Podiatry; Practical Technologist in 7066

Polygraph Examiner 5493
Polygraph Examiner Intern 5494
Pony Rider (Racetrack) 363, 5762
Practical Technologist in Podiatry 7066
Practical Technologist in Radiology 7067
Private Investigator 2323
Professional Counselor 2050
Promoter 4316
Psychologist 5661
Public Weighmaster 3506
Radiation Therapy Technologist 7068
Radiologic Technologist 7069
Radiology; Practical Technologist in 7067
Real Estate Appraiser 7135
Real Estate Broker 7136
Real Estate Sales Agent 7137
Referee 784
Registered Nurse 7332
Registered Serviceman (Weights and Measures) 5536
Respiratory Care Practitioner 7438
School Bus Driver 1599
School Librarian 4150
School Principal 2426
School Psychologist 5662
School Psychometrist (K-12) 5663
School Superintendent 2427, 3130
School Supervisor 2428
Second Manager 785
Secondary Teacher (7-12) 7616
Securities Dealer 7750
Securities Salesperson 7751
Security Guard 3253
Social Worker 7960
Special Education Teacher (K-12) 3930, 7617
Structural Pesticide Applicator 4740
Taxidermist 8260
Timekeeper 786
Track Official 787, 5763
Track Veterinarian 5764, 8348
Traffic Survival School Instructor 198
Trainer (Boxing) 3686
Trainer (Racetrack) 364, 5765
Veterinarian 8349
Veterinarian; Track 5764, 8348
Veterinary Technician 365
Wastewater Treatment Plant Operator 8499
Water Collection Systems Operator 8500
Water Distribution Systems Operator 8501
Water Treatment Plant Operator 8502
Weighmaster; Public 3506
Well Driller (Water) 4381

Arkansas

Abstractor 8573
Accountant 4
Acupuncturist 72
Advanced School Guidance Counselor 2051

Arkansas

Arkansas, continued

Advanced School Guidance Supervisor 2052, 2429
Aesthetician 1275
Agricultural Consultant 312, 4741
Agriculture Education Teacher 199
Animal Technician 366
Architect 719
Armored Car Guard 3254
Art Teacher (K-12) 3931, 7618
Asbestos Removal Worker 3719
Associate Counselor 2053
Athletic Manager 788
Athletic Promoter/Matchmaker 4317
Attorney 4102
Auctioneer 1209
Audiologist 8038
Automobile Dealer, New 7483
Automobile Dealer, Used 7484
Bail Bondsman 1247
Barber Instructor 200, 1276
Barber; Registered 1283
Barber Technician 1277
Boiler Inspector, State 1766, 3507
Boiler Installer 1586
Boiler Operator 1587
Boiler Repairer 1588
Boxing/Wrestling Referee 789
Burglar Alarm Installer 2553
Burglar Alarm Servicer, Operator 1705
Business Education Teacher 201
Career Orientation Teacher 202
Certified Court Reporter 8128
Certified Registered Nurse Anesthetist 7333
Chauffeur 8244
Chiropractor 1634
Claims Adjuster 100
Clerk of Scales 3508, 5766
Collection Agency Collector 101
Collection Agency Manager 102
Commercial Applicator 4742
Commission Clocker 790, 5767
Commission Veterinarian 5768, 8350
Contractor 1847
Coordinated Career Education Teacher 203
Cosmetologist 1278
Cosmetology Instructor 204, 1279
Custodian (Racing); Receiving Barn 376, 3894, 5803
Custom Applicator 4743
Dental Assistant 2184
Dental Hygienist 2194
Dentist 2255
Dietitian 2364
Dispensing Optician 2400
Dispensing Optician Assistant 4369
Drivers, Commercial 8245, 8276
Driving Instructor (Commercial School) 205
Early Childhood Special Education Teacher 3932, 5546
Egg Grader 3630, 8631
Electrical Contractor 1848, 2554
Electrician; Industrial Maintenance 2555

Electrician; Journeyman 2556
Electrician; Master 2557
Electrologist 1280
Electrology Instructor 206, 1281
Elementary Physical Education Teacher (K-6) 3933
Elementary Reading Teacher (K-6) 3934
Elementary School Guidance Counselor (K-6) 2054
Elementary School Principal 2430
Elementary Teacher 3935
Elevator and Lifting Device Inspector 1767, 2652
Embalmer 2901
Embalmer Apprentice 2902
Emergency Medical Technician 2676
Emergency Medical Technician Intermediate 2677
Emergency Medical Technician - Paramedic 2678
Employment Agency Counselor 4715
Employment Agency Manager 4716
Employment Agent 4717
Engineer 5573
Engineer in Training 5574
Equine Dentist 5769, 8351
Farrier (Horse Racing) 367, 5770
Fishing Guide 2809
Forester 2875
Funeral Director 2903
Funeral Director Apprentice 2904
Gas Fitter 5312
Gas Fitter Supervisor 1529, 5313
Gas Fitter Trainee 5314
General Cooperative Education Teacher 207
Geologist 3236
Grain Warehouseman 1724
Greyhound Clerk of Scales 3509, 5771
Greyhound Commission Judge 791, 5772
Greyhound Commission Veterinarian 5773, 8352
Greyhound Kennel Manager (Racing) 368, 5774
Greyhound Lead-Out (Racing) 369, 5775
Greyhound Mutuels Director 3131, 5776
Greyhound Paddock Judge 792, 5777
Greyhound Presiding Judge 793, 5778
Greyhound Racing Director 3132, 5779
Greyhound Racing Secretary 794, 5780
Greyhound Starter 795, 5781
Greyhound Trainer Assistant (Racing) 370, 5782
Greyhound Trainer (Racing) 371, 5783
Guard; Armored Car 3254
Handicapper 5784
Health Occupations Education Teacher 208
Hearing Aid Dispenser 3401
Home Economics Education Teacher 209, 7619
Horse Exerciser (Racing) 372, 5785
Horse Race Starter 796, 5786

Horse Trainer Assistant (Racing) 373, 5787
Horse Trainer (Racing) 374, 5788
Hospital Maintenance Plumber 5315
Hospital Maintenance Plumber Trainee 5316
Hospital Maintenance Plumbing Supervisor 1530, 5317
Industrial Maintenance Electrician 2555
Insurance Inspector (Boiler) 1768, 3510
Insurance Sales Agent 3782
Investment Advisor 7752
Jockey 797, 5789
Jockey Agent 798, 5790
Jockey Apprentice 799, 5791
Jockey Room Custodian 3893, 5792
Journeyman Electrician 2556
Journeyman Plumber 5318
Land Surveyor 8176
Land Surveyor in Training 8177
Landscape Architect 4053
Lead Pony Rider (Racing) 375, 5793
Licensed Certified Social Worker 7961
Licensed Master Social Worker 7962
Licensed Nurse Midwife 7334
Licensed Practical Nurse 4203
Licensed Social Worker 7963
Limited Plumber 5319
Limited Plumber Assistant 5320
Liquefied Petroleum Gas Appliance Servicer 8691
Liquefied Petroleum Gas Safety Supervisor 1531, 1725, 8692
Liquefied Petroleum Gas Truck Driver 8277
Lobbyist 4257
Manicurist 1282
Marketing and Distributive Education Teacher 210
Master Electrician 2557
Master Plumber 5321
Middle School Teacher 3936, 7620
Milk Tester 3631
Music Teacher (K-12) 3937, 7621
Notary Public 4482
Nurse Midwife; Licensed 7334
Nurseryman 3110, 4542
Nursing Home Administrator 3340
Occupational Therapist 4571
Occupational Therapy Assistant 4621
Optometrist 4665
Osteopathic Physician (D.O.) 5195
Paddock Judge 800, 5794
Pari-Mutuel Ticket Cashier 5795
Pari-Mutuel Ticket Checker 5796
Pari-Mutuel Ticket Seller 5797
Patrol Judge 801, 5798
Pest Exterminator 4744
Pharmacist 4922
Pharmacist Intern 4923
Physical Education Teacher (K-12) 3938, 7622
Physical Therapist 5062
Physical Therapist Assistant 5026
Physician/Surgeon 5196
Physician's Assistant 5130
Placing Judge 802, 5799

Plant Breeders 313
Plumber Apprentice 5322
Plumber Assistant; Limited 5320
Plumber; Hospital Maintenance 5315
Plumber; Journeyman 5318
Plumber; Limited 5319
Plumber; Master 5321
Plumber Trainee; Hospital Maintenance 5316
Plumbing and Gas Inspector 1769
Plumbing Supervisor; Hospital Maintenance 1530, 5317
Podiatrist 5428
Polygraph Examiner 5495
Private Investigator 2324
Professional Boxer 803
Professional Counselor 2055
Professional Wrestler 804
Psychiatric Technician - Nurse 4553
Psychological Examiner 5664
Psychologist 5665
Pump Installer 4382, 5323
Racetrack Steward 805, 5800
Racing Agent 806, 5801
Racing Secretary 807, 5802
Reading Specialist (K-12) 3939, 7623
Real Estate Appraiser 7138
Real Estate Broker 7139
Real Estate Sales Agent 7140
Receiving Barn Custodian (Racing) 376, 3894, 5803
Registered Barber 1283
Registered Nurse 7335
Registered Nurse Anesthetist; Certified 7333
Registered Nurse Practitioner 7336
Respiratory Care Practitioner 7439
Ring Announcer 7048
Sanitarian 3511
School Administrator 2431
School Counselor (Elementary and Secondary) 2056
School Guidance Counselor; Advanced 2051
School Guidance Supervisor; Advanced 2052, 2429
School Library Media Administrator 2432, 4151
School Library Media Personnel 4152
School Library Media Specialist 4153
School Superintendent 2433, 3133
Secondary School Guidance Counselor (7-12) 2057
Secondary School Principal 2434
Secondary School Teacher 7624
Securities Agent 7753
Securities Broker-Dealer 7754
Securities Broker-Dealer Agent 7755
Security Guard 3255
Seed Treatment Commercial Applicator 4745
Social Worker; Licensed 7963
Social Worker; Licensed Certified 7961
Social Worker; Licensed Master 7962
Soil Classifier 314
Solid Waste Facility Operator 1726
Special Education Teacher 3940, 7625

Special Gas Fitter 5324
Speech Pathologist 8039
Stable Attendant (Racing) 377, 5804
State Trooper 5477
Therapy Technician (Masseur/Masseuse) 5027
Timekeeper 808
Track Superintendent 3134, 5805
Trade and Industrial Education Instructor 211
Tree Injector (Forest Worker) 2876
Veterinarian 8353
Veterinarian; Commission 5768, 8350
Veterinarian; Greyhound Commission 5773, 8352
Wastewater Treatment Plant Operator 8503
Water Supply Operator 8504
Waterwell Driller 4383
Welder, Combination 8794

California

Acupuncturist (C.A.); Certified 73
Agricultural Pest Control Adviser 315, 4746
Alarm Company Operator 1727
Amateur Boxing Promoter 4318
Animal Health Technician 378
Announcer (Boxing, Kickboxing, or Martial Arts) 7049
Announcer (Racetrack) 5806, 7050
Apprentice Jockey (Racetrack) 809, 5807
Architect 720
Assistant Manager (Racetrack) 170, 5808
Assistant Matchmaker (Boxing, Kickboxing, or Martial Arts) 4319
Assistant to a Racing Official, Official, or Manager (Racetrack) 5809, 7729
Assistant Starter (Racetrack) 810, 5810
Assistant Trainer (Racetrack) 379, 5811
Assistant to the Veterinarian (Racetrack) 380, 5812
Athletic Promoter; Professional 4321
Attorney 4103
Audiologist 8040
Bail Bond Agent 1248
Bail Bond Solicitor 1249
Barber 1284
Barber Instructor 212, 1285
Bloodstock Agent (Racetrack) 5813
Box Office Employee (Boxing, Kickboxing, or Martial Arts) 8331
Cemetery Broker 7141
Cemetery Sales Agent 7142
Certified Acupuncturist (C.A.) 73
Certified Public Accountant 5
Certified Shorthand Reporter 8129
Chiropractor 1635
Clerical Employee (Racetrack) 5814
Clinical Lab Technician 1682
Colors Attendant (Racetrack) 5815
Cosmetician/Esthetician 1286
Cosmetologist 1287
Cosmetology Instructor 213, 1288

Custodian (Racetrack) 3895, 5816
Dental Assistant 2185
Dental Hygienist 2195
Dentist 2256
Dietitian 2365
Driver (Racetrack) 811, 5817
Educational Psychologist 5666
Electrologist 1289
Elementary School Teacher 3941
Embalmer 2905
Emergency Medical Technician 2679
Engineer-in-Training 5575
Engineering Geologist 3237
Exercise Rider (Racetrack) 381, 5818
Firearms Instructor 3687, 8643
Flagman (Racetrack) 5819
Food Service Person (Racetrack) 2850, 5820
General Building Contractor 1849
General Engineering Contractor 1850, 5576
General Teacher 7626
Geologist 3238
Geophysicist 3239, 8665
Groom or Stable Employee (Racetrack) 382, 5821
Guide Dog Instructor 383, 8669
Guide (Hunting and Fishing); Professional 2810
Hearing Aid Dispenser 3402
Horse Owner by Open Claim (Racetrack) 5822
Horse Owner (Racetrack) 5823
Horseshoer (Racetrack) 384, 5824
Insurance Adjuster 103
Insurance Adjuster; Public 104
Insurance Agent 3783
Insurance Broker 3784
Investment Adviser 7756
Jockey Agent (Racetrack) 812, 5825
Jockey (Racetrack) 813, 5826
Jockey Room/Driver's Room Attendant (Racetrack) 3319, 5827
Judge (Amateur Boxing, Kickboxing, or Martial Arts) 814
Judge (Professional Boxing, Kickboxing, or Martial Arts) 815
Land Surveyor; Professional 8178
Landscape Architect 4054
Lobbyist 4258
Locksmith 8695
Manicurist 1290
Marriage, Family, and Child Counselor 2058
Marshal (Racetrack) 816, 5828
Matchmaker (Boxing, Kickboxing, or Martial Arts) 4320
Milk Hauler and Tester 3632, 8278
Notary Public 4483
Nuclear Medical Technologist 4530
Nurse Anesthetist 7337
Nurse Midwife 7338
Nurse Practitioner 7339
Nurse; Vocational 4204
Nursing Home Administrator 3341
Occupational Therapist 4572

1263

California, continued

Officer, Director, or Partner of a Racing Association (Racetrack) 3135, 5829
Official and Manager of a Racing Association (Racetrack) 3136, 5830
Optician 2401
Optometrist 4666
Osteopathic Physician (D.O.) 5197
Outrider (Racetrack) 385, 5831
Paddock Attendant (Racetrack) 386, 5832
Parimutuel Employee (Racetrack) 5833
Pest Control Field Representative; Structural 4750
Pest Control Operator; Structural 4751
Pesticide Applicator 4747
Pesticide Applicator; Qualified 4749
Pesticide Dealer 4748
Pharmacist 4924
Pharmacy Intern 4925
Photofinish Operator (Racetrack) 4996, 5834
Physical Therapist 5063
Physical Therapist Assistant 5028
Physician 5198
Physician's Assistant 5131
Podiatrist 5429
Pony Rider (Racetrack) 387, 5835
Private Investigator 2325
Private Patrol Operator 3256
Professional Athletic Promoter 4321
Professional Boxer 817
Professional Engineer 5577
Professional Guide (Hunting and Fishing) 2810
Professional Kickboxer 818
Professional Land Surveyor 8178
Professional Martial Arts Fighter 819
Protection Dog Operator 3257
Psychiatric-Mental Health Nurse 7340
Psychiatric Technician 4554
Psychological Assistant 5667
Psychologist 5668
Psychologist; Educational 5666
Public Insurance Adjuster 104
Qualified Pesticide Applicator 4749
Racing Official (Racetrack) 820, 5836
Radiation Therapy Technologist 7070
Radiologic Technologist 7071
Real Estate Appraiser 7143
Real Estate Broker 7144
Real Estate Sales Agent 7145
Referee (Amateur Boxing, Kickboxing, or Martial Arts) 821
Referee (Professional Boxing, Kickboxing, or Martial Arts) 822
Registered Nurse 7341
Repossession Company Operator 105, 8747
Respiratory Care Practitioner 7440
Satellite Facility Supervisor (Racetrack) 1728, 5837
School Administrator 2435
School Clinical-Rehabilitative Associate 8041
School Counselor 2059
School Health Services Associate 2196, 2257, 5199, 7342
School Library Media Teacher 4154
Second (Boxing, Kickboxing, or Martial Arts) 823
Secondary School Teacher 7627
Securities Broker-Dealer 7757
Security Guard (Racetrack) 3258, 5838
Security Investigator (Racetrack) 2326, 5839
Security Officer (Racetrack) 3259, 5840
Social Worker 7964
Specialty Contractor 1851
Speech-Language Pathologist 8042
Stable Agent (Racetrack) 5841
Stable Foreman (Racetrack) 1532, 5842
Starting Gate Driver (Racetrack) 5843
Steward (Racetrack) 824, 5844
Steward's Aid (Racetrack) 5845
Structural Pest Control Field Representative 4750
Structural Pest Control Operator 4751
Superintendent (Racetrack) 3137, 5846
Tax Interviewer 8233
Tax Preparer 8234
Teacher; General 7626
Ticket Seller (Boxing, Kickboxing, or Martial Arts) 8332
Ticket Taker (Boxing, Kickboxing, or Martial Arts) 8333
Timekeeper (Boxing, Kickboxing, or Martial Arts) 825
Totalisator Technician (Racetrack) 5847
Trainer (Boxing, Kickboxing, or Martial Arts) 3688
Trainer (Racetrack) 388, 5848
Valet (Racetrack) 5849
Vendor (Racetrack) 5850, 7485
Veterinarian 8354
Veterinarian (Racetrack) 5851, 8355
Veterinarian (Racetrack); Assistant to the 380, 5812
Video Operator (Racetrack) 4997, 5852
Vocational Nurse 4204

Colorado

Acupuncturist 74
Animal Technician 389
Apprentice Jockey (Horse) 826, 5853
Architect 721
Artificial Inseminator 390, 8583
Assistant Starter (Horse) 827, 5854
Assistant Trainer (Greyhound Racing) 391, 5855
Assistant Trainer (Horse Racing) 392, 5856
Attorney 4104
Authorized Agent (Greyhound) 5857
Authorized Agent (Horse) 5858
Bailbondsman 1250
Barber 1291
Certified Public Accountant 6
Certified Shorthand Reporter 8130
Child Health Associate 5547
Chiropractor 1636
Collections Manager 106
Commercial Pesticide Applicator 4752
Cosmetician 1292
Cosmetologist 1293
Counselor; Licensed Professional 2060
Debt Collector 107
Dental Hygienist 2197
Dentist 2258
Electrical Contractor 1852, 2558
Electrician; Journeyman 2559
Electrician; Master 2560
Emergency Medical Technician 2680
Engineer-in-Training 5578
Exercise Person (Horse Racing) 393, 5859
General Teacher 3942
Groom (Greyhound Racing) 394, 5860
Groom (Horse Racing) 395, 5861
Guide (Hunting and Fishing); Professional 2812
Hearing Aid Dealer/Dispenser 3403
Insurance Adjuster 108
Insurance Broker 3785
Insurance Sales Agent 3786
Jockey Agent (Horse) 5862
Jockey (Horse) 828, 5863
Journeyman Electrician 2559
Journeyman Plumber 5325
Kennel Helper (Greyhound Racing) 396, 5864
Land Surveyor-in-Training 8179
Land Surveyor; Professional 8180
Licensed Clinical Social Worker 7965
Licensed Practical Nurse 4205
Licensed Professional Counselor 2060
Lobbyist 4259
Manicurist 1294
Manufactured Housing Dealer 7146
Manufactured Housing Salesperson 7147
Marriage and Family Therapist 2061
Master Electrician 2560
Master Plumber 5326
Milk and Cream Sampler 3633
Milk and Cream Tester 3634
Mutuel Employee (Greyhound) 5865
Mutuel Employee (Horse) 5866
Notary Public 4484
Nursing Home Administrator 3342
Optometrist 4667
Osteopathic Physician (D.O.) 5200
Outfitter 2811
Owner (Greyhound) 5867
Owner (Horse) 5868
Owner/Trainer (Greyhound) 5869
Owner/Trainer (Horse) 5870
Pesticide Applicator; Commercial 4752
Pesticide Operator 4753
Pesticide Supervisor 1533, 4754
Pharmacist 4926
Pharmacy Intern 4927
Physical Therapist 5064
Physician 5201
Physician's Assistant 5132
Plater (Horse Racing) 397, 5871
Plumber Apprentice 5327
Plumber; Journeyman 5325
Plumber; Master 5326

Plumber; Residential 5328
Podiatrist 5430
Pony Person (Racing) 398, 5872
Professional Engineer 5579
Professional Guide (Hunting and Fishing) 2812
Professional Land Surveyor 8180
Psychiatric Technician 4555
Psychologist 5669
Public Pesticide Applicator 4755
Racing Official (Greyhound) 829, 5873
Racing Official (Horse) 830, 5874
Real Estate Appraiser 7148
Real Estate Broker 7149
Real Estate Sales Agent 7150
Registered Nurse 7343
Residential Plumber 5328
Residential Wireman 2561
School Administrator 2436
School Special Service Associate 5670, 7344, 7966, 8043
Securities Broker-Dealer 7758
Securities Sales Representative 7759
Social Worker; Licensed Clinical 7965
Solicitor 7924
Teacher; General 3942
Track Veterinarian (Horse) 5875, 8356
Trainer (Greyhound Racing) 399, 5876
Trainer (Horse Racing) 400, 5877
Valet (Horse) 5878
Veterinarian 8357
Veterinarian (Horse); Track 5875, 8356
Vocational Education Teacher 214
Wireman; Residential 2561

Connecticut

Administrator (Racetrack) 171, 5879
Announcer (Boxing and Wrestling) 7051
Announcer (Racetrack) 5880, 7052
Antenna Service Dealer 1706, 7925
Antenna Technician 1707
Apprentice Television Electronics Technician 1708
Arborist 2877, 3111
Architect 722
Assistant Announcer (Racetrack) 5881, 7053
Assistant Controller (Racetrack) 2770, 5882
Assistant Director of Security (Racetrack) 3138, 5883
Assistant General Manager (Racetrack) 5884
Assistant Manager (Racetrack) 172, 5885
Assistant Operations Manager (Racetrack) 173, 5886
Assistant Plant Superintendent (Racetrack) 174, 5887
Assistant Player's Manager (Racetrack) 5888
Assistant Racing Secretary (Racetrack) 831, 5889
Assistant Starter (Racetrack) 832, 5890
Assistant Trainer (Racetrack) 401, 5891

Attorney 4105
Audiologist 8044
Authorized Agent (Greyhound Track) 833, 5892
Automobile Physical Damage Appraiser 109
Ball Boy (Racetrack) 5893
Ball Repairer (Racetrack) 5894
Ballmaker (Racetrack) 5895
Barber 1295
Bench Technician (Racetrack) 5896
Box Office Employee (Racetrack) 5897, 8334
Boxer 834
Brakeman (Racetrack) 5898
Budget Analyst (Racetrack) 2771, 5899
Business Agent (Racetrack) 5900
Cameraman (Racetrack) 4998, 5901
Casualty Adjuster 110
Certified Public Accountant 7
Cesta Maker (Racetrack) 5902
Chart Writer (Racetrack) 5903
Chiropractor 1637
Clerk of Scales (Racetrack) 3512, 5904
Commercial Pesticide Applicator 4756
Computer Analyst (Racetrack) 5905, 8610
Computer Operator (Racetrack) 5906, 8611
Concession Employee (Racetrack) 5907, 7486
Concessionaire II (Racetrack) 5908, 7487
Corporation Director II (Racetrack) 3139, 5909
Corporation Officer II (Racetrack) 3140, 5910
Cosmetician 1296
Courier (Racetrack) 5911
Customer Service Employee (Racetrack) 5912
Dealer/Repairer, Weighing and Measuring Devices 5537
Dental Hygienist 2198
Dentist 2259
Deputy Judge (Racetrack) 835, 5913
Director of Security (Racetrack) 3141, 5914
Doctor (Racetrack) 5202, 5915
Dog Owner (Racetrack) 5916
Electrical Apprentice 2562
Electrical Contractor 1853, 2563
Electrical Journeyman 2564
Electrician (Racetrack) 2565, 5917
Electrologist 1297
Elementary School Teacher (PK-8) 3943
Elevator Apprentice 2653
Elevator Contractor 1854, 2654
Elevator Craftsman 2655
Elevator Helper 2656
Elevator Journeyman 2657
Embalmer 2906
Emergency Medical Technician 2681
Engineer-in-Training 5580
Facility Supervisor (Racetrack) 175, 5918

Field Service Manager (Racetrack) 1534, 5919
Field Technician (Racetrack) 5920
Fire Protection Sprinkler Apprentice 5329
Fire Protection Sprinkler Contractor 1855, 5330
Fire Protection Sprinkler Journeyman 5331
Funeral Director 2907
General Manager II (Racetrack) 5921
General Partner II (Racetrack) 5922
General Real Estate Appraiser 7151
Group Sales Person (Racetrack) 5923, 7488
Hairdresser 1298
Handicapper (Racetrack) 5924
Harness Driver (Racetrack) 836, 5925
Hearing Aid Dealer 3404
Heating-Cooling Apprentice 3458
Heating-Cooling Contractor 1856, 3459
Heating-Cooling Journeyman 3460
Home Improvement Contractor 1857
Home Improvement Salesperson 7926
Homeopathic Physician 5203
Hypertrichologist 1683
Instructor (Racetrack) 215, 5926
Insurance Adjuster; Public 112
Insurance Agent 3787
Insurance Broker 3788
Insurance Broker (Racetrack) 3789, 5927
Insurance Consultant 3790
Insurance Investigator (Racetrack) 111, 5928, 8678
Interior Designer 2314
Intermediate School Administrator or Supervisor 2437
Internal Auditor (Racetrack) 8, 5929
Investment Advisor 7760
Investment Advisor Agent 7761
Irrigation Contractor 1858, 5332
Jockey (Racetrack) 837, 5930
Judge (Boxing and Wrestling) 838
Judge (Racetrack) 839, 5931
Kennel Helper (Racetrack) 402, 5932
Kennel Master (Racetrack) 5933
Land Surveyor 8181
Land Surveyor-in-Training 8182
Landscape Architect 4055
Laundry Employee (Racetrack) 5934
Licensed Practical Nurse 4206
Lobbyist 4260
Lure Operator (Racetrack) 5935
Maintenance Employee (Racetrack) 5936
Manager (Boxing and Wrestling) 840
Marriage and Family Therapist 2062
Masseur (Racetrack) 5065, 5937
Matchmaker (Boxing and Wrestling) 4322
Midwife 4556
Milk Hauler and Tester 3635, 8279
Mutuel Employee (Racetrack) 5938
Mutuel Manager and Assistant Mutuel Manager (Racetrack) 2772, 5939
Naturopathic Physician 5204

Connecticut, continued

Newsstand Operator (Racetrack) 5940, 7489
Notary Public 4485
Nurse Aide 4557
Nurse Midwife 7345
Nurse (Racetrack) 5941, 7346
Nursing Home Administrator 3343
Occupational Therapist 4573
Occupational Therapy Assistant 4622
Office Employee (Racetrack) 5942, 7730
Office Secretary (Racetrack) 5943, 7731
Official (Racetrack) 841, 5944
Operators Manager (Racetrack) 2756, 5945
Optician 2402
Optometrist 4668
Osteopathic Physician (D.O.) 5205
Paddock Judge (Racetrack) 842, 5946
Parking Attendant (Racetrack) 3320, 5947
Patrol Judge (Racetrack) 843, 5948
Pesticide Applicator; Commercial 4756
Pesticide Dealer 4757
Pharmacist 4928
Pharmacy Intern 4929
Photo Finish Operator (Racetrack) 4999, 5949
Photographer (Racetrack) 5000, 5950
Physical Therapist 5066
Physician 5206
Physician; Homeopathic 5203
Physician's Assistant 5133
Player Attendant (Racetrack) 5951
Player Judge (Racetrack) 844, 5952
Player Manager II (Racetrack) 5953
Player's Trainer (Racetrack) 3689, 5954
Plumber, Journeyman 5333
Plumbing-Piping Apprentice 5334
Plumbing-Piping Contractor 1859, 5335
Plumbing-Piping Journeyman 5336
Podiatrist 5431
Private Investigator 2327
Private Pesticide Applicator 4758
Professional Engineer 5581
Promoter (Boxing and Wrestling) 4323
Promoter (Racetrack) 5955
Proprietor (Racetrack) 5956
Psychologist 5671
Public Director (Racetrack) 5957
Public Insurance Adjuster 112
Public Relations Employee (Racetrack) 4324, 5958
Public Weigher 3513
Publicist (Racetrack) 4325, 5959
Publicity Director (Racetrack) 4326, 5960
Race Control Employee (Racetrack) 5961
Racing Secretary (Racetrack) 845, 5962
Radio Electronics Service Dealer 1709, 7927
Radio Electronics Service Technician 1710
Real Estate Appraiser; General 7151

Real Estate Appraiser; Residential 7154
Real Estate Broker 7152
Real Estate Salesperson 7153
Referee (Boxing and Wrestling) 846
Registered Nurse 7347
Registered Nurse (Racetrack) 5963, 7348
Residential Real Estate Appraiser 7154
Respiratory Care Practitioner 7441
Salesperson; Home Improvement 7926
School Counselor 2063
School Library Media Associate 4155
Second (Boxing and Wrestling) 847
Secondary School Teacher (7-12) 7628
Securities Agent 7762
Securities Broker-Dealer 7763
Security Employee (Racetrack) 3260, 5964
Social Worker 7967
Solar Apprentice 3461
Solar Contractor 1860, 3462
Solar Journeyman 3463
Solid Waste Facility Operator 1729
Special Subjects Teacher 3944, 7629
Speech-Language Pathologist 8045
Sportswriter (Racetrack) 5965, 8764
Starter (Racetrack) 848, 5966
Statistician (Racetrack) 5967, 8765
Storekeeper (Racetrack) 5968
Superintendent (Racetrack) 3142, 5969
Superintendent of Schools 2438, 3143
Supplier (Racetrack) 5970
Surplus Lines Broker 3791
Telephone Operator (Racetrack) 5971, 8274
Television Electronics Service Dealer 1711, 7928
Television Electronics Technician 1712
Television Electronics Technician; Apprentice 1708
Timekeeper (Boxing and Wrestling) 849
Tote Technician (Racetrack) 5972
Trainer (Racetrack) 403, 5973
Treasurer (Racetrack) 2773, 5974
T.V. Tech Cameraman (Racetrack) 5001, 5975
Usher (Racetrack) 5976, 8335
Veterinarian 8358
Veterinarian (Racetrack) 5977, 8359
Weigher; Public 3513
Weighing and Measuring Devices; Dealer/Repairer, 5537
Well Drilling Contractor 4384
Well Drilling Journeyman 4385
Wrestler 850

Delaware

Admission Employee (Racetrack) 5978, 8336
Appraiser; Motor Vehicle 114
Architect 723
Assistant Racing Secretary (Racetrack) 851, 5979
Associate Judge (Racetrack) 852, 5980
Athletic Trainer 3690
Attorney 4106

Audiologist 8046
Barber 1299
Barber Apprentice 1300
Barber; Student 1311
Breath Analyzer (Racetrack) 3514, 5981
Certified Public Accountant 9
Chiropractor 1638
Clerk of the Course (Racetrack) 5982
Commercial Pesticide Applicator 4759
Concession Stand Employee (Racetrack) 5983, 7490
Cosmetologist 1301
Cosmetologist Apprentice 1302
Cosmetologist; Managing 1308
Cosmetology Demonstrator 1303
Cosmetology Instructor 216, 1304
Cosmetology Student 1305
Cosmetology; Student Instructor in 218, 1312
Dental Hygienist 2199
Dentist 2260
Early Childhood Teacher K-3 3945
Early Childhood Teacher (Pre-K and K) 3946, 5548
Electrician 2566
Electrologist 1306
Electrologist Instructor 217, 1307
Elementary School Guidance Counselor 2064
Elementary School Principal 2439
Elementary School Teacher 3947
Emergency Medical Technician 2682
Engineer-in-Training 5582
Equipment Inspector (Racetrack) 3515, 5984
Fraternal Representative 3792
Funeral Director 2908
Funeral Director Apprentice 2909
General Contractor 1861
General Paddock Employee (Racetrack) 5985
Geologist; Professional 3240
Groom (Racetrack) 404, 5986
Hearing Aid Dispenser 3405
Heating and Air Conditioning Mechanic 3464
Horse Driver (Racetrack) 853, 5987
Horse Owner (Racetrack) 5988
Horse Trainer (Racetrack) 405, 5989
Insurance Adjuster 113
Insurance Agent 3793
Insurance Broker 3794
Insurance Consultant 3795
Investment Advisor 7764
Laboratory Official (Racetrack) 2757, 3516, 5990
Land Surveyor 8183
Landscape Architect 4056
Licensed Clinical Social Worker 7968
Licensed Practical Nurse 4207
Lobbyist 4261
Maintenance Employee (Racetrack) 3896, 5991
Managing Cosmetologist 1308
Manicurist 1309
Masseuse/Masseur 5067
Mental Health Counselor 2065

Milk Hauler and Tester   3636, 8280
Motor Vehicle Appraiser   114
Mutuel Employee (Racetrack)   5992
Notary Public   4486
Nuclear Medical Technologist   4531
Nursing Home Administrator   3344
Occupational Therapist   4574
Occupational Therapy Assistant   4623
Optometrist   4669
Osteopathic Physician (D.O.)   5207
Paddock Inspector (Racetrack)   3517, 5993
Paddock Judge (Racetrack)   854, 5994
Parking Lot Attendant (Racetrack)   3321, 5995
Patrol Judge (Racetrack)   855, 5996
Pharmacist   4930
Pharmacy Intern   4931
Photographer Assistant (Racetrack)   5002, 5997
Photographer (Racetrack)   5003, 5998
Physical Therapist   5068
Physical Therapist Assistant   5029
Physician   5208
Physician's Assistant   5134
Podiatrist   5432
Presiding Judge (Racetrack)   856, 5999
Private Pesticide Applicator   4760
Professional Engineer   5583
Professional Geologist   3240
Program Director (Racetrack)   3144, 6000
Psychological Assistant   5672
Psychologist   5673
Racing Secretary (Racetrack)   857, 6001
Radiation Therapy Technologist   7072
Radiologic Technician   7073
Real Estate Broker   7155
Real Estate Sales Agent   7156
Registered Nurse   7349
River Pilot   8476
School Administrative Assistant   7732
School Administrative Supervisor   2440
School Library-Media Specialist   4156
School Superintendent   2441, 3145
Secondary School Guidance Counselor   2066
Secondary School Principal   2442
Secondary School Teacher   7630
Securities Agent   7765
Securities Broker-Dealer   7766
Security Employee (Racetrack)   3261, 6002
Shampooist   1310
Social Worker; Licensed Clinical   7968
Speech-Language Pathologist   8047
Starter (Racetrack)   858, 6003
State Steward (Racetrack)   859, 6004
Student Barber   1311
Student Instructor in Cosmetology   218, 1312
Surplus Lines Broker   3796
Tattoo Artist   8443, 8768
Teacher of Exceptional Children   3948, 7631
Thoroughbred Jockey (Racetrack)   860, 6005

Thoroughbred Owner (Racetrack)   6006
Thoroughbred Racing Official (Racetrack)   861, 6007
Thoroughbred Racing Personnel (Racetrack)   6008
Thoroughbred Trainer (Racetrack)   406, 6009
Timer (Racetrack)   862, 6010
Totalizator (Racetrack)   6011
Vendor Employee (Racetrack)   6012, 7491
Vendor (Racetrack)   6013, 7492
Veterinarian   8360
Veterinarian Assistant (Racetrack)   407, 6014
Veterinarian (Racetrack)   6015, 8361

District of Columbia

Acupuncturist   75
Architect   724
Attorney   4107
Auctioneer   1210
Auto Repossessor   115, 8587
Barber   1313
Certified Public Accountant   10
Certified Shorthand Reporter   8131
Charitable Solicitor   7929
Check Seller   1618
Chiropractor   1639
Commercial Pesticide Applicator   4761
Dance Therapist   8624
Dental Hygienist   2200
Dentist   2261
Dietitian   2366
Electrical Contractor   1862, 2567
Electrician   2568
Elementary School Librarian/Media Specialist   4157
Elementary School Teacher (1-6)   3949
Emergency Medical Technician   2683
Employment Counselor   2067, 4718
Fire and Casualty Insurance Agent   3797
Fire and Casualty Insurance Broker   3798
Fire and Casualty Insurance Solicitor   3799
Funeral Director   2910
Gasfitter   5337
Guide (Tourist)   8670
Hearing Aid Dispenser   3406
Home Improvement Salesman   7930
Insurance Agent; Fire and Casualty   3797
Insurance Broker; Fire and Casualty   3798
Insurance Solicitor; Fire and Casualty   3799
Interior Designer   2315
Junior High School Library/Media Specialist   4158
Licensed Practical Nurse   4208
Lobbyist   4262
Master Mechanic   1236
Motor Vehicle Dealer   7493
Motor Vehicle Salesperson   7494
Notary Public   4487

Nurse Midwife   7350
Nursing Home Administrator   3345
Nutritionist   2367
Occupational Therapist   4575
Occupational Therapy Assistant   4624
Operating Engineer   4357
Optometrist   4670
Osteopathic Physician (D.O.)   5209
Parking Lot Attendant   3322
Pawnbroker   7495
Pesticide Dealer   4762
Pesticide Employee   4763
Pesticide Operator   4764
Pharmacist   4932
Pharmacy Intern   4933
Physical Therapist   5069
Physician   5210
Physician's Assistant   5135
Plumber   5338
Plumbing Contractor   1863, 5339
Podiatrist   5433
Private Detective   2328
Private Pesticide Applicator   4765
Professional Engineer   5584
Property Manager   5651
Psychologist   5674
Public Pesticide Applicator   4766
Real Estate Appraiser   7157
Real Estate Broker   7158
Real Estate Sales Agent   7159
Recreation Therapist   8744
Refrigeration and Air Conditioning Contractor   1864, 3465
Refrigeration and Air Conditioning Mechanic   3466
Registered Nurse   7351
Salesman; Home Improvement   7930
School Librarian/Media Specialist for Senior High and Career Development Centers   4159
Secondary School Teacher (7-12)   7632
Securities Agent   7767
Securities Broker-Dealer   7768
Security Alarm Agent   7931
Security Alarm Dealer   7932
Security Guard   3262
Social Worker   7969
Solicitor   116
Solid Waste Collector   1730
Steam Engineer   5526
Veterinarian   8362

Florida

Acupuncturist   76
Agent, Jockey (Racetrack)   863, 6016
Air Conditioning Contractor   1865, 3467
Alarm System Contractor   1866
Alternate Racing/Game Official (Racetrack)   864, 6017
Announcer (Racetrack)   6018, 7054
Architect   725
Asbestos Abatement Contractor   1867
Asbestos Consultant   3720
Association Manager/Supervisor (Racetrack)   176, 3146, 6019

1267

Florida, continued

Association Officer/Director/Manager (Racetrack)   3147, 6020
Athlete Agent   865
Athletic Trainer (Racetrack)   3691, 6021
Attorney   4108
Auctioneer   1211
Auctioneer Apprentice   1212
Audiologist   8048
Authorized Agent (Racetrack)   866, 6022
Barber   1314
Blacksmith/Plater (Racetrack)   408, 6023
Building Contractor   1868
Cemetery Lot Salesperson   7160
Certified Public Accountant   11
Certified Shorthand Reporter   8132
Chart Writer (Racetrack)   6024
Chiropractor   1640
Clerk of Scales (Racetrack)   3518, 6025
Clinical Lab Technician   1684
Clinical Social Worker   7970
Commercial Applicator   4767
Commercial Pool/Spa Contractor   1869
Comptroller (Racetrack)   2774, 6026
Concession Employee (Racetrack)   6027, 7496
Concession Manager/Supervisor (Racetrack)   6028, 7497
Condominium Manager   5652
Contractual Concessionaire (Racetrack)   6029, 7498
Cosmetologist   1315
Dental Hygienist   2201
Dental Radiographer   2244, 7074
Dentist   2262
Dietitian-Nutritionist   2368
Direct Disposer   2911, 8627
Doctor (Racetrack)   5211, 6030
Drywall Specialty Contractor; Gypsum   1872
Electrical Contractor   1870, 2569
Electrologist   1316
Elementary School Teacher   3950
Embalmer   2912
Emergency Medical Technician   2684
Entry Clerk (Racetrack)   6031
Exercise Person (Racetrack)   409, 6032
Funeral Director   2913
General Contractor   1871
General Employee (Racetrack)   6033
Geologist; Professional   3241
Greyhound Judge (Racetrack)   867, 6034
Greyhound Owner (Racetrack)   6035
Greyhound Trainer/Assistant (Racetrack)   410, 6036
Guidance Counselor (K-12)   2068
Gypsum Drywall Specialty Contractor   1872
Handicapper (Racetrack)   6037
Harness Driver (Racetrack)   868, 6038
Harness Owner (Racetrack)   6039
Harness Trainer/Assistant (Racetrack)   411, 6040
Hearing Aid Specialist   3407
Horse Identifier (Racetrack)   6041
Horse Show Promoter (Racetrack)   4327, 6042
Horsemen's Bookkeeper (Racetrack)   2775, 6043
Insurance Adjuster   117
Insurance Agent   3800
Interior Designer   2316
Investment Advisor   7769
Jai-Alai Judge   869
Jai-Alai Player   870
Jockey/Apprentice Jockey (Racetrack)   871, 6044
Land Surveyor; Professional   8184
Landscape Architect   4057
Licensed Practical Nurse   4209
Lobbyist   4263
Lure Operator (Racetrack)   6045
Marriage and Family Therapist   2069
Massage Therapist; Personal   5070
Master Social Worker   7971
Mechanical Contractor   1873
Mental Health Counselor   2070
Middle School Teacher (5-9)   7633
Milk Hauler and Tester   3637, 8281
Mortgage Broker   7770
Notary Public   4488
Nuclear Medical Technologist   4532
Nurse (Racetrack)   6046, 7352
Nursing Home Administrator   3346
Occupational Therapist   4576
Occupational Therapy Assistant   4625
Optician   2403
Optometrist   4671
Osteopathic Physician (D.O.)   5212
Paddock/Patrol/Placing Judge (Racetrack)   872, 6047
Paramedic   2685
Paramedic/EMT (Racetrack)   2686, 6048
Personal Massage Therapist   5070
Pest Control Operator   4768
Pesticide Dealer   4769
Pharmacist   4934
Pharmacy Intern   4935
Physical Therapist   5071
Physical Therapist Assistant   5030
Physician   5213
Physician's Assistant   5136
Physician's Assistant (Racetrack)   5137, 6049
Players' Manager/Assistant/Matchmaker (Jai-Alai)   873
Players' Trainer/Assistant (Jai-Alai)   3692, 6050
Plumbing Contractor   1874, 5340
Podiatrist   5434
Pollutant Storage System Specialty Contractor   1875
Pool/Spa Contractor; Residential   1878
Pool/Spa Servicing Contractor   1876
Private Applicator   4770
Private Investigator   2329
Professional Engineer   5585
Professional Geologist   3241
Professional Land Surveyor   8184
Psychologist   5675
Public Applicator   4771
Quarter Horse Owner (Racetrack)   6051
Quarter Horse Trainer/Assistant (Racetrack)   412, 6052
Racing Secretary, Assistant (Racetrack)   6053
Racing Secretary (Racetrack)   874, 6054
Radiation Therapy Technologist   7075
Radiologic Technologist   7076
Real Estate Appraiser   7161
Real Estate Broker   7162
Real Estate Instructor   219, 7163
Real Estate Salesperson   7164
Registered Nurse   7353
Registered Professional Reporter   8133
Residential Contractor   1877
Residential Pool/Spa Contractor   1878
Residential Solar Water Heating Specialty Contractor   1879, 3468
Respiratory Care Practitioner   7442
Respiratory Therapist   7443
Respiratory Therapy Technician   7444
Roofing Contractor   1880
School Administrator or Supervisor   2443
School Educational Media Specialist   4160
School Principal   2444
Secondary School Teacher (6-12)   7634
Securities Associated Person   7771
Securities Dealer   7772
Securities Issuer/Dealer   7773
Sheet Metal Contractor   1881
Ship's Pilot   8477
Social Worker; Master   7971
Solid Waste Facility Operator   1731
Specialty Structure Contractor   1882
Speech-Language Pathologist   8049
Stable Agent (Racetrack)   6055
Stable/Kennel Helper (Racetrack)   413, 6056
Starter (Racetrack)   875, 6057
Steward (Racetrack)   876, 6058
Thoroughbred Owner (Racetrack)   6059
Thoroughbred Trainer/Assistant (Racetrack)   414, 6060
Time-Share Agent   7165
Tote Employee (Racetrack)   6061
Tote Owner/Operator (Racetrack)   6062
Underground Utility Contractor   1883
Vendor (Racetrack)   6063, 7499
Vendor Representative/Salesman (Racetrack)   6064, 7500
Veterinarian   8363
Veterinarian Assistant (Racetrack)   415, 6065
Veterinarian (Racetrack)   6066, 8364

Georgia

Accountant; Foreign   13
Accountant; Registered Public   14
Acupuncturist   77
Adjuster; Public   119
Apprentice Auctioneer   1213
Architect   726
Athlete Agent   877
Athletic Trainer   3693
Attorney   4109

Auctioneer 1214
Audiologist 8050
Barber 1317
Barber Teacher 220, 1318
Cardiac Technician 8598
Certified Landfill Inspector 3519
Certified Landfill Operator 1732
Certified Public Accountant 12
Certified Shorthand Reporter 8134
Chiropractor 1641
Clinical Social Worker 7972
Commercial Pesticide Applicator (Certified Operator) 4772
Conditioned Air Contractor 1884, 3469
Cosmetologist; Master 1322
Cosmetology Teacher 221, 1319
Dental Hygienist 2202
Dentist 2263
Dietitian 2369
Electrical Contractor 1885, 2570
Embalmer 2914
Embalmer Apprentice 2915
Engineer-in-Training 5586
Esthetician 1320
Foreign Accountant 13
Forester 2878
Funeral Director 2916
Funeral Director Apprentice 2917
General Contractor 1886
Geologist 3242
Hearing Aid Dealer 3408
Hearing Aid Dispenser 3409
Hearing Aid Dispenser Apprentice 3410
Insurance Adjuster 118
Insurance Agent 3801
Insurance Counselor 3802
Insurance Sales Agent 3803
Journeyman Plumber 5341
Land Surveyor 8185
Land Surveyor-in-Training 8186
Landfill Inspector; Certified 3519
Landfill Operator; Certified 1732
Landscape Architect 4058
Librarian 4161
Licensed Practical Nurse 4210
Licensed Undergraduate Nurse 4211
Lobbyist 4264
Low Voltage Contractor 1887, 2571
Manicurist 1321
Marriage and Family Therapist 2071
Master Cosmetologist 1322
Master Plumber 5342
Master Social Worker 7973
Master Therapeutic Recreation Specialist 8698
Milk Hauler and Tester 3638, 8282
Motor Vehicle Dismantler 1237, 8701
Notary Public 4489
Nuclear Pharmacist 4936
Nurse; Licensed Undergraduate 4211
Nursing Home Administrator 3347
Occupational Therapist 4577
Occupational Therapy Assistant 4626
Optician 2404
Optometrist 4672
Osteopathic Physician (D.O.) 5214
Paramedic 2687

Pesticide Applicator (Certified Operator); Commercial 4772
Pesticide Contractor 4773
Pesticide Employee 4774
Pharmacist 4937
Pharmacy Intern 4938
Physical Therapist 5072
Physician 5215
Physician's Assistant 5138
Plumber; Journeyman 5341
Plumber; Master 5342
Podiatrist 5435
Polygraph Examiner 5496
Polygraph Examiner, Intern 5497
Private Detective 2330
Private Security Guard 3263
Professional Counselor 2072
Professional Engineer 5587
Psychologist 5676
Public Adjuster 119
Public Water Supply System Operator 8505
Real Estate Appraiser 7166
Real Estate Broker 7167
Real Estate Sales Agent 7168
Rebuilder 1238
Recreation Administrator 177, 8741
Recreation Leader 8742
Recreation Specialist; Master Therapeutic 8698
Recreation Supervisor 8743
Registered Nurse 7354
Registered Professional Reporter 8135
Registered Public Accountant 14
Salvage Pool Operator 8754
Salvage Yard Dealer 7501, 8755
School Administrator or Supervisor 2445
School Service Associate 2073, 2370, 5677, 7974, 8051
Securities General Dealer 7774
Securities Limited Dealer 7775
Securities Salesman 7776
Social Worker; Master 7973
Speech-Language Pathologist 8052
Teacher (K-12) 3951, 7635
Therapeutic Recreation Specialist 8779
Therapeutic Recreation Technician 5031, 8780
Used Car Dealer 7502
Veterinarian 8365
Veterinary Technician 416
Wastewater Collection System Operator 8506
Wastewater Laboratory Analyst 7600
Wastewater Treatment System Operator 8507
Water Distribution System Operator 8508
Water Laboratory Analyst 7601
Water Supply System Operator; Public 8505

Hawaii

Acupuncturist 78
Architect 727

Architect, Landscape 4059
Attorney 4110
Automobile Mechanic 1239
Barber 1323
Beauty Operator 1324
Boxer 878
Bus Driver; Motor Vehicle Operator, 1600
Certified Public Accountant 15
Chiropractor 1642
Clinical Laboratory Cytotechnologist 1685
Clinical Laboratory Technician 1686
Clinical Laboratory Technologist/ Specialist 1687
Commercial Marine License 8478
Condominium Hotel Operator 8615
Condominium Managing Agent 5653
Contractor 1888
Dental Hygienist 2203
Dentist 2264
Detective and Guard, Private 2331, 3264
Dispensing Optician 2405
Educational Administrator 2446
Electrician; Journeyman 2572
Electrician; Journeyman Industrial 2573
Electrician; Journeyman Specialty 2574
Electrician; Maintenance 2575
Electrician; Supervising 1535, 2576
Electrician; Supervising Industrial 1536, 2577
Electrician; Supervising Specialty 1537, 2578
Electrologist 1325
Elevator Mechanic 2658
Embalmer 2918
Emergency Medical Technician - Ambulance 2688
Engineer, Professional 5588
Fumigator Operator 4775
Hearing Aid Dealer and Fitter 3411
Insurance Salesperson 3804
Investment Advisor 7777
Investment Advisor Representative 7778
Journeyman Electrician 2572
Journeyman Industrial Electrician 2573
Journeyman Specialty Electrician 2574
Land Surveyor 8187
Lobbyist 4265
Maintenance Electrician 2575
Massage Therapist 5073
Mobile Intensive Care Technician (Paramedic) 2689
Motor Vehicle Operator, Bus Driver 1600
Motor Vehicle Operator, School Bus Driver 1601
Motor Vehicle Operator, Taxicab Driver 8246
Motor Vehicle Operator, Truck Driver 8283
Motor Vehicle Salesperson 7503
Naturopath 5216
Notary Public 4490
Nurse, Licensed Practical 4212
Nurse, Registered 7355

Hawaii, continued

Nursing Home Administrator 3348
Optometrist 4673
Osteopathic Physician and Surgeon 5217
(Paramedic); Mobile Intensive Care Technician 2689
Pest Control Field Representative 4776
Pest Control Operator 4777
Pharmacist 4939
Physical Therapist 5074
Physician Assistant 5139
Physician, MD 5218
Plumber 5343
Podiatrist 5436
Psychologist 5678
Radiologic Technologist 7077
Real Estate Appraiser 7169
Real Estate Broker 7170
Real Estate Salesman 7171
Sanitarian 3520
School Administrator 2447
School Bus Driver; Motor Vehicle Operator, 1601
School Counselor 2074
School Librarian 4162
Securities Dealer 7779
Securities Salesperson 7780
Shorthand Reporter 8136
Social Worker 7975
Speech Pathologist or Audiologist 8053
Supervising Electrician 1535, 2576
Supervising Industrial Electrician 1536, 2577
Supervising Specialty Electrician 1537, 2578
Tattoo Artist 8444, 8770
Taxicab Driver; Motor Vehicle Operator, 8246
Teacher (K-12) 3952, 7636
Truck Driver; Motor Vehicle Operator, 8283
Veterinarian 8366

Idaho

Advanced Emergency Medical Technician - Ambulance 2690
Apprentice Electrician 2579
Apprentice Jockey (Racetrack) 879, 6067
Architect 728
Assistant Trainer (Racetrack) 417, 6068
Associate Real Estate Broker 7172
Athletic Trainer 3694
Attorney 4111
Audiologist; School 8054
Barber 1326
Barber Apprentice 1327
Barber Instructor 222, 1328
Boilermaker 1589
Boxer 880
Certified Public Accountant 16
Certified Registered Nurse Anesthetist 7356
Certified Shorthand Reporter 8137
Certified Social Worker 7976
Chiropractor 1643
Commercial Applicator 4778
Commercial Operator 4779
Concession Employee (Racetrack) 6069, 7504
Concessionaire (Racetrack) 6070, 7505
Cosmetologist 1329
Cosmetology Apprentice 1330
Cosmetology Instructor 223, 1331
Cosmetology Student 1332
Dental Hygienist 2204
Dentist 2265
Denturist 2245
Denturist Intern 2246
Director of Special Education 2448
Donated Concession Employee (Racetrack) 6071, 7506
Electrical Contractor 1889, 2580
Electrical Contractor; Specialty 1893, 2582
Electrician; Apprentice 2579
Electrician; Journeyman 2581
Electrician; Specialty 2583
Electrologist/Esthetician 1333
Elementary School Teacher (1-8) 3953
Emergency Medical Technician - Ambulance; Advanced 2690
Emergency Medical Technician - Paramedic 2691
Engineer-in-Training 5589
Environmental Health Specialist 3521
Environmental Health Specialist Trainee 3522
Esthetician 1334
Exceptional Child School Program Supervisor 2449
Exercise Boy/Girl (Racetrack) 418, 6072
Florist 2317, 8649
Funeral Director 2919
Fur Buyer 8559, 8654
General Contractor 1890
General Real Estate Appraiser, Certified 7173
Geologist 3243
Groom (Racetrack) 419, 6073
Guide 2813
Hearing Aid Dealer 3412
Hearing Aid Fitter 3413
Insurance Broker 3805
Insurance Consultant 3806
Insurance Sales Agent 3807
Investment Adviser 7781
Investment Adviser Agent 7782
Jockey Agent (Racetrack) 881, 6074
Jockey (Racetrack) 882, 6075
Journeyman Electrician 2581
Journeyman Plumber 5344
Kennel Employee (Racetrack) 420, 6076
Land Surveyor-in-Training 8188
Land Surveyor; Professional 8189
Landscape Architect 4060
Landscape Designer 4061
Licensed Practical Nurse 4213
Limited Applicator 4780
Lobbyist 4266
Manicurist/Nail Technician 1335
Manufactured Home Broker 7174
Manufactured Home Dealer 7175
Manufactured Home Manufacturer 1891
Manufactured Home Salesperson 7176
Manufactured Home Service Company 7933
Milk Hauler and Tester 3639, 8284
Mixer-Loader 4781
Mortician 2920
Mortician Resident Trainee 2921
Mutuel Employee (Racetrack) 6077
Notary Public 4491
Nurse Practitioner 7357
Nursery Agent 3112, 4543
Nurseryman 3113, 4544
Nursing Home Administrator 3349
Occupational Therapist 4578
Occupational Therapy Assistant 4627
Official (Racetrack) 883, 6078
Optometrist 4674
Osteopathic Physician (D.O.) 5219
Outfitter 2814
Owner (Racetrack) 6079
Pest Control Consultant 4782
Pesticide Dealer 4783
Pharmacist 4940
Pharmacy Intern 4941
Physical Therapist 5075
Physical Therapy Assistant 5032
Physician 5220
Physician's Assistant 5140
Plater (Racetrack) 421, 6080
Plumber Apprentice 5345
Plumber; Journeyman 5344
Plumbing Contractor 1892, 5346
Podiatrist 5437
Pony Boy/Girl (Racetrack) 422, 6081
Private Applicator 4784
Professional Counselor 2075
Professional Engineer 5590
Professional Land Surveyor 8189
Psychologist 5679
Real Estate Appraiser, Certified; General 7173
Real Estate Appraiser, Licensed; Residential 7179
Real Estate Broker 7177
Real Estate Broker; Associate 7172
Real Estate Salesperson 7178
Registered Nurse 7358
Registered Nurse Anesthetist; Certified 7356
Residential Care Facility Administrator 3350
Residential Real Estate Appraiser, Licensed 7179
Respiratory Therapist 7445
School Audiologist 8054
School Counselor 2076
School Nurse 7359
School Principal 2450
School Psychological Examiner 5680
School Psychologist 5681
School Social Worker 7977
School Superintendent 2451, 3148

Secondary School Teacher (7-12) 7637
Securities Broker-Dealer 7783
Securities Salesperson 7784
Social Worker 7978
Social Worker; Certified 7976
Solicitor/collector 120
Specialty Electrical Contractor 1893, 2582
Specialty Electrician 2583
Stable Employee (Racetrack) 423, 6082
Standard Communications Disorders School Specialist 8055
Taxidermist 8261, 8778
Teacher of the Exceptional Child 3954, 7638
Trainer (Racetrack) 424, 6083
Trapper 2815
Veterinarian 8367
Veterinarian (Racetrack) 6084, 8368
Water Well Drilling Operator 4386
Water Well Drilling Supervisor 1538, 4387
Welder 8792
Wrestler 884

Illinois

Accident Reconstruction Specialist 5478, 8574
Accounting/Payroll Clerk (Gaming) 2987
Alarm Contractor; Private 1899
Animal Breeder (Fur Bearing) 316, 425, 8580
Animal Health Technician (Racetrack) 426, 6085
Announcer (Boxing/Wrestling) 7055
Apprentice Blacksmith (Racetrack) 427, 6086
Apprentice Jockey (Racetrack) 885, 6087
Apprentice Plumber 5347
Aquaculturist 2763, 8582
Architect 729
Asbestos Air Sampling Professional 1770, 3721
Asbestos Contractor 1894
Asbestos Inspector 1771
Asbestos Management Planner 1895, 3722
Asbestos Project Designer 1896, 3723
Asbestos Project Manager 1897, 3724
Asbestos Project Supervisor 1539, 1898, 3725
Asbestos Worker 3726
Assistant Starter (Racetrack) 886, 6088
Assistant Trainer (Racetrack) 428, 6089
Associate Director of Sales/Sales Manager (Gaming Industry) 2988, 4328, 7934
Athletic Trainer 3695
Attorney 4112
Audiologist 8056
Authorized Agent (Racetrack) 887, 6090
Automotive Parts Recycler 7507
Barber 1336

Barber Teacher 224, 1337
Bartender (Gaming Industry) 2851, 2989
Blacksmith (Racetrack) 429, 6091
Blaster 4388
Boat Operator; Passenger Boat/Charter 8481
Boiler Inspector; Deputy 1772, 3525
Boiler Inspector (Insurance Co.); Special 1773, 3530
Boxperson (Gaming) 2990
Breath Analyzer Operator 3523, 8591
Breeder; Wild Game and Bird 317, 440, 8799
Bulk Milk Hauler/Sampler 3640, 8285
Cage Credit Manager (Gaming) 2776, 2991
Casino Cage Cashier (Gaming) 1619, 2992
Casino Floor Game Supervisor (Gaming) 2993
Casino Manager (Gaming) 2994, 3149
Casino Reservations and Ticketing Manager (Gaming) 2995
Casino Shift Manager (Gaming) 2996
Certified Occupational Therapy Assistant 4628
Certified Public Accountant 17
Certified Shorthand Reporter 8138
Change Attendant (Gaming) 1620, 2997
Chef/Executive Kitchen Manager (Gaming) 2998, 8606
Chief Financial Officer/Controller (Gaming) 2777, 2999
Chief Operating Officer/General Manager (Gaming) 3000, 3150
Chief School Business Official 2452, 2778
Child Care Aide 5549
Chiropractor 1644
Clinical Social Worker 7979
Coal Mine Worker 4389
Cocktail Waitress (Gaming) 2852, 3001
Collection Agent 121
Commercial Driver (Truck or Bus) 1602, 8286
Commercial Fisherman 2816
Commercial Musseler 2817
Commercial Pesticide Applicator 4785
Commercial Pesticide Applicator For Private Company (Not For Hire) 4786
Commercial Pesticide Operator 4787
Commercial Pesticide Operator For Private Company (Not For Hire) 4788
Computer Programmer (Gaming) 3002, 8612
Cook (Gaming) 3003, 8616
Coroner; Illinois County 3526, 8675
Cosmetologist 1338
Cosmetology Teacher 225, 1339
County Corrections Officer 8621
Cross-Connection Control Device Inspector 3524, 8622
Dealer (Gaming) 3004
Deckhand (Gaming) 3005

Dental Hygienist 2205
Dentist 2266
Deputy Boiler Inspector 1772, 3525
Detection of Deception Examiner (Lie Detector Operator) 5498
Director of Marketing and Public Relations (Gaming) 3006, 4329
Director of Security (Gaming) 3007, 3151
Dishwasher/Kitchen Utility Helper (Gaming) 3008, 8628
Distribution System Operator (Water Supply) 8509
Driver (Racetrack) 6092
Driver-Trainer (Racetrack) 888, 6093
Driver Training Instructor 226
Driver Training Instructor (Third Party Certification) 227
Early Childhood Teacher PK-3 3955, 5550
Education Provider (Insurance) 228
Electrical Hoisting Engineer (Coal Mine) 4358, 4390
Electronic Criminal Surveillance Officer 5479, 8633
Elementary School Teacher K-9 3956
Emergency Medical Technician (EMT)—Coal Mine or Ambulance 2692
Emergency Medical Technician (EMT)—Intermediate 2693
Emergency Medical Technician (EMT)—Paramedic 2694
Employment Agency Counselor; Private 2077, 4720
Engineer 5591
Engineer (Riverboat Gambling) 8479
Esthetician 1340
Esthetician Teacher 229, 1341
Exercise Person (Racetrack) 430, 6094
Explosives Detonator and Storekeeper 4391
Explosives Handler (Magazine) 4392
Fee Fishing Area Operator 2818
Fire Equipment Distributor 7935
Fire Equipment Employee 2584, 2799
Firefighter 2800
First Mate (Gaming) 3009, 8480
Fish Dealer (Non-Resident) 7508
Fish Dealer (Resident) 7509
Fisherman; Commercial 2816
Food and Beverage Manager (Gaming) 2853, 3010
Food Service Sanitation Manager 2854
Food Service Sanitation Manager Certification Instructor 230
Foreman (Racetrack) 6095
Funeral Director and Embalmer 2922
Fur Buyer (Non-Resident) 8560, 8655
Fur Buyer (Resident) 8561, 8656
Fur Tanner or Dyer 8262, 8663
General Accountant (Gaming) 18, 3011
Gift Shop Manager (Gaming) 3012, 7510
Gift Shop Salesperson (Gaming) 3013, 7511
Gloveman (Boxing/Wrestling) 889
Grain Warehouse Operator 1733

1271

Illinois, continued

Groom (Racetrack) 431, 6096
Gym Owner (Boxing/Wrestling) 3152
Habilitation Aide 4629
Hard Count Clerk (Gaming) 3014
Hard Count/Soft Count Supervisor (Gaming) 3015
Hearing Aid Dispenser 3414
High School Teacher 6-12 7639
Home Health Aide 8672
Hotwalker (Racetrack) 432, 6097
Housekeeper (Gaming) 3016, 3897
Housekeeping Supervisor (Gaming) 1540, 3017
Human Resource Manager (Gaming) 3018, 4719
Hunting Area Operator (Exotic Game) 2819
Hunting Area Operator (Migratory Waterfowl) 2820
Illinois County Coroner 3526, 8675
Illinois County Sheriff 5480
Industrial Radiographer 7078
Inspector; Cross-Connection Control Device 3524, 8622
Insurance Adjuster; Public 122
Insurance Producer 3808
Interior Designer 2318
Internal Audit Manager (Gaming) 2779, 3019
Intertrack Employee (Racetrack) 6098
Invention Developer 8681
Investment Advisor 7785
Jockey Agent (Racetrack) 890, 6099
Jockey (Racetrack) 891, 6100
Laboratory Analysis Technician 1688
Land Surveyor 8190
Landfill Chief Operator 1734
Landscape Architect 4062
Law Enforcement Officer 5481
Licensed Clinical Psychologist 5682
Licensed Practical Nurse 4214
Lobbyist 4267
Maintenance Manager (Gaming) 1541, 3020, 3898
Maintenance Supervisor (Gaming) 1542, 3021, 3899
Maintenance Worker (Gaming) 3022, 3900
Marketing Assistant/Secretary (Gaming) 3023, 7733
Match-Maker (Boxing/Wrestling) 4330
Medical Radiographer 7079
Metal Mine Foreman 1543, 4393
Metal Mine Hoisting Engineer 4359, 4394
Mine Examiner 3527, 4395
Mine Manager 4396
Mine Rescue Station Assistant 4397
Mine Rescue Station Supervisor 2695, 3351, 4398
Mine Supervisor; Surface 1546, 4404
M.I.S. Manager/Technical Supports Systems Operator (Gaming) 2758, 3024, 3153, 8700

Mussel Dealer (Resident and Non-Resident) 7512
Musselor; Commercial 2817
New Vehicle Dealer 7513
Notary Public 4492
Nuclear Medicine Technologist 4533
Nuisance Wildlife Control Operator 433, 8703
Nursing Home Administrator 3352
Occupational Rehabilitation Aide 4630
Occupational Therapist; Registered 4579
Occupational Therapy Assistant; Certified 4628
Oiler (Gaming) 3025
Optometrist 4675
Osteopathic Physician (D.O.) 5221
Out-Of-State Salvage Vehicle Buyer 8562, 8708
Owner-Assistant Trainer (Racetrack) 434, 6101
Owner-Driver (Racetrack) 892, 6102
Owner-Driver-Trainer (Racetrack) 893, 6103
Owner (Racetrack) 6104
Owner-Trainer (Racetrack) 435, 6105
Paramedic (Boxing/Wrestling) 2696
Passenger Boat/Charter Boat Operator 8481
Pest Control Technician (General Use); Structural 4793
Pest Control Technician (Restricted Use); Structural 4794
Pesticide Applicator For Private Company (Not For Hire); Commercial 4786
Pesticide Dealer 4789
Pesticide Operator; Commercial 4787
Pesticide Operator For Private Company (Not For Hire); Commercial 4788
Pharmacist 4942
Pharmacy Intern 4943
Pharmacy Technician 8720
Physical Rehabilitation Aide 5033
Physical Therapist 5076
Physical Therapist Assistant 5034
Physician 5222
Physician (Boxing/Wrestling) 5223
Physician's Assistant 5141
Pit Boss (Gaming) 3026
Plumber 5348
Plumber; Apprentice 5347
Podiatrist 5438
Pony Person (Racetrack) 436, 6106
Preserve Area Operator 437, 8731
Private Alarm Contractor 1899
Private Contractor (Sewage Disposal—System Pumping) 1900
Private Contractor (Sewage System Installation) 1901
Private Detective 2332
Private Employment Agency Counselor 2077, 4720
Private Pesticide Applicator 4790
Private Security Contractor 3265
Professional Boxer 894
Professional Boxing Judge 895

Professional Boxing Manager 896
Professional Boxing Promoter 4331
Professional Boxing Referee 897
Psychologist; Licensed Clinical 5682
Public Insurance Adjuster 122
Public Pesticide Applicator 4791
Public Pesticide Operator 4792
Purchasing Manager/Agent (Gaming) 3027, 8734
Race Track Employee (Racetrack) 6107
Racing Official (Racetrack) 898, 6108
Radiation Therapist 7080
Radiation Therapy Technologist 7081
Radiographer; Industrial 7078
Radiographer; Medical 7079
Radiologic Technologist 7082
Radon Measurement Specialist 3528
Real Estate Broker 7180
Real Estate Sales Agent 7181
Rebuilder of Salvage Vehicles 1240, 8740
Regional Sales Manager (Gaming) 3028, 4332
Registered Nurse 7360
Registered Occupational Therapist 4579
Registered Serviceperson (Weighing & Measuring Devices) 5538
Remittance Agent 1621
Restaurant Bus Helper (Gaming) 2855, 3029
Restaurant Cashier (Gaming) 1622, 3030
Restaurant Hostess/Host (Gaming) 2856, 3031
Restaurant Manager (Gaming) 2857, 3032
Restaurant Server (Gaming) 2858, 3033
Ring Lessor (Boxing/Wrestling) 7936
Riverboat Senior Master/Captain (Gaming) 3034, 8482
Roofing Contractor 1902
Sales/Ticketing/Reservations Employee (Gaming) 3035
Salvage Vehicle Buyer; Out-Of-State 8562, 8708
Salvage Vehicles; Rebuilder of 1240, 8740
School Guidance Counselor 2078
School Media Specialist/Librarian 4163
School Principal 2453
School Psychologist 5683
School Superintendent 2454, 3154
School Supervisor 2455
Scrap Processor 8758
Securities Dealer 7786
Securities Salesperson 7787
Security/Emergency Medical Technician Officer (Gaming) 2697, 3036
Security Officer (Gaming) 3037, 3266
Security Supervisor (Gaming) 1544, 3038, 3267
(Sewage Disposal—System Pumping); Private Contractor 1900
(Sewage System Installation); Private Contractor 1901
Shaft and Slope Examiner (Construction and Mining) 3529, 4399

Shaft and Slope Supervisor (Construction and Mining)   1545, 4400
Shaft and Slope Worker (Construction and Mining)   4401
Sheriff; Illinois County   5480
Shot Firer (Coal Mine); Underground   4405
Slot Manager (Gaming)   3039
Slot Mechanic (Gaming)   3040, 8761
Slot Supervisor (Gaming)   3041
Slot Technician (Gaming)   3042, 8762
Social Worker   7980
Soft Count Clerk (Gaming)   3043
Solid Waste Site Operator   1735
Sous Chef (Gaming)   2859, 3044, 8763
Special Boiler Inspector (Insurance Co.)   1773, 3530
Speech-Language Pathologist   8057
Starter (Racetrack)   899, 6109
State Mine Inspector (Coal Mine)   3531, 4402
State Mine Inspector (Metal Mine)   3532, 4403
Steward (Racetrack)   900, 6110
Structural Engineer   5592
Structural Pest Control Technician (General Use)   4793
Structural Pest Control Technician (Restricted Use)   4794
Surface Mine Supervisor   1546, 4404
Surveillance Manager (Gaming)   3045
Surveillance Operator (Gaming)   3046
Swimming Pool Operator   8767
Taxidermist   8263
Teacher of the Blind and Partially Sighted   3957, 7640
Teacher of the Deaf and Hard of Hearing   3958, 7641, 8058
Teacher of the Educable Mentally Handicapped   3959, 7642
Teacher of the Learning Disabled Student   3960, 7643
Teacher of the Physically Handicapped   3961, 7644
Teacher of the Socially-Emotionally Impaired   3962, 7645
Teacher of Special Subjects K-12   3963, 7646
Teacher of Speech and Language Impaired Students   3964, 7647, 8059
Teacher of the Trainable Mentally Handicapped   3965, 7648
Third Party Safety Officer   3268
Timber Buyer   8563, 8781
Timekeeper (Boxing and Wrestling)   901
Totalizator Employee (Racetrack)   6111
Trainer (Racetrack)   438, 6112
Trainer/Second (Boxing)   3696
Transporter (Motor Vehicles)   8287
Underground Shot Firer (Coal Mine)   4405
Underground Storage Tank (UST) Worker   1903
Used Vehicle Dealer   7514
Valet (Racetrack)   6113
Vehicle Auctioneer   1215, 8786
Vehicle Dealer; New   7513
Vehicle Repairer   1241
Vendor (Racetrack)   6114, 7515
Vendor's Helper (Racetrack)   6115, 7516
Veterinarian   8369
Veterinarian Assistant (Racetrack)   439, 6116
Veterinarian (Racetrack)   6117, 8370
Vision Screening Technician   8787
Warehouse/Receiving Clerk (Gaming)   3047
Wastewater Treatment Plant Operator   8510
Water Supply Operator   8511
Water Well Contractor   4406
Water Well and Pump Installation Contractor   1904
Water Well Pump Installation Contractor   1905
Water Well and Pump Installation Contractor   4407
Water Well Pump Installation Contractor   4408
Water Well and Pump Installation Contractor   5349
Water Well Pump Installation Contractor   5350
Wild Game and Bird Breeder   317, 440, 8799
Wildlife Control Operator; Nuisance   433, 8703
Wrestler   902
Wrestling Promoter   4333

Indiana

Accountant; Public   21
Accounting Practitioner   19
Architect   730
Asbestos Contractor   1906, 3727
Asbestos Inspector   1774
Asbestos Project Designer   1907, 3728
Asbestos Project Supervisor   1547, 1908, 3729
Asbestos Waste Disposal Manager   3730
Asbestos Worker   3731
Attending Physician (Boxing)   5224
Attorney   4113
Auctioneer   1216
Audiologist   8060
Barber   1342
Barber Instructor   231, 1343
Boxer   903
Certified Public Accountant   20
Certified Shorthand Reporter   8139
Chiropractor   1645
Commercial Pesticide Applicator   4795
Cosmetology Hairdresser   1344
Cosmetology Instructor   232, 1345
Dental Hygienist   2206
Dentist   2267
Early Childhood Teacher (Pre-K)   5551
Electrologist   1346
Elementary School Administrator   2456
Elementary School Teacher (1-6)   3966
Emergency Medical Technician   2698
Engineer   5593
Engineer-in-Training   5594
Esthetician   1347
Funeral Director   2923
Health Facility Administrator   3353
Hearing Aid Dealer   3415
Insurance Adjuster   123
Insurance Agent   3809
Insurance Consultant   3810
Investment Advisor   7788
Judge (Boxing)   904
Junior High/Middle School Teacher   7649
Land Surveyor   8191
Landscape Architect   4063
Licensed Practical Nurse   4215
Lobbyist   4268
Manager (Boxing)   905
Manicurist   1348
Marriage and Family Therapist   2079
Matchmaker (Boxing)   4334
Notary Public   4493
Nurse Midwife   7361
Nursing Home Administrator   3354
Occupational Therapist   4580
Occupational Therapy Assistant   4631
Optometrist   4676
Osteopathic Physician (D.O.)   5225
Pesticide Consultant   4796
Pesticide Technician   4797
Pharmacist   4944
Pharmacy Intern   4945
Physical Therapist   5077
Physical Therapist Assistant   5035
Physician   5226
Physician (Boxing); Attending   5224
Physician's Assistant   5142
Plumber   5351
Plumber Contractor   1909, 5352
Podiatrist   5439
Polygraph Examiner   5499
Primary School Teacher (K-3)   3967
Private Investigator   2333
Private Pesticide Applicator   4798
Promoter (Boxing)   4335
Psychologist   5684
Public Accountant   21
Public Pesticide Applicator   4799
Radiologic Technologist   7083
Real Estate Appraiser   7182
Real Estate Broker   7183
Real Estate Sales Agent   7184
Referee (Boxing)   906
Registered Nurse   7362
Respiratory Care Practitioner   7446
Sanitarian   3533
School Counselor   2080
Secondary School Administrator   2457
Secondary School Teacher   7650
Securities Broker-Dealer   7789
Securities Sales Agent   7790
Shampoo Operator   1349
Social Worker   7981
Speech-Language Pathologist   8061
Time Keeper (Boxing)   907
Trainer (Boxing)   3697
Veterinarian   8371
Veterinary Technician   441

1273

Indiana, continued

Wastewater Treatment Plant Operator 8512

Iowa

Accountant (Riverboat Gambling) 22, 3048
Accounting Employee (Riverboat Gambling) 3049
Accounting Practitioner 23
Administrative Employee (Riverboat Gambling) 3050, 7734
Administrator (Racetrack) 178, 6118
Adoption Investigator 124, 8575
Advanced Registered Nurse Practitioner 7363
Alcohol Server (Riverboat Gambling) 2860, 3051
Announcer (Racetrack) 6119, 7056
Apprentice Jockey (Racetrack) 908, 6120
Architect 731
Asbestos Abatement Contractor/ Supervisor 1548, 1910
Asbestos Abatement Worker 3732
Asbestos Inspector 1775
Asbestos Management Planner 1911, 3733
Asbestos Project Designer 1912, 3734
Assistant Manager (Racetrack) 179, 180, 6121
Assistant Racing Secretary (Racetrack) 909, 6122
Assistant Trainer (Racetrack) 442, 6123
Association Member (Riverboat Gambling) 3052
Attendant (Riverboat Gambling) 3053
Audiologist/Speech Pathologist 8062
Auditing Employee (Riverboat Gambling) 3054
Auditor (Riverboat Gambling) 24, 3055
Authorized Agent (Racetrack) 910, 6124
Barber 1350
Blaster 4409
Boat Engineer (Riverboat Gambling) 3056
Boat Pilot (Riverboat Gambling) 3057, 8483
Boiler Inspector 1776, 3534
Box Person (Riverboat Gambling) 3058
Bus Driver 1603
Captain (Riverboat Gambling) 3059, 8484
Casino Clerk (Riverboat Gambling) 3060
Casino Manager (Riverboat Gambling) 3061, 3155
Casino Teller (Riverboat Gambling) 1623, 3062
Certified Nursing Assistant (Nurse Aid) 4558
Certified Public Accountant 25
Certified Respiratory Therapy Technician 7447

Certified Shorthand Reporter 8140
Chart Writer (Racetrack) 6125
Chiropractor 1646
Concession Employee (Racetrack) 6126, 7517
Concession Operator (Racetrack) 6127, 7518
Corporate Director/Officer (Racetrack) 3156, 6128
Cosmetologist 1351
Count Room Employee (Riverboat Gambling) 3063
Count Room Supervisor (Riverboat Gambling) 3064
Dealer Person (Riverboat Gambling) 3065
Deck Hand (Riverboat Gambling) 3066, 8485
Dental Hygienist 2207
Dentist 2268
Dietitian 2371
Director (Riverboat Gambling) 3067, 3157
Director of Surveillance (Riverboat Gambling) 3068, 3158
Doctor of Medicine 5227
Doctor of Osteopathic Medicine 5228
Driver/Jockey (Racetrack) 911, 6129
EDP Employee (Riverboat Gambling) 3069
Electrologist 1352
Elementary Counselor (K-6) 2081
Elementary School Media Specialist (1-6) 4164
Elementary School Principal (PK-6) 2458
Elementary School Teacher (K-6) 3968
Emergency Medical Services - Instructor 233, 2699
Emergency Medical Technician - Ambulance 2700
Emergency Medical Technician - Defibrillation 2701
Emergency Medical Technician - Intermediate 2702
Emergency Medical Technician - Paramedic 2703
Emergency Rescue Technician (ERT) 2704
Engineer, Registered 5595
Entertainer (Riverboat Gambling) 3070, 8635
Entertainment Director (Riverboat Gambling) 3071, 4336
Exercise Rider (Racetrack) 443, 6130
Farm Bulk Milk Hauler 8288
First Responder 2705
First Responder - Defibrillation 2706
Floor Person (Riverboat Gambling) 3072
Food & Beverage Director (Riverboat Gambling) 2861, 3073
Food Service Worker (Riverboat Gambling) 2862, 3074
Funeral Director 2924
Games Manager (Riverboat Gambling) 3075, 3159

Games Supervisor (Riverboat Gambling) 3076
General Contractor 1913
Groom (Racetrack) 444, 6131
Head Casino Cashier Supervisor (Riverboat Gambling) 3077
Health Service Provider in Psychology 5685
Hearing Aid Dealer 3416
Host/Hostess (Riverboat Gambling) 2863, 3078
Instructor, Community College or Vocational-Technical School 234
Insurance Agent 3811
Janitorial Employee (Riverboat Gambling) 3079, 3901
Jockey Agent (Racetrack) 912, 6132
Kennel Helper (Racetrack) 445, 6133
Kennel Owner (Racetrack) 6134
Kitchen Employee (Riverboat Gambling) 3080, 8685
Land Surveyor 8192
Landscape Architect 4064
Lawyer 4114
Lead Out (Racetrack) 446, 6135
Licensed Practical Nurse 4216
Lobbyist 4269
Maintenance Employee (Racetrack) 3902, 6136
Maintenance Supervisor (Riverboat Gambling) 1549, 3081, 3903
Manager (Racetrack) 181, 6137
Marital and Family Therapist 2082
Mental Health Counselor 2083
Milk Grader 3641
Milk Hauler 8289
Milkfat Tester 3642
Mutuel Employee (Racetrack) 6138
Mutuels Manager (Racetrack) 2780, 6139
Non-Gaming Cashier (Riverboat Gambling) 1624, 3082
Non-Gaming Change Person (Riverboat Gambling) 1625, 3083
Notary Public 4494
Nursing Assistant (Nurse Aid); Certified 4558
Nursing Home Activity Director 3355, 8704
Nursing Home Administrator 3356
Occupational Therapist 4581
Occupational Therapy Assistant 4632
Officer (Riverboat Gambling) 3084
Official (Racetrack) 913, 6140
Ophthalmic Dispenser/Optician 2406
Optometrist 4677
Osteopathic Medicine; Doctor of 5228
Outrider (Racetrack) 447, 6141
Outside Sales Representative (Riverboat Gambling) 3085, 7937
Owner/Operator (Riverboat Gambling) 3086
Owner (Racetrack) 6142
Owner-Trainer-Driver (Racetrack) 914, 6143
Owner-Trainer (Racetrack) 448, 6144

Parking/Admissions Employee 6145, 8337
Pesticide Applicator 4800
Pharmacist 4946
Physical Therapist 5078
Physician Assistant 5143
Podiatrist 5440
Polygraph Examiner 5500
Porter (Riverboat Gambling) 3087, 8725
Prekindergarten/Kindergarten Teacher 3969, 5552
Private Investigator 2334
Psychologist 5686
Racing Secretary (Racetrack) 915, 6146
Radiographer 7084
Radon Measurement Specialist 3535
Radon Mitigation Specialist 3536
Reading Specialist (K-12) 3970, 7651
Real Estate Appraiser 7185
Real Estate Broker 7186
Real Estate Salesperson 7187
Registered Nurse 7364
Registered Nurse Practitioner; Advanced 7363
Registered Respiratory Therapist 7448
Respiratory Therapist; Registered 7448
Respiratory Therapy Technician; Certified 7447
Retail Salesperson (Riverboat Gambling) 3088, 7519
School Media Specialist (K-12) 4165
Secondary Counselor (7-12) 2084
Secondary School Media Specialist (7-12) 4166
Secondary School Principal (7-12) 2459
Secondary School Teacher (7-12) 7652
Securities Agent 7791
Securities Broker-Dealer 7792
Security Director (Riverboat Gambling) 3089, 3160
Security Employee (Racetrack) 3269, 6147
Security Employee (Riverboat Gambling) 3090, 3270
Security Guard 3271
Security Supervisor (Riverboat Gambling) 1550, 3091, 3272
Service Representative (Riverboat Gambling) 3092, 7938
Sheep Dealer 2764, 8759
Shift Supervisor (Riverboat Gambling) 3093
Slot Attendant (Riverboat Gambling) 3094
Slot Change Person (Riverboat Gambling) 1626, 3095
Slot Manager (Riverboat Gambling) 3096
Slot Supervisor (Riverboat Gambling) 3097
Slot Technician (Riverboat Gambling) 3098
Social Worker 7982
Special Education Teacher 3971, 7653
Special Elevator Inspector 1777, 2659
Stock Person (Riverboat Gambling) 3099

Superintendent of Schools (K-12) 2460, 3161
Surveillance Employee (Riverboat Gambling) 3100, 3273
Tattoo Artist 8445, 8769
Taxi Driver 8247
Teacher of English As A Second Language 235, 7654
Track Superintendent (Racetrack) 3162, 6148
Tractor-Trailer Truck Driver 8290
Trainer (Racetrack) 449, 6149
Veterinarian 8372
Veterinarian Assistant/Animal Technician 450
Veterinarian (Racetrack) 6150, 8373
Wastewater Lagoon Operator 8513
Wastewater Treatment Operator 8514
Water Distribution Operator 8515
Water Treatment Operator 8516
Well Driller 4410

Kansas

Administrative Support Employee (Racetrack) 6151, 7735
Administrator (Racetrack) 182, 6152
Ambulance Attendant 2707
Announcer (Racetrack) 6153, 7057
Apprentice Jockey (Racetrack) 916, 6154
Architect 732
Assistant Funeral Director 2925
Assistant Manager (Racetrack) 183, 6155
Assistant Racing Secretary (Racetrack) 917, 6156
Assistant Starter (Racetrack) 918, 6157
Assistant Trainer (Racetrack) 451, 6158
Attorney 4115
Authorized Agent (Racetrack) 919, 6159
Barber 1353
Blacksmith (Racetrack) 452, 6160
Bloodstock Agent (Racetrack) 6161
Brakeman (Racetrack) 6162
Certified Public Accountant 26
Certified Shorthand Reporter 8141
Chart Writer (Racetrack) 6163
Chiropractor 1647
Clerk of Scales (Racetrack) 3537, 6164
Colors Attendant (Racetrack) 6165
Commercial Pesticide Applicator 4801
Concession Employee (Racetrack) 6166, 7520
Concession Operator (Racetrack) 6167, 7521
Cosmetologist 1354
Cosmetology Apprentice 1355
Cosmetology Instructor 236, 1356
Cosmetology Technician 1357
Dental Hygienist 2208
Dentist 2269
Dietitian 2372
Director of Racing (Racetrack) 3163, 6168

Director of Security (Racetrack) 3164, 6169
District School Administrator 2461
Driver (Racetrack) 920, 6170
Electrologist 1358
Elementary School Teacher 3972
Embalmer 2926
Emergency Medical Instructor-Coordinator 237, 2708
Emergency Medical Technician 2709
Emergency Medical Technician (Racetrack) 2710, 6171
Engineer-in-Training 5596
Exercise Person (Racetrack) 453, 6172
Farrier (Racetrack) 454, 6173
Flagman (Racetrack) 6174
Funeral Director 2927
Funeral Director; Assistant 2925
General Contractor 1914
Groom/Hot Walker (Racetrack) 455, 6175
Hearing Aid Fitter and Dispenser 3417
Home Health Aide 8671
Horsemen's Bookkeeper (Racetrack) 2781, 6176
Identifier (Racetrack) 6177
Insurance Agent 3812
Investment Advisor 7793
Jockey Agent (Racetrack) 921, 6178
Jockey (Racetrack) 922, 6179
Jockey Room Attendant (Racetrack) 3323, 6180
Kennel Helper (Racetrack) 456, 6181
Kennel Master (Racetrack) 457, 6182
Kennel Owner (Racetrack) 6183
Land Surveyor 8193
Landscape Architect 4065
Lead Out (Racetrack) 458, 6184
Library Media Specialist (K-12) 4167
Licensed Baccalaureate Social Worker 7983
Licensed Master Social Worker 7984
Licensed Practical Nurse 4217
Licensed Specialist Clinical Social Worker 7985
Lobbyist 4270
Lure Operator (Racetrack) 6185
Maintenance Employee (Racetrack) 3904, 6186
Managing Owner (Racetrack) 6187
Manicurist 1359
Marriage and Family Therapist 2085
Milk Hauler and Tester 3643, 8291
Mutuel Employee (Racetrack) 6188
Notary Public 4495
Nurse Aide 4559
Nursing Home Administrator 3357
Occupational Therapist 4582
Occupational Therapy Assistant 4633
Official (Racetrack) 923, 6189
Optometrist 4678
Osteopathic Physician (D.O.) 5229
Outrider (Racetrack) 459, 6190
Owner By Open Claim (Racetrack) 6191
Owner (Racetrack) 6192

Kansas, continued

Paddock Attendant (Racetrack)   460, 6193
Paddock Judge (Racetrack)   924, 6194
Parking Attendant (Racetrack)   3324, 6195
Patrol Judge (Racetrack)   925, 6196
Pesticide Dealer   4802
Pharmacist   4947
Pharmacy Intern   4948
Photo Finish Operator (Racetrack)   5004, 6197
Physical Therapist   5079
Physical Therapy Assistant   5036
Physician   5230
Physician's Assistant   5144
Plater (Racetrack)   461, 6198
Podiatrist   5441
Pony Person (Racetrack)   462, 6199
Practicing Veterinarian Assistant (Racetrack)   6200
Practicing Veterinarian (Racetrack)   6201, 8374
Private Investigator   2335
Private Pesticide Applicator   4803
Professional Counselor   2086
Professional Engineer   5597
Program Manager (Racetrack)   3165, 6202
Promotion Manager (Racetrack)   6203
Psychologist   5687
Racing Secretary (Racetrack)   926, 6204
Real Estate Appraiser   7188
Real Estate Broker   7189
Real Estate Sales Agent   7190
Registered Nurse   7365
Respiratory Care Practitioner   7449
Respiratory Therapist   7450
School Building Administrator K-12   2462
School Counselor   2087
School Nurse   7366
Secondary School Teacher   7655
Securities Agent   7794
Securities Broker-Dealer   7795
Security Employee (Racetrack)   3274, 6205
Selection Sheet Operator (Racetrack)   6206
Social Worker; Licensed Baccalaureate   7983
Social Worker; Licensed Master   7984
Social Worker; Licensed Specialist Clinical   7985
Stable Trainer/Agent (Racetrack)   463, 6207
Starter (Racetrack)   927, 6208
Supervisor of Mutuels (Racetrack)   2782, 6209
Testing Technician (Racetrack)   3538, 6210
Timer (Racetrack)   928, 6211
Totalisator Employee (Racetrack)   6212
Track Superintendent (Racetrack)   3166, 6213
Trainer (Racetrack)   464, 6214

Valet (Racetrack)   6215
Veterinarian   8375
Veterinarian Assistant (Racetrack); Practicing   6200
Veterinarian (Racetrack); Practicing   6201, 8374
Video Operator (Racetrack)   5005, 6216

Kentucky

Admission Department Manager/Employee(Racetrack)   184, 6217
Animal Technician   465
Architect   733
Assistant Trainer (Racetrack)   466, 6218
Athletic Trainer   3698
Attorney   4116
Auctioneer   1217
Audiologist   8063
Barber   1360
Blacksmith (Racetrack)   467, 6219
Boiler Inspector   1778, 3539
Boiler Installer   1590
Building Inspector   1779
Carpenter (Racetrack)   6220, 8600
Certified Public Accountant   27
Certified Shorthand Reporter   8142
Chiropractor   1648
Clerk of Scales (Racetrack)   3540, 6221
Commission Chemist (Racetrack)   3541, 6222, 8607
Commission Director of Security (Racetrack)   3167, 6223
Commission Horse Identifier (Racetrack)   3542, 6224
Commission Inspector (Racetrack)   3543, 6225
Commission License Administrator (Racetrack)   3544, 6226
Commission Supervisor of Pari-Mutuel Betting (Racetrack)   2783, 6227
Commission Veterinarian (Racetrack)   6228, 8376
Concessions Manager/Employee (Racetrack)   6229, 7522
Coroner   3545, 8617
Cosmetologist   1361
Dental Hygienist   2209
Dental Laboratory Technician   2247
Dental Technician (Racetrack)   468, 6230
Dentist   2270
Dietitian   2373
Director of Racing (Racetrack)   3168, 6231
Drinking Water Treatment and Distribution System Operator   8517
Driver Training Instructor   238
Early Childhood Teacher (K-4)   3973
Electrical Contractor   1915, 2585
Electrical Inspector   1780
Elevator Inspector   1781, 2660
Emergency Medical Technician   2711
Engineer, Professional   5598
Entry Clerk (Racetrack)   6232
Farm Manager/Agent (Racetrack)   2765, 6233

Farrier/Apprentice Farrier (Racetrack)   469, 6234
Film Patrol/Video Tape Operator and Projectionist (Racetrack)   5006, 6235
Fire Alarm System Inspector   1782
Flagman (Racetrack)   6236
Funeral Director/Embalmer   2928
Groundsman (Racetrack)   3114, 6237
Guide (Hunting and Fishing); Professional   2821
Hearing Instrument Specialist   3418
Inspector; Plans & Specifications   1783
Insurance Adjuster   125
Insurance Agent   3813
Insurance Consultant   3814
Insurance Solicitor   3815
Jockey Agent (Racetrack)   929, 6238
Jockey Apprentice (Racetrack)   930, 6239
Jockey (Racetrack)   931, 6240
Jockey Room Custodian (Racetrack)   3905, 6241
Land Surveyor   8194
Landfarming Operator   2766
Landfill Operator   1736
Landfill Operator; Sanitary   1737
Landscape Architect   4066
Law Enforcement Training Instructor   239
Lobbyist   4271
Maintenance Department Manager/Employee (Racetrack)   3906, 6242
Mechanic (Racetrack)   6243
Middle School Teacher (5-8)   3974, 7656
Milk Sampler - Weigher   3644
Milk Tester   3645
Miner   4411
Mining Blaster   4412
Mining Electrical Inspector   3546, 4413
Mining Electrical Worker   2586, 4414
Mining Emergency Medical Technician   2712, 4415
Mining Fire Boss   3547, 4416
Mining Foreman   1551, 4417
Mining Inspector   3548, 4418
Mining Safety Instructor   240, 4419
Music Teacher   3975, 7657
Mutuel Department Employee (Racetrack)   6244
Notary Public   4496
Nurse Anesthetist   7367
Nurse, Clinical Specialist   7368
Nurse, Licensed Practical   4218
Nurse, Midwife   7369
Nurse Practitioner   7370
Nurse, Registered   7371
Nursing Home Administrator   3358
Nutritionist   2374
Occupational Therapist   4583
Ophthalmic Dispenser - Optician   2407
Optometrist   4679
Osteopathic Physician (D.O.)   5231
Outrider (Racetrack)   470, 6245
Owner (Racetrack)   6246
Paddock Judge (Racetrack)   932, 6247
Paramedic   2713

Parking Manager/Employee (Racetrack) 3325, 6248
Patrol Judge (Racetrack) 933, 6249
Pesticide Applicator 4804
Pesticide Dealer 4805
Pesticide Exterminator 4806
Pharmacist 4949
Photo Finish Operator (Racetrack) 5007, 6250
Physical Therapist 5080
Physician 5232
Physician Assistant 5145
Placing Judge (Racetrack) 934, 6251
Plans & Specifications Inspector 1783
Plumber 5353
Podiatrist 5442
Police Officer 5482
Polygraph Examiner 5501
Practical Nurse and Nurse Aide Instructor 4219
Professional Guide (Hunting and Fishing) 2821
Property Valuation Administrator 8235, 8732
Psychological Associate 5688
Psychologist 5689
Racing Department Employee (Racetrack) 6252
Racing Official (Racetrack) 935, 6253
Racing Secretary/Assistant Racing Secretary (Racetrack) 936, 6254
Radiation Operator 7085
Real Estate Appraiser 7191
Real Estate Broker 7192
Real Estate Sales Associate 7193
Rehabilitation Counselor 2088, 3486
Respiratory Therapist 7451
Sanitarian, Registered 3549
Sanitary Landfill Operator 1737
School Bus Driver 1604
School Guidance Counselor 2089
School Media Librarian (K-12) 4168
School Principal 2463
School Psychologist 5690
Secondary School Teacher (9-12) 7658
Securities Agent 7796
Securities Broker/Dealer 7797
Security Department Employee (Racetrack) 3275, 6255
Social Worker 7986
Special Education Teacher 3976, 7659
Speech-Language Pathologist 8064
Stable-Area Supplier (Racetrack) 4305, 6256
Stable Employee (Racetrack) 471, 6257
Starter/Assistant Starter (Racetrack) 937, 6258
Steward (Racetrack) 938, 6259
Suppression System Inspector 1784
Teacher for Gifted Education 3977, 7660
Teacher of Vocational Education - Industrial Education 241
Testing Laboratory Employee (Racetrack) 6260, 7602
Timer (Racetrack) 939, 6261

Track Superintendent (Racetrack) 3169, 6262
Trainer (Racetrack) 472, 6263
Valet (Racetrack) 6264
Veterinarian 8377
Veterinarian Assistant (Racetrack) 473, 6265
Veterinarian (Racetrack) 6266, 8378
Veterinarian (Racetrack); Commission 6228, 8376
Wastewater Treatment Operator 8518
Water Well Driller 4420

Louisiana

Accountant/Certified Public Accountant 28
Acupuncture Assistant 79, 4370
Agricultural Consultant 318, 4807
Arborist 2879
Architect 734
Art Therapist (School) 8446
Artist (School) 8447
Assistant Starter (Racetrack) 940, 6267
Auctioneer 1218
Audiologist (School) 8065
Barber 1362
Bedding and Upholstered Furniture Repairer/Renovator 8588
Bedding and Upholstered Furniture Sterilizer 8589
Boiler Inspector/Director of Boiler Inspections 1785, 3550
Boxer/Wrestler 941
Certified Respiratory Therapist Technician 7452
Chiropractor 1649
Commercial Pesticide Applicator 4808
Contractor 1916
Cosmetologist/Beautician/Beauty Operator 1363
Cut Flower Dealer 3115
Dance Therapist (School) 8625
Dental Hygienist 2210
Dentist 2271
Dietitian-Nutritionist 2375
Early Childhood Teacher (N-K) 3978, 5553
Electrologist 1364
Elementary School Counselor 2090
Elementary School Principal 2464
Elementary School Teacher 3979
Embalmer 2929
Emergency Medical Technician (EMT) 2714
Engineer/Land Surveyor 5599
Exercise Rider (Racetrack) 474, 6268
Explosives Dealer 7523
Explosives Handler 3326, 4421
Fire Protection Sprinkler Contractor 1917, 5354
Flight Instructor (Ultralight Aircraft) 242, 353, 8647
Florist; Retail 2320, 8751
Florist; Wholesale 2321, 8564, 8797
Funeral Director 2930

Furniture Repairer/Renovator; Bedding and Upholstered 8588
Furniture Sterilizer; Bedding and Upholstered 8589
Groom (Racetrack) 475, 6269
Hearing Aid Dealer 3419
Heating and Air Conditioning Mechanic 3470
Horticulturist 319
Hot Walker (Racetrack) 476, 6270
Housing Dealer; Manufactured 7194
Housing Salesman; Manufactured 7195
Insurance Agent 3816
Insurance Broker 3817
Insurance Solicitor 3818
Interior Designer 2319
Investment Advisor 7798
Jockey 942, 6271
Jockey Agent 943, 6272
Jockey Room Custodian (Racetrack) 6273
Land Surveyor 8195
Landscape Architect 4067
Landscape Contractor 1918, 4068
Lawyer 4117
Lobbyist 4272
Manufactured Housing Dealer 7194
Manufactured Housing Salesman 7195
Milk and Cream Measurer/Sampler 3646
Milk and Cream Tester 3647
Motor Vehicle Inspector 3551
Motor Vehicle Salesperson 7524
Music Therapist (School) 8702
Mutuel Employee (Racetrack) 6274
Notary Public 4497
Nuclear Medical Technologist 4534
Nurse/Practical 4220
Nurse/Registered 7372
Nurse (School) 7373
Nursery Stock Dealer 3116, 4545
Nursing Home Administrator 3359
Occupational Therapist 4584
Occupational Therapist (School) 4585
Occupational Therapy Assistant 4634
Optometrist 4680
Osteopathic Physician (D.O.) 5233
Outrider (Racetrack) 477, 6275
Parish or City School Superintendent 2465, 3170
Parish or City School Supervisor of Instruction 2466
Pest Control Operator 4809
Pesticide Applicator; Commercial 4808
Pesticide Applicator; Private 4812
Pesticide Dealer 4810
Pesticide Salesperson 4811
Pharmacist 4950
Physical Therapist (School) 5081
Physician 5234
Physician's Assistant 5146
Pilot (Ultralight Aircraft) 354
Plant Breeder 320
Plater (Racetrack) 6276
Plumber 5355
Podiatrist 5443
Polygraphist 5502

Louisiana, continued

Pony Boy/Pony Girl (Racetrack) 478, 6277
Practical Nurse and Nurse Aide Instructor 243
Private Pesticide Applicator 4812
Psychologist 5691
Psychologist Assistant (School) 5692
Racehorse Owner 6278
Racehorse Trainer 479, 6279
Racehorse Veterinarian 6280, 8379
Racetrack Employee 6281
Racetrack Vendor 6282, 7525
Radiation Therapy Technologist 7086
Radio Technician 1713
Radio and Television Technician 1714
Radiologic Technologist 7087
Real Estate Appraiser 7196
Real Estate Broker 7197
Real Estate Salesperson 7198
Registered Respiratory Therapist 7453
Respiratory Therapist; Registered 7453
Respiratory Therapist Technician; Certified 7452
Retail Florist 2320, 8751
Sanitarian 3552
School Librarian 4169
School Psychologist 5693
School Superintendent; Parish or City 2465, 3170
School Supervisor of Instruction; Parish or City 2466
Secondary School Counselor 2091
Secondary School Principal 2467
Secondary School Teacher 7661
Securities Dealer 7799
Securities Salesman 7800
Shorthand Reporter (Certified) 8143
Social Work 7987
Solid Waste Facility Operator 1738
Speech Pathologist 8066
Sprinkler Contractor; Fire Protection 1917, 5354
Stable Foreman (Racetrack) 1552, 6283
Steward (Racetrack) 944, 6284
Teacher of Exceptional Children 3980, 7662
Teacher Vocational-Trade & Industrial (Secondary) 244
Timeshare Interest Salesperson 7199
Valet (Racetrack) 6285
Veterinarian 8380
Veterinarian; Racehorse 6280, 8379
Voice Stress Analyst 5503
Water and Wastewater Facility Operator 8519
Weighmaster 3553
Wholesale Florist 2321, 8564, 8797

Maine

Acupuncturist (L.Ac.); Licensed 80
Aesthetician 1365
Aesthetician Apprentice 1366
Amateur Boxing Promoter 4337
Amateur Kickboxing Promoter 4338
Animal Technician 480
Apprentice Electrician 2587
Apprentice Landscape Arborist 2880
Apprentice Utility Arborist 2881, 3117
Arborist (Unrestricted) 2882, 3118
Arborist; Utility 2885, 3120
Architect 735
Assistant School Principal 2468
Assistant School Superintendent 2469, 3171
Attorney 4118
Auctioneer 1219
Audiologist 8067
Barber 1367
Barber Apprentice 1368
Barber Instructor 245, 1369
Barber Student 1370
Boxer 945
Boxing Judge 946
Boxing Knock-Down Timekeeper 947
Boxing Manager 948
Boxing Referee 949
Boxing Second 950
Boxing Timekeeper 951
Certified Public Accountant 29
Certified Shorthand Reporter 8144
Chiropractor 1650
Clinical Professional Counselor 2092
Commercial Co-Venturer 7939
Commercial Driver Education Instructor 246
Commercial Pesticide Applicator 4813
Cosmetologist 1371
Cosmetology Apprentice 1372
Cosmetology Instructor 247, 1373
Cosmetology Student 1374
Debt Collector 126
Dental Hygienist 2211
Dentist 2272
Dietetic Technician 2376
Dietitian 2377
Electrician; Apprentice 2587
Electrician; Journeyman 2589
Electrician; Journeyman-in-Training 2590
Electrician; Limited 2591
Electrician; Master 2592
Elementary Teacher (K-6) 3981
Embalmer 2931
Emergency Medical Technician 2715
Engineer-in-Training 5600
Forester; Professional 2884
Fundraising Counsel; Professional 7940
Funeral Director 2932
Funeral Service Practitioner 2933
Funeral Service Practitioner Trainee 2934
Geologist 3244
Government Pesticide Supervisor 1553, 4814
Guide (Hunting and Fishing); Professional 2822
Hazardous Substance Tank Installer; Underground 1922
Hearing Aid Dealer and Fitter 3420
Helper Electrician 2588
Insurance Adjuster 127
Insurance Agent 3819
Insurance Broker 3820
Insurance Consultant 3821
Investment Advisor 7801
Journeyman Electrician 2589
Journeyman-in-Training Electrician 2590
Kickboxer 952
Kickboxing Assistant Scorekeeper 953
Kickboxing Judge 954
Kickboxing Kick Judge 955
Kickboxing Knock-down Timekeeper 956
Kickboxing Manager 957
Kickboxing Matchmaker 4339
Kickboxing Referee 958
Kickboxing Scorekeeper 959
Kickboxing Second 960
Kickboxing Timekeeper 961
Land Surveyor 8196
Landscape Arborist 2883, 3119
Landscape Arborist; Apprentice 2880
Landscape Architect 4069
Licensed Acupuncturist (L.Ac.) 80
Licensed Clinical Social Worker 7988
Licensed Master Social Worker 7989
Licensed Practical Nurse 4221
Licensed Social Worker 7990
Limited Electrician 2591
Lobbyist 4273
Manicurist 1375
Manicurist Apprentice 1376
Manufactured Home Dealer 7200
Manufactured Home Mechanic 1919
Marriage and Family Therapist 2093
Master Electrician 2592
Milk Hauler and Tester 3648, 8292
Notary Public 4498
Nuclear Medicine Technologist 4535
Nursing Home Administrator 3360
Occupational Therapist 4586
Occupational Therapy Assistant 4635
Oil Burner Technician 5356
Oil Tank Installer 1920
Optometrist 4681
Osteopathic Physician (D.O.) 5235
Osteopathic Physician's Assistant 5147
Pastoral Counselor 2094, 8714
Pesticide Dealer 4815
Pesticide Supervisor; Government 1553, 4814
Pharmacist 4951
Physical Therapist 5082
Physical Therapist Assistant 5037
Physician 5236
Physician's Assistant 5148
Plumber 5357
Podiatrist 5444
Polygraph Examiner 5504
Private Investigator 2336
Private Pesticide Applicator 4816
Professional Boxing Promoter 4340
Professional Counselor 2095
Professional Engineer 5601
Professional Forester 2884
Professional Fundraising Counsel 7940

Professional Guide (Hunting and Fishing) 2822
Professional Solicitor (Fundraiser) 7941
Professional Wrestling Promoter 4341
Psychological Examiner 5694
Psychologist 5695
Radiation Therapy Technologist 7088
Radiographer 7089
Real Estate Appraiser 7201
Real Estate Associate Broker 7202
Real Estate Broker 7203
Real Estate Sales Agent 7204
Registered Nurse 7374
Respiratory Care Practitioner 7454
School Guidance Counselor (K-12) 2096
School Library-Media Specialist (K-12) 4170
School Principal 2470
School Superintendent 2471, 3172
Secondary Teacher (7-12) 7663
Securities Broker-Dealer 7802
Securities Sales Representatives 7803
Ship's Pilot 8486
Social Worker; Licensed 7990
Social Worker; Licensed Clinical 7988
Social Worker; Licensed Master 7989
Soil Scientist 321
Solicitor (Fundraiser); Professional 7941
Solid Fuel Burner Technician 5358
Speech-Language Pathologist 8068
Time-Share Agent 7205
Transient Seller of Merchandise (Itinerant Vendor) 7526
Underground Gasoline Tank Remover 1921
Underground Hazardous Substance Tank Installer 1922
Utility Arborist 2885, 3120
Utility Arborist; Apprentice 2881, 3117
Vendor); Transient Seller of Merchandise (Itinerant 7526
Veterinarian 8381
Wrestling Manager 962
Wrestling Matchmaker 4342
Wrestling Referee 963
Wrestling Timekeeper 964

Maryland

Acupuncturist; Registered 81
Adjuster; Public 129
Air School Instructor 248, 355, 8576
Apprentice Cosmetologist 1377
Architect 736
Asbestos Abatement Worker 3735
Assistant Trainer (Thoroughbred Racing) 481, 6286
Attorney 4119
Audio-Visual/Library Associate 4171
Audiologist 8069
Bail Bondsman 1251
Barber 1378
Barber Apprentice 1379
Barber Instructor 249, 1380
Beauty Shop Manager 1381
Blaster 4422

Boxer 965
Boxing Referee 966
Cab Driver 8248
Caterer (Harness Racing) 2864, 6287
Caterer (Thoroughbred Racing) 2865, 6288
Certified Hazardous Waste Driver 8293
Certified Public Accountant 30
Certified Social Worker 7991
Chiropractor 1651
Commercial Fishing Guide 2823
Commercial Pesticide Applicator 4817
Correctional Officer 8618
Cosmetologist 1382
Cosmetologist; Apprentice 1377
Cosmetology Instructor 250, 1383
Debt Collector 128
Demonstrator Hairdresser 1384
Dental Hygienist 2212
Dentist 2273
Dietitian 2378
Driver (Harness Racing) 967, 6289
Driver Training Instructor 251
Early Childhood Teacher (N-3) 3982, 5554
Electrician 2593
Electrologist 1385
Electrology Instructor 252, 1386
Elementary School Teacher 3983
Embalmer 2935
Emergency Medical Technician 2716
Employment Counselor 2097, 4721
Engineer-in-Training 5602
Environmental Sanitarian 3554
Family Day Care Provider 5555
Farm Labor Contractor 8639
Farrier (Harness Racing) 482, 6290
Farrier (Thoroughbred Racing) 483, 6291
Fishing Guide; Commercial 2823
Forest Products Operator 2767, 8651
Forester 2886
Fundraising Counsel 7942
Funeral Director 2936
Fur Dealer 7527, 8657
General Contractor 1923
Graduate Social Worker 7992
Hairdresser; Demonstrator 1384
Hauler 8294
Hazardous Waste Hauler 8295
Health Planner 3361
Hearing Aid Dealer 3421
Home Improvement Contractor 1924
Home Improvement Salesperson 7943
Home Improvement Subcontractor 1925
Hunting Guide; Master 2824
Industrial Wastewater Treatment Superintendent 8520
Insurance Adviser 3822
Insurance Agent 3823
Insurance Broker 3824
Investment Adviser 7804
Investment Adviser Representative 7805
Jockey Agent (Thoroughbred Racing) 968, 6292
Jockey/Apprentice Jockey (Thoroughbred Racing) 969, 6293

Land Surveyor 8197
Landscape Architect 4070
Licensed Practical Nurse 4222
Lobbyist 4274
Maintenance Employee (Harness Racing) 3907, 6294
Maintenance Employee (Thoroughbred Racing) 3908, 6295
Manicurist 1387
Master Hunting Guide 2824
Midwife 4560
Milk Hauler and Tester 3649, 8296
Mining Fire Boss 3555, 4423
Mining Foreman 1554, 4424
Mortgage Broker 7806
Mortician 2937
Notary Public 4499
Nuclear Medical Technologist 4536
Nursing Home Administrator 3362
Nutritionist 2379
Occupational Therapist 4587
Occupational Therapist Assistant 4636
Optometrist 4682
Osteopathic Physician (D.O.) 5237
Owner (Harness Racing) 6296
Owner (Thoroughbred Racing) 6297
Pari-Mutuel Employee (Harness Racing) 6298
Pari-Mutuel Employee (Thoroughbred Racing) 6299
Pest Control Consultant 4818
Pest Control Operator 4819
Pharmacist 4952
Physical Therapist 5083
Physical Therapy Assistant 5038
Physician 5238
Physician's Assistant 5149
Plumber 5359
Podiatrist 5445
Police Officer 5483
Post-Mortem Examiner 3556, 8727
Private Detective 2337
Professional Engineer 5603
Professional Solicitor 7944
Psychiatrist's Assistant 4561
Psychologist 5696
Public Adjuster 129
Public Agency Applicator 4820
Pump Installer 4425, 5360
Radiation Therapy Technologist 7090
Radiologic Technologist 7091
Real Estate Appraiser 7206
Real Estate Associate Broker 7207
Real Estate Broker 7208
Real Estate Sales Agent 7209
Registered Acupuncturist 81
Registered Nurse 7375
Regulated Shooting Area Operator 2825, 8746
Respiratory Care Practitioner 7455
Salesperson; Home Improvement 7943
Sanitarian-in-Training 3557
School Guidance Counselor 2098
School Principal 2472
School Superintendent 2473, 3173
School Supervisor 2474
Secondary School Teacher 7664

Maryland, continued

Securities Broker-Dealer 7807
Securities Sales Agent 7808
Security Guard 3276
Sewage Treatment Plant Superintendent 8521
Ship's Pilot 8487
Social Worker 7993
Social Worker Associate 7994
Social Worker; Graduate 7992
Solicitor; Professional 7944
Speech-Language Pathologist 8070
Stable Employee (Harness Racing) 484, 6300
Stable Employee (Thoroughbred Racing) 485, 6301
Stationary Engineer 5527
Taxidermist 8264
Track Employee (Harness Racing) 6302
Track Employee (Thoroughbred Racing) 6303
Trainer (Harness Racing) 486, 6304
Trainer (Thoroughbred Racing) 487, 6305
Trapper 2826
Tree Expert 2887
Vendor (Harness Racing) 6306, 7528
Vendor (Thoroughbred Racing) 6307, 7529
Veterinarian 8382
Veterinarian (Harness Racing) 6308, 8383
Veterinarian (Thoroughbred Racing) 6309, 8384
Vocational Education Teacher 253
Wastewater Treatment Superintendent; Industrial 8520
Water Conditioner Installer 5361
Well Driller 4426
Whitewater Rafting Guide 8795
Whitewater Rafting Operator 8796
Wildlife Exhibitor 488, 8800

Massachusetts

Acupuncturist; Licensed 82
Aesthetician 1388
Appraiser; Motor Vehicle Damage 130
Approved Asbestos Training Provider 254
Architect 737
Asbestos Abatement Project Designer 1926, 3736
Asbestos Abatement Project Monitor 1927, 3737
Asbestos Abatement Worker 3738
Asbestos Analytical Services Provider 3739
Asbestos Contractor 1928
Asbestos Inspector 1786
Asbestos Management Planner 1929, 3740
Asbestos Supervisor-Foreman 3741
Athletic Trainer 3699
Attorney 4120
Auctioneer 1220

Audiologist 8071
Barber 1389
Barber Instructor 255, 1390
Bilingual Education Teacher; Transitional 3987, 7668
Blacksmith (Racetrack) 489, 6310
Certified Public Accountant 31
Certified Shorthand Reporter 8145
Chiropractor 1652
Commercial Pesticide Applicator 4821
Concrete Technician 8614
Construction Supervisor 1555, 1930
Cosmetologist 1391
Cosmetologist Instructor 256, 1392
Dental Hygienist 2213
Dentist 2274
Drinking Water Supply Facility Operator 8522
Early Childhood Teacher (K-3) 3984
Electrician 2594
Electrologist 1393
Elementary School Teacher (1-6) 3985
Elevator Constructor 1931, 2661
Elevator Maintenance Person 2662
Elevator Operator 4360, 8634
Elevator Repairperson 2663
Embalmer 2938
Emergency Medical Technician 2717
Fireman Engineer 2801
Funeral Director 2939
Gas Fitter 5362
General Contractor 1932
Greyhound Assistant Trainer (Racetrack) 490, 6311
Greyhound Authorized Agent (Racetrack) 970, 6312
Greyhound Owner (Racetrack) 6313
Greyhound Trainer (Racetrack) 491, 6314
Guidance Counselor 2099
Hawker/Peddler 7530
Health Officer 3558
Hearing Aid Dealer/Dispenser 3422
Hoisting Operator 4361
Home Improvement Contractor 1933
Insurance Agent 3825
Insurance Broker 3826
Insurance Inspector 3559
Jockey Agent (Racetrack) 971, 6315
Jockey Apprentice (Racetrack) 972, 6316
Jockey (Racetrack) 973, 6317
Judge (Boxing) 974
Land Surveyor 8198
Landscape Architect 4071
Licensed Acupuncturist 82
Licensed Practical Nurse 4223
Liquefied Petroleum Gas Installer 5363
Lobbyist 4275
Manager (Boxing) 975
Manicurist 1394
Marriage and Family Therapist 2100
Matchmaker (Boxing) 4343
Media Specialist; Unified 4172
Mental Health Counselor 2101
Middle School Teacher (5-9) 7665
Milk Hauler and Tester 3650, 8297

Motor Vehicle Damage Appraiser 130
Notary Public 4500
Nuclear Medical Technologist 4537
Nuclear Power Plant Engineer 5528
Nuclear Power Plant Operator 5529
Nurse Anesthetist 7376
Nurse Midwife 7377
Nurse Practitioner 7378
Nursing Home Administrator 3363
Occupational Therapist 4588
Occupational Therapy Assistant 4637
Oil Burner Technician 5364
Optician 2408
Optometrist 4683
Osteopathic Physician (D.O.) 5239
Outrider (Racetrack) 492, 6318
Pesticide Applicator 4822
Pesticide Dealer 4823
Pharmacist 4953
Physical Therapist 5084
Physical Therapist Assistant 5039
Physician 5240
Physician (Boxing) 5241
Physician's Assistant 5150
Pipefitter 5365
Plumber 5366
Podiatrist 5446
Polygraph Examiner 5505
Private Detective 2338
Private Investigator 2339
Private Pesticide Applicator 4824
Professional Boxer 976
Professional Engineer 5604
Psychiatric Nurse 7379
Psychologist 5697
Racing Official (Racetrack) 977, 6319
Radiation Therapy Technologist 7092
Radio and Television Technician 1715
Radiologic Technologist 7093
Real Estate Appraiser 7210
Real Estate Broker 7211
Real Estate Sales Agent 7212
Referee (Boxing) 978
Refrigeration Contractor 1934, 3471
Refrigeration Technician 3472
Registered Nurse 7380
Respiratory Care Practitioner 7456
Riding Instructor 257, 3700, 8752
Sanitarian 3560
School Business Administrator 2475
School Principal 2476
School Psychologist 5698
School Superintendent/Assistant Superintendent 2477, 3174
School Supervisor/Director 2478
Second (Boxing) 979
Secondary School Teacher (9-12) 7666
Securities Agent 7809
Securities Broker-Dealer 7810
Securities Issuer-Agent 7811
Social Worker 7995
Speech-Language Pathologist 8072
Stable Employee (Racetrack) 493, 6320
Stationary Engineer 5530
Teacher of Children With Special Needs 3986, 7667

Teacher of English as a Second Language 258
Thoroughbred Owner (Racetrack) 6321
Thoroughbred Trainer (Racetrack) 494, 6322
Timekeeper (Boxing) 980
Trainer (Boxing) 3701
Transient Vendor 7531
Transitional Bilingual Education Teacher 3987, 7668
Unified Media Specialist 4172
Valet (Racetrack) 6323
Vendor (Racetrack) 6324, 7532
Vendor; Transient 7531
Veterinarian 8385
Veterinarian (Racetrack) 6325, 8386
Waste Water Treatment Facility Operator 8523

Michigan

Adjuster for the Insured 131
Airport Manager 1739, 8577
Alarm System Contractor 1935
Alcoholic Beverage Worker 2866
Ambulance Attendant 2718
Animal Dealer; Research 503, 8750
Architect 738
Asbestos Abatement Contractor 1936
Asbestos Abatement Inspector 1787
Asbestos Abatement Project Designer 1937, 3742
Asbestos Abatement Supervisor 1556, 1938
Asbestos Abatement Worker 3743
Asbestos Management Planner 1939, 3744
Assessor 7213, 8236
Assistant Trainer (Racetrack) 495, 6326
Association/Track Employee (Racetrack) 6327
Attorney 4121
Authorized Agent (Racetrack) 981, 6328
Automotive Mechanic 1242
Barber 1395
Barber Instructor 259, 1396
Blacksmith (Racetrack) 496, 6329
Boiler Inspector 1788, 3561
Boiler Installer 1591
Boiler Repairer 1592
Breeder, Game Fish 2768, 8592
Breeder, Wild Animals and Birds 322, 497, 8593
Builder; Residential 1944
Building (Construction) Official 1789
Bus Driver 1605
Butter Grader 3651, 8596
Certified Industry Fieldperson 3652
Certified Public Accountant 32
Certified Shorthand Reporter 8146
(Charter Boat Operator); Operator of Vessels Carrying Passengers for Hire 8488
Chauffeur 8249
Chiropractor 1653
Clinical Laboratory Director 2759, 3175

Collection Agency Manager 132
Community Planner, Professional 8609
Construction Plan Reviewer 1790
Correctional Officer, State 8619
Cosmetologist 1397
Cosmetology Instructor 260, 1398
Dental Assistant, Registered 2186
Dental Hygienist 2214
Dentist 2275
Dewatering Well Contractor 4427
Driver; Motor Carrier 8300
Driver (Racetrack) 982, 6330
Driver-Trainer (Racetrack) 983, 6331
Driver Training Instructor (Commercial) 261
Driver Training Instructor (School) 262
Electrical Contractor (Class 1 Electrician) 1940, 2595
Electrician, Journeyperson (Class 3 Electrician) 2596
Electrician, Master (Class 2 Electrician) 2597
Electrologist 1399
Elementary School Teacher 3988
Elevator Contractor 1941, 2664
Elevator Inspector 1791, 2665
Elevator Journeyperson 2666
Emergency Medical Technician (EMT) 2719
Emergency Medical Technician (EMT), Advanced 2720
Emergency Medical Technician (EMT) Specialist 2721
Emergency Medical Technician Instructor-Coordinator 263, 2722
Employment Agency Manager 4722
Engineer, Licensed Professional 5605
Explosive Handler 3327, 4428
Farm Bulk Milk Pickup Tank Operator 8298
Farrier (Racetrack) 498, 6332
Fire Fighter Training Instructor 264, 2802, 8642
Forensic Polygraph Examiner 5506
Forester, Registered 2888
Fundraiser, Professional 7945
Funeral Goods or Services (Prepaid), Contract Seller of 7946, 8653
Fur Dealer 7533, 8658
Fur Processor 8265, 8662
Groom (Racetrack) 499, 6333
Hearing Aid Dealer 3423
Hearing Aid Salesperson 3424
Hearing Aid Trainee 3425
Horse Riding Stable Operator 500
Inspector (Building, Electrical, Mechanical, and Plumbing) 1792
Inspector, Vehicle Emission Testing 3562, 8676
Insurance Adjuster 133
Insurance Administrative Services Manager (Third Party) 185
Insurance Administrator (Third Party) 186
Insurance Agent 3827
Insurance Agent, Surplus Lines 3828
Insurance Counselor 3829

Insurance Solicitor 3830
Investment Advisor 7812
Jockey Agent (Racetrack) 984, 6334
Jockey/Apprentice Jockey (Racetrack) 985, 6335
Land Surveyor 8199
Landscape Architect 4072
Library Staff Member, Public 4173
Licensed Practical Nurse 4224
Liquid Industrial Waste Remover 8299
Lobbyist 4276
Manicurist 1400
Marriage Counselor 2102
Mechanical (Heating/Cooling/Ventilating/ Refrigerating) Contractor 1942
Medical Training Student (Postgraduate) 5242, 8699
Milk Fat Tester 3653
Mobile Home Dealer 7214
Mobile Home Installer and Repairer 1943
Mobile Home Lessor 7215
Mortgage Broker; Residential 7813
Mortician 2940
Mortuary Science Resident Trainee 2941
Motor Carrier Driver 8300
Motor Carrier of Passengers for Hire 1606, 8250
Notary Public 4501
Nurse, School 7381
Nursery Dealer 3121, 4546
Nurseryperson (Nurseryman) 3122, 4547
Nursing Home Administrator 3364
Occupational Therapist 4589
Ocularist 4684
Operator of Vessels Carrying Passengers for Hire (Charter Boat Operator) 8488
Optometrist 4685
Osteopathic Physician (D.O.) 5243
Owner (Racetrack) 6336
Parole/Probation Officer, State 7996, 8711
Personal Property Examiner 8237
Pesticide Applicator, Aerial 4825
Pesticide Applicator, Commercial 4826
Pesticide Applicator, Private 4827
Pesticide Applicator, Registered 4828
Pesticide Dealer, Restricted Use 4829
Pharmacist 4954
Pharmacy Intern 4955
Physical Therapist 5085
Physician 5244
Physician's Assistant 5151
Pilot, Ship 8489
Plant Dealer 3123, 4548
Plant Grower 323
Plater (Racetrack) 501, 6337
Plumber, Journeyperson 5367
Plumber, Master 5368
Podiatrist 5447
Police Officer; Railroad 5484, 8737
Polygraph Examiner; Forensic 5506
Private Detective or Private Investigator 2340

Michigan, continued

Private Security Guard 3277
Private Security Guard Agency Owner/Operator 3278
Professional Counselor 2103
Psychologist 5699
Pump Installer 4429, 5369
Racing Official (Racetrack) 986, 6338
Railroad Police Officer 5484, 8737
Real Estate Appraiser 7216
Real Estate Broker 7217
Real Estate Sales Agent 7218
Registered Nurse 7382
Reptile/Amphibian Catcher, Commercial 502, 8749
Research Animal Dealer 503, 8750
Residential Builder 1944
Residential Builder Salesperson 4306
Residential Maintenance and Alteration Contractor 1945
Residential Mortgage Broker 7813
Sanitarian 3563
School Administrator 2479
School Bus Driver 1607
School Guidance Counselor 2104
School Librarian 4174
School Psychologist 5700
Secondary School Teacher 7669
Securities Agent 7814
Securities Broker-Dealer 7815
Shooting Preserve Operator, Private 2827
Social Work Technician 7997
Social Worker 7998
Solicitor, Professional 7947
Stable Helper (Racetrack) 504, 6339
Taxidermist 8266
Teacher, Vocational 265
Trainer (Racetrack) 505, 6340
Truck Driver 8301
Vendor (Racetrack) 6341, 7534
Veterinarian 8387
Veterinarian (Racetrack) 6342, 8388
Veterinary Technician 506
Waste Remover; Liquid Industrial 8299
Wastewater Treatment Facility Operator, Industrial and Commercial 8524
Water Distribution System Operator 8525
Water Hauler 8302
Water Treatment Plant Operator 8526
Well Drilling Contractor 4430
Wildlife Exhibitor (Animals and Birds) 507, 8801

Minnesota

Abstracter 8569
Alarm and Communication System Contractor 1716, 2598
Alarm and Communication System Installer 1717
Architect 739
Asbestos Abatement Contractor 1946
Asbestos Abatement Worker 3745
Assessor 7219, 8238
Attorney 4122
Audiologist 8073
Bail Bond Agent 1252
Barber 1401
Barber Instructor 266, 1402
Bloodstock Agent (Racetrack) 6343
Boxer 987
Certified Public Accountant 33
Certified Shorthand Reporter 8147
Chiropractor 1654
Commercial Pesticide Applicator 4830
Concession/Vendor Employee (Racetrack) 6344, 7535
Concessionaire/Vendor (Racetrack) 6345, 7536
Cosmetologist 1403
Cosmetologist Instructor 267, 1404
Cosmetologist Manager 1405
Debt Collector 134
Dental Assistant 2187
Dental Hygienist 2215
Dentist 2276
Driver (Racetrack) 988, 6346
Electrical Contractor 1947, 2599
Electrical Lineman 2600
Electrician 2601
Elementary School Guidance Counselor 2105
Elementary School Teacher (K-6) 3989
Elevator Constructor Electrician 2602, 2667
Emergency Medical Technician 2723
Employment Agency Manager 4723
Employment Counselor 2106, 4724
Engineer 5606
Engineer-in-Training 5607
Environmental Health Specialist (Sanitarian) 3564
Equine Dentist (Racetrack) 6347, 8389
Esthetician 1406
Esthetician Manager 1407
Exercise Rider (Racetrack) 508, 6348
Farrier (Racetrack) 509, 6349
Farrier's Assistant (Racetrack) 510, 6350
Gambling Employee 3101
Gambling Manager 3102
Gate Crew (Racetrack) 6351
Groom/Hotwalker (Racetrack) 511, 6352
Hazardous Waste Disposal Facility Inspector 3565
Hazardous Waste Disposal Facility Operator 1740
Hearing Aid Dispenser 3426, 3427
Horsemen's Bookkeeper (Racetrack) 2784, 6353
Independent Insurance Adjustor 135
Insurance Adjustor; Public 136
Insurance Agent 3831
Investment Advisor 7816
Jockey Agent (Racetrack) 989, 6354
Jockey Apprentice (Racetrack) 990, 6355
Jockey (Racetrack) 991, 6356
Kick Boxer 992
Land Surveyor 8200
Landscape Architect 4073
Licensed Practical Nurse 4225
Lobbyist 4277
Manager (Boxing and Kick Boxing) 993
Manicurist 1408
Manicurist Manager 1409
Manufactured Housing Installer 1948
Marriage and Family Therapist 2107
Milk Tester 3654
Mortician 2942
Non-Commercial Pesticide Applicator 4831
Non-Hazardous Waste Disposal Facility Inspector 3566
Non-Hazardous Waste Disposal Facility Operator 1741
Notary Public 4502
Nursing Home Administrator 3365
Occupational Therapist 4590
Occupational Therapy Assistant 4638
Optometrist 4686
Osteopathic Physician (D.O.) 5245
Owner (Racetrack) 6357
Pari-Mutuel Clerk (Racetrack) 6358
Peace Officer 5485
Pest Control Applicator; Structural 4833
Pesticide Applicator; Non-Commercial 4831
Pesticide Dealer 4832
Pharmacist 4956
Pharmacy Intern 4957
Pharmacy Technician 8719
Physical Therapist 5086
Physician 5246
Physician Assistant 5152
Plumber 5370
Podiatrist 5448
Pony Rider (Racetrack) 512, 6359
Private Investigator 2341
Promoter (Boxing and Kick Boxing) 4344
Protective Agent 3279
Psychological Practitioner 5701
Psychologist 5702
Public Insurance Adjustor 136
Public Water Supply Operator 8527
Racing Official (Racetrack) 994, 6360
Real Estate Appraiser 7220
Real Estate Broker 7221
Real Estate Salesperson 7222
Referee (Boxing and Kick Boxing) 995
Registered Nurse 7383
Residential Contractor 1949
Residential Remodeler 1950
Respiratory Care Practitioner 7457
School Administrator 2480
School Media Generalist 4175
Second (Boxing and Kick Boxing) 996
Secondary School Guidance Counselor 2108
Secondary School Teacher (7-12) 7670
Securities Agent 7817
Securities Broker-Dealer 7818
Security Officer (Racetrack) 3280, 6361
Social Worker 7999
Speech-Language Pathologist 8074

Stable Foreman (Racetrack) 513, 1557, 6362
Structural Pest Control Applicator 4833
Trainer Assistant (Racetrack) 514, 6363
Trainer (Racetrack) 515, 6364
Underground Storage Tank Contractor 1951
Underground Storage Tank Supervisor 1558, 1952
Valet (Racetrack) 6365
Veterinarian 8390
Veterinarian (Racetrack) 6366, 8391
Veterinary Assistant (Racetrack) 516, 6367
Waste Disposal Facility Inspector; Non-Hazardous 3566
Waste Disposal Facility Operator; Non-Hazardous 1741
Wastewater Disposal Facility Inspector 3567
Wastewater Disposal Facility Operator 8528
Water Conditioning Contractor 1953, 5371
Water Conditioning Installer 1954, 5372
Water Supply Operator; Public 8527
Water Well Contractor 4431

Mississippi

Animal Technician 517
Architect 740
Asbestos Contractor 1955
Asbestos Inspector 1793
Asbestos Management Planner 1956, 3746
Asbestos Project Designer 1957, 3747
Asbestos Supervisor 1559, 1958
Asbestos Worker 3748
Attorney 4123
Audiologist 8075
Barber 1410
Certified Public Accountant 34
Certified Shorthand Reporter 8148
Chiropractor 1655
Counselor; Licensed Professional 2109
Dental Hygienist 2216
Dentist 2277
Dietitian 2380
Emergency Medical Technician 2724
Funeral Director 2943
Funeral Service Practitioner 2944
General Contractor 1959
Hearing Aid Dealer 3428
Insurance Sales Agent 3832
Insurance Solicitor 3833
Investment Advisor 7819
Land Surveyor; Professional 8201
Landscape Architect 4074
Landscape Horticulturist 324, 4075
Licensed Practical Nurse 4226
Licensed Professional Counselor 2109
Lobbyist 4278
Milk Hauler and Tester 3655, 8303
Notary Public 4503
Nursing Home Administrator 3366
Occupational Therapist 4591

Occupational Therapy Assistant 4639
Optometrist 4687
Osteopathic Physician (D.O.) 5247
Pest Control Operator 4834
Pest Control Technician 4835
Pesticide Dealer 4836
Pesticide Operator - Weed Control 4837
Pharmacist 4958
Pharmacy Intern 4959
Physical Therapist 5087
Physical Therapist Assistant 5040
Physician 5248
Physician's Assistant 5153
Podiatrist 5449
Polygraph Examiner 5507
Professional Engineer 5608
Professional Land Surveyor 8201
Psychologist 5703
Real Estate Appraiser 7223
Real Estate Broker 7224
Real Estate Salesperson 7225
Registered Nurse 7384
Respiratory Care Practitioner 7458
School Administrator 2481
School Teacher 3990, 7671
Securities Agent 7820
Securities Broker-Dealer 7821
Social Worker 8000
Speech-Language Pathologist 8076
Tree Surgeon 2889
Underground Storage Tank Installer 1960
Veterinarian 8392
Wastewater Facility Operator 8529

Missouri

Announcer (Boxing, Wrestling, or Karate) 7058
Architect 741
Assistant Trainer (Racetrack) 518, 6368
Association Employee (Racetrack) 6369
Attorney 4124
Audiologist 8077
Barber 1411
Certified Court Reporter 8149
Certified Public Accountant 35
Certified Shorthand Reporter 8150
Chiropractor 1656
Commercial Pesticide Applicator 4838
Concession Employee (Racetrack) 6370, 7537
Contestant (Boxing, Wrestling, or Karate) 997
Cosmetologist 1412
Cosmetology Instructor 268, 1413
Cosmetology Student/Apprentice 1414
Dental Hygienist 2217
Dental Specialist 2278
Dentist 2279
Driver (Racetrack) 998, 6371
Early Childhood Teacher (K-3) 3991
Elementary School Counselor (K-8) 2110
Elementary School Teacher (1-8) 3992
Embalmer 2945
Emergency Medical Technician 2725

Engineer-in-Training 5609
Exercise Rider (Racetrack) 519, 6372
Farrier Assistant (Racetrack) 520, 6373
Farrier (Racetrack) 521, 6374
Funeral Director 2946
Hearing Aid Fitter and Dealer 3429
Heating and Air Conditioning Mechanic 3473
Instructional School Media Technologist 4176
Insurance Agent 3834
Insurance Broker 3835
Investment Advisor 7822
Jockey Agent (Racetrack) 999, 6375
Jockey (Racetrack) 1000, 6376
Judge (Boxing, Wrestling, or Karate) 1001
Land Surveyor; Professional 8202
Landfill Operator 1742
Landscape Architect 4076
Licensed Practical Nurse 4227
Lobbyist 4279
Manager (Boxing, Wrestling, or Karate) 1002
Manicurist 1415
Matchmaker (Boxing, Wrestling, or Karate) 4345
Middle School or Junior High Teacher 4-9 7672
Milk Hauler and Tester 3656, 8304
Mutuel Employee (Racetrack) 6377
Noncommercial Pesticide Applicator 4839
Notary Public 4504
Nursing Home Administrator 3367
Occupational Therapist 4592
Occupational Therapy Assistant 4640
Official (Racetrack) 1003, 6378
Optometrist 4688
Osteopathic Physician (D.O.) 5249
Owner-Trainer (Racetrack) 522, 6379
Pesticide Applicator; Noncommercial 4839
Pesticide Dealer 4840
Pesticide Technician 4841
Pharmacist 4960
Pharmacy Intern 4961
Physical Therapist 5088
Physician 5250
Physician's Assistant 5154
Podiatrist 5450
Private Pesticide Applicator 4842
Professional Counselor 2111
Professional Engineer 5610
Professional Land Surveyor 8202
Promoter (Boxing, Wrestling, or Karate) 4346
Psychologist 5704
Public Pesticide Operator 4843
Real Estate Appraiser 7226
Real Estate Broker 7227
Real Estate Sales Agent 7228
Referee (Boxing, Wrestling, or Karate) 1004
Registered Nurse 7385
Respiratory Care Practitioner 7459
Respiratory Care Technician 7460

Missouri, continued

Respiratory Therapist 7461
School Librarian 4177
School Principal 2482
School Superintendent 2483, 3176
Second (Boxing, Wrestling, or Karate) 1005
Secondary School Counselor (7-12) 2112
Secondary School Teacher 7673
Securities Agent 7823
Securities Broker-Dealer 7824
Social Worker 8001
Special Education Teacher 3993, 7674
Speech-Language Pathologist 8078
Stable Employee (Racetrack) 523, 6380
Substance Abuse Counselor 2113, 3487
Timekeeper (Boxing, Wrestling, or Karate) 1006
Vendor (Racetrack) 6381, 7538
Veterinarian 8393
Veterinarian Assistant (Racetrack) 524, 6382
Veterinarian (Racetrack) 6383, 8394
Veterinary Technician 525
Wastewater Operator 8530
Water Supply Operator 8531

Montana

Accountant 36
Acupuncturist 83
Adjuster 137
Announcer (Racetrack) 6384, 7059
Architect 742
Asbestos Abatement Contractor/Supervisor 1560, 1961, 3749
Asbestos Abatement Project Designer 1962, 3750
Asbestos Inspector 1794
Asbestos Management Planner 1963, 3751
Asbestos Worker 3752
Assistant Trainer (Racetrack) 526, 6385
Attorney 4125
Audiologist 8079
Auditor (Racetrack) 37, 6386
Authorized Agent (Racetrack) 1007, 6387
Barber 1416
Barber Instructor 269, 1417
Bus Driver 1608
Calculator Operator (Racetrack) 6388
Certified Shorthand Reporter 8151
Chemical Dependency Counselor 2114, 3488
Chief of Security (Racetrack) 3177, 3281, 6389
Chiropractor 1657
Clerk of Scales (Racetrack) 3568, 6390
Commercial Pesticide Applicator 4844
Construction Blaster 4432
Cosmetologist 1418
Counselor; Licensed Professional 2115
Dental Hygienist 2218
Dentist 2280

Denturist 2248
Dietitian; Registered 2382
Director of Racing (Racetrack) 3178, 6391
Director at Simulcast Facility (Racetrack) 1743, 3179, 6392
Director of Simulcast Network (Racetrack) 3180, 6393
Electrician 2603
Electrologist 1419
Elementary School Teacher 3994
Emergency Medical Technician 2726
Engineer 5611
Engineer-in-Training 5612
Exercise Person (Racetrack) 527, 6394
Fur or Hide Dealer 7539, 8661
Gate Attendant (Racetrack) 6395, 8338
General Contractor 1964
Governmental Pesticide Applicator 4845
Groom (Racetrack) 528, 6396
Guide; Professional 2829
Handicapper (Racetrack) 6397
Hearing Aid Dispenser 3430
Hoisting Engineer 4362
Horsemen's Bookkeeper (Racetrack) 2785, 6398
Hot Walker (Racetrack) 529, 6399
Identifier (Racetrack) 3569, 6400
Insurance Agent 3836
Insurance Solicitor 3837
Investment Advisor 7825
Investment Advisor Representative 7826
Jockey Agent (Racetrack) 1008, 6401
Jockey Apprentice (Racetrack) 1009, 6402
Jockey (Racetrack) 1010, 6403
Jockey Room Custodian (Racetrack) 3909, 6404
Junior High School Teacher 7675
Land Surveyor 8203
Landscape Architect 4077
Lay Midwife 4562
Licensed Practical Nurse 4228
Licensed Professional Counselor 2115
Lobbyist 4280
Manicurist 1420
Milk and Cream Tester 3657
Milk and Cream Weigher, Grader, and Sampler 3658
Mortician 2947
Naturopathic Physician 5251
Noncommercial Pesticide Applicator 4846
Notary Public 4505
Nurse Anesthetist 7386
Nurse Midwife 7387
Nurse Practitioner 7388
Nurseryman 3124, 4549
Nursing Home Administrator 3368
Nutritionist 2381
Occupational Therapist 4593
Occupational Therapy Assistant 4641
Office Worker (Racetrack) 6405, 7736
Optometrist 4689
Osteopathic Physician (D.O.) 5252
Outfitter 2828
Outrider (Racetrack) 530, 6406

Owner (Racetrack) 6407
Paddock Judge (Racetrack) 1011, 6408
Parimutuel Employees (Racetrack) 6409
Parimutuel Manager (Racetrack) 2786, 6410
Parimutuel Manager at Simulcast Network (Racetrack) 3181, 6411
Patrol Judge (Racetrack) 1012, 6412
Pesticide Applicator; Governmental 4845
Pesticide Applicator; Noncommercial 4846
Pesticide Dealer 4847
Pharmacist 4962
Photo Employee (Racetrack) 5008, 6413
Photo Manager (Racetrack) 5009, 6414
Physical Therapist 5089
Physician 5253
Physician's Assistant 5155
Placing Judge (Racetrack) 1013, 6415
Plater (Racetrack) 531, 6416
Plumber 5373
Podiatrist 5451
Polygraph Examiner 5508
Pony Person (Racetrack) 532, 6417
Practicing Veterinarian (Racetrack) 6418, 8395
Principal 2484
Private Investigator 2342
Private Security Guard 3282
Professional Guide 2829
Program Employee (Racetrack) 6419
Program Manager (Racetrack) 3182, 6420
Psychologist 5705
Racing Secretary Assistant (Racetrack) 1014, 6421
Racing Secretary (Racetrack) 1015, 6422
Radiologic Technologist 7094
Real Estate Appraiser 7229
Real Estate Broker 7230
Real Estate Salesperson 7231
Registered Dietitian 2382
Registered Professional Nurse 7389
Respiratory Care Practitioner 7462
Sanitarian 3570
School Guidance Counselor 2116
School Librarian 4178
School Psychologist 5706
School Superintendent 2485, 3183
Secondary School Teacher 7676
Securities Broker-Dealer 7827
Securities Salesman 7828
Security Staff Person (Racetrack) 3283, 6423
Septic Tank Cleaner 3910
Social Worker 8002
Speech Pathologist 8080
Stable Foreman (Racetrack) 533, 1561, 6424
Stable Superintendent (Racetrack) 1562, 3184, 6425
Starter Assistant (Racetrack) 6426
Starter (Racetrack) 1016, 6427
Stationary Engineer 5531
Steward (Racetrack) 1017, 6428

Taxidermist 8267
Timer (Racetrack) 1018, 6429
Timeshare Broker 7232
Timeshare Salesperson 7233
Tip Sheet Seller (Racetrack) 6430, 7540
Tote Employee (Racetrack) 6431
Track Maintenance Worker (Racetrack) 3911, 6432
Track Superintendent (Racetrack) 3185, 6433
Track Veterinarian (Racetrack) 6434, 8396
Trainer (Racetrack) 534, 6435
Truck Driver 8305
Underground Storage Tank Inspector 3571
Underground Storage Tank Installer and Remover 1965
Valet (Racetrack) 6436
Veterinarian 8397
Veterinarian Assistant (Racetrack) 535, 6437
Veterinarian (Racetrack); Practicing 6418, 8395
Veterinarian (Racetrack); Track 6434, 8396
Vocational Education Teacher 270
Watchman (Racetrack) 3284, 6438
Water and Sewage Plant Operator 8532
Weather Modifier 7603, 8789

Nebraska

Abstracter 8570
Accountant (CPA) 38
Admissions Employee (Racetrack) 6439, 8339
Air Conditioning/Heating Contractor 1966, 3474
Animal Technician 536
Apprentice Jockey (Racetrack) 1019, 6440
Architect 743
Assistant Starter (Racetrack) 1020, 6441
Assistant Trainer (Racetrack) 537, 6442
Athletic Trainer 3702
Attorney 4126
Auctioneer 1221
Barber 1421
Boiler/Boilerhouse Inspector 1795, 3572
Boxer 1021
Boxing Promoter 4347
Chiropractor 1658
Commercial Driver 8251, 8306
Concessions Employee (Racetrack) 6443, 7541
Cosmetologist 1422
Counselor 2117
County Highway Superintendent/City Street Superintendent 1744
Court Reporter 8152
Dental Hygienist 2219
Dentist 2281
Dietitian 2383
Driving Instructor 271
Educational Media Specialist (Librarian) 4179

Electrician 2604
Electrologist 1423
Elevator Inspections Manager 1796, 2668
Embalmer 2948
Emergency Medical Technician 2727
Employment Agent 4725
Engineer 5613
Exercise Rider (Racetrack) 538, 6444
Exterminator 4848
Farm Labor Contractor 8641
Fire Protection Sprinkler System Contractor 5374
Funeral Director 2949
General Contractor 1967
Groom 539, 6445
Hawker (Peddler) 7542
Hearing Aid Instrument Dispenser and Fitter 3431
Horse Owner (Racing) 6446
Horseshoer (Racetrack) 540, 6447
Identifier-Tattooer 3573, 6448
Insurance Agent 3838
Interpreter for the Deaf 8680
Investment Advisor 7829
Jockey 1022, 6449
Jockey Agents (Racetrack) 6450
Land Surveyor 8204
Landscape Architect 4078
Law Enforcement Officer 5486
Lobbyist 4281
Massage Therapist 5090
Midwife (Nurse) 7390
Motor Vehicle Dealer 7543
Motorcycle Dealer 7544
Mutuel Employee (Racetrack) 6451
Notary Public 4506
Nurse, Licensed Practical (LPN) 4229
Nurse Practitioner (Anesthetist) 7391
Nurse, Registered Professional (RN) 7392
Nursing Home Administrator 3369
Occupational Therapist 4594
Occupational Therapist Assistant 4642
Official (Racetrack) 1023, 6452
Optometrist 4690
Osteopath 5254
Pharmacist 4963
Physical Therapist 5091
Physical Therapist Assistant 5041
Physician/Surgeon 5255
Physician's Assistant 5156
Plumber (Journeyman) 5375
Podiatrist 5452
Polygraph Examiner 5509
Pony Person (Racetrack) 541, 6453
Private Investigator 2343
Psychologist 5707
Pump Installer/Well Driller 4433, 5376
Radiologic Technologist 7095
Real Estate Appraiser 7234
Real Estate Salesperson/Broker 7235
Respiratory Care Practitioner 7463
Safety Hygienist, Industrial 3370
Sanitarian 3574
School Administrator or Supervisor 2486

School Nurse 7393
School Psychologist 5708
School Teacher K-12 3995, 7677
Securities Agent 7830
Securities Broker-Dealer 7831
Security Guard (Racetrack) 3285, 6454
Social Worker (Master) 8003
Solicitor 138
Speech-Language Pathologist/Audiologist 8081
Stable Foreman (Racetrack) 1563, 6455
Swimming Pool Operator 8766
Taxi Driver/Chauffeur 8252
Trainer (Race Horse) 542, 6456
Valet (Racetrack) 6457
Veterinarian 8398
Veterinarian's Assistant (Racetrack) 543, 6458
Water Operators/Water Treatment Plant Operators 8533

Nevada

Accountant/Auditor 39
Acupuncturist 84
Animal Caretaker 544
Animal Technician 545
Appraiser; Motor Vehicle Damage 141
Architect 744
Assistant Trainer (Racetrack) 546, 6459
Association Racing Official (Racetrack) 1024, 6460
Authorized Agent (Racetrack) 1025, 6461
Barber 1424
Bricklayer 8594
Bus Driver 1609
Carpenter 8599
Casino Management Employee 3103
Cement Mason 8602
Chiropractor 1659
Claims Adjuster/Examiner 139
Clinical Laboratory Technologist 1689
Collection Agent/Manager 140
Commercial Pesticide Applicator 4849
Concession Employee (Racetrack) 6462, 7545
Cosmetologist 1425
Cytotechnologist 1690
Dental Hygienist 2220
Dentist 2282
Electrician 2605
Electrologist 1426
Elementary School Teacher K-8 3996
Emergency Medical Technician 2728
Engineer 5614
Euthanasia Technician 547, 8638
Fishing Guide 2830
Floor and Carpet Layer 8648
Funeral Director/Embalmer 2950
General Contractor 1968
Glazier 8666
Groundskeeper/Gardener 3125, 8667
Hair Stylist 1427
Health and Safety Inspectors 3575
Health Services Administrator 3371
Hearing Aid Specialist 3432

Nevada, continued

Heating and Air Conditioning Mechanic   3475
Histologic Technician   1691
Histotechnologist   1692
Insulation Installer   3753
Insurance Agent   3839
Investment Advisor   7832
Kennel Helper (Racetrack)   548, 6463
Landscape Architect   4079
Lawyer   4127
Lead Out (Racetrack)   549, 6464
Librarian   4180
Licensed Practical Nurse   4230
Lobbyist   4282
Marriage/Family Counselor   2118
Medical Laboratory Assistant   1693, 4371
Medical Technician   1694
Milk Hauler   8307
Milk Tester   3659
Motor Vehicle Damage Appraiser   141
Mutuel Employee (Racetrack)   6465
Notary Public   4507
Nurse Practitioner   7394
Nursing Home Administrator   3372
Occupational Therapist   4595
Occupational Therapy Assistant   4643
Optician   2409
Optometrist   4691
Osteopathic Physician (D.O.)   5256
Owner (Racetrack)   6466
Owner-Trainer (Racetrack)   550, 6467
Painter/Paperhanger   8710
Pharmacist   4964
Physical Therapist   5092
Physician   5257
Physician Assistant   5157
Plasterer/Drywall Installer   8724
Plumber/Pipefitter   5377
Podiatrist   5453
Polygraph Examiner   5510
Private Investigator   2344
Psychologist   5709
Real Estate Agent   7236
Real Estate Appraiser   7237
Registered Nurse   7395
Repossessor   142, 8748
Respiratory Therapist   7464
Roofer   8753
Rotary Driller   4434
School Administrator   2487
School Counselor   2119
School Program Administrator   2488
School Psychologist   5710
Secondary School Teacher   7678
Securities Broker-Dealer   7833
Securities Sales Representative   7834
Security Employee (Racetrack)   3286, 6468
Shorthand Reporter   8153
Social Worker   8004
Speech Pathologist/Audiologist   8082
Surveyor   8205
Taxi Driver   8253
Trainer (Racetrack)   551, 6469
Trucker   8308
Veterinarian   8399

New Hampshire

Ambulance & Rescue Attendant   2729
Architect   745
Attorney   4128
Auctioneer   1222
Bail Bondsman; Professional   1253
Barber   1428
Certified Alcohol Counselor (CAC)   2120, 3489
Certified Alcohol and Drug Abuse Counselor (CADAC)   2121, 3490
Certified Drug Counselor (CDC)   2122, 3491
Certified Marital Mediator   2123
Certified Public Accountant   40
Certified Shorthand Reporter   8154
Chiropractor   1660
Clinical Social Worker   8005
Cosmetologist   1429
Cosmetology Instructor   272, 1430
Dental Hygienist   2221
Dentist   2283
Driver Education Instructor   273
Electrician   2606
Electrologist   1431
Embalmer   2951
Emergency Medical Technician   2730
Esthetician   1432
Firefighter   2803
Forester; Professional   2890
Funeral Director   2952
Hearing Aid Dealer/Dispenser   3433
Hunting & Fishing Guide   2831
Insurance Adjuster   143
Insurance Adjuster; Public   144
Insurance Agent   3840
Insurance Broker   3841
Insurance Consultant   3842
Investment Advisor   7835
Itinerant Vendor   7546
Land Surveyor   8206
Licensed Practical Nurse   4231
Lobbyist   4283
Manicurist   1433
Marital Mediator; Certified   2123
Massage Practitioner   5093
Milk Hauler and Tester   3660, 8309
Mortgage Banker; Nondepository First   7836
Nondepository First Mortgage Banker   7836
Notary Public   4508
Nursing Home Administrator   3373
Occupational Therapist   4596
Occupational Therapist Assistant   4644
Optician   2410
Optometrist   4692
Osteopathic Physician (D.O.)   5258
Pastoral Counselor   2124, 8713
Pesticide Applicator   4850
Pharmacist   4965
Physical Therapist   5094
Physical Therapist Assistant   5042
Physician   5259
Physician's Assistant   5158
Plumber   5378
Podiatrist   5454
Private Investigator   2345
Professional Bail Bondsman   1253
Professional Engineer   5615
Professional Forester   2890
Psychologist   5711
Public Insurance Adjuster   144
Real Estate Broker   7238
Real Estate Sales Agent   7239
Registered Nurse   7396
Respiratory Care Practitioner   7465
School Administrator   2489
School Teacher K-12   3997, 7679
Securities Agent   7837
Securities Broker-Dealer   7838
Security Guard   3287
Soil Scientist   325
Surplus Lines Insurance Agent   3843
Veterinarian   8400
Vocational Education Teacher   274
Wastewater Treatment Plant Operator   8534
Water Distribution System Operator   8535
Water Treatment Plant Operator   8536

New Jersey

Accountant   41
Accountant; Municipal   42
Accountant; Public School   43
Acupuncturist   85
Alcohol Counselor   2125
Animal Control Officer   3576, 8581
Architect   746
Asbestos Employee   3754
Asbestos Employer   1969
Athletic Trainer   3703
Attorney   4129
Audiologist/Speech Pathologist   8083
Authorized Agent (Racetrack)   6470
Automobile Dealer   7547
Bio-Analytical Laboratory Director   2760, 3186
Boiler Operator - Black Seal   1593
Boxer   1026
Boxing Manager   1027
Building Inspector   1797
Casino Floor Employee   3104
Casino Hotel Employee   3105
Cemetery Salesperson   7240
Check Casher   1627
Check Seller   1628
Chest X-Ray Technologist   7096
Chiropractor   1661
Clocker (Racetrack)   1028, 6471
Construction Code Official   1798
Cosmetologist/Hairstylist   1434
Cosmetology Instructor   275, 1435
Court Reporter   8155
Dental Hygienist   2222
Dental X-Ray Technologist   2249, 7097
Dentist   2284
Diagnostic X-Ray Technologist   7098

Director of Student Personnel
  Services 2490, 4726
Drug Abuse Counselor 2126, 3492
Educational Media Specialist 4181
Electrical Contractor 1970, 2607
Electrical Inspector 1799
Emergency Medical Technician 2731
Employment Agency Operator 4727
Engineer-In-Training 5616
Fire Protection Inspector 1800
Groom 552, 6472
Harbor Pilot 8490
Harness Race Driver 1029, 6473
Hearing Aid Dispenser 3434
Home Repair Contractor 1971
Home Repair Salesperson 7948
Inplant Inspector 3577
Insurance Agent 3844
Investment Advisor 7839
Jockey 1030, 6474
Laboratory Director 2761, 3187
Landscape Architect 4080
Librarian 4182
Licensed Practical Nurse 4232
Lobbyist 4284
Long Boom Crane Operator 4363
Manicurist 1436
Marriage Counselor 2127
Midwife 7397
Milk Dealer 2867, 8565
Mortgage Banker/Broker 7840
Mortician 2953
Movers and Warehousemen 1745
Municipal Accountant 42
Notary Public 4509
Nuclear Engineer - Blue Seal 5532
Nuclear Medical Technologist 4538
Nursing Home Administrator 3374
Operating Engineer - Gold Seal 4364
Operating Engineer - Red Seal 4365
Optician, Dispensing 2411
Optician Technician 8706
Optometrist 4693
Orthopedic X-Ray Technologist 7099
Orthopist 8707
Osteopathic Physician (D.O.) 5260
Pari-mutuel Employee (Racetrack) 6475
Pawnbroker 7548
Pesticide Applicator - Commercial 4851
Pesticide Applicator - Private 4852
Pesticide Dealer 4853
Pesticide Operator 4854
Pharmacist 4966
Physical Therapist 5095
Physician 5261
Physician's Assistant 5159
Pilot; Harbor 8490
Plater (Racetrack) 553, 6476
Plumber 5379
Plumbing Inspector 1801
Podiatrist 5455
Private Detective 2346
Professional Engineer 5617
Psychologist 5712
Public Health Officer 3578
Public School Accountant 43
Pump Installer 4435, 5380

Race Horse Owner 6477
Radiation Therapy Technologist 7100
Real Estate Appraiser 7241
Real Estate Broker 7242
Real Estate Instructor 276, 7243
Real Estate Salesperson 7244
Refrigeration Engineer - Blue Seal 5533
Registered Nurse 7398
Respiratory Care Practitioner 7466
Salesperson; Home Repair 7948
Sanitary Inspector 3579
School Administrator 2491
School Counselor 2128
School Principal 2492
School Supervisor 2493
School Teacher K-12 3998, 7680
Securities Agent 7841
Securities Broker-Dealer 7842
Securities Issuer 7843
Social Worker 8006
Starter (Racetrack) 1031, 6478
Steam Engineer - Blue Seal 5534
Surveyor 8207
Timer (Racetrack) 1032, 6479
Tree Expert 2891
Urban Planner 8785
Urologic X-ray Technologist 7101
Valet (Racetrack) 6480
Vendor (Racetrack) 6481, 7549
Veterinarian 8401
Wastewater System Operator 8537
Weighing or Measuring Mechanic 5539
Weighmaster 3580
Well Driller 4436
X-Ray Technologist; Diagnostic 7098
X-Ray Technologist; Orthopedic 7099

New Mexico

Acupuncturist (L.Ac.); Licensed 86
Admissions Gateman (Racetrack) 6482, 8340
Admissions Ticket Seller
  (Racetrack) 6483, 7550, 8341
Announcer (Racetrack) 6484, 7060
Architect 747
Assistant Racing Secretary
  (Racetrack) 1033, 6485
Athletic Trainer 3704
Attorney 4130
Audiologist 8084
Authorized Agent (Racetrack) 1034, 6486
Barber 1437
Barber Instructor 277, 1438
Boiler Operator; Journeyman 1594
Certified Public Accountant 44
Certified Shorthand Reporter 8156
Chiropractor 1662
Clerk of Scales (Racetrack) 3581, 6487
Clocker (Racetrack) 1035, 6488
Collection Agency Manager 145
Commercial Pesticide Applicator 4855
Concession Employee (Racetrack) 6489, 7551
Concession Operator (Racetrack) 6490, 7552

Cosmetologist 1439
Cosmetology Teacher 278, 1440
Dental Hygienist 2223
Dentist 2285
Dietitian 2384
Director of Racing (Racetrack) 3188, 6491
Electrical Contractor 1972, 2608
Electrician; Journeyman 2610
Electrician (Racetrack) 2609, 6492
Electrologist 1441
Elementary Teacher K-8 3999
Emergency Medical Technician 2732
Engineer Intern 5618
(Esthetician); Skin Care Specialist 1443
Exercise Boy (Racetrack) 554, 6493
Film Employee (Racetrack) 5010, 6494
Funeral Service Practitioner 2954
Gas Fitter; Journeyman 5381
General Contractor 1973
General Manager (Racetrack) 3189, 6495
Groom (Racetrack) 555, 6496
Hearing Aid Dispenser 3435
Horsemen's Bookkeeper
  (Racetrack) 2787, 6497
Identifier (Racetrack) 3582, 6498
Insurance Agent 3845
Insurance Broker 3846
Insurance Solicitor 3847
Interior Designer 2322
Investment Advisor 7844
Investment Advisor Representative 7845
Janitor (Racetrack) 3912, 6499
Jockey Agent (Racetrack) 1036, 6500
Jockey Apprentice (Racetrack) 1037, 6501
Jockey (Racetrack) 1038, 6502
Jockey Room Custodian
  (Racetrack) 3913, 6503
Jockey Valet (Racetrack) 6504
Journeyman Boiler Operator 1594
Journeyman Electrician 2610
Journeyman Gas Fitter 5381
Journeyman Pipe Fitter 5382
Journeyman Pipeline Welder 8683
Journeyman Plumber 5383
Journeyman Sheet Metal Worker 8684
Judge (Boxing, Wrestling, Martial Arts,
  and Kick Boxing) 1039
Laborer (Racetrack) 3328, 6505
Land Surveyor 8208
Landscape Architect 4081
Licensed Acupuncturist (L.Ac.) 86
Licensed Practical Nurse 4233
Lobbyist 4285
Manicurist 1442
Manufactured Housing Associate
  Broker 7245
Manufactured Housing Broker 7246
Manufactured Housing Installer and
  Repairperson 1974
Manufactured Housing
  Salesperson 7247
Massage Therapist 5096
Massage Therapy Instructor 279, 5097, 8697

New Mexico, continued

Matchmaker (Boxing, Wrestling, Martial Arts, and Kick Boxing) 4348
Mechanical Contractor 1975
Milk Hauler and Tester 3661, 8310
Noncommercial Pesticide Applicator 4856
Notary Public 4510
Nuclear Medical Technologist 4539
Nursing Home Administrator 3375
Nutrition Associate 2385
Nutritionist 2386
Occupational Therapist 4597
Occupational Therapy Assistant 4645
Office Worker (Racetrack) 6506, 7737
Optometrist 4694
Osteopathic Physician (D.O.) 5262
Osteopathic Physician's Assistant 5160
Outrider (Racetrack) 556, 6507
Owner (Racetrack) 6508
Paddock Judge (Racetrack) 1040, 6509
Pari-Mutuel Employee (Racetrack) 6510
Pari-Mutuel Manager (Racetrack) 2788, 6511
Pest Management Consultant 4857
Pesticide Applicator; Noncommercial 4856
Pesticide Dealer 4858
Pesticide Operator 4859
Pharmacist 4967
Pharmacy Intern 4968
Photo Employee (Racetrack) 5011, 6512
Photo Operator (Racetrack) 5012, 6513
Photographer (Racetrack Win Circle) 5013, 6514
Physical Therapist 5098
Physician 5263
Physician's Assistant 5161
Pipe Fitter; Journeyman 5382
Placing Judge (Racetrack) 1041, 6515
Plater (Racetrack) 557, 6516
Plumber; Journeyman 5383
Podiatrist 5456
Polygraph Examiner 5511
Pony Boy (Racetrack) 558, 6517
Practicing Veterinarian (Racetrack) 6518, 8402
Private Investigator 2347
Private Patrol Operator 3288
Private Pesticide Applicator 4860
Professional Boxer 1042
Professional Engineer 5619
Professional Kick Boxer 1043
Professional Martial Arts Fighter 1044
Professional Wrestler 1045
Psychological Associate 5713
Psychologist 5714
Public Pest Management Consultant 4861
Racing Secretary (Racetrack) 1046, 6519
Radiation Therapy Technologist 7102
Radiologic Technologist 7103
Real Estate Appraiser 7248
Real Estate Broker 7249
Real Estate Salesperson 7250

Referee (Boxing, Wrestling, Martial Arts, and Kick Boxing) 1047
Registered Nurse 7399
Respiratory Care Practitioner 7467
School Administrator K-12 2494
School Guidance Counselor K-12 2129
Secondary Teacher 7-12 7681
Securities Broker-Dealer 7846
Securities Sales Representative 7847
Security Chief (Racetrack) 3190, 3289, 6520
Security Staff Employee (Racetrack) 3290, 6521
Sheet Metal Worker; Journeyman 8684
Simulcast Company Employee (Racetrack) 6522
Simulcast Operator (Racetrack) 6523
Skin Care Specialist (Esthetician) 1443
Social Worker 8007
Solicitor 146
Solid Waste Facility Operator 1746
Speech-Language Pathologist 8085
Stable Area Gateman (Racetrack) 559, 6524
Stable Foreman (Racetrack) 560, 1564, 6525
Stable Superintendent (Racetrack) 1565, 3191, 6526
Starter Assistant (Racetrack) 6527
Starter (Racetrack) 1048, 6528
State Auditor (Racetrack) 45, 6529
Surveyor Intern 8209
Timekeeper (Boxing, Wrestling, Martial Arts, and Kick Boxing) 1049
Timer (Racetrack) 1050, 6530
Totalisator Operator (Racetrack) 6531
Track Maintenance Employee (Racetrack) 3914, 6532
Track Steward (Racetrack) 1051, 6533
Track Superintendent (Racetrack) 3192, 6534
Track Veterinarian (Racetrack) 6535, 8403
Trainer Assistant (Racetrack) 561, 6536
Trainer (Boxing, Wrestling, Martial Arts, and Kick Boxing) 3705
Trainer (Racetrack) 562, 6537
Veterinarian 8404
Veterinarian Assistant (Racetrack) 563, 6538
Veterinarian (Racetrack); Practicing 6518, 8402
Veterinarian (Racetrack); Track 6535, 8403
Veterinary Technician 564
Watchman (Racetrack) 3291, 6539

New York

Acupuncturist 87
Adjuster (Insurance) 147
Animal Health Technologist (Veterinary Technologist) 565
Architect 748
Asbestos Handler 3755
Assistant Trainer (Thoroughbred Racing) 566, 6540

Audiologist 8086
Authorized Agent (Thoroughbred Racing) 1052, 6541
Bail Bond Agent 1254
Barber 1444
Blaster 4437
Boiler Inspector (Boiler and Pressure Vessel Inspector) 1802, 3583
Bus Driver 1610
Certified Mobile Laser Operator 8603
Certified Motor-Vehicle Inspector 3584
Certified Nurse - Midwife 7400
Certified Public Accountant 46
Certified Shorthand Reporter 8157
Certified Social Worker 8008
Chauffer 8254
Chiropractor 1663
Cleaning Services Employee (Harness or Quarter Horse Racing) 3915, 6542
Cleaning Services Employee (Thoroughbred Racing) 3916, 6543
Cosmetologist (Hairdresser/Stylist, Manicurist, Beautician) 1445
Crane Operator 4366
Dental Hygienist 2224
Dentist 2286
Driver (Harness or Quarter Horse Racing) 1053, 6544
Driving Instructor 280
Early Childhood, Upper Elementary, and Early Secondary Teacher N-9 4000
Early Childhood and Upper Elementary Teacher N-6 4001, 5556
Emergency Medical Technician and Paramedic 2733
Engineer, Professional 5620
Farrier (Harness or Quarter Horse Racing) 567, 6545
Farrier (Thoroughbred Racing) 568, 6546
Food Services Employee (Harness or Quarter Horse Racing) 2868, 6547
Food Services Employee (Thoroughbred Racing) 2869, 6548
Funeral Director 2955
General Insurance Consultant 3848
General Service Employee (Harness or Quarter Horse Racing) 6549
General Service Employee (Thoroughbred Racing) 6550
Groom (Harness or Quarter Horse Racing) 569, 6551
Guide 2832
Hearing Aid Dealer 3436
Insurance Agent, General Property and Casualty 3849
Insurance Agent, Life Insurance, Variable Annuities, Accident and Health 3850
Insurance Agent, Mortgage Guaranty 3851
Insurance Broker 3852
Insurance Consultant; General 3848
Insurance Consultant; Life 3853
Investment Advisor 7848
Jockey Agent (Thoroughbred Racing) 1054, 6552

1288

Jockey/Apprentice Jockey (Thoroughbred Racing) 1055, 6553
Laboratory Technician, Milk 7604
Land Surveyor 8210
Landscape Architect 4082
Lawyer (Attorney, Counselor at Law) 4131
Licensed Practical Nurse 4234
Life Insurance Consultant 3853
Lobbyist 4286
Manager, Milk Gathering Plant 3193, 8696
Masseur/Masseuse 5099
Milk Tester 3662
Mutuel Employee (Harness or Quarter Horse Racing) 6554
Mutuel Employee (Thoroughbred Racing) 6555
Notary Public 4511
Nurse - Midwife; Certified 7400
Nurse Practitioner 7401
Nursing Home Administrator 3376
Occupational Therapist 4598
Occupational Therapy Assistant 4646
Ophthalmic Dispenser (Optician) 2412
Optometrist 4695
Osteopathic Physician (D.O.) 5264
Owner (Harness or Quarter Horse Racing) 6556
Owner (Thoroughbred Racing) 6557
Pesticide Applicator 4862
Pesticide Dealer 4863
Pharmacist 4969
Physical Therapist 5100
Physical Therapy Assistant 5043
Physician 5265
Physician's Assistant 5162
Podiatrist 5457
Private Investigator 2348
Psychologist 5715
Racing Official (Thoroughbred Racing) 1056, 6558
Radiologic Technologist/Radiotherapy Technologist 7104
Real Estate Appraiser 7251
Real Estate Broker 7252
Real Estate Salesperson 7253
Registered Professional Nurse 7402
School Administrator 2495
School Administrator and/or Supervisor K-12 2496
School Counselor K-12 2130
School District Administrator 2497
School Media Specialist K-12 4183
Secondary Teacher 7-12 7682
Securities Broker Dealer 7849
Securities Salesperson 7850
Security Employee (Harness or Quarter Horse Racing) 3292, 6559
Security Employee (Thoroughbred Racing) 3293, 6560
Simulcast Employee (Harness or Quarter Horse Racing) 6561
Simulcast Employee (Thoroughbred Racing) 6562
Social Worker; Certified 8008

Special Subjects Teacher N-12 4002, 7683
Speech-Language Pathologist 8087
Stable Worker (Thoroughbred Racing) 570, 6563
Track Manager (Harness or Quarter Horse Racing) 3194, 6564
Track Manager (Thoroughbred Racing) 3195, 6565
Trainer/Assistant Trainer (Harness or Quarter Horse Racing) 571, 6566
Trainer (Thoroughbred Racing) 572, 6567
Truck Driver, Heavy or Tractor Trailer 8311
Veterinarian 8405
Veterinarian (Harness or Quarter Horse Racing) 6568, 8406
Veterinarian (Thoroughbred Racing) 6569, 8407
Wastewater Treatment Plant Operator 8538
Water-Treatment Plant Operator 8539
Welder 8793

North Carolina

Acupuncturist 88
Aerial Pesticide Applicator 4864
Alarm Installer 2611
Alarm System Business Licensee 1718, 1747, 1976
Ambulance Attendant 2734
Appraiser; Motor Vehicle Damage 149
Architect 749
Armed Security Guard 3294
Attorney 4132
Auctioneer 1223
Audiologist 8088
Automobile Dealer 7553
Automobile Salesperson 7554
Bail Bond Agent 1255
Bail Bond Runner 1256
Barber 1446
Barber Instructor 281, 1447
Boiler Inspector 1803, 3585
Building Inspector 1804
Bus Driver 1611
Cemetery Broker 7254
Cemetery Salesperson 7255
Center Day Care Teacher/Caregiver 5557
Certified Public Accountant 47
Certified Shorthand Reporter 8158
Certified Structural Pest Control Applicator 4865
Chiropractor 1664
Cosmetologist 1448
Cosmetologist Instructor 282, 1449
Counselor 2131
Counterintelligence Licensee 2349, 8620
Cytotechnologist 1695
Day Care Administrator 187
Day Care Teacher/Caregiver; Home 5558
Dental Hygienist 2225

Dentist 2287
Domestic Chauffeur 8255
Driver Education Specialist 283
Electrical Contractor 1977, 2612
Electrical Inspector 3586
Electrologist 1450
Embalmer 2956
Emergency Medical Technician 2735
Engineer-in-Training 5621
Farm Bulk Milk Hauler/Sampler 3663, 8312
Firearms Trainer 3706, 8645
Food Inspector 3587
Funeral Director 2957
Funeral Service Licensee 2958
General Contractor 1978
Geologist 3245
Ground Pesticide Applicator 4866
Guard Dog Service Employee 3295, 8668
Hearing Aid Dealer and Fitter 3437
Histologic Technician 1696
Home Day Care Teacher/Caregiver 5558
Industrial Hygienist 3377
Insurance Adjuster; Self-Employed 150
Insurance Agent 3854
Insurance Company/Independent Firm Adjuster 148
Investment Advisor 7851
Investment Advisor Representative 7852
Jailer 8682
Land Surveyor 8211
Landscape Architect 4083
Librarian 4184
Licensed Practical Nurse 4235
Licensed Structural Pest Control Operator 4867
Lobbyist 4287
Manicurist 1451
Marital and Family Therapist 2132
Mechanical Inspector 1805
Medical Doctor 5266
Medical Laboratory Technician 1697
Milk Tester 3664
Motor Vehicle Damage Appraiser 149
Notary Public 4512
Nurse Practitioner 7403
Nursing Home Administrator 3378
Occupational Therapist 4599
Occupational Therapist Assistant 4647
Optician 2413
Optometrist 4696
Osteopath 5267
Pest Control Applicator; Certified Structural 4865
Pest Control Operator; Licensed Structural 4867
Pesticide Applicator; Aerial 4864
Pesticide Applicator; Ground 4866
Pesticide Consultant 4868
Pesticide Dealer 4869
Petroleum Device Technician 3665, 8715
Pharmacist 4970
Physical Therapist 5101
Physical Therapist Assistant 5044

North Carolina, continued

Physician's Assistant 5163
Plumbing, Heating, and Air Conditioning Contractor 1979, 3476, 5384
Plumbing Inspector 1806
Podiatrist 5458
Police Officer; Sworn 5487
Polygraph Examiner 5512
Practicing Psychologist 5716
Private Investigator 2350
Professional Engineer 5622
Professional Solicitor 7949
Psychological Associate 5717
Psychological Stress Evaluator (PSE) 5718
Public School Teacher K-12 4003, 7684
Real Estate Appraiser 7256
Real Estate Broker 7257
Real Estate Salesperson 7258
Refrigeration Contractor 1980, 3477
Registered Nurse 7404
Registered Professional Reporter 8159
Safety Inspection Mechanic 1243, 3588
Sanitarian 3589
Scale Technician 5540
School Guidance Counselor K-12 2133
School Media Personnel K-12 4185
School Principal K-12 2498
School Psychologist 5719
School Superintendent 2499, 3196
School Supervisor and/or Program Coordinator K-12 2500
Securities Dealer 7853
Securities Salesperson 7854
Security Guard; Armed 3294
Security Guard and Patrol Licensee 3296
Self-Employed Insurance Adjuster 150
Social Worker 8009
Solicitor; Professional 7949
Solid Waste Facility Operator 1748
Special Education Teacher K-12 4004, 7685
Speech and Language Pathologist 8089
Sworn Police Officer 5487
Taxicab Driver 8256
Taxidermist 8268
Truck Driver 8313
Veterinarian 8408
Veterinary Technician 573
Vocational Education Teacher 284
Wastewater Treatment Plant Operator 8540
Water Treatment Facility Operator 8541

North Dakota

Abstractor 8572
Addiction Counselor 2134, 3493
Announcer (Racetrack) 6570, 7061
Architect 750
Asbestos Abatement Contractor 1981
Asbestos Abatement Inspector 1807
Asbestos Abatement Management Planner 1982, 3756
Asbestos Abatement Project Designer 1983, 3757
Asbestos Abatement Project Monitor 1984, 3758
Asbestos Abatement Supervisor 1566, 1985, 3759
Asbestos Abatement Worker 3760
Assistant Veterinarian (Racetrack) 574, 6571
Associate Counselor 2135
Association Veterinarian (Racetrack) 6572, 8409
Athletic Trainer 3707
Attendant (Racetrack) 3329, 6573
Attorney 4133
Auctioneer 1224
Audiologist 8090
Auditor (Racetrack) 48, 6574
Authorized Agent (Racetrack) 1057, 6575
Barber 1452
Beauty Shop Manager/Operator 1453
Boxer 1058
Boxing Cornerperson 1059
Boxing Judge 1060
Boxing Manager 1061
Boxing Promoter 4349
Boxing Referee 1062
Boxing Timekeeper 1063
Broker; Oil and Gas 7857
Calculator Operator (Racetrack) 6576
Certified Public Accountant 49
Certified Respiratory Care Practitioner 7468
Check Seller 1629
Chief of Security (Racetrack) 3197, 3297, 6577
Chiropractor 1665
Clerk of Scales (Racetrack) 3590, 6578
Clinical Laboratory Scientist 1698, 2762
Clinical Laboratory Technician 1699
Commercial Pesticide Applicator 4870
Cosmetologist 1454
Cosmetology Instructor 285, 1455
Debt Collector 151
Dental Hygienist 2226
Dentist 2288
Dietitian 2387
Director of Racing (Racetrack) 3198, 6579
Electrician 2613
Electrologist 1456
Elementary School Principal 2501
Elementary School Teacher 4005
Embalmer/Funeral Director 2959
Emergency Medical Technician 2736
Employment Agent 4728
Environmental Health Practitioner 3591
Esthetician 1457
Exercise Person (Racetrack) 575, 6580
Fishing Guide 2833
Fundraiser; Professional 7950
Gate Admission Seller (Racetrack) 6581, 7555, 8342
Gate Attendant (Racetrack) 6582, 8343
General Contractor 1986
Groom (Racetrack) 576, 6583

Handicapper (Racetrack) 6584
Hearing Aid Dealer and Dispenser 3438
Heating and Air Conditioning Contractor 1987, 3478
Heating and Air Conditioning Mechanic 3479
Horse Identifier (Racetrack) 3592, 6585
Hot Walker (Racetrack) 577, 6586
Insurance Agent 3855
Insurance Broker 3856
Investment Adviser 7855
Investment Adviser Representative 7856
Jockey Agent (Racetrack) 1064, 6587
Jockey Apprentice (Racetrack) 1065, 6588
Jockey-Driver (Racetrack) 1066, 6589
Jockey Room Custodian (Racetrack) 3917, 6590
Kickboxer 1067
Land Surveyor 8212
Landfill Operator; Municipal Waste 1750
Licensed Practical Nurse 4236
Lobbyist 4288
Manicurist 1458
Massage Therapist 5102
Merchant; Transient 7557
Milk Hauler and Tester 3666, 8314
Monitoring Well Contractor 4438
Municipal Waste Incinerator Operator 1749
Municipal Waste Landfill Operator 1750
Notary Public 4513
Nursing Home Administrator 3379
Nutritionist 2388
Occupational Therapist 4600
Occupational Therapy Assistant 4648
Office Worker (Racetrack) 6591, 7738
Oil and Gas Broker 7857
Oil and Gas Wellhead Welder 8705
Optometrist 4697
Osteopathic Physician (D.O.) 5268
Outrider (Racetrack) 6592
Owner (Racetrack) 6593
Owner-Trainer (Racetrack) 578, 6594
Paddock Judge (Racetrack) 1068, 6595
Pari-Mutuel Employee (Racetrack) 6596
Pari-Mutuel Manager (Racetrack) 2789, 6597
Patrol Judge (Racetrack) 1069, 6598
Peace Officer 5488
Pesticide Dealer 4871
Pharmacist 4971
Pharmacy Intern 4972
Photo Employee (Racetrack) 5014, 6599
Photo Manager (Racetrack) 5015, 6600
Physical Therapist 5103
Physical Therapist Assistant 5045
Physician 5269
Physician's Assistant 5164
Placing Judge (Racetrack) 1070, 6601
Plumber 5385
Podiatrist 5459
Polygraph Operator 5513
Pony Person (Racetrack) 579, 6602
Private Detective 2351

Private Pesticide Applicator 4872
Professional Counselor 2136
Professional Engineer 5623
Professional Fundraiser 7950
Psychologist 5720
Pump and Pitless Unit Contractor 1988, 4439, 5386
Racing Secretary Assistant (Racetrack) 1071, 6603
Racing Secretary (Racetrack) 1072, 6604
Real Estate Appraiser 7259
Real Estate Broker 7260
Real Estate Sales Agent 7261
Registered Nurse 7405
Registered Respiratory Care Practitioner 7469
Respiratory Care Practitioner; Certified 7468
Respiratory Care Practitioner; Registered 7469
Sanitary Pumper (Cesspool Cleaner) 8542
School Counselor 2137
School Media Specialist 4186
School Speech Therapist 8091
School Superintendent 2502, 3199
Secondary School Principal 2503
Secondary School Teacher 7686
Securities Dealer 7858
Securities Salesperson 7859
Security Employee (Racetrack) 3298, 6605
Sewer and Water Contractor 1989, 5387
Sewer and Water Installer 1990, 5388
Social Worker 8010
Soil Classifier 326
Speech-Language Pathologist 8092
Stable Foreman (Racetrack) 580, 1567, 6606
Starter (Racetrack) 1073, 6607
Steward (Racetrack) 1074, 6608
Taxidermist 8269
Timer (Racetrack) 1075, 6609
Tip Sheet Seller (Racetrack) 6610, 7556
Totalizer Operator (Racetrack) 6611
Track Maintenance (Racetrack) 3918, 6612
Track Superintendent (Racetrack) 3200, 6613
Trainer (Racetrack) 581, 6614
Transient Merchant 7557
Truck Driver (Commercial) 8315
Valet (Racetrack) 6615
Veterinarian 8410
Veterinarian (Racetrack); Assistant 574, 6571
Waste Incinerator Operator; Municipal 1749
Wastewater System Operator 8543
Water Conditioning Contractor 1991, 5389
Water Conditioning Installer 1992, 5390
Water Distribution System Operator 8544
Water Well Contractor 4440
Weather Modifier 7605, 8790

Weighman 3593
Weighmaster 3594
Welder; Oil and Gas Wellhead 8705

Ohio

Adjuster; Public 152
Admission Employee (Thoroughbred, Standardbred, and Quarter Horse Racing) 6616, 8344
Animal Technician 582
Apprentice Jockey (Thoroughbred and Quarter Horse Racing) 1076, 6617
Architect 751
Assistant Racing Secretary (Thoroughbred, Standardbred, and Quarter Horse Racing) 1077, 6618
Assistant Starter (Thoroughbred, Standardbred, and Quarter Horse Racing) 1078, 6619
Assistant Trainer (Thoroughbred, Standardbred, and Quarter Horse Racing) 583, 6620
Athletic Trainer 3708
Attorney 4134
Auctioneer 1225
Audiologist 8093
Audiologist; School 8094
Authorized Agent (Thoroughbred, Standardbred, and Quarter Horse Racing) 1079, 6621
Automatic Sprinkler System Designer 2614
Automatic Sprinkler System Inspector 1808
Barber 1459
Blaster; Surface 4445
Boiler Inspector 1809, 3595
Boiler Operator 1595
Building Inspector 1810
Building Official 1811
Certified Public Accountant 50
Chief of Security (Thoroughbred, Standardbred, and Quarter Horse Racing) 3201, 3299, 6622
Chiropractor 1666
Clerical Worker (Thoroughbred, Standardbred, and Quarter Horse Racing) 6623
Clerk of Course (Thoroughbred, Standardbred, and Quarter Horse Racing) 6624
Clinical Counselor; Licensed Professional 2138
Concession Employee (Thoroughbred, Standardbred, and Quarter Horse Racing) 6625, 7558
Concession Manager (Thoroughbred, Standardbred, and Quarter Horse Racing) 6626, 7559
Cosmetologist 1460
Cosmetologist; Managing 1465
Cosmetology Instructor 286, 1461
Counselor; Licensed Professional 2139
Custom Applicator 4873
Custom Operator 4874
Dental Hygienist 2227

Dentist 2289
Deputy Mine Inspector 3596, 4441
Dietitian-Nutritionist 2389
Doctor (Thoroughbred, Standardbred, and Quarter Horse Racing) 5270, 6627
Driver/Trainer (Standardbred Racing) 1080, 6628
Electrical Safety Inspector 1812
Electrologist 1462
Elementary School Teacher 1-8 4006
Elevator Inspector 1813, 2669
Embalmer 2960
Emergency Medical Technician 2737
Engineer-in-Training 5624
Equine Tooth Dresser (Thoroughbred, Standardbred, and Quarter Horse Racing) 6629, 8411
Esthetician 1463
Esthetician; Managing 1466
Esthetics Instructor 287, 1464
Exercise Boy/Girl (Thoroughbred and Quarter Horse Racing) 584, 6630
Fishing Guide 2834
Funeral Director 2961
General Manager (Thoroughbred, Standardbred, and Quarter Horse Racing) 3202, 6631
Groom (Thoroughbred, Standardbred, and Quarter Horse Racing) 585, 6632
Hearing Aid Dealer and Fitter 3439
High School Teacher 7-12 7687
Horsemen's Bookkeeper (Thoroughbred, Standardbred, and Quarter Horse Racing) 2790, 6633
Horseshoer (Thoroughbred, Standardbred, and Quarter Horse Racing) 586, 6634
HVAC Inspector (Mechanical) 1814
Identifier (Thoroughbred, Standardbred, and Quarter Horse Racing) 3597, 6635
Insurance Agent 3857
Insurance Solicitor 3858
Jockey Agent (Thoroughbred and Quarter Horse Racing) 1081, 6636
Jockey (Thoroughbred and Quarter Horse Racing) 1082, 6637
Judge (Standardbred Racing) 1083, 6638
Kindergarten and Primary Grade Teacher K-3 4007
Land Surveyor; Professional 8213
Landscape Architect 4084
Licensed Practical Nurse 4237
Licensed Professional Clinical Counselor 2138
Licensed Professional Counselor 2139
Limited Commercial Applicator 4875
Lobbyist 4289
Maintenance Employee (Thoroughbred, Standardbred, and Quarter Horse Racing) 3919, 6639
Managing Cosmetologist 1465
Managing Esthetician 1466
Managing Manicurist 1467
Manicurist 1468
Manicurist Instructor 288, 1469
Manicurist; Managing 1467

Ohio, continued

Masseur/Masseuse 5104
Medical/First Aid Employee (Thoroughbred, Standardbred, and Quarter Horse Racing) 4372, 6640
Middle School Teacher 4-9 7688
Milk Hauler and Tester 3667, 8316
Mine Electrician 2615, 4442
Mine Fire Boss 3598, 4443
Mine Foreman 1568, 4444
Mine Inspector; Deputy 3596, 4441
Mutuel Employee (Thoroughbred, Standardbred, and Quarter Horse Racing) 6641
Mutuel Manager (Thoroughbred, Standardbred, and Quarter Horse Racing) 2791, 3203, 6642
Notary Public 4514
Nursing Home Administrator 3380
Occupational Therapist 4601
Occupational Therapist; School 4602
Occupational Therapy Assistant 4649
Optician 2414
Optometrist 4698
Osteopathic Physician (D.O.) 5271
Outrider (Thoroughbred, Standardbred, and Quarter Horse Racing) 587, 6643
Owner (Thoroughbred, Standardbred, and Quarter Horse Racing) 6644
Paddock Judge (Thoroughbred, Standardbred, and Quarter Horse Racing) 1084, 6645
Parking Lot Employee (Thoroughbred and Quarter Horse Racing) 3330, 6646
Patrol Judge (Thoroughbred and Quarter Horse Racing) 1085, 6647
Pawnbroker 7560
Pesticide Dealer 4876
Pharmacist 4973
Pharmacy Intern 4974
Photographer (Thoroughbred and Quarter Horse Racing) 5016, 6648
Physical Therapist 5105
Physical Therapist Assistant 5046
Physical Therapist; School 5106
Physician 5272
Physician's Assistant 5165
Piping System Inspector 1815
Placing Judge (Thoroughbred and Quarter Horse Racing) 1086, 6649
Plans Examiner 1816, 8723
Podiatrist 5460
Porter (Thoroughbred and Quarter Horse Racing) 6650, 8726
Pre-Kindergarten Teacher 5559
Private Investigator 2352
Professional Engineer 5625
Professional Land Surveyor 8213
Psychologist 5721
Public Adjuster 152
Public Operator 4877
Public School Teacher K-12 4008, 7689
Racing Secretary (Thoroughbred, Standardbred, and Quarter Horse Racing) 1087, 6651

Real Estate Appraiser 7262
Real Estate Broker 7263
Real Estate Sales Agent 7264
Registered Nurse 7406
Respiratory Care Practitioner 7470
School Administrator 2504
School Audiologist 8094
School Counselor 2140
School Nurse 7407
School Occupational Therapist 4602
School Physical Therapist 5106
School Principal 2505
School Psychologist 5722
School Social Worker 8011
School Speech-Language Pathologist 8095
Securities Dealer 7860
Securities Salesperson 7861
Security Employee (Thoroughbred, Standardbred, and Quarter Horse Racing) 3300, 6652
Security Guard Provider 3301
Social Worker 8012
Solid Waste Facility Operator 1751
Special Education Teacher K-12 4009, 7690
Speech-Language Pathologist 8096
Starter (Thoroughbred, Standardbred, and Quarter Horse Racing) 1088, 6653
Steam Engineer 5535
Steward (Thoroughbred and Quarter Horse Racing) 1089, 6654
Supply Salesman (Thoroughbred, Standardbred, and Quarter Horse Racing) 4307, 6655
Surface Blaster 4445
Teacher of Special Subjects 4010, 7691
Telephone Operator (Thoroughbred, Standardbred, and Quarter Horse Racing) 6656, 8275
Timer (Thoroughbred, Standardbred, and Quarter Horse Racing) 1090, 6657
Trainer (Thoroughbred, Standardbred, and Quarter Horse Racing) 588, 6658
Valet (Thoroughbred and Quarter Horse Racing) 6659
Veterinarian 8412
Veterinarian (Thoroughbred, Standardbred, and Quarter Horse Racing) 6660, 8413
Veterinarian's Assistant (Thoroughbred, Standardbred, and Quarter Horse Racing) 589, 6661
Vocational Education Teacher 289

Oklahoma

Accountant, Certified Public (CPA) 51
Accountant, Public (PA) 52
Administrative Employee (Racetrack) 6662, 7739
Animal Technician 590
Apprentice Jockey (Racetrack) 1091, 6663
Architect 752
Asbestos Abatement Contractor 1993
Asbestos Abatement Worker 3761

Assistant Trainer (Racetrack) 591, 6664
Athletic Trainer/Apprentice Athletic Trainer 3709
Attorney 4135
Audiologist 8097
Authorized Agent (Racetrack) 1092, 6665
Bail Bondsman 1257
Barber 1470
Blacksmith (Racetrack) 592, 6666
Blaster, Surface 4446
Bloodstock Agent (Racetrack) 6667
Broker-Dealer, Principal 7862
Building Inspector 1817
Burglar Alarm Service and Installation Company Manager 1752, 3204
Burglar Alarm Service and Installation Company Salesman 7951
Burglar Alarm Service and Installation Company Technician 2616
Chauffeur 8257
Chiropractor 1667
Concession Employee (Racetrack) 6668, 7561
Cosmetologist 1471
Cosmetology Instructor 290, 1472
Counselor, Licensed Professional 2141
Dental Hygienist 2228
Dentist 2290
Dietician; Licensed 2390
Driver Training Instructor (Commercial Driving School) 291
Early Childhood Teacher PK-3 4011, 5560
Electrical Contractor (Residential) 1994, 2617
Electrical Contractor (Unlimited) 1995, 2618
Electrical Inspector 1818
Electrical Journeyman (Residential) 2619
Electrical Journeyman (Unlimited) 2620
Electrologist 1473
Elementary School Teacher K-8 4012
Embalmer 2962
Emergency Medical Technician, Basic 2738
Emergency Medical Technician, Intermediate 2739
Emergency Medical Technician, Paramedic 2740
Engineer Intern 5626
Engineer, Registered Professional 5627
Exercise Person (Racetrack) 593, 6669
Facialist 1474
Fire Alarm Service and Installation Company Manager 1753, 3205
Fire Alarm Service and Installation Company Salesman 7952
Fire Alarm Service and Installation Company Technician 2621
Fire Alarm Sprinkler Company Technician 2622
Fire Boss (Underground) 3599, 4447
Funeral Director 2963
General Services Employee (Racetrack) 6670

Groom (Racetrack)   594, 6671
Groundwater and Observation Water Well Driller   4448
Hearing Aid Dealer and Fitter   3440
Hoisting Engineer (Underground)   4367
Horse Industry Representative (Racetrack)   6672
Insurance Adjuster   153
Insurance Agent   3859
Insurance Consultant   3860
Insurance Representative (Limited)   3861
Investment Advisor   7863
Investment Advisor Representative   7864
Issuer Agent   7865
Jockey Agent (Racetrack)   1093, 6673
Jockey (Racetrack)   1094, 6674
Land Surveyor (Intern)   8214
Land Surveyor, Registered   8215
Landscape Architect   4085
License Clerk (Racetrack)   6675
Licensed Dietician   2390
Licensed Social Worker   8013
Licensed Social Worker Associate   8014
Licensed Social Worker with Specialty Certification   8015
Lobbyist   4290
Manicurist   1475
Marital and Family Therapist   2142
Mechanical Contractor   1996
Mechanical Inspector   1819
Mechanical Journeyman   3480
Mine Foreman (Underground)   1569, 4449
Mine Shot Firer (Underground)   4450
Monitoring Well Driller   4451
Mutuel Employee (Racetrack)   6676
Notary Public   4515
Nurse Anesthetist (CRNA)   7408
Nurse, Licensed Practical (LPN)   4238
Nurse - Midwife (CNM)   7409
Nurse Practitioner   7410
Nurse Registered   7411
Nursing Home Administrator   3381
Occupational Therapist   4603
Occupational Therapy Assistant   4650
Optometrist (O.D.)   4699
Osteopathic Physician (D.O.)   5273
Outrider (Racetrack)   595, 6677
Owner/Assistant Trainer (Racetrack)   596, 6678
Owner By Open Claim (Racetrack)   6679
Owner (Racetrack)   6680
Owner/Trainer (Racetrack)   597, 6681
Pesticide Applicator, Commercial (Certified)   4878
Pesticide Applicator, Non-Commercial (Certified)   4879
Pharmacist   4975
Physical Therapist   5107
Physical Therapy Assistant   5047
Physician/Surgeon (M.D.)   5274
Physician's Assistant   5166
Plumber, Journeyman   5391
Plumbing Contractor   1997, 5392
Plumbing Inspector   1820

Podiatrist   5461
Polygraph Examiner   5514
Polygraph Intern   5515
Pony Rider (Racetrack)   598, 6682
Practical Miner (Underground)   4452
Private Investigator   2353
Psychologist   5723
Pump Installer   4453, 5393
Racehorse Trainer   599, 6683
Racehorse Trainer, Assistant   600, 6684
Racing Official (Racetrack)   1095, 6685
Real Estate Agent (Sales Associate)   7265
Real Estate Appraiser   7266
Real Estate Broker   7267
Sanitarian-in-Training   3600
Sanitarian (Registered)   3601
School Service Personnel K-12   2143, 2506, 4187, 4729, 5724, 8098
Secondary School Teacher 7-12   7692
Securities Agent   7866
Securities Broker-Dealer   7867
Security Employee (Racetrack)   3302, 6686
Security Guard/Armed Security Guard   3303
Shorthand Reporter, Certified   8160
Social Worker Associate; Licensed   8014
Social Worker; Licensed   8013
Social Worker with Specialty Certification; Licensed   8015
Special Education Teacher N-12   4013, 7693
Speech Pathologist   8099
Sports Official, High School   1096
Superintendent (Underground)   1570, 4454
Surface Supervisor   1571, 4455
Track Manager (Racetrack)   3206, 6687
Trainer (Racetrack)   601, 6688
Underground Storage Tank Installer   1998
Valet (Racetrack)   6689
Vendor Employee (Racetrack)   6690, 7562
Vendor (Racetrack)   6691, 7563
Veterinarian   8414
Veterinarian Assistant (Racetrack)   602, 6692
Veterinarian (Racetrack)   6693, 8415
Vocational Education Teacher 9-12   292
Waste Water Operator   8545
Water Operator   8546
Well Driller; Groundwater and Observation Water   4448
Well Driller; Monitoring   4451

Oregon

Accountant; Public   55
Acupuncturist (L.Ac.); Licensed   89
Adjusters; Independent   154
Agent; Non-Resident   3864
Amusement Ride Inspector   1821, 3602, 8579
Animal Health Technician   603

Apprentice Jockey (Racetrack)   1097, 6694
Architect   753
Assistant Trainer (Racetrack)   604, 6695
Association Employee (Racetrack)   6696
Attorney   4136
Audiologist   8100
Auditor; Municipal   54
Barber and Hairdresser   1476
Boilermaker   1596
Building Official   1822
Building Service Mechanic   3481
Certified Public Accountant   53
Chiropractic (Doctor of)   1668
Clinical Social Worker   8016
Commercial Driver   8258, 8317
Concessions Employee (Racetrack)   6697, 7564
Construction Contractor   1999
Consumer Electronic Entertainment Equipment Service Technician (Pick-up Point)   1719
Consumer Electronic Entertainment Equipment Service Technician (Service Dealers)   1720
Consumer Electronic Entertainment Equipment Service Technician (Technician)   1721
Consumer Electronic Entertainment Equipment Service Technician (Technician Trainee)   1722
Contractor, Registered   2000
Counselor, Professional   2144
Debt Consolidation Agent   7868, 8626
Dental Hygienist   2229
Dental Specialist   2291
Dentist, General   2292
Denturist   2250
Dietitian   2391
Electrical Contractor   2001, 2623
Electrical Contractor; Limited Energy   2004, 2632
Electrical Inspector   3603
Electrical Inspector; Family Dwelling   1823
Electrical Limited Maintenance Specialty Contractor   2002, 2624
Electrician   2625
Electrician, General Supervisor   1572, 2626
Electrician, Limited Journeyman, Elevator   2627
Electrician, Limited Journeyman (Limited Energy, Sign, and Stage)   2628
Electrician, Limited Journeyman Manufacturing Plant   2629
Electrician, Limited Residential   2630
Electrician, Oil Module   2631
Electrologist   1477
Embalmer   2964
Emergency Medical Technician   2741
Employment Agent; Private   4730
Engineer, Professional   5628
Engineering Geologist   3246
Escrow Agent   7268, 8637
Exercise Person (Racetrack)   605, 6698
Facial Technician   1478

1293

Oregon, continued

Family Dwelling Electrical Inspector 1823
Farm Labor Contractor 8640
Forest Labor Contractor 8650
Funeral Service Practitioner 2965
Geologist, Professional 3247
Groom/Hot Walker (Racetrack) 606, 6699
Hearing Aid Dealer 3441
Horseshoer/Plater (Racetrack) 607, 6700
Independent Adjusters 154
Insurance Agent 3862
Insurance Consultant 3863
Investment Adviser 7869
Jockey Agent (Racetrack) 1098, 6701
Jockey (Racetrack) 1099, 6702
Kennel Employee (Racetrack) 608, 6703
Land Surveyor, Professional 8216
Landscape Architect 4086
Landscape Contractor 2003, 4087
Lead Out (Racetrack) 609, 6704
Licensed Acupuncturist (L.Ac.) 89
Limited Building Sewer Inspector 1824
Limited Energy Electrical Contractor 2004, 2632
Limited Pump Installation Contractor 2005
Limited Sign Contractors 2006
Liquified Petroleum Gas (LPG) Fitter 5394
Liquified Petroleum Gas (LPG) Truck Equipment Operator 8318
Lobbyist 4291
Maintenance Employee (Racetrack) 3920, 6705
Manicurist 1479
Manufactured Home Installation Inspector 1825
Marriage and Family Therapist 2145
Massage Technician 5048
Mechanical Inspector 1826
Milk Grader and/or Sampler 3668
Monitor Well Constructor 4456
Mortgage Broker 7870
Municipal Auditor 54
Naturopathic Physician 5275
Non-Resident Agent 3864
Notary Public 4516
Nurse, Licensed Practical 4239
Nurse, Registered 7412
Nursing Home Administrator 3382
Occupational Therapist 4604
Occupational Therapy Assistant 4651
Official (Racetrack) 1100, 6706
Optometrist 4700
Osteopathic Physician 5276
Outfitter/Guide 2835
Owner (Racetrack) 6707
Pari-Mutuel Employee (Racetrack) 6708
Pasteurizer Operator 8712
Pesticide Applicator 4880
Pesticide Consultant 4881
Pharmacist 4976
Pharmacy Intern 4977

Physical Therapist 5108
Physical Therapist Assistant 5049
Physician 5277
Physician Assistant 5167
Pilot (River or Bar) 8491
Plans Examiner 1827, 8722
Plumber 5395
Plumbing Contractor 2007, 5396
Plumbing Inspector 1828
Podiatrist 5462
Polygraph Examiner 5516
Pony Person (Racetrack) 610, 6709
Private Employment Agent 4730
Psychologist 5725
Psychologist Associate 5726
Public Accountant 55
Public School Teacher K-12 4014, 7694
Pump Installation Contractor; Limited 2005
Radiologic Technologist 7105
Real Estate Appraiser 7269
Real Estate Broker 7270
Real Estate Property Manager 5654
Real Estate Salesperson 7271
Respiratory Care Practitioner 7471
Sanitarian, Registered 3604
Sanitarian Trainee 3605
School Administrator 2507
School Counselor 2146
School Psychologist 5727
School Superintendent 2508, 3207
School Supervisor 2509
Securities Broker/Dealer 7871
Securities Salesperson 7872
Sewer Inspector; Limited Building 1824
Shorthand Reporter, Certified 8161
Sign Contractors; Limited 2006
Speech Pathologist 8101
Starter/Assistant Starter (Racetrack) 1101, 6710
Steamfitter/Pipefitter 5397
Structural Inspector 1829
Surplus Line Agent 3865
Tax Consultant 8239
Tax Preparer 8240, 8774
Timer (Racetrack) 1102, 6711
Trainer (Racetrack) 611, 6712
Valet (Racetrack) 6713
Veterinarian 8416
Veterinarian (Racetrack) 6714, 8417
Veterinary Technician 612
Water Rights Examiner, Certified 3606, 8788
Water Well Constructor 4457

Pennsylvania

Acupuncturist 90
Adjuster; Public 155
Adjuster Solicitor; Public 156
Apprentice Jockey (Horse Racing) 1103, 6715
Architect 754
Assistant Trainer (Horse Racing) 613, 6716
Association Employee (Harness Racing) 6717

Athletic Trainer 3710
Attorney 4137
Auctioneer 1226
Audiologist 8102
Authorized Agent (Horse Racing) 1104, 6718
Barber 1480
Barber Teacher 293, 1481
Blacksmith (Harness Racing) 614, 6719
Certified Court Reporter 8162
Certified Occupational Therapy Assistant (C.O.T.A.) 4652
Certified Public Accountant 56
Chiropractor 1669
Classroom Teacher K-12 4015, 7695
Commercial Pesticide Applicator 4882
Concession Employee (Harness Racing) 6720, 7565
Cosmetician 1482
Cosmetologist 1483
Cosmetology Teacher 294, 1484
Dental Hygienist 2230
Dentist 2293
Driver/Groom (Harness Racing) 615, 1105, 6721
Driver (Harness Racing) 1106, 6722
Driver/Trainer/Groom (Harness Racing) 616, 1107, 6723
Driver/Trainer (Harness Racing) 1108, 6724
Educational Specialist 4016, 7696
Emergency Medical Technician 2742
Farrier (Horse Racing) 617, 6725
Funeral Director 2966
Groom (Harness Racing) 618, 6726
Hearing Aid Dealer and Fitter 3442
Insurance Agent 3866
Insurance Broker 3867
Investment Adviser 7873
Investment Adviser Representative (Associated Person) 7874
Jockey Agent (Horse Racing) 1109, 6727
Jockey (Horse Racing) 1110, 6728
Land Surveyor; Professional 8217
Landscape Architect 4088
Licensed Physical Therapist (L.P.T.) 5109
Licensed Practical Nurse 4240
Lobbyist 4292
Manicurist 1485
Midwife 7413
Milk Hauler and Tester 3669, 8319
Mortgage Broker 7875
Notary Public 4517
Nuclear Medicine Technologist 4540
Nursing Home Administrator 3383
Occupational Therapist (O.T.R.) 4605
Occupational Therapy Assistant (C.O.T.A.); Certified 4652
Official (Horse Racing) 1111, 6729
Officials (Harness Racing) 1112, 6730
Optometrist 4701
Osteopathic Physician (D.O.) 5278
Owner/Driver/Groom (Harness Racing) 619, 1113, 6731

Owner/Driver (Harness Racing) 1114, 6732
Owner/Groom (Harness Racing) 620, 6733
Owner (Harness Racing) 6734
Owner (Horse Racing) 6735
Owner/Trainer/Driver/Groom (Harness Racing) 621, 1115, 6736
Owner/Trainer/Driver (Harness Racing) 1116, 6737
Owner/Trainer/Groom (Harness Racing) 622, 6738
Owner/Trainer (Harness Racing) 623, 6739
Pari-Mutuel Employee (Harness Racing) 6740
Pari-Mutuel Employee (Horse Racing) 6741
Pest Management Consultant 4883
Pesticide Technician 4884
Pharmacist 4978
Pharmacy Intern 4979
Physical Therapist Assistant 5050
Physical Therapist (L.P.T.); Licensed 5109
Physician 5279
Physician's Assistant 5168
Podiatrist 5463
Private Investigator 2354
Private Pesticide Applicator 4885
Professional Engineer 5629
Professional Land Surveyor 8217
Psychologist 5728
Public Adjuster 155
Public Adjuster Solicitor 156
Public Pesticide Applicator 4886
Radiation Therapy Technologist 7106
Radiologic Technologist 7107
Real Estate Appraiser 7272
Real Estate Auctioneer 1227, 7273, 8739
Real Estate Broker 7274
Real Estate Sales Agent 7275
Registered Nurse 7414
Salesman (Harness Racing) 4308, 6742
School Administrator 2510
School Intermediate Unit Executive Director 2511
School Superintendent/Assistant Superintendent 2512, 3208
School Supervisor 2513
Securities Broker-Dealer 7876
Securities Sales Agent 7877
Social Worker 8017
Speech-Language Pathologist 8103
Stable Employee (Horse Racing) 624, 6743
Supervisor of Vocational Education 295, 2514
Track Employee (Horse Racing) 6744
Track Manager (Harness Racing) 3209, 6745
Trainer/Groom (Harness Racing) 625, 6746
Trainer (Harness Racing) 626, 6747
Trainer (Horse Racing) 627, 6748
Vehicle Salesperson 7566

Vendor Employee (Horse Racing) 6749, 7567
Vendor (Horse Racing) 6750, 7568
Veterinarian 8418
Veterinarian (Harness Racing) 6751, 8419
Veterinarian (Horse Racing) 6752, 8420
Vocational Education Teacher 296

Rhode Island

Acupuncture; Doctor of 91
Air Conditioning Mechanic 3482
Appraiser; Motor Vehicle Damage 159
Arborist 2892, 3126
Architect 755
Asbestos Abatement Contractor 2008
Asbestos Abatement Site Supervisor 1573, 2009, 3762
Asbestos Abatement Worker 3763
Athletic Trainer 3711
Attorney 4138
Auctioneer 1228
Audiologist 8104
Barber 1486
Barber Instructor 297, 1487
Blaster 4458
Bondsman; Professional 1258
Burglar and Hold-up Alarm Agent 7953
Certified Public Accountant 57
Certified Shorthand Reporter 8163
Chauffeur 8259
Check Cashier 1630
Chemical Dependency Professional 2147, 3494
Chiropractor 1670
Clinical Histologic Technician 1700
Clinical Laboratory Science Practitioner 1701
Clinical Medical Laboratory Technician 1702
Commercial Driver 1612, 8320
Commercial Fisher 2836
Commercial Trapper 2837
Concessionaire Employee (Racetrack) 6753, 7569
Cosmetologist 1488
Counselor in Mental Health 2148
Cytotechnologist 1703
Day Care Provider; Family Group 5563
Dealer (Fish) 7570
Dental Hygienist 2231
Dentist 2294
Dietitian 2392
Doctor of Acupuncture 91
Driving Instructor 298
Drug Auctioneer 1229, 8629
Drug Researcher 8630
Early Childhood Teacher (PK-2) 4017, 5561
Electric Sign Installer 2010, 2633, 8632
Electrical Contractor 2011, 2634
Electrician 2635
Electrologist 1489
Elementary School Principal 2515
Elementary School Teacher 1-8 4018
Elevator Inspector 1830, 2670

Embalmer 2967
Emergency Medical Technician 2743
Engineer 5630
Engineer-In-Training 5631
Esthetician 1490
Family Day Care Provider 5562
Family Group Day Care Provider 5563
Fire Alarm Installer 2636
Fire Extinguisher Installer/Servicer 5398
Fire Protection Sprinkler Fitter 5399
Fireworks Shooter 8646
Fisher; Commercial 2836
Funeral Director 2968
Fur Buyer; Wholesale 8566, 8798
Hairdresser 1491
Hawker/Peddler 7571
Hearing Aid Dealer/Fitter 3443
Hoisting Engineer 4368
Insurance Agent 3868
Insurance Appraiser 157
Insurance Broker 3869
Insurance Claim Adjuster/Public Adjuster 158
Insurance Solicitor 3870
Investment Adviser 7878
Investment Adviser Representative 7879
Kennel Employee (Racetrack) 628, 6754
Land Surveyor 8218
Landscape Architect 4089
Lead Hazard Abatement Contractor 2012, 8687
Lead Hazard Abatement Site Supervisor 1574, 2013, 8688
Lead Hazard Abatement Worker 3331, 8689
Lead Out (Racetrack) 629, 6755
Licensed Practical Nurse 4241
Lifeguard 8690
Live Bait Seller 7572, 8693
Lobbyist 4293
Lobster Seller 7573, 8694
Management Employee (Racetrack) 6756
Manicurist 1492
Marriage and Family Therapist 2149
Massage Therapist 5110
Milk Hauler and Tester 3670, 8321
Money and Mortgage Broker 7880
Motor Vehicle Damage Appraiser 159
Notary Public 4518
Nurseryman 3127, 4550
Nursing Home Administrator 3384
Occupational Therapist 4606
Oil Burnerperson 5400
Optician 2415
Optometrist 4702
Osteopathic Physician (D.O.) 5280
Owners (Racetrack) 6757
Pari-Mutuel Employee (Racetrack) 6758
Pesticide Applicator 4887
Pharmacist 4980
Pharmacy Intern 4981
Pharmacy Technician 8718
Physical Therapist 5111
Physical Therapy Assistant 5051
Physician 5281

Rhode Island, continued

Physician's Assistant   5169
Pipefitter   5401
Plumber   5402
Podiatrist   5464
Professional Bondsman   1258
Professional Boxer   1117
Professional Wrestler   1118
Prosthetist   8733
Psychologist   5729
Pump Installer (Drinking Water Wells)   4459, 5403
Pyrotechnic Operator   8736
Real Estate Appraiser   7276
Refrigeration Mechanic   3483
Registered Nurse   7415
Residential Building Contractor/Sub-Contractor   2014
Respiratory Care Practitioner   7472
Sanitarian   3607
School Bus Driver   1613
School Guidance Counselor   2150
School Guidance Supervisor   2151
School Superintendent   2516, 3210
Secondary School Principal   2517
Secondary School Teacher 7-12   7697
Securities Broker-Dealer   7881
Securities Sales Representative   7882
Sewage Disposal System Installer   2015
Ship Pilot   8492
Social Worker   8018
Special Subjects Teacher PK-12   4019, 7698
Speech-Language Pathologist   8105
Surplus Line Broker (Insurance)   3871
Tattoo Artist   8448, 8771
Trainer (Racetrack)   630, 6759
Trapper; Commercial   2837
Travel Agent   8783
Vendor Employee (Racetrack)   6760, 7574
Veterinarian   8421
Wastewater Treatment Facility Operator   8547
Water Treatment Plant Operator   8548
Well-Drill Operator (Drinking Water Wells)   4460
Wholesale Fur Buyer   8566, 8798
Wildlife Propagator   631, 8802

South Carolina

Accountant   58
Animal Technician   632
Architect   756
Attorney   4139
Auctioneer   1230
Barber   1493
Boxer   1119
Boxing-Wrestling Announcer   7062
Boxing-Wrestling Judge   1120
Boxing-Wrestling Matchmaker   4350
Boxing-Wrestling Referee   1121
Boxing-Wrestling Timekeeper   1122
Boxing-Wrestling Trainer   3712
Burglar Alarm Contractor   2016
Certified Shorthand Reporter   8164
Chiropractor   1671
Commercial Pesticide Applicator   4888
Contractor   2017
Cosmetologist   1494
Cosmetologist Instructor   299, 1495
Counselor, Licensed Professional   2152
Dental Hygienist   2232
Dental Specialist   2295
Dental Technician   2251
Dentist   2296
Electrician   2637
Elementary School Guidance Counselor   2153
Elementary School Principal and Supervisor   2518
Embalmer   2969
Emergency Medical Technician   2744
Engineer   5632
Engineer-In-Training   5633
Esthetician   1496
Fire Protection Contractor   2018, 5404
Forester   2893
Funeral Director   2970
Geologist   3248
Hearing Aid Dealer and Fitter   3444
Insurance Agent   3872
Investment Advisor   7883
Investment Advisor Representative   7884
Kickboxer   1123
Landfill Operator; Municipal Solid Waste   1754
Landscape Architect   4090
Licensed Practical Nurse   4242
Lobbyist   4294
Manager (Boxing)   1124
Manicurist   1497
Manufactured Housing Representative   7277
Manufactured Housing Retail Dealer   7278
Manufactured Housing Salesperson   7279
Marital and Family Therapist   2154
Milk Tester   3671
Milk Weigher and Sampler   3672
Municipal Solid Waste Landfill Operator   1754
Noncommercial Pesticide Applicator   4889
Notary Public   4519
Nursing Home Administrator   3385
Occupational Therapist   4607
Occupational Therapy Assistant   4653
Optician   2416
Optometrist   4703
Osteopathic Physician (D.O.)   5282
Percolation Test Technician   3673, 7606
Pesticide Applicator; Commercial   4888
Pesticide Applicator; Noncommercial   4889
Pesticide Dealer   4890
Pharmacist   4982
Physical Therapist   5112
Physical Therapist Assistant   5052
Physician/Surgeon   5283
Physician's Assistant   5170
Podiatrist   5465
Polygraph Examiner   5517
Private Detective   2355
Private Pesticide Applicator   4891
Professional Soil Classifier   327
Professional Wrestler   1125
Promoter (Boxing)   4351
Psychologist   5730
Public School Teacher PK-12   4020, 7699
Real Estate Appraiser   7280
Real Estate Broker   7281
Real Estate Property Manager   5655
Real Estate Salesman   7282
Registered Nurse   7416
Residential Home Builder   2019
Respiratory Care Practitioner   7473
Sanitarian   3608
School Media Communication Specialist   4188
School Media Specialist   4189
School Media Supervisor   4190
School Superintendent   2519, 3211
Second (Boxing)   1126
Secondary School Guidance Counselor   2155
Secondary School Principal and Supervisor   2520
Securities Agent   7885
Securities Broker-Dealer   7886
Social Worker   8019
Soil Classifier; Professional   327
Speech Pathologist/Audiologist   8106
Surveyor, Land   8219
Veterinarian   8422
Wastewater Treatment Plant Operator   8549
Well Driller   4461

South Dakota

Abstracter of Title   8571
Announcer (Horse Racing)   6761, 7063
Appliance Installation Plumbing Contractor   2020, 5405
Appliance Plumbing Installer   5406
Apprentice Jockey (Horse Racing)   1127, 6762
Architect   757
Assistant Starter (Horse Racing)   1128, 6763
Assistant Trainer (Greyhound Racing)   633, 6764
Associate Judge (Greyhound Racing)   1129, 6765
Association Employee (Greyhound Racing)   6766
Athletic Trainer   3713
Attorney   4140
Authorized Agent (Greyhound Racing)   1130, 6767
Authorized Agent (Horse Racing)   1131, 6768
Barber   1498
Bookkeeper (Horse Racing)   2792, 6769
Bus Driver   1614
Certified Public Accountant   59

Chart Writer (Greyhound Racing)   6770
Chiropractor   1672
Clerk of Scales (Greyhound
  Racing)   3609, 6771
Commercial Pesticide Applicator   4892
Concession Employee (Greyhound
  Racing)   6772, 7575
Concession Employee (Horse
  Racing)   6773, 7576
Concession Operator (Horse
  Racing)   6774, 7577
Cosmetologist   1499
Cosmetologist Manager   1500
Cosmetology Instructor   300, 1501
Dental Hygienist   2233
Dentist   2297
Electrical Contractor   2021, 2638
Electrical Inspector   1831
Electrician   2639
Elementary School Principal   2521
Elementary School Teacher   4021
Emergency Medical Technician   2745
Engineer-in-Training   5634
Entry Clerk (Horse Racing)   6775
Exercise Rider (Horse Racing)   634, 6776
Funeral Director   2971
Gateman (Horse Racing)   6777
Groom (Horse Racing)   635, 6778
Hearing Aid Dispenser   3445
Insurance Agent   3873
Investment Advisor   7887
Investment Advisor Representative   7888
Jockey Agent (Horse Racing)   1132, 6779
Jockey (Horse Racing)   1133, 6780
Jockey Room Custodian (Horse
  Racing)   3921, 6781
Kennel Helper (Greyhound
  Racing)   636, 6782
Kennel Master (Greyhound
  Racing)   637, 6783
Kennel Operator (Greyhound
  Racing)   638, 6784
Kennel Owner (Greyhound
  Racing)   639, 6785
Land Surveyor   8220
Land Surveyor-in-Training   8221
Landscape Architect   4091
Lead Out (Greyhound Racing)   640, 6786
Licensed Practical Nurse   4243
Lobbyist   4295
Lure Operator (Greyhound
  Racing)   6787
Manufactured and Mobile Home
  Installation Plumbing
  Contractor   2022, 5407
Manufactured and Mobile Home
  Plumbing Installer   5408
Medical Assistant   4373
Milk Hauler and Tester   3674, 8322
Mortgage Broker   7889
Mutuel Employee (Greyhound
  Racing)   6788
Mutuel Employee (Horse Racing)   6789
Mutuel Operator (Horse Racing)   6790

Notary Public   4520
Nursing Home Administrator   3386
Occupational Therapist   4608
Occupational Therapy Assistant   4654
Official (Horse Racing)   1134, 6791
Optometrist   4704
Osteopathic Physician (D.O.)   5284
Outrider (Horse Racing)   641, 6792
Owner (Horse Racing)   6793
Owner/Trainer (Greyhound
  Racing)   642, 6794
Owner/Trainer (Horse Racing)   643, 6795
Paddock Judge (Greyhound
  Racing)   1135, 6796
Parking Lot Employee (Horse
  Racing)   3332, 6797
Pesticide Applicator; Commercial   4892
Pesticide Dealer   4893
Pharmacist   4983
Pharmacy Intern   4984
Photo Finish Employee (Horse
  Racing)   5017, 6798
Photographer (Horse Racing)   5018, 6799
Physical Therapist   5113
Physician   5285
Physician's Assistant   5171
Plater (Horse Racing)   644, 6800
Plumber   5409
Plumbing Contractor   2023, 5410
Plumbing Contractor; Appliance
  Installation   2020, 5405
Plumbing Contractor; Manufactured and
  Mobile Home Installation   2022, 5407
Plumbing Contractor; Sewage and Water
  Installation   2024, 5411
Plumbing Contractor; Water Conditioning
  and Treatment   2025, 5414
Plumbing Installer; Appliance   5406
Plumbing Installer; Manufactured and
  Mobile Home   5408
Plumbing Installer; Sewage and
  Water   5412
Plumbing Installer; Water
  Conditioning   5413
Podiatrist   5466
Polygraph Examiner   5518
Pony Rider (Horse Racing)   645, 6801
Presiding Judge (Greyhound
  Racing)   1136, 6802
Private Pesticide Applicator   4894
Professional Engineer   5635
Programmer (Horse Racing)   6803
Psychologist   5731
Racing Secretary (Greyhound
  Racing)   1137, 6804
Real Estate Appraiser   7283
Real Estate Auctioneer   1231, 7284, 8738
Real Estate Broker   7285
Real Estate Property Manager   5656
Real Estate Sales Agent   7286
Registered Nurse   7417
Registered Nurse Anesthetist   7418
School Counselor   2156

School Reading Specialist K-12   4022, 7700
School Superintendent   2522, 3212
Secondary School Principal   2523
Secondary School Teacher   7701
Securities Agent   7890
Securities Broker-Dealer   7891
Security Employee (Horse
  Racing)   3304, 6805
Sewage and Water Installation Plumbing
  Contractor   2024, 5411
Sewage and Water Plumbing
  Installer   5412
Social Worker   8020
Starter (Greyhound Racing)   1138, 6806
Starter (Horse Racing)   1139, 6807
Tattooer (Horse Racing)   6808, 8772
Timer (Greyhound Racing)   1140, 6809
Trainer (Greyhound Racing)   646, 6810
Trainer (Horse Racing)   647, 6811
Truck Driver   8323
True Owner (Greyhound Racing)   6812
Valet (Horse Racing)   6813
Veterinarian   8423
Veterinarian Assistant (Horse
  Racing)   648, 6814
Veterinarian (Horse Racing)   6815, 8424
Wastewater Collection System
  Operator   8550
Wastewater Treatment Plant
  Operator   8551
Water Conditioning Plumbing
  Installer   5413
Water Conditioning and Treatment
  Plumbing Contractor   2025, 5414
Water Distribution System
  Operator   8552
Water Treatment Plant Operator   8553

Tennessee

Accountant   60
Animal Dealer, Livestock   649
Animal Technician   650
Architect   758
Assistant Trainer (Racetrack)   651, 6816
Association Employee (Racetrack)   6817
Athletic Trainer   3714
Attorney   4141
Auctioneer   1232
Audiologist   8107
Barber   1502
Boiler Operator   1597
Boxing Promoter   4352
Certified Public Accountant   61
Certified Public Weigher   3610
Certified Shorthand Reporter   8165
Chiropractor   1673
Clinical Lab Technician   1704
Collection Service Location
  Manager   160
Concession Employee (Racetrack)   6818, 7578
Cosmetologist   1503
Dental Assistant   2188
Dental Hygienist   2234
Dentist   2298

Tennessee, continued

Dietitian-Nutritionist 2393
Driver/Jockey (Racetrack) 1141, 6819
Electrologist 1504
Elementary School Counselor 2157
Elementary School Teacher K-8 4023
Embalmer 2972
Emergency Medical Technician 2746
Endodontist 2299
Engineer 5636
Exercise Rider (Racetrack) 652, 6820
Farrier Assistant (Racetrack) 653, 6821
Farrier (Racetrack) 654, 6822
Fire Protection Sprinkler System Contractor 2026, 5415
Fire Protection Sprinkler System Contractor/Responsible Managing Employee (RME) 2027, 5416
Funeral Director 2973
General Contractor 2028
Geologist, Professional 3249
Hearing Aid Dispenser 3446
Home Improvement Contractor 2029
Insurance Agent 3874
Investment Advisor 7892
Jockey Agent (Racetrack) 1142, 6823
Land Surveyor 8222
Landscape Architect 4092
Lobbyist 4296
Marital and Family Therapist 2158
Milk Sampler 3675
Milk Tester 3676
Mutuel Employee (Racetrack) 6824
Notary Public 4521
Nursing Home Administrator 3387
Occupational Therapist 4609
Occupational Therapy Assistant 4655
Official (Racetrack) 1143, 6825
Optician 2417
Optometrist 4705
Oral and Maxillofacial Surgeon 2300
Oral Pathologist 2301
Osteopathic Physician 5286
Owner (Racetrack) 6826
Pathologist; Oral 2301
Pedodontist 2302
Periodontist 2303
Personnel Consultant 2159, 4731
Personnel Service Manager 4732
Pest Control Operator 4895
Pharmacist 4985
Physical Therapist 5114
Physical Therapy Assistant 5053
Physician 5287
Physician Assistant 5172
Podiatrist 5467
Polygraph Operator 5519
Practical Nurse 4244
Professional Counselor 2160
Prosthodontist 2304
Psychologist 5732
Radiation Therapy Technologist 7108
Radiologic Technologist 7109
Real Estate Affiliate Broker 7287
Real Estate Appraiser 7288
Real Estate Broker 7289

Real Estate Sales Agent 7290
Registered Nurse 7419
Respiratory Therapist 7474
School Administrator or Supervisor 2524
School Librarian 4191
Secondary School Teacher 7-12 7702
Securities Agent 7893
Securities Broker-Dealer 7894
Security Officer 3305
Service Technician 5541
Social Worker 8021
Special Education Teacher 4024, 7703
Speech Pathologist 8108
Stable Employee (Racetrack) 655, 6827
Surgeon; Oral and Maxillofacial 2300
Time-Share Agent 7291
Trainer/Driver (Racetrack) 1144, 6828
Trainer (Racetrack) 656, 6829
Vendor Employee (Racetrack) 6830, 7579
Vendor (Racetrack) 6831, 7580
Veterinarian 8425
Veterinarian Assistant (Racetrack) 657, 6832
Veterinarian (Racetrack) 6833, 8426
Vocational Education Teacher 301
Weigher; Certified Public 3610
Weighmaster 3611

Texas

Admission Person (Racetrack) 6834, 8345
Air Conditioning & Refrigeration Contractor 2030, 3484
Air Monitoring Technician 1832, 3764, 7607
Announcer (Racetrack) 6835
Apprentice Jockey (Racetrack) 1145, 6836
Architect 759
Asbestos Abatement Contractor 2031
Asbestos Consultant 3765
Asbestos Inspector 1833
Asbestos Management Planner 2032, 3766
Asbestos Operations and Maintenance Contractor 2033
Asbestos Operations and Maintenance Supervisor 1575, 2034, 3767
Asbestos Project Manager 2035, 3768
Asbestos Project Supervisor 1576, 2036, 3769
Asbestos Training Provider 302, 3770
Asbestos Transporter 3771, 8324
Assistant Starter (Racetrack) 1146, 6837
Assistant Trainer/Owner (Racetrack) 658, 6838
Assistant Trainer (Racetrack) 659, 6839
Association Employee (Racetrack) 6840
Association Judge (Racetrack) 1147, 6841
Association Office Staff Worker (Racetrack) 6842, 7740
Association Officer/Director (Racetrack) 3213, 6843

Athlete Agent 1148
Athletic Trainer 3715
Attorney 4142
Auctioneer 1233
Audiologist 8109
Authorized Agent (Racetrack) 1149, 6844
Barber 1505
Box Person (Racetrack) 6845
Boxer 1150
Boxing Manager 1151
Boxing Matchmaker 4353
Boxing Promoter 4354
Boxing Referee 1152
Boxing Second 1153
Certified Public Accountant 62
Certified Shorthand Reporter 8166
Chaplain (Racetrack) 6846, 8604
Chart Writer (Racetrack) 6847
Child Care Administrator 3388
Chiropractor 1674
Concessionaire Employee (Racetrack) 6848, 7581
Concessionaire (Racetrack) 6849, 7582
Cool Out (Racetrack) 660, 6850
Cosmetologist 1506
Counselor, Professional 2161
Court Reporter 8167
Dental Hygienist 2235
Dentist 2305
Dietitian 2394
Embalmer 2974
Emergency Medical Technician 2747
Engineer 5637
Engineer-In-Training 5638
Entry Clerk (Racetrack) 6851
Exercise Rider (Racetrack) 661, 6852
Farrier/Plater/Blacksmith (Racetrack) 662, 6853
Fire Alarm System Contractor 5417
Fire Extinguisher System Contractor 5418
Fire Protection Sprinkler System Contractor 5419
Firefighter 2804
Fish Farmer 2769
Fishing Guide 2838
Food Service Employee (Racetrack) 2870, 6854
Funeral Director 2975
Groom (Racetrack) 663, 6855
Hearing Aid Dispenser 3447
Home Health Aide 8673
Horse Owner (Racetrack) 6856
Insurance Adjuster 161
Insurance Agent 3875
Interpreter for the Deaf 8679
Investment Advisor 7895
Irrigator 2037, 5420
Jockey Agent (Racetrack) 1154, 6857
Jockey (Racetrack) 1155, 6858
Kennel Helper (Racetrack) 664, 6859
Kennel Owner (Racetrack) 6860
Kennel Owner/Trainer (Racetrack) 665, 6861
Land Surveyor 8223
Landscape Architect 4093

Law Enforcement Officer   5489
Lead Out (Racetrack)   666, 6862
Librarian, County   4192
Lobbyist   4297
Maintenance Employee
  (Racetrack)   3922, 6863
Marriage and Family Therapist   2162
Massage Therapist   5115
Medical Radiologic Technician   7110
Medical Staff Employee
  (Racetrack)   4374, 6864
Medication Aide   4563
Midwife, Lay   4564
Mutuel Clerk (Racetrack)   6865
Mutuel Employee (Racetrack)   6866
Notary Public   4522
Nurse Aide, Long Term Care   4565
Nurse, Licensed Vocational   4245
Nurse, Registered   7420
Nursing Home Administrator   3389
Occupational Therapist   4610
Occupational Therapy Assistant   4656
Official (Racetrack)   1156, 6867
Optometrist   4706
Osteopathic Physician (D.O.)   5288
Outrider (Racetrack)   667, 6868
Parking Attendant (Racetrack)   3333, 6869
Pawnbroker   7583
Pest Control Technician; Structural   4897
Pesticide Applicator   4896
Pharmacist   4986
Physical Therapist   5116
Physical Therapist Assistant   5054
Physician   5289
Physician's Assistant   5173
Plumber   5421
Podiatrist   5468
Polygraph Examiner   5520
Pony Person (Racetrack)   668, 6870
Private Investigator   2356
Psychologist   5733
Radiologic Technician; Medical   7110
Real Estate Appraiser   7292
Real Estate Broker   7293
Real Estate Inspector   7294
Real Estate Sales Agent   7295
Respiratory Care Practitioner   7475
Sanitarian   3612
Securities Agent   7896
Securities Dealer   7897
Securities Salesman   7898
Security Guard   3306
Security Officer (Racetrack)   3307, 6871
Social Worker   8022
Solid Waste Technician   7608
Speech-Language Pathologist   8110
Stable Foreman (Racetrack)   669, 1577, 6872
Structural Pest Control Technician   4897
Tattooer (Racetrack)   6873, 8449, 8773
Tax Professional—Appraiser   8241, 8775
Tax Professional—Assessor-Collector   8242, 8776
Tax Professional—Collector   8243, 8777

Test Technician (Racetrack)   3613, 6874
Texas Public School Teacher   4025, 7704
Tooth Floater (Racetrack)   6875, 8782
Tote Technician (Racetrack)   6876
Trainer (Racetrack)   670, 6877
Underground Storage Tank Installer   2038
Valet (Racetrack)   6878
Vendor Employee (Racetrack)   6879, 7584
Vendor (Racetrack)   6880, 7585
Veterinarian   8427
Veterinarian Assistant (Racetrack)   671, 6881
Veterinarian (Racetrack)   6882, 8428
Water Well Driller   4462

Utah

Acupuncturist   92
Architect   760
Attorney   4143
Barber   1507
Blaster (Mining); Surface   4466
Boxer   1157
Certified Public Accountant   63
Certified Shorthand Reporter   8168
Certified Social Worker   8023
Chiropractor   1675
Clinical Social Worker   8024
Commercial Pesticide Applicator   4898
Contractor   2039
Cosmetologist   1508
Dental Hygienist   2236
Dentist   2306
Dietitian   2395
Driver's Education Teacher   303
Driving Occupations   1615, 8325
Early Childhood Education Teacher K-3   4026
Electrician   2640
Electrologist   1509
Elementary School Teacher 1-8   4027
Emergency Medical Technician   2748
Engineer   5639
Engineer-in-Training   5640
Fire Boss (Mining)   3614, 4463
Funeral Service Director   2976
Fur Dealer   7586, 8660
Health Facility Administrator   3390
Hearing Aid Specialist   3448
Hunting Guide   2839
Insurance Adjuster   162
Insurance Agent   3876
Insurance Broker   3877
Insurance Consultant   3878
Insurance Surplus Line Broker   3879
Investment Adviser   7899
Land Surveyor   8224
Land Surveyor-in-Training   8225
Landscape Architect   4094
Library Media Associate K-12   4193
Lobbyist   4298
Marriage and Family Therapist   2163
Massage Technician   5055
Mine Electrician   2641, 4464

Mine Foreman   1578, 4465
Motor Vehicle Dealer   7587
Motor Vehicle Salesperson   7588
Noncommercial Pesticide Applicator   4899
Notary Public   4523
Nurse Anesthetist   7421
Nurse, Licensed Practical   4246
Nurse Midwife, Certified   7422
Nurse Practitioner   7423
Nurse, Registered   7424
Nurse, Specialist   7425
Nursing Home Administrator   3391
Occupational Therapist   4611
Occupational Therapy Assistant   4657
Optometrist   4707
Osteopathic Physician and Surgeon   5290
Pesticide Applicator; Commercial   4898
Pesticide Applicator; Noncommercial   4899
Pesticide Dealer   4900
Pharmacist and Pharmacy Intern   4987
Physical Therapist   5117
Physician Assistant   5174
Physician and Surgeon   5291
Plumber   5422
Podiatrist   5469
Polygraph Examiner   5521
Pre-Need Contract Agent   2977, 7954, 8729
Preschool Special Education Teacher   5564
Private Pesticide Applicator   4901
Psychologist   5734
Radiology Technologist   7111
Real Estate Appraiser   7296
Real Estate Broker   7297
Real Estate Salesperson   7298
Recreational Therapist   8745
Respiratory Care Practitioner   7476
Sanitarian   3615
School Administrator or Supervisor   2525
School Counselor   2164
School Psychologist   5735
School Social Worker   8025
Secondary School Teacher 6-12   7705
Securities Agent   7900
Securities Broker-Dealer   7901
Security Guard   3308
Social Service Aide   3495
Social Service Worker   3496
Social Worker; Certified   8023
Special Education Teacher K-12   4028, 7706
Speech Pathologist and Audiologist   8111
Surface Blaster (Mining)   4466
Surface Foreman   1579, 4467
Teacher of Pupils with Communications Disorders K-12   4029, 7707
Veterinarian   8429
Weather Modifier (Cloud Seeder)   7609, 8791

Vermont

Accountant, Certified Public 64
Accountant, Registered Public 65
Acupuncturist 93
Adjuster; Public 165
Architect 761
Armed Courier 3309
Assistant Trainer (Greyhound Racing) 672, 6883
Association Official (Greyhound Racing) 1158, 6884
Attorney 4144
Auctioneer 1234
Audiologist; School 8112
Authorized Agent (Greyhound Racing) 1159, 6885
Authorized Agent (Racetrack) 1160, 6886
Barber 1510
Blacksmith (Racetrack) 673, 6887
Blaster 4468
Boxing, Professional 1161
Chart Writer (Greyhound Racing) 6888
Chiropractic Physician 1676
Clerk of Scales (Greyhound Racing) 3616, 6889
Clinical Mental Health Counselor 2165
Clinical Social Worker 8026
Concession Employee (Greyhound Racing) 6890, 7589
Concession Employee (Racetrack) 6891, 7590
Consulting Teacher or Learning Specialist 4030, 7708
Cosmetologist 1511
Dealer, Repairer Weighing and Measuring Devices 5542
Dental Assistant, Certified 2189
Dental Assistant, Traditional 2190
Dental Hygienist 2237
Dentist 2307
Director of Racing (Greyhound Racing) 3214, 6892
Driver Education Instructor (Public Schools) 304
Driver Instructor, Commercial 305
Electrician, Journeyman 2642
Electrician Journeyman Type S 2643
Electrician, Master 2644
Elementary School Teacher K-6 4031
Embalmer 2978
Emergency Medical Technician 2749
Engineer-in-training 5641
Engineer, Professional 5642
Exercise Boy (Racetrack) 674, 6893
Foreman (Racetrack) 1580, 6894
Funeral Director 2979
Groom (Racetrack) 675, 6895
Guard Dog Handler 676, 3310
Hearing Aid Dealer/Dispenser 3449
Hot Walker (Racetrack) 677, 6896
Installer/Seller Lightning Rods and Fire Detection Systems 2645, 7955, 8677
Insurance Adjuster 163
Insurance Agent 3880
Insurance Appraiser 164
Insurance Broker 3881
Insurance Broker, Surplus lines 3882
Insurance Consultant 3883
Jockey Agent (Racetrack) 1162, 6897
Jockey Apprentice (Racetrack) 1163, 6898
Jockey (Racetrack) 1164, 6899
Judge (Greyhound Racing) 1165, 6900
Kennel Helper (Greyhound Racing) 678, 6901
Kennel Master (Greyhound Racing) 679, 6902
Library Media Specialist 4194
Licensed Practical Nurse (LPN) 4247
Lobbyist 4299
Notary Public 4524
Nursing Home Administrator 3392
Official (Racetrack) 1166, 6903
Operator of Mechanical Lure (Greyhound Racing) 6904
Optician 2418
Optometrist 4708
Osteopath 5292
Outrider (Racetrack) 680, 6905
Owner (Greyhound Racing) 6906
Owner (Harness Racing) 6907
Paddock Judge (Greyhound Racing) 1167, 6908
Pari-Mutuel Employee (Greyhound Racing) 6909
Pari-Mutuel Employee (Racetrack) 6910
Patrol Judge (Greyhound Racing) 1168, 6911
Peddler 7591
Pesticide Applicator—Commercial 4902
Pharmacist 4988
Photographer, Itinerant 5019, 8721
Physical Therapist 5118
Physical Therapist Assistant 5056
Physician/Surgeon 5293
Physician's Assistant 5175
Pilot, Ships 8493
Plumber, Master 5423
Podiatrist 5470
Polygraph Examiner 5522
Pony Boy (Racetrack) 681, 6912
Precision Tank Tester 8730
Private Investigator (detective) 2357
Psychologist, Doctorate 5736
Psychologist, Master 5737
Public Adjuster 165
Racing Secretary (Greyhound Racing) 1169, 6913
Radiological Technologist 7112
Radiological Technologist, Limited 7113
Real Estate Appraiser 7299
Real Estate Broker 7300
Real Estate Salesperson (Agent) 7301
Registered Nurse (RN) 7426
School Audiologist 8112
School Guidance Counselor 2166
School Principal K-12 2526
School Speech and Language Pathologist 8113
School Superintendent 2527, 3215
Secondary School Teacher 7-12 7709
Securities Broker-Dealer 7902
Securities Sales Representative 7903
Security Guard 3311
Starter (Greyhound Racing) 1170, 6914
Supplier (Racetrack) 4309, 6915
Surveyor, Land 8226
Teacher of the Handicapped 4032, 7710
Tester; Precision Tank 8730
Timer (Greyhound Racing) 1171, 6916
Track Service Employee (Racetrack) 6917
Trainer/Driver (Harness Racing) 1172, 6918
Trainer (Greyhound Racing) 682, 6919
Trainer (Thoroughbred Racing) 683, 6920
Valet (Racetrack) 6921
Vendor, Itinerant 7592
Vendor (Racetrack) 6922, 7593
Veterinarian 8430
Veterinarian (Greyhound Racing) 6923, 8431
Veterinarian (Racetrack) 6924, 8432
Vocational Education Teacher 306
Wastewater Treatment Plant Operator 8554
Water Treatment Plant Operator 8555
Weighing and Measuring Devices; Dealer, Repairer 5542
Well Driller 4469

Virginia

Accountant (CPA) 66
Acupuncturist (L.Ac. or Lic. Ac.); Licensed 94
Administrative Employee (Racetrack) 6925, 7741
Apprentice Jockey (Racetrack) 1173, 6926
Architect 762
Asbestos Inspector 1834
Assistant General Manager (Racetrack) 3216, 6927
Assistant Racing Secretary (Racetrack) 1174, 6928
Assistant Starter (Racetrack) 1175, 6929
Assistant Trainer (Racetrack) 684, 6930
Authorized Agent (Racetrack) 1176, 6931
Barber 1512
Bloodstock Agent (Racetrack) 6932
Chiropractor 1677
Claims Clerk (Racetrack) 6933
Clerk of Course (Racetrack) 6934
Clerk of Scales (Racetrack) 3617, 6935
Clocker (Racetrack) 1177, 6936
Concessionaire/Vendor Employee (Racetrack) 6937, 7594
Concessionaire/Vendor (Racetrack) 6938, 7595
Cosmetologist 1513
Counselor (Licensed Professional) 2167
Dental Hygienist 2238
Dentist 2308
Director of Security (Racetrack) 3217, 3312, 6939
Driver (Racetrack) 1178, 6940

Early Education Teacher NK-4 4033, 5565
Embalmer/Funeral Director 2980
Emergency Medical Technician 2750
Engineer 5643
Entry Clerk (Racetrack) 6941
Exercise Rider (Racetrack) 685, 6942
Farrier (Racetrack) 686, 6943
Foreman (Racetrack) 1581, 6944
Gap Attendant (Racetrack) 6945
General Contractor 2040
General Manager (Racetrack) 3218, 6946
Geologist 3250
Groom/Hotwalker (Racetrack) 687, 6947
Hearing Aid Dealer and Fitter 3450
Heating and Air Conditioning Mechanic 3485
Horse Identifier (Racetrack) 3618, 6948
Horse Owner (Racetrack) 6949
Horsemen's Bookkeeper (Racetrack) 2793, 6950
Insurance Agent 3884
Investment Advisor 7904
Investment Advisor Representative 7905
Jockey Agent (Racetrack) 1179, 6951
Jockey (Racetrack) 1180, 6952
Jockey Room Custodian (Racetrack) 3923, 6953
Land Surveyor 8227
Landscape Architect 4095
Lawyer 4145
Licensed Acupuncturist (L.Ac. or Lic. Ac.) 94
Licensed Practical Nurse 4248
Lobbyist 4300
Marketing Employee (Racetrack) 6954
Medical Employee (Racetrack) 4375, 6955
Middle School Teacher 4-8 7711
Milk Tester 3677
Mutuel Clerk (Racetrack) 6956
Mutuel Manager (Racetrack) 2794, 3219, 6957
Nightwatchman (Racetrack) 3313, 6958
Notary Public 4525
Nursing Home Administrator 3393
Occupational Therapist 4612
Operations Employee (Racetrack) 6959
Optician 2419
Optometrist 4709
Osteopathic Physician (D.O.) 5294
Outrider (Racetrack) 688, 6960
Paddock Judge (Racetrack) 1181, 6961
Patrol Judge (Racetrack) 1182, 6962
Pesticide Applicator 4903
Pesticide Dealer 4904
Pharmaceutical Representative (Racetrack) 4310, 6963
Pharmacist 4989
Photo-Finish Camera Operator (Racetrack) 5020, 6964
Physical Therapist 5119
Physical Therapist's Assistant 5057
Physician 5295
Physician's Assistant 5176

Placing Judge (Racetrack) 1183, 6965
Plant Employee (Racetrack) 6966
Podiatrist 5471
Podiatrist's Assistant 4376
Polygraph Examiner 5523
Pony Rider (Racetrack) 689, 6967
Preschool Teacher of the Handicapped 5566
Private Investigator 2358
Private Security Agent 2359, 3314
Program Director (Racetrack) 3220, 6968
Psychologist 5738
Racing Secretary (Racetrack) 1184, 6969
Reading Specialist NK-12 4034, 5567, 7712
Real Estate Appraiser 7302, 7303
Real Estate Broker 7304
Real Estate Salesperson 7305
Registered Nurse 7427
Respiratory Care Practitioner 7477
School Division Superintendent 2528, 3221
School Guidance Counselor 2168
School Library Media Specialist NK-12 4195
School Principal 2529
School Psychologist 5739
School Social Worker 8027
School Supervisor 2530
Secondary School Teacher 7713
Securities Agent 7906
Securities Broker-Dealer 7907
Security Officer (Racetrack) 3315, 6970
Social Worker 8028
Soil Scientist 328
Solid Waste Facility Operator 1755
Speech Pathologist and Audiologist 8114
Staff Employee (Racetrack) 6971
Stall Superintendent (Racetrack) 690, 1582, 6972
Starter (Racetrack) 1185, 6973
Substance Abuse Counselor 2169, 3497
Teacher of the Emotionally Disturbed 4035, 7714
Teacher of the Hearing Impaired 4036, 7715, 8115
Teacher of the Learning Disabled 4037, 7716
Teacher of the Mentally Retarded 4038, 7717
Teacher of the Severely and Profoundly Handicapped 4039, 7718
Teacher of Speech and Language Disorders 4040, 7719, 8116
Teacher of the Visually Impaired 4041, 7720
Timer (Racetrack) 1186, 6974
Track Superintendent (Racetrack) 3222, 6975
Trainer (Racetrack) 691, 6976
Valet (Racetrack) 3334, 6977
Veterinarian 8433
Veterinarian (Racetrack) 6978, 8434
Veterinarian Technician 692

Veterinary Assistant 693
Video Patrol Personnel (Racetrack) 5021, 6979
Vocational Education Teacher 307
Water Treatment Plant Operator 8556

Washington

Acupuncturist; Certified 95
Amusement Ride Inspector 1835, 3619, 8578
Animal Technician 694
Announcer/Timekeeper (Professional Boxing & Wrestling) 1187, 7064
Architect 763
Attorney 4146
Auctioneer 1235
Authorized Agent (Racetrack) 1188, 6980
Barber 1514
Bingo Game Manager 3106, 8590
Blaster (Explosives User) 4470
Boiler Inspector 1836, 3620
Broker (Agriculture) 8567, 8595
Campground Lot Salesperson 7306
Cash Buyer (Agricultural) 8568, 8601
Cemetery Lot Salesperson 7307
Certified Acupuncturist 95
Certified Mental Health Counselor 2170
Certified Public Accountant 67
Certified Shorthand Reporter 8169
Chiropractor 1678
Commercial Fisher 2840
Commercial Pest Control Consultant 4905
Commercial Pest Control Operator/ Consultant 4906
Commercial Pesticide Applicator 4907
Commodity Broker-Dealer 7908
Cosmetologist 1515
Dairy Technician 8623
Debt Adjuster 7909
Deckhand 2841
Dental Hygienist 2239
Dentist 2309
Dentist (Racetrack) 6981, 8435
Dietitian 2396
Distributor's Representative (Gambling) 3107
Diver; Shellfish 2844, 8760
Driver Training Instructor (Commercial Driving School) 308
Electrical Administrator 1837, 2041, 2646
Electrical Contractor 2042, 2647
Electrician 2648
Embalmer 2981
Emergency Medical Technician (EMT) 2751
Engineer 5644
Engineer-in-Training 5645
Escrow Agent 7308, 8636
Firearms Safety Instructor 3716, 8644
First Responder 2752
Fisher; Commercial 2840
Fishing Guide 2842
Food Processor/Packer 2871

West Virginia

Washington, continued

Food Service Worker 2872
Franchise Broker/Dealer 7956, 8652
Funeral Director 2982
General Contractor 2043
General Employee (Racetrack) 6982
Geoduck Diver 2843, 8664
Hearing Aid Dispenser/Fitter 3451
Horse Owner (Racetrack) 6983
Hypnotherapist 5740, 8674
Independent Insurance Adjuster 166
Inspector (Professional Boxing/ Wrestling) 1189, 3621
Insurance Agent 3885
Insurance Broker 3886
Insurance Claims Adjuster 167
Investment Advisor 7910
Investment Advisor Salesperson 7911
Jockey Agent (Racetrack) 1190, 6984
Jockey (Racetrack) 1191, 6985
Journeyman Plumber 5424
Judge (Professional Boxing/ Wrestling) 1192
Land Development Representative 7309, 8686
Landscape Architect 4096
Librarian 4196
Library Media Specialist 4197
Licensed Practical Nurse 4249
Lobbyist 4301
Manager (Professional Boxing/ Wrestling) 1193
Manicurist 1516
Marriage and Family Therapist 2171
Masseur/Masseuse/Massage Practitioner 5120
Matchmaker (Professional Boxing/ Wrestling) 4355
Midwife 4566
Milk Hauler and Tester 3678, 8326
Motor Vehicle Wrecker 1244
Naturopath 5296
Notary Public 4526
Nuclear Medical Technologist 4541
Nursing Assistant/Aide 4567
Nursing Home Administrator 3394
Nutritionist 2397
Occupational Therapist 4613
Occupational Therapist Assistant 4658
Occupational Therapist; School 4614
Optician 2420
Optometrist 4710
Osteopathic Physician (D.O.) 5297
Osteopathic Physician's Assistant 5177
Owner/Trainer (Racetrack) 695, 6986
Pest Control Consultant; Commercial 4905
Pest Control Operator/Consultant; Commercial 4906
Pesticide Applicator; Commercial 4907
Pesticide Applicator; Private Commercial 4908
Pharmacist 4990
Pharmacy Intern 4991
Pharmacy Preceptor 309, 4992, 8716
Pharmacy Technician 8717

Physical Therapist 5121
Physical Therapist; School 5122
Physician 5298
Physician's Assistant 5178
Pilot 356
Plater (Racetrack) 696, 6987
Plumber; Journeyman 5424
Podiatrist 5472
Powder-Actuated Tool Operator 8728
Private Commercial Pesticide Applicator 4908
Professional Boxer 1194
Professional Boxing Referee 1195
Professional Wrestler 1196
Promoter (Professional Boxing/ Wrestling) 4356
Psychologist 5741
Public Card Room Employee (Gambling) 3108
Public Pesticide Consultant 4909
Public Pesticide Operator 4910
Public School Teacher PK-12 4042, 7721
Pyrotechnic Operator 8735
Radiation Therapy Technologist 7114
Radiologic Technologist 7115
Reading Resource Specialist 4043, 7722
Real Estate Appraiser 7310
Real Estate Broker 7311
Real Estate Sales Agent 7312
Registered Nurse 7428
Respiratory Care Practitioner 7478
School Communications Disorders Specialist 8117
School Guidance Counselor 2172
School Nurse 7429
School Occupational Therapist 4614
School Physical Therapist 5122
School Principal K-12 2531
School Program Administrator 2532
School Psychologist 5742
School Social Worker 8029
School Superintendent 2533, 3223
Scientific Collector 7610, 8757
Second (Professional Boxing/ Wrestling) 1197
Securities Broker-Dealer 7912
Securities Salesperson 7913
Shellfish Diver 2844, 8760
Social Worker 8030
Surveyor 8228
Taxidermist 8270
Tow Truck Operator 8327
Trainer (Racetrack) 697, 6988
Trapper 2845
Vessel Pilot 8494
Veterinarian 8436
Veterinarian (Racetrack) 6989, 8437
Wastewater Treatment Plant Operator 8557
Water Works Operator 8558
Waterfront Equipment Inspector 3622
Weigher (Dairy & Food) 3623
Weighmaster 3624

West Virginia

Accountant (CPA) 68
Animal Technician 698
Architect 764
Athletic Trainer 3717
Attorney 4147
Audiologist; Education 8118
Barber 1517
Barber and Beautician; Instructor, 310, 1519
Bulk Milk Hauler and Sampler 3679, 8328
Certified Shorthand Reporter 8170
Chiropractor 1679
Cosmetologist, Beautician, Beauty Operator 1518
Dental Hygienist 2240
Dentist 2310
Driver—School Bus 1616
Education Audiologist 8118
Electrician 2649
Electrician (Mine) 2650, 4471
Emergency Medical Technician 2753
Engineer 5646
Fishing Guide 2846
Forester 2894
Funeral Director/Mortician/ Embalmer 2983
General Contractor 2044
Hearing Aid Specialist 3452
Instructor, Barber and Beautician 310, 1519
Insurance Agent (Non-resident) 3887
Insurance Agent (Resident) 3888
Insurance Broker (Non-resident) 3889
Insurance Solicitor 3890
Investment Advisor 7914
Land Surveyor 8229
Landscape Architect 4097
Licensed Practical Nurse 4250
Lobbyist 4302
Manicurist 1520
Medical Doctor 5299
Mine Foreman 1583, 4472
Mine Surveyor 4473, 8230
Miner 4474
Notary Public 4527
Nurse Anesthetist 7430
Nurse, Midwife 7431
Nursing Home Administrator 3395
Occupational Therapist 4615
Occupational Therapy Assistant 4659
Optometrist 4711
Osteopathic Physician 5300
Pesticide Applicator 4911
Pharmacist 4993
Physical Therapist 5123
Physical Therapy Assistant 5058
Physician Assistant 5179
Podiatrist 5473
Polygraph Examiner 5524
Private Detective 2360
Professional Counselor 2173
Psychologist 5743
Public School Teacher 4044, 7723
Radiologic Technician 7116
Real Estate Appraiser 7313

Real Estate Broker 7314
Real Estate Salesperson 7315
Registered Nurse 7432
Sanitarian 3625
School Business Official 2534
School Counselor 2174
School Principal 2535
School Psychologist 5744
School Social Services and Attendance Investigator 3626, 8756
School Superintendent 2536, 3224
Securities Agent 7915
Securities Broker-Dealer 7916
Shot Firer 4475
Social Worker 8031
Speech Language Pathologist 8119
Supervisor of Instruction 2537
Veterinarian 8438
Vocational Administrator 2538

Wisconsin

Accountant/Certified Public 69
Acupuncturist 96
Aesthetician 1521
Animal Technician 699
Announcer (Racetrack) 6990, 7065
Architect 765
Assistant Racing Secretary (Racetrack) 1198, 6991
Assistant Trainer (Dog Racing) 700, 6992
Association Steward (Racetrack) 1199, 6993
Attorney 4148
Audiologist 8120
Authorized Agent (Dog Racing) 1200, 6994
Barber 1522
Bulk Milk Weigher and Sampler 3680
Butter Grader 3681, 8597
Chartwriter (Racetrack) 6995
Cheese Grader 3682, 8605
Chiropractor 1680
Clerk of Scales (Racetrack) 3627, 6996
Concession Employee (Racetrack) 6997, 7596
Concession Owner (Racetrack) 6998, 7597
Debt Collector 168
Dental Hygienist 2241
Dentist 2311
Designer 5647
Director of Racing (Racetrack) 3225, 6999
Dog Owner (Racetrack) 7000
Electrologist 1523
Elementary or Middle School Principal 2539
Elementary School Teacher 4045
Emergency Medical Technician 2754
Engineer 5648
Engineer-in-Training 5649
Film Patrol Employee (Racetrack) 5022, 7001
Fishing Guide 2847
Funeral Director 2984

General Manager/Assistant General Manager (Racetrack) 3226, 7002
Hearing Instrument Specialist 3453
Instructional Library Media Specialist 4198
Insurance Agent 3891
Investment Advisor 7917
Kennel Helper (Dog Racing) 701, 7003
Kennel Master (Racetrack) 702, 7004
Kennel Operator (Racetrack) 703, 7005
Kennel Owner (Dog Racing) 7006
Land Surveyors 8231
Lead Out (Racetrack) 704, 7007
Loan Originator 7918
Loan Solicitor 7957
Lobbyist 4303
Lure Operator (Racetrack) 7008
Manicurist 1524
Marriage and Family Therapist 2175
Medical Doctor/Doctor of Osteopathy 5301
Middle or Secondary School Principal 2540
Milk or Cream Tester 3683
Milk Distributor 8329
Mortgage Banker 7919
Mutuel Employee (Racetrack) 7009
Mutuel Manager (Racetrack) 2795, 3227, 7010
Notary Public 4528
Nurse/Licensed Practical 4251
Nurse/Midwife 7433
Nurse/Registered 7434
Nursing Home Administrator 3396
Occupational Therapist 4616
Occupational Therapy Assistant 4660
Optometrist 4712
Osteopathic Physician (D.O.) 5302
Osteopathy; Medical Doctor/Doctor of 5301
Owner/Trainer (Dog Racing) 705, 7011
Paddock Judge (Racetrack) 1201, 7012
Pesticide Applicator 4912
Pesticide Dealer 4913
Pharmacist 4994
Photo Finish Employee (Racetrack) 5023, 7013
Physical Therapist 5124
Physician's Assistant 5180
Podiatrist 5474
Practicing Veterinarian (Racetrack) 7014, 8439
Private Detective 2361
Professional Counselor 2176
Psychologist 5745
Racing Secretary (Racetrack) 1202, 7015
Real Estate Appraiser 7316
Real Estate Broker 7317
Real Estate Salesperson 7318
Real Estate Timeshare Salesperson 7319
Registered Professional Reporter 8171
Rehabilitation Counselor 2177, 3498
Respiratory Care Practitioner 7479
School Counselor 2178
School District Superintendent 2541, 3228

Secondary School Teacher 7724
Securities Agent 7920
Securities Broker-Dealer 7921
Security Employee (Racetrack) 3316, 7016
Social Worker 8032
Speech Pathologist 8121
Teacher of Special Subjects 4046, 7725
Timer (Racetrack) 1203, 7017
Tip Sheet Employee (Racetrack) 7018
Totalizator Employee (Racetrack) 7019
Totalizator Operator (Racetrack) 7020
Track Superintendent (Racetrack) 3229, 7021
Trainer (Dog Racing) 706, 7022
Veterinarian 8440
Veterinarian (Racetrack); Practicing 7014, 8439

Wyoming

Accountant, Certified Public 70
Administrator, Nursing Home 3397
Agent (Racetrack) 1204, 7023
Architect 766
Artificial Inseminator of Animals 707, 8584
Assistant Starter (Racetrack) 1205, 7024
Audiologist; School 8123
Audiologist, Speech Pathologist 8122
Barber 1525
Bus Driver, School 1617
Chemical Dependency Specialist Counselor 2179, 3499
Chiropractor 1681
Claims Adjuster 169
Commercial Pesticide Applicator 4914
Concession Employee (Racetrack) 7025, 7598
Concession Operator (Racetrack) 7026, 7599
Cosmetologist 1526
Counselor; Licensed Professional 2180
Dental Hygienist 2242
Dentist 2312
Educational Diagnostician 2542
Electrician 2651
Elementary School Teacher K-6 4047
Embalmer 2985
Emergency Medical Technician 2755
Engineer, Professional 5650
Exerciser (Racetrack) 708, 7027
Funeral Director 2986
Geologist 3251
Groom (Racetrack) 709, 7028
Guide, Professional 2848
Hearing Aid Specialist 3454
Horsemen's Bookkeeper (Racetrack) 2796, 7029
Jockey/Apprentice Jockey (Racetrack) 1206, 7030
Jockey Runner (Racetrack) 7031
Landscape Architect 4098
Law Enforcement Officer 5490
Law Enforcement Officer (Highway Patrol Officer) 5491
Lawyer 4149

Wyoming, continued

Librarian, School 4199
Licensed Professional Counselor 2180
Lobbyist 4304
Marriage and Family Therapist 2181
Middle School Teacher 5-8 7726
Mine Examiner 3628, 4476
Mine Foreman 1584, 4477
Mine Inspector 3629, 4478
Mutuel Employee (Racetrack) 7032
Mutuel Official (Racetrack) 2797, 3230, 7033
Notary Public 4529
Nurse, Licensed Practical 4252
Nurse Practitioner 7435
Nurse, Registered 7436
Nursing Home; Administrator, 3397
Occupational Therapist 4617
Occupational Therapy Assistant 4661
Optometrist 4713
Outfitter 2849
Outrider (Racetrack) 710, 7034

Owner (Racetrack) 7035
Permittee Employee (Racetrack) 7036
Permittee Official (Racetrack) 7037
Pesticide Dealer 4915
Pharmacist 4995
Physical Therapist 5125
Physician Assistant 5181
Physician, Medical and Osteopath 5303
Plater (Racetrack) 711, 7038
Podiatrist 5475
Pony Rider (Racetrack) 712, 7039
Private Pesticide Applicator 4916
Psychologist 5746
Racing Secretary (Racetrack) 1207, 7040
Radiation Technician 7117
Radiologic Technologist 7118
Real Estate Appraiser 7320
Real Estate Broker 7321
Real Estate Sales Agent 7322
Roper (Racetrack) 713, 7041
Salesperson, Insurance 3892
Salesperson, Real Estate 7323

School Audiologist 8123
School Counselor 2182
School Nurse 7437
School Principal 2543
School Psychologist 5747
School Reading Specialist 4048, 7727
School Social Worker 8033
School Speech Pathologist 8124
School Superintendent 2544, 3231
School Supervisor 2545
Secondary School Teacher 7-12 7728
Securities Agent 7922
Securities Broker-Dealer 7923
Security Employee (Racetrack) 3317, 7042
Social Worker 8034
Surveyor, Professional 8232
Trainer/Assistant Trainer (Racetrack) 714, 7043
Veterinarian 8441
Veterinarian Assistant (Racetrack) 715, 7044
Veterinarian (Racetrack) 7045, 8442

PRIMARILY FOR STUDENT USE
DATE DUE
OVER-NIGHT USE

If needed for a more extensive period, see circulation desk attendant.

GAYLORD　　　　　　　　　　　　PRINTED IN U.S.A.